THE NEW INTERPRETER'S® DICTIONARY OF THE BIBLE

D-H

VOLUME 2

EDITORIAL BOARD

THE NEW INTERPRETER'S® DICTIONARY OF THE BIBLE

D-H

VOLUME 2

ABINGDON PRESS

Nashville

THE NEW INTERPRETER'S® DICTIONARY OF THE BIBLE
D-H
VOLUME 2

Copyright © 2007 by Abingdon Press

All rights reserved.

This book is printed on recycled, acid-free paper.

Library of Congress Cataloging-in-Publication Data

The New Interpreter's Dictionary of the Bible.
   p. cm.
  Includes bibliographical references.
  ISBN 0-687-05427-3 (alk. paper)
  1. Bible--Dictionaries. I. Abingdon Press.

  BS440.N445 2006
  220.3--dc22

                    2006025839

ISBN-13: 978-0-687-33355-4

PUBLICATION STAFF

Project Director: John F. Kutsko
Project Manager: Marianne Blickenstaff
Reference Editor: Heather R. McMurray
Production Editor: Alicia Benjamin-Samuels
Contracts Manager: Linda Spicer
Production & Design Manager: Ed Wynne
Typesetter: Kathy Harding
NewInterpreters.com Web Developer: Justyn Hunter
Print Procurement: Clara Stuart
Marketing Manager: Teresa Alspaugh

EXECUTIVE STAFF

President and Publisher: Neil M. Alexander
Senior Vice President, Publishing: Harriett Jane Olson
Vice President, Abingdon Press: Tammy Gaines

1 2 3 4 5 6 7 8 9 10 – 06 07 08 09 10 11 12 13 14 15

ACKNOWLEDGEMENTS

Art Resource, NY: ELIJAH Fig. 1

Bildarchiv Preussischer Kulturbesitz/Art Resource, NY: HIEROGLYPH Fig. 2

Todd Bolen/BiblePlaces.com: DEAD SEA Fig. 1; DEAD SEA SCROLLS Fig. 1, 2; DIBON Fig. 1; DOLMENS Fig. 1; EDOM, EDOMITES Fig. 1, 2; EGYPT Fig. 2; EMIR, IRAQ EL Fig. 1, 2; EN-GEDI Fig. 1, 2; EPHESUS Fig. 1; FRANKINCENSE Fig. 1; GALILEE, SEA OF Fig. 1; GERASA, GERASENES Fig. 1; GERIZIM, MOUNT Fig. 1; GETHSEMANE Fig. 1; GLACIS Fig. 1; GOLGOTHA Fig. 1, 2; HADRIAN Fig. 1; HAZOR Fig. 1; HERMON, MOUNT Fig. 1; HERODIUM Fig. 1, 2; HESA, WADI EL Fig. 1; HOLY SEPULCHER Fig. 1

Bridgeman-Giraudon/Art Resource, NY: HURRIANS Fig. 1

Reuben G. Bullard, Jr.: GATE Fig. 1

Billie Jean Collins: HITTITES Fig. 2, 3, 4, 5, 6

Daniel Frese/BiblePlaces.com: HINNOM, VALLEY OF Fig. 1

Werner Forman/Art Resource, NY: EGYPT Fig. 3

Daniel Gebhardt/BiblePlaces.com: EGYPT Fig. 4

David W. J. Gill: GREECE Fig. 2, 3, 4, 5

Heshbon Expedition Archives: HESHBON Fig. 2, 3

HIP/Art Resource, NY: DEAD SEA SCROLLS Fig. 4

John C. H. Laughlin: DAN, TELL Fig. 1, 2, 3, 4

Erich Lessing/Art Resource, NY: DEAD SEA SCROLLS Fig. 3; EBLA Fig. 1; EGYPT Fig. 5, 6; EMBALM, EMBALMING Fig. 1; ESARHADDON Fig. 1; GLASS Fig. 1

P. L. Neville: GREEK RELIGION AND PHILOSOPHY Fig. 1

Princeton University Press/Art Resource, NY: DURA EUROPOS Fig. 1

Réunion des Musées Nationaux/Art Resource, NY: HAMMURABI, CODE OF Fig. 1

RØHR Productions Ltd.: HESHBON Fig. 1

Scala/Art Resource, NY: ESTHER, BOOK OF Fig. 1

Vanni/Art Resource, NY: HIEROGLYPH Fig. 1

John Mark Wade: DEAD SEA Fig. 1; GHAZAL, ʿAIN Fig. 1

Mattanyah Zohar: HIRI, RUJM EL Fig. 1, Fig. 2

Consultants

Archaeology Consultant

John C. H. Laughlin
Averett University
Danville, VA

Consulting Readers

Eric Elnes
Scottsdale Congregational United Church of Christ
Scottsdale, AZ

Dottie Escobedo-Frank
Cross Roads United Methodist Church
Phoenix, AZ

Renae Extrum-Fernandez
Walnut Creek First United Methodist Church
Walnut Creek, CA

Tyrone Gordon
St. Luke Community United Methodist Church
Dallas, TX

Kevass J. Harding
Dellrose United Methodist Church
Wichita, KS

James A. Harnish
Hyde Park United Methodist Church
Tampa, FL

Judi K. Hoffman
Edgehill United Methodist Church
Nashville, TN

Robert Johnson
Windsor Village United Methodist Church
Houston, TX

Chan-Hie Kim
Upland, CA

Sungho Lee
Korean United Methodist Church of Santa Clara Valley
San Jose, CA

Merry Hope Meloy
Doylesburg, PA

H. Mitchell Simpson
University Baptist Church
Chapel Hill, NC

Evelene Sombrero Navarrete
Holbrook United Methodist Church
Holbrook, AZ

Mariellen Sawada-Yoshino
San Jose United Methodist Church
San Jose, CA

CONTRIBUTORS

MARTIN G. ABEGG, JR.
Trinity Western University
Langley, BC, Canada

JUDITH Z. ABRAMS
MAQOM
Houston, TX

SUSAN ACKERMAN
Dartmouth College
Hanover, NH

SAMUEL L. ADAMS
Union Theological Seminary and
Presbyterian School of Christian Education
Richmond, VA

JOHN J. AHN
Austin Presbyterian Theological Seminary
Austin, TX

JAMES K. AITKEN
University of Cambridge
Cambridge, United Kingdom

BENNY C. AKER
Assemblies of God Theological Seminary
Springfield, MO

KAZYA AKIMOTO
Vanderbilt University
Nashville, TN

DALE C. ALLISON, JR.
Pittsburgh Theological Seminary
Pittsburgh, PA

CHERYL B. ANDERSON
Garrett-Evangelical Theological Seminary
Evanston, IL

GARY A. ANDERSON
University of Notre Dame
Notre Dame, IN

DEBORAH A. APPLER
Moravian Theological Seminary
Bethlehem, PA

WILLIAM ARNAL
University of Regina
Regina, SK, Canada

BILL T. ARNOLD
Asbury Theological Seminary
Wilmore, KY

ANDREW E. ARTERBURY
Baylor University
Waco, TX

PETER ARZT-GRABNER
Universitaet Salzburg
Salzburg, Austria

DAVID E. AUNE
University of Notre Dame
Notre Dame, IN

HECTOR AVALOS
Iowa State University
Ames, IA

ANNALISA AZZONI
Vanderbilt University
Nashville, TN

JILL L. BAKER
Albright Institute of Archaeological Research
Jerusalem, Israel

SAMUEL E. BALENTINE
Union Theological Seminary and
Presbyterian School of Christian Education
Richmond, VA

ANDREW BANDSTRA
Grand Rapids, MI

JAMES W. BARKER
Vanderbilt University
Nashville, TN

DAVID R. BAUER
Asbury Theological Seminary
Wilmore, KY

KELLEY COBLENTZ BAUTCH
St. Edward's University
Austin, TX

SHANE A. BERG
Princeton Theological Seminary
Princeton, NJ

MARIAN OSBORNE BERKY
Anderson University
Anderson, IN

MOSHE J. BERNSTEIN
Yeshiva University
New York, NY

SHARON BETSWORTH
Graduate Theological Union
Berkeley, CA

BRYAN D. BIBB
Furman University
Greenville, SC

MARK E. BIDDLE
Baptist Theological Seminary at Richmond
Richmond, VA

JULYE M. BIDMEAD
Maimi University
Oxford, OH

ROBERT D. BIGGS
The Oriental Institute, University of Chicago
Chicago, IL

BRUCE C. BIRCH
Wesley Theological Seminary
Washington, DC

BARRY L. BLACKBURN, SR.
Atlanta Christian College
East Point, GA

JEFFREY A. BLAKELY
University of Wisconsin
Madison, WI

MARIANNE BLICKENSTAFF
Abingdon Press
Nashville, TN

L. GREGORY BLOOMQUIST
St. Paul University
Ottawa, ON, Canada

MARK J. H. BODA
McMaster University
Hamilton, ON, Canada

HELEN K. BOND
New College
University of Edinburgh
Edinburgh, United Kingdom

M. EUGENE BORING
Brite Divinity School
Texas Christian University
Fort Worth, TX

ODED BOROWSKI
Emory University
Atlanta, GA

WALTER C. BOUZARD
Wartburg College
Waverly, IA

NANCY R. BOWEN
Earlham School of Religion
Richmond, IN

MARY PETRINA BOYD
Coupeville, WA

KENT V. BRAMLETT
University of Toronto
Toronto, ON, Canada

GEORGE J. BROOKE
University of Manchester
Manchester, United Kingdom

W. R. BROOKMAN
North Central University
Minneapolis, MN

MICHAEL JOSEPH BROWN
Candler School of Theology
Emory University
Atlanta, GA

SEAN D. BURKE
Graduate Theological Union
Berkeley, CA

JOEL S. BURNETT
Baylor University
Waco, TX

MARTIN J. BUSS
Emory University
Atlanta, GA

GAY L. BYRON
Colgate Rochester Crozer Divinity School
Rochester, NY

NANCY CALVERT-KOYZIS
McMaster University
Hamilton, ON, Canada

CLAUDIA V. CAMP
Texas Christian University
Fort Worth, TX

BRIAN J. CAPPER
Canterbury Christ Church University
Canterbury, United Kingdom

GREG CAREY
Lancaster Theological Seminary
Lancaster, PA

WARREN CARTER
Brite Divinity School
Texas Christian University
Fort Worth, TX

TONY W. CARTLEDGE
Biblical Recorder
Raleigh, NC

KATHY CHAMBERS
Vanderbilt University
Nashville, TN

MARK A. CHANCEY
Dedman College
Southern Methodist University
Dallas, TX

MARVIN L. CHANEY
San Francisco Theological Seminary
San Anselmo, CA

EMILY R. CHENEY
Athens, GA

SAMUEL CHEON
Hannam University
Daejon, Korea

BRUCE CHILTON
Bard College
Annandale on Hudson, NY

JULIANA CLAASSENS
Baptist Theological Seminary
Richmond, VA

TREVOR D. COCHELL
Baylor University
Waco, TX

BILLIE JEAN COLLINS
Emory University
Atlanta, GA

RAYMOND F. COLLINS
The Catholic University of America
Washington, DC

MARY COLOE
Australian Catholic University
North Sydney, Australia

EDGAR W. CONRAD
University of Queensland
Queensland, Australia

MICHAEL D. COOGAN
Concord, MA

JOAN E. COOK
Georgetown University
Washington, DC

STEPHEN L. COOK
Virginia Theological Seminary
Alexandria, VA

STEVE COOK
Vanderbilt University
Nashville, TN

ROBERT B. COOTE
San Francisco Theological Seminary
San Anselmo, CA

J. R. C. Cousland
University of British Columbia
Vancouver, BC, Canada

Cory Crawford
Harvard University
Cambridge, MA

James L. Crenshaw
Duke University
Durham, NC

Stephanie Buckhanon Crowder
Nashville, TN

Carly Daniel-Hughes
Harvard Divinity School
Cambridge, MA

James R. Davila
St. Mary's College, University of St. Andrews
St. Andrews, United Kingdom

Linda Day
Pittsburgh, PA

L. J. de Regt
United Bible Societies
The Hague, Netherlands

J. Andrew Dearman
Austin Presbyterian Theological Seminary
Austin, TX

Nancy deClaissé-Walford
McAfee School of Theology
Mercer University
Atlanta, GA

Mark DelCogliano
Emory University
Atlanta, GA

Nicola Denzey
Harvard University
Cambridge, MA

David A. deSilva
Ashland Theological Seminary
Ashland, OH

Jessica Tinklenberg deVega
Morningside College
Sioux City, IA

William G. Dever
Bedford Hills, NY

Lorenzo DiTommaso
Concordia University
Montreal, QC, Canada

Fred W Dobbs-Allsop
Princeton Theological Seminary
Princeton, NJ

Mary Kay Dobrovolny, R.S.M.
Vanderbilt University
Nashville, TN

F. Gerald Downing
University of Manchester
Manchester, United Kingdom

Jonathan A. Draper
University of KwaZulu-Natal
Scottsville, South Africa

Joel F. Drinkard, Jr.
The Southern Baptist Theological Seminary
Louisville, KY

Jean Duhaime
University of Montreal
Montreal, QC, Canada

James D. G. Dunn
University of Durham
Durham, United Kingdom

Rubén R. Dupertuis
Trinity University
San Antonio, TX

Nicole Wilkinson Duran
Villanova University
Villanova, PA

Jason C. Dykehouse
Baylor University
Waco, TX

Terry W. Eddinger
Carolina Evangelical Divinity School
High Point, NC

CARL S. EHRLICH
York University
Toronto, ON, Canada

GÖRAN EIDEVALL
University of Uppsala
Uppsala, Sweden

YOEL ELITZUR
Herzog College
Alon Shevut, Israel

JOHN C. ENDRES, S.J.
Jesuit School of Theology at Berkeley
Berkeley, CA

MILTON ENG
Rutgers, The State University of New Jersey
Newark, NJ

ESTHER ESHEL
Bar-Ilan University
Ramat-Gan, Israel

CRAIG A. EVANS
Acadia Divinity College
Wolfville, NS, Canada

KATHLEEN A. ROBERTSON FARMER
United Theological Seminary
Dayton, OH

STEVEN E. FASSBERG
Hebrew University of Jerusalem
Mt. Scopus, Israel

JOHN T. FITZGERALD
University of Miami
Coral Gables, FL

PAUL E. FITZPATRICK
Blessed John XXIII National Seminary
Weston, MA

MICHAEL H. FLOYD
Episcopal Theological Seminary of the Southwest
Austin, TX

CAROLE R. FONTAINE
Andover Newton Theological School
Newton Centre, MA

TERENCE E. FRETHEIM
Luther Seminary
Saint Paul, MN

MARK J. H. FRETZ
Messiah College
Grantham, PA

LISBETH S. FRIED
The University of Michigan
Ann Arbor, MI

STEVEN J. FRIESEN
University of Texas
Austin, TX

SERGE FROLOV
Dedman College
Southern Methodist University
Dallas, TX

RUSSELL E. FULLER
University of San Diego
San Diego, CA

SUSANA DE SOLA FUNSTEN
Los Angeles, CA

HEIDI S. GEIB
Vanderbilt University
Nashville, TN

AGUSTINUS GIANTO
Pontifical Biblical Institute
Rome, Italy

WILLIAM K. GILDERS
Emory University
Atlanta, GA

DAVID W. J. GILL
University of Wales Swansea
Swansea, United Kingdom

MARK D. GIVEN
Missouri State University
Maryville, MO

GREGORY GLAZOV
Seton Hall University
South Orange, NJ

ROBERT GNUSE
Loyola University
New Orleans, LA

PAUL W. GOOCH
Victoria University in the University of Toronto
Toronto, ON, Canada

FRANK H. GORMAN
Bethany College
Bethany, WV

NORMAN K. GOTTWALD
Berkeley, CA

DONALD E. GOWAN
Pittsburgh Theological Seminary
Pittsburgh, PA

LESTER L. GRABBE
University of Hull
Hull, United Kingdom

BARBARA GREEN, O.P.
Dominican School of Philosophy and Theology
Berkeley, CA

JOEL B. GREEN
Fuller Theological Seminary
Pasadena, CA

MARK D. GREEN
Indiana State University
Terre Haute, IN

JOSEPH A. GREENE
Harvard University
Cambridge, MA

JAMES P. GRIMSHAW
Carroll College
Waukesha, WI

MAYER GRUBER
Ben-Gurion University of the Negev
Beersheva, Israel

ESTHER GRUSHKIN
Staten Island, NY

GILDAS HAMEL
University of California at Santa Cruz
Santa Cruz, CA

MEREDITH BURKE HAMMONS
Vanderbilt University
Nashville, TN

R. JUSTIN HARKINS
Vanderbilt University
Nashville, TN

PHILLIP A. HARLAND
York University
Toronto, ON, Canada

J. ALBERT HARRILL
Indiana University
Bloomington, IN

HANNAH K. HARRINGTON
Patten University
Oakland, CA

J. GORDON HARRIS
North American Baptist Seminary
Sioux Falls, SD

AXEL HAUSMANN
Zoologische Staatssammlung München
Munich, Germany

L. DANIEL HAWK
Ashland Theological Seminary
Ashland, OH

RALPH K. HAWKINS
Bethel College
Mishawaka, IN

CHARLES W. HEDRICK
Missouri State University
(Emeritus)
Springfield, MO

CHARLOTTE HEMPEL
University of Birmingham
Birmingham, United Kingdom

ZE'EV HERZOG
Tel Aviv University
Tel Aviv, Israel

THEODORE HIEBERT
McCormick Theological Seminary
Chicago, IL

CAROLYN HIGGINBOTHAM
Christian Theological Seminary
Indianapolis, IN

CHARLES E. HILL
Reformed Theological Seminary
Oviedo, FL

CRAIG C. HILL
Wesley Theological Seminary
Washington, DC

SUSAN TOWER HOLLIS
SUNY Empire State College
Saratoga Springs, NY

PAUL A. HOLLOWAY
University of Glasgow
Glasgow, United Kingdom

MICHAEL W. HOLMES
Bethel University
St. Paul, MN

DAVID C. HOPKINS
Wesley Theological Seminary
Washington, DC

LESLIE J. HOPPE, O.F.M.
Catholic Theological Union
Chicago, IL

HEIDI J. HORNIK
Baylor University
Waco, TX

WALTER J. HOUSTON
Mansfield College
Oxford, United Kingdom

BONNIE HOWE
Oakland, CA

EDITH M. HUMPHREY
Pittsburgh Theological Seminary
Pittsburgh, PA

JEREMY M. HUTTON
Princeton Theological Seminary
Princeton, NJ

SUSAN E. HYLEN
Vanderbilt University
Nashville, TN

DAVID INSTONE-BREWER
Tyndale House
Cambridge, United Kingdom

GLENNA S. JACKSON
Otterbein College
Westerville, OH

MATT JACKSON-MCCABE
Niagara University
Niagara, NY

ROBIN M. JENSEN
Vanderbilt University
Nashville, TN

ANDY JOHNSON
Nazarene Theological Seminary
Kansas City, MO

MARSHALL D. JOHNSON
Minneapolis, MN

PHILIP S. JOHNSTON
Oxford University Wycliffe Hall
Oxford, United Kingdom

WILLIAM JOHNSTONE
Kings College
University of Aberdeen
Aberdeen, United Kingdom

A. HEATH JONES, III
Nashville, TN

BRIAN C. JONES
Wartburg College
Waverly, IA

CHRISTINE D. JONES
Baylor University
Waco, TX

F. STANLEY JONES
California State University, Long Beach
Long Beach, CA

JUDITH ANNE JONES
Wartburg College
Waverly, IA

NYASHA JUNIOR
Princeton Theological Seminary
Princeton, NJ

JOEL S. KAMINSKY
Smith College
Northampton, MA

JOHN I. KAMPEN
Methodist Theological School in Ohio
Delaware, OH

BRAD E. KELLE
Point Loma Nazarene University
San Diego, CA

WILLIAM KLASSEN
University of Waterloo
Waterloo, ON, Canada

RALPH W. KLEIN
Lutheran School of Theology at Chicago
Chicago, IL

RAZ KLETTER
Tel Aviv, Israel

SHERI L. KLOUDA
Taylor University
Upland, IN

JENNIFER L. KOOSED
Albright College
Reading, PA

ANDREAS J. KÖSTENBERGER
Southeastern Baptist Theological Seminary
Wake Forest, NC

DEBORAH KRAUSE
Eden Theological Seminary
St. Louis, MO

KAH-JIN JEFFREY KUAN
Pacific School of Religion
Berkeley, CA

ROBERT KUGLER
Lewis & Clark College
Portland, OR

ØYSTEIN S. LABIANCA
Andrews University
Berrien Springs, MI

DAVID A. LAMBERT
Yale University
New Haven, CT

NANCY L. LAPP
Pittsburgh Theological Seminary
Pittsburgh, PA

JOHN C. H. LAUGHLIN
Averett University
Danville, VA

JOHN I. LAWLOR
Grand Rapids Theological Seminary
Grand Rapids, MI

WON W. LEE
Calvin College
Grand Rapids, MI

JOEL MARCUS LEMON
Candler School of Theology
Emory University
Atlanta, GA

JUTTA LEONHARDT-BALZER
Wiesbaden, Germany

BARUCH A. LEVINE
Shelton, CT

ELY LEVINE
Harvard University
Cambridge, MA

IRINA LEVINSKAYA
Tyndale House
Cambridge, United Kingdom

JOHN R. LEVISON
Seattle Pacific University School of Theology
Seattle, WA

THEODORE J. LEWIS
The Johns Hopkins University
Baltimore, MD

GREGORY L. LINTON
Johnson Bible College
Knoxville, TN

B. DIANE LIPSETT
Wake Forest University
Winston-Salem, NC

KENNETH D. LITWAK
Asbury Theological Seminary
Wilmore, KY

JOEL N. LOHR
University of Durham
Durham, United Kingdom

LAMONTTE M. LUKER
Lutheran Theological Southern Seminary
Columbia, SC

GRANT MACASKILL
St. Andrews University
St. Andrews, United Kingdom

F. RACHEL MAGDALENE
Augustana College
Rock Island, IL

BRUCE J. MALINA
Creighton University
Omaha, NE

CLAUDE MARIOTTINI
Northern Baptist Seminary
Lombard, IL

LUTHER H. MARTIN
The University of Vermont
Burlington, VT

STEVEN D. MASON
LeTourneau University
Longview, TX

FRANK J. MATERA
The Catholic University of America
Washington, DC

VICTOR H. MATTHEWS
Missouri State University
Springfield, MO

KATHY R. MAXWELL
South Texas School of Christian Studies
Corpus Christi, TX

NATHAN D. MAXWELL
South Texas School of Christian Studies
Corpus Christi, TX

S. DEAN MCBRIDE
Union Theological Seminary and Presbyterian
School of Christian Education
Richmond, VA

BYRON R. MCCANE
Wofford College
Spartanburg, SC

P. KYLE MCCARTER, JR
Johns Hopkins University
Baltimore, MD

C. MARK MCCORMICK
Stillman College
Tuscaloosa, AL

LEE MARTIN MCDONALD
Acadia Divinity College
Wolfville, NS, Canada

STEVEN L. MCKENZIE
Rhodes College
Memphis, TN

JOHN L. MCLAUGHLIN
University of St. Michael's College
Toronto, ON, Canada

SARIANNA METSO
University of Toronto
Toronto, ON, Canada

JAMES A. METZGER
Luther College
Decorah, IA

J. RAMSEY MICHAELS
Missouri State University
Springfield, MO

JACOB MILGROM
University of California at Berkeley
Berkeley, CA

DAVID M. MILLER
Briercrest College and Seminary
Caronport, SK, Canada

MILTON MORELAND
Rhodes College
Memphis, TN

HANS-FRIEDRICH MUELLER
Union College
Schenectady, NY

E. THEODORE MULLEN, JR.
Indiana University-Purdue University
Indianapolis, IN

GÜNTER MÜLLER
Hebrew University
Jerusalem, Israel

JEROME MURPHY-O'CONNOR
École Biblique
Jerusalem, Israel

RICHARD D. NELSON
Perkins School of Theology
Southern Methodist University
Dallas, TX

CAREY C. NEWMAN
Baylor University
Waco, TX

JUDITH H. NEWMAN
Toronto School of Theology
and the University of Toronto
Toronto, ON, Canada

LAI LING ELIZABETH NGAN
Baylor University
Waco, TX

SUSAN NIDITCH
Amherst College
Amherst, MA

PAUL NISKANEN
University of St. Thomas
Saint Paul, MN

SCOTT B. NOEGEL
University of Washington
Seattle, WA

MICHAEL D. OBLATH
Pacific School of Religion
Berkeley, CA

KATHLEEN M. O'CONNOR
Columbia Theological Seminary
Decatur, GA

MARGARET S. ODELL
St. Olaf College
Northfield, MN

GERBERN S. OEGEMA
McGill University
Montreal, QC, Canada

DENNIS T. OLSON
Princeton Theological Seminary
Princeton, NJ

JAMES F. OSBORNE
Harvard University
Cambridge, MA

CAROLYN OSIEK
Brite Divinity School
Texas Christian University
Fort Worth, TX

SUSANNE OTTO
Aalen, Germany

BEN OUTHWAITE
Cambridge University
Cambridge, United Kingdom

SHARON PACE
Marquette University
Milwaukee, WI

JOHN PAINTER
St. Mark's School of Theology
Charles Sturt University
Barton, Australia

GEORGE L. PARSENIOS
Princeton Theological Seminary
Princeton, NJ

DALE PATRICK
Drake University
Des Moines, IA

DANIEL PATTE
Vanderbilt University
Nashville, TN

KIMBERLY R. PEELER
Vanderbilt University
Nashville, TN

PHEME PERKINS
Boston College
Chestnut Hill, MA

DAVID L. PETERSEN
Candler School of Theology,
Emory University
Atlanta, GA

WILLIAM L. PETERSEN[†]
Pennsylvania State University
University Park, PA

JOHN J. PILCH
Georgetown University
Washington, DC

DANIEL D. PIOSKE
Princeton Theological Seminary
Princeton, NJ

PIERLUIGI PIOVANELLI
University of Ottawa
Ottawa, ON, Canada

ELIZABETH E. PLATT
University of Dubuque Theological Seminary
Dubuque, IA

J. DAVID PLEINS
Santa Clara University
Santa Clara, CA

BEATE PONGRATZ-LEISTEN
Princeton University
Princeton, NJ

ADAM L. PORTER
Illinois College
Jacksonville, IL

STANLEY E. PORTER
McMaster Divinity College
Hamilton, ON, Canada

EMERSON B. POWERY
Lee University
Cleveland, TN

BRETT S. PROVANCE
Riverside, CA

RUTH ANNE REESE
Asbury Theological Seminary
Wilmore, KY

DAVID M. REIS
University of Oregon
Eugene, OR

BENNIE H. REYNOLDS, III
University of North Carolina at Chapel Hill
Chapel Hill, NC

VICTOR RHEE
Talbot School of Theology
Biola University
La Mirada, CA

SUZANNE RICHARD
Gannon University
Erie, PA

NEIL G. RICHARDSON
Wesley College
Bristol, United Kingdom

RAINER RIESNER
University of Dortmund
Dortmund, Germany

HENRY W. MORISADA RIETZ
Grinnell College
Grinnell, IA

ELLEN ROBBINS
Johns Hopkins University
Baltimore, MD

GREGORY ALLEN ROBBINS
University of Denver
Denver, CO

J. J. M. ROBERTS
Princeton Theological Seminary
Princeton, NJ

GARY O. ROLLEFSON
Whitman College
Walla Walla, WA

MARK RONCACE
Wingate University
Wingate, NC

CHRISOPHER ROWLAND
Queens College
University of Oxford
Oxford, United Kingdom

AARON D. RUBIN
Pennsylvania State University
University Park, PA

RODNEY S. SADLER, JR.
Union Theological Seminary and
Presbyterian School of Christian Education at Charlotte
Charlotte, NC

KATHARINE DOOB SAKENFELD
Princeton Theological Seminary
Princeton, NJ

JUDITH E. SANDERSON
Seattle University
Seattle, WA

LAWRENCE H. SCHIFFMAN
New York University
New York, NY

KARIN SCHÖPFLIN
Georg-August-Univerität Göttingen
Göttingen, Germany

ANDREAS SCHUELE
Union Theological Seminary and
Presbyterian School of Christian Education
Richmond, VA

JOSEPH F. SCRIVNER
Samford University
Birmingham, AL

JOANN SCURLOCK
Elmhurst College
Elmhurst, IL

ALAN F. SEGAL
Barnard College
Columbia University
New York, NY

RHODA SEIDENBERG
Yeshiva University Museum
New York, NY

C. L. SEOW
Princeton Theological Seminary
Princeton, NJ

ITZHAQ SHAI
Bar-Ilan University
Ramat-Gan, Israel

PHILLIP MICHAEL SHERMAN
Maryville College
Maryville, TN

YVONNE SHERWOOD
University of Glasgow
Glasgow, United Kingdom

MARY E. SHIELDS
Trinity Lutheran Seminary
Columbus, OH

JEFFREY S. SIKER
Loyola Marymount University
Los Angeles, CA

STEPHANIE SKELLEY-CHANDLER
Florida State University
Tallahassee, FL

MATTHEW L. SKINNER
Luther Seminary
Saint Paul, MN

P. OKTOR SKJAERVØ
Harvard University
Cambridge, MA

THOMAS B. SLATER
McAfee School of Theology,
Mercer University
Atlanta, GA

ABRAHAM SMITH
Perkins School of Theology,
Southern Methodist University
Dallas, TX

CHRIS M. SMITH
Bethany University
Scotts Valley, CA

DENNIS E. SMITH
Phillips Theological Seminary
Tulsa, OK

MARION L. SOARDS
Louisville Presbyterian Theological Seminary
Louisville, KY

WILL SOLL
Webster University
St. Louis, MO

SUSANNA W. SOUTHARD
Vanderbilt University
Nashville, TN

F. SCOTT SPENCER
Baptist Theological Seminary at Richmond
Richmond, VA

RICHARD A. SPENCER
Appalachian State University
Boone, NC

D. MATTHEW STITH
Community Presbyterian Church
West Fargo, ND

KEN STONE
Chicago Theological Seminary
Chicago, IL

JAMES RILEY STRANGE
Emory University
Atlanta, GA

JERRY L. SUMNEY
Lexington Theological Seminary
Lexington, KY

ROBERT C. TANNEHILL
Methodist Theological School in Ohio
Delaware, OH

JASON R. TATLOCK
Morgan State University
Baltimore, MD

EUGENE TESELLE
Vanderbilt Divinity School
(Emeritus)
Nashville, TN

ANTHONY C. THISELTON
University of Nottingham
Nottingham, United Kingdom

WESLEY I. TOEWS
Canadian Mennonite University
Winnepeg, MB, Canada

W. SIBLEY TOWNER
Union Theological Seminary and
Presbyterian School of Christian Education
(Emeritus)
Richmond, VA

PHYLLIS TRIBLE
Wake Forest University Divinity School
Winston-Salem, NC

ALLISON A. TRITES
Acadia Divinity College
(Emeritus)
Wolfville, NS, Canada

PETER TRUDINGER
Flinders University
Adelaide, Australia

PATRICIA K. TULL
Louisville Presbyterian Theological Seminary
Louisville, KY

MAX TURNER
London School of Theology
London, United Kingdom

GRAHAM H. TWELFTREE
School of Divinity, Regent University
Virginia Beach, VA

GERRIT VAN DER KOOIJ
Universiteit Leiden
Leiden, The Netherlands

EVELINE J. VAN DER STEEN
Liverpool University
Liverpool, United Kingdom

ROBERT E. VAN VOORST
Western Theological Seminary
Holland, MI

JOHANNA W. H. VAN WIJK-BOS
Louisville Presbyterian Theological Seminary
Louisville, KY

CAROLINE VANDER STICHELE
Universiteit vam Amsterdam
Amsterdam, The Netherlands

DAVID VANDERHOOFT
Boston College
Chestnut Hill, MA

JAMES C. VANDERKAM
University of Notre Dame
Notre Dame, IN

MICHAEL G. VANZANT
Mount Vernon Nazarene University
Mount Vernon, OH

ANDREW G. VAUGHN
Gustavus Adolphus College
Saint Peter, MN

T. DELAYNE VAUGHN
Baylor University
Waco, TX

RICHARD B. VINSON
Baptist Theological Seminary at Richmond
Richmond, VA

BURTON L. VISOTZKY
Jewish Theological Seminary
New York, NY

PAULINE A. VIVIANO
Loyola University of Chicago
Chicago, IL

STEVE WALTON
London School of Theology
London, United Kingdom

SZE-KAR WAN
Andover Newton Theological School
Newton Centre, MA

HAROLD C. WASHINGTON
Saint Paul School of Theology
Kansas City, MO

CECILIA WASSEN
Wilfrid Laurier University
Waterloo, ON, Canada

NANCY WEATHERWAX
University of North Dakota
Grand Forks, ND

JAMES M. WEINSTEIN
Cornell University
Ithaca, NY

STEPHEN WESTERHOLM
McMaster University
Hamilton, ON, Canada

TRISHA GAMBAIANA WHEELOCK
Gustavus Adolphus College
Saint Peter, MN

DEMETRIUS WILLIAMS
Tulane University
New Orleans, LA

TIMOTHY M. WILLIS
Pepperdine University
Malibu, CA

KEVIN A. WILSON
Lithuania Christian College
Klaipeda, Lithuania

JOHN D. WINELAND
Kentucky Christian University
Grayson, KY

DEREK E. WITTMAN
Baylor University
Waco, TX

LISA MICHELE WOLFE
United Theological Seminary
Dayton, OH

ARCHIE T. WRIGHT
Regent University
Virginia Beach, VA

BENJAMIN G. WRIGHT, III
Lehigh University
Bethlehem, PA

J. EDWARD WRIGHT
University of Arizona
Tucson, AZ

STEPHEN VON WYRICK
University of Mary Hardin-Baylor
Belton, TX

FRANK M. YAMADA
Seabury-Western Theological Seminary
Evanston, IL

SEUNG AI YANG
St. Paul Seminary School of Divinity
University of St. Thomas
Saint Paul, MN

JOHN Y. H. YIEH
Virginia Theological Seminary
Alexandria, VA

CHRISTINE ROY YODER
Columbia Theological Seminary
Decatur, GA

K. LAWSON YOUNGER, JR.
Trinity Evangelical Divinity School
Deerfield, IL

MATTANYAH ZOHAR
Maoz Tzion, Israel

SHARON ZUCKERMAN
The Hebrew University of Jerusalem
Jerusalem, Israel

GENERAL EDITOR'S PREFACE

On behalf of the Editorial Board, I welcome you to the company of users of *The New Interpreter's® Dictionary of the Bible*, a five-volume set offering the best in contemporary biblical scholarship. This new dictionary stands in the continuing tradition of the Interpreter's® series, developed for church and synagogue teachers and preachers and with the goal of supporting congregations and all students of the Bible as they seek to learn and grow.

The dictionary covers all the persons and places mentioned in the Bible. It contains a full range of articles on the cultural, religious, and political contexts of the Bible in the ancient Near East and the Greco-Roman world, and it offers many articles explaining key methods of biblical interpretation. The dictionary includes numerous articles on theological and ethical themes and concepts important to understanding the biblical witness.

The original *Interpreter's Dictionary of the Bible*, published in the 1960s, remained a key reference tool for pastors and teachers for nearly half a century. Yet it was of course a product of its time. Biblical scholarship moved an enormous distance in the intervening years, in knowledge of the literature and culture of the ancient world, and in the development of new approaches that have opened fresh horizons of interpretation, for individual books of the Bible, and for many theological concepts. Study of the Dead Sea Scrolls, of ancient Gnostic documents, and of extra-biblical prophetic texts from the ancient Near East are but a few of the many areas in which scholarship focused on extra-biblical texts has developed new data of great significance for understanding the Bible. Increased attention to gender, ethnicity, and economic class offers new insights into previously neglected aspects of the culture of the biblical world, which in some cases leads to striking new perspectives on biblical texts. Archaeology teams up with a wide range of natural sciences to develop methods that give greater insight into ancient community life, in addition to military upheavals. Newly discovered inscriptions and artifacts shed new light on biblical history and on religious beliefs and practices of ancient Israel and early Christianity. Recent progress in the analysis of Hebrew poetry, in understanding of Greek rhetoric, in theories of characterization, as well as new models of social-scientific analysis and cultural studies offer new avenues of inquiry in support of theological reading of the biblical text. To account for these and many other exciting developments, we have produced an entirely new dictionary rather than a revision of the old. While there may not be new information on certain obscure biblical persons or places, the major articles, almost without exception, introduce fresh material and even entirely new topics that were not on the 1960s scholarly horizon.

Of course these many changes in biblical studies have not taken place in a vacuum. The world itself has also changed greatly. As we move through the 21st century, we face a world grown smaller by speed of communication, yet in many ways politically and economically more fragmented (or at least we are more aware of the fragmentation) than ever before. Ecologically we face a possibly precarious future; factionalism and hostility seem on the increase within and among some religious and racial/ethnic groups, even as signs of reconciliation and search for common ground blossom in unexpected places. While such issues will not be addressed directly on every page, it is the aim of this dictionary to enable wise use of the biblical tradition in theological and ethical approaches to these difficult issues.

As the knowledge of the world surrounding the Bible and also methods for studying the Bible have expanded and changed, so also has the profile of the leaders in biblical scholarship. *The New Interpreter's Dictionary* contributors number approximately 900 women and men in more than 40 different countries from Australia to Africa, from the Americas to Europe, Asia, and the Middle East. Chosen for their scholarly expertise and publication in the areas of their articles, they are identified with Catholic, Orthodox, Jewish, and many different Protestant traditions; they range in personal commitment from conservative to liberal and come from many racial/ethnic and cultural backgrounds. The wide scope of the contributors' contexts reflects the global scope of biblical scholarship of the 21st century.

The Editorial Board took joint responsibility for nominating the wide range of authors who have contributed to this dictionary. Meetings, followed by numerous conference calls and innumerable rounds of email communication enabled comment and consensus building around the hundreds of nominees. Access to such a global span of contributors was greatly eased by computer and internet technology that could not have been feasible even a decade ago, with a website through which more than 7,100 articles were moved seamlessly and without paper from author to press and then through the various editorial stages. All but the very briefest articles were reviewed for content, balance of perspective, and accessibility by at least one member of the editorial board, and web and email facilitated discussion with authors of any proposed revisions. In addition, experienced pastors were recruited for further review of select longer articles, as an additional check on the readability and theological usefulness of the material for the intended audience.

In guidelines for authors and editors, this project has emphasized openness and generosity to various points of view. In an era when the very notion of one right answer to every question is itself increasingly called into question, we have asked our authors to offer their own perspectives on their topics while still including a clear and charitable presentation of significant alternative scholarly viewpoints. The editors are grateful to the authors for their willingness to write in this style, which will provide a fuller interpretive context for readers who are seeking an introduction to a subject.

As General Editor, it is my joy to express appreciation to the entire Editorial Board for their untiring efforts. The Board itself reflects something of the ecclesial, cultural, and racial/ethnic diversity, as well as the range of scholarly expertise that we have worked to bring to fruition in our contributing authors. Thanks, then, to Samuel Balentine, Brian Blount, Joel Green, Kah-Jin Jeffrey Kuan, Pheme Perkins, and Eileen Schuller for all that each of you has brought to our common work; and thanks to the staff of Abingdon Press, who have shepherded this long process with intelligence, imagination, and love.

KATHARINE DOOB SAKENFELD, GENERAL EDITOR

FEATURES OF
THE NEW INTERPRETER'S® DICTIONARY
OF THE BIBLE

A. The Main Entry

1. Title. Main entries are set in a bold font and highlighted in red. In most instances, where more than one person or place in the Bible shares a name, one article covers all instances of that proper name. For example, the article on JOSHUA will include Joshua, high priest and Joshua, son of Nun. However, in some instances, where the subject material is especially important, we divide articles between experts in various fields, to obtain the best treatments. For example, instead of one article on Abraham, we have ABRAHAM, NT and ABRAHAM, OT.

The articles are listed in alphabetical order, with rare exceptions; e.g., when listing all of the entries pertaining to BAAL some minor content sequencing was required.

2. Pronunciation. If the main entry is a person or place in the Bible, it is followed by a preferred pronunciation that is endorsed by the Society of Biblical Literature and derived from the *Harper-Collins Bible Pronunciation Guide* (ed. William O. Walker, Toni Craven, and J. Andrew Dearman. Revised edition, 1994). The following pronunciation key is a useful guide to the sounds that are intended.

a	cat	ihr	ear	ou	how
ah	father	j	joke	p	pat
ahr	lard	k	king	r	run
air	care	kh	ch as in German *Buch*	s	so
aw	jaw	ks	vex	sh	sure
ay	pay	kw	quill	t	toe
b	bug	l	love	th	thin
ch	chew	m	mat	*th*	then
d	do	n	not	ts	tsetse
e, eh	pet	ng	sing	tw	twin
ee	seem	o	hot	uh	ago
er	error	oh	go	uhr	her
f	fun	oi	boy	v	vow
g	good	oo	foot	w	weather
h	hot	*oo*	boot	y	young
hw	whether	oor	poor	z	zone
i	it	or	for	zh	vision
i	sky				

Stress accents are printed after stressed syllables. ´ is a primary stress. ´ is a secondary stress.

3. Biblical Languages. The editors think it is important for a dictionary to make the original biblical languages a part of appropiate entries. To satisfy those readers who are trained in

Hebrew, Aramaic, and Greek, the key terms are rendered in the original language as part of the main-entry heading. A transliteration is provided in the heading, and also with the first occurrence of any Hebrew or Greek font that is introduced in the body of an article. The transliteration style is based on the "general purpose" guide in the *SBL Handbook of Style*. For some students of the ancient languages, the transliteration style functions as a pronunciation guide, though this dictionary makes no attempt to reconcile English pronunciations with ancient-language transliterations.

4. Outline. Entries with more than 2,000 words ordinarily have an outline to help the reader navigate the information contained in the article.

5. Cross References. In the body of the main entry a reader will encounter words presented in all CAPITALS to signal that this topic exists as a separate entry in the dictionary. It would diffuse the purpose of special emphasis to signal a cross reference through capitalization for every person or place in the Bible. The capitalized cross reference means that information in another article is available to enhance the reader's understanding of a concept or to further explain the meaning of a technical term.

One of the risks of publishing five volumes over the course of several years is the potential of including "blind" cross references that lead the reader to another cross reference rather than to an article. Great care is taken in our database to prevent this frustration for the reader; if any blind references occur (perhaps if an article failed to appear), we will correct the link upon reprint.

6. Bibliography. This dictionary is not intended as a technical reference tool; therefore, entries do not contain detailed citations within the body of the article, nor footnotes at the end. However, a limited number of technical articles contain citations of an author's name, with bibliographic reference at the end of the entry. Bibliographies for articles are necessarily short and select. Works published before the mid-20th cent. generally are avoided in favor of more current works that build on earlier publications.

B. Main Entry List

The definitions included in this dictionary are written in a style that is accessible to students, pastors, and teachers of the Bible. Style decisions are based on the needs, interests, and skills in the primary audience. A group of consulting readers (all pastors of churches) aided us in vetting these articles for comprehension and usefulness in their daily tasks.

We began with the main entries from *The Interpreter's Dictionary of the Bible* (1964, 1975). We subtracted from this list several hundred King James Version spellings of persons, places, and obsolete terms, and replaced these with spellings or terms found in the *New Revised Standard Version* of the Bible. To the list of entries we added terms from other theological handbooks and Bible dictionaries, as well as topics recommended by members of the editorial board and authors. Author input was crucial as we responded to suggestions about dated topics, emerging trends, and more recently published primary sources.

The authors have moved away from the word-study approach that dominated biblical scholarship when the *Interpreter's Dictionary* was published. Scholars have learned that literary context is more important for present day Bible readers than etymology (word origins) or later theological notions of what a word means. A Bible dictionary, like any other dictionary, indexes single words or phrases that label people, places, and subjects. The challenge for the author of a Bible dictionary article is to convey (within the limited word count) the diverse range of meaning that can be represented by major terms.

C. Sources of Style

For English style (e.g., spelling and abbreviations), we relied on a blend of three sources: the *SBL Handbook of Style* (1999), produced by the Society of Biblical Literature, the *Chicago Manual of Style,* 15th Edition, and for issues unique to our project, the *New Interpreter's*® style guide.

When appropriate, we based translation of texts on the *New Revised Standard Version* of the Bible (NRSV), to promote uniformity among articles. Some familiar terms from the King James Version have been omitted, but Volume Three of the dictionary includes an article called KING JAMES VERSION, ARCHAIC TERMS. Readers are also encouraged to read the articles on BIBLE TRANSLATION THEORY; BIBLICAL INTERPRETATION, HISTORY OF; VERSIONS, AUTHORIZED; VERSIONS, BIBLE; and VERSIONS, ENGLISH for more information.

Other *New Interpreter's*® products consistently use the label "Old Testament" (OT). We decided with this dictionary to maintain the same style. Of course, when discussing the ancient languages more directly, articles refer as necessary to the Hebrew Bible (e.g., the Masoretic Text, with the abbreviation Heb.) or the Septuagint (the Greek text, with the abbreviation LXX).

We use the terms in small caps that are preferred by most scholars for identifying dates: BCE, "Before the Common Era" (in place of B.C., "Before Christ") and CE for "Common Era" (instead of A.D. for *Anno Domini*, "Year of our Lord").

For further help in navigating the dictionary, please see the list of ABBREVIATIONS at the end of each volume.

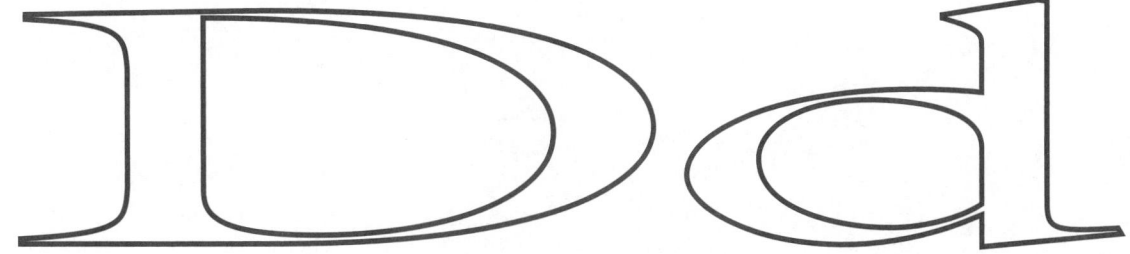

D. Fifth century manuscript containing Matthew, John, Luke, Mark, 3 John, and Acts of the Apostles. *See* TEXT, NT.

D, DEUTERONOMIC, DEUTERONOMISTIC dyoo´tuh-ruh-nom´ik dyoo´tuh-ron´uh-mis´tik. Adjectives variously used as authorial designations in critical studies since the end of the 19th cent., usually to differentiate respectively between work considered characteristic of the book of Deuteronomy (represented especially by its core legislation) and later materials in biblical literature influenced by Deuteronomy (as attested especially in Joshua, Judges, 1–2 Samuel, 1–2 Kings). *See* DEUTERONOMISTIC HISTORY; DEUTERONOMY, BOOK OF.

S. DEAN MCBRIDE

DABBESHETH dab´uh-sheth [דַּבֶּשֶׁת dabbesheth]. Means "hump." A site or geographic reference point along the southern border of the land allotted to Zebulun (Josh 19:11). Dabbesheth may be identified with Tel Shem'esh-Shammam north of Jokneam or some other site in that vicinity.

J. GORDON HARRIS

DABERATH dab´uh-rath [דָּבְרַת daverath]. A city of the Gershonite clan of Levites in the land allotted to Issachar (Josh 21:28), on the border with Zebulun. It does not appear on the list of Issachar's cities (Josh 19:17-23). RABBITH (Josh 19:20), according to the LXX, is probably a reference to Daberath. *See* GERSHON, GERSONITES; LEVITICAL CITIES, TOWNS.

Bibliography: R. S. Hess. *Joshua.* TOTC (1996).

J. GORDON HARRIS

DABRIA dab´ree-uh. In a vision, Ezra is instructed to enlist Dabria, SAREA, SELEMIA, ETHANUS, and ASIEL to write down revelatory information (2 Esd 14:24).

DAGON day´gon [דָּגוֹן daghon]. A prominent ANE deity described in the OT as the national god of the PHILISTINES.

A. Origin

Dagon probably arose as a West Semitic god, although it has also been argued that his origin was pre-Semitic. Dagan, spelled with two "a" vowels (the usual English spelling of the name), was a principal deity of the middle Euphrates region, in the third millennium and Old Babylonian periods, well attested in inscriptions and personal names from the Sargonic era and in Ebla and Mari texts, with cult centers at Mari, Tuttul, and Terqa. He has no real role in the Ugaritic myths, besides being Baal's father, but one of the two main temples there was his. He is also important in Philo of Byblos's account of Phoenician mythology, from which the Philistines apparently adopted him as their patron god. His exact nature remains elusive, though his identification with ENLIL and BAAL suggests that he was a storm god and perhaps played a role in the underworld.

B. Etymology

The origin of Dagon's name remains uncertain. The association with "fish" (dagh דָּג) made by Jerome and Rabbinic interpreters (Rashi, Kimchi) is fanciful, though it has influenced the reading of the biblical stories, since the Philistines were among the "sea peoples" and settled along the coast. First Samuel 5:4 has sometimes been taken as a reference to Dagon's ichthyomorphic nature, but the LXX offers a better reading of the verse: "only the trunk of Dagon was left." Another view derives the name from the root for "grain" (dgn דגן) and is supported by Philo's equation of Dagon with Siton, an epithet of Demeter meaning grain. A third proposal takes the Hebrew word for grain (daghan) as a secondary development from Dagon's name, which in turn derives from a root meaning "be cloudy, rainy," preserved in Arabic (dajja/dajana). If Dagon originated as a pre-Semitic deity, then it possesses no Semitic etymology.

C. Bible

The OT relates stories concerning temples of Dagon in Gaza (Samson's death, Judg 16), Ashdod (the capture of the ark, 1 Sam 5:1-5; so also 1 Macc 10:83-84; 11:4, where Azotus = Ashdod), and Beth-shan (the display of Saul's head, 1 Chr 10:10, based on the par. in 1 Sam 31:9), none of which have been confirmed by archaeology. Sites named Beth-Dagon in Judah and Asher (Josh 15:41; 19:27) suggest that other temples of Dagon once stood within those tribal territories. Theologically, the story in 1 Sam 5 is notable for establishing the power of Israel's God over Dagon, as Dagon's statue is reported to have fallen over and broken into pieces in the presence of the ark of the covenant. *See* EBLA TEXTS; MARI; UGARIT, TEXTS AND LITERATURE.

Bibliography: J. Fontenrose. "Dagon and El." *Oriens* 10 (1957) 277–79; Knut Holter. "Was Philistine Dagon a Fish-God? Some New Questions and an Old Answer." *SJOT* (1989) 142–47; J. J. M. Roberts. *The Earliest Semitic Pantheon: A Study of the Semitic Deities Attested in Mesopotamia Before Ur III* (1972).
STEVEN L. MCKENZIE

DAISAN day´suhn [Δαισάν Daisan]. One of the heads of ancestral houses that Darius sent back to Jerusalem after the exile. The descendants of Daisan were among the temple servants (1 Esd 5:31).

DALET [ד d]. The fourth letter of the Hebrew alphabet, which derives from an early Semitic pictograph of "door" (dalah דָּלָה), but the shape seems to derive from a by-form, "fish" (daghah דָּגָה). *See* ALPHABET.

DALIYEH, WADI ED. A dry steam with steep banks in the hill country, west of Samaria leading down to the Jordan Valley. The area about nine mi. north of Jericho was honeycombed with caves. In one cave called Mugharet Abu-Sinjeh, fragments of 4th cent. BCE manuscripts were found by the same bedouin who had discovered the DEAD SEA SCROLLS. When the papyrus fragments, along with some clay sealings and several coins, came to the attention of archaeologists, they were recognized as an important discovery. To confirm that the fragments came from the caves and to see if some finds may have been overlooked, Paul W. Lapp of the American School of Oriental Research in Jerusalem, conducted cave clearances in January 1963 and February 1964. In the excavations a few more papyrus fragments, clay sealings, and coins were found, along with skulls and bones, cloth, pottery, wood, a little jewelry, and remains of food. The evidence indicated this was the location of the Bedouin finds. The late fourth cent. pottery, along with the coins and 4th cent. BCE script, dated the material.

From the circumstances discovered it has been concluded that leading Samarian citizens who had rebelled against Alexander the Great left the manuscripts. Perhaps as many as one hundred of the citizens hid out in the caves, with their supplies and valuables, until they were eventually found and probably suffocated by a fire built at the entrance to the cave.

Some of the fragments contained names and dates of leaders of the community. The manuscripts represented various civil documents such as marriage contracts, loans, sale of property, and slave purchases. These manuscripts are known as the SAMARIA PAPYRI.

Only one other cave in the area, Araq en-Nasaneh, investigated by the archaeologists contained ancient remains: some complete vessels from Middle Bronze I (about 2000 BCE) and artifacts from the Second Jewish revolt (2nd cent. CE), probably also left by refugees.

Bibliography: P. W. Lapp and N. L. Lapp, eds. *Discoveries in the Wadi ed-Daliyeh* (1974); M. J. W. Leith. *Wadi Daliyeh Seal Impressions* (1997); D. M. Gropp. *The Samaria Papyri from Wadi Daliyeh* (2001).
NANCY L. LAPP

DALMANUTHA dal´muh-noo´thuh [Δαλμανουθά Dalmanoutha]. A region referenced only in Mark 8:10 (with variations such as MAGDALA and Magada). The parallel tradition in Matt 15:39 provides Magadan (or, according to textual variations, Magdala or Magdalan) perhaps as a correction to Dalmanutha. According to Mark's portrayal, the region likely lies on the western shore of the Sea of Galilee. After the second major feeding miracle on the eastern side of the sea (Mark 8:1-9), Mark portrays Jesus and his disciples traveling to the region of Dalmanutha. While there, Jesus is confronted by the Pharisees who ask him for a sign (Mark 8:11-12). According to Mark, Jesus and his disciples then depart by boat to the other side of the sea (Mark 8:14). With its variations and undetermined location Dalmanutha illustrates the challenge of charting Mark's geographical references.

Bibliography: Vincent Taylor. *The Gospel According to Mark* (1963) 360–61.
DEBORAH KRAUSE

DALMATIA dal-may´shee-uh [Δαλματία Dalmatia]. A region on the eastern Adriatic named after the Dalmatae (Delmatae), an Illyrian tribe that emerged as Rome's major regional enemy after the decline of the Illyrian kingdom. It was part of the province of Illyricum until Rome, likely in 9 CE, divided the Illyricum into two imperial provinces, Pannonia and Dalmatia (2 Tim 4:10).

Bibliography: M. Šašel Kos and J. Niehoff. "Dalmatae, Dalmatia." *Brill's New Pauly* 4 (2004) cols. 42–47.
JOHN T. FITZGERALD

DALPHON dal´fon דַּלְפוֹן dalfon]. One of HAMAN's ten sons who were hanged (Esth 9:7, 13). The etymology and meaning are uncertain.

DAMASCENE dam´uh-seen. Name used to designate the fertile area of DAMASCUS produced by the Barada River. The Ghuta oasis and the district called the Merj are found located within this area.

DAMARIS dam´uh-ris [Δάμαρις Damaris]. Pairing of Paul's female Athenian convert Damaris (Acts 17:34) with DIONYSIUS demonstrates Luke's affinity for both women and men. The name *Damaris* is unique in Greek literature and may be legendary. Ancient biblical manuscripts omit her or, conversely, indicate her high standing (Acts 13:50; 17:12). *See* AREOPAGUS.

HEIDI S. GEIB

DAMASCUS duh-mas´kuhs [דַּמֶּשֶׂק dammeseq; Δαμασκός Damaskos]. A city located ca. 150 mi. northeast of Jerusalem that became the capital of a powerful Aramean kingdom in the 10th–8th cent. BCE. The city existed as a significant regional center into the Roman period. The Aramean kingdom centered in Damascus was one of the most dominant states in Syria-Palestine during the monarchical period, especially 900–730 BCE (*see* ARAM, ARAMEANS). The city appears in the NT as the location associated with the encounter of Saul of Tarsus with the risen Jesus. Damascus sits in one of the most fertile regions in Syria-Palestine and was known in the ancient world for its waters, gardens, and orchards (see 2 Kgs 5:12). Damascus had a powerful influence on Israel and Judah. The Umayyad Mosque in present-day Damascus, e.g., likely stands on the ancient site of the temple of the god Hadad, after which Ahaz of Judah is said to have modeled an altar in Jerusalem (2 Kgs 16:10-16; compare 2 Chr 28:23). The city often competed with Samaria for control of regions like Dan (*see* DAN, DANITES) and RAMOTH-GILEAD, and at times exercised political dominance over both Samaria and Jerusalem. At other times, Damascus was Israel's strongest ally against other foes. To a certain extent, Israelite and Judean history, especially from the 10th–8th cent. BCE, can only be understood in the context of the history of Damascus.

A. Origins and Early History (Pre-10th Cent. BCE)

Damascus appears twice in the stories of Abram (Gen 14:15; 15:2), but these references may be retrojections from later periods. The earliest significant textual references to Damascus are in inscriptions of the Egyptian pharaohs Thutmose III (ca. 1482 BCE) and Amenophis III (ca. 1417–1379 BCE; *see ANET*, 242), as well as in three of the AMARNA LETTERS from the 14th cent. BCE (e.g., *COS* 3.93:243). These references consistently portray Damascus as part of a larger area that was under the shadow of Egyptian political dominance throughout the Late Bronze Age. When the Egyptian empire collapsed around 1200 BCE, the city came under the control of the Arameans. By the early to mid-10th cent. BCE, it achieved significance as one of several Aramean kingdoms around the Orontes River, Beqaʾ Valley, and northern Transjordan.

B. The Height of Power: Damascus in the Assyrian Period (10th–8th Cent. BCE)

The stories of David say that he defeated Arameans from Damascus and placed garrisons in the city (2 Sam 8:3-12; compare 1 Chr 18:3-8). During the reign of Solomon, Rezon broke away from Aram-Zobah and ruled Damascus as an independent entity, taking it from Zobah or Israel (1 Kgs 11:23-25). The OT texts depict Rezon as a persistent adversary throughout Solomon's reign. If these traditions are reliable, they provide the earliest references to a significant Aramean kingdom in Damascus.

First Kings 15:18 may give the names of Rezon's successors throughout the rest of the 10th cent.: Hezion followed by Tab-Rimmon. First Kings 15 also relates that around 900 BCE, Ben-Hadad I, son of Tab-Rimmon, attacked Basha of Israel after Asa of Judah convinced him to break a standing alliance with Israel (compare 2 Chr 16:1-6). The Aramean king then captured several cities in northern Israel. Archaeological evidence of destruction at Tell al-Qadi (Dan) may attest to this conquest, but, contrary to earlier opinion, the Melqart Stela's reference to "Ben-Hadad" probably does not refer to Ben-Hadad I or any king of Aram-Damascus (*COS* 2.33:152-153).

By the time sufficient Assyrian sources for Aramean history reemerge (ca. 860 BCE), the kingdom of Aram-Damascus, under its new king HADADEZER (Adad-idri), stands as the leading regional power in Syria-Palestine. In 853 BCE, Hadadezer led a large Syro-Palestinian coalition, which included AHAB of Israel, and defeated or at least stalled the Assyrian army of Shalmaneser III at Qarqar (*COS* 2.113A:261-264). The coalition fought the Assyrians to a similar result on three subsequent occasions between 853 and 845 BCE. The Assyrian records that portray Israel as an ally of Hadadezer of Damascus during Ahab's reign (868–854 BCE) contradict 1 Kgs 20 and 22, where the king of Damascus is called BEN-HADAD. The majority of interpreters conclude, however, that these chapters actually refer to hostilities with Damascus in the later Jehu dynasty and that Israel cooperated with Damascus throughout Hadadezer's reign.

This situation changed in 843 BCE, when HAZAEL usurped the throne in Damascus (see 2 Kgs 8:7-15; compare 1 Kgs 19:15) and began a reign that would be the apex of the kingdom's power. Through aggression against Israel at Ramoth-Gilead (2 Kgs 8:28-29; 9:14b-15a) and perhaps the killing of Jehoram of Israel and Ahaziah of Judah (*see* INSCRIPTION, TELL DAN [*COS* 2.39:161-162]; compare 2 Kgs 9–10), Hazael began to assert dominance over Syria-Palestine. When Assyria entered a period of decline for the next three decades (ca. 837–805 BCE), Damascus's expansion went virtually unchallenged. Biblical texts indicate that Hazael dominated Israel and Judah, captured Israelite territory in the Transjordan, and subjugated virtually all of the land west of the Jordan as far as Gath (2 Kgs 10:32-33; 12:17-18; 13:3). Hazael's booty inscriptions recovered from Arslan–Tash (near Til Barsip), Nimrud, and the Greek island of Samos (*COS* 2.40:162-163) may indicate that Hazael even conducted offensive campaigns into Assyrian territory across the Euphrates. Thus, the second half of the 9th cent. saw Hazael at least exert hegemony over Israel and Judah and perhaps establish a Damascus-centered empire that also included some Philistine and Transjordan kingdoms, as well as areas north of the Euphrates.

Due to an Assyrian resurgence in the west beginning around 805 BCE, Damascus's dominance eventually collapsed during the reign of Hazael's son, Ben-Hadad (II). He led a failed coalition against Zakkur, king of Hamath and Lush (*COS* 2.35:155), Jehoahaz or Joash of Israel threw off the Aramean yoke (2 Kgs 6:24–7:20; 13–14; compare 1 Kgs 20; 22), and the Assyrians subjugated Damascus (see, e.g., Rimah Stela [*COS* 2.114F:275–276]). Additionally, 2 Kgs 14:28 says that Jeroboam II (788–748 BCE) dominated Damascus and Hamath, although the historical details of this claim remain vexed.

A subsequent period of Assyrian decline in the 750s BCE, however, ushered in the final era of power for the Aramean kingdom centered in Damascus. Biblical and Assyrian texts depict REZIN, the new king of Damascus, as attempting to reassert regional dominance to match the former "house of Hazael" (2 Kgs 15:37; 16:5-6; Amos 1:3-5; *COS* 2.117F:291). When Tiglath-pileser III took the throne of Assyria in 744 BCE and revived Assyrian power, Rezin worked to construct a coalition to challenge the Assyrians in Syria-Palestine. Part of this effort was a joint campaign with Pekah of Israel to lay siege to Jerusalem and force Ahaz of Judah to join the coalition (2 Kgs 16:1-18; 2 Chr 28:1-25; Isa 7:1-17).

This attack on Jerusalem, referred to as the "Syro-Ephraimitic War" (ca. 734 BCE), would prove to be Aram-Damascus's last significant action. Tiglath-pileser campaigned down the Mediterranean coast, pushed Rezin back into Damascus, and laid siege to the city. The Assyrians ultimately destroyed the capital, deported parts of the population, and provincialized Aramean territories (*ANET*, 283; compare 2 Kgs 16:9). This destruction marked the disappearance of Damascus as a major power in the Assyrian period. When Ilu-bi'di of Hamath led another regional rebellion against Assyria in 720 BCE, the city played only a minor role and was quickly re-subjugated.

C. Damascus in the Babylonian to Roman Periods (7th Cent. BCE–3rd Cent. CE)

Although little is known about Damascus during the Babylonian period (ca. 605–539 BCE), the city became the seat of a Persian satrapy during the Achaemenid period (ca. 539–334 BCE) and had a Greek-appointed governor under Alexander the Great. After Alexander's death, the city went back and forth between Ptolemaic and Seleucid control. In contrast to the Jewish struggles with Hellenism in Jerusalem (see, e.g., the books of Daniel and Maccabees), Damascus more readily assimilated its culture and religion to Greek ideals and became an important cultural center and one-time Seleucid capital.

The city's lasting return to political prominence came during the Roman period. For a time, the NABATEANS, a people from the area southeast of Palestine, established Damascus as the capital of a semi-independent kingdom (ca. 85 BCE), but the Roman general Pompey sent troops to take it around 65 BCE. The city flourished in the Roman period, possessing a large temple; a colonnaded, cross-city thoroughfare (perhaps the "street called Straight" in Acts 9:11); and a significant population of Jews. Later centuries of Roman rule provide the context for the NT's story of Saul of Tarsus's encounter with the risen Jesus en route to Damascus (Acts 9:1-25), as well as his subsequent escape from the city (2 Cor 11:32-33). The NT's statement that a governor of the Nabatean king ARETAS IV was ruling in Damascus during these events (2 Cor 11:32) likely indicates that the Romans allowed the Nabateans to remain in control of at least a section of the city, perhaps the section where the Jewish settlement was located. *See* ASSYRIA AND BABYLONIA; ISRAEL, HISTORY OF.

Bibliography: R. Burns. *Damascus: A History* (2005); S. Hafthórsson. *A Passing Power: An Examination of the Sources for the History of Aram-Damascus in the Second Half of the Ninth Century B.C.* (2006); J. K. Kuan. *Neo-Assyrian Historical Inscriptions and Syria-Palestine* (1995); E. Lipiński. *The Arameans: Their Ancient History, Culture, Religion* (2000); B. Mazar. "The Aramean Empire and Its Relations with Israel." *BA* 25 (1962) 98–120; W. Pitard. *Ancient Damascus: A Historical Study of the Syrian City-State from the Earliest Times until Its Fall to the Assyrians in 732 B.C.E.* (1987); M. Unger. *Israel and the Aramaeans of Damascus: A Study in Archaeological Illumination of Bible History* (1957).

BRAD E. KELLE

DAMASCUS DOCUMENT duh-mas´kuhs. Early Jewish Hebrew work of which both ancient and medieval copies survive. Two medieval copies of the Damascus Document (CD) were discovered in the Cairo Genizah at the end of the 19th cent. Manuscript A (CD 1–16) contains sixteen pages and dates from the 10th cent. CE. Manuscript B dates from the 12th cent. CE and consists of two pages (19 and 20) partly overlapping with manuscript A.

The contents of CD can be divided into an Admonition (CD 1–8; 19–20) and a section of Laws (CD 9–16). The medieval manuscripts were first published under the title *Fragments of a Zadokite Work* since the document contains a number of favorable references to "the sons of Zadok" (e.g., CD IV, 1–3). The title *Damascus Document* is derived from a number of references to "the land of Damascus" and "Damascus" in the Admonition (e.g., CD VI, 5, 19; VII, 15, 19; VIII, 21; XIX, 34; XX, 12).

Ten ancient copies, ranging in date from the 1st cent. BCE to the first half of the 1st cent. CE, were subsequently discovered in Caves 4, 5, and 6 as part of the QUMRAN library (4Q266–273; 5Q12; 6Q15). The fragments from Caves 5 and 6 contain a small amount of text. The eight fragmentary manuscripts from Cave 4 provide a significant amount of text comprising both material overlapping with CD with only minor variants as well as a considerable amount of additional text relating to the Admonition and chiefly the legal part. The shorter medieval text has been explained as having been caused by accidental loss or as the result of a process of deliberate omissions.

The Admonition contains four accounts of the origins and early history of a pious reform movement. These accounts as well as references to a sojourn in Damascus (see Amos 5:26-27) and the TEACHER OF RIGHTEOUSNESS (see CD I, 11; XX, 32; see also VI, 11; XX 1, 4) have sparked a great deal of interest among scholars who have used the document as a key source in attempts to reconstruct the history of the community that resided at Khirbet Qumran from around 100 BCE–CE 68. The Admonition locates the movement's emergence around the middle of the 2nd cent. BCE. The Teacher is referred to as someone who gave guidance to the movement twenty years after its inception (CD 1) and his death is referred to in CD XIX–XX. A related figure ("the one who will teach righteousness at the end of the day") is referred to in CD VI. The legal part describes a community that dwelled in camps presided over by an overseer. The composition closes with an expulsion ceremony as well as a reference to an assembly in the third month.

A case has been made for the composite nature of the Admonition. More recently the Laws have also been subjected to source- and redaction-critical analysis. Recent years have seen an upsurge of scholarly interest in legal texts from Qumran in general and the now enlarged legal component of the Damascus Document in particular. Since the publication of the eight manuscripts of the Damascus Document from Cave 4, it has become clear that the document needs to be recognized as largely a legal work. The Damascus Documents display close links to a number of other texts from Qumran that are being investigated by scholars. For example, 4QMiscellaneous Rules (4Q265) covers a number of topics also treated in the Damascus Document such as the sabbath, the fifteen strong council of the community, and a penal code. The legal part of the Damascus Document covers a number of halakhic issues addressed in other halakhic works from Qumran (e.g., 4Q394–399 and 4Q159) such as gleanings (see Deut 23) and the ritual requirements for the red cow ceremony. The work further overlaps thematically and occasionally word for word with parts of the Community Rule, and the complex relationship of both documents lies at the heart of scholarly attempts to describe the communities reflected in the Dead Sea Scrolls (*see* RULE OF THE COMMUNITY). In short, the composition is one of the most important non-biblical works from Qumran and covers the areas of communal origins and history, organization of the communities, as well as halakhah. *See* DEAD SEA SCROLLS.

Bibliography: C. Hempel. *The Damascus Texts* (2000); M. L. Grossman. *Reading for History in the Damascus Document. A Methodological Study* (2002).
CHARLOTTE HEMPEL

DAMN, DAMNATION. *See* CONDEMNATION.

DAN, DANITES dan, dan′it [דָּן dan, בְּנֵי־דָן bene dan; Δάν Dan]. 1. The fifth son of JACOB through Rachel's servant BILHAH. The name, meaning "he has judged," is explained by the patriarch's birth narrative, during which RACHEL signifies the birth of a son born through her servant Bilhah as a divine judgment on her behalf (Gen 30:3-6). As such, the patriarchal narratives identify Dan as the first of the four sons born to the servants of Jacob's wives (the other sons are Napthali, Asher, and Gad; see Gen 35:25; 46:23; Exod 1:4).

2. The Israelite tribe that traced its descent through Dan. Tribal lists and traditions reflect the same grouping of Dan, Napthali, Asher, and Gad (Num 13:12-25; Deut 33:20-25), although the absence of Gad in many cases indicates that the organizational scheme may have more to do with geography than genealogy. This is particularly apparent in Priestly literature, where tribal Dan is most commonly grouped only with Asher and Napthali, the tribes that, with Dan, occupied the northernmost region of Israel (Num 1:38-39; 2:25-26; 7:66-71; 19:25; 26:42-43; compare 1 Chr 12:35). An exception to this scheme is Dan's grouping with the Joseph tribes, Benjamin, and Naphtali (the children attributed to Rachel) in a list of tribal leaders from David's census (1 Chr 27:22 [Heb. 27:24]).

The appearance of a people called the **Danuna** by the Egyptians and the **Danaoi** by the Greeks, near the end of the second millennium, suggests a connection with the biblical tribe, although the connection cannot be verified or defined. The population of Dan recorded in Numbers gives the impression of a very large tribe; the 62,700 enrolled members in the census are second only to Judah (1:39). Other texts, however, suggest the opposite. An account of Dan's northward migration counts only 600 fighting men among the tribe and refers to it as a **mishpakhah** (מִשְׁפָּחָה), a term that elsewhere denotes a clan (Judg 18:2, 11, 19). Tribal genealogies reinforce the sense of Dan's small size. No tribal divisions configured the tribe, a situation signaled by the listing of only one son for Dan (sons serving as eponyms for clans in genealogies). The two names given for the son, Hushim (**khushim** חֻשִׁים)

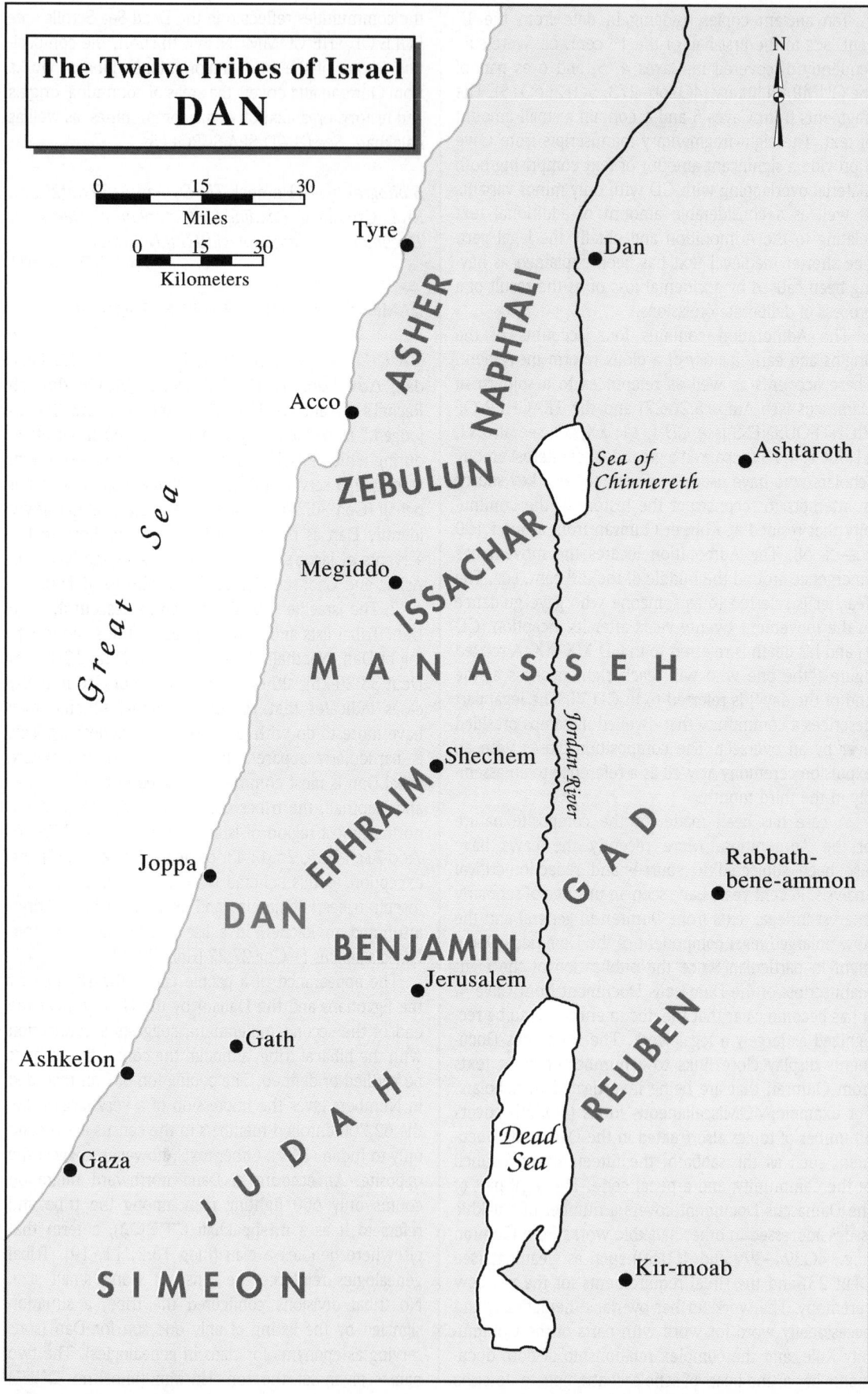

The Twelve Tribes of Israel
DAN

in Gen 46:23 and Shuham (shukham שׁוּחָם) in Num 26:42, are variants of a single name, differentiated by a metathesis (transposition) of shin (שׁ) and khet (ח).

Joshua 19:40-46 locates Dan's original settlement between the western regions of Ephraim and Judah but probably derives from the time of Solomon at the earliest. The description of the tribe's allotment consists only of a list of towns, which span a stretch of land extending westward from Benjamin and roughly equivalent to the area of Solomon's Second District (1 Kgs 4:9). Many appear also in the list of Judah's towns, namely Zorah and Eshtaol (v. 41; 15:33), Ir Shemesh (v. 41; Beth-shemesh in 15:10), Timnah (v. 43; 15:57), and Ekron (v. 43; 15:11, 45-46). Others are located within the boundaries delineated for Ephraim, notably Shaalabbim (Shaalbim in Judg. 1:35) and Aijalon. The overlap between the various tribal lists reflects fluid historical circumstances, during which Judah and Ephraim took possession of territory that had been originally claimed but later abandoned by Dan.

Early traditions associate Dan only with Zorah and Eshtaol, two towns located in the vicinity of the Valley of the Sorek. The account of Dan's migration northward explicitly situates the tribe in these two towns but also notes that it was not successful in taking territory of its own (Judg 18:1-2, 8, 11). SAMSON, the Danite judge, hailed from Zorah (Judg 13:2), which at the time was on the frontier between Israel and the newly-arrived Philistines. The stories connected with Samson reveal the precarious circumstances under which the tribe lived during this period. They portray a Danite caught between the Philistines and the Israelites and unable to fit among either. Samson's relationship with the PHILISTINES is tempestuous and marked by chicanery, retaliation, and competition. He fares little better with his kinsfolk, who view him more as a liability than a hero and seek to hand him over to his enemies (15:10-13). It is by no means insignificant, in this respect, that Samson, alone among all the judges, does not rally the tribes to overthrow Israel's oppressor but is left instead to fend for himself.

Resistance from the indigenous peoples prevented Dan from securing a possession in the land (Judg. 1:35), but encroachment by the Philistines evidently caused the tribe to abandon its allotment altogether (although elements may have remained in the region). The tribe quit its lands in the south and conquered the Canaanite city of Laish (Leshem in Josh 19:47), a city located far to the north at the juncture of major trade routes. The name "Laish" means "lion," a fact that may lie behind an ancient but cryptic reference to Dan as a "lion's whelp that leaps forth from Bashan" (Deut 33:22). In contrast to their failure to take their allotment to the south, Dan seems to have prevailed easily over the inhabitants of the town, who were unaligned and taken by surprise (Judg 18:27-29). Thereafter the tribe's pos-

session consisted of this single town, which the tribe named after its ancestor.

The city was situated on a large mound of approximately fifty acres situated in the Huleh Valley, just southwest of Mount Hermon and near a spring that constitutes one of the main sources of the Jordan River. The soil that surrounds Tell Dan is unusually fertile, while the nearby slopes offer copious and accessible grazing land. Excavations of the mound have uncovered a sequence of sizable settlements, extending back to the Pottery Neolithic period (ca. 5000 BCE), and have confirmed the site's prominence as a culture center well before Israelite occupation. The site's notoriety is confirmed by its mention, as Laish, in a number of second millennium texts, including the Egyptian Execration texts, the Mari archives, and a list of conquered cities from the reign of Thutmoses III (see DAN, TELL).

As a frontier settlement, Dan effectively marked the northern limit of Israelite settlement; the phrase "from Dan to Beersheba" functions in biblical literature as a merismus for the entire land of Israel (Judg 20:1; 1 Sam 3:20; 2 Sam 3:10; 17:11; 24:2, 7, 15; 1 Kgs 4:25 and, vice versa, 1 Chr 21:2; 2 Chr 30:5). The town's location astride trade routes, as well as its proximity to Phoenician and Aramean lands, provided the tribe with significant strategic advantages. An early poetic text characterizes Dan as a viper lurking by the roadside and throwing the rider by striking the heel of his horse (Gen 49:17), probably a reference to raiding activities along the trade routes. Another early text, the Song of Deborah, suggests that the tribe had established economic ties with the Phoenicians which it was reluctant to jeopardize (Judg 5:17). The song chastises Dan for remaining "with the ships" when DEBORAH rallied the tribes and aligns Dan with the other tribes of the north whose mercantile activities may have been imperiled by joining an attack on the Canaanite king of Hazor.

The Chronicler reports that King Huram (spelled as HIRAM in 1 Kings) of Tyre sent an artisan named Huram-abi, the son of a Tyrian father and a Danite mother, to work on the construction of Solomon's temple (2 Chr 2:13-14; see HURAM, HURAM-ABI). It is probable, however, that the report reworks a parallel note in 1 Kgs 7:13-14, where the king is described as the son of a Naphtalite women and a Tyrian father who was an artisan of bronze. The Chronicler's reworking picks up the reference to bronze working, shifts the focus to the artisan, and changes the tribal affiliation of the mother, reflecting a strategy to present "Huram-abi" as a counterpart, in the construction of the temple, to Oholiab, a Danite whose abilities and tasks in the construction of the wilderness tabernacle are described in similar terms (Exod 31:6-11; 35:30-35).

Jeroboam I established Dan as a national sanctuary during his program to reconfigure the Israelite cult after the northern tribes broke with Rehoboam (1 Kgs 12:25-33). The program entailed installing golden calves at

Dan (at the northern border) and Bethel (at the southern border) and appointing non-levitical priests, so as to reorient tribal allegiance and worship away from Jerusalem (*see* CALF, GOLDEN). While the Deuteronomist views these acts as the primal sin of apostasy that eventuated in the destruction of the Northern Kingdom (v. 30; 13:33-34; 2 Kgs 17:21-23), Jeroboam and the tribes probably understood the moves as a return to an earlier expression of Israelite worship and devotion. Later, when Jehu purged Israel of all idolatrous elements, he did not abolish the calves and yet received a divine commendation for his efforts (1 Kgs 10:28-30). By the 8th cent., however, heterodox theology and practice had made inroads; Amos castigates those who swear, "as your god lives, O Dan" (Amos 8:14).

The biblical depiction of Dan's prominence as an Israelite cultic center has found confirmation in the discovery of a large and impressive sacred precinct marked by a high place configured by ashlars, as well as four-horned altars and a sizable complex of buildings. Massive city walls testify to the city's perilous geographical situation as Israel came into conflict with the Aramean kingdom of Damascus. BEN-HADAD of Damascus captured the town during a border war, ostensibly in response to a plea from Asa for help against Baasha (1 Kgs 15:17-20; 2 Chr 16:1-4), and it may have changed hands a number of times during the 9th and early 8th cent. (2 Kgs 8:7-15, 28; 9:24-29; 13:25; 2 Chr 22:5). Fragments of a victory stela erected at Dan and dated to this period celebrate the victory of an unknown Aramean king over "the house of David" (*see* INSCRIPTION, TELL DAN).

The town of Dan's association with apostasy explains a tendency to cast the tribe Dan negatively in the editing of early traditions. The blasphemer who was stoned during the wilderness period is identified as the son of a Danite woman (Lev 24:11). The account of the Danites' migration northward has been rendered in ways that implicitly denigrate the tribe and the Danite sanctuary; they steal an idol, ephod, and teraphim made

of stolen silver, persuade a mercenary Levite to be their tribal priest under threat of force, and, after destroying and rebuilding Dan, set up the idol there (Judg 18:1-31). Dan also functions as an anti-type of Judah. The description of tribal allotments begins with the full and detailed account of Judah's possession and the exemplary faith and success of its tribal leader, Caleb (Josh 15:1-62) but ends with the report of Dan's failure to take the land the Lord has given and its conquest of a city the Lord has not given (19:40-48). Similarly, the first of Israel's judges, Othniel, is a Judahite who delivers Israel in fine form (Judg 3:7-11). The last of Israel's judges, Samson the Danite, acts in isolation, liberates by taking revenge, and is a more successful judge when he dies than when he lives (Judg 14:1-16:31).

Early Jewish and Christian literature cast Dan as an archetype of apostasy. The *Testament of Dan* declares that SATAN is the prince of Dan and that the spirits of wickedness will use the tribe to cause the Levites to sin (5:4-7). Dan is conspicuously absent from the list of the twelve Israelite tribes in Revelation (Rev 7:5-8), and patristic writers (notably Irenaeus and Hippolytus) declare that the ANTICHRIST will descend from Dan. *See* TESTAMENTS OF THE TWELVE PATRIARCHS.

Bibliography: Y. Amit. "Hidden Polemic in the Conquest of Dan: Judges xvii-xviii." *VT* 40 (1990) 4–20; M. W. Bartusch. *Understanding Dan: An Exegetical Study of a Biblical Town, Tribe, and Ancestor* (2003); A. Biran. *Biblical Dan* (1994); S. Gevirtz. "Adumbrations of Dan in Jacob's Blessing on Judah." *ZAW* 93 (1981) 21–37; Z. Kallai. *Historical Geography of the Bible* (1986); Z. Kallai. "A Note on the Twelve-Tribe Systems of Israel." *VT* 49 (1999) 125–27.

L. DANIEL HAWK

DAN, TELL. A 50-acre site some 25 mi. north of the Sea of Galilee whose monumental remains have been identified with modern Tell el-Qadi ("mound of the judge"). According to biblical tradition, in the time of

John C. H. Laughlin
Figure 1: Tell Dan from the South

Jeroboam I (late 10th cent. BCE), Dan became a cult center boasting the famous "golden calf" (1 Kgs 12:29-31; *see* CALF, GOLDEN).

After a very brief archaeological probe in 1963 by Z. Yeivin, a major excavation of the ruin was begun by A. Biran in 1966. The excavation continued until the year 2000, making it the longest continuous archaeological project ever conducted in the state of Israel. The archaeological data indicate that the site was occupied at least as early as the Pottery Neolithic period (ca. 5000 BCE) and was not abandoned until the Late Roman/Byzantine period of the 4th cent. CE. The major architectural remains belong to the Middle Bronze Age and Iron Age II.

During Middle Bronze Age I/II (2000–1800 BCE) Dan (called Laish in Judg 18:29) was a large heavily fortified city protected by a rampart wall, the core of which measured over 25 ft. thick. Associated with this wall is one of the most remarkable discoveries made at Dan C, a mud brick gate standing close to its original height. The outside of the gate was protected by two large towers and a series of arches that formed the foundation for the gate's superstructure. Each arch is composed of three radial courses of sun-dried mud brick. It has been suggested that the gate system was used for only a generation or so before being incorporated into the rampart system, which preserved the structure until its discovery in 1979. *See* ACCO, AKKO; ASHKELON; GEZER, GEZERITES. The Middle Bronze Age city came to a violent end sometime in the late 16th or early 15th cent. BCE. Many other Middle Bronze Age cities were also destroyed, most likely by the Egyptians.

ity. Evidence for a smelting industry during this last phase of the Bronze Age was found, including furnaces, slag, and muzzles of blow pipes. Another important discovery dating to the 14th–13th cent. BCE is a Mycenean tomb that contained the remains of some forty people, including men, women, and children. Hundreds of grave goods were found, the most spectacular of which is a "Charioteer" vase painted in red and black, the only complete example of this ware found to date in Israel. Such tomb goods would suggest a wealthy family lived here.

The Iron I period at Dan is identified with strata VI–V (12th–11th cent. BCE). Evidence for these periods includes pottery remains in the Late Bronze Age ceramic tradition, including the so-called collared-rim pithoi, and silos that the inhabitants may have lived in. The last phase of Iron Age I (ca. 1150 BCE) was violently destroyed. Some authorities have linked this destruction with the migration of Dan reported in the book of Judges (18:27). However, this conclusion is based more on the biblical story then on archaeology.

From a biblical perspective, the most important period of Dan's existence was during the next three phases (Strata IV–II), archaeologically known as Iron Age II (10th–6th cent. BCE). During this time Dan reached a size of 50 acres and was protected by massive defensive walls. Discoveries from this period include significant architectural remains, ceramics, small objects (many of which may have cultic significance), as well as cultic installations, including what has been identified as a **bamah** (בָּמָה) or HIGH PLACE.

John C. H. Laughlin

Figure 2: Middle Bronze mud brick gate with guard tower (right side of photo)

John C. H. Laughlin

Figure 3: "Dan High Place." Compare 1 Kgs 12:31.

While architectural remains were found dating to the Late Bronze Age, damage to these structures was widespread due to subsequent Iron Age I activ-

Dan's Iron Age II defensive system is one of the largest yet discovered in Israel. It consists of an outer and inner gate that enclosed an area of some 4,500 sq. ft. Associated with this gate is a podium or dais and a limestone bench. While their function is unclear, the podium may have been used as a seat for a visiting king, or to hold the image of a god. Most surprising are the four sets of standing stones discovered in the vicinity of the gates. Two of these installations consisted of five stones each. The other two were constructed of four stones each. Some authorities identify these installations as examples of massebot mentioned in the Bible (Gen 31:49-51; 35:19-21; Exod 24:4; 2 Sam 18:18). While the excavator concluded that these installations were cultic in nature, who used them and in what way(s) is not clear.

John C. H. Laughlin

Figure 4: Structures at Iron II Gate

Another important discovery made in 1993 is a stele fragment written in Aramaic (two other fragments were found in 1994). Dated to the last half of the 9th cent. BCE, the stele celebrates a victory over Dan by Damascus (according to 1 Kgs 15:20, Ben-Hadad captured Dan during his reign). The inscription has created something of a controversy because part of it has been translated to refer to the "House of David." This is the first clear reference to DAVID found outside the Bible.

While the city of Dan seems to have been captured during both the Assyrian (8th cent. BCE; compare Judg 18:30) and the Babylonian (6th cent. BCE) wars, it continued to be inhabited. Some significant discover-

ies have been made from later periods (including a bilingual text from the Hellenistic period that mentions "the god who is in Dan"), but the site never recovered its pre-Assyrian size. *See* DAN, DANITES.

Bibliography: Avraham Biran. *Biblical Dan* (1994); Avraham Birin, D. Ilan, and R. Greenberg. *Dan I A Chronicle of the Excavations, the Pottery Neolithic, the Early Bronze Age and the Middle Bronze Age Tombs* (1996).

JOHN C. H. LAUGHLIN

DAN, TESTAMENT OF. *See* TESTAMENTS OF THE TWELVE PATRIARCHS.

DANAOS [Δάναος Danaos]. According to Hecataeus (cited in Diodorus Siculus, *Bib. Hist.* 40.3.2), the mythical king Danaos and Kadmos (founder of Thebes) both left Egypt when Moses did. HERODOTUS (6.53) claimed that SPARTA's ancestors came from Egypt. A letter from the Spartan king Arius (1 Macc 12:19-23) also suggests a link between Spartans and Abraham's descendants. *See* GREECE.

JAMES RILEY STRANGE

DANCING [חוּל khul, כָּרַר karar, פָּזַז pazaz, רָקַד raqadh; ὀρχέομαι orcheomai, χορός choros]. Dancing is a form of religious worship and community celebration in biblical texts. Community celebrations constitute religious dance in the sense that public rituals and festivals are part of communal worship. Several Hebrew and Greek terms describe physical movements that translate as "dancing." The root khwl (חוּל) refers to "being in travail," "writhing," and "whirling," while rqd (רקד) means "to skip about." The term krr (כרר) means "whirling." It occurs only in reference to David's dance (2 Sam 6:14, 16) and is used once with pzz (פזז), which means "to be supple and agile" (2 Sam 6:16). The primary Greek terms for "dancing" are the verbal form **orcheomai** and its nominal form, **choros**.

Dancing and music form important elements of Israelite religious worship. Both singers and dancers praise God (Ps 87:7). As well, dance includes musical accompaniment (Pss 149:3; 150:3). For example, David's procession to bring the ark of God to Jerusalem includes singing, dancing, and music (2 Sam 6; 1 Chr 15). As part of this procession, David wears a linen ephod and "danced before the Lord with all his might" (2 Sam 6:14). David's wife, Michal, admonishes him for what she perceives as shameless behavior, but he rebukes her (2 Sam 6:20-22).

Dance may be employed in idolatrous worship. For instance, Joshua hears what he assumes is the noise of warfare when he and Moses return from Mount Sinai. Instead, he and Moses find the Israelites singing and dancing as they worship the golden calf (Exod 32:17-19). Also, in a contest at Mount Carmel, Elijah makes fun of the prophets of Baal who limp (pasakh פָּסַח)

about the altar as they pray to Baal to answer them (1 Kgs 18:21, 26).

While both men and women dance, women dance together as part of community celebrations. After the Israelites cross the sea and the Egyptians drown, the prophet Miriam and all of the women sing a victory song with tambourines and dancing (Exod 15:20). Also, young women dance at an annual religious festival at Shiloh (Judg 21:21; see Abel-meholah "dancing meadow" Judg 7:22; 1 Kgs 4:12; 19:16).

Dancing provides a form of greeting for returning warriors, as women dance and sing to welcome home the victors. For instance, Jephthah's daughter (unnamed in the biblical text) comes out to meet Jephthah with timbrels and dancing when he returns from war against the Ammonites (Judg 11:34). Also, when David returns from killing the Philistine, Israelite women sing and dance to honor both Saul and David (1 Sam 18:6; 21:11; 29:5).

In the apocryphal book of Judith, dance is used to greet enemy warriors and to celebrate their defeat. Seeking peace, the local population welcomes Holofernes, general of Nebuchadnezzar, with dances, garland, and tambourines (Jdt 3:7). Later, following Judith's beheading of Holofernes and the defeat of the Assyrians by the Israelites, women dance in honor of Judith for her heroism (Jdt 15:12). Then, Judith leads the women in dancing, while the men follow bearing arms, wearing garlands, and singing hymns (Jdt 15:13).

Dance also provided entertainment and was associated with playful laughter and merriment. For example, one of Jeremiah's oracles promises that Israel will again have the dance of merrymakers (Jer 31:4). Also, in describing the prosperity of the wicked, Job laments that they sing with musical instruments and that their children dance around (Job 21:11-12).

Dancing is considered to be the opposite of mourning. For example, Qoheleth contrasts weeping and mourning with laughing and dancing (Eccl 3:4). In a psalm of thanksgiving, the psalmist exclaims, "You have turned my mourning into dancing!" (Ps 30:11 [Heb. 30:12]). Conversely, in a communal lament the people ask the Lord to remember the calamities that have befallen them and complain, "Our dancing has been turned into mourning" (Lam 5:15).

Instances of dancing in the NT do not involve religious worship. Yet, as in the OT, dancing involves rejoicing and festivity. For instance, in the parable of the prodigal son, as the elder son approaches home, he hears singing and dancing in celebration of the younger son's return (Luke 15:25). Also, at the birthday party of Herod Antipas, his step-daughter, the daughter of Herodias, dances for him and his guests (Matt 14:6; Mark 6:22). Her performance leads to a rash vow by Herod and the beheading of John the Baptist (Matt 14:6-11; Mark 6:22-28). While the daughter of Herodias is unnamed in the Bible, Flavius Josephus refers to her as Salome (Josephus, *Ant.* 18.136).

NYASHA JUNIOR

DANEL. *See* DANIEL.

DANIEL dan′yuhl [דָּנִאֵל dani'el, דָּנִיֵּאל daniye'l; Δανιήλ Daniēl]. Means "El is my judge," or simply, "God judges." 1. The son of David and ABIGAIL born at Hebron (1 Chr 3:1). He is called CHILEAB in 2 Sam 3:3.

2. The head of a Levite family that returned from Babylon with Ezra. He was a descendant of ITHAMAR (Ezra 8:2). Daniel placed his seal on the covenant document (Neh 10:6).

3. The main character and hero of the biblical book that bears his name.

A. Background

Elsewhere in the OT we hear of an outstandingly righteous man named Daniel (Ezek 14:14, 20). Evidently he was thought of as an ancient Gentile worthy, for he is mentioned in the same breath with Job and Noah. In Ezek 28:3 this legendary Daniel is praised for his wisdom. Scholars generally regard Ezekiel's wise and righteous Daniel as the literary ancestor of the hero of the late OT book.

Even farther back in the ancestry of our Daniel is the king Dnil (or Danel or even Daniel) of Canaanite legend. We know him from the fragmentary *Tale of Aqhat*, a text found in the rich trove of ca. 14th cent. BCE epigraphic remains from Ugarit (Ras Shamra, on the Mediterranean coast of Syria). Aqhat, Daniel's son by his wife, Danatiya, is conceived with a kiss after the rain and fertility god Baal intercedes with the high god El on Daniel's behalf. Baal bases his plea for Daniel upon the man's piety (manifested in daily oblations to the gods) and upon his justice:

> [Daniel] is upright, sitting before the gate,
> Beneath a mighty tree on the threshing floor,
> Judging the cause of the widow,
> Adjudicating the case of the fatherless
> (*Aqhat A* 5:5-8, 22–25)

From antiquity, therefore, a Daniel existed who revered deity, showed wisdom and discretion, and led the community with justice.

B. The Daniel of the Book

It is impossible to write a biography of the Daniel of the book, as if he were an actual figure of Jewish history. This Daniel is a composite, fictional character and the stories about him and the accounts of his visions probably originated in diverse times and places. What we are given instead is an icon of Jewish piety of the 2nd cent. BCE, an exemplar of Torah-true steadfastness.

In the court tales of chaps. 1–6, the book presents an idealized literary Daniel who exemplifies the virtues of wisdom, just judgment, and able leadership. The apocalyptic section of the book, chaps. 7–12, adds the gift of vision to his portrait. Now Daniel enjoys the status of an intermediary between God and the community of the faithful, charged to convey the good news of God's imminent and final victory over tyranny and evil in the world.

The tales of Daniel (chaps. 1–6) are laid in the courts of Babylon and Persia. Their contribution to the portrait of Daniel is cumulative. In chap. 1, four exiled Jewish youths are being trained at the Babylonian academy of wisdom for service at Nebuchadnezzar's royal court. The youths, led by Daniel, refuse to drink the wine and eat the morsels of the king that are offered to them, but thrive instead on a diet of vegetables. This court tale illustrates Daniel's determination to maintain his sharp Jewish identity and moral freedom. Chapter 2 adds to the emerging picture of Daniel's skills belonging to the sage and the prophet. As a wise man, not only can he interpret the king's dream, but, with God's help, he can also recall it—an accomplishment that even that peerless Israelite courtier and sage, Joseph (Gen 41:1-36), could not match. As prophet, Daniel reveals his prescience in his sketch of human history down to its very end (Dan 2:31-45). He successfully functions a second time as dream interpreter in chap. 4, causing Nebuchadnezzar to offer a psalm of praise to "the King of heaven." In chap. 5, Daniel outshines all of the diviners of Babylon by reading and interpreting to King Belshazzar the meaning of the handwriting on the wall. The last court tale, chap. 6, portrays a pious, brave, and trusting Daniel who will not desist from praying three times each day to the God of Israel even though, by order of the Persian king, Darius, to do so meant death by lions.

These chapters render for us the outer, public history of an ideally righteous man. The remaining six chapters of the book of Daniel report the man's private and inner history. Now Daniel becomes an apocalyptic visionary whom God empowers to tell the history of the future and the promise of resurrection. His ecstatic, visionary experiences are costly to him, e.g., "my thoughts greatly terrified me, and my face turned pale" (7:28); "I . . . was overcome and lay sick for some days" (8:27). For the great vision of chaps. 10–12, Daniel prepares by mourning and fasting for three weeks (10:2-3). His experiences include observations of horrible beasts (7:1-8; 8:8:3-14), a vision of God seated upon the heavenly throne (7:9-10), and many conversations with the angelic interpreter Gabriel. In chap. 9, in the midst of his apocalyptic visions, more information about the character and personality of this literary Daniel is added. Because of his own unquestioned piety, he is able to intercede powerfully for his people (9:3). In both his prayer in chap. 9 and in the apocalyptic visions, Daniel continues to exhibit prescience, if not infallibility.

The narrative character Daniel in the book of Daniel serves, then, as a model of the lifestyle and piety of the observant Jews of the 2nd cent. BCE era of the composition of the book, as well as the mediator of the first elaborated apocalypse and the first OT figure to refer to the double resurrection of the dead (12:1-3).

C. Foreground

Two of the three additions to the book of Daniel found in the ancient Greek versions of the OT (see SEPTUAGINT; THEODOTION) further develop the character of Daniel (see DANIEL, ADDITIONS TO). In Susanna, a young lad named Daniel saves from execution a beautiful, innocent woman by proving through cross-examination that the elders who testified that SUSANNA was an adulteress had lied. Daniel ("El is my Judge") lives up to his name by being a just judge himself. A second addition to the book of Daniel is called BEL AND THE DRAGON. The first panel tells how Daniel, who abhors idolatry and trickery, demonstrates the falsity of the priests who serve the idol of the Mesopotamian god, Bel. Thereupon the king, Cyrus, executes the bad priests and gives permission to Daniel to destroy the image of Bel. In a second episode, Daniel kills a dragon that the Babylonians worshiped, is thrown into yet another lion's den, and is miraculously saved by God. These deutero-canonical additions suggest that a larger Daniel cycle was in circulation in late antiquity, and they add justice and the power of persuasion to the canonical characterization of Daniel as a man of piety, integrity, and vision.

Other deuterocanonical enlargements on the virtues of the man Daniel include the reference in 1 Macc 2:60 to the Daniel of chap. 6: "Daniel, because of his innocence, was delivered from the mouth of the lions" (see also 3 Macc 6:7; 4 Macc 16:3, 21 and 18:13). The stature of the man grows with the virtue of "innocence." The only other deuterocanonical reference to Daniel (4 Esd 12:11) reinterprets the fourth beast of his first apocalyptic vision (Dan 7:2-8) to apply to Rome, but adds nothing to the portrait of the man.

Part of the foreground of any OT character is to be found in the pseudepigraphical literature of the centuries between the OT and the NT. As a narrative person, Daniel plays a relatively minor role in these texts, though the apocalyptic ideas of the book had a major impact on the thought and literature of post-biblical Judaism and early Christianity. Whether or not the Dan'el named in Jub 4:20 as the father of 'Edni (Edna), wife of Enoch, is intended to be the same person as our hero or his ancestor cannot be determined. The same is true of the Dan'el described by *1 Enoch* as one of the fallen angels who mated with the daughters of humankind in the generation of Noah (*1 En.* 6:7; see Gen 6:1-4).

Among the Dead Sea Scrolls are fragmentary texts called PSEUDO-DANIEL (4Q243–245) and the Prayer of Nabonidus (4Q242) (see NABONIDUS, PRAYER OF). The former adds little to our cumulative portrait of the man Daniel except that by abandoning the genre of a vision in favor of a straightforward description of the culmination of history, Daniel appears more as a prophet than as a visionary. The latter text describes the success of a Jewish exorcist in ridding King Nabonidus of "an evil ulcer." The exorcist is unnamed, but the story follows the lines of Daniel, chap. 4. It suggests that later generations began to look on Daniel as a healer and wonder-worker.

The man Daniel plays no role in the NT; in fact, his name is mentioned only once (Matt 24:15). The apocalyptic imagery and theology of the book is, of course, highly influential in the Synoptic "little apocalypses" (Matt 24-25; Mark 13; Luke 17:20-37, 21:5-36) and above all in the book of Revelation.

Who, then, was Daniel? He was and is a creature of the inspired writers of his book and its subsequent interpreters. He is an icon, a paragon of virtue worthy of emulation. He is a Hasid, a holy man. Finally, he is a herald of the age to come when God will overthrow tyranny and vindicate the saints. See DANIEL, BOOK OF.

Bibliography: John J. Collins. *Daniel* (1993); André LaCocque. *Daniel in His Time* (1988).

W. SIBLEY TOWNER

DANIEL, ADDITIONS TO. Three supplements appear in the ancient Greek versions of the book of Daniel. "The Prayer of Azariah and the Song of the Three Jews" (inserted in Dan 3, between v. 23 and v. 24) records the words spoken by the young men in the fiery furnace. "Susanna" recounts Daniel's rescue of a falsely accused virgin from execution. "Bel and the Dragon" exults in Daniel's triumph over Babylonian idols.

Because these writings do not appear in the Hebrew text of Daniel, Jews and Protestants consider them apocryphal. Catholic and Eastern Orthodox Bibles, however, influenced as they are by the Greek tradition, take them as canonical Scripture.

W. SIBLEY TOWNER

DANIEL, APOCALYPSE OF. See DANIEL, BOOK OF.

DANIEL, BOOK OF dan´yuhl [דָּנִיֵּאל daniye⁾l; Δανιήλ Daniēl]. Counted among the prophets in the ancient Greek and modern Christian versions of the Bible, but included among the wisdom writings in the OT and modern Jewish translations, this work readily falls into two parts. It begins with six tales about the wise and heroic exploits of the young Jew Daniel (see DANIEL) and his three friends in the courts of Babylon and Media (see ASSYRIA AND BABYLONIA). These tales reflect a degree of acceptance of the rule of the

imperial powers, over which the book believes the God of Israel is sovereign. The work concludes with three bitterly anti-imperial apocalypses (chaps. 7, 8, 10–12) and a lengthy prose prayer of penitence (chap. 9). The tales are told in the third person about Daniel and friends, and amount to a kind of "outer history" of their lives of faithful trust and obedience. The apocalypses and prayer are first person reports by Daniel of his dream-visions and his dialogues with an angelic dream interpreter. They serve as a kind of "inner history" of the seer, whose task it is to convey to the saints the answers to mysteries that have been revealed to him (see DANIEL, ADDITIONS TO).

Readers of this somewhat baffling book have always held various understandings of its purpose. To some it provides an historiographic account of the Jewish experience of exile. Others stress its forecast of the end of time and events associated with it (see ESCHATOLOGY IN EARLY JUDAISM; ESCHATOLOGY IN THE OT). Some believe that its function is to offer encouragement to dispirited Jews victimized by foreign and domestic persecutors. Other modern readers believe that book offers an "interim ethic" as a pattern for faithful living prior to God's final victory over evil.

A. Detailed Analysis of the Book of Daniel
  1. Contents
  2. The authors and their audiences
  3. Historical setting, occasion, and date
  4. Language
  5. Versions and the evidence of a larger Daniel tradition
B. A Short History of the Interpretation of the Book
C. The Theological and Religious Significance of the Book of Daniel
Bibliography

A. Detailed Analysis of the Book of Daniel
1. Contents
The six tales that make up the first half of the book narrate the successes in the courts of Babylon and Media of the young Jewish exiles, Daniel and his three friends SHADRACH, MESHACH, AND ABEDNEGO. In chap. 1, the captive youths profit by the training they receive at the Babylonian academy of wisdom. They rise to high positions in the court of King Nebuchadnezzar (605–562 BCE) in spite of their refusal to compromise their Jewish identity and independence by partaking of the sumptuous fare of the king's table. In chap. 2, as to Joseph long before him, God gives to the ideal courtier, Daniel, the gift of dream interpretation. Daniel reveals that Nebuchadnezzar's dream of a colossus made of four metals, descending in order of value, whose feet of iron and clay are smashed by a great stone that fills the whole earth, is a summary of imperial history through four empires culminating in final and eternal fifth monarchy. Chapter 3 narrates the

heroism of the three friends who prefer being thrown into a fiery furnace to bowing down before an image of the king. Saying that they will remain faithful to God whether or not God can save them (3:16-18), they survive the ordeal with the help of a mysterious fourth man with "the appearance of a god" (3:25) who joins them in the flames. Nebuchadnezzar's second dream of his own exaltation and subsequent humiliation to animalism, Daniel's interpretation of it, its fulfillment, and the king's hymn of praise to God make up the content of chap. 4. The fifth tale recounts the interpretation by Daniel of mysterious words (*see* MENE, MENE, TEKEL, AND PARSIN) written by a ghostly hand on the wall of the banquet hall of BELSHAZZAR. Finally, in chap. 6, we hear a successor king, "DARIUS the Mede," reluctantly sentence Daniel to death in a DEN OF LIONS because he is charged with violating the royal edict that all prayers be directed to the king alone. God saves Daniel, of course, his accusers are eaten by the lions, and Darius, like Nebuchadnezzar before him, proclaims his faith in Daniel's "living god" (6:25-27).

The four visions that comprise Dan 7–12, told largely in the first person, pair the seer up with an angelic interpreter (apparently Gabriel; see 8:16, 9:21). All of these visions are expressed the three-fold structure that typifies OT: At the end of 1) the present age of tribulation and; 2) the terror of the judgment day; 3) God overcomes evil and assures a happy destiny for the saints in the new age that follows. Three of the visions are expressed in the narrative idiom of early Apocalyptic literature (*see* APOCALYPTICISM). Moving beyond the this-worldly realism of earlier prophetic eschatology, which, though it follows the same tripartite structure, is content to picture the age to come as this world in perfected form (e.g., Isa 11:1-9; 65:17-25), the three apocalypses of the book of Daniel represent the great drama of redemption as cosmic in scope. They introduce rich mythic themes of heavenly conflict and a new world order, the idea of the general resurrection of the dead, and a strict sense of the predetermination of all of history.

Daniel 7 is the best known and most vivid of the three little apocalypses in the book of Daniel. The narrator introduces the chapter (7:1) with a date that reverts to the time of King Belshazzar (chap. 5), thereby causing the apocalyptic section of the book partially to overlap the court tales. Beginning in v. 2, Daniel himself narrates his vision of four great beasts. They are a LION, a BEAR, a LEOPARD, and finally the most terrible beast of all, unidentified as to species but distinguished by its destructive iron teeth and ten horns. As the seer watches he sees a little eleventh horn appear, equipped with human eyes and "a mouth speaking arrogantly" (7:8). This visionary sequence mirrors the four-element dream of Nebuchadnezzar in Dan 2, as does the fact that the fourth member of the sequence is

the target of the judgment that now takes place. In the dramatic heavenly scene of Dan 7:9-14, the Ancient One pronounces sentence on the beasts, destroys the fourth one, and presents the "everlasting dominion that shall not pass away" (7:14) to "one like a human being [or: "son of man"] coming with the clouds of heaven" (7:13; *see* SON OF MAN). In the latter half of the chapter, the angelic interpreter tells Daniel that the four great beasts represent four kingdoms, the eleven horns are rulers of the fourth, and the "one like a human being" to whom kingship and dominion are given on the day of judgment is, collectively, "the people of the holy ones of the Most High" (7:27). The angelic interpreter's solution was no doubt understandable to the original audience of the book, but its obscurity and imprecision have been an invitation to interpreters through the ensuing millennia to consider themselves and their sects as those who receive the kingdom.

Two years pass before Daniel's second vision, recounted in chap. 8. The ram and he-goat featured in this little apocalypse represent the same historical sequence as that in chap. 7, and the arrogant little horn of the he-goat, which interferes even with the host of heaven and the "regular burnt offering" of the temple (8:11-12), is the world power that is finally subject to divine judgment.

Chapter 9, too, recounts a visionary experience of Daniel and it also deals with the question of the end of the present age of oppression and suffering, so central to apocalyptic literature. However, it is couched in the genre of a prose prayer of penitence, followed by a response by the angel Gabriel. The prayer is occasioned by Daniel's perception that the figure of seventy years, given by the prophet Jeremiah (Jer 25:11, 12; 29:10) for the duration of the exile, is key to understanding the time remaining before the culmination, the end of sin, and the advent of "everlasting righteousness" (9:24). By the simple device of reinterpreting the seventy years as weeks of years, the angel proffers 490 years as the true span of time between the destruction of the first temple and God's final victory.

The last panel in the book of Daniel is the little apocalypse of chaps. 10–12. The narrator introduces this final vision by dating it to the third year of Cyrus, the Persian king who conquered Babylon in 539 BCE. No doubt significantly, this dates the final portion of the book of Daniel seventy years after the date given for the first panel in 1:1.

The ensuing three-chapter dialogue with an interpreting angel consists of a review of ANE history. No names are mentioned, but, until near the end of it, the details fit remarkably well with what we know about late Persian and early Hellenistic imperial history. The reign of the villain ("little horn") of the two previous apocalyptic visions is recounted in 11:21-45, and his brutality toward Jerusalem and the Jewish community is spelled out. The characterization is accurate until

11:39. At that point, the author links the end of the oppressor with the end of history, and brings the vision to a conclusion with a great final tribulation and the double resurrection of the dead, "some to everlasting life, and some to shame and everlasting contempt" (12:2).

2. The authors and their audiences

No discussion of the authorship of the book of Daniel can stand alone without attention to the date and historical occasion of the writing of the book. Rather than take up all of these themes simultaneously, however, a case will be built step-by step.

First of all, we can be quite confident that the chief character of the book, Daniel, is not its author, even when he speaks in the first person in chaps. 7–12. He is an iconic sage and seer of past times to and about whom the book is credited, perhaps as part of its bid for acceptance and authority. In short, the book is pseudonymous. We must look elsewhere within the book to discern the hands that wrote it, and the audience that received it.

The behavior of Daniel and his friends in the tales of chaps. 1–6 can serve as our starting point. Even if these chapters originated separately from the apocalyptic visions of chaps. 7–12, the authors are offering the characters to their audience as ideal heroes. In the context of foreign captivity, the four young Jews are steadfast in their observance of TORAH, and in their refusal to participate in idolatrous royal cults. Their faithfulness repeatedly puts their lives at risk, and though they are not martyrs, they are certainly "saints." In the apocalyptic half the book of Daniel we learn that when God finally overcomes the oppressors of the world, the kingdom is given to "the people of the holy ones of the Most High" (7:27). Probably these heirs of the age to come are identical with "the people who are loyal to their God. . . . the wise among the people" (11:32-33) and "everyone who is found written in the book" (12:1). Since all of these epithets apply to the heroes of chaps. 1–6, we can assume that the authors are presenting a consistent picture of loyalists willing to endure suffering and persecution for the sake of their community and their God. The authors surely identify themselves with these figures that they are recommending, and are addressing themselves to an audience that shares their admiration for the fidelity of the heroes.

Date becomes important here, of course, because observant groups like this can be found in ancient Israel throughout biblical times. Suppose, however, that we can show an early 2nd cent. BCE date for the book of Daniel. This would explain why it is the most mature and elaborated OT apocalypse, for it comes at the end of literary history that includes the earlier proto-apocalyptic writings in Joel 2:28–3:21, Zech 9–14, and Isa 24–27. Furthermore, this date would offer possible authors and audience for the book. Two groups of this era that are mentioned in the apocryphal book of 1 Maccabees more or less fit the description given above. One of these is the "many who were seeking righteousness and justice" (1 Macc 1:29-41), who fled to the wilderness to escape the outrages of the Hellenists during the reign of the Greco-Syrian king Antiochus IV Epiphanes (175–164 BCE). Their piety and their pacifism seem to match the non-violent loyalty of the wise depicted in Dan 11:33-35. A discernibly separate second group is the Hasideans (1 Macc 2:42-48; 7:13-17). They were not in the vanguard of the Maccabean rebels against ANTIOCHUS, but they are said to have joined the insurgency in their zeal to recover the temple from Syrian desecration and to restore the legitimate priestly line. Modern scholarship tends to see in one or another such group of Torah-true observant Jews of the early 2nd cent. the authors and audience of the book of Daniel.

3. Historical setting, occasion, and date

Much figurative scholarly blood has been shed over the date of the book of Daniel. More traditional and conservative commentators have regarded the book's own 7th and 6th cent. BCE dates for the tales and visions as accurate; in contrast, modern critical commentators are almost unanimous in arguing that the book as we have it is the product of the early 2nd cent. BCE. Numerous historical problems in the book show its grasp of exilic history to be rather more inaccurate than would be expected from writers who had actually experienced it. For example, contra Dan 4, no record exists in Babylonian sources of a seven-year disablement of Nebuchadnezzar. A bigger problem arises with Belshazzar, who is described as son of Nebuchadnezzar and the last "king" of Babylon (Dan 5:1, 2, 30-31), even though contemporary Babylonian records prove that the last king was Belshazzar's real-life father, Nabonidus (556–539 BCE). At the most, Belshazzar served as regent during the last years of his father's reign. Furthermore, there never was a "Darius the Mede" (Dan 5:31, 9:1). For that matter, no Median empire ruled Babylon just before the Persians did, because CYRUS had subjected Media to Persian control at least sixteen years before he seized Babylon directly from Nabonidus.

Does accuracy in such details really make much difference? Much is at stake here. Not only does the book purport to offer authentic witnesses to the lives and exploits of Jews exiled to Babylon, Media, and Persia, but it also sketches out the near and distant future. If the authority of scripture depends upon the historical accuracy of its narrators as well as the ability of its prophets and seers to forecast the future reliably, then the suggestion that much of the "prophecy" in the book of Daniel took place after the fact threatens the integrity of scripture itself (*see* PROPHET, PROPHECY).

More recent critical scholarship accepts that "events taking place after the fact" is a relatively common literary convention in ancient literature, including the Bible, and that the value of a biblical book depends upon its theological truth claims and ethical values more than the verifiability of its ostensible historical setting. With that in mind, and assuming that the canonical form of the book can be treated as a theological whole even though the tales may have originated at a different time and place than chaps. 7–12, the key to dating of the final form of the book lies in the last apocalyptic vision, chaps. 10–12.

The stage for determining the date of the book of Daniel is set by the angel's specification that his survey of ANE history (the content of the concluding vision) begins with the last four kings of Persia (11:2). It is easy, then, to recognize in the "warrior king who shall rule with great dominion and take action as he pleases" (11:3) Alexander the Great, who defeated the last Persian emperor, Darius III Codomannus at Gaugamela in 331 BCE. Following the death of Alexander eight years later, his empire was divided among four of his generals, the so-called Diadochi. The two that bore most on Judean history were Ptolemy I of Egypt and Seleucus I, whose dynasty was based at Antioch in Syria. Daniel 11:5-39 follows the shifting hegemonies of these two regional powers, their elaborate interactions including political marriages (11:6, 11:17), and concludes with a detailed account of the reign of the Seleucid usurper Antiochus IV Epiphanes (175–164 BCE). The essential accuracy of this narration is accepted by later deutero-canonical (1 and 2 Maccabees) and secular (e.g., Josephus, Polybius) sources.

The brutal reign of Antiochus occasioned the issuance of the book of Daniel. The pogrom is uppermost in the minds of the writers and given the most detailed treatment in the historical review of the last apocalypse (11:21-45). The reference to "those who forsake the holy covenant" (11:30) is supported by the acknowledgement in 1 Macc 1:43 that "many even from Israel gladly adopted his religion; they sacrificed to idols and profaned the Sabbath." This party is generally accepted to be the Hellenizers, which included many of the cosmopolitan leading citizens of Jerusalem. The genuineness of the history of Antiochus can be corroborated until 11:40, which opens with the eschatological formula, "At the time of the end." That formula alone suggests that the perspective of the seer in the following verses, 11:40–12:4, turns toward the future. Although the ensuing story about the defeat and death of Antiochus, world-wide tribulation, deliverance, and resurrection continues in a history-like narrative, none of these events happened as predicted. In short, when prophecy ceased being after the fact, it missed the mark and the apocalypse failed. For dating purposes, however, the turning point is ideal. The authors must have lived in the white space between Dan 11:39 and 11:40. They knew details of Antiochus's reign after 175, including his desecration of the temple with "the abomination that makes desolate" in 167 BCE (Dan 11:31; see 1 Macc 1:54). They did not know of the recovery of the temple by the Maccabean freedom fighters and the reconsecration of the temple in 164 BCE (1 Macc 4:52-58), or they would surely have mentioned it and perhaps readjusted their timetable for the eschaton. Therefore, they must have issued the book of Daniel in something like its present form during the three-year period 167–164 BCE. This means that Daniel is the latest book of the OT canon. However, it quickly gained acceptance as scripture. Fragments of eight Daniel MSS dating from the late 2nd cent. through mid-1st cent. BCE frag. are found at Qumran along with other OT texts. Furthermore, included in a recitation of great scriptural heroes alongside the likes of Abraham, Joseph, and Elijah in 1 Macc 2:51-60 are Daniel and his three friends. A 100 BCE date for 1 Maccabees gives us a reliable date for the acceptance of the book of Daniel as scripture.

This date for the canonical form of the book of Daniel does not require that all parts of it came into existence at that time. The book certainly has a redaction history, though general agreement on the outlines of it has not been reached. The diaspora and even somewhat pro-Babylonian outlook of the tales in chaps. 1–6 suggest that these stories circulated as a separate and earlier Daniel cycle before being incorporated into the present book. They may even have originated in Jewish exilic contexts. However, the dream of Nebuchadnezzar in chaps. 2, with its four-stage symbolization of ANE history, focuses on the smashing of the feet of iron and clay by the stone that "filled the whole earth" (2:35)—interpreted by Daniel to be the coming the fifth "kingdom that shall never be destroyed" (2:44). The feet invoke the Hellenistic kingdoms of the Ptolemies and the Seleucids, who tried to keep some semblance of order through the weak bonds of marriage (2:43). It can be affirmed, then, that at least this tale from the third-person section of the book brings the time of composition down to Seleucid times. This correlation of Daniel chap. 2 with chap. 7, combined with the deep conviction radiating out of all parts of the book that God will have done with tyranny and that, with God's help, the righteous will at last be vindicated, enable us to construe the canonical form of the book as an inwardly coherent whole, even if its parts came into being over time.

As far as the little apocalypse of chap. 7 goes, the little horn on the beast that speaks enormities and in whose time God sits in judgment and awards the kingdom to the saints fits best with Antiochus IV, viewed from the perspective of the persecutions 167–164 BCE. The fact that the holy ones are "given into his power for a time, two times, and half a time" (7:25), commonly taken to mean three and a half years, corresponds well with a time of composition that knows of the desecration of the temple but not of its restoration. The event anticipated at the end of this period is the eschatological enthronement of "the people of the holy ones of the most high" (7:27), not the historical return of the legitimate high priesthood and the resumption of the Jewish cult. The latter and not the former is, of course, what actually happened. Like the resurrection of the dead (12:1-3), the kingship of the saints is the stuff of apocalyptic vision offered by someone who was looking into the future.

The apocalypse of chap. 8, too, culminates in the arrogance of Antiochus, once again in the guise of a little horn (8:9), whose actual end is not known by the seer but is confidently predicted. Finally, at the end of the angelic interpretation of the meaning of Jeremiah's seventy years, reference is made to the "abomination that desolates" (9:27; compare 11:31), but no report of the Day of the Lord and the advent of the new age is included.

In short, throughout the book of Daniel, internal evidence points to a date imbedded within the three year period (167–164 BCE) of the Seleucid persecution of the observant Jews.

4. Language

The book of Daniel is written in two languages. Dan 1:1-2:4a and chaps. 8–12 are written in Late Biblical Hebrew. The intervening passage, Dan 2:4b-7:28, is expressed in the language spoken in Judea at the end of the first millennium BCE, the so-called "Official Aramaic" (see ARAMAIC, ARAMAISM). This tongue had become the *lingua franca* of the multi-national empires of the ANE, and was used in official correspondence, court records, and inscriptions from the days of the Assyrian empire (1100–605 BCE) through the Hellenistic period (down to 30 BCE). Why the book of Daniel has this bi-lingual character continues to be debated, with no definitive answer at hand. Clearly, the more nationalistic and anti-Hellenistic factions in Judea resisted the penetration of Greek culture in various ways, and the use of indigenous Aramaic might have been one of their means of doing so. One widely held theory is that the entire book was originally written in Aramaic and that Dan 1:1–2:4a and 8–12 were later translated into Hebrew.

5. Versions and the evidence of a larger Daniel tradition

With the book of Daniel, as with the rest of the OT, the earliest external witnesses to the received Hebrew/Aramaic text (apart from a few fragments among the Dead Sea Scrolls) are the ancient Greek versions. In the case of Daniel alone, however, the Greek version received in the western church is not the Old Greek or SEPTUAGINT (LXX) but a later and more literal revision of the Old Greek attributed to a Greek-speaking Jew named Theodotion, thought to have worked ca.

180 CE. In fact, the earlier LXX text of Daniel would not even be known to us except for one complete 9th–11th cent. manuscript (based on Origen's Hexaplaric recension; see HEXAPLA) and the more recently discovered and fragmentary Chester Beatty Papyrus.

Both versions of the ancient Greek Bible supply evidence that the Daniel tradition preserved in the Hebrew/Aram. Bible, the one taken to be canonical by the synagogue and by the Protestant reformers, is only part of a larger Daniel cycle. There are three additions to Daniel in the Greek Bible (see DANIEL, ADDITIONS TO). One is the poem called "The Prayer of Azariah and the Song of the Three Jews," inserted in the Greek between Dan 3:23 and 3:24, which purports to be what the three young Jews said while they were walking amid the flames of the fiery furnace (see AZARIAH, PRAYER OF; SONG OF THE THREE JEWS. The 22 verses of the "Prayer of Azariah" take the form of a community lament (compare Pss 44, 74, 79). The "Song of the Three Jews" is a hymn of 40 verses on the refrain, "Bless the Lord," that is addressed to all of God's creatures (compare Ps 148).

The Greek Daniel also boasts two narratives not found in the Hebrew/Aram. text. One of these, SUSANNA, tells the story of a beautiful and virtuous young Jewish woman of the Babylonian exile who is helped by a wise young Daniel to escape a death sentence. The false accusation of adultery had been made against her by two wicked elders who propositioned her. In the end, as the law required for false witnesses (Deut 19:19), they were the ones who received the punishment to which the lady had been condemned. Over time, Susanna became the prototype of virtue tested by calumny. The second additional narrative, BEL AND THE DRAGON, is the two-part account of Daniel's exposure of the false claims of the Babylonian priests of Bel, followed by his slaying of a snake/dragon that the Babylonians worshiped. The conclusion bears many similarities to the canonical Dan 6, for the king (Cyrus, not the non-historical Darius of Dan 6) reluctantly allows Daniel to be thrown into a den of lions (see DEN OF LIONS). Fantasy enters this version, however, for Daniel survives the seven day ordeal on food airlifted from Judea by the prophet Habakkuk, hoisted by the hair by the angel of the Lord. Though these narratives may be regarded as apocryphal and non-authoritative, they give evidence of the popularity of the Daniel figure and the likelihood that more was told about him than the canonizers saw fit to preserve.

Different evidence of a larger Daniel cycle has also and more recently been provided by several Dead Sea scroll texts, especially the fragmentary 1st cent. BCE "Prayer of Nabonidus" (4Q242, first published in 1956; see NABONIDUS, PRAYER OF). In it, a Babylonian king Nabonidus recounts how he was afflicted "in Teiman" by God with an ulcer and how, after seven years, he was cured by an unnamed Jewish exorcist.

The healer pardoned his sins and then told him to make a written report of the events and to "glorify the name of the Most High God." There really was a Babylonian king Nabonidus (556–539 BCE), who was known even in antiquity for his curious behavior. Just when the menace of the Persian horde under Cyrus was looming, he neglected the royal Marduk cult in Babylon, turned the affairs of state over to his son and regent Belshazzar (Dan 5), and retreated to the oasis of Tema in Arabia for several years. Many scholars believe that this Qumran story about Nabonidus is an early version of the tale told about Nebuchadnezzar in Dan 4. Be that as it may, its apparent message coheres with the message of the book of Daniel as a whole, including its Greek additions, namely, that human power and pride must bow before the sovereign power of the Most High God, the God of Israel.

B. A Short History of Interpretation of the Book

Whereas the Greek OT and the Qumran manuscripts establish the existence of a larger cycle of Daniel tales extant in the 1st cent. BCE, other early refractions of Daniel elaborate the apocalyptic visions. The apocryphal work 4 Ezra (2 Esd 3–14) is a late 1st cent. CE Jewish apocalypse. The sixth vision of the seer Ezra (chap. 13) features a human figure who "flew with the clouds of heaven" (13:3) and, at the behest of the Most High, executes the judgment of the eschaton. While not an explicit interpretation of Dan 7:13, this vision, like all early Jewish apocalypses, clearly is drawing upon the book of Daniel and transforming elements of it into a larger, more radical form. The same can be said of the use of Dan 7 in the Jewish apocalypse 1 Enoch, where it provides the inspiration of the judgment scene of 14:18-22 and of the epiphany of the "son of man" in chap. 46.

The NT, too, belongs in the category of the early history of the interpretation of the book of Daniel. The tales of Dan 1–6 are alluded to only once, in a list of great heroes of faith (Heb 11:32-34). As might be expected of a people convinced they were living near the time of the Parousia, the real interest of the NT writers centers in the apocalypses of Daniel. Nevertheless, direct or indirect quotations from Dan 7–12 occur only about ten times in the NT, mostly in the so-called "little apocalypses" of the Synoptic Gospels (Matt 24–25; Mark 13; Luke 21:5-36). Though the book of Revelation rarely if ever quotes from Daniel explicitly, the imagery of Daniel is woven into its very fabric (see REVELATION, BOOK OF). Attracting special attention by the NT writers are the enigmatic image of the "abomination that makes desolate" (Dan 9:27, 11:31, 12:11—the "desolating sacrilege" of Matt 24:15; Mark 13:14; see ABOMINATION OF DESOLATION), and the "time, two times, and half a time" (Dan 12:7; see Rev 12:14. This figure equals in years the traditional 42 months or 1,260 days of tribulation preceding the culmination [Rev 11:2-3, 12:6], adjusted to 1,290 and then 1,335 days in Dan 12:11-12). Revelation 20:11-15 must surely have been shaped by the similar scene in Dan 7:9-14, especially because both mention the opening of "the books" (the record of deeds and the book of destiny). Finally, the seven-headed beast of Rev 13:1-9 (see BEAST; LEVIATHAN) is a composite of the four beasts of the last judgment scene in Dan 7:1-27, with the head and ten horns now representing Rome. The deliberate transfer of the identity of the fourth beast from the Hellenistic empire to Rome is noted in the nearly contemporary apocryphon 2 Esd 12:10-15, where the angel tells the seer, "[The vision] was not explained to [your brother Daniel] as I now explain it to you." This shift in identity served to save the apocalypses of Daniel from the stigma of a failed timetable (e.g., the last judgment should have happened during the reign of Antiochus IV Epiphanes, but did not) and, as long as Rome existed, kept the cloud-borne (second) coming of the son of man a promise for the future. (This position is pressed into service to this day by those who deny that any part of the Danielic vision failed to materialize on schedule; elaborate historical schemes are offered to prove that the Roman empire still exists in some latter-day form.)

Daniel 7:13 is the primary locus of the interest of NT writers in the book of Daniel, namely the vision of the "coming with the clouds of heaven" of "one like a human being" (or: "son of man") to receive the everlasting dominion and kingship from the Ancient One (see Matt 24:30, 26:64; Mark 13:26, 14:62; Luke 21:27). The question of whether Jesus actually spoke the words found in the "little apocalypses" of the Synoptic Gospels is much debated. Many scholars attribute the apocalyptic teachings of Jesus to the early Jewish Christian church; in turn, this raises the question of whether Jesus ever identified himself with a coming "SON OF MAN," or whether, like many other 1st and 2nd cent. CE Jews, he simply cherished this figure as the central character of the culmination promised in the apocalypse of Dan 7. The writer of Revelation, for his part, is very ready to identify the one to come on clouds of glory with the risen Christ (Rev 1:7). He also describes Christ as the glorified son of man (Rev 1:13, 14:14).

Since early Christianity was highly expectant of an early return of the Christ to complete the work of salvation and to receive the everlasting kingdom, it is no surprise that we find allusions to Daniel scattered through early Christian literature (see CHRISTOLOGY). For example, Irenaeus (ca. 130–200 CE), identifies the "stone . . . cut from the mountain not by hands" (Dan 2:34, 45) as Jesus Christ, as of course he does the "son of man" of Dan 7:13. To him, these manifestations belong not to the Judean past but to the future Parousia.

In time, a number of patristic writers contributed formal commentaries on the book of Daniel, of which that of Jerome (ca. 340–420 CE) is the most accessible. Guided by the standard set in Rev 13 and 2 Esd 12, he interpreted the four beasts of Dan 7 as Babylon, Persia, Alexander and his successors, and finally Rome. Since Rome was still extant, the appearance of the little horn, the Son of Man, and the conveyance of the kingdom to the saints must all be events of the future. Throughout his commentary, Jerome opposed the interpretation of Daniel offered by the pagan philosopher, Porphyry. Though we know Porphyry's work only through the citations of it by Jerome, we can discern that his views resembled those of modern critical scholarship more than Jerome's did. He understood the fourth beast to be the Seleucids and realized that the apocalypses of Dan 7–12 were tied to events that occurred in early 2nd cent. BCE Judea.

All of the great Jewish commentators of medieval times wrote on Daniel, including Saadia, Rashi, and Ibn Ezra. During the same centuries Christian interpreters such as Albertus Magnus and Nicholas of Lyra also contributed Daniel commentaries that drew some of their insights from Jewish scholarship.

In the Reformation of the 16th cent., commentary flourished. The magisterial work on Daniel was John Calvin's commentary of 1561. As always in his lectures on the Bible, Calvin avoided "subtle allegories" and sought out the plain meaning of the text. Of course he understood the all-important Son of Man (7:13) to be the Christ; however, in contrast to Jerome and the prevailing interpretation of his own day, Calvin interpreted the verse as referring to the first advent of Christ, an event that had already taken place. This understanding immediately raised the question of how to accommodate the angel's explanation that the "one like a human being" is "the people of the holy ones of the Most High" (Dan 7:27). Calvin solves this problem by applying the interpretive principle of *pars pro toto*: Christ and the church (that is, the body of Christ) are ways of speaking about the same thing. In the text of chap. 7 there is a sequence, all of which is manifested to the eyes of faith, of the incarnation and exaltation of Christ (7:13), followed by the adoption of the saints and the earthly reign of the church with Christ (7:18, 22, 27). Since the reign of the church in the world is not yet fully manifested, the present age must be an intermediate state prior to the Second Coming and the full inheritance of the kingdom by the saints. Such an intermediate state looks something like a MILLENNIUM (Rev 20:4-15), though Calvin himself had no use for millennialism.

Seventeenth century Calvinists, however, had a lot of use for it. English Puritans and their American contemporaries and successors often adopted a post-millennialist position, which exhibits an optimism and a dynamism that derive from the conviction that the last thousand years of this age of human history are the reign of Christ and the saints foreseen in Dan 7 and Rev 20, and that the second advent and last judgment occur only post-millennium. The trick then was to know when this millennium began, and could therefore be expected to culminate. The radical Puritans, including the Fifth Monarchy men (heirs, as they saw it, of the fifth and "everlasting kingdom" of Dan 7:27), generally pegged the beginning of the millennium to the beginning of the Protestant Reformation in 1517. They were also greatly excited by the execution of the Stuart King Charles I on Jan. 30, 1649, and the establishment of the world's first modern republic. The overthrow of papacy and monarchy alike were taken as evidence of the slow but irresistible manifestation of the polity of the new age, the rule of the saints among whom they counted themselves. Among the theological opponents of these enthusiasts were the pre-millennialists, who saw the prophecies of Dan 7 and Rev 20 as applying entirely to the future yet to come, and who anticipated no rule of the saints with Christ, themselves or anyone else, until after the PAROUSIA in a millennium that is the first thousand years of eternity.

After the restoration of the Stuart monarchy in 1669, much of the apocalyptic excitement of British Puritanism died down, though it continued to animate American self-understanding as the chosen people destined to inaugurate God's kingdom on earth. The "Cambridge Platonists" of the late 17th cent. viewed Daniel and the rest of scripture through the twin lenses of faith and reason. In 1733 another man of reason, science, and faith, Sir Isaac Newton, accepted the idea that the apocalyptic books contain valid predictions of the future. However, as a mathematician, he felt constrained to make calculations, based on the assumption that the feet made with iron and clay of Dan 2:33 and the fourth beast of Dan 7:7-8 represented the Roman empire. Counting toes and horns led him to an inventory of Rome and its successors, including Vandals, Huns, Britons, Lombards, culminating in the little horn on the fourth beast, the Church of Rome. Based on Dan 7:25 and relevant texts in Revelation, he reckoned the time of the Roman See to be 1260 years beginning in the 8th cent. CE, a time-frame that safely put disconfirming events beyond the life-span of his own generation.

Since the rise of modern biblical interpretation in the 19th cent., commentators generally have sided with or against the historical-critical approach. Among those who oppose that approach are those who affirm most or all of the following: the unity of the book, its Danielic authorship, its exilic date, the accuracy of its historical references, the Roman identity of the fourth beast, the identification of the "son of man" of Dan 7:13 with Jesus Christ, and the genuine predictive value of the book for our own future. Critically oriented commentators have tended to deny some or all of these assertions, and have looked for the theological value of the book in its faith in God's sovereignty over all times and peoples, and for God's ultimate victory over evil.

Perhaps the interpretive community with the most at stake today in the predictive value of the book of Daniel is the so-called "premillennial dispensationalists." With roots in 19th cent. Britain, their approach was enshrined in the notes of the Scofield Reference Bible (1909), fleshed out in later commentaries. The approach was popularized by Hal Lindsey in the 1970s (e.g., *The Late Great Planet Earth*), and most recently in the twelve-volume *Left Behind* series (1996–2004). Taking all of human history as a sequence of eras or "dispensations," each with its own covenant, these writers find scriptural warrant for placing us near the end of the last dispensation, counting down toward the JUDGMENT day. All apocalyptic scripture, including Daniel, is woven into one vast, composite end time scenario featuring persecution by the forces of the ANTICHRIST, the rapture of the saints in the midst of the premillennial tribulation, the last judgment and thousand-year rule of the saints, and the final destruction of the world. They have found it possible to draw a time line, to place a dot on that line, and then to say, "We are here."

Most of the other conservative writers on the book of Daniel have concentrated on defending the book's "integrity" against critical comment rather than incorporating it into a dispensationalist ideology.

C. The Theological and Religious Significance of the Book

The book of Daniel has, over the centuries, been seized upon by interpreters eager to find in it the time and manner of the end of history. In reaction to this literalism and millennialism, other students of scripture, especially in the mainstream of Judaism and Christianity, have either ignored this material or treated it as at best a highly mythic and probably very naïve attempt to write history in advance. Stationed between these two extreme understandings of Daniel and biblical apocalyptic is the interpretive stance that biblical eschatological literature is invaluable to religious thinking because its vision draws readers into the future. And that is good because, as the sage observed long ago, "where there is no vision, the people perish" (Prov 29:18).

The encompassing purpose of the book of Daniel is to offer vision and to inculcate hope, not simply for individual escape from persecution and death but for the people of God as a whole. Before addressing that large theological purpose, however, several other theological issues raised by this book should be noted. The unswerving affirmation of the sovereignty of God over all human sovereignties emerges is a theme in the first chapter and continues to be proclaimed vigorously throughout the book. The question of "interim ethics," or how to live until the DAY OF THE LORD dawns, is illustrated narratively in the tales of Dan 1–6, and vindicated in the culmination of history envisioned in Dan 7–12. The doctrine of revelation, with the corollary issues of the significance of dreams and the interpreta-

tions of mysteries, surfaces as a major issue in chap. 2. So does the difficult theological problem of determinism, sometimes shaped by the apparent conviction that what the future holds is already "appointed" or "decreed" by God (Dan 8:19, 9:26-27, 11:35). Chapter 7 provides an opportunity to think about the impact of myth on biblical literature, for surely the great beasts that appear out of the sea have their roots in the mythic theme of the warfare that the creator God must wage—at the end of time as at its beginning—against the forces of chaos.

The latter part of the book treats the difficult question of the meaning of history. Is history an incomprehensible and foreordained series of events that gain what little significance they have by merely by pointing toward the relative proximity of the end? Or do the deeds of the saints and the decisions of God actually affect the course of history and become part of its fabric? Angels and their relationship to human beings become topics of importance beginning with Daniel 8. The great prayer of Daniel 9 raises the issue of divine retribution: Must everything that happens to the people of God be interpreted as either reward or punishment? This chapter also sharpens the perennial question, voiced in many sectors of the OT, "How long, O Lord, must the righteous suffer?"

Of course, the appearance in Dan 12:1-3 of the motif of the resurrection of the dead, some to eternal life and some to eternal death, introduces into the biblical tradition for the first time (except, perhaps, for a cryptic reference in Isa 26:19), a belief that will assume major proportions in the NT (*see* RESURRECTION, EARLY JEWISH; RESURRECTION, NT; RESURRECTION, OT). Interwoven with these theological issues are problems that the book of Daniel as a whole presents. Is apocalyptic theology a "failure-of-nerve theology," written by oppressed groups who have no other hope left to them except divine intervention? If so, has it anything to say to today's affluent and secure believers? Finally, there is the nagging question, raised by the evident failure of the book to get the date of the end right: Can even an inspired book of holy writ accurately map the future in advance? Why did synagogue and church keep a failed apocalypse? Is it fair to call the book a "pious fraud," as some have done?

Overarching these significant theological issues is the problem of THEODICY, God's way of dealing with evil in the world. The book of Daniel projects a clear solution to this problem: God will not be mocked. God will achieve the divine purpose of the redemption of the world. Because this is the case, the Daniel who survives in exile and outshines the other wise men is not a passive figure who waits quietly until the Great Assize, but is one who issues forth into the fray. That is why we can speak of the first chapters of the book of Daniel as "interim ethics," that is, as instruction on how the saints should live in-between the times. The faithful friend of God does not simply hang on, observe all the strictures of the sect, and survive. The saint's courage inspires others to believe and gives hope to those who are losing their hope. The saint helps bring about a world in which God is honored, idolatry is ended, the cries of the needy are heard, and the oppressed are liberated. Like the deeds of his fictional contemporaries, Esther, Judith, and Tobit, Daniel's deeds vindicate the daring and courage of believers, grounded as they are in well-placed faith in the self-vindication of the God of Israel.

Christian readers will also recognize a similarity to the picture of the ministry of Jesus in the NT. The "little apocalypses" of the Synoptic Gospels (Matt 24–25, Mark 13, Luke 17:20-37) are to the account of Jesus' ministry what the chaps. 7–12 of the book of Daniel are to the deeds of Daniel and his friends in Daniel 1–6. Jesus' ministry of healing and of liberating persons from the bondage of sin and despair was shot through with a strong sense of the immediacy of the coming kingdom, which would vindicate God's way of combating evil in the world. His message, too, was a call not to quietism but to action, an invitation to people to offer in their own lives a foretaste of the character of the new age that is coming. His offer, like that of the book of Daniel, is of an "interim ethic," a vital and productive way of living in-between the times.

We circle back to the big vision of the book of Daniel. This book is intended to pull its readers into the future like a magnet, endowing them with hope and energy rather than leaving them terrified in the face of the end. Although God alone can cut out of the mountain that stone that fills the whole earth (Dan 2:34-35, 44-45), those who have the vision of God's coming victory can imitate in their individual and communal lives the coming reign of God. They can give foretastes of what the world will be like when justice prevails, idolatry is quashed, and the saints share rule with God.

This confidence in God's ultimate victory in the struggle with evil may be the single most profound source of hope available in our modern culture. Science and fiction alike give only ambiguous readings of the future, encouraging us when they point toward to the evolution of the human species toward ever greater capacities, but often discouraging us, as well, whey they point to totalitarian "big brothers" whose strength is underwritten by technology and nuclear threats. The most radical forms of Marxism and Islam offer to our age alternative eschatologies, but both require the destruction of significant parts of the human community in order that the purposes of emancipation be achieved. In contrast, biblical apocalyptic literature sometimes attains a vision that is universal in scope and that is rich with hope for all things. On the great day that is coming, "the creation itself will be set free from its bondage to decay and will obtain the freedom of the glory of the children of God" (Rom 8:21). On that great day, "one like a human being" will be given "dominion and glory and kingship . . . His dominion is an everlasting dominion that shall not pass away, and his kingship is one that shall never be destroyed" (Dan 7:13-14).

Bibliography: M. Casey. *Son of Man: The Interpretation and Influence of Daniel 7* (1979); J. J. Collins. *The Apocalyptic Vision of the Book of Daniel* (1977); J. J. Collins and P. W. Flint. *The Book of Daniel: Composition and Reception* (2001); J. J. Collins. *Daniel: With an Introduction to Apocalyptic Literature.* FOTL (1984); H. L. Ginsberg. *Studies in Daniel* (1948); P. Hanson. *The Dawn of Apocalyptic* (1975); L. Hartman and A. DiLella. *The Book of Daniel.* AB 23 (1978); A. Lacocque. *The Book of Daniel* (1979); C. L. Seow. *Daniel.* WBC (2003); W. S. Towner. *Daniel, Interpretation* (1984); H. Tödt. *The Son of Man in the Synoptic Tradition.* NTL (1965). W. Sibley Towner. "Book of Daniel." *The Books of the Bible*, Vol. 1. B. W. Anderson, ed. (1989) 344–346.

W. SIBLEY TOWNER

DANIEL, PSEUDEPIGRAPHA OF dan′yul, *soo′*duh-pig′ruh-fuh. A convenient but imprecise term describing the extra-biblical literature attributed to or associated with the biblical figure of DANIEL. Sometimes the designation "Daniel apocrypha" is preferred because not all the texts are pseudonymous.

The Daniel apocrypha may be divided into two categories. The first category consists of Jewish literature that was not included in the Hebrew–Aramaic book of Daniel although composed in the same era in which the book was assembled and edited (*see* DANIEL, BOOK OF). The book of Daniel in its ancient Greek versions contains several so-called "Additions": the Prayer of Azariah and the SONG OF THE THREE JEWS, inserted between what in the Hebrew is Dan 3:23 and 24; the story of SUSANNA, which precedes Dan 1 in the version ascribed to Theodotion but follows Dan 12 in the Old Greek; and the tales of BEL AND THE DRAGON, which conclude Daniel in most manuscripts (*see* DANIEL, ADDITIONS TO). The Additions date from the 3rd cent. or the first half of the 2nd cent. BCE. None survives in its Semitic original, although a claim has been made for an Aramaic copy of Susanna (4Q551).

Other pre-Christian Daniel writings, in Aramaic, were discovered among the DEAD SEA SCROLLS. Two mention Daniel explicitly. *4QPseudo-Daniel*[a-b] (4Q243–244) dates from the first decades of the 2nd cent. BCE. In form and ideology it stands between the court tales and the revelatory visions of the book of Daniel. *4QPseudo-Daniel*[c] (4Q245) is less well preserved and was written approximately fifty years later. The *Prayer of Nabonidus* (4Q242) does not refer to Daniel but appears to be an early form of the story of Nebuchadnezzar's madness that survives in different versions in the MT and LXX witnesses to Dan 4. Two other compositions—the "Son of God" text (4Q246) and 4Q*Four Kingdoms* (4Q552–553)—are sometimes considered Daniel apocrypha on the basis of shared vocabulary or themes with the book of Daniel.

The second category of Daniel apocrypha consists of Jewish, Christian, and Islamic literature composed well after the book of Daniel was assembled and edited. In this case the distinction is chronological and canonical. The corpus of these texts is large; few biblical figures enjoyed a more robust post-biblical literary afterlife than Daniel.

The Daniel legends are third-person narratives, in the mold of the court tales of Dan 1–6, that rewrote, explained, or augmented the biblical story of Daniel. They appear in multiple forms from minor elaborations of the biblical story embedded in larger works, to full-blown apocrypha such as the Old English *Daniel*. They were written mainly by Jews and Christians, though Muslim legends about Daniel are known. Some legends resolved conflicting data in the biblical story of Daniel, such as its notorious chronological inconsistencies. Others filled gaps in the narrative, for example the early life of Daniel or his last years, death, and burial (*see* LEGEND).

The Daniel apocalypses and apocalyptic oracles have remote antecedents in the revelatory visions of Dan 7–12. There are two dozen such texts, with more yet to be identified in manuscript. They date from the end of the 4th cent. through the 14th cent. CE. Extant chiefly in Greek, this apocalyptic literature also exists in Hebrew, Syriac, Coptic, Arabic, Persian, Slavonic, and Armenian; some are original compositions, while others are versions of or translations from Greek texts. The persistent coherence of discrete oracles among the texts indicates a complex history of composition and transmission similar to that of the Jewish *Hekhalot* literature. While popular among eastern Jews, Christians, and Muslims, Daniel apocalyptic literature did not circulate west of the Byzantine Empire. Their cardinal function was to reassure communities under acute distress that God still controlled history and that salvation was foreordained and imminent (*see* APOCALYPTICISM).

The Daniel prognostica are first-person forecasting treatises, which, although lacking a biblical precedent, are conceptually dependent upon the wise Daniel of the court tales. Numerous examples circulated among eastern medieval Jewish, Christian, and Muslim communities and are frequently anthological. In the west, there were two texts: the *Somniale Danielis*, the classic dream-interpretation manual, and the *Lunationes Danielis*, a prognostic based on the thirty moons of the month. Although both originally were Greek compositions of late antiquity, the Latin manuscript evidence suggests that by the 10th cent. CE they had become a regular element of the intellectual culture of western medieval Christendom. *See* APOCRYPHA, DEUTEROCANONICAL; PSEUDEPIGRAPHA; PSEUD-ONYMOUS WRITING.

Bibliography: J. J. Collins and P. W. Flint, eds. *The Book of Daniel: Composition and Reception* (2001); L. DiTommaso. *The Book of Daniel and the Apocryphal Daniel Literature* (2005).

LORENZO DITOMMASO

DANNAH dan´uh [דַּנָּה *dannah*]. A town in the hill country of Judah, probably south of Hebron (Josh 15:49). The LXX calls it **Renna** (Ρεννα), mistaking the DALET (ד) for a RESH (ר).

DAPHNE daf´nee [Δάφνη *Daphnē*]. A place near Antioch that provided asylum and to which the high priest ONIAS withdrew (2 Macc 4:33). Also known for its temple of Apollo. *See* MENELAUS.

DAPPLED [בָּרֹד *barodh*]. One of the four chariots in Zechariah's vision (6:3, 6) is drawn by dappled horses. The Hebrew root is brd (ברד), "to hail," so the meaning may derive from appearing hail-like or hail marked. *See* COLORS; HAIL, HAILSTONE.

DARA dair´uh [דָּרַע *dara´*]. Son of Zera and grandson of Judah and Tamar (1 Chr 2:6). In some manuscripts the spelling of the name is the same as DARDA (*darda´* דַּרְדַּע), so that the two are probably the same (1 Kgs 4:31).

EMILY R. CHENEY

DARDA dahr´duh [דַּרְדַּע *darda´*]. SOLOMON's wisdom was said to have surpassed the wisdom of four men, apparently noted for their wisdom (1 Kgs 4:31). Three of the four were sons of MAHOL, one of whom was Darda. Probably the same person as DARA (1 Chr 2:6).

EMILY R. CHENEY

DARIC dair´ik [אֲדַרְכּוֹן *'adharkon*]. A golden Persian coin of about 8.3 g, the daric was apparently named after DARIUS I who originated it to demonstrate his power and prestige rather than for economic reasons. One daric has been found in Samaria excavations. Among the gifts for the temple in the time of David are said to be 10,000 *'adharkonim* (אֲדַרְכֹּנִים 1 Chr 29:7). If this means darics, it is anachronistic. Ezra 8:27 refers to 20 golden vessels for the Jerusalem Temple, each worth a thousand *'adharkhonim*. The NRSV sometimes translates *darkemon* (דַּרְכְּמוֹן) as *darics*, although it may better refer to DRACHMA (Ezra 2:69; Neh 7:70-72). *See* WEIGHTS AND MEASURES.

LESTER L. GRABBE

DARIUS duh-ri´uhs [דָּרְיָוֶשׁ *dareyawesh*]. Old Persian name used by kings of the Achaemenid Empire, meaning "He who holds firm the good." 1. Darius I, the Great or the Conqueror (522–486 BCE). Darius became the legitimate king in 522 BCE when he assassinated the conspirator, Gaumata, who was pretending to be Bardiya, the younger brother of Cambyses. At least, that is the claim of the official pro-Darius account. When Cambyses died returning from campaigns in Egypt, Darius and his followers suppressed the rebellion, and he seized the throne for himself.

Specific circumstances of his rise to power are difficult to reconstruct despite native Persian sources and parallel accounts in Herodotus. Darius claimed descent from the royal family of Achaemenes, although through a different line than Cyrus. He was able to garner enough support to assassinate the imposter (whether Gaumata, or the real Bardiya), and suppress a number of revolts in several regions of the empire. After these decisive victories in 522-521 BCE, Darius himself established the official story of his ascendancy by engraving the details of his rise and military exploits in rock at Behistun, and ordering copies sent to every country in the Empire. Containing over four hundred lines of Old Persian, and paralleled by Elamite and Akkadian, it seems probable that it was originally only in Elamite, and the Persian script was invented while the work was going on. This remarkable inscription is carved in rock high above the road running from Baghdad to Teheran, accompanied with impressive iconographic representations of Darius, several defeated foes, and the god Ahuramazda. The extent to which this official propagandistic version may be trusted historically is much disputed, but it was widely disseminated throughout the empire, as illustrated by an Aramaic version in Elephantine in Egypt and by the use made of it in the account of Herodotus.

The reign of Darius the Great is characterized by territorial expansion, taking the Achaemenid Empire to its greatest geographical extent while also reforming the organizational structure of Persian authority. Indeed, by contrast with the impressive empire created by Darius, the previous period of the Medes and Cyrus may well have been little more than the holding together of diverse regional polities through military conquest, making Darius the creator of the Persian Empire.

Darius appears in the biblical sources as a supportive figure for the Persian administrative district of Judah. Work on rebuilding the temple began in the second year of Darius (520 BCE; Ezra 4:24). Simultaneously, the prophets Haggai and Zechariah (see also Isaiah 56–66) innervated the community, along with Zerubbabel the governor and Jeshua the high priest, to begin the work. When opponents petitioned Darius to stop the rebuilding efforts (Ezra 5:6-17), the king responded with Achaemenid resources to support the work (6:1-12).

2. Darius II (423–405 BCE). Ochus, the illegitimate son of Artaxerxes I, took the throne upon his father's death in 423 BCE, despite two other sons with claims as successors. After a few months of uncertainty, the two rivals were dead and Ochus took the throne and the royal name Darius II. The reign of Darius II encountered perennial difficulties with a tribal group southwest of the Caspian Sea known as the Cadusians, although we know little else about them. He also succeeded in levying tribute from the Ionian Greeks because of a weakened Athens. His son, Arses, succeeded him to the throne in 405 and assumed the throne name Artaxerxes II.

3. Darius III (336–330 BCE). Artashata, also known as Codomanus, came to the Persian throne under questionable circumstances in 336 BCE and adopted the royal name, Darius III. Often characterized as a weak dynast who is blamed for the loss of central authority and eventually the empire, Darius III had the misfortune of opposing Alexander of Macedon. Although Darius appears to have fought valiantly, he suffered repeated losses to Alexander's armies and was eventually murdered by one of his generals, bringing the Achaemenid Empire to an end.

4. Darius the Mede (דָּרְיָוֶשׁ הַמָּדִי dareyawesh hammadhi; Aram. דָּרְיָוֶשׁ מָדָיָא daryawesh madhaya'). This sixty-two year old, according to the book of Daniel, ruled the Babylonian empire upon the death of Belshazzar (Dan 5:30-31 [Aram. 5:30–6:1]), ruled at least a year, and divided the empire into 120 satrapies (Dan 6:1 [Aram 6:2]). Babylonian, Persian, and Hellenistic sources all attribute the conquest of Babylon (539 BCE) to CYRUS the Persian. No Median king Darius is attested elsewhere, and attempts to identify him historically have failed to gain wide acceptance. Perhaps he is to be identified with Gobryas (Greek sources) or Gubaru/Ugbaru (Babylonian sources), a local governor, attested as elderly (Xenophon, *Cyr.* 4.6.1), and installed by Cyrus as vice-regent over Mesopotamia soon after the capture of Babylon. *See* ALEXANDER THE GREAT; ARTAXERXES; DANIEL, BOOK OF; XERXES.

Bibliography: Pierre Briant. *From Cyrus to Alexander: A History of the Persian Empire* (2002); John J. Collins. *Daniel: A Commentary on the Book of Daniel.* Hermeneia (1993); Muhammad A. Dandamaev and Vladimir G. Lukonin. *The Culture and Social Institutions of Ancient Iran* (1989); Roland G. Kent. *Old Persian Grammar, Texts, Lexicon* (1953); Amélie Kuhrt. "Babylonia from Cyrus to Xerxes." CAH (1988) 4:112–38; Amélie Kuhrt. *The Ancient Near East, c. 3000–330 BC.* 2 vols. (1994–95); Amélie Kuhrt. "Babylonia from Cyrus to Xerxes." CAH[2] (1988) 4:112–38; Rüdiger Schmitt. *The Bisitun Inscriptions of Darius the Great: Old Persian Text. Corpus Inscriptionum Iranicarum, Part I: Inscriptions of Ancient Iran, Vol. 1* (1991); T. Cuyler Young, Jr. "The Early History of the Medes and the Persians and the Achaemenid Empire to the Death of Cambyses." CAH 4 (1988) 1–52; T. Cuyler Young, Jr. "The Consolidation of the Empire and Its

Limits of Growth under Darius and Xerxes." CAH 4 (1988) 53–111.

BILL T. ARNOLD

DARKNESS. *See* LIGHT AND DARKNESS.

DARKON dahr´kon [דַּרְקוֹן darqon]. One of Solomon's servants whose descendants are among those returning from Babylonian exile in similar lists in Ezra 2:56 and Neh 7:58. *See* NETHINIM; ZERUBBABEL.

DART [מַסָּע massaf, שְׁבָיִם shevayim; βέλος belos, δόρυ dory]. A short pointed weapon used for thrusting and perhaps thrown or blown as a projectile. In some instances it seems identical to an arrow. Job 41:26 places the dart (massaf) alongside the spear and javelin. The meaning here remains uncertain, since this is the only occurrence of massaf in the OT, and the LXX renders it *spear* (dory). Second Samuel 18:14-15 says that Joab attacked Absalom with three *darts* ("spears"), after which Joab's ARMOR-BEARERs killed Absalom. While this word may refer to mere sticks, the verb and preposition in the verse indicate "to thrust into," and the typical function of armor-bearers was to dispatch those whom their master had mortally wounded. Ephesians 6:16 uses the Greek term belos, which occurs regularly in extra-biblical literature as *arrow* or *dart*, metaphorically to represent flaming missiles that the evil one shoots at believers. This is the only occurrence of the term in the NT, but other Greek texts indicate that darts could be dipped in pitch and set on fire before being launched.

BRAD E. KELLE

DATE PALM. *See* PLANTS OF THE BIBLE.

DATES. Fruit of the palm tree or date palm (*Phoenix dactylifera*, tamar [תָּמָר]). Dates, a high-energy food source, could be eaten fresh, dried in the form of small cakes, or used for making wine and honey. Dates served as a symbol of life in the desert. In the OT, the date palm is mentioned only once as a fruit-bearing tree (Joel 1:12). However, Song 7:8 refers to the fruit of the palm tree. Also, the reference to "clusters of the vine" in this verse is taken by some scholars to refer to clusters of dates. *See* AGRICULTURE; FOOD; HONEY; PALM TREE; PLANTS OF THE BIBLE.

JULIANA CLAASSENS

DATHAN day´thuhn [דָּתָן dathan]. Dathan was the son of Eliab of the tribe of Reuben. He joined KORAH, ABIRAM, and 250 other leaders of Israel in rebelling against the exclusive authority of Moses and Aaron in the wilderness journey from Egypt to Canaan. God condemned the rebels, and the earth opened up and swallowed them as punishment (Num 16:1-40; 26:9-11).

Dathan, Abiram, and the other 250 lay leaders aimed their protest primarily against Moses' political

leadership (Num 16:12-15), while Korah, as a priestly Levite, rebelled against Aaron's unique religious authority as high priest (Num 16:16-19). The revolt of Dathan and Abiram probably existed as an earlier independent tradition since their rebellion is remembered in Deut 11:6 and Ps 106:17 with no mention of Korah the Levite. Dathan and Abiram's revolt (Num 16) is combined with Korah's rebellion as one in a series of wilderness rebellions in Num 11, 12, and 13–14.

The reduction in Reuben's census numbers from 46,500 in the first census (Num 1:21) to 43,730 in the second census list (Num 26:7) likely reflects a demotion in the tribe's status due to the guilt and punishment arising from the disobedience and rebellion of the two Reubenites, Dathan and Abiram (Num 26:9-11).

DENNIS T. OLSON

DATHEMA dath´uh-muh [Δαθεμα Dathema]. Stronghold in Gilead where Jews sought refuge from persecution by the Syrians (1 Macc 5:9, 28-34) then appealed to JUDAS Maccabeus who, after an overnight march, defeated the Syrian general Timotheus. Dathema's location remains uncertain, although it has been plausibly identified with Tell Hamad (*see* GILEAD, GILEADITES).

J.R.C. COUSLAND

DAUGHTER [בַּת bath; θυγάτηρ thygatēr]. Most commonly in the OT and NT, the word *daughter* refers to the biological female offspring of a parent.

The meaning of *daughter* in the OT is defined by complex family relationships. The common biological usage does occur frequently, for example in the descendants' lists in Genesis 5 and 11, where it is paired with *sons* to describe the totality of a father's lineage. Biblical authors also make note of female children as the "daughter of my FATHER" (bath-'avi [בַּת־אָבִי], as in Gen 20:12, and followed by "but not the daughter of my MOTHER") or "your father's wife's daughter" (Lev 18:11), suggesting that the polygamous marriages at the time made relationships between parents and female children complex. Daughters-in-law (kallah כַּלָּה) appear to have been included among the members of the family, since they are described in the Holiness Code as being among the other "daughters" (including nieces, granddaughters, and step-siblings) who are sexually unavailable to the father (Lev 18:9-17). A mother-in-law may also refer to her daughter-in-law simply as "daughter" (bath rather than kallah as in Ruth 3:16), another indication of the close familial ties, that bound extended families (*see* H, HOLINESS CODE).

The father in particular seems to have had substantial control over the life of the daughter. He could sell her as a slave (Exod 21:7), give her in marriage or for the sexual gratification of another (Gen 19:8; 34:9-21; Judg 12:9; 19:24; Neh 10:30), set a price for her marriage (called the מֹהַר mohar, Gen 34:12; Exod 22:15), and annul a vow she had made (a power transferred to the husband following her marriage, see Num 30:12-16). However, the daughter also had certain protections and rights allotted to her: she could inherit from her father, assuming he had no male heirs (Num 27:1-8, *see* ZELOPHEHAD, DAUGHTERS OF); she could participate in the Sabbath (Deut 16:11-14); and she was not to be killed as a sacrifice (Deut 12:31; 18:10; 2 Kgs 17:17 where the practice is acknowledged but condemned). The story of JEPHTHAH'S DAUGHTER (Judg 11:29-40), in which the father's ill-advised vow to the Lord results in his daughter's sacrificial death, has been discussed as an expression of fatherly love; however, her death by fire seems to fit other descriptions of child-sacrifice for which parents are condemned (Deut 12:31 and 2 Kgs 23:10 in particular).

Aside from actual parent-child relationships, the word *daughter* is frequently employed symbolically (especially in the prophets) to refer to the inhabitants of a city or land (*see* ISRAEL, DAUGHTERS OF).

In the NT, twice in the Synoptic Gospels, a parent approaches Jesus on behalf of an ailing daughter; the daughter of Jairus, the leader of the synagogue, is raised to life (Matt 9:18-29; Mark 5:22-24; Luke 8:41-56) and the daughter of the Syrophoenecian woman (Mark 7:25-30; Matt 15:21-28) has an unclean spirit that is cast out. The close kinship ties of the biological and extended family are recalled in Jesus' apocalyptic speech in which those ties are broken by the approaching end (Matt 10:35-37; Luke 12:52-53). Jesus also employs the term as one of endearment, referring to the woman with the hemorrhage as "daughter" (Mark 5:34; Matt 9:22; Luke 8:48) and by calling the woman who approached him on the Sabbath a "daughter of Abraham" (Luke 13:16). *See* FAMILY; INCEST; MARRIAGE, NT; MARRIAGE, OT.

JESSICA TINKLENBERG DEVEGA

DAUGHTER CITIES. *See* ZION, DAUGHTER OF.

DAUGHTER OF ZION. *See* ZION, DAUGHTER OF.

DAUGHTERS OF ISRAEL. *See* ISRAEL, DAUGHTERS OF.

DAUGHTERS OF PHILIP. *See* PHILIP, DAUGHTERS OF.

DAUGHTERS OF TRIBES OR NATIONS. *See* ISRAEL, DAUGHTERS OF.

DAVID day′vid [דָּוִד dawidh, דָּוִיד dawidh]. David means "beloved," probably the shortened form of a name meaning "Beloved of Yahweh" or "Yahweh is beloved." David was the second king of united Israel and the founder of the ruling dynasty of Judah, who was considered a model of kingship.

A. Biblical sources
  1. 1 Samuel 16–1 Kings 2
    a. David's rise
    b. David's reign
  2. 1 Chronicles 10–29
    a. David's reign
    b. David prepares for the Temple
  3. Superscriptions of Psalms
B. Extrabiblical Sources
  1. Inscriptions
    a. Tell Dan stele
    b. Mesha stele
    c. Sheshonq relief
  2. Archaeology
C. Historicity
  1. Jerusalem
  2. David
  3. The Bible's claims
    a. Variant traditions
    b. Anachronism
    c. Exaggeration
D. Interpretation
  1. Pre-biblical sources
    a. Ark narrative
    b. History of David's rise
    c. Succession narrative
  2. Genre and intent
    a. Historiography
    b. Entertainment
    c. Heroic legend
    d. Apology
    e. Anti-Davidic polemic
  3. A quest for the historical David
    a. David's origins
    b. In Saul's service
    c. Outlaw leader
    d. Rise to kingship
    e. Royal policies
      i. Consolidation
      ii. Capital
      iii. Harem
      iv. Cabinet
      v. Army
      vi. Taxation and forced labor
      vii. Nation
    f. The troubles of kingship
    g. Transition to Solomon
Bibliography

A. Biblical Sources

As the founder of the dynasty of Judah, a model king, and Jesus' ancestor, David's name occurs frequently in the Bible (*see* DAVID IN THE NT). Information about his life is given in three locations.

1. 1 Samuel 16–1 Kings 2

The story of David occupies the central section of the DEUTERONOMISTIC HISTORY, and in terms of volume, he is its most prominent character. The material about David in these books can be divided into two main parts—the story of David's rise to kingship and that of his reign.

a. David's rise. David first appears as the youngest son of Jesse of Bethlehem, who must be called from tending his father's sheep in order for Samuel to anoint him king (1 Sam 16:1-13). In the next scene (16:14-23), he is summoned to Saul's court to drive away the evil spirit from Yahweh with his lyre. Here, he is described as a man of strength or wealth and a warrior (16:18). The story of David's victory over GOLIATH follows (Sam 17). The popular celebration of David's victory rouses Saul's jealousy (18:6-9), so that he begins to seek ways to get rid of David (*see* SAUL, SON OF KISH).

David's popularity, even among Saul's own children, compels Saul to act subtly at first. But soon his animosity toward David becomes obvious so that David is forced to flee for his life (1 Sam 18–20). He spends most of his time as a refugee in the Judean wilderness, where he becomes the commander of a ragtag army (22:1-2). Meanwhile, Saul hounds David in an effort to kill him. David is protected by Yahweh, who gave him success against Goliath and in Saul's army. On two occasions (1 Sam 24; 26) David is presented with opportunities to kill Saul, but he refuses.

Eventually, David turns to the PHILISTINES for help and becomes a mercenary of King Achish of Gath, whom he deceives by hiding his abiding loyalty to Israel (27:1–28:2). The tension surrounding the question about whose side David would take in a battle between Saul and the Philistines is resolved when the Philistine commanders are uneasy about David's presence among them against Israel and demand that Achish send him and his men away (1 Sam 29). David returns to Ziklag, the city given him by Achish, to find it razed. While he is in pursuit of the Amalekites who raided it, Saul and his sons are losing their lives on Mount Gilboa (1 Sam 30–31). David is distraught upon learning the news of their deaths (2 Sam 1).

After Saul's death, the elders of Judah approach David to make him their king, and he reigns in Hebron over Judah for seven and one-half years (2 Sam 2:1-11). His accession over Judah leads to civil war with Ishbaal or Ishbosheth, Saul's son and successor. The conflict comes to an end with the assassinations of ABNER, Ishbaal's army commander and the power behind his throne, and of ISHBAAL himself (2 Sam 3–4). The power vacuum is filled by David, when the tribes of Israel come to Hebron to make him their king as well (2 Sam 5:1-5).

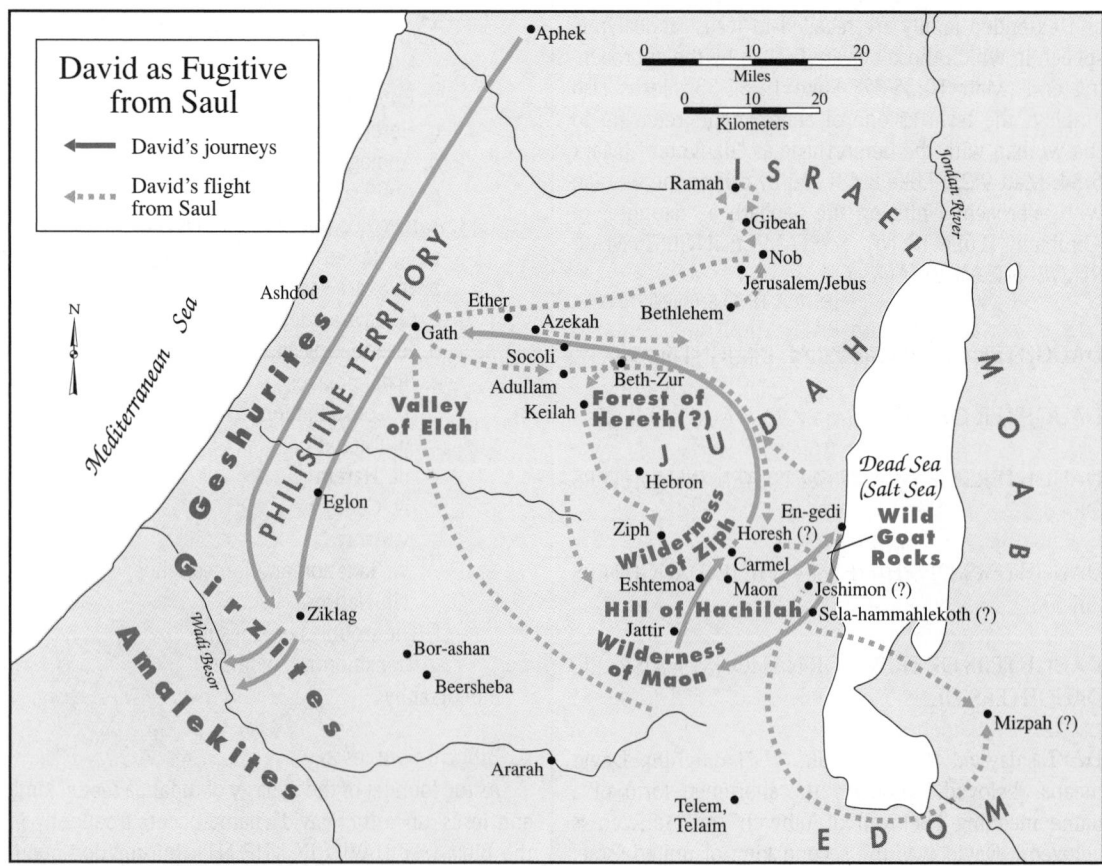

Figure 1: Map of David as a fugitive from Saul

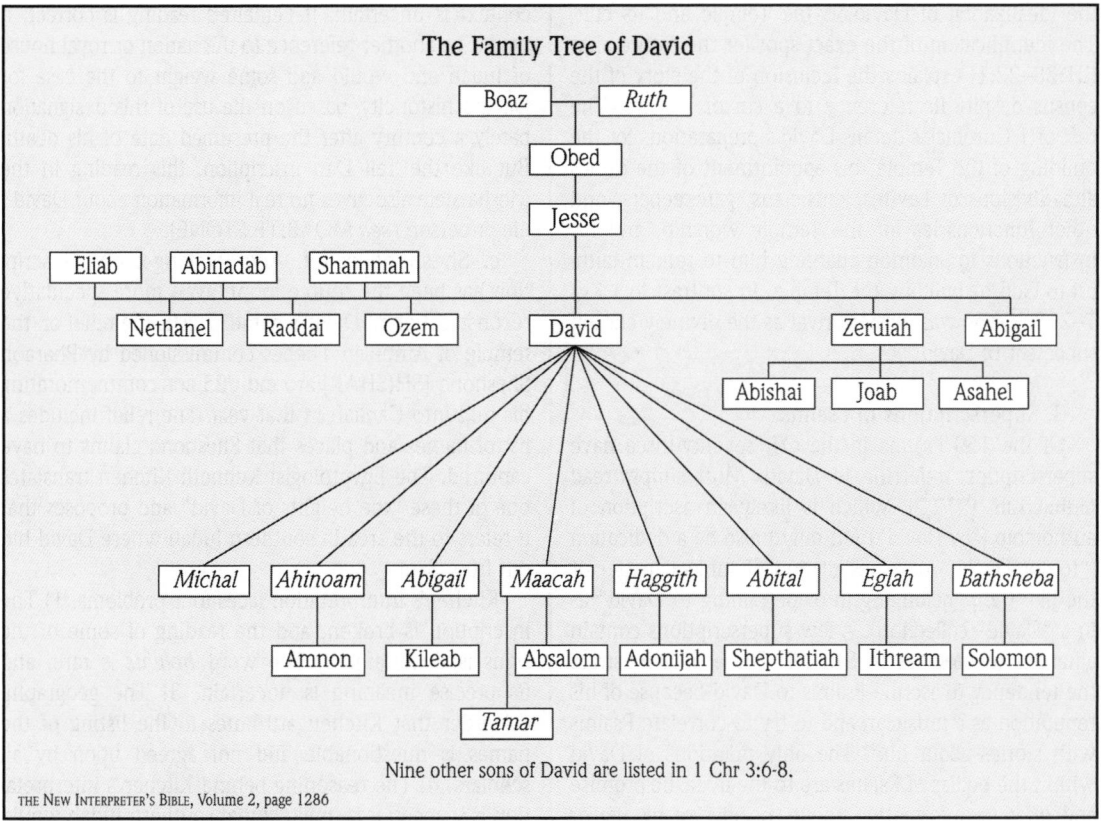

The Family Tree of David

Boaz — Ruth

Obed

Jesse

Eliab   Abinadab   Shammah

Nethanel   Raddai   Ozem   David   Zeruiah   Abigail

Abishai   Joab   Asahel

Michal   Ahinoam   Abigail   Maacah   Haggith   Abital   Eglah   Bathsheba

Amnon   Kileab   Absalom   Adonijah   Shepthatiah   Ithream   Solomon

Tamar

Nine other sons of David are listed in 1 Chr 3:6-8.

THE NEW INTERPRETER'S BIBLE, Volume 2, page 1286

Figure 2: Chart of the family tree of David

b. David's reign. As king, David conquers JERUSA-LEM and takes up residence there (2 Sam 5:6-16). He defeats the Philistines in a couple of battles (2 Sam 5:17-25) and brings the ark up to Jerusalem (2 Sam 6; *see* ARK OF THE COVENANT). Nathan delivers an oracle from Yahweh rejecting David's overture to build a temple but promising him an enduring dynasty as a reward for his faithfulness (2 Sam 7). David consolidates his empire by defeating surrounding countries, seeing to Saul's single surviving heir, and setting up a cabinet (2 Sam 8–10). His adultery with BATHSHEBA and denunciation by NATHAN (2 Sam 11–12) form a prelude to the account of ABSALOM's revolt, which is sparked by the rape of Absalom's sister, TAMAR, and David's handling of the matter (2 Sam 13–19). The story of a second revolt led by the Benjaminite SHEBA (2 Sam 20) is followed by two poems (2 Sam 22:1–23:7) sandwiched between rosters of warriors (2 Sam 21:15-22; 23:8-39), and by narratives about David's execution of Saul's heirs in appeasement of the Gibeonites (2 Sam 21:1-14) and stemming of a plague brought on by his census (2 Sam 24).

The final portion of the David story is really about SOLOMON's accession. When David is aged and can no longer function as king, wrangling among potential successors and their supporters begins. Bathsheba and Nathan successfully conspire to persuade him to name Solomon as the heir to the throne over against Adonijah (1 Kgs 1). David's final instructions to Solomon counsel him to be faithful to Yahweh and to requite or reward, as

appropriate, certain individuals for their behavior toward David (1 Kgs 2:1-9). Then David dies after a forty-year reign, thirty-three years in Jerusalem following his seven-year tenure in Hebron.

2. 1 Chronicles 10–29

With few exceptions scholars agree that Chronicles is dependent on Samuel–Kings. The major differences between them were introduced by the Chronicler for theological reasons.

a. David's reign. Chronicles omits the account of Saul's reign and begins with his death in battle (1 Chr 10//1 Sam 31) in order to show how Yahweh turned the kingdom over to David (10:13-14). Omitting the civil war, Chronicles has David's anointing and his conquest of Jerusalem carried out and celebrated by a united Israel (1 Chr 11–12). An initial, unsuccessful attempt to transfer the ark to Jerusalem (1 Chr 13) is followed by David's establishment there and his defeat of the Philistines (1 Chr 14) and then by another cultic celebration that successfully installs the ark in the city (1 Chr 15–16). Nathan's oracle articulating the Davidic promise is rehearsed (1 Chr 17) along with David's subsequent victories (1 Chr 18–20) and the story of the census and plague (1 Chr 21). However, the absence of the sin with Bathsheba and Absalom's revolt highlight the idealization of David as one of Chronicles' main themes.

b. David prepares for the Temple. The third major theme in 1 Chronicles, in addition to "all Israel" and the idealization of David, is the Temple and its cult. The identification of the exact spot for the future altar (21:28–22:1) explains the inclusion of the story of the census despite its reference to a sin of David's. The rest of 1 Chronicles details David's preparations for the building of the Temple, his appointment of the duties and divisions of Levites, musicians, gatekeepers, and other functionaries for the Temple worship, and his instructions to Solomon charging him to remain faithful to God by building the Temple. In contrast to 1 Kgs 1–2, Solomon was without rival as the divinely chosen successor of David.

3. Superscriptions of Psalms

Of the 150 Psalms in the OT, seventy-three have superscriptions referring to David. Most simply read ledhawidh (לְדָוִד), which is likely an ascription of authorship ("by David") but might also be a dedication ("to/for David") or a designation of subject matter or the like (i.e., "belonging to or pertaining to David" as in a "David" collection). A few superscriptions contain allusions to episodes in Samuel. These data illustrate the tendency to ascribe Psalms to David because of his reputation as a musician and to try to correlate Psalms with stories about him. The only mentions of David within the bodies of Psalms are to the dynastic promise and offer no information about specifics of his life or reign (see PSALMS, BOOK OF).

B. Extrabiblical Sources

Potential sources outside of the Bible for David's life are of two kinds: inscriptions and material culture or artifacts derived from archaeology.

1. Inscriptions

a. Tell Dan stele. Fragments of a 9th cent. Aramaic inscription discovered in 1993 and again in 1994 represent the first clear reference to David in sources contemporary to the Bible ever found. Even so, the reference is not to David the person but to Judah or its ruling dynasty as the "house of David." The authenticity of the inscription is established by its author's claim to have killed kings Jehoram of Israel and Ahaziah of Judah in contradiction of 2 Kgs 9–10. The inscription strongly implies that David was a historical figure whose heirs ruled in dynastic succession over Judah (see INSCRIPTION, TELL DAN).

b. Mesha stele. In the wake of the Tell Dan discovery, the French epigrapher André Lemaire has argued for the presence of the same expression, "house of David," on an inscription dating from the 9th cent. BCE. The Mesha stele is one of the few works preserved in ancient Moabite. The reading is hard to substantiate, because the line in which it purportedly occurs (31) is toward the end of the preserved document, which breaks off shortly thereafter. Some of the letters of the phrase in question are missing or partial and must be reconstructed. Yet the context is uncertain. If Lemaire's reading is correct, it would be another reference to the nation or royal house of Judah and would add some weight to the case for David's historicity, based on the use of this designation barely a century after the presumed date of his death. But like the Tell Dan inscription, this reading in the Mesha stele also gives no real information about David's life or person (see MOABITE STONE).

c. Sheshonq relief. Another long-known inscription has been the source for an even more speculative reconstruction of David's name. This is the relief on the temple of Amun in Thebes commissioned by Pharaoh Sheshonq (SHISHAK) around 925 BCE commemorating his raid into Canaan in that year. The relief includes a list of names and places that Sheshonq claims to have captured. The Egyptologist Kenneth Kitchen translates one of these "the heights of David" and proposes that it refers to the area in southern Judah where David hid out from Saul.

Kitchen's interpretation faces four problems. 1) The inscription is broken, and the reading of some of the signs is uncertain. 2) The word *heights* is rare, and its precise meaning is uncertain. 3) The geographical order that Kitchen attributes to the listing of the names is questionable and not agreed upon by all scholars. 4) The reasoning behind Kitchen's interpretation is suspect: it is unlikely that southern Judah would have borne David's name just because he spent some time there. If the area were known as the "heights of David"—and this name did not occur anywhere else—it would probably designate an area occupied or claimed by a clan or tribe. The character David would then be a hypothetical, eponymous ancestor of the tribe, rather than a historical figure.

2. Archaeology

No archaeological artifact relating directly to David has yet been found. The scarcity of 10th cent. remains from Jerusalem is troubling for historical reconstructions of David. But Jerusalem's current dense occupation and social and political complexity as well as its legacy of continual reuse and rebuilding have made it impossible to gain a complete picture of the city's occupational history.

Since the Bible credits Solomon with much more building activity than David, the two have typically been treated together as part of a package when it comes to archaeology. Similar architectural remains found at the sites of Hazor, Megiddo, and Gezer and attributed to Solomon (1 Kgs 9:15-17) betray the existence of a centralized authority that planned and executed these construction projects. David would have laid the groundwork through military conquest and the establishment of a central government that made it possible for Solomon to carry out such public works. However, some archaeologists are now lowering the dates of the city gate complexes and other features of Hazor, Megiddo, and Gezer typically associated with Solomon about a century to the Omride dynasty, ascribing even less archaeological evidence to David.

Aside from specific artifacts, however, archaeology has informed the David story in a broader sense through sociological (ethno-archaeological) parallels and a consideration of environmental factors in 10th cent. Canaan/Israel. The former have suggested on the basis of similarities with other monarchies and Middle Eastern countries that David took ancient Israel from a chieftain stage under Saul to a true nation-state. The latter has pointed to evidence of a population explosion in the central highlands at the beginning of the 10th cent. that may have put a strain on natural resources and forced youngest sons, like David, to seek out nonagricultural means of livelihood as soldiers, priests, musicians, or the like.

C. Historicity

Since the discovery of the Tell Dan fragments, the question of David's historical existence has generated a great deal of publicity. There are, to be sure, serious disagreements about the level of historicity preserved in the biblical story. But the rhetoric about and between the so-called "maximalists" and "minimalists" sometimes obscures the agreement that exists or seems to be emerging on significant points. We may highlight three of these.

1. Jerusalem

There is little doubt that Jerusalem existed long before David. So much is clear from its mention in the Amarna correspondence of the 14th cent. BCE (*see* AMARNA LETTERS). These letters from Canaanite rulers to the Egyptian court in Amarna refer to Jerusalem as a prominent city-state with a king, whatever the actual size of the site itself and its administrative domain may have been.

2. David

With some notable exceptions, most scholars seem to be persuaded by the Tell Dan inscription that David was a historical figure who lent his name to the royal house of Judah, probably as its founder. This is decidedly not to say that all of the stories about him in the Bible are historically accurate. But the bare existence of the individual seems to be supported by the extant evidence. The alternative is to regard the Tell Dan inscription as a fraud. While caution about epigraphic finds is appropriate, especially in view of recent hoaxes, the allegation of forgery in the case of the Tel Dan fragments is unfounded.

3. The Bible's claims

There is also a growing consensus, though, that the Bible's claims about the nature and extent of David's kingdom cannot be taken at face value. Thus, Finkelstein and Silberman, who might be termed "minimal-

ists," do not deny David's existence, but do question the size of his capital and his domain. Similarly, Halpern, an oft-cited "maximalist," finds a great deal of propagandistic exaggeration in the Bible's portrait to go along with the history that he sees there. There are at least three reasons, treated in what follows, for this growing consensus.

a. Variant traditions. Whatever narrative sources may underlie the biblical narrative, the story as we now have it betrays different traditions. The famous story of David and Goliath (1 Sam 17) in the Masoretic Text (*see* MT, MASORETIC TEXT) is a combination of different versions of the story, as the much shorter LXX account makes clear (compare 17:50, 51, where David kills Goliath twice). Moreover, 2 Sam 21:19, where someone else kills Goliath, suggests that the famous story was not originally associated with David. The Goliath legend is one of several stories describing David's origins and how he first came to Saul's attention. In 1 Sam 16:1-13 David is but a humble shepherd boy, while in 16:14-23 he is already an accomplished warrior. Then, at the end of the latter story, Saul brings David into his personal service, but after the slaying of Goliath, he does not know who David is (17:55-58). Similar variants appear throughout the story of David's rise, some at the textual level (in the MT but not the LXX Saul tries twice to kill David with his spear and David is promised marriage first to Merab then to Michal), others in doublets (different covenants with Jonathan, two chances to kill Saul).

b. Anachronism. The exact process by which the different traditions about David were brought together remains obscure, but it is clear that the story of David as we now have it was completed hundreds of years after his lifetime. The extent to which the story contains specific anachronisms is debated. For instance, the description of Goliath's armor (1 Sam 17:5-7) has been seen by some as an accurate reflection of actual Philistine weaponry, but by others as an anachronistic assemblage from different cultures and times or even a depiction of much later, Greek Hoplite garb. Aside from such individual anachronisms, however, there are thematic anachronisms in the David story. Nathan's oracle in 2 Sam 7 with its promise of a dynasty for David betrays a much later effort to legitimate that dynasty or to explain its longevity and that of Judah.

c. Exaggeration. It is important to distinguish between what the biblical account explicitly claims and what it may imply. Similarly, it is important to distinguish between summative generalizations, which may exaggerate, and the specific details in a given story. To illustrate, 2 Sam 5:17-25 contains accounts of just two victories against the Philistines, indeed, against two groups of Philistines. But the impression that it leaves with the reader is that David vanquished the Philistines as a whole people, and this is the force of the summary statement in 8:1. In fact, the implication of the collection of anecdotes and summaries in chap. 8 is that David defeated all of the nations around Israel and established a wide-ranging empire over them all. Such an impression exaggerates the extent of David's military successes and certainly of his actual control.

D. Interpretation

Given the length and sophistication of the David story, not to mention its central location in the OT, it is perhaps not surprising that it has been the focus of manifold interpretation, both in the popular imagination and in the academy. In addition to the historical issues treated above, critical scholarship on David has focused on the genre and intent of the Bible's story of David as well as its composition.

1. Pre-biblical sources

The modern discussion of narrative sources underlying the David story begins with Rost's 1926 monograph and has focused on three postulated works, all of which he believed were written shortly after the events they describe.

a. Ark narrative. On the basis of stylistic analysis, Rost discerned behind 1 Sam 4:1*b*–7:1 + 2 Sam 6 an originally independent document that had served as the founding tradition of the Jerusalem sanctuary and was written near the end of David's reign or the beginning of Solomon's. This basic theory has been elaborated and revised by subsequent scholars. No consensus has emerged about the beginning of this hypothetical work, and this has led one to question whether such an independent work ever existed outside of scholarly reconstruction. Still, 1 Sam 4:1*b*–7:1, where Samuel is not even mentioned, is quite distinct from both what precedes and what follows, where the prophet is the focus (*see* ARK OF THE COVENANT).

b. History of David's rise. While Rost floated the idea of this source document, he did not carry out a literary analysis of it as he did the other two. Subsequent scholars have provided such analysis, but again, they have failed to achieve any consensus about its exact beginning or ending. A common candidate for the former is 1 Sam 16:14, but some hold that his anointing in 16:1-13 is crucial for his later accession to kingship. Similarly, the work is usually ended either in 2 Sam 5 (with no agreement exactly where) or with 2 Sam 7. But many of the themes in the narrative are deuteronomistic, especially in 2 Sam 7. There were no doubt independent traditions and stories (the Goliath story is one of these) used by DtrH in composing his History, but it seems unlikely that there was an extended "History of David's Rise" previous to the Deuteronomistic History.

c. Succession narrative. The main thrust of Rost's work and the title of his book was the "Succession Narrative," which, except for a handful of DtrH glosses and an old report of the Ammonite war (2 Sam 10:6–11:1;

12:26-31), consisted of 2 Sam 9–20 + 1 Kgs 1–2. The purpose of this document was to answer the question as to who would succeed David as king of Israel.

While Rost's theory enjoyed long-standing popularity, it has come under serious challenge in recent decades. These challenges have pointed out two major problems with the theory that have sounded the death knell for it. The first is that shared by the Ark Narrative and History of David's Rise, namely, the delimitation of the source document. The story of Absalom's revolt, which is at the heart of the Succession Narrative, presupposes a great deal of material not usually included within the Succession Narrative. Thus, the references to Mephibosheth in 2 Sam 16:1-4; 19:24-30 presuppose 2 Sam 9:1 (and the rest of chap. 9), which in turn assumes 2 Sam 21:1-14. These sections then presume acquaintance with portions of 2 Sam 2:8–4:12. Finally, these narratives are themselves presupposed by 2 Sam 11–12, as observed, and by 1 Kgs 1–2. When all of these materials are included, however, the Succession Narrative loses not only its precise beginning but also its integrity and definition as an independent source.

The second major problem is that the purported Succession Narrative does not seem to be primarily concerned with the succession to David's throne. This is more than a question of semantics. Succession is the concern of 1 Kgs 1–2, but it appears to be limited as a theme to those two chapters. Neither Solomon nor succession is mentioned in the story of Absalom's revolt, leading several recent scholars to suggest that 2 Sam 13–20 was originally independent of 1 Kgs 1–2. Furthermore, the latter gives evidence of significant shaping by DtrH. The interest in how Solomon came to succeed David is deuteronomistic or later (see below). The older source, if any, that underlies these chapters can no longer be recovered.

2. Genre and intent

a. Historiography. Von Rad's assertion that the story of David's reign was the beginning of history writing in Israel was very influential in 20th-cent. biblical scholarship. This judgment was based on the paucity of references in 2 Samuel to direct divine intervention as well as the very human depiction of David "warts and all," so that the narrative was seen as a more or less straightforward reporting of historical events. Since von Rad's time, though, scholars have become more attuned to the ideological and literary creativity inherent in the biblical account of David. It has become obvious, as a result, that there is a great deal more complexity to this material than implied by von Rad's understanding. This is not to say, nevertheless, that the genre designation "historiography" is itself incorrect. Scholars such as Van Seters have only recently begun to probe the nature of ancient historiography and to realize that it entailed much more than the mere reporting of historical events and facts.

b. Entertainment. Narrative critics have ushered in a new appreciation for the literary sophistication of the David material as story. Their work represents an important move away from the historical concerns that dominated scholarly inquiry to the exclusion of literary sensitivity. Gunn hazarded the proposal that the David story was intended as pure entertainment and that questions of historical validity were misplaced and essentially irrelevant. Biblical scholars owe these critics a debt of gratitude for opening our eyes to art of the Bible's narrative. At the same time, to treat the David story only as entertainment is to dismiss a range of long-standing scholarship on other dimensions of the text and thus to be guilty of the same offense as those who long neglected its literary facet.

c. Heroic legend. Isser has recently introduced the possibility that the David story was a developing collection of popular tales about a legendary hero of the distant past similar to those from ancient Greece. The strengths of his proposal are its explanation of certain features of the stories, such as doublets and inconsistencies, and the comparability of Greek literature. There is little doubt that some of the stories of David should properly be considered legends that may have come down in variant forms. The question remains, though, whether this proposal best accounts for the David material as a whole.

Isser is less than clear about the direction and extent of influence of the Greek hero legends on the Bible. If the story about David developed during the Israelite monarchy, how were they influenced by the Greek traditions? If the influence was only during the collection stage, which Isser dates to the Persian period, then much of the comparative value of the Greek materials seems to disappear. Finally, Isser's theory does not account well for the defensive nature and tone of the materials about David—certainly those that concern his rise and likely those about his reign as well.

d. Apology. The pro-Davidic trend of the story of David's rise has long been recognized. Saul, who can do no right, is rejected in favor of David, who can do no wrong. David is Yahweh's chosen, the "man after his own heart" (1 Sam 13:14), which simply means that Yahweh favors him. David is driven out from Saul because his faithful and successful service in the army arouses Saul's jealousy. Everyone recognizes this; the army, the prophets, the priests, even Saul's own children are loyal to David. While he is in the wilderness on the run from Saul, Yahweh guides and protects him and even delivers Saul into his hand. It is hardly surprising, therefore, that a number of scholars have posited an apologetic purpose to this material. Indeed, it is hard to avoid doing so. The overall point would seem to be to explain why David succeeded Saul as king even though he had no hereditary right to the throne (though he does have an indirect claim as Saul's son-in-law!), in short, to justify David's usurpation.

Toward the end of 1 Samuel and at the beginning of 2 Samuel, the story appears to counter charges of more sinister activities. A substantial block concluding 1 Samuel seems dedicated to showing that David had nothing to do with Saul's death. Thus, he piously declines two opportunities he has to kill Saul (1 Sam 24; 26). He is prevented by Yahweh and Abigail from killing the Saul-like figure, NABAL (1 Sam 25). The latter story also explains how David acceded to Nabal's wealth and prominence among the Calebites (the leading clan of Judah) through his marriage to Nabal's widow, both of which were significant assets in his approach to the throne over Judah. When Saul dies in battle against the Philistines, among whom David had been serving after having been driven there by Saul, David is far away (1 Sam 27; 29–31). Saul's fate was sealed beforehand because of his wrongdoing (1 Sam 28). The man who claimed to have finished Saul off, though he was patently lying, was dispatched by David in short order just for making the claim that he had slain "Yahweh's anointed" (2 Sam 1:1-16). David's moving lament (1:17-27) exhibits his true feelings of love and loyalty for Saul and Jonathan.

The apologetic tone of the material continues with the deaths of Abner and Ishbaal/Ishbosheth (2 Sam 2–4). Joab assassinates Abner for personal reasons, counter to David's orders, and without his knowledge, as 3:20-30 makes clear with its repeated references to Abner departing from David "in peace." David curses Joab (though does not punish him) and laments profusely for Abner as he had for Saul and Jonathan, such that the people (army) are convinced of his non-involvement (3:37). He also vehemently denounces those who bring him the head of Ishbaal and has them ceremoniously executed, despite the fact that Ishbaal is the final obstacle to his coronation as king of Israel, which follows immediately in the narrative (5:1-5).

The apologetic flavor of the account of David's reign is more controversial but may be perceived in the story of Absalom's revolt. Here David is portrayed as a father whose only weakness is that he loves his sons (Amnon and Absalom) too much to discipline them (2 Sam 13:21). Consequently, their selfish behavior brings disaster in the form of Amnon's rape of Tamar, which sets in motion a further series of events—Amnon's murder by Absalom, Absalom's exile and return, his conspiracy and revolt against his father, David's flight from Jerusalem, and Absalom's death.

The apologetic intent of the narrative is signaled by several factors. David's gentleness is contrasted with the harshness of the "sons of Zeruiah" (16:9-14; 19:18b-23), in continuation of a theme from the story of David's rise (compare 1 Sam 26:6-11). The contrast is especially pronounced with Joab. Thus, like Abner and later Amasa, Absalom is assassinated by Joab, unbeknownst to David. As with Saul and Jonathan and Abner, David mourns profusely at the news of

Absalom's death. Yet, as with the deaths of previous individuals (Nabal, Saul and Jonathan, Abner, Ishbaal), those of Amnon and Absalom benefited David. Both appear to have been David's oldest sons and thus rivals for his throne at the time of their deaths, and Absalom was in open revolt.

A potential difficulty with the view that the David story is based on apology is that it would seem to presuppose an early (Davidic or Solomonic) date for the source material. Such is not necessarily the case, however. Since calling David's legitimacy into question is tantamount to questioning that of the entire dynasty, the apologetic theme could arise at a much later point during the history of Judah but long after David himself.

e. Anti-Davidic polemic. Another major problem with the interpretation of the account of David's reign as apology is the presence of the story of David's affair with Bathsheba and Nathan's subsequent oracle (2 Sam 11–12). This story is clearly not apologetic, as David's guilt is fully and openly acknowledged and condemned with no hint of any attempt to justify or legitimate his deeds. The contrast with the pro-David perspective elsewhere in the Deuteronomistic History is striking, though it is often overlooked in treatments of Samuel–Kings. This contrast has been emphasized by Van Seters, who proposes that the entire account of David's reign is anti-David, anti-monarchical polemic. Van Seters contends, in fact, that the "Court History," including 2 Sam 2:8–4:12 (the civil war and the deaths of Abner and Ishbaal); 6:16, 20-23 (Michal's spurning of David when he danced before the ark); all of chaps. 9–20; and 1 Kgs 2:5-9, 13-46a, was a late (postexilic) addition to the Deuteronomistic History. It highlighted the violence associated with the rise to power of both David and Solomon and was intended as an attack on monarchy as an institution and the Davidic dynasty in particular.

Many of Van Seters's literary arguments are persuasive. He is certainly correct that 2 Sam 9–20 and 1 Kgs 2:5-9 presuppose material in 2 Sam 2:8–4:12. His contention that all of the "Court History" is a post-DtrH addition is more problematic. The first two chapters of 1 Kings do indeed reflect an ambivalence about Solomon and his accession. These chapters are often read as apology for Solomon, since they legitimate the removal of his political enemies as acting on David's deathbed orders. On the other hand, the "apology" here is so paper thin as to be transparent and to lend itself easily to an anti-Solomon interpretation. For example, in 1 Kgs 1, Solomon's accession appears to result from the conspiracy of Bathsheba and Nathan, taking advantage of David's senility. Still, David's worshipful prayer thanks Yahweh for fulfilling in Solomon the promise made in 2 Sam 7.

Seibert's new proposal that 1 Kgs 1–11 represents royal propaganda that has been colored by subversive

scribes accounts for the ambiguity of the material, but seems to require a date contemporary with Solomon and does not take stock of the deuteronomistic content of these chapters. In any case, the narrative in 1 Kgs 1–2, however it was composed and whether it is pro- or contra-Solomon, is concerned with Solomon, not David and should be considered apart from the David story in 2 Samuel.

Van Seters's anti-David interpretation of the story of David's reign in 2 Samuel does not account for the apologetic notes inherent in this material and continuous with the story of David's rise, which Van Seters agrees is pro-Davidic in orientation. However, he is quite correct in his observation that the Bathsheba story clashes starkly with the depiction of David elsewhere in the Deuteronomistic History as the model king who was consistently faithful to Yahweh. Nowhere is this clash more pronounced than in the regnal formula for Abijam (1 Kgs 15:1-5), which contrasts him with David, whose heart was true to Yahweh (15:3) and who "did what was right in the sight of the LORD, and did not turn aside from anything the he commanded him all the days of his life . . . except in the matter of Uriah the Hittite" (15:5). The "except" clause is remarkable, since the Bathsheba sin rivals the worst offenses of the worst king of Israel, Ahab (compare 1 Kgs 21:1-16). It is probably a later addition, and so is the Bathsheba story, as Van Seters argues.

But this does not mean that all of the story of David's reign is secondary or anti-David. Only in 2 Sam 11–12 are David's deeds not defended. Furthermore, the allusions in these chapters to subsequent events (12:11-12) show that they presuppose the story of Absalom's revolt, but the reverse is not true. That is, there is nothing in 1 Sam 13–20 that assumes the account in chaps. 11–12. As suggested above, Absalom's revolt has its own cause in Amnon's rape of Tamar. The insertion of the Bathsheba story transformed it into a tale about moral failure and its woeful consequences, thus imbuing the former apology with a negative orientation on David.

3. A quest for the historical David

The following reconstruction is based on an apologetic interpretation of the David story in 1 Sam 16–1 Kgs 2. It is admittedly—and necessarily—speculative in some measure, and might best be termed a "plausible tale."

a. David's origins. David evidently came from the village of BETHLEHEM in the Judean highlands. His family was partially of Moabite descent, if the genealogy shared by 1 Chr 2:5-15 and Ruth 4:18-22 has any credibility. Jesse, David's father, was a prominent landholder and pastoralist and perhaps an elder of Bethlehem (1 Sam 16:4-5). David was the youngest of Jesse's sons, whether they totaled eight (1 Sam 16:10; 17:12), seven (1 Chr 2:13-15), or four (the number of those mentioned by name in 1 Sam 16–17). While David may well have tended sheep as a youth, the depiction of him in 1 Sam 16:1-13 as a humble shepherd who is anointed king is a fiction that makes use of the common image of the king as a shepherd (2 Sam 5:2).

The burgeoning population and corresponding scarcity of land resources likely forced David, as the youngest, to strike out on his own, relying on skills he cultivated. When he came to Saul's attention, he was already a warrior of some renown as well as a musician (1 Sam 16:18). This verse further describes him as eloquent and handsome, and states that Yahweh was with him. While the verse is designed to show that David was suited to be king, its implication that he was a charming and charismatic individual is borne out by the later stories about him.

b. In Saul's service. David was an adept military leader whose success on the field made him popular but also brought him into conflict with Saul. The story of his victory over Goliath is legend and may have been secondarily attributed to David (2 Sam 21:19). But there is no reason to doubt that David was a skilled and valorous warrior and strategist. He rose quickly in Saul's ranks until something poisoned their relationship and set Saul in opposition to David. The Bible attributes this change to the torment of an evil spirit from God (1 Sam 16:14) that fueled Saul's jealousy (18:9), so that he made overt attempts on David's life (18:10-11; 19:9-10).

The characterization of Saul as possessed by an evil spirit may be adapted from David's description as a musician, since music was commonly understood in the ANE to have magical powers capable of warding off demons and evil spirits (see SAUL, SON OF KISH). It would not have been anything out of the ordinary for Saul to employ a musician in his court. The evil spirit on Saul also contrasts in the writer's portrait with the charismatic spirit of Yahweh that came upon David as it had previously upon the judges and even upon Saul (1 Sam 16:13).

The biblical account emphasizes the irrational nature of Saul's jealousy by portraying him as unique in his enmity against David. Everyone else—the army, Saul's own son and daughter, all Israel and Judah (18:16)—"love[s]" David. But a critical assessment of these claims suggests that Saul's fears may have been quite reasonable. "Love" in the ANE and the Bible is language for political loyalty (see LOVE IN THE OT). The claim that all Israel and Judah were loyal to David, if only partially true, could have posed a serious threat to Saul, especially in view of David's transparent ambition. JONATHAN, Saul's son, remained loyal to his father and died at his side, despite the Bible's professions of his undying devotion to David and even his relinquishing of the throne to him. David's purported marriage to MICHAL is also a literary fiction designed to give David some claim to the throne. The story of their marriage

in 1 Sam 18:20-29 constantly refers to David becoming the king's son-in-law. The story hints at David's ambition in his willingness to risk his life to attain that position. David's insistence on having Michal taken from her husband to be with him before he moves to kingship over Israel (2 Sam 3:13-16) together with her childlessness (2 Sam 6:23) suggest that David isolated her after he had assumed the throne in order to prevent her from bearing any heirs to Saul's line.

The rift between Saul and David, then, had a cause other than jealousy on Saul's part. The real cause may well have been on David's side—perhaps even a plot against Saul in which he was involved. This is speculative, of course, but the considerations just mentioned and the vigor with which the biblical story asserts David's innocence raise it as a distinct possibility.

c. Outlaw leader. Forced to flee from Saul, David took refuge in the Judean wilderness. The account of him going first to see Samuel at Ramah (1 Sam 19:18-22) is fictional and highlights prophetic (and therefore God's) support for David over against Saul. The wilderness of Judah had long served to shelter refugees from settled society. In a short time, David was able to gather a significant force of renegades (1 Sam 22:1-2). They were freebooters who survived by raiding and pillaging. The narrative admits that David covered his tracks by systematically annihilating villages—men, women, and children—though it assures the reader that none of these were Israelite (1 Sam 27:8-12).

Perhaps the most important of David's victims was the wealthy Carmelite whom the Bible calls "NABAL." Since **naval** (נָבָל) actually means "fool," in accord with his characterization in the narrative, it seems unlikely that this was his real name. Even more significant to David than Nabal's wealth was his status as the probable leader of the Calebites, the most prominent clan of Judah (1 Sam 25). When his attempt at extortion failed, David moved to direct assault. According to the narrative, tragedy was averted when Nabal's beautiful, intelligent, and eloquent wife ABIGAIL soothed David's ego and convinced him to lift the assault. Also according to the narrative, Nabal died a short time later at Yahweh's hand. David subsequently married Abigail. Both she and the wealth she brought with her were significant assets in David's next step upward to the throne of Judah. It was no accident that David reigned over Judah for seven and one-half years in Hebron, the Calebite capital. It was also no accident that the elders of Judah who favored David as their king were the ones who received gifts from the plunder he had taken (1 Sam 30:26-31). What more could they ask for in a king than one who enriched them from the plunder of their enemies?

While in the wilderness David also became a mercenary of the Philistines. His relationship with the Philistines may actually have been more one of treaty partners than of mercenary and client. The reference to him in the mouth of the Philistines as "the king of the land" (1 Sam 21:11 [Heb. 21:12]) suggests his growing power. This might account for the discrepancy between the lengths of David's reign as king over Judah alone (seven and one-half years) and that of Ishbaal (two years, 2 Sam 2:10-11). Perhaps David became king of Judah before Saul was dead. In any case, it was an alliance with the Philistines that evidently toppled Saul, who could not hold up against formidable enemies on both his western and southern fronts.

d. Rise to kingship. Nabal was the first in a series of prominent individuals whose corpses littered the way on David's rise to the throne over Israel. Several of these individuals died violently, often at the hand of one of David's henchmen. David was the prime beneficiary, yet the narrative takes pains to demonstrate his non-involvement. Frequently, David mourns profusely and has those responsible for the killing executed.

The next victims in this list of prominent individuals, following Nabal, were Saul and Jonathan. The preoccupation noted above in 1 Sam 24–31 with defending against the charge that David was involved in their deaths leads the skeptical reader to suspect that precisely such was the case. David laments at the news that they have fallen and strikes down the Amalekite who claims responsibility. He writes a beautiful psalm commemorating them. However, his regret over their deaths does not extend to their successor, Ishbaal, against whom David initiates civil war for the throne of Israel.

David initiated the war by hemming Ishbaal in, leaving him no choice but to fight. Saul's defeat by the Philistines left little for Ishbaal to rule over—so little, in fact, that his capital over Benjamin and Ephraim was actually at Mahanaim, east of the Jordan (2 Sam 2:8-9)! It may have been at this time that David, who was already in league with the Philistines, established a treaty with the king of Geshur (essentially the Golan Heights). He then made overtures to the city of Jabesh-Gilead, one of the most loyal enclaves of Saul supporters, stating that they had paid their debt to Saul and asking them to support his kingship (2 Sam 2:4*b*-7). These moves by David left Ishbaal little room to maneuver, and he was forced to resort to war for his own survival.

The power behind Ishbaal's reign was his kinsman, Abner, who was also the next prominent victim in David's rise. Abner's assassination by Joab, according to 2 Sam 2–3, was revenge for Asahel, Joab's brother, who died in the civil war at Abner's hand. However, the occurrence of Asahel's name at the head of the list of David's honor roll (2 Sam 23:24) raises doubts about the historical validity of this episode. The Asahel who died in battle before David became king of Israel was young and out to establish a reputation for himself. How could he have been one of the best soldiers of David's reign? The story may have been contrived to provide Joab a motive for personal vengeance. In actuality Joab was probably following David's order. This is also suggested by the fact that David, despite vituperation and lamentation, never punishes Joab. His advice to Solomon (1 Kgs 2:5-6) is part of the ambiguous legitimation of Solomon and would hardly have been punishment anyway, since it is set decades later.

With Abner out of the way, the kingship was effectively David's to claim. Ishbaal was a figurehead. As with the Amalekite who killed Saul, David executes the two captains who bring Ishbaal's head to David. As also with that Amalekite, though, it is worth noting that these narrative characters perceive David as Saul's enemy. His reputation is further acknowledged later on by Shimei, the Benjaminite who derides David as he flees from Absalom, by calling him a murderer and a man of blood who is suffering God's vengeance for the blood of Saul's house (2 Sam 16:7-8).

Its army defeated, its kings dead, Israel had little choice but to accept David's lordship. While 2 Sam 5:1-5 says that the elders of Israel sought out David at Hebron and asked him to become their king, it must have been more along the lines of a capitulation. The character of David's takeover as a coup d'etat is also indicated by his subsequent dealing with Saul's remaining heirs, which likely provided additional motivation for Shimei's accusations. As with the series of royal houses in Israel during the divided kingdom narrated in 1–2 Kings, the typical practice following a successful revolt was to wipe out the males of the previous house, so one of David's first acts as king of Israel was to get rid of Saul's heirs. This was the "bottom line" result of the episode recounted in 2 Sam 21:1-9, which is apologetically cast in the guise of David acting out of compulsion to save Israel from a famine brought on by Saul himself. Jonathan's son, Mephibaal, was left alive (2 Sam 9) because his lameness prevented him from being a serious threat to David. Even so, he was kept under a kind of house arrest where he could be watched. Michal, as noted, was also isolated to prevent her bearing heirs to Saul.

e. Royal policies. David's kingship over Israel was more sophisticated than Saul's and represented a stage in Israel's development toward statehood. The trajectory of development can be seen most clearly through comparing various features of the three reigns (*see* KING, KINGSHIP).

i. Consolidation. David's first moves as king would have been aimed at consolidating his hold on Saul's former kingdom and adding it to his own domain in Judah. In addition to doing away with Saul's heirs, this would have meant dealing with the Philistines, his old allies, who now became his enemies. David's move to unite Israel and Judah was a threat to them, so they attacked (2 Sam 5:17). His victories over them secured the central highlands (from Geba to Gezer, 5:25). For the time being, he was content to leave the Philistines alone in their territory along the Mediterranean coast.

ii. Capital. While the Bible describes David's conquest of JERUSALEM as the new king's first initiative, historically it must have followed his battles with the Philistines, who would have blocked his way to the city. David's establishment of a new capital at Jerusalem was a clear change from Saul's policy of maintaining his residence on his family estates in Gibeah. The change reflected a move from a localized "chieftaincy" toward full-blown monarchy and nationhood.

Scholars have long commented on the political brilliance of David's taking of Jerusalem as his capital. Geographically, it stood roughly between Israel and Judah. Politically, it belonged to neither, since it was a Jebusite city. Its neutrality was an important asset in David's effort to unite Israel and Judah under his rule. In addition, it was an eminently defensible fortress. This asset meant that Jerusalem was not easy to conquer. Exactly how David succeeded in doing so is uncertain, because the account of the conquest (2 Sam 5:6-8) is problematic. A common interpretation has him directing his men to enter the city through its water system, and this makes good military and strategic sense. But this interpretation does not account entirely satisfactorily for the odd mention in the passage of the blind and lame and David's loathing of them.

Having established his capital, David set about to build a royal residence (2 Sam 5:11). The Bible contains no description of it other than calling it a "house of cedar." This is also the only reference to actual building undertaken by David. It is remarkable that the Bible highlights the fact that David did not build the Temple, since this is exactly what an ANE dynastic founder would typically have done. According to 2 Samuel 7, David had every intention of doing just this but was prevented by God, through the prophet Nathan, from following through. Many scholars think that an older oracle opposing the Temple does indeed underlie this chapter. However, the chapter is so thoroughly deuteronomistic that any older version of it can no longer be recovered with any certainty.

iii. Harem. Another striking development from Saul through David to Solomon was that of the harem. Only one wife (Ahinoam, 1 Sam 14:50) and one concubine (Rizpah, 2 Sam 3:7) are attributed to Saul. David, in contrast, has at least nineteen wives and concubines: In addition to Michal and Abigail, he brought Ahinoam with him to Hebron (1 Sam 25:43; 2 Sam 2:2; 3:2); Maacah, Haggith, Abital, and Eglah joined him while he was reigning over Judah in Hebron (2 Sam 3:3-5); other wives who were taken while he was king in Jerusalem are mentioned but not named (2 Sam 5:13-16); ten concubines were left behind when he fled Jerusalem (2 Sam 15:16); he married Bathsheba after Uriah's death (2 Sam 11–12); and Abishag was taken as a wife or CONCUBINE to keep him warm in his dotage (1 Kgs 1–2).

Most of these marriages were political in nature. We have seen how this was so for Michal and Abigail. Even if the marriage to Michal is fiction, the claim made thereby is political. If Ahinoam was the same as Saul's wife, her presence with David made a forceful political statement. She is said to have been from Jezreel—either the fertile northern valley, which Saul might have claimed as part of his domain (2 Sam 2:9) or, more likely in view of her appearance with David when he moves toward the throne of Judah, a site in the Negeb. Maacah was a Geshurite princess whose marriage to David likely sealed a treaty between him and her father. Absalom cuckolded his father with the ten concubines, thus asserting his political dominance and illustrating the principle that to sleep with a member of the harem was to stake a claim to the throne. Even Abishag was a test of David's virility and hence his suitability to rule. She also became a pretext for Solomon to execute Adonijah on the grounds of the principle just articulated.

The growth in David's harem compared to Saul's pales in comparison to that of Solomon's, assessed at 700 wives and 300 concubines (1 Kgs 11:1-3). The point of so large a number (almost certainly an exaggeration) was to cast Solomon as an ANE king par excellence. The fact that many of these wives are said to be from foreign countries also highlights the political nature of the marriages.

iv. Cabinet. Yet another accoutrement of monarchy that increased from Saul to David to Solomon was the personnel associated with the administration. Saul had no cabinet. Only Abner is mentioned in the post of his army commander (1 Sam 14:50-51). But as Saul's kinsman, Abner's post accords with the portrait of Saul's administration as local and family or clan based.

By contrast, there are two lists of David's cabinet (2 Sam 8:16-18; 20:23-26). These are probably variants of the same list that arose when 2 Sam 21:1-14 (the story of David's execution of Saul's heirs in order to halt a famine) was transferred to its present location from before 9:1 ("David asked, 'Is there anyone left of the house of Saul . . .'"). The list includes David's own army commander (Joab) and his priests (Zadok and Abiathar). It also lists two offices, "recorder" and "scribe," whose functions are not differentiated. The other offices will be discussed below. Solomon's cabinet was even larger (1 Kgs 4:1-6), and his administration also included officials over provinces into which he divided Israel (4:7-19).

v. Army. The story in 1 Sam 11 depicts Saul as having to call up a militia for war. It also says that he was on the lookout for worthy soldiers throughout his reign (14:52) and indicates that most of his men were of his own tribe, Benjamin (22:7).

David's army not only appears to have been a standing institution but also seems to have been much better organized. We have already seen that 2 Sam

23 provides a list of warriors in an honor guard that itself has different divisions. David's cabinet included a commander over the "Cherethites and Pelethites," apparently a kind of royal body guard consisting mainly of Philistines ("Cretans" and "Philistines") left over from David's days as a mercenary. They, along with a contingent from the Philistine city Gath, were among David's most loyal supporters when he was overthrown by Absalom (2 Sam 15:18-22).

Yet a third division of David's army may have been conscripted. David took a census (2 Sam 24), the usual purpose of which was to provide a basis for military conscription, and Solomon is said to have levied just such a conscription among the people of Israel (1 Kgs 9:22). Solomon may well have been following a practice initiated by his father.

vi. **Taxation and forced labor.** Solomon also conscripted the people of Israel into his labor force with which he built the Temple (1 Kgs 5:13-14 [Heb. 5:28-29]). The process of conscription was probably tied with that of taxation whereby SOLOMON divided Israel into twelve districts, each charged with provisioning the king and his court one month per year (1 Kgs 4:7-19). Judah, Solomon's own tribe, was exempted in both cases. It was this "yoke" that the northerners found burdensome and demanded that Rehoboam, Solomon's heir, reduce (1 Kgs 12). When he refused, they seceded, forming their own kingdom. They killed Adoram, the official over the labor force, when Rehoboam sent him to quell the revolt (12:18). That the labor force originated with David seems apparent from its mention in 2 Sam 20:24. David's appointee is also called Adoram, indicating that he continued in the post under Solomon (called Adoniram in 1 Kgs 4:6) and afterward until his death.

vii. **Nation.** Saul's domain was apparently restricted to Benjamin and the hill country of Ephraim (1 Sam 9:4). According to a certain anthropological model, he was a chieftain, not a king, and Israel was evolving toward nationhood but had not yet arrived there. It was David who first forged Israel into a nation by combining Saul's domain with his own in Judah and by annexing other tribes farther north. Aided by a power vacuum in the ANE at the time, David launched campaigns against neighboring peoples (2 Sam 8:1-14; 10; 12:26-31). However, the notion of a Davidic empire that is sometimes drawn from these texts is probably a misunderstanding. These peoples were not nations but were less developed politically than Israel. Also, David's control over these territories was likely sporadic and focused on trade routes rather than being continual and broad based.

f. **The troubles of kingship.** The Bible contains surprisingly little detail about David's reign, considering that it is purported to have lasted a total of forty years. This figure may be a round number and the actual length of his reign much shorter. The biblical account focuses on Absalom's revolt, the cause for which it attributes to David himself because of his sin with Bathsheba. If the Bathsheba story is an addition, however, and the account is read apologetically, a very different picture emerges. Absalom's revolt eventuated from frictions within the royal family, especially Amnon's rape of Tamar. But it gathered momentum because of David's unpopularity. The replacement of Saul and the policies of taxation and conscription must have generated resentment in Benjamin and the north. In Judah, David's transfer of the capital from Hebron to Jerusalem may have been unpopular. As a result, Absalom's revolt was widespread and successful; David was overthrown.

David succeeded in restoring himself to kingship through the same combination of military expertise and ruthlessness that placed him there in the first place. The duplicitous advice of his plant, Hushai, bought him time to get away and to recoup his forces. Like Ishbaal before him, David went to Mahanaim on the other side of the Jordan. But unlike Ishbaal, David was able to wait for Absalom to attack and used the terrain to counter the superior numbers of the enemy (2 Sam 18:6-8). Absalom's death at Joab's hand was likely ordered by David, who may also have been complicit in Absalom's assassination of Amnon. It seems more than coincidental that each of the sons was the oldest at the time of his death.

A second revolt led by the Benjaminite Sheba was much less of a threat (2 Sam 20). But it illustrates that David's reign was hardly a "golden age," as sectionalism, discontent, and turmoil continued even after Absalom was gone. The story of the surrender of Sheba also hints at how loose David's actual control may have been on territories removed from Jerusalem, such as the city of Abel Beth-maacah, where the citizens were unaware of Sheba's revolt and probably of Absalom's before it as well.

g. **Transition to Solomon.** The story of Solomon's succession in 1 Kgs 1 is surprisingly candid in its description of David's dotage and the uncertainty about the identity of his heir. The introduction of the virgin Abishag was a test of David's virility, an essential attribute of the king as the leader and representative of his people and nation. It was no accident that Adonijah declared himself king upon the news that David did not (i.e., could not) have sexual relations with Abishag.

In addition to being fragile and impotent, David may have been senile. In the story he is easily manipulated by Bathsheba and Nathan, who "remind" him of an oath he purportedly made to Bathsheba that Solomon would be his successor. Since no such oath is reported elsewhere, it would appear to be contrived. The rest of the story, in which David summons Zadok, Nathan, and Benaiah and orders them to install Solomon as king, may be contrived as well. But the implication that the succession was contested among David's sons seems realistic. It may even be the case that at the end of his reign David himself was manipulated as he had manipulated so many others during his lifetime. *See* CHRONICLES, FIRST AND SECOND BOOKS OF; ISRAEL, HISTORY OF; KINGS, FIRST AND SECOND BOOKS OF; SAMUEL, FIRST AND SECOND BOOKS OF.

Bibliography: Robert Alter. *The David Story* (1999); A. Graeme Auld. *Kings Without Privilege: David and Moses in the Story of the Bible's Kings* (1994); Abraham Biran and Joseph Naveh. "An Aramaic Stele Fragment from Tel Dan." *IEJ* 43 (1993) 81–98; Abraham Biran and Joseph Naveh. "The Tel Dan Inscription: A New Fragment." *IEJ* 45 (1995) 1–21; Israel Finkelstein. "The Archaeology of the United Monarchy: An Alternative View." *Levant* 28 (1996) 177–87; Israel Finkelstein and Niel Asher Silberman. *David and Solomon: In Search of the Bible's Sacred Kings and the Roots of the Western Tradition* (2006); James W. Flanagan. "Court History or Succession Document? A Study of 2 Samuel 9–20 and 1 Kings 1–2." *JBL* 91 (1972) 172–81; James W. Flanagan. *David's Social Drama: A Hologram of Israel's Early Iron Age* (1988); Frank S. Frick. *The Formation of the State in Ancient Israel: A Survey of Models and Theories* (1985); David M. Gunn. *The Story of King David: Genre and Interpretation* (1978); Baruch Halpern. *David's Secret Demons: Messiah, Murderer, Traitor, King* (2001); John S. Holladay Jr. "The Kingdoms of Israel and Judah: Political and Economic Centralization in the Iron IIA-B (ca. 1000–750 BCE)." *The Archaeology of Society in the Holy Land.* Thomas E. Levy, ed. (1995) 368–98; Stanley Isser. *The Sword of Goliath: David in Heroic Literature* (2003); Kenneth A. Kitchen. "A Possible Mention of David in the Late Tenth Century BCE, and Deity Dod Dead as the Dodo?" *JSOT* 76 (1991) 29–44; Ralph W. Klein. *1 Samuel.* WBC 10 (1981); André Lemaire. "'House of David' Restored in Moabite Inscription." *BAR* 20 (May/June 1994) 30–37; Niels Peter Lemche. "David's Rise." *JSOT* 10 (1978) 2–25; P. Kyle McCarter. "'Plots True or False': The Succession Narrative as Court Apologetic." *Int* 35 (1981) 355–67; P. Kyle McCarter. "The Apology of David." *JBL* 99 (1980) 489–504; P. Kyle McCarter. *1 Samuel.* AB 8 (1980); P. Kyle McCarter. *2 Samuel.* AB 9 (1984); Steven L. McKenzie *King David: A Biography* (2000); Steven L. McKenzie. "The So-Called Succession Narrative in the Deuteronomistic History." *Die sogennannte Thronfolgegeschichte Davids. Neue Einsichten und Anfragen.* Albert de Pury and Thomas Römer, eds. (2000) 123–35; Gerhard von Rad. "The Beginnings of Historical Writing in Ancient Israel." *The Problem of the Hexateuch and Other Essays* (1966) 166–204; Leonhard Rost. *The Succession to the Throne of David* (1982; German original 1926); Eric A. Seibert. *Subversive Scribes and the Solomonic Narrative: A Rereading of 1 Kings 1–11* (2006); Christopher Shea. "Debunking Ancient Israel: Erasing History of Facing the Truth?" *Chronicle of Higher Education* 44, 13 (1997) A12–14; Lawrence E. Stager. "The Archaeology of the Family in Ancient Israel." *BASOR* 260 (1985) 1–29; James C. Vanderkam. "Davidic Complicity in the Deaths of Abner and Eshbaal: A Historical and Redactional Study." *JBL* 99 (1980) 521–39; John Van Seters. *In Search of History: Historiography in the Ancient World and the Origins of Biblical History* (1983); John Van Seters. "The Court History and DtrH." *Die sogennannte Thronfolgegeschichte Davids. Neue Einsichten und Anfragen.* Albert de Pury and Thomas Römer, eds. (2000) 70–93; Yigal Yadin. *The Art of Warfare in Biblical Lands* (1963).

STEVEN L. MCKENZIE

DAVID IN THE NT day'vid [Δαυὶδ Dauid]. David generally refers to the dynastic promises of an eternal covenant between God and the house of David (2 Sam 7:11-14; Pss 2:7; 89; Amos 9:11; Isa 11:1-9) as promises that an anointed royal Messiah will defeat the powers hostile to God's people and inaugurate a reign of peace and justice (e.g., Luke 1:32-35, 69; Acts 13:33; 15:16-17). Genealogies affirm that Jesus belongs to the Davidic line through Joseph (Matt 1:1-17; Luke 3:31). Though the phrase SON OF DAVID, of itself, is simply genealogical, commonly referred to Solomon, its use by early Christians for Jesus (e.g., Matt 1:1; Rom 1:3) appears to signify the belief that Jesus is the agent of God's eschatological salvation. Hence its link to other christological titles derived from the same OT texts, "Son of God" or "Son of the Most High" (e.g., Rom 1:4; Luke 1:32-35). The charge of being "King of the Jews," under which Pilate executes Jesus, mocks his suffering (Matt 27:29, 36; Mark 15:18, 26; Luke 23:38) and links the anticipation of a royal deliverer with rebellion to overthrow the enemies of God's people. Luke's trial before Pilate demonstrates the malice behind that accusation (Luke 23:1-5). John's trial scene incorporates a dialogue between Jesus and Pilate over the true meaning of Jesus' claim to be "king" (John 18:33-38). Crowds hailed Jesus as the one who would inaugurate the Davidic kingdom (Mark 11:10; Matt 21:9, 15). Luke 19:27 and John 12:13 do not mention David. Unlike the Synoptic Gospels, the Fourth Gospel has no tradition of Jesus as a descendant of David or association with David's city, Bethlehem. John 7:42 has some reference to his failure to meet that criterion as a reason not to believe in Jesus.

David in early Judaism presents similar difficulties. Not all anointed or royal savior figures can be said to represent a renewal of the Davidic line. Nor do God's agents of salvation always appear as kings. Some scholars would limit Davidic messianism to those examples in which the promises to the house of David are explicitly mentioned. Others cast the net a bit wider to include anointed, royal figures who bear the epithet "son of God" or otherwise exhibit the attributes associated with the Davidic king. In either case, there is no continuous or univocal anticipation of a renewed Davidic monarchy as God's final saving act or condemnation of the evil powers that defile the earth and emergence of an order of righteousness and peace. The NT apparently draws on a particular line of Davidic speculation that may have emerged in Judean circles as late as the Herodian period. The best known example, *Pss. Sol.* 17, invokes a true Davidic king ("son of David," v. 21) in opposition to the Hasmoneans. It may represent the crisis evoked by Pompey's desecration of the Temple in 63 BCE.

The DEAD SEA SCROLLS have provided several examples of Davidic expectations and interpretation of the OT texts in question. In cases such as 4Q246 II, 1-9, the "son of God" or "son of the Most High" will bring peace and establish "an everlasting dominion." Its link to David depends upon the use of "son of God" from Ps 2:7. Some scholars find echoes of the SON OF MAN from Dan 7 in this passage as well. The text of 4Q174 1 I, 11 treats the "anointed" in Ps 2 as God's elect, but 2 Sam 7:14 as a Davidic messiah: "he shall be my son. He is the Branch of David who will arise with the Interpreter of the Law [= a priestly figure?]." The "branch of David" (Jer 23:5; 33:15) is used for a Davidic figure in 4Q161 8-10 III, 17-24 (Isa 11:1-5); 4Q252 V, 3-4; and 4Q285 5 1-6. If the "first born son" of 4Q369 1 II, 6 refers to a Davidic ruler, then the incorporation of this messianic language into Luke's infancy narrative may also be indebted to early Judean traditions.

Both the Dead Sea Scrolls and NT consider David as an inspired or prophetic figure and author of the psalms ("book of Moses, words of the prophets and David," 4Q397 14-21 10; "all those [= David's songs] composed through prophecy," 11Q5 XXVII, 2-11; "fulfill all things written in the Law of Moses, the prophets and psalms about me," Luke 24:44; Acts 2:30-31). A NT controversy story invokes this prophetic capacity to argue that David, the psalmist, refers not to himself, but to another, the "Son, my Lord" as messiah, namely Jesus (Mark 12:35-37; Matt 22:41-46; Luke 20:41-44 [citing Ps 110:1]). Whether this tradition simply presents the superiority of Jesus as SON OF GOD to a royal Son of David in view of the crucifixion and resurrection (also Rom 1:3-4) or is a rejection of the Davidic messiah tradition remains unclear. The Davidic lion/messiah who overcomes the eagle in 4 Ezra 11:37-46 (compare Rev 5:5); 12:32-33 does so in forensic terms, judgment through the word of his mouth rather than militaristic ones.

Some scholars think that Josephus crafts his story of David's reign in *Ant.* 6–7 without echoes of the militaristic defeat of God's enemies to establish a new sovereignty. Instead, his David models virtues of piety, courage, justice, and wisdom widely admired in the Greco-Roman period. David is an example of faith in Heb 11:32. His devotion to Torah study is celebrated in rabbinic texts (*b. Sukkah* 26b; *b. Shabb.* 30b). Appeals to the biblical David appear in Gospel controversy stories. David and his men eating showbread are invoked in defense of Jesus' disciples' eating grain on the Sabbath (Mark 2:23-26; Matt 12:1-8; Luke 6:1-6). The presence of David's tomb is said to show that deliverance from death must apply to another (Jesus), not David (Acts 2:25-34; on wealth in David's tomb, Josephus, *Ant.* 16.179-83; *J.W.* 1.61).

Healing miracles are attached to Jesus as "Son of David" in the NT (Mark 10:46-52; Matt 20:29-34; Luke 18:35-43), a tradition expanded in Matt (12:23; "have mercy, Son of David . . ." 9:27; 15:22). Solomon, "son of David," was reputed to be a powerful exorcist in some 2nd cent. CE traditions (e.g., *Testament of Solomon*). Christians may have created this association. *See* DAVID; MESSIAH, JEWISH.

Bibliography: J. H. Charlesworth et. al. *Qumran Messianism* (1998); K. E. Pomykala. *The Davidic Dynasty Traditions in Early Judaism* (1995).

PHEME PERKINS

DAVID, CITY OF [עִיר דָּוִד 'ir dawidh; πόλις Δαυίδ polis Dauid]. 1. Jerusalem. According to 2 Sam 5:6-9 and 1 Chr 11:4-7, the fortified city of the Jebusites, also called the "stronghold of Zion," was renamed "City of David" after David's conquest and occupation. Several biblical texts seem to refer to pre-Davidic JERUSALEM as "Jebus" (Judg 19:10; 1 Chr 11:4-5) or "the Jebusite" (Josh 15:8; 18:28). However, the pre-Davidic city was already called (u)rushalimum in the Egyptian Execration Texts from the 19th–18th cent. BCE and urusalim in the 14th cent. BCE Amarna letters (*see* JEBUS, JEBUSITES).

In post-exilic times, the term "City of David" seems to have been used of the older parts of the city (Neh 2:14; 3:15-16, 26; 12:37), located on a triangular-shaped spur on the southeastern slope of Mount Moriah (2 Chr 3:1), south of the present-day Temple Mount, bordered on the east by the Kidron Valley and on the southwest and northwest by the Hinnom and Tyropoean valleys. Josephus was the first to associate the "City of David" with Jerusalem as a whole (*Ant.* 7.3).

2. Bethlehem. The Gospel of Luke (2:4, 11) identifies BETHLEHEM as the city of David (**polis Dauid**) in order to link Jesus' birthplace with the lineage of David (*see* DAVID IN THE NT).

Bibliography: S. Ahituv. *Canaanite Toponyms in Ancient Egyptian Documents* (1984); W. L. Moran. *The Amarna Letters* (1992).

JILL L. BAKER

DAVID, DECREE OF. *See* BOOKS REFERRED TO IN THE BIBLE.

DAVID, SON OF. *See* SON OF DAVID.

DAVIDIC COVENANT. God's unilateral promise of dynastic permanence for David and his descendants, either unconditional or conditional, is often called the Davidic covenant. Some trace the Davidic covenant to promissory grants of privileges made to loyal servants by ANE kings. The validity and extent of such influence is debated.

Second Samuel 7 portrays the promise of a secure dynasty ("house") to David in unconditional terms, but without using the word *covenant*. God guarantees indefinite dynastic rule (vv. 13, 16) and pledges that David's son (singular) would receive only limited punishment for misdeeds (vv. 14-15). "Forever" implies "for an unbounded, unforeseeable duration," not the modern notion of infinite eternity (compare 1 Sam 2:30). Language of the DtrH permeates 2 Sam 7, raising the question of whether it incorporates genuinely early traditions or represents a composition by DtrH intended to explain the continued rule of David's family. In DtrH, God shows forbearance to disobedient Davidic kings (1 Kgs 11:12-13, 32-36; 15:4-5; 2 Kgs 8:19), implying that Davidic reign over Judah in Jerusalem would endure despite royal wrongdoing, but DtrH never uses *covenant* to refer to this idea. (*Covenant* does not appear in the Hebrew of 1 Kgs 8:24; translation of the verse is debated.)

A further, conditional promise involves Solomon. In 1 Kgs 2:4 David quotes a divine promise of continued rule on the "throne of Israel" (reign that incorporates the northern kingdom of Israel) if David's sons remain obedient. God directs this same pledge to Solomon in 6:12. Solomon prays that the conditional promise concerning the "throne of Israel" be kept (8:23-26). God repeats that continued rule over Israel depends on Solomon's obedience (9:4-5). Nevertheless, Solomon sinned, and rule over Israel (and the potential for an enduring dynasty) passed to Jeroboam (11:37-38).

Psalm 132 does not use *covenant* for God's promise to David and makes it conditional on his successors' obedience to covenantal law (vv. 11-12). Texts from the exilic and post-exilic periods, by contrast, explicitly mention *covenant* and speak in unconditional, open-ended terms. Psalm 89 uses language reminiscent of 2 Sam 7 to recall an unconditional covenant (vv. 30-34), then goes on to protest that God has apparently terminated it (vv. 38-45, 49). Isaiah 55:3 extends God's eternal covenant with David to the entire nation. Isaiah 55:3 and 2 Sam 23:5 apply the phrase "eternal covenant" to God's promise to David. (Otherwise this phrase is applied to God's covenants with Noah [Gen 9:16] and Abraham [Gen 17:7, 13, 19]). Abijah in 2 Chr 13:5 reminds the northern tribes of God's

"covenant of salt" (perpetual covenant; compare with Num 18:19) with David. Second Chronicles 21:7 adds "covenant" to the wording of 2 Kgs 8:19. Jeremiah 33:14-26 (a late text absent from the LXX) promises a restoration of Davidic kingship rooted in a permanent unconditional covenant (vv. 17 [compare 1 Kgs 2:4; 8:25], 21). Second Samuel 23:5 and Isa 55:3 apply the phrase "eternal covenant" to God's promise to David. The Priestly writing (P) uses this expression for God's covenant with Noah (Gen 9:16) and Abraham (Gen 17:7, 13, 19). *See* COVENANT, OT AND NT; D, DEUTERONOMIC, DEUTERONOMISTIC; DEUTERONOMISTIC HISTORY; P, PRIESTLY WRITERS.

Bibliography: Steven L. McKenzie. "The Typology of the Davidic Covenant." *The Land That I Will Show You.* J. A. Dearman and M. P. Graham, eds. (2001) 152–78.

RICHARD D. NELSON

DAVID'S CHAMPIONS. Second Samuel 23:8-39 introduces a roster of David's elite warriors with "these are the names of the warriors David had" (v. 8*a*) and concludes it with a summary total (v. 39*b*). The list also incorporates reports of heroic exploits.

First Chronicles 11:10-47 repeats the list with modifications and additions. If genuine, the list shows that some of David's most dependable followers were from the territory of Israel (e.g., Gibeah of the Benjaminites, Pirathon; vv. 29-30) and others were non-Israelites (e.g., Zelek the Ammonite, Uriah the Hittite; vv. 37, 39). Extolling David's champions served to glorify David himself (compare the four giant slayers in 2 Sam 21:15-22).

The warriors fall into two classifications: the elite Three (vv. 9, 19, 23) and the less selective Thirty (vv. 13, 23, 24). The Three were Josheb-basshebeth, Eleazar, and Shammah (vv. 8*b*–12). The Thirty are listed in vv. 24-39. Verses 13-17 recount an incident involving three unnamed members of the Thirty. Abishai and Benaiah were not part of the Three (vv. 19, 23). Benaiah was among the Thirty (v. 23), but Abishai's membership in that group hinges on textual emendation (vv. 18-19 NRSV).

Josheb-Basshebeth was the chief of the **shalish** (שָׁלִשׁ) (2 Sam 23:8), a military title apparently derived from the "third man" in a chariot squad (2 Kgs 9:25; 10:25; 15:25). The verbal similarity between **shalish** and the Hebrew words for *three* and *thirty* caused difficulties in the transmission of this list.

Bibliography: Donald G. Schley. *"The Shallishim: Officers or Special Three-man Squads?" VT* 40 (1990) 321–26.

RICHARD D. NELSON

DAWN [שַׁחַר shakhar; ὄρθρος orthros]. In the OT, *dawn* often translates shakhar, an ANE deity associated with the sun's rising (e.g., Isa 14:12; Job 41:18). In the NT, various Greek terms often refer simply to the break of day (e.g., Mark 13:35; Luke 24:1; Acts 20:11). In Luke 1:78, *dawn* is employed once to translate anatolē (ἀνατολή), a term that occasionally carries messianic overtones in the LXX (see Jer 23:5; Zech 3:8; 6:12).

JAMES A. METZGER

DAY OF ATONEMENT יוֹם כִּפֻּרִים yom kippurim; ἡμέρα ἐξιλασμοῦ hēmera exilasmou]. The Day of Atonement (Yom Kippur), celebrated annually on the tenth day of the seventh month (Tishri), comprises a series of rituals by which the high priest purifies both the SANCTUARY and the people, thereby restoring both as fitting receptacles for and agents of God's holy presence in the world.

    A. The Instructions in Leviticus 16
        1. Precautions and preparations (vv. 1-10)
        2. The ritual proper (vv. 11-28)
    B. The Structural and Theological Significance of
        the Day of Atonement in Leviticus
    C. Comparable Rituals in the Ancient Near East
    D. The Day of Atonement in Early Jewish and
        Christian Texts
    Bibliography

A. The Instructions in Leviticus 16

In the OT, the instructions for the Day of Atonement are found only in Lev 16, although various aspects related to the ceremony are mentioned elsewhere (e.g., atonement sacrifices [Lev 4:1–5:13] and calendrically fixed holy days [Lev 23; Num 28–29]). ANE parallels and later references in both Jewish and Christian sources supply additional insight (see below), but this single chapter sets the compass for understanding the importance of the day in ancient Israel's priestly theology. The final form of the chapter reflects a complex editorial process. Two originally distinct rituals—one requiring the sacrifice of a goat "for the Lord," which purifies the sanctuary (vv. 11-19), and a second, the offering of a goat "for AZAZEL," which is banished to the wilderness, thus effectively removing the impurities of the people (vv. 20-22, 26)—have been combined into one ceremony. An appendix in vv. 29-34 regularizes a ritual originally performed "at any time" (v. 2) a crisis occurred by stipulating that it be performed "in the seventh month, on the tenth day of the month" (v. 29) "once in the year" (v. 34). Working from this composite text, the instructions concerning the Day of Atonement may be outlined as follows.

1. Precautions and preparations (vv. 1-10)

The warning (vv. 1-2) that begins the chapter suggests that the precipitating crisis for these instructions is the tragic death of Aaron's sons, recorded in Lev 10. On the day of their ordination, NADAB and ABIHU

offered to God an "unholy fire" (Lev 10:1), a sin that requires not only their punishment by death but also the purification of the sanctuary, which their corpses have defiled (Lev 10:4-5; see Num 19:14-22). Leviticus 16 presents Aaron as one who now stands precariously between the words "they died" (10:2b) and the warning that he must scrupulously follow these instructions "lest he die" (16:2, 13) as well.

The preparations are set forth in two parts. First, Aaron must assemble the required materials for the ceremony (vv. 3-5). For himself and his household, he brings two animals, a bull for a "sin offering" (4:1–5:13) and a ram for a "burnt offering" (1:10-13; 8:18-21). For the people, the same offerings require two male goats. Aaron must ritually purify himself by washing, then clothing himself with linen garments—tunic, breeches, sash, and turban. The emphasis on "LINEN" conveys a mixed symbolism that is appropriate for one who is to stand between the holy and the common. On the one hand, these are not the ornate outer garments worn exclusively by the high priest but rather the ordinary undergarments common to all priests (8:6-30; see Exod 28, 39). On the other hand, linen vestments are more than ordinary; elsewhere they are the attire of angels who are privileged to appear before the throne of God (Ezek 9:2-3; Dan 10:5-6). A second section of the preparations provides the order of presentations (vv. 6-10). Aaron will offer the bull "for himself and for his house." He sets the two goats taken from the people "before the Lord" and casts lots to determine which one is "for the Lord" and which one is "for Azazel." The one designated "for the Lord" will be sacrificed as a sin offering. The goat "for Azazel" will be "presented alive" before the Lord, then sent away into the wilderness.

2. The ritual proper (vv. 11-28)

The ritual comprises three stages: the purification of the sanctuary (vv. 11-19); the purification of the people (vv. 20-22); and the sacrifice of burnt offerings and the cleansing of the participants (vv. 23-28). The first objective is to purify the sanctuary completely—inner sanctum (vv. 14-16a), outer sanctum (v. 16b), and outer altar (vv. 18-19)—of "uncleannesses" (tum'oth טֻמְאֹת), "transgressions" (pesha'im פְּשָׁעִים), and "sins" (khatt'oth חַטֹּאת, v. 16), in sum, of both ritual impurities and moral/ethical violations.

The key to this ritual is the meaning of the verb kipper (כִּפֶּר, vv. 11, 16, 17, 18). Although this verb bears the conventional translation *atone* or *expiate*, it conveys the more specific meaning of *purge* or *purify* when used in ritual texts. The blood in "sin offerings" (vv. 11, 15) acts as a ritual detergent. When its application is described with the verb kipper, the meaning is to "wipe clean" or decontaminate, that is, to purify an object that has been defiled. Aaron takes some of the blood of the slain bull he offers for himself and sprinkles (yazzeh יַזֶּה, v. 14) it before the mercy seat in the inner sanctum seven times, then repeats the process with some of the blood from the sin offering for the people (vv. 15-16*a*). He repeats the ritual once more in the outer sanctum, presumably cleansing the entire area (v. 16*b*; see Lev 4:5-7, 16-18), and then for a final time in the outer courtyard, where he daubs (nathan נָתַן, v. 18; NRSV: put) some of the blood on the horns of the altar for burnt offerings, then sprinkles (yazzeh, v. 19) some of it on the altar seven times. The number of "sprinklings" and "daubings" totals forty-nine, seven times seven, a symbolic reminder that the sanctuary has been thoroughly cleansed.

The cleansing of the sanctuary reflects the priestly understanding of sin's malignant power to infect not only persons but also institutions. Like an airborne virus, sin travels far and wide, contaminating everything in its path. The greater the sin, the more extensively the sanctuary is contaminated. An individual's inadvertent sins penetrate into the courtyard of the sanctuary, defiling the outer altar (Lev 4:22-25). Inadvertent sins by the high priest or the entire community are more serious, for their corruption penetrates into the outer sanctum (Lev 4:3-21). Most serious of all are intentional, unrepented sins, because their reach extends into the inner sanctum, thus to the ritual center of the presence of God on earth. The effects of inadvertent sins may be ritually countered on an ad hoc basis by the prescribed sacrifices in Lev 4–5. Intentional or wanton sinners, however, are prohibited from bringing offerings to the sanctuary (Num 15:27-31). The debilitating effects of their transgressions can only be addressed once a year, on the "Day of Atonement" (yom kippurim, "Day of Purification"), when the high priest dares to enter the HOLY OF HOLIES, there to risk the ritual that enacts the conviction that God will not abandon the faithful sinner.

The purification of the sanctuary was a matter of grave importance for the priests. A holy God will not reside in an unholy dwelling. Thus, if the sanctuary is not cleansed, God may leave, abandoning the community to certain destruction (Ezek 8–10). More than Israel's security is at stake, however. In the ritual world constructed by the priests, the sanctuary is a "spiritual barometer" that measures not only the community's faithfulness but also the fidelity of the entire cosmos to God's creational plan. As the only specific place in the entire creation that is said to be filled with the "glory of God" (Exod 40:35), the tabernacle concretizes God's hopes and expectations for a "very good" world (Gen 1:31). The heptadic patterning that structures God's blueprint for the sanctuary's design (Exod 25–31) and Moses' instructions for its erection (Exod 35-40), the numerous verbal links between the completion of the sanctuary and the completion of creation (see Exod 40:33 and Gen 2:2; Exod 39:43 and Gen 2:3), and the conceptualization of the sanctuary as a microcosm of an orderly world that carefully monitors the boundaries

between the sacred and the common—all these points of intersection reinforce the sanctuary's importance for sustaining the stability of creation. The ritual acts of "sevening" enacted on the Day of Atonement are a critical part of the priestly ministry. When the sanctuary is holy, God is present and the world is secure, because heaven and earth are partnered in common stewardship of God's creational intentions.

When the purification of the sanctuary is complete, a second part of the ritual effects the purification of the people (vv. 20-22). Aaron brings forward the "live goat," which has been stationed "before the Lord" and designated "for Azazel" (vv. 8, 10, 26), lays both hands on the goat's head, and confesses over it *all* the "iniquities" ('awonoth עֲוֹנֹת), "transgressions" (pesha'im פְּשָׁעִים), and "sins" (hatte'oth) of the people, presumably enumerating the sins in order to expose them to ritual expiation. After the confession, the goat is sent off to the wilderness, bearing "on itself" the people's sins (see also the "living bird" set free in Lev 14:4-7, 48-53).

The word 'aza'zel (עֲזָאזֵל) occurs only 4 times in the OT, all in this chapter (vv. 8, 10 [2x], 26). Three interpretations deserve consideration. 1) The Hebrew word may be interpreted as a combination of "goat" (עֵז 'ez) and "go away" ('azal אָזַל), thus "the goat that goes away" (LXX; Vg.). From this interpretation, we get the familiar term scapegoat (escape-goat), which first appeared in William Tyndale's 16th cent. English translation of the Bible. 2) The term may be geographical, thus a designation for the "precipitous place" or a "rugged cliff" to which the goat is sent (Rashi; *Targum Pseudo-Jonathan*; see Lev 16:10, 22). 3) A third possibility, increasingly attractive to some, but still considered as conjectural at best, is that 'aza'zel is the name of a wilderness demon, a concept that has antecedents in ANE texts and is prominent in Midrashic literature dating to the early post-biblical period.

The final part of this constructed ritual is found in vv. 23-28. Having completed his role in cleansing the sanctuary and the people, Aaron removes the linen garments he has worn, ritually washes once more, and reclothes himself, now with the more ornate vestments that signify his high-priestly status. Other participants in the preceding rituals—the one who supervised the release of the goat for Azazel (v. 26) and the one who disposed of the remains of the burnt offering (v. 28)—undergo similar ablutions. Finally, Aaron presents burnt offerings, the fat of which is "turned into smoke" (v. 25), which symbolizes the transformation the ritual has effected: places and persons once unfit for communion with a holy God have now been "turned into" an offering that is acceptable and pleasing to God.

An appendix in 16:29-34 addresses the people directly for the first time. Both the beginning and ending of the pericope designate the rituals of this day as an "everlasting statute," which future generations must observe on the tenth day of the seven month of the year. Israel's liturgical calendar is a complex amalgam composed over time (Exod 23:12-19; 34:18-26; Deut 16:1-7; Lev 23; Num 28-29). Generally speaking, the seventh month of the year (September–October) is the ritual analogue to the seventh day that anchors God's creational plan. Like the seventh day, the seventh month is a "sabbath of complete rest" (v. 31), a cessation of human labor that both celebrates what God has already provided and prepares for God's future blessings. Toward this end, the people are commanded to practice a self-denial that likely includes not only fasting, which is typically associated with repentance and seeking God's mercy (e.g., Ezra 8:21-23), but also solemn commitments to live as faithful stewards of God's justice (e.g., Isa 57:6-9).

B. The Structural and Theological Significance of the Day of Atonement in Leviticus

The final form of the book of Leviticus presents the Day of Atonement as a major rite of passage. Located at the center of the book, chapter sixteen marks the critical intersection between instructions primarily directed to the priests (Lev 1–15) and instructions principally addressed to the people (Lev 17–26, the "Holiness Code"). Inside the sanctuary, priests must bring ritual gifts (qorban קָרְבָּן, 1:2; NRSV: offering) of sacrifices that enable people to separate themselves from the world by drawing near to the presence of the holy God. In sum, the priests must "teach the people" how "to distinguish between the holy and the common, and between the clean and the unclean" (10:10-11). Outside the sanctuary, people must bring gifts (qorban, 17:4) that signal their commitment to reenter the world with lives that conform to and extend the mandate of a holy God. In sum, they must "be holy, for I the Lord your God am holy" (19:2). The journey from holy rituals to holy living is fraught with difficulty, as the book of Leviticus candidly acknowledges (Lev 8–10). On the Day of Atonement, both priests and people stand in a liminal zone, between God's expectations and human failure. The rituals that purify the sanctuary and remove the stain of human sin enact God's promise of a new beginning (*see* H, HOLINESS CODE).

The structure the book of Leviticus may convey a still larger theological truth. If, as most would agree, Leviticus was composed and edited in the exile, when the temple had been destroyed and the rituals for the Day of Atonement were no longer possible, then the book itself becomes what Mary Douglas calls a "virtual tabernacle." By faithfully attending to its instructions, a people whose hopes for new beginnings have been deadened by historical realities may remember and thereby act upon the abiding promise that God will forgive their failures and transform their world. As a literary microcosm of a world, Leviticus preserves the hope that a seemingly endless cycle of sin and punish-

ment can be interrupted. Once a year, on the Day of Atonement, the gap between what God requires and what humans offer can be overcome. Each time the instructions for the Day of Atonement are enacted, both the burden and the promise of second chances recalibrate the possibilities for the future.

C. Comparable Rituals in the Ancient Near East

Ritual purification ceremonies comparable to Israel's Day of Atonement are well attested in the ANE. Of particular significance are the rites performed during the Babylonian New Year festival (*ANET*, 331–334). The high priest washes and clothes himself in linen, sprinkles water from the Tigris and Euphrates on the sanctuary, and wipes (**kuppuru**, cognate with **kipper**) the blood of a slaughtered ram on the temple and its environs, thus purifying the whole sanctuary for the arrival of the god Nabu. When the purification rituals are complete, the high priest and the participants recite prayers of confession and penitence. While such similarities establish a clear antecedent for Lev 16, significant differences, especially the understanding of the sin, underscore Israel's particular appropriation of the rite. In Babylon, demonic (metadivine?) forces are believed to have generated the sin that defiles the sanctuary and puts the people at risk. Israel's priests, adhering to a strict monotheism, contend that humans are responsible for the sin that jeopardizes the presence of God both in the sanctuary and in the world it serves.

Ancient Near Eastern texts also contain precedents for the Azazel ritual. The closest parallels are found in Hittite banishment rituals, especially *The Ritual of Huwarlu* (CTH 398), and *The Ritual of Ambazzi* (CTH 391; compare *ANET*, 348–349). When plague threatens the land of Hatti, its effects are countered by the use of live animals, which bear the punishment, appease the angry gods, and are sent away to distant places, thus nullifying the immediate danger. The banishment to the wilderness of the goat "for Azazel" clearly functions in a similar way. The biblical rite, however, "devitalizes" the demonic aspects of Azazel and concentrates on the removal of the sins of the Israelites, not the appeasement of a supposed magical sorcerer who uses pestilence to work evil.

D. The Day of Atonement in Early Jewish and Christian Texts

Ritual and moral purity, central concerns of the Day of Atonement, receive extensive attention in post-biblical texts (e.g., Sir 50:5-21; *Jub.* 5:17-18; 34:18-19). Similarly, the ritual concerning Azazel seeds continuing interest in the scapegoat tradition in both Jewish (e.g., *1 En.* 6–16; *Apoc. Ab.* 13–14) and Greek texts (e.g., the pharmakos [φαρμακός] rituals). The *Mishnah Yoma* ("The Day") expands upon the biblical account, including, e.g., a stipulation that the high priest must prepare for the rituals of the Day of

Atonement by reading from the books of Job, Daniel, Ezra, and Chronicles (*m. Yoma* 1:1–3:2). The majority of the extant texts from Qumran address purity and impurity, which indicates these remained primary concerns for Second Temple Jewish communities (e.g., CD, 1QS, and 4QTohorot [4Q274–278]). The Temple Scroll (11Q19; 20), probably the oldest (and perhaps the "parent") text of the Qumran community, systemizes Pentateuchal legislation concerning the sanctity of the temple, accenting the demand that all who enter or live near the holy place must conform to a high standard of purity. Although the purification does not specifically require the atonement outlined in Lev 16, the trajectory of a common concern is apparent. The trajectory extends to contemporary Judaism, where the celebration of Yom Kippur climaxes the High Holy Days that begin the new year (Rosh Hashanah) with fasting, abstinence, and prayers for forgiveness.

The NT appropriates the "everlasting statute" stipulated in Lev 16:34 and extends its trajectory still further. The principal text is Heb 9–10 (see Acts 27:9), which depicts Jesus, not Aaron, as the sinless high priest who enters the heavenly sanctuary, in order to secure a once-and-for-all-eternity redemption, not only for the people but also for the entire cosmos. In Christian testimony, as in Jewish sacramental observance, the Day of Atonement seeds the hope for new beginnings. Inside the claims of this ancient priestly ritual, communion with the holy God sustains abiding covenantal promises, such that, as the author of Hebrews puts it, "those who are called may receive the promised eternal inheritance" (Heb 9:15). *See* LEVITICUS, BOOK OF; PRIESTS AND LEVITES.

Bibliography: Samuel E. Balentine. *The Torah's Vision of Worship* (1999); Samuel E. Balentine. *Leviticus.* Interpretation (2002); J. Bremmer. "Scapegoat Rituals in Ancient Greece." *HSCP* 87 (1983) 299–320; Walter Burkett. *Structure and History in Greek Mythology and Ritual* (1979); Mary Douglas. *Leviticus as Literature* (1999); Mary Douglas. *Jacob's Tears: The Priestly Work of Reconciliation* (2004); Hannah K. Harrington. *The Purity Texts* (2004); Jonathan Klawans. *Impurity and Sin in Ancient Judaism* (2000); Baruch A. Levine. *Leviticus.* The JPS Torah Commentary (1989); Hyam Maccoby. *Ritual and Morality: The Ritual Purity System and Its Place in Judaism* (1999); Jacob Milgrom. *Leviticus 1–16.* AB 3 (1991); Richard D. Nelson. *Raising Up a Faithful Priest: Community and Priesthood in Biblical Theology* (1993); R. Rendtorff and R. Kugler, eds. *The Book of Leviticus: Composition and Reception* (2003); D. P. Wright. *The Disposal of Impurity: Elimination Rites in the Bible and in Hittite and Mesopotamian Literature* (1987).

SAMUEL E. BALENTINE

DAY OF CHRIST [ἡμέρα χριστοῦ hēmera Christou]. "The day of Christ" appears in Phil 1:10 and 2:16. Closely related are "the day of our Lord Jesus Christ" in 1 Cor 1:8 and "the day of Christ Jesus" in Phil 1:6. All of these phrases derive from the prophetic idiom, "the DAY OF THE LORD," yom YHWH (יוֹם יְהוָה). Because of a desire to avoid God's sacred name, the LXX translated the Hebrew as hēmera kuriou (ἡμέρα κυρίου), "DAY OF THE LORD," and as Christians called Jesus "Lord," the transformation into "day of Christ" was natural (see also 2 Cor 1:14, "day of our Lord Jesus").

In the OT, "the day of the Lord" is typically a day of judgment, and it is the same with "the day of Christ." The Pauline letters imagine a "day" when Jesus will return and preside as the eschatological judge, determining rewards and punishments (e.g., 2 Cor 5:10).

The rabbinic "days of the messiah" is, although verbally similar, conceptually different. It refers not to the eschatological DAY OF JUDGMENT but to the happy time, thereafter, when the messiah will govern. Better parallels to the Christian expression are 4 Ezra 13:52 ("his [= the Messiah's] day") and *1 En.* 61:5 ("my Elect One's day"). *See* MESSIAH, JEWISH.

DALE C. ALLISON, JR.

DAY OF JUDGMENT. Belief in the righteousness of God is central to both Jewish and Christian theology. Being righteous, God cannot be indifferent to evil. The existence of present-day evil thus leads to an expectation of future judgment, an idea evident in a wide array of forms in early Judaism and Christianity.

In the OT prophets, the expectation of future judgment most often concerned the destiny of whole peoples, whether Israel (Amos 3:1-15; Jer 2:1-37; Ezek 6:1-7) or other nations (Amos 1:3-15; Jer 46:1-28; Ezek 29:17-20). Such oracles usually referred to a judgment that would occur at a specific moment in the future, such as "that day" (Isa 2:11-20; Jer 46:10; Ezek 30:9; Hos 1:5; Amos 8:9), "the day of the Lord" (with reference to Israel's judgment [Amos 5:18-20; Ezek 13:5] or to the punishment of other nations [Ezek 30:3-4]), or "the day of God's wrath/anger" (Ezek 7:19; Zeph 1:18). The means of judgment ordinarily took the form of human armies (Amos 3:11; Ezek 4:1-3), although God is sometimes portrayed as acting directly, e.g., through pestilence or hailstones (Isa 10:16; Ezek 38:22). The future judgment of particular individuals or groups is also found in some OT prophetic texts (e.g., Amos 4:1-3; Hos 5:1; Isa 3:10-11; Jer 17:5-11), although such occurrences are comparatively infrequent. Rarer still are references to a future judgment of "all flesh" (Isa 66:16 and Jer 25:31).

The apocalyptic perspective that became increasingly common after the exile included the expectation of a universal future judgment (Zech 14:1-21; Mal 4:1-6), usually of all individuals. This decisive event was widely conceived as a threshold moment closing the present evil age and inaugurating the new age of righteousness. It is specifically called "the day of judgment" in some early non-canonical Jewish texts (e.g., *4 Ezra* 7:36-44; Jdt 16:17; *1 En.* 22:11) and in the NT (e.g., Matt 10:15; 11:22; 2 Pet 2:9; 1 John 4:17). New Testament authors also refer to it as, among other things, the "day of the Lord" (Acts 2:20; 1 Cor 5:5; 2 Pet 3:10), the "great day" (Jude 1:6), the "last day" (John 6:40), the "day of wrath" (Rom 2:5), or simply "the day" or "that day" (Rom 2:16; Matt 24:36). The biblical portrayal of final judgment that has exercised the most influence on the popular imagination is probably that found in Rev 20:11-15, in which the dead are brought before "the great white throne" of God. "And the dead were judged according to their works, as recorded in the books" (v. 12). The idea that the works of believers will themselves be judged is found in 1 Cor 3:11-15.

The apocalyptic judge is either God (Joel 3:12; *1 En.* 91:7; *4 Ezra* 7:33; Rom 3:6) or God's agent, whether "the elect one" (*1 En.* 45:3), "the Son of man" (Dan 7:13; *1 En.* 48:2-6; Matt 13:41), the "new priest" (*T. Levi* 18:2), the "Son of God" (*4 Ezra* 13:37; Rev 2:18-29), or the "messiah" (*Pss. Sol.* 17:35-42; 2 Tim 4:1). In the Synoptic Gospels, Jesus himself refers to a future judgment to be executed by the Son of Man (Matt 25:31-32; Mark 14:62; Luke 9:26). Some scholars have interpreted these references to mean that Jesus anticipated the advent of a figure distinct from and greater than himself. Against this view, however, stands the simple fact that the great majority of Jesus' statements about the Son of Man refer unambiguously to himself (e.g., Matt 11:19; 16:13; Mark 8:31; Luke 6:5; John 6:53), some of which mention his authority to judge (Matt 9:6; John 5:27). Not surprisingly, NT authors frequently identify Jesus as God's agent of future judgment, even referring to judgment on "the day of Christ" (Phil 1:10). More surprisingly, Matt 19:28 (= Luke 22:30) assigns to Jesus' original disciples the role of judging the twelve tribes of Israel. Still more expansive is Paul's claim that Christian believers will one day judge the world and angels (1 Cor 6:2-3; but see Pauline passages such as Rom 14:10, where God acts as judge, and Rom 2:16, where the judge is Jesus Christ).

Jewish and Christian texts both differ as to whether all people or only the unrighteous will be called to account on the day of judgment. According to one view, the righteous are raised directly to eternal life and so, apparently, are not judged (Dan 12:2; *2 Bar.* 30:1-5; Luke 14:14; John 5:28-29). The most common idea, however, is that all the dead are raised and judged together, at which time the righteous and unrighteous are eternally separated (*4 Ezra* 7:32-35; Matt 13:47-50; Rom 2:16; Rev 11:18). This judgment is often thought to include those individuals still living at the time (God will judge "the living and the dead," 1 Pet 4:5).

The fate of the unrighteous was conceived in various ways. According to the Wisdom of Solomon, the unrighteous die with "no hope" of eternal life (3:18; see also 4:18-19; compare Rom 5:12-17, where death itself is the punishment for sin). Those who believe in a general resurrection logically might conclude either that such persons would be destroyed following their final judgment (possibly *1 En.* 94:6-10; Matt 10:28; Rom 9:22; 2 Pet 3:7) or that they would be eternally punished (Isa 66:24; 4 Macc 9:8-9; *1 En.* 103:8; Luke 16:23-26). The righteous, by contrast, will enjoy a blissful eternal life in the presence of God (Dan 12:3; *1 En.* 103:4; Matt 25:34; Rev 21:3). Christians today often locate this hope in a nonmaterial "heaven," but the expectation of many early believers was for a physical "new heaven and a new earth, where righteousness is at home" (2 Pet 3:13, echoing Isa 65:17; 66:22; see also Rev 21:1). *See* APOCALYPTICISM; DAY OF THE LORD; DAY, NT; DAY, OT; JUDGMENT, ESCHATOLOGICAL.

Bibliography: S. G. F. Brandon. *The Judgment of the Dead: The Idea of Life After Death in the Major Religions* (1967); John Collins. *The Apocalyptic Imagination: An Introduction to Jewish Apocalyptic Literature,* 2nd ed. (1998); Craig C. Hill. *In God's Time: The Bible and the Future* (2002).

CRAIG C. HILL

DAY OF THE LORD [יוֹם יְהוָה yom YHWH; ἡμέρα κυρίου hēmera kyriou]. The origin of "The day of the Lord," is unclear, although it goes back at least as far as the prophet Amos's "day of Yahweh" (yom YHWH) (Amos 5:18, 20). It typically refers to a dramatic intervention of God in history, a judgment that will condemn God's enemies and save God's people. In Amos, however, many within Israel are disloyal, so the prophesied theophany will mean woe for them, too. Thereafter, "the day of the Lord" is darkness and judgment not for Israel's enemies only (Isa 13:6-9; 34:8-12; Jer 46:9-12; Ezek 30:1-9; Obad 15-18; Zeph 2:1-15), but also for faithless Israel (Isa 2:6-3:15; Ezek 7:19; Joel 1:1-2:27; Zeph 1:14-18). So proclamation of "the day of the Lord" more often serves to condemn and warn than to comfort, although it can do both (Zech 14:1-21; Mal 3:13-4:6).

Scholars dispute how literally the ancients understood the catastrophic prophecies associated with the day of the Lord. Isaiah 13:9-10 envisages stars and constellations going dark and the sun and moon not giving their light (see Joel 3:14). Such cosmic forecasts, whether they occur in the OT or the NT, can be understood either as poetical or as prosaic.

In the postexilic period, when the name Yahweh was used less and less, other terms replaced it. "The day of Yahweh" (yom YHWH) becomes hēmera kyriou, "day of the Lord" in the LXX. The Greek expression "Lord" (kyrios κύριος) was popular among early Christians because they identified the kyrios with Jesus (Acts 2:20; 1 Cor 1:8; 2 Pet 3:10; *Barn.* 15:4); for them, his imminent PAROUSIA was the chief feature of the day of the Lord. But other, synonymous expressions proliferated among both Jews and Christians: "the day" (1 Cor 3:13; Heb 10:25), "that day" (Zeph 1:15; Zech 3:10; Luke 10:12; 2 Thess 1:10), "your day" (*2 Bar.* 48:47; 49:2), "the day of great judgment" or "great day of judgment" (*1 En.* 10:6; 98:10; *Jub.* 5:10), "the day of vengeance" (Isa 61:2; 1QS X, 19), "the day of visitation" (1 Pet 2:12, RSV), "the great day" (Jude 6), "the day of God" (2 Pet 3:12), "the day of the Mighty One" (*2 Bar.* 55:6), "the day of the wrath of judgment" (*Jub.* 24:30), "the day of the Lord's judgment" (*Pss. Sol.* 15:12), "the last day" (John 6:39-40), etc.

Many scholars assume that the NT associates the day of the Lord with the resurrection of the dead, the universal judgment, and the transformation of the world. But other commentators have urged that the NT uses metaphorical language to anticipate concrete historical events, such as the destruction of Jerusalem by the Romans in 70 CE. There is possible biblical precedent for identifying a catastrophe with the day of the Lord (Lam 1:21; 2:22; Ezek 34:12).

One objection to this reading is that the ancients were indisputably often literal-minded. The Qumran War Scroll prophesies a real eschatological battle, complete with literal angels. Papias (in Eusebius, *Hist. eccl.* 3.39.12), Justin Martyr *(Dialogue* 80), Irenaeus (*Adv. haer.* 5.32-36), Tertullian (*Marc.* 3.24), the Montanists (according to Epiphanius, *Pan.* 49.1.2–3), and Lactantius (*Inst.* 7.24–26) all believed, because they interpreted the OT literally, in a worldly millennium involving a far-reaching, miraculous transformation of the natural world. Commodian expected the ten lost tribes to return to the land (*Carm. apol.* 941–46). The Talmud imagines that bones will roll through underground tunnels before being reassembled for the resurrection on the Mount of Olives (*b. Ketub.* 111a).

Some early Christians nonetheless did reinterpret eschatological language in less literal ways. Second Thess 2:2 refers to someone's belief that the day of Lord is "already here." This can hardly mean that eschatological troubles had become manifest, for 2 Thessalonians itself affirms that "the mystery of lawlessness is already at work" (2:7). Something more is indicated, perhaps the presence of eschatological salvation. If so, 2 Thessalonians 2:2 may be akin to the "realized eschatology" of John's Gospel, or perhaps to the view of Hymenaeus and Philetus, who claimed (with what precise content we do not know) that the resurrection was past (2 Tim 2:17-18). The PASSION NARRATIVES are also relevant. These creatively mirror certain prophecies in the preceding eschatological discourses and so portray Jesus' end as though it were somehow the end of the age (compare Mark 13:24 with 15:33; 13:2 with 15:38; 13:35-36 with 14:34, 38; etc.). Further, the darkness at noon (Mark 15:33) seems to fulfill the day of the Lord prophecy in Amos 8:9, and Matt 27:51-53's story of resurrected saints moves an event traditionally associated with the day of the Lord into the past. These examples suggest that some people believed that the day of the Lord had already occurred or that it had been foreshadowed in the death of Jesus. *See* DAY, NT; DAY, OT; ESCHATOLOGY IN EARLY JUDAISM; ESCHATOLOGY OF THE NT; ESCHATOLOGY OF THE OT; JUDGMENT; PROPHET, PROPHECY.

Bibliography: Yair Hoffmann. "The Day of the Lord as a Concept and a Term in the Prophetic Literature." *ZAW* 93 (1987) 37–50; Marius Reisser. *Jesus and Judgment: The Eschatological Proclamation in Its Jewish Context* (1997).

DALE C. ALLISON, JR.

DAY OF YAHWEH. *See* DAY OF THE LORD.

DAY STAR [הֵילֵל helel; ἑωσφόρος heōsphoros]. This English phrase is used in the NRSV and NJB translations of helel in Isa 14:12. The KJV translates this word as "Lucifer" and uses "Day Star" in 2 Pet 1:19. In a song of joy in Isa 14, the king of Babylon is mocked for his downfall when trying to portray himself as the "Day Star" or "MORNING STAR" (ben shakhar [בֶּן־שָׁחַר], "son of the dawn," in Isa 14:12) above God in the heavens, forming an analogy between the king and, most likely, the planet Venus, which was often viewed as a god in the ancient world. The message of a fallen god is taken perhaps from the Baal myth of the Ras Shamra Texts where Athtar, the Venus-star, was placed on the vacant throne of Baal but was unsuccessful and thus had to come down to earth in order to reign.

STEVEN D. MASON

DAY, NT [ἡμέρα hēmera]. *Day* appears over 300 times in the NT, with nearly a third cited in Acts. *Day* has six meanings: 1) a temporal unit, as in a 24-hour period; 2) time of sunlight; 3) duration of an activity or state of being as in "one's days," "one's lifetime"; 4) a specific segment of time, as in "day of atonement," "day of Christ"; 5) measurement of distance, a day's journey; and 6) a non-temporal, literary device.

Day is used for daylight, in contrast to night (Mark 5:5). *Day* also refers to a period of activity, service, or an individual's lifespan. For example, Zechariah served his allotted time or days in the temple (Luke 1:23).

A fourth sense denotes a special purpose in time. An array of words is paired with *day* in the OT: Day of Atonement (Lev 16:29-31) and Sabbath (Deut 5:12-14). Each occurrence underscores time set apart for a particular occasion. The Hebrew week institutes Sabbath as a special day, a day of rest (Exod 16:22-23). Seven-day patterns are present in ANE literature, though no 7-day week or Sabbath has been found. Rich in theological import is the "day" of Yahweh. OT prophets depict this day not as reward, but as God's impending judgment upon Israel (Isa 2:6-22; Amos 5:18-20). Moreover, the DAY OF THE LORD can refer to a future judgment encompassing the entire world (Joel 3:14-21; Mal 4:5). The expression DAY OF CHRIST signifies the last day, the great day, the eschatological time of judgment and redemption of all creation. Thus, for believers in Christ the Day of the Lord becomes an anticipation of hope; for unbelievers it holds judgment. The uncertainty of the hour or day of Christ's parousia is stressed in the synoptic parable of the faithful and faithless servants (Matt 24:45-51). Of NT authors, Paul is clearest in defining the *day* of the Lord as the second coming of Christ (1 Cor 1:8; 1 Thess 5:2, 8).

A fifth use measures distance or journey length. A day's travel approximated 20 miles. Scripture refers to a day's and SABBATH DAY'S JOURNEY (Exod 3:18; Acts 1:12) (*see* DAY'S JOURNEY).

Finally, *day* occurs as a figure of speech. A day can be a millennium (2 Pet 3:8). Reminiscent of Qumran, Paul and John speak of believers, or the elect, as people of the light, of the day (1 Thess 5:5; John 11:9). *Day* can function as eternal light. Revelation 21:25 portrays the dwelling place of God's people as a shining realm of perpetual day. *See* DAY OF ATONEMENT; DAY, OT; ESCHATOLOGY OF THE NT.

CHRIS M. SMITH

DAY, OT [יוֹם yom]. *Day* refers to the period of daylight from dawn to dusk, as distinguished from night (Gen 1:14-16; Neh 4:16). The alternation of day and night, of sunrise and sunset, is fundamental to human existence and was viewed, together with the seasons and the agricultural cycle, as an enduring divine obligation (Gen 8:22; Jer 33:20-21; 31:35; Hos 6:3; Ps 89:30, 37). As the day provided the basis for orientation in time and space, it played a significant role in biblical symbolism, particularly through the opposition of night and day, darkness and light.

The inclusion of a period of darkness to constitute a day corresponding to our twenty-four hour day had not taken place in the biblical period. When the Jewish tradition developed a day/night period, the natural day was joined with the preceding night, resulting in the still-current Jewish day that begins and ends at sunset.

Times of day are indicated by reference to natural phenomena or to temple or market activities. In Israelite ritual, the cultic day was framed by the morning and evening sacrifices in the Jerusalem Temple (Exod 29:38-45; Num 28:1-8). The military division of time into watches was restricted to use at night.

The basic unit of time reckoning, the day was used to measure the passage of time. Each daylight period, or part thereof, was counted as a day. The totality of a particular span of time, whether the length of a person's life or a king's reign, was expressed in terms of

days (Gen 5; 1 Sam 2:11; Ps 90:12). This usage could extend to extraordinarily long periods of time (Gen 8:22; Deut 32:7).

In those biblical passages that refer to a specific uninterrupted interval of time, we find the idiom "x days and x nights," always with the same number of nights as of days, which serves to indicate a continuous period of time comprising *x* daylight periods, in whole or in part (Matt 12:40, referring to Jonah 1:17*b*).

Temporal adverbs, such as beyom (בְּיוֹם), "on the day," refer to a context-specific period of time, taking on the meaning "when, in the time of" (Jer 16:19), and often functioning to link two events in time. On these occasions *day* may refer to a very short time, a moment (Josh 6:10 and probably Gen 2:17) or to a definite time in the near future (1 Kgs 2:37). The emphasis in such expressions rests not on the basic meaning of *day* as a period of daylight, but rather on the close connection of events within a time frame determined by the context. Frequently these expressions convey the impression of certainty on the part of the speaker that a particular event will occur. This sense of conviction gives force to the prophetic notion of the DAY OF THE LORD (Isa 2:6–3:15; 13:6-9; 34:8-12; Jer 46:9-12; Ezek 7:19; 30:1-9; Amos 5:20; Joel 1:1–2:27; Obad 15-18; Zeph 1:14-18; 2:1-15). The Day of the Lord is always imminent, referring to events to be witnessed by the prophet's audience, often including wars and natural catastrophes extending beyond a natural day.

Bibliography: Gershon Brin. *The Concept of Time in the Bible and the Dead Sea Scrolls* (2001); John R. Wilch. *Time and Event* (1969) 89–102.

ELLEN ROBBINS

DAY'S JOURNEY [דֶּרֶךְ יוֹם derekh yom; ἡμέρας ὁδός hēmeras hodos]. The distance one might travel in the course of a day (Num 11:31; 1 Kgs 19:4; Luke 2:44; Acts 1:12). Josephus' report that the journey from Galilee to Jerusalem took three days' time (*Life* 52.269) suggests that one might travel between 32 and 40 km (20–25 mi.) in a day, dependent on the nature of the ground traversed and the condition of the traveler. *See* SABBATH DAY'S JOURNEY.

RALPH K. HAWKINS

DEACON [διάκονος diakonos]. Diakonos is used in Hellenistic Greek and occasionally in the LXX (Esth 1:10; 2:2; 6:1, 3, 5; Prov 10:4; 4 Macc 9:17) for minister, servant, agent, or representative, and in the NT with general meaning of servant or assistant (Mark 9:35; 10:43; Matt 20:26; 22:13; John 2:5; 12:26; Rom 13:4; 15:8; Gal 2:17). The term is closely related to diakonia (διακονία), the service deacons perform. The word appears as a nonspecific title in the Pauline letters, probably with stronger associations of official agent or representative of Christ and God, as well as servant (1 Cor 3:5; 2 Cor 3:6; 6:4; 11:15, 23; Eph 3:7;

6:21; Col 1:7, 23, 25; 4:7; 1 Thess 3:2; 1 Tim 4:6). But already in Phil 1:1 and Rom 16:1 the word is beginning to be used in a more specific meaning as a title for some kind of local church position, whose exact function is not clear. Perhaps at this early period, these persons were emissaries responsible for contact and communication among the various house churches in a given city and from city to city, assisting the heads of house churches who may have been acquiring the title episkopos (ἐπίσκοπος, Phil 1:1), a title that should not be translated "bishop" at this early stage of development. Phoebe from Cenchrae in Rom 16:1 is conveyor of Paul's letter to its recipients, so she seems to stand in that function as well.

By the late 1st cent. and the writing of Luke and Acts, the word group is acquiring a more specific meaning of Christian ministry of various kinds, while it is still being used in a general way. Acts 6:1-6 is often seen as foundational text for the later office of deacons, yet the word itself is never used there. The seven men are appointed with laying on of hands to minister to the material needs of the widows, specifically table service, but their work is one kind of diakonia, while the apostles' preaching is another kind (Acts 6:4). Yet in what immediately follows (Acts 6:8–7:60), Stephen, one of the seven, not one of the apostles, acts as minister of the word.

Given the early special connotations of the word group, NT texts that seem to refer to simple table service may actually carry more weight than is usually imagined, e.g., Peter's mother-in-law who serves Jesus and his friends (Mark 1:31) and especially the diakonia that Martha performs while desirous of help from her sister Mary (Luke 10:40).

At a later stage, deacons are a group of ministers who assist the episkopos (now perhaps to be understood as "bishop") in 1 Tim 3:1-13, where first the qualifications for an episkopos are discussed, then those for deacons. In both cases, the qualifications are generic and traditional with regard to virtuous behavior, but the discouragement of second marriage is indicative of the development of a quasi-"professional" group of ministers with special dedication to the church and the beginnings of asceticism with regard to marriage. The qualification of proof of good household management as preparation for leadership in the church is indicative of the common understanding from early on that the church is the larger family in which other families find their true allegiance. The women of v. 11 may be wives of male deacons, but are more likely to be themselves deacons, indicating that the role was open to both sexes. There was as yet no feminine form of the word.

In later years, the office of deacon evolved into one of direct assistance to the bishop in both social outreach and liturgy. This pattern is in place by the time of Ignatius of Antioch (early 2nd cent.). Deacons are the hands and eyes of the bishop for ministering to the needs of the poor and those who need special attention. They also stand by the bishop's side assisting him in liturgical assemblies and at the administration of baptism. Still later, deacons form part of the ordained ranks of the clergy, those who work most closely with the bishop, and therefore those from whose ranks new bishops are often chosen. See BAPTISM; BISHOP; DEACONESS; EVANGELIST; HOUSE CHURCH; LITURGY; MINISTRY, CHRISTIAN; PRESBYTER.

Bibliography: James M. Barnett. *The Diaconate: A Full and Equal Order* (1995); John N. Collins. *Diakonia: Reinterpreting the Ancient Sources* (1990).

CAROLYN OSIEK

DEACONESS dee´kuh-nis [διακονίσσα diakonissa, διακόνη diakonē]. A female DEACON, as understood after the rise of the office of deaconess in the 3rd cent. The word does not occur in the NT, in spite of the confusion caused by the sometime mistranslation of Phoebe's title in Rom 16:1. Before the 3rd cent., women serving similar functions were called by the masculine title diakonos (διάκονος, Rom 16:1; probably 1 Tim 3:11), which continued later to be used interchangeably with diakonissa. In 3rd cent. Syria, the office arose as a ministry of women to women, partly because of the impropriety of male deacons anointing the nude body of a female during BAPTISM, as baptism was still practiced by full immersion, as well as of male deacons visiting sick women in their homes. Women probably exercised these ministries earlier, but without official title or recognition. After the 3rd cent., deaconesses were usually ordained members of the clergy and, although they were in an order distinct from male deacons, deaconesses were responsible for religious instruction, pastoral visits, and other support roles to women, as well as assistance at baptism.

Numerous funerary inscriptions of deaconesses are extant, from Armenia to Gaul, mostly in the east. By the 6th cent. CE, the office included the role of liturgical leadership. The office of deaconess was sometimes combined with that of monastic superior, but nonmonastic deaconesses continued to work throughout the patristic period. Most, although not all, of the evidence suggests that deaconesses were either VIRGINs or WIDOWs. See MINISTRY, CHRISTIAN.

Bibliography: Kevin Madigan and Carolyn Osiek. *Ordained Women in the Early Church: A Documentary History* (2005); Aimé Georges Martimort. *Deaconesses: An Historical Study* (1986).

CAROLYN OSIEK

DEAD. *See* AFTERLIFE; DEAD, ABODE OF THE; DEATH, NT; DEATH, OT; SHEOL.

DEAD SEA [θάλασσα νεκρά thalassa nekra]. The Jordan River's terminal basin, a narrow, land-locked, hypersaline lake lying below sea level, near the southern end of the Syrian Rift Valley.

A. Name
B. Waters
C. Landscape
D. History and Human Settlement
Bibliography

A. Name

The expression "Dead Sea" occurs nowhere in the Bible. Biblical writers of the OT called it the SALT SEA (Gen 14:3; Num 34:3, 12; Deut 3:17; Josh 3:16, 12:3, 15:2, 5, 18:19). They also used "Sea of the Arabah," sometimes as a gloss with "Salt Sea" (Deut 3:17; Josh 3:16, 12:3); sometimes alone (Deut 4:49, 2 Kgs 14:25). Postexilic prophets knew it as the "Eastern Sea," distinguishing it from the "Western Sea," the Mediterranean (Ezek 47:18, Joel 2:20, Zech 14:8). Modern translations like the NRSV often render "Dead Sea" in place of the literal Hebrew wording.

The NT lacks any explicit reference to the Dead Sea, but the Apocrypha (2 Esd 5:7) and Josephus (*Ant.* 5.81) identify it as the "Sea (or Lake) of Sodom." Diodorus Siculus (*Bib. Hist.* 2.48), Pliny (*Nat.* 5.15), and Josephus (*J. W.* 4.476) call it "Lake of Asphaltis" or "Asphaltis" since the Dead Sea was a source of asphalt (bitumen, pitch). Strabo misnames it "Lake Sirbonis" but describes it correctly (*Geogr.* 16.2.42).

The name "Dead Sea" (**thalassa nekra**) first appears in the 2nd cent. CE in Pausanius (*Descr.* 5.7). A possible 1st cent. BCE occurrence in the *Historiae Philippicae* by Pompeius Trogus is preserved only in a 3rd cent. CE epitome by Justin (36.3.6, "*mare mortuum*"). Arab geographers from Ya'kubi (9th cent. CE) to Idrisi (12th cent. CE) called it the same in Arabic, "**albukhayra almayyita**"; but also named it the "Stinking Sea," (for its odiferous mineral springs), the "Sea of Zoghar" (for the town on its southeastern shore which produced sugar [**sukkar**]), the "Sea of Lot" (the Jordan valley was considered the "Country of Lot's People"), or the "Overturned Sea" (it lay in the land God had overturned, an evocation of the fate of Sodom and Gomorrah; *see* SODOM, SEA OF).

B. Waters

The Dead Sea receives the flow of the JORDAN RIVER and its tributaries, a catchment that stretches from the southern slopes of Mount Hermon down the entire Jordan valley. It also captures runoff from seasonal wadis on the west and from both seasonal and perennial wadis on the east, principally Wadi Mujib (Arnon) and Wadi Hasa (Zered). Fresh or mineral springs—En-Gedi and En-Feshka on the west, Zarqa Ma'in on the east—also flow into it. Subterranean mineral springs well up from the sea bed. Rainfall is sparse, however, since the Dead Sea lies in the rainshadow of

the Judean hills. Only 100 mm fall annually along its northern shore and barely half that in the south.

Although the waters feeding it are fresh or brackish, the Dead Sea itself is far saltier than the oceans, containing 30 percent dissolved minerals. These consist primarily of magnesium chloride, potassium chloride (potash), and sodium chloride (common salt). They render Dead Sea water oily to touch, bitter to taste, and poisonous to drink. The water's high specific gravity permits humans to float in it unaided, but it supports no marine life, save for infrequent blooms of salt-tolerant algae or bacteria (*see* SALT).

Todd Bolen/BiblePlaces.com
Figure 1: Dead Sea Salt Crystals

The Dead Sea's low elevation and underlying geology contribute to its hypersalinity. The sea floor is thickly coated with mineral deposits left by the drying-up of a succession of ocean lagoons and land-locked salt lakes which previously flooded the Rift. Saline springs along the shore and below the surface contribute additional minerals. High rates of evaporation promoted by the extreme aridity and high atmospheric temperatures prevailing in the Rift further concentrate the dissolved minerals. In the routine 40°C heat of summer, rates of evaporation can reach 2.4 cm per day.

Because the Dead Sea has no outlet, it loses water only by evaporation. When water entering from the Jordan River outpaces evaporation, sea level rises and the sea expands. When evaporation exceeds inflow, the level sinks and the lake shrinks. The lake has undergone prolonged but erratic cycles of expansion and contraction as regional or global climate alternated between warm, wet periods and cool, dry ones.

Changes in Dead Sea levels can be inferred from the study of lake sediments, the succession of earlier exposed shorelines, the locations and datings of archaeological sites around the water's edge, and historical texts and early travelers' accounts. From 10,000 to 2,000 BCE levels fluctuated between highs of −290 m to −355 m with an intervening low of −404 m. Less drastic oscillations, between −380 m and −395 m, took place from 2,000 BCE to the turn of the eras. By the Roman period the sea had again fallen to around −402 m, exposing a ford across the shallows between the western tip of the Lisan Peninsula and the opposite shore 4 km away. By the end of the Crusades the level had risen again to roughly –378 m, closing the Lisan ford. In 1818, the British travelers Irby and Mangles reported it was open once more to donkey caravans from Karak, but by 1848 the American explorer Lt. Lynch discovered the Lisan straights again covered by deep water.

The size of the Dead Sea has varied with its depth. For instance in recent decades, as tributaries of the Jordan River were diverted for agriculture and human consumption, the lake level fell and its length contracted from 88 to 67 km. The shallow southern basin dried out completely, replaced by artificial evaporation pans for the commercial extraction of minerals. Near En-Gedi, where the sea previously had been widest (18 km), the water retreated over a kilometer eastward. On the opposite shore where the bottom is deeper—around 400 m below the surface—the contraction is less noticeable.

C. Landscape

The same geological processes that formed the Dead Sea—downfaulting and displacement along the edges of the Rift Valley accompanied by lateral displacement within it—shaped the surrounding landscape. Steep cliffs line the lake east and west while gentle slopes approach it north and south. The eastern sandstone escarpment towers 1,000 m above the lake and plunges abruptly into the water. Consequently there is no continuous land passage along the eastern shore. On the west the limestone cliffs are lower (only 700 m above the shore) and deeply dissected by wadis draining the Judean wilderness. Along the irregular gravel beach is a broken track connecting JERICHO with the ARABAH.

Jutting into the southeast corner of the lake near the outfall of Wadi Dhra is a low-lying peninsula, the Lisan ("Tongue"). The Lisan is an upthrust halite (rock salt) dome covered with heavily eroded layers of gypsum, shale, and dolomite. On the southwestern shore is another halite dome, Jebel Usdum (Mount Sodom), 11 km long, 1.5 km wide, and about 250 m above the lake's surface and rising, owing to pressure from geological forces below. It is riddled with caves where runoff from rare rainstorms has dissolved veins of salt beneath its rocky cap. When the lake level is around –390 m or lower, a narrow beach along its foot leads the Jericho-Arabah track into the es-Sebhkah marsh fringing the southern shore. (This marsh has now dried up along with the lake's southern basin.) The prominence of Jebel Usdum and its proximity to the putative location of Sodom and Gomorrah suggests that here may be the "pillar of salt" believed to have been the fate of Lot's wife.

D. History and Human Settlement

In the OT the Dead Sea is notably associated with the story of LOT and the destruction of Sodom and GOMORRAH (Gen 19; *see* LOT'S WIFE; SODOM, SODOMITE). The text suggests the doomed cities were located on the lake's southeastern shore and there their ruins have been sought, so far in vain. The presence there of the Early Bronze Age archaeological sites of BAB-EDH-DHRAʾ and Numeirah, which were abandoned at the end of the 3rd millennium BCE, may have given rise to later legends of ancient cities obliterated by divine wrath. Whatever the biblical story's origin, the Byzantines memorialized it in the 7th cent. CE church and monastery of Saint Lot (Agios Lot) perched on the crags overlooking the southeastern Dead Sea.

John Mark Wade
Figure 2: Cave of Lot

Written accounts of the Dead Sea, both biblical and extra-biblical, have tended to emphasize the region's extremes—extreme isolation, extreme temperature, extreme dryness, and the extreme saltiness of its waters. Such a stricken landscape could readily be imagined as the setting of the divinely ordained destruction visited on Sodom and Gomorrah. By all appearances it was a land still under curse, but one whose redemption was foretold in Ezekiel's vision of the "Eastern Sea" transformed into a fishermen's paradise by miraculous freshets bursting forth beneath the rebuilt Temple (47:7-12).

The forbidding landscape around the Dead Sea notwithstanding, its isolation has encouraged fugitives to seek refuge there. At EN-GEDI David hid from Saul (1 Sam 24). At MASADA Herod built a palatial fortified retreat, where later the Zealots made their suicidal last stand against the Romans. Those who lived at QUMRAN and those who hid the DEAD SEA SCROLLS in the caves above the site sought safety at the Dead Sea, both unavailingly. During the Bar Kokhba revolt, BABATHA, daughter of Simeon, did the same; but only the scrolls containing her family archive survived.

Barren though it may appear, the land around the Dead Sea was (and still is) a source of wealth. Riches arose from asphalt seeps and salt pans, from plantations of balsam and dates and later of cane sugar and indigo, and now from industrial evaporation plants yielding potash, magnesium, and bromine from the hypersaline waters. Where fresh water was available, as at En-Gedi or around Ghor es-Safi (medieval Zoghar) on the southeast coast, the subtropical climate made land within reach of irrigation exceptionally productive.

The steep cliffs flanking the Dead Sea were obstacles to overland travel, yet the lake itself was navigable. Periodic high waters that drowned coastal roads and inundated the Lisan ford forced Dead Sea travelers into boats. Herod built a harbor at Zara on the eastern shore so he could sail from Masada to the medicinal springs at Callirhoe. Along the western shore the retreating waters exposed two composite wood-and-stone anchors, one Roman, one perhaps earlier. The Madaba mosaic map (6th cent. CE) depicts two boats on the Dead Sea carrying what appear to be cargoes of salt and grain. Medieval authors, such as the Crusader chronicler William of Tyre (writing in Latin) and the Muslim geographer Idrisi (writing in Arabic) agree that regular boat traffic linked Jericho and Kerak.

Despite its perceived isolation and manifest barreness, the land around the Dead Sea has been inhabited almost since the lake was formed 12,000 years ago. Living near the Dead Sea always carried with it certain risks: from the extreme climate, from rising or falling lake levels, or from earthquakes along the Rift's active fault lines. Nonetheless, the fitful continuity of human habitation there demonstrates the enduring, if paradoxical, appeal of this body of water and its surrounding shores.

Bibliography: Denis Baly. *The Geography of the Bible* (1974); G. W. Bowersock. *Roman Arabia* (1983); C. Clamer. "ʾAin ez-Zara Excavations 1986." *ADAJ* 33 (1986) 217–25; Herbert Donner. *The Mosaic Map of Madaba* (1992); Gideon Hadas, Nili Liphschitz, and Georges Bonani. "Two Ancient Wooden Anchors from Ein Gedi, on the Dead Sea, Israel." *International Journal of Nautical Archaeology* 34 (2005) 299–307; Barbara Kreiger. *The Dead Sea: Myth, History, and Politics* (1997); Tima M. Niemi, Zvi Ben-Avraham, and Joel R. Gat, eds. *The Dead Sea: The Lake and Its Setting* (1997); K. D. Politis. "The Sanctuary of Agios Lot, the City of Zoara and the Zered River." *The Madaba Map Centenary (1897–1997).* M. Piccirillo and E. Alliata, eds. (1999) 225–27; Walter E. Rast. "Bab edh-Dhra and the Origins of the Saga of Sodom." *Archaeology and Biblical Interpretation: Essays in the Memory of D. Glen Rose.* Leo G. Perdue, Lawrence E. Toombs, and Gary L. Johnson, eds. (1987) 185–201.

JOSEPH A. GREENE

DEAD SEA SCROLLS. The term Dead Sea Scrolls refers to all the MSS found in the wilderness of Judea since the end of the Second World War. More than 900 MSS have come from eleven caves at and near QUMRAN, on the northwest shore of the Dead Sea. There have also been significant discoveries at Wadi Daliyeh, Ketef Jericho, Wadi Murabbaʿat, Nahal Hever, and Masada, as well as less extensive MS finds at Wadi Nar, Wadi Ghweir, Nahal Mishmar, Nahal Seʿelim, Wadi Mafjar, and Khirbet Mird. Most of this article is concerned with the finds from Qumran.

A. Background Information
  1. Scholarly designation
  2. Discoveries
  3. Publication process
B. The Qumran Library
  1. General issues
    a. Overall character
    b. Date
    c. Provenance
    d. Production processes
    e. A library
  2. The manuscripts
    a. Scriptural texts
    b. Sectarian texts
    c. Other compositions
  3. Relationship to other literary corpora
    a. The New Testament
    b. Other Jewish literature
Bibliography

A. Background Information
1. Scholarly designation
The individual Dead Sea Scrolls are commonly either designated by a well-known name, such as *Rule of the Community* or *Temple Scroll*, or by a technical label. The technical label is made up of the location where the MS was found and either an abbreviated title or a catalogue number; where an abbreviated title is used the particular copy of the composition represented in the MS is designated with a raised letter. Thus 4QDeut^c is from Cave 4 at Qumran and it is the third copy of Deuteronomy (also catalogued as 4Q30). Nearly complete scrolls are referred to by column (usually in Roman numerals) and line number (usually in English numerals); more fragmentary MSS are referred to by frag. number (in English numerals), column number where more than one column is extant (in Roman numerals), and line number (in English numerals).

2. Discoveries
Origen reports a MS find near Jericho in about 217 CE. In about 800 CE Timotheus I, patriarch of Seleucia, also mentions MSS that had been found in a cave near Jericho. The initial modern discovery by

Bedouin shepherds of Cave 1 in the foothills above Qumran seems to have taken place in late 1946 or early 1947.

Todd Bolen/BiblePlaces.com
Figure 1: The Qumran Caves

In July 1947 Athanasius Samuel of the Syrian Orthodox monastery in Jerusalem acquired a copy of Isaiah (1QIsa[a]), *Pesher Habakkuk* (1QpHab), the Cave 1 version of the *Rule of the Community* (1QS), and the *Genesis Apocryphon* (1QapGen). After several months in search of an opinion as to their authenticity, he sent the first three to the American School of Oriental Research in Jerusalem where John Trever photographed them in February 1948 with the assistance of William Brownlee. Meanwhile Eliazar Sukenik of the Hebrew University in Jerusalem first became aware of the scrolls in November 1947, eventually acquiring for the Hebrew University another copy of Isaiah (1QIsa[b]), the *War Scroll* (1QM), and a copy of the *Thanksgiving Hymns* (1QH[a]). These seven scrolls were eventually brought together to form the core of the collection at the Shrine of the Book in Jerusalem.

Once it had become known that the scrolls had come from a cave near Khirbet Qumran, the Jordanian Department of Antiquities together with the Palestine Archaeological Museum and the École Biblique et Archéologique Française in Jerusalem mounted a series of archaeological expeditions to the caves (1949; 1952; and 1956) and the site of Qumran (1951; 1953–56). Many caves in the area showed signs of habitation during the late Second Temple period; eleven of them, discovered variously by the Bedouin or by archaeologists between 1947 and 1956, produced the remains of over 900 MSS. There have been several further excavations at the site of Qumran (1967–68; 1984–85; 1995–96); the exploration of the plateau in 1996 resulted in the surprise discovery of two ostraca in the wall that leads south from the main building complex.

Of the other sites Masada was surveyed in 1953 and major excavations undertaken in 1955–1956,

1963 and 1965; Wadi Murabbaʿat was examined in 1952 and 1968; Wadi Daliyeh was unearthed by Bedouin in 1962; caves in Nahal Hever were surveyed in 1953 and excavated in 1955, 1961, and 1991; and MSS were found at Ketef Jericho in 1993.

3. Publication process

All the Dead Sea Scroll frag. known to scholars have been published in some form; contrary to some reports, there never has been a conspiracy to conceal anything. In fact, nearly all of the Dead Sea Scrolls are now available in technical principal editions. First to be published in various places were six of the seven principal scrolls from Qumran Cave 1. However, once the extent of the MS finds was realized, a small international team was set up to work on their publication. This has been led by Roland de Vaux (until 1970), Pierre Benoit (1970–1984), John Strugnell (1984–90), and then Emanuel Tov.

The identification and sorting of the MSS, especially those from Cave 4, progressed rapidly in the late 1950s, but for various reasons only seven volumes of edited MSS had appeared in the Discoveries in the Judaean Desert (DJD) series by 1982.

Todd Bolen/BiblePlaces.com
Figure 2: Qumran Cave 4 interior

Through the 1980s there were calls for the process to be accelerated. Various factors resulted in the reorganization and extension of the international team and the 39-volume DJD series is virtually complete. Several of the MS discoveries from sites other than Qumran as well as some MSS from Qumran itself have been published outside the DJD series, such as the Targum of Job (11Q10), the *Temple Scroll* (11Q19), and 11Q1.

Some of the better preserved scrolls, such as the *Copper Scroll* (3Q15), *Pesher Habakkuk*, *Pesher Nahum* (4Q169), the Cave 1 version of the *Rule of the Community*, the principal copy of the *Temple Scroll* (11Q19), and the major Cave 1 version of the *Thanksgiving Hymns* have received detailed treatment in commentaries and monographs, but an enormous amount of analytical study of the frag. remains to be done. Scholarly endeavor on the scrolls continues in many forms. The Dead Sea Scrolls Foundation sponsors some major research projects. Several universities have research institutes dedicated to the study of the scrolls. International academic conferences and symposia are held regularly, particularly in association with the International Organization for Qumran Studies (established 1989). Many popular books, TV documentaries, and travelling exhibitions cater to the continuous public interest in the scrolls.

B. The Qumran Library

1. General issues

a. Overall character. The generally fragmentary remains of the more than 900 scrolls from the eleven caves at and near Qumran are mostly made of leather. About 150 of them are papyrus. One is made of three sheets of copper. A few MSS are well preserved. Perhaps surprisingly, these may well have been those that were most damaged in antiquity through regular wear and tear or by other means; as a result they were wrapped in linen and placed carefully in storage jars in a cave in a manner akin to the burial of MSS in a genizah. Those that were in good condition in antiquity were left in other caves and then were at the mercy of the climate and various animals and so reach modern times with far greater damage. For example, the approximately 600 MSS from Cave 4 are extant in more than 15,000 frag., many of which contain only a few words or letters.

Most of the Qumran MSS contain compositions written in Hebrew; some of the Hebrew imitates scriptural language, some is possibly the reflection of local spoken dialects, and some anticipates forms known in the MISHNAH. Also, 130 MSS contain Aram. compositions. Greek MSS are found only in Caves 4 (8 MSS) and 7 (19 MSS).

b. Date. Although there was some initial scepticism about dating the scrolls found in the Qumran caves to the end of the Second Temple period, they have now been dated through a combination of techniques to between the end of the 3rd cent. BCE and the middle of the 1st cent. CE. These techniques include consideration of the archaeological context, notably the way in which some scrolls were found in pottery jars of a type also found at the Qumran site where the stratigraphy, pottery typology, and coin finds point to relevant occupation between the first quarter of the 1st cent. BCE and to the third quarter of the 1st cent. CE.

Carbon[14] tests in 1990 and 1994–95 gave calibrated date ranges in the 1st cent. BCE for most of the Qumran MSS tested; significantly some frag. from MSS with internal known dates were used as a control. In addition, in the light of previously known MSS (e.g., the Nash Papyrus) and inscriptions, palaeographers have constructed typologies of writing styles and been able to suggest sequences of development for cursive, semi-cursive and formal styles of penmanship; these

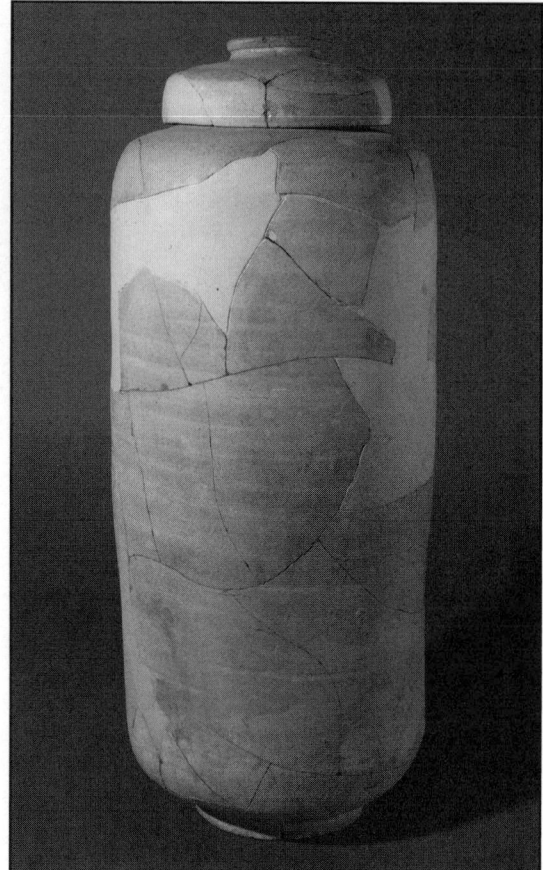

HIP / Art Resource, NY

Figure 3: Pottery lidded jar of the sort used to store the Dead Sea Scrolls, From Qumran, Israel, 1st cent. British Museum, London, Great Britain.

have enabled the dating of MSS relative to one another, though this has to be used with some caution. Only a few scrolls refer in their contents to actual historical figures; nearly all these are personages from the 1st cent. BCE (e.g., Demetrius III [reigned 96–88 BCE] in 4Q169; Salome Alexandra [reigned 76–67 BCE] in 4Q331 and 4Q332; Aemelius Scaurus [active in Syria in 66–65 BCE] in 4Q333), which is yet a further indication of the time not just of writing but also of composition, since such compositions must either be contemporary with or later than such historical figures.

c. Provenance. A few archaeologists and some textual scholars have continued to argue that the Qumran site and the scrolls found in the caves nearby have nothing to do with each other. For these interpreters all the scrolls came from elsewhere, probably the Jerusalem temple library, and were deposited in the caves, probably sometime shortly before or during the first Jewish revolt (66–74 CE). Most scholars, however, follow the opinion taken almost from the outset, that at least some of the scrolls were written at Qumran and that all of them were put in the caves by Qumran residents. Most of the MSS were brought to Qumran by those joining the community there.

The presence of at least four inkwells shows that some writing took place at the site, and the presence of several tabs and ties in Cave 8 implies that MSS were finished there. In addition from the site itself there is one ostracon with a practice alphabet on it; two other OSTRACA were discovered in 1996, though it is possible they were written elsewhere and brought to Qumran.

Erich Lessing / Art Resource, NY

Figure 4: Ink pot. Found at the Qumran excavations. Israel, 3rd cent. BCE–1st cent. CE. Shrine of the Book, Jerusalem, Israel.

Although there is great variation in writing styles amongst the more than 900 fragmentary MSS found in the Qumran caves, it is possible to discern at least two tendencies, one of which has a preference for a more full spelling system than the other. Since the majority of those compositions that have been designated sectarian are written with the spelling system that has extra vowel letters, it has been widely concluded that it is probable that many of them could have been penned at Qumran in a so-called "Qumran scribal practice." More extensive DNA analysis than has so far been undertaken might eventually be able to establish if several of the pieces of leather are genetically related, indicating their probable origin in the same local herd.

As for the caves at Qumran, it is important to appreciate that it is very likely that each cave had its own function. As a result the scrolls were placed in each cave in association with that function. So, for example, it may well be that the majority of scrolls in Cave 1 were placed there very carefully as if in a GENIZAH because they were considered beyond repair. In Cave

8 a large number of tabs and ties were discovered; perhaps that cave was some kind of workshop for finishing MSS. In Cave 7, which is at the end of the promontory on which the Qumran building is located and which can only be reached by walking through the site, all the compositions are in Greek, a special collection. In Cave 4, a man-made cave in the promontory adjacent to the site, the remains of nearly 600 MSS implies that it was probably some kind of working depository, not unlike a library stack. It is therefore very unlikely that all the MSS were deposited in the eleven caves at the same time in response to some crisis.

d. Production processes. Editions of the scrolls since 1990 have usually included some consideration of the production process of the scroll. The leather comes from goats and sheep, as well as cattle and ibex. Once the animal skins had been prepared as leather to receive writing, they were cut into pieces and then using a system of guide dots normally marked by impression with columns and lines. The scribe penned his text by hanging it from the line. Carbon-based inks were used, with varying combinations of vegetable materials. The sheets of some MSS were usually sewn together before receiving writing; others seem to have been sewn together afterwards.

There are no codices in the library; all the MSS are preserved as scrolls to be rolled, or possibly on a single sheet of leather that was folded rather than rolled (*see* SCROLL). The majority of MSS are written on one side of the leather only, but 21 are opisthographs with writing on both sides, perhaps because the scroll was reused. Some scrolls are PALIMPSESTs.

Attention to production processes has assisted in the reconstruction of some very damaged MSS. For example, where the content of a MS was previously unknown, it is possible to align fragments which have been penned by the same scribe by paying attention to the way the follicle patterns of the animal skin run (*see* WRITING AND WRITING MATERIALS).

e. A library. The Qumran scrolls are generally treated as a collection, possibly even as a library, that had been carefully assembled at Qumran over several generations. There are three prominent reasons for this. First, although there is indeed some variety of outlook that has yet to be explained fully, there is also considerable ideological coherence between the non-scriptural compositions. Second, several types of composition are conspicuous by their absence: certain contemporary Jewish compositions that one might have expected in such a library, such as the Books of Maccabees, are not there. Neither are there any non-Jewish compositions. Third, it is noteworthy that the proportion of scriptural, sectarian, and non-scriptural, non-sectarian MSS is approximately the same (25 percent; 20 percent; 50 percent; 5 percent too damaged for classification) in the three principal caves (1, 4, 11), indicating the standard make-up of the collection.

Although the scrolls may now be considered as a library, the diversity of the collection should not be forgotten. This diversity is discernible foremost in the three languages that are present; it must be assumed that the majority of the community that put the collection together were at least bilingual, perhaps using Aramaic for some purposes and Hebrew more formally as the language for prayer, for scriptural interpretation, and for community regulation. Amongst the Hebrew MSS, some are written in palaeo-Hebrew, some in cryptic alphabets perhaps designed to hide community secrets from non-members, and the majority in square Hebrew of differing cursive, semi-cursive and square styles. What the different kinds of ALPHABET indicate politically and socially has yet to be fully discerned, though it is noteworthy that part of the contemporary Hasmonean claim to legitimacy was expressed through the use of palaeo-Hebrew on coins.

Diversity in the collection is also noticeable in the different types of MS that have survived. Some are deluxe works put together from large pieces of leather with wide margins, wide columns of writing and many lines of script per column (sometimes more than 60); others are small, pocket-size MSS of only a few pieces of leather and small written columns. And there is almost everything in between. One MS, *Testimonia* (4Q175), is written on a single piece of leather and is just one column of writing. There are several tefillin, small pieces of leather written with scriptural passages in micro-writing for placing inside a small leather case for use in daily prayer.

2. The manuscripts

The contents of the Qumran library are commonly divided into three groups for ease of classification, though it is important to keep in mind that the limits of such division are under constant discussion.

a. **Scriptural texts.** About 200 of the MSS contain copies of books that eventually found their way into the three parts of the Hebrew canon (Torah, Prophets, Writings) and the OT of Christian Bibles. The term Bible is strictly anachronistic as a way of referring to the scriptural MSS found in the Qumran caves, and the label OT is even more of a distortion, forcing a later Christian label onto Jewish texts of the pre-canonical era. At the time of the Qumran community there was no list of authoritative works, nor were they available in a book or on a single scroll. Nevertheless it is evident that all the books that were later made canonical were known at Qumran, as even the phraseology of Esther is apparent in some of the sectarian compositions. Some books are better attested than others. Esther is not extant in a separate MS; perhaps its attention to the festival of Purim, which was not marked by the community who put the library together, resulted in it being largely ignored. There are surprisingly few copies of the historical books; perhaps this indicates that for the community the history of Israel was constructed largely in an alternative way from the traditions known in Joshua–2 Kings. The kings of Israel seem to have been problematic for the community, as for all who took Deuteronomy seriously. The almost complete absence of 1–2 Chronicles possibly indicates that others, probably the Hasmoneans, had adopted them to support their political propaganda as priest-kings.

Apart from possible references to the *Aramaic Levi Document* (4Q213-214b) and the book of *Jubilees* in the *Damascus Document* (CD IV, 15; XVI, 3-4) in the sectarian texts there is no explicit appeal to any written authority other than to those books that later became canonical. The book of *Jubilees* also became authoritative in the Ethiopic Church. Some of the constituent parts of *1 Enoch* have been found in Cave 4; it is possible that at some stage these were considered authoritative by some parts of the movement and by other Jews at the time, since part of the *Book of Watchers* is cited as an authority in the NT Letter of Jude (and *1 Enoch* was also authoritative later in the Ethiopic Church). The book of Tobit occurs in both Hebrew and Aramaic in Cave 4; later it was to become authoritative for much of the Christian Church, so perhaps it supported the movement behind the scrolls. The same can be said for the book of Ben Sira.

Some books are both more frequently referred to in the library as well as better represented. For those that are now found in Bibles it seems that Genesis, Deuteronomy, Isaiah and the book of Psalms were the most popular. The explicit and implicit citations of all these texts in the sectarian compositions confirms a similar picture, too. The same four scriptural books are also among the most frequently referred to in the NT, though sometimes different sections of them are used. The scriptural priorities of the movement seem to be pre-Sinaitic origins, covenantal obedience, eschatological vindication, and spiritual insight.

The variety of text-types for the various scriptural books has seemed to some to be surprising. It is important to underline first that the scriptural scrolls from Qumran show how the text of the OT has been passed on faithfully from generation to generation. Some MSS contain forms of the text of particular scriptural books that are very close to the medieval MT upon which modern editions of the OT and Jewish translations are based and which most Christian translations follow most of the time (*see* MT, MASORETIC TEXT). Furthermore, in a majority of MSS containing scriptural books with corrections, those corrections are toward a form of the text now represented by the MT. This implies that during the late Second Temple period, at least for some books, a text-type like that later authoritatively adopted by the rabbis was apparently becoming increasingly dominant.

Overall it is the variety of the variants in the texts that has to be explained and understood. None of those variants has yet been shown to be sectarian in the strict sense. Four theories have dominated scholarly discussion of the matter. At the outset, three families were proposed as the basic explanatory taxonomy, one associated with each principal region of Jewish scribal activity: with Palestine were associated the local texts, such as the Samaritan Pentateuch, for which close relations survived in the Qumran caves (notably 4Q22); with Babylon were associated the proto-Masoretic texts (e.g., 1QIsa[b]), those that anticipated the MT; and with Egypt were associated those texts that seemed to represent the kind of Hebrew that had been used by those Egyptian Jews who had translated the scriptural books into Greek (4Q71 and 4Q72a are known to have a text-type like the LXX, Jeremiah).

The second theory has argued that three local families were not enough to describe the full range of text types that exist. If anything, those three families merely represented the activities of the three most successful social groups within Second Temple Judaism. Because of the difficulties in discerning who was responsible for what, this social theory has also stressed that for several scriptural books it is no longer possible to discern the original form of the text (*Ur-text*) and that the process of authority eventually being given to one type of text over another is not simply the success of one MS family over another, but rather the narrowing down of a wide variety of textual forms to a single norm for each book.

Attention to the great number of minor variations and the smaller number of major variants has prompted a third view; this asserts the independent character of many of the scriptural MSS. 11Q1 is an example of just such an independent text, containing unique variants that imply significant scribal intervention at some time in the process of the transmission of Leviticus.

The fourth option for trying to explain something of the diversity of the evidence argues that each scriptural book has its own history of transmission that should be described before any anachronistic assertions are made about the affiliations of variant scriptural readings. As a result of this approach some scriptural books, such as Jeremiah, can be seen to have had far more complex transmission histories than others, such as Genesis. There seem to have been at least two editions of Exodus in circulation in the Second Temple period, and the story of the books of Psalms is even more complex.

Few variant readings have any doctrinal significance for Jews or Christians. But the variants as a whole actually suggest something far more important concerning the authority of Scripture for believing communities in the 21st cent. In the light of the evidence from the Qumran caves it is no longer possible to assert the divinely inspired origin of Scripture without taking into account the history of the transmission of the texts of the various books; at the least the role of the scribal communities and of those who chose one form of text over against others must be seen as part of the human collaboration with God in the production of Scripture (*see* SCRIBE). Likewise various doctrinal assertions concerning verbal inspiration now seem entirely arbitrary.

There are three further important implications of the study of the scriptural texts. First, it is clear that in many instances it is no longer possible to know with any certainty what the original text of some parts of some of the scriptural books might have been. Some variant readings are very likely to be secondary, but who is to say, for example, whether the shorter or longer form of Jeremiah was more "original." This means that it will remain preferable for scholars and Bible translators to work with diplomatic editions of the scriptural MSS rather than attempt to construct an eclectic "original." Second, it is becoming increasingly clear that each scriptural book has its own history of composition and textual transmission; it is unwise to generalize from any one set of evidence. Third, scriptural texts should not be considered apart from their ongoing social and political functions; no text (e.g., 11Q5) should be classified as non-scriptural solely because it may have had a different function from others.

Another issue also needs to be aired. It remains an open question whether modern Bible translations (such as the NRSV) should adopt readings found in the scriptural MSS from Qumran and elsewhere. For some translators the search for the "best" or "most original" reading overrides any concern for the way in which faith communities have transmitted the Scriptures for centuries; in particular this may sometimes be a factor in the historical, even historicist, concerns of Protestantism as promoted by the culture of the Enlightenment. For others there is a significant conflict of interest between the desire for intelligibility and authenticity, on the one hand, and respect for what any particular faith community has received, on the other. Some might argue that faith communities should be encouraged to make their own decisions about which text they consider should form the basis for their translations, while scholars and others can propose either eclectic or diplomatic editions of the Scriptures that take into account all the data available and try to make sense of it historically. Thus the scriptural scrolls raise questions for 21st cent. users about whose text is to be translated and why.

b. Sectarian texts. About 200 of the MSS from the Qumran caves are "sectarian." This label is a technical sociological one, implying that the members of the group or movement so designated thought of themselves as the sole and exclusive heirs of the tradition from which (as outsiders would consider) they had cut themselves off. The designation is somewhat problematic as it assumes a certain understanding of how one of the elite groups in Judaism in the three centuries before the fall of the temple in 70 CE should be modelled.

Scholars have identified which compositions merit the label sectarian, not only by discerning whether the content argues for an exclusive self-definition, but also by noting that particular technical vocabulary is used, often with a self-reference. Amongst such items of vocabulary are the labels "sons of light" and "sons of darkness", and the neologism yakhad (יַחַד), "community, union." Some scriptural terms, such as "covenant," are given a new technical meaning. The physical features of some MSS, such as being written with a cryptic alphabet, indicate that they were written for a restricted audience.

Most modern editions of texts and translations have prioritised the various rule books as best exemplifying the sect's way of life, but that can lead to a distorted view of the sect and is in any case largely an accident of the order of discovery. This brief article will order things differently in an attempt to break with a view of the sect as overly concerned with self-regulation, and in order to modify Christian misconceptions of Judaism at the time of Jesus as exclusively legalistic.

There are three kinds of sectarian composition. First, there are liturgical texts of various kinds. These are most clearly sectarian when they use both sectarian vocabulary and when they reflect a use of the 364-day luni-solar CALENDAR, but one of these factors alone might be sufficient to identify a composition as sectarian, not least because controversy over the calendar seems to have been a fundamental cause for the break with other Jewish groups. Amongst these texts are calendars and lists of priestly courses (4Q322–330), which indicate how important chronology and time were for the movement, as well as liturgical texts proper, such as the *Berakhot* (Blessings; 4Q286–290), compositions which reflect the dualistic language and cultic elements of 1QS II-III. The *Songs of the Sabbath Sacrifice* (4Q400–407; 11Q17) largely lack sectarian vocabulary, but are arranged as a set of thirteen, covering a quarter of a 52-week year. Also amongst these compositions can be included the *Thanksgiving Hymns.* Many scholars have argued that the Teacher of Righteousness composed some or all of these heavily scriptural and deeply spiritual poems to encourage the reader to identify with his experiences of rejection and suffering and his sense of the saving mercy of God in rescuing him from the hands of his enemies.

Attention to liturgical and poetic texts in the sectarian corpus has the significant effect for the modern reader of stressing the mystical and spiritual side of the Qumran community's writings and worldview. For all that the Qumran community and the movement of which it was a part was very much concerned with issues of purity and the appropriate way of living under the law, such was motivated by a profound sense of the intimate concern God had for God's elect. This spiritual intimacy can be seen in the way in which in some texts it is difficult to discern whether the worship of the community is taking place alongside the angels in heaven or is on earth with angels in its midst. The *War Rule* (1QM) has a complex redactional history but is perhaps best understood as a dramatic liturgy expressing the same proximity of God and the community as the battle against evil is fought out on the intertwined heavenly and earthly stages.

Second, there are several sectarian exegetical compositions; in fact, it seems that nearly all the explicit exegesis in the library is sectarian. Chief amongst these are those commentaries on scriptural passages that use the technical term *pesher* ("interpretation") to introduce the commentary (*see* PESHARIM). Developed from the practice of dream interpretation as evident in the book of Daniel, these commentaries take several forms. Amongst the first batch of MSS to come from Cave 1 was *Pesher Habakkuk*, a continuous running commentary on Hab 1–2; the text of Habakkuk is broken into small sense-units which are cited and then followed by brief comments, the chief hallmark of which is their atomistic identification of items in the text of Habakkuk with events in the life of the sectarian community, which views itself as living in the end-times (*see* HABAKKUK COMMENTARY, PESHER). The use of sobriquets throughout the *pesharim*, such as "Wicked Priest," makes it nearly impossible to identify the people and places involved, though this has not stopped many suggestions being made; the range of suggestions is indicative of the impossibility of identifying the characters in the play, from the 3rd cent. BCE to the 1st cent. CE. *Pesher Nahum* is also a running commentary, but other explicit commentaries take different forms, commonly combining passages from several different scriptural books into an intricately woven piece of exegesis. The *Ages of Creation* (4Q180–181) is a sectarian interpretation of scriptural history.

The *pesharim*, whether continuous or not in form, are mostly concerned in content with the correct eschatological interpretation of unfulfilled scriptural predictions, whether blessings, curses, or prophetic oracles of any kind. That concern has the effect that is made explicit in 1QpHab VII, 4-5, of affirming that the interpreter was at least as inspired as the person who uttered the original but unfulfilled text. It needs to be added that this inspired interpretation was not exercised arbitrarily without verifiable control: the Qumran commentators used a variety of recognizable interpretative tools to unlock the mysteries of the texts before them and worked as heirs of a long interpretative tradition. Nevertheless, contemporary preachers should take heed that in any age identifying unfulfilled scriptural prophecies with historical events is a hazardous pastime, however rigorous the exegesis.

There are many other kinds of scriptural interpretation in the sectarian compositions. Amongst these are compositions that seem to wrestle with problems in the plain meaning of scripture, such as the duration of the flood or the dates of Abram's travels (4Q252 I, 1–II, 3; II, 8-10). There are also exhortatory uses of scripture in which appeal is made to scriptural characters, such as Abraham, Isaac and Jacob, or the sons of Noah and the sons of Jacob as either good or bad examples (e.g. CD III, 1-5). There are also allusory anthological uses of scripture in liturgical and poetic works such as the *Thanksgiving Hymns* (1QHᵃ), a use that tends to pick the flowers of scriptural passages with awareness of their original contexts but without any explicit acknowledgement and then arranges them into a new fragrant garland with great intricacy. This kind of use of scripture recognizes the authoritative insights of earlier texts and rehearses them through aesthetic and spiritual recontextualization. Or again, in some of the legal sections of the scrolls new laws are presented through the juxtaposition of two or more scriptural passages, the alignment producing extended legislation: a clear example of this process can be seen in the *Damascus Document* where the Sabbath commandment of Deut 5:12 is extended through allusion to Exod 16:29, Num 35:4-5, Isa 58:13, and other texts all rounded off with Lev 23:38. This careful extension of scripture presupposes a coherence between the various texts that speaks of their unity. Altogether there is rich breadth to the sectarian use of scripture that can serve as an example to contemporary readers of the same ancient texts.

Third, there are the sectarian rules; apart from the parabiblical legal compositions, nearly all the rule books or lists of rules in the library are sectarian. There are far more various forms of these than there could ever have been real communities to live them out, so there is a major problem in trying to understand how the rules reflect the realities of the pluralistic character of the sectarian movement and the changes and developments that took place during its history. In addition to various collections of halakhic regulations, such as *Harvesting* (4Q284a), *Halakhah* B (4Q264a) and *Tohorot* (4Q274, 276–277), there seem to be three principal rule books: the RULE OF THE COMMUNITY, the DAMASCUS DOCUMENT, and the RULE OF THE CONGREGATION.

The *Rule of the Community* exists in at least two different forms, one shorter reflecting a more egalitarian community (e.g., 4Q256; 4Q258) and one longer reflecting a more hierarchical organization under the Sons of Zadok (e.g., 1QS); in addition all forms of the *Rule of the Community* are the result of a redactional process of several stages: in 1QS a program for a new community has been gradually expanded with practical regulations, dualistic doctrine, and liturgical framing. For text-critical and sociological reasons the shorter forms of the *Rule of the Community* may be earlier and the longer forms later: the composition becomes more elaborate as the community it represents moves from charismatic beginnings to a more institutional form.

However, the palaeographic dates of the various MSS suggest at least that the shorter form of the text was also being copied out at a later period; whether that was for academic reasons or because the community was being rejuvenated in some way it is difficult to tell.

The *Damascus Document* is known principally from its main exemplar (A; 10ᵗʰ cent. CE) discovered in the Cairo Genizah; two pages of another somewhat variant copy were also preserved there (B; 12ᵗʰ cent. CE). The Cairo *Damascus Document* has two parts, an admonitory opening section that argues for holiness, with appeal to elements of the so-called Holiness Code of the book of Leviticus, and for a moral way of life that shuns the "three nets of Belial," namely "fornication," wealth, and the profanation of the sanctuary. The faithful community established through its allegiance to the new covenant in the land of Damascus has a priestly character with Levites as members alongside the Sons of Zadok, the elect of Israel (*see* PRIESTS AND LEVITES; ZADOK, ZADOKITES). Copies of the same composition from Caves 4, 5 and 6 have shown that what is preserved in the medieval MSS is largely true to its content in antiquity, but that several sections were omitted. Amongst those are a more elaborate historical introduction, several pages of purity laws, and some other community rules that also include an allusion to the covenant ceremony that takes place at Shevuot, the Feast of Pentecost. This was probably the festival when the sectarian movement celebrated the giving of the Law and when new members were initiated into the community. The *Damascus Document* is the rule book that seems to be addressed to the wider movement of which the Qumran community was a part and it speaks of women. In 4Q270, one of the copies from Cave 4, there is a rule about what happens to the member who complains against the "fathers" and the "mothers", which shows that some women had status in the movement. The passage is also one of the few that introduces the language of fictive kinship (so common in the NT) as a descriptor of relationships within the movement. Those who identify the sectarian movement behind all these texts as Essene usually identify the community reflected in the *Damascus Document* with those Josephus describes as being of the marrying kind (*J.W.* 2.160).

The *Rule of the Congregation* is best preserved in a copy 1Q5a (1Q28a) that was originally attached to the end of the Cave 1 form of the *Rule of the Community*; it is possible that several early copies of this rule were written in a cryptic script as early as the middle of the 2ⁿᵈ cent. BCE. The principal characteristic of this rule book is its eschatological outlook; it speaks of the community of the last days when even women and children will be included in torah instruction. Though this composition might seem only to be talking of the ideal community of the end of time when the messiahs will be present, notably at mealtimes when there is bread and wine, it is very likely that some of the regulations in the text reflect actual contemporary practices (*see* ESCHATOLOGY IN EARLY JUDAISM; ESCHATOLOGY OF THE NT; ESCHATOLOGY OF THE OT; MESSIAH, JEWISH).

Setting these rule books in some kind of reconstructed social history is difficult, but it seems that there is some scholarly consensus that a movement established in the 2nd cent. BCE underwent some internal difficulties, perhaps at the end of the century. Those difficulties are probably reflected in the arguments over the calendar, purity regulations, marriage law and other matters, that feature in *Miqsat Maase ha-Torah* (4Q394–399; *see* HALAKHIC LETTER). Some part of the movement seems to have established itself at Qumran, probably in the first quarter of the 1st cent. BCE, perhaps intent on dealing with the arguments through even greater adherence to purity regulations. It is possible that external political pressures kept the fragmented movement together in some way and that it went through various changes and developments until the end of the first Jewish revolt. If this movement is to be identified with the ESSENES of Philo, Josephus, and Pliny the Elder, the majority view that is almost entirely plausible, then those who lived at Qumran were only ever a small section of a much wider group operative throughout Palestine. The discrepancies between these classical sources and the descriptions of community life in the scrolls are not insurmountable, if one acknowledges the changes that the parts of the movement described in the various scrolls must have experienced.

c. **Other compositions.** Over half of the MSS from Qumran fall into this category. It is this collection of compositions that is still the least digested by scholarly analysis and which ultimately will provide the clearest view of the late Second Temple Judaism of which Hillel and Jesus were a part. It is always difficult to classify compositions; many seem to belong to more than one category.

First, there are very many compositions that are based on authoritative scriptural books, but which develop them in various ways, not so as to replace them but to give them an appropriate contemporary reading. These kinds of composition have been labelled either as rewritten Bible or as parabiblical, to indicate their close dependence on authoritative sources. Some rewritten texts, such as Deuteronomy, were already authoritative by the 2nd cent. BCE; others, such as 1–2 Chronicles also eventually became part of the canon.

Almost all the Pentateuch is represented extensively in these kinds of rewritten paraphrases. Generally they follow the order of the source and often stay very close to its phraseology; sometimes there is greater divergence. For Genesis there are several compositions that belong in this broad category. The

Genesis Apocryphon (1QapGen) is an Aram. narrative retelling of large sections of Genesis. The extant parts of the composition are mostly concerned with Noah and Abraham. Various narrative adjustments and expansions are made to heighten the artistic effect of the story or to explain some of the elements of the storyline; e.g., a description of Sarah's beauty and wisdom (1QapGen XX, 1-8) is introduced to explain why Pharaoh was so keen to take her as his wife and perhaps to titillate the audience. The frag. of the *Exposition on the Patriarchs* (4Q464) may be another such retelling, but in Hebrew, as also the *Paraphrase of Genesis and Exodus* (4Q422), and the *Text Mentioning the Flood* (4Q577). Testamentary literature, such as the *Testament of Judah* (3Q7; 4Q484) and related compositions such as the *Aramaic Levi Document* (1Q21; 4Q213–214) can also be classified as parabiblical literature, or as sapiential or eschatological texts. Alongside Hebrew and Aramaic reworkings of scriptural books there also seems to be a similar literary phenomenon in Greek (4Q127).

For Genesis and Exodus the most through-going reworking is to be found in the book of *Jubilees*; this is a Hebrew narrative retelling of Genesis 1–Exodus 15 that introduces various halakhot, so that the patriarchs are seen to be law-abiding before ever the Law was given. Amongst other things *Jubilees* is enthusiastic about proper Sabbath observance, aligns events with the 364-day calendar, and also constructs the history of the world in jubilee periods, so that Israel comes to enter the land in AM 2450 (AM, "Anno Mundi," is based on the Jewish tradition that the universe was created in 3761 BCE), after exactly fifty jubilee periods. To assert its own authority *Jubilees* declares that its content was revealed to Moses from the heavenly tablets by the angel of the presence. Also in Cave 4 were up to three MSS that contained text close to *Jubilees* (4Q225–227).

The *Temple Scroll*, known in three or more MSS (4Q524; 11Q19; 11Q20; 11Q21), is also rewritten Bible of some sort; rather than being revealed to Moses by an angel, the TEMPLE SCROLL is made up of speeches addressed to Moses by God himself. The content of the *Temple Scroll* is of two sorts: in the first part various pentateuchal laws concerning the tabernacle and sacrifice are arranged and supplemented with texts from Ezekiel, 1–2 Kings, and 1–2 Chronicles to provide a description of the temple and what happens in each place, working with an entirely priestly perspective from the holy of holies outwards; in the second part there is an abbreviated presentation of Deut 12 onwards, the law for those who live in the land, which has an expanded section that corresponds with Deut 17:14-20, the law for the king, perhaps an expansion whose contents are directed against some contemporary ruler. *Jubilees* and the *Temple Scroll* could also be classed as non-sectarian religious law, though their outlook is taken up in several sectarian compositions;

the same goes for the *Apocryphon of Moses* (1Q22; 4Q375–376; 4Q408).

There are rewritten in parabiblical forms for several of the history books too. Dependent in some way on Joshua are the *Apocryphon of Joshua* (4Q378–379; also found at Masada [Mas11]), and the *Prophecy of Joshua* (4Q522); a form of the *Apocryphon of Joshua* seems to be cited as a scriptural authority in the sectarian *Testimonia* (4Q175), and so should perhaps be added to the list of books that were deemed authoritative at Qumran but that did not make it into subsequent Jewish or Christian canon lists. For Samuel there is parabiblical material in the *Vision of Samuel* (4Q160) and for Kings a paraphrase in the *Paraphrase of Kings et al.* (4Q382). In some instances it is difficult to tell whether the form in the Qumran library is secondary in every respect. It is possible that the freedom with which the Gospel writers rework their narrative sources is a reflection of the same scribal attitude.

There are some parabiblical forms of the prophetic books, notably the three forms of the *Apocryphon of Jeremiah* (4Q383; 4Q384; 4Q385a, 387, 388a, 389–390, 387a), the five or six copies of *Pseudo-Ezekiel* (4Q385, 386, 385b, 388, 391, 385c), and the *Daniel Apocalypse* (4Q246), *Pseudo-Daniel* (4Q243–245) and the *Four Kingdoms* (4Q552–553). Some poetic materials that are akin to the scriptural psalms could also be categorized as parabiblical or rewritten Bible (such as 2Q22; 4Q371–373; 4Q460). The *List of False Prophets* (4Q339), the *Biblical Chronology* (4Q559), and various *Narrative* works (e.g., 4Q462) can also be classed as non-sectarian parabiblical compositions.

There are many liturgical works that do not seem to have any explicit connection with the sect, but might have been used by them regularly or from time to time. There are collections of *Daily Prayers* (4Q503; 4Q504; 4Q506), *Festival Prayers* (1Q34; 4Q507–508), a *Purification Liturgy* (4Q284), an *Incantation* (4Q444), a composition with a *Lament* (4Q445), *Non-Canonical Psalms* (4Q380–381), a *Sapiential Hymn* (4Q411), and the frag. labelled *Apocryphal Psalm and Prayer* (4Q448; which mentions King Jonathan, probably Alexander Jannaeus). There is also a long list of rather fragmentary MSS containing hymns, prayers, thanksgivings, blessings, hallelujahs, and laments. It is difficult to overemphasize the rich spiritual heritage of poetry and liturgy that the community at Qumran thrived upon. In addition, those calendrical texts that seem to have some significant concern with the movements of the moon would seem to have a non-sectarian background.

There are also several compositions in the library that expand our knowledge of wisdom literature in Second Temple Judaism. Alongside the scriptural wisdom books and Ben Sira, there is the Aramaic reworking of Job (11Q10). In addition there are copies of *Instruction* (1Q26; 4Q415–418, 418a, 418c,

4Q423); this is a wisdom composition concerning the poor in which there is a mixture of instructions concerning social behaviour, economic matters, and eschatological insight into the mystery of existence. There are also collections of proverbs (4Q424), didactic speeches (4Q185), wisdom poetry (4Q411), meditations on creation (4Q303–4Q305), and parables (4Q302).

A small amount of historical literature (4Q322a; 4Q332; 4Q333; 4Q468e) includes court tales that may form part of the literary background of Esther (4Q550; 4Q550a-e) and Daniel (4Q242).

Various apocalyptic texts, such as the seven copies of the *Visions of Amram* (4Q543–549), the widely attested *New Jerusalem* text (1Q32; 2Q24; 4Q554, 554a, 555; 5Q15; 11Q18), various books associated with Enoch, the *Book of Watchers* (4Q201–202; 204–206), the *Book of Dreams* (4Q204-207; 212), non-symbolic apocalypses such as the *Apocryphon of Jeremiah* (4Q383–384; 385a; 387; 387a; 388a, 389–390), as well as several Danielic works (4Q243–245) may have been source material used by the author of the Book of Daniel. Eschatological compositions include *Words of Judgement* (4Q238), an *Eschatological Hymn* (4Q457b), the *Renewed Earth* (4Q475), and the *Messianic Apocalypse* (4Q521).

There are several unclassified and unclassifiable fragmentary compositions, though in some cases editors have attempted to name them. Chief amongst other miscellaneous compositions is the COPPER SCROLL (3Q15), a list of buried treasure, both money and other items. The text, in a Hebrew that has features of mishnaic Hebrew (also including some sets of Greek letters), almost certainly refers to real valuables, either accumulated contributions made to the community, or, more likely, part of the contents of the temple treasury secreted away before or during the first Jewish war (66–74 CE). No treasure has been found in the modern period, so it is likely that it was recovered in antiquity.

When the Qumran library is compared with the MS remains from other sites in the wilderness of Judea the distinct character of the collection is all the more apparent. From Wadi Daliyeh, Ketef Jericho, Wadi Nar, Wadi Ghweir, Nahal Mishmar and Nahal Se'elim only documentary texts survive, such as deeds of sale, receipts, lists of loans, letters, leases, and various other legal texts. From Wadi Murabba'at, Wadi Sdeir, Nahal Hever and Masada, documentary texts also predominate, but some literary texts have also survived including copies of some biblical books, most extensively the copy of the Greek Minor Prophets scroll from Nahal Hever. The presence of one copy of the quasi-sectarian *Songs of the Sabbath Sacrifice* (4Q400–407) at Masada can be explained either by suggesting that it was brought there from an independent collection in Jerusalem or by somebody from Qumran.

3. Relationship to other literary corpora

a. The New Testatment. Although some scholars have tried to suggest otherwise, there is no clear evidence that any of the NT books have been found in the caves at Qumran. Conversely, there is no clear evidence that any of the NT writings actually cite any of the non-scriptural Dead Sea Scrolls, sectarian or otherwise. Nevertheless, the Dead Sea Scrolls are the single most important textual source for understanding Palestinian Judaism at the time of Jesus. It is important not to reconstruct that Judaism as if the various religious movements within Judaism had nothing in common. For example, it seems that Jesus and the movement behind the scrolls largely shared a view on the inadmissibility of divorce, even using the same proof-texts (CD IV, 19–V, 6; Mark 10:2-12); that does not make Jesus an Essene as some have sensationally tried to argue. Jesus' practice of sharing meals with those on the edges of Jewish society and his attitude on purity would have certainly distanced him from the members of the Qumran community; that does not mean that he would never have had any contact with some of them, since it seems as if some of his teaching is indeed indirectly aimed against the "sons of light" (Luke 16:8).

The importance of the scrolls for the NT rests in at least five areas. First, it is probable that John the Baptist knew about the community at Qumran. He seems to have shared some of their eschatological outlook and to have urged his audiences to repentance that could be demonstrated through the ritual washing of baptism. According to Luke 7:18-23, when the imprisoned John sends some of his disciples to Jesus to ask him who he is, Jesus answers by referring to his actions, using passages from Isa 29, 35 and 61, but including mention of the dead being raised. A similar combination of motifs has come to light only in the so-called *Messianic Apocalypse* (4Q521). If the saying is authentic to Jesus, then it seems as if he answers John in terms John would recognize, perhaps from his knowledge of some of the texts that we now know only because they have survived in the Qumran library.

Second, it is likely that some elements in the teaching of Jesus are best understood in the light of the Dead Sea Scrolls. Some elements in the eschatological adjustment of wisdom instruction present in some of his sayings and parables are anticipated in some of the non-sectarian wisdom materials in the Qumran library. Also notable is the way that the Beatitudes, particularly in their presentation in Matt 5, can now be seen to share matters of form and content with contemporary Jewish teaching: in 4Q525 a list of nine blessings survives, the ninth of which concerns persecution, just as in Matt 5:11-12. However, apart from the *Songs of the Sabbath Sacrifice* that celebrate God as sovereign there is little on the kingship of God

in the Dead Sea Scrolls. Jesus' healing ministry may also be more clearly understood in light of the Qumran texts that refer to exorcism (4Q242; 4Q444; 4Q560), apotropaic prayer (4Q510–511; 11Q11), and healing (1QapGen XX, 28-30).

Third, it seems that, according to the writings of the second generation of Christians, some matters in the organization of the early Christian communities were similar to items now found in the scrolls. Perhaps this indicates that the second generation of Jewish Christians were those most influenced by the structures of the movement of which the Qumran community was a part. Amongst the items commonly pointed to are the casting of lots (e.g., 1QS VI, 18), the role of the "many" in community decision-making processes (1QS VI; Acts 4:32), the sharing of property (or at least the use of it; 1QS VI, 19-20), the ideology of poverty (e.g., 4Q171 II, 9), the role of the number 12 in organization (4Q164 1, 4), the function of the overseer (e.g., 1QS VI, 12), eschatological meal practice (1QSa (1Q28a) II, 11-22), and washing as part of the ritual of admission, together with confession and the gift of the Holy Spirit (1QS IV, 20-22). On the other hand, these similarities could indicate that both the community of the scrolls and the early Christian groups shared general organizational principles and religious practices common in the wider Hellenistic environment that both shared.

Fourth, the NT writers share with the authors of some of the Dead Sea Scrolls a concern with messianism. The relatively few scrolls that describe messianic figures seem to suppose that there would be two messiahs at the end time, a priestly and a royal messiah. Some compositions refer to just one of these. For example in 4Q246 there is the striking combination of the titles "Son of God" and "Son of the Most High" that seems to refer to a royal messiah (as in Luke 1:32-35). In a few earlier compositions there is reference to "the Messiahs of Aaron and Israel" (1QS IX, 11); in later compositions, there is explicit reference to the "Shoot of David," perhaps as a counterweight to the kingship of Herod the Great or the supposed divinity of the Roman emperor. The Davidic or royal messiah is not associated with suffering in any of the Qumran compositions, though the eschatological high priest seems to be (4Q541). Other uses of the term "anointed" refer to prophets in general. The NT authors play out the messianic titles in various ways: for Matthew Jesus is principally the Davidic messiah, while John the Baptist is the eschatological prophet, Elijah *redivivus* (Matt 11:14); for Luke Jesus is both a royal (Luke 1:32) and prophetic (Luke 7:16) figure; the Gospel of John portrays Jesus as prophet (John 6:14), king (John 18:36-37), and possibly as priestly (compare the seamless priestly robe in John 19:23); the author of Hebrews stresses Jesus' priesthood. The variety of messianic concerns and titles in the Dead

Sea Scrolls is suggestive of what was available to early Christian authors as they wrestled with describing Jesus against the backdrop of some Jewish expectation and the political circumstances of their times (*see* MESSIAH, JEWISH).

Fifth, both the Dead Sea Scrolls and the NT are heavily dependent on authoritative scriptures for defining the self-understandings and worldviews that they present. For the Qumran community the scriptures functioned not just as a set of prophetic predictions, but correctly interpreted they were the principal guide to a correct understanding of the justice and mercy of God as that could be appropriated and experienced in the community. For the NT authors the books of the OT, principally the prophets and Psalms, served as a source of proof-texts and as a resource for a more complete understanding of the events of Jesus' ministry. In some instances very similar uses of scriptural resources can be seen in both sets of writings. For example, in 11Q13 several allusions to Isa 61:1-3 are used to frame part of the description of what takes place at the end of the tenth jubilee period; this has enabled a fresh understanding of Jesus' use of Isa 61:1-2 (Luke 4:18-19) as an indication that, for Luke, he was declaring his ministry to be a period of jubilee release. In 1QpHab VIII, 1–2 Hab 2:4*a* is understood as concerning "all those who observe the Law in the house of Judah whom God will deliver from the house of judgment because of their suffering and their faith in the Teacher of Righteousness" (compare Rom 1:17). In *Pseudo-Ezekiel* a strikingly similar combination of Ezek 1, 10 and Isa 6 can be found as that in Rev 4.

b. Other Jewish literature. The Dead Sea Scrolls belong to the era before the fall of the Temple in 70 CE. Though rabbinic literature may contain echoes of that same time most of it comes from several decades or centuries later. There is little continuity between the kinds of Judaism represented in the Dead Sea Scrolls and those indicated in the rabbinic literature of Mishnah and Talmud. This is probably to be explained by the way in which much rabbinic material is the heir of Pharisaic traditions; the movement behind the scrolls seems to have been largely anti-Pharisaic. In fact, one of the most obvious continuities is between some of the purity regulations in 4Q394, such as the way in which liquid streams convey impurity even against the flow of the liquid, and some of the practices ascribed to the Sadducees in *m. Yad.* 4:7. This has caused some rashly to identify the Qumran group with some form of Sadduceeism. Apart from some similar concerns such as with calendrical matters, it is elsewhere in Judaism that continuities seem to exist.

In the scrolls there is considerable interest in how the community at worship can join in angelic praise of God, perhaps through some form of mystical ascent.

There is concern with angels and demons, with encouraging the presence of the former in the community while guarding against the latter. There is concern with spiritual warfare. There is concern with the divine throne chariot. These are all aspects of later Jewish mystical texts. The scrolls provide us with a link in the chain between the scriptural work of Ezekiel and Jewish mysticism as that can be found in the Heikhalot literature.

Amongst the scrolls are a few paraphrastic renderings of scriptural books in Aramaic (4Q156; 4Q157; 11Q10), some with extensive additions. These works seem akin to the later targumim, Aramaic versions of scripture used in the synagogue alongside the recitation of the week's readings in Hebrew (*see* TARGUMS). Perhaps there is a common oral tradition that lies behind these compositions. *See* APOCRYPHA, DEUTEROCANONICAL; ARAMAIC LEVI DOCUMENT; BIBLICAL INTERPRETATION, HISTORY OF; CANON OF THE OLD TESTAMENT; COPPER SCROLL; ENOCH, FIRST BOOK OF; ESSENES; JUBILEES, BOOK OF; MASADA; NAHUM PESHER; PESHARIM; PSEUDEPIGRAPHA; SONGS OF THE SABBATH SACRIFICE; TEMPLE, JERUSALEM; THANKSGIVING PSALMS; TORAH; WAR SCROLL.

Bibliography: George J. Brooke. *The Dead Sea Scrolls and the New Testament* (2005); Philip R. Davies, George J. Brooke, and Philip R. Callaway. *The Complete World of the Dead Sea Scrolls* (2002); Peter W. Flint and James C. VanderKam, eds. *The Dead Sea Scrolls after Fifty Years.* 2 vols. (1998–99); Lawrence H. Schiffman. *Reclaiming the Dead Sea Scrolls: The History of Judaism, the Background of Christianity, the Lost Library of Qumran* (1994); Florentino García Martínez and Eibert J.C. Tigchelaar, eds. *The Dead Sea Scrolls Study Edition.* 2 vols. Rev. ed. (2000); Donald W. Parry and Emanuel Tov, eds. *The Dead Sea Scrolls Reader.* 6 vols. (2004–2005); Geza Vermes. *The Complete Dead Sea Scrolls in English.* Rev. ed. (2004); James C. VanderKam and Peter W. Flint. *The Meaning of the Dead Sea Scrolls: Their Significance for Understanding the Bible, Judaism, Jesus, and Christianity* (2002); Lawrence H. Schiffman and James C. VanderKam, eds. *Encyclopedia of the Dead Sea Scrolls.* 2 vols. (2000); Emanuel Tov, ed. *The Dead Sea Scrolls Electronic Library Incorporating the Dead Sea Scrolls Reader* (2006); Michael Wise, Martin G. Abegg, Jr, and Edward Cook. *The Dead Sea Scrolls: A New Translation.* Rev. ed. (2005).

GEORGE J. BROOKE

DEAD, ABODE OF THE. Every ANE culture believed in an AFTERLIFE for the dead, who journeyed to a special abode to begin a new existence. The journey to the abode of the dead explains some of the grave goods, which are common in burials in the area, as provisions for their journey or for setting up their eternal abode.

A. Egypt
B. Mesopotamia and Canaan
C. Israel
Bibliography

A. Egypt

The pyramid texts, dynasty after dynasty, record that the Pharaoh ascends the heavens. For example: "Atum brought to [name of Pharaoh] the gods belonging to heaven. He assembled to him the gods belonging to earth. They put their arms under him. They made a ladder for [name of Pharaoh] that he m-ight ascend to heaven on it" (Pyr. Texts 1.390a).

It is unlikely that the common folk of Egypt could expect such an exalted afterlife. The pyramids themselves were oriented toward specific ikhemu-Seku, the indestructible stars (i.e., those that never set). Since we have no records of ordinary persons' aspirations from this period, we must assume that they settled for lesser rewards among the other depictions of the Duat, the Egyptian words for the afterlife. Indeed, the Egyptian afterlife could be depicted as quite a bit like affluence in this life. People with enough money to decorate a tomb depicted the joys of life along the Nile, abundant food, servants, children, wives, leisure, and comfort, which might as easily describe the afterlife as this one. People with fewer means might only have the body mummified, as biblical patriarch Joseph (Gen 50:25-26; Exod 13:19). Still others might rely on the desert sand to approximate mummification, as prehistoric graves in the Nile Valley had done. In the document known as the Amduat ("what is in the afterlife") the Pharaoh is depicted in his adventures underground in the hours from sunset to sunrise, helping the sun to be reborn.

In the New Kingdom (ca. 1540–1070 BCE), we begin to see copies of the so-called Egyptian BOOK OF THE DEAD ("the Book of Going Forth by Day"), which details the fate of courtiers or bureaucrats as well as the Pharaoh and his family. They too undergo many trials and obstacles. The climax of the story is the negative confession of sin in the "Hall of the Two Maʿats." There, the person's heart must be weighed in a balance against the feather of maʿat and found lighter. Osiris, accompanied by Isis and Nephthys, serves as judge. The proceedings are recorded by the Ibis-headed Thoth. Unsuccessful defendants are given to the Crocodile monster Sobek for a "second death." But successful candidates become an akh, a glorified body. Various other kinds of souls were posited for the individual by the Egyptians over time, including the ba, and the ka and other synecdoches like the belly, each with different functions. This reflects Egypt's long history and local traditions. It is clear though by the New Kingdom

that the akh served as the transcendent soul and the heart as the seat of morality (see EGYPT).

B. Mesopotamia and Canaan

The Mesopotamian bit ikliti, "the house of darkness," was nowhere near as much fun as the Egyptian Duat. It was a subterranean realm, really a city of the dead equipped with strong gates, not to lock out enemies but to lock the dead in. The departed were mourned with great show, somber pomp, and the loud cry of professional mourners. But, once grief was assuaged, the dead were considered more dangerous to the living than helpful. The dead became ghosts (etemmu) upon passing from this world. With proper burial, the ghosts set out for the grim city, ruled over by the mighty goddess Ereshkigal and her consort Nergal. The dead needed feeding and commemorative rites at regular intervals thereafter or they might return to do damage. The dead could be assuaged with the kispu ("sharing") ritual by which they received beer, bread, water, and the necessities of life underground, which was the responsibility of the oldest son. His double share of the estate was likely set aside for this purpose. Ereshkigal and Nergal, who were known by many different names and epithets, ruled the underworld. They also had help from the Anunnaki, a group of scholarly ancestors who acted like grim fates. Gilgamesh himself also acted as a god of equity in the underworld (see ASSYRIA AND BABYLONIA; MESOPOTAMIA; GILGAMESH, EPIC OF).

Canaan belongs to the same family of afterlife beliefs but it is far more important to the earliest periods of Israelite history. When the Canaanites died, their vital element called npsh (like Hebrew: nefesh [נֶפֶשׁ]) left the body. The soul went to the kingdom of mot ("death"; Hebrew maweth מָוֶת), where it lived on in a ghostly existence, as in Mesopotamian religion. The Canaanites also recognized the responsibilities of children to care for their parents. This included, as the Kirta legend tells us, the duty of supporting the father in his drunkenness when returning from banquets in commemoration of the dead. This is a ritual as well as a filial concern because the dead were buried and commemorated with a "wake," a great drinking party called a marzikh (see MARZEAH). Quite likely, these "wakes" abused alcohol to stimulate vision and make contact with the dead. The ghost who did come to the marzikh was called a rpʾum and was ruled by the sun goddess Shapash. Perhaps the dead were "healed" of death or persons who could heal, since that is what the root rpʾ often means, even in Hebrew where we find the word refaʾim (רְפָאִים), the ghosts (KTU 1.6: VI.45-49, 1.21; see REPHAIM).

C. Israel

Canaanite religious beliefs regarding the afterlife were abhorrent to Israelite prophets (Amos 6:4-7; Hos

7:3-7; 9:1-6; Jer 16:5-9). This suggests that the Israelites were tempted to behave as the Canaanites did and that participating in a Marzeah was considered idolatry by the prophets. There is a good reason for this caution; the biblical narrative calls the ghost of Samuel a "god" 'elohim (1 Sam 28:13), which suggests that the ritual calling him was interpreted as worship (*see* ENDOR, MEDIUM OF; NECROMANCY). To the prophets and the redactors of the Saul story, a refa' was a ghost ('ov) and it was forbidden to consult them. They were to stay resting (1 Sam 28), in a place called SHEOL, a unique proper name among abodes of the dead in the ANE. The root also signifies "ask" in the ordinary sense and probably refers to consulting the dead. The name Saul, who committed the sin of consulting the dead, also shares the same root. The denizens of this realm are the refa'im, cognate with the Ugaritic term. These ghosts keep the stations they earned in life (1 Sam 14:9-10; Ezek 32:21, 24), although they are weary (Job 3:17) or weak (Ps 88:4 [Heb. 88:5]). Synonyms for Sheol include shakhath (שַׁחַת, "ditch," Job 33:18), bor (בּוֹר, pit; Ps 28:1) maweth ("death," i.e., abode of death Job 28:22), 'erets (אֶרֶץ, "earth," Exod 15:12), 'avaddon (אֲבַדּוֹן, "perdition," Job 26:6; *see* ABADDON). All these are common nouns pressed into service as metaphors.

In the NT, the abode of the dead is almost invariably called by the Greek word HADES, where it seems to be the place of punishment, in contradistinction to resurrection as a reward for the faithful. Not so in the OT, where all go to SHEOL without distinction. So there is no question of reward or punishment. Until the Hellenistic period, there is insufficient evidence to posit a robust concept of a beatific AFTERLIFE. But after Dan 12:3, the notion of resurrection becomes indelibly part of Israelite thought, though its existence, nature, and purpose were being fiercely debated even as late as the time of Jesus. At least some of the dead in Dan 12 are said to ascend to heaven and become stars there, founding a whole new description to the abode of the dead in Jewish thought. Depictions of this process of transformation into stars or angels can be seen in *1 En.* 71 and possibly in the transfiguration of Jesus (Matthew 17:1-8; Mark 9:2-8; Luke 9:28-36). *See* ABYSS; DEATH, NT; DEATH, OT; DEITIES, UNDERWORLD; GEHENNA; RESURRECTION, EARLY JEWISH; RESURRECTION, NT; RESURRECTION, OT.

Bibliography: Elizabeth Bloch-Smith. *Judahite Burial and Practices and Beliefs about the Dead* (1992); G. F. Brandon. *The Judgment of the Dead: The Idea of Life After Death in the Major Religions* (1967); Theodore J. Lewis. *Cults of the Dead in Ancient Israel and Ugarit* (1989); John L. McLaughlin. *The Marzeah in the Prophetic Literature: References and Allusions in Light of the Extra Biblical Evidence* (2001); Dennis Pardee. *Ritual and Cult at Ugarit* (2002); Alan F. Segal. *Life After Death: A History of the Afterlife in Western Religion* (2005); Klaus Spronk. *Beautific Afterlife in Ancient Israel and the Ancient Near East* (1986); John H. Taylor. *Death and the Afterlife in Ancient Egypt* (2001).

ALAN F. SEGAL

DEAD, BOOK OF THE. *See* BOOK OF THE DEAD.

DEAD, CULT OF THE. *See* DEAD, ABODE OF THE; EGYPT.

DEAF, DEAFNESS [חֵרֵשׁ kheresh; κωφός kōphos]. These Hebrew and Greek terms describe a total lack (Lev 19:14; Mark 7:32; Luke 7:22) or partial deficiency in the sense of hearing (Ps 38:13) or understanding (Isa 42:18; 43:8). In the biblical view, God is responsible for healing and sickening (Exod 15:26), including the senses of sight, hearing, and speech (Exod 4:11). The story of Jesus healing a deaf man (Mark 7:32-37) probably reflects the folk understanding of its cause (Isa 35:5) and its proper remedy (Mark 7:33-35). Biomedical science hypothesizes these cases as dissociative illnesses or somatizing disorders. *See* DISEASE.

JOHN J. PILCH

DEATH, NT [θάνατος thanatos]. For most of humankind's history, softening the blow of death as an absolute has been a major component of all cultural thinking and philosophy; furthermore, the issue of death obviously impacts thoughts about life itself. Most important, however, the nature of God and the relationships between God and individual humans, God and the nations, and God and history are at stake. Even monotheism is in question as writers ask about the source of evil and death. New Testament writers shared these concerns, and inherited a diversity of ideas about death from Jewish and Greek worldviews, which were in turn influenced by Egyptian and other cultural notions of death (*see* AFTERLIFE).

Typically in the OT, death was simply the end of life on earth, a point at which one rejoins the ancestors, and is not a result of evil on anyone's part; however, we also find in the OT the view that humankind's propensity for evil acts resulted in death for one's self or even the community (*see* DEATH, OT). Many Jewish writers eventually developed the belief that the righteous were rewarded after death, as in the case of martyrs. The Greeks had developed a range of views, summarized by Cicero: either body and soul are annihilated at death or the soul separates from the body (*Tusc.* 1.11.23-24). The interface of Hebrew and Greek thought, as well as influences from other cultures, provided a diverse context for NT writers.

The Gospel writers use the term *death* to refer to the literal cessation of biological life. The evangelists have variant notions about the rituals of death; e.g., Jesus advises his followers to let the dead bury their own dead (Matt 8:22//Luke 9:60), but commends the woman who anoints him prior to his own death (Mark 14:3-9//Matt 26:6-13//Luke 7:36-50//John 12:1-8). In four instances, people are resuscitated from death (Mark 5:21-43//Matt 9:18-26//Luke 8:40-56; Luke 7:11-17; John 11:1-44; Acts 9:36-43), but there is no reason to believe that their physical resuscitations would be permanent.

The NT mentions some who have seemingly escaped death, such as Enoch (Heb 11:5; compare Gen 5:24); Moses, who according to tradition was assumed into heaven; and Elijah, who ascended in a whirlwind into heaven (2 Kgs 2:11). These three appear with Jesus on the mountain (Mark 9:2-8//Matt 17:1-8//Luke 9:28-36). Just prior to that story, Mark reassures the listeners that some will not die before the kingdom of God arrives (Mark 9:1//Matt 16:28//Luke 9:27), but this apocalyptic expectation does not preclude death at some point.

Paul uses the concept of death theologically in both literal and metaphorical senses. In the literal sense, death is not a natural constituent of creation and is the result of sin; Jesus saves humankind from sin and, therefore, death is overcome in the afterlife (see Rom 4:25; 5:12; 6:23; 1 Cor 15:26). In his comparison of Jesus and Adam, Paul argues that the first created human was, because of his disobedience, earthly, perishable, dishonorable, weak, and physical; Christ, on the other hand, is heavenly, imperishable, glorious, powerful, and spiritual. Jesus, according to Paul, is the "last Adam" who overcomes death (1 Cor 15:42-49). Paul assures his followers that the "dead in Christ" will rise first (1 Thess 4:16-17).

Paul's uses the concept of death to describe the metaphorical demise of one's spiritual and moral life. Sinners will not inherit the kingdom of God (1 Cor 6:9-10). In a letter probably written by one of Paul's disciples, we find a similar vice list: followers are to put to death whatever is earthly (Col 3:5-9). According to Revelation, one is to be faithful to death as a martyr, and the reward will be the crown of life (e.g., 2:10). In a vision that transcends Rome's persecution, "death will be no more" (Rev 21:4). Death is personified metaphorically in this vision as the rider on a pale green horse (Rev 6:8).

The various NT texts provide no consistent system of thought concerning death; however, the NT writers agree that death did not necessarily mean finitude. From sociological and historical perspectives, death has almost always been viewed as a transition in life rather than as final. Within that worldview, NT writers are traditional in their view that death presents the opportunity for new life. *See* DEAD, ABODE OF THE; IMMORTALITY IN EARLY JUDAISM; RESURRECTION, EARLY JEWISH; RESURRECTION, NT; SHEOL.

Bibliography: Richard Bauckham. *The Fate of the Dead: Studies on the Jewish and Christian Apocalypses* (1998); Shannon Burkes. *God, Self, and Death: The Shape of Religious Transformation in the Second Temple Period* (2003); Sarah Iles Johnston, ed. *Religions of the Ancient World: A Guide* (2004); Stanley B. Morrow. "ΑΘΑΝΑΣΙΑ/ΑΝΑΣΤΑΣΙΣ: The Road Not Taken." *NTS* 45 (1999) 571–86; Hiroshi Obayashi, ed. *Death and Afterlife: Perspectives of World Religions* (1992).

GLENNA S. JACKSON

DEATH, OT [מָוֶת maweth]. The OT represents a multifaceted portrayal of death. The writers of the OT (especially the psalmists) used the language of death to describe not just the physical cessation of life, but also as a metaphor for distress and anguish.

A. The Universality and Power of Death
B. God Victorious Over Death
C. Petitions and Expressions of Confidence
D. The Biblical Views of Death in Its World
Bibliography

A. The Universality and Power of Death

A constant theme is the universality of death. Numbers 16:29 has Moses referring to "a natural death" (moth kol-ha'adham [מוֹת כָּל־הָאָדָם] lit. "the [common] death of all humans") as well as "a natural fate" (pequddath kol-ha'adham [פְּקֻדַּת כָּל־הָאָדָם] lit. "the fate of all humans"). A psalmist reflects: "Who can live and never see death?" (Ps 89:48). The universal fate of death is the great equalizer, erasing distinctions between the wise and the fool, the rich and the poor (Ps 49:10-12; Eccl 2:14-16).

The book of Job poetically refers to death as "the house appointed for all living" (beth mo'edh lekhol-khay [בֵּית מוֹעֵד לְכָל־חָי] Job 30:23). Family terms (and with them an expression of clan solidarity) lie behind the idioms that describe death as being "gathered to one's people" (weyye'asef 'el 'ammayw [וַיֵּאָסֶף אֶל־עַמָּיו]; e.g., Gen 25:8, 17; 35:29; 49:29, 33; Num 20:24, 26; 27:13; 31:2; Deut 32:50) or "lying down/sleeping with one's ancestors/fathers" (shokhev 'im 'avoth [שָׁכַב עִם אָבוֹת]; e.g., Gen 47:30; Deut 31:16; 2 Sam 7:12; 1 Kgs 1:21; Tell Dan inscription; compare 2 Macc 12:39).

In contrast, the prophet Habakkuk alludes to a mythological portrait. His remarks about the insatiable appetite of death (Hab 2:5; compare Isa 5:14; Prov 1:12; 27:20; 30:15*b*-16; Ps 141:7) evoke myths of the deity Mot ("Death"), known, especially, from neighboring Late Bronze Age civilization of Ugarit, to have gaping jaws. With one lip to the earth, the other stretched to the heavens, Mot swallows all (compare KTU 1.5.2.2-4). Elsewhere he eats so ravenously that he has to use both hands (KTU 1.5.1.19-20; compare Job 18:13).

Thus we are presented with comforting and disturbing images of death. Whereas one psalmist refers to the "sleep of death" (Ps 13:3), others mention its "cords," "torrents," "snares," and "pangs" (Pss 18:4-5; 116:3; 2 Sam 22:5-6; Ps 116:3). Implied in each portrayal (whether using reassuring familial images or the disconcerting demonic) is the power of death. The psalmist explicitly asks: "Who can escape the power of SHEOL (// death)?" (Ps 89:48; compare Ps 49:15; Hos 13:14). Ecclesiastes likewise affirms that "No human has power . . . over the day of death" (Eccl 8:8). Adding to its inevitability is the lack of knowledge regarding when or how death arrives. Isaac acknowledges that he knows not the day of his death (Gen 27:2). Jeremiah's dirge over Jerusalem affirms that death can arrive anywhere (compare KTU 1.4.6.63-65).

"Death has come up into our windows,
   it has entered our palaces,
to cut off the children from the streets,
   and the young men from the squares." (Jer 9:21)

Moreover, the power of death strips away from the righteous their greatest joy. In the words of Ps 6:5: "in death there is no remembrance of you [God]; in Sheol who can give you praise?" To this Ecclesiastes despairingly adds the earthly counterpart: "the people of long ago [lit. "(our) predecessors"] are not remembered [by their descendants], nor will there be any remembrance of people yet to come by those who come after them" (Eccl 1:11; compare 2:16).

B. God Victorious over Death

How did Iron Age Judeans respond to their inability to control death, to its inevitability, its ubiquity, and its fateful appearance? The poet of the Song of Songs celebrates how "love is strong as death" (Song 8:6). Love is equally powerful, yet not surpassing. The OT has no language of human love being able to conquer death. Such victory is only to be found in the hands of the Almighty. Here poets and sages alike make their petition (for rescue from physical death and deathly distress) and render thankful praise that God is able and willing.

A striking passage on God's ability comes from Isa 25:8, which reverses the Canaanite imagery of the god Mot swallowing up his victims (including the storm god Baal). Here, it is Yahweh who swallows up Death. Moreover, the prophet asserts, it is a once-for-all victory and one in which God "will wipe away the tears from all faces" (Isa 25:8; compare 1 Cor 15:24-57; Rev 7:17; 21:4). God alone is the one who is able to "ransom" from the power of Sheol, to "redeem" from Death, to take away their "plagues" and "destructions" (Hos 13:14; compare 1 Cor 15:54-57). In Hannah's prayer, it is Yahweh "(who) kills and brings life, (who) brings down to Sheol and raises up" (1 Sam 2:6). Eventually, Yahweh's power over death will be articulated with the language of resurrection: "For you have power over life and death; you lead mortals down to the gates of Hades and back again" (Wis 16:13).

C. Petitions and Expressions of Confidence

In light of God's power over death, it is not surprising that the OT contains petitions seeking divine succor. For example, Ps 9:13 reads: "Be gracious to me, O LORD. See what I suffer from those who hate me; you are the one who lifts me up from the gates of death." Yet occurring far more often than the petitions themselves are expressions of confidence where the petitioner expresses his trust in God's ability and willingness to provide relief. The most famous of these types of passages is Ps 23:4, which has traditionally been translated "Though I walk through the valley of the shadow of death (tsalmaweth צַלְמָוֶת), I fear no evil, for you are with me." Moderns scholars point out that the Hebrew word behind the phrase "shadow of death" is most likely a folk etymology (tsel "shadow" + mawet "death"). Yet regardless of the "correct" linguistic etymology (most likely tsalmuth [צַלְמֻות] comes from the root tslm [צלם] "to be dark" and thus NRSV's "darkest valley"), folk etymologies resonated with readers (compare Job 38:17). Regardless, the poet of Psalm 23 is confident in Yahweh's ability to dispense fear, be it of distress, suffering, or even of death.

Petitions for future aid are anchored in the liturgy of memory, in individual and communal "salvation history." God, Judeans confessed, was their help in ages past, in deathly circumstances. Psalm 18, a royal thanksgiving psalm, depicts distress using the language of death: "The cords of death encompassed me; the torrents of perdition assailed me; the cords of Sheol entangled me; the snares of death confronted me" (vv. 4-5). To such despair, the poet responds: "In my distress I called upon the LORD; to my God I cried for help." The divine (warrior) response is overwhelmingly powerful and salvific: "Then the earth reeled and rocked; the foundations also of the mountains trembled and quaked. . . . He bowed the heavens, and came down; thick darkness was under his feet. He rode on a cherub and flew; he came swiftly upon the wings of the wind. . . . He reached down from on high, he took me; he drew me out of mighty waters. He delivered me from my strong enemy. . . . He brought me out to a broad place; he delivered me, because he delighted in me" (Ps 18:4-7, 9-10, 16-17, 19). Similar language is found in Ps 116. Here too the poet renders praise for being rescued from a situation that was so anguishing that "the snares of death" and "pangs of Sheol" had him in their grip. He reflects: "Then I called on the name of the LORD: 'O LORD, I pray, save my life!'" God was gracious in salvation. Praises burst forth: "When I was brought low, he saved me. . . . You have delivered my soul from death, my eyes from tears, my feet from stumbling." Little wonder that he then exclaims: "Precious in the sight of the LORD is the death of his faithful ones" (Ps 116:3-4, 6, 8, 15).

Other expressions of confidence with regard to Yahweh's power over death fill the psalms. Psalm 33:18-19 expresses trust that during a time of famine, Yahweh will deliver from death "those who fear him, those who hope in his steadfast love" (compare Job 5:20; Pss 34:9; 37:19). Psalm 49, a wisdom psalm, includes mention of persecutors (49:5), and how the wealthy are not to be feared, for riches cannot ransom lives from death (49:5-9). The author asserts that while the "foolhardy" may be appointed for Sheol with Death as their shepherd, he will trust that God will ransom him from the power of Sheol (Ps 49:5, 14-15). Psalm 56, a prayer of deliverance from persecution, promises to render vows and thanksgiving because "you have delivered my soul from death . . . so that I may walk before God in the light of life" (Ps 56:13). With full confidence, the author of Ps 68 praises God's salvific acts: "Our God is a God of salvation, and to God, the Lord, belongs escape from death" (Ps 68:20).

D. The Biblical View of Death in Its World

Northwest Semitic languages attest to several terms for the deceased ranging from descriptive nouns (mt "the dead") to attempts at describing their preternatural state (ilu, ʾelohim [אֱלֹהִים] "divine being, spirit," compare 1 Sam 28:13). Rephaim (refaʾim רְפָאִים) is one of the more colorful terms used widely (the cognate term rpʾm occurs in Ugaritic and Phoenician) to describe the denizens of the netherworld as well as heroes of old. In contrast to the inactive state of the dead in the biblical traditions (Ps 88:11; Isa 26:14), the ancient Syrian notion attested in the Ugaritic texts is that the rpʾm could be quite active. Three tablets known as the Rapiʾuma texts (KTU 1.20-22) have the rpʾm hitching horses, galloping on stallions, and riding for three days to reach a banquet set for them by the god ʾIlu (compare KTU 1.114). Elsewhere the royal rpʾm are invoked to give aid in an elaborate funerary ritual (see below).

Occasionally we hear of the npsh which seems to refer to the life force that at death departs like a gust of wind or a whiff of smoke (KTU 1.18.4.25, 36; compare Job 34:14; Eccl 12:7; Gen 35:18; Ps 146:4; [nefesh נֶפֶשׁ] but compare the invocation of the nbsh in a death banquet in KAI 214). In ancient Syria, the term ʾiluʾibi (reflecting the word for the divine [ʾil] in conjunction with a word for one's father [ʾib]) is used in Ugaritic deity lists and sacrificial texts to designate the deified ancestor (or one's ancestor's god). Elsewhere (KTU 1.113) ʾil is used prior to the names of departed royal ancestors to designate that they were deified in some sense. Another intriguing Ugaritic term is ʾinashu-ʾilima, which may refer to "deceased humans (who have become) divine."

That the dead were thought to continue on in the afterlife can be shown from their invocation in funerary texts and through tomb inscriptions where the dead speak from beyond the grave. An early 7th cent. BCE Aramaic inscription from Nerab (southeast of Aleppo) tells of the death of a priest named Siʾ-gabbar. He talks in the first person about the day he died, how he was still able to converse, and how he saw his children mourning over him. The dead Phoenician king Eshmunazor II (ca. 465–451 BCE) contemplates his death: "Surely I am to be pitied. I am snatched away before my time, as a son of a few days I am swept away." The story of the dead Samuel speaking from beyond the grave in 1 Sam 28 reveals that some Israelites also held the belief in a recognizable afterlife existence.

Mortuary inscriptions describe how the ancients feared the prospect of their tombs being desecrated. Attempts to discourage would-be violators included proclaiming that the tomb lacks precious metals (gold, silver, and bronze). Curses are also invoked against the person who opens the tomb. In particular, note the Nerab inscription, the Eshmunazor inscription, the inscription from the Tomb of the Royal Steward located in the Kidron Valley in southeastern Jerusalem (dated to the end of the 8th cent. BCE), and the grave malediction in Isa 14:19.

Anthropologists have long noted the diverse responses to death. A good illustration from the Syro-Canaanite world would be concepts of purity and impurity when coming into contact with the dead. Ancient Israel is known for its elaborate seven-day purification rituals (compare Num 19:13, 20; Ezek 43:7-9). Actions included cleansing with water on the third and seventh day, washing clothes, bathing, and the sprinkling of anything unclean (people, tent, and furnishing) with a mixture of water and ashes from the red cow (Num 19:11-22). While our texts from the Phoenician world are meager, archaeological evidence shows that they too buried their dead at a significant distance away from their living areas. In contrast, at the Late Bronze Age site of Ugarit in ancient Syria tombs are located underneath the houses suggesting that the dead were not thought to be polluting.

The OT describes different types of burials (e.g., in ancestral tombs, in caves, next to trees, communal burials, cremation) that are now known more fully due to archaeology. The OT has scattered passages attesting to a variety of mourning rituals. These included tearing of garments, removing sandals, wearing sackcloth, hair manipulation, fasting, sitting in dirt and ashes, and funeral meals.

Often our window into Levantine death rituals comes through royal/elite depictions (that are not representative of the entire populace). The Judean king Asa's funeral depicts a hewn tomb, aromatic spices placed on a bier, and an elaborate fire ritual (2 Chr 16:14). The commander Abner's funeral (2 Sam 3:31-36) describes several mourning rituals and carrying the body on a bier followed by a royal procession. Among Israel's neighbors, the 10th cent. BCE sarcophagus of Phoenician King Ahiram shows the dead king enthroned and receiving a banquet of some sort. A funerary text from

Ugarit (KTU 1.161) responds to the death of the king (named Niqmaddu) by invoking the ancestral royal dead (called rp'm) to take part in a ceremony to secure his transition to the underworld. Elegant poetry is used to mourn the king's absence from his throne. The Sun goddess secures his proper descent although the details of her role are debated. Some have her burning brightly while others have her escorting the dead king or the ghost throne of the king down to the netherworld. (The latter would line up with the notion that the sun deity descends into the underworld each night and thus is the proper deity to escort the dead to their final abode.) A sevenfold sacrifice accompanies the deceased king's ritual descent. The new ruler (Ammurapi) ascending to the throne then beseeches these "rpum of old" to bless his current administration with well-being (shlm).

It is clear that the dead were not thought to be cut off from the living in the world of the OT. As 1 Sam 28 reveals, some Israelites, like their neighbors, thought that the dead, with proper invocation, could be beseeched to favor the living. Yet firm voices to the contrary (e.g., Deut 18:11; Lev 19:31; 20:6, 27) taught that all forms of NECROMANCY would challenge the prerogatives of Yahweh who alone conquered and controls death. *See* AFTERLIFE; SHEOL.

Bibliography: L. R. Bailey. *Biblical Perspectives on Death* (1979); E. Bloch-Smith. *Judahite Burial Practices and Beliefs about the Dead* (1992); E. Bloch-Smith. "Life in Judah from the Perspective of the Dead." *NEA* 65 (2002) 120–30; M. Gras, P. Rouillard, and J. Teixidor. "The Phoenicians and Death." *Berytus* 39 (1991) 127–76; T. J. Lewis. "How Far Can Texts Take Us? Evaluating Textual Sources for Reconstructing Ancient Israelite Beliefs about the Dead." *Sacred Time, Sacred Space: Archaeology and the Religion of Israel.* B. M. Gittlen, ed. (2002) 169–217; D. Pardee. "Marzi u, Kispu, and the Ugaritic Funerary Cult: A Minimalist View." *Ugarit: Religion and Culture.* N. Wyatt, W. G. E. Watson, and J. B. Lloyd, eds. (1996) 273–87; H. Sysling. *Tehiyyat Ha-Metim: The Resurrection of the Dead in the Palestinian Targums of the Pentateuch and Parallel Traditions in Classical Rabbinic Literature* (1996).

THEODORE J. LEWIS

DEATH, POLLUTION OF. The corpse is the most potent source of ritual impurity in the Bible, causing an unbridgeable distance between Israelite society and the dead. This attitude stands in contrast to neighboring cultures' veneration of the dead, a practice unacceptable to Yahweh, the author of life.

No corpse-contaminated person may enter the sanctuary, which is especially vulnerable to the pollution of death (tame' [טָמֵא] "to become unclean; maweth [מָוֶת] "death"). The high priest is never allowed contact with death, even to bury his own parents (Lev 21:10-11); other priests may attend the burial of certain relatives only (Lev 21:2-3; Ezek 44:25).

Laity who have become corpse-impure, even indirectly, must undergo a week of purification (Num 19:11-20). Although corpse-contamination is not sinful, neglect of purification causes excision from Israel (Num 19:13, 20). Murder and corpses hanging overnight defile the land (Num 35:33; Deut 21:23).

Corpse-impurity concerns increase in Second Temple times. Many Jews bathed immediately after corpse contamination (Tob 2:9), hence the ritual baths found in Judean cemeteries. Herod Antipas had to bribe Jews to live in Tiberias because it was built over graves (*Ant.* 18.36-38). The Temple Scroll requires quarantine and extra purifications of corpse-contaminated persons (11Q19 XLV, 17; XLIX, 21).

According to Matthew, Jesus uses the analogy of beautiful tombs to accuse the Pharisees and scribes of hidden, inner impurity (Matt 23:27). Jews marked graves so that they could easily avoid them, but Luke compares the Pharisees' hypocrisy to unmarked graves (*m. Mo'ed Qat.* 1:2; Luke 11:44; see 10:25-37 for a possible corpse-impurity concern). Jesus' contact with the dead and his own death carry an implicit contamination that is curiously ignored, perhaps intentionally, by the Gospel writers. *See* CLEAN AND UNCLEAN; RED HEIFER.

Bibliography: Hannah Harrington. *The Purity Texts* (2004); Jacob Milgrom. "Rationale for Cultic Law: The Case of Impurity." *Semeia* 45 (1989) 103–109.

HANNAH K. HARRINGTON

DEATH, SECOND [ὁ δεύτερος θάνατος ho deuteros thanatos]. Although the "blessed and holy" will share in the first resurrection (Rev 20:6), on the day of final judgment, according to John's vision (Rev 20:11-15), all will rise from the dead to stand before the white throne and "the one who sits on it," and the books will be opened. One is the Book of Life, a heavenly registry of the righteous; the others record everyone's deeds by which they will be judged. Anyone whose name is not in the book of life will be thrown into the lake of fire to die a second and final time. Death and Hades are no longer temporary places for the dead because they, too, are thrown into the lake of fire. *See* DEATH, NT; HOLY, HOLINESS, NT; LIFE, BOOK OF.

GLENNA S. JACKSON

DEATH OF CHRIST. Jesus' crucifixion under Pontius Pilate is a historical datum with political and theological significance. Generally, for Roman authorities, it demonstrated Roman intolerance of attempts at rebellion. For the Jerusalem leadership, the cross marked Jesus' condemnation as a religious deceiver and false prophet. Among early Christians, the death of Christ served as the means by which God offered salvation and provided the pattern of discipleship.

A. Perspectives on the Death of Jesus of Nazareth

In the waning years of the 20th cent., scholarly interest in Jesus' crucifixion shifted from the question of who killed Jesus, to why he was executed on a Roman cross. What sense does the crucifixion of Jesus make within the story of his life, and within his milieu?

1. Historical evidence

Supported by testimony from Christian, Jewish, and Roman sources, the crucifixion of Jesus under Pontius Pilate is the most secure historical datum we have concerning the historical Jesus. New Testament testimony includes PASSION NARRATIVES noted for their length and detail, the speeches in Acts, and references scattered throughout the NT letters and Revelation. Although some scholars treat the 2nd cent. *Gospel of Peter* as an independent witness to the death of Jesus, most consider it dependent on the NT Gospels with little independent value. The earliest NT witnesses to the crucifixion of Jesus would be the Pauline epistles, including multiple references to the cross and crucifixion (e.g., 1 Cor 1:13, 17-18, 23; 2:2 et al.) and reminiscence of episodes related to Jesus' passion (e.g., 1 Cor 11:23-25; Gal 3:1; compare 1 Tim 6:13). For Paul, "Christ crucified" is the embodiment of the gospel (1 Cor 1:23; compare 1:18). In the speeches in Acts, Jesus' execution is a presupposition shared by speaker and audience (e.g., 2:23, 36; 3:14-15; 5:30; 13:28) and pathein ton Christon (παθεῖν τὸν Χριστον, "suffering of Christ") is a summary of the gospel (e.g., 3:18; 17:3).

First century, extrabiblical evidence is found in the Jewish historian Josephus (*Ant.* 18.63-64). Although part of the paragraph concerning Jesus is suspected of having been added by later by Christian editors, when that material has been removed we read that "when Pilate, because of an accusation made by our leaders, condemned him to the cross, those who had loved him previously did not cease to do so." Early in the 2nd cent. CE, the Roman historian Tacitus notes in his *Annals* that "Christians" take their name from "Christ, who, during the reign of Tiberius, had been executed by the procurator Pontius Pilate" (15.44). A crude graffiti cartoon, probably from the early 2nd cent., portrays a young man worshiping a donkey-headed human figure on a cross. The Greek caption mocks, "Alexamenos worships [his] god"; this may be the oldest depiction of "Christ crucified." Lucian of Samosata (b. ca. 120 CE) wrote a sneering account of a person who had converted to and then rejected Christian faith. Therein, he speaks of "the man who was crucified in Palestine because he introduced this new cult into the world," and describes Christians as "worshiping the crucified sophist" (*Passing of Peregrinus*). As the 2nd cent. Christian apologist Justin Martyr remarks, "They say that our madness consists in the fact that we put a crucified man in second place after the unchangeable and eternal God, the creator of the world" (*1 Apol.* 13.4).

The Roman practice of CRUCIFIXION was guided by its deterrent value. Quintilian (ca. 35–90s CE) observed that "whenever we crucify the guilty, the most crowded roads are chosen, where most people can see and be moved by this fear. For penalties relate not so much to retribution as to their exemplary effect" (*Decl.* 274). Variation in the manner of how victims were affixed to the cross would have provided sadistic entertainment as well as left the victim alive as long as possible for maximum deterrent effect. This means of execution resulted in little blood loss and death came slowly, as the body succumbed to shock.

The horror of the cross was drawn less from the experience of bodily torture and more from the experience of humiliation. Note the focus of the Gospels on attempts to dishonor Jesus: spitting on him (Matt 26:67; 27:30; Mark 14:65; 15:19), striking him in the face and head (Matt 26:67; Mark 14:65; Luke 22:63), ridiculing him (Matt 27:29, 31, 41; Mark 15:20, 31), insulting him (Matt 27:44; Mark 15:32, 34; Luke 22:65), and derisively mocking him (Mark 15:16-20, 29-32; Luke 22:65; 23:11, 35-37); he even suffers the humiliation of having been abandoned by his closest friends. Executed publicly, situated at a major crossroads or on a well-trafficked artery, naked, denied burial, and left as carrion for birds and wild beasts, victims of crucifixion were subject to optimal, unmitigated, vicious ridicule.

2. Roman and Jewish perspectives

Roman governors were charged with taking whatever steps were necessary to maintain the "peace of Rome." Consequently, Pilate's interest would surely have been piqued by such words as these: "He stirs up the people by teaching throughout all Judea . . ." (Luke 23:5). Add to this the teeming masses present in Jerusalem for Passover and Unleavened Bread, the scene of the Triumphal Entry, and Jesus' prophetic action in the Temple, and it is easy to see how Jesus might have seemed a threat to public order. (See Luke 23:2; John 11:47-48.)

Rome did not expose its citizens to this heinous punishment, but reserved crucifixion above all for those who resisted imperial rule. This highlights the importance of the inscription on the cross: "The King of the Jews." This placard, or *titulus*, was a stable ingredient of the passion tradition (Matt 27:37; Mark 15:26; Luke 23:38; John 19:19; compare *Gos. Pet.* 10; *t. Sanh.* 9:7). Jesus is not identified as an "insurrectionist" (compare Matt 26:55; 27:38, 44), but the claim to kingship would have been enough: "Anyone who makes himself king opposes Caesar" (John 19:12). The inscription announcing his offense marks Jesus as a pretender to the throne and thus represents first a Roman (and not a Christian) point of view: Let the cruel execution of Jesus of Nazareth be a lesson to the Jewish population, that Rome will not tolerate any attempt to incite rebellion.

From a Jewish perspective, Jesus could present several problems. 11Q19 LXIV, 6–13 designates those who betray Israel to a foreign power as deserving of the penalty of "hanging on a tree" (Deut 21:22-23). Recall John's report of Caiaphas' decision: if Jesus were allowed to continue his activites, Rome would destroy the Temple and the nation (11:47-53). Blasphemy was long regarded as an infraction punishable by death, and according to the Gospels Jesus was guilty of blasphemy (Matt 26:59-68; Mark 14:55-65). More pervasive is evidence that Jesus had to be eliminated as a religious deceiver and false prophet. This is suggested by the evaluation of Jesus as a deceiver in Matt 27:63 and John 7:11, but especially by the allegations brought against Jesus in Luke 23:2, 14, (echoing language from Deut 13, 17 regarding false prophets): he "perverts our nation/the people." Testimony from Josephus supports this picture ("he was a doer of astounding deeds"; *J.W.* 18.63-64), as do rabbinic traditions describing Jesus as a magician who deceived and led Israel astray (*b. Sanh.* 43a; 107b; compare *b. Sabb.* 104b).

It is here that Jewish and Roman narratives are most intertwined. From within the story of Israel, "leading astray" would characterize Jesus' ministry as the work of a false prophet. In Pilate's hearing, though, "leading the people astray" and "stirring up the people" would have signaled rebellion and civil unrest. Jesus had to die because he made too many enemies who opposed his ministry.

3. Jesus and his death

The possibility that Jesus contemplated his own violent death is supported by several observations. From early in his public life, Jesus was met with opposition and his ministry was enveloped in conflict. Jesus' predecessor, John the Baptist, lost his life at the hands of Herod Antipas; was this not a warning to Jesus? The tradition is clear that Jesus regarded himself in prophetic terms (Matt 11:9; 14:5; 21:11, 46; Mark 6:4; Luke 7:16; 13:33; 22:64; 24:19; John 4:19; 6:14; 7:40; 9:17), but the fate of all the prophets is rejection and death (e.g., Neh 9:26; Jer 2:30; *Jub.* 1:12). Jesus repeatedly predicts the suffering of his followers (e.g., Mark 8:34-38; 10:38-39; 14:27-28; Matt 10:25; Luke

21:12-16); would their suffering not presume his own? In addition to the explicit predictions of Jesus' suffering and death (e.g., Mark 8:31; 9:31; 10:33-34), the Gospels contain numerous, indirect sayings, and in a variety of forms (parables, aphorisms, etc.), through which Jesus anticipates a violent end (e.g., Mark 2:20; 9:12-13; 10:38, 45; 12:1-12).

If Jesus anticipated his death, would he not also have reflected on its significance? His mission in the Gospels is directed toward revitalizing Israel as the people of God. Pursuing this aim compelled him to proclaim the intervention of God's rule and to embody the ethics of this kingdom, and this practice caused conflict with his contemporaries. From this perspective, all of Jesus' activities become relevant to his execution; everything—his interpretation of Israel's Scriptures, his practices of prayer and worship, his astounding choice of table companions, his crossing of the boundaries of clean and unclean, his engagement with children, his miracles of healing and exorcism—leads to the cross. Jesus' mission led to a form of execution emblematic of a way of life that rejected the value of public opinion in the determination of status before God, and inspired interpretations of his death that accorded privilege to the redemptive power of righteous suffering.

Jesus was able to gather together Israel's history and hopes and from them forge a view of himself as the one through whose suffering Israel, and through Israel the nations, would experience redemption. In elucidating the significance of his looming death, Jesus pushed backward into Israel's history and embraced Israel's expectations for deliverance. At the table on his last night with his followers, at a meal rich with the imagery of Passover and exodus, he intimated that the new exodus, God's decisive act of deliverance, was coming to fruition in his death, the climax of his mission. (*See* LAST SUPPER, THE) Moreover, he developed the meaning of his death in language and images grounded in the constitution of Israel as the covenant people of God (Exod 24:8), the conclusion of the exile (see Zech 9:9-11), and the hope of a new covenant (Jer 31:31-33), so as to mark his death as the inaugural event of covenant renewal. How could Jesus contemplate such thoughts? Taken together with his prophetic action in the Temple, the symbolic actions at the table of Jesus' last meal with his disciples signify the disestablishment of the old ordering of Israel's life and, by means of God's great act of deliverance in his sacrificial death, the establishment of a new basis of Israel's life before God.

B. The Death of Christ in the NT

With a plethora of images, drawn from both the OT and the Greco-Roman world, early Christian interpretation of the death of Christ took many forms. These congregate around two poles: the cross as the means by which God achieved salvation (that is, the death of Jesus as an ATONEMENT) and its paradigmatic significance for Christ's followers. The saving efficacy of Jesus' death is developed in a variety of ways—e.g., in terms of sacrifice, as a demonstration of God's love, and as a conquering of evil. As a pattern of discipleship, Jesus' passion exemplified service and ennobled undeserved suffering for those who embody God's ways in a world hostile to God. When exploring the theological significance of the death of Christ, interpreters should not overlook the inescapably political nature of the cross in the NT world. It could not be forgotten then, and must not be forgotten now, that Jesus was crucified as a threat to Rome and his acceptance of his death was his rejection of the politics of coercion and violence.

1. The Synoptic Gospels and Acts

In the Gospels, the life and ministry of Jesus involve scenes of conflict, the voicing of threats, and predictions of Jesus' demise by Jesus himself and others—all by way of declaring the inseparability of Jesus' mission and his meaningful death.

For the Gospel of Matthew, Jesus' crucifixion underscores his fidelity to God, his faithfulness to his mission, and his purposeful sharing in the suffering of his people. From the Gospel's opening chapters, he is God's Messiah (1:1), Jesus ("for he will save his people from their sins" [1:21]), and Emmanuel ("God is with us" [1:23]), but as one "born king of the Jews" (2:2), he is also the focus of fear and violent hostility (2:3-18). The tension between these two assessments reaches its conclusion in the Gospel's final chapters, in which Jesus proclaims in his death the forgiveness of sins (26:28) and dies as the king of Israel who "saved others" but was unable to "save himself" (27:42). The centrality of the cross to Jesus' ministry is witnessed in 20:28, where he casts his mission in the language of sacrificial death. While presenting his death as a model of other-oriented service, Jesus sets cross-bearing as the standard for faithful discipleship. More than the other Gospels, Matthew portrays Jesus' death as an apocalyptic event, particularly in 27:51-54, which recounts cosmic portents associated with the coming of the eschaton.

The death of Jesus broods over Mark's Gospel even more than the others. This may be surprising, since the first two-thirds of the Gospel portray Jesus as a wonder-worker. Already in those early chapters, though, we find forebodings of Jesus' impending death—perhaps as early as 2:18-20, where Jesus anticipates a time "when the bridegroom is taken away" (2:20); and certainly in 3:6, where a plot against Jesus is set in motion. In a series of passion predictions (8:31; 9:31; 10:33-34; compare 9:12), Jesus demonstrates awareness of his fate and ties his suffering, death, and resurrection into the divine plan. Indeed, his death lies at the center of God's salvific plan (10:45; 14:24). At the same time, he expresses the inevitability of suffering for one so fully oriented toward the will of God in the midst of "this adulterous and sinful generation" (8:38). Jesus' suffer-ing and death come not in spite of his miracle-working and teaching, but because of them; his powerful words and deeds provide the impetus for the opposition against him. For Mark's Gospel, the connection between Jesus' mission and suffering and that of his followers is tightly drawn. On the one hand, he summarizes his mission as having come "to serve, and to give his life a ransom for many" (10:45)—this in the midst of his instruction to his disciples to extend themselves likewise in sacrificial service (10:35-45; compare 8:27-38). On the other hand, in Mark 13 Jesus predicts the impending suffering of his followers, speaking of events and using language with close parallels to the account of Jesus' own suffering in Mark 14–15. In this way, Mark shows that the suffering of Jesus' followers comprises a participation in the suffering of the Messiah.

In comparison with the other synoptic writers, Luke seems less concerned with the atoning significance of Jesus' death (though see Luke 22:19-20; Acts 20:28), but if anything is even more emphatic about the place of Christ's suffering in the divine plan. In fact, the resurrected Jesus claims that the pattern of messianic suffering and resurrection is the means by which to order a faithful reading of the Scriptures of Israel (Luke 24:25-27). Like other NT writers, Luke insists that, with the advent of Jesus, the age of salvation has dawned. However, Luke emphasizes the exaltation of Jesus (i.e., his resurrection and ascension) and Jesus' outpouring of the Holy Spirit at Pentecost as history's turning points. This does not denude the cross of significance, however, but it does refocus it. For Luke, Jesus dies as the Righteous One of God who, from the cross, is able to pronounce forgiveness and promise paradise (Luke 23:34, 43). Moreover, opposition to Jesus and, in Acts, opposition to his followers serves to promote the progress of the gospel: "It is through many persecutions that we must enter the kingdom of God" (Acts 14:22). Jesus' description of discipleship as "taking up the cross" is uniquely modified in Luke's version, with "daily" signaling the paradigmatic character of Jesus' suffering. Finally, drawing on Deut 21:23 in his representation of Jesus' execution "on a tree" (Acts 5:30; 10:39; 13:29), Luke highlights the cross of Christ as the ultimate humiliation of God's Anointed One, interpreting the death of Jesus as the center point of the divine-human struggle over how life is to be lived, whether in self-aggrandizement or humility. In his death and resurrection, then, Jesus both exemplifies and provides the basis for the way of salvation.

2. The Pauline letters

The cross is the primary point of reference in Paul's thought world, the lens through which to understand the character of God, the basis of salvation, and the nature of Christian existence. For Paul, Christ so fully identifies with God's purpose that his own self-giving in death is an expression of God's own love (e.g., Rom

5:1-10). Paul's atonement theology is highly developed, drawing together traditional formulations (e.g., 1 Cor 15:3) and a wide array of metaphors, many drawn from Israel's Scriptures but also from the wider culture. For example, in Gal 3:10-14, Paul amalgamates images of Christ as the representative of Israel in whose death the covenant culminates, justification, redemption, exodus, substitution, sacrifice, the promise of the Spirit, and triumph over the powers. The death of Christ serves for Paul also as a means for interpreting his suffering as an apostle as well as the persecution of others (e.g., 2 Cor 4:7-12; 5:10–6:13; Col 1:24) and as the model and measure of faithfulness (e.g., 1 Cor 11:17-34; Phil 2:6-11). Christ's death "for us" inaugurates new life, but, because it is "in Christ," this new life must be conformed to his.

3. The Johannine writings

For the Gospel of John, the love of God is manifest in the sending of God's Son into the world "so that everyone who believes in him may not perish but may have eternal life" (3:16)—a claim grounded in the INCARNATION but also in the sacrificial nature of Jesus' death (see, e.g., 1:29, 36; 6:51; 10:11, 15; 11:50-52; 18:14; and the portrayal of the crucifixion as a paschal sacrifice in 18:28; 19:14, 19:29 [Exod 12:22], 19:35 [Exod 12:13], 19:31-37 [Exod 12:46]). This is true in spite of the world's rejection of Jesus as the Logos of God (e.g., 1:9-13). Additionally, the Fourth Evangelist interprets Jesus' death as his "raising up" or "exaltation"—that is, as the culmination of the soteriological journey of God's Son, who came from heaven and, in his death and resurrection, returns to heaven (3:13-14, 31; 6:38; 8:23, 28; 12:32-34; 13:1-3). More than the other Gospels, John portrays Jesus as the master of his own fate; he knows his betrayer (6:70) and initiates his own betrayal (13:27), identifies himself at the scene of his arrest (18:1-11), is present before Pilate as a king and judge (18:28–19:16), bears his own cross (19:17), and dies of his own accord (19:20-33). These actions exemplify Jesus' words in 10:17-18: "For this reason the Father loves me, because I lay down my life in order to take it up again. No one takes it from me, but I lay it down of my own accord. I have power to lay it down, and I have power to take it up again."

For the author of 1 John, the significance of Jesus' death is interpreted in exemplary terms (3:16; compare 4:7-11) and as an atonement (2:2). Particular emphasis falls on the death of Jesus as a "sin offering," with the author describing Jesus' death with language from the OT (1:7, 9; 4:10; compare, e.g., Lev 16:16, 30; 25:9). This is similar to Paul's presentation of the efficacy of Jesus' blood (Rom 3:25; 5:9; Eph 1:7; 2:13; Col 1:20) as a sin offering (Rom 8:3; 2 Cor 5:21), an understanding of sacrifice in terms of exchange and representation: sin and death transferred to the sacrificial victim, its purity and life to those who receive the benefits of the sacrifice. Here, the death of Jesus wipes away sin and its effects. Substitution is clearly at the heart of sacrifice of such texts, but the metaphor is economic (exchange) rather than penal (satisfaction) (*see* SACRIFICES AND OFFERINGS).

The death of Jesus plays a pivotal role in the book of Revelation. Integrating images from Israel's experience of exodus and Isaiah's portrait of the Servant of Yahweh, Christ is the Passover Lamb of the New Exodus, whose death is key to the ransom and liberation (i.e., exodus) of God's people, and, indeed, obtains their redemption (e.g., 1:5; 5:6, 9-10; for exodus imagery, see esp. 15:1–16:21). Christ's death is the means by which Christ has conquered the forces of evil (e.g., 5:11-12)—and, then, the instrument by which his followers are likewise to engage in battle against those forces. Those who follow the Lamb do so by recapitulating in their lives his faithfulness, even to the point of their suffering like him so as to participate also in his glory: "But they have conquered him by the blood of the Lamb and by the word of their testimony, for they did not cling to life even in the face of death" (12:11).

4. Other New Testament letters

Among the remaining NT materials, the death of Christ figures centrally in two: Hebrews and 1 Peter.

Hebrews develops Jesus' death in three interrelated ways (chaps. 9–10). First, Christ's noble death is the paramount expression of his obedience. Because Jesus' obedience is representative of the obedience of all and is accepted by God as a perfect sacrifice, people are to follow Jesus, leader and pioneer, in the journey of obedience to God. Second, Jesus' death ratifies the (new) covenant between God and his people, providing the measure of faithful behavior for God's covenant partners (compare Heb 9:19-21; Exod 24:1-8). Third, the sacrificial death of Jesus echoes the annual ceremony of the DAY OF ATONEMENT (Lev 16). Focusing attention on the sacrificial goat of Lev 16, Hebrews identifies Jesus as the sinless, sacrificial victim who cleanses the sin that is an affront to God in order to lead people into God's presence.

In its major christological passages (1:18-21; 2:21-25; 3:18-22), 1 Peter emphasizes the liberating death of Christ, the paradigmatic suffering of Christ, and the character of Christ's journey through suffering to glory, all for the salvation of God's people. This accent on Christ's suffering is crucial for Peter's message to a Christian audience whose faithfulness to God has led to marginal existence in the world. Christ provides the model of innocent suffering (2:19-20; 3:16-17; 4:1-2, 13-16), exemplifying faithfulness in suffering both in his refusal to retaliate and because his suffering was undeserved. Christ provides the model of effective suffering. As his death served as the basis of liberation (1:2, 19; 3:18), so the suffering of his followers is a form of witness with the potential of turning disbelievers to God (2:12, 15; 3:1-2). Moreover, the suffering of Christ's followers is a participation in the suffering of Christ—that is, in the messianic woes by which the age of salvation is actualized (4:12-19). Finally, Christ provides the model of the vindication of the suffering righteous (1:11; 2:20; 4:13-14; 5:1, 10). His life proves that suffering on account of faithfulness to God is neither the whole nor the end of the story, but is a precursor to vindication and glory.

Bibliography: Raymond E. Brown. *The Death of the Messiah: From Gethsemane to the Grave: A Commentary on the Passion Narratives in the Four Gospels.* 2 vols. (1994); John T. Carroll and Joel B. Green. *The Death of Jesus in Early Christianity* (1995); Morna D. Hooker. *Not Ashamed of the Gospel: New Testament Interpretations of the Death of Christ* (1994); Larry W. Hurtado. "Jesus' Death as Paradigmatic in the New Testament." *SJT* 57 (2004) 413–33; Scot McKnight. *Jesus and His Death: Historiography, the Historical Jesus, and Atonement Theory* (2005); N. T. Wright. *Jesus and the Victory of God* (1996).

JOEL B. GREEN

DEATH OF JOSEPH. *See* JOSEPH THE CARPENTER, HISTORY OF.

DEBIR dee´buhr [דְּבִיר *devir*]. The meaning of the name is unclear. Most interpreters use an Arabic root meaning "to be after someone or something" and argue that the name means remote village or the like. Yet the word in Hebrew also identifies the interior of a temple, so it may refer to a city that was known for a temple.

1. A king of Eglon mentioned in Josh 10:3 who was part of an Amorite force that opposed Joshua.

2. A Canaanite city south of Hebron in the hill country of Judah that was conquered by Joshua. Joshua 10:38-39 describes how the Israelites "turned back" to the south and defeated Debir after other major cities in the Shephelah and the Judean hill country were conquered (compare also Josh 12:3). The earlier name of the city was Kiriath-sepher (Josh 15:15, 49 [with LXX], Judg 1:11). Joshua 15:15-19 specifies that Othniel (Caleb's brother) was the one responsible for the defeat of Kiriath-sepher (= Debir). As a reward, Othniel was given Caleb's daughter (Achsah) as a wife. Achsah in turn received from her father a wedding gift consisting of a field near Debir with upper and lower springs (see below for the importance of this field for the identification of Debir with Khirbet Rabûd).

For many years, William F. Albright made popular the identification of Debir with Tell Beit Mirsim. Albright pointed to the lack of cities (including those of small size) with known Canaanite remains from the Late Bronze Age south of Hebron in the Judean hill country. (Joshua is usually associated with the ending of the Late Bronze Age.) While Tell Beit Mirsim lies in the Shephelah and not the hill country, it does fit

several other aspects of the biblical description. Tell Beit Mirsim lies about 11 mi. southwest of Hebron and is on the border of the hill country. Moreover, Tell Beit Mirsim exhibited significant remains from the Late Bronze Age, and it also had a large destruction layer from that period. Albright thus claimed that the tell was physical evidence of Joshua's destruction of the Canaanite city Debir. Even though Albright's identification has been disproved with more recent data and exploration, it remains popular in some circles.

Moshe Kochavi's excavations provided evidence that biblical Debir should be associated with Khirbet Rabûd rather than Tell Beit Mirsim. Kochavi (following Galling's earlier arguments) pointed out that all of the biblical references place Debir in the Judean hill country and not in the Shephelah. Of special note is Josh 11:21, which identifies Debir as one of the cities of the Anakim in the hill country. Other references mention Debir as lying south of Hebron (again in the hill country and not the Shephelah). Kochavi's excavations at Khirbet Rabûd revealed a significant Canaanite city from the Late Bronze Age (something not known at the time of Albright's proposal), and Kochavi pointed out that Khirbet Rabûd fits the biblical picture better than Tell Beit Mirsim. Moreover, there is no other site with significant Canaanite remains in the Judean hill country south of Hebron, so Khirbet Rabûd most probably controlled all of the area south of Hebron during the time period of Joshua. Further, the water system at Khirbet Rabûd corresponds to the account of Achsah, Caleb's daughter, who is granted the upper and lower springs in the vicinity of Debir (Josh 15:13-19).

Kochavi's excavations reveal nearly continuous occupation from the Late Bronze Age through the end of the Iron Age. The excavations were limited to two trenches and an exploration of cemetery remains, so a comprehensive picture of the city is lacking. Still, erosion and large amounts of exposed bedrock allow one to trace almost all of an expansive city wall that surrounded the settlement in antiquity. Kochavi's team identified at least four major periods of occupation. The Late Bronze Age city had at least four phases and was fortified by a large city wall. The wall may have been reused in the Iron Age, and there are strata pointing to occupation during the 12th, 10th, 8th, and 7th and 6th cent. BCE. There is evidence for destruction layers in both the late 8th cent. (probably by Sennacherib in 701 BCE) and in the early 6th cent. (probably by Nebuchadnezzar in the early 6th cent. BCE). These archaeological data are consistent with the biblical references that describe Debir as being a major Canaanite city (see above) and then a district capital in the southern part of the hill country of Judah (see Josh 15:49).

3. A settlement mentioned on the northern border of Judah toward Gilgal and opposite the ascent of Adummim (Josh 15:7).

4. A city mentioned in the inheritance of Gad (Josh 13:26) in the land of Gilead.

Bibliography: W. F. Albright. *The Archaeology of Palestine and the Bible* (1932); W. F. Albright. *The Excavations of Tell Beit Mirsim. AASOR.* Vols. 21–22. (1930–43); F. M. Cross and G. E. Wright. "The Boundary and Province Lists of the Kingdom of Judah." *JBL* 75 (1956) 202–26; M. Kochavi. "Khirbet Rabûd = Debir." *TA* 1 (1974) 1–33.

ANDREW G. VAUGHN

DEBORAH deb´uh-ruh [דְּבֹרָה devorah; Δεββωρά Debbōra]. 1. Rebekah's nurse. She was a significant enough figure that her death rates mention (Gen 35:8). Furthermore, the spot near Bethel where Deborah died was named ʾallon bakhuth (אַלּוֹן בָּכוּת), or "Oak of Weeping," suggesting substantial grief at her loss.

LISA MICHELE WOLFE

2. A judge and prophet. An Israelite leader, Deborah ("honey bee") is introduced in Judg 4:4 with a string of designations: "Deborah, a woman, a prophet, the wife of Lappidoth (or "fiery woman"), was judging Israel at that time." The only female judge and the only named prophet in Judges, she is also the only biblical individual called "a mother in Israel" (5:7).

Israelites come to Deborah for judgment under "the palm of Deborah" between Ramah and Bethel. Like other prophets (1 Sam 15:3; 1 Kgs 20:13; 2 Kgs 9:7), she incites war, summoning BARAK ("lightning") from Naphtali and ordering him to fight SISERA, the general of Jabin, the Canaanite king of Hazor. Barak agrees to go only if Deborah will accompany him. She consents, warning that God will deliver Sisera to a woman rather than to him. As battle approaches, she urges Barak with assurances of God's presence. With divine assistance, Barak and the soldiers of Zebulun and Naphtali destroy the army. But Sisera seeks refuge with an ally, Heber the Kenite, whose wife JAEL lulls the exhausted general to sleep and murders him with hammer and tent peg. Thus Deborah's word is confirmed in an ironic, unexpected way. Lack of confidence in a woman's prophecy loses Barak his full victory; mistaken confidence in a woman's caregiving forfeits Sisera's life. Two women share glory—one for calling the battle, the other for concluding it.

Judges 5 consists of a triumphant song of Deborah with Barak. Generally considered one of the Bible's oldest texts, its details differ somewhat from those of the prose account. The role call of tribes mustered and missing is more elaborate and fails to correspond fully to the Pentateuch's twelve-tribe scheme. God participates with a torrent in the Wadi Kishon. Jael evidently murders Sisera while he is standing. Sisera's mother is pictured waiting at the palace window, speculating that her son is dividing spoil, including women for the soldiers and embroidery for herself. Though a product of poetic imagination, this mother elucidates the threat posed to women by callous enemies, both warriors and women. Deborah as "mother in Israel" and Sisera's mother become counterparts, while Jael, caught between the two armies, is praised for her cunning (*see* DEBORAH, SONG OF).

Though Barak is included in heroes' lists in 1 Sam 12:11 and Heb 11:32, Deborah is not mentioned outside of Judges. Historical questions regarding roles attributed to Deborah are finally unanswerable; nevertheless, readers are fascinated by the matter-of-fact recognition in Judg 4–5 of a woman who prophesied, judged, commanded a commander, and rode to war.

Bibliography: Susan Ackerman. *Warrior, Dancer, Seductress, Queen: Women in Judges and Biblical Israel* (1998); Barnabas Lindars. *Judges 1–5: A New Translation and Commentary* (1995); Klaas Spronk. "Deborah, a Prophetess: The Meaning and Background of Judges 4:4-5." *The Elusive Prophet: The Prophet as a Historical Person, Literary Character, and Anonymous Artist.* Johannes C. De Moor, ed. (2001) 232–42.

PATRICIA K. TULL

3. Mother of Tobit's father, Tobiel. She taught Tobit his scrupulous observance of tithing and instilled in him the law of Moses after his father's death had left him an orphan (Tob 1:8).

EMILY R. CHENEY

DEBORAH, SONG OF. The poem in Judg 5:2-30 (31) is commonly called the "Song of Deborah." Widely regarded as one of the oldest compositions in the OT, the song is characterized by repetitive style, vivid imagery, and a rapid montage of scenes. The related prose account in Judg 4, different in detail and emphasis, is deemed by most to be later than the poem and, at least partially, dependent upon it. A lively minority opinion disputes both the early dating and literary priority of the poem.

Numerous lines in the received text are clear to anyone knowledgeable in biblical Hebrew. Others raise grave difficulties. Extensive versional witnesses indicate that the song was popular in late antiquity and that points of clarity and obscurity coincide for ancient and modern translators. Assumptions about the overall nature of the poem inevitably influence attempts at textual and/or linguistic illumination of the obscurities.

The poem's genre has been variously characterized as victory song and thus close to the "events" it recounts: ballad, hymn of praise, and liturgy. Several more recent studies emphasize its use of taunt motifs and hypothesize that it was used before battle to muster volunteer troops. Given the song's prolonged use, not all of these suggestions are mutually exclusive.

Seemingly disparate elements in the song reveal vital connections upon analysis. The theophany in vv.

4-5 anticipates the role of the Wadi KISHON in vv. 20-21. Israelite upland peasants mustered by a female charismatic leader face the mighty lowland chariots of SISERA and the kings of Canaan. Yahweh is the great equalizer. Those who brave the odds are praised lavishly. Those less immediately threatened who cautiously sit it out are condemned. Roles of gender and power are reversed to heighten the irony. In language dripping with innuendo, the perennial victims of warfare and rape triumph over their would-be oppressors. *See* DEBORAH; JUDGES, BOOK OF.

MARVIN L. CHANEY

DEBT, DEBTOR. In the ANE debts often forced people into slavery when they were unable to repay. Hammurabi's laws indicate loan interest rates at 20% for money and 33% for grain. Loans were extended usually by temples, and sometimes by kings, for canal construction, buildings, business expansion, mortgages, and trade ventures. The recipients of such loans often could afford such high interest rates because of their own profit margin. However, peasants and middle class artisans, who were unable to repay, fell into debt slavery, and at various times up to half of the population in a Mesopotamian city could be debt slaves. In Babylon, in the early second millennium BCE, the kings intervened at irregular intervals and released debts and debt slaves with misharum or anduraru edicts in order to reinvigorate the economy (and perhaps to weaken the power of the temple priests, his rivals, who extended loans). In NT times throughout the Graeco-Roman world interest rates ran between 10% and 30%, so people also fell into debt slavery or debtor's prison (*see* SLAVERY).

Israelite society was less complex than Mesopotamian society, so there was less need for business loans. According to the OT loans were meant to help impoverished fellow Israelites; hence, interest was forbidden (Exod 22:25, Lev 25:36-37, Deut 23:19). Interest could be levied on a loan to a "foreigner," and the word may mean "merchant" (Deut 23:20), a person probably with the financial ability to repay loans with interest. Similarly creditors were limited in terms of pledges, surety, or collateral that they could require from a person when extending a loan, lest a poor person lose an item necessary for survival if the debt were not repaid (Exod 22:26-27, Deut 24:6, 10-13, 17).

The biblical text, however, implies that interest indeed was charged on loans, poor people could not repay loans, and they lost their collateral. If they had no collateral, a family member, the borrower, or the borrower's entire family might go into debt slavery. People were pressured into taking loans by the manipulation of the economy by the rich, who used questionable buying and selling practices. Debt slavery occurred both in preexilic (2 Kgs 4:1-7) and post-exilic times (Neh 5:1-13).

Ultimately, provisions were made for the periodic release of debts and debt slaves. The Deuteronomic institution of SABBATICAL YEAR (Deut 15:1-18) mandated a release of debts and debt slaves every seven years, and the Levitical institution of Jubilee Year mandated not only the release of debts and debt slaves but additionally called for the return of land every fifty years to the families who originally owned it (Lev 25:8-55, 27:16-25). Scholars compare these texts to the misharum and anduraru edicts of Mesopotamia. Scholars suspect that Sabbatical Year was practiced regularly in the postexilic era, but that Jubilee Year may have been only an idealistic vision.

The biblical text attests to the heartache experienced by people who fell into debt and debt slavery. Debtor families joined David when he was an outlaw in the wilderness (1 Sam 22:2), and narratives recall how people were lost in debt slavery (2 Kgs 4:1-7, Neh 5:5). Laws in the OT responded to this plight of the poor. Elisha (9th cent. BCE) does not know of legislation to protect the widow's sons (2 Kgs 4:1-7), so he works a wonder to help her repay her debt. But by the middle of the 5th cent. BCE, Nehemiah refers to the Sabbatical Year law (Neh 10:31). In NT times the existence of loans was assumed (Matt 25:27, Luke 16:5-7, 19:23) and Jesus spoke both of debt slavery (Matt 18:25) and debtor's PRISON (Matt 18:30).

Elsewhere in the text we hear rhetorical testimony about the evils of debt. Psalm 37:21 says the wicked borrow and do not repay. Proverbs 22:7 and Sir 18:33 warn against getting into debt. Jeremiah 15:10 and Sir 29:28 imply that lenders and borrowers cursed each other. The prophets and other religious spokespersons condemned those who manipulated people into debt and debt slavery, charged interest, and unfairly withheld pledges (Neh 5:7-11, Job 22:6, 24:3, Amos 2:8, 8:6, Ezek 18:7-17, 22:12, 33:15).

There appears to be a development in the legal tradition of Israel that increasingly championed the rights of the poor and oppressed, and this appears to be evident in laws concerning debt and debt slavery. The Covenant Code or Book of the Covenant (Exod 21:2-23:19), which is dated by scholars anywhere from the 11th to the late 8th cent. BCE, offers the basic prohibitions. Exodus 22:25 bans the imposition of interest upon a loan. Exodus 22:26-27 prohibits the creditor from retaining the cloak of a poor man overnight, if the cloak were taken as surety on a loan. Exodus 21:2-6 provides for the release of a debt slave in his seventh year of service, but he may stay a permanent slave to remain with a wife and children, if they became his family during his servitude.

The Deuteronomic Laws (Deut 12-26) emerged in the late 7th cent. BCE during Josiah's reform and they reflect prophetic influence. They appear to address some of the loopholes in the laws of the Covenant Code in protecting the weak and the poor. Deuteronomy

23:19-20 condemns a special form of interest, the neshekh (נֶשֶׁךְ) or the "bite" or "rapacious extraction," which may be a preliminary portion taken out of the loan. (I loan you $100, but only give you $90, and you repay the full $100.) This appears to have been a clever attempt to charge interest without literally breaking the law in Exod 22:25. Deut 24:6, 10-13, 17 seems to expand upon the guidelines for surety. Verse 6 mandates that millstones for grinding grain to make bread may not be taken as collateral, lest the poor person starve. Verse 17 declares that the cloak of a widow should never be taken, and that appears to build upon the cloak imperative of Exod 22:26-27. Verses 10-13 prohibit the creditor from entering the poor person's home to pick the surety of his choice, a new law altogether. Deuteronomy 15:1-11 declares that every seventh year all debts nationwide are released (Sabbath Year). Deuteronomy 15:12-18 expands upon the debt slave release guidelines of Exod 21:2-6. Because this text follows directly after the law on nationwide debt release, it may imply that debt slaves also should be released simultaneously every seven years (though v. 18 may imply otherwise). If so, all debt slaves are released every seven years to prevent dishonest counting of years for individual slaves by the slave owners, which circumvented Exod 21:2-6. This new law also applies to women slaves, not just men. Slave owners are to provide released debt slaves with provisions to prevent them from quickly returning into debt and debt slavery. Debt slaves may become permanent slaves out of love for their masters (vv. 16–17), and since reference to the slaves' families is missing as a reason for remaining, commentators assume that freed slaves could take newly acquired families with them into freedom. Thus, Deuteronomic Laws appear to build upon and move beyond the laws of Exodus.

Finally, priestly Levitical laws, dated variously from the 8th to the 5th cent. BCE, most likely took final organized and written form in the 6th cent. BCE Babylonian Exile or beyond. The laws connected to the Jubilee Year (Lev 25:8-55, 27:16-25) provide guidelines for interest, debt, and debt slaves. Leviticus 25:36-37 prohibits placing a marbith (מַרְבִּית) or a tarbith (תַּרְבִּית) on a loan. The word may mean "increase," "profit," or "gift," but it probably was another attempt to circumvent Exod 22:25 by calling this "added thing" something other than interest. Leviticus 25:39-55 mandates the release of debt slaves on the Jubilee Year every fifty years (Lev 25:39-55). Verse 41 expressly mentions that the entire family, including children, may leave at that time, another expansion of Exod 21:2-6. Jubilee Year makes the slave release more effective than the laws connected to Sabbatical Year in Deut 15 by adding land restoration to the release. Laws in Deuteronomy and Leviticus build upon the laws in Exodus, but the two codes do not seem to be aware of each other on these particular issues, for they provide different solu-

tions. (A few scholars, however, maintain that the laws complement each other by suggesting that the release of slaves in the fifty year Jubilee applied to debt slaves who had opted to become permanent slaves under Exodus guidelines, and they suggest that Deuteronomy's Sabbath Year did not really release the family created during the debt slavery experience.)

Regardless of scholarly viewpoints, all agree that throughout the law codes we see an increased attempt by legislation to help the plight of debt slaves and debt-ridden people. Whether these biblical texts were actual legal guidelines or inspirational religious rhetoric, we do not know.

In the later Rabbinic age Hillel provided a mechanism called the "prozbul" (perozbol פְּרוֹזְבּוֹל) by which debts could be carried past the Sabbatical Year of debt release: one simply turned the debt over to a court which would collect the debt later. This enabled poor persons to obtain loans just before the Sabbatical Year might arrive; otherwise credit would dry up completely in Jewish society. This, too, was a humanitarian gesture.

In the later Jewish and Christian traditions the concept of "debt" takes on figurative meanings, most often connected to the idea of sin and forgiveness. In the Aramaic TARGUMS the words "debt" and "debtor" take on meanings of "sin" and "sinner" (especially in the Targum of Isaiah), and these meanings carry over into the NT. God forgives our "debts" according to the Lord's Prayer in Matt 6:12 (though Luke 11:4 says simply that we are "indebted"). The word is also used with the nuance of religious obligation to someone: Paul was in debt to those to whom he preached (Rom 1:14) and we are all debtors to those who minister to us (Rom 15:27). *See* INTEREST; MONEY, COINS; SURETY.

Bibliography: Robert Gnuse. *You Shall Not Steal* (1985).

ROBERT GNUSE

DECALOGUE. *See* TEN COMMANDMENTS.

DECAPOLIS di-kap′uh-lis [Δεκάπολις *Dekapolis*]. Literally means "Ten Cities" and refers to a group of Greek cities located in southern Syria, northern Palestine, and the northern Transjordan. These cities are linked geographically, culturally, historically, administratively, and perhaps politically.

A. Literary References to the Decapolis
B. Cities of the Decapolis
C. Identification of the Cities
D. History of the Decapolis
Bibliography

A. Literary References to the Decapolis
The first literary reference mentioning this region of cities can be found in the Synoptic Gospels. The crowds

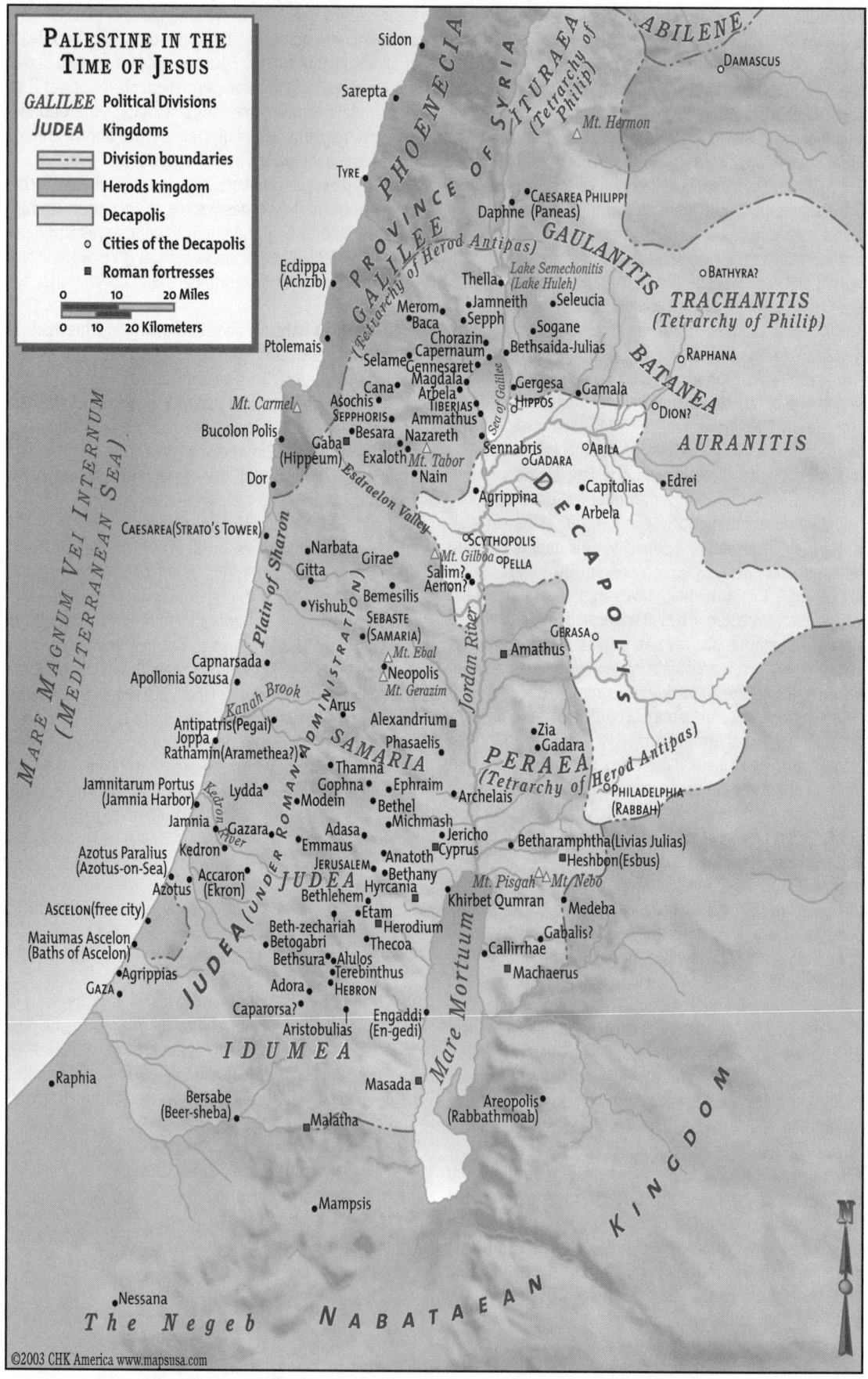

PALESTINE IN THE TIME OF JESUS

GALILEE Political Divisions
JUDEA Kingdoms

Division boundaries
Herods kingdom
Decapolis

○ Cities of the Decapolis
■ Roman fortresses

0   10   20 Miles
0   10   20 Kilometers

ABILENE

Sidon
○ DAMASCUS

PHOENECIA

Sarepta

PROVINCE OF SYRIA

ITURAEA
(Tetrarchy of Philip)

Mt. Hermon △

TYRE

GALILEE

CAESAREA PHILIPPI
Daphne (Paneas)

GAULANITIS

(Tetrarchy of Herod Antipas)

Ecdippa
(Achzib)

Thella
Jamneith
Merom
Baca
Selame
Sepph
Seleucia

Lake Semechonitis
(Lake Huleh)

○ BATHYRA?

TRACHANITIS
(Tetrarchy of Philip)

Ptolemais

Chorazin
Capernaum
Gennesaret
Magdala
Cana
Arbela
TIBERIAS
Ammathus
Nazareth

Sogane
Bethsaida-Julias

Gergesa
Hippos

Gamala

○ RAPHANA

○ DION?

BATANEA

AURANITIS

Mt. Carmel △
Bucolon Polis

Asochis
SEPPHORIS
Gaba
(Hippeum)
Besara
Exaloth
Mt. Tabor △
Nain

Sennabris

Sea of Galilee

○ ABILA

GADARA

DECAPOLIS

Capitolias
Edrei

Arbela

Dor

Agrippina

Caesarea (Strato's Tower)

Narbata
Gitta
Girae
Yishub
Bemesilis

Salim?
Aenon?

SCYTHOPOLIS
Mt. Gilboa △ ○ PELLA

Plain of Sharon

SEBASTE
(SAMARIA)

GERASA ○

Amathus

Mare Magnum vei Internum
(Mediterranean Sea)

Capnarsada
Apollonia Sozusa

Kanah Brook

Mt. Ebal △
Neopolis
Mt. Gerazim

Jordan River

Antipatris (Pegai)
Joppa
Rathamin (Aramethea?)

Arus
Alexandrium
Phasaelis
Thamna

SAMARIA

Zia
Gadara

PERAEA
(Tetrarchy of Herod Antipas)

Jamnitarum Portus
(Jamnia Harbor)

Kedron River

Lydda

Gophna
Modein
Bethel
Adasa
Emmaus

Ephraim
Michmash

Archelais

PHILADELPHIA
(RABBAH)

Jamnia
Gazara
Azotus Paralius
(Azotus-on-Sea)
Accaron
(Ekron)
Azotus

Kedron

Anatoth

JERUSALEM
Bethany
Hyrcania

JUDEA

Jericho
Cyprus

Betharamphtha (Livias Julias)
Heshbon (Esbus)

ASCELON (free city)

Bethlehem

Etam

Mt. Pisgah △ △ Mt. Nebo

Khirbet Qumran

Medeba

Maiumas Ascelon
(Baths of Ascelon)

Beth-zechariah
Betogabri
Bethsura
Adora

Herodium
Thecoa
Alulos
Terebinthus
HEBRON

Gabalis?

Callirrhoe

Machaerus

JUDEA (UNDER ROMAN ADMINISTRATION)

Agrippias

GAZA

Caparorsa?

Aristobulias

Engaddi
(En-gedi)

Mare Mortuum

IDUMEA

Raphia

Bersabe
(Beer-sheba)

Malatha

Masada ■

Areopolis
(Rabbathmoab)

Mampsis

N

NABATAEAN KINGDOM

○ Nessana

The Negeb

©2003 CHK America www.mapsusa.com

following Jesus came from Galilee, Jerusalem, Judea, the region across the Jordan, and the Decapolis (Matt 4:25). Jesus left the area of Tyre and Sidon, approached the Sea of Galilee, and then entered the region of the Decapolis (Mark 7:31). After Jesus traveled to the east side of the Sea of Galilee, he cured a possessed man living in the area of the tombs. The healed man then returned to his family and reported what Jesus had done in the Decapolis (Mark 5:20). This event took place in the region of the Gerasenes according to Mark 5:1; other variants of this text name the region variously as that of the Gadarenes, or the Gergesenes. This event or one similar to it is mentioned in each synoptic Gospel. Luke 8:26 mentions two possessed men and places the event in the region of the Gerasenes, while Matt 8:28 records just one possessed man and that it took place in the region of the Gadarenes. Textual variants of all three passages in the Synoptic Gospels mention all three cities of Gadara, Gerasa, and Gergasa as the name of the location of this event. Two of these three options, Gadara and Gerasa, are Decapolis cities (*see* GERASA, GERASENES).

Josephus claims that Scythopolis, located to the west of the Jordan River, was the largest of the Decapolis cities (*Life* 65.351). He also notes that the "first citizens" of the Decapolis came to complain to Vespasian about Jews who had been rioting in the cities and territories of the Decapolis (*Life* 74.410). This reference indicates that the Decapolis cities were well known and worked collectively in political matters.

Other authors mentioning the Decapolis include Eusebius and Stephanus of Byzantium. Eusebius, writing around 300 CE, mentions that the Decapolis was ten cities located beyond the Jordan River around Hippos, Pella, and Gadara (*Onom.* 1:16). Eusebius also records that many Christians fled from Jerusalem during the First Jewish Revolt (69–70 CE) and moved to the area of Pella of the Decapolis (*Hist. Eccl.* 3.5.3). Stephanus of Byzantium mentions Gerasa as a city of the Decapolis (*Ethnika* 135.15).

B. Cities of the Decapolis

Almost all of the Decapolis cities were located to the east of the JORDAN RIVER and the Sea of Galilee (*see* GALILEE, SEA OF); the major exception was Scythopolis (ancient Beth-Shan), which is located southwest of the Sea of Galilee. The number of the cities in the Decapolis, as the name would indicate, was originally ten, but grew with time.

Pliny the Elder (23–79 CE) in his *Nat.* (5.74) gives the earliest extant list of the Decapolis cities. He indicates that even his sources are not in agreement on which cities should be counted as members of this group, but that most sources include DAMASCUS, PHILADELPHIA (modern Amman), Raphana, Scythopolis, Gadara, Hippos, Dion, PELLA, Gelasa (most scholars believe this is a misspelling of Gerasa), and Canatha.

Ptolemy (127–148 CE), a Greek geographer, provides the only other known list of the cities in his *Geography* (5.14-22). He includes all of the cities on Pliny's list except for Raphana, but also includes HELIOPOLIS, Abila of Lysanios, Saana, Ina, Samoulis, Adra, Gadora, and another ABILA (Quailbah). Even though this Abila (Quailbah) is not mentioned by Pliny it is clear that it should be counted as one of the Decapolis cities, because Ptolemy lists it, and because there is an inscription that mentions Abila as a Decapolis city. A bilingual funerary inscription, written in Palmyrene and Greek, was found built into the wall of a mosque at Tayibeh, a village near PALMYRA. It mentions that Agathangelos of Abila of the Decapolis paid for the expenses of the construction of an arch and bench. This inscription also indicates some connection (perhaps in trade) between Palmyra and Abila.

C. Identification of the Cities

There is general agreement on the identification and location of most of these cities. It should be noted that each city controlled the surrounding territory, though the extent of this control is difficult to determine. The location of some sites can be easily identified, such as Damascus, undoubtedly the same as the modern Syrian capital. Philadelphia can be identified with Amman, the modern capital of Jordan. CAPITOLIAS has been identified with modern Beit Ras, a town located to the north of Irbid, Jordan (*see* RAS, BEIT). SCYTHOPOLIS (Nysa) is identified with Beisan (BETH-SHAN), located west of the Jordan River and southwest of the Sea of Galilee. Pella is located near the Jordan Valley at a site called Tabaqat el-Fahil. Gerasa (Gelasa) is identified with the spectacular site of Jerash in modern-day Jordan. Gadara is now known as Umm Qeis in northern Jordan (*see* GADARA, GADARENES). Hippos, which means "horse" in Greek, is located to the west of the Sea of Galilee in the Golan Heights at a site known as Qalat el-Husn (Sussiya). Abila is located at Tell Abil, also known as Quailbah (Qwelbah), which is identified from an inscription found during the excavations at the site that mentions Abila. Raphana (Raphon), which is mentioned in 1 Macc 5:37, has been identified with the site of er-Rafeh although some argue it is an earlier name for Capitolias. The location of Dion (Dium) has been linked to various sites including Kefer Abil (near Pella), Tell el-Husn near Irbid, Edun near Mafraq, but the most likely location is Tell el-Ashari in Syria near Dera. Canatha (also spelled Canata or Canotha) is usually identified with Kanawat (Qanawat) in the Jebel Arab area of southern Syria. These are the cities most often associated with the Decapolis because they appear on both Pliny's and Ptolemy's lists, or they have inscriptional evidence. The cities that remain are only identified with the Decapolis by Ptolemy's list. The best known of the remaining cities is Heliopolis, which is the spectacular site of Baalbek in the Beqa Valley of Lebanon.

Gadora is usually identified with Tell Jadur. Adra is Ed-Dera. The other Abila (of Lysanias) is normally identified with the capital of the tetrarchy of Abilene (Luke 3:1). It is located between BAALBEK and Damascus. Samoulis, Saana, and Ina remain unidentified.

D. History of the Decapolis

The Macedonians first entered this region at the time of Alexander the Great. Many of the Decapolis cities claim to be founded as colonies either by Alexander or one of his successors. However, almost all of the Decapolis cities were occupied in the pre-Classical period, and many as early as the Iron or Bronze ages. The coins minted at the cities celebrate their Macedonian connection. The Ptolemies were the first to control the Decapolis area. Philadelphia (Amman) was founded by Ptolemy II Philadelphus. Pella was certainly named for the Macedonian capital. Antiochus III in 200 BCE attacked several of the Decapolis cities, including Abila, Pella, Gadara, and Scythopolis (Polybius 5.71). Antiochus III was able to remove this territory from the Ptolemies and bring it solidly under Seleucid control. Later when Seleucid power declined, the Jewish Hasmoneans and the Arab Nabateans grew in power. Philadephia and Gerasa came under Nabatean control while the Jewish ruler Alexander Janneus took control of Abila, Scythopolis, and Gadara. The Roman general Pompey, while on his campaign to conquer the eastern Mediterranean, freed the Decapolis cities from Jewish and Arab control in 64/63 BCE. To commemorate this event many of the Decapolis cities dated their calendars to the Pompeian era, with the inscriptions and coins claiming 64/63 BCE as their year zero. During this Roman era the Decapolis functioned as an administrative unit of the Province of Arabia, not unlike Palestine under Pontius Pilate. An inscription found in the Balkans records the achievements of an equestrian official, including his tenure as prefect of the Decapolis. Trajan absorbed the Nabatean kingdom in 106 CE and created the Province of Arabia. This divided the Decapolis area between provinces of Syria and Arabia, and effectively brought an end to the Decapolis.

Bibliography: Benjamin Isaac. "The Decapolis in Syria: A Neglected Inscription." *ZPDV* 44:67–74; Carl H. Kraeling, ed. *Gerasa, City of the Decapolis* (1938); S. Thomas Parker. "The Decapolis Reviewed." *JBL* 94 (1975) 437–41; Robert H. Smith. *Pella of the Decapolis* (1973); Robert H. Smith and Leslie P. Day. *Pella of the Decapolis.* Vol. 2 (1989); Augustus Spijkerman. *The Coins of the Decapolis and Provincia Arabia* (1978); John D. Wineland. *Ancient Abila: An Archaeological History* (2001).

JOHN D. WINELAND

DECEIT [מִרְמָה mirmah, שֶׁקֶר sheqer, עָוֶל ʿawel; δόλος dolos, πλάνη planē]. Numerous Hebrew and Greek terms express the concepts of deceit and falsehood, two words used interchangeably in English translations.

God in the OT (Deut 32:4) and Jesus in the NT (1 Pet 2:22) are said to be without deceit. God may, however, employ deceit (Ezek 14:9), a lying spirit (1 Kgs 22:22-23), and even the human penchant to deceive (Rom 3:7) to serve a higher end.

Persons described as evil (Job 15:35; Prov 12:20), enemies (Prov 26:24), violent (Nah 3:1), and thieving merchants (Hos 12:7 [Heb. 12:8]; Amos 8:5) all practice deceit. Warnings abound regarding false teaching (Isa 30:12; Col 2:8), prophets (Jer 14:14; Luke 6:26; 2 Pet 2:1), believers (Gal 2:4), apostles (2 Cor 11:13; Rev 2:2), spirits (1 Tim 4:1), and messiahs (Matt 24:24). In the NT deceit occurs in several sin lists (Matt 15:19; Rom 1:29) and sin itself is deceptive (Heb 3:13).

The innocent are often falsely accused of deceit and must defend against it (Job 27:4; 31:5; 1 Thess 2:3). Deceit is also used to abuse the legal process, through false accusation (Exod 23:7), false witness (Exod 20:16; Job 13:7; Matt 26:59-60), and false swearing (Lev 6:3-5 [Heb. 5:22-24]; Zech 5:4; Mal 3:5). Persons may petition God for aid against practitioners of deceit (Ps 43:1). God hears more readily the petitions of those without deceit (Ps 17:1). *See* APOSTASY; DECEIVE; LYING.

F. RACHEL MAGDALENE

DECEIVE [נָשָׁא nashaʾ, פָּתָה pathah; πλανάω planaō, ἐξαπατάω exapataō, φρεναπατάω phrenapataō, δολιόω dolioō]. A large number of Hebrew and Greek terms express the idea of deceiving and acting falsely. Although some texts state that God is without deceit (Deut 32:4; Heb 6:18), the OT reports that God can deceive (Ezek 14:9). Jeremiah accuses God of deceiving others (Jer 4:10). Job asserts that God is behind those who deceive (Job 12:16). Jesus was also accused of deceiving (John 7:12).

Persons are admonished against cheating their neighbor (Lev 6:2 [Heb. 5:21]; Jer 9:5 [Heb. 9:4]), even in jest (Prov 26:19). Falsely accusing a person (Ps 69:4 [Heb. 69:5]; Luke 3:14), testifying falsely (Job 13:7; Mark 10:19), or swearing falsely (Matt 5:33) are all serious offenses. Specific individuals who deceive include: Laban (Gen 29:25); Jacob (Gen 31:20, 26-27); Michal (1 Sam 19:17); Saul (1 Sam 28:12); and Abner (2 Sam 3:25). Countries also deceive (Num 25:18; Jos 9:22; Obad 7). Furthermore, humans engage in self-deception (Obad 3; 1 Cor 3:18; 1 John 1:8).

False prophets and diviners are capable of deceiving people (Jer 29:8; Lam 2:14). Within the NT, sin (Rom 7:11) and Satan (Rev 12:9) can deceive. Wicked people, impostors, and the rebellious deceive believers (2 Tim 3:13; Titus 1:10). New Testament writers exhort believers repeatedly not to be deceived by false teaching (1 Cor 15:33; Eph 5:6; 2 Thess 2:3). *See* DECEIT; LYING.

F. RACHEL MAGDALENE

DECISION, VALLEY OF. *See* VALLEY OF DECISION.

DECIUS. Appointed by Emperor Philip in 248 CE to lead the army on the Danube against the Goths, Decius's troops proclaimed him emperor in 249. Then following Philip's death, the Senate recognized him. Decius instituted the first general persecution of Christians, slaughtering Fabian, bishop of Rome, in January 250. Then in June all citizens had to give evidence that they had offered sacrifice to the emperor. While some yielded and others bribed their persecutors, thousands were executed. This persecution ended in June 251, when Decius was killed by the Goths. *See* CHRISTIANS, PERSECUTION OF; PERSECUTION; ROMAN EMPIRE.

ALLISON A. TRITES

DECK [קֶרֶשׁ qeresh]. The floor or "boards" of a boat. No specific Hebrew word is used for "deck." In boats with many rowers, the deck consisted only of the stern (rear) and the bow (front). In a large boat or a ship the deck functioned as the floor but also as the ceiling or covering for the space below, perhaps decorated with ivory inlays (Ezek 27:6). Noah's ark had three decks (Gen 6:16). *See* INLAY; SHIPS AND SAILING IN THE NT; SHIPS AND SAILING IN THE OT.

EMILY R. CHENEY

DECONSTRUCTION. *See* STRUCTURALISM AND DECONSTRUCTION.

DECREE [דָּת dath, חֹק khoq; Aram. גְּזֵרָה gezerah, טְעֵם teʿem; δόγμα dogma]. Announced by an authority (human or divine), a declaration or statute directing/prescribing the actions of individuals or communities, often documented in writing. Examples include Cyrus' decree to rebuild the Temple (Ezra 5:13, 17) and Caesar Augustus' decree calling for a census (Luke 2:1) (See also Isa 10:1; 2 Chr 30:5; Ezra 6:1; Esth 1:20; Dan 3:10; Ps 2:7; Job 28:26; Acts 17:7.) *See* LAW IN THE NT; LAW IN THE OT.

TRISHA GAMBAIANA WHEELOCK

DECREE OF DAVID AND DECREE OF SOLOMON. *See* BOOKS REFERRED TO IN THE BIBLE.

DEDAN dee'duhn [דְּדָן dedhan; Δαιδάν Daidan]. 1. A son of Jokshan, son of Abraham and Keturah (Gen 25:3; 1 Chr 1:32), or a son of Raamah (Gen 10:7; 1 Chr 1:9), a descendant of Ham. Both references list Sheba as Dedan's brother.

2. Ezekiel lists Dedan in an oracle against Edom (Ezek 25:13) and pairs Sheba with Dedan as trade cities (Ezek 38:13). Dedan was a prominent commercial city

in the 7th cent. BCE located at a desert oasis in northwestern Arabia known today as Al Ula. The prophets mention Dedan as a city of caravans (Isa 21:13; 38:13), where the Dedanites traded "saddlecloths for riding" with Tyre (27:20). Nabonidus (a 6th cent. BCE Babylonian king) includes Dedan in one of his inscriptions. Dedan fell to the Persians and then to the Nabataeans under whose rule it lost its prominence.

TERRY W. EDDINGER

DEDICATION, FEAST OF. *See* FEAST OF DEDICATION.

DEED. *See* RIGHTEOUSNESS IN THE NT; RIGHTEOUSNESS IN THE OT; WORKS, GOOD.

DEEDS OF UZZIAH BY ISAIAH THE PROPHET. *See* BOOKS REFERRED TO IN THE BIBLE.

DEEP, THE [תְּהוֹם tehom]. The word *deep* translates the Hebrew word tehom for which English has no satisfactory equivalent. This problem in translation stems directly from the fact that tehom refers to an aspect of ANE cosmology which is so different from contemporary views of the universe that it is no longer a part of the modern worldview. Paired in the Bible with such terms as *water*, *sea*, and *springs*, tehom describes a vast reservoir of water that ancients believed lay below the earth's surface—hence the common translation "deep"—and which they considered the source of seas, rivers, and springs. To understand this concept and its role in biblical thought, where it has both positive and negative connotations, we must first understand the place of the deep in the biblical view of the cosmos.

In the biblical period, the earth was viewed as a stable platform at the center of the universe, resting between two great reservoirs of water, one beyond the sky that fed clouds and rain, and the other under the earth that fed the bodies of water on its surface. This cosmology is illustrated in the Bible's first story of CREATION (the Priestly version), where, on the second day of creation, God divides the primordial waters, placing some above the sky and some below, thereby clearing a space in which to form the earth on the third day (Gen 1:6-10). The lower reservoir, in which the earth's foundation rests (Ps 24:2; 104:5-9), is the biblical tehom, rendered in this article in its customary fashion, the "deep." The juxtaposition of the upper and lower bodies of water in the cosmos is reflected in the contrast many texts draw between the sky, clouds, or rain on the one hand and the deep on the other (Gen 49:25; Hab 3:10; Prov 3:20). As the world's subterranean reservoir, the deep is considered the substratum of the seas (Exod 15:4-5, 8; Ps 33:7; Job 39:16) and the source of the springs that dot the biblical landscape (Deut 8:7; Prov 8:28).

Because biblical Israel inhabited a narrow humid zone surrounded by arid deserts, and because rainfall was always erratic, the deep below the earth that fed its springs, rivers, and lakes was seen as essential to life and prosperity. It is described in the Bible as nourishing the roots of trees (Ezek 31:4), making crops grow (Amos 7:4), and providing drinking water for people (Ps 78:15). The deep, together with the waters above the sky, is believed to be a primary source of divine blessings (Gen 49:25; Deut 33:13). This life-giving character of the deep is certainly the reason the psalmist uses it as a symbol of God's justice (36:7).

The deep, as an elemental aspect of the ancient universe, occurs often in biblical accounts of creation. Occasionally it is employed for the primordial waters, the primeval ocean that existed before God separated the waters and formed the earth (Gen 1:2; Ps 104:6). These primordial waters are often thought of as chaotic forces that had to be restrained by God in order to create an ordered world, so in this sense the deep represents a dangerous power that, apart from God's control, could overwhelm the world and return it to CHAOS (Ps 33:7, 104:6-9; Prov 8:27). In the Priestly strand of the flood story, God initiates the FLOOD by allowing the two bodies of water separated at creation to engulf the earth, returning the universe to a state of chaos: the floodgates of the heavens opened and the deep erupted from below (Gen 7:11; 8:2). In some contexts, the deep even takes on the appearance of a living enemy, which God must subdue to bring order to the world (Exod 15:5, 8; Isa 51:10; Ps 77:17).

Such images of conflict between God and the deep raise the possibility that the deep is actually the biblical version of the chaos dragon of Mesopotamian lore, whose name, ti'amat, is the Akkadian equivalent of the Hebrew tehom, "deep." In the Babylonian Epic of Creation, *Enuma Elish*, the creator God Marduk kills Tiamat, "Sea," splits its watery carcass into two halves, and fashions the earth between them (compare Gen 1:2-10). In fact, the deep is often personified in the Bible, where it is pictured as crouching below (Gen 49:25; Deut 33:13), shaking (Ps 77:17), and speaking (Hab 3:10; Ps 42:8). Moreover, the Hebrew word *deep* never occurs with the definite article—though we have been using it (inaccurately from a technical standpoint) in this article—suggesting perhaps that this term is not a common noun, "the deep," but a proper noun, the name Tehom, "Deep." A number of biblical authors who employ this term (Second Isaiah, Ezekiel, the Priestly Writer) actually wrote from the Babylonian exile and may have come into direct contact with these Babylonian creation traditions. It is difficult to say how much of, and in which texts, this personal character of "deep" is intended by biblical authors. (*See* MARDUK, TIAMAT).

The identification of the deep with the primordial waters of chaos accounts for its occasional use in the Bible as a symbol of danger and death. In these contexts, the deep is sometimes used together with SHEOL, the shadowy, subterranean abode of the dead. One psalmist, who appears to be threatened by unscrupulous men, pictures his distress as a descent into the deep, from which he hopes God will rescue him (Ps 71:20). Another describes his impending death with such vivid imagery of the deep and the unruly subterranean waters that his lament has been reused for Jonah's prayer in the belly of the fish (John 2:3-10). The prophet Ezekiel describes the demise of the Egyptian Pharaoh as a descent into Sheol and into the deep (31:15).

The same dangerous and death-dealing power of the deep is present when it is employed for the waters of the sea, which spared the Israelites but drowned the Egyptians at the exodus (Exod 15:5, 8; Isa 51:10; 63:13; Pss 77:17-20; 106:9). Though all of these texts describe the historical event of Israel's escape from Egypt at the sea, God's restraint of the deep at creation is clearly in the background. In Exod 15:7-8, God's attack is directed both against the sea (and the deep) and against the armies of Pharaoh; and in Isa 51:9-10 God's victory over the chaos dragon (Rahab) is paired with God's victory at the sea (and the deep) when Israel escaped its waters. Biblical writers did not make the distinction we do between history and creation. They saw divine order as a seamless power infusing all aspects of the world, so that God's restraint of the deep and of the enemy's armies were part of the same divine work to hold back chaos and provide safety and life. *See* SEA; WATER.

THEODORE HIEBERT

DEER [אַיָּל 'ayyal]. Several wild ruminants with cloven hooves are listed among animals that may be consumed (Deut 14:5): 'ayyal, tsevi (צְבִי), yakhmur (יַחְמוּר), 'aqqo (אַקּוֹ), dishon (דִּישֹׁן), te'o (תְּאוֹ), and zamer (זֶמֶר), sometimes translated as "the deer, the gazelle, the roebuck, the wild goat, the ibex, the antelope, and the mountain-sheep." The ASV offers "the hart, and the gazelle, and the roebuck, and the wild goat, and the pygarg, and the antelope, and the chamois." *See* DOE; FAWN; ROEBUCK.

ODED BOROWSKI

DEER OF THE DAWN. *See* MUSIC.

DEFILEMENT. *See* CLEAN AND UNCLEAN.

DEIR 'ALLA, TELL. The archaeological site Tell Deir Alla is conspicuously situated in the Jordan Valley, east of the river, near the entrance of the River Zerqa (OT: JABBOK) into the Valley. Here the fertile valley-floor is several km wide and 250 m below sea level, having a warm dry climate (steppe), but with possibilities of irrigation agriculture using Zerqa water. The Valley is good for winter grazing and this part has good access to the Western (Shechem) and Eastern (Gilead, Ammon) hills.

The settlement has been inconclusively identified with SUCCOTH, a "town" connected with Jacob and Gideon, as well as with Phoenician metallurgical activities for Solomon's temple. The "Balaam inscription" from ca. 800 BCE (see below) gives the site a role in the study of this OT prophet, as well as in the study of the book of Job, having idiom with this inscription in common.

The tell is being excavated since 1960, by Leiden University and in cooperation with the Jordanian Department of Antiquities and Yarmouk University. It was used as a settlement from ca. 1700–400 BCE. The Middle Bronze IIC occupation started as a full-grown 4 ha. settlement on a low hillock with solid mud-brick buildings and soon probably a surrounding rampart wall. Some bronze objects (trident, "mono-dent" and shaft-hole thumb-axe) show the international relations of the elite. The Late Bronze Age, when this part of the Valley was connected with the Shechem city state, is specially known from its latest phase, which was destroyed by earthquake and fire. The population made use of irrigated agriculture and the settlement had industrial (metal) and trade sections as well as a religious center, privileged by having Mycenaean pottery and faience objects from Mesopotamia and Egypt. The faience drop-vase of Pharaoh Tausert dates the destruction to or after ca. 1186. Carved writing on local clay tablets from the religious and trade quarters has not yet been convincingly deciphered.

The first Iron Age settlement soon became a large "village" and probably lasted two centuries (10 phases are distinguished). From the 9th through 4th cent., a series of new villages used only the eastern half of the tell and showed varying intensities of use of site and landscape, including irrigated agriculture. The phase IX village (destroyed ca. 800 BCE) produced lots of grain and linseed (on irrigated fields) and had many domestic weaving installations, as well as the Balaam texts (Early Aramaean, ink written on a lime-plastered wall), but without an obvious cult place. The village shows connections with Phoenicia, Cis-Jordan and Amman. Phase VII has many "foreign" cultural features, including wheel-thrown pottery, and must be connected with Assyrians. Phase VI fits with Babylonians, but with strong Ammonite elements, and Phases V, IV and III fit with the Persians, including Aramaic ostraca with 5th-4th cent. writing, and 4th cent. BCE Greek pottery.

The site was deserted until a new village was established at the northeast foot in Islamic times, especially the Mamluk period largely dealing with reed sugar production for Egypt and using the main tell as a graveyard. *See* DEIR ʿALLA, TEXTS.

Bibliography: H.J. Franken. *Excavations at Tell Deir ʿAlla; the Bronze Age Sanctuary* (1992); J. Hoftijzer and G. van der Kooij, eds. *The Balaam Text from Deir ʿAlla Re-evaluated; Proceedings of the International Symposium Held at Leiden 21–24 August 1989* (1991); E. Kaptijn, *et al.* "Dayr ʿAlla Regional Project: Settling the Steppe; First campaign 2004." *ADAJ* 2005; G. van der Kooij and M. M. Ibrahim. *Picking up the Threads . . . A Continuing Review of Excavations at Deir Alla* (1989); G. van der Kooij. "Tell Deir ʿAlla: the Middle and Late Bronze Age Chronology." P. M. Fischer, ed. *The Chronology of the Jordan Valley during the Middle and Late Bronze Ages: Pella, Tell Abu-Kharaz and Tell Deir ʿAlla.* forthcoming; G. van der Kooij, Z. Kafafi. "Excavations at Dayr ʿAlla, Four Seasons 1996–2004." *ADAJ.* forthcoming.

GERRIT VAN DER KOOIJ

DEIR ʿALLA, TEXTS. In 1967, a Dutch archaeological expedition under H. Franken discovered inscribed plaster fragments at a site named Deir ʿAlla, a tell located about 8 km east of the Jordan on the northern side of the Jabbok/Zerqa river (*See* DEIR ʿALLA, TELL). These fragments were assembled and studied by J. Hoftijzer and G. van der Kooij, who published them with a forward by H. Franken in 1976. It took some years for a number of issues pertaining to these inscriptions to be clarified, mostly notably the classification of their language. Some of the fragments were subsequently re-aligned by A. Caquot and A. Lemaire, and many scholars were stimulated to study the inscriptions. In 1989 a conference was held in Leiden, the Netherlands, and a volume of papers delivered on the occasion was published in 1991. The plaster inscriptions from Deir ʿAlla have been on display in the Amman (Jordan) museum.

What makes these texts so interesting is, first of all, that they attest the name blʿm brbʿr "BALAAM, the son of Beor" (Num 22–24). There is increasing agreement among scholars that these texts are written in a local, or regional Canaanite-type language akin to classical Hebrew, but with some Aramaic-like features. In any event, they are of local, Transjordanian authorship. To the extent that they are legible and intelligible in their relatively poor state of conservation, they tell of the exploits of a seer (khozeh חֹזֵה) named Balaam, the son of Beor, who was warned by the gods of an impending calamity. The seer undertook efforts to avert it, and according to the interpretation adopted here, he was effective in doing so, thereby rescuing his land and people.

There is little doubt that the Deir ʿAlla inscriptions refer to the same person, whether real or legendary, whose orations have been preserved in the biblical Balaam tradition. The Deir ʿAlla inscriptions date from ca. 800 BCE and are probably younger than the biblical orations, which reflect the situation prior to the military ventures of MESHA, king of Moab, initiated in the mid 9th cent. BCE. The Deir ʿAlla texts may reflect, in a cryptic manner, the subsequent Moabite threat to the population of central Transjordan. At the time, the dominant population in what was biblical Gilead was Israelite, and it is decidedly possible that these texts were composed by one or more Israelites. Their content and diction bear a clear affinity to certain biblical poems in addition to the Balaam orations, principally the Sheol oracle of Isa 14:9-23. It is significant that El is the deity who appeared to Balaam, and who fashioned a netherworld, all of which associates the Deir ʿAlla inscriptions with the cult of El, and with the biblical Balaam orations.

Hoftijzer identified two principal "combinations," as he called them, as well as many loose fragments that could not be connected with any of the others. Additional columns had existed before the fragments fell to the floor when the walls on which they were written collapsed, perhaps as the result of an earthquake. The contents of Combinations I and II will first be summarized, after which selections taken from them will be presented in transcription and translation. It must be emphasized that since their discovery, the Deir ʿAlla inscriptions have been read in many different ways. What is presented here is merely one possible rendition, incorporating some textual restorations suggested by Émile Puech and others.

A. Combination I

This combination opens with Balaam's identification as a divine seer who has experienced a vision from El. Benign deities, sent by El, visited him by night and warned him that other, hostile deities, called "Shadday-gods," had established a council, and decreed that a goddess named Shagar-we-Ishtar, a Venus figure, must darken the heavens. This vision was a portent of disaster, to be accompanied by weird happenings, such as the shrieking of birds of prey, and the overtaking of grazing land by wild beasts.

From this point on, the plot is less clear. Balaam issued an admonition to these adversaries of the goddess to desist, and undertook magical methods to protect Shagar-we-Ishtar from the Shadday-gods. It is likely that he succeeded, and reversed the effects of the omen, thereby rescuing his land and people, in realistic terms, while rescuing the goddess Shagar-we-Ishtar, in mythological perspective. The displayed inscriptions celebrated this fortunate outcome on the walls of a regional distribution depot, visited by many residents and travelers.

Transcription

1. ysry [.] spr. blʿm. b[rbʿ]r. ʾš. ḥzh. ʾlhn. hʾ
2. wyʾtw. ʾlwh. ʾlhn. blylh [w]yḥz . mḥzh. kmšʾ. ʾl.
3. wyʾmrw. lb[lʿ]m. brbʿr .
4.   kh ypʿl blʾ. ʾḥrʾh.
5.   ʾš. lr[ʾ]h. mh. šmʿt
6. wyqm. blʿm. mn. mḥr. hn [——]t .
7. yzmn. [rʾšy qhl [.ʾ]lwh.

8. wlym[yn. yṣ]m. wbkh. ybkh .
9. wyʿl. ʿmh. ʾlwh. wyʾm[rw.] lblʿm. brbʿr.
10.   lm. tṣm. wlm. tbkh.
11. wyʾmr lhm .
12.   šbw. ʾḥwkm . mh. šdyn. ḥ[šbw.]
13.   wlkw. rʾw. pʿlt. ʾlhn.
14. ʾl[h]n. ʾtyḥdw. mnṣbw. šdyn. mwʿd.
15. wʾmrw. lš[gr.
16.   tpry. skry. šmyn. bʿb .
17.   ky. šm. ḥšk. wʾl. ngh. ʿtm. wʾl. smr.
18.   ky. thby. ḥtt[. bʿ]b. ḥšk.
19.   wʾl. thgy. ʿd. ʿlm

Translation

1. The misfortunes of the book of Balaam, the son of Beor, a divine seer is he.
2. Then the gods came ᵗᵒ ʰⁱᵐ at night, and he beheld a vision in accordance with El's utterance.
3. They said to Balaam, the son of Beor:
4. "So will be done, with naught surviving;
5. "No one has seen [the likes of] what you have heard!"
6. Balaam arose on the morrow, behold [
7. He summoned *the heads of the assembly* unto him,
8. And for two days he fasted, and wept bitterly.
9. Then his intimates entered into his presence, and they said to Balaam, the son of Beor:
10. "Why do you fast, and why do you weep?
11. Then he said to them:
12. "Be seated, and I will tell you what the Shadday-gods have *planned*,
13. "And go, see the acts of the gods!
14. "The gods have banded together, and the Shadday-gods have established a council.
15. "And they have said to [the goddess] Shagar:
16. 'Sew up, close up the heavens with dense cloud,
17. 'That darkness exist there, not brilliance, obscurity and not clarity
18. 'So that you instill dread in dense darkness.
19. 'And – never utter a sound again!'"

B. Combination II

This Combination is more fragmented than Combination I, and for this reason, only selected excerpts will be presented. It relates that El fashioned a necropolis, an eternal home for the dead, byt ʿlmn, which is described in the lines that follow. We read of conditions of burial in the netherworld, and of the arrival of a corpse. There is the somewhat philosophical observation that the quests of kings come to naught. The name of Balaam cannot be read in Combination II, but there are two clues suggesting that he may have been the subject of this description of the world of the dead. We first read that one who had served as a counselor would no longer be consulted, and later on, an unnamed person is addressed harshly, saying that he was being punished because of his words, and would henceforth be denied the power to pronounce execrations.

Transcription and Translation of Selected Excerpts:

1. .[ddn] yrwy . ʾl .
    wyʿbd ʾl. byt. ʿlmn.
    by[t]
    [byt]
    byt. lyʿl. hlk.
    wlyʿl. ḥtn. šm

    El satisfies himself with [lovemaking],
    Then El built an eternal home.
    A hou[se]
    [A house]
    A house where no traveler enters,
    Nor does a bridegroom enter there.

2. hlʿsh. bk. lytʿṣ.
    ʾw lmlkh. lytmlk.

    If it is for counsel, no one will consult you.
    Or for his advice, no one will take counsel.

3. [   ]h blbbm
    nʾnḥ. nqr. blbbh.
    nʾnḥ [.

    ] in their heart.
    The corpse moans in his heart.
    He moans [

4. ldʿt. spr. dbr. lʿmh.
    ʿl. lšn. lk. nšpt.
    wmlqb. ʾmr

    To know how to deliver a [divine] word to his people.
    And [banned] from pronouncing words of execration.

The citations from the Deir ʿAlla inscriptions underline their potential value for tracing religious development in biblical Israel. These inscriptions share themes and literary diction with biblical poetry, and reveal the high level of literary expression reached by Transjordanian poets, who may have been Israelites. *See* NUMBERS, BOOK OF.

Bibliography: J. Hoftijzer and G. van der Kooij. *The Baalam texts from Deir Alla Re-evaluated: Proceedings of the international Symposium Held at Leiden 21-24 August 1989* (1991).

BARUCH A. LEVINE

DEIR EL-BALAH. *See* BALAH, DEIR EL.

DEITIES, UNDERWORLD. Pantheons of underworld deities exist in a variety of literary genres (e.g., myths, rituals, administrative texts, incantations) as well as from theophoric elements in personal names. Approximately 1,550 alphabetic cuneiform Ugaritic texts from Late Bronze Age Syria, along with biblical texts, are the primary sources used below to describe the underworld deities of the ANE and ancient Mediterranean world. The various deities and related terms associated with the underworld include the following:

A. Ghosts and Spirits
B. Land, Netherworld
C. Gods
D. The God of the Fathers
E. Chemosh
F. Hades
G. Horon/Horanu
H. Molech
I. Motu, Death
J. The Shades of the Dead
K. Reshef/Rashapu/Rashpu
L. Shapshu/Shamash
M. Sheol
Bibliography

A. Ghosts and Spirits (אוֹב ʾov and יִדְּעֹנִי yiddeʿoni)

The OT uses these two terms (most often together) to refer to the SHADES of the dead and those who consult them (compare 1 Sam 28:7; Deut 18:11). The etymology of ʾov is the subject of much debate and little consensus. In contrast, the root of yiddeʿoni (from ydʿ [ידע], "to know") is certain and may reflect the notion that the dead have a type of knowledge unknown to the living. Biblical authors who argued against cults of the dead as rivals to Yahweh (e.g., Deut 18:9-14; Lev 20:6, 27) made special mention of how neither ʾov nor yiddeʿoni were to be consulted.

B. Land, Netherworld (אֶרֶץ ʾerets)

Several ANE cultures (e.g., Mesopotamia, Ugarit, Israel) used the common word for "land" to designate the netherworld. In Mesopotamia, Nergal and Ereshkigal were the king and queen of the underworld. There, the dead, according to *Ishtar's Descent to the Netherworld*, lived in darkness eating mud and filth and drinking foul water.

The Ugaritic Funerary Text (KTU 1.161.21-22) speaks of descending down to the netherworld, down to the dust. The abode of the dead was Motu's domain, a place characterized by a watery ooze, a sinking decay, and filth. The OT modifies ʾerets and sheʾol (שְׁאוֹל) with the adjective takhtith (תַּחְתִּית) ("lower, lowest") to denote "the depths of the underworld" (Deut 32:22; Ps 86:13; 88:7; Ezek 31:14-18; 32:18, 24). The earth is sometimes personified as swallowing its victims (Exod 15:12; Num 16:30-32) similar to the god Motu (compare Jer 9:21; Isa 25:8) and Sheol (Isa 5:14; Hab 2:5; Prov 1:12). *See* DEAD, ABODE OF THE; SHEOL.

C. Gods (אֱלֹהִים ʾelohim)

Occasionally the term ʾelohim, "gods," is used to refer to the preternatural state of the dead. At Ugarit, a divine determinative (il) was used with royal names in a list of dead kings (KTU 1.113). In addition, the term "gods" also seems to occur parallel to "the dead" in KTU 1.6.6.48-49. Also at Ugarit, the expression "Inashu-Ilima" refers to a group that receives sacrifices as a collective. The meaning of Inashu ("men") + Ilima ("gods") seems to refer to men who were expected to become gods in their death.

In the OT, the most famous example of ʾelohim used to designate the preternatural state of the dead comes from 1 Sam 28:13. The dead Samuel's ghost is envisioned by a necromancer from EN-DOR as an ʾelohim (NRSV: "divine being;" *see* ENDOR, MEDIUM OF) coming up from the underworld (*see* ELOHIM).

D. The God of the Fathers (אֱלֹהֵי אָבֹת ʾelohe ʾavot)

The expression "the God of the Fathers" (ʾelohe ʾavot; e.g., Exod 3:13-16) is well known from its use in the OT where it sums up the religion of the patriarchs, i.e., the deity worship   ped by Abraham, Isaac, and Jacob. A similar expression (iluibi) with the same constituent parts (ilu "god" + ib "father") refers to a deity in the Ugaritic texts.

The importance of the deity Ilu-ibi at Ugarit can be seen from his premier ranking in several deity lists as well as his appearance in a variety of literary genres (epic texts, sacrificial and offering lists). A key reference to this deity occurs in the Aqhatu story. This text describes the setting up of a stela for one's ilu-ibi as one of the duties that an ideal son does for his father. Scholars are divided as to whether ilu-ibi refers to one's deified ancestor or the patron god of one's ancestor (i.e., a family deity). The former, entailing ANCESTOR WORSHIP, would be in line with other texts that commemorate how the dead were viewed as being intimately connected to the living. In royal religion, we know from a mortuary text (KTU 1.161) that deceased kings were sought to grant blessings on the current monarchy. The frequent practice at Ugarit of locating the family tomb immediately beneath one's house also reinforced the familial bond between the living and the dead.

The latter interpretation (viewing ilu-ibi as a family's deity) argues that solidarity with one's ancestors is being expressed (and physically enacted when such a stela is erected) by the succeeding generations' worship of the same deity. This line of interpretation is more in line with the biblical "god of my/your/their father" or "the god of Abraham/Isaac/Jacob." The sense of communion and belonging that one has with his/her family (present and past) is reinforced as each generation reaffirms, practices, and hands down the same faith as one's parents, grandparents, and great-grandparents. That the deity of one's ancestor is ranked first in the ritual pantheon would be a powerful testimony to the importance of a family's ongoing confession.

E. Chemosh (כְּמוֹשׁ kemosh)

Iron Age evidence for the deity CHEMOSH is found in the 9th cent. BCE Mesha inscription (*see* MOABITE STONE), onomastica, and the OT, where the name Chemosh occurs eight times. A cognate term for the deity (Kamish) is attested at Ebla in Syria dating to the Early and Middle Bronze ages.

Readers of the OT have been influenced about the god's chthonic character due to 2 Kgs 3:26-27 where the Moabite king, in a battle context, sacrificed his eldest son (presumably to the Moabite deity Chemosh). In addition, the god Chemosh is listed next to the god Molech (1 Kgs 11:7, 33).

While child sacrifice typifies the underworld deity Molech, there is no explicit underworld reference in either of these Chemosh passages. The OT, other than labeling the deity as an "abomination" (1 Kgs 11:7; 2 Kgs 23:13), simply recognizes him as the national god of the Moabites (Num 21:29; Jer 48:46). A very positive (and again martial) portrayal of the deity is found in the Mesha inscription, which emphasizes how Chemosh successfully guided the Moabite king's military endeavors. Chemosh was used as a theophoric element in personal names. Yet it is not clear that Chemosh is an underworld deity.

F. Hades (ᾅδης hadēs)

HADES occurs as the proper name of the gatekeeper/god of the netherworld in Greek mythology (Homer, *Il.* 15.188). The Greek hadēs is the word typically chosen by LXX translators to render the Hebrew sheʾol and is the NT word that depicts either the underworld or the personified lord of the underworld. Hades is a place to which one goes down, and it too represents the lowest depths in contrast to the highest heavens (Matt 11:23; Luke 10:15). Hades has the familiar "gates" (Matt 16:18) that are prominent in the netherworlds of ANE and Greek mythology. Another reference to gates is the "keys of Death and Hades" in Rev 1:18. Hades occurs in personified form along with Death (Rev 6:8). In Rev 20:13-14, Death and Hades give up the dead and are then thrown into the lake of fire.

G. Horon/Horanu (חֹרוֹן khoron)

Horanu is attested throughout the ANE Mediterranean worlds. Though frequently invoked for healing, Horanu is often thought to be a netherworld deity.

At Ugarit he is best known for his role in magic and exorcism (KTU 1.169; compare 124.6) and has a prominent role in dealing with snakebites (KTU 1.100; 1.107). Though quite damaged, KTU 1.82 seems to list Horanu (and "the servants of Horanu") as the object of incantations along with Tunnanu, Rashpu, and Motu. At the end of the story of King Kirta, the king invokes Horanu to curse his arrogant firstborn son Yassib who is staging a revolution (KTU 1.16.6.54-58). The name Horon shows up in the OT in the city name BETH-HORON ("the temple of Horon," e.g., Josh 16:3, 5; 1 Chr 7:24). The name is also attested on an ostracon from Tell el-Qasile and in the topographical list of Pharaoh Shishak.

H. Molech (מֹלֶךְ molekh)

Molech, Malik, or Milku has historically received the most attention when it comes to biblicists investigating the topic of underworld deities (*see* MOLECH, MOLOCH). This fascination comes from what seems to be (at first glance) the OT's portrayal of child sacrifice to the deity at the "topheth" in the valley of Hinnom (e.g., Jer 32:25; compare Ps 106:37-38 *see* HINNOM, VALLEY OF). Priestly legislation demands the death penalty for people who "give" or "pass over" any of their offspring to Molech (Lev 18:21; 20:2-5). Kings Ahaz (2 Kgs 16:3) and Manasseh (2 Kgs 21:6) came under particular sanction for such activity by the Deuteronomists. In contrast, the reforms of King Josiah are praised because "he defiled Topheth, which is in the valley of Ben-Hinnom, so that no one would make a son or daughter pass through fire as an offering to Molech" (2 Kgs 23:10).

Scholars have speculated that molekh does not designate a deity but was a technical term for child sacrifice (cognate to Phoenician/Punic mulk). Other scholars emphasize how a deity by the same name is found in the cognate evidence from Mesopotamia and Syria. The god Malik is well attested in Akkadian personal names and in god lists, where he is equated with Nergal. From Ugarit we have both the deity Milku as well as the malukuma, a group of deceased kings who are invoked in the Ugaritic Funerary Text (KTU 1.161). The god Milku is often construed to be the king of the underworld presiding over the malukuma.

I. Motu, Death (מָוֶת maweth)

The Levantine underworld deity about whom we know the most is the god Motu, whose name means "Death." This ruler of the underworld is described in vivid terms as having a voracious appetite. In the most famous myth coming from Ugarit (The Baal Cycle), we read of how he consumes all, stretching one lip to the heavens, the other to the earth, and swallowing all life in between. Motu eats ravenously with both hands, having the appetite of a lion (KTU 1.5.1.14-20; RS 24.293). Even the god Balu descends into his throat

(KTU 1.5.2.2-4). This unquenchable appetite reflects the Ugaritic notion that Motu brings death to everyone, be it the storm god who secures agrarian life or the legendary King Kirta.

Motu, representing the power of death, stands apart from all other deities. Though we have extensive ritual texts at our disposal, they contain no record of any sacrifices (animal or human) presented to Motu. Nor does his name occur in any of the extant deity lists. Despite his power, victory over Motu was possible for the deities Anatu and Balu (back from the dead) who bring about his defeat (KTU 1.6.2.30-35; 1.6.6.16-35). Anatu's victory over Motu is particularly intriguing for its use of imagery having to do with grain processing: "With a knife she splits Motu, with a sieve she winnows him, with fire she burns him, with millstones she grinds him, in the field she sows him."

The OT contains imagery that resonates with the world of Ugaritic myth. The Hebrew word for death (**maweth**) can refer to the realm of death as well as the chthonic power behind death. Death's power was universal, a fate for all humans (Num 16:29; Ps 89:48), although biblical texts attest that God will have ultimate victory over death (Isa 25:8; Rom 6:9; 1 Cor 15:24-57; Rev 1:18; 7:17; 21:4). Sages, psalmists, and prophets alike used language remarkably close to that of the Ugaritic poets to describe death personified. In particular, they emphasized death's insatiable appetite (Prov 1:12; 27:20; 30:15*b*-16; Ps 141:7; Hab 2:5; compare Isa 5:14). Here the lines are blurred between using the word *death* metaphorically and referring to an underworld deity. In addition, we read of the negative imagery of "cords," "torrents," "snares," and "pangs" associated with death (Pss 18:4-5, 116:3; 2 Sam 22:5-6).

Curiously, we also find the expression **bekhor maweth** (בְּכוֹר מָוֶת) in Job 18:13. Scholars debate whether we have here an idiom for deadly disease, a reference to an offspring of an underworld deity (perhaps Resheph, because Motu is never described as having children), or as an attributive genitive ("Firstborn Death") referring to Motu himself as Ilu's firstborn).

J. The Shades of the Dead (רְפָאִים refa'im)

Refa'im is a plural term designating the shades of the dead (Isa 14:9; 26:14; Ps 88:11; Prov 2:18; 9:18; 21:16; Job 26:5) as well as groups of humans (heroic warriors?) sometimes of gigantic stature (Gen 14:5; 15:20; compare Deut 2:10; Num 13:33; *see* REPHAIM).

While the author of Prov 21:16 refers to an "assembly" of dead refa'im, the OT gives us precious little information about how such an assembly was envisioned. We occasionally read of the shades trembling (Job 26:5) and being in such an inactive state so as not to be able to render God praise (Ps 88:10). The shades are "roused" by Sheol to greet the King of Babylon when he appears in the netherworld (Isa 14:9).

A marked contrast can be found with the cognates at Ugarit. There the term *Rapiu* designates a chthonic deity, the head of the Rapiuma, a plural term designating the spirits of the dead. In KTU 1.108 we read of the full title "Rapiu, king of eternity." Scholars debate the precise identity of this deity with suggestions ranging from an independent god named Rapiu to Ilu, Balu, Motu, Rashpu, and Milku.

The royal Rapiuma (along with the deceased kings termed malakuma) are invoked during a funerary ritual (KTU 1.161) securing the descent of the deceased king to the netherworld and bringing blessing on the ascendant monarch. In the so-called *Rapiuma Texts* (KTU 1.20-22), the Ugaritic shades are hardly inactive like their biblical counterparts. Instead, they hitch horses, gallop on stallions, and ride for three days to arrive at a rich banquet thrown for them by the god Ilu.

K. Reshef (רֶשֶׁף reshef)/Rashapu/Rashpu

A deity called RESHEPH (sometimes Rashapu or Rashpu) is widely known in West Semitic religions from third millennium BCE Ebla to several manifestations at Late Bronze Age Ugarit to first millennium texts from the Syrian, Phoenician-Punic, and biblical worlds. He was adopted into New Kingdom Egypt as a war deity complete with battle-ax and shields. Though Resheph may have been the most popular of the Canaanite gods attested in Egypt in this period, he nonetheless had no primary cult center in Egypt.

It would be a mistake to summarize the multifaceted nature (both negative and positive) of Resheph into a narrow portrait. The deity had many roles: lord of the underworld, god of war, patron deity of metalworking, god of healing, and protector from disease. Some scholars have emphasized Resheph's connection to solar and astral cults.

Resheph/Rashpu is equated with Nergal in the deity lists at Ugarit and is Shapshu's "gatekeeper," presumably opening the gates of the netherworld for the sun goddess to enter when she sets in the evening (KTU 1.78). Yet in contrast to Motu at Ugarit, Rashpu (in various manifestations) is listed in the deity lists and is a regular recipient of offerings (e.g., ewes, rams, cows) in the ritual texts. Better attested are the deity's connections to disease and pestilence, that would fit well with what we know of netherworld deities elsewhere. A story from Ugarit about King Kirta's family dying from disease and sword mentions how Rashpu and Yamm were also responsible (KTU 1.14.1.16-21; compare 1.103.39-40). In one of the LB Age Amarna letters, the king of Alashiya bemoans the small amount of copper he is sending to the Egyptian pharaoh with the following excuse: "Behold, the hand of Nergal/Rashpu, my lord, is now in my country; he has slain all of the men of my country, and there is not a (single) copper-worker (left)" (EA 35:13-14).

The word **reshef** in the OT occurs only a handful of times, with quite varying translations (related to fire,

arrows, lightning, pestilence, plague). Song of Songs 8:6 complements the notion that "love is strong as death (mawet), passion fierce as the grave" with the phrase "its flashes (reshef) are flashes of fire." A psalmist writes: "[In Zion God] broke the flashing (rishefey רִשְׁפֵי) arrows, the shield, the sword, and the weapons of war" (Ps 76:3 [Heb 76:4]). Each passage can be associated with what we know of Resheph's nature from the ANE texts above. Though certainly demythologized, Ps 76:4 carries with it the imagery of Yahweh as a divine warrior defeating the war god Resheph. Scholars have highlighted two passages that retain much stronger mythic overtones. In Deut 32:22-24, we read of how Yahweh's anger will "burn to the depths of Sheol." His divine arsenal includes fire, arrows, disasters, hunger, pestilence and "burning consumption" (reshef). Similarly, Hab 3:5 mentions Yahweh marching to war with a retinue that includes pestilence and plague (reshef) marching fore and aft (compare KTU 1.82).

L. Shapshu/Shamash

Shapshu is the sun goddess at Ugarit (in contrast to the male Mesopotamian Shamash) who is called "the luminary of the gods." Ugaritic contains the idioms "to reach the sunset" and "to enter the host of the sun" to signify death. Underlying these idioms was the sense that the goddess Shapshu was intimately connected to the deceased (as was Shamash in the Mesopotamian sphere). Shapshu is prominently mentioned in the Ugaritic Funerary Text (KTU 1.161); however, her exact role is debated. Some have her burning brightly while others have her escorting the dead king or the ghost throne of the king down to the netherworld. The latter would line up with the notion that the sun deity descends into the underworld each night and thus is the proper deity to escort the dead to their final abode. In the Baal cycle (KTU 1.6.6.45-49) Shapshu leads Anatu down to the underworld to recover the slain Balu after his battle with Motu. The end of the story describes Shapshu presiding over (or "ruling" or "judging") the dead.

While the OT does employ solar imagery to describe Yahweh, it contains no emphasis on the sun's role in the underworld.

M. Sheol (שְׁאוֹל she'ol)

When personified the term she'ol can refer to the chthonic power of death. SHEOL, the place of no return (Job 7:9), is characterized by darkness (Job 17:13), dust (Job 17:16; 21:26; Ps 7:6; compare Gen 3:19), and silence (Pss 31:17-18; 94:17; 115:17; Isa 47:5). Occasionally water metaphors are used (Jonah 2:3-6) about which scholars reconstruct the backdrop of a judicial (river) ordeal. The biblical authors, like their Egyptian and Mesopotamian counterparts, used the imagery of descent and gates to describe this netherworld abode. The dead "go down" to Sheol (e.g.,

Num 16:30; Job 7:9; Isa 57:9; compare Isa 29:4; Ps 88:3-4; *KTU* 1.161.21-22; 1.5.6.24-25), the lowest place one can imagine (Deut 32:22; Isa 7:11). Its gates (Isa 38:10; Pss 9:14--Eng 9:13; 107:18; Job 38:17; compare Jer 15:7) and bars (Jonah 2:7) underscore notions of imprisonment and the inability of escape. Compare also the ropes and snares of Sheol/Death (2 Sam 22:6 = Ps 18:4-5 [Heb. 18:5-6]). Similar portrayals can be found in later Jewish (Wis 16:13; 3 Macc 5:51) and Christian (Matt 16:18; compare Rev 1:18) literature.

When personified, Sheol, like Motu (see above), was thought to have an insatiable appetite (Isa 5:14; Hab 2:5; Prov 27:20; 30:15*b*-16). It too swallows its victims (Prov 1:12; compare Ps 141:7). According to Hos 13:14, both Sheol and Death are personified as powers from which Yahweh can ransom Ephraim. The prophet Isaiah seems to depict Sheol as the personified king of the underworld rousing the shades of the dead to greet the tyrant of Babylon (Isa 14:9). Compare also Isa 28:15, 18 where the leaders are accused of making covenants with Sheol//Death. *See* AFTERLIFE; BEELZEBUL; BELIAL; BELIAR; DEAD, ABODE OF THE; DEATH, NT; DEATH, OT; GEHENNA; SATAN.

Bibliography: Bloch-Smith. *Judahite Burial Practices and Beliefs about the Dead* (1992); I. Cornelius. *The Iconography of the Canaanite Gods Reshef and Baal* (1994); J. Day. *Yahweh and the Gods and Goddesses of Canaan* (2000); B. M. Gittlen, ed. *Sacred Time, Sacred Space: Archaeology and the Religion of Israel* (2002) 169–217; G. C. Heider. *The Cult of Molek: A Reassessment* (1985); T. J. Lewis. "How Far Can Texts Take Us? Evaluating Textual Sources for Reconstructing Ancient Israelite Beliefs about the Dead." *Ritual and Cult at Ugarit.* D. Pardee, ed. (2002).

THEODORE J. LEWIS

DEITY NAMES. *See* GOD, NAMES OF; GODS, GODDESSES.

DELAIAH di-l*i*′uh [דְּלָיָהוּ delayahu, דְּלָיָה delayah; Δαλάν Dalan]. Meaning "the Lord drew up." 1. A temple priest under David allotted the twenty-third position (1 Chr 24:18).

2. One of several officials who, hearing Baruch read Jeremiah's scroll of prophecy, urged Jehoiakim not to burn the scroll (Jer 36:12, 25).

3. One of seven sons of Elioenai, a descendant of Solomon through Zerubbabel (1 Chr 3:24).

4. A family unable to prove they were descendants of Israel (Ezra 2:60; Neh 7:62; 1 Esd 5:37).

5. Father of Shemaiah who conspired to stop Nehemiah by closing the doors of the temple (Neh 6:10).

TERRY W. EDDINGER

DELICACY [מַעֲדָן ma'adhan]. Rich, expensive food eaten by kings and rulers (Gen 49:20; Prov 23:3), sometimes associated with evil (Ps 141:4) or with the deceptions of enemies (Jer 51:34; Sir 13:7). *See* FOOD; WEALTH.

DELILAH di-l*i*′luh [דְּלִילָה delilah]. A woman from the Valley of Sorek, beloved by the judge SAMSON (Judg 16:4). Unlike the former, unnamed, Philistine wife of Samson (Judg 14:1-20), Delilah bears a name but is not explicitly characterized as Philistine or Israelite. Not related to a family in the narrative, she is described as an independent individual who worked in conjunction with Samson's Philistine enemies to cause his downfall. Bribed by the PHILISTINES, Delilah tried to seduce Samson to reveal the secret of his superhuman strength. In return for obtaining this information each of the Philistine lords had promised her eleven hundred pieces of silver (Judg 16:5). Three times her attempt failed because Samson lied to her when she coaxed him to divulge his weakness. Misled, Delilah first bound him with seven fresh bowstrings that had not been dried (Judg 16:7-8), then with new ropes (Judg 16:11-12). Next she wove seven locks of hair of the sleeping Samson into her loom and fastened it with a pin (Judg 16:13-14). But when she called to her tied lover, "The Philistines are upon you, Samson," Samson freed himself easily. The Philistines, lurking in Delilah's room, were not capable of seizing him.

Finally, Delilah, blaming Samson for his threefold lie, appealed to Samson's love to weaken his resistance. Her nagging "tired him to death" so that he revealed to her the true secret of his strength (Judg 16:15-17): "A razor has never come upon my head; for I have been a Nazirite to God from my mother's womb." As long as Samson kept his hair unshorn, his strength would last (*see* NAZIR, NAZIRITE).

Recognizing the truth at last, Delilah summoned the Philistine lords, who this time carried with them the bribe money (Judg 16:18-19). Delilah made Samson sleep in her lap so that his head could be shaven. When she called again "The Philistines are upon you, Samson," Samson was not able to free himself since his strength had left him with the loss of his hair (Judg 16:20). Betrayed and delivered by his mistress, he could be overwhelmed by the Philistines (Judg 16:21).

SUSANNE OTTO

DELIVERER, THE [מַצִּיל matsil, מְפַלֵּט mefallet, מוֹשִׁיעַ moshia'; ῥυόμενος rhyomenos]. *Deliverer* translates participles of three Hebrew synonyms, ntsl (נצל), plt (פלט) and ysh' (ישע).

One meaning of the root ntsl is "rescue." The participle matsil is translated "deliverer" in one of seventeen passages, Judg 18:28: "there was no deliverer because (the city) was far from Sidon . . ." Elsewhere it is translated as a clause, often concerning rescue or deliverance from wild beasts, literal or metaphorical. In Ps 35:10: "You deliver the weak . . ." (NRSV) could be translated more literally, "You (are) the deliverer . . ."

The participle **mefallet**, from the root **plt**, means "savior" or "deliverer." We find it in a series of epithets in 2 Sam 22:2=Ps 18:2, "my rock, my fortress, and my deliverer, my God, my rock . . . , my shield, and the horn of my salvation, my stronghold," and similarly in Pss 40:17, 70:5, 144:2.

The relevant stem of **ysh**ᶜ means "help" or "save." It is used synonymously with the first verb in Ps 59:2 and with both of the others in Ps 71:2. The participle **moshia**ᶜ is translated "deliverer" in Judg 3:9, 15 and in the Qumran supplement to 1 Sam 10:27; elsewhere it is "savior." A human deliverer is a charismatic leader in the war of Yahweh, where deliverance is military. Some references to God as savior may concern enemies, but the word is more often expanded to encompass God's deliverance from sin and judgment (see Isa 43:11, 45:15, 21, etc.).

The term *deliverer* is found only once in the NRSV of the NT: Rom 11:26 cites Isa 59:20 to prove that Israel will be saved at the final judgment in spite of current rejection of Christ, "Out of Zion will come a Deliverer (**rhyomenos**); he will banish ungodliness from Jacob." The same Greek participle appears as a final clause in 1 Thess 1:9-10, "Jesus, who rescues us from the wrath that is coming." Elsewhere, **rhyomai** (ῥύομαι) is most notably used in the Lord's Prayer (Matt 6:13).

In sum, the infrequent term *deliverer* is a synonym for *savior*. It translates participles of several Hebrew words, which are also synonyms. In the early parts of the OT, deliverance is from enemies. God, who also delivers from immediate danger, often delivers from sin and judgment. In the NT, deliverance is chiefly eschatological, though it could apply to everyday situations affecting a person's ultimate destiny. *See* REDEEM, REDEEMER; SALVATION.

DALE PATRICK

DELOS dee´los [Δῆλος **Dēlos**]. A tiny, rocky island in the southern Aegean Sea at the center of the Cyclades archipelago, Delos served as the administrative seat of the Delian League, a confederacy of states aligned with ancient Athens. Greek myth (the *Homeric Hymn to Apollo*) identified Delos as the birthplace of the deities APOLLO and ARTEMIS, and their sanctuaries on the island accounted for its original renown and appeal. As it achieved great prestige as a hub of international trade during the second and early 1st cent. BCE, Delos became home to many foreign cults. The island's diverse religious context exemplified the religious mobility and syncretism that HELLENISM made possible. A Jewish community emerged there at least as early as the 2nd cent. BCE (1 Macc 15:23). A series of attacks and shifts in trade routes extinguished the prominence of Delos by the close of the 1st cent. BCE. *See* GREECE.

MATTHEW L. SKINNER

DELTA [δ d, Δ D]. The fourth letter of the Greek alphabet, derived from the Phoenician letter, **dalt** or **dilt**. *See* ALPHABET.

DELUGE. *See* FLOOD.

DEMAS dee´muhs [Δημᾶς **Dēmas**]. Paul calls Demas a "co-worker" (Phlm 24), but later says Demas has deserted him (2 Tim 4:10; *Acts of Paul and Thecla* 1, 4, 12–14). A short form of DEMETRIUS, Demas (identified as gentile in Col 4:10–14) may have been conflated with the silversmith of Acts 19:23–41.

J. ALBERT HARRILL

DEMETRIUS di-mee´tree-uhs [Δημήτριος **Dēmētrios**]. Demetrius was the name of three Seleucid kings who interacted at one time or another with Judah. 1. Demetrius I Soter (162–150 BCE) was the son of Seleucus IV (*see* SELEUCUS) who succeeded Antiochus V Eupator. The Jewish high priest Alcimus went to Demetrius for confirmation of his high priestly office and to ask for help against Judas's group (*see* JUDAS) who were still offering military opposition to Alcimus and the new Seleucid administration (1 Macc 10:37). Demetrius dispatched an army to install Alcimus in Jerusalem and to deal with the problem of Judas. Nevertheless, Judas continued his fight against Syrian rule.

Rivalry for the Seleucid throne began in Demetrius' reign and continued for much of the rest of Seleucid rule. The first was Alexander Balas (150–145 BCE; *see* SELEUCID EMPIRE) who claimed to be the son of Antiochus IV. Having received permission from the Roman Senate, he set out to try to take the Seleucid throne (Polybius 33.18). Demetrius, knowing that he needed all the allies he could get, sent an offer of peace to JONATHAN (the brother and successor of Judas. Jonathan did not believe his promises, however, and favored Alexander. The wisdom of this choice was demonstrated soon afterward when Alexander defeated and killed Demetrius in battle about the year 151 BCE.

2. Demetrius II Nicator (145–140, 129–126 BCE). In 147 BCE the son of Demetrius I sailed from Crete to attempt to take back his father's kingdom from Alexander. With the help of Ptolemy VI's forces (*see* PTOLEMY) he was able to defeat Alexander and establish his rulership in the year 145 BCE, to become Demetrius II Theos Nicator Philadelphus. Taking advantage of the struggle over the Seleucid throne, Jonathan laid siege to the Akra, which was still in Syrian hands. When Demetrius heard of this after his own position was secure, he demanded an accounting from Jonathan. The latter went boldly to

Demetrius and came away with major concessions from the king. Demetrius was soon glad of Jonathan as an ally, for troubles developed between him and his army. A force of 3,000 Jewish soldiers was dispatched to Antioch to help Demetrius put down a revolt. Shortly afterward Tryphon, a general of Alexander Balas, crowned Alexander's young son and proclaimed him king as a rival to Demetrius. In the resulting engagement, Demetrius was defeated, and the new king Antiochus VI wrote to Jonathan to confirm him in his offices.

Despite his initial defeat, Demetrius II was still alive and had not conceded the throne. Tryphon marched to Beth Shean in Judea where he was met by Jonathan. Demetrius II captured Jonathan by trickery, claiming that Jonathan was only a hostage for money owed to the Seleucid government. Simon (*see* SIMON) paid the ransom demanded but to no avail, for Tryphon executed Jonathan and retreated. Not long afterward he carried out his plan of killing Antiochus VI and taking the throne for himself (ca. 142–138 BCE). Simon negotiated with Demetrius who still sought to regain the throne. The latter made a variety of far-reaching concessions and, now under Demetrius II's rule, Judea became an independent state. After Demetrius had made concessions to Simon to enlist his friendship, he was too busy to be concerned with Judea. He marched east in hopes of gaining further assistance against Tryphon, but was taken prisoner by the Parthians. Demetrius's wife sent for his brother to marry her and take the throne as Antiochus VII Sidetes (138–129 BCE). Some years later, however, Antiochus was killed fighting the Parthians and was succeeded by Demetrius II who took the throne for a second time. But after a short second reign he was killed fighting his rival for the Seleucid throne.

3. **Demetrius III Eucaerus.** Around 90 BCE there were four claimants to the Seleucid throne. One of these was Demetrius III Eucaerus of Damascus who had been put on the throne by Ptolemy IX about 95 BCE. Alexander Janneus (*see* HASMONEANS) was now high priest and king of the Hasmonean kingdom, but he had considerable opposition from among the Jews of Palestine. Janneus' opponents called in Demetrius III against him (ca. 88 BCE; apparently mentioned in 3+4I, 2). However, when those who had asked Demetrius' aid now abandoned him, Demetrius had little choice but to retire from the country. The Parthians captured him a year or so later.

LESTER L. GRABBE

4. Demetrius the silversmith was an artisan who instigated a riot against Paul for encouraging the Ephesians to refrain from buying Artemisian shrines (Acts 19:23-41).

5. Demetrius the Chronographer was a 3rd cent. BCE historian whose work, found only in fragments in Josephus' and Eusebius' writings, is the first known writing to use the LXX.

6. Demetrius of Phalerum was an Athenian rhetorician and historian (ca. 355–280 BCE), who was instrumental in establishing the library of Alexandria with books of every known religion, including Bible translations.

EMILY R. CHENEY

DEMON [δαιμόνιον daimonion, δαίμων daimōn]. The Greek daimonion ("demon") comes from the adjective daimonios (δαιμόνιος "divine"). Related terms include daimōn (divinity, a god, goddess) or pneuma (πνεῦμα spirit). Generally, a demon is a preturnatural semi-divine entity, from the ambiguous root daiō (δαίω tear apart, divide," or, perhaps, "apportion or burn"). Although indeterminate in the OT, demons in the NT are seen as evil or unclean spiritual beings with the capacity to harm life or allure people to heresy or immorality.

A. The Old Testament
B. Greek
  1. The Septuagint
  2. Philo
  3. Josephus
C. The Dead Sea Scrolls
D. The Apocrypha and Pseudepigrapha
E. The New Testament
  1. Jesus
  2. Paul
  3. Mark
  4. Matthew
  5. Luke–Acts
  6. John
  7. Letters
    a. Ephesians
    b. Colossians
    c. 1 Timothy
    d. James
    e. 1 John
  8. Revelation
Bibliography

A. The Old Testament

No single Hebrew word exists that corresponds to *demon*, and the terms thought to represent the idea are often insufficiently represented to determine their meaning. Early traditions portray God as sending God's spirit (1 Sam 16:13) or a divine spirit (רוּחַ אֱלֹהִים ruakh 'elohim, Exod 31:3) or, on the other hand, an evil spirit (רוּחַ רָעָה ruakh ra'ah) causing personal torment (1 Sam 16:14-16, 23; 18:10; 19:9), or harm in a relationship (Judg 9:23).

A number of terms are used to designate "demons." The general noun se'irim (שְׂעִירִים, "goat-demons") occurs only 4 times. In Isa 13:21 they are (along with the wild animals, howling creatures, and ostriches), part of an apocalyptic scene of God's destruction and, similarly, in 34:14 are depicted with Lilith (see below). The seʿirim are also depicted as prohibited objects of worship (Lev 17:7) to which Jeroboam had built high places (2 Chr 11:15; 2 Kgs 23:8). The two occurrences of the noun shedhim (שֵׁדִים; plural, "demons"), which became the common term for demons (11Q11 II, 4), refer not to "no-gods" but to new or unknown gods to whom the people of God had sacrificed (Deut 32:17), including their children (Ps 106:37; see also Judg 2:11-19) when taking up the ways of the Cannanites, rendering the people polluted or unclean because of this prostitution (Ps 106:38-39 see also 1 Cor 10:20). Similarly, when God did not answer, Saul illicitly (Isa 8:19) sought the woman necromancer of Endor. In being asked to call up Samuel from the dead she is said to bring up a "god from the ground" who had the appearance of an old man (1 Sam 28:13-14).

Despite later demonization of the term AZAZEL (e.g., *1 En.* 8:1; 9:6; 10:4-8; 13:1-2; *Apoc. Ab.* 13.6-14) there is no agreement on its meaning within Leviticus, where the word azazel (עֲזָאזֵל) occurs only in the directions for the ritual for the Day of Atonement (Lev 16:8, 10, 26). While it has been proposed that azazel refers to a combination of ʿez (עֵז, "goat") and ʿazav עָזַב ("go away"), giving the meaning "scapegoat" or "for sending away," this interpretation is unlikely, because the goat is said to be for Azazel (Lev 16:8). The goat is sent (16:10) or goes to Azazel (16:26). Moreover, the phrase "for Yahweh" and "for Azazel" are in parallel (16:8), so it is unlikely that azazel is an abstract term for "entire removal." Azazel is also unlikely to mean "rocky precipice (or mountain)" (e.g., *Tg. Ps.-J* on Lev 16:10), for in Lev 16:22 the goat goes to the wilderness or "a separate place"; the parallel between Yahweh and Azazel suggests that Azazel refers to a being, perhaps a deity, rather than a location. Preternatural forces are represented by a goatlike figure in Isa 13:21. That God punishes Azazel by commanding that he be covered with rocks in the desert until the day of judgment (*1 En.* 10:4-8) contributed to the development of the idea of Azazel being demonic, even the chief demon (see the people's complaints to God against Azazel in *1 En.* 7-8). (e.g., *1 En.* 54.5; 55.4). The word lilith (לִילִית) occurring only in Isa 34:14 (and, perhaps, Job 18:15) exemplifies the uncertainty as to how far the ANE parallels are useful in determining the meaning of terms. In later texts "Lilith" was a female demon (*b. ʿErub.* 100b; *b. Nid.* 24b; *B. Bat.* 73a; *b. shabb.* 151b; also 4Q510 1 5; 4Q511 10 1), in a list with wildcat, HYENA, and goat-demon, which suggests that the lilith was a desert dwelling animal. In Mesopotamian demonology, popular imagination located the demonic not only in mythical creatures but also in animals such as dogs, snakes, and scorpions. Further, lilith is the Hebrew form of the name of an Akkadian female demon from which protection was sought (*CAD* 9:190; *RlA* 7:24-25).

Some other figures or terms in the OT have been understood to have demonic characteristics. Babylonian texts refer to demons that spill blood and suck veins; the ʿaluqah (עֲלוּקָה) mentioned in Prov 30:15 is probably a leech (*HALOT* 2.831) rather than a demonic figure. The saraf (שָׂרָף; plural serafim [שְׂרָפִים, Num 21:6, 8; Deut 8:15; Isa 6:2, 6; 14:29; 30:6]) has been understood as a demon or demonic serpent because of the association between serpents and demons among the Arabs and Egyptians, and the demonic connotations assumed inherent to the serpent in Gen 3:1-14. However, the context of all but the Isa 6 references requires that they be understood as serpents or, in Isa 14:29; 30:6, as flying or, more likely because of the context of judgment in 14:29, piercing serpents. In Isa 6:2, 6 the serafim attending the Lord on his throne would not have been considered demons but, perhaps winged figures with a human body (*ANEP*, 655). Even though the "terror of the night" and the "arrow that flies by day" as well as the paralleled "pestilence that stalks in darkness" and "the destruction that wastes at noonday" (Ps 91:5-6) are sometimes taken to refer to the feared assaults of the demonic, the meanings of the terms are, perhaps deliberately, ambiguous and metaphorical so as to embrace both the preternatural (compare Deut 28:22; Job 6:4) as well as the natural sources of threat to human existence. While earlier texts portray God as responsible for all spiritual forces (see above), only in the postexilic Ps 91 does the OT allude to protection against malevolent forces: living under the shelter of the Most High (91:1-4, 9, 14).

B. Greek

Homer, in the *Illiad*, uses atē (ἄτη, "delusion," "bewilderment") to denote a deceptive supernatural entity (*Il.* 9.21). He also gives such an explanation to a person's temporarily heightened menos (μένος, "might," *Il.* 13.61, 75), as in the case of Hector, who became manic, foaming at the mouth with his eyes glowing (15.605-610) in a way that would later came to be described as demon possession. Philostratus used daimōn to denote such superhuman overpowering of a person (Philostratus, *Vit. Apoll.* 4.44). In Homer daimonen is used of the gods assembled on Mount Olympus (*Il.* 1.222; 3.420). Further, Homer uses the term daimōn when a god acts with hostility toward a person. From the time of Hesiod the demons were the souls of the dead that kept watch over human affairs (*Op.* 120–29; Aeschylus, *Pers.* 601; Plato, *Resp.* 540c).

Aeschylus suggested that the activity of the evil demons is the omnipotent activity of Zeus (*Ag.* 160-66; 1486; 1563-66). Pindar said that Zeus directs the demons (*Pyth.* 5.12–23). Perhaps because of deteriorating social and political conditions in the 6th cent. BCE, there seems to have been an increase in anxiety and dread in relation to the demons.

For Plato demons were lesser deities (*Apol.* 27c-d; *Phaedr.* 246e), intermediaries between gods and humans (*Symp.* 202d–203a; *Tim.* 40d; *Leg.* 717a-f). This view was followed by others (Plutarch, *Def. orac.* 13.II.416e; Xenocrates, frag. 23; 225). These demons were creators (*Tim.* 42d), ruling over parts of the cosmos and protecting nations and individuals (*Phaedr.* 107d; 113d; *Resp.* 617d; 620d; *Leg.* 877a); Socrates thought that they were guiding his actions (*Theaet.* 151a; *Euthyd.* 3b). Xenocrates, a disciple of Plato, systematized demonology, distinguishing between greater and lesser (Xenocrates, frag. 225; compare Plato, *Symp.* 202d) and between good and bad demons (Xenocrates, 25), holding that the demons communicated to mortals (see Plato, *Symp.* 202e) through oracles and dreams and could be seen as a person's conscience. Because the ancients believed that the murdered could avenge themselves (Plato, *Leg.* 865d-e), and as demons were considered lower order deities and intermediaries, they became firmly associated with human suffering (*Corp. herm.* 16.10-19; Plutarch, *Quaest. rom.* 276f–277a) and possession (Porphyry, *Abst.* II.36). Eventually, demons were associated with evil, so that apotropaic activities were required (Apuleius, *De deo Socr.* 6).

1. The Septuagint

The LXX identifies pagan gods, including the spirits of popular belief, as demons (Bar 4:7) translating shedhim (שֵׁדִים, Deut 32:17; Ps 105:37 [Heb. 106:37]) and 'elilim (אֱלִילִים, "worthless ones," Ps 95:5 [96:5]) as daimoniois ("demons," Isa 65:3). Concomitantly, the se'irim שְׂעִירִים are "worthless" (mataios [μάταιος], Lev 17:7) and "worthless idols" (2 Chr 11:15). The elusive terms of threat in Ps 90:6 [91:6] are identified as demonic, and the se'irim of Isa 13:21; 34:14 are also demons. Thus, while in the monotheistic environment of the Hebrew text, it is God who is responsible for God's own Spirit as well as an evil spirit (1 Sam 16:14), in Tobit it is an evil demon (poneron πονηρόν) (3:8, 17) or spirit (6:8) that kills a woman's husbands out of envy and is sent away by the smoke of burning fish (6:8, 18; 8:3). These entities are not called daimōn, probably because of the word's positive use in popular belief.

2. Philo

In a complex, not always apparently consistent demonology, Philo uses daimōn variously: of lesser deities (*Decal.* 54); as a strong positive, even divine, adjective (*Aet.* 47, 64, 76); to refer to human fate or destiny (*Flacc.* 168, 179); to refer to the ghosts or spirits of the dead (*Legat.* 65); and of a protective genius (*Prob.* 39). He believed that daimones ("souls") filled the air, and he considered them to equal the number of the stars. Some were the words (logoi λόγοι) God used to speak to humans (*Gig.* 6–16). Some of these daimones mated with "the daughters of men" (Gen 6:2) to produce the angels of the OT (*Gig.* 6–16). Some never wanted

union with a body and are the viceroys of the Ruler of the universe, doing God's bidding (including assisting in creation, *Conf.* 171) and communicating with God's children. Philo prefers to call these entities angels or messengers rather than demons (*Somn.* 1.139–40; *see* ANGEL). Thus, Philo says that if his readers realized that souls, demons, and angels were different names for the same reality, they would be delivered of their fear of demons and superstition (*Gig.* 16). Later Philo introduces the idea that troops of evil tenants have to be ejected from the human body in order that only a single good entity may enter (*Somn.* 1.148-50). However, commenting on Exod 12:23 he says that, at birth, two powers, one salutary, the other destructive, enter a person. Should the evil in this mixture become greater, there is torment, ignominy, contention, battle, and bodily illness (*QE* 1.23). Philo's contribution to demonology is the idea of God's salvific action of sending logoi into the world, God's removal of the autonomy of demons, and subordination of demons to one deity.

3. Josephus

For Josephus, a ghost or soul of the dead could seek revenge (*Ant.* 13.317, 416; *J.W.* 1.521, 599, 607). The spirit or demon from an evil person could enter the living and kill them (*J.W.* 7.185). Good demons (*Ant.* 16.210), who helped people (*Ant.* 13.416; *J.W.* 6.47), were the souls of those killed in battle (*Ant.* 13.314; *J.W.* 1.607; 6.47). A demon could be the source of prophecy (*J.W.* 1.69; *Ant.* 13.300), protect a person (*Ant.* 16.210), and, as in the case of Saul, cause illness (*Ant.* 6.166, 168, 211). Exceptionally, Josephus uses daimonios for dreadful or calamitous acts of supranatural origin (*J.W.* 1.370, 373; 6.252). In the story of Eleazar, bad demons are shown to be removed by a professional exorcist (*Ant.* 8.45-49; also see *J.W.* 7.180–85).

C. The Dead Sea Scrolls

These texts are important in shedding light on the demonology in the NT traditions. For the QUMRAN community, a demon (e.g., 4Q510 1 5) was usually called a "spirit" (e.g., 4Q560 1 II, 6). As seen in two very brief lists of demons (4Q510 1 5-6; 4Q511 10 1-2), they could be qualified in a number of ways. As angels or messengers of destruction (4Q510 1 5 also, e.g., 1QS IV, 12; 1QM XIII, 12) they could cause people to live in darkness (1QM XIII, 12) as well as punish the wicked (1QS IV, 12; CD II, 6). The use in certain places of "bastards" (4Q510 1 5; 4Q511 2II, 3; 35 7, 48 3, 182 1; also 4Q444 2I, 4; 1QHᵃ XXIV, 3) the demonology of Qumran is seen to be informed by the *Book of Watchers* in which the spirits of the Giants (NEPHILIM, *1 En* 15.11), the dead offspring of Watchers and beautiful women, are the demons. Demons are also called "wicked" (4Q511 1 6, also, e.g., 4Q444 1 4) as well as "destroyer" (e.g., 4Q511 1 6). The lists include the names lilith (4Q510 1 5) and "howlers" or "owls," and "yelpers" or "jackals" (4Q510 1 5). In the context of the list we may speculate that these names could reflect the behavior of those afflicted by such a demon (compare Mark 1:24; 3:11; 5:7; 9:26).

For the leader of the demons (1QS III, 24; also, e.g., 11Q13 II, 12–13; 4Q387ᵃ 3 III 4) there is also a variety of descriptors, most commonly BELIAL (e.g., 1QS I, 16–II, 8; CD IV, 12-15; 1QM I, 4–5; 13–16), but also Mastema (e.g., CD XVI, 5; 1QM Xiii, 11), Melcheresa (4Q280 1 2), SATAN (11QPsᵃ XIX, 15; a name also perhaps used for demons; 1Q28b I.8) and, depending on how 4Q560 is restored, BEELZEBUL, as well as ABADDON (11Q11 IV, 10; 4Q286 7 II, 7).

Even though the Dead Sea Scrolls depict humanity as ruled by either the Prince of Light or the Angel of Darkness, the leader of the demons is both an angel (1QS III, 20-21) and under the authority of God (1QS III, 23), having been created by him (1QS III, 25). Nevertheless, 11Q13 II, 12 depicts Belial as being in rebellion against the commandments of God.

The Scrolls portray people as combating demons in a number of different ways. The Tobit fragments (4Q196–200) probably endorse the divinely ordained method of fumigation to cause potentially fatal demons to flee (Tob 6.4; 11.4, 7-8; 4Q196 14 I, XII; 4Q197 4 I, 13-14). Also, in an amulet a spirit that has entered a person (4Q560, 1 I, 3) is directly addressed and adjured in an exorcism (4Q560, 1 I, 5-6). In 11Q5 (11QPsᵃ) David is said to compose four songs for making music over the stricken or possessed (27.9-10). These were probably used in exorcisms conducted by a MASKIL, perhaps in public worship (4Q511 63 IV 1-3), who declared (hymnlike) the splendor and protection of God and angels in order to reassure the faithful as well as subdue the spirits. These exorcisms would also involve hurling abuse at the spirit and adjuring it by God (e.g., 4Q511 35; 8Q5 1; 11Q11 III, 1-12) or asking God to send a powerful ANGEL (11Q11 IV, 5), with the expectation that the demon would be sent to the great abyss (11Q11 IV, 7-9). Abraham is said to pray for the king and lay hands on his head so that the plague and evil spirit was removed from him (1QapGen XX, 28-29). The GENESIS APOCRYPHON contains examples of dealing with demons in a way similar to those in the Gospels and Acts.

D. The Apocrypha and Pseudepigrapha

Among this body of literature, the first section of *1 En.*, the *Book of Watchers* (*1 En.* 1–36), is of particular interest, for it offers a systematic demonology from the 3ʳᵈ cent. BCE that widely informed the dualism of the NT era. Interpreting the story of the sons of God in Gen 6:1-4, the book tells of some angels, the Watchers, who came down to have sexual intercourse with beautiful women (*1 En.* 6:1–7.6). Their giant offspring devoured everything, and in response

to human cries, God sent the angel Gabriel to destroy these children of adultery (*1 En.* 10:9). However, the evil spirits coming from the dead giants continued to inflict harm on people (*1 En.* 15:8-11). In this myth the diversity of demonic figures has been combined into one category. Also, in Enoch, they are not fallen angels but spirits of the giants remaining on earth causing suffering until the end (*1 En.* 16:1). In the *Similitudes of Enoch* (*1 En.* 37–71), a 1ˢᵗ cent. BCE to 1ˢᵗ cent. CE addition to the Enoch traditions, Azazel or Satan are the leaders of the evil spirits who will be thrown into the fiery abyss on the great day of judgment (*1 En.* 54:1-6).

Borrowing from Enochic traditions, Gen 6:1-5 provides *Jubilees* with the interpretive base for demonology (*Jub.* 5:1, 6-10; *1 En.* 6:1-2; 7:1-2, 5). Demons are equated with foreign gods who were alloted to the nations (*Jub.* 15:30-32). They seduce the Israelites (*Jub.* 1:7-8, 11; also 19:28) over whom the Lord alone is ruler (15:32). The leader of the spirits or demons is called Mastema (10:7-8; also 4Q225 2 II, 13; 4Q387a 3 III, 4; 4Q390 1.11; 2 I, 7) or Satan (*Jub.* 10:11). Twice he is, perhaps, called Belial (1:20; 15:33); although, as in the OT, this could mean "worthless" (e.g., Judg 19:22; 1 Sam 25:5). The polluted demons lead humans astray (*Jub.* 10:1) and cause sickness (10:12). In God's answer to Noah's prayer to restrain the demons (10:4-6), Mastema pleads for leniency. Showing that the demons and their leader are under the ultimate authority and control of God (see 10:3), and carry out his wishes (see 1QS III, 15-17, 25-26), God allows one-tenth of the demons not to be bound but remain the responsibility of their leader so they can continue to fulfill their role (10:8-9). In the meantime, Noah was taught and recorded all "the healing of their illnesses together with their seductions" (10:12). Abraham's prayer "Save me from the hand of evil spirits" (12:20), shows that the removal of or protection from demons may also have be sought in prayer.

E. The New Testament

Apart from its soteriological connections, especially in the exorcism stories of Jesus, there is little interest in demons in the NT. Nevertheless, hints of underlying views are evident: demons, the evil angels of Satan (Mark 3:22), can form a group and cooperate against a person (Matt 12:45/Luke 11:26), can be so numerous or multifaceted as to be described as "legion" (Mark 5:9), and a number of different ones can be said to possess a person (Luke 8:2), causing a wide range of sicknesses. The NT writers made a distinction between demonic and other types of sicknesses (e.g., Mark 1:32-34). Following the pattern set by the LXX, apart from Matt 8:31, daimonion is used rather than daimōn. In every case, save on the lips of the Greeks in Acts 17:18 and where Luke may have sarcastic intentions, daimonion has pejorative connotations.

1. Jesus

From what can be recovered of the historical Jesus, exorcisms were the most common form of healing or miracle he is said to have performed. He understood these exorcisms not only to be relieving suffering (e.g., Mark 5:1-20) but, as is most clearly shown in the so-called Beelzebul Controversy (Mark 3:22-27; Mark 9:32-34/12:22-30/Luke 11:14-23), to be a battle with Satan, in which he plunders his possessions. If the emphatic "I" (Matt 12:28/Luke 11:20) and the incantation in Mark 9:25 reflect Jesus' thinking, he was fully cognizant of the power of his personal force in causing a demon to leave a person (see Philostratus, *Vit. Apoll.* 4.20; Lucian, *Philops.* 16). Yet, in the style of the ancient magicians (e.g., Josephus, *Ant.* 8.46–47; *b. Me'il.* 17b), who cast out demons, Jesus also acknowledged being dependent on (or infused with) a power-authority: the Spirit (or finger) of God (Matt 12:28/Luke 11:20).

Exorcisms were a common occurrence in Jesus' time, and his contemporaries did not look on exorcism as an eschatological sign. Therefore, it is astounding that Jesus made the unique claim that his exorcisms were the operation of the kingdom of God. That is, his dealing with demons was not merely preparatory to the coming of the kingdom of God, nor a sign or even an illustration of its arrival, but the actual materialization of the kingdom of God (Matt 12:28/Luke 11:20). If the parable of the Wheat and Tares echoes the voice of the historical Jesus, it is probable that, reflecting a two-stage defeat of the demons held at the time (e.g., Isa 24:22; *1 En.* 10:4-6, 11-13), he considered his exorcisms were the first of a two stage defeat of Satan and the demons to be completed in the eschaton. *See* EXORCISM.

2. Paul

In contrast to the Gospels and Acts, Paul has little to say about evil spirits or demons. In the undisputed Pauline letters, demons are mentioned in only one place. He says that "what pagans sacrifice they offer to demons and not to God" (1 Cor 10:20; also 1 Tim 4:1; see *1 En.* 19:1; *Jub.* 1:11). Unlike his contemporary Greeks, Paul did not attribute his catalogue of troubles in 2 Cor 11:24-27 to any sinister beings of the unseen world. Only in 2 Cor 12:7 does he attribute evil, a thorn in the flesh, to such a figure that he takes to be a messenger (angelos ἄγγελος) of Satan. Nevertheless, there are a number of passages in which Paul shows the strength of his belief in the unseen evil powers of Satan (1 Cor 5:5; 2 Cor 11:14-15).

Much of what we can glean of Paul's ideas about evil spiritual beings is contained in his notion of "principalities and powers." The most obvious meaning of this language is that behind the pagan world order, where there were supernatural motivating powers (Deut 32:8; Isa 24:21-22; Dan 10:13, 20; 1 Cor 2:6-8). However, this by no means exhausts the content of Paul's use of "principalities and powers," in relation to which Rom 8:38-39 is of particular interest (see 1 Cor 15:24-25; also Eph 3:10; 6:12; Col 2:8-15). In the context of listing potential barriers between God and people, the word rulers (archōn ἄρχων) being tied to "angels" (angelos) in the phrase "nor angels nor rulers" (oute angeloi oute archai οὔτε ἄγγελοι οὔτε ἀρχαὶ) suggests both that the "rulers" are probably not intended to refer to civil authorities but to evil spiritual beings, and that, reciprocally, the "angels" are also sinister and rebellious beings in league with Satan. For, as we have just noted, in 2 Cor 12:7, Paul also expresses the view that an "angel" of Satan is responsible for harming his body (see also Col 2:18). Thus, not unlike the synoptic traditions associated with exorcism, Paul has a notion of evil spiritual beings afflicting the body and being a potential spiritual barrier, as is captured in these being called "unclean" (akathartos ἀκάθαρτος) spirits, especially in Mark's gospel.

In 1 Cor 15:24-25—"Then comes the end, when he hands over the kingdom to God the Father, after he has destroyed every rule and every authority and power"—it is not clear exactly how Paul envisages these entities save that they are preternatural enemies to be defeated before the kingdom can be handed over to God. In the post-Pauline Col 1:15 (also 2:8-15) the triumph over the rulers and authorities takes place in relation to the cross, as it does in the Fourth Gospel. That is not Paul's view in 1 Cor 15:24-25. Instead, like Jesus and the synoptic writers, Paul has linked the destruction of Satan's emissaries with the coming of the kingdom of God (Mark 3:20-27/Matt 12:22-45/Luke 11:14-23). However, for Paul, that destruction takes place at the end of time (1 Cor 15:23). Not surprisingly, then, in Rom 8:38-39 the assumption is that whatever the cross event (and the intercession of Christ Jesus) meant in relation to evil spiritual beings, Paul assumes they are still active and potentially harmful though, now, they are not able to effect a final separation between God and his people.

3. Mark

For the earliest Gospel, daimonion (eleven times, also 16:9, 17) and pneuma akatharton (πνεῦμα ἀκάθαρτον, "unclean spirit"—eleven times) are synonyms (3:22, 30; 7:25-26). Pneuma akatharton, not used in pagan literature until the 3rd cent. by Porphyry (*Christ.* 49.5, in reference to Mark 5:8), is likely to be an established term from his tradition (though see, e.g., Mark 3:11, 30; 6:7) since he only uses akathartos with pneuma. Although Mark probably has a slight preference for daimonion, in these two terms he is able to communicate to both Jews and Greeks. Against the background of the Torah teaching that the pure and the impure are not able to coexist, the Jewish readers would have been able to appreciate his message that Jesus, the "holy one of God" (Mark 1:24) has come to defeat the unclean spirits. The Greeks would have been able to understand that the feared demons were being defeated in the exorcisms, for demons are only mentioned in the context of exorcism (e.g., 1:34, 39; 3:15). They cause people to convulse and cry out (1:26), to have preternatural strength, to injure themselves (5:3-5), they throw people down, cause foaming at the mouth, grinding of the teeth (9:18) and provoke people to destroy themselves (9:22). Demons are able to enter animals as well (5:11-13).

As in the other Synoptic Gospels, Satan is the chief of demons, also called Beelzebul, who, with his minions, possesses people (Mark 3:22-27). Satan's key role is to divert Jesus from his ministry, as in the Temptation story (1:13) and through Peter's rebuke, which Mark identifies with Satan's speech (8:33). If Mark intends the sower (4:3, 14) to be Jesus then, again, Satan is depicted as destroying the work of Jesus through taking away the word planted in people (4:15). Concomitantly, throughout the first part of his story—where the question of Jesus' identity is important (1:27; 2:7; 4:41; 6:1-6, 14-16, 49-50, 54; 8:27-28) and Mark asserts from the beginning (1:1), and has God confirm (1:11), that Jesus is the Son of God—Mark shows the human character's ignorance of Jesus' true identity. It is in the cries of the demons that Mark is able to remind his readers who Jesus is (1:24-25, 34; 3:11-12; 5:7).

Nevertheless, Mark's interest in demons revolves primarily around their possession of people and their defeat in the exorcisms of Jesus. From Mark's perspective the importance of Jesus' dealing with the demons can be seen in noting that Jesus' first major public act is an exorcism. Also, of his thirteen healing stories, the largest single category is that of exorcism (1:21-28; 5:1-20; 7:24-30; 9:14-29). Then Mark heightens the importance of Jesus' exorcisms through the summaries of Jesus' ministry (1:32-34; 3:11-12).

Mark portrays Jesus using techniques of dealing with the demonic that would have been familiar to his readers from their knowledge of other exorcists. Jesus "rebukes" (1:25; 3:12; 9:25), "muzzles" (1:25-26), and "commands" (9:25) that demons never enter a person again. Jesus uses the supposed power in a name to gain ascendancy over a demon (5:9), transfers demons from one habitat to another (5:12-13) and exorcizes from a distance (7:24-29). In confronting the demons Jesus is empowered by the Spirit and is doing battle against Satan (3:22-30). Through the exorcisms (1:24, 27) and confrontations with the demons (1:34; 3:11-12, 23-27; 5:7) and the demonic (4:41), the Jesus of Mark is shown to be the Son of God (3:11; 5:7).

4. Matthew

Matthew's terminology for demons is both different and slightly more complex than Mark's. Only three times does Matthew use pneuma akatharton (plural pneumata πνεύματα) for an unclean spirit (Matt 10:1;

12:43, 45) and, in contrast to Mark, he uses pneuma for God (Matt 3:16; 12:18, 28). Perhaps only for stylistic reasons, Matt 8:16 is the only place in the NT where the unqualified use of pneumata refers to demons, so that the demonized have spirits expelled from them.

In referring to demons, Matthew prefers the term daimōn (Matt 4:24; 7:22; 8:16, 28, 33; 9:32, 33, 34; 10:8; 11:18; 12:22, 24, 27, 28; 15:22; 17:18) rather than pneuma akatharton (10:1; 12:43). Thus, in 8:28 (Mark 52–53), Matthew omits the idea of the demoniacs living in the tombs, being more interested in the ferocity of the demonic and the power-authority of Jesus. Also, Matthew is the only NT writer to use the word daimōn ("demon," 8:31). Since its only occurrence in the LXX translates gad ("fortune," Isa 65:11), a hidden reference to Gad, god of good fortune (DCH 2.325; see, e.g., Josh 11:17; 15:37). In using daimōn, Matthew may have wanted to reflect the Hellenistic setting of his exorcism story and his view that Jesus defeats such "divinities."

Matthew also shows a greater interest in the chief of demons than Mark, using the terms archōn ("ruler," 9:34; 12:24; Mark 3:22; Luke 11:15); beelzeboul (Βεελζεβοὺλ, "Beelzebul," Matt 10:25; 12:24, 27; Mark 3:22; Luke 11:15, 18-19); echthros (ἐχθρός, "enemy," Matt 13:25, 28, 39; Luke 10:19); ischuros (ἰσχυρός "strong man," Matt 12:29); peirazōn (πειράζων, "tempter," Matt 4:3; elsewhere in the NT only at 1 Thess 3:5; not in the LXX); poneros (πονηρός, "evil one," Matt 5:37 [6:13]; 13:19, 38); and, most commonly, diabolos διάβολος (used interchangeably with satan [σατάν], 4:10; 12:26; 16:23], as the opponent of Jesus (Matt 4:1, 5, 8, 11/Luke 4:2, 3, 6, 13) and his followers (13:39; Luke 8:12), as well as the chief of demons (Matt 12:24, 26), his messengers (angeloi, Matt 25:41).

Matthew's preferred term for those afflicted by demons is daimonizomai (δαιμονίζομαι, "to be demon-possessed").

The submission of the demons to Jesus and his supremacy over them is conveyed when the demons ask questions rather than make demands (Matt 8:29/Mark 5:7). Alternatively, since the earliest manuscripts have very little punctuation, Matthew may have intended the demon(iac)s to declare rather than ask: "You have come here to torment us before the time" (Matt 8:29). In "come" Matthew is probably alluding to the coming of God's kingdom and his anointed messenger (6:10; 16:28). In saying that the torment is "before time"—that is, before the final judgment—Matthew is expressing his conviction that the torment or defeat of the demons expected in the eschaton (e.g., 1 En. 10:4-6; 1QS IV, 16) has already begun in the exorcisms. The parable of the strong man (Matt 12:29) also shows that Matthew considered that in the removal of demons from individuals Jesus was engaged in the first part of Satan's defeat.

Jesus' supremacy over the demons is also seen in the dialogue between Jesus and the demon(iac)s being reduced so that all that remains is the simple authoritative command "Go"—the only time Matthew mentions Jesus' words to demons (Matt 8:32/Mark 5:13). From Matthew's perspective the Son of God does not need to use complicated techniques. In the healing of the epileptic boy Jesus suffers no ignorance of the patient's history (7:17-18) and is instantly and completely successful (17:18; compare Mark 9:24-27). In the story of the healing of the Canaanite woman's daughter, the woman kneels or worships Jesus and initially says to him: "Have mercy on me, O Lord, Son of David." She goes on to address Jesus as "Lord" three times (Matt 15:21-28). In short, for Matthew, Jesus' successful dealings with the demons reveal him to be the Son of David or of God.

Matthew has three of the four Markan stories of Jesus casting out demons (Matt 8:28-34; 17:14-21; 15:21-28; Mark 1:21-28) and duplicated one from Q (Matt 12:22-23/Luke 11:14 and Matt 9:32-34). However, he has removed exorcism from its programmatic status in the first Gospel (Mark 1:21-28), not including an exorcism story until 8:24-34, and sometimes treating them as healings (e.g., Matt 4:24; 17:14-21). Yet, as is clear from Matt 12:22-30, he maintains the view that Jesus' dealing with demons—not empowered by Satan (a blasphemous suggestion, Matt 12:32) but by the Holy Spirit (12:28)—is a messianic activity (Isa 42:7, 16; 29:18 [32:3]; 35:5; 42:18-20; 43:8; 61:1 [LXX]).

5. Luke–Acts

Although Luke has the most developed pneumatology among NT writers, and, with considerable creativity, he mentions demons more than any other writer, the range of his vocabulary for demonology is slightly more limited than Matthew's. Luke uses daimonion for an evil spiritual entity 23 times in his Gospel (Matthew 11 times; Mark 11 times; John 6 times). He uses the word only once in Acts, but in the Greek sense of a divine being (Acts 17:18). The term akatharta pneumata (ἀκάθαρτα πνεύματα, "unclean spirits") is used 5 times in Luke (4:36; 6:18; 8:29; 9:42; 11:24) and twice in Acts (5:16; 8:7). In his general avoidance of single terms to characterize the sick, he only once uses ho daimonistheis (ὁ δαιμονισθείς, "the possessed," Luke 8:36). Also, only Luke uses the exact term "evil spirits" (pneumatōn ponērōn, [πνευμάτων πονηρῶν] Luke 7:21; 8:2; Acts 19:12, 13, 15-16). He does not use the term daimōn ("demon"). In Luke 4:33, perhaps to help his Greek readers, the unique term "spirit of an unclean demon" (pneuma daimoniou akathartou πνεῦμα δαιμονίου ἀκαθάρτου) is used to equate unclean spirits with the term "demons." After this point in the narrative pneuma and daimonion are generally synonymous.

The demons are led by beelzeboul (Luke 11:15, 18, 19) the archōn diamoniōn ("ruler of the demons," 11:15) who is also called satan ("Satan," 10:18; 11:18; 13:16; 22:3, 31) for whom the terms diabolos ("devil," 4:2, 3, 6, 13; 8:12), echthros ("enemy," Luke 10:19; compare Acts 13:10) and ischuros ("strong man," 11:21) are also used for the one standing in opposition to Jesus. Luke does not use the term peirazōn ("tempter"), nor ponēros ("evil one") for the devil.

In that the devil, who first appears in the Temptation story (Luke 4:1-13), is said to leave Jesus "for awhile" (4:13), the reader anticipates Jesus continuing to contend with him (11:14-23; 13:11, 16), including, it turns out, through exorcizing his minions (e.g., 4:33-37). Like Mark, Luke depicts Satan or the devil attempting to destroy the work of Jesus; but Luke more clearly shows the devil as the enemy of the early church as well (Luke 8:11-12; Acts 6:7; 13:5). However, Satan is able to "shake in a sieve" (22:31) but not totally destroy Peter and the disciples—the church.

The eschatological significance of the casting out of demons by Jesus is spelled out in Luke 11:20. Unlike the Fourth Gospel, the cross is not associated with the defeat of Satan, though the crucifixion is a battle with Satan (Luke 22:53). Luke maintained the view that the ministry of Jesus was the first stage in the defeat of Satan, the final stage to be in the eschaton (compare 8:31). In the story of the return of the Seventy (-two) followers, where Jesus says that "I have been seeing Satan falling like lightning from heaven" (10:18), Luke is emphasizing that the eschatological expectation of Satan's downfall was not only already taking place, but that it was an ongoing process and linked to the exorcistic ministry of the church.

In retelling the exorcism stories, Luke heightens the ability and authority of Jesus over the demons. For example, in the healing of the demoniac in the synagogue the demon does not cry out after Jesus' command of submission (Luke 4:35/Mark 1:26). In the healing of the boy with the unclean spirit Jesus asks no questions; he lacks no knowledge (Luke 9:37-43; Mark 9:16, 21). In Mark the healing is protracted and seems to be in two stages—the demon leaving the boy as dead so that he has to be raised—but in Luke Jesus is immediately successful (Luke 9:42; Mark 9:20-26).

Although the first three healing stories in Luke picture Jesus dealing with demons (Luke 4:31-37, 38-41), he broadens Mark's view of the early stages of the ministry of Jesus to balance his healing and teaching (4:18). Further, unlike Mark, Luke sustains the impression that exorcism remained an important and integral part of Jesus' ministry (Luke 7:21; 13:32) and, in Acts 10:36-39, describes Jesus' healing ministry as healing all who were oppressed by the devil. This blurring of the distinction between demonic and other sicknesses, as well as how they are cured, is seen in the story of the healing of Simon's mother-in-law (Luke 4:38-39) where he says Jesus "stood over her" (Luke 4:39) in the manner of an exorcist (*PGM* IV.745, 1229, 2735). Also, Jesus is said to "rebuke" (4:39) the fever, a word used elsewhere in the Gospels to describe the action of an exorcist (e.g., Mark 1:25; 9:25). Then, in the story of the healing of the boy with an unclean spirit (Luke 9:37-43*a*), he not only says Jesus rebuked the unclean spirit, he also adds that Jesus healed (9:42) the boy. Further, in a summary Luke says that Jesus cured or healed those who were troubled or harassed (6:18) by unclean spirits. In effect Luke gives all sickness a demonic and cosmic dimension—in all HEALING God's adversary is being subdued, even though not all illness was caused by demons (e.g., the healing of the lepers, 5:12-16; 17:11-19).

The girl in Acts 16:16-18 is said to have a spirit of divination (pythōn [πύθων], 16:16) causing her to prophesy or give oracles (manteuomai [μαντεύομαι], 16:16). It was considered that Apollo, the Pythian god, incarnate in a serpent or python, inspired what Plutarch calls Pythones or "belly talkers" (engastrimythoi ἐγγαστρίμυθοι, Plutarch, *Def. orac.* 9.414e), a form of tranceinduced ventriloquism (e.g., Hippocrates, *Epid.* 5.63). That, for Luke, the girl's activity probably had strong evil connotations is seen from the LXX using engastrimythos ([ἐγγαστρίμυθος], "belly talker") of the witch of Endor (1 Sam 28:7) and from Luke describing her as "soothsaying" or "fortune-telling" (manteuomai), a word with strong negative connotations relating to false prophets in the LXX (e.g., Deut 18:10; Mic 3:11) and used for pagan ecstatic activity.

6. John

The Fourth Gospel provides an entirely different perspective on demons. The Fourth Gospel mentions demons only in the repeated and, therefore, important charge that Jesus had a demon (John 7:20; 8:48, 49, 52; 10:20, 21). These passages carry both the Fourth Evangelist's distinct understanding of the demonic and demonic possession, as well as clues to its remedy.

In the narrative leading up to John 7:20 the Jews, who are authorities (rather than the common people), and are Jesus' opponents, are looking for him, in order to kill him (John 5:18; 7:1, 11); but the crowd, who will later be shown as ignorant of the truth (12:29), knows nothing of this. Therefore, in response to Jesus asking, "Why are you looking for an opportunity to kill me?" the crowd expresses its disbelief: "You have a demon! Who is trying to kill you?" This is not a charge of madness (compare 10:20) but a way of saying that he is not believable (compare 10:20-21). Through the characteristic irony of this Gospel, where incorrect statements and unanswered questions imply unknowing truth (e.g., John 1:46; 6:42, 52; 7:20, 26, 35, 42, 48; 8:22, 53; 9:40; 18:38), readers, with their narratological advantage (compare 7:1, 20), are invited to conclude that Jesus does not have a demon, that he is

telling the truth, and that his life is being sought. Readers are given an interpretive perspective for understanding the full import of the accusation of having a demon when it is repeated and expanded.

Primarily through irony John 8:48-52 brings into play the major interpretive keys to understand the charge of demon possession brought against Jesus. As in John 7:20 and 10:20-21, Jesus is set over against the Jews as, including, having the devil as their father; the devil does not stand in the truth because he is a liar (8:42-44). Narratively, therefore, readers take up this perspective on the Jews, who are about to bring the ironic accusation against Jesus: "Are we not right in saying that you are a Samaritan and have a demon?" (8:48). This two part accusation amounts to one and the same thing, for Jesus gives a simple catchall response: "I do not have a demon" (8:49). In 8:52 the meaning of their accusation is clarified as being responsible for false prophecy. This association of the demonic or Satan with false information or prophecy embedded in his passage was well established in a Jewish context (e.g., 4Q510 1 6; *Mart. Isa.* 1:8-9) and among later Christians (e.g., Irenaeus, *Haer.* 1:23; 4). With a high view of the Samaritans in this Gospel (esp. John 4), the charge brought against Jesus turns out to be both an echo of the positive assessment of the Samaritans and a shorthand description of their own plight—liars and having the devil as their father. That is, for the readers it is the Jews, not Jesus, who are to be taken as demon possessed.

In John 10:20-21 the charge of being demon possessed is equated with being mad (mainetai, "he is mad") and unbelievable. As all other occurrences of mainomai (μαίνομαι, "mad") in the NT characterize a disbelieved message (Acts 12:15; 26:24, 25; 1 Cor 14:23), once again, the charge of demon possession is probably being associated with promulgating lies. In light of the irony already established, this would have become a signal to the readers of the very opposite conclusion to be drawn—it is Jesus' opponents who have a demon and are not to be heard.

Resembling how others understood the work of demons (e.g., *Jub.* 10:1; 1QS III, 20-26; 4Q510 1 6), in the Fourth Gospel demon possession—to be in error—meant to be of the devil, the father of lies. This enables the reader to see how demon possession was to be combated; through knowing the truth. Thus we cannot be surprised that the Fourth Gospel does not have stories of exorcism. For exorcism would belie the deep and all-encompassing hold that Satan is portrayed as having not on a few but on the many. Demon possession is, then, fought not with the hand of a healer but with accepting Jesus (1:12), his truth, and honoring God as one's Father (8:49). Johannine salvation—knowing and remaining in Jesus and the truth he brings—is the antidote to error and the demonic, not a healing encounter reserved for a few.

7. Letters

In the later Pauline epistles there is a more explicit demonology.

a. Ephesians. In Ephesians the "powers" are sometimes understood to be devilish beings under the command of Satan. There is a higher concentration of the mention of these "powers" in Ephesians than anywhere else in the NT. They are referred to by a variety of terms: archē ("ruler," 1:21; 3:10; 6:12), archōn ("lord," 2:2), dynamis (δύναμις, "power," 1:21), exousia (ἐξουσία, "authority," 1:21; 2:2; 3:10; 6:12), kosmokratōr (κοσμοκράτωρ, "world ruler," 6:12), kyriotēs (κυριότης, "dominion," 1:21), pneuma ("spirit," 2:2; "spirits," 6:12). As well as being demons, they have also been taken as "spiritual atmosphere," human and angelic powers, the structure of human existence, spiritual beings that operate in and through human structures, or the angelic host surrounding the throne of God. More likely they are—under the command of the devil (6:11, 16)—heavenly beings (3:10) influencing or controlling disobedient people (2:2-3) and, though now aware of the gospel (1:10; 3:8-11) and no longer controlling those who have been saved by grace through faith (2:8), they continue to be the opponents of Christian living (6:10-17).

b. Colossians. Colossians mentions "principalities (archai) and authorities (exousiai)" first in a list of things in heaven and on earth (Col 1:16) over which Christ is head (2:10). Although they are invisible and located in heaven (2:15; Dan 7:9; Rev 4:4; T. Levi 3:8; 1 En. 61:10; 2 En. 20:1; Apoc. El. 1:10-11), by their very names (Col 1:15) and the possibility of being captivated by them (2:8-10), they are understood to have an impact on human affairs. However, even though these forces, also called stoicheia (στοιχεῖα, "elemental spirits," 2:8), were later equated with demons (T. Sol. 8:2-4), in Colossians (and Gal 4:3) they remain cosmic beings or "elemental spirits of the universe" from where they determine sinful human activity (Col 1:21; see Jub. 2:2; 1 En. 75:1) rather than cause sickness by possessing some individual persons. Thus, the response to the activity of these heavenly forces is not exorcism but a chosen lifestyle (Col 3:1–4:6) arising out of an allegiance to Christ (3:1) who is "head of every ruler and authority" (2:10), having triumphed over them not in his ministry of exorcism but in the cross (2:14-15, 20).

c. 1 Timothy. In 1 Tim 4:1 demons (daimoniōn) and spirits that lead astray are equated and seen to be responsible not for possessing people, but those who renounce the faith will follow the teachings of demons. This associates Satan and heresy (see also 1 Tim 3:6-7; 2 Tim 2:26) in a way echoed in 1 John 4:6 and familiar more widely (see also 2 Cor 4:4; 11:3, 13-14; 1QS III, 18-19; T. Ash. 6:2).

d. James. James 2:19 says that "you believe that God is one. . . . Even the demons believe—and shud-der." The acknowledgment of God, or God's representative, by demons is reflected in the Jesus traditions (e.g., Mark 1:24-26) and Acts (e.g., 16:17; 19:15). To shudder was to respond in disabling fear to something, including to God (e.g., Mark 1:26; Pr. Man 4; Josephus, J.W. 5.438). That an exorcistic context is to be understood in James is probable in that such creedal statements as "God is one" (see Deut 6:4) found their way into the vocabulary of exorcists (e.g., Justin, Dial. 85.3) and the notion of demons shuddering is also well documented in apotropaic or exorcistic texts (e.g., PGM IV. 3014–19).

e. 1 John. In 1 John 4:1-5 the readers are warned to distinguish between the spirit of truth and the spirit of error that inspires prophecy that does not acknowledge that Jesus Christ is from God and has come in the flesh.

8. Revelation

As well as the considerable allusions to contemporary demonology in such images as falling angels and stars (Rev 8:10; 9:1; 12:4, 9) and the abyss (9:1; 20:1) as well as references to the devil or Satan (Rev 12:9; 20:2) there are three references to demons. In 9:20, recalling the lack of repentance despite the plagues in the Exodus story (Exod 8:15, 19), the writer of Revelation may be distinguishing between the worship of demons and idols. More likely they are being equated, as they had been and continued to be (Deut 32:17; Ps 95:5; Jub. 1.11; 11.4-6; 22.17; 1 En. 19.1; 99.7; Justin, 1 Apol. 5.2; 9.1; Theophilus, Autol. 1.10). Then, using the image of an animal that came to be recognized as a metaphor for filth and corruption, John sees three unclean (akathartos) frogs—a river of lying propaganda—coming out of the mouths of the devilish trinity, the dragon, the beast, and the false prophet to entice opposition to God (Rev 16:12-14; see 1 Kgs 22:20-22; 1 En. 56:5-6). As was accepted of the demonic (e.g., Sib. Or. 2.167), these unclean spirits or demonic spirits (pneumata daimoniōn, Rev 16:4) performed signs that mislead (19:20; also 13:13, 14) so that, reminiscent of Eph 6:12, though here on a cosmic stage, the battle in which Christians are involved has a demonic dimension. The third reference to demons (18:2) is part of the author's picture borrowed from Isa 21:9 (see also Jer 51:37 [LXX 28:37]) of the ruined city in which the indeterminate inhabitants are now, as with the LXX, unequivocally taken to be demons. See DEMONIAC.

Bibliography: P. S. Alexander. "The Demonology of the Dead Sea Scrolls." *The Dead Sea Scrolls after Fifty Years: A Comprehensive Assessment.* 2 vols. Peter W. Flint and James C. Vanderkam, eds. (1999) 2:331–53; C. E. Arnold. *Powers of Darkness: Principalities and Powers in Paul's Letters* (1992); W. Burkert. *Greek Religion* (1985); A. Lange, H. Lichtenberger, and K. F. D. Römheld, eds., *Die Dämone:*

Demons (2003); E. Langton. *Essentials of Demonology* (1949); J. Naveh. "Fragments of an Aramaic Magic Book from Qumran," *IEJ* 48 (1998) 252–61; D. L. Penny and Michael O. Wis. "By the Power of Beelzebub: An Aramaic Incantation Formula from Qumran (4Q560)." *JBL* 113 (1994) 627–50; R. C. Thompson. *The Devils and Evil Spirits of Babylonia.* 2 vols. (1903); G. H. Twelftree. *Jesus the Exorcist: A Contribution to the Study of the Historical Jesus* (1993); C. Wahlen. *Jesus and the Impurity of Spirits in the Synoptic Gospels* (2004); A. T. Wright. *The Origin of Evil Spirits: The Reception of Genesis 6.1-4 in Early Jewish Literature* (2005).

GRAHAM H. TWELFTREE

DEMONIAC di-moh′nee-ak [δαιμονιζόμενος daimonizomenos]. In the NT, *demoniac*, meaning a person having or possessed by a DEMON or evil spirit, is found only in the gospels (seven of thirteen occurrences in Matthew). It is considered a distinct unspecified illness (diseases and pains, demoniacs, epileptics, and paralytics in Matt 4:24) cured by Jesus, although sometimes it is associated with violence (8:28), being blind, mute (9:32), or tormented (15:22). In John, having a demon, or being a demoniac is a charge against Jesus and is equated with madness (John 10:20-21). In Mark 3:21-22, 30 a charge of madness against Jesus is associated with having a BEELZEBUL or unclean spirit. Although *demoniac* is probably an old idea (Homer, *Od.* 18:327), the word is rare before the NT period (e.g., Philemon, *Comicus* 191). The Dead Sea Scrolls (11Q5 XXVII, 10) and later Jewish literature (e.g., *y. Sabb.* 6:8b) use the term "the stricken."

GRAHAM H. TWELFTREE

DEMOPHON dem′uh-fon [Δημοφῶν Dēmophōn]. Along with TIMOTHY, APOLLONIUS, and HIERO-NYMUS, Demophon was one of the Syrian governors (stratēgoi στρατηγοὶ) in the 2nd cent. BCE in Palestine under ANTIOCHUS V, Eupator, ensuring that the Hellenistic persecution of the Jews continued unabated (2 Macc 12:2).

ALLISON A. TRITES

DEMOSTHENES. Widely recognized as the greatest Athenian orator, Demosthenes' (384–322 BCE) early successes as a public defender launched a prominent political career marked by his tireless defense of Athenian independence and his unyielding opposition to Philip of Macedon's expansion into Greek territories. By the Roman period Demosthenes became the model orator in Greek education and rhetoric; his significance and influence is suggested by the fact that only Homer is better represented in surviving papyri. Some have seen direct influence of Demosthenes in some of Paul's letters. He is an important indirect influence on NT and early Christian writings.

RUBÉN R. DUPERTUIS

DEMOTIC CHRONICLE. An early Ptolemaic oracular text on papyrus Bibliothèque Nationale Paris 215. Historical explanations attached to the oracular statements are drawn from 4th cent. BCE political events in EGYPT and serve as an important source for the chronology of Dynasties 28–30. The prediction of a ruler arising in Herakleopolis "after the Greeks" suggests it was intended as revolutionary propaganda, and it shares with Biblical literature characteristics of prophecy and a moral evaluation of kings' reigns.

CAROLYN HIGGINBOTHAM

DEMYTHOLOGIZE. A method of interpretation that attempts to liberate enduring truths from their time-bound mythological contexts. The Bible's creation narratives, prophetic oracles, miracle stories and psalms of lament illustrate that in the ancient mind, the material and spiritual worlds were always in close contact. Demythologizers seek to uncover truths in these texts that still have validity and meaning within a modern scientific world view that questions the reality of miracles and direct revelation. *See* BIBLICAL INTERPRETATION, HISTORY OF; MYTH IN THE NT; MYTH IN THE OT.

BRYAN D. BIBB

DEN. *See* CAVE.

DEN OF LIONS [גֹּב אַרְיָוָתָא gov ’aryawatha]. Various biblical texts mention that animals, especially lions, have *dens* (most often variations of the Hebrew ma‘on [מָעוֹן]; e.g., Job 38:40; Ps 104:22; Cant 4:8; Amos 3:4), but this Aramaic phrase appears in Daniel 6, where the Persian king DARIUS reluctantly orders the young Judean DANIEL thrown into a pit of hungry lions because he continues worshiping Yahweh.

Although escaped slaves and Christians were occasionally fed to beasts in the arenas of 1st and 2nd cent. CE Rome, little evidence exists that capital punishment by beasts was actually practiced in the ANE.

W. SIBLEY TOWNER

DENARII, DENARIUS di-nair′ee-*i*, di-nair′ee-uhs [δηνάριον dēnarion]. A Roman silver coin equivalent to the Greek DRACHMA. Throughout the NT, the denarius (plural denarii) is referenced as an equivalent of payment for daily wages and the Greek is sometimes translated as such (Matt 20:2; John 6:7; Tob 5:15-16). *See* MONEY, COINS.

KIMBERLY R. PEELER

DENY [ἀρνέομαι arneomai; ἀπαρνέομαι aparneomai]. The basic meanings are 1) to refuse consent to a claim or demand (e.g., Wis 12:27; 17:9; Acts 4:16; Heb 11:24); 2) to dispute that an assertion is true (e.g., Gen 18:15 LXX; Wis 16:16; John 1:20; 1 John 2:22); or 3) to repudiate, disown or renounce someone or something (e.g., 4 Macc 8:7; 10:15; Luke 9:23; 12:9; 1 Tim

5:8; 2 Tim 2:13; 3:5; Titus 2:12; Rev 2:13). There is no difference in meaning between the two verb forms. The simple arneomai appears seven times in the LXX and 33 times in the NT. The compound form appears once in the LXX (Isa 31:7) and eleven times in the NT, all in the Synoptic Gospels.

Many occurrences in the NT involve denying Christ, either in the sense of refusing to admit association with him or disowning him (e.g., Acts 3:13-14). The paradigmatic example is that of Peter (e.g., Mark 14:68, 70). As illustrated by Luke 12:8 and Matt 10:32, the opposite of denying Jesus is to confess: homologeō (ὁμολογέω, the antonym of arneomai/aparneomai). Possibly the Q saying behind Luke 12:8-9 and Matt 10:32-33 is echoed in other contexts of denial versus confession such as John 1:20 and 1 John 2:23. Finally, following Christ involves denying oneself (e.g., Mark 8:34). *See* PASSION NARRATIVES.

MARK D. GIVEN

DEPOSIT פִּקָּדוֹן piqqadhon, נוּחַ nuakh; ἀριθμός arithmos, παρακαταθήκη parakatathēkē, τίθημι tithēmi, χρῆμα chrēma]. An item entrusted to someone or placed in a location for safe keeping. Failure to restore a deposit to its owner is equivalent to oppression or robbery (Lev 6:2, 4; 5:21, 23), and good stewardship is expected of the trustee (2 Macc 3:10, 15; Sir 42:7; 4 Macc 4:3, 7; Luke 19:11-25).

Ashes were deposited outside the camp for later ritual use (Num 19:9). Ezekiel envisioned priests depositing holy offerings in temple chambers (Ezek 42:13). A decree (1 Macc 14:49) and royal archives (1 Esd 6:23; LXX 6:22) were deposited for future reference. *See* FAITH, FAITHFULNESS; MONEY, COINS; TRUST.

KENNETH D. LITWAK

DEPTHS מְצוּלָה metsulah, מַעֲמַקִּים ma'amaqqim, תְּהוֹם tehom; βυθός bythos]. Depths refer to the deepest levels of water in seas (Ezek 27:34) and rivers (Zech 10:11). "Depths" and "deep" are sometimes paired in biblical texts (Exod 15:5, Isa 51:10). As does "the deep," the depths refer not just to the substratum of seas and rivers, but more broadly to the great reservoir of subterranean waters, which are the source of seas and rivers and in which the earth's foundations rest. Also, as does "the deep," depths can refer to the chaotic waters God restrained at creation and at the exodus to bring order and preserve life (Exod 15:5, Isa 44:23; 51:10).

Most frequently, the depths are mentioned in the laments of the Psalter as a symbol of danger and death. By describing misfortune as a descent into the depths, the psalmist compares his distress to being consumed by the primordial waters of chaos God subdued at creation and restrains at the boundaries of the ordered world (Jonah 2:5; Ps 68:22 [Heb. 68:23]). In Ps 69, for example, the psalmist, who believes himself to be falsely accused and shamed by his peers, describes himself as sinking into the watery depths (v. 2) and

appeals to God to rescue him from them (vv. 15-16). Here the psalmist pairs the depths with "the PIT," another symbolic reference to the subterranean realm of death (v. 16, compare Ps 88:6 [Heb. 88:7]). Such is the despair of the author of Psalm 130, that he begins his lament with a cry: "Out of the depths I call to you, O LORD" (v. 1). In a twist on this symbol, the prophet Micah reassures his people that God will do away with their sins by throwing them into the depths of the sea (7:19). *See* DEEP, THE; SEA.

THEODORE HIEBERT

DEPUTY נִצָּב nitsav, בַּעַל־טַעַם be'el-te'em, סָגָן saghan; ἀνθύπατος anthypatos]. Someone governing on behalf of a superior (1 Kgs 22:47 [Heb. 22:48]; Ezra 4:8; Jer 51:28; Acts 13:7; 18:12). *See* GOVERNOR.

DERBE duhr'bee [Δέρβη Derbē]. A town in LYCA-ONIA, near the boundary of the Roman provinces of Galatia and Cappadocia, at or close to Kerti Hüyük, about 21 km north-northeast of Karaman (ancient Laranda) and 96 km southeast of LYSTRA. Derbe was also known as Claudioderbe, a title bestowed in honor of the Emperor Claudius around 41 CE. The town was one of Paul's destinations on his first visit to Asia Minor (Acts 14:6, 20), and a place he revisited (Acts 16:1 and perhaps 18:23; 19:1).

Paul and Barnabas preached the gospel in Derbe after fleeing Lystra, and "made disciples of many" (Acts 14:20-21). They would have spoken Greek, since they did not understand the native Lycaonian language (Acts 14:11). Little more is known of this church in the NT, save that Gaius, one of Paul's travel companions, originated there (Acts 20:4—perhaps the same Gaius as 19:29). If Galatians is addressed to the "south Galatian" churches, they may have included Derbe.

The first attested bishop of Derbe, Daphnus, attended the Council of Constantinople (381 CE), and is one of four known bishops of the city—the last died in 672 CE. Derbe was destroyed in 1402 CE by Timur Lenk, and little remains.

Bibliography: M. H. Ballance. "The Site of Derbe: A New Inscription." *Anatolian Studies* 7 (1957) 147–51; M. H. Ballance. "Derbe and Faustinopolis." *Anatolian Studies* 14 (1964) 139–40; G. Ogg. "Derbe." NTS 9 (1962–63) 367–70; E. Schnabel. Early Christian Mission. Vol. 2 (2004) 1121-22; B. van Elderen. "Some Archaeological Observations on Paul's First Missionary Journey." *Apostolic History and the Gospel.* ed. W. W. Gasque and R. P. Martin (1970) 151–61.

STEVE WALTON

DESCEND, DESCENDANT. *See* DAUGHTER; FAMILY; FATHER; GENEALOGY; MOTHER; SON.

DESCENT INTO THE UNDERWORLD. *See* UNDERWORLD, DESCENT INTO THE.

DESCENT, DESCEND [יָרַד yaradh]. The words "descent" or "descend" (or, more simply "go down") often translate various forms of the Hebrew root yaradh, whose basic meaning is movement from above to below, the counterpart of ASCENT. The verb can describe commonplace motion, e.g., one "descends" from a chariot (Judg 4:15) or a bed (2 Kgs 1:4). Rain and other forms of precipitation "descend" (Isa 55:10), as do waters of a river, e.g., the JORDAN RIVER (Josh 3:13, 16), whose name derives from yaradh.

Geographically, one "descends" to a valley (Joel 3:2) or from a city (typically situated on a higher elevation, e.g., Jerusalem, 1 Kgs 22:2). A journey southward is expressed as a "descent," e.g., "Abram went down to Egypt" (Gen 12:10). Sometimes, mere movement from one region to another can be expressed by yaradh (Gen 38:1). "Descent" can imply movement to something less desirable or honored. In particular, death is described as a descent to the underworld, as when the grief-stricken Jacob proclaims he "will go down to SHEOL" (Gen 37:35).

Descent is also part of the biblical language of theophany as God "descends" upon Mount Sinai (Exod 19:11), Mount Zion (Isa 31:4), or "the high places of the earth" (Mic 1:3-4), often in terrifying splendor (*see* THEOPHANY IN THE OT).

WILL SOLL

DESECRATE. *See* PROFANE; CLEAN AND UNCLEAN.

DESERT [מִדְבָּר midhbar; ἔρημος erēmos]. Midhbar and erēmos are frequently translated as "desert" and WILDERNESS. Although the term *desert* is often colloquially used for areas that will not sustain rain-fed agriculture, deserts are complex and diverse. Principally they vary according to altitude, temperature, precipitation, and soils, which in turn determine the amounts and kinds of plant and animal communities that inhabit these biomes. There are numerous definitions of what constitutes a desert, but essentially they include three degrees of dryness based on annual precipitation. The rainfall limits provided here are arbitrary, but they follow the general usage of archaeologists and paleoclimatologists working in the Levant.

Semi-arid deserts (often called steppes) are areas that receive an average of less than 250 mm (ca. 10 in.) a year, which is regarded as being the least absolute limit for farming. The critical word here is *average*, for there are at least as many seasons below the agricultural requirements as those that satisfy them, so reliable farming without irrigation is risky.

Arid deserts receive a mean annual rainfall of between 100 and 250 mm, although this is usually sufficient to provide substantial seasonal vegetation on plateaus and especially wadi bottoms. Arid deserts and steppes together provide the pasturage most heavily relied on by sheep and goat pastoralists in the Near East. In the past there was a wide variety of birds, mammals, and reptiles that populated the steppe and arid desert, and hunting provided important contributions to the diet of nomadic pastoralists.

Hyperarid deserts receive less than 100 mm of rainfall per year, and often many locales will experience many years of no precipitation, followed by one or two sudden cloudbursts, then several more rainless years. Nevertheless, depending on local drainage patterns, there can still be vegetation sufficient to support some degree of herding. There is a surprising array of animals in hyperarid deserts, but due to their low densities, they are generally not dependable food sources.

Much of the biblical landscape can be characterized as one kind of desert or another. Israel consists of approximately two-thirds semi-arid to hyperarid deserts, while Jordan's deserts account for approximately 85 percent of its territory. There are distinct north-south and east-west gradients: the farther south and east one goes in Jordan, the drier the terrain becomes. In the Jordan Valley there is a marked decline in rainfall from the Galilee area to the northern shore of the Dead Sea, and the Judean and Negev deserts transition from semi-arid deserts in their northern reaches to hyperarid landscapes farther south. The Sinai receives an average of 4 in. (125 mm) of rain annually along the Mediterranean coast, but the desert rapidly reaches hyperarid conditions with movement to the south.

Like all landscapes, deserts evolve so that the bleak vistas we see today belie the conditions of the terrain in the relatively recent past. The clearest example of this is reflected in the stunning rock art of Tassili n'Ajjer in the Sahara of eastern Algeria, dated variously to ca. 4000–8000 BCE. In what today is an essentially lifeless range of sand and rock, walls of caves and rock shelters show hunters pursuing wild cattle, giraffes, hippos, and other species that have since disappeared due to desertification. And in the Azraq oasis in Jordan's eastern desert archaeological excavations recovered teeth from elephants, rhinoceroses, wild cattle, and onager dating to between ca. 250,000–150,000 years ago.

Although hunter-gatherer groups had exploited deserts for at least the past three-quarters of a million years, it was not until the development of domesticated sheep and goats that these unfarmable areas of the Near East became intensively exploited, probably beginning as early as the Neolithic period some 9,000 years ago. Instead of competing with farmland for pasturage, these animals could be taken to the neighboring steppe and deserts during the rainy season to convert otherwise unusable plants into meat, dairy products, and hair or wool. Rainwater that collected in small depressions served as seasonal water sources for animals and their herders both; after the rainy season ended and the playas dried up, the herds were brought back to the farming areas where exchanges of animal products were made for farm produce. The intensification of grazing and browsing in the steppe, especially, may have been responsible for an irreversible damage to ground cover that exposed fertile soils to wind deflation, changing vast areas from seasonal grasslands to rocky, devegetated expanses that mimicked hyperarid deserts.

Since up to 28 percent of the earth's land surface comprises deserts of one kind or another, they can constitute major barriers to overland travel due to the vast expanses of waterless terrain. Two aspects of the desert environment eventually made it possible to cross many parts of deserts: subsurface water collection and the domestication of the wild desert CAMEL.

Precipitation falling in and adjacent to deserts often flows as runoff into low-lying basins, but this accumulation is unpredictable since seasonal rainfall is so sporadic in many parts of the desert. But much of the precipitation in the higher agricultural regions descends into subsurface aquifers, where water is channeled to underground basins. Where the aquifers emerge along slopes or where the basin water table intersects the land surface, artesian springs and pools appear that provide seasonal and even permanent water sources, resulting in oases that stand in stark contrast to the surrounding landscape, constituting life-saving refuges to people and animals that find themselves in an otherwise parched vastness.

But even these oases and springs were of little avail if they were inaccessible because of the long stretches of unwatered land between them. It was not until the early Iron Age (and perhaps before) with the introduction of the domesticated camel into the Near East that reliable routes for contact developed, decreasing the distance between the population centers of the ANE. Cross-desert traffic became a vital link for interregional commerce, for intercultural communication, and political and military intercourse, and the changing map of the ANE reflected these connections even after the introduction of motor transport at the end of the 20th cent.

The harsh barrenness of the desert serves as a metaphor for the need for divine protection and sustenance. During the exodus, Yahweh makes the sea as dry as the desert for the Israelites to cross (Ps 106:9) and sustains Israel in the desert land, the "howling wilderness waste" (Deut 32:10; Ps 107:4), even though the Israelites frequently rebel in their wilderness journey (Pss 78:40; 106:14). Yahweh is the one who provides life-giving rain to the empty desert (Job 38:26-27; Ps 107:33, 35), while the enemies of Yahweh will be made desolate like the desert (Zeph 2:13; Mal 1:3). The blooming of the desert is a symbol of Zion's restoration, when the wilderness and dry land shall rejoice and blossom (Isa 35:1), the wasteland will become like Eden (Isa 51:3), and the waters will break forth in streams in the desert (Isa 35:6; 43:19-20). Hope for a time of restoration and justice are likened to God's coming on a path through the wilderness, a straight highway through the desert (Isa 40:4; Mark 1:3). Building on the OT theme of God's providence and sustenance in the wilderness, the Gospels recount how Jesus provided food for the hungry crowd in the desert (Matt 15:33; Mark 8:4). *See* AGRICULTURE; ISRAEL, CLIMATE OF; ISRAEL, GEOGRAPHY OF; PASTORAL NOMADS.

Bibliography: C. B. Hunt. "Physiographic Overview of Our Arid Lands in the Western U.S." *Origin and Evolution of Deserts.* S. G. Wells and D. R. Haragan, eds. (1983) 7–63; J. D. Lajoux. *The Rock Paintings of Tassili* (1963); A. S. Leopold. *The Desert* (1962); G. O. Rollefson et. al. " 'Ain Soda and 'Ain Qasiya: New Late Pleistocene and Early Holocene Sites in the Azraq Shishan Area, Eastern Jordan." *The Prehistory of Jordan II. Perspectives from 1997.* H. G. K. Gebel, Z. Kafafi, and G. O. Rollefson, eds. (1997) 45–58.

GARY O. ROLLEFSON

DESERT OWL. *See* OWL.

DESIGN. The design of an object is determined by the original location and meaning of the work. Art that took meaning from the Bible was usually intended for churches and areas of public worship. Much of that work has lost its original context because the art now resides in museums. The composition or design of the work becomes almost entirely lost. As one looks at the design of the object (painting, sculpture, architecture, stained glass, tapestry) one must understand the original function for the audience and the intended location. *See* AESTHETICS; ARTS; CARVING; CRAFTS.

HEIDI J. HORNIK

DESIRE [אָוָה 'awah, אַוָּה 'awwah, תַּאֲוָה ta'awah, מַאֲוַיִּים ma'awiyim, הַוָּה hawwah; חָמַד khamadh, חֶמֶד khemedh, חֶמְדָּה khemdah, חֲמָדוֹת khamudhoth, חֶמְדָּן khemdan, מַחְמָד makhmadh, מַחְמֹד makhmodh, נֶפֶשׁ nefesh; βούλομαι boulomai, ἐπιθυμία epithymia, ἐπιθυμέω epithymeō, ἐπιποθέω epipotheō, ἐπιποθία epipothia, εὐδοκία eudokia, θέλω thelō]. The most common roots in the OT underlying the English *desire*, 'awah and khamadh, are basically synonyms (compare, e.g., Exod 20:17 and Deut 5:21) for something understood as fundamental to human existence. In fact, both verbal and nominal forms of 'awah are used regularly in association with nefesh, the term connoting the human "soul" or animating principle. Even nefesh itself sometimes requires the translation "desire" (Prov 13:2; Eccl 6:9).

As such, desire is frequently associated with things that are basic to the perpetuation of human life, especially food and drink (e.g., Deut 12:15, 20, 21) and sexual relationships (e.g., Gen 3:16; Deut 21:11; Ps 45:11). Other things that contribute to a pleasant life more generally also emerge as objects of desire, such as a place in which to settle (Jer 42:22), oxen and sheep (Deut 14:26), and wealth (Prov 23:3), as well as more abstract things like understanding (Dan 2:3) and wisdom (Gen 3:6; compare Prov 3:15; 8:11; Sir 24:19; Wis 6:13; 18:2). In this connection even God can be an object of desire (Ps 73:25; 2 Chr 15:15), as can God's ordinances (Ps 19:9-10) and the Temple (Ezek 24:21).

The OT contains no thought that desire per se represents a problem. Indeed, it is recognized in Proverbs that "a desire realized is sweet to the soul" (13:19; compare 13:12), while Sirach, with an eye to the finitude of human existence, counsels that one ought not "let your share of desired good pass by you" (14:16). "Desire without knowledge" (Prov 19:2) and, more specifically, pursuit of desire without regard to God's demands or at the expense of other people (e.g., Ps 10:1-4) is a problem. Thus desiring the possessions or wife of one's neighbor is forbidden in the Torah (Deut 5:21; Exod 20:17), while Micah critiques the powerful for perverting justice by dictating "what they desire" (Mic 7:3).

Desire is sometimes even attributed to God (Hos 6:6; Ps 68:16; 132:13-14), and with God the matter is simple: "What God desires, that God does" (Job 23:13). God is also frequently identified as the one who ultimately grants the fulfillment of God's creatures' desires, a theme particularly pronounced in the Psalms (e.g., 143:15-16, "You open your hand, satisfying the desire of every living thing"). Especially typical here is the notion that God grants the desires of those God finds favorable (e.g., Ps 10:17; 21:2; 37:4; 143:19) while frustrating the desires of the wicked (e.g., Ps 112:10; compare Ps 23:25; 140:8). Thus anyone who "desires life and covets many days to enjoy good" are counseled to "depart from evil and do good" and to "fear the LORD" (Ps 34:11-14). Proverbs raises the stakes beyond the mere frustration of desires to the more actively negative consequences of God's wrath for the wicked (10:24; 11:23; compare Eccl 11:9).

In the Hellenistic period desire comes to carry a much more overtly negative connotation. Particularly in Greek compositions that weave together Greek philosophical and Jewish discourse, desire (epithymia) is correlated, in the context of a mind-body dualism, with base, animalistic aspects of the human person that must be tamed by the more elevated aspect of the mind. Philo's interpretation of the commandment against "coveting" is telling in this respect (*Decal.* 142-53), as is the whole of 4 Maccabees. In the latter work, desire emerges as a power that threatens to "enslave" a person, and which must thus itself be controlled by reason, to which it stands in an antagonistic relationship (3:2-5; compare 3:11, "irrational desire"). Indeed, the basis of Jewish philosophy (i.e., the Torah) is said to be teaching "self-control, so that we master all pleasures and desires" (5:22).

When considering the significance of *desire* in the NT, then, it is important to recognize that different Greek terms underlie the English word. Forms of boulomai and especially thelō, e.g., are used of God's desire, i.e., God's will or intentions (e.g., Rom 9:22; 1 Tim 2:4; Heb 6:17), while epithymeō is never so used. In fact, forms of the latter Greek root are used overwhelmingly, even if not entirely consistently (compare Luke 15:16; 16:21), with the decidedly negative connotations familiar from other Hellenistic texts; they are therefore sometimes translated as *lust* (e.g., Matt 5:28, "everyone who looks at a woman with *lust* (epithymeō) has already committed adultery with her in his heart"). First Peter 4:2 encapsulates typical NT usage, urging its audience to live "no longer by human desires (epithymia) but by the will (thelēma θέλημα) of God."

Particularly in the epistolary literature, epithymia is typically correlated, as in 4 Maccabees, with what is perceived as a lesser and even dangerous aspect of the human being, now called "flesh" (sarx σάρξ; Gal 5:16-17, 24; Eph 2:3; 2 Pet 2:11, 18; 1 John 2:16). Though endemic to flesh generally, desire in this sense is associated particularly with (non-Christian) Gentiles (Rom 1:24; 1 Thess 4:5), women (1 Tim 5:11; 2 Tim 3:6-7) and, more generally, "the world" (e.g., 1 John 2:16 compare Jas 4:1-4; Mark 4:19). It is something to be renounced (1 Pet 2:11; 2 Tim 2:12; Titus 2:12) and, indeed, put to death (Col 3:5). Here, however, the opposite value is less often something intrinsic to the human, like reason (though compare 2 Pet 2:12, 18 and more generally, arguably, the letter of James), than an extrinsic, divine spirit that can only be obtained by participation in the Christ cult. Especially in the Pauline literature, baptism itself is construed as "crucifying the flesh with its desires" (Gal 5:24), and thus as freedom from the enslavement to sin said to characterize humans apart from possession by this spirit (e.g., Rom 6:1-14; 8:1-11).

Bibliography: Matt A. Jackson-McCabe. *Logos and Law in the Letter of James* (2001); William L. Moran. "The Conclusion of the Decalogue (Ex 20, 17 = DT 5, 21)." *CBQ* 29 (1967) 543–54; Stanley K. Stowers. *A Rereading of Romans: Justice, Jews and Gentiles* (1994).

MATT JACKSON-MCCABE

DESOLATING SACRILEGE. *See* ABOMINATION OF DESOLATION.

DESOLATION [שָׁמֵם shamem; ἐρῆμος erēmos]. In the OT desolation carries a sense of lifelessness (Isa 54:1), abandonment (Zech 7:14), ruin (Ezek 6:4), and devastation (Gen 47:19), often accompanied by astonishment or horror (Isa 52:14; Ezek 12:19; Ezra 9:3-4).

In the NT erēmos refers primarily to a deserted area (Luke 13:35; 15:4; Acts 1:20), perhaps dangerous, such as the habitation of the demoniac (Luke 8:29) or, in contrast, a quiet place, such as the refuge Jesus sought away from the crowds (Matt 14:13).

The ABOMINATION OF DESOLATION (Dan 12:11; 9:27; 11:31), a unique phrase indicating the introduction of an idol or pagan altar in the Temple and the abandonment of the daily sacrifice, is reinterpreted by the Gospels to refer to the future Temple desecration and destruction of Jerusalem in anticipation of the parousia (Matt 24:15; Mark 13:14; Luke 21:20).

Bibliography: W. A. Such. *The Abomination of Desolation in the Gospel of Mark* (1999).

HANNAH K HARRINGTON

DESSAU des´aw [Δεσσαού Dessaou; Δεεσαού Deesaou]. A village in Judea where the Jews engaged in battle against NICANOR (2 Macc 14:16).

DESTINY. 1. A widespread English translation of MENI [meni מְנִי], the name of a Babylonian god of fate (Isa 65:11).

2. A God-ordained life-role. Across a range of genres, various Scriptures reveal God destining the people for specific, sometimes momentous, callings. God singles out Abraham and his descendants for leading roles in redemption history (Gen 18:18-19; Amos 3:2). God forms Jeremiah in the womb to make him a prophet (Jer 1:5; compare Ps 139:16).

God is at work to secure God's servants' destinies, but often behind the scenes in a patient way that respects human choices and natural processes. Esther has the choice of rejecting her destiny of saving the Jews (Esth 4:14), but providentially chooses instead to embrace it. Rebekah and her family have the choice of frustrating the plans of God and Abraham (Gen 24:8, 41), but providentially they do not. *See* ESCHATOLOGY IN EARLY JUDAISM; ESCHATOLOGY OF THE NT; ESCHATOLOGY OF THE OT; FATE; PROVIDENCE.

STEPHEN L. COOK

DESTITUTE [אֶבְיוֹן ʾevyon, עָנִי ʿani]. *Destitute* aptly describes Israelites driven into debt and debt slavery by the economic policies of their age. Prophets spoke out on behalf of the POOR by condemning the rich and powerful who caused such POVERTY (Isa 1:17, Jer 5:28, Amos 2:6-7, 5:11). Biblical laws often sought to provide special protection for the poor (Exod 22:21-24, 23:10-11, Lev 25:1-55, Deut 14:28-29, 15:1-18). The condition of destitution is described in wisdom literature as something to be avoided by acting wisely (Prov 6:11, 14:23, 21:5, 24:34). In the Psalms and later Jewish literature, those who are poor (ʾevyon or ʿani) are beloved by God (Pss 132:15, 140:12, 146:7-9); herein "poor" can refer to both humble religious piety and economic poverty. Both perspectives are found in the two versions of Jesus' BEATITUDES (Matt 5:3—"blessed are the poor in spirit"/Luke 6:20—"blessed are the poor"). In his ministry Jesus believed that he was especially sent to the poor to proclaim the Kingdom of God (Matt 9:12-13; Luke 4:16-21). *See* DEBT, DEBTOR.

ROBERT GNUSE

DESTROY, UTTERLY [חָרַם kharam; ἀναθεματίζω anathematizō]. According to Deuteronomy and Joshua, the conquering Israelites were to annihilate the people of Canaan. The distinctive Hebrew verb root describing this action is khrm (חרם, NRSV: "devote to destruction" or "utterly destroy."

Deuteronomy 20:16-17 commands the slaughter of all the inhabitants of cities within Israel's territorial inheritance, and Josh 6–11 describes, in an idealized fashion, how this was accomplished. Apparently, because enemy captives were valuable as slaves, they were exclusively reserved as spoils of war for the LORD, who was the true victor in sacral war (*see* HOLY WAR). Extermination prevented any human utilization of this resource.

Nevertheless, the Canaanites were never totally exterminated (Josh 15:63; 16:10; 17:13; Judg 1). The practice of extermination conflicted with the political goals of kingship, and 1 Sam 15:8-33; 1 Kgs 9:20-21; and 20:32-42 reports royal resistance to it. Deuteronomy utilized the concept to demand the elimination of foreign religious elements (Deut 7:2, 26; 13:17, 19 [Heb. 13:16, 18]). The prophets adopted it to threaten divine punishment against Israel (e.g., Isa 43:28; Jer 25:9; Mal 3:24) and promise the destruction of Israel's oppressors (e.g., Jer 50:21, 26; 51:3; Mic 4:13). *See* ANATHEMA; BAN; DEVOTED.

RICHARD D. NELSON

DESTROYER, DESTROYERS [שֹׁדֵד shodhedh, מַשְׁחִית mashkhith; ὀλεθεύοντα oletheuonta, ὀλοθρευτῆς olothreutēs]. A destroyer is an entity that annihilates a person or thing. The Hebrew word shodhedh is translated "destroyer" when it refers to a warring nation that will bring devastation on another nation and is found mainly in Jeremiah (6:26; 15:8; 48:8, 15, 18, 32; 51:56) and Isaiah (16:4; 21:2; 33:1). Another Hebrew word, mashkhith, occurs in Exod 12:23, a passage concerning the inauguration of the PASSOVER where Yahweh informs the Israelites that "the destroyer" who is assisting Yahweh in striking down the Egyptians will pass over the Israelite houses when he sees the blood of the Passover lamb smeared on the lintel. (See also Heb 11:28.) Although other passages suggest that "the destroyer" is an ANGEL or messenger of Yahweh (1 Sam 24:16; 1 Chr 21:12, 15), "the destroying angel" affiliated with the divine is not depicted in detail, and its function and role are sketchy. First Corinthians 10:10 also mentions "the destroyer" in recalling Yahweh's destruction of the Israelites who had complained in the wilderness (*see* Num 16:13-14, 41-49). One of the locusts in Joel 2:25 is identified as "the destroyer" [hekhasil הֶחָסִיל]

but is unrelated to the destroying angel. *See* BEELZE-BUL; BELIAL; DEMON; DEVIL, DEVILS; SATAN.

EDGAR W. CONRAD

DESTROYING ANGELS. *See* DESTROYER, DESTROY-ERS.

DESTROYING LOCUST. *See* LOCUST.

DESTRUCTION, DEVOTED TO. *See* DEVOTED.

DESTRUCTION, MOUNT OF. *See* MOUNT OF DESTRUCTION.

DETAINED BEFORE THE LORD [נֶעְצָר לִפְנֵי יְהוָה ne'etsar lifne YHWH]. A phrase of uncertain meaning, apparently connected to the idea of restriction for religious purposes because of the phrase "before the LORD." First Samuel 21:7 [Heb. 21:8] indicates that DOEG the Edomite, a shepherd of Saul, was in the SANCTUARY at Nob when David made his visit there to retrieve food while fleeing from Saul. There is no purpose for his being detained, and because the root 'atsar (עָצַר) is connected to the action of retention or restraining individuals from action, scholars have concluded the phrase indicates forced detention.

C. MARK MCCORMICK

DETERMINISM. The opposite of freedom. Throughout the Bible, trust in God's sovereignty is central to understanding determinism and freedom. Some passages emphasize divine sovereignty (CREATION, PROVIDENCE, foreknowledge, ELECTION, and PREDESTINATION); others emphasize human freedom to make choices with real consequences. Many theologians argue that divine sovereignty does not deny human freedom to make real choices; others argue that God does not (or cannot) foreknow the choices that humans will freely make.

Some passages imply that God gives humans no freedom to choose or repent, raising questions about God's goodness and justice (*see* THEODICY). A classic example is the hardening of Pharaoh's heart (Exod 7: 3, 13, 22; 10:1); patristic theologians usually argued that the hardening, although foreknown by God, was the result of Pharaoh's own evil choices. Other passages suggest that God's intentions change as a result of human actions. In Exod 32:14, Moses pleads for the disobedient Israelites: "And the LORD changed his mind." (The incident may, however, be interpreted as God's foreknowledge of and permission for Moses' intercession.) Some theologians emphasize free will and human cooperation with God's GRACE in SALVATION; others emphasize predestination. Most early theologians defended human freedom to choose GOOD or EVIL. Later, AUGUSTINE argued that the fallen human will is completely dependent on God's grace; without this grace (given to those predestined for salvation without regard to merit), the will is free only to follow its own evil inclination. Protestants, especially

reformed Protestants, generally give predestination more weight than Catholics, who more often emphasize the human will's free cooperation with grace.

The OT presents God both as having a plan for history and as allowing genuine human freedom—choosing a covenant people, urging the covenant people to "choose life," not death (Deut 30:15-20), calling prophets to speak words of judgment and hope when the people fall away from the covenant, and using nations and rulers to carry out the divine purposes (Isa 45:1-4).

The NT stresses trust in God's sovereign act in Christ. Passages supporting predestination include Rom 8:28-30 (followed by Rom 9–11 on the irrevocability of God's promises) and Eph 1:4 (God "chose us in Christ before the foundation of the world"). Among challenges for those who believe only some are elect is 1 Tim 2:4 (God "desires everyone to be saved"). *See* GOD, NT VIEW OF; GOD, OT VIEW OF.

NANCY WEATHERWAX

DEUEL doo'uhl [דְּעוּאֵל de'u'el; Ραγουηλ Ragouēl]. Father of ELIASAPH, who represented the tribe of Gad during the census and the mobilization of the tribes by Moses during the Exodus wanderings in the Sinai wilderness (Num 1:14; 7:42-47; 10:20). The reading in most MSS of the LXX in these texts, however, and the Syriac, support an initial "r" instead of "d," consistent with Num 2:14, which reads "Eliasaph son of REUEL."

MARSHALL D. JOHNSON

DEUTEROCANONICAL. *See* APOCRYPHA, DEUTEROCANONICAL.

DEUTERO-ISAIAH. *See* ISAIAH, BOOK OF.

DEUTERONOMIC SOURCE. *See* D, DEUTERONOMIC, DEUTERONOMISTIC.

DEUTERONOMISTIC HISTORY. The original, unified work hypothesized to underlie the biblical books of Deuteronomy plus the Former Prophets (Joshua, Judges, 1–2 Samuel, 1–2 Kings). Sometimes called the Deuteronomic History.

    A. Noth's Theory
    B. Major Developments Since Noth
    Bibliography

A. Noth's Theory
Martin Noth first advocated the existence of the Deuteronomistic History (DtrH) in his famous *Überlieferungsgeschichtliche Studien* of 1943. Previously, scholars tended to view the Former Prophets either as originally individual compositions strung together in a final Deuteronomistic edition or as an extension of the Pentateuch—a Hexateuch encompassing Joshua or an Enneateuch extending all the way through Kings. Noth argued via tradition history that Deuteronomy–

2 Kings in the Hebrew canon (hence, without Ruth) was an original unit by a single author (*see* TRADITION HISTORY, OT).

Noth supported his theory by pointing out a series of commonalities in these books: a common structure around a set of passages, often in the form of speeches delivered by major characters, that share a common writing style and vocabulary (Josh 1:11-15; 12; 23; Judg 2:11-22; 1 Sam 12:1-25; 1 Kgs 8:12-51; 2 Kgs 17:7-18, 22-23); a common chronology; and a common theological outlook.

Noth dated the DtrH to the exile, shortly after 562 BCE, the date of the last event recorded (2 Kgs 25:27-30). He believed that a single individual, who probably lived in Mizpah, wrote DtrH. Since this individual lived in Mizpah, the administrative capital following the destruction of Jerusalem, this person had access to oral and written traditions about Israel and Judah. The Deuteronomistic Historian (Dtr) was both an editor and an author, selecting from the traditions he gathered and combining them into a unified whole through various techniques of linking and harmonization. The Deuteronomistic Historian's purpose in writing was to explain how Israel and Judah had come to naught as a direct result of habitual sinfulness, just as Deuteronomy had anticipated. Among the most important of Dtr's sources was an early form of the book of Deuteronomy, which he placed at the head of his History. The Deuteronomistic Historian, therefore, assessed Israel's history in accord with Deuteronomy's doctrine that prosperity and disaster were the inevitable results of righteousness and sin, respectively. Hence, Noth dubbed the work the Deuteronomistic History.

B. Major Developments Since Noth

Noth's theory of an original unit behind Deuteronomy plus the Former Prophets has received broad and lengthy acceptance. Within the basic contours of the theory, however, several scholars have suggested adjustments that have proven influential. Von Rad and Wolff each questioned Dtr's negative purpose as Noth perceived it. Von Rad observed that the Davidic promise (2 Sam 7) functioned in the DtrH to explain the postponement of judgment against Judah, so that the final reference to Jehoiachin's release from prison might express muted hope about where God could begin to restore his people. Wolff found hope in the recurring theme of repentance in the DtrH.

Of greater impact were the proposals of Smend and Cross. Noth found plenty of secondary additions to Dtr's work but denied any systematic redaction of it (*see* REDACTION CRITICISM, OT). Smend argued for just such redaction in Joshua and Judges. Because it reflected an interest in law, he adopted the sigla DtrN (for Nomistic) for this layer, in contrast to the basic DtrG (for *Grundschrift*). Smend's insights were developed by his students, Dietrich and Veijola, who argued

for an additional, Prophetic redaction (DtrP) in Samuel and Kings. This "layer model" of the so-called Smend or Göttingen school has become dominant in Europe. It has also become increasingly complex, as adherents have proposed additional Dtr redactors in different books as well as distinct hands within a given Dtr layer or "school" (e.g., $DtrN^1$, $DtrN^2$, $DtrN^3$).

Cross accepted certain pre-Noth arguments for a pre-exilic edition of the book of Kings. He then adduced two contrasting themes running throughout Kings: Jeroboam's sin climaxing with the fall of Samaria (2 Kgs 17) and the faithfulness of David climaxing with Josiah. Based on these two themes, Cross suggested that the DtrH was originally written as a propaganda work supporting Josiah's reform. This initial edition (Dtr^1) was revised by an exilic editor (Dtr^2) who added the current ending (2 Kgs 23:25b–25:30) and a series of glosses that presupposed the exile in some way. This "block model" has been particularly influential in North America. Its proponents have developed it in various ways, arguing for more extensive Dtr^2 influence or positing pre-Dtr^1 editions, such as a collection of northern prophetic stories or a Hezekian Dtr.

Some have attempted to combine these two models by proposing exilic (and Persian) redaction(s) of pre-exilic, independent blocks of material. Others have returned to or maintained Noth's view of a single exilic author/editor, adducing further arguments in its favor. Van Seters, in particular, has raised considerations of genre, arguing that the best analogs to the DtrH are works of history-writing by ancient Greek authors such as Herodotus. This has generated intense debate about the meaning of history and its applicability to the DtrH and other biblical literature.

Another recent trend has been a return full circle to pre-Noth scholarship by denying the existence of the DtrH as an original unit. Thus far, the number of scholars advocating this return is limited, and their argumentation is primarily a critique of the tradition following Noth, not a comprehensive alternative. The theory of an original DtrH remains dominant, though there is widespread disagreement about the specifics of its authorship, date, and purpose.

Bibliography: Antony F. Campbell, and Mark A. O'Brien. *Unfolding the Deuteronomistic History: Origins, Upgrades, Present Text* (2000); Frank Moore Cross. *Canaanite Myth and Hebrew Epic: Essays in the History of the Religion of Israel* (1973) 274–89; Walter Dietrich. *Prophetie und Geschichte. Eine redaktionsgeschichtliche Untersuchung zum deuteronomistischen Geschichtswerk.* FRLANT 108 (1972); Martin Noth. *The Deuteronomistic History.* JSOTSup 15 (1991); Thomas Römer. *The So-Called Deuteronomistic History* (forthcoming); Thomas Römer and Albert de Pury. "Deuteronomistic Historiography (DH): History of Research and Debated Issues." *Israel Constructs Its*

History: Deuteronomistic Historiography in Recent Research. JSOT 306 (1996); Rudolf Smend. "Das Gesetz und die Völker: Ein Beitrag zur deuteronomistischen Redaktionsgeschichte." *Probleme biblischer Theologie. Gerhard von Rad zum 70. Geburtstag.* H. W. Wolff, ed. (1971) 494-509. John Van Seters. *In Search of History: Historiography in the Ancient World and the Origins of Biblical History* (1983); Timo Veijola. *Das ewige Dynastie. David und die Entstehung seiner Dynastie nach der deuteronomistischen Darstellung.* AASF B 193 (1975); Timo Veijola. *Das Königtum in der Beurteilung der deuteronomistischen Historiographie.* AASF B 198 (1977); Hans Walter Wolff. "Das Kerygma des deuteronomischen Geschichtswerk." *ZAW* 73 (1961) 171–86.

STEVEN L. MCKENZIE

DEUTERONOMY, BOOK OF doo´tuh-ron´uh-mee [אֵלֶּה הַדְּבָרִים ’elleh haddevarim]. The familiar scriptural identity of ancient Israel as a people set apart among the world's dispersed nations, discretely allied with "the Lord" (Yahweh) in covenant and unified by its commitment to live in accord with a unique legacy of Mosaic Torah, comes to mature definition in the fifth and final book of the Pentateuch, Deuteronomy.

The English name derives, by way of Latin, from Gk. deuteronomion (δευτερονόμιον), a compound term meaning "Second Law-giving." This Gk. title, which already appears as an interpretative designation in the LXX of Deut 17:18 (see also the LXX of Josh 9:2c), acknowledges the book's self-referential claim to transmit a record of Moses' divinely authorized proclamation of covenantal law in the plains of western Moab, complementing the foundational policy of the Decalogue whose terms were directly addressed by the Lord to Israel through the fire on the summit of the mountain at Horeb, a generation earlier (see especially 1:3; 4:12-14; 5:1-6:3; 10:3-5; 31:24-26). The comparable Hebrew title for this Mosaic reprise and amplification of revealed legislation is **mishneh torah** (מִשְׁנֶה תּוֹרָה), "Repetition of Torah" (e.g., *b. Meg.* 31b). More often, however, classical rabbinic and later Jewish sources refer to the book by its opening phrase or incipit, ’elleh haddevarim, "These [are] the words" (1:1), frequently shortened to devarim (דְּבָרִים), "[Book of] Words."

> A. Literary Character and Principal Contents
>   1. Preamble 1:1–4:43
>   2. Covenantal law-giving in Moab: 4:44–28:68
>   3. The covenant in Moab: 29:1–32:47
>   4. Testamentary benedictions: 33:1-29
> B. Critical Analysis
>   1. Primary settings in history and scripture
>   2. The Horeb and Moab covenant traditions
>   3. Character and purpose of the Deuteronomic "Book of the Torah"
>   4. Authorship, provenance, and history of composition
> C. Theological Themes and Significance
>   1. Yahweh alone
>   2. Israel and the nations
> Bibliography

A. Literary Character and Principal Contents

As the book's initial verse announces, the text of Deuteronomy indeed consists largely of reported "words"—speech ascribed to Moses, who occasionally quotes others, including privileged communications from the Lord, and which for the most part is delivered to the people Israel, convened in plenary assembly (1:6–2:9; 2:13-19; 2:24–4:40; 5:1b–10:5; 10:10–26:19; 27:1b-8, 9b-10, 12-26; 28:1-68; 29:2b [Heb. 29:1b]–30:20; 31:2b-6, 7b-8, 10b-13, 26-29; 32:1-43, 46b-47; 33:2b-29). These longer and shorter blocks of Mosaic speaking cover a number of topics, in addition to matters of covenantal law or "Torah" in a strict sense, and they are often described as representing an amalgam or secondary archival collection of two or more originally separate addresses of Moses, with several poetic and narrative appendices attached. Yet the spare editorial frame in which the major segments of speech are set wants to coordinate them as sequential parts of an extended testament that Moses delivered to "all Israel" in immediate anticipation of his death, which is then reported, together with his epitaph, in Deut 34, bringing the PENTATEUCH to a close (1:1-5; 4:44–5:1a; 27:1a, 9a, 11; 29:1-2a [Heb. 28:69–29:1a]; 31:1-2a, 7a, 9-10a; 14-25, 30; 32:44-46a, 48-52; 33:1-2a; see also the narrator's parenthetical comments in 2:10-12, 20-23; 4:41-43; 10:6-9). Though the evidence for a more complex history of composition is quite compelling, the book's various literary components and major themes are nonetheless reasonably coherent when the testamentary character of Deut 1–33 is recognized.

The editorial frame provides a series of prefaces and briefer superscriptions that delineates the four-part structure and principal contents of Moses' testament whose centerpiece is his legacy of authoritative TORAH.

1. Preamble: 1:1–4:43

An initial preface, 1:1-5, sketches the chronological and geographical setting of Moses' valedictory address to Israel "on the other side of the Jordan" in Moab, at the end of the forty-year wilderness period; it closes by describing what will immediately follow as an explicatory preamble to the presentation of "this Torah" (hattorah hazzo’th הַתּוֹרָה הַזֹּאת)—i.e., the central component of the book, which will be specifically reintroduced by the narrator in 4:44-49. The preamble features Moses' first-person memoirs (1:6–3:29; compare 5:23-31; 9:8–10:11) and concludes with a remarkable sermonic peroration (4:1-40). The memoirs review what happened to Israel and why, during the prolonged, circuitous journey from Horeb to the final encampment in the valley below Beth-peor, east of the Jordan River. In doing so, they underscore the role of MOSES himself as the one through whom the Lord issued inviolable orders that Israel, to its detriment, did not always obey. These recollections have a somber tone; they bear little resemblance to the historical prologues of ANE suzerainty treaties (though they have often been identified with such in recent decades). On the other hand, their rhetorical character and admonitory themes suit very well the genre of testament, in this case bringing into focus the critical issue of succession to Moses' seemingly irreplaceable leadership, which topic will be treated more fully later in the book (see especially 1:9-17; 3:23-28; 31:1-23; 32:44-47; 34:9-12). The peroration takes an even more expansive and emphatically theological view: it summarizes the significance of Israel's singular transformational experiences of divine presence in the exodus from Egypt and, especially, in the fearsome revelatory encounter at Horeb; and it forecasts Israel's national destiny as an enduring witness to the Lord's demanding though compassionate sovereignty. The origins of the Torah and its unparalleled importance for Israel's national life receive insightful attention in the peroration, where the crisis of Moses' imminent death is again highlighted (4:21-24). The peroration, like the memoirs, insists that Israel's well being, now and always, requires that it heed and diligently perform everything that the Lord commands through Moses (4:1-4, 40).

2. Covenantal law-giving in Moab: 4:44–28:68

The second, conjoined preface in 4:44-49 (beginning "And this is the Torah . . .") identifies the traditions in chapters 5–28 as featuring two basic types of legislation: "the decrees [ha‘edhoth הָעֵדֹת]" (also 6:17, 20), a term that evidently identifies the oracular "words" or stipulations of the Decalogue, rehearsed in 5:2-21; and "the statutes and the ordinances [hakhuqqim wehammishpatim הַחֻקִּים וְהַמִּשְׁפָּטִים]" (elsewhere, e.g., 5:1; 6:1; 12:1; 26:16), a compound designation for the provisions articulated in 12:2–26:15. It is noteworthy that this second preface not only uses the exodus from Egypt as a point of reference (4:45), but also suggests that the beginning of Israel's settlement, attested by the successful conquest and occupation of territory east of the Jordan, was the precondition for the full promulgation of the Torah (4:46-49). This agrees with the view, expressed throughout 5:1–28:68, which understands the Mosaic legislation to configure a polity or constitutional blueprint for Israel's corporate life in its divinely granted homeland (e.g., 8:11-20; 11:31–12:1; 16:18-20; 17:14-15; 19:1-3; 26:1-3). Moreover, the structure and contents of chaps. 5–28 make clear that Moses transmits his legacy of the Torah to Israel not as

an independent lawcode, an anthology of sermons, a didactic treatise, or the like but rather as a comprehensive political charter that is integral to the completion and historical actualization of the Horeb covenant. Thus the juridical corpus proper (12:2–26:15)—which defines the national institutions, principal obligations of citizenship, offices, and social policies divinely mandated to enable Israel to live faithfully and securely in its homeland—is set in an explicitly covenantal framework. After the detailed corpus of constitutional provisions, there is a summary of the reciprocal vows that seal the covenantal relationship between the Lord and Israel (26:16-19), followed by a description of related rites of renewal and an extensive collection of sanctions (27:1–28:68).

3. The covenant in Moab: 29:1–32:47

Read as a superscription, 29:1 [Heb. 28:69] introduces the segments of Mosaic speech and related actions in chaps. 29–32 as "the words" or "matters of the covenant [divre habberith דִּבְרֵי הַבְּרִית] that the Lord commanded Moses to enact with the Israelites in the land of Moab." This covenant, which the superscription expressly distinguishes from the one enacted at Horeb, is most evident in chaps. 29–30. It is imposed by Moses as a non-negotiable loyalty oath, demanding once again that present and future generations of Israel, defined here in broadly inclusive terms, give their undivided allegiance to the Lord (29:10-15 [Heb. 29:9-14]). The crux in this formulation is Israel's accountability for renunciation of furtive as well as public acts of idolatry among all of its constituents (29:16-28 [Heb. 29:15-27]). Prominent attention is also given to the Lord's constancy and discriminating providence, exercised through the perspicuous alternatives of blessing and curse (30:1-20). Although only loosely attached to this covenant, the narrative in chaps. 31–32 interweaves several themes that directly pertain to Moses' imminent departure and succession. His military command of Israel on the Lord's behalf is transferred to Joshua, who will direct the campaign to secure and distribute tribal inheritances west of the Jordan River (31:3-8, 14-15, 23; compare 34:9). Moses' political guidance and judicial authority, now permanently encoded in the form of the transcribed "Book of the Torah" (29:21 [Heb. 29:20]), is entrusted to future generations of Israel through the oversight of the Levitical priests and the elders (31:9-13, 24-26; compare 17:8-13; 27:1, 9; 30:8-10). The capstone of this endowment of Mosaic leadership is the oracular "Song," bequeathed to Israel as a paradigmatic witness to the Lord's zealous exercise of sovereignty (31:16-22, 27-30; 32:1-47). The divine instruction to Moses in 32:48-52 is a resumptive paraphrase of Num 27:12-14, anticipating Deut 34.

4. Testamentary benedictions 33:1-29

The book's final superscription (33:1) introduces the concluding piece of Moses' testament, "the blessing [habberakhah הַבְּרָכָה]" that he bestows on the assembled hosts of Israel, just before ascending to the summit of Mount Nebo where, after surveying from afar the homeland promised to Israel's ancestors, he will die. The blessing itself is a literary collage. It consists of a collection of varied epigrammatic prognostications and petitions on behalf of the individual tribes (33:6-25) set in a hymnal frame that celebrates the Lord's conquest of Canaan (33:2-5, 26-29). There is a militant, geo-political character to both the victory hymn and the majority of the tribal benedictions. It is significant, too, that Moses acts here in a decidedly patriarchal—or even royal (compare 33:4-5)—capacity by distributing a patrimony to each of the tribes (compare Gen 27:27-40; 49:1-28). This is consonant with the paternalistic stewardship of Israel he has exercised since the departure from Egypt but especially after his successful intercession for the apostate people in the context of the golden calf affair (Deut 9:12-14; 10:10-11; compare Exod 32:7-14; 34:8-10, 27).

The testament presumes throughout that for the previous forty years the Israelites had been Moses' often unruly wards. Now, at his death, a new generation of them must come of age as his heirs, taking responsibility themselves for comprehending, sustaining, and, when necessary, repairing through repentance their distinctive covenantal relationship with the Lord.

B. Critical Analysis

Many and various features of style, design, genre, and theme attest that Deuteronomy in its received form is not a unitary literary creation but rather, as the system of editorial superscriptions itself suggests, a work of collocation and redaction. Intensive scholarly investigation and debate of these matters over the course of the past two centuries has shown the likelihood of three or four major stages in the book's development, starting in the later Judaean monarchy and culminating in the completion of the PENTATEUCH in the Persian period. Although the antecedents and origins of many of the individual traditions incorporated into Deuteronomy are probably beyond secure critical recovery, and a detailed literary stratification remains precarious, the broad outlines of the book's history of composition may be identified especially by examining how the larger components of the testament have been shaped and arranged to emphasize the constitutional character and impeccable authority of the oral and written presentations of Torah attributed to Moses. In the intertextual formation of Deuteronomy, we can discern the intentional, self-conscious beginnings of Jewish scripture and scriptural exegesis.

1. Primary settings in history and scripture

Historical-critical studies during the 19th and earlier 20th cents. brought into focus the distinctive literary profile, segmentary structure, and socio-political agenda of Deuteronomy. The results were widely understood to indicate that the book's core legislation had originated during the later 7th cent. BCE as a prophetically influenced, reformist work whose creator used the guise of Mosaic authorship to foreordain especially the normative centrality that Jerusalem's aniconic cult would acquire in the institutionalized religious practice and corporate policies of "all Israel" during the monarchy. Moreover, in the wake of the book's actualization in the reforms of King Josiah (640–609 BCE), expanded editions of it were supposed to have contributed directly to the formation of both the Pentateuch and the corpus of the former Prophets that follows it in the biblical canon. Contemporary scholarship continues to wrestle with the implications of these findings and sometimes still to question their validity.

The seminal contribution of Wilhelm M. L. de Wette, at the beginning of the 19th cent., was his renewed attention to the view—adumbrated already in Patristic literature and articulated briefly by Thomas Hobbes among others—that the legislation in Deut 4:44–28:68 preserves the document identified in 2 Kgs 22–23 as "the Book of the Torah" and "the Book of the Covenant." Ostensibly recovered from the archives of the Jerusalem temple by the priest HILKIAH, in the eighteenth year of JOSIAH's reign (622 BCE), the document is reported to have been read aloud and adopted by the king in a public ceremony of covenant-making; it was then implemented in a series of iconoclastic and liturgical reforms. As de Wette recognized, this identification has far-reaching compositional as well as historical significance. If correct, it means that the textual bridge constructed by Deuteronomy between older pentateuchal narrative sources, which it presupposes throughout, and the book of Joshua in particular is relatively late, postdating Josiah's 7th cent. Judaean reforms.

By the end of the 19th cent. other scholars, most notably Abraham Kuenen and Julius Wellhausen, had consolidated de Wette's argument through rigorous literary analysis and religio-historical synthesis. Both of them distinguished between sections of the book that, in their view, had been contributed by earlier and later "Deuteronomists" (see D, DEUTERONOMIC, DEUTERONOMISTIC). They ascribed authorship of "proto-Deuteronomy"—i.e., the Josianic lawbook, thought to be essentially preserved in chaps. 12–26—to an early "Deuteronomic" legislator, who was possibly the priest Hilkiah. They recognized the book's framework segments in chaps. 1–11 and 27–34 to be considerably more complicated, representing perhaps a composite of at least two subsequent editions of the original legislation, the second of which was contributed by an exilic

Deuteronomist whose redactional imprints could be identified as well in the former Prophets. They also defended the hypothesis, initiated by Heinrich Ewald several decades earlier, that the 6th cent. edition of Deuteronomy, with its several appendices, belonged originally to a HEXATEUCH (Genesis through Joshua) which began with the divine promises of numerous progeny and land to Abram (compare Gen 12) and concluded with the account of Israel's successful occupation of Canaan under the leadership of Moses' immediate successor. The division between the books of Deuteronomy and Joshua was understood to be the result of a subsequent postexilic redaction that accommodated the distinctive "Priestly" narrative and cultic traditions (see P, PRIESTLY WRITERS) in order to produce the pentateuchal archive that came to be known thereafter as "the Law of Moses" (e.g., Ezra 3:2; Dan 9:13; Luke 2:22).

Since Kuenen and Wellhausen, scholars have generally concurred with the view that the completed Pentateuch was, at least in large measure, identical with the authoritative work variously referred to as "the Book of the Torah" and "the Book of Moses" in reports of the 5th cent. BCE phase of the Judaean restoration, carried out under Persian auspices by Ezra and Nehemiah (compare Ezra 6:18; Neh 8:1, 3; 13:1). However, the Hexateuch hypothesis only remained in vogue until the middle of the 20th cent., even though it was brilliantly supported by the form-critical scholarship of Gerhard von Rad and still finds advocates who see the book of Joshua as providing the logical conclusion to the narrative plot and literary strata that begin in Genesis. But what came to the fore instead was Martin Noth's hypothesis of an originally independent DEUTERONOMISTIC HISTORY, designed by an exilic author whom Noth identified as the "Deuteronomistic historian (DtrH)." According to Noth, this 6th cent. work consisted of the historian's own expanded edition of Deuteronomy as an introduction, followed by the books of Joshua, Judges, 1–2 Samuel, and 1–2 Kings. Subsequently, Deuteronomy was detached from the history and incorporated into the Priestly edition of the Tetrateuch (Genesis through Numbers), creating the traditional Pentateuch.

The great appeal of Noth's hypothesis, but also its major weakness, is the parsimony of his claim that Deuteronomy through 2 Kings is the studied composition of a single historian who used a variety of sources, prominent among them being the Josianic or late monarchical edition of Deut 4:44–28:68. In effect, however, the evidence for a more complex literary stratification, discerned by earlier scholars, is relegated by Noth to a pre-compositional stage of inchoate source materials. During the last several decades some trenchant modifications of and alternatives to this aspect of his hypothesis have been proposed. These include the influential position developed by Frank M. Cross and

others identifying at least two successive stages in the composition of both Deuteronomy and the conjoined Deuteronomic or Deuteronomistic history. According to Cross' analysis of characteristic themes, the principal edition of the historical work was Josianic in date rather than exilic. It was written before Josiah's death in order to support and celebrate his achievements as at once a restoration of Israel's commitment to the obligations of the covenant supposed to have been enacted through Moses' mediation during the wilderness era and a fulfillment of divine promises made to David as dynastic founder of the united kingdom of Israel and Judah (see, e.g., 2 Sam 7; 1 Kgs 2:2-4). The exilic edition appended the account of the fall of Jerusalem and the beginning of the Judaean diaspora (2 Kgs 23:26–25:30); but it also involved at least sporadic retouching and supplementation throughout, as exemplified by passages in Deuteronomy that presuppose a setting in exile and foresee the possibility of a national restoration (esp. 4:27-31; 28:63-68; 30:1-10).

In more recent discussion, the usefulness of a distinction between discrete Deuteronomic and Deuteronomistic stages of authorship has been called into question once again, with regard to other biblical literature but also Deuteronomy itself. Some scholars now argue that work generally indicative of "Deuteronomism" was prolonged and extensive, attesting the likely existence of an on-going school of Deuteronomists, or a somewhat amorphous Deuteronomic-Deuteronomistic movement, which is implicated over the course of several generations, if not centuries, in the composition and redaction of the "Primary History" extending from Genesis through 2 Kings and perhaps also in the formation of the collection of Latter Prophets that complements it. A related critical inclination is suspicion that both the Torah articulated in Deut 4:44–28:68 and the apparent account of its discovery and promulgation in 2 Kgs 22–23 are largely fabrications of the exilic or even postexilic period, intended to create precedent for the Judaean restoration as based on some supposedly antique version of Mosaic Torah. The problem with such views is that, not unlike Noth's Deuteronomistic history hypothesis, they tend to level or amalgamate the literary evidence that points to more coherent compositional growth and redaction. To be sure, while the results of 19th cent. scholarship have not been discredited, neither can they be taken for granted in the continuing efforts to reconstruct Deuteronomy's provenance and history of composition.

Current interpretation of Deuteronomy proceeds in the midst of this critical ferment. It is therefore important to keep in view ways in which the contents of the book, though not univocal—except in the significant and no doubt intentional sense that they are ascribed to Moses—are meant to cohere, thereby comprising a programmatic statement of what the Deuteronomists understood to be ancient Israel's unique covenantal identity, normative political institutions, and orthodox theology.

2. The Horeb and Moab covenant traditions

As key geographical and temporal points of reference in Deuteronomy, Horeb and Moab define the boundaries of the wilderness interim between the exodus from Egypt and the beginning of the conquest and occupation of Israel's promised homeland west of the Jordan River. More substantively, the names denote the principal traditions of covenantal law-giving which the major literary components of the book seek to integrate into the divinely authorized and sanctioned legacy that Moses bequeaths to Israel (compare 29:1 [Heb. 28:69]; 33:4). Before the final, pentateuchal stage of the book's redaction in the earlier Persian period, the integration was apparently accomplished in the main by an exilic Deuteronomist who revised and edited together two related but originally separate compositions, which are probably of late monarchical provenance: the valedictory memoirs and testamentary depositions attributed to Moses, now incorporated into the outer framework of the book (chaps. 1–4 and 29–34); and the edition of the Torah of Moses that occupies the center of the book (4:44–28:68). A setting in exile is especially evident in the supplementary Deuteronomistic seams that hold these antecedent compositions together; these seams are most conspicuous in 4:25-40 and 28:58-68, although they are identifiable elsewhere as well.

Each of the conjoined works exhibits close familiarity with traditions preserved in the preceding books of the Pentateuch. It is, in fact, difficult to interpret the first-person memoirs of 1:6–3:29 in the way proposed by Noth, as the overture to an independent Deuteronomistic history. Rather, as earlier historical-critics maintained, the selective review of the wilderness interim provided by the memoirs assumes, and may indeed be resumptive of, a pre-Priestly narrative that continues into the book of Joshua and beyond, logically culminating in the account of Josiah's religious reforms and his territorial expansion of the Judaean kingdom (compare Josh 1:2-9). Thus 1:6-8 begins at the point in the narrative of Exodus when, after the golden calf apostasy and Moses' effective intercession, Israel is dismissed from Sinai/Horeb under his guardianship to journey toward and take possession of the homeland the Lord had promised to the ancestors (compare Exod 33:1-3; Deut 1:9-21; 10:10-11). The memoirs suggest that the covenant bond between the Lord and Israel—initiated, broken, and only partially mended at Sinai/Horeb—remains in a state of flux or probation during the rest of the wilderness interim, held together primarily through the mediating efforts of Moses (compare Exod 32:30-34; Deut 9:6–10:11). Yet the covenant-making at Horeb itself is not rehearsed until the Deuteronomistic peroration in 4:1-40, a retrospect which is clearly informed by Moses' presentation of the Torah in 4:44–28:68 (and especially 5:2-31), but which also, like the memoirs, anticipates what will follow in chaps. 29–33 (see SINAI, MOUNT).

Three matters are highlighted in the peroration that are particularly relevant to its function in the literary context. Sharply profiled is the aniconic character and theological significance of the Lord's proclamation of the covenant's substance, which is specifically identified as the Decalogue ("the ten words" [ʿasereth haddevarim עֲשֶׂרֶת הַדְּבָרִים]), also delivered to Israel in the form of tablets personally inscribed by the deity (4:9-13, 15-24; compare 10:4-5). Second, connected to the singular experience of divine speech is a renewed commission of Moses "at that time" to supplement the principal terms of the covenant with other basic provisions, which Israel would need to observe in order to secure and maintain possession of its homeland (4:14; compare vv. 1-8, 40). Third, Moses offers prophetic testimony, invoking "heaven and earth" as witnesses, that the quality of Israel's existence would remain contingent on its rejection of idolatry and its reliance upon the merciful providence of the sole God who will punish it for breech of covenant but never abandon it entirely (4:25-39).

Without discounting the presence of significant Deuteronomistic supplementation and redaction (e.g., 11:26-30; 14:4-20; 27:1-8, 11-26; 28:47-68) the Torah attributed to Moses in 4:44–28:68 seems to be substantially a Deuteronomic composition. The work is designed not only to coordinate the religious and civil provisions legislated by Moses in 12:2–26:15 but also to authorize them as integral to the covenant initiated at Horeb. The opening paragraphs in 5:1–6:3 establish the agenda (which 4:12-14 summarizes). Only the fundamental terms of the covenant were immediately addressed by the Lord to the assembly of Israel, which ostensibly included the generation to whom Moses is now speaking (5:2-22; compare also 26:16-19; 27:9). In order to avoid any further direct exposure to the terrifying divine voice, the people elected Moses to serve henceforth as interlocutor, pledging to receive and to obey what he reported to them as the rest of the Lord's own decrees, intended to regulate their corporate life in the promised land (5:23–6:3; compare 18:16-18). After a series of hortatory amplifications of this covenant's formulary (6:4–8:20; 9:1–10:11; 10:12–12:1; compare 5:6-10) Moses articulates the provisions in 12:2–26:15 as the additional terms of this covenant, mandated by the Lord. He then completes the covenant's full and formal enactment with a summary of the reciprocal oaths of ratification, sworn by the Lord and the people "this very day" (26:16-19), which is followed by a lengthy rehearsal of blessings and cursings that provide sanctions (28:1-68; see COVENANT, OT AND NT).

Although the account of the Moab covenant in 29:1 [Heb. 28:69]–32:47 seems to be a patchwork of

Deuteronomistic and older Deuteronomic materials, it exhibits a pattern of themes and emphases that parallel those of 4:1-40, formulated now with even greater urgency in view of Moses' imminent death. Both the extended loyalty oath (29:2 [Heb. 29:1]–30:20) and Moses' valedictory "Song" (32:1-47; compare 31:19-30) also invoke "heaven and earth" as witnesses (30:19; 32:1; compare 31:28); and rejection of idolatry is once again identified in both as the crux of Israel's continuing relationship with the Lord (especially 29:17-26 [Heb. 29:16-25]; 32:19-21). Woven into this vivid covenantal fabric is the recurring theme of Joshua's commission to succeed Moses in the role of divinely empowered guardian of Israel (31:7-8, 14-15, 23; 32:44; compare 3:21-28; 34:9; Josh 1:1-9). Especially noteworthy, though, is the attention focused on Moses' covenantal Torah in its definitive written form. Already in 29:2 [Heb. 29:1]–30:20 repeated reference is made to "this book" with its threatening curses (29:20, 21, 27; 30:10; compare 28:58, 61). The actual transcription by Moses—together with his instructions regarding the document's disposition, periodic proclamation, and purpose—is reported twice. In 31:9-13, the Levitical priests and elders who receive the transcription are told to read it aloud to a plenary assembly of the people every seventh year during the celebration of SUCCOTH or Tabernacles, in order to renew Israel's allegiance to the Lord and its commitment to observe the prescriptions of "this Torah." In the second report the document's Levitical custodians are expressly instructed to curate it "alongside" the ark of the covenant, apparently as an accessible counterpart to the two stone tablets within, which the Lord had inscribed at Horeb with the stipulations of the Decalogue (31:26, compare 10:1-5; also 1 Kgs 8:9; see TEN COMMANDMENTS).

In sum, an exilic Deuteronomist redesigned segments of an earlier narrative—which featured Moses' valedictory memoirs and testamentary depositions—and used them to provide a framework for a revised edition of the Torah that Moses was supposed to have delivered orally to Israel in the wilderness, thereby completing the enactment of the Horeb covenant (compare 1:3). The framework supplied a clearer, more specific context for the presentation of this covenantal Torah, and probably incorporated it into a Deuteronomistic edition of the "Primary History." However, of greatest consequence is the explicit claim, developed in the account of the Moab covenant, that Moses also promulgated this Torah in written form. His spoken "words" thus became text, not only documenting the Horeb covenant but serving as the basis for its continuing application and liturgical renewal. And his Torah thereby acquired the status of scripture, comparable in authority to and functioning as a surrogate for the Lord's own commanding presence as recorded in the venerable tablets of the Decalogue.

3. Character and purpose of the Deuteronomic "Book of the Torah"

Critical scholarship today may be no closer than it was two centuries ago to a secure identification of an original "Book of the Torah of Moses" possibly embedded in 4:44–28:68. Efforts to reconstruct such a pre- or proto-Deuteronomic composition are many and various; they have inevitably proceeded on the basis of speculative assumptions regarding what the form and contents of the work should have been, were it to be equated with the temple scroll of Josiah's time, tersely described in 2 Kgs 22–23.

One approach has supposed that the scroll must have been a charter or "code" of religious laws, promoting cultic centralization, iconoclasm, and exclusive devotion to the Lord; therefore it most likely included at least many of the prescriptions in 12:1–16:17 but possibly none of the civil legislation that follows. Similarly, it has been claimed that the parts of 5:1–11:32 and 26:1–28:68 featuring covenantal language and concepts are later accretions, perhaps reflecting post-Josianic use of the original work for instructional, homiletic, and liturgical purposes. Arguments for distinguishing between earlier and later materials in 4:44–28:68 on the basis of close stylistic and genre analysis—especially the conspicuous distinction between second-person singular and plural forms of Mosaic address to Israel—carry greater weight. However, they have not yielded consistently reliable results, if only because eclectic style is not uncommon in biblical and other ANE literatures, including legal corpora.

But if the putative temple scroll and its precise contents remain elusive, there is still probable cause to see much of the content of 4:44–28:68 rooted in ideology, institutions, and practices of the preexilic period, rather than attributing the composition to later Deuteronomistic utopianism or the like. In this regard, three perspectives on the basic character and likely sources of the Deuteronomic legislation merit particular attention.

The broad design of 4:44–28:68, as well as its chief hermeneutical claim, links together the Decalogue (5:6-21) and the legislation subsequently enacted by Moses (12:2–26:15). These corpora are treated as counterparts; though the first is brief and the second lengthy, they are equally constitutive of the Horeb covenant. It is not surprising, then, to find that earlier commentators—among them Philo of Alexandria in the 1st cent. and Luther and Calvin in the 16th—understood Moses' promulgation of Torah to provide an authoritative, if only approximate expository amplification of the Decalogue's familiar commandments. Some contemporary scholars have pressed the case further. In their view, the classical Decalogue was indeed the proto-text for the work of the Deuteronomic legislator, accounting for a topical arrangement and sequence of the code's major segments of law . One problem with such views, however, is that the supposed correlations between individual commandments and segments of exposition often lack precision and sometimes seem only tangential at best (e.g., 5:11 and 13:1–14:27; 5:20 and 24:8–25:4). Moreover, the version of the Decalogue in 5:6-21 may itself be a product of later exilic redaction, designed to serve as an epitome of basic covenantal policies and created by expanding the older formulary of the Horeb covenant as represented in 5:6-10 and elaborated in 6:4–11:25.

A strong case has been made that the Deuteronomic legislation presupposes and reworks laws preserved in the so-called Book of the Covenant or Covenant Code in Exodus 20:22–23:33 as well as the closely related cultic rules of Exod 34:11-26. The Covenant Code, which may be an Israelite composition of the Neo-Assyrian period (compare 2 Kgs 17:24-28; Ezra 4:2), is evidently familiar with the third-person casuistic style, jurisprudential conventions, and ordering of illustrative cases attested in the broadly influential cuneiform tradition of Hammurabi's laws. The signature work of the Deuteronomic legislator involved innovative redrafting, rearrangement, and extensive supplementation of selected provisions of the Covenant Code. The purpose of this recension was to create what is arguably a new literary genre of jurisprudence: a comprehensive national constitution, which is identified as the Torah of Moses. In this case, the constitution was intended to promote and regulate a revitalization of "all Israel," centered in Jerusalem, in the aftermath of the late 8th cent. BCE Assyrian destruction of the northern kingdom. The Deuteronomic revision of the Covenant Code may have commenced as early as the reign of King Hezekiah (715–686 BCE), in association with the reforms attributed to him (2 Kgs 18:3-8, 19-35; compare 2 Chr 29–31).

The most compelling argument for the preexilic origin of the Deuteronomic Torah of Moses takes into account the dramatic evidence accumulated during the past half-century from studies of ANE traditions of law and international diplomacy. Some elements in 4:44–28:68—such as the formulary in 5:6-10, the creedal declaration in 6:4-5, the reciprocal oaths in 26:16-19, and the closely parallel blessings and cursings in 28:1-6, 15-18—may reflect older traditions of covenant-making. Especially striking, however, are passages that indicate direct acquaintance with Neo-Assyrian treaty protocols, the "Vassal Treaties of Esarhaddon" (VTE) in particular: e.g., the harsh policies to root out sedition in 13:1-18 (compare VTE 108-122) and the curses in 28:27-35 (compare VTE 419-30) and 28:53-57 (compare VTE 448-50, 547-50, 570-72). The style of direct second-person address to vassals that prevails throughout Esarhaddon's treaties may even have influenced the shift to a comparable "if you . . ." formulation of laws common in the Deuteronomic legislation, accounting for one of the noteworthy differences between this corpus and "lawcodes" such as those of Hammurabi and

the Covenant Code (see HAMMURABI, CODE OF). In view of this evidence there is little basis any longer for attempting to reconstruct a "pre-covenantal" version of the 4:44–28:68. The Deuteronomic Torah of Moses was most likely drafted from the outset as a covenantal constitution that was meant to represent both the form and the substance of the treaty between the Lord and Israel, initiated at Horeb and completed at the end of the wilderness period (compare Jer 7:22-26; 11:1-5; Ezek 20:1-27; Hos 4:1; 8:1, 11-12; see COVENANT, BOOK OF THE).

4. Authorship, provenance, and history of composition

The identity of the Deuteronomists responsible for the composition and redaction of Deuteronomy is hidden behind the anonymous narrator and especially the Mosaic persona whose voice they inherited or chose to speak for them. Over the course of two centuries, perhaps less, from the late 8th or early 7th cent. BCE through the middle of the 6th, they fashioned a literate and learned work that gave normative definition to the identity of "all Israel" as the covenanted people of God and which, as such, became the cornerstone of Jewish and Christian scriptures.

The character of the work itself and its creation in several stages over an extended period should shed light on the likeliest candidates for its authorship. An interesting parallel is afforded by the book of Isaiah, which was apparently composed during much the same frame of time. Those responsible in this case may have been generations of the original prophet's "disciples" who not only guarded but continued to expound his legacy of oracular "Torah" (compare Isa 8:16, where the term is rendered as "teaching" in the NRSV). Deuteronomy is certainly familiar with prophets and prophecy. It even portrays Moses as the archetype of legitimate Yahwistic prophetism (compare Deut 1:3; 13:1-5 [Heb. 13:2-6]; 18:9-22; 32:1-47; 34:10); but there is little else in the book to suggest that the Deuteronomists considered themselves to be prophets. Another possible literary parallel is the transmission and supplementation of traditions of wisdom ascribed to Solomon, presumably collocated by scribes trained to serve as royal officials (compare Prov 1:1; 25:1). Perhaps in imitation of Deuteronomic usage, such traditions, too, could be understood to comprise "Torah" in the sense of authoritative guidance (e.g., Prov 1:8; 3:1-12; 7:1-5; 31:26; compare Jer 8:8; Deut 4:5-8). The likelihood that the Deuteronomists were at least closely associated with courtly scribes—and perhaps generations of the influential family of Shaphan in particular (compare 2 Kgs 22:3-14; Jer 29:3; 36:10-25; 40:5-12)—is supported by the access they apparently had to official chronicles and other state documents.

Still, the likeliest candidates for principal involvement in the composition and redaction of Deuteronomy are clergy belonging to the extra-patrimonial "tribe of Levi" (10:8-9; compare 33:8). They are usually identified in the book itself as the elect "priests, the sons of Levi" (21:5; 31:9) and "the Levitical priests" or, more literally, "the priests, the Levites" (17:9, 18; 18:1; 27:9). They are portrayed as officials of the state (compare 1 Chr 26:20-32); their specified duties include custodianship of the sacred ark of the covenant and cultic service at Israel's national sanctuary but also judicial review and interpretation at the highest appellate level (10:8; 17:8-12; 18:3-8; 21:5; compare Jer 33:18). Most illuminating is their close connection with Moses who is reported to have entrusted to them care for and proclamation of his legacy of Torah (17:18; 31:9, 25; 33:8-11; compare Exod 32:25-29). Moreover, Jeremiah and his father Hilkiah, who may have been the priest prominently featured in 2 Kgs 22 as discoverer of the temple's "Book of the Torah," belonged to a Levitical clan resident in Anathoth near Jerusalem that seems to have traced its ancestry to the Elide priesthood, which officiated at the ancient sanctuary of Shiloh, and ultimately back to Moses (compare Jer 1:1; 1 Sam 2:27-28; 22:20-23; 1Kgs 2:26-27). Ezra, the priestly scribe who is closely associated with Mosaic Torah in the restoration era, may have belonged to the same or to a parallel Levitical lineage (compare Ezra 7:1-26; Neh 8:1-13 (*see* PRIESTS AND LEVITES).

The portfilio of the Levitical priesthood thus appears to be an authorial hallmark in the book of Deuteronomy. Even so, given the close associations and sometimes shared roles among prophets, scribes, and Levitical priests during the later period of the Judaean monarchy, it may be unnecessary as well as impossible to exclude either of the other two groups from major involvement at one or more stages in the formation of the Deuteronomic and Deuteronomistic works.

By way of summary, the primary contexts for the composition and redaction of Deuteronomy may be reconstructed succinctly.

During the later 8th cent. BCE, Assyrian expansion to the west demolished the kingdom of Israel, deporting a substantial portion of its population and remaking the region of Samaria into a province where groups from other parts of the empire were resettled. Local Israelite shrines remained in use but were adapted to the worship of other national deities, alongside rather than replacing Yahweh. Although severely compromised, more traditional Israelite Yahwism continued to be practiced, under Assyrian sponsorship, at the former national sanctuary of Bethel (2 Kgs 17:24-33). The Covenant Code (Exod 20:22–23:33), which is a conspicuous antecedent of the Deuteronomic legislation, may have originated in this setting.

In stark contrast to the situation in the former northern kingdom, the reign of HEZEKIAH (715–686 BCE) is celebrated in biblical accounts as a time of great national resurgence in Judah, encouraged by the king's personal piety and his responsiveness to the prophectic counsel of Isaiah (2 Kgs 18–19; 2 Chr 29–32). Hezekiah's reforms and his strengthening of the nation's strategic defenses are credited with enabling Jerusalem, the capital, to withstand Assyrian siege, even though the rest of the country was decimated by Sennacherib's forces in 701 BCE. Interestingly, and consistent with his other policies, the king is remembered as having reorganized the Yahwistic clergy, regularizing especially the ranks and duties of Levitical personnel to serve the needs of a nationalized cultus now consolidated at the temple in Jerusalem (2 Chr 31:11-21). The earliest version of the Deuteronomic Torah of Moses may have been drafted in this era, as an innovative Levitical revision of the Covenant Code, intended to provide support and direction for continuing the Judaean renewal of covenantal Yahwism.

During the reign of Josiah a century later, this Levitical tradition of theTorah, whether "found" or recently rewritten, was adopted through covenant as the national polity of Judah. The brief reports of this ceremony and of Josiah's other efforts to reconstitute Judah in continuity with an idealized Davidic-Solomonic as well as Mosaic "all Israel" may have been written by royal scribes as the conclusion to a late preexilic edition of the Primary History (2 Kgs 23:1-25).

The exilic, Deuteronomistic stage of composition revised the Torah and incorporated it into the *Testament of Moses*, which may already have been part of the Primary History. In this literary context, Moses' "book" documented the charter that made David's royal successors accountable for the continuation of the dynasty and hence also for the condition and ultimate destruction of the Judaean kingdom itself (compare esp. Deut 17:14-20; Josh 23:6-8; 1 Kgs 2:1-4; 2 Kgs 14:5-6; 21:1-15; 22:11-20).

The final stage of redaction that brought the Pentateuch to completion and made it preeminent among scriptural corpora is evident in Deut 34:10-12, a colophon which, from an apparent temporal distance, declares the peerlessness of Moses and the uniqueness of his divinely orchestrated work.

C. Theological Themes and Significance

The theology of Deuteronomy is resolutely covenantal in character and purpose. There are, to be sure, witnesses in the book that can be related to a broader spectrum of scriptural reflections on the sovereignty and providence of God (e.g., 4:35-38 [compare Isa 44:6-8; Joel 2:27]; 7:10 [compare Exod 34:6-7; Dan 9:4-6; John 4:2]; 30:6 [compare Jer 31:31-34; Ezek 11:17-21]; 30:15-20 [compare Pss 111–112; Prov 14:27]); but close study of such associations only serves to the highlight the decisive significance of covenant as contextual matrix for the theological testimony that coheres in and is characteristic of Deuteronomy itself. According to the Deuteronomists, the covenantal bond, initiated at Horeb and ratified in

Moab as the denouement of Moses' work, consolidates both Yahweh's divine credentials and Israel's corporate identity as the elect people of Yahweh.

1. Yahweh alone

Confessional identifications of Yahweh as "your God," "our God," and occasionally "my God" reverberate throughout Deuteronomy in the first-person speech of Moses to Israel. The keynote declaration in 6:4, which begins the catena of passages known as the Shema in Jewish liturgy, is emblematic: "Hear, Israel! Our God is Yahweh, Yahweh alone" (shemaʿ yisraʾel YHWH ʾelohenu YHWH ʾekhadh שְׁמַע יִשְׂרָאֵל יְהוָה אֱלֹהֵינוּ יְהוָה אֶחָד). Yahweh is Israel's singular and sufficient tutelary deity, the one and only supernal being who has legitimate claim to Israel's allegiance and devotion. This creedal predication is foundational for everything else Deuteronomy has to say about Yahweh's personal character, divine attributes, accessibility, and sovereign agenda.

Yahweh is like other national deities of the ANE—Ashur of Assyria and Marduk of Babylon in particular—as regards ascriptions to them of superlative greatness and incomparability by their devotees (e.g., 3:24; 10:17-18; Exod 15:11; Ps 86:8; Dan 2:47). In the view of the Deuteronomists, what primarily distinguishes Yahweh from other divine claimants to sovereignty, whether real or imagined, is Israel's empirical knowledge of Yahweh's direct and efficacious involvement in its own history (compare 32:1-18). Uniquely demonstrative of Yahweh's power and prerogative to command are the promises of progeny and land, made to Israel's ancestors, which are already being fulfilled at the end of the wilderness era and will be fully actualized through the conquest of western Canaan (e.g., 1:7-11; 3:21-22; 7:12-14; 8:2-10; compare Josh 21:43-45; 23:14). The signature event that establishes, once and for all, Yahweh's right to govern and to expect Israel's uncompromising loyalty is, of course, the exodus from Egypt (e.g., 6:20-25; 11:2-7; 26:4-10; 29:2-6 [Heb. 29:1-5]). This comes to transactional articulation in the formulary of the Horeb covenant (5:6-10), addressed to Israel in Yahweh's own voice. The formulary identifies the exodus as the definitive exhibition of Yahweh's sovereignty over Israel and therefore demands that "other gods" and iconic surrogates for deity never be permitted to encroach on the exclusive intimacy of the covenantal relationship (5:6-9a). The formulary concludes with a declaration of the attributes of zealous, though just and patient requital and generous reward that Yahweh will henceforth exercise as Israel's only suzerain (5:9b-10; compare 4:23-24, 31; 6:14-15; 7:9-10; Exod 33:19; 34:6-7). These basic attributes have counterparts in the blessings and curses invoked in Deuteronomy 28 to indemnify the completed covenant (compare also 29:19 [Heb. 29:18]–30:10; 32:19-42). See BLESSINGS AND CURSINGS.

According to the Deuteronomists, then, the covenant relationship is predicated on Yahweh's past but also continuing attentiveness to Israel's well-being, beyond even Israel's capacity to remain faithful to its own covenantal obligations (e.g., 7:12-16; 11:8-25; 26:15; 30:1-10). Just as Yahweh's presence was the vanguard that led the Israelites out of Egypt and through the wilderness, Yahweh will be in their midst in the conquest of Canaan (1:30-33; 7:1; 9:3; 31:6, 8; compare 20:1, 4; 23:14; also Exod 14:19-20, 30-31; 33:12-16). And once the designated homeland is secured and purged of the cultic installations and practices of its previous inhabitants (7:5; 12:2-3, 29-31; compare 16:21-22; Exod 23:20-33; 34:11-14), Yahweh will remain accessible to Israel through its regularized cultic service and annual celebrations at the authorized sanctuary (12:4-19; 14:26; 15:20; 16:1-16). This single national sanctuary, actualized as the Jerusalem temple, is "the place Yahweh will choose" by establishing or putting "his name" there, which may be a sublimated reference to the status conferred on the location, or the physical structure of the temple itself, by the installation of the ARK OF THE COVENANT, exemplary of Yahweh's sovereign divine "name" (shem שֵׁם) and effective presence (compare 1 Sam 4:4; 2 Sam 6:2, 17-19; 1 Kgs 8:1-11, 27-30; Pss 78:67-72; 132:1-10; Isa 18:7; Jer 33:9; contrast Deut 12:3, 13-14; see TEMPLE, JERUSALEM). Moreover, the uniquely revelatory "voice" of "the living God" heard by Israel's assembly in the overture to the covenant at Horeb (5:22-27) and extended through Moses' constitutional legislation and thereafter preserved in his transcribed "book" (31:9-13) becomes in the Deuteronomists' view a permanent medium of Yahweh's commanding presence—divine "word" accessible in text and fixed in textual memory throughout Israel's generations (6:6-9; 30:11-14; 32:44-47; see GOD, OT VIEW OF).

2. Israel and the nations

For the Deuteronomists, the nationhood of "all Israel" is a theologoumenon of immense, preeminent, and abiding importance. Just as Israel's communal origins attest and vindicate the unrivaled providence of Yahweh, its ancestral deity, so also the Horeb covenant—formally completed by Moses' promulgation of the Torah in Moab—is supposed to transform Israel's tribal constituents and varied citizenry into a unified people, imbuing them with Yahweh's own holiness and thus also setting them apart from and above all other nations (7:6; 14:2, 21; 26:16-19; compare 29:10-15 [Heb. 29:9-14]; 33:5, 26-29; see HOLY, HOLINESS, OT). That is why Moses' Torah resists identification as a selective "lawcode" or a jurisprudential manual but rather takes the form of a comprehensive theo-political charter that defines basic national institutions (12:2–17:13), the prerogatives and limitations of extraordinary offices (17:14–18:22), and crucial policies and practices for the maintenance of communal order and well-being (19:1–26:15). Because this Torah purports to epitomize Yahweh's values, which the community is supposed to adopt willingly and to implement faithfully as its own, it makes a totalizing claim on those who comprise Israel (e.g., 6:1-15; 10:12-22; 11:18-21). Thus, while it vigorously promotes fairness and equity within Israelite society (e.g., 15:1-18; 16:18-20; 24:6-22), it leaves little if any room for tolerance of internal religious dissent and other acts deemed treasonous, pathological, or criminal (e.g., 12:29–13:18 [Heb. 13:19]; 17:2-7; 19:15-21).

No doubt the historical circumstances of fierce Neo-Assyrian and Neo-Babylonian imperialisms (e.g., 2 Kgs 18:13–19:34; 24:1-17) help to account for the intense nativism and ostensible insularity of Deuteronomy's theology. But the book's Yahwism is not narrowly provincial. The Deuteronomists understand Israel's covenantal vocation to include its witness among the world's other nations to the superlative character of Torah and of Yahweh's inalienable sovereignty (4:5-8; 9:25-29; 28:10; 29:22-28 [Heb. 29:21-27]; 32:39-43; compare Exod 19:5). Although Deuteronomy's aniconic monolatry and incipient monotheism are unalloyed, they are tempered by suggestions that other nations may also be Yahweh's vassals, at least temporally under the guidance of deputized powers (2:5, 9, 19-23; 4:19, 32-39; 10:17-18; 28:49-50; 29:26 [Heb. 29:25]); 32:8-9; compare Mic 4:5; Ps 95:3). Deuteronomy's principal agenda is covenantal particularism that neither explores nor precludes a more inclusive theological vision (compare, e.g., Isa 19:19-25; Zech 14:9; Mal 1:11). *See* LAW IN THE OT; TORAH.

Bibliography: Klaus Baltzer. *The Covenant Formulary in Old Testament, Jewish, and Early Christian Writing* (1971); Joseph Blenkinsopp. *The Pentateuch: An Introduction to the First Five Books of the Bible* (1992); Duane L. Christensen. *A Song of Power and the Power of Song: Essays on the Book of Deuteronomy* (1993); Stephen A. Kaufman. "The Structure of the Deuteronomic Law," *Maarav* 1 (1978–79) 105–58; Bernard M. Levinson. *Deuteronomy and the Hermeneutics of Legal Innovation* (1998); Norbert F. Lohfink. "Was There a Deuteronomistic Movement?" *Those Elusive Deuteronomists: The Phenomenon of Pan-Deuteronomism.* Linda S. Schearing and Steven L. McKenzie, eds. (1999) 36–66; S. Dean McBride, Jr. "The Yoke of the Kingdom: An Exposition of Deuteronomy 6:4-5." *Int* 27 (1973) 273–306; S. Dean McBride, Jr. "Polity of the Covenant People: The Book of Deuteronomy." *Int* 41 (1987) 229–44; S. Dean McBride, Jr. "The Essence of Orthodoxy: Deuteronomy 5:6-10 and Exodus 20:2-6." *Int* 60 (2006) 133–50; Patrick D. Miller. *Deuteronomy.* Interpretation (1990); Richard D. Nelson. *Deuteronomy: A Commentary.* OTL (2002); Jean-Pierre Sonnet. *The Book Within the Book: Writing in Deuteronomy* (1997); Jeffrey H. Tigay. *Deuteronomy/Devarim.* JPS Torah Commentary 5 (1996); Moshe Weinfeld. *Deuteronomy and the Deuteronomic School* (1972).

S. DEAN MCBRIDE

DEVIATE [נָטָה natah, סוּר sur, עָבַט ʿavat; ἀστοχέω astocheō]. The word "deviate(d)" is rarely used in English translations of the Bible. The NRSV uses it once for astochēsantes (ἀστοχήσαντες, 1 Tim 1:6), the NIV once for saru (סָרוּ, 2 Chr 8:15). The NJB uses it the most (Deut 17:20; 2 Chr 34:33; Prov 4:5, 5:7), usually in conjunction with sur. In all cases, the word represents diverging from commands, instructions, or the proper path of God. *See* SIN, SINNERS.

STEVEN D. MASON

DEVIL, DEVILS dev′uhl [διάβολος diabolos]. Diabolos means slanderer or false accuser (Sir 51:2; 2 Tim 3:3) and calumniator (Aristophanes, *Eq.* 44-45) and was associated with a slanderous whisper or scandal (psithyros [ψίθυρος], Pindar, *Pyth.* 2.75-76), thief (kleptēs [κλέπτης], Aristotle, *Top.* 4:5:126a:32), and enemy (diabolos; tsar [צָר], Esth 7:4).

In the OT a SATAN (satan [שָׂטָן], "the adversary" or "the accuser") is a human enemy (1 Sam 29:4) or opponent (1 Kgs 11:14), or an angelic adversary acting for God (Num 22:22). Where the LXX uses diabolos to translate the Hebrew satan, including the judicial prosecutor of the heavenly court in Job 1–2, the idea of "the satan" as a slanderer and enemy of God, inciting humans to sin, is a later introduction (1 Chr 21:1; Ps 109:6; Zech 3:1, 2) that may reflect Persian dualism (Avesta Yasna 30) or, more likely, rivalry in the Greek pantheon (Homer, *Iliad* 20.48-53).

In the NT diabolos is the accuser (1 Pet 5:8) and is a synonym for the evil one (Matt 13:19\\Luke 8:11) and is used interchangeably with the Tempter (Matt 4:1, 3), the enemy (Matt 13:39), Satan (John 13:2, 27) and, in Rev 12:7-9, is the great dragon, the ancient serpent and the deceiver of the whole world. He can be worshiped (Luke 4:7), tempts Jesus (4:2), is the enemy of the children of the kingdom (Matt 13:39), disabling their belief and salvation (Luke 8:12). Jesus is said to heal all who were oppressed by the devil (Acts 10:38) and his death destroys the devil (Heb 2:14). An eternal fire is prepared for the devil and his angels (Matt 25:41). In the gospel of John, the devil is a murderer, contains no truth, lies, and is the father of lies (John 8:44). He also motivates (13:2), fathers (8:44), or is an epithet for (6:70) Jesus' opponents. Paul uses only the term *Satan*, but in the deutero-Pauline letters the devil can snare, condemn (1 Tim 3:6-7) and capture (2 Tim 2:26) believers, who are not to make room for the devil (Eph 4:27) but to stand against his craftiness (Eph 6:11; *see* Jas 4:7). *See* DEMON.

Bibliography: P. Day. *An Adversary in Heaven* (1988); J. B. Russell. *The Devil* (1977).

GRAHAM H. TWELFTREE

DEVOTED [חרם khrm; ἀνάθεμα anathema]. The NRSV, NIV, and ASV normally use *devoted* or "devoted thing(s)" to translate the Hebrew khrm. The verbal form occurs 48 times in the hiphil (the active causative form) and three times in the hophal (passive causative). The noun kherem (חֵרֶם) occurs 29 times, 16 times in narrative texts, especially in the books from Deuteronomy through to 2 Kings. Probably the most widely known example of kherem occurs in Josh 6–7, the narrative in which Jericho is conquered and "devoted to destruction" (6:18, NSRV) and Israel warned "not to take any of the devoted thing" (6:18, NRSV). All silver, gold, and bronze are "sacred to the Lord" (v. 19). Achan, however, coveted fine clothing, silver, and a bar of gold, and kept these for himself (7:21). For this he was utterly destroyed. First Samuel 15 offers a later parallel: Saul is commanded to devote the Amalekites to utter destruction, but he spared Agag and the best of the sheep and cattle (15:9). Thereby he forfeited his kingship (15:10-33). Kherem most typically occurs in the context of war decreed by Yahweh, but also in contexts concerning the sacred. The latter occurs in Num 18:14 and Ezk 44:29: "Every devoted thing in Israel" (NRSV) is given to the priests as a sacred offering.

Nevertheless, issues about the translation and meaning of kherem remain complex and controversial. The LXX versions frequently use anathema to translate the noun (as in Jos 6:18; 7:1), and anathematizō (ἀναθεματίζω) to translate the causative hiphil verb. The AV/KJV uses "devoted things" for kherem only twice (Lev 27:28; Num 18:14), preferring normally "the accursed thing". The NJB renders kherem as "forbidden under the BAN" (Jos 6:18) or "the ban" (7:1). The REB uses a variety of renderings. Many commentators use ban, but the term is misleading. The semantic complexity of khrm is found among Israel's neighbors. The Moabite Stone (ca. 830 BCE) recounts Mesha's "devoting" the town of Nebo to destruction for his deity Chemosh. In Arabic khrm denotes sacred precincts, giving rise to the harem from which males outside the household are excluded.

To present-day sensitivities the entailments of khrm may appear merely primitive. Yet certain aspects should be kept in view. 1) Those who participate in conquest that concludes with kherem derive no personal gain from it. This conflicts with customary assumptions that conquerors would expect to acquire slaves and property from conquered peoples. War was to be carried out only in response to the will of the God of Israel. 2) Israel's identity as the people of God was not to be compromised by subsequent influence on the part of Canaanite peoples. In Deut 20:18, the reason for the kherem is "that they [Canaanite peoples] may not teach you to do according to all their abominable practices." 3) Normally a city or town suffered destruction only if it has refused terms of surrender. Whatever is holy to God cannot be retained for common use. Hence kherem follows only the command of God (Jos 11:11, 12, 20; 1 Sam 15:3-15); or Moses (Deut 2:34; 3:6; 7: 2); or Joshua (Jos 2:10; 10:35-40).

English versions of the NT render a multiplicity of Greek words as *devoted*. But these are non-technical uses and only marginal in relation to issues about kherem. Thus NRSV translates euparedron tō kuriō (εὐπάρεδρον τῷ κυρίῳ) as unhindered devotion to the Lord (1 Cor 7:35). In practice a number of Greek words denote single-minded devotion. However, in the context of kherem the most significant Greek term anathema is usually rendered *cursed* or *curse* (Rom 9:3; 1 Cor 12:3; 16:22; Gal 1:8-9), although it also more rarely may denote "votive offering" (Luke 21:5). *See* ANATHEMA; BLESSINGS AND CURSINGS; DESTROY, UTTERLY.

Bibliography: W. Horbery. "Exterpation and Excommunication." *VT* 35 (1985) 13–38; C. Sherlock. "The Meaning of ḥrm in the OT." *Colloquium* 14 (1982) 13–24.

ANTHONY C. THISELTON

DEVOUT [צַדִּיק tsadhiq; εὐλαβής eulabēs, εὐσεβής eusebēs; σέβομαι sebomai]. Tsadhiq often bears a legal connotation, denoting one who is just and whose claim is right (Ps 17:1; Isa 5:23). A devout person conducts oneself with righteousness in relationships (both human and divine), a sense that often moves into the realm of morality and is contrasted with wicked behavior (Gen 7:1). In the NT, the terms designate righteous, pious behavior. Luke–Acts singles out Jews and pagans (Luke 2:25; Acts 8:2; 10:2; 13:43; 17:4; 22:12), while other texts reserve this designation for Christians (1 Tim 4:7; Titus 2:12; 2 Pet 2:9).

DAVID M. REIS

DEW [טַל tal; δρόσος drosos]. Moisture appearing usually in the morning as minute water droplets on the surfaces of thin objects exposed to the air. As these surfaces cool overnight by radiating heat to the sky, droplets condense because the atmosphere cannot absorb the moisture at the rate at which the moisture is produced. At lower temperatures, dew becomes frost. Dew helps compensate for insufficient rain in Israel during the summer months, including the dew on Mount Hermon (Ps 133:3). In biblical times, it was viewed as falling from the sky or the heavens (2 Sam 17:12, Prov 3:20, Zech 8:12). Its quick evaporation in the morning is scientifically accurate (Exod 16:14; Hos 6:4, 13:3). Dew symbolized productivity (Gen 27; 28), renewal (Ps 110:3, Hos 14:4; 3 Macc 6:6), receptivity (Song 5:2), and things beyond human control (Mic 5:6). *See* ISRAEL, CLIMATE OF.

EMILY R. CHENEY

DHAHR MIRZBÂNEH. A rocky ridge above the springs at ʿAin es-Sâmiyeh, in the hills northeast of Ramallah. Although frequently robbed but never systematically excavated, the large region is exceptionally rich in archaeological remains, extending from at least the late third millennium to the Byzantine era. The major attraction was probably the spring itself, the largest in the Ephraim hill country, as well as the strategic location of the surrounding hills, at the head of the Wâdi ed-Dâliyeh that descends to the Jordan Valley just north of Jericho. East of the springs of ʿAin es-Sâmiyeh, a cemetery of hundreds of shaft-tombs belong to the Early Bronze Age IV period (ca. 2200–2000 BCE). *See* DALIYEH, WADI ED; MARJAMEH, KHIRBET EL.

Bibliography: W. G. Dever. "Middle Bronze I Cemeteries at Mirzbâneh and ʿAin-Sâmiyeh." *IEJ* 22 (1972) 95–112; I. Finkelstein. "The Central Hill Country in the Intermediate Bronze Age." *IEJ* 41 (1999) 17–45; P. W. Lapp *The Dhahr Mirzbâneh Tombs* (1966); P. W. Lapp and N. Lapp, eds. *Discoveries in the Wâdi ed-Dâliyeh* (1972); A. Mazar. "Three Israelite Sites in the Hills of Judah and Ephraim." *BA* 45 (1982) 107–78.

WILLIAM G. DEVER

DIADEM, DIADEMS [נֵזֶר nezer, צָנִיף tsanif, צְפִירָה tsefirah, מִצְנֶפֶת mitsnefeth; διάδημα diadēma]. *Diadem* is a transliteration of the Greek *diadēma*. The NRSV uses the word *diadem* in four OT passages. In Exod 29:6 and 39:30, *diadem* translates nezer, which is derived from nazar (נָזַר, "dedicate, consecrate"). Elsewhere, this word is translated as *crown* (2 Sam 1:10; 2 Kgs 11:12; 2 Chr 23:11; Ps 89:39; 132:18; Zech 9:16) and *turban* (Lev 8:9). In Isa 28:5, tsefirah is translated *diadem*. In Isa 62:3, *diadem* translates tsanif, which is derived from the verb tsanaf (צָנַף, "wrap together"). The same word is translated *turban* in Job 29:14; Isa 3:23; and Zech 3:5. Mitsnefeth, another derivative of tsanaf, is translated as *turban* in the NRSV (Exod 28:4, 37, 39; 29:6; 39:28, 31; Lev 8:9; 16:4; Ezek 21:26). These words suggest a piece of cloth wound around the head and fastened with a band.

The ancients applied the word to the blue band of the tiara of the Persian king. Later, it referred to the wreathlike crown of Hellenistic rulers. All three NT references are in Revelation (12:3; 13:1; 19:2) and signify royalty.

GREGORY L. LINTON

DIAL [מַעֲלָה maʿalah]. A (sun) dial is an instrument used to indicate the time of day by measuring the movement of the sun's shadow. The object creating the shadow is called a gnomon. The first gnomons were probably trees, poles or other fixed objects. The earliest extant sundial was found in Egypt and dates to circa 1500 BCE.

Reference to a sundial appears in a story about Isaiah and King Hezekiah (2 Kgs 20:8-11; Isa 38:7-8). As a sign that God will heal Hezekiah, Isaiah turns back the shadow of the "declining sun on the dial of Ahaz ten steps" (Isa 38:8). Some ancient versions apparently considered the maʿalah to be the stairs of Ahaz's house (1QIsaᵃ: "on the dial/steps of the upper story of Ahaz"; LXX: "ten steps of your father's house"). Other ancient authorities understood it to be an actual sundial (e.g., Vulgate: *horologio*).

Sundials dating to the Hellenistic and Roman periods have been found in Israel, including several in Jerusalem. Object 1229 found in locus 45 of the Qumran ruins has been identified by some as a sundial or other astronomical measuring device, though this remains controversial. *See* SUN; TIME.

Bibliography: Sharon L. Gibbs. *Greek and Roman Sundials* (1976); Uwe Glessmer and Matthias Albani. "An Astronomical Measuring Instrument from Qumran." *The Provo International Conference on the Dead Sea Scrolls.* Donald W. Parry and Eugene Ulrich, eds. (1999) 407–42.

HENRY W. MORISADA RIETZ

DIALOGUE. A conversation between two or more characters. As a literary means to achieve more drama, dialogue can be made to carry the main part of the story (Gen 23:4-15; Prov 7:14-20) and bring out a character's real disposition (e.g., Ahab in 1 Kings 22). Through dialogue an argument can be skillfully built up (e.g., 2 Sam 14, the Tekoite woman). The book of Job is a work in dialogue form, in which answers often consist of rhetorical questions (Job 38–40). *See* DIATRIBE; RHETORICAL CRITICISM, NT; RHETORICAL CRITICISM, OT.

L. J. DE REGT

DIALOGUE OF A MASTER AND HIS SLAVE. *See* DUA-KHETY, INSTRUCTION OF; JOB, BOOK OF; THEODICY.

DIALOGUE OF PESSIMISM. Also called the Babylonian Ecclesiastes, this 14th cent. BCE Mesopotamian text expresses cynicism about the gods' treating the righteous fairly and differs from the biblical Ecclesiastes in that the former views suicide as the only hope of escape. The Dialogue also has ties with the book of Job. *See* ECCLESIASTES, BOOK OF; JOB, BOOK OF.

EMILY R. CHENEY

DIALOGUE OF THE SAVIOR. *See* SAVIOR, DIALOGUE OF THE.

DIAMOND [שָׁמִיר shamir]. Judah's sin is engraved on hearts and altars with a "diamond point iron pen." (Jer 17:1) Since this particular gem was probably unknown in OT times, what stone was meant in Jeremiah's metaphor is unclear, but it evidently was very sharp and hard. Ancient references to this stone are not entirely clear until the Roman period. A diamond is composed of crystallized carbon, chemically simple, but the hardest of stones.

ELIZABETH E. PLATT

DIANA dī-an´uh. The Roman equivalent of ARTEMIS, Diana was the sister of APOLLO and daughter of JUPITER. As the virgin goddess of the hunt, she was at home on mountaintops and in groves, often accompanied by an entourage of dancing nymphs (Homer, *Hymn* 5.16-20; 27.1-22; Virgil, *Aen.* 1.498-502). While her wrath was legendary (Homer, *Il.* 9.529-542; Aeschylus, *Ag.* 134–143; Euripedes, *Bacch.* 337–340), she also protected newborn animals and children (Homer, *Il.* 21.470; Euripedes, *Hipp.* 161). Yet another portrait comes from Acts 19:23-40, where the Ephesian Artemis is primarily a fertility deity whose worship Paul's missionary activity threatens. *See* EPHESUS.

DAVID M. REIS

DIASPORA dī-as´puh-ruh [διασπορά diaspora] is the Greek term for dispersion (derived from the verb diaspeirō [διασπείρω] "to scatter"). It is used in the LXX twelve times with the meaning "dispersion of Jews among the Gentile nations" or "the Jews as thus scattered," rendering no single corresponding Hebrew term but a number of different Hebrew words. The corresponding Hebrew term golah (גּוֹלָה, plural [galuth גָּלוּת] with a meaning of "deportation" or "exile" or the state of those who were deported or exiled was translated in the LXX differently: aichmalosia (αἰχμαλωσία, "group of prisoners"), metoikesia (μετοικεσία, "captivity"), paroikia παροικία (sojourning in a foreign land). Strictly speaking, the term *diaspora* is used to denote any religious or national minority living outside its homeland. In antiquity there were other dispersions, e.g., Greek and Phoenician. In modern times there are quite a number of diasporas: Armenians, mostly in the United States and France, Turks (mostly in Germany), Palestinians in the Arab countries, Irish in the United States, Canada, or New Zealand, etc. Recently the phenomenon of population dispersal has attracted much attention, and features developed in the diasporas, such as local and translocal identities, and/or ambiguity in cultural self-expression, are widely discussed. But first and foremost the term refers to Jewish settlements outside Palestine.

Jews moved from Palestine for different reasons: some were dislocated under compulsion as war prisoners, but there also existed a voluntary immigration prompted by different economic and political motives, including overpopulation, land shortages, and internal political struggle in Palestine. Deportations of Israelites as prisoners of war possibly took place as early as the 10th cent. BCE when Judah was invaded by Egyptians (1 Kgs 14:25-28; 2 Chr 12:1-12). But the turning point in terms of dispersion was the Babylonian EXILE. In 597 BCE Nebuchadnezzar II conquered Jerusalem. Ten years later, the Temple was destroyed, and the inhabitants of the southern kingdom of Judah were forcibly exiled from their homeland to Babylonia. Cyrus (538 BCE) made it possible for them to return to Palestine, but a large proportion of Jews preferred to remain permanently in Babylonia, where throughout Hellenistic and Roman periods, flourishing Jewish communities existed. From the 3rd cent. CE, these became important centers of rabbinical learning.

From at least the 6th cent. BCE, Egypt became a popular asylum for Jewish refugees—this was one of the side effects of the Babylonian exile. At the beginning of the 6th cent. there was a military colony of Jewish soldiers in the city of Elephantine in Egypt. After the foundation of Alexandria and later in the Ptolemaic period, a new influx of Jews took place. Until the Jewish revolt of 115–17 CE, Egypt was, perhaps, the most important Jewish center. The emigration movement was fostered by some Hellenistic monarchs who found Jews to be good subjects and good soldiers, and encouraged settlements by granting privileges. Jews lived everywhere in Egypt, but the largest Jewish population was in Alexandria. According to Philo, it was as much as a million people, and though this estimate should be taken with caution there is no doubt that it was very significant: two quarters of the city, (according to Philo, *Flacc.* 8.55) or one-quarter (according to Josephus, *J.W.* 2.495; *Ag. Ap.* 2.33-35) were inhabited mostly by Jews. In Egypt, there flourished a Jewish literature in Greek, that gradually became the main language of Jewish diaspora in the eastern Mediterranean. This development began with translation of the Torah into the Greek language (*see* SEPTUAGINT), which was followed by the philosophical treatises, literary and poetical works, and scriptural exegesis.

Apart from Babylonia and Egypt, there were noticeable Jewish communities in Syria (especially in Antioch), North Africa, Asia Minor, Cyprus, Greece, and Rome. By the 1st cent. CE, Jewish communities existed in nearly all parts of the then civilized world, as far as the Crimea and Taman Peninsula. As Strabo (Josephus, *Ant.* 14.115) puts it, Jews "had already made their way into every city."

In various places in the diaspora, Jews had different degrees of self-government. In all periods of its existence, Jews were granted a right to practice their religion. Jerusalem remained a symbolic religious focus, their metropolis. Until the destruction of the Temple by the Romans in 70 CE all adult male Jews between the ages of twenty and fifty paid an annual Temple tax of half a shekel (two drachmae in Greek currency, two denarii in Roman). Many Jews traveled to Jerusalem for religious festivals. According to Acts 2:9-11, at the Feast of Weeks (Pentecost) there were Jews who came from Parthia, Media, Persia, Mesopotamia, Cappadocia, Pontus, Asia, Phrygia, Pamphylia, Egypt, parts of Lybia, Cyrene, Rome, Crete, and Arabia.

Though many Jews in the diaspora were hellenized, they managed to preserve their national identity and to resist assimilation. Their relations with the Gentile neighbors ranged from sometimes difficult to the point of anti-Jewish pogroms (for instance, in Alexandria in 38 CE), but on the whole there were long periods of peaceful coexistence and, for quite a number of Gentiles, the Judaism of the diaspora was very attractive. These formed a friendly circle of Jewish sympathizers (see GODFEARER).

The centers of Jewish community life in the diaspora was the SYNAGOGUE, which served for the economic, social, political, charitable, educational, and religious needs of community. In some places, manumissions of slaves took place in synagogues. It was in synagogues that were open for attendance for the Gentiles that Paul usually started preaching during his missionary journeys.

Bibliography: Shimon Applebaum. *Jews and Greeks in Ancient Cyrene.* SJLA 28 (1979); John M. G. Barclay. *Jews in the Mediterranean Diaspora from Alexander to Trajan* (323 BCE–117 CE) (1996); Elias Bickerman. *The Jews in the Greek Age* (1988); Erich S. Gruen. *Diaspora: Jews Amidst Greeks and Romans* (2002); R. Hachlili. *Ancient Jewish Art and Archaeology in the Diaspora.* Handbuch der Orientalistik. Erste Abteilung. Der Nahe und Mittlere Osten 35 (1998); Joseph Mélèze Modrzejewski. *The Jews of Egypt from Ramses II to Emperor Hadrian* (1995); Shaye J. D. Cohen and E. S. Frerichs, eds. *Diasporas in Antiquity.* (1993); Lester L. Grabbe, ed. *Leading Captivity Captive: The "Exile" as History and Ideology.* (1998); John M. G. Barclay, ed. *Negotiating Diaspora: Jewish Strategies in Roman Empire.* LSTS 45 (2004); Benjamin Issak and Aharon Oppenheimer, eds. *Studies on the Jewish Diaspora in the Hellenistic and Roman Periods* (1996); E. Mary Smallwood. *The Jews Under Roman Rule from Pompey to Diocletian: A Study of Political Relations.* SJLA 20 (1981); Emil Schürer. *The History of the Jewish People in the Age of Jesus Christ.* Geza Vermes, Fergus Millar, Martin Goodman III, eds. (1986) 1–186; Margaret H. Williams. *The Jews Among the Greeks and Romans: A Diaspora Sourcebook* (1998).

IRINA LEVINSKAYA

DIATESSARON. Literally "through the four," a gospel harmony, reconstructed from fragments and translations composed in Syriac (or, possibly, Greek) about 172 CE by Tatian, it wove into a single narrative material from the four (proto) canonical gospels. Duplica-

tions and contradictions were removed as the gospels were "harmonized."

The *Diatessaron* is one of the oldest witnesses to the text of the gospels. It contains material that, today, is considered "extra-canonical." Whether this is due to Tatian's use of a "fifth" (i.e., non-canonical) source, or whether the reading was then part of a proto-canonical gospel (the reading is also found in two *Vetus Latina* manuscripts of Matthew), is unknown.

The *Diatessaron* was enormously popular and was widely disseminated. Apparently, the gospels first circulated in Syria in the form of a *Diatessaron*. In the early 5th cent. it was suppressed by bishops Rabbula (Edessa) and Theodoret (Cyrrhus). Eastern witnesses exist in Syriac, Arabic, Armenian, and Georgian. In the West, Codex Fuldensis (6th cent.) appears copied from an older *Diatessaron*. Other Western witnesses exist in Old High German, Middle Dutch, and Early Italian.

Bibliography: W. L. Petersen. *Tatian's Diatessaron. Its Creation, Dissemination, Significance, and History in Scholarship* (1994).

WILLIAM L. PETERSEN

DIATRIBE. A rhetorical style of teaching employed particularly by Hellenistic philosophers for moral-pedagogical purposes in order to maintain contact with the audience. The teacher creates an imaginary dialogue partner, often answering questions and rejecting objections raised by that partner, or posing rhetorical questions to him. This style is employed in some Pauline letters (e.g., Rom 2:17-29; 3:1-9; 3:27–4:2; 11:19-24; 1 Cor 12:15-16; 15:29-35), James (e.g., 2:14-24), and already in Malachi (1:2, 6, 7; 2:14, 17; 3:7, 8, 13, 14). See DIALOGUE; RHETORICAL CRITICISM, NT.

L. J. DE REGT

DIBLAIM dib'lay-im [דִּבְלָיִם divlayim; Δεβηλαιμ Debēlaim]. Father of GOMER, Hosea's wife (Hos 1:3). Since the name means "lump of pressed figs" or "pressed fig cakes" and such food was used in fertility rites, it may metaphorically allude to Gomer's harlotry.

EMILY R. CHENEY

DIBLATHAIM. See BETH-DIBLATHAIM.

DIBON di'bon [דִּיבֹן divon]. A settlement located three mi. north of the Arnon (modern Wadi Mujib) on the plateau east of the Dead Sea, some of its ruins are located on a mound (a tell) next to the modern town of Dhiban. Dibon is referred to in biblical and extra-biblical texts. The immediate region around the settlement likely also bore the same name. It was an area claimed by both Israel and Moab. In the Iron Age inscription of King Mesha of Moab (ca. 840 BCE; compare 2 Kgs 3), there are several references to Dibon, which indicate its importance on the plateau. In line 2, Mesha identifies himself as a Dibonite, and claims credit for several construction projects in a fortified area named Qarho, which likely is his royal quarter in Dibon. Mesha also notes that the Omride dynasty in Israel had previously subjugated the Moabite population and its settlements on the plateau.

In the OT Dibon appears both as a Moabite city (Isa 15:2; Jer 48:18, 22) and as an inheritance of the Israelite tribe of Reuben (Josh 13:9, 17). Dibon's royal character and fortifications are reflected in the "woe" cast against it in Jer 48:18.

Todd Bolen/BiblePlaces.com

Figure 1: Iron Age foundation of temple

The ruins of ancient Dibon were partially excavated in a series of campaigns in the 1950s. Although there are references in Late Bronze Egyptian texts to Dibon, no LB ruins were uncovered. The main phase of occupation began in Iron Age II (9th cent. BCE). The Iron Age city showed evidence of fortifications and a number of cisterns in keeping with Mesha's description of Qarho. The stone inscription commissioned by King Mesha was discovered by a European traveler near the mound in 1868. *See* MOABITE STONE.

Bibliography: A. Dearman, ed. *Studies in the Mesha Inscription and Moab* (1989).

J. ANDREW DEARMAN

DIBRI dib´ri [דִּבְרִי divri]. A Danite whose unnamed grandson blasphemed the divine name (Yahweh) in a curse during a personal fight and, with the approval of Moses, was subsequently stoned to death. The blasphemer's mother, SHELOMITH, was the daughter of Dibri, and his father was an Egyptian. (Lev 24:10-16)

MARSHALL D. JOHNSON

DIDACHE did´uh-kee [διδαχή didachē]. Means "teaching." An early Jewish Christian community rule, titled "The Teaching of the Apostles" and subtitled "The Teaching of the Lord through the Twelve Apostles to the Gentiles [or Nations]," containing catechesis (chaps. 1–6) followed by baptismal instructions (chaps. 7–8), eucharistic prayers (chaps. 9–10), various rules concerning community leaders and their sup-

port (chaps. 11–15), concluded by a short apocalypse (chap. 16). The first title is widely attested in Patristic writings (e.g., Eusebius, *Hist. eccl.* 3.25.4; Clement of Alexandria, *Strom.* 1.20.100) though this may refer to the Two Ways only (parallel to 1–6, e.g., in the Latin *Doctrina apostolorum*). The work was lost to Western scholarship until its rediscovery in 1873 by P. Bryennios in a collection (dated 1056 CE) of early Christian writings. A heavily edited version of the complete text is taken up in book VII of the *Apostolic Constitutions* and is found in a Greek papyrus fragment from Oxyrhynchus, a partial text in Coptic and in sections in the Ethiopic *Church Order.*

There is little evidence for date and place of composition. Since the Didache draws on earlier sources and was probably edited continually while it served as the rule of a community, the dating of individual sections cannot establish the date of the final version. The key question remains whether the Didache used Matthew and/or Luke or makes independent use of the Jesus tradition since agreements are often close but not verbatim, or alternatively whether Matthew used the Didache. There is now a general consensus that the Didache should be dated no later than the end of the 1st or beginning of the 2nd cent. CE, perhaps even as early as the mid-1st cent. Egypt is sometimes suggested as the place of origin based on manuscript remains and use of the Two Ways tradition by *Barn.* 18–21, but most favor Syria, or Antioch in particular.

The Two Ways section is based largely on expansion of the second table of the Ten Commandments and shows a strongly Jewish character. There are many connections with similar material found, e.g., in the *Manual of Discipline* (1QS III, 13–IV, 26) from Qumran, the Rabbinic tractate *Derekh Eretz Zuta,* and the Greek *Testament of Asher.* It is thus likely that this material was used in catechesis and initiation by parties within Israel before it was appropriated by early Jewish Christian communities to prepare Gentile converts for admission (compare the use of "the Way" in Acts 2:28; 9:2; 19:9, 23; 24:14). Instruction in the Two Ways is required before BAPTISM in *Did.* 7:1, "having said all these things beforehand, baptize . . ."

The conclusion of the Two Ways in the Didache states that a convert only becomes "perfect" by "taking on the whole yoke of the Lord" (6:3; compare Matt 11:29-30), but the person who is unable should do as much as possible. Likewise, converts should observe the food laws, but must keep "strictly from what has been offered to idols" (6:4). In a Jewish Christian milieu it seems likely that the "yoke of the Lord" refers to the Torah and that becoming "perfect" refers to full conversion to Judaism, including circumcision on the part of Gentile converts. Circumcision and observance of the purity laws are not required for admission, but the converts should strive toward progressively fuller obedience so as to be "found perfect" on the last day (16:2).

The lack of theological development in the instruction on baptism and eucharist is significant, in comparison to Paul (Rom 6:1-14). There is no reference to forgiveness of sins or the cross of Christ in baptism. Most attention is paid to the kinds of water used, which should be pure, running ("living") water if possible (compare the six grades of water in *m. Miqw.* 1:1-8). The implication is that baptism is a ritual purification from uncleanness. Baptism is into the name of the Trinity in 7:1, 3 but into the "name of the Lord" in 9:5, an earlier practice. Fasting for one or two days by the baptisand and the officiant is required (7:4). Chapter 8 requires a weekly fast on Wednesdays and Fridays to distinguish the new member from the "hypocrites" who fast on Mondays and Thursdays (most likely Pharisaic Jews as in *b. Ta'an.* 12a) and thrice daily recitation of the Lord's Prayer (compare Matt 6:5-18).

There is no reference to the Last Supper or the Words of Institution in the instructions for the eucharist. Thanks is given to the Father for making known the "holy vine of David your servant/child" over the cup, which opens the meal as in Jewish tradition, and "life and knowledge" through "Jesus your servant/child" over the broken bread (9:1-2). The "vine" is a symbol for Israel "made known" by Jesus as David's son. After a full meal a further blessing thanks God for making the name, pronounced over them in baptism, dwell in the hearts of the participants (10:1-2) and for giving spiritual food and drink through Jesus (10:3-4). The prayers are followed by hymnic celebrations of the church gathered into the kingdom (9:4-5; 10:4-5). The Davidic Christology of the eucharistic prayers is re-enforced by the acclamation, "Hosanna to the God of David" (10:6; "house of David" in the Coptic, which is most likely original), and the section concludes with the Aramaic exclamation, **Maran atha amēn** (Μαρὰν ἀθά ἀμήν "Come Lord! Amen"; compare 1 Cor 16:22; Rev 20:20). As with baptism, the EUCHARIST emphasizes purity or "holiness" as a prerequisite for participation (9:5; 10:6). In the Coptic text and the *Apostolic Constitutions*, these instructions are followed by a prayer to be said over ointment or incense, which often accompanied a communal meal in the ancient world. It is not clear how the prayers in 9–10 relate to the weekly eucharist on the "Lord's day of the Lord" (the earliest reference to Sunday worship) described in chap. 14.

Much of the interest in the Didache has centered on the coexistence of apostles, prophets, and teachers with bishops and deacons (but not presbyters) in the community rules. Apostles are to be welcomed "as the Lord himself" and given provisions, but may not stay more than one or two days (11:3-4). Apostles should be traveling on unless they had letters of authorization for the community, and they prove themselves to be impostors if they demand money. Prophets, on the other hand, are not to be questioned when they speak "in the Spirit" (11:7), even if they enact "a worldly mystery of the church" (probably referring to symbolic prophetic acts), unless they ask for food or money for themselves. Prophets may settle in the community and share in the "first fruits" as the community's "high priests," along with teachers and the poor (chap. 13). Prophets may celebrate the eucharist "as they wish" (10:7). The high status of "charismatic" prophets and teachers threatens the position of the elected bishops and deacons (15:1-2). These officials are likely to be patrons of the community who provide financial support and open their homes for church meetings in exchange for honor.

The Didache (chap. 16) concludes with eschatological teaching referring back to the Two Ways, which it may originally have followed. The material is close to, but probably not dependent on, Luke 12:40 and more generally Matt 24. Members of the community are urged to be ready and waiting for the coming of the Lord. The "last days" are characterized by false prophecy and widespread apostasy ("sheep will be turned into wolves," 16:3) before the appearance of the "world deceiver" who does "signs and wonders" to deceive (16:4) and plunge the world into the "fire of testing" (16:5). Three signs serve as markers of the end time: the sign spread out in the sky, the trumpet sound, and the resurrection of the righteous (but not the wicked) to join the Lord when he comes on the clouds of heaven (16:6-8). Here the text breaks off; perhaps the manuscript available to the copyist was damaged.

At some stage the teaching and rules of the Didache were subordinated to the authority of the gospel tradition, though it is not certain that any particular written gospel is in mind (8:2; 9:2; 11:3; 15:3-4). It disappeared when its teaching ceased to match the practice and doctrine of the wider church, but it provides an invaluable insight into early Jewish Christianity. *See* APOSTOLIC FATHERS, CHURCH FATHERS; LORD'S SUPPER.

Bibliography: Marcello Del Verme. *Didache and Judaism: Jewish Roots of an Ancient Christian-Jewish Work* (2004); Jonathan A. Draper, ed. *The Didache in Modern Research* (1996); Clayton N. Jefford. *The Sayings of Jesus in the Teaching of the Twelve Apostles* (1989); Clayton N. Jefford, ed. *The Didache in Context: Essays on Its Text, History and Transmission* (1995); Aaron Milavec. *The Didache: Faith, Hope, and Life of the Earliest Christian Communities, 50–70* (2003); Kurt Niederwimmer. *The Didache* (1998); Huub van de Sandt and David Flusser. *The Didache: Its Jewish Sources and Its Place in Early Judaism and Christianity* (2002); Huub van de Sandt, ed. *Matthew and the Didache* (2005).

JONATHAN A. DRAPER

DIDRACHMA dĭ-drak´muh [δίδραχμα *didrachma*]. A Greek double-DRACHMA coin struck in silver. The term occurs twenty six times in the LXX as a gloss of the Hebrew SHEKEL (sheqel שֶׁקֶל) with the meaning "silver piece" (Gen 20:16; 23:16). The actual value was one half-shekel, i.e., the amount of the annual temple tax (Exod 30:13-15). In Matt 17:24, Peter is asked, "Does your teacher not pay the temple tax (didrachma)?"

BENNIE H. REYNOLDS III

DIDYMA. *See* MILETUS.

DIDYMUS did´uh-muhs [Δίδυμος *Didymos*]. A proper name meaning "twin," appearing in Greek papyri, and a nickname for THOMAS, one of the Twelve, "called the Twin" (John 11:16; 20:24; 21:2). Thomas (Thōmas Θωμᾶς) is a transliteration from the Aramaic name te᾽oma᾽ (תְּאוֹמָא), also meaning "twin." *Acts of Thomas* 11, 31, 39, calls him "the twin brother" of Christ. *See* TWINS.

JOHN Y. H. YIEH

DIE. *See* DEATH, NT; DEATH, OT.

DIET. *See* AGRICULTURE; CLEAN AND UNCLEAN; DIETARY LAWS; FOOD; MEALS.

DIETARY LAWS. Israelite dietary customs are systematized in the OT as divine commands. Of diverse origin, they form a relatively consistent system of oppositions, in which the choice of the "clean" or permitted food is an expression of the holiness of Israel and historically has been one of the most salient markers of Jewish identity. However, the prohibition of blood, which is assigned to Yahweh's altar, applies to all humanity (*see* CLEAN AND UNCLEAN).

In Deuteronomy, it is because Israel is holy to Yahweh that they are not to eat "any abhorrent thing" (or ABOMINATION, to῾evah [תּוֹעֵבָה]) (Deut 14:2-3). The text (vv. 4-21) goes on to define this (*see* 1, 3, and 5 below).

In holiness texts, the avoidance of "unclean" and abhorrent creatures (Lev 11) is an expression of the call to holiness (Lev 11:44-45; *see* HOLY, HOLINESS, OT). Discrimination between meats is an acted metaphor for Yahweh's setting apart of Israel from the NATIONS (Lev 20:25-26). At least as early as the time of the Maccabean Revolt (2 Macc 6:18-20; 7:1) the refusal to eat pork became a badge of faithful Jews against their Gentile neighbors.

Blood (Gen 9:4; Lev 3:17; 7:26-27; 17:10-14; Deut 12:16, 23-25, 27) and fat (Lev 3:16-17; 7:23-25) are to be avoided for a different reason: they are reserved for Yahweh on the altar as a ransom for human lives (Lev 17:11). Hence, to eat either fat or blood is a serious offense punished by "cutting off" (Lev 7:25, 27; 17:10, 14). The law prohibiting blood applies to all residents of the land, not only Israel (Lev 17:10-13, compare Gen 9:4). "The blood is the life" of the animal (Gen 9:4; Lev 17:11, 14; Deut 12:23). The usual interpretation is that

life belongs to God, who gave it. The key distinction symbolized here is that between humanity and God rather than between Israel and Gentiles.

Leviticus 11:2-23, 41-47, and Deut 14:4-20 identify creatures permitted and not permitted as food. Permitted are: the ruminants, which include all the species raised as food by Israelites (Deut 14:4); most fish, but not shellfish; most birds, and (in Leviticus) locusts. But the separation is less clear, since no criteria are given (except for locusts: Lev 11:20-23). The unclean birds named are probably all birds of prey or carrion eaters.

Many explanations of the origin of these distinctions have been put forward. Hygiene may be excluded, as all flesh meat presents dangers to health if not properly cooked. It has often been argued that the forbidden animals are those prominent in neighboring pagan cults, but there is no evidence for this. For example, at no time in the ANE was the pig commonly sacrificed.

The rule forbidding the fat of cattle, sheep, and goats arises from sacrificial practice, in which the fat is burnt on the altar as Yahweh's portion before the flesh is available for the worshipers to eat (Lev 3:3-5, etc.). The prohibition of blood may also be related to sacrifice: the blood of sacrificial victims is thrown against the altar or used for ritual purposes in the holy place. The method of slaughter used by Israel and by most peoples known to them ensured that the blood was drained from the body before it was used for food or sacrifice.

Because carrion could retain blood, it is prohibited for Israel as a holy people in Exod 22:31 [Heb. 22:30] and Deut 14:21 *a*; but in Lev 17:15-16 it is permitted at the cost of ritual uncleanness, which must be cleansed, perhaps in order to help the poor, who would otherwise have little access to meat.

Israelites did not eat the sciatic nerve of beasts (Gen 32:33: gidh hannasheh [גִּיד הַנָּשֶׁה]; a term the NRSV incorrectly translates "the thigh muscle"). This is not given as a law, but is enforced as one in Rabbinic Judaism.

"You shall not boil a kid in its mother's milk" (Exod 23:19 *b*; 34:26 *b*; Deut 14:21 *b*) became the basis of the separation of meat (even of fowl) from milk products both in the kitchen and at the table in Rabbinic teaching. Since Philo it has been interpreted morally, as a humanitarian teaching. There has been unfounded speculation that it refers to a Canaanite cult.

Early Jewish Christians observed the dietary laws (Acts 10:14). The Gospels interpret Jesus' teaching on purity as "making all foods clean" (e.g., Mark 7:19), but this is unlikely to have been his meaning. It was the Gentile mission that raised the question of dietary restrictions. Many Jews would not eat with Gentiles, and table fellowship between Jewish and Gentile Christians is the point at issue in Gal 2:11-14. In Acts 10:9-16, Peter's dream inverts the symbolism of Lev

20:25-26: refusing to distinguish foods symbolizes the end of the distinction between Jew and Gentile. For Paul, the issue is subsumed into the general issue of justification by faith rather than by observing the law. In Christ there is neither Jew nor Greek (Gal 3:28), and Galatians as a whole implies that believers, whether Jews or Gentiles, have no need to observe such laws (but see Rom 14). This is the position that the church generally has continued to hold.

The letter from the Jerusalem church to Gentile Christians (Acts 15:23-29) asks them to abstain "from blood and from what is strangled" (v. 29, see also v. 20). Unlike the law of "clean and unclean," the prohibition of blood is valid for all humanity. Greeks slaughtered animals in the same way as the Jews, so this would have created no significant problem for them, but would have opened the door to table fellowship between Gentiles and Pauline Jewish Christians. *See* FOOD; MEALS; SACRIFICES AND OFFERINGS.

Bibliography: Mary Douglas. *Purity and Danger* (1966); Mary Douglas. *Leviticus as Literature* (1999); Edwin B. Firmage. "The Biblical Dietary Laws and the Concept of Holiness." J. A. Emerton, ed. *Studies in the Pentateuch* (1990) 177–208. Walter Houston. *Purity and Monotheism: Clean and Unclean Animals in Biblical Law* (1993); Seth Kunin. *We Think What We Eat: Neo-structuralist Analysis of Israelite Food Rules and Other Cultural and Textual Practices* (2004).

WALTER J. HOUSTON

DIKLAH dik´luh [דִּקְלָה diqlah] Son of JOKTAN (Gen 10:27 = 1 Chr 1:21); also used figuratively to refer to a people or territory in Arabia.

DILAN [דִּלְעָן dilʿan]. A city with its villages allotted to the Judah tribe (Josh 15:38), possibly situated in the LACHISH district, but whose precise location is unknown.

DILL [קֶצַח qetsakh; ἄνηθον anēthon]. Small black seeds of this annual (*Nigella sativa*) are scattered along with cummin seed in plowed furrows (Isa 28:25, 27) and processed on the threshing floor by being beaten with sticks. It was used as a condiment. Dill was included in the tithe offered in Herod's temple by Pharisees (Matt 23:23). *See* PLANTS OF THE BIBLE; SPICE.

VICTOR H. MATTHEWS

DIMNAH dim´nuh [דִּמְנָה dimnah]. Town allocated from the Zebulun territory for the Merarite Levites (*see* MERARI, MERARITES). Variant text has RIMMON [רִמּוֹן rimmon].

DIMON di´muhn [דִּימוֹן dimon]. Dimon occurs in only one verse in the OT (Isa 15:9). Because of its obvious connection to Moab, many follow the Dead Sea Scrolls (1QIsaᵃ,ᵇ) and Vg to read "DIBON," due to the assonance of MEM and DALET throughout v. 9a. Otherwise, Dimon was one among a number of Moabite sites that are mentioned only once or twice in the OT (e.g., ALMON-DIBLATHAIM, MATTANAH, NAHALIEL).

MICHAEL D. OBLATH

DIMONAH di-moh´nuh [דִּימוֹנָה dimonah]. Located in Judah (Josh 15:22) Dimonah bordered Edom at the extreme southern end of the tribal territory. As is the case with DIMON, Dimonah is thought by some to be identified with DIBON (Neh 11:25), a site located in either Judah or Moab.

MICHAEL D. OBLATH

DINAH dī´nah [דִּינָה dinah]. The daughter of JACOB and LEAH. She is the only daughter named in the story describing the birth of Jacob's first eleven sons (Gen 29:31–30:24). Dinah is the last of Leah's progeny. She is also the only female descendant named among Jacob's children in a genealogical list (Gen 46:15), though others are also mentioned collectively as "his daughters."

Dinah is best known for her appearance in a narrative account that involves Shechem, son of Hamor, the Hivite (Gen 34). In the story, Dinah goes out to visit the women of this Canaanite land. Upon seeing the daughter of Jacob, Shechem seizes her and rapes her. Hamor, Shechem's father, proceeds to negotiate for the marriage of his son to Dinah. Though Hamor and Shechem act honorably in negotiation, the sons of Jacob deceive the two men. After Hamor and Shechem have consented to the brothers' condition that all of the city's men be circumcised, the sons of Jacob, led by Simeon and Levi, attack the town. The brothers kill all of the males and take as spoil the women, children, and livestock. The brothers' revenge angers Jacob, who fears further retaliation from the people of the land. Simeon and Levi justify their actions, saying, "Should our sister be treated like a whore?" (v. 31).

Genesis 34 is one of three OT narratives that explicitly recount the RAPE of a woman, although it must be noted that some have argued that Dinah was not raped but socially humiliated. The other two rape texts are Judg 19, the rape of a Levite's concubine, and 2 Sam 13, Amnon's rape of his half-sister Tamar. The story of Dinah and Shechem illustrates the difficult social and cultural negotiation between Israel and those perceived as outsiders. The issue of endogamous (in-group) vs. exogamous (out-group) marriage is prominent in Gen 34 (*see* MARRIAGE, OT). Simeon and Levi, and presumably their brothers, represent a party that is against marriage with those outside their group. Jacob and Dinah represent characters in the story that are open to interaction with the people of the land. Jacob makes negotiations with the men of

Shechem (Gen 33:18-20), and Dinah goes out to meet the women of the land (Gen 34:1). The brothers' excessive retaliation on the city of Shechem results in both internal and external social fragmentation. Internally, the conclusion of the story leaves Jacob's family in bitter disagreement, with sons set in opposition to their father. Externally, the sons' violence makes potential relationships with other peoples problematic. Thus, Gen 34 does not resolve the central issue in the story favorably toward endogamy or exogamy. Moreover, the account ends without adequate resolution to Dinah's desolate state.

Bibliography: Lyn M. Bechtel. "What if Dinah is Not Raped? (Genesis 34)." *JSOT* 62 (1994)19–36; Susanne Scholz. *Rape Plots: A Feminist Cultural Study of Genesis 34* (2000).

FRANK M. YAMADA

DINHABAH din´huh-buh [דִּנְהָבָה dinhavah]. City of uncertain location where apparently a non-dynastic succession of Edomite kings began with BELA (Gen 36:31-39; 1 Chr 1:43-51).

DINNER. *See* MEALS.

DIO CASSIUS [Δίων ὁ Κάσσιος Diōn ho Kassios]. Roman senator and historian from Nicea (ca. 164–235 CE), best known for his *Roman History*, spanning the time from Aeneas's arrival in Italy to his own day (229 CE), now extant only in part. He tended to emphasize the overall nature of persons and events rather than details. *See* ROMAN EMPIRE.

Bibliography: Fergus Millar. *A Study of Cassius Dio* (1964).

BRETT S. PROVANCE

DIODORUS SICULUS [Διόδωρος Diodōros]. A 1st cent. BCE historian from Sicily (hence Siculus), Diodorus settled in Rome to write his *Historical Library*, a world history in forty books, of which only books 1–5 and 11–20 are completely preserved. After examining the great civilizations prior to the Trojan War, his focus narrows to Greco-Roman history through the Gallic War. Although the early material is often unreliable, Diodorus is an important source for the Hellenistic age.

DAVID M. REIS

DIOGENES. Fourth cent. BCE philosopher who was born in Sinope on the Black Sea, but spent much of his life in Athens. He became the representative figure of Cynic philosophy. While much about him is clearly legendary, Diogenes appears to have advocated living in accordance with nature, complete self-sufficiency, with indifference to social norms and conventions, and he was known for witty sayings, an ascetic lifestyle,

and shameless acts, including inappropriately eating in the marketplace and relieving himself in public. His significance and later influence are partly due to the prominent role of chreia—brief anecdotes—in Greek rhetorical education. *See* CYNICS, CYNICISM; GREEK RELIGION AND PHILOSOPHY.

RUBÉN R. DUPERTUIS

DIOGNETUS, LETTER TO. The *Letter to Diognetus* is an apology in letter form. The author is anonymous (possibly QUADRATUS, or perhaps HIPPOLYTUS, THEOPHILUS, or Pantaenus), the recipient's identity is uncertain (if not fictional, perhaps HADRIAN), as is the date (likely between 150 and 225 CE), and the ending is missing (the last two sections are from a different document). The skilled and perceptive author, while deeply indebted to both Hellenism and Judaism, writes from a distinctly Christian perspective, offering winsome answers to basic questions about Christianity. *See* APOSTOLIC FATHERS, CHURCH FATHERS.

Bibliography: Michael W. Holmes. *The Apostolic Fathers in English.* 3rd ed. (2005).

MICHAEL W. HOLMES

DIONYSIA di´uh-nish´ee-uh [Διονύσια Dionysia]. The name of festivals of DIONYSUS celebrated at various localities in ancient Greece, including the spring celebration at Athens known as the Great Dionysia or City Dionysia (ca. 6th cent. BCE). Part of the City Dionysia was the drama competition. Contestants included the most famous tragedians, i.e., Aeschylus, Sophocles and Euripides. The plays were part of the Dionysian cult, and the theater was near Dionysus' sacred precinct on the Acropolis' southern slope.

As part of the Hellenizing measures brought about at Jerusalem under the Seleucid ruler Antiochus IV, the Jewish people were forced to participate in the Dionysia (2 Macc 6:7).

BRETT S. PROVANCE

DIONYSIUS di´uh-nish´ee-uhs [Διονύσιος Dionysios]. A theophoric name borne by many in antiquity and through the present era (e.g., *Denys/Dennis/Denise*). In the Bible, Dionysius is the name of a man present for Paul's famous AREOPAGUS speech at Athens who responded with faith (Acts 17:34), legend holding that he became the first bishop of Athens (Eusebius, *Hist. eccl.* 3.4.11). On behalf of this person, about whom nothing more historically reliable can be said, authorship was claimed of a now anonymous but significant collection of mystical treatises and letters dating to the 5th–6th cent. CE. The treatises, steeped in Neoplatonic philosophy and triadic-based categorizations, cover such themes as the divine names, angelic hierarchies, and ecclesiastical hierarchies and rites. These anonymous writings had some influence on medieval theology and literature.

Bibliography: Colm Luibheid, trans. *Pseudo-Dionysius: The Complete Works* (1987).

BRETT S. PROVANCE

DIONYSUS d *i*′uh-n *i*′suhs [Διόνυσος Dionysos; Latin *Bacchus/Liber*]. The son of Zeus and the mortal Semele, who was the Greek deity of wine and ecstasy (i.e., life, joy, and liberation). Dionysus was popular in antiquity, and expressions of interest ranged widely from revelry to dramatic performance, to afterlife concerns in ORPHISM. Biblical references directly pertaining to Dionysus are few (2 Macc 6:7; 14:33; 3 Macc 2:29).

Dionysian imagery can be compared to the Gospel of John (1:4; 10:10; 15:11), where Jesus turned water to wine (2:1-11; compare Pausanius, *Descr.* 6.26.1-2); where Jesus tied eternal life to eating the Son of Man's flesh (6:53; compare Euripides, *Bacch.* 140); and Jesus' claim to be the "true vine" (15:1).

Bibliography: Marvin W. Meyer. *The Ancient Mysteries: A Sourcebook: Sacred Texts of the Mystery Religions of the Ancient Mediterranean World* (1999) 63–109.

BRETT S. PROVANCE

DIOSCORIDES [Διοσκουρίδης Dioskourides]. In 1st cent. CE Cilicia, Pedanius Dioscorides wrote an extensive Greek work, *De Materia Medica* (The Materials of Medicine), based on his personal investigation of the medicinal uses of natural products around the Mediterranean world. Representing ancient empirical science at its best, the work is remarkable for its precision based on critical observation of the effects of the drugs when applied and for its lack of superstition and the supernatural.

MARK DELCOGLIANO

DIOSCORINTHIUS di′uhs-kuh-rin′thee-uhs [Διος Κορίνθιος Dios Korinthios]. The month name in a letter to the Jews from the Seleucid general Lysias (2 Macc 11:21). No such month name is known, although Dios is the first month (October–November) of the Macedonian CALENDAR. Various Lat. manuscripts of 2 Maccabees have *Dioscori* or *Dioscordi*, the Cretan month Dioscouros, but it is unreasonable that a Seleucid king would use a Cretan month name. Some scholars have wanted to emend the text to Dystros, the fifth Macedonian month (February–March), but in view of some other changes that Antiochus IV made, he perhaps also added "Corinthian" to the name of the month Dios.

LESTER L. GRABBE

DIOSCURI [Διόσκουροι Dioskouroi]. Castor and Pollux, semi-divine twin sons of Zeus, protectors of sailors and thus the figurehead on Paul's ship (Acts 28:11). These sons of thundering Zeus often flank a primary deity in iconography, prompting comparison with the appellation, "Sons of Thunder" (Mark 3:17).

DIOTREPHES d *i*-ot′ruh-feez [Διοτρέφης Diotrephes]. Diotrephes, meaning "cherished by God," is mentioned in 3 John 9. The author of 3 John accuses Diotrephes of putting himself first, rejecting proper authorities, spreading false charges against authorities, and dividing the church. *See* CHURCH, LIFE AND ORGANIZATION OF; JOHN, LETTERS OF.

DIPHATH. *See* RIPHATH.

DIRECTIONS. *See* ORIENTATION.

DIRGE. *See* MUSIC.

DISABILITY [מוּם mum, מְצֹרָה metsorah, פִּסֵּחַ pisseakh, חֵרֵשׁ kheresh, תֹּךְ tokh]. An impairment or blemish. Disabilities in the Bible are divided into two major categories: 1) those that touch on the sacrifices made in the Tabernacle and Temple and 2) those that concern people in non-holy situations. In the former case, blemishlessness is crucial. To create a safe interface between earth and heaven, i.e., to process sacrifices, the priest must have a perfect body as well as a perfect priestly lineage (Lev 21:16-24). Likewise, the animal to be sacrificed must also be perfect (Lev 22:21-24). It is very important to note that these requirements apply only to priests offering sacrifices. Priests who have become physically or mentally disabled can still receive the benefit of the priest's due (Deut 18:3-5) although they cannot consume it in a state of ritual impurity. Lay Israelites (and non-Israelites) bringing sacrifices may be disabled in any way except one: they must be in a state of ritual purity. The priest must also be in a state of ritual purity to offer sacrifices.

Disabilities are often used metaphorically in the Bible, especially by the prophets. For example, Isaiah's description of the "Suffering Servant" (Isa 52:13–53:5) uses disabilities as a metaphor: Israel in Babylonian exile is personified as a disabled person. Israel is likewise described metaphorically as deaf and blind because they will not heed God's words (e.g., Jer 5:2; Ezek 12:2).

Jesus' ability to cure the chronically ill and disabled is brought out most clearly in Luke (esp. chaps. 4–5; Acts 3-4). Like Elijah and Elisha, he is able to cure, bring back those who are apparently dead, and produce food when it is needed.

Biblical characters may have disabilities: Jacob becomes disabled after wrestling with an angel (Gen 32:26); Moses has a speech defect (Exod 4:10). These disabilities, however, do not prevent them from fully participating in their given roles. God tells Moses that God is the source of all abilities and disabilities (Exod 4:11). *See* BLINDNESS; DEAF, DEAFNESS; LAME, LAMENESS.

Bibliography: Judith Abrams. *Judaism and Disability* (1998).

JUDITH Z. ABRAMS

DISCHARGE [זוב zov; ῥύσις rhysis]. In men, a sexual flow refers to an abnormal urethral discharge oozing from the genitals. In women, discharges are classified as either regular, i.e., normal menstruation (Lev 15:19), or irregular, i.e., bleeding outside of the menstrual period (Lev 15:25). Anyone with such discharges is ritually impure and requires purification. *See* BLOOD, FLOW OF; CLEAN AND UNCLEAN.

Bibliography: Jacob Milgrom. *Leviticus 1–16.* AB 3 (1991).

HANNAH K. HARRINGTON

DISCIPLE WHOM JESUS LOVED. *See* BELOVED DISCIPLE.

DISCIPLE, DISCIPLESHIP [μαθητής mathētēs]. These terms involve the role of pupil or adherent. The term *discipleship* appears nowhere in the Bible, while the term *disciple* occurs roughly 260 times in the NT, exclusively within the Gospels and Acts, and (in most modern translations) once in the OT (Isa 8:16). The word derives from the Latin *disciplina*, which itself stems from *discipulus*, a learner. This emphasis on learning is reflected in the development of the Greek word usually translated "disciple," mathētēs, from manthanō (μανθάνω), "to learn." Originally mathētēs was employed among the Greeks to designate *one* "who learns," and the notion of learning continued to be present in the use of the word throughout the history of the Greek language; but the term increasingly designated an adherent, i.e., one who was committed to the teachings and ethos of a city or state, to the doctrines of a philosophical school, or to a teacher, religious figure, or great thinker who lived either in the distant past or was a contemporary of the adherent.

 A. Disciples and Discipleship in the OT
 B. Disciples and Discipleship in the NT
 C. Disciples and Discipleship in the Gospels and
  Acts
  1. Mark: Discipleship as submission to the
   powerful Jesus of the cross
  2. Matthew: Discipleship as conformity to
   Christ's example
  3. Luke–Acts: Discipleship as participation in
   eschatological mission
  4. John: Discipleship as response to Christ's
   revelation of the Father
 Bibliography

A. Disciples and Discipleship in the OT

 There is little use of *disciple* language in the OT; mathētēs never appears in the LXX, and there are only rare occurrences of talmidh (תַּלְמִיד) and limmudh (לִמֻּד), terms that later designated the master-disciple relationship in the Judaism of the inter-testamental and NT periods. The sparseness of the terms does not betoken an absence of the concept of master-disciple relationship within the OT; such a relationship did exist within ancient Israel in several forms, including those who gathered around a prophet to learn from him and carry on or develop his teachings after his death, as in the case of Isaiah (Isa 8:16; 50:4), and especially as in the relationship of Elisha to Elijah (1 Kgs 19–2 Kgs 13). The relationship between prophet and disciple may offer significant background for discipleship to Jesus in the NT, and the dynamics between Elijah and Elisha are paradigmatic for the relationship between Jesus and his disciples.

B. Disciples and Discipleship in the NT

 Perhaps the central feature of the ministry of Jesus was the calling and instructing of his disciples. In both the synoptic and Johannine traditions, the first specific act of Jesus' ministry is the calling of disciples (Mark 1:14-20; John 1:43-51). The disciples are said to be "with" Jesus (Mark 3:14; Luke 9:18; 22:56); they are the special recipients of his teaching (Mark 4:33-34; 10:23-45; 11:12-26; 13:1-37); and they are charged to perform a ministry that is an extension of his (Mark 6:7-13, 30; Matt 9:35–11:1; Luke 9:1-10; 10:1-12). The NT mentions also disciples of the Pharisees (Mark 2:18; Matt 22:16), who were apparently adherents of Pharisaic doctrine and aspired to be accepted into formal Pharisaic scribal circles; and disciples of John the Baptist (Mark 6:29), who embraced John's teaching about the impending arrival of the kingdom of God through a commitment to moral reformation and attention to fasting and prayer (Matt 3:7-10; Mark 2:18; Luke 11:1). There is a close relationship between discipleship to JOHN the Baptist and discipleship to Jesus, for both Jesus and John were eschatological prophets proclaiming the imminent appearance of the kingdom. Since John proclaimed the arrival of the "coming one" (Mark 1:7-8; compare Matt 3:11; 11:2), who John came to believe was Jesus (Matt 3:13-14; Luke 7:19; compare John 1:31-34), it is not surprising that some of the disciples of Jesus may have been erstwhile disciples of John (John 1:29-42). Yet John continued to maintain disciples even after his arrest and the inauguration of the ministry of Jesus (Mark 2:18; 6:29; Matt 11:3), and in fact there seems to have existed a John sect, a group of disciples of John who after his death believed that John was the Messiah, a view that is attacked in Luke (3:15-17; compare Acts 18:25-26; 19:1-7) and especially in John (John 1:6-8, 15, 19-28; 3:25-30).

 Although many have assumed that discipleship to Jesus involved the decision to submit to the instruction of a rabbi, in the days of Jesus there was no concept of an order of ordained Jewish rabbis who held formal positions in the Jewish religious culture; rather there were religious teachers (rabbis), mostly of the Pharisees, who on the basis of their own knowledge and embodiment of the Torah, and not on the basis of any official status, attracted groups of disciples for the study of the written Torah and especially oral Torah (the "tradition of the elders").

There were similarities between these rabbis and Jesus, which explains why Jesus is repeatedly addressed as RABBI or TEACHER (didaskalos διδάσκαλος), but one should note the differences as well. For one thing, these rabbis seem never to have approached persons with the invitation to become disciples; on the contrary, would-be disciples would implore rabbis to study under them. But the Gospels emphasize that Jesus initiated the master-disciple relationship (Mark 1:16-20; 2:13-14; John 1:43-45; 6:70; 15:16), and he did so by employing language reminiscent of the OT prophetic call formula in which God summoned select individuals to proclaim God's salvation and judgment. Moreover, discipleship to these rabbis focused upon the learning of Torah, whereas discipleship to Jesus involved a total commitment to the person and destiny of Jesus himself, even to the point of abandoning the security of vocation, possessions, and home, and repudiating family ties and responsibilities, just as Jesus had separated himself from his own family and abandoned vocation and home (e.g., Luke 9:57-62). Thus discipleship to Jesus is described as following him (akoloutheō ἀκολουθέω), used figuratively to describe the disciples' acceptance of the destiny of Jesus for themselves and their complete commitment to his person. Further, the rabbis of Jesus' day almost never ministered publicly to the crowds but focused exclusively upon their disciples, whereas Jesus repeatedly taught the crowds (Mark 2:13; 4:1-2; 7:14-16), healed them (Mark 1:32-34; Matt 11:5), fed them (Mark 6:33-44; 8:11-21), and urged them to reorient their lives to the reality of the breaking in of God's kingdom (Mark 1:14-15). The Gospels sometimes describe the crowds as following Jesus, which does not mean that they assumed the role of disciples, but rather that they were with him as those who received his ministry. Numerous persons from the crowds did commit to Jesus' teaching and destiny, and the NT sometimes designates them *disciples* in a broad sense (Luke speaks of "the seventy," 10:1; compare John 6:60-69); but from within this larger body of disciples he chose twelve (Mark 3:13-19; Luke 6:13), in analogy to the twelve tribes of Israel, in order to make clear that he, through these disciples, was calling all of Israel to repentance in the face of the arrival of the kingdom of God (Matt 9:35–11:1; *see* TWELVE, THE). Finally, disciples of rabbis hoped to become expert in the law and assume the role of teacher of the law, or rabbi, whereas the disciples of Jesus were not to aspire to such a position (Matt 23:8), but rather were to become apostles (apostoloi ἀπόστολοι) sent out (apostellō ἀποστέλλω) by Jesus to proclaim the arrival of God's kingdom (Mark 6:7-13; *see* APOSTLE). These differences with discipleship to rabbis suggest that discipleship to Jesus involved embracing him as an eschatological prophet and indeed as an apocalyptic charismatic deliverer. But in contrast to apocalyptic leaders such as Judas the Galilean (Acts 5:37), Jesus rejected the attempt to create a mass movement through urging the crowds as a whole to become disciples to a vision of political revolution.

C. Disciples and Discipleship in the Gospels and Acts

The twelve disciples play a twofold role in the Gospels. On the one hand, they are presented as historical personages who occupied a unique role as witnesses to the salvation of the Christ-event and were thus guarantors of the gospel tradition (e.g., Luke 1:2; Acts 1:21-22; Heb 2:3). On the other hand, they are examples, and sometimes even representatives, of post-Easter Christians in general (thus Acts describes Christian believers as *disciples*). In many ways, Christian readers are intended to see their own discipleship reflected in the Twelve, whether this reflection involves a warning concerning behavior readers should avoid, or encouragement toward behavior readers should adopt.

1. Mark: Discipleship as submission to the powerful Jesus of the cross

Recent Markan scholarship has acknowledged the representative character of the disciples in Mark, and some scholars have insisted that the negative portrayal of the disciples is intended to reflect certain factions within Mark's church whose perspectives are to be repudiated. Others argue that the portrayal of the disciples is not intended to target any particular group but is offered as a means of instruction—both positively and negatively—for discipleship within the church. The first view is quite speculative, while the second corresponds to the way readers throughout the centuries have actually appropriated Mark's story of the disciples.

In many respects, Mark presents the disciples in a favorable light. When called by Jesus they immediately acknowledge the authority of Jesus and obey his command to follow him, even though this means the abandonment of vocation, possessions, and family (1:16-18; 2:12-14; 10:28-30; compare 10:17-27). They are described as being "with" him as those who experience the joy of his presence and will feel the sadness of his separation (2:19-20); as those who celebrate the newness of the kingdom (2:23-28), and thus, like Jesus, have no scruples against plucking grain on the sabbath (2:23-28), or eating with unwashed hands (7:1-13), or associating with tax collectors and sinners (2:15-17); as those who are sent out to preach, to have authority over demons, and to heal, and thus continue the ministry of Jesus himself (3:13-19; 6:7-13); as those who obey the instructions of Jesus (3:9; 11:1-7; 14:12-16); and as those who suffer, in the company of Jesus, the animosity of the religious leaders (2:18, 23-24; 14:66-72).

But the disciples are also pictured as those who fail to embrace, or even to understand, the good news of the kingdom that Jesus announces, especially insofar as it demands faith in the transcendent power of Christ and submission to Christ's destiny of obedient suffering and death. Thus the disciples are afraid in the storm and receive rebuke from Jesus for the inadequacy of their faith (4:39-41); and later they fail to understand Jesus' word about the loaves because their hearts were "hardened," since they focus upon their physical lack rather than transcendent spiritual realities and Christ's sufficiency (6:51-52; compare 8:1-10). Although Jesus explains his parables to them, the disciples are still without understanding (7:18). But their lack of understanding centers especially on the necessity of Jesus' humble suffering and death and its implications for themselves. Thus even after Peter (speaking on behalf of the disciples) confesses that Jesus is the Christ, Peter repudiates Jesus' destiny of the cross (8:30-33); and when Jesus predicts his passion the Twelve did not understand what he meant, and they were afraid to ask (9:32; compare 10:23-26, 32). Their lack of understanding corresponds to their disappointing performance, and accordingly the disciples are unable to cast out a demon, lacking as they are in prayerful confidence (9:14-29); they argue about who is the greatest (9:33-37) and rebuke those who bring to Jesus children (10:13-16), who according to Jesus are in their humility truly the greatest in the kingdom (9:36-37); they aspire for the highest seats in the kingdom (10:35-45); and in the face of the cross they all fall away and Peter denies Jesus three times (14:26-31, 53-72). It is not one of the Twelve, but rather Simon of Cyrene who carries Jesus' cross (15:21; compare 8:34), and Joseph of Arimathea who buries his body (15:42-46), and the women who followed him from Galilee who attempt to anoint his body and who witness the empty tomb (15:40-41; 16:1-8). But the Markan Jesus looks beyond the failure of the disciples to the reconciliation they will experience when they encounter the resurrected Christ (14:28; 16:7), and he is confident that they will then be prepared to share in the "cup" and the "baptism" of his sufferings (10:39).

2. Matthew: Discipleship as conformity to Christ's example

Matthew is careful to draw a parallel between Jesus, who embodies the reality of God's kingdom, and the expectations for the disciples, expectations the disciples struggle unsuccessfully to realize. Thus Matthew repeatedly compares the mission of Jesus and the mission the disciples are expected to perform. For one thing, the scope of ministry is the same; the disciples are to go "only to the lost sheep of the house of Israel," reflecting

the identical limitation in Jesus' own ministry (compare 10:5-6 with 15:24). Moreover, the acts of ministry are the same in that both Jesus and the disciples (eventually) teach (compare 4:23; 5:1, 19; 9:35; 13:54; 21:23 with 28:19); both Jesus and the disciples have authority to cast out demons (8:16, 28-34; 9:32-34; 10:1, 8; 17:14-20); both Jesus and the disciples preach, and they preach the same message ("the gospel of the kingdom"; compare 4:23; 9:35 with 26:13; 24:14), namely, "the kingdom of heaven is at hand" (compare 4:17 with 10:7). And there is a parallel between persecutions attending the ministry of Jesus (12:24-42; 20:17-20; 26:3-66) and the persecution the disciples can expect in the wake of their ministries (5:10-11; 10:16-39; 23:29-36; 24:9-14; see esp. 10:24-25).

But Matthew also draws a parallel between the behavior of Jesus and the behavioral expectations of the disciples. For example, even as Jesus is meek and lowly (11:29; 21:5), so the same is expected of the disciples (18:3-4; 23:12). And as Jesus is the merciful one par excellence (9:13, 27, 36; 14:14; 15:22, 25, 32; 17:15; 20:30-34), so the disciples are to follow his example (5:7; 9:13; 12:7; 18:33; 23:23). And as Jesus was "faithful" to God's will amid persecutions by "watching" (26:40-41), so the disciples are to do the same (24:45; 25:13; 26:38). Finally, Matthew uses Father/son language to emphasize the parallel between Jesus and the disciples. Both Jesus and the disciples are "sons" of God and "know" God as Father; both Jesus (2:15; 3:17; 11:27; 14:33; 16:16; 17:5; 27:54; 28:19) and the disciples (5:9, 16, 45, 48; 6:1; 7:9; 13:43; 23:9) are identified, respectively, as "son" and "sons" of "the Father." In this way, Matthew presents Jesus as the model of discipleship in all of its major aspects—ministry, righteousness, and relationship with God.

But along with these similarities between Jesus and the expectations of the disciples Matthew emphasizes also the differences between Jesus and the actual performance of the Twelve. Matthew describes the gap that exists between Jesus who willingly accepts his destiny of suffering and death, leading finally to resurrection, and the disciples who are reluctant to accept this destiny for themselves (16:22-23; 20:20-28; 26:6-75). But in the end the failure of the disciples is met by the resurrected Christ (26:32; 28:16-20), who by the power of his continuing presence (28:20b; compare 1:23; 18:20) equips the disciples for the righteous obedience (compare 1:21-23) and vigor in mission that will lead them to make disciples of all nations through baptizing and teaching. Indeed, they will make disciples of others even as Jesus has made disciples of them.

3. Luke–Acts: Discipleship as participation in eschatological mission

At the beginning of his gospel, Luke orients his story of Jesus' earthly life (Gospel of Luke) and exalted reign (book of Acts) to the fulfillment of the divine plan (Luke

1:1-2) as set forth in the OT (Luke 1:67-79; 4:16-21; 24:25-27, 45-49; Acts 2:14-21; 3:18) to the effect that God has acted through Jesus the Messiah (Luke 2:11; 9:20; Acts 2:36) to reconstitute Israel around the righteous remnant who experience God's end-time salvation (e.g., Luke 1:32-33, 67-79; Acts 3:17-26) and to offer through this reconstituted Israel salvation to the Gentiles everywhere (Luke 24:47; Acts 22:21; 26:16-18), with the expectation that multitudes of them will be joined with the eschatological remnant of Israel to form one people who are united in their experience of the blessings of the age to come. The disciples play a pivotal role in this divine plan in that the Twelve are chosen by Jesus to be sent out as reliable witnesses of God's salvation that has come in the ministry and especially the exaltation of Christ (Acts 1:15-26; 3:15; 4:33; 10:41; 13:31). Thus throughout the Gospel the disciples are not only taught the realities of the kingdom (Luke 11:1-13; 12:22-53) but are trained for the work of global witness and proclamation that Luke describes in the book of Acts, and accordingly they are repeatedly described even in the Gospel as *apostles* (Luke 6:12-16; 9:10; 11:49; 17:5; 22:14; 24:10); in the book of Acts, the Twelve are never called *disciples* but exclusively apostles.

Yet Luke speaks not only of the twelve disciples, but employs *disciples* to describe larger groups of Jesus' followers from the Jewish crowds (Luke 6:13, 17; 10:1). These larger groups of disciples, together with the Twelve, form the critical mass of followers who will become, in Acts, the reconstituted eschatological people of God (Acts 1:15). Much of Jesus' instruction in the Gospel of Luke, therefore, is directed to the people as a whole or to these large bands of disciples. They are warned of the difficulty of the radical demands of discipleship (Luke 12:33-34; 19:11-27) and thus the necessity to "count the cost" before embarking upon discipleship (9:62; 14:25-35). But the actual experience of the disciples, and especially the Twelve, is characterized by failure: The disciples wish to call down fire upon their enemies (Luke 9:51-56); and when the women report the empty tomb to "the eleven and all the rest" the apostles did not believe them (Luke 24:8-12). It is only their experience with the resurrected Christ and the coming of the Spirit at Pentecost that transform them into effective apostles and the larger group of believers into disciples who fulfill their role as the embodiment of end-time salvation and as agents of God's salvation "to the uttermost parts of the earth" (Luke 24:13-51; Acts 1:8; 2:1-47).

4. John: Discipleship as response to Christ's revelation of the Father

The focus of John's Gospel is upon the Christ who alone reveals the Father (1:18; 10:30; 14:1-10), and to whom the Father bears witness (5:37). God effectively employs this testimony to draw disciples to Jesus (6:37, 44, 65; 10:27-29; 17:6), which involves believing in him (6:29; 20:31) and thereby experiencing both now and in the world to come resurrection (or eternal) life (3:15-16, 36; 5:19-29; 11:17-27; 20:31), i.e., the inexhaustible joyous vigor that characterizes God himself.

But this divine testimony to Jesus, which is meant to lead to discipleship, reveals a great moral divide between those who come to the light because they have oriented their lives according to God's purposes, and those who refuse to come to the light because of their commitment to evil deeds (3:18-21; 5:44; 7:7; 8:47). This repudiation of God's purposes in Christ not only created conflict between Jesus and his opponents during the period of the earthly Jesus but also will produce bitter struggle between Jesus' disciples and those who refuse the divine summons to discipleship in the post-Easter world of the intended readers of John's Gospel. These readers can expect severe persecution, including excommunication from the synagogue because of their Christian discipleship (9:22; 12:42; 16:2; compare 15:18-24; 16:33). The primary challenge these post-Easter disciples face, then, is to ABIDE in discipleship to Christ; this abiding is expressed through obedience to Jesus' commands (14:15, 18-24), especially the command to love one another (13:34-34; 15:12-13), which they will be able to accomplish through the transcendent power of the Spirit given to the disciples in the wake of Jesus' exaltation (7:37-39; 14:1–16:33). The role of the Twelve, who receive less attention in John's Gospel than in the Synoptics (6:60-71; 20:24), is essentially to bear witness in the post-Easter church to the historical manifestation of God's saving revelation in Jesus Christ and thus provide the church a solid foundation for the church's embattled belief in the redemptive effectiveness of the Christ event (15:27; 19:35; 21:24). *See* CHURCH, LIFE AND ORGANIZATION OF.

Bibliography: Ernest Best. *Disciples and Discipleship* (1986); Martin Hengel. *The Charismatic Leader and His Followers* (1981); Fernando Segovia, ed. *Discipleship in the New Testament* (1985); Michael J. Wilkins. *Discipleship in the Ancient World and Matthew's Gospel* (1995).

DAVID R. BAUER

DISCIPLINE [יָסַר yasar, מוֹסָר mosar; παιδεύω paideuō, παιδεία paideia]. The word *discipline* suggests the notion of instruction or learning. The word derives from the Latin *disciplina*, which itself comes from *discipulus*, a learner, and *discere*, to learn. Versions of the English Bible employ "discipline" to translate Hebrew and Greek terms that, in context, have to do with moral instruction.

The OT describes the concept of discipline through the use of the verb yasar ("to discipline," "to instruct") and the correlative noun mosar ("instruction," "discipline," "correction"). These terms were associated especially with the responsibility of parents toward children in the setting of the home, and came to be used as an analogy of God's actions toward individuals and toward God's covenant people Israel, and in perhaps a few passages toward the peoples of the world. The terms as employed in the Bible assume that those who administer this instruction/discipline are in positions of authority, and that the instruction is corrective. There is a consistent emphasis on the redemptive intention of such instruction, but it is stressed that persons' response to this instruction will determine its redemptive efficacy: those who respond by submitting to the positive formational purposes of instruction will experience peace, joy, and deliverance, but those who respond with stubborn resistance will experience hardship and ultimately destruction.

In the OT the most basic understanding of this concept involves parental discipline in the home. Especially as described in Proverbs, this discipline may take the form of physical correction, and indeed corporal punishment, which is actually kind insofar as it is intended to keep the child from the destructive consequences of foolishness and evil (Prov 13:24; 22:15; 23:13). But the majority of references to discipline in Proverbs describe verbal correction or rebuke; and although this correction sometimes refers to parental instruction of children (Prov 1:8; 4:1, 13) it is not limited to children but pertains to all in the community (Prov 1:2-7). Such instruction comes ultimately from Yahweh (Prov 3:11), but is communicated through the commandments of the law (e.g., Prov 6:23), through wise counsel (13:18; 19:20), and through others in the community (Prov 9:7-8; compare Job 4:3). Such instruction is of more value than great riches (Prov 8:10), since submitting to it will lead to honor (Prov 13:18), while neglecting it will lead to the utter ruin of poverty and death (Prov 5:12, 23; 13:18; 15:10, 32; compare 16:22; Job 36:10). In analogy to the discipline of children by their parents, the discipline of Yahweh sometimes assumes the form of hardships or misfortunes that Yahweh brings upon the foolish in order to lead them to the wisdom of righteousness (Prov 3:11-12).

This analogy between the physical punishment of children by their parents and Yahweh's corrective employment of hardship and distress comes to expression repeatedly in Yahweh's discipline of his people Israel, which is based upon God's covenant relationship with Israel. The connection is made explicitly in Deut 8:5: "Know then in your heart that as a parent disciplines a child so the Lord your God disciplines you." Thus God's transcendent power of destruction and deliverance throughout the wilderness experience should teach Israel to obey God's commands (Lev 26:27-28; Deut 4:36; 11:2). The prophets describe God's judgments throughout Israel's history in the land as the discipline of Yahweh, meant to correct Israel's

waywardness; but the refusal of the people to take correction will lead to exile (Hos 7:12; Jer 2:19, 30; 5:3; 31:18; 32:33), an exile that itself is God's instrument of discipline that will be finally effective in reconciling the people to God (Hos 10:10; Jer 30:11, 14; Zeph 3:7). God as sovereign creator disciplines the nations by chastising them (Ps 94:10).

Yet the discipline of Yahweh is not limited to God's punishments of whole peoples, but is directed also to individuals within Israel. Thus Job 5:17 declares, "How happy is the one whom God reproves," and the psalms repeatedly describe the discipline of Yahweh that comes through distress brought about by the opposing wicked (Pss 6:1; 38:1; 118:18). Moreover, Yahweh exercises disciplining work through the punitive casuistic consequences of violations of God's law (Lev 21:18-19; Deut 22:18).

The ultimate goal of all of this activity of discipline is that such correction should be internalized, thus leading to a "disciplined" individual (Prov 5:23; 8:10; 12:1; 15:32; see also Ps 16:7) and nation (Lev 26:27-28; Jer 32:33; 35:13; Zeph 3:7). Toward this end of a redeemed nation, reconciled to God, accepting within its own life the formative power of God's correction, the Suffering Servant of Isaiah experiences the scourging discipline that properly belongs to the nation, and through his willing and humble submission to this chastisement the nation finds healing (Isa 53:5).

The major contours of discipline/correction found in the OT were taken up and developed within the intertestamental period. Thus, e.g., ben Sira describes the importance of both parental and divine discipline for individuals (e.g., Sir 4:17; 7:23); and 2 Maccabees interprets the nation's distress at the hands of Antiochus IV Epiphanes in terms of the discipline of God intended to purify the religious life of Judah and thus deliver Judah from the destruction that will come upon the other nations (e.g., 2 Macc 6:12-15).

The LXX and NT employ the word paideuō ("to educate," "to instruct") and its noun form paideia ("instruction") to speak of discipline. In secular Greek this word referred to the education of children toward maturity, with an emphasis upon personal formation; such education could include correction and punishment.

Accordingly, Eph 6:4 admonishes fathers to raise their children in "the discipline and instruction of the Lord," emphasizing that the father is the agent of a disciplining process that ultimately is conducted by the Lord himself, and thus should reflect the gentle, non-provoking character of the Lord (here understood as Christ). And 1 Cor 11:32 and 1 Tim 1:20 speak of God's redemptive correction toward individuals within the church through distress, while Titus 2:12 describes God's instruction of Christians through the blessings of salvation. Moreover, in a manner similar to the OT insistence that God disciplines through the commandments of the law, 2 Tim 3:16 declares that the Scriptures are the means of "training" (paideia) in righteousness. Hebrews 12:5-6 quotes Prov 3:11-12, arguing that God's discipline (similar, but more gracious and effective than the discipline from earthly fathers) comes to these Christians in the form of persecution from the enemies of Christ, in analogy to Christ's own sufferings; it is only through such discipline that they will become righteous (Heb 12:11), i.e., share the holiness of God (Heb 12:10, 14) and thus "live" (Heb 12:9) in the sense of following Christ into heavenly glory (Heb 12:1-2).

DAVID R. BAUER

DISCIPLINE, MANUAL OF. *See* DEAD SEA SCROLLS; RULE OF THE COMMUNITY.

DISCOURAGEMENT. Denoting loss of courage, biblical discouragement stems from lack of faith in God's promise. The Gadites and Reubenites discourage (no' נוּא) the Israelites from entering the promised land (Num 32:1-15). This rebellious act is interpreted in Deuteronomy as a lack of trust in God: the Israelites melt (masas מָסַס) when opposed by superior enemies (1:19-40). Discouragement becomes despair upon losing hope in God (ya'ash יָאַשׁ, Isa 57:10; compare 1 Sam 27:1; Eccl 2:20). The suffering servant is not crushed (ratsats רָצַץ, Isa 42:4), because God will not abandon him.

In the NT, boldness is the result of trusting God in the eschaton, and despair is the loss of eschatological hope. Jesus counsels courage in death because God's righteous rule is already breaking in (Matt 9:2, 22), and he exhorts continual prayer "without losing heart" (mē enkakein [μὴ ἐγκακεῖν], Luke 18:1) for the same reason. Paul acts boldly because he has confidence in the final judgment (2 Cor 5:6-10; compare Heb 13:6). Mercy in his ministry also counteracts despair (2 Cor 4:1). Therefore, Paul might be discouraged (aporoumai ἀποροῦμαι) by momentary afflictions, but he does not despair (exaporoumai ἐξαπορούμαι) or "lose heart" (enkakeō ἐγκακέω) on account of the eternal weight of glory (2 Cor 4:7–5:10; compare Eph 3:13).

SZE-KAR WAN

DISCOURSE. The term *discourse* indicates either a particular text, such as a specific conversation or speech, oral or textual (e.g., Jesus' "Olivet discourse" [Matt 24:1–25:46] or Jesus' discourse called "the Sermon on the Mount"). Derivatively, the term *discourse* can also be used to mean the argument or flow within a speech or text (e.g., "the discourse of Jesus in Matthew 24–25 . . ." or "Paul's discourse in Romans functions through diatribe and other forms of logical argumentation"). Because of associations and blends of particular texts, speech modes, and arguments within particular literary genres, the term has also been used to denote complex genres of speech (e.g., poetic discourse, legal

discourse, dramatic discourse, apocalyptic discourse) or other forms of communication (e.g., iconographic discourse, architectural discourse, numismatic discourse). In linguistic usage, the term *discourse* may range from a particular speech mode within the text, that is, indirect or direct discourse (respectively, "Saul told his son to go over" [see Mark 8:30] and "Saul said to his son: 'go over'" [see also Mark 8:28]) to the very complex issues of style and textual form.

Under the influence of critical and culture theory, the term *discourse* is often used to refer to the culture out of which someone speaks or writes, the cultures that are normally associated with specific genres, or more specifically to the narrative line(s) of those cultures (e.g., political discourse, patriarchal discourse, feminine discourse, Christian discourse, Augustan discourse). Used thusly, discourse is broadly synonymous with language or perhaps dialect as a means for the articulation of culture (e.g., "the patriarchal language [discourse] in the OT has shaped our view of women"). In this context, the term is often used in association with the ideas deriving from the work of Jacques Derrida, or, more significantly, Michel Foucault. According to Foucault, discourse is part of a larger field of power and practice whose relations are articulated in different ways by different paradigms. For Foucault, culture or discourse also concerns interpretation and the culture of the world of the interpreter.

Discourse can be used to identify a particular form of analysis of texts. Discourse analysis, when applied philologically or structurally, can be understood to mean a formal analysis of narrative structure (e.g., as in the work of Vladimir Propp) or even the analysis of cognitive structures that make discourse possible (e.g., as in the work of Walter Kintsch). When applied in terms of critical or culture theory, "discourse analysis" generally means a deconstructive interpretation of language and culture, as well as the ideology (or ideologies) through which each is expressed, including the discourse or culture of the interpreter. When applied in terms of both formal and cultural uses, some authors, influenced by pragmatics or socio-rhetorical analysis, see discourse analysis as a tool for the critical analysis of the ways in which language is formally used throughout particular social, cultural, and ideological contexts. *See* RHETORICAL CRITICISM, NT; LITERARY INTERPRETATION, NT.

Bibliography: Hubert L. Dreyfus and Paul Rabinow. *Michel Foucault: Beyond Structuralism and Hermeneutics* (1982); Bryan Jenner and Stefan Titscher. *Methods of Text and Discourse Analysis* (2000); David Jobling and Tina Pippin, eds. *Ideological Criticism of Biblical Texts. Semeia* 59 (1992); Walter Kintsch. *Learning, Memory, and Conceptual Processes* (1970); Vladimir Propp. *Morphology of the Folktale.* 2nd ed. (1968); Vernon K. Robbins. *The Tapestry of Early Christian Discourse: *Rhetoric, Society and Ideology* (1996); Michael Stubbs. *Discourse Analysis: The Sociolinguistic Analysis of Natural Language* (1983).

L. GREGORY BLOOMQUIST

DISCOURSE OF CYRIL OF JERUSALEM, TWENTIETH. *See* CYRIL OF JERUSALEM, TWENTIETH DISCOURSE OF

DISCOURSE OF SAINT JOHN THE DIVINE. *See* VIRGIN, ASSUMPTION OF THE.

DISCOURSE OF THEODIUS. *See* VIRGIN, ASSUMPTION OF THE.

DISCOURSE ON THE EIGHTH AND NINTH. The *Discourse on the Eighth and Ninth*, a Hermetic tractate found in the NAG HAMMADI TEXTS (Codex VI, 6:52, 1-63, 32), takes its name from its subject matter, a description of the mystical ascent of a teacher (Hermes, also named Trismegistus) and an unnamed student. The dialogue draws upon the Hellenistic cosmological idea that the mundane world consisted of seven concentric spheres (the sun, moon, and five planets) surrounding the earth. Beyond this realm, the "Eighth" and "Ninth" (and sometimes "Tenth") spheres signified the immutable region of the divine. Advancing through the spheres, whether after death, or in the case of the *Disc. 8–9*, proleptically through mystagogical techniques, thus represented a form of spiritual progress leading toward divine illumination.

In the Hermetic tradition, instruction in basic cosmology and anthropology (the "General Exercises") and a devotion to a life of purity prepared one for the mystical experience. In the *Disc. 8–9*, Hermes acknowledges that his student has met these formal criteria and agrees to guide him into the "deeper" mysteries. Through the recitation of prayers, hymns, and magical vowel sounds, Hermes and the initiate achieve illumination, entering first into the Eighth, the place of souls and angels, and then into the Ninth, where they identify themselves with the ineffable Mind. After the initiate offers a hymn to God for providing the visionary experience, Hermes tells the student to inscribe their discourse on steles and place it in the Temple of Diospolis in Egypt. Accompanying the text is an oath warning others that a requisite spiritual development is necessary before reading its contents.

In the debate over distinct Hermetic communities, the *Disc. 8–9* provides compelling evidence that an organization centering on the figure of Hermes existed in Roman Egypt. In particular, the tractate's description of an initiation ceremony that culminates in a spiritual enlightenment suggests a ritual or liturgical setting. The *Disc. 8–9* has close parallels with other Hermetic literature, particularly *Corp. Herm.* I, IV, VI, VII, XIII, and its affinities with Middle Platonism's view of the divine and gnosticism's cosmic dualism attest to the fluidity of late ancient religious thought. *See* HERMETIC LITERATURE.

Bibliography: D. M. Parrot, ed. *Nag Hammadi Codices V,2-5 and VI with Papyrus Berolinensis, 1 and 4* (1979); D. M. Reis. "Saying as Doing: Performative Prayer and Mystical Ascent in Hermetic Hymnody." *Cauda Pavonis: Studies in Hermeticism* 20 (2001) 1–8.

DAVID M. REIS

DISCRETION AND PRUDENCE מְזִמָּה mezimmah, עׇרְמׇה ʿarmah; Aram. טְעֵם teʿem; עֵמׇא ʿemaʾ, πανουργία panourgia, βουλή boulē, γνώμη gnōmē ἔννουια ennouia]. These two English terms occur together in three places: Prov 1:4 (RSV only), 8:12, and Dan 2:14. They are among a number of terms in English, Hebrew (or Aram.), and Greek frequently used in the realm of wisdom whose concepts are close but not necessarily equal. Thus translators use a variety of related English terms for a number of Hebrew and Greek words, and the translations are not always consistent, as can be seen with the terms listed above for the few verses cited (*see* WISDOM IN THE NT; WISDOM IN THE OT).

Usually these terms indicate the ability to discern what is right and befitting. In Prov 1:2-6 and 8:10-12, *prudence* and *discretion* occur in a context of knowledge and its application. Add the context of Dan 2:14, and at the heart of all of these passages are KNOWLEDGE and the good sense to apply knowledge judiciously. The Daniel passage uses ʿemaʾ and teʿem, which can mean "counsel" and "taste." The LXX for Dan 2:14 uses boulē and gnōmē, which can mean "planning" and "knowledge." Proverbs 1:4 uses ʿarmah and mezimmah, perhaps "craftiness" and "purpose," and panourgia and ennouia, "cunning" and "insight."

Aside from these three passages where they occur together in English translations, *discretion* and *prudence* are found individually elsewhere in wisdom texts (e.g., Prov 2:11; 3:21; 5:2; 8:5; Wis 8:7; Sir 19:22) or non-wisdom texts (e.g., 1 Chr 22:12; 2 Chr 2:12; Ezra 8:18; 1 Macc 8:30). In most occurrences, discretion and prudence are understood as concrete expressions of wisdom alongside understanding, shrewdness, insight, or intelligence. They are among other character traits that are highly valued, as evidenced by their inclusion in the list of four cardinal virtues (Wis 8:7; 4 Mac 1:18 in the Greek, if not in English). The concepts are most frequently found in the book of Proverbs, and the one person who is most often characterized with them is SOLOMON (1 Chr 22:12; 2 Chr 2:12).

SEUNG AI YANG

DISCUS [δίσκος diskos]. A circular, lenticular plate usually made of stone or metal and thrown in the popular Greek game, the diskobolia (δισκοβόλια).

The athletes were frequently depicted in ancient art, most famously Myron's statue, the Discus Thrower (diskobolys δι-σκόβολυς). Shortly after Antiochus IV Epiphanes became king of the Seleucid Dynasty (175 BCE), JASON paid him for the office of high priest and the right to establish a GYMNASIUM in Jerusalem as part of an aggressive Hellenization program. According to 2 Macc 4:14-15, "Despising the sanctuary and neglecting the sacrifices, [the priests] hurried to take part in the unlawful proceedings in the wrestling arena after the signal for the discus-throwing, disdaining the honors prized by their ancestors and putting the highest value upon Greek forms of prestige."

MARK D. GIVEN

DISEASE. Contemporary Western readers of the Bible, most of whom possess a rather sophisticated knowledge of human health problems, are inclined to think that biblical reports about blindness, leprosy, paralysis, etc., name and describe familiar realities. The history of medicine, paleopathology, and similar disciplines, however, indicates that such an assumption is unwarranted and can lead to misunderstanding and misinterpretation of biblical reports. As a collection of ancient Middle Eastern documents about ancient Middle Eastern people, their culture, and values, the Bible challenges a non-Middle Eastern reader to utilize appropriate resources for respectful cross-cultural interpretation.

Cross-cultural anthropologists distinguish between emic and etic views. In anthropology, the emic view of reality is that perceived through the eyes of a people native to a particular culture. Bible readers should seek to appreciate ancient Middle Eastern views of human health misfortunes on their terms. In contrast, the etic view represents an attempt by outsiders (those not native to that culture) to make sense of what they observe in terms of their own culture. Anthropologists fully recognize the risk here; hence they distinguish between "imposed" or "pseudo" etic and "derived" etic perspectives. At the outset, the anthropologists' "imposed" perspective may well be rooted in and influenced by their own culture. The task is to keep modifying that "imposed" etic view until it fairly matches the emic viewpoint of the culture being studied. This would be a "derived" etic perspective. In this article on disease in the Bible, medical anthropology attempts to provide standard ("derived" etic) cross-cultural definitions of human health misfortunes. These definitions in turn help to better understand the emic views of disease(s) recorded in the Bible (see ANTHROPOLOGY, NT CULTURAL; ANTHROPOLOGY, OT CULTURAL.

A. Limitations of Western Points of View

The rather recent (less than two cent. old) medicocentric view of disease characterizes many sophisticated investigations of biblical reports about human health misfortunes. It is often, though not exclusively, pursued by scientists or physicians (who are sometimes also ordained clergy) in an attempt to give a modern Western scientific interpretation (an etic view) to ancient Middle Eastern pre-scientific observations (an emic view). Without adequate, modern scientific evidence (physical examination of the subject, laboratory test results, paleopathological analyses, etc.), the proposed disease identification is always purely hypothetical, as well as medicocentric (a particular form of ethnocentrism). It is an "imposed" etic view that never evolves to a "derived" etic view. In the end, as cross-culturally sensitive researchers readily admit, a modern reader simply does not and cannot know what the health problem might have been, or whether or not it was even physical.

A popular contemporary Western scientific interpretation of many of these physical problems in the Bible considers most of them to be conversion disorders (also known as conversion hysteria, conversion reaction, etc.). This means that the person who experiences a misfortune in life (whether physical, social, interpersonal, etc.) "converts" it into a physical disorder that is readily remedied by the liberating power of suggestion. It is not likely that ancient Mediterraneans interpreted their problems from this modern psychiatric perspective. The challenge therefore is to understand and appreciate the ancient Middle Eastern perspective as recorded in the Bible.

B. Terminology: Ranges of Meaning

A second source of confusion is language, whether the original ancient languages or contemporary translations. Many of the ancient lexical terms are flexible and unsystematic. These terms are commonly applied to symptoms rather than to the technical discrimination of the physical problems (often called "diseases") causing the symptoms. Thus, in the OT, the semantic field of makhaleh (מַחֲלָה "sickness," deriving from the verb khlh [חלה], to be weak or sick) is invariably glossed in dictionaries and translations as "sickness" and "disease" without distinction. The NT speaks chiefly of nosos [νόσος], malakia [μαλακία], and astheneia [ἀσθένεια], though there are dozens of words with varying nuances in the semantic domain of sickness, disease, and weakness. Ethnocentric or anachronistic interpretations are often made. For example, to claim that selēniazomai (σεληνιάζομαι, literally "moon-struck") means epileptic is a medicocentric interpretation that ignores the ancient belief about celestial bodies (including the moon) as powerful and animate forces (see Dan 12:3 where the righteous become stars in the sky after death). It is preferable to render that Gk. word literally as "moonstruck" (an emic concept, i.e., a folk illness; a culture-bound syndrome) rather than "epileptic" (an etic concept, i.e., a scientifically defined "disease"). The Gk. word selēniazomai occurs only in Matt 4:24 and 17:15 (in this latter instance associated with spirit possession) but is illuminated by Ps 121:6. Just as one could be "sunburned," so could one become "moonstruck."

In every language, words derive their meaning from the social system of speakers and writers native to a particular culture. Etymology and comparison with cognate languages sheds helpful light on the plausible meaning of a word. However, lexicographers, translators, and exegetes quite often are unaware of the social system(s) that underpin the languages they are glossing. Many if not most lexicons, Bible dictionaries/encyclopedias, translations, and commentaries reflect the unconscious ethnocentric and anachronistic perspectives of the scholars who produced or contributed to them.

Another source of confusion is the English language itself, in which terminology can be equally fluid. In the *Oxford English Dictionary*, e.g., the second definition of disease is "a condition of the body, or of some part or organ of the body, in which its functions are disturbed or deranged; a morbid physical condition; a departure from the state of health especially when caused by a structural change." The next segment (a) of the definition reports: "The condition of being (more or less seriously) out of health; illness; sickness." This ambiguity and ambivalence (disease = disturbed functions; disease = illness and sickness) also characterizes contemporary medical discourse, where medical jargon constantly changes both at the scientific and the popular level. Such fluidity of meaning relative to the English word *disease* (just like the fluidity of meaning of ancient words) leads to the problems experienced and caused by lexicographers, translators, and interpreters. These in turn contribute to the confusion and misinterpretation of biblical reports about health misfortunes that the ancients experienced.

In the NRSV and the RSV, the vast majority of occurrences of the English word *disease* are found in Lev 13–14 (NRSV: 74 of 111 total; RSV: 61 of 95 total). Significantly, the KJV translates *disease* only 29 times but—quite correctly—nowhere in Lev 13–14. Instead of "disease," KJV inserts the English word "plague" (which also does not appear in the MT of Lev 13–14). These chapters of Leviticus discuss "leprosy" (tsaraʿath צָרַעַת), which biblical scholars and paleopathologists agree is not Hansen's disease and quite likely no disease at all (*see* LEPROSY).

C. Medical Anthropology

Medical anthropology offers a way out of the problems posed by medicocentrism, anachronism, the ambiguities of the Hebrew, Aram., Gk., and English languages and their dictionaries, and modern translations. In contrast to the biomedical paradigm, medical anthropology develops and utilizes an ethnomedical paradigm, that is, a derived etic interpretation of emic data, with a set of definitions that seeks to respect what people in a given culture say about their health misfortunes (emic data). Thus, from a general, medical anthropological (derived etic) perspective, health is best understood as a condition of well-being proposed as such by a given culture. One culture's health may be another culture's misfortune and vice-versa. Medical anthropologists point out that in some societies such serious conditions as yaws, malaria, measles, whooping cough, or mumps are considered so much a part of normal, everyday life that they are not identified as a health misfortune at all. They are given no special attention. On the other hand, "cultural diseases" completely unrecognized by the West often preoccupy other cultures very much. Obviously, biblical "leprosy" preoccupied people exceedingly (see discussion above). In the biblical world, total well-being (including more than physical health) is **shalom** (שָׁלוֹם; an emic concept). While sickness has been considered a blanket term that labels human experiences of health misfortunes, it is probably preferable to consider it a process for giving worrisome physical or behavioral signs a socially recognizable meaning. Thus in the biblical world, Lev 13–14 describe the "sickness" process by which worrisome signs there described are interpreted by the examining priest as being a problem (unclean) or no problem at all (clean). In the final analysis, whatever the specific case may be this "sickness" is the reality (*see* CLEAN AND UNCLEAN). Two explanatory models or explanatory concepts help to understand sickness: disease and illness.

1. Disease

Disease is not the reality itself, but rather an explanatory model or concept that describes abnormalities in the structure and/or the function of human organs and organ systems. Disease includes pathological states even if they are not culturally recognized. This concept and the perspective upon which it is based are distinctively Western, scientific, and biomedical. The concept of disease attempts to correlate constellations of signs and symptoms for the purpose of diagnosis (explanation), prognosis (prediction), and therapy (control). These terms suggest both power and politics. Presented with a blind and mute demoniac (Matt 12:22, diagnosis–explanation), Jesus healed the man (Matt 12:22, therapy–control) and cautioned lest a worse fate follow (Matt 12:43-35, prognosis–prediction). Jesus had power (from God) to do these things (Matt 9:8), but since political authorities did not grant it (Matt 21:23), they viewed his healing activities as unauthorized political deeds deserving death (Matt 26:3-5).

2. Illness

Illness, too, is not the reality itself, but rather an explanatory model or concept that describes the human perception, experience, and interpretation of certain socially disvalued states including but not limited to disease. Illness is both a personal and social reality and therefore in large part a cultural construct. Culture dictates what to perceive and what to ignore, what to value and what to dismiss, what to express and what to overlook, then finally how to live with the illness. Illness is a sense of having lost meaning in life as a result of the sickness. Loss of meaning in life lies at the heart of illness.

Therefore, from the perspective of medical anthropology, that is, a deep respect for the ancient Middle Eastern people who wrote the Bible and described their experiences according to their culture's values, translators ought to render the Hebrew, Arama., and Gk. terms uniformly with the generic term "sickness" or "illness" in order to allow the reader to ascertain the nature of the problem that is being described or discussed (a disease or an illness). And each case, as medical anthropologists note, is highly personal, individualistic, and indeed idiosyncratic. It is difficult if not impossible to generalize. Thus, determining the nature of diseases in the modern sense would seem to be entirely out of the question in Bible translations since we simply do not have adequate information to make that determination. "Illness" would be the most appropriate translation since the Bible does indeed describe socially disvalued states (e.g., so-called "leprosy") and their social consequences (expulsion from the holy community, Lev 13:46, equivalent to a "death sentence" for a collectivistic, group-focused, and group-rooted personality).

Since Bible translations do not currently incorporate these insights, it remains for Bible readers to recognize that the terms *disease, sickness, illness,* in English translations should not be accepted as technical, medical terms and interpreted in 21st cent. biomedical categories. Bible readers are best advised to understand all of these terms as "sickness" and specifically "illness" such as it is defined and understood by medical anthropology, namely, a sociocultural construct serving as an explanatory model or concept to describe a personal and social experience that is given meaning by the culture in which it occurs.

D. Mediterranean Concepts of Sickness or Illness

Anthropologists recognize that the circum-Mediterranean region formed a culture area or culture continent both in antiquity and at the present time. What was distinctive about sickness or illness in the Mediterranean culture area is the interest in and focus upon personal causes. Every significant effect was caused by a person, whether visible or nonvisible, whether human or other-than-human (recall the comments about "moonstruck" above). The human social environment included the sky and its denizens (constellated stars, stars, planets, comets; demons, spirits, angels, and, in many cases, the dead), that showed their influence and/or presence in society. Storms and winds on bodies of water as well as fevers were believed to be caused by such entities. Thus the problem faced by any person afflicted by pain and its consequences was "Who did it?" and not "What did it?" Modern medical science offers statistical explanations concerning what percentage of people will die of cancer or diabetes or any other disease in a given population. But what contemporary people of all cultures wish to know is "Why me?" "Why did I get cancer?" Modern medicine has no answer for the "Why me?" question, while most non-Western "health care systems" incorporate much information concerning this personal question.

Clearly, then, to understand sickness or illness in the ancient Mediterranean culture area, it is essential to keep in mind that natives of that region viewed their cosmos as consisting of four interdependent elements constituting the totality of what exists: the celestial realm (person-type beings that included the high God, lesser deities, stars, planets, angels, spirits, demons, and the like), the earthly realm ("nature" apart from humans), the societal realm (the matrix in which a collectivistic person lives and breathes and derives meaning in life, often called "this world"), and the individual person (a collectivistic person embedded in some primary social group; *see* COLLECTIVIST PERSONALITY). All of these four elements played a collaborative and contributing role in the sickness experience. Thus, the ancient framework for understanding health misfortunes is not naturalistic, i.e., focused only on the person and the physical organ(s) involved, but rather it is cosmic, focused on all four of the interdependent elements.

E. Sin and Disease

All theology is based on human experience that is culturally specific. From the Middle Eastern cultural perspective, sin is shaming another person who must then take vengeance to regain honor (*see* HONOR; SHAME). This is also true of God as viewed in the Middle Eastern perspective. If Israel disobeys (= shames) God, the deity will inflict some affliction on it (Exod 15:26). The idea was debated in the book of Job (22:5-11; 34:5-9) but still widely accepted in the Hellenistic (Sir 38:10) and the NT period (Luke 13:1-5).

The case of congenital health problems was slightly different. In collectivistic culture the concept of collectivistic sin could explain why an infant who has not sinned could be afflicted with health problems (see

Ezek 18:2). The disciples' question to Jesus about the man born blind is illustrative: "Rabbi, who sinned, this man or his parents, that he was born blind?" (John 9:2). Later rabbinic opinion (*Gen. Rab.* 63:6) proposed prenatal sin. If a pregnant woman worshiped an idol, the child in her womb was presumed to do so too (*Song of Rab.* 1:41). Jesus denies both suggestions (John 9:3) and says God's healing powers will be revealed in this innocent blind man (see Exod 15:26: "I am the LORD who heals you").

The light that medical anthropology sheds on these cultural convictions is that one's belief system plays a key role in determining sickness (and health). The importance of knowing that one's life has meaning and purpose spells the difference between health and sickness. If one believes that shaming God (= sin) may bring disastrous consequences, one can either repent or suffer God's vengeance. Or, since ancient (and contemporary) Mediterranean cultures believed that a person could harm other persons simply by malicious glances (the "evil eye") accompanied by malicious intent, people did indeed become ill and even die if they believed that someone had cast the evil eye upon them.

F. Disease as Impurity

Human societies make sense out of their social living by drawing metaphorical lines around the self, others, nature, time, and space. The ancients saw these lines in terms of CLEAN AND UNCLEAN. Purity deals with the question of where persons and things belong. People and things out of place are "dirty" or "unclean." Dirt is matter out of place; a deviant person is a person out of place. To judge things and people in place or out of place requires that a person know the location of the lines that mark "in place" and "out of place." The concept of clean and unclean is part of the social system into which human beings are enculturated. The Bible locates the realities that contemporary English translators designate as "disease," "sickness," and "illness" in the realm of impurity (the out-of-bounds, the unclean) rather than in the realm of what we might call physical health. The actual, physical experience is impurity. "You are to distinguish between the holy and the common, and between the unclean and the clean" (Lev 10:10). Thus the command: "Sanctify yourselves therefore, and be holy, for I am holy" and echoes of it describe the essence of well-being (Lev 11:44-45; 19:2; 20:7, 26; 21:6-8; Num 15:40; Deut 14:2, 21; 26:19; 28:9; Luke 2:23; 1 Pet 1:16; 2:9). Holiness is a requisite for approaching and pleasing God (Num 16:5). "Disease" and its cognates in the Bible are not feared because of physical consequences but rather because they separate a person from God and restrict access to God (Ezra 9:1-2; Ezek 44:23). In other words, the Bible does not fear contagion but rather pollution. The biblical "disease" is not a physical problem that might be transmitted (contagion). It is rather an impurity that can pollute others and eventually the entire community (pollution).

Medical anthropology proposes a basic taxonomy of "diseases" in non-Western cultures: illness caused by God (or a spirit), and illnesses of the human person. In the Bible, some "diseases" are associated with a spirit agent (whether God, e.g., Exod 15:26, or another spirit, e.g., Matt 17:15 and 18), but most biblical "diseases" (impurities) that affect the human body have unknown etiologies, e.g., Mark 2:1-12; 3:1-6; etc. The skin problem called "leprosy" affecting the human person in the Bible (Lev 13) is a physical, bodily ailment not at all associated with a spirit agent. In contrast, Saul's odd and unusual behavioral problem is attributed to an evil spirit (1 Sam 19:9, even if sent by God).

The biblical diseases or impurities that affect a person's body and inhibit access to God can be clustered in another (derived etic) taxonomy based on the people's (emic) reports of these problems. According to Mary Douglas, the human body is a symbolic reality that bridges one's personal world with the sociocultural world. The individual body is a portable road map of the social body. Before Douglas, a Belgian scholar, Bernard de Gérardon, conducted a scholarly (etic) study of the human body in the Bible (emic data) and concluded that the ancients interpreted the body symbolically (derived etic). They divided the body into three zones interpreted symbolically: heart-eyes, mouth-ears, and hands-feet. The heart-eyes zone symbolizes that part of the human body responsible for emotion-infused thinking. The mouth-ears zone symbolizes that part of the human body responsible for self-expressive speech and communication. The hands-feet zone symbolizes that part of the human body responsible for purposeful action. If each part or zone of the human body is whole, and they work together in harmony, that person possesses total well-being including more than physical health (**shalom**). If any zone or part is affected by some illness, that person is no longer whole, holy, clean. That person's access to God is impeded. That person needs to be restored to well-being. In Mark (and par.), it is possible to cluster human health misfortunes ("illnesses") into two categories: those not spirit-related, and those that are spirit-related.

The illnesses that the sick people presented in Mark that are not spirit-related:

Mark 1:30-31 (mother-in-law, fever = hands-feet [bed-ridden], a bodily ailment and not a spirit inflicted ailment as reported in Luke 4:38-39)

Mark 1:40-45 (leper = hands-feet, impurity impeded access to the holy community and to God)

Mark 2:1-12 (paralytic = hands-feet)

Mark 3:1-6 (withered hand = hands-feet)

Mark 5:21-24, 35-43 (dying daughter = hands-feet)

Mark 5:25-34 (hemorrhaging woman = hands-feet, "feet" perhaps as euphemism for genitals)

Mark 7:31-37 (deaf man/speech impediment = mouth-ears)

Mark 8:22-26 (blind man = heart-eyes)

Mark 10:46-52 (blind man = heart-eyes)

Spirit-related illnesses in Mark (and par.) would include:

Mark 1:21-28 (man in synagogue)

Mark 3:20-30 (debate, Jesus accused of having an "unclean spirit")

Mark 5:1-20 (Gerasene demoniac)

Mark 7:24-30 (Syrophoenician daughter afflicted by unclean spirit/demon)

Mark 9:14-29 (deaf and possessed by a mute spirit)

Mark 9:38-40 (someone other than Jesus casts out demons)

Mark 16:9-20 (longer ending: Mary Magdalene had seven demons cast out; believers cast out demons)

Afflictions in either taxonomy render a person unclean, impure, unwhole, and, therefore, not holy as the LORD is holy. Such a person's access to God is impeded, and such persons are also a polluting threat to the community (Lev 13:46).

In the OT, these illnesses or impurities most often concern priests who serve the Temple (Lev 21:16-24). Impurity of any kind rendered the afflicted priest incapable of fulfilling his function. As an impure person, such a priest was out of place in the areas of the Temple in which sacrifices were offered. Such a priest was unfit for offering sacrifice. But impurity did not prevent him from eating the priestly portion of the sacrifice. And it did not remove him from the hereditary priesthood. The priestly line was secure (*see* PRIESTS AND LEVITES). It was with the rise of Pharisaic movement groups (about 200 BCE) and their disappointment and disillusionment with the priesthood that the concerns about purity and impurity and its consequences (apart from so-called "leprosy"; see Num 5:1-4) were extended to the ordinary Israelite.

G. Culture-Bound Syndromes

The Israelite (emic) view of its health misfortunes is quite obviously culturally perceived and interpreted. These would best be labeled as "folk conceptualized disorders." Medical anthropologists, however, commonly use the term "culture bound syndromes." No medical anthropologist identifies such human problems as misconceptions or superstitions or something "psychosomatic." Thus, the researcher interested in "diseases" in the Bible is best advised to look to other, supplementary methodologies including medical anthropology.

Attention to culture-bound syndromes invites critical Bible readers, for instance, to take the Gk. literally and translate those words in Matt 4:24; 17:15 as "moonstruck" (the emic view) instead of "epileptic" and "epilepsy" (the imposed etic medicocentric view;

see above). Simons and Hughes identify this human experience of being "moonstruck" as a "culture-bound syndrome" perhaps similar to the *gila babi* in rural Malaysia or *phii pob* in rural Thailand. Similarly, the sickness (= human health misfortune) that results from the "evil eye" belongs to this same category. Among the misfortunes of "evil eye" documented in medical literature is the sudden death of otherwise healthy individuals. It is quite plausible that the twelve-year-old girl who died before Jesus arrived (Mark 5:22-24, 35-43) was a victim of the evil eye of an envious person in the village. In the ancient Mediterranean world, 30 to 60 percent of that population did not live to the age of twelve. Hence a surviving twelve-year-old child would be an obvious target of the evil eye from anyone who had already lost a child or children (and there would be many in any village).

Though "evil eye" never appears in the NRSV or RSV (except in some footnotes), it literally appears very often in the Hebrew and Gk. texts (see Deut 15:7-11; 28:53-55; Prov 23:6-8; 28:22; Sir 14:3, 5-7, 8, 9; 31:13; 37:11; Matt 6:22-23; Mark 7:22; Luke 11:33-34; and indirectly in Gal 3:1 ["bewitched"]; 4:14 ["despise" literally means "spit," a strategy for averting the evil eye]. Each case must be judged in its context to appreciate the variety of misfortunes that the "evil eye" causes.

It is also plausible that biblical "leprosy" in the NT period might have become by that time a culture-bound syndrome. The emphasis on clean and unclean dimensions of life that emerged with strictness after the exile, the experience of acceptance in or exclusion from a selective community, and the requirement of avoiding liaisons with foreigners that also emerged in the post-exilic period (Ezra 9–10) grew stronger with each successive conquest and domination by another world power: Persia, Greece, Rome. While some Judeans under domination may have accommodated themselves and compromised their traditions, others struggled to remain observant. These observants may plausibly have developed a culture-bound syndrome affecting the skin that occasioned expulsion from the community.

H. Conclusion

Medicocentric analyses of "disease" in the Bible are plentiful but relatively worthless for historically based biblical interpretation. The final conclusion of such studies often is "we don't know" or "we can't be sure." It is preferable to adopt an alternative methodology in order to learn what ancient Middle Eastern people were experiencing and communicating in their day and age and according to their understanding. Medical anthropology is one discipline that contributes to discovering that. Surely the ancient Israelites were concerned with matters of purity and impurity. They clustered these experiences into two major categories: those that "just happened" to the body, and those caused by some spirit (including God). The concerns were pollution (impurity) rather than contagion (disease). The major consequence affected relationship with God: Was one holy, or not? Did one please God, or not? Did one have access to God, or not? Such considerations set the question on a very different and much more culturally plausible track than scientific Western medical interests. *See* BLINDNESS; BODY; BOIL; DEMON; HEALING; LEPROSY; MIRACLE; PARALYSIS, PARALYTIC.

Bibliography: John W. Berry, Ype H. Poortinga, Marshall H. Segall, and Pierre R. Dasen. *Cross-Cultural Psychology: Research and Applications.* 2nd ed. (2002); J. Keir Howard. *Disease and Healing in the New Testament: An Analysis and Interpretation* (2001); Arthur M. Kleinman. *Patients and Healers in the Context of Culture* (1980); R. E. Levine and A. C. Gaw. "Culture-Bound Syndromes." *Psychiatric Clinics of North America* 18:3 (1995) 523–36; Bruce J. Malina. *The New Testament World.* 3rd ed. (2001); Daniel Moerman. *Meaning, Medicine and the "Placebo Effect"* (2002); George Peter Murdock. *Theories of Illness: A World Survey* (1980); John J. Pilch. *Healing in the New Testament: Insights from Medical and Mediterranean Anthropology* (2000); Ronald C. Simons and Charles C. Hughes, eds. *The Culture-Bound Syndromes: Folk Illnesses of Psychiatric and Anthropological Interest* (1985); Peter Worsley. "Non-Western Medical Systems." *Annual Review of Anthropology* 11 (1982) 315–48; Allan Young. "The Anthropologies of Illness and Sickness." *Annual Review of Anthropology* 11 (1982) 257–85.

JOHN J. PILCH

DISH. *See* POTTERY; VESSELS.

DISHAN dĭ'shan [דִּישָׁן *dishan*]. One of the sons of SEIR, who in turn had two sons: Uz and Aran (Gen 36:21-30; 1 Chr 1:38-42).

DISHON dĭ'shon [דִּישׁוֹן *dishon*]. A descendant of ANAH, who is among the children of SEIR the Horite (Gen 36:21; 1 Chr 1:38). The Hebrew text of 1 Chronicles also lists Dishon's name as the father of Uz and Aran (1:42), but it probably should read "DISHAN." Dishon's clan is listed among those who inhabit the land in which Esau settles after departing from Jacob (Gen 36:6-7).

JESSICA TINKLENBERG DEVEGA

DISHONOR. *See* SHAME.

DISMEMBERMENT [קָצָה *qatsah*, קָצַץ *qatsats*]. The practice of cutting or tearing off hands, arms, or legs as criminal punishment is mentioned a few times in OT law (*see* CRIMES AND PUNISHMENT, OT AND NT). One law prescribes that a woman have her hand cut

off for seizing a man's genitals in a fight (Deut 25:11-12). Some formulations of LEX TALIONIS prescribe mutilation for acts of mutilation (e.g., Exod 21:23-25; Lev 24:19-20). In practice this probably meant legal consequences comparable to the crime, as is the case in Exod 21:26-27.

Occasionally dismemberment is mentioned as an instrument of war (2 Macc 1:16). According to Judg 1:6-7, the Israelites who captured the king of Bezek cut off his thumbs and big toes because he had done so to his royal captives.

DALE PATRICK

DISMISS, DISMISSAL. *See* DIVORCE; NUNC DIMITTIS.

DISOBEDIENCE. *See* OBEDIENCE.

DISPERSION. *See* DIASPORA.

DISPUTATION. Theological argument in a formal setting. Also a literary form of DIALOGUE on a controversial theme developed by two or more characters, who take turns in giving long presentations of various ideas. Different argumentations are thus put into the mouths of the different disputation partners. These are all characters within the text; none of them is imaginary and outside the text (as in a DIATRIBE). The book of Job, with its theme of undeserved suffering, is the clearest biblical example of a disputation. In a disputation, progression and development of the theme are much more important than the development of the characters. *See* RHETORICAL CRITICISM, NT; RHETORICAL CRITICISM, OT.

L. J. DE REGT

DISPUTE BETWEEN A MAN AND HIS BA. An Egyptian wisdom text from the Twelfth Dynasty (ca. 1990–1785 BCE). It preserves a dialogue between the man and his ba, one of the Egyptian words for the soul or spirit. The man despairs of life and wants to die. His ba threatens to leave him if he keeps complaining, explaining to him that those who have died are not happy. The man convinces his ba to stay with him until he has an heir who can bury him with the proper funeral rites. *See* WISDOM IN THE ANCIENT NEAR EAST.

Bibliography: Miriam Lichtheim. *AEL.* 1 (1973) 163–69.
KEVIN A. WILSON

DISTAFF [כִּישׁוֹר *kishor*]. A long rod, sometimes forked at the top, used for holding unspun fibers while spinning. This tool may be tucked into a belt or held in the hand. **Kishor** occurs only once in the Bible (Prov 31:19); its meaning is derived from a parallel with spindle (**palekh** פֶּלֶךְ). Thus the precise translation of **kishor** is uncertain. It is clearly a tool used in the process of spinning. However, it might be a spinning bowl, used for controlling the strands of thread when plying or twisting two threads together, or a specialized form of the spindle used in plying thread. Images of women using the distaff appear in Greek art, but they are absent from ANE images.

Bibliography: Trude Dothan. "Spinning Bowls." *IEJ* 13 (1963) 97–112; Gemma Florentine. "Spindle and Distaff." *Threads* 2 (1985–86) 33–35; Al Wolters. "The Meaning of kîšôr (Prov 31:19)." *HUCA* 65 (1994) 91–104.

MARY PETRINA BOYD

DISTRESS [צָרַר tsarar, θλῖψις thlipsis]. This is a feature of eschatological expectation in ancient Judaism and the NT. Before the messianic age would come about, a period of distress, of cosmic proportions, would have to be endured (Dan 12:1; *Jub.* 23:11; Mark 13:7-9, whereas in Rom 8:22 it is likened to childbirth; Rev 7:14, and the sequences of disasters in Rev 6, 8, 9, 16). Sometimes, as in Revelation and the Syriac Apocalypse of Bar 25–26, there is a fixed quota of messianic woes that must be completed before the kingdom finally comes. *See* APOCALYPTICISM.

CHRISTOPHER ROWLAND

DISTRIBUTION OF GOODS. *See* COMMUNITY OF GOODS.

DISTRICT [מְדִינָה medhinah, מִדָּה middah, פֶּלֶךְ pelekh, תְּרוּמָה terumah; μερίς meris μέρος meros, ὅριον horion]. The English word *district* is used for several biblical terms specifying geographical regions or units of political and religious administration. References are made to governors of the districts in Ahab's kingdom (medhinah, 1 Kgs 20:14-18); to officials of the districts of Jerusalem in post-exilic Judah (pelekh; Neh 3:9, 12, 14-18), and to the holy space reserved for the restored temple (terumah, middah; Ezek 45:1, 3, 6-7). The NT references to the "districts" (meros) of Tyre and Sidon (Matt 15:21), Caesarea Philippi (Matt 16:13), and Dalmanutha (Mark 8:10) do not cite political administrative units but rather the wide-ranging geographical regions Jesus visited in the course of teaching and healing. The district of Galilee (meros; Matt 2:22) contrasted with Archelaus's Judea carries an anti-political overtone. References in Paul's itinerary to the district of Pisidia (horion; Acts 13:14, 50) and the district of Macedonia (meris; Acts 16:12) seem to allude to their political status as Roman provinces. *See* GOVERNMENT, NT; GOVERNMENT, OT.

NORMAN K. GOTTWALD

DITTOGRAPHY. The phenomenon by which letters or words are accidentally written more than once by scribes in the process of copying manuscripts, resulting in lengthened text and possibly incorrect grammatical forms. Careful observation, sound reasoning, and knowledge of biblical languages are needed to detect such errors. *See* TEXT CRITICISM, NT; TEXT CRITICISM, OT.

R. JUSTIN HARKINS

DIVERSITY. Diversity can be dealt with at least on three different levels: ethnic diversity, religious diversity, and theological diversity.

    A. Ethnic Diversity
    B. Religious Diversity
    C. Theological Diversity
    Bibliography

A. Ethnic Diversity

On the one hand, the ancestral narratives of ancient Israel paint a simplistic picture of ancient Israelites all descending from a single family lineage, from Abraham to Isaac to Jacob to his twelve sons, who became the eponymous ancestors of the twelve tribes. The reality is much more complicated; ancient Israel was quite diverse in its ethnic composition. Communal stories trace the beginnings of ancient Israel to different places (*see* ETHNICITY). Genesis 11 connects Abraham's origin to "Ur of the Chaldeans" (v. 31), that is, in Mesopotamia. A different tradition in Deut 26:5 suggests an origin from among the Arameans: "A wandering Aramean was my ancestor." A third and more prominent tradition uses the exodus story to trace the emergence of Israel from a long period of enslavement in Egypt. Archaeological evidence traces the majority of ancient Israelites back to local Canaanite populations. Mixed with these rural Canaanites were displaced peasants and pastoralists, semitic slaves from EGYPT, and nonindigenous people like the Midianites, Kenites, and Amalekites.

In the NT, while the early followers of Jesus were primarily Galilean Jews, the early church was quite diverse. According to Acts 2, at the first Pentecost, Peter converted Jews from many nations. Luke further distinguishes Greek-speaking (Hellenist) Jews and Hebrew-speaking Jews (Acts 6:1). When Luke narrates Philip's conversion of the ETHIOPIAN EUNUCH (Acts 8), Christian membership extends beyond Israel, paving the way for the Gentile mission. Peter's conversion of Cornelius, the Roman centurion and the first Gentile convert, marks a turning point in story of inclusion and ethnic diversity in the early church (Acts 10). Eventually, Paul's missionary journeys will bring the gospel to the many parts of the Mediterranean world. *See* ANTHROPOLOGY, NT CULTURAL; ANTHROPOLOGY, OT CULTURAL; ETHNICITY; IDEOLOGICAL CRITICISM; RACISM; STRANGER.

B. Religious Diversity

On the surface, biblical narratives offer the impression that Yahweh is the only deity worshiped in ancient

Israel. Close readings reveal clues of religious diversity (*see* GODS, GODDESSES). The Deuteronomist criticizes Solomon for following "Astarte the goddess of the Sidonians, and Milcom the abomination of the Ammonites" and for building "a high place for Chemosh the abomination of Moab, and for Molech the abomination of the Ammonites" (1 Kgs 11:5-7). The Deuteronomist later blames Ahab for the introduction of Baalism in northern Israel. After taking a Sidonian princess as wife, he built a temple of Baal in Samaria (1 Kgs 16:31-34). The contest between the prophet Elijah and the priests of Baal in 1 Kgs 18:20-40 reveals the gravity of the situation. The people were hopping between Yahweh and Baal. The Deuteronomist also condemns worship of ASHERAH (1 Kgs 14:15; 16:33).

Archaeological discoveries in the northern and southern kingdoms confirm a diverse religious environment. Hundreds of excavated female figurines indicate a possible association with Canaanite religion, (but do not necessarily signify fertility cults, a phenomenon questioned by many scholars today). Of particular significance is a drawing painted on a large jar found at Kuntillet 'Ajrud with an accompanying inscription that reads: "to Yahweh of Samaria and his Asherah." While the meaning of the phrase is not entirely clear, it reveals some form of patronage to Asherah.

More importantly, Yahwism was influenced by other Near Eastern religions. The Mesopotamian combat myth between Marduk and Tiamat influenced the first CREATION story (Gen 1). In the book of Job, the prologue's divine assembly scene is common in Canaanite and Mesopotamian religions. In Ps 68:4, the reference to Yahweh as one "who rides the clouds" is a common epithet of BAAL.

The religious world of the NT was similarly diverse. In his discussion about the eating of food offered to idols in 1 Cor 8:4-6, Paul declares: "Even though there may be so-called gods in heaven and on earth—as in fact there are many gods and many lords—yet for us there is one God." Even as he argues for the worship of the one God, Paul recognizes the diversity and polytheism of his day. The MYSTERY RELIGIONS of the Greek Dionysus, the Egyptian Isis, and the Persian Mithras were quite popular. Mystery religions impacted the development of early Christianity (*see* GREEK RELIGION AND PHILOSOPHY; HELLENISM).

C. Theological Diversity

The OT narrates the covenantal relationship between Israel and Yahweh (*see* COVENANT, OT AND NT; THEOLOGY, OT). Diverse theological voices can be discerned. For example, in Proverbs and the DEUTERONOMISTIC HISTORY, a theology of RETRIBUTION is frequently evident. God will punish the wicked for their evil deeds and reward the righteous with longevity and prosperity (e.g., Deut. 30:15-20; Prov 10:30; 12:7). However, this theological construction of retribution is challenged by the writers of Job and Ecclesiastes. Job, in spite of his piety and righteousness, loses everything and offers a rebuttal to retribution theology (*see* JOB, BOOK OF; THEODICY). The prophets, Wisdom literature, and narrative history offer diverse interpretations of Israel's relationship to Yahweh, neighboring peoples, and each other. For example, Ezra and Nehemiah portray a xenophobic Israel attempting to redefine its uniqueness after the exile, while the story of Ruth and some prophetic oracles depict an inclusive vision of Israel (*see* PROPHET, PROPHECY; WISDOM IN THE OT).

In the NT, the gospel writers, Paul, the deuterocanonical and Catholic epistles, and the author of Revelation focus on the message of Jesus, but in diverse ways. The four gospels tell the story of Jesus's life, ministry, death, and resurrection, how he was affirmed as the Christ, and what it means for his followers to live a life of faith; yet the four gospel writers tell the story of Jesus from different perspectives, each with a different christological message. For example, the Gospel of Mark depicts a very human Jesus, while the Gospel of John describes a high Christology in which Jesus is pre-existent with God (*see* CHRISTOLOGY; JESUS CHRIST; REDACTION CRITICISM, NT). In contrast to the gospels, Paul rarely mentions the life of Jesus but focuses instead on interpreting the meaning of the life of faith in Jesus as the Christ for the nascent church. The deutero-canonical letters and Catholic epistles show an evolution in the church's interpretation of this faith in Christ. For example, for Paul, faith meant obedient trust in the death of Christ for salvation. For the Pastorals, it becomes either "the Christian faith" (a deposit of traditional teaching that is deemed orthodox) or the correct kind of virtue (*see* THEOLOGY, NT).

Such diversity in theological interpretation does not mean that any of the biblical writers are more accurate or truthful than others, but simply that each has a different emphasis and concern for how to relate the message. See BIBLICAL INTERPRETATION, HISTORY OF.

Bibliography: A. E. Killebrew. *Biblical Peoples and Ethnicity* (2005); L. H. Martin. *Hellenistic Religions: An Introduction* (1987); S. Niditch. *Ancient Israelite Religion* (1997).

KAH-JIN JEFFREY KUAN

DIVES d*i'* veez [Lat. *Dives*]. In Luke's parable of the rich man and the beggar (16:19-31), Jesus identifies the latter as LAZARUS, the Greek form of Eliezer ("My God helps"). Although the rich man is anonymous, the medieval church used the Latin adjective *dives* ("rich") as this figure's proper name. Older studies employed folktale motifs and Jewish literature to argue that the story condemns the rich for neglecting the poor and vindicates the faithful. Recent comparisons with Greco-Roman *Nekyiai* literature, however, suggest that the parable castigates the wealthy for their ostentation and praises the poor for their virtue.

DAVID M. REIS

DIVIDE [בָּקַע baqaʿ, פָּרַד paradh, חָצָה khatsah, חָלַק khalaq, σχίζω schizō]. Used mostly for baqaʿ, the LXX employs the verb "to divide" (schizō) 11 times with a literal meaning to "cut" wood (Gen 22:3) or "split" the Red Sea (Exod 14:21). Unlike the NT, the LXX contains neither figurative uses of the verb nor the noun form, "division" (schisma σχίσμα), in either active or passive senses.

The verb occurs twice in Acts, figuratively (14:4; 23:7), and nine times in the Gospels, all literally. Physical acts of "splitting" or "tearing" depict either natural or supernatural events. Reference to ordinary clothing that should not be "torn" can even have theological significance. In fulfillment of Scripture, Roman soldiers do not "divide" Jesus' seamless tunic, but cast lots for it (John 19:24; Ps 21:19 LXX). Supernatural events include "tearing" of the temple veil (Matt 27:51; Mark 15:38; Luke 23:45) and rocks "splitting" (Matt 27:51) at the death of Jesus. Especially striking are the heavens "torn apart" in Mark's baptism of Jesus (1:10). "Rending" of the heavens is commonplace in Jewish apocalyptic literature (*2 Bar.* 22:1; Rev 4:1).

Luke is the only author to use the verb figuratively. Both references describe how Paul's gospel "dichotomized" an entire city (Acts 14:4) and two parties within Judaism (Acts 23:6-10). The noun form (schisma) predominately occurs figuratively to convey fierce "division" or "separation" over Jesus' identity (John 7:43-44), miracle working (John 9:16), and teaching (John 10:19). Ravaged by "schisms," Paul seeks to heal Corinth's destructive social factions (1 Cor 1:10), appealing to unity in the body of Christ (12:12-25). *See* DIVORCE; EXCLUSION.

CHRIS M. SMITH

DIVIDING WALL [τὸ μεσότοιχον τοῦ φραγμοῦ to mesotoichon tou phragmou]. The Temple Mount in JERUSALEM was divided into different courtyards of increasing levels of purity. The largest, outermost area was open to Gentiles, but a low partition wall, about 1.5 m high with signs in Greek and Latin warning non-Jews not to enter further or suffer immediate execution, prevented non-Jews from entering the TEMPLE itself. Archaeologists have verified Josephus' description (*J.W.* 2.193; *Ant.* 15.417) by finding copies of the plaques while excavating Jerusalem. Some Jews erroneously thought Paul brought Gentiles into the Temple and tried to kill him (Acts 21:28*b*-31). It is also the "dividing wall" Paul uses symbolically in Eph 2:14.

ADAM L. PORTER

DIVINATION [קֶסֶם qesem, נָחַשׁ nakhash; μαντεῖον manteion, οἰώνισμος oiōnismos]. The process of discerning divine purpose or attaining supernatural knowl-

edge through various devices and stratagems. Widely practiced in the ANE, divination focuses on human schemes for uncovering divine will, in contrast with prophetic insight that derives from direct revelation (conveyed through visions, dreams, and other ecstatic experiences of the divine). While the OT retains some traces of divinatory ritual, by and large it regards manipulative approaches to God with suspicion.

For example, the authors/editors of Numbers and Deuteronomy issue strong injunctions against divination (main terms: qsm [קסם], nkhsh [נחשׁ]/manteion, oiōnismos). As the Israelites journey to the promised land, the elders of Moab and Midian approach BALAAM with "fees for divination," hoping to procure a powerful curse against the people (Num 22:7). God, however, repeatedly prohibits Balaam from casting an ominous spell, convincing Balaam that any "enchantment" or "divination against Israel" is futile (22:38; 23:23). Likewise, Moses' review of God's covenantal law, preparing Israel to possess its holy land, unequivocally forbids any engagement in sundry forms of divination, augury, and other "abhorrent practices" of the alien peoples of Canaan (Deut 18:9-14). Philistine, Babylonian, and Chaldean diviners also appear in a negative light (1 Sam 6:2; Isa 2:6; Jer 50:35-36; Dan 2:27; 4:7; 5:7). Instead, the people must continue to seek divine guidance from prophets like Moses, who mediate the very words of Yahweh (Deut 18:15-22).

On the other hand, the prophet Ezekiel endorses the use of divination by foreigners—but only in the tragic context of judgment against Judah's wickedness. Ezekiel envisions the king of Babylon (Nebuchadnezzar) standing with his sword at the fork of two roads: one leading to the capital of Ammon (Rabbah), the other to the capital of Judah (Jerusalem). Following common martial strategy in the ANE, Nebuchadnezzar decides to take the warpath to Jerusalem on the basis of four divinatory techniques: shaking arrows, consulting teraphim, inspecting livers, and casting lots. Even though the citizens of Jerusalem dismiss this threat as a "false divination," it proves to be painfully true: from Ezekiel's perspective, the people's rebellion against God merits the city's destruction by Babylon (Ezek 21:18-23). Inversely, Ezekiel chides "false" prophets among his own people—who blithely forecast peace for Jerusalem—as promoters themselves of "lying/flattering divination" (Ezek 12:24; 13:6, 7, 9, 23). Other biblical prophets also consistently expose "diviners" within Israel as worthless charlatans (e.g., Isa 3:2; 44:25; Jer 14:14; 27:9; 29:8; Mic 3:7; Zech 10:2).

The extensive repertoire of divining objects and methods employed in the ANE included the following.

1. Livers. The practice of investigating the livers of sacrificial animals for signs and omens (hepatoscopy) was widespread in ancient Babylonian (compare Ezek 21:18-21) and other Mesopotamian cultures. Although not attested among Israelites in the biblical record, the

unearthing of a clay liver model from Hazor (15th cent. BCE), inscribed with cuneiform instructions for temple diviners, attests to some hepatoscopic activity in the region. The preoccupation with the liver as a source of secret knowledge probably correlated with Mesopotamian understanding of this organ as the fountain of life-blood. The "science" of "reading" the intricate maps and grids of animal livers was typically the provenance of a highly trained, esoteric cadre of priests, whose precise techniques remain obscure. The fortuitous or disastrous omens revealed by liver analysis often determined policies for making war and peace.

2. Arrows. Flight patterns of birds and arrows were also thought to disclose good or ill fortune. The divinatory use of arrows (rhabdomancy) seems linked with the numinous quality of trees, sticks, and wood products (like rods and arrows; compare Exod 4:1-5; 17:8-13; Num 17:7-11; Judg 4:5; 6:11; 9:37 ['elon me'onenim אֵלוֹן מְעוֹנְנִים]=DIVINER'S OAK]; Hos 4:12) and may inform the mode of communication between Jonathan and David regarding David's fate. By shooting (not shaking as in Ezek 21:21) three arrows on the far side of a boy sent to fetch them, Jonathan conveys to David that he must flee the wrath of King Saul (a shot on the near side would have signaled Saul's welcome of David) (1 Sam 20:18-42). In this case, however, Jonathan controls the trajectory of arrows as a means of transmitting information, not discovering it. He learns of Saul's hostility toward David by conversation, not divination.

3. Water and oil. Some messages were decoded from various properties of water, oil, and other substances (hydromancy) mixed in a special divining vessel. During his service in the Egyptian court narrated in Genesis, Joseph possesses a personal silver cup that he claims to use for divination, particularly in forecasting judgment on evildoers (Gen 44:5, 14). He secretly plants the cup in his younger brother Benjamin's grain sack and threatens to curse the other brothers with it. However, he never follows through with the curse. Joseph simply uses the cup as a ruse to keep his brothers off balance and in his debt. In Gen 37–50, Joseph typically receives wisdom from more direct contact with God, mediated sometimes through dreams (37:5-11), but not through divinatory objects.

4. Teraphim. Figurines representing household deities were included among Neudchadnezzar's divinatory paraphernalia in Ezek 21:21, although it is not clear how they disclosed special secrets and fortunes. In some cases, the OT denounces the use of teraphim in ancient Israel ("For rebellion is no less a sin than divination [qesem], and stubbornness is like iniquity and idolatry [terafim תְּרָפִים] [1 Sam 15:23; compare 2 Kgs 23:24]), but in other cases, it takes a more neutral stance (Gen 31:19-35; 1 Sam 19:11-17; Hos 3:4). The story in Judg 17–18, featuring Micah's hiring a young Levitical priest to oversee his household shrine, hints at a consultative use of teraphim. In addition to teraphim, Micah's shrine contains a silver idol and an ephod—all of which presumably aid the priest in discerning God's blessing on the land-seeking mission of the Danite tribe. But precisely how the priest might have used these objects is never specified (17:3-5; 18:1-5, 14-20).

5. Mediums and wizards. Mediums sought oracular counsel from the ghosts and spirits of the dead. The OT consistently condemns this practice of necromancy as an "abominable" custom of Israel's pagan neighbors (Deut 18:11-12; compare Lev 19:31; 20:27; 2 Kgs 21:2, 6). Manasseh's employment of mediums in 7th cent. Judah epitomizes the "much evil" of his reign, inciting Yahweh's "anger" and Josiah's reform (2 Kgs 21:6; 23:24). Two passages provide some insight into the methods of necromancers and their clients: Isaiah speaks derisively of those who "chirp and mutter" (i.e., alter their voices and cadences) while contacting the dead (Isa 8:19-20); and Saul, panicking over an impending battle with the Philistines, seeks advice from Samuel's ghost through a female medium from Endor (1 Sam 28:3-25). In this latter incident, which only compounds Saul's fear, he is driven to NECROMANCY because Yahweh has rejected him as king and no longer speaks to him through legitimate means of "dreams, or by Urim, or by prophets" (28:6).

6. Priests and other authorized personnel determined God's purpose on various matters by means of casting lots, such as the sacred URIM AND THUMMIM dice contained in the Israelite high priest's breast pocket (Exod 28:30; Num 27:21; Deut 33:8; Ezra 2:63). By and large, the Bible approves casting lots "before the LORD our God" (Josh 18:6), not as magical objects, but as indicators of Yahweh's sovereign will (Prov 16:33). Decisions rendered through lots include assignments of territory (Num 26:55-56; Josh 18:6-10; Isa 34:17) and service (kings: 1 Sam 10:20-23; priests: 1 Chr 24:31; 25:8; 26:13-14; Neh 10:34; Luke 1:8-9; apostles: Acts 1:24-26) and assessments of guilt (1 Sam 14:38-42), judicial disputes (Prov 18:18), and causes of disaster (Jonah 1:7-10).

7. In the Greco-Roman world, seekers of divine knowledge commonly consulted mantic women inspired by the oracle at Delphi under the aegis of the god Apollo and the symbol of a snake or python. Plutarch discusses other features of the Delphic oracle, such as its emblematic association with the letter epsilon (E—representing, e.g., ei [EI, εἶ], meaning "Thou art," a signifier of divine presence) and its typical mode of operation—inspiring the essence of divine thought within a prophetess's soul, but leaving the medium to shape and deliver the message in her own voice (Plutarch, E. Delph.; Pyth. orac.). In Acts, Paul encounters a Delphic diviner (manteuomenē μαντευομένη) in Philippi, a slave girl possessed by a "pythian spirit" (pneuma pythōna πνεῦμα πύθωνα) and also by owners who profited greatly from her fortune-telling (Acts

16:16-18). Surprisingly, the girl makes a favorable announcement about Paul and associates: "These men are slaves of the Most High God, who proclaim to you a way of salvation" (16:17; compare Luke 1:76-77; 3:4-5). However, her repetition of this utterance "for many days" irks Paul to the point that he exorcises the pythian spirit from her. In turn, the slave girl's employers violently drag Paul to court, suing him for damaging their business and "disturbing our city" (Acts 16:19-21). *See* ENDOR, MEDIUM OF; EPHOD; PROPHET, PROPHECY; SOOTHSAYER.

Bibliography: Robert M. Berchman, ed. *Mediators of the Divine: Horizons of Prophecy, Divination, Dreams and Theurgy in Mediterranean Antiquity* (1998); Frederick H. Cryer. *Divination in Ancient Israel and Its Near Eastern Environment: A Socio-Historical Investigation* (1994); Ann Jeffers. *Magic and Divination in Ancient Palestine and Syria* (1996).

F. SCOTT SPENCER

DIVINE ASSEMBLY. In the ANE, a common metaphor for describing the world of the divine was the "divine assembly" or "divine council." These descriptions of gods and goddesses gathered together under the leadership of a senior deity were derived, in all probability, from the activities of the royal court. The OT provides a number of descriptions of this heavenly assembly that closely resemble descriptions in the literature of the surrounding cultures (*see* GODS, GODDESSES).

The concept of a divine assembly is attested in Egypt, Mesopotamia, Canaan, Phoenicia, and Israel. Ancient Egyptian literature reveals the existence of a "synod of the gods," though it did not play an important role in the religion. Some of our most complete descriptions of the activities of the divine assembly are found in the literature from Mesopotamia. Their "assembly of the gods," headed by the high god Anu, would meet to address various concerns, though a major activity of the assembly seems to have been feasting. It seems to have been composed of all of the major active gods and goddesses, fifty of whom were designated as "the great/senior gods," while seven were called "the gods of the fates" that they were in charge of determining. Even the active gods of the pantheon were subject to decisions of the assembly.

Similar descriptions of the divine assembly are found in the Canaanite texts from Ras Shamra (*see* UGARIT, TEXTS AND LITERATURE). There we find "the assembly of El/the gods" meeting under the leadership of the senior deity El. The exact membership of the Canaanite assembly, however, is not as clear as it is in the case of Mesopotamia. Indeed, it would seem that there were several different divine assemblies: an "assembly of the gods" and "the assembly of the sons of El." There are also references in these materials to "the assembly of Baal" and to "the assembly of the stars," among others,

suggesting possible assemblages of other deities. In the "assembly of El/the gods" it is clear that it is El who issues decrees affecting both divine and human realms.

The OT descriptions of the "divine assembly" all suggest that this metaphor for the organization of the divine world was consistent with that of Mesopotamia and Canaan. One difference, however, should be noted. In the OT, the identities of the members of the assembly are far more obscure than those found in other descriptions of these groups, as in their polytheistic environment Israelite writers sought to express both the uniqueness and the superiority of their God Yahweh. A brief consideration of the major descriptions of the council will demonstrate these similarities and differences.

Two prophetic texts present visions of the heavenly assembly. The first is the vision of Micaiah (1 Kgs 22:19-23). Micaiah describes his vision of Yahweh, seated on his heavenly throne, surrounded by the "host of heaven" (*see* HOSTS, HOST OF HEAVEN). Yahweh challenges this "host" with a task, which they debate, until one of them, a "spirit," volunteers to fulfill the challenge. Upon hearing the plan, Yahweh commissions the "spirit" to proceed, assuring its success. Isaiah 6:1-9 provides the account of Isaiah's vision of Yahweh in the heavenly council. Isaiah has his vision in the Temple, where Yahweh appears enthroned, accompanied by creatures designated as "seraphim" (*see* SERAPH, SERAPHS), who are praising Yahweh (*see* Ps 29:1-2). After having been purified by one of these creatures, Isaiah hears Yahweh's challenge to his retinue. Isaiah himself volunteers and receives Yahweh's commission. The prophet, it would seem, could be understood as the messenger of the heavenly assembly who brought Yahweh's proclamations to the human realm (*see* Jer 23:18, 22; Amos 3:7; Hag 1:13; Mal 3:1).

Another view of the divine assembly is presented in Job 1–2, when "the sons of god" (bene ha'elohim בְּנֵי הָאֱלֹהִים; *see* GOD, SONS OF) present themselves before Yahweh on the appointed day (1:6; 2:1). Among those assembled deities was one designated "the adversary" (hassatan הַשָּׂטָן; *see* SATAN), as indicated by the consistent use of the term with the definite article (see Zech 3). Only "the adversary," whose role it was to patrol the earth, is active among the members of Yahweh's council. In both meetings of the council, Yahweh gives "the adversary" the power to test Job, but not to kill him. "The adversary" develops into a demonic figure opposed to Yahweh late in the biblical period.

Yahweh's power over the members of the assembly is illustrated in Ps 82. Here Yahweh takes his place in the "assembly of El" ('adhath-'el עֲדַת־אֵל; NRSV "divine council"), in the midst of the other gods, and passes judgment on the members of the council, designated as "gods" ('elohim), "sons of Elyon" (Hebrew, bene ʿelyon [בְּנֵי עֶלְיוֹן]; NRSV "children of the Most High"; *see* EL ELYON). For their failure to dispense justice properly, they are condemned to death. Clearly Yahweh has no equal in the assembly. Two additional references in the Psalms attest to the incomparable nature of Yahweh. In Ps 29:1-2 the "sons of the gods" (bene ʾelim [בְּנֵי אֵלִים]; NRSV "heavenly beings") ascribe glory and strength to Yahweh as they bow down to him in worship. Similarly, in Ps 89:6-7, "the council of the holy ones" (qahal qedhoshim [קְהַל קְדֹשִׁים]), equated with the "sons of the gods" (NRSV "heavenly beings") emphasizes that none of the divine beings can compare to Yahweh.

While the depictions of the divine council in the OT may not be as explicit as those found in Mesopotamian or Canaanite literature, they do demonstrate that this motif had an important place in the religious worldview of ancient Israel. Not only did it provide expression for the incomparable nature of Yahweh among other divine beings, it also expressed the special nature of the prophetic word as a communication brought into the human realm by the "messenger" of Yahweh's council (*see* GOD, OT VIEW OF).

Bibliography: F. M. Cross. "The Council of Yahweh in Second Isaiah." *JNES* 12 (1953) 274–77; Lowell K. Handy. *Among the Host of Heaven: The Syro-Palestinian Pantheon as Bureaucracy* (1994); E. Theodore Mullen Jr. *The Divine Council in Canaanite and Early Hebrew Literature* (1980); H. W. Robinson. "The Council of Yahweh." *JTS* 45 (1944) 151–57; Mark S. Smith. *The Origins of Biblical Monotheism: Israel's Polytheistic Background and the Ugaritic Texts* (2001).

E. THEODORE MULLEN, JR.

DIVINE COUNSEL. *See* COUNSEL, COUNSELOR.

DIVINE MAN [θεῖος ἀνήρ theios anēr]. "Divine man" refers to a Hellenistic conception, or type, that has been used to explain the origin and meaning of certain phenomena in so-called Hellenistic Judaism and in early Christianity. Although precise definitions vary, "divine man" usually denotes a human, gifted with wisdom and supernatural powers, who is therefore regarded as divine. Representatives of this category include Epimenides, Pythagoras, Empedocles, Alexander of Abonuteichos, Peregrinus, and Apollonius of Tyana.

Working with a distinction between Palestinian Judaism and Hellenistic Judaism, some scholars argued that even before the appearance of Christianity, the "divine man" conception led principal exemplars of Hellenistic Judaism, such as Artapanus, Ezekiel the Tragedian, and Philo, to portray Israelite heroes. This was accomplished by heightening the supernatural accomplishments of these heroes and by blurring the line between their humanity and the divine nature. Moses especially emerges as a divine person.

A considerable body of 20th cent. scholarship, therefore, held that the "divine man" concept began to influence early Christians' portrayal of Jesus as soon as there was a significant influx of Hellenistic Jews into the church. One result was that Jesus' miracles were disengaged from his proclamation of the kingdom of God and were narrated in such a way to emphasize the divine power that they disclosed. Some scholars argued that tales of Jesus' miracles were collected into written catenae, or "chains," which were later incorporated into the Gospel of Mark. Moreover, in some of these miracle stories and traditions, belief in Jesus' divine nature seems to express itself (e.g., in Mark 6:45-52 Jesus' walk across the sea reads like an epiphany of Yahweh).

The "divine man" hypothesis has influenced NT scholarship in two other ways. One pertains to the question of the gospel genre. A collateral aspect of the "divine man" hypothesis has been the notion that written propaganda for a "divine man," which would include a recitation of his supernatural feats, took the form of a glorifying narrative, or aretalogy. Thus, some have argued that the Gospels, especially Mark, are essentially aretalogies for Jesus, the "divine man." On a different front, D. Georgi attempted to illumine the activities of the Jewish-Christian opponents of Paul in 2 Cor 10–13 by positing that they understood themselves to be divine men.

Recent NT study has raised serious questions about the relevance of the "divine man" concept to the NT. Although some scholars continue to defend the existence of the type in the Greco-Roman world and utilize it to elucidate the origin and meaning of the christology of the Gospels, as well as the form of the Gospels themselves, most either doubt the existence of "divine man" type in the pre-Christian Greco-Roman world or argue for various reasons that this conception is not a useful analytic tool for studying early Christianity and its literature.

Bibliography: Hans Dieter Betz. "Jesus as Divine Man." *Jesus and the Historian*, F. Trotter, ed. (1968) 114–33; Barry L. Blackburn. *Theios Aner and the Markan Miracle Traditions* (1991); Gail P. Corrington. *The "Divine Man": His Origin and Function in Hellenistic Popular Religion* (1986); Eugene Gallagher. *Divine Man or Magician? Celsus and Origen on Jesus* (1982); Dieter Georgi. *The Opponents of Paul in Second Corinthians* (1999); Carl Holladay. *Theios Aner in Hellenistic-Judaism* (1977); Erkki Koskenniemi. "Apollonius of Tyana: A Typical *Theios Aner* [Divine Man]." *JBL* 117 (1998) 455–67.

BARRY L. BLACKBURN, SR.

DIVINE NAME. *See* GOD, NAMES OF.

DIVINE PRESENCE. There is no abstraction in the biblical languages that exactly corresponds to the English word *presence.* The term most often translated by the English word is an idiomatic use of the word *face*. God may dwell, go, or be with or in the midst of those to whom he is present. *Name* and *glory* are also used to indicate the divine presence. A remarkable variety of terms is thus involved in the study of this subject.

A. God in Our Midst
B. Divine Presence in Exodus
C. The Glory of the Lord
D. Ark, Tent of Meeting, Tabernacle, and Temple
E. Name and Face as Ways of Speaking of Presence
F. "I Will Be with You"
G. The Presence of the Holy Spirit

A. God in Our Midst

During the preexilic period it is likely that every Israelite community had a sanctuary, a place believed to be holy because God was present in their midst. Although the OT writers tended to suppress much of that local worship, one sanctuary legend plays a prominent role in Genesis. It attributes the identification of Bethel as a holy place to Jacob (Gen 28:10-22). His dream taught him that "this is none other than the house of God" (28:17). The eventual triumph of the claim that there was only one legitimate place for the offering of sacrifice to Yahweh—Jerusalem—must have been hard won, for in denying the holiness of the local sanctuaries it must have challenged a profound need to know that God was very near.

B. Divine Presence in Exodus

The book of Exodus speaks of the presence of God in a remarkable number of ways. When Moses encountered God at a holy place, the first evidence of God's presence was visual, the burning bush, and fire is elsewhere associated with appearances of God on earth (Exod 3:2-6). A more enduring and significant way to refer to the divine presence appears a few verses later. When Moses protested God's commission to bring the Israelites out of Egypt, the response was, "I will be with you" (3:12), and this simple expression recurs throughout the Scriptures as a powerful promise, and in the form "God is with us" as an affirmation of hope.

Another visible indication of presence appeared as the people left Egypt, a pillar of cloud by day and of fire by night (Exod 13:21-22; 14:19; Num 14:14; Deut 1:33; etc.). Associated with the pillar of fire is the word *glory* (Exod 16:7, 10; 24:16-17; 29:43; 40:34-35), which here denotes something visual that accompanied God's appearance, a blinding light. So, the glory of the Lord which the people in Exod 16:7-10 saw in the cloud is evidently associated with the references to fire elsewhere. Cloud and fire were also part of the evidence that God was with them at Mount Sinai, with thunder and lighting, a trumpet blast, smoke, and earthquake (Exod 19:16-19).

Discussion of the presence of God in Scripture must also include the references to God's apparent absence, and this theme also appears in Exodus. After the sin of the golden calf, God informed Moses that the people were to continue to the promised land, but that he would not go with them, or "I would consume you on the way, for you are a stiff-necked people" (Exod 33:3).

In spite of God's warnings in 33:3, in 33:14 God says, "My presence [the idiomatic use of *face*] will go with you," and Exodus ends on that encouraging note. A group of visible symbols now appears: the ark of the covenant serves as a movable throne for God (Exod 25:10-22; 37:1-9); it is to be located in the tabernacle (Exod 26; 36), in and over which the presence of God is revealed by the cloud and the glory (Exod 40:34-38) which guided them through the wilderness.

Almost all of the OT's ways of referring to the divine presence thus appear in Exodus.

C. The Glory of the Lord

For the OT writers, ark, tent of meeting, tabernacle, and temple were places where the divine presence might be experienced, but *glory* was a positive, visible sign that God was indeed there. Most of the occurrences of the Hebrew kavodh (כָּבוֹד) and Greek doxa (δόξα) do not refer to anything visible and do not directly denote presence, so need not be discussed here, but *glory* as blinding light has a long history. In what appears to be a very old text, God's personal presence is indicated by a smoking fire pot and a flaming torch (Gen 15:17). Uses of the term *glory* and of *fire* and *lightning* in Exodus have already been noted. Appearances of the glory of the Lord are also described in Lev 9:6, 23; Num 14:10; 16:19, 42; 20:6, all associated with the tabernacle. God's presence in a new place, Jerusalem, was assured by the appearance of the glory that filled the Temple when Solomon dedicated it (1 Kgs 8:11; 2 Chr 5:14; 7:1-3).

The glory of the Lord appeared to Ezekiel in visions that he saw in exile in Babylonia, evidence to him that God's presence was not tied to Jerusalem (Ezek 1:28; 3:12, 23); and that was confirmed when in another vision the glory leaving the Temple and the city (Ezek 10:4, 18-19; 11:23) became a sign of God's absence. In Ezekiel's vision of a new Temple the glory appeared again as an assurance of hope for the future, when God would once again be present in Jerusalem (Ezek 43:4, 5; 44:4; compare Isa 4:5; 24:23).

The blinding light reappears a few times in the New Testament. The glory of the Lord shone around the shepherds when the angel appeared to announce Jesus' birth (Luke 2:9). Luke also uses glory to refer to the disciples' vision of Jesus' transfiguration (Luke 9:31-32). Without using the word *glory*, Paul spoke of the appearance of Christ to him as marked by a blinding light (Acts 22:6, 9, 11). John spoke of the divine presence in Jesus as seeing his glory (John 1:14), but here light is used metaphorically rather than in a physical sense (John 1:3-4, 7-9). Hebrews uses the term in a similar way: "He is the reflection of God's glory" (Heb 1:3). Usually, the NT use of glory does not point strongly toward presence.

D. Ark, Tent of Meeting, Tabernacle, and Temple

The OT authors used materials set in the wilderness era as a way of authenticating Jerusalem as the place where Yahweh's presence could be found. The series of visible indicators of the divine presence that led to Jerusalem may be said to begin with the ARK OF THE COVENANT (Exod 25:10-22; 37:1-9; Num 10:35-36). Israel learned a hard lesson about the freedom of God (the absence theme) when they took the ark into battle against the Philistines, assuming that God would necessarily be with them (1 Sam 4:3-9). But Israel was defeated and the ark itself captured. David transferred the ark to Jerusalem (2 Sam 6) and Solomon eventually installed it into the holy of holies of the Temple (1 Kgs 8:1-9). From that time on the ark seems to have become less significant than the Temple as a symbol of God's presence, so that Jeremiah could virtually dismiss it in the last reference to it in the Bible (Jer 3:16-17).

According to Exod 33:7-11 a tent of meeting was in use in the wilderness before the tabernacle was built. From time to time the Lord would appear there in the cloud, and there God spoke to Moses face to face. This may very well reflect the use of a movable sanctuary that was in existence at a very early period. The elaborate TABERNACLE with all its appurtenances, which is described twice, in Exod 25–31 and 35–40, seems likely to be a projection back into the wilderness period of the main features of the Jerusalem Temple. Tabernacle and tent of meeting are equated in Exod 40 and elsewhere (compare Num 3:38). It was the cloud within which the glory of the Lord appeared that was the evidence of God's presence, however, not the tent or tabernacle itself, according to Exod 40:34-38.

Solomon could move the ark into his new Temple of his own volition, but it was the appearance of that same cloud that validated his action (1 Kgs 8:10-13). He called the Temple "a place for you to dwell in forever" (v. 13); that this restricted God's freedom too much was acknowledged immediately afterward in his prayer: "But will God indeed dwell on earth? Even heaven and the highest heaven cannot contain you, much less this house that I have built!" (1 Kgs 8:27; *see* TEMPLE OF SOLOMON).

In spite of the destruction of Solomon's Temple in 587 BCE, hope for the future continued to focus on Jerusalem, and Ezekiel's vision of a new Temple contained reassurances concerning God's presence in the return of the glory (44:4) and in the new name that was to be given to the city: "Yahweh is there" (48:35).

In the NT, Jesus' words to the Samaritan woman spoke of a new means of access to God apart from holy places: "Woman, believe me, the hour is coming when you will worship the Father neither on this mountain [Gerizim; the Samaritans' holy place] nor in Jerusalem. . . . But the hour is coming and is now here, when the true worshipers will worship the Father in spirit and truth" (John 4:21, 23). John's choice of the Greek word meaning "tabernacled" to speak of the Incarnation emphasized that Jesus himself was now the evidence of God's presence: "And the Word became flesh and lived [tabernacled] among us" (John 1:14). The Christian conviction that God himself dwelled among them with the presence of the risen Christ was expressed with reference to the temple in Revelation's description of the New Jerusalem: "And I saw no temple in the city, for its temple is the Lord God the Almighty and the Lamb" (Rev 21:22).

E. Name and Face as Ways of Speaking of Presence

Except for the Temple as a sign of God's presence, which proved not to be as certain as many had thought, the visual signs recorded in the OT are mostly confined to records of the wilderness period, with occasional echoes in the poetry of Psalms and the prophets. Most of the OT speaks of God's presence in other ways. In 1 Kgs 8:10 the cloud fills the house of the Lord, but after that Solomon speaks of "a house for the name of the Lord" (8:16-20, 29; 11:36). In 1 Kgs 9:3 God tells Solomon that his name will dwell there forever and his heart for all time. This is the language of presence that is typical of Deuteronomy. Numerous times Moses speaks of God choosing a place "as his habitation to put his name there" (Deut 12:5), or as a dwelling for his name (12:11; 14:23; 16:2; etc.).

Studies of God's revelation of the divine name to Moses in Exod 3, and of the many references to the name of the Lord in the OT have led to the conclusion that *name* represents what human beings can know of God's character, of ways they can experience God, and the sense of God's real presence on earth. When Deuteronomy speaks of God placing his name, or making it to dwell in the place he chooses (e.g., Deut 12:5, 11), it thus offers the assurance that there is a place where God's presence can really be experienced, but it preserves the necessary distance between humanity and the fullness of divinity.

The Hebrew word panim (פָּנִים), in addition to its literal meaning *face* is used in a great variety of ways that have little or no relationship to the literal sense. Several of them are important ways of referring to the presence of God in a non-visual way. The prepositional phrase lifne (לִפְנֵי) literally "to the face of," really means "in front of, in the presence of." That idiom very likely helps to account for the use of panim to refer to God's presence in passages where any notion that God has a physical face is surely absent. So Cain went out from lifne Yahweh (Gen 4:16), and Adam and Eve hid themselves from pene (פְּנֵי) Yahweh (Gen

3:8). Yahweh promised Moses that his **panim** would go with the people when they left Sinai (Exod 33:14). These occurrences and many others are properly translated *presence*, not *face*. In the difficult passage, Exod 33:20-23, *face* and *back* are best taken to represent presence and the essential difference between God and humanity, rather than anything visual.

In spite of the warning in Exod 33:23 concerning coming too near the presence of God, some of the Psalms do speak of seeing God's face (Pss 11:7; 17:15; 42:2). Several kinds of visual experiences have been suggested to account for these passages, but it may be best to take them as just another idiomatic use of **panim** to represent presence. The hiding of God's face was thus one of the vivid ways the OT writers spoke of their sense of the absence of God (e.g., Pss 13:1; 27:9; 44:24), along with words for distance, forgetting, not seeing, and not hearing.

The NT uses the word *face* (prosōpon πρόσωπον) a few times to denote the presence of God, and it is so translated in Acts 3:20; 2 Thess 1:9; and Heb 9:24. In Rev 22:4 the servants of God will "see his face" in the New Jerusalem, echoing the language of worship that appears in the Psalms. Ordinarily, however, the NT speaks of the divine presence in other ways.

F. "I Will Be with You"

One of the most frequently appearing divine promises in the Bible is "I will be with you." To be "with" occurs in direct promises from God (e.g., Exod 3:12; Judg 6:12, 16; Isa 41:10; Jer 1:8; Acts 18:9-10), in human statements of assurance or confidence (e.g., 2 Sam 7:3; Ps 139:18; 2 Cor 13:11), and in conclusions drawn by narrators (e.g., Gen 39:2; 2 Kgs 18:7). The preposition *with* alludes to a God who is distinct from humans, yet who is near and is active on behalf of humans even when they may not realize it.

The usual OT setting for this expression of assurance is a situation of danger, or at least of risk, an uncertain future. Thus it is often paired with "Fear not" (e.g., Josh 1:9; Isa 43:5). The promise was offered to ordinary Israelites and to Israel as a whole in times of need: "Even though I walk through the darkest valley, I fear no evil, for you are with me" (Ps 23:4); "The Lord of hosts is with us; the God of Jacob is our refuge" (Ps 46:7, 11). The background of danger is clearly present in Isaiah's special use of the promise as a proper name Immanuel (Isa 7:14; 8:8; evidently not a name in 8:10). Throughout the OT, then, the statement affirmed God's powerful presence in times of need.

Matthew spoke of another kind of need: "you are to name him Jesus, for he will save his people from their sins" (Matt 1:21), but he also referred to another name, Immanuel, since it was a key to Matthew's theology. He quoted Isa 7:14 and took care to translate the name for his readers: "which means, 'God is with us'" (Matt 1:23). The old promise had new meaning for Matthew, for he claimed that God had now become present in the person of Jesus.

New Testament authors use the expression in its OT sense with reference to God being with Jesus, in John 3:2; 8:29; 16:23; Acts 10:38; and in Revelation's reiteration of the prophets' promise for the future: "God himself will be with them" (Rev 21:3; compare Isa 45:14; Jer 46:28; Ezek 34:30; Zech 8:23). The radically new thing was the claim that Jesus was God with us. Having begun his Gospel with that claim, Matthew's conclusion is thus a powerful promise, "And remember, I am with you always, to the end of the age" (Matt 28:20).

G. The Presence of the Holy Spirit

Unlike the OT, the NT uses "The Lord be with you" and variations as a general blessing, without specific reference to precarious situations (Rom 15:33; 2 Cor 13:11; Phil 4:9; 2 Thess 3:16; 2 Tim 4:22). This sense of God's continuing presence with all believers may have been based in part on Jesus' promise in Matt 28, but must also have had much to do with the experience of the presence of the Holy Spirit in their midst. John records Jesus as having said, "And I will ask the Father, and he will give you another Advocate, to be with you forever. This is the Spirit of truth . . ." (John 14:16-17; *see* PARACLETE). Although the disciples would no longer experience God's presence with them in Jesus' physical presence, they would experience it in a new way (compare John 14:25-26). They must have interpreted Jesus' promise, "For where two or three are gathered in my name, I am there among them" (Matt 18:20), with reference to the work of the HOLY SPIRIT in the church. The divine presence is referred to in terms of the Spirit in several different ways. In 1 Pet 4:14 the promise is, "If you are reviled for the name of Christ, you are blessed, because the spirit of glory, which is the Spirit of God, is resting upon you." In 1 John 3:24 the expression is, "And by this we know that he abides in us, by the Spirit that he has given us." Paul preferred to speak of the Spirit dwelling in believers (1 Cor 3:16; 6:19), or of being in the Spirit (Rom 8:9; see his frequent uses of "in Christ"). Christ and Spirit are explicitly associated in Gal 4:6: "And because you are children, God has sent the Spirit of his Son into our hearts, crying 'Abba! Father!'" *See* GLORY, GLORIFY; GOD, NT VIEW OF; GOD, OT VIEW OF; IMMANUEL; NAME, NAMING; SPIRIT; TEMPLE, JERUSALEM.

Bibliography: Pierre Benoit, Roland Murphy, and Bastiaan van Iersel, eds. *The Presence of God.* Concilium 50 (1969).

DONALD E. GOWAN

DIVINE WARRIOR. *See* WARRIOR, DIVINE.

DIVINER'S OAK [אֵלוֹן מְעוֹנְנִים ʾelon meʿonenim]. A place near SHECHEM (Judg 9:37) given as a reference point in Gaal's description of the location of Abimelech's troops. This oak was possibly a TEREBINTH, or sacred tree, perhaps the same oak mentioned in Judg 9:6. Other oak trees are also mentioned in relation to religious practice (Gen 13:8; 35:4; Josh 24:26), although the association with DIVINATION is shared only by Hosea (4:12-13).

JESSICA TINKLENBERG DEVEGA

DIVINITY OF CHRIST. Despite the overwhelming affirmation of Christ's divinity in the history of the church, there are surprisingly only three places in the NT where Jesus is quite unequivocally called "God." All are in John's Gospel. In its opening (John 1:1), Jesus is described as the pre-existent logos (λόγος)/"Word" who was ever with, and was himself also, "God." At the end of the prologue, in 1:18, he is remarkably referred to as the "only-begotten God." Then, near the Gospel's closure, Thomas addresses Jesus as "my Lord, and my God" (20:28). Beyond that, there are texts where the ascription "God" to Jesus is likely, if disputed (Rom 9:5; Titus 2:13; Heb 1:8).

Since the late 19th cent., it has been common to affirm that the cultic worship of Jesus as divine could not have developed within the rigidly monotheistic early Jewish Christianity, but only first grew in Hellenistic circles, especially under the influence of Gentile polytheistic cults of demigods and divinized heroes.

This has been shown to be mistaken, however. The "binitarian" shape of Christian worship was already well fledged in the earliest Jewish (and Gentile) monotheistic Pauline communities. That is, such worship was already established in groups many of whose members daily recited the SHEMA ("The LORD is our God, the LORD alone. You shall love the LORD your God . . ." [Deut 6:4-5]), but willingly glossed this ardently monotheistic claim to include Jesus as the one "LORD" within the self-identity of the one God of Israel (1 Cor 8:4-6). The same churches apparently anticipated that, at the eschaton, worship would finally be offered to Jesus as "Lord" with and to God the Father, within the staunchly and uncompromisingly monotheistic vision of Isa 45 (Phil 2:9-10)—all this despite the fact that in Judaism absolutely none but Israel's God may be worshiped.

Throughout the early communities, veneration apparently included such acclamations as "Jesus is Lord!" (1 Cor 12:3); invocations such as the Aram. "maranatha" ("Lord, come!"; 1 Cor 16:22; Rev 22:17), and "hymns" celebrating Christ in the most exalted Jewish terms and/ or addressed to him (e.g., Phil 2:6-11; 2 Cor 1:3-4; Rom 1:3-4; 10:9-10; Col 1:15-20; Eph 1:3-14; 5:19, etc.). Regular meetings for worship were held on "the first day of the week" now known as "the Lord's (= Christ's) day" (Rev 1:10). Jewish-styled grace-benedictions were now regularly equally both theo- and christocentric (most notably 2 Cor 13:13[14], but see also Rom 1:7; 1 Cor 1:3; 2 Cor 1:3; Gal 1:3; Phil 1:3; 2 Thess 1:2) and prayer was "in Jesus' name," even to Jesus (see 1 Thess 3:11-13; 2 Thess 2:16-17; 3:5; 2 Cor 12:8-10; Acts 7:55-56). And, remarkably, both conversion and ongoing Christian life/prayer could be summed up as "calling on the name of the Lord Jesus" (Rom 10:12-17; 1 Cor 1:2; Acts 9:14, 21; 15:17; 22:16, etc.)—a practice based on OT cultic invocation of *God* (as LORD alone), e.g., for saving intervention in Pss 99:6; 116:4; Joel 2:32, etc. Jesus had come to be regarded as the ubiquitous divine presence of God himself. In short, authentic life and worship had come to be defined, as 1 John 1:3 most succinctly puts it, as "fellowship with the Father and with his Son Jesus Christ."

So it seems there was a remarkable explosive celebration of divine christology at the very beginnings of Christianity. How should it be explained? Undoubtedly, Jesus' own expressed "self-understanding" greatly contributed. His widespread claims to personify the inauguration of the kingdom of God (forgiveness of sin, healing liberation, restoration of Israel, etc.), and in some way to be "one with God"—including "pre-existent oneness," according to the Fourth Gospel—gave considerable basis. But in his earthly life the claims were all somewhat ambiguous. However, the Christ-event, especially the resurrection, clarified and validated the claims, as far as believers were concerned. Most notably, it will have been the personal, communal, and daily experience of the risen Christ as "Lord of God's Spirit"—the dynamically, actively, self-revealing and christocentrically transforming and empowering presence of Christ—that most persuasively invited worship of him as God. After all, who but God could direct his own Spirit? *See* CHRISTOLOGY; JESUS CHRIST.

Bibliography: Richard Bauckham. *God Crucified: Monotheism and Christology in the New Testament* (1998); J. D. G. Dunn. *Christology in the Making* (1980); Mehrdad Fatehi. *The Spirit's Relation to the Risen Lord in Paul: An Examination of Its Christological Implications* (2000); Larry W. Hurtado. *Lord Jesus Christ: Devotion to Jesus in Earliest Christianity* (2003); Max Turner. "The Spirit of Christ and 'Divine' Christology." *Jesus of Nazareth: Lord and Christ: Essays on the Historical Jesus and New Testament Christology.* Joel B. Green and Max Turner, eds. (1994) 413–436.

MAX TURNER

DIVORCE [גָּרַשׁ garash, שָׁלַח shalakh; ἀφίημι aphiēmi, χωρίζω chōrizō,].

  A. Old Testament
    1. Priestly texts and Ezekiel
    2. Deuteronomic law code
    3. Prophetic texts
    4. Other

B. New Testament
1. Paul
2. Gospels
Bibliography

A. Old Testament

Two terms are used for divorce: **shalakh** in the Deuteronomic corpus, Jeremiah, Isaiah, and Malachi, and **garash** in the priestly texts and Ezekiel. Ezra 10:3 uses a different word, from the root yatsaʾ (יְצָא) to go together with badhal (בָּדַל), to separate, in v. 11, to dictate a permanent separation from foreign peoples and foreign wives.

1. Priestly texts and Ezekiel

Lev 21:7, 14; 22:13, from the Holiness Code, and Ezek 44:22 prohibit priests from marrying a divorced woman (gerushah גְּרוּשָׁה). The latter three texts pair the **gerushah** with the widow (ʾalmanah אַלְמָנָה); two add the category of prostitute (zonah זוֹנָה). Numbers 30:9 [Heb. 30:10], part of a larger text discussing the circumstances in which women are responsible for vows they have made, uses the same pairing, stating that both the widow and the divorced woman must fulfill their vows; in both cases, there is no male head of household to have jurisdiction over whether her vows can be fulfilled. **Gerushah**, like ʾalmanah, may be a technical term in writings linked with priests.

2. Deuteronomic law code

The remainder of the texts explicitly dealing with divorce in the OT use the term **shalakh**, meaning "to send away." Deuteronomy 21:14 deals with provisions for a man to marry a woman taken captive in war. If the man is not satisfied with her, he is to divorce her and set her free; he is not to sell her for money or treat her as a slave. Deuteronomy 22:19 and 22:29 deal with cases in which a man may never divorce his wife. In each case, the aggrieved party is the father of the "young woman" (Deut 22:19, 28-29), to whom the man must pay a fine. These laws may also protect the woman, who would otherwise be ineligible to marry another man.

Deuteronomy 24:1-4 address the situation of a man divorcing his wife, and then wishing to remarry her after she has married (and been divorced or widowed by) another man: the first husband is prohibited from doing so. The argument against such remarriage suggests that remarriage of one's first wife is analogous to ADULTERY. Here the divorce procedure is composed of three actions: the man gives the certificate of divorce to his wife, hands it to her, and then sends her away from his house (Deut 24:1, 3). The grounds for divorce in v. 1 are ʿerwath davar (עֶרְוַת דָּבָר), lit. "nakedness of a thing." The meaning of these words is hotly debated, the more so because this law became the basis for rabbinical law regarding divorce, and the

words are cited by Jesus in some of the Gospel texts on divorce (see below).

3. Prophetic texts

Jeremiah 3:1 cites the law described in Deut 24:1-4, and uses it metaphorically to accuse Judah of adultery. Jeremiah 3:6-11 depicts Judah and Israel as two sisters whom Yahweh married. In Jer 3:8, God, the metaphorical husband, divorced his wife Israel by sending her away and giving her a certificate of divorce. Here divorce is a metaphor for exile. In Jer 3:12-13, God overturns the law, taking Israel back under certain conditions. In Jer 3:14–4:4, the people of Judah are encouraged to repent and change their ways so they themselves will not be divorced (exiled) by God. Isaiah 50:1 picks up this metaphor: "Where is your mother's bill of divorce with which I put her away?" The reason given for her divorce is her sins. Isaiah 54:5-8 makes a move similar to Jeremiah, with God, the metaphorical husband, taking Judah back.

4. Other

It is debated whether Exod 21:10-11 deals with divorce. As part of the covenant law code, this law deals with the rights of a first wife if the husband takes a second wife. If he does not provide for her equally, then "she shall go out" (yatsʾah יָצְאָה) without debt or paying money.

The OT texts dealing with divorce are written exclusively with the men as agents and the women as objects of divorce: men are either the initiators of divorce or are prohibited from divorcing women. These texts assume that women can marry after having been divorced, although in the later texts, priests are prohibited from being joined in marriage to divorced women. The OT is silent regarding whether a wife can initiate divorce, although from Exod 21:10-11 it could be argued that a wife could divorce her husband under certain circumstances. One final text unequivocally views divorce unfavorably: Mal 2:16 says that Yahweh hates divorce. Verses 13-15 exhort men to remain with the wife of their youth, and imply that to do otherwise constitutes faithlessness both to her and to Yahweh. Together these texts give us a glimpse into what the law was on divorce, but it is full of gaps. The OT texts do not tell us how prevalent divorce was, or what the grounds for a man's divorce of his wife might be (other than the contested ʿerwath davar of Deut 24:1), e.g. The Exodus (Covenant), Deuteronomic, and Levitical (Holiness) codes also represent different time frames and thus may not speak uniformly about actual divorce practices.

The ANE context does not help us much here either. The Code of Hammurabi provides for a woman to initiate divorce, and requires that the husband return her marriage portion to her upon divorce. We do not know if those practices carried over into ancient

Israel, although we have evidence from Egypt of Jewish women initiating divorce in the Second Temple period.

In the Greco-Roman period, a Jewish divorce agreement from Egypt in 13 BCE provided for the return of the woman's dowry, and allowed for both parties to marry another. It also appears that in this period Jewish regulations for divorce were stricter than Roman practices. Both the Gospels and the rabbinic texts adhere to a restrictive view of divorce in keeping with earlier OT passages.

B. New Testament

Scholars debate every aspect of NT teachings on divorce, ranging from the terminology, to the content of the teachings, to dating, to redaction, to how to interpret the teachings themselves.

1. Paul

The earliest writing dealing with divorce is 1 Cor 7:10-16, part of a larger text on sexual morality (vv. 1-24). Two terms are used for divorce, chōrizo and aphiēmi, both of which are contested as to translation, but are technical terms for divorce in the Hellenistic world. Paul's teaching begins with an appeal to the authority of Jesus to tell the community that neither female nor male Christians should divorce. From this foundation he deals with three situations. The first deals with the woman who is already divorced, in which case Paul tells her to be reconciled with her husband, or, if that is impossible, to remain unmarried. Lest men think this is license for them to divorce, Paul addresses men next: a man ought not to divorce his wife. The final case deals with believers married to unbelievers. In this instance, Paul tells the believer not to divorce the unbeliever; however, if the unbeliever wishes to be divorced, then it is better to let the unbeliever go free for the sake of peace. The first two situations are given as Jesus' command, while the latter case is stated as Paul's own authoritative interpretation of the law.

2. Gospels

The Gospel discussions of divorce are filled with textual, redactional, and interpretational difficulties. The one thing on which all agree is that Jesus spoke against divorce.

Jesus' sayings on divorce appear only in the Synoptic Gospels. Behind these texts lie the 1st cent. CE rabbinic debate between the schools of Hillel and Shammai (see HILLEL THE ELDER, HOUSE OF HILLEL; SHAMMAI THE ELDER). The basic disagreement is on how to read the grounds for divorce given in Deut 24:1-4, ʿerwath davar (lit., "nakedness of a thing"). The school of Shammai was stricter, focusing on "nakedness," saying that the only ground for divorce was unchastity, thus reading the disputed phrase as dealing with sexual

misconduct. In contrast, the school of Hillel's reading of the expression focused on "thing," leading to a much broader interpretation: there was no limit to the grounds on which a man could divorce his wife, "even if she burned a dish." Jesus' teaching must be read in light of this debate (see LAW IN EARLY JUDAISM; LAW IN THE NT).

Jesus' teaching in Mark occurs in a debate with the Pharisees followed by instruction to the disciples. In Mark 10:2-12 the term used for divorce is apoluō (ἀπολύω). The Pharisees state that the Mosaic law allowed a man to divorce his wife. Jesus then uses a conflation of Gen 1:27 and Gen 2:24 to argue that God never intended for divorce, but that the commandment was given due to their "hardness of heart." Following this encounter, Jesus says privately to his disciples that if either a man or woman divorces his or her spouse and marries another, he or she commits adultery.

The Gospel of Matthew includes three references to the practice of divorce, beginning with a case of divorce on the basis of unchastity in the story of Joseph. Mary, his betrothed, becomes pregnant, an apparent case of unchastity. Joseph resolves to divorce her, but changes his mind when angel explains the circumstances of her pregnancy (Matt 2:18-20). This story also illustrates that betrothal was a legally binding contract that could be broken only by divorce (see BETROTHAL; BRIDE; BRIDEGROOM).

Matthew 5:31-32 cites a law that allows a man to divorce his wife by giving her a certificate of divorce (presumably a reference to Deut 24:1-4). Jesus then makes the law more stringent, saying that divorce, except on the grounds of unchastity, causes the woman to commit adultery, and, further, any man marrying a divorced woman commits adultery. Causing the woman to commit adultery presumably refers to her marrying another man after she has been divorced.

Matthew 19 likewise adds a clause specifying an exception on the grounds of unchastity (compare Matt 5:32), a clause that is not found in Mark. Here the Pharisees begin by asking Jesus about divorce from the perspective of the school of Hillel: "Is it lawful for a man to divorce his wife for any cause?" Jesus responds with a question of his own that cites the conflation of Gen 1:27 and 2:24 (that Mark also uses). He ends by drawing the same conclusion as Mark: "What God has joined together, let no one separate." The Pharisees respond with another question alluding to the text of Deut 24: "Why then did Moses command us to give a certificate of dismissal and to divorce her?" Jesus' answer is similar to Mark's rendering, saying that Moses allowed them to divorce their wives due to their hardness of heart, "but from the beginning it was not so" (v. 8). He ends with an echo of Matt 5:31-32: "And I say to you, whoever divorces his wife, except for unchastity, and marries another commits adultery."

Instead of setting Jesus' teaching on divorce in a debate between Jesus and the Pharisees, the Gospel of Luke (16:18) provides a one-verse teaching on divorce as an illustration of his assertion to the Pharisees that "it is easier for heaven and earth to pass away, than for one stroke of a letter in the law to be dropped" (v. 17). The teaching is stark, and focuses exclusively on the man: "Anyone who divorces his wife and marries another commits adultery, and whoever marries a woman divorced from her husband commits adultery." No mention is made of divorce causing the woman to commit adultery; neither is there the exception clause granting divorce in the case of the woman's unchastity; nor is there any mention of the creation texts as grounds for Jesus' interpretation of the law.

The differences among the synoptic renderings of Jesus' teachings on divorce have given rise to debates regarding which is closest to the actual teaching of Jesus. One conclusion that is inescapable, however, is that the tradition regarding Jesus' teaching on divorce was restrictive rather than expansive, and portrayed Jesus as being opposed to divorce in general, although the Gospel writers disagreed on whether divorce was allowed in certain circumstances.

Matthew and Luke see men as the agents of divorce; Mark, however, seems to suggest that women sometimes divorced their husbands (Mark 10:12). Finally, the texts restrict remarriage for both women and men; in the Gospel texts, any remarriage is seen as adulterous, with the possible exception of the man who divorces his wife on the grounds of unchastity in Matt 19. *See* BABATHA; DIVORCE, CERTIFICATE OF; FAMILY; JEALOUSY, ORDEAL OF; MARRIAGE, NT; MARRIAGE, OT.

Bibliography: Raymond F. Collins. *Divorce in the New Testament* (1992); Louis M. Epstein. *Marriage Law in the Bible and the Talmud* (1942); Carolyn Pressler. *The View of Women Found in the Deuteronomic Family Laws* (1993); Mary E. Shields. *Circumscribing the Prostitute: The Rhetorics of Intertextuality, Metaphor, and Gender in Jeremiah 3:1–4:4* (2004).

MARY E. SHIELDS

DIVORCE, CERTIFICATE OF [כְּרִיתֻת סֵפֶר sefer kerithuth; βιβλίον ἀποστάσιον biblion apostasion]. According to the deuteronomic law code (Deut 24:1, 3), a husband "writes a certificate of DIVORCE, gives it into her hand, and sends her from his house." The content of the writ is not specified, although it possibly included the formula, "She is not my wife, and I am not her husband" (Hos 2:2 [Heb. 2:4]). In both testaments, the husband alone gives a certificate of divorce. It is not known if this was always the practice or required in all cases.

In the OT, God, the metaphorical husband, divorces his wife, Israel (representing the Northern Kingdom), and gives her a certificate of divorce (Jer 3:8; for God and Judah, see Isa 50:1 [Heb. 50:6]). Notably, both texts overturn the law as set forth in Deut 24 by picturing Yahweh as remarrying Israel/Judah (Jer 3:11-13; Isa 54:5-8).

The two NT references to a bill of divorce occur in conflict texts between Jesus and the Pharisees (Mark 10:4; Matt 19:7) and allude to Deut 24:1-4. Neither text gives the content of the certificate, but both suggest that giving the certificate was separate from the act of divorcing.

Bibliography: R. F. Collins. *Divorce in the New Testament* (1992); C. Pressler. *The View of Women Found in the Deuteronomic Family Laws* (1993).

MARY E. SHIELDS

DIZAHAB diz'uh-hab [דִּי זָהָב di zahav; Καταχρύσεα Katachrysea]. A place mentioned in Deut 1:1 in relation to the location from which Moses delivers his final address to the Israelites. It means "of gold," as in Dan 2:32. Dizahab's geographical location is unknown, although the literary context suggests a location in the Transjordan, in the ARABAH, or along the route from Horeb to Kadesh-Barnea. Present-day Dahab (on the Gulf of Aqaba in the Sinai) is one possibility.

DEREK E. WITTMAN

DO, TO SHOW AND TO [עָשָׂה 'asah; show: יָדַע yadha', נָגַד naghadh; ποιέω poieō, δείκνυμι deiknymi]. A number of Hebrew and Greek words are translated as "to do" and "to show," respectively. James emphasizes that actions demonstrate faith: "Show me your faith apart from your works, and I by my works will show you my faith" (Jas 2:18). Often, the deeds of God that have been shown to the people are reviewed as the basis for following the commandments (Exod 19:4; Deut 4:3; 29:2; Josh 23:3). In John's Gospel, it is works that the "Father" is doing that show Jesus' relationship to God (John 14).

Occasionally, God is said to show individuals what they are to do, as the people's appeal in Jer 42:3, "Let the LORD your God show us where we should go and what we should do." The conjoining of these words may also be a literary device foreshadowing a later scene or heightening suspense. So, in 1 Sam 10:8, Samuel tells Saul after anointing him to go down to Gilgal and wait for seven days "until I come to you and show you what you shall do," anticipating 13:8-15, where Saul prematurely offers a sacrifice on his own accord, an action that is viewed as a rebellion against God and eventually leads to his downfall. In contrast, Samuel obeys the Lord's instructions to invite Jesse to a sacrifice "and I will show you what you shall do" (1 Sam 16:3), which sets the scene for David's anointing as king. In both cases, God is portrayed as revealing specific instructions to particular characters.

HENRY W. MORISADA RIETZ

DOCETISM. Belief that Jesus Christ only seemed to be human, suffer, and die, from the Greek dokeō (δοκέω), "seem, appear." The first explicit mention of docetic christology is by Ignatius (ca. 110–15 CE), who opposes the claim that Christ "appeared to suffer" (Ign. *Trall.* 10:1; Ign. *Smyrn.* 2). The first identification of a docetist group is around 190 CE, when Serapion opposed the *Gospel of Peter* because it was altered by those "whom we call Docetists" (Eusebius, *Hist. eccl.* 6.12). Docetism rests on a dualism between matter and spirit, a belief fully developed in Gnosticism. First John 4:2 and (less likely) the Gospel of John (e.g., 1:14) may oppose docetic tendencies.

ROBERT E. VAN VOORST

DOCTOR. See PHYSICIAN.

DOCTRINE. *See* BIBLICAL THEOLOGY; CHURCH, LIFE AND ORGANIZATION OF; LIBERATION THE-OLOGY; SACRAMENTAL THEOLOGY; SYSTEMATIC THEOLOGY; TEACHING IN THE EARLY CHURCH; TEACHING OF JESUS; THEOLOGY, NT; THEOLOGY, OT.

DOCUMENTARY HYPOTHESIS. The Documentary Hypothesis is a theory developed by scholars to explain the formation of the Pentateuch by arguing that behind the present text there were written documents that were edited together over the course of centuries. The origin of the Documentary Hypothesis is traced back to in the 17th cent., when Jean Astruc divided the biblical text on the basis of different ways of designating God (Elohim and Yahweh) and posited two sources for the book of Genesis. By paying close attention to literary features (such as repetitions and duplications, inconsistencies and contradictions, differences in vocabulary, style, and perspective), subsequent scholars built upon Astruc's work, and by the early 20th cent. there was a consensus among scholars that the PENTATEUCH (and possibly the

HEXATEUCH) resulted from the editing of four sources: the Yahwist (J), the Elohist (E), the Deuteronomist (D), and the Priestly author (P). This form of the Documentary Hypothesis, more accurately called the Newer Documentary Hypothesis, was articulated and defended by Julius Wellhausen at the end of the 19th cent. and has dominated biblical scholarship in the 20th cent.

According to this hypothesis, the Yahwist can be distinguished by the use of the name Yahweh from the beginning of the narrative, by the colorful folkloric style, and by the anthropomorphic presentation of God. The Yahwist supplies the basic narrative of Genesis, Exodus, and Numbers; thematically the work follows a pattern of promise and fulfillment (*see* J, YAHWIST; TETRAGRAMMATON).

The Elohist was initially distinguished by the use of the name Elohim for God. The Elohist's narratives have a greater moral tone than those of the Yahwist and avoid anthropomorphisms by the use of angels and dreams as a means of divine communication. E is not found in the opening chapters of Genesis, but makes its first appearance in the patriarchal stories. Having been combined with the Yahwist after the fall of the Northern Kingdom in 721 BCE, the Elohist is the most fragmentary of the sources (*see* E, ELOHIST).

The Deuteronomic source (D) is primarily, but not exclusively, identified with the law code of Deut 12–26. The Deuteronomic source has a distinctive sermonic style and stereotypical vocabulary. Its characteristic theology is that obedience to the law brings reward and disobedience results in adversity (*see* D, DEUTERONOMIC, DEUTERONOMISTIC; DEUTER-ONOMISTIC HISTORY).

The Priestly writings are characterized by an interest in priesthood and cult, ritual, and laws. Most of the genealogies and chronological details throughout the Pentateuch stem from priestly authorship as well as many of the laws found in Exodus, Leviticus, and Numbers. The style is often dry and repetitive; P is the

DOCUMENTARY HYPOTHESIS		
Source	Approximate Date	Characteristics
J Yahwistic	10th cent. BCE	Use of name Yahweh for God; Promise and fulfillment; Anthropomorphic presentation of God
E Elohistic	9th cent. BCE	Use of name Elohim for God; Use of angels and dreams instead of anthropomorphic presentation of God
D Deuteronomic	7th cent. BCE	Obedience to the law brings reward; Disobedience results in adversity; Centralization of worship
P Priestly	6th cent. BCE	Interest in priesthood and cult, ritual, and laws; The least anthropomorphic presentation of God; Unconditional, eternal covenant

least anthropomorphic in presentations of God (*see* P, PRIESTLY WRITERS).

The Yahwist and Priestly author are thought to have originated in the south (Judah); the origin of the Elohist and the Deuteronomic source is the north (Israel). The Yahwist was dated to the middle of the 10th cent. BCE, as it was thought that the author was writing at a time of great intellectual growth and national consciousness that supposedly characterized the Davidic and Solomonic age. The Elohist is dated in the middle of the 9th cent. BCE, when the Northern Kingdom was at its height. Many scholars connect the law book discovered in the Temple during Josiah's reign in 621 BCE with the Deuteronomic source, so it is dated to the mid-7th cent., at least in some form. The Priestly source is dated to 550 BCE or later, but the content of the priestly material may be quite ancient. Either the priestly author, or someone from the priestly school called a redactor (R), is responsible for combining the four sources to give us the Pentateuch in the exilic or post-exilic period. The Yahwist and the Priestly author are thought, by some, to continue into the book of Joshua, but attempts to trace the sources beyond the book of Joshua have not resulted in much agreement.

While the Documentary Hypothesis has dominated the field of biblical scholarship for much of the 20th cent., recently it has been called into question. The once secure dating of the sources has been undermined as our knowledge of ancient Israel has grown. It is difficult to argue that the Elohist narrative is a separate document, given its fragmentary nature. If the criteria used to separate the sources of the Pentateuch—repetition, contradictions, differences in style, vocabulary, and perspective—can be explained without resorting to sources, then little remains of the Documentary Hypothesis.

Bibliography: Otto Eissfeldt. *The Old Testament: An Introduction* (1965); Ernest W. Nicholson. *The Pentateuch in the Twentieth Century: The Legacy of Julius Wellhausen* (1998); Martin Noth. *A History of Pentateuchal Traditions* (1972); Rolf Rendtorff. *The Problem of the Process of Transmisison in the Pentateuch.* JSOTSup 89 (1990); John van Seters. *Abraham in History and Tradition* (1975); Julius Wellhausen. *Prolegomena to the History of Ancient Israel* (1957); R. N. Whybray. *The Making of the Pentateuch: A Methodological Study.* JSOT Sup 53 (1987).

PAULINE A. VIVIANO

DODAI doh´d*i* [דּוֹדַי dodhay]. Chief of King David's military forces in the second month (1 Chr 27:4). Perhaps a variant of DODO (2 Sam 23:9; 1 Chr 11:12). *See* AHOHI, AHOHITE.

DODANIM doh´duh-nim [דֹּדָנִים dodhanim]. In the MT (and KJV, RSV) the son of Javan and grandson of Noah (Gen 10:4). His name appears as RODANIM in

1 Chr 1:7, and in the LXX is listed as Rhodioi, a reference to his descendants in Rhodes of Asia Minor.

JESSICA TINKLENBERG DE VEGA

DODAVAHU doh´duh-vay´hy*oo* [דֹּדָוָהוּ dodhawahu]. The father of Eliezer, who spoke prophetically against Judean king JEHOSHAPHAT for his alliance with King AHAZIAH of Israel (2 Chr 20:37). According to 2 Chronicles, Dodavahu was from Mareshah, possibly one of the cities of Judea fortified by Rehoboham (2 Chr 11:8).

JESSICA TINKLENBERG DE VEGA

DODO doh´doh [דּוֹדוֹ dodho]. 1. The grandfather of TOLA and a descendant of Issachar (Judg 10:1). Tola rose to judge Israel after ABIMELECH.

2. The father of ELEAZAR, a warrior of David. Dodo was a son of Ahohi (2 Sam 23:9; 1 Chr 11:12).

3. The father of ELHANAN, a warrior of David (2 Sam 23:24; 1 Chr 11:26).

JESSICA TINKLENBERG DEVEGA

DOE [אַיָּלָה ʾayyalah, יַעֲלָה yaʿalah]. The English term "doe," applied to the adult female deer, is used by the NRSV to translate the Hebrew construct expression yaʿalath-hen (יַעֲלַת־חֵן) as "a pleasant doe" (Prov 5:19). In other locations, *doe* is used to translate ʾayyalah (e.g., Gen 49:21; Jer 14:5). Both Hebrew words are feminine forms of words used for goats and rams. *See* DEER.

ODED BOROWSKI

DOEG doh´ig [דֹּאֵג doʾegh]. The Edomite head of Saul's shepherds (1 Sam 21:7) or of Saul's guard (1 Sam 22:17); Doeg was DETAINED BEFORE THE LORD at NOB during the time that David took the bread of the presence and Goliath's sword from AHIMELECH. David, whom we know is ritually pure (1 Sam 21:5), stands in contradistinction to Doeg who will massacre the priests of Nob. Doeg reports the news of David to Saul (1 Sam 22:9-10) who orders Doeg, a foreigner, to kill all the priests, people, and animals of Nob. In contrast, Saul and his army failed to fulfill God's command to kill King AGAG and all the Amalekites (1 Sam 15).

HEATHER R. MCMURRAY

DOG [כֶּלֶב kelev; κυνάριον kynarion, κύων kyōn]. The dog was the first animal to be domesticated, between 12,000 and 10,000 years ago. The dog belongs to the order *Carnivora*, Family *Canidae*. All breeds go back to the one ancestor *Canis familiaris*. However, since then, for a variety of reasons and needs, more than 400 breeds have developed.

All ancient and modern breeds of dogs are descendants of wolves (*Canis lupus*) that were tamed in different regions by humans at the end of the last ice age. The dog is the only member of this family that can bark, the result of domestication, and this attribute was utilized in many of the chores assigned to dogs. The association between human and dog led to a special relationship, which was probably first connected with hunting activities and later, with the domestication of large and small cattle, was extended to herding.

The biblical text gives us some hints about the dog and its place in society. At times, packs of unmanaged dogs (Ps 22:17) roamed the cities (1 Kgs 14:11; 16:4), while other dogs were used by the Israelites in herding (Isa 56:11; Job 30:1) and as watchdogs (Isa 56:10). Yet, in spite of their positive contribution they were not well treated, as can be seen from Goliath's remark to David: "Am I a dog that you come out against me with sticks?" (1 Sam 17:43). Jesus alluded to the lower status of dogs when he said, "Do not give what is holy to the dogs" (Matt 7:6) and to a woman who asked him for help: "It is not fair to take the children's food and throw it to the dogs," to which she responded that even the dogs get the crumbs that fall from the master's table (Matt 15:26-27; Mark 7:27). Several biblical references to dogs have bad connotations as in the words of Hazael to Elisha: "What is your servant, who is a mere dog, that he should do this great thing?" (2 Kgs 8:13; see also Exod 22:30; Deut 23:19; 2 Sam 3:8; Prov 26:11; Eccl 9:4); bad connotations are attached especially to dead dogs as seen in the words spoken by Mephiboshet to David: "What is your servant, that you should look upon a dead dog such as I?" (2 Sam 9:8; see also 1 Sam 16:9; 24:15). Evildoers are likened to dogs in Phil 3:2 and Rev 22:15. Nevertheless, sometimes mistreating a dog possibly did not meet with the community's approval, as one proverb hints: "Like somebody who takes a passing dog by the ears is one who meddles in the quarrel of another" (Prov 26:17).

Unmanaged dogs were common in the ANE, and their presence in the urban setting as evidenced in the Bible (Ps 59:7, 15), might have caused ill feelings toward them. It is very likely that the dogs mentioned as eating bodies of the dead and licking their blood (1 Kgs 14:11; 16:4; 21:19, 23-24; 22:38; 2 Kgs 9:10, 36) were pariah dogs. In a parable, dogs lick the sores of a poor man named Lazarus as he languishes outside a rich man's house (Luke 16:21). A wall painting of Pharaoh Tutankhamen fighting Nubian enemies from his chariot shows two dogs engaged in a bloody attack on two enemy soldiers. This scene is reminiscent of the prophecies concerning the death of Jezebel: "The dogs shall eat Jezebel within the bounds of Jezreel" (1 Kgs 21:23).

Dogs also were kept as pets, and at times collars were placed on pet dogs. In the book of Tobit, Tobias's dog travels with him (Tob 6:2). The case that dogs were pets can be surmised from the way they are depicted in bronze and ivory figurines, and from their names inscribed on the collars they wore. Clay figurines from Mesopotamia showing children riding dogs add support to the notion that some of these animals were kept as pets.

Even before the advent of agriculture there were already several breeds of dogs in the ANE that are evident in skeletal remains and artistic representations. Egyptian and Mesopotamian artistic representations on cylinder seals, in paintings, statues, and figurines represent not only the roles of dogs but also the different breeds. These coupled with zooarchaeological samples show that some dogs resembled salukis or greyhounds, and mastiffs, while others were small with thick snouts and drooping ears. A terracotta plaque from the beginning of the second millennium BCE shows a child riding an Alsatian-type dog with a sharp muzzle, thick mane, pointed ears, and a bushy tail. Large sheep-dogs with flocks can be seen in outdoor scenes, and there are amulets in the form of dogs with short legs and long or short tails. Very few dog remains have been discovered in Palestine in an Iron Age context, although some have been found at Lachish, ʿIzbet Sartah, Tel Michal, Beer-sheba, and Tel Masos. The largest collection of dog remains comes from the Persian and Hellenistic strata at ASHKELON, where they were buried in a large dog cemetery. *See* ANIMALS OF THE BIBLE.

Bibliography: Oded Borowski. *Every Living Thing: Daily Use of Animals in Ancient Israel* (1998).

ODED BOROWSKI

DOGMA. *See* BIBLICAL THEOLOGY; CHURCH, LIFE AND ORGANIZATION OF; LIBERATION THEOLOGY; SACRAMENTAL THEOLOGY; SYSTEMATIC THEOLOGY; TEACHING IN THE EARLY CHURCH; TEACHING OF JESUS; THEOLOGY, NT; THEOLOGY, OT.

DOK dok [Δωκ Dōk]. A small fortress near JERICHO where, in 134/135 BCE, Ptolemy murdered his father-in-law, SIMON Maccabeus, and two of his sons (1 Mac 16:11-17; Josephus, *Ant.* 13.230; *J.W.* 1.56), probably located about 3.5 km (2 mi.) northwest of the mound of Jericho, near the base of Jebel Qarantal.

JAMES RILEY STRANGE

DOLMENS dol′muhn. Dolmens are prehistoric megalithic funerary structures, made up of very large, broad, flat slabs of unworked stone laid horizontally over wide vertical slabs of unworked stone, to form a structure in the shape of a large table. Thus the name "dolmen" comes from the Old Breton words *dol* ("table") and *men* ("stone"). Six different types have been identified, of which the simplest and by far most common is the "trilithon," in which two vertical stone slabs are spanned by one horizontal slab. A typical trilithon measures ca. 6–9 ft. long, 3–4 ft. wide, and 3–6 ft. high. Other types involve more stones in more complex arrangements. All types of dolmens were originally covered with dirt to form a tumulus, but today the tumuli have long since eroded away. Nearly all dolmens are surrounded by at least one circle of stones, some by more than one.

Todd Bolen/BiblePlaces.com
Figure 1: Dolmens near Adam

The term "dolmens" does not occur in the Bible, but they exist in biblical lands, where they are concentrated in regions immediately along both sides of the northern Rift Valley—i.e., in the Upper Galilee, the Golan Heights, and the northern Transjordan Plateau. Virtually none have been found in the hill country of the West Bank. When they appear, dolmens are frequently clustered in "dolmen fields," which may contain as many as a thousand specimens. Different types of dolmens may occur in the same field, but usually one type will dominate in any given field.

Archaeological interpretation of dolmens is extremely difficult, since they usually survive in relatively poor states of preservation, and frequently they have been reused over time for a variety of purposes. In addition, no written texts describe either the construction or the use of dolmens. Excavations indicate, however, that these structures date to the Early Bronze Age IA (3400–3100 BCE), and that they were constructed for funerary purposes, most likely to hold the burials of important individuals from nomadic pastoral tribes. Most of them, for example, are situated on hillsides and slopes of pasture land. Because of their great size, construction of dolmens would have involved significant time and effort, and in most cases they hold the burial of only a few individuals (often only one). These factors suggest that dolmens were the burial places of persons who held prominent positions in the social system of a pastoral tribe.

Dolmens are also known in some areas of Europe (France, e.g.), but there is no demonstrable connection between these structures and the dolmens of the biblical lands. Those structural similarities that do exist are the result of similar social and ecological circumstances, rather than cultural contact.

Bibliography: C. Epstein. "Dolmens Excavated in the Golan." *'Atiqot* (English Series) 17 (1985) 20–58;

M. Zohar. "Dolmens." *The New Archaeological Encyclopedia of Excavations in the Holy Land*, Vol 1. (1994) 352–56.

BYRON R. MCCANE

DOME. *See* FIRMAMENT.

DOMESTICATION OF ANIMALS. *See* ANIMALS OF THE BIBLE.

DOMINION [כָּבַשׁ kavash, מַלְכוּת malkhuth, מָשַׁל mashal, רָדָה radhah, שִׁלְטוֹן shileton; βασιλεύω basileuō, κράτος kratos, κυριεύω kyrieuō, κυριότητος, kyriotētos]. *Dominion* translates several Hebrew, Aramaic, and Greek words for control, mastery, or sovereignty. Old Testament and NT authors concur that ultimate rule and governance of humanity and of all creation belongs to God (Pss 22:28; 103:22; see also kratos κράτος in the NT doxologies 1 Tim 6:16; Jude 25; Rev 1:6). *Dominion* is also used in the OT for human rule over others, whether nations over nations (Judg 14:4; 1 Kgs 4:24; 9:19), enemies over God's people (Neh 9:28; Ps 19:13), or God's chosen king over all creation (Ps 72:8). Political and military rule, however, is relativized in light of God's supreme authority (Dan 6:26; Wis 6:3). In the eschatological visions of Dan 7–12, dominion is granted to and removed from a series of earthly rulers (Dan 7:6, 12; 11:3, 4) before God grants it eternally to "one like a human being" (Dan 7:14), who serves as a symbol for the people of God (Dan 7:26-27). Other prophetic passages envision the restoration of Israel's former dominion (Mic 4:8) or its near-universal extension through the work of a peaceful king (Zech 9:10). Two different terms for rule or mastery are used in the Gen 1 creation account as God sets humankind over the animals (radhah, v. 26) and over the earth (kavash, v. 28). Although both terms may be used to convey violent and even abusive uses of power, Gen 1 creates a context of orderliness and beneficence that seems to mitigate against such connotations (see also Ps 8:6; Wis 9:2; Sir 17:4). At times, terms translated *dominion* are used to express the need for mastery or control over sin or iniquity (Gen 4:7; Ps 119:133). Such usage then informs NT contrasts between the dominion of sin and death and the dominion of grace and resurrection (basileuō and kyrieuō, Rom 5:14-21; 6:9-14). Finally, one particular NT term (kyriotētos), also often translated *dominion*, designates a special class of angelic powers, created by and subordinate to God, but with their own influence (Eph 1:21; Col 1:16).

B. DIANE LIPSETT

DOMITIAN duh-mish´uhn. The Roman emperor Domitian (81–96 CE) enters biblical history through Irenaeus' comment dating the book of Revelation at "the end of Domitian's reign" (*Haer.* 5.30.3). That John was on Patmos for "the testimony of Jesus" (Rev 1:9) was taken to mean that Domitian had banished him (Eusebius, *Hist. eccl.* 3.20.8-9). Domitian became in Christian tradition an Antichrist figure, "a beast rising out of the sea," demanding worship from "the inhabitants of the earth" (Rev 13:1-18). He fared no better among Roman historians, such as Suetonius, Pliny the Younger, and Dio Cassius. According to Suetonius, his reign began in moderation (*Dom.* 3.2), but quickly changed so that "his savage cruelty was not only excessive, but also cunning and sudden" (11.1). He was said to have claimed the titles "Lord" and "God" (Suetonius, *Dom.* 13.2), but contemporary evidence suggests that this was more likely a whim than an official policy. He was finally assassinated, and the harsh judgments of later historians served to highlight "the uprightness and moderate rule" of his successors (Suetonius, *Dom.* 23.2).

Christian writers who blamed Domitian for the supposed persecutions in Revelation were possibly influenced by Roman historians. Yet Tertullian, who compared him to Nero, noted that "being in some degree human, he soon stopped what he had begun, and restored those he had banished" (*Apol.* 5.4). While Christians may have been among his victims, it is doubtful that they were killed or banished solely for being Christians. Hegesippus described how he tried to wipe out descendants of David (fearing, like other emperors, a Jewish "kingdom of God"), and questioned grandsons of Jude, brother of Jesus. When they said they expected a heavenly, not earthly, kingdom, he "did not condemn them at all, but despised them as simple folk, released them, and decreed an end to the persecution against the church" (Eusebius, *Hist. eccl.* 3.20.5). More popular in the provinces than in Rome, he was even celebrated in one Jewish Christian source as "a mighty warrior . . . whom all mortals will love throughout the boundless earth" (*Sib. Or.* 12.124-26; yet see 5.40, "a cursed man"). Even in Revelation, the reigning emperor is merely one in a series of seven (see Rev 17:10-11), no better or worse than the others. Nothing suggests his return as the sinister "eighth" (commonly identified as Nero). Is Revelation supporting Domitian's decree limiting wine production in favor of more grain for the poor, or protesting his failure to enforce it? (see Rev 6:8; Suetonius, *Dom.* 7.2). Although he taxed Jews heavily, including those "who without publicly acknowledging that faith yet lived as Jews" (Suetonius, *Dom.* 12.2, possibly referring to Christians), no general persecution of Christians or formal imposition of emperor worship is evident during his reign. *See* REVELATION, BOOK OF; ROMAN EMPIRE; ROME, CITY OF.

Bibliography: D. E. Aune. *Revelation 1–5.* WBC 52 (1997); J. B. Lightfoot. *The Apostolic Fathers. Part One: Clement* (1989); L. L. Thompson. *The Book of Revelation* (1990).

J. RAMSEY MICHAELS

DONKEY [אָתוֹן 'athon, חֲמוֹר khamor; ὄνος onos, ὑποζύγιον hypozygion]. A number of Hebrew and Greek terms are variously understood and translated as "donkey," "ASS," "MULE," and similar animals. In both the OT and NT donkeys appear in fables, in stories of kings, and prophecies. In the story of BALAAM, a donkey functions ironically to mock the seer Balaam's blindness to the will of God. When Balaam travels to see the Moabite king BALAK, Balaam's donkey sees the angel of the LORD in Balaam's path. Three times the donkey tries to stop Balaam, but he beats his normally obedient donkey. It is only after the LORD opens Balaam's eyes that he sees the angel (Num 22:21-35). The author of 2 Peter remembers Balaam negatively and praises the talking donkey, declaring that it "restrained the prophet's madness" (2:16).

Saul first appears in the biblical narrative on a quest to find his father Kish's lost donkeys. Instead of finding animals that could be ridden by royalty, Saul finds kingship when SAMUEL the seer anoints Saul first king of Israel (1 Sam 9-10). Later ZIBA the servant of Saul—grandfather of MEPHIBOSHETH—brings donkeys and food to DAVID the king as he flees from ABSALOM. Ziba accuses Mephibosheth, the last Saulide, of treason (2 Sam 16:1-4). Mephibosheth claims innocence and insists that Ziba was supposed to saddle the donkey for Mephibosheth, who wished to flee with David (2 Sam 19:26). Zechariah's ideal messiah will ride into Jerusalem on a donkey (9:9). It is this entry that Matthew has in mind when Jesus sends his disciples in search of a donkey and a COLT for his triumphal entry into Jerusalem (Matt 21:2//Mark 11:1-3//Luke 19:29-31; John 12:14-15). Even if Jesus did not see himself as a triumphal messiah entering Jerusalem, the Gospel writers interpreted the entry in that way. *See* ANIMALS OF THE BIBLE; SAUL, SON OF KISH.

HEATHER R. MCMURRAY

DOOMED PRINCE, THE. An incomplete Egyptian story concerning the trials of a young prince whose dire fate was predetermined. In an effort to escape danger, he travels to the land of Nahrin and wins its princess. She helps him overcome his destiny with her cunning, thus affirming shared responsibility in marriage and overturning the concept of determinism.

R. JUSTIN HARKINS

DOOR [דֶּלֶת deleth, פֶּתַח pethakh; θύρα thyra]. Modern translations distinguish between deleth ("door") and the more frequent pethakh ("entrance" or "opening"), refer to the entrance of tents (Gen 18:1), especially the tent of meeting (Exod 29:4), or the entrance to a city (1 Kgs 17:10), the opening for the city gate (Josh 8:29), the entrance to a HOUSE (Gen 19:11), a tower (Judg 9:52), or a cave (1 Kgs 19:13).

Deleth refers to hinged doors (Prov 26:14) found on houses (Gen 19:9) and rooms (2 Sam 13:17). The plural "doors" (delathoth דְּלָתוֹת), rarely referring to private houses (Judg 19:27), is common on public buildings, especially the Jerusalem Temple. Doors could be carved and plated with metals (1 Kgs 6:32).

The NT uses thyra for both the hinged door of a house (Mark 1:33) or closet (Matt 6:6) and the entrance to a tomb (Mark 15:46) or the gate of the temple (Acts 3:2). *See* ARCHITECTURE, NT; ARCHITECTURE, OT; SOCKET.

ADAM L. PORTER

DOORKEEPER שֹׁמֵר הַסַּף shomer hassaf, תַּרְעָ tara'; θυρωρός thyrōros]. Literally, "keeper of the threshold" (Jer 35:4; Ps 84:10; Mark 13:34), although similar phrases are translated either "gatekeeper" or "porter" (Ezra 7:24). This office seems to be the responsibility of PRIESTS AND LEVITES, although not limited to them entirely (John 18:16). Other than guarding the entrances to the temple, tabernacle, or other households, the only stated responsibilities for doorkeepers are collecting the silver brought into the temple and placing it in the collection box for temple repairs (see 2 Kgs 12:10; 22:4), or bringing contraband items out from the temple during Josiah's reform.

C. MARK MCCORMICK

DOPHKAH dof'kuh [דָּפְקָה dofqah]. An exodus itinerary site on the journey to Mount Sinai, described as the second stop after leaving Yam Suph, adjoining the Wilderness of Sin (Num 32:12-13). The MT clearly identifies Yam Suph as the Gulf of Elath, so Dophkah appears to be in the southern NEGEV, between ELATH and Edom.

MICHAEL D. OBLATH

DOR dor [דּוֹר dor, דֹּאר do'r; Δώρ Dōr, Δωρά Dōra]. A seaport city on the Mediterranean south of the Carmel range, probably established during the Late Bronze Age, and continuously inhabited until the 7th cent. CE.

According to the Wen-Amon tale, during the 11th cent. BCE, its residents were one of the Sea People groups named Tjeker. The term NAPHATH-DOR (Josh 11:2; 12:23; 1 Kgs 4:11) might be a Sea People derivative meaning a wooded region.

Dor joined JABIN's coalition (Josh 12:23) against Joshua, but it was not conquered until David's time (Judg 1:27). Solomon made it the center of his fourth administrative district. It flourished as a Phoenician city through most of Iron Age II. Tiglath-pileser III conquered the city in 732 BCE, making it the Duru province capital. Antiochus VII besieged Dor in an effort to capture Trypho (1 Macc 15).

ITZHAQ SHAI

DORCAS dor'kuhs [Δορκάς Dorkas]. The Greek name of Tabitha (Aram. tavithah טָבִיתָה). Both the Greek and the Aramaic mean "gazelle." She was

brought back to life by Peter (Acts 9:36-43). Although she is described as a "disciple" (μαθήτρια mathētria), scholars debate the significance of the term. She was probably a woman of some financial means and significant status in the Christian communities because she was "devoted to good works and to charity" (9:36) especially among widows for whom she provided clothing (9:39). The upstairs room in which Tabitha was laid out after death may have been a meeting place for early Christians.

NANCY CALVERT-KOYZIS

DORYMENES dor-im'uh-neez [Δορυμένης Dorymenēs]. Father of Ptolemy (2 Macc 4:45) who was governor of Coelesyria and Phoenicia (2 Macc 8:8), and whom Lysias appointed to attack Judah (1 Macc 3:38–4:25; Josephus, *Ant.* 12.298). This may be the Dorymenes mentioned by Polybius (5.61.9), an Aetolian commander who served under Ptolemy IV of Egypt.

JAMES RILEY STRANGE

DOSITHEUS, APOCALYPSE OF. This Nag Hammadi tractate (Codex VII, 5:118, 10-127, 27), better known as *The Three Steles of Seth*, purports to record the revelations of Seth transmitted to Dositheus, teacher of SIMON Magus. The text consists of three sections describing Seth's heavenly ascent to the divine triad: *Autogenes*, Barbelo, and the Unbegotten Father, each of whom Seth addresses with a hymn consisting of an invocation, glorification, and closing prayer, a model that Sethian communities replicated in their liturgies in order to experience their own mystical transformation. Close parallels with Neoplatonic thought suggest an early 3rd cent. CE date. *See* APOCRYPHA, NT; NAG HAMMADI TEXTS.

DAVID M. REIS

DOTHAN doh'thuhn [דֹּתָן dothan]. The biblical city is now identified with the site of Tell Dothan, located 22 km north of Shechem and 10 km south of Jenin. The imposing tell rises nearly 60 mi. above the eastern edge of the Dothan Valley in the Samarian Hills. The easternmost of three strategic routes through the hills to the Jezreel Valley made Dothan a vital part of the trade between Mesopotamia and Egypt. Atop a 45 mi. hill, the site reflects the military importance of the city in protecting the route. Tell Dothan contains 15 m depth of occupation levels (strata) spread over 10 acres with another 15 acres of remains on the slopes.

Genesis 37 relates the story of Joseph traveling from Hebron to Shechem to find his brothers whom he discovered near Dothan. In the story of intrigue Joseph is sold to a trade caravan of Ishmaelites and Midianites headed for Egypt through the mountain pass. Years later, marauding Arameans (possibly crossing the Dothan Pass) surrounded heavily-fortified Dothan in search of the prophet Elisha (2 Kgs 6:8-23). Other textual references to Dothan include the book of Judith 3:9; 4:6; and 7:3, and in the Onomasticon of Eusebius 76:13.

In nine seasons of excavation led by J. P. Free (1953–64) the Chalcolithic period is seen in ceramic remains. Major occupation in the Early Bronze Age included a city with walls 4 m thick. Two Middle Bronze Age strata are followed by a prosperous Late Bronze level that continued use of previous defenses. Four Iron Age II occupation strata date to the Israelite monarchy. The Israelite city was destroyed either during the invasion of the Assyrian king Tiglath-Pileser III (ca. 732 BCE) or at the fall of the Northern Kingdom in 722/1 BCE. Hellenistic, Roman, and Mameluke remains were also found on the tell.

MICHAEL G. VANZANT

DOUAY VERSION. *See* VERSION, DOUAY.

DOUBLE NAMES. *See* NAME, NAMING.

DOUBLE-MINDED [סְעִפִּים se'afim; δίψυχος dipsychos]. The OT characterizes those who waver in their commitment to God and divine law as double-minded (Pss 113; 119; 1 Kgs 18:21). This sense of doubtfulness may also imply a more deliberate vacillation closer to deceitfulness. In the NT, dipsychos is found only in James (1:8; 4:8), and it is possibly the author's neologism. James 1:5-8 addresses the proper manner of prayer, arguing that God bestows wisdom upon those who pray "in faith" rather than upon the double-minded, who are "unstable in every way." The author later asserts that the double-minded possess impure hearts, a moral judgment implying a fractured relationship with God (4:8; see 3:17). Later Christian writings follow James in connecting dipsychos with faithless prayer and an inability to trust in God (*1 Clem.* 11:2; 23:3; *2 Clem.* 11:2, 5; 19:2; *Herm. Mand.* 9:6-9; *Vis. Paul* 2.2.7; *Apos. Con.* 7:11).

DAVID M. REIS

DOUBLE-TONGUED [רָכִיל rakhil; δίγλωσσος diglōssos]. Although among some ancient Greek writers diglōssos means "bilingual," in ancient Jewish and Christian wisdom literature "double-tongued" characteristically conveys duplicity or insincerity in speech. The LXX in one instance translates rakhil (sometimes used for slander or gossip) as diglōssos (Prov 11:13). Sirach pronounces dire punishment for those who entice others with duplicitous speech (Sir 5:9, 14, 15). Although diglōssos is not used in the NT ("double-tongued" in 1 Tim 3:8 is dilogos (δίλογος), literally "double-worded"), both the Didache and the Epistle of Barnabas link being "double-tongued" with "double-minded" (*Did.* 2:4; *Barn.* 19:7), characteristics of the way of death, rather than the way of life or light.

B. DIANE LIPSETT

DOUBT [διακρίνεσθαι diakrinesthai, διστάζω distazō]. Doubt as a correlative of FAITH is characteristic of the NT, signifying not just disbelief but also partial faith. Prayer must be accompanied by unwavering faith (Jas 1:6), the opposite of being DOUBLE-MINDED (dipsychos [δίψυχος]; 1:8). If Abraham doubted God, it would be considered disbelief (Rom 4:20). The disciples have enough faith to call on the Lord, but their doubt shows them to be "men of little faith" (oligopistoi [ὀλιγόπιστοι]; Matt 14:30-31; cf. 17:20; 21:21). Peter's hesitation to follow the Spirit immediately is likewise described not as disbelief but as a lack of total submission (Acts 10:20). *See* BELIEF; UNBELIEF.

SZE-KAR WAN

DOUGH [בָּצֵק batseq; φύραμα phyrama]. A mixture of flour, water, and salt kneaded together as the basis for baked bread. For leavened bread a small quantity of fermented dough is added to serve as leavening. After the dough balls have risen, they are flattened and baked in an oven or on a heated stone, covered with ashes. In Jer 7:18 the process of kneading dough to bake bread or cakes is attributed to women (see also Tamar in 2 Sam 13:8).

In Exod 12, the people baked unleavened cakes to serve as illustration of their hasty departure. In Num 15:20-21, Israel is commanded to bring an offering of the first batch of dough (see also Ezek 44:30; Neh 10:37). The NIV translates the term 'arisah [עֲרִסָה] in these texts as "ground meal." Compare also the creative application of this metaphor in Rom 11:16).

Galatians 5:9 and 1 Cor 5:6 employ the saying "a little YEAST leavens the whole batch of dough." Dough functions here as the matter being transformed by the powerful raising agent of a small amount of yeast. In 1 Cor 5, this metaphor is used to describe the effect of unacceptable behavior on the entire community. *See* LEAVEN.

JULIANA CLAASSENS

DOVE [יוֹנָה yonah; περιστερά peristera]. The rock dove (*Columbia livia*) was probably the first bird that was domesticated in Palestine. Doves, or pigeons, were bred in dovecots (Isa 60:8), probably for meat production. In addition, the dove and turtledove had an important ritual function, which was not granted other "clean" (i.e., edible) birds: They could be offered as a sacrifice (Lev 1:14). In some cases, pigeons and turtledoves were accepted as substitutes for lambs, which the poor could not afford (Lev 5:7; 12:6). In the NT period, pigeons were sold in the courtyard of the Jerusalem Temple (Matt 21:12).

The dove was a cherished motif in ANE iconography and literature. Probably because of its billing and cooing and its alleged fidelity the dove was often associated with love, as reflected in the Song of Songs, where the woman is called "my dove" (2:14; 5:2). According to Keel, the phrase "your eyes are like doves" (Song

1:15; 4:1), exchanged reciprocally between the lovers, does not describe the color or shape of the eye. Rather, referring to the dove's messenger role within the cult of Aphrodite and other love goddesses, Keel argues that the lovers' gaze is described as conveying a message of love.

In other passages, the dove is associated with lamenting. Sick and mourning people are said to "moan like (a) dove(s)" (Isa 38:14; 59:11; Nah 2:7 [Heb. 2:8]). This simile, as well as the very name yonah, alludes to the murmuring or sighing sound made by the dove.

Highlighting its swift flight, the author of Ps 55 created a metaphor for freedom: "O that I had wings like a dove!" (Ps 55:6 [Heb. 55:7]). In Ps 68, the enigmatic dove with silver and gold on its pinions might symbolize victory (Ps 68:13 [Heb. 68:14]). Despite Hos 7:11, the dove was hardly seen as stupid. However, Jesus referred to its simplicity (Matt 10:16). In the NT and contemporary Jewish sources, the dove is associated with the Spirit. According to the Evangelists, the Spirit descended upon Jesus in the shape of a dove at his baptism (Matt 3:16; Mark 1:10; Luke 3:22; compare John 1:32). *See* BIRDS OF THE BIBLE; PIGEON; TURTLEDOVE.

Bibliography: Othmar Keel. *Deine Blicke sind Tauben.* (1984).

GÖRAN EIDEVALL

DOVE'S DUNG [חֲרֵייוֹנִים khiryownim; κόπρος περιστερά kopros peristera]. During a siege-induced famine, "one-fourth of a kab of dove's dung" (NRSV) sold for five shekels (2 Kgs 6:25). The exact meaning and amount here remain uncertain. "Dove's DUNG" was possibly used for fire fuel, as a salt substitute, or as a food source. A plant product called "dove's dung" may have served one of these purposes (e.g., NIV "seed pods"). *See* SHEKEL; WEIGHTS AND MEASURES.

LISA MICHELE WOLFE

DOWRY [מֹהַר mohar; φερνή pherne]. Dowry is a general term for various payments that are part of the marriage contract. The OT mohar, given by the groom to the bride's father (Gen 34:12), was superseded in NT times by the kethubbah (כְּתֻבָּה), which was owed to the BRIDE if she was divorced without breaking her marriage vows (*Tg. Ket.* 12:1), such as when Joseph planned to divorce Mary "quietly" (Matt 1:19). The minimum was 100 denarii (*see* DENARII, DENARIUS) for a widow or divorcée, 200 for a virgin (about a year's basic wage). It was also normal for the father to give a bride-gift, which was used by the BRIDEGROOM but reverted to the bride on DIVORCE or death. This double dowry system discouraged divorces and was insurance for the woman if she lost her husband by divorce or death. *See* MARRIAGE, NT; MARRIAGE, OT.

DAVID INSTONE-BREWER

DOXOLOGY dok-sol´uh-jee. A short poetic statement of praise to God, often expressed in parallel or balanced lines; Rev 4:8*b* and 4:11 are good examples. Doxologies (from doxa [δόξα] "glory") often seem to end or to divide longer sections of other material. For instance, Amos 4:13 interjects a word of praise to God at the conclusion of a series of oracles of doom against Israel and just before another one begins; whether original to the design of Amos or added by a compiler, the doxology lightens the gloom of Amos' words by focusing on saving aspects of God's power. Ephesians 3:20-21 marks the transition to the more instructional part of the letter, and 2 Cor 9:15 ends the "collection" section. Doxologies probably also invited the congregation to join in the praise to God, especially if (as many think) the biblical doxologies mirror prayers said by the people. Some of the psalms, for example, have repeated doxological lines, ideally suited as unison responses to the intervening stanzas; Ps 136 repeats "for his steadfast love endures forever" after every statement (see also Pss 104:1*a*, 35*b*; 107:1, 15, 21, 31). In the oldest manuscripts, Matthew's version of the Lord's Prayer ends with "deliver us from evil" (Matt 6:9-13), but early Christians added various doxologies to it. Many NT letters conclude with a doxology (Phil 4:20; 2 Tim 4:18*b*; 2 Pet 3:18*b*; Jude 25), and this may indicate the author's wish to be included with the congregation's worship, even if only through the written text.

RICHARD B. VINSON

DRACHMA drak´muh [δραχμή, drachme]. A Greek silver coin that was used in many daily transactions, but varied greatly in value and purchasing power. During the 1st cent. CE, it was generally equated with the Denarius, one day's wage for a laborer (see Tob 5:15; 2 Macc 4:19; 10:20; 12:43; Luke 15:8-9). *See* DENARII, DENARIUS.

JAMES A. METZGER

DRACO [Δράκων Drakon]. According to traditions, probably in 621 BCE, Draco introduced new criminal laws notorious for their severity (hence, "draconian") and was the first Athenian lawgiver to put laws into writing. Most modern scholars accept that Draco introduced legislation for the punishment of criminal offenses, but that the details of these laws are irretrievable, save those dealing with homicide.

Bibliography: Michael Gagarin. *Drakon and Early Athenian Homicide Law* (1981).

MARK DELCOGLIANO

DRAGNET [חֵרֶם kherem]. The Hebrew term for this type of fishing net occurs uniquely in Ezek 32:3, metaphorically in parallel with another word for NET.

DRAGON [לִוְיָתָן liwyathan, נָחָשׁ nakhash; תַּנִּין tannin, δράκων drakon]. Several ANE cultures developed myths concerning primeval chaos monsters, often depicted as dragons. Babylonians recited Marduk's defeat of Tiamat, Canaanites heralded Baal's conquest of Yamm, Egyptians chronicled Isis and Horus's slaying of Typhon, and Greeks hailed Leto's escape from the serpent Pytho.

In the LXX the Greek drakōn sometimes translates the Hebrew words tannin (e.g., Ps 73:13-14; 148:7; Job 7:12; 26:13; Jer 9:10; 51:34 = 28:34 LXX; Lam 4:3; Ezek 29:3; 32:2), liwyathan (LEVIATHAN, e.g., Ps 103:26; Job 41:1), and nakhash (Amos 9:3). The LXX of Isa 27:1 translates all three Hebrew words as drakōn individually. Elsewhere Yahweh receives praise for crushing (Ps 89:10) and dismembering the monster RAHAB (Isa 51:9). In each instance the dragon refers to a chaos monster that opposes the purposes and order of God.

Revelation 12 depicts the dragon as SATAN, the adversary who pursues God's people and empowers the Beast to make war against them. In Revelation the forces of the Lamb defeat those of the Dragon, ending cosmic conflict and preparing the way for the new heaven and the new earth. *See* COSMOGONY, COSMOLOGY.

GREG CAREY

DRAGON'S SPRING עֵין הַתַּנִּין 'en hattannin]. A place by which Nehemiah passes on his inspection of Jerusalem's walls (Neh 2:13). Mentioned only here, scholars do not know its location. The word DRAGON arises from the translation of the word tannin. (See tannin as "dragon" in Isa 27:1.) Other English translations read the word as "jackal" (ASV, NIV, RSV, JPS Tanakh [1985]).

STEVE COOK

DRAMA. Imitating real life by means of action on stage became possible once actors, with their characterizing dialogues, gradually replaced the chorus (Greece, 5th cent. BCE; already mentioned in Aristotle, *Poetics* 49a 9–19). In the early Middle Ages the Christmas, Magi, and Passion narratives were developed into drama. Some biblical texts are similar to drama: they describe turbulent situations and could, particularly where dialogue is involved, be performed by actors or voices. In Job 1, Job is hit by many disasters all at once. Unexpected reversals of roles are dramatic: having spoken, the prophet is addressed (Jer 11:21); the prophetic character becomes first-person narrator (Jer 32:6*b*, 8-13, 16; 35:3-5; also the king in Dan 4:1-13, 18, 34-37). In Jer 28:12-16, the first part of the prophetic message (vv. 13-14) is presented as received by the prophet, while the second part (vv. 15-16) of the same message is presented as passed on to the audience. The reverse occurs in Jer 21:3-7, 8-10. Moral errors, not least within close relationships, often prompt a reversal of fortune in the lives of characters and how they fare (Joseph; Saul and David). *See* COMEDY; DIALOGUE; MYTH IN THE NT; MYTH IN THE OT.

Bibliography: M. Perry, ed. *The Dramatized Bible* (1989).

L. J. DE REGT

DRAWERS OF WATER שֹׁאֲבֵי מַיִם sho'ave mayim; ὑδροφόροι hydrophoroi]. Arid biblical lands required the use of WELLS and cisterns, and drawing WATER was a predominately female task (Gen 24:11, 13, 43; John 4:7, 15). Drawers of water were considered among the lowest classes of the covenant people (Deut 29:10-11). The voluntary servant agreement between the Gibeonites and Joshua (Josh 9:21, 23, 27) declared the Gibeonites to be "HEWERS OF WOOD and drawers of water" for Israel. This duty later became related to the cultic sanctuary (1 Chr 9:2; Ezra 2:43, 70; Neh 7:46, 60). *See* SERVANT.

MICHAEL G. VANZANT

DREAD. *See* FEAR.

DREAM חִזָּיוֹן khazon; חֲלוֹם khalom, ὄναρ onar, ὕπαρ hypar]. Dreaming is a mental activity that has fascinated humans from antiquity until the present. Dreams were considered as messages from deities, demons, or the deceased or, more recently, as spontaneous if significant eruptions from the depths of the psyche. As such, dream fascination has provided scholars a basis for theories about the origin of religion. Physiologically, dreaming likely functions to protect the brain from external sensory influences during sleep. Dream images are intrinsically unintentional and indeterminate, while dream plots are fanciful constructions that integrate and explain these randomly produced images. If considered significant, dreams must be interpreted by the dreamer or by second parties, based upon the waking recall of these plots and images.

The Greeks, for whom "seeing is believing" (e.g., Aristophanes, *Eccl.* 1.772), distinguished between two modes of vision: seeing while awake (hypar) and seeing while asleep or dreaming (onar) (e.g., Plato, *Resp.* 382 E; Acts 18:9). The Hebrews distinguished between dream (khalom) and vision (khazon) but could also refer to dreaming as "a vision of the night" (khazon layelah [חֶזְיוֹן לַיְלָה] in Isa 29:7; also Dan 2:19; 7:2, 13; Job 4:13; 33:1, 5, or bemar'oth hallayelah [בְּמַרְאֹת הַלַּיְלָה] in Gen 46:2). Neither tradition, in other words, made a sharp distinction between dreams and visions and both considered these to be potentially theophanous (Num 12:6; *see* VISION).

In the biblical traditions, as in the history of religions generally, claims to theophany through dreaming must be differentiated from the deceits of false gods, demons, or evil spirits (Deut 13:1-5; Eccl 5:7; Jer 23:25-32; Zech 10:2). Further, the significance of ambiguous dreams (e.g., Isa 29:7; Job 20:8; Ps 73:20; 126:1) must be clarified and their meanings interpreted (e.g., Gen 28). Such problems and ambiguities led some, like Jeremiah, to reject dreaming altogether as a revelatory medium (Jer 27:9; 29:8-9). Others, however, believed their dreams to be messages from God (Gen 31:10-13). Joseph and Daniel's interpretative authority was claimed to be God given (Gen 41:38; Dan 2:18, 20-23), exemplified the role of "true" dream interpreter (e.g., Gen 40:5-19; 41:1-36; 42:38; Dan 2:1-45; *see* INTERPRETER). Another Joseph appears as the receiver and interpreter of dreams in the Matthean birth narrative (Matt 1:20; 2:12-13, 19).

Since any meaning attributed to dreams depends upon authorized interpretation, specialized dream interpreters inevitably arose. And since neuro-physiological variables—from diet to recent events in the life of the dreamer (e.g., during a controversial trial, Pilate's wife dreams that Jesus is innocent [Matt 27:19])—influence the phenomenology of dreaming, it is unsurprising that such specialists developed technologies for dream enhancement, e.g., incubation or dreams invoked by sleeping in sacred places (1 Kgs 3:4-5, 15). Such cultivated dreams—and their conventionalized interpretations—served the purpose of confirming and transmitting the teachings and beliefs represented by these institutional specialists and, if recorded, preserve something of their cultural assumptions.

Bibliography: L. H. Martin. "Artemidorus: Dream Theory in Late Antiquity." *The Second Century* 8 (1991) 97–108; P. C. Miller. *Dreams in Late Antiquity: Studies in the Imagination of a Culture* (1994).

LUTHER H. MARTIN

DREGS [שֶׁמֶר shemer; περίψημα peripsēma]. Sediment that settles in the skin of wine during fermentation and is thus the last part of the wine to be drunk (Ps 75:8; Isa 51:17). The term is often used poetically to describe nations who have not gone into exile (Jer 48:11) or those who grow complacent (1 Cor 4:13) and do not expect Yahweh to act (Zeph 1:12). *See* BANQUET; WINE.

TRISHA GAMBAIANA WHEELOCK

DRESS AND ORNAMENTATION. *See* CLOTH, CLOTHES; COSMETICS; JEWELRY; JEWELS AND PRECIOUS STONES; WAR, METHODS, TACTICS, WEAPONS OF (BRONZE AGE THROUGH PERSIAN PERIOD); WAR, METHODS, TACTICS, WEAPONS OF (HELLENISTIC THROUGH ROMAN PERIODS).

DRESSER OF SYCAMORE TREES [בּוֹלֵס שִׁקְמִים boles shiqmim]. One who prunes SYCAMORE trees to promote further growth or hasten ripening; self-description of Amos (Amos 7:14).

DRIED GRAPES [עֲנָבִים יְבֵשִׁים 'anavim yeveshim, צִמֻּקִים tsimmuqim; σταφίδες staphides]. A portable, nearly imperishable food in the ancient world (1 Sam 25:18; 30:12; 2 Sam 16:1; 1 Chr 12:41; Song 2:5). *See* RAISIN-CAKES.

DRINK. The primary beverages in the biblical text are WATER, WINE, and MILK (Sir 39:26). In a society with a scarcity of water resources, water (mayim [מַיִם], or the lack of water, forms a leading theme in texts like Exod 17 and Num 20–21. In John 4, the notion of "living water" builds on connotations of water to give and sustain life. Milk (khalav [חָלָב], mostly from goats) was consumed at meals and formed the basis for products like cheese and curds. Milk's significance is found in the reference to the land flowing with milk and honey (e.g., Exod 3:17. See also the idyllic description of the hills flowing with milk in Joel 3:18). Wine (yayin [יַיִן]; "new wine" tirosh [תִּירוֹשׁ]) occurs frequently in the Bible, ranging from wine for everyday consumption (Ps 104:15; Eccl 9:7; John 2) to wine as symbol of the final restoration (Isa 25:6; Amos 9:13). The misuse of wine is also noted in the biblical text. See e.g., the reference in Isa 5:11 to STRONG DRINK (shekhar [שֵׁכָר], a beverage with alcoholic content of 20–60 percent. VINEGAR (khomets [חֹמֶץ]), made from fermented wine, served as a condiment, but was also drunk in diluted form by the poor. *See* FOOD.

JULIANA CLAASSENS

DRINK OFFERING. *See* SACRIFICES AND OFFERINGS.

DROMEDARY [גָּמָל gamal; κάμηλος, kamēlos]. Both the dromedary, or one-humped CAMEL (*Camelus dromedaries*), and the Bactrian, or two-humped camel (*Camelus bactrianus*), were known in the ANE, but the dromedary, which is better adapted to hot climates, was probably the camel being referred to in the OT. The term *dromedary* does appear in the ASV (Isa 60:6; 66:20; Jer 2:23) and in the NRSV (Isa 66:20), the latter a translation of the Hebrew kirkarah (כִּרְכָּרָה).

Bibliography: O. Borowski. *Every Living Thing: Daily Use of Animals in Ancient Israel* (1998).

ODED BOROWSKI

DROPSY [ὑδρωπικός hydrōpikos]. Luke's exclusive use of this Greek word does not indicate that he was a physician, since it also appeared in nonmedical ancient literature. It describes the symptom (not the pathology) of a sick man at a dinner to which Jesus had been invited (Luke 14:2). Modern science suggests that the sick man had edema, excess accumulation of fluid in ankles, legs, or abdominal cavity. He would appear swollen, hence "swollen legs" (CEV) "and arms" (TEV) is preferable to the archaic "dropsy" (RSV; NRSV). He might have had LEPROSY (Lev 13:2). Jesus healed his problem. *See* DISEASE.

JOHN J. PILCH

DROSS [סִיג sigh]. Dross is the byproduct material extracted from alloys as they are melted down to yield pure silver. It is used in the OT figuratively to refer to Israel, as in Ezek 22:18: "The House of Israel has become dross to me." This also establishes a metaphorical contrast between Israel's impurity and the LORD's expectations: "Your silver has become dross, your wine is mixed with water" (Isa 1:22). *See* METALLURGY.

R. JUSTIN HARKINS

DROUGHT [בַּצָּרָה batsarah, בַּצֹּרֶת batsoreth, חֹרֶב khorev, תַּלְאֻבָה tal'uvah]. Prolonged dry weather (Ps 32:4; Jer 17:8), causing crop failure and scarcity of drinking water (Jer 14:1-6). Drought is one of God's curses on the Israelites for disobeying God's commandments (Deut 28:22) and neglecting the Temple (Hag 1:11). Drought symbolizes Israel's time in the wilderness (Hos 13:5) and God's defeat of Babylon on Israel's behalf (Jer 50:8-40). These dry periods produced famines, relieved by Elijah's prayer (1 Kgs 17:1; 18:1-45; Jas 5:17-18) and Joseph's grain storage (Gen 41:47-48), the latter leading to Jacob and his family's resettlement in Egypt. *See* ISRAEL, CLIMATE OF.

EMILY R. CHENEY

DROWNING [טָבַע tava'; πνίγω pnigō]. In the Bible, drowning often is associated with divine action and intervention. Because God brings order out of the chaotic sea (Gen 1) and once allowed water to FLOOD the earth to destroy living things (Gen 7), the sea becomes a symbol of a destructive power that only God can control (*see* DEEP, THE). The Egyptians who pursue the escaping Israelites are drowned when God tosses them into the SEA (Exod 14:5-31; see also 3 Macc 6:4; Heb 11:29). Jesus (whom the demons recognize as God's son) exorcises evil spirits from the Gerasene demoniac and casts them into swine that drown in the sea (Mark 5:1-13//Matt 8:32; Luke 8:33).

Passages that describe divine rescues from drowning include the story of Jonah, whom God saves from the sea by means of a great fish (Jonah 1:4-17). Peter climbs out of the boat to meet Jesus on the water and nearly slips beneath the waves, but Jesus rescues him and calms the storm, echoing stories of God's power over the deep (Matt 14:22-33).

Song of Songs (8:7) recognizes the great power of love by claming that floods of water cannot drown it (shataf שָׁטַף, literally "wash away").

MARIANNE BLICKENSTAFF

DRUM [תֹּף tof; Aram. סוּמְפֹּנְיָה sumponyah; τύμπανον tympanon]. Tof is variously translated "timbrel," "tabret," and "tambourine" perhaps indicating a hand-drum of skin stretched over a ring of wood or metal (1 Macc 9:39; 1 Sam 18:6). The NRSV translates sumponyah as "drum" in Daniel (3:5, 7, 10, 15), but may indicate a wind instrument (see RSV, KJV). *See* MUSICAL INSTRUMENTS.

RALPH K. HAWKINS

DRUNKENNESS [שִׁכָּרוֹן shikkaron; μέθη methē, οἰνοφλυγία oinophlygia]. Intoxication appears in a variety of OT contexts: as part of the sacrificial meal (Deut 14:26), a source of pleasure (Judg 9:13; Ps 104:15; Prov 31:6-7), a metaphor for human love (Song 7:9), or an indicator of excess among the wealthy and kings (1 Sam 25:26; Esth 1:8, 10; Dan 5:2; 1 Kgs 16:9; 20:16). Prophets use drunkenness as an indicator of impending destruction (Jer 13:13; Ezek 23:33), and it produces disgrace for Noah and Lot (Gen 9:21; 19:33, 35). Priests are warned against imbibing while serving in the tent of meeting (Lev 10:8-9), and proverbs caution against overindulgence (Prov 20:1; 21:17; 23:20-21, 29-35).

The NT warns against dangers associated with drunkenness: debauchery and Gentile immorality (Rom 13:13; 1 Pet 4:3), exclusion from the kingdom of God (1 Cor 6:10; Gal 5:21), and disqualification from church leadership (1 Tim 3:3; Titus 1:7). *See* STRONG DRINK; WINE.

TRISHA GAMBAIANA WHEELOCK

DRUSILLA dr*oo*-sil'uh [Δρούσιλλα Drousilla]. Mentioned as the wife of FELIX who came with her husband to hear Paul in Caesarea (Acts 24:24). According to Josephus, she was born in 38 CE (*Ant.* 19.354) and was the daughter of Herod Agrippa I of Judea. At an early age she was betrothed to Epiphanes, prince of Commogene, although the marriage never took place. She later married Azizus, who consented to be circumcised, but the marriage was dissolved by the actions of Felix who strongly desired her and was known for his own marital infidelities. She gave birth to a son named Agrippa who perished in 79 CE in the eruption of Vesuvius (*Ant.* 20.137-44). *See* HEROD, FAMILY.

Bibliography: Brian Rapske. *Paul in Roman Custody. The Book of Acts in Its First Century Setting.* Vol. 3 (1994).

NANCY CALVERT-KOYZIS

DRY BONES. *See* BONE; VALLEY OF DRY BONES.

DUAFF, INSTRUCTION OF. *See* DUA-KHETY, INSTRUCTION OF.

DUA-KHETY, INSTRUCTION OF. A Middle Kingdom text, often called the Satire on Trades and occasionally the Instruction of Khety. It opens with a narrative frame relating the words of Dua-Khety as he is taking his son, Pepy, to the Residence (the royal palace) to scribal school. Often interpreted as a tongue-in-cheek or satirical commentary on trades other than that of SCRIBE, more accurately, one should understand it as a father attempting to convince his son of the benefits of being a scribe. To emphasize his point, Dua-Khety outlines the negative points of about twenty other trades with which he contrasts the better life of a scribe, in part because a scribe is his own supervisor, although at that time scribes were officials in the government rather than being truly independent. Having presented his argument, Dua-Khety continues by instructing his son in the basic precepts for living, a combination of practical injunctions and interdictions: avoid disputes, speak cautiously, be silent in the presence of superiors, transmit messages exactly, do not gossip, eat moderately, in other words, use care and moderation in all actions. Each of these injunctions resonates with materials already known from earlier and contemporary instructional writings. This instruction, like others in general, marks the transition in the recipient's life: he is entering into a new phase, in this case schooling that will prepare him for his career. One views this particular boy as reluctant, perhaps already homesick; and the father as the one experienced in life and blessed by the gods in having lived to adulthood, is the instructor. Thus in the fitting conclusion, the elder reminds his son of the value of writing and the scribal role, a path chosen for him by his parents.

Bibliography: AEL I, 184–92; *ANET*[3], 432–34. *COS* I, 122–25. *LAE*[3], 434–37.

SUSAN TOWER HOLLIS

DUALISM. The belief that two irreductible principles, one GOOD and one EVIL, are the ultimate causes of the world and its constitutive elements. Dualism involves cosmic, ethical, and temporal dimensions. The Bible uses dualistic language but does not elaborate a dualistic system since God's ultimate authority is never challenged.

Old Testament

Dualism implies that the cosmos is divided in two opposite domains, created, respectively, by the good and the evil principle. In the creation narrative of Gen 1:1–2:4, darkness is part of the initial chaos (Gen 1:2); only light is said to be good (Gen 1:4). It may suggest that darkness is an autonomous source of evil, a possibility explicitly rejected by God's statement in Isa 45:7: "I form light and create darkness, I make weal and create woe" (compare Prov 16:4; Sir 33:14-15). There is no other principle or spirit behind the making of the world.

Dualistic systems often partition humankind into good and evil categories. In the OT, human beings are responsible for their own ethical decisions (Ezek 18; Ps 1; Prov 10:16; Amos 5:14; Sir 15:14-20). The first couple learns to know good and evil as a result of a transgression (Gen 3:22). Their descendants, giving in to an inner inclination, fill the earth with violence, so that only Noah is found worthy to escape the flood (Gen 6–9). Following Abram's positive answer to his call (Gen 17:1), Israel is urged to choose life rather than death by walking in her Lord's ways (Deut 30:15-20).

In eschatological forms of dualism the evil principle is eradicated at the end of time. In OT views, every deed, good or evil, is brought into judgment (Eccl 12:14). The righteous are to be vindicated (Ps 37). The enemies of God and the sinners among his people are to be exterminated on the "day of the Lord" (Isa 13:9; Jer 46:10; Joel 1:15, etc. Amos 5:18-20; Obad 1:15; Wis 1:7, 14) or through a large-scale final battle (Ezek 38–39; Dan 10–12). The righteous alone are promised happiness (Ps 112), resurrection and everlasting life (Dan 12:3), or immortality (Wis 2:22–3:4).

New Testament

For the NT, God is the unique creator (Eph 8:9; Rev 5:1; 10:6), through God's Word (John 1:1-3; Col 1:15-17; Heb 1:1-2). As he comes from above (John 3:31), the Word shines into darkness and brings life (John 1:5), confronting the ruler of this world (John 12:31; 14:30; 16:11). No mythology of origins presents the evil ruler as creator or explains how he came into power.

Jesus, having resisted Satan's assault (Mark 1:12-13), casts out the unclean spirits (Mark 1:23-24; compare 3:22; Acts 10:38) calls the sinners to conversion, and brings them to God (Matt 9:13; compare 1 Pet 3:18). Those who believe in him are spirit rather than flesh (John 3:6-7; 6:63; Rom 8:1-13), become children of God (John 1:11), new creatures (2 Cor 5:17), clothed with a new self (Eph 4:22-24). They reject the ways of Beliar (2 Cor 6:14-18), walk as children of light (Rom 13:12; Eph 5:8; 1 Thess 5:5) and stand against the wiles of the devil (Eph 6:11; compare Jas 4:7-8; 1 Pet 5:8-9). Nonbelievers are children of the evil one (John 8:44-45; compare 1 John 3:8-10). God's mysterious design allows both to exist side by side into the present world (Matt 5:44-45; 13:37-39).

The coming of Christ initiates the defeat of Satan and the judgment of the world (Luke 10:18; John 3:19-21). But the victory is to be completed only in the "age to come" (Matt 10:29-30; 12:32; Eph 1:20-21; Heb 6:5), when a last judgment will separate the righteous from the evil; the former will be granted eternal life, the later will depart into eternal punishment (Matt 13:41-43, 49-51; 25:31-46). In the elaborated scenario of the book of Revelation, Satan is released for a final assault and defeated (Rev 20:1-10) before the judgment (Rev 20:11-15) and the renewal of creation (Rev 21:1–22:5).

Based on this biblical language, more or less sophisticated dualistic systems were developed, through inner evolution or foreign influences, in ancient Judaism (Henochic circles, Qumran *yahad*) and in early or Middle Age Christianity (gnostic movements, manicheism, catharism).

Bibiography: Ugo Bianchi. *Selected Essays on Gnosticism, Dualism and Mysteriosophy. SHR* 38 (1978);

Mary Boyce and Franz Grenet. *A History of Zoroastrianism, I–III* (1975); Martin Hengel. *Judaism and Hellenism: Studies in Their Encounter in Palestine During the Early Hellenistic Period* (1974). Elaine H. Pagels. *The Origin of Satan* (1995).

JEAN DUHAIME

DUMAH doo'muh [דּוּמָה dumah; Ἰδουμα Idouma].
1. The sixth of twelve sons of Ishmael and eponymous ancestor of an Arabian tribe (Gen 25:13-16; 1 Chr 1:30). This Dumah likely refers to a prosperous oasis town in northcentral Arabia.

2. A town southwest of Hebron (Josh 15:52).

3. The title of an enigmatic oracle (Isa 21:11-12) set in an anti-Babylonian and Arabian context (Isa 21), possibly referencing the oasis noted in number 1 above. The LXX, however, reads Idumaia (*see* EDOM, EDOMITES), corresponding to Seir (v. 12) through Esau, Jacob's twin (Gen 25:25-26; 36:8). Dumah ("silence") also appears as a synonym for the underworld (Ps 94:17; 115:17), which might befit the oracle's context of a Judahite watchman's mysterious response to a question heard from his relative's territory about the "night" (perhaps destruction). Tentatively, Dumah could be read as a pun on Edom (ʾedhom אֱדוֹם) foreshadowing Edom's eventual status (e.g., Isa 34; 63:1-6).

JASON C. DYKEHOUSE

DUNG [דֹּמֶן domen, חֲרֵא khereʾ, חֲרִי khari, אַשְׁפֹּת ʾashpoth, פֶּרֶשׁ peresh, גָּלָל galal, גֵּל gel, צֵאָה tseʾah, צָפִיעַ tsafiʿa]. *Dung* represents numerous Hebrew words for human or animal feces. As an unclean substance, the dung inside a sacrificial animal was to be burned outside the camp (Exod 29:14; Lev 4:11), and human dung was to be buried outside the camp (Deut 23:14). A starving people under siege may have resorted to eating dung (2 Kgs 18:27) or to using human or cows' dung for cooking fuel (Ezek 4:12-15).

Similes using *dung* indicate that it was sometimes disposed of by burning (1 Kgs 14:10), and other times by decomposing in the open (2 Kgs 9:37; Jer 9:22). It metaphorically describes the transitory nature of life (Job 20:7) and moral impurity (Prov 30:12). In all cases the comparison is derogatory. While *dung* could serve as a visible curse (Mal 2:3), it does not appear to have been used as an expletive.

Jerusalem's southern gate was named the DUNG GATE (Neh 2:13; 3:13-14; 12:31). This has become the standard designation for the entry nearest the garbage dump, most certainly containing dung as well as other trash. *See* ASHES; DOVE'S DUNG; EUPHEMISM; MANURE.

LISA MICHELE WOLFE

DUNG GATE [שַׁעַר הָאַשְׁפֹּת shaʿar haʾashpoth, שַׁעַר הַשְׁפוֹת shaʿar hashafoth]. A GATE of JERUSALEM (Neh 2:13; 3:13-14; 12:31) repaired under

Nehemiah's direction. ʾAshpoth means "ash pit" or "dung heap," a likely reference to refuse discarded through the gate into the Hinnom Valley to the south of the city.

DUNGEON [בּוֹר bor, בֵּית הַבּוֹר beth habbor]. Words meaning PIT, well, or CISTERN can indicate chambers used to detain prisoners. Sometimes this vocabulary functions metaphorically (e.g., Gen 41:14; Exod 12:29). Other usage (e.g., Jer 38:6-13; NRSV *cistern*) denotes an actual subterranean container or secured room employed to incarcerate or ensure prisoners' deaths. Ancient imprisonment often did not involve buildings reserved for this purpose. The varied and nondescript characteristics of PRISON enclosures suggest that numerous structures could produce conditions harsh enough to warrant the name beth keleʾ (בֵּית כֶּלֶא), "house of restraint" (e.g., 2 Kgs 25:27). *See* CRIMES AND PUNISHMENTS, OT AND NT.

MATTHEW L. SKINNER

DURA door'uh [Aram. דּוּרָא duraʾ]. Dura represents either a toponym or an architectural element in the vicinity of Babylon in Dan 3:1. "King Nebuchadnezzar made a statue of gold sixty cubits high and six cubits wide; he erected it in the plain of the wall/fortress (duraʾ) in the district of Babylon." (Author's trans.; NRSV, "King Nebuchadnezzar made a golden statue whose height was sixty cubits and whose width was six cubits; he set it up on the plain of Dura in the province of Babylon.") A convocation followed to inaugurate the statue before all of the notables of the lands, who prostrated themselves before the image. Shadrach, Meshach, and Abednego refused, and the king had them cast into a fiery furnace (*see* SHADRACH, MESHACH, ABEDNEGO).

Duraʾ derives from the Akkadian cognate duru, "city wall, fortification wall; fortress." The text could thus mean: "in the plain of (the town of) Dura" or "in the plain of the wall/fortress."

As a toponym, duru could stand alone, but it appeared more commonly in compound place names, such as Dur-Kurigalzu. A candidate for a Late-Babylonian site called Dur in the district of Babylon includes Tell el-Lahm. A canal by this name flowed into the Euphrates south of Babylon near the site of Tell Dur.

The LXX translators used peribolos (περίβολος), "enclosure, circuit," apparently understanding the city wall. Babylon's fortifications included the inner defense wall and the adjacent outer wall; in addition, another extensive fortification wall and moat lay east of the EUPHRATES several hundred m from the outer wall. Cook identified duraʾ with the outer defense wall and located Daniel's ceremony in the plain between the outer wall and the city.

There is another possibility. A large number of cultic daises, Akkadian parakku, existed inside the city of

Babylon. Most were minor cult sites in city gates, streets and temple gateways. A prominent cult site existed along the procession route of Marduk between the Esagil temple and the extramural Akitu temple to the north of the city, the latter technically outside the outer wall in the vicinity of the great outer fortification wall and moat. This region to the north of the city, perhaps in the vicinity of the Akitu temple or Nebuchadnezzar's summer palace, would suit the "plain of the wall/fortress" very well. Moreover, such a location would be near but outside the city proper, and thus in the district of Babylon. *See* ASSYRIA AND BABYLONIA.

Bibliography: E. M. Cook. "'In the Plain of the Wall' (Dan 3:1)." *JBL* 108 (1989) 115–16; A. R. George. *Babylonian Topographical Texts.* OLA 40 (1992); K. Koch. *Daniel 1-4.* BKAT 22/1 (2005); R. Zadok. *Geographical Names According to Neo- and Late-Babylonian Texts.* Répertoire Géographique des Textes Cunéiforms 8 (1985).

DAVID VANDERHOOFT

DURA EUROPOS door´uh-yoor-oh´puhs. The 3rd cent. BCE city of Dura Europos was a Roman military outpost and port city situated on the EUPHRATES River at the eastern frontier of the Roman Syria. First a Hellenistic colony, it passed from the Seleucids to the Parthians, and then to the Romans before it finally fell to the Sassanians in 256 CE. Joint French and American archaeological excavations in the mid-20th cent. unearthed the architectural remains that had been filled in to provide more adequate defensive walls against the invading Persians in that final phase.

Excavated buildings included thirteen separate pagan temples dedicated to a variety of traditional Roman and Palmyrene deities, a Mithraeum, a Jewish SYNAGOGUE, and (to date) the earliest known and best-preserved Christian HOUSE CHURCH. Wall paintings in all these buildings combined eastern and western styles, reflecting Palmyrene or Parthian styles.

The Jewish synagogue, converted from two domestic buildings into an assembly hall in the 240s CE, is famous for its unique and extensive fresco program, painted in three registers around all of the interior walls. These frescoes illustrate biblical narratives, including scenes from the Moses cycle (the finding of Moses by Pharoah's daughter, Moses receiving the law, the Israelites crossing the Red Sea), Elijah challenging the prophets of Baal, and episodes from the book of Esther. A representation of the binding of Isaac (*see* AKEDAH) was placed above the Torah niche. The purpose of this rare figurative program—as well as the kind of community that would have commissioned it—have been much debated among scholars of Jewish art and archaeology.

The Christian building, like the synagogue, was renovated from a domestic to a liturgical space by the removal of some interior walls to create an assembly hall and separate baptismal chamber. A rectangular font was constructed at one end of the room, under a vaulted canopy supported by heavy columns. This canopy, the lunette beneath it and the side walls of the room were decorated with frescoes depicting the Good Shepherd and Adam and Eve; Jesus stilling the storm, walking on the water, and meeting the woman at the well; the healing of the paralytic, David slaying Goliath,

Figure 1: West wall of the Second Synagogue at Dura Europos. ca. 239. Torah shrine in center wall.

and an image that might be either the women arriving at the Christ's empty tomb, or the wise virgins at the door of the bridegroom.

Bibliography: C. Hopkins. *The Discovery of Dura-Europos* (1979); A. Perkins. *The Art of Dura Europos* (1973); L.M. White. *Building God's House in the Roman World: Architectural Adaptation Among Pagans, Jews, and Christians* (1989); Steven Fine, ed. *Art and Judaism in the Greco-Roman World* (2005).

ROBIN M. JENSEN

DUST [עָפָר 'afar; κονιορτός koniortos]. Genesis 2:7 emphasizes "dust" as the material from which humans come and will return. God creatively breathes life into dust. Although other Hebrew terms are related, 'afar is used over sixty times in the OT figuratively for judgment (Deut 28:24), abundance (Gen 13:16; 28:14; Job 27:16; Ps 78:27), humiliation, grief and mourning (Job 2:12; 42:6; Isa 2:10; 47:1; also Rev 18:19). Five NT texts describe shaking dust off of one's feet as a sign of repudiation (Matt 10:14; Mark 6:11; Luke 9:5; 10:11; Acts 13:51). *See* ADAM; CLAY; DEATH, NT; DEATH, OT.

MICHAEL G. VANZANT

DWARF [דַּק daq]. A category of person, generally translated as "dwarf," considered physically imperfect who, along with such others as the blind, lame, and males with crushed testicles, was therefore disqualified from "offering the food of his God" within the Israelite cult (Lev 21:17, 20).

DWELL, DWELLING. *See* ABIDE; DWELLING PLACE; HOUSE; SIT, DWELL.

DWELLING PLACE [מוֹשָׁב moshav, מָקוֹם maqom, מָעוֹן ma'on, מִשְׁכָּן mishkan; κατοικητήριον katoikētērion, σκήνωμα skēnōma]. At its most basic, a dwelling place is somewhere to live. However, most of its occurrences in the OT have a more figurative meaning. God's Temple in Jerusalem is God's dwelling place (e.g., 2 Chr 6:54; Ps 74:7; 132:5). In one passage, God becomes the people's dwelling place (Ps 90:1). In such instances, the term connotes rest and sacred communion. In Greek the term is also used to refer to the Temple in Jerusalem (1 Esd 1:50; Acts 7:46), although the NT texts do not always value this dwelling place positively. Ultimately, the body of believers is to be knit together into a dwelling place for God (Eph 2:22).

JENNIFER L. KOOSED

DYE [צֶבַע tseva']. Dye is a substance used to color raw fiber, spun yarn, or woven cloth. Canaan was well known for its dyed fabrics. Sisera's mother anticipates confiscated dyed items (Judg 5:30). Dyed textiles were used for the tabernacle and priestly garments (Exod 25–39).

Dyeing was usually done to the thread before weaving it into cloth (*see* CLOTH, CLOTHES). It was difficult to dye linen but wool took the color well. Animals or plants provided the source for most dyestuffs. The *kermes* insect produced red dyes. Saffron produced yellow. In a complex process, artisans produced purple derived from the *murex* mollusk. TYRE was known for its production of rare and expensive purple dye. Earthen materials were more likely to produce coloring for paint than for textiles.

Dyeing facilities usually were at the edges of settlements since the process could produce unpleasant odors. Dye was prepared at the facilities, using different methods for different materials. Mordants were added to the dyeing process to make the dyes more colorfast. Worldwide, the earliest known example of thread-dyed textiles was found at the Cave of the Warrior in the Judean desert.

Bibliography: E. J. W. Barber. *Prehistoric Textiles: The Development of Cloth in the Neolithic and Bronze Ages with Special Reference to the Aegean* (1991); Zvi C. Kornen. "Color Analysis of the Textiles." *The Cave of the Warrior: A Fourth Millennium Burial in the Judean Desert* (1998) 100–109; Pliny, *Nat Hist.* 9.

MARY PETRINA BOYD

DYSENTERY [δυσεντέριον dysenterion]. Luke reports how Paul, shipwrecked on Malta, healed Publius' father of "fever and dysentery" (Acts 28:8). The stem of the word enterion (ἐντέριον) indicates an intestinal problem. Invariably accompanied by diarrhea, including mucus and blood, and in this case by a fever, this case of dysentery suggests that the man likely suffered from a toxic-type illness rather than infection. He probably ate food contaminated by fly-borne toxins causing fever and dysentery, which are self-limiting within twenty-four to forty-eight hours. (Paul visited Malta for three days). This helps explain his rapid response to Paul's therapeutic prayer and laying on of hands. *See* DISEASE.

JOHN J. PILCH

DYSMAS diz'muhs. The *Acts of Pilate* identifies the penitent criminal crucified with Jesus as Dysmas, and the other criminal as GESTAS.

DYSTRUS [Δύστρος Dystros]. Macedonian name for the month of March, equivalent to the Hebrew month of ADAR (Josephus, *Ant.* 11.286). Tobit's wife Anna received payment for some weaving and a gift of a young goat on the seventh of Dystrus (Tob 2:12).

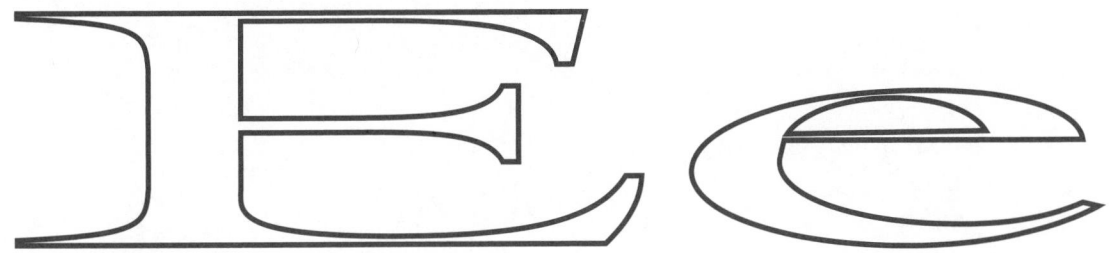

E, ELOHIST. el′oh-hist One of four principal written sources of the Pentateuch posited by the DOCUMENTARY HYPOTHESIS. This source derives its name from its so-called preference for the divine designation Elohim, "God." Scholars have long debated whether E materials represent a continuous literary strand or collected traditions supplementing the Yahwist source (J) *See* GOD, NAMES OF; SOURCE CRITICISM.

JOEL S. BURNETT

EAGLE [נֶשֶׁר nesher; ἀετός aetos]. Several eagles (species of the genus *Aquila*) can be spotted in Israel/Palestine, but they are relatively rare. The traditional translation of the Hebrew word nesher is "eagle" (this tradition was initiated by the LXX, which consistently opted for aetos, and was firmly established through the rendering *aquila* in the Vulgate). As a consequence, generations of readers have been given the impression that the biblical authors regarded the eagle as a central symbol or metaphor for human and divine power. God is thus depicted as an "eagle" carrying its young on its pinions (Deut 32:11), and the faithful ones are promised that they will experience a renewal of strength and become "like eagles" (Isa 40:31). However, some OT descriptions of the nesher do not seem to fit the eagle at all. Most evidently, the eagle is not bald on its head and neck (Mic 1:16), whereas the vulture is. Further, the eagle does not feed on carrion (Job 39:27-30), but the vulture does. In most cases, actually, "vulture" would probably be a more accurate translation of nesher (the NRSV has "vulture" in a few instances, e.g., Hos 8:1). According to a wide scholarly consensus, the reference is primarily to the majestic griffon vulture (*Gyps fulvus*). However, one cannot exclude the possibility that nesher sometimes refers to some kind of eagle, for instance the golden eagle (*Aquila chrysaetus*), the largest of the birds of prey, or the imperial eagle (*Aquila heliaca*), a bird that nests in trees.

A case in point is the description in Ezek 17:3, of a nesher "with great wings and long pinions, rich in plumage of many colors" who "took the top of the cedar." In Ezek 17, then, the eagle serves as a royal symbol, since this text is an allegorical depiction of the Babylonian ruler Nebuchadnezzar. Hence, it is reasonable to draw the conclusion that the ancient Israelites used the same term for both "eagle" and "vulture." It is, in fact, difficult to distinguish between these birds when viewed from a distance. The word

for "eagle" in biblical Hebrew is ʿayit (עַיִט), as is the case in modern usage. However, it seems preferable to take ʿayit as a general designation for all birds of prey. In the NT, the Greek word aetos (ἀετός, compare ʿayit) can designate not only eagles but also vultures: "Where the corpse is, there the vultures will gather" (Matt 24:28). Eagle symbolism is found in Revelation (4:7; 8:13; 12:14). The description in Rev 4:6-8 of four creatures, including one "like a flying eagle," is clearly influenced by the vision in Ezek 1:5-14. *See* BIRD OF PREY; BIRDS OF THE BIBLE; VULTURE.

Bibliography: G. R. Driver. "Birds in the Old Testament: I. Birds in Law." *PEQ* (1955) 5–20; J. Feliks. *The Animal World of the Bible* (1962).

GÖRAN EIDEVALL

EAR [אֹזֶן ʾozen; οὖς ous]. An organ that enables hearing and equilibrium. The ear was used to display customs and rituals and to refer symbolically to listening (or lack thereof). Piercing of the ear marked a slave as serving his master for life (Exod 21:6). Blood was placed on the ears of Aaron and his sons to consecrate them as priests (Exod 29:20; Lev 8:23). Oil was placed on lepers' ears during rituals to cleanse them (Lev 14:14-28). Most often the ear symbolically refers to how humans must be attentive, obedient, and understanding of God's commands. The commandment traditionally called the Shema (from the Hebrew shamaʿ [שָׁמַע], "hear") required the Israelites to give exclusive obedience to God. It begins with calling the Israelites to use their ears to listen (Deut 6:4-9). Ears that that do not provide human beings understanding are referred to as unopened (Job 36:10; Ps 40:6; Isa 48:8; 50:4-5), uncircumcised (Jer 6:10; Acts 7:51), heavy (Isa 6:10), and deaf (Isa 43:8). The giving of the covenant (and its renewal) involved the people publicly hearing it (e.g., Deut 31:28). Although the prophets Isaiah and Jeremiah proclaim repeatedly that God's people ought to incline their ear to God and listen (e.g., Isa 51:4; 55:3; Jer 11:8; 17:2) and the psalmist affirms that God prefers the open ear not burnt offerings (Ps 40:6), the psalmist also repeatedly pleads that God "incline" and "give ear" in order that God bring deliverance (e.g., Ps 5:1; 17:1-6; 31:2). Following the prophets, Jesus explained to his disciples that hearing God's word must bear fruit (Mark 4:13-20). Paul refers to ears as a significant body part to affirm that all the gifts of the Corinthian church members were essential (1 Cor 12:16).

EMILY R. CHENEY

EARLY AND LATE RAINS [early rains: יוֹרֶה yoreh; πρόϊμος proimos; late rains: מַלְקוֹשׁ malqosh; ὄψιμος opsimos]. Rains of Palestine occurring in autumn (October–November) and spring (March–April), marking the beginning and end of the winter rainy season, and, if timely, a sign of God's favor for Israel's covenant faithfulness (Deut 11:14; Jer 3:3; 5:24; Job 29:23; Ps 84:6; Jas 5:7). *See* ISRAEL, CLIMATE OF; RAIN.

EARRING. *See* JEWELRY.

EARTH [אֲדָמָה 'adhamah, אֶרֶץ 'erets, יַבָּשָׁה yabbashah, עָפָר 'afar; תֵּבֵל tevel; Aram. אֲרַע 'ara'; γῆ gē, οἰκουμένη oikoumenē, χοϊκός choikos]. The multiple meanings of *earth* are closely related to the diversity of meanings of the various Hebrew and Gk. words used to cover this semantic range. More than twenty-five Hebrew words are sometimes translated by the Gk. word gē in the LXX. Nevertheless, 'erets is the dominant Hebrew word. Both 'erets and gē cover a wide range of meanings from the universal sense of all the earth to a particular piece of ground, dust, or soil.

A. Terms for Earth in the Old Testament
B. Heaven and Earth
C. Earth and Sea
D. Earth as Land or Piece of Land
E. Earth as Soil or Dust
F. The Earthly Nature of Human Life

A. Terms for Earth in the Old Testament
The most common Hebrew term for earth, 'erets (e.g., Gen. 1:1), is most frequently translated in the LXX as gē. 'Adhamah ("ground") is also nearly always translated with gē.

Two other Hebrew words are worthy of note. Nearly half of the occurrences of 'afar, ("dust" or "ashes") are translated by gē. The word is consistently used to describe the dry earth in a portable form, whether as the earth used to fill wells (Gen 26:15) or the DUST used with ashes to manifest penitence (Job 42:6). Dust describes human insignificance before God, because humans come from the ground ('adhamah): "for dust ('afar) you are and to dust you will return" (Gen 3:19). Abraham remarks on the paradox that he, who is but dust and ashes, should dispute with the Lord (Gen 18:27), but he does so nonetheless. Thus 'afar is used to specify one aspect of rhe meaning of 'erets. With 'adamah it importantly draws attention to the way in which humans share in the nature of the material creation along with the other animals (Gen 2:19) that live on the face of the earth.

The Book of Daniel uses the term 'ara' for *earth* where erets might have been used to connote "all the earth," or "upon earth." The use of 'ara' in this way appears to be a Danielic characteristic (Dan 2:39; 4:1-35; 6:25-27; 7:4-23; 8:5; 12:2).

In Hebrew poetry, the term tevel is used frequently in parallel with 'erets (Pss 24:1 [Heb. 23:1]; 33:8 [Heb. 32:8]; 89:11 [Heb. 88:11]; 96:13 [Heb. 95:13]; 98:9 [Heb. 97:9]; Isa 13:11; 24:4; 26:9, 18; 34:1; Jer 10:12; Lam 4:12). In the LXX the parallelism is generally preserved by translating 'erets as gē and tevel as oikoumenē, but in Isa 26:9, 18 both terms are translated by gē, because these Hebrew words are similar in meaning. Their parallel use brings out the cosmic or global sense in which 'erets can be used. In many of these texts, tevel carries the sense of the entire populated world, a sense clearly carried by oikoumenē.

B. Heaven and Earth
The expression "heaven and earth" is found in a variety of Semitic languages and signals a fundamental aspect of the meaning of earth (*see* COSMOGONY, COSMOLOGY). Genesis 1 gives an account of the CREATION of heaven and earth by God. The understanding of this account is affected by the way Gen 1:1 is understood. If it is understood as a title, the subsequent account tells of the fashioning of the heavens and the earth from a formless void constituted by the chaotic deep waters. The fashioning was achieved by the Spirit and the Word of God (Gen 1:2-29). Understood consecutively as a sequence, v. 1 tells of the creation of the formless watery waste as a basis for the subsequent fashioning of heaven and earth. Either way, it is clear that the creation of what we might call the universe entails both the heavens and the earth. In this context it seems that the heavens are conceived as the dome over the earth, which is understood as a flat disc (Ps 24:1 [Heb. 23:1]). Here 'erets is in parallel with tevel (oikoumenē), which has the sense of both the land and the inhabited world, which God established on the seas and the rivers (Ps 24:2 [Heb. 23:2]).

The dome of the heavens contains the sun, moon, and stars and adjoins the earth at its edges. A sense of spaciousness is created by reference to the four corners or edges of the earth (Isa 11:12; Ezek 7:2; Job 37:3) or the ends of the earth (Isa 5:26; Jer 10:13; Job 28:24; Ps 135:7). In the ANE the location of the temple was often conceived to be at the center or navel of the earth. Perhaps this forms a background to the understanding of Jerusalem with its temple (and Bethel before it) at the center of the earth though the mythological elements are absent (Ezek 38:12, compare with 5:5; Gen 28:10-12, 17-18). These and other images express a sense of the expansive nature of the whole earth.

The NT builds on the OT understanding of the world with the words kosmos (κόσμος), meaning the whole world or realm of existence, and the expression panta (πάντα), "all things," each with cosmological implications (John 1:3; Col 1:16). The NT affirms God as the creator of heaven and earth (Acts 4:24; 14:15 and compare with Eph 1:10; Col 1:16, 20; Rev 5:13; 10:6; 14:7) and as Lord of heaven and earth (Luke

10:21; Acts 17:24). This might seem to guarantee that "the earth remains forever" (Eccl 1:4). But the earth is threatened because of human sinfulness. Nevertheless, there is a tradition of the restoration of the earth as a pristine paradise (Isa 11:1-10, especially 11:9), and that the creation itself hopes for redemption (Rom 8:19-23). The NT maintains the view that "heaven and earth will pass away" Matt 5:18; 24:35; Mark 13:31; Luke 16:17; 21:33. Consequently, there will be a new heaven and a new earth (2 Pet 3:13; Rev 21:1), and heaven becomes the model for life on earth (Matt 6:10; Luke 11:2). *See* NEW HEAVEN, NEW EARTH.

C. Earth and Sea

In Gen 1, the earth is distinguished, not only from the heavens, but also from the sea. The earth is defined in terms of the dry land (yabbashah), and God calls the dry land earth (vv. 9-10). In this first canonical use of yabbashah, the expression "dry land" becomes a familiar idiom. Yet, in the LXX, only in Jonah 1:13 is yabbashah translated by gē because gē defines one level of the meaning of ʾerets. Earth is the landmass in contrast to the sea. In between are the islands or coastlands (Isa 24:14-16; 42:4, 10).

Earth is suspended over the primeval ocean (Ps 24:2), perhaps on pillars (Ps 75:3 [Heb. 75:4]), though Job 26:7 portrays the earth like a garment flung out and suspended in space. Poetic imagery is evident in this portrayal of the majestic creative power of God. The variety of images reminds us of language groping to find an adequate expression to describe the mystery of the world in relation to God. Each set of images describes the earth in the context of what surrounds it: beneath it the sea and above it the heavens. *See* NEW CREATION.

D. Earth as Land or Piece of Land

Just as there is a narrowing focus from the whole earth to a particular socio-political land, so the language narrows to describe a particular piece of land. God tells Moses to take off his shoes because "the place upon which you are standing is holy ground" (ʾadhamah) in Exod 3:5. In the LXX and in Acts 7:33, the holy ground is translated by gē. A common way of showing reverence was to bow down to the ground (ʾerets and gē).

Both ʾerets and gē are commonly used for particular lands. For example, after killing his brother, Cain became a fugitive and a wanderer on the earth (beʾerets [בְּאֶרֶץ], LXX epi tēs gēs ἐπὶ τῆς γῆς). Yet it is said that Cain went and dwelt in the land of Nod (beʾerets-nodh בְּאֶרֶץ־נוֹד), East of Eden (Gen 4:12, 16). Particular places are called the "land": the land of Israel (Matt 2:20), the land of Judah (Matt 2:6), the land of Zebulon, the land of Naphtali (Isa 9:1; Matt 4:15), and the land of Egypt.

Of particular importance for OT is the theology developed on the basis of the LAND promised to Abraham (Gen 12.1-3, 6-7; 13:14-17; 15.1-7, 17-20; 17.1-14 and frequently). Although Hebrew has no vocabulary meaning promise, when God tells Abraham of the land God will give him and his descendants, this has the meaning we attribute to the promised land. The land has a central place in Jewish scriptures because it is seen to be Israel's inheritance from God and a mark of God's blessing (*see* ISRAEL, HISTORY OF). The location and extent of the land vary in particular texts. There we find a smaller (from the wadi of Egypt to Hamath and all the land between the Jordan/Dead Sea and the Mediterranean Sea, Num 34:1-12) and much larger definition (from the Euphrates to the Western Sea, Deut 3:12-20, 11:24; Josh 22). The latter might reflect the Davidic expansion of borders.

At first the land is defined as Canaan, but the boundaries grow. It is recognized that other people first dwelt in the land. Abraham did not realize the promise, but it underlies the Exodus and EXILE narratives, which resonate with the theme of return to the land. The theme of the LAND in Jewish scriptures is nuanced in a variety of ways with little reference to the extent of the land. In the NT the focus becomes the Temple and Jerusalem instead of the land. Perhaps because of the destruction of Jerusalem and the Temple in 70 CE, the NT looks for a new Temple and a new Jerusalem of a different order in a new creation (Rev 21).

E. Earth as Soil or Dust

Reference to the creation of humans out of the dust of the ground has been noted (Gen 2:7, 19), and the beasts of the field and birds of the air are also of the ground (Gen 3:19). The soil is probably in view when it is said that God cursed the ground so that it no longer produced food but weeds (Gen 3:17). Likewise in the NT, reference to the "good ground" (gē) is to be understood as "good soil" (Matt 13:5; Mark 4:8, 20; Luke 8:8, 15). Epigeios (ἐπίγειος John 3:12; 2 Cor 5:1; Phil 2:10; 3:19; Jas 3:15) and choikos (1 Cor 15:47-49) are used in the NT for "dust," in the same sense as ʿafar.

F. The Earthly Nature of Human Life

This understanding of the physical relationship of humans to the material creation, though not prominent, is presupposed in the NT, and surfaces in a distinctive way in Paul and John. In John (3:31), Jesus as the one coming from above is contrasted with the one who is of the earth (ho ōn ek tēs gēs ὁ ὢν ἐκ τῆς γῆς), probably a reference to Gen 2:7; 3;19. Two points are made about the latter. Repetitively it is said, such a one "is of the earth" (ek tēs gēs estin ἐκ τῆς γῆς ἐστιν). As a consequence, such a one speaks within the limitation of this perspective (ek tēs gēs lalei ἐκ τῆς γῆς λαλεῖ). By contrast, the one coming from heaven bears witness to what he has seen and heard (John 3:32). Thus, the earthly origin of humans is contrasted with the heavenly origin of Jesus as the revealer of God. Nevertheless, through the coming of Jesus, those who believe in him may be born from above (John 1:12-13; 3:5, 7).

Paul contrasts the earthly origin of the first Adam with the heavenly origin of the last Adam. The first Adam is of the earth, a man of dust (ho prōtos anthrōpos ek gēs choikos ὁ πρῶτος ἄνθρωπος ἐκ γῆς χοϊκός). The second man is from heaven (ex ouranou ἐξ οὐρανοῦ). Paul's contrast also involves the resurrection of Jesus. His objective is to affirm the radical difference of the resurrection life from earthly life, making clear the consequences for those who share in the resurrection of Jesus (1 Cor 15:42-50). Thus, Paul and John each affirm the understanding of the earthy origin and nature of human life but with a view to making a contrast with the new situation brought about by the coming of Jesus. *See* DEAD, ABODE OF THE; JUBILEE, YEAR OF.

JOHN PAINTER

EARTH, NEW. *See* NEW HEAVEN, NEW EARTH.

EARTHENWARE. *See* POTTERY.

EARTHLY BODIES [σώματα ἐπίγεια sōmata epigeia]. In response to the Corinthians' question about the nature of resurrected bodies, Paul states that bodies take many different forms, both on earth and in heaven (1 Cor 15:35-41). Earthly bodies are fleshly and visible, but HEAVENLY BODIES are comprised of a more refined substance. Drawing upon an agricultural analogy, he argues that resurrection involves the transformation of physical bodies into spiritual bodies (1 Cor 15:36-37, 42-44).

DAVID M. REIS

EARTHQUAKE [רַעַשׁ ra'ash; σεισμός seismos, σείω seiō, σαλεύω saleuo]. A disruptive shifting of the earth's surface, occurring throughout Mediterranean history at periodic intervals and usually at moderate levels of intensity. However, Josephus recounts a devastating earthquake that hit Judea in the seventh year of Herod I's rule (34 BCE), destroying numerous cattle in the countryside and some 10,000 people under the rubble of collapsing houses (*Ant.* 15.121-23).

In biblical literature, earthquakes typically represent intervening "acts of God" in human history, often in conjunction with other destructive natural phenomena (wind, fire, flood, ice, etc.). The effects of the Lord's "quaking" may be retributive or redemptive.

During ancient Israel's wilderness trek, the Lord decisively puts down the revolt of Korah, Dathan, and Abiram against Moses' leadership by splitting apart the ground under the rebels' feet, causing them to be swallowed up and sucked "down alive to Sheol"—"along with their households . . . and all their goods" (Num 16:30-33; Josephus, *Ant.* 3.51-53). The psalmist confirms the fear that God shakes the earth's foundations in

anger against wayward people, making them "rock and reel" and "suffer hard things" (Pss 18:7; 60:1-3).

The book of Amos (1:1) dates the prophet's mission "two years before the earthquake" during the kingdoms of Uzziah in Judah (783–746 BCE) and Jeroboam in Israel (786–746) (excavations at Hazor have uncovered evidence of an earthquake ca. 760). This chronological-geological reference has ominous theological overtones for Amos's visions of divine retribution against Israel in terms of shaken, shattered, and demolished houses (Amos 3:14-15; 6:11; 9:1). In a later, post-exilic context, Zechariah recalls the disastrous quake in Amos' day as an image of the Lord's terrible apocalyptic judgment (Zech 14:5, 14:1-21). Other OT prophets incorporate earthquakes into their forecasts of eschatological doom (Isa 29:5, 6 [with thunder, tempest, and devouring fire]; Joel 2:10 [with darkened celestial bodies]; Nah 1:5 [with melting mountains]), as do Jesus (Matt 24:7; Mark 13:8; Luke 21:11 [with famines and plagues]), the seer of Revelation (6:12; 8:5; 11:13 [7,000 killed], 19; 16:18), and the author of 2 Esdr (3:19; 9:3 [with "tumult of peoples, intrigues of nations, wavering of leaders, confusion of princes"]; 16:12 [with "sea churned up from the depths"]).

In more positive, though still fearful, terms, sudden tremulous manifestations may demonstrate God's glorious and powerful presence on behalf of his people. The wilderness theophany at Sinai, when "the whole mountain shook (kharadh חרד) violently" (accompanied by thunder, lightning, and smoke) in preparation for God's revelation of covenant law, represents a banner example (Exod 19:16-25; 20:18; compare Ps 68:7-8—"O God, when you . . . marched through the wilderness, the earth quaked [ra'ash/seiō], the heavens poured down rain, at the presence of God, the God of Sinai"). Ironically, however, when Elijah later encountered similar phenomena at the same site, "the Lord was not in the earthquake" (or wind or fire) any more than in the final "sound of sheer silence" (NRSV) or "a gentle whisper" (NIV) (1 Kgs 19:11-12; divine revelation ultimately came to Elijah in "a voice" [19:13-18]).

In the NT, Matthew associates earthquakes with Jesus' crucifixion and resurrection: when Jesus cried out and took his last breath, "the earth shook [seiō]," splitting rocks and temple veil, releasing resurrected bodies from open tombs, and inspiring soldiers' faith in Jesus (Matt 27:50-54); at Jesus' gravesite, a "great earthquake" signaled the arrival of a radiant angel who rolled back the tombstone and announced Jesus' resurrection to Mary Magdalene and another Mary (meanwhile "the guards shook [seiō] and became like dead men" [28:1-7]). In the book of Acts, a dramatic house-shaking (saleuo) in Jerusalem accompanies the Spirit's outpouring on the early church (4:31), and a foundation-shaking (saleuo) earthquake (σεισμός) in Philippi opens prison doors and loosens the shackles of the hymn-singing Paul and Silas (16:25-27).

Bibliography: D. H. Kallner-Amiran. "A Revised Earthquake-Catalogue of Palestine." *IEJ* 1 (1950–51) 223–46; D. H. Kallner-Amiran. "A Revised Earthquake-Catalogue of Palestine." *IEJ* 2 (1952) 48–65; J. L. Mays. *Amos: A Commentary* (1969).

F. SCOTT SPENCER

EARTHWORM. *See* WORM.

EAST. *See* ORIENTATION.

EAST, PEOPLE OF THE. *See* PEOPLE OF THE EAST.

EAST COUNTRY [אֶרֶץ קֶדֶם ʾerets qedhem, אֶרֶץ מִזְרָח ʾerets mizrakh]. The term likely refers to BABYLON (Ezek 47:8; Zech 8:7), east of Israel, where Abraham sends his concubines' sons (Gen 25:6).

EAST GATE [שַׁעַר הַמִּזְרָח shaʿar hammizrakh]. A GATE in the Jerusalem wall, whose only unambiguous reference is its repair by Shemaiah, who was also its "keeper" (Neh 3:29). It is possible that the "East Gate" is to be identified with the "eastern Gate of the House of Yahweh" found throughout the book of Ezekiel (10:19; 11:1; 40:6-11; 43:1-5; 44:1-3; 46:1-3), referring to the departure and return of the Presence of Yahweh from the city of JERUSALEM during the Babylonian siege.

PHILLIP MICHAEL SHERMAN

EAST WIND [קָדִים qadhim]. Torrid seasonal winds (south to southeasterly, around March and November) originating in the hot, sandy desert. These characteristically destructive winds persist in the present day and are known by several names throughout the Mediterranean, including *sirocco*, *jugo*, *khamsin*, and *ghibli*. In the OT, the qadhim is often an act of Yahweh (Exod 10:13; Ps 78:26; Jonah 4:8), having utility both for deliverance (Exod 14:21) and judgment (Hos 13:15).

NATHAN D. MAXWELL

EASTER. The English word does not occur in the Bible (except in the KJV, which translates *Passover* in Acts 12:4 as *Easter*). The NT speaks of Passover (pascha πάσχα), the Jewish holiday celebrating the liberation of Israel from slavery, which the Gospels associate with the death of Jesus (*see* PASSOVER AND FEAST OF UNLEAVENED BREAD). In the Gospels, the last supper occurs on the Day of Preparation for the Passover, and the meal Jesus eats with his disciples is a Passover meal. Jesus' words instructing his disciples to associate his body and blood with the elements of the Passover meal point to a view in which the Lord's Supper was understood in connection to Passover (see Matt 26:1, 17-30; Mark 14:1, 12-25; Luke 22:1, 7-23). In John, the last supper occurs prior to the Day of Preparation for the Passover (John 13:1), but the author explicitly associates Jesus' death with the Passover offering (John

19:14, 36). In making these connections, the Gospels point to an early Christian view in which Jesus' death was understood as being similar to the events of Passover, God's inauguration of the deliverance of Israel from slavery (compare 1 Cor 5:7). Over time, the Christian celebration of Easter developed into its own festival separate from Passover. Associations between the festivals may still be found in hymns and eucharistic prayers in some traditions. In many languages other than English, the word for the Christian holiday derives from pascha (i.e., French, *Pâques*).

SUSAN E. HYLEN

EASTERN SEA [הַיָּם הַקַּדְמֹנִי hayam haqqadhmoni]. A body of water mentioned in Joel 2:20, Zech 14:8, and Ezek 47:18, probably the Dead Sea, which lay eastward from ancient Israel. However, given its restriction to prophetic texts and the alternative translation of qadhmoni as "former," a mythical referent is plausible.

DEREK E. WITTMAN

EATING. *See* MEALS.

EBAL eeʹbuhl [עֵיבָל ʿeval]. 1. Son of Shobal, the Horite (Gen 36:23; 1 Chr 1:40; Deut 2:12).
2. Variant for OBAL, son of Joktan (Gen 10:28; 1 Chr 1:22).

EBAL, MOUNT eeʹbuhl [הַר עֵיבָל har ʿeval]. A mountain rising 3,083 ft. above sea level in the central hill country of northern Israel, adjacent to the town of Shechem and opposite Mount Gerizim (*see* GERIZIM, MOUNT). In Deut 27 Moses instructs the Israelites to construct an altar of undressed stones on this mountain when they have crossed the Jordan and entered the land of promise (compare Deut 11:29). Deuteronomy describes the elaborate covenant ceremony in which the Israelites divide themselves between the two mountains at Shechem with Reuben, Gad, Asher, Zebulun, Dan, and Naphtali standing on Ebal affirming the curses, and Simeon, Levi, Judah, Issachar, Joseph, and Benjamin on Gerizim affirming the blessings (*see* BLESSINGS AND CURSINGS). The ceremony is officiated by the Levites, who announce the curses first, hear the people's response of "Amen," then announce the blessings and again hear the people's response of "Amen." The highly structured ceremony described in Deut 27 is narrated briefly in Josh 8:30-35, where the text indicates that Joshua did all that Moses had instructed. Some scholars connect this story with the covenant ceremony at Shechem in Josh 24:1-28, which mentions setting up a stone as a witness to the affirmation of the covenant by Israel. *See* ISRAEL, GEOGRAPHY OF.

C. MARK MCCORMICK

EBED eeʹbid [עֶבֶד ʿevedh]. A proper name meaning "slave" or "servant." 1. The father of GAAL, who challenged the authority of ABIMELECH in Judg 9:26.

2. A descendant of Adin and son of Jonathan who returned from Babylonian exile under EZRA (8:6).

EBED-MELECH ee'bid-mee'lik עֶבֶד־מֶלֶךְ 'evedh-melekh]. Ebed-Melech (literally "servant of the king") was an Ethiopian EUNUCH who served in the Judahite king ZEDEKIAH's court. Ebed-Melech rescued JEREMIAH from his cistern prison (Jer 38:7-13), resulting in a promise from God of survival when the kingdom of Judah fell (Jer 39:15-18). With Mesopotamian origins, the title "servant of the king" within the royal court often referred to a paid position of service. The Assyrians developed the title Ebed-Melech into a proper name for important members of the court. The story of Jeremiah follows over 100 years of Assyrian influence in Palestine.

MICHAEL G. VANZANT

EBENEZER eb'uh-nee'zuhr אֶבֶן הָעֵזֶר 'even ha'ezer]. Means "stone of help." 1. A location associated with the Philistine defeat of the Israelites under Saul and the taking of the Ark of the Covenant (1 Sam 4:1; 5:1).

2. A stone set up by Samuel (1 Sam 7:12) following an Israelite defeat of the Philistines is also called Ebenezer, for, as Samuel explains, "Thus far the LORD has helped us." The exact location is uncertain.

PHILLIP MICHAEL SHERMAN

EBER ee'buhr עֵבֶר 'ever]. A descendant of NOAH's son SHEM representing all the Semites in J's post-diluvian Table of Nations (Gen 10:21). The Priestly genealogy (Gen 11) presents the line of Eber leading directly to Abram, suggesting Eber as the eponymous ancestor of the HEBREW PEOPLE. The Chronicler's genealogy lists Eber in two places (1 Chr 1:18, 25), apparently conflating the Genesis accounts. Other appearances of this name in the MT are not definitively supported in LXX manuscripts. First Chronicles 5:13 and Neh 12:20 have, respectively, Ōbēd (Ωβηδ) and Abed (Αβεδ), possibly translating the Hebrew 'ever.

C. MARK MCCORMICK

EBEZ ee'biz אֶבֶץ 'evets]. Ebez was a settlement mentioned in Josh 19:20 as one of sixteen towns within the territory of the tribe of Issachar. Its exact location is unknown though it is sometimes identified with the modern site of Tell el-Beida.

EBIASAPH i-bi'uh-saf. See ABIASAPH.

EBIONITES ee'bee-uh-nit [Ἐβιωναῖοι Ebiōnaioi, Ἐβιωναῖται Ebiōnaitai]. The Ebionites, whose name comes from the Hebrew 'evyonim (אֶבְיוֹנִים "the poor"), may have acquired this designation for their desire to live as those "poor in spirit" (Matt 5:3). The church fathers, who regarded them as heretics, state that they remained faithful to some aspects of the Jewish law. According to Irenaeus (Haer. 1.26.2;

3.21.1; 4.33.4; 5.1.3), they used only the Gospel of Matthew but denied the virgin birth, regarded Paul as an apostate, practiced circumcision, and prayed toward Jerusalem. Epiphanius (Pan. 30.13-14, 16, 22) records fragments of the Gospel of the Ebionites, which detail a rejection of sacrifice and the practice of vegetarianism. See EBIONITES, GOSPEL OF THE; JEWISH CHRISTIANITY.

DAVID M. REIS

EBIONITES, GOSPEL OF THE. The Gospel of the Ebionites is the scholarly title given to the gospel fragments quoted by the bishop Epiphanius (Pan. 30.13-14, 16, 22). While its relationship to the Gospel According to the Hebrews and the Gospel of the Nazoreans remains uncertain, this gospel probably originated with the Ebionites, a sect known for its observance of Jewish law. By harmonizing and transforming synoptic material, the gospel rejects the virgin birth and condemns the practice of sacrifice. The community's vegetarian outlook is apparent with the assertion that John ate "cakes" (enkris ἐγκρίς), rather than "locusts" (akris ἀκρίς), and the question about eating flesh that Jesus poses at the Passover meal. The Greek wordplay argues against Hebrew as the gospel's original language. The text's harmonization of the Synoptics, a practice known through the works of JUSTIN MARTYR and Tatian, suggests an early 2nd cent. CE date. See HEBREWS, GOSPEL OF THE; NAZOREANS, GOSPEL OF THE.

DAVID M. REIS

EBLA TEXTS eb'luh. In the years between 1974 and 1976, an archaeological expedition from the University of Rome, directed by Paolo Matthiae, discovered a huge number of cuneiform tablets (estimated to have been originally about 2,500) at Tell Mardikh (ancient Ebla or Ibla) near Aleppo in Syria. The tablets were discovered in what was called Palace G. While their precise age is still in dispute, one can say that they date to approximately 2500–2400 BCE. The tablets are overwhelmingly administrative (dealing with distribution of such things as agricultural products, metals (including precious metals), and textiles. Nevertheless, the finds included a considerable number of scholarly texts (word lists, which cuneiform scholars normally call lexical texts, both unilingual Sumerian and bilingual Sumerian-Eblaite). Many of the unilingual Sumerian texts are duplicates of texts known from Mesopotamia (principally Fara and Abu Salabikh), thought to be slightly earlier than the Ebla texts. Among these texts are such compositions as a list of names of birds (previously known from Fara, ancient Shuruppak, home of the Sumerian Noah) and a list of geographical names (previously known from Abu Salabikh, ancient name uncertain). There are also a few letters and literary texts (such as incantations and hymns).

Erich Lessing/Art Resource, NY

Figure 1: One of 15,000 tablets in the Royal Archives (2400 BCE) opposite the Audience Court of Palace G, Elba, Syria, excavated by Paolo Matthiae in 1975. Location: National Museum, Aleppo, Syria.

Interest in the new texts focused initially on the identity of the language in which they were written. It was obvious that many words were written with Sumerian logograms (word signs), especially for nouns and verbs. Most of the personal names were clearly Semitic and the words written syllabically were also obviously Semitic. The question was, what language was it and what other Semitic languages was it closest to? The initial proposal, made by Giovanni Pettinato, the original epigrapher of the expedition, was to call it Old Canaanite, an identification now largely abandoned. The language is now conventionally called Eblaite (we do not know what its speakers called it). It is generally recognized that it belongs to the eastern Semitic group that includes Akkadian and Amorite. Some scholars insist that it is really a dialect of Akkadian. No consensus has been reached on this point.

The Sumerian cuneiform writing system was created to write a non-Semitic language and was poorly adapted for writing a Semitic language, especially because of a number of Semitic consonants that do not exist in Sumerian. In addition, the Sumerian writing system (and consequently the systems derived from it used to write other languages) has the peculiarity that a number of different signs can be used to write the same syllable and additionally that a single sign can have multiple syllabic readings. An example is the sign DU (whose pictographic ancestor depicted a foot), which has a number of different readings, depending on whether it means "stand," "walk," etc. This helps to account for, as an example, an early misreading of the signs du-lu as gub-lu and a suggestion that it represented Gubla, the ancient name of Byblos.

A great many of the Ebla texts are now published (principally in Italian). While cuneiform texts of the mid-third millennium often pose problems of interpretation, it can be said confidently that we can now understand the administrative documents quite well, thanks in large measure to the overwhelming use of Sumerian logograms and our improved understanding of the Eblaite prepositions. Quite often, a document has only a few Eblaite words written syllabically (such as conjunctions and prepositions), though the logograms were clearly to be read using the Eblaite equivalents.

The initial identification of the language as Old Canaanite and the suggestion that the texts included such things as the names of the OT "cities of the plain" and personal names similar to names in the patriarchal narratives led a few scholars (and many writers in the popular press) to posit a close relationship to the milieu of the OT. Some ministers, particularly among evangelical Christians, were eager to see the Ebla texts as an affirmation of the accuracy and the antiquity of OT narratives. The principal advocate of the theory that the Ebla texts were of direct relevance for the study of the OT was the late Father Mitchell Dahood. A well-known example of his work is a text that he confidently "translated" as a proverb written in Canaanite but which turned out to be a text listing Sumerian terms for cuts of meat. Most scholars who are knowledgeable about cuneiform writing of the third millennium BCE tend to be dubious about many of his proposals and see them as early attempts to make sense of a new body of ANE textual material. Indeed, the scholarly consensus now is that the major contribution of the Ebla texts is the tremendous amount of information adding to our understanding of society and economy in third millennium Syria. As well, there is considerable evidence of the level of Sumerian scholarship in Syria at that time. The scholarly consensus now is that the importance of the Ebla texts for the study of the Old Testament is virtually nil.

Bibliography: Alfonso Archi. "The Archives of Ebla." Klaas R. Veenhof, ed. *Cuneiform Archives and Libraries* (1986) 72–86; Robert Biggs. "The Ebla Tablets: An Interim Perspective." *BA* 43 (1980) 76–87; D. N. Freedman. "The Real Story of the Ebla Tablets: Ebla and the Cities of the Plain." *BA* 41 (1978) 143–64; I. J. Gelb. "Thoughts About Ibla: A Preliminary Evaluation, March 1977." *Syro-Mesopotamian Studies* 1 (1977) 3–30; Paolo Matthiae. *Ebla: An Empire Rediscovered* (1981); Giovanni Pettinato. *The Archives of Ebla: An Empire Inscribed in Clay* (1981).

ROBERT D. BIGGS

EBONY [הָבְנִי hovni]. Tree valued for its wood, which was transported from India and Ceylon, and used for making exquisite furniture inlaid with ivory, as well as idols. It was a key trade item in the transactions that the merchants of Tyre made with the merchants of Rhodes (Ezek 27:15).

EMILY R. CHENEY

EBRON ee'bruhn [עֶבְרֹן 'evron]. A city allotted to the tribe of Asher (Josh 19:28), perhaps also spelled ABDON, a Levitical town in Asher's territory (Josh 21:30; 1 Chr 6:74).

ECBATANA ek-bat'uh-nuh [Aram. אַחְמְתָא 'akhmetha'; Ἐκβάτανα Ekbatana]. A city, near modern Hamadan located in the Zagros Mountains of modern Iran, mentioned in the books of Ezra, Judith, Tobit, and 2 Maccabees. In antiquity, Ecbatana was a major city in Median territory (see MEDES, MEDIA). When the Persian king Cyrus captured the city from Astyages in the 6th cent. BCE, Ecbatana became the capital of the new Persian province of Media. Darius could not find a record in Babylonian archives of Cyrus' decree of support for rebuilding the Temple in Jerusalem, but he was able to locate a copy in Ecbatana, which suggests the city's importance as an administrative center for the empire (Ezra 6:2). Ecbatana was the town where Tobit's brother Raguel lived (Tob 3:7; 5:6; 6:10; 7:1; 14:12, 13). Tobit's son, Tobias, stops in Ecbatana on his journey to retrieve family money in Rages, and marries Raguel's daughter Sarah. After marriage they return to live in Palestine, but upon the death of his parents, Tobias and Sarah return to her hometown of Ecbatana. Though the book of Tobit is set during the 7th cent. BCE, it was written in the 2nd cent. BCE, and the mention of Jews in Ecbatana likely reflects a lively Jewish presence in the eastern Diaspora during this time. The book of Judith mentions Ecbatana (Jdt 1:1, 2, 14) as the city in which the fictive King Arpaxhad ruled over the Medes. Arpaxhad is described as securing mighty fortifications of the city that rival those of Babylon or Nineveh; although this description appears in a work of narrative artistry, the image of Ecbatana as a major city affirms its importance as a regional capital. Ecbatana is also mentioned in 2 Macc 9:2 in connection with one of the military campaigns of Antiochus IV Epiphanes. See TOBIT, BOOK OF.

JUDITH H. NEWMAN

ECCLESIASTES, BOOK OF i-klee'zee-as'teez [Ἐκκλησιαστής Ekklēsiastēs]. The Hebrew name Qoheleth (qoheleth קֹהֶלֶת) has become more common. It is also called the Book of the Preacher.

A. Name of the Book
B. Text and Reception
C. Structure of the Book
D. Special Features
  1. Text and language
  2. Historical and social background
  3. Setting in Wisdom Literatures

E. Theological and Religious Significance
  1. Joy versus absurdities
  2. God inspires the answer
  3. Healthy religious attitude
Bibliography

A. Name of the Book

Ecclesiastes is the anglicized form of ekklēsiastēs, meaning an officer, or a person in charge of a congregation or assembly, this is, in turn, a conventional Greek rendering of the Hebrew title of the book, Qoheleth, literally, "the one who convenes an assembly." The name appears in the opening verse of the book, "The words of Ecclesiastes/Qoheleth, the son of David, king of Israel in Jerusalem (1:1, compare 1:2, 12; 7:27; 12:8, 9, 10). "The Preacher," or its equivalent in other modern languages, is also commonly found. The Hebrew name is a feminine participle of the root qahal (קָהַל) "to gather people in an assembly." A number of feminine nouns in Hebrew can denote a member (not necessarily female) of a group, thus a unit noun, as opposed to a collective noun. In this case, Qoheleth would be an individual among those who are known to be in charge of addressing the assembly. The etymological explanation, however, plays little role for the understanding of the book which contains observations, reflections, exhortations, and ruminations of a sage who was trying to enter into dialogue with the intellectual traditions known during the last stage of the formation of the Hebrew canon.

In the Hebrew canon the book belongs to the Five Megilloth, namely Ruth, Song of Songs, Ecclesiastes, Lamentations, and Esther. As such, it is located in the third part of the Hebrew canon known as the Writings (Ketuvim), after Psalms, Proverbs, and Job and before Daniel, Ezra, Nehemiah and 1–2 Chronicles. It is traditionally read during the Feast of Booths, probably because in a number of places it invokes joy (see BOOTHS, FEAST OR FESTIVAL OF). In some early Jewish traditions the book was put together with the two other books believed to be authored by Solomon, Proverbs and Canticles. In the LXX these three books are placed after Psalms, traditionally attributed to Solomon's father, David. Current English translations used in Christian churches, such as the King James Version and the Revised Standard Version, follow this arrangement.

B. Text and Reception

The modern scholarly editions of the Hebrew text known as the BHS and the BHQ are based on the Masoretic Text of the LENINGRAD CODEX (St. Petersburg) B19A from 1008 CE. The slightly older but incomplete Aleppo Codex lacks the text of Ecclesiastes and some other books. From the textual-critical points of view, the Masoretic text is in good condition. The on-going project Biblia Hebraica Quinta contains a critical edition of Ecclesiastes, published in 2004.

The book is rarely reflected in the other books in the OT, which may be due to its late composition. Two deuterocanonical books, the Wisdom of Solomon and Ecclesiasticus (also known as Sirach), seem to know of Ecclesiastes' views (e.g., Wis 2:3 and Eccl 12:7). A more accommodating view is found in the book of Ecclesiasticus. For example, in saying "Some people keep silent because they have nothing to say, while others keep silent because they know when to speak" (Sir 20:6), the author is undoubtedly paraphrasing Ecclesiastes: "A time to keep silence, and a time to speak" (3:7), while using it to support his own purposes.

The opinions shared in the book are sometimes at odds with the generally held piety in the OT, and to some extent, they are even hostile to some traditional positions. This explains the tortuous process the book had to go through before it became part of the OT. The attribution of authorship to Solomon may have paved the way for its inclusion. Similarly, the orthodox statement given in the second epilogue, 12:13-14, provides a kind of disclaimer to the generally controversial views expressed in the book: "The end of the matter; all has been heard. Fear God and keep his commandments; for that is the whole duty of everyone. For God will bring every deed into judgment, including every secret thing, whether good or evil."

It is generally held that Ecclesiastes was accepted as a sacred book by the Council of Jamnia (around 90 CE). But the decision was followed by heated disputes. Shammai's followers considered the book objectionable. On the other side, Hillel's disciples generally took a more favorable view of the book. Their more positive opinion was instrumental in the genuine appreciation of the book. An authoritative personality like Akiba, around the 2nd cent. CE, recognized its place among the sacred books. By the end of the 2nd cent., Ecclesiastes started to be read during the Feast of Booths, hence its full acceptance in the Jewish communities. Among Christians, the book is also mentioned in various lists of sacred books, for example, the early list drawn up by Melito of Sardis (about 190 CE). But as late as the early 5th cent., Theodore of Mopsuestia still expressed doubts whether the book could really be part of the sacred collection.

C. Structure of the Book

At first glance, the final form of the book seems to be a collection of loose observations, about everyday life, wisdom, and other moral teachings, sometimes on the basis of experience, sometimes on the basis of philosophical attitudes. Although one might have the impression that the book was written with no specific arrangement in mind, scholars have discerned coherence by attending to thematic statements, formulaic expressions, and delineated thought units within the book.

After the opening verse, the book begins with a motto-like statement that everything is VANITY (1:2).

The same phraseology reappears toward the end of the book (12:8). This shows that there is an effort to frame the content of the book between those two verses. This technique is usually employed to bring the reader back to the beginning, in effect to invite reading the book again. The material after 12:8 is generally held to come from a later editor and serves as an epilogue to the book. Schematically, the basic structure is: Title (1:1)—Frame (1:2)—Corpus of the book (1:3–12:7)—Frame (12:8)—Epilogue (12:9-11).

The title ascribes the work to Qoheleth ("the Teacher"), the son of David, king in Jerusalem, thus giving some authority to the book. Immediately after this, the author states the main thesis of the book: the utter futility of human existence (1:1-2) and provides evidence for this position based on the natural environments to the human life, which for the author, form an endless cycle—like the rising and setting of the sun, the wind that goes around, and the flowing of waters to the sea through rivers and back to their source (1:3-11). From this point up to 3:15, the demonstration moves from nature to civilization. The author claims that all endeavors to explain the meaning of life through wisdom or knowledge lead, in the end, nowhere (1:12-18). The sage engages in all kinds of experiments: seeking pleasure, indulging himself in wine-drinking (2:1-3), and accumulating wealth and power (2:4-11). But all this leads to the same conclusion: no matter how good or evil, no matter how wise or foolish, one's life will end in death. This is the inevitable portion of humankind. There is therefore no such thing as ultimate good, for everything belongs to hevel (הֶבֶל), to futility or vanity. Consequently, it does not make much sense to hold on to the idea of reward and punishment, which is often taken as the basis for all moral and religious reasoning. No one knows what the posterity will be like (2:18-23). However, there is some real good, albeit limited, in this life: to continue living day by day, to engage oneself in human companionship, and to do one's labor. These are to be considered gifts from God to humankind. Even the wicked can thus experience what is good in such things (2:25-26). But it should be kept in mind that in the end all this is basically absurd. In a series of antitheses (3:1-8), the author explains that any effort to achieve happiness is doomed to end in despair. But, he admits, this is the way humans think. God, for his part, must have made everything perfect, including happiness, if such a thing exists. But humankind has no way of knowing of how God works (3:9-15).

The author then observes what is happening in human society and finds more evidence for his convictions. He sees that injustice prevails over justice. He ruminates on the paradoxes in this life, especially the fact that a common fate awaits everyone—to return to dust—and thus there is nothing better for humankind than the enjoyment of the present (3:16-22). He describes various forms of social injustice, oppression of the weak by the strong, ruthless competition based on envy and greed, the impermanence of fame, being isolated, the inability to enjoy one's own wealth. Even a king cannot take for granted that his initial glory will not end in rejection (4:1-16).

At this point, Ecclesiastes introduces a series of critical observations about common piety, which sometimes grows out of ignorance. According to him, a truly wise person should not indulge in popular but empty religious practices. What makes religion true is one's reverential attitude toward the sacred (4:17–5:6). The sage resumes his observations on injustice in society, where wealth only cannot satisfy one's ultimate questions about life, and bad luck and losses deprive children of their inheritance. The only thing one should be happy with is to enjoy one's work. This is again a gift from God (5:18-20). Chapter 6 stresses the uselessness of wealth and longevity. Both wise and foolish people in fact share the same fate. There is no escape from this. It is therefore better never to be born. This is a strong challenge to the tenets of traditional wisdom (6:1-9). Again, Ecclesiastes states that human destiny was fixed long ago but hidden so that there is no way of knowing what is going to happen (6:10-12). He follows with a collection of proverbs containing the expression "something is better than" (7:1-10). To this he adds other sayings highlighting the value of wisdom (7:11-29), even if he knows that meaninglessness still lurks beneath the surface. Ecclesiastes observes that the world marches on without any coherent system. He reiterates his conviction that the same fate applies to all, no matter how careful one conducts one's life (8:1–9:6).

The understanding reached thus far is further elaborated in 9:7–12:7. Ecclesiastes recommends going on with this life, enjoying what one can enjoy. Since the end is the same for every one, it is prudent to brave life with an attitude of joy, for God has accepted one's works too. This last section develops an ethical response to the human condition hitherto observed and considered as the portion of humankind in the created world. There is also a call not to be idle, because activities in themselves are worth doing independently of their results. It is in this sense that Ecclesiastes invites one to enjoy life fully and yet responsibly while still young, before old age and death remove this opportunity.

At the end of the book (12:9-14) there are two editorial appendices, which serve as an epilogue. The first (12:9-12) commends the teaching of the book, and the second (12:13-14) encourages the reader to live according to God's commandments, i.e. traditional piety, since in the end human deeds will be judged by God. This is obviously the epilogist's effort to attenuate the book's critique of traditional wisdom.

The thematic arrangement outlined above, according to Lohfink, suggests a certain "linear-dynamic arrangement," which develops the book's argumentation: Opening (1:2-11); Narrative introduction to the primarily anthropological central thesis (1:12–3:15); Deepening through many glimpses of social experience (3:16-6:10); Refutation of contrary positions, especially of older wisdom (6:11–9:6); Application through proposals about human behavior (9:7–12:8). The arrangement within the book highlights the double critique of religion and society:

> 1:2-3—Frame
> 1:4:11—Cosmology
> 1:12–3:15—Anthropology
> 3:16–4:16—Critique of society I
> 5:1-7—Critique of religion
> 5:8–6:10—Critique of society II
> 6:11–9:6—Critique of prevailing wisdom
> 9:7–12:7—Ethics
> 12:8 Frame

Another approach is represented by Wright, who discerns the following structure, based on the the recurring words and numerology found within the book:

> I. Ecclesiastes's investigation of life and his advice (1:1–6:9)
>   A. Introduction (1:1-18)
>   B. Report of his investigation and advice (2:1–6:9)
> II. The inadequacy of other advice and of our knowledge of the future (6:10–12:14)
>   A. Introduction (6:10-12)
>   B. The development of the two topics (7:1–11:6)
>   a. No one can find what is good to do (7:1–8:17)
>   b. No one knows the future (9:1–11:6)
>   C. Conclusion (11:7–12:14)

A number of scholars (e.g., Rendtorff and Murphy) have adopted Wright's analysis. However, major commentaries by Krüger, Seow, Whybray, and Crenshaw give other assessments of the structure of the book.

D. Special features
1. Text and language
The language of Ecclesiastes exhibits peculiarities when compared to classical Hebrew. The special traits of Ecclesiastes's Hebrew cannot be considered as mere idiosyncrasies of the author. On the contrary, they often coincide with usages that emerged during the post-exilic period. One such case is the frequent use of the relative prounoun she (שֶׁ) instead of the classical form 'asher (אֲשֶׁר). Another example is the form of the demonstrative zoh (זֹה) for zo'th (זֹאת). The accusative particle 'eth (אֵת) is found in several places to introduce a grammatical subject rather than an object, a feature found in the Chronicles. These have been explained as originating from a northern Hebrew dialect that came

to be used also in Judah after the exile. It has also been suggested that the construction shabbeakh ʾaniyi (שַׁבֵּחַ אֲנִי 4:2) is a feature of northern Syria-Palestinian languages, notably Phoenician. In fact, the frequent expression "under the sun" recalls a Phoenician expression which refers to political and historical events.

Qohelet also uses a special register or style, which may explain the relatively frequent use of synonymous pairs such as "wisdom and knowledge" (1:16; 2:26); "knowledge and wisdom" (9:10); "wisdom and the sum of things" (7:25); "with wisdom and knowledge and skill" (2:21); "to know and to search out and to seek" (7:25). The author is also fond of describing key concepts in similar but not identical expressions. When describing the futility of human existence, the author uses similar but not identical expressions, such as "vanity of vanities" (1:2; 12:8); "vanity" (3:19); "this also was/is vanity" (2:1, 15, 23; 5:9; 7:6; 8:10, 14). The idea of vexation of the spirit (1:17; 4:16; 1:14; 2:11, 17, 26; 4:4; 6:9) is sometimes associated with evil things (1:13; 2:21) or affliction (6:2). In other places, the idea of vanity is connected with expressions concerning the worthlessness of "the days of one's life" (2:3; 5:17; 8:15; 9:9; 7:15).

2. Historical and social background

Taken together, the language of the book is closer to post-exilic Hebrew, and this provides strong evidence for the time of its composition. Some indirect references to the historical events also point to this period. In any case, the book must have taken its present shape earlier than the 1st cent., given that there are Qumran fragments of Ecclesiastes datable to the first half of the 2nd cent. BCE and there are allusions to Ecclesiastes in the Book of SIRACH, datable to around 175 BCE. Scholars usually agree that the book grew among the intellectual circles in late post-exilic Jerusalem and was completed slightly before 250 BCE.

This was also a period of competing foreign influences in the political sphere, which leaves their marks on the intellectual and religious life in Israel. The Ptolemaic rulers in Egypt succeeded in putting Jerusalem and Judea under their administrative control, at least during the 3rd cent. During the same period, the Seleucids in the north were trying to exercise military influence. However, neither one could take full control over the area. The political intrigues during this period settled down when the Seleucids took control of the whole region, with the support of the Tobiads, the clan of the High Priest of the time. The situation ironically favored cultural elements from Egypt and Syria to play their parts. These elements, however, had amalgamated with Hellenistic culture since roughly half a century before. These are the cultural influences often detected in Ecclesiastes.

In the sphere of economic life, the period was a prosperous one. The Ptolemaic overlords improved agricultural development through better irrigation and land contouring. But despite this, the economic growth was not enjoyed by the lower end of the social scale. Only the upper strata, together with their overlord in Egypt, could benefit from the new prosperity. Opportunity was not equally distributed. Small land holders paid rents and taxes out of their insecure business. Easy and profitable business could and did change into sudden losses and bankruptcy. Ecclesiastes's sense of an uncertain future likely reflects these economic situations.

3. Setting in Wisdom Literatures

Ecclesiastes's position within the Israelite wisdom tradition is unique. One one hand, the sage affirms the values of traditional wisdom that implement the teaching of Torah. Thus, he holds that wisdom has clear advantage over mere folly, just like light over darkness (2:13). Wisdom gives security like wealth (7:12) and health (7:19), and it helps people to conduct a serene life (8:1). On the other hand, Ecclesiastes often challenges basic assumptions of conventional wisdom. For example, good actions will be rewarded and evil deeds will be punished, but the secret to attaining success is to avoid striving for what society deems to be good and acceptable. In a number of passages, the expression "there is/are" states some conventional position and then submits it to a severe criticism. For example, he says in 1:10, "yesh davar she" (יֵשׁ דָּבָר שֶׁ, "It is said that") there exists something about which one says, ("See, this is new!")." There follows the comment that it has already been like that for ages. This use of yesh indicates that the idea being discussed is not Ecclesiastes's. Similarly, speaking about those who are privileged to be among the living, 9:4 mentions yesh bittakhon (יֵשׁ בִּטָּחוֹן), "it is said that there is hope . . ." (v. 5) "for the living know that they are going to die but the dead know nothing." Other examples include 2:21; 4:8-9; 5:12; 6:1-11; 7:15 (2x); 8:14 (3x); and 10:5. In each of these instances, Ecclesiastes cites some traditional wisdom position only to dismiss its validity.

Scholars have noted various influences from other wisdom literatures of the ANE. From Egypt, for example, "The Harper's Song" (*ANET*, 467) commends an "enjoy life while you can" attitude, and "The Instruction for Ptah-Hotep" (*ANET* 412-414) offers advice concerning one's goals in life. Texts from Mesopotamia, for example, "The Babylonian Ecclesiastes" (*ANET*, 438-440) and "The Epic of Gilgamesh," (*ANET*, 72-100) assert that human existence inevitably leads only to death. Texts from the Stoics convey philosophical, and sometimes cynical, attitudes toward widely held opinions, including the meaning of suffering. Although one can track motifs common with Qohelet in these texts from Egypt, Mesoptmia, and Greece, another text, which enjoyed long popularity in Syria-Palestine, stands closer to the world of Ecclesiastes. The bilingual Sumero-Akkadian composition called "The Human Destiny" was known within the scribal circles in Syria-Palestine, judging from the fact that copies of it were found at Ugarit (second-half of the second millennium) and in Emar (close to the beginning of the first millennium). Even if its origin is Mesopotamia, the Emar text shows local adaptations. Due to the relatively recent rediscovery of the site (in the 1970s; the text was not published until the late 1980s), this material has not been exploited in the commentaries. The composition reads as follows (author's translation, following the better preserved text from Emar).

1. Destinies have been designed by Ea. 2. Portions have been distributed according to the decree of the god. 3. It has been that way since the days of old. 4. It has been declared from the beginning. 5. Beings are different from one another. 6. Some dwell above, [some dwell below]. 7. Some are as unattainable as the faraway heavens. 8. Some are as unknown as the deep underworld. 9. The whole of life appears just like the twinkling of an eye. 10. Human life is not everlasting. 11. Where is King Alulu who lived for 36,000 years? 12. Where is King Entena who went up to the heavens? 13. Where is Gilgamesh who [managed to trace life back] like Ziusudra? 14. Where is Huwawa, who. . . . 15. Where is Enkidu who [performed] mighty deeds on earth? 16. Where is Bazi? Where is Zizi? 17. Where are the Great Kings who lived form days of old until now? 18. In fact, they have never been conceived! They have never been born! 19. A gloomy life, what advantage does it have over death? 20. O, young man, whose god . . . firmly. 21. Cast off all grief, ignore troubles! 22. Instead of joy in the heart of a single day, a period of 36,000 [years of silence will come otherwise]. 23. May Zirash (i.e., the goddess of beer) rejoice in a son like you! 24. This is human destiny.

The last line of the Emar text (line 24), together with the beginning (line 1), frame the whole text, just as 12:8 and 1:2 frame Ecclesiastes's discourses. Line 24 of the Emar text uses the singular noun "destiny" in contrast to the plural "destinies" of line 1. Ecclesiastes uses a similar technique. In 12:8 one finds havel havaliyim (הֲבֵל הֲבָלִים), "vanity of vanities," only once, not twice, as in 2:1. Ecclesiastes wants to suggest that though absurdity is still part of human life, it is not as overwhelming as it appears before he delivers his discourses.

In "The Epic of Gilgamesh," a Mesopotamian wisdom composition that deals with the futility of the search for life, the hero Gilgamesh wanted to bring his dead friend Enkidu back to life by making a journey to find the tree of life. He found it, but lost it to a snake while he fell asleep. So he went back home, vanquished, but having gained the wisdom and true knowledge of the inevitability of death. This is what makes Gilgamesh a wisdom personality in the short Emar text above (line 13). This text shares the same background with the great Mesopotamian epic though in a slightly different perspective, very much like Ecclesiastes. Both put an emphasis not on the search for life and its failure, as in the Mesopotamian epic, but on the futility of seeking the meaning of this present life in terms of the tenets of traditional wisdom (see GILGAMESH, EPIC OF).

E. Theological and Religious Significance

Ecclesiastes views any effort to see the rationality of existence as hevel ("futility" or "vanity") simply because mortals have no real control over what happens in the world. Their destiny is not in their own hand, but in God's. And there is no way of knowing what the deity has in store for humanity. The only way is to accept the portion (kheleq חֵלֶק) given by God, not stoically but serenely. Far from being insignificant or deprived of meaning, human existence is worth living despite the fact that it is beyond comprehension. Accordingly, Ecclesiastes does not attack wisdom, the wise, or the doctrines taught by traditional wisdom literature. He only observes that traditional wisdom cannot help people find the answer to the absurdities in life. Because of that he turns to his own inner experience. This is the domain in which humanity can find freedom, both intellectual and emotional. It is true that there will not be a single answer to all problems. One will have to be ready to accept "contradictions"; for example, toil and work are absurd even if they are necessary and can even provide wealth, which is a source of some happiness. Again, this happiness should not be taken as the end, since it is basically impermanent. This is the human condition, unjust as it appears, but, as Ecclesiastes believes, God has his own reasons and therefore he must be just. This is evident from Chapter 3. For everything has a season, and a time for every purpose under heaven (3:1) This means that there is a logic in creation, but the human mind cannot graasp it. And yet, as he later says, God "has made everything suitable for its time" and "has put a sense of the past and future into their minds" even though humankind "cannot find out what God has done from beginning to end" (3:11). This is where Ecclesiastes differs sharply from Job, who accuses the Creator of not taking into consideration the suffering of humankind. In Ecclesiastes's thought, God is transcendent, wholly "other," but humankind is "on earth." This does not mean that God has no concern whatsoever for what is going on in the world. God has enabled humankind to act intelligently within the limits of its possibilities and, by acting in that way, humanity will find its true self

Ecclesiastes's general world-view rests on four positions: 1) all human achievements are impermanent; 2) the life of the human being is in the end uncertain, and wealth and social position are no guarantee of success; 3) human beings have no way to attain knowledge or insight into the workings of God in the world; and 4) considering all this, the goal of human endeavors should be to experience joy, which is a divine imperative. It is customary to discuss how the book treats individual themes like futility, death, God, wealth, and so on. In what follows, these themes are discussed in their relationship with each other, with a focus on the fourth position above.

1. Joy versus absurdities

Even if the author's worldview appears negative and pessimistic, a closer look at how the author presents these thoughts reveals other facets. The argumentative style adopted in the book invites the reader to interact with the text. The reader can almost enter into a dialogue with the author while reading through the book. The author does not assume that the reader will accept everything without reserve. Thus, when Ecclesiastes says that everything is futile, readers are in fact urged to see for themselves whether this is really the case. The author deals with futility in a unique way, by placing it alongside the theme of enjoyment.

The significance of the theme of enjoyment is suggested by the frequent use of words and expressions derived from samakh (שָׂמַח) "to rejoice": 9 times as verb (2:10; 3:12, 22; 4:16; 5:18; 8:15; 10:19; 11:8, 9) and 8 times as noun (2:12; 10:26; 5:19; 7:4; 8:15; 9:7). In contrast to other typical expressions found in the book, such as hevel "futility," the phrase "there is/ there are," and the pair "to eat/to drink." The expressions with samakh have various shades of meaning. They denote some state of mind (2:10; 2:26; 3:22; 5:19; 9:7), situations that are in themselves enjoyable (4:16; 7:4; 10:19), or something in between the two (2:12; 3:12; 5:18; 8:15 2x; 11:8).

A brief comparison of Ecclesiastes' language with the rest of the OT shows that his notion of enjoyment is special. Unlike other books, the idea of enjoyment here does not cover all kinds of joy, such as those expressed by words like gil (גִּיל), ranan (רָנַן) or ʿalaz (עָלַז). In this book, it is synonymous to raʾah vetov (רָאָה בְטוֹב) "to experience what is good" (2:1; 3:13; 5:17; 6:6; 2:24). The notion of joy is evoked by Ecclesiastes precisely to counterbalance the idea that everything is hevel "vanity" (i.e., meaningless, futile). To understand this, one can look at 2:1–8:14 and 8:15–11:9, which introduce two different parts in the development of the theme of enjoyment. 2:1 presents joy as a means of testing: "I said to myself, 'Come and I will make a test of pleasure: enjoy yourself!'" Later,

in 8:15, the author says, "So I commend enjoyment" (ʾeth-hassimkhah אֶת־הַשִּׂמְחָה). The text refers to simkhah, which is mentioned for the first time in 2:1 and then developed in the ensuing verses, up to 8:14. The expression gam zeh havel (גַּם זֶה הָבֶל), "this also is vanity" in 8:14 forms an inclusio with 2:1, where the same expression occurs. This is an indication that the two verses, 2:1 and 8:14, mark the beginning and end of a long exposition in which Ecclesiastes presents the idea of joy or enjoyment as something that gradually emerges as an alternative to the absurdities in human life. Moreover, the expression "this also is vanity," or its variation, occurs only in the first section, 2:1–8:14. The absence of such expressions after 8:15 must therefore mean that from this point on absurdities cease to play a significant role in human life.

2. God inspires the answer

The passages containing the expression "nothing better" also affirm that pleasure through toil is a gift (2:24; 3:13, 22; 5:17, all in the first part above). Each affirmation occurs immediately after some statement about the futility of human efforts. Thus enjoyment gradually emerges as an alternative to the reality of hevel. This series of assertions reaches its peak in 5:20 [Heb. 5:19]: "For they will scarcely brood over the days of their lives, because God maʿaneh besimkhath libbo (מַעֲנֶה בְּשִׂמְחַת לִבּוֹ) "keeps them occupied with the joy in their heart." This usual rendering rests on the assumption that ʿanah (עָנָה) means "to be busy with," and in this context, it means "keeping someone busy." But it can also be argued that maʿaneh comes from a more familiar root meaning "to answer," which would be "making someone utter the answer." If so, the last part of 5:20 can be rendered as ". . . because God enables people to find the answer in the joy of their heart," that is, God inspires such answer. The meaning of the expression "joy of the heart" itself will become clearer if seen together with 2:1, "I said to myself (belibbi בְּלִבִּי), 'Come now, I will make a test of pleasure (vesimkhah בְשִׂמְחָה); enjoy yourself.'" Joy is therefore an intellectual condition. Ecclesiastes now realizes that this joy is the God-inspired answer to his vexing questions. This inner joy is precisely what is praised in 8:15.

Who is the God who inspires that answer? Nowhere in the book is the name Yahweh found. The deity is denoted by the generic word *God*, depicted as a God that enters the human sphere of life despite human inability to understand divine actions. God gives joy in the heart, assigns tasks, makes everything appropriate for its purpose. In Israelite tradition, God's acts are said to be marvels, or simply mighty acts. Ecclesiastes underlines this tradition and at the same time makes it clear that no one should consider this concept of God as a source of passive security and consolation. This God is not at the service of people, ready to be called upon when in distress. God is sovereign; no one knows when God will act, or under what conditions God's intervention can be expected. In this respect, Ecclesiastes's view of God is unique. This God remains elusive despite being present in all spheres of human life. No action secures divine favor and there is way to tell which actions will gain favor. Nonetheless, no one should disregard God's presence.

3. Healthy religious attitude

In the second part of his discourse, 8:15–11:9 (where joy is mentioned for the last time), Ecclesiastes is concerned with the practical application of the insight presented in the first part above; that is, Ecclesiastes commends joy as the way to respond to the experience of the futility of human efforts. The mention of God's gift of life in 8:15 deserves attention. In the first part, God is pictured as the one who gives toil (1:13; 3:10). But now, at the beginning of the second part, Ecclesiastes says ". . . for there is nothing better for people under the sun than to eat, and drink, and enjoy themselves, for this will go with them in their toil through the days of life that God gives them under the sun." Note that the antecedent of the relative clause, "that God gives them under the sun" is "the days of their life" rather than "their toil." Evidently, the picture has shifted from God as the giver of toil to God as the giver of days to enjoy in this life. Ecclesiastes believes that what is important now is the time in which one lives, where toil is no longer the lot of humankind but a gift to be enjoyed. This perspective reappears several times in the second part, all emphasizing that one's lifetime is an occasion to rejoice (8:15 2x; 11:8; 11:9).

Ecclesiastes 9:7 adds a new key statement: "Go, eat your bread with enjoyment, and drink your wine with a merry heart; for God has long ago approved what you do." This is reminiscent of a key statement in the first part, "because God enables people to find the answer in the joy of their heart" (5:20; discussed above). God's approval of human actions thus leaves no room for the idea that life is meaningless; inner joy sweeps away the pessimisms brought about by the inevitability of death. Ecclesiastes underlines this point in 11:8a and 9a when the author advises people, young and old, to rejoice in life. Again, the twofold use of "joy" and "heart" echoes the expression of "the joy of one's heart" in 5:20. The rejoicing in 11:8-9 should therefore be interpreted as the inner joy inspired by God. The distant threat of futility (see 11:8b) and the fear that everyone receives judgment before God should no longer be a source of concern; life is to be enjoyed.

In wisdom literature usage, to respect the sacred or to take religion seriously is often expressed as "fearing God." This concept appears rather frequently in Ecclesiastes and indicates how the author views the practice of religion and its place in daily life. In 3:14, to fear God is the human capacity to recognize the divine presence

despite its incomprehensibility. This idea also lies at the bottom of the warning against prounouncing empty vows in 5:6. Revering the deity by deeds is much better than by words or mere rituals. In 7:18 he suggests that those who fear God know how to deal with both traditional wisdom teaching and the critical attitude toward it. This is indeed the key to success. Nowhere in the book does Ecclesiastes disregard traditional teaching. Criticism is aimed to purify traditional teaching and to make it more consonant with the human condition. Hence in 12:13 fearing God is associated with observing the Law (torah תּוֹרָה). Even if this verse belongs to the epilogue and was written by a later editor, it reflects Ecclesiastes' view that the transcendent God can be approached by living according to the spirit of the Law. But it would be misleading to think that the Law is understood as a collection of injunctions and prohibitions. The Hebrew word for commandments, mitswoth (מִצְוֹת) is not used in the book. Ecclesiastes's concept of fearing God flows from the mystery and incomprehensibility of God. If one fails to see the rationality of existence and to perceive the ways God deals with humanity, then reverential fear is in order. This sums up the duty of humankind.

Ecclesiastes begins and ends his long discourse with a statement that everything is hevel (1:1 and 12:8). The sage does not try to do away with this reality. Rather, the author presents an alternative way of looking at it: the futility of human efforts should no longer lead to vexation of the spirit, but to joy and enjoyment instead. The author establishes that joy is a gift from God that enables humankind to deal with the reality of hevel. In 8:15–11:9, the audience is exhorted to live according to this gift.

Ecclesiastes' critique of conventional wisdom and traditional theological positions has not prevented his book from finding its way into the biblical canon. This suggests that successive communities of believers have been strong enough to accommodate divergent ways of looking at their faith. This freedom also keeps religious life healthy. But it is not the critical spirit as such that makes Ecclesiastes's views valuable. The book's strength comes from the author's integrity and seriousness. This is what the early readers respected. Ecclesiastes speaks in understandable statements, such as the sevenfold affirmation that there is nothing better for humankind than to eat and drink, since eating and drinking are also gifts from God. The emphasis on enjoyment is a message for those who view religious piety more as an exercise of asceticism than social concern and genuine love, in short, those who see enjoyment as contrary to the biblical faith. The book's critical tone toward established religious positions is sobering. Ecclesiastes manages to see the divine in the everyday realities of life. However absurd life may appear, God inspires joy of the heart. *See* WISDOM IN THE OT.

Bibliography: F. Bianchi. "The Language of Qohelet: A Bibliographical Survey." *ZAW* 105 (1993) 210–13; James L. Crenshaw. *Ecclesiastes.* OTL (1987); Michael V. Fox. *Qoheleth and His Contradictions* (1989); Agustinus Gianto. "The Theme of Enjoyment in Qohelet." *Biblica* 73 (1992) 528–32; Agustinus Gianto. "Human Destiny in Emar and Qohelet." *Qohelet in the Context of Wisdom.* A. Schoors, ed. (1998) 473–79; Thomas Krüger. *Qoheleth.* Hermeneia (2004); Norbert Lohfink. *Qoheleth.* Continental Commentary (2003); Roland E. Murphy. *Ecclesiastes.* WBC 23A (1992); Antoon Schoors. *The Preacher Sought to Find Pleasing Words: A Study of the Language of Qohelet* (1992); C. L. Seow. *Ecclesiastes.* AB 18C (1997); R. N. Whybray. *Ecclesiastes.* NCBC (1989); Addison G. Wright. "Ecclesiastes." *NJBC* (1990) 489-495.

AGUSTINUS GIANTO

ECCLESIASTICUS i-klee´zee-as´ti-kuhs. *See* APOCRYPHA, DEUTEROCANONICAL; SIRACH.

ECCLESIOLOGY i-klee´zee-ol´uh-gee. *See* BISHOP; CHURCH, IDEA OF; DEACON; ELDER IN THE NT.

ECLIPSE. *See* SCIENCE AND THE BIBLE.

ECOLOGY. There is no Hebrew or Greek notion of the modern concept of ecology, but the escalation of the ecological crisis in recent years has led to a flourishing of studies on the relationship of Christianity and ecology. The best way into a study of the Bible and ecology is through the treatment of EARTH, CREATION, or world in the text (*see* WORLD, THE). The majority of those writing have focused on the Genesis creation myths, with work on these stories having one of two foci: either a study of the meaning of radhah (רָדָה, "to have dominion"; Gen 1:26) and kavash (כָּבַשׁ, "to subdue"; Gen 1:28), or of tselem ʾelohim (צֶלֶם אֱלֹהִים, "image of God"; Gen 1:27). Studies on radhah and kavash have taken the direction of discussion of the nature of human care for the nonhuman other. The understanding of humankind as stewards, or as fellow citizens with special responsibility, has been prevalent, as has a carefully drawn distinction between domination and dominion. Work on tselem ʾelohim has sought to address human responsibility to the natural world by calling people, as those created in the image of the Divine, to model God's care for creation. More recent work, done in light of the science of ecology, focuses on the interconnectedness of the natural world. This has enabled scholars to recognize within the biblical texts the articulation of a view of the world that acknowledges the interrelatedness of all of creation. This view understands humans as part of, rather than radically separate from and ontologically superior to, this creation.

MARIAN OSBORNE BERKY

ECSTASY [ἔκστασις ekstasis]. From the verb existēmi (ἐξίστημι, "to change or displace"). This English word does not occur in the NRSV, RSV, or KJV, which prefer the word *trance*. It is, however, reported in the Kleist-Lilly translation of the NT at Acts 10:10; 11:5; 22:17 (where that Gk. word does occur) and in the NJB at Rev 1:10 (where the Gk. word does not occur). Though not synonymous, the English words are legitimately interchangeable (see alternate states of consciousness below). Philo distinguished four meanings for: 1) alienation; 2) astonishment and fear (see 2 Chr 14:13; 15:5; 17:10, all LXX); 3) perfect rest, sleep, stupor (the first creature in Gen 2:21); and 4) the context of God's self-disclosure (Abraham in Gen 15:12). His first meaning is etymologically correct, and the next three meanings concur with the contemporary understanding of the human experiences of ecstasy and trance.

Anthropologists and cognitive neuroscientists agree that human beings are capable of experiencing many different levels of awareness or consciousness other than "ordinary waking consciousness," which serves as the foundation for measuring and describing alternate (preferable to altered) states of consciousness. Ordinary waking consciousness is characterized by "rational" thought and controlled perception. Alternate states of consciousness (ASC) experiences are subjectively felt departures from ordinary waking consciousness characterized by nonsequential thought and uncontrolled perception. The human ability to experience ASC has existed at least since the upper paleolithic period (40,000 BCE) at which time the human nervous system was presumably no different from the nervous system we know today. Though Freud postulated more than 1,000 ASC, contemporary scientists are more conservative but identify more than thirty-five, which include ecstacy and trance.

Ecstacy often, though not necessarily always, includes rapture, frenzy, euphoria, extremely strong emotion, and sometimes appears to imply the loss of "rational" thought and self-control. Trance, on the other hand, suggests a hypnotic or dazed state. While the proposed characteristics are present in some experiences of ecstacy and trance, respectively, they are not always present. Thus each case needs to be examined on its own merits. Since each is an ASC, *ecstacy* and *trance* can be considered interchangeable though not synonymous terms.

Based on her cross-cultural investigations, Goodman has identified four elements in the cultural patterning of a trance experience: 1) the visionary initially experiences fright; 2) the visionary does not clearly recognize what is being seen; 3) the figure appearing in a vision offers calming assurance; and 4) the figure identifies itself. Moreover, all trance experiences are reinterpreted by the visionary with each review of and reflection upon the ASC experience. This is very likely the case with the prophets. Goodman's elements subsume three of Philo's meanings: alienation from ordinary reality;

emotional reaction; and an ASC. (His fourth meaning is explained in 1 Sam 3:1: God discloses self in ASC—khazon (חָזוֹן)—in this case a dream).

While ecstacy, or preferably trance (an ASC), would certainly describe the experience of the first creature (Gen 2:21) and Abraham (Gen 15:12), it also aptly describes the experiences of prophets, especially in hearing God's call even though those words are not used (e.g., Isa 6; Jer 1; Ezek 1–3; Amos 7–9, etc.). In these cases, God initiates the experience in the visionary. On other occasions, prophets themselves induced the ecstasy or trance (1 Sam 10:5).

Ecstasy occurs but seven times in the NT. Some instances reflect astonishment or terror with no connection to an ASC (e.g., Mark 5:42; Luke 5:16; Acts 3:10) yet nevertheless as a response to an insight into the power of God. The other occurrences are explicitly related to an ASC. The women respond to their vision of a young man at Jesus' tomb with "terror and amazement" (ekstasis, Mark 16:8), a typical response to an ASC experience. While the remaining three occurrences of ecstasy appear in Acts (10:10; 11:5; 22:17), there are actually more than twenty reports of ASC experiences in that book of the Bible alone. Anthropologists would describe these as religious ecstatic experiences. The ascension (Acts 1:3-11), the descent of Spirit (2:1-4), GLOSSOLALIA (2:5-13), and Paul's call to be an apostle (9:1-9; 22:5-26; 26:9-18) are just a few. The fact that the word *ecstasy* or *trance* does not occur in the majority of these instances offers a salutary caution against limiting one's search of the Bible about any topic to specific words whether in Greek, Hebrew, or English (e.g., ecstasy; trance). Stephen is said to have gazed into heaven and to have seen the glory of God (7:55-56). This is certainly a trance experience, a religious ecstatic trance to be precise. In most instances where the word *gaze* or *stare* occurs, it signals an ASC experience. The disciples gazed into the sky at Jesus' ascension (Acts 1:10). Peter gazed at the sheet descending from the sky (Acts 10:4). Peter also gazed at the paralyzed man before healing him (Acts 3:4) indicating—as medical and cultural anthropology confirm—that a folk healer routinely goes into trance in order to heal a client. Similarly in the book of Revelation, John specifies four times that he was "in spirit" (Rev 1:10; 4:2; 17:3; 21:10), but that phrase is more properly translated "in trance" or "in ecstatic trance." It was in trance that John took journeys to the sky and gained God's perspective on the world as well as God's will that he saw played out in the past and his present.

Bibliography: Felicitas D. Goodman. *Ecstasy: Ritual and Alternate Reality: Religion in a Pluralistic World* (1988); John J. Pilch. *Visions and Healing in the Acts of the Apostles: How the Early Believers Experienced God* (2004).

JOHN J. PILCH

ED-DALIYEH, WADI. *See* DALIYEH, WADI ED.

EDDINUS ed′uh-nuhs [Ἐδδινους Eddinous]. The Greek rendering of the Hebrew name JEDUTHUN (1 Esd 1:15).

EDEN ee′duhn [עֵדֶן ʿedhen]. A Gershonite who cleansed the Temple during Hezekiah's reign (2 Chr 29:12), possibly the same one who tended the cities of the priests (2 Chr 31:15). *See* BETH-EDEN; EDEN, GARDEN OF.

EDEN, GARDEN OF ee′duhn [גַּן־בְּעֵדֶן gan-beʿedhen]. Most readers of the Bible associate Eden with Gen 2–3, yet it is important to note that the word occurs in several other places in the OT: Isa 51:3; Ezek 31:9, 16, 18; 36:25; and Joel 2:3. From these texts one can see that Eden is a location abundantly blessed with fertility. Sterility and death have no place there.

The etymology of Eden has been the subject of considerable discussion. A common approach in the modern era has been to derive the Hebrew word from the Akkadian edinu (which, in turn, derives from Sumerian) meaning, "plain, steppe." Some have gone further and located Eden in an especially fertile area within the vicinity of the Persian Gulf. Given the deep Mesopotamian roots of much of the material in Gen 1–11, this perspective has had much to recommend it. On the other hand, there is a root ʿdn (עדן) that means, "to be fertile, luxuriant," and some believe the nominal form derives from this verbal root that is native to the Hebrew language. Those who are partial to the Akkadian etymology have argued that this particular verbal stem is denominative (i.e., a secondary formation from a pre-existing noun) and therefore sheds no light on the origin of the root itself. A bilingual Aramaic-Akkadian inscription from Tel Fekherye has provided new philological data in support of the Hebrew root with a meaning of "making luxuriant [through water]." The LXX and the Vulgate translate the phrase ganʿedhen as "garden of fertile luxuriance" (paradeisos tēs tryphēs παραδείσος τῆς τρυφῆς or in Latin, *paradisus voluptatis*).

One key to understanding the symbolic nature of Eden is the description of its location in Gen 2:10-14. The Garden is characterized by four rivers that flow from it: the Pishon, Gihon, Tigris, and Euphrates. Though the latter two are clearly identifiable with the great rivers of classical Mesopotamia, the first two are not so easy to pin down. Given that the Gihon is said to flow around the land of Cush—which in turn is frequently identified with Nubia—it may be a reference to the origins of the Nile. If so, Eden would have been the source of all the great freshwater sources known to the ancient Israelite. Because the Gihon Spring flows beneath Jerusalem (and Eden was associated with Jerusalem, see below), the Gihon River may also have been associated with this spring.

It is significant that no single geographic location can be identified as the origin of all these rivers. The function of this text is more theological than topological. The fact that the rivers are four in number points to the universal reach of Eden, for classical Mesopotamian sources frequently divide the world into four quadrants and the living waters of the earth are thought to emerge from a sacred center. And because the sources of rivers tend to be found in mountainous regions (and are so depicted in ANE art), it is likely that Eden was thought of as a cosmic mountain. The mountainous character of the Garden of God is made explicit in another Eden tradition found in the Bible: Ezekiel's famous oracle against the king of Tyre (28:11-19, esp. v. 14). We also know from Psalm 24:2-3 that there was an intimate connection between the founding of the world on top of mythic waters and the establishment of the Temple: "God has founded [the world] on the seas, and established it on the rivers. Who shall ascend the hill of the Lord? And who shall stand in his holy place?" For an Israelite reader, it must have been a commonplace to associate Eden with the sacred center of Jerusalem.

It is striking to note that kings in Mesopotamia often described themselves as great gardeners. One relief from the palace of Ashurbanipal shows a garden built on a mountaintop with irrigation channels crisscrossing its slopes and a number of different flora growing upon its slopes. This calls to mind the garden that God plants in Eden with its abundant flora (Gen 2:9) and the appointment of Adam as its steward (2:15). Given the symbolic lineage between Zion and Eden it is not surprising that recent excavations in Jerusalem have revealed that tremendous care was put into its irrigation systems such that it could be a location of an abundant variety of trees and other ornamental vegetation. The lushness of the Zion was meant to conjure the primordial abundance of Eden.

Striking confirmation of the strong affinities between the Garden of Eden and the Temple Mount in the city of Jerusalem can be found in late Biblical and Second Temple literature. In Ezek 47:1-12, the prophet is taken in a vision to the entrance of the Temple. There he is witness to an extraordinary miracle: waters issue from the threshold of the building and begin to make their way out of the city of Jerusalem. As they head toward the region of the Dead Sea and the vast desert that surrounds it, the waters gradually grow in strength and slowly turn this barren desert into a luxuriant garden. On the banks of this river "grow all kinds of trees for food. Their leaves will not wither nor their fruit fail, but they will bear fresh fruit every month, because the water for them flows from the sanctuary. Their fruit will be for food, and their leaves for healing" (47:12). This return of the wilderness to an Edenic state is picked up by the author of Revelation in the very last chapter of the Christian Bible (Rev 22:1-2). In this vision, all of creation will be returned to the paradisiacal state in which it was made through the mediation of God's appointed dwelling place in Jerusalem.

Bibliography: Gary A. Anderson. "The Cosmic Mountain: Eden and Its Early Interpretation in Syriac Christianity." G. Robbins, ed. *Genesis 1–3 in the History of Exegesis* (1988) 187–224; Richard J. Clifford. *The Cosmic Mountain in Canaan and the Old Testament* (1971); Jonas Greenfield. "A Touch of Eden." *Orientalia J. Duchesne-Guillemin emerito oblata* (1984) 219–24; Jon Levenson. *Sinai and Zion: An Enquiry into the Jewish Bible* (1985); Lawrence Stager. "Jerusalem and the Garden of Eden." *EI* 26 (1999) 183–94.

GARY A. ANDERSON

EDER ee′duhr [עֵדֶר ʿedher]. 1. A town in the south of Judah (Josh 15:21).

2. One of the sons of Elpaal (1 Chr 8:9).

3. A member of the tribe of Levi and one of the three sons of Mushi and a grandson of Merari (1 Chr 23:23; 24:30).

MARY KAY DOBROVOLNY, R.S.M.

EDER, TOWER OF ee′duhr [מִגְדַּל־עֵדֶר mighdal ʿedher]. The "tower of the flock" was a landmark (Gen 35:21), associated today with Khirbet Siyar el-Ganam, on a ridge east of Bethlehem, likely named for flocks kept in the area. During the Second Temple period, its flocks were designated for Temple service, and the site became associated with Messianic expectations.

MARK DELCOGLIANO

EDESSA [Ἔδεσσα Edessa]. A prominent ancient Mesopotamian city, with a location corresponding to modern Urfa or Orhay in eastern Turkey. Situated on the "Silk Road" between the Roman Empire and the East, Edessa was refounded by Seleucus Nicator in 303 BCE. A Nabatean dynasty ruled from the 1st cent. BCE to the early 3rd cent. CE, and the city became a major center with a varied population. Ancient traditions claim that Christianity spread to Edessa very early. According to Eusebius, Jesus corresponded with King Abgar V of Edessa; after Pentecost, the apostle Thomas sent Thaddeus ("Addai" in Syriac) to evangelize the city (*Hist. eccl.* 1.13.6-22). Other traditions venerate Thomas himself as missionary to Edessa. In the 2nd and 3rd cent., the Aram. dialect of Edessa became the literary Syriac language. The earliest Christian Syriac literature may have been written there, including the Odes of Solomon and the Testament of Adam.

B. DIANE LIPSETT

EDICT [דָּת dath, מִכְתָּב mikhtav; Aram. כְּתָב kethav, פִּתְגָם pithegham; διάταγμα diatagma]. A written order of an emperor or a king, which had been visibly approved with a seal and publicly proclaimed. Cyrus' DECREE that allowed the Jews to rebuild the Temple was found in Ecbatana, and Darius issued an edict that the decree be followed (Ezra 5:17–6:12). Because of Ahasuerus's edict, virgins were brought to him, with Esther eventually becoming a replacement for Vashti (Esth 2:8). Edicts could be revoked by another edict such as the permission given to the Jews to kill their attackers in self-defense (Esth 8:9-14) as a countermand to the previous order that ordered all Jews be killed (Esth 3:12-15; 4:8). Hebrews 11:23 credits Moses' parents for their faith and for their lack of fear of Pharaoh's edict (see Exod 1:22–2:3). *See* LAW IN THE NT; LAW IN THE OT.

EMILY R. CHENEY

EDIFICATION [οἰκοδομή oikodome, οἰκοδομία oikodomia]. To build up or to strengthen. The concept underlying these terms is the Greek word for *household*, oikos (οἶκος), which means the physical structure of the house and the network of people necessary to make it a working, livable place. When Paul writes, "Let us then pursue the things of peace and of mutual oikodome" (οἰκοδομή Rom 14:19), he is working from his understanding of Christian congregations as the household of God, in which Christians are both God's children—thus siblings (Rom 14:10, 15)—and God's household slaves (Rom 14:4). We therefore try to please each other "with the goal of oikodome" (Rom 15:2), doing those things that make us a stronger household. Paul writes to the Corinthians that they should seek the spiritual gift of prophecy even more than tongues, since through prophecy the church may receive oikodome (1 Cor 14:3, 5). Mixing the household metaphor with the image of the body, Eph 4:12 states that the gifts of apostleship, prophecy, evangelism, pastoring, and teaching were all given to persons for the oikodome of the body of Christ. As these gifts are properly exercised, the body grows and the household "builds itself up in love" (Eph 4:16).

RICHARD B. VINSON

EDNA ed′nuh [Εδνα Edna]. In the deuterocanonical/apocryphal book of Tobit, Edna is the wife of Raguel and mother of Sarah (Tob 7:2, 8). She welcomes the angel Raphael and Tobias, the son of Tobit, into her home (7:3-5), and later welcomes Tobias as her son (10:13) as he marries her daughter Sarah.

MARY KAY DOBROVOLNY, R.S.M.

EDOM, EDOMITES ee′duhm, ee′duh-m*i*ts [אֱדוֹם 'edhom, אֲדֹמִי 'adhomi]. Edom is first a geographical term, referring to the reddish brown hills of southern TRANSJORDAN, east of the Arabah rift that runs from the southern end of the Dead Sea to the Gulf of Aqabah. The etymology of the term 'edhom (red) is related to the color of the hills. The region is mountainous and semi-arid, with a tribal-based pastoralism as its economic base.

In the Iron Age I (1200–1000 BCE) an indigenous state emerged in southern Transjordan, developing to its fullness in Iron Age II (1000–586 BCE). During the 8th–6th cent. BCE, there was Edomite influence to the west of the Arabah rift, particularly in the Negev region. The Neo-Babylonian Empire brought an end to the Edomite state in southern Transjordan, and subsequently inhabitants of Edom were incorporated into the large bureaucratic structure of the Persian Empire. This latter period also marks the rise of the Nabatean culture in the region, with a political kingdom and broadly spread trading network eventually emerging in the Hellenistic period. The NABATEANS were Arab tribes who founded an imposing capital at Petra, and they assimilated much of the remaining Edomite culture.

Modern scholars have assembled a basic cultural profile of the Iron Age Edomite culture. This means that the term *Edomite* can be used in three primary senses: geographical, political, and

Todd Bolen/BiblePlaces.com
Figure 1: Mountains of Edom

Todd Bolen/BiblePlaces.com
Figure 2: Wadi Rum and Jebel Khazali

ethnic/cultural. To speak of Edom/Edomites in an ethnic sense is essentially a shorthand term for a cultural/tribal profile. It is not a racial indication. There are, of course, overlaps between the three primary senses of the term, but it is helpful to keep the distinctions in mind when something is designated as Edomite.

In the Hellenistic and Roman periods, the regions of the southern Judean hill country and the Negev were known as IDUMEA, a term derived from Edom. Edomite presence there was already influential in the later Iron Age, and it increased in the Persian and Hellenistic periods. Many inhabitants of those regions were Idumean in the ethnic/cultural sense, although they may have been Idumean, pagan, or even Jewish in religious practice. Herod the Great, e.g., was an Idumean Jew, who through Roman appointment became king of the Jews. Veneration of the Edomite deity Qos in Idumea continued during these periods.

There are extant examples of Edomite texts, but they are few and mostly fragmentary. Edomite epigraphy has been found on both sides of the Arabah (= southeastern Israel, southern Jordan). There are also a number of references to Edom in the OT and several in Egyptian and Neo-Assyrian texts.

A. Geography
B. Edomite Texts and Archaeological Research
C. Edom in the OT
D. Edom in Neo-Assyrian Texts
Bibliography

A. Geography

Perhaps it is helpful to think of a geographical core to Edom, with an oscillating Edomite cultural periph-ery, depending on the variables of climate and political fortunes. The core has a northern boundary at the Wadi el-Hesa, which runs into the southern end of the Dead Sea from the east. The semi-arid mountainous regions to the south of the Wadi el-Hesa rise to 5,000 ft. above sea level and they extend much of the way to Aqabah. The mountains are cut occasionally by valleys (wadis) for drainage of the infrequent rain. The upper elevations get some snow in the winter. In turn, Aqabah and the Red Sea are the southern border of Edom.

The eastern border of Edom cannot be easily defined, as the already arid region merges with the Arabian desert. This eastward opening provides connections, however, with the desert tribes. Similarly, the trading route that ran from Arabia to Damascus went through Edom and provided further connections with Arab tribes. Defining the western boundary of the core is most difficult because of the fluctuations in political control and the movements of tribal groups. Perhaps it is easiest to say that the Arabah rift is the western border of Edom, but that it is porous and of little political significance, so that there were continuing connections between Edom and the Negev/northern Sinai regions. These connections were the result of trade with Egypt and the broad movement of tribal-based pastoralists.

A term sometimes used in parallel to Edom is Seir or Mount Seir. According to Gen 32:3 the "land of Seir" is Edom. And there are similar references elsewhere (Gen 36:8-9; Deut 2:4-5; Judg 5:4). Some references to Mount Seir in the OT seem better suited to the hills in the southern wilderness/desert area west of the Arabah (Deut 1:2, 44), suggesting that the term *Seir* is broadly used.

Copper mining and smelting were also a part of the Edomite economy. In the area of Feinan, archaeologists have found the remains of copper slag and other indications of mining and smelting. According to carbon 14 dating, the site of Khirbet an Nahas in that region was established by the 10th cent. BCE and it remained an important place for copper production in Iron Age II.

B. Edomite Texts and Archaeological Research

Brief excavations at the site of Tell el Kheleifeh in the middle of the 20th cent. provided the first examples of material culture, including brief epigraphic remains, that can be identified with Edom (*see* KHELEIFEH, TELL EL). The site dates to Iron Age II and is located near the Gulf of Aqabah, about halfway between modern Eilat and Aqabah (*see* AQABAH, GULF OF). A seal impression discovered there contains the divine name Qos, the patron deity of Edom, or at least the patron deity of the ruling house. Subsequently, the discovery elsewhere of a few fragmentary Edomite texts confirmed the role of Qos as a cultural marker of Edomite religion. Edomite religion may well have had a pantheon of deities, but it will require further archaeological discoveries to identify its members.

Some of these texts have come from smaller Iron Age II sites in the Negev region west of the Arabah rift. They are primary evidence that Edomites (at least in the ethnic/cultural sense) lived in that region. Whatever ties these Edomites may have had politically with Edom to the east is unknown. Evidence for an Edomite-influenced cult has been found at Qitmit in the eastern Negev and at Ein Hatseva, some 25 mi. south of the Dead Sea. Over 800 cultural objects were found at Qitmit. The assemblage from the small shrine at Ein Hatseva also provides a window into an Edomite religious milieu. An ostracon found in the excavations at Tel ARAD, an Israelite fortress in the Negev, warns the fortress commander to be on the lookout for the Edomites. The ostracon dates to the time of the Babylonian campaigns against Judah in the early 6th cent. BCE.

The Iron Age site of BOZRAH was a chief Edomite city (Amos 1:12). Its ruins are located at the Jordanian settlement of Busayrah, and were the subject of excavations in the 1960s. Edomite Sela, a small, Iron Age II fortress on a steep mesa, is located near the Nabatean capital Petra. Tawilan is another Iron Age Edomite site in southern Jordan that has been excavated. Sedentary existence at all these sites is no earlier than Iron Age II.

C. Edom in the OT

Etiological accounts in the book of Genesis provide kinship links between Israel and Edom. Esau (ESAU, ESAUITES), Jacob's older brother, is identified as the father of the Edomites. Genesis 36 contains a lengthy genealogical list of Esau's descendants, and 36:1 refers to the "generations of Esau, that is Edom." In 36:43, Esau is the "father" of the Edomites. A similar connection is made in Gen 25:30, in the account of Jacob tricking his older brother, where the famished Esau asks for some of the reddish stew Jacob had prepared, so that "he (i.e., Esau) was called Edom" (i.e., "red"). The lengthy list of Gen 36 notes several links with the peoples of Canaan. Esau is reported to have married a Hittite and a Hivite woman, plus a daughter of Ishmael. The connection with Ishmael underscores the later relationship between Edom and the wandering Arab tribes traced back to Ishmael (Gen 25:13-18). Interestingly, there is a claim for kings among the Edomites before there was a king in Israel (36:31-39). This cannot be verified, and what is known so far from the archaeological record does not suggest much sedentary existence in Edom in the Late Bronze and Early Iron ages. There is the question of terminology, since the term *king* can mean a variety of things and need not refer to a ruler based in a walled settlement.

The relationship depicted for Esau and Jacob is based on both kinship and enmity. The latter is often reflected elsewhere in the biblical text in relations between Israel/Judah and Edom, but the former is still acknowledged. There are references to the "brotherhood" of Edom in Deut 2:4 and 23:7-8, and in the third generation an Edomite may be admitted to the assembly of the Lord.

In the wilderness wandering there are brief references to passing by or through the land of Edom (Num 20:14-21; Deut 2:4-8; Judg 11:17-18). Both Saul and David fought against the Edomites, with the latter subjugating them harshly (1 Sam 14:47; 2 Sam 8:13; 1 Kgs 11:15-16). A bitter opponent of Solomon was an Edomite named Hadad (1 Kgs 11:14). Solomon had occupied Ezion Geber, a port in the land of Edom (1 Kgs 9:26).

During the divided monarchy, there were both struggles and continuing relations between Israel/Judah and Edom. During the reign of Ahab a deputy ruled in Edom (1 Kgs 22:47). In 2 Kgs 3 a "king" of Edom works in concert with Jehoram and Jehoshaphat, and it is reported soon after that Edom rebelled against Judean control "to this day" (2 Kgs 8:20-22). This did not put an end to hostilities, however (2 Kgs 14:7-10).

References to the Edomites in prophetic texts reflect hostility. Amos 1:11-12 notes Edomite fury and lack of compassion, and contains a prediction of destruction for Teman and Bozrah, two Edomite towns. According to Isa 34:5-6, the Lord will destroy Edom in a sacrificial act. Jeremiah likewise contains a strong oracle against Edom (49:7-22). The prophets of the 8th and 7th cent. have oracles against a number of neighboring states, but in the aftermath of the Babylonian exile, such prophetic oracles cease for some of the neighbors. This is not the case for Edom. According to Ps 137:7, the Edomites took joy in the destruction of Jerusalem. This, and perhaps some continuing expansion in the Negev area, gave rise to continuing hatred. The short book of Obadiah, which is likely the product of the Persian period, is essentially an oracle against Edom. Joel, also likely a post-exilic composition, charges Edom with spilling innocent blood in Judean territory (4:19). In proclaiming that God had not given up on Judah during Persian reign, the prophet Malachi states that God loves Jacob (= Israel/Judah), but "hates" Esau and has judged Edom (1:3-4).

Possibly the story of Job is set in Edom. Job is explicitly described as the greatest of the sons of the east and living in the land of Uz (Job 1:1-3). A poetic couplet in Lam 4:21 refers to the "daughter of Edom who lives in the land of Uz."

There are intriguing references to Israel's deity Yahweh coming from the region of Edom to aid Israel. Deuteronomy 33:2 depicts the Lord coming from Sinai and from Seir. Judges 5:4, similarly, has the Lord marching "from Seir and the field of Edom." Yet another poem (Hab 3:3) has the Lord coming from Teman (typically an Edomite city or area, Amos 1:12) and Mount Paran. All biblical traditions locate Sinai, the "home" of the Lord, to the south of Israel, so Edom is minimally a stopping place along the way. Some scholars have suggested that Yahweh was also "at home" in Edom, and that this relationship accounts for the early tradition of Edom's "brotherhood" with Israel.

D. Edom in Neo-Assyrian Texts

In texts from the 8th and 7th cent. BCE, typically Edom is listed as a bearer of tribute. References to two Edomite kings are preserved, both of whom have theophoric names formed with Qos. Edom, like their northern neighbors Moab and Ammon, was subjugated by the Assyrians, who wanted control of the port region of Ezion geber and the trade route linking the region with Arabia.

Bibliography: John R. Bartlett. *Edom and the Edomites* (1989); Piotr Bienkowski. "Iron Age Settlement in Edom: A Revised Framework." *The World of the Aramaeans II: Studies in History and Archaeology in Honour of Paul-Eugen Dion.* P. M. M. Daviau, J. W. Wevers, and M. Weigl, eds. (2001) 257–69; Diana V. Edelman, ed. *You Shall Not Abhor an Edomite for He Is Your Brother. Edom and Seir in History and Tradition* (1995); Thomas E. Levy, R. B. Adams, M. Najjar, A. Hauptmann, J. D. Anderson, B. Brandl, M. A. Robinson, and T. Higham. "Research Reassessing the Chronology of Biblical Edom: New Excavations and 14C Dates from Khirbat en-Nahas (Jordan)." *Antiquity* 78 (2004) 863–66.

J. ANDREW DEARMAN

EDREI ed´ree-*i* [אֶדְרֶעִי *'edhre'i*]. 1. Major town of BASHAN (Num 21:33; Deut 1:4; 3:1, 10; Josh 12:4; 13:12, 31). In the OT, the Amorite king OG met defeat against Moses and the Israelites at Edrei, identfied with modern Der'a, Syria, near the Yarmuk, a major tributary of the Jordan River.

2. Town mentioned in the allotment of Naphtali (Josh 19:37), linked to a location listed in the military records of THUTMOSE III.

NATHAN D. MAXWELL

EDUCATION, NT.

A. Greek and Roman Education
  1. Family
  2. Elementary schools
  3. Higher education
  4. Academic studies
B. Jewish Education
  1. Family
  2. Religious philosophies
  3. Synagogues and schools
  4. Scribes
C. Education in Early Christianity
  1. Literacy
  2. Family
  3. Congregations and schools
D. Theological Metaphor
Bibliography

A. Greek and Roman Education

The ideal in Greek education was to have a physically and intellectually "comprehensive education" (enkyklios paideia ἐγκύκλιος παιδεία). Traditional religion played no educational role. The task of character formation was largely filled by philosophy. The classical Greek educational system was founded in the 4th cent. BCE. It spread throughout the Mediterranean with the establishment of Hellenistic cities and after Alexander's conquest, as far east as the River Indus. The Romans adopted the system during the reign of Augustus and modified it to put more stress on the study of law. Greco-Roman or Hellenistic education remained basically unaltered in the Byzantine Empire. Within the Greek Orthodox church it survived even until the 20th cent. Greek education also has deeply impressed Western civilization (*see* HELLENISM).

1. Family

In antiquity the first place of education was the extended FAMILY. The mother had the responsibility for little children and girls, and the father for older boys. Sons normally learned their profession from the father. Some trades were also taught by apprenticeship. Wealthy fathers taught their sons to read and write (Plutarch, *Cat. Maj.* 20:4-5); some of the poor did so, too (Martial, *Epigr.* 9:73.7). By the age of seven, upper class boys would attend an elementary school. Although Plato envisaged the schooling of girls, (*Resp.* 5:451D–457B), education for girls remained the exception. There is evidence that literate women were taught at home (P.Oxy. 101295). Our knowledge from ancient authors has now been supplemented by documentary evidence like school manuals and exercises. Most evidence comes from Egypt, but some educational materials have been found in such distant places as northern Britannia.

2. Elementary schools

Instruction was given either at home by a private tutor, sometimes an educated slave (Plutarch, [*Lib. ed.*] 4B), or by a teacher in school (Quintilian, *Inst.* 1:2). Some cities like MILETUS supported municipal schools, but most schools were private. The primary level comprised of sports in palaistra (παλαίστρα a sand-covered courtyard) in the latter part of the morning, and the didaskaleion (διδασκαλεῖον, reading school) for the remaining time (Lucian, *Am.* 44-45). The teaching was done by the often poorly paid grammatistēs (γραμματιστῆς) whereas the paidagōgos (παιδαγωγός Gal 3:24) was a slave for the personal care of upper class children. Reading was learned by reciting the ALPHABET forwards and backwards and by repeating syllables and whole words (Dionysius of Halicarnassus, *Comp.* 25). Fluent reading had to be done from complicated classical texts to train the stylistic sense and started with short maxims and poetical passages. After reading aloud, the pupils had to memorize texts (Quintillian, *Inst.* 1:1.25-37). Teaching to write began with copying individual letters. School exercises on OSTRACA, waxed-wooden tablets, or papyri show that the teacher wrote down an exemplary alphabet (*see* PAPYRUS, PAPYRI). The curriculum included simple arithmetic. As at home (Plato, *Prot.* 325D), discipline was very stern (Aristotle, *Pol.* 8:1139A), but some teachers like Quintillian preferred more humane methods (*Inst.* 1: 3.6-18). *See* WRITING AND WRITING MATERIALS.

3. Higher education

At the age of about fifteen, aristocratic young men could attend, for one to three years, the gymnasion (γυμνάσιον, from gymnos [γυμνός], meaning "naked," because the Greeks exercised in the nude). Every Hellenistic city had at least one. The gymnasia were sponsored by rich citizens, one of whom served as head of the institution. The pupils spent much of their time with physical education on the race-course (stadion στάδιον) and the wrestling school (palaestra), participating in the pentathlon (πένταθλον, long jumping, running, wrestling, discus and javelin throwing) and the pankration (πανκρατιον, combining boxing, kicking and wrestling). Paul testifies to the popularity of sports (1 Cor 9:24-27). Normally, the gymnasion included a lecture hall and a library, where the young men studied classical texts (Quintillian, *Inst.* 1:4-12) such as the Homeric epics *Iliad* and *Odyssey* (Dio Chrysostom, *Dic. exercit.* 8), followed by authors such as Euripides, Menander (compare 1 Cor 15:33), and Demosthenes. Latin texts included Virgil,

Terence, Cicero and Horace (*see* GREEK LANGUAGE; LATIN LANGUAGE). After grammatical analysis, often following the handbook of Dionysius Thrax, the study proceeded in four stages: 1) in textual criticism the teacher's text was meticulously compared with the pupil's copy; 2) reading aloud with attention to genre and metre was followed by memorization; 3) the exegesis of classical works included the rendering from Attic Greek to the common language and the memorizing of tables of content; 4) evaluation concentrating on ethical issues. In the exposition of Homer, allegory played an important role. The study of texts was followed by exercises in one's own literary composition. The pupils were also trained in music (mostly theory) and higher mathematics (geometry, astronomy, numbers). They formed an elitist community, prepared to become the leading class.

4. Academic studies

Only a small minority pursued academic studies. For a political career the study of rhetoric was indispensable (Quintillian, *Inst.* 3–9). Aristotle and Quintillian wrote famous rhetorical handbooks from which students started with simple compositional forms (fable, narrative, etc.). An influential collection of such studies from the 1st cent. CE was that of Theon of Alexandria. Students learned the standard speech forms (epideictic, judicial, deliberative), the five steps of preparation (invention, arrangement, style, memorization, delivery) and the four parts of a speech (introduction, narration, proof, conclusion). Students then analyzed famous speeches and tried their own compositions. Since an orator had to touch on many subjects, the study included other liberal arts. Vespasian was the first to establish chairs of rhetoric paid by an imperial salary (Suetonius, *Vesp.* 18). Philosophical knowledge could be obtained by listening to the lectures of a private teacher or attending an established institution as Plato's academy at Athens (Acts 17:18-21) or the school at ALEXANDRIA. In NT times Alexandria (Acts 18:24) housed the greatest library of antiquity and was the most important center of learning. Philosophy was not only doctrine, but a way of life; the philosophers were not only teachers, but masters of the soul, and the decision for philosophy, a kind of conversion.

B. Jewish Education

Most Jews in NT times lived in the Hellenistic cities of the diaspora. Since the 2nd cent. BCE Jewish education was influenced both by the OT and by Greek culture. Among Jews there were varying degrees of opposition against and adoption of Greco-Roman education.

1. Family

Jewish fathers took the responsibility for the education of boys when the reached the age of five (2 Macc 7:27). According to tradition, fathers were to teach their sons TORAH through learning the laws by heart (Deut 6:6-9; 11:18-21). According to the Pseudepigrapha (4 Macc 18:10-16), Philo, and Josephus, this standard was followed by most of the Jews in the Second Temple period. Sometimes reading and writing was already learned at home (*3 En.* 45:2; cf. *T. Levi* 13:2). Especially important was the duty of fathers to teach their sons a profession (*m. Qidd.* 1:11; compare Mark 6:3; Matt 13:55). Some women also were educated at home, and evidence exists that there quite possibly was a community of women who engaged in contemplation and study, such as Philo's Therapeutae (Philo, *Contempl. Life* 2).

2. Religious philosophies

Around 180 BCE the Jerusalem priest Ben Sira stood at the border between the post-Exilic hierocracy and Hellenism. He defended the privilege of priests to be scribes, but he also opened his Wisdom school and lecture hall for lay people (Sir 45:17-18; 51:23-25). The Dead Sea scrolls give evidence that there were programs for popular education (11QPsª(11Q5) XVIII, 5-8 (Ps 154)). The Essenes required not only adult men but also boys to learn, and they selected some for special training (*J.W.* 2.120; 1QHª IX, 35-36). In organizing daily study of the Holy Scriptures, the Qumran community (1QS VI, 6-8) realized an OT ideal (Josh 1:8; Ps 1:2). The Pharisees and other groups tried to persuade the whole people of Israel to study the Torah. They promoted this goal by founding synagogues where every adult Jew could read and expound the Scriptures. This democratization of education was realized in the creation of schools.

3. Synagogues and schools

Most scholars accept the existence of the SYNAGOGUE in the Second Temple period. The only extant Palestinian synagogue inscription from this time states its purpose as "teaching of the laws" (*CIJ* 2 no. 1404). The focus on reading and expounding Torah and prophets (Acts 13:15) made the synagogue service a rather intellectual affair, and Philo could call the synagogues schools, places of learning (didaskaleia διδασκαλεῖα), and the Sabbath service a kind of philosophy (philosophia φιλοσοφία), pursuit of knowledge and wisdom (*Creation* 128; *Decalogue* 98.100). The regular readings served to impress the texts into the memory of the listeners (Josephus, *Ant.* 4.210-11). During the week, the scrolls were accessible for study (*b. Qidd.* 66a; compare Acts 17:10-11). Such mid-week gatherings for study were the start of study houses (beth midrash בֵּית מִדְרָשׁ). In 66–70 CE the Zealot defenders of the Herodion built a synagogue, and at Masada they apparently altered a building into a school room. The ensemble of a hall for service and a school room can rather clearly be seen in the 1st cent. BCE synagogue of Gamla in the Golan. In the time of Queen Alexandra Salome (76–67 BCE), the scribe Shimon Ben Shatah attempted to make school compulsory for boys. This initiative failed when the Pharisees lost power and schooling remained a private initiative. There is no unambiguous evidence for girls attending schools. Evidence for a tripartite education program (Bible at age five, Mishna at age ten, Talmud at age fifteen) is found in *m. ʾAbot* 5:21 (a rather late text). In the synagogue school the attendant (Luke 4:20) often served as an elementary teacher (*m. Shabb.* 1:3-4). Learning to read started with the Book of Leviticus, because it was a text containing many rare words. As in Hellenistic education, memorization was a most important aspect (Josephus, *Ag. Ap.* 2.178; compare 1Q28a I, 6-7). In Jewish schools, the OT Scriptures served as the only school text. Other subjects were learned in connection with the Bible. Before 70 CE there must also have been Greek-speaking synagogue schools, but many Jews resented they ways in which their culture was being usurped by the dominant Greco-Roman culture and rejected non-Jewish schools for their children. (e.g., 2 Macc 4:7-17). Hellenistic Jews wishing to give their sons an education in music and sports had to hire private teachers (Philo, *Spec. Laws* 2.230).

4. Scribes

Scribes functioned as teachers in the synagogues (Matt 23:2). Apparently, some Scribes took money for their lectures and some served as judges. It is very difficult to reconstruct from late rabbinic sources the training of these "proto-rabbis." In the 1st cent. CE only a small minority belonged to one of the religious parties (compare Luke 11:45). Their study focussed on the deeper exposition of the Holy Scriptures. The hermeneutical principles they used show Hellenistic influence. Before 70 CE Jerusalem was the center of scribal training and housed the schools of such famous scholars as Hillel and Shammai (ca. 20 BCE) and GAMALIEL the Elder (Acts 5:34-39). *See* HILLEL THE ELDER, HOUSE OF HILLEL; SHAMMAI THE ELDER.

C. Education in Early Christianity

In view of Jesus' praise of the "unwise" (Matt 11:25), reflected by Paul in 1 Cor 1–2, it is understandable that one sometimes encounters an anti-intellectual bias in early Christianity. But the apostle criticized only philosophical speculation and empty rhetoric, stressing, against unintelligible pneumatic utterances, the importance of speaking "words with [the] mind, in order to instruct others" (1 Cor 14:19). He could even write, "do not be children in your thinking, rather, be infants in evil, but in thinking be adults" (1 Cor 14:20). Paul was trained as a Pharisee (Phil 3:5; see also Acts 23:6; 26:5), and traditon states that Paul was educated by Gamaliel (Acts 22:3). At the age of twelve, Jesus was able to engage learned scholars (Luke 2:46-47). Teaching and learning were not only part of family education, but also of congregational life.

1. Literacy

It is credible that Jesus received an elementary education in a synagogue school (Luke 4:16 tethrammenos τεθραμμένος) and could read (Luke 4:16-20) and write (John 8:6-8). Besides his mother tongue Aramaic, Jesus understood Hebrew, and probably also understood colloquial Greek (some of his disciples bore Greek names). Jesus left nothing written, but using mnemonic techniques like poetic forms (parallelisms, alliterations, paronomasia, etc.) he impressed his teaching summaries on the memories of his hearers. His chosen disciples he called "pupils" (mathetai μαθηταί). Jesus' disciples learned from their TEACHER (rhabbi ῥαββι, didaskalos διδάσκαλος) by word and example. He also encouraged women's education (Luke 10:38-42). A tax-collector like Matthew (Matt 9:9) must have known how to write, and church tradition connects him with the sources of the Gospel of Matthew (Papias in Eusebius, *Hist. eccl.* 3:39.16). Stemming from a higher class family, the bilingual John Mark (Acts 12:12) is traditionally identified as the author of the Gospel of Mark. With a title (hyperetes ὑπηρέτης) recalling the synagogue attendant/teacher (Luke 4:20), John Mark is depicted as a teacher in Acts 13:5, apparently handling Jesus traditions (compare Luke 1:1-4).

As a Pharisee, Paul had already received his elementary schooling (anatethrammenos ἀνατεθραμμένος) and then his higher scribal training (pepaideumenos πεπαιδευμένος) in Jerusalem (Acts 22:3; compare Gal 1:13-14). His birthplace, Tarsus, was a center of Greek culture and education. Paul's deep knowledge of the LXX was founded in a Greek-speaking synagogue (Acts 6:9; 7:58). Some Greek rhetoric and hermeneutics Paul could have learned in the school of Gamaliel the Elder, whose grandson Gamaliel II was famous for his knowledge of "Greek wisdom" (*b. Sotah* 49b). Paul's epistles are well structured, although it is disputed how far he used rhetorical conventions. Letter writing was part of some advanced study (Theon, *Progymnasmata* 10). Since the social composition of early Jewish and Gentile Christian communities reflected the surrounding society, there was a comparable spread of literacy. At least the few high class members (1 Cor 1:26, etc.) would have had some education. People like the Corinthian city treasurer ERASTUS (Rom 16:23) or the Alexandrian rhetor APOLLOS (Acts 18:24) must even have had higher learning. TERTIUS, Paul's secretary in writing Romans (Rom 16:22) might have been a professional scribe. The apostle could be sure that in his house churches there were always some able to read his letters (Gal 6:11; 1 Thess 5:27). The author of Luke-Acts, showing knowledge of medical concepts and language, is recognized, by old church tradition, as "Luke, the physician" (Col 4:14). Some ancient physicians such as the contemporary Soranus of EPHESUS also wrote historical works. The Gospels can be compared to Hellenistic biographies, and Acts to historical monographs. The Jewish Christian author of Hebrews, identified by Tertullian (*Pud.* 20) as the Cypriote Levite BARNABAS, shows a remarkable mastery of Greek language and speech forms.

2. Family

The goal of Christian education is defined in Eph 6:4: "Fathers, do not provoke your children to anger, but bring them up in the discipline and instruction of the Lord (paideia kai nouthesia kyriou παιδεία καί νουθεσία κυρίου)." The gospel of Jesus, with its emphasis on becoming like children to enter the kingdom, added a new nuance to a patriarchal system of education, although the children's duty to obey the parents is conventionally stressed (Eph 6:1). As in Judaism, Christian education was primarily religious and ethical. This education was the responsibility of both fathers (Col 3:21) and mothers (1 Tim 5:4) and was an important criterion for the selection of church leaders (1 Tim 3:4, 12; Titus 1:6). Also following the Jewish example (compare 2 Tim 1:15; Acts 16:1), the Pastoral Epistles formulate the educational ideal to "know from childhood" the "sacred writings that are able to instruct you for salvation through faith in Christ Jesus" (2 Tim 3:15).

3. Congregations and schools

In the 1st cent. the instruction of believers had no unified form. Jewish Christians followed a synagogue or even a sectarian model. The Christian episkopos (ἐπίσκοπος) had to be an "apt teacher" (1 Tim 3:2). In the Gentile Christian house churches the rich and educated hosts played a role as instructors (1 Cor 16:15-16). Apparently, some members acted as community teachers (Gal 6:6; 1 Tim 5:17). In addition, there were also the apostles and other wandering teachers (Acts 18:24-28). The community gatherings comprised readings from the OT Scriptures (1 Tim 4:13) and early Christian writings (Col 4:16; Rev 1:3), recitations of Jesus traditions (1 Cor 11:23-25) and moral instruction (1 Thess 4:1-2; 1 Cor 4:17). Probably connected with baptism there was a special catechesis (Rom 6:17) including confessional formula (1 Cor 15:3-5) and Jesus' sayings (Matt 28:19-20). Since maxims, chreias and comparisons were learned by heart already in the elementary schools, it was virtually self-evident to memorize Jesus' teaching summaries and parables and also short stories about him. Exceptions notwithstanding (Acts 18:26), teaching was primarily the duty of men, but women were encouraged to learn (1 Cor 14:34-36; 1 Tim 2:11-12). The exhortation of children and younger believers had its own place in the community instruction (Col 3:20; 1 Tim 5:1-2). Teaching/learning activities were so prominent that the early Christian groups are classified by some as "scholastic communities."

In the 2nd cent. CE the Syrian Tatian was strongly opposed to Hellenistic education (*Or. ad Graec.* 26:1-8), whereas the Alexandrian church father Clement was relatively open to it (*Strom.* 1:43-45). According to Tertullian, attendance at an elementary school was a benefit for faith, although he opposed Christian involvement as teachers because they would be involved in pagan worship (*Idol.* 10). This was probably the majority view already in the 1st cent. How strongly the Hellenistic educational system was established in society is shown by the fact that in the first centuries nobody thought of Christian elementary and secondary schools. The Christians were convinced that education in family and congregation would be enough protection against pagan influences. Only after the 6th cent. were there schools for boys in Benedictine monasteries.

The existence of Christian schools comparable to Jewish scribal schools or Hellenistic philosophical academies is a matter of definition. The Greek word for school (scholē σχολή) occurs only once in the NT. According to Acts 19:9, Paul "lectured daily in the school of Tyrannus" (author's trans.; NRSV: "argued daily in the lecture hall of Tyrannus."). It is disputed if this is an historical reminiscence or if Luke stylized the apostle as a kind of philosopher (compare Acts 17:18). Philosophical schools were characterized by some form of common life, consciousness of one's own tradition, veneration of the founder, different grades of membership, teaching/learning activities and esoteric teachings. By this wide definition one could call the Pauline and Johannine circles, and even the pre-Easter disciples of Jesus, a "school." The address of adults as "children" (1 Cor 4:17; 1 John 2:18) was typical for a teacher-student relationship.

D. Theological Metaphor

Following the OT Wisdom traditions (e.g., Prov 3:11-12), education serves as a metaphor for how God deals with believers. Concepts of education in the NT are used by Paul (1 Cor 11:32 [NRSV: "disciplined"]; 2 Cor 6:9 [NRSV: "punished"]) and Revelation (3:19 [NRSV: "discipline"]), and are especially prominent in the Pastorals (1 Tim. 1:20 [NRSV: "learn"]; 2 Tim 3:16 [NRSV: "training"], etc.) and in Hebrews (Heb 12:5-10 [NRSV: "discipline"]). The metaphor stresses aspects of education (compare Heb 12:5-10), but sometimes also recall characteristics like grace (Titus 2:12; NRSV: "training"). *See* WISDOM IN THE NT; WISDOM IN THE OT.

Bibliography: P. Balla. *The Child-Parent Relationship in the New Testament and Its Environment* (2003); A. I. Baumgarten. *The Flourishing of Jewish Sects in the Maccabean Era* (1997); S. F. Bonner. *Education in Ancient Rome* (1977); S. Byrskog. *Jesus the Only Teacher* (1994); R. Cribbiore. *Writing, Teachers, and Students in Graeco-Roman Egypt* (1996); R. A. Culpepper. *The Johannine School* (1975); R. Gehring. *House Church and Mission* (2004); B. Gerhardsson, *Memory and Manuscript with Tradition and Transmission in Early Christianity* (1998); W. V. Harris. *Ancient Literacy* (1989); M. Hengel. *The Pre-Christian Paul* (1991); C. Hezser. *Jewish Literacy in Roman Palestine* (2001); R. F. Hock. "Paul and Greco-Roman Education." *Paul in the Greco-Roman World.* J. P. Sampley, ed. (2003) 198–227; M. S. Jaffee. *Writing and Oral Tradition in Palestinian Judaism, 200 BCE–400 CE* (2001); E. A. Judge. "The Early Christians as Scholastic Community." *JRH* 1 (1960/61) 4–15, 125–37; L. I. Levine. *The Ancient Synagogue.* (2000); H. I. Marrou. *A History of Education in Antiquity* (1982); A. Mendelson. *Secular Education in Philo of Alexandria* (1982); A. R. Millard. *Reading and Writing in the Time of Jesus* (2000); T. Morgan. *Literate Education in the Hellenistic and Roman worlds* (1998); C. Osiek and D. L. Balch. *Families in the New Testament World* (1997); S. E. Porter and T. H. Olbricht, eds. *Rhetoric and the New Testament* (1993); R. Riesner. "Jesus as Preacher and Teacher." *Jesus and the Oral Gospel Tradition.* H. Wansbrough, ed. (1991) 185–210; S. Safrai. "Education and the Study of the Torah." *The Jewish People in the First Century. Volume 2.* S. Safrai, ed. (1976) 945–70.

RAINER RIESNER

EDUCATION, OT. Systematic instruction in ancient Israel and Judah took place initially in homes, with mothers and fathers assuming responsibility for teaching their children. Eventually a few young people, mostly boys from well-to-do families, went on to study in small groups under a professional teacher. While early learning shaped character for successful living, subsequent training prepared students for administrative positions at the royal court and, after its disappearance, for a scribal profession that depended on priestly benefaction and/or the needs of ordinary citizens (entrepreneurs with contractual obligations, and persons entering into daily transactions that required official documents).

A. General Observations
  1. Orality versus literacy
  2. Changes over time
  3. Influence of other cultures
  4. Scarcity of data for Israel
B. Places of Learning
  1. Home
  2. Royal court
  3. Guilds
  4. Schools
C. Teachers
  1. Parents
  2. Professional instructors
  3. God
  4. Personified Wisdom

We begin by making a distinction between learning, which takes place everywhere and under various conditions, and education, the product of intentional instruction of students by specialized teachers. This distinction corresponds to that between knowledge and wisdom, the former indicating familiarity with factual data and the latter signifying an understanding of the broader principles governing existence itself. The present discussion emphasizes the latter, while attempting to do equal justice to the former.

A. General Observations

1. Orality versus literacy

The ANE was predominantly an oral culture, with literacy ranging from less than 1 percent in Mesopotamia and Egypt to approximately 5 percent in Israel. The reasons for this low rate of literacy are many, but the chief obstacles to mass literacy were the complexity of the script (cuneiform in Mesopotamia, hieroglyphics in Egypt) and the agrarian economy in Israel and Judah. Other contributing factors were the high cost of writing materials, the absence of eyeglasses, the purposive restriction of vocational choices (a kind of managed scarcity), and the preponderance of small villages but relatively few urban settings with sufficient population to sustain a school and to employ its graduates. (The invention of the printing press and the Industrial Revolution sparked the rise of literacy in the West).

In that kind of culture writing was viewed by many as shimmering with power, hence its use in magical formulas on tombstones ("Beware! There is danger for you below.") and its presence on royal monuments and in propaganda for reigning monarchs, despite the limited number of people capable of reading the texts. Besides these magical and executive functions, writing played a universalizing role in the form of communication across vast territories; aided religious functionaries in both liturgy and dogma; served to entertain audiences and readers; and lent identification to personal items such as letters, jars (e.g., "Belonging to Yahzeyahu, wine of khl"), ceremonial gifts (e.g., "arrow of ʿabd lbʾt"), and official documents. Writing also stabilized the economy to some degree by indicating the value of weights.

2. Changes over time

With the invention of the alphabet ca. 1700 BCE in Canaan and the resulting simplification of writing, together with the emergence of Aramaic as the language of international diplomacy by the 8th cent. BCE, the stage was set for an infusion of texts in the spoken language. Biblical Hebrew and Aram. employ a simple alphabet of twenty-two consonants (the vowels were not written, although a few consonants eventually served double duty, functioning both as consonants and as vowel letters). This alphabet contrasts with cuneiform (the Sumerian, Babylonian, and Assyrian system of writing that employed hundreds of signs) and with hieroglyphics (the picture writing in Egypt), both of which could only be mastered after several years of scribal training.

Israel's beginnings were largely characterized by oral communication. Whether that situation changed dramatically under Solomon is highly controversial, like the claim that this king presided over an era of enlightenment. In any event, some progress in literacy probably took place under Hezekiah in the 8th cent.; he seems to have sponsored a group of scribes who, among other things, are said to have transcribed a small collection of proverbial sayings (Prov 25–29).

Nevertheless, the prophets of this era (Isaiah, Amos, Hosea, and Micah) and of the next century (Jeremiah) appear to have delivered their oracles orally. The Babylonian connections of Jeremiah's contemporary, Ezekiel, and the later prophet known to scholars as Deutero-Isaiah may partially explain their apparent shift to the literary side of the oral/literacy continuum. Even if the written word gained significance during the Persian and Hellenistic periods, orality continued to occupy primacy, at least for Ben Sira, a professional scribe (ca. 180 BCE). At the same time, written texts, especially those thought to derive from remote times, took on sacred character, gradually forming a CANON of Scripture. The waning of prophetic inspiration, which can be deduced from the fact that later interpreters relied on oracles by predecessors rather than proclaiming fresh words from the deity, contributed to the sense of reverence that scriptural collections came to enjoy. The extensive library at Qumran on the west bank of the Dead Sea attests to this scripturalization, as well as to the unsettled nature of the canon. Here fragments of every biblical book except Esther and a complete manuscript of a biblical book, Isaiah, were discovered, along with sectarian documents of various kinds (e.g., Hodayot [Psalms], the *War Scroll,* the Covenant Code, the *Temple Scroll*, and *Habakkuk Pesher*).

The shift from an oral to a written culture was therefore gradual and not always welcome, as Plato indicates (*Phaed.* 274C–275B). According to him, the discovery of writing threatened a time-honored reliance on memory. We might add that it encouraged elitism. Furthermore, a written text is mute before its readers and lacks the capacity of choosing discriminating ones.

3. Influence of other cultures

The durability of clay, the preferred writing material in Mesopotamia and at Ugarit, has left a permanent witness to education in these areas, and the dry climate in Egypt contributed to the survival of the much more fragile papyri used there. The result is a large collection of texts, many dealing with schools and pedagogy. In Mesopotamia the school (**edubba**, tablet house) was presided over by a teacher, called "Father," administrative assistants, and "big brothers," who monitored students' (sons') behavior. The language of instruction was classical Sumerian, and texts were bilingual, sometimes even in three or four languages. Lists of single subjects (birds, fish, cattle, trees) can be reconstructed from students' exercises dating to the Old Babylonian period. By the 11th cent. BCE fixed lists of cuneiform signs existed. Numerous clay tablets have survived on which students' exercises appear alongside a few lines of a model text from teachers. So have various school texts, which reveal a vigorous exchange between students, ironic and acerbic ridicule of students by teachers, and accounts of harsh punishment for inattention or poor performance on assignments.

These students attended class twenty-four days each month, with three days' vacation and three days off for religious festivals. Teaching was in open courtyards or in a remote area of a building. Students sat on felt cloth before sand that was used for writing sample letters; a vessel filled with water to keep clay moist lay before them. The students were an elite body, overwhelmingly male. Their instruction consisted of reciting texts from memory; students were expected to commit these recitations to writing and to copy classical texts (e.g., Atrahasis, The Gilgamesh Epic, Enuma elish). In doing so, they also translated Sumerian texts into their everyday language, Akkadian, transforming them into tragedies, and rendering episodic texts into a continuous story that presented an ethical norm for life. Death's inevitability ran through these texts as a powerful theme.

An abundance of scribal texts in Egypt points to similar professional education, with cruel discipline, student resistance, and strong reinforcement of learning from pharaohs and viziers. The number of scribes rose and fell according to the need of different pharaohs. A discovery at Deir-el-Medinah reveals flourishing scribal activity. Here an elite family held office for six generations, and a certain Kenhikhopshef occupied a position of scribe for either forty-six or fifty-four years. Like their Mesopotamian counterparts, Egyptian scribes also copied classic texts, especially Pyramid Texts, Coffin Texts, the Book of the Dead, Book of Kemit, and Instruction of Dua-Khety. At least one text from Egypt, The Instruction of Amenemope (*see* AMENEMOPE, INSTRUCTION OF), has a direct relationship with a brief section in the book of Proverbs (Prov 22:17–24:22), and another, Dua-khety (*see* DUA-KHETY, INSTRUCTION OF), is echoed in Sir 38:24-34. Likewise, the books of Job and Ecclesiastes have parallels in the BABYLONIAN THEODICY and the DIALOGUE OF PESSIMISM. Links also exist between Ecclesiastes and the Egyptian PAPYRUS INSINGER, as well as the classical Mesopotamian text, the Epic of Gilgamesh (*see* GILGAMESH, EPIC OF; compare Eccl 9:7-9). Moreover, two proverbial collections in the Bible are attributed to foreign sages, Agur and Lemuel's mother (Prov 30:1-14; 31:1-9).

4. Scarcity of data for Israel

Information about education in ancient Israel is limited to the Bible, with some exceptions (occasional inscriptions, a number of clay seals or bullae, and a few texts with letters in alphabetic sequence). Leaving aside the matter of authenticity, scholars must deduce the probable meaning of this evidence. Consequently, a disparity of views exists, ranging from positing a vast system of schools throughout Israel and Judah to the outright denial of such an institution until the time of the High Priest Joshua ben Gamla (63–65 CE) or even as late as the time of Simeon ben Shetah in the 2nd cent. CE.

The inscriptional evidence from the period of the confederacy includes an ostracon from Izbet Sartah, with the oldest twenty-two letter alphabet (ca. 1200 BCE) a text from Qubur el-Walaydah, arrowheads from el-Khadr, and some sherds. From the 8th cent. BCE and later come the Samaria ostraca and inscriptions (discovered at Kuntillet-Ajrud [a triple abecedary], Khirbet el-Qom, Khirbet Beit Lei, Silwan, and Arad), and numerous seal impressions. Inscriptions from Kadesh-Barnea indicate some knowledge of Egyptian hieratic and have been viewed as practice exercises of a trainee-scribe, unexplainably in a remote fortress. The GEZER CALENDAR that describes a year's agricultural activity has been understood as a schoolboy's practice exercise. It reads: His two months are (olive harvest), His two months are planting (grain), His two months are late planting; His month is hoeing up the flax, His month is harvest of barley, His month is harvest and feasting; His two months are vine tending, His month is summer fruit (ANET, 320). The extraordinary consistency of spelling and regularity of script (with some exceptions) is a strong argument for professional training.

The biblical evidence is difficult to assess. The narratives that suggest the presence of writing as early as Moses, with its use being later exploited by David for personal exculpation in the story about Uriah the Hittite and Jezebel for monetary gain (obtaining Naboth's vineyard for her husband, Ahab), mix fact with fiction. The astonishing silence about schools in wisdom literature until Ben Sira weighs heavily against the argument for widespread schools. So does the lack of a single student's exercise tablet, with the possible exception of inscriptions at Kadesh-Barnea. Even Ben Sira's unique reference to a school may be a metaphor for his book. The lack of a reference to a school in the book of Proverbs, where one has a right to expect it, is telling indeed, although the invitation to buy wisdom has been taken as proof of schools (Prov 4:5, 7; 17:16; compare Sir 51:23-25, 28).

B. Places of Learning

1. Home

The impression left by the book of Proverbs is that parents taught their children at home. Education during the first years probably came under the jurisdiction of mothers and in some cases wet nurses or grandmothers. For most girls, that relationship continued into their early teens when marriage normally occurred. Girls were taught varied domestic skills ranging from turning the raw into cooked, straw into baskets, flax and wool into clothes, clay into pots, and children into social beings. Like boys, they were instructed in viticulture, caring for domestic animals, and some aspects of agriculture. Boys were taught additional skills such as hunting, fighting, carpentry, and brick masonry. They also learned the rudiments of customary law. Both boys and girls received religious teaching and learned responsible behavior from their parents.

2. Royal court

The monarchy in Israel and Judah required trained personnel to maintain correspondence with rival kingdoms; to keep records of tax revenues, supplies, and names for conscription into the military; to carry out effective propaganda for the current administration; to oversee religious drama in the official cult; to train more scribes; and to create a "theological myth" for the nation. The Bible refers to guardians (ha'omenim הָאֹמְנִים, 2 Kgs 10:1, 5) in the Northern Kingdom and to Hezekiah's men in Judah (Prov 25:1). An official historiographer, often called the Deuteronomistic Historian, implies that Solomon's administrative system was modeled on that of Egypt. Modern scholars question the use of analogies with the imperial nations in Egypt and Mesopotamia, given the difference in time and in cultural advance between Israel and these two regions.

3. Guilds

In all probability, most specialized instruction took place in connection with guilds that were largely the domain of particular families. Metalworkers, tailors, jewel smiths, arrowmakers, carpenters, leatherworkers, potters, scribes, barbers, diviners, priests, magicians, and others learned their trade as apprentices working with their fathers. Exceptions to the father-son rule naturally were made, for good reasons, but the survival of the family dictated the degree to which an open-door policy applied, leading to one of managed scarcity.

4. Schools

The strongest argument for the existence of schools in Israel and Judah is the quality and quantity of the literature produced there. Much of it originated in oral delivery, but the collective memory was finally put into writing, along with a few texts that were literary from the beginning. Where did the scribes learn to read and write? One possible answer is a scribal guild, but is that explanation adequate? Perhaps not, but the few allusions to a literate populace (e.g., Isa 29:11-12; Judg 8:14), the possible mockery of school exercises in Isa 28:9-10, 13, and even the indication that heirs to the king received special training can be explained as instruction in guilds. This last text is susceptible of various interpretations. Although often interpreted in light of scribal practice in Alexandrian Egypt (the vocalizing of the alphabet and reciting it forward and backward), this text has also been seen as a linguistic distortion of a foreign language, Akkadian.

> "Whom will he teach knowledge,
>   and to whom will he explain the message?
> Those who are weaned from milk,
>   those taken from the breast?
> For it is precept upon precept,
>   precept upon precept,
> line upon line, line upon line,
>   here a little, there a little."
> Therefore the word of the LORD will be to them
>   "Precept upon precept, precept upon precept,
>   line upon line, line upon line,
>   here a little, there a little;"
> in order that they may go, and fall backward,
>   and be broken, and snared, and taken.
> Isa 28:9-10, 13

It is possible that a school was associated with the Temple in Jerusalem. That would explain the extensive religious and political propaganda in the Bible, together with the editing of proverbial collections to heighten their aesthetic appeal, the book of Psalms, and the Deuteronomic literature. Widespread schooling was unlikely, given the demands of an agrarian culture, the disruption of life from invading armies, and the Deuteronomic injunction that religion be the subject of instruction and that it take place in homes.

C. Teachers
1. Parents
The book of Proverbs uses familial language to emphasize the authority of parental teaching, which took two forms: sentential sayings and instructions. Both mothers and fathers offer advice about coping in a society afflicted with much adversity, chief of which is sexual temptation, but also laziness and drunkenness. The subject of this instruction is addressed directly as "my son" in the initial collection (Prov 1–9), in the section related to the Egyptian Instruction of Amenem-opet (22:17–24:22), in the advice to Prince Lemuel (31:1-9), and in Sirach. Although this language of father as teacher and son as student functions symbolically in both Egypt and Mesopotamia, in the book of Proverbs it is probably literal most of the time. In Sirach, the plural "sons" seems to indicate students, as also in Eccl 12:12.

2. Professional instructors
The only professional instructor whose name has been preserved in the Bible is Ben Sira, and this identification may owe something to Hellenistic pride of authorship, which has precedents in signed texts in Mesopotamia and Egypt. The unknown author of Wisdom of Solomon was a product of a Hellenistic education in Alexandria, at one point even describing the curriculum as consisting of physics, chronology, astronomy, biology, medicine, botany, and philosophy (Wis 7:17-22). Later Philo received a similar education in Alexandria; he, too, sought to combine Jewish teachings with his more philosophical Hellenistic instruction. Allegorical interpretation of the Bible became his primary means of achieving this goal. His education consisted of the encyclia or *quadrivium* (arithmetic, geometry, astronomy, and music) plus the *trivium* (grammar, rhetoric, and dialectic). Still, Philo considered these subjects inferior and seductive, particularly when contrasted with the higher stages of learning, philosophy, and wisdom, which were not based on visual perception.

The authors of the books of Job and Ecclesiastes were instructed in international wisdom, but we do not know anything about their teachers. The latter even democratized education, according to the first epilogue (Eccl 12:9, "Qoheleth taught the people," ha'am הָעָם).

3. God
Not surprisingly, some biblical authors describe the deity as teacher. That image is especially strong in the tradition ascribed to Isaiah. One of these texts mentions Yahweh's immediate instruction to prevent a dangerous misstep (Isa 30:20-21; compare 2:3), and another claims that God teaches farmers appropriate agricultural procedure (Isa 28:23-29). The idea of a divine teacher, of remote antiquity, may have originated in divination. It achieves full expression in the depiction of Moses as an extraordinary leader who received instruction directly from God. The later book of Daniel implies that the deity communicates vital knowledge to Jewish students in the king's palace (Dan 1:17). Religious leaders explained adversity as divine discipline of those whom God loved; this motif is especially prominent in the book of Job.

4. Personified Wisdom
A unique concept in biblical wisdom involves a mysterious woman, *Wisdom*, probably metaphorically personified. This extraordinary figure seems to have affinities with the goddesses Isis and Ma'at. She addresses young boys directly, advising and warning at the same time, and boasting of heavenly origin in Prov 8:22-31, Sir 24, and Wis 7:25-26. She also claims to possess life and happiness, which she offers to those who love her (Prov 8:35). The erotic emphasis of these texts seems intended to counter the blandishments of an articulate rival, *Folly*, as well as the very real allure of foreign women and adulteresses (compare Prov 9:1-12 with 9:13-18). Ben Sira's presentation of Wisdom mythicizes her and heightens her erotic appeal (Sir 24:1-23) but insists that her love must be earned (Sir 4:11-19). The author of Wisdom of Solomon legitimates the eros by means of marriage and changes the metaphorical language to something approaching an earthly divine manifestation (hypostasis). In this remarkable text, Wisdom possesses divine attributes (Wis 7:22), and she is thought to be the fashioner of all things, as well as a pure emanation of the glory of the Almighty (7:25).

D. Students
1. Boys
Formal education in the ANE was restricted to boys, with the exception of a few daughters of rulers. Even in the Greek world girls were excluded from schools until the late 4th cent. BCE. Among thousands of names of scribes in Mesopotamia only a handful are women, and these were mostly associated with Sippar and Mari. No school text mentions girls, although three or four literary tablets bear feminine names. Enheduanna, the daughter of Sargon the Great, is said to have composed hymns; Ninshatapada, the daughter of Sin-Kashib, wrote a letter prayer, and women priests/scribes existed in a cloister at Sippar. Similarly, in Egypt three extraordinary women came to prominence (Hatshepsut, Tiy, and Nefertiti). An Egyptian text even compares the instructing of women to pouring sand in a sack that is split. Ben Sira's scathing language about daughters (Sir 26:12) shows that the Egyptian sentiment was not an isolated phenomenon. This denigrating of women flourished in the Greco-Roman environment and in some rabbinic circles. The overwhelming evidence in biblical wisdom literature points to an exclusively male audience.

2. Resistance to learning

School texts from Mesopotamia and Egypt suggest that boys were often more interested in other things than an education. The Instruction of Any (*see* ANY, INSTRUCTION OF), the only surviving text in which a student responds to a teacher, reveals both the extent of students' reluctance to put forth the effort required to master a subject and the zeal with which teachers sought to overcome this resistance. Any informs his son, Khonshotep, that even domestic animals can be taught, foreigners can learn to communicate in the language of Egypt, and the shape of wood can be changed. Khonshotep argues for a softening of the requirements while diplomatically recognizing his father's extraordinary intelligence and piety.

Other scribal texts mention the appeal of the outdoors, the attraction of girls and beer, and the immediate rewards of military service, specifically booty (compare Prov 1:11-14 for the enticement of brigandage). Naturally, the harsh discipline, tiresome recitations, and endless written assignments were barely tolerated by many students. Like Egyptian scribal texts, school tablets from Mesopotamia refer to cruel punishment, ridicule, and competition that sometimes made life miserable. Biblical texts differ mainly in degree, not substance, for parental exhortations and stern warnings abound in the book of Proverbs. The author of Ecclesiastes stresses the unwelcome effect of much study, and Ben Sira uses the image of Wisdom's yoke to underline the difficulty of becoming wise at the feet of a demanding teacher. The more graphic Syriac Ahiqar text compares the positive effect of whippings to manure in a vegetable garden.

E. Curriculum

1. Life

Because biblical sages believed that Yahweh had hidden universal truths deep within the created order (Prov 25:2; Eccl 3:11), the task of humans was to search diligently for these lessons from nature and society. They could then draw analogies and apply them to their own behavior. Nothing, therefore, was outside the purview of students who hoped to profit from astute observation of plants, insects, animals, the weather, and people. The slightest gesture—a wink, the scraping of the feet, a raised eyebrow—indicated questionable character, as did laziness, drunkenness, and defiance of cultural norms when adulteresses "eat, wipe their mouths, and assert that they have done no wrong" (Prov 30:20). Presumably, the author of 1 Kgs 4:29-34 [Heb. 5:9-14] refers to this type of analogical thinking as well as the categorizing of phenomena in lists similar to onomastica (noun lists) in Egypt and Mesopotamia.

The composers of the books of Job and Ecclesiastes studied human nature and the anomalies of existence, hoping to establish reliable principles that would enable them to make sense of reality. Influenced by Hellenistic philosophy, especially Stoicism, Ben Sira continues both traditions, the careful search for analogies that illumine daily existence and the philosophical examination of the functioning universe. He also draws on the sacred narrative of his own people, a new departure among sages that in Wisdom of Solomon leads to "midrashic" treatment of the exodus from Egypt (Wis 10:15–19:22).

The curriculum in Egyptian and Mesopotamian schools included the study of languages, scientific and technical knowledge, geography, astrology, manuals, word lists, dialogues, school texts, and much more. These schools devoted considerable energy to preparing bilingual dictionaries to enable beginning students to translate classical texts into their native tongue.

2. Wisdom literature

In all probability, Israelite sages composed their own texts for use in scribal schools. That supposition applies to the latest collection in the book of Proverbs (1–9) and to the books of Job and Ecclesiastes. Ben Sira is keenly aware that he is writing inspired teachings to serve as a standard text for students, and his translator specifically mentions an even broader literary base, the canon with its three divisions (Torah, Prophets, and the other books [Writings?]). The author of Wisdom of Solomon seems to be addressing sophisticated readers who can appreciate the niceties of Greek rhetoric as well as the subtleties of a new interpretive mode, MIDRASH. Ahiqar even has a bilingual pun (lb'—lion, sea serpent, or flood).

F. Implements for Writing

1. Stylus, clay, pen, ink, and papyrus

In Mesopotamia and at Ugarit on the Phoenician coast, scribes used a stylus to form wedge-shaped characters in moist tablets of clay. The small hand-held tablets were then placed in the sun to dry or baked into terra cotta. Those hardened tablets containing classic texts and important administrative data were labeled and stored in convenient pigeonholes or stacked on shelves, many of which have been found in their original storage sites. In Egypt and Israel, pen and ink were the preferred writing implements. Papyrus, readily available through a painstaking process of pounding, pressing, layering, and drying reeds from the banks of the Nile, was widely used in Egypt and eventually in Israel. Pens fashioned from reeds, a palette, and ink of various colors (red for highlighting) were a scribe's writing instruments. (*See* WRITING AND WRITING MATERIALS). A scribal text indicates the importance of these items in the following way: "They [Scribes] gave themselves [the scroll as lector] priest/The writing-board as loving son/Instructions are their tombs/The reed pen is their child/The stone-surface their wife" (Chester Beatty Papyrus IV).

2. Other

In Israel, beginning students wrote their exercises on boards of wood or slate, sometimes on wax. Texts intended for preservation made use of leather scrolls and even copper. As papyrus became available, it was also used widely. Administrative texts (royal propaganda) were frequently incised in stone, like the Decalogue in sacred narrative. Pottery was often decorated by means of pen and ink and marked for identification (belonging to X). Broken sherds and limestone flakes provided a convenient medium for practicing the formation of letters. In a popular folktale, Ahiqar the imprisoned former advisor to King Sennacherib of Assyria (704–681 BCE), wrote his teachings on the vessels made from clay in which he was served his daily food. A 7th cent. Marsiliana board carved with ivory even has the alphabet along its edge.

G. Pedagogy

1. Goal

The primary purpose of education in Israel was to promote order and continuity in society by forming character. Its strong religious base is therefore understandable. The fear of the deity, roughly the ancient equivalent of the modern concept "religion," is said to be the first principle or premise of knowledge (Prov 1:7). This statement concerning all wisdom appears in the latest collection of proverbial sayings (Prov 1–9), but the instruction of children by parents underlying older collections rested on a religious assumption, although unarticulated. In brief, human conduct determined one's access to life's good things, and education assisted young people in their pursuit of those blessings. To this fundamental theory of knowledge the later Ben Sira added a single ingredient, Israel's unique religious tradition or mythos. Accordingly, he identified personified wisdom with the Mosaic legislation and unabashedly drew on the entire biblical narrative for inspiration, in a sense nationalizing universal wisdom. Perhaps a better formulation is that Ben Sira universalized the Mosaic legislation. We may even speak of education as enculturation, the dissemination of society's value system to each generation.

In seeking to order their lives in a beneficial way, the wise constructed a symbolic world that existed only in their imagination. They then bestowed on this imaginary world the task of ordering and explaining existence. In the end, they became subject to this symbolic world. In other words, a belief in the operative principle of reward and retribution gradually froze into dogma, which stimulated sufficient intellectual efforts to propose an alternative symbolic world. In this way, sages constantly questioned their own insights.

Central to sages was the acquisition of four virtues: self-control, restraint, eloquence, and honesty. The first virtue recognizes the enormous power of passion (fear, anxiety, and lust). The second virtue, restraint, provided a necessary balance in a culture given to rhetorical excess, elevating modesty and reticence as a desideratum to crowds in danger of losing perspective. The third, eloquence, acknowledges the persuasive power of speech for both good and evil. The fourth virtue guaranteed integrity, the tongue's use in communicating truth, especially in judicial contexts.

The different orientation in the books of Job and Ecclesiastes from that in Proverbs suggests that something other than the shaping of character is at work there. Questions are raised about the presumption that a rational order operates throughout the universe; indeed, a question mark hangs over the very meaning of existence. This interrogation of fundamental premises seems more appropriate to a learned clientele, probably professional teachers and their advanced students. This is also true of Wisdom of Solomon, for the author's fervent defense of divine justice in dealing with the Egyptians and Canaanites, his midrashic analysis of the story of the exodus from Egyptian bondage, and his wrestling with the philosophical issue of death's finality bear little resemblance to the concerns expressed in earlier parental instruction.

2. Method

Unlike instruction in Egypt and Mesopotamia, Israelite pedagogy consisted primarily of oral recitation. Memory therefore lay at the heart of education. Various aids to memory were developed, especially alphabetic poems (acrostics, compare Prov 31:10-31), numerical sayings (Prov 6:16-19; 30:15-33), lists of items in specific categories (compare 1 Kgs 5:9-14), ring compositions (inclusios, Wis 7:17-20), refrains (compare Sir 2:7-10, 12-14), chiasms, and much more. Teachers expressed their insights in one of two modes, expository and hypothetical. The first of these modes included sentential observations and admonitory imperatives. It emphasizes a teacher's authority and depends heavily on the power of example by reminding students of the high level of achievement by teachers. The second pedagogical mode subjected normal declarative speech to the interrogative. It shifts the focus from teachers to students, who are challenged to engage in a quest to discover answers to intriguing questions. Biblical wisdom employs both techniques. Aphorisms and instructions weigh in heavily on the expository side, while highly reflective texts such as Job and Ecclesiastes encourage readers to discover new insights through a rigorous process of hypothetical reflection.

Teachers endeavored to persuade students through various means: riddles, erotic language, personal example, threats and promises, and more. One of the oldest riddles from Sumer concerns the institutional school. It asks: "What does one enter with closed eyes and leave with eyes opened?" Not a single riddle has survived in Israelite wisdom, but the Samson narrative has preserved one, together with the remnants of two others.

Some numerical proverbs may conceal riddles (e.g., Sir 1:3), somewhat like the possible use of ATBaSh in Jer 25:25-26 (the equal dividing of the alphabet, correlating the first and last letters and so on). The frequent erotic imagery in biblical wisdom was intended to gain and hold the attention of young teenagers with raging hormones. Parents depended on personal authority to reinforce their promises and threats, while also hoping that respect for them would lend weight to examples from their own lives. We may therefore say that teachers appealed to the persuasive power of *logos* (logic), *ethos* (character), and *pathos* (emotions).

Persuasion by the force of logic puts the emphasis on the speech itself, even if hearers decide what passes as coherent and convincing argument. The finest example of logical persuasion occurs when teachers appeal to consensus and clothe it in rhetorical questions. For example, Job asks "Does the wild ass bray when he has grass, or the ox low over his fodder?" and follows that up with a second question of the same kind (Job 6:5-6). Bildad counters with a similar appeal to *logos*: "Can papyrus grow where there is no marsh? Can reeds flourish where there is no water?" (Job 7:8-10).

Ethos, as used here, refers to the character of speakers. In Job 8:8-10, Bildad appeals to the accumulated knowledge of past generations, to character acquired over the years. He understands this knowledge as a system of beliefs, values, and customs that had become as natural as breathing itself. The two essentials of *ethos*, therefore, are inherited tradition and personal appropriation.

When speakers move away from themselves to the audience, *pathos* becomes the dominant force and addresses human emotions. Speakers use everything within their capacity to arouse the passions of an audience, thereby enhancing the chances of action born out of emotion. Fear and awe actually play into the hands of speakers. Eliphaz stuns his audience with an account of a sinister visitor, a spirit gliding past his face and awakening him with an eerie whisper: "Can mortal man be more righteous than God; can a man be purer than his maker?" (Job 4:12-17).

3. Vocabulary

Two expressions for places where divine secrets were disclosed (the teacher's terebinth [Gen 12:6, "oak of instruction" not "oak of Moreh" in NRSV] and "hill of instruction" [Judg 7:1, not "hill of Moreh" in NRSV]) seem to indicate early divination. In Job 35:11, Eloah is described as "one who gives songs during the night, who teaches us (mallefenu מַלְּפֵנוּ) more than the beasts of the earth and bestows more wisdom than the birds of the sky." Human observation and divine instruction come together in Isa 28:23-29, where it is said that God teaches rightly (ysr יסר) and instructs the farmer (yrh ירה). Similarly, in 1 Chr 5:13 yoray (יוֹרַי) may be a short form for yoraya (יוֹרִיָה), with

the probable meaning "whom Yahweh teaches." Elihu states the idea clearly: "Look, El is sovereign in power; who is a teacher (moreh מֹרֶה) like him?" So do some psalmists (94:12 with Piel of ysr and lmd; 119:108 with lammedheni לַמְּדֵנִי; compare Sir 51:17 and 11QPsᵃ (11Q5).

The prophet Jeremiah acknowledges divine failure at teaching willful sinners (Jer 32:33 with lmd). According to Bildad, remote ancestors had more success at bequeathing their views to society (Job 8:8, 10 with hqr הֵקֶר, to inquire; yrh ירה, to teach; melibban מִלָּבָן, reasoned utterances. Elihu promises to teach Job wisdom (Job 33:33b, ʾlp אַלֵּף). Thus a broad range of vocabulary covers teaching: Piel (Intensive) forms of ʾlp, lmd, and ysr; Hiphil (causative) forms of byn בִּין, skl שָׂכֵל, ykh יכַח and yrh ירה, plus circumlocutions (e.g., yosif leqah יֹסֶף לֶקַח).

The Hebrew words for "father" and "my son" (ʾav אָב; beni בְּנִי) eventually indicated teacher and student. A single student was known as a talmidh תַּלְמִד, 2 Chr 25:8). The verb ktb כתב, to write) rarely occurs in wisdom literature (Prov 3:3; 7:3; Job 13:26; 19:23; Eccl 12:10). Ben Sira continues this reluctance to use ktb, although engaged in literary activity (Sir 39:32) and insisting that students keep reliable records of income and expenses (Sir 42:7). He never advises students to consult written texts; instead he tells them to search out intelligent people and talk to them.

The learning process began with careful observation (raʾah רָאָה, khaza חָזָה, sakhal שָׂכַל), thorough exploration (tur תּוּר, darash דָּרַשׁ, baqash בָּקַשׁ, haqar הָקַר), and assessment of data by arranging them in an orderly fashion (taqan תָּקַן). Listening supplemented ocular discovery (ʿazan עָזַן, shamaʿ שָׁמַע, nathan lev נָתַן לֵב). Reflecting on things and discussing them with others followed (shith lev שִׁית לֵב, safar סָפַר). The actual discovery of an insight was expressed by verbs for finding and knowing (masaʾ מָצָא, yadhaʿ יָדַע), attaining a full grasp of an idea by bin בִּין, laqah לָקַח, musar מָסַר, qanah קָנָה, kun כּוּן). Once a person had acquired knowledge, he was obligated to hold onto it (hazaq הָזַק), guard it (shamar שָׁמַר, nasar נָסַר), love it (ʾahav אָהַב), not abandon it (ʿazav עָזַב), or neglect it (paraʾ פָּרַא), or despise it (bazah בָּזָה, saneʾ שָׂנֵא), or let it fall (rafah רָפָה). The final result of this search for knowledge could be described as khokhmah חָכְמָה), a supernym for a host of terms (daʿath דַּעַת, musar מָסַר, torah תּוֹרָה, binah בִּנָה, tevunah תְּבֻנָה, ʾormah עָרְמָה, tushiyah תֻּשִׁיָּה, tohahath תֹּהַחַת, navon נָבוֹן, ʿarum עָרֻם, and kishron כִּשְׁרוֹן). For Qoheleth, khokhmah plus the preposition b ב, by means of) designated rational inquiry, and heshbon הֶשְׁבּוֹן stood for the entire process of thinking and its result. Anyone who possessed this knowledge was a wise person (khakham חָכָם).

Occasionally, several of these important words appear in a cluster, probably in additive fashion (Eccl

7:24-29; 12:9-10; Sir 6:27; Ps 139:1-3, 23-24; Job 28:27). The last mentioned verse covers four distinct stages in the intellectual process. The first, observation, engages the eyes as they examine observable phenomena and indicates immediate knowledge, firsthand experience, thus intimate knowledge. The second, discussion, involves the organ of speech, the agency by which individuals endeavor to articulate conclusions in a way that will communicate with others. This discussion also entails hearing with discernment. In this manner private insights become public commodity, and the collective knowledge of a society contributes to private insight.

The third stage, establishing hypotheses and reaching provisional conclusions, occurs within the mind, for the discoverer ultimately bears sole responsibility for new insights. The final stage, analytic assessment achieved by exploring every facet of an idea, returns to the earlier image of probing the recesses of earth in search of precious gems, then examining them for possible flaws. The four verbs—ra'ah, safar, kun, and haqar—nicely describe the cognitive analytic process as the poet understood it.

H. Types of Instruction

1. Religious

The Shema (Deut 6:4-9) accentuates the educational responsibility of every Israelite. Besides commanding wholehearted devotion to Yahweh, it enjoins every parent to teach the Torah, especially the Decalogue, to children from morning until evening. It specifically mentions the following times: when sitting at home, when walking on paths, when going to bed, and when rising from sleep. As aids to this instruction, the words are to be bound on the hand, placed between the eyes, and inscribed on doorposts. To this day Orthodox Jews take this command literally.

We may assume that religious instruction was much broader than the Shema, and that various traditions from local sanctuaries, especially Gilgal and Shiloh but also Dan and Beersheba, were eventually incorporated into the official "narrative" from the central place of worship, Jerusalem. Core values were transmitted through stories about ancestral worthies (and occasional unsavory characters), as well as prophets and priests. Followers of these special representatives of the deity passed along their favorite anecdotes and oracles, making essential adjustments to keep them timely as circumstances changed over the centuries. This continual updating of revered texts can easily be detected in larger prophetic compositions attributed to Isaiah and Jeremiah, and also in minor prophetic books such as Amos and Micah. An interesting example of revising earlier prophecy involves Jeremiah's oracle about a seventy-year exile in Babylon (Jer 25:11-12; 29:10), which must be reinterpreted by the 2nd cent. author of the book of Daniel

(9:24-27). Prophetic bands and priestly guilds taught each generation the vital aspects of their trades.

The importance of religious education during the rabbinic period is highlighted in *Pirqe Aboth* 5:32:

"He used to say, 'At five [one begins the study of] the Bible. At ten the Mishnah.

At thirteen [one takes on] the [responsibility for] the mitswoth (מִצְוֹת). At fifteen [one begins the study of] the Talmud. At eighteen [one is ready for] marriage. At twenty to pursue [a livelihood]. At thirty [one attains full] strength. At forty [one gains] understanding.

At fifty [one gives] counsel. At sixty [one reaches] old age.

At seventy [one reaches] the fullness of age.

At eighty [one reaches] strong old age.

At ninety [one is] bent.

And, at one hundred, it is as if one had already died and passed from the world.'"

Similar pre-Eriksonian recognition of life's stages are known from Egyptian texts. For instance, one reads this account from roughly the same time as *Pirqe Aboth.*

He [man] spends ten [years] as a child before he understands death and life.

He spends another ten years acquiring the work of instruction by which he will be able to live.

He spends another ten years gaining and earning possessions by which to live.

He spends another ten years up to old age before his heart takes counsel.

There remain sixty years of the whole life which Thoth has assigned to the man of God.

(*Papyrus Insinger* 17/22–18/3)

2. Professional

Because the duties of the priesthood involved considerable activity of a technical nature, this information had to be taught anew whenever novices joined the ranks. The topics varied from the different kinds of sacrifices together with the rituals associated with each one, the rules governing clean and unclean, the liturgical calendar and festivals, laws of all kinds and the prescribed punishment for infractions, the manipulation of special means for determining the divine will (e.g., the sacred dice, URIM AND THUMMIM), and more.

Similarly, prophetic guilds preserved for posterity the essentials of their trade (DIVINATION, diatribe, pastoral consolation, and more). The complex task of discerning the divine word and crafting it to the right audience, the poetic art of persuasion, the intercessory role, the traditions and cultic practices appropriate to the region in which they worked—all these skills were communicated from generation to generation to limmudhim (לְמֻדִּים) "taught ones," compare Isa 8:16).

Scribes, too, taught the responsibilities of their profession to apprentices. Their roles varied with the clientele; they consisted of translating diplomatic correspondence and answering it; keeping records at the royal court; overseeing simple business transactions; drawing up marriage contracts and divorce proceedings; preparing legal documents and adjudicating civil disputes; composing official letters; copying manuscripts; and so forth. Some scribes were employed largely, if not solely, as keepers of the national literary deposit, which eventually became the canon of scripture and competing deuterocanonical works. The elite status of these scribes can be detected in the only surviving biblical reflection about their activity (Sir 38:24–39:11). Unlike farmers, craftsmen, smiths, and potters who earn a living by manual labor and who are indispensable to a stable society, Ben Sira writes, scribes serve those who hold positions of power, give reasoned discourses among the learned, and travel to distant lands at their ruler's behest.

3. Enculturation

Much learning in the ancient world was instrumental; that is, it was a means of instilling cultural norms in the young. Because of competing cultures, a result of the transitory nature of life in the ANE, Israel's guardians of tradition endeavored to stamp a distinct worldview in the minds of young girls and boys. Biblical literature is replete with echoes of this struggle for the hearts of the young. The conflict between Yahweh and Baal, erroneously viewed until recently as history versus nature's cyclical repetition of the past, is but one example of this fight to control minds. Another instance of the conflict is seen in the struggle between those who championed an aniconic understanding of Yahwism and others who saw no intrinsic harm in the use of the works of human hands (called idols by critics) during worship. In this case Babylonian influence, perpetuated in later Hellenism, rivals that of earlier Canaanite religion.

Preserving national values over against the views of neighboring peoples was possibly less vexing than internal conflict. The grasping for power—political, economic, and religious—was never ending. The rivalry that is painstakingly choreographed in royal biography is easily matched by the dispute over the rightful heirs to the priesthood and its privileges. Prophetic representatives of central administration and royal ideology, concentrated in the Davidic and Zion traditions, competed with those who favored the Mosaic and patriarchal legacies. Visionaries vied with persons of a more practical bent. Sages also entered the fray, with traditionalists preferring the comfortable message of a universal divine order while radicals questioned both traditionalists' assumptions and conclusions. Evidence of editorial insertion of centrist views into liturgical texts such as the psalms, and the touching up of prophetic books

to accord with emerging dogma and to meet pressing theological needs in a community lacking hope reveal the scope of this inner struggle to capture the minds of the next generation of worshipers.

I. Restrictions on Learning
1. Controls on the intellect

Although God's knowledge, at least according to Ps 139, is complete, human discovery invariably encountered a teacher's tight fist, the restriction of knowledge. Ecclesiastes viewed every sage who claimed to have attained absolute wisdom as a liar (8:17), for the deity withheld vital information (3:11), after having planted ha'olam (הָעֹלָם) within the mind. Ironically, the exact meaning of this Hebrew word is a subject of dispute, whether a sense of duration or secrecy. The latter interpretation is in line with a text from Proverbs indicating that God's glory is to conceal while a king's glory is to search (Prov 26:2). A democratizing of the intellectual quest was accompanied by a profound sense of the unknown and unknowable in every intellectual inquiry. That awareness of limits applied especially to inquiries about time and death, for no one knows the future, and the mystery surrounding death is impenetrable.

The Niph'al (passive) form of the root hqr regularly indicates the unfathomable and immeasurable. Normally, this verb is negated, either by the particles 'en (אֵין) and lo' (לֹא) or through rhetorical questions. It refers to God's ways and deeds, with the exception of Prov 26:3, which understandably places the minds of oriental kings in the same impenetrable category. Wisdom's hiddenness is the subject of the exquisite poem in Job 28, which juxtaposes human ingenuity in extracting precious ore from the earth with the firm denial that wisdom can be discovered, save by God. Even Sheol and Abaddon, the poem insists, have only indirect knowledge of her, as if eavesdropping on a rumor. Ben Sira concurs, adding to the mystery by producing a pun on wisdom's name, presumably **musar** rather than **khokhmah**, that is not entirely clear (Sir 6:22). Furthermore, he writes: "Seek not unfathomable wonders, nor probe into things concealed from you. Attend to what is entrusted to you; hidden things are not your business. Do not talk about what exceeds your grasp, for more than you [understand] has been shown to you. Indeed, human speculations are numerous, and evil conjectures lead one astray" (Sir 3:21-24). This approach to rational inquiry echoes the sentiment expressed in Deut 29:28 ("The secret things belong to Yahweh our God, but the revealed things belong to us and to our posterity.").

This attack on the essence of rational inquiry, the desire to penetrate the unknown and make it comprehensible, does not automatically follow from humble acknowledgment that the intellect can never explain life's mystery. The necessities of polemic have forced

Ben Sira into an untenable position that because some things are not subject to cognitive analysis they should not be studied. (Perhaps he refers to Greek astrological and cosmological speculations and to Jewish apocalyptic imagination.)

It can be said that the intellect is subject to controls on every hand: deliberate ones in laws and norms imposed by society, latent controls that influence decisions unconsciously and when least expected, cognitive controls that we administer to hold things in check, and coercive or seductive controls enforced by others to restrict free expression. The language we use shapes discourse and determines thought; the myths we fabricate become the scripts in which we read the drama of our lives and the truth to which we ultimately submit; the groups to which we belong, and those to which we do not, impose hidden pressure on us in subtle and not so subtle ways; our anticipation of rejection and isolation issues in a particular code of conduct; the level of access or availability of a given choice enters heavily into our decisions; and the expected compensation for an action determines to some degree whether or not the reward justifies it.

2. Affective surprise

The marvel is that the intellectual quest is often marked by shocks of intuitive recognition of that which until the moment has been completely hidden. Given the limits on cognitive inquiry, what explanation for this surprise can be offered? Here is a paradox of learning for which society has not prepared its citizens. How can anyone recognize the radically new except through a gift of insight? It comes upon us as if bestowed by a generous but mysterious Teacher. In ancient Israel, where the *traditum* was venerated above the *novum*, this affective surprise helps to explain the combined humility of prayer and restraint of reason in discussions of the teaching enterprise.

It should not be surprising that tension arose between these very different understandings of rational inquiry. The experimental approach was based on empirical data, easily verifiable and accessible to eye and ear. By contrast, affective surprises came out of the blue as if from some mysterious but generous patron. The sages refused to choose between these views of intellectual discovery, although a later rabbinic dictum leaves no room for revelation ("No heavenly interference is allowed in the Academy"). Through analogy they arrived at fundamental insights linking nature and society.

Eyes and ears held sway in this pursuit of the reason underlying the universe, justifying the symbolic use of both organs of sight and sound (Job 42:5). Ancient Near Eastern sages were inclined to think that learning entered the ear rather than resulting from visual activity. Because instructors employed oral recitation and depended on students to memorize what they heard,

the teachers characterized model students as "hearing ones." Similarly, the servant in Isa 50:4 observes: "Morning by morning he wakens—wakens my ear to listen to those who are taught." Because reason, like its vessel, is finite, not everything succumbed to persistent inquiry. As compensation, some insights burst forth with dazzling brilliance as a gift from the unknown.

Bibliography: John Baines. "Literacy and Ancient Egyptian Society." *Man* 18 (1983) 572–99; David M. Carr. *Writing on the Tablet of the Heart: Origins of Scripture and Literature* (2005); James L. Crenshaw. "Education in Ancient Israel" *JBL* 104 (1985) 601–615; James L. Crenshaw. *Education in Ancient Israel: Across the Deadening Silence* (1998); Graham I. Davies. "Were There Schools in Ancient Israel?" *Wisdom in Ancient Israel.* John Day, Robert P. Gordon, and H. G. M. Williamson, eds. (1995) 199–211; Michael V. Fox. "The Pedagogy of Proverbs 2." *JBL* 113 (1994) 233–43; Michael V. Fox. "Who Can Learn? A Dispute in Ancient Pedagogy." *Wisdom, You Are My Sister.* Michael L. Barré, ed. (1997) 62–77; Manahem Haran. "On the Diffusion of Literacy and Schools in Ancient Israel." *Congress Volume, Jerusalem, 1986* (1988) 81–95; E. W. Heaton. *The School Tradition of the Old Testament* (1994); Alan Mendelson. *Secular Education in Philo of Alexandria* (1982); Laurie E. Pearce. "The Scribes and Scholars of Ancient Mesopotamia." *CANE* Vol. 4. Jack M. Sasson, ed. (1995) 2265–78; Nili Shupak. *Where Can Wisdom Be Found?* (1993); Stuart Weeks. *Early Israelite Wisdom* (1994); M. Young. "Israelite Literacy: Interpreting the Evidence." *VT* 48 (1998) 239–53, 408–22.

JAMES L. CRENSHAW

EGERTON PAPYRUS. The Egerton Papyrus contains the fragments of a gospel that was unknown prior to its publication in 1935. This text preserves four stories surrounding the life of Jesus: 1) a trial scene between Jesus and the "rulers of the people" over fidelity to the law; 2) Jesus' healing of a leper; 3) a controversy between Jesus and his accusers regarding the payment of tribute to Caesar; and 4) a miracle story describing the growth of seeds at the bank of the Jordan River.

While the fourth story is not found in the NT, the other three have parallels in the canonical Gospels: 1) John 5:39-47; 9:29; 10:31-39; 2) Matt 8:1-4; Mark 1:40-45; Luke 5:12-16; 17:11-14; and 3) Matt 22:15-22; Mark 12:13-17; Luke 20:20-26. Scholarship on the text remains divided over a number of issues. For instance, while many think the Egerton Gospel is dependent upon the canonical Gospels (either in their written form or through the author's recollection of their contents), others have proposed that its composition is both independent of and prior to the formation of the NT Gospels. A related issue centers on the dating of the papyrus itself: scholars arguing for NT dependence generally support a date of around 200 CE, while those who contend that the Egerton fragments represent an earlier witness to the stories found in the canonical Gospels believe that the manuscript should be placed closer to the beginning of the 2nd cent. *See* PAPYRUS, PAPYRI.

DAVID M. REIS

EGG [בֵּיצָה betsah; ᾠόν ōon]. Appearing only in the plural in the OT, eggs do not seem to have become a common food item in Palestine until ca. 5th cent. BCE. Old Testament references to eggs include bird and snake eggs. According to Deuteronomic law, someone who finds a bird's nest with young and eggs should not take the adult bird with the young; no mention is made of taking the eggs (Deut 22:6). In Job 39:14, an ostrich leaves its eggs unprotected on the warm ground, forgetting that the eggs may easily be trampled. Isaiah uses eggs figuratively to represent people's wealth (Isa 10:14) and people's evil deeds (Isa 59:5).

Luke uses "egg" and SCORPION to contrast good gifts and harmful gifts (Luke 11:12). His argument culminates in a comparison between the human ability to give gifts versus God's ability to give the good gift of the Holy Spirit.

KATHY R. MAXWELL

EGLAH eg'luh [עֶגְלָה 'eghlah]. The sixth wife of DAVID and the mother of Ithream (2 Sam 3:5; 1 Chr 3:3).

EGLAIM eg'lay-im [אֶגְלַיִם 'eghlayim]. A town of uncertain location mentioned in the oracle against Moab (Isa 15:8). The rhetorical deployment of the town in the poetical context of this verse indicates that it was situated near one of Moab's boundaries, at the point farthest from Moab's boundary at Beer-elim. *See* MOAB, MOABITES.

MARK DELCOGLIANO

EGLATH-SHELISHIYAH   eg'lath-shi-lish'uh-yuh [עֶגְלַת שְׁלִשִׁיָּה 'eghlath shelishiyah]. Usually interpreted to be the name of a Moabite town (Isa 15:5; Jer 48:34).

EGLON eg'lon [עֶגְלוֹן 'eghlon]. 1. A city in the SHEPHELAH of Judah. Many scholars locate Eglon at modern Tell 'Aitun, but this identification is not universally accepted.

Joshua 10:1-27 tells of a coalition of Amorite kings of Eglon (King DEBIR), Jerusalem, Hebron, Jarmuth, and Lachish, who joined together to attack Gibeon after it had formed an alliance with the Israelites. When they laid siege to Gibeon, Joshua came to its rescue, defeating them in the battle in which "the sun stood still." When the kings fled to the cave at MAKKE-DAH, Joshua had them brought out and killed, then he entombed them in the cave. Aside from one other

reference to this battle (Josh 12:12) and a notice that the town was assigned to Judah (Josh 15:39), the city is not mentioned again in the Bible.

2. A king of Moab during the period of the Judges whose name means "little calf," although the obesity of this Moabite king suggests a play on words with 'aghol (עָגֹל) meaning "round" or "rotund."

Judges 3:12-30 notes that when the people sinned, God gave them into the hand of Eglon of Moab. Joining with the Ammonites and Amalekites, Eglon defeated Israel and forced them to serve him eighteen years. He was eventually killed by EHUD, who hid a half-meter-long sword on his right thigh. Being a left-handed man, this was the natural place for his weapon, but the guard would not have searched there, since most people are right handed and would carry their sword on their left hip. Having gained access to Eglon under the guise of bringing tribute, Ehud stabbed the king, who was so fat that the blade and handle both went into his body. With Eglon's death, the Israelites were able to defeat the Moabites.

KEVIN A. WILSON

EGREBEH [Ἐγρεβήλ Egrebēl]. A town south of Dothan in the eastern hills of Samaria where the Edomites and Ammonites were stationed by Assyrian general Holofernes (Jdt 7:18). Many scholars associate Egrebeh with Akrabeh, north of Jerusalem, or AKRAB-ATTENE (1 Macc 5:3).

EGYPT ee'jipt [מִצְרַיִם mitsrayim; Αἴγυπτος Aigyptos]. Egypt was one of the great ancient civilizations. Located along the Nile Valley in northeastern AFRICA, the land was agriculturally rich and easily defensible. A unified state first emerged in Egypt in the fourth millennium BCE. Egypt became an empire in the second millennium BCE when its territory stretched from Syria to the fourth cataract of the Nile (in modern-day Sudan).

The English word *Egypt* derives from the name of a temple. One of the prominent structures in the ancient city of Memphis was ḥwt-k3-ptḥ, "the house of [the god] Ptah." This name came into Greek as Aigyptos and was extended to apply to the entire country. The most common designation for Egypt in Hebrew is mitsrayim (*see* MIZRAIM).

In the Bible, Egypt is especially associated with the exodus. According to the pentateuchal narratives, the family of Jacob settled in the Nile Delta during a period of famine. Their descendants were enslaved, but God delivered them through the leadership of Moses and Aaron. The exodus serves as a defining motif for the relationship between God and the people and is paradigmatic of God's saving acts. God is the one "who brought you out of the land of Egypt." In Matt 2, Egypt is also the place where the baby Jesus and his family found refuge when they fled from King Herod.

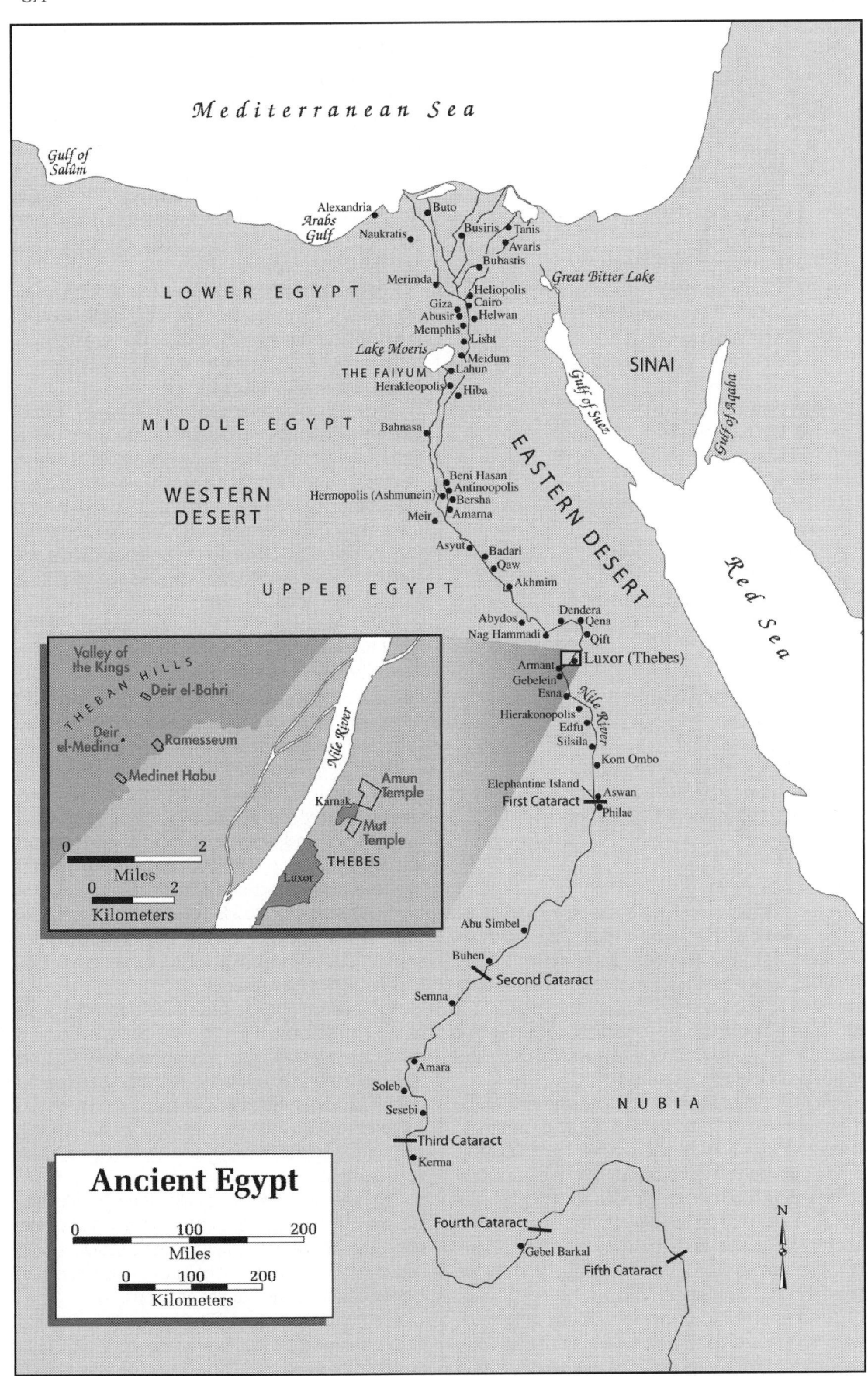

Mediterranean Sea

Gulf of Salûm

Alexandria
Arabs Gulf
Naukratis

Buto
Busiris
Tanis
Avaris
Bubastis

LOWER EGYPT

Merimda

Heliopolis
Giza
Abusir
Memphis
Helwan
Lisht
Lahun
Meidum

Great Bitter Lake

SINAI

Gulf of Suez

Gulf of Aqaba

Lake Moeris
THE FAIYUM
Herakleopolis
Hiba

MIDDLE EGYPT

Bahnasa

WESTERN
DESERT

Beni Hasan
Antinoopolis
Hermopolis (Ashmunein)
Bersha
Meir
Amarna

EASTERN DESERT

Asyut
Badari
Qaw
Akhmim

UPPER EGYPT

Abydos
Dendera
Qena
Nag Hammadi
Qift

Red Sea

Armant
Gebelein
Esna

Luxor (Thebes)

Nile River

Hierakonopolis
Edfu
Silsila

Kom Ombo

Elephantine Island
First Cataract
Aswan
Philae

Inset: Thebes

Valley of the Kings
THEBAN HILLS
Deir el-Bahri

Deir el-Medina
Ramesseum

Medinet Habu

Nile River

Amun Temple

Karnak
Mut Temple

THEBES

Luxor

0   Miles   2
0   Kilometers   2

Abu Simbel

Buhen
Second Cataract

Semna

Amara
Soleb
Sesebi

NUBIA

Third Cataract
Kerma

Fourth Cataract

Gebel Barkal
Fifth Cataract

Ancient Egypt

0   100   200
Miles
0   100   200
Kilometers

N

A. Geography

Ancient Egypt was defined by the Nile River whose waters made life possible in an otherwise extremely arid land. The river provided almost everything the Egyptians needed for life: papyrus, fish, habitat for birds and animals, and water for drinking and irrigation. It also served as the primary "roadway," especially for cargo. Of course the river held dangers like crocodiles and hippopotamuses. *See* NILE RIVER.

Prior to modern flood control dams, the level of the river fluctuated dramatically from a low point in late spring to a high point in late summer/early fall. This annual inundation was fed by monsoon rains in Ethiopia and carried with it mineral-rich silt to enrich the fields of Egypt. The fertile strip of land along the river, blackened with silt, was termed **kmt** "the Black Land" by the ancient Egyptians. The surrounding deserts were called **dšrt** "the Red Land."

The rise and fall of the river defined the agricultural seasons, of which there were three: **3ht** (inundation), **prt** (coming forth), and **šmw** (harvest). Each season comprised four months of thirty days each. Five additional days were added to bring the total up to 365.

The floodplain was cultivated intensively. The primary crops were barley and emmer wheat, which were baked into bread or brewed to make beer. Flax fibers were woven into ropes and linen cloth; flaxseed was valued for its oil. The Egyptians grew a variety of other vegetables including pulses (peas, lentils, fava beans, and chickpeas), cucumbers, melons, squash, and onions. They also raised fruits such as grapes, dates, figs, and pomegranates.

The Egyptians divided domesticated ruminants into two primary categories based on size. Cattle were an important agricultural commodity. The smaller ruminants included sheep, goats, and pigs. Two types of geese were also domesticated.

Ancient Egypt was divided into two primary administrative units: Upper and Lower Egypt. These were further subdivided into forty-two provinces known as "nomes." Upper Egypt comprised the territory south of Memphis to Aswan and the first cataract; Lower Egypt the territory from Memphis north to the Mediterranean Sea, including the Delta. To the Egyptians, south was "up" and north was "down" because the Nile flows from south to north.

Lower Egypt was "the Land of the Papyrus Plant," a broad flat wedge of land with its apex near Memphis. The branching of the Nile created a fertile delta comprising almost half the arable land of ancient Egypt. The course and number of these branches was not stable, but varied greatly over the centuries.

Upper Egypt was "the Land of the South," a long, narrow ribbon of arable land bordered by cliffs. It is often subdivided into Middle Egypt (from Memphis to Asyut), Northern Upper Egypt (from Asyut to Luxor), and Southern Upper Egypt (from Luxor to Aswan). The fertile Faiyum basin in Middle Egypt is linked to the Nile by the Bahr Yusuf. During the inundation the waters of the Nile flow into the Faiyum via this channel, filling Lake Moeris. When the level of the Nile falls, the direction of flow reverses.

Nubia refers to the section of the Nile Valley south of the first cataract. Here the river bends in broad S-curves and is broken up by several impassable stretches of rapids known as cataracts. Therefore travelers frequently preferred the shorter overland routes. Nubia's economic value lay in its mineral wealth, especially gold and high-quality stone, and its access to exotic trade goods such as ivory and ebony.

The region east of the Nile Valley is rough mountainous desert rich in minerals, especially gold and various stones used for vessels, sculpture, and building. In addition to mining expeditions, trade caravans crossed the eastern desert en route to Red Sea ports.

The region west of the Nile Valley is even less hospitable, consisting of sand plains and barren rock. Little exploited for its scarce mineral resources, the western desert's primary value lay in its five oases, which supported vineyards and date and olive groves.

The Sinai Peninsula between Egypt and Syria-Palestine gave the Egyptians access to trade and mineral resources. The Egyptians called the road across northern Sinai "The Ways of Horus" and kept well-stocked outposts along its length to supply military and trade caravans. Mining expeditions to southern Sinai brought back quantities of turquoise and copper.

B. Chronology

Historians deal with two types of chronology: relative and absolute. Relative chronology attempts to place events in sequence, identifying which occurred first, second, third, etc. Relative chronology may also address the length of time allotted to an event such as a king's reign. Absolute chronology attempts to specify the date on which an event occurred in terms of a modern calendrical system.

Developing either type of chronology for ancient Egypt is fraught with difficulties. The sources are incomplete or of dubious reliability and often are keyed to events that cannot be dated with certainty. Sufficient records survive from some periods to establish an accurate relative chronology for stretches of a few centuries, but these eras are interspersed with others for which the data are sparse and/or ambiguous. With only a couple of firm absolute dates over several millennia, the details of Egyptian chronology remain open to debate.

The primary sources for Egyptian chronology are king lists, genealogies, dated documents, archaeology, synchronisms, and astronomical observations. King lists, dated documents, genealogies, and archaeology are used in establishing relative chronology. Archaeology, synchronisms, and astronomical observations contribute to determining absolute chronology.

1. King lists

King lists are quite simply lists of kings in chronological order and often include the lengths of reigns and/or important events from each reign. The most important king lists are the Palermo Stone, the Abydos and Saqqara lists, the Turin Canon of Kings, the Demotic Chronicle, and Manetho's Aegyptiaca. Although none of these is complete, they have provided the backbone for historical reconstruction.

The Palermo Stone is a fragmentary stela, now housed in Palermo, Italy. Some smaller fragments reside in Cairo. The original stela was inscribed on both sides with a year-by-year account of each king's reign through the 24th cent. BCE. The surviving pieces are too few to allow a complete reconstruction.

The Abydos and Saqqara lists are, strictly speaking, offering lists inscribed in the mortuary temples of Seti I and RAMESSES II at Abydos and in the tomb chapel of the chief lector priest Tjunuroy at Saqqara. Their function is not historiographic but cultic, which may explain the selective nature of the lists. They prescribe offerings for the deceased kings from whom the 13th cent. BCE kings claimed succession. Kings who ruled only part of the Nile Valley or who were considered illegitimate (such as the Hyksos, Queen Hatshepsut, and the Amarna period kings) were omitted.

The Turin Canon, despite its imposing name, is not an official document, but a private text scrawled on the back of a 13th cent. BCE tax document. Originally the list included the names and lengths of reign for all the kings of Egypt through at least the middle of the 16th cent. BCE. The papyrus, now housed in Turin, Italy, is badly damaged; many names and numbers are missing. Although the text begins with gods and mythical kings, the list of kings, insofar as it is preserved, matches well with evidence available from other sources.

The Demotic Chronicle is an oracular text that cites 4th cent. BCE historical events. It is an important source for Late Period chronology. *See* DEMOTIC CHRONICLE.

The *Aegyptiaca* was a history of Egypt written in Greek by Manetho, a 3rd cent. BCE priest-historian. The work survives only in excerpts quoted by the 1st cent. CE Jewish historian, Flavius Josephus. Citations from an abridged version, known as the *Epitome*, are preserved in the works of Africanus (3rd cent. CE), Eusebius (4th cent. CE) and George the Syncellus (ca. 800 CE). Manetho's work suffered significant distortion over centuries of transmission, and even the original clearly contained inaccuracies.

2. Dated documents and genealogies

The Egyptians dated events in terms of each king's reign. Initially, each year of a king's reign was named after a significant event. Soon the biennial cattle census became the standard designation, with dates recorded in terms of the numbered census-years of a reign (in the year of the nth cattle census or in the year after the nth cattle census). Later the references to the census were dropped, and dates were reckoned strictly in terms of regnal years. Thus an event is stated to have happened in year seven or year twenty of a particular king.

Such sources allow historians to calculate the minimum length of a reign. Thus the existence of a document referring to the twenty-ninth year of Ramesses II proves that he ruled for at least twenty-nine years, but it does not establish how many additional years he reigned. Dated documents are also helpful in placing events in order within a particular reign, but do not by themselves permit absolute dates to be assigned to the events.

Because officials often named the kings under whom they served, genealogies can be important sources for relative chronology. Thus if a man served under King X and his grandson served under King Y, King X must have preceded King Y. Genealogies have been used most extensively for the Third Intermediate Period.

3. Archaeology

Archaeological excavations produce data that can be used to establish both relative and absolute chronologies. One of the most common methods for establishing absolute dates is radiocarbon (C^{14}) dating. All living organisms contain small amounts of radioactive carbon (C^{14}). When an organism dies, the radioactive carbon begins to decay. Measuring the amount of C^{14} remaining in a sample produces an approximate absolute date. Because the margin of error for this type of analysis is measured in decades, it establishes only a broad chronological framework.

Typological analysis, especially of pottery, is used to establish relative chronology. Ceramic styles, including shape, decoration, fabric, and manufacturing technique, change over time. Archaeological sites can be placed in relative chronological order based on the pottery styles occurring there. The technique was developed in Egypt by British archaeologist Flinders Petrie in the late 19th cent. CE in his study of Pre-Dynastic burials.

Archaeologists also analyze the phases of occupation and construction at a site. Egyptian kings often usurped or remodeled monuments created by their predecessors. By placing construction phases in order, archaeologists can ascertain the relative sequence of kings who made donations to a particular temple.

4. Synchronisms

Synchronisms are data that establish the contemporaneity of a person or event in Egypt and a person or event in another region. The usefulness of a synchronism for establishing absolute chronology depends on the precision with which the corresponding thing can be dated. The Royal Canon of Ptolemy establishes absolute dates for Mesopotamian kings (and their Persian and Macedonian successors) beginning with the accession of Nabonassar in 747 BCE. From the mid-7th cent. BCE on, numerous synchronisms, such as the sacking of Thebes by the Assyrians in 664 BCE, provide anchors for Egyptian chronology.

For earlier periods, both synchronisms and precise absolute dates are quite rare. For these periods the existing synchronisms are useful in establishing parameters (measured in decades or centuries) rather than exact dates. Established New Kingdom synchronisms include Amenhotep III and his son Akhenaten with the Babylonian kings Kadashman-Enlil I and Burnaburiash II (Amarna letters), and Ramesses II with the Hittite king Hattusilis III (treaty).

5. Astronomical observations

Astronomical phenomena can provide very precise dates. For ancient Egypt, Sothic dates have been used with some success. Sothic dates rely on ancient Egyptian observations of the "heliacal" rising of the star Sirius (Greek Sothis, Egyptian Sopdet). The Egyptians noticed that Sirius would disappear from the night sky during the spring only to reappear just before sunrise in the summer at the time when the Nile rose in flood. The first day on which the star became visible in the early morning sky is the heliacal rising.

Theoretically this was also the first day of the new year. In fact, New Year's Day moved throughout the seasons because the Egyptian calendar was approximately one quarter day too short, comprising 365 days with no provision for a leap day. By contrast, the heliacal rising of Sirius occurred every 365¼ days. Since the variation is one-quarter day, the heliacal rising would shift one day every four years, providing an absolute date that is precise to within four years.

Astronomical observations are affected by latitude, which complicates their use for establishing chronology. It is necessary to know the location at which an observation was made. At Memphis, Sothic cycles began in 1313 BCE and 2769 BCE. However, an adjustment of about thirty years is necessary if an observation were made in the southern city of Elephantine. Uncertainty about the location of Sothic sightings results in differing reconstructions of Egyptian chronology.

C. History

The traditional framework for Egyptian history derives from Manetho, a 3rd cent. BCE Egyptian priest and historian, who organized the king's reigns into thirty dynasties. Two criteria governed his work: the location of the capital city and presumed (but not always real) familial ties. The dynasties are grouped into longer eras known as kingdoms and periods. According this schematization, Egyptian political history in the third and second millennia BCE alternates between eras of strong centralized control (kingdoms) and eras of political disintegration (intermediate periods). Although social and cultural developments often do not fit neatly into this framework, most historical studies adopt this convention.

1. Pre- (ca. 5300–3050 BCE) and Early Dynastic Periods (Dynasties 0–2; ca. 3050–2686 BCE)

Pre-dynastic Egypt was characterized by a series of well-defined regional cultures in Upper and Lower Egypt and the western desert. Animal husbandry, specifically cattle herding, preceded agriculture, which was introduced from western Asia as were domesticated goats. In the fifth and fourth millennia BCE, Neolithic farming communities dotted the Nile Valley, including the Faiyum.

A significant transformation occurred at the end of the fourth millennium BCE as these communities were unified into a single cultural and political entity. In just a few centuries, the Nile Valley developed all of the markers traditionally associated with "civilization," including centralized state bureaucracy, writing, and monumental architecture.

The "unification of the Two Lands" became an enduring symbol of kingship. The king brought order to Egypt by unifying the two lands of Upper and Lower Egypt, represented by the White and Red Crowns, respectively. Whether that unification was originally accomplished through military force or by more gradual integration, including intermarriage between royal houses, remains uncertain.

Even as this process of unification was underway in the late pre-dynastic period, Egypt was extending its influence across northern Sinai and into southern Palestine, beginning a relationship that would continue, with a few interruptions, for millennia. Significant quantities of Egyptian and Egyptian-style pottery, tools, and other objects appear at Early Bronze IB and II sites, along with seal impressions and vessels bearing the names of Dynasty Zero and First Dynasty kings. The nature of the interaction is difficult to determine given the limited data. There is some evidence of violent confrontation: the Palermo Stone records that two First Dynasty kings engaged in "smiting the Asiatics." The primary purpose of the Egyptian presence must have been to control access to trade goods, including oil, wine, copper, and perhaps also bitumen and salt from the Dead Sea. Trade in copper seems to have been managed by the town of Arad, which served as a point of exchange between the mines in southern Sinai and Egyptian and Palestinian consumers. Arad's commercial enterprises may have included bitumen and salt.

By the Second Dynasty, the trading colonies in southern Palestine were largely abandoned in favor of sea trade with Byblos in Lebanon, which offered access to cedar wood, oils, and resin in addition to the agricultural products previously procured in Palestine. The Egyptians called the seagoing vessels used for this trade "Byblos-ships."

2. Old Kingdom (Dynasties 3–6; 2686–218 BCE)

The Old Kingdom represents five centuries of political stability and wealth accumulation and is best symbolized by the pyramid fields of Memphis. The pyramids were royal tombs, but they were also monuments to the power and wealth of kings who commanded the resources—human, material, and intellectual—for their construction. The ancient Egyptians were themselves so awed by the pyramids that they deified Imhotep, the architect of the first pyramid.

The pyramids embody many characteristics of the Old Kingdom. The precision of their design and engineering demonstrates sophistication in mathematics, surveying, and astronomy. The labor required for their construction testifies to an elaborate bureaucracy that commanded and organized the labor of large numbers of workmen and that produced, collected, and distributed agricultural surpluses to feed them. The symbolism of the pyramids points to the emerging ideology of kingship in which the king ruled by divine right as the son and earthly representative of the sun god, Re. The funerary texts inscribed in the later pyramids bear witness to religious ideas and ceremonies, including cosmology and the afterlife. *See* PYRAMID TEXTS.

The Old Kingdom brought the god Re to national prominence. The solar cult peaked in the Fifth Dynasty with the building of sun temples at Abusir and the addition of the "son of Re" name to the royal titulary. Simultaneously the Osirian cult began to grow in importance.

Figure 2: The Pyramids of Cheops, Chefren, and Mykerinos

During the Old Kingdom, the Egyptians maintained a close trade relationship with Byblos. Numerous objects from Byblos bear the names of Old Kingdom kings, especially the sixth dynasty kings Pepi I and Pepi II, and Egyptian votive offerings were offered to the city goddess, "the Lady of Byblos."

Contact with southern Palestine and Sinai seems to have been more sporadic and violent. A relief of the third dynasty king Djoser in the Wadi Mugharah indicates that the Egyptians were already mounting their own expeditions to the copper and turquoise mines of Sinai rather than trading with the locals for the ores. These expeditions continued through the Old Kingdom. The autobiography of Weni from his tomb in Abydos describes his participation in a sixth dynasty military expedition against the "sand-dwellers" of Sinai and Palestine.

3. First Intermediate Period (Dynasties 7–11; 2181–2055 BCE)

Manetho marked a division between the Eighth and Ninth Dynasties, reflecting the collapse of Memphite rule. Yet the social and cultural changes that distinguish the First Intermediate Period from the Old Kingdom were already well underway in the seventh and eighth dynasties. Their beginnings can even be seen in the late sixth dynasty as power and wealth shifted from the royal court to the nomarchs, i.e., the governors of the nomes or provinces.

Later Egyptian literature depicts the First Intermediate Period as a time of chaos, suffering, and cultural decline. Such an interpretation served to legitimate the authority of the kings of the Middle Kingdom who portrayed themselves as restoring social order through strong central government. While this period was certainly characterized by political and cultural decentralization, evidence suggests that the provinces flourished under local rule. Surpluses that previously filled the royal granaries were collected and redistributed by provincial rulers. Local artisans, freed from the constraints of royal conventions, experimented with new styles. If their works lacked technical sophistication, they expressed great creative energy.

The political history of the early First Intermediate Period is poorly recorded and little understood, but eventually two rival kingdoms emerged, one based in Thebes in Upper Egypt (Manetho's dynasty 11) and one based in Herakleopolis in Middle Egypt (Manetho's dynasties 9 and 10). If the latter ever ruled all of Egypt, effective control of the region south of Asyut was soon lost. The First Intermediate Period came to an end when the eleventh dynasty king Mentuhotep II defeated the Herakleopolitans and unified the country under Theban rule.

4. Middle Kingdom (Dynasties 11–13; 2055–1650 BCE)

The Middle Kingdom comprises the latter part of the Eleventh Dynasty, as well as the Twelfth and Thirteenth Dynasties. It was a period of strong central government and outward expansion. Egypt's reach extended from Byblos in Lebanon to Nubia and beyond. The section of Nubia between the first and second cataracts was conquered and subjected to direct Egyptian rule. Expeditions ventured as far south as Punt, probably modern Eritrea, in search of incense and other exotic goods. Newly constructed fortresses guarded the northeastern and southern borders. An additional measure of defense was provided by execration texts, clay figurines and bowls inscribed with the names of Egypt's enemies that were broken and buried to effect a curse.

Byblos, still Egypt's gateway to Syria-Palestine, became increasingly Egyptianized. Hieroglyphic inscriptions in royal tombs as well as smaller objects attest to the presence of Egyptian scribes. In these inscriptions, the rulers of Byblos refer to themselves by the Egyptian title ḥ3ty-ʿ (mayor).

Relations with Palestine and Sinai were less intensive, and there is little evidence that Egypt exercised authority over any part of western Asia other than Byblos. Periodic mining expeditions exploited the turquoise deposits in southern Sinai, and trade caravans brought Palestinian products to Egypt. One such caravan is depicted in the tomb of the mayor Khnumhotep II at Beni Hasan in Middle Egypt. The men are bearded, and both men and women wear colorful embroidered clothing.

The Egyptians themselves considered the Middle Kingdom the classical period of language and literature. The Middle Egyptian language was imitated in later centuries, and Middle Kingdom literature was copied and studied in scribal schools. The kings were also remembered with reverence. Three were deified, and their worship continued long after their deaths: Mentuhotep II at Deir el-Bahri, Senusret III in Nubia, and Amenemhat III in the Faiyum.

5. Second Intermediate Period (Dynasties 14–17; 1650–1550 BCE)

During the Second Intermediate Period the successors of the Middle Kingdom kings found themselves pressed upon from both the south and the north. The Nubian kingdom of Cush (see CUSH, CUSHITE) expanded northward from its center at Kerma, at the southern end of the third cataract. The Egyptian fortresses between the second and first cataracts were abandoned or captured, and control over that region was lost. Late in the thirteenth dynasty authority over the eastern Delta was lost to local rulers with cultural and linguistic ties to Western Asia. The Egyptian kings withdrew to Thebes, ceding control of Middle Egypt and the Delta to a line of rulers known as the Hyksos.

The four dynasties comprised in the Second Intermediate Period should be understood as contemporaneous, rather than consecutive, kingdoms. Manetho's Seventeenth Dynasty represents the continuation of kingship at Thebes; the Fifteenth Dynasty designates the Hyksos who ruled from the Delta city of Avaris. The Fourteenth and Sixteenth Dynasties are less well understood. The kings of the Fourteenth Dynasty were probably local rulers in the Delta prior to the emergence of the Hyksos. The Sixteenth Dynasty may belong with the Seventeenth in the line of Theban kings.

The term "Hyksos" derives from the Egyptian title ḥḳꜣ-ḫꜣswt, "ruler of foreign lands." The title is doubly appropriate as the Hyksos were not only of foreign descent but also claimed the allegiance of city-states in southern Palestine. Despite later descriptions of the Hyksos as foreign invaders who swept into Egypt in a devastating blitzkrieg, the evidence suggests a long and gradual process of immigration. People from Syria-Palestine began to settle in Avaris, modern Tell ed-Dab‘a, in the eastern Delta in the twelfth dynasty. The settlement served the extensive trade networks crisscrossing the Mediterranean region, by land and sea. The community developed its own culture combining Egyptian and western Asiatic elements.

The Hyksos arose first as rulers of the eastern Delta and gradually expanded their rule west and south. Although they claimed the title King of Upper and Lower Egypt, their kingdom at its largest extent was limited to the Delta and Middle Egypt. The route through the oases of the western desert allowed them to maintain trade and diplomatic contacts with the kingdom of Cush.

The Second Intermediate Period ended in violent confrontation between the Theban and HYKSOS kings lasting several decades. Ultimately the Thebans were victorious. King Ahmose captured Avaris and defeated the Hyksos. Tradition has it that Ahmose drove the fleeing Hyksos back into southern Palestine, which contributed to the end of the Middle Bronze Age there. The precise fate of the Hyksos is unknown. The post-Hyksos settlement at Avaris is entirely Egyptian in character, without the Syro-Palestinian features typical of earlier phases of occupation. Ahmose's army did push into southern Palestine, capturing the town of Sharuhen, but whether they were pursuing the remnant of the Hyksos, striking a preemptive blow against Hyksos allies, or simply raiding a vulnerable neighbor remains unclear.

The history of the Hyksos bears a surface resemblance to the biblical narrative of Joseph and the sojourn of the Hebrew people in Egypt. In both cases, Semitic peoples settle in the Delta and rise to positions of power, until a new king comes to the throne and oppresses or attacks them. Despite these similarities, we cannot equate the Hyksos or the inhabitants of Avaris with the Hebrews. The biblical account lacks the details necessary to place it in any particular historical period. In its current form the narrative is more legend than history.

6. New Kingdom (Dynasties 18–20; 1550–1069 BCE)

The New Kingdom is synonymous with empire. During this period Egyptian hegemony reached its greatest extent, eventually stretching from northern Syria to the fourth cataract in Nubia. Expansion was first southward, reaching the fourth cataract already in the reign of Thutmose I in the late 16th cent. BCE. At the same period, incursions into western Asia were limited to military campaigns, with no attempt to establish political control over the region. Nonetheless, Thutmose I penetrated as far as north as the Euphrates River where he erected a commemorative stela. His grandson Thutmose III initiated a series of military campaigns that brought Syria-Palestine into the Egyptian Empire.

The empire reached its zenith in the 14th cent. BCE under Amenhotep III, after which it contracted in stages. First to be lost was northern Syria, which fell under Hittite control; that boundary was stabilized by treaty during the reign of the 13th cent. BCE king Ramesses II. Incursions by the Sea Peoples, including the Peleset (biblical Philistines) and other groups displaced from their Aegean homeland, resulted in the loss of much of the Palestinian coast. In the mid-12th cent. BCE, the rest of Syria-Palestine slipped out of the Egyptian orbit. By the 11th cent. BCE the viceroy of Cush ceased to recognize the authority of the Egyptian king and even briefly competed for control of Upper Egypt.

Werner Forman /Art Resource, NY

Figure 3: Hatshepsut depicted as male pharoah with goddess Seshat in foundation ceremony. Relief from the Red Chapel of Hatshepsut (ca. 1479–1458 BCE). Egypt, 18th dynasty. Location: Karnak, Thebes, Egypt.

A crisis of succession occurred in the mid-eighteenth dynasty upon the death of Thutmose II. The boy Thutmose III, son of the late king and a minor wife named Isis, was crowned his successor. Because of his youth, the boy's stepmother Hatshepsut was named regent. Hatshepsut was not only the widow of Thutmose II, but his half-sister, the child of Thutmose I and Queen Ahmose. In seven years or less she had dispensed with the title regent and had herself named king alongside Thutmose III. She was the de facto ruler of Egypt for twenty years following her brother-husband's death. Thutmose III ruled in his own right for over thirty years thereafter.

The cultural and political highpoint of the eighteenth dynasty was the reign of Amenhotep III, which coincided with an era of peace and prosperity throughout the Near East. A brotherhood of "great kings" maintained an equilibrium of power through trade, intermarriage, diplomacy, and gift exchange. As a member of that "club" Egypt could focus its energies on internal affairs, including ambitious building projects and artistic works of exceptionally high quality. *See* AMARNA LETTERS.

Amenhotep III's successor, AKHENATEN, is known as the heretic king because of his religious, political, and artistic innovations. He elevated the status of a previously little-known sun god, the Aten, and suppressed the cults of all other deities. He moved his capital to a remote spot in Middle Egypt, which he christened Akhetaten, "Horizon of Aten." This experiment with monotheism, or more properly monolatry, was short lived. Soon after Akhenaten's death, the earlier religious, political, and artistic traditions were restored.

The transition from the eighteenth to the nineteenth dynasty was marked by a series of kings of non-royal blood who came to the throne by way of high administrative or military office. The kings of the nineteenth dynasty came from a northern family and Ramesses II moved the royal residence from Thebes in Upper Egypt to Pirameses in the Delta. This transition is significant for the history of Israel because the biblical account of the exodus assumes that the royal residence was located in the Delta. Although the biblical narrative refers to the Egyptian king only by title "pharaoh" and not by name, Ramesses II is most often identified as the pharaoh of the exodus. Ramesses II was certainly the most dominant figure of the dynasty, due to his sixty-six year reign and extensive building projects.

Having outlived most of his offspring, he was succeeded by his thirteenth son MERNEPTAH. The challenges Merneptah faced foreshadowed the upheaval that would overtake the entire Mediterranean region two generations later. The Sea Peoples and Libyans mounted an attack in the western Delta that he successfully repulsed. The Hittite Empire suffered a serious famine and appealed to the Egyptians for emergency

Daniel Gebhardt/BiblePlaces.com

Figure 4: Great Temple of Ramses II at Abu Simbel

supplies of grain. From this reign comes the earliest reference to Israel: on a stele celebrating his victory over the Libyans, Merneptah claims to have conquered Israel during an earlier military campaign in Palestine.

As far as can be determined, the kings of the Twentieth Dynasty were not related to the previous ruling house. Nonetheless, they legitimated their rule by modeling themselves after their predecessors. Except for the founder Sethnakhte, all took the throne name Ramesses. Ramesses III even named his sons after the sons of Ramesses II. The Twentieth Dynasty witnessed the decay of Egypt's fortunes at home and abroad. Despite some impressive construction projects, Ramesses III was barely able to hold Egypt's empire together. He successfully kept the Sea Peoples from invading Egypt, but could not prevent them from settling along the Palestinian coast. The necropolis workers staged strikes in protest over unpaid wages, undoubtedly a sign of serious shortages. The reign ended with the Harem Conspiracy, a plot to kill the king and place a lesser son (not the crown prince) on the throne.

The remaining years of the Twentieth Dynasty were characterized by serious civil disorder, including Libyan raids, workers' strikes, and tomb robberies. Finally civil war broke out as the viceroy of Cush, Panehesy ("the Nubian"), attempted to wrest control of the country, marching as far north as Middle Egypt before he was driven back by the general Piankh.

7. Third Intermediate Period (Dynasties 21–25; 1069–664 BCE)

During the subsequent 400 years the kings of Egypt rarely exerted more than nominal control over Upper Egypt. The new royal family was ethnically Libyan and had its base at Tanis in the eastern Delta, a previously minor city. Upper Egypt was effectively controlled by the high priest of Amun at Karnak, sometimes in the name of the king, sometimes more assertively in his own right. Close ties were maintained between Tanis and Thebes by the marriage of Theban high priests to Tanite princesses. The reported marriage of the Israelite king Solomon to an Egyptian princess (1 Kgs 9:16), presumably the daughter of the Twenty-First Dynasty king Siamun, indicates how far Egyptian power and prestige had fallen. In the Amarna period, Amenhotep III had refused to give a princess in marriage to the king of Babylon, proclaiming that such a thing had never been done. If in fact Solomon married an Egyptian princess and not simply an Egyptian noblewoman whom he passed off as a daughter of the king (a scam first proposed by the king of Babylon in the 14th cent. BCE), then the Twenty-First Dynasty kings were reduced to using their daughters to secure alliances with petty kingdoms in Syria-Palestine.

The Twenty-Second Dynasty king Sheshonq (biblical SHISHAK) attempted to reassert authority over Upper Egypt by installing his son as high priest of Amun.

Sheshonq also carried out a military campaign into Judah and Israel that reached at least as far north as Megiddo where he erected a commemorative stele. According to 1 Kgs 14:25-26, Sheshonq marched against Jerusalem and plundered the treasuries of the Temple and the palace. During the 8th cent. BCE, authority became increasingly fragmented, especially in the Delta. The strong unitary government of the New Kingdom was replaced by a feudal system in which local rulers exercised considerable autonomy in managing the affairs of their fiefdoms. Theoretically at least, they owed allegiance to the Tanite kings, but some of them nonetheless proclaimed themselves King of Upper and Lower Egypt.

In the midst of these political circumstances, the Israelite king Hoshea sought Egyptian assistance in a rebellion against Assyria, to which he was a pledged vassal. Hoshea withheld his tribute and "sent messengers to King So of Egypt" (2 Kgs 17:4). King So has been variously identified as the twenty-third dynasty king Osorkon or as one of the rulers of Saïs in the western Delta. The appeal was apparently unsuccessful, perhaps because the Egyptian ruler, whoever he was, faced more pressing threats at home.

Eventually, two new power centers emerged in Egypt, one at Saïs and one at Napata in Nubia (between the third and fourth cataracts). By the reign of King Piye, the Cushite kingdom had expanded north to incorporate Thebes. When King Tefnakhte of Saïs became strong enough to extend his authority south into Middle Egypt, King Piye responded with force. He marched the length of the Nile, captured Memphis, and forced the kings of the Delta to acknowledge his lordship. His successor, Shabaqa, completed the conquest of Saïs and inaugurated the Twenty-Fifth Dynasty.

The Twenty-Fifth Dynasty fell afoul of the growing might of Assyria. Shabaqa did not challenge Assyrian authority over southern Palestine and turned over the rebellious vassal Iamani, prince of Ashdod, who had fled to Egypt for refuge. Shabaqa's successors, however, supported the anti-Assyrian coalitions of vassal states on their northeastern border. King Shebitku sent an army in support of King Hezekiah of Judah in 701 BCE and engaged the Assyrians unsuccessfully at Eltekeh. Under King Esarhaddon the Assyrians determined to eliminate the Egyptian threat to their control over southern Palestine. A series of invasions by Esarhaddon and his successor, Assurbanipal, finally drove the Cushite kings out of Egypt. Memphis and Thebes were sacked, and Psamtik, ruler of the western Delta city of Saïs, was appointed to rule Egypt on behalf of Assyria.

8. Late Period (Dynasties 26–31; 664–332 BCE)

The Late Period comprises alternating periods of independence and Persian domination. Psamtik I gained control over a largely independent Egypt by careful political maneuvering. He gradually expanded his territory without ever defying the Assyrians outright. Distracted by more pressing concerns, the Assyrians allowed him to gain a foothold in southern Palestine. When Assyrian might waned, he supported them against the rising power of Babylon. In 609 BCE the Egyptian army marched to the defense of the Assyrians in northern Syria. King Josiah of Judah, siding with the Babylonians, interposed his army to block the Egyptian advance. The Egyptians quickly disposed of Josiah and his troops, but the delay spelled the doom of the Assyrians. Thereafter Egypt and Babylon wrestled for control of Palestine. According to 2 Kgs 23:31-35, the Egyptian king NECO II refused to recognize Jehoahaz as Josiah's successor and placed his brother Jehoiakim on the throne in his stead. In 601 BCE the Babylonian king Nebuchadnezzar seized control of Egypt's remaining territories in southern Palestine, but failed in his attempt to invade Egypt proper. The Egyptian kings continued to launch incursions into Syria-Palestine and to support and foment rebellion. The campaigns of Psamtik II and Apries (biblical HOPHRA) in Palestine and Lebanon encouraged King Zedekiah of Judah to rebel against Babylon. The Babylonians defeated the Egyptian army and suppressed the rebellion.

Although the Saite kings of the Twenty-Sixth Dynasty had managed to keep the Babylonians at bay, they were no match for the Persians. Cambyses conquered Egypt in 525 BCE and Egypt became a Persian satrapy (province). The Persians appointed a satrap to govern the new province, but left most of the Egyptian administrative system in place. The Persians proclaimed themselves kings of Egypt and are considered dynasty 27. Darius completed the canal, begun by Neco II, connecting the Red Sea with the Mediterranean via the Wadi Tumilat and the Pelusiac branch of the Nile.

The Egyptians briefly threw off Persian rule at the beginning of the 4th cent. BCE. Amyrtaios of Saïs led the successful rebellion and appears as the sole member of Manetho's Twenty-Eighth Dynasty. The kings of the Twenty-Ninth and Thirtieth Dynasties relied heavily on Greek mercenaries to ward off Persian attempts to reclaim Egypt. Eventually the Persians succeeded, and Egypt succumbed to Persian domination for a ten-year period sometimes labeled the Thirty-First Dynasty.

During the Late Period, Egyptian society became ever more ethnically diverse. Egypt's increasing engagement with the eastern Mediterranean brought mercenaries and traders who settled in the Delta and at military outposts along the Nile. A Greek community was established at Naukratis in the western Delta and enjoyed a monopoly on trade. The new immigrant groups included communities of Jews, the best documented of which resided at Elephantine in Upper Egypt. Aramaic papyri from Elephantine attest to the existence of a temple to Yahweh and to the observance of the Passover. *See* ELEPHANTINE PAPYRI.

9. Ptolemaic Period (332–30 BCE)

The Ptolemaic Period in its most technical sense began only after the division of Alexander the Great's kingdom among his generals. Nonetheless, the term is commonly used to refer more broadly to the period of Macedonian (Greek) domination from Alexander's conquest of Egypt in 332 BCE until the Roman conquest in 30 BCE.

Alexander the Great did not remain long in Egypt before departing to continue his conquests. His primary accomplishment during his brief stay was to found the city of Alexandria on the Mediterranean coast in the western Delta. When he died in Babylon in 323 BCE, he was succeeded by his half-brother and his infant son. Upon their deaths the empire was divided into three kingdoms, each ruled by one of Alexander's generals: Lysimachos in Macedon; Seleucos in Syria and Mesopotamia; and Ptolemy in Egypt and Cyrene (Libya).

The Ptolemies were quite successful in building upon Alexander's foundation, both literally and figuratively. They transformed Alexandria into a cultural showplace for their imperial ambitions. The lighthouse on Pharos island was one of the wonders of the ancient world. The Mouseion was a renowned center of learning and housed within its walls a library of over 700,000 volumes. Although in many ways the Greeks and Egyptians lived in separate worlds within a single country, the Ptolemaic kings paid due respect to Egyptian religious traditions. Many temples were constructed under their patronage, most notably the temple of Horus Behdet at Edfu and the temple of Isis on Philae. The priests reciprocated by endorsing the kings. The Rosetta Stone is a prime example; it records honors bestowed on Ptolemy V by a council of Egyptian priests meeting in Memphis in 196 BCE.

The early Ptolemaic kings followed an aggressive expansionist policy in both the eastern Mediterranean and Syria-Palestine. At its greatest extent, the Ptolemaic Empire incorporated Egypt, Cyrene (Libya), Cyprus, Palestine, Lebanon, and much of the Anatolian (Turkish) coastline, including the nearby islands. However, these gains could not be sustained for long. By 195 BCE, the Ptolemaic Empire had been reduced to its core: Egypt, Cyrene, and Cyprus. Syria-Palestine fell back under Seleucid rule.

Roman involvement in Ptolemaic affairs grew throughout the 2nd and 1st cent. BCE. Rome protected Egypt from Seleucid incursions and arbitrated succession disputes. The Ptolemies began to look to Rome as guarantors of succession; Ptolemy XII named Rome as executor in his will to ensure that his daughter Cleopatra VII and her brother Ptolemy XIII would share the throne as co-regents. Rome, in the persons of Julius Caesar and Mark Antony, became embroiled in the sibling rivalry among Cleopatra VII, her brothers Ptolemy XIII and XIV, and her sister Arsinoe IV. In the end Octavian conquered Egypt and annexed it to Rome.

10. Roman Period (30 BCE–395 CE)

Egypt enjoyed relative peace and prosperity under Roman rule, although most of the wealth flowed to Rome. The emperors showed little interest in Egypt, so long as taxes were promptly paid and civil unrest was minimal. The Romans retained much of the Ptolemaic administrative structure, installing a single prefect at the head of the structure. Initially three legions were stationed in Egypt, though that number was eventually reduced to one.

Alexandria maintained its status as a prominent commercial and cultural center and as an oasis of Greek culture in the land of Egypt. In many respects the city was second only to Rome itself. Alexandria boasted a prosperous and influential Jewish community, representing perhaps a quarter or more of the population. This community had produced the LXX, the Greek translation of the Jewish Scriptures, which became a foundational text for early Christianity. It also produced the philosopher Philo who synthesized Jewish and Hellenistic philosophy. However, Roman policy exacerbated tensions between the Greek and non-Greek communities. Relations between the Jewish and Greek citizens grew increasingly violent, culminating in the massacre of a large portion of the Jewish population in 117 CE.

Christianity spread through Egypt in the second half of the 1st cent. CE, facilitated especially by the Jewish communities located in Alexandria and all along the Nile. Because the early Egyptian Christian community was so closely linked to the Jewish community, it was greatly reduced in Trajan's anti-Jewish campaigns. Nonetheless, Christianity persisted and eventually flourished in both the Greek and native Egyptian communities. The evidence from the early 2nd cent. is meager, consisting primarily of papyrus fragments bearing portions of the Gospels and other early Christian writings. By the late 2nd and early 3rd cent., Alexandria emerged as a center of Christian intellectual life, both gnostic and catholic. Pantaenus, Clement, and Origen taught at the catechetical school founded by Bishop Demetrius. The city also produced the great gnostic teachers Basilides and Valentinus. The Christian community suffered greatly under waves of persecution during the reigns of Septimus Severus, Decius, Valerian, and Diocletian.

Circumstances changed dramatically in the reign of Emperor Theodosius I. In 391 CE he ordered the closing of all non-Christian houses of worship throughout the empire. Although many temples and monuments were destroyed and adherents of the old religions persecuted, traditional Egyptian religion persisted in remote areas of the country. The last holdout was the cult of Isis on the island of Philae in Upper Egypt where worship ceased in the mid-6th cent. CE.

D. Administration

Ancient Egypt developed a massive and complex bureaucracy to manage its economic, social, and foreign affairs. The king was the titular head of the government although in practice authority was delegated to the vast cadre of central, provincial, and local officials. These offices evolved over the course of the millennia in response to economic and political conditions. In general, there were three "branches" of government: the state with responsibility for internal affairs, especially agricultural production, taxation, and justice; the temples with responsibility for the performance of rituals; and the military with responsibility for security and foreign expeditions. These branches were not strictly separated, and the duties of officials often crossed over the categories. In the New Kingdom an imperial administration with close links to the military was added.

The king ruled as nfr ntr, "the good god," but the nature of his divinity remains a disputed concept. Some scholars assert that the king was only worshiped after death or, during his lifetime, outside Egypt. Certainly the king differed from other gods. He was mortal, and, unlike other gods, his vitality had to be renewed through a "jubilee" festival or *sed* fest. Yet once he acceded to the throne he was closely linked to divinity. He was the living Horus, the son of Re. The concept is made most explicit in the reliefs and inscriptions at Deir el-Bahari, which portray Amun taking human form to impregnate the queen mother.

In the New Kingdom, the term pr ʿ3, "great house" or palace, began to be used not only to designate the central bureaucracy but also as a designation for the person of the king. This term came into Hebrew as parʿoh (פַּרְעֹה) and into English as PHARAOH. Technically, then, the title pharaoh should not be used for Egyptian kings before the New Kingdom.

The state administration was headed by the vizier (Egyptian t3ty), who sometimes shared power with the overseer of works (construction projects) and the treasurer. Key departments included the royal estates, the treasury, the granary, and the archives. In the New Kingdom the office of vizier was divided, and two viziers were appointed, one for Upper Egypt and one for Lower Egypt. The next level of governance was the forty-two provinces or nomes. The nomarchs were responsible for the collection of taxes and the recruitment of corvée (forced) labor for state construction projects. Individual cities and towns had their own mayors and headmen. Justice was primarily administered at the local level by councils of local leaders. Cases could be appealed to the vizier. Accusations of official malfeasance and crimes against the state were heard by a council of prominent state officials under the oversight of the vizier.

The description in Genesis of Joseph's role in the Egyptian administration does not correspond precisely with any one office. The closest parallels are the overseer of the granary and the vizier, although there are problems with each. Joseph's primary responsibilities, the collection and distribution of grain, are those of the overseer of the granary. Furthermore, Joseph's authority extends over both halves of the country; in the New Kingdom there was a single overseer of the granary. However, the pronouncement that Joseph is to be second in command to the king with authority over the king's house (Gen 41:40) suggests that he be understood as vizier. Certainly it was possible for a foreigner to rise to high office in New Kingdom Egypt. Prime examples of Semites in high office are the vizier Aper-El in the Eighteenth Dynasty and the chancellor Bay in the Nineteenth.

Temple administration involved both the ritual functions of the temples and the management of temple estates. The temples were supported by a system of endowments, gifts of land, serfs, and raw materials. Kings frequently donated a portion of the tribute and booty acquired in foreign expeditions to one or more prominent temples. Because temple estates were often exempted from taxation by royal decree, the temples developed into powerful economic institutions. In the New Kingdom, the highest priestly title was overseer of the priests of Upper and Lower Egypt. Next in rank were the high priests of the individual cults. Beneath them were the god's servants (often misleadingly translated "prophets" in English), god's fathers, lector priests, and "pure ones." The "pure ones" served in rotation, usually one month on and three months off.

The ancient Egyptian military was not exclusively a fighting force. Rather it was an expeditionary force. The military was dispatched on trading missions and on expeditions to quarries and mines. The primary military corps was the infantry, supplemented by a small naval force and later the chariotry. The military developed its own complex of ranks and titles, ranging from generals to ordinary foot soldiers. In the New Kingdom, the crown prince was placed at the head of the army. His brothers often held ranks in the chariotry.

The New Kingdom Empire required the development of an imperial bureaucracy. Separate but parallel systems were created for Nubia and Syria-Palestine, each headed by an overseer of foreign lands. In Nubia the highest Egyptian official bore two titles: overseer of southern lands and king's son of Cush, frequently translated "viceroy" in English. He was assisted by two deputies, one for Wawat (Lower Nubia, between the first and second cataracts) and one for Cush (Upper Nubia, south of the second cataract). Syria-Palestine was somewhat more loosely administered, with much of the day-to-day responsibilities remaining in the hands of local vassal princes. Their sons were raised in the Egyptian court where they learned Egyptian culture and served as hostages for their fathers' loyalty. Upon their return they continued to emulate Egyptian ways, introducing an Egyptianizing material culture in the Canaanite city-states. The overseer of northern lands, visiting envoys, and the commanders of a small number

of garrisons oversaw the region on behalf of the crown and ensured that Egyptian sovereignty was respected.

E. Religion

Ancient Egyptian religion was polytheistic. Every aspect of life, and death, was associated with one or more deities. There were gods and goddesses for natural phenomena, including the sun, the moon, the earth, and the sky. Another set of deities was associated with life experiences, such as childbirth, illnesses, and the inundation. Abstract concepts such as order and chaos were also personified as deities. Professions had their patron gods as well.

1. Egyptian gods and goddesses

Each Egyptian god or goddess had a distinctive iconography. Most manifested themselves in animal form and/or in the form of an animal-headed human being. Thus Horus could appear either as a falcon or as a falcon-headed man, and Hathor either as a cow or as a woman with cow's ears. A few gods, such as Amun, were represented only in human form. The most restricted iconography belonged to Aten, the sun disk, which never took human or animal form. Nonetheless, the rays of the sun disk typically terminated in human hands. *See* AKHENATEN §B3.

Erich Lessing /Art Resource, NY

Figure 5: Head of the goddess Hathor with cows' ears, from the small Hathor Temple at Kalabsha (13th cent. BCE) above Lake Nasser. Location: Temples, Kalabsha, Egypt.

Gods could be worshiped in various combinations as triads or syncretistic deities. Triads were family groups consisting of a god, a goddess, and their child, such as Osiris, Isis, and Horus; Amun, Mut, and Khonsu; and Ptah, Sekhmet, and Nefertem. Syncretistic deities fused two or more deities into one composite, such as Amun-Re and Ptah-Sokar. Conversely, gods could be worshipped in particular aspects, such as Harpokrates (Horus the Child) or Horakhty (Horus of the Two Horizons).

The gods of Egypt were at once national and local. Each was associated with particular cult centers in particular cities or towns. At the same time many were known and worshiped throughout the Nile Valley. National prominence derived from both function, representing universal concerns, and politics. Gods rose to prominence along with the localities where they were revered. As political dominance passed from one region to another, the fortunes of deities waxed and waned. For example, the Upper Egyptian sun god, Montu, gained national stature when his patron Montuhotep I reunified Egypt at the beginning of the Twelfth Dynasty, only to be eclipsed later by the Theban god Amun. Similarly, the transfer of the capital to the eastern delta in the Nineteenth Dynasty raised the stature of the god Seth, who as a storm god was identified with the Semitic god Baal.

Solar deities were always important in ancient Egypt, most often a form of RE. Re tended to attract to himself other gods who could be absorbed as syncretistic deities or understood as an aspect of Re. Khepri, the scarab beetle rolling a dung ball before him, was the sun reborn at dawn. (**Kheper** means "to become," and baby scarab beetles emerged from the dung balls apparently by spontaneous generation.) The falcon, Horus, rode the distant sky like the sun and could be the sun on the horizon or the syncretistic Re-Horakhty. As Thebes rose in power during the First Intermediate Period, Re was joined with Amun ("hiddenness"), the patron of Thebes, to form Amun-Re, the hidden one made visible. By the New Kingdom Amun-Re had become the preeminent god of Egypt.

The Egyptians made no attempt to systematize or harmonize their religious traditions. Multiple traditions continued to exist and to develop despite apparent contradictions. Creation traditions arose around many of the gods and were preserved in the deities' primary cult places, particularly HELIOPOLIS, Hermopolis, and MEMPHIS. The Heliopolitan cosmogony features the self-creative sun god Re (or Atum-Re). He stands on a hill in the midst of Nun, the primeval sea, and creates the world from his own bodily fluid, either by masturbating or by spitting. First to be created are Shu (dry air) and Tefnut (moist air). Shu and Tefnut give birth to Geb (earth) and Nut (sky). The children of Geb and Nut are Osiris (god of the afterlife), Seth (god of disorder), and their wives, Isis and Nephthys, respectively. These

nine gods formed the Heliopolitan Ennead. The Hermopolitan tradition also features a primeval mound in the midst of the primeval waters. In one version the ibis-headed god Thoth lays the egg from which the world was born. Instead of nine gods, the Hermopolitan tradition has the Ogdoad, four pairs of primordial deities representing hiddenness, formlessness, darkness, and the waters. The Memphite Theology, preserved on the twenty-fifth dynasty Shabaka Stone, attributes the act of creation to Ptah who thinks and speaks the world into existence. In yet another version, the ram-headed god Khnum creates human beings on his potter's wheel.

Parallels are often drawn between the Egyptian cosmogonies and the creation stories of Genesis. In Gen 1, as in the Memphite Theology, God speaks and it is so. Also in Gen 1, God creates by separating opposites—day from night, dry land from water—much as Atum-Re creates the opposites Shu/Tefnut and Geb/Nut. In the Gen 2 account, God forms Adam from the earth, much as Khnum forms human beings on his wheel.

2. Life after death

An elaborate mythology arose around the solar cycle, describing the daily passage of Re through the sky and the underworld. Special emphasis was given to the perilous night journey through the underworld. In the New Kingdom text *Amduat*, Re's principal attacker is the serpent Apophis, and his principal defender Seth. Although Re is killed, so is Apophis and Re is reborn at dawn. The text was placed in tombs in the hope that the tomb owner might join Re in his journey and be reborn each day.

The deceased also desired to become Osiris, the god of the underworld. Osiris was slain and hacked to pieces by his brother Seth. His wife Isis collected and reunited the pieces. Osiris was restored to life, but in the underworld, not on earth. Nonetheless, Isis was impregnated by the deceased Osiris. Their son Horus inherited his father's authority over earth and became the patron god of kingship.

The emphasis given to the reassembling of Osiris' body dramatizes the importance of the preservation of the body for life after death. The afterlife was essentially a continuation of earthly existence for which one needed a body. Without a body, there was no house for the element of a person's soul or spirit known as the *ba* (associated with mobility and power). The *ba* could travel freely but should return each night to the mummy. Nourishment was provided for the deceased in the form of offerings to the *ka*, another element of the soul or spirit, associated with vitality and fertility.

Mummification developed to ensure the permanent preservation of the body. The process lasted seventy days and required the removal of all internal organs, except the heart. The four most important organs, the liver, lungs, stomach, and intestines, were preserved and placed in four canopic jars, each identified with one of the sons of Horus. The other organs were discarded, and the body was packed inside and out with natron (sodium carbonate) for up to forty days. Once the body was thoroughly dehydrated, it was prepared for burial, which included elaborate linen wrappings and the placement of protective amulets.

At first only the king could afford the elaborate funerary rituals and ongoing daily offerings that made life after death possible. Favored servants might receive the right to a proper burial as "a boon which the king gives." Later provincial and even local officials were able to aspire to become an Osiris after death in their own right.

However, physical preservation was not sufficient to guarantee access to the afterlife. New Kingdom funerary literature details the hurdles that still had to be overcome. Chapter 125 of the BOOK OF THE DEAD describes a "last judgment" in which the heart is weighed against ma'at (truth/order), shown iconographically as a feather. The chaos monster Ammamet waits to devour the unworthy. A key element is the "negative confession" in which the deceased recites a list of misdeeds not committed. The declaration includes crimes against the gods, such as blasphemy, neglect, or interference with rituals, and crimes against humanity, including robbing the poor, killing, maligning a servant to his master, and using false measures.

3. Tombs

Four primary types of burials are known from ancient Egypt: simple pit graves, bench-shaped mastabas, pyramids, and rock-cut tombs. The first three types developed progressively from one to the next through a series of stages.

The simple oval pit grave became increasingly complex both in its substructure and its superstructure. The pit itself could be lined with reed matting. The shape of the substructure changed from oval to rectangular, and the pit was enlarged to incorporate multiple chambers. Eventually a gravel or sand mound, perhaps symbolizing the primeval mound of creation, was erected over the burial.

During the Early Dynastic period the mound developed into a bench-shaped superstructure, known by the Arabic term *mastaba*. These tombs were supplied with all the goods necessary for a pleasant afterlife (food, clothing, cosmetics, etc.) either as actual funerary offerings or as images painted on the tomb walls. A statue of the deceased rested behind a "false door" through which the deceased could receive offerings. Even after the development of the pyramid for royal burials, the nobility of Egypt continued to be interred in mastaba tombs.

The pyramid developed from a series of mastabas stacked one on top of the other. The architect Imhotep designed the Step Pyramid for the third dynasty king Djoser. Built of limestone blocks, the six-level structure rose 190 ft. above the ground. The burial chamber was accessed by a shaft descending 90 ft. below ground. The first true pyramid was constructed for the fourth dynasty king Sneferu, although the best known are those of his successors, Khufu, Khafre, and Menkaure, located at Giza, on the outskirts of modern Cairo. Each pyramid was surrounded by an elaborate funerary complex comprising a mortuary temple, a valley temple, queen's pyramids, mastaba tombs for officials, and facilities for priests and servants attached to the funerary cult. Pyramids were also built by the twelfth dynasty kings.

Rock-cut tombs first appeared in the Old Kingdom. By the Middle Kingdom this style of burial had become popular for the nobility of Upper Egypt. The New Kingdom kings selected the Valley of the Kings at Thebes for their necropolis. Some of these tombs extend deep into the mountainside with many chambers and elaborately painted walls. The mortuary temples of these kings were located at some distance from their tombs, on the western bank of the Nile at the edge of the cultivated land.

4. Temples

Most Egyptian temples were enclosed structures designed to house and protect the divine image(s). The most interior space, and the most sacred, was the sanctuary (or naos) housing the image and its shrine. Most of the well-preserved temples date from the New Kingdom or later and share a similar design. They consist of three primary parts: pylon, courtyard, and sanctuary. The ground sloped upward so that the sanctuary, located in the back of the temple, was built on a high point representing the primeval mound of creation. A pylon is a monumental gateway with two large towers on either side of the doorway. The narrow gap between the towers gives the pylon a resemblance to the hieroglyph for horizon. A large temple might feature several pylons separating sections of the temple. Behind the pylon were one or more unroofed courtyards. The temple became increasingly low, narrow, and dark as one moved toward the sanctuary housing the divine image. A common feature of large temples was the hypostyle hall, so named because the roof rested on rows of colossal pillars. The pillars represented the reed marsh surrounding the mound of creation. The sanctuary itself was quite small and dark and could only be entered by the attending priest.

The Egyptian sun temple represents an entirely different type. Rather than closed and dark, it was open to the rays of the sun. A prime example is the temple of Re built by the fifth dynasty king Niuserre at Abu Ghurab southwest of modern Cairo. The temple was approached from below via a valley temple and causeway. It consisted of a large open courtyard with an obelisk at the back. In front of the obelisk was an alabaster offering table. There were two slaughterhouses with basins to catch the blood of the sacrifices.

5. Temple ritual and popular piety

The king was the primary intermediary between the realm of the gods and earthly existence. He was responsible for maintaining order (ma ͨat) in the universe through just administration, military prowess, and the performance of ritual. The rituals pacified the gods and enlisted their assistance in keeping chaos at bay. Because the king could not be everywhere at once, most religious rites were performed not by the king, but by priests acting on his behalf.

The focus of ritual was the divine image. The image was not the god, but the place where the god resided. The last step in the creation of a divine statue was the opening of the mouth ritual, which activated the statue so that the god could see, hear, and speak through it. Divine presence could not be coerced, but the consecration of the statue made it available as a vessel for the god's spirit (*ba*).

Most rituals were performed inside temple complexes to which the public did not have access. Each day the priests awoke the gods, fed and clothed them, and worshipped them. In the evening they put them to bed. The public had access to the divine images only during major festivals when they were brought out on parade. The great processional temples of the New Kingdom were designed with these parades in mind. On these occasions a person could approach the image with a question and receive a negative or affirmative response. Such oracles could be used to resolve disputes over ownership or accusations of theft.

Popular piety focused especially on the concerns of everyday living. Ordinary Egyptians called upon the gods to protect them from snakes, crocodiles, and other dangers. Pregnancy represented a particularly hazardous time and was attended by a pantheon of deities to protect mother and child. Illness and injury were treated by offering a model of the afflicted body part at the temple or by consulting a physician whose prescription included an incantation to be spoken while the appropriate medicine was administered.

F. Language

Egyptian is a branch of the Afro-Asiatic, or Hamito-Semitic, family of languages. It is distantly related to Hebrew, Aramaic, Arabic, Ethiopic, and the other Semitic languages, as well as to other African languages such as Berber and Hausa. Although Egyptian shares some grammatical features and cognate vocabulary with Hebrew and Aramaic, the languages were not mutually intelligible.

Scholars distinguish five stages in the historical development of the Egyptian language: Old Egyptian, Middle (or Classical) Egyptian, Late Egyptian, Demotic, and Coptic. The first three correspond roughly to the Old, Middle, and New Kingdoms. Middle Egyptian is sometimes termed classical because it was emulated in later periods. Demotic developed in the Late Period and overlaps historically with Coptic, the language of Christian Egypt. The latter survives as the liturgical language of the Coptic Church.

Writing developed in Egypt beginning around 3500 BCE as pictorial symbols for accounting purposes. These symbols evolved into a complex system of hieroglyphs denoting both pronunciation and meaning. One or more signs indicating the consonantal sounds were followed by a determinative specifying the classification of the word, such as animal, vegetable, or mineral. Thus the words for speaking and eating both concluded with the determinative of a man with his hand to his mouth. Hieroglyphs continued in use, especially for monumental inscriptions, through the 4th cent. CE.

Alongside the hieroglyphic script there developed a cursive script that the Greeks called Hieratic. Hieratic was widely used for texts written with brush and ink rather than inscribed in stone, although its use was restricted to religious texts in Greco-Roman times. In the Late Period a second form of cursive was developed that the Greeks called Demotic because it was used for secular texts.

Coptic is written using a thirty-one-character alphabet, the twenty-four letters of the Greek alphabet plus seven Demotic signs for sounds not represented in Greek. Coptic represents a sharp break with previous Egyptian scripts, abandoning completely the hieroglyphic principles for an alphabetic system and indicating vowels as well as consonants.

Although Coptic continued to be read and studied, the other Egyptian scripts fell into disuse and were forgotten for one and a half millennia. The key to deciphering the Egyptian scripts was bilingual (and trilingual) inscriptions that recorded the same text in Greek and either Demotic or hieroglyphs. The most famous of these is the Rosetta Stone, a trilingual inscription in hieroglyphs, Demotic, and Greek, discovered by Napoleon's expedition to Egypt at the end of the 18th cent. CE. The first breakthrough came from study of the Demotic section in which scholars were able to identify names appearing in both Demotic and Greek. The Englishman Thomas Young used cryptographic principles to identify other Demotic words based on the frequency of their occurrence in a Greek-Demotic bilingual text. He also made the first advances in deciphering hieroglyphs by proving that royal names were written phonetically and enclosed in ovals called "cartouches." History has, nonetheless, credited the Frenchman Jean-François Champollion with establishing the principles for decipherment, using both royal names and Coptic vocabulary to assign phonetic values to the hieroglyphs.

G. Literature

The surviving corpus of ancient Egyptian literature represents only a fraction of the literary output of three millennia of civilization. It includes a wide variety of religious and secular texts including funerary texts, hymns and prayers, myths, tales, love poems, and instructional literature. Many texts survive only as school exercises and are replete with student mistakes. Others have been damaged over the centuries, leaving large lacunae, especially at the end.

The definition of genres for this corpus is problematic. Differences in context, function, and literary conventions preclude the imposition of modern categories on these texts. Because questions remain about context (royal court, scribal school, cult, etc.) and function (entertainment, propaganda, education, etc.), scholarly debate over systems of categorization continues.

The best known funerary texts are the PYRAMID TEXTS, the COFFIN TEXTS, and the Book of the Dead. The names themselves indicate the developing tradition that first inscribed funerary rituals and spells on the walls of tombs, then on the coffins, and then as "books" on papyrus.

Hymns are known for virtually every deity in the Egyptian pantheon, although the most common are Osirian and solar hymns. The purpose of the hymns is praise rather than constructive theology. Nonetheless they allude to the characteristic features of the deity in question: epithets, cultic centers, associated animal forms, mythic events. Hymns were also addressed to the king.

Similarities between the solar hymns and the biblical Psalms have long been recognized, especially between Ps 104 and the great hymn to the Aten. Behind the psalmist's reference to the hiding of God's face lies the solar metaphor of the daily setting and rising of the sun that causes first distress and then rejoicing for the created world. Although there is no indication of direct borrowing, the hymns speak of divine provision for animals and humans in similar terms.

Four collections of love poems or love songs are known from New Kingdom Egypt. In these poems the lovers speak of their desire for each other and address each other as brother and sister, terms of endearment not to be taken literally. The poems are full of pastoral imagery and range in tone from tender to bawdy. Comparisons are often made to the biblical Song of Songs.

Most ancient Egyptian tales feature elements that are mythological, magical, or fantastic. Some, like the tale of Horus and Seth and the so-called Destruction of Mankind, are set entirely in the world of the gods. Others revolve around human actors whose experiences include the extraordinary. The Shipwrecked Sailor encounters a huge speaking serpent who predicts his rescue. The Doomed Prince seeks to evade the fate set for him by the Hathors.

The opening section of the Tale of Two Brothers is closely paralleled in Gen 39, the story of Joseph and Potiphar's wife. Both narratives feature handsome single men working in the household of a married man. In each case the wife of the householder seeks to seduce the youth. When he rebuffs her, she accuses

him of assault, leading to his abrupt departure from the household (to exile or prison).

The stories of Sinuhe and Wenamun, which lack the fantastic elements found in other tales, are either autobiographies or tales modeled after autobiographies. Both involve Egyptian officials who travel to Syria-Palestine. Although they cannot be taken as factual, objective descriptions of the geography and people, they do reveal Egyptian perceptions of the region in the second millennium. Sinuhe's story incorporates descriptions of Canaan and the lives of its ruling class. Wenamun recounts the perils of a trade mission by sea to Byblos, including a brief encounter with a prophet. The prophet, overcome by his god, falls into an apparent trance and pronounces an oracle. *See* WENAMON, JOURNEY OF.

The instruction was a well-developed genre in ancient Egypt. The earliest surviving instructions were probably composed in the late Old Kingdom. These texts present moral and practical instruction in the format of a father's advice to his son. The values espoused resemble those of the biblical wisdom tradition: a cool temper, silence, restraint, humility, and honesty. Sections of the book of Proverbs belong to an Israelite tradition of instructions. Proverbs 22:17–24:22 draws directly on the New Kingdom Instructions of Amenemope, albeit reworking the material to fit the Israelite context.

H. Art

The conventions or "canons" governing Egyptian art differ significantly from those that developed later in the Western world. Objects were never created for purely aesthetic reasons. Yet their functionality often included religious interests accomplished through symbolic representation.

1. Painting and relief

Two-dimensional representations were created in paint and in low relief. Raised relief was typically used outdoors and on the outsides of buildings where the sun would accentuate the effect. Sunk relief is most commonly found on interior walls. Of the three, raised relief was the most time consuming and hence most costly to produce as it required the cutting away of the entire background to a depth of about 5 mm. Sunk relief was significantly less expensive as it required only the cutting away of the edges of each figure. Painting was the cheapest of all.

Both painting and relief employed the same general principles of representation. There was no attempt at modern perspectival representation. Relative distance was indicated by overlapping objects; more distant objects were not depicted as smaller than nearer ones. Size was used instead to indicate relative importance. Thus the king and the gods were always much larger than other figures in any scene. Multiple perspectives were used simultaneously with each element portrayed from its most characteristic viewpoint.

The standardized representation of the human figure combined frontal and profile views. The head, torso (from armpit to waist, including nipple or breast), legs, and feet were shown in profile, whereas the eye, eyebrow, and shoulders were depicted in frontal perspective. In a tomb painting, it was important for objects to be visible and recognizable so that they would be magically available to the tomb owner in the afterlife. Therefore a table with objects on it was represented from the side with its legs visible. The objects on the table were depicted from whichever perspective would render them most recognizable, some in profile, others from a bird's-eye view. In a boating scene the fish were shown in profile beneath the boat.

When more than one scene was portrayed on a wall, the scenes were organized into "registers" or rows. A borderline delimited each scene with the bottom border serving as a ground line. Paintings and reliefs were accompanied by hieroglyphic captions that were integral to the depiction.

Production involved multiple phases, each employing a different specialist. Once the surface had been pre-pared, guidelines were applied in red ink. Originally six horizontal lines were used at key points of the human figure. Later a grid system was developed to control both horizontal and vertical dimensions. The guidelines were usually applied by dipping a string in red pigment and snapping it against the wall. The next step was to sketch the figures and hieroglyphs. If the wall was to be worked in relief, the carving of the background (raised relief) or figures (sunk relief) followed. The final stage was the application of paint, which was done one color at a time.

2. Sculpture

Formal sculpture, whether in stone, wood, or metal, was also subject to precise conventions. A grid system was used to control the proportions. Figures could be depicted standing, sitting, or kneeling, but the number of poses attested is quite limited. Formal sculpture always faced forward with no twisting of the body. Because statues served to house the spirit of a god or deceased human being, they were designed to be easily accessible to a living worshiper. Frontal poses facilitated the ritual functions of sculpture.

Erich Lessing/Art Resource, NY

Figure 6: Ushebtis, tomb-servants, from various periods. From left to right: painted limestone, faience, alabaster, basalt, painted wood. Front row figures: faience. New Kingdom to Greco-Roman, 14th–1st cent. BCE. Location: Aegyptisches Museum, Staatliche Museen zu Berlin, Berlin, Germany.

Stone statues bespoke stability and permanence. Limbs were kept close to the body and the stone between the legs or between the arms and the body was not carved out. The backs of standing and seated figures were often supported by a pillar or chair back. Large statues were rough cut at the quarry and finished at the site where they were to be displayed. Although figures were idealized, the artisans of each reign developed a standardized image of that king, which had distinctive features. If a king usurped a predecessor's statue, his artisans usually recarved it to reflect his image.

Statues were also made of wood, metal, ivory, and faience. Wooden statues, particularly large ones, were carved in pieces and pegged together. Metal statues could be made by covering a wood core with foil or by casting using the lost wax method. Faience objects, including statues, were made by molding and firing a silica paste.

I. Egypt and the Bible

1. Biblical perspectives on Egypt

Egypt was always in the background, and often in the foreground, of the biblical world. For millennia Egypt figured prominently in the political, economic, and cultural life of western Asia. Such dominance produced a mixture of admiration and fear. The biblical texts reflect ambivalence toward Egypt as both house of bondage and place of refuge, powerful ally and dangerous foe.

Most references to Egypt in the Bible occur in the context of the exodus. This constant refrain reinforces negative associations with Egypt as a place of slavery and oppression. The exodus motif contributes to the characterization of Egypt as at least potentially hostile.

The relationship between Israel and Egypt in the exodus narrative itself is oppositional. In the thought-world of the Pentateuch, Egypt is the primary figure over against which Israel is defined. Israelite identity is established only insofar as the people become fully differentiated from their Egyptian origins. To that end they must resist the temptation to return to the Nile Valley, and the generation that knew Egypt, including even Moses, the hero of the exodus, is barred from entering the promised land.

Relations with Egypt often dominated the foreign policy of Judah, Israel, and their neighbors. Survival required the foresight to predict the fortunes of Egypt and its rivals. Alliances had to be made and broken as an empire's power waxed and waned. Such decisions were a concern of the biblical prophets who warned of the risk of foreign entanglements.

> Oh, rebellious children, says the LORD, who carry out a plan, but not mine; who make an alliance, but against my will, adding sin to sin; who set out to go down to Egypt without asking for my counsel, to take refuge in the protection of Pharaoh, and to seek

shelter in the shadow of Egypt; Therefore the protection of Pharaoh shall become your shame, and the shelter in the shadow of Egypt your humiliation (Isa 30:1-3).

But he rebelled against him by sending ambassadors to Egypt, in order that they might give him horses and a large army. Will he succeed? Can one escape who does such things? Can he break the covenant and yet escape? As I live, says the Lord GOD, surely in the place where the king resides who made him king, whose oath he despised, and whose covenant with him he broke—in Babylon he shall die. Pharaoh with his mighty army and great company will not help him in war, when ramps are cast up and siege walls built to cut off many lives (Ezek 17:15-17).

Hosea even threatened Judah with a return to Egyptian bondage: "They shall return to the land of Egypt, and Assyria shall be their king, because they have refused to return to me" (Hos 11:5).

Yet despite the risks, relations with Egypt could be beneficial, and in the biblical texts Egypt also represents refuge and protection. The paradigmatic examples are Joseph and his family (Gen 37–50) and Jesus and his family (Matt 2), but the motif occurs repeatedly. Like Joseph's family, Abram and Sarai took shelter in Egypt during a famine (Gen 12). The OT narratives recount several instances of political refugees who sought asylum in Egypt: Hadad the Edomite (1 Kgs 11:17-22), Jeroboam (1 Kgs 11:40), the prophet Uriah (Jer 26:21-23), and the Judahites after the assassination of Gedaliah (2 Kgs 25:26; Jer 41:16-18). Of these, only Uriah did not find a safe haven.

The biblical texts associate Egypt with two other primary characteristics: wealth and wisdom. Several passages make direct references to the riches of Egypt (Isa 45:14; Dan 11:43; Heb 11:26), and in the exodus narrative the departing Hebrews despoil their former masters of enough gold to make a calf idol (Exod 12:35-36; 32:2-4). The measure of Solomon's wisdom is that it "surpassed the wisdom of all the people of the east, and all the wisdom of Egypt" (1 Kgs 4:30). The rhetoric of some texts presupposes Egypt's reputation for wisdom in order to be effective. In both the Joseph and exodus narratives, the wise men and magicians of Egypt are unable to match the discernment and skill of the representatives of God (Gen 41; Exod 7–12). In Isa 19, the prophet mocks Egypt for its lack of wisdom: "The princes of Zoan are utterly foolish; the wise counselors of Pharaoh give stupid counsel" (Isa 19:11 a).

2. Egyptian influence on the Bible

It is impossible to specify precisely the nature and extent of Egyptian influence on the Bible. Egypt and Israel were part of the same broad cultural context. They interacted almost continually for millennia, exchanging not only commodities, but people and ideas. Naturally they became aware of each other's traditions, practices, and worldviews. Some degree of borrowing and assimilation was inevitable.

The exchange was complex and had multiple dimensions. Cultural exchange occurred across the Near East and the western Mediterranean. An Egyptian concept could come to Judah by way of Cyprus or Phoenicia, in which case it would have already been modified to fit its secondary context. As a result, a biblical text may have an Egyptian air about it even when the exact link cannot be defined, or a text may bear the imprint of multiple cultural traditions simultaneously.

In Late Bronze Age Canaan, to be cultured meant to adopt certain features of an Egyptian lifestyle. The Canaanite rulers did not attempt to replicate life in the Nile Valley. Rather they adapted a select set of elements to their own cultural context. Although Egyptian military might was on the decline in the first millennium BCE, as a civilization it still offered a compelling cultural model for the rulers of Israel and Judah.

The rich iconography of ancient Egypt was mined first by the Canaanites and later by the Phoenicians, the Israelites and, to a lesser extent, the Judahites, for symbols of royalty and power. In the 8th cent. BCE, the Phoenicians and Israelites made extensive use of Egyptian solar images associated with kingship, including the winged solar disk, the winged cobra, the eye of Horus, and the falcon.

Scholars have detected reflexes of Egyptian royal practice in several biblical passages. The throne names of Isa 9:6—Wonderful Counselor, Mighty God, Everlasting Father, Prince of Peace—seem to correspond to the five-fold titulary adopted by an Egyptian king at the time of his accession to the throne that signaled the agenda for his reign. The adoption language of Ps 2:7—You are my son; today I have begotten you—has parallels in Egyptian texts from Abydos and more generally in the concept of the king as son of Re.

The full catalog of proposed influences is too great to expound in detail, but includes loan-words, idioms and metaphors, literary genres, administrative structures and practices, and religious concepts. Some of the clearest and deepest interconnections are in the wisdom tradition. The most obvious similarities are in terminology and literary genre, but the resemblance extends also to values and worldview. Yet biblical wisdom is more than a Hebrew translation of the Egyptian tradition. There are significant differences between biblical and Egyptian wisdom because in the biblical literature the values and perspectives of wisdom are fully integrated into the Israelite/Judahite context. The authors have not simply replaced references to Egyptian maʿat (order, justice) with the Israelite God. The particular mode of reflection on lived experience that constitutes "wisdom" has taken root in biblical soil and yielded a thoroughly Yahwistic vision of the good life.

3. Egyptology and biblical studies

Egyptology was born in the shadow of biblical studies. Many of the early students of Egyptian language were trained Semitists. As they formulated the grammar of Egyptian, they recognized morphological features characteristic of Semitic languages. They interpreted Egyptian in light of their understanding of those languages, importing grammatical concepts and categories developed for the study of Akkadian and other ancient Semitic languages. For example, the verbal system was divided into geminating and nongeminating forms analogous to the Semitic perfect and imperfect.

The developing body of knowledge about ancient Egypt was often interpreted with respect to the Bible—to illuminate the biblical world or to substantiate or challenge the biblical accounts. The newly accessible Egyptian texts were scoured for evidence of Joseph, Moses, and the exodus, even as the antiquity of Egyptian civilization raised questions about the age of the earth. Even scholars who were themselves interested in the study of Egypt for its own sake often found their work seized upon by biblical scholars and religious leaders.

In the early years of Egyptology it was not uncommon for scholars to work simultaneously in multiple cultural and linguistic traditions. This fostered a healthy exchange of concepts and methods, but also reinforced the link to biblical studies. The British archaeologist Flinders Petrie excavated sites in both Egypt and Palestine in the late 19th and early 20th cent. CE. He introduced his stratagraphic and sequence-dating techniques to biblical archaeology even as he investigated the cultural links between the two regions in the Second Intermediate Period/Middle Bronze Age. Similarly, William Foxwell Albright, though primarily a biblical scholar and Semitist, made significant contributions to the study of Egyptian philology and history.

Egyptology quickly emerged as a discipline in its own right. Although the fruits of Egyptological research might be of interest to scholars working in other areas, those concerns did not define the research question. The primary task was to develop as full an understanding of Egypt as possible. Egyptology and biblical studies are now pursued as quite distinct and separate disciplines.

The second half of the 20th cent. CE brought increasing specialization to Egyptology and other disciplines related to the study of the ancient world. The close association between text and image in ancient Egypt requires a certain level of integration among the subdisciplines; however, the explosion of information and developments in theory and method have rendered it impossible for any one individual to command the whole of the field.

Bibliography: James P. Allen. *Middle Egyptian: An Introduction to the Language and Culture of the Hieroglyphs* (2000); Paul S. Ash. *David, Solomon and Egypt: A Reassessment* (1999); Jan Assmann. *The Search for God in Ancient Egypt* (2005); John Baines and Jaromir Malek. *Cultural Atlas of Ancient Egypt* (2000); John D. Currid. *Ancient Egypt and the Old Testament* (1997); F. V. Greifenhagen. *Egypt on the Pentateuch's Ideological Map: Constructing Biblical Israel's Identity* (2002); Zahi Hawass, ed. *Egyptology at the Dawn of the Twenty-first Century: Proceedings of the Eighth International Congress of Egyptologists, Cairo, 2000* (2003); Miriam Lichtheim. *Ancient Egyptian Literature: A Book of Readings.* 3 vols. (1973–80); Antonio Loprieno. *Ancient Egyptian: A Linguistic Introduction* (1995); Antonio Loprieno, ed. *Ancient Egyptian Literature: History and Forms* (1996); Stephen Quirke. *Ancient Egyptian Religion* (1992); Donald B. Redford. *Pharaonic King-lists, Annals and Day-books: A Contribution to the Study of the Egyptian Sense of History* (1986); Donald B. Redford. *Egypt, Canaan and Israel in Ancient Times* (1992); Donald B. Redford, ed. *The Oxford Encyclopedia of Ancient Egypt* (2001); Gay Robins. *The Art of Ancient Egypt* (1997); Ian Shaw, ed. *The Oxford History of Ancient Egypt* (2000); Edward Wente. *Letters from Ancient Egypt* (1990).

CAROLYN HIGGINBOTHAM

EGYPT, PLAGUES IN. *See* PLAGUES IN EGYPT.

EGYPT, RIVER OF נְהַר מִצְרַיִם nahar mitsrayim]. The geographical term makes only a single appearance in the OT. The term occurs in Gen 15:18 and marks the western boundary of the land promised to Abram and his descendants. The exact geographical referent is uncertain—the Nile River being one possibility.

EGYPT, WADI OF נַחַל מִצְרַיִם nakhal mitsrayim]. The expression occurs as a geographical term for the southern boundary of the Canaanite territory (Num 34:5) and, later, of the tribe of Judah (Josh 15:4, 47; 1 Kgs 8:65; 2 Chr 7:8). It is often associated with the Wadi el-ʿArish, which abuts the wilderness of SHUR. Neo-Assyrian royal inscriptions mention the Wadi of Egypt, but how these references contribute to the identification of the brook has been disputed. Naʾaman argues that point to an identification with Wadi Bezor, while Rainey maintains that an inscription of ESAR-HADDON reinforces identification with Wadi el-ʿArish. The Wadi el-ʿArish serves as a drain for the seasonal surplus water from the wilderness of PARAN into the Mediterranean and forms a natural barrier between the NEGEB and the Sinai peninsula.

"From the Wadi of Egypt to the River Euphrates" (2 Kgs 24:7) is a synecdoche for the entire area of Syro-Palestine between its northeastern and southern borders, land included in the idyllic map of the promised land (Gen 15:18; Exod 23:31; Deut 1:7; 11:24; Josh 1:4). The borders of the Davidic-Solomonic empire may have reached this extent. The prophets envisioned a time inaugurated by the "DAY OF THE LORD" when Israel's borders would finally extend from the GREAT SEA to the Wadi of Egypt (Ezek 47:13-23, esp. v. 19).

Bibliography: Nadav Naʾaman. *Borders and Districts in Biblical Historiography* (1986); A. F. Rainey and R. S. Notley. *The Sacred Bridge: Carta's Atlas of the Biblical World* (2005).

RALPH K. HAWKINS

EGYPTIAN, THE i-jip'shuhn [ὁ Αἰγύπτιος ho Aigyptios]. A man mentioned by the Roman tribune as having recently stirred up a revolt and led 4,000 assassins into the wilderness (Acts 21:37-38).

When Paul was seized by Roman soldiers in the Temple area, the soldiers carried him to the barracks (Acts 21:32-33). Paul asked to speak to the Roman tribune, who in turn asked if Paul knew Greek. The tribune believed that if Paul spoke Greek he could not be "the Egyptian." By asking if Paul could speak Greek, Claudius Lysias implied that he views the Egyptian as a barbarian who was, therefore, unable to speak Greek. The tribune's statement stressed the likely Roman perspective that the Eyptian was a revolutionary. Both Paul and the tribune appear to know who this Egyptian is but the NT says nothing more about him.

The Egyptian's name is unknown, and he may not have been from Egypt. He was almost certainly a Jew, as inhabitants of Judea would not have followed a non-Jew into the wilderness. Josephus mentions the Egyptian along with the Sicarii and false prophets (*J.W.* 2.254-63), although Josephus does not connect the Egyptian with the Sicarii. Josephus' description of the Egyptian, however, is fairly close to that of Acts. The number of followers in Acts—4,000—is far more plausible than the 30,000 that Josephus records. Josephus provides additional information, including an account that the Egyptian and his forces marched to the Mount of Olives in order to free Jerusalem from the Romans. When they were close to attacking, Felix sent troops who slaughtered the Egyptian's followers, but the Egyptian escaped. Some years later, Josephus wrote that the Egyptian's followers did not plan to attack Jerusalem but were to seize it after the Egyptian had commanded the walls to fall down (*Ant.* 20.168-72).

KENNETH D. LITWAK

EGYPTIAN VERSIONS. *See* VERSIONS, ANCIENT.

EGYPTIANS, GOSPEL OF THE. The *Gospel of the Egyptians*, sometimes referred to as the *Holy Book of the Great Invisible Spirit*, is the scholarly title given to two untitled tractates from the NAG HAMMADI Library (Codex III, 2:40,12-69, 20 and Codex IV, 2:50,1-81,2). The text comprises four sections: 1) the unfolding of the heavenly realm, culminating with the appearance of Seth and his angelic church; 2) the origin of the world, the origin of the Sethians, and Seth's role in the protection and eventual salvation of his race; 3) two hymns of praise dedicated to the heavenly powers; and 4) a discussion of Seth's authorship of the tractate and its subsequent transmission. Despite the fragmentary nature of both versions, the contents clearly outline a cosmic drama centering on the seed of Seth. As such, it represents a Sethian form of gnostic salvation history similar to the story found in the *Apocryphon of John*. In addition, the hymnic section, which describes a mystical experience with the divine aeons, has parallels in the Greek Magical Papyri and the Hermetic literature. The developed nature of its mythology, as well as its possible knowledge of Valentinian gnostic traditions, makes a compositional date sometime between the late 2nd and 3rd cent. likely. Clement of Alexandria (*Strom.* III) and the heresiologists Hippolytus (*Ref.* 5.7.8) and Epiphanius (*Pan.* 62.2) also refer to a gospel by the same name, but the fragments and references they provide indicate that it was unrelated to this gnostic gospel. *See* JOHN, APOCRYPHON OF.

DAVID M. REIS

EHI ee′hi [אֵחִי ʾekhi]. The sixth-listed son of Benjamin (Gen 46:21). Ehi and the three names that follow should perhaps be read Ahiram, Shupham, and Hupham with Num 26:38-39.

EHUD ee′huhd [אֵהוּד ʾehudh]. 1. A left-handed Benjaminite who frees Israel from oppression by Eglon, king of Moab, whom the story indicates is a very fat man (Judg 3:15-30). Ehud's left-handedness allows him to conceal a specially made sword and to bring it into the king's chamber to stab the king without being suspected by his servants. After paying Eglon tribute from Israel and leaving with the messengers, Ehud returns to the palace and asks to speak privately with the king, saying that he has a divine message for Eglon. Once they are alone, Ehud approaches the unwary king and stabs him with the sword, leaving it embedded in the king's body, and the fat of the king's body closes around the hilt of the sword. Ehud escapes while the royal servants are in a state of confusion because they find the king's private chamber locked and do not immediately seek entry. When the servants do open the king's private chamber, they discover he is dead and sound the alarm. By then Ehud has rejoined the Israelite army, which takes control of the Jordan River crossings, and slays thousands of Moabites as they try to cross back to Moab.

2. An individual listed in the genealogy of the tribe of BENJAMIN as the son of Bilhan and great-grandson of Benjamin (1 Chr 7:10).

C. MARK MCCORMICK

EIGHT. *See* NUMBERS, NUMBERING.

EIGHTEEN. *See* NUMBERS, NUMBERING.

EIGHTY. *See* NUMBERS, NUMBERING.

ʿEIN EL-JARBA. *See* JARBA, ʿEIN EL.

EKER ee′kuhr [עֵקֶר ʿeqer]. One of the children of Ram, the grandchildren of Jerahmeel (1 Chr 2:27). His name means "offspring," and appears in a genealogical list of Judah's descendants.

EKRON ek′ruhn [עֶקְרוֹן ʿeqron; Ἀκκάρων Akkarōn]. One of the cities of the Philistine pentapolis. According to Josh 19:43 it belonged to the tribal territory of Dan, while Josh 15:11 considers "the boundary [of Judah to go] out to the slope of the hill north of Ekron." Whereas Josh 13:3 reckons it among the parts of the land unconquered by Joshua, Judg 1:18 claims it was conquered by the tribe of Judah. The Ark of the Covenant, captured by the Philistines, was brought to Ekron where it caused great suffering (1 Sam 5:10-11). Afer David's defeat of Goliath, the Israelites "pursued the Philistines as far as Gath and the gates of Ekron" (1 Sam 17:52).

After King Ahaziah of Israel was severely injured in a fall, he attempted to send messengers to "Baal-zebub, the god of Ekron" (2 Kgs 1:2, 16) to find out what his chances of recovery were. For this lack of faith in God, the prophet Elijah condemns the king to death as a consequence of his injuries. Although Baal-zebub means "lord of the fly/flies," most scholars view the name as an intentional distortion of Baal-zebul, "Prince Baal," which is a well-known epithet of the Canaanite storm-god Baal (and indeed, this form is reflected in Matt 10:25; 12:24, 27; Mark 3:22; Luke 11:15, 18). The association of Ekron with Baal is confirmed in an inscription on an ostracon found during the excavation of the site (*see* BEELZEBUL).

Ekron is also mentioned as one of the four remaining Philistine cities (Ashkelon, Ashdod, Ekron, and Gaza) in a number of prophetic oracles against the nations dating from the late 8th cent. BCE (Amos 1:8; Zeph 2:4; Jer 25:20; Zech 9:5-7).

Outside the OT, Ekron (Amqarruna) is mentioned in various neo-Assyrian royal inscriptions from the 8th and 7th cent. BCE. After Philistia came under direct Assyrian control in 734 BCE, Ekron seems to have participated in the unsuccessful revolt against Sargon II in 720. After his death in 705, Hezekiah of Judah and others including Ekron revolted against the new Assyrian king Sennacherib, who crushed their revolt in 701 and reinstated Ekron's deposed king Padi. Later Padi's son, Ikausu (Achish or Akhayush), rendered tribute to Assyria and joined in Asshurbanipal's campaign against Egypt in 667 BCE.

An Aramaic letter found at Saqqarah in Egypt indicates that king Adon, presumably of Ekron, appealed in vain for help from the pharaoh in countering the threat posed by Nebuchadnezzar of Babylon at the end of the 6th cent. In the mid 2nd cent. BCE Ekron was granted to the Hasmonean ruler Jonathan (1 Macc 10:89). A village of Ekron is last mentioned by the church father Eusebius in the 4th cent. CE (*Onom.* 11:6-7, 9-10).

Extensive archaeological excavations were carried out at the site of Tel Miqne (Khirbet al-Muqanna) in the 1980s and 1990s. The identity of the site was confirmed when a dedicatory inscription to the goddess Ptgyh, the "mistress" of Ekron, was found there. The excavation revealed the history of the site, which was a major Philistine city as of their first settlement in Canaan in the early 12th cent. It declined in the 10th cent. owing to pressure from Israel and/or Egypt, only to revive under Assyrian domination and become the ANE's largest center of olive oil production and a major producer of textiles in the late 8th and 7th cent.

Bibliography: Seymour Gitin. "Tel Miqne-Ekron: A Type-Site for the Inner Coastal Plain in the Iron Age II Period." *Recent Excavations in Israel: Studies in Iron Age Archaeology.* Seymour Gitin and William G. Dever, eds. (1989) 23–58; Seymour Gitin and Trude Dothan. "The Rise and Fall of Ekron of the Philistines: Recent Excavations at an Urban Border Site." *BA* 50 (1987) 197–222; Seymour Gitin, Trude Dothan, and Joseph Naveh. "A Royal Dedicatory Inscription from Ekron." *IEJ* 47 (1997) 1–16; Nadav Naʾaman. "Ekron Under the Assyrian and Egyptian Empires." *BASOR* 332 (2003) 81–91; Christa Schäfer-Lichtenberger. "The Goddess of Ekron and the Religious-Cultural Background of the Philistines." *IEJ* 50 (2000) 82–91.

CARL S. EHRLICH

EL el [אֵל ʾel]. ʾEl may be a common noun, "god," or, in Ugaritic literature, the name, "El," of the high god in the pantheon. In the Bible, ʾel is usually a generic term for God, although the proper name must be meant in the expression, "El, the God of Israel" (Gen 33:20; see also the Hebrew of Gen 46:3; Num 16:22; Josh 22:22; Ps 50:1). *See* GOD, NAMES OF.

C. L. SEOW

EL BERITH elʹ biʹrithʹ [אֵל בְּרִית ʾel berith; Βαιθηλβεριθ baithēlberith]. A Shechemite temple of El Berith, "god of the covenant," appears once in Hebrew (Judg 9:46) but twice in the LXX (9:46, 50). *See* BAAL-BERITH; EL.

EL BETHEL el-bethʹuhl [אֵל בֵּית־אֵל ʾel beth-ʾel]. A place name in Gen 35:7, although the name is certainly related to a similar divine epithet. It is not clear, however, if the epithet should be interpreted as "the God of Bethel" or "the God, Bethel," as suggested by the Hebrew of Gen 31:13. *See* GOD, NAMES OF.

C. L. SEOW

EL ELOHE ISRAEL el-elʹoh-heh-isʹray-uhl [אֵל אֱלֹהֵי יִשְׂרָאֵל ʾel ʾelohe yisraʾel]. This divine epithet occurs only in Gen 33:20, and means "El, the God of Israel," which suggests that El, the supreme deity of the Canaanite pantheon was regarded as the God of Israel, the northern tribes. *See* GOD, NAMES OF.

EL ELYON elʹel-yohnʹ [אֵל עֶלְיוֹן ʾel ʿelyon]. Literally means "God, MOST HIGH" or "El, Most High." This divine epithet is associated with pre-Israelite Jerusalem (Gen 14:18-20; Ps 78:35). Originally an epithet of El, the highest deity in the Semitic pantheon, the designation ʿelyon came to be associated with Yahweh. *See* ELYON; GOD, NAMES OF.

C. L. SEOW

EL OLAM [אֵל עוֹלָם ʾel ʿolam]. This divine epithet means "El, the Eternal/Ancient One." It occurs only in association with the sanctuary at Beersheba (Gen 21:33). It originally referred to the supreme deity of the Semitic pantheon, El, known in texts and iconography as an old god. *See* GOD, NAMES OF.

C. L. SEOW

EL SHADDAI el-shadʹi [אֵל שַׁדַּי ʾel shadday]. According to Exod 6, God was known as El Shaddai prior to the revelation of the name YAHWEH to Moses (Gen 17:1; 28:3; 35:11; 43:14; Exod 6:3; Ezek 10:5). The LXX and Vulgate translate the designation as "God Almighty," although other ancient translations interpreted shadday to mean "self-sufficient" (so Aquila and Symmachus). The etymology of the name is, in fact, uncertain. *See* GOD, NAMES OF.

C. L. SEOW

ELA eeʹluh [אֵלָא ʾelaʾ]. Solomon is said to have appointed Ela's son, SHIMEI, as governor over the district of Benjamin (1 Kgs 4:18).

ELAH eeʹluh [אֵלָה ʾelah]. 1. One of the eleven clans or chieftains of Esau (Edom) (Gen 36:41; 1 Chr 1:52). Possibly a place name, equivalent to Elath, used here as a personal name.

2. Site of the David/Goliath battle (1 Sam 17). *See* ELAH, VALLEY OF.

3. The fourth king of the Northern Kingdom (ca. 886–885 BCE) (1 Kgs 16:6, 8, 13, 14), successor to his father, King Baasha.

4. The father of Hoshea, the last king of Israel (2 Kgs 15:30).

5. The second son of Caleb (1 Chr 4:15).

6. A Benjaminite who lived in Jerusalem in the postexilic period (1 Chr 9:8).

WESLEY I. TOEWS

ELAH, VALLEY OF eeʹluh [עֵמֶק הָאֵלָה ʿemeq haʾelah]. The conflict between DAVID and GOLIATH (1 Sam 17) is placed within the Valley of Elah, or literally the valley of TEREBINTH (a type of large tree). Saul and the Israelites faced Goliath and the Philistines in the current Wadi es-Sant (Arabic, translated "Valley of the Acacia"). References to Socoh (probably Khirbet ʿAbad) and AZEKAH (Tell es-Zakariyeh) define the site of the Philistine forces. The Israelites' position is unclear from the text. The David-Goliath confrontation apparently took place near the small, often dry stream-bed along the northern ridge of the valley.

MICHAEL G. VANZANT

EL-AJJUL, TELL. *See* AJJUL, TELL EL.

ELAM, ELAMITES ee'luhmm ee'luh-m*it* [עֵילָם ʿelam, אֶלְמָיֵא ʿelmaye']. Elam is the name of several individuals and of a nation. **1.** The assumed eponymous ancestor of the nation Elam (Gen 10:22; 1 Chr 1:17).

2. An early Benjaminite (1 Chr 8:24), perhaps to be identified with Elam (3) below.

3. One or two ancestors of a group of returning exiles (Ezra 2:7, 31; 8:7; 10:2; Neh 7:12, 34). Though the text mentions "the other Elam" (Ezra 2:31; Neh 7:34), it gives precisely the same number of returnees from this Elam as for the first (Ezra 2:7; Neh 7:12), possibly suggesting this is the same individual and the same group of returnees.

4. A leader of the people (Neh 10:15).

5. A priest (Neh 12:42).

6. A priestly gatekeeper appointed by David (1 Chr 26:3).

7. The Elamite designation for the country was **haltamti** "the country of the lord," which was rendered in Akkadian as **elamtu**; Sumerian designated it with the ideogram NIM, "high" or "raised." Elam, located in the southwestern corner of Iran north of the Persian Gulf, was a major power during the late third millennium through the first half of the first millennium BCE, but the area controlled by the Elamites differed considerably from period to period. The Elamites were originally centered in the modern province of Fars with their capital at Anshan, 36 km northwest of modern Shiraz near Persepolis, but they controlled much of the Iranian plateau prior to the first millennium expansion of Medes and Persians into that area. From their highland center to the east, the Elamites also struggled with the Mesopotamian powers for control of the Karun River watershed in the modern province of Khuzestan, where the major city of Susa, modern Shush, was located. Eventually this lowland area, Susiana, became the new center of the Elamite kingdom.

One may divide the history of Elam into four periods: 1) Proto-Elamite (ca. 3200–2700 BCE); 2) Old Elamite (ca. 2700–1500 BCE); 3) Middle Elamite (ca. 1500–1100 BCE); and 4) Neo-Elamite (ca. 1100–539 BCE).

During the Proto-Elamite period these people of the Iranian plateau invented a still undeciphered ideographic script to write business documents on clay tablets. It is not until the early Old Elamite period, however, when the earliest mention of Elam appears in in a Sumerian inscription of Enmebaragesi, king of Kish. During this period Mesopotamian incursions into Elam, and Elamite incursions into Sumer took place, but the details are sketchy until the rise of Sargon the Great of Akkad (ca. 2350 BCE).

Sargon defeated the Elamite king Luhi-ishan of the Awan dynasty and took control of Susa. Susa remained a part of the Sargonic Empire through the reign of Naram-Sin, though Naram-Sin did conclude a treaty, the earliest extant document in cuneiform Elamite, with one of the Awanite rulers. With the collapse of Akkad under Shar-kali-sharri, Puzur-Inshushinak, the last king of the Awan dynasty, united Elam for the first time. Having subdued the plateau, he then conquered Susiana, where some of his monuments bearing bilingual inscriptions in Akkadian and linear Elamite have been found.

Following Puzur-Inshushinak's death, the Shimashki dynasty came to power on the plateau, while Susiana was once again linked to Mesopotamia, now as a province of the Sumerian Ur III dynasty. The political and economic contact between the two dynasties led to a number of dynastic marriages, but Ur fell into a steady decline under its last king, Ibbi-Sin (2028–2004 BCE), and in 2004 BCE Kindattu, the sixth king of the Shimashki dynasty, led a combined force of Elamites and Susianans in the conquest of Ur. By 1970 BCE the Elamites had occupied Susiana, and Eparti the ninth king of Shimaski took the title "King of Anshan and of Susa." His successors, however, prefered the title **sukkalmah**, "Grand Regent." Serving under the **sukkalmah**, two **sukkal** are sometimes mentioned: the **sukkal** of Elam and Shimashki, responsible for the eastern part of the empire when the **sukkalmah** was in Susa, and the **sukkal** of Susa, responsible for Susiana when the **sukkalmah** was in Anshan or Shimashki.

Following the fall of Ur, Elam continued to exercise major influence on Mesopotamia through the Isin-Larsa and Old Babylonian periods. Under Siwepalarhuppak it conquered Eshnunna on the Diyala and threatened to annex all the states in Mesopotamia, but Hammurabi of Babylon (1792–1750 BCE) with clever diplomacy and astute military maneuvers finally succeeded in turning back the Elamite threat. After that the last rulers of the Shimashki dynasty seem to have been preoccupied elsewhere, though there was some contact with the west again during the reign of Ammi-saduqa of Babylon (1646–1626 BCE).

In the following Middle Elamite period (1500–1100 BCE), three dynasties succeeded one another, the Kidinuides, the Igihalkides, and the Shutrukides. It was a period of the progressive Elamization of Susiana, particularly under the final two dynasties. There was intermittent conflict with the Kassite kings of Babylon, who probably brought an end to the Kidinuides dynasty.

There were a number of dynastic marriages between the Kassites and the Igihalkides, but that did not prevent recurring conflict between the two states. Finally under the Shutrukides (ca. 1210–1100 BCE) Elam reached the height of its power. Shutruk-Nahhunte plundered Mesopotamia repeatedly, and his son, Kutir-Nahhunte, whom some identify with Chedorlaomer (Gen 14), put an end to the Kassite Dynasty (ca. 1155 BCE). Shilhak-Inshushinak and Hutelutush-Inshushinak continued this policy of war with Mesopotamia, but the latter was defeated by the powerful Babylonian ruler Nebuchadnezzar I (1124–1104 BCE), who invaded Elam and brought back a number of captured trophies that earlier Elamite rulers had carried off.

The Neo-Elamite Period (ca. 1000–539 BCE) saw the gradual decline of Elam, particularly from the mid-8th cent. on. In the north and the east, the increasing pressure from the Medes and Persians gradually forced the Elamites off the Iranian Plateau into the lowlands, and in the west Elam's unrelenting support of Babylon in the Assyrio-Babylonian conflict led to ever more devastating Assyrian incursions into Elam.

Sargon II, Sennacherib, and Ashurbanipal all led successful campaigns against Elam, and in 640 BCE Ashurbanipal captured and sacked Susa. Nonetheless, Elam survived in Susiana until it was incorporated into Cyrus' Persian Empire as one of his provinces (Dan 8:2). Though the date of Isa 11:11 is disputed, the biblical references to Elam in Isa 21:2, 6 probably date to the period of Sennacherib's conflict with the Elamites, while the references in Jer 25:25; 49:34-39; Ezek 32:25 date to the first half of the 6th cent. prior to Elam's incorporation into Persia.

Despite the loss of their independence, the province of Elam and its Elamite inhabitants continued to play an important role in the Persian Empire. Elamite remained one of the official languages of the Persian Empire as its presence alongside Old Persian and Akkadian in Darius' Trilingual Behistun inscription indicates. Though using the cuneiform writing system, Elamite is an agglutinate language unrelated to Sumerian, Akkadian, or Old Persian, and it is still not well understood. Some scholars have suggested a relationship to the Dravidian language group, but most linguists have rejected this theory, and for now Elamite remains a linguistic orphan, with no clear connection to any other language or language group.

Bibliography: E. Carter and M. W. Stolper. *Elam, Surveys of Political History and Archaeology* (1984); D. T. Potts. *The Archaeology of Elam: Formation and Transformation of an Ancient Iranian State* (1999).

J. J. M. ROBERTS

EL-AMARNA, TELL. *See* AMARNA, TELL EL.

EL-AREINI, TELL. *See* AREINI, TELL EL.

ELASA el´uh-suh [Ἔλασα Elasa]. The location in Judea near Beth-horon where JUDAS Maccabeus was killed while leading his forces against the army of Bacchides (1 Macc 9:5).

ELASAH el´uh-suh [אֶלְעָשָׂה ’el‘asah]. A courier for King Zedekiah, and a member of the powerful scribal family of Shaphan, who took a letter from Jeremiah to the exiles in Babylon (Jer 29:3). The name means "God has made/done" and occurs in a list of the descendants of the family Passhur (Ezra 10:22/1 Esd 9:22).

PHILLIP MICHAEL SHERMAN

ELATH, ELOTH ee´lath, ee´loth [אֵילַת ’elath, אֵילוֹת, אֵילָה ’eloth]. Elath is located at the northern tip of the Gulf of Aqaba. Due to its proximity to EZION-GEBER, it was also an exodus itinerary site (Deut 2:8; 1 Kgs 9:26; 2 Chr 8:17).

The OT identifies Elath as an important port city providing access for Judah to the sea routes leading to Africa, the Arabian Peninsula, and perhaps to India. The kings of Judah built or rebuilt the site on at least two occasions. King Solomon established a fleet there (1 Kgs 9:26-27; 2 Chr 8:17-18). After recapturing Elath, perhaps from Edom or Israel, King Azariah rebuilt the port (2 Kgs 14:22; Uzziah in 2 Chr 26:2).

The city's strategic importance to other nations is evident (2 Kgs 16:6). The Arameans under King Rezin, perhaps allied with the Edomites, acquired their own control over the sea trade routes by forcing Judah to retreat from Elath.

Elath is known in Greek literature from at least the 3rd cent. BCE (Agatharchides) to the late 1st cent. CE (Claudius Ptolemy). It is referred to as Elana, from which is derived the ancient Greek name for the gulf to its south, the Laenites (Aelanite) Gulf.

MICHAEL D. OBLATH

EL-BATASHI, TELL. *See* TIMNAH, TIMNITE.

EL-BATASHI, TULEILAT. *See* BATASHI, TULEILAT EL.

ELCHASAITES. The Elchasaites was a Jewish-Christian sect that emerged under the leadership of Elchasai (or Elxai) during the reign of TRAJAN (98–117 CE). Although they originated along the Syrian-Parthian border, by the 3rd cent. their teachings had spread to Caesarea and Rome. HIPPOLYTUS (*Haer.* 9.13-27) and EPIPHANIUS (*Pan.* 19) both record fragments from the Book of Elchasai, a text containing secret revelations Elchasai received from a gigantic angelic figure called "the Son of God," whom the Holy Spirit accompanied. The book's primary teachings included the necessity of a second baptism; an emphasis on ritual ablutions, circumcision, sabbath observance, and praying toward Jerusalem; a condemnation of sacrifice; and the prediction of an apocalyptic battle against the godless angels of the north. The sect's synthesis of Jewish and gnostic ideas had a profound influence on MANI, who spent his young adulthood in an Elchasaite community before pronouncing his own teachings.

DAVID M. REIS

ELDAAH el-day'uh [אֶלְדָּעָה 'elda'ah]. One of the grandsons of Abraham and his wife Keturah, through their son Midian (Gen 25:4; 1 Chr 1:33).

ELDAD el'dad [אֶלְדָּד 'eldadh]. Eldad and MEDAD, among seventy elders chosen to help relieve Moses' burden of leadership, remained in camp prophesying under the influence of the Spirit while the others were at the TENT OF MEETING (Num 11:24-30). When Joshua complained about the usurpers, Moses defended them.

ELDAD AND MEDAD el'dad mee'dad. This apocryphal book whose remains have been lost, is about the two prophets who prophesied in the wilderness camp rather than accompanying the elders to the tent (Num 11:26-30). The only explicit quote in the apocryphal work *Shepherd of Hermas* is from this book: "'The Lord is near to those who are open to conversion,' as it is written in the Book of Eldad and Modat, who prophesied to the people in the desert" (Vis. 2.3.4). Some scholars believe that *Eldad and Medad* is quoted in 1 Clement 11.2-4; 23.3-4; James 4:5; and *Targum Pseudo-Jonathan* on Num 11:26. *See* ELDAD; HERMAS, SHEPHERD OF; MEDAD.

MARY KAY DOBROVOLNY, R.S.M.

ELDAD AND MODAD. *See* ELDAD AND MEDAD.

ELDER IN THE NT [πρεσβύτερος presbyteros]. Apart from passages where *elder* refers to older persons (Luke 15:25; John 8:9; Acts 2:17 [= Joel 2:28 (LXX)]; 1 Tim 5:1, [5:2]; Heb 11:2, "elders" in the sense of forebears), the elders of the NT fall into three distinct groups: Jewish elders, Christian elders, and the elders of the book of Revelation.

  A. Jewish Elders
  B. Christian Elders
  C. Revelation
  Bibliography

A. Jewish Elders

Jewish elders appear in the gospel when Jesus confronts the Pharisees and scribes about the "tradition of the elders" (Mark 7:3, 5; Matt 15:2). While the phrase might mean the tradition of one's forebears (see Heb 11:2), it is more likely that "elders" refers to those who enjoyed some authority in shaping the traditions of the people. Luke mentions a delegation of Jewish elders sent to ask Jesus to heal a centurion's slave. Undoubt-edly these were not simply old but were well-respected members of the Jewish community.

Philo has described what a Jewish community living in Egypt understood by "elders":

> After the prayers the seniors (presbyteroi πρεσβύτεροι) recline according to the order of their admission, since by senior (presbyterous πρεσβύτερους) they [Jews] do not understand the aged and grey headed who are regarded as still mere children if they have only in late years come to love this rule of life but those who from their earliest years have grown to manhood and spent their prime in pursuing the contemplative branch of philosophy, which indeed is the noblest and most god-like part. (*Contempl. Life* 67).

In explaining "elders" for his Greek-speaking readership, Philo talks about the study of and devotion to the way of life proposed in the Torah as the pursuit of contemplative philosophy. The elders were the revered wise men of the community, their sages. This understanding of "elders" is most likely shared by Luke and Mark.

A particular though not well-defined group of Jewish elders appears in the synoptic passion narratives. The evangelists prepare for the elders' role in the passion drama in two episodes. Jesus' first prediction of his death, says that the Son of Man will "be rejected by the elders, the chief priests, and the scribes, and be killed" (Matt 16:21; Mark 8:31; Luke 9:22). Later following the cleansing of the Temple, "the chief priests, the scribes, and the elders" confront Jesus in the Temple area with regard to his authority (Matt 21:23; Mark 11:27; Luke 20:1).

The elders appear more frequently in Matthew's passion narrative (26:3, 47, 57; 27:1, 3, 12, 20, 41; 28:12) than they do in Mark (14:43, 53; 15:1) and Luke (22:52). In Mark the elders are associated with the chief priests and scribes in Jesus' arrest (Mark 14:43; see Matt 26:47) and trial (Mark 14:53; 15:1; see Matt 26:57; 27:1; Luke 22:52). Matthew also describes the elders as joining the chief priests both in accusing Jesus (27:12) and in inciting the crowds (27:20). The Markan parallel says only that the chief priests had been involved in stirring up the crowds (15:3, 11). Mark describes the chief priests and scribes gathering in Caiphas's house (14:1); Matthew replaces the scribes by the elders (26:3) and adds the elders to the group of chief priests and scribes who mocked the crucified Jesus (27:41; see Mark 15:31). In addition, Matthew has elders involved in the deal with Judas (27:3) and in the placing of the guard at the tomb (28:12). Matthew's focus on the role that Jewish elders played in Jesus' passion undoubtedly reflects the conflict between Matthew's Jewish Christian community and other Jewish leaders.

In the Synoptics the elders always act as a group. Luke describes them as an assembly or college of elders (presbyterion πρεσβυτέριον). After the resurrection, Luke has these elders continue in their ways by conspiring with the leaders of the people and the chief priests to arrest and confront not only Peter and John (Acts 4:5, 8, 23) but also Stephen (Acts 6:12). Forty conspirators asked the chief priests and elders to join with them in their plan to kill Paul (Acts 23:14). Elders were involved with the high priest or the chief priests in accusing Paul before Felix (Acts 24:1) and Festus (Acts 25:15). These Jerusalem elders were not priests; rather, they were influential Sadducees whose voice was heeded by the Sanhedrin and the high priests.

B. Christian Elders

Ten other references to elders are to Christian elders in Jerusalem. Like their Jewish counterparts, they appear to function as a group or college of elders. Their first appearance is in Acts 11:30: the elders receive the famine relief delivered to Jerusalem by Barnabas and Saul on behalf of the church in Antioch.

Paul and Barnabas were later deputized to go to Jerusalem to discuss the question of the necessity of circumcision for Gentiles with the "apostles and elders" (Acts 15:2). Throughout Luke's account of the Council at Jerusalem the elders always act in consort with the apostles (Acts 15:4, 6, 22, 23; 16:4). The apostles and elders constitute a distinct group within the church (Acts 15:4). They serve as joint senders of the letter to Gentile believers in Antioch, Syria, and Cilicia (Acts 15:23). Luke's pairing of the apostles and the elders suggests that together they exercised a leadership function in the church. Acting in consort with the apostles, the elders are nonetheless to be distinguished from the apostles. The latter are The Twelve (Acts 1), among whom Peter and John figure most prominently in the Lukan narrative.

The Jerusalem elders appear for the last time in Acts 21:18. On his return to Jerusalem after the third missionary voyage Paul greets James and all the elders (pantes hoi presbyteroi πάντες οἱ πρεσβύτεροι). For their benefit, Paul reported on what God had done among the Gentiles. Luke provides no indication of who these elders are—although James, the brother of the Lord, certainly belongs among them—nor how the group arose and was recognized by the church. Since, the Jerusalem church was largely a community of Jewish believers, these Christian elders most likely functioned within their own community in a manner similar to that of other Jewish elders in Jerusalem. Citing James, Cephas, and John by name, Paul seems to describe the leadership cadre at Jerusalem as the "recognized pillars" of the church (Gal 2:9).

Luke twice mentions the presence of elders in communities evangelized by Paul, saying that Paul and Barnabas appointed elders in the churches of Lystra, Iconium, and Antioch (Acts 14:23) and that he summoned the elders from Ephesus to listen to his farewell discourse at Miletus (Acts 20:17). The presence of "elders" in these communities is problematic. In his letters Paul gives no indication that the leadership of his foundations was in the hands of elders. Luke may have anachronistically described the leaders of these churches as elders or he may have erroneously appropriated for them terminology in vogue for the community of Jerusalem.

The deutero-Pauline Pastoral Epistles indicate that toward the end of the 1st cent. CE, the term *elder* was emerging as a description for leaders within the church. Titus 1:5 portrays Titus as having the responsibility to appoint elders in every town (see Acts 14:23). A short catalogue of virtues (Titus 1:6) describes the kind of person to be appointed. The appointed elder's task is that of an overseer responsible for the good order of God's household; the elder is to serve as God's steward (oikonomon οἰκονόμον; Titus 1:7).

First Timothy 5:17-20 offers an elder's bill of rights, with appropriate scriptural warrants (Deut 25:4; Deut 19:15). Should the elder fulfill his responsibility with competence and preach and teach well, he is worthy of "double honor" (diplēs timēs διπλῆς τιμῆς). While some take this to mean double pay, it is preferable to understand the expression to mean the respect of the community along with sustenance. The other provision protects the integrity of the elder. The community is not to accept an accusation against the elder unless there is more than one witness ready to testify to his wrongdoing.

First Peter presumes only one form of leadership in addition to that of the apostles. This leadership is exercised by elders (5:1-5a) whose role is similar to that of Peter, the apostle (5:1a). The elder functions within the community in a role of oversight (episkopountes [ἐπισκοποῦντες], 5:2). This role, not yet an office, is comparable to that of a shepherd. The elder is to exercise his function neither authoritatively nor for financial gain. Should he exercise the function well, he will receive an eschatological reward. In the meantime, he can expect that others in the community respect his authority.

A few other NT texts indicate that "elder" was coming into general use as a title for those who exercised an authoritative leadership function by the late 1st cent. Thus, 2 and 3 John are written by "the elder" who provides directives for the church (2 John) and the beloved Gaius (3 John). James 5:14 urges that when members of the community are ill, the elders of the assembly be summoned in order to pray over those who are sick and anoint them with oil. These elders appear to act collegially as did the council of elders (tou presbyteriou τοῦ πρεσβυτερίου) who laid hands on Timothy (1 Tim 4:14).

In writing to the Corinthians, Clement spoke of "duly appointed" elders (*1 Clem.* 54:2) whose leadership role was not to be denied (*1 Clem.* 47:6). These elders are worthy of honor (*1 Clem.* 1:3) and obedience (*1 Clem.* 57:1). Writing to the Philippians, Polycarp appears to echo Titus, 1 Peter, and James as he describes the quality and functions of elders in his letter (*Phil.* 6:1). Early in the 2nd cent. Ignatius of Antioch includes the "elder" within a threefold ecclesial office: bishop, elder, and deacon.

C. Revelation

The book of Revelation provides a vision of elders who function rather differently from the elders of the NT's epistolary literature. These crowned elders take part in a heavenly liturgy. Twenty-four in number (Rev 4:4, 10; 5:8; 11:16; 19:4), they are seated on twenty-four thrones around a throne on which sits the one worthy of worship. Casting off their own crowns (Rev 4:10) and falling to the ground, the twenty-four elders worship the one who sits on the throne (Rev 4:10; 11:16; 19:4). Similarly, they fall down and worship the Lamb (Rev 5:8, 14) who stands among them (Rev 5:6). The worship of the elders includes songs of praise and thanksgiving (Rev 4:10-11; 5:8-10; 11:16-18; 19:4). These twenty-four elders are often portrayed alongside the four living creatures (Rev 4:9-10; 5:6, 8, 11, 14; 7:11; 14:3; 19:4). Twice, they are said to be surrounded by angels (Rev 5:11; 7:11).

Only twice does one of the elders speak. In Rev 5:5, one of them speaks to calm the seer's anxiety. This elder proclaims the victory and exaltation of the Messiah. In Rev 7:13-17 one of the elders engages the seer in dialogue. This elder, perhaps the same elder as the speaker in Rev 5:5, questions the seer about the identity and provenance of those clothed in white. Respectfully addressing the elder as kyrie (κύριε, the vocative of kyrios κύριος), Lord (Sir), the seer professes his ignorance and is then enlightened by the elder with regard to the identity of those clothed in white.

Opinions abound as to the identity of the twenty-four elders. They have been identified as the twenty-four astral deities of the Babylonian zodiac, angels (Roloff 1993, 69–70), biblical saints, angels representing biblical and NT saints, the patriarchs and apostles. Beale reasonably suggests that they are angels who represent the twelve tribes of Israel and the twelve apostles, thus symbolizing the entire body of the redeemed. *See* MINISTRY, CHRISTIAN; PASTORAL LETTERS.

Bibliography: G. K. Beale. *The Book of Revelation: A Commentary on the Greek Text.* NIGTC (1999); R. F. Collins. *I and II Timothy and Titus.* NTL (2002); J. H. Elliott. *I Peter* 37B (2000); J. A. Fitzmyer. *The Acts of the Apostles* (1998); D. A. Mappes. "The Discipline of a Sinning Elder." *BSac* 154 (1997) 333–43; D. A. Mappes. "The 'Laying On of Hands' of Elders." *BSac* 154 (1997) 94–97; J. Roloff. *Revelation.* CC (1993).

RAYMOND F. COLLINS

ELDER IN THE OT [זָקֵן *zaqen*]. The Hebrew term for "elder" (*zaqen*) derives from the word for "beard" (*zaqan* זָקָן). The OT writers use it more than 130 times. In a few passages it merely denotes persons of advanced years (Lev 19:32; Ezek 9:6; Joel 2:16; 2:28), but it more typically designates traditional but unofficial leaders of tribal communities or professional groups. Such individuals acquire knowledge and wisdom through years of experience; consequently, they gain the respect of—and typically exercise tacit authority over—the members of their community or group.

The most common categories of elders are national elders (usually, "the elders of Israel") and "the elders of the city" (more precisely, village elders or community leaders). Some passages mention "elders" along with other leaders (e.g., Josh 24:31; Isa 3:2; 9:15; Ezek 7:26; Joel 1:2, 14), but it is unclear whether each envisions 1) a body of traditional leaders from a specific local community, 2) a special body of traditional leaders drawn from the whole nation (i.e., national elders), or 3) a category of traditional leaders (i.e., elders of the city) inhabiting communities throughout the nation (see Deut 32:7; Job 12:20; Ps 107:32; compare "elders of the land" in 1 Kgs 20:7-8; Prov 31:23; Jer 26:17). Less common are those designated as the "elders" of a professional group (e.g., "the senior priests," 2 Kgs 19:2; Isa 37:2; Jer 19:1). Similarly, the designation "elder(s)" is occasionally applied to senior servants of a wealthy individual (Gen 24:2) or senior royal "servants" (Gen 50:7; 2 Sam 12:17; 1 Kgs 12:6, 8, 13; Ps 105:22; compare Isa 24:23).

The "elders of the city" were local leaders that typically "sat in the gate" (*see* CITY GATE), where matters of local business and law were discussed. Job's final defense (Job 29, 31) provides the fullest characterization of an "elder of the city" in the OT, though the text never uses the term *elder*. Job describes himself as a man of means, whose opinion his neighbors hold in the highest esteem, and who regularly exhibits justice, mercy, and righteousness in his dealings with others. These characteristics reflect the sources of an elder's prestige and unofficial authority. Depending on the nature of the community, these elders could function in a complementary fashion with priests and appointed judges and "officers." The Deuteronomic laws provide the most information about the common functions and powers of "elders of the city" (see Deut 19:11-13; 21:1-9,18-21; 22:13-21; 25:5-10; compare Josh 20:4; Ruth 4:1-11). They participate as adjudicators in legal disputes and notaries or witnesses in matters of business, but they also serve as representatives for their community to outsiders (1 Sam 16:4) and to the Lord (Ezra 10:14). In all these capacities, they use their economic and moral influence to promote the unity and integrity of their community.

There is scattered mention of the elders of a single clan or tribe (see 1 Sam 15:30; Judg 11:4-11), including "the elders of Judah." It is unclear whether the latter intend to portray Judah as a tribe (so perhaps 1 Sam 30:26; 2 Sam 19:11) or as a kingdom (as in 2 Kgs 23:1; Ezek 8:1). A similar ambiguity applies to the elders of capital cities, like Jerusalem (Lam 1:19; 2:10), and the elders of neighboring city-states (see Josh 9:11; Judg 8:13-16; Ezek 27:9). Such bodies of elders could have functioned as representatives of an entire nation or as traditional leaders of one city within a nation. The few references to "elders" of other nations (Gen 50:7; Num 22:4-7) likely reflect an Israelite designation ascribed to comparable groups in neighboring nations.

There are approximately three dozen references to "the elders of Israel," and another dozen passages clearly envision the same body (e.g., "elders of the people," Exod 19:7; Jer 19:1; "elders of your tribes," Deut 31:28; "elders of the congregation," Lev 4:15; Judg 21:16). A few specify the number of these elders as seventy (Exod 24:1, 9; Num 11:16-30; Ezek 8:11). The fact that the Sanhedrin of post-exilic Judea also consisted of seventy members raises the possibility that this number has been read back into early narratives on the basis of analogy. Some interpreters believe that post-exilic writers imposed this national institution in its entirety back into earlier periods of Israel's history, and that there never was such a body before the exile. Others contend that such a body functioned prior to the establishment of the monarchy, but that monarchic institutions displaced it entirely. A third and mediating position holds that traditional tribal institutions like the national elders persisted from pre-monarchic times through the monarchic period, fluctuating in strength and influence according to the political fortunes of the nation, and then resurging in the absence of the monarchy.

The "elders of Israel" serve primarily as representatives or leaders of the general population. As representatives, they make covenants on the people's behalf (Exod 24:1-11; 2 Sam 5:3; 2 Kgs 23:1-3). They bear witness to the words and actions of the Lord (Exod 17:5-6), they stand before the Lord in worship (Exod 18:12; Josh 7:6), and they stand before the king at national gatherings (1 Kgs 8:1-5). It is likely that many references to the corporate activities of "the people" actually involved the elders alone (e.g., Exod 19:7-8). The elders typically lead as well, standing alongside a national leader in worship (2 Kgs 23:1-3) or commanding the people in battle (Josh 8:10; 2 Sam 17:4, 15). They not only receive instructions from the Lord or his representative, they pass on those instructions to the people (Deut 27:1). They are responsible, along with priests and kings, for teaching the Lord's laws to the people (Deut 27:1; 31:9). On one occasion they prophesy along with Moses (Num 11:16-30), perhaps alluding to their role as administrators (Num 11:17). Finally, the elders are among those held responsible for seeing that justice is upheld in the nation (Isa 3:14).

Bibliography: H. Reviv. *The Elders in Ancient Israel* (1989); T. Willis. *The Elders of the City* (2001).
TIMOTHY M. WILLIS

ELDERS, TRADITION OF THE. *See* TRADITIONS OF THE ELDERS.

ELEAD el'ee-uhd [אֶלְעָד *'el'adh*]. A descendant of Ephraim listed in Joshua's genealogy (1 Chr 7:21) who, along with Ezel, was killed by the men of Gath following an incursion by the Ephraimites to steal cattle. His precise relationship to Ephraim is uncertain as the text lacks the phrase "son of."

ELEADAH el'ee-ay'duh [אֶלְעָדָה *'el'adhah*]. The name of this descendant of Ephraim means "God had adorned." First Chronicles 7:20 is the sole reference to this figure in the OT. The other surviving list of the descendants of Ephraim, Num 26, makes no mention of him.

ELEALEH el'ee-ay'luh [אֶלְעָלֵה *'el'aleh*, אֶלְעָלָא *'el'ale'*]. A Transjordanian city allotted to the tribe of Reuben (Num 32:3, 37), which appears in conjunction with HESHBON as a Moabite city in Isaiah (15:4; 16:9) and Jeremiah (48:34). The toponym is preserved as el-'Al, a site northeast of Heshbon (Tell Hesban).

ELEASAH el'ee-ay'suh [אֶלְעָשָׂה *'el'asah*]. Means "God made" or "God did." 1. Son of Helez and father of Sismai in the lineage of Jerahmeel (1 Chr 3:39-40). *See* JERAHMEEL, JERAHMEELITES.

2. Son of Raphah and father of Azel and the tenth generation from King Saul in two genealogical lists of the Benjaminites (1 Chr 8:37; 9:43).

ELEAZAR el'ee-ay'zuhr [אֶלְעָזָר *'el'azar*; Ἐλεαζάρ *Eleazar*]. Eleven men in the OT bear this name: "El (or God) has helped." A similar name is Eliezer, "El (or God) is help." 1. The third of four sons born to Aaron and Elisheba (Exod 6:23). The first two sons, Nadab and Abihu, died when they offered "strange fire" before the LORD (Lev 10:1-2), leaving Eleazar next in line to succeed Aaron to the priesthood. Moses effected the transfer of authority by clothing Eleazar with Aaron's vestments (Num 20:25-28). Thereafter the narrative (of the P source) frequently names Eleazar alongside Moses, where formerly it would have named Aaron (e.g., Num 26:1, 3; 27:2; etc.), yet Moses clearly has the greater authority. Just before his own death, Moses commissioned Joshua "before Eleazar" and gave him "some" of his own authority (Num 27:18-20), to inquire of Yahweh by means of Urim (sacred lots) on Joshua's behalf (v. 21). In the book of Joshua, Eleazar (named first), Joshua, and the heads of the tribes and families take responsibility to apportion the land to the tribes and families of Israel (Josh 14:1; 17:4; 19:51; 21:1).

2. The son of Abinadab who lived at Kiriath-jearim. When the Philistines returned the ark to the Israelites, the people of Kiriath-jearim brought it to Abinadab's house and consecrated Eleazar to take charge of it (1 Sam 7:1-2).

3. The second of King David's three chief warriors (2 Sam 23:9-10; 1 Chr 11:12-14), who earned his rank by fearlessly standing his ground in a battle against the Philistines.

4. A Levite, son of Mahli, and grandson to Merari the third son of Levi (1 Chr 23:21-22; 24:28).

5. One of the priests who witnessed the receipt of the treasures of silver and gold, which the exiles who returned with Ezra from Babylon brought with them (Ezra 8:33).

6. One of the Israelites who was found to have married foreign women and to have broken faith with Yahweh, according to an inquest conducted by Ezra (Ezra 10:25).

7. A priest who participated in the dedication of the wall of Jerusalem, rebuilt under Nehemiah's leadership (Neh 12:42).

8. The fourth of five sons of the priest Mattathias (1 Macc 2:5). In a battle near Beth-zechariah, Eleazar died in a heroic exploit to kill an elephant he perceived to be bearing the Seleucid king (1 Macc 6:43-46).

9. The father of Jason. Judas Maccabeus sent this Jason together with Eupolemus to Rome to negotiate an alliance against the Seleucids in 161 BCE (1 Macc 8:17).

10. An aged Judean scribe who chose a martyr's death rather than to become polluted by eating pork (2 Macc 6:18-31). The text suggests a setting in 167 BCE when Antiochus IV attempted to compel Jews to abandon the law and partake in sacrifice of swine. The same story appears again in 4 Macc 5–6, but with much more detail, including extensive speeches by Eleazar.

11. The father of Jesus who collected the proverbs in the book known as Ecclesiasticus or as the Wisdom of Jesus, Son of Sirach (Sir 50:27).

12. An elderly Jewish priest whose prayer won deliverance for the Jews in Egypt when Ptolemy IV Philopater threatened to massacre them (3 Macc 6).

WESLEY I. TOEWS

ELEAZAR BEN SIRA. *See* APOCRYPHA, DEUTERO-CANONICAL; SIRACH.

ELECT LADY [ἡ ἐκλέκτη κυρία hē eklektē kyria]. While some scholars have suggested that this is a woman who may have been the leader of a church that met in her house, the evidence suggests that she most likely represents a church whose spiritual children (2 John 1) are members of the elect congregation to which the elder directs his letter and whose sister is another community of believers (2 John 13; compare 1 Pet 5:13). Female figures were used to represent communities such as Israel (Jer 6:23; 31:21; Isa 54:1) or the Christian community in which their children are also mentioned (Gal 4:25-27) and this is probably the case here.

Bibliography: Raymond E. Brown. *The Epistles of John.* AB 30 (1982).

NANCY CALVERT-KOYZIS

ELECTION. Within the OT election signifies God's special relationship to Abraham's descendants through Isaac and Jacob. Thus the people of Israel and their physical descendants the Jewish people are commonly called the chosen people. In the NT, the church, composed of both Jews and Gentiles who proclaimed belief in Jesus as the Messiah and Son of God, came to see itself as the new Israel (Eph 2:11-22). Within most of the OT, not being among the chosen said little about one's ultimate disposition, an idea upheld by major streams of rabbinic Judaism, which affirm that righteous non-Jews have a portion in the world to come. However, the NT, and the classical Christian doctrine of election that grew from it, implies that some are predestined for eternal salvation, others for damnation. Although Jews and Christians have distinct understandings of election, it is central to the unique theological claims made by each tradition, a fact not given sufficient weight by those contemporary Christians and Jews who seek to banish the idea of divine election from Western religious discourse. *See* CHOSEN.

Bibliography: Gerrit C. Berkouwer. *Divine Election* (1960); Joel S. Kaminsky. *Yet I Loved Jacob: Reclaiming the Biblical Concept of Election* (2007).

JOEL S. KAMINSKY

ELEMENTS, ELEMENTAL SPIRIT [στοιχεῖα stoicheia]. In Aristotle (*Metaph.* 986): "that which is the primary component immanent in a thing which is indivisible into kinds different from itself." Along with the concepts of "fundamental" and "power" (dynamis δύναμις) "primary component" was the key meaning of the word. The term also developed a variety of specific meanings such as "letters" of the alphabet, "foundations" or "principles" of various sciences, arts, teaching, institutions, etc., and especially the physical elements of the world ("earth, air, fire, and water," Wis 7:17; sometimes also "ether"). Later the term took on the meaning of "heavenly bodies," "elemental spirits," and even "demons" (*T. Sol.* 8:204).

In Heb 5:12, the term refers to the "basic elements" of the oracles of God. The association with "foundation" appears in 6:1.

In 2 Pet 3:10, the term *elements* may mean "the heavenly bodies" such as sun, moon, and stars (also v. 12; compare Isa 34:4 LXX: "all the powers of the heavens will melt") contrasted with "the earth." Or one can understand "earth," metaphorically as "humankind," and interpret "elements" as the familiar "earth, air, fire, and water."

Paul uses the word four times, three times in the phrase, stoicheia tou kosmou (στοιχεῖα τοῦ κόσμου), Gal 4:3; Col 2:8, 20; and once, Gal 4:9, "the weak and beggarly stoicheia." Many hold that stoicheia refers to beings such as angels or demons, thus as "elementary spirits of the world"; the minority view adopts "rudiments of the world as a translation closer to the usual meaning of the term.

In either case, the close association of stoicheia with the Law of Moses is crucial to Paul's argument. Before faith came, Jewish Christians were imprisoned "under the law" (3:23) and as children also imprisoned "under the stoicheia tou kosmou" (4:3). The law could not give life (3:21); instead imprisoned people "under sin" (3:22). When Christians return to keeping calendar legislation, this amounts to serving those "weak and beggarly stoicheia" over again (4:9-10). On the one hand, the law is "holy, righteous, and good" (Rom 7:12); on the other it is "weak" through or because of the "flesh" (8:3). The only hope is to take part in Christ's redemption from the law and receive the status of sons in him (Gal 4:5).

The law (nomos νόμος) as such is not mentioned in Colossians, but there are references to Jewish institutions and legislation, such as "traditions of men" (2:8), circumcision (2:11), "legal demands" (2:14), calendar legislation (2:16), and ascetic regulations (2:20-22). These are involved in some measure to service of the stoicheia tou kosmou (2:8, 20). By dying with Christ, believers have been freed from the authority of the stoicheia (2:20) and live by the power of the resurrected Christ (3:1-4).

Bibliography: C. E. Arnold. *The Colossian Syncretism: The Interface Between Christianity and Folk Belief at Colossae* (1995); C. E. Arnold. "Returning to the Domain of the Powers." *NovT* 38 (1996) 55–76; R. McL. Wilson. *Colossians and Philemon.* ICC (2005).

ANDREW BANDSTRA

EL-EMIR, IRAQ. *See* EMIR, IRAQ EL.

ELEPHANT [ἐλέφας elephas]. Although not mentioned in the NT, in the books of Maccabees, elephants are among the fighting animals fielded by ANTIOCHUS (1 Macc 5:34; 2 Macc 13:15; 3 Macc 5:45). DARIUS, king of Persia, also used elephants in campaigns against ALEXANDER THE GREAT, and the Carthaginians under Hannibal used tamed African elephants during the Punic Wars.

Literary and artistic evidence suggests that elephants were prevalent in the Near East, including Syria, in early historic periods. Thutmose III hunted 120 elephants on his campaign in Syria according to his biographer Amen-

en-heb, confirmed on the Barkal Stele (*ANET*, 240). In the middle panel of Shalmaneser III's Black Obelisk, animals brought as tribute from the country Musri include elephants (*ANEP*, 353) (*ANET*, 281).

Elephants were hunted mainly for their ivory, which was used for carving jewelry, boxes, inlay pieces, handles, figurines, and other items in Syria-Palestine. Such objects were prestigious items collected by nobility, and often kept in great palaces (Amos 3:15; Ps 45:9) (Borowski 195–96). Solomon "also made a great throne inlaid with ivory and overlaid with fine gold" in his palace (1 Kgs 10:7; 2 Chr 9:17), and Ahab was singled out for " the palace he decorated with ivory" (1 Kgs 22:39) where the nobility lolled "on beds inlaid with ivory" (Amos 6:4).

Bibliography: Oded Borowski. *Every Living Thing: Daily Use of Animals in Ancient Israel* (1998).

ODED BOROWSKI

ELEPHANTINE PAPYRI el´uh-fan-tí´nee. Collective designation of a group of Aramaic documents, on papyrus and other materials, dated mostly to the 5th cent. BCE, from the Nile island of Elephantine (Upper Egypt), the seat of a military outpost of the Persian Empire, and other locations in EGYPT. The finds began to surface in the early 19th cent. in museums and collections through purchases of European travelers and were subsequently collected throughout the 19th and 20th cent. through acquisitions and archaeological excavations. The documents consist of private and official letters, legal documents, literary compositions, administrative, and other texts of varied nature. The Elephantine papyri document the life of a complex multicultural society in which Jews, Arameans, Egyptians, Persians, and other groups coexisted and interacted under the Achaemenid administration.

The private letters express the interests, concerns, and family affairs of the senders, some of which, as is the case for the so-called Hermopolis letters, appear to be away from home under military assignment. Among the official letters, the correspondence on leather and papyrus belonging to the satrap Arshama contains missives from the satrap himself as well as other Persian officers and illustrates in details Arshama's involvement in the dealings of the satrapy. Also noteworthy among the official letters is the so-called Jedaniah archive, a source of precious historical information regarding the Jewish military colony in Elephantine.

Perhaps most famous among the Elephantine papyri is a petition, of which two copies survived (TAD A4.7; TAD A4.8), from the priest Jedaniah and his colleagues, to Bagavahya, governor of Judah, reporting the destruction of the temple of Yahweh on the island, and requesting a letter to allow the community permission to rebuild its temple, so that they may reinstitute sacrifices in it. The archive also contains a memorandum rifices in it. The archive also contains a memorandum that records the joint reply (TAD A4.9) from Bagavahya and Delayah, the governor of Samaria. The officials grant permission to rebuild the temple and to resume incense and meal offerings, but they do not mention animal sacrifice, which was clearly expressed in the petition. This correspondence offers unprecedented insight in the life of this Jewish colony, and sheds light on the Jewish community's relationship with its Egyptian neighbors, the Persian administration, as well as its delicate diplomatic and religious ties with the officials in Jerusalem and Samaria.

In this archive one also finds the famous Passover letter (TAD A4.1), which appears to contain instructions regarding leavened bread. However, the text is unfortunately badly broken and, despite the title by which the letter has become known, the word *Passover* is not contained in it. The word appears instead in a private letter on ostracon TAD D7.6, where an unknown sender asks a certain Hoshayah to inform him as to when he and his family will celebrate it.

With regard to the legal documents, the private archives of Anani and Miptahiah record the legal history of two families, including most notably marriage contracts, sales or gifts of immovable property, loans, and a testamentary manumission. These documents occupy a unique place in Aramaic and Jewish law and provide invaluable data regarding the legal position and the rights of the women within these families.

Also deserving of particular attention are the story and the words of Ahiqar, preserved in a papyrus palimpsest, and constituting the earliest attestation of a literary composition that enjoyed much fame in antiquity, through its various subsequent versions in various languages. The connections between the story of Ahiqar and other biblical stories of sages at royal court is well established, and parallels between the words of Ahiqar and the book of Proverbs have similarly been drawn by scholars (*see* AHIKAR, AHIQAR). Among the papyri one also finds the Aramaic version (TAD C2.1) of the Behistun relief inscription, in which the Persian king Darius I recounts his victory over various rebels aspiring to the throne, and administrative texts, such as accounts and lists.

Bibliography: Bezalel Porten and Ada Yardeni, eds. *Textbook of Aramaic Documents from Ancient Egypt. Newly Copied, Edited and Translated into Hebrew and English* (1986–1993).

ANNALISA AZZONI

ELEUTHERUS i-loo′thuh-ruhs [Ἐλεύθερος Eleutheros]. A river in Syria mentioned in association with Jonathan's military endeavors (1 Macc 11:7; 12:30), perhaps identified with the Nahr el-Kebir or the Nahr Ibrahim. It probably formed a political boundary. Jonathan did not pursue the forces of Demetrius after they had crossed it.

DEREK E. WITTMAN

ELEVATION OFFERING [תְּנוּפָה tenufah]. This cultic term, which appears in texts from the Priestly (P) and Holiness (H) traditions, designates something that has been dedicated to the sacred realm. Following ancient rabbinic interpretation, tenufah was rendered "wave offering" in the KJV (followed by RSV and NIV). However, the verb henif (הֵנִיף), which is used in association with the nominal form tenufah, almost certainly means "lift, elevate." The texts seem to refer to a ritual gesture by which the devoted elements are held up "before the LORD" (lifne YHWH [לִפְנֵי יְהֹוָה]; see Lev 7:30; 8:27, 29; 14:12, 21, 24; Num 5:25; 6:20), that is, within the sanctuary complex, thus presenting them to Yahweh. Thus, a tenufah is something that has been elevated, an elevation offering.

In a sacrifice of well-being the breast of the animal is designated an elevation offering, and belongs to the priestly cadre as a whole (Lev 7:30-31; compare Lev 8:29; Num 6:20), in distinction from the right thigh, which is terumah (תְּרוּמָה traditionally, "heave offering") and goes to the officiating priest (Lev 7:32). However, when the right thigh of the ordination ram is burned on the altar—since Aaron and his sons cannot receive a prebend from their own offering—it is designated as an elevation offering (Exod 29:22-25; Lev 8:25-28).

Other devoted items designated as elevation offerings are the reparation offering and the log of oil brought to the shrine by a person being purified for a skin disease (Lev 14:12, 21, 24); the boiled shoulder of the Nazirite's sacrifice of well-being (Num 6:19-20); the sheaf of first-fruits of barley (Lev 23:11, 15); the two leavened loaves given at the festival of first-fruits (Lev 23:17, 20); and the gold and bronze given for the building of the Tabernacle (Exod 35:22; 38:24, 29 [NRSV: "contributed"]). What the various things referred to as elevation offerings seem to have in common is that there is some ambiguity about their sacral character, either because they are brought as the property of the offerer or because their composition varies in some fashion from cultic norms. Designation as elevation offerings makes it clear that they belong fully to the cultic realm.

While in most instances it is possible to envisage an actual ritual of elevation, the use of the verb henif and the term "elevation offering" to refer to the dedication of the Levites for service in the Tabernacle (Num 8:11, 15, 21) is almost certainly metaphorical. *See* SACRIFICES AND OFFERINGS.

WILLIAM K. GILDERS

ELEVEN. *See* NUMBERS, NUMBERING.

ELEVEN, THE [οἱ ἕνδεκα hoi endeka]. "The eleven," Jesus' twelve associates after Judas' defection from the ranks, appears in absolute form (Mark 16:14; Luke 24:9, 33) and in conjunction with "disciples" (Matt 28:16) or "apostles" (Acts 1:26). The Gospels mention the eleven only in post-resurrection narratives: receiving the risen Jesus' final commission (Matt 28:16-20); regarding the women's report of the empty tomb as an "idle tale" (Luke 24:9-11); and discussing the risen Lord's appearances (Luke 24:33-36). In the book of Acts, the Jerusalem congregation selects MATTHIAS as Judas' replacement and "add[s] [him] to the eleven apostles" (1:26). *See* APOSTLE; MINISTRY, CHRISTIAN; TWELVE, THE.

F. SCOTT SPENCER

ELHANAN el-hay′nuhn [אֶלְחָנָן ʾelkhanan]. Meaning "God is gracious." 1. A member of David's mighty men, was noted for slaying a Philistine giant. The accounts (2 Sam 21:19; 1 Chr 20:5) differ regarding the name of the giant (GOLIATH or Goliath's brother) and the name of Elhanan's father (Jaareoregim or Jair). Scholars debate whether Elhanan is actually David. Others suggest that the name Goliath was added to the David story (1 Sam 17) later.

2. Another of David's mighty men is Elhanan, son of Dodo of Bethlehem (2 Sam 23:24; 1 Chr 11:26). These two Elhanans could be the same.

MICHAEL G. VANZANT

EL-HESI, TELL. *See* HESI, TELL EL.

EL-HIRI, RUJM. *See* HIRI, RUJM EL.

EL-HUSN. *See* HUSN, TELL EL.

ELI ee′li [עֵלִי ʿeli]. Eli is the priest at Shiloh who raises Samuel to become priest in the place of his own sons, HOPHNI AND PHINEHAS. Yahweh judges the house of Eli inadequate because these two sons treat the offerings made to God with disrespect and lie with the young women who come to work at the entrance to the sanctuary. Eli himself is presented as being unacceptable as a priest because he honors his sons more than God by being unwilling to chastise them for their actions, and he benefits from their behavior regarding the meat for sacrifices (1 Sam 2:29). The judgment on the house of Eli is signaled by the deaths of both sons in a single day, and the death of old Eli when he hears that the Philistines have captured the Ark of the Covenant (1 Sam 4:13-15). The Shilonite priesthood is then replaced with Samuel, who lives at Ramah. Eli's line seems to continue in the genealogical structure in 1 Samuel as David flees from Saul. ABIATHAR, who "carries the ephod" for David, is the only survivor when Saul kills the priests at Nob. Abiathar is the son of AHIMELECH, who is the son of AHITUB, called Ichabod's brother in 1 Sam 14:3. ICHABOD is the son of Phinehas, born as his mother hears of the death of her husband (1 Sam 4:21).

C. MARK MCCORMICK

ELI, ELI, LEMA SABACHTHANI [ἠλι ἠλι λεμα σαβαχθανι ēli ēli lema sabachthani]. According to recent critical editions of the Greek NT, in Matt 27:46, Jesus' last words from the cross were ēli ēli lema sabachthani; Mark 15:34 gives them as elōi elōi lema sabachthani (ἐλωι ἐλωι λεμα σαβαχθανι). Both versions can be rendered as "My God, my God, why have you forsaken me?" Both are Greek transliterations of the first four words of Ps 22, but in Aramaic—the language Jesus spoke—rather than in Hebrew, the language in which Ps 22 was written. Matthew changed Mark's word for "my God" to one that sounded more like "Elijah" (Matt 27:47-49). There are several variant readings in the manuscript traditions of both verses; some variants show the influence of the Hebrew text (אֵלִי אֵלִי לָמָה עֲזַבְתָּנִי ʾeli ʾeli lama ʿazavtani).

One can understand the "cry of dereliction" as Mark's narrative climax. Jesus predicts his death as a divine necessity, and yet because of the crowds, his enemies cannot seize him. But then Jesus' support begins to peel away: Judas plots, the disciples flee, Peter denies, the crowds choose Barabbas, Jesus dies alone. The denouement comes after his death, when the centurion, Joseph of Arimathea, and the women disciples all turn to him. Theologically, one can understand the "cry" as an aspect of Jesus' humanity, as his agonized struggle for his last breaths. Lament psalms, such as Ps 22, were written to help the faithful express their deepest hurts to God; since Ps 22 moves from complaint to praise and statements of faith, Jesus' cry need not indicate a loss of faith. Evaluated historically, the "cry" is appropriate for a devout Jew facing a painful death, and many argue that, because it undercuts Jesus' divinity, Jesus probably said it. Others, noting how Pss 22 and 69 shape the wording of Mark 15:24, 31, and 36, believe that Mark or some earlier Christian used these psalms to construct the crucifixion narrative because they helped make sense of Jesus' death. The use of the "cry" in support of theories of substitutionary atonement—where God "turns his back on his Son" because Jesus is bearing the sins of all humanity—goes beyond Mark and Matthew and is based on medieval understandings of honor. Likewise, the problem that the "cry" presents for the doctrine of the Trinity—how could one Person be estranged from Another without damaging the singularity of God's being?—cannot be solved exegetically, since the notion of "one substance" postdates Mark and Matthew. Finally, Luke and John present Jesus as placid and composed at the moment of his death; it has always been challenging for Christian theology to do justice, in atonement theories, to the varieties of perspectives within the NT on Jesus' death. *See* GOD, NAMES OF; PASSION NARRATIVES.

RICHARD B. VINSON

ELIAB i-li′uhb [אֱלִיאָב ʾeliʾav]. A common name, meaning "God is father." 1. A leader of the tribe of Zebulun during the census of Moses and dedicatory offerings during the exodus (Num 1:9; 2:7; 7:24, 29; 10:16).

2. Father of Dathan and Abiram of the Korah rebellion (Num 16:1, 12; 26:8; Deut 11:6).

3. David's eldest brother (1 Sam 16:6, originally Elihu, 1 Chr 27:18) who fought with Saul against the Philistines and Goliath (1 Sam 17:28).

4. An ancestor of Samuel (1 Chr 6:27).

5. One of David's mighty men (1 Chr 12:9).

6. A Levite musician (1 Chr 15:18).

MICHAEL G. VANZANT

ELIADA i-li′uh-duh [אֶלְיָדָע ʾelyadhaʿ]. Means "God knows." 1. Tenth-listed of eleven sons of David born in Jerusalem (2 Sam 5:16); alternately the twelfth of thirteen sons (1 Chr 3:8). A parallel list reads Beeliada ("Baal knows" or "the lord knows"; 14:7), perhaps reflecting his original name.

2. Father of King REZON of Damascus (1 Kgs 11:23).

3. A Benjaminite commander of a large force of shielded archers serving King JEHOSHAPHAT in Jerusalem (2 Chr 17:17).

JASON C. DYKEHOUSE

ELIADAS i-li′uh-duhs [Ἐλιαδας Eliadas]. One of the descendants of Zomath who was made to divorce his wife during Ezra's expulsion of foreign women and children (1 Esd 9:28).

ELIAHBA i-li′uh-buh [אֶלְיַחְבָּא ʾelyakhbaʾ]. Means "God hides." He was a Shaalbonite and the seventeenth-listed warrior among the heroes known as David's "Thirty" (2 Sam 23:32; 1 Chr 11:33).

ELIAKIM i-li′uh-kim [אֶלְיָקִים ʾelyaqim; Ἐλιακίμ Eliakim]. Means "God raises up." 1. Eliakim, son of Hilkiah, replaced Shebna as the governor or steward of HEZEKIAH's entire house (Isa 22:15-20). His authority was second only to the king as the "father of the inhabitants of Jerusalem and to the house of Judah" (Isa 22:21). Eliakim, with Shebna now as secretary, represented Hezekiah and Judah when the Assyrian king SENNACHERIB sent his official spokesman ("the Rabshakeh," NRSV) to Jerusalem demanding surrender (2 Kgs 18:18, 26, 37; Isa 36:3, 11, 22). Eliakim approached Isaiah in sackcloth seeking prayers for the protection of Jerusalem after the Assyrian threat developed.

2. The second son of JOSIAH. Upon his father's death at the hands of the Egyptians (ca. 609 BCE), Eliakim became king and was renamed JEHOIAKIM ("The Lord [Yahweh] raises up") by Pharaoh Necco (2 Kgs 23:34).

3. A priest who helped dedicate the wall of Jerusalem rebuilt under Zerubbabel (Neh 12:41).

4. In the NT, the grandson of Zerubbabel and son of Abiud within the ancestry of Jesus (Matt 1:13).

5. The son of Melea within the genealogy of Jesus in Luke 3:30.

MICHAEL G. VANZANT

ELIALIS i-li′uh-lis [Ἐλιαλίς Elialis]. Elialis, of the family of BANI, was among those in postexilic Jerusalem who had taken foreign wives (1 Esd 9:34) and were forced to separate from their children. The parallel text in Ezra (10:34-37) does not list Elialis among the descendants of Bani.

ELIAM i-li′uhm [אֱלִיעָם ʾeliʿam]. 1. Bathsheba's father in the report to David (2 Sam 11:3). The Chronicler calls him AMMIEL (1 Chr 3:5).

2. Son of Ahithophel the Gilonite, and one of "The Thirty" warriors in David's army (2 Sam 23:34). It is unclear if these are the same man.

JESSICA TINKLENBERG DEVEGA

ELIASAPH i-li′uh-saf [אֶלְיָסָף ʾelyasaf]. Means "God has added." 1. From the tribe of Gad, Eliasaph, the son of Deuel, or Reuel (Num 1:14; 2:14; 7:42, 47; 10:20), was one of the tribal leaders who assisted Moses in taking a census of the Israelite congregation and led the Gadite offerings in the wilderness (Num 7:42, 47).

2. Eliasaph, the son of Lael, was a Levite who was head of the ancestral house of the Gershonites (Num 3:24).

STEVEN D. MASON

ELIASHIB i-li′uh-shib [אֶלְיָשִׁיב ʾelyashiv; Ἐλιάσιβος Eliasibos]. The name of a number of men in the OT, including: 1. A priest who lived during David's reign and received the eleventh lot (1 Chr 24:12).

2. Elioenai's second son, a descendant of King David through Jeconiah (1 Chr 3:24).

3. The high priest who worked with his brothers on the SHEEP GATE (Neh 3:1), lived near the ANGLE (Neh 3:20-21), and fathered Jehohanan in whose chambers Ezra slept (Ezra 10:6; 1 Esd 9:1). His provision of space in the Temple to Tobiah defiled the Temple (Neh 13:4-30).

4. The head of a priestly family who fathered Joaida (Neh 12:10, 22-23).

Three men who sent away their foreign wives and children:

5. A singer (Ezra 10:24; 1 Esd 9:24).

6. Zattu's son (Ezra 10:27; 1 Esd 9:28).

7. Bani's son (Ezra 10:36; 1 Esd 9:34).

EMILY R. CHENEY

ELIASIS i-li′uh-sis [Ἐλιασείς Eliaseis]. One of Bani's descendants indicted by Ezra's council for marrying foreign women (1 Esd 9:16-44). He does not appear in the parallel text in Ezra 10:34-37.

ELIATHAH i-li′uh-thuh [אֱלִיאָתָה ʾeliʾathah]. One of the sons of Heman, a seer of King David (1 Chr 25:4,

27). Meaning "My God comes" or "You are my God," it has been suggested that Eliathah may be an element of prayer incorporated into the genealogy rather than a proper name. This seems unlikely given that "God gave Heman fourteen sons" (1 Chr 25:5).

PHILLIP MICHAEL SHERMAN

ELIDAD i-li′dad [אֱלִידָד ’elidhadh]. Means "God has loved." A Benjaminite, the son of CHISLON, to whom Yahweh gave responsibility to represent the interests of Benjamin in the allotment of land west of the Jordan (Num 34:21). Overseeing the ten men appointed to divide the land among the Israelite tribes after the conquest were JOSHUA and the priest ELEAZAR (Num 34:17).

MARSHALL D. JOHNSON

ELIEHOENAI i-li′uh-hoh-ee′ni [אֶלְיְהוֹעֵינַי ’elyeho‘enay]. Means "My eyes are toward Yahu."

1. A Temple gatekeeper and last-listed of seven sons of Meshelemiah the Korahite, whose allotted duties would assign Eliehoenai to the East Gate (1 Chr 26:1-3, 12-14).

2. Son of Zerahiah, a descendant of Pahath-moab, and leader of an extended family returning from the exile with Ezra (Ezra 8:4; compare 1 Esd 8:31). Eliehoenai's family is among the largest recounted in Ezra 8:1-14.

JASON C. DYKEHOUSE

ELIEL i-li′uhl [אֱלִיאֵל ’eli’el]. Means "El is my God." 1. A leader within the half-tribe of MANASSEH that settled east of the Jordan (1 Chr 5:24), although other family lists (Num 26:28-34; Josh 17:2ff.) do not mention him.

2. Three of David's MIGHTY MEN (1 Chr 11:46, 47; 12:11), although the Eliel of 12:11 may be one of the two mentioned in 11:46, 47.

3. A member of the cultic musicians known as the Kohathites following the line of Elkanah and Samuel (1 Chr 6:34, possibly the ELIAB of 1 Chr 6:27).

4. Two chiefs of the tribe of Benjamin (1 Chr 8:20, 22).

5. A Levite from Hebron associated with the transfer of the Ark of the Covenant to Jerusalem (1 Chr 15:9, 11).

6. A Levite during the time of HEZEKIAH (2 Chr 31:13). *See* PRIESTS AND LEVITES.

MICHAEL G. VANZANT

ELIENAI el′ee-ee′ni [אֱלִיעֵנַי ’eli‘enay]. One of Shimei's sons whose name appears in a Benjaminite genealogy listing chiefs of clans dwelling in Jerusalem (1 Chr 8:20).

ELIEZAR el′ee-ee′zuhr [Ἐλεάζαρος Eleazaros]. 1. Ezra sent Eliezar and other leaders to find Levites to serve as priests upon the Israelites' return to Jerusalem (1 Esd 8:43).

2. One of the men compelled to put away his wife during Ezra's expulsion of foreign women and children (1 Esd 9:19). It is not clear from the text if the two Eliezars are the same person.

MARIANNE BLICKENSTAFF

ELIEZER el′ee-ee′zuhr [אֱלִיעֶזֶר ’eli‘ezer, Ἐλιέζερ Eliezer]. Means "God is help." 1. Abraham's servant, originally a resident of Damascus. Since Sarah had borne no children, Abraham assumed that Eliezer would become his heir (Gen 15:2). The NRSV translates ben-mesheq (בֶּן־מֶשֶׁק) as "heir" and damesheq (דַּמֶּשֶׁק) as "of Damascus"; but precise translation of 15:2b is difficult. The NRSV translation affirms the wordplay in Hebrew that Abraham had settled for an "heir" (ben-mesheq): his servant Eliezer of "Damascus" (damesheq).

2. Moses and Zipporah's second son. His name "Eliezer" recalled that God had helped Moses and the Israelites by delivering them from Pharaoh's sword (Exod 18:4; 1 Chr 23:15, 17; 26:25).

3. Becher's third son and one of Benjamin's grandsons (1 Chr 7:8).

4. A priest who played the trumpet during the celebration when the ARK OF THE COVENANT was brought to Jerusalem (1 Chr 15:24).

5. The chief officer of the Reubenites and Zichri's son (1 Chr 27:16).

6. A prophet who foretold that Jehoshaphat's ships would be destroyed because he had allied with King Ahaziah (2 Chr 20:37).

7. A Levite priests who had been sent to Iddo (Ezra 8:16).

8. A descendant of Jeshua who sent away his foreign wife according to Ezra's instructions (Ezra 10:18).

9. A Levite who sent away his foreign wife (Ezra 10:23).

10. Harim's descendant who sent away his foreign wife and their children (Ezra 10:31).

11. An ancestor who linked Jesus with David (Luke 3:29).

EMILY R. CHENEY

ELIEZER, RABBI. Rabbi Eliezer ben Yose ha-Galili is the name of a post-destruction leader of the early rabbinic movement. He is generally dated to the generation following the Bar Kokhba Revolt (132–135 CE) and is most famously associated with the articulation of thirty-two rules for the interpretation of Scripture. Rabbinic tradition holds that interpretive rules, or middoth (מִדּוֹת), were first specified by Rabbi Hillel (7 middoth) and subsequently by Rabbi Ishmael (13 middoth). Eliezer provides the most expansive discussion of the rules governing the interpretation of Scripture during the emerging rabbinic period. Modern scholars debate whether these middoth were normative in early rabbinic Judaism or, rather, were later reflection that attempted to codify current interpretive praxis.

PHILLIP MICHAEL SHERMAN

ELIEZER BEN HYRCANUS. A sage, active between 80–120 CE, portrayed as an important conveyer of reliable traditions from his teacher Rabbi Yochanan ben Zakkai. His frequent study partner (and intellectual sparring partner) was Rabbi Yehoshua ben Hannaniah. His closest and most notable student was Rabbi Akiba (*see* AKIVA, RABBI). In a famous dispute, resulting in his expulsion from the House of Study, a voice came out of heaven and affirmed that all his teachings were correct (*b. B. Metz.* 59b). He was tried as a Judeo-Christian because he had liked a teaching he had heard transmitted in Jesus' name (*t. Hul.* 2:24). *See* RABBI, RABBONI.

JUDITH Z. ABRAMS

ELIHOREPH el'uh-hoh'rif [אֱלִיחֹרֶף 'elikhoref]. One of the two sons of Shisha who served as SCRIBE to King SOLOMON (1 Kgs 4:3). The other was AHIJAH. Scribes are listed among the officers of many of the kings, and served as personal secretaries as well as monetary and military record keepers (2 Sam 8:17; 1 Chr 24:6; 2 Kgs 12:10; 25:19).

JESSICA TINKLENBERG DEVEG

ELIHU i-li'hyoo [אֱלִיהוּא 'elihu']. 1. SAMUEL's great-grandfather (1 Sam 1:1), called ELIAB in 1 Chr 6:12 and ELIEL in 1 Chr 6:19.

2. A "chief of the thousands" from Manasseh who joined DAVID during his flight from Saul (1 Chr 12:20).

3. A brother of David (1 Chr 27:18).

4. A Korahite who served as GATEKEEPER (1 Chr 26:7).

5. A man who responds to Job after ELIPHAZ, BILDAD, and ZOPHAR have finished their speeches. The Elihu material in Job 32–37 is generally considered to be a later insertion by an author who felt the three friends had not satisfactorily answered Job's complaint, a conclusion based on the fact that Job does not answer Elihu as he does the others, and Elihu is not among the friends God rebukes at the end of the theophany (Job 42:7-9). Elihu's arguments are similar to those of the three friends. *See* JOB, BOOK OF.

KEVIN A. WILSON

ELIJAH i-li'juh [אֵלִיָּה 'eliyah, אֵלִיָּהוּ 'eliyahu, Ἠλίας Ēlias]. Elijah ("Yahweh is my god" or "Yahweh is my strength") was an agent ("prophet") of Yahweh who lived during the dynasty of OMRI in the 9th cent. BCE and performed awesome and, at times, outrageous deeds. These deeds verified that Elijah spoke for God and so authenticated the main theme of his story: sanction for toppling the Omride dynasty.

A. The Story of Elijah (1 Kgs 17–19; 2 Kgs 1–2)
B. Elijah as a "Prophet"
  1. Names and political roles
  2. Continuing power after death
C. Legitimization of Jehuid Usurpation of Omrides
  1. Composed after Jehu's reign
  2. Structure of the legitimizing narrative
  3. Links to Moses
  4. Two related war accounts
  5. Attack on Omride-Phoenician alliance
D. The Elijah Narrative within the Deuteronomistic History
E. Elijah in Jewish Tradition, the NT, and Islam

A. The Story of Elijah (1 Kgs 17–19; 2 Kgs 1–2)

The story of Elijah begins when he declares a drought. He flees east and camps in an arroyo, fed by ravens and drinking from the stream until it fails. He then goes west to coastal ZAREPHATH, near Tyre, where he stays with a starving widow and her son, who find they have an inexhaustible supply of flour and oil. When the son sickens and dies, Elijah appeals to God and brings him back to life. Before Ahab the king and his people, Elijah arranges a contest between Baal, represented by hundreds of prophets, and Yahweh, represented by Elijah: the god who can ignite a prepared altar will prevail. Baal fails, while Yahweh's fire consumes not only the sacrifice but also the altar's wood, stones, and ground, and even the water with which Elijah has drenched it. Elijah seizes the defeated prophets and puts them to the sword. Taking Ahab to the top of Carmel and declaring the drought over, Elijah sends him home by chariot before the deluge, but is able to outrun the king's chariot and arrive first. Elijah flees JEZEBEL, Ahab's wife and the daughter of the king of Tyre, who is incensed that Elijah killed all her prophets, and after forty days he arrives at Horeb, where at the entrance to a cave he experiences a ferocious wind, earthquake, and fire and then hears Yahweh order him to anoint HAZAEL and JEHU as usurpers of the powerful ruling dynasties of Damascus and Samaria, and ELISHA as his own successor. To denounce the judicial murder of the landowner NABOTH, Elijah confronts Ahab on the way to seize Naboth's vineyard and decrees the death of Ahab and Jezebel and the end of the Omride dynasty. After Ahab's death, Elijah decrees the death of his injured successor, AHAZIAH, for attempting to consult Baal instead of Yahweh about his injury, and with fire from the sky kills two royal squadrons of fifty men each sent to arrest him. In the final episode, Elijah and Elisha together pass from Gilgal to Bethel to Jericho to the Jordan, where Elijah parts the river with his cloak and with Elisha crosses from west to east on dry land (*see* JORDAN RIVER). A fiery chariot and horses descend from the sky and in blustery gusts transport him to the sky, leaving Elisha to carry on as his successor.

B. Elijah as a "Prophet"

1. Names and political roles

Elijah is called a "man of God," a label for a type of spiritual power broker, whose influence included the political realm. Recently the term local hero, aptly borrowed from Greek tradition, was coined for such a personage. Designations for figures that overlapped with "man of God" included "seer," "commissioned" (the original meaning of the word usually translated "prophet"), "aid, messenger" (often translated "angel"), and "herald" (see PROPHET, PROPHECY). Both Elijah and Elisha are portrayed as helpers of the hungry, but it is not clear whether or not Elijah himself was poor; Elijah's interactions are almost entirely with the king of Israel and his court. Interactions between prophet and king, in which the prophet sanctions dynastic succession, the king's wars, judicial policies and actions, and state-affiliated cult shrines, are paradigmatic for the canonical books of the Prophets. All these prophetic roles figure in the Elijah story.

2. Continuing power after death

In ANE literature, typically a hero's power persisted after death. Elijah was the archetype for the hero whose power persists after death in biblical (Mal 4:5) and derived tradition. A hero was also typically venerated at his tomb. Elijah, however, was said to have been taken live to the sky, instead of dying and being buried (contrast Elisha, 2 Kgs 13:20-21), thus making tomb veneration impossible. This end Elijah shared with ENOCH (Gen 5:24; Heb 11:5; Sir 44:16), and both lived on in special roles in scripture-influenced tradition, Enoch as supplier of visions, Elijah as political wonderworker redivivus. Other than Elijah, local heroes play little if any role beyond death in scriptural tradition. The Torah and Prophets tend to disparage or ignore the veneration of departed heroes and their tomb cults, reflecting the concern of ruling courts wary of potential political opposition. The same guardedness is evident in the concept of the solitary prophet with exclusive authority that imbues the books of the canonical Prophets—a concept at odds with the social networks that likely gave support to local heroes—and it is probably reflected also in the dearth of empowering miracle accounts in the canonical Prophets.

C. Legitimization of Jehuid Usurpation of Omrides

That Elijah had no tomb may be a corollary of the synthetic make-up of his story, with its episodes prefiguring Elisha and scenes paralleling Moses laid out in an elaborately calculated literary structure. The story is crafted to legitimize the house of Jehu's usurpation of the house of Omri in 842 BCE, but probably well after the event, in the late 9th cent.

1. Composed after Jehu's reign

The individual episodes place Elijah in the time of the Omrides, but in their present form they echo the story of Elisha, even though Elisha comes after Elijah. The story of Elisha may on the whole be more folkloric than that of Elijah; but scholars now believe that it reflects the political conditions of the late 9th cent. rather than the Omride period. Since the Elijah story is fashioned in terms of the Elisha story, it was probably composed not in the time of Jehu but later, perhaps as part of a Jehuid attempt at revival in the face of Syrian incursions.

2. Structure of the legitimizing narrative

The narrative of Elijah consists of two sets of three major episodes; each of its six episodes divides into three parts. The two sets are structurally symmetrical but address two separate though related issues. The episodes of the first set (1 Kgs 17–19) confirm the exclusive authority of Elijah: he is manifestly a "man of God, and the word of Yahweh from [his] mouth true" (17:24; 18:41, 45), and of the prophets he alone remains (19:10, 14), to be commissioned at Horeb to instigate dynastic change (19:15-17). The episodes of the second set mirror the later fulfillment of Elijah's commission at Horeb, to overthrow the mighty rulers of Syria and Israel by anointing Hazael for Damascus, Jehu for Samaria, and Elisha to activate both. The second three episodes and the Elisha incidents they mirror form a chiasm or ring structure: 1 Kgs 21 goes with 2 Kgs 9–10 ("the dogs shall devour Jezebel"), 2 Kgs 1 with 2 Kgs 8:7-15 ("will I recover from this sickness?"), and 2 Kgs 2:1-18 lies at the center.

3. Links to Moses

Elijah's imitation of MOSES (the earliest clearly datable Mosaic motifs in the Bible) occurs in just two episodes, but these are critical for the narrative as a whole: the commission at Horeb (1 Kgs 19) and the anointing of Elisha that begins the carrying out of the commission (2 Kgs 2:1-18). In legitimating the Jehuid usurpation and its Syrian complement, the writer takes great care to link the dynasty's legitimizing prophet to the original champion of tribal Israel, long after the transformation of political Israel from tribal coalition to monarchy. Tribal tradition, notionally antimonarchic, remained politically vital in the 9th cent. and later, contributing both to the instability of Israelite dynasties and to efforts to bolster them nevertheless. As a monarchic expression of antimonarchic tradition, the narrative of Elijah and Elisha, like much in the Prophets, was designed to appeal to quasi-populist interests.

4. Two related war accounts

The composition of the Jehuid document also includes two stories about war between Samaria and Damascus in Elijah's time, in which Elijah does not appear. The first (1 Kgs 20) features two anonymous prophets, one of whom pronounces the end of the king of Israel. (Elijah pronounces the end of the dynasty in 1 Kgs 21.) The second (1 Kgs 22) features the prophet Micaiah, whose vision of disaster contradicts the unanimous forecast of victory by 400 other court prophets. Micaiah proves right and the king dies. These two stories do not name the king of Israel, but in their present use they imply that he is Ahab. (In the LXX, 1 Kgs 21 follows 1 Kgs 19, leaving chaps. 20 and 22 next to each other.)

5. Attack on Omride-Phoenician alliance

The dynasty of Omri included perhaps the most powerful of the kings of Israel, Ahab heading a successful anti-Assyrian coalition in Syria and Palestine. The Omrides were strengthened through an alliance with Tyre, whose expansion in the Mediterranean resulted in part from the escalating power of Assyria in the Levant (see PHOENECIA). The Omride alliance with TYRE entailed agricultural intensification and commercialization, which exacerbated economic and social stresses on the Israelite peasantry (see ISRAEL, SOCIAL AND ECONOMIC DEVELOPMENT), as reflected in the stories of Elijah and especially Elisha. The alliance also brought the cult of Baal of Tyre to Samaria. Baal stood for the alliance and its benefits for the few and burdens for the many. Elijah's scorn for Baal and Jehu's climactic obliteration of the cult of Baal (1 Kgs 19:18; 2 Kgs 10:18-28) represent attacks on the agricultural and social consequences of the alliance.

D. The Elijah Narrative within the Deuteronomistic History

The narrative of Elijah and Elisha (1 Kgs 17–2 Kgs 10) forms a mostly coherent block within the larger DEUTERONOMISTIC HISTORY, the house of David's ongoing account of its legitimization. The Deuteronomistic History formed gradually during nearly the entire period of the house of David's rule, mainly through the intermittent updating of its core account of David's usurpation of the house of Saul (roughly 1 Sam 15–2 Sam 6). The Jehuid narrative of Elijah and Elisha, which addressed a political issue—sovereignty over Israel—that was outside the scope of Davidic sovereignty, probably became a part of the Davidic history following the fall of Samaria, during the reign of Hezekiah, who wanted not only to recover the erstwhile dominion of political Israel but also to play the same dominant role in the region that the house of Omri had a century and a half earlier (see DAVID). Additions to the Elijah narrative for a probable pre-exilic edition of the Deuteronomistic History include 1 Kgs 22:37-53 and 2 Kgs 1:17-18, and additions to an exilic edition include 1 Kgs 21:27-29, highlighting repentance, an exilic deuteronomistic emphasis. The aptness of the Davidic appropriation of the block narrative is not obvious, since originally it probably negated Davidic sovereignty: Elijah's twelve-stone altar and Elisha's twelve yoke of oxen presumably

stood for the long-standing twelve-tribe concept of Israel including Judah, under the sovereignty of the king of Israel, not the house of David in Jerusalem (see ISRAEL, HISTORY OF; TRIBE).

E. Elijah in Jewish Tradition, the NT, and Islam

In the Manual of Discipline from Qumran (see DEAD SEA SCROLLS) and in Mishnaic tradition, Elijah figures as the harbinger of the coming messiah (see MESSIAH, JEWISH). In the Gospels, Jesus performs acts of power ("miracles") akin to those of Elijah and Elisha, so that some thought he was Elijah (Matt 11:14; 16:14; Mark 6:15; Luke 9:8; John 1:21). In the transfiguration stories, Elijah and Moses appear with Jesus (Matt 17:3-4; Mark 9:4-5; Luke 9:30-33). John the Baptist was said to have the spirit of Elijah (Luke 1:17). Elijah plays a significant narrative role throughout the Gospel of Mark (Mark 6:15; 8:28; 9:4-13; 15:35-36). In Luke, Jesus begins his public career as God's anointed by noting that prophets receive no welcome at home and that like Elijah and Elisha his mission will take him beyond the bounds of Israel (Luke 4:16-30; see also Luke 9:8, 19). Elijah is one of the line of prophets referred to in the Quran as precursors of Muhammad.

Bibliography: Thomas L. Brodie. *The Crucial Bridge: The Elijah-Elisha Narrative As an Interpretive Synthesis of Genesis–Kings and a Literary Model of the Gospels* (2000); Walter Brueggeman. *Testimony to Otherwise: The Witness of Elijah and Elisha* (2001); Robert B. Coote, ed. *Elijah and Elisha in Socioliterary Perspective* (1992); Marsha C. White. *The Elijah Legends and Jehu's Coup* (1997).

ROBERT B. COOTE

2. A descendant of BENJAMIN in 1 Chr 8:27. He is listed as a son of JEROHAM, but there is no indication of how Jeroham is descended from Benjamin. The genealogy in this section contains a number of family groupings assigned to Benjamin, but their relation to each other is unclear.

3. A priest in the line of HARIM in the postexilic period (Ezra 10:21). He is listed among those who took foreign wives, a practice decried by Ezra (Ezra 10:1-5). The first group of priests mentioned, the descendants of JESHUA, pledge to send away their wives and make a guilt offering. Although the text does not specifically repeat the fact that each group of priests had sent away their wives, Ezra 10:5 would suggest they did divorce the foreign women.

4. A non-priestly member of the postexilic community who had taken a foreign wife (Ezra 10:26).

KEVIN A. WILSON

ELIJAH, APOCALYPSE OF. An anonymous work known in two forms, a Coptic version (1 Elijah) and a later Rabbinic Hebrew edition (2 Elijah), different in

Figure 1: Elijah on Mount Carmel. Fresco. Ca. 239 CE. Location: Synagogue, Dura Europos, Syria.

content. First Elijah mentions Elijah twice and is, in its current form, a Christian apocalypse, likely written in the 3rd cent. CE. Most scholars believe, however, that it is based upon an earlier Jewish work now lost. It includes exhortations about fasting and prayer, an apocalyptic timetable for rulers until the ANTICHRIST, information on the Antichrist and a description of the millennial kingdom. The original Jewish work behind the Apocalypse of Elijah was referred to by Origen and the *Apostolic Constitutions*. Origen and later ecclesiastical writers thought Paul quoted this work in 1 Cor 2:9. Second Elijah, containing a vision of the Antichrist and of postmortem punishment for sin, says it was given by Michael to Elijah on Mount Carmel. *See* APOCALYPSE.

KENNETH D. LITWAK

ELIKA i-li′kuh [אֱלִיקָא ʾeliqaʾ]. Elika of Harod is one of David's "Mighty Men" (2 Sam 23:25), but his name is absent from Greek manuscripts and 1 Chr 27.

ELIM ee′lim [אֵילִם ʾelim]. A site on the exodus journey (Exod 15:27; 16:1; Num 33:9-10), Elim is, apparently, an oasis, located near or on the shore of Yam Suf (NRSV "Red Sea"). The texts describe the oasis as being particularly verdant, providing seventy palm trees and

water for twelve springs, and only a few stops short of Mount Sinai. If the exodus route was from Egypt into the southern Sinai, Elim may be on, or near, the eastern shore of the Gulf of Suez. On the other hand, if Yam Suf is the Gulf of Elath, Elim would be located in the eastern Sinai, fairly close to Mount Sinai.

MICHAEL D. OBLATH

ELIMELECH i-lim′uh-lek [אֱלִימֶלֶךְ ʾelimelekh]. Husband of Naomi and father of two sons, Mahlon and Chilion (Ruth 1:2). Elimelech's death leaves Naomi and her daughter-in-law RUTH to return to his homeland and family for protection (Ruth 1:22). Boaz, one of Elimelech's kin, marries Ruth (Ruth 4:1-13).

ELIOENAI el′ee-oh-ee′ni [אֶלְיוֹעֵינַי ʾelyoʿenay; Ἐλιωναίς Eliōnais]. Name designating six men. 1. Neariah's son, living after the exile and descending from David through Jehoiakim (1 Chr 3:23-24).

2. Leader of a clan whose members increased in numbers; settled near Gedor during Hezekiah's reign after conquering the inhabitants; and descended from Simeon, Jacob's second son borne by Leah (1 Chr 4:36).

3. One of Becher's sons who was a family head, a warrior, and a descendant of Benjamin, Jacob's second

son borne by Rachel (1 Chr 7:8). His name suggests a date for the genealogy during Hezekiah's reign.

4. Priest who descended from Pashhur and dismissed his foreign wife according to Ezra's instructions (Ezra 10:22; 1 Esd 9:22).

5. Descendant of Zattu who dismissed his foreign wife and their children (Ezra 10:27), but named Eliadas in 1 Esd 9:28.

6. Postexilic priest who played the trumpet for dedicating the Jerusalem wall (Neh 12:41).

EMILY R. CHENEY

ELIONAS el′ee-oh′nuhs [Ἐλιωνᾶς *Eliōnas*]. A descendant of Anan and a family head whose descendants sent away their foreign wives according to Ezra's instructions (1 Esd 9:32), although this name in the par. list in Ezra 10:31 is ELIEZER. Some modern translations, such as the NEB, also translate the name of the priest who was a descendant of Pashur in 1 Esd 9:22 as Elionas. He, too, sent away his foreign wife as Ezra instructed him. This name is spelled ELIOENAI in a par. list in Ezra 10:22, and thus the NRSV's use of Elioenai in 1 Esd 9:22.

EMILY R. CHENEY

ELIPHAL i-li′ fuhl [אֱלִיפָל *'elifal*]. Son of Ur and one of David's warriors (1 Chr 11:35). In the parallel text in 1 Sam 23:23-39, where these warriors are known as "The Thirty," his name is ELIPHELET, and he is identified as Ahasbai's son from the town of Maacah (v. 34). The unknown term MECHERATHITE in 1 Chr 11:36 has been conjectured as the Chronicler's faulty reading for Maacah in 1 Sam 23:34, and the words "Ur Hepher" in 1 Chr 11:35-36, for "Ahasbai" in 1 Sam 23:34.

EMILY R. CHENEY

ELIPHAZ el′i-faz [אֱלִיפַז *'elifaz*]. 1. The firstborn son of ADAH and Esau, who was father of several clans in Edom (Gen 36:4, 10). Genesis 36:12 lists Eliphaz as the father of Amalek, the eponymous ancestor of the Amalekites.

2. One of Job's three friends who argue with him concerning the reasons for his suffering and whether God is just. Eliphaz is always listed first among the three friends, is the first to speak to Job in each of the three cycles (Job 4, 15, and 22), and is the only one of the three friends whom God addresses directly (Job 42:7). He is called Eliphaz the Temanite, which connects him with the area of Edom. TEMAN was one of the clans in Edom descended from Eliphaz (1), the son of Esau (Gen 36:15-16). *See* JOB, BOOK OF.

KEVIN A. WILSON

ELIPHELEHU i-lif′uh-lee′hy*oo* [אֱלִיפְלֵהוּ *'elifelehu*]. One of the Levites of second rank installed as singers by the Levite officers under David's order when David was about to undertake his second attempt to bring the Ark of the Covenant to Jerusalem (1 Chr 15:18). His assigned instrument was the lyre (1 Chr 15:21). This list may be a later addition, and Eliphelehu is absent from the corresponding list in 1 Chr 16:5-6.

DEREK E. WITTMAN

ELIPHELET i-lif′uh-let [אֱל יְפֶלֶט *'elifelet*, אֶל יִפָּלֵט *'elifalet*; Ἐλιφάλατος *Eliphalatos*]. 1. David's son born in Jerusalem by an unnamed concubine or wife (2 Sam 5:16; 1 Chr 3:6; 2 Chr 14:7). The name repeated in 1 Chr 3:8 probably resulted from dittography.

2. Ahasbai's son, one of David's warriors called the Thirty (2 Sam 23:34).

3. Eshek's third son who descended from Saul and Jonathan, both descendants of Benjamin (1 Chr 8:39).

4. A descendant of Adonikam who camped near Ahara (Ezra 8:13; see 1 Esd 8:39-41 where the place differs).

5. One of Hashum's descendants who sent away his foreign wife and their children (Ezra 10:33; see 1 Esd 9:33 where the father is Asom).

EMILY R. CHENEY

ELISHA i-li′shuh [אֱל יָשָׁע *'elisha'*; Ἐλισαῖος *Elisaios*]. Elisha was a legendary wonderworker of the 9th cent. BCE (1 Kgs 19:16-21; 2 Kgs 2:1–10:27; 13:14-21). When such local heroes have had regional significance, as Elisha did, they often have come in pairs, one succeeding the other. Thus Elisha succeeded Elijah, and their stories in the Bible were shaped together, to support Jehu's usurpation of the Omride dynasty and founding of the longest-lasting dynasty in Israel, the house of Jehu or Nimshi (2 Kgs 9:2; *see* ELIJAH). As with Elijah, most of the tales about Elisha show him dealing with either kings or indigent folk; two linked episodes involve a well-regarded woman of Shunem, and her tale too begins and ends with reference to the king (2 Kgs 4:8-37; 8:1-6). Elisha was an Israelite, but his dealings with kings went well beyond political Israel to include Moab, Edom, and Syria.

Although the stories of Elijah and Elisha were shaped together, they show significant differences. Yahweh's conflict with Baal plays a major role in the story of Elijah, but none at all in the story of Elisha until the last scene of Jehu's coup, in which Elisha no longer appears. Resonances with the tradition of Moses play an important role in the story of Elijah; in the story of Elisha there may be only one case, 2 Kgs 4:42-44. The second half of the Elijah story appears to be based in part on the Elisha story; the Elisha story shows no comparable dependence on the Elijah story.

In a few places, Deuteronomistic writers have inserted annalistic details and rationales into the Elisha narrative (2 Kgs 3:1-3; 8:16-27; 9:29; 10:28-36; *see* DEUTERONOMISTIC HISTORY). These apart, the narrative consists of fifteen discrete episodes, which fall into two types, short and long. Most episodes of the short type tell about Elisha's miraculous relief of the poor: Elisha makes water from a spring usable by throwing salt into it; he tells a widow to use her last bit of oil to fill jar after jar with oil until she can pay her debts and save her sons from becoming debt slaves; he turns a toxic stew edible by throwing in some flour; he feeds one hundred men with only twenty barley rolls, with leftovers; he recovers a borrowed ax head from the Jordan River by throwing in a stick after it. The tales of this first type cluster mostly in the first half of the narrative. They convey the powers of Elisha that helped give him fame. These include healing, resuscitation, feeding the hungry, alleviating debt, enabling the childless to bear, and clairvoyance, and the advantage of having his prayers heard by Yahweh.

Perhaps Elisha's greatest power, and the one that plays the main role in the narrative, is his power over kings, marked by his impunity and invincibility vis-à-vis royalty and his ability to call on the supra-military force of Yahweh's chariots of fire. Indeed in the final tale—lying outside the Elijah–Elisha narrative per se—King Joash of Israel, Jehu's grandson and third-generation successor, sees the chariots of fire and calls Elisha "father," i.e., master, just as Elisha had called his master Elijah "father" (2 Kgs 2:11-12; 13:14; compare 5:13 and the expression "the sons of the prophets," 2 Kgs 2:3, etc.). The emphasis on Elisha's power over kings is fitting for a story whose purpose was to legitimate the Jehuid overthrow of the Omrides, and it is conveyed through the second, or long, type of episode. This long type dominates the narrative. There are eight such episodes, including the opening tale of succession from Elijah to Elisha, the basis for the instigation of Jehu's coup. Following this opening, the remaining seven long episodes all feature kings, and six of these (excluding the tale of the woman of Shunem) involve or imply a war or battle. (To judge from comparative evidence, "prophetic" figures often had a military aspect, as exemplified by Elijah and Elisha; the incidence of prophetic militarism in ancient Palestine may be masked in the Bible by the prevailing icon of the defenseless prophet.)

The development of these six war episodes serves the theme of the overall narrative. The first and last episodes portray the alliance of Samaria and Jerusalem, against Moab (2 Kgs 3:1-27) and then against Aram (8:28–10:27), making the allies together a target for Jehu's effort to reunite the "twelve tribes" of Israel under his rule and in alliance with, not opposition to, Damascus. The middle four episodes show a clear progression, from a background of Aramean raids and the latent Aramean humiliation of the king of Israel (5:1-27), to greater and more numerous Aramean incursions (6:8-23), to the Aramean siege of Samaria itself (6:24–7:20), to the seeming solution to the growing problem, the assassination of the Aramean king (8:7-15). In the first five of these six long episodes, Elisha appears to rescue the king of Israel from harm. The point, however, is not Elisha's solicitude for Joram, whose overthrow at Elisha's hands was fated in the commission of Elijah and Elijah's denunciation of the house of Omri, but

Elisha's power, inherited from Elijah, to make and break kings, like earlier prophets, and not just in Israel.

The narrative of Elisha in its present form locates practically all of his activity in the reign of the last Omride king, Joram, as befits the purpose of explaining his overthrow. But it has long been recognized that the Aramean invasion of Israel that pervades the narrative is more likely to reflect the political conditions of the late 9th cent., years after Jehu's coup, when Damascus reached a pinnacle of power, than the mid 9th cent., before the coup. Recently it has been plausibly suggested that the purpose of the Elijah–Elisha narrative as later Nimshid apologia, composed perhaps under Joash, was not simply to justify Jehu's revolt, but also to head off subsequent Israelite disgruntlement over the failure of Jehu's strategy of joining forces with Hazael to fend off Hamath to the north.

The tales of Elisha influenced the composition of stories about Jesus in the Gospels. An important example is the development of the feeding story in 2 Kgs 4:42-44, in which the motif of excess, already derived perhaps from the story of manna in Exod 16, receives elaborate treatment in the Gospels, each in its own way. It has been argued that the influence of the Elijah–Elisha narrative goes well beyond such individual motifs.

Bibliography: Thomas L. Brodie. *The Crucial Bridge: The Elijah–Elisha Narrative As an Interpretive Synthesis of Genesis–Kings and a Literary Model of the Gospels* (2000); Walter Brueggemann. *Testimony to Otherwise: The Witness of Elijah and Elisha* (2001); Robert B. Coote, ed. *Elijah and Elisha in Socioliterary Perspective* (1992).

ROBERT B. COOTE

ELISHAH i-li′shuh [אֱלִישָׁה ʾelishah]. The name Elishah is found in the Table of Nations list as a descendant of Japtheth (Gen 10:4) and elsewhere as the son of Javan (1 Chr 1:7).

The place Elishah is referred to as a source for acquiring purple dyes (Ezek 27:7). Residents of TYRE are mentioned as exporters of the dye from the "isles" (KJV) or "coasts" (NIV; NRSV) of Elishah (Ezek 27:7). The island/coastal reference may describe a section of Cyprus, though distinct from the KITTIM (Cyprus) of Ezek 27:6. Cuneiform inscriptions from Ugarit, Mari, Alalakh, Tel el-Amarna, and Khattushash note a place named Alashia. These inscriptions, dated to the 18th through 13th cent. BCE, lead many to connect Alashia with OT Elishah.

MICHAEL G. VANZANT

ELISHAMA i-lish′uh-muh [אֱלִישָׁמָע ʾelishamaʿ]. 1. Ammihud's son and an Ephraimite chief whose tribe camped on the west side of the tent of meeting (Num 1:10; 2:18; 10:22; 1 Chr 7:26).

2. One of David's sons born in Jerusalem (2 Sam 5:16; 1 Chr 3:6, 8; 14:7).

3. Jehoiakim's chief adviser who kept Jeremiah's scroll in his chamber (Jer 36:12, 20-21).

4. Ishmael's grandfather and a part of the royal family (2 Kgs 25:25; Jer 41:1).

5. Jekamiah's son and a descendant of Judah (1 Chr 2:41).

6. A priest who taught the people of Judah the Book of the Law (2 Chr 17:8).

EMILY R. CHENEY

ELISHAPHAT i-lish′uh-fat אֱלִישָׁפָט ʾelishafat]. One of five commanders who conspired with the priest JEHOIADA against ATHALIAH attempting to return Davidic kingship under JOASH (2 Chr 23:1).

ELISHEBA i-lish′uh-buh אֱלִישֶׁבַע ʾelishevaʿ; Ἐλισάβεθ Elisabeth]. Aaron's wife, with whom she has four sons (Exod 6:23). Elisheba was the sister of Nahshon and daughter of Amminadab, the ancestral head of Judah whose name appears in Num 2:3. In Greek her name is the same as ELIZABETH, the mother of John the Baptist.

JESSICA TINKLENBERG DEVEGA

ELISHUA el′uh-shoo′uh אֱלִישׁוּעַ ʾelishuʿa]. One of David's children born in Jerusalem (2 Sam 5:15; 1 Chr 14:5). The name means "God is salvation."

ELIUD i-li′uhd [Ἐλιούδ Elioud]. Mentioned in Matthew's Jesus genealogy (Matt 1:14-15), son of Achim and father of Eleazar.

ELIZABETH i-liz′uh-buhth [Ἐλισάβετ Elisabet]. According to the first chapter of Luke, Elizabeth was the wife of the priest ZECHARIAH and the mother of JOHN the Baptist.

The Lukan narrator initially describes her as righteous before God and blameless in following God's commandments, but she is childless and beyond child-bearing years (1:6-7). Elizabeth's story parallels the stories of childless women in the OT who, after disappointment, become the mothers of outstanding figures in biblical history. Elizabeth's story especially resembles Sarah's (see Gen 17:15-22; 18:9-15; 21:1-7) because they are both advanced in years and in both cases there is a divine announcement of the birth before the child is conceived.

As wonderful as Elizabeth's conception is, her role when she sees her relative Mary (Luke 1:36) is that of a prophetess. Elizabeth is the person who first understands and celebrates Mary's secret. Immediately following Mary's greeting, Elizabeth is filled with the Holy Spirit and speaks with prophetic insight (1:41-45). She praises Mary, blessing her because of her child (1:42) and because she responded with faith to the angel's message (1:45). In spite of the focus on Mary, the scene presents us with not one, but two, extraordinary women. With only the leaping of the child in Elizabeth's womb as a prompt, she recognizes that Mary is "the mother of my Lord" (1:43), i.e., the mother of the Messiah (see 2:11). Her prophetic power parallels that of Simeon, who later recognizes Jesus in the Temple (2:25-35). Elizabeth's words confirm for Mary what the angel told her, and Mary breaks out in a song of praise.

Elizabeth's insight and joy contrast with her husband's response when the angel tells Zechariah of John's coming birth. There is no hesitation in Elizabeth's response to Mary, but Zechariah is made mute as a rebuke for his unbelief (1:20). Furthermore, it is through Elizabeth's courage in opposing her relatives and neighbors that her son receives the name John, as directed by the angel (1:57-63). *See* MARY.

Bibliography: Raymond E. Brown. *The Birth of the Messiah* (1993).

ROBERT C. TANNEHILL

ELIZAPHAN el′uh-zay′fan אֱלִיצָפָן ʾelitsafan, אֱלְצָפָן ʾeletsafan]. 1. Uzziel's son, a Levite, and head of the Kohathite clan who had sanctuary duties and camped on the southern side of the tabernacle (Num 3:30). His son Shemaiah, along with his kinsman, carried the ARK OF THE COVENANT to Jerusalem (1 Chr 15:8) and cleansed the Temple under Hezekiah's reign (2 Chr 29:13). His name is Elzaphan in Exod 6:22 and Lev 10:4.

2. The son of Parnach and chief of the Zebulunite tribe (Num 34:25-29), whom the Lord told Moses to choose to divide the land among his tribe (NRSV, Elizaphan).

EMILY R. CHENEY

ELIZUR i-li′zuhr אֱלִיצוּר ʾelitsur]. Means "God is a rock" or "God is my rock." This Reubenite chief or PRINCE (Num 2:10) engages in military activities such as counting the people or leading large movements of people (Num 1:5; 10:18) and presents offerings at the Tabernacle on behalf of his tribe (Num 7:30, 35).

PHILLIP MICHAEL SHERMAN

EL-JARBA, EIN. *See* JARBA, ʿEIN EL.

EL-JIB. *See* JIB, EL.

ELKANAH el-kay′nuh אֱלְקָנָה ʾelqanah]. 1. Jeroham's son, an Ephraimite from Ramah in 1 Sam 1:1 but a Levite in 1 Chr 6:27, 34, with two wives: Hannah who bore him the prophet Samuel, and Peninnah who bore him several children (1 Sam 1:2, 20).

2. A Levite descended from Kohath: son of Assir (1 Chr 6:23).

3. Another Kohathite Levite, the son of Ahimoth (1 Chr 6:26).

4. Kohar's second son, descended from Levi through Kohath (Exod 6:24).

5. Two ancestors of Elkanah, father of Samuel, with the same name (1 Chr 6:35, 36).

6. A Levite who was Asa's father and lived in a Netophathite village (1 Chr 9:16).

7. A warrior among the Thirty (1 Chr 12:6).

8. A Levite, a gatekeeper for the ark of the covenant (1 Chr 15:23).

9. King Ahaz's chief minister whom Zichri killed (2 Chr 28:7). *See* PRIESTS AND LEVITES.

EMILY R. CHENEY

EL-KHALIL, RAMAT. *See* KHALIL, RAMAT EL.

EL-KHELEIFEH, TELL. *See* KHELEIFEH, TELL EL.

ELKIAH el-ki′uh [Ἐλκια Elkia]. In the genealogy of the book of Judith, Elkiah is listed as the great-great-grandfather to Merari, Judith's father (Jdt 8:1).

EL-KOM, KHIRBET. *See* QOM, KHIRBET EL.

ELKOSH el′kosh [אֶלְקֹשִׁי ʾeleqoshi]. Although other explanations have been offered, the Nah 1:1 expression, "Nahum, the Elkoshite," suggests that Elkosh was the birthplace of Nahum, the OT prophet. Two factors confront the reader regarding the gentilic "Elkoshite." First, Nah 1:1 is the only reference in the canon—including the Apocrypha—to Elkosh; second, the location of Elkosh is not known with any certainty. Multiple suggestions have been advanced, but four emerge as the most commonly encountered: 1) Al-Kush, a village about 25 mi. north of Mosul in present-day Iraq—an old Turkish tradition, based mainly on similarity of name and an apparent familiarity with Assyria reflected in the book; 2) Elcesi, a village in Galilee, a view promoted by Eusebius in his *Onomasticon*, and Jerome after him, in his commentary on Nahum; 3) Capernaum, on the northern shore of the Sea of Galilee, based on the proposal that "Capernaum" comes from Hebrew kefar nakhum (כְּפַר נָחוּם)—"village of Nahum"; 4) A Judaean location near Beit Jibrin (Betogabris–Eleutheropolis) west, southwest of Jerusalem; a view that dates as early as the mid 4th cent. CE to the time of Epiphanius of Salamis, who was born in Elueutheropolis. The Byzantine, era monk, Hesychius of Sinai, also promoted the Judean setting as the locus of Nahum's home. While none of these proposals is without its problems, the fourth view both appears to be the most viable option from a number of perspectives—but primarily, internal indicators—and enjoys widespread support.

JOHN I. LAWLOR

ELLASAR el′uh-sahr [אֶלָּסָר ʾellasar]. The territory ruled by ARIOCH, one of the four kings against whom the rulers of Sodom and Gomorrah revolt (only in Gen 14:1, 9). Numerous attempts have been made to associate the location and its ruler with a known ANE referent.

EL-LEJJUN, WADI. *See* LEJJUN, WADI EL.

ELMADAM el-may′duhm [Ἐλμαδάμ Elmadam]. Elmadam links Joseph, "adoptive" father of Jesus, to Adam (Luke 3:28), although Elmadam is not found in other biblical documentation, including Matthew.

EL-MARJAMEH, KHIRBET. *See* MARJAMEH, KHIRBET EL.

EL-MASKHUTA, TELL. *See* MASKHUTA, TELL EL.

EL-MAZAR, TELL. *See* MAZAR, TELL EL.

EL-MESHASH, KHIRBET. *See* MESHASH, KHIRBET.

EL-MILH, TELL. *See* MALHATA, TEL.

ELNAAM el-nay′uhm [אֶלְנָעַם ʾelnaʿam]. Means "God is pleasantness." Father of Jeribai and Joshaviah (1 Chr 11:46), two of David's sixteen heroes whom the Chronicler lists beyond David's "Thirty" (2 Sam 23:24-39).

ELNATHAN el-nay′thuhn [אֶלְנָתָן ʾelnathan; Ἐλλαναθάν Ellanathan]. Means "God has given." 1. Elnathan was the father of Neshushta and grandfather of her son Jehoiachin (2 Kgs 24:8).

2. Possibly the same as the Elnathan in 2 Kings, an Elnathan was involved in two important incidents during the time of JEREMIAH. He was present at Baruch's reading of Jeremiah's scroll to JEHOIAKIM (Jer 36:12). He also led a group to Egypt to extract the prophet Uriah and then violently killed him by order of Jehoiakim (Jer 26:22-23). The third ostracon from LACHISH says, "The commander of the army, Coniah son of Elnathan, has come in order to enter Egypt." Still, a positive relationship between the two is impossible.

3. The exilic return in Ezra reveals two "chiefs" and one "teacher" (person with insight) named Elnathan returning to Jerusalem from the river Ahava (Ezra 8:16). One of these may be a textual corruption (see 1 Esd 8:44 where only two are mentioned).

MICHAEL G. VANZANT

ELOAH i-loh′uh [אֱלוֹהַּ ʾeloah]. Translated "God," it is a cognate to Arabic "Allah" and occurs fifty-seven times in the Bible, mostly in late texts (forty-one in Job). The Aram. form ʾellah (אֱלָהּ) is attested ninety-six times in Aram. portions of the Bible, thus perhaps the Hebrew was derived from Aramaic. *See* GOD, NAMES OF.

C. L. SEOW

ELOHE. *See* EL; ELOHIM; GOD, NAMES OF.

ELOHIM el′oh-him [אֱלֹהִים ʾelohim]. The most common Hebrew term for "God/god," as a plural form it may also be used for "gods," hence also idols. *See* GOD, NAMES OF.

ELOHIST, ELOHISTIC. *See* E, ELOHIST.

ELOI ee'loh-*i* [Ἐλωι Elōi, ἠλι ēli]. From Hebrew ʾeli (אֵלִי) "my God." Jesus' cry from the cross, "My God, my God, why have you forsaken (abandoned) me?" (Matt 27:46; Mark 15:34) quotes Ps 22:1 in Aram., transliterated into Gk.: Elōi elōi lema sabachthani (Ἐλωι ἐλωι λεμα σαβαχθανι). *See* ELI, ELI, LEMA SABACHTHANI; GOD, NAMES OF.

MARIANNE BLICKENSTAFF

ELON ee'lon [אֵלוֹן ʾelon, אֵילוֹן ʾelon]. Literally meaning "terebinth" (oak). 1. The Hittite (or Hivite, LXX[A]) father of one of Esau's wives (Gen 26:34, although the name of the daughter is different in 36:2). Esau is depicted as the father of the Edomites whose genealogical traditions may be responsible for the differing names.

2. A son of Zebulun in the Genesis list (46:14; Num 26:26).

3. An Israelite judge from Zebulun who led for ten years before his burial at AIJALON (Judg 12:11-12). Elon and Aijalon are spelled similarly in Hebrew and the story may explain the origin of the city's name (etiology).

4. A town in the tribal territory of Dan near Timnah, currently unidentified (Josh 19:43). Possible locations include ʿAlein, which is west of Beit Mahsir, or Khirbet Wadi ʿAlin, located between Deir Aban and ʿAin Shems.

MICHAEL G. VANZANT

ELON-BETH-HANAN ee'luhn-beth-hay'nuhn [אֵילוֹן בֵּית חָנָן ʾelon beth khanan]. A city in Solomon's second administrative region (1 Kgs 4:9); the district corresponds approximately to the traditional allotment given to the tribe of Dan (Josh 19:40-48). Two cities within this tribal territory have been identified as possible candidates for Elon-Beth-Hanan: ELON or AIJALON.

JASON TATLOCK

ELON-BEZAANANNIM ee'luhn-buh-zay'uh-na'nim [אֵלוֹן בְּצַעֲנַּים ʾelon betsaʿannayim]. Means "Oak in Zaanannim." An oak located near Kedesh where the Kenites camped (Judg 4:11).

ELON-MEONENIM ee'luhn-mee-on'uh-nim [אֵלוֹן מְעוֹנְנִים ʾelon meʿonenim]. Means "DIVINER'S OAK." A tree near Shechem associated with divination (Judg 9:37). Some have equated it with the tree of v. 9.

ELOTH ee'loth [אֵילוֹת ʾeloth]. Variant of Elath. *See* ELATH, ELOTH.

ELPAAL el-pay'uhl [אֶלְפָּעַל ʾelpaʿal]. One of the two sons of Shaharaim by Hushim in Moab (1 Chr 8:11), listed among the descendants of Benjamin.

EL-PARAN el-pay'ruhn [אֵיל פָּארָן ʾel paʾran]. A Horite city that marked the southern extent of the Elamite king CHEDORLAOMER's campaign (Gen 14:6). El-paran's identification is unclear. It may be a place west of Kadesh, or it could be another name for Elath, on the Gulf of Aqaba. *See* PARAN.

RALPH K. HAWKINS

ELPELET el-pee'lit [אֶלְפֶּלֶט ʾelpelet; Ἐλιφάλετ Eliphalet]. Variant of ELIPHELET (1 Chr 14:5).

EL-QEDAH, TELL. *See* HAZOR.

EL-QOM, KHIRBET. *See* QOM, KHIRBET EL.

EL-QUBEIBEH. A modern village that is perhaps the location of the NT EMMAUS (Luke 24:13), El-Qubeibeh is located due west of Nebi Samwil and 7 mi. northwest of Jerusalem. Amwas, Abu Ghosh, and Qaloniyeh have also been proposed as the location of Emmaus.

RALPH K. HAWKINS

EL-ROI [אֵל רֳאִי ʾel roʾi]. Means "God of seeing." The name by which HAGAR identifies the divine presence in an angel (Gen 16:13). Part of an etiology explaining the name of a well, "El-roi" also connotes Hagar's surprise at experiencing benevolent attention rather than death in her divine encounter (vv. 13-14).

JASON C. DYKEHOUSE

ELTEKEH el'tuh-kuh [אֶלְתְּקֵה ʾelteqeh, אֶלְתְּקֵא ʾelteqeʾ]. A city within the original tribal area of DAN in the coastal region (Josh 19:44). Dan lost this land during the period of the judges and was forced to move to the north (Judg 1:34). The city was assigned to the Kohathites as a Levitical city (Josh 21:23). Eltekeh is also mentioned in the *Annals of Sennacherib* as the place where SENNACHERIB defeated an Egyptian force during his campaign in 701 BCE. Eltekeh has tenuously been identified with Tell esh-Shalaf, although this site is probably located too far to the south to be a viable candidate. *See* DAN, DANITES.

KEVIN A. WILSON

ELTEKON el'tuh-kon [אֶלְתְּקֹן ʾelteqon]. A town in the hill country belonging to the tribe of Judah in Josh 15:59, its only appearance in the Bible.

ELTOLAD el-toh'lad [אֶלְתּוֹלַד ʾeltoladh]. Eltolad is contained in a list of settlements of the tribe of Simeon (Josh 15:30), but also in a list of Judahite settlements (Josh 19:4).

EL-TWEIN, KHIRBET ABU. *See* TWEIN, KHIRBET ABU EL.

ELUL ee'luhl [אֱלוּל ʾelul; Ἐλούλ Eloul]. The sixth month of the Israelite religious CALENDAR (August–

September), characterized by high temperatures and no rain (Neh 6:15; 1 Macc 14:27).

EL-UMEIRI, TELL. *See* ʿUMAYRI, TALL AL.

ELUSA [Ἔλουσα Elousa]. A city in the Negev located about 20 km (12.4 mi.) southwest of Beersheba (M.R. 117056), Elusa appears to have been one of the earliest road stations founded by the NABATEANS along the trade route from Arabia to Gaza in the 3rd cent. BCE. In the 2nd–3rd cent. CE, it became one of the most important cities of the Provincia Arabia and, later, of the Palaestina Tertia. The site was abandoned by 800 CE.

RALPH K. HAWKINS

ELUZAI i-loo′zi אֶלְעוּזַי ʾelʿuzay]. Means "God is my strength." A Benjaminite warrior who abandoned Saul to join DAVID at ZIKLAG (1 Chr 12:5 [Heb. 12:6]).

ELYMAIS el′uh-may′uhs [Ἐλυμαΐς Elymais]. Elymais (one way to render the Hebrew place name Elam [*see* ELAM, ELAMITES] in Greek) was an ancient province or region in southwestern Persia (corresponding with the modern Iranian province of Khuzistan). The boundaries and relative autonomy of the region varied at different times. Ancient historians such as Strabo (2.13.6; 15.3.12; 16.1.17), Livy (37.40), and Diodorus Siculus (28.3; 29.15) describe Elymais as a hilly country, whose archers, other warriors, and residents were frequently engaged with or dominated by other Mesopotamian powers. Several OT passages suggest that the region was inhabited by descendants of Elam, son of Shem, son of Noah (Gen 10:22; see also Josephus, *Ant.* 1.143). Several later LXX texts refer in passing to Elymais (Tob 2:10; Jdt 1:6), and Dan 8:2 cites SUSA as its chief city. Elymais is called a city rather than a region in 1 Macc 6:1 (see also Josephus, *Ant.* 12.354), but scholars suggest the original text may here have read "in Elymais in Persia there was a city" rather than "Elymais in Persia was a city." Polybius (21.11) claimed that the Seleucid ruler ANTIOCHUS IV died as a result of his unsuccessful attempt to destroy a temple of ARTEMIS in Elymais. Josephus, invested in defending the greater dignity of the Jewish nation and temple, grants that the defeat at Elymais left Antiochus dispirited, but argues that plundering the temple in Jerusalem and dishonoring the Jewish God were the more decisive causes of Antiochus' death (*Ant.* 12.354-59).

B. DIANE LIPSETT

ELYMAS el′uh-muhs [Ἐλύμας Elymas]. Elymas, also called Bar-Jesus (Acts 13:4-12), is described by the narrator of Acts as "a Jewish magician, a false prophet," serving the Roman proconsul of Cyprus, Sergius Paulus. Interfering when the proconsul seeks to hear God's message from Barnabas and Saul/Paul, Elymas is vehemently denounced by Paul, then temporarily blinded in a punitive miracle. Sergius Paulus becomes Paul's first convert.

The text first calls the character "Bar-Jesus" (v. 6), then "the magos (μάγος) Elymas (for that is the translation of his name)" (v. 8*a*). Some interpreters have therefore argued that the writer assumes "Bar-Jesus" and "Elymas" to be linguistically equivalent, although how the former, which most straightforwardly means "son of Jesus or Joshua," may relate to the latter is unclear. Others hold that "Elymas" is somehow equivalent to magos and turn to Arabic or Aram. roots to try to find connections. Still others prefer a variant manuscript reading (D) that has Hetoimas (Ἑτοιμας) in place of Elymas, suggesting a connection to a magician mentioned by Josephus (*Ant.* 20.141-44). Many scholars, however, simply conclude that the meaning of "Elymas" in this passage is uncertain. What is clearer is that this character and episode contribute to a pervasive anti-magic motif that runs through Acts. Elymas in Cyprus resembles Simon the magos in Samaria (8:9-13), the fortune-telling slave girl in Philippi (16:16), and the ineffectual Jewish exorcists and others practicing magic in Ephesus (19:13-19) in their capitulation to the message and name of Jesus Christ. *See* JESUS, BAR; MAGIC, MAGICIAN; PAULUS, SERGIUS.

B. DIANE LIPSETT

ELYMEANS el′uh-mee′uhn [Ἐλυμαίων Elymaiōn]. A group of people ruled by ARIOCH who, according to Jdt 1:6, joined forces with the Assyrian army of Nebuchadnezzar against Arphaxad, king of the Medes.

ELYON el-yohn′ עֶלְיוֹן ʿelyon]. ʿElyon, "MOST HIGH," appears in the OT most frequently of God as the supreme deity. As such, it is often juxtaposed with El (Gen 14:14-18; Num 24:16; Ps 57:2 [Heb. 57:3]; 73:11; 107:11), who was the chief god of the divine council in Canaanite mythology. *See* GOD, NAMES OF.

C. L. SEOW

ELZABAD el-zay′bad [אֶלְזָבָד ʾelzavadh]. Means "God has given." 1. Ninth of eleven swift, lionlike, veteran Gadite warriors proficient in pitched combat with spear and shield who joined David at ZIKLAG against Saul (1 Chr 12:13 [12]; LXX reads Eliazer).

2. Fourth-listed son of Shemiah and a gatekeeper in the Jerusalem Temple (1 Chr 26:7).

ELZAPHAN el-zay′fan [אֶלְצָפָן ʾeltsafan]. Alternate form of ELIZAPHAN (Exod 6:22; Lev 10:4).

EMADABUN i-mad′uh-buhn [Ἡμαδαβουν Ēmadaboun]. One of those appointed to Levitical service in the newly refounded Jerusalem Temple (1 Esd 5:56). The name Jeshua Emadabun serves to differentiate him from another Jeshua mentioned in the same passage.

EMAR. Excavations conducted at Tell Meskéné (Emar) in northern Syria along the Euphrates unearthed over

1,000 tablets, predominately written in Akkadian. Emar, established in the 14th cent. by the HITTITES, was destroyed during the tumultuous days that characterized the end of the Late Bronze Age (ca. 1200 BCE).

EMATHIS em´uh-thuhs [Ἐμαθίς Emathis]. The son of a priest, Bebai, who had taken a foreign wife (1 Esd 9:29). The name is ATHLAI in the par. (Ezra 10:28).

EMBALM, EMBALMING [נָחַט nakhat, חֲנֻטִים khanutim]. To treat a dead body with preservative substances in order to stop or delay its decay. This word appears in Gen 50:2-3, where Jacob's body is "embalmed" before it is transported from Egypt to Canaan for burial, and in Gen 50:26, where Joseph's body is "embalmed" before it is placed in a coffin in Egypt.

Embalming was not generally common in the burial practices of the ANE. Mesopotamian, Phoenician, Canaanite, Philistine, Israelite, and early Jewish funerary customs did not typically include efforts to delay or arrest the natural process of decomposition. Nor did Greek and Roman customs, which entered the biblical lands during the intertestamental period. On the contrary, several ANE cultures (e.g., Canaanite, Israelite, Jewish) practiced secondary burial, the collection and reburial of human bones after decomposition of the flesh was complete. In these cultures, decay of the deceased human body was regarded as a normal part of the ritual process of death and burial. Thus the wrapping of the body of Jesus and the women preparing spices and ointments and bringing them to the tomb (Luke 23:52–24:1) are not embalming processes.

Only in Egypt was embalming common, as part of an elaborate technology of mummification. Efforts to preserve the human corpse are evident in Egypt as early as the pre-dynastic period (before 3100 BCE), but embalmers' skills appear to have reached their peak during the Twenty-first Dynasty (ca. 1000 BCE). In a process that may have lasted as long as seventy days, the internal organs were removed, and the corpse was carefully dehydrated, stuffed, and wrapped in linen.

Since embalming was distinctively Egyptian, references to it in Gen 50:2, and 50:26 emphasize that the descendants of Abraham were becoming acclimated to the society and culture of Egypt. *See* BURIAL; HEALTH CARE; TOMB.

BYRON R. MCCANE

EMBLEMS [טוֹטָפוֹת totafoth]. In Exod 13:16 and Deut 6:8 and 11:18, the Israelites are enjoined to wear "these words" as an "emblem" ("frontlets" in earlier versions) on their foreheads. It would appear that an emblem was some sort of headband. By the Second Temple Period, this commandment was interpreted to mean that certain biblical verses should be put in boxes

Erich Lessing /Art Resource, NY

Figure 1: The dead (in white) adores Osiris; Anubis embalms the mummy. From the tomb of Sennedjem, Workmen's Tombs (13th cent. BCE), New Kingdom. Deir el-Medina, Egypt. Location: Tomb of Sennedjem (Workmen's Tomb, Deir el-Medina, Tombs of the Nobles, Thebes, Egypt).

and strapped to the forehead. Thus, the ritual objects of tefillin or PHYLACTERIES developed from these totafoth. At least twenty-eight tefillin or fragments thereof were discovered at Qumran.

Bibliography: James C. VanderKam. *An Introduction to Early Judaism* (2001).

JENNIFER L. KOOSED

EMBROIDERY AND NEEDLE WORK [רֹקֵם roqem, רִקְמָה riqmah; βελόνη belonē, ποικιλτοῦ poikiltou, ῥαφίς rhaphis].

Sewing is among the earliest human skills mentioned in the Bible (Adam's and Eve's sown leaf garments in Gen 3:7). The basics of stitching together a garment might have been a part of a person's practical education (Job 16:15), and common sewing techniques even formed the basis for wisdom sayings (Eccl 3:7 and Matt 9:16) as well as admonitions against idolatrous and magical practices (see wrist charms in Ezek 13:18). Livelihoods mentioned in the Bible that were likely to have involved stitching things together include fishing (repairing nets, Matt 4:21; Luke 1:19), leatherworking or tent making (as practiced by the apostle Paul, Acts 18:3), and garment making (Acts 36:39).

On a more detailed level, trained embroiderers are listed as highly valued craftsmen in the account of the construction and embellishment of the tabernacle and its furnishings, including the curtains that separated its sacred precincts. They also were involved in the stitching together and the decoration of priestly vestments and other sacred items (Sir 45:10). These embroiderers worked with a variety of different colored threads and fabrics (blue, purple, and scarlet, and "finely twisted linen" (Exod 26:36; 35:35), either using needles or weaving (Exod 28:39; shibbatsta [שִׁבְּצְתָ]) the threads on a loom. Bronze needles used for such fine stitching were carefully stored, sometimes in ivory boxes, as prized tools. Dyed and embroidered cloth was highly regarded as a decorative touch to a woman's robe (see how Sisera's mother speculates on the rich spoil her son will bring her in Judg 5:30). Wealthier Israelites and members of the royal house could even command the use of golden threads in their richly embroidered robes (Ps 45:13-14; Ezek 16:10-18), and the best quality embroidered linen was imported from Egypt and Mesopotamia (Ezek 27:7, 23-24).

The only technical terms in the NT associated with sewing are for needle (the NRSV's translation of rhaphis [Matt 19:24] from the root of "throw/cast"; and belonē from "weave" in Luke 18:25), which appear in Jesus' saying about a camel going through the eye of a needle. The "eye of the needle" in this saying is sometimes interpreted as a narrow gate in the city wall, but others argue that the shock value of Jesus' statement is more pronounced if a sewing needle is envisioned. *See* CLOTH, CLOTHES; NEEDLE.

VICTOR H. MATTHEWS

EMEK-KEZIZ ee´mik-kee´ziz [עֵמֶק קְצִיץ ʿemeq qetsits]. Means "cut-off valley." One of the cities named among those given to the tribe of Benjamin (Josh 18:21), likely located east of Jerusalem toward Jericho, but its exact location is unknown.

EMENDATIONS OF THE SCRIBES [תִּקּוּנֵי סוֹפְרִים tiqqune soferim].

"Emendations of the scribes" is the usual English translation of the Hebrew expression, tiqqune soferim. The word tiqqune could also be translated as "corrections." The expression tiqqune soferim is used to refer to passages in the OT where the early scribes were thought to have changed the text in order to avoid expressions, which were thought disrespectful to God. The tiqqune soferim, given in the MASORA, preserve the original reading. Lists of the tiqqune soferim are found in the masora of some biblical manuscripts and in Talmudic sources. The masora of the St. Petersburg Codex, Firkovich B 19A, which serves as the base text of *Biblia Hebraica*, does not refer to the tiqqune soferim, although some are mentioned in the apparatus of *BHS*. Older lists use the term kinnah (כִּנָּה), "substitution" or "euphemism" while later lists introduce the term tiqqune. These more recent lists also give eighteen passages where the tiqqune soferim occur, older lists give fewer passages. This difference in the number of the tiqqune soferim between the older and the younger lists suggests to some scholars that the lists grew over time, perhaps in part due to exegetical activity.

The changes referred to in the scribal emendations are usually quite small, a letter or two at most and frequently concern a pronominal suffix. An example of this type of tiqqune may be found in Zech 2:12 where the MT preserves the reading "his eye." The tiqqune soferim comment in the masorah suggests the original reading was "my eye" referring to God's eye. In this case the difference between the two readings is a single letter, WAW for "his" or YOD for "my." These two letters were easily confused by ancient scribes and in this example the confusion of the letters may have been the origin of the two readings. The tiqqune, of course, suggests that the change in the text was deliberate. Sometimes the original reading preserved in the tiqqune agrees with ancient variants known from Hebrew or Gk. witnesses and thus the tiqqune may identify an actual emendation. The reading, "my eye," suggested as the original in the tiqqune soferim, may indeed have been the original reading in Zech 2:12, but sometimes the reading suggested in the tiqqune soferim was not the original, but arose through exegetical activity. Each case must be judged separately. Another well-known tiqqune refers to the text of Gen 18:22, "Abraham stood before Yahweh." This was corrected by the scribes, the original text, according to the tiqqune, read, "Yahweh stood before Abraham." The corrected text removes the theologically inappropriate idea that God might have stood waiting before Abraham.

The supposed scribal emendations indicated by the tiqqune soferim were presumed to have taken place at an early stage in the transmission of the biblical text. It is conceivable that at some early stage in the text's transmission such changes to the text were allowed, at least in some circles. With the availability of the biblical Dead Sea Scrolls, the tiqqune soferim can now be compared to the earliest forms of the Hebrew text and their antiquity examined. *See* MASORETES; MT, MASORETIC TEXT; TEXT CRITICISM, OT.

Bibliography: Carmel McCarthy. *The Tiqqune Sopherim and Other Theological Corrections in the Masoretic Text of the Old Testament* (1981); Israel Yeivin. *Introduction to the Tiberian Masorah* (1980).

RUSSELL E. FULLER

EMERALD [בָּרֶקֶת bareqeth; σμάραγδος smaragdos]. The third stone in the first row on the high priest's breastpiece (Exod 28:17; 39:10); the last stone in the Eden adornment of the king of Tyre (Ezek 28:13). The Hebrew term is related to the flashing of lightning. God's throne (Rev 4:3) has a rainbow around it resembling an emerald (smaragdinos σμαράγδινος). In the New Jerusalem the fourth foundation stone of the city wall is the same gem (Rev 21:19). Other English translations use a variety of gems in these and nearby passages for stones that might be flashing and green. Probably *emerald* represents the best choice for the Hebrew word. Geologists relate this gem to BERYL.

ELIZABETH E. PLATT

EMESA ['Εμέσης Emesēs]. The kingdom of Emesa was a city-state in western Syria, on the road between Damascus and Hama. Located on the Orontes River and the precarious boundary between Rome and Parthia, Emesa flourished during the early Roman Empire. In the 3rd cent., several Roman emperors were from the kingdom. Emesa is now the modern Syrian city of Homs.

Although older, Emesa first appears in the historical record in the early 1st cent. BCE. It emerged during the decline of the Seleucid Empire. Its first known king was Sampsigeramus I, who ruled from 69 to around 46 BCE. Emesa was a Roman ally: in 51 BCE, Sampsigeramus's son Iamblichus warned Cicero of a Parthian invasion. But the dynasty ran afoul of different factions in the Roman civil war: Iamblichus was executed by Antony before Actium, and his successor, his brother Alexander, was executed by Octavian shortly afterward.

Iamblichus II came to rule by 20 BCE, with Augustus' blessing. Emesa was connected to the other eastern kingdoms (Commagene, Cilicia, Judea) by dynastic marriage, but troops from Emesa aided Rome in the Jewish War (66–70 CE) and in subduing Commagene in 72 CE. Emesa was incorporated into the Roman province of Syria in the late 1st or early 2nd cent.

Late in the 2nd cent., Emesa achieved fame when one of its daughters, Julia Domna, married the emperor Septimius Severus (193–211 CE). Emperors from her family ruled for decades: Geta (211–212), Caracalla (211–217), Elagabalus (218–222), and Alexander Severus (222–235).

ADAM L. PORTER

EMIM, THE ee′mim [אֵימִים ʾemim]. An ancient, mythical race of GIANTS that formerly inhabited Moab (Deut 2:10). Also known as the REPHAIM but called Emim (terrors) by the Moabites (Deut 2:11), these giants were as tall as the Anakim. The Emim in Shaveh-kiriathaim were overrun by Cherdolaomer and his allies (Gen 14:5).

R. JUSTIN HARKINS

EMIR, IRAQ EL. Iraq el-Emir is an archaeological site complex in the Wadi es-Seer, about 15 km west of Amman, Jordan. The site consists of a village of undetermined size, several natural and human-sculpted caves of large dimensions, and a large building held to represent an unfinished effort to construct a temple, a tomb, or a palatial residence. The village dates at least to the Iron II period based on pottery from excavation trenches (although an Iron Age I date has also been claimed). Two inscriptions in Aramaic of "Tobiah" near the cave entrances have been variously dated as 2nd to 5th cent. BCE, but most archaeologists seem to favor a pre-3rd cent. date.

Todd Bolen/BiblePlaces.com
Figure 1: Tobiah Inscription

The caves could have served as residences or "banquet halls", but they might also have been used for storage. The majestic palace/temple (Qasr al-Abd, or "Palace of the Servant") is probably Hellenistic in age and is constructed of massive limestone blocks almost 7 m long, more than 3 m high, and circa a half-meter thick. Elegantly sculpted leopards, limestone lions, and eagles decorate the façade. The entire complex is associated with the Tobiads, a prominent Jewish landholding family, mentioned in the Zenon papyri and by Josephus (*Ant.* 12.4). The family enjoyed political

Todd Bolen/BiblePlaces.com
Figure 2: Palace south façade

power and wealth, and the Tobiads may have been military commanders and local governors as early as the Persian period, continuing to rule well into the Hellenistic period.

Bibliography: Chang-Ho C. Ji. "A New Look at the Tobaids in 'Iraq al-Amir." *Liber Annus* 48 (1998) 417–40.

GARY O. ROLLEFSON

EMISSION. *See* CLEAN AND UNCLEAN.

EMMANUEL. *See* IMMANUEL.

EMMAUS i-may'uhs ['Εμμαοῦς Emmaous]. The name Emmaous is a transliteration of the Hebrew word for "warm spring" (khammath חַמַּת). According to Luke 24:13 CLEOPAS and an unnamed disciple of Jesus met the risen Lord when going to a village (kōmē κώμη) called Emmaus. This post-resurrection encounter in Luke 24:13-35 contains a summary of Lukan theology. From a literary point of view it is one of the most charming Gospel stories. That the story includes the name of Cleopas, an uncle of Jesus (Eusebius, *Hist. eccl.* 3.11), may point to the possibility that it goes back to family tradition.

The location of Emmaus is not known for certain. Josephus sometimes gives Emmaus as the name of HAMMATH (Josh 19:35), south of TIBERIAS. Another Emmaus is located in the plain 23 km west of Jerusalem. It is first mentioned when Judah the Maccabee defeated a Syrian army in 164 BCE (1 Macc 3:27–4:25). The Roman general Varus destroyed the site in 4 BCE in revenge of an uprising. During the Jewish War of 66–70 CE Emmaus was the capital of a toparchy and the headquarters of John the Essene. In the 2nd and 3rd cent. it had a mixed population of Jews, Samaritans, pagans, and Christians. In ca. 221 CE, the scholar Julius Africanus, possibly a Jewish Christian, led an embassy to the Emperor Elgabal, who granted city rights to Emmaus, renamed Nicopolis. After an epidemic in the 7th cent. it was left uninhabited. Later the Arab village

Imwas (destroyed in 1967) took over the old Semitic name. Excavations in the late 19th and early 20th cent. unearthed a double basilica from the 5th cent. The south basilica is to be dated to the 5th cent. and the northern basilica to before 430 CE. Underneath the south basilica are older remains, possibly from a smaller 4th cent. church and a 1st cent. building. The churches possibly commemorated either a spring whose healing powers were attributed to a visit by Jesus (Sozomenos, *HE* 5:21) and/or the house of Cleopas (Jerome, ep. 108, 8). Also found were Jewish tombs from NT times and a 3rd cent. private building. Surveys show that the main city area extended west of the present excavations.

Josephus mentions a Roman veteran colony, founded by Vespasian after 70 CE, "thirty stadia" west of Jerusalem (*J.W.* 7.217). Its location was remembered by the Arab village Qaloniye (destroyed in 1948). The original Jewish name is given in the Lat. manuscripts as "Amassada" and in the Gk. manuscripts as Ammaous ('Αμμαοῦς). Both readings are corruptions by Christian copyists that go back to an original Amassa ('Αμασσα) or Amōsa ('Αμωσα). Excavations, including those of the sparse remains of a Second Temple village and a 5th/6th cent. church, confirm the uninterrupted habitation of the site from Canaanite to modern times.

With regard to the Emmaus of Luke 24, two major textual witnesses (P75 [3rd cent.], Codex Vaticanus [4th cent.]) and the majority of the manuscripts give its distance from Jerusalem as "sixty stadia" (11.5 km); however, Codex Sinaiticus (4th cent.) and others read "one hundred and sixty" (27 km). The latter reading may be a correction according to the local tradition, but the numeral sign for 100 could have been lost in the former reading. Pre-Byzantine tradition identified the Lukan place name with Nicopolis (Eusebius, *Onom.* 90). It is probable that Origen already knew of this identification (Codex 194 Tischendorf-Gregory). Josephus could describe Lydda, like Emmaus, head of a toparchy, as a village (*Ant.* 20.130). Both ancient and modern experience demonstrate that it is not impossible to go from Jerusalem to Emmaus-Nicopolis and back again in one day. The local tradition remained stable during the Byzantine period. Possibly some Crusaders identified Abu Ghosh west of Jerusalem with Emmaus. The Franciscan identification with El-Qubeiben of Jerusalem prevailed from the 13th to the 19th cent., when the site of Emmaus-Nicopolis was proposed.

Bibliography: K. H. Fleckenstein, M. Louhivuori, and R. Riesner. *Emmaus in Judäa: Geschichte–Exegese–Archäologie* (2003).

RAINER RIESNER

EMMAUS-NICOPOLIS. *See* EMMAUS.

EMOTIONS. The word *emotion* does not appear in the Bible per se, although words for individual emotions are present, such as love, hate, fear, anger, and joy. An emotion is a conscious state, behavior, or psychological event that is caused by a stimulus. Psychologists know that the pattern of arousal within the body is roughly the same for all emotions. When one experiences an intense emotion such as love, fear, or anger, bodily changes such as rapid heartbeat and breathing, dryness of the throat, increased muscle tension, perspiration, trembling of the extremities, and a sinking feeling in the stomach may occur.

Biblical writers observed personal, physical disturbances during emotional upheavals. They saw tears, pale faces, sweat, chills, shivering, and reported such physical symptoms as chest pains and gastrointestinal reactions. Biblical writers heard the sound of emotion such as laughter, wailing, cheering, bowels growling, and teeth gnashing. They describe the emotions as activity taking place within the organs. The organs of the body may ferment, boil, burn, writhe, shake, turn over, melt, roar, or rotate. In biblical poetry, very often the words heart, bowels, liver, and kidneys are parallel to one another. This correlation eliminates the precise biological meaning of these organs. Instead, they are used as metaphors for the emotions depicted.

It must be noted that in biblical times no one had a concept of the mind's role in emotions. The seat of emotions was considered to be in the heart, bowels, liver, and kidneys.

The heart was considered the most important organ, having the properties that modern scientists attribute to the mind: e.g., cognition. It was considered the real carrier of life, representing the essence of a human being. Indeed, when the heart stopped, the human died. The heart could hear, roar, scream, break, quiver, sour, melt, widen, grow, expand, rejoice, and turn to stone. But, in the Bible, the verb "to beat" does not appear with heart. The entire gamut of emotions was thought to have resided in the heart—except love.

Love, like other extreme emotions, took place in the bowels. Sorrow, agony, love, and compassion are described as whirling, roaring, boiling, and fermenting bowels. The liver is the largest and heaviest internal organ. It could sing praises in joy and pour out in sorrow. Meanwhile, deep-seated emotions such as agony and joy were thought to be located in the kidneys. Because they are covered in fat, only God could penetrate their mysteries.

In the Bible individuals, nations, and God experience emotions. Humans and God experience similar emotions the same way. For example, God longs for his beloved son Ephraim, "My bowels roar for him, I am filled with compassion toward him" (Jer 31:19). Isaiah complains to God, "Your roaring bowels and compassion have been restrained from me" (63:15). The lover in Song of Songs longs for her beloved with the same expression, "My bowels roared for him" (5:4). When God is angry at his people, literally, "his nose burns" (2 Kgs 2:23; Isa 5:25) the same way as when Job vents

his anger at his friends (23:3; 42:7). A nation's heart can melt or move with fear (Josh 7:5; 14:8; Isa 7:2) as it does in humans (Isa 13:7; Ezek 21:12). Similarly, in the NT, when Jesus feels "compassion" for someone, the Greek is splanchizomai (σπλαγχίζομαι), to feel from the gut, from splanchnon (σπλάγχνον), meaning inmost parts, entrails, the seat of emotion (Matt 9:36; 14:14; Mark 6:34; 8:2; Luke 7:13; 10:33).

Descriptions of emotions evoke empathy and humanize the Bible for the readers. To merely say that one feels sad conveys an emotion but to describe "O my bowels, my bowels! I writhe! O walls of my heart! My heart is roaring" (Jer 4:19) kindles the imagination and portrays a concrete image.

ESTHER GRUSHKIN

EMPEROR [βασιλεύς basileus, καῖσαρ kaisar, σεβαστός sebastos]. Each of these words is used in the NT to refer to the Roman emperor. Augustus (Luke 2:1) and Tiberius (Luke 3:1) are both called kaisar (from Latin *Caesar*), while Nero is called sebastos (Acts 25:21, 25). The latter word means "revered," the equivalent of "his Majesty," and is the Greek translation of "Augustus"—a title of respect for Octavian, which came to be used as if it were a proper name. Although Dio Cassius (*Roman History* 53.17) writes that Augustus tended to avoid the title "king" because it evoked unpleasant associations among Romans, Josephus and other Greek writers, including the authors of 1 Peter and Revelation, used basileus (king) to refer to the emperor (1 Pet 3:13, 17; Rev 17:9; *J.W.* 3.351; 4.596; 5.563).

RICHARD B. VINSON

EMPEROR WORSHIP. Scholars use the term "emperor worship" or, more often, "imperial cult(s)" to refer to a variety of phenomena in the Roman world that involved the emperors or members of the imperial family as recipients of honors traditionally directed at gods or goddesses, primarily sacrifice and related rituals. There was a tendency within earlier scholarship to discount the significance of these imperial cults, dismissing them as mere political flattery and characterizing them as lacking genuine religious dimensions. However, more recent work corrects this misperception and points to the thorough integration of these diverse honors for the emperors within social and religious dimensions of life in many cities of the Greek east and in western parts of the empire.

A. The Nature of Imperial Cults
B. The Roman Empire, Imperial Cults, and Early Christianity

A. The Nature of Imperial Cults
In scholarly terms, it is helpful to distinguish four levels of these rituals or cultic honors for members of

the imperial family. First, there was the official cult of deceased emperors centered at the city of Rome itself. At the death of popular emperors (though not those such as Domitian who gained the *damnatio memoriae* of the Senate), a special ceremony took place in which the Senate inducted the deceased emperor into the realm of the gods. Republican and Augustan traditions stopped short of worshiping a living emperor as a god, and this tendency was more prevalent in the western or Latin-speaking parts of the empire. In the Greek-speaking, eastern part of the Mediterranean, however, there was no such hesitancy in treating exceptional rulers—while alive—as though they were gods, particularly in the centuries following Alexander the Great (who died in 323 BCE).

Second, there were provincial imperial cults and temples organized by institutions that claimed to represent the civic communities of a given province, such as the "Council of Asia" in western Asia Minor. Imperial cult temples founded by this organization were primarily under the direction of the "high-priests of Asia." Temples established by this provincial organization in the 1st cent. or so included those for goddess Roma and god Augustus at Pergamum (founded 29 BCE), for Tiberius at Smyrna (23 CE), for Domitian at Ephesus (89 CE), and for Trajan at Pergamum (just before 113 CE). The cult for Trajan was quite typical of provincial cults, which often involved intermittent festivals and games in honor of the emperor alongside regular sacrifices in the temple. In Asia Minor, it became common in various contexts, including provincial cults, to refer to a given emperor as "god Sebastos" (Sebastos being the Greek equivalent for "Augustus") and to refer to the emperors or other members of the imperial family collectively as the "Sebastoi gods," "the revered gods."

Third, there were civic cults that were devoted to the "revered gods" collectively or to an individual emperor. These sanctuaries, such as the Sebasteion at Aphrodisias, maintained close connections with other institutions of the city and were often established using donations from prominent families. There were similar civic cults with their own priesthoods and other functionaries at various locales, including Ephesus and Laodicea, cities addressed by John's Revelation.

Fourth, there were other local shrines and expressions of honor for the emperors as gods in unofficial settings, including households and associations. Many monuments from Asia Minor attest to the involvement of local associations in honoring the emperors. Thus, a partially preserved letter from the time of Domitian shows that a group devoted to the goddess Demeter at Ephesus also included the emperors in their rituals, sacrifices, and mysteries (*IEphesos* 213). Another group near Smyrna called themselves the "Caesarists" and engaged in sacrifices for the "revered gods" and accompanying banquets (*IGR* IV 1348). At Pergamon,

the "hymn-singers" engaged in special celebrations on the birthday of Augustus, which included sacrificial banquets in honor of Augustus and the goddess Roma, offerings of sacrificial cakes and incense, and mysteries in which images of the emperor were revealed by lamplight (*IPergamon* 374). So worship of the emperors could be thoroughly integrated at the local level in areas like western Asia Minor, which was also a hub of early Christianity.

B. The Roman Empire, Imperial Cults, and Early Christianity

With the exception of John's Revelation (esp. Rev 13), there are no indisputable references to worship of the emperor in the NT. We do, however, find certain early Christian authors addressing what one's stance should be toward the empire or emperors (kings) generally. Thus, for instance, Paul calls on the followers of Christ at Rome to "be subject to the governing authorities" (Rom 13:1 RSV) and speaks of the authorities' functions in punishing evil and rewarding good conduct (compare 1 Pet 2:13-15). Similarly, the author of the Pastoral Epistles exhorts his recipient(s) to offer prayers and thanksgivings for all persons, including emperors (kings) and those in high positions (1 Tim 2:1-2). The author of 1 Peter goes somewhat further in expressly asking followers of Christ in Asia Minor to "honor the emperor," alongside others (1 Pet 2:17); this is part of his overall program to have the recipients "maintain good conduct" in the eyes of outsiders (1 Pet 2:12). Although 1 Peter comes closest to the sort of language of honor that one might encounter in imperial cults, none of these authors advocates participation in actually worshiping the emperor (e.g., through sacrifice). Still, there is a sense in which these more positive positions regarding how early followers of Christ were to relate to the Roman Empire and its rulers is in some tension with the harsh condemnations of the imperial power in John's Revelation.

In addressing the churches of western Asia Minor, Revelation strongly condemns the Roman Empire (addressed as the evil empire "Babylon") for interconnected economic, military, and religious reasons. Some aspects of the imperial cult play a role as ammunition for John's rhetorical attack (see Rev 13). In particular, John speaks of the dangers of "worshiping the beast," a phrase that offers the most direct reference to worshiping the emperor in the NT. John characterizes the Roman imperial power as a seven-headed beast rising from the sea, which derives its authority from the great red dragon, Satan himself. In light of the references to the mortal wound previously suffered by one of its heads (13:3) and to the death and subsequent return of this head (17:8-11), John probably has a returning emperor Nero in mind here. The beast was given "authority . . . over every tribe and people and tongue and nation, and all who dwell on the earth will worship it, every one whose name has not been written before the foundation of the world in the book of life of the Lamb that was slain" (Rev 13:5, 7-8).

A second beast in Revelation, this one from the earth, "exercises all the authority of the first beast in its presence, and makes the earth and its inhabitants worship the first beast" (Rev 13:12). This beast, which has sometimes been identified by scholars with the Roman governor or the high-priesthood of the provincial imperial cult, uses miracles to deceive inhabitants into worshiping the first beast and causes "those who would not worship the image of the beast to be slain" (Rev 13:15). Ultimately, "if any one worships the beast and its image . . . he also shall drink the wine of God's wrath . . . and he shall be tormented with fire and sulphur in the presence of the holy angels and in the presence of the Lamb" (Rev 14:9-10). John makes a concrete call for followers of Christ to distance themselves from any contact with imperial cults and other aspects of Roman imperialism in the cities of Asia Minor. It should be stated that although the actual imperial cult informs John's futuristic, apocalyptic imagery, Revelation is by no means a simple description of what actually went on in the cities and cults of Asia Minor in John's time.

Some scholars go beyond these certain references to the imperial cult in John's Apocalypse in order to assess other possible allusions to, or subversions of, worship of the emperors in the NT. These scholars tend to stress that imperial cults, more so than other Greco-Roman religious practices, were a primary source of conflict for early Christians. Some have emphasized a pivotal clash between the "cult of Christ" and the "cult of Caesar" (Deissmann), or that, for virtually all early Christians, "the worst abuse in the Roman Empire was the imperial cult" (Jones). Some scholars today assume a fundamental opposition between Christianity and the Roman imperial order and seek out the subtle ways in which early Christian authors, such as Paul or the author of Matthew, may have been subverting imperial cults and Roman power. There is a sense in which the question is to what degree can we assume that John the Seer's clearly expressed criticisms of imperial cults or Roman emperors are somehow representative of other early Christian authors who do not so clearly address the issue. *See* EMPEROR; MYSTERY RELIGIONS; NERO; REVELATION, BOOK OF; ROMAN EMPIRE.

Bibliography: Warren Carter. *Matthew and Empire: Initial Explorations* (2001); Adolf Deissmann. *Light from the Ancient East* (1908); Ittai Gradel. *Emperor Worship and Roman Religion* (2002); Phillip A. Harland. "Honouring the Emperor or Assailing the Beast: Participation in Civic Life among Associations (Jewish, Christian and Other) in

Asia Minor and the Apocalypse of John." *JSNT* 77 (2000) 99–121; Phillip A. Harland. *Associations, Synagogues, and Congregations: Claiming a Place in Ancient Mediterranean Society* (2003); Richard A. Horsley, ed., *Paul and the Roman Imperial Order* (2004); Donald L. Jones. "Christianity and the Roman Imperial Cult." *ANRW* II.23.2 (1980) 1023–54; S. R. F. Price. *Rituals and Power: The Roman Imperial Cult in Asia Minor* (1984).

PHILLIP A. HARLAND

EMPOWER. *See* HOLY SPIRIT; SPIRITUAL GIFTS.

EMPTIED. *See* KENOSIS.

ENAIM i-nay′im [עֵינַיִם ‘*enayim*]. Means "two springs." An unknown location between Timnah and Adullah where TAMAR disguised herself as a prostitute (Gen 38:14) to ensnare her father-in-law Judah.

ENAM ee′nuhm [עֵינָם ‘*enam*]. A village included in a list of towns in lowland Judah (Josh 15:34), usually understood to be ENAIM (Gen 38:14, 21).

ENAN ee′nuhn [עֵינָן ‘*enan*]. AHIRA, a leader of the tribe of Naphtali during the wilderness period, is always identified as the son of Enan (Num 1:15; 2:29; 7:78, 83; 10:27).

ENCAMPMENT. *See* CAMP.

ENCHANTER [אַשָּׁף ’*ashaf*, חוֹבֵר *khover*, לַחַשׁ *lakhash*]. The NRSV translates "enchanter" for three different Hebrew terms. Clearly related to the practice of magic, its precise meaning in the Hebrew text is unknown.

In Ps 58:5, enchanter is used for *khover*, which also occurs in Deut 18:11 where the NRSV translates it as "one who casts spells." The root found elsewhere (Isa 47:9, 12) is translated "enchantments."

In Isa 3:3 the underlying Hebrew word is *lakhash*, whose root, "to whisper," suggests that a *lakhash* is one who whispers incantations. In Eccl 10:11 and Jer 8:17 it refers to snake charmers.

The NRSV's most consistent use of *enchanter* is to translate Hebrew and Aram. words drawn from the root ’*ashaf* in the book of Daniel. The root occurs eight times, usually beside other words that are variously translated as magician, diviner, sorcerer, and wise man. The distinction between these terms is not always clear. *See* DIVINATION.

KEVIN A. WILSON

ENCOMIUM. A laudatory oration in praise of the superiority of a person, city, or thing (in contrast to hymns, which are in praise of a god). Pindar, a Greek lyric poet (ca. 518–438 BCE), originally used encomium to celebrate athletic and military victories. In Greco-Roman schools of rhetoric, encomia that praised persons were to include selected biographical features, referring to the subject's ancestry, to signs before and during his birth, his youthful and adult exploits and accomplishments, how he stood in death, and events or signs during and after his death. Most of these elements occur in the poetic passages of Phil 2:6-11 and Col 1:15-20 as well as in the Gospels.

Bibliography: E. Krentz. "Epideiktik and Hymnody: The New Testament and Its World." *BR* 40 (1995) 50–97.

L. J. DE REGT

ENCOURAGEMENT [אָמֵץ 'amets, חָזַק khazaq, סָמַךְ samakh; παρακαλέω parakaleō, παράκλησις paraklēsis]. In the OT, the verb *encourage* expresses the concepts of several Hebrew words. The noun *encouragement* is absent in the NRSV. The texts present both positive and negative examples of encouragement. Positively, God commanded Moses to encourage and support Joshua because he would succeed Moses (Deut 1:38; 3:28). When Sennacherib, the king of Assyria came to fight against Jerusalem, the people were encouraged by Hezekiah to trust in God (2 Chr 32:7-8). King Josiah encouraged the Levites in the service of the house of the Lord (2 Chr 35:2-6). Negatively, David encouraged Joab to continue to fight the battle after having Uriah killed (2 Sam 11:25). In Ezek 13:12 God speaks against the false prophetesses for disheartening the righteous and encouraging the wicked not to turn from their wicked ways. Isaiah speaks of the futility of artisans, encouraging the goldsmith and an anvil striker to fasten idols with nails because their gods cannot stand alone (Isa 41:7).

In the NT the terms *encourage* and *encouragement* predominately translate the verb parakaleō (Acts 15:32; Eph 6:22) and the noun paraklēsis (Acts 4:36; Rom 15:4f.; 1 Cor 14:3; Phil 2:1; Phlm 1:7); however, the verb also can be translated as "console" (Matt 2:18; 2 Cor 1:6), "appeal" (Matt 26:53; Rom 12:1), "comfort" (2 Cor 7:13; 2 Thess 2:16), "urge" (Rom 16:17; Phil 4:2), "beg" (Mark 6:56; Eph 4:1), or "exhort" (Acts 2:40; Titus 2:15; Heb 3:13). The noun can also be rendered "consolation" (Luke 2:25; 6:24; 2 Cor 1:3, 6; 7:4, 7, 13), "comfort" (Acts 9:31; 2 Cor 7:13; 2 Thess 2:16), EXHORTATION (Acts 13:15; 15:31; Rom 12:8; Heb 12:5; 13:22), or "appeal" (2 Cor 8:17; 1 Thess 2:3).

Although the sense of comfort or consolation has a slightly different connotation than encouragement, consolation may be regarded as a form of encouragement. In the NT God is the source of encouragement and comfort (Rom 15:5; 2 Cor 1:3-4; 2 Thess 2:16). The role of leaders is to encourage and comfort the believers (Acts 15:32; 1 Thess 3:2; Eph 6:22). Some believers have the gift of encouraging others (Rom 12:8 [exhorter]; Acts 4:36 [Barnabas, trans. "the son of encouragement"]). Believers are commanded to encourage one another

(Heb 3:12-13), not to forsake assembling together (Heb 10:25), and to be alert and sober in light of the return of Jesus (2 Thess 4:18; 5:11).

VICTOR RHEE

ENCRATISM. A categorization derived from Greek enkrateia (ἐγκράτεια *self-control*). The label *Encratites* (Lat. *Continentes*) was borne by a 2nd cent. group with gnostic leanings characterized by an ASCETICISM that included abstention from marriage/procreation and eating meat (Irenaeus, *Haer.* 1.28.1; compare 1.24.2) as well as wine (Clement of Alexandria, *Paed.* 2.2 [*ANF* 2:246]; Hippolytus, *Haer.* 8.13 [*ANF* 5:124]; Epiphanius, *Pan.* 47.1.7). The label was also applied to certain later groups who continued to exist outside the pale of normative Christianity (Epiphanius, *Pan.* 47.1.1-2).

Particular abstentions and self-control were encouraged in the NT (Gal 5:23; 1 Cor 7; Acts 15:20; 24:25; 2 Pet 1:6) and in early Christian texts (*1 Clem.* 35:2; 62:2; *Barn.* 2:2; *Herm. Vis.* 2.3.2). Thus, abstention is not what appears to be at the core of the tension, but the underlying theological basis (compare 1 Tim 4:3-5). *See* NAG HAMMADI TEXTS; THOMAS, GOSPEL OF.

BRETT S. PROVANCE

ENCROACHMENT [בּוֹא bo', סוּג sugh, קָרֵב qarev, קָרַב qarav]. Encroachment implies infringement upon a normal or an established boundary and is primarily an OT phenomenon. Both the state of encroachment and the act of encroaching is expressed in a variety of ways in the OT; various terms are used and the phenomenon is described against the background of understood limitations or injunctions. The possibility of movement beyond such normal or established limitations is represented in at least two domains: land boundaries and sacred boundaries.

The stipulation of Deut 19:14, "You must not move your neighbor's boundary marker . . ." (NRSV), along with Deut 27:17; Hos 5:10; Prov 22:28 and 23:10*a* addresses the first of these domains. Each of these texts employs the verb swg, "to displace." The act of removing or displacing ancient boundaries so as to enlarge one's territory constituted an encroachment. Proverbs 23:10*b*, "encroach on the fields of orphans" (NRSV) uses the common verb bw' "to enter," but it seems to suggest something more aggressive than simply the act of trespassing.

The NRSV translates the common term qrb ("draw near") as *encroach* in Deut 2:37 ("You did not encroach, however, on the land of the Ammonites . . .") when describing Israel's avoiding the territory of the Ammonites in their approach to Canaan.

Encroachment of a sacred boundary is narratively described in the 2 Sam 6:1-10 account of David's first attempt to transport the ark from the house of Abinadab to Jerusalem. Apparently Uzzah's well-intentioned act of steadying the ark when it was in danger of falling off the cart—thus touching it—constituted encroachment of a sacred boundary (compare Exod 25:12-14, poles for carrying ark). Using the term swg (סוג), Isa 59:14 indicts Israel because justice had been encroached upon.

JOHN I. LAWLOR

END, THE [τὸ τέλος to telos]. Telos can commonly mean "termination," "cessation," "outcome," or "goal," but it sometimes refers to "the last things" or the final act in the cosmic drama, as in Matt 24:6, 14; Mark 13:7; Luke 21:9; and perhaps 1 Cor 15:24. *See* APOCALYPTICISM; ESCHATOLOGY OF THE NT.

MARY KAY DOBROVOLNY, R.S.M.

EN-DOR en'dor [עֵין־דֹר 'en-dor, עֵין־דּוֹר 'en-dor, עֵין־דֹּאר 'en-do'r]. The exact location of En-dor is unknown although the town has been associated with the sites Khirbet es-Safsafeh (near Mount Tabor), Tell el-'Ajjul (also near Mount Tabor), Khirbet Jadurah, and Tell Qedesh. According to Josh 17:11 En-dor is part of Manasseh's inheritance within or near the borders of Issachar. Manassah was unable to take the city from the Canaanites.

En-dor is the home of the medium who contacts Samuel for Saul (1 Sam 28:3-25; *see* DIVINATION; ENDOR, MEDIUM OF; NECROMANCY; SAMUEL; SAUL, SON OF KISH). If En-dor is to be associated with one of the more northern sites (Safsafeh or 'Ajjul), then Saul disguised himself in order to slip through the Philistine forces. If the location is farther south (Jadurah or Qedesh), then Saul disguised himself to hide his identity from the necromancer.

Psalm 83:10 [Heb. 83:11] associates En-dor with the defeat of Sisera and Jabin (Judg 4–5).

Bibliography: Othniel Margalith. "Dor and En-Dor." *ZAW* 97 (1985) 109–11; Nehemia Zori. "New Light on Endor." *PEQ* 84 (1952) 114–17.

HEATHER R. MCMURRAY

ENDOR, MEDIUM OF en'dor [אֵשֶׁת בַּעֲלַת־אוֹב 'esheth ba'alath-'ov]. The necromancer Saul uses the Medium of Endor to contact the deceased SAMUEL when all the acceptable means of contacting Yahweh fail (1 Sam 28:7-25). Saul's expulsion of the mediums and wizards from Israel is not recounted in 1 Samuel. The exact nature of the necromantic ritual is not described, but Brian Schmidt posits that the ritual resembles late Mesopotamian necromantic practices tied to the sun god Shamash. The woman would have prepared for the ritual during the night and contacted the ghost at sunrise. This would explain why Saul had not eaten through the night.

Saul's visit to the woman is one of the reasons for his death, according to 1 Chr 10:13-14. Josephus uses the woman as an example of showing kindness because she tends to Saul, despite the fact that he is responsible for the expulsion of the mediums (*Ant.* 6.340–42). The 1st cent. CE author PSEUDO-PHILO is the only source to give her a name: Sedecla. *See* NECROMANCY.

Bibliography: Brian B. Schmidt. *Israel's Beneficent Dead: Ancestor Cult and Necromancy in Ancient Israelite Religion and Tradition* (1996).

HEATHER R. MCMURRAY

ENDURANCE [חָכָה khakhah; ὑπομονή hypomonē]. In the OT "to endure" means to remain and persevere. The former typically refers to God's throne (Lam 5:19) and righteousness (Ps 111:3); the latter to steadfastness under trial.

PERSEVERANCE in righteous adversity recurs throughout Job. Daniel's blessing for constancy in persecution (12:12) is widely developed in the NT.

The Gospels (e.g., Mark 13:13), and especially Paul, prominently depict hypomonē as a virtue necessary in the outworking of Christian salvation. Endurance is more active than PATIENCE. Thus, Paul closely associates hypomonē with the triad of Christian virtues—faith, love, and especially hope. Endurance produces hope (Rom 5:3-4); and, reciprocally, hope effects persistent endurance (1 Thess 1:3).

CHRIS M. SMITH

EN-EGLAIM en-eg'lay-im [עֵין עֶגְלַיִם 'en 'eghlayim]. Means "spring/fountain of the two calves." A place somewhere near the Dead Sea (Ezek 47:10) whose precise location is uncertain. It has been identified with sites near the northwest quadrant of the Dead Sea, and more recently within Moabite territory in the southeast quadrant.

ENEMY [אֹיֵב 'oyev; ἐχθρός echthros]. The word most often translated *enemy* in the OT is the participial form ('oyev) of the verbal root 'ayav (אָיַב). Its general meaning is "one being hostile." It is used some 270 times in the OT in a wide variety of contexts, but always of people or people groups. In 1 Sam 18:29, Saul is described as David's enemy (*see also* 1 Sam 19:17; 24:4, 19). Other references to personal enemies are found in 2 Sam 4:8 (Ish-bosheth and David), 1 Kgs 21:20 (Elijah and Ahab), and Exod 23:4 (instructions about an enemy's ox). The vast majority of the uses of 'ayav in the OT are in reference to national enemies who pursue, oppress, and fight against the covenant people (Deut 1:42; Josh 7:8; 1 Kgs 8:33; Mic 4:10). National enemies are those peoples living in the territories surrounding the Israelite nation—the Canaanites, the Midianites, the Edomites, the Amorites, the Assyrians, the Babylonians, and particularly the Philistines. In many passages, the oppression of the covenant people by these national enemies is viewed as the judgment of God, especially in the DEUTERONOMISTIC HISTORY. In the classic "framework" of the book of Judges, we read that the punishment meted out to the Israelites for worshiping Baal and the Astartes was that God "gave them over to plunderers who plundered them, and he sold them into the power of their enemies all around" (Judg 2:14; *see* 2 Kgs 21:14 and Jer 12:7.)

Other passages speak of the enemies of God who will perish or be avenged. God says in Isa 1:24, "Ah, I will pour out my wrath on my enemies, and avenge myself on my foes!" (Isa 1:24; *see* Isa 59:18; Nah 1:2; and Ps 92:9). Job accuses God of counting him as an enemy (Job 13:24), and in an interesting twist, the book of Lamentations speaks of God as enemy (ʾoyev) against the covenant people: "The Lord has become like an enemy; he has destroyed Israel" (Lam 2:4, 5).

The enemy is strikingly prominent in the book of Psalms. There, in some seventy-five instances, the psalm singers cry out to God to protect them from the enemy (Pss 25:19; 31:15; 74:3, 10; 83:2; 143:3), celebrate God's power over and protection from the enemy (Pss 8:2; 27:6; 66:3; 89:22), and praise God for delivering them from the enemy (Pss 3:7; 31:8; 106:10; 138:7). Interestingly, though, the enemy in the book of Psalms is rarely named or identified but is for the most part a general reference to an "other" or "others" who are hostile to the psalmist. The enemy, the ʾoyev, may thus be understood as the source of oppression and adversity of any who recite the words of the psalms.

A number of words are used in synonymous parallelism with ʾoyev in the OT. The most common is another participial form, tsar (צָר), translated as "adversary" or "foe." Its verbal meaning is "to surround, encircle, tie up," used some seventy times in the OT, often in parallelism with ʾoyev (Exod 23:22; Ps 27:2; Isa 1:24; Mic 5:9). Closely related to tsar is tsorer (צוֹרֵר), also translated as "adversary" or "foe." Its verbal meaning is "to envelope, to hamper, to cramp," and it too is often used in parallelism with ʾoyev (Exod 23:22; Pss 8:2; 143:12). In Ps 23:5, tsorer is the word used in the statement by the psalmist, "You prepare a table before me in the presence of my enemies." Other synonyms for ʾoyev are soneʾ (שׂוֹנֵא), translated as "hating one" or "adversary" (Deut 30:7; Ps 18:17), and various forms of qam (קָם), "one rising up" (Deut 28:7; Job 27:7; Ps 18:48).

In the NT, the word translated "enemy" is echthros, which means essentially the same as ʾoyev in the OT. The LXX translates almost all instances of the Hebrew ʾoyev with the Greek echthros. While ʾoyev in the OT refers to both personal and national enemies, echthros is used most often in the NT to refer to personal enemies rather than national ones—reflecting perhaps not so much a difference in the basic meanings of the two words as a difference in the focus of the texts in which the words occur. And the word occurs much less often in the NT, approximately only thirty times.

The few uses of echthros in reference to national enemies in the NT reflect a clear tie to the OT pro-

phetic tradition. In Luke 21:71 and 74, Zechariah commemorates the birth of John the Baptist with the following words: "We would be saved from our enemies and from the hand of all who hate us . . . that we, being rescued from the hands of our enemies, might serve him without fear." Jesus states, "Indeed, the days will come upon you, when your enemies will set up ramparts around you and surround you," in his prophecy of the destruction of Jerusalem in Luke 19:43.

Elsewhere in the NT, echthros refers to the enemy of the individual believer. In the Sermon on the Mount, Jesus says, "Love your enemies and pray for those who persecute you" (Matt 5:44; Luke 6:27). Romans 12:20 admonishes readers, "If your enemies are hungry, feed them; if they are thirsty, give them something to drink."

Several passages in the letters speak of the enemies of God. Romans 5:8-10 suggests that sinners are the enemies of God. In Jas 4:4, we read, "Whoever wishes to be a friend of the world becomes an enemy of God." And in the parable of the wheat and tares in Matt 13:24-30 and in Luke 10:19, echthros refers to satan.

The enemy, ʾoyev and echthros, is a pervasive presence in the Bible. Whether personal or national, whether sent by God or destroyed by God, whether named or only generally referred to, communities of faith throughout the millennia have told stories of their encounters with the oppressive other, the one being hostile, the one enveloping and hampering, the one hating and rising up.

Bibliography: Ingvar Fløysvik. *When God Becomes My Enemy: The Theology of the Complaint Psalms* (1997); David B. Gowler. *Host, Guest, Enemy, and Friend: Portraits of the Pharisees in Luke and Acts* (1991).

NANCY L. DECLAISSÉ-WALFORD

EN-GANNIM en-gan′im [עֵין גַּנִּים ʿen gannim]. Means "spring of gardens." En-onam, which has been identified as modern-day ʿOlam, has been suggested as the original name for En-gannim, but En-gannim may be the name of several different towns.

1. Joshua apportioned En-gannim, located northwest of Jerusalem and in the lowland (the Shephelah), to the tribe of Judah (Josh 15:34). This town has been identified with modern-day Beit Jemal and Umm Jina.

2. Joshua apportioned a town named En-gannim to the tribe of Issachar (Josh 19:21). The Chronicler's parallel list names the town ANEM (1 Chr 6:73). According to Josh 21:29, the tribe of Issachar gave En-gannim to the Gershonites, a Levite family. Modern-day Jenin, situated in the plain of Esdraelon in its southern portion, has been identified as this town.

EMILY R. CHENEY

EN-GEDI en-ged′i [עֵין גֶּדִי ʿen gedhi]. En-gedi is the largest oasis on the western shore of the Dead Sea, located about halfway between MASADA in the south

Todd Bolen/BiblePlaces.com
Figure 1: Nahal David Waterfall

and QUMRAN to the north. Its name means "spring of the young goat." It is alternately called Hazazon-tamar (2 Chr 20:2). Joshua 15:62 assigns the oasis to the territory of the tribe of Judah. It was an important source of water for those in the wilderness of Judah, which explains why David took refuge there during his flight from Saul (1 Sam 24:1). The fertility of En-gedi is reflected in the poetry of Song 1:14 and Eccl 24:14.

Todd Bolen/BiblePlaces.com
Figure 2: Chalcolithic temple from west

Archaeological digs at En-gedi have revealed its activity in different historical periods. The most impressive discovery is the Chalcolithic period (fourth millennium BCE) shrine with its associated cache of 429 copper objects from a cave at nearby Nahal Mishmar. On the hills above the oasis a fortress from the Israelite period has been unearthed that may have served as a defense against Moabites and Edomites, who would have approached Judah from the southeast. Indeed, 2 Chr 20:1-4 relates the account of an army of Moabites and Ammonites gathering against JEHOSHAPHAT at En-gedi. Another stronghold at En-gedi dates from the Herodian period, and Roman baths from the late 1st to early 2nd cent. CE made use of the spring at the oasis.

Bibliography: David Ussishkin. "The 'Ghassulian' Temple in Ein Gedi and the Origin of the Hoard from Nahal Mishmar." *BA* 34 (1971) 23–39.

KEVIN A. WILSON

ENGINES. *See* MACHINES OF WAR.

ENGLISH BIBLE. The first translation of the complete Bible into English was done by John Wycliff (first edition between 1380 and 1384), the first Reformation translation of the NT into English by William Tyndale in 1525, and the first complete printed English Bible by Miles Coverdale (published 1535). The so-called Matthew Bible (1537) is said to have been the first one that gained royal approval; the most important and influential edition among authorized versions is the King James Version (first edition 1611). Important versions to follow were the English Revised Version (1881, 1885), the American Standard Version (1897, 1901), the Revised Standard Version (1952), and the New Revised Standard Version (1989), as well as the New American Standard Bible (1971, updated 1995). Translations intended to be read easily by people of all ages and backgrounds are, e.g., Good News Bible, Contemporary English Version, Living Bible, *The Message. See* VERSIONS, ENGLISH.

PETER ARZT-GRABNER

ENGRAVING [פָּתַח pathakh; γραφή graphē]. Incising an image or lettering onto a hard surface such as metal, wood, stone, or precious stone. The stone was fixed in position and the image first etched before the actual incising was done. Various tools were used, including handheld or bow drills that used copper, emery, or iron drill bits. How this detailed work was done before the advent of magnifying aids remains an open question. Ancient jewelers did not seem to engrave metals (gold, silver, bronze), presumably because it would involve wasting some of the precious metal. Instead, engraving was done on precious stones, which made counterfeiting (e.g., of signet rings) almost impossible. In the case of a precious stone, engraving was done primarily when making seals.

The OT makes several references to engraving, most notably in reference to the engraving of the names of the twelve tribes of Israel, upon the ephod (Exod 28:9; 39:6) and high priest's breastpiece (Exod 28:21; 39:14, recalled in Sir 45:11). Engraving was also used in the construction of the Temple (1 Kgs 6:29). The specialization required of the artists who did this work is suggested by Solomon's request to HIRAM for someone skilled in engraving (2 Chr 2:7 [Heb. 2:6]). This technique is seemingly a secondary meaning of the Hebrew verb **pathakh,** "to open," but in a more intensive sense. *See* JEWELRY.

ELIZABETH E. PLATT

EN-HADDAH en-had′uh [עֵין חַדָּה ʿen khaddah]. One of sixteen cities allotted to the tribe of Issachar on the west side of the Jordan (Jos 19:21).

EN-HAKKORE en-hak′uh-ree [עֵין הַקּוֹרֵא ʿen haqqoreʾ]. A spring of water God miraculously provides SAMSON after he calls out in thirst (Judg 15:19). Etymologically a wordplay, it means "spring of the one who called" or, possibly, "spring of the partridge." A *hapax legomenon*, the former is preferred, given the context. *See* HAPAX LEGOMENA.

TRISHA GAMBAIANA WHEELOCK

EN-HAZOR en-hay′zor [עֵין חָצוֹר ʿen khatsor]. This town, whose name means "well of Hazor," was one of the fortified towns within the territory of the tribe of Naphtali, in the north of Canaan, as listed in Josh 19:37; usually identified with the modern site of Khirbet Hazireh.

ENLIL en′lil. Means "Lord Wind." Enlil was a Sumerian storm god, and the city god of Nippur, a very important religious center in northwestern Sumer. Enlil's importance accompanied that of his city. By the third millennium BCE, Enlil possessed the supreme executive power in the Sumerian pantheon under the titular leadership of An, god of heaven and city god of Uruk. Enlil's hold on the supreme executive power continued in the Akkadian tradition. Even in later periods when other deities assumed kingship over the gods, they were said to have taken over the enlilship. In some late religious texts, however, Enlil has been reduced to the level of an enemy god or demon.

J. J. M. ROBERTS

EN-MISHPAT. *See* KADESH, KADESH-BARNEA.

EN-NASBEH, TELL. *See* MIZPAH, MIZPEH.

ENOCH ee′nuhk [חֲנוֹךְ khanokh; Ἑνώχ Henōch]. 1. The first son of CAIN and the father of IRAD. The first city was named after Enoch (Gen 4:17-18).

2. In the seventh generation from Adam through SETH, Enoch was the son of JARED and father of METHUSELAH (Gen 5:18-21; 1 Chr 1:2-3; Luke 3:37). Although the text pattern in the Gen 5 genealogy says in turn that each patriarch "died," uniquely Enoch "walked with God" (Gen 5:22-24). Later interest in Enoch's non-death is apparent as when he is cited as an example of faith (Heb 11:5) or of repentance (Sir 44:16; 49:14). Much as ELIJAH's ascension stirred expectations of his return, the fact that Enoch did not die meant that he was available in the future for use by God (Jude 1:14), giving rise to an abundance of visionary and prophetic Enoch literature. *See* ENOCH, FIRST BOOK OF; ENOCH, SECOND BOOK OF; ENOCH, THIRD BOOK OF.

A. HEATH JONES, III

ENOCH, ETHIOPIC. *See* ENOCH, FIRST BOOK OF.

ENOCH, FIRST BOOK OF ee′nuhk. *First Enoch*, also referred to as *Ethiopic Enoch*, since the fullest version of this text has been preserved in Geʾez, is a collection of distinct works attributed to the biblical patriarch Enoch; these writings were composed from the 3rd (or 4th) cent. BCE to the 1st cent. BCE or CE. The unusual description of Enoch in Gen 5:24, in which Enoch is said to have walked with God, fostered speculation about the fate of the patriarch in the Second Temple period. The Enochic literature responds to the scriptural enigma by positing that the patriarch was relocated to the company of angels. By means of such illustrious companions, Enoch is taken to places throughout the cosmos ordinarily inaccessible to humankind. In addition to narrating the imaginative journeys of the patriarch, many of the works in *1 Enoch* manifest eschatological concerns. In the corpus the theme of judgment finds frequent expression in the condemnation of angelic beings (watchers) who mate with mortal women, a tradition familiar from Gen 6:1-4.

- A. Development of Enochic Literature
- B. Distinctive Sections
  - 1. The Book of the Watchers
  - 2. The Parables of Enoch
  - 3. The Astronomical Book
  - 4. The Book of Dreams
  - 5. The Epistle of Enoch and Appendices
- C. Theological and Religious Significance of the Book
- Bibliography

A. Development of Enochic Literature

First Enoch consists of five discrete works (listed in suggested order of composition): the Astronomical Book, the Book of the Watchers, the Book of Dreams, the Epistle of Enoch and the Parables (or Similitudes) of Enoch. It is commonly held that the booklets were composed in Aramaic, and then translated into Greek and finally translated from Greek to Geʾez, an early form of Ethiopic. The original language of the Book of the Parables and *1 En.* 108 is uncertain, however; these sections of the corpus have not been not discovered at Qumran and are not extant in Aramaic or Greek. The five works, each a product of a particular context and subject to redaction, contribute to a trajectory of traditions associated with Enoch, a trajectory evident also in the later books of *2 Enoch* (or the *Slavonic Apocalypse of Enoch*) and *3 Enoch* (also known as the *Hebrew Apocalypse of Enoch*).

The various works in *1 Enoch* have been associated with the genres of apocalypse and testament and with literary forms such as prophetic oracles and historical reviews. Certain selections from the corpus might be characterized as rewritten biblical narrative inasmuch as they seem to work from and attempt to clarify the brief account of the patriarch in Gen 5:21-24 or the narrative involving the sons of God who mate with the daughters of men from Gen 6:1-4. Moreover, many of the texts indicate familiarity with the Hebrew Scriptures, especially prophetic texts and wisdom literature, as is suggested by shared motifs and allusions to biblical texts. At the same time, Enochic literature reflects Near Eastern and Greek traditions as well.

B. Distinctive Sections

1. The Book of the Watchers

Although not the earliest composition in the extant collection, the Book of the Watchers (*1 En.* 1–36) is the first to be featured in *1 Enoch*. The booklet, made up of distinct literary units, is thought to have taken its current form by the 3rd cent. BCE. Chapters 1–5 approximate a prophetic oracle and contrast the orderliness of nature with the disobedience of sinners (2:1-5:4). Chapters 6–16 concern the relations of angels and mortal women, an association that has disastrous consequences. The union leads to offspring, bloodthirsty giants who consume all manner of living beings, including humans (*1 En.* 7:2-5). The angels also impart illicit teaching that leads to promiscuity and further violence (*1 En.* 7:1; 8:1-4). The archangels intervene and enlist Enoch as an intermediary to the rebellious angels (*1 En.* 12:3–13:2). After an ascent to the heavenly temple and prophetic commissioning, Enoch learns firsthand the Divine's response to the situation (*1 En.* 14:8–16:4); the patriarch then returns to earth and delivers the message of condemnation to the fallen angels (*1 En.* 13:9–14:7). In the second half of the Book of the Watchers, angels accompany Enoch on a tour of places typically inaccessible to mortals. Enoch is taken, for example, to the ends of the earth (*1 En.* 18:5, 10), to storehouses of winds and other natural phenomena (*1 En.* 18:1-4), and to the garden, former home of the primordial couple, which contains a tree of wisdom (*1 En.* 32:3-6). We are told that Enoch alone sees these sites (*1 En.* 19:3), and such wonders lead him to bless God (*1 En.* 36:4).

2. The Parables of Enoch

The Book of the Parables, or Similitudes, of Enoch (*1 En.* 37–71) is preserved in Ge'ez and is known only from *1 Enoch*. Identifying the date and provenance of the composition has proven somewhat of a challenge, yet the scholarly consensus is that the booklet derives from either the 1st cent. BCE or CE and is Jewish in origin. The work is essentially divided into three parables (*1 En.* 38–44, 45–57, and 58–69), here with the sense of revelatory discourses of Enoch, for which it is so named (*1 En.* 37:5). The most outstanding theme in the Book of the Parables is the impending judgment, when God will vindicate the elect and punish their oppressors, identified as sinners, kings, the mighty,

and those who possess the earth (e.g., *1 En.* 46:4-6; 48:8-10; 53:2, 5; 62:9). The booklet's emphasis on a final judgment is complemented by references to a certain end-time figure referred to as "the elect one" (*1 En.* 45:3-4; 51:3, 5; 52:6), "the righteous one" (*1 En.* 53:6), "the anointed one" (messiah; *1 En.* 48:10; 52:4) and "the Son of Man" (*1 En.* 46:2-4; 48:2); the individual assists God on the day of judgment as the Son of Man seated on a throne of glory to whom judgment is given (*1 En.* 69:27-29). The identity of this end-time figure is withheld until the epilogue to the Parables, where the Son of Man is revealed to be Enoch (*1 En.* 70–71; esp. 71:14).

3. The Astronomical Book

The Astronomical Book (*1 En.* 72–82), also referred to as the Book of the Heavenly Luminaries, is thought to be the earliest booklet of the corpus, from the 3rd or perhaps even the 4th cent. BCE. The book concerns the movement of the luminaries (the sun, moon, and stars) and articulates both a solar year of 364 days and a lunar year of 354 days. The book's interest in "astronomical" matters may be related to Gen 5:23 in which Enoch is said to live 365 years, a number reminiscent of the days in a solar year, though the traditions recounted in the Astronomical Book clearly extend beyond the biblical reference. Unlike the other booklets in *1 Enoch*, eschatological concerns are not primary in the Astronomical Book.

4. The Book of Dreams

The Book of Dreams (*1 En.* 83–90) is a work of the 2nd cent. BCE made up of two sections: *1 En.* 83–84, sometimes referred to simply as the "First Dream Vision," and *1 En.* 85–90, the "Second Dream Vision" or "Animal Apocalypse." Both sections culminate with a great judgment. For the First Dream Vision, judgment arrives with the deluge from which Noah is preserved; the Animal Apocalypse, however, offers a recapitulation of the history of Israel that continues until the time of the work's author, the time ordained for a second great judgment. The Animal Apocalypse is essentially an allegory in which the principal figures in the history of Israel, from the time of Adam and Eve until the 2nd cent. BCE, are recast primarily as animals and birds. The introduction of Judas Maccabeus immediately precedes God's descent and the final judgment (*1 En.* 90:8-27). Following the final judgment, Jerusalem is removed while a new city that descends to earth takes its place (*1 En.* 90:28-29; *see also* Rev 21:10-14).

5. The Epistle of Enoch and Appendices

The Epistle of Enoch (*1 En.* 91–105) is from the 2nd cent. BCE and adopts the setting of Enoch revealing to his sons his exceptional knowledge of the world and things to come (91:1-3); in this respect, the work recalls testament literature like Gen 49:1-27. The received text of the Epistle of Enoch is somewhat confused because of interpolations and dislocations of text, especially materials in chaps. 91 and 93, most likely by the editor who compiled the book. The booklet includes two distinct sections: a parenetic address to Enoch's sons (*1 En.* 91:1-10, 18-19; 92:1-10; 93:11-14; 94–105) and an apocalypse featuring a periodization of history (referred to as "the Apocalypse of Weeks"; *1 En.* 91:11-17; 93:1-10). Two appendices (the story of Noah's birth [*1 En.* 106–7] and a final chapter [*1 En.* 108]) follow the Epistle and *1 En.* 108 may have served as a conclusion to the corpus as a whole. All sections to varying degrees concern the theme of the vindication of the righteous and punishment of the wicked.

C. Theological and Religious Significance of the Book

Salient theological characteristics of the Enochic literature are its high evaluation of revelation and its apocalypticism. While the latter is muted in the Astronomical Book, other booklets in the corpus express the expectation for theophany whereby the Divine would right all wrongs. The concern for impending judgment, a temporal matter, is complemented by the literature's attention to space. Many of the Enochic works manifest special interest in places associated with the afterlife, though the realm of the dead and paradise are depicted in varying ways (e.g., *1 En.* 22:1-13; 32:3-6; 39:4-7; 61:1-5; 70:3). Moreover, the inhabited world, as well as places inaccessible to humans, contains sites related to judgment that have been established already by the patriarch's lifetime. The revelation of such sites underscores that judgment has been woven into the fabric of the cosmos. The earlier texts among the corpus, the Astronomical Book and the Book of the Watchers in particular, emphasize Enoch's access to knowledge that he then imparts to his audience. Thus, Enoch provides answers to life's most vexing questions. Even with its focus on judgment, the Enochic collection gives little insight into what constitutes sin for its authors. The literature is concerned with idolatry (e.g., *1 En.* 19:1; 99:7-9), blasphemy (*1 En.* 27:2; 94:9; 96:7) and, one infers from the story of the watchers' descent, with the crossing of boundaries (*1 En.* 7:1; 9:8; 15:3-7), warfare (*1 En.* 8:1; 15:11), use of cosmetics (*1 En.* 8:1), and popular magic (7:1; 8:3; 9:8). Abusive kings, the mighty, and the wealthy who oppress and enslave the poor are accentuated among the condemned (*1 En.* 46:7; 47:4-5; 48:8; 96:4-5, 8; 97:8-10; 99:13; 103:11-15).

A matter of ongoing debate is whether the Enochic literature challenges or takes for granted the Sinaitic covenant and torah, thought by many to be essential categories within Second Temple period Judaism. Some scholars, struck by the lack of attention the collection pays to the law, suggest that it promotes instead the revealed wisdom of Enoch. Others argue that the

literature assumes a form of nomism that remains implicit in the text and note the presence of Enochic works among the Dead Sea Scrolls, which include several compositions clearly dedicated to a very strict observance of torah.

A related question, perhaps, is the extent to which this literature reflects a unique form of Judaism, one keyed to the figure of Enoch or the sorts of revelations we find in *1 Enoch*. The many references to "the elect" (or "the righteous" or "faithful") who are addressed in the corpus indicate that authors had in mind a particular, contemporaneous audience (e.g., *1 En.* 1:1-3; 38:1; 46:8; 93:10) and such references are understood by some to suggest that the community saw themselves as distinct from other Jews during the Second Temple period. While there are scholars who have attempted to define and locate this hypothetical group vis-à-vis other streams of Judaism, given the paucity of information the consensus seems to be one of reservation in attempting to identify or delineate more precisely an alleged community. Even while reconstruction of an "Enochic Judaism" may prove elusive, it is evident that Enochic texts and significant themes associated with this literature were popular among Christians. Jude 14-15 refers to Enoch prophesying and follows with a citation of *1 En.* 1:9, and Jude 6 and 2 Pet 2:4 allude to the tradition of the angels imprisoned for their rebellion. Further, there are numerous references to the patriarch and to particular Enochic texts and motifs (e.g., the idea of the angels mating with women) in the writings of Christians until the 4th cent. CE.

In any event, even while certain interests or foci— e.g., eschatological concerns—are found throughout much of the Enochic corpus, the individual booklets emerge from different contexts and indicate development as well as attempts to nuance and perhaps even to discount theological positions taken in other of the Enochic booklets. For example, if we read the text correctly, the claim in the Epistle of Enoch (*1 En.* 93:11-14) that no one can ascend and understand the workings of the heavens (or other obscure topics) challenges the premise of the earlier Astronomical Book and Book of the Watchers, where Enoch the seer does ascend and through his marvelous journeys gains access to all sorts of otherwise inaccessible information. Likewise, while the Book of the Watchers (*1 En.* 6–16) and to some extent the Book of Dreams (*1 En.* 86–88) present the fallen watchers as the cause of the proliferation of evil on earth, the Epistle of Enoch asserts that humans alone bear responsibility for sin; no supernatural agent from heaven is to blame (*1 En.* 98:4). These incongruities suggest that were there an Enochic community, it revisited and revised in the course of time certain theological suppositions.

Bibliography: Gabriele Boccaccini. *Beyond the Essene Hypothesis: The Parting of the Ways Between Qumran and Enochic Judaism* (1998); George W. E. Nickelsburg.

1 Enoch 1: A Commentary on the Book of 1 Enoch, Chapters 1–36; 81–108 Hermeneia (2001); George W. E. Nickelsburg and James C. VanderKam. *1 Enoch: A New Translation* (2004); James C. VanderKam. *Enoch: A Man for All Generations* (1995).

KELLY COBLENTZ BAUTCH

ENOCH, SECOND BOOK OF. An apocalyptic work of unknown origins, relating the story of Enoch's ascension through the heavens, his encounter with God, and the ethical instruction he subsequently gives to his sons.

A. Plot and Structure

There are at least two recensions (long and short), possibly more, and the contents vary significantly. The outline given here is a hybrid, with the important variations mentioned in brackets after the chapter numbers. Chapters are numbered according to the convention followed by Francis I. Andersen in his English translation.

1	Introduction and titles.
2	Enoch's first instruction to his sons.
3–20	Enoch is carried through the seven heavens (the longer MSS have ten heavens).
21–22	Enoch sees the Lord and is himself gloriously transformed.
23–32	Vereveil recounts to Enoch the secrets of Creation (the longer MSS are much fuller at this point).
33–38	Enoch is commissioned to reveal these truths to his sons, that they may be transmitted to a future generation. His face is cooled in preparation for his return.
39–42	Enoch's visions are summarized.
43–66	Enoch's second instruction of his sons.
67	Enoch is taken back to heaven.
68–72	The story of Methuselah and of Melkizedek's miraculous birth (attested only by some MSS).

B. Origins and Tradition History

Second Enoch is attested by around twenty manuscripts and all written in Church Slavonic. These date from the 14th–17th cent. and reflect a number of dialects. In each case, *2 Enoch* is part of a wider work or collection.

Widely divergent dates and contexts have been proposed for its origins, from 1st cent. Palestine or Alexandria through to a 10th cent. Byzantine monastery. The evidence usually cited for an early date and Jewish authorship centers on the presence of numerous references to sacrifice and on the frequent occurrence of Semitisms in the text, but the possibility that these represent a Christian author's fictional devices cannot be excluded.

The question of whether the longer or shorter recension of the text is original remains a problem. There is evidence for a number of interpolations in the longer recension but there are also points where the shorter texts appear to have been deliberately abbreviated. At present, it seems that the best approach is a verse-by-verse comparative assessment of the witnesses, favoring neither a priori. In addition, neither recension is free of secondary additions.

C. Theological and Religious Significance

As long as uncertainty hangs over the question of the origins of *2 Enoch*, its religious significance must be assessed with caution. Some have argued that it represents a stage in the evolution of the Enoch–Metatron traditions of *3 Enoch* (*Sefer Hekalot*), though others remain skeptical of this.

The depiction of Enoch as "the one who carries away the sin of mankind" (64:5) and also the description of his transfiguration (22:8-10) have obvious similarities to the NT's depiction of Jesus. If *2 Enoch* is Jewish, then these elements may contribute to our growing knowledge of divine mediator figures in Judaism and cast light on christological elements in the NT. The fact that we have so many manuscripts in Church Slavonic attests to the ongoing transmission of Enochic ideas in Christian contexts in later centuries.

Bibliography: Francis I. Andersen. "2 (Slavonic Apocalypse of) Enoch." *OTP 1* (1983) 91-221; Andrei Orlov. *The Enoch–Metatron Tradition* (2005).

GRANT MACASKILL

ENOCH, SECRETS OF. *See* ENOCH, SECOND BOOK OF.

ENOCH, SIMILITUDES OF. *See* ENOCH, FIRST BOOK OF.

ENOCH, SLAVONIC. *See* ENOCH, SECOND BOOK OF.

ENOCH, THIRD BOOK OF. A post-biblical apocalypse, written in Hebrew, which describes Rabbi Ishmael's ascent to heaven; his encounter with Metatron, the biblical patriarch Enoch (compare Gen 5:21–24) who ascended to heaven and was transformed into an exalted angel known as the "Lesser Yahweh"; and heavenly secrets that Metatron reveals to Ishmael.

The book of *3 Enoch* is formally an "apocalypse," a revelation by a divine being or angel who grants heavenly secrets to a human recipient. It belongs to the corpus of "Hekhalot Literature," the source of MERKAVAH MYSTICISM. The title "3 Enoch" is a modern coinage; the manuscripts open with various titles and often with the text of Gen 5:24. The book describes the ascent of the 2nd cent. figure Rabbi Ishmael to the seventh celestial palace, where he encounters the angel Metatron (chaps. 1–3). Metatron tells of the early history of the world, his own fiery transformation and enthronement as the highest angel (3–15), and his subsequent demotion and punishment after Rabbi Elisha ben Abuyah ascended to heaven and mistook him for a second deity (16). Metatron then reveals minute details of the angelic hierarchy and other mysteries to Ishmael (17–40) and takes him on a tour of the universe, showing him secrets of creation, the places of the dead and the fallen angels, and the past and future history of the world (41–48).

The book survives in medieval manuscripts whose texts vary considerably. Chapters 3–15 appear on their own in one manuscript and may be the original core of the book, although this is debated. These chapters are summarized by an early 10th cent. Jewish Karaite author, and they also show knowledge of the Babylonian Talmud (edited ca. 600 CE), so chaps. 3–15 must have been composed between 600 and 900, although they clearly drew on considerably earlier traditions about Enoch and his apotheosis as well. The full text of chaps. 1–48 may have been written at the same time or may consist of later accretions around the original core. In any case the book is clearly a collection of somewhat inconsistent traditions. The surviving text lacks many typical features of Merkavah mysticism, such as magical incantations and Merkavah hymns. The earliest surviving fragment of *3 Enoch*, recovered from the Cairo Geniza repository of manuscripts, contains chaps. 1 and 43–44 as a unit and includes astrological and other magical material, indicating that the form of the book we have now has been extensively edited and purged of unorthodox elements, sometimes leaving the text incoherent.

The angel Metatron (whose name may be Greek and may have some relation to the throne of God) is constructed from traditions about earlier figures including Adam, Enoch, and the angels Michael and Yahoel. Metatron shows that Jewish tradition even in late antiquity or later could countenance the transformation of a human being into a divine being, although we have no certain evidence that Metatron, unlike Jesus, was actually worshipped.

Bibliography: P. Alexander. "3 (Hebrew Apocalypse of) Enoch." *OTP* 1 (83–86) 223–315.

JAMES R. DAVILA

ENOSH ee´nosh [אֱנוֹשׁ *'enosh*]. The father of Kenan in the Sethite genealogy of Gen 5:6-11 (also 1 Chr 1:1). The name, like ADAM, means human being. Enosh is mentioned in Gen 4:26 along with the notice that it was in his time that human beings began to worship (invoke the name of) Yahweh.

PHILLIP MICHAEL SHERMAN

EN-RIMMON en-rim´uhn [עֵין רִמּוֹן *'ayin rimmon*]. Southern Negev town. Although the two parts of the name often occur together as a compound word, some verses have a conjunction between the two elements, suggesting the translation "Ain/En and Rimmon" (Josh 15:32; 1 Chr 4:32). 'Ayin is never vocalized as a construct, as would be expected if the name meant "spring of the pomegranate tree." The town is variously assigned to the tribal allotment of Judah (Josh 15:32) or Simeon (Josh 19:7). En-Rimmon is to be distinguished from the rock of Rimmon in Benjamin (Judg 20:45-47; 21:13) and Rimmon in Zebulun (Josh 19:13).

KEVIN A. WILSON

EN-ROGEL en-roh´guhl [עֵין־רֹגֵל *'en-roghel*]. A spring just south of JERUSALEM whose name means "spring of the (clothes-)washer." From the biblical description, the spring lies in the Kidron Valley, just south of the confluence of the Kidron and Hinnom valleys. En-Rogel is usually identified with Bir 'Ayyub (Arab. "well of Job"), which still flows today. During ABSALOM's revolt, David's informers inside the city would send a messenger to En-Rogel to meet with David's messengers (2 Sam 17:17). When David was near death, his son ADONIJAH had himself proclaimed king at the stone of ZOHELETH beside En-Rogel (1 Kgs 1:9-10). The spring serves as one of the geographical markers for the boundary between Judah and Benjamin (Josh 15:7; 18:6).

KEVIN A. WILSON

ENROLLMENT [הִתְיַחֵשׂ *hithyakhes*, מִסְפָּר *mispar*; מִפְקָד *mifqadh*, פְּקֻדִים *pequdhim*; ἀπογραφῆς *apographes*, ἐπίσκεψιν *episkepsin*, ἀριθμός *arithmos*]. A public and official counting, numbering, registering, or listing of people by family, tribe, genealogy, or occupation. Such enrollments occur within various social or political contexts (e.g., membership within kinship groups in kinship-based communities— Gen 46:8-27; royal enlistments by native kings—2 Sam 24:1-9; imperial registrations of populations in vassal states—Luke 2:1-5; Acts 5:37; or enrollments for ritual purposes—Num 7:1-88).

The enrollments served different practical functions in the ancient world of the Bible, depending on the specific context, need, or occasion: collecting taxes (Exod 30:11-16), determining military strength by numbering soldiers (Num 1:1-47; 2 Sam 24:1-9), gathering workers from among resident aliens (2 Chr 2:17-18), determining eligibility for cultic service (Num 3:14-39; 26:57-62; Neh 7:63-65), apportioning land according to the size of tribal units (Num 26:1-51), determining status and eligibility within the community of returned exiles (Ezra 2:1-67; Neh 7:5-69; Ezek 13:9), and listing priests who had violated cultic regulations (Ezra 10:16-44).

Alongside these human practical registrations or enrollments, the Bible also speaks of divine enrollments of nations and people (Deut 32:8-9; Ps 87:6; Heb 12:23) as well as a divine Book of Life with a registry of names (Ps 69:28; Phil 4:3; Rev 3:5).

Some biblical traditions assume that any enrollment or counting of humans was evil and could cause a plague as divine punishment (Exod 30:12). In an enigmatic text in 2 Sam 24:1, 10-25, God first incites King David to enroll all warriors in a national census and then promptly sends a pestilence that kills 70,000 Israelites as punishment for taking the census. The human calculation of a military enrollment may have implied a trust in human strength rather than in God. The retelling of the same episode in 1 Chr 21 names Satan rather than God as the one who incited David to do the military census, thereby avoiding some of the theological difficulty.

The most significant NT enrollment is the Roman imperial census recorded as part of the birth narrative of Jesus in the Gospel of Luke. In Luke 2:1, the Roman emperor Augustus decrees that "all the world should be enrolled." The enrollment is dated to a time when "Quirinius was governor of Syria" (Luke 2:2). However, this dating creates some chronological difficulties. The birth of Jesus is usually dated to 4 BCE (the year of Herod's death; see Luke 1:5). Quirinius did not become the governor of Syria until ten years later in 6 CE (see Josephus, *Ant.* 18.3; *J.W.* 7.253; Acts 5:37). However one resolves the chronological discrepancy, the imperial enrollment enables the birth of Jesus to occur in Bethlehem, the ancestral home of Joseph and the prophesied origin of the Messiah (Mic 5:2). It also provides a political backdrop to Jesus' birth as the sign of the coming reign of God whose politics will be in opposition to the empire of Rome. *See* CENSUS; GENEALOGY; QUIRINIUS; SATAN.

DENNIS T. OLSON

EN-SHADUD. Archaeological site in the northern Jezreel Valley, apparently a small farming community in two EB I strata. Nearby Tel Shadud may be the site of SARID, part of ZEBULUN's boundary (Josh 19:10). *See* TRIBES, TERRITORIES OF.

Bibliography: E. Braun. *En-Shadud: Salvage Excavations at a Farming Community in the Jezreel Valley, Israel.* (1985).

JAMES RILEY STRANGE

EN-SHEMESH en-shem´ish [עֵין שֶׁמֶשׁ ʿen shemesh]. Not to be confused with modern Ain Shems (ancient BETH-SHEMESH), En-Shemesh ("Spring of the Sun") lay on the boundary between Judah and Benjamin (Josh 15:7; 18:17).

EN-TAPPUAH en-tap´yoo-uh [עֵין תַּפּוּחַ ʿen tappuakh]. A border town between Ephraim and Manasseh that fell to Manasseh, whereas the city of TAPPUAH belonged to Ephraim (Josh 17:7-8).

ENTHRONEMENT. *See* KING, KINGSHIP.

ENTRY, TRIUMPHAL. *See* TRIUMPHAL ENTRY.

ENUMA ELISH en-oo´muh-el´ish. The exact date for the composition of this Akkadian poem is a matter of dispute. Since the earliest copies of the work date from the 1st millennium BCE, earlier scholarship tended to link the date of its composition to the slightly earlier retrieval of the cult statue of MARDUK, the chief god of the Babylonian pantheon, from Elam under Nebuchadnezzar I (1125–1104 BCE). However, this dating has recently been challenged, and the work is now thought to have originated as early as the Old Babylonian period. The author of the Babylonian version incorporated into the poem all the available Sumerian, Old Akkadian, and West Semitic traditions of cosmology and the warrior god's struggle against the primeval sea dragon/monster. The plot of the poem is as follows. Out of the primeval duality of the freshwater ocean known as Apsu and the saltwater ocean called TIAMAT (related to the West Semitic word for *sea*, tamtu) emerge the pillars of the universe. The levels of the earth and sky then create the sky god Anu who begets Ea-Nudimmud. With Ea's defeat of Apsu, who planned to destroy the disruptive younger generation of gods in order to restore silence, the author introduces the theological motif of theomachy, a motif repeated in Marduk's battle against the sea dragon Tiamat. After Marduk vanquishes Tiamat, he splits her body into halves in order to form Heaven and Earth. Then, acting as demiurge, Marduk creates the celestial bodies and constellations and assigns the planets their courses. He designates the moon to regulate the month and the sun to regulate the day, while he assigns meteorological phenomena to himself. He fashions rivers and mountains, and creates humankind. The ordering of the cosmos is interwoven with the creation of cultic topography. Marduk establishes the temples of the chief deities Anu and ENLIL and at the same time maps them upon various levels of the heaven. His own temple, located in Babylon, represents the religious and political center. With the formation of space and time, Marduk creates not only the fundamental elements of human culture but also the necessary context for structuring the performance of the daily temple ritual and the observance of periodic festivals. Finally, Marduk creates the Netherworld as a further dimension of the cosmos that underlies the notion of the afterlife and provides a mythic space for human existence after death.

BEATE PONGRATZ-LEISTEN

ENVIRONMENT. While the meaning of the term is much more broad, *environment* is often used to refer to the earth and its processes, which constitute the natural environment for humankind. It is from treatment of EARTH, WORLD, or CREATION that we may draw a biblical perspective on the created order. *See* CREATION; ECOLOGY.

MARIAN OSBORNE BERKY

ENVOY, ENVOYS. *See* MESSENGER.

ENVY [קִנְאָה qin'ah; φθόνος phthonos]. The OT concept of envy includes rivalry and zeal (Eccl 4:4; 9:6; Ezek 35:11). Envy and JEALOUSY are also related. Envy usually connotes a desire for an object belonging to someone else (Gen 20:17), while jealousy seems to address ownership or claim on another person. Hebrew uses qin'ah to describe both aspects. Therefore envy and jealousy are tied to physical realities. Human rage from jealousy/envy is most often linked to the male/female relationship of marriage, as with the rage of a deceived husband (Num 5:14; 15, 18, 25, 29, 30). Jealousy also depicts God's claims upon Israel (esp. of God punishing evil, see Exod 20:5). The commandment to worship no other gods sets the parameters of the jealousy of God (Deut 4:24; 6:15; Josh 24:19). Proverbs defines the folly of envying the wicked though they seem to prosper (3:31; 23:17; 24:1, 19). The ill-gotten goods and power of the wicked should not be envied by the righteous.

In the NT, phthonos is often used to describe an intense emotional desire for ill will or harm to someone else (Titus 3:3). The word is found in lists defining vices to be avoided by believers (Rom 1:29; Gal 5:21; 1 Tim 6:14; 1 Pet 1:21). Envy is one cause of Jesus' trial (of the Jews, Matt 27:18; of the chief priests, Mark 15:10). Envy is divisive in the church (Gal 5:26), and results in false teachings (Phil 1:15).

MICHAEL G. VANZANT

EPAENETUS i-pee'nuh-tuhs [Ἐπαίνετος Epainetos]. A Christian greeted by Paul in Rom 16:5 as "My Beloved," Epaenetus is depicted as an émigré to Rome and the first Asian Christian convert (the Gk. text of 5*b* considers Epaenetus literally as the "first fruit in Christ"). It is possible that Epaenetus was converted by Prisca and Aquila in Ephesus and moved with the couple to Rome since they are mentioned prior to Epaenetus (Rom 16:3-5).

HEIDI S. GEIB

EPAPHRAS ep'uh-fras [Ἐπαφρᾶς Epaphras]. A Pauline associate described as a "fellow prisoner" (Phlm 23); "faithful minister of Christ" (Col 1:7); "slave (doulos δοῦλος) of Christ Jesus" (Col 4:12); and "beloved fellow slave (syndoulos συνδοῦλος)" (Col 1:7). Although Epaphras is an abridged form of EPAPHRODITUS (Phil 2:25), the two men were not the same. Epaphras established (Col 1:5, 6, 23) and correctly taught the Colossian assembly (Col 2:6) vis-à-vis others who taught unprofitable "teaching" (Col 2:22-23). He also reported their progress (Col 1:8); worked through-

out the Lycus Valley (Col 4:13); and agonized constantly in prayer for his assembly's maturity (Col 4:12).

ABRAHAM SMITH

EPAPHRODITUS i-paf'ruh-d*i*'tuhs [Ἐπαφρόδιτος Epaphroditos]. A leader in Paul's assembly at Philippi who was sent by the assembly (Phil 2:25, 30) to take gifts to the imprisoned Paul (Phil 4:18). A shorter form of his name is EPAPHRAS, but the two men were not the same, for Epaphras' work was conducted in the Lycus Valley (Col 4:13). Presumably the carrier of the letter to the Philippians (compare Phil 2:25, 28), Epaphroditus was also sent back to the assembly to relieve their anxiety about the grave illness from which he had recently recovered (Phil 2:26-28). Paul does not describe the nature of the illness but Epaphroditus' willingness to serve as the assembly's proxy, even coming "close to death" (mechri thanatou [μέχρι θανάτου], Phil 2:30), both emulates Christ's action of obedience "unto death" (mechri thanatou, Phil 2:8) and illustrates the mindset (Phil 2:5) the Philippians were being exhorted to embrace.

ABRAHAM SMITH

EPEIPH ee'fif [Ἐπιφί Epiphi]. Epeiph is the third month in the season of Shemu ("harvest" or "summer") in the Egyptian calendar. Epeiph and the month PACHON (first month of Shemu) are mentioned in the apocryphal work 3 Macc 6:38. In Aram. papyri from Elephantine, Epeiph and the Aram. month TISHRI are equated. *See* CALENDAR; TIME.

MARY KAY DOBROVOLNY, R.S.M.

EPHAH ee'fuh [אֵיפָה 'efah, עֵיפָה 'efah; οἰφι oiphi]. 1. A dry measure of capacity in the Bible (Judg 6:19; 1 Sam 1:24; 17:17; Ruth 2:17; Zech 5:6-10; etc.). According to Ezekiel (45–46) the ephah and the BATH were equal. The ephah contained ten OMER (Exod 16:36) and was smaller than the HOMER (Hos 3:2). The name probably comes from the Egyptian unit *ipt* (oiphi in Gk.). *See* WEIGHTS AND MEASURES.

RAZ KLETTER

2. One of five sons of MIDIAN (Gen 25:4; 1 Chr 1:33), a tribe well known for camel breeding during the period of the divided monarchy and later (Isa 60:6), appearing as a northwestern Arabian tribe in the Assyrian annals. Tiglath Pileser referred to Ephah with the determinative URU ("city") preceding the tribal name.

3. A concubine of Caleb (1 Chr 2:46).

4. A son of Jahdai (1 Chr 2:47).

RALPH K. HAWKINS

EPHAI ee'fi [עוֹפַי 'ofay, *Qere* עֵיפַי 'efay]. A Netophathite whose unnamed sons, among the commanders of Judean forces operating in the countryside following the fall of Jerusalem in 587 BCE, met with the Babylonian-appointed governor GEDALIAH (Jer 40:8). Second Kings 25:23 omits "the sons of Ephai," making

TANHUMETH the Netophathite. *See* NETOPHAH, NETOPHATHITE.

JASON C. DYKEHOUSE

EPHER ee´fuhr [עֵפֶר *'efer*]. The name means "young deer" or "gazelle." 1. The second son of MIDIAN and a descendant of Moses' wife KETURAH (Gen 25:4; 1 Chr 1:33) whose name was attached to a clan closely connected to the Midianites.

2. The third son of EZRA who was also a descendant of the tribe of Judah (1 Chr 4:17).

3. A chief among the "famous warriors/mighty men" of the half-tribe of Manasseh that settled east of the Jordan River (1 Chr 5:23). The term may suggest the assimilation of Midianite tribes into Israel.

MICHAEL G. VANZANT

EPHES-DAMMIM   ee´fiz-dam´im   [אֶפֶס־דַּמִּים *'efes-dammim*]. At this site the Philistines gathered for battle before David killed Goliath (1 Sam 17:1). The same place is called PAS-DAMMIM (pas-dammim פַּס־דַּמִּים) in 1 Chr 11:13. In the parallel text at 2 Sam 23:9 the place-name is lacking in the Hebrew, but is preserved in some MSS of the LXX. The site is today associated with modern Damun, about 4 mi. northeast of Socoh.

MARK DELCOGLIANO

EPHESIANS, LETTER TO THE i-fee´zhuhnz [Πρὸς Ἐφέσιους *Pros Ephesious*]. No writing in the NT contains such wide-ranging, such profound, and such celebratory theology as this relatively short writing. Not surprisingly, it has been deeply influential in the life and thought of the church. Calvin regarded it as his favorite NT book, and Coleridge perhaps gave it the ultimate accolade when he pronounced it "the divinest composition of man." Some NT scholars have hailed it as the "quintessence" and "crown" of Paulinism. Others have been less generous, judging it a distortion of what Paul would have said—or even an attempted corrective to what he taught—written by a later "disciple."

A. Authorship Issues and the Relation to Colossians/Philemon

From the time of Ignatius (martyred ca. 110 CE) until the late 18th cent. CE, Pauline authorship of the letter was assumed. But from the 19th cent. onward there have been growing doubts, if little consensus on the matter. Of the seven major commentaries listed in the bibliography, Best, Lincoln and Schnackenburg conclude against Pauline authorship, while Barth, O'Brien and Hoehner conclude in favor of authenticity, and Muddiman argues that about half of our "Ephesians" is Paul's original letter to the Laodiceans (compare Col 4:16), which has been heavily interpolated by a later writer. Monographs devoted to the matter are divided on the question as well (Mitton against Van Roon for Pauline authorship). Two questions invite attention: 1) On what basis is Pauline authorship challenged/defended? 2) What does it matter?

One cardinal observation must be made that will affect both questions: Ephesians is ostensibly (whether really or pseudepigraphically) a companion letter to Colossians and Philemon (*see* COLOSSIANS, LETTER TO THE; PHILEMON, LETTER TO). It contains one-third of the wording of Colossians, and that, in turn, comprises one-quarter of Ephesians. Thematically, Ephesians largely parallels the sequence of topics in Colossians, missing out merely the Colossian "hymn" (Col 1:15-20), and the more detailed aspects of Paul's response to the "false-teaching" in Col 2, while adding the striking eulogy (Eph 1:3-14 [partly reflecting material in the Colossian hymn]); the ecclesiology of the "one New Man" uniting Jew and Gentile in one heavenly temple (2:11-22); the remarkable teaching on the enabling nature and unifying purpose of Christ-given ministries (4:7-16); the expansion of the household codes on husband-wife relations (5:22-32; compare Col 3:18-10), and the commanding "spiritual warfare" passage, which sums up and closes the letter-body (6:10-20). The two letters are also similar in style, language and theology, and are both conveyed by the same coworker, Tychicus, who has the same remit for each letter (Eph 6:21-22 is virtually identical in its wording to Col 4:7-8). Judgment on the authenticity of Ephesians will necessarily depend in large part on whether Colossians may be judged Pauline, and whether the relationship of similarities and differences between the two letters supports or subverts such a claim on behalf of Ephesians.

Those who dispute Pauline authorship of Colossians largely do so on these grounds: 1) stylistic (arguing that the semi-liturgical long and cumbrous sentences, the heaping up of redundant synonyms and qualifying genitives, and the overloading with loosely dependent clauses contrasts too strongly with Paul's more usual argumentative rhetoric); and 2) theological, e.g., the letter's more developed cosmic christology; its emphasis on Christ as the head of the universal church, his body (unlike metaphors in 1 Cor 12 and Rom 12, which refer the "head," and its various component organs, to the local congregational "body," rather than to Christ); its spatial/above-below, and strongly "realized eschatology," rather than Paul's more normal horizontal/two-age temporal, future-orientated, emphasis, etc. Exactly the same criticisms, of course, are made of Ephesians, which shares these features.

Defenders of Colossians (and of Ephesians) respond: 1) that the style is close to that of the parts of Paul where he abandons adversarial-styled argument for more neutral forms, and where he turns to more general teaching, prayer, thanksgiving/praise, and exhortation. In fact, stylometric analysis suggests that both Colossians and Ephesians are closer to that of the center of the Pauline corpus of the thirteen letters ascribed to him than is 1 Corinthians—despite their relatively extensive use of pre-formed material (traditional confessions, hymnic material, vice/virtue lists, household codes), etc; 2) the so-called conceptual developments between the uncontested letters and Colossians (with Ephesians) are nearly always prepared for in the earlier letters, and are best accounted for as changes of emphasis elicited by the false-teaching threatening the Lycus Valley congregations. On the assumption that the latter was a brand of Jewish(-Christian?) apocalyptic mysticism that commended asceticism and rigorous nomism as a means to visionary ascent to receive heavenly wisdom and join in the "worship of angels," one may account for many of the letter(s)' moves. The cosmic CHRISTOLOGY and Christ's eschatological victory over the powers (already found in such passages as 1 Cor 8:6; 15:24-25; Rom 8:23-29; Phil 2:9-11, and in the many christological uses of Ps 110:1) is expanded, and brought into focused engagement with any speculative interest in the angelic "powers," by such passages as Col 1:15-20; 2:9-15; Eph 1:20-23. Spatial eschatology, contrasting continuing earthly/fleshly existence with the heavenly eschatological existence in which we already participate in union with Christ, was an important polemical feature of Gal 4:25-28 and Phil 3:14, 19-21. But it is hardly surprising that it receives special focus—along with strongly relational head-body/Christ-church imagery, and a striking "realized" emphasis—precisely in a context where some are advocating a quite different kind of participation in heavenly ascent and relation to the powers (one that threatens the sufficiency of Christ: Col 2:18-19; see esp. Col 2:10, 12-13; 3:1-4; Eph 1:3, 19-23; 2:1-6). On the positive side, the way Colossians meshes with Philemon, and especially the inclusion of lengthy (otherwise redundant?) greetings from named coworkers (4:10-14//Phlm 23-24), is generally understood to favor authenticity (see PAUL, AUTHORSHIP).

If Colossians is to be accepted as Pauline, then the features they share would prima facie support the Pauline authorship of Ephesians too. But it would also be possible to argue that the shared features simply show a later writer's dependence on our Colossians (though there is scant evidence of purely literary dependence in either direction), while his modulation of and additions to it reveal the writing to be post-Colossian and pseudepigraphic.

The main arguments against Pauline authorship of Ephesians may then briefly be laid out, and partly responded to, as follows.

One of the earliest and most influential objections to the authenticity of the letter was that it assumes the hearers would "surely," but crucially "may not," have personal knowledge of Paul's apostolate (3:2), and, correspondingly, that Paul has only "heard" of the readers' faith (1:15). Both points are allegedly inconsistent with his relatively long (ca. two and one-half year) ministry in Ephesus (compare Acts 19:8-10). But on an understanding that Paul wrote Ephesians from Rome (ca. 62–64; see below), there would have been many converts in Ephesus who would not have personal knowledge of Paul (which city he left some six years earlier), and Paul will have only "heard" of their then-status of faith—and that of his own erstwhile converts—from his co-workers from the Lycus Valley. But all this rather misses the real point: "Paul" matches the deliberately ironic "assuming you have heard of [my] ministry" (3:2) with a syntactically matching ironic "assuming you heard of him (= Christ) . . ." (4:20). The irony presumes that the readers know both about Christ and about Paul.

Many find Ephesians to be uncharacteristically over-dependent on another "Pauline" letter—Colossians (and to echo passages of others): the real Paul never so closely shadows himself, it is claimed. In defense of Pauline authorship one may reply that it would hardly be surprising that Colossians and Ephesians share so much in common if they were both written at the same time, and were sent to Ephesus and its hinterland of the Lycus Valley towns (see §B, below). We have no such other "paired" Pauline letters with which to compare. As Richards has shown, letters by Paul destined to be read at a public meeting for worship would be composed and also read publicly; in various drafts, with coworkers chipping in (for the impressive list of the coworkers present, see Col 4:7-14), and with preformed material added (use of which is extensive, and often parallel, in both letters; most noticeably in the *Haustafeln*, Col 3:18–4:1//Eph 5:21–6:9). In such circumstances one might expect a good deal of linguistic, thematic, and conceptual cross-fertilization, especially if the letters face analogous situations.

Ephesians is often alleged to use such key Colossian theological terms and concepts as *head, body, mystery,* and *fullness*, in different and essentially post-Colossian ways. For example, in Col 2:19 Christ is said to be the kephalē (κεφαλή, "head") from which the whole body, supported by joints and ligaments, grows with divine growth. Virtually the same is said in Eph 4:15*b*-16. But, those who argue for theological difference between the two letters allege that in Colossians Christ is "head" of the cosmic body, the universe, while in Ephesians Christ is identified as kephalē of the ecclesial body, the church (Eph 4:16) instead (*see* HEAD, HEADSHIP). This is alleged to show the use of kephalē in a new (and non-Colossian) linguistic and conceptual sense, and to reveal that author has either misunderstood Colossians, or disagreed with its cosmology and attempted to correct it by his ecclesiological counterpart. But one can argue that there is no linguistic difference in the sense of the word here: in both Colossians and Ephesians it simply means "head" (in the sense "chief, or lord, over"), and there is no reason why Christ should not be "head" of two different entities (if "head" of the cosmos, then surely also "head" of the church, as Eph 4:16 claims). Earlier in Colossians Paul says that Christ is head/Lord of both the church (1:18) and of the cosmos (1:15-17; 2:10), so in this case any linguistic argument collapses. Indeed, in my view (along with major commentaries), in Col 2:19 Jesus is not identified so much as head of the cosmic body, but more precisely as head of the ecclesial body.

It is frequently argued that the form and structure of Ephesians differ from all known Paulines in that the LETTER does not respond to specific situations/problems, and in that its first part (chaps. 1–3) is mainly eulogy, and prayer-report, not concrete theological argument or polemic. But this judgment confuses form and style with content and function. True, the style of address is not Paul's usual argument or expository discourse; rather, it is thankful, prayer-filled celebration and exhortation, written with the zeal, idealism, and enthusiasm of the visionary. The writer is convinced that he himself powerfully experiences the very "Spirit of wisdom and revelation" that he prays for his readers (1:17), and that the eyes of his own heart have thereby been opened to comprehend the rich glory of the gospel (1:18–2:8; 3:2-10). By this Spirit he is deeply united with the ascended Lord (1:3; 2:5-6). By the same Spirit (3:16) he has begun to know the depths of the love of Christ and to be filled with the eschatological fullness of God (3:18-19). And it is as one full of this Spirit (5:18) that he speaks. As for its content, the church throughout the centuries has found in Ephesians some of the apostle's most important theological teaching. As we shall see, that teaching would mesh most especially well with the situation envisaged at Colossae, or places nearby, such as Laodicea, where the Colossian false-teaching was as yet only a potential threat. Indeed, if our Ephesians also reflects the content of the lost letter to the Laodiceans, then the mutual exchange of letters (Col 4:16) could be expected to reinforce the impact of Colossians.

As for theological emphasis, it has been held that Ephesians collapses Paul's eschatological tension between present and future salvation into a purely realized version thereof. Ephesians is said to exchange final "justification by faith," and future parousia-resurrection hope, for a fully realized "salvation and co-resurrection" by faith (Eph 2:1-10), in a way that goes well beyond Colossians. Equally, Ephesians allegedly gives a centrality to the "universal church" and its "unity" unimaginable in the undisputed Pauline epistles, and barely foreshadowed in Colossians. But the view that Ephesians collapses Paul's eschatology, and thereby distorts his soteriology, is a serious misinterpretation that we must address in more detail below, and requires improbable readings of such passages as Ephesians 1:9-10, 13-14, 18, 21; 2:7, 21; 3:21; 4:13, 15-16, 30; 5:16; 6:11-14. It may be admitted that Ephesians has a more developed and pervasive concept of the "oneness" of the church across the then-known world, and of its role as "body" and "fullness" under Christ's "headship," than is explicit in previous Paulines, even Colossians. But it is clear that Paul really did from the beginning regard "the church" as fundamentally some single unified heavenly/eschatological congregation, not merely as individual local congregations (see Gal 1:13; Phil 3:6; and 1 Cor 15:9, where Paul refers to his having persecuted "the church"). Similarly he regards apostles and prophets to be appointed in "the church" (1 Cor 12:28: surely not meaning a plurality to each single congregation), and himself as part of the one "temple of God" with the distant Corinthians ("we are the temple of the living God," 2 Cor 6:16). It is equally clear, not least from his christological uses of Ps 110 and of OT Yahweh texts, that he regards Jesus as filling/controlling the church universal. One should also remember that Paul's final mission as a free apostle was to take up a collection from his Gentile congregations with the aim of publicly sealing their union with the Jerusalem church. He knew the bid was fraught with dangers (Rom 15:25-33) and those dangers materialized in the form of his arrest and prolonged (two-year?) imprisonment in Caesarea and then Rome. Given two to four years' incarceration, with little more to do than reflect and pray, it would not be surprising for him to reach the christocentric understanding of the unity of the church as Christ's body that begins to emerge in Colossians and is clearly developed in Ephesians.

The letter is claimed to evince a post-Pauline veneration for the apostle (esp. 3:5!) and perspective on Paul's ministry as completed. But while Eph 3:2-13 graphically portrays Paul's apostolic ministry and accomplishments; what is said there is not essentially different from (e.g.) Rom 15:14-21 and Col 1:23–2:5. There is no explicit indication that his task is over; in contrast see 6:19-20. The reference to "holy apostles and prophets" (Eph 3:5) in the foundation of the heavenly temple (compare 2:20) has been taken to mean those founding-generation ministries have ended. But that is an anachronistic reading. Ignatius, who knew the letter to the Ephesians, regarded prophets as ongoing, and robustly included himself as inspired by the Spirit (Rom 7:2). The language in Ephesians 3:5 is better explained as semi-polemical. The false teachers on the Colossian horizon regard themselves as holy visionaries, and look down on Gentile believers as unholy, and dub them the akrobystia (ἀκροβυστία), literally "the foreskin" (Eph 2:11). Paul's sally in 3:5 identifies those apostles and prophets who clarified the unity of Jewish and Gentile believers as God's one people as the more truly "holy" visionaries. In what ways is the question of Pauline authorship important? From a historical-critical view it is essential to isolate the discrete message of the writer's original discourse, even should it seem contrary to Paul on important issues, so the questions discussed above are critical. But what status should the possibility of an "anti-Paul" reading have for a "biblical/canonical" interpretation? Probably little. The Tychicus passage shows the writer wishes the letter to be read with Colossians (and Philemon), and its canonical inclusion with the Paulines demands it be given a Pauline reading. We may take two heuristic examples. First, the suggestion has been made that the eschatology of Ephesians is entirely "realized," and a corrective to Paul's future-orientated vision. But when Ephesians is read with its partner-letter, Colossians (esp. Col 3:1-4), let alone with the other Paulines, in some more canonical reading, then such an interpretation would be entirely subverted. (And in fact the hypothesis has been shown to be quite wrong, even on an isolated reading of Ephesians: compare 1:14, 18; 2:7; 4:30; 5:16; 6:8, 13). Second, we may take Van Kooten's view that Col 2:19 speaks of Christ as head/lord of the universal body, with its cosmic uniting joints and ligaments, while Eph 4:16 (mis-)uses the same language to "correct" the Colossian cosmic christology in favor of an ecclesial one of Christ as the head of the church-body. But, of course, any canonical reader will read the more ambiguous Col 2:19 in the light of the clear Eph 4:16, and, in our view, will be more safely guided to the meaning of each passage.

B. Destination, Occasion, and Purpose

According to most ancient manuscripts Eph 1:1*b* was addressed to "the saints who are in Ephesus, namely (= kai [καὶ] "and") those who are faithful in Christ Jesus." Some important manuscripts lack "in Ephesus," but all are headed "to the Ephesians," and in Paul's letter-addressee slot the phrase "who are" is always followed by a location, "in X." That does not mean the letter was primarily intended for Ephesus, but at least that one copy was sent there. As Paul's envoy, Tychicus, accompanying the returning slave Onesimus, and with a full letter to his master's Colossian church, could not just pass through Ephesus to the Lycus Valley towns (Colossae, Laodicea, and Hierapolis) without some communication to the major city in which Paul had had such a prolonged ministry. "Ephesians" would serve the need, and also brace them against their endemic fear of Artemisian powers (Arnold, 1989). But our "Ephesians" was probably a copy of a letter intended primarily for the church in Laodicea (why Marcion knew it as the letter to the Laodicians referred to in Col 4:16). The themes shared with Colossians suggest a prophylactic against the false-teaching incipient in Colossae (only a short day's walk past Laodicea).

The above accepts the tradition that the letters were written from Rome, during Paul's imprisonment (compare Phlm 1, 9-10, 13; Col 4:10; Eph 3:1; 6:20) there (60–62 CE), rather than from Caesarea (57–59 CE), or even from Ephesus itself (sometime within 52–55 CE?). A Roman setting might best explain the developed theology of the letter. We have no unambiguous evidence of an Ephesian imprisonment at all, let alone the lengthy one presupposed by what Paul says of his relationship with Onesimus; namely, that he became Paul's "beloved child" in prison (v. 10), had then become his very heart (v. 12), and proved himself a faithful brother and useful coworker that the apostle would dearly like to retain for the foreseeable period of his incarceration (Col 4:9; Phlm 11, 13). All this suggests a period of weeks, more likely months—and that would be more difficult to explain on the assumption of an Ephesian confinement. Paul would be bound by law to return Onesimus to his master at the first opportunity. He could return Onesimus the relatively short overland distance from Ephesus to the Lycus Valley towns (roughly five days' walk). A Caesarean or Roman imprisonment would require Onesimus to winter with Paul as shipping (and many roads over high ground) closed from late October to March/April.

The three Lycus Valley letters share a single beating heart. The one addressed to Philemon asks for a then-unbelievable level of reconciliation and new relationship with his absconded slave, Onesimus. Onesimus is to be greeted and treated as a brother; welcomed even as Paul himself would be (Phlm 17). Colossians, and especially Ephesians, paint this radical request into the broader interpretive canvas of truly and fully cosmic reconciliation and harmony inaugurated in Christ. Both letters in different ways spell out the implications for the believers' relation to the powers, and the lifestyles that should exemplify their unity with Christ and with one another. Ephesians is much fuller in the latter respect (see §D), and more suited to a plurality of audiences.

C. Analysis

No Pauline letter manifests such rhetorical discourse-cohesion as Ephesians. The key theme of cosmic reunification, inaugurated in the believers' union with Christ, dominates the horizon in virtually every section. This involves a certain level of reinforcing repetition, yet the progress from passage to passage kaleidoscopically focuses some new perspective/outworking with each move.

1. The eulogy (1:3-14)

If Galatians is theology in the boxing ring, Ephesians is theology dancing, and the berakhah (בְּרָכָה; "blessing") with which it begins is a compelling invitation onto the floor, drawing the hearers in to participate in the sequences that will follow.

Written from a Jewish-Christian perspective, it patently blesses Israel's God: the almighty author of creation and promised new creation (1:4; compare 2:15; 3:11 [compare 4:6]; 4:24), who works out his sovereign pretemporal will to the eschatological praise of his glorious grace (1:6, 11-12, 13-14). Yet that one God's identity is now supremely revealed as "the God and Father of our Lord Jesus" (1:3; compare 1:17), as that grace focuses on fulfillment in Christ of the promises made to Israel of corporate "sonship" (now, yes, but primarily eschatological: 1:5-6, as in Rom 8:23); new-exodus "redemption" from slavery/sin (1:7); "sealing" (with the Spirit: 1:13), and final "inheritance" in which God takes full possession of his people (1:14; compare 1:18 and Col 1:12) "to the praise of his glorious grace," meaning to the acclamation of all creation at the final cosmic trial (1:14*b*, but also 1:6, 12).

The eschatological chord is thus roundly struck. As yet believers only participate in "every spiritual blessing" in part, by virtue of their union with Christ in the heavenlies (let the Colossians errorists note) where their inheritance (1:14) is kept secure (a typical apocalyptic and Pauline theme; compare Col 1:5; 3:1-4). They have been chosen before the beginning of the world that they may stand blameless before God (1:4*b*//Col 1:22), and enter into full sonship (1:5) at its end. For the present they have only the "first installment" and guarantee of all of this in the gift of the Spirit (1:13*b*-14*a*). Discourse-analysis shows the climax of 1:3-14 to be 1:9-10: the revelation of the ineffable mystery of

God's majestic intent to "re-sum-up" (anakephalaioō ἀνακεφαλαιόω) all things in union/unity in Christ (compare 1:22-23; 3:3-4, 6-9, 19). The presupposition here—very much as in Col 1:15-20—is that the proto-logical unity of creation in Christ has (through the fall) fragmented into a chaos of multiple alienations (from God, from neighbor, and from authentic self), and that the Christ-event inaugurates cosmic reconciliation and harmony. This is the vision that fires the rest of the letter. But the author does not believe the vision of 1:9-10 is already fully accomplished. He looks out onto a still largely unbelieving "old" humanity, alienated from God, from the church, and from one another; dead in sin, and under the malign influence of the Evil One (compare 2:1-5; 4:17-20; 5:11-14). Even for the church itself, the days are evil (5:15; 6:13) and beset by encircling hosts of opposing powers (4:27; 6:10-17). Her day of redemption and inheritance (1:11-14, 18; 4:30) still lies in the temporal future, which readers will naturally identify (from Col 3:4, or from the Pauline tradition generally) with the parousia.

2. The prayer report begins (1:15–2:10)

After blessing God for his rich blessing of us, Paul turns to the subject of his prayer for the believers. They will undoubtedly have heard the familiar kerygma of Christ's death, resurrection, and exaltation to cosmic power at God's right hand (compare the allusion to Ps 110:1 [and Ps 8:6]) that compose 1:20-23. They will have heard too that believers are incorporated in this reality (at baptism, according to Col 2:12-13, the immediately parallel passage; and compare Rom 6:4, 8, 11, as 2:1-8 asserts. But Paul's prayer here brings new nuances. First, it is only by receiving wisdom/revelation from the Spirit (1:17) that the believer has a transformed understanding ("the eyes of the heart being enlightened," v. 18) of this proclamation (compare also 3:14-21). In a move similar to 1 Cor 2:1–3:4, Paul implies that full/mature knowledge and revelation of God takes the believer deeper into the kerygma, rather than (e.g.) leaving it behind for arcane, less christocentric "heavenly wisdom." Second, the power at work in believers (1:19) effecting the salvation spoken of in 2:1-8 is one with the power that raised and exalted Christ, and gave him plenipotentiary position over all other powers—including any that the Colossian/Laodicean and Ephesian believers might fear or unhealthily revere (1:20-21), and that could be evil-enticing powers (2:2; compare 6:13; as in Col 2). Indeed, far from being in thrall to the powers, and ruled by them, believers should recognize that in their union with Christ they share (proleptically?) in his position and rule above them and over them instead (2:6). Third, the means by which the vision of 1:9-10 is reached begins to be unveiled in v. 23: Christ will bring all things into complete harmony with himself, just as he now begins to fill the church, his body, as the head (lord) given to it.

Ephesians 2:8-10 has often been taken as non-Pauline, because it speaks of Christians as people who "have been saved by faith" in the past (using a perfect tense), and 2:5-6 because it spiritualizes Paul's resurrection hope, and locates it in the believers' conversion-initiation. But the companion letter, Colossians, uses the same "co-resurrection/made alive" metaphor (Eph 2:5-6 = Col 2:12-13; compare 3:1) for conversion-initiation without any loss of the literal resurrection hope (3:4), and so there is no reason to believe the metaphor is instead its replacement in Ephesians. And the only "salvation" that is "past" in this passage is precisely the all-changing transfer from death to life by faith union with Christ's (more starkly, Col 1:13; compare Rom 6).

3. Jew, Gentile, and cosmic reconciliation/unity 2:11-22)

This centerpiece of Eph 1–3 juts out prominently as a digression from the prayer report. It emerges from 2:11 that some are dismissively labeling Gentile believers as "the foreskin"—hardly Paul's own chosen term to address them (he uses akrobystia only in polemical Judaizing contexts). While Paul regularly faced opponents who took variations of this stance, it is most probably the Colossian false teachers he has principally in mind, and his riposte is that they are the so-called circumcision, but a quasi-idolatrous one—one merely "made with human hands," not the significant God-given circumcision of the heart (or totality of the flesh, as the par. Col 2:11 puts it).

Then, while allowing the salvation-historical privilege of empirical Israel (they are "the near" to God of Isa 57:19 in 2:12-13, 17), Paul declares Christ's death wins a double reconciliation (2:14-18). In a horizontal dimension the cross tears down (in principle) the wall of alienation/hostility keeping apart the two ancient divisions of mankind (Jew and Gentile), previously generated by the Law, and allows the former two to be re-created as one new humanity in Christ (2:14-15). But in a vertical dimension the cross also reconciles both these groups to God (2:16-17), creating a church "in Christ" that thereby already exemplifies (to the world, and even to the heavenly hosts; compare 3:10) the beginnings of the cosmic reunification promised in 1:9-10, and messianic peace (2:18) of Isa 57:19 and 52:7 (christologically interpreted). This is not a systematic theology of Israel and the church (though it comports well with Rom 9–11), but a theological account of the relationship of Jewish and Gentile believers as one body, indeed as together the one eschatological holy heavenly temple in the Lord, indwelled by God's Spirit (2:19-22). On the smooth walls of that divine edifice there is no toehold for those who regard Gentile believers as second-class citizens of God's household, excluded by their lack of holiness from the heavenly realms. Nor, for that matter, is there foothold for complacent unbelieving Jews, who thereby walk as children of wrath in the peril described in 2:1-3, and in need of the reconciliation to God described in 2:16. Defining for who belongs to the heavenly temple-city is faith in Christ and the sealing of the indwelling Holy Spirit (1:14; 2:18, 22).

4. Paul's apostolic ministry to reveal the mystery (3:2-13)

After momentarily resuming his prayer report in 3:1, Paul breaks off into a second digression. His calling is to make known the revelation of the MYSTERY of the unsearchable riches of Christ (3:8-9) and the manifold wisdom of God (3:10), he insists. What is that? It is nothing less than that the Gentiles are co-heirs, co-body members (a neologism), and co-sharers in Christ and his benefits (3:6). It is this revelation that makes the apostles and prophets the holy foundation of Christ's temple (2:20). He then makes the surprising assertion that it is the church (built on this foundation, and living as an exemplification of the cosmic unity to come) that makes known God's wisdom to the heavenly principalities and powers. This statement is best explained as delicious irony served up in a situation where some prefer to think that the angelic powers reveal heavenly wisdom to the church.

5. The prayer report resumes and climaxes (3:14-19)

The prayer is again for the revelatory and hermeneutical work of the Spirit (compare 1:17) that brings Christ (his life and molding influence) into the heart of the believers—captivating the core of their existence with love (3:17), and thereby enabling them more fully to understand the immensity of Christ's love (3:18-19). Paul uses the metaphor of a three-dimensional space, seen from the inside, and stretching out to all receding horizons. Are they the dimensions of the cosmos? The heavenly temple? The celestial body of Christ? We are not told: we are just left with the image of unfathomable vastness. To understand this love would be to be filled with all God's fullness—from which we are probably to infer that Christ filling of the church (1:23), and eventually of "all things" (1:23; 4:10), means to bring them under the power of his uniting, reconciling, and transforming love.

6. Exhortation to live out the gospel of cosmic reconciliation and unity in Christ (4:1–6:20)

The whole second part of Ephesians consists of ethical exhortation that is thoroughly grounded in the vision of the church in chaps. 1–3 (the "therefore" of 4:1 should be taken seriously), and supported by further teaching. It is clear from the extent of the material that another purpose of the letter is to provide a general ethical teaching for the predominantly Gentile addressees. The ethic promoted is decidedly community orientated, not individualistic, for the "new man" (4:23-24) is first and foremost a relational being, in counterpart to the "old man" (4:22) marked by alienations.

a. Opening exhortation to a life that expresses new creation unity (4:1-6). Following the familiar Pauline call to live a life worthy of their calling (4:1), Paul first spells this out in 4:2 as living the qualities of the new-creation personhood he explains in 4:17–5:2, and, second, as a call urgently to "maintain the unity of the Spirit in the bond of peace" (4:3). The importance of this latter call is then hammered into the drumbeat of two triads of cardinal confessional unities ("one body, one Spirit . . . one hope . . . one Lord, one faith, one baptism"), and climaxes finally with the "one God . . . in all" (4:6).

b. Ministries as Christ's victory gifts to promote united growth into Christ (4:7-16). The unity for which Paul calls is no wooden uniformity, but likened to a harmoniously growing body, where each part contributes to the whole (4:7, 16b). Yet this is not egalitarianism: a variety of church leaders—mainly those with teaching functions—are given prominence, both as Christ's ascension gifts to the church (4:8-12; using what was probably already a christological hymn based on Ps 68:19 [LXX 67:19]), and as the ligaments and sinews that hold the body together and thus shape its growth (4:16). The goal of all this is mature unity of faith and knowledge of God's Son (4:13, rather than childlike vacillation, being blown around by the contrary winds of deceitful false teaching, 4:14; compare Col 2:22), and a corporate growth into a mature man of the stature of Christ (4:13), which can also be expressed as the body growing "into" Christ, its head/lord (4:16), in love.

c. Exhortations to abandon the life of the "old man/humanity" and to live according to the new-creation humanity revealed in Christ (4:17–6:9). This does not indicate a shift away from the centrality of the theme of unity, but merely a different way of presenting it—as becomes clear in the first two subsections.

i. Exhortation to put off the old, and clothe oneself with the new man (4:17-24). The "old man"—more or less equated with their erstwhile Gentile existence—is alienated from God, and typified by callousness and lusts (4:18-19, 22). This whole type of personhood is to be "put off," like soiled clothes, and the new-creation humanity, modeled on Jesus, is to be put on. What this entails is then clarified in:

ii. Exhortation to live the truth patterned on Jesus (4:25–5:2) and to live out the light that shines from Christ (5:3-14). The ethic commended is profoundly relational, and community-building love. The first exhortation to speak only the truth with one's neighbor is thus grounded in the assertion "for we are members one of another" (4:25). The contrast with the old is clearest in 4:31-32: relationship-damaging behavior (anger, bitterness, etc.) is resolutely to be shunned;

tenderness and Godlike forgiveness to be embraced. Believers are called to imitate God, as he is revealed in the cruciform self-giving love of Christ (5:1-2). The words *unity, reconciliation*, and *peace* do not appear; but their substance is apparent throughout.

iii. Exhortation to live out the wisdom the Spirit gives in corporate charismatic worship (5:15-20) and in harmonious households (5:21–6:9). The christology of Christ filling his people to the whole fullness of God (1:23; 3:17-19; compare 4:10), which otherwise only God can do (compare 3:19), and of uniting all things in himself, so that he is all in all (1:10, 23b), as God is (4:6), includes Christ within the identity of the one God of Israel, and evokes a Spirit-led binitarian worship (5:19-20: the first explicit call to worship Christ in the Paulines [and contrast the call to the worship of angels in Col 2:18]). The same Spirit also leads in the down-to-earth cruciform commitments, and mutual submissions, that make the household an expression of the gospel of peace and cosmic reconciliation. To illustrate this, Paul uses the same preformed HOUSEHOLD CODES he incorporated into Colossians (3:18–4:1)—there probably because the return of Onesimus to his master, Philemon, made treatment of household relationships a significant agenda item for the Colossian church. In Ephesians, however, there is a new take. The *Haustafeln* (household codes) do not promote an egalitarian, strictly reciprocal mutual submission—parents are not told to obey their children; nor masters their slaves—but instead the husband-wife relationship is expanded as the prime example of what the gospel of cosmic unity looks like when earthed in human relations. The marriage envisaged is seen to mirror the Christ-church relationship between self-giving loving "head" and submissive beloved "body" in a relationship fulfilling and transcending the "one flesh" union of Gen 2:24 (*see* BODY OF CHRIST).

7. Final summons to spiritual warfare in the armor of God (6:10-20)

This is not a new "topic," but a striking military metaphor to sum up all that has been said so far. The church is addressed as cohort (this is no individualistic lone soldier facing the "hosts of wickedness"!). It holds the high ground but must withstand the attacks of the principalities and powers and world rulers of darkness (6:12). The enemy tactic (as we learn from 2:1-3, etc.) is to scatter humanity into multiple alienations. But Christ's cohort must stand unified together, with the armor of God himself (the description draws on Isa 59:17; Wis 5:17-18), and the accoutrements of the messiah (Isa 11:5): these are none other than the very righteousness, truth, hope, and faith the letter has described and urged. And, slightly ironically, the boots that will give them firm footing they need against the attack is the good news of messianic "peace" (6:15; compare 2:18) in cosmic reconciliation.

D. Theological/Contemporary Significance

Every theme/passage of the letter has been important for theology, but special mention may be made of the following: 1) the emphasis on the inaugurated eschatology of cosmic reconciliation and unity, for which the apostle suffered signally, has put the issue at the center of the gospel, rather than relegating it to a pragmatic adiaphoron. It has fueled the challenge to a culture of individualism, and encouraged new, more relational views of the nature of the self and personhood. It has also been the inspiration of the ecumenical movement, and of post-apartheid attempts at reconciliation in South Africa; 2) Ephesians 2:11-22 has provided a paradigmatic starting point for the church's attempts to address Jewish-Christian dialogue and racial hostility; 3) Ephesians 4:7-16 has played a significant role in the understanding of the purpose and facilitating functions of ministry; 4) Ephesians 5:22-32 has been one of the most influential biblical passages on Christian marriage and its relationship to the mystery of the gospel; 5) The treatment of union with Christ and the "powers" (esp. Eph 1–2, 6) has brought strength and courage to the church throughout history, not least in countries more aware of the demonic dimension of spiritual experience. *See* CHURCH, IDEA OF.

Bibliography: C. E. Arnold. *Ephesians: Power and Magic* (1989); Markus Barth. *Ephesians.* AB 34–34A (1974); Ernest Best. "Who Used Whom? The Relationship of Ephesians and Colossians." *NTS* 43 (1997) 72–96; Ernest Best. *A Critical and Exegetical Commentary on Ephesians.* ICC (1998); Ernest Best. *Essays on Ephesians* (1997); Chrys C. Caragounis. *The Ephesian "Mysterion": Meaning and Content* (1977); Harold W. Hoehner. *Ephesians: An Exegetical Commentary* (2002); Andrew T. Lincoln. *Ephesians.* WBC 42 (1990); C. L. Mitton. *The Epistle to the Ephesians: Its Authorship, Origin and Purpose* (1951); Thorsten Moritz. *A Profound Mystery: The Use of the Old Testament in Ephesians* (1996); John Muddiman. *The Epistle to the Ephesians.* BNTC (2001); Peter T. O'Brien. *The Letter to the Ephesians.* Pillar New Testament Commentary (1999); William Rader. *The Church and Racial Hostility: A History of Interpretation of Ephesians 2.11–22* (1978); E. Randolph Richards. *Paul and First-Century Letter Writing: Secretaries, Composition and Collection* (2004); Rudolph Schnackenburg. *The Epistle to the Ephesians* (1991); Ian K. Smith. *Heavenly Perspective: A Study of the Apostle Paul's Response to a Jewish Mystical Movement at Colossae* (2006); Max Turner. "Mission and Meaning in Terms of 'Unity' in Ephesians." *Mission and Meaning: Essays Presented to Peter Cotterell* Antony Billington, Tony Lane, and Max Turner, eds. (1995) 138–66; Max Turner. "Approaching 'Personhood' in the New Testament, with Special Reference to Ephesians." *EvQ* 77 (2005) 211–33 ; George H. Van Kooten. *Cosmic Christology in Paul and the Pauline School: Colossians and Ephesians in the Context of Graeco-Roman Cosmology, with a New Synopsis of the Greek Texts* (2003); A. Van Roon. *The Authenticity of Ephesians* (1974); Tet-Lim N. Yee. *Jews, Gentiles and Ethnic Reconciliation: Paul's Jewish Identity and Ephesians* (2005).

MAX TURNER

EPHESUS ef′uh-suhs [Ἔφεσος *Ephesos*]. As the capital of the Roman province of Asia, Ephesus prospered from its strategic location, banking, and commerce. It was situated at the mouth of the Cayster River, near modern Selçuk on the western coast of Turkey. Ephesus' known history begins in the 7th cent. BCE. Paul ministered in Ephesus for some three years (Acts 19:8-10; 20:31) and wrote letters to Corinth from that city.

A. Early Mythology and History
B. The Ministry of Paul and His Companions
C. Pauline Correspondence at Ephesus
D. The Ministry of John
Bibliography

A. Early Mythology and History

Both Strabo and Pausanias relate a legend that the famous female warriors, the Amazons, founded Ephesus (Strabo, *Geogr.* 11.5.1; Apollodorus 2.5.8). Hippolyte and her Amazons reportedly set up a statue of Artemis at Ephesus and established an annual circular dance with weapons and shields (Callimachus, *Hymn.* 3.110).

The name Ephesus may derive from "Apis," the word for "bee." Some early Ephesian coins had a bee on them. Pausanias claims that Coresus established a temple to the Ephesian goddess, and Ephesus "who is thought to have been a son of the river Caÿster," from whom the city received its name (*Descr.* 6.2.7). Pausanias reported that Androclus of Codrus came to Anatolia from Athens because of an oracle from Apollo. He was told to settle where he found a fish and a boar. As his company landed a boar jumped out of a thicket. On the site where Androchus killed the boar, he founded the city. That story is depicted on a frieze from the temple of Hadrian.

Ephesus may have acquired its name from the mother goddess known as Artemis Ephesia. She was the most popular goddess in Anatolia whose influence spread to Mesopotamia, Egypt, Arabia, Greece, Rome, and even Scandinavia. Pausanias claims that the "cult of Ephesian Artemis" was established before Ionians colonized the region (*Descr.* 6.2.6). Relics from a Mycenaean grave at Ephesus suggest that habitation began sometime between 1400–1300 BCE. Hittite tablets found at Miletus just south of Ephesus contain the name of a village named "Apasas" possibly an older form of the name Ephesus. The Anatolian mother-goddess Cybele later was identified with the Greek goddess

Artemis. Lydian kings ruled Ephesus, Miletus, Priene, and Didyma in the 7th and 6th cent. BCE. After Cyrus defeated Croessus, the Persians ruled the Ephesus until Alexander the Great (334 BCE) came along. The famous Artemision (or Temple of Artemis) was built in honor of Artemis in the 7th cent. BCE. and was rebuilt on a grander scale in the mid 6th cent. The temple was four times larger than the Parthenon. Croessus aided in the rebuilding by adding column capitals and reliefs along with golden statues of calves.

The city became a tributary of Athens in 466 BCE, but fell again to the Persians at the beginning of the 4th cent. BCE. In 356 BCE the Artemision was set on fire and partially destroyed by a madman. When Alexander the Great took over the city in 334 the temple had not yet been rebuilt. Lysimachus, one of Alexander's successor generals, built a 6 mi. long city wall, parts of which are still visible. The temple of Artemis was rebuilt and was an acknowledged place of asylum or refuge.

Ephesus was under Greek rule until 133 BCE when Attalus III of Pergamum bequeathed it to the Romans. At that time, Ephesus replaced Pergamum as the capital of the province of Asia. The worship of Artemis continued uninterrupted, but the residents also erected an altar to honor Augustus in the sacred precinct of the temple. At the end of the 1st cent., a temple was built to honor Domitian, but was demolished after his death.

Later in the 2nd cent. a temple was built to honor Hadrian. Strabo described Ephesus' place among the league of twelve Ionian cities as "the royal seat of the Ionians" (*Geogr.* 633). By the 1st cent. CE the city had around 250,000 citizens and was perhaps the third or fourth largest city in the Roman Empire.

B. The Ministry of Paul and His Companions

It appears from Acts 18:18-22 that Paul spoke briefly with the Jews at Ephesus on his first visit to that city, but it is not clear that he started a church. Priscilla and Aquila remained there and, along with Apollos, may have founded the church at Ephesus (Acts 18:24-28). After a lengthy stay in Corinth, Paul returned to Ephesus for some three years (Acts 19:8-10; compare 20:31).

As Acts tells the story, Paul's preaching at Ephesus so undermined devotion to the goddess that the famous temple was losing revenue. The enraged residents demanded punishment of those responsible for the loss (Acts 19:23-41). Some form of public disturbance over Paul's preaching may have led to his imprisonment in Ephesus. Paul himself states that his ministry at Ephesus was mixed with danger including his being forced to "fight with wild animals" (or fierce opponents) and "many adversaries" (1 Cor 15:32; 16:9) and that he was imprisoned at Ephesus (1 Cor 16:8-9; 2 Cor 1:8;

Todd Bolen/BiblePlaces.com

Figure 1: Celsus Library

Rom 16:3-4). Acts claims that Paul met with the elders of the Christian community at the Miletus harbor south of the Ephesus rather than risk entering the city (Acts 20:14-15).

It is likely that Ephesus was the center for Christian missionary activity in the province of Asia that led to the founding of the churches at Laodicea, Colossae, Hierapolis, and elsewhere (Col 4:13), perhaps also those at Smyrna, Pergamum, Thyatira, Philadelphia, Sardis, and elsewhere (Rev 2–3). In most of these cities, there were significant numbers of Jews where Paul launched his ministry (Rom 1:16-17; Acts 13:5, 14-16; 14:1; 16:13; 17:1-2, 10-11; 18:4-7, 19-21; 19:8). Josephus mentions a large Jewish community at Ephesus that enjoyed considerable freedom in Sabbath obesrvance and other religious practices (*Ant.* 14.262-64). Rome granted similar privileges to the Jews at Delos, Laodicea, Pergamum, Halicarnassus, and Sardis (*Ant.* 14.223-61).

C. Pauline Correspondence at Ephesus

Paul writes several letters from Ephesus: 1 Corinthians likely in 52 CE; Philemon and Philippians, from an Ephesian imprisonment; and perhaps Colossians. If a north Galatian destination for Galatians is correct, that letter may have been sent from Ephesus as well. (Some scholars argue that Rom 16 was written by Paul to the church at Ephesus.) If the greetings in Rom 16 were originally sent to Christians in Ephesus, the composition of the church was largely Gentile. Only six of the twenty-six names are likely Jewish names (Maria, Prisca, Aquila, Junia, Andronika, and Herodion).

Pauline authorship of Ephesians is disputed. The opening designation "in Ephesus" (Eph 1:1) is lacking in the most important ancient manuscripts (P[46], Codex Sinaiticus, and Codex Vaticanus or B). Since there is little in the letter that shows familiarity with the readers such as one would expect from Paul's normal practice, it is not likely that the letter was sent to Ephesus. First and Second Timothy presume that the letters were sent to Ephesus (1 Tim 1:3). Onesiphorus from Ephesus ministered to Paul both in Rome and in Ephesus (2 Tim 1:16-18). Alexander the coppersmith, about whom Timothy is warned (2 Tim 4:14-15), may be the Alexander from Ephesus in Acts 19:33, but that is not certain. Timothy's connection with the Ephesian church as its first appointed bishop is mentioned by Eusebius (*Hist. eccl.* 3.4.5). Onesimus, who fled his master (Philemon) in Colossae and was allowed to return to Paul in Ephesus (Col 4:9), may eventually have become the bishop in Ephesus at the beginning of the 2nd cent. (see Ign., *Eph.* 1:3; 6:2). The first letter to a church by the prophet of Revelation was addressed to Ephesus (2:2-3, 6). Later Ignatius of Antioch praised their diligence and love (*Eph.* 9.1; compare Acts 20:29-30; 1 Tim 1:3, 18-20; 4:1-4—compare 1 Cor 15:32; 16:9*b*; Clement of Alexandria, *Quis div.* 42; Irenaeus, *Haer.* 3.3.4). Both Acts 19 and the apocryphal *Acts of John* tell of the continual conflict between the Christians at Ephesus and those who followed the religion of Artemis.

D. The Ministry of John

There is a church tradition that connects John the apostle with Ephesus in the latter part of the 1st cent. Eusebius identifies John the apostle as the author of the fourth Gospel and 1 John (*Hist. eccl.* 3.24). He reports John's banishment to the island of Patmos (see also Rev 1:7) under Domitian and his subsequent ministry in Ephesus, but Eusebius may have confused the prophet or elder John with the apostle. Earlier Ignatius of Antioch refers to Paul's ministry at Ephesus but says nothing of John the apostle. Justin Martyr, who had stayed in Ephesus, frequently refers to the Gospels of Matthew and Luke, but does not refer to John or his Gospel (see Justin, *Dial.* 81.4). The same is true of Polycarp and Papias, both of whom had contact with the church at Ephesus. Eusebius' references to two Johns are confusing (*Hist. eccl.* 2.22.5; 3.1.1; 3.3.4; 3.23.4-5; 3.24-25). After Domitian's death, Eusebius cites both Clement of Alexandria and Irenaeus as sources for information about John's ministry in the city (*Hist. eccl.* 3.20.9–3.23.19). In the 2nd cent. (the actual date is uncertain) a small church was built over the site of the grave where John the apostle was supposedly buried. In the 6th cent., Justinian, the Roman emperor, built a major Basilica over the supposed burial place of John located under the apse of the church.

Bibliography: E. C. Blake and A. G. Edmonds. *Biblical Sites in Turkey* (1977, 1990); H. Koester. "Ephesos in Early Christian Literature." *Ephesos Metropolis of Asia: An Interdisciplinary Approach to Its Archaeology, Religion, and Culture.* H. Koester, ed. (1995) 119–40; V. Limberis. "The Council of Ephesos: The Demise of the See of Ephesos and the Rise of the Cult of the Theotokos." *Ephesos Metropolis of Asia: An Interdisciplinary Approach to Its Archaeology, Religion, and Culture.* H. Koester, ed. (1995) 321–40; R. E. Oster. *A Bibliography of Ancient Ephesus* (1987); E. Yamauchi. *Archaeology of New Testament Cities of Western Asia Minor* (1980) 79–114.

LEE MARTIN MCDONALD

EPHLAL ef'lal [אֶפְלָל 'eflal]. Mentioned only in 1 Chr 2:37, he was a descendant of Judah, Hezron, Perez, and Jerahmeel. His father was Zabad, and he was the father of Obed. A number of suggestions have been put forth concerning the meaning of the name, but there is no consensus of opinion regarding that issue.

W. R. BROOKMAN

EPHOD ee'fod [אֵפוֹד 'efodh]. Chiefly the name for an ornate garment worn by the Israelite high priest, 'efodh has cognates in other Semitic languages (e.g., Old Assyrian [epattu], Ugaritic ['ipdk]) that suggest it references a tight-fitting piece of clothing associated with cultic objects or personnel. Exodus 28:6-14 shows that the Priestly Writers understood the ephod as a specifically high priestly garment (Exod 39:2-8), but other occurrences of the term in the OT suggest related but more general meanings for the word; they also hint at the ephod's function in Israelite religion.

Exodus 28:6-14 describes the ephod as a garment worn by the Israelite high priest. It is a sleeveless top (or an apron-like piece of clothing) held on the body with shoulder straps. The elements of the ephod are finely twisted linen woven with gold thread and blue, purple, and scarlet materials. The two shoulder straps and a belt are made of the same materials. On the shoulder pieces are affixed two onyx stones, each engraved with six of the twelve names of the tribes of Israel. Mounted by gold rings to the front of the ephod was the breastplate made of the same gold, blue, purple, and scarlet materials; it contained the Urim and Thummim. The ephod was the high priest's symbol-laden ritual outerwear, a vestment (so also Lev 8:7; 1 Sam 2:28).

The comparative linguistic evidence provided above and the other uses of the term in the OT suggest that something akin to the ephod was also widely recognized as a garment covering sacred objects (idols) or persons (priests) that possessed (by contact with the priest or idol?) its own numinous qualities. Priestly Israelite religion attached to it divinatory tools (URIM AND THUMMIM), and perhaps for that reason the ephod attained a related function in Israel as well.

Used in construct with badh (בַּד "linen"), ephod refers to an unadorned linen loincloth worn by cultic functionaries; Samuel as a "priest's assistant" (1 Sam 2:18), the eighty-five priests slain by Doeg the Edomite (1 Sam 22:18), and David dancing before the ark (2 Sam 6:4; 1 Chr 15:27) all wear the linen ephod in quasi-cultic settings. Apparently "simply linen" ephods were a basic ritual garment.

A number of passages also hint that ephods served as a garment covering an idol or as some other religious object sufficiently numinous to be located in ritual or cultic settings. Gideon forms an ephod from the gold given him by grateful Israel and "all Israel prostituted themselves to it" (Judg 8:27). Within a sanctuary a priest informs David that "the sword of Goliath the Philistine . . . is here wrapped behind the ephod" (1 Sam 21:9). Ahijah, great-grandson of the priest Eli, carries an ephod in the military contingent accompanying Saul (1 Sam 14:3). In Judg 17–18 the Ephraimite Micah makes "an ephod, teraphim, and an idol of cast metal" (17:5; 18:14, 17, 18, 20) that he entrusts to a family priest; the juxtaposition of an ephod with an idol suggests its role as an idol-garment, as does the appearance of an idol and teraphim as a single grammatical unit in Hos 3:4. While this collection of references has evoked attempts to suggest that an ephod could itself be an idol, comparative philological evidence and

the prevalence of denoting an ephod otherwise as a sacerdotal garment speak in favor of seeing it as such here as well.

Two further occurrences of the term in 1 Sam 23:9; 30:7 suggest the ephod's divinatory function; twice David commands Abiathar to "bring the ephod" whereupon David seeks an oracle from God. This does not mean that the ephod is not a priestly garment; indeed, the priest Abiathar is its custodian (1 Sam 23:6). Perhaps its association with the Urim and Thummim ensured its status as a tool for divination.

A special case is 1 Kgdms 14:18, which renders the Gk. ephoud (ἐφουδ ephod) for Hebrew ʾaron (אָרוֹן, ARK OF THE COVENANT). W. R. Arnold argued that the LXX was meant to obscure the existence of multiple arks that served divinatory purposes, and that therefore all MT occurrences of ephod associated with divinatory practices should be understood to refer to arks containing divinatory devices. Similarly K. van der Toorn and C. Houtman argued in light of 1 Kgdms 14:18 that all occurrences of ephod in 1 Sam should be read as references to the ark. Most agree, however, that these readings are not necessary to explain what was probably just a translator's misreading of ʾefodh for ʾaron.

Bibliography: W. R. Arnold. *Ephod and Ark: A Study in the Records and Religion of the Ancient Hebrews* (1917); H. G. May. "Ehpod and Ariel." *AJSL* 56 (1939) 44–69; J. Morgenstern. "The Ark, the Ephod, and the Tent of Meeting." *HUCA* 17–18 (1943–44) 153–266, 1-52; Cornelis Van Dam. *The Urim and Thummim: A Means of Revelation in Ancient Israel* (1997) 141–53; K. Van der Toorn and C. Houtman. "David and the Ark." *JBL* 113 (1994) 209–31.

ROBERT KUGLER

EPHPHATHA ef′uh-thuh [Ἐφφαθα ′Ephatha]. A Gk. transliteration of the Aram. word ʾithpethakh (אֶתְפְּתַח). In its only NT usage, it is translated by dianoichtheti (διανοίχθητι), a Greek imperative meaning "be opened."

In Mark 7:31-37, a deaf man who had difficulty speaking was led to Jesus to receive healing. Jesus separated him from the crowd before he began the healing process: he stuck his fingers in his ears; he spat; he touched the man's tongue. It is unclear what Jesus did with the spittle (compare Mark 8:22), whether he rubbed it in his own hands, placed it upon the man's tongue, or simply spat on the ground (as a symbolic gesture to the deaf man of what was occurring). Following this performance, Jesus looked up to heaven, groaned, and spoke this word, "Ephphatha." Jesus' audience would probably have understood its meaning. Mark's audience, however, required a Greek translation.

In one other account (Mark 5:41), Mark portrays Jesus' use of Aramaic words during a healing episode (*see* TALITHA CUMI). Matthew and Luke, on the other hand, prefer not to use any Aramaic words during healing scenes. It is possible, but unlikely, that Mark intends to depict Jesus' Aramaic words as part of an unusual "magical" process. *See* HEALING; MIRACLE.

EMERSON B. POWERY

EPHRAEM. The preeminent figure in Syrian Christianity, Ephraem (ca. 305–73 CE) was born and ordained a deacon in Nisibis but fled to Edessa (the center of Syrian Christianity) in 363 when the Persians invaded. Many of Ephraem's works (hymns, metrical sermons, sermons, and commentaries) survive in the original SYRIAC; the translations (into Greek, Armenian) are poor and corrupted.

Ephraem's commentaries (on the DIATESSARON, and the Pauline Epistles) are valuable for reconstructing the early Syriac versions of the Bible. His *Hymns on the Nativity*, *Hymns on the Passion*, and *Nisibine Hymns* are masterpieces. He is arguably the inventor of ecclesiastical drama, for his hymns and metrical sermons sometimes dramatize biblical stories with dialogue. Later writers—notably the greatest Greek hymnographer, Romanos—plunder Ephraem for metaphors, turns of phrase, and ideas.

Theologically, Ephraem follows the doctrines of Nicea, but his exegesis and expression are Semitic. He sees the Bible as a storehouse of symbols: the burning bush is a symbol of the virginal conception (the bush/womb hosts divine "fire" without being consumed); Mary conceives through her ear (a "word" [logos λογός] enters through the ear).

Bibliography: E. Beck. Editions of Ephraem's works, published in *Corpus Scriptorum Christianorum Orientalium* (various dates); S. P. Brock. *The Harp of the Spirit* (1983); K. McVey. *Ephrem the Syrian. Hymns* (1989); K. McVey. *Selected Prose Works. Ephrem the Syrian* (1994); W. L. Petersen. *The Diatessaron and Ephrem Syrus as Sources of Romanos the Melodist* (1985).

WILLIAM L. PETERSEN

EPHRAEMI SYRI RESCRIPTUS, CODEX. One of the most valuable Greek manuscripts of the OT and NT (*see* VERSIONS, ANCIENT) and the most important PALIMPSEST. The Greek biblical text was written in the 5th cent. CE; in the 12th/13th cent. it was washed off and overwritten with thirty-eight treatises of Ephraem the Syrian in Greek translation. After the fall of Constantinople, it was brought to Florence and later on to Paris (today housed in Paris, Bibliothèque Nationale, Gr 9 [Medic-Reg C, 100, 1905] = Nestle-Aland C or 04).

By using chemical means, Constantin von Tischendorf deciphered its biblical text. Originally the codex contained the whole Bible, but in its present state only sixty-four leaves of the OT have survived, and 145 leaves (two-thirds) of the NT; no book is complete.

PETER ARZT-GRABNER

EPHRAIM, EPHRAIMITES ee´fray-im, ee´fray-uh-m*i*t [אֶפְרַיִם ’efrayim; אֶפְרָתִי ’efrathi]. Ephraim is the second son of Joseph and the eponymous ancestor of the Israelite tribe that inhabited the central hill country of Palestine. The meaning of the name cannot be ascertained with certainty. According to a folk etymology, it derives from the Hebrew root prh (פרה), which signifies fruitfulness (Gen 41:52). The ending -aim, however, suggests a toponymic designation, leading some to propose that the name refers to a geographical area, roughly cognate with Akkadian eperu ("region").

A. Ancestral Traditions
B. Territory
C. History
D. Ephraim in the Prophets
Bibliography

A. Ancestral Traditions

Patriarchal traditions locate the tribe's origins in Egypt and set Ephraim, along with Manasseh, apart from the rest of the Israelite tribes. The other tribal patriarchs were sons of Jacob, and all were born in Palestine. The tribes of Ephraim and Manasseh, however, traced their descent to grandsons of Jacob who were born to Joseph in Egypt (Gen 41:50; 46:20). The anomaly is resolved through the story of Jacob's blessing of the two sons (Gen 48:1-22), which has been rendered to explain, first, Ephraim and Manasseh's tribal status; second, Ephraim's ascendancy over Manasseh; and third, the legitimacy of the tribes' possession of Shechem. In the first section of the account, Jacob effectively elevates Ephraim and Manasseh to tribal status by declaring that "Ephraim and Manasseh shall be mine, just as Reuben and Simeon are" (v. 5). The next section relates the elevation of Ephraim over Manasseh when Jacob, against Joseph's protest, shows favor to Ephraim rather than firstborn Manasseh and declares that "the younger brother shall be greater than he" (v. 19). A third declaration concludes with Jacob granting Joseph a "shoulder" portion with respect to his brothers, a pronouncement that, in the Hebrew text, plays off the name "Shechem," a prominent town located in the middle of the hill country, near the border between the two tribes (v. 22).

An alternate tradition places Ephraim in coastal Palestine and reports the deaths of his sons, who had gone to raid cattle at Gath (1 Chr 7:21-24). The report, which has been inserted into the middle of a tribal genealogy, probably refers to a disastrous attempt to expand Ephraimite land westward during the premonarchical period. Rendered as a story of the tribal ancestor, however, it effectively counters the Pentateuchal tradition and situates Ephraim among the other Israelite tribes in Palestine who, in the person of "his brothers," provide comfort. The discrepancy between the two traditions prompted rabbinic speculation that the Ephraimites had undertaken an early exodus.

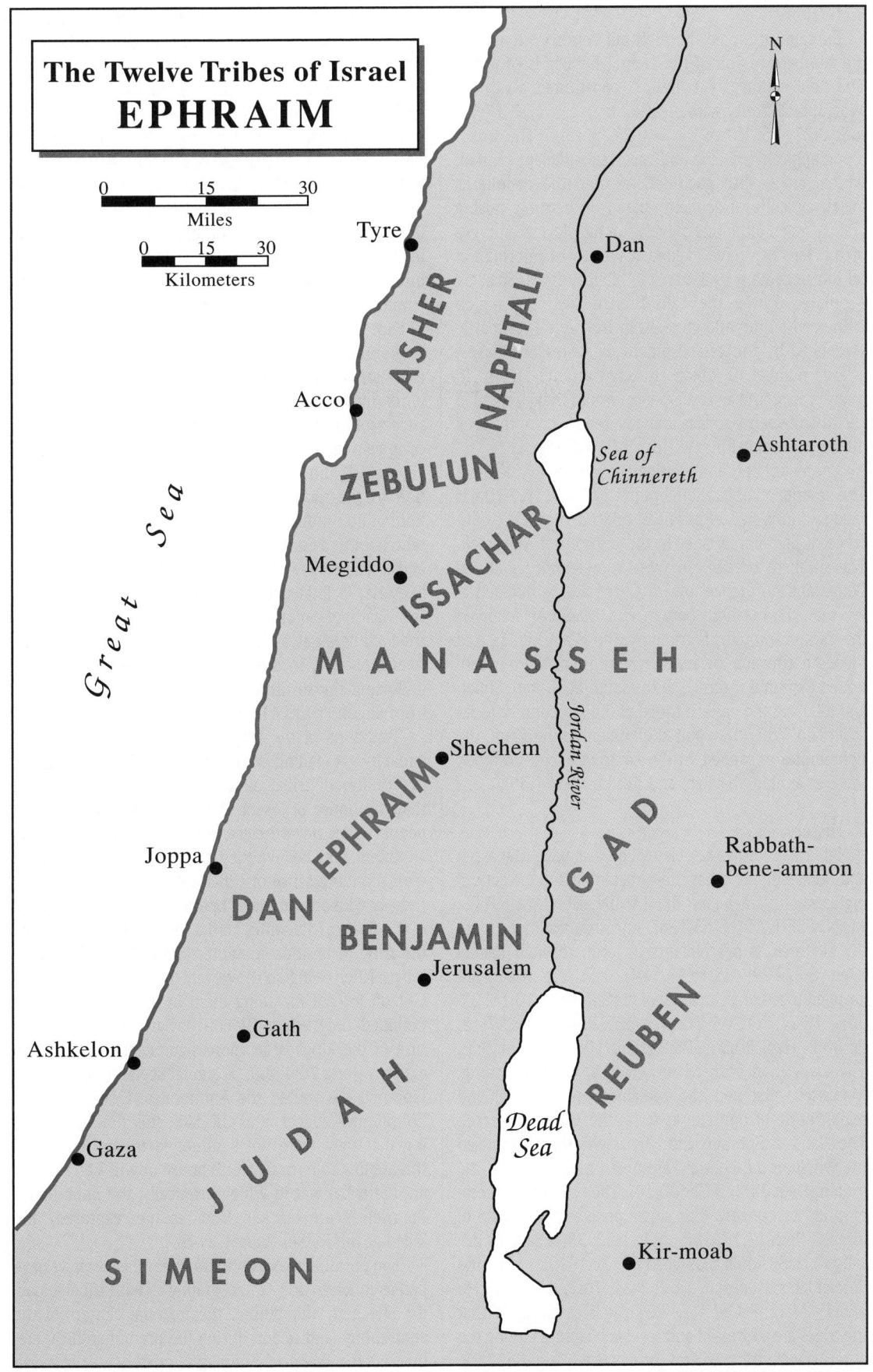

The Twelve Tribes of Israel
EPHRAIM

B. Territory

Ephraim occupied the high hill country situated in the southern region of the central highlands of Israel. The "hill country of Ephraim" constituted a distinct geographical entity within early Israel (e.g., Josh 17:15; Judg 3:27; 4:5; 1 Sam 1:1; 9:4; 2 Chr 13:4). The area is topographically diverse and receives sufficient rainfall, which, along with good soil, created the conditions for an agricultural economy based on herding, raising grains, and cultivating olives. Archaeological surveys of the territory have yielded a wealth of information on the settlement of the area in biblical times. Sparsely populated during the Late Bronze Age, the region witnessed a dramatic increase in Iron Age I, primarily evidenced by the establishment of scores of villages, a large number of which clustered around Shiloh. In many cases, these settlements would have entailed clearing the dense forests that covered much of the area during the biblical period (Josh 17:14-18).

The area of Ephraim's settlement was vaguely defined. The description of its allotment (Josh 16:5-9; 17:7-10a) is rendered in broad terms and specifically notes the existence of Ephraimite cities in the territory of Manasseh. The southern border ran west from Jericho, south of Bethel and Ai, thence toward Gezer, and terminated at the sea. The northern border with Manasseh followed the Yarkon through its tributary, the Wadi Kanah, and thence northward toward Shechem. From there it continued east until it turned to the south at Taanath-Shiloh and followed the eastern fringe of the hill country as far as Jericho. When Dan quit its allotment in the south, the Ephraimites expanded to the southwest and absorbed the area around Shaalbim and Aijalon (Judg 1:35).

C. History

Biblical literature associates Ephraim with Manasseh and Benjamin, the other tribes that inhabited the central highlands of Israel (see BENJAMIN, BENJAMINITES; MANASSEH, MANASSITES). Ancestral traditions identify all three as descendants of Jacob through Rachel (Gen 30:22-24; 35:16-18, 24), and the tribes are grouped together in an array of texts (Num 1:10-11, 32-36; 2:18-24; 7:48-65; 10:21-24; 26:28-41; Deut 27:12; Ps 80:2 [Heb. 80:3]; 108:8 [Heb. 108:9]; 2 Chr 9:3). The association with Manasseh is particularly strong. Manasseh inhabited the remainder of the highland region north of Ephraim as far as the Valley of Jezreel. The "land of Ephraim and Manasseh" thus comprised the whole of the central Palestinian massif west of the Jordan (Deut 34:2; 2 Chr 30:10). The two tribes together could be conceived as single people, "the house of Joseph" (Josh 17:17; 18:5; Judg 1:22, 35; 2 Sam 19:20; 1 Kgs 11:28; Amos 5:6; Obad 18; Zech 10:6) and "the descendants of Joseph" (Josh 14:4; 16:1, 4; 17:14, 16; 18:11; 24:32; 1 Chr 5:2; 7:29). It is as "Joseph" that the tribes are addressed and receive blessings among the other Israelite tribes in two early poems (Gen 49:22-27;

Deut 33:13-17). The former begins by calling Joseph "a fruitful bough," a pun on Ephraim's birth narrative (Gen 41:52), and both acclaim Joseph's fecundity, blessedness, military prowess, and preeminence.

Associations with Benjamin to the south are also indicated by various biblical texts. Ephraimites joined Benjaminites in defeating oppressing powers (Judg 3:27-29; 5:14). Shimei the Benjaminite attempted to curry favor from David by declaring that he was "the first among all the house of Joseph" to meet the king on his return (2 Sam 19:20). And Sheba, who led an insurrection against David, is identified both as a Benjaminite and a man from the hill country of Ephraim (2 Sam 20:1, 21).

Ephraim's preeminence among the tribes as a whole is attested by the presence of Ephraimite leaders at key junctures in Israel's history in the land. Joshua, the successor of Moses and the central figure in Israel's conquest and settlement traditions, was an Ephraimite chieftain (Num 13:49-50; Josh 19:49-50). The transition to the monarchy was facilitated by Samuel, an Ephraimite judge, priest, and seer (1 Sam 1:1-28), who anointed Saul (a Benjaminite) as Israel's first king, and later rejected him in favor of David. Ephraimites, likewise, facilitated the division of the monarchy after the death of Solomon. Jeroboam rallied the Israelite tribes to break away from Rehoboam and established a rival monarchy in the north, after receiving an oracle endorsing the insurrection through Ahijah, a prophet from Shiloh (1 Kgs 11:26-40; 12:1-33).

Traditions of the tribal period confirm Ephraimite audacity. A telling vignette embedded within the description of tribal allotments has Joshua affirming that the house of Joseph is a numerous and powerful people who, nevertheless, may not receive the extra allotment they believe they deserve (Josh 17:14-18). A corresponding sense of tribal entitlement extends into Judges. Gideon summons Ephraim to block the escape of the fleeing Midianites across the Jordan, thus placing the tribe in position to capture and kill the Midianite kings. After doing so, however, the Ephraimites chide Gideon for not including them in the muster and are mollified only when Gideon declares that their capture of the kings is far more significant than his own exploits (Judg 7:24–8:3). A similar scenario recurs after Jephthah has routed the Ammonites. Once again the Ephraimites appear after the fact, this time complaining that they were not summoned to the battle and threatening to burn Gideon's house down. The result is an intertribal war in which, ironically, the Ephraimites themselves are blocked from escape, captured, and killed at the Jordan (Judg 12:1-6).

The prominence of Ephraim in early Israel may have had as much to do with geography as with tribal audacity. Shechem and Bethel, the regional centers of the central highland region during the premonarchical era, marked the limits of Ephraim's territory to the north and the south, respectively. In addition, Shiloh, one of the most important shrines in early Israel, was located in the heart of Ephraim.

Shiloh, however, was destroyed by a massive conflagration ca. 1050 BCE, and Shechem declined in importance with the rise of the Israelite monarchy. Although the town was briefly the center of Jeroboam's kingdom (1 Kgs 12:25), regional economic and political power eventually shifted northward to Tirzah and finally to Samaria. The establishment of the northern monarchy, however, also precipitated another dramatic period of settlement. Population growth, primarily rural in character, exploded during Iron Age II in all areas except the border region around Bethel, an area vulnerable to conflict with Judah (2 Kgs 14:30; 23:15-20; 1 Chr 15:8; 17:2).

By the 8th cent. BCE "Ephraim" denoted the entire central hill country, with Samaria at the center, and, with the loss of much of Israel's territory to surrounding powers, served as a designation for the Northern Kingdom as a whole (Isa 7:2, 5; 9:8-9; 17:3; Hos 5:3, 5; 6:10; 10:6). The rump state of Ephraim, which comprised this highland region, was torn by internal strife and was caught up in the regional turmoil precipitated by the resurgence of Assyrian imperialism that began with the accession of TIGLATH-PILESER III (745–727 BCE). The death of Jeroboam II ca. 746 BCE ushered in a period of political instability, marked by assassinations and coups, as competing factions within Israel pressed the nation to accept vassalage to Assyria or to align with regional coalitions intent on opposing Assyrian expansion. With the assassination of Pekahiah, whose father Menahem was an Assyrian vassal, Ephraim was drawn into the orbit of Rezin of Damascus, the ringleader of opposition in the area (2 Kgs 15:8-26). Pekah, likely a puppet ruler, joined Rezin in a campaign to besiege Jerusalem and remove Ahaz from the throne (the so-called "Syro-Ephraimite War," see Isa 7:1-6). The siege, however, was broken off when Tiglath-Pileser III campaigned down the Mediterranean coast in 734 BCE. Subsequent campaigns in 733–732 resulted in the destruction of Damascus, the assassination of Pekah, and the transformation of erstwhile Israelite territory into Assyrian provinces (2 Kgs 15:29). Ephraim alone retained a measure of autonomy under the reign of Hoshea, an Assyrian vassal, and survived until Hoshea rebelled. After a three-year siege, ending in 722, Sargon II destroyed Samaria, exiled the population of Ephraim, and resettled the region with exiles from distant parts of the empire (2 Kgs 17:5-6). Thereafter, Ephraim formed part of the Assyrian province of Samaria.

D. Ephraim in the Prophets

Ephraim's audacity becomes arrogance and apostasy in the prophecies of Hosea and Isaiah. Tribal and national identity coalesce in the prophecies of Hosea, which associate Ephraim with archetypal symbols of

corruption (9:6-10) and indict Ephraim for apostasy and idolatry (4:18-19; 5:3-4; 6:10; 13:1), arrogance and obstinacy (5:5; 9:16-17), and oppression (12:8). In a twist on its etiological association with fruitfulness, Hosea characterizes Ephraim as once fruitful but no longer able to bring to birth or to sustain life (9:11-14; 13:12-13). Isaiah, for his part, takes the opposite tack on the association, declaring that Ephraim has gorged itself on its overabundant fruitfulness (Isa 28:1-4). Conversely, Ephraim remains the object of Yahweh's affection and thus provokes divine ambivalence about judgment (Hos 6:4; 11:1-9). This latter sense is picked up in later prophetic literature, where divine compassion resolves divine ambivalence (Jer 31:18-20) and Ephraim embodies the hope that Yahweh will bring back the exiles and establish a reunified and restored Israel in the land (Jer 31:7-9; Ezek 37:15-23; Zech 10:6-7).

Bibliography: I. Finkelstein. *The Archaeology of the Israelite Settlement* (1988); Z. Kallai. "The Settlement Traditions of Ephraim." *ZDPV* 102 (1986) 68–74; J. M. Miller and J. H. Hayes. *A History of Ancient Israel and Judah* (1986);

L. DANIEL HAWK

EPHRAIM, FOREST OF ee'fray-im [יַעַר אֶפְרַיִם ya'ar 'efrayim]. Located in the Transjordanian territory of Gilead, the Forest of Ephraim apparently stretched northward from the Jabbok, roughly between Manhanaim and Zaphon. It was here that David's generals meted a disastrous defeat to Absalom's army. The battle account (2 Sam 18:6-8) notes that of the 20,000 men who perished, the forest "devoured" more victims than did the sword. Likewise, Absalom was there captured and killed by Joab, who found the usurper hanging by his own hair in a tree (2 Sam 18:9-15). Centuries later, Jeremiah (Jer 22:6) and Zechariah (Zech 10:10) favorably compared this region with the famously forested LEBANON.

WALTER C. BOUZARD

EPHRAIM GATE ee'fray-im [שַׁעַר אֶפְרַיִם sha'ar 'efrayim]. A pre and postexilic Jerusalem gate (2 Kgs 14:13; 2 Chr 25:23; Neh 8:16; 12:39), piercing the northern city wall (thus facing Ephraim) west of the Temple courts and perhaps east of the BROAD WALL uncovered by N. Avigad. *See* GATE; JERUSALEM.

Bibliography: N. Avigad. *Discovering Jerusalem* (1980).

JAMES RILEY STRANGE

EPHRATH ef'rath. *See* EPHRATHAH, EPHRATHITES.

EPHRATHAH, EPHRATHITES ef'ruh-thuh, ef'ruh-th*i*t [אֶפְרָתָה 'efrathah, אֶפְרָת 'efrath, אֶפְרָתִי 'efrathi; Ἐφραθα ephratha, Ἐφραθ Ephrath, Ἐφραθί Ephrathi]. 1. A town identified with BETHLEHEM (Gen 35:16, 19; 48:7; Mic 5:2 [Heb. 5:1]; Ruth 4:11; LXX Josh 15:59*a*). In Ps 132:6 [Heb. 131:6], the toponym may, but does not have to, refer to a different location. Several scholars have argued that Bethlehem, aka Ephrathah, was not identical with Bethlehem of Judah because Jer 31:15 allegedly situates Rachel's burial place, associated in Gen 35:19; 48:7 with both Ephrathah and Bethlehem, near RAMAH in Ephraim.

2. The father of HUR who was called "father of Bethlehem" (1 Chr 4:4).

3. The wife of CALEB, mother of Hur (1 Chr 2:19, 50; 4:4). According to LXX 1 Chr 2:24, Caleb married Ephrathah after the death of his father HEZRON.

4. "Ephrathite" is gentilic of Ephrathah in 1 Sam 17:12 and Ruth 1:2, and of Ephraim in Judg 12:5 and 1 Kgs 11:26 (where the proper translation is, accordingly, "Ephraimite"). In 1 Sam 1:1, the meaning of the term is uncertain: it may identify SAMUEL's ancestor Zuph as either an Ephraimite (in which case it would contradict Samuel's Levitic genealogy in 1 Chr 6:18-23) or a resident of Ephrathah, that is, Bethlehem.

SERGE FROLOV

EPHRON ee´fron [עֶפְרוֹן 'efron]. 1. Ephron son of Zohar, the Hittite; the individual from whom Abraham bought land to bury Sarah. All 12 references to Ephron occur in Gen 23–50 (23:8, 10, 13, 14, 16, 17; 25:9; 49:29, 30; 50:13) and relate to the land transaction. Initially identified as "Ephron, the son of Zohar" (23:8), his identification as a "Hittite" is expressed in two ways; bene-kheth (בְּנֵי־חֵת, sons of Heth—Gen 10:15 names Heth as a son of Canaan) and hakhitti (הַחִתִּי the Hittite). The former expression occurs only in Gen 23:3, 5, 7, 10, 16, 18, 20; 25:10; and 49:32, and always in the context of Abraham's purchase of property. The latter expression is used together with the former in Gen 23:10, but is used more broadly in the OT as a gentilic.

2. Cited in Josh 15:9; 18:15 as a mountain (har הַר) on the border between Judah and Benjamin, near the Waters of Netophah—approximately 7 km northwest of Jerusalem.

3. A city taken from Jeroboam by Abijah, according to 2 Chr 13:19.

4. A fortified city in Gilead of the Hellenistic era, according to 1 Macc 5:46 and 2 Macc 12:27.

JOHN I. LAWLOR

EPIC OF GILGAMESH. See GILGAMESH, EPIC OF.

EPIC OF KIRTA. See KIRTU, KERET, KIRTA, EPIC OF.

EPICTETUS. Originally from Hierapolis in Phrygia, Epictetus, who lived in the 1st/2nd cent. CE, was raised as a house slave to Epaphroditus, a freedman in the upper echelons of Nero's secretarial services. Epictetus enjoyed an excellent education under Musonius Rufus, a Stoic philosopher. Epictetus nevertheless suffered the common indignities of his servile status, including tor-

ture. Eventually set free, Epictetus was banished from Rome along with other philosophers by Domitian, who saw a political threat in their philosophical activity (89 CE). Epictetus spent the rest of his life in Nicopolis in Epirus where he ran a well-attended school. What we know of his teaching derives from the notes of his erstwhile student, the historian Arrian, who recorded his teacher's lectures in eight books of *Diatribae* or *Discourses* (we possess four) as well as a handy compendium in one book (the *Enchiridion* or *Manual*). The social categories of our own day fail to find a match for Epictetus, and it is here that we may locate a portion of his importance for the NT. Epictetus was materially prosperous, well educated, and socially well connected, but, because an ex-slave, he was excluded by his status from the privileges enjoyed by Rome's free-born citizenry. Men like Epictetus, along with others made marginal by sex, geography, ethnicity, or class filled Paul's audiences. Epictetus provides an important glimpse into a nonsystematic, passionate, practical, and religiously inspired Stoicism. A wise god, according to Epictetus, created the universe, and, whether or not it may seem so to human beings, all things have been created according to this god's will to work for the good of all. Our freedom (and we do have free will) consists in our willingness to accept or reject this god's plan, and either work for it or against it. Similarities of Epictetus' precepts to Christian teachings have led some scholars to look for evidence of direct Christian influence on Epictetus' thought. Almost all scholars reject this possibility. Although one may assume that Epictetus had knowledge of the existence of Christians, he did not address the group in his work. Epictetus' work, despite any similarities to contemporary Christian thought, remains thoroughly grounded in the pagan culture of Greco-Roman antiquity.

Bibliography: Adolf Friedrich Bonhöffer. *The Ethics of the Stoic Epictetus.* William O. Stephens, trans. (2000); A. A. Long. *Epictetus: A Stoic and Socratic Guide to Life* (2002); Douglas S. Sharp. *Epictetus and the New Testament* (1914).

HANS-FRIEDRICH MUELLER

EPICURUS, EPICUREANISM ep´uh-kyoor´uhs, ep´uh-kyoo-ree´uhn-iz-uhm [Ἐπίκουρος Epikouros]. Epicurus was a Greek philosopher from Samos (b. 341 BCE; d. 270 BCE), and the philosophy of life he introduced bears his name as Epicureanism. He received some of his training as a youth in Athens, and later, after establishing schools on Lesbos and at Lampsacus, he went to Athens and founded his school, the Garden. Though he is said to have written voluminously, much of Epicurus's surviving work is only found in secondary sources (esp. Diogenes Laertius, *Lives* 10). His followers, however, have shed additional light on his philosophy, including his most famous admirer, the Latin poet Lucretius (b. ca. 94 BCE; d. ca. 55 BCE), whose long poem, *De rerum natura* (*On the Nature of Things*), declares his debt to Epicurus.

Epicureanism is a personally appropriated philosophy, the goal of which (telos τέλος) is pleasure (hēdonē ἡδονή, from which comes our *hedonism;* see Laertius, *Lives* 10.11; 10.131), and ataraxia (ἀταραξία), that is a calm or undisturbed state in the individual, is a prime component of a happy life (Laertius, *Lives* 10.128; compare 10.80). According to the Epicureans, one was to prefer that which brings pleasure, and to shun that which causes pain (Laertius, *Lives* 10.34, compare 10.136; Lucrecius, *De rerum natura* 2.16-19), including false opinions that trouble souls (Laertius, *Lives* 10.132). In all, Epicurus' goal was a therapeutic wellness.

Yet pleasure was not to be simply equated with personal gratification, for many things that personally gratify also come with a personal cost or pain. Rather, pleasure involves a trouble-free state of mind (Laertius, *Lives* 10.131-32; compare 10.129). Serious Epicureans certainly would not have approved of the licentious gratification the name of their philosophy now evokes (as it did then as well). In determining one's approach to life, Epicurus also emphasized the use of reason (logismos λογισμός) (Laertius, *Lives* 10.144; compare 10.140).

Cosmologically, Epicurus was influenced by Democritus's atomism (ca. 5th cent. BCE), the position that everything that exists is made up of small particles called atoms (from atomos ἄτομος—indivisible; Laertius, *Lives* 10.41). Epicurus considered matter eternal, and thus he was a materialist (Laertius, *Lives* 10.44). Lucretius emphasized that the earth had a beginning and will have an end (Lucrecius, *De rerum natura* 5.235-46), and this imperfect world was neither the work of any deity (5.198–99), nor made with any intention (5.419). As to the origin of living organisms, they arose from the earth (5.783–820).

In Epicureanism the existence of the individual soul is not denied, but since it too is also composed of atoms, it dies along with the body at death, the soul's atoms dispersing (Laertius, *Lives* 10.65). Therefore, death is not to be feared; conversely, to fear death is to suffer (Laertius, *Lives* 10.124–26), a particular point Lucretius pressed hard (Lucrecius, *De rerum natura* 1.104-11; 3.1018-23). There is no divine retribution after death (Lucrecius, *De rerum natura* 3.966, 978–81, 1011–13), and the attempt of Epicurus to overthrow of old fears won him the praise of Lucretius (3.1-30), who thought traditional religious beliefs dreadful (1.146).

Contemplation of the cosmos is the key to overcoming baseless fears, such as the attachment of malicious intentions to heavenly phenomena (Laertius, *Lives* 10.81-82; compare Lucrecius, *De rerum natura* 1.127-28; 3.14-22). The individual's opinions are to be in harmony with what is observed (Laertius, *Lives* 10.87; Lucrecius, *De rerum natura* 2.1090-94),

not succumbing to mythos (μῦθος Laertius, *Lives* 10.87) nor speculations concerning astral phenomena (Laertius, *Lives* 10.79). Correct understanding of the cosmos is thus foundational to personal blessedness (Laertius, *Lives* 10.78), as it also is to personal tranquility (ataraxia Laertius, *Lives* 10.85), or as Lucretius put it, an unpolluted conscience (*De rerum natura* 5.18). It should be noted that methodologically, Epicurus rejected skepticism, emphasizing a more inductive approach through sense-perceptions (aisthēsis αἴσθησις) and feelings (pathos πάθος) (Laertius, *Lives* 10.31-32; 10.38).

Sociologically, Epicureanism was counter-cultural, and Epicureans were known to gather in communities. Epicureans embraced all members of society, whether free or slave, man or woman (compare Gal 3:28). Epicurus downplayed education (Laertius, *Lives* 10.6), and followers were encouraged to critically consider traditional family life, as well as to avoid politics (Laertius, *Lives* 10.119; compare Lucrecius, *De rerum natura* 3.78). One was to "live unnoticed" (lathe biōsas λάθε βίωσας; Epicurus, *Fragment* 551; compare *Gos. Thom.* 42). On the other hand, Epicurus considered possessing friends as of the highest degree for a happy life (Laertius, *Lives* 10.148; compare Mark 3:31-35).

In the Bible, Epicureans are only mentioned in Acts 17, where they and the Stoics disputed with Paul (17:18), resulting in Paul's famous speech on the Areopagus at Athens. Consistent with Luke's strategic preference for divided audiences, some elements of Paul's speech run counter to Epicureanism and some elements of the speech are agreeable to the Stoics. For example, Paul affirms that the cosmos was created by God (v. 24), that there will be a divine judgment after death (vv. 30-31; compare 10:42), and that resurrection from the dead is a reality (vv. 31-32; compare v. 18), a theology that contradicts Epicurean thought.

Recent NT scholarship has also directed attention to the Epicurean poet and philosopher Philodemus (b. ca. 110 BCE; d. ca. 40/35 BCE), whose work was recovered in papyri from Herculaneum. Philodemus was born in Gadara of Syria (Matt 8:28) and was a student of the renowned ZENO of Sidon. His work *De morte* presents Epicurean attitudes concerning death. It is in a work of Philodemus that the Epicurean approach to life is famously stated:

> God is not to be feared,
> Death holds no surprises.
> The good is readily accessible,
> The horrible is easy to patiently endure.
> (Philodemus, *Against the Sophists* 4.9-14)

See GREEK RELIGION AND PHILOSOPHY.

Bibliography: Diogenes Laertius. *Lives of Eminent Philosophers.* R. D. Hicks, trans. Vol 2. (1925); Epicurus. *The Epicurus Reader: Selected Writings and Testimo-*

nia. Brad Inwood and L. P. Gerson, trans. (1994); John T. Fitzgerald, Dirk Obbink and Glenn S. Holland, eds. *Philodemus and the New Testament World* (2004); Lucretius. *De rerum natura*. W. H. D. Rouse, trans. (1937); Jerome H. Neyrey. "Acts 17, Epicureans, and Theodicy: A Study in Stereotypes." *Greeks, Romans, and Christians: Essays in Honor of Abraham J. Malherbe*. David L. Balch, Everett Ferguson, and Wayne A. Meeks, eds. (1990) 118–34.

BRETT S. PROVANCE

EPIGRAPHY. *See* ALPHABET; INSCRIPTIONS.

EPILEPSY. The contemporary Western medical understanding of epilepsy includes a wide range of physical disorders characterized by disturbed electrical rhythms of the central nervous system. The British neurologist John Hughlings Jackson (1835–1911) discovered that epilepsy was caused by brain and spinal cord injury. The ancients may have known its symptoms but not the cause. There is no Hebrew or Greek word in the Bible that can be translated "epilepsy." The ancient interpretations are culture-bound syndromes. Thus, the psalmist affirmed the potentially harmful effects of the moon (and sun; 121:6), and Matthew identified its victims as "moonstruck" (not "lunatics," much less "epileptics," NRSV) who sought healing from Jesus (4:24). When a demon caused the syndrome by "seizing" a victim (*see* Luke 9:39), exorcism healed it (Matt 17:18). Another culture-bound syndrome, "falling out," explains the behavior of the youth in Matthew's report (17:15; *see also* Mark 9:18) or the behavior of Saul (1 Sam 19:24) more plausibly than epilepsy in that culture. While the human body has basically functioned consistently over millennia, societies have interpreted physical disorders in different but rarely scientific ways.

Bibliography: Ronald C. Simons and Charles C. Hughes, eds. *The Culture-Bound Syndromes: Folk Illnesses of Psychiatric and Anthropological Interest* (1985).

JOHN J. PILCH

EPIMENIDES. Epimenides of Crete was a miracle worker active during the archaic period, reported to be from Knossos. He is said to have been invited to Athens by the prompting of the Delphic oracle after the murder of the potential tyrant Kylon when he had sought sanctuary on the Athenian acropolis (probably around 600 BCE). Epimenides was given the task of purifying the city; such a role is attributed to other Cretans.

Diogenes Laertius, writing in the 3rd cent. CE, included Epimenides among his lives of philosophers. Epimenides was reported as writing poetic and legal texts, although these have only survived as quotations in other sources; one poetic work was on Jason and the Argonauts. Epimenides was reported to have been long lived; ages suggested in ancient sources include 157–299.

In the letter to Titus, a Cretan prophet is quoted, "Cretans are always liars, vicious brutes, lazy gluttons" (1:12). Later Christian commentators considered this to be a quotation from Epimenides.

Bibliography: T. Nicklin. "Epimenides' Minos." *Classical Review* 30 (1916) 33–37; J. U. Powell. "On an Alleged New Fragment of Epimenides." *Classical Review* 30 (1916) 139–42; E. W. Brooks. "Epimenides and 'Maxinidus.' " *Classical Review* 33 (1919) 100.

DAVID W. J. GILL

EPIPHANES i-pif'uh-neez ['Αντίοχος 'Επιφανής Antiochos Epiphanēs]. The Seleucid ruler ANTIOCHUS IV Epiphanes (175–164 BCE) has become one of the most notorious figures in history. He was possibly one of the most able of the Seleucid rulers; however, circumstances allowed him little room to maneuver. His was not a mission to spread Hellenism to the native peoples, but when Jason offered him a large sum of money to take the office of high priest, Antiochus was happy to accept, a question not of ideology but valuable resources (*see* MACCABEES, MACCABEAN REVOLT).

He spent the first five years preparing to extend the Seleucid Empire. Antiochus successfully invaded Egypt in 170 BCE, but during a second invasion in 168, the Romans intervened and forced him to withdraw. When he heard of fighting between JASON's and MENELAUS's forces in Jerusalem, he sent an army to put a stop to it, and then, for reasons that are still unclear, he authorized attempts to suppress the practice of Judaism. Thwarted by the power of Rome, Antiochus could do little in the western part of his empire. He began a series of campaigns toward the east, during which he died in late 164 BCE.

LESTER L. GRABBE

EPIPHANIUS ['Επιφάνιος Epiphanios]. Epiphanius (315–403 CE) was one of the most vocal defenders of orthodoxy during his tenure as bishop of Salamis. In addition to helping instigate the Origenist controversy, he played a central role in condemning the Tall Brothers for their subordinationist Christology and views on pre-existence and the resurrection. Epiphanius earned his reputation as one of the early church's great "heresy hunters" for his Panarion ("Medicine Chest"), which attempts to provide a theological "antidote" for the eighty "poisonous" heresies he examines. Although his dependence upon earlier authors, combined with his uncritical and confusing attempt to establish heretical genealogies, limits its historical value, the Panarion nevertheless preserves important information about 2nd-cent. Jewish-Christianity, in particular the Gospel of the Ebionites and the Book of Elchasai (both of which he quotes), as well as the Nazoreans and the Gospel of the Nazoreans. *See* EBIONITES, GOSPEL OF THE; ELCHASAITES;

HEBREWS, GOSPEL OF THE; NAZOREANS, GOS-
PEL OF THE.

DAVID M. REIS

EPIPHANY i-pif′uh-nee [ἐπιφάνεια epiphaneia]. In
the Hellenistic world, epiphaneia (meaning an appearing or a manifestation of an ordinarily invisible power)
was used as a religious term for the helpful intervention
of divine beings in human affairs. In Christian tradition
epiphany is used to describe both the incarnation of
Christ and occasions when the manifestation of God
in Christ has become (or is expected to become) easily
recognizable.

In the LXX, the verb from which the noun comes
is used to describe God's self-revelation (Gen 35:7) and
appears in contexts that compare God's favorable manifestations to the shining of the sun (e.g., Num 6:25;
Deut 33:2; Pss 31:16; 80:3). This seems to be the sense
in Luke 1:78-79 as well.

In the NT both the noun (epiphaneia) and the verb
(epiphainō ἐπιφαίνω) can be used to refer to revelation that has already happened (as in 2 Tim 1:10; Titus
2:11 and 3:4). However, the noun is used more frequently to refer to the SECOND COMING (the future
eschatological appearing of Christ). This is clearly the
case in 2 Thess 2:8; 1 Tim 6:14; and Titus 2:13 (where
the NRSV translates epiphaneia as "manifestation")
and in 2 Tim 4:1, 8 (translated as "appearing").

The Christian feast that celebrates the manifestation
of God in Christ has focused predominantly on Christ's
birth (in the western church) or on his baptism (in the
eastern church). In the western church, Epiphany is
commonly observed on January 6 as a commemoration
of the coming of the Magi. The three "kings" or wise
men are seen as the first representatives of the wider
world to recognize the appearance of God in the birth
of the child. The "Twelve Days of Christmas" run from
December 25 to January 5, which is sometimes called
"Twelfth Night," or the eve of Epiphany.

KATHLEEN A. ROBERTSON FARMER

EPISTLE. See LETTER.

EPISTLE OF BARNABAS. See BARNABAS, EPISTLE
OF.

EPISTLE OF THE APOSTLES. See APOSTLES, EPIS-
TLE OF THE.

EPISTLE TO THE LAODICEANS. See LAODICEANS,
EPISTLE TO THE.

EPISTLES, APOCRYPHAL. Pseudonymous letters
written by or to personalities of biblical times and/or
concerned with events or personalities of these times,
including several by the Virgin, the Letter of Christ
about Sunday, Paul to the Laodiceans, Paul to the Alex-
andrians, the Correspondence of Paul and Seneca,
James to Quadratus, the Ap. Jas., the Letter of Lentu-
lus, several involving Pilate, Pseudo-Titus, possibly the
Epistle of the Apostles, and others contained in narrative works (e.g., two in 4 Baruch, the Correspondence
of Abgar and Christ, 3 Corinthians in the Acts of Paul,
several in the Pseudo-Clementines, etc.).

F. STANLEY JONES

EPISTLES, CATHOLIC. See CATHOLIC EPISTLES.

EPITHETS, DIVINE. See GOD, NAMES OF.

EPSILON [ε e, Ε E]. The fifth letter of the Greek alphabet, derived from the Phoenician letter hē, a sound not
needed in Greek, so the sign was used as a vowel letter.
See ALPHABET.

EQUALITY. The modern ideal that all persons have
the right to pursue happiness without discrimination
regardless of race, gender, class, age, and sexual preference. Biblical texts do not uniformly or clearly provide
a stance. The idea that God created humankind, male
and female, connotes equality (Gen 1:1–2:3). Genesis
2:4-25, however, relates woman's creation from man's
rib. This can be read as subordination of the woman to
the man, though some disagree with this reading. First
Corinthians 12:4-26 refers to each person's important
role in the Christian community, although this is complicated by Paul's ranking of roles (1 Cor 12:27-30).
Paul discounts differences between Jew and Greek,
slave and free, and male and female (Gal 3:26-28), but
he instructs people to remain slaves (1 Cor 7:21) and
for the slave Onesimus to return to Philemon (Phlm
17). Paul's stance, perhaps, is influenced by his view
that Jesus' return was near (1 Cor 7:26, 29-31). See
EXCLUSION.

EMILY R. CHENEY

ER uhr [עֵר ‘er; ″Ηρ Ēr]. 1. Judah's eldest son by the
Canaanitess Shua (or Bath-Shua) (Gen 38:3-7; Num
26:19; 1 Chr 2:3). Er married Tamar (Gen 38:7), but
the Lord took Er's life because of Er's unspecified evil
deeds.

2. Judah's grandson through Shelah (1 Chr 4:21).

3. A third Er appears in Jesus' genealogy (Luke
3:38), twenty-five generations removed from Judah,
through Judah's son Perez.

KATHY R. MAXWELL

ERAN ihr′an [עֵרָן ‘eran]. A son of SHUTHELAH and
grandson of Ephraim whose name may mean "protector" or "watcher," Eran is the eponymous ancestor of
the Eranites clan, a subclan of Ephraim (Num 26:36),
although he is absent from the corresponding list in
1 Chr 7:20-29. The LXX (26:40), Syriac, and Samaritan
Pentateuch read "Eden," "joy," instead of Eran, probably as a result of scribal confusion of the DALET (d ד)
with the RESH (r ר). See EPHRAIM, EPHRAMITES.

RALPH K. HAWKINS

ERASTUS i-ras′tuhs [Ἔραστος Erastos]. This name appears three times in the NT (Acts 19:22; Rom 16:23; 2 Tim 4:20), in each case referring to the same associate of Paul. In Rom 16 Paul sends greetings from several persons, among whom is Erastus, "the city treasurer" (oikonomos οἰκονόμος). If Paul wrote Romans from CORINTH, Erastus is most likely the treasurer of that city. Of special note is 2 Tim 4:20 (considered deutero-Pauline), which states, "Erastus remained in Corinth." Such clues indicate that Erastus was perhaps a person of reputable status in Corinth and a follower of Paul.

DEMETRIUS WILLIAMS

ERECH ee′rik [אֶרֶךְ ʾerekh]. Erech is the biblical name of the ancient city of Uruk (modern Warka) on the lower Euphrates River. In Gen 10:10, it is listed, along with Babylon and Akkad, as ruled by the primeval king NIMROD in the land of SHINAR (Babylonia). In Ezra 4:9, it is one of the places from which Ashurbanipal (Osnapper) (668–627 BCE) deported people to Samaria.

Excavations at Uruk took place intermittently for thirty-nine seasons between 1912 and 1989. The site was occupied from the fifth to first millennia BCE, being the center of one of the major early phases of civilization known as the Uruk period (4000–2900 BCE), a phase in which writing was invented (ca. 3300 BCE). In Sumerian, the city's name was Unug, and it was one of the largest cities in the world (400 hectares or 988 acres). According to the Sumerian King List, the First Dynasty of Uruk included the semi-legendary characters Enmerkar, Lugalbanda, Gilgamesh, and Dumuzi (Tammuz) who play prominent roles in Mesopotamian epics. In the second millennium, Uruk declined in importance, but during the first millennium it was renovated by the Assyrian king Sargon II (721–705 BCE), only a few generations before Ashurbanipal's deportations from the city.

K. LAWSON YOUNGER, JR.

ERI ee′ri [עֵרִי ʿeri]. Means "roused." Among the seven sons of Gad (Gen 46:16); the eponymous founder of the Erites clan (Num 26:16). *See* SHUNI.

ERIDU. Means "the good city." Eridu, located 7 mi. southwest of Ur at modern Abu-Shahrain in Iraq, was one of the oldest, and the southernmost major city of ancient Sumer. It was the city of Enki (Akkadian Ea), the Sumerian god of wisdom and freshwater lagoons. His temple in Eridu, E-abzu (house of the apsu), was built on the edge of a lagoon (apsu). The Sumerian king list names Eridu as the site of the first kings before the rule moved farther north. Eridu figures prominently in several Sumerian myths involving Enki. Some are creation accounts, and some reflect the close trade and cultural connections between Eridu and Dilmun (modern Bahrain). One tells how Inanna, city goddess of Uruk (Erech), took the powers of civilization from

Enki, a mythological reflection of the shift of power from Eridu to the north. By the beginning of the 2nd millennium BCE Eridu had declined, never to regain its early importance.

J. J. M. ROBERTS

EROS [ἔρως erōs]. *Eros* is the Greek word for sexual love or desire. It is also the name of the god of love represented as shooting golden love arrows. Ancient Greeks understood *eros* as a destructive passion associated with the uncontrolled longing to make love to another person. This passion is attributed to the gods Aphrodite and Eros. The gods were not always good or benevolent, so persons might fall in love with people whom they would not have chosen if they were "in their right mind." At the same time, resisting the will of the gods only brought one harm. Thus, when struck by the arrows of Eros, it was better to give in. In contrast, some Stoics suggested that *eros* was not an uncontrollable passion but rather a force that could be controlled with reason. These Stoics proposed that the gods were good and benevolent toward humanity and that sexual love was a means for promoting friendship and relationships among people. They advocated a life of sexual restraint, moderation, and responsibility. The word *eros* is not used in the LXX or in the NT despite its importance in 1st cent. culture. The biblical texts mainly use the Greek words agapē (ἀγάπη) and phileō (φιλέω) to describe love.

Bibliography: Kathy L. Gaca. *The Making of Fornication: Eros, Ethics, and Political Reform in Greek Philosophy and Early Christianity* (2003).

RUTH ANNE REESE

ERR, TO [שָׁגָה shaghah, תָּעָה taʿah; πλανάω planaō]. To err is to stray from the right path. In its literal sense, straying is like missing the mark (hamartanō ἁμαρτάνω, to sin). In ethics, these terms may be thought to differ: sinning is culpable, whereas some errors, innocent mistakes, are not. However, this difference is not fully present in biblical usage.

The straying of sheep is a common biblical topos, mentioned literally (Exod 23:4; Matt 18:12), and applied figuratively (Ps 119:176; Isa 53:6). Lost animals are pitied rather than blamed, so the metaphor mitigates human responsibility. Nevertheless, even when biblical authors treat error as inadvertent through ignorance (Lev 4:13; Num 15:25), these errors are also sins requiring expiation. The psalmist's question, "Who can detect their errors?" (19:12), is accompanied by a plea for cleansing; James' wanderer is also a sinner (5:20).

Predominantly, erring is culpable and avoidable. Those who err wander from the truth (1 John 4:6). Although error may attach to belief (e.g., resurrection, Mark 12:27), it usually describes godless or immoral ways of living. A graphic instance is Paul's view of the "due penalty of their error" for those who, denying their natural knowledge of God, surrender to lust (Rom 1:27).

The faithful themselves are prone to err. The geographical wilderness wandering of Israel is paralleled by the erring "in the heart" of those who do not know God's ways (Ps 95:10; Heb 3:10). False prophets lead Israel astray (Jer 23:32), and may deceive Christians (2 Pet 2); animal-like, they live by base instinct and greed, straying from the "straight road" and following Balaam's road (2 Pet 2:15); unlike sheep, they deserve judgment (2:3). Hence the explicit injunction against being led astray (1 Cor 6:9; Jas 1:16). The faithful, in need of divine forgiveness, must not too humanly excuse their erring. *See* CONSCIENCE; SIN, SINNERS.

PAUL W. GOOCH

ERRA EPIC. This unusual Babylonian epic, composed by Kabti-ilani-Marduk, and dated to either the 11th or 8th cent. BCE, portrays the irrationality of violence and its threat to world order. The text narrates, primarily in direct address, how Erra (Scorched Earth), the Babylonian god of war and pestilence, convinces MARDUK, king of the Babylonian gods, to leave his throne in order to have his statue refurbished. Erra offers to maintain order in Marduk's absence, but this is a ruse. Once Marduk steps down, Erra and his subordinates go on a murderous rampage, justifying their violence by claiming that humans have shown a lack of respect for the gods. In the ensuing chaos, however, righteous and unrighteous alike perish. Babylon itself is polluted by indiscriminate bloodshed. Only when Ishum (Fire), Erra's vizier, manages to calm Erra's rage, and Marduk resumes his place on the throne, is peace and world order restored.

J. J. M. ROBERTS

ERUBIN. A tractate of the MISHNAH, with interpretations and commentaries on it in the GEMARA of the Jerusalem and Babylonian TALMUDs. The rabbinic concept of Erubin deals with the prohibition against carrying things in a public domain on the Sabbath. The ʿeruv (עֵירוּב; plural ʿeruvin [עֵירוּבִין]) is a means of transforming public or shared property into private domain by delineating the territory according to rabbinic practice (*see* HALAKHAH). Another mode of transforming public domain into private domain for the sake of carrying on the SABBATH was through sharing food.

BURTON L. VISOTZKY

ERUPTION [מִסְפַּחַת mispakhath, סַפַּחַת sappakhath]. These Hebrew words describe a skin condition often associated with "LEPROSY" (not Hansen's disease). They refer primarily to a swelling or raised lesion but could include a SCAB (Lev 13:2, 6, 7, 8; 14:56). The priests examined such conditions to confirm or deny the "leprosy." *See* ITCH; SCURVY.

JOHN J. PILCH

ESARHADDON ee´suhr-had´uhn. Esarhaddon was king of Assyria (680–669 BCE). His Assyrian name, Ashur-akha-iddina ("Ashur has given a brother"), implies

that he was a younger son of SENNACHERIB, perhaps the youngest. But, due in part to the urging of his formidable mother, one of Sennacherib's queens, Sennacherib unexpectedly passed over older sons to name Esarhaddon as heir apparent. Although he attempted to strengthen Esarhaddon's position, SENNACHERIB was assassinated by another son, Urdu-Mullissu, and his accomplices (2 Kgs 19:37 = Isa 37:38), and a battle over the succession ensued. In a daring march, Esarhaddon led his troops down mountain passes in mid winter to surprise and defeat resoundingly his brothers' troops, securing his throne.

While throughout his life he was plagued with a chronic illness, Esarhaddon proved to be a very successful ruler, particularly in foreign affairs. Reversing his father's policy, he rebuilt Babylon, which his father had only recently destroyed, and won decades of relative peace from the long-rebellious Babylonians (*COS* 2:306). In 676, he succeeded in quelling a western revolt with a campaign against Sidon and its northern allies. Demonstrating his violent tendencies, he had the two ringleaders, Abdi-Milkuti of Sidon and Sanda-uarri of Cilicia, decapitated and hung their heads from the necks of their magnates to display throughout the streets of Nineveh.

Erich Lessing Art Resource, NY
Figure 1: Stone prism of Esarhaddon, Neo-Assyrian, 680–660 BCE. British Museum, London, Great Britain.

Attested in various letters and oracles, Esarhaddon constantly worried about internal matters, particularly the loyalty of his officials. In 670, he even took the extreme measure of assassinating many of his own magnates, suggesting that even after ten years of rule he still seriously feared an uprising. Thus the loyalty of vassal kings was a major concern as witnessed by the many vassal treaties dating to his reign. As a genre, these are an important component in understanding the OT's covenant/treaty form (*see* ALLIANCE; COVENANT, OT AND NT). The payment of tribute by vassal kings was a tangible evidence of their loyalty as seen in the mention of Manasseh's payment along with other kings of the Levant. This loyalty issue is probably behind the story of Manasseh's captivity to Babylon (2 Chr 33:11-13).

Esarhaddon's greatest military achievement came in 671 when he successfully invaded EGYPT on his second attempt. His inscriptions give a detailed description of the capture and looting of Memphis. However, very soon after his departure from Egypt, the Egyptians under Taharqa (biblical TIRHAKAH) revolted, thereby precipitating another campaign by Esarhaddon, who died, however, while in route.

Although not mentioned in Assyrian inscriptions, Esarhaddon apparently sent deportees into SAMARIA (Ezra 4:2), just as his son Assurbanipal did a generation later (Ezra 4:9-10). *See* ASSYRIA AND BABYLONIA.

Bibliography: Israel Eph'al. "Esarhaddon, Egypt, and Shubria: Politics and Propaganda." *JCS* 57 (2005) 99–111; Tae-Hun Kim. *Assyrian Historical Inscriptions and the Syro-Palestinian States in the Eighth–Seventh Centuries BCE* (2005); S. C. Melville. *The Role of Naqia/Zakutu in Sargonid Politics* (1999); S. Parpola and K. Watanabe. *Neo-Assyrian Treaties and Loyalty Oaths* (1988); Frances Reynolds. *The Babylonian Correspondence of Esarhaddon, and Letters to Aššurbanipal and Sin-Šarru-Iškun from Northern and Central Babylonia* (2003).

K. LAWSON YOUNGER, JR.

ESAU, ESAUITES ee´ saw עֵשָׂו ʿesaw, בְּנֵי עֵשָׂו bene ʿesaw, בֵּית עֵשָׂו beth ʿesaw; Ἠσαῦ Ēsau]. Esau is the brother of Jacob (*see* JACOB), the son of ISAAC and REBEKAH, ancestor of the people of Edom (*see* EDOM, EDOMITES).

The struggles of Esau and Jacob in their mother's womb distressed her so she besought God, learning that she was carrying two contending nations. The elder (Esau) would serve the younger and stronger (Jacob). Esau emerged first, red and hairy (his names plays on the Hebrew words *red* and *hairy*) with his brother close behind and grasping Esau's heel. The brothers had different temperaments: Esau was a hunter, while Jacob preferred to stay home and cook. Each son was preferred by a different parent: Esau by his father, and Jacob by his mother. Once, claiming to be famished, Esau traded his birthright to Jacob for a bowl of pottage his brother was cooking (Gen 25:21-34).

Subsequently, Esau's father assigned him to prepare wild game for a meal, at the conclusion of which Isaac would bless his son. While Esau was hunting, his mother and brother deceived the old and blind Isaac into thinking that meat served by a disguised Jacob was wild game served by Esau. Fooled, Isaac gave Jacob virtually all the blessing (to Esau's consternation and anger). Jacob fled to his maternal kin (Gen 27). After his brother had been there for some years and returned

with wives, children, and substantial property, Esau met Jacob in Edom and they were reconciled. Refusing Jacob's gifts, Esau indicated that he had plenty of goods already himself (Gen 32:1–33:16). Esau and his family moved to SEIR of Edom, dispossessing the indigenous Horim. Elsewhere Esau is paired with Jacob when fraternal strife is alluded to: in Mal 1:2-3; Rom 9:13; Heb 12:16; once when both brothers are blessed (Heb 11:20).

Esau married two Hittite women (Judith and Basemath) and Canaanite women, Mahalath (a daughter of his father's half-brother, Ishmael), Adah, and Oholibamah, also of Canaan though not kin to Ishmael. (Adah and Judith may be the same person, since they have the same father, Elon the Hittite) (Gen 26:34; 28:8-9; 36:1).

To Esau's wives were born descendants who became the nation of Edom: Though individual names are provided, the key heir is Edomites in general (Gen 36; 1 Chr 1:34). Edom is named as adversary to Israel/Judah (Jacob's descendants) on various occasions: First, as the exodus survivors approach the land promised them, they are instructed to pass peaceably by the people of Edom, who also received their land from God (Deut 2:4-12, 22, 29; Josh 24:4). Second, Edom is intermittently hostile to Israel (2 Kgs 3; 8; 2 Chr 20–21; Amos 1:11-12). And third, when Judah was suffering at the hands of the Babylonians in the early 6th cent., the prophets Obadiah (1:6-9, 18-21) and Jeremiah (49:8-10) and also Ps 137:7 accuse the Edomites of increasing Judah's distress; revenge is anticipated (see also Lam 4 and Ezek 25). In the 2nd cent., the Edomites were defeated by Judas the Maccabee (1 Macc 5:3).

Bibliography: Hershel Shanks, ed. *Abraham and Family: New Insights into the Patriarchal Narratives* (2000).

BARBARA GREEN, O.P.

ESCAPE, ROCK OF. *See* ROCK OF ESCAPE.

ESCHATOLOGY IN EARLY JUDAISM. The term *eschatology* designates the ensemble of doctrines a specific group holds about the "last things" (eschatoa ἔσχατοα, from eschaton ἔσχατον), i.e., the end of the existing world and the ultimate destiny of humankind. Often, eschatological beliefs exert a beneficial influence on religious communities, especially (but not exclusively) in times of crisis, by providing them with the comforting expectation of relief from situations they perceive to be extremely difficult. However, under the combined pressure of economic, political, social, and psychological factors, a people who perceive themselves to be in a time of great hardship can develop more radical views of the "last things" as a time for divine justice and wrath. The last days and all the cataclysms surrounding them (wars, massacres, famines, epidemics, earthquakes, and other catastrophes) are then perceived as dramatically imminent and revealed in certain signs (*see* APOCALYPTICISM). In the face of the imminence of the eschaton, the faithful can adopt either a passive, nonviolent posture or a more proactive, revolutionary plan of action. Such an evolution of the eschatological discourse can be discerned through the history and literature of Second Temple Judaism, from the Macedonian conquest, in 333 BCE, to the end of the Second Jewish War, in 135 CE.

A. Characteristics of Early Jewish Eschatology
B. Early Jewish Eschatological Literature
  1. The books of Enoch and Daniel
  2. The Dead Sea Scrolls
  3. Psalms of Solomon and Parables of Enoch
  4. Post–70 CE eschatological works
Bibliography

A. Characteristics of Early Jewish Eschatology

During the Hellenistic and Roman periods, many inhabitants of Judea and Galilee experienced feelings of anxiety and frustration under the rulers whom they judged to be illegitimate, imperialist, and oppressive. One of the aspects of Jewish resistance to these rulers was the burgeoning of eschatological and apocalyptic hope. From the images inherited from prophets, wisdom, and other traditional lore, the Jewish theologians of the Second Temple period derived a wide spectrum of symbols and ideas that would subsequently become shared by both Judaism and Christianity. Among them are: 1) the subdivision of history into a sequence of different periods; 2) the turmoil of the "end of days"; 3) the coming of an eschatological prophet; 4) the advent of the Messiah, a charismatic leader sent by God to usher in the end times (*see* MESSIAH, JEWISH); 5) the return of the lost tribes to the land of Israel; 6) the waging of a HOLY WAR against the hostile nations; 7) the descent on earth of the heavenly Jerusalem and its holy Temple; 8) the final triumph of the God of Israel, who will reign over the pacified and renewed "world-to-come" ('olam habba' עוֹלָם הַבָּא); 9) the resurrection of the righteous; and 10) the JUDGMENT of sinners. These eschatological ideas led people to found sectarian communities that attempted to live in preparation for the end times (as the Community of the Renewed Covenant at QUMRAN) or who organized groups that fought for freedom (as did the Sicarii, the ZEALOTs, and Bar Kochba's partisans; *see* BAR KOCHBA, SIMON). When the end times did not come, Jewish and Christian theologians eventually tried to discourage any speculation about the exact date of the end and any active attempt to hasten it. As Rabbi Yohanan ben Torta told his colleague Rabbi Akiva, "Grass will grow from your cheeks, and still the son of David will not come" (*y. Taʿan.* 68d).

B. Early Jewish Eschatological Literature
1. The books of Enoch and Daniel

The historical roots of Jewish eschatology and apocalypticism lie in the oldest strata of the Enoch literature circulating in Aramaic by the 3rd cent. BCE or earlier. The story of the rebellion of the WATCHERs (Shemihazah, Asael, and the other fallen angels) and its devastating consequences lays the ground for further developments of supernatural and eschatological beliefs. Thus, in the Book of Watchers (*1 En.* 1–36), the contamination provoked by the union of heavenly beings with the daughters of men and the birth of the giants (also briefly mentioned in Gen 6:1-4) leads the Lord to purify and renovate the earth by means of the deluge (*see* FLOOD). The patriarch Enoch is "the righteous scribe" who acts as a mediator between the fallen angels and the Lord. More than half the Book of Watchers is devoted to the visions that Enoch sees concerning not only the decree pronounced against the watchers but also meteorological and astronomical phenomena (*see* ENOCH, FIRST BOOK OF; WATCHERS, BOOK OF THE). The Maccabean crisis in 167–164 BCE witnessed an impressive outburst of eschatological and apocalyptic new ideas (*see* MACCABEES, MACCABEAN REVOLT). Theologians belonging to the Enochic movement expressed their hopes for a radical change in the course of human history in some revelatory tracts later inserted in the Book of Dreams and the Epistle of Enoch (*1 En.* 83–90 and 91–105; *see* ENOCH, FIRST BOOK OF). The Animal Apocalypse (chaps. 85–90), written shortly before 160 BCE, symbolically shows Adam and the first patriarchs as white bulls, while their descendants (from Jacob onward) as a flock of sheep persecuted by wild beasts and (in the aftermath of the Babylonian exile) watched over by seventy merciless shepherds. The Lord of the sheep intervenes by condemning the evil shepherds together with the blind sheep (i.e., the Jewish collaborators), and then by inaugurating a new house (i.e., the New Jerusalem and/or the eschatological Temple). There will gather not only all the surviving sheep but also those who had died or had been dispersed, together with Enoch himself and "all the animals on earth and all the birds of heaven." In the end, the birth of a young, white, large-horned bull that inspires the respect of the wild beasts and birds will usher in the metamorphosis of all the animals into white bulls. The Apocalypse of Weeks (*1 En.* 93:1-10 + 91:11-17) adopts an alternative approach to such an allegorical understanding of human history and destiny and prefers to organize it chronologically into ten periods of weeks (of years). A reference to the Maccabean uprising is probably to be found at the end of the description of the seventh week; the following two weeks are depicted as an era of political and religious restoration, while the judgment of the fallen angels, the passing away of the first heaven, and the renewal of creation will not happen until the seventh part of the tenth week.

The main features of these Enochic pamphlets (i.e., the allegorization and periodization of history) are also present in the book of Daniel, the only truly apocalyptic text to have been included in the OT (*see* DANIEL, BOOK OF). A wisdom tale based on the traditional schema of the four kingdoms (chap. 2) is transcoded into a visionary experience of four dreadful monsters emerging from the sea and struggling for supremacy (chap. 7). As for "the One like a son of man," the supernatural character that comes with clouds to receive "an everlasting dominion" on all the nations of the earth, he has the same appearance as his angelic colleagues of the Animal Apocalypse. Daniel also displays a distinctive chronology that should go on not for "seventy years" (as in the original prophecy of Jer 25:11-12; 29:10), but for "seventy weeks of years," that is, ten jubilees or 490 years (chap. 9). Accordingly, the profanation of the Temple by Antiochus IV Epiphanes will happen in the middle of the seventieth week and will last for three and a half years (Dan 9:27; compare 7:25; 8:14; 12:7, 11-12). After the death of this evil king, Michael will set the people of Israel free and "many of those who sleep in the dust of the earth will awake, some to eternal life, and some to shame and everlasting contempt" (chap. 12). Such a reinterpretation of the length of the Babylonian exile implies that, in spite of the return of the deportees and the rebuilding of the Temple in 525–515 BCE, more than three centuries later the true restoration of Israel was thought to be still ahead. It is from this feeling of dissatisfaction for the political and religious institutions of the day that more radical and sectarian expectations will develop during the 2nd and the 1st cent. BCE.

2. The Dead Sea Scrolls

The DEAD SEA SCROLLS illustrate the variety of eschatological and apocalyptic beliefs at the end of the Second Temple period. Both the Enochic and Danielic literature are well represented in the QUMRAN libraries. A periodization of history is found in the *Ages of Creation* (4Q180-81), while the eschatological pesher called *Melchizedek* (11Q13; *see* MELCHIZEDEK TEXT) and the DAMASCUS DOCUMENT (CD) offer a chronology of the exile similar to that of the book of Daniel. The TEACHER OF RIGHTEOUSNESS supposedly began his career some 410 years after the destruction of the First Temple and died forty years later, which would approximately leave forty additional years before the inauguration of the eschaton expected by his followers. The testimony of other documents, such as the HALAKHIC LETTER (4Q394–399), the RULE OF THE CONGREGATION (1QSa [1Q28a]), or the *Eschatological Midrash* (4Q174 + 4Q177), demonstrate that the members of the community felt that they were actually living at the "end of days," a time of testing and refining that precedes the messianic age. Concerning the expectation of an eschatological

leader, the *Commentary on Genesis A* (4Q252) is probably the oldest witness of a messianic interpretation of Gen 49:10 ("the scepter shall not depart from Judah, nor the ruler's staff from between his feet"), the *Damascus Document* and the *Eschatological Midrash* read, respectively, Num 24:17 ("a star shall come forth from Jacob, a scepter shall rise from Israel"), and 2 Sam 7:12-14 ("I will raise up your descendant after you [...]; I will be a father to him, and he will be a son to me") as proof-texts for the coming of "the Interpreter of the Law" and "the PRINCE (nasiʾ נָשִׂיא) of the whole Congregation" (in the *Damascus Document*) or "the BRANCH of David" (in the *Eschatological Midrash*). Even if the *Damascus Document* has these two figures grouped together under the designation of "the Messiah (singular) of Aaron and Israel," the mention of "the Messiahs (plural) of Aaron and Israel" in the RULE OF THE COMMUNITY (1QS), as well as the reference to "[the] chief [priest] of all the congregation of Israel" and "the Messiah of Israel" in the *Rule of the Congregation*, confirm that the Qumranites were waiting for two distinct anointed leaders. The priestly Messiah would take precedence over his royal colleague. Such a bi-messianic belief was probably the result of the rejection of both the priesthood and (after 104 BCE) the monarchy held in Jerusalem by the Hasmonean rulers. In the last days, the priestly Messiah of Aaron will have the responsibility of re-establishing the true HALAKHAH and the legitimate cult in the restored Temple. Before entering into the eschatological blessings, the members of the community were expecting to endure a forty-year war against the "Kittim" (i.e., the Romans) until the final victory of light over darkness, of good against evil. This highly ritualized series of battles to be fought at the side of the angelic hosts was described in the WAR SCROLL. Other fragments of the War Scroll, especially 4Q285, reveal that the Prince of the Congregation, explicitly identified with the Branch of David, is expected to be the commander of the Jewish liberation army and that, in such a role, he will execute the chief of the Kittim. Another fragment applies to the Kittim defeated by the Prince of the Congregation the prophecy against Gog of Ezek 39:4 ("you shall fall on the mountains of Israel, you and all your troops"). Josephus's description of the eschatology of the ESSENES (*J.W.* 2.154-56) has been influential in attributing to the Qumranites a strong belief in judgment after death and immortality of the soul. These ideas were quite widespread among the Jews living in the Greco-Roman diaspora, esp. in Egypt (see, e.g., the Wisdom of Solomon), and evidence of hope for eternal life has been detected in the major sectarian writings, such as the *Rule of the Community*, the *Damascus Document*, and the *Hodayot* (1QHᵃ; *see* THANKSGIVING PSALMS). However, the publication of the integrality of the Dead Sea Scrolls has shown that the belief in bodily resurrection was also represented at Qumran, not only in the "classical" Enochic and Danielic texts but also in other documents of probably nonsectarian origin, such as the *Pseudo-Ezekiel* (4Q385–88; 391) and the so-called *Messianic Apocalypse* (4Q521). This contradiction is only apparent because resurrection and eternal life are but two sides of the same coin for an apocalyptic group such as the Community of the Renewed Covenant at Qumran. The SONGS OF THE SABBATH SACRIFICE (4Q400–407; 11Q17) and other mystical texts clearly demonstrate that the members of the congregation felt that they were already living in communion with the angels of heaven. Yet, the limits of any realized eschatology become apparent when the first-generation believers begin to die. At that point, the time and modalities of the end need to be renegotiated and other means of reward for the departed members of the community have to be envisioned. The inhabitants of Qumran were so concerned by the fate of the physical remains of their dead that they allocated to their burials a large part of the plateau on which the settlement was built. It was no wonder that they came to imagine that the deceased Sons of Light would be brought back to life in order to share with the living (possibly) the duties of the war against the Kittim and (more probably) the rights of the eschatological blessings.

3. Psalms of Solomon and Parables of Enoch

In Second Temple Judaism, as in other historical contexts of colonization and oppression, eschatological discourses and apocalyptic writings primarily functioned as forms of political resistance. This is especially true for the *Psalms of Solomon* (*see* SOLOMON, PSALMS OF) and the Book of Parables (*1 En.* 37–71), two PSEUDEPIGRAPHA written in the years that followed Pompey's conquest of Jerusalem, in 63 BCE, in reaction to the turmoil provoked by the fall of the HASMONEANS and the ascension to power of the Idumean Herod, king of Judea from 37 to 4 BCE (*see* HEROD, FAMILY). The *Psalms of Solomon* expresses the concerns of the members of the "congregations of the devout" for what they perceived as a severe corruption of the traditional values of Judean society. The only solution to that crisis was deemed to be a divine intervention that would put an end to the Hasmonean and Herodian usurpations. The only legitimate rulers can be Davidic, and a Messiah "son of David" is expected to purify Jerusalem from all the foreigners and their Jewish collaborators. Then, "he will shepherd the flock of the Lord faithfully and righteously" (17:40), in conformity with the prophecy of Isa 11.

In the Book of Parables, the patriarch Enoch is supposed to report about a new series of eschatological visions that he saw in the course of his otherworldly journey. At the beginning of the second parable, a mysterious creature that God calls "my Chosen" is explicitly identified with the Son of Man of Dan 7. This preexisting Messiah will sit on a throne of glory to execute the last judgment over the sinners, esp. "the kings, the mighty, and all who possess the earth" that are depicted as the worst enemies of the righteous (chaps. 46, 48, and 62–63). In the end, the latter will be saved and, having received a new covenant, they will inherit the earth and accede to everlasting life. Thus, the Book of Parables can be interpreted as an invitation to the faithful to take courage and not abandon hope in spite of the difficult times they are experiencing. The text ends by describing the apotheosis of Enoch, who is identified with the heavenly SON OF MAN (chap. 71). This is the supreme reward that the Book of Parables promises to any practitioner who would engage in the patriarch's mystical path.

4. Post-70 CE eschatological works

During the last century of the Second Temple period, the hope for alternative social and religious structures progressively turned into a radical negation of existing institutions. Ultimately, The Romans destroyed the Holy City and its Temple in 70 CE (*see* TEMPLE, JERUSALEM). Jewish theologians adjusted their eschatological worldviews in order to reduce the terrible cognitive dissonance provoked by the catastrophe. Some interpreted the second destruction as a repetition of the first one, which had occurred at the hands of the Babylonians in 587 BCE. Jeremiah's prophecy about the length of the exile was read in a more literal way as announcing a restoration after (only) seventy years of punishment. This is the message of hope delivered by the *Coptic Jeremiah Apocryphon*, a narrative midrash that retells the story of the prophet JEREMIAH from the destruction of Jerusalem and the deportation of its inhabitants to their triumphal return at the end of the exile (*see* JEREMIAH, APOCRYPHON OF). Of particular interest is the presence of EZRA among the Judeans exiled in Babylon: after two miracles that reveal his extraordinary charisma to his schoolteacher, God accepts Ezra's sacrifice for the renewal of the covenant, thus bringing the captivity to an end (chaps. 32 and 34). If the "prophet" Ezra was considered as a younger contemporary of Jeremiah, then it is not so surprising to find him in the role of the protagonist of *4 Ezra*, an apocalyptic text purportedly written thirty years after the destruction of the First Temple.

Fourth Ezra and its literary twin *2 Baruch* (ascribed to the scribe BARUCH, Jeremiah's closest collaborator) are the two most representative apocalyptic responses to the fall of the Second Temple, written at the end of the 1st cent. CE. In both writings, the seers complain about the desolation of ZION and the apparent absence of divine justice. The angels reply that all the promises of God will be fulfilled, not in this age but after the coming of the Davidic Messiah. The meaning of the vision described in Dan 7 is reinterpreted and actualized: the ROMAN EMPIRE is going to be destroyed by the Messiah, who will wage war against the nations and will gather the surviving faithful and the lost ten tribes of Israel in the heavenly Jerusalem. According to *4 Ezra*, his glorious reign will last four hundred years and will be followed, after his death, by the general resurrection and the last judgment (chap. 7). While waiting for the Messiah, both *4 Ezra* and *2 Baruch* exhort the righteous to obey the Torah, because this is the only way to be saved. These apocalypses and other related writings probably played a role in sparking Bar Kochba's insurrection, and, in the long term, they made a significant contribution to the development of Jewish and Christian eschatological beliefs. *See* DAY OF THE LORD; RESURRECTION, NT; RESURRECTION, OT; RIGHTEOUSNESS IN EARLY JEWISH LITERATURE.

Bibliography: Alan J. Avery-Peck and Jacob Neusner, eds. *Judaism in Late Antiquity. Part Four: Death, Life-After-Death, Resurrection and the World-to-Come in the Judaisms of Antiquity* (2000); Richard Bauckham. *The Fate of the Dead: Studies on the Jewish and Christian Apocalypses* (1998); Jan N. Bremmer, *The Rise and Fall of the Afterlife* (2002); James H. Charlesworth, ed. *The Messiah: Developments in Earliest Judaism and Christianity* (1992); James H. Charlesworth. Hermann Lichtenberger, and Gerbern S. Oegema, eds. *Qumran-Messianism: Studies on the Messianic Expectations in the Dead Sea Scrolls* (1998); John J. Collins. *The Scepter and the Star: The Messiahs of the Dead Sea Scrolls and Other Ancient Literature* (1995); John J. Collins. *Apocalypticism in the Dead Sea Scrolls* (1997); John J. Collins. *The Apocalyptic Imagination: An Introduction to Jewish Apocalyptic Literature.* 2nd ed. (1998); Casey D. Elledge. *Life After Death in Early Judaism: The Evidence of Josephus* (2006); Martha Himmelfarb. *Tours of Hell: An Apocalyptic Form in Jewish and Christian Literature* (1983); George W. E. Nickelsburg. *Resurrection, Immortality, and Eternal Life in Intertestamental Judaism and Early Christianity.* 2nd ed. (2007); Gerbern S. Oegema. *The Anointed and His People: Messianic Expectations from the Maccabees to Bar Kochba* (1998).

PIERLUIGI PIOVANELLI

ESCHATOLOGY OF THE NT es´kuh-tol´uh-jee. *Eschatology* (from eschatos ἔσχατος, "last") is traditionally that area of theology concerned with the last things—the Second Coming, the resurrection of the dead, the final judgment, and attendant and subsequent events. In the NT, however, many of the eschatological expectations of Judaism are understood as fulfilled in the life, death, and resurrection of Jesus as well as in the experience of the church, so that eschatology becomes past, present, and future.

A. Realized Eschatology
  1. The phenomenon
  2. Explanations
B. Present Suffering and Future Expectations
  1. Tribulation
  2. *Parousia*
  3. Resurrection
  4. Judgment
  5. The final state
C. Contingent Eschatology
D. Personal Eschatology and the Intermediate State
Bibliography

A. Realized Eschatology
1. The phenomenon

While one must be cautious in making broad generalizations, it is fair to claim that a number of NT books look into the future and foresee a series of preternatural occurrences: there will be signs in the heavens and supernatural portents on earth; the Messiah will return; the dead (or the righteous dead) will be raised; people will be judged; Satan, sin, and death will be defeated; there will be a renewed world or new creation. Most of these expectations appear in Paul, and the Gospels and Revelation attest to all of them.

These expectations did not originate with Christianity but were inherited from pre-Christian Judaism. Although again one must be careful of generalizations, because there was a diversity of eschatological beliefs, it is easy enough to find Jewish texts that expect signs and wonders, eschatological redeemers, resurrection, judgment, the defeat of evil, and a utopian realization of God's will.

The NT, taken as a whole, judges these and related expectations as having been partly fulfilled in the history of Jesus as well as in Christian religious experience and yet, at the same time, deems them to be outstanding events. The tension cannot be explained away by claiming that some books have a "realized eschatology" (C. H. Dodd's term) whereas others do not, for both perspectives on eschatology often appear in the same author.

Concerning "realized eschatology," every NT writer who uses the word **Christos** (Χριστός) of Jesus of Nazareth implicitly asserts that a messianic redeemer has already entered the world. Similarly, affirmation of Jesus' post-mortem vindication conveys that at least one dead individual has been raised. Matthew 27:51-53, in which dead saints exit their tombs and enter Jerusalem, even has it that more than one person has been raised. Related is 1 Cor 15:20, which calls Christ "the first fruits of those who have died" (compare 15:23). This metaphor not only unites Jesus' resurrection with the resurrection of others but presumably implies that, with his resurrection, the general resurrection has begun. Second Timothy 2:17-18 refers to some who went a step further, claiming that the resurrection was past.

Whatever precisely they believed, other Christians thought of the resurrection of the spiritually dead as already raised to new life (John 5:25; Eph 2:1).

In addition to proclaiming that the Messiah has come and the resurrection has commenced, the NT contains texts which speak as though God has already judged the world. In John 12:31, the sentences of life and death have already been passed and, in 5:24, those who hear and believe already possess eternal life and so will not come under judgment. Other passages, moreover, have it that Satan and sin have already suffered defeat (e.g., Mark 3:23-27; Luke 10:18; John 12:32; Rom 8:1-4). 2 Cor 5:17:15 can even speak of the old things passing away and of a "new creation" in Christ (so too Gal 6:15). In short, as Matt 12:28 par. Luke 11:20 has it, the kingdom of God has somehow come (compare Luke 17:20-21).

The influence of realized eschatology on the NT is so pervasive that it even structures certain narratives. Mark 13 is a prophecy about the visible coming of the Son of Man on the clouds of heaven and the events leading up to that climax. Yet many of its prophecies and admonitions have parallels in the passion narrative, which Mark 13 introduces. Mark 13:24 prophesies that the sun will be darkened, and in Mark 15:33 the sun goes dark when Jesus is crucified. Mark 13:2 foresees that the Temple in Jerusalem will be destroyed, and in Mark 15:38 the Temple is symbolically destroyed when its veil is torn. Mark 13:35-36 warns hearers to "keep awake" lest the master find you asleep when he comes, and in Mark 14:34, 38 Jesus tells his disciples to "keep awake" and then he comes and finds them asleep. Mark 13:9 foretells that his disciples will be "hand[ed] over" and will appear before Jewish councils, and in Mark 14:10, 21, 41, 53-65 Jesus himself is "handed over" (author's trans.; NRSV: "betrayed.") and appears before a council of Jewish elders. In Mark 13:9 Jesus tells his disciples that they will be beaten and will stand before governors and kings, and in Mark 14:65 he himself is beaten while in Mark 15:1-15 he appears before Pilate the governor.

Such parallelism implies that the crucifixion and the events leading up to it are akin to the end of the world in miniature. The passion anticipates the end of the age or inaugurates the end. Jesus himself experiences tribulation and is then vindicated, so that his history is the history of the last things.

2. Explanations

The habit of interpreting Jesus' appearance as an eschatological event could be partly explained by reference to Jewish texts that apply eschatological language to past events in order to magnify their significance. Wisdom 19:6 hyperbolically affirms that, at the exodus from Egypt, "the whole creation in its nature was fashioned anew," and *L.A.B.* 11:5 declares that, when God gave the Law to Moses, mountains caught on fire, and

the earth was shaken, and the depths boiled, and the sky was folded up, and rain went up instead of down.

One problem with understanding early Christian texts that wrap past events in eschatological language as simply another instance of Jewish rhetoric is that many early Christians expected the consummation to be near (see below). Given this belief, they necessarily saw OT prophecy as looking forward to one grand event, not two. For them, everything was eschatological, that is, everything had to do with the end. They did not think of some messianic prophecies as clustered around the middle of history, others around the end of time. They instead saw a time line that had ended in their own era. This is why the NT regularly describes Jesus' ministry in eschatological terms. Messianic prophecies were eschatological prophecies, and messianic fulfillment eschatological fulfillment.

In searching for the origin of realized eschatology, one can observe that Jesus himself may well have spoken of God's kingdom as already entering the present (Matt 12:28//Luke 11:20), and further that cultic worship created and maintained experience that was conceived as proleptic participation in the golden age (see Aune). But one is still left wanting to know why the passion in particular drew to itself eschatological language. One good explanation is that Jesus himself anticipated suffering and even death in the eschatological crisis and looked beyond that to the resurrection of the dead, and that some of his followers were then able to correlate his expectations with his passion and vindication. This meant, for them, that the expectations of Jesus had, at least in part, come to fulfillment.

B. Present Suffering and Future Expectations

Despite its partially realized eschatology, the NT also features an unrealized eschatology. The reason is that believers in Jesus did not, after his departure, find themselves living in the world of their hopes and dreams, which is precisely what the world of eschatological promise is supposed to be. God's will was not being done everywhere on earth as in heaven; the last had not become first. Much of eschatology remained promise, not reality.

1. Tribulation

Jewish eschatology has always envisaged eschatological salvation as coming to birth amid terrible tribulations: the worst of times will precede the best of times. The rabbis spoke of the "birth pains of the Messiah," and several Jewish apocalypses outline the trials and tribulations of the latter days (see Pitre). Already Dan 12:1 prophesies "a time of anguish, such as has never occurred since nations first came into existence."

This belief belongs also to the NT, whose eschatological logic is this: if the kingdom is at hand, then the tribulation that introduces it must have begun already or be near to hand. Jesus himself foresaw not just the golden age but its prelude, the final cataclysm. Just as he thought of the kingdom as already manifesting itself, so too did he think of the painful eschatological necessity as having arrived or shortly to be inaugurated (Matt 6:13//Luke 11:4; Matt 10:34-36//Luke 12:51-53; Matt 11:12-13//Luke 16:16; Mark 9:49; Luke 12:49-50).

Parts of the NT follow suit. In addition to offering a proleptic realization or inauguration of utopia, they also offer a proleptic realization or inauguration of the time of eschatological woe. They do not just construe the present as though the kingdom has come; they also construe the present as though the great tribulation has begun. Mark's audience would have read itself into Mark 13:5-13, which foresees the "beginning of the birth pangs." First Corinthians 7:26 makes "the present crisis" as a motivation for the unmarried to stay unmarried. Colossians 1:24 says that what is lacking in "Christ's afflictions" is even now being filled up (compare 1 Pet 4:12-19 and see Dubis). Revelation 7:14 characterizes Christian martyrs as those who have come out of "the great ordeal," that is, the messianic tribulation (compare 3:10).

2. Parousia

The word parousia (παρουσία), which literally means "presence" (2 Cor 10:10), designated both the official arrival of a high-ranking person, especially king or emperor, as well as the manifestation of a hidden deity. The word came into Judaism with reference to the entries of God in history (as in Josephus, *Ant.* 3.80, 203; 9.55) and may, in pre-Christian times, have already been used of God's eschatological coming (*T. Jud.* 22:2; *Jer* 10; *2 En.* 32:1). In the NT, the word is applied to Jesus' eschatological coming: Matt 24:1; 1 Cor 15:23; 1 Thess 2:19; 5:23; 2 Thess 2:1, 8, 9; Jas 5:7-8; 2 Pet 1:16; 1 John 2:28.

Three characteristics mark the Parousia in the NT. First, the focus is not on God's appearance but on Jesus' return: the risen Lord who has left and gone to heaven will come again (comapre Acts 1:11). Second, the Parousia is near: Acts 3:19-21; Rom 13:11; 1 Cor 16:22; 1 Thess 5:1-11; Heb 10:37; Jas 5:8; 1 Pet 4:17; 1 John 2:8; Rev 22:20. The sense of near expectation goes back to the proclamation of John the Baptist (Matt 3:7-12//Luke 3:7-17) as well as to Jesus' own sense of God's impending apocalyptic vindication of his cause. Third, the relevant NT texts have been greatly influenced by OT prophetic oracles that portray the coming judgment and salvation of God. Daniel 7:13-14, with its depiction of the last judgment and the coming of one like a son of man, is the most influential (Mark 13:26; 14:62; Rev 1:7); but other texts also played an important role in imagining the Parousia. For instance, part of LXX Isa 2:10, 19, 21 has been taken up into 2 Thess 1:9 while Isa 66:15 is close to 2 Thess 1:8; and Zech 14:5 has influenced Matt 25:31 (compare 1 Thess

3:13). Further, the oracle in Isaiah 26–27 contains the chief elements of the Parousia in the NT: God's coming (26:21), judgment (26:21), resurrection (26:19), the gathering of the saints (27:13), and a trumpet (27:13).

The imminence of the Parousia has created problems for Christian interpreters. Some have accordingly referred many of the relevant prophecies, especially those in the gospels, to the resurrection of Jesus, Pentecost, or the destruction of Jerusalem in 70 CE (e.g., Wright). Such readings reckon with a large measure of metaphor. Mark 13:26, on this view, is not about employing clouds as a novel means of transport. The language rather confers theological meaning on a forthcoming historical event.

One problem for such less-than-literal readings of NT language about the Parousia is the similarity between Mark 13:24-27 and the closely related tradition in 1 Thess 4:13-18. Paul writes about the coming of the Lord Jesus who will meet the saints in the clouds. The synoptic Jesus similarly speaks of the Son of Man coming on clouds and of the elect being gathered to him. The point is that 1 Thess 4:13-18 lends itself to being understood neither as metaphor nor as a prophecy about 70 CE. One has great difficulty imagining that Paul was not referring to literal clouds in the atmosphere—he speaks of people being "in the air"—or that his first readers might have given his words a figurative sense. So an appeal to metaphor when pursuing the meaning of the closely related Mark 13:24-27 seems equally out of place (compare Acts 1:11: Jesus "will come in the same way as you saw him go into heaven").

3. Resurrection

Belief in the resurrection of the body is attested in pre-Christian Judaism (Dan 12:2; 4Q521; *1 En.* 62:15; Josephus, *J.W.* 3.362; *4 Ezra* 7:31-44). The belief arose, probably under Zoroastrian influence, because of the conviction that disembodied life must mean a miserable, shadowy existence in Sheol, and that a physical body will be needed for full participation in a redeemed world. In the NT, the belief is prominent, appearing in the synoptics (Mark 12:18-27 par.), John (5:28-29), Acts (23:6), Paul (1 Corinthians 15), Hebrews (6:2), and Revelation (20:4-5). Jesus himself shared the expectation (Matt 10:28; Mark 12:18-27; Matt 12:41-42//Luke 11:31-32), which became central with the early proclamation of his rising from the dead.

Several NT texts reflect a very literal understanding of resurrection. The story of Jesus' empty tomb implies strict physical continuity between Jesus of Nazareth and the risen Jesus. Similarly, Matt 27:51-53 recounts the story of dead saints exiting their tombs and walking around in Jerusalem while John 5:28-29 moves the mind's eye to picture graves, skeletons, and decaying flesh.

Other texts, however, may suggest something less obvious. Mark 12:18-27 prophesies that the resurrected saints will be "like angels in heaven," and Matt

13:43 has them shining like the sun (compare *2 Bar.* 50:2). Both texts imply more than a resumption of mundane existence. So too Paul's difficult notion of a "spiritual body" (1 Cor 15:35-57), which posits significant discontinuity between pre- and post-resurrection states. Origen's interpretation of this in *Cels.* 7.32, which minimizes physical continuity and envisages a new body, is not without justification.

The gospels are also relevant here, for in them the body of the risen Jesus possesses properties not associated with physicality. Although he can be touched (Luke 24:39; John 20:20, 27) and although he eats (Luke 24:41-43), yet he also appears suddenly out of nowhere, and he disappears into thin air just as abruptly (Luke 24:31, 36, 51; John 20:19, 26; Acts 1:9). In Matt 28:1-10, he seems to be gone before the angel rolls away the stone, which implies that his resurrected body has passed through the solid rock. There is also the odd circumstance that the post-Easter Jesus is sometimes not recognized (Matt 28.16-20; Luke 24:13-27; John 20:14), as well as the facts that the appearances in the gospels are intermittent, not continuous, and that, in Acts 9:7, Paul sees something others do not. Mark 16:12, which says that Jesus "appeared in another form," seems to express what is assumed elsewhere: his resurrection body was transformed into a new state of being.

In many ways, the NT's expectation of the resurrection of the body functions like belief in a blessed existence immediately after death: both bring life with God. There are, however, at least two ways in which resurrection and life immediately after death are not functionally equivalent. First, the general resurrection of the just and unjust (Luke 11:31-32; John 5:28-29; Acts 24:15; Rev 20:11-15) is a collective affair: everyone rises at once, at the end. This means that no one is fully redeemed until everyone is redeemed, and that the story of the individual is not complete until the larger human story is complete. Second, resurrection language has a christological dimension, because it gives believers the same fate as Jesus. He is the "firstborn" (Rom 8:29) or the "first fruits" (1 Cor 15:20), so that his resurrected existence is the prototype of Christian eschatological existence.

4. Judgment

The NT's texts about judgment serve several functions. The prospect of reward and punishment—whether immediately after death (Luke 16:19-31; Heb 9:27) or at the end (Rev 20:11-15)—aims to motivate the righteous to obedience. It also functions to comfort the godly in their suffering and to summon the wayward to repentance. Beyond these practical and motivational ends, the expectation of judgment serves certain theological purposes. It is a way of justifying God, of declaring that the judge will not be in recess forever, that the good, that is, God, will win in the end.

The NT offers a variety of different images of the future judgment. No coherent picture emerges because the texts are designed to foster right behavior, not to offer a cartography of future states. Matthew 25:32-33 uses the image of a shepherd dividing sheep from goats. In 1 Cor 3:10-15, eschatological fire alternately purifies and destroys human works. Matthew 7:13-14 depicts people going through two different gates to two different fates whereas 25:1-13 portrays people being included in or excluded from a wedding celebration. Second Corinthians 5:10 envisages a courtroom with a king serving as judge, an image recurring in Matt 25:31 and elsewhere. Sometimes God is on the throne (Rom 14:10), other times Jesus (Matt 25:31; 2 Cor 5:10). But in Luke 12:8-9, Jesus is not on the judgment seat but rather takes the role of advocate or adversary, confessing and denying others before the angels in heaven. In this scenario, angels are the judges on the last day (*1 En.* 1:9; 11Q13 II 9, 14; *T. Levi* 3:2-3; Matt 13:41-2, 49; Rev 14:15-19).

Commentators since Origen have fretted over the presence in Paul's letters of justification by faith and judgment by works. Some have espied here a contradiction, others a paradox. Still others have tried to eliminate or reduce the inconsistency. The truth is, however, that, when the apostle refers to the eschatological judgment, he speaks in two different ways, according to his rhetorical needs. Grace gets emphasized in one circumstance (esp. in Rom 1–8 and Galatians), judgment and human responsibility in another (Rom 14:10-12; 1 Cor 3:5-17; 2 Cor 5:10).

The tension is not unique to Paul. Matthew 7:24-27 and 25:31-46 (where Christian affiliation seems irrelevant) assume that judgment will be according to works (compare 5:18-20). But in the parable in Matt 20:1-16, all the workers in the vineyard receive equal pay for unequal work. Here there is a strong doctrine of grace. Again, rhetorical need drives the Matthean texts, not curiosity about the literal future.

Most of the NT tends to be dualistic; that is, it foresees two disparate eschatological fates. The saints will be in paradise (Luke 23:43) or in Abraham's bosom (Luke 16:22) or will inherit life (Matt 7:14; Mark 9:43, 45) or be "with Christ" (Phil 1:23). The unrighteous will instead go to Gehenna (Matt 10:28; Mark 9:43, 45, 47) or be destroyed (Matt 7:13; 2 Thess 1:9) or perish (1 Cor 1:18). In 1 Cor 15:22, however, Paul says that, just as all die in Adam, so in Christ will all be made alive. Romans 5:18 similarly declares that, just as Adam's trespass led to the condemnation of all, so Jesus' "act of righteousness leads to justification and life for all" (compare Rom 11:25-36). Most exegetes, seeking to harmonize these texts with others that envision limited salvation (1 Thess 1:10; 4:13-18), have maintained that Rom 5:12-21 and 1 Cor 15:22 cannot mean what they appear to mean. But it is plausible that, as with what he has to say about justification by faith and judgment by works, Paul is not consistent and, according to his rhetorical needs, maintains now one view, now another, even if they are contradictory.

5. The final state

Revelation 20–21 draws a distinction between a millennial kingdom and the subsequent final state (*1 En.* 93.3-10; 93:11-17; *4 Ezra* 7:26-44; 12:31-34; *2 Bar.* 29:3-30:1; 40:1-4; 72:2-74:3). This scheme is not obviously adopted anywhere else in the NT, although some have found it in 1 Cor 15:23-28.

By and large the NT reflects little interest in what the kingdom will be like. The focus is instead on the fact of its coming and on the transition between the evil present and the eschatological world, that is, on Parousia, judgment, resurrection. What matters is that death and evil will be no more and that God will be all in all (1 Cor 15:28). Beyond that, the general impression is that the kingdom will be realized not in some other world but on this earth made new—a revised, second edition with the earlier deficiencies corrected. Second Peter 3:10-13, however, foretells the destruction of the world by fire, and Rev 21:1 prophesies the passing away of heaven and earth and their replacement by a new heaven and new earth (compare Isa 65:17; 66:22; *1 En.* 91:16; *L.A.B.* 3:10).

C. Contingent Eschatology

The numbers in Dan 9:24-27 and 12:7-12 imply that there is an eschatological calendar and that God has set a date for the end. Several extracanonical apocalypses leave the same impression. Biblical prophecies, however, often present themselves as contingent, or conditional upon this or that human response (Jer 12:14-17; 18:5-11). This explains Jonah's prophecy that Nineveh will be destroyed in forty days, which fails to come to pass because the people of Nineveh turn from their evil ways, after which God repents of harming them (3:10; compare Judg 2:1-3; 2 Kgs 20:1-6; 1 Sam 2:27-36).

The idea of contingency was eventually applied to eschatological expectation. Some rabbinic passages have it that the Son of David will not come until Israel changes for the better (e.g., *b. Sanh.* 97b, 98a; *b. Sabb.* 118b; *b. B. Bat.* 10a; *b. Yoma* 86a). Earlier pseudepigraphical texts make repentance usher in the consummation (*T. Dan* 6:4; *T. Sim.* 6:2-7; *T. Zeb.* 9:7-9; *As. Mos.* 1:18; *2 Bar.* 78:7) or assume that the time before the end, although predetermined, can be cut short (e.g., 4Q385 frag. 3; *Pss. Sol.* 17:45; *L.A.B.* 19:13; *2 Bar.* 20:1-2). But when the end is conceived primarily in terms of judgment instead of salvation, hope for its delay, occasioned by repentance, may arise (*Sib. Or.* 4:162-7; 5:357-60; *Gk. Apoc. Ezra* 3:6). Tertullian assumes this when he prays for "the delay of the final consummation" (*Apol.* 39; compare Exod 15:5-6, where God gives "an extension of time" to wicked people).

The NT also knows of the contingency of eschatological expectation. In Acts 3:19-21, Peter invites his audience to repent and turn again so that God will send the Messiah. Second Peter 3:11-12 speaks of holy lives "hastening" the coming of the day of God. In Luke 18:1-8, the widow's persistence in gaining a hearing means that God will vindicate the elect who cry out day and night and will not delay long over them. In this way God's eschatological act is an answer to the saints' cry that justice be done. Perhaps the same thought lies to hand in the Lord's Prayer (Matt 6:9-13//Luke 11:2-4). "Your kingdom come" may presuppose that the coming of God's kingdom is, like bread, forgiveness, and deliverance from evil, a proper object of petition, so that to utter the words is to hope that God will hear and hasten salvation? However that may be, Mark 13:10 makes the completion of the eschatological prophecies wait upon the completion of the Christian mission, and Mark 13:20 speaks of God abbreviating the days of eschatological terror.

If several NT texts assume that God's mercy can hasten the speed with which the kingdom comes, Luke 13:6-9 on the contrary assumes that God's mercy may delay the end. In this parable, a man is about to cut down his unfruitful fig tree, but his gardener begs him to leave it alone another year, because maybe it will yet produce fruit. Here the patience and mercy of God are reflected in the action of the gardener, who gains another year for the tree, which is a transparent symbol for Jesus' hearers or Israel. God, in mercy, has not rendered immediate judgment but rather a period of respite.

That God has delayed or will delay the end is in tension with the notion that God will hasten it. But the two disparate hopes share two presuppositions. First, both imply that there is no fixed date for the end, or that if there is a fixed date, it can be changed. Second, both assume that whatever God does is the consequence of mercy.

D. Personal Eschatology and the Intermediate State

By the first century, belief in a soul or spirit that can survive bodily death had become widespread within Judaism, as had the conviction that the soul or spirit of a righteous individual goes to a desired place; see *1 En.* 22:1-14; 60:8; *Jub.* 23:31; Tob 3:6; 4 Macc 14:6; Bar 2:17; *L.A.E.* 13:6; 31:4; 32:4; Wis 15:8; Josephus, *J.W.* 2.154; 3.362; *2 Bar.* 30:25. Such hope, moreover, often existed beside expectation of bodily resurrection, despite the tradition of speaking of the dead as asleep (John 11:11; Acts 7:60; 1 Cor 15:51; 1 Thess 4:14; the idiom really says nothing about the state of the dead).

It is, then, no surprise that the NT often sounds dualistic in its anthropology. Examples include Matt 10:28 (opponents can kill the body but not the soul); 14:26 (the disciples think they might be seeing Jesus' "ghost"; compare Luke 24:37, 39; Acts 12:15); 2 Cor

12:1-4 (Paul while yet alive could visit the third heaven, and he can conceive of this as an ascent "out of the body"); 1 Pet 3:18-22 (Jesus "in the spirit" preached to the spirits in prison); 2 Pet 1:13 (Peter is for now "in his body"); and Jas 2:26 (the body apart from the spirit is dead).

Given this anthropology and Jewish precedent, it is understandable that early Christians, when not hoping for the Parousia to take place within their lifetimes, often assumed that the righteous dead are in a better place. This is the assumption of Luke 16:19-31, the parable of the rich man and Lazarus. Although one cannot comb this morality tale for details about the afterlife, the story does take for granted both an afterlife and postmortem reward and punishment. Also from Luke is the account of the good thief on a cross (23:43). To his request to be remembered, Jesus says, "Today you will be with me in Paradise." Acts 7:59 ("Lord Jesus, receive my spirit") and 2 Cor 5:6-9 (Paul speaks about being away from the body and at home with his Lord) probably have something similar in mind. So too Phil 1:21-24, where Paul says that death will put him in a better state because then he will be with Christ, and Rev 6:9-11, which depicts martyrs under the heavenly altar who are aware of what is happening on earth. The notion, found in Ephrem the Syrian, that the dead sleep, or that they dream in Sheol, a place where the righteous and unrighteous are not clearly distinguished, goes against several NT texts.

Once one comes to believe in a conscious interim state, and even if one simultaneously believes in a final judgment at the resurrection, there must be some sort of judgment at death, so that one goes to the right place. This seems implicit in all of the texts just cited, which thus move the idea of a corporate judgment at the end to the individual's fate immediately after death. In this the NT anticipates subsequent patristic interpreters, who so often apply to individuals and their deaths biblical texts and expectations that were once about collective eschatology.

Bibliography: Dale C. Allison, Jr. *The End of the Ages Has Come: An Early Interpretation of the Passion and Resurrection of Jesus* (1987); Dale C. Allison Jr. *Jesus of Nazareth: Millenarian Prophet* (1998); David E. Aune. *The Cultic Setting of Realized Eschatology in Early Christianity* (1972); Vicky Balabanski. *Eschatology in the Making: Mark, Matthew and the Didache* (1997); Richard Bauckham. *The Fate of the Dead: Studies on Jewish and Christian Apocalypses* (1998); John T. Carroll, Alexandra R. Brown, Claudia J. Setzer, and Jeffrey S. Siker. *The Return of Jesus in Early Christianity* (2000); Martin C. de Boer. *The Defeat of Death: Apocalyptic Eschatology in 1 Corinthians 15 and Romans 5.* (1988); C. H. Dodd. *The Parables of the Kingdom* (1963); Mark Dubis. *Messianic Woes in First Peter: Suffering and Eschatology in 1 Peter 4:12-19* (2002); T. F. Glasson. *The Second Advent: The Origin of a New Testament Doctrine* (1963); R. Barry Matlock. *Unveiling the Apocalyptic Paul: Paul's Interpreters and the Rhetoric of Criticism* (1996); C. Marvin Pate, and Douglas W. Kennard. *Deliverance Now and Not Yet: The New Testament and the Great Tribulation* (2003); Brant Pitre. *Jesus, Tribulation, and the End of Exile: Restoration Eschatology and the Origin of Atonement* (2006); Alan F. Segal. *Life after Death: A History of the Afterlife in Western Religion* (2003); H. M. Shires. *The Eschatology of Paul in the Light of Modern Scholarship* (1966); N. T. Wright. *Jesus and the Victory of God* (1996).

DALE C. ALLISON, JR.

ESCHATOLOGY OF THE OT es´kuh-tol´uh-jee [ἔσχατος eschatos]. *Eschatology,* from the Greek term for "last" or "final," is a modern scholarly term covering perspectives on final, culminating events or "last things" found within the Scriptures. Broadly understood, this term may encompass any biblical or cognate expectation that present experience, in all its complexity, will find a definitive resolution or culmination in God's time. In many biblical texts, such a denouement ushers in a revolutionary new reality, where God has seized the initiative and redefined the parameters of existence. Eschatology provides the faithful with a sense of an ending to current experience and a firm confidence in the ultimate fruition of God's work. It offers assurance that that God's activity on behalf of God's people, humanity, and creation has a definite direction and goal (telos). God's purposes for God's people and their world are both good and definitive, and God will bring them to consummation.

A. Definition and Scope
B. The Day of Yahweh; The Latter Days
C. Inclusive ("Universal") Salvation
   1. God's commitment to all earth's nations
   2. The roots of Israel's inclusive eschatology
D. Apocalyptic Eschatology
E. The Social Location of Israelite Eschatology
F. The Exile and the Blossoming of Eschatology
G. Resistance to Eschatology
H. God's Prerogative and Its Relation to History
I. Personal Eschatology
J. Resurrection
Bibliography

A. Definition and Scope

Some scholarship uses the term *eschatology* narrowly, with reference only to ideas of the world's ultimate destiny and a finishing point to history. An eschatological "sense of an ending," however, need not involve any such overtly cosmic and apocalyptic expectations or beliefs. Often, biblical eschatologies describe more or less circumscribed *eschatons* ("endings," "finales"), bringing relatively localized sequences of events to a head. Psalm 137:7, for example, refers to the destruction of Jerusalem in 586 BCE as an eschatological event, "the day of Jerusalem." Referring to the same occurrence, Obadiah reprimands Edom for gloating over "your brother's day" (v. 12). On this "day," Judah experienced the unloosing of God's presence and power and was never again the same.

The prophet Amos warned the Northern Kingdom of a coming "end" (qets קֵץ), by which he meant that their days were numbered, doomsday had come (Amos 8:2). Like ripe fruit, their time was ripe; there would be no more forgiveness from God. Ezekiel later applied the same term in a highly similar way, speaking in no uncertain terms of Judah's "end" (Ezek 7:6). For him, this end would spell dissolution of normal life, the joys and sorrows of which would be rendered moot by the approach of the day of the Lord (7:12). Israel's various prophets anticipate different sorts of definitive eschatological interventions of God, many of which, like that of Amos, are envisioned as lying within the scope of ongoing, proximate history. They neither stand outside of history nor bring it to a halt, but represent climactic break points or inaugural moments within it. Among many examples, one should mention God's definitive protection of Jerusalem amid Assyrian invasion (Isa 37:35-38; 38:6) and God's long-awaited retribution on Edom, which abetted Babylonia at Jerusalem's destruction (Jer 49:14-16; Obad 8-10). Not to be overlooked, as well, is God's triumphant guidance of the people home from foreign exile (Isa 45:13; 52:12; Mic 4:10).

Other biblical texts reveal a sweeping eschatology, highlighting God's concern with humanity as a whole and with the direction and goal of global history. Upon reflection, it appears obvious that eschatological expectations about such matters inevitably emerged within the Scriptures. Indeed, it is fair to say that such expectations are a necessary consequence of the biblical understanding of Yahweh, creation, and humanity. God's nature sets God at work on behalf of creation (Hab 3:2). If God were not about this work, how could the faithful speak of God's goodness?

In the biblical perspective, God is about the business of perfecting humanity and the cosmos as a whole. In this regard, it is far from surprising that the J and P strands of the Pentateuch begin with a primeval history detailing God's creation of the world and God's trenchant concern for all nations. The storyline of these strands emphasizes for all to see that Israel's particular relationship with God was never about this one people alone. Israel's history with God arose as part of God's universal work with all peoples, the biblical story insists, and it is all about God's universal plans for creation. This is apparent from many texts of varying provenance, including Gen 12:3 (J); 17:5, 23 (P); 22:18 (RJE); Exod 9:16 (E); 19:5-6 (E); Pss 47:9; 72:17. See CREATION; NATIONS; UNIVERSALISM.

Biblical eschatology does not always concern collective humanity. There is much "personal eschatology" within the Scriptures. Biblical faith prioritizes communal wellbeing but does not neglect the worth and responsibility of each individual. Thus, Scripture often warns the haughty of an inevitable end (telos) in Sheol, where strength fails and prayers go unanswered (Ps 101:5; Prov 6:17; 16:18; 18:12). Such warnings do not preclude a cosmic "last judgment" of evildoers, such as we find in Joel 3:1-2; Zech 14:2-3; and Dan 7:9-10, but neither do they concern themselves with this type of apocalyptic eventuality.

B. The Day of Yahweh; The Latter Days

Israel's life with Yahweh entailed a wait for God's arrival to set things right, an incursion of God's awesome presence known idiomatically as "the day of Yahweh" (yom YHWH יוֹם יהוה). God's people should practice disciplined readiness for "the day," the time of God's concrete advent (see DAY OF THE LORD). When it comes, earth will experience the destabilizing, transformative appearance of the Lord, who comes to defeat evil and establish justice. At that time, humanity will feel the full heat of the fiery, inscrutable divine presence. The experience will be nothing short of cataclysmic, leaving nothing unchanged (Zeph 1:14-18). From before the time of Amos—the first prophet that we know of to speak specifically of the day of Yahweh (Amos 5:18-20)—Israel oriented itself on God's epiphany "on that day" (bayyom hahu' הַהוּא בַּיּוֹם). The people trusted that it would be a day of rejoicing and salvation (see Isa 25:9). In speaking of the day of Yahweh, Amos must have been using a concept familiar to his audience, or he could hardly have called it something they desired (5:18).

Amos 5:18-20 attempts a dramatic reversal of popular conceptions about the day of Yahweh. The prophet affirms the people's belief in a coming eschatological judgment of God's enemies, but immediately shocks them with his proclamation that they, the chosen people, are among God's foes. Due to their flouting of God's standards of economic and social justice, the day of Yahweh means terror and disaster for them, not light and safety.

The expression "the day of Yahweh" and closely related phrases occur over two dozen times in the OT, not to mention the hundreds of occurrences of related terms, such as the idiom "on that day." Very likely, the concept of Yahweh's "day" developed within multiple Israelite settings. One source of influence must have been the people's folk traditions of Yahweh as the divine warrior. Past victories of God in "Yahweh war" surely encouraged an expectation of God's return to defeat present enemies. As in bygone days, the Cosmic Victor would meet them in battle, accompanied by the heavenly host (as in Judg 5:20).

In addition to the traditions of the wars of Yahweh, Israel's liturgy vibrantly preserved poetic and mythic images of God as "strong and mighty," "mighty in battle" (Ps 24:8). These warrior images—many co-opted from the myths of surrounding peoples—must also have strongly informed both prophetic and apocalyptic descriptions of the day of Yahweh. God already lays claim to the world and to cosmic victory in Scripture's liturgical images (e.g., Ps 24:1-2). Thus, it is difficult to agree with scholars who maintain that Israelite eschatology developed global and cosmic dimensions only after the exile. Israel's eschatological views certainly developed over time, but from long before the exile the divine warrior laid claim to cosmic victory over chaos and sole prerogative to rule earth's nations and peoples.

Certain biblical texts speak of God's promised future with Israel using the phrase "days to come/latter days" (ʾakharith hayyamim אַחֲרִית הַיָּמִים). The phrase does not generally refer to the end of time as such, but to the farthest reaches of the given speaker's perspective. In the era associated with this horizon, God's ultimate hopes for Israel on earth may find definite realization. According to texts in Deuteronomy, Micah, Hosea, and other books, the latter days will see the redemptive-historical process moving through the biblical story achieving substantive fulfillment. In contrast to apocalyptic thinking (see §E), this era will not necessarily arrive any time soon. In fact, the latter days are conceived of as "not now," "not near" (Num 24:17), but for generations yet unborn.

In the redemptive era, some texts project that God's people will return to the Lord with all their heart (Deut 4:29-30; Hos 3:5). Others prophesy that many nations of the world will orient themselves around Israel and its God (Mic 4:1-5; Isa 2:2-5). Still others speak of a muster of the forces of evil in the latter days (Ezek 38:16; Dan 10:14). God's decisive defeat of these forces will usher in salvation.

When panoramas concerning the latter days appear in Scripture, they are generally presented in ways that have immediate, practical relevance for their first audience. The vision of Zion's ultimate glory in Mic 4:1-5, for example, is presented neither as a curiosity nor an opiate. Rather, it provides a powerful impetus for Judah to follow the covenant in the here and now, despite the present foolishness of other nations (4:5).

Any vision of a coming utopia provides an implicit critique of the world's current imperfect state. Present reality reveals its ugly warts when compared to God's promised future. Biblical visions of the latter days have the intention of evoking the reader's concern with the world's blemishes and the reader's involvement in healing them.

C. Inclusive ("Universal") Salvation

The eschatology of the Scriptures is remarkable for its grand, world-encompassing scope. The prophets, especially, see themselves as charged with a global task. Isaiah, for example, addresses himself to "all you inhabitants of the world, you who live on the earth" (Isa 18:3). By the same token, Jeremiah wields the divine word "over nations and over kingdoms" (Jer 1:10). So too, the prophets "from ancient times" who came before him "prophesied war, famine, and pestilence against many countries and great kingdoms" (Jer 28:8).

Isaiah's and Jeremiah's perspectives are not idiosyncratic within the Scriptures. The scope of each of the major prophetic books is international in its proportions, and each has a section of detailed prophecies about foreign kingdoms and their faults. The Book of the Twelve also maintains a global purview. Each individual book of the Minor Prophets collection has its own unique theological perspective, but they all understand God's sovereignty to extend universally over all peoples, places, and times.

1. God's commitment to all earth's nations

At critical points, the Scriptures remind us that all nations are under God's control. Israel must not believe it is the only people in which God takes an active interest. As God puts it in Amos, "Did I not bring Israel up from the land of Egypt, and the Philistines from Caphtor and the Arameans from Kir?" (Amos 9:7). Even more striking, in Jonah God speaks of Assyria as God's own handiwork (Jonah 4:10). And in Isa 19:24-25, God speaks of Egypt and Assyria as destined to become blessings on earth alongside of Israel. Here again, foreign nations are pictured as God's own people. These texts are not isolated aberrances. For similar perspectives elsewhere in biblical literature, see Gen 16:10 (J); 20:11 (E); 21:18 (E); 1 Kgs 5:1; Ps 82:8; Isa 10:5; 16:3-4; Jer 27:3-6; Ezek 28:18. From early on, Yahweh makes clear that Yahweh is not confined by geography but reigns supreme (1 Kgs 20:28; Ps 76:12; Zeph 2:11). The deity who is enthroned on the ark's cherubim reigns over all nations (Pss 47:8; 80:1).

God's global sovereignty, in the end, will not be subject to humanity's veto. The will of God will be done on earth, as it is in heaven. Using metaphorical terms of expression, Scripture insists that the gods of the nations must die (Ps 82:6-8; Zeph 2:11). All claims on human community, especially those that degrade some members' full humanity, must collapse before God's ultimate prerogative. A death sentence, however, is not God's last word for those who do not recognize the Lord's rule. Beyond judgment, God's program for earth's peoples issues in blessing.

Biblical salvation is not indiscriminate, and no biblical texts offer solace to the obdurate. Yet, the eschatological vision of the Scriptures is often sweepingly inclusive. The divine offer of salvation is open—radically open. Especially in 2 Isaiah (see ISAIAH, BOOK OF), we see God's desire to extend God's promised shalom to any of the world's people who are willing to accept it (Isa 42:6; 44:5; 45:20, 22; 49:6; 55:5; 56:6-7; 66:18-21). Here, the Lord's eschatological plans manifestly entail international justice and world harmony (viz. universal salvation).

Few texts of the OT go as far as to explicitly welcome foreigners into Israel's sacrificial worship, and even its priesthood, as Isa 56:6-7 and 66:21 appear to do. Such eschatology must have radically tested the limits of Israel's self-conception as God's chosen people. The position was certainly controversial within Israel, and appears to have been contested (by Ezek 44:6-9, on the basis of Num 16:40; 18:4, 7).

A hierarchical and restrictive view of Israel's cult, however, need not imply a theology of hostility toward strangers. Even Ezekiel's relatively conservative eschatological program is stunningly generous in welcoming outsiders into Israel. It offers foreign sojourners the unprecedented provision of a permanent allotment of family land within Israel's borders (Ezek 47:22-23).

Second Isaiah's vision of inclusive salvation is more radical than Ezekiel's, but it is by no means unique within Scripture. In Zech 2:11, for example, God declares that at the eschaton, "Many nations shall join themselves to the LORD . . . and shall be my people; and I will dwell in your midst." A similar vision is found in multiple other texts, including 1 Kgs 8:41-43; Ruth 1:16; Pss 22:27; 67:2; 68:31-32; 102:22; Isa 18:7; 19:19-22; Jer 3:17; 4:2; 12:16; Zech 8:20-23; 14:16; and Mal 1:11.

2. The roots of Israel's inclusive eschatology

God's international salvific concern was not a late development within biblical history. Second Isaiah's inclusive vision of salvation has older roots, predating the Babylonian exile.

First, 2 Isaiah's eschatology betrays the strong influence of the psalms of the Jerusalem Temple, which had long attributed a magnetic, mesmeric quality to Zion. Zion, the city of the Great King, evokes the yearning of all nations according to the psalms. It irresistibly draws them in as pilgrims (see especially Pss 47:9; 65:2, 5; 72:11, 17; 86:9; 96:9-10). The magnificence of the God of Zion, other psalms proclaim, inspires the awe and praise of the entire world (Pss 66:4; 67:3, 5; 68:32; 98:4, 7; 99:3; 117:1; 138:4-5).

Given the nature of this expansive theology associated with Zion, it was inevitable that various psalms would come to describe Zion as a center of new life for all nations by their worship of the Lord. This flowering of a veritable universalism in the Psalter reached a zenith in the composition of Ps 87. Since Zion is God's city, Ps 87 depicts all peoples claiming it as their true spiritual home. Even Israel's classic enemies, Egypt and Babylonia, Philistia and Tyre, eventually turn there in yearning for God (87:4). God claims them as God's own people, giving them honorary birthright status in Zion (87:6). Accepting this new status, God's traditional enemies become Yahweh's people (compare Isa 44:5; 56:5).

Beyond the psalmists, Judean prophetic circles well before the writings of 2 Isaiah likewise embraced an expansive vision of Zion as a global center of salvation. Micah 4:1-4, especially, presents a positive eschatological picture of the world's nations orienting themselves around Zion. Isaiah 2:2-5 is a closely parallel text.

Like Mic 4, Zeph 3:9-10 speaks of the transformation of the world's peoples into worshipers of Yahweh. They will praise the true God with one accord and from beyond the rivers of Ethiopia bring offerings to Jerusalem. Fascinatingly, the special mention of Ethiopia here may reflect an African heritage of Zephaniah ben Cushi. (Zeph 1:1 suggests such an ancestry.)

Jeremiah 16:19-21 is yet another preexilic prophetic reference to God's planned salvation of the nations. The text looks beyond the coming judgment on Judah to contemplate the goal of history in the nations rallying around Yahweh. Converting to Yahweh, earth's peoples make the astounding confession that their traditional gods were never gods at all.

Finally, certain priestly themes and traditions within the Pentateuch also reemerge in expanded form in the texts of 2 Isaiah. According to the Priestly Torah, God chose Abraham as a vehicle for blessing the entire created order, purposing to use him to animate the world with divine power and witness (see especially Gen 1:28; 9:7; 17:2, 6). Repeating loaded keywords from the Priestly Torah, Isa 51:1-3 prophesies that Abraham's descendants shall finally find themselves "blessed" and "multiplied." God, in 2 Isaiah, promises to fulfill in God's people the world-transforming work that was begun in their great progenitor according to Genesis.

D. Apocalyptic Eschatology

Scholars continue to debate the meaning of the term *apocalyptic* and the extent of biblical material that may fall under the rubric. Many would agree, however, that apocalyptic perspectives differ from prophetic ones in at least three main ways. 1) An apocalyptic worldview leans toward metaphysical and moral dualism; 2) it expects God's promised utopia to be supernatural and transcendent in character; and 3) it is highly energized by the prospect of a radical, imminent eschaton. It is the latter eschatological dimension of apocalypticism that is of most interest here.

In the context of an apocalyptic symbolic universe, eschatology takes on great significance and urgency. The end times are not put off to a distant, abstract future. Rather, apocalyptic visionaries view the eschaton's arrival as imminent, about to come upon them unexpectedly with bewildering force.

The apocalyptic imagination understands that earthly history will neither prepare for God's in-breaking nor cause it to occur in any way. In the perspective of apocalyptic texts, historical processes are going nowhere, accomplishing nothing (e.g., Zech 1:11). To accomplish God's goals, heaven will have to break into the course of history from the beyond and bring its progress to a screeching halt (e.g., Zech 1:13-16; Dan 7:26-27; 2 Esd 11:44).

In apocalyptic eschatology, literal cosmic disturbances along with world wars and other terrible tribulations mark history's break point (e.g., Joel 2:10; 3:15; Zech 14:6; Isa 13:10; 34:4; Dan 8:10). Indeed, primordial chaos breaks loose in the end days, returning earth to its original dark and formless condition (Gen 1:2). Scholars commonly refer to this foundational apocalyptic scenario with a German phrase coined by Hermann Gunkel: *Endzeit wird Urzeit*, the end will be the beginning having come back again. God, the divine warrior, must conquer primal chaos—the great archenemy—once again (e.g., Joel 3:11, 13; Isa 63:1-6). This time it will be once and for all.

The divine warrior is also the Cosmic Victor. As in the original creation, God's defeat of chaos paves the way for beauty, harmony, and human community. The eschatological hope of apocalypticism centers on God's renewal of the cosmos, nature, and humanity, thus establishing perfect shalom and joy. The renewal is physical and material, not symbolic and ethereal. It ushers in a marvelous world beyond what humans have ever known (e.g., Zech 14:6-7; Isa 25:8; 26:19). Apocalyptic literature is domesticated when its radical, beatific expectations are downplayed.

E. The Social Location of Israelite Eschatology

Israelite eschatology emerged from many different places in ancient society. It was at home within circles of power as well as within peripheral groups. Isaiah, with his eschatology of a remnant and a messiah, was at home in Jerusalem and had ready access to the king. He traded in eschatological concepts out of a central societal position. Micah, by contrast, came from Judah's villages, representing the concerns of the countryside. Yet, as easily as Isaiah, he bore eschatological messages about the Messiah and about a coming doomsday.

Sometimes in past biblical scholarship, Temple worship was characterized as lacking in eschatology, focusing on cycles of ritual and cultic myth. However most scholars now have a more critical and elastic view of Israel's traditions of worship and priestly officials, which includes a place for eschatology.

The psalter gives us a window into the themes of Israel's worship, and eschatological perspectives are well represented. The conclusion of Psalm 82, for example, calls on God to arise and establish God's reign on earth. God has the responsibility to do so, "for yours are all the nations" (Ps 82:8). Other examples of pronounced eschatology in the psalter include Pss 68:20-35; 76:12; 97:1-6; 104:31-35; 108; 144. Some of this eschatology can even be characterized as apocalyptic.

Like prophets and priests, Israel's sages and purveyors of wisdom are known to have developed eschatological perspectives. An apocalyptic worldview could even take shape among them. Thus, mantic sages appear to have been the authors of the apocalyptic visions of the book of Daniel. It was no huge step for such sages, skilled in figuring out hidden or obscure revelations, to turn their talents to mining the unfulfilled ideals and prophecies of Scripture in order to piece together God's ultimate plans for the cosmos.

F. The Exile and the Blossoming of Eschatology

The exilic period brought an intense, focal concentration of Israel's eschatological hopes. It provided the occasion for archiving earlier prophetic promises as written Scripture, susceptible to learned study and radical new future-oriented interpretations. It saw the development of fixed eschatological terms out of earlier prophetic concepts.

The exile was also a period conducive to the crystallization of many traditional Israelite motifs into a detailed eschatological drama. As such a standard, fixed drama developed, it became a repeating construct in postexilic prophecy and early Israelite apocalypticism.

The burning of Jerusalem and the collapse of the Judean state necessitated new expanded understandings from the biblical authors. It required new divine initiatives if God's work with Israel was to find its way forward.

During the exile, the schools of Deuteronomy, Jeremiah, and Ezekiel began to come to terms with the people's historic inability to uphold God's covenant. They announced prophecies of a new covenant, with built-in guarantees against dissolution. In God's promised future, they proclaimed, God's people will be empowered with a new transformed nature, hardwired for faithfulness (Deut 30:6; Jer 31:31-34; Ezek 11:17-20; 16:60; 36:24-28).

The exilic authors of 2 Isaiah, for their part, came to see the whole era of Israelite history from the conclusion of the covenant on Mount Sinai to the destruction of the monarchy in 586 BCE as an unmitigated disaster (Isa 43:18). They declared that God's way forward with Israel must now be based entirely on the model of God's earlier friendship and steadfast commitment to the ancestors (Isa 41:8; 51:2). Now, God was creating a new history with Israel, which would finally fulfill God's specific promises to Abraham and Sarah.

Ezekiel, in his first vision in Babylonian exile, was shocked to experience first hand how the reality of God far transcended the manufactured icons and symbols of Jerusalem's finite Temple. He learned that Jerusalem's destruction would not, and could not, contradict the reality of God's sovereign enthronement atop the cosmic center (Ezek 1:22-28).

The exile had a serious impact on the development of biblical eschatology, but it hardly birthed eschatology as such. By the time of Jerusalem's fall, biblical thought had long known a belief in history's orientation towards a telos determined only by God's sovereign will. It was well familiar with God's summons to the faithful to orient their lives on this coming telos and on a new pure era beyond the catastrophe.

Certain theological constructs employed by the pre-exilic prophets nurtured the idea of a new era of restoration and purity beyond the "end" of Israel and Judah as independent nations. The prophetic image of a remnant that would survive the coming visitation of God was one such construct (see, e.g., Zeph 2:9; Ezek 9:8; Isa 6:13; 7:3). Though conveying the threat of mass casualties, the thought of a remnant also upheld the promise of God's commitment to preserve God's people.

The same can be said for the image of divine judgment as a time of birth pangs. Like the idea of a remnant, this construct helped foster eschatological hope amid threatened retribution. The image of the pain of childbirth in Mic 4:9, for example, certainly preserves the possibility that new life could be birthed for Judah out of the people's present cataclysm.

So too, the ideal of a new exodus arose in Israel well before exilic times. Already in Hosea, in the 8th cent., God appears planning a new love affair with Israel that would restore the couple's lost state of intimacy. In Hos 2:14-15, God announces this new beginning with the people, and specifically includes a promise of resettlement within God's good land.

Messianism was alive and flourishing in the eighth century as well, and not only within the orbit of Jerusalem's royal court. (Messianism is a particular form of eschatology that entails the expectation of a coming savior figure to inaugurate God's ideal future.) In the north, Hosea conceived of a future eschatological leader who specifically lacked the trappings of monarchy. Unlike a king, this figure would be modeled along the lines of village Israel's tribal judges (Hos 1:11).

In Judah, long before the fall of Jerusalem, the prophet Isaiah began to cultivate a royal, Zion-oriented messianism (Isa 7:14, 16; 9:6-7; 11:1-5). He spoke of God's ideals for the Davidic line coming to fruition with the advent of a wondrous, transcendent monarch dispensing peace and justice from Jerusalem.

Micah and his circle presented a counter messianic vision. Micah 5:2-3 abandons Jerusalem as the coming Messiah's royal seat, siding instead with Hosea in favoring a decentralized, humble, and rural leadership of future Israel.

A final word is in order about the argument that apocalyptic eschatology derived out of the frustrations and deprivations of Israel's experience of exile. Such a deprivation theory is is reductionistic, making apocalypticism look like a psychological coping mechanism—an opiate for the persecuted and peripheral. What is more, it is circular in its reasoning and unable to account for significant bodies of biblical and social-scientific data.

Newer anthropological and cross-cultural study of apocalypticism has demonstrated that one must look elsewhere than to contexts of alienation and oppression to explain this phenomenon's rise.

The experience of exile did contribute to apocalypticism's rise, but not because of its purported deprivations. Rather, the exile entailed clear positive motivating factors that facilitated a worldview change to apocalypticism.

First, the exile signaled the ending of an era, which raised expectations of a coming radical transformation of the world. Second, the captivity in Babylonia meant tremendous changes for people to absorb, shaking their beliefs and ways of thinking. This type of shake up is certainly able to predispose people to accept a new universe of meaning, such as the one provided by apocalypticism. Third, many Israelites likely interpreted the exile as a major portent or harbinger, presaging the eschaton. Given its symbolic association with God's cosmic mountain, the destruction of Jerusalem's Temple Mount must have terrified some Judeans into an apocalyptic state of mind. The burning of God's Temple likely appeared to them to be the beginning of the collapse of the universe and the inauguration of an entirely new reality.

G. Resistance to Eschatology

It is a common human trait to be dismissive of eschatology. Human beings tend to assume that everyday life is steadfast and enduring, that the world around them represents hard, dependable fact. Often, they suppose that God stands at some distance from experience and history, that "The LORD will not do good, nor will he do harm" (Zeph 1:12). History, they assume, is shaped primarily by earth's superpowers, or else it is like a sea cliff or a canyon wall, shaped only by wind, water, and time.

The biblical texts are unsupportive of such resistance to eschatology. True, not all biblical texts are eschatological. Some, indeed, are resigned to a foreseeable future where history remains stagnant and alienated from Yahweh (compare Deut 4:19-20; 2 Kgs 5:18; Ps 82:1-4; Mic 4:5; Eccl 1:7; 8:14). But a focus on the hard realities of the here and now is a far cry from a conviction that God is uninvolved with the world or that whatever eschaton there might be has already been realized.

Anti-eschatological views are far more typical of the addressees of God's servants than of the servants themselves (see Mic 2:7; Ezek 8:12; 9:9; 12:22, 27; 13:10-11; Mal 2:17; 3:15; Ps 10:4, 11). The prophets' opponents were known to ridicule their messages of a coming eschaton. For examples, see especially Jer 20:10; Isa 5:19; and Isa 66:5.

In almost all biblical perspectives, eschatological skepticism is a foolish stance. It robs one of orientation, impetus, and hope. It is precisely the sense of an ending—the knowledge of a telos—that should shape and energize life in the present. Without such a perspective, one can too easily land in complacency or despair. That is, a focus on eschatological justice does not undermine ethics and activism in the here and now (as has sometimes been claimed). Zephaniah 1:12 describes God ominously searching Jerusalem with lamps on the day of judgment, ferreting out those with no eschatological sensibility. These people are so skeptical and cynical that they have sat life out, decadent and indolent. They believed that God was not involved in life, did not care enough to enact justice, so they were not bothered with justice either. They lived a life of indifference and stagnation, becoming like spoiled wine standing too long with the dregs. Beyond outright skepticism, another common way to resist eschatology is to put off the existential decision of responding to God and God's coming. There is a natural human tendency to put off hard decisions, especially in the face of uncertainty. Why not wait to make one's choice until God's sovereignty is revealed in power?

Several biblical texts show awareness of this tendency, but suggest it is an extremely unwise gamble. There is a restricted window of opportunity for seeking the Lord according to these texts (see Isa 55:6). A point may come when judgment is inevitable and the Lord will not be found (Hos 5:6; Jer 7:16; 14:12; Ezek 8:18; 14:12-23). Here and now is the time for making existential decisions, assuming it is not already too late.

At the eschaton, according to several texts, each person's true colors will be revealed (Isa 4:3; Ezek 9:4; Dan 12:1). Only those aligned with God and God's work may survive the firestorm, exiting the purge with their lives intact (Isa 33:14; Zeph 2:3; Zech 13:9). The eschaton will be a time for awestruck silence (Zeph 1:7; Zech 2:13), not for making one's pleas to God (Ezek 7:25-27).

There will be no point trying to choose sides or switch allegiances at God's arrival, confronted with God's burning glory. The epiphany on earth of God's scorching otherness is at issue. Decision-making is meaningless at such a time, when everyone necessarily falls prostrate in dread (Nah 1:6; Mal 3:2). Even in the aftermath of the dreadful day, survivors will not dare to invoke the name of the Lord. Rather, they will avoid attracting God's attention in any way, lest they too be struck down (Amos 6:10; 8:3).

H. God's Prerogative and Its Relation to History

The biblical traditions agree that God is at work in history, directing it toward a telos in accord with God's will. Though often awkward and messy, history is subject to God's guiding vision, not controlled by chance, fate, or the tyranny of humanity.

This basic truth is captured dynamically in Jeremiah's image of history as a clay vessel and God as a potter (Jer 18:1-12; compare Isa 29:16; 45:9; 64:8). Like a pot taking shape on a wheel, history may wobble and bend, testing God's patience. Ultimately, however, it must yield to its maker's skillful control.

The short book of Habakkuk reveals that God shapes and directs the progress of history in intricate, obscure, and surprising ways. It also reveals a divinely appointed stance for living on this side of the eschaton. In the ambiguous and painful period before the arrival of God's justice, "the righteous live by their faith" (Hab 2:4).

The five "woes" of Hab 2:6-20 reveal a sense in which meaning can be understood to subsist within the flow of human history. The woes are proverb-like utterances—wise observations about how God has hardwired life on earth so as to favor respect and friendship. They are aimed obliquely, operating under the principle that if the shoe fits, then one must wear it. In the present canonical shape of Habakkuk, however, they clearly find their target in the Babylonians, who for the time being seem to mete out treachery with impunity.

With time, according to the woes, evil corrects itself. Corruption and cruelty eventually boomerang on their perpetrators. Such life choices are self-defeating, inherently destined for frustration. In the theological perspective of Israelite wisdom literature, God not need physically intervene in the world for history to continually "list" towards its necessary end.

While some biblical texts, such as Hab 2:6-20, reveal a sense of meaning within the long haul of time, the focus of many others is on how often God and history appear to be completely out of sync. What humanity in its blindness is making of life on earth simply does not jive with God's good intentions for creation. History in this sense of what humanity makes of the world is a tremendous frustration for God, a cause of genuine divine agony.

Historical experience as created by human beings is full of tragedy, defiance of God, and injustice. From this perspective, history is fundamentally contradictory to the divine will and a poor overall indicator of earth's final destiny. For real insight into the telos of history we must look beyond what humanity is doing with the world. That is why at Hab 2:3 God instructs the prophet to wait for an appointed time. If the vision seems to tarry, he must nevertheless wait patiently for its sure arrival.

What is this vision, this appointed time, for which Habakkuk must wait? It is nothing less than the cataclysmic day of Yahweh, the tangible, transformative advent of the divine warrior. When the revelatory moment arrives, everyone will know it, and it will clarify God's intentions for history (Hab 3:6-7).

Biblical faith encompasses a sense of meaning and teleology in human history, despite perplexity and ambiguity, but also hopes for something more from God. The faithful look for a new beginning direct from the hand of God, which will resolve their frequent experience of contradiction between the ways of God and the ways of history.

God reveals to Habakkuk another deep truth beyond the fact of a promised future: a way to participate in the eschaton's promised salvation even while awaiting it. As Habakkuk's anger and fear collide with God's difficult and alien plan, he is challenged to adopt a new form of life. He is confronted with the need for selfless trust and suffering servanthood (Hab 2:4).

Embracing an existence of suffering trust, he discovers the norm of a new life. The old self, which insists on control and its own understandings, is destroyed. In its place, a new self is born.

I. Personal Eschatology

Ancient Israel shared with its Near Eastern milieu a lively belief in the existence of departed shades (i.e., disembodied spirits of the dead). The term REPHAIM—the Ugaritic and Phoenician word for shades—occurs with the specific meaning of "departed spirits" in such texts as Ps 88:10; Isa 26:19; and Prov 9:18. Other biblical texts refer to the shades as "preternatural beings" (Num 25:2; 1 Sam 28:13) or as "ghosts," and "familiar spirits" (Deut 18:11; Isa 8:19; 19:3).

Though confined and enfeebled, cut off from hope, the shades of the dead have neither lost their identity nor faded away according to a variety of biblical texts. Rather, they form a great assembly (Prov 21:16), a veritable silent majority. They are often asleep, but are able to be roused and interact with others (1 Sam 28:15; Isa 14:9-10). They are able to reason and to ponder what they see around them (Isa 14:16), and they are capable of intense emotion (Job 26:5 refers to them as trembling in fear). They speak audibly to one another (Isa 14:9; Ezek 32:21), and humans can overhear them. To the living, they often appear to mutter, chirp, and whisper (Isa 8:19; 29:4; compare Isa 45:19).

Fresh data and discoveries are constantly enlarging our understandings of the ancient world's preoccupation with the shades of the departed. As the twenty-first century gets underway, archaeologists are unearthing a royal "palace of the underworld" in the ancient Bronze Age city of Qatna in Syria. Evidence from the complex's main chamber attests to periodic ceremonial dining with the dead (the kispum).

Much more was going on in the *kispum* than merely honoring and commemorating the dead. Stacked dishes and the remains of numerous animal bones scattered about the underground chamber point to periodic family feasts in the actual presence of the bones and spirits of the deceased. A separate throne chamber formed a space for the ghost of the reigning king's father to appear, to be offered food and drink and to commune with the living.

Israelite religion existed within the same ancient cultural milieu as Qatna, and was well aware of its powerful preoccupation with the spirit world. In fact, they undertook a variety of religious practices in connection with these beliefs, some of which were opposed and censured by the proponents of the traditions that eventually formed the Scriptures.

Necromancy and mortuary cults are manifestly offensive to God's spokespersons (see Lev 19:31; 20:6, 27; Deut 18:1011; 2 Kgs 21:6; Isa 8:19-20; 57:56; 65:4). More offensive still, however, was the very existence of Sheol itself. The biblical writers were repulsed and terrified by Sheol, given its relentless claim on all living creatures, its insatiable appetite for all human souls (e.g., Hos 13:14; Hab 2:5; Job 24:19; Ps 18:45; Prov 27:20).

The idea that Sheol is God's planned eschatological *telos* for each soul is simply contradictory to the great theological themes of the OT. It does not fit in with the most rudimentary of biblical tenets about God's will for humanity, human community, and the inner harmony of each person. Sheol is a scandal, for which God must somehow answer. The offence at Sheol is readily observable in the biblical texts. One is hard pressed to find even a single biblical passage where Sheol appears neutrally as a peaceful resting place. Rather, the texts portray Sheol as the unwelcome fate of the boastful and wicked (e.g., Job 24:19; Ps 9:17; 49:14; Isa 5:11-14; 14:15). There is no justice in the righteous falling prey to its power. Faithful psalmists repeatedly cry out to God for deliverance from its terrors (e.g., Ps 6:4-5; 9:13; 55:4; 69:1-2; 88:4-5).

Must the clutches of Sheol forever threaten and demoralize even the most faithful of God's followers? Over time, biblical eschatology became increasingly articulate that the answer to this question is no.

Psalm 16:10-11 expresses hope of not being given up to Sheol, of not seeing the Pit. Rather, the psalmist aims his hopes heavenwards, towards "fullness of joy" and "pleasures forevermore." Psalm 49:15 also presents an eschatology alternative to a destiny in the underworld. It understands God as able to ransom its speaker from Sheol's grasp and "receive" him or her into the divine presence. Psalm 73:24-26 also speaks of God receiving the soul into heaven, and it is rather less ambiguous about this hope than Ps 49 is.

Various texts of the OT affirm that Sheol is well within God's reach (e.g., Ps 139:8; Amos 9:2; Isa 7:11; Prov 15:11; Job 11:8; 26:6). Other texts, such as Hos 13:14, go farther and suggest that Sheol's days are numbered. Hosea 13:14 understands that God is not only able to reach into Sheol and rescue its prisoners but also capable of subduing and destroying Sheol as an extant reality. If it were not for Israel's apostasy, God would be about this work.

At the eschaton, according to Isa 25:7-8, God finally feels free to accomplish what could not be done at the time of Hosea: a victory over Sheol. In that day, God will exercise God's prerogative to remove Death permanently from the realm of reality. At history's end, this text announces, the Lord will "swallow up death forever." God will destroy "the shroud that is cast over all peoples."

J. Resurrection

Resurrection as presented in the Scriptures is a physical, material, fleshy phenomenon, to be rigorously distinguished from notions of a disembodied soul rising to an ethereal, spiritual existence in heaven. In contrast to notions of a spiritual afterlife, concepts of bodily resurrection entail the rising to new, beatific life of the deceased corporeal human being. Key words to keep in mind here are *physical, bodily,* and *corporeal.*

Specific descriptions of bodily resurrection in association with the end times appear only at the tail end of the history of OT eschatology. When these descriptions do start to occur, however, they are riveting. They are wondrous, awe-inspiring visions, which, at the same time, feel peculiarly contiguous with the development of God's history with God's people.

Daniel 12:2 is by far the most celebrated proclamation of resurrection in the OT. The verse prophesies the awakening to life of multitudes that have been long dead and buried. The puzzling use of the term "many" in the verse is clarified by cross-reference to Isa 53:11 (compare Mark 10:45).

Other overt visions of eschatological resurrection occur in Isa 26:19 and in Ps 22:27-29. In Isa 26:19, God promises the faithful that "Your dead shall live, their corpses shall rise." Indeed, God summons the dead and buried, the "dwellers in the dust" to arise and rejoice, to "awake and sing for joy!"

Late eschatological redaction of Ps 22 describes a universal embrace of the Lord at the eschaton, which includes all nations of earth and all peoples in the underworld (vv. 27-29). The thought of 22:29 is captured well by the NAB version: "All who sleep in the earth will bow low before God; All who have gone down into the dust will kneel in homage."

The feeling of contiguity of the OT's resurrection descriptions with what has come before in the Scriptures is powerfully bolstered by preceding occurrences of individual instances of resurrection. Old Testament individuals who actually rose from the dead are few in number, of course, and their experiences are admittedly non-eschatological. Nevertheless, their stories attest to the reality of resurrection within the experience of God's people and prepare us for its appearance as a phenomenon of late biblical eschatology.

The protagonists of certain well-known psalmic and prophetic poems experience bodily resurrections from death (Ps 22:15, 24; Isa 53:9-12). The Scriptures also know of two renowned persons who avoided death entirely by being translated bodily directly into God's presence: Enoch (Gen 5:24) and Elijah (2 Kgs 2:11; compare Mal 4:5).

Israel's lawgivers, prophets, and sages were always partially in the dark about God's thoughts and plans in directing history. They confessed that God's work is often strange, marvelous, and extraordinary (see Isa 28:21). A few of them believed this work extraordinary enough to permit humans to entertain the possibility of an eschatological resurrection.

In his celebrated vision of dry bones filling a valley, the exilic prophet Ezekiel comes face to face with resurrection (Ezek 37:1-14). For the first ten verses of Ezek 37, the prophet is contemplating nothing other than a literal, bodily rising of the dead. This fact is obvious from 37:10, where Ezekiel mistakes the human remains that he sees for fallen warriors on a deserted battlefield. Up through this point in the chapter, the prophet has absolutely no idea that the skeletons of his vision are mere metaphors for the despondent exilic community.

In 37:3 God confronts Ezekiel with the question, "Mortal, can these bones live?" Ezekiel's response is at once diplomatic and faithful: "O Lord GOD, you know." The rabbis recognized the genius of the answer. It recognized the stupendous power of God even to effect the inconceivable, for which one dare not hope. Ezekiel appreciated God's sovereignty over reality, including sovereignty over life and death.

The biblical figure of Job likewise wrestled hard with the idea of bodily resurrection. Like Ezekiel, he was able to imagine it primarily as an impossible possibility. Particularly in Job 14:13-17, he states that if he could hope that beyond Sheol there was some sort of resurrection, then he could endure his present problems.

Job entertains the idea of a resurrection hope again in Job 19:23-27. The passage is admittedly opaque, but it appears to reference a time after the deterioration of Job's body to "earth" (19:25) when he nevertheless encounters God "in my flesh" (19:26), as "I myself" (19:27), using "my eyes" (19:27*b*). He confesses that he pines and yeans at the prospect of this miraculous eventuality (19:27*c*).

It has rightly been said that long before it made its overt appearance, the concept of resurrection was etched in the logic of Scripture. In other words, resurrection faith is no incongruous add-on to biblical eschatology, but is existentially and morally correlative to canonical Yahwism's core values. If earth is ever to see these values realized in fullness, then Sheol must surrender its prisoners and be forever abolished.

The values at issue would include at the least the following: the embrace of harmony and shalom over against the aqueous, suffocating chaos of Sheol; the embrace of vibrant, spirit-directed life over against the path of disobedience leading to destruction; the embrace of public, corporate worship over against stillness and thanklessness; the embrace of loving, nurturing community over against loneliness and exile; and the embrace of purity and holiness over against uncleanness and corpses. *See* AFTERLIFE; APOCALYPTICISM; DAY, NT; DAY, OT; DAY OF JUDGMENT; DAY OF THE LORD; DEATH, NT; DEATH, OT; LIFE; RESURRECTION, NT; RESURRECTION, OT; SHEOL.

Bibliography: James Barr. *The Garden of Eden and the Hope of Immortality.* (1992); Elizabeth M. Bloch-Smith.

Judahite Burial Practices and Beliefs About the Dead (1991); Stephen L. Cook. *The Apocalyptic Literature.* (2003); Stephen L. Cook. *Prophecy and Apocalypticism: The Postexilic Social Setting* (1995); William J. Dumbrell. *The Search for Order: Biblical Eschatology in Focus* (1994); Lester L. Grabbe and Robert D. Haak, eds. *Knowing the End from the Beginning: The Prophetic, the Apocalyptic and their Relationships* (2003); Craig C. Hill. *In God's Time: The Bible and the Future* (2002); Philip S. Johnston *Shades of Sheol: Death and Afterlife in the Old Testament* (2002); Brian B. Schmidt. *Israel's Beneficent Dead: Ancestor Cult and Necromancy in Ancient Israelite Religion and Tradition* (1996).

STEPHEN L. COOK

ESCHATON. es´kuh-ton *See* ESCHATOLOGY IN EARLY JUDAISM; ESCHATOLOGY OF THE NT; ESCHATOLOGY OF THE OT.

ESDAR, TELL. A small agricultural village sharing a common culture with larger nearby sites, it is located on 5 acres in the northern Negeb desert approximately 18 km east-southeast of BEER-SHEBA. It has five occupation levels: two Early Bronze Age, two Iron Age I, and a Roman level. The earlier Iron Age I ruins are domestic buildings arranged in a defensive circle and violently destroyed in the late 11th cent. The 10th cent. village was strictly a small farm site. Avraham Biran identified the site with AROER of David's time since no Iron Age I remains were found at nearby Tell Aro'er. *See* NEGEB, NEGEV.

TERRY W. EDDINGER

ESDRAELON ez´druh-ee´luhn [Ἐσδρηλών Esdrēlōn]. An expanse of land stretching from the Jordan River to the Mediterranean Sea, separating the mountains of Carmel from those of Galilee, and including the Plain of Megiddo. This designation occurs only in the book of Judith (3:9; 7:3). This area in the OT is Jezreel. *See* JEZREEL, JEZREELITE.

STEPHANIE SKELLEY-CHANDLER

ESDRAS, FIFTH BOOK OF. *See* ESDRAS, SECOND BOOK OF.

ESDRAS, FIRST BOOK OF ez´druhs [Ἔσδρας Esdras]. The name Esdras is the Greek form of Ezra. The book Esdras A, or 1 Esdras, appears in the LXX just before the book Esdras B. Esdras B is a literal translation of the canonical books Ezra–Nehemiah. Esdras A appears in the Apocrypha, but unlike most books of the APOCRYPHA it is not included in the Roman Catholic OT.

First Esdras overlaps in the gist (but not in every detail) with the end of Chronicles, with part of Nehemiah, and with Ezra (*see* CHRONICLES, FIRST AND SECOND BOOKS OF; EZRA AND NEHEMIAH, BOOKS OF). It can be considered "rewritten Bible." It reorders the chapters in Ezra–Nehemiah, omits the story of

Nehemiah, and adds a story about Zerubbabel, all in an attempt to make better sense of the very difficult canonical text. Josephus (writing between 70–95 CE; *see* JOSEPHUS, FLAVIUS) uses the text of 1 Esdras for this portion of his history of the Jews, not the canonical Ezra–Nehemiah. The order of chapters compared to the canonical Chronicles–Ezra–Nehemiah is as follows:

1 Esdras	Canonical Chronicles, Ezra, Nehemiah	The Episode
1:1-33	2 Chr 35:1-27	Josiah celebrates the Passover, battles Pharaoh Neco, dies, and is mourned.
1:34-58	2 Chr 36:1-21	Presents the last kings of Judah and the fall of Judah and Jerusalem to Babylon.
2:1-15	Ezra 1:1-11	Cyrus, king of Persia, permits the Jews to return to Judah and to build a temple for YHWH in Jerusalem. Sheshbazzar (Gk. Sanabassaros) brings the temple vessels back to Jerusalem.
2:16-30	Ezra 4:7-24*a*	A letter to King Artaxerxes from satrapal officials complaining that the Jews are rebuilding Jerusalem and its walls (1 Esdras adds "and laying the foundations for a temple"). The officials warn the king that if the city is rebuilt and the walls finished, they will not pay tribute. The king orders the building stopped, and building is stopped until the second year of Darius.
3:1–5:6	No Parallel	Darius' three bodyguards debate what the strongest thing in the world is. One picks wine, one picks the king, and one, Zerubbabel, says that a woman is stronger than a king, but truth is strongest of all. Darius rewards Zerubbabel with anything that he wishes. Zerubbabel wishes Jerusalem and the Temple to be rebuilt. Darius orders Zerubbabel to lead the Jews back to Jerusalem and to rebuild the Temple. Funds are to be furnished from the satrapal treasury.
5:7-46	Ezra 2:1-70 (= Neh. 7:6-73*a*)	A list of the returnees who came up to Jerusalem with Zerubbabel and Joshua the priest.
5:47-65	Ezra 3:1-13	An altar is set up for sacrifices and the Temple foundations are laid.

5:66-73	Ezra 4:1-5	Enemies of Judah and Jerusalem offer to help them build the Temple, but the offer is refused. The enemies connive to prevent the completion of the building until the second year of Darius.
6:1-22	Ezra 4:24*b*–5:17	The prophets Haggai and Zechariah encourage the people to continue work on the Temple. Sisinnes (Tattenai in Ezra), governor of Syria and Phoenicia, investigated the Jews who were building and wrote to Darius detailing his findings.
6:23-34	Ezra 6:1-12	Darius searches in the royal archives for proof that Cyrus had given permission for rebuilding the Temple. Finding Cyrus' document, Darius orders the Temple's rebuilding, ordering funds to be provided from the tribute due the satrapy.
7:1-15	Ezra 6:13-22	The Temple is completed and dedicated in the sixth year of Darius. The Passover is celebrated.
8:1-27	Ezra 7:1-28	Ezra the scribe arrives in Jerusalem from Babylon in the seventh year of Artaxerxes. He comes bearing a letter from that king releasing cultic personnel from tribute and other taxes.
8:28-67	Ezra 8:1-36	This section lists the people who went up with Ezra to Jerusalem. The priests carry the gold and silver vessels donated for the temple by the king and his friends.
8:68-90	Ezra 9:1-15	Soon after he arrives, local rulers come to Ezra complaining that the people Israel are intermarrying with the foreign peoples of the land. Ezra tears his garments and prays.
8:91-96	Ezra 10:1-5	The people Israel take an oath to separate from their foreign wives with their children.
9:1-36	Ezra 10:6-44	The men assemble in Jerusalem and all those with foreign wives separate from them.
9:37-55	Neh 7:73*b*–8:13	On the new moon of the seventh month, the people Israel gathers before the East Gate of the Temple and Ezra reads them the Law of Moses. The people rejoice and give gifts to one another and portions
		to those who had none. The ending of 1 Esdras is lost; it ends in mid-sentence: "Then they assembled. . . ."

The questions confronting readers of this book are many: Is this Greek text a translation from a Hebrew or Aramaic original, or was it originally written in Greek? Does 1 Esdras contain the original order of the chapters, or is the original order that of the canonical Ezra–Nehemiah? When and why was 1 Esdras written? What is the intended ending? Is its beginning the original beginning, or is that too lost? If we are missing both the beginning and the end, is 1 Esdras simply a fragment of a much larger work?

The purpose and theological import of the book must be sought in the order of the chapters, since this is the only difference between the versions. First Esdras ends with the reading of the law, and this reading is immediately preceded by the mass separation from foreign wives. In canonical Ezra–Nehemiah, the mass divorce is followed not by the law-reading but by the story of Nehemiah's wall. The divorce and law-reading are separated by eight full chapters. By immediately preceding the law-giving by the divorce, 1 Esdras stresses the holiness of the law. Now all who hear the law are bound by it. Passive observers, not under the strict command of the Mosaic covenant, are excluded from hearing it.

Bibliography: R. J. Coggins and M. A. Knibb. *The First and Second Book of Esdras.* CBC (1979); Jacob M. Myers. *I and II Esdras.* AB 42 (1974); Zipora Talshir. *I Esdras: From Origin to Translation* (1999).

                            LISBETH S. FRIED

ESDRAS, FOURTH BOOK OF. *See* ESDRAS, SECOND BOOK OF.

ESDRAS, SECOND BOOK OF ez′druhs. The Second Book of Esdras is a composite book including a pseudonymous Jewish apocalypse (written near the end of the 1st cent. CE), a Christian preface, and a Christian appendix, both added some time later. The entire complex is characterized by the theme of faithfulness and judgment, with the central apocalypse addressing the thorny problem of human and Jewish suffering by means of dialogue with a heavenly being, the transformation of the seer, and a series of eschatological visions. Though visionary in impulse, the book is canonically oriented, directing its readers to the OT, and alluding to both testaments in its Christian sections.

    A. Reception
    B. Genre, Structure, and Function
    C. Debates Concerning Interpretation
    D. Theological and Hermeneutical Issues
Bibliography

A. Reception

Second Esdras is an anomaly, both in terms of its character, and in terms of its reception within the Jewish and Christian communities. It is extant in Latin (our most reliable text), Syriac, Georgian, Ethiopic, Armenian, and Arabic, but was (at least so far as its central core is concerned) first written in Hebrew, or possibly, Aram. Quotations from the Gk. version, and a fragment in Coptic also survive. Now appearing regularly in extended versions of the Christian Bible as part of the Apocryphal/Deuterocanonical section, it is unique among these texts in that it was not originally grouped with the extended OT writings, but rather was appended to some ancient versions of the NT, notably the Vulgate. Within its complex history of reception, 2 Esdras has sometimes been titled 3 Esdras and 4 Esdras. The core of the book (i.e., chaps. 3–14) was apparently written in the late 1st cent. or early 2nd cent. CE by an anonymous Jewish seer, who gives voice to communal lament for the destroyed Temple, while offering an articulate theodicy and a visionary glimpse of hope. It is by far the most philosophical of the Jewish apocalypses. To this original apocalypse, the Christian community appended two other texts, placing one of these pieces at the beginning, and the other at the end, so that the Jewish work has been set in a Christian frame. The central (Jewish) composition (chaps. 3–14) is commonly referred to as *4 Ezra*. he Christian texts found in chaps. 1–2 and 15–16 are referred to as *5 Ezra* and *6 Ezra*, respectively. When the entire corpus is intended, the term Second Esdras is most commonly used. We will treat the central Jewish apocalypse separately, then consider the Christian additions, and the difference that the Christian framework makes in reading the apocalypse.

This apocalypse has been read seriously by Christian theologians throughout the ages, including such noteworthies as Clement of Alexandria, Cyprian and Ambrose. In the English world, the book made an impression upon Spencer, who alludes to it in his *Faerie Queene,* as well as on Milton, who specifically mentions it in the introduction to the *Deucalion.* Christopher Columbus appealed to its description of the globe (6:42) in his exploratory efforts. In the 18th cent. some people noted the detailed "signs" of the closing age (e.g., 2 Esd 5:8), believed that these signs were fulfilled in their century, and argued that the end was at hand.

B. Genre, Structure, and Function

Certainly this piece is an apocalypse in every sense of the word, and has sometimes even been called *The Apocalypse of Ezra*. The Christian frame complicates the classification, since especially the closing chapters (15–16), and to a lesser extent the first two chapters resemble prophecy more than apocalypse. That is, the emphasis on these chapters is upon the oral, rather than the written word, whereas the genre apocalypse has a distinct "scribal" characteristic—scrolls are eaten, the seer is commanded to write down or to seal up the vision, and so on. Indeed, the closing chapters present an unspecified series of judgment oracles, without specific reference to Ezra as the recipient of these words from God; Ezra is, however, the prophetic intermediary in the first two chapters, where he receives not simply divine words, but also a vision (a strong component of apocalypse) of the heavenly Zion.

The generic characteristics of apocalypse are wholly apparent in the original Jewish *4 Ezra*. Comparison of this piece alongside other Jewish apocalypses puts it firmly in the tradition, and other analyses since that time (*see* APOCALYPSE; APOCALYPTICISM). Along with other apocalypses, the book is written pseudonymously—the "prophet" is of course not the historical Ezra of the rebuilt Jerusalem, but an anonymous seer from the late 1st cent. CE, writing in lament for the destroyed second Temple. The book also includes a mediating angel, a series of visions, oracles from God, involved and poetic discourse concerning mysteries, preparation for and reaction to the visions on the part of "Ezra," and *ex eventu* prophecy ("prophecy" written after the events) which heralds judgment and the imminent coming of a Messiah. Mostly concerned with the historical dimensions of past and future (the "temporal" axis), the apocalypse also hints at some of the mysteries of the heavens (the "spatial" axis). Linked to these mysteries of time (when?) and space (where?) is the mystery of the identity of God's people (who?), which comes to the fore in the very center of the work. Unique among the apocalypses, this one is philosophical, spending as much time in weighty dialogue between the seer and angel as it does in the visionary and the oracular. Sometimes, in the midst of a lengthy interchange, a reader may well forget that "Ezra" is in conversation with a heavenly being—one envisions the classroom, the courtroom, or the deliberating assembly.

The mystery of identity, and the theme of transformation are carefully prepared for by these dialogues, and built into the very structure of the work. Given the strong rhetorical impact of *4 Ezra's* structure, it is hard for us to imagine the consensus of the nineteenth and twentieth centuries when many scholars considered that this book was composed of various sources. Scholars today tend to champion the book's unity and literary coherence. Especially convincing to the case for integrity is a glimpse of the book's literary structure:

Vision 1 (3:1–5:20)	Setting, lament, appearance, dialogue, conclusion
Vision 2 (5:21–6:34)	Setting, lament, appearance, dialogue, conclusion
Vision 3 (6:35–9:25)	Setting, lament, appearance, dialogue, conclusion

Vision 4 (9:26–10:59)	Altered setting, dialogue, vision, interpretation, mystery
Vision 5 (11:1–12:51)	Setting, vision and interpretation
Vision 6 (13:1-58)	Setting, vision and interpretation
Vision 7 (14:1-48)	Setting, call, exhortation, vision and inspired writing, instruction

Visions 1 through 3 and visions 5 through 7 surround the central vision 4 (9:26–10:59), in which a turn-around takes place: Ezra, the plaintiff, is transformed into Ezra the spokesman of God. These first three "visions" (actually, each is an angelophany followed by a dialogue) are carefully set up by a series of characteristics, including description of setting, lament, question, wise reply, discussion, eschatological teaching, and conclusion. At the beginning of each section, we note Ezra's troubled agitation, and his careful ascetic preparations to receive God's word and vision. That pattern is accentuated at 9:26, where Ezra is instructed to leave his room, not to fast but eat flowers, and wait for God to reveal truth in the isolated "field called Ardat." The vision that follows is entirely unlike anything the Ezra has witnessed so far. Ezra plays host to a lamenting "woman." In trying to comfort her, he assumes the role that the angel Uriel has played up until this point. Though their conversation is somewhat didactic, we are transported when Ezra takes up the lament for Jerusalem in a beautiful lyrical passage:

> For you see that our sanctuary has been laid waste, our altar thrown down, our temple destroyed, our harp has been laid low, our song has been silenced, and our rejoicing has been ended; the light of our lampstand has been put out, the ark of our covenant has been plundered, our holy things have been polluted, and the name by which we are called has been profaned; our free men have suffered abuse, our priests have been burned to death, our Levites have gone into captivity, our virgins have been defiled, and our wives have been ravished; our righteous men have been carried off, our little ones have been cast out, our young men have been enslaved and our strong men made powerless. And, what is more than all, the seal of Zion—for she has now lost the seal of her glory, and has been given over into the hands of those that hate us. (10:21-23)

Under the misapprehension that the woman he is comforting is simply pining for personal losses. Ezra offers her a larger perspective, then, he is startled. For this is no ordinary woman, but a representation of Jerusalem. Uttering a huge cry, like a birth-pang, she is transformed into a city that is being built, with huge foundations. So shaken is our seer that he calls out to the angel Uriel, who tells him what the reader has already suspected—Ezra has been standing on holy ground, unaware that he has been conversing with an embodiment of the holy people. Uriel decodes every detail of the woman's lament, showing that she and Ezra have been lamenting the same dire state of Jerusalem. Ezra's lament of the first three visions is thus confirmed, even while he is moved into a different mode. As a climax, the seer is invited to explore the heavenly city. What he sees, we are never told—for the reader is to be tantalized concerning this, the mystery of the identity of God's people. This is, presumably, a mystery that they must discover for themselves. Or, perhaps, there remains just a touch of the esoteric, as Ezra is privileged beyond ordinary folk, privy to God's greatest mysteries. (Certainly this is consonant with the closing vision, in which Ezra rewrites, by inspiration, the twenty-four books of the OT for the sake of all the people, while rewriting seventy books of mystery intended only for the wise.)

After this strange encounter, the apocalypse is entirely altered. Gone is the question of theodicy, no longer heard are the philosophical dialogues and the complaints before God concerning suffering and the state of God's people. In their place, Ezra receives, understands by interpretation, and relates visions of a great eagle (vision 5), and of an anointed Man from the Sea (vision 6). These visions are followed by a direct encounter with the Almighty, in which he Ezra is given the explicit command to comfort and warn Israel, drinks a cup of inspiration from the hand of God, and re-dictates the destroyed holy books (both "canonical" and esoteric) to five assistants, recorded for the benefit of people and sages, respectively. He is now the great Scribe of the faithful. Where once he had questioned the ways of God to the angel, now Ezra justifies the ways of God to Israel: "Take courage, O Israel; and do not be sorrowful, O house of Jacob; for the most high has you in remembrance, and the Mighty One has not forgotten you in your struggle" (12:46-7). The close of the book, with its emphasis upon God's inspired word, implies that the greatest answer God can give is to be found in the holy writings: "for in them is the spring of understanding, the fountain of wisdom, and the river of knowledge."

The clearest function of *4 Ezra*, then, is that of consolation and encouragement. The experience of Ezra traces for the questioning reader a movement from skepticism and distress to a final state of confidence and hope. Dramatically, the theodicy is set up to be resolved in Ezra's own lament, his visionary crisis, and his transformation into one who knows God's ways, plans and character. Though the book is by no means "equalizing" in its vision of the faithful—some are "wise" and some are not—the gift of faith, knowledge and hope is for all of the faithful. The book, even while it hints at Ezra's superior visionary knowledge, does not encourage such speculation on the part of "the people," who are to be content with the twenty-four ordinary books of the Lord. Yet they are to be encouraged that some of their company have been shown more secrets of the future, and of the heavenly regions, and that the very books they hear read have been inspired by God's. Their hope for God's judgment at the hand of Messiah is not in vain, and it is incumbent upon them to "set their house in order" (14:14). The apocalypse functions, then, as a vindication for those who are lamenting the downfall of Jerusalem, as an encouragement for them to see beyond the tragedy to the heavenly Zion which God is preparing, as an exaltation of the holy books by which the identity of the faithful is marked, and as an exhortation for them to live in the light of what they have learned: "if you, then, will rule over your minds and discipline your hearts, you shall be kept alive, and after death you shall obtain mercy" for "He is a righteous judge" (14:32).

To this well-structured piece, the Christian community added its preface, and a conclusion. The preface (chaps. 1 and 2) identifies Ezra, and describes the seer's call to declare judgment, rehearses the mercies of God throughout Israel's history, condemns Israel ("this" people) alongside of Sodom and Gomorrah, and transfers Israel's glory to "others"—namely, Gentile believers. These words of oracular judgment are confirmed by Ezra's visionary sight of a great white-clad multitude that worships and stands around the crowned "Son of God." Ezra praises these valiant saints, and then is told by the angel to go and tell all the wonders of the Lord that he is seen. This preface leads into the apocalypse proper, in which Ezra moves from lamenter to God's spokesman. The final section (chaps. 15–16) is less skillfully attached, and seems like an afterthought. The role of the appendix is to strengthen those who are being persecuted, and to declare judgment against unbelievers and unfaithful Christians. Not a few phrases in the appendix echo the gospels and Revelation, in their more picturesque parts. If the preface acts as an encouragement to the new Christian community, the prologue serves to guard against presumption: "Woe to those who sin and want to hide their sins!" (16:64).

It is interesting to note that the question of identity—"who are the people of God"—set up in the Jewish apocalypse through the transformed Ezra and the lamenting woman/heavenly Zion, is retained in the Christian appendix. Suffering, we are told, is important to the forging of a true identity (16:73). One of the greatest mysteries of God is the identity of God's true people, an identity connected with lament, suffering and judgment.

C. Debates Concerning Interpretation

On the whole, most of the scholarly debate concerning this book has circled around source criticism, and whether the book may be read as a unity. Certainly, a consensus exists with regards to the discrete nature of the Christian preface and appendix. With a few notable exceptions, scholars seem more prepared today to read the Ezra Apocalypse as a unity. Moreover, there is an almost unanimous opinion regarding the dating of the Jewish core, on the basis of a literal reading of 3:1 (30 years after the destruction of the Temple in 70 CE, that is ca. 100 CE).

Of more interest is the interpretive debate concerning the "message" of Second Esdras. It is important to note from the first that apocalypses tend, by their nature, to be "centrifugal," that is, encyclopedic and addressing multiple issues and mysteries, rather than "centripetal," that is, seeking a center of meaning. Nevertheless, the structure of this piece, centered around its central vision, and its stable appeal to the canon, render the search for a main message plausible. Unlike, for example, the Enoch corpus, this piece is more concerned with the dealings of God with humankind than with the mysteries of the heavenly realms for the sake of esoteric knowledge. Even the privileged seer, like Ezra, is vouchsafed his experience for the sake of the community, who are gathered together around a common history, a common book, and a common eschatological hope.

Some have thought that the book presents a legalistic foundation for personal salvation, and that its major purpose is to elicit good behavior through glimpses of a horrendous or hopeful future. While this charge may have be pronounced by some critics because of a certain understanding of Jewish identity, it should be noted that the "Christian" portions of the book are more liable to be legalistic and personally salvific than the dynamic Jewish core. Though the central section certainly configures the identity of God's people in a way particular to Judaism, and differently from, for example, Revelation, it is hard to see a frank "legalism" here. Ezra debates with the angel, in Job-like fashion, balking at platitudes and "correct" answers from Torah; the seer shows compassion for the lot of humanity, and not simply for Israel; there is wonder, and not simply relief, at the prospect of the visionary City; suffering is embraced as the means by which the faithful are transformed, and not simply dismissed as a present situation that will be transcended. The focus of the piece seems not, as some have suggested, to be on the eschatological hope only, but on the identity of God's people, and the part that suffering plays in that identity.

Readers of the text have questioned, as they have with the complex dynamics of that Biblical theodicy, Job, *how* it is that the book comes to its resolution. Some have resolutely continued to insist that the book makes no dramatic sense in its current configuration, and that Ezra is simply a skeptic who has been softened, by the addition of more material, into one who trusts. Some have believed that Uriel is the orthodox theologian, who uses Ezra as a "foil" to be stymied: in this scenario, Ezra is seen as eventually converting to the angel's divine wisdom. Others have suggested that the piece works through catharsis, as Ezra articulates the lament of the community, is given no real intellectual answer to his questions, but is nonetheless consoled by a series of supernatural experiences. Some have insisted that the book leaves its tension unresolved, uttering irreconcilable statements that should not be softened. Others have said that the tension is resolved, if not by offering intellectual answers, by experience, so that there is a satisfactory dramatic conclusion even while the questions may remain. All these perspectives, though very different, point to the complex character of a text which is structured around a central turning point, but which leaves mysteries unsolved.

D. Theological and Hermeneutical Issues

The tension between resolution and suspense is consonant with the Pauline dynamic of "already-not yet" and with the flavor of the NT apocalyptic, which gives a hopeful resolution, even while the human plight (particularly, the plight of the suffering faithful) is recognized. Christian readers might resonate with the manner in which suffering and identity are linked. For those whose identity is formed by the one who died and so is Lord, this bond of suffering with significance should be compelling. The Jewish context of *4 Ezra* means that the dynamic between suffering and identity will not be worked out to any great extent, in terms of doctrine—or at least, in terms of Christian doctrines of KENOSIS, ATONEMENT, and the imitation of Christ. Yet, the story of Ezra and his people is a poignant one, calling readers to enter into the tragedy of loss along with the lamenting seer, to rejoice in God's provision of a representative who moves from deep sorrow to a divinely-offered understanding of reality, and to a hope that God is at work through and not simply despite the brokenness of this world.

In terms of understanding the NT world, that world into which Jesus, Paul, and the others spoke and wrote, this piece is invaluable. The lament over Zion is such as to quicken our imaginations, so that we understand the shock of 70 CE, and its attendant events. The vision of the Man from the Sea reminds us of the 1st cent. hope for Messiah, and the biblical focus upon justice. Ezra's glimpse of the Holy City provides a context for the new covenant, in which "God . . . has shone in our hearts to give the light of the knowledge of the glory of God" (2 Cor 4:6). If the "lamp" of *4 Ezra* is the inscribed word of God, the light of the Christian community is the Word (John 1:1-5). Ezra knows that the lamenting Zion is to be identified with the glorified Zion. Christian writers will explain how it is that glory comes from lament.

All this being said, there is ample room for contrition as the Christian community reads this tome, in its final form. Onto this wonderfully allusive and sensitive dialogue founded upon revelation open to mystery, the Christian community has placed a literary millstone. Ezra's view of the heavenly Zion was of a city in the process of being built, the extent of which could hardly be imagined—is there room in the seer's imagination for "the nations" alongside the people who possess Torah? The Christian preface to *4 Ezra* leaves no room for imagination by saying that God's first people are "forsaken" (1:25) and have forfeited their inheritance, since "the blood . . . of [God's] servants" will be required of them (1:32). This prefaced indictment adds an air of cynicism to the deep lament and the hopeful visions that follow. The final shape of this piece is barely saved from spitefulness by the concluding reminder to the reader that only "the Lord knows all the works of men, their imaginations and their thoughts and their hearts" (16:54).

The book teaches both directly and inversely, offering a salutary, imaginative, and faithful vision of reality.

Bibliography: John J. Collins. "The Jewish Apocalypses." *Semeia* 14 (1979) 21–59; David A. De Silva. "2 Esdras: The Mighty One Has Not Forgotten." *Introducing the Apocrypha: Message, Context and Significance* (2002) 323–51; Lorenzo DiTommaso. "Dating the Eagle Vision of *4 Ezra*: A New Look at an Old Theory." *JSP* 20 (1990) 3–38; Edith M. Humphrey. *The Ladies and the Cities: Transformation and Apocalyptic Identity in Joseph and Aseneth, 4 Ezra, the Apocalypse and The Shepherd of Hermas* (1995); Bruce W. Longenecker. *2 Esdras.* Guides to the the Apocrypha and Pseudepigrapha (1995); B. M. Metzger. "The Fourth Book of Ezra." *OTP* 1. (1985) 516–59; Michael Edward Stone. *Fourth Ezra; A Commentary on the Book of Fourth Ezra* (1990).

EDITH M. HUMPHREY

ESDRAS, SIXTH BOOK OF. *See* ESDRAS, SECOND BOOK OF.

ESDRAS, THIRD BOOK OF. *See* ESDRAS, FIRST BOOK OF.

ESDRIS ez´dris [Ἔσδρις *Esdris*]. A Jewish division leader in the battle against Gorgias mentioned in 2 Macc 12:36.

ESEK ee´sik [עֵשֶׂק *ʿeseq*]. The well of springwater dug by Isaac's servants somewhere between Gerar and Beersheba (Gen 26:20). The name means "contention." According to the biblical account it is so named because of the quarrel over its water rights that occurred between Isaac's servants and the herders of Gerar.

STEPHANIE SKELLEY-CHANDLER

ESHAN ee'shuhn [אֶשְׁעָן 'esh'an]. A town in the hill country of Judah, somewhere near Hebron, listed among the towns that are the tribal inheritance of Judah (Josh 15:52). This is its only reference, and, thus, its exact location remains unknown. The LXX includes an alternate reading of Soma for this place. *See* HEBRON, HEBRONITES.

STEPHANIE SKELLEY-CHANDLER

ESH-BAAL. *See* ISHBAAL.

ESHBAN esh'ban [אֶשְׁבָּן 'eshban]. A son of Dishon and grandson of Seir appearing among members of a Horite clan in Edom (Gen 36:26; 1 Chr 1:41). *See* EDOM, EDOMITES.

ESHCOL esh'kol [אֶשְׁכֹּל 'eshkol]. An ally of Abram and brother to MAMRE and Aner (Gen 14:13, 24). Since both Eshcol and Mamre appear to have been places located in the Hebron vicinity (Num 13:22-23; Gen 23:17-19, respectively), the names are likely personifications of places.

WESLEY I. TOEWS

ESHCOL, WADI [נַחַל אֶשְׁכֹּל nakhal 'eshkol]. A wadi, or dried out riverbed, near Hebron, that received its name (Eschol means "cluster") from the extraordinary cluster of grapes the Israelite spies brought from there after having spied out the land of Canaan (Num 13:22-24; 32:9).

The area around Hebron has been well suited to viticulture in both the past and the present, especially to the north. This has led to an association of the modern site of Burj Haskeh with the Wadi Eshcol, since it is just north of Hebron (3 km), at the head of a wadi, and rich in vineyards.

RALPH K. HAWKINS

ESHEK ee'shik [עֵשֶׁק 'esheq]. A Benjaminite descended from Saul who was the father of Ulam, Jeush, and Eliphelet (1 Chr 8:39). He and his sons are absent from a similar list in 1 Chr 9:35-44.

ESHMUNAZAR. The name of several kings of SIDON, most notably the 5th cent. BCE king Eshmunazar II. This dynasty helped the Persians conquer Egypt in 526 BCE. The Phoenician name most likely means "Eshmun is a helper," referring to the healing deity Eshmun centered in Sidon and sometimes identified with Asclepius. Inscriptions of Eshmunazar II's reign state that Sidon had been given control of Dor and Joppa, and that he built many temples. Eshmunazar II's sarcophagus, unearthed in 1855 and now in the Louvre, contains a twenty-two-line inscription revealing contemporary attitudes toward death.

R. JUSTIN HARKINS

ESHNUNNA LAWS. A collection of cuneiform laws composed in the kingdom of Eshnunna (modern Tell Asmar on the Diyala) during the reign of Dadusha, an early contemporary of HAMMURABI of Babylon. The laws are similar to the later collection produced by Hammurabi. The Eshnunna collection is preserved on two large tablets excavated at Harmal and on a student exercise tablet containing extracts of the laws, found at Tell Haddad. The collection begins with a date formula in Sumerian, then switches to Akkadian for a list of values for basic commodities and services, and continues in Akkadian with laws formulated in the familiar "if . . . then" pattern. *See* HAMMURABI, CODE OF.

J. J. M. ROBERTS

ESH-SHUNA, TELL (NORTH). *See* SHUNA (NORTH), TELL ESH.

ESHTAOL esh'tay-uhl [אֶשְׁתָּאוֹל 'eshta'ol]. A city in the Judean low country belonging to the tribe of Dan (Josh 19:41). The Samson narrative is situated in this area where the spirit of the Lord began to stir in Samson (Judg 13:25), and where he was buried (Judg 16:31). Eshtaol is also listed as a place from which the Danite tribe began their campaign to take LAISH (Judg 18:2). It was identified as Judahite territory in Judg 15:33.

STEPHANIE SKELLEY-CHANDLER

ESHTEMOA esh'tuh-moh'uh [אֶשְׁתְּמוֹעַ 'eshtemo'a].
1. A descendant of Caleb, the son of Ishbah (1 Chr 4:17). The text may imply that Ishbah was head of a city named Eshtemoa. *See* CALEB, CALEBITES.

2. A Maacathite of the tribe of Judah, the son of Hodiah (1 Chr 4:19). *See* JUDAH, JUDAHITES.

3. One of the cities of refuge assigned to the Levites (Josh 21:14; 1 Chr 6:57 [Heb. 6:42]) located in the mountains of Judah near Hebron. Some of David's loot captured from the Amalekites at ZIKLAG was sent to Eshtemoa in appreciation for help he received while fleeing from Saul (1 Sam 30:28).

MICHAEL G. VANZANT

ESHTON esh'ton [אֶשְׁתּוֹן 'eshton]. The son of Mehir and father of Bethrapha, Paseah, and Tehinnah in the lineage of Judah (and perhaps Caleb) (1 Chr 4:11-12).

ESLI es'li [Ἐσλι Hesli]. Father of Nahum and son of Naggai in Luke's genealogy of Jesus (Luke 3:25), Esli connects Joseph, "adoptive" father of Jesus, to Adam.

ES-SAIDIYEH, TELL. *See* SAIDIYEH, TELL ES.

ES-SAMRA, KHIRBET. *See* SAMRA, KHIRBET ES.

ESSENE GATE es'een [Ἐσσηνῶν πύλη Essēnōn pylē]. South of Herod's tower, Jerusalem's western wall ran through an area called Bēthsō (Βηθσώ) to the Gate of the Essenes (Josephus, *J.W.* 5.145), probably named after an adjacent Essene community. Essenes lived in "no one city," but settled "in large numbers in each one" (*J.W.* 2.124); Philo limited their communities to Judea (*Hypoth.* 11.1). The gate's remains on the southwest hill, present-day Mount Zion, are in a section of wall that bounded the southwest corner of the city. Its lowermost threshold dates from Herod the Great's reign, coinciding with the gap in occupation at Qumran and Herod's esteem for Essenism (Josephus, *Ant.*, 15.372–79), when its Jerusalem community throve. Essene graves have been discovered in nearby East Talpiot. *Bethso* ("house of going forth," i.e., sanitary block) reflects the *Temple Scroll's* sanitation legislation (11Q19 XLVI, 13-46) and Essene scrupulosity (compare *J.W.* 2.147–49). Proximity to the traditional site of the Upper Room (Acts 1:13; 2:1; Mark 15:15; Luke 22:12) suggests Essene influence on the community of goods of Acts (2:42–47; 4:32–5:11; 6:1–6). The mysterious water jar carrying male who led Jesus' disciples to the room for his last supper (Mark 14:13–16) may have been an Essene novice, since women normally carried the water jar. Jesus' host, the Beloved Disciple of John's Gospel (13:21–30), who took Jesus' mother, Mary, into his Jerusalem premises (19:26), may have administered the Upper Room and Essene novice- and guesthouse near the gate.

Bibliography: Brian J. Capper. "'With the Oldest Monks . . .' Light from Essene History on the Career of the Beloved Disciple." *JTS* 49 (1998) 1–55; Bargil Pixner. "Jerusalem's Essene Gateway. Where the Community Lived in Jesus' Time." *BAR* 23 (1997) 22–31, 64, 66–67; Rainer Riesner. "Jesus, the Primitive Community, and the Essene Quarter of Jerusalem." *Jesus and the Dead Sea Scrolls.* James H. Charlesworth, ed. (1992) 198-234.

BRIAN J. CAPPER

ESSENES es´een ['Εσσαῖος Essaios, 'Εσσηνός Essēnos]. The Essenes, a Jewish group attested in the last two centuries BCE and the 1st cent. CE, are mentioned by several ancient authors, with Philo and Josephus offering the earliest extensive accounts of them. The community of the Dead Sea Scrolls may have been a small branch of the larger Essene movement.

A. The Sources
B. The Term and Its Egymology
C. Traits
D. The Essenes and the Community of the Dead Sea Scrolls

A. The Sources

The earliest writer to mention the Essenes is PHILO OF ALEXANDRIA (ca. 20 BCE–50 CE), and he does so in two passages: *Good Person* 75–91 and *Hypoth.* 11.1-18. After Philo, PLINY the Elder, in *Natural History* (completed in 77 CE) provides a much briefer description (5.15, 73) in the context of mentioning towns

from Jericho south down the western side of the Dead Sea. His famous location of a community of Essenes (**Esseni**) north of En Gedi has played an important role in identifying the community of QUMRAN as Essenes.

Around the same time Josephus wrote several statements about the Essenes in his *Jewish War*, with the 2.119-61 being the most extensive (also 1.78-80; 2.113, 567; 3.11; 5.145; *see* JOSEPHUS, FLAVIUS. In his *Antiquities of the Jews* (from the 90s CE) he provides additional information about them (especially in 18.18-22; also 13.171-72; 15.371-79; *Life* 10-11). In his major sections regarding them, Josephus lists them as one among several Jewish groups, including the Pharisees and the Sadducees (first referring to the three in the time of the Hasmonean Jonathan [ca. 150 BCE in *Ant.* 13.171-72]), although he has far more to report about the Essenes than about any other group. There are later sources of information about the Essenes, but they are probably derivative from the earlier ones. For example, Dio of Prusa (in Synesius, *Dio* 3.2) seems to draw on Pliny in locating Essenes near the Dead Sea, while *Haer.* 9.18-28 by Hippolytus of Rome (ca. 170–236) closely parallels the report in Josephus but may have some more accurate readings.

B. The Term and Its Etymology

It is likely that the spellings of *Essene* in the Greek and Latin sources transliterate a Semitic word (either Hebrew or Aram.), just as the associated names Pharisee (**Pharisaios** Φαρισαῖος) and Sadducee (**Saddoukaios** Σαδδουκαῖος) do, but there is uncertainty about what that Semitic word was. Philo uses the plural spelling **Essaioi** (so too Hegesippus) as does Josephus who records the singular form as well (**Essaios** [e.g., *J.W.* 1.78]); for the group he also employs **Essēnoi** ('Εσσηνοί, e.g., *J.W.* 2.160; likewise Hippolytus and Dio). Josephus even resorts to the two different plural forms in the same context (see *Ant.* 15.371, 373). Pliny uses **Esseni**, the Latin equivalent of **Essenoi**. Epiphanius, in his *Pan.* 10.1-5, also refers to **Essenoi** (as a Samaritan group) and in 19.1, 1-4, 10; 5, 1, 6-7; 20.3, 1-4 to Jewish people he calls **Ossaioi** or **Ossenoi**, placing them near the Dead Sea.

The question of etymology was of interest to Philo. In both his descriptions, he suggests that *essaioi* was related to the word for holiness (**hosiotēs** ὁσιότης [*Good Person* 75; *Hypoth.* 11.1]). He was aware, however, that *essaioi* was not actually a Greek word. Modern scholars have offered several proposals for the derivation of the name. One is that it as an Aramaic term equivalent to Syriac khs' (pious one). The element essen- would reflect the absolute plural, while essai- would arise from the emphatic plural. The standard objection to the proposal has been that the word is not attested in a Jewish Aram. work. It has, however, been found in 4Q213a 3-4 6, but the occurrence may not be helpful as it is in an early text (Aramaic Levi), possibly antedating the formation of the Essenes, and is not used there as a designation for a member of a group. Another possibility is to relate *Essene* to Aramaic ʾsyʾ (healers); in this connection, scholars often refer to the Therapeutai (healers) who are described by Philo in *On the Contemplative Life* and closely resemble the Essenes (and see Josephus, *J.W.* 2.136). However, Philo seems to distinguish the two groups, not identify them. A plausible case can be made that *Essene* is an Aramaizing spelling of the Hebrew word ʿosim (עֹשִׂים, "doers" [from ʿasah עָשָׂה]) in the sense that they are doers of the Torah. This is a phrase attested in Qumran texts (1QpHab VII, 10-12; VIII, 1-3). No explanation is, however, free of difficulties.

C. Traits

Philo and Josephus, though each perhaps shaped his accounts of the Essenes for his own purposes, highlight a number of the same characteristics. Both report that the Essenes, who numbered more than 4,000 (*Good Person* 75; *Ant.* 18.20), cultivated a holy form of life (*Good Person* 75, 83-84, 88-91; *Hypoth.* 11.2, 18; *J.W.* 2.119, 128, 133, etc.). They also place emphasis on the specific nature of that sanctified way: they lived together and had no private property but rather a community of goods such that everything was placed at the disposal of each member of the group. In this manner they met the needs of all, including the sick and aged (*Good Person* 77, 85-87; *Hypoth.* 11.1, 4, 5, 10, 11, 13; *J.W.* 2.122, 124-27; *Ant.* 18.20). Both also note that the Essenes were found in many towns (*Good Person* 76; *Hypoth.* 11.1; *J.W.* 2.124) and that they were industrious workers who shunned luxury, aiming only for what was necessary (*Good Person* 76, 78; *Hypoth.* 11.6, 8, 10-11; *J.W.* 2.120, 122, 129, 131; *Ant.* 18.19). They comment that the Essenes avoided marriage in view of their low estimate of women's ways (*Hypoth.* 11.14-17; *J.W.* 2.120-21, 161; *Ant.* 18.21), although Josephus adds that there was a group of Essenes who did marry (*J.W.* 2.160). Philo says that the Essenes avoided philosophy apart from the teaching about God's existence and creation of the world (*Good Person* 80); Josephus, in what seems a related vein, highlights their understanding of fate—that all happens according to her decree (*Ant.* 13.172). Both speak of the Essene views about sacrifice, with Philo saying they did not sacrifice animals (*Good Person* 75) and Josephus indicating there was something unusual about their practice in this regard but a textual difficulty renders the passage difficult to understand (*Ant.* 18.19). They also say the Essenes had no slaves (*Good Person* 79; *Ant.* 18.21).

Josephus has more to say about the admission procedures and other rules of the group (especially *J.W.* 2.125-48). He also describes their eschatology at some length (an immortality of the soul [*J.W.* 2.151-57]), although the closely parallel version of Hippolytus attributes to them a belief in resurrection of bodies (*Haer.* 9.26-27). Josephus adds the comment that the Essene regimen resembles that of the Pythagoreans (*Ant.* 15.371)—a claim that can to some extent be documented from sources about the Pythagoreans. In his narratives Josephus also mentions several Essenes, some of whom were accurate predictors—Judas (*J.W.* 1.78-80), Simon (*J.W.* 2.113), Manaemus (*Ant.* 15.371-79; because of him Herod treated the Essenes well)—a trait that he attributes to the Essenes (*J.W.* 2.159). He names John the Essene as a commander over a toparchy during the Jewish revolt against Rome (*J.W.* 2.567) and praises him highly (3.11); moreover, he records that Essenes were tortured by Romans at that time but would not blaspheme the lawgiver or eat forbidden foods (2.152).

D. The Essenes and the Community of the Dead Sea Scrolls

A number of the first experts to see the texts from Qumran cave 1 proposed that the community associated with the scrolls was a group of Essenes (*see* DEAD SEA SCROLLS). Not only are there striking similarities between the ancient descriptions of the Essenes and the contents of the scrolls but Pliny the Elder wrote that Essenes lived on the west side of the DEAD SEA north of EN-GEDI. The Roman geographer added a brief description of those Essenes that mentions their community of goods (they are without money) and their practice of celibacy (they are without women). The texts from QUMRAN, especially ones dealing with the organization and practices of the group (e.g., the *Rule of the Community*, the *Damascus Document*), evidence a number of close parallels with the ancient descriptions. They too speak of a community of goods (see 1QS V, 2-3; VI, 18-23) and a belief in pre-determinism (e.g., 1QS III, 13–IV, 26). A lengthy series of weighty parallels emerges, while there are also agreements on minor points such as the prohibition of spitting in a community meeting (1QS VII, 15; *J.W.* 2.147). As a result, a large number of scholars, though not all, have identified the scrolls community as Essene. One can at least say they more nearly resemble the Essenes than any other group identified in the ancient sources.

Bibliography: A. Adam. *Antike Berichte über die Essener* (1972); T. Beale. *Josephus' Descriptions of the Essenes Illustrated by the Dead Sea Scrolls* (1988); R. Bergmeier. *Die Essener-Berichte des Flavius Josephus: Quellenstudien zu den Essenertexten im Werk des Jüdischen Historiographen* (1993); J. Taylor. *Pythagoreans and Essenes: Structural Parallels* (2004); G. Vermes and M. Goodman. *The Essenes According to the Classical Sources* (1989).

JAMES C. VANDERKAM

ESTHER es´tuhr [אֶסְתֵּר ʾester; ᾽Εσθήρ Esthēr]. An orphan adopted by her cousin Mordecai, Esther appears in the book that bears her name as Mordecai's ward and as one of many virgin girls rounded up as potential replacements for the exiled Queen Vashti. Vashti's crime—refusing to appear before King Ahasuerus—and the unnerved response of the king's advisors (1:16-18) set off the gender dynamics of Esther's rise to the court and her actions there. She is singled out by the eunuch Hegai, in charge of the virgins' harem, apparently for her malleablility (2:9, 15). Mordecai seems to have recommended this strategy of chameleon-like malleability (though he uses no such strategy himself) in instructing her not to reveal her Jewishness to the court (2:10, 20).

Esther's emergence as a character in her own right occurs only as she moves toward the strategic revelation of her ethnicity to Ahasuerus and to Mordecai's (and by extension, the Jews') mortal enemy, Haman. Her initial incomprehension to Mordecai's act of public protest (4:4) suggests that in the process of being accepted as a Gentile at the court, Esther has lost touch with the concerns of her people. Interestingly, although the decree that the Jews be annihilated comes from the court, Mordecai hears it outside the king's gate before Esther, tucked away under the court's wing, knows of it. She has in effect traded her ethnic identity for an intimate knowledge of how to survive at the court itself. In her exchange with Mordecai, he tells her the status of their people and she tells him the laws of entry to the court—each information of which the other was heretofore apparently ignorant (4:7, 11). The drama of Esther's character resides in her risky but successful efforts to regain her hidden Jewishness while maintaining her proximity to power.

Like most courageous survivor-saviors, however, Esther's methods are not morally innocent. While Vashti refused for reasons of personal dignity to go in to the king's banquet at his invitation, Esther must put all dignity aside and go uninvited to the king to invite him to the banquet/s she prepares. All of this food, humility, and service turn out to be a kind of long-term seduction, by means of which she gains control over the king's fickle decrees.

Unlike the threatening Vashti, Esther, because of the demands of her minority ethnic identity, uses her sexuality in ways that are very compatible with the patriarchal system in which she lives. Tellingly, the only man to whom she talks back is Mordecai, who is also the only Jew with whom she speaks. She allows the eunuchs (those useful gender go-betweens) to show her what will please men, and she proceeds to please men. Through her exploitation of her sexuality, the king not only executes Haman, but endorses a reversal of his thoughtless decree that the Jews be annihilated. The king's earlier thoughtless decree on the subordination of women (1:19) stands, in some

sense reinforced by Esther's pleasing manipulation of her husband, the king.

NICOLE WILKINSON DURAN

ESTHER, ADDITIONS TO es´tuhr. Along with the Hebrew (MT) version of Esther there exist two Greek versions of the story in the Septuagint (LXX) and the A Text. Common to these two Greek texts are six blocks of material absent from the Hebrew, commonly termed the Additions and identified by the letters A through F. The Additions were clearly introduced at a later time, and the fact that Hebrew was the original language gives an impression of differing origins for their composition. That this book exhibits such a complicated textual history suggests how significant the Esther story must have been in early Judaism, as various communities reworked and adapted the story for their use. The extra details depict the inner emotions and piety of the characters and portray the events and outcome as under divine direction. As Hebrew Esther does not mention God, the Additions make the Greek versions overtly religious.

Additions A and F describe a prophetic dream. Addition B follows Esth 3:13 and provides a verbatim text of Haman's edict; similarly Addition E follows Esth 8:12 with Mordecai's counter-edict. Lengthy and heartfelt prayers, first of Mordecai and then of Esther, comprise Addition C (following Esth 4:17). Addition D (which replaces Esth 5:1-2) presents a significantly more dramatic version of Esther's entrance before the king. A colophon appended to the LXX version attributes the translation to Lysimachus. *See* ESTHER, BOOK OF.

LINDA DAY

Scala/Art Resource

Figure 1: Megillat Esther in Silver Container. Museum of the Old Jewish Cemetery, Prague, Czech Republic.

ESTHER, BOOK OF es´tuhr [אֶסְתֵּר ʾester]. A narrative book in the Ketuvim (Writings), the third section of the TANAKH. Its title derives from Queen Esther, the story's main protagonist, and it is one of three books in the biblical tradition (along with the books of Ruth and Judith) to have been given a female name (*see* ESTHER). Set in the Persian Empire, the book describes the Jews' endangerment and subsequent deliverance,

through Esther's initiative and ingenuity, from the genocide plotted against them. It is one of the five Megilloth, or scrolls, in the Hebrew Scriptures and is often
referred to simply as "the Megillah" ("the Scroll"; see
Fig. 1). The book of Esther explains the origins of the
Jewish festival of PURIM, which is celebrated annually
in the springtime on the 14th and 15th of Adar.

A. Division and Contents
B. Literary Qualities
C. Motifs
D. Original Context
E. Cultural Concerns
F. Theological Significance
Bibliography

A. Division and Contents

The book represents a well-unified narrative, exhibiting a cohesive plot and a linear structure.

1:1-9—The story opens with the descriptions of two
glamorous parties, one for kingdom officials and the
other for all the people in the citadel of SUSA, thrown
by the Persian King AHASUERUS. Queen VASHTI also
gives a separate party for all the women.

1:10–2:4—At the second party's conclusion, the
inebriated king commands Vashti to come to the men's
party so that he might show off her great beauty. She
refuses. The royal advisors suggest, first, that Vashti
be banished for her disobedience and a kingdomwide
decree asserting male domestic authority be disseminated, and second, that all the kingdom's beautiful
young women be brought to Susa so that Ahasuerus
might choose a new queen.

2:5-20—Two Jews are introduced, Mordecai and
his foster daughter Esther. Esther is taken into the selection process, quickly becomes a favorite in the palace,
and is selected by the king.

2:21–3:15—Mordecai refuses to bow down to
HAMAN, the king's second-in-command, which enrag-
es him. Vowing revenge, Haman casts lots to determine
an auspicious date, then bribes King Ahasuerus to issue
a decree for the Jews' destruction.

4:1-17—Esther and Mordecai converse about what
is to be done, and Esther agrees to risk her life to
request an audience with the king.

5:1-8—Three days later Esther approaches Ahasuerus to request that he and Haman attend a party.

5:9–6:14—Seeing Mordecai on his journey home,
Haman again becomes angry and, in consultation with
his friends, determines to hang him on a high gallows.
In a series of coincidences in the royal bedchamber, Ahasuerus is read an account from the royal annals about
how Mordecai once foiled an assassination attempt
and vows to recognize Mordecai's loyalty at the very
moment when Haman is seeking audience with him for
permission to kill Mordecai. Instead, Haman ends up
leading a grand procession to publicly honor Mordecai.

7:1-10—At Esther's second party she reveals that
she herself is one of the Jews whom Haman's edict
would kill. At this news Ahasuerus becomes angry with
Haman and orders his execution.

8:1-17—Ahasuerus grants Esther and Mordecai
permission to write a counter-decree allowing the Jews
to defend themselves against their enemies.

9:1-19—When the fateful day arrives, the Jews
suffer no casualties but all who choose to attack them
are killed.

9:20–10:3—Mordecai and Esther send letters to all
Jews, establishing that henceforth the holiday of Purim
be celebrated as a commemoration of their redemption.

B. Literary Qualities

The book is aesthetically composed, an example of
fine literature. The narrative is presented in a straightforward style with relatively little direct dialogue. The
plot does not have a single climax but a series of
defining pivotal moments (e.g., Esther's decision to act
at 4:15-16; the prefiguration of the changing status of
Mordecai and Haman at 6:11-13; the summarizing
statement of final reversal and Jewish victory at 9:1).

The book reflects aspects of various genres of biblical
and ancient literature: folklore, court legend, wisdom
literature, the establishment and celebration of a new
holiday of a festal etiology, and the farce, parodies, and
exaggerations of carnivalesque literature. On the whole,
the book can best be classified as an example of the genre
of Jewish novel (see LITERARY INTERPRETATION, OT).

The tone of the book is ironic and humorous
throughout. Many of its details are unbelievably incongruous and exaggerated. The plot progresses by means
of a series of highly improbable events. Some of the
characters function more as types than as full-fledged
characters: Haman as the quintessential villain, Ahasuerus as the dim-witted foreign ruler, Memucan as the
loyal servant. Esther is the only character who is multi-
dimensional and who exhibits change and growth.

C. Motifs

The book exhibits several themes, all interconnected and dependent upon the others, that lend a sense
of symmetry to the narrative. A series of ten parties
occurs, culminating in Purim, the ultimate celebration. Almost half of the instances of the term mishteh
(מִשְׁתֶּה, "party") in the Bible appear in this book. The
focus of these parties is not on food but on drink (1:7-
8; 3:15; 5:6; 7:2), the ensuing inebriation illustrated
by the resultant illogical actions of the characters, and
significant shifts in fortune take place during them.
Reversals of circumstances are frequent, when that
which occurs is the direct opposite of what is expected.
For example, the Jewish underdogs come out on top,
grief turns into joy, the gallows intended for Mordecai is
used instead for Haman. Writing reflects the kingdom's
bureaucracy, as decisions do not remain oral but must

be written down, and even rewritten again and again into multiple languages. A series of several letters is written and sent throughout the land (1:22; 3:12-15; 8:8-14; 9:20-23, 29-32) and events are recorded in the official annals (6:1-2; 10:2). The book emphasizes laws, as numerous official commands and edicts are promulgated. Obedience and disobedience to these commands also function as a theme, as the choices a character makes either to obey or to disobey drives the progression of events and their outcomes. For instance, Esther obeys Mordecai's instructions (2:10, 20); then he later obeys her (4:16-17); the Jewish community obeys them both (9:23-32); they both disobey royal commands (3:2; 4:11), and it is Vashti's initial blunt disobedience that throws the events into motion (1:10-12). Concern for HONOR pervades the book, which reflects the shame and honor codes of ancient society. Especially Haman, but also to a lesser degree Ahasuerus, is concerned for personal honor; though not seeking it, Mordecai receives public honor; the Jews' shame turns to ultimate honor with their final victory.

D. Original Context

The book is set in the Persian Empire and it contains many details that correspond to what we know about the history of this time and place (*see* PERSIA, HISTORY AND RELIGION OF). Ahasuerus is commonly thought to reflect the Persian king XERXES I (486–465 BCE). The city of Susa served as his winter residence and the administrative capital of the empire, and inscriptional evidence testifies to its luxurious and costly construction. The book portrays further aspects of the Persian Empire, including its geographical extent, its equine postal system, its seven-member advisory council, and its maintenance of official written records. There is also evidence to suggest that the Persian political administration, especially during the earlier stages of its history, showed a significant degree of tolerance toward the local languages, laws, customs, and religious practices of the various ethnic groups in its population, a tolerance that appears also in the book of Esther as non-Persians (Esther, Haman, Mordecai) are promoted to high positions and laws are translated into local dialects (1:22; 3:12; 8:9). Many of the story's details, however, are historically improbable, e.g., selection criteria for its queens, the number of provinces, the concept of unalterable laws, and numerous personal names. In sum, the book is certainly a fictional story, but one in which the author(s) incorporated details that were known at the time about Persian history and culture. Because of its Persian setting and its lack of interest in Israel, Jerusalem, or temple, the provenance of the book is most certainly not Palestine but elsewhere in the Jewish DIASPORA. Most scholars generally date the book's composition to the 4th or 3rd cent. BCE.

Along with the Hebrew version (the MT), the story has survived in two other (Greek) versions. Both of these versions contain six segments of material (traditionally designated as the "Additions") not included in the Hebrew version, and in one of the Greek versions (the A, or Alpha, text) the details vary so significantly from the Hebrew that it probably represents a different tradition of the story altogether. In addition, it is possible that chaps. 9–10 are the work of one or even two later authors. These numerous reworkings suggest that the story was well used and popular in its time. As it was written explicitly to portray a time after the exile (2:6) when many Jews were living away from their homeland of Judah, the book must have successfully addressed the challenges of diaspora life in a foreign environment experienced by its original audiences (*see* ESTHER, ADDITIONS TO).

E. Cultural Concerns

Inherent in the book are issues of cultural identity and minority survival, presenting the situation of those who live within a culture that is not their own and the prejudice and persecution that can arise in such circumstances (*see* FOREIGN, FOREIGNER). At its center is an ethnic conflict that begins on a personal level but escalates to involve the entire kingdom. The book portrays varying degrees of both cultural assimilation and the maintenance of ethnic community. An individual who is known by two different names (2:7), Jewish "Hadasseh"/Persian "Esther" is a prime example of persons who learn how to live between two cultures. Gender identity is also a significant issue. VASHTI, Esther, and ZERESH are representatives of strong women who are forced to make their choices within the limits of a patriarchal system, and the eunuchs, likewise, are marginal figures who bridge male and female realms. In the book ethnic and gender identities do not remain stable but shift as individuals encompass multiple identities (*see* ETHNICITY; EUNUCH; GENDER; PATRIARCHAL LANGUAGE).

F. Theological Significance

Any reader may well be warranted in wondering whether the book even holds any theological or religious import. God is not active in the events, nor even mentioned. In addition, other elements typical in biblical literature that might suggest a religious interest (Torah observance, prayer, temple worship, covenant language, etc.) are also not part of the book's concern. The emphasis is instead on human initiative, responsibility, and accountability, for it is through the direct action of human individuals that the successful outcome is achieved. The Greek versions of the story address the issue of divine absence by directly writing God into the events, presenting the victorious outcome as divine design, and portraying Esther and Mordecai as pious persons. Scholars are divided on the question of whether the book is religious or secular in orientation. Some do find it to suggest a God who is present but chooses to remain hidden. They maintain that the many reversals of fortune are not due to chance alone but reflect a divine hand guiding the process. Yet one might argue that the book's theological ambiguity, the absence of any reference to God, is not a problem but a benefit. This characteristic reflects well the ambiguities inherent in living a faithful life, recognizing that often God cannot be seen clearly and that it can be impossible from a human perspective to know with certainty, in any given situation, if or how God might be active.

The book stands squarely within the biblical tradition, as other parts of the canon are echoed in it. It exhibits a strong intertextuality with Israel's ongoing story of its origins and history. Esther reflects MOSES in the exodus, delivering her people and establishing a festival, and the book shares a similar court setting, plot, and linguistic expressions with the Joseph story (Gen 37–50). First Samuel 15, the story of the battle between Saul and the Amalekite king Agag continues in the ethnic rivalry between Haman and Mordecai. The book of Esther also shares details with the books of Daniel, Ruth, and Judith.

The holiday of Purim includes strong ethical components. It is a celebration not of national victory but of the time of rest that follows that victory, the Jews' release from danger (9:18-19, 22). Jews of every generation are charged not only to rejoice but also to observe charity and generosity, to give to the poor in their midst. Reading the book after the Shoah, or Holocaust, brings added responsibilities to theological interpretation. The genocidal horrors it portrays can no longer be treated as only part of a work of fiction but are real and experienced, and Jewish victory cannot be unquestioningly asserted. Those in the Christian tradition are further obligated to acknowledge the anti-Semitism that has frequently been a part of the interpretation of this story throughout many centuries. A post-Shoah understanding of this book must find theological meaning not in terms of ultimate triumph over persecution but at the level of human resistence, of individuals courageously coming forward to try to prevent evil from running its course (*see* HOLOCAUST AND BIBLICAL INTERPRETATION).

Bibliography: Timonty K. Beal. *The Book of Hiding: Gender, Ethnicity, Annihilation, and Esther* (1997); Carol M. Bechtel. *Esther.* Interpretation (2002); Adele Berlin. *Esther.* JPS Bible Commentary (2001); Linda Day. *Esther.* AOTC (2005); Michael V. Fox. *Character and Ideology in the Book of Esther* (2001).

LINDA DAY

ETA [η ē, H Ē]. The seventh letter of the Greek alphabet, based on the Phoenician khet, which became the vowel letter eta, representing long e in contrast with epsilon, the short e. *See* ALPHABET.

ETAM ee′tuhm [עֵיטָם ʿetam; Ἠτάμ Ētam, Ἀιτάμ Aitam]. 1. One of the towns in the territory of Simeon (1 Chr 4:32). Its location is unknown.

2. A town mentioned in Josh 15:59*a* of LXX (not in MT) as being in the region of biblical Judah, near Bethlehem. Its exact location and identity are unknown, but it may be identified with the town mentioned by Josephus (*Ant.* 8.186) as the place to which Solomon would go in the morning. Josephus describes the spot as approximately 6 to 8 mi. from Jerusalem and characterized as being pleasant with gardens and streams of water. This town may be the same one mentioned in 2 Chr 11:6 (compare Josephus *Ant.* 8.246) as having been fortified by REHOBOAM, since it occurs between Bethlehem and Tekoa in the list of fortified cities and is described by Josephus as not far from Jerusalem.

3. Father of Jezreel, Ishma, and Idbash, among the descendants of Judah (1 Chr 4:3). Other place names occur as personal names in this genealogy, indicating that Etam, here, may be the town rather than the person. *See* ETAM, ROCK OF.

C. MARK MCCORMICK

ETAM, ROCK OF [סֶלַע עֵיטָם selaʿ ʿetam]. After Samson's wife and father-in-law were burned by the Philistines, Samson struck them down "hip and thigh," and withdrew to the cleft of rock of ETAM (Judg 15:8). There, too, the men of Judah bound him to deliver him to the Philistines (Judg 15:11-13).

STEPHANIE SKELLEY-CHANDLER

ETERNAL LIFE. *See* IMMORTALITY; LIFE.

ETERNAL PUNISHMENT. *See* HELL.

ETERNITY [עַד ʿadh; αἰών aiōn]. An infinite length of time (Isa 57:15; 2 Esd 8:20). *See* TIME.

ETHAM ee′thuhm [אֵתָם ʾetham]. Etham, rarely mentioned in the Bible (Exod 33:20; Num 33:6-8), is identified as the second itinerary site visited by the Israelites; first SUCCOTH, then Etham. The exact location of Etham or the Wilderness of Etham is highly speculative. Its proximity to Succoth would appear to many to locate Etham in the Nile Delta region (assuming that Tjeku is indeed Succoth). Since the Masoretic Text locates Succoth solely in the Jordan River valley (Gen 33:17; Josh 13:27; Judg 8:4-9; 1 Kgs 7:46), it would render an exact location of Succoth, and thus Etham, difficult. *See* EXODUS, ROUTE OF.

MICHAEL D. OBLATH

ETHAN ee′thuhn [אֵיתָן ʾethan]. 1. An adjective referring to water and streams that are continuous and ever flowing, permanent or enduring (Amos 5:24; Ps 74:15).

2. A wise man called the Ezrahite and used as a comparison for Solomon's wisdom in 1 Kgs 5:11, and for whom Ps 89 is dedicated (v. 1).

3. The son of Zerah, son of Judah and his daughter-in-law Tamar (1 Chr 2:6, 8).

4. An ancestor of Asaph (1 Chr 6:42).

5. A son of Kish (1 Chr 6:44).

C. MARK MCCORMICK

ETHANIM eth´uh-nim [אֵתָנִים ’ethanim]. The pre-exilic name of the seventh month of the Hebrew year, corresponding approximately to September/October (1 Kgs 8:2). ABIB (Exod 13:4), ZIV (1 Kgs 6:1, 37), and BUL (1 Kgs 6:38) are the only other month names extant from the preexilic period, probably derived from the Canaanite calendar.

RALPH K. HAWKINS

ETHANUS i´thay´nuhs [Lat. **Ethanus**]. One of the five scribes trained to write rapidly who accompanies Ezra for forty days to rewrite the law that was previously burned (2 Esd 14:24).

ETHBAAL eth-bay´uhl [אֶתְבַּעַל ’ethba‘al]. King of TYRE (ca. 887–856 BCE) who obtained kingship around age thirty-six through a coup d'état. In his time, Tyre was the preeminent Phoenician city, partly through his bringing SIDON under his control. Ethbaal, "Baal is with him," is referred to as the father of JEZEBEL, who married King AHAB of Israel (1 Kgs 16:31). The description "king of the Sidonians" derives either from his control of Sidon or the fact that "Sidonians" was a general term for Phoenicians.

Bibliography: H. Jacob Katzenstein. *The History of Tyre* (1997).

KEVIN A. WILSON

ETHER ee´thuhr [עֶתֶר ‘ether]. A town in the lowlands of Judah, somewhere near Libnah. In Josh 15:42 it is listed among the towns in the tribal inheritance of Judah. A second reference (Josh 19:7) identifies Ether as part of the inheritance of the tribe of Simeon. Since these lists differ slightly, there is some confusion over their relationship. However, Judg 19:1 explains that the inheritance of the tribe of Simeon lies within that of Judah.

STEPHANIE SKELLEY-CHANDLER

ETHICAL LISTS. *See* LISTS, ETHICAL.

ETHICS IN THE NON-CANONICAL JEWISH WRITINGS. The topic "Ethics in the Non-Canonical Jewish Writings" cannot be dealt with in the same way as ethics in the OT or in the NT, as the Apocrypha and PSEUDE-PIGRAPHA neither represent a specific religious group nor sociological movement, nor do they all originate from the same geographical area and period in history. Instead they come to us from different life settings and represent many different, often unknown, groups and socioreligious traditions in Second Temple Judaism

(538 BCE to 70/135 CE). Some of the main themes of these writings, as far as they relate to ethical questions, are: 1) the Torah and wisdom; 2) divine revelation and intervention; 3) the origin of and ways to deal with evil; 4) human responsibility and one's role in society; and 5) the love command and the "Golden Rule."

A. The Non-Canonical Writings
   1. Apocrypha
   2. Pseudepigrapha
      a. Historiography and legend
      b. Ethical writings in narrative form
      c. Ethical writings in pedagogical form
      d. Poetic writings
      e. Apocalyptic
   3. Dead Sea Scrolls
   4. Philo and Josephus
B. Theological Themes
   1. Torah and wisdom
   2. Divine revelation and intervention
   3. The origin of evil and how to deal with it
   4. Human responsibility and society
   5. The love command and the Golden Rule
Bibliography

A. The Non-Canonical Writings

1. Apocrypha

First and Second Maccabees, Wisdom of Solomon, and Sirach are substantial writings with clearly distinguishable ethics representing religious and philosophical views held in Judaism during the early Hellenistic periods (3rd cent. BCE–1st cent. CE). The books of First and Second Maccabees were commissioned by the Hasmonean rulers in the century after the Maccabean Revolt (164 BCE) and represent an inner-Jewish ethic focused on national unity and a fight against Hellenistic-Syrian culture and religion (*see* MACCABEES, FIRST BOOK OF; MACCABEES, SECOND BOOK OF). Their ethics highlight the values that are connected with Judaism as a way of life and are most visible in their identity markers, such as dietary laws, circumcision, and Temple worship. The example of martyrdom for the Jewish cause is employed to stress the importance of keeping God's commandments, as preserved and handed down by ancestral traditions. Moral and, above all, military resistance against the Syrian occupancy is glorified using vivid descriptions of the God-given success of the Maccabean brothers in the war with Antiochus IV Epiphanes. The ethics of First and Second Maccabees are therefore national, social, and inner-Jewish at the same time, all subordinated to the concept of Jewish identity and the struggle for the survival of the Jewish nation. Even the Mosaic laws are subject to this, as the example of the temporary abolishment of Sabbath laws during the war in order to save Jewish life shows (1 Macc 2:41).

Wisdom of Solomon from 1st-cent. CE Egypt represents a synthesis between biblical teaching and Greek philosophy in its treatment of the concept of wisdom (*see* SOLOMON, WISDOM OF). The first six of its nineteen chapters are addressed to the ungodly rulers of the earth and urge them to love justice and avoid perverse words and deeds, as God sees everything and no one escapes final judgment. It describes two opposing ways of life: the just life and the ungodly life. Solomon is the perfect example of the wise person or sage, and personifies wisdom, which existed since the creation of the world and is its ruling principle (chaps. 7–9). Although there are few examples of practical wisdom or ethics, it is obvious that all ethical principals are to be derived from the leading principle of God's wisdom and righteousness, which rules this world.

In SIRACH, the Greek translation of an originally Hebrew work ascribed to Ben Sira around 200 BCE and written down by his grandson in the year 132 BCE, we find the commandment to love oneself connected with the command to love (and free) one's slave (7:21). It has also been linked to the Golden Rule with the anthropological argument that the neighbor, including the slave, is a human being too (31:15). As in Tobit, but more explicitly employing Greek philosophical concepts as in the Wisdom of Solomon, the author of Sirach equates the divine teaching found in the "books of Moses" with the Greek concept of wisdom. In both cases, divine teaching and wisdom include the practical call to act righteously. Believing and acting are here seen as two sides of the same coin. If you believe that a human being is like you, that is to say, that others have been created in the image of God in just the same way as you, you will love them like yourself, whether they are slave or free. This is simultaneously found in Torah and in the Hellenistic principle of the Golden Rule.

2. Pseudepigrapha

The Pseudepigrapha are usually considered to belong to the conceptual world of the latter parts of the OT and of early Judaism, but are seen by some as presenting more of the early Christian and Patristic traditions. Christianity, indeed, has preserved most of these writings, as the emerging church had an interest in them, whereas rabbinic Judaism rejected the Pseudepigrapha or was even unfamiliar with them. Despite their large number (over seventy) and diverse character, for which reason they cannot be summarized under one title or theology, the Pseudepigrapha can be arranged, though imperfectly, by genre, as is done here, namely, in: 1) Historiography and Legend; 2) Ethical Writings in Narrative Form; 3) Ethical Writings in Pedagogical Form; 4) Poetic Writings; 5) Apocalyptic.

a. Historiography and legend. The *Fourth Book of Baruch (Paraleipomena of Jeremiah)* and LIVES OF THE PROPHETS, in particular, give examples of the lives of the prophets, which because of their martyrdom are worthy to be held in memory, and because of

their exemplary lives, are worthy to be followed (*see* BARUCH, FOURTH BOOK OF). Although they do not elaborate on ethical themes in a systematic or even practical way, these texts call, e.g., for the graves of the prophets to be kept in honor, and, in the *Fourth Book of Baruch*, underline the importance of remembering the horror of the destruction of Jerusalem and the Temple.

b. Ethical writings in narrative form. In the apocryphal legendary book of Tobit (*see* TOBIT, BOOK OF) from the 3rd cent. BCE dealing with Tobit, Sara, and their son Tobias, Tobit teaches his son to live a righteous life after his father's death and gives a number of examples from practical wisdom, of which one is the Golden Rule: "And what you hate, do not do to anyone" (4:15). Although the booklet gives no explanation of it, it is the oldest example of the use of the Golden Rule in Judaism, a popular ethical maxim taken over from the Greek world (*see* ARISTEAS, LETTER OF). The context of the book of Tobit is that of diaspora Judaism and the need to find a middle way between the adoption of foreign customs and philosophical/ethical principles and at the same time the keeping of the Torah. It is easier to find this middle way in the realm of ethics than in the observance of the more specifically Jewish customs.

Jewish identity—or, more generally speaking, the question of what constitutes Jewish practice—remains the ruling principle behind this cultural mediation, but as the example of the Golden Rule shows, non-Jewish ethical principles do not have to threaten this identity, as they are of a more universal nature and can also be found in the Books of Moses. Understood in this way, Tobit reveals its deeper meaning as it points to the Torah as source of all moral guidelines. The book of Tobit, theologically and anthropologically speaking, then emphasizes three main concepts and employs them as keywords throughout the book: truth, righteousness, and mercy.

These concepts are first of all attributed to God, but are also expected from humans as a response to God. Righteousness is understood in a very practical way as being merciful and doing good deeds (4:7), and it is in the end Tobit himself who gives the best example of how to act righteously in a foreign land (1:17-20; 2:1-8). Finally, the didactic parts of the book underline the importance of righteousness toward especially the needy, one's brothers, and one's parents (4:3.7-13:16).

In the *Letter of Aristeas*, written between 127 and 118 BCE and narrating the Greek translation of the OT produced in commission for the Ptolemaic king Ptolemaeus II Philadelphus, the king asks, "What does wisdom teach?" The thirteenth of the seventy-two Jewish translators answers with the Golden Rule: "Insofar as you do not wish evils to come upon you, but to partake of every blessing (it would be wisdom), if you put this into practice with your subjects, including the wrongdoers, and if you admonished the good and upright also mercifully. For God guides all men in mercy" (§ 207). This is one of the earliest examples of the Jewish use of the Golden Rule in its negative and positive form, here understood against the background of the command to love one's neighbor and argued for with the theological concept of *Imitatio Dei*: Loving one's neighbor is a way of following, obeying, and imitating God. At the same time the author shows that as far as ethics are concerned he considers Greek philosophy and biblical teaching to say basically the same thing.

In the book of *Jubilees* (see JUBILEES, BOOK OF) an example of the "Rewritten Bible" genre from between the Maccabean Revolt in 164 BCE and 150 BCE that divides Israel's history into periods of fifty-year jubilees, we find the Golden Rule in its most popular context, namely, as practical wisdom teaching from parents to children: Love your brothers like someone loves his own soul and do good (36:4). The command to love one's neighbor is listed here among other commandments, equated with the Golden Rule, and defined as doing good. At the same time it is presented as biblical teaching and as the wisdom taught by life itself; in other words, neighbor love is part of human and natural law.

In this context, PSEUDO-PHILO or *Liber antiquitatum biblicarum*, written after 70 CE, is of interest too, because it employs a style and expresses a point of view that is also found in other writings, though much less consistently used, i.e., than of ideal or exemplary biblical figures, who, because of their exemplary lives or righteous deeds or moral behavior, are worthy of imitation.

Finally, the romance of JOSEPH AND ASENETH gives an impressive and entertaining example of how Judaism seems to have attracted non-Jews, as it tells the story of chaste Joseph and the Egyptian princess Aseneth, who falls in love with him and, after a mysterious transformative experience, takes over all the practices and beliefs taught by Moses.

c. Ethical writings in pedagogical form. In the Testaments of the Twelve Patriarchs, a collection of twelve single smaller works, of which some go back to a Jewish source from the 2nd and 1st cent. BCE, but which as a whole have been edited in final Christian form in the 1st and 2nd cent. CE, we find the commandment to love one's neighbor combined with the commandment to love God (*T. Iss.* 7:6), a combination otherwise found only in the NT (Mark 12:28-34 and par.), but as such going back to the OT, where the commandment to love one's neighbor (Lev 19:18) is argued for with the call of *Imitatio Dei* (Lev 19).

In other passages, the Love Command is connected with the promise of blessing (*T. Sim.* 4:6), with a call to show mercy to those who are poor and ill (*T. Iss.* 5:2), with the call to include the animals in one's neighbor love (*T. Zeb.* 5:1), and with the call to do good (*T. Benj.* 4:3). Whereas there is no systematic treatment of ethics or a connecting with philosophical reasoning or Greek philosophy, ethics is very much understood in its practical form as moral teaching with an emphasis on doing good and being merciful, much in line with the teachings of the OT.

All testaments, but especially the *Testament of Joseph*, consider the patriarchs to be exemplars due to their behavior and high moral standards. For this reason the patriarchs are narrated here giving farewell speeches while lying on their deathbeds. Within this framework a life according to the Torah is depicted, and lists of practical ethics form the main content of these moral teachings from parents to children.

Other testaments, such as the *Testament of Job*, employ more or less the same technique and share a similar theology and ethic (see JOB, TESTAMENT OF; PATRIARCHS, TESTAMENTS OF THE TWELVE).

d. Poetic writings. Among the Poetic Writings most relevant from an ethical point of view are the *Psalms of Solomon* and *Pseudo-Phocylides*. The *Psalms of Solomon* are a compendium of (wisdom-) theological and anthropological beliefs of Pharisaic origin in the form of psalms dating from the second third of the 1st cent. BCE. The ethics in these eighteen psalms are shaped by the eschatological expectations of the author, who expected that, at the end of days soon to come, the sinners would be punished and the righteous would be rewarded. Until then, education about righteousness plays an important role and at the end of days a Davidic messiah is expected to play a leading part.

In the description of the importance of righteousness, education, and the punishment of the sinners and rewards of the righteous at the end of days (in order to do justice to their present suffering), the author reflects what Pharisaic circles had considered to be important since the 2nd cent. BCE, and much ethical teaching would be derived from this basic way of thinking: God's teachings are not only mediated through the Law of Moses but also revealed directly. God is judge and king, is merciful and loves God's people, helps the needy, and is thus the perfect exemplar. However, in all of this, humanity has a free will to choose to follow or not, and the righteous one has the ability to ask for forgiveness, to repent, to fast, etc. The fact that humankind is divided at all into righteous and sinners is partly due to God's *providentia*. In the background stands a concept of God as ruling king, who allows the righteous to suffer only in order to try them, and an understanding of punishment as a means for God to express his love (see *Pss. Sol.* 3:3-10; 10:1-3; 13:8-10; 16:14; and 18:4).

PSEUDO-PHOCYLIDES is a Jewish writing dating from the 1st cent. BCE or very early 1st cent. CE dedicated to ethical teaching, as it consists of *sententia* or *gnomai* in the form of a moral poem in 219 hexameters later divided into 230 verses. It epitomizes the teaching of the Torah for Hellenized Jews by incorporating non-biblical material, both post-biblical wisdom literature and Greco-Roman popular ethical and philosophical concepts. However, it also has parallels with the rabbinic writing of *Derekh Eretz Zuta*, as it employs the seven Noachidic laws. Its main ethical teachings can be divided systematically into: 1) sexual ethics; 2) mercy toward the weak; and 3) sincerity toward the neighbor. The ethics of Pseudo-Phocylides is furthermore universalistic in outlook and consists of practical rules for everyday life, both personal and social.

The teachings of this writing can be divided as follows: Prologue (1–2); Summary of the Decalogue (3–8); Exhortations to Justice (9–21); Admonitions to Justice (22–41); Love of Money and Its Consequences (42–47); Honesty, Modesty, and Self-Control (48–58); Moderation in All Things (59–69); The Danger of Envy and Other Vices (70–96); Death and Afterlife (97–115); The Instability of Life (116–121); Speech and Wisdom, Man's Distinction, Avoidance of Wickedness, and Virtuous Life (122–152); The Usefulness of Labor (153–174); Marriage, Chastity, and Family Life (175–227); Epilogue (228–230).

Behind the book stands a concept of God as someone who is creator and king of the universe, who is mighty and wise, whose universe exists in harmony, who judges humankind after death, and who is the ruler of everyone's soul. As far as moral behavior is concerned, one is expected to honor God in everything and above everything, share everything God has given with those in need, use the ability to reason with wisdom and to acquire wisdom, and to avoid evil, especially sexual sins (vv. 177–94). Furthermore, one is expected to labor in honesty (153–74), limit oneself and be modest, execute justice and mercy, and have stable social relationships, i.e. between husband and wife, parents and children, masters and slaves, and even between friends and enemies (see, respectively, 195–97, 207–9, 223–27, 142, 218, 140–42).

e. Apocalyptic. The most important apocalyptic writings in early Judaism also mark the beginning and end of Apocalyptic thinking in Judaism: the books of *1 Enoch* partly going back to the 4th/3rd cent. BCE, but mostly from the 1st cent. BCE and CE; the canonical book of Daniel from the 2nd cent. BCE; and *4 Ezra* as well as *2 Baruch* from the beginning of the 2nd cent CE. They all, though in theologically different ways, have the origin of evil as their main topic and attribute evil to either the fallen angels, to foreign powers, or to the first human beings and see humankind's possibilities to act ethically as rather limited.

Most of the apocalypses have developed a detailed system and explanation of how evil came into the world, how evil has influenced the course of history, and how evil will do so until the end of this world.

Evil is mostly represented in the oppression of Israel by cosmic and/or foreign powers as well as in a variety of sins that come with this. In this respect they differ from the Prophets, who blame mankind and the evil heart—and not the heavenly or other powers for bringing sin and destruction upon the world. The teaching of the authors of the apocalypses basically consists of giving to humankind the knowledge of its origin, how to follow the path of righteousness, and how to develop patience in times of distress.

The ethics found in these writings are principally interim ethics, i.e., ethics for the period between the presence of the authors and the end of days, and are meant for a minority group, not developed for the members of society at large, but for a group of persecuted martyrs and saints. This "holy remnant" still lives according to the Laws of Moses in a basically vicious and violent environment with no hope for survival. The goal of this kind of interim ethics is to help the group endure the final days of humanity, which will be a time of wars, famine, and global destruction, in order to prepare for the days of the Messiah. He is about to come soon and bring a new law and a time of righteousness to the world.

Understood within the context of early Jewish society, the followers of these apocalyptic thinkers did not consider themselves obliged to uphold the moral standards and ethical rules of the society in which they lived, as they were basically opposed to this society and everything that it represented, including its ethics and morals. The apocalypticists considered society's *mores* and ethics to be expressions of wickedness, and offered many examples of this. The holy remnant they thought themselves to be would endure until the time of distress was over, when they could give up their "interim ethics" and begin to live according to the new or newly explained Torah of the Messiah.

First Enoch has a long history and the origin of some of its oldest parts may date back to the 4th and 3rd cent. BCE. Like no other apocalypse before or after, the Ethiopic book of *1 Enoch* sees only one reason for the origin of evil in the world in that it blames the fallen angels and the Great Adversary for having brought destruction in all of its forms to the world and humankind. Between God and God's angels, and the Adversary and the fallen angels, there is an ongoing cosmic battle, in which the nations of the world are mere marionettes (*see* ENOCH, FIRST BOOK OF).

Here, there is more distance between God and humankind, with hardly any room left for human free will, as everything depends on the outcome of this cosmic battle. What awaits human beings, who possess an eternal soul, is the final judgment and, with it, either reward or punishment depending on which side of the battle they stood. As everything had been determined and evil existed before creation, it is predestination that defines one's fate and hardly anything can be done on the basis of moral reasoning.

Also for the author of *2 Baruch* one of the main reasons to employ a strict eschatological interpretation of Israel's origin, history, and future is to find an answer to the question of the origin of evil (*see* BARUCH, SECOND BOOK OF). He finds it in the first sin committed by Adam, which since then has inhabited human hearts, and has led to death and destruction. With this worldview there is little space left for human action; only a holy remnant has remained to live according to the Law and it is only at the end of time that God will intervene by sending a Messiah, not only to save Israel but also to punish the nations of the world. In this sense the author considers it crucial to teach his audience about the origin of evil, to call for repentance like the biblical prophets, and to comfort the people in times of distress.

Even stronger and with more impact than *2 Baruch* is the theology of *4 Ezra*, who also uses the genre of apocalyptic visions to draw a picture of Israel's history as defined by the evil heart of humankind. This evil heart since Adam is the source of all destruction and because of it the course of history cannot be changed anymore until the very end of days. Then, God will intervene by sending a Messiah. Until then the ethical imperative is to return and repent from doing evil (*see* ESDRAS, FOURTH BOOK OF).

3. Dead Sea Scrolls

Among the DEAD SEA SCROLLS we find Essene and non-Essene writings, the latter being, e.g., biblical manuscripts and writings the Qumran community collected and copied but did not write itself. The former writings were the result of a longer tradition and redaction process during the existence of the community at the shore of the Dead Sea from the mid-2nd cent. BCE–68 CE, for which reason it is difficult to get a clear and compete picture of the ethics of the Essenes.

Already Philo and Josephus praised and admired the high moral standards of the ESSENES, and the Essene writings, such as the RULE OF THE COMMUNITY, the DAMASCUS DOCUMENT, and the RULE OF THE CONGREGATION as well as the *Hodayot* seem to confirm this (*see* THANKSGIVING PSALMS). They describe an abstemious, moderate, and simple life of a community shunning pleasure and passions and nourishing themselves only to beat hunger. Their members did not amass any richness, but shared everything among themselves, and used their clothes until they were completely unusable.

Apart from their practical way of life, they also had an ethical theory, in which they taught their pupils and one another: no slavery, no swearing, no anointing, bathing in cold water before every meal as well as after contacts with nonmembers, wearing white clothes, being extra modest with regard to their natural functions, no marriage, no animal offerings for the Temple, and sharing common meals. It is not clear whether they were also abstemious of wine and meat. In all, the members were called to live a righteous life, be meticulous in their daily practice, separate themselves from the surrounding world and search the Scriptures.

Behind their ethics lies a theology, dualistic in nature and with a clear idea of predestination. God had created man and had appointed two spirits to rule over him: the good spirit of light, truth, and righteousness, and the evil spirit of darkness, error, and perversity, both limited in power until the end of this age (*Rule of the Community*). It is only through discipline and cooperation with the good spirit that man can improve himself. More about this Essene theology, without which the Essene ethics is unthinkable, is found in the *Hodayot*, though not in a systematic but in a more poetic language. Furthermore, there are specific rules for becoming a member of the Community or entering the covenant, both ritualistic and moral in nature (*Damascus Document*). And finally, many of the rules were stricter than generally accepted in the world of the OT, early Judaism, or the NT, such as those connected with keeping the Sabbath or those relating to wars. This set them apart in the eyes of everyone else.

4. Philo and Josephus

The ethics of PHILO OF ALEXANDRIA (ca. 10 BCE–45 CE) depend on his anthropology, which on its turn largely depends on Platonic views. In this sense, humankind lives in a dual world. On the one hand, the human's divine soul belongs to the spiritual world and the realm of angels and demons, whereas the mortal and more animal-like body is part of the earth and the world of the senses. Individual human beings can live closer to the one or to the other world, the latter being the case with the majority of mankind, and the former more rarely taking place in the lives of the truly wise and righteous men, such as Abraham. From this it follows for Philo that man's spirit is close to reason and righteousness, whereas his body is the source of all evil and for the soul a mere prison.

Consequently, the ethics derived from this is an emphasis of shunning every desire, passion, and sensuality, an effort to achieve complete liberation from emotions and the world of the vices and at the same time being taught in how to live a life defined by the cardinal virtues, in all quite similar to the way the Stoics taught. For Philo, however, there was one important difference with Stoic ethics, namely that for him this liberation comes from God and not from humans themselves. Openness toward the Word of God and the final surrender to God enables humans to see their true nature and to have faith in their own destiny, being that of a divine soul, whose world belongs to God. The goal of Philo's ethics, therefore, seems to be the return of the soul to its original bodiless and transcendent condition.

It is not clear where to situate the ethics of Flavius Josephus (ca. 37/38–100 CE; *see* JOSEPHUS,

FLAVIUS). According to his own account he had the background of a Sadducee, but by choice had become a member of the party of the Pharisees. In his youth he had stayed with the Essenes, whereas before and during the First Jewish War against Rome (66–70 CE) he was the leader of a resistance movement in Galilee and closely related to the Zealots and *Sicarii*, but at the end of that war he would turn to the Romans, where he would stay until his death. With such a *Vita* the right label for his ethics seems to be that of an opportunist. And still, his *Jewish War* contains many theological reflections and questions about responsibility and Jewish suffering, whereas the *Antiquities* contain elements of morality and Jewish rights.

From the perspective of the conclusions he reaches at the end of his life, Josephus argues that it is best to accept the fate bestowed by God, even if this means the victory of Rome, the loss of a Jewish state, and the destruction of Jerusalem and the Temple. Those who have not only resisted this fate but have also actively fought against Rome are the revolutionaries, the Zealots and the *Sicarii*, whom Josephus blames for almost everything, not least for their violation of the Law of Moses and the desecration of the Temple. In this sense, the good resides with the Romans, as God is on their side, and evil and suffering is caused by the revolutionaries, who act against God's will and against fate and destiny, as Josephus often puts it. Behind Josephus' reflections lies the concept of divine guidance, divine providence, as well as the language of destiny, in which Hellenistic historiographers often expressed how God controls everything in history. At other times he uses the language of prophecy applied by the historical authors and prophets of the Bible.

It is in his *Jewish Antiquities* that Josephus is more explicit about the practical side of the belief in divine providence. In writing his history of the Jewish people, he emphasizes the importance of piety, courage, wisdom, humanity, and other virtues, and shows this in great detail in the exemplary life of individual leaders and other central figures in biblical history, such as that of Moses. At the same time he can use selected biblical stories to moralize against vices, such as pride, greed, corruption, etc. By using these literary techniques Josephus follows a didactic purpose, for which he clearly had a Jewish audience in mind, whereas for the purpose of an apology of the Jewish rights in the context of the Roman Empire audience (see *Against Apion*) he may also have written for a non-Jewish audience.

B. Theological Themes
1. Torah and wisdom
In a number of noncanonical Jewish writings, especially the Apocrypha and Pseudepigrapha, we find evidence that the TORAH is philosophically equated with the Greek concept of Wisdom and that divine teaching is identified with the law of nature or of the cosmos (*see* WISDOM IN THE OT). In both cases, Torah/Wisdom functions as the foundation of all of the laws of society and consists of many moral teachings for humanity. Furthermore, in connection with the philosophical concept of Wisdom, we find a frequent employment of practical wisdom, specifically in the form of wisdom sayings, and most notably formulated as the pedagogical teachings of parents to their children or in general of an older generation to a newer one. It is repeatedly stated that it is never enough to simply know what is wise, but one should also act wisely, that is to say, with mercy and righteousness. A popular example in this is the employment of the Golden Rule, as it best exemplifies the philosophical equation of Torah and Wisdom and at the same time is the epitome of practical wisdom. Ethics is thus embedded in a philosophical and theological system.

2. Divine revelation and intervention
For most Jews in antiquity it was unquestionably true that all knowledge comes from God and that revelation is therefore divine. However, that God still intervened in history was a view held mostly by the Prophets; as for the apocalyptic thinkers and also for the Essene community there was a second power in heaven capable of influencing humankind, but in a negative way: God's Adversary and his helpers or the fallen angels. Although few doubted that God would prevail in the end, it was indeed only at the end that God would intervene through a Messiah. Until then, humanity would be the victim of a cosmic battle, a war between good and evil (either personified, or as abstract powers): a clash between God's angels and the fallen angels.

Although there was some room for human action and responsibility, the course of history was, in principal, predetermined as a sequence of good and bad periods and as a constant influencing of the one and of the other side of the cosmic battle, heading toward a catastrophic climax. Even in the end, God would not intervene directly, but send an Anointed or Messiah together with a host of angels to speak and execute the final judgment (*see* MESSIAH, JEWISH).

With this concept in mind, human responsibility is by nature limited and ethical teaching consists mainly of a call to follow the laws of the course of history and of the cosmos. Within the microcosmos of the individual's place in the family, clan, or smaller society, various wisdom sayings and collections of teaching that had been growing throughout history and that had come from the whole of the ANE environment to enter Judaism during its postexilic period as Wisdom theology, would give one meaning and direction in life. The authors of the apocalyptic writings would see ethics limited in time and subject: they developed an interim ethics for a minority.

3. The origin of evil and how to deal with it

Human responsibility, the need to act morally wise, and the necessity of developing moral teaching begins with accepting that there is at least some room for human action. This room had been limited by the answers given to the question on the origin of evil and whether and how to deal with it. The prophets of Israel considered the wicked human heart to be the origin of evil, and without interruption had called people to return to the moral teaching of the God of Abraham, Isaac, and Jacob. However, in the Persian period, the apocalyptic authors of especially the early parts of *1 Enoch* blamed the fallen angels for having brought about evil on earth and divided humankind into two groups: those under influence of these fallen angels and acting accordingly wicked, and those under the influence of the angels of God and acting righteously. Wise was the one who had the knowledge of where humankind came from and belonged, but, as a whole, human action was seen to be limited due to a lack of human responsibility.

In the Hellenistic period, under the influence of both Stoic philosophy and apocalyptic thinking, the various Jewish groups in society (esp. after the Maccabean Revolt of 164 BCE) were divided on questions of the interaction of fate and human responsibility. As Flavius Josephus later reports, the Sadducees thought everything to be dependent on fate and left no room for human action. As they also didn't believe in a life after death, their maxim was to enjoy life as long as it was possible, but that there was nothing one could do to change one's fate.

Contrary to the SADDUCEES, the ESSENES and PHARISEES believed in the possibility of interaction between fate and one's own action and responsibility, with the Pharisees giving somewhat more room to human action than the Essenes. For the Essenes, it was clear that one could know one's fate by studying Scripture and reading it through the lens of their apocalyptic worldview: a cosmic battle was going on between the good and evil angels, who influenced humankind in both directions. For the Pharisees, it was more important to develop a strategy for making the best of one's place in society and acting politically wise by choosing and supporting the right party.

For both Essenes and Pharisees it was clear that one can decide which direction to take by acting either wickedly or righteously. Knowledge of one's fate and destiny and teaching right action were therefore of the utmost importance. Again, for the Pharisees there was more room for human acting than for the Essenes, who believed that, through predestination, every man had a given portion of good and evil parts in him, and it was difficult, though not impossible, to change one's course in life.

Therefore, the Pharisees were best prepared to develop a more advanced ethics and moral teaching for society at large, which they were also able to adjust to the needs of society by constantly updating their interpretation of the Mosaic Law. It was the Pharisees, then, who laid the foundations of the ORAL TORAH and later rabbinic Judaism, whereas the Essenes developed only a group ethic with an emphasis on social values, and the Sadducees an ethic that served only themselves and was meant to allow them to survive as best as possible.

4. Human responsibility and society

The idea of human responsibility goes back to the authors of the books of Moses and the Prophets and especially their Deuteronomistic editors during and after the Babylonian exile. Ezra and Nehemiah would renew and implement this concept in postexilic Jewish society and base every moral teaching on the Laws of Moses. The authors of *1 Enoch* would question this idea of human responsibility and point to the fallen angels as the cause of all evil, until, much later, the Maccabees would take a reverse turn, and again stress the need for human action in order to defend divine teachings and especially the freedom to live according to one's own religion.

Thus, between the 5th/4th cent. BCE and the Maccabean Revolt in 164 BCE as well as during the following period of the independent Jewish state ruled by the Hasmoneans until the coming of the Romans and the Herodian rule at the end of the 1st cent. BCE, the ethical values of Judaism in the Persian and Hellenistic period developed from a post-prophetic apocalyptic denial of human responsibility to a more balanced approach between the need for human action, a call for religious freedom, and the fight for what by then would be called "Judaismos," a set of Jewish values simply called the traditions of the ancestors and, as such, consisting of the essence of Mosaic teachings. Man's principle obligation in society was therefore to defend these traditions against anyone endangering them, whether from the outside or the inside. In sum, ethics often functioned to define and defend Jewish identity with or against the definitions of other groups within Jewish society.

5. The love command and the Golden Rule

The concept of love in the OT ('ahavah אַהֲבָה; God's love, love for God, love for others, erotic love) is distinct from that of Greek thought (eran ἐρᾶν, philein φιλεῖν, agapan ἀγαπᾶν; passionate love, love of people/friends, honor, etc.). However, in Hellenistic Judaism, efforts are made to combine the two, in that it stresses the love of or for God and the love for others as the faithful fulfillment of the biblical commandments, even if this requires suffering and unconditional martyrdom, as love is the ultimate response to God's love (*see* LOVE IN THE OT).

Furthermore, the importance of the commandment to love one's neighbor, often linked with philanthropy, is stressed again and again and often combined with or understood as an example of the originally Greek Golden Rule. Finally, authors like Philo underline the importance of both commandments for the well-being of humanity, and it should also be noted that wisdom or God's teaching can be the object of love. However, eros is typically downplayed as being important only to the "unchaste" Greeks.

Theologically, the ethical maxim of either the love command or the Golden Rule or both can be founded on three arguments: 1) equality (because everyone as God's creature is equal, everyone, even the slave, deserves the same treatment and respect); 2) the importance of doing good and being merciful (this is especially expected from those in a higher position); and 3) the call for *Imitatio Dei* (as God is good and does good, one should follow this). In the later rabbinic literature, the first and third aspect are also found to be based on the biblical teaching that humanity is created in the image of God (and for that reason everyone is equal) and that one should be holy, because God is holy (Lev 17–26; *t. Sanh.* 9:11; *Lev. Rab.* 24:7), whereas the second aspect becomes a cornerstone of rabbinic ethics (see esp. *b. Sotah* 14a). Both rabbinic Judaism and early Christianity would employ all three reasons to stress the importance of the commandments to love God and the neighbor at the same time. *See* APOCRYPHA, DEUTEROCANONICAL; RIGHTEOUSNESS IN EARLY JEWISH LITERATURE.

Bibliography: R. Bauckham. "The Conflict of Justice and Mercy: Attitudes to the Damned in Apocalyptic Literature." *Apoc* 1 (1990) 181–96; A. P. Bloch. *A Book of Jewish Ethical Concepts: Biblical and Postbiblical* (1984); S. Burkes. "Wisdom and Law: Choosing Life in Ben Sira and Baruch." *JSJ* 30 (1999) 253–76; J. J. Collins. "Ben Sira's Ethics." *Jewish Wisdom in the Hellenistic Age* (1997) 62–79; J. J. Collins. "Jewish Ethics in Hellenistic Dress: The Sentences of Pseudo-Phocylides." *Jewish Wisdom in the Hellenistic Age* (1997) 158–77; A. Cronbach. "The Social Ideals of the Apocrypha and Pseudepigrapha." *HUCA* 18 (1944) 119–56; J. G. Gammie. "Spatial and Ethical Dualism in Jewish Wisdom and Apocalyptic Literature." *JBL* 93 (1974) 356–85; P. Gray. "Points and Lines: Thematic Parallelism in the Letter of James and the Testament of Job." *NTS* 50 (2004) 406–24; W. Harrelson. "The Significance of 'Last Words' for Intertestamental Ethics." *Essays in Old Testament Ethics: J. Philip Hyatt, in Memoriam.* J. L. Crenshaw and J. T. Willis, eds. (1974) 203–13; Marinus de Jonge. "The Two Great Commandments in the Testaments of the Twelve Patriarchs." *NovT* 44 (2002) 371–92; H. C. Kee. "Models of Community in the Literature of Postexilic Judaism." *Who Are the People of God? Early Christian Models of Community* (1995) 17–54; H.-J. Klauck. "Brotherly Love in Plutarch and in 4 Maccabees." *Greeks, Romans, and Christians* (1990) 144–56; G. S. Oegema. "Love Your Neighbour as Yourself: Jesuanic or Mosaic?" *BN* 116 (2003) 77–86; E. J. Schnabel. *Law and Wisdom from Ben Sira to Paul: A Tradition Historical Enquiry into the Relation of Law, Wisdom, and Ethics* (1985); H. D. Slingerland. "The Nature of *Nomos* (Law) within the Testaments of the Twelve Patriarchs." *JBL* 105 (1986) 39–48; G. M. Zerbe. *Non-retaliation in Early Jewish and New Testament Texts: Ethical Themes in Social Contexts* (1993).

GERBERN S. OEGEMA

ETHICS IN THE NT. Although the NT does not develop a systematic ethical theory, its writings are filled with moral exhortations rooted in Jesus' gospel of the Kingdom and in the church's preaching about Jesus Christ. Accordingly, even when it makes use of insights from philosophical ethics, the ethical teaching of the NT is profoundly theological in origin and content.

A. The Gospels and the Acts of the Apostles
  1. The Gospel of Mark
    a. The ethic of the Kingdom
    b. The ethic of discipleship
  2. The Gospel of Matthew
    a. A greater righteousness
    b. Good works and judgment
  3. Luke–Acts
    a. Jesus' ethical teaching
    b. The moral life of the early church
B. The Pauline Letters
  1. Paul's letters
    a. The moral imperative
    b. Sin, law, and the flesh
    c. Life in the Spirit
    d. An ecclesial ethic
    e. An eschatological ethic
  2. Letters written in Paul's name
    a. Colossians and Ephesians
    b. The Pastoral Epistles
C. The Johannine Writings
  1. The Gospel of John
  2. First John
D. From Hebrews to Revelation
  1. The Letter to the Hebrews
  2. The Letter of James
  3. First Peter
  4. The book of Revelation
E. Unifying Themes
Bibliography

A. The Gospels and the
Acts of the Apostles
The Gospels are the church's primary witnesses to the ethical teaching of Jesus. Each Gospel, however, describes Jesus' teaching in a distinctive manner. The Gospel of Mark presents Jesus' ethic in light of the in-breaking kingdom of God. The Gospels of Matthew

and Luke do the same, but in the former Jesus' ethic is described in terms of doing a greater righteousness, whereas in the latter there is an emphasis on the need for repentance in light of the reversal of fortunes the kingdom is bringing. Finally, Luke's account of the early church in the Acts of the Apostles provides an insight as to how disciples practiced the ethic of the Kingdom in the period after Jesus' death and resurrection.

1. The Gospel of Mark

The Markan Evangelist outlines the structure of Jesus' ethical teaching in his initial description of Jesus' ministry. After John's arrest, Jesus proclaims the gospel of God: God's own good news that, in Jesus' ministry, the time is fulfilled and the Kingdom is at hand (1:14-15). Two consequences follow from this proclamation. First, people must change their former way of life in light of the in-breaking kingdom of God; they must repent. Second, they must adopt a new way of life characterized by faith in the good news that Jesus proclaims; they must believe in the good news of the kingdom.

a. The ethic of the Kingdom. The Kingdom of God is a dynamic reality that refers to God's rule over history and creation. The gospel about the Kingdom announces that, through Jesus' ministry, God is re-establishing God's rule over history and creation, which have fallen under the power of Satan. Jesus' gospel, then, forebodes a conflict of kingdoms, and it summons humanity to submit to God's reign rather than to the rule of Satan. Jesus' authority to forgive sins and his power over demons, sickness, the chaotic forces of nature, and death itself show that the Kingdom is making its appearance in his ministry, but only those who believe in the good news of God that Jesus proclaims can understand this. Faith, then, which brings understanding, is the indispensable virtue for the moral life. Unless one believes the gospel that Jesus proclaims, it is impossible to see the hidden presence of the Kingdom in his ministry.

Although the Kingdom is already present in a hidden manner in Jesus' ministry, it will not arrive in power until he returns at the end of the age as the glorious Son of Man. Consequently, in addition to faith, the ethic of the Kingdom requires perseverance and vigilance: perseverance because there will be severe persecutions before the final appearance of the Kingdom; vigilance because the manifestation of the Kingdom in power will come suddenly and unexpectedly.

b. The ethic of discipleship. Jesus proclaims the gospel of the Kingdom to all Israel and summons people to follow him as his disciples, among whom the Twelve play a central role. Jesus' disciples are given the mystery of the kingdom of God (4:11) and are expected to understand the hidden presence of the Kingdom in his ministry. Jesus' disciples are his brothers and sisters, the members of a new family who do God's will (3:35).

They are to be servants to one another, following the model of the Son of Man who came not to be served but to serve and give his life as a ransom for many (10:45). Unfortunately, Jesus' disciples often become fearful and fail to understand him (4:40; 8:14-21). They, therefore, function as a negative as well as a positive example of the ethic that Jesus proposes.

Jesus' teaching about the Mosaic law does not play a central role in the Markan narrative since the Gospel was written for a Gentile community for whom the dietary prescriptions of the law were no longer in force (7:19). Nevertheless, it is apparent that Jesus affirms the importance of the commandments, identifying the love of God and the love of neighbor as the most important (12:28-34). He insists that God's commandments have precedence over human traditions (7:8), and in the case of divorce he calls people to observe God's original will (10:6-9). The essential conflict between Jesus and his contemporaries is not over whether the law should be observed but how it should be observed now that the Kingdom has appeared. Jesus does not so much develop a new ethic as he calls people to a radical way of life in light of the in-breaking Kingdom. He summons them to repentance, faith in the gospel of the Kingdom, utter devotion to God's will, selfless service to others, perseverance in the face of persecution, and vigilance for the Parousia of the Son of Man.

2. The Gospel of Matthew

The Gospel of Matthew also presents Jesus' moral demands in light of the in-breaking kingdom of God, which Matthew prefers to call the kingdom of heaven. People must repent, "for the kingdom of heaven has come near" (4:17). Matthew, however, gives greater attention to the content of Jesus' ethical teaching and the need to do good works because of the impending judgment all must face.

a. A greater righteousness. The Sermon on the Mount is the most comprehensive presentation of Jesus' ethical teaching, although it should not be construed as a compendium of his ethical teaching. The sermon occurs after Jesus' initial proclamation of the Kingdom and the call of his first disciples (4:18-22). It is addressed to the disciples in the hearing of all Israel (5:1-2; 7:28), indicating that it is intimately related to Jesus' proclamation of the Kingdom and intended for disciples and all who wish to become disciples. Jesus insists that he has come to fulfill rather than to abolish the law and the prophets. He warns his disciples that if they do not practice a righteousness that exceeds that of the scribes and Pharisees, they will not enter the kingdom of heaven (5:17-20).

In the body of the sermon, Jesus provides three teachings on this greater righteousness. In the first (5:21-48), he establishes six contrasts between what has been said in the past about murder, adultery, divorce, oaths, revenge, and love and the greater righteousness to which he calls his disciples. Jesus' disciples must be perfect (undivided in their allegiance to God) as their heavenly Father is perfect (5:48). In a second teaching (6:1-18), he instructs his disciples not to do their righteous works of almsgiving, prayer, and fasting for others to see, as the hypocrites do, but in secret for God to see. In a third (6:19–7:12), he calls upon his disciples to be single-minded in their devotion to God by seeking the Kingdom and its righteousness above all else (6:33). In the conclusion of the sermon, Jesus warns his disciples about the importance of doing God's will and acting on the words of the sermon (7:13-27).

Matthew's understanding of righteousness can be summarized as behavior that accords with Jesus' interpretation of the Mosaic law in light of the in-breaking kingdom of heaven. It is a righteousness that Jesus exemplified in his own life, which was characterized by obedience to God's will (3:15; 4:1-11). This is not to say that the sermon provides a complete commentary on the law or a new law, but it does reveal how Jesus interpreted salient aspects of the law in light of the in-breaking Kingdom. For Jesus, the key to interpreting the law and the prophets is the love commandment (7:12; 22:34-40) and the exercise of mercy (9:13; 12:7).

b. Good works and judgment. According to Matthew, Jesus places a high priority on doing God's will (7:21). It is not enough to call Jesus "Lord." Those who do God's will are like good trees that bear the fruit of righteousness, whereas those who do not do God's will are like bad trees that will "be cut down and thrown into the fire" (7:19). Jesus criticizes the behavior of the scribes and Pharisees because, in their zeal for their ancestral traditions, they "make void the word of God" (15:6). In the parable of the two sons, he compares the religious leaders to the son who said that he would go into his father's vineyard and work but did not (21:28-32). In a series of seven woes, which stand in sharp contrast with the Beatitudes, Jesus denounces the scribes and Pharisees as hypocrites because they do not practice what they preach (23:3). They neglect the weightier matters of the law (23:23). They appear righteous but are filled with hypocrisy and lawlessness (23:28). In his final discourse (24:1–25:46), he warns his disciples about what will happen in the period before his Parousia. Lawlessness will increase and "the love of many will grow cold" (24:12). The parable of the ten bridesmaids and the parable of the talents exhort disciples to be like vigilant and industrious slaves who employ the period before the Parousia as a time to produce works of righteousness (25:1-30).

God's final judgment plays an important role in Jesus' teaching. On the day of judgment, people will be required to give an account for every careless word they uttered. By their words they will be justified or condemned (12:36-37). In another parable with ethical implications, the weeds among the wheat, Jesus explains that at the end of the age the Son of Man will send his angels to separate those who are evil from those who are righteous (13:36-43). And in his description of the final judgment that the Son of Man will render, Jesus teaches that people will be judged on the basis of the mercy they have, or have not, extended to others (25:31-46).

Although Jesus' teaching places a premium on doing righteousness in light of impending judgment, his ethic remains firmly rooted in God's grace. The greater righteousness he requires is possible because of the power unleashed by the in-breaking kingdom of heaven. And the judgment all must face is the inevitable outcome of God's kingdom, which destroys Satan's power. The graciousness of this kingdom is manifested in the Beatitudes, which proclaim that the kingdom is God's gift to the poor in spirit and those who hunger and thirst for righteousness (5:3-12). It is clear from the parable of the unforgiving servant, therefore, that human forgiveness ought to be the response to God's gracious forgiveness (18:23-35). And it is evident from the parable of the laborers in the vineyard that God's generosity is not a payment for work done (20:1-16). The ethic of the Matthean Jesus, then, is a subtle interplay of moral responsibility and divine mercy.

3. Luke–Acts

Luke's double work, which comprises nearly one-fourth of the NT, provides an insight into the way in which the ethical teaching of Jesus was appropriated and put into practice by the early church. As in the Gospels of Matthew and Mark, the in-breaking kingdom of God is the motivating factor for Jesus' ethical teaching. The concepts of righteousness and law, however, do not play the prominent role in this Gospel that they do in the Gospel of Matthew. Instead, Luke presents Jesus' ethic of the Kingdom in a way that is more accessible to a Gentile audience; he focuses on love, the correct use of possessions, and life in community. These topics are presented in light of the great reversal that the kingdom of God is effecting and the need to repent and follow Jesus in the way of discipleship.

a. Jesus' ethical teaching. Luke's account of Jesus' ethical teaching occurs in two places: Jesus' Sermon on the Plain and his great journey to Jerusalem. Jesus delivers the Sermon on the Plain (6:20-49) to his disciples in the presence of a great crowd. The contrasting Beatitudes and woes (6:20-26), which introduce the body of the sermon, highlight the reversal of fortunes that the Kingdom is bringing for rich and poor alike, and indicate that the instruction that follows is an ethic for those who embrace the Kingdom. The central theme of the sermon is twofold: the command to love one's enemies and the injunction not to judge others. On the one hand, when commanding his disciples to love their enemies, Jesus rescinds the principle of reciprocity. He argues that it is not sufficient for disciples to love those who love them since even sinners do the same. The true test of discipleship is to love one's enemy rather than to retaliate in kind. On the other hand, in his injunction not to judge others, Jesus invokes the principle of reciprocity, arguing that if disciples do not judge others, they will not be condemned, and if they forgive, they will be forgiven. Jesus' disciples are to be merciful as their Father is merciful (6:36). As in the Sermon on the Mount, Jesus warns disciples that it is not enough to call him Lord. They must put his words into practice (6:46-49).

Luke recounts a great deal of Jesus' ethical teaching in his account of Jesus' great journey to Jerusalem (9:51–19:44). Four themes are especially important: the radical demands of discipleship, the need for repentance, the danger of greed, and Jesus' definition of the neighbor. First, since the kingdom of God is at hand, those who follow Jesus must lead an itinerant life that will separate them from family (9:59-62). The radical nature of the demands Jesus makes is shown in his refusal to allow a particular disciple to bury his father, one of the most serious obligations of the law (9:57-60), and in his challenging statement that those who do not renounce all of their possessions cannot be his disciples (14:33; see also the response to the rich ruler, 18:22). Second, Jesus warns people that if they do not repent, they will perish (13:1-5). He admonishes that the kingdom of God is about to effect a great reversal in their lives: the first will be last and the last first (13:30), and the humble will be exalted (14:14). Third, in the parables of the rich fool (12:16-21), the dishonest steward (16:1-9), and the rich man and Lazarus (16:19-31), Jesus warns people of the danger and folly of greed. He summons all to use their possessions wisely for the sake of the Kingdom and for those in need. The way disciples employ their possessions, then, is a measure of their discipleship. Fourth, Jesus uses the parable of the good Samaritan to redefine the neighbor as anyone who is in need (10:29-37).

Finally, any discussion of Jesus' ethical teaching in the Gospel of Luke should take into consideration the example of Jesus' life. In no other Gospel is Jesus so consistently presented as being in the company of sinners, the dispossessed, women, and those on the margin of society. By associating with such people, Jesus exemplifies the ethical implications of the gospel he preaches. He sides with the poor and downtrodden because the kingdom of God is effecting a reversal of fortunes.

b. The moral life of the early church. In the Acts of the Apostles, the one who proclaimed the kingdom becomes the content of the gospel the church proclaims. Jesus called people to repentance because the kingdom was making its appearance in his ministry. The church calls people to repentance because God has vindicated Jesus, establishing him as Lord and Messiah, thereby making him the source of salvation. All who formerly rejected Jesus and his message must now repent and be baptized in his name if they hope to share in this salvation. After Peter's sermon on Pentecost, then, when the crowd asks, "What should we do?" Peter responds, "Repent, and be baptized every one of you in the name of Jesus Christ so that your sins may be forgiven; and you will receive the gift of the Holy Spirit" (2:37-38). Those who repent and are baptized enter the community of the church as disciples.

According to Luke's portrayal of the early church, the disciples held all things in common and "would sell their possessions and goods and distribute the proceeds to all, as any had need" (2:44-45). Barnabas provides an example of such discipleship when he sells his field and lays the proceeds at the feet of the Apostles (4:36-37). In contrast to him, Ananias and Sapphira, who secretly withhold some of the proceeds of their sale from the Apostles, are examples of disciples who have not understood the ethical demands of the gospel (5:1-11). Although disciples can no longer physically follow Jesus in the manner his first disciples did, they find new ways to apply his teaching to changing circumstances. Somewhat surprisingly, Acts does not invoke Jesus' teaching on the need to love one's enemy.

The proclamation of the gospel to the Gentiles raises the issue of the Mosaic law. Must Gentiles be circumcised and adopt a Jewish way of life to share in the blessings of Israel's messiah? The conversion of the household of Cornelius teaches Peter that no one is profane or unclean (10:28) and that "God shows no partiality" (10:34). At the conference of Jerusalem, Peter reminds the church that all are saved "through the grace of the Lord Jesus" rather than through the law (15:11). Although Acts reveres the role of the Mosaic law in Jewish life and is at pains to show that Paul was not an apostate from Judaism, the law is no longer the guiding ethical principle for the early church. Disciples are those who have repented, been baptized, and now live within a community of like-minded disciples in a way that reflects Jesus' ethical teaching.

B. The Pauline Letters

New Testament scholars distinguish between those letters whose Pauline authorship is not disputed (Romans, 1–2 Corinthians, Galatians, Philippians, 1 Thessalonians, Philemon) and those that appear to have been written by others in Paul's name (Ephesians, Colossians, 2 Thessalonians, 1–2 Timothy, Titus). Although not accepted by all scholars, this distinction can be helpful in highlighting different accents in the ethical teaching of the Pauline letters.

1. Paul's letters

Since Paul responds to particular issues and questions as they arose in his churches, his letters do not present a systematic moral theology. Instead, he engages in moral exhortation or parenesis, reminding his Gentile converts of the gospel they already know, or should know, and he urges them to live in a way that coheres with that gospel. In his exhortations, Paul presupposes the moral teaching of the OT, especially the Decalogue, and he shows an acquaintance with Jesus' teaching on divorce (1 Cor 7:10-11). He is also acquainted with certain aspects of Hellenistic moral philosophy such as the importance of conscience (Rom 2:15; 9:1) and imitation in the moral life (1 Cor 11:1; Phil 3:17). The genius of Paul's moral reasoning, however, is not so much the teaching he has left behind; it is the incisive manner in which he makes moral decisions in light of the gospel he proclaims. Just as Jesus called his disciples to live in a particular way because the kingdom of God was making its appearance in his ministry, so Paul summoned his converts to live in a way that accords with the ethical implications of Christ's death and resurrection. By that death and resurrecton, they were justified and reconciled to God, and so enabled to live in and by the power of God's Spirit.

a. The moral imperative. One of the most distinctive aspects of Paul's letters is the relationship they establish between the indicative of salvation (what God has done in Christ) and the moral imperative (how believers ought to respond to the gift of salvation). This relationship can be seen in the structure of Romans and Galatians, as well as in a number of statements Paul makes when he exhorts his converts to live a morally good life. For example, after his exposition of the righteousness of God in the first eleven chaps. of Romans, Paul embarks upon an extended moral exhortation in which he summons the justified to present their bodies to God as living sacrifices by conducting themselves in accord with the gospel they have received (Rom 12:1–15:13). And in Galatians, after arguing that a person is justified on the basis of faith rather than on the basis of doing the works of the law, he exhorts his converts to live in and through the power of the Spirit they received when they were justified (Gal 5:13–6:10). The structure of both letters indicates that the morally good life is made possible by, and is the outworking of, the gospel Paul preaches.

This relationship between the indicative and the imperative is evident in Paul's moral reasoning. He argues that since believers died to sin when they were baptized into Christ's death, they are not to persist in sin (Rom 6:1-11). And, since Christ's death transferred them from the realm of sin to the realm of grace, they are to present themselves as slaves to righteousness rather than as slaves to sin (Rom 6:12-23). Likewise, when exhorting his Corinthian converts to shun immorality, Paul reminds them that their bodies are members of Christ and temples of the Holy Spirit. Consequently, immorality is incongruous with their new life.

The precise relationship between the indicative of salvation and the moral imperative is difficult to define since Paul often exhorts his converts to do what God has already accomplished in them. For example, whereas in Gal 3:27 he says that they were clothed with Christ, in Rom 13:14 he exhorts them to put on Christ. The tension between the new creation God has already established in Christ and the continuing power of sin reminds believers that they must work out their salvation "with fear and trembling," remembering that it is God who is at work in them, enabling them "both to will and to work for his good pleasure" (Phil 2:12-13).

b. Sin, law, and the flesh. Paul's ethic is informed by an incisive analysis of the human condition. Previous to his call, he thought of himself as blameless "as to righteousness under the law" (Phil 3:6). But when God revealed his Son to him, it became necessary for Paul to reassess his former understanding of the law and the righteousness he had attained under it. Concluding that if justification could have come through the law then the death of God's Son was of no account (Gal 2:21), Paul reevaluated his former righteousness as inadequate when compared to the righteousness that comes from God (Phil 3:7-11). In light of what God accomplished in Christ, Paul now understands that humanity was in far more dire straits than he previously realized. Everyone, Jew as well as Gentile, is under the power of sin (Rom 3:9). Paul understands and personifies sin as a power that entered the world through Adam's transgression, bringing with it the power of death (Rom 5:1-12). Because all are under the power of sin, all have sinned, and no one is justified "by deeds prescribed by the law" (Rom 3:20).

The law had played a central role in Paul's life when he was a Pharisee, and he continued to revere it as an expression of God's will. Thus Paul writes, "the law is holy, and the commandment is holy, just and good" (Rom 7:12). Nevertheless, even though the law codified God's will in its commandments, it did not possess the inner power to enable people to follow its prescriptions. The law is spiritual because it comes from God, but humanity dwells in the sphere of the flesh, a realm that is mortal, perishable, and so subject to sin and death. Consequently, when those who are not in Christ strive to do God's will, as expressed in the law, the power of sin frustrates their attempt to fulfill the just requirements of the law. The culprit, then, is not the law but the power of sin that dwells in and rules over humanity, which lives in the realm of the flesh. Writing from the perspective of redeemed humanity, Paul summarizes the plight of unredeemed humanity when he says, "For I do not do the good I want, but the evil I do not want is what I do" (Rom 7:19).

c. Life in the Spirit. For Paul, believers fulfill the just requirements of the law when they are transferred from the realm of the flesh to the realm of the Spirit. This transferal has been effected by God's redemptive work in Christ. Paul presents Christ as a new Adam, in whom the new creation has already appeared. Consequently, those who have been baptized into Christ belong to this new creation and are in the realm of the Spirit: "But you are not in the flesh; you are in the Spirit" (Rom 8:9). Transferred to the realm of the Spirit, believers are no longer under the power of sin, nor are they "subject to the law" (Gal 5:18). This is not to say that the moral life has become an effortless task, or that believers can do whatever they want. It is still possible for those who have been transferred to the realm of the Spirit to fall back into the ways of the flesh. Thus Paul refers to his Corinthian converts "as people of the flesh" because of their jealousy and quarreling (1 Cor 3:1-4). And he must remind his Galatian converts not to use their freedom in the Spirit "as an opportunity for self-indulgence" (Gal 5:13). Although life in the Spirit is a reality made possible by God's redemptive work in Christ, it does not do away with human failure or free will. Those who live by the Spirit must continually respond to the urging of the Spirit. If they do, the Spirit will produce its singular fruit in their lives: "love, joy, peace, patience, kindness, generosity, faithfulness, gentleness, and self-control" (Gal 5:22-23). The moral life, then, must be lived in and through the power of the Spirit, which enables believers to do what they could not formerly do when they were in the realm of the flesh, under the power of sin, subject to the law.

Although believers are no longer subject to the law, Paul insists that they "fulfill" the law, which is summed up in the commandment, "You shall love your neighbor as yourself" (Lev 19:18, quoted in Gal 5:14; see also Rom 13:8-10). Consequently, just as love plays a central role in the ethical teaching of Jesus, so it plays a central role in Paul's moral teaching. Love "builds up" the community of believers (1 Cor 8:1) and is the "more excellent" way (1 Cor 12:31) that is available to all who live in the realm of the Spirit. The paradigm for this love is the self-sacrificing love of Christ, "who gave himself for our sins to set us free from the present evil age" (Gal 1:4). Accordingly, Paul speaks of "the law of Christ" (Gal 6:2), by which he means the law as lived out and expressed in Christ's life. Although believers are no longer subject to the law, they fulfill its deepest requirements when they follow the example of Christ, who fulfilled it through his life of self-effacement and sacrifice for others.

d. An ecclesial ethic. Apart from his letter to Philemon, Paul addresses his correspondence to communities of believers rather than to individuals. Even though it is the individual who must put Paul's teaching into practice, Paul is deeply concerned to form the moral life of the community within which the individual works

out the ethical implications of the gospel. It is appropriate then to speak of Paul's ethic as an ecclesial ethic. This ecclesial ethic can be viewed from two vantage points: the need to preserve the holiness of the community, and the need to build up and preserve the unity of the community.

The church is not a sanctified community because its members already lead exemplary ethical lives but because God has called it into existence and sanctified it through the death and resurrection of Jesus Christ. Therefore, just as Israel of old was commanded to be holy because God is holy, so the church must be holy because it has been purchased and sanctified through the blood of Christ. Paul's understanding of the church as a sanctified community is reflected in the way he identifies those who are in Christ. They are "the saints" or "the holy ones" (hoi hagioi οἱ ἅγιοι), who have been washed, sanctified, and justified "in the name of the Lord Jesus Christ and in the Spirit of our God" (1 Cor 6:11). The church is the "temple of the living God" (2 Cor 6:16), a community of believers, which Paul has promised to present as "a chaste virgin to Christ" (2 Cor 11:2). Because the church is the sphere in which God's holiness dwells, Paul is especially concerned that his converts avoid immorality and idolatry, for God's will is their sanctification, which requires them to abstain from fornication (1 Thess 4:3). Because sexual immorality and idolatry defile the sanctified community, Paul commands the Corinthians to expel a man who has committed a gross act of sexual immorality lest he defile the sphere of God's holiness. The community is a fresh batch of unleavened dough because Christ, its Passover, has been sacrificed. The presence of the immoral man in their midst is like yeast that threatens its holiness (1 Cor 5:1-8). Paul makes a similar argument when he exhorts the Corinthians to avoid fornication (1 Cor 6:12-20); for inasmuch as they belong to Christ, they must not give themselves to another.

Paul is especially concerned to preserve the unity of the church, which he views as the body of Christ. In 1 Cor 8–10 he encourages those who have a robust conscience not to scandalize those whose conscience is weak by eating food that has been sacrificed to idols. In Philippians he calls upon the community to be of one mind and not to do anything from selfish ambition (Phil 2:1-4). And in Rom 14:1–15:13, he exhorts the strong in conscience to put up with the failings of the weak, calling upon all to welcome one another as Christ welcomed them. By being of one mind and heart the church reflects what it is in Christ, and it becomes the sphere where all can live out the moral imperatives of the gospel.

e. An eschatological ethic. Paul's ethic can be described as eschatological inasmuch as it calls upon believers to live with a certain tension in their lives.

Although they have already been justified and reconciled in Christ, they have not yet been saved. Consequently, they must live between two ages with a certain reservation about the present age. On the one hand, they are already living in the new age of the Spirit. On the other, they are still living in the old age, the realm of the flesh, which has not yet passed away. They are to be blameless before God at the coming of the Lord (1 Thess 3:13; 5:23), and they are to live with a profound sense that the "present form of the world is passing away" (1 Cor 7:31). The old age is passing away, and they are not to be conformed to this world (Rom 12:2), for the day of the Parousia is near (Rom 13:11-12). Paul's ethical teaching, then, is marked by a keen awareness that the end of the age has already made its appearance and that the final consummation of all things is at hand. Those who live according to this ethic must walk between the old age, which is passing away, and the new age, which has already appeared.

2. Letters written in Paul's name

Colossians, Ephesians, and the Pastoral Epistles provide a good insight as to how Paul's moral legacy was preserved and developed in new ways by those who wrote in his name. On the one hand, these letters continue to ground the moral imperative in the indicative of salvation. On the other, they develop an ethic that allows the church to live in the world without compromising its distinctive Christian character.

a. Colossians and Ephesians. The first two chaps. of Colossians explain the mystery of Christ: because they have been transferred from the power of darkness into the kingdom of Christ, believers are no longer subject to cosmic powers. In the last two chaps., the letter draws out the practical implications of this mystery in order to show believers how to lead a life worthy of the Lord. Thus Colossians, like Romans and Galatians, affirms that the morally good life is the outworking of the gospel. This intimate connection between the mystery of Christ and the moral life of the believer is presented at the beginning of the letter's moral exhortation: "So if you have been raised with Christ, seek the things that are above, where Christ is, seated at the right hand of God. Set your minds on things that are above, not on things that are on earth, for you have died, and your life is hidden with Christ in God" (3:1-3). Through baptism, believers have stripped off "the old self" and clothed themselves with "the new self, which is being renewed in knowledge according to the image of its creator" (3:9-10). Therefore, they must live in accordance with the new self with which they have been clothed. Although this process of renewal is not yet finished, the social distinctions that once separated people from one another no longer matter in Christ: "There is no longer Greek and Jew, circumcised and uncircumcised, barbarian, Scythian, slave and free"

(3:11). Accordingly, Colossians calls upon believers to put to death whatever is still of this earth in their life (3:5) and to clothe themselves with those virtues that are appropriate for God's elect (3:12-17).

Ephesians also draws an intimate connection between the indicative of salvation and the moral imperative. But whereas the moral indicative of Colossians is rooted in the believer's baptismal union with Christ's death and resurrection, the moral indicative of Ephesians is grounded in the new humanity that has been granted to believers within the sphere of the church, the body of Christ. Therefore, Ephesians begins its moral exhortation by summoning believers to lead a life worthy of the calling to which they have been called by maintaining "the unity of the Spirit and the bond of peace" (4:1-3). Since there is one body, the body of Christ that is the church, the overriding moral imperative is to maintain the unity of the church so that all will be built up into the head, who is Christ. For Ephesians the moral life is a struggle against cosmic powers, and believers must equip themselves with "the whole armor of God," which is truth, righteousness, the gospel of peace, faith, salvation, and the Holy Spirit (6:13-17).

One of the most distinctive aspects of the ethical teaching of Colossians and Ephesians is the use and adaptation of household codes (Eph 5:21–6:9; Col 3:18–4:1). In the Hellenistic world these codes regulated the social relationships in the household between husbands and wives, parents and children, masters and slaves. But in adopting the structure of these codes, Colossians and Ephesians emphasize that these human relationships must be understood in light of the new relationship that believers enjoy in Christ. Thus Ephesians establishes an intricate analogy between the relationship of husband and wife on the one hand, and Christ and the church on the other (5:22-33).

b. The Pastoral Epistles. The ethic of the Pastoral Epistles is intimately related to the sound teaching of the gospel that Paul entrusted to Timothy and Titus. Adherence to sound teaching leads to good works, and to a life of piety, devotion, and godliness (εὐσέβεια eusebeia), whereas digression from sound teaching results in a godless life (ἀσέβεια asebeia) devoid of good works. The eusebeia with which the Pastorals are concerned is rooted in the mystery of faith. Apart from this mystery, which was manifested in the epiphany of Jesus Christ (1 Tim 3:16), godliness cannot be practiced.

First Timothy provides a great deal of practical instruction about living a morally good life. Some of that instruction is culturally conditioned. Women are to adorn themselves with good works, to be submissive, and to live lives of faith, love, holiness, and modesty (2:9-15). Believers are to provide for relatives, especially for their family members (5:8). Younger widows are to marry and manage their households (5:14). Slaves are to regard their masters "as worthy of all honor, so that the name of God and the teaching may not be blasphemed" (6:1). And those who are rich are "to be rich in good works, generous and ready to share" (6:18). The picture that emerges is that of a well-ordered household in which each member knows his or her place and performs good works that bring credit to the faith. Family relationships, marriage, and the goodness of creation are affirmed.

Despite this emphasis on doing good works, the Pastorals are profoundly aware that salvation is the result of God's grace (2 Tim 1:9-10; Titus 3:4-7). This grace made its appearance in the epiphany of Christ, and it enables believers to perform good deeds: "For the grace of God has appeared, bringing salvation to all, training us to renounce impiety and worldly passions, and in the present age to live lives that are self-controlled, upright, and godly, while we wait for the blessed hope and the manifestation of the glory of our great God and Savior, Jesus Christ" (Titus 2:11-13).

C. The Johannine Writings

When compared with the synoptic and Pauline tradition, the ethical teaching of the Johannine writings is somewhat abstract. The specific moral teaching of Jesus and Paul is replaced by the injunction to believe in the one whom God sent into the world and by the "new commandment" to love one another.

1. The Gospel of John

The ethical teaching of the Fourth Gospel is grounded in a profound theological analysis of the human condition: the world dwells in a darkness of which it is not even aware. This darkness is the sin of the world, which the Lamb of God takes away (1:29). Alienated from God, the world prefers the darkness in which it dwells to the light of God, lest its sin be exposed. Consequently, the world does not know the truth, which is God. Because the Father loves the world, he sends the Son to reveal the Father to the world. Those who believe that Jesus comes from God have passed from death to life because they know the truth. They no longer dwell in the darkness of sin but in the light of God, which is life. Consequently, when the crowds ask Jesus what they must do to perform the works of God, he replies, "This is the work of God, that you believe in him whom he has sent" (6:29). For the Fourth Gospel, ethics has become christology, and it is fulfilled in a single work: to believe in Jesus as the one whom the Father sent into the world. Those who believe know the true condition of the world, and they live accordingly.

In his farewell discourse (13–17), Jesus leaves his disciples with a new commandment: they should love one another as he has loved them (13:34; see also 15:12, 17). The commandment is new because it comes from Jesus, who gives it at the eschatological hour, the last and newest hour. The disciples must love one another just as the Son loved them and laid down his life for them (15:13). Inasmuch as it is focused on the community, this love commandment is more limited in scope than the commandment to love one's enemy. But when the community of disciples makes the Father known to the world, the community's love embraces the world.

The ethical teaching of the Fourth Gospel assumes an intimate union between Jesus and those who believe in him. He is the vine, his Father is the vinegrower, and those who believe in him are the branches (15:1-11). So long as they abide in him by keeping his commandments, they will produce the fruit of a morally good life. But if they do not abide in him, they will be cut off and destroyed. Jesus' "commandments" are disclosed in his revelation of the Father. If the disciples live in the truth, which is the revelation Jesus has brought from the Father, they will keep his commandments and bear fruit. The morally good life, then, requires an intimate union with Jesus, which is expressed by faith in his word and love for the disciples.

2. First John

The most specific ethical teaching of the Johannine tradition is found in 1 John. It serves as a corrective to an erroneous interpretation of the Gospel that led some to claim that they were without sin. This problem is apparent in the opening chapters of 1 John, where the author warns his readers not to deceive themselves by saying that they are sinless (1:8, 10). One cannot claim to have fellowship with Christ and continue to walk in the darkness (1:6), to know him without obeying his commandments (2:4), or to be in the light while hating the members of the community (2:9). The true test of the moral life is to do Jesus' new commandment, which is "an old commandment," the love commandment the community has heard from the beginning (2:7; 3:11). First John relates this love to God's own love and to the believer's love for God. Believers love one another because God first loved them (4:19); therefore, those who say they love God but do not love their fellow disciples, whom they see, cannot love the God whom they have not seen (4:20-21). The true test of the moral life, by which believers know they are God's children, is to love God and obey his commandments (5:23). Precisely what these commandments are, apart from believing in the name of his Son, Jesus Christ (3:23), is not specified.

Although 1 John warns its readers not to claim that they are sinless, it affirms that those who abide in Christ do not sin (3:6). Sin is lawlessness, and those who sin are children of the devil (3:4, 8). Those who are born of God do not sin "because God's seed abides in them"; and if they are truly born of God, they cannot sin (3:9). Sin, then, is an indication that one is a child of the devil rather than a child of God. But despite its perfectionist language, 1 John is aware that believers sin, and it distinguishes between sin that is mortal and sin that is not. Whereas one who sins in a mortal way (by apostasy) is beyond prayer, one should pray for those whose sin is not mortal (5:16-17).

D. From Hebrews to Revelation

The Letter of James is the most explicitly ethical writing of the NT, urging readers to be doers of the word. The Epistle to the Hebrews, 1 Peter, and the book of Revelation offer moral guidance to believers whose original fervor has begun to wane, or whose faith is in danger of failing because of revilement or persecution.

1. The Letter to the Hebrews

Hebrews describes itself as a "word of exhortation" (13:22). Written to a community that has grown lax, it provides its readers with an exposition of the high priesthood of Jesus in order to dissuade them from forsaking their original confession of faith and to persuade them to follow the faithfulness of Jesus and of the cloud of witnesses described in chap. 11. To accomplish this goal, Hebrews juxtaposes its doctrinal exposition with a series of moral exhortations. In doing so, it establishes an intimate connection between its exposition of Jesus' priesthood and sacrifice on the one hand, and its exhortation that the community return to its original fervor and confession of faith on the other. Moral exhortations occur throughout the letter and are always related to the doctrinal expositions that precede and/or follow them. For example, the first moral exhortation (2:1-4) occurs in the midst of a section in which Hebrews explains why Jesus is a suitable high priest (1:5–2:18). On the basis of this exposition, Hebrews admonishes its readers that they must pay greater attention to what they have heard (2:1-4) because they have received a greater salvation, which comes from the Son who is greater than the angels (1:5-14). Other moral exhortations follow a similar pattern (see 3:7–4:11, 14-16; 5:11–6:20; 10:19-39; 12:1-13, 14-29). In the midst of these exhortations, Hebrews introduces three severe warnings that there is no second repentance for those who apostatize since there is no further sacrifice for sins (6:4-6; 10:26-31; 12:16-17). This teaching presented a problem for the early church's doctrine of penance, but it is no more severe than the statement of 1 John that discourages prayer for those whose sin is mortal, a reference to apostasy from the Johannine community (5:16-17).

The connection Hebrews draws between exposition and exhortation is not quite the same as the relationship Paul establishes between the indicative and the imperative. Whereas for Paul, the indicative of salvation provides the inner power for the moral life, for Hebrews doctrinal exposition is primarily a way of motivating believers to maintain their original confes-

sion of faith. Believers should act in a particular way because they know that their sins have been forgiven, and there will be no further sacrifice for sins.

2. The Letter of James

Like the Sermon on the Mount, the Letter of James highlights the importance of being doers of the word and not merely hearers of it (1:22). It emphasizes the importance of the law and the need to do works of mercy that show one's faith. For James the law consists of the moral prescriptions of the Mosaic law. He refers to the Mosaic law as the perfect law, the law of liberty (1:25; 2:12), because it is the perfect expression of God's will for the moral life, and its fulfillment leads to freedom. Like Jesus and Paul, James highlights the importance of the love commandment, identifying the commandment to love one's neighbor as "the royal law" (2:8). But unlike them, he never sums up the law in the love commandment. James insists upon doing all of the commandments of the law, which he views as a totality. A violation of a single commandment is a violation of the whole law (2:10).

Like the Gospel of Luke, James is partial to the poor and the oppressed. Religion is a matter of caring for orphans and widows (1:27). Because God has chosen the poor to be heirs of the kingdom, believers are not to show favoritism to the rich (2:1-5). James blames the rich for oppressing the poor (2:6), and he excoriates them for withholding the wages of laborers (5:4). Accordingly, judgment plays a central role in his letter. Those who do not show mercy will be judged without mercy under the law of liberty (2:12-13). Since God is the sole lawgiver and judge, believers are not to judge their neighbors (4:12). Rather, they are to be patient until the coming of the Lord. The Lord is near, and the divine judge is standing at the door (5:7-11).

The premium James places on doing works of mercy is important for understanding its teaching on justification (2:18-26). Reacting against a distortion or a misunderstanding of Paul's teaching on justification by faith, James argues that "faith by itself, if it has no works, is dead" (2:17). James maintains that Abraham was justified by works, adding that faith was active along with his works and was brought to completion by his works (2:21-22). This tension between the teaching of James and Paul is explained, in part, in light of their different approaches and concerns. Whereas Paul views faith as an act of submission to God's will and reacts against using the Mosaic law as a means of salvation, James understands works as deeds of mercy and kindness and reacts against a purely formal faith that that is not expressed in deeds of loving-kindness.

The ethic of James is concrete, and it does not allow compromise between friendship with God and friendship with the world (4:4). Apart from its reference to the birth that believers have received by the word of truth (1:18) and its discussion of wisdom from above (3:13-18), this letter rarely draws a connection between the indicative of salvation and the moral imperative (but see 1:18).

3. First Peter

Written for Gentile believers in Asia Minor who were experiencing suffering and revilement for their faith, 1 Peter portrays its recipients as if they were exiles in a foreign land (1:1), exhorting them to live "in reverent fear" during the time of their exile (1:17). To support its recipients during this time of trial and exile, the letter reminds them of their new status in Christ and exhorts them to associate their sufferings with those of Christ. In this way, the letter establishes an intimate relationship between the indicative of salvation and the moral imperative.

The recipients of the letter have been chosen, destined, and "sanctified by the Spirit to be obedient to Jesus Christ" (1:2). They have been given a new birth through Christ's resurrection (1:3). Therefore, they are no longer to be conformed to their former desires but to be holy just as God, who called them, is holy (1:14-15). Because they have been born anew, they are to rid themselves of malice, guile, insincerity, envy, and slander and, like newborn infants, they are to long for spiritual milk so that they may grow into the salvation that has been granted to them (2:1-2).

In the ethical vision of 1 Peter, believers are like living stones who are being built up into a spiritual house, whose cornerstone is Christ (2:4-8). Echoing the language once applied to Israel of old (Exod 19:6), 1 Peter identifies believers as "a chosen race, a royal priesthood, a holy nation, God's own people" (2:9), who have been called out of darkness into the light. Consequently, they must view themselves as aliens and exiles from their true homeland and abstain from the desires of the flesh (2:11).

During the period of their exile, believers still live in the world. Accordingly, 1 Peter provides its recipients with specific guidelines that accept the political and social structures of the day without question. Believers are to submit to the authority of the emperor and governors for the sake of the Lord, fearing God and honoring the emperor (2:13-17). Those who are slaves should accept the authority of their masters and find an example in the suffering of Christ who suffered for them (2:18-25). Wives are to accept the authority of their husbands so that spouses who do not believe will be won over by their conduct (3:1-6). Husbands are to honor their wives, who are also heirs "of the gracious gift of life (3:7), and all are to seek unity and avoid repaying evil with evil (3:8-9). Many of these injunctions are conditioned by the social structures and ethos of the day, and so should not be used to justify slavery or the subordination of women today.

Finally, 1 Peter consistently relates its moral exhortations to the suffering of Christ. For 1 Peter, the suffer-

ing of Christ provides a model for Christians, who will always be aliens and exiles in the world. Therefore, inasmuch as Christ did not retaliate when he suffered and was abused (2:23), believers must imitate his example, realizing that if they suffer for what is right (3:14), or if they are reviled for the name of Christ (4:14), they will be blessed. It is better to suffer for doing good than to suffer for doing evil (3:17; 4:15). Rooted in the example of Christ and aware that Christians are aliens and exiles from their heavenly home, the ethical vision of 1 Peter is ultimately christological and eschatological in nature.

4. The book of Revelation

Written to dissuade believers from submitting to the cult of the emperor, the book of Revelation exhorts it audience to worship God alone (19:10; 22:9). In a series of messages to the seven churches (2:1–3:22), the risen Christ warns certain congregations, who have lost their original fervor and who participate in idolatrous worship, to repent. Christ threatens punishment to those who do not repent and promises vindication to those who endure. Next, the risen Lord reveals the eschatological judgment of God that is about to come upon the world (5–16), the punishment of Babylon/Rome (17–20), and the new creation that will emerge (21–22).

Revelation views the ethical life as a cosmic struggle between the adherents of the Lamb (Christ) and the adherents of the Beast (the Roman Empire), which is the representative of the Dragon (Satan). Although Christ has already won the victory, Satan continues to exercise his power through the Roman Empire, which requires people to worship the emperor. Consequently, whereas Rom 13 and 1 Pet 2 exhort believers to obey the authority of the emperor, Revelation warns its listeners not to worship the Beast. In doing so, it establishes a salutary tension within the NT. So long as rulers legitimately exercise their authority, believers should obey them; but whenever rulers assume the prerogatives of God, believers must not submit to them. Although Revelation does not present specific moral instructions, it provides a fitting conclusion to the study of ethics in the NT by reminding its readers that the sum of all ethics is obedience to God.

E. Unifying Themes

Although there are a variety of ethical visions in the NT, there are a number of unifying themes that occur in most of its writings. First, the ethical teaching of the NT is essentially theological in nature inasmuch as it is grounded in what God has done in Christ. The ethic of the NT begins with the proclamation of the gospel of the Kingdom and the gospel about God's redemptive work in Jesus Christ. Second, the theological nature of this ethic leads most NT writings to ground the moral imperative in the indicative of salvation. The gift of salvation provides believers with a motive and, more important, with the power of the Spirit to live a morally good life. Third, the ethical teaching in the NT is ecclesial in nature inasmuch as it is primarily addressed to the community of believers and is intended to be lived within the community of the church. Apart from the community of believers, many of these ethical injunctions have little meaning and are impossible to practice. Fourth, the love commandment, although often expressed in different ways, plays a central role in the ethical teaching of the NT. In several writings it is portrayed as the summit of the moral life and/or as the key to interpreting the ethical demands of the gospel. Fifth, the ethical teaching of the NT is eschatological in nature inasmuch as it reminds believers that there will be a final reckoning when they must give an account for what they have done. Although believers will not be justified on the basis of their works, they will be judged by them.

Bibliography: Brian K. Blount. *Then the Whisper Put on Flesh: New Testament Ethics in an African American Context* (2001); Jean-François Collange. *De Jésus à Paul: L'éthique du Nouveau Testament* (1980); T. J. Deidun *New Covenant Morality in Paul.* (1981); Victor Paul Furnish. *Theology and Ethics in Paul* (1968); Victor Paul Furnish. *The Moral Teaching of Paul: Selected Issues.* 2nd rev. ed. (1985); A. E. Harvey. *Strenuous Commands: The Ethic of Jesus* (1990); Richard B. Hays. *The Moral Vision of the New Testament: Community, Cross, New Creation: A Contemporary Introduction to New Testament Ethics* (1996); Eduard Lohse. *Theological Ethics of the New Testament* (1991); Eugene Lovering Jr., and Jerry L. Sumney, eds. *Theology and Ethics in Paul and His Interpreters: Essays in Honor of Victor Paul Furnish* (1996); Willi Marxsen. *New Testament Foundations for Christian Ethics* (1993); Frank J. Matera *New Testament Ethics: The Legacies of Jesus and Paul* (1996); Wayne A. Meeks. *The Origins of Christian Morality: The First Two Centuries* (1993); Robert F. O'Toole. *Who Is a Christian? A Study in Pauline Ethics* (1990); Brian Rosner, ed. *Understanding Paul's Ethics: Twentieth Century Approaches* (1995); J. Paul Sampley. *Walking Between the Times: Paul's Moral Reasoning* (1991); Rudolf Schnackenburg. *Die sittliche Botschaft des Neuen Testaments.* Vol. 1. *Von Jesus zur Urkirche.* Vol. 2. *Die urchristlichen Verkündiger* (1986–88); Wolfgang Schrage. *The Ethics of the New Testament.* David E. Green, trans. (1988); Siegfried Schulz. *Neutestamentliche Ethik* (1987); Jeffrey S. Siker. *Scripture and Ethics: Twentieth-Century Portraits* (1997); Allen Verhey. *The Great Reversal: Ethics and the NT* (1984).

FRANK J. MATERA

ETHICS IN THE OT. Ethics connotes critical reflection on the moral dimensions of human experience. Related to the OT, ethics may focus on the moral character and conduct of any of the communities reflected in the collected texts that make up the Hebrew canon. This may include reflection on those who produced the texts, those who collected and edited the text in the process of canonical formation, and those who have appealed to the canon in its various forms as a moral resource through generations to the present.

A. The Diverse Meanings of Old Testament Ethics

The literature relating the field of ethics to the OT has suffered from some confusion of definition and inconsistency of terminology. It is best to think of several different arenas where the texts of the OT can be meaningfully related to the concerns of ethics and morality. Each frames and focuses that relationship differently and in so doing faces different sets of problems and challenges.

1. The world behind the text

Some investigations of OT ethics have focused on discovering, understanding, and critically assessing the morality of ancient Israel. Since the OT is the product of many different voices and communities within Israel over a period of many centuries there is no unified system of morality to describe. The work of Johannes Hempel through the mid-20th cent. sought to describe the roots of Israelite morality in the various social contexts within Israel. He attempted to wed an historical framework reflecting the social contexts of different periods in Israel's history with attention to the various social strata within Israel at any given historical moment (e.g., peasants, pastoralists, urban dwellers, royal noble classes). Each of these would face a different set of conditions in the various historical periods of Israel's life (e.g., semi-nomadic tribal society, agrarian tribal federation, urbanizing monarchy, destroyed homeland and scattered exile, rebuilding provincial outpost in a larger empire).

Hempel and those he influenced still felt they could describe, through these varied social contexts, a developing Israelite morality. This has since be rightly criticized as failing to account for the complex diversity of the OT. It cannot be assumed that every text is typical, even of its own social class or historical context. Some may reflect a widely influential popular morality while other texts represent a minority voice declaring the popular morality bankrupt or unfaithful. Few texts represent more than a witness out of a particular segment of ancient Israel and cannot reflect every class or social segment. We simply do not have in the OT evidence for the morality of all social groupings in every historical period. Particular texts may not be typical or complete in their witness to ancient Israelite morality. The moral world of the OT is a complex world.

More recent use of social scientific methods have recognized this problem and been content to describe the morality reflected in particular sets of texts and to set that as concretely as possible within the social and historical context reflected behind the text (Knight; Wilson). These efforts enrich our understanding of the morality in given times and places within particular societal contexts without trying to synthesize these into some larger consistent or developmental moral framework. Such studies give depth to our understanding of the moral world that produced the witness of particular texts while recognizing that we cannot create a typical or complete history of ancient Israelite ethics. We catch glimpses of the moral world behind the text of the OT, with each glimpse reflecting a different strata of Israelite life or a different moment in the experiences of Israel's story.

Recent attention to the moral address of particular genres of OT literature have produced helpful insights into ancient Israelite morality (Otto; Barton 2003). While recognizing development over time within particular genres (e.g. law, wisdom) such studies have helped develop a clearer portrait of the particularity of Israel's moral vision. A closer look at some of these genres follows below.

2. The world of the text and the formation of canon

The very fact that a text with its attendant moral witness and vision has taken written form and been passed on to succeeding generations creates a new context within which to assess the nature of OT ethics. At root these texts are witnesses to Israel's lived experience in the world in relationship to God drawn from different social and theological perspectives and reflecting different historical contexts. These witnesses have taken written form, been edited and added to as books, collected into larger units, and eventually fixed as canon in three major groupings: Law, Prophets, and Writings. This canon which Christians call the OT and Jews call TANAKH was never intended or claimed as a systematic treatment of Israel's history, theology, or ethics (see CANON OF THE OLD TESTAMENT).

Another way of understanding OT ethics is to understand it as the study of the ethical dimensions of the world of the text created by the formation of the canon. Individual books can be studied for their moral witness and at times the dialogues and tensions of moral voices within a particular book. But also subject to study and reflection is the moral dialogue created within the canon: the convergences, tensions, juxtapositions, continuities and contradictions created by fixing the moral witness of these texts in an authoritative collection handed on from one generation to the next. The moral vision of the redactors may become a subject of reflection as well as the witness of individual texts or collections.

The nature of the moral conversation created within the canon and its various arrangements can differ greatly. For example, what are the moral implications for reading first of God's universal creation and relationship to all of humanity in Gen 1–11 before beginning the story of God's particular relationship to Abraham and Sarah and their descendants (Gen 12)? The inclusion of the exclusivism of Ezra and Nehemiah must be in moral conversation with the more expansive view of Jonah. Sometimes the canon preserves what must have been a minority voice in ancient Israel (Jeremiah) while clearly giving us no texts from a more popular figure (Hananiah). The ethical perspectives of some books may be in adversarial conflict (Proverbs and Job) while other books may reflect a continuity of moral perspective over generations within the same book (Isaiah and its exilic and post-exilic additions). The study of OT ethics as the study of the texts in their particularity and arrangement in the canon may be informed by what we can know or discover about the world of Israel from which they came, but the canon itself forms a new context within which further ethical conversation takes place and the moral vision of the text may or may not be capable of connection to particular moral worlds behind the text. The canon is to some degree an artificial construct that transcends the reality of historical and empirical Israel at any period. OT ethics in the context of the canon focuses the theological witness and moral implications of a collection of texts that have finally been claimed as scripture by both Christianity and Judaism. Studies of OT ethics based on such canonical perspectives, informed by but not dependent on recovering ancient Israelite morality, have become more common in recent years (Birch 1991; Clements; Wright; Janzen).

3. The text as scripture through generations

Although the canon of the OT originated in ancient Israel it remained an authoritative collection as scripture for the faith and ethics of Christian and Jewish communities down to the present. The moral witness of the OT is not simply a witness to ancient character and conduct but remains a shaping moral influence in the life of ongoing communities today. Thus, OT ethics may also properly refer to critical reflection on how texts regarded as scripture can become active moral resources for reflecting on contemporary ethical issues and challenges. Such studies reflect on the methodologies and perspectives associated with reflection on biblical texts regarded not simply as ancient witnesses but as authoritative resources to help contemporary confessional communities to reflect on who God would have them be and what God would have them do (Birch and Rasmussen; Birch 1991; Ogletree; Janzen). *See* AUTHORITY OF SCRIPTURE.

Such a use of the canon requires honest and critical reading of texts and not a superficial imposition of some moral system formed outside the text and forced upon the canon. Such an effort will yield diverse outcomes—illumination and insight in one instance, struggle and dialogic tension in another. If the OT does not give us some simplistic moral template to apply, it has nevertheless proven a source of insight drawn from its diverse witness that has distinctively shaped generations of those communities that claim these texts as scripture. It may well be that the canon invites readers into a process of moral discernment more than into a ready-made set of moral rules, norms and conclusions.

It serves that process well to recognize that our modern use of the OT as a resource for ethics faces an impediment in the recognition that these texts are rooted in a world utterly alien to and unlike our own. Moral assumptions and categories used in the OT are often alien and sometimes repugnant to us. Some texts reflect practices as unexamined realities that we no longer regard as morally acceptable even if still practiced to some extent, e.g,. polygamy, slavery, holy war, kingship, patriarchal treatment of women as property. Systems taken for granted in the OT are almost incomprehensible to many in the modern world, e.g., ritual defilement and purity. As much as possible these matters need to be understood in their own social context, but it is important for ethics to understand that the canon of the OT has not primarily functioned in religious communities as a model of normative behavior to be merely emulated. Israel is not presented as the consistent model of moral community. There are texts reflecting Israel's sinful behavior (e.g., excessive nationalism and idolatry), texts presented as Israel's failure to properly discern God's will (e.g., the request for a king), and texts that simply suggest unexamined ancient social practice (e.g., patriarch, slavery, practices of war).

Differences between the world of Israel and our own must be faced honestly and the texts that reflect these differences cannot be ignored or explained away. Such use of the OT as a moral resource of ongoing ethical reflection in communities of faith does not require recovery and emulation of the actual practices of ancient Israelite morality. What we can recover of ancient social, historical, and faith contexts in ancient Israel will, of course, enrich our understanding of the texts, but will not reveal some consistent pattern of morality with which contemporary communities simply align themselves. The ethical perspectives within the totality of the OT canon will be diverse and incapable of being encompassed in any single system of morality. Yet, the presence of such divergent moral voices in the canon represents the judgment of the ongoing community that first shaped and then handed on these texts that they are worthy of moral contemplation and ethical reflection in our own deliberations to meet the moral challenges of being God's people in our own time.

B. Foundations in Community Witness

The OT assumes that all persons are moral agents. Who we are and how we act is considered to be a matter of moral accountability. The collection of witnesses that form the canon of the OT presumes to affect moral agency. The Hebrew canon is not just the fortunately preserved literature of interesting ancient communities. It seeks to form communities of moral agency within which individuals are brought into relationship with the character, activity, and will of God as witnessed by these collected testimonies from ancient Israel. Such communities are then to understand themselves and to act, individually or corporately, as moral agents in the world. Furthermore, the formation, preservation and transmission of this literature as canon imply that its intention is to form communities of moral agency in relationship to God through succeeding generations.

Recent work in ethics has placed a new stress on formation of communities of moral agency, both as reflected in the formation of the canon and in the use of that canon as scripture through generations (Birch and Rasmussen; Cahill; Fowl and Jones). It is the community that serves as the necessary context for understanding the ethical dimensions of the biblical text.

1. Text as formed in community

One of the fortunate developments in recent scholarship on the OT has been the full recognition that every text originates out of a social context. Ethical insight cannot be legitimately abstracted from the text as timeless truths or principles, nor attributed to the genius of individual witnesses in isolation from the community. In the OT there is no private and individual morality that is not also related to important public moral commitments.

To form criticism's early concern with *Sitz im Leben* ("situation in life") has now been added scholarly work employing such tools as sociology, social history, cultural anthropology, and socioeconomics (*see* FORM CRITICISM, OT). Such work has begun to add significantly to our understanding of particular social contexts that gave rise to the voices of the biblical witness and gave impetus to the preservation of those witnesses beyond the social context within which they originated.

For those interested in the ethics of ancient Israel and of the OT, this affords new possibilities in the area of descriptive biblical ethics. A more complex and less artificial phenomenological description of Israel's social behavior and moral attitudes is emerging. Avoided are the broad, synthetic or developmental attempts to draw generalizations concerning all Israel with respect to ethical norms from the OT. Many more concrete investigations of the particular morality reflected in specifics texts are enriching our understanding of the social contextuality of every text. This includes important work on the historical development of moral norms in legal and wisdom texts (Otto); prophetic and narrative texts (Barton 2003); the background for laws and moral attitudes on adultery (McKeating); the moral norms reflected in the Deuteronomic literature (Wilson); or the morality reflected in the structures of political power in text from monarchic Israel (Knight).

2. Community as context for moral formation

Throughout the text of the OT the witness of the text is directed to the formation of a community in relation to God that is not limited to Israel or any subgroup of Israel at any given historical time or place. Drawn from many times and social contexts, the text of the OT constitutes the story that shapes a faith community and its moral identity.

It is thus the narrative texts of the OT that receive priority as the formative influence on the shaping of community identity. Of course, the OT contains more than narrative, but it is the narrative framework that still serves to relate the community of faith, ancient and modern, meaningfully to other types of biblical material. Law, prophecy, wisdom and apocalyptic literature all are preserved and handed on by a community formed by the story of relationship to God reflected in the narrative traditions that tell a story of promise, deliverance, covenant making, nation building, prophetic confrontation, exile, restoration and eschatological hope. The story even came to understand the God of Israel as one who created the world, and, when that world became broken, desired redemption of all creation and peoples. The story is added to and developed in particular ways but is assumed as the identity-forming, narrative-shaped

reality of the community's life. Even wisdom literature, the least reflective of Israel's story, uses Israel's name for God, finds contact with Israel's story in the role of God as Creator, and finally relates wisdom to Torah in Sirach.

Hauerwas (1983) argues that narrative is the most suitable form for the community to remember and reinterpret its own past. In so doing, a community of character is formed. Character refers to the form our moral agency takes through our beliefs and intentions as those are shaped by the remembering and reinterpreting of the biblical story. Israel's remembering and reinterpreting of God's actions on its behalf is not without its tensions. There is no harmonious, single, official version of Israel's remembered story. In fact, the text shows the importance of such character formation in relation to the narrative tradition as a dynamic process. For example, the centrally important text of Exod 1–15 gives evidence not only of originating memory but of community reclaiming and reinterpreting of that memory through the incorporation of liturgical Passover practices into the narrative and the reclaiming of the story in new ways by a generation in Babylonian exile (Exod 6).

3. Canon as conveyor of moral witness

The canon itself is testimony to the intention of the biblical text as we now have it to transcend its originating social contexts and undertake the dynamic task of community formation through succeeding generations. The fact that the literature of Israel is preserved and transmitted in a canonical collection serves to guard against abstracting the text of the OT from the communities of faith that have preserved, transmitted and valued it.

The arrangement of the Hebrew canon does not seem related to realities in the historical life of Israel so much as to the need to make Israel's story, as shaped by the canon, available to future generations. This means that the theological and ethical function of the canon for the church may be enriched by historical and sociological insight into the originating contexts of particular texts, but that function does not depend on detailed descriptive knowledge of the ethics of ancient Israel. Such knowledge, due to the nature of textual resources, will only be partially available in any case. Thus, the task of OT ethics is to recognize that the canon is a theological construct that does not directly relate to an historical Israel (Childs).

The Hebrew canon only functions as a moral resource to the degree that it is reflected upon and appropriated by communities of faith. Nowhere does it give rise to autonomous rules and principles, or independent systems of philosophical ethics directed to individual well being. The canon of the OT functions as a moral resource only when communities of faith identify themselves in some authoritative way with the story of Israel as made available by the Hebrew canon.

C. Foundations in Divine Reality

The relationship between text and community is not only historical and sociological. The relationship is theological, and the moral authority of the text is a function of the text as the story of God and God's community, not a function of the community in and of itself. Israel's story and the texts that transmit it do not themselves provide the bases for the shaping of moral community through subsequent generations. These texts and the story of Israel have been handed on as witnesses to a divine reality that entered into relationship with Israel and is still available in relationship to subsequent generations. The bases for ethics in the OT, both for the originating communities and the communities who have received the texts that tell the story, rest in the reality of the God witnessed there.

1. Knowledge of God: divine character and conduct

The focus of the Hebrew canon and of the community formed by the witness of its texts is, at every level, in response to the reality of God. Israel as a community of faith is formed in response to its understanding of what God has already done, and who God has already revealed the divine self to be. Israel has "seen what I did to the Egyptians, and how I bore you on eagle's wings and brought you to myself." Now arises the possibility of a new identity as God's "treasured possession out of all the peoples." Now Israel can be shaped in response through covenant to become "a priestly kingdom" and a "holy nation" (Exod 19:4-6).

For the OT the community receives its identity from divine initiative and the establishment of ongoing relationship with God in creation, promise and covenant. The shaping of community is not a human achievement but is a divinely initiated gift that calls for response. Moral character is not the autonomous creation or possession of the community but an ongoing response in relationship to the reality of God. Ethics in the OT is not a cultural phenomenon. Both human character and conduct are morally judged in relation to the community's knowledge of God and what relationship to God demands as faithful response.

The knowledge of God in the OT is prior to and encompasses the knowledge of God's will. Traditional treatments of ethics in the OT focused on the revealing of the divine will as the basis of ethics. This meant that moral norms were primarily located in commandment, law, or explicit moral admonitions, as in the prophets. Certain "ethical" texts were abstracted from their context in the story of Israel's relationship to God. At its worst, this reinforced caricatures of the OT as rigid law over against NT gospel. Even more sophisticated treatments, however, tended to characterize ethics in the OT as primarily focused on commandment and therefore deontological in character (Ogletree).

Although obedience to God's revealed will and the role of commandment are important in the OT, a singular focus here separates moral demand from the person of God. In the OT ethics arises not as a matter of obedience to an external model or code of morality, but as a result of entering into the life of God. A number of scholars have argued similar points in the recent literature and a much richer picture of the bases for OT ethics is emerging. Barton (1982) suggests that the OT is not primarily a moral guide but rather suggests a way of life lived in the presence of God. Ethics is not a list of obligations but a means of having communion with God. Childs argues that God's commandments rest on the people's prior understanding of God. God continues to make God's will known.

In the terms of recent discussions in Christian ethics, we are being called to attend more carefully to the character of God alongside the conduct of God. Who God is becomes important alongside what God does. The activity and revealed will of God are expressive of the character of God, and knowing God becomes as important as being acted upon or commanded by God (see Jer 22:16). The text of the OT invites us to enter into the life of God as the supreme moral agent in the biblical story. The divine reality over against which community is formed becomes known in character and conduct.

Such attention to the moral significance of the character of God can significantly enrich our understanding of key moments in the biblical story. For example, the theological and ethical significance of the exodus from Egypt is usually discussed in terms of what God has done. But God's act of deliverance is preceded by two remarkable accounts of self-disclosure in Exod 3–4 and 6 that make clear that what God does in deliverance is expressive of crucial qualities of God's character, which both Israel and Pharaoh, although in different ways, will come to "know" (note the importance of the knowledge of God throughout the plague stories).

2. Bases of ethical norms

Moral norms in the OT arise not only from discerning and attending to God's revealed will, but from imitating God's character and conduct and from fitting one's life to the natural patterns of order in God's created world.

a. *Imitatio Dei*. The importance of the imitation of God as a basis for ethics in the OT was seen early by scholars such as Buber and Rowley. More recently a number of scholars have given new attention to this important theme.

The life of God models the moral life. God as experienced by Israel and mediated to subsequent generations through the canon is to be imitated as moral agent, in both character and conduct. Israel's identity is shaped by its imitation of God who has invited them into relationship.

This *imitatio dei* can be in reference to particular divine actions in the salvation story or in creation. For example, the legal codes urge Israel to act the way God has already acted toward them. "[God] executes justice for the orphan and the widow, and . . . loves the strangers, providing them with food, clothing. You shall also love the stranger, for you were strangers in the land of Egypt" (Deut 10:18-19). The dramatic climax of Micah's oracle in 6:1-8 ("He has shown you, O mortal, what is good . . .") does not seem to imply commandment so much as a divine demonstration of justice, kindness, and humility that Israel is to emulate. The entire central metaphor in Hosea implies that God's treatment of Israel is to model how Israelites are to treat each other.

This already suggests that we imitate God not only in actions of significant ethical importance but in qualities of life that are ethically significant. "You shall be holy, for I the Lord your God am holy" (Lev 19:2). Israel is asked to love God (Deut 6:4) and the neighbor (Lev 19:18) even as God has already loved Israel (Deut 7:8). The prophets in urging justice, righteousness, and compassion as attributes of the moral life under covenant also attribute such qualities of character to God (Jer 22:16). As God's actions reflect and flow out of these qualities of character, so too should Israel's (and the readers of these texts in subsequent generations). This is in great contrast to patterns in the ANE cultures surrounding Israel. The gods might command ethical behavior in human society on some minimal standard as reflected in law codes, but the gods do not model such behavior and are often depicted as acting in willful and self centered ways.

There are, of course, limits to the community's imitation of God. We cannot duplicate God's deeds of sovereign power; we cannot perfectly embody the moral attributes toward which we strive. We strive to imitate God as moral agents and covenant partners, but we do not become God. It is in part the revealed will of God as seen in explicit moral texts of law and precept that helps guide the community and hold it accountable when its attempts to emulate divine moral agency fall short.

b. Revealed divine will. A large part of the OT reflects an understanding that Israel was formed as an ongoing community in a covenant at Mt. Sinai that established a relationship with God. This relationship, in Israel's story, was initiated by God and anticipated by divine promise first given to Abraham (Gen 12:1-3). But the covenant relationship implied commitments from God and Israel to relationship and the obligations to moral behavior that maintained the wholeness of covenant and the mutual joining of God and Israel in larger mission within creation and history. God makes these obligations known in explicit expressions of the divine will through commandment and law code, through the guidance and admonition of priests and

prophets, and through God's raising up of leaders for particular moments in Israel's history. None of these function autonomously but point to the God whose revealed will may be discerned in laws and leaders, but who holds accountable those who distort the purposes of covenant law or pervert the trust of covenant leadership.

Obedience to God's revealed will is not blind obedience, but is rooted in trust that God is faithful to the divine commitments to steadfast love, justice, righteousness and compassion. It is noteworthy that even the decalogue, one of the most foundational expressions of divine will for the moral life of the community, begins with a reminder of God's prior demonstration of God's commitment to Israel's well-being, "I am the Lord, your God, who brought you out of the house of slavery . . ." (Exod 20:2). The prophets, in reminding Israel that they have broken covenant, testify to God's faithfulness in covenant relationship (as in Mic 6:1-8). Yet, even the prophets' confrontation with Israel is not for the sake of punishment as an end in itself, but for the renewal of covenant and the restoration of relationship (see Hos 11). God's people can be renewed as moral agents in obedience to covenant and in some sense the OT suggests a continual process of commitment, accountability, and renewal of covenant partnership. God's commitment to moral partnership with those who would be God's covenant people is ongoing. Obedience is not to an arbitrary power but grows out of enduring relationship in a life lived by the community in the presence and purpose of God. Thus, even obedience to divine will in the OT has both deontological (duty oriented) and teleological (purpose oriented) elements, and both are encompassed in a theology of shared relationship and moral agency.

c. Natural law. Barton (1982) has argued convincingly that alongside the imitation of God and obedience to God's will there is a third basis for ethics attested in the OT which is akin to philosophical notions of natural law. He describes it as conformity to the patterns and orders of the world, and although God created the world, this moral order operates as a given framework into which one can place the moral life without reference to revealed morality. It has been often noted that OT witnesses to creation attribute it to Israel's God but with no particularity in respect to Israel. God created all humans, declared them good (Gen 1), gave them the gift of moral choice (Gen 2), considers them the crown of creation only a little lower than heavenly beings (Ps 8:5), and manages its complexities without obligation to privilege Israel or any other (Job 38–41). Thus, wisdom literature notably appeals to a divinely created moral order that can serve as a standard to wise and righteous behavior completely apart from any tradition of revealed divine will or any particular history of experience with a God to be morally emulated. The assumption of these creation and wisdom texts is that God's created world embodies a moral order that is part of the fabric of all human existence and can be appealed to apart from the particular moral traditions of a God revealed in relation to the life of Israel.

This assumption of an ethical order built into the fabric of creation sometimes appears outside creation and wisdom texts. Abraham, in bargaining with God over the fate of Sodom and Gomorrah, can appeal to a moral standard that can presumably even hold God accountable ("Shall not the judge of all the earth do what is just?" Gen 18:25). Amos' oracles against the nations (chaps. 1–2) indict the nations for atrocities by presumably appealing to standards of moral behavior that would be known and acknowledged by all peoples without reference to the moral traditions of Israel or any other particular revealed tradition. Patterns of behavior that make for a "good person" and for the just treatment of all persons are reflected in Job 31 without reference to any particular religious tradition. It seems clear that future work in OT ethics must give fuller attention to the notion of moral dimensions common to all human life, and as built by God into the fabric of creation without necessary reference to particular revealed traditions.

D. Ethics as Explicit Norms for Morality

The recent work of Eckart Otto has already been widely recognized as establishing a new standard and important new perspectives in the study of OT ethics. In this masterful work, he has concentrated only on legal and wisdom texts as the major concentration of texts dealing with explicit systems of moral norms in ancient Israel. Although it is puzzling and has been singled out for some criticism (Barton 2003), Otto defends his focus on explicit moral texts as a protection from the collapse of OT ethics into the history of Israelite religion and the theology of the OT. He also argues against any sort of "application" of insights from OT ethics on any direct line to ethical concerns today. Nevertheless, his work has greatly advanced our understanding of the moral dimensions of Israelite law and wisdom.

1. Ethics in law

Otto begins his work on the ethics of Israelite law with an analysis of Israel's oldest law code, the Book of the Covenant (Exod 21–23), which he confidently traces through several editions. Even in its earliest form this legal code is seen as interested in the connections of community more than the defense of abstract legal principles. It shows a major interest in the rights and the needs of those whom society relegates to the economic or social margins. The containing of conflict is more important than the maintenance of privileges for an upper class, which is relatively absent in the Book of the Covenant. Even in its early expressions Israelite law had important distinctions from the legal traditions of surrounding cultures and these remained visible through subsequent developments in the legal

traditions. Although the legal traditions are viewed as God-initiated, in Israel they place high value on human responsibility since there is no world of the gods to blame for evil deeds or the progression of events, only the one God who has given humans great responsibility in creation and in covenant partnership has enlisted Israel into the divine moral vision.

Building on a wealth of recent work on Israelite law, Otto sees the subsequent development visible in the Book of the Covenant as moving Israel's moral vision from law to ethics, or to put it another way from a focus on enforceable standards of minimal acceptable behavior to the inclusion of unenforceable ethical principles. This can be seen in the inclusion of apodictic laws alongside the more common ANE casuistic laws, and the use of motive clauses to argue theological for the moral value of behavior that is not in principle enforceable. Pragmatic legal standards for minimizing conflict are expanding from the strictures of law to the appeal of moral vision—from law to ethics.

Otto argues that the ethical ideals of early Israelite law inevitably fail; they fall short of the moral vision. This resulted the development in the later Israelite monarchy of a more thoroughly theologized expression of Israelite law integrated into the story of Israel's salvation history. Law and ethics were grounded in God's actions toward Israel in history—delivering, revealing, covenanting. This is seen first in Deuteronomy and then in the final redaction of the Covenant Code, as both are related to the Decalogue and God's covenant with Israel on Sinai. In Deuteronomy law and ethics are seen as a response to God's grace in delivering, covenanting with, and guiding Israel through the wilderness. This trend to theologize the law is continued in the Priestly Code. Here a system of sacrificial atonement represents God's initiative to provide a way to live in relationship to God's moral demands in spite of human sin and failure. In the ethical demands of the law God expresses the divine will, but recognizes that humans are always sinners and will fall short of the unenforceable moral demands of the law. In Deuteronomy and the Priestly Code God's grace provides a means to live with the human failure to fully embody the ethical imperatives of the divine will, through God's grace and the provision of a means to atone for sin. Israel moves from distinctive legal beginnings to expressions of moral vision that are centrally important to Israel's identity but legally unenforceable. With the recognition that this makes human moral efforts necessarily fall short, Israel's legal traditions turn to reliance on God's trustworthiness and redeeming grace along with a system of God-initiated atonement for sin, allowing new beginnings.

In the end, OT law and its development through Israel's history manifest some distinctive features of OT ethics. The laws of Israel rest on a positive view of human beings as created by God as good and able to engage cooperatively in seeking the common God.

This is a contrast to Mesopotamian views of humanity as inferior beings tied to evil and chaos. Israelite legal traditions stress human capacity for solidarity with God and others. Law in the OT stresses the sanctity and dignity of human life and has little by way of a class ethic although women are still subordinate to men and limited forms of slavery are sanctioned. This can be clearly seen in allowing no penalty for murder except capital punishment and this applies regardless of status, gender, or nationality of the victim. All human lives are equally valued before the law.

2. Ethics in wisdom

Wisdom literature stands alongside Israel's legal codes as sources of explicit ethical guidance in the OT. Although less theologized wisdom literature does attribute the order of the world to God's creation and present a portrait of the wise and righteous person as contrasted to the fool and sinner. This body of ethical teaching reflected in Proverbs, some Psalms (e.g. 73) and by implication in Job (esp. chap. 31) is, of course, paralleled in ANE wisdom texts, and at one time was considered tangential to Israel's tradition. Current scholarly opinion recognizes a more central role for wisdom in Israel's tradition, although its grounding is in traditions of God's creation and not in Israel's experience of God in its own history. The emphasis is on the order which God has created and with which wisdom seeks to guide readers to live harmoniously. Wisdom puts forward an ethic rooted in the natural order of the world and offers aphorisms and essays that seek to align human behavior with the order God created. Although it runs the risk of materialism with an emphasis on rewards and punishments, the successful life is also one lived in harmony with neighbor and in society so it is not simply an individualistic and materialistic ethic. The moral life is not described in totally secular terms either. It is lived in conscious recognition of God as the source of the created order and the ground of the moral life. "The fear of the Lord is the beginning of knowledge" (Prov 1:7).

Since the ethic of wisdom is rooted in nature and experience its literature is pragmatic and down to earth, reflecting on behavior that seeks the good in nearly every realm of human life. But human life is not tidy, so within the wisdom tradition there did come a recognition that moral behavior and the untroubled life were not always and inevitably partners. The Book of Job struggles with the problem of righteous suffering and Ecclesiastes with the elusive nature of meaning in spite of attentive pursuit of the avenues recommended to bring success and well-being. The moral life is not simply achieved in relation to one's own human effort. Wisdom is not so easily found and has its limits (Job 28).

Otto treats wisdom's discovery of its own limitations as akin to the development in legal traditions that recognized human failure and the need for a more direct relationship to God and revealed traditions of divine will and grace. For wisdom he sees this development reflected beyond the canon in the Book of Sirach where wisdom is identified with Torah and a connection is made to Israel's historical traditions. The God who makes wisdom possible in the created order of the world is also the God who has called Israel into special partnership and revealed the divine nature and will in Israel's story. A life of wisdom and a life informed by Torah are identified. Both become associated with "teaching" and related to the notion that the moral life is one lived in harmony with the life of God as that is known in the many modes of Israel's witness.

E. Ethics as Implicit Witness to Morality

As important as the legal and sapiential traditions are to OT ethics, their explicit moral guidance does not exhaust the moral resources of the Hebrew canon. Far larger portions of the texts of the OT are taken up by narrative and prophetic traditions. These are not ethically irrelevant, but set forth a moral vision that is not explicit in commandment or proverb, but lived out in relation to the complexities of divine and human experience in a world where both divine and human choices really do make a difference and the moral character of God and humans are shaped in relationship that began with creation itself.

1. Ethics in creation

Hebrew concepts of creation as compared with those of their ANE neighbors makes a great difference in the conception of ethics in the OT. In Mesopotamia human beings are created out of the blood of a traitorous god who aligned himself with the power of chaos. Thus, humans are the product of guilt and punishment and assigned to do the work of the world and relieve the gods of such labor. They are the slaves of the gods. How different in Israel is the conception of human life as a divine creation. Male and female are created in the image of God (Gen 1:26) and along with all creation are pronounced good (1:31); humankind are seen as created for relationship with God, others and nature and are given the gift of free will, the capacity to make free moral choices (Gen 2). Humans are created "a little lower than divine beings" and "crowned with glory and honor" (Ps 8). Even when creation becomes broken, God is portrayed as committed to the restoration of relationship. How could such a view of humans created with dignity, freedom and honor and gifted with the desire for relationship by God's own self not have implications for the moral life. Human ethical responsibility matters to God and to the life God intended in community and creation. Some of this is reflected in the legal and wisdom material discussed above where human life and dignity seems given stronger place than in surrounding ancient cultures. But much more is reflected in the mass of narrative traditions that tell Israel's story and its narrated experience of relationship with God, and in the prophetic literature with its voice raised to confront and renew that relationship when it becomes broken. Such texts are not morally explicit legal claims or wise aphorisms, but it is increasingly recognized that the shaping of moral character in all of its complexity is often through the stories that communities tell, and their ability to convey meaning while reflecting the complexity of human experience.

2. Ethics in narrative

A large portion of the OT is taken up with narrative texts that tell the story of Israel's encounter with God and the manner in which this shaped the ongoing life and experience of Israel as the people of God. Earlier in this article we shared the growing body of work by ethicists and theologians noting the important shaping role of story in human experience. This relates directly to the moral importance of biblical narrative and the shaper of community moral identity. A good deal of work has been done on the role of narrative texts in NT ethics, but in spite of some significant voices on the moral value of OT narrative, much remains to be done.

The rich stories of the Pentateuch, the historical books, and the stories in Daniel, Jonah, Ruth and Esther are not primarily for entertainment or information. They are the stories that have shaped the identity of a community and that community understands its story to be one of relationship to God. Such stories shape communities and individuals as moral agents whose character and conduct are affected by their own conscious incorporation into the story.

Such narratives find their ethical function in several ways. First, the stories approximate the moral complexities of human life. We do not exercise our role as moral agents in the neat frameworks of separate laws or aphorisms but in overlapping claims and values in social contexts. Narratives approximate this messiness of human life yet show models of central characters making their way, not without mistakes and repercussions, but nevertheless living out a moral vision that has dignity and integrity. Second, this complexity of ethics in the midst of life is not lived alone but in relationship to a God who is engaged in the processes of historical experience with us. The portraits of this engagement vary from period to period of Israel's storytelling life, but the overall picture is of a God that values human beings and has made a special partnership with Israel for wider purposes than mere gratification or self serving purposes. From creation, to promise, to deliverance, to covenant, to settlement, to kingship, to judgment, to exile, to restoration—the sum of Israelite narrative traditions is a story that communicates God's valuing of human life in general and Israel as divine partner in particular. How that relationship is lived and understood varies greatly in the telling

but reflects the complexity that rings true for human experience in general. Third, the narratives have a power to transform and call persons and communities beyond the minimum ethical standards that might be defined by law codes or wise teachings. Qualities of love, justice, righteousness and compassion surprise us in the actions of God and the characters of the story and inspire readers of these stories through the generations to a similar pondering of the ways in which their own lives might reach beyond the ethical minimum. We might forgive as did Joseph. We might be willing to sacrifice all as was Abraham. We might aspire to be persons after God's own heart as was David, and be willing to repent when confronted by our own violence and its effect on our families and others—as was David. The characters of the narratives are both more and less than commandment demanded, and God in these stories is both agent of accountability and unrestrained lover and renewer of relationship. Each of the great themes of these narratives is deserving of full treatment as ethically significant, and this article cannot do them justice. It can only point to the growing recognition of the power of narrative to shape community moral identity as through the canon handed on to the generations it yet does today.

3. Ethics in the prophets

Again, the brief section of this article cannot do justice to the ethical significance of the prophetic texts in the OT. However, it is important to see them in the context of the entire OT. In the past the prophetic books have received attention for their ethical significance almost as if they could be abstracted from their Israelite and OT context as the voicers of timeless moral truths that they somehow discerned as individuals of unusual moral insight.

It is important to note that the prophets served as moral agents to express both God's judging and redeeming message for Israel precisely within the context of the traditions considered above. They knew and referenced the narrative traditions indicating that they also were shaped by them. They knew the lawcodes and the covenant understanding on which they were based and they confronted Israel with the breaking of covenant and the failure to uphold their responsibilities within it. They even drew on the aphorisms of the sapiential traditions and the liturgical songs of the temple. They were extensions of the moral identity of Israel as God's covenant partner.

But they also spoke for God—they spoke God's word. The prophets understood themselves to be called, compelled to speak. They boldly announced "Thus says the Lord" and spoke in the first person as if God was speaking. They were deeply informed in the particulars of their own contexts.

In many ways the prophets were models of the ethical life demanded by covenant partnership with God.

They not only announced God's judgment and hope for the people they were obedient to God's calling and the demands of covenant often at cost to themselves. They pointed to the qualities of divine character which demanded imitation (steadfast love, justice, righteousness, compassion) by God's people and often summoned them to knowledge of such a God (e.g. Hosea, Jeremiah). But they were also reminders and renewers of the moral demands of covenant as an expression of divine will and a requirement of partnership with God. This could be particularized in very concrete socioeconomic and political contexts (e.g. Amos, Isaiah, Ezekiel).

The prophetic indictment and call to renewed commitment focused broadly across the spectrum of Israel's life. In the realm of the cult they focused both on the idolatries that displaced Israel's God in favor of other loyalties (e.g. Hosea), and on the hypocrisy that divorced cultic ritual practice from moral lives of covenant obedience marked by justice and righteousness and care for the marginal (e.g. Amos). In the sociopolitical realm they denounced the exploitation of the weak and poor and the seduction of material wealth (Amos, Isaiah, Micah). They denounced political leadership that sought personal and nationalistic power but disregarded the covenant principles and failed to trust in God over their own power (see Hosea, Isaiah, Jeremiah). They pointed to the corruption of leadership and institutions when these should have been guarding the integrity of covenant (see Hosea, Micah, Jeremiah, Ezekiel, Malachi).

Interestingly the prophets often addressed messages of judgment and calls to accountability for the nations. Since the nations knew nothing of the specific channels through which God had made known the divine character and will this suggests that the prophets understood some notion of moral vision as inherent to being human and a part of God's creation. Some actions are ethically abhorrent to all nations and persons and the demands of behavior and character which eschews such practices is understood by the prophets to be universal. This relates to the discussion of natural law above.

The prophets not only spoke God's judgment but God's hope. Because the prophet's ethical message rests on relationship to God it is dynamic and not static. God is not bound to automated enforcement but loves, forgives, and renews (e.g. Hos 11). Thus, ethics in the prophets is never a mechanical application of legal demands for obedience. God models the very qualities in renewing relationship with Israel that the people of God are to show to one another in renewing and healing their own broken relationships. After the destruction of Jerusalem and the deportation into exile entire prophetic messages were given over to hope and renewal (compare with Ezekiel and Deutero-Isaiah). If kings and leaders had broken covenant the proph-

ets could imagine a renewed moral vision in which faithful rulers arise (Isa 9; 11) and a New Jerusalem becomes possible (Ezek 40–48). Failure of present moral vision is transcended by eschatological visions of renewed moral life in relation to God.

F. The Old Testament as a Resource for Contemporary Ethics

Because the OT is not an ancient collection of documents newly discovered in modern times, its interest for ethics cannot be limited to what we can learn about the ethical understandings of ancient Israel. The canon of the OT has been handed on and claimed as ethically foundational for generations of Christians and Jews down to the present day.

A rich discussion on the issues involved in the use of scripture in contemporary ethics has developed in recent years. A rehearsal of that discussion goes beyond the bounds of this article but it is important to note that the moral vision of the OT is a living tradition and not a mere antiquarian interest. The OT continues to play a formative and normative role in the lives of contemporary communities of faith who see themselves in continuity with the identity of the biblical communities that gave us the canon of the OT. The very richness and diversity of the discussion on how these texts continue to serve as moral resources in the ethical issues of our own time is a part of the ongoing gift of these texts of moral testimony.

Bibliography: John Barton. "Approaches to Ethics in the Old Testament." *Beginning Old Testament Study.* John Rogerson, ed. (1982) 113–130; John Barton. "The Basis of Ethics in the Hebrew Bible." *Ethics and Politics in the Hebrew Bible.* Semeia 66 (1994) 11–22; John Barton. *Ethics and the Old Testament* (1998); John Barton. "Understanding Old Testament Ethics." *JSOT* 9 (1978) 44–64; John Barton. *Understanding Old Testament Ethics: Approaches and Explorations* (2003); Bruce C. Birch. "Divine Character and the Formation of Moral Community in the Book of Exodus." *The Bible in Ethics: The Second Sheffield Colloquium.* J. Rogerson, M. Davies, M. D. Carroll R., eds. (1995) 119–35; Bruce C. Birch. *Let Justice Roll Down: The Old Testament, Ethics, and Christian Life* (1991); Bruce C. Birch. "Moral Agency, Community, and the Character of God in the Hebrew Bible." *Ethics and Politics in the Hebrew Bible.* Semeia 66 (1994) 23–41 [portions excerpted with permission for use in this article]; Bruce C. Birch, "Old Testament Narrative and Moral Address." *Canon, Theology, and Old Testament Interpretation.* G. Tucker, D. Petersen, R. Wilson, eds. (1988) 75–91; Bruce C. Birch and Larry L. Rasmussen. *Bible and Ethics in the Christian Life, rev. ed.* (1989); Lisa Sowle Cahill. "The New Testament and Ethics: Communities of Social Change." *Interpretation* 44 (1990) 383–95; Brevard S. Childs. *Biblical Theology of the Old and New Testaments: Theological Reflections on the Christian Bible* (1993); Ronald E. Clements. *Loving One's Neighbor: Old Testament Ethics in Context* (1992); Stephen E. Fowl and L. Gregory Jones. *Reading in Communion: Scripture and Ethics in Christian Life* (1991); Stanley Hauerwas. *A Community of Character: Toward a Constructive Christian Ethic* (1981); Stanley Hauerwas. *The Peaceable Kingdom: A Primer in Christian Ethics* (1983); Johannes Hempel. *Das Ethos des Alten Testaments* (1938); Waldemar Janzen. *Old Testament Ethics: A Paradigmatic Approach* (1994); Douglas A. Knight. "Political Rights and Powers in Monarchic Israel." *Ethics and Politics in the Hebrew Bible.* Semeia 66 (1994) 93–118; Henry McKeating. "Sanctions Against Adultery in Ancient Israelite Society, with Some Reflections on Methodology in the Study of Old Testament Ethics," *JSOT* 11 (1979) 57–72; Harry P. Nasuti. "Identity, Identification, and Imitation: The Narrative Hermeneutics of Israelite Law." *Journal of Law and Religion* 4 (1986) 9–23; Thomas W. Ogletree. *The Use of the Bible in Christian Ethics* (1983); Eckart Otto. *Theologische Ethik des Alten Testaments* (1994); C. S. Rodd. *Glimpses of a Strange Land: Studies in Old Testament Ethics* (2001); G. J. Wenham. "The Gap Between Law and Ethics in the Bible." *Journal of Jewish Studies* 48 (1997) 17–29; G. J. Wenham. *Story as Torah: Reading the Old Testament Ethically* (2000); Robert R. Wilson. "Approaches to Old Testament Ethics." *Canon, Theology, and Interpretation.* G. Tucker, D. Petersen, and R. Wilson, eds. (1988) 62–74; Robert R. Wilson. "Sources and Methods in the Study of Ancient Israelite Ethics." *Ethics and Politics in the Hebrew.* Semeia 66 (1994) 55–63; Christopher J. H. Wright. *An Eye for an Eye: The Place of Old Testament Ethics Today* (1983).

BRUCE C. BIRCH

ETHIOPIA ee´thee-oh´pee-uh [Αἰθιοπία *Aithiopia*]. Ethiopia and Ethiopian(s) are terms that occur approximately forty times in the NRSV. Their use in biblical studies principally is based upon the use of the term (Aithiopia) in the LXX. In the LXX, Ethiopia is the translational equivalent to the Hebrew term **kush** (כּוּשׁ; see CUSH, CUSHITE), a reference to the great riparian nation that flourished between the 1st and 6th cataracts of the Nile, to the south of EGYPT covering roughly the same territory as the Sudan. The terms *Cush* or *Cushites* are sometimes used for a nonpersonal entity, i.e., not the eponymous ancestor, Cush (**Chous** Χους) as in Gen 10:6, but as a national reference, as in Isa 18:1, "Ethiopia" (Aithiopia Αἰθιοπια). This nation was populated by a people described in Isa 18 as "tall and smooth" and known to have been characteristically dark skinned (see Num 12:1 and Jer 13:23). Cush and Egypt had enduring ties that are evident in the OT; often when Egypt is mentioned, it is found in conjunction with Cush(ites) (see Ps 68:31[Heb. 32]; Isa 20:3, 5; 43:3; 45:14; Ezek 30:4; Nah 3:9).

A. Meaning of the Greek Term
B. Biblical Ethiopia (Cush)
C. Ethiopia as Modern Nation
D. Ethiopia as a Metonym

A. Meaning of the Greek Term

The English word *Ethiopia* derives from a composite Greek term meaning "burnt face." This term is used in the Bible to describe the general phenotype of people from Cush, a nation in the northeastern quadrant of the African continent, populated by a people from that sub-Saharan region. The OT does not use the term "burnt face" to describe anyone; the Hebrew uses specific ethnic/national designations, such as Cush. When the OT was translated into Greek, one of the unintended consequences was that the people of Cush (and likely other sub-Saharan African nations like Sheba, Saba, Put, etc.), were identified in Greek by a common phenotypic description: "burnt face" (Aithiops Αἰθίοψ).

B. Biblical Ethiopia (Cush)

Biblical Ethiopia (Cush, or the Egyptian spelling Kush), also called Nubia, was governed from three capital cities along the serpentine course of the Nile at different periods; Kerma in pre-biblical times, Napata during the time of the OT and NT, and Meroe in the subsequent Christian era. These cities served as central cites for administration and commerce for this nation except for a period of about a century from the mid 8th to the mid 7th cent., when Ethiopia exercised direct hegemony over Egypt. During this period, Cushite kings reigning in Thebes ruled Cush from that city.

Ethiopia occurs numerous times in English translations of the OT describing a nation rich in natural resources (Job 28), whose population consisted of mighty soldiers of fortune (2 Sam 18; 2 Kgs 19; 2 Chr 12; 14; 16; 21; Zeph 2; Isa 20; 37; 43; 45; Jer 46; Ezek 29; 30; 38; Nah 3; Dan 11), who would eventually worship Yahweh (Ps 68:31[32]; Isa 11; 18; Zeph 3).

In the NT, there is a reference to an unnamed Ethiopian courtier of the CANDACE (queen) of this great nation. Acts 8:26-40 describes the story of the ETHIOPIAN EUNUCH, whom the text assumes is either a Jew or a proselyte ("God-fearer") by the matter-of-fact declaration that the man had "had come to Jerusalem to worship." Such a statement supposes that a community of Yahwists persisted in Nubia as is also suggested in such passages as Ps 68:32; Isa 11:11; 18:7; and Zeph 3:10 and by the fact that Beta Israel, or Ethiopian Judaism, is still extant in sub-Saharan Africa.

C. Ethiopia as Modern Nation

Ethiopia also has a modern referent: an Eastern African nation in the highlands and plateaus of the

"Horn of Africa." It is separated from the "Horn" by the Great Rift Valley. The capital city is Axum (the place where the ark of the covenant is said to reside). This modern entity represents what is likely a a nation that is distinct from biblical Cush. According to the narratives of the *Kebra Nagast*, the book of the origins of the people of contemporary Ethiopia, this nation is the biblical SHEBA, the land from which the Queen of Sheba made her trek northward to learn of the glory of Solomon and his kingdom (1 Kgs 10:1-13; 2 Chr 9:1-12). The *Kebra Negast* describes the history of this ancient nation that developed from the "Queen of Sheba" and was governed by Menelik, her son by King Solomon. Perhaps the most fascinating aspect of this story is the account of the ARK OF THE COVENANT. As told in this book, Menelik went to Israel to meet his father and learn of the glories of his kingdom. When he arrived, Solomon wanted to make him his successor, but Menelik refused, pledging to go back to succeed his mother. After a time, when his son was determined to return home, Solomon sent the sons of the high priests and a replica of the ark with Menelik's entourage. The young priests, however, decided that they should not be sentenced to live in a strange land with a replica of the ark, which was their birthright. They switched the replica for the original and fled. When the deception was discovered, Solomon sent his armies to capture the authentic ark, only to find that Menelik's fleet had already departed from Ezion-Geber/Elat. Thus, Ethiopian legend holds that the actual ark of the covenant resides to this day in an Orthodox church in Axum.

D. Ethiopia as a Metonym

Ethiopia is also a term that has been employed to refer to the entire continent of Africa. For the Ethiopianist, African American authors inspired by Ps 68:31 [Heb. 68:32] and writing at the latter part of the 19th cent., the term *Ethiopia* referenced the entire continent and all of its people. In fact, these recently freed African Americans viewed themselves as "Ethiopians" brought for a time to the Americas to learn about God before returning to their homeland to usher in a pan-African renaissance where Ethiopia soon will "stretch out its hands to God" (Ps 68:31).

RODNEY S. SADLER, JR.

ETHIOPIAN EUNUCH [Αἰθίοψ εὐνοῦχος Aithiops eunouchos]. The Ethiopian eunuch's encounter with the evangelist PHILIP is found in Acts 8:26-40. Luke's description of the Ethiopian EUNUCH is compact yet evocative. "Now there was an Ethiopian eunuch, a court official of the Candace, queen of the Ethiopians, in charge of her entire treasury. He had come to Jerusalem to worship and was returning home; seated in his chariot, he was reading the prophet Isaiah" (Acts 8:27-28).

In the ancient world, ETHIOPIA was a region of Africa in southern Egypt along the Nile. The Ethiopian's position as treasurer to the CANDACE identifies him

with the capital of her kingdom, Meroe. The crown prince of ancient Meroe was considered divine and unsuitable for day-to-day rule in the kingdom. His mother was given the title "Candace" (Kandakē Κανδάκη), and she ruled the kingdom in his place. The Candace's eunuch treasurer was a prestigious person for his political relationships as well as his obvious proximity to the kingdom's financial resources. Meroe was a distant but nonetheless interesting locale for Luke's contemporaries. Gaius Petronius led a late 1st cent. BCE Roman military campaign against Meroe, and Dio Cassius reports Nero planned, but never carried out, an invasion in 62 CE. Luke's audience was familiar with Ethiopia but nevertheless viewed it as near the end of the known world.

In addition to unusual geographic and social connections, the Ethiopian treasurer is described as a eunuch. In the ancient world castrated males lived a precarious existence—considered neither fully masculine nor feminine in social or gender roles. Males castrated prior to puberty appeared softer, free of body hair, had a high-pitched voice, and evidenced a sallow complexion. Their "unmanly" appearance made them targets of criticism, ridicule, and anger. Despite this, eunuchs were sold as slaves throughout the ancient world and appeared in royal courts in positions of trust.

Modern interpreters often minimize the Ethiopian treasurer's status as a castrated male. Some translate the Greek **eunouchos** as "chamberlain" instead of eunuch thus avoiding any discussion of castration and gender. Others acknowledge the Ethiopian's castration, but believe Luke mentioned it only as it informs the man's religious affiliation. Deuteronomy 23:1 indicates that a eunuch could not enter the interior courts of the Temple. Interpreters have used this passage along with Josephus (*Ant.* 4.290-91), to argue that a eunuch could not convert to Judaism. It remains unclear what associations Luke intends by describing the Ethiopian as a eunuch; at the very least, his identification as such makes the treasurer and the story all the more unusual.

Traditional interpretations of the story understand its significance to be twofold. It is a graphic illustration of the fulfillment of Jesus' pre-ascension prophecy to the apostles in Acts 1:8 that "you will be my witnesses in Jerusalem, in all Judea and Samaria, and to the ends of the earth." Ancient church legends presume the Ethiopian eunuch returned home to found the Ethiopian church (Eusebius, *Hist. Eccl.* 2.213-14; Irenaeus, *Haer.* 3.12.8).

The passage is also significant for its obvious similarities to the story of Peter's conversion of the Roman centurion Cornelius in Acts 10:1-33. Their conversions are compared to identify the first Gentile convert. The Ethiopian eunuch is an enigmatic figure in this debate because of his castration; Luke's account does not specify the eunuch's religious affiliation. We are told the eunuch "had come to Jerusalem to worship and was returning home" (8:27c-28a). Scholars argue that despite his pilgrimage to Jerusalem, the Ethiopian must be a Gentile and not a Jew because a castrated male would not be allowed into the assembly (Deut 23:1). Given later details about the Ethiopian's interest in Isaiah, the man is probably a God-fearer, one interested in Jewish religious life and practice but not a convert.

Comparisons between the Ethiopian and CORNELIUS also hint at a larger historical debate among early Christians about the genesis of each of these conversion accounts. Scholars suspect that rival factions of Philip and Peter's disciples each told a story of the first Gentile convert in order to further the status of their respective evangelist.

The Ethiopian eunuch emerges as an inquisitive and confident figure seeking a relationship with Philip's Jesus. The eunuch demands baptism and his joy-filled CONVERSION prefigures the later receptiveness of God-fearers and Gentiles alike to the good news.

HEIDI S. GEIB

ETHIOPIC ENOCH. *See* ENOCH, FIRST BOOK OF.

ETHIOPIC VERSION. *See* VERSION, ETHIOPIC.

ETH-KAZIN eth-kay´zin [קָצִין עִתָּה 'ittah qatsin]. One of the towns allotted to the family of Zebulun (Josh 19:13). Zebulun's allotment was in the northwest of Canaan, between the tribal lands of Issachar and Asher, but the exact location of Eth-Kazin is unknown. *See* ZEBULUN, ZEBULUNITE.

ETHNAN eth´nuhn [אֶתְנָן 'ethnan]. One of the three sons of Ashhur with his wife Helah. Ethnan is among those listed in the Chronicler's genealogy of Judah (1 Chr 4:7).

ETHNARCH eth´nahrk [ἐθνάρχης ethnarchēs]. An official or dependent ruler. The exact meaning can vary because the title could cover a range of responsibilities related to the governance of an ethnic group or a subservient nation. The title could refer to an overseer of ethnic affairs in a large city, since the Jews of Alexandria had their own ethnarch who oversaw some legal affairs (Josephus, *Ant.* 14.117; 19.283). Ethnarch could also refer to a client ruler of a semi-autonomous people (e.g., several Hasmonean monarchs were granted the status of ethnarch by the dominant Syrian rulers [*Ant.* 14.148; 1 Macc 14:47]; ARCHELAUS, son of Herod the Great, was given the title of ethnarch by Augustus [*J.W.* 2.93]). The only reference to an ethnarch in the NT, however, comes in 2 Cor 11:32, where Paul seems to use the term for a governor or official in charge of Damascus under the Nabatean king ARETAS IV. *See* TETRARCH, TETRARCHY.

STEVEN J. FRIESEN

ETHNI eth´ni [אֶתְנִי 'ethni]. The son of Zerah and the father of Malchijah (1 Chr 6:41 [Heb. 6:26]) in the genealogy of Asaph, one of the Levitical singers appointed by David who are said to have served in the Tent of Meeting and later in the Temple built by Solomon. *See* PRIESTS AND LEVITES.

DEREK E. WITTMAN

ETHNICITY [גּוֹי goy, גּוֹיִם goyim; ἔθνος ethnos, ἐθνικός ethnikos]. Ethnicity is used throughout the Bible in a variety of semantic contexts and rhetorical situations to indicate nations, groups of people, foreigners, Gentiles, and "others." Throughout the different periods of biblical history, ethnicity is a defining marker for understanding the different cultures and worldviews that gave rise to the multitextured narratives in the Bible. There is no single definition for ethnicity. Many traditional studies define ethnicity through what may be considered an "essentialist approach," which focuses on what are considered fixed or observable qualities inherent in a particular ethnic group. In this way, ethnicity is understood in biological terms of descent or ancestry, referring to blood, seed, kinship, or genealogy. Cultural anthropologists and sociologists define ethnicity as a social construct subject to change depending on historical time and circumstances. Still others note that ethnicity is an "invented term," the product of modern scholarship. Ethnicity is also closely related to race inasmuch as it is a social construct. In this regard, Greek terms such as laos (λαός, "people, nation"), phylē (φυλή, "tribe, nation, people"), genos (γένος, "family, nation, people, descendants"), and syngeneia (συγγένεια, "kindred, relatives"), and Latin terms *genus* ("descent, family, tribe, nation, people"), and *natio* ("tribe, nation, people") are often interchangeably associated with ethnicity. Most scholars, however, deal with race and ethnicity as separate entities, while others see a symbiotic relationship between the two. In either case, both terms are ultimately social constructs that say as much about present concerns as they do about ancient conditions and circumstances. For reading the Bible and other extrabiblical writings, ethnicity should be understood as a social and political construct for designating groups of people, as well as a rhetorical strategy for boundary-making and self-definition.

A. Ethnicity in the Old Testament
B. Ethnicity in the New Testament
C. Interpretive Implications
D. Summary
Bibliography

A. Ethnicity in the Old Testament

In the OT, goy and goyim are used to refer to clearly defined ethnic, political, and geographical identities, often understood as foreigners. Both terms are used to refer to specific "NATIONS" or "people" who are recognizably distinct from the more general understanding of people ('am עַם). For example, in Gen 10, the descendants of Noah's sons are listed (Shem, Ham, and Japheth) by way of the "nations" associated with them (Gen 10:5, 20, 31). In this table, the geographical references should not be understood solely in a literal sense as ethnicity can often function as a symbolic rhetorical marker to signal certain attitudes, values, and beliefs about those writing the narratives as opposed to those mentioned in the narrative. The term goy is used when God promises to make the offspring of Abraham a great "nation" (Gen 12:2; 17:20; 21:18). Moses refers to Israel as a "nation" (goy) that is also a distinct body of people (Exod 33:13; Deut 4:6-7). The plural form, goyim, is used to refer to a number of specific nations in the case of Gen 10:31; Judg 2:23; and Isa 61:11. The plural form also refers to the people dwelling in and around the land of Canaan (Deut 4:38; Josh 23:13). Throughout the OT goy and goyim indicate a specific covenant relationship with Yahweh (Josh 5:8).

B. Ethnicity in the New Testament

In the NT, ethnicity is usually connected with texts that attempt to demonstrate the universal inclusive impulse of early Christianity, i.e., that Christianity is to extend to the ends of the world (Acts 1:8c). The ultimate end of the world in this case is represented by the ETHIOPIAN EUNUCH, serving as the ideal exemplar of one who could be converted to Christianity (Acts 8:26-40; see ETHIOPIA). Ethnicity is also used to isolate some of the intra-Christian disputes in early Jewish-Christian communities, whereby practices such as circumcision and dietary customs were identified as differences between Jews (Ioudaios Ἰουδαῖος) and Gentiles (ethnos) (that is, non-Jews) and became hallmarks for representing insiders and outsiders (see, e.g., 1 Cor 7:17-24). It is this ethnic binary and other polarities of difference that Paul and his followers seek to overcome in their teachings (e.g., Gal 3:28, "There is no longer Jew (Ioudaios) or Greek (Hellēn Ἕλλην), there is no longer slave (doulos δοῦλος) or free (eleutheros ἐλεύθερος), there is no longer male (arsēn ἄρσην) and female (thēlys θῆλυς); for all of you are one in Christ Jesus"; Col 3:11 "there is no longer Greek and Jew, circumcised (peritomē περιτομή) and uncircumcised (akrobystia ἀκροβυστία; see CIRCUMCISION), barbarian (barbaros βάρβαρος), Scythian (Skythēs Σκύθης), slave and free; but Christ is all and in all!" Among the Gospel writers, Jesus is depicted as one who associates with a Samaritan (John 4:1-42; see SAMARITAN WOMAN; SAMARITANS) and a SYROPHOENICIAN WOMAN (Mark 7:24-30; compare Matt 15:21-28), yet instructs his followers not to pray as the ethnē (Matt 6:32).

C. Interpretive Implications

Ethnicity is best understood in biblical writings as an interpretive category for raising questions about differences and boundaries that exist among groups of people, as well as the distinctive values, beliefs, and attitudes certain groups may hold. The interpretive import goes beyond the mere surface identification of groups of people (e.g., Egyptians, Babylonians, Cretans, Jews, etc.), but in actuality may serve as a rhetorical strategy for calling attention to certain dangers that the author takes particular groups to represent. For example, when the writer of Titus refers to Cretans as "liars, vicious brutes, and lazy gluttons" (Titus 1:12-13), this is not simply directed at the Cretans, but rather at those who "must be silenced . . . teaching for sordid gain what it is not right to teach" (Titus 1:11). In this regard, it is useful to examine the symbolic use of ethnicity in biblical writings through the lens of what is referred to as "ethno-political" rhetoric.

D. Summary

By analyzing biblical writings through the lens of ethnicity, one must reckon with the complex and often hidden or masked ideological assumptions that are implicit in ancient texts and complicit in the methods that are utilized to interpret the texts. Ethnicity offers a framework for exposing some of the unrelenting realities related to race that invariably influence how interpreters of the Bible read ethnic differences in biblical writings. See ANTHROPOLOGY, NT CULTURAL; ANTHROPOLOGY, OT CULTURAL; IDEOLOGICAL CRITICISM; RACISM; STRANGER.

Bibliography: F. Barth. *Ethnic Groups and Boundaries* (1969); P. Bilde et al., eds. *Ethnicity in Hellenistic Egypt* (1992); B. Braxton. "The Role of Ethnicity in the Social Location of 1 Corinthians 7:17-24." *Yet with a Steady Beat.* R. Bailey, ed. (2003) 19–32; M. Brett, ed., *Ethnicity and the Bible* (1996, 2002); D. Buell. *Why This New Race? Ethnic Reasoning in Early Christianity* (2005); G. Byron. *Symbolic Blackness and Ethnic Difference in Early Christian Literature* (2002); J. Curtis and N. Tallis. *Forgotten Empire: The World of Ancient Persia* (2005); S. Fenton. *Ethnicity* (2003). J. Hall. *Ethnic Identity in Greek Antiquity* (1997); D. Redford. *From Slave to Pharaoh: The Black Experience of Ancient Egypt* (2004); R. Sadler. *Can a Cushite Change His Skin? An Examination of Race, Ethnicity, and Othering in the Hebrew Bible* (2005); W. Sollors. *The Invention of Ethnicity* (1989).

GAY L. BYRON

ETHNOGRAPHY AND ETHNOLOGY. *See* ANTHROPOLOGY, NT CULTURAL; ANTHROPOLOGY, OT CULTURAL.

ETIOLOGY. The study of a phenomenon's cause or origin (aitia αἰτία). As a critical term applied to narrative, *etiology* refers to stories that tell how something came to be or came to have its definitive characteristics. In Scripture such stories are typically told about names of persons and places, rites and customs, ethnic identities, and natural phenomena.

Ostensibly etymological explanations of personal and place names, actually based on wordplay, are a frequent type of etiology. Personal names explained by etiology include El-roi (Gen 16:13), Esau and Jacob (25:25-30), Jacob's sons (29:31–30:24), 32:24-38), Moses (Exod 2:10*b*), Peter (Matt 16:18-19), etc.

With place names, sometimes continuity to the present is implicit (Gen 16:14; 32:30), while other place names are explicitly said to be used "to this day" (Josh 5:8-9; 7:26*b*; Judg 18:12; 2 Chr 20:26; Matt 27:3-8, etc., though the phrase "to this day" does not always signal an etiology). Monumental stones also mark "to this day" places where eventful things happened (Gen 35:20; Josh 4:9; 7:26*a*; 8:29; 1 Sam 6:18*b*; 2 Sam 18:18).

Etiologies also explain the origins of various rites and customs, sometimes with the phrase "to this day" (Gen 32:32; Josh 9:27; 1 Sam 5:5) but not always (Exod 12:21-27*a*; Judg 11:39*b*-40). An etiological connection is also implied when a rite or custom is called a "sign" of its original precedent (Gen 17:11; Exod 13:6-10; 13:15*b*-16, etc.). Etiological explanation is sometimes associated with answering children's questions (Exod 12:26-27*a*; 13:14-15; Deut 6:20-25; Josh 4:6*b*-7, 21-24, etc.).

Etiological stories trace Israelite attitudes toward other peoples back to events involving eponymous ancestors. For example, the Ishmaelites' antipathy toward the Israelites comes from the conflicted relationship between Hagar and Sarah, and their respective sons, Ishmael and Isaac (Gen 16:11-12; see also Gen 9:18-27; 19:30-38, etc.).

Myths of origins generally have an etiological function whether or not they expressly make an etiological claim. The rainbow is created to be a perpetual sign of Yahweh's post-flood covenant with "all flesh" (Gen 9:8-17; compare Gen 2:18-24). Although Gen 1:1–2:4*a* does not explicitly state that Sabbath observance originated in God's rest on the seventh day of creation, this is how the story was understood (see Exod 20:8-11; 31:12-17). Stories that are not purely mythic may also have an etiological function without making claims to this effect. The Pentateuch's portrayal of Israel as a covenant people with one central sanctuary provides an etiology for the kind of religious community formed by Second Temple Judaism, as do accounts of the Last Supper for the rites of eucharist (Luke 22:14-20; see 1 Cor 11:23-26) and foot washing (John 13:1-15). The renaming of Simon as "Peter," the "rock" on which the church was founded, is an etiological account of Simon Peter's authority in the early church (Matt 16:18).

In view of this complexity, a monolithic approach to etiological stories is unwarranted. Earlier scholarly discussion focused on their use of formulaic language, their intention, and their historicity. It is now clear that the overall structure of the narrative, and not formulaic language itself, is the definitive trait. Moreover, narratives can be etiological in different ways, depending on how etiological elements shape their overall structure, and the etiological elements can have different rhetorical effects.

For example, in the story of Jacob at the Jabbok (Gen 32:22-32) the "etymological" (wordplay) etiologies of the names Israel and Peniel are integral parts of the narrative spoken by the main characters, but the dietary etiology (for not eating the thigh muscle) is an afterthought spoken by the narrator. By telling Jacob that he is now to be called "one who strives with God" (Israel), the anonymous attacker intimates that this crippling struggle is in effect an encounter with God, and by calling the place "face of God" (Peniel) Jacob signals that he retrospectively recognizes this to be the case. The narrative itself actually has nothing to do with the origins of a dietary custom, but the concluding etiology serves to link the narrative's characterization of Israel's identity—as a people whose struggle with God is crippling yet still promising—with a practice that will continually remind them of it. The narrative invites those who identify with Jacob to characterize themselves with a theological insight that their history hints at, and to internalize this self-characterization with a symbolically corresponding food taboo.

Etiological thinking may or may not be speculative. Mythic reflection and historical investigation can both take an etiological form. And when etiological thinking is speculative, it may or may not be fanciful. When inquiring about things that happened before recorded human witnesses, modern cosmologists and paleoanthropologists are engaged in etiology, just as were their ancient counterparts. Both start from an assessment of the way things presently are, and then ask from what hypothetical starting point they could have come to be this way, given what is known about natural and social developmental processes. From an assessment of the extent to which a biblical narrative is etiological, one can draw no direct conclusion regarding its historicity. As the story of Jacob shows, the function of etiological elements may have little or no bearing on the question of historicity, and undue preoccupation with this question would miss the main point. *See* LEGEND; NAME, NAMING; NARRATIVE CRITICISM; RHETORICAL CRITICISM, NT; RHETORICAL CRITICISM, OT; WORDPLAY IN THE OT.

Bibliography: B. O. Long. *The Problem of Etiological Narrative in the Old Testament* (1968); P. J. Van Dyk. "The Function of So-Called Etiological Elements in Narratives. *ZAW* 102 (1990) 19–33.

MICHAEL H. FLOYD

ET-TELL. *See* AI.

ET-TWEIN. *See* TWEIN, KHIRBET ABU EL.

EUBULUS yoo-byoo′luhs [Εὔβουλος Euboulos]. Paul's companion (2 Tim 4:21), likely present during the confinement from which 2 Timothy was written. Eubulus was a common Greek name.

EUCHARIST [εὐχαριστία eucharistia]. The term *eucharist* derives from the Greek term eucharistia, which means "thanksgiving," from eucharisteō (εὐχαριστέω, "to give thanks"). It came to be used in the early church as the primary technical term for its ritual meal of bread and wine. In the NT, however, it was used only in a generic sense, never in a technical sense.

A. Background of the Term
B. New Testament Usage
C. The Old Paradigm
D. A New Paradigm
   1. The banquet tradition
   2. Eucharist vs. agape?
   3. Eucharist in the New Testament
   4. Transition to a token meal
Bibliography

A. Background of the Term

The semantic background for the term "to give thanks" is most likely to be found in the patronage or benefactor social system of the ancient world. The appropriate response to a benefactor was to show gratitude, which was expressed in various ways including "thanksgiving." This usage appears in Acts 24:3, where Tertullus addresses his superior, "most excellent Felix," with the appropriate "utmost gratitude" (or "with all thanksgiving"). The religious usage, in which one would direct thanksgiving to one's deity, probably developed first in the Hellenistic ruler cult before being adopted into Greco-Roman religious language including that of Hellenistic Judaism. In the LXX, the standard prayer term is "bless" (eulogētos εὐλογητός; barukh בָּרוּךְ), but in the later apocryphal writings eucharistia/eucharisteō occur, both in reference to thanksgiving given to men (2 Macc 12:31) and to God (2 Macc 10:7). Philo makes extensive use of "thanksgiving" in his prayer language as the appropriate response to the gifts given by God (*Plant.* 130).

B. New Testament Usage

In the NT, eucharisteō simply means thanksgiving offered to God as a response to God's gifts. It is Paul's standard term for introducing the "thanksgiving" section of his letters (Rom 1:8; 1 Cor 1:4; Phil 1:3; 1 Thess 1:2; Phlm 4). It is also a standard term for thanksgiving offered in a variety of contexts in the Gospels (Luke 17:16; 18:11; John 11:41). Its most influential usage, however, is found in the last supper texts, in which Jesus "gives thanks," over the bread in Paul's version (1 Cor 11:24) and over the cup in Mark's version (Mark 14:23). In these accounts, eucharisteō is often used interchangeably with eulogeō (εὐλογέω "to bless"), indicating that neither term had yet become the dominant prayer term for the Lord's Supper tradition. For example, in 1 Cor 10:16, "the cup of blessing" is "blessed." Similarly, in Mark 14:22, the prayer over the bread is "to bless," but over the cup, it is "to give thanks" (see also Matt 26:26-27; Luke 22:17, 19 has eucharisteō for both cup and bread). In the NT, rather than "eucharist" the ritual meal is called LORD'S SUPPER in Paul (1 Cor 11:20) and "breaking of bread" in Acts (2:42; 20:7).

C. The Old Paradigm

According to a traditional reading of the evidence, there were two forms of ritual meals that developed in early Christianity, namely the eucharist and the AGAPE (or love feast; see Jude 12; Tertullian, *Apol.* 39.16-18). Paul's version of the Lord's Supper in 1 Cor 11:17-34, since it included a full meal (11:21) as well as the last supper institution narrative (11:23-25), is seen in this model to represent an early combination of the two. Many scholars conclude that the two forms of meal became separated as a direct result of the problems at the Corinthian meal. The *agape* continued to retain the form of a full meal while the eucharist became only a token meal of BREAD and WINE. The last supper tradition, with its emphasis on the death of Jesus as interpreted in the words of institution, came to be connected with the eucharist, while the *agape* lacked that emphasis. Scholars who follow this paradigm tend to assume a fairly direct line of development from the command of Jesus ("Do this in remembrance of me," 1 Cor 11:24-25) to the practice of the later church. Some scholars would then use the term *eucharist* to refer to all forms of the ritual meal in the NT that are deemed implicitly "sacramental." Others would reserve the term *eucharist* for the later codified form of ritual meal with its specified prayers, token portions of bread and wine, change of location from table to altar, and explicit sacramental theology.

D. A New Paradigm

1. The banquet tradition

The early Christian ritual meal developed out of the social institution of the ancient banquets. According to this model, early Christians ate together ritually as all groups did, whether they were Greek, Roman, Jewish, or early Christian in their religious identity. The basic cultural structure of the meal was that of the reclining banquet, a meal tradition that was rich in religious and cultural symbolism (*see* BANQUET; MEALS). Like other groups of their day, early Christians adapted their meal practices to fit their specific identity. One implication of this model is that it does not require an account for the early Christian ritual meal as directly based on a command of Jesus. Rather the occurrence of a ritual meal is seen to be an expected outcome of social formation.

2. Eucharist vs. agape?

Many scholars are now convinced that the evidence for Christian meal practices is too complex to be categorized under two forms of meal, one "sacramental" in meaning and token in form (the eucharist), the other more secular in meaning and a full meal in form (the agape). Rather one should emphasize the great variety to be found in early Christian meal forms.

When eucharistia first began to be used in a technical sense, it referred to a ritual meal tradition that was still fluid. Ignatius in the early 1st cent. urged that "one eucharist" be observed and defined it as a celebration of the "one flesh of our Lord Jesus Christ and one cup which brings the unity of his blood" (Ign., *Phld.* 4.1) yet made no reference to the last supper or words of institution. Ignatius also used both "eucharist" and "agape" to refer to the same ritual meal, which therefore must have been a full meal, not a token meal (Ign., *Smyrn.* 8). At about the same time in Syria (ca. 100), the *Didache* provided official prayers for what it termed the *eucharistia*; these prayers make no reference to the death of Jesus and its meaning nor to the last supper nor to any meal traditions of Jesus (9–10). The eucharist of the *Didache* was also a full meal (10:1), and was celebrated with the cup first then the bread (as seen also in Luke 22:17-19 and 1 Cor 10:16). Throughout the 2nd and 3rd cent., there continued to be variations in early Christian ritual meal traditions in regard to terminology, theology, order (bread-cup or cup-bread), form (full meal or token meal), and even types of food (e.g., some sources specify bread and water rather than bread and wine). It was not until the 4th cent. that the standard liturgical form of the eucharist had taken shape.

3. Eucharist in the New Testament

Scholars often use the term *eucharistic* rather loosely in describing the NT, but it can be misleading to do so. While it is true that the NT is a primary resource for eucharistic language and imagery, it is incorrect to read later eucharistic theology and practice back into the NT documents.

The "institution narratives" (i.e., the last supper narratives: Matt 26:26-30; Mark 14:22-26; Luke 22:14-23; 1 Cor 11:23-25) have often been read as straightforward historical accounts in which Jesus instituted what the church continues to practice today. But read in their contexts, these narratives do not lend themselves easily to such interpretations. Above all, it is unclear how they might have functioned as liturgical texts. Although it is often assumed that the narrative

and words of Jesus would have been liturgically performed or recited in some way, there is no record of this ever having taken place in Christian communities until the 3rd cent. It is only at this point that the narrative is actually included in a liturgical prayer (*Apostolic Tradition* 4). Rather than being liturgical texts, it is more likely that the institution narratives functioned as etiological texts or cult legends, explaining where the rite came from, rather than as rubrics outlining how it was to be practiced.

The "words of institution" in the last supper narratives (e.g., "This is my body. . . . This is my blood of the covenant," Mark 14:22, 24) tend to be interpreted with the highly developed sacramental meaning of later church traditions. But in the contexts of the NT writings themselves, such interpretations would be anachronistic. While scholars have often interpreted the words of Jesus in these narratives according to the categories of ritual sacrifice, it is more likely that the correct semantic background for these phrases is that of martyrdom, especially as it is expressed in 4 Maccabees (e.g., 6:27-29; 17:20-22).

The "Lord's Supper" in 1 Cor 11:17-34, which is the most detailed account of a ritual meal in a NT community, is clearly a full meal (11:21), as is the meal envisioned in the institution narrative Paul quotes in which the cup is blessed "after supper" (11:25); here the narrative reflects the normal order of a Greco-Roman banquet in which the first course, the deipnon (δεῖπνον) or "supper," was followed by the second course, the symposium or the wine-drinking part of the meal. Contrary to the old paradigm, there is no compelling reason in the text of 1 Cor to assume that Paul intended to separate a "sacramental meal" from a full meal. Rather it is more likely that Paul's advice to "wait for one another" (11:33) simply means to eat together, not separately, and in doing so one would "discern the body" (11:29), namely the community as "body" (10:16-17; 12:13). According to this reading, Paul's advice assumed that Christians in Corinth would continue to eat a full meal together.

4. Transition to a token meal

It is unclear exactly when or under what circumstances the primary ritual meal in early Christianity became a token meal of bread and wine with an accompanying sacramental theology. This development may have been at least partially a result of the change in social location for the early Christian communities from the house church, with its tradition of hospitality centering on the dining room, to the basilica, which brought with it another form of social formation and social organization, a process that mushroomed in the 4th cent. This new context generated the standard liturgical form for the eucharist. Prior to that, however, early Christian ritual meals took on a wide variety of forms and, while eucharist was a generally used name for the communal meal, it had not yet developed a standardized meaning. *See* DIDACHE.

Bibliography: Paul F. Bradshaw. *Eucharistic Origins* (2004); Dom Gregory Dix. *The Shape of the Liturgy* (1945); Andrew McGowan. *Ascetic Eucharists: Food and Drink in Early Christian Ritual Meals* (1999); Andrew McGowan. "Is There a Liturgical Text in This Gospel?: The Institution Narratives and Their Early Interpretive Communities." *JBL* 118 (1999) 73–87; Andrew McGowan. "Food, Ritual, and Power." *A People's History of Christianity, Vol. 2: Late Antique Christianity.* Virginia Burrus, ed. (2005) 145–64; Dennis E. Smith. *From Symposium to Eucharist: The Banquet in the Early Christian World* (2003); L. Michael White. "Regulating Fellowship in the Communal Meal: Early Jewish and Christian Evidence." *Meals in a Social Context: Aspects of the Communal Meal in the Hellenistic and Roman World.* Inge Nielsen and Hanne Sigismund Nielsen, eds. (1998) 177–205.

DENNIS E. SMITH

EUERGETES yoo-uhr´juh-teez [εὐεργέτης euergetēs]. Euergetes literally means "BENEFACTOR." It was a title of honor given to persons who had "done the state some service." In the prologue to Sirach, Ben Sira's grandson uses the reign of the Ptolemaic ruler in Egypt, Euergetes, as a reference for dating his translation.

MARY KAY DOBROVOLNY, R.S.M.

EUGNOSTOS, LETTER OF. A non-Christian Gnostic tractate probably originating in Egypt in the later part of the 1st or 2nd cent. CE. Written in Sahidic Coptic, *Eugnostos,* likely the source for the Christian Gnostic tractate *The Sophia of Jesus Christ,* features a description of the nonvisible heavenly realm the writer believed to be mirrored in the visible world, which can be known through a divine principle called Thought (ennoia ἔννοια). *See* APOCRYPHA, NT; JESUS, WISDOM OF.

SUSANA DESOLA FUNSTEN

EUMENES II OF PERGAMUM yoo´muh-neez [Εὐμένης Eumenēs]. Eumenes II Soter was king of PERGAMUM (ca. 197–158 BCE). His father had attempted to turn the capital into the Athens of Asia, and Eumenes made the city a center of Greek culture and learning, with the country organized as a Greek state. He sided with Rome against ANTIOCHUS III and was rewarded with a large slice of Seleucid territory, but he later helped Antiochus IV gain the Seleucid throne. His army stopped the invading Gauls in central Asia Minor, giving the name GALATIA to the region. Eumenes commemorated the victory in the famous Pergamum altar.

LESTER L. GRABBE

EUNICE yoo´nis [Εὐνίκη Eunikē]. Eunice, whose name means "good victory," was the mother of TIMOTHY,

one of Paul's closest friends and co-workers. She was from Lystra or Derbe in Galatia and had been converted to faith in Christ from Judaism, although she was apparently married to a Gentile (Acts 16:1, 3). According to some Lat. MSS on Acts 16:1 and Origen on Rom 16:21, she was a widow, and it is possible that she had improved her family's status through marriage. Eunice was known for pious faith, which she received from her mother LOIS and passed on to Timothy (2 Tim 1:5).

NANCY CALVERT-KOYZIS

EUNUCH yoo´nuhk [סָרִים saris; εὐνοῦχος eunouchos]. Although the term saris can designate a married royal official (POTIPHAR, Gen 39:1), eunouchos often suggests a castrated figure attending female rulers (JEZEBEL [2 Kgs 9:30-32], ESTHER [Esth 4:4-5], CANDACE [Acts 8:27]) or overseeing the king's harem (Esth 2:14-15). The emasculated condition of eunuchs could include a range of physiological characteristics (defective, damaged, or dismembered testicles and/or penis) resulting from inherited nature ("eunuchs who have been so from birth"), imposed mutilation ("made eunuchs by others"—often a casualty of war or slavery), or self infliction (as with ascetics "who have made themselves eunuchs for the kingdom of heaven") (see Matt 19:12).

While eunuchs could enjoy considerable political and economic influence (Acts 8:27), in ancient societies that placed a high premium on male virility, the effeminate eunuch embodied shame, impotence, and social deviance. His ambiguous, abnormal sexuality marked him as a threatening liminal figure, "no man . . . a thing of nought" (Herodotus, *Hist.* 8.106); "neither man nor woman but something . . . monstrous, alien to human nature" (Lucian, *Eunuch.* 6-11; compare Josephus, *Ant.* 4.290-91). In the Bible, the eunuch's alienation is compounded by his disability (lack of wholeness) and inability to transmit covenant status through circumcision (in the case of dismemberment) and procreation. Biblical law excludes men with damaged genitalia from the worshiping assembly in general (Deut 23:1) and the holy priesthood in particular (Lev 21:17-21; compare Philo, *Spec. Laws* 1.324-25). In the Wisdom similes of Ben Sira, eunuchs exemplify frustrated desire and anguished futility (Sir 20:4; 30:20).

Other traditions, however, paint a more hopeful picture. Isaiah and the Wisdom of Solomon envision an honored and fruitful place for faithful eunuchs in the Lord's house (Isa 56:3-8; Wis 3:14-15); Jeremiah reports the noble efforts of EBED-MELECH, an Ethiopian eunuch serving the king of Judah, to rescue Jeremiah from unjust imprisonment (Jer 38:7-15; 39:15-18); and Acts 8:26-40 recounts the baptism of a Scripture-reading, God-fearing eunuch from Candace's Ethiopian court. In this latter text, the eunuch's prominent status as a chief financial officer is balanced by his apparent identification with the shorn and scorned figure from Isa 53:7-8 and his implied experience of religious ostracism ("What is to prevent me from being baptized?" Acts 8:30-36).

Bibliography: Mathew Kuefler. *The Manly Eunuch: Masculinity, Gender Ambiguity, and Christian Ideology in Late Antiquity* (2001); F. Scott Spencer. "The Ethiopian Eunuch and His Bible: A Social-Science Analysis." *BTB* 22 (1992) 155–65.

F. SCOTT SPENCER

EUODIA y*oo*-oh′dee-uh [Εὐοδία Euodia]. Paul urges this Christian woman to agree with fellow believer SYNTYCHE so that they may live in harmony in the church in Philippi (Phil 4:2), continuing the tradition of women leaders in the church in Philippi (compare Acts 16:40). They are included in the group of "fellow-workers" having previously helped Paul in his evangelistic endeavors (Phil 4:3). It is likely they are Paul's close friends because in such letters enemies were left unnamed and denigrated by anonymity.

Bibliography: Gordon D. Fee. *Paul's Letter to the Philippians.* NICNT (1995); Gerald F. Hawthorne. *Philippians.* WBC 43 (1983).

NANCY CALVERT-KOYZIS

EUPATOR y*oo*′puh-tor [Εὐπάτωρ Eupatōr]. The surname of the Seleucid king ANTIOCHUS V (1 Macc 6:17; 2 Macc 10:10, 13:1). It means "of a good father," likely a reference to Antiochus IV Epiphanes.

EUPHEMISM. A socially proper word or expression substituted for one that is considered offensive or inappropriate. Biblical authors and editors often used euphemisms to express things they perceived to be socially sensitive, taboo, or dangerous. Sexual intercourse is described through verbs such as "to know" (yadha‛ [יָדַע], Gen 4:1; gnōskō γνώσκω) or "to go in" (bo᾽ [בּוֹא], Gen 16:2). Body parts such as the hand or feet are used to describe genitalia (Ruth 3:4; Isa 6:2). Excretory functions (1 Sam 24:3, lit. "to cover his feet"), death, and illness are also frequently euphemized in the biblical material.

FRANK M. YAMADA

EUPHRATES RIVER y*oo*-fray′teez [פְּרָת perath]. In the Bible, the Euphrates is one of the rivers of paradise (Gen 2:14). It formed the northeastern boundary of territory promised by Yahweh to Israel (Gen 15:18, Deut 1:7; 11:24; Josh 1:4) and of the Israelite kingdom at its peak (2 Sam 8:3; 10:16; 1 Kgs 4:24; 1 Chr 18:3). The Euphrates and Egypt were used as idealized boundary markers of the kingdom God gave to Solomon (1 Kgs 3:13; 4:21). It is sometimes known simply as "The River" (Num 22:5; Josh 24:3, 14) as in the province "Beyond the River" (Ezra 4:10-22; Neh 2:7-9). The

river's two branches flow westward through the highlands of eastern Anatolia, join and flow southward past ancient Kummuh (classical Commagene), Carchemish, and Til Barsip (*see* TARTAN).

It was at Carchemish in 605 BCE that Babylonian crown prince Nebuchadnezzar II defeated Pharaoh Neco II and drove him back to Egypt (2 Kgs 24:7; Jer 46:2). The river turns southeastward at Emar, collecting the waters of the Balih and Habur, and passing ancient Dura-Europus, Mari, and Hit (famous for bitumen). At ancient Sippar (city of sungod Shamash) it reaches the Mesopotamian plain, dividing into many shifting branches that provided water, irrigation, and transport for the ancient cities of Sumer and Babylonia. Among these was Babylon, seat of Marduk, where Nebuchadnezzar II settled the lion's share of Jews carried off from Jerusalem and Judah, and which became a center of postexilic Judaism. Jeremiah's book of prophecies was sunk in the Euphrates opposite Babylon (Jer 51:60-64). Also dependent on the river were Nippur, seat of Enlil, chief god of the Sumerian pantheon; Shuruppak, where Ziusudra, the Sumerian Noah, built his ark; Uruk, city of Anu and the goddess Ishtar and home to the hero Gilgamesh; and Ur, city of moon god Nanna/Sin and original home of Abraham (Gen 11:28-31). The various river branches emptied into extensive marshes at the head of the Persian Gulf until the Roman period when today's Shatt-al-Arab was formed.

JOANN SCURLOCK

EUPOLEMUS y*oo*-pol′uh-muhs [Εὐπόλεμος Eupolemos]. A diplomat sent by Judas Maccabeus to establish a relationship with Rome after the defeat of NICANOR (1 Macc 8:17; 2 Macc 4:11). Identified as the son of John and the grandson of Accos he is likely the same Eupolemus who was a Jewish historian at that time.

DEREK E. WITTMAN

EUPOLEMUS, PSEUDO-. *See* PSEUDO-EUPOLEMUS.

EURIPIDES. Athenian tragic playwright, who was born probably in the 480s BCE and died between 408 and 406 in Macedon, while the guest of King Archelaus. Euripides wrote some ninety plays, of which nineteen survive, including *Medea, Bacchae, Hippolytus,* and *Trojan Women.* During his lifetime, he won only four victories at the Athens dramatic competition called the DIONYSIA (and one posthumously), far fewer than his contemporaries Sophocles and Aeschylus. Nevertheless, he attracted strong interest in his time. Euripides was known for being willing to portray women and slaves in unconventional ways, for critiquing traditional religion and representing the gods engaged in morally questionable actions, and for confronting darker aspects of social and psychological experience. Aristotle in the *Poetics* called him the "most tragic of the poets."

DIANE B. LIPSETT

EUROPEAN INTERPRETATION. Bible interpretation in Western Europe was shaped since the Enlightenment by struggles between churches and their critics, fought in academic denominational theological departments controlled by state churches (e.g., Lutheran in Germany), with little dialogue with lay groups and independent churches rooted in faith-based readings of Scripture and the confessions. Historical-critical studies, including social-historical studies, predominate; scientifically establishing "what the text meant" precedes theological interpretation, "what the text means."

With the decline of state churches, and in countries with clear church/state separation (e.g., France), "reception history" and academic ahistorical literary studies of the Bible (structuralist, deconstructionist, narrative, philosophical) developed in dialogue with lay groups and through greater ecumenical interaction. Academic biblical interpretation became more contextual through its role in inner-church conflict (ordination of women, gays and lesbians) and through the ecumenical acknowledgment of "ecclesial interpretations"—Roman Catholic (flowering after Vatican II), Lutheran, Methodist, and Pentecostal (holiness tradition), Reformed (Evangelical, InterVarsity Fellowship)—and of liberationist interpretations in feminist and contextual Bible study.

DANIEL PATTE

EUSEBIUS yoo-see´ be-uhs. Fourth-century historian of the early church, bishop during the Council of Nicea, and Christian apologist, Eusebius of Caesarea is often overlooked as biblical scholar. During his forty-year career (ca. 290–339 CE), Eusebius presided over a library at Caesarea originally cultivated by Origen and later Pamphilus, and served as "corrector" of the OT manuscripts of Origen's *Hexapla*. A Christian chronicler, he sought to synchronize biblical and extrabiblical events. In his geographical *Onomasticon*, Eusebius surveyed biblical place names. The *Prophetic Ecologues*, the *Demonstration of the Gospel*, and *On Isaiah* reveal his abilities as a commentator. Eusebius also distinguished himself as a scholar of the Gospels, producing a cross-referencing system (called *Sections and Canons*) for comparing the Gospels. Around 320, he composed a two-part work entitled *Questions and Answers on the Genealogy of our Savior* and *Questions and Answers on the Resurrection of our Savior*. When Constantine commissioned Eusebius to produce "fifty copies of the sacred writings" for use in the new churches he proposed to build in Constantinople, the result was probably Gospel books, not complete Bibles. These "magnificent and elaborately-bound" volumes likely included his *Sections and Canons*. In *Ecclesiastical History* (3.25.1-7), Eusebius produced the first datable (ca. 303–326) list in the history of the Christian canon of Scripture, whereby he sought to distinguish between writings that were to be deemed authoritative for the Christian community ("encovenanted"), and those that, because they were heretical, pseudepigraphical, or both, were not. The catalog suggests that Eusebius had in mind a twenty-two-book NT that included four Gospels, Acts, fourteen letters of Paul (including Hebrews), 1 Peter, 1 John, and the Apocalypse. A twenty-two-book list of Christian Scriptures, "covenantal writings," held out a certain attraction for Eusebius. Accepting Origen's reckoning of the number of books constituting the Hebrew Scriptures, Eusebius saw an obvious symmetry between the number of books in the old and new covenants, a symmetry lending further support to the doctrine of providence propounded throughout the *Ecclesiastical History*. Thus, Eusebius played an instrumental role in the process of canonization. He deserves not only the moniker "the father of Church history" but "the father of the Christian Bible" as well.

Bibliography: Harold Attridge and Gohei Hata, eds. *Eusebius, Christianity, and Judaism* (1992); T. D. Barnes. *Constantine and Eusebius* (1981); G. F. Chesnut. *The First Christian Histories: Eusebius, Socrates, Sozomen, Theodoret, and Evagrius.* 2nd ed. (1986); G. S. P. Freeman-Grenville, R. L. Chapman III, and J. E. Taylor. *The Onomasticon by Eusebius of Caesarea* (2003); R. M. Grant. *Eusebius as Church Historian* (1980); M. J. Hollerich. *Eusebius of Caesarea's Commentary on Isaiah* (1999); A. A. Mosshammer. *The Chronicle of Eusebius and Greek Chronographic Tradition* (1979); Gregory A. Robbins. "Fifty Copies of the Sacred Writings" (*VC* 4:36): Entire Bibles or Gospel Books? *Studia Patristica* 19 (1989) 91–98; Gregory A. Robbins. "Eusebius' Lexicon of 'Canonicity'" *Studia Patristica* 25 (1993) 134–41.

GREGORY ALLEN ROBBINS

EUTYCHUS yoo´tuh-kuhs [Εὔτυχος Eutychos]. In Acts 20:7-12, a young man who attended an evening meeting between Paul, his missionary associates, and the leaders of the Christian movement in Troas. The hour grew late; there were many lamps in a small upstairs room; Eutychus sat in the window, presumably seeking air, but "fell into a deep sleep while Paul kept on talking longer." He fell from the window and was gathered up for dead, but Paul, holding him, said, "Don't worry—the life is still in him." The story illustrates well Luke's dry wit: Paul's loquacity nearly killing the lad (whose name means "lucky"); Paul's breezy bedside manner, saying "he's fine—rub some dirt on it," and then going back upstairs for yet more talk and a midnight snack; and the home folks' relief at being able to take Eutychus away alive.

RICHARD B. VINSON

EVANGELISM. *Evangelism*, a modern term, never used in the NRSV, denotes the proclamation of GOOD NEWS or "Gospel," derived from the Greek verb euangelizō (εὐαγγελίζω) and noun euangelion (εὐαγγέλιον).

In the OT, heralded good news often concerns the death of an enemy ruler or victory in battle (1 Sam 31:9; 2 Sam 1:20; 4:10; 18:19-31; 1 Kgs 1:42; Ps 68:11-14; Nah 1:15). Jeremiah references his own birth announcement by a "man who brought [glad] news to my father"(Jer 20:15): however, in light of the Babylonian threat against Judah, Jeremiah "curses" this messenger for "not kill[ing] me in the womb" (20:15-18).

Certain texts in Psalms and Isaiah 40–66 extol in more cosmic and spiritual terms the "evangelical" tidings of God's restoration (salvation) of creation and people (Pss 40:9; 96:2; Isa 40:9; 52:7; 60:6; 61:1). The Isaiah passages especially trumpet the good news of Israel's joyous return from exile. Paul cites part of Isaiah 52:7 to describe those who proclaim the gospel of God's salvation realized by faith in the Lord Jesus whom God raised from the dead (Rom 10:9-17), and the Lukan Jesus cites Isa 61:1-2*a* as a programmatic statement of his Spirit-directed mission (Luke 4:18-19).

Typically, the synoptic narratives feature Jesus' (and sometimes his disciples') heralding the good news of God or God's kingdom, often in conjunction with supernatural acts of healing and deliverance (Matt 4:23; 9:35; 11:5; 24:14; Mark 1:14-15; Luke 4:40-44; 7:22; 8:1-2; 9:1-6; 16:16). Luke (1:19 and 2:10) reports Gabriel's good news announcements of the births of John and Jesus. In Acts and the Pauline letters the focus shifts to the living Lord Jesus Christ as the prime subject (substance) of God's redemptive gospel (Acts 5:42; 8:12; 11:20; 13:32-33; 15:7, 35; Rom 1:1-6; 2:16; 10:15-16; 15:19-20; 16:25; 1 Cor 9:12-23; 15:1-7; Gal 1:6-9; Phil 1:12-16; 1 Thess 3:2). An exception appears in 1 Thess 3:6, where Timothy brings good news to Paul about the Thessalonians' "faith and love."

F. SCOTT SPENCER

EVANGELIST i-van'juh-list [εὐαγγελιστής euangelistēs]. One who proclaims the good news (euangelion εὐαγγέλιον). The three biblical uses of the term appear in Pauline-related writings and refer to preaching the gospel of Jesus Christ (Acts 21:8; Eph 4:11; 2 Tim 4:5).

Although many spread the Christian gospel in Acts, only Philip is specifically designated "the evangelist" in 21:8. This label aptly recalls Philip's itinerant preaching and baptizing mission in 8:4-40 and may be used to distinguish this Philip from his apostle namesake (compare Luke 6:14; Acts 1:13). Moreover, the fact that Philip emerges as "the evangelist" when the missionary/apostle Paul and the prophet Agabus visit Philip's

Caesarean home (21:8-14)—and just after Paul had instructed the elders/presbyters (20:17), overseers/bishops (20:28), and shepherds/pastors (20:28-29) of the Ephesian church (20:17-38)—may reflect a special "evangelist" vocation in Pauline circles distinct from other "offices" or ministries.

The deutero-Pauline letter of Ephesians distinguishes evangelists from apostles, prophets, pastors, and teachers in a list of gifted leaders in the body of Christ (4:11). Since the church rests upon "the foundation of the apostles and prophets" (2:20)—direct emissaries of the risen Christ, including the twelve apostles, presumably, and Paul, certainly (1:1; 3:1-6)—"evangelists" may represent second-generation preachers who carry on the apostolic-prophetic mission. Their distinction from pastors and teachers may intimate their primary calling to attract, rather than to instruct, new converts.

Paul exhorts Timothy to "do the work of an evangelist," focusing more on the functional than official role of evangelistic ministry (2 Tim 4:5). In 2 Timothy, such work is closely related to "proclaim[ing] the message" and offering pastoral instruction (4:2-4). Again, the relationship between apostle and evangelist appears to be successive: Timothy, the "beloved child" of Paul the "apostle of Christ Jesus," is charged with faithfully guarding and passing on Paul's gospel (1:1-2, 6-14; 2:1-2; 3:10-14; compare 1 Tim 1:18; 4:11-6; 6:20).

Early church fathers typically used euangelistēs as a technical title for the authors of gospel books (ta euangelia τὰ εὐαγγέλια; compare Hippolytus, *Antichr.* 56; Tertullian, *Prax.* 21.23). Eusebius, however, also refers to "evangelists" engaged in itinerant missionary work and gospel proclamation. Numbered among the "shining lights" of the 2nd cent., evangelists were "pious disciples of great men" who "built in every place on the foundations of the churches laid by the apostles" (*Hist. eccl.* 3.37). Eusebius cites a particular evangelist named Pantaenus, formerly a venerable philosopher in the Alexandrian tradition, who "was appointed as a herald for the gospel of Christ in India," furthering the mission begun by the apostle Bartholomew (*Hist. eccl.* 5.10). *See* GOOD NEWS; MESSAGE; MINISTRY, CHRISTIAN.

F. SCOTT SPENCER

EVE eev [חַוָּה khawwah]. The name Eve, meaning "life," appears but once in the story of Eden (Gen 2–3), near the end (3:20). Elsewhere, the generic "woman," prefaced in places by the possessive "his" or the article "the," identifies the primal female figure.

A. The Life of Eve

In the beginning (Gen 2:7), the LORD God "forms the earthling (ha'adham הָאָדָם) dust from the earth (ha'adhamah הָאֲדָמָה)." Despite the common view of this creature as "man," nothing in the text requires such a reading. An ecological pun, not sexual identity, grounds the first creature. In time, the LORD God observes that the singularity of the earthling is not "good" and decides to make for it an ʿezer keneghdo (עֵזֶר כְּנֶגְדּוֹ, Gen 2:18-20). Most often in the Bible the noun ʿezer refers to God and so connotes superiority (e.g., Exod 18:4; Deut 33:7, 26, 29; Ps 115:9-11). Here the accompanying word keneghdo, meaning "like unto" or "corresponding to," tempers the connotation to indicate equality (contra the traditional understanding of helper or subordinate). Translations such as "companion" or "partner" best convey the sense.

God's first attempt to provide the earthling with a companion fails. Among the animals is found no ʿezer kenegdo. God then puts the earthling to sleep, takes a part from its side (tselaʿ [צֵלָע], often rendered "rib"), and closes up the place with flesh (Gen 2:21-25). God "builds" (banah בָּנָה) the part removed into "woman." The verb suggests considerable labor, but the process remains unknown. Woman emerges in mystery. With her advent, the sexually undifferentiated earthling is no more. Instead, from the leftovers of the divine surgery, man the male emerges. Quoting a poem (which varies in details from the narrative), the man recognizes the simultaneity, similarity, and difference of the sexes (Gen 2:23). He uses a formula of mutuality to describe his companion as "bone of my bones and flesh of my flesh" (compare Gen 29:14; 2 Sam 5:1; 19:12). Further, the pun he evokes in calling (not naming) her "woman" (ʾishah אִשָּׁה) and himself "man" (ʾish אִישׁ) attests their continuity and their contrast.

In the subsequent scene of disobedience (Gen 3:1-7), the woman figures prominently. As spokesperson for the human couple (a departure from the strictures of patriarchy), she replies to the devious question that the serpent asks about God's command not to eat the fruit of a particular tree. To the command she attaches the prohibition, "neither shall you touch it." Thereby she becomes a faithful interpreter of divine law, building around it "a fence" that promotes obedience. She shows intelligence and thoughtfulness as she ponders the wholesome possibilities that the fruit offers: physical nourishment ("good for food"), aesthetic pleasure ("delight to the eyes"), and sapiential acquisition ("desired to make one wise"). Without consulting the man, "who is with her," she eats. Then, behaving like a faithful wife, she "gives" (ntn נתן) him some of the fruit. (The verb connotes neither trickery nor seduction.) Unlike her, he ponders not at all but simply eats. Throughout the scene the strong, active, and independent role of the woman contrasts with the weak, passive, and acquiescent role of the man.

The contrast continues in a trial, with God questioning the couple (Gen 3:8-19). Though asked only about *his* disobedience, the man answers by betraying the woman and blaming both her and God. In her answer, the woman does not implicate the man but blames the serpent for beguiling her. God proceeds to describe (not prescribe) the consequences of disobedience. (Contrary to translations, the Hebrew verb forms are not imperatives.) The deity curses (ʾarur אָרוּר) the serpent directly and the man indirectly through the ground (Gen 3:14, 17). But never does God curse the woman. The consequences (not commands) for her consist of increased pain in childbirth (a physical sign) and rule by the man (a cultural sign). Neither consequence defines her in creation.

After the divine judgments, the narrator secures male rule. "The man called the name of his woman Eve because she was the mother of all living" (Gen 3:20). In contrast to the poem quoted by the man, this report uses a naming formula (the verb "call" plus the noun "name"), not just the verb "call" alone (compare, e.g., Gen 2:19; 4:25, 26); it assigns the man the verb "call" in the active voice, not in the passive "is called"; and it specifies for her the proper name Eve (khawwah), not just the generic noun "woman." The explanation of the name yields a wordplay on the verb hyh (היה) or hwy (חוי), to live. Although the connection is positive, irony prevails. In naming the woman, the man rules over her. In controlling Eve, he robs her of life.

Eve appears once more in the story, identified not by her name but as "his woman" for whom God makes clothes (Gen 3:21). In the closing scene no gender reference of any kind specifies her. Instead, the narrator employs the single word haʾadham as a generic identity for the human couple whom God expels from the garden (Gen 3:22-23).

But Eve returns in the next story, about Cain and Abel. Using a conventional expression for sexual intercourse, the narrator says that "the man knew Eve his woman [or wife]," and "she conceived and bore Cain" (Gen 4:1). Her account differs. "I have created (qnʾ [קנא], also "made" or "acquired") a man (ʾish)," she says, "with [or together with] the LORD." Besides forming a wordplay with the Hebrew name qayin (קַיִן, Cain), the verb qnʾ links her labor to the creative work of God (compare Gen 14:19, 22; Exod 15:16; Deut 32:6). She says nothing about her husband's participation. These extraordinary words, coming in a first-person declaration, conclude Eve's life in the OT.

B. The Foreshadowing of Eve

The portrayal of Eve in Genesis resembles goddess figures in the ANE, particularly the Canaanite goddess ASHERAH (also called Athirat). Various sources call her "the creatress of the gods," the consort of the creator god El; also "the mother of the gods," who are her seventy sons. Depicted as an erotic figure among sacred trees, indeed as a fertility deity, she holds snakes in her hands, representing immortality or healing. A wooden pole (a cult object) symbolizes her. This pole, plus specific references to her, appears in biblical texts (e.g., 1 Kgs 14:15; 18:19; 2 Kgs 18:4).

Echoes of Asherah in the figure of Eve include Eve's place among trees in a sacred garden, her involvement with the serpent who offers immortality, her role as childbearer, the explanation of her name as "mother of all living," and her creative relationship with the creator God Yahweh. Yet these echoes reverse for Eve. The sacred garden becomes the site of temptation and disobedience. One tree holds forbidden fruit and another represents life denied. The serpent's promise of immortality leads to the prospect of death. Enmity between her and the serpent replaces intimacy. The fertility of childbearing becomes increased labor and pain. God exiles the "mother of all living" from the tree of life, indeed from the sacred garden. And the "man" whom she created alongside Yahweh becomes the first to murder life. In short, all that works well for Asherah works adversely for Eve. No doubt an anti-Canaanite polemic lurks in her portrayal. If this foreshadowing is foreboding, her future looms yet more threateningly.

C. The Afterlife of Eve

Early Jewish and Christian texts hold Eve responsible for sin. They include the apocryphal book of Sirach (early 2nd cent. BCE), which, without naming her (compare Gen 3:2-6), asserts that sin began with "a woman" (25:24). The pseudepigraphic book 2 Enoch (1st cent. CE) quotes God as creating a wife (Euva) for Adam so that death might come (30:17). The Apocalypse of Moses (1st cent. CE) has Adam call Eve "evil woman" and ask why she has brought destruction and death upon them (14:2). In the NT, 2 Corinthians (1st cent. CE) cites Eve's deception by the serpent as a warning for Christians not to be led astray (11:3). First Timothy (early 2nd cent. CE) deems Eve second in creation and uses that status to instruct women in being submissive to men. It convicts Eve (but exempts Adam) as a transgressor who was deceived (2:11-15).

With rare exception, commentators throughout the ages have continued to espouse negative views of Eve. Feminists who accept these views reject, in turn, the story of Gen 2–3 as misogynist; other feminists propose counter interpretations (see above). Despite the overwhelming judgments of history, the life of Eve remains unsettled. *See* WOMEN IN THE OT.

Bibliography: James L. Kugel. "Adam and Eve." *Traditions of the Bible* (1998) 93–144; Kristen Kvam, Linda S. Schearing, and Valarie H. Ziegler, eds. *Eve and Adam: Jewish, Christian, and Muslim Readings on Genesis and Gender* (1999); Carol Meyers. *Discovering Eve: Ancient Israelite Women in Context* (1988); Phyllis Trible. "A Love Story Gone Awry." *God and the Rhetoric of Sexuality* (1978) 72-143; Howard N. Wallace. *The Eden Narrative* (1985).

PHYLLIS TRIBLE

EVENING. *See* NIGHT; TWILIGHT.

EVENING SACRIFICE. *See* SACRIFICES AND OFFERINGS.

EVERLASTING. *See* TIME.

EVERLASTING GOD. *See* ESCHATOLOGY OF THE NT.

EVI ee´vi [אֱוִי ʾewi]. One of the five kings of Midian killed by the Israelites as an act of the Lord's vengeance for the Midianite influence over the Israelites (Num 31:8; Josh 13:21). According to Num 31, the conflict is linked to the incident in which the Israelites entered into sexual relations with the women of Moab, who in turn invited the Israelites to sacrificial rites in honor of their gods (Num 25:1-3). In Josh 13:21, however, their defeat is part of the victory over King Sihon of the Amorites.

STEPHANIE SKELLEY-CHANDLER

EVIDENCE [עֵד ʿadh; μάρτυς martys, μαρτύριον martyrion]. Evidence is almost always interpreted in relationship to the validity of the witness. The Hebrew root ʿadh primarily means "perpetuity," or passing on through time. Evidence is expected to promote a deeply felt conviction that something is either true or false. Most often the term is used in legal terminology where evidence is provided to give grounds for believing testimony. Simply, evidence consists of proofs or statements presented as truth within a legal setting. Therefore, evidence and witness are entwined. Within the post-NT church, those who died for their faith were called "martyrs"; death was evidence of faith.

Evidence may be presented in several ways. First, it may be brought through the oral testimony of individuals. Giving evidence and testimony was considered a duty within the religious context of Israel (Deut 17). Numbers 35:30 literally reads evidence is "by the faces/mouths of witnesses." Invoking the death penalty required the evidence of more than one witness (Deut 17:6). In fact, any charge against another must be supported by at least two witnesses (Deut 19:15; Matt 18:16; 2 Cor 13:1; compare 1 Tim 5:19). The integrity of the witness is of highest concern (Prov 12:17). Responsibility came with testimony, especially in death penalty cases where witnesses were required to "cast the first stones" (Deut 17:2-7). In the event of false testimony the accuser received the punishment the accused was to receive (Deut 19:15-21).

Material evidence is also seen in the biblical text. Within the wedding event, evidence of the bride's virginity was expected. Lack of the evidence was grounds for annulment (Deut 22:14-22). Written evidence provided grounds for lawsuits. God's written copy of the Law of the covenant given to Moses (Exod 31:18) served as the grounds for God's lawsuit against Israel (Hos 4:1-6). See COURT OF LAW; JUSTICE.

MICHAEL G. VANZANT

EVIL [רַע ra'; κακός kakos; πονηρός ponēros]. The concept of evil in the OT is not limited to moral categories, but embraces a much larger concept of misfortune including natural disasters, e.g., plagues and famines, attacks by foreign enemies, and defeat in battle. Because of this disconnect from the moral overtones, biblical authors could ascribe such evil events to God without impugning God's righteousness. God sent evil spirits to people (1 Sam 16:14), brought evil upon a nation (Isa 49:11), and caused the destruction of a city (Jer 21:10). Despite this, many biblical writers avoided ascribing evil to God, proclaiming instead that evil has no place with God (Ps 5:4).

More often, however, evil is considered an attribute of humans, though humans are not considered to be inherently evil. Judges repeatedly reproves the Israelites because they did evil in the sight of the Lord (2:11; 3:7, 12; 4:1; 6:1; 9:23; 10:6; 13:1). Each of the rulers in 1–2 Kings is judged based on whether he did good or evil in the sight of the Lord, i.e., whether he followed the law as set out in Deuteronomy (see e.g., 1 Kgs 15:25-26). In wisdom literature, evil is seen as the path that leads to ruin and death (Prov 11:19; 12:13; Eccl 8:12).

In the NT, evil remains a characteristic of humans, but is never attributed to God (Jas 1:13). Evil comes from within a person, not only because of actions but also because of humanity's fallen condition (Matt 15:19; Rom 7:14-25). For Paul especially, we must be saved from our evil nature (Rom 1:28-32). Because of the new life they have been granted in Christ, Christians are to turn away from evil and pursue good (Heb 5:14; 1 Pet 3:11; 3 John 11) because their evil deeds will be judged at the end of time (2 Cor 5:10). See SIN, SINNERS; SUFFERING AND EVIL.

KEVIN A. WILSON

EVIL ONE, THE [ὁ πονηρός ho ponēros]. A NT and early Christian term equivalent to "the devil" or "Satan." In one parable, e.g., Matthew uses "ho ponēros" (13:19) precisely where Mark uses "SATAN" (4:15) and Luke "the devil . . ." (8:12). Translating "the evil one" rather than "an evil person" or "evil" must be based on both grammar (the form must be masculine, substantive) and context. Several examples of ho ponēros in 1 John seem best translated as "the evil one" (1 John 2:13-14; 3:12; 5:18-19). In other passages, however (when the grammatical case is dative or genitive), the form may be either masculine or neuter, and interpreters must decide whether "the evil one" or "evil" is appropriate (Matt 5:37; 13:38; John 17:15; Eph 6:16; 2 Thess 3:3). For example, the final petition of the Lord's Prayer may be translated "deliver us from evil" or "deliver us from the evil one" (Matt 6:13).

DIANE B. LIPSETT

EVIL SPIRIT. See DEMON.

EVIL-MERODACH ee'vuhl-mer'uh-dak [אֱוִיל מְרֹדַךְ 'ewil merodhakh]. Son of Neo-Babylonian king Nebuchadnezzar who succeeded his father in 562 BCE and is credited with releasing King JEHOIACHIN of Judah from prison in the first year of his reign (2 Kgs 25:27; Jer 52:31). Evil-Merodach was assassinated by his brother-in-law, Neriglissar, who subsequently assumed the throne. His Babylonian name, Amel-Marduk, means "man of Marduk," but biblical Hebrew 'ewil means "foolish," suggesting a double entendre.

R. JUSTIN HARKINS

EVODIUS, HOMILY OF i-voh'dee-uhs. Two Coptic homilies, one Bohairic and one Sahidic, composed before 565 CE, and falsely ascribed to Bishop Evodius of Rome, describe closely related but different versions of the events surrounding Mary's death, or Dormition. In the Sahidic version, Evodius claims to be an eyewitness to the events described. See VIRGIN, ASSUMPTION OF.

SUSANA DE SOLA FUNSTEN

EWE. See SHEEP, SHEEPFOLD; SHEPHERD.

EX VOTO. From the Latin ex voto suscepto "from the vow made." Greco-Roman and ancient Christian devotees commonly offered material goods or promised future actions should a god fulfill their wishes, often safe travel or healing from illness. Romans summarized the logic of votives as da ut dem "give so that I might give." Devotees often adorned sacred sites with votive inscriptions, providing a record of their requests and the gods' miraculous deeds. See INSCRIPTIONS.

CARLY DANIEL-HUGHES

EXACTOR OF TRIBUTE [נוֹגֵשׂ noghes; πράσσων prassōn]. "Exactor of Tribute" may refer to various types of officials whose task it was to procure taxes or labor from subjugated peoples. In Hebrew, noghes denotes the underlying verbal root "to press," which is used in contexts of physical (e.g., Exod 3:7; 5:6, 10, 13, 14; Job 39:7) or fiscal (e.g., Deut 15:2, 3; 2 Kgs 23:35) oppression. The term may thus be variously translated as "driver," "oppressor," or "taskmaster" as well as "exactor of tribute." The latter has been used in English translation of the Bible (RSV) only in Dan 11:20.

In the symbolic narrative of Dan 11, this title is used to describe a person sent on a mission by one of the kings of the north. The fairly clear allusions in the preceding and following verses to ANTIOCHUS III and ANTIOCHUS IV of Syria make it plain that the king in question is SELEUCUS IV whose reign (187–175 BCE) fell between those of his better-known father and brother. It is virtually certain that the exactor of tribute would then be Heliodorus who, according to 2 Macc

3:7-40, was sent by Seleucus to Jerusalem to expropriate the wealth from the treasury of the Temple. Such a mission of exacting tribute (or to put it less politely, "robbing temples") of subjugated peoples had become a major preoccupation of Antiochus III and his successors since the Romans defeated him at Magnesium (190 BCE) and demanded as terms of peace the payment of an exorbitant indemnity.

PAUL NISKANEN

EXALTATION [גָּבַהּ gavah, גָּדַל gadhal, נָשָׂא nasaʾ, רוּם rum, רָמַם ramom; ὑπερύψοω hyperypsoō, ὑψόω hypsoō, ὕψος hypsos]. Act of exalting; state of being exalted. The words have both literal (tall or high) and figurative (being of high status) meanings. Old Testament texts criticize self-exaltation (Deut 8:14; Ps 66:7); God alone exalts the righteous (Pss 37:34; 75:10). God also exalts individuals (e.g., Joshua, Josh 3:7; David, Ps 89:19; God's servant, Isa 52:13). Above all, it is the LORD who is exalted (Ps 99:2), and whose name is exalted by worshipers (Ps 34:3). The OT motif of reversal (i.e., exaltation of the lowly, Ps 35:26; Ezek 21:26) is carried over to the NT (Matt 23:12 par.; Luke 1:52). In the NT Jesus is the one whom God has exalted (Acts 2:33; Phil 2:9). In John (3:14; 8:28), exalt (NRSV, "lifted up") has a dual meaning, referring simultaneously to Jesus' crucifixion and glorification.

SUSAN E. HYLEN

EXCAVATE, EXCAVATION. *See* ARCHAEOLOGY.

EXCELLENT [אַדִּיר ʾaddir; Aram. יַתִּיר yattir; κράτιστος kratistos, διάφορος diaphoros, ὑπερβολή hyperbolē]. "Excellent" (ʾaddir) is used relative to Yahweh, "how excellent is your name in all the earth" (KJV; NRSV "majestic," Ps 8:1, 9), and in Ps 76:4, where Yahweh is considered "more excellent than the everlasting mountains" (KJV; NRSV "majestic").

An "excellent spirit" and "excellent wisdom" (yattir) were found in Daniel (Dan 5:12, 14; 6:3), where the idea of "skillful" is often used instead of "excellent." The meaning of yattir includes the idea of "in excess" or "in abundance."

Kratistos is a form of address for persons in positions of authority, e.g., "most excellent" Theophilus (Luke 1:3); Felix (Acts 24:3); and Festus (Acts 26:25). This address is unique to the Lukan narratives within the NT, although it is common in Josephus' and Philo's writings.

The author of Hebrews utilizes **diaphoros** to compare Christ to the angels: his name is "more excellent" (or "more distinct") than theirs (Heb 1:4); and he has been granted a "more excellent ministry" (Heb 8:6).

Paul uses **hyperbolē**, which literally means "thrown beyond," to describe a "more excellent way," the way of "greater gifts" to be used for the body of Christ (1 Cor 12:31; 27–31).

EMERSON B. POWERY

EXCITEMENT [זְגֹר zeghor; θόρυβος thorybos] A variety of Hebrew and Greek words meaning excitement include a connotation of turmoil, disquiet, uproar, and unrest (4 Macc 8:26). The cause of the agitation can be the rumor of war (e.g., Matt 24:6; Mark 13:7). Conversely, it can take on the sense of being "beside oneself with joy" as in conjunction with the "day of the Lord" (2 Thess 2:1) *See* JOY.

MARY KAY DOBROVOLNY, R.S.M.

EXCLUSION. The notion of exclusion carries a strongly negative connotation for contemporary readers who often associate it with intolerance. As will be seen below, modern categories sometimes obscure the Bible's very different worldview.

A. Old Testament
B. New Testament
C. Conclusion
Bibliography

A. Old Testament

The idea of exclusion can be explored in relation to the Israelite community or to those outside of it. The Priestly texts of the OT touch upon ideas of exclusion, though not always in a negative or ethically freighted manner. For example, all Israelites except the high priest are excluded from entering the Holy of Holies. Only priests and Levites are permitted general access to certain precincts of the sanctuary. These exclusions concern ancient notions of graded holiness and are not connected to one's ethical disposition. Thus, e.g., there is nothing wrong ethically with a menstruant. In spite of the strong tendency within such texts to create hierarchies, this same corpus contains some of the most open and inclusive ideas in the whole OT. For example, Exod 12:48-49 allows a resident alien to participate in Israel's cultic celebration of Passover if he circumcises the males in his household.

One clear example in which the Bible challenges the contemporary belief that exclusion is equivalent to intolerance can be seen in the differing ways Leviticus and Deuteronomy treat the question of resident aliens eating meat from an animal that died rather than was slaughtered. According to P, resident aliens are prohibited from eating such meat because to do so endangers the purity of the land (Lev 17:15). Deuteronomy 14:21, on the other hand, permits resident aliens to eat such meat because they are fully excluded from the norms governing the community. Here, Deuteronomy appears more tolerant than P, because it does not require aliens to observe Israel's basic purity rules. Sometimes inclusion leads to greater intolerance than exclusion.

A more radical form of exclusion concerns either those external to the community who are annihilated at God's command (*see* BAN) or those internal to the community who violate major norms resulting in their being killed or cut off from the community. The former applies to the Canaanites and Amalekites (Exod 17:8-16; Josh 6–10), the latter to Achan whose cultic violation resulted in the death of him and his immediate family (Josh 7). While such radical exclusion does occur, it is more the exception than the rule. Israelites did not generally view the external other as a threat that needed to be eliminated aside from the few groups whose behavior was viewed as a direct affront to the deity (Deut 25:17-19; *see* CHOSEN).

Many regard Ezra 9–10 and Neh 13 as some of the most ethnocentric passages in the OT and some link them to the priestly group that produced the final editions of Leviticus and Ezekiel. Texts such as Isa 56 and Ruth supposedly represent a more inclusive strand of the tradition. Deuteronomy is often characterized as falling between these two polar views in that it contains both tolerant and intolerant passages.

Such schemata tend to distort ancient Israelite ideas by simply evaluating them against modern standards, doing a disservice to those seeking to understand the Bible's conceptual framework. The context of the above-mentioned so-called exclusionary passages indicates that marital purity likely received a greater emphasis at this time because the survival of the small, near extinct, postexilic Israelite community was at stake. Texts such as Isa 56 and Ruth may be more inclusive than Ezra and Nehemiah, but they are far from universalistic or non-ethnocentric. Isaiah 56 does not call for the inclusion of all Gentiles. Rather it allows those few Gentiles who wish to participate in the cult of Yahweh to do so. Furthermore, even in texts like Ruth and Isa 56 in which foreigners are joined to Israel's life, it is not at all clear that these outsiders ever became full-fledged Israelites (Ruth 4:10; compare Josh 6:25).

B. New Testament

For many contemporary Christians, Jesus becomes the paradigm of inclusion and tolerance. Jesus' teaching on love of neighbor, in harmony with OT texts like Lev 19:18, 34 and Prov 19:17, is seen to support this view, along with his openness to sinners, tax collectors, lepers, and prostitutes. However, Jesus was not inclusive without limit. Jesus' primary concern in his ministry was the "lost sheep of Israel," not the larger world, or Gentile population (Matt 10:5-6). Stories such as the Syrophoenician woman (who uses her wit to overturn Jesus' guiding principle—Matt 15:21-28; Mark 7:24-30), and the faithful centurion (who initially seems to gain Jesus' attention because of his love for the Jewish people—Luke 7:3-6) underline this idea. Jesus does not directly counter or oppose the OT's teaching on purity, but rather regularly tells those he heals to show themselves to the Temple priest in order to be pronounced clean (e.g., Mark 1:44, in accordance with Lev 14). Further, Jesus instructs various sinners to turn from immoral behavior and follow his commandments.

Those who continue in sin are liable to exclusion from the Kingdom, a consequence described metaphorically as a place of darkness, where there is weeping and gnashing of teeth.

This last point raises interesting questions about biblical views of inclusion or exclusion in "the world to come," or what is commonly called "heaven" in Christian vocabulary. The OT's notion of salvation is national and this-worldly oriented; if the nations are addressed in this context, it is usually with respect to God's dealings with his people, Israel. Particular strands of later Christian tradition have made much of a dichotomy between the elect and the damned, an idea difficult to find in the OT and not altogether an emphasis of the NT. Paul's periodic language of ELECTION as an eternal decree (Eph 1) or of divine hardening of the heart (Rom 9) could lend itself to such ideas though here modern individualistic perspectives, and remnants of Luther's personal salvation struggle (acutely problematic in readings of Rom 9–11), often cloud the discussion. If, e.g., we take Matt 25:31-46 seriously, participation in the world to come appears dependent upon one's treatment of the other. Revelation 20:12-15 likewise suggests that one's deeds affect the final judgment. Such texts challenge narrow views that advocate a binary opposition between the elect and the non-elect, where the latter is perceived as automatically damned.

While contemporary Christians often see their religion as more open-minded and less exclusionary regarding membership than texts like Ezra and Nehemiah, a number of NT texts call this into question. Many of Paul's arguments regarding Gentile inclusion suggest that boundaries were important. The issue was not whether there should be boundary markers, but rather what constituted an appropriate boundary. Marriage to nonbelievers is regulated (1 Cor 7:12-16) and Christians are warned against close associations with non-Christians (2 Cor 6:14–7:1). Further, those who were part of the community but who persisted in sin were to be excluded (Acts 5; 1 Cor 5)—something later to be termed *excommunication* in Christian practice.

C. Conclusion

For documents produced in the ancient period, both sections of the Bible contain some astonishingly inclusive notions. In the OT, God's plans for Israel are set against a larger cosmic scheme of bringing blessing to all the nations of the world. Furthermore, provided certain conditions were met, outsiders could participate in Israel's religious life. In the NT, certain requirements for Gentile inclusion are negotiated and there was not to be distinction between race, gender, or social status within the Christian community (Gal 3:28). The picture is multifaceted and complex, and one must remember that exclusion takes many forms, many of which do not equate with being beyond the pale of

God's workings. Nevertheless, all religious communities have boundaries and thus exclusion is inevitable. This is all the more true of the Bible that countenances a community founded on the notion of being God's holy people. To obscure this is to disregard key tenets of the biblical worldview, no matter how incompatible with contemporary sensitivities.

Bibliography: Mark G. Brett, ed. *Ethnicity and the Bible* (1996); Shaye J. D. Cohen. *The Beginnings of Jewishness: Boundaries, Varieties, Uncertainties* (1999); Joel S. Kaminsky. "Did Election Imply the Mistreatment of Non-Israelites?" *HTR* 96 (2003) 397–425; Frank Anthony Spina. *The Faith of the Outsider: Exclusion and Inclusion in the Biblical Story* (2005); Miroslav Volf. *Exclusion and Embrace: A Theological Exploration of Identity, Otherness, and Reconciliation* (1996).

JOEL S. KAMINSKY
JOEL N. LOHR

EXCOMMUNICATION. Excommunication is a late Latin word (*excommunicatio*) not used in the Vulgate. It denoted expulsion from the church, exclusion from its sacraments and from the salvation thought to be available only through them. Technically the term is not biblical. However, it is still appropriate to examine any precedents, which are to be found in the biblical and related texts, without reaching any judgment as to the biblical warrant for the later practice of excommunication.

The two key presuppositions of such discipline are 1) a community with clearly defined boundaries, and 2) an acknowledged authority to determine whether any member of the community has transgressed these boundaries.

The understanding of the "holy" in the OT includes the corollary that infringements of the holy will be punished: examples include Nadab and Abihu (Lev 10:1-3) and Achan (Josh 7). Indeed, we could extend the parallel to Adam and Eve (Gen 3:23-24), the worshipers of the golden calf (Exod 32:15-29), and the wilderness generation (Num 26:65). *Mishnah Sanhedrin* 10:1 extends the list of those excluded from the world to come to include those who deny the resurrection of the dead, those who read heretical books, etc.

These ways of protecting the holy from all that is impure can generate an exclusionary discipline marking off the chosen people from outsiders, but do not count as precedents for excommunication. The laws of ritual purity, which temporarily excluded the impure (from corpse uncleanness, menstrual bleeding, and the like) from the sanctuary (Lev 12–15), provide another possibility. Here the boundaries were clear and the authority (the priest) unquestioned. More serious failures warned against in Deut 27–28 would result in exclusion from the land; the curses were in effect exclusionary. Prob-

ably the nearest we come to excommunication as such in the OT is Ezra's campaign against mixed marriages; failure to conform was to be punished by confiscation of property and expulsion from the congregation of the (returned) exiles (Ezra 10:8).

In Ezra's policy we are not talking about excommunication as such. The key term was *separate*, separation to be holy, separation to God, which also meant separation from others. This was the basic logic of the laws of clean and unclean, as Lev 20:24-26 indicates. It was the logic of both Pharisees ("the separated ones") and the Essenes, who "separated" from the bulk of the people (4Q397 14-21 7). The point, however, is that separation from others (as unclean, a threat to the group's holiness) included a judgment on the others, in effect an exclusion of the others from the more narrowly defined Israel (*see* CLEAN AND UNCLEAN). The exclusionary force is clearly recognizable in such a group's dismissal of other Jews as "sinners" (as in *1 En.* 1:7-9; 5:4-7; 1QS V, 7-13; 1QH^a XV, 12; CD IV, 6-8; *Pss. Sol.* 3, 13). And Qumran's own tight discipline included a more rigorous disciplinary exclusion of failing members (1QS V-VII).

Jesus rejected that kind of "label-and-dismiss" policy toward others who differed in matters of halakhah. A notorious fact was his consorting with "sinners" and others who by virtue of lifestyle or practice were deemed to be "outside" (Matt 11:19; Mark 2:16-17), as also his openness to the other who potentially threatened his own space (Mark 9:38-40). His exhortation to invite the maimed, the lame, and the blind (Luke 14:13, 21) could have been an implicit criticism of Qumran's exclusion of just such persons from their midst (1QSa (1Q28a) II, 3-10). Equally, it was the recognition that no one should be deemed common or unclean. The recognition that Gentiles were acceptable to God as Gentiles was the key turning point in the earliest Christian mission (Acts 10:28; 11:17; Gal 2:15-16; 3:2-5). In an important sense, therefore, Christianity began as an objection to defining the people of God and maintaining its status as God's holy people by a policy of exclusion/excommunication, though 2 Cor 6:14–7:1, which quotes Isa 52:11, is a reminder that the distinction can be overdrawn.

Many of the new believers evidently experienced exclusion from their local synagogue communities. According to Acts several of Paul's churches began as breakaways from the local synagogue (Acts 18:6-7; 19:9). Paul complains that some missionaries in Galatia want to exclude (ekkleiō ἐκκλείω) the Gentile believers in order to make them enter fully into Israel's heritage by accepting circumcision (Gal 4:17). John's Gospel points to situations where the Jesus Messianist Jews were expelled from the synagogue aposynagōgos (ἀποσυνάγωγος; John 9:22; 12:42; 16:2); "the Jews expelled" (exebalon ἐξέβαλον from ekballō ἐκβάλλω) the blind man (9:34-35). This expulsion is a reminder that the diaspora synagogue was often well established, its members highly regarded in the Mediterranean cities, and that it retained the right to discipline its own members—as Paul knew only too well (2 Cor 11:24). The small groups of Christians meeting in members' flats or houses were only beginning to draw boundaries and to develop authority structures (*see* CHURCH, LIFE AND ORGANIZATION OF).

Nevertheless, disciplinary procedures are beginning to develop in the NT period. There are echoes of the infringement of the holy in the death of Ananias and Sapphira (Acts 5:1-10); and Peter's condemnation of Simon Magus in Acts 8:20-23. The falling away of many believers is envisaged as a possibility in Galatians, and subsequently becomes a reality in cases like Demas (2 Tim 4:10). First John looks back to the departure of many from the congregation, where, evidently, the disagreement between the baptized as to whether "Christ has come in the flesh" became too sharp for them to remain together (1 John 2:18-19; 4:1-3). The clash between "the elder" and Diotrephes in 3 John sounds like rival leaders using exclusionary measures against each other (ekballō). The emergence of the Nicolaitans in the churches of the apocalypse (Rev 2:6, 15) and the denunciation of Jezebel that smacks of excommunication (2:20-23) indicates a desire on the part at least of the writers for congregational boundaries to be more tightly drawn and disciplinary authority exercised.

Matthew gives the clearest signs of a developing internal discipline, in the rule that the offending brother should be admonished first privately, then in the presence of two or three witnesses and finally before the church as a whole (Matt 18:15-17; similarly Titus 3:10; compare 1QS V, 26–VI, 1). But the talk of "binding and loosing" in Matt 16:19 and 18:18, which was traditionally thought to be the granting of such disciplinary power to ecclesiastical officials, is better understood in terms of teaching authority.

Paul's letters give the clearest examples of disciplinary measures: withhold a share in the common meal from those who refused to work (2 Thess 3:10); disown those who ignore or disobey his instructions (3:14-15). He is fiercely dismissive of others who presumably regarded themselves as Christians (2 Cor 11:13-15; Gal 1:9—"let him be anathema!"; Phil 3:17-19). He does not hesitate to quote Deut 24:7 in calling for the Corinthians to "Drive out (exarate ἐξάρατε from exairō ἐξαίρω) the evil man from among you" (1 Cor 5:13), and Gen 21:10 in urging the Galatians to "Drive out (ekballō)" the other missionaries from their midst as excluded from the heritage of Abraham (Gal 4:29)!

Most striking is the strong line Paul takes, and expects the Corinthians to take, against the man living with his father's wife (1 Cor 5:1). When they have assembled they are "to hand this man over to Satan for the destruction of the flesh, in order that his spirit may be saved in the day of the Lord" (5:5). Similarly,

it would appear, Hymenaeus and Alexander have been "handed over" to Satan, "so that they may learn not to blaspheme" (1 Tim 1:19-20). What is envisaged in 1 Cor 5:5 is hard to discern, and though it seems to be ultimately positive in intent, if the spirit to be saved on the day of the Lord belongs to the one who suffered exclusion. The possibility that reconciliation was in fact achieved (as was the case in 2 Cor 2:5-11), however, warns against being misled by the rhetoric of the earlier passage. *See* ANATHEMA; DEVOTED; HERESY.

JAMES D. G. DUNN

EXECRATION. Execration refers to the Egyptian practice of formally and preemptively cursing places, groups of people, or individuals perceived as threats, or to the texts containing these curses. The curse is pronounced and/or inscribed upon terra cotta, stone, or wooden figurines, often in the form of bound prisoners, representing the target individual or group, or on pottery jars, or, in at least one instance, on a human skull. The representatively accursed objects were ceremoniously shattered and buried as a magical enactment of victory over the subjects mentioned in the verbal pronouncement or listed in the inscribed text. The rite of "breaking red jars," the color of blood, provides a parallel example of the apotropaic magic involved. The curse inscriptions follow a general formula evidenced on the so-called Berlin bowls (no earlier than the mid-Twelfth Dynasty): after naming the subjects, a summary statement directs the curse against "all the [inhabitants] of [place names and] their [warriors] . . . who may rebel, plot, fight, talk of fighting, or talk of rebelling—in this entire land."

Objects probably associated with the rite appear beginning in the Old Kingdom and continuing into the early New Kingdom period. Excavations of nearly all the pyramid temples from the Old Kingdom period have revealed figurines of bound prisoners. These figurines include only one group of inscribed statuettes, however, while, in later periods, especially the Middle Kingdom and the Second Intermediary periods, inscribed objects become much more common. Concentrations of items bearing execration texts have been discovered near the tombs at Thebes and Saqqara and at the Middle Kingdom border fortress of Mirgissa in Nubia.

Texts sometimes name specific enemies of state, providing Egyptologists with important information concerning domestic and international affairs at a given moment. Spell 37 of the Coffin Texts indicates that execrations could be addressed to the dead who were considered particularly dangerous because they lay entirely beyond the control of earthly agents. In other instances, the texts employ stock, sometimes clearly anachronistic, lists. Still other texts seem to strive for universality, listing groups of nine (three triads, the familiar ennead, representative of completion and perfection). The three most frequent subjects of execration are individual Egyptians, the Nubians and their chieftains, and certain West Asiatic groups. Over 400 figurines placed in rough pottery found in the Giza cemetery include figurines inscribed mostly with Nubian names. The Berlin and Brussels texts mention, among other sites, Ashkelon, Byblos, Migdol, Shechem, Pella, Apheq, Rehob, Hazor, Acco, Ekr(on), Laish, Beth-Shemesh, and, perhaps, Jerusalem.

Biblical scholarship is particularly interested in execrations targeted at West Asiatic groups and territories. According to one view, once widely accepted but now increasingly questioned, the execration texts provide a glimpse into social organization in the Middle Bronze Age I (2000–1800 BCE) era in Syria-Palestine. According to the argument, the Berlin texts reflect a tribal societal order while the predominance of town names in the Brussels texts, dated about fifty years later, indicate an ongoing process of urbanization. Both sets of texts contain Semitic personal names typical of the Middle Bronze Age II period. *See* CURSE; EGYPT; OATH; SIN, SINNERS.

Bibliography: James Pritchard, ed. *ANET* (1950) 328–29.

MARK E. BIDDLE

EXECUTION [מוּת muth]. Execution is killing as the result of the death penalty for a judicial offense (Exod 21:14). In biblical times, three types of judicial executions were permitted, the first being the most prevalent: stoning, burning, and hanging. STONING was the punishment exacted for several offenses, most notably idolatry or the seduction of others to idolatry (Lev 20:2; Deut 13:6-10), BLASPHEMY (Lev 24:14), and Sabbath profanation (Num 15:32-36). Both burning (Lev 20:14; 21:9) and hanging (impalement on a gibbet for a limited period of time, Deut 21:22-23) were usually deployed intra-communally as post-execution penalties (e.g., Josh 7:15; 8:29). Apart from ancient Israelite society and later Second Temple Judaism, stoning was a prominent form of execution (e.g., with the Persians and Greeks). In republican and imperial times, beheading and CRUCIFIXION were prominent among the Romans. In post-biblical times, moreover (e.g., *Tg. Ruth* 1.17), death by sword (including beheading) and STRANGLING were also permitted. *See* MARTYR; STEPHEN.

ABRAHAM SMITH

EXECUTIONER [σπεκυλάτωρ spekylatōr]. The person responsible for carrying out capital punishment. In Israelite society, no exclusive term was used for the executioner (Ezek 9:1; Dan 2:14), although the captain of the guard (1 Kgs 2:25, 34) could be assigned the role. In Roman society, this person (in Latin, the *spekoulator:* Tacitus, *Ann.* 1.24-25; 2.73) was deployed within the praetorian guard and some provincial administrations. His tasks included spying and executing. An executioner (spekylatōr) beheaded John the Baptist. In

the case of Jesus' execution, the role was assigned to Pilate's soldiers and a CENTURION (Matt 27:27, 54; Mark 15:16, 39; John 19:23).

ABRAHAM SMITH

EXEGESIS ek´suh-jee´suhs. An interpretive method that establishes the meaning of a biblical text or passage by studying its historical context and making application of that study to the contemporary situation and environment. Described as being derived from the Gk. exagein (ἐξάγειν, "to lead out"), this hermeneutical approach to biblical literature assumes an essential meaning within the text that can be isolated and explained through philological and historical methods that establish a literary contemporaneity between the community that produced the text and the reading community.

Some identify the earliest exegetical work to be in biblical or pseudepigraphal literature. The narratives of Exodus and Numbers, in many instances, expand and further explain elements of stories that appear in much more truncated form in the book of Deuteronomy. Some scholars describe the materials of Exodus and Numbers as a kind of exegesis of the briefer narratives of Deuteronomy. By the same token, the books of Chronicles modify the presentations we find in the books of Samuel and Kings. In both of these examples, the secondary writers, considered by some to be exegetes, clearly modify the primary narratives with which they work.

There are several instances in the Pseudepigrapha in which brief biblical narratives are expanded and explained in a manner that is closer to contemporary notions of exegesis than the examples in Exodus–Numbers and in Chronicles. While the biblical materials change and reshape the earlier narratives, in the Pseudepigrapha the relationship with the biblical materials is more one of expansion and explanation. Just one example of this relationship is available in the *L.A.E.* 9 and 10, where Eve explains to her children just how it was that the serpent had tricked her into eating the forbidden fruit and the results of that mistake. This material clearly expands the impact of the story in Gen 3 and offers an interpretive position on the impact of the serpent in the garden. *See* BIBLICAL CRITICISM.

C. MARK MCCORMICK

EXHORTATION. A general term describing language addressed to an individual or group with the goal of persuading the addressee(s) to act or think in a particular way. Various terms refer to its different aspects: ysr (יסר)/musar (מוּסָר) and paideuō (παιδεύω)/paideia (παιδεία) when the speaker exercises disciplinary authority over the addressee(s); yrh (ירה)/torah (תּוֹרָה) and parakaleō (παρακαλέω)/paraklēsis (παράκλησις) when adherence to precepts is at issue; ʿwd (עוד)/ʿeduth (עֵדוּת) and noutheteō (νουθετέω)/nouthesia (νουθεσία) when the address is framed negatively as an admonition, etc. The semantic fields of these terms include but often extend beyond exhortation itself, and thus they can be translated in diverse ways. The word *parenesis* (parainesis παραίνεσις), although rare in Scripture, is gaining recognition as a common term that aptly covers all such discourse in both Hellenistic and ANE contexts.

Parenetic exhortation basically takes the form of commands, or when negatively formulated as admonition it takes the form of prohibitions, together with a supporting rationale expressed in subordinate clauses. The rationale can incorporate a wide variety of forms including wisdom sayings (e.g., proverbs, precepts, similitudes, and riddles), illustrative narratives (e.g., parables, fables, and didactic tales), model cases (e.g., anecdotal CHREIA and exemplary *paradeigmata* [paradeigmata παραδείγματα]), prophetic oracles, laws (both apodictic and casuistic), and historical surveys, etc. When the argumentation aims to motivate action, it may assume the rambling dialogical style of disputation or diatribe; and when it aims to motivate reflection, it may take on the closely logical style of protreptic (protreptikos [προτρεπτικος]; a style of instruction or persuasion). Such exhortation typically pertains to occasions when social and/or personal identities are undergoing transformation, as a response to life cycle transitions faced by individuals or historical crises faced by communities. It can serve either to subvert or affirm the social order and/or the social roles played by individuals, depending on whether it intends to foster socializing transformation or foment countercultural resistance.

Exhortation can be a dominant or prominent rhetorical element in different genres: wisdom instructions (e.g., Proverbs), prophetic books (e.g., Zephaniah), legal and testamentary literature (e.g., Deuteronomy), and letters (e.g., 1 Thessalonians, Hebrews, and James), as well as sections of the Gospels (e.g., the Sermon on the Mount in Matt 5–7 and Jesus' testamentary address in John 14–16). The study of prophetic exhortation has become entangled in the question of whether prophets urged repentance to avoid the punishments they announced, but it may not be possible to tell whether calls for repentance were originally spoken by the prophet or added in the book's reinterpretation of his message. *See* FABLE; LAW IN EARLY JUDAISM; LAW IN THE NT; LAW IN THE OT; PARABLE; PROVERB; WISDOM IN THE ANCIENT NEAR EAST; WISDOM IN THE NT; WISDOM IN THE OT.

Bibliography: A. V. Hunter. *Seek the Lord! A Study of the Meaning and Function of the Exhortations in Amos, Hosea, Isaiah, Micah and Zephaniah* (1982); A. J. Malherbe. "Exhortation in 1 Thessalonians." *NovT* 25 (1983) 238–56; A. J. Malherbe. *Moral Exhortation: A Greco-Roman Sourcebook* (1986); L. G. Perdue. "Paraenesis and the Epistle of James." *ZNW* 72 (1981) 241–56; L. G. Perdue and J. G. Gammie, eds. *Paraenesis: Act and Form. Semeia* 50 (1990); M. A. Sweeney. "A Form-Critical Reassessment of the Book of Zephaniah." *CBQ* 53 (1991) 388–408.

MICHAEL H. FLOYD

EXILE. The biblical exilic period begins with the Babylonian deportations of Judahites in the early years of the 6th cent. BCE. While Assyria, beginning with TIGLATH-PILESER III (745–727 BCE) had deported many people from the Northern Kingdom in the 8th cent., including 27,290 from Samaria alone, according to the claims of SARGON II, those exiles disappeared from history. The Judean exile, by way of contrast, played a profound role in shaping the literature and theology of the OT, and those who returned from exile exerted primary leadership in the post-exilic community.

　　A. Three Deportations
　　B. Conditions in the Land and in Exile
　　C. Literature of the Exile
　　Bibliography

A. Three Deportations

The Bible mentions three Judean deportations: 597 BCE, when Nebuchadnezzar exiled King Jehoiachin, members of his family, other officials, representatives of the upper classes, military personnel, craftsmen and smiths, and installed Mattaniah as puppet king, changing his name to Zedekiah (2 Kgs 24:14-17); in 586 BCE, when Nebuzaradan, an official of Nebuchadnezzar, responded to a revolt by Zedekiah by destroying the temple and much of Jerusalem and capturing and deporting King Zedekiah and others while Nebuchadnezzar himself got no closer than Riblah in Syria, some 175 mi. away (2 Kgs 25:1-21//Jer 52:4-27); and 582 BCE, when Nebuzaradan again sent Judahites into exile (Jer 52:30). A fourth deportation dating to the reign of Jehoiakim, antedating the three noted above, is reported in 2 Chr 36:6-7 and Dan 1:1-7, but seems unlikely to modern historians.

The Bible reports inconclusive figures for these deportations. For the 597 deportation 2 Kings mentions the numbers 10,000 and 8,000 (2 Kgs 24:14-16), but it is not clear whether these round numbers are to be taken as alternate amounts or whether they should be totaled together. In Jeremiah we find the following figures: in the 597 campaign: 3,023 Judeans; in the 587/586 campaign: 822 Jerusalemites; and in the 582 campaign: 745 Judeans, or 4,600 altogether (Jer 52:28-30). Blenkinsopp and Albertz estimate those exiled from Judah to be about 20,000, of a total population of 200,000 (Blenkinsopp) or of 80,000 (Albertz), thus representing 10 percent or 25 percent, respectively, of the population of Judah during its final years. Albertz estimated that an additional 25 percent of the population may have been killed in battle or fled to Egypt so that the population of Judah was halved in the series of Babylonian attacks. All these numbers are far less than the 200,150 Judeans that Sennacherib claims he exiled in 701 BCE.

The Chronicler suggests that the land of Israel lay empty during the exile, enjoying its Sabbaths (2 Chr 36:20-21), and this interpretation might also be drawn from Jer 13:19 and 2 Kgs 25:21 (compare 2 Kgs 17:23). The author of 2 Kings indicates that only the poorest people of the land were left after the first deportation (2 Kgs 24:14). But the discussion above suggests that 50 to 90 percent of the population remained, and Barstad has argued that the Babylonian conquerors might have wanted to retain the agricultural economy because of their desire for taxes and such products as grapes and olives. Nebuzaradan left vinedressers and tillers of the soil in 586 (2 Kgs 25:12), and some Judean refugees returned from Moab, Ammon, and Edom after they heard about Gedaliah being appointed as governor (Jer 40:11-12).

At least three dates have been assigned to the end of the exile: 539 BCE, when Babylon fell to the Persian Cyrus, who gave the Jews permission to return home and build the Temple (2 Chr 36:22-23; Ezra 1:1-4); 520 BCE, when a substantial number of exiles, under the leadership of Zerubbabel and Joshua, returned during the reign of Darius I; or 516 BCE, when the rebuilt Temple in Jerusalem was dedicated. For many Jews the exile had no ending since they continued to live in Egypt, Mesopotamia, and other parts of the diaspora.

After the second deportation, the Babylonians installed Gedaliah son of Ahikam son of Shaphan as governor, with provincial headquarters at Mizpah (2 Kgs 25:22-26; Jer 40:5–41:18). Inscriptions on two seals indicate that he had been a high royal official. A number of people joined Gedaliah in Mizpah, including the prophet Jeremiah, who had declined an invitation to go to Babylon (Jer 40:1-13), and his secretary Baruch (Jer 43:3, 6). Gedaliah ignored warnings about Ishmael, the son of Nethaniah, a member of the Judean royal family, who had been sent by Baalis, king of the Ammonites, to assassinate him, and he and a number of other Judeans fell victim to him (Jer 40:14–41:3; 2 Kgs 25:25). This happened in the seventh month, but no year is specified in the biblical record. Some scholars conclude that the third Babylonian deportation was in reprisal for this assassination, and this would suggest that Gedaliah may have governed for at least four years. Ishmael also killed seventy of some eighty pilgrims from Shechem, Shiloh, and Samaria who were coming to present grain offerings and incense at the temple of Yahweh. This temple may have been at or near Mizpah or the neighboring town of Bethel. When Ishmael was later confronted by troops led by Johanan at Gibeon, many of his followers deserted him, and he fled to the Ammonites (Jer 41:11-15).

B. Conditions in the Land and in Exile

The infrastructure of Judah was not completely destroyed by the Babylonian attack. While archaeology has shown that Jerusalem and a number of towns to the south of it were severely damaged, the towns in Benjamin, north of Jerusalem, such as Gibeah, Gibeon, Mizpah, and Bethel, escaped relatively unscathed. It is not surprising that a dozen or more towns in Benjamin are listed as settlements for those who returned from the Babylonian exile (Ezra 2:21-35//Neh 7:25-38). Edomite encroachment in the southern part of Judah in the 6th cent. suggests that Babylonian control did not extend that far south. Enough of the civic, religious, and cultural life continued to make it possible that some of the theological literature during the exile was produced in the land.

The exiles in Babylon were settled on apparently vacant land in the vicinity of Nippur. The river Chebar, mentioned by Ezekiel, makes a loop through Nippur. The Judean exiles may have served as tenant farmers, which the Babylonians may have considered a more beneficial way to treat them than to turn them into slaves. The elders played a major role in the exilic community (Ezra 5:5, 9; Jer 29:1; Ezek 8:1; 14:1; 20:1, 3; 6:7-8) and may have sought Ezekiel's approval for building a temple in Babylon (Ezek 20:1-3, 32). Ezra recruited cultic personnel (Levites and Nethinim) at a "place" called Casiphia, which may have been the site of a sanctuary of some sort. Jeremiah was able to communicate with the exiles by letter (29:1-23; compare 51:59-64), and he was critical of prophets in Babylon, namely Ahab and Zedekiah, who apparently predicted trouble for Nebuchadnezzar and thus would be roasted in fire by him (Jer 29:21-23; compare Hananiah, a prophetic opponent of Jeremiah in the land [Jer 28:1-14]), and Shemaiah, who had attempted to have Jeremiah imprisoned (29:24-32). The custom of praying toward Jerusalem may have begun at this time (1 Kgs 8:30, 35; Dan 6:10). Practices such as circumcision, Sabbath-keeping, and many of the dietary laws became marks of Jewish identity during the exile, particularly for those who lived outside the land. There is frequent reference to water near the settlements of the exiles (Ezek 1:3; Ezra 8:15; Ps 137:1), suggesting that they may have practiced rites of purification. Some seventy Jewish names appear in the archives of the Murashu business firm in the vicinity of Nippur, although these documents date about a century after the end of the exilic period. A cuneiform text mentions a "city of Judah" near Sippar in 498 BCE, demonstrating the continuing presence of Jews in Babylon after the "end" of the exile.

Little is known about Jewish interaction with the Babylonian government. After the long reign of Nebuchadnezzar (605–562 BCE) there were three rulers in the next six years of the Neo-Babylonian Empire (Amel-Marduk [biblical Evil-Merodach], 562–560; Neriglissar,

560–556; and Labashi-Marduk 556), a sign of great instability, before Nabonidus (556–539), the last Neo-Babylonian king, came to the throne. The report that Evil-Merodach released Jehoiachin from prison in his accession year (2 Kgs 25:27-30//Jer 52:31-34) ends the DEUTERONOMISTIC HISTORY on a positive note, but this apparently led to no other political changes. According to the Weidner Tablets, Jehoiachin had originally lived at the Babylonian court and was well provided for and even given the title "king of Judah." The reason for his later imprisonment is unknown, but may be related to the murder of Gedaliah by Ishmael, a member of the royal family.

Another place of exile in the 6th cent. was Egypt. A group led by Azariah and Johanan inquired of Yahweh through Jeremiah about whether they should flee to Egypt after the murder of Gedaliah. Jeremiah received a divine oracle forbidding their flight to Egypt, but Johanan and the rest denounced Jeremiah's oracle as a lie, and took him and many others to Egypt (Jer 42:1–43:7). Through a symbolic action Jeremiah announced Nebuchadnezzar's forthcoming invasion of Egypt (Jer 43:8-13; Nebuchadnezzar did attack in 568–567 BCE). Jeremiah also announced a judgment oracle against the Judeans in Egypt because of their continuing idolatry (Jer 44:1-14). The exiles in Egypt refused to listen to Jeremiah and claimed that their troubles started when they stopped making offerings to the queen of heaven (Jer 44:15-19). Jeremiah then announced an additional judgment oracle and predicted that those who did not die violently would only be a tiny remnant when they returned to Judah (Jer 44:20-30).

Another Jewish group in Egypt in the 6th cent. was the Jewish military colony at Elephantine, which even erected a temple to Yahweh in Egypt sometime before the invasion of Cambyses in 525 BCE. Exactly when these Jewish families came to Egypt is uncertain, with one scholar dating this to the reign of Manasseh, ca. 650 BCE. In any case, these Jews, like those mentioned in the book of Jeremiah, went to this exilic land by choice rather than deportation. The Aramaic documents surviving from this site, however, date to the late 5th cent. (COS 3.46-3.153, 116–32).

C. Literature of the Exile

A number of biblical books or writings were composed or edited during the period of the exile. The prophet Jeremiah prophesied during the last forty years of the Judean kingdom, and he lived for a time in post-monarchical Judah before being taken to Egypt. Both in words stemming from this prophet himself and from the Deuteronomistic redaction of his book come words accepting the exile as God's will (the good figs were those who had already gone to Babylon while the bad figs referred to the doomed King Zedekiah and the remnant in the land [Jer 24:1-10]), but recognizing that exile is not the final destiny for God's people

(purchase of the field of his cousin during the siege of Jerusalem [Jer 32:1-15], the promise of a new covenant [Jer 31:31-34], and the promise of a legitimate "branch" from the house of David [Jer 23:5-6; compare 33:14-26]). The prophet Ezekiel was taken into exile in 597 BCE and lived out his career in Babylon. Until 586 he was unrelenting in foreseeing the inevitability of the destruction of Jerusalem, but his book also contains sixteen chapters of hope, including his vision of a renewed temple in a renewed land and a stream coming from that temple that would bring life to the Judean desert and even the Dead Sea (chaps. 40–48). Yahweh, according to Ezekiel, is faithful to his old promises, but free to adapt them to this new situation. Second Isaiah (chaps. 40–55) announced a new exodus from Babylon to Jerusalem and called Israel to take up the role of servant, trusting in God's promises in spite of suffering. The prophet in Second Isaiah may have modeled this vocation in his personal life. Lending authority to his message in Isa 40:8 and 55:10-13 was the effective power of Yahweh's word. Yahweh, according to Second Isaiah, was willing and able to save Israel.

The book of Lamentations and some of the community laments (Pss 44, 74, 79, and 102; compare Ps 137) express Israel's deep sorrow over the severe damages experienced in the Babylonian attack and an appeal for Yahweh to act. The final form of the Deuteronomistic History (DTR), consisting of part of Deuteronomy and the books of Joshua through 2 Kings, offers a theodicy by attributing the cause of the defeat of the northern and southern kingdoms to the worship of other gods and violation of the principle of one central sanctuary. It also encourages readers to repent, like King Josiah who was unparalleled in his turning to Yahweh (2 Kgs 23:25), and DTR ends with the release of Jehoiachin from prison (2 Kgs 25:27-30) and the assurance that the promise to David (2 Sam 7) is still alive. The Priestly Source in the Pentateuch records the everlasting covenants made with Noah (Gen 9) and with Abraham (Gen 17) and assures readers that Yahweh will remember his covenant as he did in Egypt and therefore the everlasting promise of the land will become again a reality. Yahweh will tabernacle with the people as he did in the desert, and P suggests that the ancient promises will become reality when an appropriate sanctuary is established, with an Aaronic priesthood, and an elaborate sacrificial system. The priestly narrative is notoriously difficult to date, but it was likely put together in the 6th or 5th cent., in Babylon, and therefore is an exilic product.

The exile had the effect of validating the judgmental message of prophets like Amos, Hosea, Isaiah, Micah, Zephaniah, and Jeremiah, and all of these books were updated during the exile, with words of judgment against Babylon, words of hope, or other materials. Some scholars believe that the ancestral narratives in Genesis were composed or given a completely new redaction in the exile, when their recurrent theme of the divine promise of the land would have been particularly relevant. The story of the book of Daniel is set in the exile, although there is a critical consensus that the book was composed in the 3rd and 2nd cent. BCE and addresses issues of that time. *See* ASSYRIA AND BABYLONIA; BABYLON, OT; CYRUS; DOCUMENTARY HYPOTHESIS; EZEKIEL, BOOK OF; ISRAEL, HISTORY OF; JEREMIAH, BOOK OF; MURASHU, ARCHIVES OF; NEBUCHADNEZZAR, NEBUCHADREZZAR; NIPPUR; P, PRIESTLY WRITER.

Bibliography: Rainer Albertz. *Israel in Exile: The History and Literature of the Sixth Century BCE.* D. Green, trans. (2003); Hans M. Barstad. *The Myth of the Empty Land: A Study of the History and Archaeology of Judah During the "Exilic" Period.* (1996); Ralph W. Klein. *Israel in Exile: A Theological Interpretation* (1979, 2002); Oded Lipschits and Joseph Blenkinsopp, eds. *Judah and the Judeans in the Neo-Babylonian Period* (2003); J. B. Pritchard, ed. *ANET* (1969) 84–85, 222–23, 288, 491–92; 548–49; Daniel L. Smith-Christopher. *The Religion of the Landless: A Sociology of the Babylonian Exile* (1989); Daniel L. Smith-Christopher. *A Biblical Theology of Exile* (2002).

RALPH W. KLEIN

EXISTENCE [אַיִן ʾayin, הָיָה hayah, יֵשׁ yesh; βίος bios, γένεσις genesis, ἐιμί eimi, ζωή zōē]. Existence is the fact of being. The word can be used to refer to any entity or object whether animate or inanimate, natural or supernatural—as long as the entity or object is known to be or considered to be real. Since there is no present-tense form of the verb "to be" (hayah) in Hebrew, rarely does one find the English word "existence" in translations of the OT. Greek, on the other hand, expresses the idea of existence more directly with various forms of the verb "to be" as well as words that can also be translated as "life." Because of this lack in the Hebrew language, there was a tendency in biblical theology and interpretation to believe that the ancient Israelites did not have a notion of existence as such. Biblical theologians would then infer some essential difference between Hebrew and Greek ways of thinking. However, James Barr's trenchant critique of such linguistic-theological studies demonstrates that conclusions about ways of thinking cannot be drawn from peculiarities of grammar and morphology. Moreover, the OT does express ideas of "existence" and "being" through other forms of the verb "to be" and the words "there is" (yesh) and "there is not" (ʾayin) (e.g., Dan 12:1 and Ps 14:1).

In the NT, Paul uses the present active participle of "to be" ("I am," eimi) in order to discuss God's creative and salvific powers (Rom 4:17). God has the power to call "into existence the things that do not exist." Even though the idea that God created the world is a central theological concept in the OT, the idea that God created *ex nihilo* (from nothing) developed later in the context of Hellenistic Judaism. It is most clearly expressed in this Romans passage.

"Existence" is sometimes used as a synonym for life or living, usually in reference to human life. Examples of this usage occur primarily in the apocryphal wisdom literature. Sirach warns that a life of begging is an existence (sometimes translated as "a life") not worth living (40:29). In the Wisdom of Solomon, the writer, in Solomonic guise, muses on the equal beginning and end of existence for all people (7:5).

Bibliography: James Barr. *The Semantics of Biblical Language* (1961).

JENNIFER L. KOOSED

EXISTENCE OF GOD. For many people, the reality of *mana*, personal deities, or God is evident from the power, unpredictability, and human impact of what happens in the world. Perhaps, then, there is a universal human awareness of the divine (Ps 19:1-4; Rom 1:19-20). Philosophers of religion speak generically of "the holy," "absolute dependence," or "ultimate concern," understood in various ways in different religions.

The radical diversity of religious beliefs may suggest, however, that this universal sense of divinity is erroneous, or at best distorted (Rom 1:21-23; Acts 17:22-31). If so, God is properly known only through revelation, not through general human experience (Matt 11:27 // Luke 10:22; John 1:18). A classic Christian debate is whether there is not only a "revealed theology" but a "natural theology," and, if so, whether the two are mutually reinforcing.

Anselm's "ontological argument" combines the two approaches. He begins with what is believed about God on the basis of revelation, but he then seeks understanding, which is more than mere belief. God is believed to be "that than which nothing greater can be conceived"; but when this is understood, one recognizes that God "cannot not be," for God is "Being Itself" (compare Exod 3:14) or "necessary being." Anselm quotes the Psalms: "The fool says in his heart, 'There is no God'" (Ps 14:1; 53:1). To deny God seems absurd. But Anselm wants to explain the possibility of the fool. Denial of God is possible as long as one's thinking is based on the finite world, where everything we experience might either exist or not exist. But the same does not apply to God. "Existence" is contingent; God's "being" is not.

Thomas Aquinas took this insight a step farther. It is true "in God" that God cannot not exist; but "for us" it is not so. Indeed, for Aquinas God is beyond any direct experience. If we want to argue convincingly that God exists, we must start from the finite world.

Thus he formulates his "five ways" to God, which have been characterized as a "cosmological argument" for God. Each "way" begins with some feature of the finite world (change, causality, being, degrees of perfection, goal-seeking); each feature, he argues, is not self-explanatory but depends on a cause or origin that is like it but different in degree, being perfect and not contingent; "and this," he concludes at the end of each way, "all people call God." For Aquinas the way of reason converges with the way of faith; although they use different methods, they cannot conflict, and misunderstandings in one realm may be corrected by insights gained in the other.

Philosophers and theologians have disagreed for centuries over the logical validity of arguments for God's existence—and over their compatibility with what Christians believe about God. After Descartes revived the ontological argument, Pascal spoke contemptuously of "the God of the philosophers." The Protestant Reformation emphasized revelation; but by the 18th cent. there was widespread emphasis on "natural religion" and even "deism," reliance only on what could be known about God by reason (see THEISM). Although Kant thought that the ontological and cosmological arguments were not valid, he himself affirmed God as one of the "postulates" supporting a moral life; pragmatism and existentialism have taken similar perspectives. One view of modern culture is that these various attempts to prove God's existence encouraged people to begin doubting it.

Those who affirm some kind of natural theology tend to emphasize the similarities between God and the world, viewing God as the fullness of those positive qualities that we experience in the finite realm, so that words like "being," "truth," "goodness," "power," and "wisdom" apply most properly and fully to God. The progress of modern science has encouraged arguments for "intelligent design" by God as traditionally understood; it has also stimulated new approaches to natural theology, looking for ways God acts upon a world of constantly evolving change. In process theology, God is even said to change, though without the tragic conflicts involved in finite change.

Those who are more skeptical about natural theology tend to emphasize God's difference from the world and the freedom of God's will. The only "existence" that we directly experience, they point out, is the existence of finite things, which might not have been, are vulnerable to constant change, and at some time will no longer exist; obviously God cannot be said to "exist" in this sense. When we try to speak about God on the basis of the world of our experience, they say, we must speak in terms of what God is *not*, and this "negative" or "apophatic" theology is appealing to many because it respects God's mystery. From this perspective God is known adequately only on the basis of God's own self-knowledge as the TRINITY, disclosed through God's own Word and Spirit. *See* ATHEISM; GOD, NT VIEW OF; GOD, OT VIEW OF.

EUGENE TESELLE

EXODUS, BOOK OF ek′suh-duhs [שְׁמוֹת shemoth; Ἔξοδος exodos]. The book of Exodus tells the story of the origins of the people of Israel through the power of Yahweh their God: how God heard their cry as slaves in Egypt, made Godself known to them through Moses, God's appointed leader, freed them, revealed the law to them, made a covenant with them, and, in spite of their apostasy, came to dwell among them.

The names by which the book is known give clear indications about its content. *Exodus*, "going out," is its common name in English, derived from the Gk. translation of the OT from the last centuries BCE. It stresses freedom (see Exod 19:1, where exodos translates Hebrew tse′th [צֵאת], "going out, release from slavery").

In the OT, the book is called **shemoth**, "names," from its opening phrase, "Now these are the names of the children of Israel." This title emphasizes the identity of God's people and continuity in their history: it links back to the promises of descendants, nationhood, and land, which God made to their forefathers, Abraham, Isaac, and Jacob/Israel, in Genesis; it points forward to stages in the realization of these promises in the rest of the OT.

Exodus is the second of the first five books of the Bible, the PENTATEUCH. The common Hebrew term for this collection is the TORAH, "law, instruction." As part of Torah, Exodus is not simply a story about the past but is intended to provide a pattern and a guide for all time.

A. Structure of Exodus

Exodus can be divided into sections by topic:

B. Detailed Analysis: Expectations and Discoveries

1. The exodus and history

A running narrative such as is contained within Exodus may create the expectation that what is being told is a straightforward account of what actually happened. There can be no doubt that what Exodus relates does reflect actual events in the history of the ANE. Historians can document how from the 12th cent. BCE EGYPT, which had been a great power in its New Kingdom period from the 16th cent. BCE, with an empire spreading at times up through the land of Canaan to the borders of modern Syria, was in decline and gradually withdrew from southwest Asia. This decline enabled small nations like Israel to emerge.

But the Bible is concerned with international politics only insofar as they affect Israel's destiny. If one turns to Exodus with purely a historian's interests, one finds oneself told too little—and too much. The book relates to Egyptian history but only in a vague way. Not a single Egyptian is identified by name, not even the pharaohs, despite the fact that two of them, the pharaohs of the oppression and the exodus, are involved. The only specific reference, the place names Pithom and Raamses (Exod 1:11), suggests that the period envisaged is the 19th, "Ramesside," Dynasty (14th–13th cent. BCE). Historians acknowledge that, after more than two centuries of archaeological research, there is still an absence of evidence for the presence of Israel in Egypt. This is a disappointing result only if highest value is placed on the reconstruction of past events for their own sake on the basis of contemporary records, as would be expected in the work of a modern historian. But Exodus should not be expected to carry out tasks for which it was never intended. Events are narrated from Israel's point of view and in miraculous terms as a confession of faith: "This is the LORD's doing and it is marvelous in our eyes" (Ps 118:23). True to its nature as Torah, Exodus recounts Israel's experiences in generalized terms—"Pharaoh," for instance, as emblematic tyrant—for edification and instruction.

Thus a puzzling feature of the literary presentation of Exodus can be explained: narrative is interspersed with law, not least laws about religious rites commemorating the exodus. Through the observance of these rites the particular story transcends the limits of a historical past and becomes accessible to succeeding generations as part of their story. As Deut 5:3 puts it: "Not with our fathers did the LORD make this covenant, but with us, who are all of us here alive today."

2. The unity of the account

A further initial expectation may be that the account in Exodus is unitary and uniform. This would be particularly the expectation if Exodus were a running transcript of events with MOSES as its author. Certainly within Exodus and elsewhere in the Pentateuch it is stated that Moses wrote down materials (e.g., Exod 24:4). But it can hardly be the case that Moses wrote the whole Pentateuch. These statements that Moses wrote are in third-person accounts written by someone else about him; it is difficult to imagine that Moses himself wrote such passages as the account of his own death in Deut 34:5-10. It is likely then that the Pentateuch was written sometime after the death of Moses—but how long after and by whom? These are questions that have exercised generations of scholars.

In recent times, many interpreters have preferred to leave the question of the history of the composition of Exodus to one side and to read the book as a summated unity. The final form of the text as it now stands is, after all, the received Scripture of synagogue and church, and it should be interpreted at that completed level.

Nonetheless, interpreters find themselves, in however limited a way, constrained to acknowledge evidence of more than one level within the book that suggests that it has passed through a history of composition. A view that has prevailed widely since the 1870s states that the Pentateuch comprises four literary sources, labeled J, E, D, and P, from different periods. Scholars, particularly in Germany, where that DOCUMENTARY HYPOTHESIS arose, are now more likely to affirm that the Pentateuch, Exodus included, comprises P and non-P materials, but that each of these broad groupings has passed through long and complicated historical development from originally independent traditions to finally "redacted" editions.

In the analysis of Exodus below, a combination of methods will be followed. It is intended that full justice be done to the final form of the work. But it will be agreed that the book of Exodus is composite, and it will be presumed that, if the work is indeed composite, full justice can only be done to its richness by making use of the interplay between P and non-P. Complex theories about the growth of earlier collections and associated editorial procedures will, however, be avoided; the stress will be on verifiable outcomes rather than hypothetical processes. It is hoped thus to strike a balance between "synchronic," final form approaches and "diachronic," analytical methods. The view will be taken below that Exodus indeed comprises two levels, an earlier version and a final edition of it, each of which has to be studied synchronically in its own terms; in the case of the later edition these terms include a diachronic relation to the underlying version that it presupposes and with which it interacts. Before exploring the theology thus developed in section C below, some justification for that view of the dynamics of the composition of Exodus must now be offered. For this analysis it will be suggested that the Bible itself provides both an analogy and an instrument.

3. A biblical analogy for parallel accounts

It is clear that the OT provides two accounts of the history of Israel. The Chronicler's work, beginning with Adam in 1 Chr 1:1 and ending in 2 Chr 36 with the Babylonian exile, covers much of the same ground as the earlier account that runs from Genesis to 2 Kings. But these accounts offer different explanations for the course of Israel's history. The earlier, it may be argued, uses especially the concept of covenant as expounded in Deuteronomy to explain events; the later reuses that earlier history especially in Samuel and Kings but applies the doctrine of holiness as expounded in Leviticus (*see* HOLY, HOLINESS, OT). Harmonies of these two compositions have often been produced (as they have of the four Gospels in the NT). But the production of a single consistent history does not seem to be the Bible's aim: it is more likely that justice is done when each of these versions is studied on its own terms and in the light of its differing emphasis.

It will be argued below that the Pentateuch presents a somewhat analogous phenomenon: there are two principal accounts, each covering much of the same ground, from creation at the beginning of Genesis to the death of Moses at the end of Deuteronomy. But unlike the histories, in the Pentateuch these two accounts are closely interwoven. Yet, it will be argued, they are still relatively clearly separable, and it is when they are first separated that the dynamics of their combination can be fully appreciated. The appropriateness of the analogy is perhaps confirmed when, as in the histories, the earlier of the two accounts in the Pentateuch is seen to be dominated by the concept covenant, and the later by holiness.

4. A biblical instrument for separating the accounts

A key for unlocking the history of the composition of Exodus is provided by Deuteronomy. The material in Deuteronomy varies sometimes very strikingly from the account in the final edition of Exodus (and Numbers). One of the most obvious differences is that there is no reference in Deuteronomy to the TABERNACLE in the midst of the camp that is the subject of more than one-third of the material in Exodus (chs. 25–31 and 35–40). Where Deuteronomy does refer to a sanctuary, it is in terms of the Tent of Meeting, pitched outside the camp (Deut 31:14-15, as in Exod 33:7-11). It is striking that, if the chapters on the tabernacle in Exod 25–31 are for the moment set aside, the narrative carries straight on from the last verse of Exod 24 to the first verses of Exod 32 (Exod 31:18 is a hybrid verse providing a link between the two). It is equally striking that this continuous narrative sequence closely matches the sequence in the reminiscence in Deut 9:9-14. It would seem to be a reasonable deduction that the tabernacle material now in Exod 25–31; 35–40 has been added to a narrative in Exod 24 and 32–34, the original content of which can be confirmed from the reminiscences in Deut 9–10.

There are a great number of other such matches between Exodus and Deuteronomy. These matches enable the reconstruction of a version underlying the final edition of Exodus that corresponds to the view of matters in Deuteronomy. Because of the instrumentality of Deuteronomy in reconstructing this matching version, this version is here called the "D-version." In continuity with the conventional view of scholarship that the final edition of the Pentateuch reflects the interests of Priestly circles, that final edition in which the D-version is embedded is called the "P-edition." It is appropriate to call it an "edition" since it seems clearly to have known and interacted with that earlier D-version. *See* P, PRIESTLY WRITERS.

5. Separating the earlier version and the final edition

There is space here to give only four samples and a summary table of the detailed argumentation required to separate the underlying D-version from the final P-edition in Exodus with the help of Deuteronomy.

a. Two laws for Passover. There is a striking divergence between Deuteronomy and the final edition of Exodus on how to celebrate Passover. Legislation on Passover is given in Exod 12:1-28 and Deut 16:1-8. In Deut 16:1-8 Passover is celebrated in the Temple and is therefore legislated for in Temple vocabulary. It is one of the three annual pilgrimage festivals to the central sanctuary; it lasts for a week; the victim may be chosen from the cattle as well as the sheep and goats; its slaughter is described as a sacrifice (zevakh זֶבַח); it is boiled (see PASSOVER AND FEAST OF UNLEAVENED BREAD). There are parallels to this Deuteronomy legislation in Exod 13:3-10. But in Exod 12:1-28 Passover is envisaged in entirely different terms: it is a one-night ceremony in the homes of the Israelites. As a lay ceremony, Temple sacrificial terminology and practice are inappropriate: the victim, now just a lamb or goat, is slaughtered (shakhatu שָׁחַטוּ), not sacrificed, and roasted whole on a spit.

Like the tabernacle material in Exod 25–31, noted above, Exod 12:1-28 not only follows practices not found in Deuteronomy, it also interrupts the connection in the narrative. Exodus 11:8, which ends Moses' announcement of the tenth and final plague, the death of the Egyptian firstborn, is continued by the narrative of that plague in Exod 12:29-36. That connection produces a logical sequence: the threat to the firstborn is directed only against the Egyptians (elsewhere in the plagues narrative, Israel is protected from the plagues by living apart in Goshen); it is the death of the Egyptian firstborn that forces the Egyptians to release Israel. Passover is to be observed as a memorial and celebration of that release only when Israel has entered the land (Exod 13:5). With the insertion of Exod 12:1-28, Passover becomes, somewhat illogically, a means of protection for Israel against the plague that was designed for its benefit. Observed by Israel on the very night of the tenth plague as an apotropaic rite, it introduces an inconsistency. No Israelites are allowed to leave their houses until the morning (v. 22); but in the narrative in Exod 12:29-36 the expulsion of Israel takes place at midnight.

With the insertion of Exod 12:1-28, the final editor, P, has redefined the significance of Passover. The extent of that redefinition becomes clear in the next example.

b. The route of the exodus. There is a further striking divergence between Deuteronomy and the final edition of Exodus on the question of Israel's route from the sea to the mountain of God. In the reminiscences in Deuteronomy several events now portrayed in Exod 15:22–18:27 as happening before Israel reached the mountain happen only after the Israelites' arrival at the mountain. In Exod 18, for example, Moses' father-in-law Jethro comes to give Moses advice about the appointment of judges. This happens on the eve of Israel's arrival at the mountain (Exod 19:2). By contrast, in the reminiscence in Deut 1:6-18 the appointment of judges takes place on the eve of departure from the mountain.

A similar transposition seems to have occurred in Exod 17:1-7. The people murmur against Moses because they have no water to drink. Moses strikes water from the rock and calls the place Massah-Meribah. But in the reminiscence of Deuteronomy no murmuring takes place in the wilderness before the arrival at the mountain. In Deut 9:22 the incident at Massah occurs after departure from the mountain between two other incidents of complaining by the people at Taberah and Kibroth-hattaavah, as told in Num 11. The transposition of the Massah-Meribah incident in the present final edition of Exodus is part of a symmetrical pattern of incidents of murmuring in the wilderness that takes place both before and after the mountain. The striking of water from the rock recurs again at Meribah after the mountain in Num 20:2-13. The incident of manna and quails in Exod 16 is matched symmetrically in Num 11:4-35 where it is located at Kibroth-hattaavah, its original location according to the reminiscence in Deut 9:22.

That it is the final editor of P who has created this symmetrical pattern of murmuring both before and after Sinai by means of reuse and transposition of material that Deuteronomy recalls as having occurred only after departure from the Mountain of God is confirmed by the list of place names that now occur on Israel's route from the sea to the mountain in Exod 15:22–19:2: Marah, Elim, Sin, Rephidim. None of these place names occurs in Deuteronomy.

In the light of the reminiscences of Deuteronomy that there is a direct journey from the sea to the mountain with no period of murmuring before the mountain, it is likely that the D-version in Exodus ran directly from Exod 15:22*b*, "they [Israel] went three days in the wilderness," to Exod 19:2*b*, "and encamped there before the mountain," and that the intervening material, Exod 15:22*b*–19:2*a*, is another long insertion by P. This three days' journey is precisely what Moses requests of Pharaoh in Exod 3:18; 5:3; 8:27 [Heb. 8:23]. Highly significant consequences then follow for the chronology of the D-version of Exodus. Between the night of escape from Egypt in Exod 12:29-36 and the conclusion of the covenant in Exod 24:7, seven days elapse. The three days' journey to the mountain is followed by three days of preparation (Exod 19:10-15). On the sixth day, therefore, Yahweh appears and reveals the TEN COMMANDMENTS (Decalogue) in the sight of the people and the content of the Book of the Covenant to Moses, which Moses then writes (Exod 19:16–24:4*a*). On the seventh day, Moses builds an altar, promulgates the Book of the Covenant, and makes a covenant between Yahweh and his people on its terms (Exod 24:4*b*-8; see COVENANT, BOOK OF

THE). In the D-version this seven-day period must coincide with the seven-day Passover of Deut 16:1-8. This conclusion is confirmed by the terms of Moses' request to Pharaoh in Exod 3:18, etc.: that Israel hold a festival in which a zevakh will be sacrificed, precisely the view in Deut 16:1-8 of Passover as a Temple pilgrimage festival of which sacrificial language may be used. An echo of the Deuteronomy legislation is embedded even in the text of Exod 12:27 where the slaughter of the Passover victim is called a zevakh.

With the insertion of Exod 15:22*b*–19:2*a*, the P-edition has radically revised the timetable of Israel's route to Sinai (the P-edition's name for the mountain in contrast to "Horeb" in the D-version), and thereby the festival with which the revelation at Sinai is related (*see* SINAI, MOUNT). Instead of reaching Horeb on the third day as in the D-version, Israel now comes to Sinai in the third month (Exod 19:1). Instead of Horeb marking the culmination of the exodus in the making of the covenant on the seventh day, as commemorated by Passover, Sinai now stands centrally in the Pentateuch as the place of the revelation of Law as commemorated in the Festival of Pentecost. Interestingly enough, in post-biblical Hebrew Pentecost is referred to as ʿatsereth hafesakh (עֲצֶרֶת הֶפֶסַח), "the conclusion of Passover," picking up the term ʿatsereth for the last day of Passover in Deut 16:8.

c. The law codes. It is frequently argued that the collections of law in Exodus, the Decalogue in 20:1-17 and the "Book of the Covenant" in 20:22–23:33 ("B"; the title is derived from Exod 24:7) are easily separable from their present contexts and may therefore have had independent origins and histories before being edited into the present book; Exod 34:17-26, sometimes referred to as the "Law of Yahweh's privileges" (also, the "J-Decalogue"), which closely parallels Exod 23:14-19, is often added to the discussion. This seems a very convincing view; after all, law by its very nature is under constant development and extension. Thus, from a study of their content, a great variety of occasions for the composition and collection of the laws in the Ten Commandments and the Book of the Covenant has been suggested, from the pre-settlement period, through the early monarchy, to the flourishing of prophecy in the 8th cent., to the fall of Samaria in 722 and the influx of refugees in Jerusalem, to the work of reforming kings like Hezekiah or Josiah, down to the exile and beyond. It cannot be denied that there is plausibility in all of these proposals. Nonetheless, the view taken here is that, whatever the origins and development of the individual laws or law codes, the law collections as they stand now in Exodus are literary compositions, selected no doubt from a large pool of available traditional materials but created for the purpose and integral to their present contexts (*see* LAW IN THE OT).

This conclusion is suggested by the content of the biblical law codes, by analogy with other Near Eastern law codes, and, above all, by the reminiscence of Deuteronomy. It is often observed that the biblical law codes are not exhaustive; many areas of life are not covered. The biblical law codes are not practical legal manuals that can be appealed to by the courts and applied. Only examples, sometimes extreme cases, are given in the laws, which must be assumed to provide illustrative materials from which analogies may be drawn; e.g., in Exod 21:22-25 the presumably rather rare case of a pregnant woman injured while intervening in a brawl, perhaps involving her husband, is the trigger for the listing of a whole—but incomplete—list of laws of retaliation, beginning with "an eye for an eye and a tooth for a tooth." Analogy suggests that a law code can be composed and copied unchanged for centuries (e.g., there are more than fifty copies of the famous law code of HAMMURABI, king of Babylon, composed about 1700 BCE, spanning a millennium).

But the most important argument that both Decalogue and the Book of the Covenant belong integrally to the D-version of Exodus is provided by the reminiscence in Deut 4:9–5:31 that both were revealed at Horeb: a version of the Decalogue is given in Deut 5:6-22; the Book of the Covenant is referred to in Deut 4:14; 5:31. On this argument, where the Decalogue in Exod 20:1-17 diverges from the Decalogue in Deut 5:6-22, it is Deut 5:6-22 that provides the original version. This is the case above all in the chief difference between these two versions of the Decalogue, the motive for observing the Sabbath. In Deut 5:12-15 it is to commemorate the exodus; in Exod 20:8-11 creation. But the phrase "as Yahweh your God commanded you" in Deut 5:12 (also 5:16) must be cross-referring to the matching (but now altered) command in the original D-version of Exod 20:8-11.

If both Decalogue and the Book of the Covenant were indeed composed together specifically for their present context in the D-version of Exodus, many features of their content can be clarified synchronically by virtue of that fact. Thus, in the case of the Decalogue, the "Prologue," "I am the LORD your God," specifically relates to God's action just demonstrated in Exod 1–19, "who has brought you out of the land of Egypt." This act of liberation provides the basis for the claim to exclusiveness in the relationship between God and Israel made in the first four commandments; the quality and defense of freedom from SLAVERY determine the content of the remaining six. In the case of the Book of the Covenant, it is arguable that its sacral framework in Exod 20:22-26; 23:10-19 is an exposition of the first four commandments of the Decalogue and that the intervening social commandments are an extended exposition of the remainder. It is notable that these social commandments begin in 21:1-11 with precisely the legislation for the freeing of debt slaves, the condition of the Israelites as initially indigent clients of the Egyptians as portrayed in the last chapters of

Genesis (see DEBT, DEBTOR). The motif of "spoiling the Egyptians" on Israel's release, Exod 3:22; 12:35-36, is explained by the development of the law of slavery in Deut 15:13-15, where the released slave is to be festooned with goods in compensation for his labor and to enable him to resume an independent life. Recalling that they were once SOJOURNERs in Egypt is the motivation for the protection of the vulnerable in society that frames the last section of the social legislation in Exod 22:21 [Heb. 22:20]–23:9. Even the retaliation law, "an eye for an eye," can be illuminated in the light of the wider Exodus context: Israel in Exod 4:22-23 is declared to be Yahweh's FIRSTBORN; if the Egyptians do not release Yahweh's firstborn they will pay in retaliation the penalty of the loss of their own firstborn, in the tenth plague. The pregnant woman caught in the brawl bringing forth a dead fetus resonates with the command of Pharaoh to the midwives to slay all the sons of Israel as the mothers squat on the birthing stool (Exod 1:16) and the perilous floating of Moses by his own mother in a straw ark on the crocodile-infested Nile (Exod 2:3).

Read within the context of Exodus as a whole, the "law of Yahweh's privileges" in Exod 34:17-26 is not to be taken as an earlier or rival version of the Book of the Covenant. It should be seen in relation with the preceding verses, Exod 34:5-16, which may be interpreted as a rerun of the events surrounding the original promulgation of the Decalogue as described in Exod 19:11-19, with a free play on the first two commandments of the Decalogue in Exod 20:2-6, concerning the name of God, the exclusiveness of God's worship, and the covenant relationship with God. It is then clear that Exod 34:18-26 is a free repetition of Exod 23:14-19, the conclusion to the legislative section of Book of the Covenant. It never existed as an independent law code; rather, Exod 34:5-26 alludes to the beginning of the Decalogue and the end of the Book of the Covenant to imply the inclusion of all the material in between in order to affirm that the covenant unilaterally abrogated by Israel in the golden calf incident has been remade on identical terms. This conclusion is supported by the paragraph markers in the Hebrew text: the whole of Exod 34:1-26 is treated as one long paragraph comparable to other narrative sections in Exodus; it is not subdivided into a myriad of short paragraphs as in the legal sections (Exod 20–23 is demarcated into fifty-five separate paragraphs).

d. The golden calf narrative. It has already been noted that Deuteronomy has no knowledge of the Tabernacle material in Exod 25–31; 35–40. On the other hand, the reminiscences in Deut 9:7–10:11 show virtually word-for-word correspondences in the chain of passages Exod 24:12, 18; 31:18; 32:8-21; 34:1, 4, 27-29, which provides the coherent narrative thread for the golden calf narrative (see CALF, GOLDEN). Where that correspondence is lacking, the hand of the P-editor may

be identified. Exodus 24:14-18a reflects P's concern with order in the recalcitrant community while Moses is absent on Sinai. Moses' intercession in Deut 9:26-29 in the second period of forty days and nights has been transposed into the first period of forty days and nights in Exod 32:11-14, to allow space for the punitive action by the Levites in Exod 32:25-29, which has no parallel in Deuteronomy. In Exod 34:2-3 the construction of the ark (expected from the reminiscence in Deut 10:1-3) is suppressed because the P-edition has already given specifications for the ark in Exod 25:10-22 (carried out in 37:1-9) and replaced with the P-editor's preoccupation with hierarchy within the community (as in Exod 19:20-25).

6. The date of the earlier account

A connected narrative is only as early as the latest material it contains. There are several features in the earlier account embedded in the text of Exodus that link it to events later than the exodus itself. Perhaps the clearest of these links occurs in the golden calf incident in Exod 32:4, the statement of Aaron to the apostatizing people, "These are your gods, O Israel, which have brought you up out of the land of Egypt." This statement matches the proclamation of Jeroboam about his golden calves in 1 Kgs 12:28. The fact that the plural "gods" fits the two calves in 1 Kgs 12 rather than the single calf in Exodus suggests that the writer of Exodus had the situation of 1 Kings in mind. Since, further, these golden calves are identified in the theological reflection in 2 Kgs 17 as the leading cause of Israel and Judah's exile (vv. 16, 19-20), the narrative may have been composed as late as the exile of Judah, post-587 BCE. A cryptic reference to that exile probably occurs in Exod 32:34—at some time after their settlement in the land, the consequences of Israel's sin with the golden calf will be visited upon them.

Other themes connect Exodus with that wider narrative: e.g., the motif of the bones of Joseph that occurs in Gen 50:25; Exod 13:19; and Josh 24:32; and the parallel between Solomon's construction of "store cities" in 1 Kgs 9:19 with Pharaoh's in Exod 1:11, as part of the negative portrayal of Solomon in 1 Kgs 10:26–11:40 where his trading with Egypt and multiplication of wives are specific violations of the law of monarchy in Deut 17:16-17. There is allusion to the exodus in the great programmatic speeches that interlink that wider narrative in Josh 24:5-10; 1 Sam 12:6, 8; 1 Kgs 8:52, 53.

On the basis of such observations, many interpreters now relate Exodus to a vast narrative running from creation to exile that begins in Genesis (usually from Gen 2:4b) and stretches down to the end of 2 Kgs. If so, then the date of the composition of the D-version of Exodus cannot be earlier than the last event recorded in 2 Kgs 25:27-30, the freeing of King Jehoiachin in 561 BCE. Sufficient time after that event must be allowed for the composition of the work. A general consideration supports this contention: in the time of exile when Israel had lost all its key possessions (Temple, monarchy, and land), it was essential to compose a comprehensive account of Israel's past to preserve Israel's identity and to provide guidance for an uncertain future. The run-up to the rebuilding of the Temple in 520–16 BCE (Ezra 6:15), with all its hopes of providing a new national and religious focus for the ingathering of all Israel into its land from exile among the nations, seems an entirely appropriate context for this massive work of theological reconstruction. The central themes of Deuteronomy, identified as "one God, one people, one sanctuary," and its affiliated D-version are a faithful articulation of such hopes. A date in the third quarter of the 6th cent., between the rise of Cyrus and the rebuilding of the Temple, seems appropriate for the composition of the D-version.

7. The P-edition

The remainder of the material in Exodus, especially the alternative version of the call of Moses and the genealogy of Aaron the "father" of the priesthood in chap. 6, elaborations in the plague and exodus stories in chaps. 7–14, drastic rearrangement of material in the middle section, chaps. 15–18, and the huge amount of materials on the Tabernacle in chaps. 25–31, 35–40, noted above, besides many adjustments in detail, is contributed by the P-edition. As for the date of the P-edition, it has been suggested that its chronology of the founding of the Tabernacle in the year 2666 from creation, that is, two-thirds through a period of 4,000 years, points to its expectation of a climax of history around the beginning of the 2nd cent. BCE. Such a date would again fit with a period of threat to Israel's religious institutions (see Dan 11:29-35; 1 Macc 1:45-61). But the circumstances giving rise to the P-edition were not simply external; factors internal to the life of Judaism may be inferred. The domestication of the Passover rite, argued above, is a significant indicator. The D-version's hopes of universal ingathering of Israel were never likely to be realized; Diaspora proved irreversible. The P-edition, describing Jewish life as centered round an idealized Tabernacle in "the wilderness of the nations" (Ezek 20), is concerned with the practice of holiness for a people for whom the sanctuary has begun to be spiritualized in the heart and in the home.

It should be noted that strong lines of, esp., Israeli, scholarship argue for an earlier date for P, and of German scholarship for dividing P into P[G], the *Grundschrift*, which provides the basic framework of the Pentateuch, and P[S], its later supplements. But from the argument above it seems clear that the P-edition presupposes, and is, therefore, later than, the D-version. The P-edition may well witness to ancient religious practice and contain early material, but history of material has to be distinguished from history of composition.

It would indeed suit the above argument very well if it could be established that P (and, indeed, D) represents a written tradition progressively elaborated over many centuries. That vigorous dialogue was conducted between differing theological positions is an essential presupposition of the above presentation, but one may be skeptical whether analysis of the present literary form of the material allows a running reconstruction of the preliminary stages of that debate.

C. Theological and Religious Significance

On the above argument, the book of Exodus represents the interaction between two compositions that freely draw upon reservoirs of tradition and living religious practice. Both begin from the revelation to Moses of the name of God (Exod 3:14-15; 6:2-3; *see* GOD, NAMES OF; TETRAGRAMMATON; YAHWEH). Yahweh is the English transliteration of the Hebrew consonants of the name: in Jewish tradition it is ineffable, exceptionally pronounced once annually on the Day of Atonement by the High Priest. For normal reading the name was provided with the vowels of the Hebrew word for "my lord" (ADONAI) to remind the reader to use "LORD" as a substitute (the traditional English "Jehovah," never used in Hebrew, is a combination of the consonants of the original and the vowels of the substitute). This name is explained in 3:14: "I am the one who is/shall be"; Yahweh is the living, eternal God. But it is a name that is full of possibility. The name is actually a third-person verb, "He is," or, because it is in the causative conjugation, "He brings into being." He is objectively the one who is not only eternal in himself but is the creator. But the name is explained in the first person, "I am": he is also subjectively the one who says "I," a God of relationship who addresses his people as "Thou." Strikingly, the name has only a pronoun, I/ he, for subject and no complement/object. Who I am/ he is and what I/he am/is/will be/bring into being is dynamically open to the future and requires unfolding events to reveal. The rest of Exodus is thus an exposition of this name in terms of who God discloses Godself to be and what God discloses God will do. The focal point of this exposition is the Decalogue where the opening of the Prologue, "I am," picks up the divine name; as the reason for keeping the SABBATH in the Fourth Commandment makes clear, the D-version expounds this name in covenantal terms, the P-edition, without abrogating the covenant, in universal.

For both compositions, religious institutions practiced regularly by the community provide the means through which the truths of God's being and action are expressed and appropriated generation by generation. The two compositions express their respective theologies through narrative accounts of these institutions, in some cases viewed quite differently. For the D-version these institutions are Dedication of Firstborn, Circumcision, Passover/Unleavened Bread, Covenant, and

Sanctuary; for the P-edition, Covenant, Circumcision, Passover, Sabbath, Pentecost, Torah, and Sanctuary.

1. The theology of the earlier version

a. Dedication of firstborn. Israel, the descendants of the seventy-strong family of Jacob are declared to be the LORD's firstborn son (4:22). Their destiny is to be his "treasured possession"; his elect "out of all peoples, for all the earth is mine" (19:5). This election means that they are to become "a kingdom of priests," a blessing among the nations (taking the promises to Abraham, Gen 12:3, to be integral to the D-version); "a holy nation" consecrated to serve God (19:6). But Israel are utterly powerless themselves to realize this status. Tyrannically reduced to perpetual slavery by the Egyptians, only an intervention by Yahweh himself, his "signs, wonders, strong hand and outstretched arm," displayed in the plagues and at the Red Sea, can rescue Israel and constitute them as his people, his "firstborn." In thankful recognition of this act of Yahweh in bringing them into their status of unique privilege, they dedicate their firstborn (13:1-2, 11-16).

b. Circumcision. The absolute requirement for the dedication not just of the firstborn but of all the male children by CIRCUMCISION, and the life-maintaining function of this rite as a sign and vehicle of dedication of Israel to Yahweh, is vividly conveyed in the incident immediately following the declaration of Israel as Yahweh's firstborn: the assault of Yahweh on Moses and his rescue by the speedy circumcision of his son by his wife (4:24-26). Moses, the agent of Israel's redemption, had himself to be redeemed by the dedication of his own son. The redemption of self is prior to the redemption of others (a point made strongly in the P-edition in 30:11-16 on the pre-emptive redemption of males of age to serve in the army).

c. Passover/unleavened bread. The chronology of the exodus in the D-version matches the chronology of Passover in Deut 16:1-8, as argued above. It is probable that, as many have argued, in origin Unleavened Bread was an agricultural festival, marking the beginning of the grain harvest in spring, a time of new beginnings with the "purging out of the old leaven" (Exod 13:3; 23:18). In D, the agricultural aspect is firmly subordinated to the seven-day Passover, the annual commemoration of Israel's definitive new beginning through Yahweh's act of deliverance. The cycle of the seasons is taken up into Yahweh's goal-directed program for history. Past memory, present experience, and future hope are, as in the Christian celebration of the Lord's Supper, integrated with one another.

d. Covenant. The culmination of the original D-Passover in Exod 24:3-8 is the conclusion of the covenant between Yahweh and Israel. By obedience to the terms of the covenant Israel is locked into the freedom with which Yahweh has made them free. The terms are laid down in the Decalogue and the Book of the Covenant. The privileged position of the Decalogue, revealed in the hearing of the people and written with the finger of God on two tablets, is made clear in the Exodus narrative. That public manifestation of the will of Yahweh in the Decalogue provides the framework for the Book of the Covenant. The heart of the Book of the Covenant, 21:1–22:20 [Heb. 22:19], is made up of a law code, a combination of "statute" and "ordinance," expressed mainly in the objective third person; God rarely appears, except as witness of oaths. But, by the framework, law code has been enfolded in a covenant code couched in second-person address. Thus law, governing especially interhuman relations, is taken up into the relation of Yahweh and Israel as covenant partners.

The climax of the D-version is the breaking and remaking of the covenant in Exod 32–34. With great irony and pathos, it is during Moses' absence for forty days and nights to receive the tablets of the Decalogue that Israel immediately falls into breach of the First and Second Commandments: "Thou shalt have no other gods....Thou shalt not make any image." Conforming themselves to long-standing ANE representations of the supreme deity, they make the image of a "golden calf." The penalty for such idolatry is death (22:20 [Heb. 22:19]). Moses the mediator becomes Moses the intercessor pleading for the lives of his people. On the assumption that the wider D-version begins with Gen 2:4*b*, it is striking how Exod 32 corresponds to Gen 3; the "fall" of humanity in general is replicated in the "fall" of God's people, Israel. The fate of the human race ejected in consequence of disobedience from the Garden of Eden is matched by, and begins to find its solution in, the fate of the covenanted people spared but bearing the penalty of exile from their land for their disobedience. As in Gen 3 God cannot apply the full force of a sentence of death on human creation without destroying his own handiwork, so here he cannot frustrate his own purposes by the annihilation of his "kingdom of priests."

e. Sanctuary. Nonetheless, as in Eden, the immediacy of relationship between God and Israel is impaired. The question of how such a God can relate to such a people dominates Exod 33. God does go in their midst; only God's presence, God's "angel," God's "face," represented by the ark with the tablets, or by the pillar of cloud intermittently descending upon the Tent of Meeting pitched outside the camp of the Israelites, accessible only to Moses the mediator and Joshua his successor, can be granted to them, for guidance in the course of their wanderings. But both God and people remain bound by covenant: Exodus 34 describes how the covenant is remade on precisely the same terms as before. The Decalogue as epitome of these terms is duly inscribed on two new tablets (34:28).

Despite the loss of all the emblems of freedom, land, statehood, capital city, monarchy, even the cherished centralized cult, God's commitment to his people remains constant; he has not abrogated their status. Beyond the ruins of the present time, the prospect of perhaps even imminent restoration beckons. The conclusion in the D-presentation in 34:29*a* is thus departure from the mountain toward the promised land.

2. The theology of the final edition

The P-edition presents a theological critique of the D-version, partly by engaging directly with its concepts, partly through new or alternatively understood institutions. P comes from the post-exilic period, perhaps from long after the "restoration." Many years of partial return from exile have been experienced, but still the long-expected ingathering of Israel from the nations has not taken place, the definitive "Jubilee" of restoration to land and full realization of status (Lev 25–26). Meantime, in coping with life now and in anticipation of that dawning end-time, how is Israel to organize itself? Israel's appropriate response is to get ready for the dawning of the new age by living an active life of holiness now, of according to God all that is due to him, of "realized eschatology," the pre-emptive experience of the quality of that end-time; thus the "enabling environment" for the coming of that time will be prepared. P's concern is to show how Israel may become what it is, may truly realize the status it already possesses.

a. Covenant. The free grace dimension of covenant is extended. The covenant is no longer tied to the decision of the present generation of the people, as in the D-version in 19:3-8; 24:3-8; it has been in being since the time of the ancestors of Israel, Abraham, Isaac, and Jacob (6:2-5). Through the "merits of the fathers" it has endured since time immemorial and stands unconditionally for all time beyond cancellation.

b. Circumcision. Circumcision is the sign of the covenant already instituted with Abraham and is, accordingly, indelibly engraved on the flesh of all Israel's male descendants virtually from birth as a token of their inalienable status (Gen 17).

c. Passover. For the community of Israel, whether gathered in the land or dispersed throughout the world, Passover, the feast of liberation, has still to be observed even by those who no longer have access to the central sanctuary. It becomes a decentralized domestic rite and assumes an apotropaic character as a rite of defense against destructive forces in an alien environment. The three annual pilgrimage festivals in the Temple in Jerusalem (beginning with Unleavened Bread, now distinguished from Passover), in principle remain as rites of communal solidarity.

d. Sabbath. But if observance of pilgrimage festivals to Jerusalem is no longer possible for all Jews scattered in the Diaspora, the weekly Sabbath is practicable for all Jews wherever they live. Sabbath punctuates the action of the P-edition of Exodus: before Sinai in Exod 16; in P's Decalogue in Exod 20:8-11 as a creation ordinance (compare Gen 2:1-4*a*); in connection with the Tabernacle both as the last element in its specification, 31:12-17, and as the first act of its institution, 35:1-3.

e. Pentecost and Torah. If the covenant is of age-old institution, then events at the Mountain of God cannot concern the making of the covenant between Yahweh and Israel. The significance of Mount Sinai is that it now becomes the place of the revelation of Torah, not simply of the Decalogue and the Book of the Covenant, but of the specification for the Tabernacle that will henceforth take over from Sinai as the location of the indwelling glory of God and of all further revelation (see Lev 1:1–Num 10:11). On the P-edition's chronology this revelation of Torah is now associated with PENTECOST. It is through the revelation of Torah that Israel learns the full apparatus of the life of holiness to which it is called.

f. Sanctuary. Through the life of obedience to Torah, Israel aims at nothing less than the remaking of the cosmos. Kearney pointed out that there is a correspondence between the seven speeches of Yahweh on the specification of the Tabernacle in Exod 25–31 and the seven days of creation in the P account of creation in Gen 1:1–2:4*a* (there is a huge insistence on the verb "to make" in Exod 25–31: some 106 times; compare Gen 1:7, 11, 12, 16, 25, 31; 2:2-4). Cosmic imagery has been noted in the structure and decoration of the Tabernacle since Josephus. The cosmic dimension has been anticipated by the three additional plagues of the P-edition culminating in darkness (10:21-29) and the showdown with the gods of Egypt that the plagues and the exodus imply (12:12; see 6:6; 7:4); the "sea," a branch of the deified Nile, as the site of the exodus in the P-edition (14:1-2), has cosmic overtones (compare Gen 1:10), as opposed to the "Red Sea" of the D-version which simply marks the southern boundary of the promised land (23:31).

The appropriateness of this cosmic message for a community living in worldwide dispersion is obvious. In the Tabernacle, the idealized sanctuary in the midst of the people, the new age is already dawning; the preparation for that new age is enabled by the adornment, furnishing, rites and personnel of that sanctuary; it is already fit to receive the indwelling presence and glory of Yahweh, the climax of the book in the P-edition (40:34-38).

D. Applications

There is a long history—and large literature—of oppressed peoples and groups, from, say, the pilgrim fathers (who also crossed a sea) to civil rights movements, who have identified themselves with the Israelites of the book of Exodus as victims of political, military, social, economic, or religious oppression and who have found in them a consolation in their suffering and an inspiration and warrant for resolute action in their struggle for liberation. This inspiration cannot be drawn in any facile way; the non-Jewish reader must be aware with unmitigated horror that the history of pogrom and genocide with which Exodus begins has continued in modern times with unparalleled ferocity for the descendants of the first audience of the book.

A fundamental principle should govern the application of the Exodus narrative to modern life: an awareness of the uniqueness of Moses and of the authority and completeness of the system that he has mediated. The events recorded are once for all: the objective fact of the making of Israel God's people, as immutably as the covenant with Abraham. The unequaled status of the mediator, who spoke with God, as it were, face to face, lends unsurpassed authority to the material mediated. Moses and Torah provide the criteria by which subsequent leaders and teaching are to be measured (Deut 18:15-22).

The Christian appropriation of the Exodus narrative has traditionally read it in suitably holistic terms as part of the history of salvation. The story of Moses with regard to the people of Israel is taken up into the action of Jesus with regard to the nations of the world. Already in Matthew's Gospel the story of Jesus is seen as a recapitulation of the history of Israel (e.g., Herod's slaughter of the innocents; the flight into Egypt; forty days in the wilderness; the Sermon on the Mount; twelve disciples); in Paul's Epistles, the crossing of the Red Sea and the striking of water from the rock become types of baptism; the Last Supper with the institution of the new covenant is the fulfillment of the first covenant and its ritual laws; in Acts 2 universalization of the original Pentecost takes place.

It is by reading these narratives in OT and NT as part of whole that dangers in interpretation can be avoided: e.g., on the one side, quietism and individualistic pietism; on the other, political zeal without a rounded view of responsibility. "Stand still and see the salvation of God" (Exod 14:13) is a favorite text of pietism: the hearer is invited to stand back and view at a distance—or wait for—the unrepeatable act of God. That ignores the fact that Israel went up from Egypt "equipped for battle"; their response was one of preparedness and participation, "standing still" in the sense of presenting themselves ready for action as "co-workers" with God. Such are the ambiguities in any human action that history is littered with examples of those who regarded themselves as liberators of their people but left others as victims. The kingdom of God is for all; it is not to be taken by storm but realized by patient commitment, individual and communal, to the pattern laid down by the mediator. *See* EXODUS, ROUTE OF; HAMMURABI, CODE OF; PLAGUES IN EGYPT; SANCTIFY, SANCTIFICATION.

Bibliography: F. Crüsemann. *The Torah* (1996); W. G. Dever. *Who Were the Early Israelites and Where Did They Come From?* (2003); W. Johnstone. "The Use of Deuteronomy in Recovering the Two Main Phases in the Production of the Pentateuch." *Abschied vom Jahwisten.* Jan Christian Gertz, Konrad Schmid, and Markus Witte, eds. (2002) 247–73; P. J. Kearney. "Creation and Liturgy: The P Redaction of Ex 25–40." *ZAW* 89 (1977) 375–87; R. G. Kratz. *The Composition of the Narrative Books of the Old Testament* (2005); B. M. Levinson. "Is the Covenant Code an Exilic Composition? A Response to John Van Seters." *Search of Pre-Exilic Israel* (2004) 272-325; Michael Walzer. *Exodus and Revolution* (1985).

WILLIAM JOHNSTONE

EXODUS, ROUTE OF. The exodus from EGYPT is a topic around which whirl controversy, debate and heated argument. There is no consensus regarding the date of the Israelite slavery, nor its nature, nor even its historicity. The route of the Israelite journey is also called into question in many circles. It is an area where archaeological interpretation and biblical narrative collide.

A. Location of Slavery and Traditional Route
  1. Raameses to Yam Suf
  2. Yam Suf to Sinai
  3. Sinai to Kadesh-barnea
  4. Kadesh to Moab
B. The Exodus Route Reconstructed
  1. Goshen
  2. Succoth
  3. Yam Suf
  4. Mount Sinai
  5. Exodus from the Negeb

A. Location of Slavery and Traditional Route

As the narrative setting of the Israelite slavery is within Egypt, the biblical presentation of the exodus route begins there. When Joseph brings his family to Egypt, the text relates that they settled in Goshen (Gen 45:10; 46:28-29, 34; 47:1, 4, 6, 27). Because of these verses, it is generally assumed that Goshen is to be found within the Nile Delta region of Egypt.

After their enslavement the Israelites worked on two store-cities (*see* STORE-CITIES, STOREHOUSES) mentioned in Exod 1:11. PITHOM is named only here in the OT. RAAMESES (NRSV "Rameses"), on the other hand, is identified as the place from which the Israelites began their exodus journey (Exod 12:37; Num 33:5).

The biblical texts that describe the exodus route are primarily in the books of Exodus (12:37-19:25), Numbers (parts of chaps. 10, 20, 21 and 33:1-49) and brief statements in Deuteronomy (chaps. 1 and 2). The itinerary in Numbers is in much greater detail, *vis-à-vis* sites mentioned. As many of these sites are listed exclusively in the OT, their exact locations remain a mystery. Nevertheless, archaeologists and biblical scholars have suggested the geographical identifications of a number of them. Most of the scholarly effort, it seems,

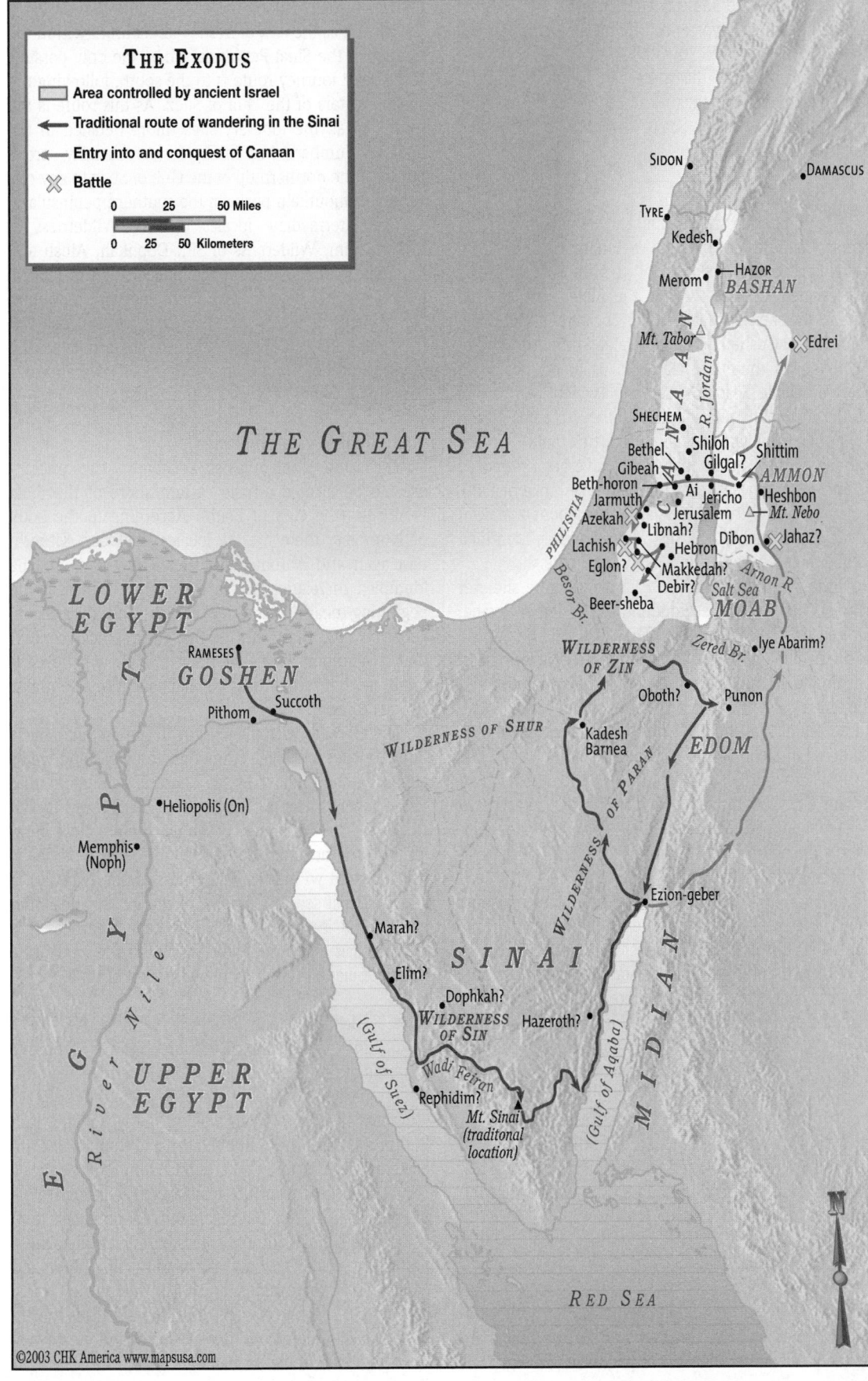

THE EXODUS

Area controlled by ancient Israel

Traditional route of wandering in the Sinai

Entry into and conquest of Canaan

Battle

0   25   50 Miles

0   25   50 Kilometers

SIDON

DAMASCUS

TYRE

Kedesh

Merom   HAZOR

BASHAN

Mt. Tabor   Edrei

C A N A A N

SHECHEM

R. Jordan

Bethel   Shiloh   Shittim

Gibeah   Gilgal?

Beth-horon   AMMON

Jarmuth   Ai   Jericho   Heshbon

Azekah   Jerusalem   Mt. Nebo

Libnah?   Dibon   Jahaz?

Lachish   Hebron

Eglon?   Makkedah?   Arnon R.

Debir?   Salt Sea

Beer-sheba   MOAB

Besor Br.

THE GREAT SEA

Zered Br.   Iye Abarim?

WILDERNESS
OF ZIN

LOWER
EGYPT

Oboth?   Punon

RAMESES

GOSHEN

Succoth   Kadesh
Pithom   Barnea   EDOM

WILDERNESS OF SHUR   WILDERNESS OF PARAN

Heliopolis (On)

Memphis
(Noph)

Ezion-geber

Marah?

SINAI

Elim?

Dophkah?

WILDERNESS   Hazeroth?
OF SIN

Wadi Feiran

River Nile

Rephidim?

Mt. Sinai
(traditonal
location)

UPPER
EGYPT

(Gulf of Suez)

(Gulf of Aqaba)

MIDIAN

PHILISTIA

E G Y P T

N

RED SEA

is directed toward identification of the sites visited between leaving Egypt and arriving at Kadesh-barnea (*see* KADESH, KADESH-BARNEA).

The beginning of the route can be divided into a few convenient groupings: Raameses to Yam Suf (commonly translated "Red Sea"), Yam Suf to Sinai, and Sinai to Kadesh-barnea.

1. Raameses to Yam Suf

The itineraries in Exodus and Numbers are the same: Raameses to Succoth to Etham to Pi-hahiroth (with Baal-zephon and Migdol) to Yam Suf. Raameses is presented in three ways in the Bible. First, in Gen 47:11, the land of Raameses is located in the same place as is Goshen. The general assumption is that Goshen (and therefore Raameses) is to be located in the Nile Delta. Second, Raameses is identified as one of the two store-cities built by the Israelites (Exod 1:11). Third, Raameses is the starting point for the exodus journey. While many sites have been proposed as ancient Raameses (e.g. Tell er-Retabe, ancient Pelusium, Tanis and Qantir), the large area (about 9 sq. km) north of the ancient Hyksos town of Avaris, identified as Pi-Raameses, is the most likely candidate.

Pithom is never mentioned as an itinerary site, yet scholars have attempted to identify it as Tell er-Retabe, located west of Pi-Raameses. Thus, it would be outside of the path taken by the fleeing Israelites. Nevertheless, heading toward the east, they would have encountered the ancient Egyptian region and/or site of Tjeku (located at Tell el Maskhuta), generally accepted as what is rendered in Hebrew as Succoth.

After leaving SUCCOTH, the Israelites traveled to Etham and Pi-hahiroth (which is located adjacent to Baal-zephon and Migdol). These locations are completely unknown to archaeology. According to the biblical narrative, however, they are located near "the sea" (Exod 14:2, 9; Num 33:7). This is the same sea against which the Egyptian army cornered the Israelites (Exodus 14–15). It is assumed, therefore, to be Yam Suf.

Within the traditional understanding of the exodus, it is also suggested that the waters of the Gulf of Suez (sometimes identified as Yam Suf) extended farther north than they do today. The region between the gulf and the Bitter, Ballah, or Timsah Lakes would have thus been more extensively covered with water. In particular, this water is also assumed to be fresh, allowing the growth of grass reeds. Hence, the identification as Yam Suf, the Sea of Reeds (*see* RED SEA, REED SEA). This, therefore, is the region containing the waters that the Israelites must have crossed.

2. Yam Suf to Sinai

There are, in general, three routes proposed from Yam Suf to the eastern Sinai Peninsula: northern, middle and southern. The northern and middle routes are severely discounted due to, respectively, the Egyptian

military presence along the coastal route (Exod 13:17-18) as well as the lack of fresh water sources within the interior of the Sinai Peninsula. Thus, the only possible escape and journey route is to the south, following the coastal waters of the Gulf of Suez. As this route is the most logical, the itinerary sites (more detailed in the book of Numbers than in Exodus) are usually spread out from the northern tip of the Gulf of Suez to any of a variety of mountain peaks in the southern peninsula.

The intermediate locales (Marah, Wilderness of Etham, Elim, Wilderness of Sin, Dophkah, Alush and Rephidim) are not mentioned outside of the biblical text. They are, nevertheless, identified with any number of wells or wadis present in the western coast of the Sinai Peninsula. This southern route also favors the identification of Mount Sinai with one of several peaks, commonly Gebel Musa or Mount Serbal.

3. Sinai to Kadesh-barnea

The same problem exists relative to the itinerary sites to be located on the eastern shore of the Sinai Peninsula (the Gulf of Elath). According to the book of Numbers, there are 21 locales. Between Kibroth-hattaavah and Abronah (19 sites), they can only be identified in relationship to each other, except at the beginning (near Mount Sinai) and the end (near Ezion-geber). Thus, they only fit the geographical context that is assumed as the working model, whichever it might be, but in the most popular scenario, a southern exodus route.

Therefore, as with the journey to Mount Sinai, these itinerary sites are divided amongst the wells and wadis alongside the Gulf of Elath. There is agreement that Ezion-geber is near, or the same as, Elath (*see* ELATH, ELOTH). The Wilderness of Zin lies then in close proximity to the northern tip of this gulf. Kadesh-barnea is to be located within the Wilderness of Zin (Num 20:1; 33:36). Most scholars agree that the fortress near 'Ein el Qudeirat is to be identified as Kadesh-barnea. It is a large oasis and would have furnished the needs of a large population for an extended period of time.

4. Kadesh to Moab

Outside of the biblical account, little is definitive in terms of the identification of the itinerary sites from Kadesh-barnea to Moab. According to the book of Numbers the route taken was southerly, toward Yam Suf (in this case, the Gulf of Elath), and then in a northeastern direction to travel around Edom into Moab.

What is clear from the biblical text (although most of the sites listed in Num 33 are only found in this text) is that the biblical authors consistently identified these particular locales as only associated with Edom and Moab. Thus, their understanding of the journey was a movement from the Negeb, south toward Elath, northeast around Edom and finally north and northwest through Moab to the Arabah.

B. The Exodus Route Reconstructed

The physical locations of specific, critical sites are crucial to an understanding of the exodus route. The arguments tend to focus on the actual whereabouts of the early itinerary sites, those involved with the slavery, and the locales visited up to, and including, Mount Sinai. It is generally admitted that sites such as Pithom, Raameses and Succoth, although identified archaeologically (if Succoth is indeed to be identified as Tjeku) only circumstantially point to the biblical exodus story. Moreover, the exodus is primarily, if not exclusively, a story deriving solely from the biblical sources. These sources, no matter how defined, present a consistent geographical picture of the itinerary sites. This observation is true especially regarding the initial sites of Goshen, Succoth, Yam Suf and Mount Sinai.

1. Goshen

Identified in only two books, Genesis and Joshua, GOSHEN is only clearly localized in Joshua (10:41; 11:16; 15:51). These texts locate a Goshen within the region of the Negeb. At the same time, it is not clear within the Bible just where the eastern border of Egypt is to be situated. From the perspective of the biblical authors, the eastern border is found at the "wadi of Egypt," located approximately at the southern border of today's Gaza Strip. This then, brings the references in Genesis (45:10; 46:28, 29, 34; 47:1, 4, 6, 27) into a much clearer light. They indicate that Goshen is located outside of Egypt proper (46:34; 47:6), and from the ancient Israelite geographical perspective, quite reasonably in agreement with the Joshua passages.

2. Succoth

The OT identifies Succoth in only one locale, somewhere within the Arabah (Gen 33:17; Josh 13:27; Judg 8:4-9; 1 Kgs 7:46; Pss 60:6 [Heb. 60:8]; 108:7 [Heb. 108:8]). On no occasion do biblical sources locate Succoth within Egypt itself.

3. Yam Suf

Verses within the OT that mention Yam Suf in relation to other known geographical areas, are consistent in identifying Yam Suf as the Gulf of Elath (Exod 23:31; Num 14:25; 21:4; 33:11; Deut 2:1; 1 Kgs 9:26). Since no texts locate Yam Suf in association with the Gulf of Suez, or any part of Egypt proper, there is every reason to accept the consistency of the biblical sources, and to identify Yam Suf as only the Gulf of Elath.

4. Mount Sinai

Even with all the controversy and discussion concerning the location of Mount Sinai, it would appear to be very easily located just based on biblical references (see SINAI, MOUNT). Whenever Mount Sinai is mentioned in association with known locales, it is clear where the biblical sources understood it to be.

Mount Sinai is within the Wilderness of Sinai and near the Wilderness of Paran (Exod 19:1-2; Lev 7:38; Num 10:12), both associated with the region of the eastern Negeb and Edom. It is also specifically identified as within the region of Edom (Deut 33:2; Judg 5:4-5). Mount Sinai is never associated with today's Sinai Peninsula (itself, never actually mentioned within the Bible).

5. Exodus from the Negeb

According to the biblical sources, the initial exodus itinerary sites (from Succoth to Kadesh-barnea) are to be located outside of Egypt. They appear to be found within the eastern Sinai region (with Succoth in the Arabah), indicating an exodus from the Negeb and not Egypt. See EXODUS, BOOK OF; NUMBERS, BOOK OF; WANDER; WILDERNESS.

MICHAEL D. OBLATH

EXORCISM. The supernatural expulsion of harmful spirits or demons from afflicted (possessed) persons or places. In the ANE, evil spirits were widely regarded as principal causes for physical and psychological maladies, as well as natural and environmental disasters. To ameliorate these calamities, certain sacerdotal officials and charismatic figures functioned as exorcists (exorkistēs ἐξορκιστής), invoking divine power against malignant forces through various magical incantations and demonstrations. Some Mesopotamian priests, e.g., liberated a demon-possessed person by smashing a miniature model of the nefarious spirit, after reciting special apotropaic formulas.

Other exorcising techniques appear in biblical (and related) literature associated with David, Solomon, Tobias, Jesus, and Paul.

A. Saul
B. Tobias
C. Solomon
D. Jesus
E. Paul
Bibliography

A. Saul

Tormented by "an evil spirit from the Lord," King Saul hired the young Bethlehemite David to bear his armor and strum the lyre. At first, the evil spirit left Saul whenever David played in his presence (1 Sam 16:14-23). But David's music achieved only a temporary exorcism. Eventually, the evil spirit assaulted Saul "while David was playing music," impelling the raving king to hurl his spear (with intent to kill) at the increasingly popular David (1 Sam 18:10-11; 19:9-10). Josephus describes Saul's demonic disorder as choking fits that court physicians could not cure; only David could cast out (ekballō ἐκβάλλω) the strangling spirit through his hymn-singing and harp-playing (Ant. 6.166-69). Qumran's *Psalms Scroll*[a] recounts that David composed four psalms to be sung specifically over those harassed by demons (11QPs[a] XXVII, 2-4, 9-11).

B. Tobias

On his wedding night with Raguel's beautiful daughter Sarah, whose seven previous husbands had all been murdered by a vicious demon, Tobias protected himself by burning portions of a fish's heart and liver on the incense embers in the bridal chamber. The odor from the smoke so repulsed the demon that "he fled to the remotest parts of Egypt," where the angel Raphael bound him hand and foot. To ensure that the demon would not return, the couple offered special supplication for the Lord's "mercy and safety" (Tob 6:3-8, 14-18; 8:1-18).

C. Solomon

In the *Testament of Solomon*, King Solomon deals in a similar fashion with the homicidal demon Asmodeus, known for "hatching plots against newlyweds." In this case, Solomon thwarts the evil spirit with the smoking liver and gall of a sheatfish, burned with a branch of storax (*T. Sol.* 5.1-13). Solomon's reputation as an exorcist is attested in other extrabiblical materials. Josephus credits him with formulating powerful incantations to drive away wicked spirits and recounts the exorcising feats of a contemporary Jew named Eleazar, who used Solomon's name and magical words as well as a special root prescribed by Solomon to deliver possessed members of Vespasian's family and army. Placed under the seal of Eleazar's ring, the root emitted an odor that extracted demons through the afflicted person's nostrils (*Ant.* 8.42-49).

D. Jesus

The Gospels report several examples of Jesus' exorcising ministry, focusing primarily on his authoritative verbal control over demonic forces.

When an evil spirit infesting a man in the Capernaum synagogue recognizes Jesus as "the Holy One of God" and queries, "Have you come to destroy us?" Jesus promptly responds, "Be silent, and come out [exelthe ἐξελθε] of him!" The demon duly obeys, sparking the audience's amazement at Jesus' authority (Mark 1:21-28; Luke 4:31-31).

As a severely afflicted demoniac from the region of Gerasa recognizes Jesus as "Son of the Most High God" and implores Jesus ("I adjure you [horkizō ὁρκίζω] by God," Mark 5:7) not to torment him, Jesus again orders the evil spirit "to come out [exelthein ἐξελθειν] of the man"; on this occasion, however, further conversation ensues, in which Jesus secures the demon's name ("Legion," a symbol of oppressive Roman military occupation) and grants its wish for transfer to a nearby herd of swine, which then stampedes into the sea and drowns. By contrast, the former raving demoniac is now described as "sitting, clothed, and in his right mind" (Mark 5:1-20; Luke 8:26-39; compare Matt 8:28-34).

When Jesus encounters a boy possessed by a tormenting spirit that caused convulsive fits (and also made him a deaf mute in Mark 9:17, 25), he rebukes the spirit (and orders it to "come out [exelthe] of him, and never enter him again!" in Mark 9:25). Previously, the boy's father had asked Jesus' disciples to cast out the evil spirit, but to no avail. After Jesus cures the child, he explains privately to his befuddled disciples that their exorcising failure was due to their lack of prayer (and possibly fasting) in Mark 9:28-29 and their "little faith" in Matt 17:19-20 (see Mark 9:14-29; Matt 17:14-21; Luke 9:37-43).

When a distraught Syrophoenician (Mark 7:26) or Canaanite (Matt 15:22) woman beseeches Jesus to heal her demon-possessed daughter, he does not immediately respond as she wishes. After she presses him, however, revealing her "great faith" (in Matt 15:28), Jesus pronounces the daughter free from her debilitating demon. Mark's account makes clear that Jesus never actually encounters the afflicted girl. Only when the mother returns home does she find "the child lying on the bed, and the demon gone" (Mark 7:30).

In a story unique to Luke 13:10-17 set in a synagogue, Jesus meets a chronically bent-over woman "whom Satan bound for eighteen long years." Taking the initiative, Jesus declares her "free from [her] ailment" and also lays hands upon her to restore her to full (upright) health. The woman's release from Satan's grip triggers not only her praising God and the audience's rejoicing, but also the synagogue leader's criticizing Jesus for healing on the Sabbath.

Accused by certain critics of expelling demons through the agency of Satan or Beelzebul, Jesus counters by exposing the logical fallacy of this charge ("How can Satan cast out Satan?" [Mark 3:23]) and explaining the grounds of his authority: "But if it is by the Spirit [Matt 12:28]/finger [Luke 11:20] of God that I cast out demons, then the kingdom of God has come to you" (Mark 3:22-27; Matt 12:22-29; Luke 11:14-22). In Matthew and Luke, Jesus elaborates on the hazards of controlling evil spirits, given their sinister attempts, once exorcised, to repossess their victims with reinforcements (seven more demons, more diabolical than the first) (Matt 12:43-45; Luke 11:24-25).

E. Paul

As Eleazar invoked the name of Solomon (exorcists often recited the name of some powerful hero or deity), Jesus' followers invoked his name while casting out evil spirits. As well as exulting before Jesus in the power they exerted over demons "in your name" (Luke 10:17), his disciples also complain about a maverick exorcist (not in their circle) whom they discovered "casting out demons in your name" (Mark 9:38; Luke

9:49). In the first case, Jesus both affirms and redirects their enthusiasm ("rejoice [rather] that your names are written in heaven" [Luke 10:18-20]); in the second, he discounts their concern and affirms the independent exorcist ("Whoever is not against us is for us" [Mark 9:39-40; Luke 9:50]). When a Philippian slave-girl and fortune-teller, possessed by a "Pythian" (serpentine) spirit associated with the Roman god Apollo and Delphic oracle, annoys Paul with her persisting chatter, he successfully orders the offending spirit "in the name of Jesus to come out (exelthein) of her" (Acts 16:16-18).

But all exorcists invoking Jesus' name are not so fortunate. In Matthew, Jesus warns that some who claim to expel demons in his name will find themselves rudely exposed "on that day" of reckoning as charlatans whom Jesus "never knew" (Matt 7:21-23); and in Acts, a group of itinerant exorcists (seven sons of a Jewish priest called Sceva) who attempt "to use the name of Jesus"—just as Paul did—find themselves embarrassingly discomfited by a wicked, yet perceptive, spirit who knows the authority of both Jesus and Paul better than they do (Acts 19:13-16). *See* DEMON; DEMONIAC; HEALING; MAGIC, MAGICIAN; MIRACLE.

Bibliography: H. D. Betz, ed. *The Greek Magical Papyri in Translation (including the Demotic Spells)* (1986); Susan R. Garrett. *The Demise of the Devil: Magic and the Demonic in Luke's Writings* (1989); H.-J. Klauck. *Magic and Paganism in Early Christianity: The World of the Acts of the Apostles* (2003); T. E. Klutz, ed. *Magic in the Biblical World: From the Rod of Aaron to the Ring of Solomon* (2003); T. E. Klutz. *The Exorcism Stories in Luke-Acts: A Sociostylistic Reading* (2004); M. E. Meyer and R. Smith, eds. *Ancient Christian Magic: Coptic Texts of Ritual Power* (1994); E. Sorensen. *Possession and Exorcism in the New Testament and Early Christianity* (2002); P. A. Torijano. *Solomon the Esoteric King: From King to Magus, Development of a Tradition* (2002); G. H. Twelftree. *Jesus the Exorcist: A Contribution to the Study of the Historical Jesus* (1993).

F. SCOTT SPENCER

EXPIATION [כפר kpr; ἱλάσκομαι hilaskomai]. God's freeing and cleansing people from the onus and blemish of sin.

Modern discussion has focused on whether the biblical materials concerned with the ATONEMENT refer to expiation or propitiation (sacrifice as a means of appeasing God's wrath), or whether expiation is separable from some notion of propitiation. The linguistic evidence for use of kpr in the OT prioritizes a definition of atonement as "to wipe away" or "to cleanse." Moreover, theologically, the need of sinful humanity is not so much a transformation in God's self or in God's attitude toward humanity but rather the metamorphosis of humanity's sinful existence before God.

Among the OT sacrifices, the most important for our purposes is the purification offering (khatta'th חַטָּאת e.g., Lev 4:1–6:7; 6:24-7:10; see Lev 16), which focuses on cleansing the effect of sin: cultic impurity. Jacob Milgrom has argued for this explanation of atonement persuasively, though that view could reduce the purification offering to a concern only with contamination of the temple. Clearly, however, this rite cannot be segregated from forgiveness of sins (e.g., Lev 4:20, 26, 31; 16:16). Milgrom also interprets atonement as redemption through the substitution of an animal for a human being (Lev 16), as well as purification of the sanctuary and, by extension, of the community of God's people (e.g., Lev 15:31; 16:19). In this context, we find no explanation of the sacrificial act as "satisfaction" or "penalty"; rather, sacrifice addresses the proclivity and effects of sin to pollute, stain, and spoil.

In the NT, expiation is central to Paul's exposition of the death of Jesus in Rom 3:25 (hilastērion ἱλαστήριον; NRSV: "sacrifice of atonement"), though scholars debate whether Paul's language supports the idea of assuaging God's wrath and whether "place of atonement" (that is, "MERCY SEAT") should also be understood here. The importance of expiation is pervasive in Hebrews, which describes the action of God to initiate covenant relations with humanity, the work of God in Christ to provide a forerunner who, through his suffering and death, not only enters the presence of God before us but wipes away all barriers so that we might enter with him, and so God's initiative to transform the human condition (esp. Heb 9–10). If, from the perspective of Israel's Scriptures, sin rendered people unclean and thus excluded them from God's presence, for Hebrews the institution of sacrifice was largely concerned with the removal of this impediment (*see* CLEAN AND UNCLEAN). In the Fourth Gospel, John the Baptist identifies Jesus as "the Lamb of God who takes away the sin of the world" (John 1:29). Similarly, 1 John emphasizes the expiatory significance of Jesus' death: "the blood of Jesus his Son cleanses us from all sin" (1:7). *See* SACRIFICES AND OFFERINGS; SIN, SINNER.

Bibliography: Daniel P. Bailey. "Jesus as the Mercy Seat: The Semantics and Theology of Paul's Use of *Hilasterion* in Romans 3:25." Ph.D. diss. (1999); John Goldingay. "Your Iniquities Have Made a Separation Between You and God." *Atonement Today* (1995) 39–53; Jacob Milgrom. *Leviticus.* AB 3–3B (1991–2001).

JOEL B. GREEN

EXTERMINATE [בָּעַר ba'ar, חָרַם kharam, שָׁמַד shamadh]. The verb shamadh (NRSV: usually "destroy") is often used in contexts of warfare or punishment (Josh 11:20), while ba'ar implies sweeping away or purging evil (1 Kgs 22:46 [Heb. 22:47]). The distinctive verb kharam (NRSV: usually "utterly destroy" or "devote to destruction") describes killing or destroying persons, animals, and other booty captured in holy war (1 Chr 4:41). *See* BAN; DESTROY, UTTERLY; HOLY WAR.

RICHARD D. NELSON

EXTORTION [בֶּצַע betsaʿ, עֹשֶׁק ʿosheq; ἁρπαγή harpagē, ἅρπαξ harpax]. These and other terms are variously translated "extortion," "oppression," "fraud."

The acquisition of property, goods, or money, perhaps with consent or even legally but through abuse of authority, wealth, or force is condemned in the Bible and often is equated with robbery (Lev 6:2, 4; 19:13; Ps 62:10; Ezek 22:7, 12, 29; 1 Cor 6:10). Those without power (the poor, aliens) were particularly vulnerable and were to be protected (Jer 21:12; Ps 72:4; Prov 14:31). Extortion incurs punishment (Ezek 18:18; Amos 4:1; Zech 7:10; contrast Eccl 4:1; 5:7), but as a metaphor for powerlessness it may represent punishment (Deut 28:29, 33; Hos 5:11). Some stories suggest extortionate practices (1 Sam 2:15; 8:10-18; 25:2-13; 2 Sam 12:1-4; 1 Kgs 21:1-16; Luke 19:12-27). Jesus accused the Pharisees of outwardly pious behavior combined with enthusiasm for extortion (Matt 23:25; Luke 11:39; compare Matt 7:15; Luke 18:11). *See* CRIMES AND PUNISHMENT.

PETER TRUDINGER

EYE [עַיִן ʿayin; ὄμμα omma, ὀφθαλμός ophthalmos]. Most frequently "eye" refers to the physical organ. David's eyes were beautiful (1 Sam 16:12), while Leah's eyes were "weak" (Gen 29:17; or "tender, delicate"). Warfare often resulted in the defeated enemy's eyes being gouged out (Judg 16:21; 2 Kgs 25:7; Jer 39:7). Loss of the right eye made one militarily worthless (1 Sam 11:2).

Eyes reveal arrogance (Prov 6:17), pity (Ezek 16:5), scorn (Prov 30:17), and respect (Ps 123:2). Bright eyes are signs of "shalom," health and well-being (Ps 38:10 [Heb. 38:11]), while dim eyes reveal ill health and age (Deut 28:65; Job 17:7; Ps 69:3 [Heb. 4]). Eyes are the portals for greed (1 Sam 2:29, 32) and lust (Ps 73:7 [Heb. 73:8]; Prov 17:24; 27:20; 2 Pet 2:14; 1 John 2:16). Open or lifted eyes symbolize alertness (Gen 13:10, 14; 18:2) while closed eyes represent lack of concern (Prov 28:27; Matt 13:15). The eyes produce tears (Ps 119:136). ʿAyin is also translated "spring," relating the eyes to the "well of the soul."

Spiritual perception and comprehension are increased when the eyes are opened through God's law (Ps 119:18) or by the Holy Spirit (Eph 1:18). John relates "seeing" to "believing" (John 1:50). *See* APPLE OF THE EYE; GOUGING EYES; SEEING.

MICHAEL G. VANZANT

EYELIDS OF THE MORNING [עַפְעַפֵּי־שָׁחַר ʿafʿappe-shakhar]. In Job 3:9, this image can be understood as symbolically referring to night that awaits the eyes of its partner, the DAWN; but Job's curse threatens this bond and the alternation of day and night, and so also threatens the foundation of creation that God had promised to maintain after the FLOOD. Metaphorically, the phrase, rendered as "eyelids of the dawn" in Job 41:18, also refers to the eyes of the LEVIATHAN, a sea monster, where the projection of the reddish rays of dawn is used to describe the inner fire of Leviathan that is emitted through its glance. This image is used to emphasize God's power over Leviathan's glance and inner fire (Job 42:1-2). In Egyptian hieroglyphics, crocodile eyes also symbolize dawn. *See* JOB, BOOK OF.

EMILY R. CHENEY

EZBAI ezʹbi [אֶזְבָּי ʾezbay]. Ezbai was father of Naari, one of David's MIGHTY MEN (1 Chr 11:37). The parallel list (2 Sam 23:35) hints that Ezbai may be the result of a textual corruption, a scribe mistaking the letter resh (ר) for the letter zayin (ז). The list of David's warriors is inconsistent in its characterization: some warriors are listed by a gentilic, others are identified through familial relationships (brothers or fathers).

PHILLIP MICHAEL SHERMAN

EZBON ezʹbon [אֶצְבֹּן ʾetsbon]. 1. One of Gad's seven sons (Gen 46:16); supplanted by OZNI in Num 26:16.

2. A son of Bela and grandson of Benjamin (1 Chr 7:7), although this list may be Zebulun's genealogy, given the different Benjaminite list in 1 Chr 8 and the Chronicler's omission of Zebulun otherwise.

DEREK E. WITTMAN

EZEKIEL, APOCRYPHON OF i-zeeʹkee-uhl. The name "Apocryphon of Ezekiel" generally refers to five citations preserved in Christian sources, all of which bear the prophet Ezekiel's name somewhere in the tradition, which presumably belonged to a longer work no longer extant. Possibly several other anonymous citations could have originated in this work. Not all scholars agree, however, that they must have come from a single apocryphon. They are: 1) Epiphanius of Salamis (4th cent. CE; *Pan.* 64.70) says that he found "in Ezekiel's own apocryphon," a parable that narrates a story about two men, one blind and one lame, who cooperate to despoil a king's garden out of anger at not being invited to his son's wedding feast. Versions of the same parable also appear in several rabbinic sources; 2) 1 Clement 8:3 quotes a short saying about repentance, which Clement of Alexandria (*Paed.* 1.10) later attributes to Ezekiel; 3) Tertullian (*Carn. Chr.* 23) knows a saying "in Ezekiel" about a heifer that "has given birth but has not given birth," which he employs in arguments about the virginity of Mary; 4) Evagrius of Antioch (Lat. trans. of Athanasius *Vit. Ant.* 15) cites a short "prophetic word" about judgment that came "through Ezekiel," which appears in at least eighteen other Christian sources. 5) Papyrus Chester Beatty 185

(4th cent. CE) preserves fragments of what is most likely a manuscript copy of at least part of the apocryphon. Clement of Alexandria (*Paed.* 1.9) knows some of this same material, which he says came "through Ezekiel." The sections in common between Clement and Chester Beatty 185 bear a resemblance to Ezek 34 (*see* CHESTER BEATTY PAPYRI).

Based on the testimony of Epiphanius, the appearance of an Ezekiel "pseudepigraphon" in the *Stichometry of Nicephorus* (8th–9th cent. CE), Josephus's mention of two books of Ezekiel (*Ant.* 10.79), and the evidence of Chester Beatty 185, scholars do not generally doubt the apocryphon's existence as a Second Temple Jewish work. Although its scope and contents remain unknown, it was clearly popular with Christians for a long time. The surviving fragments indicate that it probably focused on eschatological themes of divine judgment, the necessity of repentance, and the hope of resurrection. Its original language, most likely Hebrew or Greek, and place of origin are unknown.

In connection with this apocryphon, Cave 4 from QUMRAN revealed several copies of a Pseudo-Ezekiel work (4Q385, 385b, 385c, 386, 388, 391) written in Hebrew that take the form of a first-person dialogue between the prophet and God. *See* EZEKIEL, BOOK OF.

Bibliography: James R. Mueller. *The Five Fragments of the Apocryphon of Ezekiel* (1994); James R. Mueller and S. E. Robinson. "The Apocryphon of Ezekiel." *OTP* (1985) 487–95; Michael E. Stone, Benjamin G. Wright, and David Satran. *The Apocryphal Ezekiel* (2000).

BENJAMIN G. WRIGHT, III

EZEKIEL, BOOK OF i-zee´kee-uhl [יְחֶזְקֵאל *yekhezqe'l*]. The third book of the major prophets and attributed to the priest Ezekiel, son of Buzi, one of the Judeans deported to Babylonia in 597 BCE (*see* EXILE). The book's date notices, themes, and historical allusions reflect the Judean political situation leading up to the deportation and Nebuchadnezzar's subsequent destruction of Jerusalem in 586 BCE. The book employs a number of formulas normally associated with prophetic speech and presents the prophet Ezekiel as actively engaged in announcing oracles of judgment and restoration (*see* PROPHET, PROPHECY). However, other features, including its well-planned structure, complex development of metaphors, and coherent theological program suggest that it was produced largely as a literary composition. Through its elaborate visions of the glory of God, preoccupation with the fate of Jerusalem, and repetition of key themes, the book argues that the rebellious and now defeated house of Israel would come to recognize the power, sovereignty, and covenantal loyalty of their God Yahweh in the events that had so devastatingly overturned their assumptions about national security and privilege.

A. Structure and Outline of Book
B. Detailed Analysis
  1. Historical background
    a. Date notices in Ezekiel
    b. Ezekiel's understanding of Judean political alliances
  2. Literary analysis
    a. Judean prophetic and priestly traditions
      i. Proof sayings
      ii. Disputations
      iii. Symbolic acts
    b. Ancient Near Eastern traditions
C. Theological Significance
Bibliography

A. Structure and Outline of Book

The book of Ezekiel exhibits a degree of literary coherence unmatched in the prophetic canon. Early Jewish interpreters noted a division of the book into two sections treating doom and consolation respectively (1–24, 25–48); some modern interpreters continue to treat the organization of the book in this way. Chapter 24 does dwell at length on the destruction of Jerusalem and thus gives the impression of a definitive end to the period of judgment; whether this event signals a turning point in the book is another question. Framing devices in chapters 24 and 33 suggest that at the very least chapters 25–33 constitute a transitional stage in the movement from judgment to restoration. Yet even this observation does not take into account other features that argue against a bipartite division of the book. Since the nations in chaps. 25–32 are presented elsewhere as Judean allies, their judgment can hardly be construed as salvation for Judah. Nor does chap. 33 signal the advent solely of salvation: Ezekiel must still call the exiles to repentance, and the remnant in Jerusalem remains under judgment. Moreover, the designation of the material in chapters 34–39 as restoration oracles may be overly simplistic. These oracles are primarily concerned with establishing the honor of Yahweh's holy name; whatever salvation is proclaimed in these latter chapters is oriented toward that goal. Finally, the program of restoration in chapters 40–48 has as part of its goal the prevention of any further abuses of power. It is therefore more accurate to suggest that the theme of chapters 25–48 is the assertion of the divine will to rule over Israel and to establish its distinctiveness over against the nations. In this respect, chapters 25–48 constitute the fulfillment of the divine oath in 20:33 to be Israel's king.

The book's three great visions of the glory of God (1, 8–11, 40–48) also argue against the traditional bipartite division of the book. Although it is well known that the visions are literarily linked to one another, interpreters do not always treat them as significant structuring elements. On the contrary, the visions do appear to delineate distinct stages in the prophet's work. The first stage is introduced by the vision in chapter 1 and continues through chapter 7. This section introduces the key characters in the book, establishes the relationships between them, and announces the theme of irrevocable judgment. While much of the material in these chapters, particularly the symbolic acts (3:22–5:4) and the oracles of judgment against Jerusalem and Judah (5:5–7:27), may have originally been associated with the prophet's public ministry, their placement at this point in the book draws attention to an extended process of Ezekiel's preparation to declare the divine message. The interval between the dates in 1:2 and 8:1 corresponds almost exactly to the number of days that Ezekiel must lie on his side (4:4–8), suggesting that in their present literary context the symbolic acts now function as a type of ordeal preparing the prophet for his role among the exiles. Furthermore, the exiles do not appear as an audience either for the symbolic acts or for the oracles of chaps. 5–7. In 5:5 and 7:1, the oracles are introduced as God's own direct speech, presumably to the prophet alone, while in 6:1 the prophet is instructed to speak to the mountains of Israel.

It is only with the second great vision (8:1–11:25) that the prophet begins to interact directly with the exiles. While elders sit with him in his house (8:1), Ezekiel is carried away in "visions of God" to Jerusalem, where he becomes a direct witness to abominations in the Temple, its destruction by heavenly executioners, and the deity's departure from the Temple and city (*see* TEMPLE, JERUSALEM; VISION). At the end of this extended vision, Ezekiel reports what he has seen to the elders, thus indicating the first time in the book that he speaks to the exiles (11:25). From this point on, the prophet has an audience. The exiles come to inquire of him, and God commands him to engage his audience directly: to announce their abominations, judge them, refuse their inquiries, explain his symbolic acts, and call them to repentance.

In chaps. 1–7 and 8–39, the figure of the prophet plays a key role in structuring the material. Immediately after the visions of chaps. 1 and 8–11, the prophet not only performs signs but becomes one, an incarnate testimony to the hidden work of God in the unfolding events. Although the symbolic act of 12:1–6 is not dated, its juxtaposition with the dated vision of chapters 8–11 suggests a close association with the period of ZEDEKIAH's rebellion (8:1; compare Jer 27–28). Ezekiel's symbolic act suggests that Zedekiah's rebellion will end in a cowardly yet futile attempt to escape, leaving the city to destruction and famine. When the actual siege of the city begins in chapter 24, the prophet acts again as a sign, this time by foregoing the normal mourning rites when his wife dies (24:18). Though this sign remains open to a variety of interpretations, it is explicitly linked to the next phase of the prophet's ministry (24:25-27; 33:21-22). It is only in

this latter phase of his ministry (i.e., chaps. 33–39) that Ezekiel is actually called a prophet (33:33).

The third and final vision (40–48) presents yet a third stage in Ezekiel's ministry, as he receives instructions to become the founder of the newly established (if visionary) kingdom of God in the land of Israel. Although the language of signs is not used in this section, Ezekiel's active involvement in the vision rounds out the book's extensive development of his persona. In the vision, Ezekiel walks through the courts of God's new temple, measures its foundations, establishes its sacrifices, and bathes in the living stream that brings healing to the land. Throughout, the prophet is instructed to take careful note of what he sees so that he may report what he sees to the exiles. Despite the vision's emphasis on restoration in the land of Israel, certain features of the vision make it unlikely that it was ever intended as an actual model of restoration; for example, the allocation of the land to the twelve tribes in exactly equal parcels defies the geographical realities of the region. Once again, the figure of Ezekiel may hold the clue to the significance of this vision for the exiles. Though both he and they remain absent from the land, the prophet becomes a testimony to the experience of divine presence and thereby offers that same experience to the exiles through the medium of his vision.

In addition to the development of the prophetic persona, other structuring elements establish coherence in smaller sections of the book. One of the most striking is the framing device of chaps. 16 and 23. Both chapters develop at length the metaphor of JERUSALEM as the adulterous wife of God (*see* ADULTERY). Within this frame, chaps. 17–22 examine the multiple modes of Jerusalem's rebellion, which encompass political and familial betrayal as well as religious apostasy. The pornographically charged invective of chapter 23 rounds out the disclosure of Israel's guilt and leads ineluctably to the siege of Jerusalem in chapter 24. Other types of rhetorical strategies function as structuring devices in other units; for example, the concluding summary statements in chaps. 34–39 employ a handful of key phrases and terms such as the covenant of peace (34:25; 37:26) and the enumeration of eschatological blessings (34:25-31; 36:33-38; 37:24-28) in order to establish a consistent emphasis on the divine intention to restore Israel.

More than simply a collection of collections, the book exhibits dramatic movement from crisis to resolution. The principal characters are Yahweh, Ezekiel, and the house of Israel. The book sustains an autobiographical perspective throughout, as the prophet reports that he sees visions, sits among the exiles, is carried to worlds both defiled and cleansed, witnesses and performs unspeakable acts, and even occasionally objects to divine commands. Yet the driving force is Yahweh, the God who refuses to abandon the ancient promises despite Israel's numerous rebellions, which technically cancels out any obligation on God's part to abide by these promises. The so-called recognition formula, "and they shall know that I am the Lord," which appears more than 70 times throughout the book, leaves no question as to the purpose of the book: to give witness to the sovereignty and power of God in such a way that Israel can have no other recourse than to submit to the divine will (*see* GOD, OT VIEW OF; PROMISE). The book's conviction that God will succeed is suggested at the level of motifs: a prophet made dumb during judgment has his mouth opened to proclaim salvation (3:26; 33:22); hearts of stone are replaced with hearts of flesh (3:7; 36:26); the shame of exile and betrayal (16:59-63) becomes a source of self-knowledge before it is forgotten in the restoration (36:31; 39:25-29); the mountains and valleys of Israel are destroyed and then reclaimed (6; 35:1–36:15); and the bloody city of Jerusalem becomes supplanted by a city and temple of God's own design and making, ready to be inhabited by quiet people dwelling securely in the presence and protection of God (38:8, 10).

The complex nature of these structuring elements suggests that the book was composed over an extended period of time. At least two oracles are concerned with the succession of generations (18, 20), and the date in 40:1 suggests that the book may have been published for the second generation of exiles. Whether this publication was undertaken by the prophet himself or by a disciple cannot be determined, though the relatively narrow time frame of two decades between the prophet's first and last visions helps to explain the book's theological coherence. Although some features of the book do suggest subsequent reworkings, none is of necessarily post-exilic origin, and there is no reason to deny that the book acquired its present form during the exile. These considerations are reflected in the following outline:

B. Detailed analysis

1. Historical background

a. Date notices in Ezekiel. One of the distinctive features of Ezekiel is the attachment of a number of date notices to visions and oracles (*see* ORACLE). The dates are not evenly distributed throughout the book, nor are they evenly spaced over the book's time frame. The earliest dates fall in the fifth to seventh years of the deportation (593–591 BCE; 1:2; 8:1; 20:1) and roughly coincide with Zedekiah's conference with emissaries of neighboring kingdoms to plot rebellion against Babylon (Jer 27–28). Half of the dated oracles are concentrated in the years of the siege of Jerusalem (588–586 BCE; 24:1; 26:1; 29:1; 31:1; 32:1; 33:21). Nearly all of these dates are found in the oracles against the foreign nations, though one notice draws explicit attention to the beginning of the siege of Jerusalem (24:1-2), and another records the date on which the prophet learns that the city had fallen (33:21). The remaining two dated oracles are assigned to the twenty-fifth and twenty-seventh years (40:1; 29:17). The latter date introduces an oracle that revises the timetable of salvation for the exiles and may be associated with Nebuchadnezzar's last known campaign against Egypt (29:17-21; *ANET*, 308). The former date, which introduces Ezekiel's third and final vision, is not as easily tied to historical events, though it may have symbolic significance.

Ezekiel 40:1 explains the twenty-fifth year as exactly fourteen years after the destruction of Jerusalem, suggesting that Ezekiel's final vision came in a year that was theologically significant because of its relationship to the year of Jerusalem's destruction. One is tempted to interpret the period of fourteen years, or two times seven years, in light of Deutero-Isaiah's remark that Jerusalem has paid double for all its sins (Isa 40:2). Even though the reasoning behind the figure of fourteen years cannot be determined with certainty, the span of time between judgment and restoration is remarkably short. By contrast, Jeremiah proclaimed that Jerusalem would be subject to Babylon for a full seventy years (Jer 29:10). The time span is short even for Ezekiel, who elsewhere proclaims a forty-year period of judgment for Egypt (Ezek 29:13).

b. Ezekiel's understanding of Judean political alliances. All of the dates in Ezekiel encourage reading the book in light of what is known of the first decades of the reign of King Nebuchadnezzar of Babylon (605–556 BCE). From Ezekiel's perspective, these decades are but the dead end of a long history of political alliances that had only weakened the kingdoms of Israel and Judah. In an allegory of Yahweh's "marriage" to the sisters

Oholah (Samaria) and Oholibah (Jerusalem), Ezekiel presents Jerusalem's current crisis as the result of its long and fitful search for powerful "lovers" (Ezek 23; *see* OHOLAH AND OHOLIBAH; SAMARIA). Although the biblical motif of going after other lovers is associated with idolatry (e.g., Deuteronomy, Hosea), Ezekiel's use of the term reflects the political idiom of his day, in which treaty partners considered one another "friends" ('ahev [אָהֵב], 1 Kgs 5:1 [Heb. 5:15]) and expressed commitment to treaty obligations in comparable language. Ezekiel's allegory reflects his understanding of Judah's attempts to secure its political position by forging alliances with stronger nations. Although the younger sister Jerusalem sees her older sister destroyed by her lovers the Assyrians, she not only lusts after them but seeks other lovers as well. The strategy traps the kingdom in conflicting allegiances from which it cannot hope to extricate itself. Having violated all of her allegiances, she suffers a devastating and terrifying public ravaging at the hands of all of the allies she had so desperately played off against one another.

Ezekiel's allegory mirrors what is known of the history of Israel and Judah. Biblical accounts indicate that kings of both kingdoms sought alliances with Assyria in the mid-8th cent. BCE (2 Kgs 15:19; 16:7). The Israelite and Judean kings entered these alliances voluntarily, but they could not freely leave them, and subsequent attempts to extricate Israel and Judah from Assyrian control were costly. By 722 BCE, the Assyrians had destroyed Israel, deporting and resettling Israelites throughout the empire while settling peoples from other regions in the land around Samaria (2 Kgs 18:9-11). Sennacherib's invasion in 701 BCE put down Hezekiah's attempted revolt of 705 and resulted in the loss of forty-six fortified Judean towns and the imposition of steep penalties on top of an already crippling tribute (*ANET*, 288; 2 Kgs 18:13-16). The archaeological evidence suggests that the kingdom only gradually recovered from this assault (*see* ASSYRIA AND BABYLONIA).

Assyria continued to dominate Judean affairs for much of the next century. Esarhaddon reports that Manasseh (ca. 686–642 BCE) was a dutiful vassal who contributed both labor and materials for rebuilding Nineveh (*ANET*, 291). Despite the absence of reliable written accounts for the period after 639, historians suggest that Assyria continued to exercise influence in Syria- Palestine well into the 620s. Even though pressures from the east forced Assyria to turn its attention away from Syria-Palestine in the latter part of that decade, Assyria may not have left a power vacuum but may instead have ceded this region to Egypt in exchange for military assistance. The report that Pharaoh Neco went up to Assyria at Harran in 609 (2 Kgs 23:29) suggests not only that Egypt remained a loyal partner to the bitter end, but also that Assyria remained a significant player in Syria-Palestine even after the fall of Nineveh in 612. Whether Josiah's death at Megiddo was due to rebellion against Egypt or Assyria remains unclear, but if Assyria had already ceded Judah to Egypt, then the pharaoh's imposition of heavy tribute on Josiah's successor may have been understood not as a new obligation but rather as the punitive reinforcement of an older alliance that traced its authority back to Assyria. Ezekiel's condemnation of Egypt's attempt to succeed Assyria as the great cosmic tree in whom all nations take their shade may partially corroborate this construal of events (Ezek 31).

In Ezekiel's allegory, Jerusalem's interest in the Babylonians begins while Judah is a vassal of Assyria. No sooner has Jerusalem made Assyria her lover than she begins to lust after the Chaldeans, with whom she first becomes acquainted by gazing at magnificent wall carvings (23:14-15). Ezekiel's reference to wall carvings is a crux, since it is not clear where they are seen. The account may preserve a memory of diplomatic visits to Assyria, where Assyrian palace reliefs relayed the message of Assyria's indomitable strength in subduing the rebels in its empire. Ezekiel's allegory does reflect what is known of Judean contacts with Babylonia during its attempted rebellion against Assyria in the late 8th cent. Hezekiah entertained envoys from Merodach-Baladan of Babylonia (2 Kgs 20:12-15//Isa 39:1-4), who is described in Assyrian inscriptions as a particularly intractable rebel. The Assyrians may have taken Manasseh in chains to Babylon to force Manasseh to renounce his father's alliance with Babylon (2 Chr 33:11). That Manasseh was subsequently able to reinforce Judah's military strength suggests that he did affirm his loyalty to Assyria and was rewarded for doing so (2 Chr 33:14).

After Babylon threw off its Assyrian yoke in the 620s, it proceeded to launch a remarkably successful assault on the Assyrian empire itself. Nebuchadnezzar's defeat of Egypt at Carchemish in 605 brought an end to the Assyrian control of Syria-Palestine, and Judah became a Babylonian vassal in 604. Subsequent Judean rebellions, apparently based on Egyptian promises of aid, resulted in Nebuchadnezzar's invasion of Judah in 597, the deportation of the Judean king and three thousand leading citizens to Babylonia, and the installation of Zedekiah as regent of Judah. When Zedekiah rebelled a few years later, Nebuchadnezzar laid siege to Jerusalem in 588, and the city fell in 586.

Yet by Ezekiel's account, if Egypt does not succeed Assyria as the cosmic tree, neither does Babylon. In contrast with Jeremiah, who encourages the exiles to settle down in Babylon, build houses, and pray for the peace of that city (Jer 29:4-9), Ezekiel presents a more guarded assessment. He may concede that God regards Nebuchadnezzar as a faithful servant (Ezek 29:17-20), but he does not claim, as Jeremiah does, that God has allowed Nebuchadnezzar to set up his throne in Jerusalem (Jer 1:15). Rather, Ezekiel presents Babylon as the enraged lover who is allowed to wreak vengeance against the "adulteries" of its unfaithful vassal. Far from being a divinely ordained agent of cosmic order, Babylon is simply the chaos that Jerusalem has invited in to its own destruction. Indeed, the mysterious oracle against Gog of Magog may hint that any Babylonian attempt to act beyond the limits of the divine commission will be met with a battle of apocalyptic proportions (Ezek 38–39; *see* GOG AND MAGOG).

2. Literary Analysis

In the first decade of the 21st cent., the literary analysis of Ezekiel draws on a wide array of methods. Form and tradition criticism, which had been developed in the 20th cent. in order to identify supposedly oral features and contexts of prophetic books (*see* FORM CRITICISM, OT), have been combined with other methods more suited to the analysis of the book's compositional dimensions. Accompanying this trend has been a shift away from treating the book as a record of the prophet's ministry to regarding it an aspect of the ministry itself. An earlier search for the prophet's original oracles endeavored to extract individual units from their literary contexts; a more recent emphasis on the book's final form regards these units as elements of a literary whole. An example of the shift in methodology can be seen in the treatment of the book's frequent use of introductory and concluding prophetic formulas (e.g., the word-event formula, "the word of the Lord came to me"; the messenger formula, "thus says the Lord"; concluding oaths such as "I have spoken," and so on). Both methods treat these formulas as seams joining discrete elements; whereas the former rips the seams apart to focus on the individual units, the latter traces their design as literary elements contributing to an organic whole. The former method tends to regard these prophetic formulas and genres as records of Ezekiel's activity as a prophet, the latter as literary reflexes of an older tradition of prophecy. The present discussion adopts the latter stance and assumes that the book of Ezekiel represents a complex melding of originally oral genres from a variety of ANE and Judean priestly and prophetic sources.

a. Judean prophetic and priestly traditions.

The pervasive use of prophetic formulas gives the book of Ezekiel the appearance of a prophetic memoir. Ezekiel reports significant interaction with his fellow exiles; however, the book does not document this activity so much as it presents the words of God as they came to him. The frequently occurring word event formula focuses on the prophet's experience of receiving these messages. Other formulas direct him to perform tasks that are characteristic of prophetic activity; he must prophesy, speak, set his face against God's enemies, announce abominations, judge, and so on. Often these commands are doubled: "prophesy, and say to them." Occasionally instructions to prophesy are omitted, as if the divine communication is intended for the prophet alone (23:1, 36), and reports that Ezekiel did as he was commanded are the exception rather than the rule (11:25; 12:7; 24:18). Similarly, chapters 40–48 are structured as a report of Ezekiel's visionary experience. Even though the vision includes further instructions to the prophet to describe the measurements of the Temple (43:10), take note of the Temple ordinances (44:5), and also, somewhat surprisingly, to consecrate the altar (44:18-27), it is understood that the prophet does not carry out these tasks.

Whether or not the book yields evidence for recovering the historical Ezekiel, it does present a compelling portrait of a prophet in exile. The opening superscription identifies Ezekiel as a priest, the son of Buzi. The curious "thirtieth year" of 1:1, which is correlated with the fifth year of Jehoiachin's exile in 1:2, may refer to Ezekiel's age when he received his first vision. The dates mentioned in 40:1 and 29:17 would thus indicate a period of some twenty years of prophetic activity. This interval between the first and last dates in the book has suggested a comparison with Num 4:3, which reports that the Kohathites served in the sanctuary for twenty years, that is, from the age of thirty until their retirement at fifty. The author's acquaintance with priestly traditions is evident throughout the book in traditions of legal argument (3:17-21; 33:1-9; 18; 22:6-12); technical knowledge of 6th-cent. cult practices (6:4; 8; 43:7-9); and acquaintance with the Holiness Code (Lev 17–26). Whether the figure of Ezekiel is presented as a priest or a prophet, he is addressed throughout the book as ben ʾadham (בֶּן אָדָם), "son of man." Ancient Near Eastern usage frequently indicates a contrast between ʾadham and royalty, thus suggesting that the primary meaning of the term is not mortality (e.g., NRSV: "mortal") but the status of a subject before his king. As it is used in Ezekiel the title ben ʾadham connotes both the prophet's obedience to Yahweh and, consequently, his essential difference from his fellow exiles (*see* ADAM; SON OF MAN).

Beyond the reports of Ezekiel's prophetic activity, little else is known of his personal life, other than that his wife died during the siege of Jerusalem (24:18); yet even her death is significant only because Ezekiel's reaction becomes a sign for the exiles. Against tendencies in the mid-20th cent. to psychoanalyze or to romanticize the prophetic personality, form and redaction critics have emphasized the formal aspects of these narratives and urged that they be interpreted in terms of the prophet's theological message. Ezekiel's failure to mourn the death of his wife thus need not signify blocked emotions or more extreme forms of psychic withdrawal or dissociation but should be understood as part of his prophetic message.

In keeping with the portrayal of Ezekiel as a prophet to the exiles, the book employs a number of prophetic genres. The following are just a few illustrative examples:

i. Proof sayings. The form-critical analysis of oracles of judgment draws attention to a basic two-part structure consisting of an indictment or announcement of the reason for judgment, and an announcement of the judgment itself. In some announcements of judgment, a proof saying is added, thereby creating a three-part oracle of judgment. Proof sayings assert that the subject of the judgment oracle will come to a new awareness of the nature of his or her opponent. The use of the three-part proof saying in 1 Kgs 20:28 suggests that it originated in the war traditions as a means of reassuring vulnerable Israelite troops that they would successfully repel aggressors with the help of their God. The proof saying thus challenges the arrogance of enemy attacks against God's people while also reassuring the Israelite army of victory. Israel will share God's victory when God gives the enemy into its hand or otherwise reverses Israel's humiliation by showering them with the spoils of war.

In Ezekiel, the clearest examples of the three-part proof sayings are in the oracles against the foreign nations (25; 35:5-9, 10-15), though they appear elsewhere as well (13:1-16, 20-23). The genre is relevant to the exilic experience, which Ezekiel characterizes primarily as the experience of shameful humiliation in the eyes of the nations, and the oracles cite the nations' taunts of the defeated Judah as the reason for judgment. Although the older examples of these oracles anticipated a reversal of fortunes for Israel's sake, Ezekiel's adaptation of the genre focuses primarily on the nations' acknowledgment of the power of God. Ezekiel's appropriation of the genre thus underscores his theological agenda.

ii. Disputations. Complex adaptations of older genres are also evident in disputation speeches, in which the deity quotes a popular saying in order to refute it (11:3-21; 12:21-25, 26-28; 18; 33:10-16, 23-29). The popular sayings disclose a range of exilic and Judean responses to the crisis. Those who remain in Jerusalem express complacent security (11:3) and even self-congratulation for surviving the destruction (33:23); they blame others for the disaster, be they the ancestors who have "eaten sour grapes" or fellow exiles who have "gone far from" Yahweh (18:1; 11:15); or they acknowledge the veracity of Ezekiel's visions but consider them irrelevant for the present time (12:22, 27). From the exiles, one hears genuine despair (33:10; 37:11).

The clear differentiation between the voices of the exiles and those of the remnant in Jerusalem suggests a fundamental problem of injustice within the community, which the disputations resolve by exposing the false assumptions underlying the respective proverbs of the Jerusalem remnant and the exiles. In a few cases, a word of God decisively refutes the proverb (e.g., 12:21, 26; 33:25-29). In other instances, the disputation concretizes an underlying metaphor, thereby exposing the proverb's absurdity (11:3; see 24:3-13). Ezekiel

thereby demonstrates a penchant for exploiting the visual imagery inherent in the proverbs. The complaint that "our bones are dried up" (37:11) is answered in an extended literary unit that combines elements of vision and symbolic act while concretizing the saying by envisioning a valley filled with dry bones. The image of a battlefield strewn with bones is unique in the biblical tradition and is most likely derived from the Near Eastern tradition of treaty curses. Assyrian kings would allude to these curses in their reports of subduing rebels who were so roundly defeated that no one was left to bury the dead. Ezekiel's answer to the exiles' complaint thus subtly invokes the book's theme of rebellion even as it seeks to console the exiles.

Other disputations reflect comparably complex literary strategies. For example, the disputation in chap. 18 refutes the popular proverb, "The fathers have eaten sour grapes, and the children's teeth are set on edge." The disputation poses the question about intergenerational responsibility by examining the relationship between not two generations but three, thus forcing the readers to determine just which generation to which they belong. Whereas the involved discussion of case law in this same chapter urges the present generation to take responsibility for its plight, the same mode of argumentation is used in chap. 33 to console the exiles overly burdened by guilt (18; 33:10-16).

iii. Symbolic acts. The reports of the prophet's symbolic acts further indicate the book's adaptation of prophetic genres. In critical studies of the past century, questions have revolved around the performative character of symbolic acts designed to capture the interest of the audience in other than oral ways. Prophetic narratives thus generally include instructions to perform the symbolic act along with a narrative account of the prophet's performance and subsequent dialogue with the audience about its meaning.

Some of Ezekiel's symbolic actions bear out this interpretation. At numerous points, Ezekiel employs physical gestures: he "sets his face against" an enemy to announce judgment (6:1; 21:2 [Heb. 21:7]; 25:2; 35:2; 38:2); performs a sword dance (21:14–17 [Heb. 21:19–22]); sets up a signpost marking Nebuchadnezzar's advance (21:18–19 [Heb. 21:23-24]); and joins two sticks together to signify the reunification of Israel and Judah (37:16). The report of a symbolic act in 12:1-16 fully conforms to the above description of the nature and function of prophetic symbolic acts.

However, other reports of symbolic acts appear to have been adapted so as to reflect on the meaning of the prophet's involvement in the message. Central to this development is the notion of the prophet as "sign" (12:6b; 24:24; see 4:3), a term that in other contexts connotes the mysterious irruption of divine power into the profane realm (Exod 10:1-2). While the term can certainly suggest that the prophet's actions rhetorically stand for or point to something else, the narrative sequence suggests something else. To say that Ezekiel becomes a sign is to suggest that Ezekiel himself embodies and endures the reality of judgment, and the symbolic acts of 3:22–5:4 and 24:15-24 convey this sense of complete immersion in the exiles' experience of judgment.

Along with his extensive use of prophetic formulas and genres, Ezekiel is also adept at exploiting the ironic dimensions of non-prophetic genres and metaphors. The use of metaphors in prophetic speech is not unique to Ezekiel, but it is characteristic of Ezekiel that he develops them so extensively.

At sixty-three and forty-nine verses respectively, the allegories of Jerusalem and Samaria as wives of God rival some prophetic books in length (chaps. 16, 23). Ezekiel's revisionist history of the Exodus pushes the theme of Israel's rebellion to absurd lengths (chap. 20), and songs of lament ironically underscore the frailty of human achievements (27; 28:15-23; 31). One nation's symbol of strength is another's emblem of chaos: thus the lion of the tribe of Judah, long a symbol of the strength of the Davidic dynasty, becomes a ravening beast of chaos to be caught and subdued by its frightened neighbor-prey (19:1-9). Even a trade list can serve Ezekiel's rhetorical ends (27:12-25).

b. Ancient Near Eastern traditions. During the 20th cent., significant gains were made in the identification of Near Eastern traditions in Ezekiel, but often these traditions were treated as supplemental coloring rather than as significant elements of meaning. For example, interpretations of the vision of chap. 1 drew parallels with other prophetic call visions, as if the genre of the call narrative were the predominant element to be explained. Thus even though interpreters acknowledged the unusual character of Ezekiel's prolonged account of the four living beings in 1:5-21, it was assumed that the meaning of the vision lay primarily in its association with the ensuing account of Ezekiel's call. Similar generic complexity is evident in the third great vision in chaps. 40–48, which, while it is labeled a vision, presents an elaborate integration of priestly, legal, architectural, and political materials. Especially for this latter vision, the question of coherence remains a crux: were these chapters composed over time, as some have argued, or does the unit contain its own compositional coherence?

The book's use of disparate materials requires a more sophisticated analysis of its integration of biblical and Near Eastern genres. In nearly every chapter of the book, readers encounter adaptations and inversions of traditional forms, metaphors, and conventions. It has been argued that the transition from oral to written forms allowed for extensive manipulation of a genre's elements, and some examples of this process have been described in the above section. But other combinations, particularly those that graft Judean forms onto Near Eastern patterns, may also have contributed to the compositional design and theological coherence of the book.

While some scholars explain the presence of Near Eastern materials as the influence of Babylonian culture on the exiles, the great preponderance of imagery suggests a deeper and more penetrating acquaintance with Assyro-Babylonian influence than can have occurred within the first several decades of exile. One alternative explanation is that the nature and frequency of these motifs reflects Assyria's centuries-long dominance that had established a common cultural matrix in which at least the elite populations of vassal kingdoms sought to participate. The mechanisms for participating included diplomatic visits to Assyria, where public buildings were designed to impress Assyrian ideology upon its visitors. As noted above, Ezek 23:14-15 may preserve a memory of such diplomatic visits. In addition, Assyrian letters indicate that foreign scribes and vassal princes received their training at the Assyrian court. Although there is no direct evidence that Judean princes or scribes participated in such training, Assyrian culture has left its mark on the traditions and culture of Israel and Judah.

In Ezekiel, Assyrian influence is most evident in the visions. The magnificent account of the four living creatures in chap. 1 is replete with both imagery and vocabulary from Assyro-Babylonian aesthetic traditions. Other motifs, such as the departure of the deity from the profaned Temple in chaps. 8–11 and the deity's return to the land and a new temple in chaps. 40–43; the nine heavenly executioners in chap. 9; and the measurements of perfectly square structures in chaps. 40–43, all indicate a thorough acquaintance with Assyro-Babylonian iconography. The influence may also be evident in the overall structure of the book of Ezekiel, which resembles the Assyrian building inscription genre, in which kings gives autobiographical accounts of military battles and building projects. Ezekiel bears fruitful comparison with the Babylonian inscriptions of Esarhaddon which, unlike most examples of the genre, focus on the fortunes of a single city, Babylon. If this genre lies behind the overall structure of Ezekiel, then Ezekiel has of course appropriated it for theological purposes.

Within such a framework, many of Ezekiel's motifs of rebellion and restoration become intelligible. Like Deuteronomy, Ezekiel demands that the house of Israel demonstrate unswerving loyalty to its God. But Ezekiel differs from Deuteronomy somewhat in showing a much closer connection to the political realm from which this notion of loyalty is derived. Whereas Deuteronomy focuses squarely on the "love" that Israel is to have for its Lord, Ezekiel delves more deeply into the nation's infidelity. Ezekiel presents Jerusalem's harlotries not simply as theological apostasy but also as political duplicity. His characterization of Israel as the house of rebellion is drawn primarily from political discourse

(Gen 14:4; 2 Kgs 18:7, 20; 24:1, 20; Ezek 17:15) and bears interesting comparison with Assyria's assessment of rebellious vassals. Ezekiel condemns Zedekiah for violating his oath of allegiance to Babylon and possibly also for deceiving his Ammonite allies (21:25-32 [Heb. 21:30-37]). Many of Ezekiel's symbolic acts—being bound in his house, setting siege to a city, attempting escape—have formulaic parallels not only in Assyrian inscriptions but also in wall reliefs commemorating royal victories over rebellious kings and cities. Other features, including the composition of Gog's army and the resuscitation of dry bones, can be interpreted in light of Assyrian inscriptional motifs.

Finally, Ezekiel's presentation of the God of Israel as a God who establishes his kingship by force over a rebellious people and then graciously provides for them in a city of his own making seems to owe much to Assyrian inscriptional traditions. It has been said that in the OT the God of Israel often sounds like an Assyrian potentate; nowhere is this more true than in Ezekiel, where conceptions of loyalty and rebellion, covenant and kingship, exhibit an especially close relationship to the political idioms of the 7th and 6th cents. BCE. At the same time, the theological appropriation of these idioms constitutes a radical critique of the empires of Ezekiel's day. In characterizing the other empires as "lovers" and as foolishly hubristic rivals of God, Ezekiel relativizes all human claims to power and presents the God of Israel as the only true shepherd of Israel.

C. Theological Significance

As Ezekiel's preoccupation with the siege of Jerusalem suggests, the looming military crisis evoked profound questions about the reliability of God's promises. The exiles' shame at having been abandoned by their god is public, as neighboring nations are said to rejoice in the kingdom's downfall: "These are the people of the Lord, and yet they had to go out of his land" (36:20; see 25:3, 8; 26:2; 36:2, 4). Multiple complaints voiced in the book place the blame for disaster squarely on the God of Israel: "The Lord does not see us; the Lord has forsaken the land" (8:12); "The way of the Lord is unfair" (18:25; 33:17); "Our bones are dried up and our hope is lost; we are cut off completely" (37:11). Other traces of complaint in the ritual scenes of chap. 8, the allegory of the abandoned child Jerusalem (chap. 16), and the divine refusal to accept the inquiries of the exiles (14:3; 20:2-3), suggest that the entire book is written to explain the apparent absence of God (39:28-29). From the splendid vision of chap. 1 to the final declaration of the new name for the new city (**YHWH shammah** [יְהוָה שָׁמָּה] "the Lord is there," 48:35) the book declares that the God of Israel has by no means abandoned his people but has, rather, remained ever present.

Yet Ezekiel does not simply reassure the exiles that their national deity has taken up residence along with them in exile—indeed, such a claim would have little power to console, since the peoples of that time were well acquainted with the notion of gods being forced into exile. Rather, Ezekiel declares that the God of Israel is not merely present but omnipotent, who sends mighty empires into oblivion and is the sovereign lord even of Nebuchadnezzar (29:17-20). This display of power is not intended simply to impress; rather, it is motivated by God's intention to honor the ancient promise to settle Jacob's descendants in the land (37:25). The notion of divine omnipotence is thus inextricably bound up with notions of Yahweh's fidelity and integrity.

Occasionally biblical interpreters define the theological innovation of the exilic period as a breakthrough to monotheism, the conviction not only that the God of Israel is the only God for Israel, but that he is the only God; occasionally, credit goes to Ezekiel's younger contemporary, the anonymous poet of Isa 40–55, for this insight. While it can be argued that Ezekiel anticipated this development, it is more likely that Ezekiel continued to acknowledge the existence of other gods. In chap. 21, for example, Nebuchadnezzar consults multiple oracles, as if to seek concord among the respective national deities of Judah and Ammon before embarking on his campaign (21.18-23 [Heb. 21:23-28]). Even so, Ezekiel's theology is a kind of practical monotheism, since in his view there may be other gods but no other gods that matter. Ezekiel's majestic vision in chap. 1, in which the deity is enthroned upon and supported by four living beings that symbolize the totality of the created order, presents the God of Israel not simply as a mobile deity but as the God of the universe. In this connection it is worth noting that Ezekiel's favorite terms for Israel's idols, gillulim (גִּלּוּלִים, "dung balls") and shiqqutsim (שִׁקּוּצִים, "worthless things"), deny any reality to the divine beings they are intended to represent. Whether the Judean worshipers venerated these images as representations of deities or not, these pejorative epithets indicate that Ezekiel regarded them as utterly worthless in mediating divine power (*see* IDOL; IDOLATRY).

Ezekiel's understanding of divine omnipotence is as much a will to relationship as it is a will to power. Throughout the book, the covenant formulary "I will be their God, and they will be my people" exists as an as-yet unrealized promise (11:20; 34:31; 36:28; 37:23). Yet Ezekiel is at pains to point out that God's failure to make good on this covenant is not for lack of divine intention or ability. Despite Israel's repeated rebellions, which have continually jeopardized the divine oath, God intends to establish the bonds of the covenant (*see* COVENANT, OT AND NT). The final chapters suggest that the goal of the entire process of judgment is to fulfill the promise made to "my servant Jacob" (37:25). The people will be brought back into the bond of the covenant, cleansed and given new hearts so that they may obey God's statutes, all so that God can fulfill this ancient promise.

On the question of divine ELECTION, the Babylonian deportation generated deep conflicts between the exiles and those who remained in Judah. What was the status of the exiles? Did their deportation signify a divinely sanctioned expulsion? The question of election runs sharply through Ezekiel, as it does through the book of Jeremiah and the later narratives of the return (Ezra, Nehemiah). Jeremiah raises the question in terms of moral distinctions between good and bad figs; Ezekiel expresses a more painful rupture of bonds of kinship, a rupture that reflects the exiles' sense of having been betrayed by the Jerusalemites simply for the sake of financial advantage (11:14-21).

One of the difficult questions to untangle is whether Ezekiel sides with one group over another in this dispute. On the one hand, Ezekiel quite literally presents the God of Israel abandoning Jerusalem to become a "small sanctuary" for the exiles (miqdash meʿat [מִקְדָּשׁ מְעַט]; 11:16); moreover, he condemns the Jerusalemites for their complacent self-identification with Abraham (33:23-24). These texts, along with others that speak of exclusion (13:9) or utterly purging rebels from the community (20:38), establish clear distinctions between not only the exiles and the Jerusalemites but also between the purged exiles and everyone else. Other texts, however, speak of the divine intention that all should live (18:32) and that none be left behind (39:28). Moreover, Ezekiel's proclamations of restoration often revolve around symbols of unity: the exiles and Jerusalemites will have "one" heart (11:19; see "new" heart, 36:26); the two nations will be brought together into one nation (37:15-23); and the twelve tribes will share equally in the inheritance (47:13-14).

In light of Ezekiel's emphasis on corporate regeneration, it is worth noting that older interpretations of Ezek 18 as a breakthrough to supposedly more advanced conceptions of individual responsibility are no longer compelling. The question of moral regeneration does, however, remain a perennial question in Ezekiel studies. Acknowledging that human regeneration is made possible by divine grace alone (see, e.g., 36:26-27; 37:9-10, 14; 39:29), some commentators also suggest that the book's frequent references to shame point to the inner dynamics of moral transformation.

In addition to being concerned with matters of the heart, Ezekiel is also interested in the transformation of behaviors affecting the community. Ezekiel's vision of the Temple abominations culminates with a disclosure of ethical abuses—as if cultic abomination and communal betrayal went hand in hand. Moreover, Ezekiel's criteria for righteousness are as concerned with economic and social justice as they are with proper forms of worship (18:5-9; 22:7-12); even the preoccupation with sexual morality may indicate a concern to honor sacred familial bonds (18:6; 22:10-11). Ezekiel pursues this interest in social justice into the restoration: as Good Shepherd, God rescues the flock from caretakers who feed off the flock (34), and provisions for restoration to the land of Israel dwell at length on the just division of economic resources (45:9-12; 47:14).

The influence of Ezekiel in subsequent Jewish and Christian tradition is somewhat ambivalent. Outside of his book, Ezekiel is not mentioned elsewhere in the OT, and no NT writing quotes the book, though the Gospel of John and Revelation do allude to it. Whereas modern readers tend to find the book's oracles of judgment repellent, ancient Jewish and Christian interpretations tended to draw in rich and creative ways on the book's transcendent visions of divine and human reconciliation.

The earliest known quotations of Ezekiel in the Jewish tradition are in DEAD SEA SCROLLS fragments designated the SONGS OF THE SABBATH SACRIFICE. Although these texts are so fragmentary as to be virtually unintelligible, they suggest that Ezekiel's vision of the new temple provided the basic framework for imagining a heavenly, angelic liturgy. Other documents from the Dead Sea suggest that Ezekiel had a profound impact on the community's self-understanding.

Although Ezekiel cannot itself be said to be an example of apocalyptic literature, it has had a significant impact on the development of apocalyptic imagery. Whereas Ezekiel only intimates that the kingdom of God supplants human pretensions to rule the world (as in the case of Gog and possibly also Egypt; see 31–32), both Daniel and Revelation envision a decisive break between human history and divine rule. One may therefore suggest that both Daniel and Revelation make explicit Ezekiel's view of history. Moreover, despite the absence of any direct quotations of Ezekiel, Revelation is in many respects an apocalyptic retelling of Ezekiel, complete with the reappearance of angelic executioners, the "woman" Israel, Gog, and the transformed city of God. See APOCALYPTICISM.

Less well known is Ezekiel's influence on developments in early Christology. Appropriating the imagery of God as the good SHEPHERD who rescues the flock from wicked shepherds who serve their own interests (Ezek 34), John 10 applies this imagery to Jesus. A more intriguing but less well-known iconographic tradition draws on the vision of chap. 1 and equates Christ with the four living creatures that accompany the throne of God. This tradition of identifying Christ with the living creatures survives in the practice of employing the four faces of Ezekiel's living creatures as emblems of each of the four gospels. In its earliest form, this tradition emphasized the fourfold unity of the gospels, which served to reveal Christ in the world (Irenaeus, *Haer.* 3.11.8). The iconographic representation of Christ as one of the living beings suggested that Christ's status, albeit an exalted one, was understood to be more angelic than divine (*see* CHRISTOLOGY). By contrast, a post-Nicene appropriation of the iconography of Ezek 1 suggests a much closer identification of Christ with God. In the Rabula Gospel (6th cent. CE), Christ is no longer portrayed as one of the living creatures but takes the place of the enthroned deity as the "appearance of the likeness of the Glory of God" (1:28). Ezekiel's unusual phrase thus came to be understood as a reference to the person of the Trinity who reveals God to humankind.

Ezekiel's influence can also be gauged in the appropriation of motifs that have subsequently become important elements of the Christian tradition. It remains an open question whether early Christians drew on Ezek. 37 as a symbol of resurrection. The evidence is thin, and it has been suggested that the chapter was understood more literally to refer to the national revival of Israel. On the other hand, the chapter holds an important place in Easter liturgies. In African-American folk traditions, Ezekiel's vision of the VALLEY OF DRY BONES is also an important symbol of liberation. Other uses of Ezekiel have been less happy. Bernard of Clairvaux (12th cent. CE) used Ezekiel's vision of the abominations in Jerusalem (and, ironically, the offer of repentance and life in chap. 18), to urge Europeans to join the crusades to rescue Jerusalem from the so-called "infidel."

Bibliography: Leslie C. Allen. *Ezekiel 1–19.* WBC 28 (1994); Leslie C. Allen. *Ezekiel 20–48.* WBC 29 (1990); Joseph Blenkinsopp. *Ezekiel.* Interpretation (1990); Daniel I. Block. *The Book of Ezekiel, Chapters 1–24.* NICOT (1997); Daniel I. Block. *The Book of Ezekiel, Chapters 25–48.* NICOT (1998); Lawrence Boadt. *Ezekiel's Oracles against Egypt: A Literary and Philological Study of Ezekiel 29–32* (1980); Daniel Bodi. *The Book of Ezekiel and the Poem of Erra* (1991); Keith W. Carley. *Ezekiel Among the Prophets: A Study of Ezekiel's Place in the Prophetic Tradition* (1974); Stephen L. Cook and Corrine L. Patton, eds. *Ezekiel's Hierarchical World: Wrestling with a Tiered Reality* (2004); Katheryn Pfisterer Darr. *The Book of Ezekiel.* NIB 6 (2001) 1072-1607; Ellen F. Davis. *Swallowing the Scroll: Textuality and the Dynamics of Discourse in Ezekiel's Prophecy* (1989); Iain M. Duguid. *Ezekiel and the Leaders of Israel* (1994); Walther Eichrodt. *Ezekiel: A Commentary.* OTL (1970); Kelvin J. Friebel. *Jeremiah's and Ezekiel's Sign-Acts: Rhetorical Nonverbal Communication* (1999); Julie Galambush. *Jerusalem in the Book of Ezekiel: The City as Yahweh's Wife* (1992); Moshe Greenberg. *Ezekiel 1–20.* AB 22 (1983); Moshe Greenberg. *Ezekiel 21-37.* AB 22A (1997); Ronald F. Hals. *Ezekiel.* FOTL 19 (1989); Paul Joyce. *Divine Initiative and Human Response in Ezekiel* (1989); S. Tamar Kamionkowski. *Gender Reversal and Cosmic Chaos: A Study on the Book of Ezekiel* (2003); Ralph Klein. *Ezekiel: The Prophet and His Message* (1988); Risa Levitt Kohn. *A New Heart and a New Soul: Ezekiel, the Exile and the Torah* (2002); John F. Kutsko. *Between Heaven and Earth: Divine Presence and Absence in the Book of Ezekiel* (2000); Jacqueline E. Lapsley. *Can These Bones Live? The Problem of the Moral Self in the Book of Ezekiel* (2000); Jon D. Levenson. *Theology of the Program of Restoration of Ezekiel 40–48* (1976); Johan Lust, D. Baltzer et al., eds. *Ezekiel and His Book: Textual and Literary Criticism and their Interrelation* (1986); Henry McKeating. *Ezekiel.* Old Testament Guides (1993); Gary T. Manning, Jr. *Echoes of a Prophet: The Use of Ezekiel in the Gospel of John and in Literature of the Second Temple Period* (2004); Gordon Matties. *Ezekiel 18 and the Rhetoric of Moral Discourse* (1990); Margaret S. Odell. *Ezekiel.* Smyth and Helwys Bible Commentaries 16 (2005); Margaret S. Odell and John T. Strong, eds. *The Book of Ezekiel: Theological and Anthropological Perspectives* (2000); Thomas Renz. *The Rhetorical Function of the Book of Ezekiel* (1999); Kalinda Rose Stevenson. *The Vision of Transformation: The Territorial Rhetoric of Ezekiel 40–48* (1996); Steven Shawn Tuell. *The Law of the Temple in Ezekiel 40–48* (1992); Walther Zimmerli. *A Commentary on the Book of the Prophet Ezekiel, Chapters 1–24.* Hermeneia (1979); Walther Zimmerli. *A Commentary on the Book of the Prophet Ezekiel, Chapters 25–48.* Hermeneia (1983); Walther Zimmerli. *I Am Yahweh* (1982).

MARGARET S. ODELL

EZEKIEL THE TRAGEDIAN i-zee´kee-uhl. A Hellenistic Jewish poet, likely in the 2nd cent. BCE, who wrote a tragedy, *Exagōgē* (Ἐξαγωγή) based on the Exodus. Ezekiel may have written other plays, but only fragments of this work remain, primarily from EUSEBIUS (quoting ALEXANDER POLYHISTOR), and fragments in CLEMENT OF ALEXANDRIA. The reconstructed play is incomplete and focuses upon Moses recounting the events of the book of Exodus and nonbiblical material, such as a dream in which God tells Moses to sit on God's throne on Mt. Sinai.

Bibliography: Carl R. Holladay. *Fragments from Hellenistic Jewish Authors Volume 2: Poets* (1988); Howard Jacobson. *The Exagoge of Ezekiel* (1983).

KENNETH D. LITWAK

EZEM ee´zuhm [עֶצֶם *'etsem*]. A town in the territorial allotment to Simeon in Josh 19:3. First Chronicles 4:29 also lists it as a Simeonite town. Simeonite territory lay entirely within the territory of Judah, and Josh 15:29 lists Ezem among Judahite towns. Its precise geographical location is unknown.

DEREK E. WITTMAN

EZER ee´zuhr [אֵצֶר *'etser,* עֵזֶר *'ezer*]. Six men carry the name Ezer. 1. Sixth son of Seir and a Horite chief whose name may represent a clan who lived in Edom (Gen 36:21, 27, 30; 1 Chr 1:38-42).

2. Etam's son who founded the town Hushbah (1 Chr 4:4).

3. Ephraim's son whom the Gittites killed when he attempted to steal their cattle (1 Chr 7:21).

4. A Gadite chief who joined David's warriors at Ziglag (1 Chr 12:9).

5. Son of Jeshua, the ruler of Mizpah, and a repairman of a section of the Jerusalem wall (Neh 3:19).

6. A priest who celebrated the dedication of the rebuilt Jerusalem wall (Neh 12:42).

EMILY R. CHENEY

EZION-GEBER ee´zee-uhn-gee´buhr [עֶצְיוֹן גֶּבֶר ‘etsyon gever]. Ezion-geber is cited seven times in the Bible (Num 33:35, 36; Deut 2:8; 1 Kgs 9:26; 22:48 [Heb. 22:49]; 2 Chr 8:17; 20:36) and is believed to have been a port city located on the north shore of the present-day Gulf of Aqaba (see AQABA, GULF OF). According to Numbers and Deuteronomy, Ezion-geber was a place of encampment for the Israelites while on their journey from EGYPT to Canaan (see EXODUS, ROUTE OF). Kings and Chronicles also name Ezion-geber as a strategically important city for trade and commerce and report that Solomon constructed a fleet of ships at Ezion-geber and, by way of the seaport, imported luxury goods from Ophir (1 Kgs 9:26-28; 2 Chr 8:17-18). The biblical writers state that Jehoshaphat attempted to initiate a similar system of trade through Ezion-geber in partnership with Ahaziah, but the ships were destroyed at the port, and Jehoshaphat discontinued his commercial activity there (1 Kgs 22:47-49; 2 Chr 20:35-37). After the reign of Jehoshaphat Ezion-geber receives no further mention.

The modern location of Ezion-geber continues to be debated by scholars. In 1933 F. Frank discovered Tell el-Kheleifeh 556 m inland from the Gulf of Aqaba and suggested that this site was biblical Ezion-geber (KHELEIFEH, TELL EL). N. Glueck excavated Tell el-Kheleifeh over three seasons (1938–40) and confirmed Frank's earlier hypothesis. Glueck contended that the city was founded in the 10th cent. BCE by Solomon, was subsequently destroyed twice, and then rebuilt by Uzziah and renamed as Elath in the early 8th cent. BCE. The five destruction layers of Tell el-Kheleifeh therefore served as the location of both Ezion-geber (I and II) and Elath (III–V). This highly influential view, however, soon proved insufficient. Although Tell el-Kheleifeh may have participated in maritime industries, the coast near the site could not support a port or shipyard and no material evidence pertaining to either was ever recovered near the tell. Moreover, biblical references always named Ezion-geber and Elath as two separate cities. In light of this evidence, B. Rothenberg asserted that the offshore island Jezirat Fara'un (Island of Pharaoh) situated 7 mi. southwest of Tell el-Kheleifeh be identified with Ezion-geber. Recent underwater excavations by A. Flinder have

identified at this site the only natural anchorage for ships in the region, an artificially enclosed harbor, and the remains of Iron Age I pottery.

Regardless of its precise location, a port at the head of the Gulf of Aqaba would have been a valuable asset for any of the political powers of the region. Such a location would have been the focal point of trade and commerce, including that of luxury goods, from those shipping vessels sailing from the south and east. If the ancient Israelites had the capacity to build or secure a port in this region, then it would have also controlled the shortest trade routes between the Mediterranean Sea and the Indian Ocean. For this reason one can understand the struggle witnessed in the Bible between Israel and its neighbors, particularly Egypt, for control of the area. See ELATH, ELOTH.

Bibliography: Alexander Flinder. "Is This Solomon's Seaport?" *BAR* 15 (1989) 30–43.

DANIEL D. PIOSKE

EZORA i-zor´uh [Ἐζωρά Ezōra]. The leader of a family that heeds Ezra's call to banish non-Israelite wives and children (1 Esd 9:34; absent in the parallel version, Ezra 10:39-40).

EZRA ez´ruh [עֶזְרָא ‘ezra’]. The story of Ezra is told in a first-person account (Ezra 7:27–8:34; 9:1-15) and a third-person account (Ezra 7:1-11; 8:35-36; 10:1-44; Neh 7:73*b*–8:18 [possibly also 9:1-5; the reference to Ezra in Neh 9:6 NRSV is incorrect and not supported in the Heb. text]), although it is unclear whether the change in person represents use of an independent source or the decision of the narrator. Ezra is called a priest and a scribe of the law of the God of heaven (Ezra 7:12). Despite the genealogy connecting him to the high priestly line in Ezra 7:1-5, he was not a high priest. As a SCRIBE he was no doubt an expert in the law, but some have seen in this title an indication that he was a commissioner for Jewish affairs in the Persian government.

Ezra came to Jerusalem at the direction of the Persian king Artaxerxes and in his seventh year (458 BCE if this was Artaxerxes I; 398 BCE if it was Artaxerxes II). The order of the canonical text favors Artaxerxes I; the later date is favored by some who point to the mention of a wall in Ezra 9:9, the reference to Jehohanan the son of Eliashib in Ezra 10:6, and the involvement of Nehemiah with the mixed marriage question that does not seem to presuppose Ezra's actions. An Aram. document whose authenticity is contested (Ezra 7:12-26) gave him four assignments: to return to Jerusalem with a number of Israelites, to determine whether the community in Judah and Jerusalem was in conformity with the law, to take a series of contributions to Jerusalem and spend them on sacrificial offerings, and to appoint judges in the province of Beyond the River who were to regulate Jewish life outside of Jerusalem in an appropriate manner. Ezra's mission has been compared to that of Udjahorresnet, whom Darius I sent to Egypt to establish a temple cult and reorganize the legal system.

Ezra's journey from Babylon to Jerusalem began on the first day of the first month, and his entourage arrived on the first day of the fifth month. Many scholars believe that the account of Ezra's reading the law, now located at Neh 8:73*b*–8:18, should be placed between Ezra 8 and 9 because it took place in the seventh month. The incident with the mixed marriages was the occasion for an assembly in the ninth month (Ezra 10:9), and the divorce commission finished its work on the first day of the first month (Ezra 10:17). This ordering of the materials means that Ezra completed his work within a year. Otherwise he would have delayed reading the law, surely his most important assignment, for thirteen years. This also suggests that the terms of Ezra and Nehemiah did not overlap, and that the notices that Ezra participated in the dedication of the walls repaired by Nehemiah are secondary (Neh 12:26, 36; the Ezra mentioned in Neh 12:1, 13, and 33 is a different individual).

Ezra's most important action was his reading of the law in Neh 8. This law was probably a nearly final edition of the Pentateuch (scholars have detected allusions to Deuteronomy, the Holiness Code, and the priestly code), and the reaction to this reading of the law and the influence of the law on the decisions on mixed marriages are indications of its canonical authority. Some scholars have seen in the degree of Artaxerxes Persian authorization of the Pentateuch. Ezra's presiding over the forced divorces of 110 or 111 men who had married women from "the peoples of the land" is his most controversial action. These women are probably not true foreigners, but rather people who were not considered to be full members of the community, perhaps because they had not been in exile or had not been fully accepted into the Golah community for other reasons. The decision to divorce these women is based on a halachic midrash of Lev 18:3; 19:19; Deut 7:1, 3; 23:3. A much more open attitude toward mixed marriages is found in Ruth and in the books of Chronicles.

Historical and chronological issues, including the historicity of Ezra, continue to be debated. Some have argued that Ezra is a fictional character, others that there is solid historical evidence for his existence. Still others advocate a mediating position, which recognizes a "historical Ezra" whose portrayal has been ideologically and theologically embellished. *See* EZRA AND NEHEMIAH, BOOKS OF.

Bibliography: Joseph Blenkinsopp. "The Mission of Udjahorresnet and Those of Ezra and Nehemiah." *JBL* 106 (1987) 409–21; Tamara C. Eskenazi. "Cur-

rent Perspectives on Ezra-Nehemiah and the Persian Period." *CurBS* 1 (1993) 59–86; Lester L. Grabbe. *Judaism from Cyrus to Hadrian: The Persian and Greek Periods* (1992); James W. Watts, ed. *Persia and Torah: The Theory of Imperial Authorization of the Pentateuch* (2001).

RALPH W. KLEIN

EZRA, APOCALYPSE OF. *See* ESDRAS, SECOND BOOK OF.

EZRA, FIFTH. *See* ESDRAS, SECOND BOOK OF.

EZRA, FOURTH. *See* ESDRAS, SECOND BOOK OF.

EZRA, GREEK APOCALYPSE OF. *See* ESDRAS, SECOND BOOK OF.

EZRA, QUESTIONS OF. *See* ESDRAS, SECOND BOOK OF.

EZRA, REVELATION OF. *See* ESDRAS, SECOND BOOK OF.

EZRA, SIXTH. *See* ESDRAS, SECOND BOOK OF.

EZRA, VISION OF. *See* ESDRAS, SECOND BOOK OF.

EZRA AND NEHEMIAH, BOOKS OF ez´ruh, nee´huh-mi´uh [עֶזְרָא נְחֶמְיָה ʿezraʾ nikhemyah]. Ezra and Nehemiah were originally considered one book, under the name of Ezra. In the Greek tradition they were considered two books as early as the 3rd cent. CE, by Origen, and the Latin Vulgate followed this tradition in the 4th cent. The division into two books does not appear in Hebrew manuscripts until the 15th cent. CE, and even today the *masora finalis* in the Masoretic Text appears only at the end of Nehemiah. The name Ezra or Esdras is also applied to a number of other works: 1 Esdras (also known as Esdras α in the LXX, 2 Esdras in the Slavonic version, and 3 Ezra in the Vulgate). This is a Greek translation of 2 Chr 35–36, Ezra 1–10, and Neh 8:1-13, plus an apocryphal story about three pages, one of whom is Zerubbabel.

Second Esdras (also known as 3 Esdras in the Slavonic version and 4 Esdras in the Vulgate), is an apocalyptic work from the end of the 1st cent. CE. The introductory and concluding chapters of 2 Esdras are Christian works: 5 Ezra (2 Esdras 1–2); 6 Ezra (2 Esdras 15–16). The translation of Ezra and Nehemiah in the Septuagint is called Esdras β and Esdras γ.

A. Division of the Book
B. Detailed Analysis
 1. Introductory issues in Ezra–Nehemiah
 2. Date of the persons Ezra and Nehemiah
 3. The relationship of Neh 8 and Ezra 7–10

4. Ezra 1–6: return from exile and rebuilding of the Temple

5. Ezra 7–10: the initial work of Ezra

6. Neh 1:1–7:73a: return of Nehemiah and rebuilding of the wall

7. Neh 7:73b–10:39: a firm agreement to keep the Torah

8. Neh 11–13: the climax of Nehemiah's work and related matters

C. Theological Issues

Bibliography

A. Division of the Books

1. Ezra 1:1–6:22, return from exile and rebuilding of the temple

   a. 1:1-11, imperial permission to go home

   b. 2:1-70, the list of those who returned

   c. 3:1-13, erection of altar and foundation of the temple

   d. 4:1-24, opposition to the Jewish community

   e. 5:1-17, a challenge to the temple rebuilding

   f. 6:1-22, the Temple is authorized and completed

2. Ezra 7:1–10:44, the initial work of Ezra

   a. 7:1-10, Ezra comes to Jerusalem

   b. 7:11-28, the Persian authorization of Ezra

   c. 8:1-36, Ezra's trip to Jerusalem

   d. 9:1-15, Ezra faces a community challenge

   e. 10:1-44, the great divorce proceedings

3. Nehemiah 1:1–7:73a, return of Nehemiah and rebuilding of wall of Jerusalem

   a. 1:1-11, Nehemiah prays for help
     2:1-20, the beginning of Nehemiah's efforts in Jerusalem

   b. 3:1-32, workers on the Jerusalem wall

   c. 4:1-23, Nehemiah's provisions for the defense of Jerusalem

   d. 5:1-19, internal threats to the community

   e. 6:1-10, the wall is completed despite attempts to intimidate Nehemiah

   f. 7:1-73a, next steps after the completion of the wall

4. Nehemiah 7:73b–10:39, Torah, confession, and firm agreement

   a. 7:73b–8:18, Ezra reads the Torah to the people

   b. 9:1-37, a great day of repentance

   c. 9:38–10:30, a firm agreement to keep the Torah

5. Nehemiah 11:1–13:31, the climax of Nehemiah's work and related matters

   a. 11:1-36, the new settlers in Jerusalem

   b. 12:1-26, lists of Priests, Levites, and High Priests

   c. 12:27-43, the dedication of the city wall

   d. 12:44–13:3, the people solidify the reform measures

   e. 13:4-31, Nehemiah's corrective measures

B. Detailed Analysis

1. Introductory Issues in Ezra–Nehemiah

Since the early part of the 19th cent., Ezra and Nehemiah have often been considered to be part of the Chronicler's history (1 and 2 Chronicles; Ezra and Nehemiah). This was based on the overlap between 2 Chr 36:22-23 and Ezra 1:1-3a, the arrangement of the text behind 1 Esdras (where 2 Chr 35–36 is followed by the story of Ezra, and Neh 8 follows Ezra 10), the vocabulary and style of these works, and their theology or ideology. The first two of these factors can be explained in other ways, and a lengthy debate about the vocabulary and style has proved to be inconclusive. Differences in theology—the doctrine of retribution is more evident in Chronicles than in Ezra–Nehemiah, kings are prominent in Chronicles, but not in Ezra, there is a different concept of prophets and prophecy in the two works—suggests that Ezra and Nehemiah should be considered as a work distinct from Chronicles.

As with the book of Daniel, parts of Ezra are written in Aramaic (4:8-6:18; 7:12-26) and the rest in Hebrew. The reason for this probably results from the author including a number of Aramaic source documents in the account: 4:8-16, a letter from Rehum to Artaxerxes; 4:17-22, the reply of Artaxerxes to this letter; 5:6-17, a letter from Tattenai the governor of the province Beyond the River to Darius, of which 5:13-15 is a paraphrase of the decree of Cyrus; 6:3-17, the reply of Darius, of which 6:3-5 is the citation of the decree of Cyrus; 7:12-26, the decree of Artaxerxes, authorizing the return of Ezra. The parts of Ezra 4:8–6:18 not attributable to source documents are probably written by the author of Ezra 1–6. It is not necessary to reconstruct a pre-canonical Aramaic Chronicle in 4:8–6:18 that has been included in its entirety in the book of Ezra.

Hebrew sources used by the author of Ezra include: 1:9-11, an inventory of the Temple vessels (compare 5:14-15; 6:5); 2:1-3:1, the list of those who returned from Babylon (//Neh 7:7-6–8:1); 4:6-7, summaries of letters from the adversaries of the Jews in the time of Xerxes and Artaxerxes; 8:1-4, the list of those who returned to Jerusalem with Ezra (10:8-43).

2. Date of the persons Ezra and Nehemiah

The date for Nehemiah's coming to Jerusalem is fixed at 445 BCE, the 20th year of ARTAXERXES I (Neh 1:1; 2:1; 5:14). Nehemiah's first term as governor lasted for twelve years (Neh 5:14). After a trip to see the Persian king, of an unspecified duration, Nehemiah returned to Jerusalem for a second term (Neh 13:6-7), again for an unspecified length of time. Far more controversial is the date for EZRA (the seventh year of Artaxerxes; Ezra 7:7-8), since it is unclear whether Artaxerxes I or Artaxerxes II is meant. In the former case, Ezra came in 458 BCE, thirteen years before Nehemiah; in the latter case, he came in 398 BCE. Although the MT portrays Ezra and Nehemiah as contemporaries in Neh 8:9 (the reading of the law), 12:26 (the days of the governor Nehemiah and of the priest Ezra, the scribe), and 12:36 (Ezra participated in the dedication of Nehemiah's walls), all of these joint appearances are suspect, and Nehemiah acts by himself in Neh 1–7 and 13. In Neh 8:9 the name Nehemiah does not appear in the corresponding place in 1 Esd 9:49, and the word governor does not appear in Ezra LXX, suggesting that the reference to Nehemiah the governor is a conflation of two different glosses. The arrangement of the canonical books suggests that Ezra came first, in 458 BCE. (For the date of his reading of the law, see below.) This traditional date might suggest that Ezra failed, at least in some matters, since Nehemiah repeats his efforts to remedy the situation dealing with mixed marriages. The high priest at the time of Nehemiah was Eliashib (Neh 3:1, 20; 12:10, 22-23; 13:4, 7, 28), but in Ezra 10:6 Ezra went to the chamber of Jehohanan the son of Eliashib. This would put Ezra later than Nehemiah and since a Johanan is mentioned as a high priest in the Elephantine papyri in 407 BCE (AP 30.18), a date during the reign of Artaxerxes II would be required. It is not clear, however, that either Eliashib or Jehohanan in Ezra 10:6 was a high priest. In addition, Johanan is the grandson, rather than the son, of Eliashib in Neh 12:22 (but see 12:10-11). A reference to a wall in Ezra 9:9 is not a reference to the wall Nehemiah rebuilt, but the word wall here is a metaphorical reference to the protection supplied by the Persians. While the evidence is not conclusive, the rest of this article assumes that Ezra preceded Nehemiah. The books of Ezra and Nehemiah were substantially complete by the end of the 5th cent. BCE.

3. The relationship of Neh 8 and Ezra 7–10

If Ezra's main assignment is fulfilled by his reading of the law in Neh 8, it seems strange that he would wait thirteen years to do this since the context in Nehemiah suggests a date no earlier than 445 BCE. There have been various attempts to fit the events of Nehemiah into the chronology of Ezra 7–10 by placing Neh 8 after Ezra 8 (or after Ezra 10), with the result that Ezra's work is completed within one year: month one, day one or twelve: Ezra leaves Babylon (Ezra 7:9; 8:31); month five day one: Ezra arrives in Jerusalem (Ezra 7:9); month seven day one, Ezra reads the law; month nine day twenty, assembly called to address question of mixed marriages (Ezra 10:9); month ten day one to month one day one of the next year, commission deals with those who have married foreign wives (Ezra 10:16-17). While this rearrangement of the material eases the historical or chronological problem,

it is also clear that Neh 8–10 has been designed as a literary unity, and these chapters need to be understood theologically as part of that unit (see the discussion of them below).

4. Ezra 1–6: return from exile and rebuilding of the Temple

Ezra 1 begins by recording a decree of CYRUS that reports that Yahweh had instructed Cyrus to build the temple and that Cyrus was authorizing the Jews to return to Jerusalem, aided by financial support of their neighbors in the Persian Empire (1:2-4, in Hebrew; compare 6:3-5. See also the Cyrus Cylinder, ANET 315-316; COS 2.124). The gifts of the neighbors resemble the contributions of the Egyptians to the Israelites at the Exodus (Exod 11:2-3; 12:35-36). Cyrus sent along with Sheshbazzar, the leader of the returnees, the Temple vessels taken by Nebuchadnezzar. The list of returnees in Ezra 2 takes the place of the account of the return and indicates the whole-hearted response to the invitation to return home. Originally it may have recorded the results of a series of returns in the 6th or 5th cent. may reflect a census of the community in the 5th cent. It lists laity (vv. 3-20, a list of people by family names, and vv. 21-35, a list of people by city names), priests (vv. 36-39), Levites (vv. 40-42), temple servants (vv. 43-54), and servants of Solomon (vv. 55-57). In Ezra 3, Jeshua and Zerubbabel are the leaders of the community, with no mention of the fate of Sheshbazzar, and they mark the erection of an altar by celebrating the Feast of Booths (compare Neh 18:13-18). According to Hag 1:1, 14, Zerubbabel was the governor of Judah and a descendant of David, but neither of these factors is mentioned in Ezra. Jeshua and Zerubbabel also laid the foundation of the Temple, which may represent a foundation deposit ceremony, in which a stone from the old Temple was placed in the new (compare Zech 4:9). According to Ezra 5:16, Sheshbazzar had already laid the footings for the Temple. The text of Ezra 3 gives the impression that these events happened under Cyrus, but it is much more likely that they took place during the reign of Darius.

In Ezra 4 the leaders of the Jewish community refuse the offer of their "adversaries" to help with building the Temple. After a summary of hostile letters that were sent to Persian authorities in 4:6-7, an Aram. letter by Rehum and his authorities is recorded in vv. 11-16, protesting Jewish work on the walls and indicting Jerusalem as a perpetually rebellious city. While the context implies that this is opposition to the Temple, it actually is opposition to the walls and may reflect an incident from the 5th cent. In his reply (vv. 17-23), Artaxerxes orders the Jewish work to stop, and the editor interprets this as stoppage of the work on the temple (v. 24).

The work on the Temple resumes in Ezra 5, thanks to the prodding of Haggai and Zechariah (compare Ezra 6:14). A letter from Tattenai, the governor of the province, and his associates cites at length the Jews' defense of their building project, appealing especially to its authorization by the decree of Cyrus. The letter asks DARIUS whether such a decree had actually been issued. Darius found the decree in Ecbatana, the summer residence of the Persian kings (6:3-5), and ordered Tattenai not to interfere with the work of the Jews, but rather their work is to be supported by royal revenues (6:6-12). This letter presumes that prayers will be offered by the Jews on behalf of the Persian king and his family (v. 10). The Jews finished the work (vv. 13-15), dedicated the Temple (vv. 16-18), and celebrated the Passover (vv. 19-22). With the report of the Passover celebration, the language of Ezra returns to Hebrew from Aramaic.

5. Ezra 7–10: the initial work of Ezra

There is a 57-year gap between the completion and dedication of the Second Temple in Ezra 1–6 and the activities associated with Ezra. The account of the work of Ezra is a combination of first person (7:27–8:34; 9:1-15, an Ezra Memoir) and third-person narratives (7:1-11; 8:35-36; 10:1-44; compare Neh 7:73–9:18). The genealogy in 7:1-5 shows that Ezra is a descendant of the high priest's family, although there are major gaps in that genealogy. Ezra's trip to Jerusalem is authorized by the Aramaic firman (royal decree) of Artaxerxes (7:12-26), which most scholars hold to be authentic, even though it is conceded that some Jewish coloring may result from Jews who had access to the Persian court or from the redactor who included the firman in his story of Ezra. This document authorizes Israelites—priests, Levites, and laity—to return to Jerusalem with Ezra (v. 13); empowers Ezra to make inquiries in the community about conformity to the law that he is bringing to Jerusalem (v. 14); commissions Ezra to take contributions from the king, his counselors, and the people of the province with him and spend them on sacrificial offerings; and orders Ezra to bring cultic vessels contributed by Artaxerxes to Jerusalem (8:26-27, 33-34; compare 1:7-11; 6:5). The firman excuses the Temple personnel from taxes (v. 24) and commissions Ezra to appoint judges in the province (vv. 25-26). The amount of silver and gold mentioned in this document—estimated by Grabbe as about 25 metric tons—seems unrealistic, and it is hard to believe that the Persian king would have let Ezra carry this much wealth without an appropriate bodyguard (Ezra 8:21-22). Herodotus reports that the satrapy of Ebir-nari produced tribute of 350 talents of silver in a year, and the whole Persian empire yielded 14,560 talents of silver annually, 15 percent of which, according to this account, would go to the Jewish province of Yehud. The mission of Ezra has been compared to that of Udjahorresnet, an Egyptian priest and scribe who was sent back to his home country by the Persians to restore the cult and to reorganize the institutions of scribalism and religious learning.

The author of the book of Ezra understands the book brought by Ezra to be the Pentateuch (7:6, 10). Modern scholars have noted a number of minor differences with Pentateuchal laws in Neh 8–10, and this suggests that the law brought by Ezra was not the final form of the Pentateuch, but it may have consisted either of Deuteronomy, the priestly document in the Pentateuch, or an undefined groups of laws now contained in the Pentateuch. Some even believe that Ezra's law book has been lost. Fried denies the equivalence between the "law of God" and Jewish law.

According to 8:1-14, Ezra's entourage numbered 1,513 men, not counting women and children. When it was discovered that there were no Levites in the group, Ezra sent a delegation to a sanctuary, CASIPHIA, and obtained 38 Levites to go with him to Jerusalem (8:15-20). Ezra arrived safely in Jerusalem and delivered to the priests the gold, silver, and Temple vessels he had brought with him (8:24-36) (see PRIESTS AND LEVITES).

Ezra was told that some members of the community had married "foreign wives," whose abominations were considered like those of the pre-Israelite inhabitants of the land (9:1-4). Gathered around Ezra at this time of crisis is a support group who trembled at the words of the God of Israel (Ezra 9:4; 10:4; compare Isa 66:2, 5). The foreign wives are apparently women from the group of people who did not go into exile or from the residents of Samaria. In a prayer, Ezra confessed the sins of the people during the history of Israel, not least by marrying foreign women (9:5-15). At the suggestion of Shecaniah, Ezra leads the people to make an oath to divorce the foreign wives (10:1-5). All members of the community met in assembly at Jerusalem and appointed a commission to handle the matter. When the commission completed its work in two months, the wives of 27 clergy and 83 laity were divorced, with their children (10:18-44, a list that seems to be dependent on Ezra 2//Neh 7). This represented less than one percent of the population.

6. Neh 1:1–7:73a: return of Nehemiah and rebuilding of the wall

The bulk of the book of Nehemiah is made up of a first person narrative called the Nehemiah Memoir (1:1–7:73a; 12:31-32, 37-40; 13:4-31). Ezra 3 (the list of those who worked on the wall) and 7:6-73a (the list of those who returned home [//Ezra 2:1-70]) were not written by Nehemiah but may have been included in his Memoir. Scholars have sought parallels to Nehemiah's Memoir in ANE royal inscriptions narrating the king's deeds in the first person, in Egyptian tomb and temple inscriptions in which officials report their faithful carrying out of duties, and in the biblical prayers of the falsely accused. None of the parallels is completely satisfactory, and the Memoir also may not be preserved in its original form or extent. The materials in 5:14-19 belong with those in Ezra 13. One of the most characteristic features of the Memoir is the prayer for God to remember Nehemiah (5:10; 13:14, 22, and 31; compare other short invocations in 4:4-5; 6:9, 14; and 13:29). Williamson has proposed that these petitions may have been added in a second edition, with the first edition being a report to the Persian king. In the present form of the narrative, however, Nehemiah does not address the Persian king at all.

Nehemiah, a Jewish official of Artaxerxes, located in Susa, the Persian king's winter residence, was informed by his brother Hanani of the bad conditions in Jerusalem, including its destroyed walls and gates. This seems to refer to recent events (compare Ezra 4:23), and not to the destruction inflicted by the Babylonians in the early 6th century. In a prayer, Nehemiah confessed the sins of the people and asked for divine support (chap. 1). Later, Nehemiah obtained permission from Artaxerxes to rebuild Jerusalem, with lumber supplied by provincial authorities (2:1-10). Upon his arrival in Jerusalem, Nehemiah inspected the walls by night and secured the agreement of Jewish officials to participate in the project. SANBALLAT; TOBIAH, and GESHEM mocked the Jews and accused them of rebelling against the king (2:11-20), and their opposition continues throughout the book. Nehemiah 3, which does not mention Nehemiah, describes the various groups and individuals who worked on different sections of Jerusalem's fortifications. Much can be learned about the geography and administration of post-exilic Judah from this chapter. The plots of Sanballat and Tobiah were frustrated by the strategies of Neh 4.

Economic hardship resulted from drought, work on the wall, and the king's tax, which led to large indebtedness and debt slavery. Nehemiah demanded the restoration of property to its original owners and the end of charging interest for loans (5:1-13). Nehemiah refers to himself as governor of Judah and mentions his predecessors in this office (Neh 5:14, 15), some of whose names have turned up in inscriptions (e.g., Elnathan, Yehoezer, and Azai. Sheshbazzar is called governor in Ezra 5:14 and ZERUBBABEL is called governor in Hag 1:1, 14; compare Ezra 6:7). Nehemiah claims he did not accept the food allowance of the governor and was a generous host to guests at his table (5:14-19). This paragraph was written after Nehemiah's first term as governor and so should be associated with the materials in Neh 13.

Sanballat accused the Jews of rebelling and Nehemiah himself of wanting to be king. Nehemiah rejected this charge and also the invitation of the prophet Shemaiah to meet with him in the temple. Shemaiah had been hired for this task by Sanballat and Tobiah. Nehemiah uttered an imprecation against them and against the prophetess Noadiah (6:1-14). The wall was completed in only 52 days (Neh 6:15), but the

wrangling with Tobiah continued (6:15-19). When the construction of the walls was complete, Nehemiah appointed his brother Hanani and a certain Hananiah to administrative responsibilities in Jerusalem, but he also noted the city's sparse population. The list of returnees in 7:6-72a may once have served as a transition to Nehemiah's own account of the transfer of people to Jerusalem. It attested to the purity of descent for those moving to Jerusalem, and demonstrated that those who transferred to Jerusalem were dedicated to the Law. Nehemiah's account of the transfer has been lost and is replaced by the account of a lot-casting ceremony in 11:1-2. In its present location, the list of returnees suggests that the whole community was present for Ezra's reading of the law in Neh 8.

7. Neh 7:73b–10:39: a firm agreement to keep the Torah

Nehemiah 8 reports Ezra's reading of the TORAH (Law) to the people. This event may have been the climax of his mission and belongs historically between Ezra 8 and Ezra 9. In 1 Esdras, it follows Ezra 10. An earlier form of Neh 9:1-5 may also once have been placed between Ezra 10:15 and 10:16. In the present context, however, Neh 8 shows that the people who would transfer their residence to Jerusalem had dedicated themselves completely to the Law. Nehemiah 9 may have been written in part to modify Neh 8. While true Israel in Neh 8 included primarily only those who had returned home from the exile, true Israel to the writer of Neh 9 consisted of all those who had agreed to separate themselves from non-Israelites and who confessed their sins and showed true repentance. The sequence of reading the Law (chap. 8), confession of sin (chap. 9), and the Firm Agreement (chap. 10) displays an ideal response to the Law. Ezra read the Law to the assembly on the first day of the seventh month, known elsewhere in the OT as a convocation commemorated with trumpet blasts (Lev 23:23-25), and later as New Year's day. The Levites helped people understand what was read to them. On the second day of the assembly, they discovered in the Law the requirement that people should live in booths during the festival of the seventh month. The people carried out this requirement, which had not been so observed since the days of Jeshua (=Joshua; compare 2 Chr 30:26, there had been no Passover like Hezekiah's since Solomon; 35:18, there had been no Passover like Josiah's since Samuel), and they celebrated the festival for eight days (Neh 8). The festival of booths was also observed at Solomon's dedication of the Temple (2 Chr 5–7) and at the erection of the altar in Ezra 3:1-4.

After separating themselves from foreigners, the people confessed their sin and read from the book of the law (9:2-3). The prayer in Neh 9 begins with a call to praise (v. 5b; the MT needs correction) and ends with a petition, confession of sins, and complaint

(vv. 32-37). In between, comes a historical retrospect recounting creation, the election of Abraham, the exodus, the wilderness wanderings, and life in the land. The rebellions of the people began during the wilderness wanderings and continued during the history in the land. The people acknowledged that their punishment had been just: God's generosity had been met with their disobedience. The last two verses of the prayer show frustration over the Jewish enslavement to the Persians, an opinion not clearly voiced elsewhere in Ezra and Nehemiah. This prayer is similar to Ezra 9:6-15; Dan 9; and Bar 2:11–3:8.

The Firm Agreement in Nehemiah 10 begins with a list of those who endorsed this document (10:2-8, priests [related to or derived from the lists in 12:1-7, 12-21]; 10:9-13, Levites [all but two of the Levites are known from elsewhere]; 10:14-27, lay leaders [only one name does not appear also in the lists of those who returned]). The Firm Agreement itself deals with mixed marriages, Sabbath observance, the wood offering, first fruits, levitical tithes, and proper care of the Temple. These pledges are logically and chronologically subsequent to Neh 13 and make Nehemiah's decisions there permanent; their location in this literary context forms a sequel to the reading of the law and the confession of sins (Neh 8–9).

8. Neh 11–13: the climax of Nehemiah's work and related matters

According to Neh 11:1-2, ten percent of the people were designated by lot to live in Jerusalem. The list in Neh 11:3-19 names those who settled in Jerusalem at the time of Nehemiah; when this was taken over and revised in 1 Chr 9:2-17, it names those who returned to the land right after the exile. Typologically, this list is later than Ezra 2//Neh 7, since singers are now included among the Levites, though gatekeepers have not yet attained levitical status. Verses 21-24 (additional information about Temple servants and Levites), 25-30 (villages in Judah) and 31-35 (villages in Benjamin) are secondary. The lists of towns in the latter two paragraphs describe a much larger territory for Judah and Benjamin than was occupied by the post-exilic province.

Nehemiah 12:1-26 presents lists of priests (vv. 1-7, 12-21) and Levites (vv. 8-9, 24-25) from two different periods, as well as important information about the post-exilic high priestly line (vv. 10-11, 22-23). Verses 12-21 consist of a master list of twenty-two priestly houses, followed in each case by the name of the head of that house in the time of the high priest Joakim. From this list was derived the list of priests from the time of Jeshua, Joiakim's father, in vv. 1-7. Thus the list of the priestly houses in vv. 12-21 is treated as if these houses were individuals. Verses 12-21 are also the source used to develop the roster of priestly signatories to the firm agreement in Neh 10:2-8. Nehemiah 12:27

was once joined to Neh 11:20, with Neh 11:21–12:26 comprising a series of supplements. Nehemiah 12:27-43 recounts the dedication of the wall and is a combination of words from the Nehemiah Memoir (vv. 31-32, 37-40) and other material. Nehemiah 12:44–13:3 is secondary and indicates that the actions by Nehemiah in regard to separation from foreigners and the tithe in 13:4-13 were done in conformity with the already constituted theocracy and its laws and decisions.

The last section of Nehemiah consists of units from the Nehemiah Memoir: vv. 4-9, the misuse of the Temple chambers by Eliashib to house Tobiah, who was then expelled by Nehemiah; vv. 10-14, measures taken by Nehemiah to restore the full payment of tithes and to give compensation to the Levites; vv. 15-22, correction of Sabbath abuses; vv. 23-29, controversies with those who had married foreign women and whose children could no longer speak the language of Judah and expulsion from the community of the grandson of the high priest who had married the daughter of Sanballat; and vv. 30-31, establishment of the duties of the priests and Levites and provision for wood offering and first fruits.

C. Theological Issues

The books begin with an announcement that Yahweh has remained faithful to the promise spoken by Jeremiah and brought Israel back to its land, with permission to rebuild the Temple in Jerusalem. Despite external opposition, the Temple is completed, with prophetic support. A joyful observance of Passover marks this occasion, and recognition is given to divine intervention exercised through Persian authorities (Ezra 1–6). This Temple is the focus of the religious life of post-exilic Judah, and its importance continues until the destruction of the Temple, that had been greatly enlarged by Herod, in 70 CE (see TEMPLE, JERUSALEM).

In chaps. 7–10, Ezra himself comes to Jerusalem, thanks to God's influence on the Persian king. His mission is to support the Temple and to teach the law of the God of heaven, which he brings with him. Ezra addresses the issue of mixed marriages, which he perceived as an internal threat to the community. His drastic solution to this problem by forced divorces is quite controversial, and a more inclusive view of Israel's relationship to outsiders is presented in the nearly contemporary Books of Chronicles and Ruth. If Ezra deals primarily with the restoration of the Temple and the establishment of the community, the first seven chapters of Nehemiah report efforts to provide safety for the city of Jerusalem. The support of Artaxerxes for this project is in response to the prayers of Nehemiah, so that once again Persian political support represents divine intervention.

Ezra's reading of the Law is followed by repentance and a firm commitment to it and to the Temple service (Neh 8–10). The central role of the Pentateuch in the canons of later Judaism and Christianity is here given a firm grounding. Nehemiah then sees to the repopulation of Jerusalem, which is followed by dedication of the walls he has rebuilt (Neh 11–12).

In recognizing the role of the Persian authorities in these events, the books of Ezra and Nehemiah assume that faithful living can take place under foreign rule. Clearly the books are deeply concerned about Jewish identity and the danger of its loss. One can sympathize with this concern if not always with the means chosen to achieve it. The books reassure the community of its legitimacy by comparing the return to the exodus, by reporting the presence of Temple vessels from the preexilic Temple, by comparing the Temple to that of Solomon (see TEMPLE OF SOLOMON), and by linking the people genealogically to their ancestors. Above all, the presentation and acceptance of the Law (some form of the Pentateuch) provides cohesion and direction for the community.

Two passages in Nehemiah recognize that the accomplishments reported in these books are not the final end for God's people. While the books recognize in general the benevolent rule of the Persians, the prayer in Neh 9 ends with a poignant lament: "[The] rich yield [of the land] goes to the kings whom you have set over us because of our sins . . . and we are in great distress" (v. 37). The final reforms of Nehemiah in chap. 13, even after the establishment of the Temple, the community, and the city, indicate a situation which is "already and not yet." *See* EXILE; EZRA.

Bibliography: Joseph Blenkinsopp. *Ezra-Nehemiah.* OTL (1988); Lisbeth S. Fried. *The Priest and the Great King: Temple-Palace Relations in the Persian Empire* (2004); Lester L. Grabbe. *A History of the Jews and Judaism in the Second Temple Period.* Vol. 1. *Yehud: A History of the Persian Province of Judah* (2004); H. G. M. Williamson. *Ezra, Nehemiah.* WBC 16 (1985).

RALPH W. KLEIN

EZRAHITE ez′ruh-h*i*t [אֶזְרָחִי ʾezrakhi; Ἐζραΐτης Ezraites, Ἰσραηλίτης Israēlitēs]. Ethan the Ezrahite and his brother, Heman, are identified as men of wisdom and composers of songs (1 Kgs 4:31 [Heb. 5:11], Pss 88:1; 89:1). *Ezrahite* could be a familial name based on Zerah (zerakh [זֶרַח]; 1 Chr 2:6) or a derivative of ʾezrakh (אֶזְרָח), meaning a native-born individual.

JASON R. TATLOCK

EZRI ez′r*i* [עֶזְרִי ʿezri]. The son of Chelub and the agricultural official in charge of field workers, Ezri is listed among officers in David's bureaucracy (1 Chr 27:26).

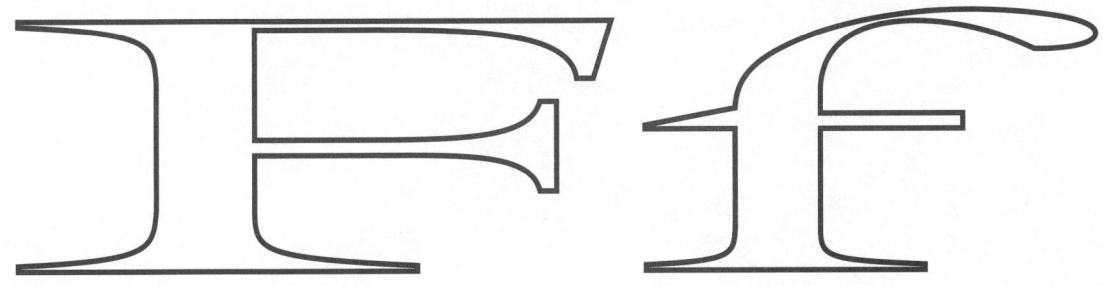

Ff

FABLE. A fable is a genre of narrative literature usually involving animals or inanimate objects who possess or exhibit human traits and interests, such as speaking and reasoning. Fables function on two levels—as short folktales to provide entertainment and as vehicles to convey moral instruction. In the OT the story of Balaam's talking DONKEY (Num 22:21-35) illustrates the longest example of a fable. Another famous example of a talking animal is the crafty serpent in Gen 3. In Judg 9:7-15 a conversation between three noble trees and a useless bramble illustrates Jotham's negative attitude toward Abimelech's kingship. King Jehoash of Israel (2 Kgs) sends a message to his enemy King Amaziah of Judah recounting a story of a talking thornbush who arrogantly demands an alliance with a particular cedar. The thornbush, symbolic of Amaziah's arrogance and subsequent defeat, is then trampled by a wild beast. *See* ALLEGORY; PARABLE.

JULYE M. BIDMEAD

FACE [אַף ʾaf, פָּנֶה paneh; πρόσωπον prosōpon]. *Face* is used literally and metaphorically in the Bible. **Paneh,** the most common Hebrew word for *face*, always appears in the plural (panim פָּנִים) and refers to one face.

People "fall on their faces" or do obeisance with the face to the ground before God or others in humility, prayer, or worship (Num 20:6; 22:31; Ruth 2:10; 1 Sam 24:8; 1 Kgs 1:23; Dan 2:46; Ezek 9:8). Abraham fell on his face before God (Gen 17:3, 17). The angels and other heavenly beings bow their faces before God (Rev 7:11).

The word is also used for *surface*, such as the face of the deep (Gen 1:2), earth (Gen 1:29; 8:9), and moon (Job 26:9). To "set one's face" is to decide to go in a particular direction (Gen 31:21) or take a particular course of action (Isa 50:7; Luke 9:51). To seek God's face is to seek God (Ps 24:6).

Face is also used as metonymy to refer to a person or the person's presence. The most common usage is for God's acceptance or rejection of a person or group. If one is rejected or abandoned by God, he or she is hidden from God's face (Gen 4:14; Deut 31:17; Mic 3:4). Job and many psalmists ask why God has hidden his face (Job 13:24; Ps 13:1). When God sets his face against someone, God acts against that person (Lev 17:10; 26:17), but when God hears someone's cries, it is the opposite of God hiding God's face (Ps 22:24;

compare Isa 59:2). When God's face does not turn away from the people, God is gracious and compassionate, indicating acceptance (2 Chr 30:9).

To ask God to hide God's face from a person's sins is to ask God to ignore or forget about the sins (Ps 51:9). People ask for the light of God's face to shine upon them (Ps 4:6), which means to have God act favorably toward them. Moses hid his face because he was afraid of God (Exod 3:6). In another passage Moses asks to see God's face, but God refuses because no one can see his face and live (Exod 33:20; compare Judg 6:22). The upright are promised that they will see God's face (Ps 11:7), which means that they will be acceptable to and find favor with God. On the new earth, believers will see God's face (Rev 22:4).

KENNETH D. LITWAK

FACETS [עֵינָיִם ʿenayim]. A metaphorical translation of "eyes," indicating the fullness of the glory of Yahweh's servant, the BRANCH, described as "a single stone with seven facets" (Zech 3:9).

FAIENCE. A glazed, non-clay pottery made from silica. The blue or green glaze of faience is obtained through the mixing of alkali salts with the original silica or through the silica being buried in lime, ash, and charcoal. Both of these techniques produce a natural glaze after firing. Faience was generally used for jewelry, decoration, and figurines.

KEVIN A. WILSON

FAIR HAVENS [Καλοὺς Λιμένας Kalous Limenas]. The author of Acts is the only ancient writer to mention Fair Havens, modern Kali Lemenes (also Limeonas Kalous, Kalus Limeonas, Kaloi Limenes, or Kalous Limionas), on the southernmost tip of the island of Crete, near ancient Lasea, 12 mi. east of Matala. Paul's Rome-bound transport stopped at this bay, made up of four or five small harbors, for protection from unfavorable winds (Acts 27:8). If the fast mentioned (Acts 27:9) is the DAY OF ATONEMENT, Paul was probably at Fair Havens in October or November 60 CE. Against Paul's advice, the ship leaves Fair Havens and sails toward Phoenix, likely searching for a larger city in which to winter, but wrecks at the island of Malta.

KATHY R. MAXWELL

FAITH, FAITHFULNESS [אֱמוּנָה ʾemunah, אֱמֶת ʾemeth; πίστις pistis].

A. Range of Meaning
B. Old Testament
  1. The faithful God
  2. The faith of Abraham
  3. Faith as righteousness
C. New Testament
  1. Paul
    a. The faithfulness of God
    b. The faith of Abraham
    c. Faith as righteousness
    d. Faith vs. the law
    e. Faith vs. works of the law
    f. The obedience of faith
    g. Faith as assent and commitment
    h. Faith and faithfulness
    i. Pistis Christou
    j. The faith
  2. New Testament usage apart from Paul
    a. Faith in the Synoptic Gospels
    b. Believing in the Gospel of John
    c. Faith in Acts
    d. Faith in James
    e. Faith in Hebrews

A. Range of Meaning

The two words ("faith, faithfulness") provide the simplest rendering of the Greek pistis and the basic spectrum of its meaning both in wider Greek usage and in the NT in particular.

The basic range of the term in its actual usage, then, is from the sense of subjective confidence in someone/something else, to the objective basis for such confidence: a subjective believing on the basis that the one/object trusted is reliable—"trust, confidence, faith"; and that which evokes trust—"faithfulness, reliability, fidelity, commitment." The Latin *fides* has the same basic range—"trust" in a person or thing, and "that which produces confidence or belief, trustworthiness, faithfulness, credibility." This was the range of sense that use of the word pistis by Paul and others would have evoked among those who heard them.

The nearest equivalent term in the OT is ʾemunah or ʾemeth. The basic idea in ʾmn-rooted words was "constancy" (of things) and "reliability" (of persons); the more frequently used ʾemeth as "that on which others can rely." From "stability" through "reliability," ʾemeth acquires the meaning of "truth," while ʾemunah conveys more the idea of "conduct that grows out of reliability," i.e., faithfulness. This is reflected in the Greek translation, for while the LXX translators preferred to translate ʾemunah by pistis (20 times), they preferred to translate ʾemeth by alētheia (ἀλήθεια), "truth," (87 times), though alētheia is the preferred translation of ʾemunah some 20 times in Psalms. Notable too is the fact that ʾemeth is occasionally translated by dikaiosynē (δικαιοσύνη), "righteousness" in the LXX (5 times). The point is that these rather differ-

ent terms in Greek (and English) all merged into one another in Hebrew usage: "truth" and "righteousness" as well as "faithfulness" were rooted in the thought of constancy and reliability.

It is important to appreciate two immediate corollaries. One is that the Hebrew and Greek terms clearly overlap, but do not overlap completely. The Hebrew terms are weighted to the more objective end of the two English words—"stability, reliability, faithfulness," whereas in Greek usage pistis extends more into the subjective sense of "trust in, believing, *faith*." The other is that the range of meaning should not be treated as though the two senses, "faith, faithfulness," were quite distinct and discrete; on the contrary, it was the fact that the two senses ran into each other that was a major factor in the earliest disputes about "faith" in embryonic Christianity.

Both points need to be borne in mind before extending the overview to include the related verbal usage—pisteuō (πιστεύω) and ʾmn. The basic meaning of the Greek verb is simply "trust, put faith in, rely on a person, thing or statement." The Hebrew also indicates "trust in, reliance on," but basically is an expression of confidence in the object of the trust. In the Hebrew usage, trust includes a recognition and affirmation of the trustworthiness of the one trusted; the stability and security of believing ("faith") as predicated on the stability and reliability ("faithfulness") of the one relied on. A rather crucial question is whether and to what extent the Hebrew heʾemin (הֶאֱמִין) and ʾemeth have influenced the NT use and understanding of pisteuō and pistis.

B. Old Testament

1. The faithful God

Yahweh is ʾel ʾemeth (אֵל אֱמֶת) "faithful God" (Ps 31:5), one who can be utterly relied on. This is true not least of God as creator: "As creator, God "keeps ʾemeth," and humankind can rely on God forever (Ps 146:6). "The works of his hands are faithful and just" (Ps 111:7). But it is true particularly of God as the God of Israel: "All the paths of Yahweh are steadfast love and faithfulness, for those who keep his covenant and his decrees" (Ps 25:10). Significant here is the frequent linking of ʾemeth with khesedh (חֶסֶד), God's "steadfast love" (*see* LOVE, OT). Thus Abraham's servant blesses the God of Abraham "who has not forsaken his steadfast love and his faithfulness toward my master" (Gen 24:27). And Micah ends on the note of assurance: "You will show faithfulness to Jacob and steadfast love to Abraham, as you have sworn to our ancestors from the days of old" (Mic 7:20).

Similarly with ʾemunah: "The word of the Lord is upright and all his work is done in faithfulness. He loves righteousness and justice; the earth is full of the steadfast love of the Lord" (Ps 33:4-5); Yahweh says to Israel, "I will take you for my wife in faithfulness; and you shall know the Lord" (Hos 2:20); "The steadfast love of the Lord never ceases, his mercies never come to an end; they are new every morning; great is your faithfulness" (Lam 3:22-23).

The verb is occasionally used of Israel trusting in Yahweh, that is, gaining confidence in his faithfulness (Exod 14:31), and in Moses' reliability as one who enjoys intimacy with Yahweh (Exod 19:9). More often Israel is rebuked for failing so to trust (Num 14:11; Deut 1:32; 2 Kgs 17:14; Pss 78:22, 32; 106:24). More astonishing is the fact that the people of Ninevah respond to Jonah's preaching in the way Israel should: they "believed God," that is, relied on him, and took Jonah's message as indeed a message from God.

In the OT, then, Yahweh the faithful God looks to his creatures and his people to recognize, to rely on, and to reflect his faithfulness in their own lives. Two texts in particular became significant in spelling out what this response involved.

2. The faith of Abraham

God promised Abraham that he would have as many descendants as the stars in the sky, and Abraham "believed (he'emin) the Lord and the Lord reckoned it to him as righteousness" (Gen 15:6). This promise and Abraham's response, coming immediately prior to the solemn ritual of sacrifice by which the Lord made his covenant with Abram (Gen 15:7-21), was evidently seen as characterizing the covenant relation between Yahweh and Abraham and his descendants. It was given by divine initiative, an act of unsolicited generosity; and the appropriate human response was to believe (he'emin), to respond with matching 'emeth.

Here at once it is important to recognize that Hebrew thought engaged the full range of the believing response. From early days Abraham was seen as the type or model of the covenant member, his response as the response appropriate to God's faithfulness. Already in Gen 26:5 the promise of offspring "as numerous as the stars of heaven" is being matched by talk of Abraham's obedience and keeping of the Lord's commandments, statutes, and laws. And this thought, that Abraham's trust in God's promise was, of course, of a piece with his accepting what God commanded him to do and his doing it, is a consistent motif thereafter. For example, Jubilees has the Lord saying to Isaac: "All the nations of the earth will bless themselves by your seed because your father obeyed me and observed my restrictions and my commandments and my laws and my ordinances and my covenant" (*Jub.* 14:11). And according to the Damascus Document, Abraham "was accounted a friend of God because he kept the commandments of God" (CD III:2).

More frequently recalled was the folk memory of how Abraham had been tested and yet found faithful, with particular reference to the sacrifice of Isaac in Gen

22 (Jdt 8:26; *Jub.* 17:15-18; 18:16; 19:8; *m.* 'Abot 5:3). Particularly noteworthy is Sir 44:19-21:

Abraham was the great father of a multitude of
     nations,
   and no one has been found like him in glory;
He kept the law of the Most High,
   and entered into covenant with him;
he certified the covenant in his flesh,
   and when he was tested he proved faithful.
Therefore the Lord assured him with an oath
   that the nations would be blessed through his off-
        spring;
that he would multiply him as numerous as the dust
        of the earth,
   and exalt his offspring like the stars . . .

Here clearly the weight of Abraham's 'emeth is being understood in terms of his faithfulness, the faithfulness expected of the devout Israelite.

Equally striking is the way the second half of Gen 15:6 was taken up to ascribe the Lord's reckoning righteous in reference to an act of such faithfulness. With reference to Abraham's offering Isaac, 1 Maccabees recalls that "when he was tested he was found faithful [the same phrasing as Sir 44:20], and it was reckoned to him for righteousness" (1 Macc 2:52). Psalm 106:31 describes Phinehas' heroic zeal in staying the plague that had followed from the sin of Baal Peor, and concludes: "and that has been reckoned to him as righteousness from generation to generation forever." The action of Simeon and Levi in avenging the defilement of their sister Dinah by killing the Shechemites (Gen 34) receives the same accolade: "and it was a righteousness for them and it was written down for them for righteousness" (Jub 30:17-19). In a Qumran letter to Jewish leaders, justifying their separation from the multitude of the people, a list is given of the halakhic interpretations distinctive of the sect ("some of the works of the law"), and the letter recipients are invited to agree with (and follow) these halakhoth with the closing promise: "And this will be counted to you for righteousness, since you will be doing what is righteous and good in his eyes" [4Q398 14-17 II, 7 (4QMMT C31).]

It should be emphasized that there was absolutely no sense of forcing a meaning upon the text (Gen 15:6) by understanding it so. Of course, Gen 15:6; 17:1-14; and 22:1-19 were all of a piece. Abraham's trust in God was embodied in and expressed by his obedience. His faith and faithfulness were two sides of the same coin; it was the same word, and the same attitude and action expressed by that word.

3. Faith as righteousness

"The righteous live by their faith ('emunah)" (Hab 2:4). The text was evidently understood in Israelite and early Jewish praxis as describing the righteous one, the tsaddiq (צַדִּיק), that is, the one who is a faithful member of the covenant people, who fulfills the obligations required by the law of the covenant as a loyal Jew. This self-understanding of "the righteous" is particularly prominent in the Psalms (1:5-6; 5:12; 7:9-10; 14:5), in the Wisdom literature (e.g., Prov 3:32-33; 4:18; 9:9; 10:3, 6-7; Wis 2:10, 12, 16, 18; in *1 Enoch* (e.g., 1:8; 5:4-6; 82:4; 95:3; 100:5), and in the *Psalms of Solomon* (2:38-39; 3:3-8, 14; 4:9; etc.). The same understanding of the Hebrew of Hab 2:4 is evident in the Qumran *pesher*: "The interpretation of it concerns the observers of the law in the house of Judah, whom God shall deliver from the house of judgment because of their struggle and their fidelity to the Teacher of Righteousness" (1QpHab 8:1-3). So too in the Targum of Habakkuk.

Notable is the LXX rendering of Hab 2:4: "the righteous out of my faith(fullness) shall live." Again the variant translation is not a sign of any difference of opinion, but more a recognition that the faith envisaged by Habakkuk was an affirmation of and response to God's faithfulness: to trust was to reckon God faithful, to live faithfully in response to God's words/commandments. Righteousness embraced both (or all) facets.

Worth noting finally is the double use in Isaiah: 7:9—"If your faith is not firm you will not stand firm"; 28:16—"he who believes need not hasten/be anxious." Implied is the same combination of attitude and act: a trust (in God), in God's reliability and faithfulness, and a living out that trust in a (feeble human) attempt to mirror that faithfulness.

C. New Testament

1. Paul

Of the NT writings, the letters written by Paul in the 50s, that is, within the beginnings of Christianity, and the only certain first-generation Christian writings still available to us, call for consideration first. Two other factors underline the importance of Paul's letters for the present subject. One is that the theme of "faith/faithfulness" is a predominantly Pauline concern. The other is that Paul's letters also show immediate interaction with the OT and Jewish traditions just examined. Their main emphases mirror those of Paul's Jewish forebears and clearly indicate the developments in earliest Christian thinking that pulled embryonic Christianity more and more apart from Second Temple Judaism.

a. The faithfulness of God. Paul echoes Israel's confidence in God as "faithful" in several contexts: "God is faithful" in caring for the first believers (1 Cor 1:9; 10:13; 1 Thess 5:24), as is also the Lord (Christ) (2 Thess 3:3; also 2 Tim 2:13), a pattern that Paul seeks to emulate in his own dealings with his converts (2 Cor 1:18). The same thought is implicit in Paul's confidence in God, in the outworking of God's purpose, and in the unveiling of the divine mystery hidden from the

generations. But the theme becomes a central feature in Paul's theology only in Romans. There, however, it is a major secondary theme of his most theologically discursive letter.

Its importance is indicated already in the letter's thematic statement: "I am not ashamed of the gospel, since it is the power of God for salvation, to all who believe, Jew first but also Gentile. For the righteousness of God is being revealed in it from faith to faith—as it is written, "The one who is righteous will live by faith" (Rom 1:16-17; citing Hab 2:4). We shall return to the role of human believing and of Hab 2:4 below. Here it is important to note that the principal theme of the letter, "the righteousness of God," correlates closely with the theme of God's faithfulness to the people chosen by God to be his special people—Israel. For here Paul is clearly assuming the idea of God's *saving* righteousness—that is, God's commitment to be Israel's God and to exercise saving grace to Israel, even when Israel fails in its covenant obligations before their God. It is this theme, drawn particularly from the Psalms and Second Isaiah, where God's dikaiosynē is regularly to be translated as God's "salvation" or "vindication" of Israel (*see* RIGHTEOUSNESS IN EARLY JEWISH LITERATURE; RIGHTEOUSNESS IN THE NT; RIGHTEOUSNESS IN THE OT), which Paul clearly assumes here, though without ignoring the obverse side of God's righteousness in opening his indictment in the following verses (1:18). The faithfulness of God to Israel becomes the main thrust of the climax of the letter's theological exposition in Rom 9–11, even though pistis language is not explicit. There Paul insists that "the word of God" (to and for Israel) has not failed (9:6), and rounds off the reflection by insisting that "the gifts and calling of God are irrevocable" (11:29). Significantly, the last word is "mercy" rather than "faithfulness" (11:30-32), but echoes the passage that most characterized Israel's understanding of God's motivation and commitment to his covenant people (Exod 34:6-7).

That climax to the letter is already foreshadowed in Rom 3:1-8, where Paul touches on the issues he is to develop later in the letter, and does so by playing on the theme of God's ʾemunah/pistis. Paul has included the "Jew" in his indictment of humanity (2:1-29), which naturally raises the question whether there is any advantage in being a Jew (3:1). His answer in effect is that the key factor is not the Jews' unfaithfulness (apistia ἀπιστία), but God's faithfulness (pistis). And in making the point he draws out the full force of the Hebrew motif:

> What if some were unfaithful? Will their faithlessness (apistia) nullify the faithfulness (pistis) of God? By no means! Although everyone is a liar, let God be proved true [Ps 115:2], as it is written, "So that you may be justified by your words and prevail in your judging" [Ps 50:6]. But if our injustice (adikia ἀδικία) serves to

confirm the justice (dikaiosynē) of God, what should we say? That God is unjust to inflict wrath upon us? . . . By no means! For then how could God judge the world? But if through my falsehood God's truthfulness (alētheia ἀλήθεια) abounds to his glory, why am I still being condemned as a sinner?

The full force of the theme would be evident only to those conscious of the Hebrew background of Paul's line of argument. For, as we have seen, 'emeth and 'emunah were translated both by pistis and by alētheia in the LXX. Similarly "the righteousness of God" (dikaiosynē theou [δικαιοσύνη Θεου]) often functions as a synonym for "the faithfulness of God" (pistis theou [πίστις Θεου]). So here, Jewish "unfaithfulness" is evidently of a piece with human "unrighteousness," and as the one is met by God's "faithfulness" so the other is met by God's "righteousness," just as "my lie" is met by God's "truth." Despite the large-scale rejection of Messiah Jesus by his fellow Jews, Paul was still confident that God remained faithful to the people he had chosen and to whom he had "entrusted the oracles of God" (Rom 3:2). God remains true (alēthēs ἀληθής) despite human lies. That God remains faithful includes a readiness to overlook human unrighteousness. But it does not change God's obligation also to judge the world and to "inflict wrath." The faithfulness of God in Paul's eyes is always tempered by both sides of God's righteousness—salvation-effecting and wrath-bestowing.

b. The faith of Abraham. It should not surprise us that Paul regarded Gen 15:6 as crucial to his exposition of h]]is gospel and theology. As we have seen, the text was regarded as a central element in Jewish understanding of Israel's covenant obligation—to live faithfully before Yahweh in accordance with his law, the law given as part of God's covenant with Israel, at Sinai, just as Abraham had lived faithfully. Paul's coming to believe in Jesus as Messiah, Son of God, and Lord, evidently gave him a new appreciation of Gen 15:6, or fresh insight—an insight that shifted the emphasis from faithfulness to faith.

It may be possible, indeed, to trace the process by which Paul worked out this differently weighted exposition of Gen 15:6. It is quite likely that the issue of how Gentile believers may be reckoned as "sons of Abraham" was not one that he first introduced in his evangelistic or follow-up preaching. A plausible hypothesis is that it was the incoming (Christian Jewish) missionaries to the churches of Galatia who first posed the challenge: if Gentiles are indeed to share in the blessings promised to Abraham and his seed, they must do as Abraham did, and be circumcised; only the circumcised are the descendants of Abraham. Whatever the precise sequence of events and arguments used by the incoming missionaries, it is abundantly clear that they were pressuring Paul's converts to be circumcised, and

thus (presumably) to become true heirs of Abraham.

Significantly, Paul begins his response, after a more wide-ranging defense of his gospel and reminder of how the Galatians became Christians (by receiving the Spirit), by immediately quoting Gen 15:6—"Abraham believed God and it was reckoned to him for righteousness" (Gal 2:6). The conclusion Paul at once draws is that it is Abraham's thus believing that characterizes the relationship Abraham exemplifies for his descendants: "Those of faith (ek pisteōs ἐκ πίστεως), they are Abraham's sons" (Gal 3:7). At this point Paul's concern was evidently to focus on the promise that in Abraham all the nations/Gentiles would be blessed (3:8), and that is the line that his exposition follows. Whether he knew that the other missionaries had been pressing Abraham as an example of circumcision, or was at this point concerned about moving along the faith-faithfulness spectrum that the example of Abraham invited is not clear. Rather strikingly, Paul ends this paragraph by reiterating 2:6 but in terms of Abraham's faithfulness—"Consequently, those of faith are blessed with faithful (**pistos**) Abraham" (2:9)—which suggests that the natural corollary (to share the faith of Abraham is also to be faithful to the command for circumcision like Abraham) had not yet entered into the debate.

Whether that is the case or not, the corollary had certainly been drawn by the time Paul wrote Romans. Here again, after setting out in succinct terms his understanding of the gospel (3:21-31), the first scriptural passage to which he turns is Gen 15:6. Once again the debate was framed in terms of faith versus works of the law (Gal 3:2-5; Rom 3:27-4:2) (see below), but on this occasion Paul addresses head-on the obvious point (obvious to anyone familiar with Jewish tradition) that Abraham acted out his faith in the faithfulness of his obedience to the command to be circumcised (and to offer up his son Isaac). What follows (4:3-22) is one of the best examples of Jewish exposition of a biblical text available to us from these centuries.

Paul begins by expounding the significance of "reckoned"—as carrying the meaning not of having wages counted out in return for services rendered, as in a contract between two human beings, but as meaning "granted" as a gift (4:4-8). Then Paul turns to expound the meaning of "Abraham believed" (4:9-21), first, from the order of events in Abraham's case (4:9-12). Here he uses the same tactic as in Gal 3, by noting the time difference between what had been granted/promised to Abraham, and the giving of the law. But in this case the time gap is that between Abraham's believing (Gen 15:6) and the subsequent command that he be circumcised (Gen 17). Paul's point is that righteousness had already been fully reckoned to believing Abraham prior to and independent of his being circumcised. Second, Paul underscores the link between faith and promise in Abraham's case (4:13-17)—again a link he had highlighted but not as such developed in Gal 3.

But the third step in the exposition is the most crucial (4:17-21), for here Paul presses the character of Abraham's faith, as sheer and total reliance and trust, unable to perform anything (what hundred-year-old man could make his aged, barren wife pregnant?). The trust is in the creator God, not simply in the one "who gives life to the dead" (the deliverance of Isaac from the knife might have provided a more suitable type of the resurrection of Jesus, as in Heb 11:17-19), but in the God "who calls things which have no existence into existence," the very creation of a son. This is what it means to "believe": Abraham's trusting hope in the existence-creating, life-giving God when there was nothing in himself or his circumstances to give grounds for that hope. The empty hand of impotent trust was quite distinct from the faithful obedience of circumcising the males of his household or subsequently offering up Isaac in sacrifice—things he could and did do. It was this faithful trust of Abraham "which God reckoned to him for righteousness," not his faithfulness (4:22).

c. Faith as righteousness. It is equally unsurprising that the second text on which Paul bases so much of his gospel is the other great "faith" text that provoked reflection among his contemporaries. Its centrality to Paul's own gospel is indicated by the fact that it is precisely Hab 2:4 that Paul appends to his thematic statement at the beginning of Romans (Rom 1:16-17). What is noticeable, however, is that Paul seems to have avoided choosing between the two variant versions of the Hebrew and the Greek:

> Hebrew—"the righteous (one) by his faith(fulness) shall live"
> Greek (LXX)—"the righteous out of my faith(fulness) shall live"
> Paul—"the righteous out of faith/faithfulness(?) shall live"

That Paul intended the ek pisteōs to be read as "out of/from faith" is most likely, since he has already commended the Romans' pistis ("faith") (Rom 1:8, 12), and his main theme in the letter is that the gospel is for "all who believe" (1:16; 3:22; 10:4). Indeed, the theme of "faith" dominates key sections of the argument of Romans: 3:21–5:21 (3:22, 25, 27-28, 30-31; 4:3, 5, 9, 11-14, 16-20; 5:1-2), chaps. 9–11 (9:30, 32, 33; 10:4, 6, 8-9, 11, 14, 17; 11:20) and chaps. 12–15 (12:3, 6; 14:1, 2, 22-23).

At the same time, however, it could be that Paul still wanted to retain the force of the LXX version. For Hab 2:4 is appended to the assertion that "the righteousness of God is being revealed from faith to faith" (1:17). The double phrase is regularly understood as Paul insisting that human response to the gospel is and can only be faith from beginning to end. But possibly Paul was implying that the gospel came from God's faithfulness to human faith. In this way he would be answering the Jewish understanding of the integral nature of faith and faithfulness by affirming it for himself, but as primarily a spectrum not so much from human faith to human faithfulness (like Abraham's faith/faithfulness), but from God's faithfulness to human trust. Salvation (1:16), a righteous status before God (1:17), depends primarily and definitively on the outreaching movement of God's righteousness/faithfulness finding its appropriate response in human faith/trust.

Unsurprisingly, Hab 2:4 also features in the earlier, less well-developed argument of Galatians, though not at all in such a prominent place as in Romans, or as Gen 15:6 in both Galatians and Romans. It comes instead within the argument that develops from Gen 15:6 in Gal 3: that by the law no one is justified before God is plain, because:

> "The righteous from faith (ek pisteōs) shall live" [Hab 2:4]. But the law is not from faith (ek pisteōs) rather "The one who does them will live by them" [Lev 18:5] (Gal 3:11-12).

The decisive clue here is the repetition of the phrase ek pisteōs. This is a phrase that more than any other in Galatians expresses Paul's gospel, as its regular repetition indicates (2:16; 3:7-9, 11-12, 22, 24; 5:5). "Those from faith" (hoi ek pisteōs [οἱ ἐκ πίστεως]) are those defined, given their identity by their believing, sons of Abraham, believing as he believed (3:6-9). Like Abraham, they are (reckoned) righteous (ek pisteōs); their living grows out of and expresses their trustful relationship with God. The contrast Paul makes with this life of faith, however, deserves separate treatment.

d. Faith vs. the law. In his exposition of Gen 15:6 and Hab 2:4 Paul set his face against the usual interpretation of these verses of his contemporaries: that faith and faithfulness hung together, that reception of promise and obedience to command naturally went together, that faith and law were mutually integrated. It is in Galatians that Paul began to make his case that the two needed to be held apart, otherwise the latter would corrupt both the understanding and reality of the former. To regard Torah-obedience as integral to faith, rather than as an outworking of faith, meant that human doing and achievement entered into the heart of the relation between God and humankind. Contrast this with Paul's view that all that the creature could do before the Creator was to believe, to trust, to worship, to glorify, to give thanks (Rom 1:21). It was essential, therefore, to restate the relation between trust and Torah, between faith and faithfulness, if that on which all else depended was not to be obscured and lost.

Galatians 3:11-12 sets out Paul's point in epigrammatic form. The relationship with God (being accounted righteous by God) is dependent on faith as first and last, the bottom line (ek pisteōs). In contrast, the law spells out a different aspect of that relationship. It is not ek pisteōs; it is not integral to the defining identity of believers, hoi ek pisteōs. Instead, its role is to chart the path of life, to define how "those of faith" should live: "he shall live by them" (Lev 18:5). This was certainly the original import of Lev 18:5, as its earliest commentary (Ezek 20:5-26) shows: "You shall keep my statutes and my ordinances; by doing so one shall live." That God's people should live their lives in accordance with God's laws was why God had given the Torah in the first place, as Deuteronomy insists repeatedly (e.g., Deut 30:15-20). Paul drives home the same point later in the same chapter (3:21). The law is not against the promises, because their roles were different: the law does not make alive. By implication, the promise does (Paul already anticipates the argument of Rom 4:17); the promise gives life, the law orders the life given.

The law versus faith theme runs through Gal 3. Promise and faith are what stand in symbiotic relationship: the promise to Abraham of seed and to be a blessing to the nations is received by faith (3:6-9); the promised blessing is received by these nations through such faith (3:11, 14, 22). That relationship is unaffected by the later coming of the law (3:17-18). Its role in relation to Israel (by implication, including circumcision as limiting the scope of the promise to the circumcised), was temporary, a guardian or custodial role until "the coming of faith" (3:23-24). By this remarkable way of referring to the coming of Christ Paul presumably implies that during the rule of the law the promise-faith nexus of Abraham's righteousness was hidden and incompletely realized. Only with the coming of Christ, Abraham's promised "seed" (3:16), has the basic promise-faith dynamic reemerged and become active and effective again in the preaching of the good news of Jesus Christ to Gentiles as well as Jews. This coming of faith offers release from the rule of the law, and the transition (for Jew as well as Gentile) to the full sonship of those who believe as Abraham believed and who receive the Spirit of the Son (3:25–4:7).

In Romans Paul develops the equivalent argument differently, and in two stages. First, in Rom 4 he does not press for such a sharp either-or of faith and law. The argument ("what came later cannot alter the earlier being reckoned righteous through faith") is put in terms of the time-gap between Abraham's believing (Gen 15) and his being circumcised (Gen 17; Rom 4:10-11), rather than the 430-year gap between promise and Torah (Gal 3:17). And although Paul presses the point that the inheritance from Abraham comes through faith and not the law (Rom 4:13-15), he puts the contrast more as a rather-than and not as an either-or. The promise of Abraham is guaranteed to all Abraham's descendants, "not only to the one who is of the law but also to the one who is of the faith of Abraham" (4:12, 16).

More striking is the Romans equivalent to Gal 3:11-12, which comes later in the argument of Romans (Rom 10:5-13). Here again Paul uses Lev 18:5 to contrast law-righteousness with faith-righteousness. "The righteousness that comes from the law" (10:5) is a matter of doing what the law demands, and thus maintaining life within the covenant and (initially) securing life within the land and (later) life in the age to come. But "the righteousness that comes from faith" (10:6-13) is not to be thought of as narrowly tied down to Israel or its law. Here Paul cites Deut 30:12-14: "Do not say in your heart, 'Who will go up into heaven?' or 'Who will go down into the abyss?' But what does it say? 'The word is near you, in your mouth and in your heart.'" In fact, the Deuteronomy passage is similar to the Leviticus passage: Paul breaks off his quotation of the former at the point where it continues, "so that you can do it" (Deut 30:14). However, the talk of going up to heaven and descending into the depths (or crossing the sea) invited a more cosmic perspective on what was being said; so that it is no surprise that 2 Bar. 3:29-30 interprets the passages as speaking of divine Wisdom (subsequently identified, of course, with "the book of the commandments of God"—4:1). It was presumably this wider perspective that prompted and enabled Paul to interpret the Deuteronomy passage as speaking about the word of faith, the preaching of Jesus as risen from the dead and exalted to Lord. As Baruch heard a more profound and universal word from the creator God coming through the Torah, so Paul heard the word of faith coming through the words of Moses. The gospel of faith/to faith was not in antithesis to the law but transcended it, as the revelation of Christ transcended the revelation of Moses.

e. Faith vs. works of the law. A variant of the faith/law contrast is that between faith and "works of the law," and this is the sharper contrast for Paul, more of an antithesis than a contrast. It appears in Paul's first definitive assertion regarding "justification by faith" (Gal 2:16), and he repeats it in a further variation in 3:2-5, though thereafter he opts for the balder faith/law antithesis. But in Romans the main proponent set over against faith is "works of the law" (Rom 3:27-28; 4:2-3; 9:32).

By "works of the law" Paul presumably means, as the phrase itself indicates, doing what the law requires, observing its statutes and commandments. In Galatians in particular the phrase was evidently prompted by the insistence of Peter and the other Christian Jews that Gentile believers had, in effect, to "judaize," to adopt a Jewish life-style, to observe the characteristic Jewish food laws if they were to share the same meal table (and Lord's Supper) with Jewish believers (2:11-14). Paul robustly responded by setting such "works of the law" in antithesis to faith, to believing in Christ Jesus (2:16). The point is the same as he expressed in more general terms later in chap. 3, but with the added implication that Jewish believers could no longer shelter behind the barricade of the law and separate themselves from other believers. Justification was by faith alone, which meant that all such discrimination and sectarian withholding oneself from full fellowship with other believers was destructive of their common foundation—the promise to faith, the gospel of faith. An instructive comparison here is with 4Q394-399: the letter to the Jewish leadership used the phrase ("some works of the law") to denote the interpretations of the law (halakhic rulings) over which they had separated from the mass of the people. Paul uses the same phrase to denote the interpretations of the law being insisted on by the Jewish believers. Whereas Qumran chose to define themselves by their works of the law, Paul saw the first Christians, Gentiles as well as Jews, defined by their faith in Christ.

The point is pressed home at the beginning of Gal 3. Paul could remember how the Galatians had received the Spirit—evidently an (almost) tangible experience in the lives of these Galatians. "Was it by works of the law that you received the Spirit, or by hearing with faith?" (3:2). The last phrase, "hearing with faith" (ex akoēs pisteōs ἐξ ἀκοῆς πίστεως)" is ambiguous. Most prefer to take akoēs in the sense, "that which is heard, message"—so, "by believing what you heard" (NRSV, NIV, NJB), "by believing the gospel message" (REB)—though in the nearest parallel Paul stresses the importance of "hearing" (Rom 10:14-18). At any rate, it had been their trustful acceptance of the message of Christ crucified (3:1) (and commitment to this Christ as Lord), and that alone, that had resulted in their receiving the Spirit, the promised blessing of Abraham (3:14). That alone should be enough to make it clear to the Galatians (and to the incoming "troublemakers") that were already sons of Abraham, and that any further rules and commandments of the law were both unnecessary and a distraction from the central and solely sufficient factor of faith.

In Romans the phrase "works of the law" is introduced in the final summing up of the indictment in 3:19-20. The antithesis to "faith" is unstated, but implicit, in that 1:16-17 and 3:19-20 form an *inclusio*—the righteousness (of God) "from faith to faith" (1:17) set in contrast to the "not being reckoned righteous before God from works of the law" (3:20). The indictment is universal not because Gentiles as well as Jews might think to claim a righteousness before God on the basis of Torah-obedience, but because "no flesh" includes Jews and signifies that Torah-obedience in itself is not the basis for acceptance by God. From 2:1 onward Paul's concern was primarily to ensure that his fellow Jews should be aware that their privileges under the law did not guarantee them a favorable verdict in the final judgment (2:6-13); the condemnatory catena of texts in 3:10-18 spoke directly "to those within the law, so that every mouth (Jew as well as Gentile) might be stopped and all the world become liable to God's judgment" (3:19). The "works of the law" in view presumably refer primarily not to Israel's failure to obey the law (2:21-24; 3:3), but to Israel's presumption of

a "favored nation" status before God, as illustrated both by the "Jew's" boasting (over other nations) in the privilege of having and being instructed by the law (2:17-20), and the (misplaced) confidence arising out of his having obeyed the fundamental covenant command to be circumcised (2:25-27).

The antithesis between faith and "works of the law" reemerges in 3:27–4:2. The "boasting" (referred to in 2:17, 23) is excluded not by "works of the law" but by faith (3:27). Works of the law would seem rather to strengthen or at least be a ground for such boasting—as the case of Abraham illustrates (4:2): his works would have documented that he was "a friend of God" (CD III, 2), the one chosen to fulfill God's purpose, and could therefore be seen as a ground of boasting. But such an emphasis on works of the law in actual fact narrows the purpose of God down to Israel; it implies that God is God of Jews only, when he is also God of Gentiles also (3:29). That is why the basic statement of the gospel is in terms of faith, and not works of the law—"a person is justified by faith apart from works of the law" (3:28)—so that the one God of Jews and Gentiles might justify both Jew and Gentile in the same way, "from faith," "through faith" (3:30). Were justification by works of the law, then only the people of the law would be justified, and if Gentiles were to be justified it would be necessary for them to become members of the people of the law (Jews). But a relation with God in which a person is reckoned righteous, acceptable to God, is more fundamental than the Jew/Gentile divide; it operates at a deeper level of divine-human relationship, prior to and indeed independent of any or particular works of the law (like circumcision). It operates through and is dependent only on faith, the trust of the creature on the Creator, the human non-entity relying wholly on the life-giving God (4:17). In Paul, the antithesis between faith and works of the law is nowhere so profound as in 3:27–4:25.

The antithesis reemerges one more time in Romans—in Rom 9:32. Romans 9:30–10:4 is Paul's final exposition of "the righteousness which is from faith." Here once again he picks up the contrast between the Israel that had failed to appreciate the fundamental character of God's righteousness and the Gentiles who had experienced that righteousness. He elaborates the contrast in terms of his favorite race metaphor. "Gentiles who do not pursue righteousness have attained it, the righteousness which is from faith" (9:30). In contrast, Israel pursuing the goal set by God has not attained it. Somewhat confusingly, Paul describes the goal as "the law of righteousness" (9:31); the point should be held in mind for a moment. In what lay the difference between the two "contestants" and their goals? The answer, once again, is in terms of the faith/works of the law antithesis (9:32). Israel made the mistake of understanding righteousness in terms of the works demanded by the law. Consequently they mistook the character of that righteousness, as though God's acceptance began from their law-obedience; in focusing on works of the law they mistook the basis of their covenant relation with God. That relationship is based only on faith.

The picture of Israel failing to reach the goal being pursued easily translates into the image of Israel stumbling, which allows Paul to draw in one of the two somewhat enigmatic Isaiah references to "believing" (Isa 28:16) but using the LXX version (Rom 9:33): "Behold, I place in Zion a stone of stumbling and a rock of offence; and he who believes in him/it shall not be put to shame." The goal that is the law of righteousness can be transposed into Christ the stone of stumbling, just as in the following paragraph the word of the law can be transposed into the word that speaks of Christ (10:6-13). In both cases, it is a matter of pressing behind works of the law to the more fundamental matter and basis of faith. The law as understood and implemented in terms of works, the way of life demanded by the law (9:32), is of a piece with the unenlightened zeal that counts righteousness as exclusive to Israel (10:2-3), and with the righteousness of the law summed up by Lev 18:5 (10:5). But that law properly understood points rather to Christ and calls for faith in that Christ: the righteousness "attained" through faith (9:30, 32), the righteousness of God to all who believe (10:3-4). The invitation to faith in him is for all (10:11-13), for all who believe, without regard to the demands of the law hitherto so definitive for Israel: "Everyone who believes in him shall not be put to shame" (Isa 28:16); "Everyone whoever calls upon the name of the Lord shall be saved" (Joel 3:5).

f. The obedience of faith. The care with which Paul makes his case for faith over against the law (and works of the law) strongly suggests that the antithesis between faith and the law is not so sharp as it has often been presented. Here we must recognize a major and regrettable tendency in Christian theology at least from the 2nd cent. on. Evidently in these early days of Christianity it was found necessary to establish and reinforce the identity of nascent Christianity by setting it in antithesis to the rabbinic Judaism emerging at the same time. Since Judaism is so defined by the law, and since Christianity is readily defined in terms of faith, it was natural to pose the antithesis in terms of law and faith. And following the Reformation, when justification by faith became "the article by which the church stands or falls," the antithesis between the gospel and the law easily transposed into an antithesis between Christianity and Judaism, each part of the double antithesis reinforcing the other. This polarization of law and faith not only had horrific consequences in the outworking of 20th cent. anti-Semitism, but reading Paul in the light of that polarization resulted in a misperception of Paul's teaching at this point.

One mistake has already been hinted at: because of the tradition of negativity attaching to the Torah/law in Christian perception, it was too readily assumed that Paul was much more hostile to the Jewish law than was actually the case. Thus far we have observed that Paul's critique of the law in Galatians was quite narrowly focused—on Christian Jewish missionaries' attempt to require Gentile believers to be circumcised and to "judaize"; that is, from Paul's perspective, their failure to recognize that the protective role of the law for Jews was no longer in operation now that faith had come. And with regard to Romans in particular we have noted that Paul's critique is directed against a wrong evaluation of the law, in terms of "works of the law," in place of or subordinating faith, and that otherwise the law can be seen to speak of Christ and of faith in him.

There are other passages where Paul does not hesitate to juxtapose law and faith in a positive way that have always puzzled those who approach Paul with the assumption that faith and law are polar opposites for Paul.

One is the fact that Paul could describe his commission as bringing Gentiles "to the obedience of faith" (Rom 1:5). The thought that faith could "obey" rather than simply "trust" comes with something of a jolt for some. The apparent dissonance is softened by realization that the Greek verb "to obey" (hypakouō ὑπακούω) is derived from the verb "to hear" (akouō ἀκούω) and that LXX uses hypakouō to translate the Hebrew shamaʿ (שָׁמַע), since the latter regularly denotes a heedful or responsive hearing (and so "to obey"). We may therefore presume that Paul simply had in mind the character of response that would demonstrate the success of the gospel—not a mere hearing, but a responsive hearing, a hearing that was also an accepting of the gospel and an acting on its challenge and its promise. The faith in view, in other words, was not passive, but an engagement with the gospel, a response expressed in commitment in baptism to Jesus as Lord, and a life ordered by this new commitment. Nor, on the other hand, should Paul's language be drawn back into Reformation polemics by denigrating "obedient faith" as an "achievement." Paul's "obedience of faith" is responsive not self-asserted. It would probably not escape the notice of the audiences to whom the letter was read that only a few paragraphs later Paul makes a similar but more explicit contrast between a mere hearing of the law and a doing of the law (2:13) and appends that to the sharp contrast between doing evil and doing good as the basis of final judgment (2:6-10). The faith to which Paul's gospel called Gentiles like them (1:5-6) was a faith that expressed itself in obedience, that is, in terms of 2:7 and 10, in the commitment to persevering good-doing. Elsewhere Paul does not hesitate to speak of "the work of faith" (2 Thess 1:11). How this "obedience of faith/work of faith" related to doing/the works of the law is not made clear in these passages.

The relation of the two (faith and law) does become clearer in the second passage, a few paragraphs farther on in Romans—3:27. In the light of the gospel just stated in epigrammatic form (3:21-26) Paul concludes that boasting is excluded—not by "the law of works" but by "the law of faith." Here again the dissonance is so strong for many commentators that they find it necessary to infer that Paul is here using the term nomos (νόμος) not in the sense of "law," but rather in the sense "principle or order." But the paragraph ends with precisely the assertion that such commentators are unwilling to hear encapsulated in the phrase "the law of faith": "Do we then make the law invalid through faith? Not at all. On the contrary, we establish the law" (3:31). The nomos to which Paul refers at the end of the paragraph is certainly to be understood as the Jewish law/Torah, so it is very unlikely that he shifted the sense of nomos between 3:27 and 3:31. It is much more likely that "the law of faith" is a summary statement of his claim that "faith establishes the law": he can speak of "the law of faith" precisely because and only insofar as faith does "establish" the law.

The obvious inference to be drawn from this is that Paul saw faith as justification for the law, as the positive outcome of the law, as the means by which the law achieves its intended end. Here again, the sequel, the example of Abraham, demonstrates what Paul presumably had in mind (Rom 4): a life lived out of absolute trust in God and expressive of that trust is what God is looking for, and through it he can achieve his purposes. Such a life finds expression in and through the law; Abraham's acceptance of circumcision was "the seal of the righteousness of the faith which he had in his uncircumcision" (4:11). But the *basis* of that life is faith and only as the expression of that faith are the actions of the life acceptable to God as measured by the law given by God. The engagement with God is always "through faith," "from faith," "by faith," as the only channel through which God can effectively operate (4:11-20). In short, "the law of faith" denies that law and faith are mutually hostile opposites. It affirms rather that the law can only be explicated in faith terms and only be lived out through faith.

The equivalent in Galatians was Paul's rebuke in Gal 3:3: "Are you so foolish? Having begun with the Spirit are you now made complete with the flesh?" The beginning determines the ongoing and the end: as Spirit is the beginning and the end, so faith is the beginning in the end. To reduce the outworking of faith to particularly prescribed "works of the law" is the same as abandoning the Spirit for the flesh. At the same time, Paul can describe the outcome of a life led by the Spirit as "fulfilling the requirement of the law" (Rom 8:4), and in the same context can even speak of "the law of the Spirit" (8:2) just as he had spoken of "the law of faith" (3:27). Paul does not speak in terms of "faith" at these points (pistis does not occur between Rom 5:2 and 9:30), but the theological logic is the same.

The third striking passage is Gal 5:6: "In Christ Jesus neither circumcision counts for anything, nor uncircumcision, but faith operating effectively through love." Here it is impossible to see faith as something inactive or solely receptive. Paul clearly had in mind an active faith, a working faith. This is the same faith as the obeying faith, the faith that establishes the law. The point becomes clearer when it is recalled that Paul uses the same "neither circumcision, nor uncircumcision" formula in 1 Cor 7:19: "circumcision is nothing and uncircumcision is nothing, but keeping God's commandments." "Keeping God's commandments" is evidently the equivalent in Paul's thought to "faith operating effectively through love." In 1 Cor 7:19 there is an astonishing juxtaposition of commandments discounted and commandments affirmed; only someone who was able to discern that some commandments had been relativized, but without relativizing the commandments as a whole, could have so spoken. Similarly, the relativizing of circumcision as a divine requirement did not set faith operating through love over against the law as a whole, but rather indicated how the commandments that were still in force could/should be kept.

The point becomes clear a few verses later when Paul boldly affirms that "the whole law is fulfilled in one word, in the well known, 'You shall love your neighbor as yourself'" (Gal 5:14). Here, as in Rom 13:8-10, Paul evidently drew on the corporate memory of Jesus' teaching on the preeminence of the commandments to love God and the neighbor as oneself (e.g., Mark 12:28-31). Like Jesus, Paul does not set the love command over against the law, but sees the law as "summed up" (Rom 13:9), as "fulfilled" (Gal 5:14) in the love command. Moreover, most see a link in Paul's thought between Gal 5:14 and 6:2 (as between the talk of "the neighbor" in Rom 15:2 and the only other reference to "the neighbor" in 13:9-10): "the law of Christ" (Gal 6:2) is the love command, is the life lived out in embodiment of the love command in living for the neighbor as Jesus did (Rom 15:2-3). This can only be a further expression of what Paul meant by "faith operating effectively through love," the love that fulfils the whole law in a way that demonstrates the relative unimportance of the works of the law insisted on by his Christian Jewish opponents.

g. Faith as assent and commitment. Faith for Paul included both an assent to the claims made by the gospel and a commitment to the one proclaimed in the gospel. The assent is referred to several times: "that we will also live with him [Christ]" (Rom 6:8); "that God raised him from the dead" (10:9); "that Jesus died and rose again" (1 Thess 4:14). This content of faith is also alluded to in the many creedal formulations that Paul echoes, even when the term "faith" does not appear: "God raised him from the dead" (Rom 4:24-25; 7:4; 8:11; 10:9; 1 Cor 6:14; 15:4, 12, 20, etc.); "Christ died for us" (Rom 5:6, 8; 14:15; 1 Cor 8:11; 15:3; 2 Cor 5:14-15; 1 Thess 5:10); "he was handed over (for our sins)" (Rom 4:25; 8:32; 1 Cor 11:23; Gal 1:4; 2:20); "Christ died and was raised" (Rom 4:25; 8:34; 1 Cor 15:3-4; 2 Cor 5:15; 13:4; 1 Thess 4:14). Abraham also believed "that he would become the father of many nations" (Rom 4:18); Abraham "believed God" (Gal 3:6).

The commitment is expressed in various "believe in" formulations: believe "in (epi ἐπί) him" (Rom 4:5, 24; 10:11; also 1 Tim 1:16), "believe in (eis εἰς) him" (Rom 4:18; 10:14; Gal 2:16; Phil 1:29), and was probably acted out in the initiate's confession that "Jesus is Lord" in handing himself/herself over to that Lord in baptism (Rom 10:9; also 1 Cor 8:6; 12:3; 2 Cor 4:5; Phil 2:11; Col 2:6). This gives rise to the single most common reference of pistis, notably when Paul is recalling his audiences to their conversion and their ongoing commitment (Rom 1:8, 12; 1 Cor 2:5; 15:14, 17; 2 Cor 1:24; 13:5; Gal 3:14, 24, 26; Phil 1:25, 27; 2:17; Col 1:4, 23; 2:5, 7, 12; 1 Thess 1:3, 8; 3:2, 5-7; 2 Thess 1:4; 2:13; Phm 5-6). Paul is not alone in this as the other NT writings not otherwise covered in this article attest (1 Pet 1:5, 7, 9, 21; 5:9; 2 Pet 1:1, 5; 1 John 5:4; Jude 20; Rev 2:13, 19; 13:10; 14:12).

h. Faith and faithfulness. We have already observed that the ek pisteōs in Rom 1:17 might refer to God's faithfulness, and that it certainly has that sense in 3:3. We will see below that other usages of pistis can refer to Christ's faithfulness, as in Rom 3:25, or as a quality of "faithfulness, reliability, fidelity." Thus as one of the fruits of the Spirit (Gal 5:22), and elsewhere also linked with love (1 Thess 3:6; 5:8; Phlm 5; also Eph 6:23; 1 Tim 1:14; 2 Tim 1:13) or with patience (2 Thess 1:4) and with other virtues (2 Cor 8:7; also 1 Tim 2:15; 4:12; 6:11; 2 Tim 2:22; 3:10; Titus 2:2), the triad of faith, hope, and love appears in 1 Cor 13:13; Col 1:4-5; 1 Thess 1:3; 5:8.

It is important to observe that faith in Paul's theology is not simply the starting point for the Christian. The discussion of faith and law already is sufficient to demonstrate that Paul saw faith as the continuing basis for relation with God and for the ongoing life of faith. Here it is also important to grasp that he never saw faith as a formal thing, but always as the living expression of a life dependent on God and on Christ. A notable expression of this is Rom 14:22-23, where Paul makes it clear that all Christian conduct is to be seen as an expression of faith. Conduct, even somewhat controversial conduct, is acceptable to God when it is an expression of faith; but whatever is not done ek pisteōs is self-condemned; "for whatever is not of faith (ek pisteōs) is sin" (14:23). Here faith can stand, as elsewhere Spirit and love, as providing the spring and motivation for action. Christian conduct, not least in relation to fellow believers, should grow out of that

same relation of trust in God and submission to Christ the Lord, otherwise it will inevitably be divisive and self-destructive. No doubt Paul has the same perspective in mind when he asserts that "we walk by faith and not by sight" (2 Cor 5:7).

Equally significant is the clear implication of the passage as a whole (Rom 14) that different believers' faith will come to expression in different ways, different attitudes toward controversial issues and different patterns of conduct. This does not trouble Paul so long as the different patterns are truly expressive of faith, of trust in and submission to Jesus the Lord (14:4). The test is whether thanks can be given *ex anima* to God for the different and disputed actions (14:6), whether thereby is expressed the true submission of the proud creature to its Creator (1:21).

A similar implication as to differing levels or measures of faith is probably indicated in Paul's exhortation: "you [the Roman believers] should not think too highly of yourselves beyond what you ought to think, but observe proper moderation, as God has measured to each a measure of faith" (Rom 12:3). The implication of the compressed thought is that each has been doled out a measure of faith—different measures of faith. The thought, in fact, is similar to that expressed in 1 Cor 12:9: there is a gift of faith granted to some and not others. Again we should not see this faith as distinct from the faith that is salvation. The spectrum is unbroken: it is the same faith, the same openness to and trust in God that is in view. It is often attested in Christian communities that there are some who seem to have a deeper or more profound faith than others, whose conduct is more fully an expression of their faith. Paul's counsel, then, is that whatever a person's level of faith, the awareness of each person's dependence on Christ should be sufficient to prevent him or her from thinking of himself or herself too highly and disregarding fellow believers. Paul looks for faith to "grow, increase" (2 Cor 10:15; 2 Thess 1:3) and is concerned for the Thessalonians' "lack of faith" (1 Thess 3:10).

i. *Pistis Christou.* No one can doubt that for Paul, faith, the attitude and action of believing, is the medium through which God's saving righteousness came to effect. ". . . to all who believe" is one of the leitmotifs of Romans (1:16; 3:22; 10:4). Abraham is the paradigm of the one who believes and so is reckoned righteous (4:3-24). Salvation comes to those who respond to the gospel preaching by believing in their hearts that God raised Jesus from the dead and by confessing him as Lord (10:9-10, 14). Similarly, in Galatians, it is the believing that has been decisive (Gal 2:16; 3:6, 22). And the same emphasis is clear elsewhere (particularly 1 Cor 15:2, 11). In all these passages the verb pisteuō is used. It would seem obvious that pistis is the noun equivalent to the verb, as denoting the faith (pistis) of those who believe (pisteuō). And so it appears in many of the passages already examined: Paul's gospel seeking to educe "the obedience of faith" (Rom 1:5); Paul commending the "faith" of the recipients of his letters (Rom 1:8, 12); God who justifies circumcision "from faith" and uncircumcision "through faith" (3:30); Abraham's faith (4:5, 9-20); justified from faith (5:1-2); the misunderstanding of Israel as a goal to be pursued "from works" and not "from faith" (9:30, 32); the righteousness from faith and the word that effects faith (10:6, 8, 17); the faith by which they stand, contrasted with unfaith (11:20); and so on.

However, there has always been a minority opinion that by the phrase pistis Christou (πίστις Χριστοῦ) Paul meant to refer not to the believer's faith but to Christ's faith or faithfulness. And since the argument for this interpretation was restated by Hays it has gained a considerable following, notably in Martyn's *Galatians* commentary. The disputed verses are:

> Rom 3:22—"the righteousness of God through pisteōs Iēsou Christou (πίστεως Ἰησοῦ Χριστοῦ) to all who believe";
> Rom 3:25—where "through faith" seems to hang awkwardly in the sentence;
> Rom 3:26—God who "justifies the one from pisteōs Iēsou";
> Gal 2:16—"no one is justified from works of the law but only through pisteōs Iēsou Christou, and we have believed in Christ Jesus, in order that we might be justified from pisteōs Christou and not from works of the law";
> Gal 3:22—"in order that the promise might be from pisteōs Iēsou Christou to those who believe";
> Phil 3:9—"not having my own righteousness which is from the law, but the righteousness which is through pisteōs Iēsou Christou, the righteousness from God to the/that pisteis (epi tē pistei ἐπί τῇ πίστει).

The grammatical form does not tell either way. Pistis plus the genitive can either mean "faith of" (subjective genitive) or "faith in" (objective genitive). What seems to be the most natural in English ("faith of") is not determinative for the Greek—as other formulations indicate: pistis theou "faith/trust in God" (Mark 11:22); "the knowledge of Christ Jesus" (Phil 3:8).

The case for reading the genitive as a subjective genitive has several strong features: 1) It puts the weight on God's action in Christ; God justifies on the basis of Christ's faithfulness on the cross; the emphasis rules out any hint that human faith might be a "work" of self-achievement; 2) It fills out what otherwise is a rather sparse sequence of references to Christ's action in accepting death on the cross; the only other near equivalent is the description of Christ's death as an act of "obedience" (Rom 5:19). Hays makes much of the

narrative structure encapsulated for him in the phrase "the faith of Christ;" 3) In several of the references listed above the phrase pistis Christou is complemented by human believing; to take pistis Christou as referring to the same believing would be tautologous.

On the other hand, the emphasis on God's action in and through Christ does not depend on reading a subjective genitive. Although Paul otherwise does not elaborate the point (and "the faith of Jesus Christ" itself is not much of an elaboration), it is clear enough in passages like Rom 5:8; 8:3, 34; and 15:3, and is generally implicit in any of Paul's references to Jesus' death. It is worth observing that "the faith of Christ" has no verbal equivalent in talk of Christ "believing," and that the narrative of Jesus most likely in mind (synopticlike Jesus tradition) does not make anything of Jesus believing or of Jesus' own "faith/faithfulness." Moreover, the repetition of pistis and pisteuō in referring to human response to the gospel can without strain be understood as repetition for effect, especially when (as in Rom 3:22) the verb enables Paul to repeat one of his major themes —"to all who believe."

The case for reading the genitive as an objective genitive is basically that in most of Paul's argumentation in the relevant letters pistis obviously serves as the noun equivalent to the verb describing the believing or act of believing of those who respond to the gospel. Particularly noticeable is the key assertion in Paul's exposition in Gal 3:6-9, where, as already noted, Paul takes up from Gen 15:6:

> Just as "Abraham believed (episteusen ἐπίστευσεν) God, and it was reckoned to him for righteousness." Know then that those of faith (hoi ek pisteōs οἱ ἐκ πίστεως), they are Abraham's sons. . . . Consequently, those of faith (hoi ek pisteōs) are blessed with faithful (pistō πιστῷ) [that is, presumably, trusting] Abraham.

Here it is clear that hoi ek pisteōs denote those who believe as Abraham believed. Their identity derives from that faith, that is, from their believing as Abraham believed. A reference to "those who derive identity from faithful Jesus" would make no sense of the sequence of Paul's exposition.

The importance of recognizing this reference in the phrase ek pisteōs lies in the fact that it probably carries the other ek pisteōs phrases with it (2:16; 3:7-9, 11-12, 22, 24; 5:5). In other words, ek pisteōs probably defines the state or individuals referred to as derived "from faith," whose status or identity is determined "from faith," that is, the faith with which Abraham believed, as also those who are sons of Abraham in that they believe as he did and are thereby counted righteous as he was counted righteous. To be noted at once is the fact that the first ek pisteōs reference is the crucial Gal 2:16, and that Gal 3:6, in effect, elaborates the first of the ek pisteōs references and so also the first and second of the pistis Christou references. If these first two pistis Christou references were ambiguous for the recipients of Paul's letters (dia pisteōs Iēsou Christou διὰ πίστεως Ἰησοῦ Χριστοῦ, and ek pisteōs Iēsou Christou), then the exposition of Abraham's faith would surely have indicated to them that what Paul had in mind was "(their) faith in Jesus Christ."

In addition, it must be judged unlikely that in the course of his exposition in Gal 3 Paul varied the referent of his several pistis and ek pisteōs references between the Galatians' faith and Christ's faith. When Paul sums up the argument running from 3:6, "in order that we might receive the promise of the Spirit through faith" (3:14), he is clearly referring back to the same faith as that which Abraham exercised, the same faith to which the blessing of Abraham was promised (3:6-9). Likewise, when Paul sums up the fuller sweep of the argument (3:6-26) by claiming that "you are all sons of God, through this faith, in Christ Jesus" (3:26), it is hardly likely that by "this faith" he means "this faith of Christ Jesus," since the "in Christ Jesus" would follow exceedingly awkwardly. The "in Christ Jesus" obviously refers to the position into which "this faith" sets them; that is, the faith that has determined Paul's converts to be Abraham's seed (3:29), 3:26 referring back to the crucial definition of 3:6. Again, it would be very odd if Paul had intended to refer two or three of the sequence of pistis references to Christ's faithfulness, when the thrust of the passage is that faith like Abraham's believing is what has served to bring Gentile believers into the blessing promised to Abraham and his descendants.

The problem, rarely faced up to by the proponents of the "faith of Christ" reading is that in order to sustain that reading in a few crucial cases they virtually have to read all the supporting pistis references in the same way. But then that leaves Paul's verb (pisteuō) with virtually no noun partner or equivalent. The result is a major skewing of the exposition away from its most obvious line of thought, which leaves the means through which the Galatians receive the blessing of justification unspoken, apart from the occasional use of the verb (2:16; 3:22).

The same is true of the equivalent passage in Rom 3–4. Here again the ek pisteōs motif runs through the central line of argument like a silver thread (1:17; 3:26, 30; 4:16; 5:1; 9:30, 32; 10:6; 14:23). And here again the critical parallel is between Abraham's believing and being counted righteous (4:3, 5) and the faith through which or from which the first Christians were justified (3:30; 5:1). "The righteousness of faith" (4:13) is, of course, the righteousness promised to faith, to those who are "of the faith (ek pisteōs) of Abraham."

In short, the subjective genitive reading of the pistis Christou texts ("the faith of Christ") involves a good deal of reading into Paul's argument and makes too little sense of Paul's regular ek pisteōs motif. In contrast, the objective genitive reading ("faith in Christ") fits well with the flow of Paul's argument in both Romans and Galatians and provides a noun phrase equivalent to Paul's call to "believe in" Christ.

j. The faith. Pistis as denoting a "body of belief or teaching," that which is believed rather than the act/attitude of believing, may already be in view in Gal 1:23, itself a statement stretching back to the first decade or so of emergent Christianity: the report of the Judean churches that "he who was formerly our persecutor now preaches the faith which he once tried to destroy." But at such an early stage of the emergence of "faith" as a key marker of the new sect it is more likely that pistis still carries the primary sense of "believing": Paul had tried to destroy the movement based on belief in Messiah Jesus, and thereafter preached the need so to believe. The same sense is probably foremost in Gal 3:3, 2, 5 ("the hearing of faith") and Gal 3:23-25 ("the coming of faith"), since what Paul had in view was probably the realization of the possibility for Gentiles to become heirs of Abraham's blessing simply through faith. Sometimes mentioned under this heading are Rom 1:5 and 12:6; but again the former probably means "faith's obedience," and the latter "the measure of trust."

What cannot be disputed, however, is that pistis in the sense of a "faith to be believed, a body of belief/teaching" is well established in the Pastoral Epistles (1 Tim 1:19; 3:9; 4:1, 6; 5:8; 6:10, 12, 21; 2 Tim 2:18; 3:8; 4:7; Titus 1:13; also Jude 3). Indeed, pistis as "the faith" is such a dominant emphasis in the Pastorals that it probably influences several of the other more ambiguous usages (1 Tim 1:2; 3:9, 13; Titus 1:4). In itself the usage is somewhat ambiguous. But in the Pastorals "the faith" is of a piece with "the teaching" (1 Tim 4:16; 6:1; 2 Tim 3:10; Titus 2:7, 10), "sound teaching" (1 Tim 1:10; 2 Tim 4:3; Titus 1:9; 2:1), "the good teaching" (1 Tim 4:6), "the teaching which accords with godliness" (1 Tim 6:3), "sound words" (1 Tim 6:3; 2 Tim 1:13), and "that which has been entrusted" (1 Tim 6:20; 2 Tim 1:12, 14). A notable feature of the Pastorals is the sequence of "faithful sayings" (pistos ho logos πιστὸς ὁ λόγος) (1 Tim 1:15; 3:1; 4:9; 2 Tim 2:11; Titus 1:9; 3:8). So it is hard to escape the conclusion that a more formalized sense of pistis has emerged by the time of the Pastorals, and that the Pastorals were intended to reinforce that sense. And this remains true even if the Pastorals still retain much of the earlier Pauline sense of pistis as the vital and defining (Christian) act/attitude of believing (1 Tim 1:4, 5, 14; 2:7, 15; 4:12; 6:11; 2 Tim 1:5, 13; 2:18, 22; 3:10, 15; Titus 1:1; 2:2; 3:15). Repeated characterizations of believers as "faithful" (pistos) are also a step beyond the earlier Paul (1 Tim 3:11; 4:3, 10, 12; 5:16; 6:2; 2 Tim 2:2; Titus 1:6). In view of the discussion of the repeated use of the formulation "faith which is in Christ Jesus" (pistis en Christō Iēsou) is particularly noticeable (1 Tim 1:14; 3:13; 2 Tim 1:13; 3:15).

2. New Testament usage apart from Paul

Although it is Paul's usage that gives "faith" its most distinctive Christian imprint, pistis/pisteuō are by no means absent elsewhere in the NT.

a. Faith in the Synoptic Gospels. The majority of references to faith (or lack of faith) in the Synoptic Gospels occur in relation to miracles—nearly two-thirds, and in Mark eight of thirteen. Typically the tradition recalls Jesus as making statements like, "Do not fear, only believe" (Mark 5:36), "All things are possible to him who believes" (Mark 9:23), and, most frequent, "Your faith has saved you/made you well" (Mark 5:34//Matt 9:22: Luke 7:50; 17:19). The encounter with the centurion at Capernaum is recalled as notable for the great impression that his faith made on Jesus (Matt 8:10//Luke 7:9); and Matthew draws the same point from Jesus' other known encounter with a supplicating non-Jew (Matt 15:28). The motif is so regular and consistent that it must derive from a shared memory of Jesus' mission: that he called for and evoked such faith.

The Evangelists do not attempt to portray the faith as faith in Jesus himself (the only exception is Mark 9:42/Matt 18:6). What the tradition envisages is faith in God, reliance on the power of God to heal (e.g., Mark 2:5-12), or to answer prayer (Mark 11:22-24//Matt 21:21-22; Matt 17:20//Luke 17:6), or generally trust in God's care and provision (Matt 6:30//Luke 12:28)—though only Mark 11:22 explicitly speaks of "faith in God." If we assume that behind Jesus' usage lay the Hebrew ʾemunah or ʾemeth and the Hiphil (heʾemin) of ʾmn, it should be noted that the concept would be of "firm faith," faith that is steady and committed in its reliance on God. It was the firmness of the faith of the centurion (Matt 8:10/Luke 7:9), the boldness of the faith of the friends of the paralyzed man (Mark 2:1-12) and of the woman with the hemorrhage (Mark 5:34//Matt 9:22), and the persistence of the faith of Bartimaeus (Mark 10:52) that impressed Jesus. It was to an unyielding trust in God that Jesus gave assurance of answered prayer (Mark 11:22-24//Matt 7:7-11//Luke 11:9-13). In contrast, the condemnation of a "faithless (apistos ἄπιστος) generation" (Mark 9:19) probably echoes Deut 32:20—"a perverse generation, sons in whom there is no faithfulness."

Equally striking is the complete absence of any reference to Jesus' own faith, or to Jesus as "believing." The one exception might be Mark 9:23—it is because Jesus has faith that "all things are possible" to him; but the primary function of the reference is to encourage the father of the boy to believe (9:24). Elsewhere the adjective "faithful" (pistos) appears only in reference to characters in Jesus' parables (Matt 24:45//Luke 12:42; Matt 25:21, 23//Luke 19:17; Luke 16:10-12). Jesus is presented not so much as the one who trusts in God/is faithful to God as the medium of God's healing power to those who trust in God. In short, Jesus is presented neither as the example of one who believed, nor as the one in whom subsequent hearers (of the Gospels) should believe. This both confirms the pre-Easter content and character of this Synoptic material and undermines the view that the story of Jesus was told as a narrative of Jesus' faith/fullness.

b. Believing in the Gospel of John. John's Gospel never uses the term pistis; in the Johannine writings the word appears only in 1 John 5:4. In some distinction from Paul, John prefers to use action verbs rather than the more static nouns. For example, he uses *seeing* (blepō βλέπω, theaomai θεάομαι, theōreō θεωρέω, idein ἰδεῖν and horan ὥραν, from horaō—together more than 110 times), rather than *sight*. He prefers *knowing* (ginōskō γινώσκω—56; eidenai, from [horaō] ὁράω—85) to *knowledge*. He uses *abiding* (menō μένω) and "coming to" (erchomai pros ἔρχομαι πρός). So it is perhaps less surprising that John prefers the verb *believe* (pisteuō—98) rather than the noun pistis (never used).

The importance of the theme is evident from John's own stated objective in writing:

> in order that you may (come to) believe that Jesus is the Messiah, the Son of God, and that in believing you may have life in his name (20:31).

This objective is clear from the beginning and is frequently alluded to (1:7; 6:29, 69; 8:31; 9:35-38; 11:27; 12:36, 46). Such believing exempts from judgment (3:18), frees from sins (8:24), is promised sight of the glory of God (11:40), and, most commonly, is promised eternal life (3:15-16, 36; 5:24; 6:35, 40, 47; 11:25-26). Equally prominent is the repeated rebuke of failure to believe (5:38, 44-47; 6:36, 64; 7:5, 48; 8:45-46; 10:25-26; 12:37-39; 26:9).

John's assumption is that the signs that Jesus did are sufficient in themselves to win such believing; he narrates his sequence of signs precisely with that in view—as 20:30-31 makes clear (2:11; 4:53; 6:64, 69; 10:37-38, 42; 11:15, 42, 45, 48; 12:11, 37; 13:19; 14:11; 20:8, 25, 29). Yet at the same time he makes a point of warning that a faith based on miracles as such is inadequate: initially the people believe in his name because of his signs, "but Jesus did not entrust himself to them, because he knew everyone" (2:23-24); he rebukes or challenges the royal official from Capernaum, "Unless you see signs and wonders you will not believe" (4:48); the crowd in Galilee obviously needs to move on from a faith that looks only to satisfaction of everyday hunger (6:30).

This pressing for a faith that sees beyond the actions of Jesus, or the testimony of the Evangelist himself, is a recurring theme in the central chapters of the Gospel. The light having shone in the darkness (1:9; 3:19-21) begins a process of separating shallow or merely inquiring faith into a faith truly in Jesus as the one sent from God: Nicodemus who has still to gain basic insight (3:12); the Samaritans who grow in faith (4:39-42); the crowds who need to move on from belief in Jesus as another Moses to recognition that he himself is the bread from heaven (6:30, 36); the Jerusalem crowds who hesitate between belief and unbelief (7:31, 48; 8:30-45); the blind man as characterizing the movement from blindness to sight (9:35-38); the authorities who believed in him but did not confess it for fear of being expelled from the synagogue (12:42). The disciples themselves are those who have moved on to that deeper faith (2:22; 7:38-39; 13:19; 14:29; 19:35; 20:8-9, 26-29). John's hope evidently was that the words of Christian testimony (his own words) would bring such waverers to full faith and any such secret disciples to open confession (17:20-21; 19:35).

A marked distinction from the Synoptics is that in John the belief is in Christ; the formula pisteuein eis (πιστεύειν εἰς "believe into") occurs no less than 35 times (usually "believe in him"). To believe in Jesus was to believe in God, the Father who had sent him (12:44; 14:1, 10-11; 16:27, 31; 17:8). It is equally clear from passages like 2:22 and 7:38-39 that John understands faith as Easter faith, faith in the full light of the complete revelation that was the mission, death, and resurrection of Christ. This is the primary reason why John's Gospel is so different in its presentation of Jesus from the other three.

In 1 John there is again the warning against a wrong or inadequate belief (4:1), and a clear statement of what "right" belief is—in Jesus as the Christ, the Son of God (5:1, 5, 10). Proof of this right belief is the evidence of being loved and loving one another (3:23; 4:16). The aim of the letter is similar to that of the Gospel: "I write these things to you who believe in the name of the Son of God, so that you may know that you have eternal life" (5:13).

c. Faith in Acts. As John is written to bring audiences to believe, so Acts is written to record how the first preachers and missionaries brought many to belief, in widening circles: the initial expansion (4:4; 5:14), the Samaritans (8:12-13), the coastal region (9:42), Cornelius (11:17; 15:7), the breakthrough in Antioch (11:21), and consistently during Paul's mission as a mark of his success (13:12, 48; 14:1, 23; 16:31, 34; 17:12, 34; 18:8; 19:18; 21:25). As in John the primary object of such believing is Christ (9:42; 10:43; 11:17; 14:23; 16:32; 18:8; 22:19), "faith" in Christ (20:21; 24:24; 26:18). Luke makes a point of including the words of James to indicate that the gospel was successful not only among Gentiles—"many thousands of believers among the Jews" (21:20). The most poignant of Paul's appeals is to King Agrippa when Paul is on trial: "King Agrippa, do you believe the prophets? I know that you believe" (26:27).

A striking feature that becomes most obvious in Acts is that faith soon became the principal identifying characteristic of nascent Christianity, at least from

within the new movement. The first Christians can be described simply as hoi pisteuontes (οἱ πιστεύοντες), "those who believe" (Acts 2:44; Rom 3:22; 1 Cor 14:22; 1 Thess 1:7; 2:10, 13), or hoi pisteusantes (οἱ πιστεύσαντες), "those who believed/became believers" (Acts 4:32; 2 Thess 1:10), or hoi pepisteukotes (οἱ πεπιστευκότες), "those who had become (and remained) believers" (Acts 15:5; 18:27; 19:18; 21:20, 25); or indeed as (hoi) pistoi, "(the) believers/ faithful" (Acts 10:45; 16:1, 15). Luke can also speak of "the faith" in the same connection, but with the same issue unclear as to whether the thought is of the movement characterized by such believing or a body of belief (6:7; 13:8; 14:22; 16:5).

As in his Gospel Luke portrays a strong link between faith and miracle (3:16; 14:9) and does not hesitate to portray miracles as faith-producing (8:13; 13:12; 19:18). But his account is more ambiguous as to the link between believing and the Spirit: Stephen and Barnabas are "full of the Holy Spirit and faith" (6:5; 11:24); Cornelius receives the same gift as the first disciples received at Pentecost "when we believed in the Lord Jesus Christ" (11:17); at the same time, however, Luke seems to envisage situations where individuals have believed and have not yet received the Spirit (8:12-13, 16; 19:2).

d. Faith in James. James' talk of faith resonates with other NT writings, but has some distinctive elements. The one reference to faith in respect of Christ could be read either as "faith in Christ" or "the faith of Christ" (2:1), the latter being that much more likely than in the Pauline Letters, since James is so evidently echoing Jesus' own concern for the poor (2:5-8). Like Jesus he calls for a faith that is firm and does not doubt God's generosity (1:5-8), and his talk of "the prayer of faith as effective in saving/healing the sick" (5:15) presumably likewise harks back to the mission of Jesus. And like Paul, he sees that the testing of faith produces patience and patience maturity (1:3; compare Rom 5:3-4).

The most distinctive feature of James in regard to faith, however, has always been seen as his treatment of faith and works (2:14-26). It is hard to escape the strong impression that James is reacting either to Paul himself on the subject or to some report of Paul's teaching. The degree to which James matches the line of argument in Rom 3:27–4:22 is uncanny otherwise and hard to explain:

	Romans	James
The issue posed in terms of faith and works	3:27-28	2:18
Significance of claiming "God is one"	3:29-30	2:19
Appeal to Abraham as test case	4:1-2	2:20-22
Citation of proof text, Gen 15:6	4:3	2:20-22
Interpretation of Gen 15:6	4:4-21	2:23
Conclusion	4:22	2:24

What is also striking is that James reproduces what seems to have been the familiar line of Jewish interpretation of Abraham and Gen 15:6, and almost certainly represents how many Jews, including Christian Jews, must have responded to Paul.

As a Christian statement either in counter to Paul or to complement Paul, James is a reminder that Christians should not assume a too sharp antithesis between faith and works, and that interpretations of Paul that make that assumption need to be corrected, not so much by James, but in the light of Paul's own fuller treatment of Christian obligation and responsibility. In other words, the key treatment of justification by faith (by Paul) needs to be more carefully nuanced than has too often been the case, rather than James simply being dismissed as failing to see Paul's point.

e. Faith in Hebrews. The only other NT writing for which faith/faithfulness is of major significance is Hebrews, though in contrast to John, use of the noun (32) far exceeds that of the verb (2). Like the rest, Hebrews regards faith as the basic starting point for his readers (4:2-3; 6:1). Indicative of the influence of Hab 2:4 in shaping early Christian thought is its use (with a slightly different text form) in Heb 10:38-39, obviously understood in a "Pauline" way. Characteristic of Hebrews is the exhortation that the recipients of the letter should "approach [into the very presence of God within the heavenly holy of holies] with a true heart in full assurance of faith" (Heb 10:22).

One of the most distinctive features of Hebrews is the emphasis on being "faithful" (**pistos**). True to his Jewish heritage, God is the one who above all is "faithful," whose promise can be utterly relied on (10:23; 11:11). Moses was faithful as a servant in God's house (3:2, 5). And past heroes and current leaders are held out as examples of faith to be imitated (6:12; 13:7). But the primary pattern is provided by Christ himself—the "merciful and faithful high priest" (2:17), worthy of more honor than Moses, as a son is worthy of greater honor than a servant (3:3-6). Hebrews does not hesitate to describe Jesus as "the pioneer and perfecter of (our) faith" (12:2). In all this the emphasis is not so much on the faithfulness of Christ in the terms usually argued for **pistis Christou** in Paul, as on Jesus who as one entirely like us has opened the way through death to lead God's children through to glory (the theme of 2:9-18), or, alternatively, as the one who has already run the race from beginning to end and is already seated at God's right hand to inspire and encourage those still in the midst of the race (12:1-2).

This last comes as the climax to one of the most famous chapters in the NT—the roll call of heroes of the faith, from Abel to the nameless martyrs of the more recent past (11:4-40). In the midst comes the stark observation that "without faith it is impossible to please God (though the emphasis is on belief rather than belief in), for whoever would approach him must believe that he exists and that he rewards those who seek him" (11:6).

Before Abraham, it is Noah who "became an heir of the righteousness that is in accord with faith" (11:7). But Abraham is central in the roll call, as we might expect from both Jewish tradition and Paul (11:8-19). Notably, however, it is the full sweep of his faith that is highlighted: his obedience in setting out for the land of promise (11:8-10), his trust in the faithful God to provide an heir (11:11-12), and his readiness to offer up his son Isaac (11:17-19). In some contrast to Paul, it is not only the life-giving power of God in enabling procreation that foreshadows the resurrection of Jesus, but Abraham's trust that Isaac would be restored to him if he went through with the sacrifice (11:19). And Moses too is remembered as an example of faith rather than for his giving the law (11:23-28).

In some ways the most distinctive but also intriguing and puzzling feature of Hebrews on this subject is the definition the unknown author provides of faith —11:1-3:

> faith is the **hypostasis** (ὑπόστασις) of things hoped for, the **elenchos** (ἔλεγχος) of things not seen. . . . By faith we understand that the worlds/ages were prepared by the word of God, so that what is seen was made from things that are not visible."

By **elenchos** he presumably means "proof (or conviction)," faith as being sure about things unseen, in contrast to confidence in what can be seen and controlled. The heroes of faith well exemplified this confidence in the face of the unknown. More problematic is the **hypostasis**, which normally denotes the essence or basic nature of an entity, its essence or reality. Here it trades on the Hebrew notion of hope, not as in Greek with a note of uncertainty (as in English usage), but as expectation of good, confidence in God: faith is the basis, or guarantee, or even realization of that hope. The closest parallel in the NT is Rom 8:24-25, coming as it does at the end of the paragraph 8:18-25.

Bibliography: H. W. Attridge. *Hebrews.* Hermeneia (1989) 308–14; C. K. Barrett. "The Allegory of Abraham, Sarah, and Hagar in the Argument of Galatians." *Essays on Paul* (1982) 154–70; D. A. Campbell. "The Meaning of *PISTIS* and *NOMOS* in Paul: A Linguistic and Structural Perspective." *JBL* 111 (1992) 91–103; J. D. G. Dunn. *Romans.* WB 38 (1988); J. D. G. Dunn. ed., *Paul and the Mosaic Law* (2001); J. D. G. Dunn. *The Theology of Paul the Apostle* (1998); J. D. G. Dunn. *The New Perspective on Paul* (2005); D. G. Garlington. *Faith, Obedience and Perseverance* (1994); R. B. Hays. *The Faith of Jesus Christ: The Narrative Substructure of Galatians 3:1–4:11* (2002); B. W. Longenecker. "*Pistis* in Romans 3.25: Neglected Evidence for the "Faithfulness of Christ."

NTS 39 (1993) 478–80; B. W. Longenecker. *The Triumph of Abraham's God: The Transformation of Identity in Galatians* (1998); C. D. Marshall. *Faith as a Theme in Mark's Narrative* (1989); J. L. Martyn. *Galatians.* (1997); D. Moo. *The Epistle to the Romans.* NICNT (1996); H. Räisänen. "The 'Law' of Faith and the Spirit." *Jesus, Paul and Torah: Collected Essays* (1992) 48–68; V. Rhee. *Faith in Hebrews: Analysis within the Context of Christology, Eschatology, and Ethics* (2001); R. Schnackenburg. *The Gospel According to St John Vol. 1* (1968) 558–75; M. Silva. "Faith Versus Works of Law in Galatians." *Justification and Variegated Nomism. Vol. 2: The Paradoxes of Paul* (2004) 217–48; I. G. Wallis. *The Faith of Jesus Christ in Early Christian Traditions* (1995); S. K. Williams. "The Hearing of Faith: *AKŌ PISTĒS* in Galatians iii." *NTS* 35 (1989) 82–93.

JAMES D. G. DUNN

FALCON [אַיָּה ʾayyah]. Several kinds of falcons are found in Palestine. Thus, a reference to "the falcon of any kind" would make perfect sense in the lists of unclean birds (Lev 11:14 = Deut 14:13; NRSV has "the kite of any kind"). However, it is uncertain which bird the onomatopoeic word ʾayyah actually designated: the falcon, the HAWK, the BUZZARD, or the KITE. Arguably, the keen-eyed falcon is a strong candidate, at least in the case of Job 28:7, where NRSV translates: "That path no bird of prey knows, and the falcon's eye has not seen it." *See* BIRDS OF THE BIBLE.

GÖRAN EIDEVALL

FALL, THE. The identification of the story of ADAM and EVE as an account of "the fall" in Western civilization is largely due to the influence of Paul and the way he was read by Augustine. In Judaism, the story of the garden of Eden does not carry quite the same weight. Nevertheless, it is clear from the final canonical form of Israel's Scriptures that the stories of human rebellion in Gen 1–11 constitute the background against which God's election of Abraham (and eventually that of Israel) takes place. Because the account of the fall is the first narrative of disobedience in this literary unit, it warrants careful attention.

    A. Adam and Eve in the Book of Genesis
    B. Genesis 2–3 in the Context of Genesis 1–11
    C. Adam and Eve in the Christian Bible
    Bibliography

A. Adam and Eve in the Book of Genesis

The narrative begins with the creation of Adam, his being led into the garden, and being told that he may eat from all the trees in Eden save one, the tree of the knowledge of good and evil. Should he eat from this single tree he will surely die. Surprisingly, no explicit reason is given as to why this tree, out of all the others, should be forbidden. After this brief account of the

giving of the commandment, the narrative takes a brief detour to describe the naming of the animals and the creation of Eve. Then the story comes to a full stop before it begins again in a new scene with only Eve and a serpent on center stage. This crafty animal questions Eve about the nature of the garden. Eve discloses to the snake that should they eat or even touch the forbidden tree they will die. The snake then interrupts and corrects Eve's construal: there is no such penalty for eating of the tree. Rather, God is simply jealous and knows that should she eat of the fruit she herself will become divine-like, knowing both good and evil.

The biggest challenge for the reader of this story is making sense of the snake's intervention. At first glance, it looks as though the snake is correct. After all, Adam and Eve do not die after they consume the fruit (and the threatened penalty—you shall surely die—no doubt connotes a swift physical death at the hand of heaven); indeed Adam continues to live until the ripe old age of 930. And the snake's impugning of God's motives also seems to be—quite strikingly and surprisingly—confirmed (Gen 3:22). No doubt for these reasons among others, the ancient Gnostics saw the snake as the hero of the story.

How does one account for these difficulties? Some scholars have pointed out that there are a number of affinities between this tale and wisdom traditions. In those materials the keeping of commandments is tied to the notion of "life" whereas disobedience is framed as "death" (compare Prov 5:5; 20–23; 7:21-27). A similar trope can be found near the conclusion of Deuteronomy when Moses sums up the terms of the covenant to the Israelites who are about to enter the promised land, "I call heaven and earth to witness against you today that I have set before you life and death, blessings and curses. Choose life so that you and your descendants may live, loving the Lord your God, obeying him, and holding fast to him; for that means life to you and length of days, so that you may live in the land that the Lord swore to give to your ancestors, to Abraham, to Isaac and to Jacob" (Deut 30:19-20). Here we can see a striking overlap between the condition established in Eden at the beginning of the Torah and the nature of the promised land that concludes the Torah. Entrance and abiding within these localities conveys "life" to those so blessed. And most significantly, their continued presence there depends on the observance of a command or set of commandments. Their exile from the land is accompanied with the threat of death. In this light, it is certainly key that the terms used to describe the sending forth of Adam and Eve from Eden (Gen 3:24) are words that elsewhere connote nations being driven from their lands.

Nevertheless, there still remains the problem of why God prevents Adam and Eve from consuming the tree of the knowledge of good and evil. Does consuming this fruit really make one like God (Gen 3:22)? Some solve this problem by arguing that the clause "good and evil" is a merism that connotes a totality of knowledge. In others words, Adam and Eve wish to rise above their status as finite human beings and approach the level of divinity. Yet, given other usages of this phrase in the OT, it is more likely that the term refers to the type of knowledge associated with human maturation. Indeed, many have compared the story of Adam and Eve to that of Enkidu in the Gilgamesh epic (*See* GILGAMESH, EPIC OF). For in that tale, Enkidu becomes fully human through having sexual intercourse with a woman, bathing, anointing, and putting on clothes. He is also said to become godlike in the human wisdom he has attained. And like Adam and Eve, the curse of acquiring such knowledge is that he becomes aware of his mortality. By becoming a mature human being Enkidu is made aware of the death sentence that stands over every living thing, a detail that never bothered him when he was an animal. In a sense, as Irenaeus noted already in the 2nd cent. CE, by eating from the forbidden tree, Adam and Eve grow up.

Yet there is one dramatic difference between the story of the humanization of Enkidu and the maturation of Adam and Eve. For Enkidu, the means by which he achieves this end are undeniably good. To be sure, his becoming human includes the tragic feature of learning about death, but his newfound knowledge will also empower him to do things he never imagined before. The story of Adam and Eve is not ambiguous in this fashion. Here the progress of the human race is also a regression.

B. Genesis 2–3 in the Context of Genesis 1–11

It should be noted that precisely this sort of tragic flaw will accompany all the stories of human advancement in Gen 1–11. It is a striking fact that the development of many of the cultural skills that serve to distinguish the place of the human person within the world is associated with some sort of rebellion. The dawning of agriculture, e.g., that begins with the expulsion of Adam and Eve, is not seen as a blessing bestowed by God but as a punishment for the disobedience of a command. Similarly, the account of the beginning of metal casting, the manufacture of musical instruments, and the skills of animal husbandry all take place within the line of CAIN, a line that begins with a single murder and concludes with Lamech's boast of even greater violence (Gen 4:17-24). All of these skills, which remain human inventions within the book of Genesis, were construed as benefactions given to humanity in Mesopotamian tradition. There, the humanization of the human race takes place by the gift of special knowledge bequeathed to specific guilds. So precious is this knowledge that Atrahasis, the hero of the flood story in the Mesopotamian story, takes all sorts of craftsmen on board so that these skills are not lost as a result of the impending deluge. What was once given by the gods should not be taken lightly. The Bible's own approach

to these inventions could not be more different. Noah, unlike Atrahasis, takes no interest in these crafts and the descendants of Cain and all they had learned perish in the turbulent waters.

The key to seeing why the Bible takes this particular approach to this matter becomes clear in the story of the origin of the great city of Babylon. In the Gilgamesh epic, the building of the great city of Uruk is seen as the crowning achievement of this great king's life. The reader is exhorted to gaze upon the greatness of the city walls and the temple built therein. By this great architectural feat Gilgamesh has secured the only sort of immortality known to the ancient world—he has left behind a monument that will perpetuate the memory of his great name. The account of the building of the city of BABEL in Gen 11 is a conscious inversion of the Gilgamesh epic. Many readers have focused undue attention on the tower of Babel and have understood the hubris that lies at the root of this story to be the desire to storm the heavens. But the description of the tower is part of a grammatical construction known as a hendiadys (two words that convey one thought). Thus the phrase "city and tower" conveys the sense of an enormous city (compare Deut 1:28, which describes the large cities of Canaan in terms strikingly similar to the city and tower of Babel).

But if this is the case, what is wrong with building a great city? The hymns to Zion in the biblical Psalter look strikingly similar to the hymn to Uruk that graces the opening lines of the Gilgamesh epic. In Ps 48 the Israelite pilgrim is exhorted to enter the gates of the city and gaze upon its wall and fortifications as a way of honoring God. But there is a difference between Zion and Babel. Babel is a city that is built by human design and for specific human ends ("to make a name for ourselves," 11:4). Jerusalem, on the other hand, is a city founded by God. To be sure, human beings assist in its construction, but the city comes solely from the design and intention of God. So it should not be surprising that the error of the builders of Babel is the subject of a dramatic theological inversion at the turn of Gen 12. Here God enters into human history to stop the avalanche of sin that has been growing over the previous eleven chapters and to call Abraham forth from Babylon to journey to a land that God will reveal. In return for the faith Abraham will show in this mission, God promises to make his name great (Gen 12:2).

Greatness depends, then, not on specific human achievements but unqualified obedience to a divine command. And in this fashion, we can better appreciate why the story of Adam and Eve proceeds in the manner it does. It is not the case that the knowledge that Adam and Eve acquire is in itself bad or inappropriate to human beings; the issue is the manner by which it has been achieved. Indeed, this is one of the central themes of the entire primeval cycle. The story of those great moments of culture-founding that were so celebrated in the ANE is highly qualified in the Bible's own telling. The specific ends that are accomplished are not evil in and of themselves (knowledge of good and evil, forging of metal instruments, the construction of an enormous city); rather, the problem lies in the means by which they are carried out. In God's design all of these and more are the proper patrimony of humanity provided that they attend carefully to their Lord's commands and render him the obedience that he is due.

C. Adam and Eve in the Christian Bible

As we have seen, the fall of humanity in the OT begins with the story of Adam and Eve and culminates in the building of the city of Babylon. With the call of Abraham, God begins to set aright the world that has steered so far off course. The entrance into the promised land is construed to be a fitting consolation for the loss of Eden. In the writing of Paul, however, this bigger frame is reduced to a single snapshot—the story of the single transgression by Adam and Eve. Though there may be multiple reasons for this adjustment, no doubt one explanation was certainly central: for Paul the antipode to the disobedience of the first man was the saving activity of the last man.

Crucial for Paul, as indeed for all the writers of the NT, was the dramatic intervention of God to raise and vindicate his son who suffered a horrific and ignominious death on the cross. This act was, from the very beginning, construed in such a way as to go far beyond the saving of a single person. In order to underscore the cosmic significance of the event, Paul contrasted the work of Christ to that of Adam, "But in fact Christ has been raised from the dead, the first fruits of those who have died. But since death came through a man, the resurrection of the dead has come through a man; for as all die in Adam, so all will be made alive in Christ" (1 Cor 15:20-22). Paul was certainly aware that the word ʾadham (אָדָם) in Hebrew was both a personal name of a figure in Genesis and a designation of all humanity. And so, Paul reasoned, if what happened to the first Adam was passed on to all humanity then all the more so for the second or last Adam. *See* SECOND ADAM.

It is precisely this sort of argument to which Paul returns in his last and most mature letter, the Epistle to the Romans. Now, however, his point is slightly different. His interest is in contrasting the baneful effects of what the first man did with those of the last man. Through Adam comes sin and ultimately death to which all humanity has become an heir, but through Christ comes justification and life, which will accrue to all who persevere in the faith.

The history of Christian reflection on the fall of Adam and Eve follows exactly on the footprints left by Paul. Christian writers from Irenaeus to John Milton would compare the story of Adam and Eve with that of Christ in order to tease out hundreds upon hundreds of textual correlations, for in the Christian imagination,

the understanding of the one necessarily presumes a grasp of the other. *See* EDEN, GARDEN OF.

Bibliography: Gary Anderson. "Biblical Origins and the Problem of the Fall." *Pro Ecclesia* 10 (2001) 1–14; Gary Anderson. *The Genesis of Perfection: Adam and Eve in Jewish and Christian Imagination* (2001); James Barr. *The Garden of Eden and the Hope of Immortality* (1993); Joseph Blenkinsopp. *Pentateuch* (1992); Robert Di Vito. "The Demarcation of Divine and Human Realms in Genesis 2–11." *Creation in the Biblical Tradition.* R. J. Clifford and J. J. Collins, eds. (1992) 39–56; R. W. L. Moberly. "Did the Serpent Get It Right?" *JTS*, NS 39 (1988) 1–27.

GARY A. ANDERSON

FALLOW GROUND [נִיר nir]. Soil that has been broken up through plowing so that weeds and harmful insects are destroyed but has been left unseeded, so it can regain its nutrients. According to Exod 23:11, every seventh year (similar to the seventh day of rest), the Israelites were mandated to let their land rest and remain unseeded after plowing it. Their orchards and vineyards were to remain uncultivated, so animals and poor people would have access to eat whatever grew. This process of replenishing the soil referred metaphorically to the renewal of the Israelites' relationship to the Lord (Jer 4:3; Hos 10:12).

EMILY R. CHENEY

FALSE APOSTLES [ψευδαπόστολος pseudapostolos]. "False apostles" and "super apostles" are the derogatory terms Paul uses to characterize his rival missionaries in Corinth (2 Cor 11:5, 13; 12:11). Paul's sharp critique provides the only clues about them: they appear to have boasted of their Jewish heritage (2 Cor 11:22) and ability to perform "mighty works" (2 Cor 12:12; see 10:12; 11:18). They also criticized Paul for his inferior rhetorical ability and his refusal to accept the Corinthians' financial support (2 Cor 10:10; 11:5-11; 12:13). Paul denounces these missionaries as ministers of Satan for proclaiming "another Jesus" and a "different gospel" (11:4, 13-14)

DAVID M. REIS

FALSE CHRISTS. *See* FALSE MESSIAHS.

FALSE GODS [כָּזָב kazav]. The phrase is infrequent in English translations of the OT and never appears in the NT. The NIV offers five such translations (Ps 4:2; 40:4; Jer 13:25; 16:19; Amos 2:4); the RSV three (Ps 40:4; Jer 14:22; 18:15); the NRSV only one (Ps 40:4).

In no case does the Hebrew text actually use the term *god* or *gods*. Rather the nouns that lie behind these translations, kazav (Pss 4:2; 40:4; Amos 2:4) and sheqer (שֶׁקֶר, Jer 13:25; 16:19), primarily mean "lie" or "deception." Only the literary context allows the translation "false god(s)." The Hebrew text often leaves room for more than one interpretation as in Jeremiah 13:25, "because you have forgotten me and trusted in lies (NRSV)/false gods (NIV)."

These texts are commonly poetic, literature in which words are used in a creative and allusive fashion. For example, in Jer 16:19-20, the poem begins by referring to general and negative nouns ("lies," "worthless things" [v. 19 NRSV]), which are then identified more specifically as "gods" in v. 20. One could, with the NIV, translate "lie" (the noun is singular in Hebrew) as "false gods," but to do so obscures the move from the general to the specific in this poem. Therefore, it is probably best to think that a noun such as "lie" could be used to allude to deities other than Yahweh, implying that they are false things, but not that there is a concept of "false gods" per se in the OT. *See* APOSTASY.

DAVID L. PETERSEN

FALSE GOSPEL [ἕτερον εὐαγγέλιον heteron euangelion]. For Paul the gospel was God's revelation of the truth given to humanity for its salvation (Rom 1:16; 1 Cor 15:1-2; 2 Cor 6:7). This good news of Christ's redemptive activity in the world, however, was received with scorn by non-Christians (1 Cor 1:23), and even followers of Jesus disagreed about the content and significance of the gospel. In 2 Corinthians, Paul confronts the activity of rival missionaries (the "super-apostles"), whose message consisted of appeals to their Jewish heritage, their rhetorical finesse, and demonstrations of spiritual power (10:10; 11:18, 22; 12:12). Paul chides the Corinthians for being susceptible to affirming "another Jesus than the one we proclaimed" and receiving "a different (heteron) gospel from the one you accepted" (11:4). To counter this opposition, the apostle reminds the Corinthians of the truth of his gospel, upon which his authority rests, and disparages his opponents as FALSE APOSTLES aligned with Satan (11:7-10, 13-15; 13:8; see 1 Thess 2:2-4; 3:2). Deviating from this gospel thus risks a spiritual enslavement and jeopardizes the Corinthians' status as people of God (11:20).

In Galatians, Paul confronts another group of rival missionaries proclaiming a "different gospel" (1:6). Their teachings centered on the observance of at least some aspects of the Jewish law, particularly circumcision (5:2, 12, 24). Paul emphasizes that there is in fact only one gospel, which he received in a revelation from Christ and had faithfully transmitted to the Galatians during his original visit (1:1, 7-8, 11-12; 4:13-14). Because the power of this gospel supersedes the law's effectiveness for attaining righteousness, Paul chastises the Galatians for their foolish decision to become "enslaved" into a mode of life that Christ's entrance into the world rendered ineffectual, and encourages them instead to live under the power of the Spirit (3:1-5, 10-26; 4:1-11; 5:16-26). *See* CORINTHIANS, SECOND LETTER TO; GALATIANS, LETTER TO THE.

DAVID M. REIS

FALSE MESSIAHS [ψευδόχριστος pseudochristos]. Jesus mentions a time when "false Messiahs and FALSE PROPHETS" will appear, producing signs and wonders to demonstrate that the PAROUSIA has arrived (Matt 24:24; Mark 13:22). Although these individuals will lead many astray with their messianic claims, Jesus cautions his disciples to resist their deceptive calls (Matt 24:4-6; Mark 13:5-6; Luke 21:8) and to wait for the cosmic signs that will accompany his return (Matt 24:29-31; Mark 13:24-27; Luke 21:25-28). The relationship among false messiahs (Christs), antichrists (1 John 2:18, 22; 4:3; 2 John 7), and the ANTICHRIST (Rev 13:1-10) remains unclear, but all share an antagonism toward the redemptive plan of Christ.

DAVID M. REIS

FALSE PROPHETS. *See* PROPHECY, FALSE; PROPHET, PROPHECY.

FALSE TEACHERS [ψευδοδιδάσκαλος pseudodidaskalos]. This epithet appears in the NT only at 2 Pet 2:1, opening a polemical section wherein a group is denounced for sexual immorality, greed, deeds of exploitation, and perverting the truth. These are standard, almost boilerplate accusations; the real issue seems to be the interpretation of Jesus' second coming, which the author explains may be delayed but will happen literally, as promised (2 Pet 3:1-10). Only Christians would debate over more or less literal understandings of the second coming. "False teacher," then, is what one Christian might call another when their understandings of doctrine differed. Similarly the author of Revelation denounces Christians who ate food sacrificed to idols, calling this practice "the teaching of Balaam" (2:14) and calling one of the leaders of the opposition group "Jezebel" (3:20). The letter of Jude castigates a group of "intruders" for altering the true apostolic teaching; Jude's language is colorful but imprecise, and it is hard to pinpoint where the opponents have become unorthodox. The first two letters of John, arguing against Christians who doubted the physical reality of Jesus' body (i.e., a docetic christology; *see* DOCETISM), called them ANTICHRIST and forbade any contact with them.

RICHARD B. VINSON

FALSE WITNESS. *See* TESTIMONY; WITNESS.

FALSE WORSHIP [שָׁוְא shawe', מַעַל ma'al; ψευδο pseudo (prefix)]. A wide variety of Hebrew and Gk. terms describe "false worship," as worship of gods other than Yahweh. One of the most descriptive scenes of false worship is at the foot of Mount Sinai (Exod 32:1-6). Elements included molten "gods," a priest, a proclamation "this is your god, O Israel" (32:4), an altar with burnt offerings, and a festival. Worshiping other gods was frequently confronted in the OT (Deut 11:16; 17:3; 29:26; Judg 2:19; 3:7; 10:6; 1 Kgs 9:9;

2 Kgs 19:37). Canaanite religious practices infiltrated worship in Israel (1 Sam 1–3; 9–10). Emblems of false worship were condemned by the prophets (2 Kgs 18:4; Isa 2:8, 20; Hos 8:4-6; 13:1-2). False prophets/apostles tempted the faithful (Ezek 13:7, 9; Matt 24:24; Acts 13:6; 2 Cor 11:13; Gal 2:4; Rev 16:13). *See* APOSTASY; FALSE GODS; FALSE GOSPEL; FALSE MESSIAHS; FALSE TEACHERS.

MICHAEL G. VANZANT

FAMILY [מִשְׁפָּחָה mishpakhah; οἶκος oikos]. Critical analysis of the Israelite and early Christian conceptions about family is based on a triangulation of data: 1) biblical and other written records from that time and area, 2) archaeological findings, and 3) ethnological analogies. Several different Hebrew and Greek words and expressions are translated with the term *family* in modern translations of the Bible. This demonstrates fluidity in their concept of family and the fact that modern conceptions about family differ from those of the biblical world. In the societies of the ANE and Mediterranean regions, factors such as geographical proximity, economics, and religion appear to have been just as significant as kinship ties (blood descent and marriage) to their concepts of the family. Many ideas about family are reflected in settlement patterns and the architecture of houses. Comparisons with similar societies today bring these data together with relevant linguistic and archaeological data to produce a reasonable sketch of how they understood this fundamental institution.

A. Family in the Old Testament
    1. Kinship terms and Israel's lineage structure
    2. Archaeology and Israelite families
    3. Historical developments
B. Family in the New Testament
    1. Terms
    2. Early Christian families and Greco-Roman society
Bibliography

A. Family in the Old Testament
1. Kinship Terms and Israel's lineage structure
The term *family/-ies* is found approximately 200 times in the OT. It most commonly translates the Hebrew word mishpakhah (in about 60 percent of the occurrences); however, translators render that word CLAN more often than *family*. In the majority of the remaining instances, *family* translates beth ʾav (בֵּית־אָב, FATHER'S HOUSE), beth ("house/household"), beth ʾavoth (בֵּית־אָבוֹת, "ancestral house"), or ʾavoth ("fathers"). More than a half dozen other terms (e.g., ʾakhim [אַחִים, "brothers"], zeraʿ [זֶרַע, "seed"]) are rendered *family* in at least one instance each.

It is helpful to consider Israel's lineage structure in order to understand how all these terms can be used to mean *family*. Joshua 7 and 1 Sam 10 provide an ideal

picture of this lineage structure. The first text speaks of identifying a guilty person by separating out his tribe, his clan within the tribe, his household within the clan, and then the man (gever גֶּבֶר) within the household. The selection of Saul to be king in 1 Sam 10 presents a slightly modified sequence of separations; there are references here to Saul the man within his tribe and clan, but there is no mention of his household.

The wording of certain laws demonstrates the breadth of what the term *man* implies within this lineage structure. Moses regularly addresses his audience with the pronoun *you* (masc. sg.) in a distributive sense; but in a few passages, he specifies that this singular "you" implies more than just individual adult males. For example, the law of Sabbath-years states, "You may eat what the land yields during its Sabbath—you, your male and female slaves, your hired and your bound laborers who live with you" (Lev 25:6). He elaborates in similar fashion in the laws on annual festivals, telling them, "[You shall] rejoice before the LORD your God, you and your sons and daughters, your male and female slaves, the Levites resident in your towns, as well as the strangers, the orphans and the widows who are among you" (Deut 16:11, 14; see 5:14; 12:12, 18). Each "you/your" refers to a man, but more specifically to an adult male with property. These texts suggest as well that the designation "man" includes not only an adult male but also his wife or wives, because wives are not specifically mentioned in these texts. For some, this omission reflects a profound understanding of the Eden pronouncement, "The two shall become one flesh" (Gen 2:24). On the other hand, polygamy seems to have been well accepted (Deut 21:15-17), and that tends to undermine such a direct interpretive connection. Ethnological analogies support the implication that "you" here also includes the man's children and slaves, even though they are explicitly mentioned.

A reference to all these family members and slaves with the singular *you* does not mean that any of them loses his or her identity as an individual; rather, it reflects their legal status in comparison with others in their community. A man's wife, children, and servants or slaves (biblical Hebrew does not distinguish the two) are considered part of the man or an extension of the man in legal matters. They are one with the man, but each has the potential to separate from him. Sons become adult males with property (men), and daughters marry and join themselves to another male. The situation of slaves and hired laborers is more complicated, as there are distinctions between Hebrew slaves and foreign slaves, and between slaves and hired laborers. Masters are to free Hebrew slaves after six years and give them material goods with which they might reestablish their own house (Deut 15:12-18; see Exod 21:2-6). The Passover laws distinguish between slaves and hired laborers, allowing only slaves to share the meal with their masters (Exod 12:43-45). Meanwhile, a hired laborer can be redeemed from his servitude by a relative (Lev 25:39-43). Such passages reflect fluidity in their concept of who makes up a family, but all point to a sense of oneness revealed in mutual obligations.

This sense of oneness represents their basic understanding of family. Typically, it is the man who collects and distributes the family property, oversees the family farm or business, adjudicates intramural disputes, arranges marriages, and represents the family to the community; but there are occasions where a widow/wife will perform these duties instead (see Judg 4:5; Ruth 1:8; 4:3; Prov 31:10-31). The behavior of each individual in the family affects the reputation of the others, but particularly the status of the man in the community. Others in his community judge him, not only in light of his own behavior but also in light of the behavior of his wife and children and slaves, unless he does something to distance himself legally from them. This sense of oneness also means that actions taken by others against a man's wife or children or slaves are considered actions against him, and he will respond as if he personally has been wronged.

Levites are obviously independent, and yet their inclusion in delineations of family members reflects the notion that they are also reliant on another man for their protection and livelihood (Num 18:20; 35:1-3; Deut 18:1-5; Josh 13:14; 14:1-4; 21:1-3; see PRIESTS AND LEVITES). The same applies to "the alien, the orphan, and the widow." A man has taken on the responsibility of providing for them as a husband/father normally would provide, but he also enjoys the benefits of having their help in the work of the home.

The same principle of mutual responsibilities and benefits applies to lesser and lesser degrees as one moves to broader levels of the lineage system. A group of men who claim descent from the same father a few generations earlier would make up a household (see HOUSEHOLD, HOUSEHOLDER). These men could come together to confront the men of another household, the households of one clan could come together to confront the households of other clans, etc. It is in this vein that David speaks of the men of Judah as "my bone and my flesh" (2 Sam 19:12-13; see Gen 2:23), vis-à-vis the members of the other tribes.

Ethnological studies show that we should expect to find flexibility in family ties at these broader levels (among clans and tribes). Over time, environmental and political circumstances would make it increasingly difficult to be rigidly exclusive about family affiliations solely on the basis of blood descent, particularly at the tribal level. For these reasons, many modern researchers conclude that tribal designations in the OT might have been based more on geography than blood descent. The presence of purely geographical names in some genealogies lends some support to this conclusion (e.g., 1 Chr 2:50-51). Numerous texts voice concerns about foreign threats to family solidarity, but other tribes

could have been just as threatening to the ideal composition of any given tribe. War, disease, and natural disasters could influence a group's demographics (see Dan and Benjamin in Judg 17–21), so various mechanisms existed to counteract these destructive influences and preserve some level of stability. For example, regular religious ceremonies promoted clan solidarity (1 Sam 20:6), and conventions such as endogamy at the tribal level reinforced tribal identity (as with the daughters of Zelophehad, Num 27:1-11; 36:1-12). Laws regarding homicide, marriage, boundaries, community discipline, etc. served in part to maintain stability and a balance between the desires of individual family units and the welfare of the broader family in which they existed.

Another way one can see flexibility in the concept of family is in the use of the terms *household* and *people* in the OT. Different texts speak of collections of individuals at each lineage level as a household. Joshua's famous declaration of faith ("as for me and my household, we will serve the Lord," Josh 24:14) probably indicates that he is speaking on behalf of his father's house (beth 'av; see Exod 12:3-4) or his clan (mishpakhah; again see 1 Sam 20:6). Members of the same clan or tribe can constitute one "house" (Judg 1:23, 35; 2 Sam 3:19; Zech 12:12-14), and writers often refer to the entire nation as "the house of Israel" (2 Sam 6:5; Jer 2:4). The flexibility in their use of this term suggests that they were utilizing the concept of family as the conceptual basis for their political unity.

We can derive similar conclusions from biblical references to one's people. The context would determine how a speaker who uses the term *people* is viewing others and his/her relationship to them. The primary principle is one of "us vs. them." For example, Saul speaks of the elders of his clan or tribe as "my people" in contrast to the other clans/tribes in Israel (1 Sam 15:30), but the Philistine Achish refers to the whole nation of Israel as David's "people" (1 Sam 27:12). To refer to others as one's house or people is to say they are family, along with all the privileges and obligations that go with it.

2. Archaeology and Israelite families

Consideration of Israelite houses and settlement patterns enhances this picture. The typical Israelite dwelling is known as a "four-room HOUSE." Small columns divided the space into four areas, and also supported a structure two to three stories high. Archaeological remains indicate that these homes were designed especially for agricultural households, with small livestock inhabiting the central ground floor and the upper floor(s) reserved for sleeping. Each house could serve as a residence for a nuclear family and those directly attached to them. Several of these four-room houses would be conjoined, sharing a common courtyard and walls. Ethnological analogies suggest that such groupings constituted a minimal lineage, probably a "father's house." Several of these houses might occupy the same town, and those who claimed common descent would make up a clan. The names of some clans are identical to the names of some of the larger towns in Israel (e.g., Hebron). The Samaria Ostraca contain the names of several clans associated with Manasseh and Ephraim, showing that each of these clan territories included several settlements. This indicates that a clan basically consisted of several households in close geographical proximity to one another, probably with one larger settlement as its head (father or mother) and satellite settlements as the sons or daughters. Conversely, there is no indication that a clan was ever smaller than a single town or city, with the possible exception of very large cities, such as Jerusalem. References to "the cities of Judah and the streets of Jerusalem" (Jer 5:1; 7:17, 34; 11:6, 13; 44:6, 9, 17, 21) suggest that the latter were neighborhoods roughly equivalent in size and administration to towns or villages in the countryside. Connections between streets and professional guilds probably reflect a common practice of referring to one's professional associates with kinship terms (Jer 37:21; see "sons of the prophets" in 2 Kgs 6:1).

The SAMARIA OSTRACA also point to the collective nature of a family's economic obligations. They imply that the various components of a clan cooperated to provide goods to the central authorities. Similarly, the men, women, and children within a house would have contributed to their house's efforts in fulfilling the clan's obligations. Cultural convention prescribed different tasks and functions to the various family members, according to natural abilities and the needs of the agricultural calendar. Everyone would have shared some tasks, while others would have been gender or age specific. Still, immediate circumstances might have altered this. For example, a widow might take on some of the tasks more commonly performed by a husband, or an unmarried man might perform tasks more commonly performed by a wife.

In sum, the concept of family involves mutual assistance and responsibilities. An individual's people or house (i.e., family) consists of those from whom he/she can expect assistance and those for whom he/she feels obligated to render assistance. These feelings derive from a combination of blood, marriage, territorial, economic, religious, and professional ties. The strength of these feelings was greatest at the level of one's immediate blood kin, becoming increasingly weaker as one moved farther out and up the social structure to the clans and tribes. One of the primary purposes of many social and religious institutions was to reinforce a sense of family among these larger groups.

3. Historical developments

The size and strength of a family would have fluctuated over the years, as births, marriages, deaths, ecological conditions, and economic fortunes changed the configuration of the families within each father's house, clan, and tribe. Laws and customs favored the older son over his siblings, so intramural friction could cause brothers in one house to split and form two houses. The nuclear family of a younger brother might choose to attach itself to the house of his wife's father (Jacob is close to this while he works for Laban). Slaves could be adopted as sons (so Eliezer in Gen 15:2), and a son could leave or be forced out of his family to found his own house or become a slave in another house (see the status of Jephthah in Gilead; Judg 11:1-11). A father's house could expand until it became its own clan, while another might be absorbed into a different house or clan. One father's house might become dependent on another, causing the latter to become a clan and the former its son. Changes in clan names and their genealogical placement reflect such shifts (see the lists in Num 26 and 1 Chr 1–9). The division of the tribe of Joseph into the two tribes of Ephraim and Manasseh is a classic example of lineage bifurcation. The references to Machir and Gilead alongside tribes in the Song of Deborah (Judg 5:14-18) might preserve the memory of a time when those clans held the status of tribes.

These observations about fluctuations in the tribal structure raise some questions about the reliability of the biblical picture of Israel's tribal/family structure over the entire history of Israel. Some believe that this picture represents an idealization that developed during and after the Babylonian exile and that writers superimposed it back onto pre-exilic events. Power struggles recorded in the history of preexilic Israel actually serve to address post-exilic conflicts. Such a view is problematic, however, because there is no real correlate to the entire Israelite tribal structure in post-exilic Judea. It seems unlikely that postexilic writers would impose a *post facto* idealization of conditions that serve no real purpose in a postexilic context. Other historians believe the kinship-based structures existed in pre-monarchic Israel, but the centralizing bureaucracies of the monarchies dismantled those kinship-based structures because they posed a direct threat to royal authority. Such historians often associate ideas about royal authority with Canaanite influences. Thus, the evil innovations of the nations are seen to be anti-family as well, and family values become the values espoused by the orthodox biblical writers in opposition to abuses by the royal establishments. Ethnological analogies provide a third alternative. These suggest that there could have been fluctuations in the strength of kinship groups from generation to generation, as tribal and kinship-based powers operated in a complementary fashion with royal powers. This view accounts for the criticism one finds in the OT for abuses of power by both official and traditional leaders, while at the same time allowing for the differences between pre-exilic kinship groups and post-exilic kinship groups.

B. Family in the New Testament

1. Terms

The term *family* is used in one of three ways in the NT: 1) to denote a living domestic group (oikos [more commonly, "house"], 1 Tim 5:4, 8; Titus 1:11; or in the Greek phrase "those of," Mark 3:21; Acts 16:33; Rom 16:10-11); 2) to designate an extended lineage, such as Abraham's descendants (genos [γένος, Acts 4:6; 7:13; 13:26] or patria [πατριά, Luke 2:4; Acts 3:25; Eph 3:15]); and 3) in reference to Christians as a "spiritual family" (adelphoi [ἀδελφοί usually, "brothers"]; Matt 25:40; Rom 8:29; 1 Cor 8:12; Gal 1:2). It is clear that the latter intends to draw on common feelings about family to build a sense of mutual and personal obligation among individuals from diverse social backgrounds. The use of such nomenclature begins with Jesus (Matt 25:40) and is grounded in two related notions. One is that Christians share a common father in God (2 Cor 6:17-18; Gal 3:25-26; 1 John 3:1) and a common brother in Christ, who is the "firstborn within a large family" (Rom 8:29; see 1 Cor 8:12; Gal 1:1-2). The other notion is that Christians are the true descendants of Abraham and heirs of the divine promises to him and his seed (Rom 4:9-25; Gal 3:27-29). In this, Christians perpetuate and take upon themselves the idea of Israel as a single people (2 Cor 6:16; 1 Pet 2:9-10) or house (Gal 6:10; Heb 3:5-6). The price they pay for doing this is that their new church family takes priority over their natural families, requiring a shift in familial responsibilities and benefits (Luke 14:26; 18:28-30).

2. Early Christian families and Greco-Roman society

Research into the Greco-Roman world reveals that NT writings reflect some specifically Jewish beliefs about family, but the writers are also sensitive to assumptions held by the broader society. For example, only Christian and Jewish writers draw a direct connection between idolatry and sexual immorality. Furthermore, they tend to view sexuality and marriage in general in relational terms, while Roman and Hellenistic laws demonstrate a basic desire to regulate social status through marriages and sexual mores. For example, Paul imitates the convention of his day when he uses HOUSEHOLD CODES to prescribe morals and ethics for Christian homes (Eph 5:21–6:9; Col 3:18–4:1), yet the specific standards he calls for (such as monogamy) derive from distinctively Jewish-Christian ideals. These codes show that Christian families typically consisted of a husband and wife, children, and slaves. Paul does not prescribe a wholesale overthrow of this system, but he does realign his readers' view of it on the basis of their relationships with God and with one another as Christians. Husbands are to imitate Christ's love for the church in their love for their wives (Eph 5:25), and slaves are to serve their masters "as slaves of Christ" (Eph 6:5-8).

Christian worship took place almost entirely in private homes for at least the 1st cent. of Christianity's existence. Many of the prescriptions for early Christian worship flow out of common conceptions about proper life in the home. There is evidence that there were slight regional differences, which reflect competing Hellenistic and Roman practices. There are indications, e.g., that women were more involved in public life in the Roman West than the Hellenistic East, and there was less separation of roles along gender lines in the West. The expectations the NT writers express to different communities regarding Christian women in worship and society seem to parallel these competing cultural norms. Again, however, the writers justify their instructions on the basis of a Christian worldview.

The Christian practice of sharing a common meal would have made a more radical statement in some areas than others. Meals were a clear representation of a community's social hierarchy, with precise rules of inclusion and exclusion. Again, there were regional differences, as Roman homes were seen as more welcoming to visitors. In some areas and times, there was a clear separation at meals by gender. The Christian practice of full inclusion at meals might have been seen as a threat to this hierarchy and the social structures it supported, particularly regarding slaves and free; but the concept of a common family with one father—God—would have been compromised without such inclusion. *See* CHILD, CHILDREN; DAUGHTER; FATHER; GOD THE FATHER; MARRIAGE, NT; MARRIAGE, OT; MEALS; MOTHER; SERVANT; SLAVERY; SON.

Bibliography: Ken M. Campbell, ed. *Marriage and Family in the Biblical World* (2003); Shaye J. D. Cohen, ed. *The Jewish Family in Antiquity* (1993); Norman K. Gottwald. *Tribes of Yahweh* (1979); Joseph H. Hellerman. *The Ancient Church as Family* (2001); Wayne A. Meeks. *The First Urban Christians* (1983); Halvor Moxnes, ed. *Constructing Early Christian Families* (1997); Carolyn Osiek and David L. Balch. *Families in the New Testament World* (1997); Leo G. Perdue, ed. *Families in Ancient Israel* (1997); Lawrence E. Stager. "The Archaeology of the Family in Ancient Israel." *BASOR* 260 (1985) 1–36; Michael L. White and O. Larry Yarbrough, eds. *The Social World of the First Christians* (1995).

TIMOTHY M. WILLIS

FAMINE [רָעָב ra'av; λιμός limos]. The OT offers vivid descriptions of the suffering people experience when the food bins run dry (e.g., Joel 1–2; Lam 2:11-12; 4:3-4). In a subsistence society with limited food supplies, events such as drought, locusts, fire, and enemy invasions could be responsible for wide-ranging famine.

On the one hand, famine was seen as a natural event that together with war, pestilence, and earthquakes, fell with little discrimination upon both the just and the unjust, affecting humans, animals, and all the earth. In such instances, the effects of famine had to be mitigated and, where possible, overcome. However, the prophets in particular portray famine as a sign of the sin and failure of humans. In Amos 4:6-12, God sends afflictions such as famine, drought, mildew, blight, and pestilence upon people as a summons to repent and return to God. *See* BREAD; FOOD.

JULIANA CLAASSENS

FARA (NORTH), TELL EL. *See* TIRZAH.

FARA (SOUTH), TELL EL. Located in the northwestern Negev about 18 mi. southeast of Gaza and 16 mi. west of Beersheba, on the west bank of the Wadi Gaza (Nahal Besor). The large (15 acre) mound is strategically situated along the routes connecting the coast to Beersheba and Arabia, and is near the international route linking Egypt to Syria and Mesopotamia.

The ancient name of the site is uncertain. W. M. F. Petrie, who excavated Fara in 1928–29, misidentified it as biblical Beth-Pelet. W. F. Albright subsequently identified the site as Sharuhen, an Asiatic stronghold captured by the Egyptian king Ahmose at the beginning of the Eighteenth Dynasty (ca. 1540 BCE), and equated with Shilhim in Josh 15:32 and Shaaraim in 1 Chr 4:31 in the lists of cities of Simeon. In the 1970s Aharon Kempinski and James Stewart suggested that Sharuhen was located at Tell el-ʿAjjul, southwest of Gaza, leaving Fara with no identification. In 1980, Nadav Naʾaman proposed that Fara was the site of biblical Shur (mentioned in Gen 16:7; 20:1; 25:18; Exod 15:22; 1 Sam 15:7; 27:8). Naʾaman's identification has gained some adherents, but Anson Rainey has recently argued for a return to Albright's view while contending that the Egyptian name of the site was Sharhan, not Sharuhen.

Archaeological remains at the site cover the period from the second half of the Middle Bronze Age (17th–first half of 16th cent. BCE) to early Roman times (1st cent. CE). The site's most prominent feature is a late Middle Bronze Age wall, glacis, and trench fortification system on the west side of the mound (the site was otherwise protected primarily by steep natural slopes). The next major period of settlement activity was the 13th cent. BCE, when a large square brick building (the "Residency") at the north end of the mound, and an adjoining smaller structure, were used by the Egyptian colonial rulers of Canaan in the Late Bronze Age. Finds associated with this administrative complex included a jar fragment inscribed with the name of the Nineteenth Dynasty king Seti II (1200–1194 BCE), as well as hieratic ostraca. Philistine settlement at Fara is attested for the late 12th–11th cent. BCE.

The limited evidence for the history of Fara in the 1st millennium BCE suggests occupation at least in the 10th–9th and 7th–6th cent. BCE, with perhaps a settle-

ment gap in between. An ostracon inscribed "to our Lord," discovered in 1999 by a joint Israeli-American re-excavation of the site probably dates to the late 10th–early 9th cent. BCE. Later occupation of Fara is attested for Persian and early Roman times. *See* SHUR, WILDERNESS OF.

JAMES M. WEINSTEIN

FARE [שָׂכָר sakhar]. Several Hebrew and Gk. terms are translated "fare" in the sense of "See how your brothers fare" (1 Sam 17:18; e.g., Gen 18:25; 30:29; 2 Sam 11:7; Esth 2:11; Hag 1:5, 7; Rom 9:29). As wages or payment, sakhar occurs only in Jonah 1:3.

FARMER [אִכָּר ʾikkar; γεωργός geōrgos]. One who cultivates crops or breeds and raises livestock (e.g., Isa 28:24-28). The Gezer Calendar lists eight farming periods in a twelve-month cycle. The farmer planted cereals (e.g., wheat and barley) during the early sowing season and legumes and vegetables in the late sowing season. The farmer is used in the NT as a metaphor for ministerial leadership (1 Cor 9:7-10) and proverbial images of endurance (2 Tim 2:6) and patience (Jas 5:7). *See* AGRICULTURE.

RALPH K. HAWKINS

FAST, FASTING [הִתְעַנָּה hithʿannah; עִנָּה נֶפֶשׁ ʿinnah nefesh, צוּם tsum, צוֹם tsom, νηστεύω nēsteuō, νηστεία nēsteia, ταπεινοφρονέω tapeinophroneō, ταπεινοφροσύνη tapeinophrosynē]. Fasting refers to a practice common in ancient Israel and post-biblical Judaism to abstain from nourishment, usually over the course of a day. In the Bible, it generally serves as a form of mourning and indicates that the individual or community is in some state of distress.

- A. The Nature and Scope of Fasting in the Old Testament
- B. The Meaning of Fasting in the Old Testament
- C. Measuring Fasting's Effects
- D. Special Instances of Fasting in the Old Testament
- E. Post-Biblical Continuities and Developments
- F. Fasting in the New Testament
- Bibliography

A. The Nature and Scope of Fasting in the Old Testament

Fasting in ancient Israel involved abstention from food and often, if not always, water (Jonah 3:7; Esth 4:16). It was accompanied by other physical performances: weeping, lament, tearing one's clothing, donning sackcloth, applying ashes to one's head, and/or lowering oneself to the ground (e.g., Esth 4:1-3). All these practices are closely associated with mourning, and fasting should be classified with them as an act of mourning. The presence of a technical vocabulary for referring to "fasting" suggests that the act was indeed conceived of as a discrete, coherent ritual, though there are instances in which the refusal of food is presented as a natural response to a given situation, rather than the decision to engage in a ritual act (e.g., 1 Sam 1:6). In all other respects, the effects of such reflexive abstinence resemble those of a formal fast. The duration of fasts varied; they could be set for a particular period of time (e.g., 2 Sam 3:35), culminate in a process of prayer or sacrifice (e.g., Judg 20:26), or simply come to an end when their purpose was met or became obsolete (e.g., 2 Sam 12:16-20). Individuals could embark upon a fast, or communal fasts could be initiated by the leadership, usually a royal but sometimes a priestly figure (Joel 1:13-14). Though it is poorly attested as a practice elsewhere in the ANE, the testimony of the OT suggests that it must have been a rather common phenomenon in that area of the world. A reference to fasting and weeping in the Deir Alla Texts, found in the eastern Jordan Valley, shows that these practices were not the province of Israelites alone.

B. The Meaning of Fasting in the Old Testament

Fasting always appears in situations of real or threatened loss. Sometimes the loss concerned is final, as when fasting appears in mourning the dead. At other times, fasting occurs in close proximity to prayer, and it seems to aid in reversing an evil decree. How the same rite can appear in both contexts, be both efficacious and not, requires some thought. Perplexity regarding the meaning of fasting also follows from another angle. Formative Judaism and Christianity both tend to regard fasting as a penitential act, viewing it either as a physical expression of internal contrition or a way of atoning for sin by anticipating punishment and preemptively inflicting it upon oneself. However, in the OT, fasting frequently appears in situations in which there is no evidence of sin. Scholars have responded to these difficulties by positing the existence of different kinds of fasts. While the exact enumeration varies, one usually finds included within such lists: 1) fasting as an act of MOURNING the dead, 2) fasting as an act of penitence, 3) fasting as an auxiliary to PRAYER, and 4) fasting as a preparation for encountering the divine. This view of the diversity of fasting within the Bible is partially inspired by the results of ethnographic research. Early ethnologists studied the fasting practices of various peoples around the world and indeed found that fasting could be practiced for a wide variety of motivations.

While this view still has adherents, it should be questioned on a number of scores. Lists of fasting practices culled from multiple cultures would not seem to furnish an ideal paradigm for classifying the phenomenon within a single culture. More to the point, however, is the way in which the reigning classification undercuts the deep points of connection that exist between the different "types" of fasting in the OT. Running throughout all of these supposedly separate categories is the fact that fasting serves as a physical manifestation of distress, usually a type of distress that is not plainly evident upon the body of the one fasting because it has actually befallen others (e.g., the dead), because it is only potential (i.e., in the future), or because its lacks a visible bodily effect (e.g., barrenness or failure of crops). Fasting makes that distress evident. It allows the one who refrains from eating to assume the persona of someone who is actually afflicted. In those instances where suffering is already in physical evidence, fasting is rarely, if ever, employed.

It is for this reason that fasting as part of mourning the dead should not be seen as different in essence, only different in circumstance, from the sort of fasting that attends prayer. Within a social entity with shared interests, the diminishment wrought by death upon one member is felt by others and compels them to experience loss themselves through self-affliction (e.g., 2 Sam 1:12). Likewise, fasting constitutes a natural response to threatened affliction, preemptively reflecting upon the body future loss. Doing so can help move the deity to pity and thus frequently accompanies prayer, but it does not change the basic mechanism at work: the actualization of distress through the cessation of the normal bodily function of eating—only one step away from death itself.

C. Measuring Fasting's Effects

While the difficulty of interpreting ritual has long been noted, the biblical text offers us real evidence concerning the meaning of fasting. One passage gives us an unusually clear statement of fasting's intent. When asked by his courtiers why he fasted before (rather than after) the death of his child, David explains: "While the child was still alive, I fasted and wept; for I said, 'Who knows? The Lord may be gracious to me, and the child may live'" (2 Sam 12:22). David has transposed the usual practice of fasting as part of mourning the dead and chosen to display his grief preemptively, in the hope that God may take pity upon him.

Fasting here, and in innumerable other instances, appears in the context of prayer and must therefore be said to possess a degree of efficacy. The question is whether we can be more precise about why fasting, of all things, is used to express grief and hence why it elicits divine pity. To answer this question, it is useful to look beyond fasting, for the moment, to the broader theology of ancient Israel. Like any good ANE emperor, it was the province of the God of Israel to look after the afflicted. The covenant code formulates it the following way: "You shall not abuse any widow or orphan. If you do abuse them, when they cry out to me, I will surely heed their cry" (Exod 22:22-23). There is great potential power that stands to be unleashed by the cry of the poor. Now the widow and orphan both present rather obvious portraits of suffering. What though of the individual (a king, say) whose table is well stocked and roof firm, but who nevertheless stands to suffer some great, as of yet unrealized loss? Fasting proves to be a solution; it allows those who have not yet experienced loss to number themselves among the afflicted by embodying the diminishment they will soon undergo.

Just how such a process works is amply demonstrated in both psalms and narrative. Other human beings recoil at the sight of one who fasts and engages in its concomitant rites: "My knees are weak through fasting; my body has become gaunt. I am an object of scorn to my accusers; when they see me, they shake their heads" (Ps 109:24-25). An attempt is made to prevent others from entering into that state. Thus David's courtiers encourage him to cease from his fast (2 Sam 12:17), and Esther, without even first inquiring as to the reason for her uncle's behavior, sends Mordecai proper clothing to replace his mourner's garb (Esth 4:4). Fasting disturbs—there is an unseemliness to it—and hence provokes a superficial attempt to remove its traces. The afflicted persist in seeking a real solution. We lack, of course, any depiction of how fasting affects the deity. But it seems likely that we may use these instances of human response as a register of fasting's effects. Affliction is distasteful, even painful to its beholder; it incites God to remove its root cause before the threatened diminishment attains permanence.

D. Special Instances of Fasting in the Old Testament

The most famous instances of fasting in the OT are the fasts that tend to be closely associated in people's minds with repentance. By the post-exilic period, fasting had taken a step toward the penitential, or, to put it more accurately, the fast day seems to have broadened its scope to incorporate a process of turning away from sin. The book of Jonah provides a case in point. The people are told to refrain from all food, to cry out to God, and to turn away from their evil ways (3:7-8). Fasting continues to be closely related to crying out (at least, that's what the sequence of commands in Jonah would suggest), but there is a new requirement for the fast day. And its fulfillment is said to be the most effective element in moving God to pity: "When God saw what they did, how they turned from their evil ways, God changed his mind . . ." (3:10). The same might be said for the well-known passage from the book of Joel: "Yet even now, says the LORD, return to me with all your heart, and with fasting, with weeping, and with mourning; rend your hearts and not your clothing" (2:12-13). That bodily affliction, tears, and, what is most likely, some form of moaning or lament should attend a "return" to the LORD provides us with no grounds for reducing them to external manifestations of repentance; they may very well continue to be efficacious in their own right as forms of appeal.

Like the passage from Jonah, the discussion of fasting in Isaiah (58:2-7) expands upon the traditional confines of the fast. Here, too, there has been widespread misunderstanding over the basic topic of the prophet's exhortation. The prophet does not condemn the way people fast, i.e., without sincerity or contrition, but their failure to incorporate a key element in their fast day proceedings. Nowhere does the prophet call on the people to repent; rather, he demands that they turn their fast days, when they afflict themselves, into days of economic release, when they alleviate the suffering of those who are afflicted quite without the artifice of fasting. While those who fast suppress their immediate physical needs to secure their long-term welfare, Isaiah argues that they must also suppress the pursuit of their own welfare and turn instead to furthering the material state of the downtrodden. Only then will they reap the benefit of their fasts (58:8). In any event, Isaiah does not argue for a "spiritual" fast; his concerns remain firmly rooted in the material.

Though in subsequent Jewish tradition, the fast of the DAY OF ATONEMENT comes to be seen as a time for repentance, the depiction of the day in the priestly account (Lev 16) gives no indication of that meaning. That said, there is also no act of communal prayer, which raises the question of fasting's purpose in this unusual, fixed day of fasting. To begin with, it is important to recognize that there is very little direct connection between the priestly proceedings of the day (vv. 1-28) and the community's accompanying actions (vv. 29-31). It is possible that communal fasting adds an element of implicit entreaty that the high priest's purificatory rituals prove successful. More likely is the possibility that fasting provides individuals with a way of participating in the events unfolding within the sanctuary by showing that members of the community share in the negative circumstances engendered by sin and its resultant impurities. Fasting thus continues to function as a form of mourning.

E. Post-Biblical Continuities and Developments

The situation with regard to fasting becomes considerably more complicated within post-biblical Judaism. On one hand, there is a strong degree of continuity with biblical tradition. Well into late antiquity, communal fasts very much like those in the OT continue to be observed on occasions of disaster. The entire community would assemble and cry out to God (e.g., 1 Macc 3:44-54 and m. Ta'an. 2:1-4). So too, in keeping with its function as an act of mourning, regular fasting was used as a way of marking grief over exile and the loss of the Temple, a practice already alluded to in Zech 8:19. On the other hand, interaction with Hellenism and its traditions led to real changes in the meaning of fasting and an all-around greater diversity of purpose.

Fasting becomes a form of piety, a good deed for which an individual might expect to accrue a degree of merit or atone for some sin (e.g., Tob 12:8; *Pss. Sol.* 3:7-8). Fasting is also considered an aid to piety, protecting the mind from impure thoughts (e.g., *T. Sim.* 3:4). In some accounts, fasting proves to be a way of attaining revelation (e.g., *2 Bar.* 9:2–10:1). None of these perspectives on abstinence from food resound with biblical theology, and they are not to be found within the OT, with the probable exception of its very latest book, the book of Daniel (9:3-23; 10:2-6). All of these new conceptions of fasting are notable for their focus on the human individual and his or her spiritual needs, whereas the OT tends to focus on fasting as a way of communicating with God. Changing notions of individual eschatology are probably responsible for the view of fasting as atoning. The other powers attributed to fasting, purification of thought and initiation of revelation, are attested in Greek literature.

Another important development in this period is the penitential fast. Here we encounter a peculiar combination of the emerging importance of repentance, that is to say regret for sin, and the biblical practice of mourning over sin (e.g., *T. Reu.* 1:9-10). Whereas the latter (e.g., Deut 9:18-20), true to other biblical examples of fasting, represented a form of grief over loss occasioned by sin and figured in petitionary contexts, it provided a vocabulary that could suggest repentance and an accepted practice that could be used to embody physically internal contrition, which by the post-biblical period had become an effective means of atoning for certain sins. It is most likely through the idea that fasting constitutes mourning over sin that the DAY OF ATONEMENT came to be seen as a day of repentance (*Jub.* 34:19 and *m. Yoma* 8:8).

F. Fasting in the New Testament

Fasting in the NT conforms to the patterns of fasting within post-biblical Judaism, both in terms of its continuities with earlier biblical tradition and its newer developments. Confusion has been caused by the peculiar assumption that Jesus' approach to fasting must have been distinct from his late Second Temple surroundings. Some scholars have therefore concluded that Jesus rejected the practice of fasting, a view that suits certain anti-ritual biases latent in modern scholarship. The position that would seem to emerge from the fasting controversy in Mark (2:18-20) and a statement presumably originally from the Sayings Gospel (Matt 11:16-19 and Luke 7:31-35) fits in quite well with the traditional view of fasting (*see* Q, QUELLE). Fasting is an act of mourning and is antithetical to rejoicing. John and his followers followed a pious practice of mourning for the distraught state of the Jewish nation and therefore fasted regularly. Jesus and his followers conceived of themselves as participating already (in some fashion) in the kingdom of heaven. Fasting in such circumstances would be inconceivable—rather like fasting at a wedding; Zechariah had already made clear that fasts would turn to feasts when the moment of redemption came. The difference between Jesus, on

one hand, and John and the Pharisees, on the other, is not over the value or nature of fasting, but over eschatology, whether Israel has indeed entered the period of redemption (*see* ESCHATOLOGY OF THE NT).

In the NT, there was a continued appreciation of fasting's ability to help ensure successful prayer (e.g., Acts 13:3), though it is no longer clear whether the original reason for this connection was understood, namely the abjectness that fasting imposes upon the supplicant. We also find the view that fasting and prayer are good deeds, signs of individual merit. Thus the righteousness of Anna is bound up in her continual fasting and praying in the Temple (Luke 2:37). The Sermon on the Mount (Matt 6:16-18) encapsulates the change in the nature of fasting, from a method of manifesting and communicating need to a good deed. The entire context of the passage is, of course, the standard threesome of good deeds: almsgiving, prayer, and fasting. With the performance of each, the individual accrues merit in heaven. This concept of individual eschatology and the new sense of fasting as meritorious leads to a rejection of the ostentation that was at the very heart of fasting in the OT: in the world of ancient Israel, God must see their distress and hear the articulation of said distress. The conception of fasting in the Sermon on the Mount clashes significantly with the more traditional fast of mourning undertaken by John the Baptist. This diversity within the NT is fully in line with the multiplication of meanings undergone by fasting within post-biblical Judaism. *See* ASCETICISM.

Bibliography: Rudolf Arbesmann. "Fasting and Prophecy in Pagan and Christian Antiquity." *Traditio* 7 (1949) 1–71; Hendrik A. Brongers. "Fasting in Israel in Biblical and Post-Biblical Times." *Instruction and Interpretation: Studies in Hebrew Language, Palestinian Archaeology and Biblical Exegesis: Papers Read at the Joint British-Dutch Old Testament Conference Held at Louvain, 1976, from 30 August to 2 September.* Joint British-Dutch Old Testament Conference, ed. (1977) 1–21; David Lambert. "Fasting as a Penitential Rite: A Biblical Phenomenon?" *HTR* 96 (2004) 477–512; S. Lowy. "The Motivation of Fasting in Talmudic Literature." *JJS* 9 (1958) 19–38; John B. Muddiman. "Jesus and Fasting." *Jésus aux origines de la christologie.* Jacques Dupont (1975) 283 –301; Saul M. Olyan. *Biblical Mourning: Social and Ritual Dimensions* (2004).

DAVID A. LAMBERT

FAT. *See* SACRIFICES AND OFFERINGS.

FATE [מִקְרֶה miqreh; ἀνάγκη anankē]. Any end or outcome viewed as inevitable may be termed a *fate*, especially an adverse outcome. Wickedness seals one's end-fate, but in the here and now the folly of wickedness becomes apparent only through revelation (Ps 73:17-20; "end" NRSV). The righteous often get saddled with the same fate as the wicked, death being foreordained for both (Eccl 2:14; 3:19).

As a philosophical principle, *fate* implies that chains of causality or hidden patterns of God determine experienced events. Diviners rely on causality in their claim to have access to the necessary course of the future (Isa 47:13; Jer 10:2; Ezek 21:21; Matt 2:2). Astrologers read the heavens to determine fate on earth (Dan 2:27; 4:7; 5:7, 11).

The notion of an impersonal, metadivine fate is lacking in biblical faith, but God does predetermine happenstances and outcomes (Pss 16:5; 31:15; Prov 16:33). Interpreters from Augustine to Calvin have embraced a strong doctrine of PROVIDENCE based on key biblical evidences (e.g., Gen 50:20; Acts 2:23) while sharply distinguishing providence from fate.

Biblically, a notion of fate is developed most explicitly in Qoheleth for whom fate is happenstance directly from the hand of God that is unintelligible and disorienting, having no discernible connection to human behavior or will (Eccl 9:1-3). Further, Qoheleth suggests that overarching God-determined designs circumscribe human existence (Eccl 3:11, 15; 7:13; 8:17). (See, similarly, 1 Sam 16:14; 1 Kgs 22:22; Rom 9:18; 2 Thess 2:11). Qoheleth's recommendation for living under determinism is to grit our teeth, accept responsibility, and take charge of what we can (Eccl 2:24; 3:12-13; 5:18-20; 8:15; 9:7-10; 11:9).

In *fatalism* the tyranny of forces beyond their control renders people impotent, devoid of responsibility (Rom 9:19), and shrugging their shoulders at life, as among the exiles (Ezek 18:2) whose wrongheaded perspective Ezekiel blasts.

Divine determinism looms large in apocalyptic literature: Ezek 38–39 and Dan 7 reveal a detailed divine plan for the ages and especially the eschaton. However, God's fixed blueprint for history leaves space for human freedom, and apocalyptic visions become guides for discerning the times and reacting appropriately.

An ideology of fatalism stands in tension not only with Scripture's stress on human moral responsibility but also with its admissions about chaos, which adheres persistently to the cosmos, threatening its patterned, God-ordained course (e.g., Ps 46:2-3; Jer 4:23). Job, especially, attests that chaos (radical arbitrariness and contingency) lies inextricably embedded within God's free creation (Job 3:8; 7:12; 41:1-10*a*), plainly calling fatalism into question, implying that until the eschaton there are no sure bets about the details of human experience. For the time being, chaos continues to exercise a mysterious tempering effect on God's bright providential work and on fate's dark assaults on human freedom. *See* DESTINY; ESCHATOLOGY OF THE NT; ESCHATOLOGY OF THE OT; LAMENT.

Bibliography: Richard A. Hughes. *Lament, Death and Destiny* (2004); Jon D. Levenson. *Creation and the Persistence of Evil: The Jewish Drama of Divine Omnipotence* (1988); Peter Machinist. "Fate, *Miqreh,* and Reason: Some Reflections on Qohelet and Biblical Thought." *Solving Riddles and Untying Knots: Biblical, Epigraphic, and Semitic Studies in Honor of Jonas C. Greenfield.* Z. Zevit, S. Gitin, and M. Sokoloff, eds. (1995) 159-75.

STEPHEN L. COOK

FATHER [אָב *'av;* πατήρ *patēr*]. The concept of father in the Bible includes not only the immediate male ancestor but also more distant ancestors. In a metaphorical sense, father may refer to a founder or an authority figure. Analogically, the term is applied to God, esp. in the contexts of creation and covenant.

    A. Father in the Old Testament
      1. Social context
      2. Theological context
    B. Father in the New Testament
      1. Greco-Roman background
      2. Jesus in the Gospels
      3. Paul's Letters
    Bibliography

A. Father in the Old Testament
1. Social context

In ancient Israel the father played a very significant role in the structuring of the family, which formed the basis of the larger tribal organization of Israelite society. The smallest familial unit is typically referred to as the FATHER'S HOUSE (beth *'av* בֵּית אָב; e.g., Josh 6:25; *see* HOUSEHOLD, HOUSEHOLDER). This would generally include more than one generation of family members living together under the authority of a father or grandfather. Above this basic social unit one finds the extended FAMILY or CLAN (mishpakhah מִשְׁפָּחָה) and ultimately the TRIBE (shevet שֵׁבֶט or matteh מַטֶּה). The significance of the father can be seen in the patrilineal structure of biblical genealogies in which it is the male ancestor who gives his name to a tribe or family. When used in the plural, "fathers" is a reference to ancestors in general (e.g., Zech 1:2-6) who are deceased as evidenced in the circumlocutions used to describe death: "being gathered to one's fathers" (e.g., Judg 2:10) and "sleeping with one's fathers" (e.g., 1 Kgs 2:10).

The role of the father within this family structure was primarily that of protector, being the one most responsible for the welfare of the family members. This function is revealed in frequent references to the plight of those without this family member (e.g., Lam 5:3). The precarious position of the widow and the orphan in Israel points to the essential role of the father in Israelite society (*see* FATHERLESS; ORPHAN). Along with the role of protector comes that of educator. This aspect of fatherhood is emphasized in the wisdom literature, which speaks of the duty of a father to educate and discipline his children (e.g., Prov 4:1-4). These responsibilities are shared with the MOTHER as well (e.g., Prov 1:8; 6:20).

Metaphorically, the concept of father is extended to include a variety of authority figures. It is used with reference to prophets (e.g., 2 Kgs 2:12), priests (e.g., Judg 17:10), and kings (e.g., 1 Sam 24:12), and even more generically as an address of respect to a superior (e.g., 2 Kgs 5:13). Frequently, such usage emphasizes the role of protector or teacher that belongs to the natural usage of the term *father*. It may be used to indicate the founder of an occupation, an institution, or an identifiable group (e.g., Gen 4:20-21), and in this way acts as the counterpart to the Hebrew idiom "son of" referring to one who belongs to such a designated group.

2. Theological context

The commandment to honor one's father and mother (Exod 20:12) reinforces the importance of both male and female parents, not only within the social order but also as an integral aspect of Israel's covenant with Yahweh. It is rooted above all in the gift of LIFE that parents, with God's help, impart to children (Gen 4:1; 5:1-3; *see* CHILD, CHILDREN). The connection between the commandment and this incomparable gift is made in later wisdom literature (Sir 7:27-28). Among the implications of this commandment is the duty of children to obey their parents (Deut 21:18).

While human parenthood is thus theologically important in its own right, it takes on added significance when it is the image or analogy by which God is understood. When used with reference to God, the term *father* almost always appears in the context of Yahweh's covenant relationship to either Israel or Israel's king. This usage is rooted in the covenantal function of creating a bond of KINSHIP between two parties. Thus, Yahweh directs Moses to tell Pharaoh that "Israel is my first-born son" (Exod 4:22). Similarly, in the account of the Davidic Covenant, Yahweh declares concerning King David's offspring: "I will be his father, and he shall be my son" (2 Sam 7:14). Such a father-son relationship between Yahweh and the king is also expressed in some of the royal psalms (e.g., Ps 2:7; *see* COVENANT, OT AND NT). Although the familial language emphasizes an interpersonal bond of care and concern (e.g., Isa 63:16; 64:7-8; Hos 11:1-4), the generational inequality stresses God's authority over Israel or the king and the honor due to God as father (Mal 1:6).

The association of God with the figure of a father in Israel is further illustrated through the not infrequent usage of theophoric names containing ʾav (e.g., Abiel, Abijah, Eliab, Joab). Although the direct appellation of God as father is relatively rare in the OT, its usage becomes more common in the post-exilic period both in biblical (e.g., Isa 63:16; 64:7; Mal 1:6; 2:10) and deuterocanonical texts (Tob 13:4; Wis 2:16; 14:3; Sir

23:1, 4). One can note a development in the later wisdom texts, Wisdom of Solomon and Sirach. In these, the references to God as father are not tied explicitly to Israel as a whole or Israel's king, but the appeal to God as father is made on a personal and individual basis.

The image of God as father is often connected to the theme of creation in the OT (e.g., Isa 45:9-12; 64:7). The father's role in begetting provides a fitting image for the act of creation. Although this usage suggests a more universal understanding of the fatherhood of God, it should also be noted that what is created or begotten is frequently specified as Israel itself (Deut 32:6; Isa 45:11; 64:7) thus returning to the covenant context for use of the term *father* for God. While the two usages are not mutually exclusive, God's particular fatherhood with regard to Israel has priority over a universal fatherhood with respect to all of creation (*see* GOD, METAPHORS FOR; GOD, NAMES OF; GOD THE FATHER).

B. Father in the New Testament
1. Greco-Roman background

The use of the Greek term patēr throughout the Hellenistic World is not radically different from the biblical usage of the Hebrew ʾav. In both contexts the father was understood to be the head and protector of the household and a teacher to his children. Also, father may refer to other ancestors, be used metaphorically as a title of respect, and be an epithet for the deity (e.g., Zeus as "father of humans and gods"). Jew, Greek, and Roman alike would view piety toward one's father as a moral and religious obligation. In Roman law there was a heightened sense of the power a father exercised over his descendants and other dependents by virtue of his paternal authority. Although not absolute, this *patria potestas* (power of the father) was significant, even extending to the power of determining whether an infant should be allowed to live or exposed. While there are some OT parallels to the *patria potestas* with regard to pronouncing a death sentence (Gen 38:24), selling children as slaves (Exod 21:7), or determining one's heir (1 Kgs 1:33-35), there appears to be more of a balance struck between the rights of a father and those of his children (Deut 21:15-17), as well as a greater co-authority shared by father and mother (Deut 21:18-21).

2. Jesus in the Gospels

The social context for NT usage of the term *father* follows closely upon that of the OT. Jesus reaffirms the binding nature of the commandment to honor one's father and mother in opposition to more recent interpretations that would limit the obligations of this commandment (Matt 15:3-6; Mark 7:10-13). Jesus concurs that the commandment extends beyond the obedience of minors to their parents and includes the financial support of parents by adult children (Sir 3:11-14; Mark 7:10-12). At the same time, obligations to parents and family are relativized with reference to the greater good of following Jesus (Matt 10:37-38; Luke 14:26). Even the gravest obligations of piety (e.g., burial) toward one's father are not to come before the demands of discipleship (Matt 8:21-22) and the proclamation of God's kingdom (Luke 9:59-60).

The most prominent usage of the term *father* in the NT is Jesus' practice of referring to God as father, which is attested in all of the canonical Gospels. There are approximately 150 instances in the Gospels in which Jesus refers to God as Father. The Gospel according to Mark (Mark 14:36) as well as Paul's letters (Rom 8:15; Gal 4:6) preserve in Greek transliteration (abba ἀββα) the Aramaic word for father (ʾabbaʾ אַבָּא) that was spoken by Jesus (*see* ABBA). The only instance in the Gospels where Jesus addresses God other than as "Father" is in the cry of abandonment from the cross ("My God, my God . . ." Matt 27:46; Mark 15:34), which is itself a quotation from Ps 22:2.

Both Matthew's and Luke's Gospels (Matt 6:9-13; Luke 11:2-4) contain an account of the LORD'S PRAYER in which the disciples also are instructed to address God as father. While at times Jesus appears to refer to God as father for a relationship that is either exclusive to him (e.g., Matt 7:21; 10:32; 11:27) or in opposition to the paternity of others (John 8:41-42), there are numerous instances in which Jesus refers to God as "your father" when addressing his followers, especially in Matthew's Sermon on the Mount and the corresponding passages in Luke. In the resurrection appearance to Mary Magdalene, Jesus speaks of God as "my father and your father" (John 20:17). The distinction and identity in this usage may indicate a relationship of Jesus to the Father that is at once unique from yet in some sense shared with that of his followers. When Jesus refers to God as "the Father" (with the definite article), there is an indication of a unique relationship between Jesus and the Father (e.g., Matt 11:27; Mark 13:32; Luke 10:22; John 3:35).

3. Paul's Letters

In the Pauline literature, the HOUSEHOLD CODES (Col 3:18–4:1; Eph 5:22–6:4) describe the roles of family members, including fathers, according to the general expectations of Jewish and Hellenistic ethics. They emphasize, however, the role of Christian love in familial relations (Col 3:19; Eph 5:25-33), and caution fathers against provoking their children to anger, while reminding them of their obligation to raise their children "in the discipline and instruction of the Lord" (Eph 6:4). Thus the *patria potestas* is mitigated somewhat, and the religious aspect of education is highlighted.

Paul uses the term *father* in describing his own role as an apostle. Through his ministry of preaching the gospel, Paul becomes the spiritual father of those who come to believe (1 Cor 4:15; Phlm 10). He also refers to his junior collaborators in the ministry as his children (2 Tim 1:2; Titus 1:4).

Paul describes God as Father approximately forty times, usually in the context of liturgical formulas and in the salutations of his letters. He identifies "God our Father and the Lord Jesus Christ" as the source of the grace and peace that he extends to the various recipients of his letters (Rom 1:7; 1 Cor 1:3; 2 Cor 1:2; Gal 1:3; Eph 1:2; Phil 1:2; 2 Thess 1:2; Phlm 3). In addition to calling God our Father, and witnessing to the early Christian usage of abba (Rom 8:15; Gal 4:6), Paul also points to the distinctive relationship that Jesus has to the Father by referring to "the Father of our Lord Jesus Christ" (e.g., Rom 15:6; 2 Cor 1:3).

In Eph 3:14-15, God is called the Father from whom every patria (πατριά fatherhood, family, or nation) takes its name. The passage emphasizes both the honor due to God as Father (Eph 3:14) and the benevolence and graciousness of the Father in lavishing his gifts and love upon his children (Eph 3:16-20).

Bibliography: John W. Miller. *Calling God "Father"* (1999); Carolyn Osiek and David L. Balch. *Families in the New Testament World* (1997); Leo G. Perdue, Joseph Blenkinsopp, John J. Collins, and Carol Meyers. *Families in Ancient Israel* (1997).

PAUL NISKANEN

FATHER IN HEAVEN [ὁ πατήρ ὁ ἐν τοῖς οὐρανοῖς *ho patēr ho en tois ouranois*]. Matthew's Jesus calls God "my (or your) father in heaven" fourteen times (Matt 5:16, 45; 6:1, 9; 7:11, 21; 10:32, 33; 12:50; 16:17; 18:10, 14, 19; 23:9), Mark's Jesus once (Mark 11:25). *Father* is a common address to God in Jewish prayers of the period (Tob 13:4; Sir 51:10a; 3 Macc 6:2-3; 4Q372). "In heaven" locates God as creator and ruler of the universe. Early Christians might also have heard "father in heaven" as a counter-claim to "father of his country," one of the emperor's typical honorifics.

RICHARD B. VINSON

FATHERLESS [יָתוֹם *yathom*, אֵין אָב *ʾen ʾav*]. The term *yathom*, rendered "fatherless" in older English translations, is consistently translated "ORPHAN" in the NRSV. The only occurrence of "fatherless" in the NRSV is a translation of *ʾen ʾav*, literally "no father," as a further description of being orphaned (Lam 5:3).

FATHER'S HOUSE [בֵּית אָב *beth ʾav*; οἶκος τοῦ πατρός *oikos tou patros*]. In the OT, the phrase designates the smallest familial unit, a kinship designation below both tribe and clan and headed by a patriarchal figure (Gen 12:1). It occurs in the plural in census lists (e.g., Num 1:2; Ezra 2:59). In the NT, the most common referent for Father's House is the Temple in Jerusalem (John 2:16/Luke 2:49). An alternate usage points to heaven (John 14:2).

PHILLIP MICHAEL SHERMAN

FATHERS, APOSTOLIC. See APOSTOLIC FATHERS, CHURCH FATHERS.

FATHERS, CHURCH. See APOSTOLIC FATHERS, CHURCH FATHERS.

FATHOM [ὀργυιά orguia]. A nautical unit of depth equivalent to 6 ft. (1.83 m), roughly measured by stretching a lead-weighted length of line between two outstretched arms. Acts 27:28 refers to this unit within the context of Paul's travels at sea.

FATLING [מֵחַ meakh, מְרִיא meri']. As the choicest animal among bovines, it was raised for its use as a sacrifice or for a special celebration and therefore well fed. Other animals were sacrificed alongside it (2 Sam 6:13); however, Ezekiel uses fatling to refer not only to sacrificed cattle (34:3) but also to all the sacrificed animals (39:18). Fatlings were offered as burnt offerings (Ps 66:15) and peace offerings. Fatlings were among the animals that Saul and the Israelites failed to utterly destroy when they defeated the Amalekites (1 Sam 15:9). David sacrificed a fatling in the celebration of bringing the ark of the covenant to Jerusalem (2 Sam 6:13). According to Isaiah's prophecies, fatlings will feed on the ruins of Jerusalem (5:17) and lie down with the lion when the Davidic king rises from the "stump of Jesse" (11:1-6). See FATTED; SACRIFICES AND OFFERINGS.

EMILY R. CHENEY

FATTED [אָבוּס 'evus, אָבַס 'avas, מַרְבֵּק marbeq, מְרִיא meri'; σιτευτός siteutos]. The terms marbeq (lit. "stall-fed," 1 Sam 28:24), 'evus ("trough-fed," Prov 14:4), siteutos (Luke 15:23) and others are used to designate livestock whose value for sacrifice was increased because fullness was associated with wealth and well-being. "Fatted" may be applied to a wide variety of sacrificial animals, including fowl (1 Kgs 4:23), calves (1 Kgs 1:25) and oxen (Prov 15:17). See SACRIFICES AND OFFERINGS.

R. JUSTIN HARKINS

FAWN [עֹפֶר 'ofer; νεβρός nebros]. The NRSV uses "fawn" when translating generic Hebrew words that refer to offspring or children of a DEER or GAZELLE (Gen 49:21; Jer 14:5). Fawns are mentioned twice in the Song of Songs in metaphorical allusions to the beautiful body of a beloved woman (Song 4:5; 7:3) where the Greek term nebros, which actually means "fawn," is used in the LXX to translate 'ofer (STAG). See ANIMALS OF THE BIBLE.

ODED BOROWSKI

FAYUM FRAGMENT. A tiny papyrus fragment from the Fayum in Egypt dated to the late 3rd cent. CE. It contains a poorly preserved text parallel to Matt 26:31-34 and Mark 14:27-30. Because it was discovered in the collection of Archduke Rainer in Vienna, it is also known as the Papyrus Vindobonensis (Vienna) Greek 2325 or the Rainer Gospel Papyrus. G. Bickell found the fragment in Vienna in 1885 and published it in 1887. Scholars from the late 19th cent. forward have proposed that it was a fragment of a gospel that was independent of the canonical Gospels. Though this theory is not without merit, it is now generally thought to be an abbreviated account of the canonical sources, rather than an independent source. The text contains a portion of the story of Jesus referring to Zech 13:7 ("I will strike the [shepherd and the] sheep will be scatter[ed]), followed by a short dialogue between Peter and Jesus. The preserved text is too fragmentary for a definitive reading, though it is typically reconstructed in line with the texts of Mark and Matthew. The fragment was once part of a larger gospel text, though it is too poorly preserved to reveal any significant details about its original context.

MILTON MORELAND

FEAR [אֵימָה 'emah, יִרְאָה yir'ah, פַּחַד pakhadh; φόβος phobos, εὐσέβεια eusebeia]. Fear in the Bible has many generic senses, varying in degree and in object. These range from everyday frights to terror for one's life, from fear of immediate, specific dangers to dread of unknown harm or evil. Most prominent, however, is the biblical conception of fear as a religious disposition, reflected in the expressions, "fear of God" and "fear of the Lord." This complex field of meaning includes the seemingly contradictory responses of, on the one hand, dread before divine holiness, power, and mystery; and, on the other, a reverential awe that trusts in God's graciousness. Pious fear, or reverence, inspires grateful worship, ethical obedience, and the pursuit of wisdom.

A. Terminology
B. Old Testament
  1. Mundane fears
  2. Religious meaning
C. Second Temple Judaism
D. New Testament
  1. Mundane fear
  2. Religious meaning
Bibliography

A. Terminology

The Hebrew language of fear is vivid and concrete. From the verbal root yr' (יָרֵא), "to fear, be in awe," which may retain an elemental association of "trembling" (Gen 3:10), derives the basic noun yir'ah, "fear, awe" (Deut 2:25), and the term mora' (מוֹרָא), "divine terror" (Jer 32:21). The noun pakhadh, "terror" (Job 22:10), derives from the root pkhd (פָּחַד), "to tremble in fear" (Isa 19:16). Also noteworthy are the verbal root b't (בָּעַת), "to startle, terrify" (Job 7:14), and its cognate noun be'athah (בְּעָתָה), "terror" (Jer 8:15). There are two additional nouns signifying "terror," 'emah (Exod 23:27), and maghor (מָגוֹר, Jer 6:25); and several forms derived from the root khtt (חתת) "to be shattered" (Isa 7:8), denoting "overwhelming dismay," e.g., khittah (חִתַּת, Gen 35:5).

Old Testament usage frequently evokes the physical symptoms of fear, sometimes in explicit detail, e.g., Job 4:14, "dread came upon me, and trembling, which made all my bones shake." The vocabulary above is complemented by expressions conveying bodily effects of fear, such as shuddering or creeping flesh (Job 21:6), writhing in distress (Exod 15:14), pounding heart (Jer 4:19), and hair standing on end (Job 4:15). The Hebrew semantic field therefore most closely resembles the English term *trepidation*, "trembling fright or dread." In OT contexts where fear principally signifies respect (Lev 19:3), or piety (Ps 147:11), the physical manifestations of fear are not in the foreground. Rarely, however, is the language of fear totally removed from these corporeal associations.

The LXX usually translates the Hebrew verb yr' with Gr. phobeomai (φοβέομαι), "to fear." In as few as five instances, the Hebrew noun yir'ah is rendered by eusebeia, "reverence" or "piety" (1 Esd 1:23; Prov 1:7; 17:11; Isa 11:12; 33:6). Similarly, in the NT the verb phobeomai and the related noun phobos, "fear," are most frequent, referring to worldly fears (Matt 14:5), respect for persons (Rom 13:7), and also reverence toward God (Acts 9:31). Other derivatives of phobeomai appear a few times: emphobos (ἔμφοβος), "terrified" (Luke 24:5, 37; Acts 10:4; 24:25; Rev 11:13); aphobōs (ἀφόβως), "without fear" (Luke 1:74; 1 Cor 16:10; Phil 1:14; Jude 12); phoberos (φοβερός), "terrifying" (Heb 10:27, 31; 12:21); phobētron (φόβητρον), "terrors" (Luke 21:11); ekphobeō (ἐκφοβέω), "to frighten" (2 Cor 10:9). An infrequent usage in the NT is eusebeia, "respect, reverence, piety" (Acts 3:12; 1 Tim 2:2; 4:7, 8; 6:5; 2 Tim 3:5; 2 Pet 1:3, 6). Related terms are eusebeō (εὐσεβέω), "to act reverently" (1 Tim 5:4) or "to worship" (Acts 17:23); and eusebēs (εὐσεβής), "pious" (Acts 10:2, 7; 2 Pet 2:9). The noun eulabeia (εὐλάβεια) denotes piety (Heb 5:7) or reverence (Heb 12:28); the related adjective eulabēs (εὐλαβής) refers to the devout (Luke 2:25; Acts 2:5; 8:2; 22:12). Finally, the terms deiliaō (δειλιάω), "to be timid" (John 14:27); deilia (δειλία), "timidity" (2 Tim 1:7); deos (δέος), "awe" (Heb 12:28); and ptyrō (πτύρω), "to be frightened, intimidated," each occur once in the NT.

B. Old Testament

1. Mundane fears

The natural world in the OT can display fear (Ps 76:8), and animals are instilled with dread of people (Gen 9:2), although Behemoth and Leviathan are impervious to fright (Job 40:23; 41:33; compare 39:16). Most frequently, however, it is humans who are subject to fear in the OT. This includes fear of lions and other wild beasts (Amos 3:8; Job 5:22). One might be fearful for the security of the household (Prov 31:21), or afraid of everyday threats such as heights and dangers in the streets (Eccl 12:5). Eerie encounters with the unknown provoke fear, e.g., Eliphaz's night vision and the necromancer's summoning of Samuel's spirit (Job 4:12-16; compare 1 Sam 28:12-13).

People in danger, such as the storm-tossed sailors on Jonah's ship, fear for their lives (Jonah 1:5). The greatest source of mortal fear, however, is human enmity. Cain fears vengeance for the murder of Abel (Gen 4:14). Jacob fears the vengeful wrath of Laban and Esau (Gen 31:31; 32:8, 12), and Isaac fears that the men of Gerar will kill him in order to seize Rebekah, his wife (Gen 26:7). Dread of kings' deadly anger is common: Moses fears Pharaoh's reprisal for the killing of an Egyptian (Exod 2:14-15); Adonijah fears Solomon (1 Kgs 1:50); Ahab's princes are justly terrified of Jehu (2 Kgs 10:4); and the prophet Uriah flees for his life from Jehoiakim (Jer 26:21). Nebuchadnezzar's palace master fears for his head (Dan 1:10), and Nehemiah is "very much afraid" of Artaxerxes (Neh 2:2).

The terrors of war loom large in the OT, hence fear of the enemy in battle is often evoked (Deut 20:8; Judg 7:3). The Israelites are terrified by the Egyptian army (Exod 14:10); they are also greatly afraid of the Canaanites (Num 14:1-9), and the Philistines, esp. Goliath (1 Sam 7:7; 17:11, 24). Gideon fears the Midianites (Judg 7:10-12); Saul the Philistines (1 Sam 28:5); and David is very much afraid of Achish of Gath (1 Sam 21:12). It is also reported that their enemies fear Israel: the people of Jericho dread the invading Israelites (Josh 2:8; compare Deut 2:4), as do the Gibeonites (Josh 9:34) and King Adoni-zedek in Jerusalem (Josh 10:1-2). The Syrian kings, frightened by the success of David's campaigns, abandon their alliance with the Ammonites (2 Sam 10:19).

A formulaic expression of assurance, "Do not be afraid," occurs in the everyday language of the OT. Joseph's brothers receive this encouragement from Joseph's servant and from Joseph himself (Gen 43:23; 50:19-21). A midwife tells Rachel, about to die in childbirth, "Do not be afraid; for now you will have another son" (Gen 37:17); and the women attending the wife of Phinehas, also in mortal travail, tell her the same thing (1 Sam 4:20). Jonathan assures David, fearing death at the hand of Saul, "Do not fear" (1 Sam 23:17); and David gives the same assurance to Abiathar and Meribaal, each fearing for their lives (1 Sam 22:23; 2 Sam 9:7). Jael makes treacherous use of the phrase, inviting Sisera in to be murdered (Judg 4:18). Boaz assures Ruth that he will deal with her honorably (Ruth 3:11). For other examples of this expression in commonplace speech, compare 2 Kgs 6:16; 25:24; Jer 40:9; Ps 49:16.

2. Religious meaning

Of the many references to fear in the OT, the great majority (about four-fifths) have God as their object. The OT understanding of fear of God underscores human fragility and vulnerability before the divine. People are tremulous in their approach to God, seized with an intense combination of fear and awe. God, however, demonstrates a gracious character, and human fright becomes worshipful reverence, trusting in God's mercy and gratefully obeying God's commands.

The OT gives ample witness to the notion that encounters with God, or the presence of divine holiness, can be dangerous, even deadly. One cannot see God and live (Exod 33:20; compare Gen 16:13; 32:30; Judg 6:22-23; 13:22; Isa 6:5), and hearing God's voice presents a similar peril (Exod 20:19; Deut 4:33; 5:23-26). The adjectives "terrible," "awesome," are used dozens of times as an attribute of the Lord (Exod 15:11; Deut 7:21; 10:17; Zeph 2:11; Pss 47:2; 68:35; 76:7, 12), God's name (Deut 28:58; Mal 1:14; Pss 99:3; 111:9), and God's deeds (Exod 34:10; Deut 10:21; 2 Sam 7:23; Isa 64:3; Pss 65:5; 66:3; 106:22; 145:6). Persons and things, by cause of their proximity to God's holiness, may likewise inspire fear: e.g., Moses, descending from Sinai; Samuel, calling upon the Lord; and the ARK OF THE COVENANT (Exod 34:30; 1 Sam 12:18; 2 Sam 6:6-10; compare Josh 4:14; Ezek 1:22; Lev 19:30).

Primordial religious dread is often described as fear of the "numinous," a profound unease stirred by God's otherness, mystery, and power. This uncanny sense of the divine is widely known among the religions of the ANE, and is sometimes at play in biblical fear of God. For example, a sense of the numinous perhaps lies at the origin of the appellation, "the Fear of Isaac," for the God of Israel's ancestors (Gen 31:42, 53). But in the OT a more important motive for fearfulness before God is awareness of sin. Already in the garden, the first human is afraid of God (Gen 3:10). Moses fears God's anger after the apostasy of the golden calf (Deut 9:19). The OT anticipates universal judgment, the great and terrible "day of the Lord," when humanity will cower and flee from the "terror of the Lord" (Isa 2:10, 19, 21; compare 13:6-8; Joel 2:1; Amos 5:18).

God's disposition, however, is not determined by wrath. In the aftermath of Israel's great apostasy at the foot of Sinai, God declares to Moses the divine name and character: "The Lord, the Lord, a God merciful and gracious, slow to anger, and abounding in steadfast love and faithfulness, keeping steadfast love for the thousandth generation, forgiving iniquity and transgression and sin" (Exod 34:6-7a). To be sure, the Lord here also is "by no means clearing the guilty" (v. 7b), but the formulation of divine mercy in Exod 34:6-7 (compare Exod 20:5b-6; Num 14:18) becomes a leitmotif of the OT, appearing in psalms of praise (Pss 103:3-4, 8-10; 111:4; 112:4; 116:5; 145:8-9) as well as lament (Ps 86:5, 15; compare Lam 3:22, 32); in Hezekiah's passover decree (2 Chr 30:9) and Ezra's penitential prayer (Neh 9:17, 31); in the prophetic writings (Isa 54:9-10; Jer 32:18; Joel 2:13; Jonah 4:2; Mic 7:18-20), and in apocalyptic writings (Dan 9:4).

As this refrain develops through the OT, there is relatively more emphasis on God's merciful qualities. Fear of God in the OT, therefore, is never removed from the gracious God whose original creative impulse is for good, making the world and blessing it (Gen 1:22, 28; 2:3); the God who keeps the divine promises to the ancestors, Abraham, Isaac, and Jacob; who creates Israel as a people by freeing them from slavery and bestowing upon them the covenantal relationship; and whose relation to humanity is characterized by mercy.

Although theophany in the OT has a terrifying dimension (e.g., Exod 20:18), regularly God's self-disclosure calls people to a response of grateful worship. At the burning bush, Moses is "afraid to look at God" (Exod 3:6), but the encounter results in revelation of the divine name and the promise to free Israel, after which the people will "worship God on this mountain" (Exod 3:12).

Jacob's vision at Bethel stirs fear, but in gratitude for God's promises, Jacob institutes worship of the Lord there (Gen 28:17-22).

Frequently in the OT, human fright meets with the divine response, "Do not fear." This is characteristic of theophanies (Exod 20:20; Judg 6:23; Dan 10:12, 19; Gen 15:1; 21:17; 26:24; 46:3), and is also prominent in the sacral war traditions, where God assures Israel of deliverance from enemies (Exod 14:13; Num 14:9; 21:34; Deut 1:21, 29; 3:2, 22; 7:18; 20:1-3; 31:6, 8; Josh 8:1; 10:8, 25). Second Isaiah makes extensive use of this motif (41:10, 13, 14; 43:1, 5; 44:2; 54:4; compare 44:8; 51:12).

Worshipers in the OT declare that God's mercy makes possible their approach: "But I, through the abundance of your steadfast love, will enter your house, I will bow down toward your holy temple in awe of you" (Ps 5:7); or again, "If you, O Lord, should mark iniquities, Lord, who could stand? But there is forgiveness with you, so that you may be revered" (Ps 130:3-4). Genuine reverence in worship means approaching God with confidence, yet humble gratitude.

To "fear the Lord" can be a technical designation for participation in the cult. This is made clear in the account of 2 Kgs 17, where peoples in the former Northern Kingdom, after the Assyrian destruction, worship the Lord but also other gods (2 Kgs 17:23-41; compare vv. 25, 28, 32, 35). Properly, however, to "fear the Lord" means to worship the Lord exclusively and to live in righteousness. These elements are integrated seamlessly in Deuteronomy, where covenantal loyalty entails sole worship of the Lord and faithful obedience. The central demand of Deuteronomy, for absolute and exclusive love of God (Deut 6:4-5), is framed by the call for fear of the Lord (6:2, 13). Repeatedly Deuteronomy exhorts the people to love God, keep God's command-ments, walk in the Lord's ways, serve and hold fast to the Lord (10:12-13, 20; 11:1, 13, 22; 13:4; 19:9; 30:6, 16). Fear as worshipful reverence and as obedience are inseparable here. Fear of God and striving to live a righteous life are emphatically associated with just liv-ing and kindness to the stranger or resident alien (e.g., Deut 10:18-20; 25:18).

In the wisdom literature, fear of the Lord is "the beginning of wisdom," a central concept (Prov 1:7; 9:10; Ps 111:10; Job 28:28). For the book of Proverbs, this means that fear of the Lord and wisdom have a complementary, even reciprocal, relationship. Rever-ence toward God is the prerequisite to true wisdom (1:7; 9:10; compare 15:33), yet the sages teach critical reflection on religious matters; hence embracing their instruction affords deeper understanding of the fear of the Lord and knowledge of God (2:1-7). Fear of the Lord is also here a moral category, motivating righ-teousness and the avoidance of evil (2:9-10; 3:7; 16:6). Qohelet's reference to fear of the Lord is more austere, usually focused on God's total sovereignty (Eccl 3:14; 5:7; 8:12-13). In the final analysis, the whole duty of humanity is to fear God and keep God's command-ments (Eccl 12:13).

In the Psalms, "those who fear the Lord" is a dis-tinctive usage with several possible meanings. In some contexts the phrase appears to designate the congrega-tion at worship in the Temple (Pss 22:23, 25; 31:19; 66:16). Elsewhere it may refer to the entire people (Pss 60:4; 61:5; 85:9), or to those who are faithful, "the pious" (Pss 25:14; 33:18; 34:7, 9; 103:11, 13, 17; 111:5; 145:19; 147:11). In Pss 115:11, 13; 118:4; 135:20, "those who fear the Lord" are not Gentile con-verts, but simply members of the post-exilic worshiping community.

In some wisdom psalms, fear of the Lord is closely associated with devotion to Torah. The sage of Ps 1:2 extols delight in the Lord's "teaching" (torath תּוֹרַת). Psalm 19:7-9 puts fear of the Lord on a par with the Lord's "teaching," "statutes," "instruction," and "judg-ments." Elsewhere fear of the Lord is linked with keep-ing the Lord's commandments (Ps 112:1), walking in the Lord's ways (Ps 128:1), and following the Lord's precepts (Ps 119:63). This Torah piety flourishes in early Judaism and also anticipates the ethical dimension of fear of the Lord in the NT.

C. Second Temple Judaism

The Apocrypha and Pseudepigrapha generally do not dwell on the themes of worldly and religious fear so frequently as the canonical books of the OT. The important exception to this is Sirach, where fear of the Lord and wisdom are leading theological motifs, virtually identified with each other (Sir 1:11-20; 25:10-11). Sirach also presents a more developed form of the

Torah piety, joined with wisdom and fear of the Lord, known already in the OT (Sir 2:15-17; 21:11; compare 2:7-11; 40:26-27). Elsewhere in the Apocrypha, fear of God refers to the piety of diaspora Jews: a God-fearer is a righteous person (Jdt 8:8; Sus 2). In some Pseudepig-rapha, fearing God amounts to loving God (*Let. Aris.* 159, 189; *T. Benj.* 3:3, 4*b*). The apocalyptic texts relate fearful reactions to revelatory events such as visions, divine messengers, and heavenly signs (*1 En.* 14:13-14; 15:1; 21:9; 60:3).

The Dead Sea Scrolls contain only a few of the numerous OT expressions for fear. "One who fears God" appears to designate a person deemed admissible to the cult (1QHᵃ XX, 3; CD X, 2; CD XX, 19). The War Scroll draws on the OT sacral war tradition in exhorting the children of light not to fear their enemies (1QM X, 3; XV, 8; XVII, 4), and terror at the judgment of God is evinced in the Rule of the Community (1QS IV, 2) and in the Hodayot (1QHᵃ XVIII, 34).

Philo widely follows the common OT and Jewish usage for fear of God (*Migr.* 21). He casts God in philo-sophical terms as a solution for fear and distress (*Somn.* 1.173). The righteous therefore are distinguished more by love than fear (*Spec. Laws* 1.300), and fear must be complemented by courage (*Her.* 28). The writings of Josephus contain many references to fear, but usually not related to God. Worldly dangers are most in view for Josephus, especially the terrors of war. The linking of fear of God and loving God in Deut 6:5, 13 gener-ates a vigorous debate in the rabbinic literature over the relative merit of the two. Simeon ben Eleazar declares, "Greater is the one who acts from love than the one who acts from fear (*m. Sotah* 31a). There is also debate whether Job's piety is motivated by fear or love of God (*m. Sotah* 5:5).

D. New Testament

1. Mundane fear

Rarely does fear figure in the NT apart from religious or theological associations. In such cases, it usually concerns fear of other persons. In the parable of the talents, a slave fears his harsh master (Matt 25:25; Luke 19:21). Joseph, seeking to return to Judea, is afraid of the new ruler, Archelaus (Matt 2:22). Herod fears John the Baptist and is reluctant to execute him (Mark 6:20). The Jewish religious leaders fear Jesus (Mark 11:18); and in Acts, the Jerusalem disciples are afraid of Saul (Acts 9:26).

Frequently, religious and civil authorities are afraid of angry crowds. Matthew depicts the Jewish religious leaders as stymied by fear of the crowd in their conflict with Jesus (Matt 21:26, 46). Pilate, seeking to release Jesus, is intimidated by the crowd (John 19:8). Accord-ing to Matthew, Herod fears not John the Baptist but the crowd (Matt 14:5). In Acts, the Jerusalem Temple police are inhibited by fear of an angry mob (Acts 5:26), and a Roman tribune fears that a violent crowd will tear

Paul to pieces (Acts 23:10). Finally, Roman magistrates and a tribune fear punishment from their imperial superiors for mistreating Paul, a Roman citizen (Acts 16:38; 22:29).

2. Religious meaning

Fear of God is less prominent in the NT than in the OT, but many of the OT religious motifs do appear here. The Gospel narratives know well the intense combination of fear, wonder, and worship that can issue from an encounter with divine power or presence. Zechariah in the Temple, e.g., and the shepherds in the field, are terrified by the appearance of angels (Luke 1:12; 2:9), but God's messengers give the reassuring words, "Do not be afraid" (Luke 1:13; 2:10; compare 1:30; Matt 1:20; 28:5; Acts 27:24). The disciples, at sea in the storm, are terrified to see Jesus walking on the water, but he replies, "It is I, do not be afraid" (Matt 14:26; Mark 6:50; John 6:20). By all accounts the disciples are terrified at the transfiguration; the Matthean account reports Jesus' assurance, "Do not be afraid" (Matt 17:6-7; Mark 9:6; Luke 9:34). Events such as Jesus' healings of the demoniac, the woman with a hemorrhage, and the paralytic stir fear but also a wondrous awe, praise of God, and faith (Mark 5:15; 33; Matt 9:8; compare Luke 7:16). At the cross, the centurion is terrified, yet confesses Jesus a "son of God" (Matt 27:54); and the women at the tomb respond to Christ's resurrection with fear, great joy, and worship (Matt 28:8-9).

Fear of divine judgment is clearly evinced in the NT (e.g., Heb 10:27-31), and uncomprehending fear can be a sign of weak faith (Mark 4:40). But reverential fear of God is a remedy for the fears of this world: suffering (1 Pet 1:6), want (Luke 12:32-24), opposition (Phil 1:28), persecution (Rev 2:10), and death (Heb 2:15). Faithful fear of the Lord has a moral dimension (2 Cor 7:1). It characterizes the life of the church (Acts 9:31), and of individual believers who, confident that God is at work for good in them, work out their own salvation "with fear and trembling" (Phil 2:12-13). The expression here conveys not frightfulness but fervency (compare 2 Cor 7:15). For the author of 1 John, God's perfect love, realized among the faithful, banishes anxious fear entirely: "There is no fear in love, but perfect love casts out fear; for fear has to do with punishment, and whoever fears has not reached perfection in love" (1 John 4:18).

In certain contexts the fear of the Lord entails respect for the social authorities of the day: "Honor everyone. Love the family of believers. Fear God. Honor the emperor" (1 Pet 2:17; compare Rom 13:1-7). In similar fashion, pious slaves respect their masters (Eph 6:5; Col 3:22; 1 Pet 2:18-25); wives their husbands (Eph 5:22-24; 1 Pet 3:1); and children their parents (Eph 6:1-2; Col 3:20).

A special usage occurs in Luke–Acts: "those who fear God" can refer simply to the faithful (Luke 1:50; compare 18:2, 4); but in Acts, the GODFEARERS (10:2, 22, 35; 13:16, 26) or "worshipers, pious ones" (13:43; 16:14; 17:4, 17; 18:7), appear to be a special class of non-Jewish persons who are not full converts, but believe in the biblical God, worship at the synagogue, and live in close relation to the Jewish community. *See* ANXIETY; HOLY, HOLINESS, NT; HOLY, HOLINESS, OT.

Bibliography: Walther Eichrodt. *Theology of the Old Testament.* Vol. 2 (1967) 268–77; Mayer I. Gruber. "Fear, Anxiety and Reverence in Akkadian, Biblical Hebrew and Other North-West Semitic Languages." *VT* 40 (1990) 411–22; A. Thomas Kraabel. "The Disappearance of the 'God-fearers.'" *Numen* 28 (1981) 113–26; J. Andrew Overman. "The God-Fearers: Some Neglected Features." *JSNT* 32 (1988) 17–26; J. Reynolds and R. Tannenbaum. *Jews and God-fearers at Aphrodisias: Greek Inscriptions with Commentary* (1987).

HAROLD C. WASHINGTON

FEAR OF ISAAC [פַּחַד יִצְחָק pakhadh yitskhaq]. Appearing only in Gen 31:42 (though see also the related designation in Gen 31:53), the divine designation "fear of Isaac" alludes at once to the awe that the deity engenders in the devotee and to the terror that is manifested in the protection of the devotee.

C. L. SEOW

FEAST OF DEDICATION [חֲנֻכָּה khanukkah; τὰ ἐγκαίνια ta enkainia]. Commonly known by its Hebrew designation, HANUKKAH, this festival may be referred to in the title of Ps 30, "A Song at the dedication of the Temple." This title may reflect the practice of singing that psalm in the Second Temple during Hanukkah, which begins on the twenty-fifth day of Kislev (November–December). The festival was inaugurated by Judah Maccabee in 165 BCE (1 Macc 4:36-51; 2 Macc 10:5-8) at the rededication to God of the Temple on Mount Moriah. The Temple had been turned into a temple of the Olympian Zeus by Antiochus IV Epiphanes three years before (1 Macc 3:54; compare 2 Macc 6:2; 10:5). Second Maccabees 10:6 explains that the holiday is celebrated for eight days "like a feast of tabernacles." This simile treats the seven days of Tabernacles and the additional "eighth day" of Lev 23:36 and Num 29:35 as a single festival. Moreover, 2 Macc 10:6 indicates that at the initial celebration of Hanukkah in 165 BCE the people marched with the festival bouquet consisting of the palm frond and the additional plants prescribed in Lev 23:40. The festival originated as a postponed Festival of Tabernacles. Because of Antiochus's decrees outlawing Judaism, Tabernacles could not be observed that year in the month of Tishri. The precedents for a make-up holiday are the make-up Passover in the second month of the year (Iyar) for those who are unclean or "far away" during the regular Passover in the first month (Nisan) (Num 9) and the public celebration of the Passover in the second month in the reign of Hezekiah (2 Chr 30).

The current practice of each Jewish family or individual lighting oil lamps or candles on each night of Hanukkah beginning with one light on the first evening and increasing the number of lights by one each night (*b. Sabb.* 21b) is traced variously to 1) the Maccabees having lit lamps in the Temple court on the twenty-fifth of Kislev 165 BCE (the Jewish prayer "for the miracles" recited in each prayer service and in the Grace After Meals throughout the festival); 2) the account of the miraculous occurrence that a vial containing enough pure olive oil for one day kept the Temple candelabrum burning for eight days (scholium to Scroll of Fasts; and *b. Sabb.* 21b); and 3) the perception that both Hanukkah candles and Christmas lights incorporate the lighting of lights to commemorate the winter solstice or Saturnalia. In fact, the Talmud (*b. ʿAbod. Zar.* 8a) contends that the latter eight-day festival was originally a monotheistic rite established by Adam and that only later was it adopted by polytheists. Josephus (*Ant.* 12.323-26) calls Hanukkah "the Festival of Lights," explaining the latter designation as a metaphor for liberty.

According to John 10:22-42 it was during a pilgrimage to the Temple to celebrate the festival of Dedication (ta enkainia) that Jesus was challenged by the Jews, "If you are the Christ, tell us plainly." According to the apocryphal *Gospel of the Birth Mary*, it was at the Dedication that an angel appeared to Joachim and his wife, Anna, in the Temple and told them that she would conceive and bear Mary, who would give birth to Jesus, Son of the Most High God (*Gos. Bir. Mary* 1–2).

Bibliography: Elias J. Bickerman. *The God of the Maccabees* (1979); Vered Noam. "The Miracle of the Cruise of Oil: The Metamorphosis of a Legend." *HUCA* 73 (2002) 191–226; Gale A. Yee. *Jewish Feasts and the Gospel of John* (1989).

MAYER GRUBER

FEAST OF WEEKS. *See* WEEKS, FEAST OF.

FEAST OR FESTIVAL OF BOOTHS. *See* BOOTHS, FEAST OR FESTIVAL OF.

FEASTS AND FASTS. Both feasts (festivals) and fasts were occasions for religious rites in response to events, whether favorable or unfavorable. While there were spontaneous times for celebration and grief, there were also set times for communal observances. The DAY OF ATONEMENT falls into both categories in that it is termed a festival and a fast.

A. Feasts/Festivals
  1. Lists of holidays
    a. Lists of pilgrimage festivals

    b. Priestly sources
    c. Ezekiel's list
    d. The book of Esther
  2. Sources outside the Old Testament
    a. List in 1 and 2 Maccabees
    b. Greek texts from Egypt
    c. Festivals listed in the Dead Sea Scrolls
    d. Festivals in the NT
B. Fasts
  1. Fasting by individuals
  2. Fasting by groups
  3. Attitudes toward fasting
  4. Fasting and special experiences
  5. Dated fasts
Bibliography

A. Feasts/Festivals

1. Lists of holidays

a. Lists of pilgrimage festivals. In one category of these texts, there are short statements about three pilgrimage festivals, times when males were to appear before God at the sanctuary with an offering (Exod 23:14-17; 34:18, 22-23; Deut 16:1-17 [here Passover is included in the Festival of Unleavened bread, vv. 1-3*a*, 5-7]; *see* PASSOVER AND FEAST OF UNLEAVENED BREAD); in the immediate context of the first two of these passages the SABBATH is mentioned as well (Exod 23:12; 34:21). In Exod 23, part of the covenant code (Exod 20:22–23:33), there are no specific dates for the three occasions. It calls the first of the pilgrimage holidays "the festival of unleavened bread" and stipulates that Israelites were to eat unleavened bread for seven days "at the appointed time in the month of Abib, for in it you came out of Egypt" (23:15). The second is "the festival of harvest, of the first fruits of your labor, of what you sow in the field" (v. 16). Nothing is said about the duration of the festival or the month it which it occurs. The third is "the festival of ingathering at the end of the year, when you gather in from the field the fruit of your labor" (v. 16). That this last harvest season coincided with the end of the year suggests an autumnal beginning of the year in the calendar that underlies the list. Exodus 34, which offers the contents of the new set of tablets that God gave Moses, provides similar information about the three pilgrimage holidays. It differs from the one in chap. 23 in that it calls the second holiday "the Feast of Weeks" which was associated with "the first fruits of wheat harvest" (34:22), although it too fails to specify a date and does not give a reason for the name. The third festival is dated to "the turn of the year," which may mean the same as the "end of the year" in chap. 23. Deuteronomy 16 is more detailed and also introduces some concerns characteristic of the book. It orders the Israelites to "observe the month of Abib by keeping the Passover" (v. 1) and commands them to offer the Passover sacrifice (from flock or herd) "at the place that the LORD will choose as a dwelling for his name" (v. 2; see vv. 5-6). The Passover sacrifice was to be eaten with no leaven, and the rule was that unleavened bread ("the bread of affliction" [v. 3]) be eaten for seven days (vv. 3-4, 8). For the second of the three holidays Deuteronomy offers an explanation for why it was called the "festival of weeks": "You shall count seven weeks; begin to count the seven weeks from the time the sickle is first put to the standing grain. Then you shall keep the festival of weeks . . ." (vv. 9-10a). An offering was to be made at the one place, and the time was to be marked by rejoicing (vv. 10-11). The passage thus furnishes the first rough approximation of when the Festival of Weeks was to take place. The third holiday is for the first time called "the Festival of Booths" (or, "Festival of Tabernacles") in v. 13 and, like the Festival of Unleavened Bread, it was to last for seven days (v. 15; see BOOTHS, FEAST OR FESTIVAL OF). It too was a joyful time associated with a harvest season: "when you have gathered in the produce from your threshing floor and your wine press" (v. 13). The seven-day celebration was to take place at the sanctuary.

b. Priestly sources. A second category of lists, commonly attributed to priestly sources, finds expression in Lev 23 (see H, HOLINESS CODE) and Num 28–29 (see P, PRIESTLY WRITERS). The two provide fuller enumerations that also incorporate the three pilgrimage festivals of the shorter summaries; they also date most of the festivals to specific times. They use a system of numbered, not named, months, with the sequence beginning in the spring. Leviticus 23 places its list of holidays under the rubric of "holy convocations, my appointed festivals" (v. 1), whereas Num 28–29 prefaces the schedule with the words "My offering, the food of my offerings by fire, my pleasing odor, you shall take care to offer to me at its appointed time" (28:2). As a consequence, this latter listing includes many details about the appropriate sacrifices for each occasion, most of which are not found in Lev 23. Combining the information from the two lists, the full pentateuchal set of special occasions results:

Daily offering, morning and evening (only in Num 28:3-8; see also Exod 29:38-42)

Sabbaths on the seventh day (Lev 23:3; Num 28:9-10)

First day of each month (only in Num 28:11-15)

Passover (month 1/day 14 at twilight; Lev 23:5; Num 28:16): Although neither of the two lists includes it, Num 9:6-13 gives rules for a second Passover on 2/14, one month after the normal time for the festival. The second possibility for keeping Passover was for the convenience of an individual who "is unclean through touching a corpse, or is away on a journey" (v. 10) on 1/14.

Festival of Unleavened Bread (1/15-21; Lev 23:6-8; Num 28:17-25): The two lists explicitly separate the week of unleavened bread from the Passover that falls on the previous day.

Waving of the Sheaf (1/?): Only Lev 23:9-14 mentions the ceremony in which the priest waves the sheaf of the first fruits of the harvest. Verse 11 dates the occasion to "the day after the sabbath," but it does not specify which Sabbath it intends or in which sense it is using *Sabbath*. An ambiguity could arise in a context where *Sabbath* refers not only to the seventh day of each week but also to days of convocations on which no work was permitted (see 23:32 for the Day of Atonement). The difficulty presented by the phrase "the day after the sabbath" gave rise to differences in figuring the date of the waving ceremony and consequently of the Festival of Weeks, the date for which is calculated from the time of the wave offering.

Festival of Weeks (3/?): Both priestly lists include the holiday (Lev 23:15-21; Num 28:26-31), but only Lev 23 treats the issue of when it occurs. It says: "And from the day after the sabbath, from the day on which you bring the sheaf of the elevation offering, you shall count off seven weeks; they shall be complete. You shall count until the day after the seventh sabbath, fifty days; then you shall present an offering of new grain to the LORD" (vv. 15-16). A period of fifty days from some point after Passover entails that the Festival of Weeks would be in the third month.

Trumpets (7/1): Both lists also refer to a festival for blowing trumpets (Lev 23:23-25; Num 29:1-6). The fact that the first of the seventh month is singled out from the other first days of months indicates that it had a special status, but blowing of trumpets is the only characteristic of it in the lists, apart from its offerings. Later this date was to be called ROSH HA-SHANAH or NEW YEAR.

Day of Atonement (7/10): The two lists (Lev 23:26-32; Num 29:7-11) include among the provisions for the day that the Israelites were to deny themselves (as the NRSV translates) or, in another interpretation, were to fast, on the tenth day of the seventh month (Lev 23:27, 29, 32; Num 29:7). Leviticus 23:32 adds that the self-denial or fasting was to extend from the evening of 7/9 until the next evening, a full day. The ceremonies involved in the Day of Atonement are described in much more detail in Leviticus 16. There, among the rituals at the sanctuary, one reads about the two goats, one offered to the deity, the other sent to the wilderness, to Azazel, bearing the sins of Israel.

Festival of Booths/Tabernacles (7/15–21 [with an eighth day, 7/22]): The two lists devote sizable sections to the last holiday of the year (Lev 23:33-36, 39-43; Num 29:12-38 [the length of this section is due to the fact that it enumerates the offerings for each day of the festival]). Both stipulate a seven-day festival but make reference to an eighth day as well (Lev 23:36, 39; Num 29:35-38). The reason for the name of the holiday is given in Lev 23:42-43 which explain that the Israelites were to live in booths during those seven days to recall that the LORD made their ancestors live in booths when he led them out of Egypt.

c. Ezekiel's list. The prophet Ezekiel, in his vision of the restoration (chaps. 40–48), includes a section in which he speaks about offerings, and in it he emphasizes the responsibility of the prince to provide the ingredients for the sacrifices. As one might expect, the prophet who was also a priest was familiar with a range of special days (45:17: "the festivals, the NEW MOON, and the sabbaths, all the appointed festivals of the house of Israel"), but in the only place in which he lists holidays (45:18-25) he compiles a short and in part unusual schedule. He makes reference to an offering of a bull on 1/1 to purify the Temple and adds that the same procedure was to be followed on 1/7 to effect atonement for "anyone who has sinned through error or ignorance" (v. 20). Following these instructions, he deals with Passover, dated to 1/14, the seven days of eating unleavened bread (v. 21), and an unnamed seven-day festival beginning on 7/15 (v. 25), that is, the Festival of Booths in the priestly lists.

d. The book of Esther. The table of holidays in the Pentateuch was lengthened in later times by many Jews. The book of Esther, which narrates a story set in Persia times, explains the origin of the Festival of PURIM or Lots (3:7; 9:24). The new holiday celebrated the triumph of the Jews in the Persian empire over their enemy Haman and his forces who had intended to annihilate them on Adar (the twelfth month) 13, the date designated by casting the lot. With royal permission, the Jews defended themselves and in fact slaughtered their enemies on that date. The Jews in Susa the capital did so on both the thirteenth and the fourteenth of the same month, resting on the fifteenth, while Jews in the provinces rested on the fourteenth (9:1-17). "Therefore the Jews of the villages, who live in the open towns, hold the fourteenth day of the month of Adar as a day for gladness and feasting, a holiday on which they send gifts of food to one another" (9:19). Mordecai, however, is said to have ordered that Adar 14 and 15 be celebrated as an annual holiday, "as the days on which the Jews gained relief from their enemies, and as the month that had been turned for them from sorrow into gladness and from mourning into a holiday; that they should make them days of feasting and gladness, days

for sending gifts of food to one another and presents to the poor" (9:22; for the plural "days" see vv. 26, 31 ["days" of Purim] 27 ["these two days]" 28 ["these days of Purim]). Nevertheless, only Adar 14 came to be regarded as a holiday. Second Maccabees 15:36 is the earliest evidence for the festival other than the book of Esther; it refers to Adar 14 as "Mordecai's day."

2. Sources outside the Old Testament

a. List in 1 and 2 Maccabees. First and Second Maccabees increased the roster of holidays by introducing the Festival of HANUKKAH (the word means "dedication"), an eight-day festival beginning on 9/25. The holiday took its origin in the act of cleansing and dedicating the Jerusalem Temple after it had been defiled by order of the Seleucid King Antiochus IV in 167 BCE (1 Macc 1:41-59; 2 Macc 6:1-6). Judas the Maccabee, the leader of the military response to the king's policies, and his forces were able to gain control of the Temple Mount and repair and consecrate the sanctuary in 165 or 164 BCE (1 Macc 4:36-58; 2 Macc 10:1-8). Judas, his brothers, and "all the assembly of Israel" decided that the occasion ("the dedication of the altar") should be memorialized by an eight-day festival, beginning on Chislev (the ninth month) 25 (1 Macc 4:59; see 2 Macc 10:6-8). Several times Second Maccabees associates Hanukkah with the Festival of Booths (10:6; see also one of the letters prefixed to the historical narrative, 1:9). The precise significance of the association is not clear, although both were eight-day events. Second Maccabees also advocates a second holiday in the month Adar. After Judas and his forces had defeated the Seleucid general Nicanor, who had threatened to raze the temple and build one to Dionysus on that very spot (14:33), they voted "never to let this day go unobserved, but to celebrate the thirteenth day of the twelfth month . . ." (15:36). This Day of Nicanor is, as the text observes, falls one day before "Mordecai's day," that is, Purim.

b. Greek texts from Egypt. Some other Jewish texts written in Greek mention festivals that, like the Day of NICANOR, did not survive antiquity. Philo of Alexandria (ca. 20 BCE to 50 CE) wrote that the completion of the work of translating the Torah into Greek was still celebrated in his time in Alexandria by an annual holiday at Pharos where, according to the traditional story, the translation had been prepared several centuries earlier (Philo, *Mos.* 2.41-42). He claims that not only Jews but many others as well celebrated the occasion. Third Maccabees 6:36 speaks about a festival to mark the deliverance of Jews in Egypt at the time of Ptolemy IV Philopator (221–204 BCE) but does not offer a specific set of dates for it. It may be that 6:39-40 imply a seven-day celebration (Epiphi [April to May] 8–14, the seven days after Epiphi 5–7 when the destruction was to occur). Later in the same book one reads about a festival (7:19) but it is not clear whether the same or a different one is meant.

c. Festivals listed in the Dead Sea Scrolls. The community associated with the Dead Sea Scrolls was in possession of a series of texts that mention the festivals. Those texts list and date the pentateuchal holidays (including the second Passover) but never mention Purim and Hanukkah, the extra-pentateuchal celebrations. A category of texts that have been labeled calendrical by their editors (especially 4Q319, 320, 321, 324, 325, 326, and 327 [or 394 1-2]) provide varied lists, often mentioning the twenty-four groups of priests who each week rotated service at the Temple (see 1 Chr 24:7-18) as a way to name weeks. The kinds of information embodied in these texts allow one to infer the dates even for the festivals not dated in the Bible. So, e.g., the date for the waving ceremony of Lev 23:9-14 is 1/26 (a Sunday and thus the day after the Sabbath [4Q320 4 III, 3, 13; 4 IV, 8; 4 V, 2, 11; 4 VI, 6; 4Q321 2 II, 9; 2 III, 3, 7; 4Q325 I, 3; 4Q326 4]), and the Festival of Weeks, 50 days later, falls on 3/15 (4Q320 4 III, 5; 4Q321 2 II,5). These dates are calculated on the 364-day annual calendar used by the group for its sacred festivals. In these lists, the scriptural Festival of Trumpets is called the Day of Remembrance [4Q319 13 5 (4Q259+4Q319 VIII, 5); 4Q320 4 III, 6; 4 IV, 2; 4Q321 2 II, 2,6] . A second relevant classification of texts found among the scrolls—often called Rewritten Bible or, better, Rewritten Scripture—includes different kinds of writings that offer information about the festivals. The Temple Scroll and the *Book of Jubilees* are the most prominent examples. *Jubilees* explicitly dates the Festival of Weeks to the middle of the third month, which, according to 44:1-5, must fall on 3/15 (see also 14:10; 15:1). In the book it is the time for covenant making and renewal, just as may have been the case at Qumran. The Temple Scroll, in a rather fragmentary section (cols. XIII-XXIX), seems to treat the pentateuchal festivals but adds several others to them. It lists the daily offerings (XIII, 10-17), the Sabbath offering (XIII, 17-XIV, 7), the first day of each month (XIV, 7–XV, 3), the days of consecration of priests (XV, 3–XVII, 4; perhaps 1/1–1/7), Passover (XVII, 6-9 [1/14]), the Festival of Unleavened Bread (XVII, 10-16 [seven days, beginning on 1/15]), the waving ceremony (XVIII, 2-10 [the date is not preserved]), the Festival of Weeks (XVIII, 10–XIX, 9 [the date is not preserved]), a festival of the first fruits of wine (XIX, 11–XXI, 10 [no date preserved but it is 50 days after the Festival of Weeks]), a festival of the first fruits of new oil (XXI, 12–XXIII, 2 [no date preserved]; see 4Q365 23 9), a festival of the wood offering (XXIII, 3–XXV, 1 [possibly 6/23-29]; see 4Q365 23 5-11), the day of remembrance (XXV, 3-10 [7/1]), the Day of Atonement (XXV, 10–XXVII, 10 [7/10]), and the Festival of Booths (XXVII, 10–XXIX, 1 [eight days, beginning on 7/15]). The waving ceremony, the Festival of Weeks, the festival of wine, and the festival of oil form a series in which each holiday after the waving ritual is separated from the previous one by fifty days. For example, 4Q329 1 II(4Q394 1-2 v) dates an oil festival to 6/22; extrapolating from that date, the waving ceremony would take place on 1/26, the Festival of Weeks on 3/15, and the festival of wine on 5/3.

d. Festivals in the NT. In the NT there are a few references to the Jewish festivals. Passover is familiar from the Gospels, especially the passion narratives (but see also Luke 2:41-52), while Pentecost (the Festival of Weeks) is the setting for the outpouring of the Holy Spirit in Acts 2. Jesus celebrated Passover (John 2:13-25), the Festival of Booths (John 7–8), and Hanukkah (10:22-39), and Paul seems to have observed the Festival of Unleavened Bread (Acts 20:6) and Pentecost (20:16). The Day of Atonement is a very important thematic element in Hebrews (see chap. 9).

B. Fasts

Fasts and fasting receive fairly frequent mention in the Bible and could take the form of either personal or communal exercises.

1. Fasting by individuals

Named people denied food to themselves in times of great crisis or need. King David fasted as his and Bathsheba's first child, a product of their adulterous union, struggled for life (2 Sam 12:16, 21-23; see also 1 Kgs 21:27; Ps 35:13), while Ezra fasted when he heard about mixed marriages (Ezra 9:5; compare 8:21, 23). Nehemiah did the same when he learned of Jerusalem's devastated condition (Neh 1:4). The extraordinarily pious Judith was exceptional in that she regularly fasted more days than she ate—every day other than Sabbaths and festivals and the days before them (Jdt 8:6; but compare the elderly Anna who "never left the temple but worshiped there with fasting and prayer day and night" [Luke 2:37]).

2. Fasting by groups

Spontaneous communal exercises in fasting are attested for times of military crises (1 Sam 7:6; Jer 36:6, 9; Bar 1:5; Jdt 4:9, 13; 1 Macc 3:47; 2 Macc 13:12), natural disasters such as invasion by locusts (Joel 1:14; 2:12, 15), and danger of annihilation (Jonah 3:5; Esth 4:3) or shipwreck (Acts 27:9). In the days of Ezra and Nehemiah, the people fasted and dressed in sackcloth as they gathered for the purposes of separating themselves from foreigners and confess their own sins (Neh 9:1). David and his men are said to have fasted as part of their mourning after the deaths of Saul and Jonathan (2 Sam 1:12), while David alone is supposed to have refused food at the death of Abner (3:35).

3. Attitudes toward fasting

Depriving oneself of food was regarded as a valuable religious exercise, one that many Jews appear to have practiced. The Pharisees and their disciples are said to have fasted (Matt 9:14; Mark 2:18) as are John (Matt 11:18) and his disciples (Mark 2:18; Luke 5:33); they are contrasted with Jesus' disciples who surprisingly did not follow this custom. When questioned about this strange state of affairs, Jesus explained that while the bridegroom was with the disciples, they could not fast but they would fast when he is taken away from them (Mark 2:19-20//Matt 9:14-15//Luke 5:34-35). In fact, Luke quotes a Pharisee as saying he fasted twice per week (18:12). According to Tob 12:8, prayer is good when accompanied by fasting although proper almsgiving is better (see also Sir 34:26; Luke 2:37; Acts 13:2, 3; 14:23). Sincere fasting is mentioned by psalmists (69:10; 109:24), and if the desired outcome of fasting did not occur, those who were denying themselves in this way could be disappointed (Isa 58:3; Jer 14:12). The prophets were critical of some ways of fasting, and one of them defined a true fast, not as bowing "the head like a bulrush" and lying in sackcloth and ashes, but as doing away with injustice and sharing food with the hungry, houses with the homeless, and clothing with the naked (Isa 58:3-7; Isa 58 later became the prophetic reading for the Day of Atonement, a day of fasting). In the Sermon on the Mount, Jesus assumed that his followers would fast but warned against hypocritical forms of fasting. He urged a more private approach to the discipline—one in which others will not be able to see what was happening; the heavenly Father would, however, observe it and give a reward (Matt 6:16-18; see also *T. Jos.* 3:4-5). Jesus himself, like Moses on Mount Sinai, fasted forty days during the temptation (Matt 4:2//Luke 4:2).

4. Fasting and special experiences

There is some evidence that fasting could be employed as a means to induce unusual religious experiences. At any rate, the practice is mentioned in several such contexts. So, e.g., Daniel prayed and fasted as he made confession to God after reading and puzzling over the meaning of Jeremiah's seventy-year prophecy (Dan 9:3). His prayer was interrupted by the appearance of the angel Gabriel who explained the prophet's words to him. In 2 Esd 5:13 the seer is told to fast for seven days, after which he would see greater things (a second vision) than the angel had already revealed to him. He received the same order before his third vision (6:31), but the angel commanded him not to fast before vision 4 (9:23).

5. Dated fasts

Two kinds of communal fasts are connected with specific dates. The first is the Day of Atonement (7/10), which became associated with fasting. The practice of fasting is related to the command that the Israelites "deny" themselves (Lev 16:29, 31). Whatever may be the full range of meaning for this phrase, the understanding of it as meaning *fasting* came to characterize

the day. In the Qumran commentary of Habakkuk, the Wicked Priest attacked the Teacher of Righteousness and his community of the Day of Atonement, which is called a fast day (1QpHab XI, 8; see also CD VI, 19). The only other dated fasts figure in the book of Zechariah. Zechariah 7:3, 5; 8:19 mention a fast in the fifth month, the month in which Babylonians destroyed Jerusalem and the Temple in 587/86 (2 Kgs 25:8), and Zech 8:19 makes reference to other fasts in the fourth, seventh, and tenth months. In none of these instances does the text specify a date.

The Scroll of Fasting (*Megillat Taᶜanit*), dating from Tannaitic times, lists thirty-five dates when fasting was forbidden, while the scholion to it provides explanations for the events that occurred on those days and that rendered fasting inappropriate on them. The *Mishnaic tractate Taᶜanit* explores times when fasting was practiced (e.g., when rain was needed) and the proper ways for carrying it out. *See* CALENDAR.

Bibliography: J. van Goudoever. *Biblical Calendars* (1961); J. Milgrom. *Leviticus 1–16.* AB 3 (1991) 1009–84; J. VanderKam. *Calendars in the Dead Sea Scrolls: Measuring Time* (1998).

JAMES C. VANDERKAM

FEINAN, WADI. PUNON (Num 33:42-43) is one of the places where the Israelites camped on their journey through the Wadi Arabah. It is identified with Wadi Feinan, located ca. 45 km south of the Dead Sea on the east side of the Wadi Arabah.

Wadi Feinan, although in a dry area, had a considerable permanent water source in the form of springs, which made it suitable as a temporary campsite. However, the most important asset of the Wadi Feinan is its substantial copper ore fields, the largest in the region. It is because of these ore fields that the wadi has been exploited from the Chalcolithic onward. The famous copper treasure of the Nahal Mishmar cave near En Gedi was made from copper mined in the Wadi Feinan. Copper mining and smelting continued into the Early Bronze Age.

Renewed activity in the Wadi Feinan seems to have started at the beginning of the Iron Age (12th cent. BCE) on the site of Khirbet en-Nahas. Here evidence is found of copper mining and smelting, probably by a semi-nomadic group or tribe. An extensive cemetery was found in the Wadi Fidan, an offshoot of the Wadi Feinan, that may have been created by the same semi-nomadic population. They were probably involved in a trade route between the coast and the Wadi Arabah, trading the copper mined in the Wadi Feinan. A fortress built at Nahas around the end of the 10th cent. is evidence of the growing importance of the metal trade. This fortress was short lived, but metal production continued, reaching its zenith in the Assyrian period.

It was again exploited in the Roman period. In the

3rd and 4th cent. CE Feinan was a considerable town, surrounded by cultivation, and famous as the center of copper production in the region. *See* COPPER.

EVELINE J. VAN DER STEEN

FEJJA. A ruined Arab village situated about 5 km (3 mi.) from the mound of APHEK (*see* ANTIPATRIS). The name Fejja is similar to the Greek name of the Hellenistic site, Pegai (Pēgai Πηγαὶ), meaning "springs," mentioned for the first time in the Zenon papyri (259 BCE) as a frontier post, most likely to be found between Samaria and the region of the Greek polis on the coastal plain.

Archaeological surveys and small-scale excavations conducted by J. Kaplan in 1951 showed that Fejja was built on virgin soil. Ancient ruins were found approximately 12 m north of the village, but, while excavations there revealed occupation in the Middle Bronze Age, Iron Age II, and Persian periods, there were no Hellenistic remains. Because of the absence of both springs and archaeological remains, it appears that Fejja and the Pegai of the Zenon papyri are two different sites.

RALPH K. HAWKINS

FELIX fee'liks [Φῆλιξ Phēlix]. Roman procurator of Judea, from 52–59/60 CE who tried Paul in Caesarea (Acts 24).

Felix was the only procurator of Judea of servile origin (Tacitus, *Hist.* 5.9.3; Suetonius, *Claud.* 28), having formerly belonged to Claudius' mother Antonia (his name was probably Antonius Felix, as suggested by Tacitus and *CIL* 5.34, rather than Claudius Felix, as suggested by Josephus, *Ant.* 20.137). He succeeded Ventidius Cumanus in 52, owing his appointment to Claudius' favor, the recommendation of Jonathan the high priest (*J.W.* 2.240; *Ant.* 20.137-62), and perhaps a prior appointment over part of Jewish territory (Tacitus, *Ann.* 12.54).

Josephus regarded Felix's administration as a significant step in the nation's descent into revolt. He began energetically, attempting to stamp out banditry, and succeeded in sending a rebel chief named Eleazar to Rome (*J.W.* 2; *Ant.* 20.161). But Felix was powerless to stem the surge of rebellion and was completely unable to tackle more insidious threats. His administration saw the emergence of the *sicarii* [sikarioi σικάριοι]; taking their names from short swords, *sicae* (Lat.), these men mingled with the crowds and assassinated their victims (*J.W.* 2.254-57). Political murder became commonplace, though Josephus' claim that Felix bribed the *sicarii* to murder Jonathan (*Ant.* 20.161-63) is improbable. Felix also had to contend with the appearance of a number of "desert prophets" promising the end of Roman domination (*J.W.* 2.258-60; *Ant.* 20.67-168). One of these, "the Egyptian," assembled a large crowd of supporters in the desert, claiming that God would enable them to take Jerusalem. Felix sent his troops, killing many and taking prisoners, but the Egyptian

himself escaped (*J.W.* 2.261–63; *Ant.* 20.169-72). Josephus's account is doubtlessly exaggerated, but his contention that by the time Felix left it appeared "as if no one was in charge" (*Ant.* 20.180) may be true.

It is against this tense background that Paul was arrested in Acts, the Roman tribune initially taking him for the Egyptian (Acts 21:38). Paul was sent to Felix in Caesarea (23:23-35), and given the opportunity to defend himself (24:10-21). The author of Acts suggests (improbably) that Felix possessed "an accurate knowledge of the way" and allowed Paul to have certain liberties (24:22-23). However, he showed a reluctance to come to any decision, putting off the case for two years, during which time he often conversed with Paul, at least once in the presence of his Jewish wife, Drusilla, (the daughter of Agrippa I, whom he enticed away from her husband, King Azizus of Emesa, and married unlawfully, *Ant.* 20.141-44). Luke suggests that Felix's dilatoriness was not interest in Paul's message but hope for a bribe (Acts 24:26). Recalled by Nero in 59 or 60 CE, Felix left Paul in prison for his successor, Festus, to deal with.

On Felix's return to Rome, his brother Pallas, a favorite of Nero's, is said to have saved him from Jewish charges of maladministration (*Ant.* 20.182).

HELEN K. BOND

FELLOWSHIP. *See* COMMUNION.

FEMINIST INTERPRETATION. Feminist interpretation makes gender and gender relations a central subject matter of biblical interpretation. A feminist is someone who adheres to or advocates feminism. Feminism is a political stance that claims that the full humanity of women makes them equal to men; it therefore advocates for legal, political, and economic equal rights for women and for the full inclusion of women in all levels of leadership within society. Feminism critiques and resists social systems and structures that deny, diminish, suppress, or subordinate women's full humanity. As a liberation movement, it calls for the transformation of relationships and society. This emphasis on liberation originates outside the Bible in women's experiences of subjugation and struggles for emancipation, although it also has a foundation in the Bible. The creation of both male and female in the image of God (Gen 1:26-27), the story of the liberation of the oppressed Hebrews from slavery (Exod 1–15), the pouring out of the Holy Spirit on "both men and women" (Acts 2:18), and Paul's assertion that in Christ there is "neither male nor female" (Gal 3:3-28) are texts that provide a vision of relationships between men and women.

Feminist interpretation, therefore, approaches the biblical text from this political stance and queries both the biblical text and interpretations of the biblical text as to whether they promote or deny women's liberation and well-being. Feminist interpretation recognizes that one's experiences as a gendered being makes a difference in interpretation. Therefore, gender analysis, a systemic analysis of how the text constructs masculinity and femininity, is a foundational element of feminist interpretation. A central concern is to privilege women's experiences, voices, values, concerns, and differences.

It is common to speak of multiple feminisms or feminist interpretations for two reasons. First, feminist interpretation is not itself a method of interpretation, but is engaged with various critical interpretive approaches including, but not limited to, canonical, ideological, narrative, reader response, rhetorical, social scientific, and text criticisms. Second, feminist interpretation has increasingly recognized that women's lives consist of intersecting identities and thus acknowledges other forms of oppression. Critiques of particular feminist interpretations arise when exclusive focus on gender and sexism overlooks or diminishes the significance of other systems of dominance. Gender, race, religion, ethnicity, sexual orientation, age, class, physical abilities, education, nationality, and colonialism or imperialism are also forms of dominance that oppress those who are Other than the dominant identity. Women committed to feminism, but who also experience other forms of oppression, developed other interpretive strategies including Jewish feminist, lesbian, mujerista, postcolonial, and womanist interpretation.

There is no single way to categorize the results of feminist interpretation nor can they all be enumerated here. Two important emphases have been recovery and challenge to patriarchy. Projects of recovery have been central because women's experience of invisibility and marginalization makes them aware of the absence of women in biblical interpretation. The most direct recovery involves identifying stories and texts about women in the Bible. The recovery of both named and unnamed women such as Shiphrah and Puah (Exod 1:15-22), Jephthah's daughter (Judg 11), the Syrophoenician woman (Mark 7:25-30) and Junia (Rom 16:7) makes evident the presence of women in the text and their significance for the histories of Judaism and Christianity. This also includes identifying texts that portray God using female imagery, e.g., Isa 42:14; Luke 15:8-10. Recovery more broadly undertakes feminist historical reconstruction where the aim is to place women in the center of the histories of ancient Israel and Christianity. Focus is placed on the social roles fulfilled by women within the biblical text such as wife, mother, priest, and prophet. Another focus describes a particular time, movement, or group such as the role of women in households in Israel or in the early Jesus movement. This often requires going beyond the canonical text to include extra-canonical and cross-cultural research.

Women's experiences of oppression make the study and understanding of the role of patriarchy a central concern. Patriarchy refers to the systems of legal, social, economic, and political relations that validate and enforce the sovereignty of male heads of families over dependent persons in the household. Feminist interpretation has made it clear that the Bible came into being in patriarchal societies, cultures, and religions and is written in masculine-centered language and serves patriarchal interests. If patriarchy is a defining feature of the biblical text and ancient cultures, then a critical concern is to identify and challenge what in the text has encouraged or allowed men's exploitation of women throughout history. A significant challenge has been to "texts of terror" that portray physical and sexual violence against women, e.g., Judg 19–21; 2 Sam 13:11-14; Ezek 16. Many studies have demonstrated the intertwining of the Bible, sexual violence, and patriarchal gender constructs. A related task is to analyze where patriarchal bias appears in interpretations and to challenge where interpretations may be more oppressive to women than the biblical text itself.

Two other issues in feminist interpretation are translation and appropriation. The issue of translation is how to render gendered source languages. The exclusive use in the Bible of masculine forms for God functions to engender God only as male. Masculine plural forms in the source language, such as "brothers," may obscure the presence of women in a group. Should the translator highlight the patriarchal norms of the language or change them to make the text more inclusive?

Appropriation concerns biblical authority. Feminist interpreters recognize that the same text that has oppressed also inspires and authorizes women and men in their struggles for full humanity. Feminist interpretation rejects claiming as Word of God or authoritative Scripture a text identified as oppressive. Some feminist interpreters reject all biblical material outright, while others, through different strategies, find ways the Bible is still useful and authoritative. One strategy is feminist midrash, which retells biblical stories in ways that promote egalitarian and nonhierarchical paradigms. *See* BIBLICAL INTERPRETATION, HISTORY OF; GENDER STUDIES; IDEOLOGICAL CRITICSIM; JEWISH BIBLICAL INTERPRETATION; LATINO-LATINA INTERPRETATION; LESBIAN INTERPRETATION; MUJERISTA INTERPRETATION; PATRIARCHAL LANGUAGE; POSTCOLONIAL BIBLICAL INTERPRETATION; READER RESPONSE CRITICISM; RHETORICAL CRITICISM, NT; RHETORICAL CRITICISM, OT; SOCIAL SCIENTIFIC CRITICISM, NT; SOCIAL SCIENTIFIC CRITICISM, OT; TEXT CRITICISM, NT; TEXT CRITICISM, OT; WOMANIST INTERPRETATION.

Bibliography: Bible and Culture Collective. "Feminist and Womanist Criticism." *The Postmodern Bible* (1995) 225–271; Musa W. Dube. *Postcolonial Feminist Interpretation of the Bible* (2000); Elisabeth Schüssler Fiorenza. *Wisdom's Ways: Introducing Feminist Biblical Interpretation* (2001).

NANCY R. BOWEN

FENCE [גָּדֵר gadher גְּדֵרָה gedherah; φραγμός phragmos]. A stone-built wall encircling a village, field, or vineyard, intended to provide protection (Ezek 42:7; Num 22:24) and mark boundaries. Professionals (godhrim גְּדֵרִים) were often employed to construct fences (e.g., 2 Kgs 12:13; 22:6; Ezek 22:30). *See* BOUNDARY STONES; WALLS.

FERTILITY CULT. Matters of fertility—both human fecundity and the agricultural fertility of crops and herds—were of significant concern to most ANE cultures, including Israel. After all, the first commandment found in the Bible is God's instruction to humanity to "be fruitful and multiply" (Gen 1:28), and despite the Bible's claims that Israel is a "land flowing with milk and honey" (Exod 3:8), Israel's central hill country—the heartland of ancient Israel—was in large part an agriculturally marginal environment, in which it was often challenging to wrest enough produce from the land to survive. The lowlands that were the primary location of pre-Israelite settlement in Canaan were more forgiving but still could suffer from hardships such as droughts, which may have been as frequent as three or four years in ten. Further east, in Mesopotamia, while human fecundity may not have been a problem (indeed, one of the Mesopotamian versions of the ANE flood myth has been interpreted to suggest a Mesopotamian concern with overpopulation), the harvest of croplands was frequently threatened by the unpredictable flooding patterns of the TIGRIS RIVER and EUPHRATES RIVER; these floods also could cause the over-salinization of Mesopotamian fields with a corresponding decrease in productivity. Even in Egypt, although the Nile's flood was far more predictable and the land's fecundity thus far more assured (as indicated, e.g., by the famous description of Egypt as the "breadbasket" of the Roman world), harvests could on occasion fail. Indeed, some have speculated that agriculturally devastating climatological changes were one of the factors that caused the collapse of the Egyptian Old Kingdom in ca. 2130 BCE (*see* AGRICULTURE; BARREN, BARRENNESS; CHILD, CHILDREN).

Scholars have long suggested that a primary means by which the inhabitants of ANE cultures addressed these vulnerabilities was religion and especially rituals that sought to encourage the gods responsible for fertility to shower their beneficence on the land. Many scholars have argued, e.g., that in MESOPOTAMIA, an ancient ritual of sacred marriage, dating from the third millennium BCE, brought together in sexual union a priestess of Inanna (in later tradition, ISHTAR), the culture's goddess of fertility, and a city-state's king, who represented Inanna's mythological consort, the fertility god Dumuzi (later TAMMUZ), so that this king and priestess might, through their intercourse, imitate their divine counterparts who bestowed agricultural bounty. Many scholars have maintained that a feature

of this cult was the mythological account of Dumuzi's untimely death, followed by rebirth, which was taken to correlate with the natural cycle of seasonal change and more specifically with the withering away of vegetation in the hot Mesopotamian summers and its reappearance in the cooler seasons of fall, winter, and spring. This motif was also found in Egyptian traditions of ISIS and OSIRIS (*see* EGYPT) and Canaanite traditions of the demise and subsequent return to life of the storm god BAAL (*see* CANAAN, CANAANITES).

Likewise in Canaanite tradition, it was therefore surmised, older Mesopotamian traditions of sacred marriage and sacralized sexual intercourse must have persisted and must even have persisted into the late second and first millennium BCE, as the Israelites emerged in Canaan. Biblical texts that accuse the Israelites of "playing the whore" on "every high hill and under every green tree" (Jer 2:20; 3:6) were thus taken literally and interpreted to mean that the Israelites engaged in sacral sexual intercourse at open-air sanctuaries, especially intercourse with sacred prostitutes of both sexes (*see* HIGH PLACE; PROSTITUTION). Other scholars pushed still further to argue for an Israelite ritual of sacred marriage involving Jerusalem's king.

Recent scholarship finds unconvincing the theory that a royal ritual of sacred marriage once existed in ancient Israel, and, indeed, multiple aspects of the older understandings of ANE "fertility cults" have now been called into question. Jerrold S. Cooper has noted, e.g., that, despite the earlier consensus that the Mesopotamian sacred marriage had as its purpose promoting agricultural fertility, the goddess Inanna actually embodies power in the ritual, meaning that for the king to participate in the rite is to become socially and politically tied to her divine power and, moreover, to become her kin. Consequently, the king becomes able to properly regulate relations between the divine realm and the human and thus to properly regulate the very order of the cosmos. Cooper also points out that it is unclear, despite the claims of older generations, that the woman who represents Inanna in the sacred marriage rite is her high priestess; it may rather be the queen. Furthermore, direct evidence for the sacred marriage in Mesopotamia can be found only in Ur III and early Old Babylonian texts (ca. 2100–1800 BCE), making it difficult to propose that Mesopotamian sacred marriage traditions persisted in late second millennium and first millennium BCE Canaan and Israel.

Many scholars now agree that the sources that speak of sacred prostitution in the ANE (e.g., Herodotus, *Hist.* 1.199) must be dismissed as late and possibly polemical. Biblical texts that characterize sacralized sex as a part of Canaanite ritual practices, and likewise biblical texts that denigrate some Israelites for engaging in these rituals, should similarly be seen as stemming from the biblical writers' polemical attempts to define

Canaan as a degenerate "other," attempts that were probably driven in part by the fact that—as an abundant amount of archaeological evidence now suggests—the people who became Israel were themselves originally Canaanite and so sought to distinguish themselves from their mother culture. Even when these origins were no longer remembered, the drive for such cultural distinction would continue to engender such polemic. *See* SACRIFICES AND OFFERINGS; SEX, SEXUALITY.

Bibliography: Jerrold S. Cooper. "Sacred Marriage and Popular Cult in Early Mesopotamia." *Official Cult and Popular Religion in the Ancient Near East.* Eiko Matsushima, ed. (1993) 81–96; Robert A. Oden. *The Bible Without Theology: The Theological Tradition and Alternatives to It* (1987).

SUSAN ACKERMAN

FESTAL GARMENT חֲלִפֹת בְּגָדִים khalifoth beghadhim, שְׂמָלֹת חֲלִפֹת khalifoth semaloth מַחֲלָצוֹת makhalatsoth]. Festive occasions required the use of one's best clothes. The quality of garments was determined by the type of fabric, excellence of the dye (for wool), and brilliance (especially for linen). Abundance and ability to change one's clothes also denoted power and festive quality. This was ideally a change of the customary wool MANTLE and tunic, as indicated by the expressions **khalifoth semaloth** (Gen 45:22) and **khalifoth beghadlim** (Judg 14:12-13, 19; 2 Kgs 5:5, 22-23), which mean "changes of garments," or "festal garments." In the Genesis passage, Joseph gives such a set of garments to each of his brothers, but five sets to Benjamin. In Judg 14:12, Samson promises "thirty linen garments and thirty festal garments" to the Philistines of Timnah if they solve his riddle.

The clothes of Jehu and other vassals bringing tribute in the 8th cent. BCE to the Assyrian king Shalmaneser III on a black basalt stela (the "Black Obelisk") give an idea of what festal garments might have looked like in ancient Israel and Canaan, as Assyrian artists are considered accurate in their depiction. The list of articles of tribute from the kings of Samaria and other realms mentioned in the annals of Tiglath-Pileser III (744–727 BCE) includes linen garments with multicolored trimmings, probably similar to those of the stela above, with their long fringed tunics and mantle.

Women's "festal robes" (**makhalatsoth**) are mentioned along mantles and cloaks in Isa 3:22. These are perhaps fine, white robes, as the Gk. version indicates. The "festal apparel" (NRSV) or "rich apparel" (RSV) of Zech 3:4 (**makhalatsoth**), in contradistinction to "filthy clothes" of the past (3:3), refers symbolically to the ceremonial use of especially fine, brilliantly white garments for the Jerusalem high priest.

Dress style evolved over time. The fine garments of Jews in Hellenistic and Roman Palestine are similar in many respects to a more general Greco-Roman standard but still include tunic and mantle. They are expected in festive occasions, as in the story of a king who gave a wedding banquet for his son (Matt 22:11) but notices a man who was not wearing a wedding robe (endyma gamou ἔνδυμα γάμου). *See* BRIDE; BRIDEGROOM; CLOTH, CLOTHES.

GILDAS HAMEL

FESTIVALS. *See* FEASTS AND FASTS.

FESTIVALS, GRECO-ROMAN [ἕορται heortai; Lat. *feriae*]. Greek festivals were annual, biennial, and quadrennial religious rituals performed in honor of various gods and goddesses. They typically featured a procession (pompē πομπή), communal sacrifices, feasts, fellowship, and entertainment. There were no clear distinctions between religious and secular activities. For example, Athena was honored by games during the *Panathenaia*, the greatest of the Athenian festivals, and DIONYSUS was honored by all manner of theatrical performances throughout Attica during the *Dionysia*. Festivals were celebrated at least sixty days out of the year in Athens.

Roman festivals were holidays on which religious rites were performed. Many were accompanied by public games (*ludi*), which also had religious origins and rituals. Most festivals were celebrated annually on a fixed date (*feriae stativae*), but some annual festivals were celebrated on movable dates set by the magistrates and priests (*feriae conceptivae*). Irregular holidays could also be proclaimed to appease the gods in response to a prodigy such as an earthquake or to celebrate a victory (*feriae imperativae*). There were both public festivals paid for by the state, and private festivals commemorating family events such as birthdays and deaths. In the imperial period, however, the emperor's birthday was celebrated as a public holiday.

The origins of many of the oldest Greek and Roman festivals were in such matters as agriculture, fertility, and rites of passage. Some festivals were modified in response to urbanization and others invented or imported in response to new trends such as the mysteries. Eventually the number of Roman holidays outnumbered work days, but it should be remembered that there were no weekends. Free Romans and slaves were expected to rest from work and legal disputes on all holidays. Priests made rulings on what sorts of work were and were not permissible.

The only mention of a particular Greek festival in biblical literature is in 2 Macc 6:1-7. The Syrian Greek ruler Antiochus IV Epiphanes sent an Athenian elder to Jerusalem to rededicate the temple to Zeus and force the Jews to give up their laws. Then, "on the monthly celebration of the king's birthday, the Jews were taken, under bitter constraint, to partake of the sacrifices; and when a festival of Dionysus was celebrated, they were compelled to wear wreathes of ivy and to walk in the procession in honor of Dionysus" (6:7). Such demands were very unusual for a Greek ruler, but the episode anticipates difficulties Christians would face under Roman rule, especially with respect to the festivals of the imperial cults. *See* EMPEROR WORSHIP; GREEK RELIGION AND PHILOSOPHY; ROMAN RELIGIONS.

Bibliography: Steven J. Friesen. *Imperial Cults and the Apocalypse of John: Reading Revelation in the Ruins* (2001); H. W. Parke. *Festivals of the Athenians* (1977); Noel Robertson. *Festivals and Legends: The Formation of Greek Cities in the Light of Public Ritual* (1992); H. H. Scullard. *Festivals and Ceremonies of the Roman Republic* (1981).

MARK D. GIVEN

FESTUS, PORCIUS fest′tuhs por′shuhs [Φῆστος Phēstos]. Roman procurator of Judea from 59–62 CE, and the judge who sent Paul to Nero (Acts 25:11). He is known only from Josephus and Acts.

Unlike that of his predecessor, Felix, Josephus' assessment of Festus is relatively positive. Finding the country overrun with brigands, the new procurator took measures to pacify the region, capturing and killing a number of insurgents (*J.W.* 2.271, *Ant.* 20.182, 185–88). Later a dispute arose over the Jewish leaders' extension to a Temple wall designed to prevent Agrippa II from overlooking cultic activities from his palace. Despite his own annoyance (the wall also blocked the Roman guard's view of activities), Festus allowed a Jewish delegation to petition Nero who, on this occasion, upheld their wishes (*Ant.* 20.189–96).

In the NT, Festus appears in Acts 25–26 where he succeeds Felix as Paul's judge. The apostle had been in prison for two years (24:27), and Acts suggests that the Jewish authorities attempted to put pressure on the new procurator to transfer the case to Jerusalem (25:1-3). At first, Festus refused, insisting that the Jewish leaders bring their case to Caesarea (25:4-5), but after hearing the case he tried to persuade Paul to consent to trial in Jerusalem (Acts claims he wished to do the Jewish authorities a favor). Paul's only hope of a fair trial was to appeal directly to Caesar (25:11). Soon after, Agrippa II and his sister Berenice arrived in Caesarea to welcome the new procurator and heard Paul's defense (25:23–26:32). Acts makes it quite clear that Paul was found innocent, first by Festus (25:25, though he later suspected that Paul was mad, 26:24) and then by all of Paul's judges (26:30-31). Although there is probably some historical fact behind this account, the narrative in Acts exhibits strong theological tendencies and apologetic motifs: the account makes it abundantly evident that Paul was not guilty of any crime under Roman law, and clearly draws parallels between the trial of the great apostle and that of Jesus in Luke 23:1-25.

In order to date Paul's trial, it is necessary to know exactly when Festus arrived in the province. He died in office (*Ant.* 20.197) and his successor, Albinus, was in post by 62 (Jesus ben Ananias was brought before him four years before the revolt, i.e., 62, *J.W.* 6.300–309), but the date of his arrival is unclear. According to Jerome's Chronicle of Eusebius, Festus arrived in the second year of Nero (ca. 56), which would give him a six-year term of office. Eusebius' dates, however, are derived entirely from Josephus, and the latter's brief account of Festus' administration suggests a much shorter term. A coin issue of October 59 may suggest the arrival of a new procurator, thus a date of 59 or 60 seems most likely for both Festus' arrival and the final stages of Paul's trial in Caesarea.

HELEN K. BOND

FETTER [אֵסוּר ’esur, כֶּבֶל kevel; δεσμός desmos, χειροπέδη cheiropedē, πέδη pedē]. A fetter is a constraint that encircles the wrists or ankles, also known as a shackle. In the OT, people are occasionally bound in fetters: Samson (Judg 15:14); Zedekiah (2 Kgs 25:7; Jer 39:7); Jeremiah (Jer 40:1, 4); Jehoiakim (2 Chr 36:6). Fetters are sometimes employed poetically as in Eccl 7:26 where women's hands are likened to these constraints. In the NT, too, people are bound with fetters, although the same Greek words are variously translated "shackles" or "chains." For example, the Gerasene demoniac (Mark 5:4) is bound by the people of his community but he keeps breaking free. Paul is arrested on several occasions and is fettered in prison (Acts 16:26; Col 4:18). Occasionally, the fetters are only metaphorical. For the writer of Second Timothy, the word of God is unfettered (2:9). *See* CHAINS, IMPRISONMENT.

JENNIFER L. KOOSED

FEVER [קַדַּחַת qaddakhath; πυρετός pyretos]. Since the ancients did not have thermometers, this abnormal bodily state (fever) was identified by the emanation of bodily heat beyond the customary experience. The judgment was quite subjective but certainly correct when the fever was "high" (see Job 30:30 where the word does not occur, yet the experience is surely a raging fever). Indeed, the ancients distinguished between major (see Luke 4:38) and minor fevers, although Galen thought this simplistic and inadequate (*De differentiis febrium* 1).

In the OT, God sent fever as punishment for disobedience (Deut 28:15, 22), a fever sometimes so severe it affected vision (Lev 26:16). In the NT, Jesus and Paul heal fevers (e.g., John 4:52; Acts 28:8; *see* DYSENTERY). Of special interest is the report of Jesus' healing of Peter's mother-in-law. Two Synoptics (Mark 1:30-31; Matt 8:14-15) simply report that she was suffering from a fever. Jesus touched or took her by the hand and her condition was relieved (therapeutic touch). But Luke (4:38-39) presents a strikingly different scenario. Instead of touching her hand, Jesus "rebukes" her fever just as he "rebukes" demons (4:41), the wind (8:24), and an unclean spirit (9:42). Since the Hebrew (ruakh

רוּחַ) and Greek (pneuma πνεῦμα) mean "spirit," "wind," and "breath" interchangeably, Luke apparently interpreted the problem as spirit possession, and Jesus cast out of Peter's mother-in-law a demon named "fever."

Bibliography: John J. Pilch. "Spirits." *The Cultural Dictionary of the Bible* (1999) 161–162.

JOHN J. PILCH

FIBULA. *See* JEWELRY.

FIELD [שָׂדֶה sadheh; ἀγρός agros]. A general term that can refer broadly to the open field or narrowly to a specific area of land. In its broadest sense, the uses of the term range from open country outside a walled city (e.g., Judg 9:32) to country inhabited by wild animals (Exod 22:31 [Heb. 22:30]). In its narrower sense, uses range from cultivated ground (e.g., Gen 37:7) to tribal territories (e.g., Josh 21:12).

Metaphorically, the destruction of Zion, due to its corrupt leadership (Mic 3:9-12), was to be like the plowing of a field (v. 12). In the parable of the weeds among the wheat (Matt 13:24-30), the field represents the entire world (v. 38), for sowing the seeds of the Kingdom. These fields are "ripe for harvesting" (John 4:35), illustrated by the multitude of villagers that came to Jesus following his encounter with the woman of Samaria (John 3:35), building upon the OT image of the harvest as eschatological fulfillment (compare Isa 27:12; Joel 3:13). Paul describes the extent of his own mission as the borders of a farmer's field (2 Cor 10:13) and envisions the care of the church as nurturing a field (1 Cor 3:9). *See* AGRICULTURE; FULLER'S FIELD.

RALPH K. HAWKINS

FIELD OF BLOOD [χωρίον αἵματος chōrion haimatos, ἀγρός αἵματος agros haimatos]. The potter's field purchased with the silver Judas Iscariot received for betraying Jesus (Matt 27:3-10; Acts 1:16-19) and linked in Acts to Judas' wickedness and death. In Matthew the purchase fulfills Jeremiah's prophecy (see Zech 11:12-13; Jer 18:1-19; 32:6-15). *See* JUDAS.

HEIDI S. GEIB

FIERY SERPENT OR POISONOUS SNAKE [נָחָשׁ שָׂרָף nakhash saraf]. "Fiery" (Isa 14:29) is probably a reference to the burning of the venom of poisonous snakes, such as snakes associated with scorpions (Deut 8:15) or those that God sent among the Israelites as punishment for their grumbling (Num 21:6, 8). In order to heal people who were bitten, God commanded Moses to craft a bronze serpent. Those who looked at the bronze serpent were healed from the SERPENT bites. The plural form (serafim שְׂרָפִים), usually transliterated as *seraphs* (*see* SERAPH, SERAPHS), refers to some sort of mythical flying beings with serpentlike bodies (Isa 6:2, 6, 7).

C. MARK MCCORMICK

FIFTEEN. *See* NUMBERS, NUMBERING.

FIFTY. *See* NUMBERS, NUMBERING.

FIG TREE, FIGS [תְּאֵנָה te'enah; συκῆ sykē, σῦκον sykon]. One staple of the ancient diet that provided a sweet accompaniment to other foods was the fig (*Ficus carica*). Cultivated at least since the Early Bronze Age (ca. 3000 BCE), the tree could take root in rocky soil and within seven years bear fruit for as many as fifty years. The many place names associated with fig trees (Bethany = "house of figs"; Bethphage = "house of unripe figs," Mark 11:1) testify to their importance to the economy. The fig tree's pride in its flavor is chronicled playfully in its refusal to rule the other trees in Jotham's parable (Judg 9:10-11). In fact, newly ripened figs were so loved that Isaiah describes the zest with which they were eaten (Isa 28:4). Other prophets use the fig as an analogy for Israel (Hos 9:10; Amos 8:1-2; Nah 3:12). The budding or barren fig tree is a symbol of fruitfulness in some of Jesus' parables (Matt 24:32; Mark 13:28; Luke 13:6-9; 21:19-31). The fig tree begins to put on its leaves in spring and is quite lush by summer when its shade is a relief from the sun (John 1:48-50). It is also paired with the grape vine as a symbol of prosperity and peace for the farmer (Mic 4:4). Fig cakes served as rations for soldiers that could be carried on campaign or stored for later consumption in camp (1 Sam 25:18; 30:12), and were also used medicinally as a poultice for boils (2 Kgs 20:7). *See* AGRICULTURE; FOOD; PARABLE; PLANTS OF THE BIBLE.

VICTOR H. MATTHEWS

FIGHT, TO [לָחַם lakham; ἀγωνίζομαι agōnizomai]. To engage in struggles against one's enemies either defensively or offensively. Fighting was often understood as needing God's sanction beforehand. Moses assured the Israelites that God would fight for them against the Egyptians (Exod 14:14). Battling against the Amalekites was successful for the Israelites whenever Moses' hands were raised (Exod 17:11). Deuteronomy recalls God's actions against the Egyptians on behalf of the Israelites (Deut 1:30) and their defeat in battling against the Amorites because the Israelites refused to listen to God (Deut 1:41-45). According to Deut 20:10-14, victory in battle required the Israelites to kill all the men and take the women, children, and livestock as spoil (*see* DESTROY, UTTERLY; HOLY WAR). Jesus describes defensive and offensive battling as characteristic of earthly rulers (John 18:36). Fighting refers metaphorically to the struggle to be faithful to God (1 Tim 6:12; 2 Tim 4:7).

EMILY R. CHENEY

FIGURED STONE [אֶבֶן מַשְׂכִּית 'even maskith]. Stones carved to resemble people, animals, or other objects are regularly found in archaeological excavations in the Middle East. Given the biblical injunction against making idols, including figured stones (Lev 26:1; Num 33:52), they are relatively rare in the Iron Age in Israel. Standing stones were used as cultic objects, although only a few standing stones with any decoration have been discovered. Stones were also used for the creation of stelae and other monumental inscriptions. Carved stones became more frequent in Palestine in the Greek and Roman periods with the import of Hellenistic artistic ideas.

KEVIN A. WILSON

FIGUREHEAD [παράσημος parasēmos]. A carving on a ship's stemhead. This practice began with the ancient Chinese and Egyptian seafarers who painted eyes on the bows of their ships, believing the oculi would help them find their way. Among later civilizations the adornments became carved likeness of deities, animals, and serpents, signifying religious beliefs and serving to frighten the enemy. Acts 28:11 describes an Alexandrian ship with a figurehead of the twin gods Astor and Pollux.

KATHY CHAMBERS

FILIGREE. See JEWELRY.

FIND, TO [מָצָא matsa'; εὑρίσκω heuriskō]. "To find" is the act of locating a person, place, or thing. Find can also indicate a human leader or God's act of determining fault or favor in a person. The word appears in instances where people are unable to locate God (Job 23:3) because of God's immense power and righteousness (Job 37:23) or human faithlessness (Hos 5:6-7). On the other hand, those searching diligently (Prov 8:17) for God or with all their heart (Deut 4:29; Jer 29:13) are promised success. Symbolically and theologically *finding* refers to receiving and experiencing God's blessings after one has asked God for them (Matt 7:7-11; Luke 11:9-13). Locating a missing sheep (Matt 18:13; Luke 15:3-7), a coin (Luke 15:8-10), and a son (Luke 15:11-32) after searching for them refers figuratively to God's joy when humans are forgiven and restored to God, especially when they turn toward God. A person who attempts to look for one's own life (Matt 10:39*a*), however, will fail. Those who give up their lives for Jesus truly experience or discover life (Matt 10:39*b*).

EMILY R. CHENEY

FINE. See CRIMES AND PUNISHMENT, OT AND NT.

FINE LINEN. See LINEN.

FINGER OF GOD. See GOD, FINGER OF.

FIR TREE [בְּרוֹשׁ berosh]. An evergreen tree of the pine family. The Hebrew word could also be translated as pine (Isa 41:19), cypress (1 Kgs 5:8), or juniper, but the context has led to the selection of "fir tree" in a few instances. While praising God for providing grass for the cattle and plants for human consumption, the psalmist expresses the wide range of God's provisions for the world by referring to the generous watering of fir trees in which storks make their home (Ps 104:17). Fir trees are also used to highlight the surpassing greatness of Egypt (Ezek 27:5) and Assyria (Ezek 31:8). See PLANTS OF THE BIBLE.

EMILY R. CHENEY

FIRE [אֵשׁ 'esh; πῦρ, pyr]. The phenomenon can also be described by words such as *flames*, or *torch*, etc., and it is sometimes closely related to *light*. Both in the OT and NT fire is part of everyday life. On the one hand, fire is a useful, beneficial element providing light and warmth (Isa 44:15-16; Acts 28:2), and heat for cooking (Exod 12:8; Jer 7:18) or for the work of craftsmen (Ezek 22:20). On the other hand, fire has a destructive quality and is therefore employed in war (Judg 20:48; Jer 21:10), and sometimes, though seldom, as a means of execution (Gen 38:24; Lev 20:14; 21:9; Josh 7:15). It may also refer to the scorching heat of the sun (Joel 1:19; Amos 7:4). In a figurative sense or as a metaphor it describes feelings such as extreme pain (Ps 39:4), passion of love (Song 8:6), malice (Isa 9:17), or anger (Zeph 3:8; Sir 28:10-14).

That fire plays an important part in the practice of the Israelite cult is indicative of its symbolic and theological meaning. Offerings are burned in fire (Lev 1–7, esp. 1:1-17) that has to be taken from the altar (illicit fire: Lev 10:1; Num 3:4). It seems that Israel's neighbors offered children to their gods (2 Kgs 17:31), a practice forbidden in Israel (Deut 12:31; Jer 7:31). The phrase "to make son/daughter/children pass through (the) fire" (Deut 18:10; 2 Kgs 16:3; 17:17; 21:6; 23:10; Ezek 20:31) refers to this. A special aspect of sacrificing is annihilating with fire the property and places of residence of those defeated in battle (Deut 13:17) and burning their idols (Deut 7:5, 25; see also 2 Kgs 23:11). Priestly contexts employ the purifying effect of fire (Lev 13:52, 55, 57; Num 31:23). The ever-burning fire on the altar (Lev 6:12-13) indicates the continual presence of God. This practice marks a bridge to the predominant usage of fire as an explicit or implicit reference either to God himself or to phenomena belonging to the divine sphere.

Fire accompanies theophany (*see* THEOPHANY IN THE NT; THEOPHANY IN THE OT), thus indicating God's presence. God appears within a burning bush (Exod 3:2); as this fire does not consume the plant it must be of a special, supernatural quality. God leads the Israelites through the desert in a pillar of fire by night (Exod 13:21-22; 14:24; 40:38; Num 9:15-16; 14:14; Deut 1:33; Neh 9:12, 19). God's appearance on Mount Sinai seems to combine two aspects of fire, volcanism (Exod 19:18; Deut 4:11-12; 5:23) and lightning in a thunderstorm (Exod 24:17; see also Ezek 1:4, 13; Pss

18:8; 29:7; 97:3). God speaks out of the fire (Deut 4:12, 15, 33, 36; 5:4; 9:10; 10:4). Fire represents divine presence when God makes a covenant with Israel at Mount Sinai or Mount Horeb, respectively; when he enters into a covenant with Abraham by night, God shows himself as a smoking fire pot and a flaming torch (Gen 15:17). It is remarkable that 1 Kgs 19:12 explicitly denies the prevailing tradition that God is in the fire.

God's throne and environment are (like) fire (Ezek 1:27; Dan 7:9-10). God may even be identified with devouring fire (Exod 24:17; Deut 4:24; 9:3; Isa 10:17). When divine fire kindles flames on an altar and consumes the offering, this means that God is present and accepts the sacrifice (Lev 9:24; 1 Kgs 18:38; in Judg 6:21 an angel evokes such a fire). Fire is also characteristic of celestial beings attending on God: the Seraphs (that is, literally, "the burning ones," Isa 6:2) flying about God's throne are an example of this. The angel who announces the birth of Samson ascends toward heaven in the flames of the fire burning on the altar (Judg 13:20). A chariot of fire with horses of fire takes Elijah to heaven (2 Kgs 2:11). Before the battle against the Arameans Elisha asks God to make a servant see horses and chariots of fire in a vision (2 Kgs 6:17); these are divine supporters of the Israelite army. Psalm 104:4 says that God makes fire and flame his ministers.

Since there is also a dangerous quality of divine presence and hence of God's appearance in fire, it is perilous for any human being to approach such a fire (Deut 5:5; 18:16). In addition, fire often represents God's wrath (Pss 79:5; 86:46; Jer 4:4; 15:14; 21:12; Ezek 22:31; Nah 1:6), and the effect of this, i.e. JUDGMENT. Fire as punishment comes about as part of a natural catastrophe as fire from heaven (Gen 19:24; 2 Kgs 1:10-14; Job 1:16; as hail with fire, Exod 9:24). More often divine punishment occurs in the course of a military campaign leading to defeat and destruction (Num 11:1; 16:35; Hos 8:14; Amos 1:4, 7, 10, 12, 14; 2:2, 5; Jer 17:27; 49:27; Zech 9:4; Lam 1:18; 2:3); war and its effect on the defeated are described as fire and interpreted as divine action, as a theophany of the judging deity. In Jeremiah God declares that his word is like fire (Jer 23:29), and he decides to turn the divine message uttered by the prophet into fire that will devour the people who are compared to firewood (Jer 5:14). The forest fire is a common metaphor of divine judgment in the Writing Prophets (Ezek 15:2-7; 21:3; Jer 11:16). In late texts of the OT God's judgment gains an eschatological touch (Deut 32:22; Isa 33:11-12; 66:15-16; Ezek 38:22; 39:6; Dan 7:11; Joel 2:3; Zeph 1:18); sometimes the final judgment through fire has at least in part a purifying effect (Zech 13:9; Mal 3:2). Isaiah 66:24 foreshadows the idea of a permanent fire tormenting evildoers after death. This concept is intensified in the Pseudepigrapha (see for instance, *1 En.* 18:11; 21:7; 90:23-26; 91:9; 100:9; 102:1; 4 Macc 12:12).

The writings of the NT carry on two theological functions of fire, namely, indicating divine presence or action on the one hand, and describing judgment and punishment on the other. The focus is clearly on the latter aspect. Stubborn sinners will experience punishment through fire; this process is compared to the burning of wood (Matt 3:10; 13:40; John 15:6). The (eternal) fire of judgment is burning, often it is explicitly situated in hell (Matt 3:12; 5:22; 13:42; 18:8-9; 25:41; Mark 9:43, 47-49; Rev 8:7; 9:18; 11:5; 14:10; 19:20; 20:9-10, 14-15). What happened to Sodom will be repeated at the end of time (Luke 17:28-30). Faith will be tested by fire then (1 Pet 1:7).

Quoting the OT, God is again identified with consuming fire (Heb 12:29; Heb 1:7 quotes Ps 104:4, referring to flames and fire as God's ministers). God's throne emanates flashes of lightning and has seven fiery torches burning before him (Rev 4:5). The vision of the Son of Man includes a description comparing his eyes to a flame of fire (Rev 1:14). The connection between the HOLY SPIRIT and fire is a peculiarity in the NT, which is nevertheless in line with older tradition because the Holy Spirit is of divine, heavenly origin. John the Baptist announces someone coming after him who will baptize with the Holy Spirit and fire (Matt 3:11). That the Holy Spirit fills the members of the earliest congregation on Pentecost is illustrated by tongues as of fire resting on each of the assembled persons (Acts 2:3).

KARIN SCHÖPFLIN

FIRE, PILLAR OF. *See* PILLAR OF CLOUD AND FIRE.

FIREBRAND [אוּד ʾudh, זִיקוֹת ziqoth, זִקִּים ziqqim]. Burning wood used metaphorically by Isaiah to describe two foreign kings derisively as "smoldering stumps of firebrands" (Isa 7:4) and to describe Israel in Amos 4:11 and Zech 3:2 (NRSV, "brand"). Isaiah calls for those who have lit firebrands to walk among those brands (50:11). Firebrands and arrows are hurled by a "maniac" who is like a duplicitous neighbor (Prov 26:18).

R. JUSTIN HARKINS

FIREPAN [מַחְתָּה makhtah]. An implement mentioned in Leviticus and in the Priestly texts of Exodus and Numbers as being made of bronze (e.g., Exod 38:3), and in 1 Kgs 7:50 as being made of gold. The root khathah (חָתָה) means "take up, collect," typically with fire as its object (Prov 25:22; Isa 30:14). Based on this and its function in Num 16, where Korah and his followers in opposition to Aaron and Moses are told to bring their incense before Yahweh in their makhtah, it is translated either "firepan," something to carry hot coals, or as "CENSER," something to carry burning incense.

C. MARK MCCORMICK

FIRM, TO BE. *See* STEADFASTNESS.

FIRMANENT [רָקִיעַ raqiʿa; στερέωμα stereōma]. Derived from the Lat. *firmamentum*, in Hebrew cosmology, it is a dome or vault that God created on the second day to separate the waters in the heavens from the waters of the earth (Gen 1:6-8), containing small openings to allow water to fall through as rain. On the fourth day, God placed the sun and moon in this dome (Gen 1:14-19). Described as glittering crystal (Ezek 1:22), it shone mightily (Dan 12:3) and revealed God's handiwork (Ps 19:1). The firmament is occasionally seen as God's abode (150:1; Pr Azar 1:34). *See* HEAVEN.

EMILY R. CHENEY

FIRST AND LAST [רִאשׁוֹן riʾoshon ("first"), אַחֲרוֹן ʾakharon ("last"); πρῶτος prōtos ("first"), ἔσχατος eschatos ("last")]. 1. A divine self-name. Three occurrences in Second Isaiah emphasize might (41:4), oneness (44:6), and power to deliver from captivity (48:12). The author of Revelation uses the term to refer to Christ's coming reign and power over death (Rev 1:17; 2:8; 13:22).

2. *First* and *last* are terms Jesus uses to describe the reversal of status in the kingdom of God/Heaven between those who have power and those who serve: "Some who are first shall be last and the last first" (Matt 19:30; 20:16; Mark 10:31; Luke 13:30). The one who wishes to be "first" must become a slave to all (Mark 10:44). *See* ALPHA AND OMEGA; GOD, NAMES OF; KINGDOM OF GOD, KINGDOM OF HEAVEN; SERVANT; SERVE, TO; SLAVERY.

JESSICA TINKLENBERG DEVEGA

FIRST FRUITS [בִּכּוּרִים bikkurim, רֵאשִׁית reʾshith; ἀπαρχή aparchē]. Two words in the OT bikkurim and reʾshith, correspond to the English term "first fruits." They appear separately and in combination (and sometimes with the word *fruit* [peri פְּרִי]) to refer to the first portion of grain (Deut 18:4), fruit (Neh 10:38), oil and vegetable harvests (2 Chr 31:5), and the first (or best) of batches of dough (Num 15:20-21), wine, and honey (2 Chr 31:5). The related term, bekhor (בְּכוֹר) denotes the FIRSTBORN among Israel's human and animal populations.

The terms are used in three distinct ways. One cluster of references denotes the offering accompanying celebrations of the feasts of Passover and of Weeks or Pentecost (*see* PASSOVER AND FEAST OF UNLEAVENED BREAD; WEEKS, FEAST OF). Exodus 23:16 requires the presentation of the first fruits of the first harvest before the Lord as a wave offering at Passover (compare Lev 23:16). Presumably this was a sheaf of barley, since it was the first crop to ripen (compare the Gezer Calendar [*ANET* 321]). The second festal occasion for presenting first fruits is the Feast of Weeks (Pentecost); here the offering must be wheat in accord with the normal agricultural calendar (Exod 34:22; compare Num 28:26, where the day of offering is referred to as the "day of first fruits").

Another group of references to first fruits requires their offering to the Lord without connection to a particular feast. Grouped with three negative sacrificial stipulations (not to mix the blood of a sacrifice with leavened goods, leave the "fat of the festivals" until morning, or boil a kid in its mother's milk), there is a straightforward command to provide as an offering to God "the choicest (reʾshit) of the first fruits (bikkurim)" (Exod 23:18-19; 34:26; compare Lev 2:12, 14; 23:10; Deut 26:2).

A third cluster of references demands that first fruits be given to the priests and/or Levites for their sustenance (Num 15:20-21; 18:12-13; Deut 18:4; Neh 10:38 [Heb. 10:37]; 12:44; 13:31; Ezek 44:30). Whether such offerings are different from the first two kinds of first fruit gifts described above, or are the same ones, is not entirely clear from a straightforward reading of the text (*see* SACRIFICES AND OFFERINGS).

Of course, reading the references to first fruits or to the "first of the first fruits," according to various theories of the Pentateuch's compositional history, might provide some solution to the latter quandary (as well as others relating to the proper calendrical reckoning for occasions of first fruit offering), but with little firm result since the references are well mixed among the usual "sources" including the Yahwist, Deuteronomic, and Priestly strata (*see* J, YAHWIST; D, DEUTERONOMIC, DEUTERONOMISTIC; P, PRIESTLY WRITERS). In fact, one might expect the Priestly passages to be most concerned with the delivery of offerings into the sacerdotal leadership's hands, but that is not the case. The precise relationship among these three ways of conceiving of first fruits thus remains open to interpretation. So it is not surprising that in early Jewish literature there are implicit reflections on some of these questions, as well as explicit expansions on the notion of first fruit offerings (see, e.g., the introduction of a festival of the first fruits of wine in 11Q19 XI-XXI, 10 [compare *Jub.* 7:1-6; 1QapGen XII, 13-16; *T. Levi* 9:14]).

In addition to the first fruits listed above, Exod 13:2-16 requires that the firstborn of any womb, human or animal, be dedicated to God; along with Num 3:12-16 the latter passage provides for the redemption of the firstborn, allotting in particular the Levites to God's service as a replacement for the firstborn male of all Israelite families.

Quite apart from an inventory of the uses of the term "first fruits," the hermeneutical key for understanding the phenomenon of first fruits and firstborn in Israelite religion is perhaps a prophetic text, Jer 2:3. There Israel is described as the first fruits of the Lord's harvest, and in turn as holy to God, sacred in a way that the rest of creation is not apart from God's designation. Read in light of this equation of holiness with the status of being first fruits the rest of the OT's statements on the latter topic take on a more substantial meaning as offerings to God: they are the part of the fullness of creation that mark all the rest as belonging to God as well (compare Rom 11:16).

New Testament uses of the term are exclusively metaphorical: according to Rom 8:23 the Holy Spirit provides the first fruits of the spirit (*see* FRUIT OF THE SPIRIT), and in 11:16 the holiness of the first of a batch of dough is used to signal that the whole must be holy as well (compare Num 15:20-21). In a discourse on resurrection Paul describes Jesus resurrected as the first fruit of God's plan to raise all to new life (1 Cor 15:20, 23). Second Thessalonians 2:13 names the letter's recipients as the ones God chose to be the first fruits of salvation (compare Jas 1:18; Rev 14:4).

ROBERT KUGLER

FIRSTRIPE [בִּכּוּרִים bikkurim; ἀπαρχή aparchē]. The term describes the first vegetables, fruits, and grains to ripen (Num 13:20; 18:13; Isa 28:4; Jer 24:2; Mic 7:1; Nah 3:12). The "first-ripe," along with the first-born of humans, were to be offered or dedicated to the Creator of all living things. Corporate worship included first-ripe offerings (Lev 23:9-21), as did individual worship (Exod 23:19; Deut 26:1-11). New Testament writers gave the term metaphoric theological meaning (Rom 8:23; 11:16; 16:15; 1 Cor 15:20, 23; 16:15; Jas 1:18; Rev 14:4). *See* FIRST FRUITS; SACRIFICES AND OFFERINGS; WORSHIP, OT.

MICHAEL G. VANZANT

FIRSTBORN [בְּכוֹר bekhor, פֶּטֶר peter; πρωτότοκος prōtotokos]. Throughout the OT the two terms bekhor and peter refer to the firstborn of humans and animals alike. The plural form bekhorim (בְּכוֹרִים) refers to the first fruits of labor (e.g., Exod 23:16; 34:22; Lev 2:14). When combined with reʾshith (רֵאשִׁית) it is describing the first fruits brought into the sanctuary during the first pilgrimage festival (Exod 23). In this sense it is given to the priest as a tax (Lev 2). Peter identifies the "first to come out of the womb" that is to be devoted to the Lord; the firstborn of Israel are redeemed through the dedication of the Levites to the Lord (Num 3:12). The Greek term for firstborn in the LXX, prōtotokos (approx. 130 times for the Hebrew bekhor), is a derivative of prōtos (πρῶτος; first) and the root word tek- (having to do with bearing children or the children themselves).

A. Old Testament Interpretation
B. New Testament Usage
Bibliography

A. Old Testament Interpretation

The primary use of the term in the OT is simply to identify the firstborn of individuals, primarily the patriarchs, but is often used to describe the firstborn of the animals. Israel (the nation) is identified as the firstborn son of God (Exod 4:22; compare Jer 31:9). Every first-born male must be dedicated to the Lord. In the case of the children of Israel, the firstborn son is redeemed through the Levites (Num 3:12, 13, 45; 8:18). The firstborn male of cattle, sheep, and goats must be offered up to the Lord as a burnt offering (Exod 13:12, 15); the firstborn of unclean animals must be redeemed by a lamb (Exod 34:20). A similar line of thought is presented in the OT Apocrypha and Pseudepigrapha (e.g., Tob 5:13; Wis 18:13; Sir 17:18; 36:12; 2 Esd 6:58; 4 Macc 15:18; Jub 24:3; 26:27; 36:14).

According to Gen 49:3 (compare Deut 21:17), the firstborn is the "procreative strength" (reʾshith ʾoni רֵאשִׁית אוֹנִי) of the father, i.e., the life of the father is continued on through the son. This concept of inheritance rights (bekhorah בְּכֹרָה) has been the focus of research concerning the firstborn in the OT.

Deuteronomy 21:15-17 sets out the procedures to fulfill the primogeniture rights of inheritance for the firstborn son (compare Num 27:7-8, which passes the rights to the daughters of a sonless man). The firstborn son is to receive a "double portion" of the inheritance being passed on by the father (perhaps because he was to become the head of the family). However, this does not appear to be a guaranteed right. In fact, in the case of several of the patriarchs this firstborn right is overlooked or circumvented. The birthright of Abraham's firstborn goes to Isaac rather than the eldest son Ishmael (Gen 21:8-21); Jacob acquires the birthright from Esau (Gen 25:31-34); and Joseph obtains the birthright that belonged to Reuben (Gen 48:22). Some scholars argue these apparent violations are due to the principle of *patria potestas*; the father has the right to choose which son will receive the "double portion." As a result, it is thought that the Deuteronomy law was established to ensure the inheritance be passed to the rightful son. However, these particular instances are hardly the reason for the establishment of Deut 21:15-17. Each of the patriarchal narratives provides legitimate reasons for the circumvention of the firstborn rights. In the case of Abraham, Ishmael is the son of his concubine—in other cases found in the Near East, the son of a concubine has no inheritance rights unless otherwise granted by the father (compare Code of Hammurabi §§170-71). Genesis 27 indicates that Isaac was deceived into granting the blessing of the firstborn to Jacob rather than to Esau the rightful heir. The disinheritance of Reuben, the firstborn of Jacob, is brought about by his own act of serious disobedience in Gen 49 rather than by the choice of his father.

Many scholars have turned to the ANE in search of comparisons to determine the development of the primogeniture rights. The Code of Hammurabi offers little light by which to understand the issue. Generally speaking, the property of the deceased father is to be divided up in equal portions (§§167, 170). However, it appears the father was allowed to show favor to a beloved son by giving him a gift from the estate or allowing him the first choice of the inheritance (§165). There is no indication that this particular son is the firstborn, rather he is just the favored one. Other Old Babylonian texts found at Tel Harmal indicate the inheritance should be divided equally among the sons but that the eldest would receive an extra portion; although it is unclear what that portion would equal (IM 51190). Similarly, in texts found at Nippur and Ur in southern Babylonia, the firstborn son was granted an additional 10 percent of the inheritance. The 14th cent. BCE Nuzi texts indicate that the firstborn natural son was granted an honored position in the distribution of the estate. In addition, the father could pass down his inheritance to an adopted son should there be no natural-born son.

Much discussion has been undertaken as to the actual meaning of the amount of the firstborn's inheritance, the "double portion" (pi shenayim פִּי שְׁנַיִם) found in Deut 21:17. The phrase is translated literally "mouth of two," perhaps suggesting enough for two people. Pi senayim occurs in two other places: Exod 22:3 and 2 Kgs 2:9 translated in various English versions as "double portion" (compare Zech 13:8—translated "two-thirds"). The LXX is helpful in translating this difficult phrase. The translators of the LXX have used the term dipla (διπλᾶ), which is defined as double (twice as much).

Additional understanding of this phrase may be gleaned from ANE texts. An adoption contract from Mari suggests that the adopted son is to receive "two-thirds" of the estate of his father. However, there is no indication that this is the firstborn son. The Akkadian term found in the passage (aplum) is defined as "heir" or "son." Another Old Babylonian text from Kutalla suggests the firstborn son was given a double portion of the inheritance. Another text from the same collection indicates the eldest son's portion was 10 percent of the estate. Texts from Nuzi that deal with inheritance rights indicate that the firstborn son will receive a double portion of the property (HSS V 7). Other Nuzi texts suggest that the eldest son only receives the first choice from the property of his father (HSS V 21). The ANE texts offer a varied opinion as to the rights of the firstborn, as a result they do not provide a great deal of help in determining the meaning of pi shenayim in Deut 21:17; as suggested above, the best alternative for defining the term can be found in the OT and LXX.

B. New Testament Usage

The Greek term prōtotokos (or a form of it) is found just nine times in the NT. In its primary use it identifies Jesus as the firstborn. He is the firstborn son of Mary (Matt 1:25; Luke 2:7—indicating that Mary had no previous children, though not necessarily identifying her as a virgin). As the firstborn son, Jesus was taken to the Temple on the eighth day by Mary and Joseph to be redeemed according to the Law of Num 3:13 and 45 (Luke 2:22-24). There is no indication as to the price of redemption and the ceremony should be considered a dedication of the child to the Lord (compare 1 Sam 1:11).

Jesus is identified as the firstborn of creation (Col 1:15, 18). As a result he is considered the mediator of all creation and the one who holds all things together (vv. 16-17). He is called the firstborn of the dead in Col 1:18 and Rev 1:5 (compare Heb 12:23). Jesus is also identified as the firstborn among many of the prōtotokōn (πρωτότοκων) "assembly of the firstborn" in Heb 12:23 (compare Rom 8:29). Some argue that this raises the believer to a position alongside Christ; however, they do not possess the rank of firstborn as does Christ, but merely enjoy the place of brother or sister alongside their archēgos (ἀρχηγός), the originator of their salvation. His role as the Passover lamb should also be taken into consideration in the concept of firstborn (1 Pet 1:19; John 1:29). As the lamb he is the substitutionary firstborn sacrifice for those who are unclean (Exod 34:20), i.e., all of humanity. See INHERITANCE IN THE OT; PASSOVER AND FEAST OF UNLEAVENED BREAD; SACRIFICES AND OFFERINGS.

Bibliography: Eryl W. Davies. "The Inheritance of the Firstborn in Israel and the Ancient Near East." *JSS* 38 (1991) 175–91; M. de J. Ellis. "The Division of Property at Tell Harmal." *JCS* 26 (1974) 135–36; I. Mendelsohn. "On the Preferential Status of the Eldest Son." *BASOR* 156 (1959) 38–40; Roland de Vaux. *Ancient Israel* (1961); Paul Watson. "A Note on the 'Double Portion' of Deuteronomy 21:17 and II Kings 2:9." *ResQ* 8 (1965) 70–75.

ARCHIE T. WRIGHT

FISH [דָּג dagh, דָּגָה daghah, ἰχθύς ichthys, ἰχθύδιον ichthydion, ὀψάριον opsarion].

    A. Fish in Egypt
    B. Fish in the Old Testament
    C. Fish in the New Testament
    Bibliography

A. Fish in Egypt

When the Israelites remembered their time in Egypt, they often reminisced about the ready availability of fish in their diet. The bounty of the Nile River valley created the image of an "easy" existence that haunted the Israelites in the wilderness (Num 11:4-6; see also Ps 78:18). In fact the Nile does contain a wide variety of species of fish, many of which have been identified from their appearance in tomb paintings (*mugils* = mullets are the most often depicted). Many of these species (i.e., *tilapia* and *clarias*) have adapted to the annual inundation of the NILE RIVER that leaves them in the shallow waters of marshland and irrigation canals where they breed. Their vast numbers and the practice of holding their young in their mouths contributed to a connection between fish and fertility in Egyptian culture. New Kingdom (1550–1070 BCE) records demonstrate the importance of fish to the Egyptian economy and to the diet of every class of people. Among these records are ration lists indicating that the most common fish supplied to workmen in Egypt were *tilapia* (a mouth-brooding red fish), *synodontis* (an omnivorous bottom-feeder), and *mormyrus* (a species with an elongated body and snout generally caught off shore). Fish imagery is used in Ezekiel's oracle against Egypt and its pharaoh, whom the prophet refers to as the "great monster" (hattannim haggadhol הַתַּנִּים הַגָּדוֹל; 28:3), a title similar to other chaos beasts and gigantic sea creatures like RAHAB (Ps 87:4) and LEVIATHAN (Job 41:1-11 [Heb. 40:15-31]; Ps 74:14). The biblical text is quick to show that each of these monsters, including the "large fish" in Jonah 1:17 [Heb. 2:1] (dagh gadhol, kētos κῆτος; Matt 12:40) were always subject to the power of Yahweh.

B. Fish in the Old Testament

Once the Israelites settled in Canaan, fish are seldom mentioned. Without ready access to the sea, since the coastline was controlled by the Philistine city-states, fishing would have been confined to streams, the Jordan River, and the Sea of Galilee. In no instance, except perhaps the oblique references in the Holiness (Lev 11:10) and Deuteronomic codes (Deut 14:10) forbidding the consumption of fish that lacked fins or scales, is there a distinct description of a particular species of fish in the text. Even Ezekiel's Edenlike vision of the restored Temple and the rejuvenation of the land with many streams of water only speaks in general terms of "a great many kinds" of fish (Ezek 47:7-10). Still, the existence of a FISH GATE in the north wall of Jerusalem in both the pre- and postexilic periods (2 Chr 33:14; Neh 3:3; Zeph 1:10) and the sale of fish in the market (Neh 13:16) demonstrate that fish and fish products had a place in Israelite meals and homes.

C. Fish in the New Testament

Greater attention is given to the harvesting of fish in the NT, first because of their importance to the general economy of the Galilee area, and second because of the allegorical equivalence between fishing and evangelism in the early Christian movement. The image of the disciples as "fishers of people" (Mark 1:17) rings true to people whose occupation has been to work in cooperative associations (Luke 5:7-10) that daily drew in the nets filled with fish from the sea. Thirteen harbors like CAPERNAUM and BETHSAIDA served as homes for the fishing boats and their crews. The name of one of these harbors, Taricheae (lit., "fish factory") or Magdala, suggests that it functioned as a central processing center for pickling the catch from throughout the lake. The process included gutting the fish, rubbing them with salt, and laying them for three to five days in layers between dry matting. The drying process drained away their body fluids while permeating them with salt. This may explain John's use of the term opsarion to describe the two "small [dried] fish" brought forward by the disciples (John 6:9).

There are eighteen indigenous species of fish in the Sea of Galilee, ten of which have some commercial value. The catfish (*Clarias lazera*) is physically the largest species (growing to 4 ft. and 25 pounds), but it is forbidden in the Holiness Code (Lev 11:9-12) and therefore may have not been eaten by the Jews in antiquity. Among the most prolific of the commercial species is the Kinneret sardine (*Acanthobrama terrae sanctae*). Large quantities were caught at night by fishermen using seine nets and they were then pickled in brine and transported throughout the country. Several members of the carp family (*Cyprinideae*) are indigenous to the Sea of Galilee, including the Long-Headed Barbel (*Barbus longiceps*, which can grow to 30 in. in length and weigh as much as 15 lbs.) and the *Barbus canis*, both of which are well fleshed and predatory, feeding off the schools of sardines. A third category of indigenous fish is the musht, particularly the *Tilapia galilea* ("St. Peter's Fish") that can grow to 18 in. and weigh as much as 4.5 lbs. Its silvery body and comblike dorsal fin is easily distinguishable, and its flat shape makes it suitable for frying or broiling (Luke 24:42). The musht is the only fish in the lake that swims in shoals (see Luke 5:1-7), congregating in the northern portion of the lake in the winter and then dispersing into mating pairs as the waters warm up in summer. The preference for eating freshly caught fish may be the basis of Jesus' request in John 21:10-11 that Peter "bring some of the fish (ichthys) you have just caught" despite the fact that bread and dried fish (opsarion) were already cooking on the charcoal fire (John 21:9). *See* FISHERMEN; FISHING.

Bibliography: D. J. Brewer and R. F. Friedman. *Fish and Fishing in Ancient Egypt* (1989). J. Murphy-O'Connor. "Fishers of Fish, Fishers of Men: What We Know of the First Disciples from Their Profession." *BRev* 15 (1999) 22–27, 48–49; M. Nun. "Cast Your Net upon the Waters: Fish and Fishermen in Jesus' Time." *BAR* 19 (1993) 46–56, 70.

VICTOR H. MATTHEWS

FISH GATE שַׁעַר הַדָּגִים sha'ar haddaghim]. GATE of pre and postexilic JERUSALEM, mentioned as part of Manasseh's refortification project (2 Chr 33:14), and repaired under Nehemiah's governorship (Neh 3:3; 12:39). This gate may have pierced the wall near the northwest corner of the Temple Mount, west of the SHEEP GATE.

FISHERMEN [דַּיָּגִים dayyaghim; ἁλιεῖς halieis]. While the occupation of fisherman may not have been as "miserable" as the Egyptian sage Khety suggests ("Satire of the Trades," *ANET*, 433; *see* DUA-KHETY, INSTRUCTION OF), it certainly was backbreaking labor with a relatively small reward. At least in ancient Israel, the fish catcher did not have to contend with crocodiles or marshlands drying up (Isa 19:8). However, the only reliable body of fresh water was the Sea of Galilee and some stretches of the Jordan River. As it flowed south the water became increasingly saline, eliminating fish habitat (note Ezekiel's eschatological vision of a rejuvenation of the Dead Sea with fishermen casting their nets from its banks from En-gedi to En-eglaim [47:8-10]). Most of what is known of the practical aspects of fishing come from the accounts in the NT about Jesus' recruiting of his disciples from the men working the boats in the Sea of Galilee (Matt 4:18). The discovery of a 26.6 ft. long, wooden fishing boat near the village of Magdala provides a glimpse into the daily struggle that teams of five men (sometimes family members as in Mark 1:19-20 and sometimes day laborers) faced sailing out each morning or evening to cast their linen nets (John 21:3). The forming of fishing cooperatives allowed families to work together and share the risks and burdens of the sea (Luke 5:7-10). Their labors did not always result in a catch (Luke 5:5), and they would have had to share what they did pull in with family members, those who provided them with loans, and the tax collector (*see* Levi's "tax booth" set near the shore in Mark 2:14). There were also the ongoing tasks of repairing, cleaning, and weaving their nets (Mark 1:19; Luke 5:2), maintaining their boats, and sorting and processing their catch. *See* SHIPS AND SAILING IN THE NT; SHIPS AND SAILING IN THE OT.

VICTOR H. MATTHEWS

FISHHOOK [חַכָּה hakkah]. Ancient fishermen used hooks, nets, and baskets (Job 41:1; Hab 1:15). Their implements were emblems of their profession (Isa 19:8).

FISHING [דָּגִים daghim, ἁλιεύω halieuō]. Information about fishing practices or implements, prior to the NT period, is confined to a few metaphorical references in the prophets (Isa 19:8; Jer 16:16; Hab 1:15) and in wisdom literature (Eccl 9:12). The most detailed source for fishing techniques is found in God's interrogation of Job (41:1-7 [Heb. 40:25-31]) about LEVIATHAN. This latter passage does include references to a variety of items employed by fishermen: FISHHOOKs (khakkah חַכָּה), HARPOONs (sukkah שֻׂכָּה), and fish spears (tsiltsal צִלְצַל). Unfortunately, examples of these implements, made of both bone and metal, have only been recovered in excavations in Egypt. This may be due to the fact that the Philistines

and the Phoenicians controlled the Mediterranean seacoast and the Israelites were limited to fishing in the Jordan River and the Sea of Galilee. However, the inclusion of a "FISH GATE" in Jerusalem (Neh 3:3) and the prohibition in the dietary laws against eating fish that lack scales or fins (i.e., catfish; Lev 11:9-12; Deut 14:9-10) indicate a familiarity with fishing and the inclusion of fish in the local diet and economy. Individual fishermen, who did not own a boat or were not part of a fishing cooperative (Luke 5:7-10), could stand on the shore with line and hook (Matt 17:27) or wade into the shallows and cast a small net about 20–25 ft. in diameter (see the expression amphiblēstron [ἀμφίβληστρον], in Matt 4:18). Large-scale fishing, as depicted in the Prophets and the Gospels, was done with drag or seine nets (Hab 1:15 [khērem חֵרֶם]; Matt 13:47 [sagēnē σαγήνη]). This large net (750–1,000 ft. long and 25 ft. high), made of interwoven linen threads (similar to a net discovered in a cave near En-gedi), was attached to ropes and held to the bottom with sinkers. It would be carried approximately 100 yds out into the lake in a boat and then its wings were expanded, forming a wall in the water that trapped the fish as the team of men dragged it back toward the shore. Continual maintenance, including washing the nets (Luke 5:2) and spreading them out to dry (Ezek 26:5), prevented deterioration and the expense of making new ones. Fishermen who had boats that could sail out into the Sea of Galilee (based on a recovered boat from Magdala they were 26.5 ft. long and 7.5 ft. wide) deployed a trammel net (John 21:6; Luke 5:4; diktyon δίκτυον). This consisted of several attached sections forming a three-layered trap as much as 500 ft. long that was dropped from the side of the boat to create circular or spiral shapes in which to enmesh the fish. When the men created a commotion, the fish were frightened through the outer portion of the net and into the inner, tightly woven sections that had now taken on the form of an encircling bag under the pressure of the fleeing creatures. The catch (principally barbell, musht, and sardines) was then pulled into those boats cooperating in this joint enterprise (Luke 5:6-7). Once they reached the shore, the rest of the night and early morning would be spent in the process of disentangling and sorting out the commercially valuable and the forbidden fish (Matt 13:48). Of course, the tax collectors also took note of the success of the night's work and were ready to take their portion of the catch (Mark 2:14). *See* FISH; GALILEE, SEA OF; LEVIATHAN.

Bibliography: K. C. Hanson. "The Galilean Fishing Economy and the Jesus Tradition." *BTB* 27 (1997) 99–111; M. Nun. "Cast Your Net upon the Waters: Fish and Fishermen in Jesus' Time." *BAR* 19 (1993) 46–56, 70.

VICTOR H. MATTHEWS

FIVE. *See* NUMBERS, NUMBERING.

FIVE SCROLLS, THE. *See* MEGILLOTH.

FLAGON [קַשְׂוָה *qaswah*; σπονδεῖον *spondeion*]. One of the ritual vessels of the tabernacle and temple, a flagon was a container (jug, cup, etc.) for drink offerings (Exod 25:29; 37:16; Num 4:7; 1 Chr 28:17; Isa 22:24; 1 Macc 1:22; 1 Esd 2:9), but not limited to ritual use (Esth 1:8 NRSV).

STEVE COOK

FLAGSTAFF [תֹּרֶן *toren*]. The NRSV's translation of *toren* in a simile (Isa 30:17), otherwise translating the word as "MAST" (Isa 33:23; Ezek 27:5).

FLAMINIUS, CIRCUS. Constructed toward the end of the 3rd cent. BCE and located in the southern part of Campus Martius, this ovoid arena was one of several in Rome, the largest and most famous of which was Circus Maximus, designed specifically for the sport of chariot racing.

JAMES A. METZGER

FLASK [פַּךְ *pakh*; ἀγγεῖον *angeion*, καψάκης *kapsakēs*]. A small container for fluids. A number of Hebrew words could be translated *flask*, although the precise distinction between these words is not clear. The NRSV renders *pakh* as *flask* in 2 Kgs 9:1-3, but uses the translation *vial* in 1 Sam 10:1. In the apocrypha, a *kapsakēs* of oil is translated *flask* (Jdt 10:5). In the NT, *angeion* is rendered *flask* (Matt 25:4). In each case, the container holds oil. The difficulty with such translations is that ancient terminology for pottery does not always match modern terms for such vessels, so the correspondence is not always precise. From an archaeological standpoint, a flask is often defined as a small vessel with a rounded body and small neck. It often has two small handles on either side of the neck. It is used for the storage and transportation of liquids. Other objects, such as skins and horns, could fulfill the same purpose (1 Sam 1:24; 1 Kgs 1:39).

KEVIN A. WILSON

FLAVIUS JOSEPHUS. *See* JOSEPHUS, FLAVIUS.

FLAX [פִּשְׁתָּה *pishtah*]. Common flax (*Linum usitatissimum* L.) is an annual plant that grows from seed in about 100 days to a height of 12 to 36 in. and has blue flowers that produce seed pods. The medicinal properties of linseed oil that is extracted by crushing flax seed may have been known to the ancient Egyptians since archaeologists have recovered crushed flax seeds from Badari in Middle Egypt (dated to ca. 4000 BCE). Although there is no mention of its use in the biblical narrative, it seems likely that the properties of linseed oil were known. Flax was cultivated in fields alongside barley and wheat (Exod 9:31). Its importance to the village economy is seen in its inclusion in the GEZER CALENDAR, which states that the flax harvest took place in February and preceded the wheat harvest. Since flax required richer soil and a ready water supply, it was primarily grown in marshy or irrigated lowland areas rather than in the hill country of Israel. When fields of flax were grown primarily for their fiber, the immature, green stems were pulled from the ground, not cut. The stems were soaked in water for several days. This softening process allowed the long "bast" fibers that lay between the skin of the flax stalk and its woody core to be separated out or combed (Isa 19:9). They were then beaten into threads and woven on a loom into LINEN cloth (Hos 2:5, 9). An alternative to soaking the stems was to leave them out in the sun to partially rot, like those left on Rahab's roof (Josh 2:6). Half-ripe stems were used to create the best quality thread for garments (see Prov 31:13), while the more mature stems were twisted to make mats and very strong ropes (see Judg 15:14). Since washing loosened the fibers, linen garments had to be dried carefully and repleated to restore their shape. One sign of the strength of flax even while wet is the interchangeable use of the Hebrew term for a lamp "wick" in Isa 42:3. *See* CLOTH, CLOTHES.

VICTOR H. MATTHEWS

FLEAS [פַּרְעֹשׁ *par'osh*, ψύλλος *psyllos*]. A parasitic insect of the order *Siphonaptera*, it is unlikely that the ancients understood much about their behavior and physiology. In exchanges with Saul, David twice refers to himself as a flea (1 Sam 24:14; 26:20 NRSV), professing his insignificance relative to Saul. History has shown that fleas can be effective transmitters of disease, and they surely were in the ancient world. *See* ANT; INSECTS OF THE BIBLE.

R. JUSTIN HARKINS

FLEE, TO [בָּרַח *barakh*; φυγέω *phygeō*]. "To flee" means to run away to find safety from an oppressive, frightening, or threatening situation, sometimes because of God's direction. Jacob ran away from Laban (Gen 31:20-22) as God commanded him (Gen 31:13). The Egyptians failed in their attempt to escape the water of the Red Sea when they realized they were in danger (Exod 14:25-28). *Fleeing* symbolically refers to seeking security in a source other than God (Ps 11:1) or wrongly assuming one can flee to a place where God does not exist (Ps 139:7; Jonah 1:3, 10). *Fleeing* also refers to the diminishing of sorrow (Isa 51:11) and the rapid passing of time (Job 9:25; 14:2). *Fleeing* can refer to an attempt to escape judgment—either divine or human. The messengers order Lot and his family to flee the distruction of Sodom, and they flee to Zoar (Gen 19:15-23). Jesus refers to the attempt of the scribes, the Pharisees, and the Sadducees to escape judgment (Matt 3:7//Luke 3:7). Jesus' disciples ran away when Jesus was arrested (Matt 26:56). Paul instructs people to flee from worshiping idols (1 Cor 10:14).

EMILY R. CHENEY

FLEET [אֳנִי 'oni; ναῦς naus, στόλος stolos]. A group of ships operating under one authority (e.g., 1 Kgs 9:26-27; 10:11, 22; 1 Macc 1:17). *See* SHIPS AND SAILING IN THE OT.

FLESH IN THE NT [σάρξ sarx]. *Flesh* typically translates sarx in the NT, and refers basically to the material substance that covers the bones of humans or animals—as clearly in Luke 24:39 and 1 Cor 15:39—and in the regular phrase to describe humankind as "flesh and blood" (Matt 16:17; 1 Cor 15:50; Gal 1:16; Eph 6:12; Heb 2:14). Paul was not physically known to most of the Colossians; they had not seen his face "in the flesh" (Col 2:1); in Col 1:22 and 2:11 "the body of flesh" is intended precisely to underline the physicality of the human body. Marriage has an inescapably physical character, as the union of two to become "one flesh" (Matt 19:6//Mark 10:8; 1 Cor 6:16; Eph 5:31). Paul's "thorn in the flesh" (2 Cor 12:7) was evidently a painful physical affliction. That circumcision was "in the flesh" emphasized its outwardness and visibility in the male human body (Rom 2:28; Gal 6:13; Col 2:13). The point of John 6:51-56, which uses the term *flesh* rather than *body*, was to emphasize the manifest physicality of the incarnate Word (and the basic physicality of "eating" this flesh).

"In the days of his flesh" Jesus learned obedience by what he suffered (Heb 5:7-8; 1 Pet 4:1). In the normal course of events, flesh decays and corrupts (Acts 2:31); the Son shared flesh and blood so that he might share death (Heb 2:14). In a word, flesh is essentially weak (Matt 14:38//Mark 14:38). So the description of humankind as "all flesh" is a basic assertion of humankind's weakness and inadequacy (as flesh) before God (Matt 24:22//Mark 13:20); "no flesh shall (all flesh shall not) be justified from works of the law" (Rom 3:20; Gal 2:16); "no flesh can (all flesh cannot) boast before God" (1 Cor 1:29).

Consequently, *flesh* also stands in contrast to *spirit*, the spirit as a countering, positive force, but inhibited or restricted by the flesh (Matt 14:38//Mark 14:38; 1 Cor 5:5; Col 2:5). A spirit by definition does not consist of flesh and bones (Luke 24:39). There is a fundamental distinction between birth from the flesh and birth from the spirit (John 3:6). This is precisely the wonder of the incarnation: that "the Word became flesh" (John 1:14; 1 John 4:2). But although it is the flesh of the Son of Man, as bread of life, which must be chewed (John 6:53-54), it is also important to grasp that "it is the Spirit that gives life, the flesh is of no value" (6:63). Jesus' own transposition from the realm of flesh to Spirit (Rom 1:3-4; 1 Tim 3:16) is also the pattern for human salvation (1 Pet 3:18; 4:2). But the reconciliation takes place precisely in and through Christ's flesh (Eph 2:14; Heb 10:20).

Sarx is one of Paul's key terms (used ninety-one times in the Pauline corpus). In his usage the range

of signification reviewed above is extended and deepened. It still denotes the physical body, or physical relationship, or kinship, without any negative connotation (Rom 11:24; 1 Cor 6:16; 15:39; Eph 5:29, 31; Col 2:1). But that sense naturally elides into the thought of human weakness, liable to affliction and weariness, "mortal," subject to corruption, and therefore incapable of inheriting the kingdom of God (Rom 6:19; 1 Cor 15:50; 2 Cor 4:11; 7:5). As also for Paul, relations "in the flesh" stand in some contrast to relationships in Christ and to the power that comes from Christ (2 Cor 12:7-9; Gal 2:20; Phil 1:22-23; Phlm 16).

In Paul, however, the moral connotation of flesh becomes markedly stronger. It is precisely as sarx that no one can be justified before God or boast before God (Rom 3:20; Gal 2:16; 1 Cor 1:29). The flesh weakens and incapacitates the law (Rom 8:3; similarly 7:13-14). "Those who are in the flesh are not able to please God" (8:8). Still more alarming is the fact that the sarx is the sphere of sin's operations (7:18, 25; 8:3—"sinful flesh"), whereby natural human appetites are corrupted into sinful passions (7:5). Most striking is the regular Pauline antithesis between flesh and Spirit. "The flesh's way of thinking is death, whereas the Spirit's way of thinking is life and peace" (8:6; see further Gal 3:3; 5:16-17, 19-23; Phil 3:3).

This explains the outright opposition to sarx in some of Paul's exhortations (Rom 8:7; 13:14; Gal 5:24; 6:8), and the striking way in which Paul expresses his concerns about "flesh" by using the phrase kata sarka (κατὰ σάρκα), "according to the flesh." Kata sarka denotes an attitude shaped and determined by the flesh, by the priorities of the flesh (again human appetites). A kata sarka attitude is simply inadequate to appreciate God's priorities (1 Cor 1:26; 2 Cor 1:17; 5:16; 10:2-3; 11:18). To live kata sarka is a self-afflicted sentence of death (Rom 8:5, 13; Gal 4:23, 29). In all this it is important to recognize that Paul is not working with a physical dualism between matter and spirit or between flesh and Spirit. Rather his concern is that the weakness of the flesh leaves the believer all the time vulnerable to the power (sin) that excites the human appetite for envy, acquisitiveness, and self-satisfaction ("sinful desires"). He recognizes that the always pressing threat of human mortality pushes the human being toward short-term gratification and power plays. For Paul, therefore, it was imperative that believers be resolute in resisting such temptations, in looking to the Spirit for priorities and enabling, and in endeavoring ever to follow Christ's example.

An important aspect of Paul's view of sarx is that it was a major component in his argument that the gospel for Gentiles did not require them to become proselytes. It was precisely Israel's emphasis on the need for "circumcision in the flesh" that was focusing Jewish believers' attention too much on the outward and visible and causing them to miss the fact that the relation of Gentile believers with God was already sealed by the Spirit without circumcision (Rom 2:28-29; Gal 3:3; 6:12-13; Phil 3:3-4).

It should also be noted that Paul did not think that receiving the Spirit delivered the believer/baptisand from the flesh. The process of salvation, the life of the Spirit still had to be lived out "in the flesh" (Gal 2:20; Phil 1:22). That process would not be complete until the resurrection (1 Cor 15:42-54; 2 Cor 4:16–5:5). In the meantime the life of Christ could only be manifested in and through the mortal flesh (2 Cor 4:11) and in the tension between flesh and Spirit (Gal 5:16-17; Rom 7:14–8:25). See BODY; CIRCUMCISION; INCARNATION.

Bibliography: J. D. G. Dunn. *The Theology of Paul the Apostle* (1998) 62–67, 477–82.

JAMES D. G. DUNN

FLESH IN THE OT [בָּשָׂר basar; שְׁאֵר she'er]. Biblical Hebrew and Aram. employ the term basar and the much rarer she'er in the meaning "flesh, body." Patterns of OT usage best indicate the profile of the biblical concept. The predominant usage of basar/she'er in the OT refers to the soft (muscle) tissue of the body, human or animal, living or dead (basar—Gen 2:21; Exod 4:7; Lev 6:3; etc.; she'er—Prov 5:11; 11:17; Ps 73:26), sometimes as distinct from 'atsam (עֶצֶם) "bone" (Job 10:11), 'or (עוֹר) "skin" (Job 10:11) or dam (דָּם) "blood" (Isa 49:26). In a few instances, it designates the tissue of a specific organ such as the heart (Ezek 11:19; 36:36), the foreskin (Gen 17:11, 13), the "folds" of Leviathan's flesh (Job 41:15), or, euphemistically, the male member (Lev 15:2, 3; Ezek 16:25; 23:20; 44:7, 9). In one instance, "flesh" refers figuratively to some component of a wheel (Ezek 10:12). Varieties of the idiom, "bone of my bone, flesh of my flesh," which many modern European languages have adopted from Scripture, denote consanguinity or kinship (basar—Gen 2:23, 24; 29:14; 37:27; Lev 18:6; 25:49; etc.; she'er—Lev 18:6, 12, 13, 17; 20:19; 21:2; 25:49; Num 27:11; Jer 51:35).

Flesh for consumption is "meat" (basar generally—Exod 12:8, 46; Deut 12:15, 20; etc.; she'er—Exod 21:10; Ps 78:20, 27). Not surprisingly, priestly discussions focus on the suitability of specific categories of flesh for consumption, i.e., whether they are "clean" or "unclean." Flesh containing blood, the source of life, may not be consumed (Gen 9:4; Lev 17:11; etc.), nor may the flesh of animals gored or mangled (Exod 22:30), nor, of course, the flesh of animals that does not conform to any of the several kosher requirements (pork, e.g., see Lev 11:8, 11; Deut 14:8; Isa 65:4; etc.). Animal sacrifice involves the consumption of the meat through fire on the altar or by the priestly class (Exod 29:31, 32, 34; Lev 4:11; etc.). Those not qualified by virtue of both holy office and holy life consume sacri-

ficial flesh inappropriately and risk consequences (Lev 7:18, 20, 21; Deut 16:4; 1 Sam 2:15). References to cannibalism or animals consuming human flesh in time of distress/judgment occur in grotesque portrayals of the horrors experienced by evildoers (Gen 40:19; Lev 26:29; Deut 28:53, 55; 1 Sam 17:44; Isa 9:20; etc.; she'er—Mic 3:3). The longing to return to Egypt and its regular supply of meat also plays a central role in the Torah's thematic treatment of the murmuring of the Israelites during the exodus generation (Num 11:33; Exod 16:3, 8, 12; etc.).

Since corporality characterizes creaturely existence, "flesh" can designate classes of beings. Thus, in contrast with God's spirit/breath (ruakh רוּחַ) or God's mighty arm, "flesh" emphasizes human mortality (Gen 6:3; Ps 78:39 and Deut 5:26; Jer 17:5; Ps 56:4; 2 Chr 32:8, respectively). Humans share this corporality with animals such that references to "all flesh" or the like can refer to animals collectively (Isa 31:3), human beings as a class (Ps 65:2; Isa 40:5, 6; 66:23; Joel 2:28), or animals and human beings together (Gen 6:12, 13, 17, 19; etc.). A significant group of texts ambiguously refers to "all flesh" such that human beings alone or humans and animals together may be in mind (Num 16:22; 27:16; Isa 49:26; 66:16; Jer 12:12; etc.). Significantly, in contrast to Greek idealism, the OT does not view corporality per se as evil and inferior to spirituality. In fact, although corporality implies weakness, it does not involve sinfulness. Instead, since it manifests vitality Ezekiel (11:19; 36:26) can speak of God's intention to replace the unresponsive "heart of stone" with a vital "heart of flesh." Humans are corporeal beings; life is in the blood that invigorates the flesh (Lev 17:11), not in an ephemeral spirit. See BODY; CLEAN AND UNCLEAN; FAMILY; SOUL.

Bibliography: H. W. Wolff. *Anthropology of the Old Testament* (1974).

MARK E. BIDDLE

FLESHPOT [סִיר הַבָּשָׂר sir habbasar]. The Hebrew word sir can denote a POT, CALDRON, or KETTLE, any VESSEL used for cooking, washing, and ritual purposes. In Exod 16:3, the Israelites speak of the "fleshpots" (NRSV) from which they ate in Egypt before their wandering in the wilderness. See COOKING AND COOKING UTENSILS.

STEVE COOK

FLINT, FLINTY [חַלָּמִישׁ khallamish, צֹר tsor]. The stone, composed of impure quartz, is abundant in the Middle East and is known for its hardness and durability (Ezek 3:9, Ezekiel's determination is harder than flint). When fractured the stone produces sharp, elongated edges suitable for use as cutting tools. In Neolithic Age Palestine the production of various flint tools influenced all aspects of life. The flint knife was used for ceremonial "cuttings." Zipporah used a tsor to circumcise her son (Exod 4:25), while the Israelite men's circumcision entering the promised land (Josh 5:2-3) was accomplished with "knives of flint." Flint represents the steadfast determination of the Servant of the Lord (Isa 50:7). Psalm 114:8 alludes to the exodus event where the Lord "turns . . . the flint into a spring of water."

MICHAEL G. VANZANT

FLOAT [צוּף tsuf]. By throwing a stick into water Elisha miraculously retrieves an iron ax, making it float to the surface (2 Kgs 6:6). *See* RAFT.

FLOCK. *See* SHEEP, SHEEPFOLD.

FLOG [נָכָה nakhah; δέρω derō, μαστιγόω mastigoō]. A method of punishment in which a person is beaten with a lash or flexible rod across the back. It was intended to be non-lethal. Deuteronomy 25:1-3 places a limit of no more than forty lashes in legal cases where flogging is used. This limitation does not seem to be for the physical protection of the criminal. Instead, more than forty lashes would cause the criminal, a fellow Israelite, to be degraded. Flogging continued in the NT period, although the Romans apparently did not impose a limit on the number of lashes. It is commonly assumed that Jesus received thirty-nine lashes from the Romans before his crucifixion, but none of the Gospels indicate how long he was beaten. Acts records that a number of early disciples were flogged for their proclamation of the gospel (Acts 5:40; 16:23; 22:24). According to 2 Cor 11:23-24, the prohibition against more than forty lashes was still followed by Jews in the 1st cent. CE.

KEVIN A. WILSON

FLOOD [מַבּוּל mabbul; κατακλυσμός kataklysmos]. The biblical flood story of Gen 6–9 forms a key component of the Bible's primordial history (Gen 1–11). The flood story represents an ancient Israelite adaptation of time-honored Near Eastern lore and establishes the core theological theme of God's governance over a conflicted world.

A. The Place of the Flood Story in Genesis
B. The Biblical Flood Narrative
C. Diverging Theological Trajectories in the Flood Narrative
D. Flood Traditions
  1. Ancient Near Eastern myth
  2. Biblical and Rabbinic reuse of the flood story
  3. Flood, science, and biblical interpretation
E. The Flood and Natural Evil
Bibliography

A. The Place of the Flood Story in Genesis

The four major scenes of the primordial history in Genesis—the Eden betrayal (Gen 2:4–3:24), Cain's murder of Abel (Gen 4:1-16), the global corruption that occasions the flood (Gen 6:1-7), and the Babel hubris (Gen 11:1-9)—demarcate a line of despair that runs like a thread through these early chapters of Genesis. Each scene adds to a complex layering of deceit, jealousy, destruction, and self-puffery that mar God's world. The stories present a series of corrupt deeds that consign humans to an endless cycle of familial pain, fraternal strife, divine displeasure, and wanton conspiracies. Against the literary backdrop of the spread of sin in the world, the flood story is emblematic of the corruption that taints the entire created order.

Yet this reading of the early chapters of Genesis is incomplete. Crucially, each scene is laden with a redemptive motif, indicating that no matter how far or how deep human sin runs, God stands ready to repair the world. Thus, the Edenic couple is clothed by God (Gen 3:21); Cain receives a protective mark (Gen 4:15); a new covenant is instituted after the flood (Gen 9:8-17); and Abraham hears the clear voice of God after Babel's babble of languages (Gen 11:27–12:5).

The final shape of Gen 1–11 takes an even more positive tone. Genesis 1 sets the stage with its message of creation's inherent goodness and human fruitfulness. The flood story, in this larger literary context, accents the cleansing of creation and the renewal of God's commitment to life. Despite the dire character of the flood and the other stories in the primordial history, Gen 1–11 underscores hope amid desolation.

The final version of these chapters reinforces a message of divine compassion for a world wrenched by dislocation and destruction.

B. The Biblical Flood Narrative

Before comparing the flood story with its precursor sources, we should take stock of the total narrative, since this is the canonical version that has been handed down throughout the centuries and has exerted the greatest influence on Jewish, Christian, and Islamic tradition.

Chapter 6 opens with the fateful decision by God to send the flood as a punishment for human wrongdoing and violence (Gen 6:1-13). This story line follows a pattern established by the stories of Adam, Eve, and Cain, but now the punishment is global in scale. The catastrophe of the flood reintroduces the chaos out of which the original creation emerged in Gen 1. Ancient Mesopotamian and Canaanite myths about warrior gods battling sea gods to create new world orders would suggest that the biblical flood story is a type of creation story. Presumably God intended to use the flood's chaos as the cauldron in which God would fashion a revivified world order.

The story proceeds from divine regret over evil to a plan of action to clean up creation. Noah is selected out from among mortals to craft a boat that will carry representative animals to repopulate the earth after the flood purifies the world (Gen 6:13). God's imparting of the boat's blueprint to Noah becomes the occasion for God to institute an agreement—a covenant—assuring that Noah and his family will survive the catastrophe (Gen 6:14-22). Likewise, the survival of ritually pure animals ensures that the sacrificial system, so dependent on animal offerings, would endure.

After Noah has been shut up in the boat (Gen 7:1-16), the next scene describes the swelling of the waters from below and the torrential storms from above (Gen 7:17-23). While the text states that all land life was destroyed, no indication is given of Noah's condition onboard the ark. Noah reappears on the scene when the flood ends and the water recedes (Gen 8:1-15), whereupon birds are sent forth to find dry land and eventually make their way into the revived world (Gen 8:6-12).

God calls Noah out of the ark with the covenant inducement to multiply and fill the earth (Gen 8:15–9:11). For his part, Noah offers sacrifices on an altar, pleasing God who promises not to send another such flood in the future (Gen 8:20-22).

As in ANE warfare iconography, the story ends with the cosmic war ended and the world at peace, as signified by God at rest in victory with God's war bow inactivated in the sky (Gen 9:12-17).

This idyllic moment is shattered by the tale of Noah's drunkenness in his newly planted vineyard (Gen 9:18-27). Noah's subsequent cursing of his heirs ensures the world will continue to face the challenges of evil.

C. Diverging Theological Trajectories in the Flood Narrative

Our discussion has already hinted at the theological richness of the flood story. Yet as biblical scholars have long recognized, the Genesis flood story represents the interweaving of two originally separate flood tales, each bearing its own unique theological stamp.

Carefully inspecting the literary patterns of the biblical text, the French court physician Jean Astruc (1684–1766) identified two memoirs adapted by Moses that served as sources for the flood story. The clue was provided by the variation in divine names in various segments of the narrative. Memoir A made use of the name Elohim (God), while Memoir B spoke of Jehovah (Yahweh). Untangling the strands, Astruc discovered two variant flood stories in Genesis.

Further inspection revealed that the distinction in divine names went hand in hand with differences in detail between the memoirs.

In Memoir A, one pair of each kind of animal board the ark; the timing of the event is far more "realistic" than in the more stylized Memoir B; Noah sends out a raven at the end of the flood; and the God of Memoir A is rather dispassionate in meting out judgment. This same God gives detailed instructions for the construction of the ark, indicative of patient planning and forethought on God's part.

By contrast, Memoir B's Lord has one pair of each unclean animal plus seven pairs of clean animals enter the ark. The story uses the stylized phrase of forty days and forty nights to calibrate time; Noah sends out a dove at the end of the flood; and Memoir B presents a judgmental deity who changes his mind, regrets creating the world, and is angered at humans for their evil ways. In Memoir B, the flood appears to be sent more out of spite than for any serious moral consideration or with much foresight.

In delineating the two sources, Astruc advanced scholarship toward unpacking the divergent theologies or proclamations of the Priestly (Memoir A) and Yahwist (Memoir B) strands of the Pentateuch. (*See* DOCUMENTARY HYPOTHESIS; J, YAHWIST; P, PRIESTLY WRITERS).

When woven together, the Priestly and Yahwist flood stories complement each other to achieve a deeper theological insight not achieved by either story in isolation. In the primordial history of Gen 1–11, it is the Yahwist source that presents the marred tales of garden rebellion, murder, and tower construction that plunge humanity into chaos. In this source, despite the Lord's efforts at ameliorating the circumstance (e.g., by making garments for Adam and Eve, marking Cain, and calling Abraham), sin becomes an intractable force in the world. On the other hand, the Priestly writer supplies the initial seven-day creation story and the genealogies that unfold a "productivity" thesis that works more expansively to undo the global corruption identified by the Yahwist source.

Yahwist realism and Priestly optimism imbue Genesis with an overall trajectory of tempered hopefulness. The theological whole is more than the sum of its literary parts.

D. Flood Traditions

1. Ancient Near Eastern myth

A proper appreciation of the literary and historical significance of the flood story is best gleaned by comparison with its ANE forbears.

If geophysicists William Ryan and Walter Pitman are correct, the flood tradition owes its start to the cataclysmic events in the Neolithic Period (5500 BCE), when, with the melting of the polar ice caps, the Mediterranean Sea rose to catapult water across the Bosporus, turning a freshwater lake into the Black Sea. The population displaced by that catastrophe is presumed to have carried memories of this flood to the wider ANE and beyond.

Ryan and Pitman are not the only ones to suggest that a historical event lies behind the flood tradition, Sir Leonard Woolley and his protégé Max Mallowan postulated, on the basis of flood layers in lower Mesopotamia, that river floods in the mid-fourth millennium BCE or early third millennium BCE are precursors to this tale.

Regardless of the precise historical spark behind the tale, its obvious literary embellishments and variant versions attest to a lively storytelling tradition that made the flood a centerpiece among myths orienting ANE peoples to a tumultuous natural order.

We are fortunate to possess a number of ancient flood stories that bear striking relationship in outline and detail to the biblical text.

In addition to the Sumerian King List, which mentions the flood, mythic texts from that region (ca. 2000 BCE) present the tale of King Ziusudra ("Life of Long Days"). Following the creation of the Sumerians and the rise of their main cities, the gods send a seven-day flood from which Ziusudra escapes by boat. When the flood ceases, life is renewed as the sun-god's rays stream in through one of the boat's windows. Rewarded with immortality, Ziusudra departs to live in the idyllic land of Dilmun.

The Akkadian Atrahasis tale (ca. 1700 BCE) tells of a time when overworked gods went on strike. Their human replacements, made from clay, multiply greatly and overpopulate the region. To cut down the burgeoning brood and to end their noisy antics, the gods send in succession a plague, a drought, and finally a flood. The man Atrahasis ("Exceedingly Wise One") is spared when Enki, the god of wisdom and water, warns him to build a boat. Despite the wind-god Enlil's anger over Atrahasis' escape, Atrahasis manages to survive.

The most noteworthy version is that found in the Gilgamesh Epic (ca. 13th cent. BCE and 7th cent. BCE). This version presents an expansive story that bears strong resemblance to the biblical tale.

Folded inside an extensive account of the heroic exploits of King Gilgamesh and his companion, Enkidu, the flood tale is narrated by Utnapishtim, the man immortalized by the gods for surviving the flood. Gilgamesh traveled to meet the survivor of the flood in an effort to gain the knowledge of immortality. In his tale, Utnapishtim recounts the seven-day construction of a cubic boat, the seven-day storm, and the seven-day drying of the land. Utnapishtim sent out a series of birds as the flood receded and upon disembarking, he made a sacrifice to the gods, an offering around which the gods gathered "like flies." Utnapishtim and his wife were granted immortality, a signal to the reader that Gilgamesh would not achieve the immortality he sought so fervently.

Whether we follow Carl Jung to tease out psychological artifacts from myth or turn to Bronislaw Malinowski to appreciate the living cultural canopy beneath which myth flourishes, it is readily apparent that the flood tale spoke to the ancients on many levels. It is a tale, at its heart, about death and renewal. The story underscores human limitations and divine grace, even as the latter is mixed with divine vengeance. This myth taps immortal yearnings, and enables believers to come to grips with the contingent instability of the natural order.

In short, the Bible's precursors focus attention on the themes of tragedy and hope found also in the Gen-esis flood story. This is the legacy of the flood tradition. In the Bible, of course, the vivid depiction of flood survival balances out the unmitigated disaster described at the end of 2 Kings, namely the story of Judah's exile to Babylon. Through the lens of the flood story, the Bible sees hope for the exiles, the very community responsible for the final production of the Pentateuch.

2. Biblical and rabbinic reuse of the flood story

Outside of Genesis, Noah and the flood story receive only scant attention in the OT. First Chronicles 1:4 simply mentions Noah and his sons in a genealogical list. Ezekiel invokes Noah along with Daniel (or Danel) and Job as great figures of the past whose legendary merit would not be sufficient to save the people of Israel from God's wrath, given the depths of the nation's corruption (Ezek 14:14, 20).

The flood story gains a little more theological traction in Isaiah in a segment devoted to reflecting on the exile in Babylon. The prophet affirms that in those dark days God would adhere to the covenant just as God did after the flood (Isa 54:9-10).

Psalm 29:10 may, perhaps, be read as a reference to God's triumph over the flood, though this psalm more likely reflects the myth of the divine warrior, the combat motif that we have seen underlies the Genesis flood story.

A number of NT texts make varying theological use of the flood story. The writer of Hebrews presents Noah as one of a line of faithful ancestors who heeded God's call and, despite appearances to the contrary, built the ark, saved his family, and went down in history as an heir of righteousness (Heb 11:7).

Making complex associations, First Peter states that in his death Christ descended to preach for those who died in their disobedience as God waited patiently for Noah to build the ark (1 Pet 3:18-20). The saving through water becomes emblematic of baptism (1 Pet 3:21).

Second Peter continues with the flood theme, suggesting that the story confirms that God is able to rescue righteous people while still holding the unjust accountable (2 Pet 2:5).

Though the Synoptic Gospels all share material concerning signs of the tumultuous end of the age (Matt 24; Mark 13; Luke 17), Matthew and Luke invoke as parallels references to life just before Noah's flood raged. In Noah's day, people continued to eat, drink, and marry, thoroughly oblivious to their impending doom. The same state of affairs will obtain when the Son of Man appears. In the context of Matthew and Luke, these Gospel references to the flood do not focus on dividing the corrupt from believers; rather the focus is that no one knows when the turning of the age will take place.

The hints about Noah's generation provided by the Gospels are fleshed out in greater detail in the Qumran texts. There, the pre-flood world is depicted as a place of violence and forbidden knowledge, a land terrorized by the Watchers—offspring of wicked angels who mated with mortal women (*1 En.* 15, 86, 106; *Jub.* 7). Their half-breed children devastated the earth. Only the miraculous birth of Noah and the building of his boat brought relief to a torn world (*1 En.* 106).

By far the greatest literary and theological exploration of the flood story is found in Talmudic and Midrashic lore. Scattered amid the vast cargo hold of rabbinic legal debate and theological speculation are retellings of various aspects of the flood story.

Some texts focus on the corruption of the pre-flood world. Shamhazai, an angelic being permitted by God to inspect the good world that God created, quickly became sexually involved with mortal women and bore children by them.

Noah's role as deliverer is debated by the rabbis, with most doubting that Noah did anything on his own to merit God's saving action. Regardless of his moral worthiness, Noah is depicted as righting the curses of the ground. His farming labors yielded harvests amid thorns. He also gave humankind the tools that made the burdens of agriculture less troublesome.

Noah's story becomes the occasion for the rabbis to highlight God's compassion. Taking 120 years to build the ark, Noah has ample time to warn his hard-hearted compatriots of their doom. In hopes they would repent, God even tacks on an additional week at the end to give one last chance for repentance. Yet there are limits to God's patience.

The rabbis embellished the details of the ark. No lamps were needed, since a great pearl illuminated the boat. Feeding the animals would no doubt be exhausting, but Noah was energized by God, so he never needed to sleep. Nevertheless, one tradition does suggest Noah fell ill under the stress of this labor.

The rabbinic imagination even wondered where the garbage was kept on the ark. Some thought it was stashed on the lowest level, others on top. For the latter, speculation about trapdoors and Noah's shoveling labors complete the rabbinic portrait of waste management aboard the ark.

After the flood, the male raven quarrels with Noah, fearing that Noah wanted him off the ark to seize his mate. Consistently, the rabbis berate Noah for planting a vineyard after disembarking, rather than cultivating a more useful plant.

By expanding on the flood story's details, the rabbis suggest a way to live inside the story. By animating the human foibles of Noah, succeeding generations are called to ponder the enduring meaning of the story and find wisdom in Noah's harrowing experience.

3. Flood, science, and biblical interpretation

During the medieval period, Western Christian interpreters recast the flood story in much the same fashion as Jewish interpreters. The precise shape of the ark was a topic for discussion. Suggestions ranged from a pyramid, chest, and sarcophagus, to a sailing ship, houseboat, and even a castle at sea.

Did carnivores eat meat during the voyage? One interpreter speculated that, as the carnivores devoured the numerous sheep on board the ark, the boat would progressively get roomier.

Another writer suggested the odor of the animal dung would have been transported away by miraculous intervention, sparing the ark's passengers much distress.

A big question was whether there was sex on the ark. Some held that its human occupants abstained out of grief for the world but allowed that the animals continued breeding. This was held to explain Noah's son Ham's troubles, since he was said to have mated with animals during the voyage bringing curses down upon himself.

Centuries of unfettered realism in interpretation ran aground on the advances in knowledge and cultural interchange brought by European exploration.

As adventurers from Europe entered the New World in the 16th and 17th cent., the flora and fauna they observed raised perplexing questions. Discoverers quickly ran up against more types of animals than might have fit on the ark. Why, after the flood, did Noah's heirs take different creatures to different parts of the world?

Further, difficulties were raised by the diverse peoples these explorers encountered. Were the Native Americans really Noah's descendants? If so, why did it seem that the New World's inhabitants had forgotten not only the flood story but also the language and customs of the early Israelites?

A commitment to the historical character of the story eventually collided with the findings of modern geology and paleontology, but at first every effort was made to unify Genesis with science.

Sir Walter Raleigh and the Jesuit scholar Athanasius Kircher, e.g., sought to breathe life into biblical literalism by scientifically calculating the amount of water required to cover the entire earth and by charting deck by deck the engineering requirements of the ark.

During the 17th and 18th cent., geological theorists like Thomas Burnet, William Whiston, John Ray, and Richard Kirwan made the flood event a key component in the history of God's mechanical shaping of the earth. How else, except with reference to Noah's flood, could one explain the presence of marine fossils on mountaintops?

Yet by the 1820s, too much was known about the deep age of the earth and about long-extinct fossil worlds to believe the flood was a major player in earth's geohistory. The Rev. William Buckland at Oxford sounded the death knell of flood geology when he taught that the flood was a great event, which, while it did occur, left no trace in the geological record. The

Englishman John Pye Smith and the American Edward Hitchcock followed suit with the suggestion that the flood was a localized event, a view that continues to be held by many today.

Gone were the days when the flood could be viewed scientifically as a significant global catastrophe.

In the 1960s, under the auspices of hydrologist Henry Morris and conservative theologian John Whitcomb, flood geology was resuscitated in the form of what was called "Creation Science." Current religious debates over "intelligent design" and Darwinian evolution, however, avoid any reference to the Garden of Eden, Noah's flood, and the Tower of Babel, thus suggesting that the commitment to a literal reading of the flood story may be languishing in conservative Christian circles.

As the historicity of the literal story continues to be undermined, the mythic view of the flood will serve to invigorate the theological imagination of the story. In that sense, ANE myths serve as a better guide to the reading of the tale than appeals to supposed geologic flood layers.

E. The Flood and Natural Evil

Does the flood story shed light on the question of suffering and natural evil? The Bible's view that God uses nature's fierce elements to mete out judgment against corrupt humanity continues to have appeal in some quarters. For centuries, biblical interpreters have suggested that natural disasters are signs of God's displeasure with corrupt humanity.

However, this aspect has become problematic in light of modern science's naturalistic view of the workings of hurricanes, volcanoes, earthquakes, and devastating floods. Ever since the disastrous earthquake and tsunami flooding of Lisbon in 1755, theologians have been divided over looking to the Bible for insight into God's wrath.

While some might continue to invoke the flood story as proof that nature's God works justice against corrupt nations by sending disasters, others find the divine vengeance motif problematic not only scientifically but ethically and theologically. The idea that God judged pious Lisbon while letting corrupt Paris party away was anathema to Voltaire, whose novel *Candide* was a spirited indictment against this view of God. In a post-Holocaust age, the more pressing issue of moral evil has come to the fore, even as the question of God's authorship of natural evil recedes into the background.

The notion that God uses nature as a divine weapon to wage war against hated human foes has become a problematic element of the tradition. Time will tell whether and how the flood story will survive as more than an artifact of ANE and biblical lore. At the very least, our effort to reclaim an image of a compassionate God from the biblical text needs to remain cognizant of the judgmental character of God as portrayed in the flood story. *See* CREATION; DEEP, THE; MARDUK; SEA; TIAMAT; WATER.

Bibliography: D. C. Allen. *The Legend of Noah: Renaissance Rationalism in Art, Science, and Letters* (1963); B. F. Batto. *Slaying the Dragon: Mythmaking in the Biblical Tradition* (1992); H. N. Bialik and Y. H. Ravinitsky. *The Book of Legends* (1992); D. J. A. Clines. *The Theme of the Pentateuch* (1982); S. Neiman. *Evil in Modern Thought: An Alternative History of Philosophy* (2002); J. D. Pleins. *When the Great Abyss Opened: Classic and Contemporary Readings of Noah's Flood* (2003).

J. DAVID PLEINS

FLOODS [מַבּוּל mabbul; κατακλυσμος kataklysmos]. "Flood" is the translation for several Hebrew and Greek words, which are not all connected with the story of the FLOOD in Gen 6–9. The Hebrew mabbul is used almost entirely to refer to the flood of Genesis, the one exception being Ps 29:10, "the LORD sits enthroned upon the flood," which refers to the primordial flood. The Genesis flood story lies behind the use of the Greek kataklysmos in Matt 24:38; Luke 17:27; and 2 Pet 2:5, all of which refer specifically to the flood story of Noah in Gen 6–9. In other occurrences *flood* is often the translator's word for an abundance of waters, or a torrent of rain.

The Red Sea drowning of the Egyptians pursuing Moses and the fleeing people is sometimes described as a flood (Exod 15:5, 8). In all cases, God is the one who is able to create floods (Gen 6:17; Isa 8:6-8) and save people from them (Ps 124:4; Nah 1:7-8), but the floods can also praise God (Ps 98:8).

Flood is often used metaphorically (e.g., 2 Sam 5:20; 1 Chr 14:11; Job 22:11, 16; Pss 69:2; 88:17; Song 8:7; Luke 6:48).

C. MARK MCCORMICK

FLOOR [קַרְקַע qarqaʿ]. This term is a reference to the bottom or the lower extent of a specific spatial domain, and therefore often refers to the floor of a building or other structure [*see* ARCHITECTURE, NT; ARCHITECTURE, OT; HOUSE], or may refer to the bottom of the sea. In 1 Kings the floor of the Temple of Solomon in Jerusalem is covered with cypress boards, and plated with gold (1 Kgs 6:15, 16, 30; also Ezek 41:16, 20). In 1 Kgs 7:7, the term is used in the description of the HOUSE OF THE FOREST OF LEBANON as an expression of the extent of the use of cedar in the Hall of Judgment. The same term is used for the tabernacle floor, which is earthen (Num 5:17). In Amos 9:3 it is used as an expression of extent; the bottom of the sea as the opposite point from the top of Mount Carmel.

C. MARK MCCORMICK

FLORA. *See* PLANTS OF THE BIBLE.

FLORILEGIUM, CAVE 4. *See* DEAD SEA SCROLLS; QUMRAN.

FLOUR [סֹלֶת soleth; σεμίδαλις semidalis]. Fine flour or groats, ground from only the inner kernels of the WHEAT and sifted twice to eliminate large pieces and bulkier meal, is to be differentiated from MEAL (qemakh קֶמַח; aleuron ἄλευρον), which was ground from the whole kernels and the bran. Fine flour is described as "the finest of the wheat" (e.g., Deut 32:14; Ps 81:16), and was served as a luxury (e.g., Gen 18:6). The most frequent use of fine flour in the OT was as a cereal offering, for which it was mixed with oil (e.g., Exod 29:2; Lev 2:1-7, 11). *See* GRAIN; THRESHING.

RALPH K. HAWKINS

FLOW OF BLOOD [זוֹב zov "flow, discharge," דָּם dam "blood"; ῥύσις τοῦ αἵματος rhysis tou haimatos "flow of blood"]. "Flow of blood" describes the female discharge of blood—women with regular flows, i.e., menstruants, and those with irregular or extended flows, i.e., bleeding outside of MENSTRUATION. A menstruant is ritually contagious for one week (Lev 15:19), and sexual intercourse with her is defiling (Lev 15:24) and forbidden (Ezek 18:6).

A woman with a flow of blood outside of menstruation has a disease (*see* CLEAN AND UNCLEAN). The desperate woman who touched the hem of Jesus' garment is probably in this irregular status (Matt 9:20; Mark 5:29; Luke 8:43). Scripture does not prescribe any cure but gives instructions for ritual purification after healing. Like the menstruant, the woman is ritually contagious. If healed, she waits one week and offers sacrifices to Yahweh (Lev 15:29-30).

Although this point is debated, women with blood flows were, at least in some communities, probably secluded. The Torah bans individuals with flow of blood from the Israelite camp (Num 5:2-3; Josephus, *Ant.* 3.261). The Temple Scroll and the Mishnah mention special areas for women during impurity (11Q19 XLVIII, 14-17; *m. Nid.* 7:4).

HANNAH K. HARRINGTON

FLOWER [צִיץ tsits; ἄνθος anthos]. The landscape of ancient Canaan was brightened by the colorful blooms of olive and pomegranate trees as well as by blooming plants growing throughout the Shephelah, the hill country, and the plains. In the spring the steppe regions and hillsides would have been covered with flowers. Curiously, other than the blossoms on flowering shrubs and trees such as the almond (Exod 25:33), there are only three flowers mentioned by name in the biblical text: the LILY (Hos 14:5; Matt 6:28), the rose (Song 2:1), and the camphire (= henna; Song 1:14).

There are many references to flowering plants whose products (dyes, spices, fragrances) were imported, such as spikenard (from the Himalayas, Song 1:12-13), cro-

cus (from Asia Minor, Isa 35:1), and saffron (from India, Song 4:14), but these were not native to Syria-Palestine. The henna plant is a shrub that bears fragrant clusters of small white or yellow flowers. Its leaves were dried and transformed into a paste that was used as a cosmetic and hair dye. There is a generic use of the term *rose* in some passages that may variously refer to the crocus or narcissus (*Narcissus tazetta*), which grows wild and has a yellow bloom (khavatseleth [חֲבַצֶּלֶת], Isa 35:1), or to a bulb-based plant like the tulip (*Tulipa sharonensis*, Song 2:1) with its silver gray-green leaves and bright red flowers. The lily also refers to a variety of different plants species: the "lilies of the field" (Luke 12:27) may be identified as the daisy-like chamomile (*Chamaemilum nobile*) while the lilies (shoshannim שׁוֹשַׁנִּים) referred to in the Song of Songs (6:3; 7:3) are quite likely the hyacinth (*Hyacinthus orientalis*) that has fragrant blue flowers.

The delight that the ancient Israelites took in flowers can be seen in their use as part of the decorative design of the cedar wall coverings and doors in the Jerusalem Temple (1 Kgs 6:18, 32). However, their brief period of natural beauty and inevitable fading under the relentless rays of the sun also served in Job's complaint as a metaphor for short time span allotted to humanity (Job 14:2).

The writer of James (1:10-11) applies this same principle in his discourse on faith to the rich, who, like flowers, must eventually wither and die. Isaiah draws on flower imagery as well in his mocking of the "drunkards of Ephraim" referring to their "fading flower of glorious beauty" that could not withstand the "tempest" of Assyrian invaders (Isa 28:1-4). Second Isaiah employs this metaphor again as he draws a comparison between the people, who like grass or the flower of the field, are short-lived while the "word of God" endures forever (Isa 40:6-8; 1 Pet 1:24-25).

The psalmist plays on this same theme, but chooses to compare mortals, who may flourish "like a flower" but must ultimately pass away, while the Lord's "steadfast love" is everlasting to those who keep the covenant (103:15-18). *See* PLANTS OF THE BIBLE.

VICTOR H. MATTHEWS

FLUTE. *See* MUSICAL INSTRUMENTS.

FLY [עָרֹב 'arov, זְבוּב zevuv; μυῖα muia]. Flies are insects in the order Diptera. Since there are over 120,000 different species within this order, thousands coexisting in any given area, it is impossible to determine the specific type of fly in the Bible. In Ecclesiastes, a dead fly ruins the perfume (10:1). Flies constitute the fourth Egyptian plague (Exod 8:24). Flies kill people by biting (Wis 16:9). The Egyptian army is likened to a swarm of flies (Isa 7:18). A Philistine deity is called "Lord of the Flies" (2 Kgs 1:2), a phrase that appears in the NT as BEELZEBUL, and, more popularly, Beelzebub (*see* BAAL-ZEBUB). This "Lord of the Flies" is no longer god of the Philistines, but is identified with SATAN. Taken together, these verses imply a type of fly more destructive than the common housefly, which generally is aggravating but not dangerous. *See* INSECTS OF THE BIBLE.

JENNIFER L. KOOSED

FODDER [בְּלִיל belil, מִסְפּוֹא mispo᾽]. Food, often a mixture of grains such as barley, wheat, and vetches seasoned with salt, provided for oxen, cattle, and donkeys (Gen 24:25, 32; Judg 19:19; Job 6:5; Sir 38:26), or food sought by cattle themselves in a field, especially for their offspring (Job 24:5). Symbolically, this plentiful silage making them productive work animals or a good meat source points to God's rewards to the people for their obedience (Isa 30:23-24).

EMILY R. CHENEY

FOLD. *See* SHEEP, SHEEPFOLD.

FOLKLORE IN BIBLICAL INTERPRETATION. To paraphrase a question posed by the great biblical scholar Hermann Gunkel, "What has the Bible to do with folklore?" For contemporary westerners the term *folklore* evokes certain types of activity and artistic creations—perhaps the music of the Appalachians or the patterned quilts of American Shaker communities, the Child ballads of the 19th cent., or the tales collected by the brothers Grimm. When thinking specifically of folk literature, certain genres come to mind such as proverbs, riddles, folktales, legends, myths, and epics. Folklorists argue about the definition of folklore itself and about whether terms such as *riddle* or *folktale* are relevant to the lore of one or another cultural, linguistic, or ethnic tradition. Nevertheless, a preliminary overview of materials in the Bible reveals a corpus rich in stories of various kinds and variations upon them, heroes and heroines who look very familiar to readers of other traditional literatures, ritual descriptions that partake of recurring symbolic structures, telegraphic sayings, and verbal puzzles. The nature of this corpus seems to suggest that the Bible might have a good deal to do with folklore.

A. Definitions, Past and Present
B. Context
C. Texture and Text
D. Variation and Multiplicity
E. Performance
Bibliography

A. Definitions, Past and Present
Folklorists of the 19th cent. viewed folklore in romantic, nationalistic, and antiquarian terms and sought to collect or reconstruct the orally produced lore of rural, peasant "folk" cultures and of "primitive," pre-modern societies. In a similar fashion, Gunkel

pictured ancient Israelite shepherds sitting about the fire, sharing simple tales that would become the basis for the more sophisticated, written stories of Genesis. These limited notions are largely passé in the field of folklore and in applications of the field to the study of biblical literature. Folklore may be rural or urban, written or oral, created by literate or illiterate people, and the folk group, which shares a cultural frame of reference and identifies with the folk product, may be large or small. Folklore may be verbal like the proverbs and tales of the Bible, silent and dramatic like the ritual actions described in Numbers or Leviticus, or an item of material culture, like the many artifacts, unearthed by ANE archaeologists, that were a part of Israelite religion as lived.

B. Context
Folklore is always set in culture, in a social context, but also derives meaning and substance from humanly shared deep-seated themes, from specific performance settings, and from the contribution of the individual folk artist who renders a particular piece in a particular way. Bible readers encountering the flood story of Gen 6–9 thus might consider psychoanalytical dimensions that associate water with chaos and creation; also relevant are the specific ANE cultural contexts that make flood accounts meaningful in Israel and Mesopotamia; finally one needs to explore the literary setting of the flood account in Genesis and the special messages and meaning with which an individual author, set in time and place, has endowed the story.

C. Texture and Text
Texturally, all folk literature partakes in traditional-style composition, evocative of but not necessarily produced by oral composition. In traditional folk forms, repetition is valorized. Whereas a modern novelist or poet varies his or her language, that process of finding new ways to say things being a part of his or her craft, the folk artist works creatively within certain conventions understood, expected, and shared by his audience. Formulaic means of expression and variations upon these formula patterns, both in the very language chosen and in the arrangement of pieces of content, serve to emphasize key themes and messages. The Bible is rich in recurring topoi. Its many "literary forms" and "type scenes" are indicative of traditional style literatures. Economy of expression and culturally shared expectations concerning content unify and reflect the larger tradition in a process that John Foley, the scholar of oral literature, has called "immanent referentiality." Foley suggests that the repetition of language from work to work and the resulting evocation of pieces of content that they signify bring to bear on one piece the larger tradition of which it is a part. Thus in the OT mere mention of the "Bull of Jacob" invokes the divine warrior with all its associations of virility, warrior prow-

ess, and the rescue of Israel—all the stories told about him. This "metonymic" style of narration whereby the part speaks to the whole is critical to the biblical corpus and to an understanding of Israelites' conception of their tradition.

D. Variation and Multiplicity

There are no "original" versions of a traditional story; rather there are variants and multiplicity. We might assume therefore that Gen 6–9, the story of the flood, is but one version of a fund of such stories extant in ancient Israel; indeed the Genesis account itself appears to combine two versions (see FLOOD). Genesis 12, 20, and 26 preserve actual variants of the tale about the patriarch who tells the foreign ruler that his wife is his sister. Genesis 41 and Dan 7 share with the ANE tale of Ahiqar the same essential conventionalized pattern of content involving the rise in status of the wise hero who is able to answer the ruler's seemingly impossible question. The Synoptic Gospels might be approached as traditional-style variants of the story of Jesus, while the parables and sayings found in multiple versions in the tradition provide further evidence of traditional-style variation in the biblical corpus. Awareness of the importance of multiplicity and variation in traditional literature warns the biblical scholar against searching for the "original" version or assuming that the presence of multiple variants of a tale or formula in the Bible means one biblical writer "borrowed" material from another. This approach also alerts the reader of the Bible to be sensitive to specific variations on the shared pattern, for herein lies information about the setting and date of any particular version, and about audiences and authors to whom the tale was meaningful.

E. Performance

Understanding biblical texts as folklore is intimately related to appreciating performance settings. Prophets are portrayed delivering prophetic oracles to groups or performing symbolic actions. Forms like the mashal, whether a parable or a saying, are delivered and performed, and instructions given for symbolic action imply planned ritual performances. Increasingly, students of early and oral literatures also emphasize the performance qualities of traditional literature with its texture of formulaic expression, repetition, and metonymy. The writers are to be regarded as creative composers and performers who work in a traditional setting. Written texts capture the cadences of oral literature and may have been meant to be read aloud, and audiences have certain expectations for the way heroes should act or wives are wooed. In this way, the receivers of the literature are participants in the creation and performance of the literature.

To view biblical material as folklore is to be concerned not only with the form and setting of the many types of biblical literature but also to treat biblical texts

as one means by which Israelite or early Christian identities, in their interesting complexity and variation, were reflected and constructed. Expressed in traditional media, many texts offer a window into the ways in which a variety of contributors and receivers participated in that process of self-definition.

Bibliography: Dan Ben Amos. "Toward a Definition of Folklore in Context." *Toward New Perspectives in Folklore.* A. Paredes and R. Bauman, eds. (1972) 3–15; Alan Dundes. *Interpreting Folklore* (1980); John Miles Foley. *Immanent Art: From Structure to Meaning in Traditional Oral Epic* (1991); Hermann Gunkel. *The Folktale in the Old Testament* (1987); Patricia G. Kirkpatrick. *The Old Testament and Folklore Study* (1988).

SUSAN NIDITCH

FOLLY [אִוֶּלֶת ʾiwweleth, כֶּסֶל kesel, נְבָלָה nevaʿlah, סֶכֶל sekhel, סִכְלוּת sikhluth; ἄνοια anoia; ἀφροσύνη aphrosynē]. The translation of several terms used in the Bible and particularly in the wisdom literature of the OT (Proverbs, Job, Ecclesiastes) for lack of good sense. Folly may describe people with distorted judgment and/or specific imprudent behaviors. The causes of folly are manifest variously among fools, such as youthful naiveté (pethi פֶּתִי), brutishness (baʿar בַּעַר), flightiness (khasar lev חֲסַר לֵב), arrogant mental laziness (כְּסִיל kesil), impertinence (לֵץ lets), and willful disregard of discipline (אֱוִיל ʾewil). Shared in common is the rejection of wisdom and, as a result, dire individual and communal consequences.

Folly connotes being misguided, taking the wrong path in life (Prov 14:8). Fools are undisciplined (Prov 5:23) and stubborn (Prov 27:22). Spurning instruction, they live by their wits alone (Prov 12:15a; 28:26a), complacently and carelessly (Prov 14:16b). Their emotions are unrestrained (Prov 12:16a; 14:17a, 29b; 29:11a) and skewed: they loathe right objects (e.g., wisdom, Prov 1:7b; 15:5a) and esteem wrong ones (e.g., wickedness, Prov 2:14). Folly itself is their joy (Prov 15:21a). Their speech is similarly distorted. They talk too much (Prov 15:2b, 28b; Eccl 10:12b-14a) and without listening (Prov 18:13), and their words are malicious, false, and intended to provoke (Prov 10:11b, 18; 11:12a; 18:6; 22:10). Finally, their actions are at best senseless (Prov 7:6-23; 12:11b) and at worst immoral and unjust. Fools excel at wickedness (Jer 4:22; Prov 13:19b; Eccl 7:25). Doing wrong is their sport (Prov 10:23a; Isa 32:6) and, in their arrogance, they do not think themselves accountable (Prov 14:9a). Rather they persist in their folly, like a "dog that returns to its vomit" (26:11). Such callousness is exemplified by Nabal ("fool") who "returned evil for good" by refusing hospitality to David (1 Sam 25:21).

Folly is expressed theologically when one rejects "the fear of the LORD," namely, reverence for God and acknowledgment of one's place within God's creation. Fools may deny God's existence outright, saying in their hearts "there is no God" (Ps 14:1*a*; Jer 4:22). They may scoff at God and those who believe in God (Pss 74:18, 22; 119:51*a*). Or they may preach about God falsely, as when Job's friends did not speak about God "what is right" (Job 42:8; Isa 32:6). Several texts explicitly associate folly with guilt, sin, and godlessness (Ps 69:5 [Heb. 69:6]; Prov 24:9; Isa 32:6; 2 Tim 3:1-9). Not surprisingly, God finds foolish behavior repugnant (Prov 12:22*a*; 15:26*a*; 16:5). In the NT, Mark includes folly in his list of vices, those "evil things" that defile a person (7:20-23).

The consequences of folly are disastrous. For the fool, the consequences result in shame and ruin that may be experienced as poverty, loss of social status, anguish, physical illness, and/or premature death (Prov 1:26-32; 5:7-14; 8:36; 18:7, 13; 19:3*a*; Ps 38:5-8 [Heb. 38:6-9]). For the community, folly threatens stability and prosperity. Ecclesiastes likens it to dead flies in a bowl of perfumer's oil: even "a little folly outweighs wisdom and honor" (Eccl 10:1). Elsewhere, the sages caution that a fool is more dangerous than a mother bear deprived of her cubs (Prov 17:12; see 26:10). Hence parents are distressed by foolish children (Prov 10:1*b*; 17:21, 25), the public despises any lack of good judgment (Prov 12:8*b*; 14:17*b*), and everyone is urged to discipline folly immediately (Prov 19:29)—not only for the fool's sake (if he or she is receptive to wisdom) but as a warning to others (Prov 19:25*a*; 21:11*a*).

The opposition of folly and wisdom is perhaps most vivid in Prov 9, where both are personified as women who issue (nearly) identical invitations to "those without sense" (9:1-6, 11, 13-18). Folly, whose description resonates with that of the "stranger woman" elsewhere in Prov 1–9 (2:16-19; 5:1-14; 6:20-26; 7:6-27), is loud, thoughtless, and comparatively lazy, sitting at the door of her house at the high places so that she might easily get the attention of passersby (9:13-15). Although her invitation begins exactly like that of personified wisdom (9:16; see 9:4), she soon whispers about "stolen water" and "bread eaten secretly" (9:17; see 5:15-19). Lest the naive seize on her promises of an illicit, erotic banquet, the text abruptly concludes with a stern warning: Folly's house is not a haven but the underworld. To choose folly is to choose death (Prov 8:36; 21:16). *See* FOOL, FOOLISHNESS; LISTS, ETHICAL; PROVERBS, BOOK OF; WISDOM IN THE OT.

Bibliography: Michael V. Fox. "Words for Folly." *ZAH* 10 (1997) 4–17.

CHRISTINE ROY YODER

FOOD. Since the beginning of time, food has been considered one of the essential elements necessary to sustain life. Something of this view is reflected in the very first chapter of the OT when God is said to give both humans and animals food to eat (Gen 1:29). Food has found its way into virtually every part of the biblical traditions, holding a range of connotations and associations.

    A. The Biblical Menu
      1. The bounty of the land
      2. Meat and dairy products
    B. The Significance of Food in Biblical Literature
      1. Symbolism of food
      2. Hospitality and table fellowship
      3. Food prohibitions
      4. Food and gender
    C. Theology of Food
      1. The God who provides
      2. Food as a curse
      3. Eschatology
      4. Food and the cult
  Bibliography

A. The Biblical Menu

Food's most important connotation is surely its ability to sustain life. Starting with the daily milk that sustains a newborn baby, people need their daily bread (see the Lord's Prayer in Luke 11:3). This connotation is reflected in the Hebrew term lekhem (לֶחֶם), "bread" that is often used to refer to food in general. Daily meals and the need to produce enough food for all to eat thus frequently feature in the biblical text. In reflecting on the daily diet as portrayed in the biblical traditions, we encounter multiple references to the foods people ate.

1. The bounty of the land

A central part of ensuring adequate food was the ability to cultivate the land. So we read in Deut 8:8-9 how Israel viewed the land as a gift of God, "a land of wheat and barley, of vines and fig trees and pomegranates, a land of olive trees and honey, a land where you may eat bread without scarcity, where you will lack nothing." This list includes some of Israel's most important foods, which together form part of the bounty of the land.

For most people in the Mediterranean world, food constituted BREAD or cereal in some other form. According to one reference in the Mishnah, bread made up more than 50 percent of the daily menu (*Ketub.* 5:8). Bread could be either leavened or unleavened, and was made from wheat or barley. As meat was considered a luxury food and only consumed on special occasions, bread, together with other cereals like parched grains, formed the basic fare consumed by people at every meal accompanied by smaller amounts of vegetables and fruits, legumes, oil and other condiments.

Fruit made up a large percentage of the daily fare in the biblical traditions and was highly valued for its versatility. The value of fruit trees in the biblical traditions is particularly evident from the command against cutting down fruit trees in Deut 20:19. So olive orchards and vineyards are often cited in the biblical traditions (1 Sam 8:14; 2 Kgs 5:26; Neh 9:25). Both olives and grapes had a multipurpose value—olives being used for food and pressed for oil (1 Kgs 17:12-16), and grapes being eaten in the form of fresh fruit (Num 6:3), dried as raisins (1 Sam 30:12), and pressed into wine (Deut 32:14; Ps 104:15). Moreover, as the first fruits to ripen, figs were considered a delicacy (Isa 28:4). Dried figs pressed into cakes constituted part of the standard provision for travelers (1 Sam 25:18). Finally, although it is likely that dates formed a large part of Israel's diet, the OT alludes to this fruit only once (Joel 1:12; "palm"). Dates formed a high-energy food source in the ANE and could be eaten fresh, dried in the form of small cakes, or used for making wine and honey.

Because the land Israel is typically quite dry, vegetables were less commonly cultivated. In Num 11:5-6, Israel longs for the variety of fruits and vegetables they had to eat in Egypt: the cucumbers (more precisely muskmelons), melons (likely the watermelon that grew in Egypt), leeks, onions, and garlic. Nevertheless, it was for a vegetable garden that Ahab killed Naboth in 1 Kgs 21:1-5, and Elisha performs a miracle on a pot of poisonous gourds in 2 Kgs 4:38-41.

With regard to condiments, salt was by far the most important seasoning in biblical times (Job 6:6; Mark 9:50). Sweetness was provided by honey—either from bees found in the field or honey made from dates and other fruits (Judg 14:8-9; 1 Sam 14:25-27; Prov 24:13). Imported spices such as cinnamon (Exod 30:23-25; Prov 7:17-19), cumin (Isa 28:27), dill (Matt 23:23), and saffron (Song 4:13-14) were considered luxury items, highly valued for improving the taste of foods. Finally, bitter herbs formed a regular addition to the Passover meal, together with the roasted lamb and unleavened bread.

2. Meat and dairy products

A second important source of food came from livestock such as sheep, goats, and cattle. Goat's and sheep's milk formed an important part of the biblical diet (Prov 27:27; Deut 32:14). However, as milk cannot be preserved for a long period of time without refrigeration, milk was often turned into other dairy products such as curds (Gen 18:8; Judg 5:25) and cheese (2 Sam 17:29).

According to Deut 14:4-6, the animals that Israelites were allowed to eat were the ox, the sheep, the goat, and venison (like the gazelle and the antelope). Goat's meat was prized in Israel's early pastoral history (Gen 27:6-10; Judg 6:19-20; 13:15). By NT times, goat meat perhaps was of lesser value, as reflected in the parable of the prodigal son (Luke 15:29-30), where the elder son complains that in contrast to his brother for whom was prepared the fatted calf, he did not even receive a

kid. Roasted lamb served a central part of the Passover meal (Exod 12:3-4).

Because most people could not afford to eat meat on a regular basis, the consumption of meat was either associated with festive occasions or accompanied a sacrifice of some sort. This stands in sharp contrast to the eating habits of the wealthy; it is reported, e.g., that the daily meat consumption in King Solomon's court constituted ten fat oxen and twenty pasture-fed cattle (1 Kgs 4:23). Moreover, as there was no refrigeration, meat had to be consumed on the same day it was prepared, which resulted in meat being served at festive occasions where the whole community could share (see, e.g., Solomon's inaugural festival in 1 Kgs 8:63-65 as well as the wedding meal in Matt 22:4).

Fish plays a much more central role in the NT than in the OT (compare Num 11:5 where Israel yearns for the fish they had to eat in Egypt, in contrast to the many NT stories where fish feature prominently, e.g., Matt 14:16-19; 15:34-37; John 21:9-10, 12).

B. The Significance of Food in Biblical Literature
1. Symbolism of food

Food in the biblical literature did not merely function to satisfy hunger. Images of food entered Israel's discourse and held rich symbolic value. Throughout the OT, milk and honey became symbols of the fruitfulness of the land, when the promised land is described as a land flowing with milk and honey (Exod 3:17; Num 13:27; Deut 6:3; Josh 5:6). The OT ideal of peace and prosperity was expressed by the desire that every person would sit under his/her own vine and fig tree (1 Kgs 4:25).

Symbolic references to food abound in the NT. Many of Jesus' parables and his teaching use food as means of illustration. Examples include the woman kneading bread as illustration of the kingdom of heaven (Matt 13:33; compare Luke 13:21), and believers being described as the salt of the earth (Matt 5:13; compare Mark 9:50; Luke 14:34).

In several post-biblical texts food is used as a symbol of teaching or learning—a connection already found in Deut 8:3 where bread is equated to the word of God (compare also the use of milk in 1 Cor 3:2 and 1 Pet 2:2 as an image for elementary teachings that serve the function to nourish new Christians). These associations build on the fact that the act of learning is not passive, but like food, the learners have to make the knowledge part of themselves in order to receive the gift of life. The connection between food and learning is at the heart of the food language in the Gospel of John, where Jesus identifies himself as the Bread of Life (6:35, 51) and as the living water (4:14-15). The act of ingesting food and drink becomes an important metaphor for believing when Jesus is portrayed not just as the provider of food and drink, but as the food and drink itself that needs to be ingested by the believer. Building on the image of the Passover lamb, Christians are to eat of the flesh of Christ and drink of his blood, thereby receiving the gift of life (John 6:51, 53). *See* PASSOVER AND FEAST OF UNLEAVENED BREAD.

2. Hospitality and table fellowship

A central aspect of food's significance in the biblical traditions is the notion of sharing a meal, often described in the terms of breaking bread together (Exod 2:20; Luke 24:35; Acts 2:42; 27:35). This relates to the act of social bonding that forms a key aspect of meals in the biblical tradition, particularly in terms of food's capacity of defining various social groups (*see* MEAL CUSTOMS; MEALS). Where people met for meals for social or religious purposes, certain customs and rules applied that inform our understanding of the function of meals and food in the biblical traditions.

The early Christian communal meals became the setting for the regular celebration of the LORD'S SUPPER during which time bread and wine became the vehicle of the proclamation of Christ's death. We read though how the early Christian communities faced obstacles when socioeconomic factors impacted the way the communal meals were conducted, causing schisms between believers. In 1 Cor 10, Paul emphasizes the importance of overcoming these divisions, using the symbol of a singular bread to describe the unity that should exist among Christians who are part of the one body of Christ.

Related to the notion of table fellowship is the act of sharing one's food with the STRANGER or foreigner. This expectation of hospitality is illustrated well in Gen 18 when Abraham and Sarah provide an elaborate feast that includes cakes, a roasted calf, curds and milk to the three strangers. And in 1 Kgs 17:13, the widow prepares for her visitor, Elijah, a flat bread or pita with her last bit of flour and oil.

This emphasis on hospitality continues into the NT when Jesus' act of multiplying the bread and fish to feed a whole crowd serves as an important reminder that hospitality ought to form a central characteristic of this new community.

3. Food prohibitions

In both the OT and NT, food plays a central role in identity formation, particularly the laws of CLEAN AND UNCLEAN food that serve as a boundary marker between "us" and "them." Leviticus 11 and Deut 14 present two almost identical lists of animals that were either considered to be clean food and therefore permitted to be eaten by those who associate themselves with the Israelites, or alternatively forbidden because of their unclean nature.

Furthermore, in Lev 7:26-27 Israel is explicitly prohibited from eating blood, saying that all blood needs to be drained from the meat. Similarly, in Exod 23:19; 34:26; Deut 14:21 one finds the prohibition of boiling a kid in its mother's milk. These food prohibitions continue today as part of kosher rituals (e.g., the custom of separating dairy and meat products).

In the NT different interpretations of these dietary laws led to all sorts of practical problems that had to be addressed by Paul in his letters to the early churches. A central question relates to the way the Jews and the new converts should interact, i.e., whether the new Gentile converts should hold to traditional Jewish food customs. Peter's vision in Acts 10:10-13 reflects something of the early church's decision to relax the food laws that eased social interaction between Jews and Gentiles.

Rethinking food laws in the newly conceived Christian community is also at the heart of Paul's advice to the Corinthians in 1 Cor 8:10-11. Here the issue is whether meat that has been sacrificed to idols should be consumed by the believers or not. Once more we see how the new social unit has to create a new identity where diverse groups come together. The ethos of this new community is to mirror their founder's eating habits. In the Gospels, Jesus is portrayed as frequently eating with people who are considered by society as sinners and outcasts, thereby breaking social boundaries. Thus, food creates a new religious identity according to which believers from all walks of life gather to eat together, celebrating the Lord's Supper.

4. Food and gender

Several studies have highlighted intricate connections between symbols of food and feeding and women's experience. Women play an active role in producing, distributing and preparing food resources. Moreover, women's bodies produce food to sustain the new life they bring forth. Especially in antiquity, a child did not live unless a woman nursed it at her breast.

It is these associations that underlie some intriguing rabbinic interpretations that use the metaphor of a mother nursing her baby to describe God's care for Israel in the wilderness (*Sifre Num.* 89; *b. Yoma* 75a; *Exod. Rab.* 1:12; *b. Sotah* 11b). Israel's daily dependence on the manna in the wilderness is imaginatively expressed by the image of a baby drinking every day from her mother's breast, completely satisfying the child's nutritional needs. These interpretations build on a number of biblical texts that make a connection between nursing imagery and God's provision of food (Num 11:11-12; Deut 32:13-16; Isa 66:11-13). Biblical women associated with food include Eve, whose decision to eat the fruit leads to expulsion from the garden (Gen 2–3); Abigail, who, in 1 Sam 25, provides a feast for David and his people in order to keep her household alive; and Woman Wisdom who in Prov 9 hosts a banquet inviting people to share in the gift of life by enjoying her abundant gifts of food and wine.

C. Theology of Food

1. The God who provides

From the various parts of the OT, we see how Israel deeply believed that God is the gracious provider of food. This belief is shaped by the paradigmatic story of God providing manna for Israel in the wilderness during its journey to the promised land (Exod 16; Num 11; Deut 32:10-13).

Moreover, Israel held that God continued to provide nutrition once Israel reached the promised land. Deuteronomy 8:7-10 states that it is God who brought Israel into the good land, a land of plenty where the Israelites were able to eat more than enough. Israel believed that God dispenses the rain that makes the earth fruitful, thus supplying food to humans and animals alike (Ps 104:10-13; Lev 26:4).

The image of the God who provides is firmly rooted in the conviction that God wills life for all of God's children. God, the Giver of life, knows that food is essential to sustain the lives of all of God's creatures. Accordingly, Israel perceived God's provision of food to fully satisfy their needs. In light of this, it is no wonder that some interpreters regarded an image of nursing as a wonderful illustration of God's love for God's people.

Moreover, God's profound commitment to life is also seen in the emphasis on joy that forms part of God's provision of food (Ps 104:15; Eccl 9:7; Joel 2:21-23). God wants God's children to enjoy life, to fully live and delight in the gifts of creation. This is evident from the fact that God's provision of food does not merely consist of basic nurturance to sustain the body, but rich delicacies whose distinct purpose it is to create happiness.

It is further important to note that Israel did not merely believe that God only provided food for the children of Israel, but that God's provision of food extends to all of creation, including the animals (e.g., in Psalm 104 the cattle are fed right next to the humans [vv. 14-15] and the young lions seek their food from God [vv. 21-22]).

Moreover, God's provision of food is strongly connected to the belief that God executes justice for the oppressed. God's provision of food extends to *all* people, especially those who are hungry (Ps 146:7-8). This relates to the biblical claim that God is in a special way the God of the poor and the oppressed. As Deut 10:18 says: "God executes justice for the orphan and the widow, and loves the strangers, providing them food and clothing."

Finally, God's provision of food extends into the NT where Jesus' ministry becomes a concrete expression of the belief represented in Luke 1:53 that God fills the hungry with good things. We see this vividly illustrated in the Gospel texts that present Jesus as feeding the hungry (Matt 14:15-21; Mark 6:35-44; Luke 9:10-17; John 6:5-15), Jesus as eating with sinners (Luke 5:29-32; 15:1-2; 19:5-7), and Jesus serving as host at the Last Supper (Matt 26:26-29; Mark 14:22-25; Luke 22:17-20; see also 1 Cor 11:23-25 and the Supper at Emmaus in Luke 24).

2. Food as a curse

The image of the God who provides is not without complexity. Particularly in the prophetic literature, one finds the reversal of this provider image in a number of biblical texts that present descriptions of the suffering people experience when there is famine in the land (Joel 1; Lam 2; 4). In terms of the theological framework of the time, believers perceived God to be withholding food. Moreover, in Num 11, God uses food that ordinarily is considered to be a blessing as punishment. So God provides Israel plenty of meat to eat in the form of quail (vv. 19-20, 31), which at first seems to be a gracious response to the needs of God's children. But then while the Israelites are eating, disaster strikes and they become gravely ill (v. 33). The notion of food as punishment is further evident in the troubling image in Jer 8:14 and 9:15 where God is depicted as providing "poisoned water" to the people and giving them "wormwood" to eat.

However, these theological formulations reflect something of Israel's struggle to reconcile an imperfect world of famine and war with the image of God who provides food. Although people of faith may give varying theological answers, we can still learn from these believers' honest expression of pain and lament before God who has been their refuge in the past.

3. Eschatology

The significance of food in the biblical traditions is further evident from the fact that believers portrayed the dawning of a new age in terms of a rich, ongoing banquet where everybody has enough to eat—often while they were still caught in the ravages of food shortage. So in Isa 25:6-8, God is portrayed as hosting a festival to celebrate this victory over the forces of chaos—a banquet where God is the host who presents "a feast of rich food, a feast of well-aged wines" (v. 6).

The notion of God hosting a glorious banquet took on a life of its own in many Jewish and Christian texts (2 Bar 29:5-8; b. Ketub. 111b; Sifre Deut. 316) and is often linked to a messianic expectation. The NT writings build on traditions of the eschatological banquet when people from all the corners of the earth will come to eat at the banquet that is used to envision the kingdom of God (Luke 13:29; Matt 8:11). The parable of the great banquet in Luke 14:15-24 realizes something of the all-inclusive nature of the banquet in Isa 25, when the outsiders of society—the poor, the disabled, and the blind—are invited to the banquet. Moreover, the fact that the invitations to the banquet go out beyond the city reflect something of the community's emerging understanding that the Gentiles ought to be included in the "all" who look to God for food.

4. Food and the cult

Building on food's central importance in daily life and the comprehensive theology that developed around food, the biblical traditions attest to the significant role food played in the cult of Israel and in the emerging NT church's religious practices.

So one finds in the Pentateuch extensive instructions of various fruit, grain, and meat sacrifices that Israel had to bring to the Temple (e.g., the sacrifice of well-being or the peace offering in Lev 3:1-9; the thanksgiving sacrifice in Lev 3:12-15 and the sin offering for atonement in Exod 29:36. In addition to its theological significance, the sacrifices had the further function of providing in the upkeep of the Levites as the priests were entitled to a part of the food offering (Deut 18:1-3; Lev 24:9). *See* SACRIFICES AND OFFERINGS.

These sacrifices, in conjunction with the yearly festivals like the PASSOVER AND FEAST OF UNLEAVENED BREAD (Exod 34:18) and the Feast of Weeks (Exod 34:22), formed part of the covenant obligations according to which Israel promised to respond to the God who has liberated them from Egypt, who has led them through the wilderness, who has provided in all their needs, and who has brought them into the promised land (*see* FEASTS AND FASTS). So, after the harvest, Israel brought their first fruits to serve as a thanksgiving offering (Lev 23:10-20; Exod 23:19) to God for abundantly providing the rain for the harvest. And particularly in the Passover festival, the food of roasted lamb, unleavened bread, and bitter herbs serves as a mnemonic device, reminding Israel of their story as God's chosen people (Exod 12; Num 9).

The central role of food in Israel's liturgical practices was continued in the early church in the Lord's Supper, built in the context of the Passover meal, with bread and wine serving as reminders of Christ's death and resurrection. The symbol of the paschal lamb is given new meaning in connection with Christ's death in 1 Cor 5:7; 1 Pet 1:18-19. *See* AGRICULTURE; DRINK; MANNA; MEAT; MILK; WEEKS, FEAST OF.

Bibliography: Athalya Brenner and Jan Willem van Henten, eds. *Food and Drink in the Biblical Worlds* (1999); L. Juliana M. Claassens. *The God Who Provides: Biblical Images of Divine Nourishment* (2004); Daniel S. Cutler. *The Bible Cookbook* (1985); Mary Douglas. *Purity and Danger: An Analysis of Concepts of Pollution and Taboo.* 2nd ed. (1984); Philip J. King and Lawrence E. Stager. *Life in Biblical Israel* (2001); Carol Meyers. *Discovering Eve: Ancient Israelite Women in Context* (1988); Dennis E. Smith. *From Symposium to Eucharist: The Banquet in the Early Christian World.* (2003); Jane Webster. *Ingesting Jesus: Eating and Drinking in the Gospel of John* (2003); John Wilkins, et al., eds. *Food in Antiquity* (1995).

JULIANA CLAASSENS

FOOD, CLEAN AND UNCLEAN. *See* CLEAN AND UNCLEAN.

FOOL, FOOLISHNESS [אֱוִיל 'ewil, אִוֶּלֶת 'iwweleth, כְּסִיל khesil, נָבָל naval, נְבָלָה nevalah, סִכְלוּת sikhluth; ἀφρός aphros, ἀφροσύνη aphrosynē, μωρία mōria, μωρός mōros]. *Foolishness* has a range of meanings that include "FOLLY," "vile thing," "outrage," and "stupidity." The noun is applied to the threatened rape of the Levite and the actual rape of his concubine (Judg 19:23, 24; 20:6, 10), Dinah (Gen 34:7), and Tamar (2 Sam 13:12). In addition, it is frequently contrasted with wisdom, especially in the wisdom literature. As foolishness is contrasted with wisdom, the fool is contrasted with the sage. Succinctly, a fool is everything a sage is not—imprudent, stupid, lazy, perverse in speech, even wicked (see, e.g., Prov 1:7; 14:16; 19:1; Eccl 7:25). And as wisdom is understood as divinely bestowed, the quintessential fool is the one who does not believe in God (Pss 14:1; 53:1). NABAL, *fool* (naval), is even the name of one poor character who dares to defy David (1 Sam 25). Laban's name is *fool* spelled backward (lavan [לָבָן], Gen 24, 28–31).

In the NT, the word is also used in contrast to wisdom. For example, in Matthew, Jesus tells a parable of ten virgins—five who are wise and five who are foolish (Matt 25:1-13). In his epistles, Paul uses the word in a variety of ways including as a rhetorical device. In 2 Cor 11, Paul mounts a defense of his own authority by asking the community to "bear with [him] in a little foolishness." Then, he proceeds to speak "as a fool" by boasting of his credentials, the suffering he has borne, and the dangers he has braved. Both the writers of the Gospels and Paul use the epithet "fool" and "foolish" to rebuke those who stray from the right path (Matt 23:17; Gal 3:1). *See* WISDOM IN THE NT; WISDOM IN THE OT.

JENNIFER L. KOOSED

FOOT [רֶגֶל reghel; ποδός podos]. In ancient societies where walking was the most common means of transportation, feet were one of the dirtiest parts of the body. Thus hospitality demanded that visitors be provided with water to wash their feet (Gen 18:4; 19:2; 24:32). In wealthy homes, servants would wash their masters' and guests' feet. Jesus' washing of the disciples' feet (John 13:1-11) was intended to show that the gospel is about service, not about being served. Despite the dirtiness of feet, Moses was required to take off his sandals when he stood on holy ground (Exod 3:5). A number of idioms involve feet. For example, "to be under someone's feet" was to be under the power of that person (Ps 8:6; Eph 1:22), while "to sit at the feet" implied learning from someone (Luke 10:39; Acts 22:3). The Hebrew word for "feet" may also be a euphemism for genitalia (Exod 4:25).

KEVIN A. WILSON

FOOT WASHING. Biblical and Greco-Roman hospitality dictated that hosts should provide water for washing guests' feet (Gen 18:4; Luke 7:44). Typically, the washing was done either by a slave (1 Sam 25:41) or by the guests themselves.

Exodus 30:17-20 requires priests to wash their feet before approaching the altar, and acting "with unwashed feet" came to suggest inadequate preparation, especially in a cultic setting (e.g., Philo, *QE* 1, 2).

In John 13:4-20, Jesus washes his disciples' feet, an act without recorded parallel in antiquity, where superiors did not willingly wash the feet of inferiors. Interpretations of Jesus' action differ, including: foot washing provides spiritual purification or forgiveness of post-baptismal sins; it symbolizes baptism and eucharist; it represents welcome into God's household; and it is a call to follow Jesus in humble service or in fulfilling the love commandment by laying down one's life for another.

According to 1 Tim 5:10, widows were expected to wash the saints' feet. Augustine (*Letters* 50.33) says that some Christians practiced foot washing during Lent, and others rejected the ritual to avoid confusing it with baptism. The 7th cent. liturgy of the church in Spain provides the first evidence for foot washing on Maundy Thursday.

JUDITH ANNE JONES

FOOTSTOOL [הֲדֹם רֶגֶל hadhom reghel, כֶּבֶשׁ kevesh; ὑποπόδιον hypopodion]. These terms are rarely used as a literal reference to an object of furniture. In 2 Chr 9:18, kevesh is used to refer to the footstool of Solomon's throne. The term is late and is derived from the word for "lamb," which may have been an alteration of the misunderstood term ro'sh 'aghol (רֹאשׁ עָגֹל, rounded top) used in 1 Kgs 10:19. The LXX reads as though the Hebrew was "heads of calves" (ra'she 'aghol רָאשֵׁי עָגֹל), and identifies the back of the throne of Solomon as having been decorated with a calf's head.

More often, references to a footstool (hadhom regel) are metaphorical and in the context of the proper attitude of worshipers toward the deity or of dominance over enemies. In Ps 99:5 and 99:9, Yahweh's footstool is identified with "his holy mountain," a reference to Zion (compare also Lam 2:1). In Isa 66:1, the term is a metaphor for the earth, contrasted with the heavens as Yahweh's throne. Jesus cites this metaphor (Matt 5:34-35) as he instructs against making oaths. Stephen cites Isa 66 to illustrate his point that God does not need a physical structure in which to dwell (Acts 7:49).

Psalm 110:1 is a metaphor for dominion over enemies, which is cited in the NT several times. In Mark 12:36 (Matt 22:44; Luke 20:43), Jesus quotes this Psalm, focusing on the first phrase of the psalm to illustrate the misidentification of the Christ as literally a descendant of David. Peter quotes Ps 110:1 as proof of Jesus' ascension (Acts 2:35), and it is used again in Heb 1:13 and 10:13.

When the OT references a footstool as a piece of furniture, it uses a term connected with animal imagery. When the actual term that means "footstool" is used, it is a poetic and metaphorical reference to the appropriate attitude toward the deity. These references are cited in the NT to illustrate the identification of the Messiah, or to support the assertion that Jesus of Nazareth has ascended and is at the right hand of God.

C. MARK MCCORMICK

FORBEARANCE [חָדַל khadhal; ἀνεξίκακος anexikakos]. As a translation of khadhal, *forbear* sometimes means "cease" or "desist from" (or refers to the exercising of patience or self-restraint, by human beings or God, in a variety of contexts. Where "forbearance" (in the sense of "patience" or "self-restraint") is demonstrated, the implication is that the situation might legitimately, naturally, or at least understandably provoke a forceful response or display of emotion. Though the declining strength and understanding of an aged parent might tempt one to irritation, one ought rather to show "forbearance" (syngnōmē [συγγνώμη] "fellow-feeling," "allowance," Sir 3:13). Controversies and quarrels are apt to arise even in the community of God's people; but even with the quarrelsome, servants of the Lord are to be "forbearing" (anexikakos, "patient" and "tolerant," 2 Tim 2:24 [compare Wis 2:19, where it is a characteristic expected of the righteous]); their reputation for "forbearance" (makrothymia μακροθυμία, patience in the face of provocation) commends their message to others (2 Cor 6:6). Every believer, in fact, should have a reputation for "forbearance" (to epieikēs [τό ἐπιεικής], gentleness or graciousness, shown in situations where a different reaction might be anticipated, e.g., Phil 4:5). When wronged by fellow believers, followers of Christ are to forbear (anechomai [ἀνέχομαι] "bear with") and forgive those who wrong them (Col 3:13). The general admonition to "forbear" (anechomai) one another in love (Eph 4:2, "bearing with one another in love") implies that in the life of a community irritation is inevitable; but the love that is not easily provoked (compare 1 Cor 13:5), that "covers a multitude of sins" (1 Pet 4:8), will resist the temptation.

God's people are to show "forbearance" inasmuch as their God is forbearing. Claims to this effect are of course accompanied by a sense that it is the prerogative of the Creator to judge his creatures, of Israel's God to judge his covenant people. That he does so with justice is also presupposed (Gen 18:25; Ps 96:13; etc.). Yet God's compassion for all that he has made, his understanding of human frailty, his love for his people, and faithfulness to the promises he made to their ancestors (Pss 103:13-1; 145:9; Deut 7:8, etc.) all find expression in the forbearance with which he delays the execution of judgment or reduces its severity. God's reputation for forbearance (compare Wis 12:18) is naturally appealed to by those who sense that their deeds merit divine punishment (Pr Azar 1:19 where "forbearance" (epieikeia ἐπιείκεια) is parallel with "abundant mercy"; also 2 Macc 10:4). Jeremiah's plea that God, in his "forbearance" ('erekh 'appekha [אֶרֶךְ אַפֶּךָ] or "slowness to anger") will not take him away (Jer 15:15) may be just such an appeal for divine clemency; but the request has also been understood as a plea that God will not, by showing forbearance toward Jeremiah's foes, give them opportunity to destroy him.

According to 2 Pet 3:9, God's forbearance (makrothumeō μακροθυμέω) is mistaken by some as laxity in keeping his promises; in fact, however, God is motivated by a desire that none "should perish, but that all should reach repentance." God's forbearance is to be understood as providing opportunity for salvation (2 Pet 3:15). Along similar lines, God's forbearance (anochē ἀνοχή, here parallel with kindness and patience) in Rom 2:4 is intended to give opportunity for repentance, though it is disregarded by those who store up wrath for themselves on the day of wrath (2:4-5).

In Rom 3:25-26, the time of God's forbearance is contrasted with the "present time." The former period was one in which sins were passed over (paresis πάρεσις, meaning "deliberate disregard," or "letting go unpunished"), whereas in the present God's righteousness is demonstrated: now that he has "put forward" Christ Jesus "as a sacrifice of atonement by his blood," God may rightly "justify" the one (i.e., the sinner) who has faith in Jesus. The point appears to be that, prior to Christ's sacrifice for sin, God, in his forbearance, did not prosecute sins (see also Acts 14:16; 17:30).

According to the apostle Paul, the passing over of sins was only temporary, since God's intention from the beginning was to provide a means for their atonement in the sacrifice of Christ; God is manifestly shown to be righteous when he declares righteous those sinners who believe in Jesus.

STEPHEN WESTERHOLM

FORD [מַעֲבָר ma'avar, מַעְבָּרָה, ma'varah עֲבָרָה 'avarah]. A ford is a crossing place through a river or stream. All of the Hebrew terms are derived from 'avar (עָבַר), "to pass over or through." The JORDAN RIVER was the main flowing water source in Israel and separated it from the Israelite tribes east of the river (TRANSJORDAN) and the nations of Moab, Ammon, and Edom (see Josh 2:7; Judg 3:28; 12:5-6; 15:28; 19:18). The ancient river was approximately 90–100 ft. wide and 5–12 ft. deep, but erosion and flooding changed its contour frequently, requiring the discovery of new fords. Jacob and his family forded (passed over) the Jabbok River (Gen 32:22 [Heb. 32:23]). Moab fled

to the fords of the Arnon (a massive valley in Transjordan) to escape an attacking enemy (Isa 16:2). The fords of Babylon are noted in Jer 51:32, probably referring to crossings over the Euphrates River.

MICHAEL G. VANZANT

FOREHEAD [מֵצַח metsakh; μέτωπον metōpon]. The location of both marks of blessing and curse (Exod 13:9; 2 Chr 26:19; Ezek 9:4). In Revelation, both the blessed (9:4) and the cursed (13:16) receive identifying marks on the forehead. Jeremiah 3:3 suggests that a "woman of fornication" was marked on the forehead as well. Other prophetic passages use a "hard forehead" as a metaphor for stubbornness (Ezek 3:7-8; Isa 48:4).

PHILLIP MICHAEL SHERMAN

FOREIGN, FOREIGNER [בֶּן־נֵכָר ben nekhar, זוּר zur, נָכְרִי nokhri; ἀλλότριος allotrios, ἀλλογενής allogenēs, ξένος xenos]. Land, customs, or people outside the land, customs, or people of context, as other than Israel or the Christian community, e.g., invaders of Israel (e.g., Obad 1:11), foreign gods (e.g., Jer 5:19), and non-Israelites (Exod 21:8). Foreigners had few rights in ancient Israel (Exod 12:43; Deut 15:2-3; 17:15; 23:20 [Heb. 23:21]), in contrast to the SOJOURNER (ger [גֵּר], NRSV "alien"), who lived in Israel and was subject to and protected by the law (e.g., Exod 12:19, 48ff.; Num 9:14; Deut 31:12).

In the NT, *foreigner* occurs less frequently (Acts 17:21; Heb 11:9, 34; Luke 17:18) due to the internationalization of Judaism. According to Eph 2:11-19, Christ has broken down the "dividing wall" between Jew and Gentile, so that "aliens" or "sojourners" and "strangers" can now be assimilated into the covenant by the blood of Christ (v. 13). *See* ESTHER, BOOK OF; EZRA AND NEHEMIAH, BOOKS OF; IDOLATRY; IDOL; LAND; RUTH, BOOK OF; STRANGER.

Bibliography: J. McRay. "Christianity: Judaism Internationalized." *ResQ* 32 (1990) 1–10.

RALPH K. HAWKINS

FOREKNOWLEDGE. *See* KNOWLEDGE; PREDESTINATION.

FORERUNNER [πρόδρομος prodromos]. The word *forerunner* derives from two Greco-Roman contexts: athletic contests and the office of the herald. In the Greek Scriptures, the word is employed metaphorically on four occasions. In a passage that discusses God's punishment of the Canaanite peoples for unacceptable religious practices, the writer of the Wisdom of Solomon suggests that God punishes people in incremental stages in order to allow them time to repent. In the time of the conquest, then, wasps were sent as "forerunners" of the Israelite army (Wis 12:8). In the Letter to the Hebrews, rich in athletic metaphors, Jesus acts as a "forerunner," entering into the inner sanctum of the Temple on behalf of his believers (Heb 6:20). In the LXX, the word is also used to describe the first-ripe fruits, "forerunners" of the grape harvest (Num 13:20) and the fig harvest (Isa 28:4).

JENNIFER L. KOOSED

FORESAIL [ἀρτέμων artemōn]. The lowest sail at the ship's bow used for maneuvering the ship as well as controlling speed. Acts 27:40 refers to the foresail within the account of Paul's shipwreck.

FORESKIN. *See* CIRCUMCISION.

FOREST [יַעַר yaʿar; ὕλη hylē]. Except for the fabled Forests of Lebanon (1 Kgs 7:2; Zech 11:1-2) that contained magnificent stands of choice CEDAR (*Cedrus libani*; ʾerez [אֶרֶז]) and lofty PINE, PINE TREE (*Pinus pinaster*; berosh [בְּרוֹשׁ]; 2 Kgs 19:23; Ezek 31:3), most trees in the "forests" of ancient Syro-Palestine consisted of evergreen, woodland thickets of Kermes OAK (*Quercus coccifera*; Isa 6:13; ʾallon [אַלּוֹן]), and the TEREBINTH (*Pistacia Terebinthus*; ʾelah [אֵלָה]). The largest stands of trees south of LEBANON would have been in the Sharon Plain and Shephelah foothills. The southern areas of Canaan would have been too dry to support large forests. Thus only when its longevity and great height gave a particular oak tree some distinction in its area did it serve as a landmark (Judg 6:11) or as a place to bury the dead (Gen 35:8). The thick undergrowth and interwoven branches were safe havens for the wild animals of the land, including lions (Ps 104:20; Jer 5:6). Such thickets could prove to be difficult ground if an army were unlucky enough to blunder into them (2 Sam 18:6-8).

Small forested areas were lumbered for building materials and charcoal, and this eventually contributed to the deforestation of the hill country as it became more of a population center for the Israelites. Since there were increasing demands for arable land, it is no wonder that Isaiah (32:19-20) speaks of an idyllic future when God's reign over the land means that the "forests disappear" and farmers can "sow beside every stream," presumably without having to share space or water with unwanted trees such as poplars (Job 40:22) and bushes. This attitude could also explain Joshua's admonition to clear the forests of the hill country and "possess it" (Josh 17:18). The pattern of opening up all of the land that was suitable for cultivation and the addition of terraces on hillsides to increase available cultivation of vines and more profitable olive and fig trees (Judg 9:8-11) led to the shrinking of the forest lands of that region (see the reversal image in Hos 2:12, where God threatens to destroy the vines and replace them with a wild forest).

Drawing on a natural occurrence that would have thinned the forest, the biblical writers crafted metaphorical images of forest fires. The psalmist compares the conflagration to God's implacable and relentless wrath as the deity pursues the enemy and casts them about like "chaff before the wind" (83:14). Isaiah likens the blaze that begins among the undergrowth and gradually spreads to the trees to the insidious nature of wickedness that consumed the nation in its flames (9:18-19). Realizing that an empty, infertile land is one without hope, Second Isaiah crafts one of his restoration visions detailing how God will bring life back to the wilderness by opening up rivers and foundations and planting cedar, acacia, myrtle, olive, pine, and cypress trees together in an Eden-like paradise so "all will see . . . that the hand of the Lord has done it" (Isa 41:17-20). *See* AGRICULTURE; PLANTS OF THE BIBLE.

VICTOR H. MATTHEWS

FOREST OF EPHRAIM. *See* EPHRAIM, FOREST OF.

FOREST OF LEBANON. *See* HOUSE OF THE FOREST (OF LEBANON).

FORGE. *See* FURNACE.

FORGERIES. An archaeological forgery is the manufacture and representation of a supposedly ancient artifact as though the artifact is genuine. Forgeries surface in many forms, such as inscriptions, papyrus, bullae, and as ivories. A forged artifact may be sold on the antiquities market or displayed in a museum collection. Unfortunately, hundreds of forged artifacts exist in museums around the world. Several reasons motivate individuals to engage in the forgery of antiquities. Some persons seek financial reward from their forgery. The monetary value of an ancient item exceeds the value of a replica sold as a souvenir. Production, distribution, and consumption drive this fraudulent business.

A forger may use a forged artifact to enhance his or her appearance as an authority. Or, a forger may seek to gain fame and prestige by producing artifacts that appear old and obscure and by providing a setting for tales that capture the public's imagination. Still other forgers may enjoy the thrill of creating historical fiction by means of forgeries. An individual may forge artifacts to prove a particular theory because the scientific data are not sufficient to support the theory. When a person is convinced of the truthfulness of a religious theory and seeks to create the proof for that particular religious view, then he or she commits religious fraud. Detection of a forged artifact presents a special challenge to archaeologists who employ the same scientific techniques used at excavation of sites. Chemical analysis of forged materials often reveals the fraud.

Prior to the emergence of archaeological research in the 18th cent., forgery of archaeological artifacts was virtually unknown. Moses Shapira forged several Moabite artifacts in the late 1800s and sold them on the antiquities market in Jerusalem. He even buried some of his work at various Moabite sites in the Transjordan. Rumors spread in 2000 about the discovery of a Persian princess mummy that dated to ca. 600 BCE. It had been wrapped in a traditional Egyptian manner and placed in a wooden coffin that rested inside a stone sarcophagus. However, modern dating techniques later proved that the coffin was only 250 years old. Linguists also demonstrated that the inscription on the breastplate was forged. Finally, computed tomography (CT or CAT scans) confirmed that the process of mummification had not followed the Egyptian custom, e.g., the brain remained inside the skull.

In 2002, several scholars proclaimed the so-called James Ossuary as the first archaeological evidence that Jesus existed (*see* OSSUARIES). The first announcements indicated that the ossuary belonged to an anonymous antiquities collector. Later reports identified the owner of the ossuary who claimed he had purchased the object from an Arab antiquities dealer in Jerusalem. The inscription on the ossuary reads "ya'akov bar yosef akhui diyeshua" and is translated as "Ya'acov or Jacob [James] son of Yosef [Joseph] brother of Yeshua [Jesus]." The Geological Survey of Israel dated the limestone ossuary to the 1st cent. CE; but what about the inscription? Analysis of the patina in the inscription led the Israeli Antiquities Authority (IAA) to proclaim the inscription a modern forgery. However, several authorities have questioned the methods used by the IAA to examine the inscription on the ossuary.

In 2003, a report spread that workers discovered an inscription (dubbed the Jehoash Inscription or the Bedeq Habbayit Inscription) while working near the Temple Mount in Jerusalem (*see* INSCRIPTIONS). The inscription reports repairs made to the Temple during the reign of Jehoash, son of Ahaziah, king of Judah. Interestingly, the owner of the James Ossuary also had possession of the Jehoash Inscription. Examination of the inscription indicated that the forger had used a mixture of ancient alphabets to create the inscription.

Forgers often con unsuspecting buyers out of millions of dollars. Forgery damages the science of archaeology as a legitimate discipline. Since most forgeries occur in the context of genuine archaeological investigations, authentic artifacts may come into question because of a forged artifact. Forgery casts doubt in the eyes of the public on the conclusions drawn from archaeological excavations. Forgery exploits the deep faith of individuals who seek tangible evidence for that faith and is a form of fraud perpetrated upon the public.

The forger creates history, which is dangerous. Museums and collections often contain a certain number of unidentified forgeries. Forgery also damages efforts for legitimate fund-raising. The scientific community must examine unprovenanced artifacts with great care and apply the latest scientific tools to the analysis of these artifacts. Owners of unprovenanced discoveries need to allow experts to examine the artifacts. Finally, archaeologists should refuse to publish unprovenanced material without collaborating documentation of the artifact's authenticity. *See* ARCHAEOLOGY.

STEPHEN VON WYRICK

FORGETFULNESS, LAND OF. *See* LAND OF FORGETFULNESS.

FORGIVENESS. Forgiveness is the act by which an offended party removes an offense from further consideration, thereby reestablishing a basis for harmonious relations with the offender.

Forgiveness is called for when humans wrong one another (Gen 50:15-21; Matt 18:21-22). Ultimately, however, all sins—including wrongs done to other human beings—are committed against God (Ps 51:4; compare Mark 2:7) inasmuch as they represent a violation of the good order of God's creation and (in the case of those to whom God's law has been entrusted) a transgression of God's stated will. Divine forgiveness is thus a precondition for good relations between God and God's erring creatures.

A. Forgiveness in the Old Testament
  1. The root ns' (נשׂא)
  2. The root slkh (סלח)
  3. The root kpr (כפר)
  4. The root ksh (כסה)
B. Forgiveness in the New Testament
  1. Terminology
  2. The Synoptic Gospels and Acts
  3. The Gospel and Epistles of John
  4. The Pauline corpus
  5. Hebrews and other writings
Bibliography

A. Forgiveness in the Old Testament
  1. The root ns' (נשׂא)
When used of the committing or forgiving of sin, the term ns' ("take," "carry") reflects the understanding of wrongdoing as a burden taken on and necessarily borne by the evildoer unless relieved by the forgiveness of the offended party. In a number of passages (e.g., Lev 19:17; 22:9; Num 18:22, 32), the NRSV translates "incurring" guilt where the Hebrew ns' refers more pictorially to "taking on [the weight]" of the offense. The force of the Hebrew is better captured in renderings that speak of wrongdoers as "bearing" their iniquity (Num 5:31; 14:34), sin (Lev 24:15), guilt (Lev 17:16), or punishment (Ezek 14:10; 44:12; compare also Num 9:13; Ezek 23:49). The same Hebrew verb underlies the NRSV when it describes the offender as being "subject to punishment" (Lev 5:1, 17; 19:8; 20:17, 19, 20), or simply "pay[ing] the penalty" (Prov 19:19).

Implicit in each of these texts is the notion that wrongdoing, as a violation of what ought to be, inevitably leads to disaster. The disastrous consequences are an outworking of what is inherent in the act itself: what disturbs cannot but lead to disturbance.

Forgiveness occurs when those who are offended "bear away" or "remove" (the verb here is also ns'; LXX commonly aphiēmi ἀφίημι; see §B1 below) the burden of the offense. The forgiving party may be human. Joseph was greatly wronged by his brothers, but the plea of Gen 50:17 is that he will "forgive" (lit., "bear away") their crime. Similarly, Abigail pleads with David to forgive the insolence of her husband, Nabal, rather than act vengefully (1 Sam 25:28). In both cases, the alternative to forgiveness is due punishment. Pharaoh, who is already experiencing the consequences of his sin against Yahweh and against Moses, confesses his wrongdoing and asks Moses both to forgive his sin and to beseech Yahweh to remove the plague brought on by his willfulness (Exod 10:12-17). Saul requests that Samuel "pardon" his sin in transgressing Yahweh's commandment and Samuel's words (1 Sam 15:24-25).

Usually, however, it is Yahweh whose forgiveness (i.e., Yahweh's "bearing away," "removing," or "pardoning" of sins) is celebrated (Pss 32:1, 5; 85:2; 99:8; Isa 33:24; compare Mic 7:18) or implored (e.g., Exod 32:32). In the latter case, the afflictions of the petitioner may be mentioned to prompt Yahweh's compassion (Ps 25:18; compare Job 7:21). That acknowledgment of sin on the part of the sinner precedes God's granting of forgiveness is at times explicit in the context (Exod 32:31; Ps 32:5). In Gen 18:24, 26, Abraham pleads with God to "forgive" (here, however, the verb may simply mean "bear" in the sense "put up with") Sodom if fifty righteous people can be found in the city; the motivation given is that the Judge of all the earth would not be so unjust as to destroy the righteous with the wicked.

The decision to forgive lies with the offended party, and several texts indicate that God's forgiveness is not to be presumed; God may be provoked to the point that God is unwilling to forgive (compare Exod 23:21, where it is Yahweh's "angel" who will not "pardon" Israel's rebellion). It lies in Yahweh's "jealous" nature that Yahweh will not forgive an Israel that forsakes Yahweh to worship foreign gods (Josh 24:19-20; compare Isa 2:8-9). The implication of Hos 1:6 is that Israel has continued so long in sin that Yahweh is no longer prepared to forgive them. Indeed, the very text that affirms that God is One who "forgiv[es] iniquity and transgression and sin" (thus expressing God's nature as "merciful and gracious, slow to anger, and abounding in steadfast love and faithfulness") goes on to say, "yet by no means clearing the guilty, but visiting the iniquity of the parents upon the children and the children's children, to the third and the fourth generation" (Exod 34:6-7; compare Num 14:18). The point seems to be that Yahweh's mercy, expressed in Yahweh's willingness to forgive, far outweighs but does not eliminate Yahweh's prerogative and responsibility to punish sin (compare Exod 20:5-6). Punishment rather than forgiveness is

operative where Israel persists in egregious sin; and even where Yahweh's willingness to forgive means that sinners do not bear the full brunt of their sin, they may nonetheless experience a measure of punishment (Num 14:17-23, where the NRSV's translation "forgiving" [v. 18] and "pardoned" [v. 19] reflect Hebrew ns', though "forgive" [vv. 19, 20] reflects Hebrew slkh discussed below; compare also Ps 99:8). In these cases, sin is shown to have consequences, even though the merciful Yahweh does not allow sin to sever Yahweh's relationship with Yahweh's people.

2. The root slkh (סלח).

Many of the above points are evident also in texts where the NRSV uses "forgive" to translate slkh (note the parallel use of the two verbs in Num 14:19, as discussed above). In rendering this term, the LXX employs a variety of Greek verbs and expressions, including aphiēmi (ἀφίημι "cancel," "forgive"), katharizō (καθαρίζω, "cleanse"), ou mimnēskomai (οὐ μιμνήσκομαι "do not remember"), and epilanthanomai (ἐπιλανθάνομαι, "forget"); most frequently we find hileōs einai (ἵλεως εἶναι "be merciful"). When the root slkh occurs, however, God alone is the one who forgives. Human forgiveness is not expressed with this root. The alternative to forgiveness is that Yahweh should "mark (and see that the evildoer suffers the consequences of) iniquities" (Ps 130:3-4; compare Jer 36:3). Yahweh's readiness to forgive is frequently celebrated (Neh 9:17; Pss 86:5; 103:3; 130:3-4; compare Isa 55:7), or implored (e.g., Exod 34:9 and Ps 25:11). In the latter case, the request is often accompanied by a reminder that Yahweh has the reputation, history, or nature of being a merciful God, and hence one willing to forgive (Num 14:19; Dan 9:9). A confession of sin may accompany the petition for forgiveness (Dan 9:5-14, 19).

That sin leads to disaster is implicit in texts that associate forgiveness with deliverance from sickness (Ps 103:3), plague (Amos 7:1-3; compare "forgive their sin and heal their land," 2 Chr 7:14), devastation, and exile (Dan 9:7-19). Accordingly, those who experience the judgment of devastation and exile may acknowledge that God has not forgiven their sin (Lam 3:42). Sirach warns against presuming on God's forgiveness (Sir 5:5-6; 16:11; compare Deut 29:19-20 and 2 Kgs 24:4).

Forgiveness of sin is a presupposition for the return of God's favor to those experiencing divine judgment (Jer 31:34; 33:8). In Solomon's prayer at the dedication of the Temple, various scenarios are depicted in which the sin of an individual Israelite or of the people as a whole has led to disaster, but they turn in their need to Yahweh and pray toward the "house (i.e., the Temple) . . . built for (Yahweh's) name"; Solomon prays that God will then forgive the penitent ones and deliver them from their afflictions (1 Kgs 8:30, 33-50//2 Chr 6:21, 24-39).

Vows and pledges made to Yahweh are to be fulfilled, whether made by a man (Num 30:2) or a woman (30:3-4, 6-7, 9, 10-11, 13-14). An exception, however, is made for cases in which the father of a woman in her youth or the husband of a married woman hears of the woman's vow and expresses immediate disapproval. (The point, at least in part, may be that since the man's resources are at stake in the commitments of his daughter or wife, he is entitled to disallow such vows.) In these cases Yahweh is said to "forgive" (slkh) the woman her vow (30:5, 8, 12). Release from her commitments is obviously intended (note the alternative "her vows shall stand," 30:4, etc.), though forgiveness from failure to carry out what has been promised may also be in view.

A number of texts drawing on priestly tradition speak of forgiveness (slkh) granted after certain cultic rites of atonement (involving a "sin" or "guilt" offering) are performed. The wrongs for which forgiveness is required in these texts are often explicitly unintentional (Lev 4:13, 22, 27; 5:15, 18; Num 15:22, 24, 25, 27, 28; contrast what is said about intentional ["high-handed"] sin in Num 15:30-31). In each case the agent of forgiveness, left unstated ("they/he/you shall be forgiven"; more lit., "it shall be forgiven to them/him/you"), is God (Lev 4:20, 26, 31, 35; 5:10, 13, 16, 18; 6:7; 19:22; Num 15:25, 26, 28).

3. The root kpr (כפר)

In the cultic texts just cited, forgiveness (slkh) is linked to a procedure by which priests make atonement (kpr, "cover," or perhaps "wash off," "cleanse," and hence "expiate"; the LXX generally has a form of hilaskomai (ἱλάσκομαι, "propitiate," "expiate," "atone") for sin. The provision for atonement is itself instituted by Yahweh, so that, like forgiveness, it is to be seen as a divine gift and means by which humans may be delivered from the consequences of their wrongdoing. At times God is the subject of the verb kpr, and no reference is made to sacrifices; in such cases the NRSV sometimes renders this verb, too, as "forgive" (e.g., Pss 65:3; 79:9; Ezek 16:63; compare "absolve" in Deut 21:8; "pardon" in 2 Chr 30:18). That such forgiveness on God's part is an act of compassion and an alternative to the justified destruction of God's people is stressed in Ps 78:38. Conversely, Isa 22:14 insists that the iniquity of a people who have persisted in sin and refused calls to repentance will not be forgiven (kpr); and in Jer 18:23, the prophet prays that God will not forgive (kpr) those who have plotted to kill him in spite of the good he has done them.

4. The root ksh (כסה)

Finally, the NRSV translates the Hebrew root ksh ("cover"; LXX kryptō κρύπτω, "conceal") as "forgives" in Prov 17:9, where the reference is to a human who, by disregarding an affront, allows a friendship to develop.

B. Forgiveness in the New Testament

Several OT texts indicate that God's forgiveness is an essential element in God's people's restoration to favor and their enjoyment of a blessed future (e.g., Jer 31:34; Ezek 16:63; compare 36:25, 29, 33). The early Christians shared the vision that lay at the heart of Jesus' mission, that the day of fulfillment and salvation had come and that God now offered, through Jesus, forgiveness to all. Inevitably, forgiveness plays a prominent role (much greater than a concordance would suggest!) in a number of NT writings.

1. Terminology

The Greek terms most frequently rendered by "forgiveness" and its cognates are the various forms of the verb aphiēmi and the noun aphesis (ἄφεσις). In nonbiblical Greek the verb commonly means "release, let go, send away, relinquish, discharge." It is used in similar ways in a number of NT texts: e.g., for the divorcing of a spouse (1 Cor 7:11) and the canceling of a debt (Matt 18:27). In Luke 4:18, the related noun aphesis is used for release from captivity. But in the LXX the verb was used for forgiveness (i.e., release from the "indebtedness" toward God that results from one's sin; e.g., Exod 32:32; Josh 24:19; Sir 2:11; 28:2); both the verb and the noun are commonly used in this sense in the NT. (Note that the verb takes as its object "debts" in Matt 6:12 [i.e., forgiving sins is spoken of metaphorically as discharging debts], and that it is used both for the canceling of a debt in a parable [Matt 18:27, 32] and for the forgiving of a wrong in its interpretation [18:35].) The noun is occasionally used for "forgiveness" without further qualification (Mark 3:29; Heb 9:22), but is usually followed by that which is forgiven (e.g., Matt 26:28; Mark 1:4; Acts 2:38; Eph 1:7; Col 1:14). The verb is used mostly but not exclusively (compare Matt 6:12; 18:35) for divine forgiveness.

In Luke 6:37, the NRSV renders Gk. apoluō (ἀπολύω, a verb whose range of meaning overlaps substantially with that of aphiēmi: "release," "dismiss," "send away") "forgive/forgiven."

In a few texts in the Pauline corpus (2 Cor 2:7, 10; 12:13; Eph 4:32; Col 2:13; 3:13), "forgive" (and cognates) represents charizomai (χαρίζομαι, "bestow freely," "give graciously"). The connotation is no doubt present that such forgiveness results from the gracious disposition of the one who forgives.

Finally, we may note in this context that the Gk. verb exilaskomai (ἐξιλάσκομαι) is rendered "forgive" in the NRSV in Sirach (5:6; 16:7; 34:23); such a rendering perhaps loses the connotation of the Greek that divine forgiveness is linked to the expiation of sins. The (compound) verb is not found in the NT; where hilaskomai occurs, the NRSV renders differently ("be merciful," Luke 18:13; "make a sacrifice of atonement," Heb 2:17).

2. The Synoptic Gospels and Acts

In the Synoptic Gospels, John the Baptist functions as a forerunner and herald of the coming Messiah and of the judgment that will attend his appearing. Those who heed his message confess their sins and are baptized in preparation for the pending events. According to Mark 1:4 (followed by Luke 3:3), the baptism of John is one "of repentance for the forgiveness of sins"; such forgiveness is a prerequisite for surviving the judgment and participating in the kingdom to come. Matthew notes the confession (3:6), the repentance (3:2, 8, 11), and the baptism (3:6, 7, 11), but does not explicitly link John's baptism to the forgiveness of sins.

The focus of Jesus' message in all three Synoptic Gospels is the coming of the kingdom of God (in Matthew, usually "kingdom of heaven"; Matt 4:17; 10:7; Mark 1:14-15; Luke 10:9, 11). Given human sinfulness, admission to the kingdom is not possible apart from divine forgiveness. (Note the presupposition of human sinfulness in Matt 7:11//Luke 11:13; also Matt 6:12//Luke 11:4; Matt 6:12-14; and compare Matt 15:19-20//Mark 7:21-23; Luke 13:3, 5.) God's willingness to forgive all—even the most notorious of sinners—and welcome them into his kingdom is the thrust of a number of Jesus' parables: the feast to which all are invited (Matt 22:1-10//Luke 14:16-24); the tax collector's humble prayer (Luke 18:9-14); most famously, the parables of the lost sheep and coin and that of the prodigal son (Luke 15:3-32). God's willingness to forgive sinners is demonstrated when Jesus calls a tax collector to be his disciple (Matt 9:9//Mark 2:14//Luke 5:27-28) and when he associates with other tax collectors and sinners (Matt 9:10-13//Mark 2:15-17//Luke 5:29-32; see also Luke 19:1-10; note the reputation Jesus has, according to Matt 11:19//Luke 7:34, of being "a friend of tax collectors and sinners"). When a woman known to be a "sinner" bathes Jesus' feet with her tears and an ointment and dries them with her hair, Jesus sees in her actions an expression of the love of one who has been forgiven much (Luke 7:47). Even Simon Peter, in Luke's Gospel, is called to follow Jesus after acknowledging himself to be "a sinful man" (5:8, 10-11); the resurrected Jesus' renewed acceptance of Peter after Peter has denied him, and of the other disciples after they have forsaken him, are further examples of the boundless forgiveness offered by Jesus and displayed in his activities (see also Luke 23:34).

On two occasions in the Synoptics, Jesus himself pronounces the forgiveness of sins (Matt 9:2-8//Mark 2:3-12//Luke 5:18-26; also Luke 7:48). On the first occasion, certain scribes (and Pharisees, according to Luke) interpret his actions as blasphemous, since forgiveness is a prerogative of God alone; Jesus' right to forgive is brought in question in the second incident as well (Luke 7:49). Neither here nor in passages where Jesus demands the absolute loyalty and love of his disciples (e.g., Matt 10:37-39)—a loyalty and love due God alone—does Jesus provide verbal legitimation for his activities. (Similarly, he declines to spell out the source of his authority in Matt 21:23-27//Mark 11:27-33//Luke 20:1-8.) But he does follow up his pronouncement of the paralytic's forgiveness with a healing that demonstrates his authority to forgive (Matt 9:4-8//Mark 2:8-12//Luke 5:22-26).

Forgiveness, according to the synoptic Jesus, is available for every sin but one: blasphemy against the Holy Spirit. Mark (3:28-30) sees such a sin in those who attribute Jesus' miraculous powers to Satan rather than to God's Spirit, thus signaling their unalterable opposition to God's kingdom. Matthew 12:31 is placed in the same general context and immediately after the insistence that those who are not "with" Jesus are "against" him; probably the saying here has the same meaning as in Mark, though no interpretation is attached. Matthew 12:32 = Luke 12:10, in distinguishing between things spoken against the Son of Man (and therefore forgivable) and those directed against the Holy Spirit (and therefore unforgivable), perhaps allows for the forgiveness of sins that spring from a failure to recognize Jesus' divine mission because of his unpretentious appearance, while declaring willful opposition to the presence and power of God to be unforgivable.

Along similar lines, Mark 4:12 sees God's mysterious purpose being fulfilled in those who, when confronted by Jesus and the message of the kingdom, "look" without "perceiving" and "listen" without "understanding": their closed minds and hearts rule out the possibility of a true repentance that would bring the forgiveness of sins.

Though the demands Jesus places on his disciples are stringent (e.g., Matt 5:17-48), he himself (as we have seen) demonstrates an ongoing willingness to forgive their failings, includes a petition for forgiveness in the prayer he teaches them (Matt 6:12//Luke 11:4), and assures them of God's forgiveness—provided that they extend the same forgiveness to others. Such forgiveness is to be granted as often as it is requested (Matt 18:21-22; Luke 17:3-4); indeed, as Jesus' way of life is an active demonstration of God's willingness to forgive, the same is to be true of his disciples (see Matt 5:43-48). The merciful will obtain mercy (Matt 5:7); and those willing to forgive will be forgiven (Matt 6:14; Mark 11:25; Luke 6:37; compare Sir 28:2). Conversely, forgiveness is emphatically denied those unwilling to extend it to others (Matt 6:15; 18:23-35).

Finally, we should note that Matthew explicitly identifies the forgiveness of sins as the purpose behind Jesus' outpouring of his blood in death (26:28). That purpose and that sacrifice are in view already in 1:21, where it is said of Jesus that he "will save his people from their sins," and in 20:28, which speaks of the Son of Man "giv[ing] his life a ransom for many."

In the Acts of the Apostles, the forgiveness of sins is repeatedly associated with Christian conversion (involving repentance and baptism; see Acts 2:38; 5:31; also Luke 24:47) for Jews (Acts 5:31) and Gentiles (26:17-18) alike. The expression is, for Luke, closely linked with "salvation" (see Luke 1:77); like salvation, forgiveness is only possible through the name of Jesus (Acts 2:38; 5:31; 10:43; 13:38; compare 4:12).

3. The Gospel and Epistles of John

Forgiveness plays little explicit role in these writings. The darkness that, according to John's Gospel, prevails in the world (compare 1:5; 3:19-21) is doubtless that of sin, so that entrance into the light (8:12; 12:46) must mean (among other things) forgiveness of sin; but the point is not made explicit. (Compare, however, John 1:29 and 8:36 [following v. 34]; and note that those who refuse to believe in Jesus remain, and will die, in their sins [8:24; 9:41].) In the one text in the Gospel where forgiveness is mentioned, the resurrected Jesus declares to his disciples, who have just received the Holy Spirit: "If you forgive the sins of any, they are forgiven them; if you retain the sins of any, they are retained" (20:23; compare Matt 16:19; 18:18). Presumably the disciples are being given a power to exercise in Jesus' absence that he himself has possessed while with them; in that case, the forgiveness or retention of sins that has hitherto been linked to believing or refusing to believe in Jesus (compare 15:22; 16:9) will now be linked to positive and negative responses to the disciples' post-Easter witness to their Lord (compare 20:21).

The readers to whom 1 John is written have experienced the forgiveness of sins (2:12; the distinction between the "little children" of whom this is said and the "fathers" and "young people" of v. 13 seems only rhetorical; what is said of each group individually is true of all). They may also experience forgiveness should they sin even now, provided they confess the sins they have committed: God is faithful in forgiving (1:9), Jesus Christ is the advocate for his people even when they sin (2:1), and his death has atoned for all sins (2:2; compare 1:7; 4:10). Nonetheless, as the Synoptic Gospels talk about unforgivable sin (Matt 12:31-32//Mark 3:28-29//Luke 12:10), so 1 John can talk of "mortal sin" (5:16). In the light of what John has already said about the atoning death of Christ and God's faithfulness in forgiving, mortal sin can only be behavior, consciously and deliberately adopted, that expresses one's rejection of God and his provision, in Christ, for forgiveness.

4. The Pauline corpus

Language of forgiveness is rare in the Pauline corpus as well. Most examples come from letters whose authorship is disputed. Ephesians (1:7) and Colossians (1:14) identify the forgiveness of sins as the substance of the "redemption" enjoyed by believers (Ephesians adds "through [Christ's] blood"); i.e., through Christ's atoning death, believers enjoy deliverance from the judgment that awaits unforgiven sin. Colossians 2:13 sees in the forgiveness of trespasses (here the verb for "forgive" is charizomai, suggesting that forgiveness is a gift of God's grace) the granting of new life; the forgiven were formerly "dead in trespasses." Ephesians 4:32 and Col 3:13 enjoin believers to (graciously) forgive (again, charizomai) those who wrong them just as God (Ephesians adds "in Christ") has forgiven them.

Paul himself models a willingness to forgive in 2 Cor 2:10, and requests that the Corinthians join him in forgiving and restoring one whom they, as a community, had disciplined (2:6-7). Elsewhere he ironically begs the Corinthians to forgive him the "wrong" of not requiring them to support him (12:13). The only other reference to forgiveness in the acknowledged Pauline epistles comes in the form of a quotation from the Psalms (Rom 4:7, citing Ps 32:1).

In part, the infrequency of references to forgiveness in Paul's writings reflects his concept of sin and its rule over unredeemed humankind ("in Adam"; compare Rom 5:15-21; 1 Cor 15:21-22). Humans, who have chosen not to give God due honor (Rom 1:21), have become "futile in their thinking," "their senseless minds" have been "darkened," they have been "given up" to "impurity," "degrading passions," and a "debased mind" (1:21, 24, 26, 28). They live "under the power of sin" (3:9; 5:21), as "slaves of sin" (6:17, 20). In itself, forgiveness of sins would do nothing to transform their plight; Paul speaks rather of the need to "die" to sin and enjoy a new life with Christ (Rom 6:1-11).

On the other hand, Paul sees the reference in Ps 32 to the forgiveness of sins (by God) as an equivalent to what happens when "God reckons righteousness apart from works" to those who believe (Rom 4:6-7). The equivalence suggests that what others refer to as "forgiveness" overlaps substantially with what Paul means by "justification." In principle, those who do what the law requires are righteous, and will be found righteous by God when he judges humankind (Rom 2:13; compare 2:6-11). But since no human being does the righteous works on which such a declaration of righteousness could be based (Rom 3:9-20, 23), God has revealed a "righteousness . . . through faith" for "all who believe" (3:21-22): those without righteous works of their own may be declared righteous on the basis of their faith in Christ Jesus. God is righteous even when he declares sinners to be righteous, since he has provided in Christ a "sacrifice of atonement" for their sins (3:24-26). Such a declaration may well be thought an equivalent to the forgiveness of sins. Note should also be made of Paul's language of reconciliation: in order to reconcile sinners to God's self, God does not count "their trespasses against them." Christ is, again, the means of reconciliation: though knowing no sin himself, he was charged with our sin, "so that in him we might become the righteousness of God" (2 Cor 5:19-21; compare Rom 5:10).

5. Hebrews and other writings

The writer of Hebrews finds God's revelation through God's Son superior to earlier revelations, the mediation of Christ superior to that of Moses, Christ's priesthood superior to the levitical priesthood, his sacrifice of himself superior to the sacrifices of the old order. The latter, he argues, could not have effected true forgiveness since they had to be repeated over and over again, whereas the forgiveness God promises banishes all memory of misdeeds (10:11-18, citing Jer 31:34; see also Heb 10:4). Yet though the sacrifices ordained by the law could not themselves bring forgiveness of sins, they foreshadowed, and provided an interpretive framework for, the truly effective sacrifice of Christ (compare 10:1). In particular, the earlier sacrifices made clear that "without the shedding of blood there is no forgiveness of sins" (9:22, where exceptions, such as that made for impoverished Israelites [Lev 5:11-13], are acknowledged in the beginning of the verse but then disregarded in a statement of the general principle; compare Lev 17:11); it is through the blood of Christ that the very consciences of his followers are cleansed (Heb 9:13-14). On the other hand, to persist willfully in sin after one has come to a knowledge of the truth is to turn one's back on the Son of God and profane the only blood by which wrongdoing can be cleansed. For such a person only judgment can remain (10:26-31; compare 6:4-8).

A number of OT texts link sickness with sin (e.g., Deut 28:22, 27-28; Ps 38:3; see also 1 Cor 11:30) and forgiveness with healing (Ps 103:3). The tentative wording of Jas 5:15 makes clear that such a linkage is not applicable in all cases; but where it is, the prayer that brings healing to the sick will also lead to the forgiveness of their sins. *See* ATONEMENT; CLEAN AND UNCLEAN; HEALING; JUSTIFICATION, JUSTIFY; RECONCILE, RECONCILIATION; REDEEM, REDEEMER; SACRIFICES AND OFFERINGS; SALVATION; SIN, SINNER.

Bibliography: Gary A. Anderson. "From Israel's Burden to Israel's Debt: Towards a Theology of Sin in Biblical and Early Second Temple Sources." *Reworking the Bible: Apocryphal and Related Texts at Qumran.* Esther G. Chazon, Devorah Dimant, and Ruth A. Clements, eds. (2005) 1–30; Walter Brueggemann. "The Travail of Pardon: Reflections on slh." *A God So Near: Essays on Old Testament Theology in Honor of Patrick D. Miller.* Brent A. Strawn and Nancy R. Bowen, eds. (2003) 283–297; Baruch J. Schwartz. "The Bearing of Sin in the Priestly Literature." *Pomegranates and Golden Bells: Studies in Biblical, Jewish, and Near Eastern Ritual, Law, and Literature in Honor of Jacob Milgrom.* David P. Wright, David Noel Freedman, and Avi Hurvitz, eds. (1995) 3–21.

STEPHEN WESTERHOLM

FORK [מַזְלֵג mazlegh, מִזְלָגָה mizlaghah, מִזְרֶה mizreh; πτύον ptuon]. 1. A "three-pronged fork" (mazlegh), used by priests of the tabernacle to extract their portion of a sacrifice (1 Sam 2:13-14).

2. A gold or bronze sacrificial instrument (mizlaghah) at the altar of the tabernacle (Exod 27:3; 38:3; Num 4:14) and Temple (1 Chr 28:17; 2 Chr 4:16).

3. A six-pronged winnowing fork (mizreh) for removing CHAFF from grain (Isa 30:24), used figuratively for chastisement (Jer 15:7).

4. A winnowing fork (ptuon) often used figuratively for chastisement of people (Matt 3:12; Luke 3:17).

5. The NRSV interprets "the head of the road(s)" to mean "fork in the road(s)" (Ezek 21:19, 21).

MICHAEL G. VANZANT

FORM CRITICISM, NT. "Form" refers to the established structure of a communication, which informs the hearer about its meaning. Knowledge that a given set of words constitute, e.g., a poem or a chronicle or a law determines how those words are evaluated.

Biblical scholars began sorting out the forms in biblical texts to avoid the misconceptions about the types of speech and written tradition found in the Bible. Though "form," as synonymous with "genre" could be used for the structure of an entire text, such as the Pauline "letter form," the term came to be used for oral traditions incorporated with the written biblical texts. This distinction between "forms" as units of oral tradition and genre as the applicable to written composition was central in early 20th cent. form criticism, which emphasized the communal "setting in life" (*Sitz im Leben*) in which the different forms originally arose. Contemporary scholars are skeptical about the possibility of detecting specific settings for each type of material.

Studies of the sources of the OT and the NT had sensitized scholars to the possibility of oral traditions behind the texts. Forms involving law (Exod 20:1-17 and Matt 5:17-48), announcement (1 Kgs 17:1 and Mark 1:15), prayer (1 Kgs 8:12-54 and Luke 11:1-4), proverb (Prov 9 and Matt 25:31-46), poetry (Song 2 and Col 1:12-20), instruction (Gen 17:9-14 and Gal 4:1-11), epic (Judg 5 and Heb 11), and philosophical argument (Wis 2 and Rom 9–11) were readily identified. All of these involved identifiable patterns of speech.

Though a long period of oral development for sources that were written down and then incorporated into the received texts, was characteristic of the OT, the NT texts were composed within a century of the events in question. The relationship between oral and written textuality must be quite different in that case. Bifurcation in study of "the OT" and "the NT" resulted in marked contrasts in the craft of form criticism. In the case of the OT, investigators stressed the similarity of forms to other literatures and their progressive incorporation within the texts. New Testament studies took a different tack, especially after Rudolf Bultmann's seminal work. It posited autonomous, individual forms of tradition that were taken up directly by the evangelist and, to a lesser extent, elsewhere in the canon.

Bultmann's approach to form criticism and his historical conclusion that the NT, composed by the Christian community, did not provide evidence about Jesus himself, but reflected later faith in Jesus. For Bultmann, study of the historical Jesus was, strictly speaking, impossible and in any case beside the point. The issue for faith was whether or not one accepted salvation through Jesus' death on the cross, not the historical veracity of specific facts about his life. The picture of evangelists collecting anonymous Christian traditions supported such a historical view.

After the end of the Second World War, study of Jesus as a figure in history resumed. During the same period, scholarly attention employed redaction-critical, rhetorical-critical, structuralist, deconstructionist, and postmodern approaches to describe NT documents as a whole rather than as collections of earlier oral and written materials.

Although form critics quickly identified different types of spoken tradition, the description of biblical narratives proved especially contentious. Bultmann distinguished between legends (that is, stories designed to teach faith) and miracles further divided between healings and nature prodigies. But those categories broke down on analysis. All stories have some sort of instructional value, an issue Bultmann attempted to address by referring to the allegedly "kerygmatic" content of many stories in the Gospels. That understanding, however, requires that an external factor, the "preaching" (the KERYGMA), determines the form of the material in question, rather than considering forms genuinely comparable from one culture to another. Similarly, the category of "miracle" imports a post-Enlightenment definition (namely, of miracles as abrogations of natural law) into the study of ancient texts.

Yet since the rise of new understandings of history, beginning with the work of R. G. Collingwood prior to the Second World War, form criticism has seen a revival. Collingwood stressed the vital connection between history as narrative and the meaning attached to events by those who referred to these accounts. History on Collingwood's understanding emerges as perspective as well as record, and that view has emerged with new force with the ebb of postmodernism. The shape of traditions prior to the written text of the Bible has accordingly reemerged as a productive line of inquiry. The distinction between "written" and "oral" forms has been softened by the many examples that have emerged in the study of rabbinic literature of both kinds of tradition existing alongside and enriching each other. By the same

token, the symbiotic relationship between forms and sources has been acknowledged, as well as the capacity (as in the case of the Mishnah) for a tradition that is oral in principle quickly to reach written form.

Perhaps most important, form criticism as presently practiced assumes neither that only the faith of communities is reflected in traditions (as Bultmann claimed) nor that there must be a one-to-one correspondence between every statement in the Bible and what actually happened in the past. Accordingly, Bultmann's form of "miracle" can be refined so as to be a genuinely literary tool, comparable to the other forms. What the Enlightenment called miracles were, in ancient texts (not only the Bible), stories of exorcism, healing, visions, and signs. Similarly, the idea of the "legend" need no longer obscure the underlying issue of form or eliminate historical judgment: stories from the ancient world exert paradigmatic value, illustrating the power of a given teaching, or of exorcistic, therapeutic, or visionary capacities. With such corrections, form criticism appears poised for a return to a central position in critical reading of the Bible. *See* MIRACLE; REDACTION CRITICISM, NT; REDACTION CRITICISM, OT; SOURCE CRITICISM.

Bibliography: Rudolf Bultmann. *The History of the Synoptic Tradition.* John Marsh, trans. (1994 [from 1921]); Martin Dibelius. *From Tradition to Gospel.* Bertram Lee Woolf, trans. (1971) [from 1919]); Klaus Koch. *The Growth of the Biblical Tradition: The Form-Critical Method.* S. M. Cupitt, trans. (1969).

BRUCE CHILTON

FORM CRITICISM, OT. "Form criticism" is a term that was first used in NT studies but is now also used widely for the study of the OT. In transiting between the two fields, its meaning has changed somewhat. In OT studies, the term now commonly refers to a recognition of the dynamic structure of a text.

In order to understand this way of operation, it is necessary to see that the word *form* is used in different senses. In some contexts, it refers to an external aspect of a text in contrast to its deeper meaning. In other contexts, it refers to a text's inner structure in opposition to its more incidental features. In form criticism, both internal and external aspects are considered in their relation to each other.

Another ambiguity that needs to be noted is that for some writers, the word *form* designates a stable pattern, whereas, for others, it represents something purely particular, so that every object has its own special form. The discussion to follow takes an intermediate position. It assumes that forms are shared, but also flexible. For instance, houses share much of their structure without any being exactly the same. Applied to biblical texts, this means that the structure of a given text can be similar to, although not identical with, that of another text in the same or in a different religious tradition and thus also similar to what you or I may want to say.

There is then a contrast between historical criticism and form criticism. Historical criticism looks primarily at the particularity of a text in its own special situation. It is true, historical criticism makes use of comparative data, but its focus is on what the text meant at one particular time. Conversely, while form criticism takes account of historical conditions and of the particular meaning of a text in the past (insofar as these can be recovered), it focuses on how basic considerations of human life are embodied in the text. In its practical application, historical criticism is negative. By limiting the meaning of a text to the past or to a single tradition, it frees one to follow a different path. Form criticism puts more emphasis on commonality, including the commonality of past and present, although it also recognizes differences.

In older scholarship, there were attempts to employ form criticism as a means for dealing with historical issues, such as the oral prehistory of a text or its date. However, such efforts turned out to be problematic, since forms cannot be readily assigned to a specific time. Instead, form criticism deals effectively with the interrelation of "life," "content," and "language." Human life, as it is expressed in language, includes many different processes. These might include greeting a friend, expressing sexual or other love, making a purchase, establishing a social rule, giving practical advice, announcing an occasion, and so on. The verbal pattern of each of these represents a genre. More specifically religious genres include prayer (petition or praise), ritual and ethical instruction, and stories of origin.

In order to live effectively in society, it is necessary to learn ways of acting and speaking that are appropriate for these various genres. Most important, each kind of speaking calls for a type of content, including both thought and emotion. For instance, a simple greeting expresses interest but does not probe for information ("How are you?" generally requires no answer). A social rule points to an act valuable for society in general, while practical advice has in mind more immediately the concern of the individual addressed. The content that is considered to be appropriate for each genre is quite similar cross-culturally, but it also varies in more or less important ways from society to society.

Thoughts (and, to some extent, moods) are conveyed by means of language. Linguistic expressions are to some extent arbitrary. Yet a number of linguistic forms are inherently appropriate for a given genre. For instance, love poetry around the world often features dialogue, just as it tends to express a high degree of personal equality in its content. In the OT, second-person address ("you shall [not]") exhibits the personally responsive character

of many directives. That linguistic pattern is not strictly necessary, yet it does have a certain fit for directives to which no express penalties are attached.

Form criticism needs to start with language forms since they are audible or visible and thus immediately available. With the help of linguistic aids, one can move from observing linguistic forms to a recognition of the thoughts and feelings they express. Next, with the help of a general knowledge of human life, together with an awareness of local conventions as they appear in various parts of the OT, one can move from the thoughts and feelings expressed—and sometimes directly from the linguistic forms themselves—to the personal and social dynamics of the text.

This kind of analysis does not require a high degree of specialization. On the contrary, it gains from interdisciplinary and intercultural perspectives and can also be pursued effectively by persons who are interested primarily in practical application. These can ask, "Does a recognition of the variety of genres help me to gain an understanding of how life operates in its different facets, so that I will not attempt to deal with all problems in the same way?" More specifically, "Does the dynamic structure of a given text shed light on how I might pursue my own life?" Form criticism by itself does not provide theological or ethical answers, but it provides a path toward them. *See* BIBLICAL CRITICISM; BIBLICAL INTERPRETATION, HISTORY OF; FOLKLORE IN BIBLICAL INTERPRETATION; MYTH IN THE OT; POETRY, HEBREW.

Bibliography: Martin J. Buss. *Biblical Form Criticism in Its Context* (1999); Marvin A. Sweeney and Ehud Ben Zvi, eds. *The Changing Face of Form Criticism for the Twenty-first Century* (2003).

MARTIN J. BUSS

FORMER PROPHETS. *See* CANON OF THE OLD TESTAMENT.

FORNICATION [πορνεία *porneia*, πόρνος *pornos*]. *Fornication* (porneia) is not specifically defined in the Bible. The term refers to inappropriate sexual behavior. Some argue that fornication is sexual relations between unmarried persons; however, the concept is broader than ADULTERY and includes INCEST (Sir 23:16).

Paul refers to fornication as first among the works of the flesh (Gal 5:19; see also Col 3:5; Eph 5:3), and he defines it as a sin against the body as well as the body of Christ (1 Cor 6:12-20). Jesus argues that fornication, not improper washing, is an act that produces defilement (Matt 15:18-20; Mark 7:22-23).

Fornication applies metaphorically to IDOLATRY (Wis 14:12; Rev 2:14, 20). The corruption of Babylon is symbolized as fornication (Rev 17:2, 4; 18:3, 9; 19:2). *See* CLEAN AND UNCLEAN.

EMILY R. CHENEY

FORSAKE, FORSAKEN. *See* ABANDON.

FORT. Used in the NRSV to translate a variety of Hebrew and Greek words that refer to defense structures during war (2 Chr 27:4; Nah 3:14; 2 Macc 10:33). Other translations of the same terms include siege wall, siege work, STRONGHOLD, FORTIFICATION, and FORTRESS.

FORTIFICATION [מִבְצָר mivtsar; καταφυγή kataphygē]. Syro-Palestinians utilized several techniques to secure their cities, including an artificial slope, earthen rampart, wall system, or combination thereof. A CITY was most vulnerable at its GATE, thus, most were protected by TOWERs. Extensive water systems located within towns helped prolong the inhabitants' survival when besieged. *See* WAR, METHODS, TACTICS, WEAPONS OF (BRONZE AGE THROUGH PERSIAN PERIOD); WAR, METHODS, TACTICS, WEAPONS OF (HELLENISTIC THROUGH ROMAN PERIODS).

JASON R. TATLOCK

FORTRESS [בִּצָּרוֹן, bitsaron מִבְצָר mivtsar, מְצוּרָה metsurah]. Various Hebrew terms are translated "fortress" as a walled and fortified site providing defense of an area in time of trouble. Fortresses were often positioned on hilltops and had high walls, double gates, and bars (Deut 3:5) but were less than an acre in size. They were abundant in the Negev and in Jordan. These fortresses were often located near borders and along significant roads. Fortified cities could also be called fortresses (2 Chr 11:10-11). Metaphorically, God is called a fortress, a refuge in a time of distress (Ps 59:16). *See* CASTLE; FORT; FORTIFICATION.

JOEL F. DRINKARD, JR.

FORTRESSES, HERODIAN. *See* HERODIAN FORTRESSES.

FORTUNATUS for′chuh-nay′tuhs [Φορτουνᾶτος Phortounatos]. One of three long-standing Christian converts from Corinth (1 Cor 16:17). He traveled with ACHAICUS and STEPHANAS from Corinth to Paul in Ephesus, perhaps bringing the letter to which Paul alludes in 1 Cor 7:1. Significantly, since Corinth was a Roman colony, the name is a Latin one, denoting "prosperous" or "lucky," and was found frequently among freedmen or slaves. Paul states that the arrival of these three delighted him, and they raised or refreshed his spirits. Indeed they made up for his being absent from Corinth.

ANTHONY C. THISELTON

FORTUNE. *See* DESTINY.

FORTY. *See* NUMBERS, NUMBERING.

FORUM [φόρον phoron]. A center of civic life and economic exchange (Acts 28:15).

FORUM OF APPIUS for′uhm uhv ap′ee-uhs [τὸ Ἀππίου Φόρον to Appiou Phoron]. A market town along the APPIAN WAY approximately 40 mi. southeast of Rome, possibly founded when the road was built in 312 BCE. By the 1st cent. CE it had become an important town, as it was about a one-day journey from Rome and thus a natural first or last stop on the way to or from the imperial capital. The Roman poet, Horace, describes it as an unpleasant and crowded place (*Sat.* 1.5). In Acts 28:15 Christians from Rome travel as far as the Forum of Appius to meet Paul as he journeys to their city.

RUBÉN R. DUPERTUIS

FOUNDATION [יָסַד yasadh; θεμέλιος themelios, καταβολή katabolē]. The Hebrew root yasadh has the basic meaning of foundation and laying a foundation. A strong foundation is an essential part of any building. Foundations were sunk into solid ground, preferably on bedrock, to make sure a structure was stable (Luke 6:48-49).

The foundation of Solomon's palace had large stones of eight to ten cubits (1 Kgs 7:10). Massive ashlar foundations have been discovered in excavations of the walls of Samaria. The platform supporting the Herodian Temple has foundation stones as large as 45 ft. x 10 ft. x 10 ft., estimated to weigh over 450 tons. The OT mentions the foundation of a wall (Ezek 13:14), a house (Hab 3:13), a city (Josh 6:26; 1 Kgs 16:34), Solomon's Temple (1 Kgs 6:37) and the Second Temple (Ezra 3:10). The NT mentions the foundation of the walls of New Jerusalem (Rev 21:14, 19).

Figuratively, the word is used of Yahweh as creator laying the foundations of the earth (Job 38:4; Ps 102:25; Isa 48:13), the world (Ps 24:1-2; 89:11), and the heavens (Ps 89:11). These same foundations shake or tremble when Yahweh is angry (Ps 18:8 [Heb. 18:7]).

JOEL F. DRINKARD, JR.

FOUNDATION, GATE OF THE. *See* GATE OF THE FOUNDATION.

FOUNTAIN [מַבּוּעַ mabbuʿa, מַעְיָן maʿyan, מָקוֹר maqor, עַיִן ʿayin; πηγή pēgē]. A fountain was a flow or spring of fresh water from a cavity in a hillside or valley, in contrast to a perennial stream or to a WELL or CISTERN used to catch rainwater. Water was a crucial factor for survival in ancient Palestine, where rainfall is limited to half the year. Ancient peoples often settled their villages based on the location of water sources. The soft limestone rock of Palestine is favorable for the natural formation of fountains, which are therefore numerous. Where fountains existed, settlements were usually established around them. The addition of the prefix "en" (i.e., ʿayin, "spring, fountain") to numerous place-names attests to the significance of fountains (e.g., EN-DOR; EN-EGLAIM; EN-GANNIM; EN-GEDI; EN-HADDAH; EN-RIMMON; EN-ROGEL; EN-SHEMESH; EN-TAPPUAH).

The fountain provided a rich metaphor for biblical writers. The Lord is a fountain (Ps 68:26), specifically the "fountain of life" (Ps 36:9) or "living water," in contrast to a cracked cistern that holds no water (Jer 2:13); the mouth of the righteous is a fountain (Prov 10:11), and the teaching of the wise (Prov 13:14), the fear of the Lord (Prov 14:27), and wisdom (Prov 16:22; 18:4) are all fountains of life. In the Minor Prophets fountains are signs of eschatological fulfillment, flowing directly from the house of the Lord (Joel 3:18) and providing pardon for the royal family and the residents of Jerusalem, "to cleanse them from sin and impurity" (Zech 13:1).

RALPH K. HAWKINS

FOUNTAIN GATE שַׁעַר הָעַיִן sha'ar ha'ayin]. Gate of Jerusalem (Neh 2:14; 3:15; 12:37), likely located at the south end of the city above the juncture of the Central (Tyropoean) and Kidron valleys, probably named because a Pool of Siloam overflow channel ran beneath it. See GATE BETWEEN THE TWO WALLS.

FOUR. See NUMBERS, NUMBERING.

FOURTEEN. See NUMBERS, NUMBERING.

FOWL [זַרְזִיר zarzir, צִפּוֹר tsippor; ἀλέκτωρ alektōr, ὄρνεον orneon]. Surprisingly few biblical texts mention fowl, i.e., domestic poultry (Neh 5:18). It is thus uncertain whether the Hebrew word zarzir, which occurs in Prov 30:31 a, denotes the cock or some other animal. The translation "strutting rooster" (NRSV) rests, moreover, upon a textual reconstruction. However, it would be premature to draw the conclusion that domestic fowl were totally unknown in Palestine during the OT period. Iconographic evidence indicates otherwise. A fighting cock is, for instance, represented on an onyx seal from ca. 600 BCE, which was discovered at Tell en-Nasbeh. Later, in the NT period, poultry had been introduced on a larger scale. According to rabbinical sources, it was prohibited to keep fowl in Jerusalem. Nevertheless, the crowing of a cock (alektōr) was probably quite a common sound in the city, as implied by the episode recounting Peter's denial (Mark 14:30, 68, 72). Mention should also be made of a remarkable saying, directed to the city of Jerusalem, where Jesus speaks metaphorically of himself as a hen (orneon): "How often have I desired to gather your children together as a hen gathers her brood under her wings" (Matt 23:37; Luke 13:34). As with many Hebrew and Greek terms for birds and animals, it is often difficult to determine what specific bird corresponds to which term. See BIRDS OF THE BIBLE; COCK; FOWLER; HEN.

GÖRAN EIDEVALL

FOWLER [יָקֹשׁ yaqosh, יָקוּשׁ yaqush]. Someone who captures fowl. Indirectly, via proverbs and metaphors, the biblical texts provide information concerning fowlers' techniques. Using bait or decoys, the fowler lured small birds into a snare or trap (Amos 3:5; Ps 124:7). Alternatively, he caught them in his net (Hos 7:12). Hence, it is not surprising that cunning enemies were portrayed as fowlers (Job 18:8-10; Ps 91:3; Prov 6:5; Jer 5:26-27; Hos 9:8).

GÖRAN EIDEVALL

FOX [שׁוּעָל shu'al; ἀλώπηξ alōpēx]. The fox (Vulpes palaestinus), a burrowing animal, is a small canid, related to the domestic dog. Foxes are widespread all over the Middle East and prey on rodents and other small creatures. The Song of Songs considers the fox a menace to vineyards, where it destroys the grapes (Song 2:15). The fox's habitat often makes it a symbol of destruction and desolation as in Ezek 13:4 (see also Ps 63:10). The Bible relates that Samson captured 300 foxes, tied them in pairs, attached a burning torch to the tails of each pair, and sent them free to burn the Philistines' fields as revenge (Judg 15:4-5).

Bibliography: O. Borowski. *Every Living Thing: Daily Use of Animals in Ancient Israel* (1998).

ODED BOROWSKI

FRACTURE [שֶׁבֶר shever]. Any sort of physical injury involving breaking, most famously used in a passage about restitution: "fracture for fracture, eye for eye, tooth for tooth" (Lev 24:20). A fractured arm or leg disqualifies a descendant of Aaron from priestly functions (Lev 21:20). Shever also refers to the interpretation of a dream (Judg 7:15).

PHILLIP MICHAEL SHERMAN

FRAGRANCE. See ODOR; PERFUME.

FRAME [מוֹט mot, מִסְגֶּרֶת misgereth, קֶרֶשׁ qeresh, שָׂחִיף sakhif, שְׁלַבִּים shelabbim שֶׁקֶף sheqef]. Several Hebrew words are translated "frame" or "rim," indicating the edge around something. 1. Mot (Num 4:10, 12) refers to a carrying frame for TABERNACLE implements.

2. Misgereth (Exod 25:25, 27; 37:12, 14) refers to the border or rim, and therefore the framework for the table in the tabernacle. It is also used for the borders of the framework of the bases of the bronze sea in the Temple in Jerusalem (1 Kgs 7:28-36).

3. Qeresh indicates the framework upon which the curtains of the tabernacle are hung (Exod 26:15-16; Num 3:36; 4:31).

4. Shelabbim (1 Kgs 7:28) refers to the framework of the base of the bronze sea.

5. Sheqef is used in 1 Kgs 6:4; 7:4-5, and sakhif in Ezek 41:16 to refer to the framework around the window of the Temple in Jerusalem.

6. Other words are used to refer to human or animal frames: 'etsem (עֶצֶם) "bone, framework" (Ps 139:15); 'erekh (עֶרֶךְ) "order, arrangement, frame" (Job 41:12 [Heb. 41:4]).

C. MARK MCCORMICK

FRANKINCENSE [לְבֹנָה levonah; λίβανος libanos]. A prized incense in the Near East and the Mediterranean prepared from the gum of several species of *Boswellia* (*Burseraceae*) trees and shrubs native to the Arabian peninsula (*Boswellia sacra*) and North Africa (*Boswellia papyrifera*, native to Ethiopia). The range of the frankincense tree in southern Arabia in the Hadhramaut and Dhofar follows the rain shadow of the current southwest monsoon. To obtain its resin, a deep, longitudinal incision is made in the trunk of the tree; below it a narrow strip of bark 5 in. in length is peeled off. The secreted milk-like juice hardens when exposed to the air, and within three months it is transformed into yellowish "tears" that are scraped off into baskets.

Todd Bolen/BiblePlaces.com

Figure 1: Frankincense on display at Avdat

The numerous references to frankincense in the Pentateuch detail its use in the formula for sacred incense in the Tent of Meeting (Exod 30:34), in combination with grain offerings (Lev 2:2), and with the bread offering (Lev 24:7). Its aromatic values are highlighted in references to sweet fragrances (Song 3:6; 4:6), and its high price and value as a kingly gift is demonstrated in its inclusion among the gifts of the magi to the infant Jesus (Matt 2:11). *See* ALTAR; INCENSE; SACRIFICE AND OFFERINGS; SPICE; WORSHIP, OT.

VICTOR H. MATTHEWS

FREE CHOICE, FREE WILL. *See* DETERMINISM.

FREEDMEN, SYNAGOGUE OF THE [συναγωγὴ Λιβερτίνων synagōgē Libertinōn]. A Jerusalem assembly of Diaspora Jewish immigrants, some of whom argued with Stephen and instigated his arrest and interrogation by the high council (Acts 6:9-15). "Freedmen," from Latin *libertine*, denoted native or proselyte Jews formerly displaced and enslaved by Roman conquerors (Philo, *Legat.* 155; Tacitus, *Ann.* 2.85). In Acts 6:9, they are identified most closely with North African (Cyrenian, Alexandrian) Jews resettling in Jerusalem; but they may also include "others . . . from Cilicia and Asia" in the same or an affiliated synagogue. A Greek inscription attests to an ancient Jerusalem SYNAGOGUE founded by the family of Theodotos, son of Vettenus, whose Latin name may suggest a history of ownership and manumission by the Roman *gens Vettena*. Theodotus, a possible descendant of "Freedmen," refurbished the synagogue as a center for studying Jewish law and a dormitory supporting "those in need [coming] from abroad."

Bibliography: C. K. Barrett. *The Acts of the Apostles.* Vol. 1 (1994) 323–25.

F. SCOTT SPENCER

FREEDOM. *See* LIBERTY.

FREEWILL OFFERING. *See* SACRIFICES AND OFFERINGS.

FRIEND, FRIENDSHIP [אֹהֵב ʾohav, סוֹד sodh, רֵעַ reʿa; ἑταῖρος hetairos; φίλος philos]. *Friend, friendship* communicates a warmth of emotional closeness and common goals.

In the OT, a friend (reʿa) is a COMPANION or ally (Gen 28:12), or someone who is trusted like a family member (Deut 13:6). Song of Songs 5:16 describes the lovers as friends (reʿa).

Abraham is described as a *friend* (ʾohav) of God, from the root word ʾahav (אָהַב) for "love" (2 Chr 20:7; Isa 41:8; compare Jas 2:23 where Abraham is described as a friend [philos] of God).

Sodh has the nuance speaking with someone in a friendly way, in confidence. Job remembers that when he was in his prime, the friendship (sodh) of God was upon him (Job 29:4).

In the NT, Jesus calls his disciples "my friends" (philoi [φίλοι], Luke 12:4; John 15:14), and he is described as a friend (philos) of sinners (Matt 11:19; Luke 7:34). The early church treated this sort of intimate association with sinners as a unique feature of Jesus' behavior. As God incarnate, Jesus became a healing and forgiving presence among those who were most open to it.

The most striking use of *friendship* appears in the Fourth Gospel, when Jesus says that his disciples will no longer be called servants or slaves but friends whenever they do as he commands them; moreover, the greatest love (AGAPE) is to lay down one's life for one's friends (John 15:12-14).

The Greek term hetairos often denotes a relationship of lesser intimacy than philos (Matt 20:13; 22:12) and describes a working relationship that comes from common, shared tasks. However, in ancient Greek, philos and hetairos were often used as cognates with no discernible difference.

There is only one disciple whom Jesus addresses personally as "Friend" (hetairos), and that is JUDAS (Matt 26:50), at the time of Jesus' arrest when Judas has embraced him warmly (kataphileō καταφιλέω, meaning fervent embrace). Jesus' words to Judas: eph ho parei (ἐφ ὃ πάρει, "this is why you have come" or "do what you are here to do") need not be interpreted as recognition of betrayal, but as a renewal of Jesus' invitation to his friend Judas to drink the cup with him (Matt 26:27-28). These words were commonly found on blown-glass drinking vessels in Galilee. Therefore, this scene is not necessarily a display of irony or satire on the part of Jesus, as most scholars interpret. Jesus did not need to be ironic, but could be genuine and forthright in his last encounter with Judas. As Jesus affirms his friendship with Judas and offers him thanks for his obedience, the nature of friendship, as Jesus practiced it with his disciples, becomes more transparent. See LOVE IN THE NT; LOVE IN THE OT.

Bibliography: John F. Fitzpatrick. *Friendship, Flattery and Frankness of Speech* (1996).

WILLIAM KLASSEN

FRINGE [גְּדִלִ ים gedhilim, צִיצִת tsitsith]. The edge of a cloth garment. The fringe on one garment had great symbolic importance in the ancient world. God commands the Israelites to make a fringe on the corners of their garments and to attach to them a thread of blue (tekheleth תְּכֵלֶת) to remind them of the commandments and the exodus from Egypt. This distinctive blue dye is enormously expensive to produce, and its salient characteristic is that it never fades. The tassels on the fringe are to serve as a safeguard from sin; a visible reminder that one is a part of the "kingdom of priests" (Exod 19:6). The practice of wearing fringes with these threads in them continues to this day and the main scriptural passage mandating their use (Num 15:37-41) is a prominent liturgical component of Jewish evening and morning services. The wearing of these fringes is also called for in Deut 22:12. The High Priests' garments had a distinctive fringe containing bells and pomegranate of blue, purple, and scarlet linen (Exod 29:24-26).

The hem of one's garments could serve as a marker of one's identity. David cuts off a corner of Saul's hem to prove that he had been in a position to kill the king but refrained from doing so (1 Sam 24:3-11). The prophet Zechariah (8:22-23) foresees that, in messianic times, each Jew will raise the hem and corner of his garment as an identity marker. Indeed, the fringe

on one's garment could be pressed into clay as a kind of signature. *See* TASSELS.

JUDITH Z. ABRAMS

FRIT. *See* GLASS; GLAZE, GLAZING; JEWELRY; POTTERY.

FROG [צְפַרְדֵּע tsefarde'a; βάτραχος batrachos]. A frog is an amphibian. The most common frogs in Israel are *Rana esculenta*, popularly known as green or water frogs. These frogs are also common in Egypt and may be the type of frog to which the biblical writers refer. Frogs appear in the Bible only in reference to the second plague visited upon Egypt (Exod 8:2-15; Pss 78:45; 105:30; Wis 19:10) and metaphorically in one of John of Patmos' visions (Rev 16:13).

Bibliography: G. S. Cansdale. *All the Animals of the Bible Lands* (1970).

JENNIFER L. KOOSED

FROST. *See* ISRAEL, CLIMATE OF; SNOW.

FRUIT [פָּרָה parah, פְּרִי peri; καρπός karpos, ἀπαρχή aparchē]. The fleshy and edible pulp that covers the seed of the plant or tree. The most common fruits were the olive, grape, and fig (Judg 9:7-15; Deut 8:7-8), but a rich variety of fruits was available including the almond, apricot or quince, citron, date palm, mulberry, muskmelon, myrtle, pistachio, pomegranate, olive, sycamore fig, walnut, and watermelon.

The nutrition, variety, and diverse uses of fruits made them a central part of the ancient diet. Fruits were eaten fresh, but many fruits like figs, dates, grapes, apricots, and mulberries could be dried and stored for future needs (1 Sam 25:18). Honey was produced from date palms and wine from grapes. Olive oil was used for cooking and lighting (Matt 25:1-13). As medicine, dried figs were used to heal ulcers (Isa 38:21), watermelon as a laxative, quince as skin lotion, and wine for relief from suffering (Mark 15:23).

Fruit was also integral to economic, political, and religious life. Wine and olive oil were chief exports for international trade and political alliances (1 Kgs 5:10-12). Kings and priests were anointed with oil (1 Sam 10:1), as were the sick (Jas 5:14). The Festival of Booths celebrated the ingathering of the fruit harvest (Lev 23:33-43), and tithes of fruit supported the Temple (Lev 27:30; *see* BOOTHS, FEAST OR FESTIVAL OF).

Fruit was a valued gift from God to be shared with others. Fruit was not to be collected for the first three years after planting, and in the fourth year fruit was set apart for God (Lev 19:23-25). Every seventh year, vineyards and olive orchards were to be left fallow so the land could rest, and poor people and wild animals could be fed (Exod 23:10-11). To preserve God's fertile land, fruit trees were not to be destroyed during war (Deut 20:19).

The abundant use of fruit made it ripe for symbolic meaning. Fruit symbolizes offspring. Children are the "fruit of the womb" (Gen 30:2; Luke 1:42) and the first humans are to "be fruitful and multiply" (Gen 1:28; 8:15-17).

Fruit is a sign of God's reward and punishment. The righteous are rewarded for good work or speech; they will "eat the fruit of their labors" (Isa 3:10; compare Prov 12:14). God punishes the disobedient according to the "fruit of their doings" (Jer 21:14; Mic 7:13; compare Matt 3:10). Similarly, fruit represents the natural growth that follows from a life with God. Those who delight in the law of the LORD are like "trees planted by streams of water which yield their fruit" (Ps 1:1-3). The branches joined to the true vine will bear much fruit (John 15:1-17). Those who live by the spirit will bear the FRUIT OF THE SPIRIT (Gal 5:16-26). The FIRST FRUITS are the first converts in a certain geographical area (Rom 16:5; 2 Thess 2:13). As first fruits, Jesus and the first converts represent all humankind who belong to God (Rom 11:16; 1 Cor 15:20-23).

Specific fruits also carry symbolic meaning. The olive is a symbol of restoration and hope (Gen 8:11; Hos 14:6). The vine is a symbol for Israel and indicates both God's blessing (Gen 49:11-12) and curse (Isa 5:1-7). The vine and fig both signify peace and security (1 Kgs 4:24-25; Mic 4:4). *See* AGRICULTURE; PLANTS OF THE BIBLE.

JAMES P. GRIMSHAW

FRUIT OF THE SPIRIT [καρπὸς τοῦ πνευματός *karpos tou pneumatos*]. This phrase is found only in Gal 5:22, though different terms and partial parallels exist in other places (compare Eph 5:9; Phil 1:11; 4:8; Col 1:6, 10; 3:12-15; 2 Pet 1:5-7). Nine qualifiers follow "fruit of the Spirit," concretely defining "fruit." These terms represent the ethical characteristics of life in Jesus through the Spirit: love, joy, peace, longsuffering, kindness, goodness, faith/faithfulness, gentleness, and self-control.

These fruit are contrasted with "works of the flesh" in Eph 5:19-21. Similar virtues and vice lists occur in other NT works and in Hellenistic (esp. Stoic thought) and Roman literature, including Jewish Hellenistic literature. Lists such as these also played a role in the literature of the church fathers and Gnosticism. The nature of these fruit in the NT takes on a significant ethical tone quite different from similar lists in Hellenistic and Roman sources.

Fruit is a "generic" metaphor. Though singular in nature, it suggests a number of attributes that more concretely identify it. Moreover, the qualities for which it stands contain a center of coherence that derives from the Spirit's nature and work, noting results that come from one's association with the Spirit through Jesus. This association is contained in the syntactical relationship between "fruit" and "of the Spirit." "Of

the Spirit" means that the Spirit produces these kinds of qualities in the believer.

The fruits of the Spirit, in Gal 5:22-23, are coupled with the works of the flesh in vv. 19-21. Both lists occur in a larger section (5:13-26) in which Paul exhorts his readers to ethical behavior, characterizing the crucified life (5:24) under the rule of God by the Spirit (5:21). Verses 13-15 provide summary statements of this section; the remaining verses detail the exhortation of v. 13*b*: "through love serve one another." "Walk/live by the Spirit" in vv. 16 and 25 frame Paul's exhortation for believers to live in freedom as slaves of Christ. The paradox of freedom/slavery in (v. 13) provides further emphasis. Thus, the fruits of the Spirit are set in bold contrast to the works of the flesh and show how believers are to live out this freedom.

Increasingly, scholars trace the fruit metaphor back to Isaiah's theology of restoration and new exodus, esp. chaps. 32 and 57. The wording of the LXX that provides a suitable linguistic and theological basis for future Pauline reflection and application. Though all the nouns in Gal 5:22-23 do not occur in these places, the metaphor "fruit" and some of the qualifiers do, such as righteousness and peace. Also, Isa 27 contributes to the setting of Paul's use of "fruit." This chapter sets forth judgment and salvation in military and agrarian metaphors. Israel will be like a fruitful vineyard (vv. 2-3; compare 32:12). In parallel structure, Jacob will take root, Israel will bud and blossom. They will then fill the world with fruit (v. 6). In more literal and explicit terms, it is the Spirit who creates and works in his people to make them righteous (32:12-17). This promise is couched in such key terms as new creation, new exodus, and fruitfulness. Paul particularizes this time of the Spirit's activity in the new age as the new life in the Spirit. The coming of Jesus and the Spirit has thus fulfilled these and other Isaianic texts. *See* HOLY SPIRIT.

Bibliography: G. K. Beale. "The Old Testament Background of Paul's Reference to 'the Fruit of the Spirit' in Galatians 5:22." *Bulletin for Biblical Research* 15 (2005) 1–38; Richard N. Longenecker. *Galatians.* WBC 41 (1990).

BENNY C. AKER

FRUITS, FIRST. *See* FEASTS AND FASTS; FIRST FRUITS.

FRYING PAN [דּוּד *dudh*, מַרְחֶשֶׁת *markhesheth*, מַשְׂרֵת *masreth*; τήγανον *teganon*]. Cookware specialized for deep frying (Lev 2:7; 7:9; 1 Sam 2:14; 2 Sam 13:9; 2 Macc 7:5). *See* COOKING AND COOKING UTENSILS.

FUEL [אָכְלָה *'akhlah*; κατάβρωμα *katabroma*]. Many different kinds of material were used for fuel. Wood was the most common (e.g., Gen 22:3; Lev

1:7; Ezek 15:4, 6), although with the development of metallurgy, charcoal became more popular in later antiquity (e.g., John 18:18; 21:9). Other fuels included thorns (Ps 58:9; Eccl 7:6; Nah 1:10), grass (Matt 6:30), animal bones and excrements (Ezek 4:15; 24:10), and stubble (Exod 15:7). The law prescribed a continual fire on the altar (Lev 6:8-13), thus a constant supply of fuel (wood) was necessary (Neh 10:34). Figuratively, the Ammonites would be "fuel for the fire" (Ezek 21:32). *See* FURNACE.

MARK RONCACE

FULFILL, FULFILLMENT כָּלָה kalah, מָלֵא male᾽, עָשָׂה ᾽asah; πίμπλημι pimplēmi, πληρόω plēroō, τελέω teleō]. Christians have often associated the notion of fulfillment with the accomplishment or completing of God's purposes in Jesus. Yet the concept of fulfilling or enacting God's promises and appointed purposes, whether by God or humans, is widely present in the OT. The concept was also known among other Jewish groups in various forms (e.g. Qumran, CD 4:13-14; 1QM 11:5-6; 14:4-5; 1QS 3:16-18, 2314:4-5).

A. Fulfillment in the Old Testament and Apocrypha
  1. Fulfillment of a period of time
  2. Humans fulfilling God's will
  3. God fulfilling God's will
B. Fulfillment in the New Testament
  1. Fulfillment of a period of time
  2. Humans fulfilling God's will
  3. Jesus' fulfillment of the Scriptures
C. Hermeneutical and Theological Considerations
  1. Continuity
  2. Christological and eschatological convictions
  3. Perspectives and polemic
  4. Incarnation
  5. Interplay of the human and divine
  6. Proof-texts
Bibliography

A. Fulfillment in the Old Testament and Apocrypha
In the OT and Apocrypha, fulfillment language commonly denotes three meanings (verbs: male᾽, kalah, ᾽asah).

1. Fulfillment of a period of time

One sense of fulfillment concerns the accomplishment of a period of time. The completed time period can involve pregnancy (Gen 25:24), contracted work (Gen 29:21), days of liturgical service (Lev 8:33) and purification (Lev 12:4), a Nazirite's vows (Num 6:5, 13), one's life (2 Sam 7:12; Wis 4:13; Sir 26:2), and Babylonian exile (Jer 23:12; Tob 14:5).

2. Humans fulfilling God's will

A second sense concerns humans fulfilling, carrying out, or accomplishing God's purposes. In the Deuter-

onomistic History, Solomon banishes Abiathar from the priesthood, fulfilling God's threat of judgment (1 Kgs 2:27, recall 1 Sam 2:27-36; 3:10-14). Cyrus enacts or fulfills God's promise that the exiles will return from Babylon and rebuild the Temple (2 Chr 36:22; Ezra 1:1). Sirach knows that without the deceptions of divination, omens, and dreams (except those sent from God—how does one know?), "the law will be fulfilled." This fulfillment comprises humans living or performing the law's stipulations for worship and justice (Sir 34:8). Because Joshua "fulfilled the commandment, [he] became a judge in Israel" (1 Macc 2:55). The seven brothers, martyred by Antiochus Epiphanes, "fulfilled their service to God" in faithful obedience, even to death. The opposite sense of not performing or accomplishing God's purposes appears when Jeremiah condemns those who "accomplish" idolatry (Jer 44:25).

3. God fulfilling God's will

A third more common meaning comprises God fulfilling or accomplishing God's will. This usage appears in a general sense in Ps 20:4, where the psalmist prays for God to perform or enact the king's petitions. More often, the usage involves God performing or fulfilling what God has previously declared. In dedicating the Temple, e.g., Solomon blesses God for fulfilling God's promise to and covenant with David that David's son (Solomon) would build a house for God (1 Kgs 8:15, 24, and par., 2 Chr 6:4, 15). Often this sense of God accomplishing God's previously declared purposes concerns the Babylonian exile. In exiling the people as punishment, God accomplishes purposes of judgment (2 Chr 36:21, fulfilling Jer 25:11-12). "The Lord has done what he purposed, he has carried out/accomplished/fulfilled his threat" (Lam 2:17). But God also fulfills God's gracious promises to bring the people home. In underlining certain return from Babylonian exile, Isa 46:10 declares, "I am God . . . declaring the end from the beginning and from ancient times things not yet done, saying, 'My purpose shall stand, and I will fulfill my intention'." Isaiah 55:11 emphasizes the efficaciousness of God's declared purposes for the return: "my word . . . shall not return to me empty; but it shall accomplish that which I purpose and succeed in the thing for which I sent it." Perhaps Tob 14:5 captures both dimensions of punishment and salvation in presenting the return to and rebuilding of Jerusalem as happening when "the times of fulfillment shall come." *See* WILL OF GOD.

B. Fulfillment in the New Testament
These same three meanings of fulfillment appear in the NT:

1. Fulfillment of a period of time

The first meaning concerns the fulfillment or completion of a period of time. The passive construction is common and in some instances seems to underline

God's ordering of the time. New Testament writers, esp. Luke, use several verbs: plēroo, Luke 1:20 (Zechariah's silence until the angel's words are fulfilled); Acts 7:30 (Moses' exile in Midian); 9:23 (Saul/Paul in Damascus); 19:21 (Paul in Macedonia and Achaia); 24:27 (Felix's governorship); pimplēmi, Luke 1:23 (Zechariah's Temple service); 1:57 (Elizabeth's pregnancy); 2:6 (Mary's pregnancy); 2:21 (birth to circumcision); 2:22 (days of purification); Acts 7:23 (Moses' forty years); teleō, Luke 2:43 (end of Passover).

Several instances place greater emphasis on God's ordering of the time to accomplish/fulfill God's purposes. Mark begins Jesus' public activity with Jesus declaring, "the time is fulfilled" (Mark 1:15). In the absence of a verifiable widespread and unilateral 1st cent. messianic expectation, the verb emphasizes more the significance of the present as a time of God's activity rather than as the fulfillment of a long-awaited expectation. Luke depicts Jerusalem "trampled on by the Gentiles" (Rome's destruction of the city and Temple in 70 CE "until the times of the Gentiles are fulfilled" (Luke 21:24). These "times" seem to embrace a double significance involving both the Gentiles (= Rome) as God's agents in punishing Jerusalem, and as objects of the church's mission activity until the establishment of the eschaton. Also important is Luke 22:16 where Jesus declares he will not eat the Passover "until it is fulfilled in the kingdom of God." The future focus suggests an eschatological framework, while the link with Passover colors the coming establishment of God's purposes as liberation from oppressive powers. John 7:8 ("my time has not yet fully come") belongs with John's other indications of divinely ordained time ("my hour," 2:4; 12:23), particularly emphasizing Jesus' departure to the Father through crucifixion, resurrection, and ascension.

2. Humans fulfilling God's will

A second usage concerns humans fulfilling or performing or accomplishing God's will. One significant instance appears in Jesus' declaration in Matt 5:17 that "I have come not to abolish [the law and the prophets] but to fulfill them." The meaning of Jesus' claim is much debated, but some things are clear. The contrast with "abolish," repeated from 5:17a, indicates an ongoing significance for the law and prophets. To fulfill them cannot mean to supersede or replace them. The subsequent teaching of 5:21-48 ("You have heard it said . . . but I say to you . . .") confirms this, since in at least five of the six instances Jesus upholds in some way what was previously taught (the exception concerns revenge in 5:38-42). This teaching about practices of discipleship indicates that part of the fulfillment of the law and prophets involves doing their teaching. But while obedience is important, Matthew employs other language for doing Jesus' teaching (7:24) and keeping the/his commandments (28:20).

The use of other language suggests that "something more" is involved in fulfilling the law and prophets. The structure of 5:21-48, wherein Jesus quotes the tradition and interprets it, suggests that part of this "something more" involves Jesus' definitive interpretation and elaboration. He fulfills or completes the law and prophets by providing their definitive interpretation. Disciples are to live the law and prophets as interpreted by Jesus. Significantly, Jesus' interpretation is not alien to the tradition but derives from it. Twice Jesus quotes Hos 6:6 in Matt 9:13 and 12:7 to emphasize doing mercy. He declares the two greatest commandments of the law require love for God and humans (Matt 22:37-39). Again Jesus quotes the law, notably Deut 6:5 and Lev 19:18. Also comprising the "something more" is Matthew's understanding of the tradition's anticipatory or predictive function. In 11:13 the phrase "law and the prophets" forms the subject for the verb *prophesied*. This suggests that "fulfilling" the law and prophets involves the understanding that Jesus completes or accomplishes God's previously revealed purposes. I will return to this sense below in considering Matthew's fulfillment sayings in the discussion of the term's third meaning.

These factors also clarify Jesus' statement to John in Matt 3:15 that Jesus' baptism is necessary "to fulfill all righteousness." The verb *fulfill* at least includes the meaning "to do" since the baptism follows, and "obey" since God voices approval in v. 17. But something more than obedience again seems to be implied, because of the verb *fulfill* and its anticipatory or predictive sense. God's words in 3:17 concerning Jesus as God's beloved son echo Isa 42:1-4 (just and suffering servant), Ps 2 (king as God's agent), and Gen 22 (Abraham offering Isaac), suggesting that these references in some way anticipate Jesus' baptism. The baptism fulfills or performs or completes or accomplishes that anticipation.

Jesus is also presented as accomplishing or fulfilling God's purposes in the Gospels of Luke and John. In the transfiguration (Luke 9:31), Moses, Elijah, and Jesus discuss the latter's "exodus/departure that he was to accomplish/fulfill at Jerusalem." The term "exodus" denotes liberation from Egypt (Exod 19:1) and personal death (Wis 3:2; 7:6), suggesting that the conversation concerns Jesus accomplishing or performing God's purposes in his death, resurrection, and ascension (Luke 24:50-51). Twice in John's passion narrative, Jesus fulfills his own sayings. His betrayal by Judas in 18:5-9 performs or fulfills his statement about betrayal (17:12; also 6:39). His crucifixion performs or fulfills his claim of being lifted up (12:32-33).

Paul also emphasizes that humans fulfill or do God's purposes. God's will is made known in the law. In Rom 8:4 "the just requirement of the law" is fulfilled in those who "walk" (a Deuteronomic metaphor for living faithfully to covenant requirements) "according to the Spirit." The sending of the Son to condemn sin in the flesh and the coming of the Spirit provide empowerment for doing or fulfilling the law. This fulfilling centers for Paul, as for Jesus, on loving one's neighbor (Rom 13:8; Gal 5:14). Bearing another's burdens fulfills (anapleroō ἀναπληρόω, a compound of plēroō) "the law of Christ." The writer of 2 Thess 1:11 prays that God may "accomplish" or "fulfill by his power every good resolve and work of faith." Three instances use the verb *fulfill* for living out or accomplishing specific service for God. Barnabas and Saul "complete/accomplish/fulfill" their mission work (Acts 12:25) as do Paul and Barnabas (Acts 14:26). Archippus is urged to "see that you complete/fulfill the task that you have received in the Lord" (Col 4:17). James 2:23 sees expressions of faith in works as fulfilling Gen 15:6. Humans fulfill or accomplish God's will in living or doing it.

3. Jesus' fulfillment of the Scriptures

The third meaning of the term concerns the fulfillment or accomplishment of the Scriptures especially in the life of Jesus. This usage appears most frequently in Matthew and John, occasionally in Mark and Luke–Acts, but not in Paul. Some instances assert a generic claim that a particular act fulfilled, lived out, or was consistent with God's purposes previously made known or anticipated in the Scriptures. These usages do not specify or quote particular Scriptures. Examples include Mark 14:49, (Jesus' arrest ["But let the scriptures be fulfilled"]; compare Matt 26:56); Matt 26:54, (Jesus' arrest); Luke 21:22, (Jerusalem's impending fall in 70 CE [this happens in "days of vengeance as a fulfillment of all that is written"; the phrase "days of vengeance" derives from uncited Deuteronomic and prophetic declarations of judgment]; Deut 32:35; Hos 9:7); Luke 24:44, (all Jesus' activity); John 17:12, (Judas' betrayal); Acts 3:18, (Jesus' suffering ["God fulfilled what he foretold through all the prophets"]); Acts 13:27, (the Jerusalem leaders reject Jesus). Significantly, these unspecified and uncited passages especially concern aspects of Jesus' death. This focus suggests significant effort to interpret Jesus' death as expressive of God's will, consistent with the Scriptures, anticipated by them, and hence a fulfillment of them.

Matthew's Gospel includes at least ten declarations introduced with some variation on the formulaic, "this happened that what was spoken by the Lord/prophet might be fulfilled." The verb *fulfilled* is commonly passive to express divine action. These statements provide explicit scriptural reflection on an event in the Gospel story. Four appear in the birth narrative: Matt 1:22-23, (conception, citing Isa 7:14); Matt 2:15, (flight to and from Egypt, citing Hos 11:1); Matt 2:17-18, (grief after Herod's slaughter of the Bethlehem infants, citing Jer 31:15); and Matt 2:23, (Jesus in Nazareth, citing Isa 4:3). Four refer to Jesus' Galilean activity: Matt 4:14-16, (his whole ministry, citing Isa 9:1-2); Matt 8:17, (Jesus' healings, citing Isa 53:4); Matt 12:17-21, (Jesus'

ministry of justice, citing Isa 42:1-4, 9); Matt 13:35, (parables, citing Ps 78:2). Two appear in the passion narrative: Matt 21:5, (entering Jerusalem, citing Isa 62:11 and Zech 9:9); Matt 27:9-10, (the potter's field, citing Zech 11:13, influenced by Jer 18–19; 32). The cited texts variously resemble both the LXX and MT forms. Most (except Isa 53:4 and Zech 9:9) are not quoted in other NT writings. Matthew is especially reliant on the prophets (six from Isaiah, two cite or mention Jeremiah, two use Zechariah, one from Hosea) with only one drawn from the Psalms and none from the Pentateuch. Eight of the ten directly refer to Jesus.

Luke–Acts frames Jesus' ministry with a fulfillment claim. In the Nazareth synagogue, Jesus begins his ministry by reading from Isa 61:1-2 and declares, "Today this scripture has been fulfilled in your hearing" (Luke 4:18-21). Unlike Matthew, Luke's Jesus, rather than the narrator, makes the claim. The Isaiah text, part of a Sabbath-Jubilee tradition that envisioned a just society, sets the agenda for Jesus' Spirit-directed activity throughout the gospel and Acts. Acts similarly begins with a fulfillment text but it concerns Judas directly and Jesus indirectly (1:16-20). Judas' betrayal is seen to be consistent with and to enact Pss 69:25 and 109:8. A subsequent sermon from Paul in 13:32-33 sees God raising Jesus as fulfilling what "God promised to our ancestors . . . in the second psalm" (Ps 2:7).

John's Gospel cites Scriptures in five fulfillment statements. John 12:38-40, using an introductory formula similar to Matthew's, explains failure to believe in Jesus by citing Isa 53:1 and 6:10 to emphasize God's (non)revealing activity. John 15:25 cites Ps 69:4 to explain it as hatred. John 13:18 interprets Judas' imminent betrayal by citing Ps 41:9. Two aspects of Jesus' crucifixion, taking his tunic (John 19:24) and not breaking his legs (19:36) fulfill Ps 22:18 and Exod 12:10, 46, respectively. The latter incident is linked with a second Scripture (Zech 12:10) though fulfillment language is not used. Whereas Matthew and Luke use fulfillment statements for all of Jesus' activity, John focuses only on aspects of the passion, Jesus' rejection (twice), Judas's betrayal (also Matthew and Luke–Acts but with different texts), and aspects of the crucifixion (twice). Unlike Matthew, John's OT texts appear elsewhere in NT writings (except Ps 41:9).

C. Hermeneutical and Theological Considerations

How are we to understand the claim that in these various events God fulfills or performs or completes God's purposes? The issues are complex. At least six dimensions can be briefly noted.

1. Continuity

That the NT employs similar uses of fulfill/fulfillment as the OT is significant for understanding the relationship of the two testaments. The OT is not a book of promises whose accomplishment or fulfillment must await the coming of Jesus and the NT. The OT shows the dynamic of proclamation or declaration of God's purposes and their subsequent accomplishment already operative. The presence of this dynamic reminds us of the historical and theological indebtedness of NT writers to the Hebrew tradition and identifies an element of continuity between the testaments.

2. Christological and eschatological convictions

But similarity and continuity are not the only elements. The NT writers read the OT through a particular lens not shared by other readers either before or during the 1st cent. They read the Scriptures and wrote the NT texts with hindsight, several decades after Jesus' ministry. They read as part of a protracted process of reflection on and discernment about God's purposes manifested in Jesus. They read from the distinctive perspective of commitment to Jesus. They understood him as the definitive agent of God's purposes, the one in whom God's purposes were definitively revealed and enacted in anticipation of their eschatological completion. Moreover, they read with the conviction that God had raised Jesus from the dead. Claims of resurrection belong to a cluster of eschatological motifs and express the conviction that the new era in which God's purposes of justice and life were to be established was underway. That is, the fulfillment language used by NT writers reflects christological and eschatological convictions. *See* CHRISTOLOGY; ESCHATOLOGY OF THE NT.

3. Perspectives and polemic

These christological and eschatological perspectives are often forgotten or misunderstood when Christian discourse blames Jews, past and present, for not understanding the supposedly "obvious" references in the Scriptures to Jesus. It must be remembered that these references were not obvious to anyone without christological and eschatological perspectives. The Qumran community, e.g., also read the Scriptures but through the perspective of their own experiences and history. Not surprisingly, they found their own story anticipated in the Scriptures and interpreted the Scriptures in that light. Similarly, NT writers, looking back on the ministry of Jesus, saw references in the Scriptures to Jesus where no other readers had seen them.

4. Incarnation

The Christian tradition, borrowing Jewish convictions, has affirmed the central importance of encountering God within human experience and history. Jesus "enfleshes" God's words, actions, purposes, will (John 1:14). Accordingly, to claim that the OT comprised predictions or promises that no one understood for hundreds of years until Jesus came seriously violates the Judeo-Christian affirmation of human history as the locus of God's revelation. Rather, texts that NT writers cite in relation to Jesus had functioned for faithful communities in different contexts for hundreds of years with quite different meanings. Hosea 11:1 (Matt 2:15) refers to Israel; Ps 2:7 (Acts 13:32-33) refers to Israel's king. The promise of a child in Isa 7:14, cited in Matt 1:23, did not lie dormant for some 800 years but addressed its own 8th cent. context of fear and threat from Israelite-Syrian and Assyrian imperialism. The child is the future of Judah, indicating that Judah will not be destroyed if it trusts God. Matthew sees his own situation under Roman imperialism post-70 CE as analogous, thereby interpreting the Isaiah text as anticipating and promising God's salvation from Rome. Matthew claims the promise as christological and eschatological, and celebrates God's accomplishment or fulfillment of it in Jesus. Matthew again cites Isa 7–9 in 4:15-16 to interpret or frame Jesus' ministry as another act of God in saving the people. These rich and multivalent texts have multiple meanings for diverse contexts and perspectives.

5. Interplay of the human and divine

The fulfillment language raises the question of the interplay of divine DETERMINISM and human free will. Does God accomplish God's purposes in disregard for or in relation to human agency? Though the NT language often emphasizes divine work, the role of human agency is important.

6. Proof-texts

Scholars have debated whether the NT writers selected proof-texts or "one-liners" from the OT without regard for contexts, or whether the cited verse refers to larger passages and traditions. Often the latter occurs. Both spoken and written texts in oral societies frequently employ "metonymic" citation, whereby a small part of a larger tradition or text is cited to evoke the larger text. The audience uses the small part to recall and elaborate the larger tradition. For instance, in citing verses from several lament psalms (Ps 69:4 in John 15:25; Ps 22:18 in John 19:24; Ps 69:25 in Acts 1:16-20), NT writers evoke the much larger paradigm of the righteous sufferer vindicated by God to explain Jesus' death. *See* PLEROMA; PROMISE.

Bibliography: Warren Carter. "Evoking Isaiah: Why Summon Isaiah in Matthew 1:23 and 4:15-16?" and "'To Save His People from Their Sins.'" *Matthew and Empire: Initial Explorations* (2001) 75–107; W. D. Davies and Dale C. Allison. *The Gospel According to Saint Matthew.* Vols 1–3. (1997); J. D. G. Dunn. "The Law." *The Theology of Paul the Apostle* (1998) 128–61; C. F. D. Moule. "Fulfillment Words in the New Testament: Use and Abuse." *NTS* 14 (1968) 293–320; C. M. Tuckett, ed. *The Scriptures in the Gospels* (1997).

WARREN CARTER

FULL, TO BE OR TO FILL [מָלֵא male', שָׂבַע sava'; μεστός mestos, πίμπλημι pimplēmi, πλήρης plērēs, πληρόω plēroō]. To be occupied or to occupy plentifully. At God's command animals plentifully occupied the waters and the skies; and humans, the earth (Gen 1:22-28). *To be full* or *to fill* refers to the bountiful manner in which God bestows blessings (Deut 33:23; Pss 65:9; 81:10), wisdom (Deut 34:9; Jas 3:17), glory (Isa 6:3; Ezek 43:5), knowledge (Isa 11:9), justice (Isa 33:5), God's spirit (Luke 4:1), children (Ruth 1:20), and joy and peace (Rom 15:13). The concept also refers to the glory dwelling in Jesus (John 1:14), amazement at Jesus' miracles (Luke 5:26), and the indwelling of power in Jesus' followers (Acts 2:4; 6:8; 13:52; Eph 5:18). Negatively, the concept refers to an abundance of material possessions (Prov 30:9) and lies (Acts 5:3). Metaphorically, the concept refers to murder (Isa 1:15) and adultery (2 Pet 2:14). *See* FULFILL, FULFILLMENT.

EMILY R. CHENEY

FULLER [כֹּבֵס koves; γναφεύς gnapheus]. Raw fibers contain oily and sticky substances that must be removed to make clothing. A fuller prepared cloth in a process that includes cleaning by beating or rubbing, and washing in detergents like LYE (Mal 3:2). The fabric was then spread out to be bleached by the sun. Consequently, the process became a symbol for purity. For example, during the transfiguration, Jesus' cloak is described as whiter than any fuller (RSV) could make it (Mark 9:3).

Bibliography: Philip J. King and Lawrence E. Stager. *Life in Biblical Israel* (2001).

JENNIFER L. KOOSED

FULLER'S FIELD [שְׂדֵה כֹבֵס sedheh khoves]. A location south of Jerusalem between the Kidron and Hinnom valleys reached by way of a road near the conduit of the Upper Pool. Associated with Isaiah's encounter with Ahaz (Isa 7:3), it was also the Assyrians' encampment as Sennacherib approached Jerusalem (2 Kgs 18:17; Isa 36:2).

DEREK E. WITTMAN

FULLNESS OF TIME [πλήρωμα τοῦ χρόνου (τῶν καιρῶν) plērōma tou chronou (tōn kairōn)]. Rooted in APOCALYPTICISM, this term designates the completion of one preordained historical period and the dawn of a new era, often characterized by the redemption of God's elect. In the NT, the visitation of God's Son on earth marks the transition between these two ages (Gal 4:4; Eph 1:10). *See* ESCHATOLOGY OF THE NT; FULFIL, FULFILLMENT; PLEROMA.

JAMES A. METZGER

FUNERALS. Although there is no Hebrew or Greek equivalent, the NRSV uses "funeral" with reference to burial rites and procedures (Tob 14:11; 1 Macc 9:41; 2 Macc 4:49; 5:10). *See* BURIAL; MOURNING; TOMB.

JAMES A. METZGER

FURNACE [כּוּר kur, כִּבְשָׁן kivshan, תַּנּוּר tannur; Aram. אַתּוּן 'attun; κάμινος kaminos]. Used to translate the Hebrew kur and kivshan, and the Aramaic 'attun. It means an enclosed chamber where FUEL is converted into heat for the purpose of smelting or refining ore or to make lime. *Furnace,* meaning OVEN, is used to translate tannur. In the NT, kaminos is translated *furnace*. The infrequently used Hebrew words 'alil (עֲלִיל) and moqedh (מוֹקֵד) are also rendered *furnace*, as is the LXX chōneutērion (χωνευτήριον). *See* REFINING.

References to furnace are most often used metaphorically to indicate God's judgment or testing. In the account of the destruction of Sodom and Gomorrah, the intensity of the cities' destruction is likened to "the smoke of a furnace" (Gen 19:28). This same image of destructive fury is alluded to by the prophet Isaiah, who indicates that unjust Assyrian conquerors have much to fear from God's judgment, "whose fire is in Zion, and whose furnace is in Jerusalem" (Isa 31:9, see also Ps 21:9). In addition, the refining of metals can serve as a metaphor for the people Israel, as God chastises them for their failures to seek righteousness (Ezek 22:20, 22). When such biblical texts stress Israel's failures, the nation is likened to dross (Ezek 22:18). Nonetheless, sometimes the metaphor is used to show that Israel has more than passed God's trial. For example, Second Isaiah remarks that Israel's refining surpasses that of fine metals: "See, I have refined you, but not like silver; I have tested you in the furnace of adversity" (Isa 48:10).

Allusions to the refining powers of furnaces are found in contexts that anticipate the Israelites' repentance or deliverance. The experience of slavery in Egypt is referred to as an iron crucible (furnace) from which God redeemed the people (Deut 4:20; 1 Kgs 8:5). These texts emphasize that suffering was part of God's plan so that the people would learn to obey the covenant and would be bound to God as a beloved people (Jer 11:4). It is interesting to note that the awesome effects of refining may be invoked here, for even God's own promises are described as being refined by a furnace (Ps 12:6).

There are occasions when the image of smoke and a furnace is used in the context of the language of theophany, in which God's presence is made known on earth by natural phenomena. When God makes a covenant with Abraham, promising him land and descendants, the patriarch responds by preparing animals for sacrifice. The animals are cut in two. In this covenant ratification ceremony, God signifies acceptance of Abraham's offering by passing through the pieces of the animals by "a smoking firepot (furnace), and a flaming torch" (Gen 15:17). The transcendence of the scene is underscored by its mysteriousness. The theophany occurs at night. Abraham is in a "deep sleep," and he is overcome by terror (Gen 15:12). Similarly, when God gives the Israelites the covenant at Mount Sinai, the theophany is the presence of smoke, fire, and an earthquake (Exod 19:18). The scene is so overwhelming that God warns Moses to alert the priests and people to keep away, lest they die (*see* THEOPHANY IN THE OT). In the book of Revelation, the arrival of the Son of Man who comes in judgment also uses the language of theophany: "his feet were like burnished bronze, refined as in a furnace, and his voice was like the sound of many waters" (Rev 1:15). *See* THEOPHANY IN THE NT.

Perhaps it is the overpowering nature of the furnace that lies behind the depiction of its ashes in the plague narratives of Exodus. When God commands Aaron and Moses to scatter "handfuls of soot from the kiln (furnace)" in front of Pharaoh, the plague of boils descends upon man and beast (Exod 9:8, 10).

The fiery furnace in the book of Daniel (Dan 3) is the place of the trial and miraculous deliverance of three Jewish captives, Hananiah, Mishael, and Azariah, known in this narrative by their given Babylonian names, Shadrach, Meshach, and Abednego. Nebuchadnezzar's henchmen set them up for a test; they goad the king to issue a decree that whoever does not bow to the golden idol will be cast into a fiery furnace. Given a final chance to comply by the king, the three testify to their unwavering faith in God—regardless of God's decision to save them. The fiery furnace becomes a showcase for God's divine justice as well as the exiles' courage: an angel appears alongside the Jews, they remain completely unharmed. Nebuchadnezzar acknowledges God and rewards his captives. This image of the fiery furnace as a polemic against IDOLATRY is also found in the midrash that tells of Abraham being cast into the fiery furnace on the orders of King Nimrod when he refuses to honor Nimrod's gods (*Gen. Rab.* 38.13). As are Shadrach, Meshach, and Abednego, Abraham emerges unscathed, testifying to the one God (*see* DANIEL, BOOK OF).

When referring to the future judgment that the Son of Man will accomplish on earth, the author of the book of Matthew includes the image of a furnace of fire, the place of punishment for sinners (Matt 13:42, 50). Similarly, the book of Revelation includes this terrifying scene of the bottomless pit of divine punishment: "from the shaft rose smoke like the smoke of a great furnace, and the sun and the air were darkened with the smoke from the shaft" (v. 9:2).

SHARON PACE

FURNITURE [כְּלִי keli; σκεῦος skeuos, κατασκεύασμα kataskeuasma]. The Hebrew word refers to any item that is manufactured for a specific purpose. While it is usually translated "article, utensil, implement, vessel," it often refers generally to items whose use is specified by modifying words, e.g., weapons for hunting or war (Judg 18:11, 16, 17), the equipment of oxen (2 Sam 24:22), musical instruments (Amos 6:5; 1 Chr 15:16), various implements made of metal and used as tools (1 Kgs 6:7), or the equipment used with a chariot (1 Sam 8:12). It is translated "furniture" when referring to the implements and furnishings of the tabernacle (Exod 25:9; 40:9), of the Temple in Jerusalem (1 Chr 9:29), and of Tobiah's or Holofernes's home furnishings (Neh 13:8; Jdt 15:11). The Greek words are used most often to mean "vessel." *See* VESSELS.

C. MARK McCORMICK

FURROW [גְּדוּד gedhudh, מַעֲנָה maʿanah, נִיר nir, תֶּלֶם telem]. A furrow is a shallow trench dug in the soil for planting. The OT presents different terms for furrows depending on their function and role. The term nir (Jer 4:3; Hos 10:12) designates a furrow in a virgin field. Maʿanah (1 Sam 14:14) was a furrow that marked the distance the seeds could be broadcast. Telem was a generic term for a furrow, though actually it referred to the ridge of the furrow, while gedhudh referred to the depression (Ps 65:11 [Heb. 65:10]). *See* PLOW; TOOLS.

Bibliography: O. Borowski. *Agriculture in Iron Age Israel* (2002).

ODED BOROWSKI

GAAL gay´uhl [גַּעַל ga'al]. Gaal challenged ABIM-ELECH's attempt to establish a hereditary monarchy during the period of the judges (Judg 9:26-41). When Gaal, an outsider, moved into Shechem, the people put their trust in him. During a festival in the temple while Abimelech was away, Gaal challenged his right to rule. ZEBUL, the governor of the city, reported it to Abimelech, who defeated Gaal and his men the next morning in battle, and they were forced to leave Shechem. *Gaal* means "dung-beetle," which may be a slur on his inability to rule the city. *See* SHECHEM, SHECHEMITES.

KEVIN A. WILSON

GAASH gay´ash [גַּעַשׁ ga'ash]. A mountain, probably 30 km to the southwest of Shechem, to the north of which Joshua is said to have been buried in Timnath-serah in the hill country of Ephraim (Josh 24:30; Judg 2:9). One of David's fighting men hailed from the nearby wadis of Gaash (2 Sam 23:30; 1 Chr 11:32).

DEREK E. WITTMAN

GABAEL gab´ay-uhl [Γαβαήλ Gabaēl]. Son of Gabreas and brother of Gabri from the region of Rages in Media (Tob 1:14; 4:20). Tobit entrusts him with the care of ten talents of silver (Tob 1:14), which he later sends his son TOBIAS to reclaim (Tob 5:3). *See* TOBIT, BOOK OF.

GABATHA gab´uh-thuh [Γαβάθα Gabatha]. One of two eunuchs, the other being Tharra, who conspired against King Ahasuerus until MORDECAI intervened (Add Esth 12:1). The name BIGTHAN appears in the MT instead (Esth 2:21; 6:2).

GABBAI gab´i [גַּבָּי gabbay]. One of the Benjaminite leaders who settled in Jerusalem when Judahites and Benjaminites were repopulating it during the Persian period (Neh 11:8).

GABBATHA gab´uh-thuh [Γαββαθά Gabbatha]. Gabbatha is the Greek transliteration of an Aramaic word that refers to the elevated stone pavement upon which Pilate sat when he dispensed public judgment. The name is used only in John 19:13, a passage describing Jesus' trial before Pilate, and corresponds to the Greek name **Lithostrōtos** (Λιθόστρωτος). The Aramaic word is from a root meaning "to be high." Textual investigation (references from Philo and Josephus) as well as archaeological excavation suggest that Pilate's Gabbatha was outside of Herod's palace (south of the Jaffa Gate). Archaeologists uncovered a podium that stands twelve ft. higher than the foundations of the palace. If their inferences are correct, then the pavement was approximately 1,100 ft. long and 200 ft. wide. Most archaeologists dismiss the claim by the Sisters of Zion Convent that the stone pavement beneath their building is the site of Jesus' confrontation with the Roman ruler.

Bibliography: John McRay. *Archaeology and the New Testament* (1991).

JENNIFER L. KOOSED

GABRIAS gay´bree-uhs [Γαβριάς Gabrias]. Also spelled Gabri. He appears as the brother of GABAEL in Tob 1:14, but is later described as his father (4:20).

GABRIEL gay´bree-uhl [גַּבְרִיאֵל gavri'el; Γαβριήλ Gabriēl]. Angel named twice in Daniel (8:16; 9:21) and in Luke (1:19, 26). According to several Second Temple Jewish documents, Gabriel ("God is my mighty one") was one of the four archangels, along with Michael (Dan 10:13, 21; 12:1; Jude 9; Rev 12:7), Sariel, and Raphael (named twenty times in Tobit). In Daniel, Gabriel functions as interpreter of the prophet's vision (8:15-26) and of Scripture (9:20-27, wherein the angel ex-plains Jeremiah's "seventy weeks"). In Luke, his role is to bring news of the impending births of John and Jesus to Zechariah and Mary. When Zechariah asks for proof, Gabriel, citing his rank as one who stands before the Lord, lays a temporary curse on the aged priest. The Book of the Watchers (*1 En.* 1–36) names Gabriel as the angel in charge of Eden, the cherubim, and the serpents (20:2), and he is both intercessor for the persecuted (9:1) and ultimate executioner of the wicked (9:9-10). According to the War Scroll from Qumran (1QM), the names of the four archangels appear on the shields of the towers of God's army; presumably they are the spirits who fight for the sons of light in the decisive battle. *See* ANGEL.

RICHARD B. VINSON

GAD THE SEER, WORDS OF. *See* BOOKS REFERRED TO IN THE BIBLE.

GAD, GADITES gad, gad´it [גָּד gadh, גָּדִי gadhi; Γάδ Gad, Γαδδί Gaddi]. 1. Gad is the seventh son of Jacob and eponymous ancestor of the tribe of Gad. Gad's mother, ZILPAH, the maidservant of LEAH, bore Gad on behalf of Leah. Leah named the child "Gad" (Gen 30:11), a name meaning "good fortune." The name's

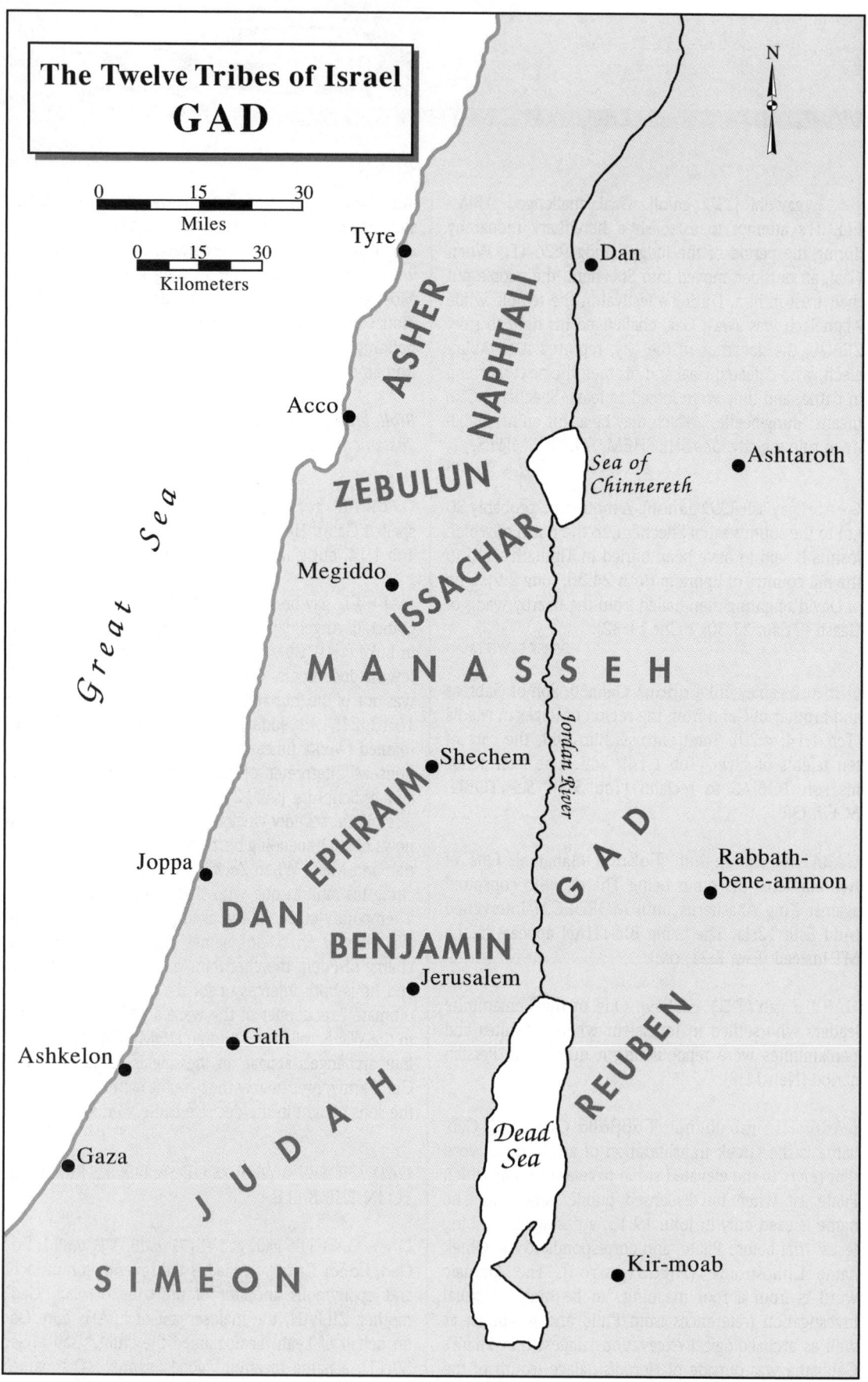

The Twelve Tribes of Israel
GAD

meaning may derive from its association with a deity of good fortune also named "Gad" (see Isa 65:11) who is well known from ancient Aramaic, Syriac, and Arabic texts. No actions of the man Gad are recorded; the Bible focuses exclusively on the tribe. Jacob's blessing suggests that Gad's history will be marked by episodes of violence (Gen 49:19). Moses' blessing upon Gad also forecasts a violent future, but it adds the positive note that Gad will receive "a commander's allotment" of "the best of [the land]" and will take a leading role among its people (Deut 33:20–21). Most of what we know about Gad we learn from Israel's entry and settlement stories in which Gad plays a prominent role alongside Reuben. The key texts may be summarized in seven scenes.

a. Gad and Reuben's petition (Num 32). Gad and Reuben petition MOSES to assign them territories east of the Jordan, a land with good pastures for their many cattle (see TRIBES, TERRITORIES OF). Moses assumes they are refusing to cross the Jordan with the other tribes and accuses them of committing again the sin of the faithless spies who hesitated to enter Canaan. Gad and Reuben promise to help the other tribes conquer Canaan before settling in their land; Moses relents and grants them the recently conquered land of kings Sihon of Heshbon and Og of Bashan. Gad rebuilds eight cities that lie in two separate areas, one located between the Arnon River and the Wadi Wala and the other in the area extending from Heshbon about 16 mi. northeast to Jogbehah and including part of the southern Jordan Valley (see REUBEN, REUBENITES).

b. Moses' recapitulation of the allotments and obligation to assist (Deut 3:8-22). Moses reminds Israel of the tribal allotments of Gad, Reuben, and the half-tribe of Manasseh and of their obligation to participate in the conquest of Canaan (see MANASSEH, MANASSITES). The territory allotted to the three tribes east of the Jordan is here defined more expansively than in scene one; it now includes the Jordan Valley, "the Arabah," between the Dead Sea and the Sea of Chinnereth. Reuben and Gad are treated as a single unit in the description of their territorial inheritance.

c. Joshua's recapitulation of the obligation to assist (Josh 1:12-18). Preparatory to crossing into Canaan, JOSHUA reminds Gad, Reuben, and the half-tribe of Manasseh of their obligation to help the other tribes conquer Canaan. Their compliance is briefly noted in Josh 4:12 (see CANAAN, CANAANITES).

d. The list of conquered kings (Josh 12:1-6). The narrator recounts all the kings that Israel has defeated, beginning with the two kings east of the Jordan: King Sihon of Heshbon who ruled the territory from the Arnon to the Jabbok River, including the Arabah from the Sea of Chinnereth southward to the Dead Sea, and King Og of Bashan who ruled the territory from Hermon southward to the Jabbok. Again, the territory allotted to the tribes east of the Jordan is defined more expansively than in scene one.

e. Joshua's recapitulation of allotments (Josh 13:8-33). Moses' allotments to Gad, Reuben, and the half-tribe of Manasseh are defined by a list of cities for the second time. Significant differences between this list and the list in scene one are apparent. The southern territory around Dibon, Ataroth, and Aroer as well as all Mishor (the tableland around Madaba) up to the banks of the Jordan is assigned to Reuben rather than to Gad. Gad's territory now includes the area from Heshbon northward to approximately the Jabbok River. The border between Gad and Reuben is located just north of Heshbon.

f. Release from obligation (Josh 22:1-9). Joshua releases Reuben, Gad, and the half-tribe of Manasseh from their obligation to assist in the conquest of Canaan.

g. The altar at the border (Josh 22:10-34). On their way home, Reuben, Gad, and the half-tribe of Manasseh build an altar near the Jordan. The Israelites judge this an act of apostasy. A delegation of Israelites accuses the eastern tribes of rebellion against the LORD and likens their act to "the sin at Peor" (Num 25) and to the sin of Achan (Josh 7). The accused tribes respond saying they have built a "copy of the altar of the LORD" not for sacrifice, but as a "witness between us that the LORD is God" to remind Israel that the tribes east of the Jordan have a legitimate "portion in the LORD." This answer satisfies the delegation, and war is averted.

Several things are immediately apparent. First, almost everywhere in the entry and settlement narratives Gad acts in concert with Reuben and, often, the half-tribe of Manasseh. Only in the city lists defining tribal allotments is Gad sometimes treated as a separate entity (Num 32:34-36; Josh 13:24-28). The shared fate of Gad and Reuben arises from their both having large herds of cattle for which the land east of the Jordan is well suited (a circumstance incongruous with the depravations suffered during the wilderness wanderings; Num 32:1; Deut 3:19). Second, the city lists in scenes one and five disagree about Gad's allotment. The list of Gadite cities in Num 32:34-36, which is considered to be the oldest source, places Gad both south and north of Reuben, but the Deuteronomistic (see DEUTERONOMISTIC HISTORY) sources consistently support the list in Josh 13:24-28, which places Gad's territory north of Reuben's (see Deut 3:17; 4:43; Josh 12:1-6; 20:8; 21:38). Third, the two longest scenes, one and seven, share similar themes. Both raise the possibility that the eastern tribes will forget their national identity and act in disregard of their obligations to the tribal confederacy, and both are concerned that the eastern tribes will act as earlier faithless Israelites have acted and bring divine wrath upon all the tribes. Together scenes one and seven suggest that the tribes east of the Jordan symbolize a threat to Israel's national unity and religious institutions.

Determining the earliest location of Gad's tribal inheritance requires that one resolve the conflict between Num 32:34-36 and the Deuteronomistic texts (scenes two through five). One must consider the possibility that the geo-political realities of the author's world have been retrojected into the world of the text. The biblical writers sometimes borrowed from earlier lists and narratives to create literary composites, thereby distorting earlier historical and geographical realities. This appears to be the case in Num 32:34-36, where an original list of Gadite cities that included Dibon, Ataroth, Aroer, and Atroth-shophan has been augmented with cities drawn from Josh 13. The addition to the list of these final four cities results in the odd picture of Gad inhabiting territory both north and south of Reuben. Joshua 13 appears also to be a combination of several texts the author/editor had available. The late date usually assigned to Deuteronomistic texts casts doubt on the reliability of their historical geography. For this reason, the expansive picture of Gad's territory is often judged a late idealization of doubtful historical value. Thus, the list of cities in Num 32:34-35*a*, which defines Gad as the area around Dibon, Ataroth, and Aroer provides the most reliable witness available to Gad's earliest territory. These cities all lie in an area extending north about 10 mi. from the Arnon Gorge. Support for this location comes from the place name "Dibon-gad" (Num 33:45-46), from 2 Kgs 10:33 in which the ordering of names implies that Gad's territory lies south of Reuben's and includes Aroer, and from the Mesha Stele, a memorial inscription describing the accomplishments of King MESHA who reigned over Moab from Dibon in the later part of the 9th cent. BCE (*see* MOAB, MOABITES). The Mesha Stele states, "Now the men of Gad had lived in the land of Ataroth from ancient times" (10).

One must consider, however, the possibility that the discrepancy in the city lists derives from historical change as much as from literary borrowing and editing. The conflict may be resolved by assuming that the tribe of Gad migrated northward at some point. In this case the depiction of Gad inhabiting territory from Heshbon northward would have historical value as a testimony to Gad's location at a time later than the story world. Evidence to support this hypothesis includes the following: Jer 49:1-6 and Josh 21:38-39 both mention Heshbon as a Gadite city; lists of Levitical cities and cities of refuge name RAMOTH-GILEAD as a Gadite city (Deut 4:43; Josh 20:8; 21:38); and Gad is frequently associated with Gilead (e.g., 1 Sam 13:7; *see* GILEAD, GILEADITES).

The association of Gad and Gilead might, however, date from early in Israel's history. In a post-battle roll call of Israelite tribes, the Song of Deborah lists Gilead where one expects to find Gad (Judg 5:15-17). Significantly, the disloyalty theme prominent in scenes one and seven appears here also. After reproaching Reuben for dithering in indecision and "tarrying among the sheepfolds," Deborah reproaches Gilead/Gad because it "stayed beyond the Jordan" while other tribes helped rout the Canaanite oppressor.

The question of religious fidelity dominates scene seven. The altar built by the Jordan constitutes apostasy, since by Deuteronomistic reckoning, sacrifices may be offered only at the central tabernacle/temple (Deut 12:1-12). The story also expresses concern that future generations of Israelites might one day reject their religious unity with the tribes east of the Jordan and refuse them participation in Israelite worship (Josh 22:24-25). Perhaps, for the narrator, this projected future in which tribes east and west of the Jordan are alienated has arrived. This would explain the narrator's rendering of "the Reubenites and the Gadites in the land of Gilead" as distinct from "the land of Canaan . . . the Israelites" (22:32). Indeed, the land east of the Jordan may even be "unclean"; at the least, it is a realm distinct from "the LORD's land" (22:19).

Gad's earliest territory lay in a region often dominated by Moab, and the history of Gad must, therefore, be mapped against the background of Moabite history. The entry and settlement narratives present conflicting information about Moab's presence in the territory assigned to Gad and Reuben. Some texts state that Israel conquered the territory given to Gad and Reuben by the Amorite king, Sihon, who reigned from Heshbon (Num 21:21-31; 32:33; Deut 1:4; 2:31-37; 4:46; 29:7-9; Josh 12:1-6; 13:8-11, 21). Other texts use the term "the plains of Moab" to describe the area northwest of Mount Pisgah (Num 26:63; 31:12; 33:48-50, etc.) and suggest that during the settlement period Moab controlled this area (Num 22–24; compare Judg 3). Additionally, archaeological work has shown that HESHBON, Sihon's supposed capital, was largely unoccupied during the entry and settlement period. The SIHON story thus appears the less reliable of the two pictures and may in fact have served polemically to undercut Moab's claim that Israel had poached its land (the Sihon story is similarly used against an Ammonite claim, see Judg 11:12-28). In short, it is probable that Israel encountered a Moabite presence when they entered the land Gad and Reuben would inherit (*see* MOAB, MOABITES).

Outside the entry and settlement narratives, we hear of Gad several times. During the reign of King Saul, we learn that the Ammonite king Nahash oppressed Gad and Reuben, gouging out their right eyes to weaken their resistance (1 Sam 10: lines following v. 27; text restored based on 4Q51; *see* DEAD SEA SCROLLS), and, later, we learn that some of the Israelites fled across the Jordan into Gad to escape Philistine oppression (1 Sam 13:7). David was able to conquer Moab early in the 10th cent. BCE (2 Sam 8:2, 12), but apparently Israel's control of the area slipped soon after Solomon's death. King Omri reasserted Israel's dominance about 880 BCE. We know this from the Mesha Stele that records that Israel exercised control over the land of Madaba (*see* MEDEBA) during the reign of Mesha's father (Mesha Stele, 4-6) but that about thirty years later, Mesha rebelled against Israel and reestablished control over the land of Madaba. The rebellion occurred toward the end of King Ahab's reign (ca. 853 BCE), and the Bible confirms its success (2 Kgs 1:1; 3:4-5). How long Moab continued to control the land allotted to Reuben and Gad is unclear, but this probably occurred sometime after the Mesha Stele was written (ca. 840 BCE) and before the end of Jehu's reign (ca. 816 BCE). Second Kings 10:32-36 reports that toward the end of Jehu's reign Israel lost control of the Transjordan to the Syrian king Hazael. But by the time of Isaiah, it seems that Moab had again asserted its authority between the Arnon and Heshbon, only to lose it again, not to Israel, but to an unnamed nation. Isaiah 15–16 (compare Jer 48–49) laments, possibly with deep sarcasm, Moab's loss of at least eight cities that were once assigned to Gad and Reuben. Presumably, the nation responsible for this attack remained in control of the territory until the destruction of Israel in 722 BCE. Whatever remnant of Gad remaining after 722 probably migrated into the area north of Heshbon, where the Deuteronomistic editors locate the Gadite homeland in their own time.

Gad appears once in the NT in a list of tribes marked for protection from the plagues of the apocalypse (Rev 7:5).

Bibliography: J. A. Dearman, ed. *Studies in the Mesha Inscription and Moab* (1989); R. Nelson. *Joshua.* OTL (1997); J. Van Seters. "The Conquest of Sihon's Kingdom. A Literary Examination." *JBL* 91 (1972) 182–97.

BRIAN C. JONES

2. Gad the "seer" or prophet is prominent in the David narratives. He advised David to leave Moab (1 Sam 22:3-5). Gad was God's spokesperson concerning the sin of David's census (2 Sam 24:11; 1 Chr 21:9-10). Gad instructed David to purchase the threshing floor of Araunah and build an altar on it when the plague against Israel ended (2 Sam 24:18; 2 Chr 21:18). Gad participated in the formation of Levitical music (2 Chr 29:25). According to Chronicles, the "Chronicles of Gad the Seer" were used in the compilation of the Chronicler's history (2 Chr 29:29).

MICHAEL G. VANZANT

3. A deity of good luck. Isaiah 65:11-12 condemns a group in post-exilic Judah for participating in libation rituals in worship of the deities Gad and MENI. Gad was also worshiped by the Phoenicians and is identifiable with the Greek Tyche and the Latin Fortuna.

TREVOR COCHELL

GAD, VALLEY TOWARD [הַנַּחַל הַגָּד hannakhal haggadh]. The area of the Gadites (Gen 35:26) in Gilead, and starting place for the census David commands Joab to undertake (2 Sam 24:5).

GADARA, GADARENES gad´uh-ruh, gad´uh-reen [Γαδαρά Gadara, Γαδαρηνός Gadarēnos]. A town of the DECAPOLIS, about 6 mi. southeast of the Sea of Galilee. According to Matt 8:28, two DEMONIACs living among the tombs met Jesus there, but Mark 5:1, Matthew's probable source, names the place "Gerasa," (so also Luke 8:26; *see* GERASA, GERASENES). Gerasa, also part of the Decapolis, was over 30 mi. from the lake in the same direction. The manuscript tradition of all three Synoptics is tangled; some texts read "of the Gergesenes." If "of the Gerasenes" is the correct reading for Mark 5:1, then presumably "of the Gadarenes" is Matthew's attempt to move the episode closer to the lake, sparing the pigs a thirty-mile jog to their drowning and making the story geographically more plausible. From the time of Pompey's campaign (63 BCE), Gadara was a Gentile city. Herod the Great included it in his territory, but after his death it was an independent part of the province of Syria. Although Jewish soldiers occupied Gadara at the beginning of the War of 66–70, Vespasian's arrival liberated the city (Josephus, *J.W.* 4.413-35); the Jewish troops tried to escape but were all killed, some of them by drowning in the Jordan.

RICHARD B. VINSON

GADDI gad´i [גַּדִּי gaddi; Γαδδί Gaddi]. 1. The spy from the tribe of Manasseh, one of twelve spies Moses sent into the land of Canaan (Num 13:11).

2. The surname of John, eldest son of Mattathias (1 Macc 2:2), who apparently played a relatively minor role in the Maccabean revolt.

GADDIEL gad´ee-uhl [גַּדִּיאֵל gaddi'el]. Means "God is my luck." The son of Sodi and a chieftain from the tribe of Zebulun, listed among the twelve spies whom Moses sends into Canaan from the wilderness of Paran (Num 13:10).

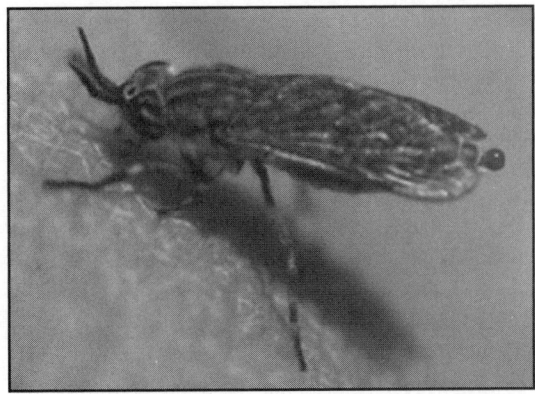

Dr. Dan Simon, Tel Aviv

Figure 1: *Haematopota* spec. (*Tabanidae*), Israel. Feeding on human.

GADFLY [קֶרֶץ qerets]. Both "gadflies" and "horse-flies" refer to the same order of insects (*Tabanidae*) whose bite may cause pain to humans and cattle. Although "gadfly" occurs in English only in Jer 46:20, a number of Hebrew terms could refer to gadflies. Isaiah 7:18 says that the Lord will "whistle for the fly" (zevuv זְבוּב) from the upper Nile, which will sit down in the wetland, a typical behavior of gadflies. Zevuv may be etymologically related to the Arabic *t'uban* and the Latin *Tabanus* (= gadfly). *See* FLY; INSECTS OF THE BIBLE.

AXEL HAUSMANN AND GÜNTER MÜLLER

GADI gay´di [גָּדִי gadhi]. The father of the Israelite king MENAHEM, who came to the throne after killing his predecessor SHALLUM (2 Kgs 15:14, 17).

GAHAM gay´ham [גַּחַם gakham]. Of the twelve sons of NAHOR, Gaham is the second-listed of four by the concubine REUMAH (Gen 22:24) in REBEKAH's genealogy (vv. 20-24).

GAHAR gay´hahr [גַּחַר gakhar]. One of several temple servants in a list of those whose descendants returned with Zerubbabel from the exile (Ezra 2:47; Neh 7:49).

GAI gi [Γαί Gai]. The eunuch in charge of the king's harem who treated ESTHER with "special favor" (Add Esth 2:9). She "found favor" in the eyes of the king and received the queen's diadem (2:17), apparently due to her adherence to Gai's guidance.

GAIUS gay´yuhs [Γάϊος Gaios]. The Greek simply transcribes the Lat.]. 1. One of the first people baptized by Paul in Corinth (1 Cor 1:14). Probably of pagan origin, his wealth enabled him to receive "the whole church" (Rom 16:23; compare 1 Cor 14:23) for the liturgical assembly. The adjective "whole" indicates that the large community of at least fifty believers also met (perhaps more frequently) in smaller house churches. The greeting in Rom 16:23 might suggest that Paul lodged with him when he was writing Romans. His identification with Titius Justus (Acts 18:7) is highly speculative.

2. Gaius of Macedonia (Acts 19:29) was a travelling companion of Paul.

3. Gaius of Derbe (Acts 20:4) was also a travelling companions of Paul. Nothing else is known of them. .

4. The apparent leader of a congregation, addressed as "beloved" in 3 John 1. *See* CORINTH; PAUL, THE APOSTLE; ROMANS, LETTER TO THE.

JEROME MURPHY-O'CONNOR

GALAL gay´lal [גָּלָל galal]. 1. One of the Levites returning to Jerusalem after the Babylonian exile (1 Chr 9:15).

2. Descendant of Jeduthun, whom David set apart as a temple musician (1 Chr 16:1-2; 25:1-8), and ancestor to one of the Levites returning to Jerusalem after the Babylonian exile (1 Chr 9:16; Neh 11:15).

NATHAN D. MAXWELL

GALATIA guh-lay´shuh [Γαλατία Galatia]. The Roman province of Galatia lies in central Anatolia or modern Turkey. To the west was the province of Asia, to the southwest, Lycia and Pamphylia, to the south Cilicia, to the east Cappadocia, to the north Pontus, and to the northwest Bithynia. The historic area of Galatia should be distinguished from the later Roman province of Galatia, which included other regions. The northern part of Galatia consisted of three tribal areas (from west to east): the Tolistobogii, the Tectosages, and the Trocmi; lying to their north was the area of Paphlagonia. The Tolistobogii were located to the west of river Sangarius, with Phrygia to the west and Bithynia to the north. The Tectosages were located in the region round Anycra (the modern Ankara). The Trocmi lands included the fort of Tavium whose western frontier was the river Halys, the border with the Tectosages. To their south was the area of Lycaonia; to the south west Pisidia, and to the southeast parts of western Cilicia. One of the features of the province was the great central Anatolian plain, which stretches from the area to the east of Iconium to the mountains bordering Pontus in the north.

A. History
B. Topography
C. Paul in Galatia
D. Religion and Cult
Bibliography

A. History

The area of Galatia takes it name from the European Gauls who crossed into Asia in 278 BCE; in the previous year they had reached as far as Delphi. Initially their presence was encouraged by Nikomedes of Bithynia in northwestern Anatolia. They came into contact with the kingdom of Pergamum in northwest Anatolia; their defeat by Attalos I was marked in the city in a number of structures including the monumental altar of Zeus (now largely in Berlin), and displays of defeated Gauls placed in the vicinity of the temple of Athena (and known from Roman copies). The Gauls settled into a social framework of three tribes, each subdivided into three, a structure described in detail by the Augustan geographer Strabo (*Geogr.* 12.5.1). Onomastic studies have shown that Celtic personal names continued in use into the Roman period.

Rome gained a greater role in Anatolia when the kingdom of Pergamum was bequeathed to her in 133 BCE forming the basis of the province of Asia. The challenge to Rome's authority came from Mithridates VI (132–63 BCE), the ruler of Pontus. Galatia seems to have been under the effective authority of the kingdom of Pontus from 120 until about 96 BCE. During the First Mithridatic War (89–85 BCE), Asia was attacked. Ancient sources indicate that Gauls fought on both sides of the conflict, with the Roman army and

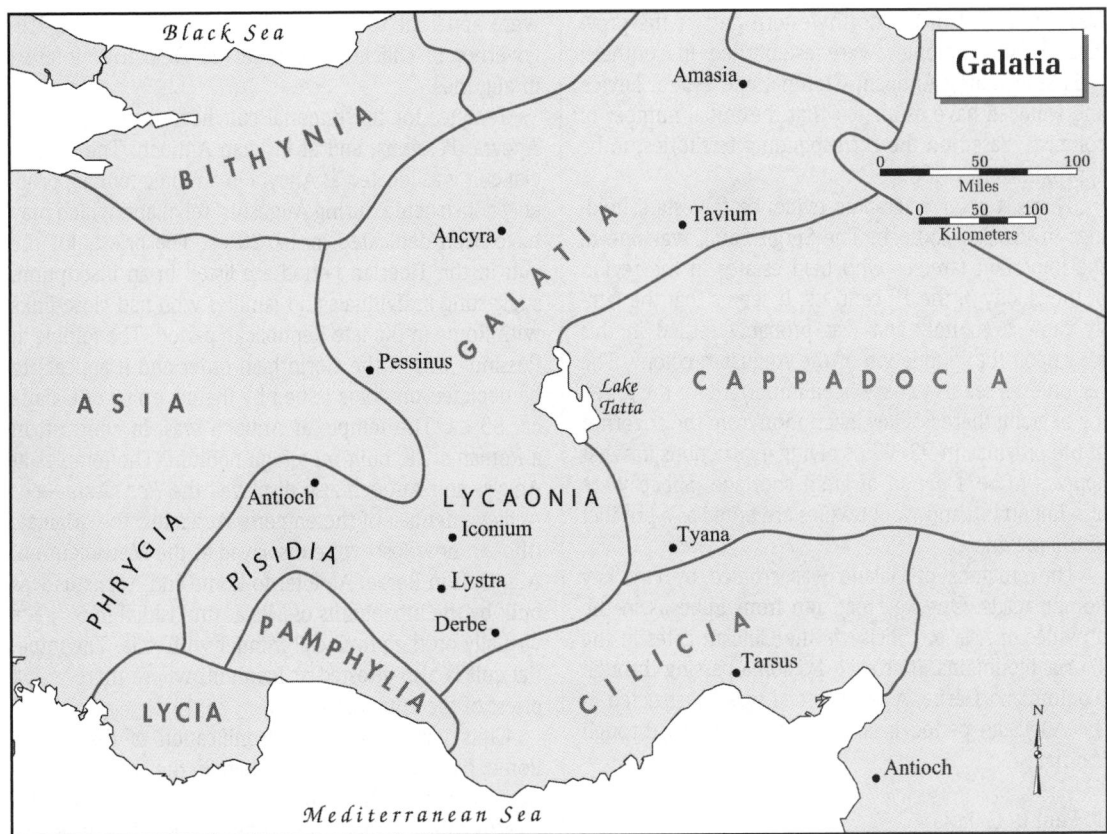

in Mithridates' invasion of mainland Greece. These divided loyalties, made more acute when Mithridates was defeated in Greece by Sulla, may explain the killing of 57 leading Galatians at Pergamum in 86 BCE by Mithridates. The Roman general Sulla brought stability to the region in 85 BCE.

One of the survivors of Mithridates' massacre was Deiotarus, who became an ally of Rome. Rome is likely to have used this friendship to create a base in Galatia from which to attack Pontus (84–82 BCE). Galatians are regularly mentioned in the campaigns against Mithridates until his flight to Armenia in 69 BCE. In 63 BCE Pompey assigned Galatia to the control of three rulers, or tetrarchs, including Deiotarus, who was awarded the title king, or *rex*, by the Roman Senate in 59 BCE. During the 50s BCE there are clear links between one of the other Galatian kings, Brogitarus, who seems to have been involved in a bribery scandal. Thus Galatia became in effect a client, though not a province, of Rome. One of the noticeable effects during this period was that the kings of Galatia had in effect absorbed the Hellenistic culture. On Brogitarus' death, Deiotarus consolidated his territory and sphere of influence.

During the civil wars of Rome, Galatians were noted fighting for Pompey at Pharsalus (in 47 BCE); Deiotarus was forced into supporting Julius Caesar in his campaign against Pontus in 47 BCE. With Caesar's assassination in 44 BCE, Deiotarus found himself first on the side of Brutus and Cassius, and his troops fought at Philippi

(in 42 BCE). Deiotarus died around 40 BCE, and was succeeded by Castor. Control of Galatia (and indeed much of central Anatolia) seems to have been given to Amyntas, who had been a member of Deiotarus' inner circle, around 36 BCE. Galatians found for Mark Antony at Actium (in 31 BCE). Amyntas continued as a client king of Rome but was killed, with the result that in 25 BCE Augustus annexed the region, thereby forming the imperial province of Galatia. The first governor appointed was Marcus Lollius, who returned to Rome in 21 BCE to hold the consulship. The administrative center of the province was located at Anycra.

The province continued to expand. It incorporated the former kingdom of Paphlagonia lying on its northern boundary when its ruler, Deiotarus Philadelphus, died in 6/5 BCE. It was further extended to the northeast with the incorporation of Pontus Galaticus. Further changes to the area of the province were made in the 2nd cent. CE.

B. Topography

The creation of the province of Galatia brought with it the creation of new cities in northern Galatia. These included the cities that mapped onto the three former tribal areas: from west to east, Pessinus, Ancyra, and Tavium. All three date their foundation to the Augustan period, probably in the late 20s BCE. The Roman names for these communities also demonstrate that they were intended to be tribal capitals. A new colony of Germa was established in the northwestern part of the province. Further colonies were established in southern Galatia including Antioch, Cremna, and Lystra. Levick and Mitchell have estimated that the initial number of colonists, based on the corresponding territories, to be approximately 15,000.

There is good epigraphic evidence for estate holdings in Pisidian Antioch. The Sergii Paulli was one of the important families who held estates in the region of the colony in the 1st cent. CE. It seems that the family came from Italy and was probably settled in this area upon the foundation of the Augustan colony. The region itself seems to have been important for the growing of grain; there is a key inscription from the governor of the province in 92/93 CE giving instructions in what appears to be a period of grain shortage. Sheep were also important, and wool textiles are noted as a product of the province.

The province of Galatia was crossed by two key Roman roads. One key road ran from Ephesus in the province of Asia to Cilicia via the Cilician gates in the Taurus mountains. It crossed Lycaonia passing through Iconium and Derbe. A second road was constructed in the Augustan period from Side in Pamphylia through Isauria.

C. Paul in Galatia

Paul and Barnabas traveled through the southern part of Galatia. They had traveled up from the coast of Pamphylia (Perge in Acts 13:13) using the newly constructed Roman road, the *via Sebaste*. Their starting point for the work in Galatia was the Roman colony of Pisidian Antioch where they had probably been given an entrée by Sergius Paulus, the Roman governor of Cyprus (ca. 46–48 CE; Acts 13:7-12) whose family estates lay there. They then traveled southeastward using the Roman road network to Iconium (Acts 13:51), Lystra, and Derbe (Acts 14:6), part of the province known as Lycaonia.

It is this route, with the creation of a series of churches along the main routes of the southern part of the Roman province, which probably provides the setting for the epistle to the Galatians. If this is the case Paul would have been writing to Christian communities set in Roman or Hellenistic urban populations with a mix of Roman, even Italian, and Jewish members. If, however, the epistle was sent to churches in the northern part of the province, the area settled by the Gauls, there is no evidence of previous contact with Paul. The southern Galatian theory thus makes better sense for the topography of the province.

D. Religion and Cult

Religion in Galatia can be found to have several different strands: those derived from the Gauls, the indigenous Anatolian peoples, cults of the Hellenistic east, and then those of Rome. Aspects of Gallic religion

were apparent to Cicero (*Div.* 1.26-27; 2.20, 76-79), governor in Cilicia, who observed Deiotarus' interest in auguries.

Temples for the imperial cult have been located at Ancyra, Pessinus, and at Pisidian Antioch. The provincial cult was located at Ancyra in an Ionic temple, probably constructed during Augustus' reign and which may have been dedicated in 19/20 CE. The priests for the cult in the Tiberian period are listed in an inscription, suggesting individuals and families who had close links with Rome in the late Republican period. The temple at Pessinus was of the Corinthian order and it appears to be depicted on coins issued by the governor of Galatia ca. 35 CE. The temple at Antioch was, in contrast, in a Roman style, built on a high podium. The temples at Ancyra and Antioch also displayed the *Res Gestae*—or Achievements—of the emperor Augustus; the originals (though now lost) were displayed at the Mausoleum of Augustus in Rome. An altar to Rome and Augustus was built by the inhabitants of Milyas (in Pisidia) in 5/4 BCE virtually on the provincial frontier with Asia. The imperial cult is also attested at Iconium, where there was a priest of the emperor Tiberius.

Cults for Roma, the personification of the city of Rome, have been found elsewhere in the province, such as at Attaleia on the Pamphylian coast; interestingly, the cult has the epithet *archegetis*, a title often given to Apollo in Greek colonies, indicating the guiding hand of the deity (usually through the Delphic oracle).

Agonistic festivals for Galatia were held at Ancyra and Tavium. Details of the games at Ancyra in the Tiberian period reveal public banquets and spectacular games including gladiatorial fights (one set of games in 30/31 CE had fifty pairs of gladiators), bullfights, and wild-animal hunts. *See* ANTIOCH, PISIDIAN; DERBE; ICONIUM; LYSTRA.

Bibliography: W. M. Calder, et al., eds. *Monuments from Lycaonia, the Pisido-Phrygian Borderland, Aphrodisias* (1962); D. H. French. *Roman Roads and Milestones of Asia Minor, fasc. 2: An Interim Catalogue of Milestones* (1988); D. W. J. Gill and C. Gempf, eds. *The Book of Acts in Its Graeco-Roman Setting.* Vol. 2 (1994); B. Levick. *Roman Colonies in Southern Asia Minor* (1967); B. Levick. *Anatolia. Land, Men, and Gods in Asia Minor.* Vol. 1. The Celts in Anatolia and the Impact of Roman Rule (1993); D. Mitchell, D. French, and J. Greenhalgh. *Regional Epigraphic Catalogues of Asia Minor 2: The Ankara District, the Inscriptions of North Galatia* (1982); S. Mitchell and M. Waelkens. *Pisidian Antioch: The Site and Its Monuments* (1998).

DAVID W. J. GILL

GALATIANS, LETTER TO THE guh-lay´shuhn [Γαλάται Galatai]. Paul's Letter to the Galatians is one of the most significant documents in the Christian

Scriptures. Paul's vigorous discussions of justification and faith are at the heart of the letter's concerns.

This letter reflects an intramural debate in early Christianity. Galatians is not Paul's assessment of Judaism as a social and religious community but the apostle's response to certain Jewish Christians who sought to require observance of traditional Jewish Law in the life of the church.

A. Detailed Analysis

1. Backgrounds

In the original sense of the designation, Galatia was a territory in northern Asia Minor. Originally the region was populated by Celts who migrated there from Gaul in the first half of the 3rd cent. BCE. In Greek, **Galatai** (Galatians) is a variant of **Keltoi** (Κελτοί, Celts). In 25 BCE the last of the Galatian kings died, leaving his kingdom in the hands of the Romans, who reorganized the area into a province by adding other districts (Isauria, parts of Lyconia, Paphlagonia, Pisidia, Phrygia, and Pontus) to Galatia. *See* GALATIA.

Paul does not name any cities or towns of Galatia, so that it is impossible to determine whether the churches to which he wrote were in the old territory of the ethnic Galatians (North Galatia) or in the Roman provincial Galatia (South Galatia). If Paul's letter addressed residents of North Galatia, there is little information in the NT to fill out the picture of who the Galatians were; but if Paul addressed the inhabitants of South Galatia,

then Acts 13–14 may give data to assist reading Paul's letter to the Galatians.

Similarly, it is difficult (if not impossible) to determine approximately when Paul composed his letter to the Galatians. At the heart of this matter is the problem of trying to coordinate portions of Galatians with seemingly parallel portions of Acts. In particular is the matter of whether 2:1-10 refers to the same events recounted in Acts 15. Disagreements among scholars result in some interpreters dating Galatians as early as 49 CE (usually those arguing against identifying Gal 2 with Acts 15) and others as late as 56 CE (predominantly those contending that Gal 2 and Acts 15 are variant accounts of one incident).

Paul says of his original dealings with the Galatians, "You know it was because of an illness of the flesh that I preached the gospel to you at first" (4:13). He continues, "You would have plucked out your eyes and given them to me—if possible" (4:15). These lines and the mention of the "large letters" of Paul's handwriting (6:11) lead some interpreters to conclude Paul had problems with his vision, and this forced him to reside among the Galatians. Perhaps this is true, though one cannot say with certainty. We do, however, know that Paul traveled in Galatia more than once, although from the account in Acts 16–19 we know few details of his trips. Nevertheless, the reader of Galatians may infer that Paul's first contact with the Galatians was in a time of personal crisis. Scholars have come to recognize that Paul's letters are written using rhetorical devices and styles that were typical for the 1st cent. Greco-Roman world. Paul and his readers would have been familiar with such devices from their use in general education and daily life. Scholars have suggested that Paul's letter to the Galatians is an apology written in the form of judicial rhetoric and that it is an attempt to persuade using predominantly deliberative rhetoric. Still other scholars have argued that Galatians is a sermon that declares or re-presents the gospel that Paul proclaimed.

2. Problem eliciting the letter

According to 1:6, Paul wrote to the Galatians because they were deserting their confidence in his preaching and turning to what he caustically calls a "different gospel." This other gospel was proclaimed among the Galatians by a group of outsiders who came among them after Paul's departure and who were probably in Galatia when Paul wrote. Paul says the Galatians were seeking to receive the Spirit out of the works of the Law rather than out of the hearing of faith. In other words, under the influence of those who have come among them, the Galatians were moving toward Law observance. This is clear from the references in 4:10 to the calendar, in 5:2 to circumcision, and in 5:3 to the "whole Law."

In order to understand what Paul is saying in Galatians, it is necessary to gain some idea of who the outsiders who have come among the Galatians are and what they have said that has caused the problem. Paul records three relatively neutral pieces of information about those who came among the Galatians after his departure. Of them he says:

a. They preach "another gospel," different from that preached in Galatia by Paul; he says it is a perversion of the gospel (1:6-7). This is Paul's description, however; and an unbiased reader of the letter should infer that in the minds of these preachers, the gospel they proclaim is the gospel, not a perversion.

b. They "trouble" the Galatians (1:7). The message of these preachers disturbs or frightens the Galatians; it "upsets" them (5:12).

c. The preachers in Galatia are themselves circumcised (6:13).

From Paul's letter, one learns something of the content of the Galatian preachers' proclamation: The Law is their point of departure and the heart of their theology (5:1-4). They probably speak of "the Law of Christ" (6:2)—for this is not a Pauline phrase. They probably teach that God's Law was affirmed and interpreted by God's Messiah, so that Jesus is the Messiah of the Law. Their theology has an additive pattern: they view the Law as primary and add Christ to it as the authoritative interpreter. They probably teach that to obey the Law as interpreted by Christ is to become "Abraham's offspring" (3:6-18).

The "good news" is good for the Gentiles. This is obvious since the preachers are in Galatia, advocating the Law among Gentiles.

The "good news" proclaimed by the preachers was conditional. At 4:17 Paul employs the image of the gate and gatekeepers. The preachers at Galatia have threatened to shut the Galatians out if they failed to comply with the admonition to Law observance. The preachers must have understood the Law as the narrow gate to salvation and themselves as the gatekeepers who guarded the way of righteousness. The preachers appear to have taught that the "key" to the gate was Law observance (4:17), especially circumcision (5:2, 13).

3. Content of the letter

a. **Galatians 1:1-5, Salutation.** Paul identifies himself as an "apostle," as one who was sent by God. Paul aims, even in this opening, to establish his independence from other human agents. Paul states that he was not called by a human but by the same power of God that raised Jesus Christ from the dead. One should notice at the outset of this letter that Paul's perspective and remarks are profoundly theological. Paul's CHRISTOLOGY is evident in his understanding that Jesus is both the Messiah and the Lord. Paul's soteriology comes through as he refers to the Lord Jesus Christ's having given himself for the sins of humans in order to deliver them. Paul's eschatological worldview is clear from the mention of "the present evil age," and the thoroughly theological cast of Paul's thinking is seen

as he explains that the saving work of Christ occurred "according to the will of God" (*see* ESCHATOLOGY OF THE NT). His ecclesiology is evident as he views the congregations of Galatia together and as recipients of divine grace and peace.

b. **Galatians 1:6-10, Rebuke and statement of thesis.** The Galatians were turning away from the gospel Paul preached to a different gospel. One should notice that according to Paul the Galatians were turning from the "grace" of Christ and from "the one who called" them, that is, God. Yet Paul insists there is no other gospel than the one he proclaimed in Galatians; there is otherwise only perversion. Moreover, Paul reports that this turning on the part of the Galatia occurred at the instigation of some troublesome preachers. From Paul's comments throughout the letter, we find a Jewish cast to the concerns and activities of these preachers—at 4:10 we find they focused on the calendar of Jewish religious observances; at 5:2-3 we find they emphasized circumcision and the Law; at 6:13 we learn that they are circumcised. Yet these are not Jewish missionaries who are simply trying to convert Christians to Judaism. Both they and Paul refer to their message as the gospel, albeit a different gospel, so that we should understand the preachers to be Christian Jews. Paul says, "Let them be anathema."

In v. 10 Paul's question reflects what the newly arrived preachers said about him, namely, that he was just a "people-pleaser." But, according to Paul, preaching about the Law is itself pleasing people, as one offers legal norms that bring a sense of security to those who observe the Law.

c. **Galatians 1:11-12, Thesis concerning the gospel.** From his strenuous protest in 1:10, Paul moves briefly to explicate his assessment of what was happening in Galatia. Paul's gospel was good news, and the primary reason it was good was that the news was not a message that came from humanity. Paul's gospel came by revelation of Jesus Christ.

d. **Galatians 1:13–2:21, Autobiographical information.** This section of the epistle, retrospective as it is, picks up the thought from 1:10 concerning Paul's "still pleasing people." From beginning to end Paul is illustrating his independence in order to show the error of the Galatians' tendency toward taking up Law observance.

Paul tells of his past in Judaism. He also recalls his call to be an apostle. As Paul tells the story, the reader learns that Paul experienced an act of divine intervention; and that interruption by God came according to God's own preordained will. It is striking to compare Paul's words with those of the prophets Isaiah (Isa 49:1-5) and Jeremiah (Jer 1:4-5). Paul paraphrases the lines of the calls of the prophets to establish his independence and to document his direct call by God. The one truly new element in Paul's report is the reference to God's Son, so that we see Christology at the forefront of Paul's theological reflection. Paul reports, moreover, his early work in order to corroborate further his independence from other human agents. He reports a visit to Jerusalem that is meant to confirm that at the outset of his work he was barely known to the apostles and to those in Jerusalem.

In 2:1-10 Paul refers to a second visit to Jerusalem. Scholars debate exactly what and when the incident reported here took place. Some interpreters contend that Paul is referring to the events that are reported in Acts 11:30, while others argue that Paul has the incident from Acts 18:22 in mind. The majority or consensus of NT interpreters, however, relates the remarks here to the events that are reported in Acts 15, the so-called Apostolic Council in Jerusalem. If there is a chronological difficulty with this correlation, scholars judge that Luke (in Acts) was not clear or precise about the exact sequence of events in the life of the early church.

Although Paul is adamant about his independence and explains that early in his ministry he had only minimal relations with the church in Jerusalem and its leaders, he recalls here that later in his ministry he did have dealings with Jerusalem; but even then he says that he moved as a result of divine revelation, not in accordance with human volition. In turn, 2:3 scores a major point in Paul's argument against the Galatians being concerned with observance of the Law: Titus, a Gentile like the Galatians, had accompanied Paul on the trip to Jerusalem, and he was not required by the Jerusalem leaders to be circumcised. Indeed, at Jerusalem when the "false believers" tried to impose the observance of the Law on the mission to the Gentiles, they failed. They did not gain support from the Jerusalem leaders, who embraced the Law-free mission to the Gentiles in warm fellowship. Then, in a closing note to this memory, Paul recollects only that at Jerusalem there was a request that he should remember the "poor."

In 2:11-14 Paul recalls a difficult situation in the life of the early church that occurred at Antioch. The key to the crisis in Antioch was that the problem arose over table fellowship, the very place where Christians came together to eat and to celebrate the Lord's Supper. In the debate we see that Peter (Cephas) and those who took his side chose to favor a pre-Christian Jewish tradition that labored to preserve Jewish dietary regulations in the context of a gathering of Jewish and Gentile Christians. Peter and his companions withdrew from table fellowship with Gentile Christians. Paul, on the other hand, and whoever agreed with him, chose to embody Christian unity that is declared dramatically in 3:28, "In Christ there is no Jew or Greek!" From Paul's perspective, Peter's maintaining distance from the Gentiles set the Law over Christ.

Galatians 2:15-21 is one of the most difficult passages in all of Paul's epistles. It presents problems for translation and, in turn, for interpretation. Commentators disagree sharply about what Paul is saying here, and all who study the passage admit its ambiguity.

A summary of Paul's line of thought in 2:15-21 runs as follows: The Galatians, who are Gentiles, are moving toward Law observance as a way of maintaining their good standing with God. To discourage them, Paul says that he and his companions, Jews who once did observe the Law, now know that no one is set right or stays right with God by Law observance. People are only right with God by virtue of what God did in the cross of Jesus Christ and by what God does through the Holy Spirit. If this is not true, Christ died for nothing. If people who hear the gospel and believe subsequently seek to maintain their relationship to God by Law observance, they deny God's grace and back away from their calling in and by faith.

e. Galatians 3:1-5, A further rebuke. Paul debates sarcastically and ironically with the apparent contention of the Galatians that they will profit from observance of the Law. The basic issue is this: How did the Galatians receive the Spirit? Paul presents two options. They either received the Spirit out of the works of the Law or out of the hearing of faith.

It is instructive to notice here that Paul juxtaposes, first, Law and faith and, then, Spirit and flesh; in turn, he creates rhetorical parallels between, first, Spirit and faith and, then, flesh and Law. As Paul creates these pairs of opposites and equals he makes an important point: the Spirit comes only by the hearing of faith. As the Spirit works and faith comes into the world by the work of God in Jesus Christ, humans believe in the Gospel, and the Spirit takes hold in their lives and brings them into a relationship with God.

f. Galatians 3:6–4:7, An extended argument from Scripture. In order to prove his point about the needlessness of Law observance among the Galatians Paul launches an exegetical argument. The form is midrashic (*see* MIDRASH). Abraham was the first Jew, himself a convert from a pagan background. Paul's point in this discussion for the sake of the Galatians comes in 3:7, "Thus you know that the ones out of faith, these are the children of Abraham." The Law is nowhere in sight and, for Paul, it is irrelevant for the life of persons called through faith to a relationship to God.

In 3:10-14 Paul again offers a midrashic argument. He still sharply contrasts or juxtaposes Law and faith. But now the apostle elaborates his thinking: the Law curses while faith blesses. Indeed, Christ himself was cursed by the Law in order to redeem humanity from the curse of the Law. Paul is arguing that God's action in Christ is the realization of God's promise that was made to Abraham (*see* ABRAHAM, NT AND EARLY JUDAISM).

Paul next argues by analogy in 3:15-18 to a legal matter, a will. This is imaginative exposition, although perhaps not strictly midrash. Paul's logic, although related to Roman law, is quite clear: a will stands;

anyone other than the one who makes the will cannot amend it once it has been set; and a will is intended to be (necessarily) fulfilled. Thus, Paul argues that God's promise to Abraham is really like a will. First, there are terms to the will; it is set for "Abraham and his offspring [seed]." The word for "offspring" or "seed" in Greek is sperma (σπέρμα), a singular collective noun. Paul makes a significant point from the use of the singular sperma ("seed") rather than the plural spermata (σπέρματα, "seeds") in the LXX, arguing that God's promise was not given to Abraham and all those who are Law observant ("seeds"); rather, God made a promise only to Abraham and one other (his "seed"), namely, Jesus Christ. Second, there is no amending God's promise. The Law (and Law observance) came 430 years after the promise of God to Abraham. Therefore, the Law cannot amend the promise of God to Abraham and his "seed."

Paul declares in 3:19-20 that God who made the promise to Abraham did not give the Law to Israel. Rather, angels did. How does Paul know this astounding piece of information? Clearly there was a Jewish legend current in Paul's time that suggested that angels delivered the Law to Moses on Sinai. One sees the idea in a variety of places: here in Galatians; in Acts 7:53; in Josephus, (*J.W.* 15.136); and perhaps in Deut 33:2. Through creative logic Paul puts the idea of the angelic deliverance of the Law to a very different use from any of his contemporaries. He argues that the angelic delivery of the Law means that Moses was a mediator. Moses mediated the Law to Israel; so that he was the representative of one group (the angels) to another group (the people of Israel). Yet, God is one, not a group in need of a representative.

If the Law did not come directly from God, then why was it given? In response to this question we see that even though he argues against God's giving the Law, Paul still maintains a high view of the Law. The angels gave the Law as helpful guidelines, because humans transgressed God's will.

While Paul insists in 3:21-22 that the Law is not inherently contrary to God's will, nevertheless, he contends that the Law did not come directly from God with God's own power; and so, the Law is impotent. At most, according to Paul, the Law revealed the sinfulness of humanity. The Law served to unite humanity in the common condition of sinfulness, so that the promised blessing of God to Abraham could be given out of faith, the faith of Jesus Christ, to all those who believe.

Paul declares in 3:23-29 that the Law confined or constrained humanity until faith came, which faith did in Jesus Christ. The Law was a pedagogical supervisor that served until Christ. The Law served in this capacity so that humanity "might be justified out of faith." But, now, Paul insists that faith has come, so there is no more need for the former supervisor. Now

all are children of God through faith in Jesus Christ. All this means that there is no division in Christ, be it in terms of ethnicity, social status, or sexual-social roles. Interpreters often suggest that behind 3:28 lay an early Christian confessional or baptismal formula that expressed the transformation of human existence and the new relationships brought into existence through Jesus Christ. Whether or not that is correct, the sense of Paul's statement epitomizes his understanding of the meaning of the Christ-event at the level of human life.

Paul offers by analogy another argument concerning the irrelevance of the Law for those who have received the Spirit of God's Son (Gal 4:1-7). The analogy builds off the matter of minors who become heirs before they reach the age of their majority. He identifies the "heirs" as those of faith who were like minors before God sent Christ. In turn, the "guardians" of humanity prior to the advent of Christ were "elemental spirits of the universe": for Gentiles, Paul means to name lesser gods, demons, etc.; and for Jews, he means the Law.

Paul continues by focusing on the matter of the appointed time of inheritance. He identifies that time with God's sending of Christ. The idea of God's sending his Son, Christ, for the purpose of saving humanity occurs here and in Rom 8:3-4. Paul is actually taking up a motif from Hellenistic Judaism of God's sending a savior for humanity's sake. Outside the OT, in the Jewish writings of the Hellenistic period, one sees the idea that God acted by sending a savior in order to bring salvation, although in these places God sent "Wisdom" or the "Logos" as the agent of salvation (Philo, *Dreams* 1.69; Sir 24; Bar 3; and Wis 9). Paul picks up this abstract, mythical theme and makes it concrete by reference to Christ.

g. Galatians 4:8-20, Discussion of Paul's distress. Paul's remarks in these verses extend from the last analogy. Prior to their conversion the Galatians were pagans who would most likely have worshiped idols. As Christians, Paul informs them that they are freed from idols as they are freed in Christ. Paul identifies the desire of the Galatians to become Law observant as nothing but a desire to return to bondage.

In 4:12-20, with rhetoric, Paul transports the Galatians back to a moment in their past, to the origin of their faith. He reminds them of their reception of the Gospel, and he reminds them of their gracious reception of the apostle himself (despite his troublesome condition at the time). Then, Paul makes an emotional appeal for the Galatians to remember and reaffirm the Gospel as they first heard and believed it.

h. Galatians 4:21–5:1, A second argument from Scripture. Paul declares that his argument in these verses is an allegory (4:24). Again, he takes up material from the story of Abraham, but now Paul considers the larger family story by focusing on the two sons and the two "wives" of Abraham. Once again, Paul creates sets of opposites: flesh/Spirit; slave/free; flesh/promise.

He allegorizes the story of Abraham's family as he interprets and applies the account to the situation in Galatia. Paul also gives an overt proof-text for his advice that follows: "Cast out the slave and her son"; that is, Paul admonishes the Galatians be done with Law observance and the preachers.

Finally, Paul moves forcefully in 5:1 from allegory to state his point directly: Christians are freed by Christ for freedom, but they must guard against taking on a yoke of slavery.

i. Galatians 5:2–6:10, Parenesis or discussion of Pastoral concerns. Paul says that moving toward Law observance denies Christ and the freedom he grants. Paul sharply juxtaposes justification "by Law" with justification "by grace." Verse 6 summarizes Paul's thematic concern, "For in Christ neither circumcision not uncircumcision matters anything, but faith is working through love." In 5:10 Paul expresses his confidence in the Galatians; and then, suddenly he becomes obviously impassioned in v. 11, declaring that Law observance removes the scandal of the cross. At last, in v. 12 Paul utters a crude wish for his adversaries in Galatia.

j. Galatians 5:13–6:10, A spiritual meditation and Pastoral exhortations. Called to freedom, the Galatians are told they can use their freedom as an opportunity either to focus on themselves or to focus on others. In 5:14 Paul repeats a well-known line from Lev 19:18. Paul's fondness for this portion of the OT is clear, for the line from Leviticus also lies behind his remarks in Rom 13:8-10. The popularity and importance of this line in early Christianity may stem from the use of Leviticus by Jesus himself, who is found uttering this line at Matt 22:39 and Mark 12:31; compare Luke 10:27. Then in v. 15 Paul seems to warn against bickering in the life of the church.

In 5:16-24 Paul ponders the Spirit and the Flesh in opposition to each other. Then Paul makes two lists, "the works of the Flesh" and "the FRUIT OF THE SPIRIT." Such catalogues were the stock materials of the moral teachings of Hellenistic philosophers. Galatians 5:25 employs technical terminology for the formation of a line by a military unit, and v. 26 plainly says that Christian freedom is not anarchy; rather, the Spirit frees and forms according to the parameters of God's will. In turn, 5:26 is an exhortation in negative form that builds off the previous statement. Furthermore, Paul's directions become remarkably practical as he reasons about the life of the members of the Galatian congregations in 6:1-5, instructing the Galatians to "be gentle" and to "bear one another's burdens." Finally, 6:6-10 offer more observations about inner-church relations.

k. Galatians 6:11-18, Closing with Paul's autograph and conclusions. Paul brings the letter to a conclusion with his own hand rather than by continuing to use the services of the secretary (amanuensis). Paul puts a new twist on opposition to Law observance, stating that concern with Law observance is a style of living

that actively avoids the danger and the scandal of the cross of Christ. Paul says the practice of circumcision is truly vain in comparison with the new creation that had come through the cross of the Lord Jesus Christ. In a penultimate remark (6:17), Paul disavows those who oppose him, and then, in 6:18 he ends the letter as he began it, with a thoroughly theological statement, a benediction.

B. Theological and Religious Significance of Galatians

Paul insists that the gospel he preached among the Galatians is the only gospel. Anything else, no matter what it is called or who preaches it, is a perversion. Paul states boldly that his apostolic commission and the origin of his message were the results of divine revelation. He did not learn his message from any human. In contrast, he suggests the preachers in Galatia are concerned only with "the flesh." This is seen in their focus on keeping the Law, especially in their concern with CIRCUMCISION. They are bound up with human activity in the present evil age, not with the Spirit who is known and experienced by the power of God—the same power that raised Jesus from the dead.

One of the main lines of Paul's argument in Galatians is his juxtaposition of faith and the Law. This contrast reflects Paul's apocalyptic mind-set, for he thinks of faith and the Law as elements in two opposing realms, one potent and the other impotent (3:21). One sees this at 2:16 where Paul speaks of "the faith of Christ" and "the works of the Law." Literally, his phrases in Greek say, "out of the faith of Christ" and "out of the works of the Law." He thinks here of two realms from out of which powerful results emanate.

For Paul these words (along with others like SPIRIT and flesh) function as technical terms that describe two opposing realms, one God's and the other in opposition to God. They are cosmic in scope, and humans are in either one realm or the other. Persons in God's realm are being saved, whereas those in the other realm are lost, cursed. Accordingly, those "in faith" are saved and those "under the Law" are cursed, for Jesus Christ rescued those "in faith," whereas those "under the Law" are caught up in the Law's impotence. *See* FLESH IN THE NT; GRACE.

The good news for those under the Law is that Jesus Christ gave himself, invading the realm of the Law and becoming cursed as he died crucified. And then God revealed his power, overcame the curse, and saved humanity by raising Jesus from the dead. Moreover, from "the faith of Christ" comes faith itself (5:22), by which humans, like Abraham, are set right with God. Contrary to the claim of the preachers in Galatia, SALVATION is not tied to human actions (the workings of the Law). For saving faith is not a human product; it is a fruit of the Spirit (5:22), a gracious gift from God. In contrast, from "the workings of the Law," the system of righteousness-maintenance advocated by the preachers, comes "the curse of the Law" (3:13), whereby all things are "consigned to/under sin" (3:22).

In 3:15-18 Paul shows the problem of the additive pattern (Law + Christ = new Law) advocated by the preachers in Galatia. He says that attempts to add Christ to the Law show ignorance of the priority of God's promise to Abraham. One cannot add Christ to the Law because the promise and its fulfillment stand above the Law and coexist apart from the existence of the Law.

Paul perceives that salvation comes through the power of God: Paul was called by this power; Jesus Christ was raised by it; and the Galatians have faith because of God's power. From this starting point Paul argues that the Galatians have made a dangerous mistake in turning to the Law, for humans are cursed by the workings of the Law. Since salvation is based in God's promise to Abraham and the fulfillment of the promise in Jesus Christ, the Law has nothing to do with the promise. In Christ, the fulfillment of the promise, God acted to save humanity from its involvement with the impotent, "elemental spirits of the universe," one of which was the Law. Christ himself became cursed by the Law. Nevertheless, God raised Jesus from the dead and thereby demonstrated God's power, that Jesus Christ is God's Son, and that the Law is impotent.

Paul's message to the Galatians is that involvement with the Law is enslavement to the flesh. He calls for the Galatians to abandon the error of their ways and to stand fast "in Christ" (not "under the Law"), for Jesus Christ, and he alone, means freedom (5:1). *See* ANTI-JUDAISM; FAITH, FAITHFULNESS; LAW IN EARLY JUDAISM; LAW IN THE NT.

Bibliography: J. M. G. Barclay. *Obeying the Truth: A Study of Paul's Ethics in Galatians* (1988); C. K. Barrett. *Freedom and Obligation: A Study of the Epistle to the Galatians* (1985); Hans Dieter Betz. *Galatians: A Commentary on Paul's Letter to the Churches in Galatia.* Hermeneia (1979); F. F. Bruce. *The Epistle to the Galatians: A Commentary on the Greek Text.* NIGTC (1982); Charles B. Cousar. *Galatians.* Interpretation (1982); James D. G. Dunn. *The Epistle to the Galatians.* BNTC (1993); Richard B. Hays. "The Letter to the Galatians: Introduction, Commentary, and Reflections." *NIB* 11 (2000) 181–348; Richard N. Longenecker. *Galatians.* WBC 41 (1990); J. Louis Martyn. *Galatians: A New Translation with Introduction and Commentary.* AB 33A (1997); Frank J. Matera. *Galatians.* SP 9 (1992).

MARION SOARDS

GALBANUM gal'buh-nuhm [חֶלְבְּנָה khelbenah; χαλβάνη chalbanē]. Used in making sacred incense for the holy precincts of the TENT OF MEETING (Exod 30:34-35). A green resin is produced by the giant fennel (*Ferula galbaniflua*; a perennial, with smooth stem, and shining leaflets growing to 6 ft. in height) that is native to the high mountains of northern Iran. The dried sap was transported by traders. Personified wisdom compares herself to the smell of the incense (Sir 24:15). *See* INCENSE; PLANTS OF THE BIBLE; SPICE; WISDOM IN THE OT.

VICTOR H. MATTHEWS

GALEED gal'ee-ed [גַּלְעֵד gal'edh]. Means "heap of witness," a stone-heap marker built somewhere in Gilead by Laban and Jacob, one of two witnesses of their non-aggression (if not mutual protection) covenant (Gen 31:44-54). Laban's Aramaic name for Galeed, JEGAR-SAHADUTHA, likewise means "heap of witness." Covenants often included multiple witnesses, yet the two witnesses in this narrative might also recall the deception Laban and Jacob had each manifested (e.g., Gen 29:25; 31:20).

JASON C. DYKEHOUSE

GALILEE, GALILEANS gal'uh-lee, gal'uh-lee'uhn [גָּלִיל (הַגּוֹיִם) galil (haggoyim), גְּלִילָה gelilah; Γαλιλαία Galilaia, Γαλιλαῖος Galilaios]. 1. The term *Galilee* is derived from the Hebrew galil, referring to a ring, pivot, or rollers. This meaning is generalized to refer to a district generically (e.g., Josh 13:2; Ezek 47:8). Its application as a proper name to the area proximate to the west side of the Sea of Galilee may be a function of the roughly circular shape of the lake or of the ringlike shape of the area in question. The primary importance of Galilee to biblical scholarship is as the location of Jesus' hometown and much of his activity.

 A. Boundaries
 B. History
 C. Economics and Society
 Bibliography

A. Boundaries

The boundaries of Galilee were in flux, or vaguely delineated. The core region corresponds roughly to territories on the west side of the lake, comprising the lower hill country and plains west and southwest of the lake—including the Beth Netofah Valley, the Tir'an Valley, and the Nazareth ridge—and the higher hill country to the northwest, beginning with the Meiron massif. By the Roman period, Galilee was divided into two or three subregions. Josephus attests to a division between Lower Galilee and Upper Galilee, the former including the valleys and low hill country south of Kefar Hananya and the Meiron Massif, and the latter including the more rugged hill country at the southern reaches of the Lebanon mountains, north of Kefar Hananya and Meiron (Josephus, *J.W.* 3.35-40). The Mishnah adds a third category, "The Valley," comprising the land immediately along the western rim of the lake (*m. Shev.* 9:2).

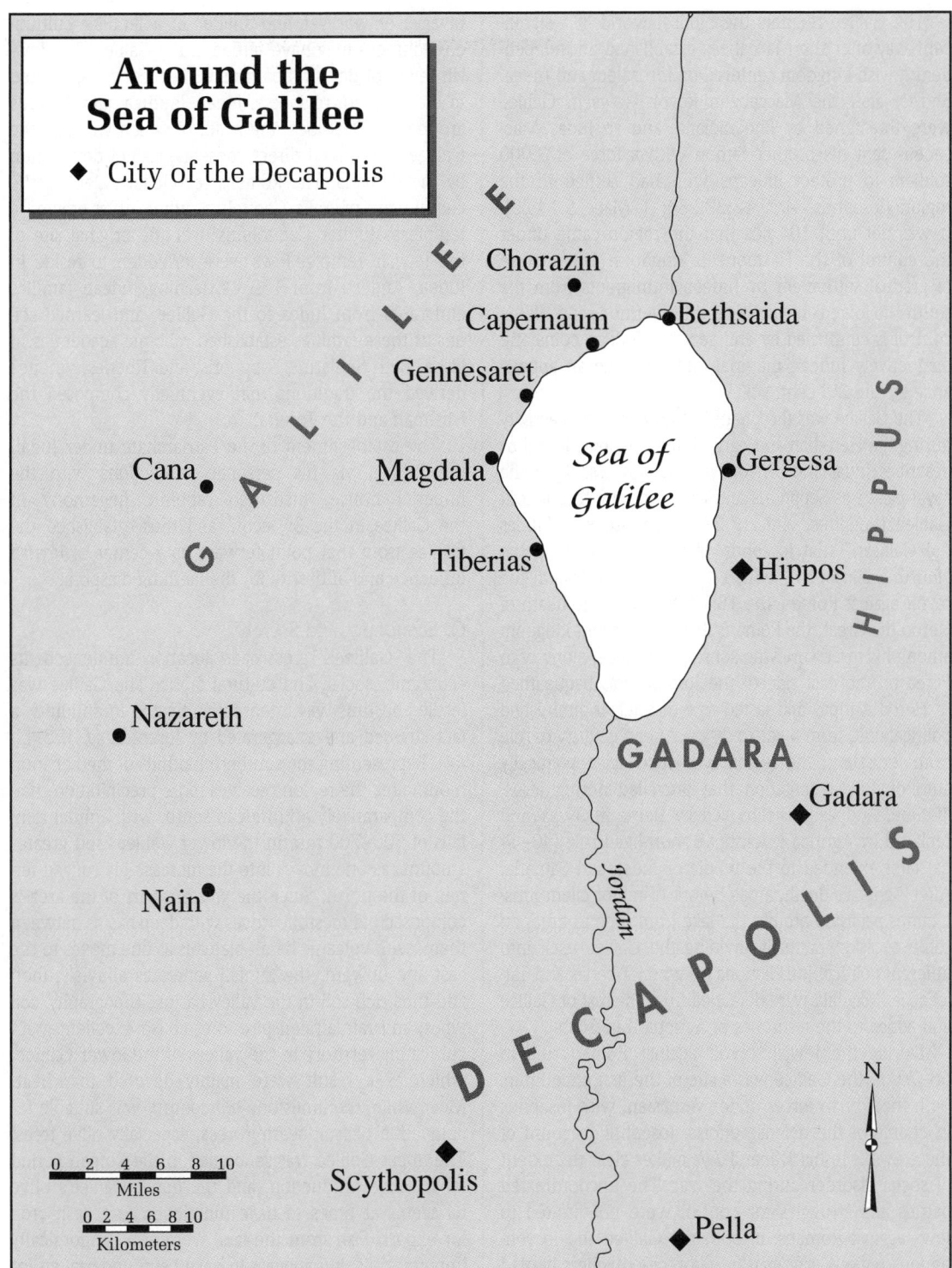

B. History

In the OT, the Galilee is the northern extent of the settlement of the twelve tribes, corresponding roughly to the territory of the tribe of Naphtali (see, e.g., Josh 19:32-39), but at times also including (parts of) the territories of Zebulun, Asher, and/or Issachar. References to the area in the OT reinforce the impression of the Galilee as a crossroads, with a confluence of Israelite, Phoenician, and

Aramean cultural influences and political hegemonies (see 1 Kgs 9:11). When the Israelite kingdom split after the death of Solomon, the Galilee and its tribes were included in the Northern Kingdom. The Assyrian invasion of Israel in 732 BCE resulted in the area coming under Assyrian rule, with at least some of the population deported (2 Kgs 15:29). It remains debated to what extent the region was depopulated as a result of the Assyrian deportations.

The Galilee reenters the biblical world in a significant way after the Maccabees established an independent Jewish kingdom centered on Jerusalem and Judea. Shortly after the Maccabean Revolt, Jews in Galilee were threatened by Phoenicians, and so Judas Maccabeus sent his brother Simon with a force of 3,000 soldiers to protect Judeans who had settled in the region (Josephus, *Ant.* 12.332-34; 1 Macc 5:14-23). It was not until 104 BCE that the region came under the control of the Hasmonean kingdom. This picture of gradual settlement by Judean immigrants from the south, followed by political intervention and, later, control is confirmed by archaeology: Judean coins and distinctively Judean material culture make an appearance by late 2nd cent. BCE.

The Galilee was the site of banditry and rebel activity during the Herodian and early Roman periods. Josephus describes Judas the son of Hezekiah as assaulting the royal palace at Sepphoris and as plundering throughout Galilee (Josephus, *Ant.* 17.271); likewise it is "Judas the Galilean" that Josephus describes as founding the "fourth philosophy" which he claims instigated the revolt against Rome (*Ant.* 18.23-24). After the death of Herod the Great, the Romans divided his client kingdom among his three surviving sons. The Galilee, along with Perea on the east side of the Jordan, was bequeathed to Herod Antipas and lasted as a distinct, if diminished political unit, from 4 BCE to 39 CE. After a century of rule from Jerusalem, the region was once again politically autonomous, a condition that prevailed during Jesus' lifetime. Antipas was removed by Rome in 39 CE and replaced by Agrippa I. Agrippa's short-lived rule (40–44 CE) later extended to the whole of Judea and Samaria. After Agrippa's death, a patchwork of minor client jurisdictions persisted around the lake from time to time, on some occasions actually dividing the Galilee itself into different political jurisdictions (as when Tiberias and Tarichaeae/Magdala were detached from the rest of Galilee and added to the territories of Agrippa II in 54 CE).

During the Jewish revolt against Roman rule in 66–70 CE, the Galilee was a site of the first encounters with the Roman forces under Vespasian, with Josephus in charge of the defense efforts. Josephus' account of these events in his *War* and *Life* makes clear the extent of social disorder during the war. The uncoordinated battles and struggles for control were not limited to Jews against Romans; in both the Galilee and in contiguous regions, rich battled poor, city-dwellers battled peasants, individual cities declared for different sides in the struggle or rebelled against particular military commanders, Jews and Gentiles slaughtered one another, and powerful individuals used the war as a stage on which to enact personal rivalries (most notably, the personal rivalry between Josephus and John of Gischala; see, e.g., Josephus, *J.W.* 2.285-94).

After the Romans suppressed the great revolt of 66–70 CE, some Judean Jews seeking to escape the ravages of war yet find shelter in a familiar cultural environment may have settled in the Galilee. The Jewish revolt of Bar Kochba from 132–135 CE was limited to the southern regions of Judea, Idumea, and the area around the Dead Sea, the result of which was that the Galilee was spared direct consequences of devastation by the Romans. The Romans rebuilt Jerusalem as the Gentile city of Aelia Capitolina, where they erected a temple to Jupiter Capitolinus over the original site of the Jewish Temple. Jews were forbidden to reside in Judea. And so from 135 CE, leading Judean families emigrated from Judea to the Galilee, and learned scions of these families established rabbinic academies in Usha, Beth She'arim, Sepphoris, and Tiberias, whence derived the traditions that eventually composed the Mishnah and the Tosefta.

The establishment of the Patriarchate under Judah the Prince, via his personal connections with the imperial house, instituted rabbinic hegemony in the Galilee in the 3rd cent., and thus established the Galilee from that point forward as a center of Jewish influence and authority for the far-flung diaspora.

C. Economics and Society

The Galilee's crossroads location influenced its economic, social, and cultural fabric. The Galilee was fertile and thus was intensely cultivated in antiquity, a fact stressed and exaggerated by Josephus (*J.W.* 3.42-44). Representing the southern foothills of the Lebanon mountains, the region receives more precipitation than the comparatively arid Judean south, with annual rainfalls of 500–700 mm in the lower Galilee, and greater amounts as one moves into the increasingly rugged terrain of the north. Since the western part of the area is composed of limestone ridges with deep basins between them, with volcanic basalt plateaus as one moves to the east and upward, the rainfall generates alluvial runoff and thus rich soil in the valley basins. Topography, soil types, and rainfall conspire to establish excellent grain cultivating territory in the valleys of the lower Galilee, which as a result were mainly devoted to wheat. Meanwhile, the limestone hill country was suitable for cultivation of fruit-bearing trees, especially olive trees. The upper Galilee was renowned in the Roman period for its olive production, and the upper Galilee's olive oil seems at times to have functioned as a cash crop for export. Fish from the lake were also economically important; fishing appears to have been undertaken for profit, and a complex network of regulations and taxes was imposed on fishing by the state.

Such an agriculturally productive area could support dense settlement. Current population estimates for early Roman Galilee range from about 150,000 to 500,000, depending on what estimates are given for the city populations of Sepphoris and Tiberias. Major roads move through and around the region (e.g., the road from Damascus to the coastal plain), and the area is but a short distance from a variety of different urban centers and cultural influences, including the prominent port cities of the Phoenician coast: Tyre, Sidon, and Ptolemais, as well as Caesarea farther south. The cities of Gaulanitis and the Gentile settlements of the Decapolis sit immediately on the east side of the lake, while Damascus and Jerusalem are each a little over 100 km away. "Galilee of the Gentiles" supported a multiethnic populace with multiple social and cultural ties to a diverse range of urban centers. The primary language of administration and trade was Greek. Even rural villagers were likely to have had some knowledge of the cultural currents of the "pagan" Greco-Roman world outside their borders, whether as a result of encountering urban institutions and culture directly in Tyre or Ptolemais, or as a result of the proximity of pagan temples, various Gentile expressions of piety, and Roman troop garrisons in the Galilee itself, or merely through the more passive agency of Tyrian coins with their images of Melqart. In addition, since Hasmonean times the Galilee's large Jewish population ensured cultural contacts with Jerusalem as well as the cultivation of local forms of Israelite piety.

Trade in valuable and easily transportable luxury items by itinerant peddlers was probably prevalent throughout Galilean history; likewise, an inner-regional trade in both agricultural goods and bulky items like pottery can be documented archaeologically. At the beginning of the 1st cent., however, the Galilee did not provide easy access for bulk transportation, and thus the exploitation of its resources for export or profit was difficult. The difficulty was caused not only by the rugged topography of the hill country, which esp. inhibited north-south travel, but also by the absence of navigable waterways leading to the markets and ports of the Phoenician cities. In antiquity, bulky goods—among which Galilee's abundant foodstuffs must be included—were difficult to transport overland. In the absence of any easy transportation of large quantities of products like grain, olives, or olive oil from the Galilee to major areas of consumption or distribution, the region's productive capacity was not effectively exploited until the early Roman period. At the beginning of the 1st cent. Galileans were probably not deeply integrated into the economy of the Roman world. The effects were likely positive for the majority of Galileans: their produce remained largely their own, and dues of various sorts were difficult to extract.

The situation changed when Herod Antipas became tetrarch of Galilee and Perea. Antipas rebuilt or expanded Sepphoris shortly after its destruction by Varus in 4 BCE, and built an entirely new city, Tiberias, as his new capital, on the shore of the lake, around 19 CE. These new urban foundations served as centers of consumption in the Galilee itself. Sepphoris was in a position to consume surplus from the fertile plains of lower Galilee. Later, with the establishment of Tiberias, the entire area around the lake could also be exploited. The latter city also boasted a mint, and it is from this point forward that the Galilee came to be effectively monetized. This process of "urbanization" (not to be thought of in modern terms, but simply as the establishment of elite consumer cities in hitherto underexploited hinterlands) appears to have been a matter of Roman political and economic policy: it brought marginal regions under more direct Roman control, and allowed elites more effectively to tap the surplus of local economies, monetize the region, and more easily collect taxes, rents, and other dues. The "urbanization" of the Galilee began in earnest under Antipas at the beginning of the 1st cent., continued throughout the Roman period, and resulted in the progressive expansion of such cities as Sepphoris, Tiberias, Capernaum, and others.

It is in the context of this process of "urbanization" that the two most dramatic ancient Galilean religious phenomena—the Jesus-movement, and, later, the development of rabbinic Judaism—should be understood. The Jesus-movement, or at least some early expressions of it, seems to have reflected Galilean Israelite piety, identified with local traditions and was not especially engaged with Judean institutions or movements such as the Temple or the Pharisees. Antipas' initiation of a process of urbanization brought with it not only a novel and potentially disruptive orientation of local agricultural production toward profit, export, and urban consumption, to the detriment of the peasantry, it also imported urban retainers like the Pharisees and other hallmarks of elite culture. Regardless of the actual message of the historical Jesus (and it is notable that the Synoptic Gospels never mention Sepphoris or Tiberias), some Galilean Jesus-people appear to have reacted negatively to both socioeconomic and cultural aspects of Antipas' program. The Q document probably composed in Galilee promotes an agenda of local self-sufficiency, and satirizes urban retainers like the Pharisees (see Q, QUELLE). In the shadow of Antipas' rebuilding of Sepphoris and establishment of Tiberias, it is difficult to see such a program as anything but a reaction to a loss of autonomy among rural or village functionaries. Later rabbinic literature stems from a different stage in the process, and reflects the urban location and perspective of dislocated Judean sages. A rift between the urban rabbis and the rural "people of the land" is reflected in numerous Mishnaic passages. The rabbinic academies do not seem to have exerted any direct authority over most of the people, and the traditions that were codified in the Mishnah reflect an imaginary situation in which Jerusalem and the Temple remain the center of Jewish life; one assumes that this utopian orientation reflects a lack of influence on daily life in Galilee during the early 2nd cent. By the beginning of the 3rd cent., however, the Patriarchate of Judah the Prince gave more official patronage to the rabbis, and it may have been in Sepphoris, during the early 3rd cent., that the Mishnah was compiled. Both the increasing influence of the rabbis and the increasing urbanization of Galilean Jewish life in the following centuries led to a shift in emphasis in the Tosefta (comprising 3rd cent. rabbinic traditions of interpreting Mishnah). Here Mishnaic materials are reinterpreted with relatively more emphasis on the city as a meaningful sphere of human activity. Thus the religious expressions ranging from Q through the Mishnah to the Tosefta reflect the progressive urbanization of the Galilee and accompanying shifts in its religious culture. *See* HEROD ANTIPAS; ISRAEL, HISTORY OF; MISH-NAH; SEPPHORIS; TIBERIAS; TOSEPHTA, TOSEPTA.

Bibliography: S. Freyne. *Galilee from Alexander the Great to Hadrian* (1980); R. A. Horsley. *Archaeology, History, and Society in Galilee* (1996); L. I. Levine, ed. *Galilee in Late Antiquity* (1992); J. Lightstone. "Urban (Re-)organization in Late Roman Palestine and the Early Rabbinic Guild." *SR* (2006); J. L. Reed. *Archaeology and the Galilean Jesus* (2002); Z. Safrai. *Economy of Roman Palestine* (1994); M. Sawicki. *Crossing Galilee* (2000); E. Schürer. *The History of the Jewish People in the Age of Jesus Christ 175 B.C.–A.D. 135* (1973).

WILLIAM E. ARNAL

2. A Galilean (**Galilaios**) is a resident or native of Galilee; despite Isaiah's phrase "Galilee of the Gentiles" (Isa 9:1), all the NT uses of "Galileans" refer to Jews. Jesus is once identified as "Jesus the Galilean" (Matt 26:69), and the bandit "Judas the Galilean" (Josephus, *Ant.* 17.271) is named in Acts 5:37. The original core of Jesus' disciples are twice called Galileans (Acts 1:11; 2:7), and could be so identified by their accents (Mark 14:70; Luke 22:59). Since in Jesus' lifetime Galilee fell under the jurisdiction of Herod Antipas, in Luke Pilate transfers Jesus to him upon learning that Jesus was from Galilee (Luke 23:6). Luke also refers without explanation to a group of Galileans "whose blood Pilate mingled with their sacrifices"—an otherwise unattested, but plausible, action by the Roman procurator (Luke 13:1-2). According to John 4:45, the Galileans welcomed Jesus upon his return from Jerusalem, because they had witnessed his activities during the Passover festival (i.e., the Temple incident, John 2:13-25).

RICHARD B. VINSON

GALILEE, SEA OF [θάλασσαν τῆς Γαλιλαίας **thalassan tēs Galilaias**]. The Sea of Galilee is a freshwater lake located in northern Palestine. At its greatest length, the present-day lake stretches approximately 13 mi.; at its widest point, it is approximately 7 mi. across. Its primary source is the Jordan River, which flows into it from Mount Hermon to the north and exits to the south toward the Dead Sea, though it is also filled by other streams and springs. Fig. 1 Northern end of Sea of Galilee from the west Todd Bolen/BiblePlaces.com

By the early 1st cent. CE, the coast of the lake was dotted by villages and small cities. On the western coast

Todd Bolen/BiblePlaces.com
Figure 1: Northern end of Sea of Galilee from the west

stood Capernaum, Ginnesar, Magdala (also known as Taricheae), and Hammath, famous for its hot springs. Around 20 CE, Herod Antipas built his capital city Tiberias on the lake side, naming it after the current emperor. Another city, perhaps Philoteria, was located at Beth Yerah on the southern shore. The southeastern portion of the lake adjoined the Decapolis, an administrative district within the province of Syria, and the Decapolis city of Hippos stood directly across the lake from Tiberias. The northeastern portion of the lake, including Bethsaida, was included within the territory of the Herodian client king, Philip. Territorial boundaries changed throughout the 1st cent.; at the time of the first Jewish Revolt, e.g., Tiberias, Magdala, and the former territory of Philip belonged to Agrippa II. The area west of the lake was predominantly Jewish; that to its east was mostly Gentile. Thus, Jesus likely would have encountered Gentiles in his travels around the lake.

The lake was known by a variety of names. The OT refers to it as the Sea of Chinnereth (*see* CHIN-NERETH, CHINNEROTH; Num 34:11; Josh 12:3, 13:27). Later names include the Lake of Gennesar (Josephus, *J.W.* 2.573), the Lake of Gennesaritis (Josephus, *Ant.* 18.28), the Lake of Taricheae (Pliny, *Nat.* 5.71), and the Lake of Tiberias (Josephus, *J.W.* 3.57). Luke refers to it as the Lake of GENNESARET (5:1) and John as the Sea of Galilee of Tiberias (6:1) and the Sea of Tiberias (21:1). Mark (1:16; 7:31) and Matthew (4:18; 15:29) used the name more familiar today, the Sea of Galilee. One scholar has suggested that Mark referred to the body as a sea (**thalassa** θάλασσα) rather than a lake (**limnē** λίμνη) to evoke the LXX connotations of the sea as a chaotic and dangerous force, that had now been mastered by Jesus.

Josephus describes the lake in glowing prose ("its water is sweet to the taste and excellent to drink, clearer than marsh water . . . perfectly pure") and the area around it as especially fertile. In his view, nature had so blessed the surrounding territory that "each of the seasons wished to claim this region for her own" (*J.W.* 3.516-21). The area's fertility can be attributed to its volcanic soil and to Galilee's rainfall, which is greater than that of most of Palestine.

According to the Gospels, Jesus spent considerable time in the area of the Sea of Galilee. Four of his disciples (Andrew, Simon, James, and John) were fishermen from surrounding villages. Mark identifies Capernaum as their hometown (1:29), while John states that Andrew and Philip were from Bethsaida. All of the Gospels relate stories of Jesus' activity in Capernaum; Matthew suggests that the town served for a while as his base of operations (4:13, 9:1; compare 9:7).

Many of the fish species that currently populate the lake, such as catfish, sardines, barbels, and tilapia (often called "Saint Peter's fish"), appear to have been present since antiquity. Gospel stories make ample use of fishing imagery, such as Jesus' promise to Simon and Andrew that he would make them fishers of people (Mark 1:17//Matt 4:19//Luke 5:10) and his comparison of the Kingdom of Heaven to a cast net that captures fish that then must be sorted between good and bad (Matt 13:47-50). The Gospels refer to multiple fishing methods—the use of hooks (Matt 17:24-27) and nets (Luke 5:1-11), including both seine nets (dragnets) (Matt 13:47-50) and cast nets (Mark 1:16-18//Matt 4:18-20; John 21:4-14). Several miracle stories involve fish, such as Peter's discovery of a coin for the temple tax in one's mouth (Matt 17:24-27), the multiplication of the loaves and fish (Mark 6:32-44//Matt 14:13-21//Luke 9:10-17; Mark 8:1-10//Matt 15:32-39; John 6:1-15), and massive catches by net (Luke 5:1-11; John 21:4-14).

The lake also provides the setting for other miracle stories, including Jesus' stilling of the storm (Mark 4:35-41//Matt 8:23-27//Luke 8:22-25), his walking on water (Mark 6:45-52//Matt 14:22-33; John 6:16-21), and his casting of demons into swine that leap into the lake (Mark 5:1-20//Matt 8:28-34//Luke 8:26-39). The Gospels also often depict Jesus and his disciples traveling by boat. The image of a lake bustling with boats is corroborated by numerous references in Josephus and the rabbinic writings.

Archaeological evidence—breakwater walls, piers, promenades, anchors, mooring stones, hooks, and net sinkers from at least sixteen sites confirms the importance of fishing and boating. The most famous discovery is a 1st cent. CE wooden fishing boat, extracted from the mud approximately 1.5 kms north of ancient Magdala in 1986. With a capacity of fifteen passengers, it is likely comparable in size to the vessels that carried Jesus and his disciples. *See* FISH; FISHING; SHIPS AND SAILING IN THE NT; SHIPS AND SAILING IN THE OT.

Bibliography: Mark A. Chancey. *The Myth of a Gentile Galilee* (2002); Sean Freyne. *Jesus, A Jewish Galilean: A New Reading of the Jesus-Story* (2004); Mendel Nun. "Cast Your Net upon the Waters: Fish and Fishermen in Jesus' Time." *BAR* 19.6 (1993) 46–56, 70; Mendel Nun. "Ports of Galilee." *BAR* 25.4 (1999) 18–31, 64. Elizabeth Struthers Malbon. "The Jesus of Mark and

the Sea of Galilee." *JBL* 103 (1984) 363–77; Shelley Wachsmann, ed. *The Excavations of an Ancient Boat in the Sea of Galilee (Lake Kinneret)* (1990).

MARK A. CHANCEY

GALL, HERB [רֹאשׁ ro'sh; χολή cholē]. The Hebrew word ro'sh is used to refer to a bitter tasting herb, such as wormwood (see Deut 29:18 [Heb. 29:17]) and is applied metaphorically for a tragic or sorrowful condition (Lam 3:15, 19; NRSV, "wormwood"). There is no certain identification of the plant, although the most popular suggestion is poisonous hemlock (Hos 10:4*b*). The opium poppy (*Papaver somniferum*) and *Hyoscyamus reticulates* (a toxic plant related to the tomato) have also been suggested. The vinegar mixture offered to Jesus on the cross (Matt 27:34) was designed to soften the sufferer's pain and cloud the senses. *See* PLANTS OF THE BIBLE; SPICE.

VICTOR H. MATTHEWS

GALL OF LIVER [מְרֹרָה merorah, מְרֵרָה mererah; χολή cholē]. Derived from the verbal root meaning "to be bitter," this originally meant "bitterness" as an abstraction or "poison" (Matt 27:34; Acts 8:23), but later was a specialized term for the gallbladder (Job 20:25) and bile (Job 16:13), sometimes used for divination and medicine in the ancient world (Tob 6:7-8).

R. JUSTIN HARKINS

GALLERY [אַתִּיק 'attiq]. An architectural term used only in Ezekiel's description of the future temple (Ezek 41:15; 42:3, 5). The term appears to describe passages, walkways, or streets that abut the sides of the Temple and its secondary buildings. The location and appearance of the secondary buildings are unclear.

RALPH K. HAWKINS

GALLEY [אֳנִי 'oni]. A large, narrow, seagoing vessel, propelled by oars (Isa 33:21) that composed a fleet (1 Kgs 9:26-27; 10:11, 22; NRSV "ships"). Solomon built such vessels, that his servants used for importing gold, silver, ivory, apes, and peacocks. Hiram, king of Tyre, supplied Solomon oarsmen. References in Ezek (27:6, 8, 26, 29) to the oars and rowers used to move the ships of Tyre and Tarshish imply these were galleys. The late date of the reference to the galley in Isa 33:21 may suggest the war ships of Hellenistic kings. *See* SHIPS AND SAILING IN THE NT; SHIPS AND SAILING IN THE OT.

EMILY R. CHENEY

GALLIM gal'im [גַּלִּים gallim]. 1. The city of origin for PALTI son of Laish. Saul gave his daughter MICHAL, who had been married to David, to Palti while David was hiding from Saul (1 Sam 25:44).

2. Isaiah also mentions a Gallim as a city on the route of an army invading Judah from the north (Isa 10:30). There is no way to know with certainty whether Samuel and Isaiah refer to the same Gallim.

TREVOR D. COCHELL

GALLIO gal´ee-oh [Γαλλίων *Galliōn*]. L. Iunius Gallio Annaeanus was PROCONSUL of ACHAIA while Claudius was emperor. Gallio was the adopted son of Seneca the Elder. An inscription at Delphi dates Gallio's tenure to 51–52 CE; Acts 18:12-17 describes Paul being brought before Gallio by Jews and accused of encouraging worship practices contrary to the law. According to Luke's narrative, Gallio dismissed the case on the grounds that it was an affair entirely internal to the Jewish community, involving no breach of public order. Given that Paul's eighteen-month stay in Corinth (Acts 18:11) must overlap with Gallio's dates in office, one can then construct approximate dates for 1 Thessalonians (written from Corinth) and the Corinthian letters (written from Ephesus, where Paul went next). Gallio died in 65 CE, most likely by suicide, after being accused of being involved in a plot against Nero.

RICHARD B. VINSON

GALLON. The NRSV renders the phrase **metrētas duo ē treis** (μετρητὰς δύο ἢ τρεῖς, "two or three measures" John 2:6) as "twenty or thirty gallons." A liquid measure, **metrētēs** (μετρητής), is roughly 9 gallons.

GALLOWS. *See* HANGING.

GAMAD gay´mad [גְּמָדִים *gammadhim*]. The sole reference to this otherwise unknown location (Ezek 27:11) occurs within a lamentation intoned by the prophet Ezekiel over TYRE, which is imagined as a ship. Various groups of people take metaphorical roles on this ship: the "men of Gamad" are assigned to staff the watchtowers.

PHILLIP MICHAEL SHERMAN

GAMAEL gam´ay-uhl [Γάμηλος *Gamēlos*]. Appears in 1 Esd 8:29, but is called DANIEL in Ezra 8:2.

GAMALIEL guh-may´lee-uhl [גַּמְלִיאֵל *gamli'el*; Γαμαλιήλ *Gamaliēl*]. 1. Son of Pedahuzur and head of the tribe of Manasseh (Num 1:4, 10, 16; 2:20; 7:54, 59; 10:23).

2. Gamaliel I. The grandson of Hillel, Gamaliel was a prominent 1st cent. CE Pharisaic teacher (*Sotah* 9.15; Acts 5.34) and is known for a number of rabbinic rulings (*m. Git.* 4.2-3; *m. Yebam.* 16.7; *T. Sanh.* 2.6).

In Acts 5:33-40, he urges a Jewish council to show moderation toward the disciples. The historicity of this speech has been questioned. First, it is a perfect statement of the theology of Acts. Second, Gamaliel cites the examples of Theudas (executed in 44 CE) and "after him" Judas the Galilean (executed in 6 CE). Besides the chronological problem, Theudas' rebellion had not yet taken place in the mid-30s when Gamaliel made his speech. While some intervention by Gamaliel is possible, the present speech is clearly Lukan.

Acts 22:3 claims that Gamaliel educated Paul. Some have doubted this: Paul's exegesis in his letters is not rabbinic in character, and Acts is keen to link Paul with Jerusalem. Yet it is quite possible that a zealous young man (Gal 1:14) would have sought out the most prominent Jewish teacher of his day. *See* AKIVA, RABBI; HILLEL, THE ELDER, HOUSE OF HILLEL; RABBI, RABBONI; SAGE.

HELEN K. BOND

GAME [טֶרֶף *teref*, צַיִד *tsayidh*]. Since eating meat generally meant slaughtering a valuable sheep or goat from the flock, it was only eaten on festive occasions (1 Sam 1:3-5) or as part of the hospitality ritual (Gen 18:7). People supplemented this shortage of protein by HUNTING wild animals (ROEBUCK, DEER, and GAZELLE). The role of game hunter is not mentioned outside of Genesis (Nimrod, Gen 10:9; Esau, Gen 25:27), although the Holiness Code does enjoin hunters to drain the blood from their game (Lev 17:13), and hunters are cautioned not to be lazy (Prov 12:27). Metaphorically, *game* or *prey* is often associated with hunting lions (Num 23:24; Isa 5:29). *See* COOKING AND COOKING UTENSILS; FOOD.

VICTOR H. MATTHEWS

GAMES, NT. Though infrequent in the NT, examples include a game played by children in the marketplace mentioned by Jesus (Matt 11:16-17) and what amounts to a game of chance that takes place as soldiers cast lots for Jesus' garments (Mark 15:24). Despite their absence in the NT, archaeological evidence suggests that ball and board games were part of the world of early Christianity. More common in the NT are allusions to Greek athletic competitions, such as might be seen at the games in Olympia or the Isthmian games in Corinth. Paul uses imagery of a runner striving for victory and a well-trained boxer prepared for the fight as metaphors for the Christian experience (1 Cor 9:24-27). This is similar to the widespread use of the athlete as a metaphor for the pursuit of truth and wisdom in Hellenistic philosophical writings. Elsewhere, Paul challenges Christians in Galatia for having fallen off the pace (Gal 5:7), and makes reference to not running in vain (Gal 2:2; Phil 2:16). Images of athletic competition are also used in 2 Tim 2:5 and Heb 12:1-2.

Bibliography: Sean Freyne. "Early Christianity and the Greek Athletic Ideal." *Sport.* Gregory Baum, ed. (1989) 93–100.

RUBÉN R. DUPERTUIS

GAMES, OT. The discovery of board games, rattles, whistles, and pull toys at various archaeological sites throughout Israel demonstrates that its people, as elsewhere in the Near East, enjoyed a variety of playful activities. However, the OT is rather mute on the subject, and of the few references that exist to games and other amusements, many appear in contexts that are unclear or open to interpretation. For example, Gen 21:9 informs us that Ishmael "played" with Isaac, but many commentators understand the word for "play" here (metsakheq מְצַחֵק) to mean "mock, make fun of." Similarly, some see God's question to Job, "Will you play with him (Leviathan) like a bird, and tie him down for your girls?" (40:29), as implying the use of caged birds as playthings. Others understand Isa 22:18 as a metaphorical reference to playing with a ball, but the passage may refer to winding a turban. The only clear references to play appear in Isa 11:8, which mentions an infant playing near a viper's hole, and Zech 8:5, which speaks generally of boys and girls playing in the squares of Jerusalem.

Elsewhere, we must infer information concerning games. For example, challenging one another with riddles likely served as a form of amusement, though the contexts in which they appear in the Bible (i.e., Samson in Judg 14:12-19 and the Queen of Sheba in 1 Kgs 10:1) are far from amusing.

Similarly, a number of competitive sports probably provided diversion for members of the military, though again the evidence for this is indirect. One such sport was belt wrestling, also attested elsewhere in the Near East. God's challenge to Job in 38:3 may allude to this sport, but the verse may simply mean "prepare yourself." A clearer reference to wrestling (apparently without a belt) appears in 2 Sam 2:14 in the report of a competitive match between Saul and David's men that escalated into a war. Wrestling techniques may inform the idiom "leg upon thigh" used in reference to Samson's smiting of the Philistines (Judg 15:8), and the manner in which the angel defeats Jacob by wrenching the "socket of his thigh" (Gen 32:24). Though these references appear in serious contexts, we can infer that other occasions provided moments when such activities could be engaged in for sport.

It is likely that military training integrated competitive sports. Foot racing is a case in point. A number of military figures are described as fleet of foot including Saul and Jonathan (2 Sam 1:23); Asahel (2:18); Ahimaz (18:23; 18:27); and the Gadite warriors in David's employ (1 Chr 12:8). That these are not merely references to these figures' military prowess seems assured in that competitive foot racing is implied elsewhere in the Bible. Thus, Ps 19:6 uses racing as a metaphor for the sun's movement, and Ps 119:32 employs a similar metaphor for running the course of God's commandments (see also Jer 12:5; Eccl 9:11).

Other competitive sports are mentioned only parenthetically in the Bible, and again, mostly in serious contexts. These include horseback riding (Jer 12:5), sword fighting (2 Sam 2:12-16); archery (1 Sam 20:20, 35-38); hunting (Gen 21:20; 27; Lev 17:13; Deut 12:15; 14:5); and stone slinging (Judg 20:16; 1 Sam 17:34-36, 40, 49; 1 Kgs 3:25; 1 Chr 12:2; 2 Chr 26:14).

SCOTT B. NOEGEL

GAMMA [γ g, Γ G]. The third letter of the Greek alphabet, derived from the Phoenician letter gaml. *See* ALPHABET.

GAMUL gay′muhl [גָּמוּל gamul]. A priest recorded as receiving the twenty-second lot in the list of apportionments amongst the Aaronites (1 Chr 24:17).

GANGRENE [γάγγραινα gangraina]. Putrification of flesh due to infection. 2 Timothy 2:17 warns that profane words spread "like gangrene" to decay the faith of others. This passage accuses Hymenaeus and Philetus of proclaiming that the resurrection has already occurred, a stance 2 Timothy deems heretical and, therefore, as potentially destructive as a gangrenous infection.

MARIANNE BLICKENSTAFF

GARDEN [גַּן gan, גַּנָּה gannah; κῆπος kēpos]. An enclosed space for cultivation, especially herbs, vegetables, and fragrant plants. The most famous biblical example is the Garden of Eden, in which God planted every nutritious and beautiful plant, as well as the tree of life and the tree of the knowledge of good and evil. Eden was watered by a river, and so "like the garden of the Lord" is a metaphor for well-watered and fertile land, especially after God restores the land's fortunes. In Song of Songs, the nubile but virtuous bride is a locked garden full of the most fragrant and delicious fruits. Most actual gardens had to be irrigated, and so "you shall be like a watered/waterless garden" is a prophetic trope for Israel's weal or woe (Isa 1:30; Jer 31:12). Luke's version of the mustard seed parable has it planted in a garden, where the aggressive plant would be troublesome even before the birds nested in it (Luke 13:19). According to John, Jesus was arrested, crucified, and buried in a garden (18:1; 19:41), setting up the scene where Mary Magdalene mistakes the risen Jesus for the gardener (20:15).

RICHARD B. VINSON

GARDEN OF EDEN. *See* EDEN, GARDEN OF.

GARDEN OF GETHSEMANE. *See* GETHSEMANE.

GARDEN OF GOD [גַּן־אֱלֹהִים gan-ʾelohim]. Ezekiel 28:13 speaks of the placement of a primal-being in "Eden, the Garden of God." A second occurrence (Ezek 31:8-9) compares Pharaoh, imagined as a tree, with the trees in the Garden of God. Both contexts draw on mythological themes known from other ANE texts and the second creation account of Genesis. A similar phrase, Garden of the LORD, occurs in Gen 13:10 and Isa 51:3. *See* EDEN, GARDEN OF.

PHILLIP MICHAEL SHERMAN

GAREB gair′ib [גָּרֵב garev]. 1. Gareb the Ithrite is listed among the warriors of David known as the "Thirty" in 2 Sam 23:38 and in the parallel text 1 Chr 11:40.

2. In Jer 31:39 the extent of the city to be rebuilt in the restoration prophecy is identified as going farther from the Corner Gate to the hill Gareb, apparently a boundary marker. Its actual location is unknown.

C. MARK MCCORMICK

GARLAND [לִוְיָה liwyah, פְּאֵר pe'er, עֲטָרָה 'atarah; στέμμα stemma]. A wreath worn either around the neck or the crown of the head during special occasions such as weddings (Isa 61:10), feasts (Isa 28:1, 3), receptions held in honor of a dignitary or civic leader (Jdt 3:7), or celebrations following a military victory (Jdt 15:13). Garlands frequently adorned sacrificial animals as well (Acts 14:13).

JAMES A. METZGER

GARLIC [שׁוּם shum]. Garlic (*Allium sativum*) was among the savory Egyptian foods the hungry Israelites missed during their trek in the wilderness (Num 11:5). Native to Iran and central Asia, cloves of garlic were common offerings in Egyptian tombs, including that of Tutankhamen. The plant, which is cultivated by separating and planting its cloves, was used as a spice in cooking, to preserve meat, and for medicinal purposes. *See* AGRICULTURE; FOOD; PLANTS OF THE BIBLE.

VICTOR H. MATTHEWS

GARMENT. *See* CLOTH, CLOTHES; FESTAL GARMENT; LINEN GARMENT.

GARMITE gahr'mit [גַּרְמִי garmi]. Keilah the Garmite appears in a Judahite genealogy (1 Chr 4:19). The term is derived from the word for "bone."

GARRISON [מַצָּבָה matsavah, נְצִיב netsiv]. A military force stationed to control a conquered area or defend a frontier or a border region. The word is based upon natsav (נָצַב), "to make a stand." Philistine garrisons of the 10th cent. BCE were found within Israel at Bethlehem (2 Sam 23:14; 1 Chr 18:13), Gibeathelohim (1 Sam 10:5), and Geba (1 Sam 13:3). David's conquest and expansion of Israel produced Israelite garrisons in Edom (2 Sam 8:14; 1 Chr 18:13) and Aram (2 Sam 8:6). Jehoshaphat of Judah garrisoned cities in the northern kingdom Israel (2 Chr 17:2, though see 1 Kgs 15:16-24). *See* WAR, METHODS, TACTICS, WEAPONS OF (BRONZE AGE THROUGH PERSIAN PERIOD); WAR, METHODS, TACTICS, WEAPONS OF (HELLENISTIC THROUGH ROMAN PERIODS).

MICHAEL G. VANZANT

GAS gas [Γάς Gas]. The purported head of a family that originally returned from exile in Babylon (1 Esdr 5:34, but absent in corresponding lists, e.g., Ezra 2:57).

GASHMU gash'myoo. *See* GESHEM.

GASPAR. According to legend originating in the Armenian Infancy Gospel, Gaspar was one of the

MAGI who visited Jesus' manger in Bethlehem (Matt 2:1). *See* GOSPEL OF THE INFANCY, ARMENIAN; MELKON.

GATAM gay'tuhm [גַּעְתָּם ga'tam]. A clan chief and son of Eliphaz and grandson of Esau (Gen 36:11, 16; 1 Chr 1:36). The name's meaning remains uncertain.

GATE [שַׁעַר sha'ar; πύλη pylē, θύρα thyra]. A gate is an entrance into a walled enclosure. It is used of gates into a city, and gates into a temple or sanctuary, gates to sheepfolds, and gates to houses.

A. Gates in the Old Testament
  1. Defense
  2. Site of justice
  3. Place of assembly
  4. Cultic activity
B. Gates in the New Testament
  1. City gates
  2. House gates
  3. Narrow gate and sheep gate

A. Gates in the Old Testament
1. Defense.
The gates of a city were most important for they controlled access into the CITY. The earliest gates were simple openings in a wall and are found by the Chalcolithic period (5th–4th millennium BCE). A Chalcolithic temple at 'En Gedi has a gatehouse, basically a two-chamber gate and a second postern gate that led to the spring. By the Early Bronze Age simple gates often had projecting towers with thick walls to protect the entrance.

In the Middle Bronze Age city gates were clearly designed primarily for a defensive function. The gate was always a weak point in the defenses, so the Middle Bronze gate complex often incorporated towers into the gate. The two- and four-chamber gates had rooms on each side of the passageway. Pier walls served to constrict the width of the passageway as well as providing a location for multiple sets of doors. The side rooms could serve as guardrooms; they also often had stairs to provide access to a second story or roof for further defense in the event of attack.

A fully preserved Middle Bronze Age gate was found at Tell Dan. The mud-brick gate had four chambers; it also had a true arch across the entryway and each set of pier walls. Just in front of the gate was a series of cobblestone steps that possibly led to a pedestrian entrance or served as part of a revetment wall.

In the Iron Age city gate complexes were designed more for multiple purposes. Obviously defense was still a concern. But the presence of open plazas, administrative buildings, storehouses or warehouses, and even cultic installations in or adjacent to the gate complex indicates a much larger social context for it.

Reuben G. Bullard, Jr.
Figure 1: Four-chamber Iron II Gate; Mudaybi, Jordan

The Iron Age gate complexes had two-chamber, four-chamber, or six-chamber gates. A number of sites such as Tell Dan and Megiddo had an inner and outer gate and indirect entry to the inner gate. Gate complexes served a variety of functions. The first and primary function was defensive. The gate controlled entry into the city. It had doors that could be closed and bars to secure it at night and at times of attack. Towers often flanked the gates and provided additional defensive positions, as well as guardrooms.

2. Site of justice.

The gate complex was also the locale of the court and the administration of justice. Thus the prophets could call for justice at the gate (Amos 5:15). The elders of the city sat in the gate to dispense justice (Deut 21:9; 22:15). The discovery of benches in chamber rooms of gates and in the area between inner and outer gates has been interpreted as the place the elders sat. Executions also took place at the gate complex (Deut 22:24), probably just outside the gate. Related to the administration of justice, the gate was also the place where legal transactions were conducted such as the buying and selling of property (Gen 23; Ruth 4:1-11).

3. Place of assembly

The threshing floor was often located just outside the gate and was also a place of assembly. According to 1 Kgs 22:10, the kings of Israel and Judah met at the threshing floor at the gate of Samaria and the prophets prophesied to them there. At Tell Dan in the area between the inner and outer gate, there was a canopied platform that probably held a throne, again possibly indicating royal activity.

Because the gate complex was a place for public assembly, the prophet Jeremiah delivered his oracles to the people there (Jer 17:19). Similarly Ezra read the law to all the people gathered in the plaza at one of the city gates (Neh 8:1).

Just inside or outside the gate was often a plaza where merchants sold their goods (2 Kgs 7:1). Here the people of the city regularly gathered for commerce and social interactions. Storehouses and warehouses were also located near the gate.

4. Cultic activity.

The gate complex was also a location for cultic activity. At Mudayna on the Wadi Thamad, a sanctuary was discovered just inside the gate complex. And at Tell Dan four sets of massebot were found in the gate area. The strongest evidence of cultic activity within the gate complex comes from Bethsaida. This site had several cultic installations in front of the inner gate. Most impressive was a bamah or high place just to the right of the inner gate. Two steps led to the top of the bamah. The top was a smooth basin in which two incense burners were found. A stele originally sat at the rear of the bamah; it was discovered broken in several pieces nearby. The stele had a bull-headed figure probably representing a moon deity. To the left of the inner gate was a plain niche also apparently for cultic purposes. Four additional stelae, benches, and a shelf within the gate complex indicate other cultic activity.

Bibliography: C. H. J. de Geus. *Towns in Ancient Israel and in the Southern Levant* (2003); Aharon

Kempinski and Ronny Reich. *The Architecture of Ancient Israel* (1992); Ephraim Stern, ed. *New Encyclopedia of Archaeological Excavations in the Holy Land.* 4 vols. (1993).

JOEL F. DRINKARD JR.

B. Gates in the New Testament

1. City gates.

The NT also refers to city gates (pylē; e.g., Luke 7:12; Acts 12:10; Heb 13:12). The city gates are depicted as a place of execution when Stephen is dragged outside the city to be stoned (Acts 7:58). A place of assembly outside the gates, where people came to pray (possibly a synagogue), is the site where Paul and Silas spoke with Lydia (Acts 16:13-14).

2. House gates.

Courtyard entrances to the homes of the wealthy had gates, variously called both thyra and pylē. In a parable (Luke 16:20), Lazarus sits outside the rich man's gates (pylē). Peter stands outside the gate (thyra) of the high priest's courtyard after Jesus' arrest (John 18:16). Cornelius' men wait outside the gate to Simon Peter's house (pylē) in Acts 10:17, and Paul knocks at the house gate (thyra) of Mary, mother of John Mark (Acts 12:13).

3. Narrow gate and sheep gate.

Gate refers metaphorically to the difficulty of following the path to new life as a follower of Jesus. The Beatitudes describe the "wide gate" that leads to destruction, easily entered by many people, and to the "narrow gate" that leads to life, entered by few (pylē; Matt 7:13-14).

"I am the gate" (thyra; John 10:9) is one of the Johannine "I am" sayings. Jesus likens himself to the gate of the sheepfold through which the sheep enter and exit; they follow and trust him because they know his voice. There is no other legitimate entrance to this sheepfold (John 10:1-3, 7, 9).

MARIANNE BLICKENSTAFF

GATE BETWEEN THE TWO WALLS [שַׁעַר בֵּין הַחֹמֹתַיִם sha'ar ben hakhomothayim]. Gate of pre- and postexilic Jerusalem, route of ZEDEKIAH's failed escape in 587 (2 Kgs 25:4; Jer 39:4; 52:7), and located perhaps about 150 m south of the FOUNTAIN GATE. It is probably the DUNG GATE (Neh 2:13; 3:13-14; 12:13), and may also be the POTSHERD GATE (Jer 19:2).

JAMES RILEY STRANGE

GATE OF SAMARIA. *See* SAMARIA, GATE OF.

GATE OF SHALLECHETH. *See* SHALLECHETH, GATE OF.

GATE OF THE FOUNDATION [שַׁעַר הַיְסוֹד sha'ar haysodh]. Speculations based on 2 Chr 23:5 (LXX "Middle Gate"; compare Jer 39:3) place this preexilic GATE in the north/northwest section of an inner defensive enclosure around the Temple courts and the adjacent palace. The earlier parallel passage in 2 Kgs 11:6 calls it the "SUR GATE." *See* ATHALIAH; GUARD, GATE OF THE; JEHOASH; MUSTER GATE; TEMPLE, JERUSALEM.

JAMES RILEY STRANGE

GATE OF THE GUARD. *See* GUARD, GATE OF THE.

GATEKEEPER. *See* DOORKEEPER; GATE.

GATH gath [גַּת gath; Γέθθα Geththa]. One of the cities of the Philistine pentapolis, Gath plays a particularly important role in the stories about King David. It appears first, however, in the book of Joshua, where it is listed as one of the cities where the Anakim, presumably a primordial race of giants, remained after the conquest. Later, the Ark of the Covenant was brought to Gath after it was captured by the PHILISTINES (1 Sam 5:8-10). During his ministry, the prophet Samuel is supposed to have restored cities lying between Ekron and Gath on the border between Israel and Philistia to Israel (1 Sam 7:14). Gath's association with giants is continued in the story of David and Goliath (1 Sam 17), the latter a man of immense proportions from Philistine Gath. After the Israelites' rout of the Philistines subsequent to David's defeat of Goliath, the Israelites pursued the Philistines as far as Ekron and Gath (1 Sam 17:52), which is later the location of a series of anecdotes about the exploits of David's heroes in battle against fearsome Philistines (2 Sam 21:15-22 //1 Chr 20:4-8).

Even though his story began with the defeat of a Gittite champion, David subsequently had very close relations with Gath. During his flight from his rival Saul, the first king of Israel, David tried to find refuge with Achish, the king of Gath. The first time he approached Achish, he was rejected (1 Sam 21). Yet, after his second attempt, David became a vassal of Achish, who presented him with the city of Ziklag as his personal fiefdom (1 Sam 27). That David's alliance with the Philistines is embarrassing to the biblical authors is demonstrated by the care they took in claiming that David actually worked against Philistine interests. First Samuel 29 is an effort to show that while David was correct in his dealings with Achish and trusted by him, he nonetheless was relieved of the necessity of accompanying the Philistine lords into battle against Saul. Hence, contrary to rumors that must have circulated in antiquity, the text claims that David bore no responsibility for the death of Saul. Indeed, in his lament over Saul and Jonathan, David is said to have coined the phrase "Tell it not in Gath" (2 Sam 1:20). Significantly,

Gittite mercenaries, whom he probably acquired during his days as Achish's vassal, played a major role in David's inner circle throughout his reign. Before David brought the ark to Jerusalem, he entrusted it to Obededom the Gittite (2 Sam 6:10-12; 1 Chr 13:13-14; 15:24-25). Surprisingly, Ittai the Gittite was one of the few people who supported David at the time of the revolt of his son Absalom, along with the Cherethites and Pelethites and 600 men of Gath (2 Sam 15:17-22; 18:2). In spite of this relationship with Gath, it was perhaps inevitable that David and the Philistines should eventually come to blows. Second Samuel 8:1 relates that David defeated the Philistines and took the otherwise unknown Metheg-ammah from their hands. Although the parallel in 1 Chr 18:1 claims that David took "Gath and its villages from the Philistines," this text probably represents a late attempt to make sense of an otherwise incomprehensible passage and ascribes to David a mastery of the Philistines he was probably unable to realize.

The close relationship between Israel and Gath continued during the reign of David's successor Solomon. At that time the slaves of a certain Shimei escaped to Gath, from whence they were returned to Jerusalem, thus indicating the existence of cordial relations between the two cities (1 Kgs 2:39-41). Although Rehoboam, Solomon's son, is supposed to have fortified Gath (2 Chr 11:8), many scholars correct the text to Moresheth-gath, the hometown of the prophet Micah. In addition, the ascription of this passage to the time of Rehoboam is a source of dispute.

In the late 9th cent. BCE, King Hazael of Aram-Damascus is said to have captured Gath on his way to threaten Jerusalem (2 Kgs 12:17 [Heb. 12:18]). In the early part of the following century King Uzziah (Azariah) of Judah allegedly broke down the walls of Gath, Jabneh, and Ashdod (2 Chr 26:6). However, in this case as in so many others, the historical reliability of Chronicles is questionable. Subsequently, Gath pretty much disappears from the biblical text and is conspicuous by its absence in prophetic oracles against the nations. Only the late 8th cent. prophets Micah and Amos refer to it, the former in a passage (Mic 1:10) that alludes to David's lament (2 Sam 1:20), and the latter in a controversial passage in which Israel is warned by allusion to the fates—past or future—of the cities of Calneh, Hammat, and Gath (Amos 6:2).

Gath appears occasionally in extra-biblical sources. In Amarna Letter 290 from the mid 14th cent. BCE Gath's (gimtu/gimti) king Shuwardata is embroiled in a conflict with Abdi-Heba, the king of Jerusalem. In 712/711 BCE Assyrian king Sargon II lists Ashdod, Gath, and Ashdod-Yam (asdudimmu) among his conquests, which indicates that Gath was subsumed under Ashdod's authority at that time. In the 4th cent. CE the church father Eusebius located Gath at the site of a village called Saphita. The latter presumably gave its name

to Tell es-Safi, which is where most scholars now locate the site of ancient Gath (see SAFI, TELL ES).

Although Tell es-Safi had been excavated briefly in 1899, it was was not until the commencement of a major archaeological project under the direction of Aren Maeir at the site, beginning with a surface survey in 1996, that the identification of Tell es-Safi with ancient Gath has generally become accepted. Preliminary results of the excavation appear to show that Gath was a major Philistine city from the mid to late 12th until the late 9th cent. BCE. Evidence of a massive destruction level on the tell itself, combined with an enormous and unique siege trench surrounding the city on three sides, seems to solve the mystery of Gath's disappearance from the historical record as a result of the campaign of Hazael mentioned in 2 Kgs 12:17 (Heb. 12:18). It also allows us to speculate that the enigmatic reference to Gath in Amos 6:2 alludes to this shocking destruction of one of ancient Palestine's major cities, which subsequently was reduced to an insignificant village.

Bibliography: Aren M. Maeir. "Notes and News: Tell es-Safi/Gath 1996–2002." *IEJ* 53 (2003) 237–46; Aren M. Maeir. "The Historical Background and Dating of Amos VI 2: An Archaeological Perspective from Tell es-Safi/Gath." *VT* 54 (2004) 319–31; Aren M. Maeir and Carl S. Ehrlich. "Excavating Philistine Gath: Have We Found Goliath's Hometown?" *BAR* 27 (2001) 22–31; Anson F. Rainey. "The Identification of Philistine Gath: A Problem in Source Analysis for Historical Geography." *ErIsr* 12 (1975) 63–76; William M. Schniedewind. "The Geopolitical History of Philistine Gath." *BASOR* 309 (1998) 69–77.

CARL S. EHRLICH

GATHAS. Five poems of the AVESTA, dating to the second millennium BCE and containing the story of Zarathustra's appointment by AHURA MAZDA as first human sacrificer. *See* ZOROASTRIANISM.

GATH-HEPHER gath-hee'fuhr [גַּת הַחֵפֶר gath hakhefer גִּתָּה חֵפֶר gittah khefer,]. A town marking the eastern boundary of the land that Joshua and the priest Eleazar apportioned to the tribe of Zebulun (Josh 19:13). Also, the hometown of the prophet Jonah who lived during the reign of the Israelite king Jereboam II (2 Kgs 14:25). Khirbet ez-Zurra, situated northeast of Nazareth, has been suggested as its current site, especially since excavations have demonstrated its occupation during Iron I and II periods, the time during which Jonah lived. The town el-Meshed has also been suggested.

EMILY R. CHENEY

GATH-RIMMON gath-rim'uhm [גַּת רִמּוֹן gath rim-mon]. A town within the land that Joshua and the priest Eleazar apportioned to the tribe of Dan (Josh 19:45) that they were required to give to the

Kohothite families of the Levites (Josh 21:24). Also, the name of a town from the half-tribe of Manasseh that Joshua and Eleazar were required to give to the Kohathite families (Josh 21:25), but identified as the town BILEAM (IBLEAM) in the par. list in 1 Chr 6:70. According to the later list in 1 Chronicles, the tribe of Ephraim, not the tribe of Dan, allotted this town to the Kohathites (6:69). The Chronicler has possibly omitted the connection of Gath-Rimmon to the tribe of Dan because that tribe had built an idolatrous sanctuary (Judg 18:14-31). This town may be synonymous with Tell ej-Jerisheh. *See* KOHATH, KOHATHITE.

EMILY R. CHENEY

GAUGMELA [Γαυγαμήλα *Gaugamēla*]. The location near present-day Mosul where ALEXANDER THE GREAT's vastly outnumbered Macedonian forces defeated Persian forces under the command of Darius III in 331 BCE. Eventually, DARIUS was forced to flee the field along with a remnant of his army, effectively ending his rule over Persia.

DEREK E. WITTMAN

GAULANITIS gawl'uh-ni'tis [Γαυλανίτις *Gaulanitis*]. The name in the Hellenistic and Roman periods for the area (now called the Golan) to the northeast of the Sea of Galilee, roughly from Caesarea Philippi in the north to the Wadi Yarmuk in the south. When narrating biblical history, Josephus often links Gaulinitis with Gilead, the area just to its south (*Ant.* 4.96; 8.36). The Seleucids controlled Gaulinitis for most of the 2nd cent. BCE, but in 83–80 BCE, Alexander Janneus annexed it and held it under Hasmonean rule for twenty years. Pompey's military campaign put an end to that; control passed to the Itureans from 64–20 BCE, when Herod the Great was able to secure it as part of his kingdom. Upon Herod's death in 4 BCE, his son Philip was made tetrarch of Gaulinitis and Trachonitis (the area farther east). After Philip died (34 CE) Gaulanitis was ruled by Agrippa I and II, and then much of the territory revolted in the War of 66–70 (Josephus, *Life* 1.187). There were some early battles for control of the Golan, but the Jewish troops decided to make a stand at Gamla, a walled and fortified city built into a rocky hill. Vespasian's troops destroyed the city and all its inhabitants in 67 CE.

RICHARD B. VINSON

GAULS gawls [Γαλάται *Galatai*]. The Gauls were also referred to as Celts in both Latin and Greek. They originated in the Danube River basin and migrated into central and western Europe. In 278–277 BCE three tribes numbering about 20,000 people migrated eastward to the central part of Anatolia. They harassed their neighbors until their defeat by Attalus I of Pergamum in 232 BCE confined them to the eastern part of Phrygia. In 25 BCE, Augustus reorganized their client kingdom as the province of GALATIA. Later emperors added territory

to the province so that in Paul's time it extended south to the Mediterranean Sea and included other peoples who were not Gauls.

First Maccabees 8:2 probably refers to the Roman conquest of Cisalpine Gaul. Second Maccabees 8:20 probably refers to the Galatians of Asia Minor, who had hired themselves out as mercenaries.

GREGORY L. LINTON

GAUZE, GARMENTS [גִּלָּיוֹן *gillayon*]. A luxury item of the daughters of Zion (Isa 3:23). The same Hebrew word is used of a writing surface in Isa 8:1. *See* TABLET.

GAY INTERPRETATION. Gay biblical interpretation can be defined initially as interpretation of the Bible carried out by readers who identify themselves as gay. Several developments during the latter part of the 20th cent. led to the emergence of such interpretation. Under the influence of feminism and movements for gay and lesbian rights, questions about gender and sexuality assumed greater significance in many religious communities as in the wider society, especially in the United States and Europe. These questions often led to reexamination of biblical views on gender and sexual practice, as did increased attention by biblical scholars to the social worlds of ancient Israel and early Christianity. At the same time, trends in hermeneutics and literary theory, and studies of the relationship between biblical interpretation and social location, led to greater recognition of the fact that the meaning and significance of biblical texts cannot be reduced to a single content. Rather, readers derive a range of meanings from biblical texts on the basis of, among other things, their own social affiliation and identification. Thus, in a world structured in part by gender and sexuality, readers who identify as lesbians, gay men, or bisexuals sometimes read the Bible with distinctive results.

Such readings may begin by challenging the ways in which a handful of biblical texts are often used to condemn homosexuality. However, to focus only on those few biblical texts that can be read as referring to same-sex sexual contact may be too narrow an approach to biblical interpretation. In any case, the original meanings of the texts in question can only be understood against the background of a thorough knowledge of ancient assumptions and practices pertaining to gender, kinship, sexual reproduction, and a host of other factors. Such knowledge can be pursued by many educated readers of the Bible, and not only by gay readers.

Thus, more positively and more broadly, gay biblical interpretation also produces readings of the Bible that utilize the Bible as a resource for lesbians, gay men, and others who are marginalized on the basis of gender and sexual practice. For example, some of these readings have explored the biblical tradition of lament as a resource for communities wrestling with the impact of the HIV/AIDS pandemic. Other readings examine the contemporary significance of biblical characters who in one way or another can be interpreted as transgressing norms of gender and sexuality (e.g., Jacob, Deborah, Ruth and Naomi, David and Jonathan, Vashti, biblical eunuchs, Jesus, etc.). In such instances, gay and lesbian readers refuse to allow homosexuality to serve only as an object of interrogation and instead use their own association with homosexuality, and hence with the margins of dominant views on gender and sexuality, as a strategic perspective from which the Bible can be reexamined.

Once prevailing assumptions about gender and sexuality begin to be interrogated, however, some of the assumptions supporting the idea of gay biblical interpretation also become available for critical reexamination. For example, the use of "gay" as an inclusive term for men and women is now considered inadequate, since it obscures the very different relations that men and women have to codes of gender and sexuality, today as in the ancient world. Experiences of bisexuality in the modern world as well as the study of bisexual practice in many times and places (including the ancient Greco-Roman world that gave us the NT) indicate that humans cannot be divided neatly into two categories of sexual orientation, "gay" and "straight." Moreover, binary categories of male and female, which are presupposed when defining such terms as gay, straight, bisexual, and so forth, seem unable to account for the complexities of gender identification and lived bodily experience that are often referred to under the rubric "transgender."

Because of these and other complications, many readers now speak about "queer biblical interpretation" instead of "gay biblical interpretation." "Queer," here, uses a former term of abuse as both a rallying point for activists and academicians and as a way of referring to a diverse group of individuals and interpretive approaches. Instead of being grounded in a presumption of gay identity shared among gay readers, queer readings of the Bible challenge a wide range of ways in which normative conceptions of sex, gender, and kinship are used to simplify the complexities of sex, gender, and kinship found in the Bible, modern society, and contemporary religious communities. Gay biblical interpretation can thus be understood as one example of this larger set of queer approaches to the Bible, social analysis, theology, and religious life. *See* BIBLICAL INTERPRETATION, HISTORY OF; GENDER STUDIES; IDEOLOGICAL CRITICISM; LESBIAN INTERPRETATION; SEX, SEXUALITY.

KEN STONE

GAZA, GAZITES gay´zuh, gay´zit עַזָּה ʿazzah, עָתִי ʿazzathi, עַתִים ʿazzathim; Γάζα Gaza, Γαζαῖος Gazaios, Γαζαῖοι gazaioi]. **1.** A city in southwest Palestine, about 4 km (2.5 mi.) from the sea. Although the shoreline in the area is unsuitable for a seaport, the site

was economically and militarily important in antiquity because it controlled a narrow passage between the sea and the desert, through which ran a major international highway (one of the earliest and most significant of its kind), connecting Egypt with Syria and Mesopotamia. Fertile and abundantly supplied by fresh water from wells, the coastal plain around Gaza was well suited for agriculture.

The city is mentioned for the first time in an Egyptian document dating from 1468 BCE, where it is referred to as royal property through conquest (*ANET*, 235). In the period covered by the Amarna letters, Gaza was the administrative center of Egyptian-controlled Palestine and perhaps of the entire Canaan, as Egyptians called their Asian empire, which also included parts of Syria and Lebanon; in the documents of Dynasties Nineteen and Twenty, possibly including the Merneptah stele (*ANET*, 378), the city is often called "The Canaan." In the so-called Table of Nations (Gen 10), Gaza demarcates the southwest boundary of the "territory of the Canaanites" (v. 19).

After 1200 BCE, Gaza became one of the five city-states of the Philistines; the statement of Deut 2:23 that "Caphtorim, who came from Caphtor" destroyed and supplanted "Avvim, who had lived in settlements in the vicinity of Gaza," probably refers to Philistine migration to the area. According to Josh 10:41, Joshua's conquests in the southern part of Canaan extended "from Kadesh-Barnea to Gaza," but Josh 11:22 admits that he failed to dislodge Anakites (i.e., giants; *see* ANAKIM, ANAKITES) from Gaza, Gath, and Ashdod (the tradition of Philistine giants also underlies the Goliath episode in 1 Sam 17 and the brief heroic tales in 2 Sam 21:15-22), and Josh 13:3 lists Gaza and other Philistine cities among the areas that remained to be conquered as of Joshua's retirement. An alternative or complementary conquest tradition includes Gaza and its dependencies in the allotment of Judah (Josh 15:47) and claims that after Joshua's death the tribe captured the city (Judg 1:18) but did not drive out "the inhabitants of the plain," presumably including the residents of Gaza (Judg 1:19). Since the narrator of Judges consistently distinguishes between the conquest of Canaanite cities and the expulsion of Canaanite populations (contrast, e.g., Judg 1:8 and 1:21), Judg 1:18-19 is not self-contradictory, and the MT of v. 18 should be preferred to the LXX, which attempts a redundant harmonization by having Judah fail to capture Gaza and other Philistine cities. The SAMSON narratives, where Gaza plays a prominent role, clearly presuppose that it was under uncontested Philistine control. The city's residents try to ambush Samson when he visits a local prostitute, forcing him to escape by tearing off the door off its gate (Judg 16:1-3), and after his capture he is jailed in Gaza and forced to grind at the prison mill (16:21). Put on display in the temple of Dagon in Gaza, Samson brings the building down, killing himself together with 3,000

Philistines (16:23-30). The same presupposition underlies 1 Sam 6:17 that lists Gaza among the cities whose rulers made offerings of gold when Philistines returned the Ark of the Covenant to Israel.

In 1 Kgs 4:24 (Heb. 5:4), Gaza appears as the southern terminus of Solomon's dominion. Even if the note (which sounds anachronistic, given that it describes the kingdom of Solomon as coterminous with the Neo-Babylonian and later Persian province Abar-Nahara) reflects the actual fact of Gaza's incorporation in the United Monarchy (as suggested also by 2 Sam 8:1), there is no doubt that later, perhaps right after Solomon's death, it again became an independent city-state. The prophet Amos (mid 8th cent. BCE) denounces Gaza alongside other political entities of the region, accusing the city of deporting "entire communities" and selling them into slavery in Edom (1:6). Amos's prediction that Gaza's fortifications will be destroyed by fire (1:7) may have come true already in 734 BCE when Tiglath-pileser of Assyria attacked the city, forcing its king Hanno to flee to Egypt (*ANET*, 282-83). In 720 BCE, Sargon II apparently recaptured Gaza (*ANET*, 284). Its king Silli-Bel did not join the regional anti-Assyrian coalition formed early in Sennacherib's reign; probably in response to this decision Hezekiah, a prominent member of this coalition and perhaps its leader, attacked Gaza (2 Kgs 18:7-8). After defeating the coalition, Sennacherib rewarded Silli-Bel by giving him parts of Hezekiah's kingdom (*ANET*, 288). Under Esarhaddon (681–669 BCE), the same king (or his successor by the same name) was ordered, together with Manasseh of Judah (2 Chr 33:11) and other vassal rulers, to do corvée work for Assyrians (*ANET*, 291), and in 669 BCE he was required to assist Ashurbanipal in the invasion of Egypt.

After Assyria's collapse in the late 7th cent. BCE, Gaza was caught, together with Judah and other minor states of Palestine, in the struggle between Egypt and Babylon for domination in the region. The cryptic statement of Jeremiah that "baldness has come upon Gaza, [because?] Ashkelon is silenced" (47:5) may refer to the capture and sack of Ashkelon by Nebuchadnezzar in 604 BCE. The dating of this pronouncement to the time "before Pharaoh attacked Gaza" (Jer 47:1) suggests, in agreement with Herodotus (*Hist.* 2.159), that at one point, probably after Nebuchadnezzar's defeat by Necho II in December 601 BCE, the city was overrun by Egyptian forces. The prophecies of Jeremiah (25:20) and Zephaniah (2:4) envision Gaza's total destruction, perhaps during one of Nebuchadnezzar's campaigns in the 590s or 580s BCE. Whether or not it actually happened, there is little doubt that Babylonians retook the city from Egyptians, as suggested above all by the presence of the king of Gaza in the list of minor rulers held hostage in Babylon (*ANET*, 308).

With Cyrus' takeover of Babylon in 539 BCE, Gaza became a part of the Persian Empire. Herodotus, who visited Gaza around 450 BCE, describes it as a large city, comparable in size to Sardis, and reports that it belonged to "the Arabians" (*Hist.* 3.5; concerning the city's size, see also 2.159). The prophecy of Deutero-Zechariah that "the king shall perish from Gaza" and it will "writhe in anguish" (Zech 9:5), as well as Polybius's comment that the city offered strong resistance to a "Persian invasion" (16.22a.4), may indicate that in the 4th cent. BCE it supported a revolt against Persian domination in Egypt and was severely punished for that.

Gaza was the only Levantine city to remain loyal to the Persians after Alexander's victory at Issus in 333 BCE. Led by the eunuch Batis, its garrison and residents withstood a two-month siege; after the city's fall, all men were slaughtered and women and children sold into slavery. Rebuilt and repopulated soon thereafter, Gaza changed hands several times following Alexander's death, until the battle of Ipsus in 301 BCE left it under Ptolemaic rule. Ptolemy IV Philopator defeated the Seleucid king Antiochus III in the battle of Raphia near Gaza (217 BCE), but after winning the battle of Paneion Antiochus III managed to take over the entire Palestine, including Gaza (198 BCE). Under both Ptolemaic and Seleucid rule, the city enjoyed broad autonomy as a Hellenistic polis. During the Maccabean revolt, Gaza resisted Jonathan's onslaught but surrendered hostages to him after he devastated the surrounding countryside (1 Macc 11:61-62; Josephus, *Ant.* 13.150–53). The city Gazara that is reported in 1 Macc 13:43-48 to have been captured and cleansed by Simon is most likely Gezer, although the text erroneously calls it Gaza (contrast Josephus, *Ant.* 13.215). In 96 BCE, Alexander Jannaeus captured Gaza after a yearlong siege, massacring its inhabitants and destroying most of the city (Josephus, *Ant.* 13.357–64).

In 62 BCE, Pompey proclaimed Gaza a free city (Josephus, *Ant.* 14.76), and in 57 BCE Gabinius, the Roman governor of Syria, rebuilt it, according to some ancient sources at a new site. According to many commentaries and translations, the parenthetic note at the end of Acts 8:26 describes the city's pre-96 BCE site as a "desert" (thus KJV), but it is equally possible that the reference is to the road from Jerusalem to Gaza as running through the wilderness, i.e., crossing the Negev (thus NRSV). Herod received Gaza in 40 BCE and established control over it in 37 BCE, but a year later Mark Anthony gave the city to Cleopatra. In 30 BCE, Octavian returned Gaza to Herod; after his death, it became a semi-autonomous polis under the overall jurisdiction of the Roman governor of Syria. In 66 CE, Jewish rebels attacked Gaza (Josephus, *J.W.* 2.460; his claim that the city was razed is contradicted by numismatic evidence). Under Vespasian, Gaza was included in the province of Judea. The city flourished economically through most of the Roman and Byzantine periods and remained an important center of polytheistic Greco-Roman culture until around 400 CE. In the reign of Julian (361–63 CE), anti-Christian riots broke out, with mobs sacking and destroying the local monastery. There were also thriving Jewish and Samaritan communities in Gaza; archaeological excavations uncovered ruins of a large synagogue with mosaic floors (one of which depicts King David playing a lyre), dedicated in 508 or 509 CE. The city fell to Muslim Arab troops in 634 CE.

The KJV rendering of ʿayyah (עַיָּה) in 1 Chr 7:28 as Gaza (NRSV, Ayyah) is incorrect and does not fit the context.

2. Gazites, is the gentilic of Gaza (Judg 16:2).

Bibliography: Aryeh Kasher. "Gaza During the Greco-Roman Era." *The Jerusalem Cathedra.* Vol. 2. Lee I. Levine, ed. (1982) 63–78; H. J. Katzenstein. "Gaza in the Egyptian Texts of the New Kingdom." *JAOS* 102 (1982) 111–13; H. J. Katzenstein. "'Before Pharaoh Conquered Gaza' (Jeremiah 47:1)." *VT* 33 (1983) 249–51; Aharon Kempinski. "Some Philistine Names from the Kingdom of Gaza." *IEJ* 37 (1987) 20–24; Martin A. Meyer. *History of the City of Gaza* (1907); Asher Ovadiah. "Excavations in the Area of the Ancient Synagogue at Gaza." *IEJ* 19 (1969) 193–98; Asher Ovadiah. "Gaza Maiumas." *IEJ* 27 (1977) 176–78; Asher Ovadiah. "The Synagogue in Gaza." *Ancient Synagogues Revealed.* Lee I. Levine, ed. (1982) 129–32; Uriel Rappaport. "Gaza and Ascalon in the Persian and Hellenistic Periods in Relation to Their Coins." *IEJ* 20 (1970) 75–80; Keith N. Schoville. "A Note on the Oracles of Amos Against Gaza, Tyre, and Edom." *Studies on Prophecy* (1974) 55–63; Hayim Tadmor. "Philistia Under Assyrian Rule." *BA* 29 (1966) 86–102; Donald J. Wiseman. *Chronicles of Chaldaean Kings* (1956).

SERGE FROLOV

GAZARA. *See* GEZER, GEZERITES.

GAZELLE [צְבִי tsevi, δορκάς dorkas]. Bones of several species of this deerlike animals have been found in Iron Age strata at many sites and indicate that gazelles were a supplementary meat source in parts of the country. In poetic texts the gazelle is often a symbol of beauty (Song 2:9, 17; 4:5; 7:3; 8:14). *See* ANIMALS OF THE BIBLE.

Bibliography: O. Borowski. *Every Living Thing: Daily Use of Animals in Ancient Israel* (1998).

ODED BOROWSKI

GAZEZ gay'ziz [גָּזֵז gazez]. A name possibly meaning "shearer." 1. Gazez was a son of Caleb through a concubine named Ephah.

2. A grandson of Caleb named Gazez whose father was Haran (1 Chr 2:46).

GAZZAM gaz'uhm [גַּזָּם gazzam; Γαζέμ Gazem, Γηζαμ Gēzam]. Head of a family of Nethinim among the returnees from Babylon (Ezra 2:48; Neh 7:51).

The RSV substitutes Gazzam for Gazera in a similar list (1 Esd 5:31).

GEAR [מִלְחָמָה milkhamah; σκεῦος skeuos]. The term *battle gear* refers to equipment used by soldiers, with the exact meaning dependent on context (Deut 1:41).

GEBA gee'buh [גֶּבַע gevaʿ]. A town given to the Levites (Josh 21:17) in the territory of the tribe of Benjamin (Josh 18:24), Geba is identified with modern Jabaʿ, northeast of Jerusalem, across the valley from Michmash. During the battle of Michmash, in which Saul's army defeated the Philistines, the Israelites camped at Geba (1 Sam 13:6). In the divided monarchy Geba was on the boundary between Israel and Judah. King Asa fortified Geba, apparently to guard that border (1 Kgs 15:22). Scholars debate whether GIBEAH and Geba are two separate towns or two versions of the same name (both words mean "hill"). If they are the same, Geba would have been Saul's home town and the capital during his kingship (1 Sam 10:26).

KEVIN A. WILSON

GEBAL, GEBALITES gee'buhl, gee'buh-lit [גְּבָל geval, גִּבְלִי givli, גְּבָלִים givlim]. 1. A seaport city in LEBANON, best known by its Greek name Byblos (modern Jubail, about 20 mi. north of Beirut). Byblos was continuously occupied from around 5000 BCE until after the Arab conquest in the early 7th cent. CE. Throughout the Bronze and Iron ages the city was a cultic center and a major hub of commerce and craft, especially known for its production of paper from Egyptian papyrus (hence the Greek name, probably derived from Western Semitic geval, but phonetically proximate to biblos (βίβλος "book"). Byblos is mentioned in numerous Near Eastern documents of the 2nd and 1st millennia BCE, including Egyptian execration texts (*ANET*, 329), campaign reports of Egyptian and Assyrian kings (*ANET*, 229, 240–43, 275, 276, 280, 282, 283, 287, 291, 294, 301), *The Story of Sinuhe* (*AEL* 1:222–25), and the *The Report of Wenamon* (*AEL* 2:224–30). Byblos is called Gubla in several Amarna letters. Alphabetic inscriptions discovered in Byblos are among the world's oldest; the most important of them, on the sarcophagus of King Ahiram (early 10th cent. BCE), is accompanied by an engraving that shows him seated on a throne with cherubim for armrests.

Psalm 83:7 [Heb. 83:8] accuses Gebal of participating in a conspiracy of nations against Israel and its deity. Since the list of conspirators (Ps 83:6-8) places Gebal after Edom and Moab, but before Ammon and Amalak, here Gebal may refer here to a region south or southeast of the Dead Sea that Josephus mentions as Gobolithis (*Ant.* 2.6); significantly, the LXX does not identify Gebal of Ps 83:7 with Byblos. However, given that the verse also refers to Philistia and Tyre, Byblos is not out of place. Josephus and the LXX may reflect a late Second Temple period reinterpretation, when neighboring Idumea was of much greater interest for Jewish audiences than relatively distant Byblos.

2. The Gebalites were the residents of Gebal portrayed in the Bible as highly skilled masons. They are among those who hewed stone blocks for the foundation of Solomon's Temple, but they are distinct from "Solomon's builders" (1 Kgs 5:18 [Heb. 5:32]). Ezekiel 27:9 places "the elders of Gebal and its artisans" in charge of building repairs for the king of Tyre. Joshua 13:5 includes "the land of the Gebalites" in the list of areas that Israelites failed to conquer under Joshua.

SERGE FROLOV

GEBER gee´buhr [גֶּבֶר gever]. A son of Uri; he was one of the twelve officials Solomon appointed over Israel (1 Kgs 4:19). See BEN-GEBER.

GEBIM gee´bim [גֵּבִים gevim]. A town whose inhabitants fled the approaching Assyrian army according to Isa 10:31. In the poem, the town is listed between Anathoth and Nob, suggesting that it was located between those two places, but the exact location is uncertain.

T. DELAYNE VAUGHN

GECKO gek´oh [אֲנָקָה 'anaqah]. Listed among swarming creatures that transmit uncleanness when dead, its precise identification is unclear. The other animals listed in Lev 11:30 and Syriac texts suggest a reptile. Its groaning cry, emphasized by its name (from the verb 'anaq [אָנַק] "groan"), suggests specifically the gecko. See ANIMALS OF THE BIBLE.

EMILY CHENEY

GEDALIAH ged´uh-li´uh [גְּדַלְיָה gedhalyah]. 1. Son of Ahikam and grandson of Shaphan (2 Kgs 25:22). Nebuchadnezzar appointed Gedaliah governor of Judah (2 Kgs 25:22-26). Ishmael, an opponent of Babylonian sovereignty, killed Gedaliah (2 Kgs 25:24-26; Jer. 40:13-16).

2. Son of Amariah, father of Cushi, and grandfather of the prophet Zephaniah (Zeph 1:1).

3. Son of Pashhur and one of the officials of Zedekiah who conspired to accuse and imprison Jeremiah (Jer 38:1).

4. A temple singer and one of the six sons of Jeduthun; one of the temple musicians who, accompanied by lyre, sang songs of praise and thanksgiving to God (1 Chr 25:3, 9).

5. A descendant of Jeshua, the high priest, and one of the priests who divorced his foreign wife after return from Babylonian captivity (Ezra 10:18).

CLAUDE MARIOTTINI

GEDER gee´duhr [גֶּדֶר gedher]. A city of unknown location in a list of Canaanite cities defeated by Joshua (Josh 12:13). Further, Baal-hanan (1 Chr 27:28) is

described as a Gederite. The name is related to the term for "wall." Some have suggested the city may be GERAR due to scribal confusion between the letters dalet (d ד) and resh (r ר).

PHILLIP MICHAEL SHERMAN

GEDERAH gi-dee´ruh [גְּדֵרָה gedherah; Γαδηρά Gadēra]. 1. A town in the lowland region of the territorial allotment of the tribe of Judah (Josh 15:36), most likely the same town from which potters in the king's service are said to have come (1 Chr 4:23). Its geographical location is the subject of some debate.

2. The Benjaminite hometown of Jozabad, one of the warriors who joined with David at Ziklag (1 Chr 12:4).

DEREK E. WITTMAN

GEDEROTH gi-dee´roth [גְּדֵרוֹת gedheroth]. One of the towns listed in the lowland region of the territorial allotment to the tribe of Judah (Josh 15:41). According to 2 Chr 28:18, it was among the towns the Philistines captured when they expanded into that region during the reign of Ahaz. See KEDRON.

DEREK E. WITTMAN

GEDEROTHAIM gi-dee´ruh-thay´im [גְּדֵרֹתָיִם gedherothayim]. Ostensibly a town in the tribe of Judah's lowland territory (Josh 15:36). Alternatively, the LXX reads kai hai epauleis autēs (καί αἱ ἐπαύλεις αὐτῆς), "and its [Gederah's] farms," thus suggesting the Hebrew reading weghidhrotheha וְגִדְרֹתֶיהָ, "and its [Gederah's] sheepfolds." This reading is preferred, reducing the number of towns in the list to the MT's stated count of fourteen.

DEREK E. WITTMAN

GEDOR gee´dor [גְּדֹר gedhor]. 1. Gibeon's son and a descendant of Benjamin, whose name may also represent his family (1 Chr 8:31). In 1 Chr 9:37, he is Jiel's son.

2. A town in Judah's hill country (Josh 15:58). The Chronicler names its founder Penuel (1 Chr 4:4).

3. A city in Judah founded by Jered. The warriors Joelah and Zebadiah were Benjaminites from Gedor, but whether the Chronicler is referring to the same city previously mentioned is uncertain (1 Chr 12:7).

4. A city that marked the boundary of the tribe of Simeon (1 Chr 4:39).

EMILY R. CHENEY

GE-HARASHIM gi-hair´uh-shim [גֵּיא הֲרָשִׁים ge' harashim]. Ge-harashim appears only twice in the OT. In 1 Chr 4:14, he is listed in a genealogy as the son of Joab. The name means "Valley of Artisans." Because of the literal meaning of the name, it is possible that Joab is not the biological father of an individual son, but the founding father of a geographical area known for an abundance of craftsmen. The word does seem to refer to a place in Neh 11:35, as it appears in a list of cities. See CRAFTS.

JENNIFER L. KOOSED

GEHAZI gi-hay´zi [גֵּחֲזִי gekhazi]. The servant of Elisha (2 Kgs 4:12), portrayed as a man of dubious character, Gehazi appears three times in the ELISHA stories, first in the story of the wealthy Shunammite woman (2 Kgs 4:8-37) where Gehazi serves as a go-between.

When Elisha heals Naaman's leprosy (2 Kgs 5:1-27), Naaman desires to reward the prophet, but Elisha declines. Gehazi runs after Naaman telling him that his master has changed his mind, and Naaman gives Gehazi two talents of silver, for which the prophet punishes him with the leprosy that had afflicted Naaman.

Finally, Gehazi tells Joram, king of Israel, about Elisha's great deeds (2 Kgs 8:1-6).

CLAUDE MARIOTTINI

GEHENNA ei-hen´uh [γέεννα geenna]. The Latin and English term *Gehenna* comes directly from the Greek geenna, itself a form of the Hebrew (ge hinnom גֵּי הִנֹּם), which means "Valley of Hinnom." In the OT the term occurs thirteen times and only geographically, usually as haggevul ge en-hinnom (הַגְּבוּל גֵּי בֶן־הִנֹּם), "valley of the son of Hinnom" (though twice without ben, "son"). This valley was almost certainly located to Jerusalem's immediate southwest. It is mentioned both as a simple place name (Josh 15:8 [x2]; 18:16; Neh 11:30), and as the location of abhorrent child sacrifice by Ahaz (2 Kgs 23:10 // 2 Chr 28:3), Manasseh (2 Chr 33:6), and generally (Jer 7:31, 32; 19:2, 6; 32:35). This sacrifice was reportedly offered to the underworld deity Molech at the TOPHETH altar, and would provoke dire punishment (Jer 19), even a name change to "Valley of Slaughter" (Jer 7:32). The Hinnom Valley may be the implied location for the Assyrian king's predicted funerary pyre (tofteh תָּפְתֶּה], possibly "to Molech," Isa 30:33), and for the unquenched fire in the eschatological display of corpses (Isa 66:24; compare Jer 7:32). Zion's godless fear fiery punishment (Isa 33:14). These Isaianic texts contributed to the term's later conceptual development.

Intertestamental Jewish literature testifies to a growing belief in postmortem punishment of the wicked by fire (e.g., *1 En.* 90:25-26; Jdt 16:17; 1QHᵃ XI, 29). However, this place of punishment is not named as Gehenna until the NT and the later Latin *2 Esd* (7:36). Gehenna then occurs frequently in other early Jewish and rabbinic writing, essentially as a place of punishment, though with different nuances.

In the NT, geenna occurs twelve times, and always as postmortem punishment. Except for Jas 3:6, where it metaphorically sets the tongue on fire, geenna occurs always in the Synoptics and in sayings of Jesus. There are three contexts: 1) sin leads there (Matt 5:22), to unquenched fire (Matt 5:29-30; Mark 9:43-48); 2) disciples must fear him who can throw or destroy them there (Matt 10:28; Luke 12:5); and 3) some

scribes and Pharisees and their converts are destined there (Matt 23:15-33).

The NT has other portrayals of postmortem fate, notably Hades. In the LXX, hadēs (ᾄδης HADES) translates she'ol (שְׁאֹל SHEOL), while in intertestamental literature it often represents a holding place for the dead before the final judgment (notably in *1 En.* 22, which uniquely suggests more than two compartments). However, in the NT Hades also connotes punishment. While it might be possible to make a distinction between Hades as a provisional, disembodied state and Gehenna as eternal destruction of body and soul, most scholars argue instead for a substantial overlap of the terms, since Luke associates Hades with judgment and fire (Luke 10:13-15; 16:23-28). Other congruent NT images include John the Baptist's warning of unquenchable fire (Matt 3:12) and the fiery lake in the book of Revelation, which will consume human and superhuman forces, along with death and Hades (Rev 20:10, 14; 21:8).

The exact process by which a geographical toponym became the locale of postmortem punishment is obscure. The clear association with abhorrent sacrifice and subsequent slaughter, and the possible further links with fire and corpses are perhaps sufficient links. It is often suggested that the Hinnom Valley became Jerusalem's garbage dump, and that it constantly smoldered. Alternatively, the association to the cult of the underworld deity Molech seems to contain a link between a fiery altar and the entrance to divine realm. *See* AFTERLIFE; DEAD, ABODE OF THE; HINNOM, VALLEY OF; MOLECH, MOLOCH; UNDERWORLD, DESCENT INTO THE.

Bibliography: L. R. Bailey. "Gehenna: the Topography of Hell." *BA* 49 (1986) 187–91; R. Bauckham. *The Fate of the Dead* (1998); J. Boyd. "Gehenna—According to J. Jeremias." E. A. Livingstone, ed. *Studia Biblica 1978.* Vol. 2 (1980) 9–12; C. Milikowsky. "Which Gehenna? Retribution and Eschatology in the Synoptic Gospels and in Early Jewish Texts." *NTS* 34 (1988) 238–49.

PHILIP S. JOHNSTON

GELILOTH gi-li´loth [גְּלִילוֹת geliloth]. 1. Means "circles," a locale on the Benjamin–Judah border (Josh 18:17).

2. A place in Canaan (Josh 22:10). *See* GILGAL.

GEMALLI gi-mal´i [גְּמַלִּי gemalli]. Father of Ammiel, the spy from the tribe of Dan who was sent with eleven others to reconnoiter the land of Canaan (Num 13:12). The name Gemalli has been understood as meaning "camel owner" or "my completion."

GEMARA guh-mah´ruh [גְּמָרָא gemara']. Rabbinic commentary on the MISHNAH. Mishnah and Gemara combine to make up a tractate of the TALMUD. These commentaries were compiled by rabbis during the two to three centuries following the "publication" of the Mishnah, ca. 200 CE. Not all of the sixty-three tractates of the Mishnah have accompanying Gemara. The Jerusalem Talmud, redacted ca. 425 CE, comments on only thirty-nine Mishnaic tractates, with a focus on the orders of Mishnah dealing with agriculture (eleven tractates), festivals (twelve tractates), women (seven tractates), and torts (eight tractates). The Babylonian Talmud, redacted ca. 525 CE, comments on thirty-seven Mishnaic tractates, omitting Gemara on the agricultural Mishnah, yet offering Gemara on Mishnah tractates dealing with the Jerusalem Temple. The Babylonian Talmud's Gemara is extensively dialectical in its treatment of the Mishnah.

Bibliography: H. L. Strack and G. Stemberger. *Introduction to the Talmud and Midrash* (1992).

BURTON L. VISOTZKY

GEMARIAH gem'uh-ri' uh [גְּמַרְיָה gemaryah, גְּמַרְיָהוּ gemaryahu]. 1. Son of HILKIAH and emissary from ZEDEKIAH to Nebuchadnezzar (Jer 19:3).

2. Son of the powerful scribe Shaphan, and brother of ELASAH. Jeremiah 36 recounts the reading of a scroll of the prophet by BARUCH in 604 BCE in the temple chamber of Gemariah. The son of Gemariah, Micaiah, spread word of the scroll to other officials. Extrabiblical evidence confirms the existence of a historical Gemariah.

PHILLIP MICHAEL SHERMAN

GEMATRIA. *See* NUMBERS, NUMBERING.

GEMS. *See* JEWELS AND PRECIOUS STONES.

GENDER. The term has two apparently distinct fields of use, in grammar and in concepts of human difference. Languages typically indicate gender, either in a binary system, wherein all objects are either masculine or feminine (so Hebrew), or adding neuter as a third possibility (so Greek and English). Unlike English, the biblical languages do not associate the gender of a noun with biological sex, a fact that sometimes creates interesting translational or interpretational issues. For example, to what extent is the female personification of wisdom in Prov 1–9 a function merely of the grammatical feminine gender of the Hebrew hokhmah (הָחְמָה), and to what extent does it represent an actual female being? Similarly, is the masculine ho logos (ὁ λόγος, the Word) at the beginning of John best referred to as "he" (so NRSV) or "it," as we would normally translate it in other contexts (John 1:1-5)? On this level we find that matters of grammar and of human difference are not always entirely distinct.

"Gender" is typically distinguished from "sex" in contemporary theory to designate the socially constructed, as opposed to the biological, aspects of human sexual difference. Differentiating the gender terms "masculine/feminine" from the more physiological "male/female" can draw attention to social variation in the traits associated with men and with women that are often assumed to be innate. "Gender roles" indicates sets of behaviors expected of men and women; they likewise vary from one context to another, though they are often rationalized as "natural" and universal. More recent gender theory, however, contests the binary presupposition inherent even in this more critical approach to gender (*see* GENDER STUDIES).

In the Bible, as in most traditional societies, the creation of humans as biologically male and female (Gen 1:27) was understood as the basis for important gender role distinctions. By virtue of being male, men held the dominant hereditary roles of head of household, king, and priest. Women were not entirely excluded from public offices and activities: they were judges, prophets, wise women, and entrepreneurs, as well as, predominantly, wives and mothers. Neither men nor women, however, fulfilled his or her gender-based social roles until he or she produced a male child. Men needed to pass on their names and inheritances through male offspring; women were the vessels of this need and in this respect the property of their men. Evident here is the intimate ideological linkage of gender and sex, with the biological process of reproduction seamlessly undergirding male and female identities and power inequality (*see* SEX, SEXUALITY).

The gender of God is also an important issue in biblical translation, interpretation, and theology. The divine name, Yahweh, is grammatically masculine; thus, so are all its pronouns. The most common metaphorical images for God are male (lord, king, husband, divine warrior, father). Some images are non-personal, however (rock, fortress, shield), and, rarely, female (nursing mother [Isa 49:15], mother hen [Luke 13:34]). The regular depiction of the God-Israel relationship as that of husband and wife suggests that the biblical authors understood their God as male.

CLAUDIA V. CAMP

GENDER STUDIES. Gender studies is an academic discipline that understands all concepts of human sexual difference as the product of ideologies rather than of nature, analyzing how these concepts shape social and psychological worlds so as to be taken for granted as "natural" and universal (*see* IDEOLOGICAL CRITICISM). Gender studies arose as one aspect of the feminist critique of patriarchy, but now encompasses as well the study of masculinity and homosexuality.

A. Gender Studies: An Emerging Field
B. Gender Studies and Biblical Studies
Bibliography

A. Gender Studies: An Emerging Field
Feminists identified the problem of androcentrism, the tendency in a male-dominated world to define,

implicitly or explicitly, the human being as the male human (notably evident in the use of man or mankind to mean humankind). While early feminist work tended to focus on women, this insight led to critical thinking on maleness/masculinity as well as femaleness/femininity and, thus, to gender as a category in itself. It became commonplace to observe that masculinity and femininity were socially constructed ideas, culturally variable, rather than innate traits inherently connected to physiological sex (see GENDER; SEX, SEXUALITY). But further complications then emerged. What about gays, lesbians, and bisexuals, whose sexual desires do not correspond to conventional expectations about gender difference; or persons with mixed anatomical traits (hermaphrodites); or those who feel trapped in a body of the wrong sex and perhaps seek surgical and hormonal change (transsexuals)? More generally, if culturally assigned gender characteristics were absent, what meaning, if any, still resides in biological sexual differences?

On a different front, feminism as a political movement also encountered difficulty with the assumption that "women's experience" was the single, unifying reality that early feminists—almost all white, heterosexual, and middle-class—had taken it to be. Given the importance of differences in race, class, and sexual orientation, among other things, binary thinking about gender is as inappropriate politically as it is theoretically. There is no "essential" woman or man; both gender and sex are cultural constructions.

In spite of these considerations, we all are culturally conditioned by societies that have traditionally taken gender for granted. It is difficult to escape the subjective experience of being a man or a woman, even if that experience is complicated or challenged by other social, psychological, or physiological factors, including a critical perspective on gender itself. Since people who experience themselves as women often experience oppression in this name, it is also difficult to imagine a political movement without at least some provisional gender categories.

Gender studies offers at least three approaches to wrestling with this paradox: 1) The sense of being a gendered subject seems natural because of our repeated performance of behaviors that are culturally regulated in such a way as to unify gender, anatomical sex, sexual desire, and sexual acts into a binary system of males and females. The experiences of non-heterosexuals, however, presents resistance against the enforced heterosexuality of the majority culture (see GAY INTERPRETATION; HOMOSEXUALITY; LESBIAN INTERPRETATION). 2) Gender theorists agree that gender is the product of discourse, the ideological language that rationalizes and thus naturalizes the ways we think and live. The less gender calls attention to itself as part of a language system, the more natural it seems. Critical study must then focus on the ways that we "learn gen-

der" through cultural products and discourse that seem to be about other issues. 3) Politically, one may adopt the identity of "woman" as a position within a set of power relationships in order to effect change in those relationships. The gender designation, however, is understood as a political or functional construct within the fluid reality that is gender.

B. Gender Studies and Biblical Studies

An assumption existed within some early feminist biblical criticism and persists today within evangelical feminism, that biblical female figures, while newly emphasized, were valued for their traditional roles or conventional gender traits. Recent feminist criticism is decidedly constructionist, looking at the ways gender functions as part of the Bible's ideological programs. Most of this work focuses on female representations, with attention to the power relations encoded in the Bible. Notable, then, is the relatively few but growing number of works that examine the Bible's construction of masculinity and/or utilize queer theory.

Texts about homosexuality in the Bible indicate clearly the anxiety that existed about masculinity. In the ideology of the biblical world, genitalia defined gender. Forbidding a man to "lie with a man as with a woman" (Lev 18:22), however, implicitly acknowledges that a man could indeed perform the defining sexual role of a woman.

The gender irony of the "husband-wife" metaphor for the God-Israel relationship, frequent in the prophets, renders Israel (usually defined by its male members) as female. More playfully, trickster figures like Samson (Judg 13–16) mix traditional male and female characteristics, raising questions about polarities that pervade biblical thought, especially that of Israelite versus foreigner. Recent deconstructive readings of biblical texts, including studies of God's gender, increasingly point to such ironies and ambiguities latent within the Bible. See FEMINIST INTERPRETATION; MASCULINITY STUDIES.

Bibliography: Cheryl B. Anderson. *Women, Ideology, and Violence: Critical Theory and the Construction of Gender in the Book of the Covenant and the Deuteronomic Law* (2004); Roland Boer. *Knockin' on Heaven's Door: The Bible and Popular Culture* (1999); Judith Butler. *Gender Trouble: Feminism and the Subversion of Identity* (1990); Claudia V. Camp. "Riddlers, Tricksters, and Strange Women in the Samson Story." *Wise, Strange and Holy: The Strange Woman and the Making of the Bible* (2000); David J. A. Clines. "David the Man: The Construction of Masculinity in the Hebrew Bible." *Interested Parties: The Ideology of Writers and Readers of the Hebrew Bible. JSOTSup 205* (1995); Howard Eilberg-Schwartz. *God's Phallus: And Other Problems for Men and Monotheism* (1994); J. Cheryl Exum. *Fragmented Women: Feminist Subversions of Biblical Narratives* (1993); Stephen Moore. *God's Gym: Divine Male Bodies of the Bible* (1996); Deborah F. Sawyer. *God, Gender and the Bible* (2002); Ken Stone, ed. *Queer Commentary and the Hebrew Bible* (2001).

CLAUDIA V. CAMP

GENEALOGY. Biblical genealogies, intergenerational lists of purported KINSHIP among persons, tribes, and other groups, are clustered in the J and P material in the Pentateuch and in 1 Chronicles, Ezra, and Nehemiah. Apart from these there are sporadic lists or allusions to parentage that serve to identify or enhance the dignity of an individual in a narrative or the presumed author of a prophetic book (e.g., Zeph 1:1; 1 Sam 1:1; 9:1; see also the tribal identifications in Luke 2:36; Rom 11:1; Phil 3:5; Acts 4:36). The pedigree of David in Ruth 4:18-22, noteworthy for its length, connects the king to the earliest period of Israelite life in Canaan.

A. Genealogies in the Pentateuch
  1. Tribal genealogies
  2. Genealogies in P
B. Genealogies in Chronicles, Ezra, and Nehemiah
C. The Functions of the Biblical Genealogies

A. Genealogies in the Pentateuch
1. Tribal genealogies
Apart from the genealogy of Cain in Gen 4:17-22, the genealogical material in J is essentially a classification of Semitic tribes around Palestine as descendants or kinfolk of Abraham, the Semite par excellence. In addition to classifying the Moabites and the Ammonites as descendants of the sons of Lot, the sons of Nahor are said to be the ancestors of a group of twelve Aramaic tribes that lived in the northeast and east of Palestine (Gen 22:20-24). Similarly, the descendants of Abraham's second wife, Keturah, are eponyms of a group of northwest Arabian tribes (Gen 25:1-6). A comparison of these J passages with names in the Table of Nations (Gen 10) demonstrates that several attempts at a genealogical classification of the same tribes were made in the early sources of the Pentateuch (compare the ancestry of Aram, Uz, and Dedan and Sheba in the J texts with statements in Gen 10). A feeling of kinship among tribes was traced back genealogically to a common eponym as an expression of existing community. By this means even a non-Israelite clan like Caleb (a descendant of Esau, Num 32:12; Josh 15:17; Judg 1:13; Gen 36:11) could be incorporated into an Israelite genealogy in the P source (Num 13:6; 34:19).

Unlike the branching genealogies in the rest of J, the Cainite genealogy of Gen 4:17-22 is linear in form, proceeding from father to son without naming siblings until it reaches its climax in the children of Lamech. Although this list was taken up and given new meaning by the priestly author of the Sethite genealogy of Gen

5, it is probable that the genealogy of Cain (qayin קַיִן) originally was a tradition of the Kenites (qeni קֵינִי), who lived in the south of Judah. The weight of the list, however, is directed toward its culmination in the three sons of Lamech, who are said to be the creators of the three "callings" of the inhabitants of the steppe: sheep breeders, musicians, and smiths. The prehistory of the Kenites is given in genealogical form.

2. Genealogies in P
Much of the genealogical material in the Priestly source of the Pentateuch is prefaced by the phrase *elleh toledhoth* (אֵלֶּה תּוֹלְדוֹת, "these are the begettings of . . ." or "these are the descendants of . . . "). The opening words of Gen 5, "This is the book of the toledhoth [NRSV list of the descendants] of Adam," suggest that these genealogies came originally from a compilation prior to the work of the editors of P. In the current form of the text, the toledoth begin with the "begettings" of Adam, running in linear form through ten antediluvian patriarchs down to Noah and the flood, ending with Noah's three sons (Gen 5:1-32; 6:9-10). The "Table of Nations" in Gen 10 intends to show how "the whole earth was peopled" (Gen 9:19) from the three sons of Noah—seventy nations. The toledhoth continue from Shem to Terah (Gen 11:10-26, 27), and from there through Abram to confederacies of twelve tribes, each that stem from Ishmael (Gen 25:12-16), Isaac (Gen 25:19-20), and Esau (two toledhoth, Gen 36:1-6, 36:9-43). Toledhoth also are provided for Jacob (Gen 37:1-2), Aaron and Moses (Num 3:1-3) and Perez (Ruth 4:18-22). The toledoth compilation therefore not only functioned to categorize tribes, as in J, but also created a link between the narratives of primeval history and the stories of the Hebrew patriarchs and matriarchs, while also providing a framework for the latter narratives themselves.

In the toledhoth the first name in each list was the last in the preceding list, and the sequence runs in an unbroken line. By utilizing both linear genealogies (as in Gen 5 and 11) and branching pedigrees, the toledhoth compilation accomplished the first overall classification of previously existing lists in the Pentateuch—a real family tree.

Linked to the genealogies of Adam (Gen 5) and Shem (Gen 11) is a carefully calculated chronology of the primeval period that shows signs of awareness of various forms of the Sumerian king lists. Some of these Sumerian lists have ten names before the flood, the last being the hero of the flood. Fantastically long life is attributed to these kings, and in one list the seventh figure, like Enoch in Gen 5, has special wisdom concerning the gods. In Genesis the life span of individuals from Adam to Noah (except for Enoch, a special case) ranges from 750 to 1000 years and from Noah to Abraham 148 to 600; the life span of the patriarchs is 100 to 200 years.

By some interpretations of Gen 5 and 11, the age of the father at the birth of his first son enables the reader to calculate the number of years after creation (AM, *Anno Mundi*) when each of the individuals was born—and also the year of the flood. The various textual traditions—the Hebrew text, the Samaritan Pentateuch, the LXX, Josephus, the book of Jubilees, and the Assumption of Moses—have widely diverging chronologies. In the MT of the Hebrew Bible, however, the flood occurs in the year 1656 AM, the same year in which Methuselah died. Adding statements from other parts of the Pentateuch, we find that the P sources calculated the date of the exodus at 2666 AM, which is two-thirds of a so-called Great Year of 4,000 years—a rather widespread tradition in the ANE. It is possible that subsequent calculations dated the rededication of the Jerusalem Temple by the Maccabees to the year 4000 AM.

Detailed genealogies of the twelve tribes of Israel are found in Gen 46:8-27; Exod 6:14-27; Num 26:5-61; and 1 Chr 1–9, while Gen 29:31–30:24 (including Dinah); 35:16-20 offers a narrative list of the birth of the twelve tribal ancestors, and unexpanded lists occur in Gen 35:22-26; 46:8-27 (including Dinah); and 1 Chr 2:1-2. All lists agree on the names of the tribes assigned to the two wives of Jacob, Leah and Rachel, and the two concubines, Zilpah and Bilhah, respectively, an assignment that appears to reflect the relationships among the tribes during the period of the monarchies. *See* TRIBE.

B. Genealogies in Chronicles, Ezra, and Nehemiah

Of utmost concern in Ezra and Nehemiah is the demonstration of legitimacy and continuity between the restoration community in Jerusalem and that of pre-exilic Judah. At the end of a lengthy list of names of clans who returned from Babylon are six clans, three of them priestly, who "could not prove their families [Heb.: father's houses] or their descent, whether they belonged to Israel" (Ezra 2:59). The judgment in the case of the non-priestly clans is not stated, but of the priests it is said, "These looked for their entries in the genealogical records, but they were not found there, and so they were excluded from the priesthood as unclean" (Ezra 2:62). The books of Ezra and Nehemiah present the idea of genealogical purity more explicitly than any other biblical material. The author was appalled that the "the holy seed (zeraʿ haqqodhesh זֶרַע הַקֹּדֶשׁ) has mixed itself with the peoples of the lands" by intermarriage (Ezra 9:2; see also 9:8, 11; 10:10; Neh 9:2; 13:1-3). Genealogical continuity between the pre-exilic community the restoration community had to be demonstrated not only by the returning exiles but also by the remnants of Israel left in the land.

The most extensive collection of genealogical data in the Bible is 1 Chr 1–9, which consists of genealogies of the twelve tribal patriarchs (1 Chr 2–8), prefixed by a collation of genealogical data derived from the book of Genesis (1 Chr 1). This material introduces and reinforces the emphasis on the unity of Israel found in the narrative sections of Chronicles ("all Israel," repeated thirty-four times in Chronicles in addition to construct forms like "all the elders of Israel," "all the congregations of Israel," "all the tribes of Israel," etc.). The compiler of 1 Chr 2–9 painted a genealogical picture of "all Israel," the Israel of the Davidic era, preceded by a sketch of its antecedents. Moreover, geographical data included in these lists point to the importance to the author-compiler that the territory occupied under the united monarchy be retained by the restoration community. The Chronicler drew from all available sources—biblical, military, folk-traditional, cultic—to express in genealogical form several theological and nationalistic concepts that are prominent in the narrative. Within this sketch the author emphasized the preeminence of Judah—the tribe of David—and also Levi, from whom came the cultic leaders of the restoration. Chronicles as a whole thus presents the picture of the ideal theocracy of Israel.

In the genealogies of Chronicles the phrase "heads of fathers' houses" (roʾsh beth ʾavoth [רֹאשׁ בֵּית אָבוֹת], NRSV: "heads of their ancestral houses," "chief in their clan," or similar expressions) recurs often. One of the characteristics of such persons is that they are military commanders: "mighty warriors," "famous men," "units of the fighting force," or "ready for service in war." Such persons could command "the thousands and the hundreds." Military associations can be seen also in other OT lists, for example in the tribal genealogy of Num 26—which serves as the core of 1 Chr 1–9 and which refers to "everyone in Israel able to go to war" (v. 2; see also Num 1:3). It therefore seems that the Chronicler (or earlier compiler) used the list in Num 26 as the basic information and then added names from actual lists of military leaders and war heroes as needed, especially for the genealogies of Issachar, Benjamin, Asher, and the tribes east of the Jordan. That the "heads of fathers' houses" are alluded to in genealogical fashion in Numbers and elsewhere suggests the possibility that such military offices were in some cases hereditary and thus amenable to genealogical treatment.

In only four genealogies of 1 Chr 2–9 are there no military allusions, namely, those of Judah, Levi, Manasseh, and Ephraim, the core tribes of historic Israel, both north and south. The Chronicler apparently had richer genealogical material available for these tribes than for the others. For the two lengthiest genealogies, those of Judah and Levi, the compiler's purpose is clear. These tribes constituted the bulk of the restoration community, supplying both the political and the religious leadership—a priest and a (lay) governor. Within the genealogy of Judah, the bulk of detail is given to descendants of Hezron (1 Chr 2:9–4:20), allowing the Chronicler to insert a linear list of ancestors of David (1 Chr 2:10-17).

C. The Functions of the Biblical Genealogies

Biblical genealogies were adaptable to widely varied literary and ideological purposes. With respect to language, structure, and themes, they are closely attached to their contexts and to the narratives in which they occur.

The genealogical system of the priestly narrative of the Pentateuch reflects the priestly concern for order and purpose in history—even in the prehistory of Israel. This concern extends to the genealogical relationships among the various Semitic tribes and peoples, and also to the division of history into well-ordered epochs by chronological speculation attached to the genealogies. Moreover in the toledhoth compilation there is an interest in the cultus, the foundation of which by Aaron is thought to be the culmination of the divine purpose in all history up to that time.

Likewise in the Chronicler, the genealogical data reflect the major theological motifs and tendencies discernible in the narrative. In Ezra-Nehemiah, which stands in close relationship to Rabbinic genealogical interest, the genealogical data are so closely woven into the fabric of the books as a whole that it becomes difficult to determine precisely the boundaries between genealogy and narrative. The strong interest in a genealogical structuring of society in Judaism subsequent to the OT, however, seems not to have resulted in generally available family pedigrees, except for the priests. It is nonetheless striking that there are tribal identifications in the NT in Luke 2:36; Rom 11:1; Phil 3:5; and Acts 4:36.

The two genealogies of Jesus in the NT (Matt 1:1-17 and Luke 3:23-38) are examples of the tendency toward the historification of traditional motifs in the Gospel tradition. This means that the genealogies in Matthew and Luke do not come from the earliest strata of the Gospel tradition, although the orthography and the form itself suggest that they stem from Jewish-Christian circles rather than the Hellenistic Christian communities. Both lists fall into the category of midrash and provide support for the application of the titles Messiah and Son of God to Jesus. *See* GENEALOGY, CHRIST.

In general, the genealogical form—both linear and branching—was used by biblical writers to serve the interpretation of history and, as such, illumines the authors' view of historical relationship more than the actual course of historical events itself. *See* CHRONOLOGY OF THE OT.

Bibliography: Oded Borowski. "The Table of Nations (Genesis 10): A Socio-Cultural Approach." *ZAW* 98 (1986) 14–31; Marshall D. Johnson. *The Purpose of the Biblical Genealogies.* 2nd ed. (1989); Ralph W. Klein. "Archaic Chronologies and the Textual History of the Old Testament." *HTR* 67 (1974) 255–63; Abraham Malamat. "King Lists of the Old Babylonian Period and Biblical Genealogies." *JAOS* 88 (1968) 163–73;

Robert R. Wilson. *Genealogy and History in the Biblical World* (1977).

MARSHALL D. JOHNSON

GENEALOGY, CHRIST. Extensive genealogies of Jesus are found only in Matt 1:1-17 and Luke 3:23-38. Both lists are linear, proceeding in Matthew from father to son and in Luke from son to father.

> A. Matthew 1:1-17
> B. Luke 3:23-38
> C. Comparison of the Two Lists
> D. Conclusion
> Bibliography

A. Matthew 1:1-17

The Matthean genealogy, running from Abraham to Jesus, uses data from the LXX for names from Abraham to Zerubbabel (vv. 2-12), with deletions in the list of kings between Joram and Uzziah and a few apparent discrepancies (compare 1 Chr 3:9 and Matt 1:12). The derivation of the nine names between Zerubbabel and Joseph is unknown.

Verse 17 creates a periodization of Israel's history by finding three groups of fourteen generations between Abraham and Jesus. That the author was thinking of the numerical value of Hebrew letters in the name David (fourteen) is untenable, because the genealogy was composed in Greek. In Matthew's genealogy and in the periodization of history in Jewish apocalyptic writings, a fixed number of periods of equal length elapses before the beginning of the age of fulfillment. The structure has eschatological significance: history is in order, the time is fulfilled, and the messianic age has dawned.

Matthew's genealogy mentions four women (in addition to Mary), a rarity in Hebrew and Jewish records. According to the OT, Tamar and Rahab were harlots, Bathsheba an adulterer, and Ruth a Moabitess. In some postbiblical Jewish writings, all four were considered Gentiles. This might reflect the evangelist's concern for Gentiles and sinners. More significantly, these four women had become involved in Jewish disputes between Pharisaic proponents of the Davidic Messiah and those who looked for a priestly Messiah. Including the four women demonstrates that the Pharisaic expectation of the Messiah had been fulfilled in Jesus of Nazareth, son of David and therefore a descendant of these four women.

Many think that Matthew's account of the virginal conception of Jesus (1:18-25) is irreconcilable with a genealogy that traces Jesus' descent through Joseph, and that the genealogy, therefore, cannot be the work of the evangelist. But the genealogy's distinctive features—numerical structure, dependence on data from the LXX, "son of David" christology, eschatological tone—are consistent features of Matthew as a whole.

Both the genealogy and the virgin birth story describe who and what Jesus is on the basis of his ancestry, and both use the title "son of David." *See* VIRGIN BIRTH.

B. Luke 3:23-38

After a comment that Jesus was about thirty years old when he began his work, Luke inserts a genealogy of names with the genitive article that proceeds from Joseph back to Adam or, more precisely, to God. The names from Nathan back to Adam are derived from Genesis; Ruth 4:18-22; and 1 Chr 1:1-4, 24-26, with the addition of Cainan and with Arni and Admin replacing Ram (Ruth 4:19). The only other identifiable names until Joseph are Salathiel and Zerubbabel (v. 27). The remaining names include several repetitions (five of Mattathias, two of Simeon, two of Levi, two of Melchi, three of Joseph, and two of Jesus). Moreover, Luke's use of the names of Israel's tribal fathers (Levi, Simeon, Judah, and Joseph) in the preexilic section has no parallel elsewhere for preexilic times.

Luke's comment in 3:23 that Jesus "was the son (as was thought) of Joseph" may reflect awareness of the difficulty of tracing descent from Joseph while holding to belief in virginal conception, or it might simply indicate uncertainty of the historical accuracy of the list itself. The mention of Jesus' sonship from God in the baptism story suggested to Luke the idea of grounding this sonship in the historical succession from God through Adam.

The most puzzling feature of Luke's genealogy is the deviation from Judah's royal line to proceed instead through David's son Nathan (2 Sam 5:14; 1 Chr 3:5; 14:4) and from him through a series of otherwise unknown names to Shealtiel and Zerubbabel. Luke might have been aware of an esoteric Jewish tradition that identified David's son Nathan with David's court prophet of the same name, which would comport with Luke's references to Jesus as prophet (7:16, 39; 13:33; 24:19).

C. Comparison of the Two Lists

The two genealogies differ in form (ascending from Abraham in Matthew; descending to Adam and God in Luke) and content. From Zerubbabel to Joseph the two lists are composed of otherwise unknown names, different from each other until they meet again in Joseph. Thus Joseph's father in Matt 1:16 is Jacob but in Luke 3:23 Matthew follows the royal line from David to Jechoniah, while Luke traces Jesus' descent from David's son Nathan through a series of otherwise unknown names until the two lists meet again in Salathiel. Matthew has thirteen names from the exile to Jesus (despite the assertion in 1:17 that there are fourteen) while Luke has twenty-two for the same period. There also are minor differences in orthography and form in the two lists. The history of interpretation evidences numerous attempts to harmonize the two lists—e.g., one Gospel provides Joseph's legal lineage and the other his natural, or one Gospel outlining Joseph's ancestry and the other Mary's—but none have proved satisfying.

D. Conclusion

The two genealogies of Jesus are examples of the tendency in the gospel tradition to historicize traditional motifs. Along with early Christian literature generally, they presuppose the Davidic ancestry of Jesus. They arose in Jewish-Christian circles from the need to historicize this belief and to express in a distinctive way the Christian conviction that Jesus is the fulfillment of the hope of Israel.

Bibliography: François Bovon. *Luke: A Commentary on the Gospel of Luke 1:1–9:50.* Hermeneia (2002); Raymond E. Brown. *The Birth of the Messiah.* 2nd ed. (1993); Joseph A. Fitzmyer. *The Gospel According to Luke.* Vol. 1. AB 28 (1981); Joachim Jeremias. *Jerusalem at the Time of Jesus* (1969); Marshall D. Johnson. *The Purpose of the Biblical Genealogies, with Special Reference to the Setting of the Genealogies of Jesus.* 2nd ed. (1989); Marshall D. Johnson. "Genealogies of Jesus." Forum 2/1 (1999) 41–55; Ulrich Luz. *Matthew 1–7: A Commentary* (1989); Geoffrey Parrinder. *Son of Joseph: The Parentage of Jesus* (1992); Jane Schaberg. "The Foremothers and the Mother of Jesus." *Concilium* 206 (1989) 112–19; Ann Belford Ulanov. *The Female Ancestors of Christ* (1993).

MARSHALL D. JOHNSON

GENERAL [שַׂר sar; στρατηγός stratēgos]. These terms and several others refer to a high-ranking military officer (also translated as CHIEF, officer, or tribune) and are used for such officers of the Canaanites, the Assyrians in Judith (probably not the historical Assyrians since their king is identified as Nebuchadnezzar), the Greeks, the Medes and Persians, and the Romans. Famous named generals include Sisera (Judg 4), Holofernes (Judith), and Lysias (Acts 21–24). *See* CAPTAIN.

KATHY R. MAXWELL

GENERATION [דּוֹר dor, תּוֹלֵדוֹת toledhoth; γενεά genea, γένεσις genesis]. A generation is a group of people all around the same age. One generation gives birth to the next; genealogies recount these successive generations. The word can also refer to the interval of time roughly equivalent to a human lifespan. The phrases "throughout their generations" (Exod 27:21) and "generation to generation" (Ps 106:31) are poetic ways of indicating forever. In the OT, the word is first used in the phrase concluding the first creation story (Gen 2:4*a*) and refers to the universe generated by God. Human genealogies then go on to structure the entire book of Genesis—five in the primeval history (Gen 1–11) and five in the ancestral stories (Gen 12–50)—implying that human procreation is in imitation of God's creative powers. In addition, Abraham is promised progeny (Gen 12:2), and having children becomes the manifestation of God's covenant and the fulfillment of God's promises. The OT genealogies are attributed to the Priestly source and the Chronicler, both of whom wrote around the time of the Babylonian exile when family lines were disrupted and the community was concerned about inheritance and identity.

In the NT the word is used in similar ways. Matthew 1:1-17, e.g., contains Jesus' genealogy. In the Gospels, Jesus frequently condemns his age by labeling it an "evil and adulterous generation" (Mark 8:38; Matt 16:4), or a "faithless and perverse generation" (Matt 17:17; Luke 9:41). *See* GENEALOGY.

JENNIFER L. KOOSED

GENEROSITY [ἀγαθωσύνη agathōsynē, ἁπλότης haplotēs]. The term *generosity* does not occur in the OT, although its practice is widely encouraged. For example, God expressly commands Israel to "open her hand" to the needy (Deut 15:7-11).

Throughout the NT, Christian generosity figures prominently as a selfless response. The NT assumes the common OT practice of almsgiving, and teaches its proper implementation (Matt 6:1-6). Rather than greed, "giving freely," materially or spiritually (Acts 10:2-4; Luke 11:41; Rom 12:8), is both spiritual gift and Christian virtue (Gal 5:22; Eph 5:9). Paul depicts generosity as a concrete sign of divine grace (2 Cor 8–9). *See* ALMS, ALMSGIVING.

CHRIS M. SMITH

GENESIS APOCRYPHON. One of the first seven scrolls discovered in Cave 1 at Qumran, and the final one to be unrolled, the *Genesis Apocryphon* (1Qª Gen) is an Aramaic parabiblical work that relates, with additions, omissions, and expansions, some of the stories from early chapters of Genesis (5–15). The scroll, opened in 1956, contains the remains of twenty-two columns, but was originally longer; the sheet to the right of column 22 was clearly cut away in antiquity and the text of column 22 breaks off in the middle of a sentence. It is now generally accepted that text survives from at least one column before column 1, which has been labeled column "0." The document is generally believed to have been composed in the 1ˢᵗ or 2ⁿᵈ cent. BCE.

Genesis Apocryphon interprets the Bible as it rewrites, rearranging material in order to tell the story more smoothly, and embedding answers to unasked questions within its narrative. The nature of the rewriting is uneven, with much more extra-biblical material and much less actual biblical interpretation being furnished in the earlier portions than in the final four columns.

The central character in each section narrates in the first person, a storytelling technique that contributes to the vividness of the narrative. Only in the last segment of the *Apocryphon*, beginning with the material parallel to Gen 14, does the narration move to third person. Another stylistic hallmark of the *Apocryphon* is its employment of biblical idiom in its composition, but not necessarily in the contexts where the idiom occurs in the Bible. At times the use of biblical language indicates a harmonization or rearrangement of material to resolve exegetical or interpretive difficulties.

The first section of the *Apocryphon*, from column 0 through column 5, focuses on the generations before Noah, i.e., Enoch-Methuselah-Lamech. The very fragmentary columns 0 and 1 seem to refer to the Watchers and their offenses, while column 2 describes Lamech's alarmed reaction to the wondrous appearance of his newborn son, Noah, and his accusation of his wife Bitenosh of having borne the child of one of the Watchers. The meager remains of columns 3–5 tell that his fears are eventually allayed after his father, Methuselah, visits Enoch and is informed about the nature of the child and of some of the adventures that he will experience.

In column 6, the *Apocryphon* moves to Noah as its central figure, and he experiences the first of several extra-biblical visions. Most of the preparations for the flood and the whole of the flood narrative itself do not survive, but the narrative following the flood expands on the sacrifices that Noah offers and the promises that God makes to him after the flood. Noah receives several symbolic dreams referring to both near and distant future, including the End of Days. One of the dreams is later fulfilled by Noah's division of the earth among his sons (cols. 16–17). The transition from the Noah portion to the Abram portion apparently occurred in the now unreadable column 18.

The portion of the *Apocryphon* devoted to the early adventures of Abram (cols. 19–22) is far better preserved than the segment dealing with the earlier material in Genesis, and it also differs from it in its handling of the biblical material, adhering much more closely to the biblical storyline. The visit of Abram and Sarai to Egypt is expanded at a number of points, but the story retains its fundamental shape. Once again, Abram dreams a symbolic dream, which warns of impending danger to Sarai when they enter Egypt and thus serves as a justification for his subsequent deceptive behavior. The *Apocryphon* supplements the biblical account further, presenting a poetic description of Sarai's beauty. Her stay with Pharaoh is specified as two years in length, and Pharaoh's afflictions are said to be due to an evil spirit that smote him and his household. Only after Abram lays hands upon him and prays for him is Pharaoh relieved of divine punishment. Abram then returns to Canaan, views the entire land, and traverses it.

With the beginning of the equivalent of Gen 14 (*Apocryphon* 21:23), the narrative shifts from Abram speaking in the first person to a third-person narrator telling the story of the war of the kings. This portion of the *Apocryphon* is closer to the biblical text of Genesis than any other, and there are points at which it resembles an Aramaic Targum of Genesis. With the progress of the story into Gen 15 at the bottom of column 22, the third-person narration continues. The text of the *Apocryphon* breaks off in the middle of its rendition of Genesis 15:4.

The differing natures, styles, and narrators of the diverse parts of the *Apocryphon* have led scholars to postulate that it was not composed as a unity, but that its author put together pieces from earlier works that focused on individual figures. This notion is supported by the appearance of the words "[Copy of] the book of the words of Noah" toward the end of column 5, just before Noah speaks. Features such as vivid dialogue and the employment of dreams and visions, however, seem to be common to all parts of the work, and some of the connections between different segments of the narrative may be evidence either of one author or of a careful editor.

The first sections of *Apocryphon* appear to be closely related to the books of Enoch and to Jubilees, but their generic relationships need to be studied further. It is generally agreed the Qumran sect did not compose the Aramaic texts found at Qumran, and on those grounds the *Apocryphon* might belong to common Jewish literature of the Second Temple era. When describing Noah's celebration of the production of wine from his new vineyard in the fifth year, rather than the fourth (column 12), the *Apocryphon* coincides with sectarian, rather than later rabbinic, practice. On the other hand, the reference to endogamy in Noah's choosing his children's spouses (column 6) may point to general Second Temple, and not necessarily sectarian, practice.

Bibliography: N. Avigad and Y. Yadin. *A Genesis Apocryphon: A Scroll from the Wilderness of Judaea* (1956); J. A. Fitzmyer. *The Genesis Apocryphon of Qumran Cave I: A Commentary* (2004); J. C. Greenfield and E. Qimron. "The *Genesis Apocryphon* Col. XII." *Abr-Nahrain Supplement* 3 (1992) 70–77; M. Morgenstern, E. Qimron, and D. Sivan. "The Hitherto Unpublished Columns of the *Genesis Apocryphon*." *Abr-Nahrain* 33 (1995) 30–54.

MOSHE BERNSTEIN AND ESTHER ESHEL

GENESIS, BOOK OF jen´uh-sis, בְּרֵאשִׁית bere᾽shith; Γένεσις Genesis]. Genesis contains a sprawling collection of stories, poems, and genealogies organized by the theme of generations to make a kind of genealogy of all that is. These varied pieces of literature form a loose but vivid narrative of the ancient beginnings of Israel's life and of faith against the background of all creation. Peopled by patriarchs and matriarchs, often of dubious character, dramatic events from murder to flood, barrenness to birth, and betrayal to reconciliation punctuate the stories.

After telling of the cosmos' beginnings and the spread of its inhabitants across the earth (chaps. 1–11), the book turns to the story of the one family of Abraham over four generations through its fractures, troubles, and betrayals, overcome repeatedly by the promises of God and ending in the unity of the family Israel (chaps. 12–50). The book concludes with the survival and flourishing of the continuously threatened family. The first eleven chapters, often called the "primal history," set the sweeping horizon of the family stories. Through Abraham's family, the book testifies about divine concern for all the peoples of the earth. Its vision is global and its God is the creator and sustainer of all peoples.

A. Name and Division of the Book
  1. Questions about the book's origins
  2. Literary features
    a. Source criticism
    b. Form criticism
      i. Etiologies
      ii. Genealogies
      iii. Poetry
      iv. Myth
      v. Narratives
    c. Thematic and literary unity
    d. Folkloric aspects
  3. Setting and context
B. Narrative and Thematic Development
  1. Genesis 1–11: The generations of the heavens and the earth
    a. Creation in seven days
    b. Harmony and disruption in the garden
    c. Violence, protection, and fruitfulness
    d. Ten generations from Adam to Noah
    e. The Flood and new creation
    f. Seventy nations descended from Noah
    g. Confusion of languages
    h. Ten generations from Shem to Abram
  2. Genesis 12–50: The four generations of Israel
    a. Family of Abraham, Sarah, and Hagar
    b. Family of Isaac and Rebekah
    c. Family of Jacob, Rachel, Leah, Bilhah, and Zilpah
    d. The Family of Joseph
C. Theological and Religious Significance of the Book
  1. God of all
  2. God the Creator
  3. Call to worship
  4. Interconnection of life
  5. God the keeper of promises
  6. Responsibility and reconciliation
  7. The chosen people
  8. God's presence, hidden and revealed
Bibliography

A. Name and Division of the Book

Genesis is the name of the first book of the Bible. Called bere'shith in Hebrew, its English name comes from the Greek word genesis "origins." Genesis is the book of origins, of the beginnings of the physical world, its inhabitants, and especially of the people of Israel. Divine promises to Abraham (12:1-3) structure the stories and serve as thematic threads across the main body of the book (chaps. 12–50).

The book divides into accounts about each of four generations of the family, preceded by stories with a much broader scope that concern the creation, spread, and growing diversity of humankind within in its cosmic habitat. This first section (chaps. 1–11) is joined to the larger unit (chaps. 12–50) in a number of ways, including the statement, "These are the generations of the heavens and the earth" (2:4a).

Although the stories focus on one generation of the family at a time, the stories of the generations interlace, overlap, and echo one another. God's promises of land, progeny, and blessing to Abraham and his family (12:1-3) create a thematic ribbon, uniting the stories across the four generations. In each generation those promises seem impossible from a human viewpoint. The promises face threats and impediments from both outside and inside the family, but they also receive partial fulfillment in gradual steps and anticipatory ways across the book. By the book's end, many conflicts and hurdles are overcome, and the family faces its future in Egypt, reassured by a promise of return to the land of Canaan and of divine presence in their midst.

1. Questions about the book's origins

The book of Genesis has been a kind of laboratory for the development and practice of modern approaches to biblical interpretation. The beginnings of modern biblical criticism coincided with the rise of scientific and historical thinking, and those shifts in understanding of knowledge and of the world were brought to the study of Genesis. There is at present a wide range of approaches to the book's interpretation and a great deal of controversy focused on particular sections such as the creation stories of Gen 1–11 and the story of the destruction of Sodom and Gomorrah (chaps. 18–19.)

2. Literary features

a. Source criticism. Among the first modern interpreters were source critics, scholars who noticed repetitions and contradictions, as well as multiple names for God across the book. They speculated that Genesis comprises three separate written sources of documents from various times that were woven together to create the book in its present form. These different written sources help explain some oddities in the text, such as the presence of multiple names for God, repetitions of events, and seeming differences in styles of speaking about God. For example, Gen 1–2:3 calls God by the general Hebrew word for God (Elohim), whereas Gen 2–3 adds the proper name Yahweh, usually translated "Lord," to produce the name "Lord God." An example of repetitious stories in Genesis occurs when Abraham twice endangers his wife's life by lying to a monarch (12:10–13:1; 20), and his son Isaac does the same thing with Rebekah (26:1-11).

The source critical theory, often called the DOCUMENTARY HYPOTHESIS, articulated most fully by Julius Wellhausen, applies not only to Genesis but to all five books of the Pentateuch. These documents include the Yahwist (J), from the mid-10th cent. BCE, the Elohist (E) from a century later, and the Priestly writer (P), writing during the sixth or fifth century. The theory also includes the Deuteronomist (D) source, but that material has more importance for other books of the Pentateuch, most notably Deuteronomy. Subsequent generations of interpreters have modified the hypothesis in a number of ways, but the theory remains in place as a general description of how Genesis came to its present form (see D, DEUTERONOMIC, DEUTERONOMISTIC; E, ELOHIST; J, YAHWIST; P, PRIESTLY WRITERS).

Although this theory of composition is not pursued with the same intensity as it was earlier, it has left an important legacy with theological implications. Whether and how written sources are visible in the text, there is a strong interpretive consensus that Genesis was composed from many pre-existing materials by many people over a long period, stretching from the time of the united monarchy to the Babylonian and Persian periods centuries later. This means that Genesis is the written testimony of the people, testimony embraced and retold over the centuries for new situations. The book imparts their faith in the one God, Creator of all, whom they meet over and over in the crises of their existence as a people. Rather than being the work of one inspired moment, or one angelic revelation to one human being, Genesis is a book of the people that comes into existence over a long process of inspiration.

There are two ancient traditions regarding authorship of Genesis and the Pentateuch. One holds that Ezra, a leader during the time of the restoration from Babylon during the 4th cent. BCE, was the author of the Pentateuch, a tradition that arises from the reading of the law in Nehemiah (8:1-12). The other more prominent tradition concerns Moses's authorship. In light of modern theories of composition, the tradition of Mosaic authorship of the Pentateuch stands as a theological claim rather than as a literary one. Moses appears for the first time in the book of Exodus, not Genesis, but he is a central human figure in the formation and deliverance of Israel. His spirit of worship, obedience, and courage stands over the five books symbolically. Traditions of his authorship probably served as a way for the ancients to gain authority for their writings by attaching his name to them. His importance as the liberator and covenant mediator between God and Israel grows through the generations and makes him symbolic author of the book.

Present scholarship focuses on the narrative construction of the book as whole, the way its parts fit together to create a certain thematic and narrative coherence despite the compilation of Genesis from many kinds of literature. Interpreters generally maintain that the final version of the book was shaped by the priests concerned with the rebuilding of the Judean community after its destruction by the Babylonians. For them, worship of the one God, faithful to the divine promises of progeny, land, and blessing, would enable the community of Israel to find its true identity and its proper relationships with other peoples. Related to the book's composition is the modern discovery of ancient texts that exhibit many affinities with stories in Genesis. These include the Babylonian Creation Epic (ENUMA ELISH), ATRAHASIS MYTH, the Gilgamesh Epic, and others that have similar accounts of creation and of a disastrous flood (see GILGAMESH, EPIC OF). These similarities reveal that the writers of Genesis drew upon the oral and written literature of their time and culture, but often they altered the perspectives of their neighbors, recasting the borrowed tradition to tell of the one God who creates and sustains the cosmos (see SOURCE CRITICISM).

b. Form criticism. Another fruitful approach used to study Genesis has been the study of oral traditions that lay behind the written sources. Herman Gunkel gave this line of interpretation definitive expression. Gunkel proposed that pre-written traditions of oral societies gave texts their literary shape. The oral performance of texts according to conventional patterns underlay the written documents. Examples of these literary patterns or genres in Genesis include genealogies, sagas or stories of heroes, and etiologies, stories of the origins of things, place, and practices. According to form critics, repeated events in life, such as worship rituals, legal settings, and communal gatherings, gave rise to these conventional patterns of conveying material. Because oral traditions were publicly performed and preserved ancient memories, they provide a partial window into the world of the society that produced the biblical texts (see FORM CRITICISM, OT).

Form critical interpretation remains a significant approach to the study of Genesis. There is now a consensus among interpreters that literary genres not only structure texts but are also a major aspect of how a text communicates meaning. If readers recognize, for example, that cosmogonies (creation accounts) are neither histories nor modern scientific accounts of how things came to be, but rather are theological texts that explain the world as it is, then readers avoid misinterpreting the text and forcing it to say things it does not convey. See COSMONOGY, COSMOLOGY.

Recent study of oral traditions somewhat complicates understandings of the origins of Genesis. Whether specific forms arise from oral or written traditions is no longer clear because processes of both speaking and writing probably interact with each other across a long process of composition, rather than occurring in separate stages of production. Genesis welds together oral and written materials that mutually shape each other. The legacy of form criticism remains central to interpretation of Genesis because the study of genres helps to illuminate the text's purposes.

i. Etiologies. Among the genres or literary forms that appear in Genesis are etiologies. An ETIOLOGY is a story that explains why things are they way they are. In one sense, the whole of Genesis is an etiology of Israel. It tells how the nation came to be from its beginnings among the people of the world as co-descendants of Adam and Eve, to its particular origins in the family of Abraham and Sarah, and its survival and triumph in Egypt under Joseph. The book also explains how Israel's relations with neighboring peoples came to be. The enmity between the Ishmaelites and Israel, for instance, has its roots in Hagar's enslavement to Abraham and Sarah, who mistreat her and send her and her child away into the wilderness (chaps. 16 and 21). The conflict between Edom and Israel arises from the original struggles between Esau and Jacob, eponymous ancestors of the two nations (Gen 25:23).

The book contains smaller etiologies, as well, such as the story of the Garden of Eden (Gen 2:4b–3:23; see EDEN, GARDEN OF). The first part of the story (2:4b-24) explains the origins of sexual attraction and marriage. "Therefore a man leaves his father and mother and clings to his wife, and they become one flesh" (v. 24). The second part (3:1-23) names disobedience as the cause of discord between man and woman, animals and humans, and humans and God. It also tells why men labor fruitlessly and women experience pain in childbirth and become subordinate to their husbands (3:16). These and other etiologies explain the social realities of the hearer by telling of events in the mysterious past that directly shape the present.

The story of BABEL is another example of an etiology (11:1-9). Although the genealogy of the previous chap. 10 reports that the descendants of Noah spread across the earth and spoke their own languages, the Babel story provides a narrative explanation of the confusion of tongues. The inability of peoples to speak to one another is God's response to human efforts to build a city and a tower. "Therefore it was called Babel, because there the Lord confused the language of all the earth" (11:9).

Other etiologies explain how places and shrines got their names and, in the process, draw attention to important things that happen there. Hagar's experience of the God who sees (El-roi) gives the well where the event occurs its name, Beer-lahai-roi (16:14). Acts of naming in these etiologies help underscore the significance of events that occur there. Jacob's dream of the ladder extending between heaven and earth with the angels of God ascending and descending, for instance, becomes the occasion to name the place "Bethel," that is, the "house of God" (28:12-18). Some stories are etiologies of Israelite practices. Circumcision arises as a sign of God's covenant with Abraham (17:10-15). Similarly, Israelites do not eat "the thigh muscle" because the angel who wrestled with Jacob until dawn injured his thigh, but not until after he changed Jacob's name to Israel (32:22-32).

ii. Genealogies. Genealogies are another major literary form that appears in Genesis, usually considered the product of the priestly writers who put the book into its final form. The book itself is a kind of loose GENEALOGY, because it establishes relationships of birth among all the family of Israel, between Israel and its neighboring peoples, and among all the peoples of the earth descended from the first couple in Eden. But this theological claim emerges also in part from the genealogical lists that join major parts of the book. To modern western readers, the genealogies ("the begats") might seem unimportant, but they not only serve important literary purposes like bridging time and generations and so structuring the book, they also connect everyone and everything to each other. From Adam and Eve down through the generation to the family of Joseph, every one is related to everyone else. All are brothers and sisters both in the family and among the peoples, and all are part of God's creation of the earth and its animal inhabitants.

iii. Poetry. Although Genesis largely comprises narratives, poetry appears frequently and draws attention to various important moments in the overall story (*see* POETRY, HEBREW). When God creates the woman in the garden and brings her to the man, the man bursts out in poetic joy of recognition:

This at last is bone of my bones and flesh of my flesh;
This one shall be called Woman, for of Man this one
was taken (2:23).

The condensed language and balanced, parallel phrases of this poetic verse accent the moment of climax in the creation account when the human is no longer alone.

Likewise, the poetic structure of God's address to the serpent and the humans (3:14-19) highlights the disintegration of harmony and interrelationship among animals, humans, and the earth that chap. 2 establishes. Another example of poetry used to highlight important moments in the narrative is Jacob's blessing of his twelve sons (chap. 49). There poetry portrays the tribes and their fates according to the character of each son. It is as if Jacob prophesies what happens much later in the nation's history to predict the relationships

of disharmony, stuggle, and domination that occur among them.

iv. Myth. The first CREATION story falls somewhere between poetry and prose (Gen1–2:4a). Its repetitious patterning of particular phrases from day to day—"and God said," "and so it was evening and morning," and "God saw it was good"—create a poetic orderliness built from imagery of the natural world. Many interpreters identify the text as a hymn-like narrative in praise of the God of creation. But this first creation account, like the second one (2:4a–3:24) also falls under the literary category "myth of creation." As a literary form, myth does not mean "false." It refers rather, to any story in which gods interact with humans. Although much of Genesis might be called "mythic" in this sense, a prime example of "myth" is the peculiar story where the sons of God intermarry with the daughter of humans (6:1-4). The sons of God are heavenly creatures whose marriages to human women produce giants, called the "nephilim." This mythic material may be included in this section of Genesis to demonstrate the spread of sinfulness and what ancients might think of as perverse mixing of creatures from different spheres of existence (*See* MYTH IN THE NT; MYTH IN THE OT).

v. Narratives. The predominant genre of the book of Genesis is narrative, the telling of stories in prose (*see* NARRATIVE LITERATURE). These include narratives of patriarchs and matriarchs, often called "sagas." A SAGA is a loosely constructed account of a hero or a family facing many struggles. The stories of Abraham, SARAH, ISAAC, HAGAR, and Ishmael, for example, can be considered a saga containing a collection of smaller narratives. The saga begins with Abraham's calling (12:1-9), followed by a journey to Egypt where his wife Sarai faces a threat to her life and status at the hands of Pharaoh and with Abraham's complicity (12:10-20) Often called "the imperilment of the matriarch," the basic story outline also occurs in chap. 20 and 26:1-11. *See* ABRAHAM IN THE OT; ISHMAEL, ISHMAELITES.

A conflict narrative depicts Abraham's encounter with LOT when the two divide the land between them because the land cannot support both large families (13:1-18). A battle story follows as Abraham encounters four local warrior kings (14:1-24). A story portrays the ritual sealing of the covenant between God and Abraham. These various types of narrative are set next to each other with little literary connection, but their juxtaposition creates the impression of continuity and development in the lives of the characters. By contrast, the story of Joseph's rise, fall, and rise again (chaps. 37–50) is more tightly structured. Characters develop in complex ways and plot lines are clearer. The tighter narrative form causes interpreters to refer the Jospeh stories as a "novella," or little novel.

Among the literary components of the Genesis narratives are their attention to character development. Abraham, for example, begins as a meddling figure who tries to control his own destiny by adopting Eliezar of Damascus as his heir (15:1-6) and by taking Hagar to be the mother of the promise (16:1-6). By chap. 22, however, he trusts God enough to bind his son Isaac for sacrifice at God's command.

Jacob, too, changes from being an arrogant and conniving trickster who always gets his own way in the early stories about Esau and his family (25:23-34) to become a humble, generous, and peace-seeking brother (chap. 33). Jacob's character, though, remains complex and contradictory. He does not interfere when his sons retaliate for DINAH's rape by massacring the men of Shechem (chap. 34). And his favoritism for RACHEL's sons, Joseph (37:2-4) and Benjamin (chap. 42) causes great damage to the family. His stubborn grief for Joseph endangers the family's future (42:36-38). Circumstances intervene, however, and he accepts risk (43:11-14) and finds new life (45:25-28).

Narrative characterizations not only enable the book to present main characters as models of faith and obedience, but also as flawed human beings who struggle with others and with God and who come to clarity and wholeness in their vocations on a long, arduous path.

c. Thematic and literary unity. The multiplicity of literary forms in Genesis may make the book look like a hodge-podge of unrelated pieces, but that is not the case. Common themes of promises join the stories into a larger narrative of one family and its survival. The promises to Abraham (12:1-3) serve as an overarching theological structure for the body of the book (chaps. 12–50). When God calls Abram to leave his father's house for an unknown land, God also promises to make of him a great nation, to bless him, to make his name great, and through him, "all the families of the earth shall be blessed" (12:3). From generation to generation, the fulfillment of these promises appears to be impossible. Family members betray and trick one another; the families of the earth do battle with and thwart the life of Israel and even attempt to enslave them. But despite these many obstacles, the divine promises reach fulfillment gradually, incrementally, until the whole family finds partial reconciliation and lives peacefully among the nations at the end of the book.

Another element of the book's unity occurs in the interrmingling of the stories of the generations. Just as with the lives of any multi-generational family, accounts of the generations do not form discrete story units; rather the boundaries between the generations are fluid and overlapping. It is hard to tell, for example, where the story of Abraham ends and Isaac begins because Isaac's birth (chap. 21), near sacrifice (chap 22), betrothal (chap. 24), and presence at Abraham's burial (25:8) occur as central events in Abraham's story. Stories of Isaac's adulthood, in turn, overlap with the lives of Jacob and Esau, who become more prominent characters than he (chaps. 26–27).

By far the most intergenerational stories of all revolve around Jacob whose actions impinge upon the lives of his parents, Isaac and Rebekah, and set in motion the troubles of the next generation of thirteen children whom he begets. These are the twelve sons, each of whom becomes the eponymous ancestor of one of the twelve tribes of Israel (29:31–30:24; 35:16-31) and a daughter, Dinah (chap. 34). Finally, Jacob presides as the patriarch in the background of the stories of Joseph. Events in Joseph's life slip similarly back and forth between events in Egypt where he is the principal character and events in Canaan where Jacob continues to preside over the family.

At the literary level, these interlocking stories create significant threads across the generations where actions of betrayal, dysfunction, and trickery repeat themselves as if the fracturing of relationship begun in the garden continues to be reenacted among the children of Abraham. Abraham and Sarah abuse and expel Hagar and her son (21:8-14). Abraham nearly takes the life of Isaac under divine command (chap. 22). Jacob tricks his brother and his father Isaac, thereby stealing Esau's blessing for himself (27:1-38). His father-in-law Laban, in turn, deceives him by switching Rachel, the promised bride, with her sister Leah and so gaining Jacob's indentured labor (29:15-20). Finally, Joseph's brothers sell him into slavery after they nearly kill him (ch. 37).

The interconnected generational stories also show a movement toward reconciliation and healing. Sarah's laughter (18:12-15) replaces her bitter envy of Hagar (16:1-6). Both Abraham's sons Isaac and Ishmael gather in peace to bury him (25:9). Rachel and Leah join together in support of Jacob against the control of their father (31:14-16). Jacob and Esau reunite in peace and generosity (33:1-15), and Joseph makes peace with his brothers (45:1-15).

Finally, the literary intermingling of the stories of the generations and thematic patterns indicate that Genesis holds a view of reality in which everything and everyone is related to each other. Not only are the generations of Israel intimately connected with one another, but all the nations and the non-human creation itself are connected in a web of life, a matrix of relationship and interconnection created by the one God, Yahweh.

d. Folkloric aspects. A final literary feature of Genesis is the folkloric nature of some of the narratives. The stories tell of underdogs like Jacob who use wit and cunning to outwit those with power over them. Jacob tricks his brother and his father. Later his father-in-law Laban tricks him into marrying both his daughters and working as his indentured servant for years. Jacob's deceit marks him as a flawed character, but it also presents him as one engaged in wily tactics to survive life-defeating circumstances. This makes him what folklorists call "a trickster," a stock figure in literature who uses the only power available to him to survive. He deceives those with power over him to make his way in the world. That Genesis presents Jacob, the father of Israel, in such a way makes it a remarkable story of origins. Rather than speaking of him as a virtuous hero, without fault or deceit, Genesis portrays the nations's eponymous ancestor as one who betrayed, is betrayed, and slowly moves toward wholeness and healing in the midst of his struggles with people and with God.

Another folkloric feature of Genesis appears in the ways several stories mock and subtly make fun of other nations. The neighboring nations of Moab and Amon, for example, derive from incestuous relations between Lot and his daughters (19:30-38). Although they are related to Abraham's family, they are illegitimate children. Esau, father of the nation of Edom and named with a word related to the word for red, sells his heritage for red stew (25:30-34). Likewise, the Pharaoh, who raises Joseph to the highest place in Egypt next to himself, virtually abdicates responsibility to Joseph who, in effect, rules Egypt (41:41-45).

With delicious irony for hearers whose ancestors were once enslaved in Egypt, the story presents Joseph enslaving all the Egyptians, taking their money, their land, and, finally, their labor in payment for the food he supplies (47:13-26). The triumph of Joseph over the Egyptians would be heard both as a turning of the tables on the Egyptians and perhaps as a theological promise of a similar reversal for captives much later in Babylon. The less powerful characters (like Jacob among Laban's family, or Abraham with Pharaoh and Abimilech, or Joseph before Potiphar the jailor and Pharaoh) survive by their cunning, their clever outwitting of their overlords and captors, finally to make their way toward new life. Readers facing threatening futures can find examples of both divine faithfulness and human ingenuity in cooperation with God's promises. (*See* FOLKLORE IN BIBLICAL INTERPRETATION)

3. Setting and context

The book's many literary layers address multiple audiences in various contexts across the centuries, but the people for whom the material was gathered were probably those who had just returned from exile in Babylon, as well as those who remained in the land. The Babylonian invasions of Judah during the 6th cent. BCE virtually destroyed Judah as a nation. Leaders were deported to Babylon, invasions left Jerusalem in ruins, and the Babylonians occupied the land for fifty years. In the aftermath of the destruction, the nation's future was at stake. Not only was Judah no longer an independent nation, but God seemed to have abandoned them or even to have lost the war to Babylonian deities. Redactors of Genesis responded to this theological crisis by emphasizing God's faithfulness to the promises made to Abraham

Shortly after Babylon fell to the Persians in 538 BCE, King Cyrus of Persia issued an edict to permit the exiles to return to Judah. Although the the prophet Second Isaiah had promised exiles a glorious return

and a rebuilt people, the return itself was less than wonderful. The books of Ezra and Nehemiah portray a reality of conflict and quarrelling inside the community, with those who had remained in the land, and with neighboring peoples. Genesis takes on additional layers of meaning in view of this context. It points to the possibility of reconciliation within and names the nation's call to be a blessing to the peoples of the world.

The book's attention, therefore, to themes of conflict and competition within family groups, and of the renewal of divine promises to Abraham from generation to generation would assure this once shattered people that they would survive their present struggles. Despite bitter troubles and long conflict between Jacob and Esau, the two brothers manage to meet again in peace, humility, and generosity. Similarly, despite Jacob's preference for Joseph and hatred among the brothers, despite their plans to kill him and sell him into slavery, and despite his later distrust of them, the whole family reaches peaceful accommodation and reunites.

The themes of divine PROMISE that bind the book together offer the rebuilding community a renewed vision of its identity. The people of Judah are children of Abraham and Sarah, called by God to the land of promise. God, not they, will make of them a great nation, give them a name, and will make them a blessing to the nations around them. The God who regathers them is the Creator of the cosmos, the Governor of all peoples, and the one who not only commands them to be fruitful and to multiply, but guides that fruitfulness. (*See* COVENANT, OT AND NT)

Other themes of Genesis also contribute to the rebuilding of the community after its invasion, occupation, and deportation by Babylon. The prominence of God's word in the first creation account, for example, offers hope that the divine word is still powerful, creative, and the producer of order regardless of the chaos the community faces. Moreover, the creativity of that word that brought forth the cosmos and all its creatures implies that the word of the same God can recreate Israel. Similarly, the theme of worship, anticipated in the first creation account when God rests on the Sabbath, is reiterated in stories of worship to call the community to a renewal of itself as a worshiping people.

B. Narrative and Thematic Development
1. Genesis 1–11—The generations of the heavens and the earth

Genesis 1–11 is a narrative of beginnings. Often called the "primeval history," it is history before "history" in any modern sense. Most national and tribal peoples have stories of beginnings to explain who they later become. Israel's stories of origin begin not with the chosen people themselves but with God's creation of and interaction with the cosmos and all its inhabitants. These chapters introduce Genesis and the whole

Bible with an unmistakable faith claim; Israel's God is the God of everything and everyone.

The primeval history contains its own various literary genres. Two CREATION accounts open the book. The first account of creation in seven days (1–2:4*a*) is usually considered poetic prose, hymn-like in style, probably from the Priestly writer. The second creation account, from the Yahwhist or J writer, is prose narrative that takes place in the Garden in two scenes. The first scene (2:4*b*-24) establishes harmony and interrelationship among the human characters, animals, the earth and God. The second scene (3:1-24) describes the dissolution of that harmony. Genealogies link the mythic story of giants and humans, and stories about fractured relations among peoples (4:23-24). Loose thematic threads connect the passages to form a prologue for stories of God's engagement with the family of Abraham which forms the body of the book (12–50:26).

While there are many ways to interpret these beginning chapters, one central approach is to see them presenting God's efforts to create a whole and harmonious world, efforts that are thwarted repeatedly by human violence and division. Episodes in these chapters anticipate major themes of the book, ranging from God's concern for all peoples to conflict among kinfolk and with other peoples. Many interpreters believe these conflicts prepare the way for another creative beginning when God's chooses Abraham and his family to be a blessing for the nations.

a. Creation in seven days. The book's first words are remarkably difficult to translate. It is not clear from the Hebrew whether "in the beginning," God creates from nothing or if the text plunges into the first of a series of creative acts "when God began to create." Perhaps the ambiguity in the Hebrew is deliberate so as to honor the mysteries of creation and the human inability to fathom it. What is incontestable is that God is Creator. Genesis does not answer modern theological or scientific questions, though some traditions hold that it does. Instead, it imagines a world before God speaks, a world of "waste and void," chaos and emptiness. Into that abyss comes the "breath" or "spirit" of God, hovering over the waters when God's creative word brings forth the world (1:1-2).

Interpreters note the beautiful orderliness of this creation account, hymn-like in its repetitive, rhythmic structure. For each of the first six days, a narrator reports God's speech. "God said, 'let there be . . . ,'" and God's words produce the desired effects. God sees that the work is "good," and the narrator numbers the day, "And it was evening and morning of the first day." The six and seventh days alter the repetitive patterns and so draw attention to specific moments of the creative process.

During the first three days (1:3-13), God creates a habitat, beginning with light and darkness, and provides a "dome" or roof-like structure to keep waters above and below separate from one another. Next, God brings forth dry land, separates and names the elements of the world, and on the third day calls forth vegetation. The habitat is thus ready for occupants whom God creates during the next three days (vv. 14-31). Even though God created light on the first day, God makes heavenly bodies to govern the seasons, including the sun and the moon; modern scientific knowledge of the cosmos was not available to the ancients. God creates and blesses fish and birds and commands them to be "fruitful and to multiply" (1:22).

On the sixth day, God creates animals, but when God creates humans, the verbal pattern changes (1:24-31). The "us" in "Let us make humankind in our image" (1:26) may reflect God's speech to lesser beings in the heavenly court or may simply be the royal plural; whatever its source, the distinct verbal pattern draws attention to the creation of humans. They alone are made in the divine image, male and female. How humans represent the divine image is unclear, but the divine image sets humans apart and emphasizes their dignity among God's creatures. God blesses them and commands them to be fruitful and multiply like the animals and to have dominion over the living things. God sees that everything is "very good." On the seventh day God rests from creative work (2:1-4*a*).

Although affirmation of the creative power of the divine word is central to this creation hymn, God's rest may be of equal importance, for it invites humans to do likewise. The chapter from the priestly writers encourages the Israelites to celebrate the SABBATH at a time when the community's identity was threatened by foreign powers.

b. Harmony and disruption in the garden. Most interpreters think the next two chapters form a second creation account, a different story about how creation occurred from the Yahwist, or J writer. The text speaks of Yahweh (LORD) God instead of using the general term Elohim for God. Although it may be possible to see chapter one as a God-centered account of creation and chapters two and three as human-centered, efforts to turn them into one continuous story require one to set aside disconnections. Chapter one is poetry, and two and three are largely prose; the two accounts use different names for God and have different starting points and purposes.

Genesis 2:4*b*–3:24 has two scenes. Chapter 2 establishes harmony in creation and among all creatures, and chapter 3 tells of its dissolution. The setting is a barren desert where water wells up from ground and trees. God's first act is to create "the human" (ha'adham הָאָדָם). When God forms adham from the earth, wordplay suggests close links between humans and the earth (ha'adhamah [הָאֲדָמָה], v. 7). God plants a garden for the human to till the soil (*see* ADAM). Surrounding rivers make the garden a lush paradise, but there is a problem; the human is alone.

God solves the problem in two steps. First, God creates animals but finds no "helper as his partner" (v. 20), so God creates woman from Adam's rib. Using the rib ensures that his companion is made of the same substance. Adam declares "This is at last is bone of my bones and flesh of my flesh" (v. 23; see 2 Sam 5:1; *see* EVE). This story tells of the divine origins of sexual attraction (v. 24), but it also establishes a harmonious paradise. Animals, humans, and even naked individuals live together and feel no shame.

As in the first creation story, chapter two also connects all creatures to one another. Animals and humans share origins in the dust of the ground; the human names the animals, perhaps implying control, but also relationship; and the woman is taken out of the man, and the two become one. These themes of interconnectedness among all creation receive development later in the book through genealogical connections.

Peaceful relations in Eden collapse in the next chapter (3:1-24). A serpent appears in the Garden and tells the woman that she and Adam will not die, as God said, from eating from "the tree of knowledge of good and evil"; instead, their eyes will be opened and they will know good from evil (3:5). The woman finds the tree desirable, so she eats of it and gives some to her man. This disobedience opens their eyes to brokenness in the world and fractures the harmonious relations of the first scene. Is this wisdom? When God questions them, they each deny responsibility. He blames her, and she blames the serpent as the relationship between humans and animals disintegrates. God curses the serpent and puts "enmity" between the serpent and the woman's offspring. Her punishment is to suffer pain in childbirth and be ruled over by her man. He will suffer from tilling the soil, and the ground, too, will be cursed.

Language of sin does not appear here, although this story later becomes the basis for theological views of original sin. It does assert that life is the way it is because humans seek wisdom their own way rather than God's way. Because humans disobey God, alienation pervades the cosmos. Even though the couple now faces expulsion and death, God makes clothing for them. In whatever way various religious traditions understand this story, it offers a powerful interpretation of unredeemed human life as alienation from God, self, others, and the created world. This fracturing of relations sets out a major theme of the book.

c. Violence, protection, and fruitfulness. Immediately the story of CAIN and ABEL expands the theme of broken relationship within the family (4:1-15). When they become enemies, alienation spreads to the next generation. Each brother brings an offering to the Lord from his own labors. The text gives no reason why God is pleased with Abel and has "no regard" for Cain's offering, though this preference introduces the motif of the mystery of divine choice. The story is more concerned with disharmony among brothers. A Hebrew word for "sin" appears here for the first time. Sin is not simply infraction but a personified force, "lurking at the door," and needing overmastering (4:7). The sin of violence toward a brother echoes ominously through the book. Cain kills Abel and, when interrogated by God, responds churlishly, "Am I my brother's keeper?" (4:9). The implied answer is a resounding, "Yes! You are." The story anticipates discord between Sarah and Hagar, Isaac and Ishmael, Jacob and Esau, Rachel and Leah, and Joseph and his brothers.

Like the story of creation in the garden, this one also ends with God protecting the miscreant, thus expanding the theme of divine protection to the sinner. The story is not troubled by the illogical presence of other people because it is not tracing biological continuity; it focuses, instead, on the spiraling of violence and alienation in God's creation. God puts a mark on Cain, probably a tribal tattoo. The mark is not a curse but protection from being killed, for anyone who kills Cain will "suffer a sevenfold vengeance" (4:15).

God's protection of Cain enables him to be fruitful and multiply, He finds a wife who has a child named Enoch, who has a long line of offspring among whom is Lamech. Lamech and his two wives have children of many accomplishments: herding, creating musical instruments, and making tools. But even as the family multiplies, Lamech's mocking song multiplies vengeance from the sevenfold promised to Cain to seventy-sevenfold (vv. 23-24). Vengeance among groups is not yet controlled by the law of an eye for an eye.

Adam and Eve, too, remain fruitful. They have another child and grandchild and, according to this tradition, Yahweh's name comes into use with the grandchild (v. 26). Another tradition places revelation of the sacred name at the burning bush (Exod 3:13-15; 6:2-3).

d. Ten generations from Adam to Noah. Genealogies might bore modern Western readers, but they are critical components of the book of Genesis. Probably supplied by a Priestly writer (P), they provide structure for the loosely connected stories, bridge time gaps, and bring ancestors of multiple groups together in a linear relationship. Chapter 5 reprises the creation of humans in the divine image, showing that this status was not limited to the first couple but includes all humanity (5:1-2). The ancestral notices have a common pattern: the age of the ancestor when he became a father, the name of the offspring, and the ancestor's age at death. The ages are preposterous and keep building up to the oldest ancestor, Methuselah (5:25-27), after which they begin to decrease. The age decline may suggest the increasing sinfulness of humans who die sooner than the blessed ones, or inflated ages may reflect practices of Babylonian writing about ancient heroes. This first genealogy underlines the fruitfulness of humans and their interconnectedness. It ends with Noah and his three sons who become central characters for the next three chapters.

e. The Flood and new creation. The FLOOD story has two introductions (6:1-8 and 6:11-13). The first is a strange account of heavenly beings called "sons of God" who have intercourse with human women and produce offspring called "the Nephilim," that is, giants. Whatever the meaning of the story, God repents of creating humans and plans to blot them out, "for I am sorry that I have made them" (v. 7). The violence and disharmony begun in the garden has spread to all creation. NOAH, by contrast, is "blameless" and "walks with God."

The second introduction continues the theme of human sinfulness (6:11-13). It offers a general assessment of the earth as "corrupt in God's sight" because it was "filled with violence" engulfing "all flesh" (vv. 11,13). Interpreters explain contradictions in details across the story as the product of the weaving together of two different literary traditions. There is also a Babylonian tale of a great flood with similar detail to this story. Surely massive devastation from flooding waters lies behind the stories.

God tells Noah of divine plans to destroy the earth and promises to make a covenant with him (6:18). God orders him to bring two of each living creature into the ark (6:14-21). Chap. 7 also tells about the flood, but there God orders Noah to bring seven pairs each of "clean" animals and only one pair of each "unclean" animal. (Clean animals are animals suitable for sacrificial worship according to priestly tradition; "clean" does not refer to physical or moral qualities. *See* CLEAN AND UNCLEAN.) Seven days later, with Noah and family aboard the ark, the rains begin. A second account of the entering of the ark by Noah and family follows, and pairs of "all flesh" come aboard, two by two (7:17-24). Waters swell and creation is obliterated, except for occupants of the ark (*see* ARK OF NOAH).

Themes of creation and fruitfulness reappear in chap. 8 where new creation emerges after watery chaos. God sends all the creatures out of the ark to begin again (8:13-19). God promises never again to destroy the whole earth, "as long as earth endures" (v. 22). The covenant with Noah and the shaky new beginnings appear in chap. 9. In this new world, the command to be fruitful and multiply remains primary, but now animals fear humans and humans may eat them, unless their blood is in them. Blood was understood to carry the gift of life, so animals to be eaten must be separated from it. Human blood may not be spilled at all. In an allusion to the murder of Abel, God prohibits the taking of human life because humans are made in the divine image (9:4-6).

God's covenant with Noah is the first covenant in the Bible. A covenant is a legal agreement in which two parties agree to be loyal to one another by following agreed stipulations. Signified by the rainbow, this covenant embraces the whole of creation—the living creatures from the ark and the earth itself. The rainbow will remind God of the covenant and the promise never to destroy the earth again with water (9:8-17). But the new creation is not trouble-free, as the story of Noah's sons, SHEM, Ham, JAPHETH, and Ham's son Canaan shows (9:18-28). Noah lies naked and drunk in a tent. Ham sees Noah's nakedness (perhaps a sign of dishonoring him) and Noah curses Ham's son Canaan, not Ham, the forefather of Africans (as some past interpreters held in support of the enslavement of black people; *see* CANAAN, CANAANITES; HAM, HAMITES). The Canaanites were the natives of Canaan or Palestine. This curse is an etiology that anticipates later life in the land when the Israelites enslave some Canaanites (Judg 1:28; *see* SLAVERY).

f. Seventy nations descended from Noah. This genealogy of the descendants of Noah is often called "the table of the nations" because it depicts all known nations of the ancient world as descended from Noah's sons. The number seventy signifies a complete list and demonstrates again that humans have been fruitful and multiplied. Though the genealogy does not mention God, it furthers the theme that God is God of all peoples. Each has its own land and language. Nimrod appears as the founder of the kingdom of Babel or Babylon (v. 10), anticipating the setting of the next chapter, with which this text stands at odds because multiplicity of language is a simple fact here and a new event there.

g. Confusion of languages. The story of BABEL begins with everyone speaking the same language and ends with a profusion of languages, a point already made in the previous chapter. The people settle in Babel and decide to build a city and a tower. The tower with "its top in the heavens" may not be an effort to be like God but a desire to build a protecting fortress. The people fear being scattered (v. 4). The building efforts displease God, who comes down, confuses their language, and scatters them over all the earth. The very thing that humans fear happens.

The story is an etiology. It explains the origins of languages and cultures. God's discontent with human efforts to build may be because settling in one place violates the command to "fill the earth" (1:28). Or the story may imply other kinds of disobedience resulting in further fracturing of relations among creatures. The scattering of peoples becomes the occasion to turn attention to one group among them, the people who will become Israel.

h. Ten generations from Shem to Abram. Noah's son Shem, the father of Semites, is the starting point of this genealogy that traverses ten generations and climaxes with Abram and Sarai (11:26-32). Terah, Abram's father (vv. 26-27) is the first in the list to be located geographically, in Ur of the Chaldeans, a name for Babylon (vv. 28, 31). And Sarai, Abram's wife, is notable for being barren (v. 30). Terah takes his family and plans to migrate to Canaan but settles, instead, in Haran in northwest Mesopotamia. The story of Israel begins with the theme of displacement.

2. Genesis 12–50—The four generations of Israel

These chapters form the heart of the book. Some interpreters call them a "history of blessing" set over against the primeval history, sometimes called "a history of cursing." The blessings promised to Abraham and his descendants are set out at the beginning of the section (12:1-3) and mark an altered narrative reality. Here God actively promises new life despite the pre-history of human violence and sin. But the body of the book is not utterly distinct from the primeval history. The primeval history lays out major themes and patterns of life that receive specificity and enactment in the story of God's particular relationship with Israel. Abraham's family turns out to be no less sinful and violent than the other children of Adam and Eve. What separates them is their calling to be a blessing to the nations.

Across the chapters, the family confronts threats to these promises from within the family and from without. Quarrelling, violence, and distrust within the family and without nearly destroy it.

a. Family of Abraham, Sarah, and Hagar. Genesis 12:1-3: Promises and Blessings. God's promises to Abram (12:1-3) set forth major themes for the rest of the book. The series of promises in this key text begins with the promise of land. God tells Abram to leave his father's house for a land still to be revealed. Second, God will make Abram into a great nation, bless him, and make his name great, unlike the citizens of Babel who wanted to make a name for themselves (11:4). Finally, God promises to make him a blessing for all the families of the earth. Abram's call is not for his family's sake alone but for the benefit of all the families of the earth. The promises bring moral responsibility in relation to the world. In their old age Abram and Sarai break with all they know to obey God's call. The fulfillment of the promises will seem increasingly impossible but will result in the creation of a people and a nation.

Because of a famine Abram and Sarai go down to Egypt, foreshadowing Israel's sojourn in Egypt that begins with Joseph (Gen 37–50) and ending in the release of slaves (Exod 1–15). Often called the "endangerment of the matriarch," the story tells of Pharaoh's attraction to Sarai's beauty and Abram's fear for his own life (12:4-20). This situation endangers the promise because, as will become clearer later, the promise includes Sarai, who alone is to be mother to a great nation. God protects her by afflicting Pharaoh with plagues, and Pharaoh lets them go (see Exod 7:8–10:11). Similar stories of threats to a matriarch occur two more times (Gen 20; 26:1-11).

When the family returns to the Negeb, Abram averts a potential crisis with his nephew Lot. Abram models generous behavior by offering Lot his choice of land for his household. Abram serves a blessing to the nations by choosing Canaan (13:1-8).

A mysterious battle between Abram and four kings concludes when another mysterious figure, King MELCHIZEDEK brings bread and wine, blesses Abram and God the Most High (14:1-24).

Abram laments that he does not yet have a child and proposes to adopt Eliezer of Damascus as his legal heir. God rejects Abram's controlling efforts, repeats the promise, and shows him uncountable stars of heaven as a sign. God brought him here "to give you this land." A covenant ceremony follows (15:1-21).

The barrenness of Sarai seems an impossible barrier to the realization of God's promises (see BARREN, BARRENNESS). She takes matters into her own hands by giving her Egyptian slave Hagar to Abraham to produce a child (16:1-15). Abram's age of ninety-nine years makes the birth of a child appear ridiculous, but the story repeats the promises in covenantal terms (17:1-27). Three mysterious strangers confirm that Sarah will bear a son and she laughs (18:1-15).

The story of Lot's family resumes in the story of Sodom and Gomorrah account (18:16–19:38). Sarah is endangered again. This story repeats the general plotlines of 12:10-20, though with a different king, place, and outcome (20:1-18).

God's promise that Sarah will give birth to a child comes to fulfillment despite its unlikelihood from a human point of view (21:1-21).

God tests Abraham by commanding him to take his son Isaac to Mount Moriah and bind him for sacrifice (see AKEDAH). Just as Abraham is about to kill the son upon whom the covenant rests, God intervenes and provides a ram instead (22:1-23).

Sarah's death in Canaan becomes the occasion for Abraham to purchase land from Hittite natives before whom he bows down. He now legally owns a tiny piece of the promised land (23:1-20).

b. Family of Isaac and Rebekah. Abraham tells a servant of God's promises and sends the servant to his brother's family to get a wife for Isaac. Abraham sends a servant to his brother's family to get a wife from his own kin for Isaac rather than from among the natives who worship other deities. REBEKAH is the chosen bride (24:1-67).

Rebekah becomes pregnant with twins who fight in her womb. The two sons, JACOB and Esau, are brother nations (25:1-34). See ESAU, ESAUITES.

Another famine sends Isaac to Gerar where King Abimelech of the Philistines rules and desires Rebekah. God presents Isaac with promises given to Abraham (26:1-34).

With the help of Rebekah, Jacob deceives his aging, sight-impaired father into giving him Esau's blessing (27:1-46).

c. Family of Jacob, Rachel, Leah, Bilhah, and Zilpah. As Jacob journeys to Haran in another story of displacement, Jacob dreams of angels going up and down a ladder. The dream implies that Jacob's sojourn will reveal a connection between the transcendent and the earthly. God appears and identifies the divine self as God of Abraham and Isaac and repeats the ancestral promises to Jacob (28:10-22). *See* BETHEL, SHRINE.

The story of Jacob's four marriages is an etiology of the twelve tribes of Israel and the creation of a nation. His attraction to Rachel resembles Isaac's betrothal to Rebekah (see 24:10-51), but the tale becomes a complex story of multiple wives who give birth to sons who will form the twelve tribes of Israel. Conflict among the wives repeats the pattern of discord among the other family members (29:1–30:24).

After Joseph's birth, Jacob yearns for his own home apart from his father-in-law LABAN. Jacob's increasing wealth causes discontent among Laban's sons, but the Lord urges him to return to his kinfolk (31:3). Peaceful agreement between LEAH and RACHEL foreshadows reconciliation between Jacob and Laban and among brothers in later stories (30:25–31:55).

Jacob's encounter with Esau begins with an encounter with the "angels of God" (32:1). A humbled Jacob now hopes to "find favor" in Esau's eyes. An unnamed man wrestles with him all night, dislocates Jacob's hip, and gives him the name, Israel. Jacob meets Esau and the two part in peace (33:1-20). Like Abraham, Jacob purchases land and builds a shrine to the God of Israel, signifying partial fulfillment of God's promise of land to Abraham's offspring (32:1–33:20).

Following is a horrifying account of the rape of DINAH, Jacob's daughter, by a man of Shechem who wants to marry her. Her brothers slaughter the Shechemites in sharp contrast with the reconciliation between Jacob and Esau (34:1-31).

God dislocates Jacob again by sending him to BETHEL to build an altar to the God "who appeared to you when you fled . . . Esau" (35:1; see 28:20-21), Isaac dies, "old and full of days," and the reunited brothers Jacob and Esau bury him. This genealogy traces the line of Esau's Edomite descendants, again claiming family connections between the offspring of Abraham and Cannanite peoples (36:1-43).

d. The Family of Joseph. The Joseph story continues the account of Jacob's family but with Joseph as the primary figure (*see* JOSEPH). There is rancor among Jacob's sons who cannot speak "peaceably" to Joseph (37:4). Conflict among brothers appears to destroy God's promises of life in the land. Joseph's first dreams contribute to increased hatred among brothers. After trying to kill him, they sell him and he becomes a slave to Potiphar, an Egyptian official of Pharaoh in another story of displacement.

Judah fails in his responsibility to give his daughter-in-law TAMAR to his son to fulfill the levirate duty. Disguised as a prostitute, she tricks him into fulfilling the levirate duty and gives birth to twins. The fruitfulness of the family continues despite Judah's initial lack of cooperation (38:10-30).

POTIPHAR puts Joseph in charge of everything of the Egyptian's household (*see* EGYPT). POTIPHAR'S WIFE sexually desires Joseph, but he refuses. Potiphar jails him in another "pit" (see 37:24). But within the prison Joseph rises because "the Lord is with him" (39:1-23). Joseph changes from a dreamer to a dream-interpreter when two of his prisonmates have dreams related to their work in Pharaoh's court (vv. 1-8). Joseph's interpretations come true, but the restored cupbearer forgets Joseph, and tension grows (40:1-23). Pharaoh tells his disturbing dreams to Joseph, who interprets them as predictions of seven years of plenty followed by seven years of drought. Pharaoh puts Joseph in charge (41:1-57).

Famine in Canaan prompts Jacob to send his sons to Egypt for food, but he does not send beloved Benjamin. Joseph recognizes his brothers, but they do not recognize him. Joseph remembers his dreams (37:5-11). He accuses them of spying and imprisons one brother, while sending the others to get Benjamin. Jacob initially refuses to send Benjamin to Egypt (42:1-38). Jacob changes his mind and sends Benjamin. When Joseph sees his younger brother approaching, emotion overtakes him but the brothers remain blind to his identity (43:1-34). Joseph wants to know if his brothers have changed, so he tests them again by making Benjamin appear guilty of theft. Judah responds by telling of the famine, of his father's grief over Joseph's death, of his father's affection for Benjamin, and of the delicate conditions of Jacob's health (vv. 18-34). Judah and his brothers are changed people (44:1-34). Joseph bursts out, "I am Joseph. Is my father still alive?" (45:3). His brothers are astonished but Joseph urges them not to be distressed for "God sent me . . . to preserve life" (45:5). Joseph has found his brothers at last (compare 37:16), and his high office in Egypt saves the family from famine. Foreshadowing Exodus, Joseph's declares that God brought the family to Egypt to preserve a remnant (45:1-28).

Jacob/Israel goes to Egypt and on his journey, encounters God who repeats the promises and pledges to go with him to Egypt and to bring him back again. The entire family, whose names appear in the genealogy, set out on the journey. In a tearful reunion, Joseph meets his father (46:1-27). Joseph enables his community, Egypt and the world to survive the famine. He swears he will bury his father with their ancestors in Canaan when the time comes (47:1-31).

Jacob's poetic blessings of his grandsons (chap. 48) and his sons (49:1-28) anticipate later events in Israel's history. Jacob declares that Joseph's sons born in Egypt are members of the family and his true heirs (48:1-7). The chapter closes with Jacob's death.

Jacob's burial in the land signifies the later return of the nation from Egypt to the promise land. The brothers worry that Joseph will retaliate against them without their father to restrain him but Joseph restates his belief that "God intended it" to preserve life (50:20). Joseph asks to be buried in the land, and assures his brothers that "God will surely come to you, and bring you up . . . to the land he swore to Abraham, to Isaac and to Jacob" (50:24). This promise is fulfilled in Exodus. (Exod 13:9).

C. Theological and Religious Significance of the Book

The theological claims of Genesis, the Bible's first book, stand as an introduction to the Jewish and Christian canons.

1. God of all

Genesis testifies that its God is the God of all peoples and of the whole created order. The power of God's creative word brings the world and its peoples to life and continues its work in the creation and recreations of the people of Israel. The first creation account (Gen 1:1-2:4*a*) opens the book and the Bible with the faith claim that there is one God whose all powerful word brings into being all that is. This God does not belong to Israel alone, nor is this God concerned with Israel alone. Even as the focus of Genesis moves from cosmic concern for all humanity (chaps. 1–11) to concern for one people (chaps. 12–50), the book maintains its global perspective. The family of Abraham is called to be a "blessing to the nations" (12:3), a vocation announced in the promises to Abraham and repeated across the book. Abraham's call to be "a blessing to the nations" reveals Israel's God to be the God of the nations. This international horizon has particular resonance for our time, politically and religiously.

Major characters in Genesis confront and usually find reconciliation with the eponymous leaders of the nations around them, revealing divine concern for all peoples. Abraham, Sarah, and Hagar, for example, are foreparents not only of Israel but also of the Ishmaelites. God gives promises to Hagar, foremother of the Ishmaelites, that parallel promises to Abraham. Her offspring will multiply so "that they cannot be counted for multitude" (16:10, 17:20; 22:17), and her son Ishmael will become a "great nation" (21:13, 12:2). Abraham becomes "the ancestor of a multitude of nations" (17:4), referring not only to numerous children by Sarah but also to family connections with other peoples.

That God cares for all peoples is a major assertion of the book. When Abraham and Lot, an ancestor of Moab, face the problem of insufficient land to support both their families and livestock, Abram actively keeps the peace. He lets Lot choose the fertile plain of Jordan, while he, in turn, chooses the leftover land of Canaan (ch. 13). While this story is an etiology that explains how two peoples came to live next to each

other, the story also tells of divine care for people other than Israel. Even more explicitly, when Abraham and Sarah journey to Gerar and King Abimelech "takes" Sarah into his household, God appears to Abimelech in a dream and answers Abimelech's question about divine justice. God affirms Abimelech's innocence and protects him from the consequences of his unwitting actions (20:5-7). The story contradicts Abraham's own negative assessment of Gerar as a place where "there is no fear of God at all" (20:11). At the story's conclusion, Abraham prays for Abimelech, and God responds by healing infertility plaguing the land (20:17).

Divine concern for people other than Israel appears even in the story of Jacob. His brother Esau is forefather of the neighboring nation of Edom. Their relationship reprises the Cain and Abel conflict but with a different outcome. Jacob's life centers on this relationship, its many conflicts and their resolution. Accounts of Jacob's youth show him tricking his brother and stealing both his brother's birthright and the blessings intended for the firstborn son, Esau (25:23-31; 27:1-40). The two brothers hate each other, and Jacob flees for his life (27:41).

Jacob's relationship with Esau creates a literary frame around Jacob's marriages and his begetting of his thirteen children (chaps. 29–30). When he flees from his father-in-law Laban to return to his family, he encounters Esau in fear and trembling, uncertain if his brother will harm him and his family. When the two meet again, however, both are changed characters. They reunite humbly and go their separate ways in peace (32:1–33:20). This story sets forth a partial fulfillment of the call to Abraham to be a blessing to the nations because God is God of all.

After many trials and tribulations, Joseph, too, becomes a blessing to the nations when he rescues the Pharaoh (41:1-57) and the Egyptians from famine, although not without folkloric exaggerations (47:13-16). Jews, Muslims, and Christians today trace their faith story back to Abraham, Sarah, and Hagar. Although Genesis recognizes and presents accounts of conflicts, hatred, and jealousy among peoples, it moves finally toward shalom or well-being among the nations because God is God of all.

2. God the Creator

That God is Creator in Genesis is not a scientific declaration in any modern sense; it is a theological assertion expressed in multiple literary forms in the long course of the book's story. Genesis expresses faith in the one God who, by the power of the word, brings all things into being and sustains and recreates life in many forms over and over again. By creating the world in seven days, God transforms chaos into order and beauty, populates the earth, and extends divine creativity to living creatures and human beings, who are called to be fruitful and multiply. God also creates more directly and concretely in the second creation narrative (2:4*b*-25). Rather than simply by the power of the creative word, God appears here in more human terms, planting a garden, sculpting Adam from the earth, breathing life into him, creating the animals and finally performing surgery on Adam to create Eve and sexuality. Then God creates life anew and reconstitutes the human family after the destruction and chaos of the flood. Noah and his family begin again and humans, made in the divine image, grow in creative accomplishments, planting vineyards, making wine, and speading throughout the earth in all their mulitiplicity of peoples and languages (10:1-32).

Divine creation and recreation concerns the people of Israel. God alone creates the family and the nation. The birth of Isaac, child of the promise, is a miraculous birth, unthinkable because of the ages of both parents, a birth delayed and unlikely in view of Sarah's lifetime of barrenness (11:30). Rachel too is barren and envies her sister Leah who gives birth with ease (29:31-35). Underscoring the inadequacy of human efforts to make the family fruitful, Rachel begs Jacob to give her children. His reply is a question that echoes across the family stories: "Am I in the place of God?" (30:2). No, he is not; only God can give her children and bring the promises to fulfillment.

The barrenness of the matriarchs emphasizes divine action in the birth of the children and the creation of Israel. That creation occurs despite conflicts among them. Like Sarah, Rachel gives Jacob her slave to bear a child for her (30:8). In a competition for offspring, Leah also gives Jacob her slave Zilpah (30:9-13). Rachel and Leah argue over Leah's mandrakes, a root thought to confer fertility. Rachel wins the mandrakes in exchange for giving Leah her turn to sleep with Jacob. At the climax of this story of wives and children, God remembers Rachel who gives birth to Joseph (30:25). The conclusion of all these struggles is the birth of the twelve sons who will becomes eponymous ancestors of the twelve tribes of Israel and a daughter.

Behind the scenes, God guides this family, recreating them from generation to generation. These stories are clearly etiologies, explaining how the nation of twelve tribes came into being from the one father, that is, how they are all related to one another. But in addition to Rachel's barrenness, the conflict and struggles among the mothers threaten the future of the family. Finally the women urge their husband Jacob "to do whatever God has said to you" (31:16). They interpret Jacob's new wealth as God's gift to them.

The Creator God forms, speaks, and guides Israel into being. The story of Joseph is a long narrative about stress on the family, its strife from inner quarrels, and the threat to its suvival from famine. But again God recreates the family as Joseph acknowledges, "God sent me before you to preserve life, . . . to preserve for you a remnant on earth, to keep alive for you many survi-

vors" (45:5, 7). The God of continuous creation offers hope to the book's audience, the nation struggling to begin life after its destruction by the Babylonian Empire. It will survive because God continually recreates them.

3. Call to worship

The book's first chapter is filled with awe at the wonder of the created world. It concludes in rest and implicitly calls its readers to weekly rest, a day of sabbath like God's rest (2:3). The text suggests that worship is the vocation not only of the people of Israel but of all peoples; worship is what makes us human. This invitation to worship is not stated as law but as the consequence of dwelling within God's world.

Interpreters often overlook the significance of worship in Genesis, emphasizing the etiological aspects of events at shrines more than their importance for worship. But worship is enacted again and again across the body of the book. Noah's priestly sacrifice of clean animals pleases God (8:21). Abram offers a heifer in a covenant ceremony during which God renews promises concerning the land and seals the promise with a torch passing through the cut pieces of sacrificed animals (15:1-24). Hagar, too, worships after she conceives and escapes from Sarah's cruelty into the wilderness. An angel appears to her, tells her to return, and blesses her offspring in terms similar to the promises to Abram (16:10; see 15:5). God names the child Ishmael, a play on the Hebrew verb, "to hear," for God hears the affliction of the foreigner, the slave, the Egyptian, the woman. Hagar responds worshipfully by naming God El-roi, the one who sees. She asks in astonishment, "Have I seen God and lived?" (see Exod 33:20; Judg 6:22-23; 13:22).

Events of worship both structure and comment upon the life of Jacob. As he leaves his family to go to Laban, Jacob dreams of the ladder, with angels ascending and descending. In fear he wakes and declares the place to be the house of God, that is, Bethel (28:16-17). Despite the awesomeness of encountering God, Jacob sets conditions on his loyalty. "If" God will keep him, feed him and bring him "in peace to his father house," then God will be his God (28:18-22). Later, when Jacob leaves Laban's household, the two enter into a covenant (31:44-54). The covenant takes the form of worship and is symbolized by a stone pillar and a pile of stones. They are to be a "witness between you and me" (31:44, 48). Laban asks that the Lord "watch" them when they are not together (v. 49). This may be a prayer for divine protection or for divine judgment, if one of them misbehaves. A covenant meal seals their agreement, and Laban blesses his daughters and departs.

As soon as Jacob survives his altercation with Laban, he worships because his pending encounter with his brother Esau promise even greater danger (32:9-12). He prays to the God of his ancestors who has sent him back to his "country and kinfolk." With newfound humility, he speaks of his unworthiness before God's "steadfast love and faithfulness" (v. 10). He begs God to deliver him from Esau and reminds God of the promise to make his offspring like "the sands of the sea" (v. 12). During the night, he encounters a man who "wrestled with him until daybreak" (32:23-32). In this all night struggle, the stranger changes his name from Jacob to Israel (v. 28). He then testifies, "For I have seen God face to face, and yet my life is preserved" (v. 30). The creation of the nation occurs symbolically in this worshipful encounter with the divine. When Jacob arrives in Bethel, he builds an altar and God appears, confirms Jacob's name change, and restates the promises (35:9-12).

Even though the book's final worship events occurs in the Joseph story, Jacob is still their focus (46:1-4; 50:7-14). Before Jacob sets out to join his son in Egypt, he offers sacrifice and speaks with God in terms of call narratives. He replies to God, "Here I am," marking his obedience and commitment as God promises to go with him to Egypt (v. 4). Finally, when Joseph and his brothers bury their father Jacob, "they held a very great lamentation" (50:10). Laments are prayer forms that cry out to God in the midst of suffering. The book ends, therefore, in lamentation at the death of Jacob and points toward the laments of the enslaved nation in Exodus (2:23).

Worship events form a thematic ribbon across Genesis, interpreting and commenting on the story of the people as guided by interaction with the divine. They evoke from readers a similar worshipful awareness of the numinous places and events in life. For the book's audience attempting to rebuild after the Babylonian period, Genesis calls them to their fundamental identity as a worshiping people.

4. Interconnection of life

Genesis declares the created world to be a sacred place even before shrines are built or people worship. Step by step God declares the process of creation to be "good," and when it is complete, "very good" (Gen 1–2:3). Genesis affirms not only that humans are joined to the earth itself, but also that interconnections are equally strong among human neighbors on this planet. The text presents humanity united with inanimate and animate creation, related as kin to the animals and the birds, to the trees and the stars in the "generations of the heavens and the earth" (2:4a).

The network of life in which humans abide is itself a temple of worship, a sacred place, a cosmos bursting with beauty and revelatory power. And though the text gives humans a role to govern, "to have dominion" over the fish, birds, the wild animals, and every creeping thing (1:28), they are to do so as participants in the process of creation, guided by a God's-eye view of things. Made in the divine image, all humans partici-

pate in the creative life of God and, like the fish and the birds, the beasts and the creeping things, they are blessed and commanded to continue the creative process by being fruitful and multiplying. From one angle, Genesis is the story of that fruitfulness in the face of all odds against it. This fruitfulness itself creates a wide and flowing matrix of connection.

The garden story (chaps. 2–3) affirms linkages within the creation in different ways. Hebrew wordplay connects adam ('adham) to the earth ('adhamah) from which he is made (2:7). The narrative shows Adam in relationship with the animals when he names them and with the woman ('ishah אִשָּׁה) for she is taken from man ('ish [אִישׁ] 2:23). No aspect of creation is excluded or isolated from any other. This interlocking of life forms has ethical implications for humans who alone are made in the divine image and who are given dominion over all living things (1:28).

The theme of the interconnectedness of all things does not disappear from Genesis after the creation stories. All humans are connected by their common origins from the first couple (chaps. 2–3). The earth and all living things suffer the same fate as humans because of human violence (chaps. 6–8). The stories of the four generations of the family of Israel unfold within the broader story of the cosmos and its human inhabitants. Never are the descendants of Abraham exempt from participation in God's plan to bless the nations through them. And even when the various generations of the family are bitterly divided, the book asserts interrelatedness because everyone in the family descends from Abraham and Sarah.

Interconnection among human generations appears clearly in the genealogies that link episodes in the primal history. The list of Adam's descendants (5:1-32) ends with the introduction of Noah (v. 32). Noah's descendants, in turn, connect the story of the flood with the spread of humanity across the earth in their multiplicity of culture and language (10:1-32). This "table of the nations" asserts that all peoples on the earth are brothers and sisters to one another. The narrative of Israel's beginnings occurs within this wider horizon, and its calling to be "a blessing to the nations" keeps that horizon in view (12:3).

The book's narrative device of interlocking of stories of the generations further amplify inter-relatedness within the family. Boundaries between the generations are far from clear. Isaac's birth (21:1-5) and his betrothal to Rebekah (24:1-67), for example, are major events in the life of Sarah and Abraham (11:27–25:11). Isaac then emerges as the central character in the narrative (25:19), but immediately his twin sons Jacob and Esau are born and the stories of generations again intertwine (25:21).

Repetitions of events and story types within subsets of the family further connect generations. Abraham's untruthfulness that twice imperils his wife, Sarah, reappears in the lies of his son Isaac who betrays Rebekah according to the same story pattern (12:10-20; 20; 26:1-11). Conflicts between Rachel and Leah (29:21–30:24) echo disputes between Cain and Abel (4:1-16), Jacob and Esau (25:23–27:45), and Joseph and his brothers (chap. 37). Similarly, the movement toward reconciliation between Rachel and Leah (31:14-35) anticipates reconciliation between Jacob and Esau (32:9-17) and between Joseph and his brothers (45:1-15; 50:15-21). The patterns of interlocking stories reveal that the generations share both similar failures and similar transformations.

And the intermingling of stories across generations reveals divine presence and consistency in creating and recreating life in the midst of struggle, false starts, deceit, and betrayal. God is with them, guides them, and creates them as one family and nation again and again.

5. God the keeper of promises

The God of Genesis is not only the creator and speaker of world-making words, but also the one who keeps promises. The promises uttered to Abraham set forth the organizing themes of the family stories (12:1-3). Each generation hears the promises, and each generation creates major obstacles to their fulfillment (*see* PROMISE). Yet the promises come to fruition anyway. Abraham and Sarah attempt to enact the promises according to their limited insight regarding how to overcome Sarah's problematic infertility. They substitute Eliezer for Abram's promised heir (15:1-6) and use Hagar as Sarah's surrogate (chaps. 16, 21). Abraham and Isaac endanger the lives of their wives of the promise (12:1-20; 20; 26:1-11); Jacob creates enmity in his family even at birth (25:23-26) and meets impediments to the promises in his confrontations with Laban and his sons (chap. 31). Rachel is barren initially and later struggles with her sister for priority, threatening family stability (chap. 30). Finally, Joseph confronts the hatred and envy of his brothers, and comes close to death in the pit (chap. 37). He is enslaved, betrayed, and imprisoned (chaps. 39–40). Tamar is nearly burned to death by Judah (chap. 38).

Despite this long story of threats to the survival of the family and divisions among them, God's fidelity to the promises saves them repeatedly. After reiterating the promises to Jacob, God reassures him: "Know that I am with you and will keep you wherever you go, and will bring you back to this land; for I will not leave you until I have done what I have promised you" (28:15). When Joseph dramatically reveals himself to his brothers, he interprets his life's suffering and implicitly comments on the entire life of Israel as God's faithfulness to the promises. He declares that God intended all these things for good in order to save a remnant for Israel (45:5, 7). Despite their unrighteousness, the nation survives because God is the faithful keeper of promises.

And although the story ends in Egypt not in Canaan, Jacob's burial in Canaan points symbolically to the nation's return to the land (49:28–50:13), and Joseph himself asks to be buried there (50:25).

Divine faithfulness to the promises occurs despite their delay in coming to fulfillment. The promises do indeed take a very long long time to come to realization, and the delays make any fulfillment seem hopeless. Jospeh's story provides a good example because he consistently faces the end of possibility. First, his brothers put him in the pit to die and then take him out only to sell him into slavery (chap. 37). When he is a slave in Potiphar's house, his master's wife attempts to seduce him, falsely accuses him, and gets him thrown into prison (chap. 39). In prison, he successfully interprets the dreams of the cupbearer and baker, but the cupbearer forgets him when he returns to power (chap. 40). Only "two whole years later," does Joseph gain the opportunity to interpret dreams for Pharaoh and begin life anew in the court (chap. 41). Only then does the claim that God is "with Joseph" (39:2, 21) result in new life for him.

If the audience of Genesis is Judean deportees who reside in Babylon or among the surviving remnant who struggle to rebuild Jerusalem, then the book's portrayal of God as faithful keeper of the promises stands as both solace and hope for the future of the nation. Their current struggles, whatever they may be, do not mean the end of the promises, despite the long the delay. For, if God was faithful to four generations of patriarchs and matriarchs with their massive human failings, hatreds, and sinfulness, then God will continue to keep the promises and bring them to fruition anew. God, not they, is in charge of ensuring the survival and continuation of the family. God will provide posterity, land, and a great name. God will bless them and bless the nations through them despite circumstances that appear deeply, impossibly hopeless. God's fidelity to the promise in the past assures the continued survival of the family of Israel.

6. Responsibility and reconciliation

Beginning with Cain's question, "Am I my brother's keeper?" (4:9), the book calls the family repeatedly to responsibility and reconciliation. From the spread of sin and alienation among peoples (chaps. 1–11) to the seeming destruction of the family when Joseph's brothers place him in mortal danger and then cover-up their crime (chap. 37), the book explores relationships in conflict.

Abraham and Lot compete for land, Sarah and Hagar struggle for inclusion and inheritance for their sons, Jacob and Esau live in enmity, Rachel and Leah fight over Jacob, and Joseph is cast off by his brothers.

These characters are individuals who also stand for nations; hence, the relationships among them are many-layered, concerned both with life within the family and with relations among the nations. And, in every case, the major characters meet God or become aware of God's action in their lives and are then able to move toward responsibility and reconciliation. Hagar, for example, sees God and so is able to return to Abraham's household to raise her son Ishmael (16:13-15). Abraham encounters God repeatedly (12:1-3; 15; 17:1-22; 18:22-33; 22:15-18). Sarah experiences God in the birth of Isaac (21:1-8). Jacob meets God at major turning points of his life: before meeting Rachel and Laban's family (28:10-17) and as he flees and anticipates his meeting with Esau (32:9-30). Even Laban alters his selfish, controlling behavior and reconciles with Jacob in light of God's watching presence (31:48-50).

The narratives are deeply human and moving because they capture jealousy, deceit, betrayal and slowly move toward love, shalom, or the well-being not of an individual alone but for the whole family of peoples. Characters suffer for long periods of time but eventually have experiences that alter their selfishness as in the case of Jacob, or remind them of their true identity as God's instrument for the rescue of all as in the case of Joseph (50:15-21). Genesis invites readers to such awareness of the holy in their lives and of their responsibility to be the "keeper" of brother and sister, reconciled and peaceful.

7. The chosen people

The theme of God's choice of the people of Israel and of leaders runs through the book. In the thick of family intrigues and battles, and in the face of external threats from other peoples, God acts in the life of this chosen family. God chooses without explanation. Without expressing a reason, God favors Abel's animal offering over his brother's offering of fruit from the ground (4:3-4). God chooses Noah to begin life anew because Noah found favor in God's eyes (6:8-9). But Noah and his offspring prove to be little better than others before them (9:20-28). God calls Abraham and Sarah for no reason except perhaps for Sarah's barrenness. God's choice of this couple begins in impossibility, but Sarah's infertility merely emphasizes divine activity in the birth of the child of the promise.

Fairly consistently, God chooses the younger over the older and so inverts the social expectations of the patriarchal culture. God chooses Jacob over Esau (25:23) although it sometimes appears as if Jacob chooses himself. He clings to Esau's heel at birth (25:26), tricks Esau out of his birthright (25:31-34), and deceives his father Isaac to steal the blessing that belongs to Esau the first born (27:1-41). But Jacob, the conniver, is God's choice to be the father of the nation, the eponymous ancestor of Israel. And God chooses Joseph over his older brothers, continuing the theme of social inversion by highlighting the family's uncomprehending shock in response to Joseph's dreams of future power over them (37:5-11).

God's choice is not only mysterious but flouts the expectations of the society where the eldest son has an assured inheritance as the leader and patriarch. This means that leadership can arise in unexpected spheres of the community. When God chooses Abraham and Sarah, it is not on the basis of their human capacities, since they are beyond child-bearing ages. By implication, when God chooses Israel from all the peoples of the earth, God chooses for reasons other than this people's human achievements. And always in the stories of individuals and of Israel, their chosen status is for the sake of God's plan to make them a blessing to all the nations of the earth. Israel's election as God's special people, therefore, does not exalt them over the other peoples of the world. Instead, it gives underscores their responsibility to be a "blessing to the nations" (12:3).

8. God's presence, hidden and revealed

God's presence in these narratives of origins is both hidden in the stories of the generations and revealed in key moments at shrines and dramatic intersections of life. God does not always manifest the divine self through explicit miracles that interfere with the created world, such as in the rolling back of the sea in Exod 14, or in the stopping of the sun in Josh 10:13. Rather God often works in hidden ways as Abraham and Sarah face the barrenness of their lives and the distance they stand from the promises' fulfillment, or as Hagar faces death in the wilderness after her abuse in the family, or as Jacob suffers from the trickery and greed of Laban, or as Joseph is falsely accused, imprisoned, and alienated from his kinfolk and homeland, almost assimilated into the Egyptian culture.

Within most of these generational stories God seems hidden. This is because the stories show God at work in daily life, in deep suffering, and in fractured relationships. Narrative literature shows, enacts, and performs God's presence and often leaves readers to assess its significance. It invites us in to interpret these lives ourselves. Through much of the book the main characters speak little of God. Only occasionally do they see the larger meaning of their struggles within the divine place as Joseph does when he reveals himself to his brothers (chap. 45).

But punctuating these stories and framing the main action are theophanies in which God appears to some of the characters who in turn build shrines, name God, and are altered by their encounters. Abraham, Hagar, Isaac, and Jacob meet God on their journeys into and out of danger. When things seem hopeless, they each encounter the One who blesses their lives, urges them forward, and reveals transcendent meanings hidden within their ordinary lives. These appearances of the divine interpret the stories in which they appear and call readers to openness to the manifestations of God in their own lives. The book of Genesis points to the luminous world in which human life transpires and reveals its sacredness even in the midst of loss, conflict, and darkened hopes.

Bibliography: Robert Alter. *Genesis: Translation and Commentary* (1996); Athalaya Brenner, ed. *A Feminist Companion to Genesis* (1993); William P. Brown. *The Ethos of the Cosmos: The Genesis of Moral Imagination in the Bible* (1999); Walter Brueggemann. *Genesis*. IBC (1982); David W. Cotter. *Genesis*. Berit Olam (2003); Terrence Fretheim. "The Book of Genesis." NIB 1 (1994) 321–674; John Kaltner. *Inquiring of Joseph: Getting to Know a Biblical Character through the Qur'an* (2003); Carol Meyers. *Discovering Eve: Ancient Israelite Women in Context* (1988); Susan Niditch. *Underdogs and Tricksters: A Prelude to Biblical Folklore* (1987); Jacob Neusner. *Confronting Creation: How Judaism Reads Genesis: An Anthology of Genesis Rabbah* (1991); Naomi Steinberg. *Kinship and Marriage in Genesis: A Household Economics Perspective* (1991); W. Sibley Towner. *Genesis*. WBC (2001); Gerhard von Rad. *Genesis*. OTL (1972); Claus Westermann. *Genesis 1–11: A Commentary*. CC (1984); Claus Westermann. *Genesis 12-36: A Commentary*. CC (1985); Claus Westermann. *Genesis 37–50: A Commentary*. CC (1986).

KATHLEEN M. O'CONNOR

GENEVA BIBLE. A Bible produced among English exiles in Geneva during the reign of Mary Tudor, as a result of continued translation and revision in Tyndale's tradition. William Whittingham edited a revised NT in 1557, using Theodore Beza's Latin NT of 1556 and introducing the verse divisions of Stephanus' Greek NT of 1551. The original edition is the total Bible of 1560. During the reign of Elizabeth several editions followed. Some were printed in Geneva, others in England. The Scottish edition of 1579 was the first Bible ever printed there. In England editions of the Bible continued up to 1644. *See* VERSIONS, ENGLISH.

PETER ARZT-GRABNER

GENITALIA [אֵשֶׁךְ 'eshekh, מָבוֹשׁ mavosh, שָׁפְכָה shafekhah]. Genitalia refers to the external sex organs, both female and male. Genitalia that were damaged or produced an emission rendered one unholy or unclean (Deut 23:1 [Heb. 23:2]; Lev 15:2-30; 21:20). The same principle applied to sacrificial animals (Lev 22:24). The Abrahamic covenant mandated male circumcision (Gen 17:11-14, 23-25). Exposure of the genitals was to be avoided, particularly in holy places (Exod 20:26; 28:42).

The Bible usually avoids referring to these body parts directly, and instead employs euphemisms. In many instances the Hebrew word used for "genitalia" is simply the generic word "flesh" (basar בָּשָׂר), where the context provides clarification (Gen 17:11; Exod 28:42; Lev 15:2; Ezek 23:20; 44:7, 9). Other euphemisms for genitalia include "feet" (reghalim רְגָלַיִם,

as in Exod 4:25; Deut 28:57; 2 Sam 11:8; Ruth 3:4, 7, 8, 14; Isa 7:20; Ezek 16:25) and "hand" (yadh יָד, Isa 57:8).

In Lev 21:20 'eshek indicates "testicles." In Deut 23:1 [Heb. 23:2], shafekhah refers to "penis"; in Deut 25:11, mavosh is rendered "genitals" (all NRSV). The root of mavosh means to "be ashamed." Each of these Hebrew words appears only once in the biblical text; all three relate to the injunction against damaged genitalia. *See* CIRCUMCISION; EUPHEMISM.

LISA MICHELE WOLFE

GENIZAH guh-neet'suh. A repository for worn-out sacred texts that, according to rabbinic law, should be hidden away or buried rather than destroyed. The root gnz (גנז), "to hide, store," is probably of Semitic origin, but seems to have entered Hebrew from Persian (e.g., Esth 3:9 ginze hammelek גִּנְזֵי הַמֶּלֶךְ, "the king's treasuries").

The most famous example was the "Cairo Genizah," the storeroom of the Ben Ezra Synagogue in Fustat (Old Cairo). Among countless treasures, it preserved medieval copies of the book of SIRACH (Ecclesiasticus) in Hebrew, the Damascus Rule, and the ARAMAIC LEVI DOCUMENT.

Bibliography: Stefan C. Reif. *A Jewish Archive from Old Cairo: The History of Cambridge University Library's Genizah Collection* (2000).

BEN OUTHWAITE

GENNAEUS gi-nee'uhs [Γενναῖος Gennaios]. The father of Apollonius. His son is listed among five governors who troubled the Jews under ANTIOCHUS V (2 Macc 12:2).

GENNESARET gi-nes'uh-ret [Γεννησαρέτ Gennēsaret]. The term may refer to either the Sea of Galilee (Luke 5:1; 1 Macc 11:67) or to a plain on its northwest side (Matt 14:34; Mark 6:53). In the latter case the area is associated in the Gospels often with the ministry of Jesus.

PHILLIP MICHAEL SHERMAN

GENRE. The Bible presents a range of literatures, comparable to those of the ANE and the Mediterranean Basin. Scholars call these different sorts of literature *genres*, to indicate their characteristics, styles, topics, and approaches to their audiences. Typical genres include, but are not limited to, APOCALYPSES, BIOGRAPHY, chronicle, commentary, epic, history, INSCRIPTION, legal code and judgment, LEGEND, LETTER, Myth, novel, philosophy, poetic composition (with subgenres of poetry for lament, love, music, royal decrees, and worship), prophecy, and RITUAL—all of which the Bible represents.

Although genres from the ancient world come to us by means of written evidence, many of them originated as oral performances. (Commonly, oral traditions incorporated within written documents are identified according to their "form," a term that relates to the genre of originating performance.) Throughout the Bible, differing genres often appear within individual works, which indicates that genres do not represent fixed types of communication to which biblical books can be made to conform. Rather, genres and generic hybrids emerged from particular social interactions, which generated the texts as we have them from traditions behind them. *See* FORM CRITICISM, NT; FORM CRITICISM, OT; HISTORY, HISTORIOGRAPHY, NT; HISTORY, HISTORIGRAPHY, OT; LITERATURE, THE BIBLE AS; NARRATIVE LITERATURE; POETRY, HEBREW; PROPHET, PROPHECY; TRADITION, ORAL.

Bibliography: Kenton L. Sparks. *Ancient Texts for the Study of the Hebrew Bible: A Guide to the Background Literature* (2005).

BRUCE CHILTON

GENTILES jen′t*i*ls [גּוֹיִם goyim; ἔθνος ethnos]. When these words are translated *gentiles* (from the Lat. word for NATIONS), they refer to all ethnic groups besides Jews, as in Ps 2:1, "Why do the nations (or gentiles) rage . . . against the Lord and the Lord's anointed?" Goy [גּוֹי] means "a people," so it often does refer to Israel, as in Exod 19:6, "a holy people." Some NT uses of ethros clearly mean non-Jews (e.g., Luke 2:32; Rom 2:14; 1 Cor 1:23), but others—Matt 28:19, which reads panta ta ethnē [πάντα τὰ ἔθνη], "every nation"—include the Jews. Paul sometimes uses "Greek" to mean "non-Jew" (Gal 3:28).

RICHARD B. VINSON

GENTILES, COURT OF THE. *See* COURT OF THE GENTILES.

GENTLE, GENTLENESS. *See* MEEKNESS.

GENUBATH gi-ny*oo*′bath [גְּנֻבַת genuvath]. HADAD, a member of the royal house of Edom, found favor in the eyes of Pharaoh, who gave him the sister of his own wife. The queen's sister gave birth to a son, Genubath, who grew up in the king's palace among Eyptian princes (1 Kgs 11:17-20).

CLAUDE F. MARIOTTINI

GEOGRAPHY. *See* ARAB, ARABIA, ARABIANS; ASIA; ASSYRIA AND BABYLONIA; CANAAN, CANAANITES; EGYPT; ISRAEL, GEOGRAPHY OF; MESOPOTAMIA; SAMARIA; SUMER, SUMERIANS; SYRIA.

GEOLOGY. *See* ISRAEL, GEOLOGY OF.

GEOMETRY. As a system of logic, geometry is frequently traced to Euclid (ca. 325–265 BCE) in Alexandria and was current in the biblical region and time, but influences of geometry in the Bible are peripheral. Geom-

etry was certainly used in architecture and construction (Ezek 40:47; 41:21; 43:16-17; 1 Kgs 7:23), and simple geometric shapes appear in various descriptions (Exod 39:9; Job 26:10; Prov 8:27). Logic of the type involved in geometry is exemplified by various proverbs, but more prominent were interests in numbers themselves and in number patterns (e.g., Prov 30:15, 18, 21). *See* NUMBERS, NUMBERING; SCIENCE AND THE BIBLE; SCIENCE, EGYPT; SCIENCE, MESOPOTAMIA.

A. HEATH JONES, III

GEORGIAN VERSION. *See* VERSION, GEORGIAN.

GER guhr. *See* SOJOURNER; STRANGER.

GERA gee′ruh [גְּרָא gerah]. 1. Benjamin's fourth son (Gen 46:21).

2. One of Benjamin's grandsons through his first-born, BELA (1 Chr 8:3-5). The name appears twice in this genealogy, indicating either two sons by the same name or a textual repetition. Unlike Gen 46:21, the genealogy in 1 Chr 8:1-2 does not mention that Benjamin had a son named Gera.

3. A son of EHUD, also called HEGLAM (1 Chr 8:7).

4. The father of the judge Ehud (Judg 3:15).

5. The father of SHIMEI, who cursed DAVID when he fled from ABSALOM (2 Sam 16:5-8).

KEVIN A. WILSON

GERAH gee′ruh [גֵּרָה gerah]. The twentieth part of a SHEKEL (Ezek 45:12), appearing largely in association with the shekel of the sanctuary in the Priestly Code (e.g., Exod 30:13; Lev 27:25; etc.). *See* MONEY, COINS.

GERAR gee′rahr [גְּרָר gerar]. Gerar was in the southern periphery of Canaan somewhere in the Negev between Gaza and BEER-SHEBA (see NEGEB, NEGEV). After the Sarah and Abimelech event (Gen 20:2), Abraham received resident status in Gerar (Gen 20:15). Isaac sought resident status there during a severe famine (Gen 26:1). Rebekah's familiar problem with Abimelech (Gen 26:7-11) and jealousy of the inhabitants resulted in Isaac's moving out of the city into the "wadi of Gerar" (Gen 26:17). Conflict with Gerar's inhabitants forced both Abraham and Isaac to relocate to Beer-sheba at the kingdom's border. Yet, they made a treaty relationship with the king (Gen 21:31-34; 26:26).

The king of Gerar is also called king of the Philistines (Gen 26:1). The identification between the Philistines and residents of Gerar (Gen 21:14-15, 34) is anachronistic due to the much later conquest of the region by the Philistines (Deut 2:23; CAPHTOR, Amos 9:7; Jer 47:4). Gerar is missing in the list of conquered city-states in Josh 12 due to Israel's inability to subdue Philistia (Josh 13:1-4). Asa of Judah routed invading Ethiopians as far as Gerar (2 Chr 14:13-15). During

Hezekiah's reign, men of Simeon drove out tent-dwelling MEUNIM from the "wadi of Gerar" (1 Chr 4:39-41).

MICHAEL G. VANZANT

GERASA, GERASENES ger´uh-suh, ger´uh-seen [Γερασηνός Gerasēnos]. Gerasa (Jerash) is one of the three names given in manuscripts of the NT to the town in which Jesus met two people (one in Mark) possessed by demons. He exorcised the demons, sending them into a herd of pigs that rushed off the side of a cliff into the Sea of Galilee (Matt 8:28-34; Mark 5:1-17; Luke 8:26-39). Other names for this town occurring in MSS of the Gospels are Gadara and Gergesa (see GADARA, GADARENES). The biblical texts, however, do not name these towns directly, but speak of their citizens in whose territory the exorcism took place, i.e., Gerasenes, Gadarenes, Gergesenes.

It is likely that the best reading in Matthew is "Garadenes" (8:28). The town of Gadara is 5 mi. southeast of the Sea of Galilee. Josephus (Life 9.42) notes that the town possessed villages on the shore of the Sea of Galilee. Coins bearing the name Gadara sometimes bear the image of a ship. The reading in Matthew, then, is a plausible setting for the miracle story.

"Gerasenes" is the best reading found in the MSS of Mark. Like Gadara, Gerasa was a city of the Decapolis. Identified with the modern Jordanian city Jerash, Gerasa was located 37 mi. southeast of the Sea of Gali-lee—a full two days' journey. Origen noted that Gerasa was the least likely setting for the exorcism involving drowned swine (Comm. Jo. 6.41).

"Gergesa" is a variant reading found in each Gospel. Eusebius (Onom. 74.13) names this as the setting of the miracle of the swine, noting that the village still existed in his day (4th cent. CE). The village that Eusebius identified is located on the eastern shore of the Sea of Galilee. Origen also favored Gergesa as the setting, citing a local tradition Gergesa has been identified with the modern Tel el-Kursi. The site was excavated in 1971–74 and again in 2001–2. Excavation revealed a monastery built in the 5th cent. CE and abandoned after an 8th cent. CE earthquake. Nothing was found at Kursi that indicates that the site was venerated in connection with the exorcism though the excavator suggested that a chapel on a hill about the monastic church was built in the 6th cent. CE to commemorate the miracle.

Neither study of the textual variants nor the results of excavation has been successful in identifying the setting for the exorcism narrated in the Synoptics. Gerasa (Jerash) is, nonetheless, a very important archaeological site. It has been excavated and is remarkably well preserved.

Inscriptions on the site indicate that people believed that the town was built by Alexander the Great for his soldiers who settled in the area. "Antioch on the Chrysorrhoas," the town's original name, however, suggests that the town was founded by the Seleucids.

Todd Bolen/BiblePlaces.com
Figure 1: Oval Forum

The Jewish king Alexander Yannai captured it from the Seleucids in 85 BCE (Josephus, *J.W.* 103–06). Jewish rule ended in 63 BCE when Pompey brought the region into the Roman orbit. At this time, the city's name was changed to Gerasa, and it was remodeled into a Roman city, the basic plan of which is still visible today. After Trajan absorbed the Nabatean region into the Roman sphere, the southern Decapolis cities including Gerasa were split off from the Roman province of Syria and were formed into the new province of Arabia. Gerasa was at its height in the 1st to 3rd cent. CE as a Roman city, with some continuing Nabatean influence. It continued to prosper later as a Christian Byzantine city, with episcopal representation at the councils of Seleucia (359) and Chalcedon (451). Its many early churches (at least thirteen) attest to its Christian prosperity; seven are known to have been built during the reign of Justinian alone (527–65). By the middle of the 8th cent., Gerasa/Jerash had gone into decline, though there continued to be some occupation until about the 13th cent. The site was rediscovered in 1806, and the modern town dates from 1878. Much of the site was previously buried under debris, which helped preserve it. Though excavation began in the 19th cent., most work has been conducted in the 20th.

Excavation revealed a city wall that was 10 ft. thick. It was built in the 1st cent. CE and enclosed a 2-mi. circle with a diameter of 3,500 ft. In front of the southern gate of the city, there is a triumphal arch built to commemorate Hadrian's visit in 130 CE. Also outside the walls are the remains of a 15,000-seat hippodrome. The south gate of the wall led into the city's oval forum, a design unique for a Roman city. Ionic columns line the edges of the forum, and in its center is a base that probably held a dedicatory statue. The city's streets were arranged in Hippodamian fashion with streets meeting to form right angles. East of the forum are stairs that lead up to the 1st cent. CE Temple of Zeus Olympius. Only a few walls of the temple have been restored. It was built on the site of an earlier temple. Just behind the temple is the South Theater, which has been partially restored. Seating capacity was about 5,000.

The forum opens to the *cardo*, or main north-south street, which in Jerash is oriented slightly to the northeast, so that it aligns perfectly with the entrance to the Zeus Temple. The street runs 1,665 ft. to the north gate of the city. To the left on the way is an unusually shaped octagonal market area identified as a meat market. The cardo was intersected by two *decumani*, or major east-west cross streets. At each of the two intersections of a decumanus stood a tetrapylon, or four-based ornamental structure. The southern one was later made into a circular area in the 3rd cent. The southern decumanus continued to the east down the hill and across the river into what is now the modern town.

At the center of the ancient city, there is a massive temple dedicated to Artemis, the patron of the Roman city. Two more theaters and a large bath complex are located in the northern part of the city.

The oldest church in the city is known as the cathedral, an impressive structure though there is no evidence that it was an episcopal one. This church was in use in the mid 4th cent., an indication of the early and large Christian presence in the city. It is built in classical basilica style, with rectangular nave, apse on the eastern end, roof supported by two rows of columns that create two side aisles, and entrance through three doors from an atrium to the west. From the *cardo* one ascended through a monumental gateway up a flight of stairs. These structures cover the site of an earlier temple that was perhaps dedicated to a Nabatean god. Though the church is to the west of the *cardo*, still the architects preserved the early Christian custom of orienting the church with its apse to the east, so that worshipers facing the altar would face the rising sun. This means that at the top of the stairs, one arrives not at the entrance to the nave, but at the back of the church, behind the apse. A walkway on either side enabled worshipers arriving from the cardo to traverse the length of the nave on the outside, and so enter the church through the atrium on the west side.

Toward the end of the 5th cent. the Church of St. Theodore was built just above the cathedral to the west. Its apse actually cut into the atrium of the cathedral, the new church also being oriented with apse facing east. This new church, dated to 496, also had its own atrium farther to the west, and a baptistery on the south side. Immediately behind the Church of St. Theodore is the triple church complex of Sts. Cosmas and Damian, John the Baptist, and George, all built together about 530. They share a common narrow atrium and connecting doors. All had fine mosaic floors.

To the right at this point is the Viaduct Church, built in the 6th cent. Its nave was originally part of a colonnaded passageway leading from the east side of the city to the Temple of Artemis. On the left or west, an imposing gateway from the cardo leads up a flight of stairs to a plaza with the foundations of the altar. Another flight of stairs leads to the entrance of the temple. The temple was built on a platform constructed of vaulting, 131 ft. long, 74 ft. wide, and almost 14 ft. high. It was built in classic style with an inner walled cella containing the statue of the goddess, surrounded on all sides by columns, here of the Corinthian order. Many of the columns are still standing, but precariously. Guides encourage visitors to insert a narrow object or even a finger in the cracks between a base and column to actually feel the movement of the column as it sways in the wind. Like most Greek temples, the temple is oriented to the west, so that the approach is from the east and the rising sun could illumine the inside and the statue of the goddess that stood at the west end.

West of the temple of Artemis is a 6th cent. church known as "the synagogue church" since it was built above a 4th cent. synagogue. The synagogue had a narthex, which had three doors that opened to the main hall. It was a basilica with a central nave and aisles set off by two rows of columns.

LESLIE J. HOPPE, O.F.M.

GERISA, TELL. An ancient mound located in the Yarkon Valley at the fork of the Yarkon and Ayalon rivers as an inner-port city. The identification of the site with Gath-Rimmon is refuted on both geographical and archaeological grounds.

The first village on the site was in the Early Bronze Age III and early Middle Bronze Age IIA. The main urban stage began during the Middle Bronze Age IIA. Archaeological digs unearthed two superimposed fortification systems of mud-brick walls reinforced by an impressive GLACIS, with a third city wall and glacis dating from the Middle Bronze Age IIB. A large shaft hewn into the bedrock was exposed to a depth of 6.2 m in the eastern side of the mound, as were twenty-seven narrow stairs carved out of the rock of the sidewalls, a water system apparently built in the Middle Bronze Age IIA when a fortified city occupied the mound. The system was reused in the Iron Age I, with a stone-lined well incorporated into the shaft.

During the Late Bronze Age II the fortifications were neglected, and a large building was erected in the center of the mound, apparently the palace of the local ruler. Many objects, including imports from the Aegean, Cyprus, and Egypt, were unearthed in and around the building. In Iron Age I the center of the mound was left unoccupied (and possibly was cultivated) while two farmsteads were constructed at both ends of the hill. Pottery discovered associates the settlement with the Philistines. Finally, the site was sporadically inhabited in the Early Arab period (10th cent. CE), observed mainly in numerous refuse pits.

Bibliography: Z. Herzog. "Gerisa, Tel." *The New Encyclopedia of Archaeological Excavations in the Holy Land 2* (1993); B. Mazar. "Jaffa and the Yarkon Area During the Biblical Period." *Israel: People and Land: Ha-Aretz Museum Yearbook* (1984); A. F. Rainey. "Tel Gerisa and the Danite Inheritance." *Israel: People and Land: Eretz Israel Museum Yearbook* (1989).

ZE'EV HERZOG

GERIZIM, MOUNT ger′uh-zim [גְּרִזִים‎ הַר‎ har gerizim]. Now called Jebel et-Tur, located on the southwest side of the city of Shechem, the mountain stands at 868 m, rising 500 mi. above Shechem. According to Deuteronomy, the Israelites were to hold a ceremony on Mount Gerizim after they had conquered the land (Deut 11:29; 27:12). Half of the tribes were to stand on Mount Gerizim while Joshua read the blessings of the law, while the other half were to stand on Mount EBAL to hear the curses (Josh 8:30-35). A cultic site dating from the mid 13th to late 12th cent. BCE has been excavated on Mount Ebal. Mount Gerizim was also the site from which JOTHAM told the parable of the trees when Shechem proclaimed his brother ABIMELECH as their ruler (Judg 9:7-21).

Josephus (*Ant.* 11.306–12) states that the Samaritans established a temple at Mount Gerizim during the Persian period (4th cent. BCE). While no remains of such a temple have been found, objects excavated from Gerizim indicate that some form of cultic site was situated there from at least the time of Nehemiah. It is clear that during the Persian period Mount Gerizim became the central religious site for the Samaritans. The worship of God at Mount Gerizim derived its authority through connection with relatively old traditions within Israelite religion, including the stories that mention both Abraham and Jacob building altars in Shechem (Gen 12:6-7; 33:18-20). The question of whether to

Todd Bolen/BiblePlaces.com
Figure 1: Mount Gerizim, Shechem, and Mt. Ebal from east

worship at Gerizim or Jerusalem was still debated in the 1st cent. CE, as can be seen by the Samaritan woman's question to Jesus at the well (John 4:20). A Samaritan synagogue on Mount Gerizim is still in use today. *See* ISRAEL, GEOGRAPHY OF; SAMARIA; SHECHEM, SHECHEMITES.

Bibliography: Ingrid Hjelm. *Jerusalem's Rise to Sovereignty: Zion and Gerizim in Competition* (2004).

KEVIN A. WILSON

GERON. *See* SENATOR.

GERSHOM guhr´shuhm [גֵּרְשֹׁם gereshom]. 1. Moses gave this name to his elder son born in Midian by his wife ZIPPORAH to commemorate that he was "an alien in a foreign land" (Exod 2:22; 18:3; 1 Chr 23:15-16; 26:24). According to Judg 18:30, Gershom's son Jonathan and Jonathan's sons served as priests for the Danite tribe.

2. Levi also gave this name to his elder son (1 Chr 6:1-2, 5, 16-17, 20, 43), whose descendants are referred to as Gershomites or the sons of Gershom (1 Chr 6:62, 71; 15:7). His name is spelled Gershon in 1 Chr 23:6-7. *See* GERSHON, GERSHONITES.

3. A descendant of Phinehas, who returned with Ezra from Babylon to Jerusalem, also bears this name. He is Aaron's grandson and a priest (Ezra 8:2; 1 Esd 8:29).

EMILY R. CHENEY

GERSHON, GERSHONITES guhr´shuhn, guhr´shuh-nit [גֵּרְשׁוֹן gershon, גֵּרְשֻׁנִּי gershunni]. 1. The eldest of Levi's sons and the eponymous ancestor of one of the three branches of Levites (Gen 46:11; Exod 6:16; Num 3:17), Gershon was the father of Libni and SHI-MEI, who probably represented two branches within the Gershonites (Exod 6:17; Num 3:18). In 1 Chr 6 he is called GERSHOM. A variant tradition contends Gershon's first son was named Ladan (1 Chr 23:7).

2. According to the schema of Leviticus and Numbers, the Gershonites were one of the three divisions of the Levites. Gershon was the firstborn, which probably reflects an early period in Israelite history when the Gershonites were the most important priests. In Leviticus and Numbers, however, the Gershonites are subordinated to the Kohathites, the descendants of Levi's second son (*see* KOHATH, KOHATHITES). The Kohathites were in charge of the most holy things in the tabernacle (Num 4:4), while the Gershonites had lesser duties, such as carrying the curtains, hangings, and coverings of the tabernacle (Num 4:24-28). To facilitate this work, they were provided with two carts and four oxen (Num 7:7). During the wilderness wanderings, the Gershonites were to camp immediately to the west of the tabernacle, forming a boundary between the tabernacle and the non-priestly tribes (Num 3:23). The book of Joshua assigns thirteen Levitical towns to Gershon out of the tribal possessions of Issachar, Asher,

Naphtali, and Manasseh (Josh 21:6, 27-33). According to the Chronicler, David preserved the threefold division of the Levites in the Jerusalem Temple (1 Chr 23:6) *See* LEVI, LEVITES.

KEVIN A. WILSON

GERUTH CHIMHAM gihr´ooth-kim´ham [גֵּרוּת כִּמְהָם geruth kimham]. A place near Bethlehem where Ishmael, son of Nethaniah, and his men stopped while fleeing to Egypt after assassinating GEDALIAH (Jer 41:17). The name may mean "lodging place of CHIMHAM."

GESHAN gesh´uhn [גֵּישָׁן geshan]. A Calebite of the tribe of Judah and the third son of Jahdai. His name appears only in 1 Chr 2:47.

GESHEM gesh´uhm [גֶּשֶׁם geshem]. Along with SAN-BALLAT the Horonite and TOBIAH the Ammonite, Geshem opposed Nehemiah's plans to reconstruct the wall of Jerusalem. With the others, he ridiculed Nehemiah (Neh 2:19), attempted to entrap him during a meeting in a village in the plains of Ono (Neh 6:1-2), and threatened to report to the Persian king that Nehemiah was leading a rebellion against the king (Neh 6:4-9). His title, "the Arab," identifies him as the official with the highest rank in the section of the province south of Judah. A Lihyanite Arabian inscription with this name may be a reference to him.

EMILY R. CHENEY

GESHUR, GESHURITES gesh´uhr, gesh´uh-rit [גְּשׁוּר geshur, גְּשׁוּרִי geshuri]. 1. One of the areas not conquered by Joshua (Josh 13:8-13), east of the Sea of Galilee in the southern Golan Heights, Geshur remained independent during the time of David. David's marriage to Maacah, daughter of King Talmai, probably indicates a treaty between the two kingdoms (2 Sam 3:3). Absalom fled to Geshur after his failed revolt (2 Sam 13:37).

2. Inhabitants of an area near Philistia not conquered by Joshua (Josh 13:2) where David made raids while living with the Philistines (1 Sam 27:8-11). Some scholars emend these two references from "Geshurites" to "Gezerites."

KEVIN A. WILSON

GESTAS [Γεστας Gestas]. *Acts of Pilate* identifies the thieves crucified with Jesus as Gestas and DYSMAS. Gestas tells Jesus, "If you are the Christ, save yourself and us" (*Acts of Pilate* 10.2).

GESTURES. Gestures are facial expressions, postures, and body movements that 1) express physiologically-rooted emotional states and 2) convey symbolic meanings in conventionally ritualized patterns. Ancient Near Eastern and biblical literatures invoke gestures literally, to describe the gestures in question (e.g. 1 Kgs 8:54) and idiomatically, to convey the attitudes that such gestures represent (e.g., Gen 4:5-6; Exod 9:28-29; Isa 1:15). Recent advances in the analysis of gesture in biblical literature are distinguished by a systematic description of their semantic parallels in other Semitic languages, and by social scientific insights into nonverbal communication.

Gestures expressing emotion must be interpreted in context for setting can nuance similar body movements while different movements of the same body part may occasion homophonous expressions. Thus bending over can connote greeting (Gen 33:3), gratitude (Gen 48:12), entreaty (2 Sam 16:4), or grief (Job 1:20). Again, extending the hand(s) can connote rebellion (2 Sam 18:28), violence (2 Sam 20:21-22), oath-taking (Ezek 20:6), begging (Ps 88:10), blessing (Lev 9:22), supplication (Isa 1:15), and praise (Ps 28:2). Physiological studies help to limit the meanings of expressive emotional gestures. For example, they exclude the proposal that Job put his hand on his mouth in Job 40:4 out of disgust with God's first speech since such is not a gesture of disgust. Literary context, on the other hand, helps to define Job's reaction as an expression of fear regarding confrontation with God (compare Job 9:20). Divine hand gestures in biblical narratives, e.g., those featuring prophetic commissions and healing, may be interpreted in the context of the wider canon in a way that link such acts, and in turn the sacramental rites based on them, to biblical creation theology and eschatology (compare Exod 4:15; Deut 18:18; Isa 6:7; Jer 1:9; Dan 10:16; Matt 8:3; 20:34; Mark 1:41; John 9:6).

Since symbolic actions belonging to specific contexts, such as the temple, the law-court and the army, speak clearly to their participants, the interpretation of biblical gestures is facilitated when the literary references may be correlated with ancient iconography or with the reenactments in traditional Jewish and Christian liturgical acts (compare John 13:5-14; Acts 2:42-46). In art, gestures are identified with body movements specifically intended to convey meaning. Thus the representation of captives as stooping invokes a gesture indicating submission or humiliation, but the representation of workers as stooping does not. This definition breaks down when narrative context endows such postures with their intended meaning as in Jesus' stooping to wash his disciples' feet (John 13:5-14), or in the extension of his hands on the cross, to convey, in the context of the Gospel, a supreme divine gesture of salvation.

Bibliography: Uri Ehrlich. *The Nonverbal Language of Prayer: A New Approach to Jewish Liturgy* (1999); Gregory Glazov. "The Significance of the 'Hand on the Mouth' Gesture in Job XL 4." *VT* 70, 1 (2001) 30–41; Mayer Gruber. *Aspects of Nonverbal Communication in the Ancient Near East* (1980).

GREGORY GLAZOV

GETHER gee´thuhr [גֶּתֶר *gether*]. A descendant of SHEM and son of Aram and progenitor of the Arameans or Syrians in the Table of Nations (Gen 10:23; 1 Chr 1:17).

GETHSEMANE geth-sem´uh-nee [Γεθσημανί *Gethsēmani*]. Derived from gath shemane [גַּת שְׁמָנֵי], which means "oil press." An olive orchard located within the Mount of Olives.

Todd Bolen/Biblplaces.com

Figure 1: Gethesemane and the Mount of Olives from west

In the Gospel tradition, there is only one reference to Gethsemane (Mark 14:32//Matt 26:36). It is the site for the depiction of Jesus' agonizing prayer, Judas' betrayal, and Jesus' arrest. Both Mark and Matthew refer to it as a chōrion (χωρίον, a "plot of land"; diminutive of "field"). Luke prefers a broader reference, the "Mount of Olives" (22:39; compare Mark 14:26), perhaps as an allusion to this "mount" as a traditional place of mourning (compare 2 Sam 15:30). John refers to Judas' betrayal and Jesus' arrest scene occurring in "a garden" (across the Kidron Valley) without any other specific designation (John 18:1). The phrase "garden of Gethsemane" is derived from combining the synoptic and the Johannine traditions. Apparently, it was a place Jesus visited frequently (Luke 22:39), which may explain why Judas knew where to find him (John 18:2).

Prior to Jesus' arrest, it was the courtyard in which Jesus expressed his deepest struggle with God's will for his life and mission. The "cup," which Jesus desires to have "removed," is the symbol of his fate (compare Mark 10:38-39). A Jesus fraught with indecision over his mission does not fit into the larger theological agenda of the fourth Gospel, in which his struggles are resolved more abruptly: "What shall I say? 'Father, save me from his hour'? No, for this purpose I have come to this hour" (John 12:27). In addition, this latter saying occurs at a different narrative location in John. In the synoptic depiction, Jesus resolves the tension with a confession of dependence on the sovereignty of God: "Yet, not my will but yours be done" (Mark 14:36//Matt 26:39// Luke 22:42). Nevertheless, Jesus offers this prayer repeatedly before any apparent resolution (Mark 14:32-34), hinting at the resistance of the earlier temptation scene (compare Matt 4:1-11//Luke 4:1-13).

In Christian tradition, Gethsemane has come to represent Jesus' lowest moment in life, the one occasion when the synoptic authors depict him hesitant about his purpose. In modern-day Jerusalem, the historical site of Gethsemane is debated, although several religious traditions promote specific sites for the purpose of holy pilgrimages and symbolic places of prayer.

EMERSON B. POWERY

GEUEL gyoo'uhl [גְּאוּאֵל ge'u'el]. One of twelve spies Moses sent from the wilderness of Kadesh to explore the land of Canaan. This son of Machi of the tribe of Gad was among ten who advised Moses against going into Canaan.

GEZER CALENDAR gee'zuhr. A small (approximately 7 × 11 cm) chalk slab, crudely inscribed with seven lines in the Paleo-Canaanite (or "early Hebrew") alphabetic script, found in 1908 by R. A. S. Macalister in his "Fourth Semitic" level, dated roughly to Iron I–II (11th–6th cent. BCE). A date more precisely in the 10th cent. BCE, however, is suggested by paleography (the

relatively primitive form of the letters), making it possibly our earliest Hebrew inscription.

Most scholars regard the Gezer "calendar" as a schoolboy's practice text, i.e., a mnemonic poem something like "Thirty days hath September. . . ." The order of the months and the specified agricultural activities correspond roughly with the ancient Canaanite and Israelite seasonal year, which the liturgical calendar followed, beginning in the fall with the onset of the winter rains.

Bibliography: W. F. Albright. *ANET* (1969) 321; K. A. D. Smelik. *Writings from Ancient Israel. A Handbook of Historical and Religious Documents* (1991) 18–28.

WILLIAM G. DEVER

GEZER, GEZERITES gee'zuhr [גֶּזֶר gezer]. The prominent 33-acre mound of Tell el-Jezer near Ramleh, at the juncture of the Shephelah/central hills and central coastal plain, is to be identified with ancient Gezer. The site was excavated by British archaeologists in 1902–09 (R. A. S. Macalister) and 1934; and again by an American team in 1964–74, 1984, and 1990, directed by W. G. Dever and J. D. Seger.

The combined excavations have revealed twenty-six strata, dating from the late Chalcolithic (3400–3300 BCE) to the Herodian era (1st cent. CE), more than almost any other site in ancient Palestine.

The Bronze Age strata, while they are confined to the pre-biblical era (i.e., pre-Israelite), indicate that Gezer gradually became one of the most strategic sites in an increasingly urban Palestine. The Middle Bronze Age is particularly noteworthy, boasting massive city walls (the "Inner Wall"), a triple-entryway gate, and a citadel, among the most impressive anywhere in the country. Also significant is the famous Field V "High Place" consisting of ten enormous aligned standing stones and a large basin, probably a Canaanite forerunner of the biblical **bamoth** (בָּמוֹת) or HIGH PLACES. A heavy destruction ends this era, no doubt part of the well-documented Egyptian campaign of Thutmosis III in 1468 BCE.

Following a partial gap in occupation in the 15th cent. BCE, Gezer became one of the Palestinian city-states known from the 14th cent. AMARNA LETTERS found in Egypt. These texts, which include nearly a dozen letters from three successive kings of Gezer, illuminate socioeconomic conditions in Palestine during the beginning of New Kingdom pharaohs. The American excavations attributed the impressive "Outer Wall" to this period, although others disagree. Disruptions of the very end of the period may be the result of the campaign of Pharaoh MERNEPTAH, whose "Victory Stela" of ca. 1207 mentions Gezer.

Gezer was apparently not taken during the early Israelite settlement in the 13th–12th cent. BCE, in keeping with biblical sources (Josh 10:33; 12:12; 16:10; Judg 1:29). The 12th–11th cent. BCE levels (Str. XIII–XI) represent a continued Canaanite occupation, but with Bichrome pottery and other elements that indicate some Philistine presence. At least two destructions punctuate the 12th–11th cent. BCE levels. There follows a "post-Philistine/pre-Israelite" horizon (Str. X–IX: late 11th–mid-10th cent. BCE) characterized by red-slipped unburnished wares (see POTTERY).

In the stratum dated to the mid-late 10th cent. BCE (Str. VIII) is the rebuild of the "Outer Wall," with the addition of a series of Phoenician-style ashlar (dressed) masonry towers; and on the south side of the mound (Field III) a gatehouse, a four-entryway upper city gate, and a stretch of casemate or double city wall. These well-planned and constructed monumental structures are very similar to those found in Hazor and Megiddo, and they are thus taken by the majority of scholars to reflect Solomon's building activities described in 1 Kgs 9:15-17 (see TEMPLE OF SOLOMON). Red slipped and hand-burnished pottery characterizes this horizon. Domestic structures are not well attested. Gezer may have served largely as a fortified outpost on the Judean-Israelite border, perhaps the capital of one of Solomon's twelve administrative centers (1 Kgs 4:7-19). A few tombs belong to this horizon. Heavy destruction in Str. VIII gives evidence of the well-known raid of the Egyptian Twenty-second Dynasty Pharaoh Sheshonq ca. 925 BCE (the SHISHAK of 1 Kgs 14:25). The Shishak stela apparently names "Gezer" in topographical order in listing campaigns in the Shepelah district, although the text is partially broken at this point.

Israelite occupation at Gezer in the 9th–8th cent. BCE (Str. VII) is not especially well attested. The upper city gate is now rebuilt following its destruction (above) as a three-entryway gate, similar to that of Megiddo Str. IVA. A series of well-constructed private houses was found northwest of the gate area (Field VII), many of them rebuilt and used until the destruction of the site in the Neo-Assyrian period (below).

Stratum VI marks the 8th cent. BCE occupation, brought to a fiery end in a destruction that is surely to be attributed to TIGLATH-PILESER III in his campaigns of 734/733 BCE. A relief found long ago in the ruins of his palace at Nimrud (now lost) depicts an Assyrian battering ram drawn up against the tower of a city wall, its defenders on top surrendering. The accompanying cuneiform inscription specifies gazru (Gezer). Evidence of just such a breach was found immediately to the east of the Field III city gate. Iron arrowheads and pottery covered by calcined (burnt limestone) were found in one of the casemate chambers to the west of the gate.

Stratum V belongs to the post-Assyrian horizon, when Judah was now reckoned as a Judean site. Evidence comes chiefly from Macalister's "royal stamped jar handles" and a few cuneiform tablets. The city gate is now converted into a rather flimsy two entryway gate. In several places debris witnesses the Neo-Babylonian destruction of 587/586 BCE, after which Gezer sinks into decline. There are few stratified levels of the Persian epoch (Str. IV), although Macalister's rich "Philistine Tombs" belong here.

Stratum III–II illustrate the Hellenistic era. The Field III gate is finally rebuilt in Str. II, no doubt in connection with the efforts of the Maccabean insurgents, who came from nearby Modin. The "Outer Wall" was also reused for a final time, with the addition of semicircular ashlar bastions surrounding the towers. Coins of Demetrius II (ca. 144 BCE) and Antiochus VII (ca. 138–129 BCE) confirm the dates.

The scant remains of Str. I are Herodian, but the site was largely deserted by this time. Nearly a dozen "boundary inscriptions" carved into the bedrock in an arc some distance away read in archaizing Hebrew "boundary of Gezer," and in Greek "Alkiou" (Ἀλκιου), the genitive of "Alkios," (Ἀλκιος) probably the landowner of a large estate including the largely abandoned site. A few Byzantine tombs and traces of medieval activity in the vicinity attest to some lingering occupation in the general area. Then Tell el-Jezer was forgotten, and the location of Bronze Age and biblical Gezer lay unknown until Clermont-Ganneau's discovery of some of the boundary inscriptions in 1870. The name, however, was preserved in a corrupted version on the medieval tomb of a Muslim holy man on the highest rise of the mound (as Tell ej-Jezairli, "Tomb of the Algerian").

Bibliography: W. G. Dever. "Late Bronze Age and Solomonic Defenses at Gezer: New Evidence." *BASOR* 262 (1986) 9–34; W. G. Dever. "Further Evidence on the Date of the Outer Wall at Gezer." *BASOR* 289 (1993) 33–54; W. G. Dever, ed. *Gezer IV: The 1969–71 Seasons in Field VI, the "Acropolis"* (1986); W. G. Dever, et al. *Gezer II: Report of the 1967–70 Seasons in Fields I and II* (1974); W. G. Dever, H. D. Lance, and G. E. Wright. *Gezer I: Preliminary Report of the 1964–66 Seasons* (1970); S. Gitin. *Gezer III: A Ceramic Typology of the Late Iron II, Persian and Hellenistic Periods at Tell Gezer* (1990); H. D. Lance. "Gezer in the Land and in History." *BA* 30 (1967) 34–47; R. A. S. Macalister. *The Excavation of Gezer*, Vols. I–III (1912); J. D. Seger. *Gezer V: The Field I Caves* (1988).

WILLIAM G. DEVER

GHASSÛL, TELEILÂT EL. Teleilât el-Ghassûl is a Chalcolithic settlement (4500–3400 BCE) east of the Jordan River. Most Chalcolithic settlements in the region lined dry riverbeds (wadis) in peripheral, arid areas. Copper ore was first mined along the Wadi Arabah south of the Dead Sea during this era. The population of the region lived primarily in unfortified villages and with an agricultural and pastoral economy during the Chalcolithic period. Tools were generally a mix of copper (Chalco) and stone (lithic) objects. The Chalcolithic

Age is considered prehistoric with no societal records in existence.

The 50-acre site of Teleilât el-Ghassûl was abandoned at the beginning of the Early Bronze Age I (3300–3000 BCE). Excavation of the site revealed ten levels of occupation covering close to a thousand years (ca. 4400–400 BCE). Artifacts discovered in excavation provided the basis for defining a Ghassulian culture found in numerous Chalcolithic settlements. Due to its location overlooking the southeast end of the Jordan Valley, its size, and long occupation, the site was probably the main administrative and economic center for the area.

Teleilât el-Ghassûl provides a glimpse at early village planning. The un-walled village contained densely built clusters of dwellings arranged around streets and alleys. Planning requires cooperation between inhabitants and usually points toward a central authority of some type. Religious activity included use of small temples, the only civic structures. Belief in an afterlife is evident with individual burials complete with votive vessels. Pottery discovered includes various types of cups, bowls, and storage jars with only slight variations through the years. Painted red bands serve as a simple decoration for the vessels, while a few smaller items display delicate geometric triangles and stripes.

Material uncovered throughout the Chalcolithic period in the region represents innovative and vivid art objects that rival any prehistoric collections in the area. Artistic abilities revealed in wall paintings at el-Ghassûl represent outstanding talent. The paintings depict an artistic tradition based upon development of professional artists. The works include pictures of a religious ceremonial procession and numerous animals, including a kneeling leopard. The Ghassulian culture is unique in the implementation of copper technology, religious art, and burial customs. *See* COPPER; PREHISTORY IN THE ANCIENT NEAR EAST.

MICHAEL G. VANZANT

GHASSÛL, TULEILÂT EL. *See* GHASSÛL, TELEILÂT EL-.

GHAZAL, ʿAIN. Located near Amman, Jordan, ʿAin Ghazal is the largest-known Neolithic site in the Near East, covering approximately 35 acres and numbering several thousand inhabitants at its height. Founded around 8500 BCE (calibrated), it is also the longest-lived Neolithic settlement, spanning an uninterrupted occupation for 2,700 years until ca. 5800 BCE (calibrated), and its succession of habitation episodes has been an encyclopedia of developments during one of the most revolutionary periods of cultural development: the emergence of farming, the development of animal husbandry, and an increasingly complex social structure. Excavations from 1982 to 1998 demonstrated that although Palestine was abandoned for more

John Mark Wade

Figure 1: Plaster statues in Amman Museum; Amman, Jordan.

than a thousand years, highland Jordan thrived, leading to unprecedented population growth and density. Like Jericho, ʿAin Ghazal's religious sphere centered for a time on a cult that recreated "portraits" on the skulls of certain people associated with links to ancestral origins, both in terms of known personalities and of mythical ancestors. The latter were depicted in the form of large (approximately 1 m high) plaster statues with brilliant artistic capabilities. After 7500 BCE, ritual shifted from a kinship-based ancestral basis to a community-wide religious focus represented by some of the earliest-known temples and shrines south of Turkey.

GARY O. ROLLEFSON

GHAZZA, KHIRBET. *See* UZA, HORVAT.

GHOSH, ABU. The small (ca. 9 acres) Neolithic village of Abu Ghosh is located on a broad terrace about 7 mi. west of Jerusalem, only a few hundred yards from biblical Tel Qiryat Yeʿarim. Despite the lack of radiocarbon dates, the main occupation of the village was by early farmers during the Middle Pre-Pottery Neolithic B period, sometime between 8500 to 7500 BCE, based on stone tool technology and morphology. Plant remains were not recovered during the two major excavations, but the dominance of sickle blades and milling stones indicate a heavy reliance on domesticated plants found at other sites in the region at this time. In addition, there is also evidence suggestive of the earliest stages of goat domestication. The site was reoccupied on a smaller scale during the Pottery Neolithic period, probably sometime between 5500 to 4500 BCE.

Bibliography: Hamoudi Khalaily and Ofer Marder. *The Neolithic Site of Abu Ghosh. The 1995 Excavations.* IAA Reports, No. 19. (2003); Monique Lechevallier.

Abou Gosh et Beisamoun. Deux Gisements du VIIe Millénaire Avant l'Ère. Chrétienne en Israël. Mémoires et Travaux du Centre de Recherches Préhistoriques Français de Jérusalem. No. 2 (1978).

GARY O. ROLLEFSON

GHOST [אוֹב ʾov; φάντασμα phantasma]. An apparition or spirit of the dead. NECROMANCY is condemned in the OT. In the NT, the disciples mistake Jesus for a ghost (Matt 14:26; Mark 6:49; Luke 24:37-39). *See* SHADES.

GHOST, HOLY. *See* HOLY SPIRIT.

GIAH gi'uh [גִּיחַ ghiakh]. A site, perhaps in the territory of Benjamin, used to specify the route taken by Joab and Abishai in their pursuit of Abner (2 Sam 2:24). The LXX renders the name of this otherwise unknown site as Gai (Γαί), "valley," although this does not provide any additional information since Gaih is unknown as a site name. The Hebrew ghiakh may be related to the verb guakh (גּוּחַ), "to burst forth," perhaps meaning "spring."

RALPH K. HAWKINS

GIANTS [רָפָא rafaʾ, רָפָה rafah; ραφά rapha, γίγαντες gigantes]. The REPHAIM were individuals of immense size and strength. GOLIATH, the Philistine giant slain by David, was noted for extraordinary height (1 Sam 17:23-54). Archaeological evidence of a giant race is minimal. Biologists note that abnormal size consistently results in sterility, thus a large assemblage of bone specimens from a race of giants is unlikely. The giant with six fingers on each hand and six toes on each foot (2 Sam 21:20) is consistent with the genetic abnormalities known in people with anterior pituitary hypertrophy.

Two types of giants are seen in the text. The NEPHILIM were offspring from divine and human relations such as the union in Gen 6:1-4 ("heroes that were of old"). A second group were giants born of human parents, such as the Rephaim (Deut 2:11, 20; 3:11, 13; Josh 12:4; 13:12; 17:15). *See* REPHAIM, VALLEY OF.

MICHAEL G. VANZANT

GIBBAR gib'ahr [גִּבָּר gibbar]. Family name of a group of people returning from exile in Babylon mentioned in Ezra 2:20. A corresponding list preserved in Neh 7 records Gibeon in the place of Gibbar, leading some to suggest that the list preserved in Ezra 2 is textually corrupt.

GIBBETHON gib'uh-thon [גִּבְּתוֹן gibbethon]. A city originally assigned to the tribe of Dan in west-central Palestine (Josh 19:44) before they moved north. Also, the city was assigned to the Levite clan of Kohath (Josh 21:23) along with Elteke, Aijalon, and Gathrimmon. The Philistines soon captured all of these cities. Baasha

assassinated Nadab while Israel besieged Gibbethon (1 Kgs 15:27). Later Omri, commander of the Israelite army, attacked the city. But when Elah was killed by Zimri, Omri withdrew to Tirzah (1 Kgs 16:8-20) and became king of Israel. Tel el-Melat, 3 mi. east of Gezer, may be the site of ancient Gibbethon.

MICHAEL G. VANZANT

GIBEA gib'ee-uh [גִּבְעָא givʿaʾ]. The grandson of Caleb by his concubine Maacah (1 Chr 2:49). His father was Sheva.

GIBEAH gib'ee-uh [גִּבְעָה givʿah]. Several places names mentioned in the OT. Givʿah means "hill." 1. A town in the territory of Judah listed as being south of Hebron (Josh 15:57). The location of Gibeah in Judah is unknown.

2. A town in the territory of Ephraim that is the burial place of Eleazar the priest who helped Joshua make the tribal allotments (givʿath pinekhas [גִּבְעַת פִּינְחָס] Josh 24:33). The town's location is unknown, but Jibia and et-Tell have been suggested as possible locations.

3. A town in Benjamin (givʿath benyamin [גִּבְעַת בִּנְיָמִין]; 1 Sam 13:2), which appears prominently in Judg 19–21 (compare Hos 9:9; 10:9) and has been associated with the seat of Saul's kingship (givʿath shaʾul [גִּבְעַת שָׁאוּל]; 1 Sam 11:4; 15:34). Scholars disagree as to whether Gibeah was the hometown of Saul or only his seat of power. There is also disagreement concerning Gibeah's location and about whether it is the same as GEBA (gevaʿ גֶּבַע), Gibeon (givʿon [גִּבְעוֹן]; *see* GIBEON, GIBEONITES), or GIBEATH-ELOHIM (givʿath haʾelohim [גִּבְעַת הָאֱלֹהִים]; 1 Sam 10:5). This confusion stems from the fact that all of these place names contain the root for "hill."

Regardless of the location of Gibeah, what is clear are the connections drawn between the rape of the LEVITE'S CONCUBINE at Gibeah (Judg 19) and Saul's reign from Gibeah; these connections were possibly made to denigrate traditions about Saul's kingship. After the men of Gibeah rape the Levite's concubine, the Levite dismembers her and sends the twelve pieces throughout Israel. The tribe of Benjamin, however, chooses to stand with Gibeah (Judg 20). It is the tribe of Judah, David's ancestors, that goes up first against Gibeah and the Benjaminites (Judg 20:19). The story shows the tribe of David leading the other tribes nearly to eradicate the tribe of Saul. In 1 Sam 10–11 after Samuel anoints Saul the Benjaminite as king of Israel, the Ammonites lay siege against Jabesh-Gilead, the town whose virgin daughters where taken to provide wives for the six hundred Benjaminites who survived the slaughter of their tribe (Judg 20:46-21:23). When word reaches Saul at Gibeah, he dismembers a yoke of oxen and sends the pieces to the tribes to call them into battle against the Ammonites (1 Sam 11). The image of carving someone or something and using the pieces to call Israel into battle and Jabesh-Gilead appears in the Saul cycle and connect the two Gibeah stories. The Judges account can be read to undermine Saul's early success against Israel's enemies by calling into question the morality of his Benjaminite forebearers. The story of Judges seems more ideologically than historically driven. Some argue that the story in Judges is an exaggeration, while others argue that the story is not historically a part of the period of the Judges, but relates instead to the war between David and the Saulides after Saul died at Gilboa. How one resolves the question of historicity of the Judges account directly affects the debate surrounding the location of Gibeah (see below).

In other traditions about Gibeah, ITTAI, a Benjaminite from Saul's seat at Gibeah chose to fight with David, and he is listed as one of David's MIGHTY MEN (in 2 Sam 23:29//1 Chr 11:31 he is listed as ITHAI). First Chronicles 12:3 shows other Benjaminites from Gibeah joined David and serves the purpose of illustrating that David was accepted by some of Saul's own people as well as all of Israel. According to the Hebrew text of 2 Sam 21:6, the last of the Saulides were to be put to death at Gibeah of Saul because of his otherwise unknown massacre of Gibeonites.

In the 1840s Edward Robinson identified Gibeah of Saul with Jabaʿ, a position followed by J. M. Miller and P. M. Arnold, who also assert that Gibeah and Geba are variants of the same name. Robinson later associated the town with Tell el-Ful, a position echoed by W. F. Albright and followed by most scholars. The site of Tell el-Ful is roughly 5 km north of Jerusalem's Damascus Gate on the road from Judah to Mount Ephraim. Strategically the site offers an excellent view in all directions save the northwest. The site was occupied between the 12th cent. BCE and the 1st cent. CE. There is evidence of a tower dated to the 11th–10th cent. BCE which has been associated with Saul.

The alternate site for Gibeah, Jabaʿ, is located 9 km northeast of Jerusalem. A surface survey revealed Iron Age and Persian pottery shards, but without excavation the precise nature of the site and how to date it cannot be determined. Those who connect Jabaʿ with Gibeah believe that Judg 19–21 shows that Gibeah must have been a flourishing town with walls, homes, and roads prior to Saul's rise to power. The remains at Tell el-Ful do not show evidence of such a city.

There are two points that argue against the identification of Gibeah with Jabaʿ: 1) according to Isa 10:29, Geba and Gibeah are separate locations that an enemy will march through from the north to Jerusalem. Gibeah (Heb. givʿah) along with Geba and Gibeon are listed as separate locations in Benjamin (Josh 18:21-28). These two texts lead some to believe that Geba and Gibeah must be separate towns. 2) If the story of the Levite's Concubine in Judg 19–20 is either an exaggeration or was written to discredit the Saulides then the fact that Tel el-Ful was not a major city in the 12th–11th cent.

BCE does not disprove that Tell el-Ful is Saul's Gibeah (Judg 19:15, 21).

Bibliography: William F. Albright. "A New Campaign of Excavation at Gibeah of Saul." BASOR 52 (1933) 6–12; William F. Albright. *Excavations and Results at Tell el-Ful (Gibeah of Saul)* (1924); Patrick M. Arnold. *Gibeah: The Search for a Biblical City* (1990); Simcha Shalom Brooks. "From Gibeon to Gibeah: High Place of the Kingdom." *Temple and Worship in Biblical Israel.* John Day, ed. (2005) 40–59; Aaron Demsky. "Geba, Gibeah, and Gibeon—An Historico-Geographic Riddle." BASOR 212 (1973) 26–31; Nancy L. Lapp, ed. *The Third Campaign at Tell el-Ful: Excavations of 1964* (1981); Amihai Mazar. *Archaeology of the Land of the Bible 10,000–586 bce* (1990); J. Maxwell Miller. "Geba/Gibeah of Benjamin." VT 25 (1975) 145–66.

HEATHER R. MCMURRAY

GIBEATH-ELOHIM   gib´ee-uhth-el´oh-him [גִּבְעַת־הָאֱלֹהִים givʿath haʾelohim]. A place whose name means "the hill of God." Samuel told Saul he would meet a group of prophets there coming down from the sanctuary (lit. "high place"), and that the spirit of Yahweh would come upon him, and he would be a changed man (1 Sam 10:5-7). The exact location is difficult to identify, partly because of the ubiquitous use of the term givʿah (גִּבְעָה, "hill") and forms of it in place names in the region of Benjamin. Some have identified it with Gibeon, where there was apparently a significant sanctuary (1 Kgs 3:4), but this identification is difficult to maintain without independent evidence of Philistine presence because of the notice in 1 Sam 10:5 that there was a Philistine garrison at Gibeath-elohim. Others consider GIBEAH, the hometown of Saul (1 Sam 11:4), as a better candidate. The predictions of Samuel are fulfilled when Saul arrives at Gibeah (1 Sam 10:10). The story of the attack on a Philistine garrison at GEBA, carried out by Jonathan (1 Sam 13:3), is then attributed to Saul (13:4). J. M. Miller explained it as a story originally about the completion of Samuel's instructions that Saul do whatever seems appropriate when the signs are fulfilled, for God is with him (1 Sam 10:7).

Bibliography: J. M. Miller. "Geba/Gibeah of Benjamin." *VT* 25 (1975) 145–66; J. M. Miller. "Saul's Rise to Power: Some Observations Concerning 1 Sam. 9:1–10:16; 10:26–11:15; and 13:2–14:46." *CBQ* 36 (1974) 157–74.

C. MARK MCCORMICK

GIBEATH-HAARALOTH   gib´ee-uhth-hay-air´uh-loth [גִּבְעַת הָעֲרָלוֹת givʿath haʿaraloth]. Means "hill of foreskins." This is where Joshua circumcised with flint knives the Israelites who had been born after leaving Egypt (Josh 5:3).

GIBEON, GIBEONITES gib´ee-uhn, gib´ee-uh-n*it* [גִּבְעוֹן *giv´on*, גִּבְעֹנִי *giv´oni*]. Gibeon is referred to primarily as a place name in the OT. It is a strategic city in the territory of Benjamin. The Gibeonites feature prominently in the conquest narratives of the book of Joshua. While the city remains significant during the united monarchical period, it receives only scant mention in later historical periods. There are also two references to Gibeon as a personal name in the genealogies of Saul (1 Chr 8:29; 9:35).

    A. Gibeon in the Old Testament
    B. Gibeon in Non-biblical Texts
    C. Gibeon in Archaeology
    Bibliography

A. Gibeon in the Old Testament

Canonically, the earliest mention of Gibeon in the OT is in the book of Joshua (chap. 9). According to the narrative sequence of the book of Joshua, the story of the Israelites' encounter with the Gibeonites comes at a point after the Israelites have defeated and taken the cities of Jericho and Ai (*see* JOSHUA, BOOK OF). When the kings in the region west of the Jordan heard what happened to Jericho and Ai, they formed an alliance to do battle with the Israelites. The Gibeonites were not willing to risk being conquered, however, so seek a different course of action. They decide to trick Joshua and the Israelites into making a treaty with them by posing as travelers from a faraway land. Setting out to meet Joshua and the Israelites, they make the ruse work by taking with them worn-out items: sacks for their donkeys, torn and mended wineskins, patched sandals, clothes, and dry and moldy food. Having succeeded in tricking the Israelites, the Gibeonites submit themselves to servitude to the Israelites and secure a treaty with them, thereby escaping annihilation. When the Israelites discover that they have fallen prey to a ruse, it is too late since they had sworn an oath to the Gibeonites in the name of Yahweh. The Israelites decide to let the Gibeonites live "so that wrath may not come upon [them]" (9:20).

This narrative serves at least two purposes. First, it is an etiological story that explains how the Gibeonites become "hewers of wood and drawers of water" in service to the Temple. Such a status comes as a result of a curse that Joshua imposes on them. Second, the story deals with the complexity of the Israelites' relations to the NATIONS. The Gibeonites, as a subgroup of the HIVITES (9:7; 11:19), are designated for annihilation (Deut 20:17). Yet, out of fear for Israel's God and having heard of Yahweh's mighty deeds, they are willing to take a different route for their communal survival. Like the story of Rahab, the story of the Gibeonites deals with the intricacies of how some "outsiders" become "insiders" among the Israelites. It cautions readers against a simplistic thinking that the Israelites were

to have nothing to do with the people in their midst except to obliterate them.

Perhaps the more challenging theological issue in this text is the response of Yahweh. In 9:14, the text notes that the Israelite leadership "did not ask direction from the Lord" when confronting the Gibeonites. The implication seems to be that Yahweh would have said "no," that Yahweh would not have let the Gibeonites live, since the command to annihilate the Hittites, the Amorites, the Canaanites, the Perizzites, the Hivites, and the Jebusites had come directly from Yahweh.

After entering into the treaty with the Israelites, the Gibeonites immediately find themselves the target of an impending attack from the "five kings of the Amorites," a powerful coalition led by Adoni-zedek, the king of Jerusalem (Josh 10). As a result, the Gibeonites seek the help of Joshua and the Israelites, who inflict a devastating defeat on the coalition force. The text reports that Yahweh is actively involved on behalf of Israel in this battle. Yahweh "threw [the enemy] into a panic" and "threw down huge stones from heaven on them" (10:10-11). It is in this context that the well-known text of the sun standing still at Gibeon occurs (10:12). The short poetic couplet has generated much discussion. Much more important than the extended daylight for the battle is the suggestion that the sun and moon are called upon to stand still in amazement of the awe-inspiring victory that Yahweh has wrought.

According to the tribal allotments, Gibeon falls under the territorial configuration of Benjamin (18:25; *see* BENJAMIN, BENJAMINITES). It is, however, designated as a Levitical city to provide residence for the Aaronic priestly families who are dispersed throughout Israel, as well as grazing land for their livestock (21:17).

During the historical periods covered in the OT, Gibeon figures prominently as the site of battles and massacres. Gibeon is first mentioned as the site of a battle for the struggle of the Israelite throne following the demise of Saul (*see* SAUL, SON OF KISH). According to the narrative in 2 Sam 2, upon the death of Saul, the Judeans made David king over Judah. At the same time, Abner, Saul's military commander, made Saul's son Ishbaal a rival king over Israel. What began as a battle by proxy at the "pool of Gibeon" (2 Sam 2:12-17) eventuated in a long and protracted battle between the forces of David under the command of Joab and the Saulide forces under Abner. The "pool of Gibeon" evidently remained in use and of significance into the 6th cent. BCE when it was mentioned again in the book of Jeremiah (41:12). This is very likely the pool uncovered in archaeological excavation at Gibeon.

Gibeon is mentioned again 2 Sam 20:8-13 as the location in which JOAB murdered Amasa, whom David had earlier appointed as his military commander in place of Joab (19:13). The meaning of the reference to the "large stone that is in Gibeon" is not certain.

Gibeon surfaces a third time as the locus of massacre in 2 Sam 21:1-9. The narrative begins by relating a three-year famine during David's reign. David seeks out the Lord to understand the reason for the famine and is told that the famine is the consequence of Saul's slaughter of the Gibeonites (an event unattested elsewhere in the OT) in violation of the oath the Israelites made to the Gibeonites (Josh 9). To make restitution to the Gibeonites, David allows the Gibeonites to execute seven of Saul descendants at Gibeon (in the Heb., the spelling is Gibeah). The historical nature of this narrative is not clear. What is clear, however, is the emphasis of the Israelite-Gibeonite relationship, whereby the Gibeonites as a distinct ethnic group fall under treaty protection of the Israelites.

After Jerusalem fell to the Babylonians, an insurgence broke out against the Babylonian-appointed governor, Gedaliah, and Gedaliah was murdered along with many others. This rebellion was led by a member of the royal household named Ishmael. When Johanan, a military leader and supporter of Gedaliah, heard what had happened, he pursued Ishmael and came upon him at the "great pool that is in Gibeon" (Jer 41:12). Ishmael, however, managed to escape.

In addition to its notoriety as a place of battles and murders, there is a positive side to Gibeon as a locale in biblical history. After Solomon succeeds to the throne and secures his kingdom, he goes to Gibeon to offer burnt offerings and to pray (1 Kgs 3:3-15; 2 Chr 1:5-13). Gibeon is referred to as "the principal high place." It is here that Solomon prays for and is granted wisdom. It is likely that Gibeon continues to serve as the primary sacred center until the construction of the Temple in Jerusalem. The sacred significance of Gibeon is expanded by the Chronicler, who suggests that, in addition to the altar of burnt offering, the Tabernacle of Moses (1 Chr 16:39; 21:29) and the Tent of Meeting are both located (2 Chr 1:3, 13) there during the reigns of David and Solomon. It is here that David appoints Zadok as priest and other cultic personnel and musicians to oversee regular worship and sacrifices (1 Chr 16:37-42; see ZADOK, ZADOKITES). If Gibeon's listing among the Levitical cities dates to the exilic or post-exilic period, it may have been included because of the memory of these sacred associations.

Beyond these considerable references to Gibeon and the Gibeonites, there are only a few other less significant mentions of the city or the people in the later periods. In Jer 28:1, Gibeon is identified as the hometown of Jeremiah's prophetic opponent, Hananiah. Neh 7:25 lists 95 Gibeonites among the returnees to Judah from exile in Babylon, some of whom may have participated in the rebuilding of the city wall of Jerusalem (3:7).

B. Gibeon in Non-biblical Texts

There are two references to Gibeon in extra-bibli-

cal texts. The first is in an Egyptian text of Pharaoh Sheshonq I (SHISHAK in 1 Kgs 14:25), where Gibeon appears among the roughly 150 cities that Sheshonq listed in conjunction with a campaign into Palestine during the reign of Rehoboam of Judah. A second mention comes from Josephus, who reports that the Roman general Cestius Gallus encamped at Gibeon on his way to Jerusalem in October 66 CE to put down the Jewish Revolt (*J. W.* 2.513–16).

C. Gibeon in Archaeology

Gibeon is identified with modern-day Arab village of el-Jib, 9 km north-northwest of Jerusalem. The identification of Gibeon with el-Jib was made in the 19th cent. by E. Robinson on the basis of topography and the Arabic name, which preserves the Hebrew givʿon. Later archaeological excavations by J. B. Pritchard at el-Jib in the 1950s uncovered thirty-one jar handles inscribed with the name "Gibeon" (givʿon) in ancient Hebrew script, confirming this identification. The strategic location of Gibeon at the crossroads of the central hill country, where a north-south trade route passes, is borne out by the archaeological evidence. Among the discoveries at el-Jib are sixty-three wine cellars dated to the 8th–7th cent. BCE, revealing Gibeon as a major wine-producing center. Excavations there also uncovered two water systems. The first is a massive circular pool hewn out of limestone, measuring 11.3 m in diameter and 10.8 m deep, connected to a freshwater source by means of a sloping tunnel. This is very likely the "pool of Gibeon" mentioned several times in the OT. A second system is an impressive stepped tunnel that leads from inside the city wall to a water source outside the city. This second system is particularly important in time of siege during war.

Bibliography: J. Blenkinsopp. *Gibeon and Israel* (1973); R. D. Nelson. *Joshua.* OTL (1997).

KAH-JIN JEFFREY KUAN

GIDDALTI gi-dalʹti [גִּדַּלְתִּי giddalti]. One of the sons of Heman who, along with the sons of Asaph and Jeduthun, was commissioned by David to prophesy to the accompaniment of musical instruments (1 Chr 25:4). The name means "I have magnified." The twenty-second of twenty-four lots cast to assign shifts of service fell to him (1 Chr 25:29). His name appears among the last nine names in 1 Chr 25:4, which are commonly regarded as a liturgical prayer.

DEREK E. WITTMAN

GIDDEL gidʹuhl [גִּדֵּל giddel]. 1. Progenitor of a family of temple servants returning after Babylonian captivity (Ezra 2:1-2, 43-54; Neh 7:49).

2. Progenitor of a family of Solomon's servants returning after Babylonian captivity (Ezra 2:1-2, 55-57; Neh 7:58).

NATHAN D. MAXWELL

GIDEON gid´ee-uhn גִּדְעוֹן gidheʿon]. The story of Gideon and his family is the fourth of six told in the central section of the Book of Judges (3:7–16:31). Gideon follows Othniel, Ehud, and the team of Deborah and Barak; after him will come Jephthah and Samson. The traditional translation "judge" is unfortunate, since the leaders do much more than adjudicate. They negotiate with foreign kings, lead armies to battle, liberate and govern their people. The term "chieftain" will be used here (see JUDGE; JUDGES, BOOK OF).

Gideon's position is pivotal in the book. The chieftains who precede him are exemplary characters who succeed in bringing "rest" to the land (Judg 3:11, 30; 5:31). Gideon's story begins on a high note suggesting that he will rank not only with Othniel, Ehud, and Barak, but even with Abraham and Moses. His end, however, represents a nadir that places him instead with King Jeroboam, "who caused Israel to sin" (1 Kgs 14:16). After Gideon's death his son Abimelech only makes things worse. And the last two chieftains, Jephthah and Samson, follow him in his successes and especially his failures. The "rest" brought by the first four chieftains will not appear again in the book. Thus Gideon experiences a turning point in his own life and represents a turning point in the book.

Gideon's story begins as the others' do, with the Israelites doing evil in Yahweh's eyes and Yahweh's giving them into the power of an oppressor, this time the Midianites and other eastern groups (Judg 6:1-6; compare Judg 2:11-15; 3:7-8, 12-14; 4:1-3; 10:6-9; 13:1; see MIDIAN, MIDIANITES). The Israelites cry out for help against the incursions at every harvest (6:6-7; see 2:18; 3:9, 15; 4:3; 10:10). Until now Yahweh has responded favorably to these cries, but this time something completely different happens. Instead of raising up a chieftain, Yahweh sends a prophet to remind them of all the times their God has already delivered them and how ungratefully they have responded (6:7-10).

But then Yahweh commissions Gideon, the son of Joash, of the tribe of Manasseh, to deliver Israel from Midian's power. Of the biblical stories which have been grouped together as "call narratives," none are so much alike as those of Moses (Exodus 3–4) and Gideon (see CALL, CALLING, CALL STORIES). Yahweh's messenger appears to each man where he is hiding from oppressors, while he is carrying out a daily task for his father/father-in-law near a sacred place. Shared distinctive expressions include "all [Yahweh's] wonderful acts," "I send you," "but/excuse me, sir," and most significantly, "I/I AM will be with you." Moses and Gideon respond with objections of inadequacy and receive a "sign" (Exod 3:12; Judg 6:17, 21). Moses receives three more signs in the same long conversation (Exod 4:2-9), while Gideon receives three more over several days (6:36-40; 7:9-15). A staff (of Moses, of God, or of Yahweh's messenger) plays a significant role. Fire symbolizes Yahweh's presence, at which each man

expresses profound fear. Neither man can carry out his commission yet, since the covenant is being broken in his household (Exod 4:24-26; Judg 6:25-32). This breach must be healed before Israel can be delivered.

Gideon's call narrative also shares much with the theophany to Abraham in Genesis 18 (see THEOPHANY IN THE OT). Shared distinctive expressions include "appeared to him," "the oak," "if I have found favor in your eyes," "please do not," and a seldom-used phrase for "since." Both Abraham and Gideon prepare meat and flour as a meal for the divine visitor(s), although the reception of the meal differs starkly. Abraham's visitors eat it, but Gideon's guest turns the meal into a burnt offering (compare Judges 13). Like Jacob, Gideon renames the place of theophany (Gen 28:11-22; 32:24-30; Judg 6:19-24).

After such an auspicious beginning, we expect great things, and indeed Gideon's first action accomplishes a great deal (6:25-32). His own father owns an altar to BAAL and a wooden pole used for worshiping ASHERAH. At Yahweh's command Gideon tears down both, builds a new altar, uses the pole as fuel and his father's own bull as a burnt offering, initiating the altar as Yahweh's. Thus he has cleansed his father's household of evil and is ready to proceed. His acting at night and with the help of ten servants is often taken as a sign of cowardice, but the determination of the townspeople to kill him in revenge suggests that he is rather acting prudently. Presenting the town with a *fait accompli* gives his father the opportunity to defend him, saving his life. Gideon receives a new name in honor of Joash's challenge: JERUBBAAL, interpreted as "Let Baal plead his case against him."

In response to the next invasion and with the power of Yahweh's spirit, Gideon musters the men of his own village and tribe, Ophrah and Manasseh, and three northern tribes (6:33-35). Gideon then asks God for a sign of victory involving DEW. When God fulfills the terms impressively, Gideon realizes he has asked for a relatively easy sign and proceeds to ask for the opposite and more difficult sign. Once again God does as requested. The language in vv. 38 and 40 is similar to that of the creation tale in Genesis 1, and God is manipulating the dew, which is supposed to belong to Baal (compare 1 Kgs 18).

But just when Gideon is sure his army is ready, Yahweh objects that 32,000 are too many (to battle 135,000; 8:10). Yahweh insists that any who are afraid must leave. When "only" 10,000 leave, Yahweh orders a second reduction based on how the men drink water. Now Gideon is down to 300 men, a number that presumably will preclude Gideon's army from taking credit for the victory themselves, and thus forcing acknowledgment of Yahweh's role.

Immediately after the reduction in force Yahweh orders him on a private reconnaissance mission, where he overhears a Midianite reporting his dream and his comrade interpreting it to mean that Gideon will win the battle. At the high point of his story, Gideon prostrates himself in worship. Returning to his camp, he calls the men to battle. In three companies of 100 each, they surround the camp on three sides in the pitch-dark night, and produce a light and sound show of 300 torches, 300 trumpet blasts, 300 shouts, and 300 jars smashing. Awakening suddenly, the Midianites panic and lash out at each other as they try to flee back to safety on the eastern side of the Jordan.

Now Gideon calls for the first time on a tribe to the south, Ephraim, to capture Jordan's fords and cut off the Midianites' escape (Judg 7:24–8:3). The Ephraimites comply and even kill two Midianite princes, but they attack Gideon furiously for not involving them from the beginning. When Gideon diplomatically minimizes his own accomplishment and exaggerates theirs, they are mollified. This is the second of three episodes involving Ephraim and Jordan's fords that together demonstrate the downward spiral of both this major tribe and the quality of leadership provided by the chieftains (Judg 3:26-30 and 12:1-6; see EPHRAIM, EPHRAIMITES).

Gideon proceeds far eastward against two kings who have killed his brothers (Judg 8:4-21). On his return, he viciously attacks two Israelite towns which have refused to aid his men on this trip, Succoth and Penuel. No longer a diplomat, he has become a destroyer of his own people.

Thankful to see the end of seven years of Midianite oppression, Israel requests its chieftain to become its king, establishing a dynasty for the first time. Gideon's refusal is as hollow as it is theologically correct. His words attribute kingship to Yahweh alone (see Exod 15:18), but his actions claim the privileges of kingship—and even, perhaps, of priesthood—for himself. He takes the royal crescents, pendants, and purple garments of Kings ZEBAH AND ZALMUNNA after killing them, plus one golden earring from each Israelite's loot (Judg 8:21, 24-26). Also in royal fashion, he has many wives and seventy sons (Judg 8:30; see 2 Kgs 10:1).

With the spoils Gideon makes an EPHOD, probably a priestly garment worn when seeking an ORACLE (see Exod 28:6-35; 1 Sam 2:27-28). He establishes the ephod in Ophrah, to which "all Israel" comes—as if his home town is their capital—to "prostitute themselves" to it, a very problematic metaphor for worshiping other gods, thereby breaking the covenant (Judg 8:27; 2:17). The one who has "prostrated himself" to Yahweh (Judg 7:15) has now become, with his family, ensnared in "prostitution" ("snare," Judg 8:27; 2:3; another ephod, Judg 17–18).

Despite the trouble he causes Israel, Gideon is credited with establishing forty years of "rest" for the land (Judg 8:28) like Othniel, Ehud, and Deborah before him. Gideon is allowed to die peacefully at a ripe old age and be buried in his father's tomb. He is included in the list of chieftains in 1 Sam 12:11 and the cloud of witnesses in Heb 11:32.

Bibliography: Daniel I. Block. *Judges, Ruth.* NAC (1999); Judith E. Sanderson. *Judges.* Smyth & Helwys Bible Commentary (forthcoming).

JUDITH E. SANDERSON

GIDEONI gid´ee-oh´ni [גִּדְעֹנִי gidhʿoni]. Father of ABIDAN, the leader of the tribe of Benjamin in the wilderness (Num 1:11; 2:22; 7:60, 65; 10:24).

GIDOM gi´duhm [גִּדְעֹם gidhʿom]. The farthest place to which the Israelite army pursued the Benjaminites into the wilderness east of Gibeah toward the rock of Rimmon (Judg 20:45). The Hebrew word might be an infinitive rather than a place name (NEB, "until they had cut down").

GIFT, GIVING [מַתָּן mattan, מַתָּת mattath, נָתַן nathan, קָרְבָּן qorban; δῶρον dōron, δωρεά dōrea, δώρημα dōrēma, χάρισμα charisma]. A *gift* is an object or attribute freely bestowed upon another without the expectation of compensation or return. *Giving* is the action of bestowing a gift. The Hebrew and Greek words that are translated "gift" and "giving" are multiple, and the above list is only a brief sampling. Not only are there multiple words associated with giving but also each word appears in a variety of contexts. The words, like the concept, are multivalent. There are three primary contexts in which gifts are given in the Jewish and Christian Scriptures. First, God is a giver of gifts to humanity. Among God's gifts are sustenance (Gen 1:29-30), work (Eccl 3:13), the priesthood (Num 18:6), the Holy Spirit (Acts 10:45), and grace (Rom 5:15). In Paul's letters, God also gives a variety of spiritual gifts including wisdom, healing, and the ability both to speak in tongues and interpret such speech (1 Cor 12:4-11). Second, humanity gives gifts to God as a symbol of appreciation of and thankfulness for God's gifts. The sacrificial system as outlined in Leviticus and Numbers can be understood within this economy of the gift. Third, people give each other gifts. Gifts are bestowed by kings upon subjects who have performed some service and as a mark of honor (Dan 2:6). Kings will also present gifts to each other as signs of goodwill between their nations, and as a part of covenant making. This type of gift giving appears in the prophetic books where it is criticized as a violation of the people's covenant with God (Ezek 16:33). People of comparable rank give gifts to each other as a sign of friendship (Prov 19:6), although gift giving is condemned if it is done in order to gain influence and power (Prov 6:35). Gifts can strengthen social and familial bonds. For example, gifts are given to one's children, sometimes in lieu of inheritance (Gen 25:6) and sometimes as part of inheritance (Ezek 46:16-17). In marriage arrangements, the man's family may give gifts to the woman's family (Gen 34:12). Gifts can also be given to people who are poor as an act of mercy and justice (Sir 4:3; Matt 6:2-4). *See* GIFTS OF HEALING; SACRIFICE AND OFFERINGS; SPIRITUAL GIFTS.

JENNIFER L. KOOSED

GIFTS OF HEALING [χαρίσματα ἰαμάτων charismata iamatōn]. The phrase "gifts of healing" appears in the Bible only in 1 Cor 12:9, 30, but must be understood under the larger canopy of the Bible's interest in HEALING. Yahweh's role as healer is paramount in the OT (e.g., Exod 15:26; 2 Kgs 5:7). In the NT, divine healing is typically mediated through God's envoys. The Synoptic Gospels present healing as a sign of the inbreaking Kingdom of God—a reminder that behind the healing ministry of Jesus and his followers stands Yahweh the healer (*see* KINGDOM OF GOD, KINGDOM OF HEAVEN). During Jesus' ministry, his disciples participate in his ministries of healing and EXORCISM (Mark 6:7-13 par.), and in Acts the ministries of the apostles and other witnesses include healing. Both Peter and Paul repudiate any notion that they have power to heal apart from Jesus (Acts 3:12-16; 14:14-15). Their healing activity conveys the blessings of SALVATION now available through the risen Lord (e.g., Acts 3:1-10; 9:34; 16:16-18) and proves that they are the Lord's authorized emissaries. James directs those who are sick to call for the elders of the church to anoint and pray for them (5:14-15).

In 1 Cor 12, Paul lists "gifts of healings" as manifestations of the HOLY SPIRIT's work in the church's life. The use of the plural, "gifts of healings," suggests that each occasion of healing is a manifestation of this gift, as opposed to individuals possessing permanently the power to heal. In 2 Corinthians, Paul speaks of his having performed "the signs of an apostle" (12:12; compare Rom 15:18-19). These would have included healing, but Paul is generally reticent to speak of such matters autobiographically. His own weakness is an occasion for identifying with the suffering of Jesus and for communicating the power of the gospel (e.g., Gal 4:13; 2 Cor 12:7).

JOEL B. GREEN

GIFTS, SPIRITUAL. *See* SPIRITUAL GIFTS.

GIHON, RIVER gi′hon [גִּיחוֹן gihon]. The mythological second river flowing from EDEN (Gen 2:13). *See* GIHON, SPRING.

GIHON SPRING gi′hon [גִּיחוֹן gikhon]. Ancient JERUSALEM's only permanent water source, located outside the fortified city in a cave in the Kidron Valley. The name "Gihon" may be derived from the verb, guakh (גּוּחַ), "to burst forth," which would reflect its nature as a siphon type-spring, fed by ground water that

sporadically "bursts forth" through cracks in the cave's floor. Depending on the season of the year, Gihon may provide enough water to supply about 2,500 people in a day.

Solomon's coronation occurred at this site (1 Kgs 1:33, 38, 45). Later, in the face of the impending Assyrian invasion of 701 BCE, HEZEKIAH sought to enlarge the city and improve its defenses and facilities. Because the first water system (the SILOAM Channel) lay outside the city wall, Hezekiah built the Siloam Tunnel (aka Hezekiah's Tunnel) to divert the waters of the Gihon into the fortified area of the city, where it emptied into the Siloam Pool (2 Kgs 20:20). The Siloam Inscription, discovered near the southern end of the tunnel, dates the tunnel paleographically to the 8th cent. BCE. In the following century, Manasseh built an outer wall west of the Gihon to further strengthen Jerusalem's defenses (2 Chr 33:14). *See* SHELAH, POOL OF.

RALPH K. HAWKINS

GILADI, KEFAR. In northern Israel, two mounds near Kibbutz Kefar Giladi are candidates for biblical ABEL-BETH-MA'ACAH and JANOAH, conquered by Tiglath-pileser III in the 8th cent. BCE (2 Kgs 15:29). Because Tell Abil, north of the kibbutz, preserves the initial component of the toponym, it may be identified with Abel-beth-ma'acah. Moreover, a 4th cent. CE Greek inscription on a boundary stone, found 3 km away, possibly retains the second part of the name if reconstructed as Beth[m]achōn. The other mound, which has remains from the Early Bronze, Iron Age II, and Persian eras, is south of Kefar Giladi near Givʿat ha-Shoqet. It could be biblical Janoah inasmuch as 2 Kings locates the city between Abel-beth-maʿacah and Kedesh and since nearby Khirbet Nikha might preserve the name.

Bibliography: Jacob Kaplan. "The Identification of Abel-Beth-Maachah and Janoah." *IEJ* 28 (1978) 157–60.

JASON R. TATLOCK

GILALAI gil′uh-li [גִּלֲלָי gilalay]. A priest and musician who participated in the consecration of the rebuilt wall around Jerusalem (Neh 12:36).

GILBOA, MOUNT gil-boh′uh [הַר הַגִּלְבֹּעַ har haggilboaʿ]. Mount Gilboa ("mountain of the bubbling spring") is a ridge of limestone hills in the northern reaches of the central hill country extending into the eastern Jezreel Valley. Modern Jebel Fuquʿah rises over 1,600 ft. above sea level and is south of the Hill of Moreh. Near the mount lies Ain Harrod spring, the traditional site of Gideon's selection of men for battle against the Midianites (Judg 7). The main OT narrative concerning Mount Gilboa relates the battle between Israel and the Philistines who were encamped in the Jezreel Valley. Israel gathered on Mount Gilboa. Saul was defeated and his three sons died with him at the hands of the Philistines (1 Sam 28:1-4; 31:1-13). Saul's headless body was hung on the walls of Beth-Shean about 7 mi. away. David's lament (2 Sam 1:17-27, esp. 21) memorializes the death of Saul and Jonathan.

The Jezreel Valley's eastern entrance allowed a lucrative trade route to run west to Megiddo and then Phoenicia. Mount Gilboa experienced numerous military conflicts over control of this route. Reference to Gilboa (1 Sam 28:4; 2 Sam 21:12) may indicate a village existed near Mount Gilboa.

MICHAEL G. VANZANT

GILEAD, BALM IN gil′ee-uhd [צֳרִי בְּגִלְעָד tsori beghil‘adh]. The aromatic ointment of an unidentified plant, known in ancient times for its presumed medicinal qualities (Jer 46:11) and exported from Gilead to Egypt and Phoenicia (Gen 37:25; Ezek 27:17). Gilead's association with healing BALM became well known in the African American spiritual based on Jeremiah's rhetorical question (Jer 8:22).

RALPH K. HAWKINS

GILEAD, GILEADITES gil′ee-uhd, gil′ee-uh-dît [גִּלְעָד gil‘adh, גִּלְעָדִי gil‘adhi]. The name of three individuals in the OT, a tribal designation for the inhabitants of the territory of Gilead (Gileadites, Gadites), and a place centrally located east of the Jordan between the river Yarmuk and the DEAD SEA. The name derives from gal‘edh (גַּלְעֵד, "hill of witness"), that originally referred to the pile of stones commemorating Jacob's covenant with Laban at Gilead (Gen 31:44-48); however, a recent proposal suggests that Gilead's "rugged country" describes a highland region divided by the Jabbok River, consisting of well watered forests and pastures suitable for nurturing olives and grapes.

1. The son of Machir and grandson of Manasseh (Num 26:29-32; 36:1, 2; 1 Chr 2:21, 23), who fathered six sons: Iezer, Helek, Shechem, Asriel, Shemida, and Hepher—all significant clan leaders.

2. The father of JEPHTHAH, a son born of a prostitute (Judg 11:1-2). Jephthah was exiled from his homeland by his brothers, who sought to divide his inheritance between themselves. Following the invasion of the area by the Ammonites, Jephthah was called back to Gilead years later to deliver the people from foreign oppression (Judg 10–11).

3. An ancestor of ABIHAIL and a descendant of Gad mentioned in 1 Chr 5:11-14.

4. Gilead's descendants, also called Gileadites or Gadites, dwelt in the region bounded by the Arnon in the South, the Jordan Valley on the West, Jabbok at the north and south, and the desert in the east (see GAD, GADITES). In many cases, the biblical text remains unclear whether the designation *Gilead* refers to the territory itself or to the Gadites. Gilead, mentioned along with Reuben and Dan in Judg 5:16-17, represents only the northern area and seems to be the equivalent of Gad.

5. Northern Gilead had a permanent settlement as early as 2200 BCE, while the southern area remained unoccupied until the 13th cent., when the Moabites and Amorites shared control of the region. According to the biblical text, Jacob settled in Gilead (Gen 31:23). Moses defeated Og and Sihon, two Amorite kings controlling all Gilead and Bashan (Deut 4:47-49). Following the Israelite conquests, the tribes of Reuben and Gad (sometimes referred to as Gilead) settled in the eastern portion, while the half-tribe of Manasseh remained in the western sect. Despite Gilead's unwillingness to come to Manasseh's aid following the battle with Sisera (Judg 5:17), Gideon, a Manassite, helped Reuben and Gad defeat the invading Midianites and Amalekites.

DAVID found refuge in Gilead from his son Absalom, who rebelled against him, and, following a pivotal attack in Gilead, David regained his throne (2 Sam 15–19). Gilead served as a strategic commercial location, motivating David to take over the region and secure trade along the KING'S HIGHWAY. Following the expansion of Solomon's empire and the division between Israel and Judah, control of Gilead remained important to the Northern tribes for economic reasons. A coalition with Assyria enabled Israel to defeat the Arameans; however, during the reign of Jeroboam II internal conflict threatened possession of the territory. Eventually, Gilead was conquered by Tiglath-Pileser and became an Assyrian province (2 Kgs 15:29; Isa 8:6-8), following the attempt by Pekah, son of Remaliah, to form an alliance with neighboring regions against Assyria.

SHERRI L. KLOUDA

GILGAL gil′gal [גִּלְגָּל gilgal; Γάλγαλα Galgala] is a shrine in the early pre-monarchic period and the early monarchy.

Based on the Hebrew root gll connoting roundness or rolling, **gilgal** is usually translated as a circle of stones. The word itself makes no mention of stones, but the association is made based on Josh 4:19-20. In all but one of the thirty-eight instances of this place name, it appears with the definite article, **haggilgal** (הַגִּלְגָּל)—a rare, but not unheard of phenomenon. It may suggest that the word refers to any circle of stones, with the definite article indicating which one is meant.

The clues in the Bible concerning the location of Gilgal are somewhat contradictory. While most of the references are consistent with a location on the eastern border of Jericho (Josh 4:19), geographical clues in Deut 11:30; Josh 12:23 (Heb.; NRSV following LXX: Galilee); Josh 15:7; and 2 Kgs 2:1 do not agree with this placement. For this reason, many scholars posit at least three and up to five different sites named Gilgal. Other scholars, claiming that the different geographical markers are due to the complex compositional and transmission history of the text, interpret all of the occurrences of Gilgal as the same place.

The site near Jericho, which accounts for all of the references to Gilgal except those noted above, serves the Israelites as a national shrine and sanctuary. It is here that Joshua sets up the first national monument in the promised land—the twelve stones taken from the bed of the Jordan River (Josh 4:19-20), likely a reference to the stone circle that gave the place its name. This is also the site of the communal circumcision and the Passover celebration (Josh 5). Gilgal serves as the Israelites' base camp during their conquest of Canaan, and the people return to divide the land (e.g., Josh 10; 14).

Gilgal apparently lost importance during the period of the Judges, and may have been outside Israelite territory for a time. Judges 2:1 describes the abandonment of Gilgal by an angel of the Lord in favor of Bochim ("Weepers"). In Judg 3:19, during the campaign of Ehud, the narrative passes through Gilgal, describing it as territory controlled by the Moabites. It is likely that the angel's abandonment of Gilgal is an account of the loss of territory near the Jordan to the Moabites.

Gilgal was a cult site for the Israelites, as Samuel assembles the Israelites to make burnt offerings and well-being sacrifices as part of other rituals. Saul's confirmation as king occurred at Gilgal (1 Sam 11) as did Samuel's ultimate rejection of him as king (1 Sam 15). In between, Saul uses Gilgal as a base of operations in battle with the Philistines. In some of the contexts, it appears that Gilgal, located in the Jordan rift valley, is used because the Philistines have overrun the prominent sites in the hill country (1 Sam 10; 13).

It may be that the rejection of Saul at Gilgal led to the disgrace of this cult center. In the 9th cent. BCE, the prophets Amos and Hosea condemn Gilgal and other shrines as sites of apostasy or at least unacceptable worship. For Amos, Gilgal is paired with Bethel, emblematic of the corruption of the (northern) Israelite cult.

Based on its prominence in the narrative of Saul's reign, in particular, form critics identify Gilgal as a major center of the tribe of Benjamin that was prominent before the time of the tribal league. Gilgal may also be the site of a ritual commemoration of the Jordan crossing, where the crossing was reenacted (compare 2 Sam 19:15, 40; Mic 6:5). Once the history of Israel became standardized and applied to the twelve-tribe confederation, Gilgal became important to the whole people; its history and existence were extended to and attributed to the actions of the whole confederacy (Josh 4). With the rise in power of the tribes of Ephraim and Manasseh in the north and Judah in the south, Gilgal's honor and reputation declined.

Archaeologists have attempted to identify the site of ancient Gilgal but have been unsuccessful despite excavations and surveys at several sites in the Jordan Valley near Jericho. None of these sites has produced solid evidence either for a large cult center or an early Iron Age occupation that fits the settings in the Bible.

Suggestions have also been made for identifying other sites for Gilgal based on the conflicting geographical notes mentioned above. These have been based, in large part, on similarity between Arabic place names like Jiljuliyeh and Gilgal.

Nowhere in the Bible is Gilgal clearly described. It is not identified as a city, nor is there any description of habitation after the temporary sojourn of the whole people there under Joshua. Not even the location is clearly given—all we know is that it was somewhere to the east of Jericho. Such issues, coupled with the problematic nature of the source texts, frustrate the attempt to find Gilgal archaeologically. It is unlikely that archaeologists would be able to securely identify Gilgal without additional epigraphic evidence.

At the same time, there is an archaeological site called Gilgal. This site consists of six separate locations in the lower Jordan Valley, north of Jericho. Excavation and surface survey at these sites have revealed them to have been Late Natufian and Pre-Pottery Neolithic A settlements. The only connection with biblical Gilgal is the approximate location.

Bibliography: Boyce M. Bennett Jr. "The Search for Israelite Gilgal." *PEQ* 104 (1972) 111–22; Hans-Joachim Kraus. "Gilgal: A Contribution to the History of Worship in Israel." *Reconsidering Israel and Judah: Recent Studies on the Deuteronomistic History.* G. N. Knoppers and J. G. McConville, eds. (2000) 163–78; George M. Landes. "Report on Archaeological 'Rescue Operation' at Suwwanet eth-Thaniya in the Jordan Valley North of Jericho." BASORSup 21 (1975) 1–22; James Muilenburg. "The Site of Ancient Gilgal." *BASOR* 140 (1955) 11–27.

ELY LEVINE

GILGAMESH, EPIC OF. By far the longest and most famous work of Mesopotamian literature, this epic included twelve tablets in its final Standard Babylonian version. Five Sumerian tales about Gilgamesh, a perhaps historical king in Uruk in the first half of the third millenium, provided the basic material for narrative poems written in the Babylonian language around 1700 BCE. Different versions of the epic have been recovered from Mesopotamia, Syria, the Levant, and Anatolia. The Standard Babylonian version of the first millennium is associated with the name of Sin-leqe-unninni, an incantation priest from Uruk. Gilgamesh later became a legendary figure, eventually regarded as divine judge of the underworld. While the Old Babylonian version opens with the words "Surpassing all other kings" emphasizing the heroic aspect of the king as warrior, the late version's "He who saw the deep" adds the component of a more human and wise Gilgamesh who bore hardship and had to pay a price for his knowledge. As Gilgamesh is driven by superhuman energies and has turned into an oppressor of his people, the gods create Enkidu as a counterpart to match his strength. They become friends and embark on a journey to the Cedar Forest to battle Huwawa in order to gain immortal fame. On their return Gilgamesh repudiates the goddess Ishtar, and, with Enkidu's help, kills the Bull of Heaven sent by Anu to exact her vengeance. In response to their misdemeanor, the gods decide that one of them must die and sentence Enkidu to death. Deeply troubled by the death of his friend, Gilgamesh journeys to Utnapishtim, the survivor of the FLOOD, to ask him how he obtained eternal life. Utnapishtim challenges him with several tests, and, recognizing his own failures, Gilgamesh returns to Uruk to write down his story for the benefit of future generations.

Bibliography: B. R. Foster. *The Epic of Gilgamesh* (2001); A. R. George. *The Babylonian Gilgamesh Epic* (2003).

BEATE PONGRATZ-LEISTEN

GILOH gi'loh [גִּלֹה giloh]. 1. A village in the hill-country of Judah, in the district of Debir (Josh 15:51). Although usually associated with Khirbet Jala, northwest of Hebron, this identification would place Giloh in the district of Beth-zur (Josh 15:58).

2. The site of an Iron Age I settlement located at the center of a suburb of the same name SW of Jerusalem (M. R. 1676 1264). Long walls divided the site into what appear to be family units connected with animal pens. An early example of a four-room house was uncovered, and the material culture corresponds with that of other sites of the central hill-country in Iron Age I.

One particular structure discovered at Giloh is unique in Iron Age I. Designated Building 105, it was built directly on bedrock and has been interpreted as a raised platform or the foundation of a tower (Mazar 1994, 83). The only comparable structure is at Mount Ebal. These two are the sole public buildings known from any of the Iron Age I settlement sites of the central hill country. Instead of a tower, Building 105 might be a BAMAH or other cultic structure.

Giloh may be speculatively associated with Baal Perazim, based on David's defeat of the Philistines at BAAL-PERAZIM, said to be near the Valley of Rephaim (2 Sam 5:20; 1 Chr 14:11). A "Mount Perazim" is also mentioned in Isaiah in association with the Valley of Gibeon. Giloh is on the summit of a major ridge overlooking the Valley of Rephaim and contains remains from the time of the Judges or the time of David. The theophoric component "Baal" may signifiy a cult of Baal which took place here and left its traces in the name (89–90).

Bibliography: A. Mazar. "Jerusalem and Its Vicinity in Iron Age I." *From Nomadism to Monarchy: Archaeological and Historical Aspects of Early Israel.* I. Finkelstein and N. Naʾaman, eds. (1994) 70–91.

RALPH K. HAWKINS

GIMEL gim'uhl [ג g]. The third letter of the Hebrew alphabet, which derives from the Semitic word, *gaml, meaning "throw-stick." *See* ALPHABET.

GINATH gi'nath [גִּינַת ginath]. The father of TIBNI, the failed rival of OMRI for the throne in Israel after the death of ZIMRI (1 Kgs 16:21-22).

GINNETHOI gin'uh-thoi [גִּנְּתוֹי ginnethoy]. A priestly leader who returned to Jerusalem with ZERUBBABEL; helped purify the people, gates, and walls (Neh 12:4).

GINNETHON gin'uh-thon [גִּנְּתוֹן ginnethon]. 1. One of the priestly signatories to the covenant drawn up by Ezra (Neh 10:6).

2. Head of a priestly family listed during the tenure of Joiakim (Neh 12:16), probably a reference to the same family as Neh 10:6.

GIRGASHITE guhr'guh-shit [גִּרְגָּשִׁי girgashi]. The Girgashites were a western tribe descended from Canaan (Gen 10:16; 1 Chr 1:14) but whose exact location is unknown. God's promise of land to Abraham included the territory of the Girgashites (Gen 15:21). An additional five times in the OT the tribe is listed as being dispossessed by the Israelites (Deut 7:1; Josh 3:10; 24:11; 1 Chr 1:14; Neh 9:8). Scholars have tied the tribe to the Qaraqisha of Hittite and Egyptian inscriptions. Others connect the Girgashites to various names found in Punic and Ugaritic texts. The tribe might have Phoenician associations if these links are correct.

The Gerasenes, Gadarenes, and Gergesenes of the NT (Matt 8:28; Mark 5:1; Luke 8:26) may be related to the ancient Girgashites. *See* GADARA, GADARENES; GERASA, GERASENES.

MICHAEL G. VANZANT

GIRZITES guhr'zit [גִּרְזִי girzi]. A people located somewhere between Philistia and Egypt whom David attacked from ZIKLAG (1 Sam 27:8). That the Girzites are otherwise unknown has led some scholars to doubt their existence. The MT contains notations indicating the text should read "Gezrites" instead of Girzites, although Gezer is not in the region described in 1 Sam 27:8. Girzite may instead have been a scribal dittography for Geshurite (Josh 24:11).

RALPH K. HAWKINS

GISHPA gish'puh [גִּשְׁפָּא gishpaʾ]. Mentioned along with ZIHA as having been in charge of the NETHINIM, a relatively low-ranking order of temple functionaries (Neh 11:21).

GITTAIM git'ay-im [גִּתַּיִם gittayim]. The town to which the Canaanite inhabitants of Beeroth are said to have fled permanently (2 Sam 4:3). It is listed in Neh 11:33 among the various towns that some Benjaminites inhabited after they returned from exile during the Persian period. The name means "two winepresses."

GITTIN [גִּטִּין gittin]. The name of the sixth tractate of the third order (Nashim/"On Women") of the MISHNAH. The tractate presents legal interpretation (HALAKHAH) on issues surrounding the granting of a DIVORCE based on the text of Deut 24:1-4. The tractate is named after the certificate of divorce. *See* DIVORCE, CERTIFICATE OF.

PHILLIP MICHAEL SHERMAN

GITTITE. *See* GATH.

GITTITH. *See* MUSIC.

GIZONITE gi′zoh-nit [גִּזוֹנִי gizoni]. Hashem the Gizonite is listed as one of David's warriors (1 Chr 11:34). The notice should point to Gizo as Hashem's place of birth, but no such place is known. The parallel notice (2 Sam 23:32) omits any mention of Hashem's (there Jashen's) place of birth.

PHILLIP MICHAEL SHERMAN

Todd Bolen/BiblePlaces.com
Figure 1: Beersheba Iron Age Glacis

GLACIS. Defensive slopes of consolidated earth and other materials outside of and leading up to a fortification wall, glacis were utilized throughout the history of walled settlements and fortresses. Stone and especially brick fortification walls were vulnerable to erosion and attack, whether by battering or sapping. The glacis helped protect the wall from attack by distancing the enemy from the cover of the wall base and placing them within the sweep of defensive fire.

KENT V. BRAMLETT

GLAPHYRA. The title, meaning "Elegant Comments," of a work on the PENTATEUCH by CYRIL OF ALEXANDRIA, whose interpretation is predominantly christological. Cyril devotes seven books to Genesis, three to Exodus, and treats Leviticus, Numbers, and Deuteronomy in a single volume, an emphasis typical of early interpreters in the church.

RALPH K. HAWKINS

Erich Lessing /Art Resource, NY
Figure 1: Glass Vase from Egypt, found in a burial cave at Gezer. New Kingdom. (1500-1400 BCE). Location: Israel Museum (IDAM), Jerusalem, Israel.

GLASS [זְכוֹכִית zekhokhith; ὕαλος hyalos]. Glass (often rendered "CRYSTAL," KJV; NEB) consists of silica or sand mixed with lime and soda, heated to allow the materials to fuse into a liquid that cools into a rigid, translucent substance. Old Testament poetry reveals the Israelites considered glass to be a valued and precious material equal in value to gold and rubies (Job 28:17). New Testament apocalyptic poetry also reveals the sacred beauty and luminescence of glass (Rev 4:6; 15:2; 21:18, 21). *See* SEA OF GLASS, GLASSY SEA.

Production processes capable of making large items came only in the Roman era. The production purity and temperature required for consistent glass quality apparently was not available in OT Israel. Artifacts from ancient Israel include small glass beads and vases, probably imported from Phoenicia and Egypt. No ancient glass industry has been discovered in Israel.

Roman Period tombs often contain glass pearls, necklaces, and small glass vials used for oil and perfumes to anoint the body. The production of such items through heating rods of glass and shaping them around a core of clay and dung was known in Iraq by the 15th cent. BCE. Greek tradition claims Phoenicia as the birthplace of glass production and design.

MICHAEL G. VANZANT

GLASSY SEA. *See* SEA OF GLASS, GLASSY SEA.

GLAZE, GLAZING [כֶּסֶף סִיגִים kesef sighim; χρῖσμα chrisma]. The application of a layer of finish to earthenware that makes its surface glossy and resistant to moisture. Proverbs 26:23 contains an analogy between glaze (literally "silver dross") laid over a piece of pottery and fervent lips on a person with an evil mind. Ben Sira identifies setting his heart to finishing the glazing as one aspect of the handiwork of the skillful potter (Sir 38:30).

DEREK E. WITTMAN

GLEANING, GLEANINGS [לָקַט laqat]. The act or resulting product of gathering remnants from a harvested field. The Torah prohibits a landowner from reaping the entire harvest of a field. Instead, the harvester must leave a portion for those unable to provide for themselves: widows, orphans, and foreigners in the land (Lev 19:9, 23; Deut 24:21). Ruth, a widow, gathered the gleanings from the barley and wheat harvest for herself and her mother-in-law, Naomi, in the fields of Boaz (Ruth 2:2-23).

JESSICA TINKLENBERG DEVEGA

GLORY, GLORIFY [כָּבוֹד kavodh; δόξα doxa, δοξάζω doxazō]. Glory-language in the Bible has both subjective and objective senses. Subjectively, glory refers to the act of worship (e.g., "give glory to God"). Objectively, glory denotes the object of worship (i.e., God's revealed presence, God's glory). In both its subjective and objective senses, glory-language became an important marker in the development of Israel and the church's faith (monotheism) and practice (worship). What was once reserved for Israel's one true God ("giving glory to God," "glorifying God"), early Christians ascribed to the resurrected Jesus. Further, Christians claimed that Jesus was the glory of God, God's revealed presence. Glory-language was thus an important way for conveying the Christian understanding of God.

A. Semantic Observations
B. Glory as Divine Presence in the Old Testament and Second Temple Judaism
C. Glory, the Son of Man, and Jesus
D. Glory in Early Christianity
   1. Glory as God's presence
   2. Glory and the future
   3. Glory as resurrection
   4. A glory christology
E. Conclusion
Bibliography

A. Semantic Observations

The root of kavodh (kbd כבד) appears about 400 times in the OT. The noun, verb, and adjective are all used to signify culturally positive values—e.g., "bounty," "wealth," "respect," "intelligence," "beau-

ty," "greatness," and "strength" (noun); "multiply," "give respect/be respected," "succeed," "reward," and "be well known" (verb); and "rich" (adjective). Culturally neutral meanings include "weight," "possessions" (noun), "be heavy," "thicken," "test" (verb), and "heavy," "abundant" (adjective). Culturally negative uses of the word group include "burden" (noun), "make difficult," "sin," "harden" (verb), and "difficult," "weary," "grievous," "troublesome," and "aged" (adjective). Kbd thus possesses an extraordinarily wide range of meaning and overlaps the semantic fields of a large number of Hebrew words.

Most significant are the instances when kavodh signifies divine presence. The phrase "Glory of Yahweh" appears thirty-six times in the OT and can be divided into two mutually exclusive semantic profiles—constructions that employ "movement" terminology and constructions that employ "appearance"/"sight" terminology. In the first, the Glory of Yahweh is said to "fill"/ "settle," "rise/go up," "come/arrive," "enter/depart," or merely "stand still/be over." The "Glory of Yahweh" is also said to "appear." Glory "appears" in and at places where Yahweh's presence is expected—i.e., in a cloud, on top of Mount Sinai, at the door of the Tent of Meeting, and over the Temple—and "appears" to the whole assembly or congregation, all the children of Israel, to others outside of Israel, or, more generally, to all flesh.

Because the "Glory of Yahweh" is associated with either "movement" or "appearance" terminology, it does not denote an attribute of Yahweh's character (like mercy or love, which cannot be "seen" and does not "move"). Neither is the meaning of the Glory of Yahweh exhausted by "fire" or "brightness"—terms used to describe its appearance. Rather, in the OT the Glory of Yahweh signifies the visible divine presence. To see/experience Yahweh's Glory is to see/experience Yahweh.

The Greek noun doxa designates either a person's favorable status, reputation, or position, or the person's vanity and conceit. Doxa is used as a term of measurement—i.e., the "brightness" of a light; the "beauty" of a flower; the "wealth" of the nations. Doxa can even refer to heavenly, angelic figures. The verb doxazō can mean "appoint," "exalt," "honor," and "worship." By far, however, the most theologically important use of doxa is as a way to characterize God. In these passages glory is contextually coordinated with other nouns like "wisdom," "spirit," "image," "word," "name," and "power." Glory thus formed part of the semantic field of words signifying God's revealed presence.

B. Glory as Divine Presence in the Old Testament and Second Temple Judaism

The theophany to Moses at Mount Sinai functions paradigmatically for the "Priestly" tradition's technical use of Glory of Yahweh (Exod 24:16-18). Although the narrative goal is to build the tabernacle, the place for Yahweh's Glory to dwell (Exod 29:43; 40:34-35; Lev 9:6, 23; Num 14:10; 16:19, 42; 20:6), the revelation legitimized Moses, and him alone, as the sacred mediator. Only Moses is allowed to experience Yahweh's divine presence, his Glory. Yet, the parenthetical description of Glory as a devouring fire (Exod 24:17) delimits Yahweh's approachability, even for a legitimized mediator like Moses. Glory is to be feared and respected. Inclusios to Exod 24 are found in Exod 40 and Lev 9. The Glory of Yahweh exchanges the mountaintop for the newly completed tabernacle and in so doing a sign of legitimacy and approval is granted to the new place of worship (Exod 40:34-35) and the group of legitimized mediators widens to include Aaron and his sons (Lev 9:6, 23). Glory in Exod chaps. 24, 40, and Lev 9 establishes sacred office, time, mediator, and order.

The hallmark of a royal theology is the kingship of Yahweh. Yahweh was celebrated as the sustainer king of ancient Israel, the one who blesses and prospers his people. A second, related theme is that the human king of Israel is Yahweh's vice-regent on earth. To the king, the divinely elected representative, Yahweh promised protection and through the king Yahweh mediated blessing. It is not surprising, then, to find Glory connected with both Yahweh as king and the human king as the representative. Psalm 24 celebrates the movement of the ark to Jerusalem and the establishment of the sanctuary. The high point of the procession is the theophany of Yahweh's Glory. The antiphonal cries for the Temple doors and gates to open is so that Yahweh may appear. After a triad of requests, Yahweh Sabaoth (the warrior) is identified as the "King of Glory" (Ps 24:10). The royal hymns on creation also speak pointedly about Yahweh's Glory. Whether one views the "son of man" in Ps 8 as a primal/archetypal human (compare Gen 1:26), there is no denying that royal theology pervades the psalm and Yahweh's crowning of a "human" with Glory (Ps 8:5) as the high point of creation mirrors Yahweh's special relationship with the king. The regular enjoyment of Yahweh's divine presence, his Glory, forms a central part of Temple liturgy and democratizes the unqualified blessing of God upon king, Temple, nation, and world. Glory in a royal context assures of Yahweh's rightful and benevolent control over all.

Divine presence can also connote judgment. Jeremiah indicates that Yahweh will punish his people for their infidelity. In the appalling abandonment of Yahweh, the nation exchanged glory for something that can never bring life (Jer 2:11-13). Hosea confirms yet another consequence of defiant and promiscuous behavior (Hos 10:5-6). By alluding to the capture of the ark by the Philistines (2 Sam 4), Hosea foresees that Yahweh's Glory will once again be "exiled." When this "deportation" occurs, the creative processes of life cease (Hos 9:11-12). In all likelihood, standing behind—and

uniting—glory as divine presence, in all its ramified uses, is an old theophanic tradition that associated glory with the appearance of a storm-god, an echo of which can still be heard in Ps 29:3: "Glory thunders upon the waters." Here Glory defeats the powers of chaos and subdues enemies. Whether associated with Sinai, monarchy, or a prophetic judgment oracle, glory never lost its theophanic power to signify Yahweh's presence. That the prophets adopted the theophanic tradition as a strategic subgenre ensured that glory was destined to become a sign of eschatological divine presence.

The exile forced Jews to rethink their tradition and what they understood about their God. While, for the prophets, exile equals punishment, the texts do look through, and beyond, judgment for a day of forgiveness, deliverance, restoration, and even eschatological transformation. Glory plays a key role in this view of the end: it signs the transforming eschatological presence of Yahweh.

Second Isaiah opens with a vision that mixes Sinai, exodus, and royal motifs.

"And the glory of the Lord shall be revealed, and all flesh shall see it together" (Isa 40:3-5). The appearance and subsequent royal parade of glory in the plain sight of "all flesh" not only secures release but telegraphs the news of Yahweh's solidarity with his people. To evoke eschatological finality, Isa 35 employs imagery of creation's renewal and unprecedented abundance. The oppressor nations shall have their "glory" and "majesty" given away. In contrast, the revelation of glory (as the visible presence of Yahweh) enacts a joyful return for the "ransomed of the Lord" (Isa 35:10).

The prophetic hope for the future often centers in the symbol of Jerusalem/Zion. Through one of his "visions" Zechariah paints an eschatological picture of Jerusalem. The transformed city will be immeasurable, possess no walls, and experience abundance. Yahweh, the great warrior, will protect the city with fire and be the glory within it (Zech 2:5). Isaiah 2:4-6 echoes the same theme. The arrival of Yahweh not only restores what once was—the glories of a Davidic kingdom—but also amplifies. Mixing Sinai with royal imagery, the prophet speaks of a day when the Lord will once again "tabernacle" in Zion. This time, however, Yahweh will "create" a new (and permanent) place for his Glory to rest. From "Mount Zion and in Jerusalem" the Lord will reign, and there Yahweh again will "manifest his Glory" (Isa 24:23). Although the "kingdom of God" is not a prominent theme in the OT, it is connected to the traditions of Zion/Jerusalem—and thus to glory. Yahweh as "King" (of the world) could be used as a shorthand expression for summing up prophetic assurances about the future of the world (Ps 145:10-13).

The eschatological enthronement of Yahweh in Zion inaugurates a new age for Israel and initiates the conversion of the nations. In passages saturated with exodus, Sinai, and royal images, Isaiah describes just such a new day. Isaiah 60:1-3 describes a grand theophany, a revelation of glory, with two, coterminous consequences—the transformation of Zion so that it becomes the (unique) bearer of Yahweh's glory ("Glory shall be seen upon you") and the in-gathering of the nations ("all the nations shall come to your light"). In Isa 62:10-11 and 66:18-19, Zion is not only the bearer of glory, but the instrument by and through which the nations will enjoy Yahweh's presence. Glory begins to function as an archetype of eschatological conversion and forms the leading edge of glory's participation in Second Temple Judaism's traditions of transformational mysticism.

Glory also formed part of the characteristic field of signifiers used in "throne visions" of Second Temple Jewish apocalypses. Throne visions are indebted, in both content and form, to visionary material within the OT, particularly the inaugural call of Ezek 1 and the vision of Dan 7. Ezekiel describes Yahweh as having a human-shaped form and seated upon a throne-chariot (Ezek 1:26-28). This remarkable anthropomorphic depiction of Yahweh's presence wielded a powerful influence upon other visions of God and, most interesting, the throne visionary characterization of a/the chief mediator figure who often does God's eschatological bidding. The throne vision of *1 En.* 14 displays the influence of Ezek 1 (and to a lesser extent Isa 6). Both visions make references to wheels (Ezek 1:16; *1 En.* 14:18), a throne (Ezek 1:26; *1 En.* 14:18; compare Isa 6:1), God's garment (Isa 6:1; *1 En.* 14:20), and cherubim (Isa 6:2; *1 En.* 14:11, 18). Further, the visionary depiction of Yahweh in a human shape in Ezek 1:26-28 explains the anthropomorphic description of God in *1 En.* 14. The enthroned "Great Glory" should be read as a pure and unmediated manifestation of God himself.

Daniel 7 also possesses ties with Ezek 1. Whereas in Ezek 1 there is but one heavenly, human-shaped figure (understood to be the Glory of Yahweh), Dan 7:13-14 adds a second heavenly figure—the one like a Son of Man. The addition of a second figure caused no small amount of confusion, esp. from the Jewish perspective. When considered on purely form and tradition grounds, the text borders dangerously on ditheism, since the second figure acquires the anthropomorphic description reserved for Yahweh in Ezek 1:28. Daniel 7 effects both a semiotic shift and semantic reinvestment of Glory. Glory thus becomes a symbol of divine investiture that demonstrates the exalted position of Son of Man.

The same sort of shift can be detected in Similitudes of Enoch, another area in which the influence of Ezek 1 can be detected (*1 En.* 45:1-3c; 55:3-4; 61:8; 62:1-6; 69:29). Like the Son of Man in Dan 7, the Elect One/Son of Man in Enoch acquires the descriptors reserved for Yahweh in Ezek 1. Glory thus forms part of the divine equipment that the Son of Man possesses. The placement of the Elect One/Son of Man upon the "throne of Glory" is for the sole purpose of eschatological judgment—something traditionally reserved for God.

C. Glory, the Son of Man, and Jesus

Of particular interest are the sayings within Matthew, Mark, and Luke that depict the Son of Man coming "in glory" or "on the clouds with glory" to occupy the "throne of glory" (Mark 8:38//Matt 16:27; 19:28; Luke 9:26; Mark 13:26//Matt 24:30; 25:31; Luke 21:27). In these texts the figure of Jesus intentionally echoes Dan 7 and thereby places these Son of Man sayings squarely within the throne vision tradition stemming from Ezek 1. Jesus thus provocatively identifies himself with Yahweh's heavenly agent of Dan 7. Jesus depicts his own future return as the Son of Man in the language of an eschatological theophany. At this eschatological apocalypse the Son of Man will sit upon the "throne of glory." The Son of Man's sitting upon the throne of glory is for the purpose of eschatological judgment and thus signals the functional transference of the duties of Yahweh to himself. In his eschatological theophany, Jesus, as the Son of Man, will come "in Glory" and "with Glory." Both phrases refer to the divine presence that will accompany the Son of Man at his "coming": Jesus will come shrouded, draped, and encompassed by Yahweh's presence, his glory. These astounding statements, by asserting that Jesus will participate in Yahweh's eschatological presence, boldly and scandalously move beyond any imaging of a divine agent within Second Temple Judaism. Jesus' Son of Man in/with glory sayings not only defined his own future role as God's chief, singular agent (i.e., the one who will do Yahweh's eschatological bidding) but also so closely identified him with Yahweh's glory that the two can no longer be separated. These sayings effectively open a breach in the wall of Jewish monotheism and may well have been a/the contributing reason for his execution.

D. Glory in Early Christianity
1. Glory as God's presence

Early Christianity continued to use *glory* to describe God's revealed presence. When Acts records that Stephen looked into heaven and saw the "glory of God and Jesus standing at his right hand" (Acts 7:55), the echoes of Jesus' Son of Man sayings and the throne vision tradition of Ezek 1 and Dan 7 can be clearly heard. Hebrews' description of the ark also mentions the "cherubim of glory" positioned over the mercy seat (Heb 9:5). The cherubim, together with the seat, had always been associated with tabernacle and Temple theophanies (Exod 25:22; Num 12:89; Deut 33:26; 1 Sam 4:4; Ps 18:10; Ezek 9:3; 10:4). Second Peter's description of Jesus' transfiguration stands squarely in prophetic-call/throne theophany tradition. God is the "Majestic Glory" who spoke to Jesus (2 Pet 1:17). Indeed, any past appearance of God could be legitimately construed as an appearance of his glory. Although Acts has Stephen proclaiming that the "God of glory appeared to our fathers" (Acts 7:2), the patriarchal narratives are silent about such an appearance of glory.

2. Glory and the future

Early Christianity also laid claim to the mantle of the prophets. Thus, not surprisingly, God's glory figures prominently in the description of the future. Even though all believers will undergo judgment at the throne of God, Jude assures its readers of God's commitment and ability to make them "stand in the presence of his glory" (Jude 24; compare 1QH^a XII, 28-29; Rom 3:23). Revelation combines theophanic, royal, and prophetic imagery in the description of the eschatological, heavenly temple that will be filled with the smoke "from the glory of God and from his power" (Rev 15:8). Glory also describes the new, creative powers God unleashes. On that great day a new city will descend from heaven awash in the glory of God (Rev 21:11). In that new city there will be no need for sun or moon, "for the glory of God will be its light" (Rev 21:23). Present suffering stands in direct contrast to the "hope of the glory of God" (Rom 5:2). The afflictions associated with "this age" pale in comparison to the apocalypse of Glory that awaits at the Parousia (Rom 8:18; 1 Pet 5:1). Christians themselves can expect transformation into glory in the eschatological age. The goal of God leads believers "to Glory" (Heb 2:10). Those who endure will receive the promised "crown of glory" (tēs doxēs stephanon τῆς δόξης στέφανον, 1 Pet 5:4; compare 1 Cor 9:25; 2 Tim 2:4; Jas 1:12). Indeed, unjust suffering for the Name of Jesus ensures a "certain Glory" (doxan tina δόξαν τινά) for the faithful (Herm., *Vis.* 3.2.1; compare 2.6.6). These texts demonstrate that Christians, like the prophets, continued to hope for an age ushered in and defined by Yahweh's glory.

Although glory continued to signify the end, a profound and controversial referential shift began to take place. No longer is the eschatological age simply defined as the apocalypse of Yahweh's glory; it is the advent of Jesus and his glory. Christ is the "hope of glory" (Col 1:27), and believers are to appear "with him in glory" (Col 3:4). Titus 2:13 exhorts believers to sobriety and patience in light of "the appearing of the glory of our great God and Savior Jesus Christ." Despite vigorous debate over how to construe the Greek of this verse, one can say that Jesus—who is both God and Savior—will bear the eschatological divine presence (i.e., glory) at his Parousia. Peter encourages believers in their sharing of Christ's sufferings so that they "may also rejoice and be glad when his glory is revealed" (1 Pet 4:13). The future apocalypse is not defined by the revelation of the Father's glory; nor does Jesus share it with the Father. Glory belongs to Jesus.

The way in which Jesus substitutes for Yahweh and the way in which glory, as a sign of Yahweh's presence, is applied to Jesus in eschatological settings can be seen in 2 Thessalonians. Oppressors will be excluded from the Lord's glory and the saints will experience glorification (2 Thess 1:9-10). Although echoing Dan 7 generally (and the gospel Son of Man tradition in particular), the passage substitutes "Lord Jesus" for the Son of Man in an almost verbatim quote of Isa 2:10 (LXX). This text effects a controversial referential transference: quoting an OT passage emphasizing the eschatological "Day of the Lord," the juridical functions reserved for Yahweh are now said to be executed by Jesus. First Peter states that believers should joyfully share in Christ's sufferings in this life so that they may also rejoice "at the revelation of his Glory" (1 Pet 4:13; compare 2 Thess 1:7). This clear referential shift from Yahweh to Jesus reflects early Christianity's redefinition of the godhead via an eschatological christology (or a christocentric eschatology). And it is precisely here, in an eschatological context, that glory stands for Jesus when he stands for Yahweh.

3. Glory as resurrection

Hebrews 2:9 not only scandalously reapplies Ps 8 to Jesus (thus making this a psalm celebrating Jesus), but it also retrofits the psalm in light of the crucial events of Jesus' life. When read through the lens of Jesus' life, "to be made lower" refers to his incarnation, while his crowning with glory refers to the resurrection/exaltation. To be "crowned with glory" is to be raised from the dead, an act that commences eschatological subjection. The "crowning with glory and honor" parallels the ascription of glory to the resurrected Jesus in the hymnic fragment of Rev 5:12-13 and the investiture of Jesus with "the name above every name" (i.e., the name, the LORD) in the hymn of Phil 2:5-11. First Peter 1:21 also textually and theologically juxtaposes glory and resurrection: "Through him you have confidence in God, who raised him from the dead and gave him glory, so that your faith and hope are in God." There can be no doubt that "raised him from the dead" formed part of early Christianity's confession of faith, while "and gave him glory" could be part of the earliest confessional formulae (which does not appear elsewhere) or the author's own addition. In either case, the phrase structurally parallels "crowned with glory" of Ps 8:7 (LXX) and Heb 2:9 and isolates the resurrection as the moment of Jesus' investiture with eschatological glory.

In Phil 3 Paul affirms that the resurrected already possess a body of glory, an eschatological, transformed body. Believers, too, will undergo a final act of transformation into conformity with this eschatological glory of Jesus. This metamorphosis will occur at the Parousia, which early Christianity depicted as an apocalypse of glory. The striking new piece of information is the means by which Jesus obtained this eschatological transformed body of divine presence. The phrase "by which he is able to subject all things unto himself" recalls Ps 8:7 (LXX) and its common use in earliest Christianity (1 Cor 15:25; Eph 1:22-23; Heb 2:5-9; 1 Pet 3:22) to refer to the resurrection of Jesus. In fact, the parallels with Eph 1:20 are so striking that it is hard not to conclude that a confessional fragment stands behind both passages. Both Phil 3:21 and Eph 1:20, 22 isolate the resurrection of Jesus as an apocalyptic power unleashed to subdue all enemies. "Taken up in glory" of 1 Tim 3:16 equally designates the resurrection/exaltation/enthronement of Jesus.

When Paul writes, "We were buried therefore with him by baptism into death, so that as Christ was raised from the dead by the glory of the Father, we too might walk in the newness of life" (Rom 6:4), he witnesses to the early Christian practice of baptism and to the early confession that "Christ was raised from the dead." The activity of the father and passivity of the Son was a common feature of resurrection formulas employing "to raise up." These formulas sometimes included a reference to the means by which the raising of Jesus took place—e.g., the "Spirit" (Rom 8:11), "power" (1 Cor 6:14), "strength" (Eph 1:19), or divine "energy" (Col 2:12). Glory thus becomes one of the apocalyptic symbols announcing the eschatological triumph of God in the resurrection of Jesus. The resurrection of Jesus, then, is the in-breaking of eschatological glory—a prolepsis of the final apocalypse of glory that will transform all those who share in Christ and finish the process of cosmic subjection.

4. A glory christology

The depiction of the final day as an apocalypse of Jesus' glory (and not Yahweh's) implicitly witnesses to early Christianity's belief in the divinity of Jesus. What was implicit in the eschatological appropriation of glory becomes explicit when glory is deployed in a decidedly christological way.

The hymnic/confessional fragment preserved at Heb 1:1-4 describes Jesus as the "radiance of his glory" and the "exact representation of his very being" (Heb 1:3). The juxtaposition of glory with essence in the ontological characterization of Jesus clearly articulates Jesus' status. Jesus is God's glory, God's very being. This hymn/confession formed part of the author's strategy to distinguish between Jesus and angels, as the catena of OT texts and the sustained midrash on these texts proves (see Heb 1:5–2:18). The binatarian shape and content of the hymn/confession—i.e., its focus upon Jesus and God and Jesus as God—alleviates potential confusion between Jesus and powerful angelic figures. Jesus is ontologically superior to any and all angelic agents; Jesus is equal with God; Jesus is God.

Paul uses a technical title "Lord of glory" (compare Eph 1:17) for Jesus. The phrase "Lord of glory" is quite rare, only occurring here and in *1 Enoch* (*1 En.* 22:14; 25:3; 63:3). Paul also identifies the moment of Christian conversion as discovering "the light of knowledge of the glory of God in the face of Jesus Christ" (2 Cor 4:6). In 2 Cor 3:18 Paul characterizes the process of transformation into the resurrection likeness/image of Christ as a metamorphosis into glory. For Paul, both conversion and subsequent spiritual transformation is glory centered. The revelation of Christ as glory inaugurates a process of transformation that ultimately resolves into a final transformation in the glory of Christ.

James, too, directly connects Jesus with glory, but does so in a passage beset with grammatical ambiguity. James 2:1 warns the Christian community about showing partiality in expressing their "faith in our Lord Jesus Christ of glory." The awkward separation of "of glory" from "in the Lord" by the words "our Jesus Christ" has led to interpretive difficulties. The best option is to understand "of glory" in apposition to the phrase "Lord Jesus Christ," i.e., "faith in our Lord Jesus Christ, [who is] the glory."

E. Conclusion

Glory's most significant theological usage was as a sign of divine presence. As such, Glory: 1) legitimized sacred leaders, time, and space; 2) communicated the unqualified blessing of God; 3) helped define what the eschatological future with God was to be like; 4) described the anthropomorphic depictions of Yahweh in apocalyptic visions; and 5) was employed by Jesus to define his own future role as the Son of Man. 6) Earliest Christianity took over the hope for a future age defined by eschatological glory, and 7) effected a profound referential shift by replacing the expectation for an apocalypse of Yahweh's glory with Jesus with and as the glory of Yahweh. Such a shift took place because both 8) Jesus and 9) Jesus' resurrection were interpreted as an apocalypse of God's presence.

Bibliography: G. B. Carid. *The Language and Imagery of the Bible* (1980); C. C. Newman. *Paul's Glory Christology: Tradition and Rhetoric* (1992); Christopher Rowland. *The Open Heaven: A Study of Apocalyptic in Judaism and Early Christianity* (1982).

CAREY C. NEWMAN

GLOSSES, TEXTUAL. *See* TEXT CRITICISM, NT; TEXT CRITICISM, OT.

GLOSSOLALIA. *See* TONGUES, GIFT OF.

GLUTTON, GLUTTONY [זוֹלֵל *zolel*; φάγος *phagos*]. A person who eats to excess. Fourth Maccabees 1:3, 27 categorizes gluttony as a passion that, like lust, interferes with reason. The glutton, like the drunkard, can expect to fall into poverty (Prov 23:21) and should anticipate insomnia, colic, and nausea (Sir 31:20). "He is a glutton and a drunkard" ends the parents' curse on their disobedient son just before he is stoned (Deut 21:20); it was also a derisive comment made about Jesus (Matt 11:19; Luke 7:34). Diligent study of the Law and the cultivation of reason can cure gluttony (4 Macc 1:3; 2:7).

RICHARD B. VINSON

GNASH, GNASHING. *See* TOOTH.

GNAT [כֵּן ken; κώνωψ kōnōps]. The third Egyptian plague (Exod 8:16-19) was an abundance of kinnim (כִּנִּים), although the exact insect is impossible to discover (NKJV, "lice"; NIV, "flies"; NEB, "maggots"). Origen and Philo suggest the Arab midge, a small gnat whose sting causes painful skin irritation around the eyes, ears, and mouth. Others posit the malaria-ridden anopheles mosquito or the sand fly (*Psychdidae*) known to carry dengue fever. Isaiah 51:6 may understand ken as the singular "gnat," although it is sometimes translated "thus" (as KJV).

"Strain out the gnat" describes meticulous obedience by the Pharisees of ceremonial law requirements for cleanness and ritual purity (Matt 23:24). *See* FLY; PLAGUES IN EGYPT.

MICHAEL G. VANZANT

GNOSTICISM. From the Greek word gnōsis (γνῶσις) (knowledge), the broad classification, a genus, for a collection of religious sects that flourished in early Christian circles from the 2nd to the 5th cent. CE. Some of the speculative elements that remythologize Genesis traditions and Jewish wisdom materials or adapt Platonic topics and items from astrological and magical texts probably had developed by the 1st cent. CE. Adherents of these groups claim revealed insight (gnōsis) into ancient traditions. This knowledge requires a radically different understanding of those traditions from that commonly available in the churches or philosophical schools. Often it is obtained by ritual acts as well as instruction. Only an elite few attain such knowledge. Christian opponents of such sects used the expression "gnostics" of their adherents in a mocking or satirical way. Those groups closely tied to Christian circles would have spoken of themselves as true or spiritual Christians.

A. Defining Gnosticism
  1. Worldview
  2. School, sect, or heresy
  3. Famous gnostic teachers
  4. Related movements
B. Sources for Gnostic Teaching
C. History of Gnosticism
  1. Early speculative traditions (1st cent. CE)
  2. Flourishing gnostic sects (2nd to 3rd cent. CE)
  3. Decline in the West (4th to 5th cent. CE)
D. Key Themes in Gnostic Texts
  1. Unknown Father and the divine world
  2. Wisdom, the Jewish God, and creation
  3. Reinterpreting Genesis
  4. Divine revealers and salvation
  5. Elitism and ethics
E. Gnosticism and the New Testament

A. Defining Gnosticism

Such broad classifications as "Judaism," "Christianity," and "Gnosticism" embrace wide ranges of individual variation in the surviving examples. Referring to a text as "Jewish," "Christian," or "Gnostic" provides little specific information about content, social location or ideology. Some scholars have tried to find a replacement for "Gnosticism" that would delimit sets of texts or groups more precisely. As long as the term "Gnosticism" is used for a grouping of related though diverse phenomena, it remains serviceable.

1. Worldview

The history-of-religions movement in the early 20th cent. led to descriptions of a gnostic view of the world, which found its way into political philosophy. The negative view of the material world and hostility toward its governing authorities found in gnostic texts was interpreted using philosophical categories of alienation. Gnostic enlightenment provided a healing integration for persons who were (are) in some sense powerless in a larger social context.

2. School, sect, or heresy

Irenaeus (180 CE) composed a refutation of gnostic views because Christians confused such opinions with true faith. Somewhat later (245 CE) Origen insists that the anti-Christian views of Celsus (178 CE) were based on gnostic sources, not the Christian gospels. Irenaeus provided readers with a complicated genealogy of teachers and sects that traced this multi-faceted heresy back to Simon Magus (Acts 8:4-25). Thus gnostic claims to possess a secret teaching that the risen Jesus had given to one or more of the Twelve are shown up as lies. Until the 20th cent. there was little reason to question the view of Christian authors who presented Gnosticism as a deviant sectarian form of Christianity.

Two developments in the 20th cent. changed the landscape. New Testament scholars came to recognize the diversity of belief and practice in the first century, and newly discovered manuscripts provided access to actual gnostic texts. Creating the boundaries which would marginalize some groups as "heretics" was part of a complex process that is just beginning in the 2nd cent. In addition, a number of gnostic texts have few Christian features. They are engaged with a new mythologizing of Genesis materials, with philosophic topics concerning the divine, the cosmos and human nature or with other traditions about the soul's ascent.

Thus not all gnostic sects associated themselves with Christianity. Some interpreters prefer to think of gnostic groups along the lines of the philosophical schools.

3. Famous gnostic teachers

Ancient philosophical schools would trace their roots back to the founder through a succession of teachers. Christian opponents provided similar lists of gnostic teachers and disciples. Bibliographical notes intended to discredit an individual cannot be trusted. However several individuals were prominent gnostic teachers in the 2nd cent. and appear to have been well-known in Christian intellectual circles. Only summaries, brief quotations or extracts of their writings preserved by opponents survive. Basilides was active in Alexandria (ca. 132 CE; Irenaeus, *Haer.* 1.24.3-7; Hippolytus, *Haer.* 7.20-27). He is reported to have composed 24 books of commentary on the gospels as well as odes or hymns. His son or successor, Isidore, is credited with writing on ethics. Though patristic summaries suggest a gnostic view of the origins of the world, Basilides comments on the gospels of the Christian canon. He advised followers to deny their faith rather than be martyred, and apparently celebrated the baptism of Jesus on Epiphany. The most famous gnostic teacher, Valentinus, also from Alexandria, founded a distinctive school. He taught for several decades in Rome (ca. 140–160 CE). Significant extracts from three of his followers are preserved in Christian authors: Ptolemy's *Letter to Flora* excerpts from Heracleon's commentary on John in Origen's own commentary, and extracts from Theodotus in Clement of Alexandria. Irenaeus derived much of his first hand information from followers of Ptolemy.

4. Related movements

Christian writers link Marcion with 2nd cent. gnostic teachers. He shared their scorn for the god depicted in Jewish scriptures but not their complex mythology and allegorical exegesis. In the mid-3rd cent., the prophet Mani inaugurated a distinctive, new form of gnostic religion in Persia. Manichaeism spread East as far as China. It was a strong competitor to Christianity in the Christian West during the 4th cent. CE.

B. Sources for Gnostic Teaching

Until the 20th cent. reports from those opposed to gnostic teaching provided the only sources of information about their views. Even the continued discovery of new manuscripts such as the *Gospel of Judas* cannot erase the need to consult patristic summaries. The Christian paraphrases often underline structural elements in gnostic mythologizing that are difficult to situate in the primary sources. Christian writers also provide at least half of our evidence for gnostic interpretation of the canonical gospels and Pauline epistles.

Gnostics wrote in Greek. All that survives of their original language are selections in Christian authors and a few papyrus fragments. Greek was the language of the educated in Alexandria but not of the Egyptian populace. From the late 2nd to the mid-3rd cent., a large number of gnostic texts were translated into Coptic, the language of the people. Books from the 4th to 6th cent. containing copies of these writings form the basis for our first hand knowledge of Gnosticism. Some texts such as the Apocryphon of John have turned up in more than one codex, which suggests that they may have been particularly important. There is no evidence for a fixed group of gnostic texts that always appear together. Therefore it would be wrong to think of these books as a "bible" intended to replace the canonical scriptures.

The most important find were texts from thirteen codices found near Nag Hammadi (1946). The volumes include gnostic and non-gnostic texts, copied in the mid-4th cent. CE and apparently assembled from different parts of Egypt. None of these works are attributed to one of the famous teachers. Most are either anonymous or pseudepigrapha attributed to one or more of Jesus' followers or to some ancient prophet. Based on information from earlier sources, it is possible to identify Valentinian teaching in a number of these writings. The best known work among them is a collection of Jesus' sayings that has been overlaid with some gnostic interpretation, *The Gospel of Thomas*. Those sayings which appear to be alternate versions of 1st cent. synoptic material have been incorporated in recent editions of the gospel synopsis.

C. History of Gnosticism

Often the details of persons, customs or events mentioned in Biblical texts provide the clues that scholars use in connecting them with a particular socio-historical setting. Gnostic writings engage in a level of abstract mythologizing and discourse that is almost entirely disengaged from such realism. Consequently scholars have proposed histories of Gnosticism based on notices in patristic sources and formal features of the surviving texts. Only a very general outline can be suggested.

1. Early speculative traditions (1st cent. CE)

Early speculative traditions that form the building blocks of gnostic mythological systems probably belong to the same environment as Jewish Enoch traditions, speculation about the fallen angels, the ordering of the heavens, Adam, Eve, their offspring, Noah, the flood, and Wisdom's role in creation. Some scholars see the ironic skepticism directed at the creator's self-predications as hints of disenchantment with Judaism after the disaster of 70 CE.

2. Flourishing gnostic sects (2nd to 3rd cent. CE)

Whether or not a form of gnostic speculation had emerged in Jewish circles, there is no doubt that gnostic groups were established in the Christian communities of Alexandria, Rome and other cities by the 140s. Foundational texts like the *Apocryphon of John* had been composed and edited in multiple versions. Teachers like Valentinus adapted and reinterpreted earlier gnostic material. They also began to comment on the gospels being read in Christian churches. Some gnostic texts appear to be composed in response to the criticisms of Christian leaders like Irenaeus. The diverse dialects into which the texts from Nag Hammadi were translated shows that gnostic groups existed up and down the Nile valley in the 3rd cent.

Scholars have suggested four sub-categories of Gnosticism based on the Coptic texts. A group, which may have originated in Syria, follows the lead of *Gospel of Thomas* in adapting Jesus sayings to a gnostic milieu with Thomas as its authority. Another group of texts highlight the figure of Seth as the heavenly revealer. Gnostics belong to the seed of this figure. Baptism(s) and sealing with five seals as well as certain angel names recur throughout this group. Therefore scholars speak of a "Sethian" type of Gnosticism. A third set of texts present Valentinian teaching. Some such as the *Tripartite Tractate* do so in conversation with 3rd cent. Christian christological and trinitarian debates. In the mid-3rd cent. the neo-Platonist teacher Plotinus opposed gnostic views held by some of his students in Rome. Versions of texts they were reading were found at Nag Hammadi. This form of Gnosticism incorporates neo-Platonic speculation about the divine and claims to facilitate the soul's upward ascent to union with the divine.

3. Decline in the West (4th to 5th cent. CE)

Decline in the West should not be attributed to the anti-gnostic polemics of Christian officials. Significant changes in the socio-religious setting must have been involved. Some of the Nag Hammadi books were manufactured at or near Egyptian monastic centers in the mid-4th cent. The monks may have been collecting such materials as contributions to individualized ascetic piety. At the same time, Manichaean teaching was gaining a foothold in the region. The more elaborate social and religious organization of Manichaean groups along with their devotion to unique texts, made them a more formidable alternative than the earlier gnostic sects. Individuals who might have been drawn to Gnosticism at one time now have such alternatives as neo-Platonism, monastic asceticism or Manichaeism. The socio-political implosion of the Roman empire in the West also contributed to the decline of Gnosticism.

D. Key Themes in Gnostic Texts

Gnosticism did not originate as a well-defined philosophy or set of religious doctrines. Nor did its teachers compose authoritative texts to replace the traditional Jewish and Christian scriptures. Therefore the themes which recur from one text to the next are subject to considerable variation. The following catalogue refers to examples from the version of *Apocryphon of John* in Nag Hammadi Codex II.

1. Unknown Father and the divine world

God as the source of true being is an "unknown Father" whose self-contemplation brings forth the Mother, her offspring and then a series of paired, male-female divine beings. Among them one finds the archetypal human (*Ap. John* 2,26–9,24).

2. Wisdom, the Jewish God, and creation

Wisdom, last of the aeon-pairs to emerge, attempts to create without her male counterpart. A bizarre lion-faced, serpent-like creature appears whom his mother hides from the divine world with a luminous cloud. This figure begins to create his own aeon pairs, seven rule the planetary spheres and five the abyss. He boasts of being the sole god only to be countered by a divine voice and appearance of the first Human in the light-waters above (9,25–14,34).

3. Reinterpreting Genesis

A repentant Wisdom is the Spirit moving across the waters. The demonic powers created by Wisdom's offspring begin to shape Adam according to the image they saw. Unknown to them, the divine Mother-Father has slipped in a luminous being to assist Adam and provoke rebellion against the creator. Struggles ensue as the creator attempts to prevent Adam from knowing the true God. Adam is cast out of paradise into a material body driven by sexual desire. Divine providence removes life from Eve before she is raped by the creator. Adam (and Eve) lapse into forgetfulness until the gnostic race descended from Seth comes into being (15,1–25,16).

4. Divine revealers and salvation

Those who belong to the gnostic race receive the Spirit, are purified from all contamination and will return to their divine source. Other souls who require repentance will reach a lower level of the divine because they can still be led astray. Still others will be sent back for reincarnation until they become capable of knowledge (25,17–27,21). Jesus is the final manifestation of these providential Wisdom figures who descend to enlighten humanity (30,12–31,28). Salvation is awakening to the light captured from the divine realm and the eventual return to one's roots there.

5. Elitism and ethics

Apocryphon of John counters the charges that gnostics think of themselves as an elite who are saved by nature and even violate ethical codes to demonstrate the point. Though there is a special endowment to the gnostic race, they require divine revelation, spiritual anointing and ritual practice. They practice ordinary virtues. Vices are the result of passions manipulated by demons to imprison humanity. Consequently an ascetic renunciation of sexuality, wealth and other pursuits were represented as chains of Hades (25,23–27,11). Valentinian teaching adopts and reformulates the distinction between those saved through a spontaneous reaction to gnostic revelation, and a different path for souls led by way of repentance and ordinary Christian praxis.

E. Gnosticism and the New Testament

For the first half of the 20th cent., interest in gnostic texts was fueled by the hypothesis that John's gospel had adopted a gnostic myth in which the primordial revealer descends into the world of darkness to enlighten the elect. The evangelist had reinterpreted both this pre-Christian gnostic mytheme and the story of Jesus in bringing the two together. Echoes of John's prologue occur in such texts as *Trimorphic Protennoia*. However there is no clear evidence for gnostic redeemer myths in the 1st cent.

Though gnostic authors often frame their works as revelation discourses between the Jesus who has returned to his divine glory and one or more disciples as is the case with *Apocryphon of John*, they have no place for a redemptive death or bodily resurrection. The eternal Savior does not suffer or die. The *Gospel of Judas* treats all sacrificial cults, even the Passover and Eucharist, as the creator's rules, which gnostics will disobey. Attempts to discern a proto-gnostic influence behind the interest in wisdom, rejection of the cross and resurrection, deviant behavior at the Lord's Supper, rejection of marriage and moral improprieties in 1 Corinthians have not proved persuasive.

Gospel of Thomas has preserved variants of Jesus' sayings and parables. Some scholars have attempted to mine other gnostic writings for additional Jesus traditions with little result. The Jesus teaching conveyed by Mary Magdalene in the *Gospel of Mary* is a standard gnostic exposé on the soul's ascent past the demonic guardians of the planetary realms and their associated passions. It contributes nothing to understanding what the historical Jesus taught or the role of Galilean women in his entourage.

Gnostic texts are marketed by many today as though they embodied the earliest, authentic form of Jesus' teaching subsequently suppressed by orthodox bishops determined to safeguard their authority over the faithful. However gnostic mythology and interpretation require a general acceptance of the Jewish and emerging four gospel canon to be effective. Valentinians appear to have an elaborate sacramental praxis, but there is no evidence until Mani of gnostic interest in taking on established religious institutions. Consequently gnostic groups are closer to schools or sectarian options within a larger religious tradition than

they are to churches. *See* ADAM, APOCALYPSE OF; IRENAEUS; JOHN, APOCRYPHON OF OR SECRET BOOK OF; MARY, GOSPEL OF; NAG HAMMADI TEXTS; PHILIP, GOSPEL OF; THOMAS, GOSPEL OF; TRUTH, GOSPEL OF.

Bibliography: W. Barnstone and M. Meyer, eds. *The Gnostic Bible* (2003); A. D. De Conick. *Recovering the Original Gospel of Thomas* (2005); H. Jonas. *The Gnostic Religion* (1958); K. L. King. *The Secret Revelation of John* (2006); B. Layton. *The Gnostic Scriptures* (1987); A. Marjanen and P. Luomanen, eds. *A Companion to Second-Century Christian "Heretics"* (2005); E. Pagels. *The Gnostic Gospels* (1979); P. Perkins. *Gnosticism and the New Testament* (1993); J. M. Robinson, ed. *The Nag Hammadi Library in English* (1988); K. Rudolph. *Gnosis* (1983); J. D. Turner. *Sethian Gnosticism and the Platonic Tradition* (2001); M. A. Williams. *Rethinking Gnosticism* (1996).

PHEME PERKINS

GOAD [דָּרְבָן darevan, מַלְמָד malmadh; κέντρον kentron]. A long-handled, pointed instrument utilized by plowmen when driving or guiding their oxen. Sometimes it was tipped with metal to clean the plough (1 Sam 13:21). Shamgar used a goad to kill the Philistines (Judg 3:31).

The word is also used metaphorically. The reference to "the sayings of the wise" as goads (Eccl 12:11) means they lead people to live righteously. The expression "it hurts you to kick against the goads" (Acts 26:14) connotes the idea of futile and harmful resistance to a higher authority, signifying the futility of Paul's persecuting the church.

Bibliography: Stanley D. Toussaint. *Acts* (1983).

VICTOR RHEE

GOAH goh´uh [גֹּעָה go'ah]. A place near Jerusalem, perhaps to the south and east of the hill GAREB (Jer 31:39).

GOAL. *See* MARK, GOAL, SIGN.

GOAT SKIN. Goat skin had multiple uses such as material for clothes (Gen 3:21) and writing. DNA studies of parchment fragments of Dead Sea Scrolls indicate the wide use of goat skins in parchment. Skins were also used as containers for liquids such as water, milk, and wine (no'd [נֹאד] 1 Sam 16:20; khemeth [חֵמֶת], Gen 21:14-15; nevel [נֶבֶל], 1 Sam 1:24). If present-day practices are an indication, goat skins were likely used as churns to make butter. Rules applied to goats used for sacrifice specify that the skin should be burned along with the whole animal (Lev 16:27). Hebrews 11:37 describes the faithful in desperate times as going about in skins of sheep and goats (en aigeiois dermasin [ἐν αἰγείοις δέρμασιν] "in skins of goats"). *See* SKIN.

Bibliography: O. Borowski. *Every Living Thing: Daily Use of Animals in Ancient Israel* (1998).

ODED BOROWSKI

GOAT, GOATHERD [עֵז 'ez; תַּיִשׁ tayish]. The goat (*Capra aegagrus*) was as important an animal for Israelite economy and culture as the sheep. Goats are kept in herds the size of which depends on available space and resources such as water and grazing lands. Goat herders reside in villages and towns as well as pursuing a semi-nomadic life. Two main types of goats are extant in the region: the Bedouin or black goat is raised mostly in the Negev and Sinai; the hill country or Damascene goat, which has reddish-brown hair, is raised near permanent settlements in the Judean hills, Samaria, and Galilee. A third type of goat, Baalbek, with black and white hair, is kept mostly in the Golan and Hermon mountains.

The black goat produces an average of 75 L milk per year while the Damascene goat produces about 400 L milk per year. The latter, similarly to the Near Eastern Awassi sheep, needs to drink twice a day, while the Bedouin goat can go without drinking for as long as four days. This trait enables the Bedouin goat to survive and flourish in semiarid and arid areas where other small cattle cannot. The black goat is fed mostly by grazing, while the Damascene goat is kept near the home and feeds on greens and feed.

Although goats are not very selective in their diet, they mature quickly, and are a good source of milk, meat, and hair. Goats are shorn once a year usually from May to June. In recent history, goat hair has been used mainly for making Bedouin tents and sacks for transport. It is highly possible that in biblical times goat hair was used for the same purposes or, at least, for rope making.

The importance of the goat in the Israelite economy is exemplified by the multiple terms related to it and recorded in the Bible. A female goat (doe) is an 'ez (Gen 15:9); a male goat tayish (Prov 30:31) and 'ottudh (עַתּוּד, Gen 31:10). The book of Daniel presents another term, tsafir (צָפִיר, Dan 8:21) or tsefir-ha'izzim (צְפִיר־הָעִזִּים, Dan 8:5). A young he-goat is sa'ir (שָׂעִיר, Lev 16:20) or se'ir 'izzim (שָׂעִיר עִזִּים, Lev 4:23); a young she-goat is se'irath 'izzim (שְׂעִירַת עִזִּים, Lev 4:28). Another term for a young he-goat is gedhi (גְּדִי, Judg 13:19) or gedhi 'izzim (גְּדִי עִזִּים, Gen 38:17). The term seh (שֶׂה, Exod 12:5) is sometimes used for a young he- or she-goat as well as young sheep.

Young male goats played an important role as part of the sin-offering (Lev 4:23; 16:5; Num 7:16; 2 Chr 29:21; Ezek 43:22, 25; 45:23), and also in burnt offerings (Lev 1:10; 22:19) and peace offerings (Lev 3:6, 12; 17:3; Num 7:17). Under special instructions, apparently for the DAY OF ATONEMENT, two goats were selected, one to be sacrificed to Yahweh and the other to AZAZEL: "Aaron shall present the goat on which the lot fell for the LORD, and offer it as a sin offering; but the goat on which the lot fell for Azazel shall be presented alive before the LORD to make atonement over it, that it may be sent away into the wilderness to Azazel" (Lev 16:9-10).

In the NT, the goat (the self-centered, cursed sinner) is not favored over the sheep (the generous, merciful giver of food and drink) when the righteous and the wicked are separated on the day of judgment (Matt 25:31-46). The early Christian resistance toward the goat as a symbol of the sacrificial cult also surfaces in Heb 9, where Christ's blood substitutes for the blood of goats.

Goats must have been included in herds offered as tribute or taken as war booty. Numerous Assyrian kings, among them SHALMANESER III, TIGLATH-PILESER III, and SENNACHERIB, boast of getting tribute of such herds from Israel or Judah. *See* ANIMALS OF THE BIBLE.

Bibliography: O. Borowski. *Every Living Thing: Daily Use of Animals in Ancient Israel* (1998).

ODED BOROWSKI

GOB gob [גּוֹב gov]. Site of two of four legend-making battles between Davidic forces and the Philistines, whose named slain heroes were descended from Gittite giants (2 Sam 21:15-20; compare 1 Chr 20:4-8).

GOBLETS [כְּלִים kelim; ποτήριον potērion]. In Esth 1:7, Ahasuerus serves drinks in golden goblets of varying kinds. The word can also mean article, utensil, or vessel.

GOD, CHILDREN OF. *See* CHILDREN OF GOD.

GOD, FINGER OF [אֶצְבַּע אֱלֹהִים 'etsba' 'elohim; δάκτυλος θεοῦ daktylos theou]. This expression can signify God's presence, agency, care, and authority. By it, Pharaoh's magicians admit the LORD's superior power (Exod 8:19 [Heb. 8:14]; see Ps 8:3). The Mosaic Covenant is two "tablets of stone, written with the finger of God," bearing God's character and ultimate authority while assuring God's people of intimate care (Exod 31:18; Deut 9:10). When Jesus says, "But if it is by the finger of God that I cast out the demons" (Luke 11:20), he claims and displays that same divine presence and power, authority and care. *See* ANTHROPOMORPHISM; GOD, METAPHORS FOR.

BONNIE G. HOWE

GOD, HOUSEHOLD OF [οἶκος τοῦ Θεοῦ oikos tou theou]. The household was the basic social and economic unit of ancient Israel. The household was also a primary location for living out covenantal relationship with God, and household language was employed to articulate the activity of God and ways of living appropriate to this relationship.

The nation is presented as the "household of Israel" that developed from the ancestral household of Jacob/Israel (Jer 2:4). The "household of Israel" originated from and belonged to God in covenant relationship (Exod 16:31; 40:38). The covenant formula "I will be the God of all the clans of Israel and they shall be my people" denotes Israel's identity in this covenant relationship (Jer 31:1, 33). Israel was "the household of God," as both the recipient of Moses' leadership (Num 12:7-8) and the breaker of the covenant (Jer 12:7; Hos 8:1). God creates this household in delivering the people from "the household of slavery" in Egypt (Deut 5:6; 6:12; 7:8).

In the NT, the phrase "household of God" is not common but appears in some later writings. These writings relate the claim of the church as the household of God to Israel's identity in various ways. The post-Pauline Ephesians sees the inclusion of Gentiles into a new household comprising Jews and Gentiles, and constituted by Christ's death (Eph 2:19). Gentiles were "aliens from the commonwealth of Israel" (2:12) but through Christ's death, animosity between Jew and Gentile has been overcome to form one humanity, the household of God (2:19). Hebrews sees some continuity in God's work with Israel and the church, but asserts the superiority of the household of God, the church, created by Christ (Heb 3:1-6). First Peter employs numerous images from the OT including a number of terms associated with households ("father," 1:3; "children," 1:14; "stranger/sojourner," 2:11). Not surprisingly the church is identified as "the household of God" in which God's judgment will be experienced (1 Pet 4:17).

Also evident in the NT usages is cultural influence from the household codes of Hellenistic world. In the post-Pauline 1 Timothy, the writer is concerned that the readers "know how one ought to behave in the household of God" (1 Tim 3:15). The church is presented as a household in relationship with the living God experienced through the incarnated, risen, and ascended Christ (1 Tim 3:15-16). This household of God is accommodated to social structures living "a quiet and peaceable life" (1 Tim 2:2). The church imitates (elite) patriarchal household structures with men exercising leadership roles (1 Tim 3:1-13). Men prove themselves for ecclesial leadership by ruling their own households well, having submissive children, and one wife (1 Tim 3:4-5, 12), "for if someone does not know how to manage his own household, how can he take care of God's church?" Women are to be silent, submissive, taught, fertile, and modest (1 Tim 2:13-15). Such a vision of the church and its leadership differs from the charismatic structure of ministry in Paul's letters (Rom 12; 1 Cor 12–14, treating 14:34-36 as an interpolation). *See* CHURCH, IDEA OF THE; FAMILY; GOD THE FATHER; HOUSEHOLD CODES; HOUSEHOLD, HOUSEHOLDER.

WARREN CARTER

GOD, METAPHORS FOR. All language for God, including biblical language, is metaphorical. That is to say it works by comparison. In the process of comparing God to beings and entities from the world familiar to humanity, three steps may be discerned. First, in naming God shepherd, or king, or judge, known occupations and roles from the social context are used to establish a connection with the Deity. Second, while this connection is made, it becomes apparent also that the comparison does not fit completely. God is *like* a human shepherd, a king, or judge but cannot be identified with these figures entirely. Something always falls short in the comparison. As the comparison is made, it thus becomes clear that there is something wrong as well as something right about naming God in this way. God may be called a judge, but God is not altogether like a human judge. Third, the familiar basis for the comparison itself undergoes change: through the naming of God as king, e.g., the concept of human kingship changes as it is submitted to the criterion of God's kingship. It is essential that the first step of this process remains operative in order for the entire process to function. A metaphor that is based on an unfamiliar occupation or title or entity will gradually be a dead metaphor.

The Bible shows an understanding of the difficulty of naming God in terms that are familiar to humans and at the same time exhibits great daring in its naming of the Almighty. Isaiah 40:12 shows clearly the insight into the difficulty:

> To whom then will you liken God
> Or what likeness compare with him?
> (Isa 40:18)

And further:

> To whom will you compare me, or who is my equal?
> says the Holy One.
> (Isa 40:25)

These are rhetorical questions to which the appropriate response must be that God is not comparable to anyone or anything. Yet elsewhere the biblical writers unhesitatingly compare God to a ruler, a potter, a father, a woman in childbirth, a bear, a lion, an eagle, a rock, and a brook. There exists a remarkable fluidity and flexibility in the various images and names for God used in the biblical text.

Some metaphors for God are more dominant in the Bible than others. First there are those that draw from the sphere of human power and authority. Two of the most familiar are the titles "king" and "lord." "King" was a common way to indicate the deity in southwest Asia of ancient times, including ancient Israel. "King," to indicate the God of Israel, occurs roughly forty times in the OT with more than half of the occurrences clustered in a group of psalms that celebrate God's kingship over God's people, the entire earth, and the cosmos (e.g., Pss 93; 95–99; 145 and 149). God is also referred to by this title in some prophetic material but rarely in the Torah. Clearly kings were a known entity in those days, and the threefold process described above would include a reshaping of the idea of kingship in the image of God's kingship. God is, after all, the ideal king who cares for the needy and the poor, who delivers the weak and those who have no helper (Ps 72:12-14). The title "lord" for God comes from the same metaphorical field as that of king. Lord occurs over 6,000 times in the English versions of the Bible as it renders the unpronounceable proper name of God, in Hebrew written with four consonants, represented in English with the letters YHWH. Because the pronunciation of the name fell out of use very early on, the four consonants received the vowels that literally mean "lord" in English (Hebrew ʾadhonay אֲדֹנָי). Hence a proper name was transformed into a title that became the dominant one in the Bible, first in the OT and subsequently in the NT where the title predominates for Jesus and the risen Christ. In fact, "king" as a designation for God or Christ is infrequent in the NT and is replaced by "lord" (Gk: kyrios κύριος). Both these titles constitute the human community as a realm under the rule and also the care and the protection of the divine lord (*see* ADONAI, ADONAY; JESUS, METAPHORS FOR; KING, GOD AS; KING, KINGSHIP; LORD).

Today both titles are problematic as the reality of kingship and lordship recedes from human cognizance and where they are still known have lost much of their power. In addition, they are exclusive male metaphors that identify the male with authority, so they do not easily open up into a possible female pairing. When metaphors die off as a result of increasing unfamiliarity with the human phenomenon, i.e., when they become fossilized by loss of step one in the comparison process, they are in danger of being taken literally. Then a total identification of God with the metaphor may take place (a loss of step two), which in this case may lead to a masculinization of metaphors for God.

Another cluster of comparative language is embedded in the metaphors for God as kinsman, mainly FATHER, but also, lover, BRIDEGROOM, or husband (*see* FAMILY; MARRIAGE, NT; MARRIAGE, OT). In the OT the term *father* for God is only rarely used, possibly because the main deity of the Canaanite pantheon was termed the "father of the gods." The power of the comparison lies in the family relationships from which the images are drawn. God may thus be compared to a lover forsaken by his bride (Jer 2:1), to a husband left by his wife (Hos 2:1), or to a father/parent with faithless children (Deut 32:6; Jer 3:19; Isa 1:2). A few times the appellation "father" is used in the OT when God's saving activity is called on (Isa 63:16; 64:8; Mal 2:10). In the NT, the cluster of royal relationships is no longer active and the dominant image for God becomes "father." Jesus called God "my father" and "our father," and God is described as "the father" in the Gospels, "the father of our kyrios (κύριος "lord") Jesus Christ" and "the father" in the rest of the NT. While it could be that this imagery comes mainly from the early church rather than from the immediate context of Jesus, as some scholars maintain, the dominance of the metaphor is undeniable. According to a feminist critique of metaphors for God, all family relationships must be viewed critically as belonging to a network of patriarchal social relations, for contemporary contexts no less than those of the past. Thoroughgoing analyses and critique have revealed these networks as potentially and often actually violent and abusive toward women. For metaphors drawn from the family sphere, the problem with the comparison is not a lack of familiarity but the negativity that colors the relationships embedded in the images. Thus Brian Wren correctly observed that the name "father" no longer has the power to subvert the patriarchal order in our context but that it is rather invoked to defend this same order.

Less familiar than the metaphors listed above is one not directly used for God but used for Jesus and perhaps his original title: TEACHER. As God provides TORAH, instruction, for the covenant people, God is certainly perceived as teacher even if not so named. From the Gospels of the NT it is clear that the rav (רַב), or rabbi (ῥαββι), rabbouni (ῥαββουνι), or didaskalos (διδάσκαλος), had an original place in the naming of Jesus (e.g., Matt 8:19; 12:38; 19:16; 22:16, 24, 36; Mark 4:38; 5:35; 9:17, 38; 10:17; Luke 9:38; 11:45; John 1:38; 20:16). This metaphor goes clearly to the heart of one of the most important functions of Jesus' ministry (*see* RABBI).

The inanimate metaphor of "rock" occurs more than forty times for God in the OT and has survived in the liturgy but is today not much alive in the Christian context. With rock was meant a place of refuge and safety that additionally had the connotation of holiness and the miraculous. God in the Bible is actually compared to a "rock that gave birth" (Deut 32:18).

Uncommon, but rich in diversity and imagery is the metaphor of MOTHER for God. God is said to be like a woman in labor (Isa 42:14; 45:10; compare also Ps 90:2); a healing, nourishing motherly presence (Hos 11:3-4); a compassionate mother who will never forget her child (Isa 49:14-17); and a comforting presence as a mother can be comforting (Isa 66:13; *see* CHILD, CHILDREN). More inclusively parental are metaphors for God that draw on animal imagery as that of the eagle (Exod 19:4; Deut 32:11), continued in the protecting metaphor of God's wings (Pss 17:8; 57:1; 61:4; 63:7; 91:1; and Ruth 2:12). In the NT this image is present in words attributed to Jesus that declare how Jesus longed to gather Jerusalem's children as "a hen gathers her brood under her wings" (Matt 23:37 and Luke 13:34).

A last and powerful metaphor for God is found in the personification of wisdom. Although initially most likely intended to personify an aspect of God, in later literature wisdom became a full-fledged image for God or the Torah, as in the books of Wisdom of Solomon and Sirach. Wisdom (sophia σοφία), was certainly an original title for Jesus, although eventually the "word" or logos (λόγος) metaphor became dominant (see Luke 7:35; 1 Cor 1:23-24; compare John 1:1-3, 14). *See* GOD, NAMES OF; METAPHOR IN THEOLOGY; THEOLOGICAL HERMENEUTICS; WISDOM IN THE NT; WISDOM IN THE OT.

Bibliography: Johanna W. H. van Wijk-Bos. *Reimagining God—the Case for Scriptural Diversity* (1995); Brian Wren. *What Language Shall I Borrow? God-Talk in Worship: A Male Response to Feminist Theology* (1991) 187.

JOHANNA W. H. VAN WIJK-BOS

GOD, NAMES OF. The question of divine identity is a theologically critical one in the Bible, because the people of the OT and NT worshiped neither an inanimate object nor an impersonal being, but someone with whom they related. Since in ancient Israel the name of a person signified that person's nature and character, a survey of the various names of God will give some insights about how God was understood. While Yahweh ("the LORD") is the distinctive name by which Israel's God was known, there are numerous other designations that must be considered.

A. Significance of Names
B. God
  1. Elohim
  2. Eloah
  3. El
C. Yahweh (יהוה YHWH)
D. God/Lord of Hosts
E. Lord
  1. Baal
  2. Adon/Adonai
F. El Epithets
  1. El Shaddai
  2. El Elyon
  3. El, Creator of Heaven and Earth
  4. El Roi
  5. El Olam
  6. El Berit

G. Kinship Terms
  1. Father, Mother
  2. Brother
  3. Uncle
  4. Husband
H. Other Designations of God
  1. Holy One
  2. Jealous
  3. Mighty One
  4. Fear of Isaac
  5. Shield (of Abraham)
  6. Rock
Bibliography

A. Significance of Names

In ANE culture, a name was not merely a label one attaches to a person or an object. Rather, a name implies existence, identity, and character. Thus, in the Babylonian epic known as the *Enuma Elish*, the primal state of the cosmos was characterized as a time when heaven and earth were not yet named and "no gods whatever had been brought into being, uncalled by name" (*ANET*, 60–61). The opening chapter of the Bible, too, begins with the naming of day and night, heaven, earth, and seas, and so on (Gen 1:1-31). And the first human gave the animals names, thus establishing the nature of the relationship between the two orders of creation (Gen 2:19-20).

The name of a person signifies the person's existence, nature, and character (see, e.g., Gen 27:36; 1 Sam 25:25). Thus, when Moses was sent to his people to declare God's intended deliverance of them, Moses was certain that they would want first to know the name of that God (Exod 3:13), that is, to know that such a God exists and what the nature and character of that God are. Indeed, the name of God often meant the very presence of God. Thus, the ark of covenant, which symbolized the presence of God was, according to the Hebrew text of 2 Sam 6:2, "called by name, 'the Name of Yahweh Sabaoth, who sits enthroned upon the cherubim.'" And when the Deuteronomistic theologian wanted to speak of the presence of God in the temple, without implying that the deity was somehow tied to the edifice or its location, the theologian spoke only of God causing God's name to dwell there, while God is so transcendent that even the highest heaven cannot contain God (1 Kgs 8:14-64). In the OT, believers are said to know (Pss 9:10 [Heb. 9:11]; 91:14), rejoice in (Ps 89:17), love (Ps 5:11 [Heb. 5:12]), or trust (Ps 33:21) God's name, while those outside the fold do not "call on the name" of God (Ps 79:6; Jer 10:25). The fact that the name of God was equated with the presence of God itself seems to be corroborated by personal names like Shemida (probably "the Name Knows"), Samuel (possibly "the Name [Yahweh] is El"), or simply, Shem (a theophorous name that has been abbreviated).

Since the name of God is associated with the presence, character, and identity of God, it is understood to be as authoritative and as holy as the very presence of God itself.

B. God

The English noun "God" renders Hebrew ʾelohim (אֱלֹהִים), ʾel (אֵל), and ʾeloah (אֱלוֹהַ), Aramaic ʾelah (אֱלָהּ), as well as Greek theos (θεος) in the LXX and the NT. Like English "God," these are originally common nouns ("god") that, when applied to a particular deity by adherents, have the force of a proper name ("God").

1. Elohim

The Hebrew term ʾelohim, a plural form, may be used of gods in general (i.e., as a common noun) and, by extension, also images representing the gods. When the plural form is used of a single deity, Hebrew grammarians call that form "plural of majesty."

As a common noun, the Hebrew term may occur in genitive constructions, thus forming divine epithets like, "God of the Hebrews," "God of Israel," "God of the ancestors," "God of the covenant," "God of gods," "God of Hosts," "God of heaven," "God of heaven and earth," "God of salvation," "God of glory," and so on. The noun, whether conceived as common or proper, occurs over 2600 times in the Bible. In the so-called "Elohistic Psalter" (Pss 42–83), Elohim may have been deliberately used instead of Yahweh, the distinctive name of Israel's God. Psalm 53, for instance, has Elohim, whereas Psalm 14, which parallels it, has Yahweh. Similarly, in many passages in Chronicles, which is dated to the post-exilic period, Elohim appears instead of Yahweh in the parallel pages in Kings. This preference for Elohim over Yahweh was due in part to an increasing reticence to pronounce the proper name of Israel's God and in part to a conscious theological generalization of God in the post-exilic period, a movement from an emphasis on a national God to a God of the entire universe. The latter explanation may also account for the predominance of the designation in Israel's wisdom literature, which is concerned not so much with a covenant people as with the experience of all people.

2. Eloah

Related to the plural form ʾelohim is the singular ʾeloah. The Hebrew term appears far less frequently than the plural form, occurring only 57 times in the Bible; its Aramaic equivalent, ʾelah is attested 96 times in the Aramaic portions of the Bible. As a divine name, Eloah occurs most frequently in late texts, the overwhelming majority, 41 times, being in the book of Job. The significance of this distribution is unclear. It is possible that the term, though present already in archaic Hebrew poetry (Ps 18:31 [Heb. 18:32]; Hab 3:3), may

have become more common as a result of foreign influences, particularly Aramaic. The preponderance of the name in the book of Job, though, may be explained differently. The book is set somewhere in the Transjordan, in the region around Edom and North Arabia, and this particular name for the deity may have been chosen to give the speeches a foreign flavor. The ancient poem in Hab 3, after all, declared that Eloah came from Teman (Hab 3:3).

3. El

The noun ʾel is the common Semitic term for "god." In ancient Canaan, however, ʾel became the name of the chief deity of the pantheon. In Canaanite mythology, El was portrayed as a god senior not only in rank but also in age—an ancient god. He is known in Ugaritic literature as ab shnm "Father of Years" (CTU 1.4.iv.24), characterized as the progenitor of gods and humans and portrayed as having a grey beard (CTU 1.3.v.2, 25; 1.4.v.4). He was also seen as a gracious figure, frequently called "Beneficent El, the Compassionate" (CTU 1.4.iv.58; 1.6.iii.4, 10, 14; 1.16.v.23). He presides over the divine council and is called king (CTU 1.2.iii.5; 1.3.v.36; 1.4.i.5; iv.24, 38) and judge, as also evident in the personal name "El is (my) Judge." In Ugaritic mythology, he is known by the epithet "Bull El" (CTU 1.2.i.33, 36; 1.3.v.35; 1.14.1.41), a designation signifying virility. Much of the characterization of El as a benign old king is corroborated by iconography, where the deity is typically depicted sitting on a cherubim-throne, with a long beard, right hand raised in benediction, and sometimes with horns on his head, which recall his designation as "bull." El was thought to have had his abode in the remote mountains, at "the source of the double deep" (CTU 1.2.iii.4, 3.v.7, 4.iv.22)—the Tigris and Euphrates.

Many of the traits of Canaanite El are associated with the deity in the Bible, although, as one might expect in ancient Israel, Yahweh has taken over the role of El in many instances. As 2 Sam 22:32 has it, "Who is ʾel but Yahweh?" The scene in Psalm 82 of God (ʾel) presiding over the divine assembly and judging errant divine beings, for instance, is certainly reminiscent of the role of El in Canaanite mythology (see also Pss 89:7-8; 29:1). The depiction of Yahweh as "the Most High," assigning options to the "sons of El" (so Deut 32:8b, according to 4Q37 and LXX) recalls the role of El, an allusion corroborated by the reference in verse 6 to the deity as one who created people and formed them, with terms that echo the depiction of El in Ugaritic literature. Yahweh is revealed to Moses as "gracious and merciful God" (Exod 34:6; Deut 4:31), a characterization reminiscent of Canaanite depictions of El. In many cases, when ʾel is used in the Bible, the context suggests God's role as king, supreme ruler of the divine council, and creator. Thus, in depicting the myth of an attempted coup d'etat in heaven, Isaiah claims that the rebel meant to elevate his throne above the "stars of El" to sit on the "mount of assembly in the far reaches of the north" (Isa 14:13).

The deity, when known as El, was originally associated with the north, as the name Israel suggests, particularly in cities taken over from the local "Canaanite" populations.

C. Yahweh (יהוה YHWH)

Occurring 6,828 times in the Bible, this is by far the most common designation for God in the OT. The name appears over 40 times in the inscriptions of the monarchical period, as opposed to 2 times for Elohim and 5 times for El. It is the distinctive name of Israel's God; no other deity is known by it.

The earliest epigraphic evidence of the name Yahweh is in the Moabite Stone from the mid-9th cent. BCE (*KAI* 181). The earliest Hebrew evidence comes from eighth-century inscriptions from KUNTILLET ʿAJRUD in the Sinai Peninsula, where the form yhw (יהו *HI*, KAjr 9, 20.2) is probably to be vocalized as yahwē, since it occurs at the site along with YHWH (יהוה *HI*, KAjr 20.1). Outside the Bible and these inscriptions, the name is not found elsewhere. Claims that the name is found among the tablets of Ebla, Ugarit, or in Old Aramaic inscriptions cannot be sustained.

The precise pronunciation of the name is lost. Beginning at least in the post-exilic period, the name was deemed too sacred to pronounce. Hence, ʾadhonay (אֲדֹנָי, "my Lord") was articulated in its place, or, where the name is already preceded by ʾadhonay YHWH, ʾelohim was the substitute pronunciation (hence, "the Lord God"). As one reads in the Talmud, "the Holy One, blessed be He, said, 'I am not pronounced as I am written; I am written with YOD HE but pronounced by ALEF DALET'" (*b. Qidd* 71a). The ancient versions followed this convention, with the Septuagint generally rendering the name as Kyrios (Κυριος) and the Vulgate as *Dominus*, as do most modern English translations, which have "the LORD," with all letters in upper-case. In some Hebrew manuscripts from Qumran, which had no vowel points, four dots representing ʾdny or five dots representing ʾdwny (אדוני) were introduced to cue the reader to say ʾadhonay. Other manuscripts write the four letters, YHWH, in Paleo-Hebrew ("Phoenician") script, instead of the standard Aramaic square script of that time in order to give the name an archaic feel and indicate that the name should not be pronounced as written. Some Greek manuscripts also follow this method, writing the name in Hebrew script instead of Greek. When the Jewish scribes known as the "masoretes" began inserting vowel points to the manuscripts some time before the 10th cent. CE, they simply introduced the vowels for ʾadhonay, using the simple vocal shewa (ְ) underneath the initial letter (y) instead of the composite shewa (ֲ) that is required for the guttural alef

of ʾadny, followed by o and a. Beginning perhaps as early as the 12th cent., but certainly by the early 16th cent., Latin transcriptions of the name simply merged the consonants YHWH with the masoretic vowels for ʾadōnāy/ʾadonāy, thus giving us the forms Iehoua, Iehovah, or Jehovah. The last of these forms appeared a few times in the King James Version of 1611 and subsequent translations till the American Standard Version of 1901 increasingly rendered the divine name so. Modern scholarly reconstruction, however, suggests that the name was most probably pronounced as "Yahweh." This reconstruction is based on the Greek transcriptions of the name as Iaoue/Iaouai (Clement of Alexandria in the 3rd cent. CE) or Iabe/Iabai (known to the Samaritans, Theodoret of Cyrrhus and Epiphanius of Salamis, both of the 4th cent. CE). Complicating the matter are variant spellings of the name, yah (יָה)and yahu (יָהוּ), along with the theophoric element in proper names, yo ([יוֹ] going back to earlier *yaw-, as we know from cuneiform transcriptions of names) and yeho ([יְהוֹ] from earlier yahu). These have been transcribed Iao, Iaou, and Ia, the first two of these Greek transcriptions representing Hebrew yahu and yaw [יָו], while the last corresponds to Hebrew yah. Although scholars have reached a consensus about the pronunciation of the name, it is still the convention, whether following tradition or in deference to religious sensibilities, to render the name as "the LORD" or simply transcribe the letters Yahweh, leaving readers to pronounce the name according to their own scruples. Many Jews simply refer to the TETRAGRAMMATON as HA SHEM ("the Name").

Related to the issue of its pronunciation is the question of the name's etymology. The folk etymology is provided in Exod 3:14. In response to the suggestion of Moses that the Israelites would want to know the name of the deity who was sending Moses to them, God said, "ʾeheyeh ʾasher ʾeheyeh" (אֶהְיֶה אֲשֶׁר אֶהְיֶה 'I am who I am or 'I will be who I will be'). Thus you shall say to them, ʾehyeh has sent me to you." Hosea, too, records this etymology when he has Yahweh declaring to Israel, "and I will not be ʾehyeh to you" (Hos 1:9), meaning God will not longer be with them (compare 2:23 [Heb 2:25]). One might infer, therefore, that God's name must have been yihweh (יְהוֶה, "He is" or "He will be"). This etymology assumes that the root hwy (הוי) in the divine name is a by-form of hyy (היי), the more common verb for "to be" in Hebrew, a reasonable assumption, since hwy is used in that sense in a few passages. Still, the name is cryptic, and perhaps intentionally so. It could mean that the deity is inscrutable, indefinable, or Wholly Other. It could also be understood as a promise of divine presence: "he will be (present)." If this etymology is original, however, one has to account for the evidence that suggests that yahweh (יְהוֶה, the causative form) is the pronunciation of the name, rather than yihweh.

Assuming that yahweh is the primitive pronunciation, one might consider the form to be causative, "he causes to be," thus, "he brings into being" or "he creates." Some scholars, therefore, imagine an original sentence name, such as "El Creates (Israel or the winds), "El Who Creates", or "El Who Creates the Hosts," and so on. In support of such reconstructions, scholars note analogues from the Amorite onomasticon, like yakhwi-ilum ("May God Preserve"). Others, however, doubt the reliability of the folk etymology's connection of the root hwy to the root hyy and question the relevance of the Amorite parallels (Knauf 1984; van der Toorn 1999). Rather, they relate the divine name not to hwy/hyh (היה) "to be" but to hwy "to fall" or "to blow," hence the causative form yahweh would mean "he causes (rain) to fall" or "he causes (the wind) to blow" or simply, "he blows," all appropriate names for a storm deity. Yet, there is no evidence that the ancient Israelites ever associated the name with any other verb except the verb "to be." Moreover, a strong argument can be made that as far as the significance of the name within the Bible is concerned, the only etymology that matters is the theological one.

Some, who challenge the Israelite or even West-Semitic origin of the name, argue that the earliest occurrence of the name is, in fact, in two Egyptian inscriptions from temples in Nubia, in modern Sudan. The first dates to the time of Amenophis III, around 1400 BCE. The second, in part a copy of the first, is from the reign of Ramses II in the 13th cent. Both inscriptions contain a list of place-names, each preceded by the designation "land of Shasu," the term Shasu being Egyptian for Semitic nomads from the Transjordan, anywhere from Syria to the Sinai. Among the places mentioned as belonging to the territories of these nomads is one called yhw3, which many have related to the name Yahweh. To be sure, yhw3 is not a divine name but a place name in these inscriptions. Still, scholars imagine that the divine name Yahweh might have been related to the place name somehow. The early identification of the name with Yahweh of the Israelites gained traction because one of the other toponyms in the later list mentions another place name, s'rr (שערר), which has been identified as biblical Seir, that is, Edom. That identification, if correct, corroborates the linkage of the place yhw3 to Israel's deity, since Yahweh is said to have come from that region "Yahweh, when you proceeded from Seir // when you marched from the country of Edom" (Judg 5:4; compare Deut 33:2). Though tantalizing, the connection between the name yhw3 and Yahweh, who came from Seir, is not certain.

Several lines of evidence point to a southern desert origin of Yahweh. A number of archaic poems suggest that Yahweh originated from the region. The ancient Song of Deborah, which recounts Yahweh's going forth from Seir // the country of Edom, calls the deity zeh sinay (זֶה סִינַי) "the one of Sinai" (Judg 5:4-5; see also Ps 68:8-9, 18). The Song of Moses, also an archaic text, refers to the deity appearing from Sinai // Seir and shining forth from Mount Paran // Meribat Kadesh (Deut 33:2), while the ancient poem of Yahweh's theophany in Hab 3 speaks of Eloah coming from the south // Mount Paran (Hab 3:3). The inscriptions from Kuntillet ʿAjrud, too, mention "Yahweh of Teman" (HI, KAjr 14.1-2) and "Yahweh of the Teman/the South" (HI, KAjr 20.1), names that may suggest local Yahwisms, in this case, northern and southern. Moreover, biblical sources affirm that the Israelites came to know Yahweh through a revelation to Moses in the Sinai desert (Exod 3:9-15; 6:2-9). Some scholars in the 19th cent. proposed that Yahweh might have originally been a "Kenite" or "Midianite" deity introduced to Moses by his father-in-law, who is identified as a Kenite in some sources (Judg 1:16; 4:11) and a Midianite in others (Exod 2:16; 3:1; 18:1; Num 10:29). Bracketing the question of the role of Moses, a few more recent scholars still deem it likely that the deity Yahweh originated among southern desert nomads. If Yahweh of the southern desert was indeed a storm deity, as the evidence suggests, it is easy to see how that tradition could have been adapted to Canaanite tradition of the storm deity, Baal (Hadad). That view of God would also merge with the tradition of God as El, a tradition at home in the settled cities of Canaan.

Despite the difficulty of corroborating many historical details about the priestly version of the Mosaic origin of Yahwism (Exodus 6), the southern desert provenance of Yahweh seems reliable enough. Even though other sources presume knowledge of Yahweh from the beginning (Gen 4:26), P suggests that Yahweh had hitherto been known to Israel's ancestors as El Shaddai, but the name Yahweh was revealed first to Moses (Exod 6:2-3), while a parallel account suggests that God was simply known as the deity of the ancestors (Exod 3:14-15).The claim gains credence when one notes that among the proper names from the ancestral period of Israel's history, not a single one is Yahwistic (that is, having Yahweh or some form of it as part of the name), with Joshua being the first indisputable Yahwistic name. Moreover, the sanctuaries from the period are often associated with El, including the designations ʾel ʿelyon (אֵל עֶלְיוֹן), ʾel bethʾel (אֵל בֵּיתאֵל), ʾel ʿolam (אֵל עוֹלָם), El-Creator of Heaven and Earth, and ʾel roʾi (אֵל רָאִי), while the God of the ancestors is often depicted as having El traits.

D. God/Lord of Hosts

The English designation "LORD of Hosts" translates Hebrew YHWH tsevaʾoth (יהוה צְבָאוֹת), an epithet that occurs 261 times in the Bible, along with the variants "Yahweh, God of Hosts" (19 times), "God of Hosts" (19 times), and, the syntactically anomalous forms, yahweh ʾelohim tsevaʾoth (4 times) and ʾelohim tsevaʾoth (1 time). The name is typically rendered in the Septuagint as kyrios pantokratēr (κυριος παντοκρατηρ, "Lord Almighty") or tseva'oth is simply transcribed, thus, kyrios sabaōth (κυριος σαβαωθ, 56 times), the form found in the NT (Rom 9:29; Jas 5:4).

The epithet does not occur in the Pentateuch or in Joshua and Judges. Its first appearance in the Bible is in connection with the sanctuary at Shiloh in association with the ark, which was associated with the enthroned presence of God (1 Sam 4:4). The notion of Yahweh as an enthroned king recalls the Canaanite perception of El. Indeed, there are reasons to believe that the cult at Shiloh was connected with Yahweh as El (Seow 1989). It has been suggested, therefore, that the epithet of the deity was originally 'el tseva'oth ("God of Hosts"), the hosts referring at once to the celestial hosts (the luminaries of the heavens) that represent the armies that accompanied the divine warrior (e.g., 1 Sam 17:45) and to the hosts of divine beings that attend the divine council (e.g., Ps 89:5-11 [Heb. 89:6-12]).

E. Lord

The epithet "Lord" is a virtual name of God in many instances.

1. Baal

Though most commonly associated with the Canaanite deity known as Baal Hadad (ba'al hadhadh [בַּעַל הֲדַד] "the lord Hadad"), the term ba'al ("lord") must once have applied to Israel's God (see BAAL). This is evident in the fact that some children and grandchildren of Yahwists like Saul and David were given ba'al names like Ishbaal (2 Sam 4:1, 5; 1 Chr 8:33), Mephibaal (1 Chr 4:4), Meribbaal (1 Chr 8:34), and Beeliada (1 Chr 14:7; 2 Sam 5:16 LXX). In all these cases, ba'al in the name simply referred to Yahweh as "Lord." Moreover, just as the traits of El were assumed by Yahweh in Israelite religion, so too were many of the traits of the Canaanite "Lord" (that is, Baal Hadad) applied to Yahweh, notably the notions of the deity as divine warrior and life-giving rain. The danger of Yahweh being given the precise title and bearing the traits of the Canaanite god, however, is that the two "lords" were too easily identified with one another. Thus, in the face of syncretism in 8th-cent. Israel, the prophet Hosea declared that henceforth, Yahweh would no longer be called ba'li (בַּעְלִי) "my Baal" (Hos 2:16 [Heb. 2:18]). In due course, the ba'al element in the personal names from the early monarchy was changed to the more acceptable term, 'el, so that Beeliada was called Eliada (2 Sam 5:16; 2 Chr 3:8), or, in a polemic against Baalism, the term bosheth (בֹּשֶׁת "shame") substituted for ba'al (thus Ishbaal, Mephibaal, and Meribbaal became Ishbosheth, Mephiboshet, and Meriboshet).

2. Adon/Adonai

Unlike ba'al, known above all as the honorific of the Canaanite god Baal Hadad, the term 'adhon (אָדוֹן), a synonym of ba'al, did not carry such theological baggage. Hence, 'adhon ("lord") was an acceptable alternative, as in the epithet, "Lord of all the earth" (Josh 3:11, 13; Ps 97:5; Mic 4:13; Zech 4:14; 6:5). The term, together with the more common form, 'adhonay ("my lord"), was used in apposition with Yahweh (thus, "[my] Lord Yahweh," so especially in Ezekiel), in parallelism with Yahweh (e.g., Exod 15:17; Isa 3:17), and as a substitute for Yahweh (Isa 6:1). Indeed, the usage of this designation became common due to theological scruples associated with the sacred name, Yahweh.

F. El Epithets

In addition to the general designation, the term 'el is specified in names like 'el shadday (אֵל שַׁדָּי), 'el 'elyon, 'el 'olam, 'el berith (אֵל בְּרִית), and 'el ro'i, some of which may have been tied to particular sites where the deity was venerated.

1. El Shadday

This divine name occurs 7 times in the Bible, while the shorter form, shadday by itself, appears 38 times. The name is not unique to Israel, for an analogous form of it appears in Ugaritic, il shd (CTU 1.108.102), and apparently as a theophoric element in Egyptian transcriptions of West Semitic names, Ugaritic, Phoenician, and Thamudic (an old South Arabian dialect). Its etymology is uncertain and various conjectures have been made by scholars. The most widely-accepted is the view that shadday is related to Akkadian shadu "mountain" and, hence, 'el shadday would mean "El, the One of the Mountain(s)," the ending –ay being adjectival. Accordingly, Hebrew shadday is connected: 1) with Old Babylonian references to the god of the Amurru as bel shade "lord of the mountains," 2) with the fact that the gods are frequently called "mountain" in the ANE, a phenomenon reminiscent of the divine epithet "Rock," properly "Mountain," in the Bible (note the personal name, surishadday [צוּרִישַׁדָּי] "shadday is my Mountain"), and 3) with the cosmic mountain, where El was believed to have resided, the mountain where El presided over his assembly (see Isa 14:13). Pertinent, too, is the fact that the gods of the divine council in the plaster inscription from Deir 'Alla in the Transjordan are called both 'lhn "gods" and shdyn, perhaps so named because of the locus of the divine assembly—in the cosmic mountain. The supreme deity of the assembly would, thus, be the quintessential shadday. Yet, the etymological connection of shadday with Akkadian shadu is not without problems, since Akkadian shadu corresponds phonologically to Hebrew sadheh (שָׂדֶה) or sadhay (שָׂדַי not shadday) and the Thamudic personal name 'lsdy would suggest Hebrew 'lsdy (אֵלְשֵׂדִי) instead of 'lshdy (אֵלְשַׁדִּי).

The Septuagint typically renders the name as pan tokratōr "almighty" and the Vulgate usually has omnipotens, though the latter may reflect an explanation, evident in Jewish exegesis (b. Hagg. 12a), that shadday is derived from sha + day (שַׁ + דַּי), "the one who is (self) sufficient." Indeed, Aquila and Symmachus, Jewish translators of the Hebrew scripture into Greek, rendered the name as hikanos (ἱκανός "sufficient, able"), as does LXX in a few instances. That is unlikely to have been the original meaning of the name. The divine name shadday appears in wordplays with shadayim (שָׁדַיִם) "breast" (Gen 49:25-26) and shodh (שֹׁד) "destruction" (Isa 13:6 = Joel 1:15), but neither of these represents viable etymologies.

Regardless of its true etymology, what seems clear is that shadday is an epithet of El. Hence, shadday is associated with blessings (Gen 28:3; 48:3; 49:25), fecundity (Gen 28:3; 35:11), mercy (Gen 43:14), which in Canaanite mythology was a gift of El, and visions (Num 24:4, 16), a mode by which El was known. The name is also associated with the function of God as divine warrior (Ps 68:14 [Heb. 68:15]; Isa 13:6; Ezek 1:24; Joel 1:15; Job 6:5) and protector (Ps 91:1). Naomi's complaint of having been dealt with bitterly by shadday (Ruth 1:20-21) is, therefore, probably meant to be ironic.

According to the priestly tradition source in Exod 6:3, God was known to the ancestors of Israel in pre-Mosaic times as ʾel shadday (see also Gen 17:1; 28:3; 35:11; 43:14, 48:3). Despite the preponderance of the name in exilic and post-exilic contexts, that priestly claim should not be dismissed as a later invention. The name shadday is, after all, a divine element in personal names of West Semites from the second millennium BCE onwards, and the priestly work manifests other many archaisms. The frequent usage of shadday in the book of Job may, similarly, be explained as an archaism, for the tale presumes a setting like that of Israel's ancestors. Perhaps not coincidentally, shadday is a theophoric element in personal names for three individuals from the Mosaic period (Num 1:5, 6, 12), but not later, although the ancient name would reappear as a Jewish name in documents from Elephantine in the post-exilic period.

2. El Elyon

This specific formulation, meaning "El, the (Most) High," occurs in Gen 14:18, 19, 20, 22 and Ps 78:35, but ʾel and ʿelyon appear together as parallel terms in Num 24:16; Pss 57:2 [Heb. 57:3]; 73:11; 107:11. The passage in Genesis 14 suggests that ʾel ʿelyon was the designation of pre-Israelite (Canaanite) Jerusalem, called Salem in that passage. The context points to the deity as superior to others. Elsewhere, too, ʿelyon suggests God's supremacy over others (Deut 32:8; Isa 14:14) and, not surprisingly, the epithet is applied to Yahweh (1 Sam 22:14; Pss 7:17 [Heb. v. 18]; 18:13 [Heb. v. 14], etc.).

3. El, Creator of Heaven and Earth

Appearing only in Gen 14:19, 22 (where it is juxtaposed with ʾel ʿelyon), this formulation is expanded from the more common epithet, ʾl qn(h) ʾrts "El, Creator of the Earth," attested on a fragmentary inscription from Jerusalem (*HI*, Jslm 78.3), in Phoenician, Punic, Palmyrene, and Greek inscriptions, as well as in the Hittite story Ilkunirsa (= West Semitic ʾl qn ʾrts).

4. El Roi

This designation is attested only in Gen 16:13 and associated with Beer-Lahai-Roi ("Well of the Living One Who Sees Me"), the "Living One" being an epithet of El (Josh 3:10; Hos 1:10 [Heb. 2:1]; Pss 42:2 [Heb. v. 3]; 84:2 [Heb. v. 3]). Taking the masoretic vocalization of the name at face value, the name may be explained to mean "God of Seeing" or, if one accepts the folk etymology in the passage and revocalizes the Hebrew slightly, "God Who Sees Me."

5. El Olam

The designation ʾel ʿolam—meaning, probably, "El, the eternal one" or "El, the Ancient One"—appears as an epithet of Yahweh in Gen 21:33, a story set in Beersheba. The epithet is reminiscent of the assumption in mythology about the antiquity of El, as suggested also by the designation of God as "the Ancient of Days" (Dan 7:9). By itself, ʿolam may refer to the deity, as in Dan 12:7, which refers to an oath sworn in the name of haʿolam (הָעוֹלָם), "the Eternal One" or "the Ancient One." Dan 4:31 also refers to praise given to Most High, who is known as "the Eternal/Ancient Living One."

6. El Berit

Judg 9:46 mentions a temple of ʾel berith in Shechem, which has been associated with the il brt mentioned in a Hurrian hymn, a tantalizing connection, since the Amarna letters record that there was a sizable Hurrian presence in Shechem. See also LXX of Gen 34:2, where the Greek has "the Hurrian" instead of "the Hivvite" in MT in the description of the ethnic origin of the city. Yet the local deity of Shechem is called baʿal berith in 8:33 and the local temple is "the temple of Baal Berit" (9:4), which is certainly the same as "the temple of El-Berit." Hence, ʾel berith may be interpreted as meaning "god of the covenant," namely for Shechem, Baal.

G. Kinship Terms

A number of terms derived from familial structures signify God's intimate relationship with people.

1. Father, Mother

Expressing convictions about God as giver or life, provider, and protector, God is addressed as father in Jer 3:4, 19; Isa 63:16; 64:8 (Heb. 64:7). This view is corroborated by the fact that many personal names in the Bible have "father" as a theophoric element:

e.g., Eliab ("My God is Father"), Abijah ("Yahweh is Father"). In the NT, too, God is addressed as "Abba, Father"—a redundant name, with the Aramaic and Greek equivalents occurring together (Mark 14:36; Rom 8:15; Gal 4:6) and Jesus taught his disciples to pray to "our Father in heaven" (Matt 6:9; *see* ABBA). Biblical imagery of God is also maternal: God is described as conceiving, giving birth, and nursing Israel (Num 11:12; Deut. 32:18; Isa 46:3-4). *See* GOD THE FATHER.

2. Brother

The term "brother" (ʾakh אָח) designates God in personal names like Ahijah ("yh is my [divine] Brother") and Ahimelech ("My [divine] Brother is King"). Such names suggest that God is one's next-of-kin, the one who redeems and protects.

3. Uncle

Also appearing as a kinship term for God is ʾam (עַם), a term for one's father's brother (as opposed to a mother's brother), as in Ammiel ("ammiʾel עַמִּיאֵל "ʾel is my [divine] Paternal Uncle").

4. Husband

Hosea, who uses the relationship between a man and a woman as a metaphor for the covenant relationship between Yahweh and Israel, records that Israel once called baʿali "my lord" (meaning also "my husband") but would, because of the confusion. Israel had between Yahweh as "lord" and Hadad as "lord," no longer call God that way. Rather, God would be known not as baʿali but as ʾishi (אִישִׁי "my husband"; Hos 2:16). This designation suggests covenant relationship between God and people as one involving love and faithfulness.

H. Other Designations of God

1. Holy One

The designation, qadhosh (קָדוֹשׁ "Holy One"), appears as a free-standing form for God in the archaic poem in Hab 3, where it parallels ʾeloah, and is said to have come from the south (Hab 3:3; see also Isa 40:25). The plural form, qedhoshim (קְדֹשִׁים with the "plural of majesty"), is also used to mean God in a few instances (Hos 12:1; Prov 9:10; 30:3). More common is the designation "Holy One of Israel," which occurs 31 times (the vast majority being in Isaiah), along with its variations, "Holy One of Jacob" (Isa 29:23) and "my/their/your [i.e., Israel's] Holy One" (Isa 10:17; 43:15; 49:7; Hab 1:12). These designations point to the deity as the wholly transcendent one (see Isa 6:3; 55:8; Hos 11:9), though in the NT, Jesus, the manifestation of divine presence on earth, is called "the Holy One" (Mark 1:24; Luke 4:34; John 6:69; Acts 3:14; Rev 3:7). The "Holy One" in 1 John 2:20 is perhaps deliberately ambiguous, possibly meaning both God and Jesus.

2. Jealous

Exod 34:14 refers to Yahweh as a God whose name is "Jealous," but elsewhere "jealous" is an adjective applied to the deity, as in the phrase ʾel qannaʾ (אֵל קַנָּא), "a jealous God" (Exod 20:5; Deut 4:34; 5:9; 6:15). This designation of God appears to be at home in the northern kingdom, Israel. It suggests that God is one who demands absolute allegiance and will brook no compromise.

3. Mighty One

The epithet, ʾavir yaʿaqov (אֲבִיר יַעֲקֹב) was originally associated with the ark of covenant, an emblem of the north, Israel (Gen 49:24; Ps 132:2, 5), though it is found in later texts as well (Isa 49:26; 60:10; Sir 51:12). A variant form of the epithet, ʾavir yisraʾel (אֲבִיר יִשְׂרָאֵל) is found alongside the name Yahweh Sabaoth, a name that is also linked to the ark (Isa 1:24). Since these epithets seem to be associated with the north and tied to the notion of God as King, it is likely that ʾabir originally meant "bull," a term reminiscent of El's designation as "bull" in Ugaritic literature. The term was originally a metaphor for the might of the deity.

4. Fear of Isaac

The epithet pakhadh yitskhaq (פַּחַד יִצְחָק "fear of Isaac") appears only in the Bible (Gen 31:42), though it is obviously related to the variant form, pakhadh ʾaviw yitskhaq (פַּחַד אָבִיו יִצְחָק "fear of his father, Isaac," Gen 31:53). An older argument—on the basis of cognates in Ugaritic, Palmyene, and Arabic—that the term pakhadh means "kinsman," hence "kinsman of Isaac," once widely accepted, has been effectively challenged on philological grounds. Other derivations of the term have failed to convince. When all is said and done, it is unlikely that the ancient readers of the story in Genesis would have connected pakhadh with anything other than the primary meaning on the term in the Bible: fear. The term probably alludes at once to the awe that the deity engenders in the devotee and to the terror that is manifested in the protection of the devotee.

5. Shield (of Abraham)

The designation, "Shield of Abraham," is attested only in the Hebrew text of Sir 51:12, though it is certainly related to the claim in Gen 15:1 that God is a shield (maghen מָגֵן) to Abram. The designation suggests God's role as protector and deliverer (see Deut 33:29; 2 Sam 22:3, 31).

6. Rock

The word tsur (צוּר "rock"), a synonym of "mountain" (har [הַר], Job 14:18) and "crag" (selaʿ [סֶלַע], Deut 32:13; Isa 2:211; Ps 71:3), which are places of refuge, is used of God both as a metaphor and as an appellative. The former is evident in personal names like Elizur ("My God is a Rock," Num 1:5) and Zurishaddai ("My Rock is Shadday," Num 1:6). The latter is corroborated by the name Pedahzur ("The Rock has Redeemed," Num 1:10).

In the metaphorical usage, God is called "the rock of salvation" (Deut 32:13; 2 Sam 22:47; Pss 89:26 [Heb. 89:27]; 95:1), "the rock of refuge" (Pss 31:2 [Heb. 31:3]; 91:3; 94:22; Isa 17:10), "rock of strength" (Ps 62:8), or "the rock of (one's) heart" (Ps 73:26), in all cases suggesting stability, strength, or reliability. It is in that sense that God is called tsur 'olamim (צוּר עוֹלָמִים "everlasting rock" Isa 26:4). The KJV interprets the expression as "everlasting strength," though a marginal note suggests "Rock of Ages," an epithet that has been popularized in Christian hymnody. Thus, "Rock" could be used as a synonym for God (Deut 32:4, 18, 30) and God is addressed directly as such (Hab 1:12). Hence, Deut 32:18 speaks of Rock that has begotten a people, along with God who has birthed them (Deut 32:18; compare Ps 89:26). In most of these cases, where Rock is a name for God, LXX typically renders Rock as theos ("God").

In the NT, Christ is said to be the rock, though the allusion there is to the incident at Meribah, where water was miraculously made to flow from a rock (Num 20:2-8).

Bibliography: M. C. Astour. "Yahweh in Egyptian Topographic Lists." *Festschrift Elmar Edel.* M. Görg and E. Pusch, eds. (1979) 17–34; J. Barr. "The Symbolism of Names in the Old Testament." *BJRL* 52 (1969) 11–29; F. M. Cross. *Canaanite Myth and Hebrew Epic* (1973); W. H. Brownlee. "The Ineffable Name of God." *BASOR* 226 (1977) 39-46; O. Eissfeldt. "El and Yahweh." *JSS* 1 (1956) 25–37; D. N. Freedman. "The Name of the God of Moses." *JBL* 79 (1960) 151–56. D. N. Freedman. "Divine Names and Titles in Early Hebrew Poetry." *Magnalia Dei: The Mighty Acts of God.* F. M. Cross, et al., eds. (1976) 55–107; J. A. Hackett. *The Balaam Text from Deir ʿAlla* (1984); D. Hillers. "Paḥad Yiṣḥaq," *JBL* 91 (1972) 90–94; A. Klawek. "The Name Jahveh in the Light of Most Recent Discussion" *FO* 27 (1990) 11–12; T.N.D. Mettinger. *In Search of God: The Meaning and Message of the Everlasting Names* (1988); C. L. Seow. *Myth, Drama, and the Politics of David's Dance* (1989); M. S. Smith. "Yahweh and Other Deities in Ancient Israel: Observations on Problems and Recent Trends." *Ein Gott Allein?* W. Dietrich and M. A. Klopfenstein, ed. (1994) 198–234.

C. L. SEOW

GOD, NT VIEW OF [θεός theos]. The NT view of God reflects both continuity and discontinuity with the OT. God's love is now revealed in a new way in Jesus. The cross and resurrection are the heart and climax of this revelation, making possible and universalizing a new experience of God as Father, through the Son, in the Holy Spirit (see GOD, OT VIEW OF).

A. Methodologies
  1. Literary and linguistic
  2. Social scientific
  3. Historical-critical
  4. Reflexive
  5. Canonical
B. The Old Testament and Its Fulfilment
C. God and Jesus
  1. God
  2. Gospels
  3. Jesus and the kingdom of God
  4. The Father and the Son
D. The Resurrection and "New Creation"
  1. Eschatology and christology
  2. Pneumatology and missiology
  3. Ecclesiology and ethics
E. God Is Love
F. Jewish Monotheism and the New Testament View of God
G. New Testament Writers and Their Understanding of God
  1. The Gospels and Acts
  2. Paul
  3. Other New Testament letters
  4. The Apocalypse
H. Interpretation
Bibliography

A. Methodologies

For undertaking a study of God in the NT, several methodologies are necessary: literary and linguistic, social scientific, historical-critical, reflexive, and canonical.

1. Literary and linguistic

Literary and linguistic methods examine the words used about God, and the sentences, contexts, narratives, and literary genres (esp. the four Gospels), in which they are used. In view of the ubiquity, both explicitly and implicitly, of "God" in the texts, very little is excluded from our enquiry. Theology embraces at least eschatology, christology, pneumatology, missiology, ecclesiology, and ethics, since theology, as expressed in the NT, is concerned with a revelation that changes human lives, creates new communities, and foreshadows the destiny, in the purpose of God, of creation itself.

2. Social scientific

New Testament language about God is refracted through the lenses of particular cultures, societies, and traditions. Three socio-cultural themes especially concern us: the fundamental importance of honor, the patron and client system that provided the social cement of the ancient world, and Judaism's concern for purity and holiness.

3. Historical-critical

The texts point to a revelation rooted in history,

and the documents themselves, with their authors and intended readers, were grounded in specific, historical contexts. Jesus of Nazareth, and all that flowed from him, is the heart of this history.

4. Reflexive

The texts describe divine "imprints" on human lives, especially the life of Jesus "the Son" and his apostle, Paul, but also on the life of ecclesial communities, even if the imprint was, at times, more a vocation than a reality.

5. Canonical

We need to consider the witness of all the writers, giving due weight to the distinctiveness of each, and attempting a theological synthesis. Finally, the God of the NT cannot really be viewed from the outside, but only from the perspective of faith.

B. The Old Testament and Its Fulfilment

The God of the NT is not different from, or other than, the God of the OT, but rather the same God (e.g., 2 Cor 4:6). Specifically, in the NT, as well as in the OT, God creates and calls into existence both a world and a people (e.g., Gen 1-2; 12:1-3; Rom 4:17); God, in God's holiness and righteousness, acts to redeem God's people, and God's covenant with them is the very foundation of their life (e.g., Deut 29:1-3; Josh 24; Heb 12:18-24); God entrusts God's name (i.e., God's very being) to God's people (Exod 3:13-15; John 17:26); God's glory also signifies his presence with them (e.g., Ezek 8:4; Luke 2:9); that glory is associated especially with the divine light and its transforming power, and with God's sovereignty and victory, both now and in the future (e.g., Isa 40:5; Phil 2:9-11); although God is already king, God's kingship is not universally acknowledged, but on the Day of the Lord it will be (e.g., Ps 96:10-13; 1 Pet 4:13; Rev 21:23); God loves God's people, and, in this love, also judges them—i.e., both refines and vindicates them (e.g., Deut 4:37; Hos 11:1; Col 3:13; Prov 3:12a; Heb 12:6). God's faithfulness is expressed through God's promises (e.g., Gen 12:7; Acts 13:32-33), God's will and purpose through his word, and his law (Exod 20:1-17; John 1:17a). Thus the same actions are predicated of God in the OT and NT: God creates (calls), speaks and promises, loves and saves, judges and vindicates. In more personal terms, God remains the God of Abraham, Isaac, and Jacob (Mark 12:26 and par.), of Moses (Heb 11:23-24) and of the prophets (Luke 1:70). Finally, the OT unwearyingly repeats: beside God there is, and there must not be, any other god. That is a truth that becomes increasingly clear, and at the same time, comprises a command (e.g., Isa 44:6; Ex 20). So, in the NT, although Paul acknowledges contemporary polytheism (1 Cor 8:6), the reality is "one God."

The NT witness to God rests on these foundations. Yet there is development, and even discontinuity. Chris-

tology cannot simply be bolted on to the OT. Something new has happened. The songs of Mary and of Zachariah (Luke 1:46-55, 69-79)—both mosaics of OT imagery and allusions—bear witness to God's "new thing." God fulfils the promises to redeem, and to be with, the people drawn now, in the light of the new revelation, from all nations. So God brings into being a "new creation" in Christ, and, consequently, major biblical themes—notably the divine righteousness, holiness and glory—are developed and changed.

In the OT, particularly in Deutero-Isaiah, God's holiness and saving action on behalf of Israel belong together (e.g., Isa 43:3; 47:4; 48:17). God's holiness is to be authentic always and everywhere in God's love for God's people and in opposition to evil. God, in God's action for Israel and the world, is not compromised or corrupted. In the NT, however, the word "holy" is only rarely (e.g., Rev 4:8) used of God, and infrequently of Jesus (e.g., John 6:69). But it occurs frequently with reference to the Holy Spirit, and is used of new Christian communities ("the holy ones"—e.g., Rom 1:7; 1 Cor 1:2). This shift in language suggests that there has been inaugurated a relocation of, and a wider participation in, the holy (see HOLY, HOLINESS, NT; HOLY SPIRIT).

Similarly, God's righteousness is now understood in a new light. God's righteousness in the prophets comes to fruition in right relationships among humans, between humans and their Creator, and in the healing of creation (e.g., Isa 11:1-9; 58:2-6). In the NT specific references to God's righteousness are confined almost entirely to the Pauline writings (Matt 6:32; Jas 1:20; and 1 John 3:10 are rare exceptions), corresponding, theologically, to "the kingdom of God" in the synoptic teaching of Jesus. According to Paul, God's righteousness has been revealed "apart from the law" (Rom 3:21), so that here, too, there is both continuity and discontinuity.

Thirdly, there is development as well as fulfilment in the understanding of the divine glory. Paul argues that the brilliance of the new revelation exceeds the old, but also implies that the divine glory, like the divine holiness, is both relocated and more widely shared (2 Cor 3:7, compare John 17:22; see GLORY, GLORIFY).

Finally, the development and change in the NT understanding of God is reflected in a spatial and geographical shift, from the land of Israel and its Temple to new communities both within in and beyond Israel.

In biblical theology this image and truth belong together. In the OT two interacting stories unfold: the story of God and the human story (e.g., the story of Adam, Abraham, Israel). The two stories converge in the NT in the person who is God's Son. The destiny of Adam finds its fulfillment in Jesus, the last Adam (1 Cor 15:45; Luke 3:23-38), and the very image of God (e.g., John 1:14; 2 Cor 4:4). Thus the central message of the NT is that the Son of God is both the image of God and the truth about human existence. But at the heart of this revelation is a God who is "for us" and "with us" in a way that fulfils yet transcends the old. The interaction between the theology inherited from Israel's heritage, and what is now said about Jesus is crucial for the NT view of God. But we can only do justice to that view of God by telling the story of Jesus.

C. God and Jesus

1. God

The word theos was not a distinctively Christian word. But in contrast with contemporary writers, both Jewish and Greco-Roman, NT writers rarely qualify theos with an adjective. Theos occurs in combination with other concepts such as "the Kingdom," "the Son," "the Word," and "the righteousness" of God. Most significant of all is "the God and Father of our Lord Jesus Christ," and its cognate expressions.

2. Gospels

The Gospel of Mark moves quickly to summarize the message the Son brings: "the kingdom of God ēngiken (ἤγγικεν "has drawn near/arrived"). Luke expresses at greatest length the continuity with the old, but the celebration of what is new is also clear (e.g., 1:31-2, 68). Matthew proclaims God's presence in a new way ("Emmanuel," "God with us," 1:23), while John writes of the Word that was in the beginning with God, and was God (1:1), now "made flesh" (1:14; see INCARNATION).

3. Jesus and the kingdom of God

The kingdom of God, as proclaimed and lived by Jesus, is crucial to the NT view of God. "The kingdom" means God in God's self-revelation and sovereign presence, and so it is necessary to say both that "the kingdom" brought Jesus, and that Jesus brought "the kingdom." What the Synoptic Gospels for the most part imply, and John's Gospel more explicitly says, about "the Father" and "the Son" explicates the meaning of the kingdom and Jesus' relation to it (see KINGDOM OF GOD, KINGDOM OF HEAVEN).

Jesus specifically linked his exorcisms with the kingdom (Luke 11:20; Matt 12:28). More generally, his healing miracles, demonstrating the bias of Israel's God toward the poor, the least and the marginalized, are the well-nigh ubiquitous accompaniment of his proclamation of the kingdom. Other miracles ("mighty deeds," or, in John's Gospel, "signs"), recall the God of Israel, and, sometimes, his prophets: the God who feeds his people in the wilderness (Mark 6:34; Exod 16; 2 Kgs 4:42-44), who rescues his own from the chaos of the sea (Mark 4:34 and par.; Exod 14:21-31; Ps 107:23-32), who raises the dead (Luke 7:11-17; 1 Kgs 17:17-24; 2 Kgs 4:18-37), and who promises a superabundance of wine in the coming new age (John 2:1-11; compare Isa 25:6; Joel 3:18).

Yet the relationship with the old is stretched to breaking point. Jesus transgressed Jewish maps of holiness and of the purity system by touching lepers and other unclean people (e.g., Mark 1:39-45; 5:25-34 and par.). His meals with sinners and the failure of his disciples to fast, together with Sabbath controversies (Mark 2:13) provoked angry responses from the religious leaders

The teaching of Jesus, similarly, recalls OT teaching about God, but, at the same time, strikes a new note of authority and fulfillment. Leading characters in the parables are especially important, contravening by their behavior socio-cultural norms and expectations: a king forgives a slave (Matt 18:27), a vineyard owner sends his son into a dangerous situation (Mark 12:6), a patriarch acts in an unpatriarchal way by running to meet his wayward son (Luke 15:20); an employer pays his eleventh-hour workers with a generosity that was economic madness (Matt 20:8), a departing émigré disburses huge sums of money to his servants (Matt 25:15), and a sower sows seed with careless profligacy (Mark 4:3). All these figures in the parables of Jesus are germane to the NT view of God. Other images are surprising, if not iconoclastic. Contrary to expectations, the kingdom is hidden, insignificant, and small (Mark 4:30; Matt 13:33/Luke 13:20-21), but it will not always be so. In the end, the most unlikely people will be invited to the banquet of the kingdom (Luke 14:15-24). Even now, through his son Jesus, God is showing his concern for lost individuals (Luke 15).

The so-called divine passives in the teaching of Jesus also comprise an important part of his understanding of God. Many hint at a future sifting or reversal: "For all who exalt themselves will be humbled, and those who humble themselves will be exalted" (Luke 14:11). Others reflect a measure-for-measure theology: so "the instruments of someone's sin are the instruments of that person's punishment (Wis 11:16, Matt 7:1). Yet other divine passives express the overwhelming generosity of God (Luke 6:38; Matt 7:7//Luke 11:9).

4. The Father and the Son

Jesus may have spoken infrequently about "the Father." But, even if John's Gospel is, in part, an expansion of Jesus' original words, and some of Matthew's references to the Father are redactional (e.g., Matt 12:50; contrast Mark 3:35), we are still left with the Lord's Prayer, the father/son logion of Matt 11:27 and Luke 10:22, the parable of the Prodigal Son or Waiting Father (Luke 15:11-30), and the Abba-prayer of Jesus in Gethsemane (Mark 14:36; see GOD THE FATHER). The importance of the Aram. word ABBA, used by both adults and children of their earthly father, must not be overstated. Nevertheless, its occurrence, not only at Mark 14:36, but also at Gal 4:6 and Rom 8:15, suggests that it was remembered by the early church as a word used characteristically, if not uniquely, by Jesus, as a warm and intimate mode of address to God.

The OT uses the word *father* of God, though much less frequently than the NT. In the OT, God is the father of Israel, or of Israel's king (e.g., Isa 64:8; 2 Sam 7:14); in the NT, God is first and foremost the God and Father of Jesus, and, secondly, of those who come to God through Jesus. God has not changed, but now God has a Son "in whom God is pleased" (Mark 1:11; Matt 3:7). Only this Son knows the Father, who has entrusted "all things" to him (Matt 11:27; Luke 10:22), and, therefore, the Son, and only the Son, reveals the Father in a way that was not possible before (John 1:14-18; *see* SON OF GOD). Thus Jesus brings no new information about God, but a new view of God, in that by looking at, or through, this image, we may see God (John 14:9). But this is not possible without the mysterious alchemy of grace and obedient faith. People may look and look, and not see God at all, (Mark 4:12 and par.; John 6:36). Rather, they must hear God's Son, (Mark 9:7 and par.), follow (Mark 8:38), and believe, in order to see the glory of God (John 11:40). Yet even this happens only by divine agency: "No one knows the Father but the Son, and those to whom the Son chooses to reveal him" (Matt 11:27; Luke 10:22; compare John 6:44).

The teaching of Jesus about God, and the life that exemplified it, come to a crisis in the journey to Jerusalem, punctuated in the synoptics by a recurring prediction: "the Son of God must undergo great suffering" (Mark 8:31; 9:31; 10:33). Passive verbs, denoting divine agency, and the impersonal dei, ($\delta\epsilon\hat{\imath}$ lit. "it is necessary"), signifying the divine will and purpose, are used. The PASSION NARRATIVES of the Gospels, therefore, also contribute to the NT view of God. John offers a summarizing statement of the revelation that is about to take place: "Now the Son of Man has been glorified, and God has been glorified in him. If God has been glorified in him, God will also glorify him in himself, and will glorify him at once" (John 13:31-2). As often, John makes explicit, or recapitulates, theological themes implicit in the synoptics. In the synoptic passion narratives, references to God are infrequent, and God is nowhere the explicit subject of any verb. Jesus, too, is no longer the agent of action, but the passive recipient of it. He speaks infrequently, although even his silence is eloquent. The taunt of the high priests (Mark 15:31; Matt 27:42), or the elders (Luke 23:31), "he saved others, he cannot save himself" encapsulates the paradox of the divine revelation in the cross. (The taunt, "Save yourself" is specifically linked by Matthew with Jesus' status as Son of God [27:40, 43]). Important, too, is the darkness (Mark 15:33; Matt 27:45; Luke 23:44). It is a theological darkness. God's "face" in the OT is the source of light and well-being for humankind and the world (Num 6:25-26). Conversely, when God hides God's face, humankind are delivered "into the hand of our iniquity" (Isa 64:7; Rom 1:18). According to Mark and Matthew, none feels the darkness more acutely

than God's Son (Mark 15:34; Matt 27:46), and yet, is God absent?

The death of Jesus is inseparable from his resurrection; they are not two consecutive events, since Jesus died "to God," and therefore neither evil, nor the suffering inflicted by evil, separated the Son from the Father ultimately and irrevocably. On the far side of the darkness, a disciple will be enabled to say, "My Lord and my God" (John 20:28). This is why, according to several writers, the cross is the heart of the revelation (John 13:1-2; Rom 5:8; 1 John 3:16). So the Father and the Son were "glorified." The death of Jesus marked the Son's ultimate obedience to the Father (Phil 2:8; Heb 5:8; 12:2), the final surrendering of the Son by the Father (Rom 8:32), and the defining summary, climax and fulfillment of Jesus' revelation of God.

D. The Resurrection and "New Creation"

The claim "God raised Jesus from the dead" becomes as foundational for the NT understanding of God as the assertion "the Lord brought us out of Egypt" (Deut 26:8) was for the OT. The resurrection revealed the truth of the cross: not only that Jesus was God's loving, obedient Son, but also that God was Jesus' loving, faithful Father. The cross and resurrection, therefore, interpret each other, and in this reciprocal interpretation two kinds of language have especial significance: the language of sacrifice ("hand over" "send," "surrender") and the language of victory ("raised," "created," "glorified"). God's sacrifice and victory together make possible a new creation (e.g., Gal 6:15; 2 Cor 5:17; John 20:22; Gen 2:7), establish his kingdom, and release God's Spirit into human life and the world in a powerfully new way (John 19:30; 20:23 Acts 2:1-11; Rom 1:3-4).

In this new world eschatology, christology, pneumatology, missiology, ecclesiology, and ethics, all shed light on, and help to explicate the NT understanding of God in ways that confirm, illumine and transform "the old."

1. Eschatology and christology

God's kingdom or kingship is entrusted to "the Lord" who is now at God's right hand as God's vice-regent (e.g., Acts 2:33). (This is why "kingdom" language is infrequent outside the synoptics). Because the Son will hand over the kingdom to the Father at the End (1 Cor 15:24), "the DAY OF THE LORD" acquires the twofold meaning of the day of God and the day of the Lord (Jesus). "The Lord," in fact, is a title that, more than any other, expresses the interplay of theology and CHRISTOLOGY. Its frequency in the OT means that it is often not possible to determine whether "the Lord" in the NT, particularly in Acts and the letters, refers to God or to Jesus. It is a title that both identifies Jesus with God, and differentiates Jesus from God. Above all, against the socio-political background of "lords" as the source of patronage, and of Caesar's imperial lordship, the proclamation that the crucified Jesus was Lord was deeply counter-cultural and theologically iconoclastic (see ESCHATOLOGY OF THE NT).

2. Pneumatology and missiology

The Spirit in the NT is an eschatological phenomenon (2 Cor 1:23; Rom 8:23; Acts 2:17). The Spirit, in both Jewish and Christian understanding, is the dynamic power of God, creating, encountering, and transforming human beings. New Testament pneumatology fills out what OT and NT writers alike mean by calling God "the living God." God moves where God wills—not arbitrarily or randomly, but from a human perspective, unpredictably and surprisingly (John 3:8; Acts 10:45). God spoke—and speaks—through patriarchs, prophets, and apostles (e.g., Luke 1:67; Acts 1:16), God's Spirit endowed the ministry of Jesus with power (Luke 4:16; Mark 1:9-11 and par.), and equips his church for mission, propelling the church beyond familiar boundaries (John 20:19-23; Acts 1:8;13:2;16:7). In this mission, God's Spirit continues to embrace the outcast, as in the ministry of Jesus (Luke19:9; Gal 3:1-6). Thus, the Spirit now makes a home in mixed communities of Jews and Gentiles beyond the boundaries of "the holy land." In all of this, the Spirit exposes life, religion, and even scriptural interpretation that lack the Spirit's light and power (e.g., 2 Cor 3:4 -11).

So there is something surprising, even shocking, about the God of the NT. The offense of the gospel disturbs religious convictions (Matt 11:4-6//Luke 7:22; compare 1 Cor 1:23); "the more sin, the more grace" (Rom 5:20) is perhaps its most striking expression. Consequently, there is a marked reduction in the particularist language of the OT. For example, the expression "our God," so frequent in the OT, is almost entirely absent from the NT, and, at John 8:54, is criticized by Jesus. God remains God of the Jews (above all, Rom 11:26-29), but is God of the Gentiles also (Rom 3:29). Their territory is God's, as much as the land of Israel (Acts 7). All this was known to writers of the Jewish scriptures, and to later Jewish writers also, but now the universality of Israel's God finds new, practical expression in the law-free mission of the church to Gentiles in Gentile lands (see GENTILES; NATIONS).

Movement and mission are thus central components of the NT view of God (as they were, in a less overt way, in the OT). It is a mission that is no longer bound to a particular culture, nation or country. God's mission to the Gentiles, foreshadowed in the OT, and, perhaps, in the ministry of Jesus, becomes a major outcome of his resurrection.

3. Ecclesiology and ethics

The church is the outcome of the mission of the Son and the Spirit, and therefore contributes, however indirectly and imperfectly, to the NT view of God (see CHURCH, IDEA OF). Both its multi-racial membership, and the conduct enjoined upon it, bear witness to the God who does not discriminate (Rom 2:11; Jas 2:1-9). The unity to which it aspires points to the God who is One (Gal 3:20, 28; John 17:21; Eph 4:3), and the love and humility, especially, that should mark its life, are the imprint of God's own character (Phil 2:1-11; Eph 5:1-2). AGAPE, a word almost entirely absent from the OT outside the Song of Songs (though the OT, of course, testifies to the divine love for Israel), becomes pivotally important (e.g., Rom 13:10; Gal 5:22; Col 3:14; 1 John 3:16). Also, the church's members belong to each other (Rom 12:5; 1 Cor 12:27) and this, together with the "each other" commands of the NT Gospels and letters (e.g., Mark 9:50; John 13:34; Gal 6:2), hint at a mystery in God that was to find later doctrinal expression in the TRINITY.

E. God Is Love

Jesus, the only-begotten Son, brings us to the heart of the matter: God is love (1 John 4:8, 16). The NT does not say that love is God. Nor does the NT simply say, "God loves," in a way that allows for other actions and attitudes to be predicated of God. Rather, God is love: there is nothing other than, additional to, or contrary to love, as the ultimate reality called God (see LOVE IN THE NT).

But still more needs to be said. God loved us while still "far off" (Luke 15); God loved us while we were still weak, godless, sinners and his "enemies" (Rom 5:6-10); and that love was expressed in the Son's "handing himself over for me" (Gal 2:20). Thus charis (χάρις grace), God's unmerited favor, comes to prominence in most of the epistles of the NT, especially their opening greetings (e.g., Rom 1:7; 1 Cor 1:3). Divine power is experienced as GRACE (and vice versa, 2 Cor 12:7-10), and love is the key to both the transcendence and the power of God: the divine love is "perfected"—i.e., it comes to its appropriate completeness—in us (1 John 2:5).

The FORGIVENESS of God, and the peace that flows from it, are, similarly, central to the NT view of God (e.g., Matt 26:28; Luke 24:47, and the opening greetings of most of the NT letters). The testimony of the OT, and of Jesus' own life and teaching, show that the death of Jesus did not make possible the forgiveness of God (as often asserted by later Christian theology). Rather, Jesus' death and resurrection, and the gift of the Spirit revealed God's forgiveness with new, transforming power—actualized in "peace with God" through our Lord Jesus Christ (Rom 5:1; see JESUS CHRIST).

F. Jewish Monotheism and the New Testament View of God

New Testament writers very rarely call Jesus "God." Several texts (Rom 9:5; 2 Thess 1:12; Titus 2:13; Heb 1:8; 2 Pet 1:1) are, in varying ways, ambiguous. In two other texts (John 1:18 and 1 Tim 3:16) not all the

MSS have theos. So the theological *inclusio* that frames John's Gospel (1:1 and 20:28) is especially important, even though the phrase in 1:1*c* lacks a definite article in the predicate, kai theos ēn ho logos (καὶ θεὸς ἦν ὁ λόγος) and is therefore sometimes translated "the Word was divine" rather than "the Word was God."

Other texts very closely identify Jesus with God: the SHEKINAH-like language used by Jesus of himself at Matt 18:20, the revelation of God's name (John 17:26*a*), the opening greetings of the epistles, the "name of Jesus" that, at Phil 2:10-11, becomes the new way of acknowledging Yahweh (Isa 45:24-5) "to the glory of God the Father"; the prayer-wish of 1 Thess 3:16, where God and "our Lord Jesus" share a singular verb, the description in Revelation of "one like a son of man" in terms reminiscent of the Ancient of Days in Daniel (Rev 1:13-16; Dan 1:9), and the symbolism of God and the Lamb sharing one throne (Rev 22:3, though 3:21 should also be noted).

These texts (and others), together with the varied, even flexible, character of Jewish monotheism, means that the emergence in a largely Jewish context of claims that Jesus was divine cannot be ruled out. Some scholars still hold to the view that that development can only have occurred on Gentile soil. Yet the building blocks of NT christology lay to hand in, particularly, the OT and Jewish concepts of the divine wisdom, and the divine order (logos). (The 1st cent. Jewish philosopher Philo's references to the logos offer some striking parallels with NT christology). This may have made it easier to accommodate christological developments without serious discontinuity with Jewish monotheism. But, finally, we should note that, in the OT and NT, God and humans are not, so to speak, antithetical. Rather, humans are made in God's image (Gen 1:26), a little lower than a god (Ps 8:5), and humans at their most exalted (e.g., the high priest, Sir 50:1), and responsible (Ps 82:6) reflect God's glory, and share in God's divinity. The controversy behind the NT, therefore, may have been, not so much Jesus' "divinity," but the fact that it was the crucified Jesus of Nazareth for whom these claims were made.

G. New Testament Writers and Their Understanding of God

1. The Gospels and Acts

The four evangelists' views of God must be read out of the totality of their narratives, and, above all, out of the interplay between their language about Jesus and their language about God. For Mark the load-bearing phrases are "the Son of God" (1:1; 15:39), and "the kingdom of God" (1:15). Each sheds light on the other. The mission and destiny of the Son of God (and Son of Man) can be understood more fully in the light of Jesus' words and deeds explicating the kingdom, and vice versa.

This theological infrastructure remains in Matthew and Luke, although it is overlaid and developed by much new material, and, at times, considerable editing. In Matthew the twofold affirmation of the divine presence in Jesus (1:23 and 28:20) form an *inclusio* for almost the whole Gospel. Within this *inclusio* the character of God-with-us is presented more fully than in Mark. To love one's enemies is to imitate God's perfection in its all-embracing love (5:43-48). This "Emmanuel" is both gentle (11:29, 21:5—as his followers must be (5:5)—and humble (12:18-21). The character and mission of the Son of God can be seen most clearly in his forgoing power, rather than exercising it (26:53; 27:40, 43). At the same time, the gentle, unassuming presence of Emmanuel brings judgment (8:12; 10:15; 11:24; 12:45; 13:42, 50; 18:35; 24:51; 25:30, 46).

Luke, too, fills out the new understanding of God reflected in Mark's narrative, notably in the parables of the Lost Sheep, the Lost Coin and the Waiting Father (chap. 15), though, once again, the proximity of the OT and NT (see especially Ezek 34:11) should be noted. Luke appropriates, to a greater extent than the other evangelists, OT theological expressions such as "before God" (e.g.. 1:6, 8; 24:19), and, in both the Gospel and Acts, uses more frequently the impersonal dei (δεῖ) particularly with reference to the sufferings of the Messiah, and the fulfillment of Scripture (e.g., Luke 22:37; Acts 17:3). Thus, Luke's writings convey, not unlike the writings of Josephus, a sense of the overarching providence of God. But even in Luke-Acts there are harsher notes: for example, the twofold reference to "enemies" in the Song of Zacharias (1:70, 74), the uniquely harsh conclusion to Luke's version of the Wicked Husbandmen (20:18), and the fate of Ananias and Sapphira (Acts 5:1-11).

In Matthew and Luke-Acts we find an implicit theme of relocation. The shekhinah (שְׁבִינָה) resides in Jesus, rather than the Temple (Matt 18:20). Luke's narrative in his first volume begins and ends in the Temple (1:18; 24:50-53), but while his second volume also opens in Jerusalem (1:12), the programmatic prediction of Jesus in 1:8 makes clear that it will not end there. Throughout Acts God is portrayed as the God who vindicated Jesus (e.g., 2:24, 36), and as the God who, through his Spirit, inaugurates, authorizes, and enables the developing mission of the church. Yet this same God is not unknown to the Gentiles, whose poets have reached out towards him (17:28), and whose peoples already know of his goodness (14:15-17). At the same time the author is careful to emphasize that this same God is the God of the patriarchs (e.g., 3:13), and the God of the Jewish people (e.g., 24:14).

In John "kingdom" language is displaced and reinterpreted by Father/Son language and references to "eternal life." ("Kingdom of God" occurs at 3:3 and 5, but not thereafter.) The Father and the Son together (e.g., 5:19-20; 10:30; 17:21), are the joint agents of the kingdom; eternal life, defined as knowing God and "the one whom you have sent" (17:3) is the inheritance of those who come to the Father through the Son.

All of this falls within another *inclusio:* two of the clearest statements in the NT about the "divinity" of Jesus (1:1; 20:28). Within this *inclusio,* all statements about "God," if explicitly or implicitly linked to the Son, are correct (including 1:18 and 4:24), but those which are not so linked are mistaken (e.g., 8:41-42, 54; 9:16; 16:2), or inadequate (9:29).

The Gospel unfolds the intimate relationship of the Father and the Son: the Father knows (10:15), loves (3:35; 5:20; 10:17), and sends (3:17) the Son, entrusting "all things" to him (3:35), and bearing witness to him (8:18). Similarly, the Son knows the Father, has seen the Father (3:11), shares his glory (17:5), comes from the Father (3:16), bears witness to the Father (5:37), makes the Father known (1:18), perfectly reflects him (1:14; 14:9), completes his Father's work (17:4), and returns to the Father (e.g., 13:3), exalted (12:32), glorified (13:31-32), and ascended (20:17).

The significance of the so-called "I am" sayings (6:35, 41, 48, 51; 8:12; 10:7, 9, 11, 14; 15:1, 5) of the Gospel is disputed. It is not obvious that they should be linked with the revelation of Yahweh in Exod 3:14*a* ("God said to Moses, 'I am who I am'"). The Greek phrase ego eimi (ἐγὼ εἰμί) could be simply a means of identification or recognition, as it clearly is on the lips of the once-blind man (9:9). The occurrences of ego eimi without a predicate should also be noted (e.g., 8:24, 28, NRSV "I am he," REB "I am what I am"). Yet in the scene of Jesus' arrest, the three-fold use of ego eimi (18:5, 6, 8) seems to have, in the manner so distinctive to this evangelist, a deeper meaning. An echo of the revelation of Yahweh in Exodus therefore seems probable. Thus God now feeds his people, enlightens the world, raises the dead etc. through his Son, Jesus. But this Gospel is under no illusions: "the world" prefers the darkness of not knowing and not believing in God (e.g., 3:19).

Of all the NT writers, it is John who comes closest to the church's later doctrine of the Trinity. What Jesus was, the Spirit is—e.g., as PARACLETE and bringer of truth (14:16 and 14:6, 17). Through the work of the Son and the Spirit, a person may come to eternal life, to share the glory, the unity, and the mission of the Father and the Son, the holiness of the Son (17:17), the knowledge of God's name (17:26), and, even the very status of "god" (10:34).

2. Paul

The heart of the Pauline understanding of God can also be found in the interplay between theology and christology. All comes from God, whether it is our creation or re-creation in Christ (1 Cor 8:6; 2 Cor 5:18). Similarly, all things are directed to God, and to the glory of God through Christ (e.g., Rom 15:6). First Corinthians 8:6 may well be said to summarize Paul's

view of God: "Yet for us there is one God, the Father, from whom are all things and for whom we exist, and one Lord Jesus Christ, through whom are all things, and for whom we exist." In between the "from God" and the "to God" of this formula, a divine interchange has taken place: God in Christ became what we are, that we might become what he is (e.g., 2 Cor 5:21; 8:9; Phil 2:5-11; 3:4-11). This interchange reveals the righteousness of God (Rom 1:16-17), sets us free from the imprisoning impotence of the Law (Rom 8:3-4; Gal 4:4-6), and makes possible a new life in the Spirit (Gal 5:16; Rom 8:3), characterized by a threefold experience of God (2 Cor 13:13; Rom 8:9; 1 Cor 12:4-6). Paul, therefore, emphasizes not so much what God is but what God has done in Christ.

The Pauline interplay of theology and christology, focused in this interchange, is marked by paradox and antithesis. The apostle bears in his own person the dying and rising of Jesus, and, by so doing, becomes the channel of God's life to others (1 Cor 4:9-13; 2 Cor 4:12; 6:3-10). This power/weakness dialectic reflected in Paul's life is fundamental to the way in which God is both perceived and experienced after the Christ-event. Despite the undoubted continuity with the OT and Judaism in the themes of the divine pathos (especially in Hosea), in God's choice of the lowly, and even, in later Judaism, God's humility, Paul's rhetorical phrases, God's "foolishness" and God's "weakness" (1 Cor 1:25), coined to express the paradox of the cross, have no precedent in the apostle's Jewish heritage.

Paul also makes use of traditional theologoumena: e.g., "God is not mocked" (Gal 6:7), and "God shows no partiality" (Rom 2:11; compare Deut 10:17), the latter, however, now with reference to Jew and Gentile. Other theological themes have deep roots in the OT and Jewish understanding of God: the measure-for-measure concept of God's judgment, (1 Cor 3:17*a*; compare Mark 4:24-25 and par.); the wrath of God, revealing itself in the dehumanizing and socially destructive effects of idolatry (Rom 1:18-31; Ps 115:3-8); the revelation of God in creation (Rom 1:19-20; Job 12:7-9); a future divine judgment, though now the "judgment-seat of God" (Rom 14:10) may also be called the judgment-seat of Christ (2 Cor 5:10); God is frequently the warrant for ethical conduct in Pauline paranesis as in Jewish paranesis (e.g., Rom 13:1; Exod 20:2), although now Christ may be the warrant (e.g., Rom 15:7), or God in Christ (e.g., Rom 14:3; 1 Thess 5:17). Finally, Paul inherits the Jewish understanding of God's predestining grace. Grace works within human responsibility and freedom; no one is predestined to destruction. The difficult Rom 9:22 has no pro prefixed to the verb; all such pro verbs in Paul (and deutero-Paul) are positive (e.g., Rom 8:29; 1 Thess 5:9; Eph 1:4). Crucially, "God has imprisoned all in disobedience so that he may be merciful to all"

(Rom 11:32; 1 Tim 2:4). This verse, along with others in Paul (2 Cor 5:14-15; 1 Cor 15:22), comes close to expressing a kind of universalism, but references elsewhere to "those who are perishing" (1 Cor 1:18; 2 Cor 2:15; 4:3; 2 Thess 2:10), though present tenses, caution against this view. The strongest warnings in the Pauline corpus of the consequences for unbelievers come in the doubtfully Pauline 2 Thessalonians (1:12), referring, however, to the penalty they will pay, rather than that God will inflict.

3. Other New Testament letters

Other letters affirm the view of God to be found in the Gospels and in the letters of Paul, although always in new contexts, and, frequently, with new expressions. So the Pastorals (though this has been disputed), reflect the same understanding of God as the genuine Paulines—e.g., God is "immortal" and "invisible" (1 Tim 1:17; Col 1:15; Rom 1:23). The Pastorals, almost uniquely in the NT, refer to God as savior (e.g., Titus 2:11, and six times in all; elsewhere in the NT only at Luke 1:47 and Jude 25). James reaffirms God's election of the poor (2:5; Luke 6:20), Hebrews that God is the cause and reason of everything (2:10; Rom 11:36), and the notably theocentric 1 Peter that God is the Father of our Lord Jesus Christ (1 Pet 1:3), although of these (probably) later letters only 1 John has much to say about God as Father (1 John 1:2-3; 2:1). Divine judgment and punishment are reaffirmed by two later writers (Jude 3; 2 Pet 2:1) in critical times for the churches here addressed. First John, building, it seems, on Johannine tradition, whether before or after the Gospel of John, twice affirms "God is love" (1 John 4:8, 16), and "those who abide in love abide in God, and God abides in them" (v. 16*b*).

4. The Apocalypse

Some scholars have questioned whether Revelation is entirely reconcilable with the NT. A central interpretative issue is whether the image of the "slaughtered" lamb at 5:5 is the key to the Apocalypse's understanding of God. It is not self-evidently so. Yet details which may read like divine punishments are, in fact, contemporary or recent events, theologically interpreted (e.g., 6:6), and "the kings of the earth," erstwhile opponents of God come, in the end, to the heavenly Jerusalem (compare 19:19 and 21:24) while, despite much severe language (not without parallels elsewhere in the NT), the most severe is reserved largely for "the Beast" and for Satan (exceptions are 14:9-11 and 21:8).

The Apocalypse, like other apocalyptic writings of the time (e.g., 4 Ezra and 2 Baruch) was a response to an historical crisis, conveying the powerful message that God, despite appearances to the contrary, is the God of history, "King of kings, and Lord of lords" (17:14; 19:16; compare 1 Tim 6:15).

H. Interpretation

Biblical language about God is both sufficient and insufficient. It is sufficient in the same way that the Bible itself is sufficient. But it does not say all we need or want to say about God, and it has to be interpreted. Its language has to be supplemented by, and translated into, other terms, deriving from other languages and cultures. The NT period left the church with unfinished business: a theological task that culminated eventually in the formation of the doctrines of the Incarnation and the Trinity, and an apologetic task that involved engaging with fundamental philosophical questions about God and human existence. Yet extensions of biblical language need to be consonant with central biblical insights. The interpreter cannot engage in generalizing abstractions about God that neglect the gritty, contextualized narratives in which the NT story about God is embedded. Within this tension of contextualizing evangelism and contextualized, historical texts, the interpretative task must be attempted.

In this task preconceptions about God can hardly be avoided. The 21st cent. interpreter is likely to bring to the text a Christian (or sub-Christian) theism that has to be corrected, refined, and deepened by Scripture. For example, many widely accepted dualisms and antitheses are foreign to the NT: natural and supernatural, God's love and God's justice, even belief in God and atheism. Absent, too, are the concepts of contemporary and subsequent philosophical discourse: God's immutability, omniscience, transcendence, and impassibility. All of these need to be rethought in the light of the NT, rather than read into it.

At the same time, a biblicism that accepts biblical language at face value and thus, for example, makes God a personal agent, intervening in his world, makes the NT themes of wrath and judgment, and of God "hardening" human hearts, particularly problematical. God does not "intervene"; God is always present, ever active. Many strands of NT language—Jesus' teaching about the kingdom, Paul's frequent references to "before God," the Spirit who blows where it wills, the effects of divine wrath—all show that the apparently panentheistic statement in Acts 17:28*a* (". . . in him we live and move and have our being") is not an isolated Hellenistic intrusion into Scripture, but as fundamental to it as "God is love" and "God is Spirit."

Our interpretation of the Bible's personal theism requires us to interpret the OT in the light of the NT, where the divine kenosis (κενόσις lit. "emptying"), adumbrated particularly in the prophets, can now be seen in the remarkable linguistic developments: God hands over all things to his Son; the cross and resurrection reveal a divine "foolishness" that is wiser than human wisdom, giving rise, not only to a deeper understanding of agapē (ἀγαπή love), but also to a faith that God is AGAPE. And the ever-extending work of the Holy Spirit shows that, while Israel's privileges have not been revoked (Rom 9:1-5), no land or city is privileged any more.

This divine KENOSIS, or "emptying," can be seen in the relative infrequency of theos as subject, and the far greater range of genitives (e.g., kingdom, Son, Spirit, church, Word). All of this suggests that a theism that conceives of a god at the expense of humans (e.g., the more power and freedom God has, the less power and freedom humankind has) is unbiblical. Expressed christologically, this means that the sonship that the believer inherits through the Son is not an inferior or pale reflection of the sonship of Jesus (Rom 8:32).

The fatherhood of God (and Athanasius' insight that God, unlike human males, is father wholly, entirely, and uniquely), must be interpreted in the light of the male-dominated cultures of the ancient world. NT teaching about the fatherhood of God, in fact, contains the seeds of patriarchy's overthrow. God is called "father," not because he is a male patriarch, but because he loves and has children, supremely Jesus the Son. That is why subsequent Christian tradition, notably in Julian of Norwich, has rightly called God—and even Jesus—our "mother." In the use of theological language, and particularly the personal theism of the Bible, it needs to be remembered that it is easier to say what God is not than to say what God is.

In summary, each text or passage must be interpreted with reference both to their own context and to other texts or passages in a way which allows the cross and resurrection to be the canon within the canon. But the interpretative task is best undertaken also in dialogue with Christian tradition and experience, and in wider conversations with, e.g., science, not excluding its understanding of chance and randomness in the universe. Last but by no means least, all authentic interpretation of the NT view of God is self-involving. The observation that hermeneutics is not so much a problem to be solved as a mystery to be contemplated is especially apposite here. *See* BIBLICAL THEOLOGY; CHRISTOLOGY; GOD, NAMES OF; THEOLOGY, NT.

Bibliography: Jerome H. Neyrey. *Render to God: New Testament Understandings of the Divine* (2004); I Howard Marshall. *New Testament Theology: Many Witnesses, One Gospel* (2004); Neil G. Richardson. *God in the New Testament* (1999); Neil G. Richardson. *Paul's Language about God* (1995); Marianne Meye Thompson. *The God of the Gospel of John* (2001); N. T. Wright. *The New Testament and the People of God* (1996).

NEIL G. RICHARDSON

GOD, OT VIEW OF. The word "God" is used to translate the three common generic names for the deity in the OT (ʾelohim אֱלֹהִים; ʾeloah אֱלֹהַּ; ʾel אֵל). At the same time, "God" is a word commonly used to refer to Israel's deity, regardless of the underlying Hebrew name.

God is the central subject of the OT and a character in every biblical tradition (except Esther). God's existence is assumed throughout (though not unchallenged, Ps 14:1) and God's core character and salvific purposes are constant across its pages (though not always free from question, e.g., Job). God is a living reality for Israel, about whom basic confessions are made (e.g., Exod 34:6-7). At the same time, Israel's God is presented in a way that is not free from ambiguity and, finally, impenetrable complexity. The effect of such a presentation is that the reader will be challenged to make clear sense of the God of the OT and, inevitably, new interpretations will be made available for study and review.

    A. The Word of God and the Knowledge of God
    B. Names/Epithets/Metaphors for God in the OT
        1. ʾelohim, ʾeloah, ʾel
            a. ʾel ʿelyon
            b. ʾel ʿolam
            c. ʾel shadday
            d. ʾel roʾi
        2. Yahweh; Yahweh Sebaoth
        3. Various Epithets/Metaphors
            a. ʾadhon, ʾadhonay
            b. qadhosh
            c. ʾavir
            d. pakhadh
            e. baʿal
            f. ʾav
            g. Other metaphors for God
    C. A Relational God
    D. God as Present and Active
    E. Images for Divine Activity
        1. God creates
        2. God blesses
        3. God elects
        4. God makes (covenant) promises
        5. God judges
        6. God saves
    Bibliography

A. The Word of God and the Knowledge of God

The God of the OT is one who speaks, and speaks in such a way as to be understood, if not finally fathomed. Israel's God is not a silent God (contrast the idols, 1 Kgs 19:26-29; Pss 115:5; 135:16; Jer 10:5). The divine word is never unambiguously divine, however; human beings can mistake it for a human voice (e.g., 1 Sam 3). The word of God is believed to be from God and sufficiently clear and effective to shape faith and life, but no criteria are available to demonstrate beyond a reasonable doubt that such speech had a divine origin. Moreover, God's speaking invites human (and nonhuman; compare Ps 19:1) response and engages in genuine interaction with the parties addressed.

God is thus presented as one who is spoken to; indeed, God is desirous, even eager for creaturely communication (e.g., Gen 18:17; Isa 65:1-2; Jer 33:3; Amos 3:7), and is genuinely affected by such engagement. God is also presented as one who is spoken about; indeed, every reference to God in the Old Testament is a word about God, even those words that God is said to speak. At the same time, God's speaking conveys more than a certain content; the speaking in itself is important as integral to God's faithfulness within the relationship. Such knowledge of God and of God's ways is deemed essential if the relationship with God's people is to be genuine.

Bible readers are introduced to a speaking God on the first page of the OT. This Creator God continues to speak in the texts that follow—to Adam, Eve, Cain, and Noah. The God who speaks to the pre-covenant people in Gen 1–11 provides a pattern for the continuation of God speaking with "outsiders" in the rest of the OT. Using the Pentateuch as an illustration, God has a speaking relationship with outsiders such as Hagar (Gen 16; 21), Laban (Gen 30:27; 31:24, 29), Abimelech (Gen 20), the Egyptians (through dreams; Gen 40-41), and Balaam (Num 22–24). Such texts witness to Israel's conviction that God's word is not silent in the life of the nonchosen world. Israel's recognition of the range of God's audience means that they also recognized that God's knowledge was not confined to them. They could, therefore, learn about God from those outside of their own community. The common reflection of ANE traditions in OT texts is testimony to this witness.

The content of God that is revealed to people ranges widely, from factual information to innermost divine thoughts. God does not simply speak about more objective realities, as if the word of God were merely a matter of data. The texts reveal a divine concern about a considerable range of matters that bear on the relationship (see Gen 35:10; Num 12:5-8; Zech 7:9-10), including divine emotions or feelings (see Num 14:10-11; Jer 31:20; Hos 11:8), even inner divine reflections (Gen 2:18; 8:21; Num 14:11; Ps 95:10-11; Jer 3:7, 19-20). God's own self is not removed from the word—for the sake of fullness in relationship.

The basic structure of this word of God involves a relationship (as with human words more generally), which Israel's God takes seriously. God's word is usually an initiating word, but may also be a responding word in interaction with human parties (e.g. Abraham; Moses; Jeremiah). In the call of Moses, for example, God interacts in an extended dialogue wherein Moses is taken seriously by God. Moses' responses lead to new divine speech (Exod 3–7). Moses' recognition of God's holiness (Exod 3:6) does not lead to passivity in the divine presence. God does not demand a self-effacing Moses. Indeed, Moses' questions find an openness and willingness in God and lead to fuller knowledge of God and God's ways (see Jer 33:3). Moses' persistence in pressing the issues with God increases the revelatory possibili-

ties; simple deference would tend to close them down. Human alertness and faithfulness may occasion genuine insight; finitude and sin may lead to misunderstanding.

God's way into the future is thus not dictated solely by the divine word and will; God's word interacts with the human word and together their words and actions shape the future (though not in a way that can be factored out). This also means that, though God's word is powerful (e.g., Jer 23:29), it is generally resistible (see Ezek 2:5, 7; 3:11). For example, in response to God's word, Israel can doubt (Judg 6:12-13), object (Moses, Exod 3–7), challenge (Exod 32:11-13), question (Jer 1:6-7), reject (Zech 7:11-12), ridicule (Gen 18:12-13), scorn (Jer 6:10), despise (Jer 23:17), and disbelieve (Ps 106:24). The word of God is therefore not only powerful, it is vulnerable. Such a seeming contradiction can only be made coherent if the word of God is understood fundamentally in relational terms.

Moreover, God does not speak the word and then leave, but God goes with that word, working in ways to make it effective. It is God, who has an ongoing relationship with the word, who brings about the effects of a word, not the word itself in some autonomous fashion (see Isa 44:26; 48:3). The fulfillment of a divine word is fundamentally a testimony to God's work, not to a word's mysterious power. At the same time, the word once given is now not only in God's hands; it is also in the hands of those who can misuse it or ignore it. God's word in the world is not inevitably successful. This is the case for all divine acts, both words and deeds. No good reason exists to deny that God's activity in non-verbal ways would be any less resistible than the word.

Israel's knowledge of God was received from various sources, each having its ultimate origin in the word of God. At the same time, this knowledge was always mediated in and through creaturely agents, whose imprint is always left on the end result. For the last century and more, scholarly interest was focused primarily on divine revelation in and through historical events, particularly dramatic events such as the Exodus. This emphasis has now given way to a more comprehensive understanding of the vehicles in and through which Israel gained new knowledge of God. They include historical events, natural events, dreams, visions, theophanic encounters, creation/wisdom, encounters with strangers, individual and communal verbal communications, liturgical experience, and interactions with ANE literature and religion. Such varied experiences with God generated Israel's theological reflection and the development of new language for God. Human language (embodied or not) is the chief vehicle in and through which the knowledge of God is transmitted to human beings. Indeed, there is no word of God to human beings apart from the words and related symbols by which human beings communicate. There is thus no pure, unmediated word of God. But the finite is capable of the infinite; human words can bear the divine word. One cannot finally sort out the divine word from the human word, however; they are bound up together in every reported word of God in the OT. Nonetheless, the word is called the word of God.

The typology of a typical word event may be outlined as follows (prompted by texts such as Exod 3–15): 1) the religious heritage in which the recipient stands; 2) the experience/reception of the word of God; 3) key events that fill out and confirm the spoken word; 4) the interpretation by the receptor to the larger community (the last two matters would generally be reversed with reference to prophetic speech).

The knowledge Israel gains about God is presented in a variety of types of literature, ranging from narrative to poetry to law. The so-called credal statements—the more generalized claims regarding God—are particularly important when analyzing Israel's understanding of God. These generalizing statements are of two basic kinds: summaries of God's actions ("historical recitals"; e.g., Deut 26:5-9; Josh 24:2-13) and more abstract claims about the nature of God (e.g., Exod 34:6-7). The former highlight those events that are constitutive of Israel's faith and its life with God, including the exodus from Egypt, the wilderness wanderings, and the entrance into the land of promise. These events are more translucent with respect to God's purposes and bring sharper coherence and clarity to the larger range of divine purpose and activity. The latter provide central claims about the God who was believed to be active in those (and other) events: gracious, merciful, slow to anger, abounding in steadfast love, forgiving iniquity, and judging the guilty. These two types of confessional statements (integrated in Neh 9:6-31, compare 9:17, 31) represent Israel's mature understandings of God (though dating is uncertain); at the same time, they do not close down Israel's ongoing theological reflection. Israel's historical experience occasions ever-new questions about God and, over time, the summative statements may be revised to take this reflection into account. Examples include the addition of divine repentance to the confession of Exod 34:6-7 (Joel 2:13; Jonah 4:2) and the expansion of God's constitutive actions to include creation (Neh 9:6).

These confessional statements may provide the reader with an inner-biblical basis for evaluation of statements about God that occur in other types of biblical literature. The regular appeal of many Psalms to these generalizations about God may provide an indication of Israel's own evaluative practice (e.g., over half of the uses of "gracious" in the OT occur in the Psalms). At the same time, narrative portrayals of God may not entirely "fit" the summative claims (e.g., Gen 22:1-19) and certain psalms (especially laments, e.g., Ps 44:23-24 [Heb. 44:24-25], where God is said to sleep and forget) may challenge those basic claims. The rhetorical and metaphorical character of such theological

language must be considered in any evaluation of these texts for Israel's understanding of God. At the same time, readers should not try to "force" such portrayals of God into a fixed mold thought to be provided by the basic confessional claims. These "edges" in the canonical imaging of God should be allowed to stand as an ongoing challenge for the interpreter, which may in turn prompt new directions of reflection about God for ongoing communities of faith.

The language used to speak of God is primarily analogical or metaphorical (names of God are an apparent exception) and fundamentally relational.

B. Names/Epithets/Metaphors for God in the OT

God always reveals God's own name to Israel (except in Gen 16:13). In seeking to discern what divine name-giving entails, two extremes should be avoided. On the one hand, a name is not a mere badge of identity; on the other hand, a name does not belong to the sphere of magic, as if by knowing or pronouncing the name one has control over the deity. Hagar's naming of God (ʾel roʾi [אֵל רֳאִי]; Gen 16:13) does not thereby mean that she has control over God. The oft-cited Gen 32:29, where Jacob's request for the name of his assailant is not granted, is not pertinent here, for God had already given Jacob the name (Gen 28:13).

Divine name-giving involves the following understandings: 1) It entails distinctiveness, setting God off from others who have names, including gods. 2) In giving the name, God becomes a distinctive member of the community of those that have names; God thereby chooses to join the historical community. Even more, to give the name Yahweh with reference to the God of the ancestors (Exod 3:14-17) ties God to this particular history, to which God remains committed. 3) Naming entails a certain kind of relationship. It opens up the possibility of, indeed admits a desire for hearing the voice of the other (Isa 65:1-2). A relationship without a name inevitably means some distance; naming the name is necessary for closeness. And so naming makes true communication and deeper encounter possible (in the OT period, the divine name was pronounced). Naming entails availability. By giving the name, God becomes accessible. God and people can now meet and address each other. Yet, because name is not person or identity or character, there remains an otherness, even a mystery about the one who is named. 4) Naming entails vulnerability. In becoming so available to the world, God is to some degree at the disposal of those who can name the name. God's name may be misused as well as honored. For God to give the name is to open the divine self up to the abuse of the name. Naming entails the likelihood of divine suffering (compare Exod 3:7). This is probably a factor that undergirds the giving of the commandment regarding the name of God (Exod 20:7).

Names, though not fully revealing of person or character, may give insight into God, as does other language

God uses about the divine self (though we do not know the precise meaning of any name of God). In any case, names provide some continuity in God-talk across the generations The most basic names for God in the OT are below.

1. 'elohim, 'eloah, 'el

The generic names for God in the OT are 'elohim, 'eloah, and 'el. 'Elohim occurs over 2,570 times in the OT. The name is not attested outside of the OT. 'Elohim is generally used interchangeably with 'el and Yahweh. The discrete use of 'elohim in some Psalms (compare Ps 14 with Ps 53) and in some Pentateuchal texts (e.g. Gen 20–22), indicates that this name for God may have been preferred by a distinctive group within Israel with particular interests (the northern kingdom?). In some cases, the use of 'elohim may be intended to resonate with the God worshiped by non-Israelites, and hence its use may have an apologetic interest.

'Elohim, a plural form, is sometimes used for other gods (Exod 20:3), when it may take the definite article (Exod 18:11) and plural adjectives/verbs (Ps 97:7). Its plural form may mean it had polytheistic (or less than fully monotheistic) overtones at one time. Yet, its use in the OT for Israel's God (always with singular verbs) may mean that the plural has reference to intensification, universality (say, God of gods) or, less probably, majesty.

The OT begins with reference to 'elohim rather than Yahweh (Gen 1:1), which may indicate that it more readily carried a universal sense than other names. The addition of Yahweh to 'elohim, "Lord God," in Gen 2:4–3:23 may claim that this universal creator God is none other than Israel's personal God. The constant interchange between Yahweh and 'el in the following Genesis narratives, particularly with their lively interest in the interaction between the chosen family and surrounding peoples, may carry this universal intention forward. Abraham was chosen for the sake of "all the families of the earth" (Gen 12:3).

'Eloah, which may be the singular of 'elohim, occurs 57 times in the OT and is used mostly in Job (41 times), perhaps to avoid specifically Israelite associations.

'El is a generic name for God in Israel and in the ANE, with a more specific reference to the high god in Israel and some other cultures (e.g., Ugarit). The name 'el is occurs over 200 times in the OT; it is often used with descriptors (a righteous God, Isa 45:21) and with compounds that speak more specifically in terms of places or themes (e.g., 'el berith [אֵל בְּרִית]), probably understood as local manifestations of 'el. The name Israel is formed with the theophoric element 'el. This link suggests that the relation between Israel and 'el is historically prior to the link with the name Yahweh. 'El seems to be used more often in older (or archaizing) texts.

'El (with compounds) is especially prominent in Gen 12–50, and may reflect the language for God most prominent in the pre-Mosaic era. The use of the personal name Yahweh in these same narratives may constitute a theological claim: the God whom Israel's ancestors worshiped under the name 'el is no other than Yahweh (compare 'el 'elohe yisra'el [אֵל אֱלֹהֵי יִשְׂרָאֵל], "'el, the God of Israel," Gen 33:20). Another case is Gen 14:22, where Abraham's use of Yahweh with 'el 'elyon [אֵל עֶלְיוֹן], "Most High God," implies that Yahweh is the same as 'el, and Melchizedek's god is to be so identified. This extends the claim regarding Yahweh; the 'el worshiped by the Canaanites is none other than Israel's God. The phrase, "the God of my (your) father" (e.g., Gen 49:25), a special reference to the God of Israel's ancestors, also links the God of the ancestral period with later Israel (see Exod 3:6).

a. **'el 'elyon.** Commonly translated "Most High God," it may reflect the use of the name 'el for the high god in Canaanite religion. The adjective with superlative force is derived from a noun meaning "height," and may place stress on the incomparability of Yahweh in relation to other gods. Used primarily as a name or a divine epithet ("the exalted one"), it occurs almost exclusively in poetic literature (e.g., Ps 9:2), most often in the Psalms; it may be especially associated with temple worship. Most High is commonly used in apocryphal and pseudepigraphical literature (e.g., Sir 7:9; 3 Macc 6:2), as well as the Dead Sea Scrolls and is reflected in the NT (e.g., Luke 1:35; Mark 5:7). 'El 'elyon and Yahweh are often parallel in poetic texts (e.g., Ps 73:11; 107:11). Its use by Melchizedek may specify the name of the God worshiped in pre-Davidic Jerusalem. The relation of 'el 'elyon to creation and to the Davidic kingship is evident in Gen 14 and in texts such as 2 Sam 22:14 (compare 1 Sam 2:10; Ps 47:2), suggesting a use of this name when more universal claims for Israel's God made. In Deut 32:8-9, Yahweh is placed in relation to Israel, and the Most High in relation to all other peoples.

b. **'el 'olam.** 'El 'olam (אֵל עוֹלָם) usually translated "the Everlasting God," is a name used in apposition with Yahweh as well (only in Gen 21:33, linked with the Philistines). This name, more than a simple temporal reference, may refer to the fullness of God. The use of 'olam for the king (1 Sam 20:42; 2 Sam 7:13, 16) suggests that the name was oriented to royal themes.

c. **'el shadday.** The name 'el shadday (אֵל שַׁדַּי) is linked to the ancestral traditions (e.g., Gen 17:1; 28:3, texts often associated with the P tradition), with roots in Canaanite religion. The identification of this name with Yahweh is evident in Exod 6:3. Its common usage in poetic texts is especially evident in Job, a book without specific Israelite references. The name also occurs in association with the non-Israelite Balaam (Num 24:4, 16), where it is parallel to 'el 'elyon (elsewhere only in Ps 91:1). The precise sense of the name remains uncertain. The name is associated with creation and blessing in Gen

49:25, a text which suggests the meaning "God of the breasts." Most often it is linked to mountains (hence, "God, [one] of the mountain[s]"), as gods often were in the Near East. The common translation "God Almighty"; an abstraction of an originally concrete image, is based on the LXX; this may reflect an educated guess as to meaning on the part of the LXX translators.

d. 'el ro'i. This name is used only in the story of Hagar (Gen 16:13) and again links an 'el name to a non-Israelite figure. This is the only text where a human being specifically names God; that it is a woman who does so, and an Egyptian woman at that, makes an interesting point for reflection as to how particularities of the human experience of God can lead to new names for God.

2. Yahweh; Yahweh Sebaoth

Yahweh, the personal name for Israel's God, occurs about 6,800 times in the OT , in every book but Esther and Ecclesiastes. It is called the Tetragrammaton for its four Hebrew consonants (YHWH [יהוה]). A shortened form (yah [יה]), used mainly in poetry, occurs some fifty times. The name also occurs nineteen times in various inscriptions dating from 9th–5th cent. BCE—all with reference to Israel's God.

The history of the name Yahweh is complex; indeed, no clear historical lines can be drawn. Some texts claim that the name Yahweh was divinely revealed to Moses (Exod 3:14-15; 6:2-3), yet its use throughout Genesis (from 2:4) suggests that the name had a pre-Israelite life. Efforts to find such a "home" for the name (e.g., among the Midianites, Exod 3:1; 18:10-12) have not proved successful, though some have been eliminated (e.g., Canaan). That the name Yahweh was invoked already in Gen 4:26, and by non-Israelites in a setting that has all of humankind in view, may reflect a belief that Yahweh is universally worshiped (though other names are used). Yahweh is a God for all people and may be prayed to and worshiped by all (see 1 Kgs 8:41-43).

Exodus 3:14 is a most puzzling verse. The name given by God upon Moses' request ('eheyeh 'asher 'eheyeh אֶהְיֶה אֲשֶׁר אֶהְיֶה) consists of a repeated form of the Hebrew verb "to be" (hayah [הָיָה]) in the first person singular Qal Imperfect, bracketing the relative particle. Yahweh itself may be a third person imperfect form (the a vowel suggests a hiphil form, but that aspect is not attested in the OT or in Northwest Semitic). The most common translation is that given in the NRSV: "I AM WHO I AM." Some scholars suggest that this divine response is a refusal to give the divine name, out of a belief that knowing the name necessarily gives some control over the one named: in effect, "I am who I am" and it is not your business to know my name. This, however, is a counsel of despair and stands at odds with God's regularly giving a name when appearing to Israel's ancestors (Gen 35:11; Exod 3:6). Indeed, God does reveal divine names even though

that entails vulnerability in that the name could be misused. Moreover, that Yahweh is immediately used in apposition to "the God of your fathers/ancestors" in 3:15-16 suggests a more positive meaning. It is difficult to believe that the 6,800 uses of the name Yahweh are only testimony to God's refusal. There is, of course, a lack of final definition in the name Yahweh. But, as with all names, this simply recognizes the limits of drawing inferences from the name regarding the nature of the one whose name it is.

Other possible translations of the divine name include "I will be what (who) I will be"; "I will cause to be what I will cause to be"; "I will be who I am/I am who I will be." The last-noted may well be the best option, in essence: I will be God for you. The force of the name is not simply that God is or is present, but that God will be faithfully God for them in the history that is to follow (see Exod 3:16-17). The use of the same verbal form in 3:12; 4:12, 15 (compare 6:7; 29:45) also implies this. God will be God with and for this people at all times and places; the formula suggests a divine faithfulness to self. Israel need not be concerned about divine arbitrariness or capriciousness; God can be counted on to be who God is. This name will shape Israel's story, but the story will also give greater texture to the name. This understanding means that there are stakes in God's name-giving; God now must live up to the name given.

The "translation" LORD (capitalized in the RSV/NRSV) is something of a problem. LORD obscures the fact that Yahweh is a name and not a title/epithet. The use of LORD is based on the post-OT Jewish practice of reading 'adhonay (אֲדֹנָי "Lord") for Yahweh, because of an increased sense of distance associated with Yahweh's relation to the world (followed by the LXX's kyrios [κύριος], and the NT). To facilitate this reading, the vowels for the Aram. word meaning "the Name" (HA SHEM), synonymous with Yahweh in post-biblical Judaism, have been superimposed on the consonants for Yahweh in the Hebrew text (or, these are the vowels for 'adhonay, though the initial a vowel is not thereby accounted for). With the phrase 'adhonay YHWH (which occurs 305 times, e.g., Gen 15:2), the vowels of 'elohim are imposed on the consonants YHWH In these cases, many translations use the phrase "Lord God" (implicitly recognizing that the meaning of YHWH is not Lord, for a literal rendering would be "Lord LORD"). In view of this reality, it could be argued that, as with other personal names, we simply transliterate what the original Hebrew was thought to be—Yahweh (this pronunciation is only an educated guess, constructed largely from early Christian references). The transliteration of the present Hebrew form, "Jehovah," does not represent any known ancient pronunciation; such a form emerged in the Middle Ages and has had a hallowed usage in Christian hymnody (also in the ASV). An alternative practice would be to follow the common NT practice of using "God." This would also meet the concern of some that the word LORD brings into thousands of texts a masculine metaphor that is not present in the original Hebrew (*see* TETRAGRAMMATON; YAHWEH).

YHWH tseva'oth (יְהוָה צְבָאוֹת) occurs 284 times (including eighteen times with 'elohe (אֱלֹהֵי) added to YHWH and five times in place of it). It is usually translated "Lord of Hosts." The word "hosts" (tseva'oth) is a plural of the noun tsava' (צָבָא), often translated as "army" (Judg 4:2, 7) or a "host" of human or nonhuman, earthly or heavenly creatures (Gen 2:1). More abstractly, it can refer to service assigned or undertaken, military or cultic. The identification of the "hosts" in the epithet is difficult; suggestions include Israel's armies, the angelic host, and celestial bodies.

Regarding armies, see 1 Sam 17:45, "the Lord of hosts, the God of the armies of Israel." In contexts of judgment, even foreign armies are God's hosts (Isa 1:24-25). Regarding the celestial bodies (especially stars), God involved them in battle against Israel's enemies (Judg 5:20). In view of Job 38:7, this heavenly host symbolized the other heavenly host, namely, the angelic messengers (or divine council) that God "recruited" for divine service in the world (Ps 103:20-21). All "the host of heaven" is explicitly identified as this divine council in 1 Kgs 22:19; other texts refer to these figures as "sons of God" (Ps 29:1) and "holy ones" (Ps 89:5-7).

The predominance of the name in prophetic texts (251 times) suggests a specific linkage between this divine council and the prophet's role as a messenger of the word of the Lord. As such, the name may reflect the understanding that the prophet was a member of the divine council (Jer 23:18, 22; 1 Kgs 22:19); the word of God thus becomes a divine instrument, often for purposes of judgment (Jer 23:29), diminishing the military/royal links. The prophet was understood to be a member of the heavenly host, whose responsibility was to speak the word of God. In such a case, the name focuses on the God-Israel relationship, with the "hosts" (including angelic figures and prophets) being those who mediated the word of God (e.g., Jer 6:6). Isaiah 21:10 makes the prophetic point well: "What I have heard from the Lord of hosts, the God of Israel, I announce to you."

Interpreters need not choose among these options. Because sava' in the human sphere has reference not only to armies (1 Sam 8:11-12) but to other workers in the service of God (Exod 38:8), indeed to Israel as a whole (Exod 12:41), it may be that each option could be in view in one or another context. As such, "Hosts" has reference to any group, human or divine, called upon by God to mediate a divine objective, which may or may not be military in nature. Another approach would take "hosts" as a plural of intensification or majesty, particularly in view of the LXX translation as "Lord Almighty." But such an abstraction lacks convincing evidence.

3. Various Epithets/Metaphors

Whether one or more of the following epithets/metaphors constituted an actual name for Israel's God is not clear. It is possible for a metaphor to be elevated to the status of name, and that may have occurred with 'adonay (compare also the fivefold use of "Rock" in Deuteronomy). But it seems clear that the meaning of God's name is not to be found in some abstract notion of, say, monotheism. In any case, all such epithets/metaphors have a "Yes" and a "No" with respect to God. That is, they have continuity with the reality which is God, but they do not have a one-to-one correspondence, for no metaphor can fully capture the reality of God.

a. 'adhon, 'adhonay. The epithet/name for God as "Lord" ('adhonay, 449 times) may be a plural form of 'adhon (אָדוֹן "lord"; forty times) with a first person singular suffix; the vocalization is changed slightly (long final *a*) so as not to be confused with "my lords." In a majority of instances, 'adhonay is directly linked to the name Yahweh (315 times) and replaces Yahweh in later texts. It is rarely used in divine speech (five times). Cognates exist in other Semitic languages with essentially the same meaning for both gods and human beings.

The human analogy may have more to do with authority than rule or power in itself (compare Abraham, Gen 18:12; Laban, Gen 31:35; Joseph, Gen 45:8; Eli, 1 Sam 1:15). 'Adhonay is especially common in the prophets (320 times, 217 in Ezekiel) and the Psalms (fifty-five times). Featured in prophetic messenger formulas (Isa 3:15; 10:24), it may be especially associated with the authority of the word of God. In some texts, 'adhonay has a more universal reference, the "Lord of all the earth" (Josh 3:13; Ps 97:5; Mic 4:13) or "Lord of lords" (Deut 10:17: Ps 136:3); such usage and other factors have led to the suggestion that 'adhonay means "Lord of all." The universal authority of God may carry its basic sense.

b. qadhosh. Qadhosh (קְדֹשׁ) means "Holy One." God as the "Holy One of Israel" is especially prominent in Isaiah (1:4; 5:19, 24). This language expresses the "otherness" or transcendence of God; God is not a human being (Num 23:19; Hos 11:9). At the same time, this Holy One dwells in the midst of Israel (Isa 12:6; Hos 11:9), and hence holiness does not express aloofness or distance. God is revealed as the transcendent one precisely in his immanence, by the way in which God is present and active among the people. God is both far off and near at hand, indeed God "fills" the earth (Jer 23:24), as does God's glory (Isa 6:3) and love (Ps 33:5).

c. 'avir. 'Avir (אֲבִיר, "Mighty One), usually is used in the phrase "the Mighty One of Jacob" (Gen 49:24; Isa 49:26; 60:16), may also occur alone in Ps 78:25 (the "bread of the Mighty One"). It occurs in parallel with Yahweh in Psalm 132 and with such metaphors as Shepherd and Rock (Gen 49:24) and Redeemer and Savior (Isa 49:26). The word is used for human beings, especially heroic figures (Ps 76:6 [Heb. 76:5]), and also animals known for their strength (e.g., stallions, Judg 5:22).

d. pakhadh. Pakhadh (פַּחַד, "Fear [of Isaac]") usually is associated with the ancestral era (Gen 31:42, 53). The use of pakhadh in 1 Sam 11:7 for the dread that Yahweh causes to fall on Israel's enemies suggests that the issue of divine protectiveness of the chosen family is the foremost theme, though reverential awe is possible.

e. ba'al. Ba'al (בַּעַל, "lord") was an everyday word for a human head of the family (Gen 20:3), and it often was used as a metaphor for deity throughout the ANE where it became a name for the storm god of fertility in Canaan. Early Israelites may have appropriated that epithet for Yahweh (as with El), evident in the use of ba'al in the names of some Yahweh-worshipers (e.g., sons of Saul and Jonathan, 1 Chr 9:39-40). But, due to the development of sharp religious conflict with the Canaanites, especially in the face of a developing syncretism (compare 1 Kgs 18:21), this epithet was deemed unsuitable. For example, the ba'al element in the name Ishbaal was changed by later editors to bosheth (בֹּשֶׁת), "shame" (1 Chr 8:33-34; 2 Sam 2:8; 4; see Jer 11:13). The relation of Baal-berith (Judg 9:4) to El-berith (9:46) has not been satisfactorily resolved.

At the same time, the Israelites did appropriate language and themes from that Canaanite tradition and openly used them to fill out their way of speaking about Yahweh (e.g., storm imagery, Ps 18:14-15; conflict with sea/dragon, Ps 74:12-15; "Ancient of Days," Dan 7:9-14; marriage and death/resurrection imagery in Hosea). This practice did not constitute a "baalization" of Yahweh in any theoretical sense, but recognized (as with El) that non-Israelite understandings had at least some grasp of the truth about God (through general revelation). The use of such imagery may have proved helpful for polemical purposes in staking out claims regarding Yahweh (see Hos 2:8), perhaps even for efforts to establish links with the thought world of Baal adherents. In Hosea's promised future the marriage imagery remains intact, but it is expressly stated that Yahweh will be called "husband," not ba'al (2:18 [Heb. 2:16]).

f. 'av. 'Av (אָב), "father," is an infrequent metaphor with reference to God (twenty-one times). Though God could be addressed as Father (Jer 3:4, 19), its usage makes it difficult to claim as a name for God. It is striking that Father is used mostly in texts that have to do, not basically with power and authority, but with creation (Isa 64:8), intimacy (Jer 3:19), compassion (Ps 103:13; Jer 31:9), even friendship (Jer 3:4), and it is used in parallel with metaphors such as Savior and Redeemer (Isa 63:16; *see* FATHER; GOD THE FATHER).

g. Other metaphors for God. Numerous, often neglected metaphors for God are found in the OT; over fifty such metaphors occur in the book of Psalms alone. The use of such images—which are relational, ordinary, earthly, secular, concrete, and usually personal—links God closely to the everyday life of individuals and communities. These metaphors are drawn primarily from the following seven spheres, though they are not strictly limited to a single sphere:

1. Human personality: thinking, feeling, willing, self-awareness, spirit.
2. Personal activity: communicating, showing compassion, loving, bringing justice; using the mouth, hand, arm, ears, eyes. These first two spheres have been called anthropomorphic metaphors, recognizing that the only appropriate image for God in the life of the world is the human being (Gen 1:26-28; compare the NT reference to Jesus as "the image of the invisible God," Col 1:15).
3. Family: husband, father, mother, redeemer, creator, provider, helper, comforter. Though God is never called mother, female images are used for God, which reflect the special experiences of women, such as seamstress (Ps 139:13), midwife (Isa 66:7-9), creator (Gen. 1; 5:1-3), and especially motherhood (Isa 42:14; 66:13). The image of a child in its mother's womb or at its mother's breast is capable of conveying a sense of closeness with God that is unique.
4. Socio-political: friend, king, judge, warrior, preserver, savior, enemy.
5. Human vocations: shepherd, teacher, seamstress, tailor, lawgiver, advocate, midwife, homemaker, nurse, physician, healer, potter, farmer (e.g., vine grower; planter; reaper), metalworker, gardener, composer, singer, guide, builder, tentmaker.
6. Objects people have made: fortress, shield, lamp, fountain. Viewed as extensions of their makers, these metaphors are not impersonal (see Ps 31:2).
7. Nonhuman: rock, sun, fire, light, dew, spring rain, insects (e.g., maggots), animals (e.g., lion, leopard, eagle, bear, hen). These metaphors are not personal, but they are clearly relational (e.g., Deut 32:18; Exod 19:4; Deut 32:18; Ps 31:2-3).

Generally, these names and metaphors used for God in the OT interact with one another in various ways in different periods of Israel's history and are used by Israelite thinkers to develop fresh theological perspectives.

C. A Relational God

Through the lens provided by these various images, the God of the OT is seen to be a highly relational God. Most basically, God is present and active in the world, enters into a relationship of integrity with the world, especially with Israel, and both world and God are affected by that linkage. In this relationship, God has chosen not to stay aloof, but to get caught up with the creatures in moving toward the divine purposes for creation, and in such a way that God is deeply affected by such engagement. The following dimensions of divine relationality may be noted.

The God of the OT is a relational being. Such realities as the divine council, the sons of God, and the heavenly messengers witness that Israel's God is a social being, functioning within a divine community (e.g., Gen 1:26; 6:1-4; Isa 6:8; Jer 23:18-23; Prov 8:22-31). These texts and others witness to the richness and complexity of the divine realm. God is not in heaven alone, but is engaged in a relationship of mutuality within that realm, and chooses to share the creative process with other divine beings (Gen 1:26). In other words, relationship is integral to the identity of God, prior to and independent of God's relationship to the world. The reference to a divine community in association with the creation of the human community is especially to be noted (Gen 1:26). Human beings are created in the image of a God who is engaged in a relationship of mutuality and who chooses to create in such a way that creative power is shared with those who are not God.

The witness that God is one and unique (Deut 6:4-5; Isa 40:18, 25) is not compromised by this recognition of the sociality of God. God is God and other members of the divine council are not. Unlike other deities in Israel's environment (such as Baal), Israel's God is not divided into various divinities or powers. While the language of "monotheism" may be too theoretical (and dependent upon certain philosophical perspectives), some such formulation is in order. Developments in Israel's understanding of the oneness of God may certainly be discerned; Isa 40–55 provides the clearest formulations (e.g., Isa 43:10-13).

This relational God freely enters into relationships with the creatures. As noted, biblical metaphors for God, with few if any exceptions, have relatedness at their very core. These kinds of relational images for God were believed to be most revealing of a God who had entered deeply into the life of the world and was present and active in the common life of individuals and communities. The pervasive use of anthropomorphic/anthropopathic language is especially significant. This language stands together with the more concrete metaphors in saying something important about God. God is a living and dynamic being, whose ways of relating to the world are best, if not exclusively, conveyed in the language of human personality and activity.

The importance of such relational language is sharply evident in the prohibition of images. The basic concern of this prohibition is to protect God's relatedness. In the words of Ps 135:15-18, the idols "have mouths, but do not speak; eyes but do not see. They have ears but do not hear; noses, but do not smell. They have hands, but do not feel; feet, but do not walk" (see also Ps 115:5-7; Jer 10:4-5). With the idols there is no deed or word, no real presence, no genuine relationship. This relational understanding is continuous with that point where the OT does speak of a legitimate concrete image, namely, the human being (Gen 1:26). The human being, with all of its capacities for relationships, is believed to be the only appropriate image of God in the life of the world. This relational God of the OT is not, first and foremost, the God of Israel, but of the world. God was in relationship with the world before there ever was an Israel, and so God's relationship with Israel must be understood as a subset, albeit a deeply significant one, within this more inclusive and comprehensive divine-world relationship. God's acting and speaking are especially focused in Israel, but this divine activity is a strategic, purposive move for the sake of the world (Gen 12:3).

The opening chapters of Genesis are illustrative: God involves the creatures in creational tasks (1–2); God walks in the garden and engages the human (3:8-13); God ameliorates Cain's judgment (4:15); God suffers a broken heart (6:6); God limits the divine options in relating to sin and evil (8:21-22). And readers are not yet to Abraham and Israel! The rest of Genesis witnesses to this kind of God. God genuinely interacts with "outsiders," including Hagar (16:7-13), Abimelech (20:3-7), and Pharaoh (41:15-36); God responds to the prayers of the chosen on behalf of the unchosen (18:22-33; compare Exod 32:7-14; Num 14:19-20). For both chosen and unchosen, this divine-human relationship has a genuinely interactive character.

This relational God has created a world in which all creatures are interrelated. The world of the OT may be imaged as a spider web. Interrelatedness is basic to this community of God's creatures. Each created entity is in symbiotic relationship with every other and in such a way that any act reverberates out and affects the whole, shaking this web with varying degrees of intensity. Being the gifted creatures they are, human beings have the capacity to affect the web in ways more intense and pervasive than any other creature, positively and negatively.

Such an understanding of interrelatedness stands over against any notion of a static or mechanistic world. Given the genuineness of these relationships, there is a degree of open-endedness in the created order, which makes room for novelty and surprise, irregularities and randomness (see Job 38-41). "Time and chance happen to them all" (Eccl 9:11). To be sure, there are the great rhythms of Gen 8:22 (see Jer 31:35-37): seedtime and harvest, cold and heat, summer and winter; day and night. But, there is play in the system; one might speak of a complex, loose causal weave. Job 38–41 constitutes God's own imaging of the creation; things do not all fit into a neat little schoolroom of nature. Recent learnings from the scientific community demonstrate the rightness of this vision, revealing a cosmos of great complexity, remarkable openness, and a genuine interplay of law and chance.

That the world is so interrelated makes attempts to understand how God relates to its creatures more complex. To speak very generally, God so relates to this interrelated world that every movement in the web affects God as well; God will get caught up in these interconnections and work with them for the sake of the future of all creatures. Or, in other terms, God honors this interrelatedness and, in acting, takes into account both the order and the play of the creation. God works from within a committed relationship with the world and not on the world from without in total freedom. For example, God's faithfulness to promises made entails the limiting of divine options (e.g., Gen 8:21-22). Indeed, such is the nature of divine commitment that God's relationship with Israel (and, in a somewhat different way, the world) is now constitutive of the divine identity. The life of God will forever include the life of the people of God and the life of the world.

Most basically, the OT urges readers to think of God as being in a genuine relationship with every aspect of the creation and intimately involved with every creature. In short, the God-world relationship in the OT takes the word relationship seriously, which will in turn necessitate some re-characterization of traditional portrayals of the God of the OT. Remembering that the God-world relationship is asymmetrical, that God is God and creatures are not, what might a genuine relationship entail? Among other divine commitments, the following seem especially pertinent:

1. God so enters into relationships that God is not the only one who has something important to say. The OT will speak of divine-human communication that honors and values what the human has to say (e.g., Exod 32:7-14).
2. God so enters into relationships that God is not the only one who has something important to do and the power with which to do it (e.g., Gen 1:28). Given the divine faithfulness to such a relationship, God will exercise constraint and restraint in the exercise of power in the world.
3. God so enters into relationships that God is genuinely affected by what happens to the relationship. For example, the flood is introduced by a grieving God (Gen 6:6-7) and later, in prophetic texts, God will lament over what has happened to both people (Jer 9:17-18) and environment (e.g., Jer 9:10; 12:7-13).
4. God so enters into relationships that the human will can stand over against the will of God (e.g., Isa 30:1; Ezek 2:5; Zech 1:15). The divine will is resistible. God does not always get God's will done in the world, evident in the divine expres-

sion of anger, most especially because of continuing human resistance.
5. God so enters into relationships that the future is not all mapped out (e.g., Jer 22:1-5 speaks of two possible futures for Israel). The people of God, and indeed the larger creation, through the powers they have been given, are capable of shaping the future in various ways, indeed the future of God (note the two possible futures for God in Jer 22:4-5). The future is not simply in God's hands, though that is ultimately the case.

In sum, God has taken the initiative and freely entered into relationships, both in creation and in covenant with Israel. Having done so, God—who is other than world—has decisively and irrevocably committed the divine self to be in a faithful relationship with that world. Because God will certainly honor commitments made—because of who God is—God will not suspend these commitments, not even for short periods.

D. God as Present and Active

God is present and active in all creation (*see* PRESENCE OF GOD). God "fills heaven and earth" (Jer 23:24; see Ps 139). God is part of the map of reality and is relational to all that is not God. The earth is also "full of the steadfast love of God" (Ps 33:5; 36:5). God is not simply "here and there," God is always lovingly present, in every divine act, whether of judgment or salvation. Hence, God's presence is not a static or passive presence; it is a presence in relationship, profoundly grounded in and informed by steadfast love and working for the good of all, even in the midst of judgment.

The numerous active verbs of which God is the subject demonstrate that Israel's God is an acting God; indeed God is active in every event. No full account of any event is possible without factoring God into the process. Such divine activity includes speaking; no wedge should be driven between a speaking God and an acting God. At the same time, God's special presence is associated with certain times and places (e.g., tabernacle, Exod 40:34-38) and the chosen people (Exod 29:45-46).

According to Ps 104:1-3, God has made the spaces of this world God's very own dwelling place. The result, to use the language of Isa 66:1, is that heaven is God's throne and the earth is God's footstool. Hence, any movement of God from heaven to earth is simply a movement from one part of the created order to another. God—who is other than world—works from within the world, not on the world from without.

Scholarly focus on history and on decisive events in that history has tended to narrow the range of God's activity. While God's acting is focused in Israel, and God's speaking is especially articulate there, the divine activity is not limited either to Israel or to historical events. Genesis 1–11, for example, portrays a God whose universal activity includes creating, grieving, judging, saving, electing, promising, blessing, covenant-making, and law-giving. God's actions in and for Israel thus occur within God's more comprehensive ways of acting in the larger world and are shaped by God's overarching purposes for that world. Other texts (e.g., Amos 9:7) reinforce the understanding that even God's salvific actions, as well as a knowledge of God, are not confined to Israel or effected only through Israel's mediation.

God's actions are an activation of the divine will, not idle or accidental. Every divine act is an act of will and always stands in service of God's purposes in the world. God's speaking, for example, represents a decision by God to accomplish God's will in a given situation. The divine word does not make God present, but seeks to clarify and direct God's will within an already pervasive presence. Every divine action is informed by God's ulti-mate salvific will for the world, by God's faithfulness to promises, and by God's steadfast love for all.

Distinctions within the will of God are recognized. On the one hand, God's will for salvation is absolute and ultimate (e.g., Gen 12:3). On the other hand, God's will for judgment is contingent and circumstantial, and always stands in the service of God's salvific will (e.g., Jer 26:2-3; compare divine repentance). Unlike divine love, divine wrath is not an attribute of God; if there were no sin, there would be no wrath.

God's acting in the world is always situationally appropriate, fitting for specific times and places. God's seeing often precedes the divine acting (Exod 3:7-10; compare 2:24-25). God is a master at discernment, seeing what is needed and acting in a way that fits the needs of that moment. God's actions are always related to particular situations in the world and are designed to make a difference in that situation. At the same time, within those focused actions, God has the more com-prehensive divine purposes in view (e.g., Exod 9:16).

Using Exod 1–15 as illustrative, God's acts are related to the specifics of Israel's situation. Hence, God does not respond to human oppression of a socio-political sort by ignoring those realities in the shape that God's salvation takes. God here acts to save Israel from the effects of other people's sins; God does not act to save Israel from its own sins. God's saving actions in connection with the return from exile, however, have different needs of Israel in view; Israel is forgiven its sin and saved from the effects of its own sinfulness (see Isa 43:25; 40:1-11).

God's activity is effective in the world, from the creation of the world to the deliverance of Israel from Egypt to judgment on Israel by various foreign armies. God does get things done in the world, though, as noted, God's work is not always successful.

Two comprehensive outcomes might be noted. For one, God's acts issue in new knowledge of God and God's purposes in the world. New promises are stated, responsibilities delineated, and religious issues clarified and judged. Given the experiential character of knowing for Israel, this divine action affects not simply 'head knowledge,' but the entire relationship between the knower and the known. The importance of verbal events for such new knowledge should be highlighted more than has commonly been the case. Meaning is not simply "inferred" from historical events. For example, God's verbal encounter at the burning bush gives Moses the capacity to see the "something more" in the events, and the events' occurrence confirms and fills out that knowledge.

God's acts also issue in a becoming. Divine actions have not simply to do with revelation. God's actions effect a new relationship with God and a changed sta-tus for human beings and communities (e.g., freedom from oppression). God also acts to this end in and through various forms of Israel's worship life. The dra-matized festivals (Passover, Weeks, Tabernacles) are considered vehicles for God's ongoing salvific activity among the people; God's saving activity in historical event is made newly available to Israel in liturgical event. Israel's sacrificial system has a sacramental structure in and through which God acts to forgive the penitent worshiper. Israel's worship constitutes an important matrix for Israel's becoming as well as for Israel's reception of new knowledge of the God who acts therein.

God's actions may also issue in new knowledge and becoming for God. Human responses to God's actions may lead to a new level of divine knowing (see Gen 22:12; Deut 8:2), which can lead to new directions in divine action (see the possible futures for God in Jer 22:1-5). New divine commitments made and new relation-ships established make for a changed situation for God. In some sense one must speak of newness in God as well.

God works through human language and various human and nonhuman agents to get things done in the world. God acts directly, but always through means. And the variety of means is impressive. God works through that which is already created to bring about new cre-ations (Gen 1:2, 11, 20, 24); God works through human language to call Abraham as well as through the dynamics of his interrupted journey to Canaan (Gen 11:31–12:3); God works through nonhuman agents in the plagues, at Passover, and at the Red Sea (the nonhuman is the savior of the human!); God works in and through the sacrificial rituals to bring about forgiveness of sin and reconciliation with God; God works through prophets to speak God's word of judgment and grace; God works in and through the moral order—a loose causal weave of act and conse-quence, which can be named the judgment of God.

God's use of, even dependence on human agents in both judgment and salvation is especially prominent. For example, God works through non-chosen, non-Israelite kings and armies to send Israel into exile and to bring them home again, amply demonstrated in Isa 10:5 ("Assyria, the rod of my anger") and Isa 45:1 (God's "anointed," Cyrus of Persia). God even refers to Nebuchadnezzar as "my servant" (Jer 25:9; 27:6; 43:10).

In such divine activity, creaturely agency is not reduced to impotence; God's activity is not all-determining. There is neither a "letting go" of the creation on God's part, nor a divine retention of all power. Both God and creatures are effective agents. Because God does not perfect the agents before using them, God's actions through them will always have mixed results. As an example, force and violence are associated with God's acts in the world at least in part because they are characteristic of those in and through whom the work is being carried out. Harsh words are used with God as subject because they depict the actions of those in and through whom God mediates judgment. The portrayal of God's violent action is conformed to the means that God uses.

For these reasons, interpreters must not diminish the distinction between God and God's agents or discount the very real power of these human armies. God uses the means available in that time and place, but does not necessarily confer a positive value on the violent means in and through which God works (see Isa 47; Zech 1:15). This decision to work through such means is a risky move for God because God thereby becomes associated with the agents' (often violent) activity.

In sum, consideration of God's work through human agents must steer between two ditches of deism and determinism. God neither remains ensconced in heaven watching the world go by nor does God micromanage the world to "control" (a much abused word) its every move so that creaturely agency counts for nothing. But between these two ditches, the biblical texts do not always provide clear direction.

While all of God's acts are related to worldly situations in a meaningful way, some divine actions are more significant than others (see Deut 26:5-9). These greater levels of significance may be, but are not necessarily, related to the events being "extraordinary" or "miraculous." Where these elements do occur in the texts they are not easily sorted out. The following matters may be noted:

1. The extraordinariness is not understood in terms of divine intervention or intrusion, as if God were normally not present and then intervenes at certain moments to make things happen. God is present on every occasion and active in every event. God is likely understood to act in and through the means provided by the causal continuum; sufficient "play" exists in it to allow for God to work and the unusual event to occur.

2. Issues of genre and rhetoric. The language used for the exodus events includes extraordinary features, from the plagues to the Passover epidemic to the sea crossing. Isaiah 40–55 also uses extraordinary images to speak of a future return (including changes in nature), and links this extraordinariness to God's new work. Yet, the fall of Jerusalem and the return of the exiles are described in the more mundane terms of Babylonian army movements and Persian royal policies (see Jer 39; 52; Ezra 1–2). This distinction of the event itself and the rhetoric of extraordinariness regarding the divine action is different from the exodus account, where they are integrated (Exod 7–14). A liturgical setting for the exodus complex of events (compare Passover, Exod 12) may inform and heighten the dramatic character of the telling. We have here to do with an act of God, but the function of the text's extraordinary features may have to do more with rhetorical strategy and liturgical drama than with literal description, and so, finally, not dissimilar from that used by Deutero-Isaiah.

The extraordinariness in Deutero-Isaiah's testimony regarding the return from exile need not be literally descriptive of Israel's actual history in order to speak the truth about God's acts and be theologically and religiously significant. Yet, if no links exist between the confession and Israel's actual life, at least in its broad strokes, then the confession does become problematic. The 'happenedness' of those events that Israel has confessionally interpreted as constitutive of its identity is indispensable for faith, even if they cannot finally be verified. But divine activity should be linked not only to the events themselves but also to the confessional activity which interprets them. They belong together in any statement about the God who acts; only God's act in the gift of faith enables the confession that God has acted in Israel's external world (see Exod 14:31 and what follows).

3. God is not the only agent associated with certain of the extraordinary elements. Both human and nonhuman agents are engaged. In the plagues, for example, divine agency is explicitly associated with only six plagues (1, 4, 5, 7, 8, and 10); Aaron/Moses are involved in three of these in a dual role (1,7, and 8), and a nonhuman agent is cited in the eighth plague. In four cases, only human agency is cited (2, 3, 6, 9). Both God and Israel recognize this dual agency (Exod 3:8-10; 14:31), but the texts do not factor out just how this duality works.

4. Efforts have been made to explain the extraordinary elements in natural terms. For example, in the plagues, the frogs leave bloody water, flies are drawn to dead frogs, etc. The gifts of manna, quail, and water have also been so interpreted. Such reflections need not "explain away" the

divine factor, however, if God is kept in the picture (not always done). Consideration of divine providence should not be divorced from recognition of nature's God-given potentialities. To cite one example (Exod 17:1-7): God is here not creating water out of thin air, nor is nature disrupted. Water does course through rock formations; the actions of both God and Moses enable their hidden potential to surface. God works in and through the natural (and the human) to provide water for the people, as God does throughout the exodus complex of events.

5. God acts differently in some events. How to articulate this difference is difficult, but may be due to variations of intensification in divine action. In some texts, God's presence is more unobtrusive (e.g., God never appears to Joseph or his brothers, yet is an effective agent, Gen 50:20). In other texts, God's presence is more intense (e.g., Exod 40:34-38). In developing a typology of divine presence one might speak of variations in intensification in comparing God's general presence, God's accompanying presence, God's tabernacling presence, and God's theophanic presence.

These distinctions no doubt relate to the needs of the situation, and God's purposes related thereto. One might also speak about God's concern for human life and freedom in the face of too sustained a divine intensity ("you cannot see God and live"). But such differences also involve the dynamics of the God-world relationship and God's commitments related thereto. For example, God's promise at the end of the flood never to act in that way again (Gen 8:21-22; 9:11) limits the divine options with respect to any related matter. One could say something comparable with respect to all of God's promises. Or, the intensity of the divine presence may be affected by the depths of human sinfulness. So, e.g., God is driven from the temple by Israel's abominations (Ezek 8:6) and its iniquities "make a separation between you and your God" (Isa 59:2). Negative human response can push God back along the continuum of presence so that it becomes less intense, and hence less felt and effective. Positively, human need and powerlessness may call forth intensity in God's presence (see Deut 32:36). God's possibilities are closely related to the nature of the situation. So for a variety of reasons God does act differently in events, but one cannot finally sort out the factors at work within these differences.

In sum, the present and active God acts in the world within committed relationships in accordance with the divine will. God's actions are always situationally appropriate and effect new knowledge and becoming, though that divine action in both word and deed is resistible and hence may not always be successful. God acts directly through various means, both human and nonhuman, so that the world is not only dependent upon God, God has also chosen to be dependent on the world. God's actions may be of varying intensities and some acts are more significant than others, but their import is not necessarily related to the extraordinariness of events.

E. Images for Divine Activity

The most basic images for God in the OT are introduced in Gen 1–11, before there ever was an Israel. As such, they witness to a God who is present and active in the world more generally, not just in Israel. The way God is imaged in pre-Israel narratives also prompts readers to be on alert for how this God continues to be present and active among other peoples.

1. God creates

The importance of creation theology in biblical-theological reflection has been slow to be appreciated in the modern period. The causes are many and complex, but an anthropocentrism has certainly been at work. One could also cite an emphasis on (salvation) history and the history/nature split.

God's creative activity is a theme that pervades the biblical narrative and has three interrelated points of reference: the beginning and the end of the world and the times in between.

Most fundamentally, creation is an act of God whereby "heaven and earth" are originally brought into being. The creation accounts in Gen 1–2 are the primary witness to this creative activity and provide a universal frame of reference in terms of which the entire Bible is to be interpreted. Several other texts witness to this originating creative action of God (Pss 33; 104; Prov 8:22-31).

Genesis 1–2 and other texts speak of the modes of creation from several (overlapping) perspectives. 1) God creates by means of the word (Gen 1:9; Ps 148:5; Heb 11:3). 2) God creates by means of the word, followed by deeds of separation or other creative actions (Gen 1:6-7; Ps 33:6). 3) God speaks with others (divine beings or creatures) and invites their participation in the creative process (Gen 1:11, 26). 4) God uses that which has already been created as "raw material" to bring still other creatures into being (Gen 2:7; Ps 8:3; 2 Pet 3:5). 5) God creates some creatures out of nothing (Gen 1:14-16). Later texts will extend this point to encompass all of God's creative activity (2 Macc 7:28; Rom 4:17; Heb 11:3). 6) God and humans name creatures, thereby bringing further order to the creation (Gen 1:5-10; 2:20). 7) God evaluates what has been created, the results of which could entail further creative work on the part of either God or creatures (Gen 1:4-31; 2:18). 8) God creates by bringing order to that which already exists (the earth in Gen 1:2, 9). 9) God creates by spirit and by wisdom (Gen 1:2; 2:7; Prov 8:22-31). Some scholars would add still another mode of creation: God creates through combat with chaotic forces and victory over them (compare Ps 74:12-17; 77:12-21; 89:10-15). But this view is unlikely.

Creation refers to God's continuing creation, that ongoing activity of God in every sphere of life whereby the world is ordered and maintained (Ps 104:30; the theme of blessing). This focus of creational activity has to do not only with God's continuing work in nature, but also with the ordering of families and nations (Gen 4–11), including the development of law (Gen 9:1-7). That Isa 40–55 can so readily use the language of creation for God's salvific action in the return from exile is a signal of God's continuing creative work between the beginning and the end (e.g., Isa 41:20). What God does in Israel's redemption stands in the service of endangered divine goals for life in creation.

Creation is that divine eschatological action whereby a new heaven and a new earth are brought into being (Isa 65:17; Dan 12:2); this consummation reveals the direction for all of God's prior work, whether in creation or redemption. This creational theme has a universal frame of reference, revealing a God who is present and active in the world beyond Israel. The larger world, human and nonhuman (e.g., Isa 11:6-9), is always included in God's purposes. One might speak generally of an open future, within which human response participates in shaping life in the world, but God works purposefully within the complex of worldly events in such a way that the promise of a new heaven and a new earth will be brought into being.

Two important conclusions may be drawn regarding the creation accounts:

1. The creation is not presented as a finished product; rather, a certain open-endedness characterizes the created order that leaves room for further developments. God gives the command to humans to "subdue the earth" (Gen 1:28); "good" does not carry the sense of "perfect." For humans to subdue the earth means that, in time, creation would look other than the way it did on the seventh day. Ironically, God gives humans this "natural law" so that the created order would not remain the same. Development and change are what God intends for creation. Genesis 1–2 presents readers with a dynamic situation in which the future is open to a number of possibilities and in which creaturely activity is crucial for the proper becoming of the creation.

2. God is not the only subject of creating activity. Genesis 1–2 does not present God's creating as a unilateral act. Rather, God speaks with that which has already been created and involves them in further creative activity (Gen 1:11-12,

20, 24). Moreover, God shares the creation of human beings with that which is not God (Gen 1:26, "let us"). Humans are created in the image of this kind of God; this implicitly entails a sharing of the creative process with them. The texts that follow report this kind of human involvement (see Gen 2:18-25). Human decisions regarding the animals and the woman are honored by God and are taken into account in moving into new stages of creaturely development.

These texts thus witness to a relational model of creation, wherein both God and creatures participate in the becoming of creation. God is not simply independent and the creatures simply dependent; God has chosen to enter into an interdependent creative process. Amid all the order of the creative process God builds in a degree of open-endedness and unpredictability, leaving room for genuine creaturely decisions and actions regarding developments in the created order. This is a risky move for God, for the creatures may misuse their God-given power; yet, even when they do, God exercises constraint and restraint and continues to engage humans in this process (see Ps 8).

2. God blesses

Blessing is a gift of God, usually mediated through human or nonhuman agents, that empowers recipients to bring forth and experience life, goodness and well-being, including spiritual and more tangible expressions. God's blessing is given creation-wide scope from the beginning (Gen 1:22, 28), and continues in the post-sin, pre-Abrahamic world (9:1). Through acts of blessing, God provides a life-giving, life-enhancing context for all creatures within every sphere of their existence. As such, blessing belongs primarily (but not exclusively) to the sphere of creation. This means that non-elect peoples are not dependent upon the elect for many forms of blessing; it rains on the just and the unjust, and families who have never heard of Abraham thrive. God is active for good in every human life. The genealogies of the non-elect demonstrate this (e.g., Ishmael, Gen 25:12-18; Esau, 36:1-42).

This understanding of blessing in universal terms stands in some tension with Gen 12:3, "in you all the families of the earth shall be blessed." This language suggests that blessing shall be mediated by the Abrahamic family (see 30:27; 39:5; 47:7, 10). Yet, Gen 12:2, "I will bless those who bless you" (see 27:29) recognizes that the non-chosen can also mediate blessing to the elect. This point is illustrated several times in Genesis (12:16; 14:18-20; 20:14; 26:12-14) and elsewhere (Num 22–24). But, if God as Creator already blesses the world independent of the chosen family, and if the non-elect can mediate blessing to the ancestral family, of what purpose is Abraham's election?

Blessing encompasses two different, though not unrelated experiences:

1. The general, creational realities such as fertility, prosperity, and success in the sociopolitical sphere, which all of God's creatures can mediate and experience independent of their knowledge of God. The texts noted above illustrate this type of blessing.
2. God's specific, constitutive promises to the elect family, initially through Abraham (son, land, many descendants, nationhood; Gen 12:1-3, 7; 13:14-18; 15:4-5, 18-21), and never mediated by the non-elect. They are "constitutive" because they are community-creating, without which Israel would not have come to be. These promises, called "the blessing of Abraham" in 28:4, are repeated to Isaac (26:3-4, 24), and commended by Isaac to God on behalf of Jacob (28:3-4), who extends them to Jacob (28:13-15; 35:10-12).

The creational blessings are life-enabling and life-enhancing, but they are finally not sufficient for the fullest possible life. The constitutive blessings mediated through the elect are essential if the best life possible is to be experienced. They bring focus and intensity to the blessings of creation, making them more extensive and abundant, and decisively give new shape to individuals and communities; thereby they can become even more correspondent to God's will for goodness and well-being in creation (see Gen 20:17-18; 30:27-30). The larger issue at stake in the divine choice of this family is a universal one: the reclamation of the entire creation in view of sin and its deleterious effects upon life.

As for the chosen family, it is not as if, given God's blessing to Abraham initially, they stand in no further need of divine creational blessings along the way. Blessing is not a one-time gift; the chosen and redeemed people of Israel are in need of continuing blessing all along their journey for the sake of continuing life, health, and well-being (see Num 6:22-27). Moreover, while God sets an "agenda" for the chosen family to be a blessing to all families; God remains engaged in the lives of "outsiders," often in ways independent of their relationship to the chosen ones.

3. God elects

In Gen 1–11, God's electing is set as a basic way in which God chooses to work in the world. God chooses Abel's offering rather than Cain's (Gen 4:4-5); this divine choice of the younger over the older brother sets a pattern for the chapters that follow (Isaac rather than Ishmael; Jacob rather than Esau; compare also 38:27-30; 48:13-14). Moreover, God chooses Noah (6:8-9) as the one to be saved from the flood. With him, God begins again with the human family and, at the end of the flood, enters into covenant with "all flesh." This divine electing activity is thus not an end in itself; God elects for the purpose of preserving the creation alive in a reasonably stable world environment.

Such purposes of life and well-being for the entire creation are continued and brought into sharper focus in God's election of Abraham/Israel. The purpose of God's loving choice of Israel in keeping the oath to its ancestors (Deut 7:6-8), as well as in giving the law, has a creational focus: so that "you may live, and that it may go well with you, and that you may live long in the land you are to possess" (Deut 5:33; compare 6:24). In other words, God's objectives in choosing Israel are fundamentally creational in their most basic concerns: creational stability and communal stability.

As we have seen, this divine purpose for Israel is not simply for the sake of the chosen; God has God's world in focus (Gen 12:3). God's exclusive move in choosing Abraham/Israel is not an end in itself, but a divine strategy for the sake of a maximally inclusive end. The blessing of Israel's ancestors for the sake of all the families of the earth (including the non-human family, given 9:8-17) is in tune with the universal divine purposes of life and well-being. Divine election does not entail having a corner on participation in the goodness of God's creation but a charge to extend those gifts to all.

4. God makes (covenant) promises

The God of the covenant promise, integral to the rhythm of Gen 1–11, constitutes a basic image for all that follows. After the flood, God makes a covenant with Noah and all flesh (9:8-17; compare 8:21-22). In this unilateral, unconditional covenant with the entire creation God binds the divine self with respect to the future—thereby limiting the divine options: I will never destroy the earth again. God decides to go with the world—come what may in the wake of continuing sin and evil. Notably, God makes this promise precisely because humankind is sinful through and through (8:21). Sinfulness so defines humanity that, if human beings are to live, they must be undergirded by the divine promise. Only God can assure the future of creation.

Covenant is thus introduced into the biblical narrative as a word with universal associations. Apart from Israel, God has established a promissory relationship with creation, revealing God's most basic way of relating to the world—in commitment, patience and mercy, not in anger or capriciousness. The covenants that God proceeds to make with Abraham/Israel are grounded in this prior promise and can be confidently assumed to be as good as this prior promise; the God with whom Israel has to do is as trustworthy as God here is revealed to be (see Jer 31:35-37; 33:14-26; Isa 54:9-10).

The covenant with Noah and all flesh is also revealing of the basic structure within which subsequent covenants are framed, which, in turn, has theological implications. God elects (Gen 6:8); God saves (6:18; 8:1); human beings respond in worship and faith (8:20), and only then does God establish covenant. This fourfold structure is characteristic of God's covenants with Abraham (12:1-3; 12:10-20 and 14:20; 15:6; 15:18 and 17:1-8), with Israel (the covenant is not made until Exod 24), and with David (2 Sam 7).

While God does not explicitly "make a covenant" with any non-chosen people, God does make repeated promises regarding Ishmael (Gen 16:10-11; 17:20; 21:13, 18), in language remarkably similar to the covenants with Abraham, Sarah, and family (compare 12:2; 17:15). These stories carry an image of God as Creator who makes promises to those who do not belong to the "people of God." This divine pattern continues in other texts (e.g., Isa 19:18-25). The chosen people are thereby reminded that they cannot confine God's promising activity to their own precincts.

Interhuman covenants between insiders and outsiders are also made in the Genesis narrative (e.g., 21:22-34; 31:44). Such human commitments may be said to stand in the tradition of a God who makes promises; human faithfulness to promises made is a possibility for those who stand outside of the explicit covenant promise. Such promising is again a witness to the work of God the Creator. Promise gives basic shape to the life of all human beings, chosen or not.

5. God judges

The image of God as judge is already evident in Gen 1–11. God does not treat the sin of Adam and Eve (and their descendants) lightly. Such divine action proves to be the case throughout the OT. The judgment of God, which may be defined as the mediation of the moral order—seeing that sins do have consequences, plays a key role so that sin and its effects do not have the last word. In other words, this divine move is made not simply because God is offended, but also because social and cosmic stability is at stake.

To that end, God announces and mediates the effects of sin on the primary spheres of human life and vocation (3:14-19), indeed upon the natural order (6:5-13). At the end of the flood story, God promises never to destroy the earth again (8:21-22; 9:8-17); this promise builds into the very structures of the world a limitation with respect to the range of God's judgment: never again will its scope be universal. This promise does not mean, however, that God will not judge in less thoroughgoing ways, in which both chosen and nonchosen may participate (e.g., Gen 18–19; the fall of Jerusalem).

Exactly how God relates to the movement from sin to consequence is not easy to sort out. Generally speaking, the relationship between sin and consequence is conceived in intrinsic rather than forensic terms; that is, consequences grow out of the deed itself rather than as the imposition of a penalty. At the same time, Israel insists that God not be removed from this sin/consequence "journey." God mediates the consequences of sin in and through the working out of sin's effects so that sin and evil do not go unchecked in the life of the world. The point may be illustrated by Ezek 22:31: God declares, "I have consumed them with the fire of my wrath." What that entails is immediately stated: "I have returned (nathatti נָתַתִּי) their conduct upon their heads." This moral order, however, does not function in any precise or inevitable way; it is not a tight causal weave, and so the treacherous may thrive (Jer 12:1).

In sum, Israel's sin generates certain effects in a snowballing, act-consequence schema. At the same time, God is active in the interplay of sinful actions and their effects and uses "third parties" as agents for that judgment. Both divine and creaturely factors are interwoven to produce the judgmental result. In modern terms, our own sin, as well as the sins of our forebears, presses in upon us, but no less the hand of God. For history is our judgment and God enables history, carrying the world along, not in mechanistic ways, but with a personal attentiveness in view of the relationship. God's salvific will remains intact in everything, and God's gracious concern is always for the best; but in a given situation the best that God may be able to offer is burning the chaff to fertilize the field for a new crop.

6. God saves

Already Gen 1–11 introduces the image of God as Savior, seen especially in God's deliverance of both human beings and animals from the flood (e.g., 8:1). Given human sinfulness and the dire effects let loose in God's creation, God chooses to be savior. This divine move demonstrates that God is active in saving activity out and about in the creation independent of Israel and the mediation of the community of faith (see Gen 16:7-14; 21:15-21; Amos 9:7). God here acts in both word and deed outside the boundaries of the "community of faith" (see also Gen 20:17-18; 18:22-33; 41:57).

This God, shown to be savior of the world, becomes the savior of the progenitors of Israel (e.g., Gen 14:20) and that activity will come to a climax in God's delivering Israel from slavery in Egypt (Exod 3:8; 6:6; 14:30; 18:11) and beyond. Importantly, these saving activities of God are not narrowly spiritual in character; as is evident in Exod 15:2. Salvation language is used with respect to social and political matters as God enables deliverance from the world's oppressors. This divine concern is so wide-ranging that God will bind the divine self to the Torah to act in saving ways on behalf of those who have been abused, whether Israelite or "resident alien," even if Israel itself proves to be the perpetrator (Exod 22:21-27). The concern for the stranger and alien is particularly evident in the laws (e.g., Deut 24:19-22) and Israel is commanded to follow God's ways in extending justice and love to them (Deut 10:19), even to "love the alien" (Lev 19:34). Israel's experience of the effects of God's saving deed is to be extended to all others.

A more specific divine act of salvation is forgiveness of sin. God's forgiving activity is claimed in Israel's basic confessional statements, "forgiving iniquity and transgression and sin" (Exod 34:7; compare Neh 9:17). God not only forgives, but is eager to do so (Isa 55:6-7; Jer 36:3; Ps 32:5). This divine action is integrated into the heart of Israel's life of worship—its sacrificial structures (Lev 4–5). At the same time, forgiveness becomes available independent of those structures to those who are repentant (e.g., 2 Sam 12:13; Ps 51). The prophets, envisioning God's future actions on behalf of the people of God, understand that forgiveness grounds that new life (Isa 43:25; 53:10-12; Jer 31:31-34). Forgiveness is understood to be basic in the ways that God responds to the sin and evil of the world, both in the present and the future. *See* COVENANT, OT AND NT; ELECTION; FORGIVENESS; GOD, METAPHORS FOR; GOD, NAMES OF; PROMISE.

Bibliography: Samuel E. Balentine. *The Hidden God* (1983); Walter Brueggemann. *Old Testament Theology: Testimony, Dispute, Advocacy* (1997); Brevard Childs. *Biblical Theology of the Old and New Testaments: Theological Reflection on the Christian Bible* (1993); Terence E. Fretheim. *God and World in the Old Testament: A Relational Theology of Creation* (2005); Terence E. Fretheim. *The Suffering of God: An Old Testament Perspective* (1984); John Goldingay. *Old Testament Theology: Israel's Gospel* (2003); Abraham J. Heschel. *The Prophets* (1962); Phyllis Trible. *God and the Rhetoric of Sexuality* (1978); Claus Westermann. *What Does the Old Testament Say About God?* (1979).

TERENCE E. FRETHEIM

GOD, SON OF. *See* SON OF GOD.

GOD, SONS OF בְּנֵי־הָאֱלֹהִים bene ha'elohim; υἱοί θεοῦ huioi theou, τέκνα θεοῦ tekna theou]. Several passages in the OT refer to divine beings other than Yahweh, testifying to the polytheistic world in which the OT materials were produced. Three different phrases, all of which share the common plural noun "sons," designate these beings. The most common is "sons of god" (bene ha'elohim, Gen 6:2, 4; Job 1:6; 2:1; 38:7; Deut 32:8 [LXX], and bene 'elim אֵלִים בְּנֵי], Pss 29:1; 89:7), which are comparable to the designation found in the Ugaritic materials (bn 'ilm), and can be understood as either "sons of god" or "sons of El." The OT designates them as "sons of the Most High/Elyon" (bene 'elyon בְּנֵי עֶלְיוֹן], Ps 82:6) once. Each occurrence should be taken simply as a generic designation, "gods" or "divine beings."

The first reference to these beings is found in the mythological piece in Gen 6:1-4. This introduces the flood story with an account of the breakdown of the order of creation when "the divine beings" (bene ha'elohim; 6:2, 4) co-mingled with women of earth, producing the ancient heroes. This same phrase is used in Job 1:6; 2:1, designating the members of Yahweh's

heavenly assembly (*see* DIVINE ASSEMBLY). Only "the adversary" (*see* SATAN), who is allowed by Yahweh to test Job, is explicitly identified. Another reference to "divine beings" (bene 'elohim) occurs in Job 38:7, where they parallel the morning stars, suggesting astral connections (see 1 Kgs 22:19; 2 Kgs 21:5).

These same divine beings are called bene 'elim in Pss 29:1 and 89:7. In the former, these deities give praise to Yahweh, while they serve to illustrate Yahweh's incomparability in the latter. Both instances presume the setting of the divine assembly. This is noted explicitly in Ps 82:1, where God condemns the "divine beings" called "sons of the Most High/Elyon" (82:6) for their failure to perform their proper duties. Scholars also reconstruct a reference to these divine figures in Deut 32:8, reading "sons of God" in place of "sons of Israel," based on evidence found in other versions. This passage reflects the belief that the Most High, Elyon, allotted nations among various deities.

The NT adopts this concept to designate the community of believers, called "sons" (huioi theou; Matt 5:9, 45; Luke 20:36; Gal 4:5; Eph 1:5; etc.) or "children" (tekna theou; John 1:12; 11:52; Rom 9:8; 1 John 3:1-2, 10; 5:2; etc.) of God. Paul suggests that "sonship," a trait associated with the Israelite concept of election, is a status available to Jew and Gentile (Rom 9:4-8; Gal 4:5), which would be revealed through the anticipated resurrection (Rom 8:19-23). In Luke 20:36 Jesus proclaims that those who participate in the resurrection will be "like an ANGEL." A different understanding is reflected in 1 Pet 3:18-22, possibly derived from the Enochic traditions, which present the resurrected Christ preaching to the "spirits in prison," who may have been connected with the "fallen" angels of Gen 6:1-4 and who are now subject to his authority (1 *En.* 15:8-12). The NT usages are consistent with Jewish traditions of that period. *See* ADOPTION; PEOPLE OF GOD.

E. THEODORE MULLEN JR.

GOD MOST HIGH. *See* ALMIGHTY.

GOD OF GODS אֱלֹהֵי הָאֱלֹהִים 'elohe ha'elohim]. Used of God as supreme deity, ruler of all beings, human and divine (Deut 10:17; Josh 22:22; Ps 84:7 [Heb. 84:8]; 136:2; Dan 2:47; 11:36). *See* GOD, NAMES OF.

GOD OF HOSTS אֱלֹהֵי צְבָאוֹת 'elohe tseva'oth]. A variant of the more common epithet, LORD OF HOSTS, as the numerous attestations of the form "Yahweh, God of Hosts" suggest. *See* GOD, NAMES OF; HOSTS, HOSTS OF HEAVEN.

GOD OF THE COVENANT אֵל בְּרִית 'el berith]. The designation, 'el berith, "God of the Covenant," occurs only in reference to a "temple of 'el berith" at

Shechem (Judg 9:46), also called "the temple of Baal Berith" (Judg 9:4).

GOD SOWS [יִזְרְעֶאל yizreʿeʾl]. This meaning of the name JEZREEL, Hosea's first son (Hos 1:4), serves as a warning to Israel, recalling the violence done by King Ahab (1 Kgs 21:1-10) in the valley of Jezreel. Later, God promises to sow Jezreel's restoration (Hos 2:23). *See* GOMER; HOSEA, BOOK OF.

JESSICA TINKLENBERG DEVEGA

GOD THE FATHER. This metaphor, not common in the OT, presents God in anthropomorphic or human-like terms. It compares human fathers and God's actions. Just as a human father has compassion for or reproves a child in love, so God (Ps 103:13; Prov 3:12; Deut 8:5). The father image denotes God's covenant relationship with Israel (Deut 32:6; Exod 4:22). As Father, God created or established the people (Mal 2:10), loves them as children (Hos 11:1), and expects their obedience (Deut 14:1). More often than not, Israel, depicted as a son (Hos 11:1) and daughter (Isa 1:8), is a disobedient child (Isa 1:2). The estranged people remind God that "you, O Lord, are our father; our Redeemer from of old" and beg God to turn back to them (Isa 63:15-19). Jeremiah presents God as a father who laments the people's faithlessness yet calls them to repent. The people turn to God as penitent children (Jer 3:19-25). Jewish prayers of the second temple period address God as "father" (4Q372).

Maternal imagery is also used. God gives birth to and sets limits for the sea, clouds, darkness, and ice and hoarfrost (Job 38:8-11, 29). God also conceives, gives birth to, and nurses the child Israel (Num 11:12; Deut 32:18; Isa 46:3-4). Though a divine warrior, God cries out like a woman in labor against Israel's enemies (Isa 42:14). God's sovereign ways are no more to be questioned than a woman in labor (Isa 45:10-11). The maternal image highlights God's compassion for the child Israel; the Hebrew word compassion (rkhm רחם) is from the same root as "womb" (Isa 49:15; 66:13).

The NT uses this metaphor more frequently. Paul identifies God as the father of Jesus to denote their close relationship. As God's agent or son, Jesus' liberating work expresses the Father's will (Gal 1:3-4). The Father raises Jesus from the dead (Rom 6:4; Gal 1:1), who will hand the Kingdom to the Father (1 Cor 15:24). Paul prays that believers will be blameless before the Father (judge) at Jesus' coming (1 Thess 3:13). As in the OT, the Father creates everything (1 Cor 8:5), shows mercy (2 Cor 1:3), and receives the people's praise (Rom 15:6; Phil 4:20). Through Jesus God becomes Father of believers through adoption (Rom 8:23). They cry out to him as "abba" (Rom 8:15; Gal 4:6; *see* ABBA).

The Synoptic Gospels present the Father as authoritative (Matt 11:25), loving (Luke 15:11-32), impartial (Matt 5:45), forgiving (Matt 6:14-15), judge (Matt 18:23-35; 25:31-46), provider (Matt 6:8, 25-32), and hearer of prayers (Matt 6:9). Jesus exists in intimate relationship with and reveals God as father (Luke 10:21-22), whose mercy for all believers should imitate (Luke 6:36).

John's Gospel uses the metaphor about 120 times. Jesus' revelation of God through words and works is rooted in the intimate relationship of the Father and Son from before creation (John 1:1-18). It is marked by oneness (10:30, 38) and love (3:35). The Father sends Jesus to reveal God's life-giving and judging activity (5:19-30). To see, hear, know, or honor Jesus is to encounter the Father (5:23; 12:45; 14:7-10). In receiving Jesus, believers are begotten (1:12; 3:3-10) as God's children, who form a community of love and service (13:13-17, 34-35), and to do the Father's works revealed by Jesus (14:12). *See* FATHER; GOD, HOUSE-HOLD OF; GOD, METAPHORS FOR; GOD, NAMES OF; MOTHER; SON OF GOD.

WARREN CARTER

GODFEARER [φοβούμενοι τὸν θεόν phoboumenoi ton theon "those who fear God," σεβόμενοι τὸν θεόν sebomenoi ton theon "those who revere God," θεοσεβεῖς theosebeis]. A term that designates Gentile sympathizers with Judaism. Jewish, classical, and Christian literary texts, as well as documentary evidence of inscriptions, show that in the Hellenistic-Roman period a significant number of Gentiles in different parts of the ancient world were either interested in or sympathetic toward, Judaism. According to Josephus (*Ag. Ap.* 2.282), "there is not one city, Greek or barbarian, not a single nation, to which our custom of abstaining from work on the seventh day has not spread, and where the fasts and the lightning of lamps and many of our prohibitions in the matter of food are not observed." The forms of union of Gentiles to Judaism and the degree of their involvement were varied: many Gentiles adopted Jewish customs, such as Sabbath observance and dietary laws; others had close relations with Jewish communities and were only one step from becoming proselytes (*see* NATIONS; PROSELYTE). It was from their ranks that at least some of the converts to Judaism were drawn. In the fourteenth satire of Juvenal, in which he describes the harmful effect of the bad example of parents on their children, he says that if the father is idle on every seventh day, abstains from the flesh of pig, and worships nothing but the clouds and the spirit of the heavens, then the son will not only follow his example, but will go further and will allow himself to be circumcised, i.e., will become a proselyte. In some places, Godfearers formed a defined group. Until the 1930s, this category was called in scholarly literature "semi-proselytes," but since Jewish law knows no semi-proselytes, and a pious sympathizer was not expected to become a full convert, this term gradually fell out of use.

The existence of Gentile adherents to the Jewish cult was of great importance for Jews who lived in the DIASPORA. Godfearers belonged to different social groups. From the inscription in Aphrodisias (Caria, modern Turkey), we know that among them were craftsmen. But among Godfearers there were also people of prominence whose social links with Jewish communities could secure Jewish life in the Gentile milieu. Dio Cassius (*Roman History* 67.14.1-3) testifies that in Domitian's reign many people "drifted into Jewish ways," including Domitian's first cousin, consul Flavius Clemens. There are some indications that among Godfearers there were many women. Josephus (*J.W.* 2.560) reported that almost the whole female population in Damascus was devoted to Judaism. In the time of Nero, the empress Poppaea may have been attracted to Judaism (Josephus, *Ant.* 20.195). Some Godfearers were benefactors of Jewish communities and participated in charitable activities. From epigraphical evidence we know that a certain Capitolina, who belonged to a well-known family, decorated a synagogue in Tralles (Caria) and Julia Severa, a member of the local aristocracy of Acmonia in Phrygia and the priestess of a pagan cult, built a synagogue. In Aphrodisias, town counselors were among subscribers to a Jewish charitable institution. In Panticapaem (Bosporan Kingdom, modern Kertch in the Crimea), the Jewish prayer-house was built by a highly placed official (*see* SYNAGOGUE).

A paradigmatic description of a model Gentile sympathizer with Judaism is given in Acts 10. A Roman centurion from the Italian cohort, Cornelius, is pious—his piety being expressed through the Jewish practices almsgiving and prayer, and he enjoys a good reputation among Jews. Nevertheless, he is not a member of the Jewish community—he is a Gentile who holds an official position and in such capacity is obliged to participate in the official state pagan cult. The Jewish Christians who came with Peter to Cornelius' house were astonished that Cornelius was qualified to receive the Holy Spirit (Acts 10:41).

Luke devoted a substantial part of Acts to the Godfearers (Acts 10; 13:16, 26, 43, 50; 16:14; 17:4, 17; 18:6-9), who played an important role in his theology. These Gentiles stood on the boundary between God's people and the pagan world. Though pagans, they were accepted by God, since they feared him and worked righteousness, and thus their right to be accepted into Christian community was justified. The conversion of Cornelius marked a new departure in the policy of the Christian mission: assurances were given that this new turn was validated by God. The Godfearers were the first group among the Gentiles to hear the Christian message and, on the whole, showed themselves to be receptive to it, though in some places, Jewish communities took measures to fight for influence over the Godfearers. The more widespread Christian teaching became, the more actively Jews looked for the support of Jewish sympathizers. Godfearers could be either the backbone of the Gentile Christian communities or the greatest impediment to the spread of the Christian mission.

Patristic literature preserves information about the existence of Godfearers who neither remained close to the synagogue nor became Christians. They formed separate religious groups such as the Hypsistarii and Messalians. Later, some of them gave rise to Christian sects.

In the talmudic period, the rabbis started to determine the status of Godfearers. The term they used is *heaven-fearers*, where heaven is a traditional substitute for God. This term, however, appears only in later writings, and is not found in MISHNAH.

Bibliography: Louis Feldman. *Jew and Gentile in the Ancient World: Attitudes and Interactions from Alexander to Justinian* (1993); Martin Goodman. *Mission and Conversion: Proselytizing in the Religious History of the Roman Empire* (1994); Irina Levinskaya. *The Book of Acts in Its Diaspora Setting* (1996); Joyce Reynolds and Robert Tannenbaum. *Jews and Godfearers at Aphrodisias* (1987); Paul R. Trebilco. *Jewish Communities in Asia Minor* (1991); Max Wilcox. "The 'God-Fearers' in Acts—Reconsideration." *JSNT* 13 (1981) 102–22.

IRINA LEVINSKAYA

GODLESS [אוֹנִים ʾonim בְּלִיַּעַל beliyaʿal, זֵדִים zedhim, חָנֵף khanef, ; ἄθεος atheos, ἀνόσιος anosios, ἀσεβής asebēs, βέβηλος bebēlos]. The khanef is a person who ignores God, God's rules, and the threat of punishment for so doing (Job 8:13; Isa 10:6; 33:14), and the khanef harms others through slander (Isa 9:17; Prov 11:9). Job's friends imply that he is such a person, while he maintains he is not (Job 8:13; 13:16; 15:34; 17:8; 20:5; 27:8; 34:30; 36:13). The zedhim are haughty, insolent persons who do not submit to God (Ps 119:122). The beliyaʿal is a worthless person, "godless" in the sense of bringing only harm to others. The ʾonim are the powerful who believe they can create their own future (Prov 11:7). An asebēs is impious—a person who does not practice the virtue of eusebeia (εὐσέβεια), normally expected religious behavior (Rom 4:5; 5:6; 1 Tim 1:9; 1 Pet 4:18; 2 Pet 2:5, 6; 3:7). An anosios (1 Tim 1:9; 2 Tim 3:2) stands or acts against things set apart for God (holy things, such as temples, priests, or sacrifices). An atheos is without the one true God, and thus has no hope (Eph 2:12). The bebēlos focuses on worldly rather than spiritual things (1 Tim 1:9; Heb 12:16).

RICHARD B. VINSON

GODLY [אֱלֹהִים ʾelohim, חָסִיד khasidh; εὐσεβής eusebēs, εὐσεβῶς eusebōs]. The khasidh lives by God's khesedh (חֶסֶד, *see* KHESED), the aspect of God's nature that keeps God well disposed toward humanity and faithful to the covenant. The khasidh is "godly" in the sense of living in a way that pleases God (e.g., Pss 31:23 [Heb. 31:24]; 32:6; Hos 6:4, 6); the word appears often in the Psalms as a term for God's people as opposed to sinners (e.g., Pss 30:4 [Heb. 30:5]; 37:28; 85:8 [Heb. 85:9]; 97:10; 116:15). The Hebrew word for God, ʾelohim, is once used as an adjective to mean "godly" (Mal 2:15, "godly offspring"). The eusebēs is a person who lives a eusebōs life, or according to eusebeia (εὐσέβεια). Outside the NT, eusebeia is the virtue of displaying appropriate respect to the gods; Christian writers would substitute "God" for "the gods" in that definition. According to Titus 2:11-12, devotion to God teaches us to lead lives that are self-controlled, just, and godly; any Greco-Roman philosopher would agree (see also Acts 10:7; 2 Pet 2:9). Paul writes of "godly grief" in 2 Cor 7:9-11, or grief "in accord with God." He means that his hard words to them brought sorrow but also repentance and better behavior.

RICHARD B. VINSON

GOD'S ONLY SON [μονογενής υἱός τοῦ θεοῦ monogenēs huios tou theou]. A Johannine phrase (John 1:14, 18; 3:16, 18; 1 John 4:9). The Greek monogenēs, "only, unique," is sometimes translated "only-begotten" (i.e., KJV, NKJV, NAS), a decision based on the VULGATE, Jerome's 4th cent. Latin translation of the Bible. Jerome chose the word *unigenitus*, "only-begotten," to translate monogenēs in instances when the word was applied to Jesus (i.e., John 1:14; compare Zech 12:10). Elsewhere he translated *unicus*, "only" (i.e., Luke 7:12; 8:42; 9:38). His choice was not a grammatical one, but a reflection of the church's rejection of the Arian position on the nature of Christ and the subsequent language of the Nicene Creed identifying Jesus as "begotten, not made" (*see* CHRISTOLOGY). While the Father/Son relationship of God and Jesus is important to John's Gospel, the word monogenēs should not be interpreted in light of these later debates about the nature of Christ as "begotten." The Johannine phrase speaks instead to Jesus' unique relationship to the Father, something John expresses in a number of ways (compare 5:19-21; 14:10-11). As God's only Son, Jesus comes to the world, a reflection of God's glory (John 1:14), bringing both life and judgment (John 3:14-19).

SUSAN E. HYLEN

GODS, GODDESSES. The first commandment of the Decalogue states that Israel "shall have no other gods before" YHWH (Exod 20:3). Taken at face value, the commandment does not deny the existence of other gods. It does even insist on an exclusive relation with other deities. It may be understood as merely emphasizing the priority of Yahweh before others; Yahweh is the deity with whom Israel is to relate primarily.

The Song of the Sea, arguably among the earliest texts in the Bible, too, implies that other gods exist, though none of these others is comparable to Israel's God (Exod 15:11), a claim that would be reiterated in later passages as well (2 Sam 7:22; Ps 89:8-9; Jer 10:6; 2 Chr 6:14). The sense one gets in most of the OT is that Yahweh is the superior deity who presides over the council of the gods, a role that EL plays in Canaanite mythology. Thus, Israel's God is called EL ELYON ("Most High") and is portrayed as the one who parcels out the nations "according to the number of the gods" (Deut 32:8 in NRSV, which follows the Greek and evidence from Qumran), in particular choosing Jacob as his own (Ps 47:4). Thus, the OT recognizes that the nations have their own gods—"foreign gods" (Gen 35:2, 4; Deut 31:16; 1 Sam 7:3), like CHEMOSH of the Moabites (Num 21:29; 1 Kgs 11:7), MILCOM of the Ammonites (1 Kgs 11:5, 7), RIMMON of the Arameans (2 Kgs 5:18), BAAL-ZEBUB of Ekron (2 Kgs 1:2-3), DAGON of the Philistines (Judg 16:23; 1 Sam 5:2), ASTARTE of the Sidonians (1 Kgs 11:5; 2 Kgs 23:13), and BEL and NEBO of the Babylonians (Isa 46:1), and so on—but Yahweh, the God of Israel is superior to them all.

Yahweh is also the supreme deity in the divine council, indeed, the "GOD OF GODS" (Deut 10:17; Josh 22:23; Pss 84:7; 136:2; Dan 2:47; 11:6). Yahweh is the deity before whom the other gods bow down (Ps 97:7) and the gods are called upon to praise Yahweh (Ps 29:1). He is one feared in the divine council (Ps 89:8). Indeed, Israel's God is understood to be the one who presides over the council, issuing judgments against the gods of the nations, casting them out from the realm of the divine when they do not do their duties in maintaining justice on earth (Ps 82; *see* DIVINE ASSEMBLY).

In theory, then, it was possible for someone in Israel to worship other gods, and some must have done so, or else there would have been no need for the first commandment or for the prophetic injunctions against IDOLATRY. The problem appears to have been particularly acute in the Northern Kingdom, where prophets like Elijah, Elisha, and Hosea, as well as the Deuteronomists, warned against following other gods, notably BAAL and ASHERAH. The danger that Baalism posed for ancient Israel comes in part from the fact Yahweh was portrayed as a storm deity, like the Canaanite deity known properly as baʿli-haddu ("the lord Haddu"), and, indeed, that Yahweh was early on identified with that deity and was even called baʿal (בַּעַל "lord"), as evident from names with the Baal-element given to children of Yahwists. As for Asherah, though the common noun came to refer to a cultic symbol and representation of divine presence in Israel, it once represented the goddess who was the consort of the Canaanite high god, El, and may even have been understood as least by some to have been the consort of Yahweh, as some Hebrew inscriptions imply. The Northern Kingdom seemed more susceptible to such association of Yahweh with these other gods, as the Bible itself as well as epigraphic evidence suggest. The biblical polemics against the worship of other deities, though, may have exaggerated. The preponderance of Yahwistic personal names in the pre-exilic period indicates that Judah and Israel were largely committed to Yahweh as their God.

By the mid-6th cent. BCE, we find the first direct denial of the existence of other deities (Isa 44:6; 45:5, 14). Though the divine council is still mentioned in the prologue of Job (Job 1–2), it may in fact be a literary trope, for no other god plays a role in the rest of the book, and Job indeed reckons that God alone is accountable for Job's sufferings. Moreover, in Daniel's vision of the heavenly court, one finds the mention of a plurality of thrones, though Daniel does not describe a divine council in place, but only a single deity is enthroned (Dan 7:9-10). *See* DEITIES, UNDERWORLD; GOD, NAMES OF; GOD, OT VIEW OF; GREEK RELIGION AND PHILOSOPHY.

Bibliography: John Day. *Yahweh and the Gods and Goddesses of Canaan* (2002); Patrick D. Miller. *The Religion of Ancient Israel* (2000); Jeffrey H. Tigay. *You Shall Have No Other Gods: Israelite Religion in the Light of Hebrew Inscriptions* (1986).

C. L. SEOW

GOEL [גֹּאֵל goʾel]. Often translated "redeemer," the "goel" is the individual responsible for providing some form of justice for a dead family member (Num 35:16-21; Deut 25:5-6; Ruth 4:1; Isa 48:17). *See* REDEEM, REDEEMER.

GOG gog [גּוֹג gogh]. A descendant of Reuben listed only in a genealogical list in 1 Chr 5:1-10 in some unclear connection with Joel, Shemaiah, and Shemei.

GOG AND MAGOG gog, may'gog [גּוֹג גֹּוֹג gogh, מָגוֹג maghogh; Γὼγ Gōg, Μαγώγ Magōg]. Gog from the land of Magog first appears in Ezek 38–39 as the archetypal evil force rising up in the eschatological age, marshaling all the enemies of Israel to attack this peaceful and defenseless people. Yahweh defeats Gog and his hordes, establishing the promised Covenant of Peace (Ezek 34:16; 37:28). Gog and Magog also appear in Rev 20:7-10, where Magog has become a general, fighting alongside Gog. In both cases, Gog is the antagonist in a plotline following the ANE Combat Myth.

Some who see a historical figure in Gog settle on Gyges of Lydia, but Gyges' military career is not that of an archetypal enemy. The Gyges of legend, also proposed, achieves success through artifice, not military victory. The Sovereignty of the Creator, so central to Ezekiel, suggests a more menacing opponent. Others see the name derived from the Sumerian gug, meaning "darkness." The Gog of Ezek 38–39 is presented as a trans-historical representative of the cosmic powers of chaos, the ultimate symbol of anticreation, in opposition to the divine

sovereign. The disorder and darkness need to be undone if the promised Covenant of Peace is to be established.

PAUL E. FITZPATRICK

GOIIM goi'im [גּוֹיִם goyim]. Often translated as NATIONS or Gentiles. Specifically, the region reigned over by King Tidal, who, along with kings Amraphel, Arioch, and Chedorlaomer, defeated kings Bera, Birsha, Shinab, Shemeber, and the king of Bela in the Siddim Valley (Gen 14:1, 9). The similarity of the name Tidal to the Hittite royal name Tudhaliash has led some scholars to suggest that this group were Hittites. The people with this name in Josh 12:23, whose king Joshua defeated, were either associated with Gilgal (MT) or Galilee ("nations of Galilee," LXX). They were possibly a migrating people related to the Philistines.

EMILY R. CHENEY

GOLAN goh'luhn [גּוֹלָן golan]. Moses chose the city of Golan as one of three cities of refuge east of the Jordan in the territory of Bashan allotted the half-tribe of Manasseh (Deut 4:43; Josh 20:8). Golan became a Gershonite Levitical city (Josh 21:27; 1 Chr 6:71 [Heb. 6:56]). The area around the city was also known as Golan. The Golan Heights is a flat, fertile tableland bounded by the Sea of Galilee/Rift Valley on the west, the Yarmuq River on the south, and Mount Hermon in the northeast. Early Middle Bronze Age megalithic DOLMENS, stone burial cairns, are scattered upon the plateau. Josephus called this region Gaulanitis, the eastern boundary of Galilee under the tetrarchy of Philip in NT times. According to Eusebius, the city and plateau was densely populated. The location of the city of Golan is unknown, although one suggestion is Sahem el-Jolan, nearly 17 mi. from Galilee.

MICHAEL G. VANZANT

GOLD [זָהָב zahav; χρυσός chrysos]. Gold, one of the most precious of metals, is cited frequently in the Bible, both in a literal and a metaphorical sense. The traditional source of gold was OPHIR (1 Kgs 9:28, probably south Arabia or Yemen). PARVAIM is also mentioned as a place of origin (2 Chr 3:6), but this has not been identified and may well be another name for Yemen, or the term may simply mean "from the east."

Gold was a synonym for wealth: Abraham was rich in gold, and Solomon was said to be so rich that he did not have silver drinking vessels, but only gold ones (1 Kgs 10:21). Because it is relatively soft, gold was often used in the form of gold leaf, covering objects made of wood, bronze, or silver. Gold leaf was used to cover statues and idols, and this was probably the case with the golden calf. The Ark of the Covenant was overlaid with gold leaf (Exod 25:11-18). Much of the temple furniture was made at least partly of gold.

JEWELRY made of gold has been found in archaeological contexts all over the Levant, mainly in burials and in hoards. Earrings were particularly popular.

Because of its intrinsic value, gold was also used as currency, although it seems to have been largely replaced by SILVER as the more common currency in the later Iron Age. So-called chocolate bar ingots (bars pre-shaped to be broken or cut into equal portions) of gold have been found in Iron Age Amathus, on Cyprus, and in Beth Shean A in an 11th cent. BCE context. Unmixed hoards of gold are relatively rare in the southern Levant in the Iron Age, but a famous hoard of fine jewelry, mostly earrings, probably unworn, and of high quality and craftsmanship was found in Tawilan in southern Jordan, dated to the 10th or 9th cent. BCE.

It is likely that gold jewelry for women had a double function, being both an ornament and a source of wealth, a form of insurance in case of divorce. Until very recently (and in some cases even today) gold and silver jewelry had this same double function in many Near Eastern societies. On the other hand, the wearing of gold jewelry was clearly not limited to women in the biblical period. The Midianites, e.g., wore golden earrings (Judg 8:24).

EVELINE J. VAN DER STEEN

GOLDEN CALF. *See* CALF, GOLDEN.

GOLDEN RULE. In the SERMON ON THE MOUNT, the following words are attributed to Jesus, "In everything do to others as you would have them do to you" (Matt 7:12//Luke 6:31). Within the context of the first Gospel, this "golden rule" (a phrase with 17th cent. origins) appears as an isolated verse within Matthew's collection of sayings that comprise the Sermon on the Mount. As a summary of the law and the prophets, this saying functions as a concise abridgment of Jesus' message, similar to the "double commandment" in Matt 22:40. The Golden Rule and the "double commandment" each function as a succinct summation of the TEN COMMANDMENTS (Exod 20:13-17; Deut 5:17-21). Indeed, in Matthew, Jesus' use of panta (πάντα, "in everything") hints at a more general principle rather than at a specific moral exhortation.

This rule appears to have a more fitting literary context within Luke's version of Jesus' sermon (see Luke 6:27-36). It falls within a series of sayings in which "loving enemies," "blessing persecutors," "giving to beggars" are all part of what it means to be "merciful" even as God is merciful. This rule comprises what it means to take the correct course of action, that is, "to do unto others." Some scholars argue that Luke's version of the saying is closer to Q than Matthew's (*see* Q, QUELLE). In any case, both Matthew's and Luke's depictions encourage an active way of living in the world.

Some historical Jesus scholars question the historicity of these words due to numerous parallels in the wider Jewish tradition, including its negative equivalent (i.e., "do not do to others, what you do not want done to you"). This latter saying is attributed to Rabbi Hillel, among others, who was an early contemporary of Jesus. Apparently, Hillel spoke this saying, as a summary of the entire TORAH, to a potential proselyte (*b. Sabb.* 31a), in a context similar to Matthew's version of Jesus' saying (*see* HILLEL THE ELDER, HOUSE OF HILLEL). The negative parallel, however, is not exclusive to Jewish tradition, as early Christian sources such as the *Didache* (1:2) also include this adaptation of the rule. Nor is the positive form exclusive to Jesus: "That which a person makes request from the Lord for his/her own soul, in the same manner let that person behave toward every living soul" (*2 En.* 61:1-2).

In the history of interpretation, this pithy saying has often been viewed as the entire "gospel" in sum (*see* GOSPEL, MESSAGE). It is not, however, unique to ancient Judaism or Christianity; the idea of reciprocal morality occurs in various ancient Eastern traditions. According to an ancient Buddhist saying, "Comparing oneself to others in such terms as 'Just as I am so are they, just as they are so am I,' he should neither kill nor cause others to kill" (*Sutta Nipata* 705 (see also Confucius' philosophy, *Anelects* 15.23).

As a fundamental teaching of the Jesus of the Gospels, the Golden Rule is one of Jesus' most memorable sayings and has had great influence on the history of Christian interpretation.

EMERSON B. POWERY

GOLDSMITH [צוֹרֵף tsoref]. The Hebrew word appears a number of times in Isaiah and Jeremiah, mainly in relation to idols (Isa 40:19; 41:7; 46:6; Jer 10:9) made of SILVER, often overlaid or decorated with gold leaf. The goldsmith worked both in silver and in GOLD. In Judg 17:4 tsoref is translated "SILVERSMITH."

Gold earrings, pendants, and beads are found regularly in archaeological contexts from the biblical period (Iron Age II), showing that goldsmiths were familiar with a wide variety of techniques, including lost wax casting, filigrain, cloisonné, and granulation. Gold leaf was often used for jewelry or for gilding.

EVELINE J. VAN DER STEEN

GOLGOTHA gol'guh-thuh [Γολγοθᾶ Golgotha]. Luke calls the place of Christ's crucifixion simply "Skull" (Κρανίον Kranion 23:33), whereas the three other evangelists give both this Greek name and its Semitic equivalent Golgotha. Matthew (27:33) and Mark (15:22) give the Greek name "Skull Place" (Kraniou Topos Κρανίου Τόπος) first and then the translation Golgotha. This order is inverted in John 19:17, which speaks of "the Skull Place which is called in Hebrew Golgotha." In fact Golgotha sounds closer to the

Todd Bolen/BiblePlaces.com
Figure 1: Garden Tomb

Aram. gulgalta> (גּוּלְגָּלְתָּא) than to the Hebrew gulgoleth (גֻּלְגֹּלֶת), but to call Hebrew what was is in fact Aram. is common in the NT (e.g. John 19:13; Acts 21:40; 22:2; 26:14).

The site may have received its name because of a topographical feature such as holes reminiscent of a pair of eyes. This interpretation is followed by those that connect the location of Jesus' crucifixion and burial to a cliff that resembles a skull and a nearby rock cut tomb outside the old City near the Damascus Gate. But a more generic explanation is also possible. In Arabic ras "head" is frequently applied to a ridge jutting out from a range, e.g., Ras Feshkha just south of Qumran. The site traditionally identified as Golgtha was in fact a section of poor rock left projecting from the east wall of the quarry beneath the Holy Sepulchre.

This mundane explanation did not satisfy Christian piety. Origen (185–254 CE) claimed, on the basis of Jewish tradition, that the skull was that of Adam who had been buried there. This interpretation became dominant in the Eastern church because of its theological potential. The Western church, however, tended to follow Jerome (331–420 CE), who refused the Adamic interpretation, and maintained that the name derived from an execution ground on which the skulls of the condemned lay scattered. The unexplained shift from the singular ("the Skull") to the plurality of many skulls is just one of the flaws in this speculative suggestion. Not only did capital trials and executions take place in Caesarea Maritima from the imposition of direct control by the Romans in 6 CE, but the presence of Jewish tombs in the immediate vicinity of the traditional site of Golgotha clearly indicate that it was not a Jewish place of execution. In fact there is no documented place of execution in 1st cent. Jerusalem. Golgotha was simply the arbitrary choice of the centurion on duty.

The north and west sides and the summit of the rock venerated as Golgotha are visible today under protective glass in the Holy Sepulchre. The rock rises some 11 m above the bed of the quarry, and there is a vertical earthquake crack in the west face. It was cut on the south to take the temenos wall of the Capitoline temple erected in 135 CE, and probably also on the east when it was incorporated into the southeast corner of the open courtyard that separated the Rotunda from the Basilica in the Constantinian Holy Sepulchre. *See* CROSS; CRUCIFIXION; HOLY SEPULCHRE; JERUSALEM.

Bibliography: C. Coüasnon. *The Church of the Holy Sepulchre in Jerusalem* (1974); J. Jeremias. *Golgotha* (1926).

JEROME MURPHY-O'CONNOR

Figure 2: Holy Sepulchre edicule

GOLIATH gul-li´ uhth [גָּלְיָת golyath; Γολιαθ Goliath]. Philistine champion defeated by David in single combat (1 Sam 17). Though Goliath is well armed and described as a giant, David defeats him with one stone and a slingshot. First Samuel 17:4 (MT and translated as such in the NRSV depicts Goliath as six cubits and a span tall, which would make him over 9 ft. tall. Other manuscripts (Lucianic recension of LXX, 4Q51, and Josephus, *Ant.* 6.171) all indicate four cubits and a span, which would still make him over 6 ft. tall. In either case, within the context of the battle, Goliath is a more than formidable opponent. Anachronistically, after defeating Goliath and cutting off his head with his own sword, the story says that David took the head and the weaponry of Goliath to Jerusalem (1 Sam 17:54). However, in another instance it seems that David had dedicated the sword of Goliath to the sanctuary of Yahweh at Nob (1 Sam 21:10; 22:10). Second Samuel 21:19 identifies Goliath's slayer as ELHANAN of Bethlehem, while 1 Chr 20:5 says that Elhanan killed Lahmi, the brother of Goliath. This has led some to consider Elhanan as an alternate name for David, or to conclude that an achievement of Elhanan was later attributed to David. Sirach praises David for removing Israel's disgrace by killing Goliath (47:4; see also Ps 151:7; *L.A.B.* 61:4).

C. MARK MCCORMICK

GOMER goh´muhr [גֹּמֶר gomer]. 1. Gomer the daughter of DIBLAIM was the wife of the prophet Hosea (*see* HOSEA, BOOK OF). She is described as an 'esheth zenunim (אֵשֶׁת זְנוּנִים, "wife of harlotries" or "promiscuous wife") at the point of marriage rather than a wife who subsequently became "promiscuous" (Hos 1:2). The root znh (זנה) refers to any kind of pre- or extra-marital intercourse and zenunim seems to refer to habitual behavior rather than a profession (as a prostitute). Gomer is taken by the prophet as a living sign and becomes the mother of three symbolic children: Jezreel, LO-RUHAMAH ("Not Loved") and LO-AMMI ("Not My People"). Her role in this respect is similar to the "prophetess" in Isa 8:3 who also conceives a symbolic child. In the poetic passage of Hos 2 she runs away after her "lovers" (representing the Baals) and is stripped and punished and recaptured/restored by God/her husband. Gomer may or may not be the unnamed woman "loved" and "bought" by Hosea who is described as "having a lover" and being an "adulteress" (Hos 3:1).

The harlot-nation is often employed in the Prophets as a metaphor designed to shock a male audience by calling them "whores" (compare Ezek 16; 23; Jer 22:20-23; Nah 3:5-6). However, Gomer is the only incidence of the metaphor being applied to a living symbolic person. Traditionally, her story has been read as a divine love story, but increasingly her graphic punishment has been seen as a problem by biblical critics and Christians concerned with how the text might have an impact on women and victims of sexual abuse within the church. Gomer also scandalized traditional interpreters who found it difficult to accept God's instruction to a prophet to marry a woman who is already promiscuous. Targum Jonathan interpreted Diblaim [divlayim דִּבְלַיִם] as a derivative of "fig," and turned God's command to "Take a wife of harlotry" into a prophecy from Hosea that if the people repented, they would be forgiven, but if not they would fall "as the leaves of the fig-tree fall." Augustine argued that she abandoned her life of harlotry before her marriage; Jerome claimed that her marriage to Hosea remade her "chaste." Luther stated that she was a pure woman who only took on the name of "harlot" as a metaphor.

2. Oldest son of Japheth and grandson of Noah, and the father of Ashkenaz, Riphath, and Togarmah according to the table of nations (Gen 10:2-3; compare 1 Chr 1:5-6). Ezekiel names "Gomer and all its troops" among the nations to be defeated as part of God's judgment on Gog, king of Magog (Ezek 38:2-6).

YVONNE SHERWOOD

GOMORRAH guh-mor´uh [עֲמֹרָה 'amorah, Γόμορρα Gomorra]. One of the five "cities of the plain" destroyed by God (Gen 19:24-25), information in Genesis indicates that Gomorrah was located in the Jordan Valley in the Dead Sea area (Gen 13:10), although its precise location remains unknown. Gomorrah is never mentioned alone in the biblical material but always occurs alongside SODOM (Gen 18:20; Isa 1:9) or with the other cities of the plain (Deut 29:23).

In Gen 14, King BIRSHA of Gomorrah joins other cities in the area in an unsuccessful revolt against CHEDORLAOMER of ELAM. Gomorrah is later destroyed after Yahweh sends two angels to Sodom to find out if the wickedness of these cities is as great as he has heard (Gen 18:16-21). Sodom and Gomorrah are mentioned frequently in both the OT and NT as paradigms of wickedness (Jer 23:14) and examples of God's punishment (Isa 13:19; Matt 10:15; 2 Pet 2:6).

KEVIN A. WILSON

GONG [χαλκός chalkos]. A percussive musical instrument made of copper or brass. In 1 Cor 13:1 prophecy without love is compared to a noisy gong. *See* MUSIC; MUSICAL INSTRUMENTS.

GOOD [טוֹב tov; ἀγαθός agathos, καλός kalos, χρηστός chrestos]. "Good" in the Bible expresses a satisfying experience of reality, rather than defines an abstract idea or moral norm. It is most commonly used as an adjective to describe or appraise the beautiful feature, desirable quality, or useful purpose of a person, a thing, or an event. For example, God saw the light as good (Gen 1:4), promised the Hebrews a good land to inhabit (Exod 3:8; Deut 1:25), and gave them the law that is good (Ps 119:39; Rom 7:12). Jesus said that the seed in the good soil yields grains thirty-, sixty-, and hundredfold (Mark 4:8), and he is the good shepherd who lays down his life for the sheep (John 10:11). Paul contended that the spiritual gifts were given for the good benefit of the church (1 Cor 12:7) and urged his readers to share good things with the teachers of the word (Gal 6:6). Thus, "good" is an expression of a favorable judgment on aesthetic, practical, and moral grounds.

Most significant is the exclusive use of agathos in reference to God, when Jesus said to the man asking about eternal life: "No one is good but God alone" (Mark 10:18). To say "God alone is good" is to profess the Lord God as the only (Mark 12:29; Deut 6:4) almighty creator who made everything good (Mark 13:19; Gen 1:4, 10, 12) and a loving savior ready to rescue God's people from any danger (Mark 11:12; 13:40; Deut 23:14; 2 Sam 22:3; Isa 25:9). Jesus has indeed healed the sick and cast out demons (Mark 1–2) and will give up his life as a ransom for many (Mark 10:45). However, he does all these to proclaim the good news of God's kingdom and he serves as God's agent at God's will (Mark 11:34), so he gives all honor to God alone.

In the OT, God's goodness is expressed in actions of mercy and justice. God's protection and assistance are extended especially to the orphans, the widows, the weak, and the poor. There is no wonder that the psalmist praised God: "O how abundant is your goodness that you have laid up for those who fear you, and accomplished for those who take refuge in you, in the sight of everyone! In the shelter of your presence you hide them from human plots; you hold them safe under your shelter from contentious tongues" (Ps 31:19-20), and exclaimed: "O taste and see that the Lord is good; happy are those who take refuge in him" (Ps 34:8).

God's goodness is so abundant that even sinners, if willing to repent, can count on God's readiness to forgive their sins. Thus, the psalmist pleaded: "Do not remember the sins of my youth or my transgressions; according to your steadfast love remember me, for your goodness' sake, O Lord! Good and upright is the Lord; therefore he instructs sinners in the way" (Ps 25:7-8), and again, "Before I was humbled I went astray, but now I keep your word. You are good and do good; teach me your statutes" (Ps 119:67-68).

The most spectacular goodness that God has shown is liberating the suffering Hebrews from the slavery in Egypt, providing for them in the desert, making covenant with them on Mount Sinai, and giving them the Torah to live by. As Moses said to Hobab, "God has promised good to Israel" (Num 10:29). The story of exodus is the best evidence of God's gracious election of the former slaves as God's people (Exod 6:6-8), and it reveals God's special concern for the deprived and the downtrodden. Having experienced divine care, protection, guidance, and rescues, God's people ought to give

thanks, sing praises, and bear witnesses to God's glory, "for God is good" (Pss 100:5; 106:1; 107:1; 136:1).

In the NT, God's goodness is likewise demonstrated by the indiscriminate care that God as creator provides to all people. As Jesus taught, God makes the sun shine and the rain fall on the evil and the good (Matt 5:45), feeds the birds in the sky, clothes the lilies of the field, and meets people's daily needs (Matt 6:26, 30, 32). God's goodness is further revealed in the gracious release that God as savior offers to the oppressed, as Mary confessed in the Magnificat, "he [God] has brought down the powerful from their thrones, and lifted up the lowly; he has filled the hungry with good things, and sent the rich away empty" (Luke 1:52-53).

God's goodness is culminated in the granting of eternal life to all believers through Jesus Christ. God shows no partiality, as Paul proclaimed, in giving "eternal life" to all who patiently do good and in casting wrath on all who do evil, "the Jew first and also the Greek" (Rom 2:7-11; John 3:16). And it is written that "when the goodness and loving kindness of God our Savior appeared, he saved us, not because of any works of righteousness that we have done, but according to his mercy" by the Holy Spirit and through Jesus Christ, so that "having been justified by his grace, we might become heirs according to the hope of eternal life" (Titus 3:4-7).

God's goodness is so reliable that, even in the face of persecutions, Paul could claim with confidence: "We know that all things work together for good for those who love God, who are called according to his purpose" (Rom 8:28). In response to God's goodness, then, believers should do good works because "He [Jesus Christ] it is who gave himself for us that he might redeem us from all iniquity and purify for himself a people of his own who are zealous for good deeds" (Titus 2:14; 3:8). Leaders of the church, in particular, should be "rich in good works" (1 Tim 6:18) and serve as "a model of good works" in all respects (Titus 2:7).

Thus, the third use of "good" in the Bible has to do with moral character and charitable deeds. In the OT, doing good means to obey the law of God: "Be careful to obey all these words that I command you today, so that it may go well with you and with your children after you forever, because you will be doing what is good and right in the sight of the Lord your God" (Deut 12:28). To do good is the guarantee to live in security and to abide forever (Ps 37:3, 27). In the NT, goodness in a moral sense is a fruit of the HOLY SPIRIT (Gal 5:22, agathōsynē [ἀγαθωσύνη] "goodness or generosity"; Rom 15:14), and doing good is the purpose of Christian life, "for we are what he has made us, created in Christ Jesus for good works, which God prepared beforehand to be our way of life" (Eph 2:10).

It should be emphasized that doing good works is motivated by the experience of God's goodness and is supposed to imitate God's benevolence. Surely, believers are encouraged to behave in a way that most people consider good, truthful, honorable, and commendable (Phil 4:8). But Jesus called his followers to forego the customary principle of "an eye for an eye" and love their enemies, so that they may be perfect as their "heavenly Father is perfect" (Matt 5:48). Paul urged the Christians in Rome to "bless those who persecute you; bless and do not curse them" (Rom 12:14) and to "overcome evil with good" (Rom 12:21), because God has loved them and sent Jesus to die for them while they were still sinners (Rom 5:8). Such a counterintuitive idea of ethics is modeled on the gracious God who extends goodness to the unworthy.

In order to do good works, people need to be able to tell good from evil. The story of Adam and Eve eating the fruit of the tree in the garden hoping to "be like God, knowing good and evil" (Gen 3:5), other interpretations notwithstanding, indicates that exercising moral autonomy to make ethical choices, if misled by evil, may lead to disobedience against God and collision with God's will. Therefore, the Bible is full of exhortations about seeking good and resisting evil (Pss 34:14; 37:27; Amos 5:14-15; 1 Pet 3:11). The definitions of good and evil can be very confusing and moral options ambiguous, so Paul offered this advice: "Do not be conformed to this world, but be transformed by the renewing of your minds, so that you may discern what is the will of God—what is good and acceptable and perfect" (Rom 12:2). In Paul's view, the renewing of minds by the Holy Spirit is the first step to a right discernment.

The Bible also recognizes that to do good works is a constant struggle with the power of sin that controls the flesh. We cannot do the good that we want to do; instead, we do the evil that we hate, even though we like the law of God (Rom 7:14-24). The only help comes from Jesus Christ (Rom 7:25), Paul argued, through whom God will empower believers "to will and to work for his good pleasure" (Phil 2:13). *See* ETHICS IN THE NT; ETHICS IN THE OT; EVIL.

JOHN Y. H. YIEH

GOOD NEWS [בָּשַׂר basar; εὐαγγελίζω euangelizō]. From Hebrew and Greek verbs meaning "to preach/ bring glad tidings"; also translated "good tidings" or "glad tidings." In the OT's historical books, the phrase refers to news of military victory (excluding 1 Sam 4:17 in which basar is negative). The prophets develop theological nuances for the phrase, using it in reference to God's activity, especially God's faithfulness to God's people in exile (e.g., Isaiah). In the NT, the phrase usually indicates the activity or message of God, specifically the gospel of Jesus Christ. Reports of good news are brought by various agents including prophets, angels, Jesus, apostles, and other messengers. *See* GOSPELS.

KATHY R. MAXWELL

GOPHNA [Γοφνά gophna]. A mountainous region (1 Macc 2:28) within Samaria (2 Macc 15:1) where Mattathias and his followers hid during the Has-

monean struggle for independence (167–142 BCE). Josephus wrote that Judas Maccabeus later took refuge specifically in the district of Gophna (*J.W.* 1. 45). Judas' defensive battles were mostly on the roads leading north and west from Jerusalem, suggesting the Hasmonean base may have been located in the mountains within the quadrilateral delineated by Gophna, Modeïn, Ammaus, and Jerusalem.

RALPH K. HAWKINS

GORGIAS gor´juhs [Γοργίας Gorgias]. Gorgias was a Seleucid general and friend of King ANTIOCHUS IV (1 Macc 3:38; 2 Macc 8:9). During the Maccabean revolt, he went to Judea to lead the Syrians against Judas Maccabeus' forces. Gorgias set out at night from Emmaus to surprise the Jewish army, but he found an empty camp because Judas, having heard of their plan, had fled. Early the next morning, however, Judas routed the Seleucids, driving them as far as Jamnia (1 Macc 4:1-25; compare 2 Macc 8:12-29; Josephus *Ant.* 12.298-312). Gorgias then became governor of Idumea (2 Macc 10:14; 12:32), where he engaged the Jews in numerous skirmishes (1 Macc 10:14). He defeated a Jewish offensive at Jamnia (1 Macc 5:55-62, 65-68; compare Josephus, *Ant.* 12.350-53), but 2 Maccabees reports that he was nearly captured before managing to escape to Marisa (12:35). *See* MACCABEES, FIRST AND SECOND BOOKS OF.

DAVID M. REIS

GORTYNA gor-ti´nuh [Γόρτυνα Gortyna]. A city located in south-central Crete on the Letheus River and listed as one of the locations to which the Roman consul Lucius sent copies of a letter in support of the Jews and their high priest Simon (1 Macc 15:23). Among Cretan cities, it was second in significance to Knossos. Gortyna was known for its 5th cent. BCE law code inscribed on a wall within the city.

DEREK E. WITTMAN

GOSHEN goh´shuhn [גֹּשֶׁן goshen; Γέσεμ Gesem]. 1. Goshen is the name given to an area believed to be in the eastern Egyptian Delta region where the Israelites resided from the time of Joseph until their sojourn from Egypt. The land of Goshen is described in Gen 46–47 as an area within EGYPT where Jacob and his sons were allowed to settle and, importantly, a region that was suitable for raising and shepherding livestock. Goshen is twice characterized as "the best part of the land" (Gen 47:6, 11) on which the Israelites, as pastoralists, could care for both their own flocks and those of the pharaoh (47:6). In Gen 47:11 the narrative appears to suggest that Goshen be equated with the "land of Rameses." (LXX Gen 46:28 renders "land of Ramessē" [Ραμεσση] instead of "land of Goshen"). Of Goshen little more is said other than that the descendants of Jacob prospered in the region and remained there until the time of the exodus (Exod 8:18; 9:26).

The specific location of Goshen is an enigma that continues to be debated by scholars. One attempt at determining Goshen's location stemmed from exploring different designations for the region in the LXX, wherein Goshen is twice supplanted by the phrase **Gesem Arabias** (Γέσεμ Ἀραβίας; Gen 45:10; 46:34). This regional appellation was also used by the geographer Ptolemy to denote the 20th Lower Egyptian nome, or administrative district, on the eastern Delta whose capital was Phacusa—or modern Faqus. Moreover, the discovery of the Egyptian place name **Gsm.t** on a number of geographical lists from the area led to the speculation that this toponym was synonymous with biblical Goshen. Two major difficulties arose, however, with this hypothesis. First, the philological connection between the Egyptian **Gsm.t** and the Greek **Gesem** proved dubious under further scrutiny. And second, extant archaeological data provided no other evidence for a village or area named **Gesem** or **goshen** in the region. An alternative name offered in the LXX occurs in connection with the 5th cent. BCE Arabian ruler Geshem, the same antagonist of Nehemiah (Neh 2:19; 6:1-2, 6), whose notable kingdom extended from southern Judah and into the eastern Delta region. Rabinowitz conjectured that the translators of the LXX substituted "the land of Geshem (of Arabia)" for the Hebrew Goshen since the former toponym would have been more recognizable to its intended audience.

If the biblical record does indeed preserve a historical connection between Goshen and the land of Raamses, then Goshen would have been positioned near the Egyptian cities of PITHOM and RAAMSES mentioned in Exod 1:11. Such a location still poses complications, however, as these appellations were common to dozens of Egyptian sites. Continuing excavations in the region have pointed to three possible sites for biblical Pithom: Tell el-Maskhuta, Tell el-Retabeh, and Heliopolis. None of the locations, however, can be conclusively identified with the Pithom referred to in Exod 1. Raamses, in contrast, has been convincingly connected to Avaris, the royal city of RAMESSES II, built on the old Hyksos capital at Tell ed-Dabʿa-Qantir. This city of the Nineteenth and Twentieth Dynasties was situated in the northeast Delta region and, according to historical records, contained monumental architecture comparable to that of Thebes and Memphis.

Evidence gleaned from biblical and archaeological evidence suggests that the land of Goshen existed in the eastern Delta region of Egypt, situated near the modern sites of Faqus and Tell ed-Dabʿa-Qantir. This region was known to have been populated by Semitic peoples, and the name Goshen itself is of Semitic origin. No Egyptian parallel, however, has yet to be discovered in connection with the Greek and Hebrew designations for the area. *See* EXODUS, ROUTE OF.

2. The land of Goshen (LXX **Gosom** Γόσομ) occupied by Joshua's forces (Josh 10:41 and 11:16) is located in the southern hill country of Canaan between Hebron and the Negeb.

3. A city of Judah referred to in Josh 15:51, located in the hill country. Goshen is rendered by the LXX as **Gosom**, perhaps reflecting this tradition's distinction between these locations and that of the Goshen in Egypt.

Bibliography: R. North. *Archeo-Biblical Egypt* (1967); I. Rabinowitz. "Aramaic Inscriptions of the Fifth Century BCE from a North-Arab Shrine in Egypt." *JNES* 15 (1956) 1–9; A. Rainey, ed. *Egypt, Israel, Sinai: Archaeological and Historical Relationships in the Biblical Period* (1987); E. Uphill. "Pithom and Raamses: Their Location and Significance." *JNES* 27 (1968) 291–316; E. Uphill. "Pithom and Raamses: Their Location and Significance." *JNES* 28 (1969) 15–39.

DANIEL D. PIOSKE

GOSPEL, MESSAGE [εὐαγγέλιον euangelion, κήρυγμα kērygma]. In the NT, *gospel* is never used for a written document, but is the comprehensive term for the good news of God's saving act in Jesus Christ, communicated in a variety of images and concepts.

A. Terminology
  1. The English word
  2. New Testament usage
  3. Old Testament and Jewish background
  4. Hellenistic context
B. The "Beginning of the Gospel"
  1. John the Baptist
  2. Jesus and the pre-Easter disciples
  3. The resurrection
C. The Gospel in the Pre-Pauline Christian Communities
  1. Sayings of Jesus
  2. Stories about Jesus
  3. The cross/resurrection kerygma
D. The Pauline Gospel in the Epistolary Tradition
  1. The gospel as the power of God
  2. The gospel as Christian freedom
  3. The Christ-event as the climax of the cosmic drama
E. Mark and His Successors in the Gospel Tradition
Bibliography

A. Terminology
1. The English word
The modern English word *gospel* is derived from the Old English *gódspel*, a combination of *gód* (good) and *spel* or *spiel* (news, tidings). The ambiguity of its later written form led to a false etymological explanation of *gódspel* in terms of "God" and "story, narrative," as though the English word meant "a story about God." The original English word, however, was a proper translation of the Latin transliteration (*evangelium*) of the original NT term euangelion, "good news."

2. New Testament usage

Early Christianity utilized a broad terminological spectrum to express the good news of God's saving act in Jesus Christ. A number of verbs were used for the act of communicating the gospel, including euangelizomai ([εὐαγγελίζομαι], to announce good news, e.g., Matt 11:5; Luke 1:19; 2:10; 4:18; Acts 5:42; 8:4; Rom 1:15; 1 Cor 1:17; 15:1; Gal 1:8; Eph 3:8; Heb 4:2; 1 Pet 1:12; Rev 10:7), kērysso ([κηρύσσω], to announce, proclaim, 61x NT—e.g., Matt 3:1; 10:7; Luke 4:18; 9:2; Acts 10:42; Rom 10:15; 1 Cor 1:23; 1 Pet 3:19; Rev 5:2), didaskō ([διδάσκω], to teach, 97x NT, in parallel with euangelizomai or kērysso Matt 4:23; 9:35; 11:1; Acts 5:42; 15:35; 28:31); diamartyromai ([διαμαρτύρομαι], to testify, bear witness, 15x NT—e.g., Acts 8:25; 20:24; 1 Thess 4:6). Sometimes quite commonplace words are used for the act of communicating the gospel, e.g., laleō (λαλέω), the ordinary word for "speak" (e.g., 1 Thess 2:2, 4; Acts 4:31; 13:16; Heb 13:7). This cluster of words, along with others, are used almost interchangeably. Although there was a fundamental difference between the church's initial missionary preaching to outsiders and its continuing instruction to converts, this difference was not bound to the vocabulary of kērygma for the former and didache (διδαχή) for the latter (compare, e.g., Acts 17:18-19; 28:31). No technical vocabulary was exclusively associated with preaching the gospel.

Likewise, the gospel message itself could be designated by a broad spectrum of terms, including to euangelion (the good news), either used absolutely (e.g., Mark 13:10; 14:9), or further specified by such phrases as tēs basileias ([τῆς βασιλείας], of the kingdom, e.g., Matt 4:23; 9:35), tou Christou ([τοῦ Χριστοῦ], of Christ, e.g., Mark 1:1; Rom 15:19), tou theou ([τοῦ θεοῦ], of God, e.g., Mark 1:14), tēs charitos tou theou ([τῆς χάριτος τοῦ θεοῦ], of the grace of God, Acts 20:24), to kērygma (the message, Matt 12:41//Luke 11:32; 1 Cor 1:21; 15:14), or by general terms such as ho logos tou theou ([ὁ λόγος τοῦ θεοῦ], the word of God, e.g., Acts 8:14; 1 Thess 2:13; Col 1:25) or simply ho logos ([ὁ λόγος], the word, the message, e.g., Mark 4:14-20; 2 Tim 4:2). Thus, while the Christian gospel was designated by a broad range of words and expressions, to euangelion (the gospel, the good news) was such a key term for much of early Christianity that the whole realm of the Christian life and mission could simply be called "the gospel" (e.g., Rom 1:1, 9). This was distinctive of early Christianity; no other religious movement in the Hellenistic world so identified itself with having a gospel to preach, teach, and by which to live. This does not mean that the early church's preaching of the gospel was bound to this particular word. Nonetheless, euangelion was so central to the early Christian movement that the character of early Christianity is illuminated by exploring the connotations associated with the key terms euangelion and euangelizomai. Like all the religious terminology of early Christianity, these words had ordinary, secular meanings before they were adopted and adapted by the church to express its faith in God's saving act in Jesus Christ. The church's gospel vocabulary had roots in both its OT and Jewish background and its first-century Hellenistic context.

3. Old Testament and Jewish background

New Testament authors found *gospel* terminology in their Bible. The OT authors had adapted a vocabulary already ancient in their situation. At Ugarit, the term "good news" (bshrt) was used in the fertility cult to announce that Baal had again become alive. Biblical authors used the verb basar (בָּשַׂר) and its cognate noun besorah (בְּשׂרָה) to represent primarily good news from the battlefield (e.g., 1 Sam 31:9; 2 Sam 4:10; 18:19, 20, 25, 26) and, derivatively, Yahweh's victory and saving acts (e.g., Ps 40:9 ["the glad news of deliverance"]; 68:12; 96:2). Especially the later Isaiah tradition uses this terminology to speak of the good news of God's saving act at the exodus, now eschatologically fulfilled in the "new exodus" from Babylon. This announcement of God's liberating act from Babylonian captivity expresses the good news that God's kingdom has been inaugurated (Isa 40:9; 41:27; 52:7; 60:6; 61:1). This Jewish tradition continued into the time of the early church. The Targums document that the Palestinian Judaism of Jesus' time still used the basar terminology for the good news of the messianic age to come, and such texts as Isa 52:7 were widely used to express the eschatological victory of God. This is also illustrated by the Qumran scrolls, where forms of the verb basar are found 15 times, sometimes specifically as a designation for the good news of eschatological salvation (e.g. 1QHᵃ XXIII, 14; 4Q440 3 I, 16). The corresponding noun besorah is not documented at Qumran, however; the Qumran community had no message they designated *gospel.*

4. Hellenistic context

The LXX translators represented this terminology by the noun euangelion and the cognate verb euangelizomai, words that had already been used in secular Greek to proclaim the good news of victory, for a wedding or the birth of a child. The writings of Philo and Josephus show that by NT times, this vocabulary could be used by Hellenistic Jews for political and religious good news. Not only the birth of the emperor, but the beneficent course of his life and his ascent to the throne could be described as euangelia (εὐαγγέλια e.g., Josephus, *J.W.* 4.656). Gentile culture in the Greco-Roman world was familiar with the terminology to express the politico-religious claims of the empire, as illustrated by the famous Priene inscription (9 BCE) lauding the birth of Augustus as the beginning of a new age of peace and salvation:

Since the Providence which has ordered all things and is deeply interested in our life has set in most perfect order by giving us Augustus, whom she filled with virtue [divine power] that he might benefit humanity, sending him as a savior (sōtēr σωτήρ), both for us and for our descendants, that he might end war and arrange all things, and since the Caesar through his appearance (epiphanein [ἐπιφανεῖν], compare "epiphany," often used of Hellenistic rulers) has exceeded the hopes of all former good messages (euangelia), surpassing not only the benefactors who came before him, but also leaving no hope that anyone in the future would surpass him, and since for the world the birthday of the god (Augustus) was the beginning of the good tidings (euangeliōn εὐαγγελίων) that came by reason of him. . . .

Like parousia (παρουσία), epiphaneia (ἐπιφανεία) (epiphany), and sōtēr (savior), euangelion had overtones of the language of the emperor cult. Thus when the early Christian missionaries addressed the world with its gospel message, it both made the claim to announce the fulfillment of the hopes of the OT and Judaism and presented an alternate, competing message to the ideologies of the dominant culture.

B. The "Beginning of the Gospel" (Phil 4:15)

The gospel vocabulary was used prior to Jesus and the church, in both Jewish and Gentile contexts, and in a variety of senses. But so far as we know, no pre-Christian group identified itself as essentially commissioned to preach a or the gospel. Yet our earliest Christian document, 1 Thessalonians (ca. 50 CE), repeatedly uses euangelion not only as a term for the Christian message (1:5; 2:2, 4, 8, 9), but to designate the whole sphere of Christian life and mission (3:2; compare Phil 1:5; 4:15; 2 Cor 10:14; Rom 1:1, 9; 11:28; 15:16). What was "the beginning of the gospel" in this sense (Phil 4:15), and with whom did it begin?

1. John the Baptist

The NT references all present John from the Christian point of view, as the one sent by God to announce the "mighty one" to come, but not as a preacher of the Christian gospel. Luke 7:28 proclaims John to be the greatest of the old era, and Luke 16:16 makes clear that John's ministry was completed before the gospel began. This is typical of the Evangelists, each of whom has his own way of distinguishing the message of John from that of Jesus and the early church (compare Mark 1:4-14; Matt 3:1-15; 11:18-19; Luke 1:5–2:52; 3:15-22; 7:18-34; 16:16; Acts 18:24–19:7; John 1:19-27, 32-34; 3:26-30). Even the redactional Matt 3:1, which parallels John's preaching to that of Jesus (compare Matt 4:17), does not portray John as

preaching the gospel. The gospel did not begin with John the Baptist.

2. Jesus and the pre-Easter disciples

Though the message of Jesus himself was in many ways different from that of the later church, we have good reason to claim that the gospel began with Jesus' own preaching. All the Gospels—but not Acts or any of the Letters—present Jesus as proclaiming the good news of God's saving act. The Synoptics, following Mark, specifically use the gospel vocabulary of Jesus and his disciples (euangelizomai; kēryssō; euangelion; kerygma; compare Matt 4:23; 9:35; 10:7; 11:5; Mark 1:14-15; Luke 4:18, 43-44; 7:22; 8:1; 9:2, 6; 10:9; 20:1). The Fourth Gospel, though not using the explicit vocabulary associated with Christian proclamation, clearly presents Jesus—but not his disciples—as proclaiming the message of God's saving act (e.g., 3:1-21; 4:7-26; 5:19-47; 6:22-58; 10:1-18; 11:17-44; 12:20-36, 44-50). Yet all these portrayals are influenced by the church's own preaching of the gospel in its post-Easter situation. The message of Jesus cannot be read directly off the pages of the NT; any representation of the message of the historical Jesus must necessarily be a reconstruction. This task requires careful scholarship and can be done with some degree of probability, but will always fall short of certainty. The following summary is representative of a large number of centrist interpreters of the NT's manifold witness to Jesus' own message:

1. Jesus saw his own ministry as the time of the fulfillment of God's promises of eschatological salvation. Mark's summary of the gospel proclaimed by Jesus (1:14-15) begins "the time is fulfilled," i.e., the time of waiting is over, the promised time of God's ultimate salvation begins. Although the formulation is Markan, the substance very likely represents Jesus' own message.
2. This means that Jesus' message was centered on announcing the act of God, not on presenting ideas about God. The gospel is act, not idea. The historical Jesus, and the Jesus portrayed in the variety of NT interpretations, was not a purveyor of religious ideas that may be evaluated as better or worse than other such ideas. The gospel cannot be expressed without utilizing a spectrum of religious ideas, i.e., the gospel necessarily requires theological conceptualization, implicit or explicit, intended or not, for its communication. But the gospel itself, from its inception in the life and message of Jesus throughout the NT, is not basically an idea, but the good news of God's saving act.
3. For Jesus, God's saving act was expressed primarily in the symbol of the kingdom of God. God's sovereign action is represented not by a concept, but by the tensive symbolic language that evokes

the grand narrative of God's saving acts. The drama has three acts: 1) God the creator and ruler of all, 2) who has been active in history to preserve God's own people, 3) and who will act definitively to reassert the divine rule over a rebellious creation that is at present de jure God's kingdom. Since God is the Creator, the universe will become de facto the kingdom of God only through this eschatological act. Jesus was not an apocalypticist in the sense of having a detailed plan for the end of history, but Jewish apocalyptic eschatology provided the theological context within which these images function. For Jesus, God's decisive act was not yet fully present, but was already on the near horizon, so close and so real that it already influenced the present (Mark 1:15 ēngiken [ἤγγικεν], "has come near").

4. Hearing Jesus' proclamation of the dawning kingdom was a call to decision: Would the hearers continue to live as though the darkness prevailed, or reorient their lives to the new reality that was already dawning? This reorientation was called teshuvah (תְּשׁוּבָה), metanoia (μετάνοια), traditionally translated "repentance." The gospel is not a command, something else to do, another worthy cause to support. But the indicative of God's gracious, unilateral act necessarily involves the imperative of human response. The dialectic of indicative/imperative was inherent in the gospel from the beginning and continued through all its NT forms.

5. Though this call to decision was ultimately serious business, it was not grim. Jesus' message was the announcement of good news that generated joy and celebration. God's act meant that, despite the continuing evil in the world and without fleeing from it or ignoring it, Jesus' message created a community of celebration pervaded by joy (Mark 2:19; Matt 13:44-46). The Beatitudes are not moralizing exhortations to "be happy," but pronouncements that declare the blessedness of those to whom God's kingdom belongs, a blessedness filled with joy and laughter, a call for dancing in the streets and permission to go ahead and celebrate in the light of the dawning kingdom (Luke 6:20-23; 11:31-34).

6. Jesus' proclamation of the gospel was thus theocentric. As in Mark's summary, it was the "gospel of God" (Mark 1:14). The operative word in the phrase "kingdom of God" was God. Though the historical Jesus saw himself as playing a key role in God's eschatological saving act, Jesus did not proclaim himself as Messiah or Savior. In the language of later theology, his gospel focused on the Father, not the Son. While all the Gospels represent post-Easter Christian interpretations of the Christ event, the message of the Fourth Gospel in which Jesus proclaims himself expresses the Christology of the later church. The Synoptic Gospels' portrayal of Jesus whose gospel announces the kingdom of God is closer to historical reality. Yet in the earliest proclamation of the church, Jesus the proclaimer became Christ the proclaimed, and this message of the church was in historical continuity with the gospel proclaimed by Jesus. The Christian gospel began with Jesus, but in what sense?

3. The resurrection

Jesus proclaimed the good news of the coming kingdom of God that already impinged on the present and called for response. Although some did respond, most rejected his message, including the religious and political leadership, and Jesus was killed as a threat to pure religion and a stable society. In view of the fate of the prophets of Israel, Jesus must have reckoned with the probability of his own violent death (compare 1 Kgs 19:10; Luke 11:47; Acts 7:52; 1 Thess 2:15). His trust in God, conceptualized within the framework of Jewish apocalyptic theology, means he must also have believed that God would not let his death be the last word about his life. Although Jesus foresaw the likelihood of his own violent death and believed in God's vindication even beyond his death, the specific passion predictions (Mark 8:31, 9:31, 10:33-34 and their parallels) are in their present form retrospective formulations of the early church. Jesus did not include his death and resurrection in the gospel he proclaimed. Yet one of the earliest, perhaps the earliest, formulation of the Christian gospel centers on God's act in the death and resurrection of Jesus (1 Cor 15:3-5). How did the proclaimer become the proclaimed?

The resurrection of Jesus is central in the formation of the Christian gospel. This event can be conceptualized and narrated in a variety of forms already found in the NT, but the event itself, however conceptualized, is pivotal in the transformation of Jesus the proclaimer into the Christ-event as itself the content of the gospel. This is manifest in at least three ways: 1) The resurrection itself was a constituent element of the earliest, pre-Pauline declarations of the Christian gospel (1 Thess 1:10; 1 Cor 15:4; Rom 1:3-4; 4:24-25; 10:9), and continued to be prominent in NT authors' summaries of the Christian proclamation (e.g., Acts 2:32; 3:15; 10:40; 13:32; 17:18). 2) The resurrection was the basis for continuing the message from and about after his death. Jesus' disciples did not continue Jesus' teaching on the basis of idealism or admiration, continuing the cause of a dead teacher of important values. His teachings had challenged the common-sense, everyday cultural values, and could not validate themselves. Jesus' death seemed to demonstrate their unreality. God's act in raising up Jesus vindicated him as God's messenger and as himself part of God's eschatological saving event. The resurrection was thus not an optional appendage to Jesus' life and message, but the essential basis for their continued affirmation. 3) The resurrection meant that Jesus the proclaimer had not been left behind in history, but was a living reality. In the proclamation of his followers, he himself continued to speak. The resurrection meant that there was a middle term between Jesus the proclaimer and Jesus the proclaimed: Jesus the self-proclaimed, who continued to speak in the preaching of the church, accompanying his church through history. To hear and respond to the preaching of Jesus' post-Easter disciples is to hear and respond to Jesus himself. This reality is conceptualized in a variety of ways by NT authors, but Matthew is typical: Jesus accompanies his church through history (Matt 28:18), is himself the one who is present and active in the sowing of the word (Matt 13:37), identifies himself with his missionaries (Matt 10:40), and himself builds the church (Matt 16:18). The church did not simply continue to repeat the message of the pre-Easter Jesus—the historical Jesus preached the gospel of the kingdom; the church preached the gospel of God's act in Jesus. It is true that Jesus did not make himself the content of his own message; he preached about God, and the post-Easter church preached about Jesus. This must be seen in christological perspective, so that the church's preaching Christ is not an alternative or replacement for Jesus' preaching about God. Mark, for instance, is fully aware of this. As a Christian, he presents the "gospel of Jesus Christ" (1:1), which is not only in continuity with, but continues to represent Jesus' preaching of the "gospel of God" (1:14).

C. The Gospel in the Pre-Pauline Christian Communities

The event of God's saving act was itself the good news. The apprehension, expression and communication of this good news required language and theology. While the event cannot be communicated apart from some theological framework, no particular theology should be identified as the gospel itself. Earliest Christianity utilized a wide linguistic and conceptual spectrum in order to express the gospel. As one would expect, the first Christians adopted biblical and Jewish categories. Jesus' language of the kingdom of God as the primary symbol and summary of the good news was continued in the early church, but was no longer central (compare Acts 8:12; 20:25; 28:23, 31; Rom 14:17; 1 Cor 6:9-10; 1 Thess 2:12; Jas 2:5; Rev 12:10). The fundamental good news was that the Messiah had come, the deliverer promised by God who would make life and the world what God intended them to be. In this context, the content of the gospel could be simply and clearly expressed: Jesus is the Christ, or better, the Christ is Jesus (e.g., Luke 2:11; Acts 5:42; 8:5; 17:3; 18:5, 28). The Christian gospel was that the Christ was no longer a hoped-for future figure, but had become concrete reality in Jesus. In contexts where Jewish tradition and

its biblical categories were known, the gospel could be expressed in metaphors such as the death of Jesus as a sacrifice that accomplished forgiveness of sins (e.g., Luke 24:47; 1 Cor 15:3). In broader contexts, metaphors that transcended the original biblical and Jewish context were used to conceptualize God's saving act in the Christ-event. The gospel could be portrayed as good news to the poor, deliverance from captivity, healing of blindness (Luke 4:18-19), as God having provided the ransom from slavery or imprisonment (Mark 10:45; 1 Tim 2:6), as reconciliation that healed estrangement and restored the relationship between God and human beings (2 Cor 5:18-19), as the establishment of Jesus as Lord of the universe, the one who has defeated all humanity's enemies, cosmic and earthly (Phil 2:5-9). Particularly in the Johannine community, the Christ-event could be portrayed as the concrete appearance in this world and the availability through faith in Christ of those universal human values symbolized by the way, the truth, the life (John 14:6), bread (John 6:1-59), water (4:7-15; 7:37-38), light (8:12), eternal life (3:16; 11:1-44).

All the varieties of early Christian proclamation of the gospel were fundamentally christological. Christology, however, is not centered on Jesus, but on God. This is indicated by the word itself; the term christos (χριστός) is an adjectival form, "anointed," representing the perfect passive participle. Jesus is the anointed; God is the anointer. To confess that Jesus is the Christ is not to say something special about the person of Jesus per se, but to point to God as the one whose act is embodied in Jesus. God's act in Christ created the gospel (2 Cor 5:19). In the earliest days of the church, the salvific act of God in Christ was conceptualized in basically three ways: 1) The continuation of Jesus' message by collecting, amplifying and interpreting Jesus' sayings; 2) by telling stories of Jesus' deeds that became transparent to the presence and act of God in him, and 3) by proclaiming Jesus' death and resurrection as God's definitive saving act.

1. Sayings of Jesus

After the crucifixion, some of Jesus' disciples continued his proclamation of the kingdom, with the difference that now Jesus himself was seen to play the central role in God's inauguration of the kingdom. This mode of proclamation is represented by the hypothetical document Q (see Q, QUELLE). This document, in the belief of many scholars, is no longer extant but can be reconstructed from the elements common to Matthew and Luke not derived from Mark. This postulated document of ca. 250 verses is composed almost entirely of sayings of Jesus, and presumably represents the "Q community" of Palestine about the middle of the 1st cent CE. There is no evidence that the "Q community" referred to the document as a "Gospel." Referring to Q as a "Sayings Gospel" is a somewhat misleading modern designation. Specific gospel vocabulary in Q is minimal: euangelion occurs not at all, euangelizō only once (Q 7:22; Jesus is the subject [Scholarly convention now designates Q texts by their chapter and verse location in Luke), kērygma and kērussō once each (Q 11:32, Jonah the subject; Matt Q 12:3, Jesus' disciples the subject). Yet it is clear that the postulated "Q community" regarded both Jesus and his disciples as proclaimers of the gospel. The content of the gospel message in Q is the coming kingdom of God (Q 6:20; 7:28; 9:60; 10:9, 11:2; 12:31; 13:18, 20; 13:28, 29; 16:16; 22:29-30), with one saying possibly indicating the presence of the kingdom (11:20). The Q document had no passion story, and has no sayings in which the death and resurrection of Jesus are explicitly represented as God's saving act. Thus some interpreters have seen Q as representing a form of the gospel that continued Jesus' own preaching, an explicit rejection of the christological kerygma that focused on Jesus' death and resurrection. Yet Q does have an explicit christology in which Jesus as the Son of Man will function as the final judge (Q 12:8, 10; 17:24-30; 22:28-30), which seems to require something like the death and resurrection/exaltation of Jesus. It is also clear that Q does not proclaim Jesus' death on the cross as God's saving act, and that neither the Jesus of Q nor his disciples proclaim his death and resurrection as the gospel message. The saving act of God seems to be mediated by the word of Jesus as his sayings are circulated and proclaimed by his followers.

2. Stories about Jesus

Some streams of earliest Christianity embodied the gospel message in stories of Jesus' mighty deeds. There may have been written collections of such stories that circulated in pre-Pauline, pre-Gospel Christianity, but such documents as may have existed are no longer extant and cannot be reconstructed with any confidence. Although such miracle stories had several similarities to the variety of popular magicians and thaumaturges in the Hellenistic world, as told by the early Christians such stories were an eschatological genre, a means of communicating the gospel that in the Christ-event God had acted for the salvation of the world. They were intended not merely to recount some amazing deed of Jesus in Galilee or Jerusalem, but to point to the Christ-event as a whole. Each story portrayed some fundamental human need, the human plight in which authentic life as God the Creator willed it was frustrated by some adversary: sin and guilt, sickness, leprosy, meaninglessness, "natural" evil of storms and the like, loneliness, isolation, hunger, demons, and death. In each story, what people are unable to do for themselves, Jesus does for them. He heals the sick and restores them to themselves, their family, society, and authentic human life (e.g., Mark 1:29-31; 5:21-34); he acts in God's place to forgive sins (e.g., Mark 2:1-12);

he cleanses lepers and restores them to life in human community (e.g., Mark 1:40-45); he overcomes enslaving demonic power and sets people free for the abundant life God intends (e.g., Mark 5:1-20); he overcomes the destructive forces of nature so that they no longer dominate human life (e.g., Mark 4:35-41); he frees people from the dehumanizing power of hunger and in an impossible situation provides a banquet where people eat and drink together (e.g., Mark 6:30-44); he gives ultimate meaning to life by calling ordinary people to discipleship (e.g., Mark 1:16-20; 2:13-14). Even the last enemy of life, death itself, is overcome, and when it is already too late, it is not too late for the good news of resurrection (Mark 5:21-43). Though the specific gospel vocabulary (euangelion, euangelizomai, kerygma) was only rarely associated with such stories (but compare Matt 4:23; 9:35; 10:7-8; 11:5; Mark 1:39, 45; 5:20; 7:36; Luke 4:18-19; 7:22; 9:2), it is clear that they were not mere reports of incidents in the life of Jesus, but vehicles for communicating the saving act of God in the Christ-event as such, seen in the light of the church's resurrection faith.

Yet such stories involved an inherent christological problem. The Jesus they portrayed acted with the power of God and was himself sometimes portrayed as the epiphany of a divine being, but did not share the weakness and victimization intrinsic to a truly human life. Could such a being suffer and die? Or did he only appear to be human? In the language of the later creeds, he was "truly divine," but was he "truly human?" The version of the gospel expressed by the miracle stories could not be readily combined with the kerygma of Jesus' suffering and death, and found its eventual deposit in the docetic Gospels of the second and later centuries in which the powerful, miracle-working Jesus only appeared to suffer and die.

3. The cross/resurrection kerygma

In this version of the gospel, the Christian message was focused in the death and resurrection of Jesus, with its significance seen in the framework of a cosmic drama of salvation. In some formulations, Jesus' death was itself seen as the saving act of God, revealed as such by God's act in raising him from the dead (e.g. 1 Cor 15:3-5). In other credal or hymnic expressions of this understanding of the gospel, Jesus' death was seen as representing his obedience to God or the results of human sin and ignorance, reversed by God's act in the resurrection (Acts 2:36). The hymns and confessional formulae quoted in the Pauline tradition are all of this type (e.g., Rom 1:2-3; Phil 2:5-9; Col 1:15-20; 1 Tim 2:5; 3:16). The earliest Christian creeds—like the later ecumenical creeds—did not elaborate the "life and teachings of Jesus" as the content of the gospel; indeed there was no place for such affirmations within a framework that focused on the death of Jesus as central to the meaning of the gospel. Our earliest

NT documents, the letters of Paul, represent only this third type of gospel message. This does not mean that Paul was unaware of the tradition of Jesus' sayings and the stories of his miracles, but that he saw no way of combining these forms of gospel proclamation with the theology of the cross without making unacceptable compromises. Paul initiated the epistolary tradition that made letters a didactic means of bearing witness to the gospel. Except for the four canonical Gospels, all the NT documents stand in this tradition, and present the Christian message within the framework of a cosmic drama focusing on the incarnation, death and resurrection, with minimum or no reflection of the life and message of Jesus.

D. The Pauline Gospel in the Epistolary Tradition

Paul placed his distinctive stamp on the gospel that has been influential in every age of church history. Paul did not invent the gospel message or terminology. In many ways, he took up the earlier proclamation, continued and developed it. Yet the gospel vocabulary is particularly dense in his writings (of 134 instances of euangelion, its cognates and variations, more than half occur in the undisputed letters of Paul).

Though Paul was not an eyewitness of the ministry of Jesus, he had ample opportunity to learn from Peter the sayings of Jesus and stories about him (Gal 1:18). Yet Paul insisted that his gospel did not consist of what he had learned from human beings, but had been revealed to him by the risen Christ (Gal 1:11-12). This did not mean that the content of Paul's gospel was information from the heavenly world transmitted in ecstatic experiences; Paul had such experiences, but spoke of them only reluctantly (2 Cor 12:1-10). Rather, Paul's gospel was focused on God's act in the death and resurrection of Jesus (e.g., Rom 5:1-11; 2 Cor 5:11-21). This perspective was not original with him. He had received it from the earliest Christians, and when challenged cited the creed of 1 Cor 15:3-5 as normative for his proclamation of the gospel. But neither does this mean that Paul merely went about repeating that Jesus had died for human sins and God had raised him from the dead. He adapted and elaborated this basic affirmation according to the needs of each situation, so that his understanding of the gospel continued to grow in response to new needs.

In Paul's view, the Christian message could be expressed in a variety of ways, but not an unlimited variety. He could enthusiastically affirm other versions of the gospel than his own, so long as they focused on Christ as crucified and risen (1 Cor 1:10–3:23; note esp. 3:21-22; 15:11). Yet, near the end of Paul's missionary career, the preaching of "false apostles" who visited Corinth and the crisis among the Galatian Christians caused by Christian missionaries preaching "another gospel" forced Paul to think through the implications of the gospel afresh. Paul's sharp response to what he perceived as a false version of the gospel are found in 2 Cor 10–13 and the letter to the Galatians. His more reflective teaching, providing something of a summary of the Pauline gospel in the last period of his life, is found in Romans, so that Christian theology has rightly turned to Galatians and Romans for the most profound statement of the Pauline gospel.

1. The gospel as the power of God

While the gospel announces God's act in the death and resurrection of Jesus, it is no mere report. As the "gospel of God" (Rom 1:1; 15:16; compare 1 Thess 2:2, 8-9; 2 Cor 11:7), it not only has God's act as its content, but has both its origin and its authority in God. Though expressed in human words, language, and concepts, it is the word of God that is heard when the gospel is preached (1 Thess 2:13; 1 Cor 1:8; 2 Cor 4:4-6; 5:20). This gospel is not a mere word, but is communicated in the power of the Holy Spirit and mediates God's own power that generates faith and effects salvation (Rom 1:16-17; compare 1 Thess 1:5; 1 Cor 4:20). Paul can thus speak of those who came to faith by means of his preaching as having been begotten by the gospel (1 Cor 4:14; compare Phlm 10). Though dependent on human preachers for its articulation, the gospel is an independent power operative even in the preaching of those who have false motives (Phil 1:12-18). Even in Paul's own ministry, he does not regard the power effective in his work as the result of his own efforts or faithfulness—though he considers himself as a slave to the gospel with an inescapable obligation (1 Cor 9:19-23)—but considers the gospel as divine treasure in earthen vessels, clay jars, "so that it may be made clear that this extraordinary power belongs to God and does not come from us" (2 Cor 4:7).

2. The gospel as Christian freedom

The Galatian crisis brought into sharp focus one major implication of the Pauline gospel, that God's salvation was a matter of justification by faith apart from works of the law (Gal 2:15-16; 3:19–4:5; 5:1-5). The gospel was seen to be the gospel of freedom. So regarded, freedom is not a subjective idea or ideal, but the objective reality of God's liberating act. God's act in Christ not only meant that believers are set free from the law, but are delivered from the oppressive cosmic powers, the "elemental spirits of the world" that held human life in bondage (Gal 4:3). This insight into the nature of the gospel as Christian freedom, born of the Galatian controversy, was deepened and elaborated in Paul's reflections summarized in Romans. The insight that God's liberating act sets believers free from the law means that acceptance by God is in no way conditioned by human obedience to law, Mosaic or other, but is a matter of the free grace of God (Rom 3:21-31; 5:1-11; 7:1-25). The gospel thus sets believers free from all efforts to justify themselves; God is the one who justifies (Rom 8:33). The gospel as the power of God for salvation means deliverance from the guilt and power of sin (Rom 3:21-26; 5:1-11; 6:1-23), from the coming wrath (Rom 5:9), from condemnation and death (Rom 8:1-25), and from the cosmic powers, the structures of systemic evil to which all these enemies of life belong (Rom 8:31-39). This liberating act representing God's own love sets the believer free to love others, as God's love becomes effective in the life of the believer (Rom 5:1-5). The freedom of the gospel is not only freedom-from, but freedom-for. The indicative of God's saving act contains the imperative of the believer's response.

3. The Christ-event as the climax of the cosmic drama

Paul's focus on the death and resurrection of Christ does not mean that he restricted the gospel to this one event. Paul understands the gospel of Jesus' death and resurrection to be the definitive climax of the mighty acts of God from creation to eschaton. The salvation of the world through the Christ-event had been intended by God from eternity, and Christ himself had been preexistent (1 Cor 2:7; 8:6; 2 Cor 8:9; Rom 16:25; Phil 2:6). The gospel of God's salvific acts to be climaxed in Christ was already announced through the prophets, Christ himself was already active in the OT story of God's people, and the Scripture had already proclaimed the gospel to the OT people of God (Rom 1:2; 16:26; 1 Cor 10:4; Gal 3:8). The gospel thus did not represent a change in God's plan, but the fulfillment of God's purpose from eternity. In the fullness of time, God sent forth his Son who by his death and resurrection brought salvation to the sinful world (Gal 4:4-5; Rom 1:3-4; 15:8; 2 Cor 1:20). Paul never pictures the earthly Jesus as preaching the gospel himself, though the gospel now proclaimed by the church represents the message of the risen Christ. It is Christ who speaks in the Christian mission, so that the gospel, now being proclaimed to Jew and Gentile alike, is the saving gospel from Christ (Rom 9:1; 15:8; 2 Cor 13:3). Since the resurrection of Jesus was not seen as an isolated event but the beginning of the general resurrection (1 Cor 15:12-57), for Paul the gospel had an inherent eschatological dimension. The gospel includes the final coming of the kingdom of God, the parousia of Christ, the resurrection, and the judgment (1 Cor 6:9; 15:23-24, 50; Gal 5:21; Rom 2:16; 1 Thess 2:19; 3:13; 4:15; 5:23). For Paul, the gospel is not the story of Jesus' life, nor is it limited to the singular event of the cross and resurrection. The gospel is the story of Jesus Christ, but this story is set in a cosmic framework stretching from creation to eschaton, to which the Christ-event is the defining center and hermeneutical key to the lordship of God the Creator over all history.

E. Mark and His Successors in the Gospel Tradition

It is widely, though not universally, accepted that the author of Mark was the first to compose a Gospel. Although Mark has been increasingly appreciated as an early Christian teacher with a profound theology and therefore much more than a reporter, collector, or editor, his achievement in creating the Gospel form itself has not been sufficiently appreciated. Prior to Mark the gospel message was expressed either in sayings and stories ostensibly portraying incidents from the life of Jesus or in the kerygma of Jesus' crucifixion and resurrection. These two central genres of Christian confession and proclamation seemed to be logically incompatible. How could the Jesus of the miracle stories who was master of wind and wave (Mark 4:35-41) also die in human weakness (2 Cor 13:4)? No doubt many accepted both versions and did not reflect on how they could be combined, but sometimes they were consciously opposed to each other and considered to be mutually exclusive. Yet each form of the gospel is vital, and the church needs both forms of proclamation. Mark was the first to think through a theology in which both versions of the gospel could be combined, a literary-theological construct that contained the good news of the miracle stories within a narrative framework dominated by the kerygma of the death and resurrection, portraying Jesus in terms of both true humanity and true deity. Mark thus opened the way for Matthew, Luke, and John to combine various expressions of the gospel within the narrative framework of Gospel. When combined with the epistolary form Paul and his successors had made into the standard form of Christian teaching, the way was prepared for the formation of that collection of documents that would become the norm for the church's proclamation of the gospel: epistle and gospel, the NT canon.

Bibliography: M. Eugene Boring. *The Continuing Voice of Jesus* (1991); M. Eugene Boring. *Truly Human/ Truly Divine: Christological Language and the Gospel Form* (1984); Rudolf Bultmann. *Theology of the New Testament* (1955); C. H. Dodd. *The Apostolic Preaching and its Developments* (1937); William Horbury. "Gospel' in Herodian Judaea." *The Written Gospel.* Marcus Bockmuel and Donald A. Hagner, eds. (2005) 7–30; Larry W. Hurtado. *Lord Jesus Christ: Devotion to Jesus in Earliest Christianity* (2003); Leander Keck. *Who Is Jesus? History in Perfect Tense* (2000); Helmut Koester. "The Term 'Gospel." *Ancient Christian Gospels: Their History and Development* (1990); Klyne Snodgrass. "The Gospel of Jesus." *The Written Gospel.* Marcus Bockmuel and Donald A. Hagner, ed. (2005) 31–44; Georg Strecker. "Das Evangelium Jesu Christi." *Eschaton und Historie: Aufsätze* (1979); Georg Strecker. *Theology of the New Testament.* Friedrich Wilhelm Horn, ed. M. Eugene Boring, trans. (2000).

M. EUGENE BORING

GOSPEL ACCORDING TO THE HEBREWS. *See* HEBREWS, GOSPEL OF THE.

GOSPEL HARMONY. In the history of Christianity, reading the Synoptic Gospels in harmony—as if they relay historical information about the same fundamental story—has been common. The approach is to interpret these stories in light of each other—at times supplying information to fill in the gaps of specific gospel passages. In light of this interpretive method, some created actual reconstructed harmonies. Tatian's 2nd cent. *Diatessaron* (lit. "through the four"), which maintained influence in Syrian Christianity for several centuries, was the first one developed. In the early 19th cent., Thomas Jefferson (the third President of the United States of America) created "The Life and Morals of Jesus of Nazareth," which was published posthumously because it revealed Jefferson's enlightenment bias against the supernatural. In fact, in the history of Christian tradition, most major commentaries on the Gospels have assumed the interpretive basis of a gospel harmony approach for their reflections.

The origins of the development of the synopsis, a presentation of the gospel stories in par. columns, initially depended on the understanding of the gospel harmony. These research tools, however, eventually complicated the assumptions behind the idea of a harmonized gospel account.

In contemporary gospel research since the mid-19th cent., this interpretive approach has become rare. It is still common only among more popular approaches to the interpretation of the Gospels, which tend to assume fewer discrepancies among gospel accounts. *See* SYNOPTIC PROBLEM.

EMERSON B. POWERY

GOSPEL OF BARTHOLOMEW. *See* BARTHOLOMEW, GOSPEL (QUESTIONS) OF.

GOSPEL OF BASILIDES. *See* BASILIDES, GOSPEL OF.

GOSPEL OF JUDAS. *See* JUDAS, GOSPEL OF.

GOSPEL OF PETER. *See* PETER, GOSPEL OF.

GOSPEL OF PHILIP. *See* PHILIP, GOSPEL OF.

GOSPEL OF THE EBIONITES. *See* EBIONITES, GOSPEL OF THE.

GOSPEL OF THE HEBREWS. *See* HEBREWS, GOSPEL OF THE.

GOSPEL OF THE INFANCY, ARMENIAN. Edited so far in two recensions, the *Armenian Gospel of the Infancy* is a combination and expansion of the *Protoevangelium of James* and the *Infancy Gospel of Thomas*. P. Peeters

postulates that it was translated from Syriac prior to the 9th cent. and revised thereafter. In notes to his French translation, Peeters identifies further parallels with the *Arabic Infancy Gospel, Pseudo-Matthew*, and the *Six Books History of the Virgin*. The exact genesis of this writing awaits further clarification.

Bibliography: Paul Peeters. *Évangiles apocryphes II: L'Évangile de l'Enfance* (1914).

F. STANLEY JONES

GOSPEL OF THE NAZARENES. *See* NAZOREANS, GOSPEL OF THE.

GOSPEL OF THE NAZOREANS. *See* NAZOREANS, GOSPEL OF THE.

GOSPEL OF THE SAVIOR. *See* SAVIOR, GOSPEL OF THE.

GOSPEL OF THOMAS. *See* THOMAS, GOSPEL OF.

GOSPEL OF TRUTH. *See* TRUTH, GOSPEL OF.

GOSPELS. The word *gospel* is based on the Old English term *god spel*, "good news" or "good tidings," in turn a translation of the ecclesiatical Latin terms *bona annuntiatio* and *evangelium* ("good news"), one a translation and the other a transliteration of the Greek term euangelion (εὐαγγέλιον "good news"). The first occurrences of the Greek word euangelion in the NT occur in the Pauline Letters and constitutes a terse abbreviation for "the good news [of the saving significance of the death and resurrection of Jesus]" (Gal 1:11; Rom 1:9; 1 Cor 9:23). Paul also used the fuller expressions "gospel of God," referring to God as the source or authority for his message (1 Thess 2:2; Rom 1:1; 15:16), and "gospel of Christ," emphasizing Christ as the content of the message (Rom 15:19; 1 Cor 9:12). The term *gospel* occurs in the opening sentence of the Gospel of Mark: "The beginning of the gospel of Jesus Christ, the Son of God" (1:1), though the author of this work probably intended the phrase "the beginning of the gospel of Jesus Christ" to refer only to the opening section of the work (1:2-15 or perhaps 1:4-8). Nevertheless, since a short opening section is described as the "beginning," the author is characterizing the entire work as "the gospel of Jesus Christ." The little word *of*, however, is ambiguous, and this phrase can mean either "the gospel about Jesus Christ" (an objective genitive) or "the gospel proclaimed by Jesus Christ" (a subjective genitive). Since Jesus does not speak until 1:15, and what he says is described in 1:14 as "preaching the gospel of God," the opening phrase must mean "the gospel about Jesus Christ." The phrase "the gospel of Jesus Christ" in Mark 1:1, then, describes the content of the following work as gospel. Unlike Paul, for whom the gospel centered on the saving significance of the death and resurrection of Jesus, Mark used the term to include the public life of Jesus, a major theological contribution.

Sometime during the 2nd cent., based on Mark's use of the term *gospel* to describe the content of his work, the term came to be applied to works like Mark, Matthew, Luke, and John, which were narratives of the life and teachings of Jesus. The oldest use of "gospel" for a type of literature may be the titles of the canonical Gospels themselves. These four Gospels were given similar titles when assembled in a fourfold collection, ca. 150 CE. While there is some evidence that they were initially labeled "According to Matthew," "According to Mark," etc., the preponderance of manuscript evidence suggests the longer, more familiar titles "The Gospel according to Matthew," "The Gospel according to Mark," etc. Evidence outside the canonical Gospels for the use of the term *gospel* as a literary form appeared in Christian writings by the middle of the 2nd cent., such as the works of Marcion (surviving only in fragments), Justin Martyr (*1 Apol.* 66.3), and *2 Clement* (8:5).

For much of the last century, the canonical Gospels were widely regarded as *sui generis*, i.e., as a unique literary genre that had organically emerged when the oral proclamation of the Christian gospel first began to be presented in written form as the Gospel of Mark (ca. 70 CE). Many modern scholars were convinced that the Gospels were *sui generis* because of their dissimilarity to typical ancient biographies, such as the Greek biographies found in Plutarch's *Lives* or the Latin biographies found in Suetonius' *Lives of the Caesars* (both late 1st cent. and early 2nd cent. CE). Oddly, the very scholars who emphasized the uniqueness of the canonical Gospels were form critics who tended to argue that the constituent oral forms that were incorporated into the written Gospels were conventional oral genres found in both the Hellenistic world (e.g., apophthegmata or pronouncement stories, miracle stories) and the Jewish world (e.g., parables). The reason why the Gospels did not have parallels and their constituent oral forms did was because of a broad consensus that both the Gospels and their constituent oral forms belonged to *Kleinliteratur* (i.e., "popular literature," frequently oral in origin and transmission), while conventional Greek and Latin biographies were considered *Hochliteratur* (i.e., "cultivated literature," produced by and for educated members of the upper classes). The parallels between Peter's proclamation of the gospel to the Roman centurion Cornelius in Acts 10:34-43 are virtually an outline of Mark, suggesting the oral origins of the Gospels. While Peter's speech itself is probably not based on actual historical memory, it has been crafted to resemble the kind of oral proclamation of the gospel known in the author's own day. Matthew and Luke, each of which reflect literary dependence on Mark, show signs of literaturization, i.e., of transforming the relatively unliterary style and

form of Mark into literary productions of a more sophisticated character. While Mark began his narrative with the beginning of Jesus' public ministry, Matthew and Luke fashioned more complete lives of Jesus including birth narratives and genealogies at the beginning, and concluding with resurrection stories and appearances and even, in the case of Luke, the ascension of Jesus to heaven.

The view that the canonical Gospels are not *sui generis*, but rather have generic affinities with ancient biographical literature is more popular now than a generation ago. Several factors have convinced many that the Gospels are indeed a distinctive type of Greco-Roman biography: 1) Since a literary genre is both a social convention and a communication code, the notion of a unique genre is a contradiction in terms. 2) Though the "literary qualities" of the Gospels were previously impugned, in reality a text is "literary" when a given society regards it in such a way that the immediate context of its origin is ignored or regarded as irrelevant; "literature" is no longer regarded as having "instrinsic literary qualities." 3) The recognition of the theological and narrative skills of the Gospel authors was ignored during the heyday of form criticism (1920–60), and only fully appreciated with the development of redaction criticism (1960) and narrative criticism (1970). 4) Greek and Roman biographical literature had been studied and typed in ways that both masked and restricted the great variety of styles and linguistic registers they exhibited as well as the variety of social levels where they circulated. The great variety of types found in ancient biography has become increasingly evident with the recent publication of fragments of ancient biographical literature. *See* APOPHTHEGM; JESUS; SYNOPTIC PROBLEM.

Bibliography: Richard A. Burridge. *What Are the Gospels? A Comparison with Greco-Roman Biography.* (1992).

DAVID E. AUNE

GOSPELS, APOCRYPHAL. A general description of a large body of anonymous (i.e., the *Gospel of the Ebionites* and the *Gospel of the Hebrews*) or pseudepigraphal (i.e., the *Gospel of Thomas* and the *Gospel of Peter*), popular, extra-canonical Jesus literature that arose from the early 2nd–5th cent. CE (and even later). They typically present themselves as apostolic and implicitly equal in authority to the canonical Gospels. Many of these gospels are popular in the sense that ordinary Christians wrote them, rather than scholars, and they were based on popular Jesus traditions or tried to fill in lacunae in the canonical Gospels, such as Jesus' childhood or events between his resurrection and ascension. A very few, like the *Gospel of Thomas*, probably preserve authentic sayings of Jesus not found elsewhere. *See* APOCRYPHA, NT.

Bibliography: J. K. Elliott, ed. *The Apocryphal New Testament.* Rev. ed. (1999).

GOSSIP [רָכִיל rakhil; φλύαρος phlyaros, ψιθυρισμός psithyrismos, ψιθυριστής psithyristēs]. A gossip (rakhil, psithyristēs, or phlyaros) spreads gossip (psithyrismos) about someone—false information and malicious opinions, especially when offered in secret (psithyrismos and psithyristēs come from the verb psithyrizō [ψιθυρίζω], "I whisper"). The Hebrew word, often translated "slanderer," understands the gossip as one who travels around bearing tales about another, or as an informer who may profit by harmful information. Gossips reveal secrets, so the wise do not trust them (Prov 11:13, 20:19). In Jeremiah's gloomier moments, he declares that all the neighbors are gossips (Jer 6:28; 9:4 [Heb. 9:3]). Gossip shows up in two NT vice lists (Rom 1:29; 2 Cor 12:20); the purported tendency of young widows to gossip is one of the pastor's reasons why only widows at least sixty years of age should be supported by the church (1 Tim 5:13).

RICHARD B. VINSON

GOTHIC VERSION. *See* VERSION, GOTHIC.

GOTHOLIAH goth´uh-li´uh [Γοθολία Gotholia]. Called ATHALIAH in Ezra 8:7, he is the father of Jeshaiah, the family head of Elam who returned with Ezra from Babylon (1 Esd 8:33).

GOTHONIEL goh-thon´ee-uhl [Γοθονιήλ Gothoniēl]. Gothoniel was the father of Chabris, a magistrate of Bethulia, who heard the testimony of Achior against Holofernes (Jdt 6:15).

GOUGING EYES [נָקַר naqar; ἐκκόπτω ekkoptō]. This verb means "bore, pick, dig," and is often used with the object "eyes," where it means "gouge out." Dathan and Abiram accuse Moses of planning to gouge out the eyes of those challenging him (Num 16:14). The Philistines gouge out Samson's eyes after they capture him (Judg 16:21). Nahash the Ammonite king, who had been oppressing the Transjordanian groups, agrees to a covenant with the people of Jabesh-gilead. The sign of the covenant is that he will gouge out the right eye of all the men (1 Sam 11:1-4). The people of Jabesh-gilead agree, but request permission to send messengers to the people of Israel to see if anyone will come to their aid. Saul hears about the situation from his home in Gibeah and leads an army to deliver them from Nahash.

C. MARK MCCORMICK

GOURDS [פַּקֻּעִים peqa'im, פַּקֻּעֹת paqqu'oth]. The Hebrew word for gourd means "to burst open" and this may refer to the common property of ripened fruit to split apart. There are only two instances in the OT in which gourds are referenced. The first (1 Kgs 6:18) deals with the decorative motif carved into the cedar-covered walls of the Jerusalem Temple. The intertwining images of gourds on a vine and flowers would create a pleasant effect. In the other case, the "company of the prophets" that served Elisha had been forced by famine conditions to gather some wild gourds to add body to their stew. Their lack of basic plant lore lead them to include several specimens of the poisonous colocynth (*Citrullus colocynthis*), which produces small melon-like fruit. This vine trails along the sandy ground and resembles a cucumber with its well-cut palmate. Its bright colors that range from clear yellow to bright orange with green markings may look inviting; however, it is intensely bitter, and is a powerful cathartic that can cause a drastic purgative effect and dehydration. It has been suggested that this was the plant additive used by the Roman emperor Claudius' wife to slowly debilitate and ultimately eliminate her husband. *See* PLANTS OF THE BIBLE.

VICTOR H. MATTHEWS

GOVERNMENT, NT. In broad terms, government refers to the institutions, processes, and individuals through which order is created and maintained in a given society. These institutions and processes deal primarily with the creation and enforcement of legislation, taxation, control of the economy, and military mobilization.

The word *government* does not appear in the NRSV NT because there is no equivalent word in Greek, which reminds us that ancient ideas about social organization were quite different from modern ideas about government. Modern western notions of government tend to assume that all people are equal in the eyes of the law, that political officials are regular individuals who receive their power from the people, and that inhabitants of a nation-state have a responsibility to participate in the process of governance (even if that only means casting a ballot in elections). All of the texts of the NT were written within the context of the Roman Empire, and none of the three assumptions in the previous sentence characterized the Empire. People were considered unequal from birth, leaders were thought to be exceptional individuals who received their authority from divine sources, rulers were often worshiped as deities, and most of the population had no method for participating in the broad organization of society. Thus, in the NT we encounter very different conceptions about governance.

This difference is reflected in the vocabulary for discussing the institutions, processes, and individuals that promoted legislation, military power, and economic control in the Roman Empire. The primary NT terms are basileia (βασιλεία, kingdom, empire), exousia (ἐξουσία, authority), basileus (βασιλεύς, king, emperor), hegemōn (ἡγεμών, ruler), despotēs (δεσπότης, master), kyrios (κύριος, lord), archō (ἄρχω, to rule), and hypotassō (ὑποτάσσω to submit, to be subject to, to obey). This vocabulary surfaces in various ways with distinct nuances in the NT texts, and so this article begins with an overview of Roman imperial government and then summarizes the range of attitudes and ideas about "government" in the NT.

A. The Roman Imperial System

The long reign of AUGUSTUS (30 BCE–14 CE) initiated a new public order in the Mediterranean world and Europe, an order known as the ROMAN EMPIRE. From his capital in Rome, Augustus was able to consolidate control of huge territories through conquest, diplomacy, and political manuevering. The ruling structures he established survived several crises and lasted approximately three centuries. The primary goals of the Augustan system were the extraction of wealth (mostly through taxation and plunder) and the suppression of opposition. In comparison with other ancient empires the Augustan strategy for accomplishing this was minimalist: after conquest, only enough bureaucracy and administration was used in order to control and to profit.

The empire was divided into approximately forty provinces. Stable provinces had proconsuls appointed by the Roman Senate, while provinces requiring military occupation had legates and procurators appointed by the emperor. These Roman officials normally relied on local aristocracies—and pressured local aristocracies—to keep the population under control, using regional and local institutions for these purposes whenever possible.

In addition to the provinces, Rome exercised control over some areas through semi-autonomous client rulers like King Herod the Great in Palestine or the tetrarch Herod Antipas who inherited Galilee and Perea (*see* HEROD, FAMILY). Client rulers had a good deal of discretion over internal affairs but no freedom in foreign affairs. These rulers maintained their own military and taxed their own subjects. They were expected to use these resources to assist the Empire when Rome requested it.

The Roman army was the main means for bringing territories and people under control, and the threat of military force was needed in most provinces to maintain that subjection. In the 1st cent. CE there were about twenty-five Roman legions, each composed of approximately 6,000 Roman citizens, and at least an equivalent number in the auxilia (units made up of non-citizens). In addition, there were between 5,000–10,000 members of the praetorian guard who comprised the emperor's personal militia. So the armed forces of the Empire included more than 300,000 professional soldiers, in addition to local police forces and armies of client rulers.

These political and military institutions allowed the imperial government to extract resources from the provinces. The main forms of taxation were a land tax (on public and private properties), a poll-tax on individuals, and indirect taxation (such as import duties at frontiers, 5 percent inheritance tax, 4 percent sales tax on slaves, etc.). At the end of the Roman Republic such taxes were mostly farmed out to publicani, who contracted to provide a fixed amount to Rome. The publicani then charged higher fees in their region in order to make a profit. Augustus and his successors moved away from the publicani system. In its place the cities of the provinces were required to collect the taxes from their territories, with the Roman provincial officials overseeing the operations of the cities. Thus the tax collectors (telōnēs τελώνης) mentioned in the gospels were probably not publicani, but rather local employees involved in the collection of tribute.

The official justification for this imperialist system was that it provided the civilized world with *pax et securitas*, "peace and security." The basis for this was the claim that the whole world had benefited from the actions of Augustus and his successors: the emperors brought an end to war, rid the land of brigands, cleared the sea of pirates, and reestablished order.

B. The Historical Jesus

Jesus lived within this Roman imperial context. He spent most of his life working in Galilee, which was governed by the client ruler HEROD ANTIPAS. Jesus traveled at least once into Judea after the Romans turned the region into a province. It was in Judea that he was executed ca. 30 CE by the prefect PONTIUS PILATE with the approval of some members of the local Judean aristocracy. The method of execution was crucifixion, which was normally reserved for insurrectionists, bandits, disobedient slaves, and others who challenged Roman rule. In the case of Jesus, the verdict was that he had claimed to be king of the Jews (e.g., Mark 15:26; John 19:19-22).

Did Jesus' ideas about government include the claim that he was the rightful king of the Jews? Modern scholars are divided regarding the exact teachings of the historical Jesus and the scope of this article does not allow for a full discussion of these complex issues. Scholars are nearly unanimous, however, that the central feature of Jesus' mission was the proclamation that God's kingdom was present or about to arrive. Scholars also tend to agree that Jesus thought he played, or would play, a special role in God's rule, although probably not as king. Modern interpretations of the historical Jesus diverge at this point, with many scholars arguing that Jesus presented himself as an eschatological prophet announcing the arrival of God's kingdom, while other scholars portray Jesus as a counter-cultural philosopher who prodded listeners to seek the reality of God's kingdom in everyday life. In either case, the focus on God's rule in the midst of Roman rule left Jesus open to the charge that he was a revolutionary. Some audiences would have welcomed such a revolution (John 1:49; 6:15) and others would have opposed it (Matt 27:11-14; Luke 23:3).

C. Paul

Paul's experience of Roman government was mostly harsh. In one highly-charged rhetorical setting he recalled numerous imprisonments and floggings, and then specifically mentioned that he was beaten with rods by governing authorities on three occasions (2 Cor 11:23-25). The Acts of the Apostles records three actions against Paul by municipal authorities (Pisidian Antioch, Iconium, and Philippi), plus one unsuccessful attempt to have him arrested or lynched in Ephesus and one unsuccessful accusation before a Roman proconsul (Gallio at Corinth). One imprisonment and flogging at the hands of local government is recorded in Acts (Philippi) and the narrative ends with Paul under arrest by imperial authorities for over two years.

Paul's message was at least partially responsible for his arrests, beatings, and trials, for he taught that God would soon bring all government—including Roman imperialism—to an end. Paul thought that the return of Christ was near (1 Thess 4:15) and would come suddenly, when people were declaring "peace and security" (1 Thess 5:3, a Greek translation of *pax et securitas*). When Christ returned, Christ would hand over the basileia to God, "after he has destroyed every ruler and every authority and power. For he must reign until he has put all his enemies under his feet" (1 Cor 15:24-25). Since this world was about to pass away, the major social structures of this world—marriage, sexuality, possessions, religious observances such as circumcision, even proper respect for the dead—were no longer important (1 Cor 7, esp. v. 29-31). The true citizenship of believers was in heaven (Phil 3:20).

In his extant letters, Paul did not lay out a theory of governance. His only extended discussion of these issues is found in the moral exhortation section of his letter to the Roman believers. Here Paul provided some assertions and arguments that hint at his thinking on the relation of governance and apocalyptic expectation (Rom 12:9–13:10). Four observations on this text are in order. First, the discussion is framed at beginning and end by the command to love. This is the highest ethical principle. Second, love is defined in a specific way: the negative injunction to renounce vengence, and the positive injunction to show kindness to enemies. Third, within this ethic of love for enemies, the role of authority (exousia) and those who rule (archontes ἄρχοντες) is twofold: government is a servant of God that praises those who do good and punishes those who do evil. A fourth observation follows from this: believers were to be subservient (hypotassō) to any authority and not to resist it. The motivation for subservience was also twofold—to avoid punishment and to have a clear conscience. The section concludes with a restatement of the basic principle: love that cares even for enemies is the fulfillment of God's requirements for human behavior. Believers should pay what they owe: tribute to foreign rulers (phoros φόρος), taxes (telos τέλος), respect (phobos φόβος), and honor (timē τιμή).

This description of the role of rulers and authority in Rom 13 is surprising because it contradicts aspects of Paul's own experience. When he composed these lines he had scars on his body from unjust floggings by rulers and authorities. The idealized view of authority, however, allowed Paul to transition into a series of apocalyptic exhortations. Within the context of an ethic of love for all (including enemies), Paul's apocalypticism is described in terms of sober living in the daylight, not the drunken revelry of the night that has passed. His gospel about the approaching kingdom of God was not supposed to foster disorder but rather a morality that surpassed the ethics of those who did not embrace his teachings.

D. The Gospels and Acts
1. Mark

In the earliest of the canonical gospels, the author of Mark presented Jesus' public career as a challenge to the governments of the region. According to Mark, the proclamation by Jesus that God's kingdom was near comes after Herod Antipas arrested John the Baptizer (Mark 1:14-15). Popular support for Jesus grows along with opposition to him. In Mark 6 Herod Antipas hears about Jesus and wonders about his connection to John, whom Herod had executed. In Mark 8, Jesus warns his disciples that he is taking them into a confrontation with Roman authority and with the Judean aristocracy, so they need to pick up their crosses if they would follow him. Jesus heads to Jerusalem, where the crowds welcome him with hopes for the restoration of David's kingdom (Mark 11:1-10). There Jesus challenges the authority of the Judean aristocracy at the center of national life, the Jerusalem temple. The Judean aristocracy arrests him and hands him over to the Roman prefect Pilate. Pilate is unimpressed by the case against Jesus, but orders his crucifixion to satisfy the aristocracy and the crowds. The charge is that Jesus had royal aspirations. Throughout the gospel, however, the author has been careful to redefine the concept of **basileia**. The kingdom of God is a radically different type of society, where leaders serve rather than dominate and where humility is the definition of greatness (Mark 10:41-44). It is especially hard for the wealthy to enter this kingdom, for it requires a renunciation of possessions, family, and security (Mark 10:17-31).

2. John

The Gospel of John records a different tradition about the life of Jesus that portrays Roman government more positively and the Judean aristocracy more negatively. The author of John affirms the kingship of Jesus early in the narrative (John 1:49) and Jesus finally acknowledges the charge before Pilate (18:33-38). But in the same text the concept of **basileia** is again redefined: Jesus' kingdom is not "of this world," which is seen by the fact that his followers do not fight to release him. His followers are to distinguish themselves instead by their love for each other (13:34-35; 14:21). The role of the Roman government in the death of Jesus is deemphasized in John. The major antagonists here are not the Romans but rather "the Jews," a frequently-used phrase in this gospel that can have several overlapping meanings. When used for opponents of Jesus, "the Jews" often refers to members of the aristocracy centered primarily in Jerusalem (5:1-18; 7:1). It is this aristocracy that is said to have plotted Jesus' death after the raising of Lazarus (11:45-53) and that harrasses Pilate into condemning Jesus. The Roman prefect makes repeated protestations about Jesus' innocence but finally acceeds to their demands when "the Jews" label Jesus as an enemy of the emperor (19:12-16).

3. Matthew

Even though Matthew and Luke both follow the Markan storyline, the role of government is handled quite differently. The Gospel of Matthew adds elements that highlight the kingship of Jesus and that blame the Jewish people for his death. Matthew's gospel immediately goes beyond Mark by adding a genealogy that organizes Israel's history around four events: Abraham, the establishment of David's rule, the destruction of the Davidic kingdom, and the coming of Jesus (presumably as the restoration of the Davidic kingdom). Then come birth narratives that have foreigners recognize Jesus as king of the Jews and an attempt by the reigning king, Herod the Great, to kill Jesus as an infant. The Matthean narratives of Jesus on trial before Pilate also have new elements that heighten the guilt of the Judean aristocracy: Pilate's wife has a dream about Jesus' innocence (27:19); Pilate washes his hands to show his own innocence (27:24); and then, "the people as a whole answered, 'His blood be on us and on our children'" (27:25). In addition, the author of Matthew adds a story about the Judean aristocracy bribing the Roman soldiers not to reveal that Jesus had risen

from the dead (28:11-15). But ultimately, all authority is given to the risen Jesus (28:18). *See* ANTI-JUDAISM; ANTI-SEMITISM.

4. Luke and Acts

The Gospel of Luke takes the Markan storyline in a different direction, playing down the royal implications of the Jesus traditions and accepting the presence of Roman imperialism. One strategy for accomplishing this was to refocus the narrative around the Jerusalem temple rather than around the conflict with aristocracy or with the empire: the birth of John, the birth of Jesus, and the story of Jesus at age twelve make the temple a central concern at the beginning of the text; the temptations of Jesus end with the rejection of a miraculous display at the temple (4:1-13); the middle of the text is dominated by Jesus' journey to Jerusalem (from 9:51 on); and the text ends with the disciples rejoicing and worshiping in the temple after the ascension of Jesus. The author of Luke also makes several other editorial decisions that cast the Roman Empire as an acceptable political framework. For example, the births of John the Baptizer and of Jesus are both introduced with references to the current emperor and regional officials (2:1; 3:1). In addition, when John is asked for advice by tax collectors and soldiers—representing the two crucial features of Roman imperialism—John only instructs them to do their jobs well without engaging in extortion (3:12-14) rather than criticizing Roman rule itself. When Jesus does finally face trial before Roman authorities, both Pilate and Herod Antipas pronounce him innocent, and Pilate suggests that flogging and/or release would be more appropriate than crucifixion. Pilate is finally swayed by the aristocracy and the crowd, however, and Jesus is condemned to death (23:13-25). Primary responsibility resides with the Judean aristocracy and the author notes that some Jews (and at least one Roman) were shocked by the execution (23:27, 47-48).

The Acts of the Apostles develops and expands the relatively positive appraisal of Roman government found in the Gospel of Luke, which was written by the same author. The ascension of Jesus is narrated again at the beginning of Acts and then the author lays out an interpretation of the expansion of the churches within the framework of Roman imperialism. Roman officials and military men have their flaws in the narrative (Acts 18:17; 24:26), but they are mostly benign or positive toward the churches in Acts (10:44-48; 16:18-33; 27:42-43). The author shifts most of the blame for problems on Jews (7:54-60; 9:23-25; 13:50; 14:2, 19; 17:5-13; 21:27-30) or on venal gentiles (16:19; 17:5; 19:23-38), and points out several high-status gentiles who join the movement (13:12). Paul is the main character for most of Acts, and he is portrayed as a Roman citizen who interacts easily with some of the most powerful aristocrats in the Empire. The story ends with the apostle under lenient house arrest in Rome, and readers never learn the verdict of his trial in Rome.

E. The Pastoral Epistles

First Timothy, 2 Timothy, and Titus show great concern for proper, respectable behavior on the part of believers. In 1 Timothy there are signs that this concern is related to problems that arose from a fundamental disagreement between the churches and dominant society over the claims of rulers. The disagreement was about who is the king of kings and lord of lords, and so the author of 1 Timothy twice contrasts Roman rulers with God as the only one who rules over all. The first contrast comes in 1 Tim 2:1-6. This text implies that rulers and officials are not allowing churches to lead quiet lives (2:1-2). Three assertions follow that are at odds with dominant society: God is their savior, there is only one God, and Jesus is the only mediator between God and humanity. Each of these three assertions contradicted imperial propaganda, which claimed that the emperors were humanity's saviors, that the emperors were divine, and that the emperors were mediators for the grace of the other deities toward humanity (*see* EMPEROR WORSHIP). The author exhorted the audience to pray for all kings and dignitaries so that these rulers will allow the dissenting churches to live in peace.

The second contrast comes in 1 Tim 6:12-16. The author wrote that the audience made the "good confession" and that Jesus also made the good confession before Pontius Pilate (the only reference to Pilate outside the gospels and Acts). The confession of Jesus probably alludes to the gospel traditions in which Pilate interrogates Jesus about whether he is a king (Mark 15:2-5//Matt 27:11-14//Luke 23:2-5; John 18:33-38). In 1 Tim 6 the author goes on to assert that God is the "only Sovereign, the King of kings and Lord of lords. It is he alone who has immortality . . ." (6:15*b*-16*a*). This statement also contradicts normal imperial claims about the emperors, indicating a basic ideological disagreement with mainstream society.

The Letter to Titus adds one extra responsibility of the believers in relation to rulers in addition to praying that rulers allow believers to live in peace. Titus 3:1 exhorts the audience also to submit (hypotassesthai [ὑποτάσσεσθαι], from hypotassō [ὑποτάσσω]) and to obey (peitharcheō πειθαρχέω) rulers and authorities. Thus the Pastoral Epistles do not lay out an extensive discussion about government. Rather, the author assumes a fundamental disagreement about the ultimate authority in world, and urges believers to obey rulers and to pray that these rulers will permit believers to live without harassment.

F. First Peter

First Peter was written to churches under severe pressure (1 Pet 4:12) but the source of the pressure is unclear (perhaps popular disapproval or local governmental harassment). In this context, we find another example of early believers trying to articulate their difficult relationship with the institutions and processes of governance. The author asserts a Pauline view of the responsibilities of rulers—to punish evildoers and to praise those who do good (2:13-17). The text also exhibits an understanding of the way the empire operated, describing the emperor (basileus) as one who is at the top of the hierarchy and other rulers (hēgemōn ἡγεμών) as those who are sent by the emperor in order to do the punishing and praising. The author refers to any of these as a human authority or human institution (anthrōpinos ktisis ἀνθρώπινος κτίσις), and advises readers to submit (hypotassesthai) to them for the Lord's sake. The exhortation concludes with a hierarchy of responsibilities for believers that also has a Pauline tone: honor all people, love fellow believers, fear God, and honor the emperor.

Later in 1 Peter the author engages in a long discussion of how the audience should react when the ideal does not match reality and they suffer for doing good (3:8–4:19). The readers/hearers were instructed to bless those who abused them and to be ready to explain their hope. Jesus Christ is presented as the role model for those who suffer unjustly: they should imitate his endurance and his commitment to do the will of God. Such suffering was a sign that the Spirit of God is with believers; it was also a process by which they were being purified.

In this context the author mentions the possibility that his audience might suffer for being Christians. At the time when 1 Peter was written, believers did not yet call themselves "Christian." This term was used by outsiders, often in a derogatory fashion. In some instances the label could result in capital punishment (see Pliny the Younger, *Ep.* 96).

G. Revelation

The final book of the NT provides a trenchant critique of government and imperialism. The author recounts visions that describe his audience as a kingdom (Rev 1:6) and government as a demonic entity that opposes God. The primary symbol of Roman imperialism is the beast with seven heads and ten horns (Rev 13:1-8). This beast received its power and authority from Satan, and was using this power to destroy all opposition. It blasphemed God and conquered God's people. All inhabitants of the realm had to worship it. The beast was assisted by a second beast that is probably to be associated with the local aristocracies who supported Roman imperialism and enforced its rule (13:11-18). The second beast controlled the economy, deceived the people, and killed anyone who would not worship the beast of Roman imperialism.

This denunciation of the Roman Empire was expanded in Rev 17–19 to reveal the web of economic and political exploitation that formed the basis of imperial rule. Here the empire is portrayed as a 7-headed, 10-horned beast carrying a prostitute drunk on the blood of the saints (Rev 17). A series of oracles in Rev 18:1-19:8 then provides a sarcastic description of the fate of this imperial system. The prostitute who called herself a queen is destroyed in a day. Pestilence, famine, and fire consume her. The kings of the earth who committed fornication with her and lived in luxury wail at her torment. The merchants who became fabulously wealthy from her mourn the loss of such riches. The sailors and shippers weep at the loss of their ill-gotten gains. But heaven bursts into song, rejoicing over the empire's demise and praising God for judging the system that corrruped the earth (Rev 19:1-8).

If there is anything positive to be said in Revelation about the rulers of this world, it is ambiguous and comes near the end. As the author describes the new Jerusalem after the old heavens and earth have passed away, he writes this. "I saw no temple in the city, for its temple is the Lord God the Almighty and the Lamb. And the city has no need of sun or moon to shine on it, for the glory of God is its light, and its lamp is the Lamb. The nations will walk by its light, and the kings of the earth will bring their glory into it. Its gates will never be shut by day—and there will be no night there. People will bring into it the glory and the honor of the nations" (21:22-26). In the visionary logic of the Apocalypse this is perhaps a statement of what the author thought governance ought to be, and what it someday might be.

H. Summary

The NT does not provide one coherent description or evaluation of government. If the texts are arranged according to their evaluation of the Roman Empire, Luke-Acts comes out at positive end of the scale with its optimism about the possibilities for churches in the empire, and Revelation comes out at the opposite end because of its extreme denunciation of empire.

At a general level, however, the texts all share a common conviction that the God of Israel is the ruler above all rulers, the King of kings. Another common element is the assumption that there is tension or hostility between government and the churches. Finally, most of the texts also instructed believers to be subordinate to governmental authorities, expecting that one day all government would be destroyed so that God and Christ could reign over all.

Bibliography: Ernst Bammel and C. F. D. Moule, eds. *Jesus and the Politics of His Day* (1984); Warren Carter. "Vulnerable Power: The Roman Empire Challenged by the Early Christians." *Handbook of Early Christianity: Social Science Approaches.* Anthony J. Blasi, Jean Duhanime, and Paul-André Turcotte, eds. (2002) 453–88; Everett Ferguson. *Backgrounds of Early Christianity.* 3rd ed. (2003); Steven J. Friesen. *Imperial Cults and the Apocalypse of John: Reading Revelation in the Ruins* (2001); Peter Garnsey and Richard Saller. *The Roman Empire: Economy, Society and Culture* (1987); Richard A. Horsley, ed. *Paul and Politics: Ekklesia, Israel, Imperium, Interpretation* (2000); Walter E. Pilgrim. *Uneasy Neighbors: Church and State in the New Testament* (1999).

STEVEN J. FRIESEN

GOVERNMENT, OT. *Government,* in its narrow sense, refers to the political apparatus that administers affairs of state. More comprehensively, *government* refers to the polity or state as institution, encompassing the foundation of its authority, the shape of its policies, its several branches, and its administrative mechanisms (i.e., government in the narrow sense). This entry follows the broader usage as it traces the historical course of Israel's political experience, in the first instance as the OT tells the story and, secondly, according to a critical reconstruction of Israel's political history in the ANE context, followed by a synoptic view of foreign and domestic affairs under the monarchy.

A. Israelite Government According to the OT
   Canon
B. Israelite Government Critically Understood
C. The Succession of Israelite Forms of Government
   1. Independent tribal government
   2. Independent monarchic government
      a. United Kingdom
      b. Divided kingdoms
   3. Dependent colonial government
D. Israelite Government in Its Near Eastern
   Context
E. The Many Facets of Israelite Monarchic Government
   1. Foreign affairs
      a. Relations between Israel and Judah
      b. Relations with neighboring states
      c. Relations with the great powers
   2. Domestic affairs
      a. Relations within the political center
      b. Relations between the political center and
         its primary beneficiaries
      c. Relations between the political center and
         the populace at large
F. The Legacy of Israelite Government
Bibliography

A. Israelite Government According to the OT Canon

In its first manifestations as a people, the polity of Israel is a theocracy in which MOSES, the mouthpiece of God, combines all the offices and functions of government. He has charismatic authority that is valid so long as the people will do as he says. Leadership of the community passes to Joshua who continues in a theocratic mode. His major role is commander-in-chief of the Israelite army that successfully conquers Canaan. In the process of occupying the land, Israel is viewed as a unified people but the assignment of land is awarded to sub-sections of the people that we generally designate as TRIBEs. The authority of Joshua is said to consist in his adherence to the law of Moses.

Following Joshua, a succession of spirit-inspired military leaders assumes authority (see JUDGES, BOOK OF). The separate tribes emerge as discrete units, sometimes acting alone and sometimes cooperating. The theocratic theme that ran through the leadership of Moses and Joshua is attenuated to the breaking point by the loose loyalty of these leaders to the religious beliefs and practices set forth in the law of Moses. Apart from the attention to religion, there are few indications of how social and economic life was organized.

Pressure from the Philistine city-states prompts Israel to appoint a strong military leader in the person of Saul who is described as Israel's first king. Saul dies in battle and is replaced by David who creates the rudiments of a state apparatus and establishes a long-lasting dynasty. The pioneer work of David in shaping the state is expanded by Solomon who enlarges the bureaucracy, encourages inter-state trade, and engages in a large-scale building program, including a temple for the national deity. Nonetheless Solomon worships other gods and arouses opposition to his forced labor policies. At his death, Israel splits into two polities: Judah remains with the Davidic dynasty and the northern tribes create their own state which retains the name of Israel (see ISRAEL, HISTORY OF).

For the next three hundred years, the history of these two kingdoms is told in a cursory manner that focuses primarily on the religious infidelity of most of the rulers of the Northern and Southern kingdoms. Both kingdoms are destroyed, the north by Assyrians and the south by Neo-Babylonians, and the former kingdoms of Israel and Judah are absorbed into the conquering empires. Details about the regimes of these kings are largely either military or cultic, with only a few side glances at social and economic conditions and a smattering of information about state administration (See CHRONICLES, FIRST AND SECOND BOOKS OF; KINGS, FIRST AND SECOND BOOK OF).

Once the Northern Kingdom falls, Israel disappears from the narrative altogether and the focus shifts to Judah whose populace, apart from some of the poor, is deported to Babylonia from whence they are released by Persian king Cyrus after fifty years of servitude. Some thousands of Israelites previously deported to Babylonia return to Judah, repatriated to a province of the Persian empire with a governor and high priest exerting secular and religious authority under the watchful eye of the Persians (see ZERUBBABEL). The

Jerusalem temple is rebuilt and Nehemiah strengthens Jerusalem as the capital of the Persian province of Judah (See TEMPLE, JERUSALEM).

This ends the political history of Israel/Judah as described in the Jewish and Protestant OT canon. The Roman Catholic OT includes the books of 1-2 Maccabees which tell of an uprising in Judah against the Seleucid ruler and his Judahite supporters who prohibited observance of the law of Moses and profaned the temple with a bastardized mixture of Greek and Yahwistic religions. After a fierce guerrilla war, Judah gains religious independence and, shortly thereafter, political independence. A Judahite dynasty, established by a faction of those who had prevailed in the guerrilla war, lasted about eighty years before the Romans conquered Judah (see HASMONEANS; MACCABEES, FIRST BOOK OF; MACCABEES, SECOND BOOK OF).

Summing up the biblical version of Israelite governance, the politics of Moses lack both structural clarity and historical veracity. Moreover, the governmental modes of Israel touched on in the tribal and colonial sources can be reconstructed only in broad outline, principally because the tribal accounts present no comprehensive depiction of how tribal society and governance were organized and the colonial accounts, while more detailed than tribal reports, suffer from huge temporal gaps.

The biblical record leaves us with the accounts of the united monarchy and the rival kingdoms as the fullest information we have about Israelite governance. Although the history of the kings over several hundred years is continuous, it is often sketchy in the extreme (see KING, KINGSHIP). More importantly, the highly moralistic account of the monarchy is severely critical of nearly all the kings, judging them "good" or "bad" depending on whether they did or did not confine all worship to Jerusalem. The exclusivity of worship at Jerusalem, however, was introduced so late in the monarchy that it is grossly misapplied to all the kings preceding Josiah. In the eagerness to pass judgment, the non-religious dimensions of governance are given short shrift. In other words, not only is religion invoked as the sole criterion for assessing kings but the rulers are unfairly judged for violating a religious requirement that was not in force during their reigns!

In short, incomplete and late sources, an overemphasis on religion compared to other factors in political history, and a slant on pre-exilic Israel that misconstrues its social and religious circumstances, render the Bible by itself of limited value for grasping the actual governance of ancient Israel. The OT requires the assistance of archaeology, extra-biblical documents, and a study of comparative social and political institutions, beginning with the ANE and extending to wherever in time and space conditions similar to those in ancient Israel are perceived to have prevailed (see ARCHAEOLOGY; SOCIAL SCIENTIFIC CRITICISM, OT).

Politically relevant archaeological discoveries, beginning around the middle of the tenth century, give ample evidence of developing cities with walls and fortifications, public buildings, water tunnels, workshops, shrines, and residential quarters. Much of this construction, especially in the administrative-military complexes, is on a sufficient scale to have required organized labor that only a central authority could have mustered. Governmental structures, separated from the rest of the city, together with larger dwellings distinguishable from the majority of modest housing, indicate the presence of an elite set off symbolically and socio-economically from the populace at large. Excavations of the royal acropolis in Samaria and of secondary administrative centers in both kingdoms, such as Dan, Megiddo, Lachish, and Beersheba, richly supplement biblical information on state institutions and practices.

The political economy of Samaria in the late ninth or early eighth century is illuminated by receipts written on broken pottery that record consignments of oil and wine, either as taxes for the royal coffers or as delivery of produce to officials from the estates granted them as perquisites of office (see SAMARIA OSTRACA). A late eighth-century dedicatory inscription carved into a rock-cut tunnel to bring water within Jerusalem's walls is identifiable as part of Hezekiah's preparations against an Assyrian siege (see SILOAM). From the same period an elaborate rock-cut tomb outside Jerusalem belonging to a steward whose name is only partially preserved may well be that of the royal steward SHEBNA condemned by Isaiah for making just such extravagant preparations for his burial. Standardized storage jars with the names of four towns stamped on their handles may have been assigned to, or manufactured at, those locations as a measure of state control of the economy in late eighth-century Judah. The Lachish letters from 588–586 BCE dramatically attest to the sharp divisions within Judahite ruling circles concerning the proper policy to pursue in the face of Neo-Babylonian domination (See LACHISH). Numerous carved seals and seal impressions used to stamp papyrus documents illustrate details of state administration. The seals frequently name their owners, and sometimes their official titles. These names and titles correspond closely to the personal names and offices of government personnel cited in Samuel, Kings, Isaiah and Jeremiah.

B. Israelite Government Critically Understood

Politics and religion were so closely woven in the ancient world that descriptions of religious developments as reported in the OT frequently carry political significance, or at least useful political inferences and implications. That these data on government usually appears as a "sideshow" to the main narrative about religious happenings speaks convincingly for their overall reliability. It appears that the biblical writers are often unaware of what they are disclosing about the flow of political events, especially when their inadvertent political disclosures are in conflict with their claims about religion.

Fortunately, it turns out that the archaeological record and the extra-biblical writings are broadly congruent with much of the biblical depiction of the history related in the OT, although this in no way "proves" the Bible to be true in all matters it touches on. As the material remains are cautiously connected to the biblical record, they do imply modes and circumstances of government of the sort claimed by the OT for the tribal era onward. There is, however, no archaeological support for the Moses traditions, which reinforces the impression they give of being legendary in origin (See PENTATEUCH).

Yet even when we lack archaeological evidence and extra-biblical writings that directly link to the OT, there is a huge body of information concerning government in the ANE, including extensive data on the ideology, organization and administration of the very empires that dominated Israel for centuries. Finally, a corpus of social and political theory analyzes world-over tribal, statist and colonial types of government found in ancient Israel. In addition, social history and comparative social studies document societies and polities that bear certain resemblances to ancient Israel and thereby suggest hypotheses about the history and structure of governance in Israel for which we have only limited biblical evidence.

C. The Succession of Israelite Forms of Government

1. Independent tribal government

Agrarian and pastoral highlanders bearing the communal name "Israel" emerged in Canaan by the end of the 13th cent. BCE, and their village settlements spread over the central highlands during the following two centuries. There are strong indications that these folk were indigenous to Canaan and are best understood as a socioeconomically disadvantaged sector of the populace, principally peasants, who formed a movement that asserted its independence from the lowland city-states. Although some of the clans and tribes may have been headed by chieftains, their social arrangements were far more egalitarian than prevailed in the city-states. In taking up residence in the highlands beyond the reach of the hierarchic city-states, emergent Israel opted out of a centralized mode of government and developed socioeconomic policies and practices that spread the communal distribution of wealth and power far more widely than in statist polities (see ISRAEL, ORIGINS OF).

The first form of government among these associated peasants was decentralized self-rule embedded in and diffused throughout its social institutions. The populace was grouped in "tribes" that were allied for purposes of military defense, economic cooperation, domestic law and order, and religious ritual (*see* AMPHICTYONY; TRIBE). Lacking state officials, all self-governing functions were carried out by elders, priests, and military "judges," who were recognized leaders in their respective tribes. Archaeological findings are broadly congruent with the biblical sketch of an agrarian populace inhabiting villages and working the land with a labor-intensive technology that remained vulnerable to the erratic rainfall and unexpected foreign attack The biblical record contains no comprehensive description of social and religious arrangements. However, some features of the Israelite polity can be plausibly conjectured from a study of other decentralized polities known the world over, such as the Icelandic Commonwealth, the Swiss Confederation, and the Iroquois Five Nations of New York State.

The primary forms of social interaction occurred at the local level, involving village and lineage groupings, and were focused on maintaining an adequate subsistence level and on defending against outsider threats to their independence. Wider circles of social interaction and cooperation, extending from village to village and reaching across tribal and regional boundaries, were secured by covenanted alliances that entailed social, economic, and religious commitments and obligations dependent on voluntary consent of the parties as "comrades in oath" (*see* ALLIANCE). Lacking state enforcement, the terms of cooperation depended on consensus, custom, negotiation, honor and shame rituals, and religious sanctions. The cult of the god Yahweh was a strong force in promoting a specifically Israelite identity, although it was not the sole form of worship practiced and it contained elements (such as goddess worship, magic, divination and necromancy) that were repudiated in post-exilic times (*see* ISRAELITE RELIGION, HISTORY OF; GOD, OT VIEW OF).

As a workable mode of self-rule, the Israelite confederacy was strong and effectual to the degree that the associated tribes found their self-interests served by its cooperative agreements. Over all, in spite of internal friction and open conflicts among the covenant partners, the confederation's "regulated anarchy" proved viable for two centuries.

2. Independent monarchic government

In the transition to centralized governance, Israel adopted state institutions whose officials claimed a monopoly of domestic power and reserved the right to tax, wage war, and control aspects of domestic life deemed vital to the welfare of the state. In return for these powers, Israelite state institutions promised defense of their subjects from outside powers and the maintenance of internal peace and justice. The balance between the gains and losses of state government was a matter of constant dispute among sectors of Israelite society that did not feel greatly rewarded by the claimed benefits bestowed by the crown.

a. United Kingdom. The steps to statehood as described in Samuel-Kings show a steady increase in the extension and consolidation of state powers, in a process of "creeping monarchism." Saul was made commander of the tribal levies in order to expel the encroaching Philistines from the hill country, but his non-military powers were so little developed that he is more nearly regarded as the last of the charismatic military leaders than as a person with customary royal powers. In contrast, DAVID's reign contained several marks of unambiguous state power, especially his establishment of a state capital, recruitment of a professional army, and enlistment of a body of officials to conduct affairs of state. He is reported to have appointed commanders of the citizen army and of the professional army, a manager of forced labor, a herald or protocol officer, secretary or chief scribe, and two priests representing royal and more traditional forms of religion (*see* ABIATHAR; PRIESTS AND LEVITES; ZADOK, ZADOKITES).

On the other hand, David's government lacked certain customary features of statist politics. He did not build lavishly, and it seems he did not tax his subjects to raise state revenue, depending rather on booty from his military campaigns abroad and on the fostering of interstate trade. In spite of his manifest successes, David's rule was shaken by two revolts, one within his own household and the other an uprising of the northern tribes, each foreshadowing structural weaknesses that were repeatedly to plague Israelite governance: on the one hand, illicit seizures of the throne from within the royal family or by officers of state, and, on the other hand, local resentment of royal favoritism toward one or another region or faction within the state.

In consolidating state power, the major undertakings of SOLOMON lay in royal building projects, notably of temple and palace, enlargement of the military, systematic taxation, expanded interstate trade, diplomatic ties to surrounding states, and enhancement of the royal ideology. To implement his aggressive expansion of state powers, Solomon's bureaucracy was both altered and enlarged beyond David's. Significantly, he introduced two new offices, that of director of internal revenue and steward of the palace and royal estates, clear evidence of his intensification of state control of the economy by heavy taxation and expansion of royal estates (*see* TAXES, TAXATION). Solomon consolidated the citizen levy and standing army under one command, and he expelled from office the priest who favored traditional religion and a less heavy-handed government.

Solomon is said to have divided his kingdom into twelve administrative districts. Each district was to provision the royal court with abundant food on a monthly rotation. The roster of these districts and the names of their overseers is thought by some scholars to belong to the reign of a later king, but such a rigorous tax system accords well with the political ambitions attributed to Solomon. Although the geographic layout of the districts is sketchily described, it appears that at least in some instances the new districts cut across old tribal territories, possibly for reasons of economic rationality with the added intent of weakening tribal loyalties. Judah is not named in the redistricting. If Judah is included, as the LXX does, there are thirteen districts rather than the twelve stated at the beginning of the roster. This omission may signal that Judah was exempted from the food levy altogether, or that Judah was taxed on a different basis.

In recent years doubts have arisen concerning the magnitude of the kingdom of David and Solomon. Indeed, some have gone so far as to dismiss their regime as a political fiction. Certainly the grandiosity of the description of Solomon's reign needs to be deflated but, although contested, the biblical and archaeological data speak for a modest first step toward statehood that failed when it overreached itself. ANE history and political anthropology attest to small states arising on a slender demographic and social infrastructure, especially when power shifts occur in larger states in their vicinity. It is plausible that David —and Solomon in particular—may have aimed for a strongly centralized state but were unable to realize it, both because of their limited resources and because their political aspirations collided with the stubborn resistance of a large part of the populace whose loyalties were tenaciously local and thus only tenuously committed to supporting a centralized polity, especially when the state intruded sharply on their local customs and on their subsistence economy.

b. Divided kingdoms. In his bid for optimal power, Solomon strained the productive capacity of his subjects and exacerbated the social and cultural divisions that David had managed to contain. His heavy reliance on the forced labor of Israelites was the immediate cause of the break away of the Northern Kingdom at Solomon's death (*see* LABOR; SLAVERY). This rupture of united Israel made it necessary for the northern tribes to provide for their own instruments of government.

With the choice of JEROBOAM I as their ruler, the northerners appear to have opted at first for a reduced bureaucracy and an attendant softening of the tax and corvee burdens. The new regime in the north retained the cult of Yahweh as the official religion, but provided for its own temples, priesthood, and festivals entirely independent of the Yahwism of Judah. The capital city was located successively at three different sites in the first decades of northern rule. This shifting of the administrative center, along with a series of military coups that seized political power, probably reflected a struggle among sectional interests in the ecologically and culturally diverse north, as well as class divisions between the powerful and the powerless.

After a series of unstable regimes, civil war split the northern populace into two factions, one apparently favoring a less centralized state and the other a strongly centralized governmental apparatus, whose leader OMRI emerged as the founder of the first stable northern regime. Omri established a new capital city, Samaria, and he and his son AHAB launched building projects rivaling those credited to Solomon in Jerusalem. Trade with Tyre and Damascus flourished. Ahab joined a coalition of Syro-Palestinian states that blocked the westward expansion of Assyria, an event that turned out to be the highwater mark of Israelite leadership in inter-state matters. The JEHU dynasty that followed in a more isolationist mode was compelled to acknowledge Assyrian power, but the Northern Kingdom remained independent for more than a century, until it was engulfed by renewed expansion of the Assyrian Empire. In the half century prior to the fall of the Northern Kingdom, Jeroboam II presided over a period of peace and prosperity that coincided with a similarly strong regime in the Southern Kingdom. Within decades, however, the renewed expansion of Assyria destroyed the Northern Kingdom and carved up its territory into provinces of the Assyrian empire.

The Northern Kingdom was a larger, more economically diverse and more multicultural and cosmopolitan state than was the smaller, more insular Southern Kingdom. When the north withdrew from the Davidic dynasty, Judah was left with a capital and an administrative apparatus but with a severely reduced population and fragile economic infrastructure. The one cohesive force in the south was the Davidic dynasty that proved more enduring than the regimes of the Northern Kingdom.

Unlike the Northern Kingdom, Judah escaped catastrophe by capitulating to Assyrian hegemony without a fight and accepting a vassal status. Apart from one unsuccessful attempt to shake loose from Assyrian domination, Judah remained under Assyria's thumb for a century. Although subject to Assyrian suzerainty, the polity of Judah experienced little change, being allowed limited self-rule as long as it paid obeisance and tribute to Assyria. The main effect of Assyrian hegemony was to deny Judah any autonomy in foreign affairs. Later, as the Assyrian Empire was crumbling in Syro-Palestine, Judah expanded territorially under JOSIAH who also launched draconian policies of fiscal and cultic centralization that prospered Jerusalem at the expense of the economic viability and the religious loyalties of the rural population (*see* DEUTERONOMISTIC HISTORY). In the final two decades before its political demise, Judah was riven by factional infighting in highest government circles between those who favored submission to Neo-Babylonia and those who argued for revolt with reliance on help from Egypt (*see* JEREMIAH, BOOK OF).

3. Dependent colonial government

With the dissolution of the vassal kingdom of Judah, its territory and inhabitants were under the direct control of Neo-Babylonia. The political leadership of Judah was deported to Babylonia and authority passed to a colonial regime headed by an Israelite official loyal to Babylonia. The hiatus of biblical information concerning the exercise of governmental authority in Judah following the death of GEDALIAH contributes to the notion of Judah as a virtually uninhabited land during the exile, and thus generating "the myth of the empty land" (see DIASPORA; EXILE). The reality is that a considerable population remained within Judah, including settlements around the destroyed sections of Jerusalem.

When, a half century later, Persia replaced Neo-Babylonia as the ruling empire in the ancient Near East, its policy of restoring deported leaders to their homelands and fostering a revival of local culture and religion was favorable to a restoration of Judah. A successful restoration of Judah depended greatly on cooperation between the returning "exiles" and those who had remained in the homeland, each group believing itself best qualified to revive the domestic life of Judah. Ultimate authority lay with the Persian court, but this authority was exercised in Judah by two simultaneously ruling colonial officers, the one serving as civil governor (see NEHEMIAH; ZERUBBABEL) and the other as high priest (see EZRA; JOSHUA). Aspirations for restoring the Davidic dynasty failed to materialize. On the other hand, the upper classes of Judah benefited economically from Persia's policy of strengthening the province as a bulwark against Egypt.

Local leadership divided between governor and priest was continued under subsequent Ptolemaic and Seleucid empires. The turmoil of the Maccabean War issued in Judah's independence, with the native ruler assuming the title of Davidic heir and high priest. The Hasmonean line of native Judahite kings was active in promoting prosperity through foreign trade and conquest of regions adjacent to Judah which spawned "new wealth" in commerce over against "old wealth" in land. Nonetheless, the Hasmoneans' assumption of Davidic prerogatives, their arbitrary rule and their severe repression of dissent, as well as an acquired taste for the ostentation of Hellenistic culture, fomented internal strife that eventually provided an opening for Rome to intervene and thereby extend its rule over Palestine.

The Judahite elite who served as administrators in the imperial systems of Persia and the Hellenistic empires were severely constrained both by their obligations to the empire and by the need to remain in as favorable a position as possible with their fellow Judahites. The local governing elite were deemed successful by the empires when they kept Judah politically pacified and economically profitable, but they were deemed successful by Judahites only when they were able to gain concessions from the empires to preserve or expand socio-cultural and religious spheres of self-determination and to improve the economic lot of the province. Obviously these two desiderata were not easily reconciled, and we can observe the "push and pull" of these exigencies in the biblical reports about the governorship of Nehemiah and the priesthood of Ezra.

Most of our information about government in ancient Israel stems from an exilic and post-exilic literary matrix. In other words, the OT as a canonical whole comes from the period after the loss of independent statehood and was compiled by state-less people in deported and restored communities who survived as religio-cultural enclaves within the great empires (see CANON OF THE OLD TESTAMENT). Unintentionally, the colonial imperial order as imposed on the province of Judah proved to be an incubator for Judahite culture and religion to prosper under the aegis of reformist groups who re-drew the identity of Israel in essentially "apolitical" or "trans-political" terms, but not in "non-political" or "anti-political" terms. At the same time local political activity was vigorously pursued, to the extent allowed by empire, in the process of giving internal definition to the restored community, as is evident in the disputes among civil and religious leaders reported in the books of Haggai; Zechariah, Ezra, Nehemiah.

Ideologically, the restored Judahite leadership claimed continuity with the larger Israelite past rooted in territory, history, and tradition. Judah was the "homeland" of all dispersed Judahites, initially in a geographical sense and subsequently in a metaphorical sense. Pragmatically, restored Judah could offer particular institutional, ritual, and literary achievements as models for how dispersed Judahites might organize their cultural and religious life. Nonetheless, the geographical distance and differences in local conditions meant that the communities of the dispersed charted their own courses without slavish imitation of the homeland.

D. Israelite government in Its Near Eastern Context

The governments of monarchic Israel, both Northern and Southern Kingdoms, form a subset within the larger family of regional states. A circumspect comparative study of Israelite government with other polities in the ANE provides an indispensable perspective that is lacking when Israelite politics is seen solely in terms of its textual description or in terms of generalized political theory.

In temporal terms, Israelite politics fall with the last one-third of ANE history. States had existed in the region for nearly two thousand years before the emergence of Israel. Territorially, demographically, and economically, the Israelite polity was among the small to mid-sized states of the region, comparable to most other Syrian and Palestinian states, commanding limited natural and human resources for mounting major military or diplomatic initiatives with or against other regions. Israel's freedom to function as an unfettered sovereign power lasted only for about four centuries (during the tribal era, the united monarchy, and the first hundred years or so of the divided kingdoms). From the late 8th cent. BCE onward, Israelite politics were played out within the shadow, and often under the thumb, of much stronger powers.

Geopolitically, however, Israel enjoyed a military and commercial importance out of proportion to its fragile political strength. Palestine lay at the center of a nexus of land routes running north-south between Egypt and Mesopotamia and east-west between the Mediterranean and the Arabian desert that provided an avenue for interstate trade, conquering armies, and the spread of new ideas and technologies (see ISRAEL, GEOGRAPHY OF). As a consequence of their strategic location, influence on or actual domination of Israel and Judah was a prime goal of imperial powers seeking to gain a "choke-hold" on the network of routes that converged and crossed in this narrow Syro-Palestinian corridor.

Not only were ANE states repeatedly threatening one another, but internal stability was at risk during the transition from one ruler to the next. Even in the great empires, dynastic continuity was by no means assured in the rough and tumble of domestic politics. Dynastic disruption is prominent in the Northern Kingdom. Even though the Davidic dynasty endured through more than four hundred years, it was not without precarious moments in the shaky passage from one ruler to the next. Assassinations and military coups, frequent in the north, also disturbed the south.

As for legal institutions, the judicial role assigned to the king in both Israelite states accords with the ANE custom of regarding the king as "chief judge," with responsibility to see that all parties uphold justice in the realm through wise appointments and exemplary conduct. In Israel, as elsewhere, most judgments were carried out through existing civil administration, reaching down to the level of the village councils, with the king serving symbolically, if not often in practice, as the court of highest appeal. In the administration of justice, Israel and Judah were very typical Near Eastern states in many respects. Interestingly, however, contrary to the law codes in the wider Near East, none of the bodies of law in the OT are attributed to kings. Instead, they are credited to Moses as the mouthpiece of God and thereby stake out the claim that Israel's laws pre-dated the monarchy (see LAW IN THE OT). This decisive privileging of the pre-monarchic era as the defining moment for Israelite governance found fruitful resonance in the last decades of the Southern Kingdom when the Deuteronomic Reform attempted to subject state politics to the dictates of the law of Moses.

Royal ideology is the point where the domain of government and the domain of religion intersect and generate "theo-politics," a mode of religious justification and glorification of statist regimes in the ANE (see MESSIAH, JEWISH). It appears that the cult of Yahweh was the "official" religion of both kingdoms, but still allowed for various forms of Yahwism and alternative cults during the reigns of most kings, with perhaps Jehu in the north and Hezekiah and Josiah in the south as sole exceptions. In any case, the central thrust of royal ideology was to surround the monarch with unchallengeable sanctity, such that opposition to, or even criticism of, the ruler could be branded as both treason and blasphemy. The Israelite rulers, as throughout the Near East, were lauded as the dispensers of peace and justice validated and empowered by the national deity. In practice, this flowery rhetoric gave way to justification of the fiscal burdens of government and to government's penchant for directly supporting or simply allowing big landholders and merchants to bilk and dispossess the already marginal peasants. Israel's prophets, ardent critics of the social, political and religious institutions, do not so much deny the grandiose claims of theo-politics as they expose the hubris and hypocrisy of leaders who insist that they are defenders of the very theo-politics of peace and justice that their policies and practices systemically sabotage (See JUSTICE; PROPHET, PROPHECY)

The one respect in which ancient Israel stands apart from the rest of the ANE is in the great prominence that its literature gives to the periods before and after the monarchy. Elsewhere in Israel's environment there are exceedingly few references to pre-state conditions other than in the form of mythological idiom or in dismissal of pre-state conditions as barbaric and chaotic. Moreover, the literature of the ANE has no real parallel to the OT grounding in post-monarchic Israel as a stateless ethnic enclave within empires that carefully preserves its memories of both a tribal and a monarchic past, and in which the decisive formative and ongoing charter of the people is Mosaic-tribal and not Davidic-monarchic. This canonical literary "bracketing" of kingship between a tribal beginning and a state-less ethnicity throws into sharp relief the way in which the final editors of the OT trace their roots to tribal Israel and treat the monarchy as a straying from the path of religious rectitude, a path to which they are committed to return even though they are denied political autonomy by alien powers.

E. The Many Facets of Israelite Monarchic Government

The goals of the centralized state in ancient Israel were generic to the ANE. The routines and episodic crises that occupied political leaders required the marshaling of sufficient means to preserve, expand and exploit the natural and human resources that formed their wealth and power base. The primary agenda of Israelite governments consists of foreign and domestic concerns that involve six distinguishable but interconnected sets of political relationships extending outward from the political center in widening circles.

1. Foreign affairs

a. Relations between Israel and Judah. Once separated, Israel and Judah were in frequent conflict and less frequent cooperation. A crucial point is that for the most part these two states did not make their decisions on the basis of their commitments to different forms of Yahweh worship, but rather with reference to political pragmatics. Briefly under Omri and Ahab, Israel and Judah were joined in an alliance that was shattered by the northern usurper Jehu. It also appears that the two kingdoms were on cordial terms under the simultaneous prosperous reigns of Jeroboam II in the north and Azariah (=Uzziah) in the south, but whether there was a formal alliance is unknown. Tension and conflict more often prevailed. The Northern Kingdom generally held the upper hand in these contests of power, even to the extent of breaking down the walls of Jerusalem on one occasion and laying protracted siege to the city on another. Nevertheless, there appears to have been no attempt by either state to incorporate the other by conquest. Judah, clearly the weaker party, lacked the means to conquer Israel, and Israel itself possessed a sufficiency of resources that it stood to gain little by seizing Judah, although it did not hesitate to exert its influence on the south. In at least one case Israel attempted to install its own choice of the king in Judah, but the effort failed. After the fall of the Northern Kingdom and the withdrawal of Assyria, Josiah of Judah attempted to reconquer northern territory and impose his version of Jerusalem-centered Yahwism on northerners.

b. Relations with neighboring states. The hostility between Judah and Israel is duplicated in their relations with other Syro-Palestinian states. Sometimes one or the other Israelite state was in alliance with nearby states, but it was extremely difficult for these kingdoms to align their diplomatic and military strategies in order to cooperate over any extended period of time. The primary issue that divided these small states was how they should relate to the far bigger powers of Egypt, Assyria, and Neo-Babylonia, whether to submit to their dominion or to oppose them, or to find some "third way." Under the Omrides, commercial ties with Tyre and Damascus greatly prospered the northern kingdom, but Jehu cut these ties and before long the Northern Kingdom was in a protracted war with Damascus. The Trans-Jordanian states of Ammon, Moab and Edom were important for Israel and Judah in that they lay astride north-south and east-west routes that carried inter-regional trade (*see* TRADE AND COMMERCE). David and Solomon had dominated these regions but the rulers of the twin kingdoms had mixed success

in continuing this legacy. The Philistine city-states of Gaza, Gath, Ashkelon, Ashdod, and Ekron, located on the coast to the southwest of Judah, their power broken by David, nonetheless remained independent and were from time to time at war with Judah over control of overland trade and access to the sea (*see* PHILISTINES).

The role of religion in the politics of Syro-Palestine was considerable in that all the states had their own patron deities who promised victory in battles but who for the most part could be worshiped alongside the cults of other gods. There is little indication that any of the wars were religious in the sense of attempting to impose one state's religion on another. Technically, in trying to impose Jerusalem-based Yahwism on the north, Josiah was not acting against another state because the imperial rule of Assyria was retreating from its Israelite holdings and there was as yet no government in its wake.

c. Relations with the great powers. During the periods when the great powers were absent from Syro-Palestine, its regional states were able to pursue their goals without interference from imperial powers. It was in just such a "great-power vacuum" that tribal Israel emerged and eventually became a state. Similar recessions of foreign power permitted Israelite political ascendancy under Omri and Jeroboam II and a Judahite florescence under Azariah (=Uzziah), and yet again under Josiah. The neo-Assyrian empire intruded into Syro-Palestinian affairs for more than two hundred years, beginning in the mid-9th cent. and continuing until the collapse of Assyrian dominion with only brief periods of respite. Control over Israel and Judah passed for a time to Egypt and then to Neo-Babylonia, followed by Persia, the Ptolemaic and Seleucid empires, and lastly Rome. At first, the Northern Kingdom bore the brunt of the Assyrian onslaught; but it was not long before Judah fell into subjection to Assyria and was eventually destroyed by Neo-Babylonia.

The impact of the great powers on the domestic fortunes of Israel and Judah was momentous. The most obvious impact was the annual payment of tribute required of subject states by their imperial overlords. These payments laid waste the royal treasury which was filled from a variety of sources such as royal investment in inter-state trade, tolls on transit trade, taxation of subjects, and produce from the royal estates. When Israel and Judah rebelled, heavy indemnity payments were added to the annual tribute. In large measure, the burden of tribute and indemnity was passed on by the crown to the general populace. Imperial control over Israel and Judah disrupted agriculture and stock breeding. Amid the turbulence of invasion and siege, it was difficult to tend fields, orchards and flocks when villagers fled to walled cities or were impressed into military service. Likewise, the flow of trade was often drastically interrupted The domestic politics of the subject states were thrown into turmoil as factions within the state establishment opted for divergent strategies in opposing or collaborating with the hegemonic states. The several short reigns and assassinations in the closing decade of the Northern Kingdom, as well as the shifting loyalties and tenuous power of the Judahite kings following Josiah, amply illustrate the difficulty of sustaining continuity and coherence of leadership in Israel and Judah when they were under severe external pressure.

2. Domestic affairs

a. Relations within the political center. The political center was composed of those who made the principal decisions and fashioned the policies that sought to secure, defend, replenish, expand, and legitimate the governing institutions. They composed no more than one percent of the population. In the absence of written constitutions and a dearth of archival records, the scope and configuration of the political centers in Israel and Judah can only be estimated.

The political center will have included the monarch, members of the royal family, the chief officers of the major branches of government responsible for the chains of command that carried out state decisions and policies, state-appointed judges, upper echelons of the priests, top level military officers, the royal body guard, and advisors to the court who might have held official assignment or were consulted on an ad hoc basis. Influential members of the royal family will have included sons of the monarch, one of whom may have been co-regent in certain reigns, other close male relatives, and queen mother (*see* QUEEN). The salient state offices reported in the reign of David and Solomon apparently continued intact with few modifications. The chief officers reported to the king, at times consulted with one another, but seem not to have formed a cabinet that met with regularity and adhered to stated rules and fixed agendas.

It is often claimed on slender evidence that under the monarchy there existed a council or assembly of distinguished citizens with consultative or legislative powers. The collectivity referred to in the OT as "the PEOPLE OF THE LAND," who have political clout at certain junctures in Judahite politics, is not depicted as a state institution but rather as an influential bloc of citizens, varying in composition from time to time, who acted in concert to shape the state in line with their convergent interests. In the public face they presented, the political centers of Israel and Judah employed "spin" in order to project a unity of viewpoint and action which they often simply did not possess. This highly desired unity of government purpose and policy rose and fell erratically, if only because the multiple social and economic interests represented in the political center and in its supportive power base were not easily prioritized and, in fact, were at times openly contradictory.

Each new challenge to state authority and power might precipitate realignment of cliques or factions within the bureaucracy. Many political narratives in the OT reveal frequent tensions and conflicts within the ruling center over such issues as the choice of successors to the throne of David, the proper state religious policy, and the correct stance to adopt toward threats from foreign powers, notably during the last decades of Israel's and Judah's independence. Many of the assassinations and power coups related in the OT are depicted as originating within the political center by army commanders, "servants" of the king, or even by member of the royal family. In short, the authority and effective power of the political center could not be safely taken for granted by any ruler, but had to be constantly reassessed, redeployed, and shored up in the face of changing circumstances within and beyond state boundaries.

b. Relations between the political center and its primary beneficiaries. Insofar as the state prospered in achieving its goals, sectors of the populace wielding social power and commanding wealth stood to benefit appreciably from governmental policies and projects. Chief among these beneficiaries were big landholders and merchants, some of whom were simultaneously state officials. In addition to the estates assigned them in compensation for their service, some enterprising officials engaged in land acquisition and commercial ventures "on the side." These state beneficiaries constituted at best no more than three to five percent of the population. Social, economic, and political networks were sufficiently enmeshed that they could reinforce one another through a strong state apparatus, but, in a weakened regime or in time of crisis, the divided loyalties of state officials and the diverse interests of state beneficiaries could undermine and even neutralize the capacity of the political center to take actions that would be widely obeyed.

All in all, persons of substantial wealth and high social standing prospered from a burgeoning state but suffered loss or decline when the state languished. The amount of available human and natural resources was a key variable in the relation between the political center and its principal beneficiaries. In good times there might well be adequate resources to enrich both the state and a wider circle of wealthy landholders and merchants, but in times of war, natural disaster or a weak or incompetent monarch, the division of diminished resources could become an arena of acute struggle between the political center and its dependent beneficiaries. Whether in good times or ill, however, the usual "losers" were the small peasants whose standard of living was in danger of precipitous decline whenever tax and debt became too onerous.

In short, the political center required the consent and cooperation of its leading citizens, and the leading citizens depended on state structure to protect and enhance their wealth and status. However, when the interests of center and its beneficiaries clashed, there was fertile soil for political instability and for the emergence of peripheral domestic power centers and court cabals. These could enfeeble the central regime to the point of near collapse or, if strong enough, actually topple the regime in power, as a result of an alliance between disaffected leaders in civil society and those in governmental service.

c. Relations between the political center and the populace at large. We have little information about the impact of central government on the majority of its subjects who lacked wealth and social status. There is little foundation for the common claim that a covenant between God, the king, and the people as a whole regulated Israelite politics and that every Israelite subject of the state stood under the protection of the terms of the covenant (*see* COVENANT, OT AND NT). To be sure, there was covenantal thought in ancient Israel, probably stemming from tribal times, that projected both religious and civil implications, but such thought was unable to shape government in any decisive way. Although Deuteronomy contains a sketch of how a religiously-based society would comport itself, including a radical scaling back of kingship and some limited protections for ordinary folk, it does not detail rights and duties of all Israelites, and there is no sign that all of its terms were ever put into practice. To be sure, rulers would now and then appropriate covenant thought to their advantage, as seems the case with Hezekiah and Josiah, but it is highly doubtful that they subjected themselves unequivocally to covenantal restraints dictated by religious tradition, such as those set forth in the book of Deuteronomy. It is, in fact, questionable whether any of the Syro-Palestinian tributary states, dependent as they were on capturing the surpluses of their overwhelmingly agrarian and pastoral producers, could have prospered or survived, had they adhered to policies of social and economic justice advocated by prophets and priests, as also by the covenant-oriented "laws" in the OT.

In sum, the great majority of subjects in Israel and Judah, who constituted at least ninety-five percent of all Israelites, are little evident in biblical traditions. As is characteristic of ANE states, these subjects of the crown do not possess any direct voice in government. Nonetheless, they are the routine targets of government actions that require of them taxes, forced labor, and participation in wars, as they also suffer the neglect of governments that for the most part "look the other way" when the socially and economically powerful landholders and merchants plundered and dispossessed the poor through harsh debt foreclosures (*see* AGRICULTURE; ISRAEL, SOCIAL AND ECONOMIC DEVELOPMENT OF). Although we have few details of how these state exactions were organized and administered, or at what levels of demand they operated from king to king, it is certain that the governments could not have functioned without considerable demands on their subjects and without at least a moderate level of compliance. According to the OT, insofar as the common people had voice at all, it sounded forth in the words and deeds of a line of prophets who condemned their victimization at the hands of the very leaders who were pledged to protect and support them. The scattered and largely indirect evidence on the degree of the actual consent and compliance granted to the political center by the general populace points in two directions: on the one hand, general compliance, whether due to actual consent or to fear and inertia; on the other hand, noticeable disquiet, resistance, and support for regime change which lay behind at least some of the assassinations and coups that punctuated the history of both kingdoms.

F. The Legacy of Ancient Israelite Government

In spite of frequent claims that ancient Israel was an early model of "proto-democratic" government, the legacy of ancient Israel provides no distinctive politics and no template for translating culture and religion into a satisfactory polity. To be sure, ancient Israel's politics have been mined for the support of divine right of kings, revolution against unjust authority, covenanted commonwealths, liberal democracy, nationalism, capitalism, socialism, and Zionism. This astonishing diversity in reading biblical politics stems in part from the scriptural authority invested in the OT, an authority that has repeatedly tempted proponents of socio-political systems to claim support in the biblical heritage. These strikingly divergent political programs can plausibly claim a biblical ancestry only because the unsystematized and unreconciled political structures, practices, and viewpoints expressed in the OT contain elements that appear to have affinities with a wide spectrum of modern political systems and programs without being at all identical with any one of them.

None of the OT political forms is transferable into contemporary politics. They cannot be transplanted as a whole, or in selected parts, for two reasons. Government in ancient Israel is never reduced to a single system, and the course of world history has unfolded far beyond the adequacy of ancient models to do more than inform us of the sources of some of our notions and sentiments about politics and to highlight political dilemmas that have been with us since political centralization arose. The modern state of Israel, claiming biblical roots, has not been able to recuperate a coherent biblical politics that can resolve the conflicting claims of religious nationalism and liberal democracy. Similarly, various attempts to conceive the United States theo-politically as a "New Israel" have foundered on the shoals of religious diversity and liberal democracy. The most that can be said for Israel's unoriginal and undistinguished political life is that it did manage to preserve a record of early Israel's tribal origins and to provide monarchic cover for the people's rich cultural and religious life, from which the remarkable literature and thriving religion of multiple colonial "Judah-isms" eventually issued in a more unitary Rabbinic Judaism (*see* JUDAISM; LAW IN EARLY JUDAISM; RABBINIC LITERATURE).

Bibliography: David Biale. *Power and Powerlessness in Jewish History* (1986); Martin Buber. *The Kingship of God* (1967); Norman K. Gottwald. *The Tribes of Yahweh. A Sociology of the Religion of Liberated Israel 1250-1050 BCE* (1979, 1999); Norman K. Gottwald. *The Politics of Ancient Israel* (2001); Ann E. Killebrew. *Biblical Peoples and Ethnicity: an Archaeological Study of Egyptians, Canaanites, Philistines, and Early Israel [ca. 1300-1100]* (2005); Oded Lipschitz. *The Fall and Rise of Jerusalem: Judah Under Babylonian Rule* (2005); Tryggve N. D. Mettinger. *Solomonic State Officials. A Study of the Civil Government Officials of the Israelite Monarchy* (1971); Tryggve N. D. Mettinger. *King and Messiah. The Civil and Sacral Legitimation of the Israelite Kings* (1976); John Middleton. *Tribes Without Rulers: Studies in African Segmentary Systems* (1958); Robert D. Miller II. *Chieftains of the Highland Clans: A History of Israel in the 12th and 11th Centuries BC* (2005); Ira Sharkansky. *Israel and Its Bible* (1996); John T. Strong and Steven S. Tuell, eds. *Constituting a Community: Studies on the Polity of Ancient Israel in Honor of S. Dean McBride, Jr.* (2005); Michael Walzer, Menachem Lorberbaum, and Noam Zohar, eds. *The Jewish Political Tradition, Vol. 1: Authority; Vol. 2: Membership* (2000, 2003).

NORMAN K. GOTTWALD

GOVERNOR. An official empowered by a king or by an emperor with responsibilites for a particular region. The governor's responsibilities depend on the political and economic needs of the kingdom or empire in question.

When Nebuchadnezzar conquered Jerusalem (586 BCE), Judah became a province of the Babylonian Empire and the Babylonians appointed Gedaliah as the area's first governor. His father and grandfather had been royal officials during the reign of Josiah. Gedaliah pursued a policy of reconstruction through collaboration with the Babylonians from his provincial capital at Mizpah. Gedaliah was soon assassinated by nationalists who then fled to Egypt. Very little is known about the administration of Judah under the Babylonians after this.

The Persians assimilated the territories of the Babylonian Empire and reorganized it after Cyrus's triumphant entry into Babylon (539 BCE). Many details of the Persian administration are unclear from the available evidence; assimilation and reorganization probably took place in stages. In time, however, the area west of the Euphrates became the satrapy of Beyond the

River, which was subdivided into provinces. It appears that Samaria and Judah were separate provinces, each with its own governor. Three governors of the Persian province of Yehud are known to us from biblical texts: Sheshbazzar, Zerubbabel, and Nehemiah. Sheshbazzar helped implement the Persian policy of supporting national religious institutions within the empire. He returned the holy vessels to Jerusalem that the Babylonians had removed, and initiated the reconstruction of the Jerusalem Temple (538 BCE; Ezra 5:14-16). About fifteen years later Zerubbabel was admonished to start or to restart the Temple reconstruction effort (Hag 1:1, 4). Nehemiah's service came in the 5th cent. BCE and was part of a local effort to make Jerusalem and the Temple the center of Jewish life (445–433 BCE; Neh 5:14-15, 18; 12:26).

Alexander the Great destroyed Persian imperialism in the late 4th cent. and for much of the 3rd cent. BCE, Judea, Samaria, and the Transjordan came under Ptolemaic control. Little is known with certainty about Ptolemaic administration of the area. There was probably a financial administrator over the area as was the case throughout Egyptian territories. The high priest of the Jerusalem Temples seems to have maintained some authority for the nation, perhaps in place of a governor. The centrality of the high priest and the Jerusalem Temple for administration of Judah probably began in the Persian period.

Judah, Samaria, and the Transjordan came under Seleucid control at the beginning of the 2nd cent. BCE. At first the Seleucids probably maintained the Ptolemaic administrative structure for Judah, with most of the administration centered in the Jerusalem Temple and the high priest functioning in some ways as a governor of the region. The Maccabean Revolt and the rise of the Hasmonean dynasty in the middle of the 2nd cent. decreased Syria's direct control of the area. These developments also centralized power in the hands of the Hasmonean ruler, who soon held both the post of high priest in Jerusalem and the office of ethnarch (which included responsibilities and status beyond that of a governor).

The creation of the Roman Empire under Augustus initiated a new governmental structure for the Mediterranean world. The Romans tended to administer their empire with minimal bureaucracy or interference, as long as the territories remained subservient and produced taxation. Local aristocracies were allowed to run most local and regional affairs if these two criteria were met. The governors of the provinces, however, tended to come from the Roman aristocracy.

There were two types of provinces under the Romans. One group of about ten provinces did not require military occupation and was administered by the Roman Senate. The Senate appointed proconsuls who normally served as governors of a province for one year after a distinguished career in service to the empire. In fact, the proconsulships of Asia and Africa were considered the crowning achievements of a senatorial career. A proconsul was normally assisted by a quaestor—a younger senator who oversaw provincial finances—and at least one legate (also a senator).

The second type of Roman province included about thirty imperial provinces that were under the jurisidiction of the emperor. These tended to be the provinces that required permanent military occupation. For the larger imperial provinces the emperor normally appointed a legate with senatorial status as his governor and a procurator with equestrian status to oversee financial affairs. Some of the smaller imperial provinces like Judea only received an equestrian official to oversee all military, financial, and judicial matters. This official had the military title of prefect from the time of Augustus, but Claudius changed it to the civilian title of procurator.

Most of the NT references to governors are to these prefects/procurators of Judea: PILATE (Matt 27:2, 11, 14, 15, 21, 27; Luke 3:1 and 20:20); FELIX (Acts 23:24, 26, 33; 24:1, 10); and FESTUS (Acts 26:30). The NT authors did not use technical terms for these officials, however, preferring in all cases the general noun hēgemōn (ἡγεμών, "ruler") or a form of the cognate verb hēgemoneuō (ἡγεμονεύω, "rule"). This same Greek root could be used for QUIRINIUS the legate of Syria (Luke 2:2) and even the emperor TIBERIUS (Luke 3:1). Thus from the perspectives of the NT texts, the fine distinctions of governmental status were in some circumstances unimportant.

Other NT texts, however, reflect more precise distinctions in the imperial hierarchy. First Peter 2:13-14 urged its audience to recognize "the authority of every human institution, whether of the emperor as supreme, or of governors, as sent by him to punish those who do wrong and to praise those who do right." Moreover, the precise term is used for proconsuls of senatorial provinces—Sergius Paulus in Acts 13 and GALLIO in Acts 18 (see PAULUS, SERGIUS).

Thus, the biblical tradition covers more than a millennium of history and at least a half dozen distinct royal and imperial systems. In most of the texts, the particular details of administration and governance are less important than the actions of the governors. The roles played by governors varied greatly. Sometimes he was a foreigner imposing authority from outside, sometimes an insider collaborating with foreign domination, and other times an aristocrat defending a region from foreign encroachment. See GOVERNMENT, NT; ROMAN EMPIRE; SANHEDRIN.

STEVEN J. FRIESEN

GOZAN goh´zan [גּוֹזָן gozan]. A region and river in northwest Mesopotamia where Tiglath-Pileser III (744–727 BCE) exiled the Transjordanian tribes (1 Chr 5:26). Then Shalmaneser V (726–722 BCE) or Sargon

(721–705 BCE) also deported some Israelites there (2 Kgs 17:6; 18:11). Urging Hezekiah to surrender to Assyrian domination, Sennacherib listed Gozan among several nations Assyria had dominated (2 Kgs 19:12). Gozan has been identified with modern Tell Halaf, where texts containing Israelite personal names have been found.

RALPH K. HAWKINS

GRACE [חֵן khen; χάρις charis]. Rarely found in the OT, the word *grace* is employed frequently in the NT writings, particularly in the letters of Paul, to designate the signal demonstration of God's goodwill toward humankind in the person of Jesus Christ and the effects of that goodwill in human lives. That God shows himself gracious in his dealings with human beings is a central theme in OT and NT alike.

A. Grace in the Old Testament
  1. Terminology
  2. The Concept of grace
B. Grace in the New Testament
  1. Terminology
  2. The notion of grace
    a. The Gospels and Acts
    b. The Pauline corpus
    c. Other writings
Bibliography

A. Grace in the Old Testament
1. Terminology

The noun *grace* occurs in three verses in the NRSV OT, each time representing the khen ("attractiveness, charm, favor, grace"; LXX commonly charis). In Ps 45:2, it refers to the gracious speech of the king. The "grace" that the remnant of God's people is said to have "found . . . in the wilderness" in Jer 31:2 refers to a renewed experience of God's favor following an outpouring of divine judgment. Whether the cry "Grace, grace to it!" that greets the completion of Zerubbabel's temple in Zech 4:7 expresses admiration for its beauty or a prayer that God's favor will rest upon the building is not clear.

Much more frequent is the adjective *gracious*. Though generally used in the NRSV for Hebrew khen or its cognates, at times other roots lie behind the rendering. For example, the "gracious hand" of God, a phrase used repeatedly in Ezra–Nehemiah (Ezra 7:9; 8:18; Neh 2:8, 18) for the divine blessing evident in the success of an undertaking, is more literally God's "good (tovah טוֹבָה) hand"; similarly, Yahweh's "gracious" words in Zech 1:13 are, more literally, "good." The "gracious" words of Prov 15:26 are, literally, words "of pleasantness" (no'am נֹעַם); the adjective related to this latter noun (na'im נָעִים, "pleasant") is rendered "gracious" and applied to God in the NRSV of both Pss 135:3 and 147:1, though an alternative rendering of these verses sees the act of praising God itself as "pleasant" (compare NEB, NIV).

Where the NRSV's "gracious" represents khen and its cognates, a human subject is occasionally described ("a gracious woman," Prov 11:16; people "gracious in speech," 22:11; note Ps 112:4, where the combination "gracious" and "merciful," widely used of God, is applied to those who fear him). The related Hebrew verb khanan (חָנַן, "show favor, demonstrate goodwill, be gracious"; LXX generally eleeō [ἐλεέω], "feel pity, show mercy"), however, is rendered "be gracious" only with God as the subject. (Job 33:24 is an apparent exception, though the angel spoken of is presumably a messenger of God.) A few of these texts affirm that God has (2 Kgs 13:23), may (2 Sam 12:22; Amos 5:15; Mal 1:9), or will (Exod 33:19; Isa 30:18-19) show himself gracious; conversely, Ps 77:9 represents the cry of one whose circumstances suggest that God has "forgotten to be gracious." More commonly the verb is used in prayers that God will deal favorably with the one(s) praying (so esp. in the Psalms) or with those on whose behalf prayer is offered (Gen 43:29; Num 6:25). In a few texts the request that God will show himself gracious is general (e.g., Gen 43:29; Num 6:25; Ps 67:1); usually, however, the request springs from a particular situation of need (Pss 6:2; 9:13; 25:16; 31:9, etc.). Situations and needs vary considerably, but in each case appeal is made to the compassion of the One on whose favor human well-being is utterly dependent. Though the decision whether to show favor rests with God alone (note Exod 33:19), both his promise to be gracious (Ps 119:58) and his custom of being so (119:132) may be cited as the basis for an appeal.

That God is "gracious" by nature is affirmed in a number of texts in which the Hebrew adjective khannun (חַנּוּן; LXX eleēmōn [ἐλεήμων], "merciful, compassionate") underlies the NRSV. The foundational self-characterization of God in Exod 34:6-7 portrays Yahweh as "a God merciful and gracious, slow to anger, and abounding in steadfast love and faithfulness, keeping steadfast love for the thousandth generation, forgiving iniquity and transgression and sin, yet by no means clearing the guilty." The words are frequently echoed in other OT texts, both those celebrating the goodness of God (Pss 103:8; 145:8; see also the ironic reference in Jonah 4:2) and those that cite that goodness to explain the survival of his sinful people in the past (Neh 9:17) or to motivate their repentance in the present (Joel 2:13). The combination "gracious and merciful" (Hebrew khannun werakhum [וְרַחוּם חַנּוּן]; LXX regularly eleēmōn kai oiktirmōn [ἐλεήμων καὶ οἰκτίρμων], "merciful and compassionate"; the order of the two adjectives may be reversed) is also found where God is praised (Ps 111:4; compare 116:5), sinful Israel's continued existence is explained (Neh 9:31), repentance is encouraged (2 Chr 30:9), and appeals are made for fresh demonstrations of God's favor (Ps 86:15-16).

2. The concept of grace

A study of grace in the OT should include such overlapping terms as "goodness," love, and mercy as well. Here we simply observe that the notions that we commonly associate with divine grace—that human beings owe the blessings of life to the goodwill of their Creator, and that the origins of the people of God, the privileges they enjoy, and their continued existence in spite of their own sinfulness are all to be ascribed to the goodwill of their God—are amply attested in the OT.

"The LORD is good to all, and his compassion is over all that he has made" (Ps 145:9). He "upholds all who are falling, and raises up all who are bowed down" (v. 14); he opens his hand to give to all their food, "satisfying the desire of every living thing" (vv. 15-16); he "is near to all who call on him" (v. 18). The perspective of Ps 104 is similarly universal, noting the provisions of God's providence for all his creatures; and Ps 107, citing a variety of examples of God's help for the needy, calls on all people to "thank the LORD for his steadfast love, for his wonderful works to humankind" (vv. 8, 15, 21, 31). The attentive will find evidence on all sides of "the steadfast love of the LORD" (v. 43).

Yet among the peoples of the world Yahweh chose "[the descendants of] Jacob for himself, Israel as his own possession" (Ps 135:4; compare Deut 32:8-9). Nothing but divine compassion and love can explain the choice and the blessings and privileges that followed upon it—certainly not the numbers or the righteousness of the chosen people (Deut 7:7-8; 9:6; compare Ezek 16:1-14; Hos 11:1). Nor did God treat his people as their deeds deserved. Their continued existence is a testimony to his willingness to forgive (Neh 9:31), and that same willingness inevitably provides the basis for a renewed relationship with him (Jer 31:31-34; compare Ps 130:7-8).

B. Grace in the New Testament
1. Terminology

In the NT, NRSV, "grace" translates charis. Charis is also behind NRSV "gracious" in Luke 4, Col 4, and 1 Pet 3:7. But "gracious will" in Matt 11:26 = Luke 10:21 renders Greek eudokia (εὐδοκία), "good will, good pleasure."

In classical Greek, charis was used in a variety of senses, including each of the following: 1) that which pleases, or brings delight (chara [χαρά], "delight, joy"), namely, "beauty, attractiveness, loveliness, winsomeness"; 2) that which makes a disposition attractive or winsome, namely, "goodwill, graciousness"; 3) the manifestation of a disposition of goodwill, namely, "favor [shown], kindness [done], beneficence, boon"; and 4) the appropriate response to a kindness done, namely, "gratitude, thankfulness."

In the LXX charis is found most frequently in the expressions "grant" or "find favor with [or "before," or "in the eyes of"]" someone (LXX, Gen 6:8; 18:3; 30:27; etc.). (The underlying Hebrew for "favor" is generally khen, though, exceptionally, in Esth 2:9, it is khesedh [חֶסֶד], "kindness [where a relationship is presupposed between the source and the recipient of the kindness]," a term usually rendered in the LXX by eleos [ἔλεος], "mercy, compassion.") Occasionally it means "charm, attractiveness" (LXX, Ps 44:3; Prov 3:22) or "gift [indicative of favor]" (LXX, Esth 6:3). A significant parallel to NT usage—one that would doubtless resonate with readers of the NT epistles—was the use of charis in contemporary inscriptions for a favor (or favors, for which the plural charites was used) bestowed by a benefactor (divine or human) on a beneficiary (typically a city or institution); the same word was used for the thankfulness of the beneficiary. Philo is among the Jewish authors (compare also Wis 3:9; 4:15) who by the 1st cent. had begun to use charis of divine beneficence and of the gifts of that beneficence.

In the NT, charis is used in each of the classical senses listed above. 1) Occasionally it means "attractiveness, winsomeness" (compare the "gracious" speech, or speaking "with grace," of Col 4:6; perhaps also the "gracious words," or "words of grace," of Luke 4:22; see below). 2) In a number of texts it refers to an attitude or disposition of "goodwill, graciousness." In these cases the NRSV shows a variety of renderings: "favor" (Luke 1:30; 2:40, 52; Acts 7:10, 46); "goodwill" (Acts 2:47); "grace" (Acts 4:33, probably referring to the popular favor enjoyed by the believers, though favor with God is also possible); and "credit" (Luke 6:32, 33, 34; 1 Pet 2:19, 20, where the word means "that which brings God's favor"). 3) The term means "favor" (i.e., a favor that has been granted), and is so rendered by the NRSV, in Acts 24:27; 25:3, 9; 2 Cor 1:15. Similar usages of charis are rendered "gift" (1 Cor 16:3) and "blessing" (2 Cor 9:8). The "grace" of Acts 6:8 seems to be a divine endowment by which Stephen was enabled (in response to the prayer of 4:29-30) to perform miracles. 4) The term means "gratitude, thankfulness" where it is rendered "thanks" (Rom 6:17; 7:25; 1 Cor 15:57; 2 Cor 2:14; 8:16; 9:15), "thankfulness" (1 Cor 10:30), and "gratitude" (Col 3:16). "Thank" in Luke 17:9; "[be] grateful" in 1 Tim 1:12; 2 Tim 1:3; and "give thanks" in Heb 12:28 all reflect the Greek idiom "have thankfulness [again charis]."

Worth mentioning here are two Greek words related to charis with important usages in the NT. The verb charizomai (χαρίζομαι) means "to show kindness, be gracious, give as a favor." At times it means "forgive," underlining the generous treatment reflected in the act of forgiveness (2 Cor 2:7, 10; Eph 4:32; Col 2:13; 3:13; see FORGIVENESS). Elsewhere the use of the verb reflects the benevolence on display, e.g., in Jesus' acts of healing (Luke 7:21; NRSV: "had given") and in the gifts that God, who gave "his own Son . . . for all of us," grants—together with Christ—to his people (Rom

8:32; NRSV: "gives"; compare also "bestowed" in 1 Cor 2:12). Also related to charis is the noun charisma (χάρισμα), used (generally in the plural) for the "(spiritual) gift(s)"—with which believers serve one another in the community of faith (e.g., Rom 12:6; 1 Cor 1:7; 12:4, 9; 1 Tim 4:14; 1 Pet 4:10).

Most frequently, and most characteristically, charis is used in the NT (in a sense related to [2] above) for the demonstration of God's goodwill toward humankind in Jesus Christ and (in sense [3] above) for its beneficial effects on human beings. We will approach this distinctive focus of grace by looking individually at the NT writings.

2. The notion of grace

a. The Gospels and Acts. The word *grace* does not appear in any of the Synoptic Gospels in the NRSV. Luke's is the only Synoptic Gospel to use charis, and it follows conventional usage in doing so: in no case is the word used to signal the decisive manifestation of God's grace in the activity of the Messiah Jesus. (Luke 4:22 is a possible exception, if the "gracious words" [lit., "words of grace"] of Jesus that astonish his listeners are taken to mean his message of salvation. The point may simply be that his speech was attractive or winsome.) But, as in the OT, the notion of grace is abundantly present even where the word is not used. When Jesus brings healing to the sick and oppressed, divine compassion and grace are on display. Equally expressive of divine grace is the forgiveness that Jesus offers in words (Mark 2:5; Luke 7:48) and enacts in deeds when he accepts the frailties of his disciples (Luke 5:8-11) and seeks out the company of the notoriously sinful (Matt 9:10-13; 11:19; note also Luke 23:34; and see FORGIVENESS); the divine consolation that he offers the "poor in spirit," "those who mourn," the "meek," "all . . . that are weary and are carrying heavy burdens" (Matt 5:3-5; 11:28-30); the invitation that he extends to all to participate in God's kingdom (Luke 14:15-24). Without using the abstract term *grace*, Jesus gives the notion its most memorable expressions in his parables of the father who welcomes home his prodigal son (Luke 15:11-32) and of the tax collector who returned home "justified" after offering the simple prayer, "God, be merciful to me, a sinner!" (18:9-14). If Paul sees in the sacrificial death of Jesus the decisive demonstration of God's grace for human salvation (Rom 3:24-26), the latter chapters of each of the Synoptic Gospels tell the story of that sacrifice, offered, consciously and deliberately, by Jesus as "a ransom for many" (Matt 20:28//Mark 10:45).

In John's Gospel, charis occurs only in the prologue (1:1-18), though its appearance here seems programmatic. That the Word made flesh was "full of grace" (1:14) suggests that in Jesus God's goodwill toward human beings was perfectly expressed and graciously offered. Those receptive of his person and message tap into the "fullness" of that grace, experiencing an unending stream of divine blessings ("grace upon grace," v. 16). Thus, the decisive intervention of divine grace, as well as the perfect revelation of divine truth, took place in the person of Jesus (v. 17).

In the body of the Gospel, the word *grace* does not appear, though its NT significance is captured in the famous text: "For God so loved the world that he gave his only Son, so that everyone who believes in him may not perish but may have eternal life" (3:16). That the Son of God came into the world to take away its sin (1:29), to offer salvation (3:17), "living water" (4:10, 13-14; compare 7:37-38), life from the dead (5:24), the bread (6:32-35, 50-51) and light of life (8:12), and the way to God (14:6) are all Johannine expressions of the NT theme that God's grace is decisively offered to humankind in Jesus Christ. John stresses, too, that Jesus voluntarily gives his life for others' good (10:11, 17-18).

In Acts, the Christian message is repeatedly designated "the word [or "good news," or "message"] of [God's] grace" (Acts 14:3; 20:24, 32): it is "through the grace of the Lord Jesus" that Jews and Gentiles alike "will be saved" (15:11). Moreover, it is only by God's grace that converts come to believe the gospel message (18:27). Those who respond to the message with faith then experience the grace of God in their lives; its effects can be seen by others (11:23), presumably through evidence of transformed lives and of the presence of God's Spirit in their midst. To continue in the faith is "to continue in the grace of God" (13:43). It is natural, then, for believers to "commend" one another in prayer to the "grace of God" (or "of the Lord [Jesus]") for guidance, provision, and protection (14:26; 15:40; compare 20:32).

b. The Pauline corpus. Already in 1 Thessalonians (judged by most scholars to be the earliest of Paul's extant letters, and thus the earliest NT writing), we find the distinctive greeting of most NT epistles, "Grace to you and peace" (1:1; expanded elsewhere to include "from God our Father and the Lord Jesus Christ" [Rom 1:7; 1 Cor 1:3; etc.]); and the letter closes with the typical Pauline benediction, "The grace of our Lord Jesus Christ be with you" (5:28; compare Rom 16:20; 1 Cor 16:23; etc.). Here already is suggested something of the centrality of grace in Paul's understanding of the Christian message: God's goodwill is demonstrated and made available to all in Jesus Christ and is effective in the lives of believers, not simply in their initial coming to faith, but also in the strength they need for their daily lives.

Charis occurs nowhere else in 1 Thessalonians. What emerges clearly from the letter is that Paul's message when he came to Thessalonica centered on the outpouring of divine wrath that, when the full "measure" of human sinfulness had been reached (compare 2:16), would be poured out upon humankind, and on

the deliverance from that wrath that God offers in Jesus Christ to those who believe in him (1:9-10; 5:2-10; *see* WRATH). Such salvation from merited judgment is thus, in its essence, a gift of divine grace, though the word is not used.

In 2 Thessalonians (whose Pauline authorship, however, is disputed), "grace" appears again in the prescript (1:2) and closing benediction (3:18) as well as in the reminder (2:16) that God's blessings—here specifically "eternal comfort and good hope"—are gifts of divine "grace" granted jointly (as in 1:2) by "our Lord Jesus Christ himself and God our Father." Similarly, it is "according to the grace of our God and the Lord Jesus Christ" that the faithful lives of believers will bring honor to the name of their Lord and that they themselves will share in his glory (1:11-12).

It is clear that Paul's message in Corinth, as in Thessalonica, was one of salvation offered in Christ (1 Cor 1:18; 9:22; 10:33) in view of the judgment that awaits all human beings (1 Cor 4:5; 2 Cor 5:10) and the condemnation that awaits the "world" (1 Cor 11:32; compare references to "the perishing" in 1 Cor 1:18; 2 Cor 2:15; 4:3). Again, we may say that salvation from merited condemnation is a gift of God's grace, but the term itself is used in this way only in the plea made by Paul, as an "ambassador" for Christ, that the Corinthians must not "accept the grace of God in vain" (2 Cor 5:18–6:2). What we otherwise find are further reminders that God's grace is the source of every spiritual endowment enjoyed by believers (1 Cor 1:4-7) and of the strength by which every trial is endured (2 Cor 12:9) and every task done in God's service (1 Cor 3:10; 15:10; 2 Cor 1:12; compare 3:5). Of particular interest are the various usages of charis in 2 Cor 8. The grace (NRSV: "generous act") of the Lord Jesus Christ in abandoning his riches to become poor for the sake of human beings (8:9) is cited as a motivation for the Corinthians to complete their own "generous undertaking" (so NRSV renders charis in 8:6, 7, 19; but the rendering does not capture the connotation of the Greek that the undertaking itself was inspired by God's grace [9:14]; the latter point is explicit also in the reference to the "grace" given the Macedonian believers [8:1], who saw the opportunity to contribute as a "privilege" [8:4]) to contribute some of the goods that they possess in abundance to meet the needs of others (8:10-14).

There are seven explicit references to charis in Galatians. These include the customary prayers for grace in the prescript (1:3) and closing benediction (6:18) of the letter and the familiar acknowledgment in 1:15 and 2:9 that divine grace lies behind both Paul's commissioning as an apostle and the strength with which he carries out his appointed task. The reference in 1:6 is ambiguous (in Greek as in English). The point may be that "the grace of Christ" was effectively at work when the Galatians heard and heeded the call of God in the proclamation of the gospel. More likely, Paul is saying that they were brought by the call of God in the gospel into a state of grace: whereas formerly they belonged to the "present evil age" (1:4) that is destined for destruction, now as God's children (4:5-7) they enjoy God's favor. Toward the end of the argument of the epistle, however, Paul indicates that their enjoyment of God's favor would be jeopardized were they to submit to the rite of circumcision (5:4). Only in Christ, Paul suggests, is grace to be found. Implicit in the claim is the notion that the subjects of the law are all liable to its curse on transgressors (Gal 3:10; compare 3:13; 4:5). Inasmuch as all human beings are "imprisoned . . . under the power of sin" (3:22), no one complies with the requirements of the law; hence "no one will be justified [found righteous] by the works of the law" (2:16), and neither justification nor life can be achieved under the law's regime (2:21; 3:12, 21). The gospel is able to offer deliverance from the curse of the law, however, inasmuch as Christ took upon himself that curse (3:13); it offers righteousness and life to those who respond in faith—"just as Abraham 'believed God, and it was reckoned to him as righteousness'" (3:6, quoting Gen 15:6). Faith thus represents an alternative path to righteousness to that spelled out in the requirements of the law, and it is the only path viable for sinners (2:16-21; 3:11-12). For sinful human beings, the law brings a curse; the same sinners find in the path of faith enjoyment of God's grace (1:6; 2:21; 5:4).

Like the other Pauline epistles, Romans begins (1:7) and ends (16:20) with prayers that its readers will continue to experience God's grace. The epistle also contains reminders that Paul owes his apostleship and the strength to carry out his divine commission to God's grace (1:5; 12:3; 15:15-16), and, indeed, that God in his grace has granted to all believers gifts by which they can serve in the community (12:6-8). Other references to grace focus on God's gift of salvation in Jesus Christ (as in 2 Cor 6:1), often (as in Galatians) contrasting the path of faith and grace to potential alternatives that prove unable to reach the same end.

In all his writings Paul presupposes that human beings are moral creatures who must choose in their actions between good and evil and who are held responsible by God for their choices. That the sinful actions of all human beings render them liable for divine condemnation is also presupposed in Paul's message of salvation by grace for those who believe the gospel. These convictions, presupposed everywhere, are articulated clearly in Paul's letter to the Romans. Here the "wrath of God" is said to be revealed from heaven against "all ungodliness and wickedness" of human beings (1:18). The latter have suppressed what they know about God, refusing to honor him and give him thanks, choosing to worship parts of the created realm rather than the Creator himself, practicing and applauding deeds they know to be wrong (1:18-32). Jews have been given the law, spelling out the good

they are required to do; for Gentiles, the requirement of the law is written on their hearts (2:14-20). For all, the same standard applies: "the doers of the law . . . will be justified [i.e., found righteous by God]" (2:13; compare vv. 6-11). But since "there is no one who is righteous," and "all have turned aside," it follows that "the whole world" is guilty before God (3:10-19). And though the law promises life to those who do its commands (2:13; 7:10; 10:5), in the absence of any who show such obedience, "'no human being will be justified in [God's] sight' by deeds prescribed by the law" (3:20). If any are to be found righteous, it must be "apart from law" (3:21).

The righteousness of faith, spoken of in "the law and the prophets" (3:21)—particularly in the declaration that "Abraham believed God, and it was reckoned to him as righteousness" (4:3, citing Gen 15:6)—has now been decisively revealed in the gospel of Jesus Christ, and its operative principle is that of grace. If sinners (the "ungodly" of 4:5; 5:6) are paradoxically declared to be righteous, such a declaration of "righteousness" can hardly be due recognition of the way they have lived; it can only be a gift of God's grace made possible by the sacrificial death of Jesus that atoned for their sins (3:24-25; 4:4-5; note that "as a gift" in 4:4 [NRSV] is, more literally, "according to grace [kata charin κατὰ χάριν]"; compare "free gift of righteousness" in 5:17). Such righteousness is granted "apart from works" (i.e., apart from the righteous deeds that one would normally expect of any who are to be declared righteous) to those whose sins God forgives (4:6-8; note also the insistence of 11:5-6 that, where divine grace is in operation, human "works" cannot be a factor). It is gratefully received by faith: "faith" and "grace" go together (4:16). Hence those who are "justified [declared righteous] by faith" have thereby found "access to this grace in which [they] stand" (5:1-2; compare the discussion of Gal 1:6 above).

In Rom 5:12-21, Paul declares that the obedience of Christ more than offsets the disobedience of Adam. The latter made sinners of all Adam's descendants and subjected them to God's condemnation; the former "leads to justification and life for all" (5:18), and does so by the grace of God and of Jesus Christ (5:15, 17). The result is that (a personified) Grace now "reigns" where (a personified) Sin once held dominion (5:21).

Yet the reign of Grace must not be thought to legitimate or excuse further indulgence in sin (Rom 6:1-23). Grace prevails among those who have died to sin and now live for God; to continue sinning would be to revert to slavery under Sin's rule. In this context Paul again contrasts the law and grace (6:14-15): those who live under Grace have been set free from the slavery to Sin that marked life under the law. In Rom 7, Paul will grant that the law itself is "holy," its commands "holy and just and good" (7:12). But it was introduced to a world already ruled by Sin (5:20-21), a rule it has no power to overthrow (compare 8:3). Its commandments, though good, provoke disobedience on the part of rebellious human beings (5:20; 7:5, 7-13). Only through grace is sin overcome.

In Philippians, Paul again contrasts the path of righteousness through the law with that of faith (3:4-11). The latter is not here explicitly linked with grace; but the point of the linkage is clear when Paul characterizes the righteousness that "comes from the law" as his "own" righteousness and contrasts this with the righteousness "based on faith" that comes (as a gift) "from God" (3:9).

Something of the centrality of faith is retained in the disputed letters of the Pauline corpus, not only in the pre- and postscripts to the letters (Eph 1:2; 6:24; Col 1:2; 4:18; etc.) and in reminders that it is by gifts of God's grace that the church is equipped and God served (Eph 3:2, 7, 8; 4:7; in 4:29, the speech of believers is to be a means by which God's grace is brought to others), but above all in the insistence that salvation (or justification) and all the blessings that attend it are gifts of God's grace (Eph 1:6-7; 2:4-9; 1 Tim 1:14; 2 Tim 1:9; Titus 2:11; 3:7). Retained, too, is the insistence that human works play no role where divine grace is effective (Eph 2:8-9; 2 Tim 1:9; Titus 3:4-7). In Titus 2:11-13, grace is assigned an educative role as well: those to whom God's grace brings salvation learn thereby that they must "renounce impiety and worldly passions" and live appropriately while they await the return of their "great God and Savior, Jesus Christ."

c. Other writings. Distinctions between law and grace, or between grace and human "works," are not found in the other writings of the NT; these emphases seem characteristically Pauline (compare, however, John 1:17). Prayers for continued experience of divine grace are routinely found in the greetings and closing benedictions of (even the non-Pauline) NT epistles (Heb 13:25; 1 Pet 1:2; 2 Pet 1:2; 3:18; 2 John 3; Rev 1:4; 22:21). Like Paul, 1 Pet 4:10 uses "grace" of the particular gifts given by God to individual believers by which they serve the community. Jude 4 reflects the same concern as Rom 6, that the grace of God may be used as an excuse for sinful behavior. The assurance of Prov 3:34 that God gives grace to the humble is quoted in Jas 4:6; 1 Pet 5:5. First Peter 5:10 characterizes God as the source of "all grace." Hebrews 4:16 finds his "throne" to be one of grace; with Jesus, God's Son, as their "great high priest," believers may boldly approach God's throne to "receive mercy and find grace to help in time of need" (4:14-16).

Both Hebrews and 1 Peter stress that the decisive revelation of God's grace is found in Jesus Christ. Prophets foretold the coming of this grace (1 Pet 1:10). It was by God's grace that Jesus "taste[d] death for everyone" (Heb 2:9). Believers have received the "gracious gift of life" (1 Pet 3:7), the "Spirit of grace" (Heb 10:29), and "stand" in "the true grace of God" (1 Pet

5:12). And while they await the grace that represents the consummation of all that salvation brings at the coming of Jesus Christ (1 Pet 1:13), their hearts are to be "strengthened by grace" (Heb 13:9).

Bibliography: Darrel J. Doughty. "The Priority of ΧΑΡΙΣ." *NTS* 19 (1972–73) 163–80; James D. G. Dunn. *The Theology of Paul the Apostle* (1998) 319–23, 707–8; Brad Eastman. *The Significance of Grace in the Letters of Paul* (1999); R. H. Gundry. "Grace, Works, and Staying Saved in Paul." *Bib* 66 (1985) 1–38; James R. Harrison. *Paul's Language of Grace in Its Graeco-Roman Context* (2003); Judith M. Lieu. "'Grace to You and Peace': The Apostolic Greeting." *BJRL* 68 (1985) 161–78; Andrew T. Lincoln. "Ephesians 2:8-10: A Summary of Paul's Gospel?" *CBQ* 45 (1983) 617–30; Howard I. Marshall. "Salvation, Grace and Works in the Later Writings in the Pauline Corpus." *NTS* 42 (1996) 339–58; James Moffatt. *Grace in the New Testament* (1931); J. Nolland. "Luke's Use of ΧΑΡΙΣ." *NTS* 32 (1986) 614–20; Stephen Westerholm. "The Righteousness of the Law and the Righteousness of Faith in Romans." *Int* 58 (2004) 253–64; Michael Winger. "From Grace to Sin: Names and Abstractions in Paul's Letters." *NovT* 41 (1999) 145–75.

STEPHEN WESTERHOLM

GRACIOUS [חַנּוּן khannun; χάρις charis]. A merciful, forgiving, or caring manner. In the OT graciousness is most often an attribute of God, and is consistently used in conjunction with "mercy" and "LOVING-KINDNESS" (Exod 34:6; Pss 86:15; 103:8; Joel 2:13; Jonah 4:2). God's graciousness is sometimes understood as liberating or redeeming (Ps 26:11; Neh 9:17), or as a sign of God's covenant relationship with Israel (2 Kgs 13:23). Less often in the OT, graciousness is attributed to humans (Ruth 2:13; Prov 11:16).

The term *gracious* appears in the NT as a variant of **charis** or of several other terms referring to God's grace (Matt 11:26; Luke 10:21; 1 Pet 3:7), the grace of Jesus (Luke 4:22), or human acts of grace (Col 4:6). *See* GRACE.

JESSICA TINKLENBERG DEVEGA

GRAFT [ἐγκεντρίζω enkentrizō]. Splicing a plant onto the stock of a similar plant to create a new or stronger plant. Paul uses "graft" as a metaphor to describe the incorporation of the Gentiles into Israel, a wild olive shoot grafted into the olive tree (Rom 11:17, 19, 23, 24).

GRAIN [דָּגָן daghan]. Grain can denote any number of seed-bearing grasses and their edible seeds, or cereals. Cereals supplied by far the largest proportion of the diet of the ANE. These annual grasses were likely the first plants cultivated for food. Signs of domestication appear earliest for WHEAT and barley, followed by rye, oats, and MILLET (*see* SPELT). Diffusion transplanted two other cereals, rice and sorghum, from Asia and Africa, respectively, during Hellenistic and Roman centuries.

Humans gathered grain from bounteous naturally occurring stands for thousands of years prior to domestication. Gathering selected for ears that resisted shattering, a crucial characteristic for seed dissemination among wild grains. Human sowing, harvesting, and threshing brought about the shift to nonshattering ears and brought about other changes in growth habit and morphology. Morphological changes permit paleoethnobotanists to differentiate between wild and domesticated types in the archaeological record. Distinct cereals appear at about 9000 BCE at sites in the Jordan Valley (barley) and in Syrian steppe region sites (wheat). By the end of the third millennium, barley and wheat had spread throughout the western Mediterranean basin, the Nile Valley, and central Europe.

The production characteristics of wheat and barley nicely complement each other, and the two frequently appear as a word pair in the OT (e.g., Deut 8:8; Isa 28:25; Job 31:40). Both cereals are broadcast sown or deposited by dibbling or seed plow, usually after the tilling of the field in early winter (*see* SOW, SOWER). Repeated irrigations follow in Mesopotamia, while rainfed agriculture hopes for abundant and well-timed precipitation. Weeding heightens yields, reduces undesirable seeds in the harvest, and provides a fodder resource. Harvest takes place by uprooting or by reaping with a sickle. Barley matures more rapidly than wheat, and its harvest is first (Ruth 2:23). Thus, sowing both barley and wheat can serve to stretch the harvest season in order to better accommodate the labor supply. Workers transport sheaves to the threshing floor, where the stalks are beaten, trampled, or sledged in order to separate ears from straw and to disarticulate the ears. Raking and winnowing ensue, successively refining the product, followed by various grades of sieving. Workers then pack the grain for transport and storage (*see* WINNOW).

Archaeology can identify numerous tools and installations employed in grain growing. These include the PLOW, HOE, SICKLE and sickle blades, THRESHING FLOOR, and storage facilities such as pithoi, stone-lined or plastered grain pits, silos, and GRANARIES. Depending upon the species of grain, a variable number of other processing steps are required before sieving. Kernels of glume wheats (e.g., emmer) must be removed from the spikelets. This process normally involves parching in an OVEN. The brittle CHAFF is then broken away by pounding in a mortar. Free-threshing wheat (durum) and barley do not require parching and pounding. The most common species of barley, however, requires de-hulling for most foods. The hull is removed by pounding moistened kernels. Cereals are processed into a huge variety of foodstuffs, from bulgur to BREAD and porridge to beer. Mortars and pestles, cooking pots, ovens, bread molds, beer strainers, and

saddle querns are notable artifacts of grain processing (*see* COOKING AND COOKING UTENSILS).

The ANE's preoccupation with cereals extends beyond their cultivation, of course, to their control. These agrarian societies stood chiefly upon the wealth of cereal fields. Grains were the fundamental building block of the economy and principal medium of taxation as well (e.g., the cereal offering). As the disenfranchised complain to Nehemiah (5:2), "We must get grain, so that we can eat and stay alive." Cereal production and distribution underlie an enormous field of ideas and their literary and artistic expression. The Psalms often acknowledge human dependency upon God in terms of the productivity of cereal fields (e.g., Psalm 65:13 and 72:12). The paradoxical and essentially mysterious germination of grain seed once cast onto a bed of earth provides the foundation for early Jewish and Christian exposition of the resurrection (1 Cor 15:37). *See* AGRICULTURE; PLANTS OF THE BIBLE.

DAVID C. HOPKINS

GRANARIES [מַאֲבֻס ma'avus, מְגוּרָה meghurah; ἀποθήκη apothēkē]. The storage of grain was a critical link to life in the marginal environment of ancient Israel. Regular droughts lead to famine. The only safeguard against this possibility was to store wheat and other agricultural products in granaries and silos to tide the people over during difficult periods, but prolonged drought or insect infestations could leave these granaries empty and their villages abandoned by the starving people and animals (Joel 1:17). Underground pits lined with stones or plastered with lime and large storage jars were common in small villages. The wealthiest could have several barns to store their grain (Luke 12:18). Massive silos with staircases were built to meet the needs of urban settlements, as well as temple communities, or as reserves for governmental distribution (e.g., the 346 m ton silo from Iron II Megiddo). Invading armies regularly broke open granaries to feed their soldiers or to deny the populace the strength to resist (Jer 50:26). The metaphorical value of storage facilities is made clear in John the Baptist's description of God's gathering "his wheat" into the granary (Matt 3:12) and in Jesus' injunction to the faithful not to worry since God would provide for their needs (Matt 6:26). *See* CISTERN; STORE-CITIES, STOREHOUSES.

VICTOR H. MATTHEWS

GRANULATION. *See* JEWELS AND PRECIOUS STONES.

GRAPES [עֲנָבִים 'anavim, אֶשְׁכּוֹל 'eshkol; σταφυλή staphylē]. The widespread cultivation of domestricated grapes (*Vitis vinifera*) in vineyards indicates how important they were to the local diet (Isa 65:21), as fresh fruit or raisins (1 Sam 30:12), and to the wine-making industry (Neh 13:15; Rev 14:17-20). Sour grapes (Isa 5:2; Jer 31:29; boser [בֹּסֶר]) figure as a metaphor for unfaithfulness while an empty vine represents a land lacking in righteousness (Mic 7:1). *See* PLANTS OF THE BIBLE; VINE, VINEYARD.

VICTOR H. MATTHEWS

GRASP, TO [אָזַר 'azar, חָזַק khazaq, לָקַח laqakh, לָפַת lafath, קָרָא qara', תָּפַשׂ tafas; ἀντέχω antechō, συνίημι syniēmi]. This verb has two general uses in the Bible: to grasp someone or something physically, and also to grasp mentally or to understand. In the first use, Moses is commanded to grasp his staff (Exod 4:4). Samson grasps the pillars of the Philistine building in order to kill the crowd (Judg 16:29). One can grasp in the sense of "capture" (Prov 30:28; compare Ezek 21:11; 29:7). In its second sense of *grasp* as "understand," suniēmi expresses the disciples inability to "grasp" Jesus' prediction of his death (Luke 18:34).

KENNETH D. LITWAK

GRASS [דֶּשֶׁא deshe', חָצִיר khatsir, יֶרֶק yereq, עֵשֶׂב 'esev; χόρτος chortos]. Grass is a ground-covering plant, which grows in a spear-like shape and ranges in color through various greens and browns. The words translated "grass" can also refer to vegetation more generally, as in Gen 1:11-12. Usually, the words indicate plants grazed upon by livestock (Deut 11:15; 1 Kgs 18:5), but can also occasionally indicate vegetables and grains eaten by people (Gen 3:18; Matt 13:26). In addition, "grass" is used poetically as a metaphor for human frailty and mortality (Isa 40:6; 1 Pet 1:24). The grasses native to the land of Israel include marram grass, triple-awned grass, and panic grass.

Bibliography: Michael Zohary. *Plants of the Bible* (1982).

JENNIFER L. KOOSED

GRASSHOPPER [אַרְבֶּה 'arbeh, חָגָב khaghav]. The words *grasshopper* and LOCUST are used interchangeably (Nah 3:15, 17 NRSV, KJV, NIV). Both are declared clean for eating (Lev 11:22). The locust is understood as a gregarious, swarming, and destructive short-horned grasshopper (*Acrididae*). "Swarms of locusts" are used to describe countless numbers, especially of the enemy (Judg 6:5; 7:12; Jer 46:23). Grasshoppers eat vegetation throughout their lifespan (Judg 6:5; 2 Chr 7:13; Eccl 12:5), although very few species actually form destructive swarms.

Metaphorically, Israel's spies were like grasshoppers in the sight of the Canaanites (Num 13:33) The earth's peoples are as insignificant as grasshoppers (Isa 40:22). The enemies of Israel destroy like grasshoppers (Amos 7:1). Ninevah's enemies, like grasshoppers, appear, destroy, and quickly disappear (Nah 3:15-17). *See* INSECTS OF THE BIBLE.

MICHAEL G. VANZANT

GRATING [מִכְבָּר mikhbar]. The meaning of this term is obscure, but it is used in tandem with the Hebrew term resheth (רֶשֶׁת), which means "net," so it is understood as a netting made of bronze for the tabernacle ALTAR in the instructions and completion of the TABERNACLE (Exod 27:4; 35:16; 38:4-5, 30; and 39:39). The bronze netting is under a ledge on the altar and extends halfway down. There are rings at its four corners, and, as with other tabernacle furniture, poles are placed through the rings so that the altar can be lifted and carried (Exod 38:4-7).

C. MARK MCCORMICK

GRATITUDE. The social ethos of gift-giving and reciprocity is perhaps best captured by the image of the "Three Graces," dancing in a circle, hand-in-hand (an image derived from Greek mythology, persisting into the Roman period). Seneca explained this image as an allegory for gift-giving: there is one "Grace" for giving well, another for receiving the gift well, a third for returning the gift well. Gifts passing through different hands nevertheless returned to the giver, and if the circle was broken at some point the beauty of the dance was destroyed (*Ben.* 1.3.2-5). Initiating the circle with a gift was a matter of choice on the part of the giver; showing gratitude and returning the favor for a gift one accepted was an absolute moral obligation (Aristotle, *Eth. nic.* 1163b12-15; Seneca, *Ben.* 1.4.3; Isocrates, *Demon.* 26; Sir 35:2).

In the LXX and NT, the word translated "grace," (charis χάρις), actually encompasses the entire cycle of gift-giving and response. In some contexts, the word emphasizes the favorable disposition of the giver (e.g., Gen 6:8; 18:3; Exod 33:13; Prov 3:34; 22:1; Luke 1:30; Rom 5:15, 17; Heb 4:16; Jas 4:6), in others the gift given (e.g., Esth 6:3; Sir 3:31; Wis 3:14; 8:21; 4 Macc 5:9; 11:12; Rom 12:3, 6; Heb 12:15; 1 Pet 1:10, 13; 3:7; 4:10; 5:15), and in still others the response of gratitude on the part of the recipients of favor (e.g., 2 Macc 3:33; 3 Macc 1:9; Luke 17:9; Rom 6:17; 7:25; 1 Cor 10:30; 2 Cor 8:16; 9:15; 1 Tim 1:12; 2 Tim 1:3; Heb 12:28). The OT uses different words to capture the favorable disposition of the giver and the response of the recipient, but the latter is no less connected to the former. Thus offerings are still gifts "given back" (shuv שׁוּב) to God in acknowledgment of God's gifts (Num 18:9), and the psalmist muses at length how he will make a "return" to God for all God's benefits (Ps 116:12-19).

Failure to show gratitude was considered an act of injustice, even sacrilege against divine laws (Seneca, *Ben.* 1.4.4). It was also highly imprudent. Affronted benefactors could become dangerous enemies (Aristotle, *Rhet.* 2.2.8; 3 Macc 3:20-22a; 4 Macc 8:5-8; 9:10; compare Heb 10:26-31). Moreover, even though patrons and benefactors were to give in the interest of the recipient and not in their own interest (Seneca,

Ben. 1.2.3; 4.29.3), they had limited resources and needed to give wisely—that is, to individuals or groups that understood how to be grateful (Sir 12:1; Seneca, *Ben.* 1.1.2; 3.11.1; Isocrates, *Demon.* 24). The person who understood how to show gratitude developed a kind of "good credit rating" for future benefactions (Sir 3:31; compare Seneca, *Ben.* 4.18.1; Anaximenes, *Rhet. Alex.* 1421*b*33–1422*a*2).

A city expressed its gratitude for public benefactions with the conferral of public honors, whether recognizing the generous act by crowning the benefactor at a public event, commemorating the gift with an inscription, or perhaps by erecting a statue of the giver. The extreme expression of such gratitude was worship. When the gift was of such magnitude as to match the gifts besought by the gods (deliverance from a foreign enemy, the enjoyment of peace and security, relief of a city or region from famine), the response of gratitude could take the form of cultic honors, as it did in the Roman imperial cult.

In personal relationships of friendship, where the parties were social equals, gratitude manifested itself chiefly in displaying appreciation for the gift, acknowledging the gift and one's association with the giver, and returning the kindness as and when appropriate. In personal relationships of patronage, where one party was socially and/or economically inferior to the other, gratitude would take the form of increasing the honor of the giver through personal testimony and, in Roman contexts, being visible among the giver's entourage (Aristotle, *Eth. nic.* 1163b1-5, 12-18; Seneca, *Ben.* 2.22.1; 2.24.4); showing loyalty to the patron in his or her conflicts with others, even when costly (Seneca, *Ep.* 81.27); and offering whatever service might be needed or requested by the patron (Seneca, *Ben.* 6.41.1-2).

The dynamics of reciprocity are frequently evident in human interactions, as when Ahasuerus seeks some way to honor Mordecai for the latter's timely service, or when Paul makes Philemon mindful of the former's many benefits when asking for a favor from the latter. These texts are primarily concerned, however, with guiding worshipers of the One God to be grateful recipients of God's gifts. In line with sociocultural practice, gratitude toward God is expressed through expressions of honor, thanksgiving, and testimony to the goodness of the Patron, whether through speech (Pss 103:1-6; 116:12-19; 2 Cor 1:9-11; Eph 1:6, 12, 14; Col 1:12; 2:7; 3:15, 17; Heb 13:15; 1 Pet 2:10) or deeds (Matt 5:16; 2 Cor 9:11-12; 1 Pet 2:11-12; 4:10-11); loyalty to God, even at the cost of life itself (4 Macc 13:13; 16:18-19; 1 Cor 10:14-21; 1 Pet 1:6-9; Rev 14:6-13); and living with a view to making a fair return to God (1 Cor 6:19-20; 2 Cor 5:14-15), including "returning" gifts and services to God in the person of those whom God wishes to benefit (e.g., the poor in general or among the faith community, Matt 25:31-46; Eph 5:2; Heb 13:16; 1 John 3:16-18).

Worshipers are especially warned against acting ungratefully, bringing contempt upon their Patron or Mediator by their failure to show honor and loyalty (see esp. Heb 6:4-8; 10:26-31), or by a display of distrust toward the provisions God or Jesus has made for them (Gal 5:2-4; Heb 3:12, 19), which results in endangering their access to God's favor. Such warnings are in keeping with ancient social codes of reciprocity according to which the patron is never limited in regard to showing favor anew even to those who have acted ungratefully, but recipients are instructed never to presume upon such favor, attending fully instead to responding nobly to gifts that have been given, even when gratitude is costly.

Bibliography: Frederick W. Danker. *Benefactor: Epigraphic Study of a Graeco-Roman and New Testament Semantic Field* (1982); David A. deSilva. *Honor, Patronage, Kinship and Purity: Unlocking New Testament Culture* (2000); David A. deSilva. *Perseverance in Gratitude* (2000); Ronald M. Hals. *Grace and Faith in the Old Testament* (1980); Richard P. Saller. *Personal Patronage under the Early Empire* (1982); Andrew Wallace-Hadrill, ed. *Patronage in Ancient Society* (1989).

DAVID A. DESILVA

GRAVE [קְבוּרָה qevurah, קֶבֶר qever, שְׁאוֹל she'ol; τάφος taphos]. The grave is a cave or an excavated area for burial of the dead (Gen 23:8-9; Deut 10:6; 34:6; 2 Kgs 13:21), also called a TOMB. Family tombs were common ("gathered to one's people," Gen 25:8; 49:33). Fear of ceremonial uncleanness through decomposition required a quick burial, usually on the same day as the death (Num 19:11-19; Deut 21:22-23; Ezek 43:6-9; Acts 5:5-6; and Jesus' burial, Matt 27:57-61). SHEOL as "the grave" (Ps 49:14 [Heb. 48:15]; Hos 13:14) represents the place where the dead reside. *See* DEAD, ABODE OF THE.

MICHAEL G. VANZANT

GRAVEL [חָצָץ khatsats]. Used figuratively in Prov 20:17 of food gained through deceit and in Lam 3:16 of Yahweh's disposition toward the lamenter. Although the Hebrew form occurs in Ps 77:17, it is translated "arrow" in that instance. Both terms derive from a Hebrew verb meaning "divide" (i.e., comminute).

NATHAN D. MAXWELL

GRAVING TOOL [חֶרֶט kheret]. 1. Aaron uses this scoring or cutting instrument on gold to form the representation of a calf (Exod 32:4 NRSV, alternate reading).

2. A stylus in one possible rendering of Isa 8:1: Yahweh gives the instruction to inscribe a clay tablet "with a stylus of ordinary men."

NATHAN D. MAXWELL

GRAY [שֵׂיבָה sevah; πολιά polia]. The color of hair of elderly persons, such as Jacob in his old age (Gen 44:29, 31). Proverbs claim that gray hair is a crown of glory and the beauty of the aged (Prov 16:31; 20:20). God's care extends throughout life, including the time of gray hair (Ps 71:18; Isa 46:4). The gray horse of Zech 6:3 uses another Hebrew word that is more accurately translated "dappled."

MARY PETRINA BOYD

GREAT [גָּדוֹל gadhol, כָּבַד kavadh, מְאֹד me'odh, רַב rav; μέγας megas, πολύς polys]. The English translations for a number of Hebrew and Greek words. In Hebrew these include rav, often denoting great quantity (Gen 36:7); me'odh, which can mean "very" (Gen 13:13); and kavadh, which can mean heavy or numerous (Ps 38:5). Most common is gadhol and related terms, which typically denote magnitude and extent. The term appears in God's promises of a great nation (Gen 12:12; Jer 6:22), the recital of God's great acts in history (Deut 4:37), and in descriptions of the future day of the Lord (Joel 2:11). In Greek megas and related words, which in the LXX often translate gadhol, have a similarly broad range of meanings, and appear in the NT in typical Greek and Hellenistic usage. Significantly, megas can be a title for God or gods (Exod 18:11; Titus 2:13; Acts 19:28, 34); in this context the claim that Simon was "the power of God that is called great" has been understood as a claim to divinity or at least a special relationship with the divine (Acts 8:10; see MAGIC, MAGICIAN; SIMON MAGUS). Polys, typically referring to great number or size, is also often translated as "great."

RUBÉN R. DUPERTUIS

GREAT ASSEMBLY. A rabbinic institution mentioned first in a MISHNAH passage (m. 'Abot 1:1) as the repository of the Oral Torah given to Moses by God at Sinai. According to Rabbinic Judaism, the Oral Torah provided both authoritative interpretation as well as the necessary rules of interpretation (hermeneutics) for the Written Torah. There is no historical evidence for such an institution, which many scholars view as an ideological production creating continuity between pre-exilic Israel and postexilic Judaism.

PHILLIP MICHAEL SHERMAN

GREAT BIBLE, THE. An edition of the Bible resulting from diocesan and national injunctions in 1536, 1537, and 1538, ordering the provision of English Bibles in all the churches. Most important was the 1538 injunction, calling for "one book of the whole Bible of the largest volume in English," and finally causing Miles Coverdale to arrange a new and larger edition of the MATTHEW BIBLE. This revision was published in Paris in 1539 and became known as the Great Bible. A revised edition, with royal approval and a preface by Archbishop Cranmer, followed in 1540. See VERSIONS, ENGLISH.

PETER ARZT-GRABNER

GREAT COMMISSION. The closing pronouncement in the Gospel of Matthew (28:18-20). This is but one post-resurrection directive found in the NT (see also Mark 16:15; Luke 24:47-49; John 20:21-23; Acts 1:8). Its significance in Matthew marks the shift from the ministry of Jesus to the ministry of the church, and implies an indefinite time-period before the PAROUSIA. The universal character of the Great Commission is equivalent to Luke 24:47 and Acts 1:8. However, the procedure used in this evangelism effort is distinctly Matthean. Instead of instructing his closest disciples to preach as he did (e.g., Matt 4:17; 11:1), Jesus tells them to teach and baptize, a directive that stands in contrast to some early Christian practice (see e.g., 1 Cor 1:17). See BAPTISM.

Bibliography: M. J. Wilkins. *The Concept of Disciple in Matthew's Gospel* (1989).

MICHAEL JOSEPH BROWN

GREAT SEA. See SEA, GREAT.

GREAT SYNAGOGUE. See SYNAGOGUE, THE GREAT.

GREAVES [מִצְחָת mitskhath]. The legging armor worn by the Philistine GOLIATH as he fought young David (1 Sam 17:6). This protective gear covered the wearer from knee to ankle, clasping at the ankle. Although Goliath's greaves were made from copper or bronze, greaves were often made from animal hide.

GREECE grees [יָוָן yawan; Ἑλλάς Hellas]. Greece forms the southern part of the Balkans. To the east of the mainland lies the Aegean Sea, and to the west the Adriatic. The mainland stretches from Macedonia in the north down to Attica in the south; to the west, joined to the mainland by the narrow isthmus of Corinth is the Peloponnese. Greece itself contains a large number of islands, such as Euboia lying just off the coast of the mainland.

A. Topography and Landscape
B. The Ancient Concept and History of Greece
C. The Roman Province
D. Greece in the Bible
E. Cities
F. Sanctuaries
G. Communications
H. Visual Arts
Bibliography

A. Topography and Landscape

Mainland Greece is dominated by a series of mountain ranges encircling plains. The Pindos range dominates northwestern Greece, and the mountains continue down the spine down to Mount Helikon in Boiotia which lies on the north side of the Saronic Gulf. The

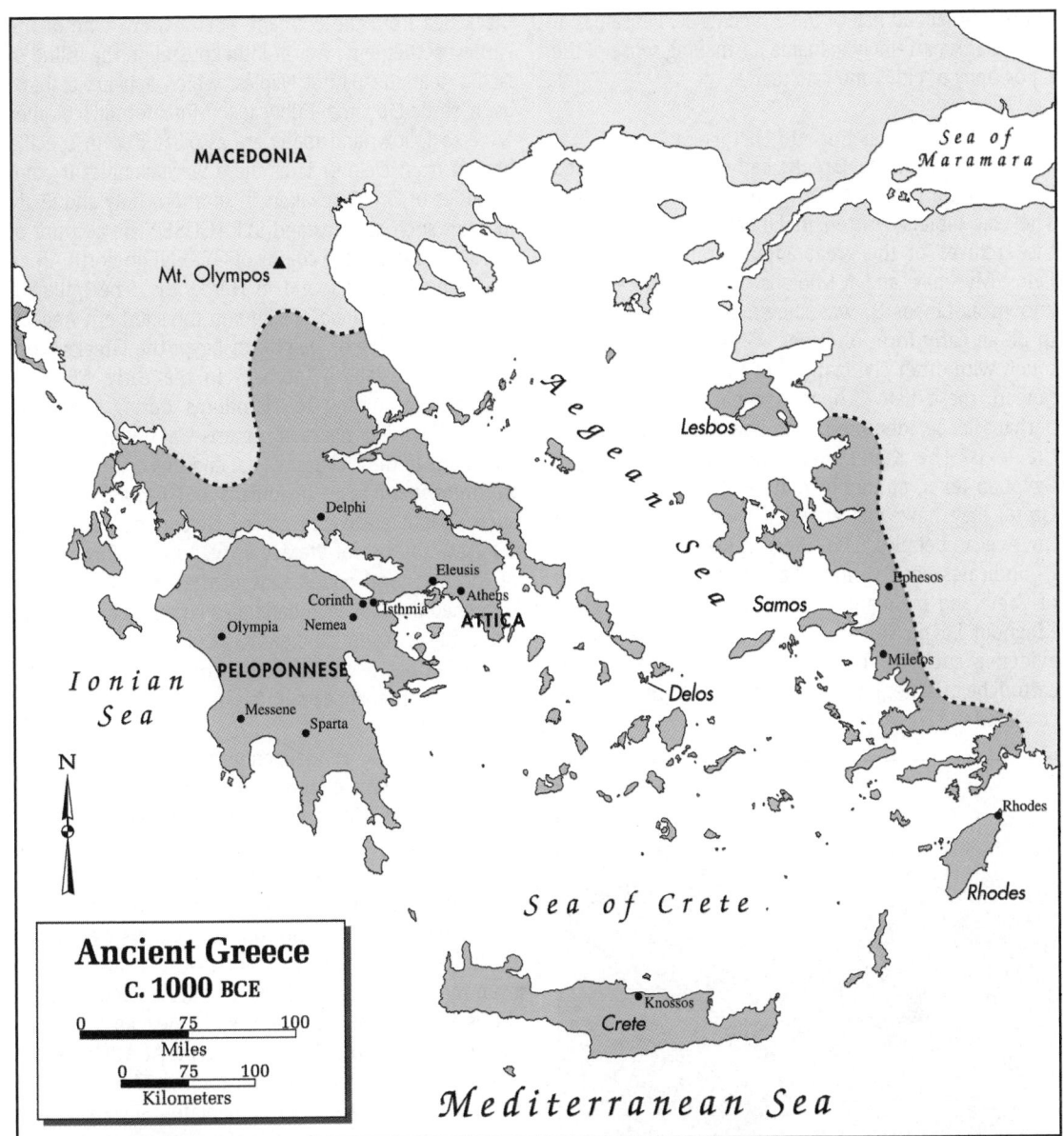

Ancient Greece
C. **1000** BCE

0   75   100
Miles
0   75   100
Kilometers

highest point is Mount Olympos at 2,917 ft. There are also major plains such as in Macedonia and Thessaly. The Peloponnese is joined to mainland Greece by a narrow isthmus (now cut by the Corinth Canal). The Peloponnese is equally mountainous; there is good agricultural land such as around Argos, and the Eurotas Valley of Laconia in the southern Peloponnese. In the eastern Peloponnese is the dormant volcano of Methana, which erupted during the Hellenistic period, but was known for its thermal baths in the 2nd cent. CE.

Archaeological field surveys in Greece have started to give indications about the use of the land in the Roman period. There seems to have been a trend in the late Hellenistic period, perhaps starting at the end of the 3rd cent. BCE, for a reduced number of rural, and therefore presumably agricultural, sites. Examples of this can be found in Boiotia and the southern Argolid. This reduc-

tion may be linked in part to the growing attraction of life in the city. The paucity of rural sites continued right through the 1st cent. BCE. Judging by field surveys in Boiotia, this century also seems to have been a time when some of the smaller urban settlements were shrinking. This may be paralleled by literary texts, such as Strabo and Dio Chrysostom, which hint at the decay of Roman cities at this time. It is only during the 2nd and 3rd centuries, a time when there is a growing Roman interest in the Greek east, that the number of rural sites increases, perhaps in part due to the growing need to supply the means to meet Roman taxation.

Two ancient texts help to shed light on the landscape and cities of ancient Greece in the imperial period. Strabo was a geographer writing during the reign of the emperor Augustus. Pausanias was essentially writing a travel guide for Roman visitors to Greece during the second half of the 2nd cent. CE. Pausanias in particular is extremely valuable for making sense of the topography of cities and sanctuaries.

B. The Ancient Concept and History of Greece

The origin of the Greeks can perhaps be traced back into the Late Bronze Age or Mycenaean period. The clay tablets written in Linear B were found in the archives of the great administrative palaces of Pylos, Mycenae, and at Knossos. The deciphered text, known as Linear B, was shown by Michael Ventris to be an early form of Greek. Greece was clearly in touch with other civilizations of the eastern Mediterranean; these Late Bronze Age palace societies are perhaps to be identified with the Ahhiyawa of Hittite texts. The Keftiu mentioned in New Kingdom Egyptian texts, although traditionally identified with Crete, may have had a wider meaning to embrace the Aegean peoples. The "Aegean list" of Amenhotep III indicates that various Late Bronze Age palaces of Crete and mainland Greece were known to New Kingdom Egypt; this is supported by archaeological evidence such as the faience plaques bearing the cartouche of Amenhotep III found in Late Bronze Age contexts at Mycenae.

David W. J. Gill

Figure 2: Pylos

The collapse of the palace societies at the end of the Late Bronze Age took Greece into a dark age, illuminated to some extent by archaeological finds. The apparent hero shrine at Lefkandi on the island of Euboia is one of the earliest examples of a religious shrine with the focus on the buried remains of a wealthy individual. However, during the 8th cent. BCE the distinctive political map of the Greek world began to emerge with the formation of independent city-states or poleis (πόλεις). Some of the key cities included Miletos in Ionia, the island of SAMOS in the eastern AEGEAN, CORINTH, and SPARTA in the Peloponnese, and ATHENS on the mainland. The western coast of Anatolia, modern Turkey, was the homeland of the Ionian Greeks with cities such as EPHESUS and MILETUS. Various Greek cities had colonized the shores of the Mediterranean and the

Black Sea from the 8th cent. BCE onward. One of the earliest settlements was at Pithekoussai on the island of Ischia near the Bay of Naples, which appears to have been settled by the Euboeans. More formal colonies were to follow, and many are associated with specific oracles from Delphi. Thus there were significant communities of Greek speakers in southern Italy and Sicily in cities such as Taras and SYRACUSE. The account of the foundation of the colony of CYRENE in north Africa (modern Libya) is found in Herodotus. The initiative came from the island of Thera in the southern Aegean at the prompting of Delphi. In Egypt the Greeks were allowed to establish, perhaps in the early 6th cent. BCE—and according to Herodotus during the reign of the Egyptian pharaoh Amasis—a trading base at Naukratis in the western Delta, and this complemented the mercenary bases of Ionians and Carians in Egypt such as that excavated at Tell Defenneh. This period also saw the rise of literacy as well as the formulation of the first legal codes. One of the earliest texts was scratched in a Euboean hand on a cup from an 8th cent. BCE context at Pithekoussai. One of the earliest extant law-codes has been recovered from Dreros on Crete, and Crete often appears in the historical sources as the origins of laws.

The network of independent cities that emerged during the archaic period continued down to the Roman period. Cities had a wide variety of constitutions. These included the two kings of Sparta who formed part of a constitution reputedly given to the law-giver Lykourgos by the Delphic ORACLE. Other cities such as Corinth, Sikyon, and Athens were ruled by individuals, literally tyrants, who seized power from the local ruling families. Polykrates, the tyrant of the island of Samos in the eastern Aegean, famously had an alliance with Amasis of Egypt. At Athens social reforms were carried out by Solon in the early 6th cent. BCE. These were not immediately successful and for part of the 6th cent. BCE the city was dominated by the Peisistratid tyranny. However, following the expulsion of the tyrants, the Athenian constitution was transformed by Kleisthenes who helped to create a democracy.

The growth of Persia during the 6th cent. brought the Ionian Greeks (in what is now western Turkey) under direct control of the Persians. Their revolt at the end of the 6th cent. BCE brought assistance from cities such as Athens. After the destruction of Ionian cities such as Miletos, Persia turned against the cities of the mainland. In 490 BCE the city of Eretria was razed to the ground and the Persians landed on the plain of Marathon in Attica with the intention of destroying Athens. The Athenian force, assisted by the polis of the Plateians, defeated the Persian force, and the 192 Athenian dead were buried under a great mound. The Athenians were said to have built their treasury at Delphi from the booty seized at Marathon.

David W. J. Gill
Figure 3: Messene

The Persians invaded mainland Greece in 480 BCE, by building a bridge from Asia to Europe and then marching across northern Greece; they even cut a canal across the neck of the Athos Peninsula to secure the safe passage of the fleet. The Greek alliance made a valiant defense at the narrow pass of Thermopylai where the Spartan contingent under Leonidas was killed. The Persian army marched as far as Athens, which was destroyed, but the Persian force received a major setback at the naval battle of Salamis. The Greek alliance defeated the Persian army at Plataia, and the Persian invasion was thrown back. The Persians received a further defeat at Mykale in Ionia. These events, described in detail by the 5th cent. BCE Greek historian HERODOTUS, became important landmarks in the Roman cultural map of Greece from the 1st cent. CE.

The 5th cent. BCE was dominated by the growing tension between Sparta and the development of a league with Athens at the head (and which became the Athenian Empire). War broke out in 431 BCE, and for the first part of the campaign Sparta made regular invasions of Attica while the citizens of Athens sat behind their city walls and were decimated by plague. After ten years of conflict a truce was negotiated, in part because of the Athenian capture of Spartan forces in the campaign of Pylos and Sphacteria in the southwestern Peloponnese. However, Athens was drawn into involvement with the interpolis disputes among the Greek cities of Sicily. Athens sent substantial forces to the island in 415 BCE, which, after a lengthy siege of

Syracuse, were eventually destroyed or captured in 413 BCE. In spite of this disaster Athens struggled on, but the Spartans eventually won the upper hand, in part by securing a base in Attica and by enlisting Persian support. Athens was finally defeated and her walls pulled down by Sparta.

During the 4th cent. BCE Greece was dominated by the rise of Macedonia, which dominated the Greek poleis during the reign of Philip II. The Greeks were suppressed and bound to Philip by treaty. During this time Sparta's position was curtailed and a ring of fortified cities, such as Messene and Megalopolis, were built around Laconia to contain her power. After Philip's assassination his son Alexander III ("the Great") came to the throne of Macedon (see ALEXANDER THE GREAT). His conquests led to the destruction of the Persian Empire, and brought about the establishment of Greek cities as far afield as Afghanistan and the Indus Valley. His death, and the division of the territory among Alexander's generals, brought about the creation of a number of kingdoms such as the Seleucids and Ptolemies. The Seleucids controlled the area of Palestine and their rule forms the backdrop of 1–2 Maccabees (see HELLENISM; SELEUCID EMPIRE).The Ptolemies established a number of bases in the Aegean during the 3rd cent. BCE, including the Methana peninsula (renamed Arsinoe) in the Peloponnese (see PTOLEMY). This common cultural unity with a common use of Greek as a language forms the backdrop for the NT period.

By the NT period two distinct parts of Greece could be recognized, the provinces of ACHAIA and MACEDONIA. The island of CRETE lying to the south of the Peloponnese was part of a separate Greek-speaking province of Crete and Cyrenaica.

C. The Roman Province

Rome had taken an interest in Greece from the beginning of the 2nd cent. BCE, and in 196 BCE T. Quinctius Flaminius had in theory set the Greek states free. However Rome continued to interfere in the internal politics of Greece, not least in her interference over the membership of the Achaean League. In effect Greece, or more properly southern Greece, was incorporated into the ROMAN EMPIRE in 146 BCE when Mummius defeated the Achaean League of Greece, captured the city of Corinth, and quite literally razed it to the ground. Pausanias (7.16.9) also suggests that the cities of Greece were then subject to taxation.

In the following years mainland Greece was in effect perceived as an extension of the province of Macedonia. This is hinted at by an inscription erected at Delphi ca. 100 BCE and relating to piracy in the Aegean; responsibility was seen as belonging either to the magistrate in charge of either the province of Macedonia or Asia (which included some of the Aegean islands). Other inscriptions from the 1st cent. BCE also suggest the influence of the Roman governor of Macedonia. However, there are hints that there was some opposition: the council building and records of the city of Dyme in the northern Peloponnese were destroyed by fire ca. 137 BCE. This action brought the intervention of Q. Fabius Maximus.

In the late Republican period Greece became the battleground in the conflict between Mithradates of Pontos and the Roman general Sulla. Sulla captured the harbor of Piraeus and the city of Athens in 86 BCE. Archaeologists working in the Kerameikos area of the city have found examples of the catapult balls that were used. It was here in the vicinity of the Sacred Gate that Sulla is said by the biographer Plutarch—a Greek born at Chaironeia—to have entered the city.

Greece became the setting for the civil wars that ravaged Rome at the end of the Roman Republic. Julius Caesar clashed at Pharsalos in Thessaly in 48 BCE, then, following Caesar's assassination in 44 BCE, Marc Antony and Octavian defeated the assassins Brutus and Cassius at Philippi. Perhaps the most significant battle was the sea battle of Actium off the west coast of Greece where in 31 BCE Octavian defeated the fleet of Marc Antony and Cleopatra. This key event was marked in Greece as the starting point for the new calendar (the Actian era) for cities in Greece; one of the examples of this was an honorific inscription from the Methana Peninsula in the Peloponnese granting the right of grazing sheep to a Roman living at Corinth.

In 27 BCE Augustus (as Octavian had become) reorganized the provinces of the Roman Empire. Southern Greece was turned into the senatorial province of Achaia, now separate from the province of Macedonia. This new province included the Peloponnese, and its northern frontier was formed by the regions of Aitolia, part of Epirus, and Thessaly. The provinces of Achaia, Macedonia, and Moesia were combined as a single imperial province under the control of the emperor in 15 CE, in part in response to complaints of the heavy taxation (Tacitus, *Ann.* 1.76.4). This arrangement was short lived and Achaia reverted to a senatorial province in 44 CE. The province was governed by a proconsul, or *anthypatos* in Greek (see Acts 18:12).

The province was granted special status by the emperor Nero in 67 CE who had even taken part in the Olympic games. The announcement giving Greece both freedom and exemption from taxation was made at the Isthmian games. One of his ambitious plans, unfulfilled until the 19th cent., was to cut a canal across the isthmus of Corinth thus making the Peloponnese an island. Greece's independence came to a swift end when Vespasian came to power in the aftermath of Nero's death.

The growing interest in the Greek world, esp. in the 2nd cent. CE, brought educated Romans to Greece in search of the origins of classical culture. One manifestation of this was the writing of travel guides, such as that made by Pausanias, to cater for their needs. Another was the creation of the Panhellenion by Hadrian, and based in Athens, which brought together the Greek cities in a single organization focused on the temple of Olympian Zeus.

Greece was also the source for specialist marbles in use for building projects in other parts of the Roman Empire. Among them were the quarries of Karystos on the island of Euboia, where there is epigraphic evidence of Roman centurions located there. This was the source of the prized *cipollino.* The quarries of Attica, esp. those on Mount Pentelikon, were also in use during the Roman period.

Greek continued to be the main language of the province of Achaia. One exception to this was the Roman colony at Corinth where Latin appears to have been used for public inscriptions until the early 2nd cent. CE. However some of the graffiti found on Roman *terra sigillata* pottery were in Greek suggesting that Latin was not necessarily in everyday use. An unusual example of Latin being used in a historic Greek sanctuary was at Eleusis for the benefaction inscription of Pulcher on the propylon.

D. Greece in the Bible

Greece figures in the OT only in apocalyptic oracles in response to persecution of Jews under Hellenistic rule. Daniel denigrates the "king of Greece" (whom some scholars think refers to Alexander the Great) as a shaggy goat (Dan 8:21); the reference to Greece is continued in 10:21; 11:2 (see DANIEL, BOOK OF). The prophet Zechariah envisions the day when Zion's king will come and defeat "Greece," a possible reference to war between Greece and Persia (Zech 9:13). First and Second Maccabees recount Jewish resistance during the reign of the Seleucids (see MACCABEES, MACCABEAN REVOLT).

Greece is the setting for parts of the NT. Paul arrived in the province of Achaia after leaving Macedonia. His first stop was the historic city of Athens, which had fallen out of favor under the emperor Augustus as it had supported Brutus and Cassius, the assassins of his adopted father Julius Caesar. However, the place of Athens in classical Greek history allowed it to have a special role as a cultural center in Greece. From Athens Paul moved to Corinth, the administrative heart of the Roman province and it was here that he was brought before the Roman governor, Gallio (Acts 18:12), the adopted son of L. Junius Gallio and the brother of Seneca. The mention of Gallio helps to pinpoint Paul's activity in Corinth as the governor's period of office was mentioned in a letter of the emperor Claudius and inscribed at Delphi; Claudius is noted as being *imperator* for the twenty-sixth time which places the inscription before August 1, 52 CE. The governor may have held office for up to two years, and so Paul may have been in Corinth from the end of 50 CE just after the governor took up his office.

Paul may have traveled in northwestern Greece after a second visit to Macedonia (Acts 20:1; see also 19:21), before traveling to Greece, presumably the province of Achaia distinct from Macedonia, where he stayed for three months (Acts 20:2-3). It may have been at this point that he reached Illyricum (Rom 15:20), the province created by Augustus on the Adriatic coast. If so, Paul is likely to have crossed over from Macedonia along the Egnatian Way, which linked Macedonia (and the eastern provinces) with the Adriatic. From the Adriatic he would have been able to take a ship down the west coast of Greece, down the Corinthian Gulf, passing colonies like Patras, and arriving at Lechaeum the harbor of Corinth.

The two Corinthian epistles provide important insights into life in the Roman colony during the mid 1st cent.; the second epistle is in fact addressed to the Corinthians and Christians through the province of Achaia (2 Cor 1:1; see CORINTHIANS, FIRST LETTER TO; CORINTHIANS, SECOND LETTER TO). The Epistle to the Romans appears to have been written from Corinth, and names members of the Corinthian church in its valedictory section. Other epistles to the Greek world, but in fact the province on Macedonia, were to PHILIPPI and THESSALONICA (see PHILIPPIANS, LETTER TO; THESSALONIANS, FIRST LETTER TO; THESSALONIANS, SECOND LETTER TO). Churches in the provinces of Macedonia and Achaia sent contributions "for the poor among the saints at Jerusalem" (Rom 15:26). This linking of these two Greek-speaking provinces is found elsewhere in the NT (1 Thess 1:8).

E. Cities

The well-established *poleis* of the Hellenistic era continued to survive into the Roman period. Corinth also served as the base for the governor of the province. This may explain the actions of a resident of Corinth, L. Licinnius Anteros, who acted as the ambassador for the *polis* of Methana near Epidauros during the Augustan period. The subsequent honor awarded to Anteros may be explained by a successful bid by the city to the governor, through Anteros, to have their tax burden lifted. The cosmopolitan nature of Corinth is reinforced by the series of inscriptions celebrating Junia Theodora who was a resident of Corinth in the mid 1st cent. CE. Her family originally came from Lycia in Turkey, and a monumental base—rebuilt into a late antique tomb—recorded a series of letters from individual cities. Military tombstones from the colony probably indicate troops attached to the governor's headquarters. They include Caius Valerius Valens, apparently from the Alps, an ordinary solider of the Eighth legion during the 1st cent. CE. His legion is known to have formed part of the garrison of Moesia (on the Danube frontier) from ca. 45 CE. In 70 CE the legion moved to Germany which provides a likely *terminus ante quem* for the Corinth inscription. A second tombstone belongs to an officer, *optio*, Aurelius Nestor, of the Fourth Flavian legion. This legion was based in Moesia Superior from the late 1st cent. CE.

Athens entered the imperial period by making a number of political miscalculations. Among them was the erection of a pair of statues representing Brutus and Cassius alongside the historic group of the Tyrannicides—the Harmodios and Aristogeiton who traditionally brought the tyranny of Athens to an end in the late 6th cent. BCE—in the Athenian agora. Such a move celebrating the assassins of the emperor Augustus' adopted father left Athens isolated. However, in 15 BCE the city received a major benefaction from Agrippa, the son-in-law of Augustus, who erected a concert hall (Odeion) in the open space of the Athenian agora. A further major benefaction followed in 11/9 BCE when a new market was erected to the east of the agora.

Sparta had been one of the few cities of Greece to support Octavian, the future emperor Augustus. A member of its social elite, Eurycles, assisted Octavian at the battle of Actium and was rewarded not only with Roman citizenship but also with the island of Kythera off the southern Peloponnese. Augustus himself visited the city in 21 BCE. The Euryclid family seems to have gravitated toward Corinth, the provincial capital, and are known from inscriptions as well as mentioned by Pausanias as being benefactors of a set of baths in the city. It was one of the cities identified in the province as both free and immune from taxation. The Euryclid family also tried to establish links with King Herod of Judea, and Herod did show his generosity toward Sparta, among other cities in Greece (Josephus, *J.W.* 1.425). Pausanias (3.11.4) also records a temple of the deified Julius Caesar in the agora at Sparta which is likely to reflect the links between the city and Augustus.

Argos was the focal point for the Achaean League and the imperial cult for the province. It received a number of benefactions during the Roman period, not least the construction of the Odeion adjacent to the earlier classical theater which itself was adapted in the Roma period. Augustus established two cities in the province: the colony of Patras (Colonia Aroe Augusta Patrensis) in 14 BCE and the "free city" of Nikpolis located near Augustus' key victory at Actium in Epirus. Nikopolis was also the location of the quinquennial Actian games, i.e., held every four years, to celebrate Augustus' naval victory. Augustus gave the Spartans the responsibility for organizing the games.

F. Sanctuaries

Each Greek city had a sanctuary dedicated to its patron deity as well as a range of other sanctuaries dedicated to the Olympian gods. One of the most famous urban sanctuaries was that of Athena on the Athenian acropolis. Dominating the skyline was the 5th-cent. BCE temple of Athena Parthenos. This building, known as the Parthenon, contained the colossal gold and ivory ("chryselephantine") statue of Athena made by the sculptor Pheidias. Also on the acropolis was the Erechtheion, which housed many of the sacred spaces associated with Athens' early history, such as the mark where Poseidon's trident struck the ground in his contest with Athena for control of the city. At the entrance, marked by a monumental gateway, the Propylaia, was the small temple of Athena Nike ("Victory") built in the early 420s BCE during the early part of the Peloponnesian War. During the Roman period the sanctuary had attracted other buildings, notably the circular structure linked to the cult of Roma and Augustus, which stood next to the Parthenon. Its architecture seems to pick up deliberately Ionic architectural elements of the Erechtheion lying just to the north. Dominating the skyline was the warlike Athena Promachos, probably erected in the 430s BCE, and whose spear-tip could be seen glinting in the sun as ships came round the tip of Attica off Cape Sounion.

Some sanctuaries served a much wider group than worshipers from a single city. One of the most popular spots was the sanctuary of Demeter and Kore at Eleusis. This mystery cult celebrated the capture of Kore by Hades and the underworld, as well as the giving of grain. The secrets of the cult are still largely unknown but foundations of the large covered hall, the Telesterion, have been uncovered. Elsewhere in the sanctuary were silos for holding grain made as an offering. The cult retained its popularity in the Roman period. In the late Republican era a new monumental gateway or propylon was provided for the sanctuary, decorated

David W. J. Gill

Figure 4: Erchtheion

David W. J. Gill
Sanctuary of Demeter and Kore at Eleusis

with colossal caryatids (thus mirroring the more famous sculptures on the Erechtheion on the Athenian acropolis). The frieze also carried symbolism relating to the Eleusinian cult including baskets for offerings made during the mysteries. This was dedicated by Claudius Appius Pulcher, the governor of the Roman province of Cilicia, the structure was completed in 48 BCE after Appius' death (see MYSTERY RELIGIONS).

Some of the key sanctuaries that continued to flourish through the Roman period were those that hosted the Panhellenic games; in other words, the participants were Greeks from across the Mediterranean and Black Sea regions. Three of these sanctuaries—Olympia, Isthmia, and Nemea—were located in the Peloponnese, and the fourth, Delphi, on the mainland. Olympia itself had been damaged in the late Republican period, but received a number of imperial benefactions; the emperor Nero took part in the games held there. At Olympia the Metroon—the temple to the Mother of the gods—located near to the entrance to the stadium, was the place where statues of the members of the imperial were displayed.

Delphi's position as a leading oracle in the Greek east meant that it attracted dedications from Greek poleis from around the Mediterranean. One of the early acts by Rome was to replace the statue of Perseus of Macedonia with that of the Roman commander Aemilius Paullus who annexed Macedonia following the battle of Pydna in 168 BCE. Continuing Roman interest in the oracle is reflected by Plutarch's work on the Delphic Oracle.

Such sanctuaries had helped to forge a Hellenic identity as they embraced Greeks from mainland Greece, western colonies, Ionia, and beyond. This iden-

tity was formalized in the 2nd cent. CE by the emperor Hadrian who established the Panhellenion at Athens with a focus on the sanctuary of Olympian Zeus, which he completed.

During the Roman period the worship of the emperors developed in Greece as in other Greek-speaking provinces of the eastern Mediterranean (see EMPEROR WORSHIP). One of the best documented examples is at Gytheion, the harbor town for Laconia in the southern Peloponnese. At Sparta a set of games, the Kaisarea, was initiated, probably in celebration of the emperor Augustus. At Messene in the southwest Peloponnese, two former dining rooms on the north side of the sanctuary of Asklepios were turned into a shrine for the imperial cult. This was the location for the display of letters to the emperor Tiberius on his accession, which also recorded the establishment of an agonistic festival in honor of the emperor, tellingly called the Romaia.

At Athens during the Augustan period a 5th cent. BCE temple, originally dedicated to Ares at Acharnai in the countryside of Attica, appears to have been carefully dismantled and reerected in the space of the Athenian AGORA (marketplace) to house the cult. The cult name is attested by Pausanias' topographical description of the agora, while the move itself is indicated by the Roman mason marks on the blocks. Visually it linked the cult with the contemporary buildings of Pericleian Athens. Another focus for the worship of members of the imperial family was the temple of Nemesis at Rhamnous in rural Attica, which was rededicated to Livia the widow of Augustus in 45/46.

The cult is found elsewhere in the Greek world. Altars and statues dedicated to Augustus have been found distributed across the Peloponnese, through Boiotia, and on some of the Aegean islands. One of the most unusual settings for the imperial cult appears to have been in the reused Mycenaean tholos tomb at Orchomenos in Boiotia, the so-called "Treasury of Minyas."

G. Communications

The topography of Greece meant that there were few substantial roads; one of the few existing in the early imperial period was the Via Egnatia that traversed the province of Macedonia. One road seems to have been established along the southern shore of the Gulf of Corinth linking the two colonies of Corinth and Patrai, with another road heading north from Naupaktos on the north side of the Gulf of Corinth for the city of Nikopolis.

The numerous islands also encouraged the use of maritime transport. One of the key sea routes was from the Aegean into the Saronic Gulf, where ships could transfer cargoes either at the Piraeus (the port of Athens) or at Cenchreae, the eastern harbor of Corinth. Cargoes that were transferred at Cenchreae could be taken over the relatively narrow Isthmus of Corinth and placed on ships at the equally important harbor of Lechaeum on the Corinthian Gulf. This allowed ships access to the Adriatic, and across to Italy.

The Piraeus was an important stopping-off point for military movements to the eastern provinces. This is in part reflected by the large number of Roman military inscriptions from Athens and its environs, in particular to the Trajanic period.

H. Visual Arts

The visual richness of the Greek world is hinted at by the 2nd cent. CE travel writer Pausanias who was eager to point out sculptures and other sights that were "well worth seeing" (see ARTS). This is in spite of the clear evidence of looting that took place in the early Imperial period. Key sculptures by well-known artists, as well as panel-paintings were carried off to Rome. Indeed some of the finest 5th- and 4th-cent. bronzes may owe their survival to the fact that the Roman ships carrying them off to Italy sank with their loot still on-board.

It is striking that when Paul was in Athens he observed that it was a city "full of idols" (Acts 17:16). These would no doubt have included the statues displayed in the sanctuaries of the city as well as in the public spaces. By the 2nd cent. CE Roman visitors to the city were known to marvel at the colossal gold and ivory statue of Athena Parthenos displayed inside the Parthenon. This had been created by the celebrated sculptor Pheidias and completed during the 430s BCE. The richness of the iconography was so admired by Roman visitors that small-scale replicas were made. Moreover, a series of marble slabs quoting elements from the battle between the Amazons and Greeks from

the shield of Athena were found in the Piraeus. These appear to have been made in an Attica marble workshop for export probably to provide decoration in a villa perhaps in Italy. The companion statue to the Athena was the chryselephantine statue of Zeus Olympios displayed within the temple of Zeus at Olympia. The Roman geographer Strabo, writing during the reign of the emperor Augustus, made the comment that the seated Zeus would have removed the roof of the temple if he had stood.

The agora ("marketplace") where Paul disputed with people every day while he was in Athens (Acts 17:17) was itself an area in which sculptures were displayed. One of the most important groups was the Tyrannicides showing the men who initiated events to remove the Peisistratid tyranny from Athens. In Paul's day there would have been a pair of statue groups showing Harmodios and Aristogeiton, since the original group, made by the 6th-cent. BCE sculptor Antenor, had been returned to Athens by one of the Hellenistic rulers—several are named in the sources—after the fall of the Persian Empire; the Persians had removed the statues when they sacked the city in 480 BCE, and the Athenians had replaced them with a further group in the 470s. This same public space included a long base displaying the statues of the heroes after which each of the tribes of Athens was named. Elsewhere he would have seen sculptural groups of the Hellenistic benefactors of the city.

Although sculpture is one of the main groups of visual arts to have survived from the Roman period, Greek cities would have displayed a series of paintings. In the agora itself one of the open colonnades facing the open space was known as the Stoa Poikile ("Painted Stoa"). This had been created in the early 5th cent. and had been decorated on the inside with a series of panel paintings recalling the great Athenian victory at the Battle of Marathon in 490 BCE. On the slopes of the Akropolis was a remarkable tomb to the hero Theseus who was reputed to have unified Attica and whose bones had been recovered from the island of Skyros and placed in Athens in the 470s. This was decorated by a famous series of paintings showing events in the mythology of Theseus. Finally at the entrance to the acropolis itself, as part of the monumental gateway complex (the Propylaia), was a large dining room known as the Pinakotheke or painting gallery; some paintings could still be viewed there in the 2nd cent. CE.

Other aspects of funerary art that would have been prominent at Athens and elsewhere in the Greek world would have been funerary sculptures. Cemeteries were usually placed outside the city walls of cities and markers or stelai were placed on the graves. Although during the Hellenistic period there had been a move toward much simpler forms of tomb marker, during the 1st cent. CE there appears to have been a move toward the type of high relief stelai that had last been used in the late classical period. *See* GREEK LANGUAGE; GREEK RELIGION AND PHILOSOPHY; HELLENISM.

Bibliography: S. E. Alcock. *Graecia Capta: The landscapes of Roman Greece* (1993); S. E. Alcock. *Archaeologies of the Greek Past: Landscapes, Monument, and Memories* (2002); J. M. Camp II. *The Archaeology of Athens* (2001); P. Cartledge and A. Spawforth. *Hellenistic and Roman Sparta: A Tale of Two Cities* (1989); D. Engels. *Roman Corinth: An Alternative Model for the Classical City* (1990); D. W. J. Gill. "Corinth: A Roman colony in Achaea." *BZ* 37 (1993) 259–64; J. M. Hurwit. *The Athenian Acropolis: History, Mythology, and Archaeology from the Neolithic Era to the Present* (1999); M. H. Jameson, C. N. Runnels, and T. van Andel. *A Greek Countryside: The Southern Argolid from Prehistory to the Present Day* (1994); N. Kaltsas. *Sculpture in the National Archaeological Museum, Athens* (2002); M. S. Kos. "A Latin Epitaph of a Roman Legionary from Corinth." *JRS* 68 (1978) 22–25; C. B. Mee and H. A. Forbes, eds. *A Rough and Rocky Place: The Landscape and Settlement History of the Methana Peninsula, Greece. Results of the Methana Survey Project Sponsored by the British School at Athens and the University of Liverpool* (1997); R. K. Sherk. "Roman Imperial Troops in Macedonia and Achaea." *AJP* 78 (1957) 52–62; A. J. S. Spawforth. "Corinth, Argos, and the Imperial Cult: Pseudo-Julian, Letters 198." *Hesperia* 63 (1994) 211–32; G. Speake, ed. *Encyclopedia of Greece and the Hellenic Tradition* (2000); A. Stewart. *Greek Sculpture: An Exploration* (1990); J. Travlos. "The Topography of Eleusis." *Hesperia* 18 (1949) 138–47; T. van Andel and C. N. Runnels. *Beyond the Acropolis: A Rural Greek Past* (1987); M. E. H. Walbank. "The Foundation and Planning of Early Roman Corinth." *Journal of Roman Archaeology* 10 (1997) 95–130.

DAVID W. J. GILL

GREED [בֶּצַע batsa'; πλεονεξία pleonexia, πλεονέκτης pleonektēs]. The term *greed* occurs throughout the OT as covetousness, avarice, or insatiable desire, typically regarding love of money. Selfish gain or longing to be rich conveys greed's idolatrous essence. Israel, and especially Levitical priests, was forbidden to covet or crave anything (Exod 20:17), including food (1 Sam 2:29). The psalmist warns that greed leads to apostasy (Ps 10:3). The prophets repeatedly admonish Israel that greediness is a chief cause of her spiritual decline and impending judgment (Jer 8:10; 22:17). Individually, greed destroys one's life (Prov 1:19). Thus, the model prayer in Ps 119 petitions God's deliverance from pleonexia (LXX, 118:36). Greed is classified as a heinous vice in both the OT and NT (Isa 57:17; Rom 1:29).

The antonym of generosity, greed figures prominently in the NT and always in association with material gain. Apart from idol worship itself, the NT views idolatry as only one thing: greed (Col 3:5; Eph 5:3, 5). The NT abounds in tragic examples of excessive desire: Ananias and Sapphira, Judas Iscariot, false leaders within Israel, and false teachers within the church (Acts 5:1-10; Matt 26:14-16; Mark 7:1-23; 2 Pet 2:14-15; Jude 11, respectively). Mark strikingly juxtaposes greed's destructive nature with related human vices: envy, coveting, deceit, and evil desire (7:22-23). Unsurprisingly, therefore, in Jesus' and Paul's teachings believers are warned to shun greed and to avoid those within their community who pursue insatiate desires, and thereby forfeit claim to the kingdom of God (Luke 12:15; Eph 5:3-5; 1 Cor 5:11; 6:10). *See* COVET.

CHRIS M. SMITH

GREEK BARUCH. *See* BARUCH, THIRD BOOK OF.

GREEK LANGUAGE. The Greek used in the NT and in the SEPTUAGINT (LXX) is a variety of "common" (koinē [κοινή], pronounced koi'nay) Greek used in the Hellenistic and Roman periods.

    A. History of the Language
    B. Greek of the Hellenistic and Roman Periods
    C. Significant Features of Biblical Greek
      1. LXX
      2. Greek NT
        a. Matthew
        b. Mark
        c. Luke-Acts
        d. Paul and his letters
        e. Hebrews
        f. James
        g. Peter and Jude
        h. Johannine writings
    D. NT Greek
      1. The Greek of the NT
      2. Semitisms in NT Greek
      3. Greek and the language of Jesus
    E. Issues in NT Greek Language Study
      1. Linguistic approach
      2. Verbal aspect theory
      3. Discourse analysis/textlinguistics
    Bibliography

A. History of the Language

Ancient Greek, an inflected language from the Indo-European family, has a history of over 3500 years. Greek is similar to other languages based around inflectional morphology. That is, words usually consist of two or more morphemes, with morphemes changed to indicate differences in word forms.

Indo-European is a large family of languages thought to originated near the Black Sea. There is evidence for the western branch by 3500 BCE. Scholars refer to the earliest form of Greek as Common Greek. This

Common Greek made its way from the Balkans down through Macedonia into the Greek mainland and islands, where it was developed further before being spread in a common (koinē) form by Alexander the Great and his entourage throughout the Mediterranean world. This Greek became the Greek of the NT and of the LXX (*see* HELLENISM).

The history of the Greek language can be divided into the following periods: the Mycenean period (ca. 1600-1200 BCE), the so-called Dark Ages (1200–900 BCE), the Archaic period (900-600 BCE), the Classical period (600–332 BCE), the Hellenistic period (332–63 BCE), the Roman period (63 BCE–4th cent. CE), the Byzantine period (4th–15th cent.), the Turkish period (15th–19th cent.) and the modern period (19th cent. to the present).

There are at least three theories regularly presented regarding the entrance of Greek into the mainland around 2000 BCE and surrounding islands. The first, not widely held, is the successive-wave hypothesis. It contends that there were three waves of migration by Greek-speaking peoples (Ionian in 2000 BCE, Achaean in 1700 BCE and Dorian in 1200 BCE). These waves supposedly account for the irregular distribution of Greek dialects during the dialect period of Classical Greece. Most scholars today accept a two-migration hypothesis. The first wave of what is now identified as East Greek entered in 2000 BCE. A second migration occurred around 1200 BCE with the western migration. A third hypothesis contends that there was never a second migration, but that the West or Doric Greek represents an uprising of previously settled indigenous people who spoke a dialect of Greek that emerged when the Mycenean kingdoms weakened. The script of the earliest Greeks was linear A, a pictographic language so far undeciphered. During the Mycenean period, linear B was the script used for this incipient form of Greek. Linear B is an administrative script. It appears that the literature of Greece at this time was entirely oral. The Doric invasion of 1200 BCE may have been related to the collapse of the Mycenean period, which led to the so-called Greek Dark Ages. During this period we have little evidence of civilization or literature. Also during this period the Greek dialects continued to develop, so that by 1000 BCE the major dialects were firmly established in the Greek territories.

By the beginning of the Archaic period in around the 9th cent., most scholars recognize four major Greek dialects: 1) Aeolic, in the regions of Thessaly and Boeotia; 2) Ionic, along the eastern edge of the Greek mainland, including Attica (within which Attic developed), as well as on the western coast of Asia Minor; 3) Arcado-Cypriot, spoken on the island of Cyprus and the Peloponnese; 4) Doric, also in the Peloponnese, though the Doric invasion was never able to penetrate its innermost areas, leaving the older Arcado-Cypriot dialect in the heart of the territory. Though the dialects were all recognizably Greek, they had a number of phonological, morphological, lexical and syntactical differences that probably made mutual spoken understanding difficult, even if reading comprehension was possible.

The first Greek literature was an epic variety of Ionic found in Homer's *Iliad* and *Odyssey*. Herodotus wrote the first western history in Ionic. With the growth of Athenian importance the Attic dialect grew in significance, especially as a literary language. Attic became the established dialect of Greek literature of the Archaic and Classical periods, though literature was written in other dialects in such places as Lesbos and Boeotia (Aeolic) and Syracuse (Doric). Attic Greek was a form of Ionic Greek with a number of its own peculiarities in pronunciation, morphology, lexicon, and syntax. At least two major forms of Attic Greek were in use. One was literary, used by the various authors, and the other was spoken Attic, which had features that distinguished it from the written language.

With the rise of Alexander the Great in the late 4th cent., the language of Greece became that of the Hellenistic world. The language used by Alexander's army and entourage was a form of the most significant Greek dialect of the time, Attic. Scholars have called this Great Attic. It is the basis for the koinē Greek of the Hellenistic and Roman periods (Hellenistic Greek). However, it was a form of Attic spoken by a much more diverse group than the native Greek speakers of Attica. It included the first language used by Greeks and others that also served as a second language for anyone who wanted to communicate with, do business with, or increase one's political or social status with the Greek-speaking conquerors. That Greek underwent phonological, morphological, lexical, and syntactical changes as it was used by non-native speakers in a variety of new contexts.

After Alexander's death Greek continued as the administrative language of the Mediterranean world, even where an indigenous language was being spoken, such as in Egypt (Demotic was used, though Greek became widespread, certainly as the administrative language). Demotic eventually adopted a form of the Greek alphabet and became Coptic. Similarly, at least in the eastern part of the Roman Empire, the Romans retained Greek as an administrative language. The influence of Greek was such that Juvenal even called Rome a Greek city, on the basis of the amount of Greek spoken. As the center of the Roman Empire moved further east, the influence of Greek diminished in the west. During the Byzantine period, Greek continued to flourish as the language of the eastern Empire.

A broadly used literary koinē developed as well, with authors such as Polybius, Plutarch, scientific writers and philosophers, and Jewish authors such as Philo and Josephus—not to mention the authors of the Greek Bible. There were some who noted what they thought were decadent tendencies in this koinē Greek, and sought a return to Attic standards. This Atticistic Revival probably began during the 1st cent. BCE and is found in such writers as Dionysius of Halicarnassus, Plutarch, and Lucian. We have evidence from lexica of the period of comments about what constituted standard Greek, although these standards often hyper-corrected the Greek of the time to an idealized Attic standard.

B. Greek of the Hellenistic and Roman Periods

The lexical changes characteristic of **koinē** included semantic shifts in the meanings of words, the creation and addition of new words (neologisms), the falling out of use of other words, the incorporation of words from other languages into Greek (loanwords), and semantic borrowing, where the meaning of a Greek word shifted in the light of the use of an indigenous word. Shifts in meanings of words were motivated by a number of factors, including application of Greek to new contexts (e.g. religious) encountered as the language was spread throughout what became the Hellenistic world. In some instances, Greek speakers simply adapted words that were already found in indigenous languages.

The phonological changes included what is called itacism, a shift in pronunciation of vowels, perhaps encouraged and accelerated by encounter with a variety of indigenous languages possessing other phonological systems. Nevertheless, there was a tendency to move toward pronouncing more vowels with the *i* (*ee*) sound. Itacism is reflected in numerous papyri where words with vowels such as *eta iota*, later *eta*, and other vowels became *iota*. There were other phonological changes as well. These include diphthongs becoming monophthongs, so that some diphthongs began to be spelled with single vowels. There was also a large number of vowel and consonant interchange, especially the loss of distinction between long and short vowels (e.g. long and short *o*), but also consonant interchange (e.g. *lambda* and *rho*). There were also various assimilations, so that rough breathing was lost, or consonants were changed to accommodate a following consonant (e.g. *nu* becomes *mu* before another *mu*). A number of these phonological changes reflect the use of the Ionic rather than the Attic spellings of words (e.g. double *sigma* instead of double *tau*), including the curtailment of the Attic declension.

Morphological changes included alterations of the forms of noun and verb endings. Endings tended to become more regularized, such as retaining the same vowel in all of the endings of a noun, using *nu* as the accusative singular ending for nouns that had not previously had a consonant ending, creating pronoun forms to match others, and the replacement of irregular forms with regular ones in both nouns and verbs. Thus the *mi* verbs were replaced by *omega* forms, and aorist verbs were given sigmatic endings.

Changes also occurred in syntax. The dative case was retreating in use before the accusative. There was an increased use of prepositions to clarify case usage, including en ἐν with the dative. The dual had disappeared. Compound word forms were created, perhaps to reinforce the meaning of a changing word. There was a tendency to use the conjunction hina ἵνα ("in order that," "so that") and the subjunctive mood form instead of the infinitive. The optative mood-form virtually disappeared (apart from Atticistic hypercorrection), in the light of the use of the subjunctive as the form to indicate semantic projection. The use of parataxis, including usage with the conjunction kai καί ("and"), rather than hypotaxis and elaborate periods, increased.

The changes in the language of the time have not been fully appreciated in either textual criticism or grammatical study. The standard Greek NT text of today has regularized spellings that do not show the potential confusion that an ancient author and reader would encounter when reading or hearing the text. Grammars all too frequently use as their point of comparison the supposed standards of Attic Greek, rather than noting that Attic Greek was far from being universal or widespread (or reflective of the supposed rule). The koine of the Mediterranean world was more widely spoken and required to do far more than the Greek that had come before it, and in that sense established its own norms for communicative competence.

C. Significant Features of Biblical Greek

The **koinē** Greek of the Hellenistic and Roman periods is represented in the Old Greek version of the OT, usually referred to as the Septuagint (LXX), and the NT. Because the LXX is for the most part a translation, it is less significant for our discussion than are the authors of the NT composing in Greek. The Greek of the NT and the LXX is a variety of **koinē** found in a variety of sources from the non-literary sources of the papyri to the literary and even Atticistic writers. The **koinē** Greek of the Hellenistic and Roman periods has a large amount of coherence and consistency throughout the period. The written **koinē** (no descriptions of spoken **koinē** exist) can be classified according to categories of fixed register. Register is the concept that language is used in various situations, that linguistic features are chosen according to the particular context, and that knowledge of these features allows reconstruction of the context of situation.

There are four major fixed registers in the written **koinē** Greek of the Hellenistic and Roman periods. These include the vulgar, non-literary, literary, and Atticistic, and all but the vulgar are part of the so-called literary **koinē**. The following table illustrates these levels.

Vulgar	Documentary papyri of various types
Non-Literary	Non-documentary (official and some business) papyri, inscriptions, scientific texts, authors such as Epictetus, Apollodorus, Pausanias

Literary	Authors such as Philo, Josephus, Polybius, Strabo, Arrian, Appian
Atticistic	Authors such as Dionysius of Halicarnassus, Plutarch, Lucian

1. LXX

The Greek of the LXX is a translational form of koinē Greek (*see* SEPTUAGINT). Regardless of what one thinks of the legends about its origins (in such authors as Aristeas, Josephus and Philo), the LXX was probably created because of linguistic necessity. The majority of Jews who wished to use the holy text of the OT could not understand the original language. This major translation project appears to have begun with the Pentateuch, and then extended to other books. The final form of the LXX includes books that were probably not translations at all. At various times, translators, whose knowledge of Hebrew varied considerably, rendered the source text into Greek. The Greek that was the basis for their work was the koinē which reflects accommodations made to the original sacred language, mostly in terms of lexicon and syntax. There are instances of loanwords, semantic borrowing, and loan translations, where the Hebrew words are translated into unnatural Greek. There are also instances of syntactical influence, such as increased use of parataxis with kai ("and"). For the most part, the language reflects the same kinds of developments found in other koinē Greek of the time, with increased use of certain types of constructions (e.g. en and the dative), and decreases in others (such as periodic style).

2. Greek NT

The NT remains one of the most important corpora of original koinē Greek. Most scholars would place the vast majority of NT writers in the category of non-literary authors. However, some would argue for Hebrews and parts of Luke-Acts, as well as sections in Paul and possibly 1 Peter and James, as reflecting literary characteristics, and the book of Revelation perhaps being vulgar. In any case, the individual writers of the NT have peculiarities of their own that are worth noting.

a. Matthew. If we assume that Matthew used Mark, there are a number of characteristics of Matthew's style which stand as distinct in relation to the Second Gospel. These include: the tendency to abbreviate the wording of individual episodes (where synoptic comparison is possible) by using a more compact and less redundant style; selection of more literary rather than the less literary or even vulgar vocabulary of Mark; tempering of the exuberance of Mark's narrative by replacing narrative present tense-forms with imperfect or especially aorist tense-forms; stylistic elevation of Mark's text; and use of parallelism, perhaps reflective of the OT (mediated in most instances in Matthew's Gospel by the LXX). Matthew's Gospel is written in a non-literary style that at times reflects literary influences.

b. Mark. Mark's Gospel is considered the most Semitically influenced of the Gospels, although many of the supposed Semitic elements are at best Semitic enhancement. Mark's syntactical variation and vocabulary choice are limited. However, Mark's style is also typified by a high proportion of narrative present tense-forms, typical of historical writers of the time and used in an emphatic way in discourse. Mark also has a higher proportion of compound words and a more frequent use of periphrastic tense-forms instead of simple verb forms. Mark's style uses conjunctions less and asyndeton more, apart from the widespread use of kai ("and") in keeping with much other Greek of the time as a discourse marker to introduce paragraphs or pericopes. Mark's style is non-literary, though not vulgar.

c. Luke-Acts. The author of Luke-Acts displays the widest range of styles of any of the evangelists. Luke has such typical characteristics as a vocabulary that at times reflects Attic style and the use of the optative mood-form. One of the distinct characteristics of Luke's writing is adjustment of his style to the narrative context. Thus the prologue to Luke's Gospel (1:1-4) is written in what comes close to a periodic classical sentence typical of Greek historians. He then changes to a more Septuagintally influenced style in the birth narrative, including instances of Semitic poetic style in the hymns. In Acts, there is a more Semitically reflective style used in the early chapters when the action focuses upon Palestine, which becomes more thoroughly Hellenistic when Christianity moves westward into the Greco-Roman world. Though mostly written in non-literary Greek, there are a number of places where a firm literary style is used in Luke's writings (e.g. Luke 1:1-4; 15:11-32).

d. Paul's Letters. Perhaps Paul's style consistently comes closest to spoken Greek of the time, because Paul's letters were dictated to a scribe for subsequent reading. This style is embedded within a modified version of the contemporary LETTER form, possibly modeled on the official letter. Although his vocabulary is consistently drawn from the spoken Greek stratum, there are times when Paul uses language influenced by the literary writers or the philosophers, such as the Stoics and Epicureans, both in some direct quotations and in allusions. Paul's syntax is occasionally given to hypotaxis or at least lengthy clause complexes (Eph 1:3-14), often found with compounded word groups with accumulated modifying words. Paul sometimes (e.g. Romans, 1 and 2 Corinthians) uses the DIATRIBE style, including the dialogical use of rhetorical questions, apostrophe, short clauses, parallelism, and even parataxis or asyndeton. Paul's language is probably functionally labeled as non-literary, although passages such as 1 Cor 13 and Phil 2:5-11 (if written by him) certainly attain literary status.

e. Hebrews. Hebrews consistently attains the highest literary level in the NT. The language is marked by more complex syntax and vocabulary, sometimes creating periods. This higher level may reflect the possibility that Hebrews was written as either a literary letter or even a sermon. In many instances, Hebrews seems to reflect some of the aspirations of classical prose in its attention to rhythm, hiatus, alliteration, and parallelism. Hebrews should be considered an example of an aspiring non-literary koinē that often touches the literary level.

f. James. James is characterized by features of paraenetic and diatribal style. This includes the dialogical use of questions and answers, short sentences, and parallelism. The author often selects lexical items from the literary stratum. The quality of writing has led to some skeptical wondering about the possibility of the text's author coming from 1st cent. Palestine, but given the region's bilingual—if not multilingual—environment, it remains a possibility. James may also be an example of an essay letter, which would explain its linguistic level. James is an example of an aspiring non-literary koinē.

g. Peter and Jude. The differences in style between the Petrine letters points to either different authors or different scribes (Sylvanus/Silas in 1 Pet 5:12). Scholars have noted features of the language of 1 Peter that aspire to a literary and even Atticistic character, such as the use of rhythm, possibly patterning usage after other literary authors, choices in vocabulary, and use of the optative mood-form. 2 Peter and Jude have linguistic features in common characterized by a vigorous style with some literary characteristics, such as attention to rhythm and lexical choice. These would have been possible for writers native to a bi- or multilingual Palestine, especially if they were a type of literary letter, as has been suggested.

h. Johannine writings. Despite speculation about sources in John's Gospel, most linguistic investigations are not conclusive that linguistic criteria exist for such differentiation. The style of the Gospel and letters is typified by a paratactic style (the use of "and") while also using a number of sentences without conjunctions (asyndeton); the use of the narrative present; use of **hina** and the subjunctive mood-form in a variety of ways; limited vocabulary choice; apparent redundancies (such as "answered and said"); provocative lexical alteration, suggesting either stylistic variation or subtle semantic variation. The book of Revelation is known for a number of departures from standard written Greek, despite knowledge of a wide vocabulary. This has led to much speculation as to the cause—some elevating these solecisms to the status of theological significance, with others denigrating the level of Greek to that of the vulgar. There are indisputable characteristics of vulgar Greek found in Revelation, but the vast majority of the questionable constructions are also found in the contemporary papyri, while the author also shows knowledge of standard Greek on other occasions. This non-literary Greek sometimes falls into vulgar characteristics.

D. NT Greek

1. The Greek of the NT

With the rise of study of ancient languages in the Enlightenment, questions were raised about NT Greek. Rather than simply disparage the Greek of the NT, some posited that the recognizably different Greek of the NT was a special inspired form of Greek (so-called Holy Ghost Greek). Others attempted to establish the Semitic basis of the Greek from parallels in Semitic texts. It is out of this background that the four major periods of discussion emerge.

The first major period in recent discussion resulted from the discovery of documentary papyri. In the late 19th cent., archaeologists discovered huge caches of papyri (*see* PAPYRUS, PAPYRI). These caches contained non-documentary papyri, including manuscripts (fragmentary and some intact) of ancient authors, including NT texts. At least as important were the thousands of documentary papyri also discovered. These documentary papyri, some of them including archives of correspondence (such as the Zenon papyri, and later the Babatha archive), often represented individual correspondence. They included tax accounts, receipts, records of transactions, wills, personal letters, and the like. Adolf Deissmann was one of the first to recognize the significance of these finds for NT study. His analysis of these documentary papyri was instrumental in showing that supposed unique biblical usage of Greek words was the usage found in these papyri. Deissmann's research was extended by James Hope Moulton, who also investigated grammatical correspondences between the papyri and the NT. The papyri had shown through numerous examples that both the lexicon and grammar of the NT found many of its closest parallels, not in the Greek of the Classical period (which had already been recognized), but in the Greek of the documentary papyri. Hence, this position held that the koinē Greek of the time was the result of linguistic development. The Greek of the NT was a form of this variety of Greek, even if influenced by Semitic contact, such as through the LXX.

The second major period in study of NT Greek, the so-called Aramaic hypothesis, considered it a Semitized form of Greek. The main proponents of the koinē Greek hypothesis passed off the scene between the two world wars, and this, combined with the discovery of Semitic documents from the Hellenistic and Roman period such as the Dead Sea Scrolls, revived the hypothesis that NT Greek was heavily influenced by Aramaic. Such scholars as C. C. Torrey, Matthew Black, and, more recently, Maurice Casey have attempted to place the theory on firmer comparative linguistic ground, appealing to apparent mistranslations, Greek ambiguities, and better Aramaic texts for comparison. Torrey went so far as to contend that the Gospels, Acts 1–15 and Revelation were direct translations from Aramaic. Later scholars have been more cautious, seeing less direct translation and more lexical and syntactical influence. These theories point out that 1) the NT was written in a highly Semitized environment; 2) the Greek itself points to the influence of Semitic languages; 3) the kind of linguistic crossover posited is linguistically defensible and quantifiable; 4) specific sources, such as in Aramaic, can be identified.

The third period attempts to revive the theory of a form of special Jewish Greek. Such scholars as Henry Gehman and Nigel Turner (whose several volumes on Greek grammar have had widespread influence) have argued that there was a form of Jewish-Greek dialect used in 1st cent. Palestine. They reach this conclusion because the Semitic language hypothesis seems inadequate to explain what they see as widespread use of this Greek in the NT, the LXX, and even in the language of Jesus and his disciples. Gehman considered this a temporary, transitional dialect; Turner argued that it was neither a temporary nor artificial form of language, but that it was the one in use by Jews and Christians of the time. This hypothesis holds that such a blending of Greek and Semitic languages is a linguistic possibility that occurred in Palestine and Egypt.

The fourth position revives the Deissmann-Moulton hypothesis while attempting to pull back from what are perceived as its extremes. In reaction to the various Semitic hypotheses (Aramaic and Semitic Greek), a number of scholars have made proposals regarding the Greek of the NT as a form of koinē Greek. Such hypotheses consider that there may be more strata of language use than simply the documentary papyri versus Classical Greek. Some have posited that the Greek of the NT is closest to a scientific or popular level language. Others have tried to get away from the manifest disjunctions in such discussion. Sometimes the discussion is about the Greek language system itself; at other times it asks how this system is used in particular instances. So, it is possible to say that an author might display Semitic linguistic features (on the basis of first language, education, context, content, etc.) in a particular example, with that usage not necessarily reflecting the system of the Greek language itself. The multilingual milieu of Palestine and the rest of the Hellenized Mediterranean was more complex than is often realized. It is possible to hold that a given linguistic feature might evidence Semitic influence while the language of the NT is still seen to be an instance of written koinē.

2. Semitisms in NT Greek

In the past, there have been two differing approaches to Semitisms in the Greek of the NT. One is to assume the priority of the Semitic languages and require that the Greek of the NT justify itself as Greek. This tendency unfortunately still continues, where individual linguistic features (e.g. the narrative present tense-form, parataxis with "and," etc.) are selected with the presumption that such a feature is Semitically induced. The other approach is to assume that the Greek of the NT is a variety of the koinē Greek of its time, and require that posited Semitisms be defended as such. This requires substantial quantification, not merely the citation of a particular instance (though a single instance of a phenomenon in extra-biblical Greek would tend to show that this is at least Greek usage). The latter is the sounder method, because the documents of the NT are Greek documents, the environment in which they were written was a bi- or even multilingual one with Greek widespread even in many Jewish circles, and the authors of the NT—though mostly Jewish—came from backgrounds where Greek would have been the primary language of communication (e.g. Paul and Luke).

As a result, one should consider three possible levels of Semitic influence: 1) interlingual translation (as in Mark when instances of Aramaic are translated into Greek, or most of the books of the LXX); 2) intervention, when a decidedly non-Greek structure used in the Greek of the NT must be recognized as due to the intrusion of a Semitic structure; 3) enhancement, when a recognizably Greek structure is used more frequently possibly because of a parallel Semitic form. Level 3 is of interest, not because it addresses the issue of Semitisms, but because it helps to chronicle the diachronic development of the language. Language is changed by its users as they adapt to differing linguistic contexts. Thus, enhancement is one of the factors that plays a part in language development in a context where a language is being used by a wide range of speakers or writers in ever-expanding social, cultural and geographical contexts.

Level 2 is of interest because it represents an instance when there is an unanticipated intrusion of another language into the base language. One of the factors that scholars who posited such examples have failed to take into account is how languages relate to each other in terms of prestige. Greek was the prestige language in the wider Mediterranean world in the 1st cent., necessary for trade, communication and commerce. This status was true even in Palestine, apart from particular religious contexts. One of the patterns in use of prestige languages is that they tend to influence non-prestige languages, rather than the reverse, as the users of non-prestige languages adapt their language to the dominant language. These findings indicate that it is in the area of lexicon where there is the most crossover between languages. This is understandable in the light of the fact that when a language is being used for phenomena that is has not encountered before there is a need to find a suitable word, and sometimes the local or indigenous language can provide that lexical item. The grammar of a language, especially a prestige language, is far less susceptible to the impact of non-prestige languages. This seems to be the case with the Greek of the NT. There may well be lexical items used that were Semitically influenced. However, there are few instances of grammatical influence. The long-term diachronic influence of Semitism intervention on koinē Greek was minimal, as seen in the Greek of the second and 3rd cent. Christian writers.

3. Greek and the language of Jesus

A last issue is the relation of Jesus to the Greek in which the NT is written. Though Aramaic was almost assuredly Jesus' first language, the linguistic diversity of Palestine has raised the question of whether Jesus may have spoken Greek. The evidence suggests that Jesus followed a trade that would have required contact with non-Jews; a number of Jesus' closest followers came from the area of Galilee (which was thoroughly Hellenized) and had Greek names (e.g. Andrew, Philip); Jesus said to converse with people who quite possibly spoke Greek, some with no Semitic language (e.g. the Syrophoenician woman of Mark 7:25-30; the centurion in Capernaum in Galilee in Matt 8:5-13; Herodians; a Samaritan woman in John 4:4-26; Levi/Matthew a tax collector in Mark 2:13-14; the Samaritan leper in Luke 17:11-19; and Pilate in Mark 15:2-5); there is widespread evidence of use of Greek in 1st cent. Palestine; the Jews composed some of their texts in Greek, even in Palestine; and the early church made a transformation to a Greek-speaking church, possibly as early as Paul, and at least by the time of the early church writers (e.g. the entire NT, the *Didache, Epistle of Barnabas, Shepherd of Hermas, 1 Clement*, Greek church fathers, etc.).

Recent research has posed two further questions. The first is whether we can find particular instances in which Jesus actually spoke Greek, and the second is whether, in the light of the likelihood that Jesus spoke Greek, he actually used it in his teaching at any point. The first question asks whether any particular passage reflects such usage. Many of the passages noted above have been cited as possible instances where Jesus spoke Greek. The one passage for which there is clearly the most contextual evidence for Jesus speaking Greek and having a record of what he said is Jesus' conversation with Pilate recorded in all four of the Gospels (Mark 15:2-5; Matt 27:11-14; Luke 23:2-4; John 18:29-38). The second question shifts the evidence to see if Jesus' use of Greek goes beyond a functional competence to a communicative competence, such that he could give an extended content-filled discourse. Scholars are far less certain that we have evidence of Jesus teaching in Greek, although the so-called Sermon on the Mount might be such an example (Matthew 5–7). The circumstances that drew people together from such diverse ethnic and possibly linguistic groups would have required speaking in a common language, such as Greek.

E. Issues in NT Greek Language Study

The last thirty years have brought renewed interest in the linguistic character of the Greek of the NT. As a result, there are a number of areas where there has been more intense research into the study of Greek, influenced by developments in linguistic methodology. There are three areas that merit brief discussion.

1. Linguistic approach

The field of modern linguistics is fairly new when compared with traditional study of Greek language. One of the hindrances in the utilization of modern linguistic methods in the study of ancient Greek is that many of the standard scholarly resources, which were valuable in their time and encyclopedic in their knowledge, are outdated in their methodology and do not reflect recent linguistic advances. A modern linguistic approach, as opposed to earlier, traditional grammatical approaches, does not approach Greek in the same way, rejecting such practices as: using Classical Greek as a normative form for comparison with NT Greek; relying upon comparative study of the best literary texts (the purview of classical philology), instead studying the range of written remains available; treating study of the history of the language as determinative for studying usage at a given time and in a specific author; relying upon etymologies of words as determinative of meaning; theologizing the meanings of words and treating lexical items as ciphers for theological concepts; utilizing the framework of traditional grammar with its tendency to prescribe usage.

A modern linguistic approach to the study of an ancient (or, as it has sometimes been called, epigraphic) language requires the utilization of a suitably well-developed linguistic model. Most of the models applied to ancient Greek share the following characteristics in common: an explicitly empirical bias allowing for criteria to be tested against usage; reliance on the reasonable assumption that language is structured in its parts and susceptible to systematic examination; recognition that the most useful results are descriptive rather than prescriptive; consideration of all of the various levels of language usage, from the morpheme to the discourse, to provide a complete analysis. The result of such an approach is to develop models that account for language usage. These models are then tested against actual usage and corrected so that the model is as inclusive in its explanation of the data as possible.

A number of different models have been applied to ancient Greek. These include formalist models that draw upon the psycho-linguistic theories of Noam Chomsky and his followers, and functionalist models. Most have not followed the path of formalist models, although there is work in case theory that utilizes formalism. Recent linguistic study of Greek has drawn predominantly upon functionalist models, whether linked to the work of the Summer Institute of Linguistics or a variety of discourse-based models. As modern linguistics itself moves away from its early structuralist roots to consider larger units of analysis—discourse analysis is based upon the assumption that the major unit of analysis is beyond the sentence—a variety of working linguistic models continues to be developed for study of the Greek of the NT.

2. Verbal aspect theory

One of the major areas of linguistic research has been in the area of verbal aspect theory, and this work has been applied to the study of Greek as well. The history of study of Greek verbal usage indicates three distinct stages. In the rationalist period of linguistic study (18th and 19th cent.), each tense-form was equated with a distinct time-based function. The present tense-form was seen to refer to present time, the aorist to the past, and the future to the future, etc. Any apparent variations from this pattern were only that—apparent, and not indicative of the true function of the verbal tense-form. With the results of comparative philology came the ability to recognize that verbs performed other functions in language than simply referring to time.

Aktionsart theory claimed that verbs in Greek and some other languages were concerned not with when an action took place, but how it took place. As a result, research turned to studying the various types of action and how these were grammaticalized by the limited choice of tense-forms in any language, Greek included. *Aktionsart* theory placed emphasis upon a complex relationship between the action itself, the kind of action reflected in the root of the verb and the kind of action reflected by the various tense-forms. The most recent scholarship has concluded that Greek verbal structure is not based primarily upon time as a feature of the individual tense-forms or word roots, or around an attempt to objectively characterize actions as they actually occur, but around the notion of verbal aspect. Verbal aspect theory argues that the use of the Greek tense-forms does relate to the kind of action, but in terms of the author or writer characterizing the action of the lexeme in a particular way by choosing one tense-form over another. Recent research has extended the significance of verbal aspect by realizing that the various choices of aspect are made by authors to shape the interpretive parameters of their discourse. For example, the narrative present may be used not just to highlight a particular event, but to introduce a new character, change a scene, open or close a paragraph or the like.

A number of issues in aspect theory continue to be discussed. The first is how to characterize the aspects. Some wish to retain the traditional tense-form labels, such as present, imperfect, aorist, perfect, pluperfect, etc. However, these are not descriptive, consistent or free from previously prescribed values. Others wish to define the aspects in terms of descriptive characteristics, such as the aorist as perfective, the present/imperfect as imperfective, and the perfect/pluperfect as stative

aspect. Others wish to develop their own terminology. Finally others are more concerned with describing their relationship with each other, given that choice of one aspect implies not choosing another. Besides definition of the aspects, other questions concern the following issues. One is the relation of aspect to time. Some wish to show that the Greek tense-forms as verbal aspect markers do not grammaticalize any temporal reference, while others wish to retain relative temporal reference in the indicative mood, and some even in the other moods. A third issue is the relation of choice of aspect to conscious choice. In some occasions it may be possible to attribute a conscious choice to the author, while in others the choice must be un- or subconscious. A fourth issue is the relation of aspectual semantic categories to the meanings of individual lexical items, and whether the lexical item has an inherent aspect to it, or even constrains the choice of verbal aspect. Recent research has shown that the aspectual system of Greek is independent of other verbal systems. A final issue is whether the Greek perfect tense-form constitutes a verbal aspect in its own right (Greek would then have three aspects) or whether it is a tense-form or some composite form of tense and aspect.

3. Discourse analysis/textlinguistics

Discourse analysis, sometimes referred to as textlinguistics, is an area of increasing interest in recent study of the Greek of the NT. Various forms of discourse analysis first developed in the study of conversation, but recent work has developed principles suited to the study of written discourses. Discourse analysis was developed out of the growing recognition that meaningful language usage takes place at levels larger than or beyond the sentence. Previous linguistic study had been concerned with units at the sentence and below, such as morphology, clause structure and the like. However, over the last forty years there has been increasing recognition that units such as these were always used in terms of larger units, with the largest unit of language representation being the discourse itself.

There are at least five major groupings of scholars concerned with discourse study of the NT: 1) Summer Institute of Linguistics discourse analysis, influenced by linguists who have developed graphic forms for languages without a previous written form; 2) South African discourse analysis, which has traditionally focused upon the colon (consisting of a predicate/subject unit) as the most meaningful unit for discussion; 3) Continental European textlinguistics, which has had major work done in Scandinavia and in Germany, and has brought together rhetorical theory, communications theory, and the traditional linguistic distinction between syntax, semantics and pragmatics; 4) Systemic Functional discourse analysis, which often utilizes the notion of register (see above) to study the various levels of language use within a context of the textual, interpersonal and ideational dimensions of language; and, as some have recently proposed, 5) an eclectic category of discourse analysts who often drawn on various discourse models, as well as various literary and rhetorical models, in their research.

As can be seen from this brief taxonomy of discourse analysts, just as modern linguistics is not a single thing per se, so discourse analysis is not a thing, but a term used to describe a number of different approaches to a common concern for study of language at the discourse level. There are a number of issues that differentiate various discourse models. One is whether a given discourse model is a top-down or a bottom-up approach. A top-down model begins with the discourse type as an entity and then differentiates its smaller units of structure as the interpreter moves down, while a bottom-up approach begins with smaller units of structure, such as the word group or clause, and builds up increasingly larger units until the discourse is reached. The top-down model is required to make assumptions about the shape of a discourse before studying its particulars, while the bottom-up model assumes that a discourse is the composite of its individual parts. Another issue is how one moves beyond the clause or sentence. Some discourse analysts believe that the unit beyond, such as a paragraph, is a further unit of structure in a similar way as the sentence is a unit of structure (so that the paragraph is a sort of super-sentence). Other discourse analysts believe that linguistic units beyond the sentence do not have structure in the same way as the sentence, and require a different type of analysis. This indicates that one of the reasons that linguistics has often not progressed beyond the sentence is that there is something about the sentence that seems to constitute a natural barrier to further analysis. A third area of exploration is identifying and then defining the units beyond the clause or sentence, such as the clause or sentence complex, the sub-paragraph, paragraph, and others. Some identify these units on the basis of function or even type (procedural, expositional, etc.), while others identify them on the basis of formal features, such as conjunctions. Even though there are a number of issues still to be resolved in discourse analysis, there is a growing sense among linguists that discourse analysis is a necessary approach to the study of language.

Bibliography: Francisco Rodriguez Adrados. *A History of the Greek Language: From Its Origins to the Present* (2005); Procope S. Costas. *An Outline of the History of the Greek Language, with Particular Emphasis on the Koine and the Subsequent Periods* (repr. 1997); David Crystal. *A Dictionary of Language. 2nd ed.* (1999); Geoffrey Horrocks. *Greek: A History of the Language and its Speakers* (1997); Karen H. Jobes and Moisés Silva, *Invitation to the Septuagint* (2000); James Hope Moulton. "New Testament Greek in the Light of Modern Discovery." *Essays on Some Biblical Questions of the Day.* Henry Barclay Swete, ed. (1909) 461-505; Stanley E. Porter. *Verbal Aspect in the Greek of the New Testament, with Reference to Tense and Mood.* Studies in Biblical Greek 1 (1989); Stanley E. Porter. "Studying Ancient Languages from a Modern Linguistic Perspective: Essential Terms and Terminology." *Filología Neotestamentaria 2* (1989) 147-72; Stanley E. Porter, ed. *The Language of the New Testament: Classic Essays* (1991); Stanley E. Porter. *The Criteria for Authenticity in Historical-Jesus Research: Previous Discussion and New Proposals* (2000); Henry St. John Thackeray. *A Grammar of the Old Testament in Greek according to the Septuagint* (1909); Nigel Turner. *Style: A Grammar of New Testament Greek, v. 4* (1976).

STANLEY E. PORTER

GREEK RELIGION AND PHILOSOPHY. This essay explores trends in religion and philosophy of the Hellenistic era (323–31 BCE) and early Roman period (63 BCE–132 CE). Although the philosophy portion of the essay addresses exclusively the Hellenistic and early Roman periods, the religion portion emphasizes equally classical religion (490–323 BCE). This is not a distraction from the period that matters most, however. Previous generations assumed dramatic distinctions between Classical and Hellenistic religion. That there were changes is obvious. But the assumption of decline and corruption in Hellenistic Greek religion is no longer credible. Some important things resisted change, and some things that changed did so less than scholars previously supposed. Given stability in key areas, information about the Classical period is equally relevant for the Hellenistic period. Furthermore, attention to Classical religion prepares one to evaluate more clearly changes in the Hellenistic period. Any number of other topics might have been covered here (purity; superstition; domestic religion; relation of religion to magic) but space did not permit it. Entries in the bibliography will facilitate study in excluded topics.

    A. Greek Religion: The Classical Period
        (490–323 BCE)
      1. Panhellenic religion and polis religion
      2. Panhellenic religion: Deities
        a. Panhellenic myth: Homer and Hesiod
        b. Panhellenic myth: Eastern antecedents
      3. Panhellenic Religion: Sanctuary and ritual
        a. Altars and sacrifices
        b. Temenos and votive offerings
        c. Panhellenic sanctuaries: The example of Delphi
        d. Panhellenic festivals: The example of Olympia
        e. Women and the Thesmophoria
      4. Polis religion: Deities at Athens
      5. Polis Religion: Sanctuaries and ritual at Athens

A. Greek Religion: The Classical Period (490–323 BCE)

1. Panhellenic Religion and Polis Religion

The first step in understanding Classical Greek religion is to grasp that no such thing existed. The Greeks shared no single religion. Greek religious life tied people to their respective city-state (polis πόλις). Non-citizens participated in the religion of another polis only under certain circumstances.

Even so, one can speak in a qualified way of Panhellenic religion. Indeed, the Greeks themselves became more aware of this in the 400s BCE, if not sooner. In the midst of the Peloponnesian War, for instance, when the Plataeans appeal to the Spartans for protection, they entreat the Spartans to consider "the gods whose altars are common to all Greeks" (Thucydides, 3.59.2). Half a century earlier, when the Persians were bearing down on mainland Greece, the rest of the Greeks feared that the Athenians would abandon the joint Greek effort to repel the Persian invaders. The Athenians promised that they would, however, fight alongside their neighbors, and they provided several bases of their union with the rest of Greece. They referred to shared blood and language, but also, and more important for present concerns, to common temples and rituals (Herodotus, *Hist.* 8.144; see also 7.132, 8.121, 9.81). In common to all Greeks, therefore, are certain gods, certain altars at which to worship those gods, and certain festivals and rituals to accomplish this worship. In the latter part of this section we will explore religion, as it was unique in a particular city. And, although we will first explore the character of Panhellenic religion, we will occasionally be reminded that the polis πόλις was the primary religious institution.

2. Panhellenic Religion: Deities

a. Panhellenic Myth: Homer and Hesiod. Herodotus identifies HOMER (ca. 8th cent. BCE) and HESIOD (ca. 700 BCE) as the definitive tellers of stories about Greek divinities (2.53). Homer's epics, the *Iliad* and the *Odyssey,* are stories about two men. The *Iliad* opens with the wrath of Achilles, while the *Odyssey* begins with that versatile man, Odysseus. Yet, the gods are equally present as each poem begins. Apollo appears in *Il.* 1.9-10 as the god who inspires Achilles' wrath, and the will of Zeus appears in line 6.

These are poems, then, about the interaction between humans and deities who are presented in anthropomorphic terms (as human beings). The deities are a family whose father, Zeus, rules from his palace on Mt. Olympus. Hera is Zeus' wife and sister. The siblings and children of Zeus are Aphrodite, Apollo, Ares, Artemis, Athena, Demeter, Dionysus, Hermes, Hephaestus and Poseidon. Driven by human concerns, Athena and Hera despise the Trojans because the Trojan prince Paris (*Il.* 24.31-36) claimed Aphrodite was more beautiful. Aphrodite, conversely, is equally loyal to the Trojans. Gods and goddesses also act on their loyalties. Apollo attacks Patroclus (*Il.* 16.778). Athena advises the son of Odysseus, Telemachus, until Odysseus returns (*Od.* 178–323).

In other ways, however, the gods are not at all human. They do not die. They do not age. They do not change. They do, however, have an origin and a history. These are the topic of Hesiod's *Theogony.* The poem describes the origin and family tree of all the gods and powers, as well as how Zeus and the Olympians overthrew Cronus and the Titans in order to rule, the so-called Succession Myth.

Homer and Hesiod, then, provide a Panhellenic image of Greek deities. For centuries to come, sculptors fashion statues of the gods and goddesses faithful to the depictions in Homer and Hesiod. This respect for the grand old masters has its limits, though. The Greeks did not give to Homer and Hesiod the respect accorded to the Bible. Literary portraits throughout antiquity tell new and different stories, like the genealogical tales in *The Library* of Apollodorus (1st or 2nd cent. CE). In the *Dionysiaca* of Nonnus of Panopolis (5th cent. CE), Dionysus, relatively insignificant in Homer, has become a universal and omnipresent god. It is wrong, therefore, to sketch strict genealogies of Greek deities, as though the Greeks had only one way of describing the relationships between them. This appears even more profoundly in *polis* religion.

Finally, between immortals and mortals were heroes—human beings who had performed feats greater than other mortals. After death, their tombs became sites of veneration and worship similar to that given to gods (*see* GODS AND GODDESSES).

b. Panhellenic Myth: Eastern antecedents. Nothing comes from nothing, and Greek religion received influences from the antecedent civilizations to the East. Assumptions about Greek borrowing can go too far, of course, but borrowing there certainly was. Various aspects of the Homeric epics recall the Akkadian epics and *Gilgamesh*. In a similar way, the Succession Myth in Hesiod's *Theogony* parallels Babylonian, Hittite and Phoenician writings. Such influences have received scant attention until recently due to the desire to set off Classical Greece as a perfect, unique world unto itself. The Greeks, however, were never fully isolated from the East, a fact that will gain importance when we discuss the Hellenistic period.

3. Panhellenic religion: Sanctuary and ritual

a. Altars and sacrifices. Temples were not the center of Greek religious life. The altars mattered most, and they were not housed in the temples, but usually outside. Among all the festivals, games, processions and prayers in honor of the deities, sacrifice at an altar was the core of Greek religion.

Different deities desired different sacrifices. *Chthonic* (earthly) gods were those who either dwelt in the underworld, or who tended the things of the earth like agriculture. To them was given sacrifice on low altars, *bothroi*, so that the sacrifice would descend below, or liquids like milk or honey were poured into pits in the ground. Heroes, entombed in the ground, received the same sacrifice. *Ouranic* (heavenly) deities ruled over matters related to life and affairs above earth. *Bomoi,* high altars that sent sacrifices upward, were for these deities. Also, animal sacrifice for a chthonic god would burn the whole offering, but for an ouranic god, only portions would be burnt, and a meal would follow the sacrifice. Archaeological evidence shows that the distinction in altars was not always followed, but the Greeks made the distinction in theory.

More important is noticing the fact that one deity could serve multiple functions, and may even receive chthonic worship at one place, ouranic elsewhere. Responsibility for various functions by one deity is important to note in general. Poseidon Soter (Savior) in his sanctuary at Sunium was thought by the Athenians to protect sailors. But, there was also within the city of Athens a sanctuary dedicated to Poseidon Hippios (of horses). Both of these are dedicated to Poseidon, but one would not take a horse related issue to the sanctuary of Poseidon Soter, nor would one take a sailing related issue to the sanctuary of Poseidon Hippios. Both deities were Poseidon, in some sense, but served different functions. Each altar would have been served by different priests and would have had its own day of celebration, apart from the other altars dedicated to the same god under a different epithet. The typical Greek city would have been populated with sanctuaries devoted to various gods who oversaw the various public and private matters of the city, and the location of these temples often corresponded to the function of the deity. The temples of Zeus Polieus and Athena Polias, for instance, would have been in the center of town indicating their central importance for civic life. In addition to certain daily observances at a given shrine, each city would have had a unique calendar of festivals, with any given day a celebration of different deities.

b. Temenos and votive offerings. Altars were surrounded by an area "cut off" for special devotion to the god or goddess and hence named temenos (τέμενος from temnō τέμνω, to cut). The temenos could be demarcated in any number of ways, from a simple, low wall with an open end, to something as elaborate as the walls around the Athenian acropolis, which was a temenos. Everything within the temenos belonged to the god.

To win the favor of a deity before a difficult undertaking, or to thank a deity after surviving some hazard, a person might install in the temenos some offering of thanks and honor, such as a vase, a statuette, etc. The presence of many such votives indicates a deity's power and attentiveness. These votives could also be monumental items. After defeating the Persians, the Greeks offered captured Persian warships as thank-offerings to various gods throughout Greece (Herodotus, *Hist.* 8.121). Temples and statues dedicated to the gods fall under the heading of dedications to the deities.

c. Panhellenic sanctuaries: The example of Delphi. In addition to sharing common deities and common ways to worship them, the Greeks also shared certain places for this worship, especially at Delphi, Olympia, Isthmia and Nemea. Although this sense of commonality may not have been true before the Persian Wars (490–479 BCE), it was true afterward. Precisely within these shrines for Panhellenic religion, however, we see especially clearly the structure of polis religion.

P. L. Neville
Figure 1: Temple of Apollo, Delphi

Legendary stories about the foundation of the sanctuary of Apollo at Delphi connect the site with Panhellenic worship from its origins. When he sought to make the will of heaven known to all humanity, Apollo needed a home for his oracle. He went to the side of Mount Parnassus, and slew the dragon Python that dwelt there. He then established a priesthood from a group of Cretans whom he met while disguised as a dolphin. It was from this site that Apollo made his will known through his oracular priestess, the Pythia. The Panhellenic character of the shrine is obvious in the numerous treasuries set up there from all of the cities of Greece, to win the favor of Apollo, or to thank him for oracular guidance. Not only Greeks, but people from all over the world consulted this oracle, and they did so throughout antiquity, until the Christian Emperor Theodosius the Great finally closed the shrine in the late 4th cent. CE.

But Panhellenic religion at Delphi was mediated through the ideals of the polis. All of the religious functionaries and priests at the shrine were Delphians. The preliminary sacrifice that preceded consultation of the oracle could only be offered by Delphians. Each Greek city had proxenoi (πρόξενοι plural, from singular proxēnos πρόξενος), or ambassadors, between cities, and these proxēnos helped citizens of one city participate in the cult of another. Serving in this way,

Delphians would offer sacrifice on behalf of foreigners. So, the same polis structure that prevailed elsewhere prevailed also at Delphi. For, although Greeks consulted the oracle before non-Greeks each day, Delphians consulted first among the Greeks. Thus, the shrine of Apollo was treated like a civic organization of Delphi, to which outsiders were granted special privileges of participation according to the dictates of polis religion. The same principles apply at Panhellenic festivals as well.

d. Panhellenic festivals: The example of Olympia. The four Panhellenic sanctuaries (Isthmia, Delphi, Olympia, Nemea) provided a regular circuit of athletic contests. They had not always been Panhellenic. Olympia first developed a Panhellenic status near the end of the 8th cent. BCE. The others slowly followed suit: Delphi in 582 BCE; Isthmia, 581 BCE; Nemea, 573 BCE. At Delphi, not only athletic contests, but also musical contests took place. Local games for local citizens continued, of course, in dozens of cities, but the four festivals mentioned here were Panhellenic contests and were completely connected to devotion to their respective local deities: to Apollo at Delphi; to Poseidon at Isthmia; to Zeus at Nemea and Olympia. A very important fact distinguishes these games from the consultation of the Delphic oracle. In the Classical period, only Greeks could participate in these games. When Alexander 1 of Macedon tried to compete at Olympia, he was at first prevented, only later to be admitted because he could demonstrate Greek ancestry in his Argive descent (Herodotus, *Hist.* 5.22). The games were for all Greeks, but only Greeks.

The myths associated with the games suggest their origin was in funerary games like those described in Book 23 of the *Iliad* in honor of Patroclus. The games at Delphi are connected to the death of Python. The games at Isthmia are connected to the hero Palaemon. The games at Nemea are connected to the hero Opheltes. Traces of this significance survive in later practices and myths, but the games came to be celebrations in honor of the local god. The games, however, are only one aspect of the activity of these sanctuaries. We must look at the total sanctuary to understand the significance of the place for Greek religion. Olympia will provide our example.

The **temenos** of Zeus at Olympia, dubbed the Altis (Grove) was enormous, over 200 m on a side. The **temenos** contained numerous altars and buildings, as well as the stadium wherein the games were conducted. All of these structures, and more, were within the **temenos** and belonged to the god. Another sacred area, however, around the Altis, is attested in the poems of Pindar about Olympia, and has been uncovered by archaeologists. Here were housed pilgrims and visitors to the games.

The altar was of monumental size, over 20 ft. high with two levels. Victims slaughtered at the lower level were carried to the upper level to be burned. Equally enormous were the great temple of Zeus at Olympia and the statue of Zeus Olympius. Surrounding this central altar were numerous other altars dedicated to numerous other deities, including other altars of Zeus. So, at each individual altar, some unique aspect of Zeus was worshiped. At the altar of Zeus Herkeios, he was worshiped for his protection of homes (**herkeios** ἑρκεῖος means the wall around a house), while at the altar of Zeus Agoraios, he received sacrifice as overseer of the marketplace (agora ἀγορά). Based on dedications made by victors in war and the games, we can surmise that in his primary function at Olympia, that of Zeus Olympius, Zeus was honored for his power as king and for victory.

A celebration of the Olympic games would have taken place every four years in August or September. All wars, it was agreed, would cease in honor of the games. In 472 BCE, the format of the games took a definitive shape. The pentathlon and horse races came on day one. The following day saw the sacrifice of 100 bulls at the altar of Zeus Olympius, and a great feast that night. More athletic events followed over the next three days. Other events would have taken place at the same time as the games, given the vast numbers in attendance. For instance, the historian Herodotus first read his *Histories* at Olympia during the days of the festival in honor of Zeus.

What was true at Delphi, however, held true also at Olympia. Panhellenic games were circumscribed by the limits of polis religion. The sanctuary of Zeus at Olympia was controlled by the nearby city of Elis. The Eleans were the judges of the games, and they were the ones who determined who was able to participate in the games and in the sacrifices. When the Spartans did not act according to the desires of the Eleans in the midst of the Peloponnesian War, the Eleans banned Sparta from the temple, from the sacrifice and from the games for that year (Thucydides, *History of the Peloponnesian War* 5.50).

e. Women and the Thesmophoria. As in all aspects of Greek life, religious observance distinguished sharply between men and women. Women were considered more likely to be ritually impure, especially because of childbirth, and could be excluded from temples especially associated with masculine deities like Poseidon or Heracles. Even when included in many rituals, women were assigned different roles than men. Certain festivals, however, were confined exclusively to women, such as the *Thesmophoria*. The *Thesmophoria* was Panhellenic inasmuch as it was celebrated in numerous cities, but Panhellenic in this sense differs from what we have just seen in regard to Delphi and Olympia, where all Greeks go to one place and do the same thing. Applied to the *Thesmophoria*, Panhellenic implies variety, because the festival had different accents in different cities.

Aristophanes' fanciful comedy *Thesmophoriazusae* pretends to depict women at the festival, but cannot be taken seriously except in its emphasis on the secrecy of the festival's conduct. The festival was celebrated in honor of the goddess Demeter prior to sowing in the Fall. Demeter, of course, mourns the loss of her daughter Persephone (or, Kore), who was kidnapped by the god Hades. Due to an arrangement, Persephone can return to earth for a limited time each year, and these are the seasons in which Demeter is happy and the earth has temperate seasons. When Persephone returns to Hades, bad weather returns.

At ATHENS, each deme (civic subdivision) chose women to represent it at the festival, and the women would congregate first at the sanctuary of Demeter. This was near the Pnyx where the Athenian assembly met. The business of the assembly, however, was suspended during the *Thesmophoria*. The congregation of women in some sense mirrored the city's male governing assembly. Because Demeter and Persephone were especially prominent in Sicily's pantheon, the festival there lasted ten days, but in Athens it ended after three. The first day, the *Anodos* (ascent) included the ascent of the women just described as well as the slaughter of baby pigs, and their burial in pits. This evoked the mythical loss of Euboleus' swine when Kore was kidnapped. The second day, *Nesteia* (fasting) was a fast day evoking the sadness of Demeter at Kore's departure. On the third day, *Kalligenia*, the women honored the goddess of Good Birth with sacrifices and feasting. The festival is, thus, associated not only with the fertility of crops about to be planted but with the birth of future Athenian citizens.

4. Polis religion: Deities at Athens

Xerxes sacked Athens in 480 BCE, but Athena signified her continued protection of the city when her sacred olive tree, although burned, pushed forth a new shoot. Because the tree lived, Athena still protected the city (Herodotus, *Hist.* 8.55).

As Athena went, therefore, so went Athens. Although the Athenians were not alone in devotion to Athena, their devotion to her was unique. We understand Athenian worship of Athena Polias (of the city) by recognizing her relation to two other deities, the god Poseidon and the hero Erechtheius. When the gods chose which cities they would rule, Athena and Poseidon raced toward Athens. Athena arrived first, and demonstrated her claim by planting an olive tree. Poseidon, moments later, struck the earth with his trident and salt water flowed from ground, but too late to win the race. Athena was patron of Athens.

But the Athenians made room for Poseidon. The two deities were paired, for instance, at Cape Sunium. On the Acropolis a pool for Poseidon stood next to an olive tree of Athena. Athena and Poseidon are further connected in Athenian cult by another figure, the hero Erechtheius, who was born from the soil of Athens itself. Athena adopted him as her son, and he became the firstborn Athenian. Athenians placed great pride in their intimate connection, through Erechtheius, to the land of Attica, and attributed their strength and democratic life to their intimate connection with their territory. They could not themselves be the children of Athena, but were at least the children of Athena's son. When supporting opposing sides in a war, Poseidon slew Erechtheius, and to resolve the conflict Athena herself established a cult for Erechtheius and Poseidon together within her temple. Furthermore, Poseidon and Erechtheius shared a priest taken from the old, aristocratic Eteobutadae family, the same family that provided the priestess of Athena Polias.

Thus, the central cult of Athena Polias at Athens had a unique character shared nowhere else in Greece. Interestingly, devotion to Athena at Troezen also tells of her contest with Poseidon for reign over the land, and is even connected to the hero Sthenias. But, each story is unique and each city has its own myth of origins unconnected entirely to the literary portrayals of the gods in Homer.

5. Polis Religion: Sanctuaries and ritual at Athens

The original temple of Athena, burned by the Persians, was replaced in the middle of the 5th cent. by the temple we call the Erechtheion. The monumental altar of Athena Polias, the Erechtheion and the area around the sacred olive tree were the center of the cult of Athena Polias on the Acropolis. The entire Acropolis, of course, was a *temenos* dedicated to Athena Polias, and the other monuments on the Acropolis were subsidiary elements of the cult of Athena Polias. The enormous statues of Phidias—the bronze Athena Promachos that could be seen from the port of Piraeus, and the renowned Athena Parthenos within the Parthenon— were not the centers of cult activities, nor even was the unparalleled Parthenon itself. Indeed, the epithet Parthenos "Virgin," was subsumed under the title Polias. Athena Parthenos had no altar or priesthood. Another statue, however, far less imposing than Promachos and Parthenos statues, was critical for Athenian religion.

This statue played a key part in the Panathenaic procession celebrated each year on the 28th of the month Hekatombaeon, the birthday of Athena. Celebrations spanned the days before after the 28th, but the main events were the sacrifices made to Athena on her monumental altar, and the gift to Athena of a new *peplos*, a sacred robe placed on the statue of Athena Polias inside the Erechtheion. Life-sized and made of olive wood, its workmanship was so unusual that it was assumed that it had fallen from the sky. The *peplos* was decorated with the scenes of the battle between the gods and the giants that led to the kingship of Zeus, and was presented to Athena Polias at the end of the huge procession that culminated on the Acropolis.

The procession began at dawn at the main gate of Athens, and, led by the priestess of Athena and priest of Poseidon-Erechtheius, wound its way through the city to the Acropolis. Behind the priestess and priest and the other religious attendants would follow civic dignitaries, indicating the centrality of the cult in the life of the city. The political dimension of the procession expressed itself in other activities as well. For, not only Athenians participated in the procession. Athens used the festival and procession to express the status of its allies, vassals and resident aliens. Representatives of other cities supplied a cow and panoply of armor. Even more interesting, the daughters of resident aliens (metics) carried parasols and stools for the daughters of Athenians. These parasol-bearers are often thought to express the openness of Athenians toward outsiders, but another explanation is more likely. The parasol is a symbol of elite status in Classical Athens, as is the luxury of having a servant to carry one. Having the daughters of metics carry parasols for the daughters of citizens transmits this social elitism to the civic realm. In Classical Athens, even the poorest citizens were still superior to foreigners. The inferiority of metics is on parade at the central religious festival of the city, reinforcing the city's social hierarchy, as well as the relationship of Athens to its allies and vassals. In every respect, therefore, Athena and Athens are completely intertwined.

Emphasizing the unity of politics and religion introduces a corrective note as well. The survey of religion in this essay has presented a largely static portrait of religion in Classical Athens. But these were times of change no less than any other time. In the events leading to Athenian democracy, the tyrant Hipparchus was assassinated while leading the Panathenaic procession. Control over the festival passed to a democratic body after his death. Further, as the government in Athens transitions from aristocratic to democratic models, more inclusive priesthoods appear next to those controlled by old aristocratic families. Religion, then, changes with the changing political life of the city.

There were also changes in the deities worshiped at Athens and elsewhere. Innovations were common, either as modifications of existing cults or the addition of new cults. For instance, as early as the mid-6th cent. there had been an altar for Athena Nike on the Acropolis. Only in the middle of the 5th cent., however, was a temple added to it, together with a priestess. Likewise, although hero cults were often confined to the tomb of the hero, one city could try to suborn the hero of another city. Thus, before Athens went to war with Aegina (ca. 505) the Athenians built a shrine to Aegina's hero Aeacus in order to steal his favor from the Aeginetans. Changes in the pantheon and the changing tide of politics bring us finally to the Hellenistic and Roman periods, which will occupy the remainder of this essay.

B. Greek Religion: The Hellenistic Period (323–31 BCE) and the Coming of Rome

What historians call the Hellenistic era begins when ALEXANDER THE GREAT dies in 323 BCE, after having conquered an empire from Greece to India (*see* HELLENISM). At his death, this Empire was divided among his successors into various kingdoms. The successors of Alexander's successors continued to rule these kingdoms until the coming of Rome. Indeed, the Hellenistic period closes with the victory in 31 BCE of Octavian (soon to be Augustus Caesar) over his fellow Roman Mark Antony and Antony's ally, Cleopatra, the last successor of the Greek Ptolemaic dynasty in Egypt.

The Greek world changed dramatically under Alexander's successors. The hundreds of independent city-states from the Classical period were reorganized and unified under the rule of a few kings. Furthermore, the Greek world now spread far beyond its historic homeland well into Asia and North Africa. More than ever before, Greeks were influenced by and influencing their neighbors. These political and social changes were accompanied by changes in religion, and standard narratives about Hellenistic religion once assumed that religion in this period differed radically from Classical religion. Scholars also viewed this change as decline from the Classical ideal. Eastern cults muddied the pure Greek stream of the Classical period. Or, changes

were seen as preparation for Christianity, with the demise of traditional polytheism in favor of a devotion to individual deities like the Egyptian Isis. Whether scholars applauded or lamented the change, however, the overriding assumption was that the change was nearly total.

Recent scholars no longer hold this view, or else hold it in a less absolute way. Change there was, to be sure, but not everything changed, and not everything that changed did so as drastically as once thought. As stated in the first lines of this article, the Classical period was covered at some length in order to assess properly what did and what did not change in the Hellenistic period. For, long after the Classical period, the Greeks continued to punctuate the year with religious observances and feasts, and they continued to consult the oracle at Delphi. They also continued to celebrate the Panhellenic games in honor of the gods. But in these very signs of continuity, we also see change. For, although the Greeks continued to celebrate Panhellenic games, and these games continued to be open only to the Greeks, the boundaries of Greekness had expanded. In about 200 BCE, a man from Sidon was able to enter the Nemean games because the town of Sidon appeared in Greek mythology. From the 2nd cent. BCE onward, even the Romans could claim Greek ancestry through connections in mythology. But Greek religion had always changed, a fact noted above. There was nothing new, therefore, about the mere fact of change in the Hellenistic period. Furthermore, from before the Classical period, Greek religion was infused with Eastern elements (see section 2.b., above).

When discussing the evolution of Greek religion in this period, therefore, a helpful phrase is "selective continuity." We focused above on the formative aspect that the polis had on Greek religion. Even Panhellenic religion was mediated through the machinery of polis religion. This continues to be the case, but in a selective way. Whether or not one experienced such changes is a function partly of geography, partly of socio-political standing. We will first explore degrees of change in light of geography.

1. The geography of continuity and change

a. Athens. If someone had gone to sleep in Athens in the 5th cent., and awoken in the 2nd cent. BCE, the religious life of the city would have changed little. The annual celebrations processions and festivals would have remained largely the same. New heroes were added, such as Attalus I, who had saved the city from the attacks of Philip V, and earned for it hero status. But the general religious structure was largely the same.

In addition to signs of continuity, however, some features of Hellenistic religion would have been surprising, such as the appearance of personal portrait statues on the Acropolis and at other shrines. In the Classical period, one demonstrated munificence or gratitude by erecting statues of deities. In the Hellenistic period, it became more and more popular to signal one's gratitude by erecting a statue of one's own likeness. Perhaps even more shocking would have been the ruler-cults for Hellenistic monarchs. This, and a few other signs of the time, will be dealt with more below. For Athens, therefore, and for much of mainland Greece, the signs of continuity were more prominent than the signs of change.

b. Delos. Not all Greeks remained at home, however. On the island of DELOS we find the interaction of travelers and immigrants from all over the Mediterranean, and we see as well the intersection of several pantheons, not only the traditional Greek gods of the island, but also the Egyptian deities Isis, Anubis, Harpocrates and others. More important, for our purposes, is the manner in which this mingling of deities is matched by a mingling of worshipers. People of a great many cities worshiped together in the various sanctuaries of Delos regardless of the fact that some were Athenian expatriates, some Greeks from elsewhere, some were Romans, and others were even slaves. The requirements of the Classical polis that generally barred slaves (as non-citizens) from public cult, and separated foreigners from locals do not seem to hold so tightly on Delos. Furthermore, when Athenians who had lived for a time on Delos, and had served even as priests in the island's various shrines, returned to Athens, they did not bring their Delian worship with them, but resumed participation in Athenian religious life. The dominant role of the polis, then, on a person's public religious life has dimmed somewhat.

2. Mystery cults

We can also speak of change apart from the cult life of specific cities. For, we see in the Hellenistic period the rapid rise of universalist cults, into which people can enter regardless of ethnicity or citizenship. Especially popular were those forms of religiosity we commonly call MYSTERY RELIGIONS. The category is problematic for various reasons. First is the assumption that mystery cults develop only during the Hellenistic or Roman periods, and their irrational, ecstatic experience of the divine was a salve for the soul in an uncertain world no longer stabilized by **polis** structures. But mystery cults like that of Dionysus and Demeter flourished in Greece before the Hellenistic age. Second is the related assumption that mystery religions are eastern. This, again, ignores the cults of Dionysus and Demeter, which appear actually to have been the models for the cults of figures like Isis when they entered the Greek world. The third error attempts to explain mystery cults in relation to Christianity, wherein personal salvation takes the place of other pagan religious concerns. The mysteries are viewed as attempts to leave behind typical religion and to "convert" to mystery cults in the way that one would convert to Christianity, thereby

rejecting all other religious observance. This is not generally the case at all, and initiation into a mystery cult was simply a supplement to standard religious observances, not a replacement. More important, any supposed emphasis on life after death in the mystery cults is a mistake. Like other religious observance surveyed above, mysteries secured the special favor of a deity in this life. Even blessings promised after death were not immortality in the Christian sense.

The Greek term mystērion (μυστήριον), the basis of the English "mystery," implies secrecy, though not every cult required the secrecy of its members. What the mystery involved was the initiation of a person into a special, more intimate relationship with that deity. To discover how different cults functioned, and to allow for variety, we will survey three mysteries, even though the rites were often secret and our knowledge is often imperfect. Also, for the sake of space, some cults, like the popular devotion to Mater Magna (Cybele) have been left out. General works in the bibliography provide further reading.

a. Demeter at Eleusis. The cult of Demeter at Eleusis could be covered in Classical religion, or earlier, and likewise, could have fit neatly into this essay's sections on either Panhellenic or *polis* religion. The Eleusinian mysteries were a major festival in the religious calendar of the city of Athens, but they were open to non-Athenians as well, both men and women, and even slaves. As with Panhellenic rites at Delphi and Olympia, however, local Athenian officials oversaw the mysteries, and the festival that initiated the mysteries at Eleusis began with a procession in Athens.

The *Hymn to Demeter* from the 7th cent. BCE describes the origin of the cult at Eleusis, based on the myth of Demeter and Persephone, called Kore in the Eleusinian cult (see above, Women and the Thesmophoria). Demeter mourned the initial loss of her daughter within her sanctuary at Eleusis. When she was reunited with her daughter, she assembled the Eleusinian leaders and described to them mysteries not to be violated, which promised bliss in this life and hereafter. This promise of eternal blessings, however, was not a promise of immortality as such, but merely a softening of the conditions that all shared in Hades.

We do not know, however, exactly what happened when one received this special knowledge on initiation. The mysteries were to be kept secret, and they were so kept under penalty of death. The tragedian Aeschylus ran into trouble, for instance, when he inadvertently alluded to the mysteries in a play.

Initiates performed sacrifices and purified themselves and then, individually, were led into a dark room lit by torches and shown the sacred objects of Demeter. Christian writers say that the initiated were shown a stalk of grain. If accurate, this implies a connection to Demeter's concern for agriculture, but the precise significance is unclear. Since men and women alike were initiated into the cult, a strict connection between Demeter and fertility is unlikely.

The mysteries of Demeter at Eleusis were not late, therefore, were not developed in the East, nor did participation in them imply a rejection of traditional civic religion. Indeed, initiation into the mysteries of Demeter was a standard festival each year on the Athenian public calendar.

b. Dionysus. The mysteries of DIONYSUS also developed very early. Unlike the mysteries of Demeter, however, the mysteries of Dionysus were not tied to one city, nor did they occur at a standard time on a particular calendar. This variety in time and place accompanies the variety in forms that Dionysiac mysteries would assume. By and large, they involve a lapse in reason. This is in accord with the fact that Dionysus has a peculiar standing even when included in standard religious observance apart from his mysteries. Not only is he the god of wine, but he is never the principal deity of a city. His shrines were often outside of a civic center, indicating his outsider status. Even in Athens, where a shrine to Dionysus sat on the side of the Acropolis, the statue of Dionysus housed there was said to have been brought from outside the city. So he is to be contrasted, for instance, with Zeus Polieus or Athena Polias. Their shrines are centrally located. Dionysus is on the fringe.

A story in Herodotus describes the mania associated with devotion to the cult of Dionysus (Herodotus, *Histories* 4.78-80). When the Scythian King Scylas is initiated into the mysteries of Dionysus, a Greek mocks the Scythians. Whereas the Scythians had previously reviled the Greeks for being possessed by the spirit of Dionysus in rites dedicated to the god, now their King was so possessed. When the Scythians see the spectacle of their King caught up in a Dionysiac frenzy, they drive him from power and eventually kill him. A powerful expression of the heights of madness to which Dionysus can drive his worshipers is reflected in Euripides' *Bacchae*. When Demosthenes portrays his opponent Aeschines in an unfavorable light in his speech *On the Crown* (18.259-60), he describes how Aeschines participated in ecstatic rites that involved garlanded people brandishing snakes through the streets and shouting chants. Thus, the rites were thoroughly Greek and preceded the Hellenistic era by all accounts, but there was some ambivalence about the utterly irrational possession by the god that the rites induced.

Dionysus received great dignity even in pre-Classical times in works that revised the standard theogonies like Hesiod's *Theogony*. In the Derveni Papyrus, assumed to be from the 4th cent. BCE, a succession of chief deities rules the heavens in the manner of Hesiod's Succession Myth. The Derveni Papyrus is fragmentary, and the fragment ends at the point when Zeus fathers Persephone. Interestingly the same succession pattern continues in a poem from late in the Hellenistic period called the *Rhapsodies*. This work continues to circu-

late until the 6th cent. CE, and in it, after Zeus fathers Persephone, he mates with her and she gives birth to Dionysus who becomes the chief of all deities. In some traditions in the Roman period, Dionysus embodies all the deities and is a universal and omnipresent god.

c. Isis. ISIS was worshiped in Greece first among Egyptians who had moved to Greek cities. In Athens, for instance, we know from an inscription in 333 BCE, when Alexander was only beginning his conquest of Persia, that Egyptians were permitted a temple to Isis. In the 5th cent. Herodotus referred to Isis as the basis for the mysteries of Demeter at Eleusis (2.58-9). The association is an obvious one, given the Greek habit of seeing a unity underlying all deities in all places, and especially because in Egyptian religion, the functions of Isis overlapped with those of Demeter.

The Egyptian version of her myth opens with the murder of Osiris, the brother and husband of Isis, by Set. Through her ritualized grief, she revives Osiris, and then bears a son with him, Horus, who then turns on Isis and beheads her. Undeterred, she cuts off his hands (*see* EGYPT).

In the Egyptian New Kingdom she is assigned various functions. She protects the coffins of the dead. She protects women in giving birth. She is the goddess who ensures that each year the Nile floods, fertilizing the earth. She is, thus, also goddess of the harvest. This latter duty is a particular connection with Greek Demeter. In Greek stories about Isis, Osiris was replaced by Sarapis, under the influence of the Ptolematic kings. They had founded this cult and had made it a central feature of their kingdom. For a Greek description of Egyptian traditions about Isis, see Plutarch's *Isis and Osiris*.

The passage of Isis into the Greek world turns Herodotus' claim on its head in at least one sense. Isis did not provide a model for the cult of Demeter. Rather, when Isis entered the Greek world, she was given mysteries, rites of initiation, on the model of Demeter's cult at Eleusis. A prominent expression of the popularity and allure of these rites is depicted in the novel by Apuleius, *The Golden Ass*. The degree to which the novel is a religious tract is unclear, but many read it thus. The character Lucius becomes overly interested in magic, and is turned into an ass. Only through the inspiration of Isis does he return to being a man. He is then initiated into the cult of Isis, thus overcoming his brutish character through the inspiration of Isis. Lucius lives the rest of his life devoted to Isis. By the close the Hellenistic period, the cult of Isis is omnipresent throughout the Greco-Roman world.

People, thus, turn more and more to deities that bring them personal benefit, and not necessarily benefit for the whole city. Likewise, these deities are open to anyone, regardless of citizenship. On the other hand, this does not imply the total abandonment of civic cults, at least not in any wholesale fashion. Prominent people still adorn their cities with festivals in honor of the city's deities as they always had done. Given the connection between the city's powerful members and the city's religious life, perhaps the mysteries are especially attractive to those excluded from positions of power and, thus, cults: the urban poor, non-citizens and women. Seen this way, the mysteries are not a new, more spiritual religion, as opposed to Classical polis religion. They participate in, or complement, polis religion, both in the Classical and later periods. Over time, mysteries do come to sever cult life from a single city, and reflect the renegotiation of the relationship between religious involvement and socio-political standing within a city. Here, the phrase "selective continuity" has significance again, where we see continuity in religious expression among the elite from the Classical to the Hellenistic period inasmuch as they continue to oversee civic cult. The mysteries do not replace the civic cults, but function in addition to civic cult, and perhaps provide options for those whose socio-economic position does not provide full participation at major civic festivals (Shipley 2000, 175–76).

3. Associations

In the Hellenistic and Roman periods, we also see the spread of private associations dedicated to a particular deity, a phenomenon not unheard of in the Classical period but appearing with increasing frequency in the later periods. The chief function of the associations was the sacrificial feast and meal that accompanied the regular celebration of whomever received the association's adoration. The organization of this meeting, as well as monthly or more frequent gatherings, required the appointment of officers and various functionaries. This is one reason why these groups are important for the study of early Christianity and Judaism, because even in non-Jewish sources an association can be labeled a συναγωγή synagōgē (*see* SYNAGOGUE). In such associations in Egypt, some offices are defined as "the elders," presbyteroi (πρεσβύτεροι from πρεσβύτερος presbyteros) Extremely rarely, the associations refer to themselves as an ekklēsia (ἐκκλησία "church, congregation, assembly").

The growth and spread of these associations is often linked to the decline in polis religion in a manner reminiscent of arguments about mystery cults. As was said in regard to the mysteries, however, civic cults remained active. It is better to see in these private associations, as with the mysteries, something in addition to civic religion.

4. Ruler cult

Civic cults in earlier centuries had centered on the welfare of the city. Honor was given to deities to thank them for past protection and to ensure future protection. In the Hellenistic period, when the welfare of the city depended on the warring and heavily armed Hellenistic monarchs, it was not surprising for cities

to grant divine honors to their kings. Cities regularly established a cult with an altar, temple and priesthood for their king. In earlier times, certain human beings attained hero status, the midpoint between humanity and divinity, after death. Now, divine honors were given to living human beings, a practice that modern scholars have labeled "ruler cult."

The practice had sparse precedent in the pre-Hellenistic period. With the Spartan victory in the Peloponnesian War, for instance, the Spartan King Lysander received divine honors. The institution only took its definitive shape, however, when Alexander was apparently addressed in 331 BCE by the Egyptian priest of Ammon at Siwa as the son of Ammon-Ra. This experience probably led Alexander in 324 to order Greek cities to perform cultic activities toward him.

The precise significance of the procedure has been disputed. To some, ruler cult signals the devaluation of traditional religion. Since the gods matter so little, the argument goes, the Greeks offered their kings divine honors. It has been shown above variously, however, that theories about the devaluation of the gods rest on tenuous evidence. It is best to see in the practice the resolution of a tension on the part of cities that had always been fiercely independent but now must reconcile themselves to outside control. The traditions of the polis had no place for a king, and needed to accommodate their life to the presence of a being on whom they depended for ultimate survival. This was the role of the gods, and so into the ranks of the gods the kings were enrolled. As cities passed back and forth in the struggles between kings to the polis would discontinue the cult of the old king in favor of the new.

5. The coming of Rome

As the Romans extended their control over the Mediterranean in the 3rd cent. BCE, they slowly gained greater and greater control over mainland Greece and, eventually, much of the empire of Alexander's successors. Control over Greek cults passes, therefore, into the hands of Roman governors. No effort was made to apply Roman religious law outside of Italy, but attention was paid to the proper maintenance of shrines and money in the service of religion. Greek cities also establish cults for powerful Romans.

In spite of certain similarities, we should not assume that Greek and Roman religion are identical. The Romans themselves speak of "Greek rites" indicating differences in conducting sacrifices. Romans also occasionally suppress Greek cults like those of Dionysus for causing public disturbance.

Even in the Roman period, however, we see patterns of strong continuity in Greek religion. When Pausanias (ca. 150 CE) describes in his *Descriptions of Greece* travels throughout the Greek world, he mentions the past life of the places that he visits, but also describes a living, vibrant religious life, with local cult myths and local festivals continuing to be told and celebrated. Greek religious life continued, therefore, well into the 4th–6th cent. CE when the combination in Constantinople of Roman authority and Christian belief led to the discontinuation of pagan cults, most especially at Olympia and Delphi.

C. Greek Philosophy

1. Religion and Philosophy: From mythos to logos?

This essay treats religion and philosophy separately, but the two are closely related in both ancient sources and modern scholarship. In modern scholarship, a persistent assumption has held that Greek civilization in the 6th to 4th cent. transitioned to a greater or lesser degree from mythological to rationalistic explanations of reality, from myth to reason, (in Greek terms, from mythos μῦθος to logos λόγος). This assumption has been labeled the "from . . . to . . ." thesis, and it applies to more than religion, embracing history, philosophy, medicine and several sciences. Herodotus (or Thucydides) undertook the first rational history, while Hippocrates introduced into magical medicine an empirical, scientific quality.

This thesis is today challenged by many Hellenists. Although there were clearly rejections of the mythical worldview, these did not apply to all social classes. Furthermore, were rationalizing trends in philosophy always opposed to mythology? As late as the 200s BCE, well into the supposed era of rationality, Apollonius' *Argonautica* seamlessly unites magical stories from mythology and the atomic theories of the Presocratic Democritus. When Medea saves the Argonauts from Talos the giant by bewitching him with her eyes, Apollonius' description of the Evil Eye relies on Democritus' opinions about material effluences from objects that resemble the objects from which they come. Thus, Democritus' rational science stands alongside the mythical story of Medea. Likewise, we see the very philosophical Demetrius of Phalerum creating liturgies for the god Sarapis. The picture is, thus, more complicated than the "from . . . to . . ." thesis allows. These insights apply generally to the philosophers covered in the following pages. For, the philosophical schools surveyed below (Cynics, Stoics, Epicureans and Sceptics) all critique traditional religion in one way or another, so that historians have understood the Hellenistic age as a time of creeping atheism. The preceding discussion of religion indicated the vibrancy of religious life throughout the Hellenistic period, however. The opinions of each school on religion do deserve attention, but they are best addressed individually. Each school's religious teaching makes most sense within a distinctive system.

2. School philosophy

The word "school" has appeared several times in the previous paragraph. What is a school of philosophy in this era? Nineteenth century scholars sought to trace parallels with modern universities, but this effort is anachronistic and discredited. It is easier to say what schools are not, but harder to say what they are, especially because each school changed over time in both teaching and structure. And a movement like Cynicism qualifies as a school according to no one's definition. Even the functioning of the more institutional schools is unclear. Plato's Academy, so named because Plato met students outside Athens near the shrine of the hero Hekademos, survived its founder's death (see PLATO, PLATONISM). Plato was succeeded by Speusippus, who was in turn succeeded by Xenocrates, and so on until 88 BCE, when Athens was sacked. Succession was often marred by secession, though, at the Academy and elsewhere. Aristotle, Plato's most famous student, might have headed the Academy if he had not founded his own school, the Lyceum, named for the shrine of Apollo Lykeion near where it met (also called the Peripatos, The Walk, from a nearby gathering place). Around 300 BCE, Zeno of Citium founded yet another Athenian school. Because he taught in the Stoa Poikilê ("Frescoed Stoa") his followers were the Stoics. Epicurus founded a group of followers in Athens which at gathering place called the Garden either in 305/4 or 307/6. Like Plato's Academy, each of these schools also had a history of stability and disruption, as when Aristo of Chios left the Stoa and joined the Garden.

It is very difficult to know the form of instruction and structure of each "school." One suspects that each was unique, but how much so is difficult to say. We have only the doctrines with little description of teaching methods, and cannot infer from doctrines how those doctrines were taught, though some have tried. What it meant to be a school, at least to the ancients themselves, is suggested by various works entitled *On Sects* (*Peri Haireseōn*). None of these works survives completely, but fragments and comments of earlier works are preserved in authors like Diogenes Laertius and Sextus Empiricus. These works dealt with the doctrines of important philosophical and medical schools or **haireseis**. The word **hairesis** (αἵρεσις) has less the sense of the English "heresy," and more the sense of "sect" or "school of thought" in this context. Two features marked a legitimate **hairesis** to Sextus Empiricus (*Pyr.* 1.16-17). First, the group must adhere to various beliefs, and explain how the various beliefs are mutually supportive of, and related to, one another. Or, second, a school is a group that bases the appearance of living correctly on a philosophical principle.

This latter point deserves attention because Hellenistic philosophy emphasizes questions of ethics, and of how to live life a certain way. Plato was not unconcerned with ethics, but his heirs in the Academy were more exclusively concerned with ethics. Other schools reflect the same trend. Some see this philosophical posture as an emotional salve for the anxiety-ridden Hellenistic era, when the polis no longer provided a stable basis for life. But, other eras were perhaps even more anxious than the Hellenistic one. The practical bent in Hellenistic philosophy may derive from the growing association of philosophers with kings and leaders, whose questions and concerns are better resolved with practical answers than with philosophical abstractions. Furthermore, these philosophical trends do not arise from nothing, and it is perhaps best to begin this survey by noting earlier influences on the character of Hellenistic philosophy.

3. The Socratic tradition in ethics

Scholars often connect Hellenistic ethics to ARISTO-TLE, and it is true that later thinkers followed Aristotle in many ways, especially in making the goal of life (telos τέλος) the center of ethical theory. This survey, however, will follow a different path, the Socratic tradition in ethics. One of Socrates' chief concerns is to center philosophy in the pursuit of rational bases for personal happiness (eudaimonia εὐδαιμονία). Aristotle follows him in this, and subordinates even the broadest scientific study to this end. But, in the realm of ethics, we see differences between the Socratic tradition and the tradition represented by Aristotle. Aristotle's ethics, after all, derive many of their values and principles from the behavioral norms and prejudices of the Athenian social and political elite. Socrates is different. He scorned the conventional aspirations for wealth and power that concerned the leaders of Athens, and sought happiness instead in the freedom from such cares and personal autonomy. This same renunciation of conventional goods characterizes the Cynics, Stoics, and Epicureans. Although Cynic and Stoic writers intentionally trace their origins to Socrates, and some Epicureans actively oppose Socrates, they are all united by their attention in ethics to a life that transcends conventional behavior. Other points of contrast and comparison will also arise, but noting this disposition introduces nicely the following discussion. The Cynics, as an extreme example of non-conventional living, offer an appropriate place to begin.

4. The Cynics

Ancient writers established perhaps dubious lines of succession to trace philosophical influence. Diogenes Laertius (1.13-20) breaks the world of philosophy into two broad streams, an Ionian that begins with Thales, and an Italian that includes Pythagoras and Parmenides. The Ionian school eventually arrives at Socrates. The Cynics, an extension of this Ionian school, trace their succession to Socrates through Antisthenes (444–365 BCE) and Diogenes (d. 323 BCE—no relation to Diogenes Laertius).

It is hard to know whether Diogenes or Antisthenes was first called Cynic, but the paradigmatic Cynic for the later tradition is Diogenes. The term "Cynic"

(Kynikos Κυνικός) derives from the Greek word for dog and means literally "Canine". Antisthenes was perhaps so named because he taught at the gymnasium named Kynosarges (Ἰ Κυνόσαργες, "White Dog"?). Or, and perhaps more plausibly, the Cynics took their name from their particular philosophy. What philosophy, then, inspired people to call them canine?

a. Cynicism: A Philosophical school? Answering this requires one first to recognize that the title "philosophers" was regularly denied to the Cynics (see CYNICS, CYNICISM). Discussing the work On Sects by Hippobotus, Diogenes Laertius notes Hippobotus' exclusion of the Cynics from the ranks of philosophical sects (1.19). This exclusion is not surprising, given the definition of a school or sect from Sextus Empiricus above. The Cynics proposed no positive doctrines and so could not be classed among the philosophical schools. And that is precisely what the Cynics wanted—to avoid conventional philosophy. The character of this un-philosophical philosophy can be surveyed under three headings.

b. Defacing the currency. The Cynics lived the by the motto "Deface the Current Coin," which refers to the event that initiated Diogenes' philosophical career. The story explaining how Diogenes and/or his father adulterated or defaced coins of Sinope has several versions (Diogenes Laertius, Vit. phil. 6.20-21). Whatever the case, it appears that he had to go into exile from Sinope, and then began to live in a way that ignored social custom and public norms. As he watched a mouse go about its daily life, Diogenes "discovered the means of adapting himself to circumstances . . . He used any place for any purpose, for breakfasting, sleeping or conversing" (Diogenes Laertius, Vit. phil. 6.22). He thus rejected all polite or typical behavior, and lived, like a mouse—or, better, a dog—according to nature. Connected as it is with the origin of Diogenes' philosophical life, the story about chiseling the face off of coinage resonated through Cynic traditions. Cynics saw it as their goal to chisel away, as one would the impression on a coin, all social customs about where to eat, where to sleep, where, even, to relieve oneself, and hence, to live like a dog. The goal is not, however, to reduce human beings to the level of beasts. Rather, Diogenes insists that one must live according to reason (Diogenes Laertius, Vit. phil. 6.24). The typical conventions of urban society are what is unreasonable and irrational. Animals are only a model to the degree that they live according to nature and have no choice to do otherwise. Human beings must train themselves to live according to nature and reason.

c. Emphasis on Ethics. The Cynics also reject conventional philosophy, especially such abstract argument as ancients and moderns associate with philosophy. Several conversations, likely fictional, between DIO-GENES and Plato reflect the Cynics' view. Diogenes Laertius writes (Vit. phil. 6.40):

"Plato had defined man as an animal, biped and featherless, and was applauded. Diogenes plucked a fowl and brought it into the lecture-room with the words, 'Here is Plato's man.'"

Diogenes calls Plato's lectures a complete waste of time (*Vit. phil.* 6.24) and mocks Plato in other ways as well, mostly for having valuable things or expensive tastes (*Vit. phil.* 6.26). It is no wonder, then, that Plato is said to have called Diogenes "A Socrates gone mad" (*Vit. phil.* 6.54). If he is mad, however, there is method to Diogenes' madness, as his twin criticisms of Plato demonstrate. Diogenes had no time for lectures on philosophy. He pursued a wisdom (sophia σοφία) that issued forth in a life lived a certain way. To Diogenes, Plato talked, but did not live, according to this form of wisdom.

These conversations also reflect Cynic aggressiveness. In order to provoke people to live their lives more philosophically, Diogenes regularly insulted them. "He was great at pouring scorn on his contemporaries" (Diogenes Laertius 6.24), the goal of which was to rouse people to recognize the degree to which they had departed from natural living. A particular tool in this arsenal is boldness, frankness of speech. The Cynic prized above all freedom (6.69, 71), and especially freedom to say whatever was necessary.

d. Self-discipline. One achieved this freedom only through ascetical exercise (askēsis ἄσκησις). The goal of the Cynic was to accommodate oneself to whatever life brought, whether exile, hunger or poverty. Any of life's privations or struggles the Cynic was prepared to meet without fear. When one is prepared for hunger, the lack of food does not disturb one's serenity. When one is prepared to sleep on the ground, the lack of a house does not disturb one's serenity. The askēsis of the Cynic was the so-called shortcut to this virtue (Diogenes Laertius, *Vit. phil.* 7.122). By accepting to live with a rough cloak, a bag and a stick, like a beggar, the Cynic has total independence from social norms. And this self-mastery, defined by freedom from others and self-control over one's desires, is more powerful than political mastery. Whether it is true that Diogenes had several encounters with ALEXANDER THE GREAT, his reported conversations with Alexander reflect the power of self-mastery. Alexander approached a reclining Diogenes and offered whatever Diogenes requested. Diogenes asked Alexander only to stop blocking the sun (*Vit. phil.* 6.38). The Cynic is the only true ruler because he rules himself.

The principles outlined here all motivated Diogenes to reject conventional religion as much as any other aspect of conventional life. Although it is a mistake to call him an atheist, since he regularly refers to the gods, it is also true that he has no interest in conventional religion. A passage from Tertullian is telling (*Nat.*, 2.2). When asked about heaven, Diogenes refuses to say anything about the matter. Why? Because he has never been to heaven. Thus, Diogenes has rid himself of concern for the gods because he cannot know anything about them. What passes as religion and devotion to the gods, in his mind, is really superstition that impedes the self-sufficiency, freedom and detachment that he pursues.

e. Roman cynicism and the ideal cynic. The characters and character of Cynicism in the Roman period are usually not described by Cynics themselves. Lucian mocks Peregrinus (*On the Death of Peregrinus*) and lauds Demonax (*The Life of Demonax*) as two people living the Cynic life. The Stoics Seneca and Epictetus write on Cynicism in such a way that they reconcile it with Stoicism. Their motivation in doing so will become clear below in the discussion of Stoicism. The two valuable sources of information on Cynicism by Cynics are the work *Charlatans Unmasked* by Oenomaus of Gadara (2nd cent. CE) and the fictitious *Cynic Epistles*, which were composed anywhere between the 3rd cent. BCE to the 2nd cent. CE. Even the Epistles, however, seem to reflect a taming of Cynicism in order to make it an acceptable way of life, not entirely unlike the work of Epictetus.

f. Cynics and the New Testament. Scholars discern Cynic elements in the ministries of Jesus and Paul. Paul's language in 1 Thess 2 recalls Dio Chrysostom's Discourses 4 and 32 about Cynics who show boldness (parrēsia παρρησία), do not flatter nor seek glory, and who adaptively move from harshness to the gentleness of a nurse to ensure receptivity to their teaching. Historical Jesus research debates connections in both the itinerant preaching style of Jesus and the content especially of the Q Source (*see* Q, QUELLE), as when Jesus in Luke 6:27-30 urges the disciples to love their enemies, turn the other cheek and give freely to beggars, each of which has parallels in the Cynics. Such hypotheses, however, are often wedded to the pursuit of a non-eschatological Jesus.

5. The Stoics

Stoics differ dramatically from Cynics, but in ways that evoke Cynicism. Although they reject Cynic rudeness and filthiness, the Stoics cannot dispense altogether with the Cynics. Zeno's lineage to Socrates runs through Diogenes and Antisthenes in the progression: SOCRATES–Antisthenes–Diogenes–Crates–ZENO.

Stoics also follow Cynics in pursuing a life lived according to nature, physis (φύσις). Unlike the Cynics, however, this turn to nature is not cast in the negative terms of rejection nor is it oriented only around ethics. The Stoics define their ethical devotion to nature within a broader systematic account of reality. Several similes express the relationship of ethics to physics and logic, such as that philosophy is an animal in which logic is the bones, ethics the flesh and physics the soul. (Diogenes Laertius, *Vit. phil.* 7.40) Whatever the precise meaning of such similes, they make it clear that ethics are wedded to logic and physics in a systematic and inherent fashion. The following paragraphs will give an account of this system to prepare for discussing Stoic ethics, as well as to establish points of comparison and contrast with Epicureanism (see STOICS, STOICISM).

a. Physics: Nature and corporeal reality: everything that exists, exists bodily. What the Stoics mean by nature (physis φύσις) includes far more than any modern conception of that English word. Nature is that power that shapes everything, unifying and giving coherence to the world.

To see how this works, we must recognize that Stoics distinguish between things that "exist" (einai [εἶναι] from eimi [εἰμί]) and things that "subsist" (hyphistasthai [ὑφίστασθαι], from hyphistēmi [ὑφίστημι]). Both of them fall under the general category of being "something" (ti τί), but they differ in a key respect. Things that only "subsist" are things that can be spoken of (lekton λεκτόν), like a centaur, but which do not have any independent existence. The centaur, for instance, has no existence beyond a person's mental image of a centaur. Also under the category of subsistence are such things as time, place and the void. That such a thing as void does not exist for the Stoics will be important below with the Epicureans. It also helps to explain the difference between subsisting and existing. For, in order to exist, something must be corporeal, which means that it must have length, breadth and depth and offer resistance. Since the chief quality of existence is the ability to act upon something, or to be acted upon, and only bodies can so act or be acted upon, it follows that only bodies exist. Void does not exist.

This is a radical move because it leads the Stoics to argue that god exists as a body. Moreover, god is immanent throughout all creation in this form. For, if god is to affect the world, and only bodies can affect other bodies, then god must be in bodily form. God interpenetrates all matter and ". . . extends to every part of it, just as soul does with respect to us" (Diogenes Laertius, *Vit. phil.* 7.138). This assumption presents problems, for it seems to suggest that god, a body, is present within matter, another body, such that two bodies occupy the same space at the same time. How the Stoics address this issue can be explained after one further matter is clarified.

Two basic principles underlie all existence one of them an active principle and one a passive principle. God is associated with the divine reason (logos λόγος) or the "artistic fire" (pyr technikon πῦρ τεχνικόν) which orders the universe. The passive principle, matter, is ethically neutral, and waiting to be acted upon. The Stoics also express this relationship between active and passive principles in the language of the four basic elements of earth, water, air and fire. Fire and air are active principles, which together form "breath" (pneuma πνεῦμα). Pneuma gives coherence to earth

and water. Pneuma is the active principle that enables earth and water, the passive principle, to cohere and to be what they are. Every individual thing that exists, then, is a compound of **pneuma** and matter. One can speak of **pneuma** as the vehicle of the **logos** since **pneuma** is that entity that makes raw matter into the various elements of the cosmos. **Pneuma** is present throughout the whole cosmos and provides a divine order to reality. This function of **pneuma** in the entire cosmos is its same function within every individual entity. As different proportions of **pneuma** are blended with matter, what issues forth is either an animal's soul or a blade of grass or a rock.

What, then, of the problem noted above? If **pneuma** exists as a body, and the matter that it animates exists in the same way, how do the Stoics escape the charge that two bodies seem to occupy the same space at the same time—an impossibility even in ancient science? The resolution of this problem appears to come from the idea of "mixture." Wine and water can mix, with one fully permeating the other, but an oiled sponge could still separate out one from the other. This is how **pneuma** permeates all things that exist, even though it has length and breadth and width of its own.

What this philosophy of nature accomplishes is the rational ordering of all existence. All things are explained as the intelligent activity of an underlying rational principle that animates all matter. This rational principle is signified by many different names. We have already seen **pneuma**, **logos** (reason), **physis** (nature), and god, but the Stoics will also call it necessity, destiny and the "artistic fire" (**pyr technikon**). The artistic fire is especially intriguing for two reasons. The first issue develops from the fact that fire is an active principle animating the world. For, the world goes through stable periods, as well as periods of conflagration when all things become fire. At these times of the conflagration, god possesses all substance, while during the stable times of the cosmos, god serves only as the animating part of matter in the manner described above.

Second, the term "artistic" underscores the fact that nature has a purpose for its activity. Nature is like an artist fashioning a work of art. All of its designs are good, even if they do not appear so at first. Stoics allow for moral weakness, but things like illness or natural disasters only appear to be bad due to our limited perspective. A fuller view of reality would allow us to see the guiding purpose behind everything.

The Stoics, thus, have a keen sense of divine providence. God shapes every aspect of reality. This does not mean, of course, that the Stoics accept the traditional practice of religion any more than the Cynics do when it comes to sacrifices and divine images. What they did was associate various deities with the names of natural phenomena, so that Hera was "air," for instance. The various deities all manifest the supreme deity, Nature, which the Stoics called Zeus.

b. Nature and human nature. All things that are vivified by pneuma have different levels of what the Stoics call "tension." The degree of tension will determine whether something is a plant or animal or human being. Only human beings and animals are so disposed as to have a soul. The Stoic soul has eight parts or qualities: the five senses of sight, hearing, smell, touch and taste as well as speech, reproduction and what the Stoics call a "governing principle" (hēgemonikon ἡγεμονικόν). This governing principle accomplishes everything that we might associate with the brain, but in a qualified sense. The governing principle leads a given animal to select from its environment those things that it needs to survive. A dog will run to a bone with meat on it, for instance, and not a stone. This governing principle, however, is not the same as reason. Only human beings are endowed with reason, and this only after maturity. Reasoning, logos, develops over time, and only in human beings. As it does develop, it does not erase the faculties listed above, but governs them in such a way that impulses are now directed in a new way, a "natural" way that accords with reason.

c. Stoic Logic. The Stoics meant by "logic" the twin subjects of rhetoric and dialectic. If nature is a rational power that underlies everything, Stoic theories about rhetoric and dialectic explore how it is that people can grasp this rational power and express it, to themselves and to others, through language.

d. Stoic ethics. Most important of all, however, is that a person should live in accord with the reason that pervades the universe, that is, according to nature. In this, the Stoics echo the Cynics, as we saw above. But they do so in a far more systematic way, which is entirely un-Cynic. This systematic character continues in the realm of ethics, where the Stoics distinguish between virtue, vice and things that are indifferent. Conventional thinking attaches happiness (eudaimonia εὐδαιμονία) to things like health, reputation and wealth. For the Stoics, happiness is connected to things that are morally good, unhappiness to things that are morally bad. Things that make no difference to goodness or badness are labeled indifferent (adiaphthoros ἀδιάφθορος). The pursuit of health may be according to nature, and part of the world, but it is indifferent. This does not mean, however, that one should actively avoid being healthy. Rather, it means that when making a moral judgment, one should not make health the primary determining factor in how to act. In such a case, health is indifferent. Like the Cynics, the Stoics emphasize the importance of self-mastery and training to develop the skills necessary to live according to nature no matter what one encounters.

In regard to things that are indifferent, it is important that one can choose to let them be determinative if the general circumstances allow nothing important to be compromised. This approach to decision making provides the entry point for Stoics into the larger society and even into the world of politics. The Cynics viewed political life in all of its forms as unnatural. Not the Stoics. One *can* choose to participate in public life if circumstances allow (Diogenes Laertius, *Vit. phil.* 7.121). In the 1st cent. CE we see the Roman Stoics Musonius Rufus and Seneca intimately connected to Roman imperial power, and Epictetus was visited by the Emperor Hadrian. The Stoic philosopher-king Marcus Aurelius actually was Roman Emperor from 161–180 CE.

e. Stoics and the New Testament. Paul's writings reflect Stoic influence variously, as when he speaks of living according to nature (Rom 1–2). Engberg-Pedersen has compared the pattern of conversion to Stoicism to the pattern of conversion to Christianity in Paul's letters.

6. The Epicureans

If ancient writers describe lines of succession through the Ionian school from the Cynics and Stoics back to Socrates, the Epicureans follow a different succession, through the Italian line (Diogenes Laertius, *Vit. phil.* 1.15). This genetic separation from Socrates reflects as well the antipathy that some Epicureans had for Socrates, thought they may actually not have had Socrates as their primary target. Because Cynics and Stoics so associated themselves with Socrates, Epicureans may have hit the teacher to hurt his disciples. Regardless, the Epicureans share with both Cynics and Stoics a rejection of conventional values, as well as the connection between happiness and self-mastery, and, in general, the internalization of happiness regardless of external circumstances. Unlike the Cynics, however, and just like the Stoics, the Epicureans establish a coherent system to ground their way of life (*see* EPICURUS, EPICUREANISM).

a. Physics: Corporeal existence—atoms and the void. Stoics and Epicureans share a basic physical doctrine about bodily reality, but it is precisely in this agreement that one sees how radically the two differ. The following survey of Epicurean physics will especially compare the Epicureans to the Stoics, and derives from Epicurus' epitome of his philosophy in his *Letter to Herodotus* (not the historian) preserved in Diogenes Laertius, *Vit. phil.* 10.35-73.

Epicurus first introduces his completely empiricist approach (Diogenes Laertius, *Vit. phil.* 10.38) and bases his arguments on the perception of the senses (aisthēsis αἴσθησις). Referring to the universe as "the all" (to pan τό πᾶν), he insists that the sum total of the parts that make up the universe is always the same. It is not that the universe does not change, but the sum of what constitutes the universe is always the same amount. Of what does this sum consist? What is the "stuff" that makes up the universe? Epicurus writes,

"Moreover, the all is bodies and void. That bodies exist is universally witnessed by sensation itself

. . . And if place, which we call "void" . . . did not exist, bodies would not have anywhere to be or to move through, as they are observed to move" (Diogenes Laertius, *Vit. phil.* 10.39-40).

Here we see how the Epicureans are in the most basic sense like the Stoics, and how they are also unlike the Stoics. Like the Stoics, they insist on a corporeal model of all reality. They differ, however, in believing that bodies move through void, and that void even exists at all. For the Stoics, recall, void subsists, but does not exist. There is no void in the universe. For the Epicureans, on the other hand, the universe is comprised of void and bodies.

"Bodies, in addition, can be further subdivided into atoms. Epicurus writes, Of bodies, some are compounds, others the things from which the compounds have been made . . . The primary entities, then, must be atomic kinds of bodies" (Diogenes Laertius, *Vit. phil.* 10.40-1).

The basic bodies out of which all bodies are created, the primary entities of reality are atoms (literally, in Greek, "uncuttable things"). The universe, then, consists of atoms and the void. Composite bodies arise from the atoms and return to the atoms when the composites dissolve. The atoms are an indefinite number of shapes, since the great variety of composite bodies in the universe could never have arisen if all atoms were the same shape. The atoms rebound off of one another and are divided by the void until they form aggregates, which become the visible elements of the universe. Thus, in the Epicurean universe, all change arises from the coming together of an infinite supply of atoms into bodies and their eventual separation again. In the Stoic universe, on the other hand, the properties of a given body develop under the influence of **pneuma**, which provides a rational order for the universe.

This Stoic idea—that the universe is driven by a single rational purpose—would also not appeal to the Epicureans. For the Epicureans, there was no such thing as providence. Although they, oddly enough, believed that the gods exist, they asserted that the gods have no concern whatsoever for humans and for worldly affairs. The gods, rather, live in a state of contentment and happiness, detached from our existence. Whatever happens in our world is not due to providence, but to chance, to the coming together and the separation of atoms as they collide with one another in the void. This rejection of the gods does not mean that the gods have no place in Epicurean ethics, for they have a central role to play. What this role is will become clear below.

b. **Epicurean ethics.** The goal of life is pleasure (hēdonē ἡδονή) to the Epicurean. Athenaeus quotes the following statement of Epicurus (Diogenes Laertius 12.546): The beginning and root of all good is the plea-

sure of the stomach; even wisdom and refinements (of culture) are to be referred to this." This quotation, and others like it, of course, makes the Epicureans look very much like our modern sense of an Epicurean—someone devoted wholly to the pleasures of the body. But that does not seem at all to be what Epicurus had in mind. Pleasure involves erasing pain, whether physical or mental pain, as Epicurus asserts in the third of his Principle Doctrines, *Kyriai Doxai* (Diogenes Laertius, *Vit. phil.* 10.139):

"The magnitude of pleasure reaches its limit in the removal of all pain. When pleasure is present, so long as it is uninterrupted, there is no pain either of body or of mind or of both together."

The Epicurean eats, then, in order to remove the pain of hunger, and will enjoy eating. The Epicurean is not a rigorous ascetic. On the other hand, one may cause greater pain by eating too much, either because of health problems, or because one will always want to eat in such a way. This desire will cause one to be anxious about maintaining such a standard of eating, precisely the thing that the Epicurean wants to avoid by eating. The content of pleasure, then, is tranquility, of both mind and body.

This tranquility is what the gods possess, and human beings should try to imitate that tranquility (Diogenes Laertius, *Vit. phil.* 10.121). Recall, however, that the gods' tranquility is founded on their total disinterest in and separation from the world. We must imitate this tranquility precisely by putting away any fear of the gods, that they are cruel or vengeful. It was such fear that gave rise to the superstitions of conventional religion. The Epicurean must put aside this fear of the gods along with all other fears, especially the fear of death. Epicurus writes in his *Letter to Menoecus* (Diogenes Laertius, *Vit. phil.* 125) that "life has no terrors for him who has thoroughly apprehended that there are no terrors for him in ceasing to live." What such insight provides is a lack of fear regarding death, as well as the anxiety that comes with trying to avoid death.

This desire to put away anxiety and fear motivates the retreat from worldly cares that Epicurus urges on his followers, and it was this impulse that led him to found the Garden. Epicurus' Principle Doctrine 14 (Diogenes Laertius, *Vit. phil.* 10.143) refers to "the security of a quiet private life withdrawn from the multitude." The Epicurean does not engage in politics or public life, but withdraws from society and its disturbances.

The wise person does not live alone, however, but is surrounded by like-minded friends. Principle Doctrine 27 (Diogenes Laertius, *Vit. phil.* 10.148) reads, "Of all the means which are procured by wisdom to ensure happiness throughout the whole of life, by far the most important is the acquisition of friends." A friend, of course, could easily upset one's tranquility, but friendship is also an essential component of the happy life.

c. Romans and Epicureanism: Philodemus. In the 50s CE, Lucretius presented the teachings of Epicurus in verse, providing a poetically powerful form for Epicurean teaching. Although ethical concerns appear in the prologues to the six books of the poem, the primary concern is with physical theory, especially the argument that deities are unconcerned about human beings.

Epicureanism among Romans has begun to focus attention on Philodemus (ca. 110 BCE–40 BCE). Long neglected, he has received renewed attention with the recent editing or reediting of all the papyri of his works from the Villa of the Papyri in Herculaneum that was destroyed with the city of Pompeii in 79 CE. He is an important source for his teacher Zeno of Sidon, who is second only to Epicurus himself among Epicureans. Philodemus has also been discovered to be a creative thinker himself.

d. Epicureans and the New Testament. Philodemus has been useful especially for illuminating Paul's pastoral work. Philodemus' writings reflect a communal psychagogy in which all members mutually admonished one another, much like Paul's letters mention mutual encouragement (Rom 1:12; 1 Thess 5:14). Paul urges his congregations to imitate his own adaptability (1 Cor 8:1-11:1) in guiding one another.

7. Scepticism

In addition to dividing philosophers into the two Ionian and Italian branches, Diogenes Laertius also divides philosophers into dogmatists and sceptics (1.16). Dogmatists assert arguments and believe that things can be known. Sceptics, on the other hand, suspend their judgment in the belief that nothing is knowable. The idea that knowledge was fragile or limited has a long history in Greek philosophy, but the distinctive philosophical tradition of Skepticism is associated with Pyrrho of Elis (ca. 360–270 BCE). The stories about Pyrrho's internal peace mirror those told of other wise men (compare Diogenes Laertius 9.68). Pyrrho arrived at this state of tranquility, however, not by discerning the underlying truth of reality, but by recognizing that no such truth could be discerned. The Sceptics suspended judgment on all matters and asserted no positive doctrines. They would often alternately defend and attack the positions of other schools in order to show "that every saying has its corresponding opposite" (Diogenes Laertius, *Vit. phil.* 9.75). It was only when Pyrrho assented to this reality that he achieved internal peace, and it was this peace that his followers pursued. Skepticism dominated Plato's Academy under Arcesilaus (316–242 BCE) and Carneades (214–129 BCE), and was appreciated in Rome by Cicero (106–43 BCE), who believed that the exercise of arguing for and against a teaching prepares one well for public oratory (*Tusc.*, 2.9).

8. Middle Platonism

Although Plato's Academy was for a time imbued with skepticism, the tenor of Platonism between Antiochus of Ascalon (130 BCE–68 BCE) and Plotinus (205–270 CE) was hostile in rejecting the posture of the Sceptics. This, the period of so called Middle Platonism, was one in which Platonists borrowed extensively from other schools, from Pythagoreans as well as from Aristotle and the Stoics.

a. Plutarch. PLUTARCH of Chaironeia (ca. 46–127 CE) was an incredibly prolific writer on many subjects. His central concern in philosophy, the *telos* of this thought, is likeness to God, a standard theme of Middle Platonism since Eudorus in the 1st cent. BCE. In keeping with the agonistic spirit of philosophy of the time, many of his philosophical writings are polemical, directed especially the Stoics and Epicureans.

Most famous are his *Parallel Lives*, of which 23 survive. His purpose in writing the *Lives* was not, as a historian, to record every fact in perfect order, but, rather, to provide snapshots of an individual's character as a model for imitation or avoidance (*Alexander*, 1). This ethical purpose is reflected as well in his numerous works on moral philosophy. Precisely because he is not especially unique, but reflects contemporary attitudes, his works are a valuable tool for popular opinions on various issues, as in the work *How to Tell a Flatterer from a Friend*.

Plutarch is also important for assessing attitudes to traditional religion because for the last thirty years of his life he was a priest at Delphi, and wrote a work important for the study of Isis, *On Isis and Osiris*. In his tract *On Superstition* he explains the middle road between superstition and atheism. Superstition, he explains, is a fear based on misapprehension about the gods, that they are vengeful and cruel, and have anything to do with the anthropomorphic deities of poetry.

b. Philo of Alexandria. PHILO OF ALEXANDRIA also falls under the heading of Middle Platonism, even though have some have seen him eclectically drawing from any number of philosophical traditions. Philo was operating well within the bounds of the Middle Platonism of his time in Alexandria, which was influenced by Stoicism and Pythagoreanism. He adapts this Platonism to his exegetical efforts. As an Alexandrian Jew, almost three quarters of his works are devoted to explanation of the Pentateuch. It is difficult, as well, to distinguish always at what point he draws on Jewish influences, at what point on Platonic influences.

Philo, too, contributes to the philosophical discussions about true religion. The Cynics, Stoics and Epicureans reject ritual, and Philo is like them in his emphasis on interior religion, on religion as an affair of the heart. But he also makes room for the temple in Jerusalem, which was ordained by the Law of God. Here we see the twin influences of his Jewish faith and the Greek philosophical tradition in which he worked. *See* GREECE; HELLENISM.

Bibliography: Kempe Algra, et al. *The Cambridge History of Hellenistic Philosophy* (2005); H. W. Attridge. "The Philosophical Critique of Religion under the Early Empire." *ANRW* 2.1.6.1 (1978) 45–78; H. D. Betz. "Jesus and the Cynics: Survey and Analysis of a Hypothesis." *JR* 74 (1994) 453–75; R. Bracht Branhma, et al., eds. *The Cynics* (1996); Jan Bremmer. *Greek Religion* (1994); Walter Burkert. *Ancient Mystery Cults* (1987); Walter Burkert. *Greek Religion* (1985); R. Buxton, ed. *From Myth to Reason?* (1999); John Dillon. *The Middle Platonists* (1996); P. Eddy. "Jesus as Diogenes? Reflections on the Cynic Jesus Thesis." *JBL* 115 (1996) 449–69; Troels Engberg-Pedersen. *Paul and the Stoics* (2000); John Fitzgerald, ed. *Friendship, Flattery and Frankness of Speech* (1996); John T. Fitzgerald, et al. *Philodemus and the New Testament World* (2004); Clarence Glad. *Paul and Philodemus* (1995); R. Gordon. "Fear of Freedom? Selective Continuity in Religion During the Hellenistic Period." *Didaskalos* 4 (1972) 48–60; A. A. Long. *Hellenistic Philosophy: Stoics, Epicureans, Sceptics* (1986); A. A. Long and David Sedley. *The Hellenistic Philosophers.* 2 vols. (1990); Abraham Malherbe. *Paul and the Popular Philosophers* (1989); J. L. Martyn. "De-apocalypticizing Paul: An Essay Focused on Paul and the Stoics by Troels Engberg-Pedersen." *JSNT* 24 (2002) 61–102; Jon Mikalson. *Ancient Greek Religion* (2005); S. Price. *Religions of the Ancient Greeks* (1999); R. W. Sharples. *Stoics, Epicureans and Sceptics: An Introduction to Hellenistic Philosophy* (1996); Graham Shipley. *The Greek World after Alexander* (2000).

Translations from Loeb Classical Library, Long and Sedley (1990), and, for *Letter to Heraclitus*, Cambridge History of Hellenistic Philosophy, 362–382.

GEORGE L. PARSENIOS

GREEK VERSIONS. *See* VERSIONS, GREEK.

GREEN [יֶרֶק yereq, עֵשֶׂב 'esev, רַעֲנָן ra'anan; χλωρός chlōros]. A color term most often describing growing vegetation. God gave humans green plants for food (Gen 1:30; 9:3). Green can refer to vegetation in general (Rev 9:4), such as the plants destroyed in the plague of locusts (Exod 10:15) or pastures or grass (Ps 23:2; Joel 2:22; Mark 6:39). The green tree may be symbolic of idolatrous worship (1 Kgs 14:23; Jer 2:20; Ezek 6:13). Yet the vitality of the green tree is symbolic of those who trust in the Lord (Jer 17:8; Ps 92:14; Prov 11:28). Green modifies animals only in Ps 68:13 (dove's feathers) and Rev 6:8 (horse). *See* COLORS.

MARY PETRINA BOYD

GREETING [בָּרַךְ barakh; ἀσπασμός aspasmos, χαίρειν chairein]. The Bible records the use of greetings in both letters and conversation. Gehazi is told not to greet anyone (barakh, "to salute or greet with a blessing," 2 Kgs 4:29). Mary is perplexed by Gabriel's greeting (Luke 1:29). John, within Elizabeth's womb, responds to Mary's greeting (Luke 1:41, 44). Paul greeted the church in Jerusalem (Acts 21:19), and he regularly mentions that he is writing the greeting in his letters in his own hand, suggesting that the rest of the letter was written by an AMANUENSIS (see 1 Cor 16:21; Col 4:18; 2 Thess 3:17). James 1:1 and 1 Esd 8:9 use chairein for *greeting. See* BLESSINGS AND CURSINGS.

KENNETH D. LITWAK

GREGORY OF NAZIANZOS [Γρηγόριος Ναζιανζοῦ Grēgorios Nazianzou]. From Nazianzos in Cappadocia, Gregory was summoned to Constantinople in 379 CE where he preached five influential pro-Nicene sermons called the "Theological Orations" and became archbishop during the Council of Constantinople in 381. His writings display keen awareness of the nature of scriptural language and careful theological exegesis. Along with his friend GREGORY OF NYSSA, he is considered one of the "Cappadocian Fathers" noted for their contribution to the development of Trinitarian doctrine.

MARK DELCOGLIANO

GREGORY OF NYSSA [Γρηγόριος Grēgorios]. Gregory (b. ca. 335–340 CE; d. after 394), along with his brother BASIL of Caesarea and friend GREGORY OF NAZIANZOS, was one of the three so-called Cappadocian Fathers. Basil oversaw Gregory's education in the Greco-Roman classics, and as a young man Gregory embarked upon a career as a rhetor and got married (a decision his ascetic sympathies caused him later to regret). Through the efforts of Basil and Gregory of Nazianzos, Gregory accepted ordination as a lector in 360, and in 372 Basil appointed him bishop of Nyssa. Gregory's support of Nicene theology led to conflicts with the Arians, who succeeded in deposing him in 376. This was only a temporary setback, however, and he returned to his see in 378 when the Arians lost imperial support. Thereafter, he was an influential voice for Nicene orthodoxy at the councils of Antioch (379) and Constantinople (381).

Gregory's theology weaves together ideas from the classical tradition, particularly Platonic philosophy, and Christian writers such as Origen. Representative examples of his Christian Platonism appear in *On the Soul and the Resurrection*, a Christian reworking of Plato's *Phaedo*, as well as *On the Life of Moses* and *Commentaries on the Song of Songs*.

DAVID M. REIS

GREGORY THE GREAT. Bishop of Rome (Pope) (590–604 CE) and author of several commentaries: the massive *Moralia*, a threefold literal, mystical, and moral exegesis of the entirety of Job; forty homilies on the Gospels and twenty-two on the book of Ezekiel; and an allegorical exposition of Song 1:1-8.

GRIDDLE מַחֲבַת makhavath]. A plate with depressions used for cooking (Lev 2:5; 6:21; 7:9); the Hebrew word seems to be of relatively late derivation.

GRIEF. *See* EMOTIONS; MOURNING; SORROW; SUFFERING AND EVIL.

GRIESBACH HYPOTHESIS. Named after J. J. Griesbach, an 18th cent. biblical scholar who developed the first modern synopsis as a tool for Gospel research (1776). This theory is also called the Two-Gospel Hypothesis, in which the Gospels of Matthew and Luke precede chronologically and serve as sources for the Gospel of Mark. Mark is thereby considered third in origin among the Synoptic Gospels, combining the Palestinian Gospel (i.e., Petrine/Jewish) of Matthew with the Hellenistic (i.e., Pauline/Gentile) Gospel of Luke. Proponents of this theory suggest that it allows scholars to explain the historical implications of early Christianity in a more reasonable manner. Griesbach himself developed this theory in response to the dominant position that the canonical order was also the chronological order, a traditional view of Gospel origins in place at least since Augustine.

The revival of the Griesbach Hypothesis supports this solution over any theory that necessitates the creation of hypothetical (i.e., nonextant) sources to explain the origins of the narratives. Indeed, the Two-Gospel Hypothesis should be clearly distinguished from the Two-Source Hypothesis, which refers to the most popular solution of Gospel origins: the Gospel of Mark and the hypothetical *source* "Q" function as sources for Matthew and Luke (*see* Q, QUELLE).

Proponents of Griesbach Hypothesis view the facts differently. In terms of the order of the stories, Mark preserves the same order as the others when all three Gospels report the same story. Additionally, when all three do not agree, Mark usually preserves the same order of the pericope in either Matthew or Luke. The majority of scholars assume these facts support Markan priority. Greisbach proponents assume these observations express Mark's own editorial work. *See* SYNOPTIC PROBLEM.

EMERSON B. POWERY

GRIFFON. Mythological creature sometimes identified with the VULTURE but having the head of a lion and wings of an eagle; associated with royalty in Egypt and Mesopotamia.

GRIND, GRINDING טָחַן takhan]. The pulverizing of grain between two stones in order to process it into flour, a task generally carried out by women, servants, or slaves (Exod 11:5), prisoners (Judg 16:21), or war captives (Lam 5:13).

GRUMBLING רָגַן raghan; διαγογγύζω diagonguzō]. Complaining with a churlish attitude (e.g., Wis 1:10, 11; Sir 46:7; 1 Macc 11:39; Luke 15:2), often rendered as "murmuring" or "whispering." The Israelites grumbled in the wilderness (Deut 1:27). Isaiah looks to a time when "those who grumble will accept instruction" (29:24). In the NT, Jesus' teaching and actions elicit grumbling (Luke 15:2; 19:7) and grumbling appears as a threat to the Christian community (Jas 5:9; Jude 1:16). *See* MURMUR.

RALPH K. HAWKINS

GUARD טַבָּח tabbakh, מַטָּרָה mattarah, מִשְׁמַעַת mishma'at, מִשְׁמָר mishmar, רָצִים ratsim; κουστωδία koustōdia, σπεκουλάτωρ spekoulatōr, φυλακή phylakē, φύλαξ phylax, ὑπηρέτης hypēretēs]. In both the OT and NT, several terms are translated "guard," meaning a person or group of persons who protects or watches over a place or person. Mishmar refers to the place where someone is confined (Gen 40:3; Lev 24:12), a guard-post (1 Chr 9:23; Neh 4:3, 16-17; 7:3), or a division of the temple service (Neh 12:24; 13:14). Mattarah is used frequently in Jeremiah to refer the guard's courtyard (32:2; 38:28; 39:14; Neh 3:25; 12:39). Tabbakh, suggesting the idea of an executioner or guardsman, is used for the bodyguards of the Egyptian pharaoh (Gen 37:36; 39:1; 40:3; 2 Kgs 25:8-10) and of the Babylonian king (Jer 39:9–52:30; Dan 2:14). Ratsim refers to the bodyguard or couriers of the king (1 Kgs 14:27-28; 2 Kgs 10:25; 11:6). Mishma'at also indicates bodyguards (1 Sam 22:14; 2 Sam 23:23; 1 Chr 11:25).

In the NT the Latin loan-word koustōdia is used for the group of soldiers who guarded Jesus' tomb (Matt 27:65, 66; 28:11). Spekoulatōr, a Latin loan-word that may mean "executioner," is used for the bodyguard of Herod Antipas (Mark 6:27). Phylax refers to sentinels (Acts 5:23; 12:6, 19), as does the related word phulakē (Acts 12:10). Hypēretēs has the basic meaning of "assistant," but in some contexts refers to the guards attending a court (Matt 5:25; 26:58; Mark 14:54, 65; John 7:32, 45; 18:3, 12, 22; 19:6; Acts 5:22, 26).

GREGORY L. LINTON

GUARD, COURT OF THE חֲצַר הַמַּטָּרָה khatsar hammattarah]. During the Babylonian siege of Jerusalem, an area within the palace complex used to detain prisoners (Neh 3:25). Jeremiah was confined there, but during that time was allowed to prophesy and conduct business (Jer 32:2, 8, 12; 33:1; 37:21; 38:6, 13, 28; 39:14-15).

TREVOR D. COCHELL

GUARD, GATE OF THE שַׁעַר הַמַּטָּרָה sha'ar hammattarah]. Mentioned as the terminus of a procession around Jerusalem's walls (Neh 12:39). Associations with "the gate behind the guards" (2 Kgs 11:6) and "the court of the guard" of Jeremiah's confinement (Jer 32:2; 33:1; 37:14-21; 38:6-28; 39:11-18) may place it inside the city, south of the Temple, between the temple courts and the palace. *See* GATE OF THE FOUNDATION; GUARD, COURT OF THE; JERUSALEM; MUSTER GATE; SUR GATE.

JAMES RILEY STRANGE

GUARD, TO BE ON [שָׁמַר shamar; φυλάσσω phylassō, προσέχω prosechō]. The Hebrew verb shamar occurs hundreds of times in the OT, primarily with the meanings "keep," "watch," "preserve," or with the associated meanings of "keep watch over" or "guard." The particular admonition "to be on (one's) guard" against someone or something is an exhortation used to refer to guarding against an adversary (1 Sam 19:2) or against an enemy (2 Kgs 9:19). In the NT the verbs phylassō and prosechō carry the meanings "to guard, to keep," "to keep watch," or "to keep guard." The use of these words to express the admonition "to be on (one's) guard" against sin, worries, and greed appears three times, all in Luke (12:15; 17:3; 21:34).

DEMETRIUS WILLIAMS

GUARDIAN [ἐπίσκοπος episkopos, ἐπίτροπος epitropos, παιδαγωγός paidagōgos]. A paidagōgos was usually a male slave who accompanied well-to-do boys outside the house, walking with them to school, to the gymnasium, or to the military training grounds, protecting them from danger from others or from their own youthful lack of judgment. When the boy came of age, he became responsible for himself. Paul compares the Mosaic Law to a paidagōgos in Gal 3:24; we were properly guarded by the Law until Christ came, but now no longer need it, he argues. He uses epitropos just a few verses later (4:2) with the same sense. Writing to the Corinthians, he claims the singular role of a father; they might have 10,000 paidagōgoi, but only one father (1 Cor 4:15). An episkopos was an officer in a temple or private association who had defined responsibilities to the group. It is often translated "bishop" (1 Tim 3:1-6; Titus 1:7-9), but in 1 Pet 2:25, Christ is called the "shepherd and episkopos of your souls/lives," and "guardian" or "overseer" possibly conveys the sense better. *See* CUSTODIAN.

RICHARD B. VINSON

GUDEA. A governor of the southern Mesopotamian city-state Lagash (ca. 2100 BCE), Gudea is well known for his literary, artistic, and architectural achievements. The *Gudea Cylinders* relate how the deity Ningirsu, appearing in a dream, asked Gudea to build a temple in the capital city of Girsu (modern Tello) and how he dutifully responded. Statues of Gudea further contribute to his cultural legacy and reputation as a pious ruler. *See* INSCRIPTIONS.

STEVE COOK

GUDGODAH. *See* HOR-HAGGIDGAD.

GUEST [קְרֻאִים qeru'im; ἀνακειμένων anakeimenōn].

A visitor or traveler to whom HOSPITALITY is extended. Guests were dependent on the care and protection of the host (Judg 19:23). Both the OT and NT describe guests as those invited for meals or celebratory feasts (1 Sam 9:24; 2 Sam 12:4; 1 Kgs 1:41, 49; Zeph 1:7; Matt 22:10-11), but a guest might also be anyone who needs lodging or a place to rest (Gen 18:3; 19:3). Jesus utilizes the Greco-Roman convention of "places of honor" in seating dinner guests to discuss the reversals of the kingdom of God (Luke 14:7). *See* MEALS.

JESSICA TINKLENBERG DEVEGA

GUEST ROOM [κατάλυμα katalyma, ξενία xenia]. Kataluma is used in Mark 14:14; Luke 2:7; 22:11 for the room borrowed by Jesus and his disciples for the Passover meal. Usually a katalyma was a single room where travelers could stay overnight, which is the connotation in Luke 2:7 of the occupied room in Bethlehem. In Phlm 22, Paul asks Philemon to prepare a guest room (xenia) for him.

MARY KAY DOBROVOLNY, R.S.M.

GUIDEPOST [תַּמְרוּר tamrur]. A word appearing only in Jer 31:21, the meaning and derivation of which are uncertain. Because it appears in parallel with the term ROAD MARKER, the two are usually considered synonymous and may represent stones piled along a path to mark the way.

GUILE, GUILELESS [מַשָּׁאוֹן masha'on, שֶׁקֶר shereq; ἀκέραιος akeraios, δόλος dolos]. Guile is synonymous with cunning or DECEIT. One who is not deceitful and is not treacherous or crafty or cunning in dealings with others is guileless. In the Scriptures of Israel, shereq represents acting or speaking with guile, deceit, or falsehood, as in Ps 119:78: "Let the arrogant be put to shame, because they have subverted me with guile." Proverbs 26:26 employs mashsha'on to refer to guile: "though hatred is covered with guile, the enemy's wickedness will be exposed in the assembly."

Romans 16:19 uses akeraios to refer to being guileless in respect of evil. The NT often uses dolos, which means guile or deceit; 1 Pet 2:1 exhorts believers to rid themselves of all guile.

KENNETH D. LITWAK

GUILT. *See* CONSCIENCE; ERR, TO; SIN, SINNERS.

GUILT OFFERING. *See* SACRIFICES AND OFFERINGS.

GULF. *See* CHASM.

GULF OF AQABA. *See* AQABA, GULF OF.

GULL. *See* SEA GULL.

GULLIBLE. The term is never used in the Bible, but

the concept is present, as in "The simple believe everything . . ." (Prov 14:15) and "For this reason God sends them a powerful delusion, leading them to believe what is false" (2 Thess 2:11). Religious people have been accused of being gullible.

MARY KAY DOBROVOLNY, R.S.M.

GULLOTH, UPPER AND LOWER [גֻּלֹּת תַּחְתִּית gulloth takhtith; גֻּלֹּת עִלִּית gulloth ʿillith]. Part of the land near Hebron given to Caleb by Joshua, which he in turn gives to his daughter Achsah and her husband Othniel at her request (Josh 15:18; Judg 1:15). Gulloth likely means *basin*, and Achsah's request for the land plays on the notion that she had already been given dry, parched land as an inheritance (neghev [נֶגֶב], *desert*), and thus needed basins of water (gulloth mayim גֻּלֹּת מָיִם) as well (Judg 1:15). The name for this location is translated "upper springs" and "lower springs" in Josh 15:19.

JESSICA TINKLENBERG DEVEGA

GUM [בְּדֹלַח bedholakh, נָטָף nataf, נְכֹאת nekhoth]. From the root for *drop* suggesting the gathering of light-colored, secreted sap (Num 11:7) from trees or shrubs that have been pruned or sliced. One suggestion for gum, based on its aromatic and healing properties, is opobalsamum (*Commiphora gileadensis*). This is a resin extracted from the sliced branches of a shrub found in southern Arabia that was a common item listed in caravan inventories (Gen 37:25). It also recommended it as a worthy gift to be included among other spices (Gen 43:11). It could be distilled by dissolving it in warm olive oil, or it could be ground into a powder. *See* BALM; MASTIC; MYRRH; PLANTS OF THE BIBLE; SPICE.

VICTOR H. MATTHEWS

GUNI gyoo'ni [גּוּנִי guni]. 1. The second of the four sons of Naphtali (Gen 46:24; 1 Chr 7:13); eponymous ancestor of the tribe of Gunites (Num 26:48).

2. The grandfather of AHI, chief of a Gadite clan (1 Chr 5:15).

GUR guhr [גּוּר gur]. An ascent near IBLEAM where Jehu's men mortally wounded Ahaziah king of Judah (2 Kgs 9:27).

GUR-BAAL guhr-bay'uhl [גּוּר־בָּעַל gur baʿal]. Arab-inhabited city against which King Uzziah of Judah warred (2 Chr 26:7). The LXX reads epi tēs petras (ἐπὶ τῆς πέτρας) "(the Arabs living) on the rocks,"

presupposing that gur is a scribal error for tur (טוּר). The preferred reading is probably with the Targum, which reads gerar (גְּרָר, GERAR).

GYMNASIUM [γυμνάσιον gymnasion]. The gymnasium, where upper- and middle-class Greek and Macedonian boys were educated, had three functions over time: education, social interaction, and social integration. It was especially important outside Greece and Macedonia, enabling a minority ruling class to maintain and sustain its distinct cultural identity in a larger, indigenous, non-Greek society.

Education normally included Greek literature, rhetoric, music, mathematics, and athletics. Greek literature, rhetoric, and music reinforced a sense of cultural identity and pride. Athletic training fed upon the Greek love for athletic competition and the notoriety it brought to individual and community alike and was conducted in the nude, hence the name gymnasion, from gymnos (γυμνός), meaning "naked." (Coeducational programs were not the norm.) The programs of the gymnasium were often subsidized by the king or wealthy local citizens. The gymnasium bolstered the sense of cultural and ethnic superiority among the Greco-Macedonian ruling class.

Subsequently, the gymnasium became a center for social gatherings. Similar to contemporary alumni of a given institution who might gather socially, graduates of the gymnasium interacted socially, in political as well as commercial circles, further reinforcing their sense of uniqueness in non-Greek contexts.

With the rise of the *polis*, ancient non-Greek cities restructured as Greek cities, the gymnasium became an integral element in bringing non-Greeks into Greek culture. Usually after a Greek city was chartered, thereafter only persons educated in the gymnasium could hold citizenship and influence municipal affairs. Thus, an indigenous ruling elite could perpetuate economic and political power in a few families. For Jewish boys, this meant neglecting their temple training, reading Homer and not the prophets, and being embarrassed in athletic training by their circumcision. Such training made Jewish young men more Greek and less Jewish. More traditional Jews, like the Maccabees, bristled at these developments (1 Macc 1:24; 2 Macc 4:9, 12).

Bibliography: F. W. Walbank. *The Hellenistic World* (1993).

THOMAS B. SLATER

Hh

H, HOLINESS CODE. The siglum used in Pentateuchal scholarship to refer to the second portion of Leviticus (chs. 17–26), which A. Klosterman (1893) designated the Holiness Code (German: *Heiligkeitsgesetz*). H is believed to be separate from the larger Priestly Source (P) although the exact relationship between the two sources is an issue of on-going debate. The material is called the Holiness Code due to the frequent refrain, "You shall be holy, for I the LORD, your God, am Holy." *See* LEVITICUS, BOOK OF; P, PRIESTLY WRITERS.

PHILLIP MICHAEL SHERMAN

HA SHEM hay′shim [הַשֵּׁם hashem]. Leviticus 24:11 already refers to "the Name" (hashem), the pronunciation of which was blasphemy and Deut 28:58 refers to "the honored and awesome name, Yahweh." Hence, the term *Adonai* (and sometimes *Elohim*) came to be pronounced wherever Yahweh appears. By rabbinic times, however, even Adonai was deemed too holy a name and so the TETRAGRAMMATON was simply referred to as "the Name." *See* ADONAI, ADONAY; GOD, NAMES OF.

C. L. SEOW

HAAHASHTARI hay′uh-hash′tuh-r*i* [הָאֲחַשְׁתָּרִי ha’akhashtari]. A Judahite, the son of Ashhur by his wife Naarah (1 Chr 4:6). The name may also refer to a tribe, the AHASHTARITES.

HABAIAH huh-bay′yuh [חֲבַיָּה khovayyah; Οββια Obbia]. A priest (Hobaiah, Neh 7:63) whose descendants were among postexilic returnees to Jerusalem prevented from serving as priests due to a lack of records establishing their lineage until a priest was available to determine their ancestry by lot (Ezra 2:61; 1 Esd 5:38).

HABAKKUK. *See* HABAKKUK, BOOK OF.

HABAKKUK, BOOK OF huh-bak′uhk [חֲבַקּוּק khavaqquq]. The 8th book among the twelve Minor Prophets in the OT canon (*see* BOOK OF THE TWELVE). Nothing is known of Habakkuk except that he is identified as a prophet in 1:1 and 3:1. His book differs from the other prophetic books in that it deals with a single subject, the question why God, whom Habakkuk believes to be the upholder of justice, seems to allow injustice to flourish without doing anything about it.

A. Structure and Unity
  1. Structure
  2. Unity
B. Date and Setting
  1. Date
  2. Setting
C. Text and Translation Problems
D. Genres
E. Traditions
F. Message
G. Influence
Bibliography

A. Structure and Unity

1. Structure

The book is usually divided into three parts, although some read the first two as a single unit: the dialogue (1:2–2:5), the so-called "woe (or alas) oracles" (2:6-20), and the prayer of Habakkuk (3:1-19). Although there are no indications of changes of speaker, it is clear that 1:2-3 is a speech of the prophet, that God is the speaker in 1:5-11, and that 1:12-17 contains the prophet's rejoinder. The only narrative fragment in the book appears in 2:1, the prophet's insistence that he will persist in his search for an answer. A somewhat cryptic word of assurance from God is the result (2:2-5), and 2:6*a* introduces a new major section, vv. 6*b*-20, a poem of five stanzas marked by the appearance of hoy (הוֹי, "woe," "alas"). Chapter 3 is clearly marked off by a title and a concluding technical note similar to those found in the Psalms.

2. Unity

Although the book in its present form can be read as a consistent message concerning a prophet's personal struggle with the problem of the justice of God, many questions have been raised about its unity. Chapter 3 has its own introduction and might well have been a part of the hymnody of the temple, and this led a good many earlier scholars to question whether it was part of the original book. The fact that the commentary on Habakkuk found at Qumran dealt only with the first two chapters seemed for a time to support that conclusion, but Hab 3 would not have fit the interests of the commentator, and the general opinion now is that although the chapter may have existed separately at one time and may have been added to the book, either by Habakkuk himself or by a later editor, it forms an appropriate conclusion to the book.

Much discussion pertains to the unity and chronology of the dialogue in Hab 1. The speech of the Lord in vv. 5-11 does not answer any of the questions in vv. 2-4. Efforts to account for that have involved rearranging the text and suggesting that redactors have added material, but these proposals have no support in the ancient manuscripts and have been found to be too subjective for any of them to be widely accepted. Less subjective is the suggestion that vv. 5-11 are not a response but are Habakkuk's quotation of an oracle he had received earlier, a part of, or even the basis for his complaint. In that case, 1:2–2:1 contains a single speech by the prophet. The reading offered below (*see* §F. Message) will take vv. 5-11 to be a response to vv. 2-4, however.

Other questions concern the identity of the oppressor (one or two?) and chronology. Must there have been an interval between vv. 11 and 12, to allow time for Habakkuk to realize conditions were becoming or had become worse, because of the Chaldeans? That does not seem to be necessary. Several approaches to the book have claimed it deals with a single oppressor throughout, but the book provides more support for the conclusion that Habakkuk first complains about injustice within Judah, and then protests the violence of the Chaldean army in vv. 12-17. The reference to the weakness of TORAH in v. 4 seems appropriate only if the prophet complained about his own people, for the word is never used elsewhere of the affairs of the nations.

B. Date and Setting

1. Date

The only clue to the date of this book is the reference to the Chaldeans in 1:6. This suggests that it must have been produced at the time when Nebuchadnezzar's forces had begun to move toward Judah, but before the fall of Jerusalem in 597 BCE. Several scholars have insisted on questioning the reference to the Chaldeans, however, and the book has been dated as early as the time of Hezekiah (701 BCE) and as late as the time of Alexander the Great (late 4th cent. BCE). There seems to be no good reason not to take the text as it stands, and recent commentators find the reign of Jehoiakim (608–598 BCE) to be the likely period for the production of the book. The evidence from history and the book itself do not seem specific enough to confirm the efforts of several scholars to date it more exactly.

2. Setting

The Assyrians, who had ruled the Middle East for over a century, had been weakened by attacks of the Medes and the Chaldeans, the latter having become the ruling class in Babylon. In 612 Nineveh fell, and subsequently Pharaoh Necho moved north to hold back the advance of Nebuchadnezzar's army by strengthening what was left of the Assyrian forces. He killed King Josiah of Judah at Megiddo on his way north in 609, and

soon deposed Jehoahaz, who had succeeded his father, replacing him with Jehoiakim (2 Kgs 23:34–24:6). After the Egyptians had been defeated at Carchemish in 605, Jehoiakim offered his allegiance to Nebuchadnezzar, but rebelled in 598, leading to the siege and fall of Jerusalem, and to his death. Both 2 Kings and the book of Jeremiah rate him as a poor ruler, so his reign may have produced the kinds of ills Habakkuk complains of in his first speech (see Jer 22:18-23; 36:1-32).

C. Text and Translation Problems

There are some very difficult verses in the book, especially in Hab 3, and often the ancient manuscripts offer little help in determining their meaning. Two early Hebrew texts of Habakkuk are now partially available. Among the first scrolls to be found at Qumran was a commentary on the first two chaps. of the book (1QpHab; 1st cent. BCE). The text it quotes varies only a little from the MT. The parts of Habakkuk that are preserved in the scroll of the Twelve Prophets found in the Wadi Murabbaʾat (Mur 88; 2nd cent. CE) are almost identical to the MT.

The earliest known manuscript of a Greek translation is a scroll of the Minor Prophets found at Nahal Hever (8Hev 1). It contains parts of each chapter of Habakkuk, and also is close to the Hebrew text in most respects.

The most interesting variant reading appears in the central verse of the book, Hab 2:4*b*. The Hebrew text reads "but (the) righteous one will live by his faithfulness," and the same reading appears in the Greek translation of the Nahal Hever scroll. The LXX, however, in most of its manuscripts, reads "but the righteous one will live by my faithfulness," but in MSS A and C it reads "but my righteous one will live by faithfulness." These are likely to be interpretations, rather than representing a different Hebrew text, but the reading of A and C is of interest since it reappears in Heb 10:38. Paul omits the possessive pronoun entirely in Rom 1:17 and Gal 3:11. The text of Hab 3 is virtually impossible in several places, and translators can do little more than guess at verses such as 9 and 14.

D. Genres

The book begins with a complaint, of the type that appears often in the Psalms and Job, and also in the complaints of Jeremiah (see Jer 12:1, 4; 20:8). Habakkuk's cry, "How long?" and "Why?" appears also in Pss 13:1-2; 22:1-2; 74:10; 88:1, 13; 89:46, and elsewhere. "Why?" is repeated in Job 3:11, 12, 20, 23; 7:20-21; 10:18, and "How long?" in 7:19. In 18:7 he cries out "Violence!" but finds no justice, as Habakkuk did. The prophet thus used a form of prayer that was well known in his time, but his complaint focused not on his own suffering, as in these parallels, but on the righteous in general. The resumption of the complaint in 1:12-17 repeats the "Why?" question in v. 13, and follows the pattern found in the Psalms, with its description of the violence of the enemy (see Ps 79:1-4), and vv. 12-13*a* begin to sound like the expressions of confidence that are another common feature of the genre (e.g., Ps 22:3-4), but for Habakkuk this affirmation of what he believes is no basis for confidence but is the source of his problem, as the succeeding verses reveal.

A poem of five stanzas appears in 2:6*b*-19, each stanza marked by the exclamation hoy (vv. 6, 9, 12, 15, 19). The first four speak of the sins and resulting punishment of an unnamed tyrant, but the subject matter of the fifth is different, for it ridicules idolatry. This may account for the appearance of hoy in the middle of the stanza rather than at the beginning, or it may be that lines became displaced in the copying of an early manuscript. The use of the word hoy in the OT has been the object of extensive study in recent years. Theories that claimed it was used as a curse-formula, that it originated in wisdom-teaching as the opposite of ʾashre (אַשְׁרֵי) "happy," and that it was just a cry to get attention, like "Hey!" have been shown to be without adequate support in the OT evidence. Most scholars conclude from its appearance in 1 Kgs 13:30; Jer 22:18; 30:7; 34:5; and Amos 5:16 that the word was typically a cry of grief or dismay. The familiar translation, "Woe to . . ." has thus been misleading. The word is not followed by a preposition but is an outcry followed by a third-person reference to the person and the event that have produced the cry. This suggests a modification of the way several prophetic texts should be read, but vv. 6-19 certainly contain nothing of dismay. A few scholars have thus suggested that the poem is an imitation of a funeral song, celebrating the death of a tyrant and using the cry in a mocking way. This is based in part on the appearance of hoy, and in part on the use of the theme of reversal of fortune in vv. 8, 11, and 16, which in the true funeral song (e.g., 2 Sam 1:19-27) was emphasized as one of the reasons for lamentation, and which appears in a prophetic poem concerning the death of a tyrant in Isa 14:4-21. If the poem in Habakkuk has thus turned grief-language into language of rejoicing, it explains why the prophet has introduced it as not only a "taunt" but also as a "mocking riddle" (v. 6). Interpreting the poem as a parody of a funeral song has not been widely accepted, but if it is read that way it means that Habakkuk has chosen a brutal way to celebrate in advance the death of a tyrant.

The prayer of Habakkuk in Hab 3 has been identified as a lament and as a thanksgiving, for there are parallels with both types of Psalms (e.g., Pss 18; 44; 75; 76). Some have called it the description of the vision that the prophet was instructed to write in 2:2, but the poem as a whole is not closely paralleled elsewhere, especially because of vv. 16-19. The central part, vv. 3-15, is a theophany, a description of the effects of the coming of God making use of the most awe-inspiring natural events (see Pss 18:7-16; 29:3-10; 77:16-20; Nah 1:2-8). The suggestion that this powerful language was chosen in the effort to convey something of the emotional experience of a visionary who had sensed the presence of God in a truly daunting way has much to commend it.

E. Traditions

The book makes use of prophetic, cultic, and wisdom traditions of Israel. Habakkuk is identified by the title as a prophet and a visionary (and see 2:2). God's announcement of the coming of an enemy army is similar to the messages of other prophets, such as Zeph 1:14-18 and Jer 4:11-18; 5:15-17; 6:22-26. The idea that God would use such an army to punish injustice among his own people, then judge the foreigners for the excesses of their cruelty had appeared earlier in Isa 10:5-19. Prophets before Habakkuk had taken up the outcry hoy as an instinctive reaction to the abuses they saw and the terrible messages they had to offer.

The prophet, like others (e.g., Amos 4:13; 5:8-9; 9:5-6), uses literature drawn from the cult for his own purposes. He produces his own psalm of complaint in 1:2-4, 12-17, as noted above, and his prayer in Hab 3 is reminiscent throughout of the Psalms. The rubrics at the beginning and end suggest that it was used in worship at some time.

Parallels to the wisdom literature are also prominent. Favorite words of the sages appear frequently, and the concern about the justice of God raises questions also found in Job and Ecclesiastes. There are other relationships with Job. Much of Job takes the form of a dialogue, between Job and his would-be comforters, and Job longs for dialogue with God. The first part of Habakkuk is dialogue also, and the prophet does engage in a short debate with God. Habakkuk ends with theophany, and he acknowledges that his experience of the nearness of God has changed him, even though his questions have not been answered. The book of Job ends in a similar way. God speaks "out of the whirlwind" (38:1; 40:6), certainly an allusion to theophany, and answers none of Job's questions, but Job also acknowledges he has been changed (42:5-6).

Earlier studies of the cultic material in the book led several scholars to the conclusion that Habakkuk was a cult prophet who produced this material for use in the Temple service. His title, "prophet," in 1:2 offers some support for that, but when it is observed that the book draws from wisdom and prophetic traditions as well, it may be safest to conclude that all this material would have been a part of the daily life of anyone in Judah who had the ability to produce a work of such depth.

F. Message

The book begins with a question that has disturbed those who believe in God from Habakkuk's time to the present: How can a righteous God do nothing about wrongdoing, treachery, and wickedness? The prophet puts it as bluntly as possible: "you will not listen"; "you will not save"; "you make me see wrongdoing." But it is a challenge to God based on faith, not unbelief, as vv. 12-13 indicate. What Habakkuk believes and what he sees are starkly opposite, but he insists that there ought to be a reason for that which God can explain.

God responded, but with no answer to Habakkuk's questions. He said nothing about justice, offered no hint of comfort, explanation, or assurance. Instead he announced the coming of another invader, even using the word **khamas** (חָמָס) "violence" of that army, a word Habakkuk had used twice in his complaint. It is a warning, not an answer, but God's responses to prayers elsewhere are also not what had been hoped for (Job 38–41; Jer 11:18-23; 12:1-6). God does not say, as God did to other prophets, "I am sending the Chaldeans to punish the sins of my people." God just says that what Habakkuk complains of will soon get worse.

The prophet persists with the justice-question, however, in vv. 12-17, expressing as forcefully as possible the contrast between what he believes and real life. "Your eyes are too pure to behold evil, and you cannot look on wrongdoing; why do you look on the treacherous, and are silent when the wicked swallow those more righteous than they?" He acknowledges in v. 12b the traditional prophetic explanation of Israel's sufferings under foreign oppressors, but this does not answer his questions. He emphasizes the wickedness of these agents of judgment by adding to God's description even more details of the terror brought by an invading army. Then he reports that he waited for another response from God, using the imagery of a watchtower to emphasize his persistence (2:1).

The remainder of the book says nothing about why the righteous suffer in a world ruled by a just God. The message that follows contains an assurance that evil will not prevail forever, and two words about how the righteous cope in the meantime. "The righteous live by their faith [faithfulness]" (2:4b) is both a challenge and a promise. Those who do not lose faith, who remain faithful, even when there seems to be no reason to do so, will be justified by God (declared righteous), and will receive the gift of life, which in the OT means not mere existence but full vitality.

The taunt song that follows is neither a word of God nor of the prophet. It will be sung by "everyone," rejoicing that the suffering the tyrant has inflicted on others now rebounds upon him. Efforts to identify him as Sennacherib or Jehoiakim or Nebuchadnezzar or Alexander have not been successful, for the sins described have been committed again and again. This is an "all-purpose" condemnation of tyranny, and if the scholars who call it a parody of a funeral song are correct, it means that God is authorizing the oppressed to celebrate, for the death of the tyrant is certain.

Habakkuk's prayer begins with a plea for mercy, but then, the description of theophany indicates a powerful personal experience of the presence of God, for 3:16 records the physical effects it had on him—both trembling and a sense of blessing: "I wait quietly." The question whether it might be possible for the righteous to live by their faith when nothing is going right was answered in a personal way for Habakkuk by the experience of the nearness of God, for in vv. 17-18 he announces that even though things get far worse— v. 17 contemplates the possibility of starvation—he has now found a remarkable gift, the ability to rejoice. The book thus makes a major contribution to the message that appears numerous times in Scripture: God has not explained how evil can exist in a world governed by a good and powerful God but has instead given to believers the strength to prevail (and rejoice) without the answer.

G. Influence

Legends about Habakkuk developed during the postexilic period and may be found in the apocryphal addition to Daniel called Bel and the Dragon, as well as in the Lives of the Prophets, one of the Pseudepigrapha. They are of no historical or theological value. The writer of the commentary on Habakkuk found at Qumran used the text of Hab 1–2 for his own purposes, interpreting it all as predictions of events of his own time, without any interest in the original intent of the book. In rabbinic Judaism, the book was cited frequently in the discussion of important theological topics. The rabbis concluded that all the commandments of the Torah were based on Hab 2:4b: "but the righteous shall live by his faith" (b. Mak. 24a; Midr. Tann. 17:25). Chapter 3 was read in the synagogue service for the Feast of Weeks, when the giving of the Torah was celebrated, since the poem was associated with the revelation at Sinai (b. Meg. 31a).

Paul quoted Hab 2:4b twice, in Rom 1:17 where it serves as the theme-verse for the letter, and in Gal 3:11. In both cases he omitted the pronoun "his." The verse does not mean quite the same thing for Paul as it did in the Hebrew, where 'emunah (אֱמוּנָה) essentially means "faithfulness." His Greek word pistis (πίστις) can mean both faithfulness (Rom 3:3; Gal 5:22; 2 Thess 1:4; Titus 2:10) and faith, but Paul's use of Hab 2:4b makes it clear that he is emphasizing faith. The author of Hebrews uses 2:3-4 in a different way, with a quotation in 10:37-38 that is significantly different from the MT. The author commends endurance during a time of waiting, and uses Hab 2:3 to promise "the coming one," rather than the coming vision, then reverses the order of 4a and 4b. Despite these variations the original sense of faithfulness is preserved.

Later Christian writers also worked with Hab 2:3 as they tried to understand the fact that the Second Coming of Christ had been long delayed. The reference to "coming one" in Heb 10:37 seemed to make the Habakkuk text a key reference for them.

The conclusion of the book seems not to have been used as much as it might have been, but it was paraphrased in an interesting way as the last verse of the hymn "Praise to God, Immortal Praise," by Anna L. Barbauld. The last two lines are a striking summation of Habakkuk's message: "And when every blessing's flown, Love Thee for Thyself alone."

Bibliography: Francis I. Andersen. *Habakkuk: A New Translation with Introduction and Commentary.* AB 25 (2001); Kenneth L. Barker and Waylon Bailey. *Micah, Nahum, Habakkuk, Zephaniah.* NAC 20 (1999); Michael H. Floyd. *Minor Prophets, Part 2.* FOTL 22 (2000); Donald E. Gowan. *The Triumph of Faith in Habakkuk* (1976); Robert D. Haak. *Habakkuk* (1991); Theodore Hiebert. "The Book of Habakkuk." *NIB 7 (1996) 623–65;* J. J. M. Roberts. *Nahum, Habakkuk, and Zephaniah* (1991); O. Palmer Robertson. *The Books of Nahum, Habakkuk, and Zephaniah.* NICOT (1990).

DONALD E. GOWAN

HABAKKUK COMMENTARY, PESHER. The Habakkuk Commentary (1QpHab) is one of the most important exegetical writings from Qumran, since it illuminates methods of biblical interpretation employed by Second Temple Jewish communities. The commentary has a distinct structure: each small section of biblical text from Habakkuk is followed by an explanation introduced by a formula including the term *pesher* (interpretation), e.g., "its interpretation concerns . . . " (psrw ʿl), "the interpretation of the word is . . ." (psrw hdbr), or "its interpretation is that . . ." (psrw ʾsr). Twelve and a half columns of text are preserved, providing a continuous commentary on the first two chaps. of the book of Habakkuk. The manuscript is dated paleographically to 30–1 BCE. The text appears to have been composed earlier, since there are marks indicative of the copying process preserved in the margins of the manuscript.

The biblical text quoted in the Commentary displays traditions other than that of the Masoretic text in several places, which is reflective not so much of sectarian variants as of the great textual diversity attested among the biblical manuscripts found at Qumran. The sections of interpretation, on the other hand, show how the Essene community idiosyncretically interpreted the words of the prophets from their own viewpoint, in the light of contemporary historical events and of events relating to the community. They interpreted the prophetic text as though the full significance of the prophecy was not known to Habakkuk but only to the Essene commentator, in particular to the TEACHER OF RIGHTEOUSNESS (1QpHab VII, 4-5). The historical references included in the Commentary are often veiled, however, and apart from the identification of the Kittim with the Romans, the text itself gives little support for identifying the Teacher of Righteousness or his opponents the WICKED PRIEST and the Liar.

Bibliography: M. Bernstein. "The Contribution of Qumran Discoveries to the History of Early Biblical Interpretation." *The Idea of Biblical Interpretation: Essays in Honor of James L. Kugel.* H. Najman and J. H. Newman, eds. (2004) 215–38; G. Brooke. "Qumran Pesher: Toward the Redefinition of a Genre." *RevQ* 10 (1979–81) 483–503; T. Lim. *Pesharim* (2002).

SARIANNA METSO

HABAZZINIAH   hab´uh-zi-n*i*´uh   חֲבַצִּנְיָה khavatsinyah]. The grandfather of the Rechabites whose faithfulness Jeremiah tested by offering them wine to drink (Jer 35:3).

HABIRU, HAPIRU hah-bee´roo, hah-pee´roo. A socially and politically marginal population group appearing throughout much of the ANE from ca. 1850 to 1150 BCE. They appear prominent in pre-Israelite Canaan and are thought by many scholars to be connected in some manner with the early Israelites = Hebrews (*see* HEBREW PEOPLE).

Although the etymology of the word continues to be in dispute, the contexts in which the habiru appear often portray them as unsavory and even seditious objects of social disdain and fear. The one trait that best comprehends all the habiru—a diverse populaton both enthnically and occupationally—is that of an outsider status they occupy from the perspective of the dominant social and political order. The term *outlaw* conveniently catches the double nuance of the habiru as those who stand recognizably outside the prevailing order, whether as fugitives or refugees in flight or expelled from the dominant order, or as soldiers of fortune, brigands, or rebels who prey upon or threaten the dominant order.

The heterogeneity of the habiru is attributable to the fact that they left their home societies either by free choice or expulsion, and for differing reasons, whether legal, social, economic, or political. To their new social locations they brought a great variety of skills, which both benefited and threatened the status quo. They appear in many occupational niches, primarily as mercenaries, brigands, agricultural workers, and construction laborers. The habiru/outsider label was carried across language fields, embracing Akkadian, Hittite, Ugaritic, and Egyptian (the term appears as ʿapiru in Egypt), and quite possibly in some occurrences of the biblical term *Hebrew* (although the formal Hebrew linguistic equivalent would probably be ʿapiru). The temporal persistence and geographical spread of the term *habiru* for this decentralized ragtag population group is probably best explained on the hypothesis that the "outlaws" who first took on, or were given, the name *habiru* passed it along to other outlaw groups as some of the habiru moved from country to country across the ANE.

In pre-Israelite Syro-Palestine, habiru were enlisted as auxiliaries in the armies of warring city-states, on occasion planted on land grants in return for their service, or were encouraged as brigands to harass enemy states. It is striking that the habiru are more frequently attested in mountainous regions than in the lowlands, presumably because their weaponry and manner of fighting were more suited to free booting and guerrilla warfare than to the clash of large armies. In the reign of Pharaoh Amenhotep II in the late 15th cent. BCE, large numbers of habiru are listed as prisoners of war put to work on state projects. In the Amarna letters, written by Canaanite rulers to the pharaoh in the 14th cent. BCE, references to armed groups of habiru are abundant, but habiru is also freely employed as an epithet (not unlike "subversives" or "terrorists") to vilify enemy rulers and anyone who angers or threatens someone in power. It is evident that habiru served as a disruptive "wild card" within a highly volatile imperial/feudal system that was not to last for much more than another century or so.

This much can be said about the similarity between the Amarna habiru and the first Israelites: they both represented a trajectory leading to the disruption of imperial control in Canaan. Although it now appears that biblical 'ivrim (עִבְרִים) is likely to be linguistically equivalent to habiru, a number of the OT occurrences of "Hebrew/s" appear in social, political, and military contexts that show affinities with the habiru as described in extrabiblical texts. Abraham, called "the Hebrew," commands a band of 318 warriors, contrary to his peaceful role elsewhere in tradition (Gen 14:14); the pharaoh who knows not Joseph fears "the Hebrews" as rapidly breeding vermin who threaten to destroy Egypt (Exod 1:8-22); the terms of service for the biblical Hebrew slave may have a parallel in contracts from the Mesopotamian city of Nuzi (*see* NUZI) in which habiru attached themselves in servitude to Nuzi citizens (Exod 21:2-11); and in the battle that Saul and Jonathan wage against the Philistines, a group of "Hebrews"—distinguishable from Israel and the Philistines—wavers in its allegiance until it sees that Israel is prevailing (1 Sam 13:3-7a; 14:21-23a).

In sum, while no direct line of continuity is traceable from the heterogeneous Amarna habiru to the early Israelites, themselves composed of heterogeneous elements, it is reasonable to suppose that early Israel included Amarna-type habiru elements. One explanation of the Israelite success in fending off the city-states that tried to abolish their movement is that habiru recruits to the Israelite movements provided strategic and tactical military skills that might not have been in the repertoire of peasants, of the sort, e.g., that, by carefully choosing time and place to surprise

the enemy, could lead to Israelite victories against Canaanite chariots and infantry equipped with the compound bow.

In short, while not all Israelites were habiru, it is quite possible that a fair number of them were habiru and were so regarded by Egyptian and Philistine enemies of the Israelites when they refer to them derisively as "Hebrews." By contrast, in later biblical parlance, "Hebrew/s" serves as an ethnic synonym for "Israel/ites" without any social derogation. It has been suggested that the heavy tax and debt burdens imposed by officials and landlords drove peasants off the land and into the ranks of rootless habiru composed of fugitives and refugees from various walks of life. The disappearance of the term from historical records after 1150 BCE may be due to a lightening of the debt burden in many of the early Iron Age states such as Israel itself, as well as the opening up of new social and economic opportunities in these new "multipower-actor states," with the consequence that habiru were largely absorbed into these Iron Age communities and polities that replaced the older Late Bronze Syro-Palestinian city-states. *See* ISRAEL, ORIGINS OF; SHASU.

Bibliography: M. L. Chaney. "Ancient Palestinian Peasant Movements and the Formation of Premonarchic Israel. Excursus: The *'Apiru* and Social Unrest in the Amarna Letters from Syro-Palestine." *Palestine in Transition. The Emergence of Ancient Israel.* D. N. Freedman and D. F. Graf, eds. (1983) 39–90; N. K. Gottwald. *The Tribes of Yahweh* (1979); M. Greenberg. *The Hab/piru. AOS 39.* (1955); M. Mann. *The Sources of Social Power. Vol. 1* (1986); M. B. Rowton. "The Topological Factor in the *hapiru* Problem." *AS* 16 (1965) 375–87; M. B. Rowton. "Dimorphic Structure and the Problem of the *'apiru-'Ibrim*." *JNES* 35 (1976) 13–20.

NORMAN K. GOTTWALD

HABOR hay'bor [חָבוֹר *khavor*]. A tributary of the EUPHRATES RIVER along which the inhabitants of Samaria were settled following its conquest by the Assyrians in 721 BCE. The Bible identifies the Habor as "the river of GOZAN," one of several cities in which the Israelites were also settled (2 Kgs 17:6; 18:11; 2 Chr 5:26). The river Habor has been identified as the modern Nahr el-Khabur originating near Haran and entering the Euphrates north of Mari.

RALPH K. HAWKINS

HACALIAH hak'uh-li'uh [חֲכַלְיָה *khakhalyah*]. The father of Nehemiah (Neh 1:1; 10:1 [Heb. 10:2]). Some scholars have suggested that the name derives from the verbal root **khakhal** (חָכַל) and means "wait for Yahweh." However, others counter that the use of an imperative form of a verb is uncharacteristic of Hebrew nomenclature.

DEREK E. WITTMAN

HACHILAH huh-ki´luh [חֲכִילָה khakhilah]. A hill in the wilderness of ZIPH where David took refuge from Saul (1 Sam 23:19; 26:1). Saul also encamped on this hill during his pursuit of David (1 Sam 26:3). The hill is described as being south of JESHIMON, but the exact location is unknown.

HACHMONI hak´moh-ni [חַכְמוֹנִי khakhmoni]. 1. The father of Jashobeam, one of DAVID'S CHAMPIONS (1 Chr 11:11).

2. The father of Jehiel, a court official who later attended the king's sons (1 Chr 27:32). The final Hebrew characters of the name suggest that both occurrences should be translated "a Hachmonite," indicating membership in the Hachmonite family, which is not mentioned elsewhere.

RALPH K. HAWKINS

HADAD hay´dad [אֲדָד ʾadhadh, הֲדַד hadhadh, חֲדַד khadhadh]. 1. Hadad, an ANE storm god, is often depicted holding a lightning bolt and/or a mace, while standing on the back of a lion or bull. At Ugarit he was known by the name BAAL (see UGARIT, TEXTS AND LITERATURE). Ugaritic texts provide the most complete mythology of Baal/Hadad who rose to power by defeating MOT (death) and the sea god Yam. In the Iron Age, Baal became primarily a Canaanite god, while Hadad became the chief god of the Arameans. Personal names containing Hadad are known in all ancient periods in Mesopotamia and Syria but are particularly common after the 9th cent. BCE in Syria, as, e.g., the Aramean kings HADADEZER and BEN-HADAD, both of whom appear in the Bible (2 Sam 8:3, 10:16; 1 Kgs 20:1). The god Hadad is also mentioned in the Tell Dan inscription as having provided victory to the king of Damascus (see INSCRIPTION, TELL DAN). Hadad-names from Edom and Arabia are also preserved in the Bible, including one of ISHMAEL's descendants (Gen 25:15) and an Edomite who rebelled against Solomon (1 Kgs 11:14-22). Aside from such personal names, the god Hadad is mentioned by name only once in the OT (Zech 12:11). References are also made to RIMMON, which means "thunderer," one of the epithets of Hadad (2 Kgs 5:18).

KEVIN A. WILSON

2. One of Ishmael's sons (Gen 25:15; 1 Chr 1:30).

3. The son of Bedad and one of the kings of Edom. He defeated the Midianites in the land of Moab and established the center of his government in the city of Avith (Gen 36:35; 1 Chr 1:46).

4. An Edomite king who succeeded Baal-hanan (1 Chr 1:50). In the Gen 36 list of the Edomite kings his name appears as HADAR (Gen 36:39).

5. A prince from the royal house of Edom, who became an adversary of Solomon (1 Kgs 11:14-22). When the army of David conquered Edom and Joab killed many of the men of Edom, Hadad escaped to Egypt with some of his father's servants where the Pharaoh provided him with royal treatment and gave him his sister-in-law in marriage. See EDOM, EDOMITES.

CLAUDE MARIOTTINI

HADADEZER hay´dad-ee´zuhr [הֲדַדְעֶזֶר hadhadh ʿezer]. Hadadezer was king of ARAM-ZOBAH in the 10th cent. BCE. Zobah was likely centered in the northern Beqa Valley in what is now Lebanon. Hadadezer is only known through references to his conflicts with Israel under DAVID.

It is likely that the events described in 2 Sam 10 should be construed as having occurred prior to those described in 2 Sam 8, despite their current arrangement. Thus, the first phase of Hadadezer's conflict with Israel came about when Zobah's forces involved themselves in a dispute between Israel and Ammon. Although 2 Sam 10:6 claims that the Ammonites "hired" the army of Zobah, it is quite possible that the arrangement involved the Ammonites as vassals to Hadadezer. The first phase of the engagement took place in Ammonite Transjordan, and saw the Israelite army, under JOAB, outmaneuvered and forced to face the Ammonites in front and the Arameans in the rear. By dividing his forces and leading his elite troops against Hadadezer, while his brother Abishai engaged the Ammonites with the remainder of Israel's army, Joab managed a stalemate, and all three armies withdrew.

When Hadadezer mustered a large, all-Aramean force (including elements from east of the Euphrates) for a return engagement, he was decisively beaten by the Israelite army, this time under David's command (2 Sam 10:16-19). The location of this battle, Helam, is unknown. After this battle, many of Zobah's vassals defected to Israel.

The final engagement between David and Hadadezer (2 Sam 8) was a surprise thrust by David into the territory of Zobah, possibly while Hadadezer was occupied near the Euphrates (2 Sam 8:3). David's success, including the seizure of considerable plunder and the decimation of Hadadezer's chariotry, signaled the end of Hadadezer's, and Zobah's, ascendancy.

The last mention of Hadadezer in the biblical record is in 1 Kgs 11:23, where Rezon, the new king of Aram-Damascus, is identified as a former servant or vassal of Hadadezer.

D. MATTHEW STITH

HADAD-RIMMON hay´dad-rim´uhn [הֲדַד־רִמּוֹן hadhadh-rimmon]. A compound name for the ANE storm god. Hadad and Rimmon both mean "thunderer." In Ugaritic mythology Hadad, who is most often referred to by his title BAAL, rises to power by defeating the deities Yam (the sea) and Mot (death). Mot, however, overcomes Baal and it appears that Baal is dead for some time. The goddess Anath travels to the underworld to rescue Baal. Zechariah 12:11 refers to "the mourning for Hadad-Rimmon in the plain of Megiddo." In the Ugaritic text, Anath mourns over the death of Baal. Zechariah's mention of mourning probably refers to prayers and rituals performed by worshipers imitating Anat's mourning, perhaps with intentions of reviving Baal. *See* UGARIT, TEXTS AND LITERATURE.

TREVOR D. COCHELL

HADAR hay′dahr [חֲדַר hadhar]. 1. The eighth king of Edom, he succeeded Baal-hanan (Gen 36:39). The Edomite king list in 1 Chr 1:50-51 reads HADAD instead.

2. The eighth son of Ishmael (Gen 25:15); the NRSV, following the Hebrew, reads "Hadad."

HADASHAH huh-dash′uh [חֲדָשָׁה khadhashah]. Town listed in the allotment to the tribe of Judah (Josh 15:37). Although Josh 15:33 indicates a location within the Shephelah (lowland) of Judah, and scholars have suggested a general vicinity between Lachish and Gath, the exact site of the town is unknown.

HADASSAH huh-das′uh [הֲדַסָּה hadhassah]. The initial name the narrator supplies to identify ESTHER (Esth 2:7). The common interpretation is that Hadassah was her given Hebrew name, but that she was subsequently known as Esther. Hadassah means MYRTLE. A previously conjectured connection to ISHTAR is no longer advocated.

TRISHA GAMBAIANA WHEELOCK

HADES hay′deez [ᾅδης hades]. In Greek mythology, Hades is the god of the underworld. *See* DEAD, ABODE OF THE; DEITIES, UNDERWORLD; SHEOL.

HADID hay′did [חָדִיד khadhidh]. A town in the northern Shephelah settled by those who returned from the exile (Ezra 2:33; Neh 7:37). The returnees who settled there were from the tribe of Benjamin (Neh 11:34), although it earlier fell within the boundaries of Ephraim. The connection of Benjamin with this area may have occurred when the tribe of Benjamin expanded its territory following the destruction of the Northern Kingdom in 721 BCE. It is unclear whether the town fell within the boundaries of Yehud during the Persian period or whether returning Jews settled there even though it belonged to another province. Hadid is identified with modern el-Haditheh. Although the town is not mentioned in the Bible as being occupied during the pre-exilic period, surface surveys of el-Haditheh have yielded sherds from the Late Bronze and Iron ages. The town may also appear in the topographical list of Thutmose III.

During the Hasmonean period, the city was fortified by Simeon to serve in defense of the kingdom. Alexander Jannaeus lost in a battle near Hadid against Aretas III, a Nabatean king who attacked Judea. During the

Roman period, Hadid was captured by Vespasian, who built a camp there.

KEVIN A. WILSON

HADLAI had′li [חֶדְלָי khadhlay]. Either the father or the family name of Amasa, an Ephraimite chief during Pekah's reign (2 Chr 28:12).

HADORAM huh-dor′uhm [הֲדוֹרָם hadhoram]. 1. A descendant of Joktan (Gen 10:27; 1 Chr 1:21). Hadoram has been associated with Dauram, listed in an Old Sabean inscription as a town in the south Arabian kingdom of SHEBA (modern Yemen). *See* SABEANS.

2. The son of King Tou of HAMATH, sent by his father to congratulate David following his defeat of the Aramean king Hadadezer (1 Chr 18:10). Hadoram is a theophoric name meaning "Hadad is exalted," replaced in the parallel account (2 Sam 8:9-10) with the Israelite theophoric name Joram ("Yahweh is exalted").

3. King Rehoboam's administrator of the department of conscript labor (2 Chr 10:18), called Adoniram in 1 Kgs 4:6; 5:14 [Heb. 5:28] and Adoram in 1 Kgs 12:18.

RALPH K. HAWKINS

HADRACH had′rak [חַדְרָךְ khadhrakh]. A city once located between Damascus and Aleppo. An 8th cent. BCE inscription describes Hadrach as the capital of King Zakir of Luas, also King of Hamath, who withstood a siege by a coalition of neighboring kingdoms. Some also identify Hadrach with Hatarikka mentioned in Assyrian records as an object of several 8th cent. campaigns. Any connection between the siege and these Assyrian interventions is uncertain.

Zechariah 9:1-2a describes Hadrach and Damascus as the center of a divine initiative that begins with Aramean and Phoenician cities, ranging northward to Hamath and southward to Tyre and Sidon. From there Yahweh marches down to Philistia, pacifying threats to Yahweh's sanctuary by destroying enemy cities and assimilating their people (vv. 2b-8). Attempts to identify this prophecy with particular military campaigns have not been persuasive. It probably describes a typological pattern of divine activity, based on prophetic interpretation of past campaigns as initiatives of Yahweh but not specifically referring to any of them.

Bibliography: J. C. L. Gibson. *Textbook of Syrian Semitic Inscriptions. Vol. 2: Aramaic Inscriptions* (1975); P. D. Hanson. "Zechariah 9 and the Recapitulation of an Ancient Ritual Pattern." *JBL* 92 (1973) 37–60; J. K. J. Kuan. *Neo-Assyrian Historical Inscriptions and Syria-Palestine* (1995).

MICHAEL H. FLOYD

HADRIAN. Publius Aelius Hadrianus, born in Italica, Spain (76–138 CE), was proclaimed emperor of the Roman empire in 117 in Antioch two days after his

Todd Bolen/BiblePlaces.com
Figure 1: Triumphal Arch erected for Emperor Hadrians's visit to Gerasa in 129/130 CE

days after his alleged deathbed adoption by TRAJAN. Hadrian traversed the path from provincial, to emperor, to god with the assistance of real ability, favorable circumstances, and family connections.

Upon his father's death when Hadrian was ten, he became the ward of his mother's nephew Trajan and Caelius Attianus. Hadrian further enjoyed the lifelong devotion of Trajan's influential wife Plotina, who assisted with the proclamation of Hadrian's adoption. Upon his accession, Hadrian faced internal and external military threats. He spent much of his reign touring provinces, inspecting and improving fortifications, founding cities, and initiating building projects throughout the empire. Surviving Roman coins commemorate his various visits, allowing historians to retrace his steps. Hadrian also extended Trajan's *alimenta* system (state support for poor children), codified centuries of praetorian edicts in the *edictum perpetuum*, and introduced legislation to protect slaves from inhumane treatment. Hadrian extended a general ban on genital mutilation to include circumcision (*Historia Augusta*, Life of Hadrian 14.2). This latter ban infringed on a fundamental ancestral practice of the Jews, one contributing cause to their third and catastrophically disastrous revolt (132–135 CE).

In 130 Hadrian founded *Colonia Aelia Capitolina* on the ruins of Jerusalem which was sacked by TITUS at the end of the first Jewish revolt in 70 CE. The colony's name came from Hadrian's own family name "Aelius" together with one of Roman Jupiter's primary epithets. Hadrian dedicated a temple to Jupiter on the site of the Temple. Across the Mediterranean, Jews were outraged and supplied material support to the rebels who rose up to fight a guerrilla

war in Judaea under the leadership of Simon (*see* BAR KOCHBA, SIMON). The Romans fought a war of extermination, reducing some thousand towns and villages, killing or enslaving the inhabitants. Over half a million died on the battlefields alone. At the end of this war, Jews were prohibited from entering or coming within sight of Jerusalem; Judaea ceased to exist, and became Syria Palestina. The permanent exile of the Jews until modern times may be dated from this defeat.

One must also consider the complicated impact of these struggles on the divergence and separation of Jews, Jewish Christians, and gentile Christians as distinct groups. (For Hadrian's specific policy towards Christians, *see* TRAJAN, to whose precedents Hadrian closely adhered.) Also difficult for Jews and Christians was Hadrian's methodical cultivation of EMPEROR WORSHIP. He founded numerous temples for this purpose (later Christian legend maintained—falsely—that he built these temples for Christ) in addition to consecrations of imperial family members (e.g., Plotina) and temples for traditional deities (e.g., the temple of Venus and Rome, the Pantheon in Rome, the temple of Jupiter [Olympian Zeus] in Athens). Hadrian was deeply interested in religion, and was initiated into the Eleusinian Mysteries in Athens. An odd innovation was Hadrian's consecration of his extraordinarily beautiful young male lover Antinoos after he drowned in the Nile. Worship of Antinoos was particularly popular in Greece, and led to a new style in sculpture.

Hadrian ensured a smooth succession when his health began to fail, first by adopting Lucius Aelius Caesar, who, however, predeceased him. Hadrian then adopted Antonius Pius. After his death, Hadrian was consecrated as the state god *Divus Hadrianus* by Antonius Pius. *See* ROMAN EMPIRE; VESPASIAN.

Bibliography: Anthony Richard Birley. *Hadrian: the Restless Emperor* (1997); Mary Taliaferro Boatwright. *Hadrian and the Cities of the Roman Empire* (2000).

HANS-FRIEDRICH MUELLER

HAELEPH hay-ee'lif [הָאֶלֶף ha'elef]. Eleventh in a list of fourteen west Benjaminite towns comprising that tribe's inheritance (Josh 18:28). Listed between ZELA and Jebus (Jerusalem) and meaning "The Thousand," the toponym occurs only here and lacks an expected conjunction. Septuagint versions omit it or conflate it with Zelah, Saul's burial place.

JASON C. DYKEHOUSE

HAGABAH hag'uh-buh [חֲגָבָה khaghavah; Ἀγγαβά Hangaba]. The head of a family of relatively low-ranking temple functionaries, the NETHINIM, who are listed among those returning to Jerusalem from Babylon with Zerubbabel (Ezra 2:45; 1 Esd 5:29; Hagaba in Neh 7:48). The name is distinct from Hagab (Ezra 2:46; 1 Esd 5:30).

DEREK E. WITTMAN

HAGAR hay'gahr [הָגָר haghar; Ἀγάρ Hagar]. Hagar's story is found in the OT in Gen 16:1-16 and 21:8-21. She was Sarai's Egyptian maid. It is not clear when she began to serve her mistress, but possibly she was one of the female slaves acquired as part of the gifts that Pharaoh gave to Abram for taking his wife (Gen 12:16). Since Sarai was barren and old, she gave Hagar to Abram to be his second wife in order to fulfill Yahweh's promise that a son would come from Abram's own issue (Gen 15:4) and in order that Sarai might obtain children (lit. "be built up," 16:2) by her. The arrangement resulted in the maid's pregnancy and elevated Hagar's status; this carried with it unforeseen consequences.

The theme of "see" (ra'ah [רָאָה]) and "sight" is prominent in the Hagar story. When Hagar saw that she was pregnant, her mistress became slight in her eyes. Sarai also saw correctly that her status had been lowered; she complained to Abram that he was responsible for her plight and called upon Yahweh to be the judge in this situation. Abram promptly gave Hagar back into Sarai's hand as a maid and to do whatever was good in her eyes. Hagar was so severely afflicted by her mistress that she ran away into the wilderness. She was the first runaway slave. But how was a lone pregnant woman to survive in the wilderness? God did not leave her to die in the desert; the messenger of Yahweh found her by a spring of water on the road to Shur. He called Hagar by name, something that Sarai and Abram never did; she was always "maid" or "slave" to them. Yahweh recognized her status as Sarai's maid and told her to return and submit to her mistress. It is troubling that God would tell her to return to an abusive situation. This instruction is not a prescription for counseling abused persons but should be read as God's way to ensure Hagar's and the child's survival. She would return to suffer under Sarai's hand, but in the meantime she had access to Abram's resources and protection. In due time, she gave birth to Ishmael, Abraham's firstborn son. She was the ancestress of the Ishmaelites and probably also the Hagrites. God promised that her son would be "a wild ass of a man" (Gen 16:12), living free and defiant among his kin.

Hagar was the first woman to have a theophany (the other person was Samson's mother, Judg 13:2-24). She conversed with God and received a promise from Yahweh that her descendants/seed would be innumerable, a promise otherwise only given to males. She was the first person to receive a birth annunciation of her son from the messenger of Yahweh. She was the only person to name God, not just the place of God's appearance. She named Yahweh "El Roi," "the God who sees me," and the well where she encountered God "BEER-LAHAI-ROI," the "well of the Living One who sees me." Her story foreshadowed Israel's later experience of slavery and affliction in Egypt, deliverance by Yahweh's intervention, and wandering in the wilderness.

While Gen 16 presents a Hagar who was defiant and self-determined, Gen 21 presents a Hagar who was passive and vulnerable. At the feast celebrating the weaning of ISAAC (yitskhaq [יִצְחָק]), Sarah saw Ishmael "Isaac-ing" (metsakheq [מְצַחֵק], NRSV, "playing"), and, perceiving that he would be a threat to Isaac as the heir of Abraham, she demanded that the slave woman and her son be cast out. Abraham obeyed Sarah with God's affirmation to expel mother and son. The two castaways wandered in the wilderness of Beer-sheba until the small provision of food and water were gone and the child was dying of thirst. Hagar set the boy under a bush at a distance of a bowshot so as not to see her son die. Apparently both mother and son wept and cried out, for the messenger of God called to Hagar from heaven in response to the boy's voice. God intervened at the critical moment, telling her to take the child by the hand and assuring her that her son would become a great nation. God opened her eyes and she saw a well from which she drew water for the child to drink. Ishmael grew, became an expert bowman, and lived in the wilderness of Paran. His mother got a wife for him from Egypt, making Hagar the only woman in the Bible to arrange for her son's marriage.

The Hagar story has been read by feminists, womanists, and Third World theologians through the lenses of their lived experiences and social locations. The issues that have been highlighted by these scholars include surrogate motherhood; slavery and poverty; polygamy and concubinage; single mothers and their struggle to raise children; homelessness; women's oppression of other women; sexual and physical abuse; racism, classism, sexism, and patriarchy; survival and liberation; whether God sided with the oppressed or the oppressor; and Jewish-Muslim-Christian dialogue. *See* CONCUBINE; POOR; RACISM; SEXUAL ABUSE; SLAVERY.

In the NT, Hagar appears in Gal 4:21-31. She is the only named woman in the book of Galatians. Paul used her and the "free woman," i.e., Sarah, in an allegory to represent the Judaizing Christians who were slaves to the Law and the Gentile Christians who were free children through the promise. Hagar was equated with Mount Sinai and the earthly Jerusalem, but the free woman Sarah was Jerusalem from above. Paul wanted to refute the claims of those who insisted that circumcision and obedience to the Law were required for becoming a Christian.

Bibliography: Alan Cooper. "Hagar in and out of Context." *USQR* 55 (2001) 35–46; Susan Elliott. *Cutting Too Close for Comfort: Paul's Letter to the Galatians in Its Anatolian Cultic Context* (2003); Elsa Tamez. "The Woman Who Complicated the History of Salvation." *New Eyes for Reading: Biblical and Theological Reflections by Women from the Third World.* John Pobee and Barbel von Wartenberg-Potter, eds. (1986) 5–17; Phyllis Trible. *Texts of Terror: Literary-Feminist Readings of Biblical Narratives* (1984); Phyllis Trible and Letty Russell, eds. *Hagar, Sarah, and Their Children: Jewish, Christian, and Muslim Perspectives* (2006); Delores Williams. *Sisters in the Wilderness: The Challenge of Womanist God-Talk* (1993).

LAI LING ELIZABETH NGAN

HAGGADAH huh-gah´duh. Also spelled *aggadah*, lit. means "narrative" or "telling," haggadah was defined by the 11th cent. CE rabbi of Grenada, Shmuel ibn Naghrela, as "everything that is not HALAKHAH." In particular, haggadah is rabbinic lore, falling into two branches: 1) expansive stories about biblical characters and narratives; and 2) didactic legends, often hagiographic in nature, about the rabbis themselves (*see* RABBI, RABBONI).

In regard to the biblical text, haggadah is a mode of MIDRASH dedicated to the transmission (and invention) of traditional stories and ideas. Fanciful details of the "lives" of biblical characters may be found in rabbinic haggadah, such as the notion that Abraham's father, Terah, was an idol manufacturer, or that the fruit that Adam and Eve consumed from the tree of knowledge of good and evil was an apple (or more commonly in rabbinic literature, a fig or a citron). Rabbinic narrators could invent entire conversations between biblical characters, such as the debate between the brothers Ishmael and Isaac over who would inherit from their father Abraham, which precipitated the trial recounted

in Gen 22. Authors of haggadah also expressed their theology through the invention of dialogue, even for God. Haggadah was also a vehicle for the teaching of rabbinic ethics.

Narrative portions of the Torah engendered many generations of haggadah, which were ultimately collected in rabbinic midrash, and there are compendia of haggadah on Genesis such as *Genesis Rabbah* or *Midrash Tanhuma* to Genesis. The first eleven chapters of Exodus and the narrative sections of Numbers and Deuteronomy also attracted a great deal of haggadah. There is even a rabbinic collection of haggadah ostensibly centered on Leviticus, although fewer than 20 percent of the verses of that biblical book are commented upon. Often, midrashic works on the Torah combine both Halakhah and Haggadah, depending on the nature of the biblical verses under rabbinic scrutiny. The legends about the rabbis, or sage tales, are often midrashic in character in that they, too, are based upon a verse of Scripture that is either manifest or embedded in the narrative. Many of these sage tales follow the format of the Greco-Roman CHREIA or pronouncement story. As such, there are many narratives that recount the exploits of a certain rabbi that share structure and detail with the "lives" of Hellenistic philosophers or saints of the early church. One of the great compendia of sage tales is the TALMUD that revels in recounting these legends. Since these stories are didactic narrative, the haggadah is no longer deemed to be a reliable source of history or biography about the rabbis. Rather, the rabbis of the haggadah are treated as fictional characters.

The term *Haggadah* is also used for the *Seder Haggadah Shel Pesach*, the rabbinic expansion of Deut 26 that serves as the liturgy for the evening festive meal on PASSOVER. *See* JEWISH BIBLICAL INTERPRETATION; RABBINIC INTERPRETATION; RABBINIC LITERATURE.

Bibliography: Burton L. Visotzky. *Reading the Book: Making the Bible a Timeless Text* (2005).

BURTON L. VISOTZKY

HAGGADHAH. *See* HAGGADAH.

HAGGAI. *See* HAGGAI, BOOK OF.

HAGGAI, BOOK OF hag´i [חַגַּי khaggi]. The tenth book of the Minor Prophets (Book of the Twelve) in the OT. The book of Haggai addresses issues related to the reconstruction of the Second Temple in the early Persian period (520 BCE) in the province of Yehud. It traces the impetus of the project to the prophetic voice of Haggai and the response of the key leaders ZERUBBABEL (Davidic governor) and JESHUA (Zadokite priest) and of their community. This rebuilding project is understood as inaugurating an era of peace and prosperity for the people of God that is but a prelude to the commencement of the universal reign of Yahweh through a Davidic royal figure.

A. Structure

B. Detailed Analysis

1. Form and history

The book of Haggai clearly reflects and may also be structured according to the pattern of rituals used for the reconstruction of temples throughout the ANE. The temple restoration process can be divided into four phases: first, the decision to build; second, the preparation of the building site and materials; third, the laying of the foundations; and finally, the latter stages of construction that included dedication festivities. The book of Haggai ends at the third phase, suggesting that the book may have also served as a text deposited in the foundations of the Second Temple (see TEMPLE, JERUSALEM).

The project is undertaken near the outset of Darius' reign in 520 BCE. The book of Ezra offers evidence that Cyrus had given permission for Temple reconstruction at the outset of his reign (Ezra 1:1-4; 5:13-16; 6:3-5), an action consistent with his treatment of other sub-jects in this early period (e.g., *ANET* 315-16). However, the book of Ezra shows that little was accomplished during the reigns of Cyrus and Cambyses, so that at the outset of Darius' reign there was a need for a renewed effort. In the wake of the unsettled transition of power from Cambyses to Darius (522–519 BCE), such a project on the western frontier of the Persian Empire by individuals from the heart of the empire, may have been seen as advantageous to the new regime.

2. Haggai 1:1-15: Exhortation to rebuild the Temple

As is typical of temple restoration rituals, the decision to build must be linked to a divine source and here the prophet Haggai provides this impetus for the project. In a chiastic scheme that surrounds the entire chapter (1:1, 15), the prophecy is dated according to the reign of the Persian emperor, even though the prophetic message is directed to Zerubbabel and Joshua, respectively the Davidic governor and the Zadokite high priest of the province of Yehud (see ZADOK, ZADOKITES). In the temple restoration rituals the divine message was related to the royal figure, here the dating by Persian emperor and inclusion of the priestly figure reveals the shifting realities of the Persian period Jewish community. The message reveals to the new leadership the failure of "these people" to focus attention on the Temple project (1:2). Two issues are introduced in the first half of the message (1:2-7), the construction of the Temple and the poverty of the people, but these two issues are not connected directly. It is only after crossing the climactic center point in v. 8, with the direct calls to action reminiscent of the building of the First Temple by Solomon ("Go up to the hills and bring wood and build the house," 1 Kgs 5:1-6 [Heb. 5:15-20]) and linked to the purpose of Yahweh's pleasure and honor, that the two issues are then connected in v. 9. The poverty of the people (v. 9a) is directly linked to the people's lack of attention to the construction of the Temple (v. 9b) and this poverty is identified as a divine discipline (vv. 10-11). The chapter ends with a narrative description of the obedient response of the people who are now no longer "these people" (v. 2; compare Isa 7:16; 8:11), but rather "the remnant of the people" (v. 12). At the heart of this concluding narrative lies the promise of God's presence for this remnant: "I am with you" (v. 13).

3. Haggai 2:1-9: Encouragement for restoring the former glory

The second oracle comes nearly a month after work began on the project, a period associated with the preparation phase in ancient temple reconstruction. This phase was probably the most difficult of the entire project as the builders excavated the old site in search of the original foundations of the Temple. The rhetoric of this passage creatively draws in the audience by naming the various addressees (Zerubbabel, Joshua, Remnant; compare 1:12, 14) and then using three questions that communicate that the prophet empathizes with the potential discouragement of his hearers (vv. 2-3). The passage creates a rhetorical shift by using the term "but now" (wiʿattah וְעַתָּה, author's trans.) to introduce a prophetic speech form often called "encouragement for a task" (e.g., Josh 1:6-9). The message addresses each party (Zerubbabel, Joshua, People) as it encourages them to continue the work with the repeated promise of 1:13, "I am with you" (2:4). The allusion to the "covenant" in 2:5 reminds the hearers of God's promise after the golden calf incident in Exod 32–34 to remain with them. The prophetic message ends with the promise of a cosmic upheaval enacted by Yahweh that will provide the material resources necessary for the present glory of the Temple to exceed the former glory of the pre-exilic Solomonic Temple.

4. Haggai 2:10-23: Prophetic messages on the day the foundation was laid

The book closes with a literary complex that extends from 2:10-23, providing two prophetic oracles delivered on the twenty-fourth day of the ninth month in the second year of Darius. The significance of this day is identified in 2:18 as "the day that the foundation of the LORD's temple was laid." The two oracles are addressed to priestly (2:10-19) and royal figures (2:20-23), suggestive of the personnel involved in ANE foundation-laying ceremonies. While some have suggested that the first oracle (2:10-19) contains two unrelated prophetic pieces (2:10-14, 15-19), this is not the case for ritual as well as rhetorical reasons. First, the concern over purity and defilement in 2:10-14 was a regular component in temple reconstruction. Second, the key rhetorical signal "but now" (wiʿattah) appears in 2:15, and this term always appears midway through a speech rather than at the outset. This unified oracle begins by rehearsing the past in terms of a ritual impurity that has spread from disobedient hands to sacrificial offerings to the sacred altar that was in use on the site prior to the construction of the Temple (see Ezra 3:1-6).

The focus of this day of foundation laying, however, was not to be on the past, but rather on the obedience of the present and the promise of the future. The prophet employs creative rhetoric in vv. 15-19 to force the hearers to think of past, present, and future at the same time. This is accomplished by leaving his initial sentence incomplete and returning to that unfinished sentence at key intervals, completing it only in the closing words of the pericope: "But now, consider what will come to pass from this day on. Before a stone was placed upon a stone in the LORD's temple. . . . Consider from this day on, from the twenty-fourth day of the ninth month. Since the day that the foundation of the LORD's temple was laid, consider . . . from this day on I will bless you." What lies in the spaces between these repetitions of the initial incomplete sentence are references to the curse they have experienced in the past. By not finishing the sentence until the final words the hearers consider their past, while simultaneously reflecting on the hope this present day will bring for their future. It is that hope of blessing that is the reward of their obedience, a hope suggested from the outset in 1:1-11.

The book ends with a second oracle delivered on that day of foundation laying. This oracle in 2:20-23 is closely linked with the previous pericope in 2:10-19 on ritual and rhetorical grounds. First, royal and priestly figures are essential in ANE rites related to temple reconstruction and the superscription reveals that these were delivered on the same day. Second, the superscriptions at 2:10 and 20 ("the word of the Lord came to [ʾel אֶל] the prophet Haggai . . . ," author's trans.) use a slightly different wording from the one employed in 1:1; 2:1 ("the word of the Lord came through [beʾ adh בְּיַד] the prophet Haggai . . . ," author's trans.) and the rhetorical shape of the two superscriptions (2:10, 20) are arranged chiastically (2:10—date formula, messenger formula; 2:20—messenger formula, date formula). However, although linked to vv. 10-19, 2:20-23 does emphasize the role of Zerubbabel and extends the promise of blessing in v. 19 beyond mere agricultural bounty to include the fulfillment of the ancient Davidic hopes for universal dominion. The political and military upheaval envisioned in 2:22 is linked to the work of Yahweh alone and not to a popular uprising by the Jewish community. Nevertheless, great hopes are attached to Zerubbabel as Davidic heir, using language associated with David in the past: "take" (2 Sam 7:8; 2 Kgs 14:21; 23:30), "my servant" (2 Sam 3:18; 7:5, 8; Pss 78:70; 89:3; 132:10), "signet ring" (Jer 22:24), "chosen" (1 Sam 16:8-10; 2 Sam 6:21; Ps 78:70). Ancient Near Eastern foundation-laying ceremonies were often opportunities to showcase royal authority and success and this section is no exception. This conclusion to the book reveals that the obedience of the community and its leaders, which was celebrated at the foundation-laying ceremony, had cosmic implications.

C. Theological and Religious Significance of the Book

Haggai is a witness to the focus of the early Persian period community on its core symbol of identity: the Second Temple. While chronicling the key role of a faithful community and its leadership including the prophet Haggai, it consistently highlights the role of the divine in providing the impetus, empowerment, and encouragement to restore the sacred site and the promise of the divine to reward the community with renewed blessing and empire. Allusions to earlier traditions of Israel (those related to David and Moses) provide further legitimacy to the activities encouraged by the prophet.

Bibliography: Mark J. Boda. *Haggai, Zechariah*. NIV Application Commentary (2004); John Kessler. *The Book of Haggai: Prophecy and Society in Early Persian Yehud* (2002); Carol L. Meyers and Eric M. Meyers. *Haggai, Zechariah 1-8*. AB 25b (1987); David L. Petersen. *Haggai and Zechariah 1-8: A Commentary*. OTL (1984); Paul L. Redditt. *Haggai, Zechariah and Malachi*. NCB (1995); W. H. Rose. *Zemah and Zerubbabel: Messianic Expectations in the Early Postexilic Period* (2000); Marvin A. Sweeney. *The Twelve Prophets*. 2 vols. Berit Olam (2000); Pieter A. Verhoef. *The Books of Haggai and Malachi*. NICOT (1987); Hans Walter Wolff. *Haggai: A Commentary* (1988).

MARK J. H. BODA

HAGGEDOLIM hag´uh-doh´lim [הַגְּדוֹלִים *haggedholim*]. The father of Zabdiel (Neh 11:14), the official in charge of the priests who settled in Jerusalem after the Babylonian exile. The name means "the great ones" and may indicate Zabdiel's descent from high priests rather than from a particular individual of that name.

DEREK E. WITTMAN

HAGGI, HAGGITES hag´ee, hag´it [חַגִּי *khaggi*]. 1. The second-listed of seven sons of Gad and grandson of Jacob and Zilpah (Gen 46:16). Haggi was one of Zilpah's sixteen descendants among the seventy who arrived with Jacob in Egypt (Gen 46:18, 27).

2. An Israelite clan whose ancestor was Haggi (Num 26:15).

JASON C. DYKEHOUSE

HAGGIAH ha-gi´uh [חֲגִיָּה *khaggiyah*]. A Levite among the descendants of MERARI in a genealogical list in 1 Chr 6:30 [Heb. 6:15]. He is listed as the father of Asaiah and the son of Shimea. The name probably means "festival of Yahweh," although some have questioned whether it is theophoric.

HAGGITH hag´ith [חַגִּית *khaggith*]. A wife of David and mother of Adonijah, the fourth son of David born at Hebron (2 Sam 3:4; 1 Chr 3:2), who failed to seize the throne (1 Kgs 1:5–2:25). Some Greek manuscripts occasionally omit her name, but the context of interfamily rivalry suggests the original reiterated the prospective queen mother's name.

JASON C. DYKEHOUSE

HAGIGAH [חֲגִיגָה *khaghighah*]. The twelfth and final tractate of the second order of the Mishnah, *Mo´ed*. This order deals with regulations pertaining to biblically mandated religious festivals. The biblical basis for the *Hagigah* is Deut 16:16 (as well as Exod 23:14), which requires that "all your males shall appear before the LORD your God in the place that He will choose" three times annually. *Hagigah*, derived from the Hebrew term for pilgrim-feast (khagh חַג), lays out the precise details related to the three festivals in ancient Judaism

where participants were required to be present in Jerusalem: Passover (Pesah), Feast of Weeks (Shavuot), and the Feast of Booths (Sukkot).

PHILLIP MICHAEL SHERMAN

HAGIOGRAPHA [כְּתוּבִים *kethuvim*; ἁγιογράφα *agiographa*]. Hagiographa means "holy writings." The Jewish canon is divided into three sections; the Hagiographa is the third and final collection of sacred Scriptures after the Torah ("Teachings") and the Nevi'im ("Prophets"). The Writings consist of the Psalms, Proverbs, Job, the Megillot (Song of Songs, Ruth, Lamentations, Ecclesiastes, and Esther), Daniel, and 1 and 2 Chronicles. As evidenced by this list, the collection contains a wide variety of materials—poems, songs, philosophical musings, maxims, short stories, histories. Some of the material may date from the monarchical period; however, in its final form, the Hagiographa is postexilic. It is also possible that the three divisions within the Jewish Scripture are the result of a three-stage canonical process. The Torah would have been the first collection to come together as authoritative, and the Hagiographa would have been the last. *See* CANON OF THE OT.

JENNIFER L. KOOSED

HAGRITE, HAGRITES hag´rit [הַגְרִי *haghri*, הַגְרִים *haghrim*]. David's warrior Jaziz, who tended David's flocks, has the epithet Hagrite that identifies his residence (1 Chr 27:30). According to 1 Chr 5:10, 19-20, the Hagrites lived east of Gilead and were defeated by the tribe of Reuben during Saul's reign. Psalm 83:7 (Heb. 83:6) lists them with the peoples of Moab, Edom, and the Ishmaelites, who were Israel's enemies.

EMILY R. CHENEY

HAIL, HAILSTONES [בָּרָד *baradh*; χάλαζα *chalaza*]. Hailstorms are uncommon in Syria-Palestine, although they do occur during severe thunderstorms in the spring or summer. Hail is formed when raindrops freeze after having been lifted to colder regions by upward air currents. When their masses have increased to an extent that air currents can no longer support them, they fall to the ground, sometimes doing great damage.

The plague of hail (Exod 9:18-33) reflects the phenomenology of hailstorms in terms of the limitation of its scope. However, the fact that the hailstorm strikes all of Egypt except Israelite-inhabited Goshen marks it as exceptional. The unusual concentration of the hail was perceived by the Israelites as having been an act of Yahweh, and one of such importance that, of the twenty-nine occurrences of hail in the OT, twenty-two of these are in connection with the sixth plague (Exod 9; Pss 18:13-14; 78:47; etc.). The plague of hail was unusually severe: "there was hail with fire flashing continually in the midst of it, such heavy hail as had never fallen in all the land of Egypt since it became a nation" (Exod 9:24).

Hail appears elsewhere in both literal and figurative usages. In literal usages, hail serves as a means by which Yahweh aids Israel in battle (Josh 10:11), punishes the wicked (Isa 28:2, 17), expresses anger (Ezek 13:13; etc.), and manifests divine glory (Ps 148:8), all of which occur in the apocalypse (Rev 8:7; 11:19; 16:21). Figuratively, hail describes the destructive consequences of covenant violation by Israel (Isa 28:2). *See* ISRAEL, CLIMATE OF; PLAGUES IN EGYPT.

RALPH K. HAWKINS

HAIR, HAIRS [שֵׂעָר *seʿar*]. Semitic men are depicted in Egyptian art as having curly hair of moderate length. They would have favored the Mesopotamians, who described themselves as "the black-headed people" in reference to their typical hair color.

The norm was for men to cut or clip their hair periodically, though probably more often than Absalom, who reportedly cut his hair once each year (2 Sam 14:25-27). The narrator emphasized the weight and luxuriance of Absalom's hair, perhaps to suggest handsomeness or virility, or to foreshadow Absalom's death, which involved getting his head entangled in a tree (2 Sam 18:9-15).

Persons who made Nazirite vows demonstrated devotion to God by letting their hair and beards (for men) grow long, to be shaved when the votive period was completed (Num 6:5, 18), a practice that continued into the NT period (Acts 21:24). Some appear to have lived as life-long Nazirites: Samson's long hair was described as a sign of life-long devotion (Judg 13:5) and a key to his superhuman strength (Judg 16:17-20). Likewise, Hannah vowed that Samuel's hair would never be shorn (1 Sam 1:21). Priests were prohibited from shaving bald spots on their heads and from trimming the corners of their beards (Lev 21:5), perhaps to preserve a distinct appearance.

New Testament evidence suggests that women typically wore their hair long. The woman who anointed Jesus' feet with oil dried his feet with her hair (Luke 7:38). Paul reflected a belief that it was shameful for a woman to shave her head (1 Cor 11:5-6), and considered it a lesson of nature that men should maintain short hair rather than wearing it long, like women (1 Cor 11:14-15).

While Paul considered a woman's long hair to be her "glory" (1 Cor 11:15), NT writers advised women against braiding, plaiting, or adorning their hair with jewelry, regarding such efforts as excessive vanity (1 Tim 2:9; 1 Pet 3:3).

How one's hair was treated could have symbolic significance in a variety of ways. Priests were consecrated via anointment of the head with oil (Exod 28:41; 29:7), and kings were designated in similar manner (Judg 9:8; 1 Sam 10:1; 16:12). Likewise, rejoicing or blessing could be conveyed by the application of oil to the head (Ps 23:5).

In contrast, sorrow or repentance was expressed by SHAVING the head (Isa 15:7), pulling out the hair (Ezra 9:3), or imposing dust or ashes (Josh 7:6; Job 42:6; Ezek 27:30). A woman accused of adultery could be tested by a trial in which the priest publicly disheveled her hair before requiring that she drink bitter water (Num 5:18).

Prophets used the image of shaving the hair as a metaphor for judgment. Isaiah predicted a time of baldness instead of "well-set hair" (Isa 3:24), and predicted that Yahweh would shave the Israelites with an Assyrian razor (Isa 7:20). Ezekiel symbolically shaved his head and beard, dividing the hair as a sign of impending judgment (Ezek 5:1). *See* BALDNESS; BEARD; NAZIR, NAZIRITE; SAMSON.

TONY W. CARTLEDGE

HAKKATAN hak'uh-tan [הַקָּטָן *haqqatan*; Ακαταν *Akatan*]. The father of clan chief Johanan, listed as a descendant of Azgad (Ezra 8:12; 1 Esd 8:38) and, along with 110 other descendants of Azgad, among the returnees who left Babylon with Ezra during the reign of Artaxerxes. The name means "the small one."

DEREK E. WITTMAN

HAKKOZ hak'oz [הַקּוֹץ *haqqots*; Ακκως *Akkōs*]. 1. The head of a clan of priests, descendants of Aaron upon whom the seventh lot fell when David, Zadok, and Ahimelech organized the priests for their liturgical duties (according to 1 Chr 24:10).

2. A priestly clan head whose descendants were among the returnees who left Babylon with Zerubbabel but were unable to provide documentation establishing their genealogy and were thus disqualified from serving as priests until another priest could determine their ancestry through use of the URIM AND THUMMIM (Ezra 2:61; Neh 7:63; 1 Esd 5:39). Eupolemus, an envoy of Judas Maccabeus to Rome, appears as a son of Accos (perhaps the same family) in 1 Macc 8:17. *See* KOZ.

DEREK E. WITTMAN

HAKUPHA huh-ky*oo*'fuh [חֲקוּפָא *khaqufaʾ*; Αχιβα *Achiba*]. The head of a family of relatively low-ranking temple functionaries called the NETHINIM who were among those who returned to Jerusalem from Babylon with Zerubbabel during the reign of Cyrus (Ezra 2:51; Neh 7:53; 1 Esd 5:31).

HALAH hay'luh [חֲלַח *khalakh*]. The location where the Assyrian king deported the inhabitants of Samaria during the reign of King Hoshea (ca. 722 BCE; 2 Kgs 17:6; 18:11). According to 1 Chr 5:26, the Assyrian king TIGLATH-PILESER III deported the Transjordanian tribes of Reuben, Gad, and the half-tribe of Manasseh to Halah (ca. 733 BCE). The NRSV emends the Hebrew of Obad 1:20 (hakhel-hazzeh [הַחֵל־הַזֶּה], "this army") to read khalakh. According to this reading, the exiles in Halah will take over areas of Phoenicia. The location of Halah is unknown.

HEATHER R. MCMURRAY

HALAK, MOUNT hay'lak הָהָר הֶחָלָק hahar hekhalaq]. A mountain, with a name meaning "smooth mountain" (i.e., without foliage), rising toward SEIR and marking the southern limit of Joshua's conquest (Josh 11:17; 12:7). As Seir (se'ir שֵׂעִיר]; hairy [i.e., with foliage]) is understood as being located west of the Arabah, Mount Halak occupies a location somewhere between Kadesh-barnea and the Dead Sea. Genesis depicts Jacob (Israel) as "smooth-skinned" (khalaq חָלָק) and Esau (Edom), who is associated with Seir, as "hairy" (sa'ir שֵׂעָר; 27:11; 36:8). A "smooth mountain" rising toward Seir fittingly separates these brother-nations.

JASON C. DYKEHOUSE

HALAKAH. *See* HALAKHAH.

HALAKHAH הֲלָכָה halakhah]. Jewish rabbinic law, lit. "going [on the way]." Rabbinic law can derive directly from the Torah, can be interpreted from the Bible, or can be passed down in the rabbinic community as "Oral Law." Scripturally derived law is called *midrash halakhah* (*see* MIDRASH). Oral legal traditions were collected topically initially as MISHNAH and attributed to rabbinic authorities. Commentaries on the Mishnah, such as the GEMARA (*see* TALMUD) also serve as sources for rabbinic halakhah. By the Middle Ages, halakhah was organized in formal codes such as that of Maimonides (*Mishneh Torah*, ca. 1177–87 CE) or Joseph Karo (*Shulchan Aruch,* ca. 1564 CE), which covered every aspect of Jewish behavior and ethics. *See* RABBINIC INTERPRETATION.

Bibliography: Burton L. Visotzky. "The Literature of the Rabbis." *From Mesopotamia to Modernity: Ten Introductions to Jewish History and Literature* (1999) 71–102.

BURTON L. VISOTZKY

HALAKHIC LETTER מִקְצָת מַעֲשֵׂי הַתּוֹרָה miqtsath ma'ase hattorah]. Also known by the Hebrew name, as "Some of the Works of the Law," or the abbreviation 4QMMT. None of the six copies of the document discovered in Cave 4 in 1952 (4Q394-99) is complete, but together they preserve perhaps as much as 50 percent of the original. Although two of the manuscripts (4Q394-95) have been dated paleographically to the mid 1st cent. BCE, many researchers believe that the document dates to the very origin of the QUMRAN sect (ca. 160 BCE).

The document can be divided into three parts: a calendar, a list of legal rulings, and an admonitory conclusion. One of the six manuscripts contains the remains of a 364-day sectarian calendar, which preceded the legal document. As the remainder of the work does not mention calendrical matters and instead deals only with issues related to purity, it remains doubtful whether the calendar is an integral part of 4QMMT.

The main body of 4QMMT lists some two dozen matters of Jewish law that give evidence of having been composed by the leadership of the Qumran sect for the purpose of warning the addressee, who had come under the influence of a third party (perhaps the PHARISEES) concerning purity restrictions that he was violating. Although Jewish law and various discussions pertaining to it are ubiquitous in the DEAD SEA SCROLLS, only 4QMMT directly challenges the position of another religious party. Because of the potentially defining nature of such a challenge, scholars have hoped to find in 4QMMT a basis for a definitive identification of the group behind the sectarian scrolls. In this regard, it has been noted that some of laws echo halakhic rulings in the MISHNAH that are attributed to the SADDUCEES.

The exhortation that makes up the final portion of the text urges the addressee to do "what is right and good" for his own benefit and that of Israel. Contextually, "doing what is right and good" refers to the two dozen or more legal rulings in the body of the document. These are called "works of the Law," the very phrase that gives the composition its name. According to the author of the letter, right conduct regarding these laws "will be reckoned . . . as righteousness." Thus 4QMMT appears to be in direct opposition to Paul's letters to the Galatians (e.g., Gal 2:16) and Romans. It is of note that the expression "works of the law" is found in antiquity only in Romans, Galatians, and 4QMMT.

Bibliography: Elisha Qimron and John Strugnell. *Qumran Cave 4.V: Miqṣat Ma'ase ha-Torah* (1994).

MARTIN G. ABEGG, JR.

HALF-TRIBE חֲצִי שֵׁבֶט khatsi shevet]. A term used to describe the two portions of the TRIBE of Manasseh because they settled in separate locations. When the tribes of Gad and Reuben requested to settle east of the Jordan River, half of the tribe of Manasseh made the same request (Num 32:33-42; 34:13-15). This half of the tribe drove out the Amorites (Num 32:39) and took the land located in Gilead and Bashan (Deut 3:13-15; 29:8), where the men built sheepfolds and fortified towns for their families, but they themselves did not settle there until after they had fought and acquired the land west of the Jordan for the rest of the tribes (Num 32:16-33; Josh 1:12-18; 4:12-13; 12:6; 13:29-31; 18:17). The other half of the tribe of Manasseh did not make this request and received its portion after the conquest in central Palestine, a portion that, according to Josh 17:5-10, was located north of Ephraim's, southwest of Issachar's, and southeast of Asher's portions. Elsewhere these boundaries differ (Josh 16:19; 17:11).

EMILY R. CHENEY

HALHUL hal'huhl [חַלְחוּל khalkhul]. A town 6 km north of Hebron in the hill country of Judah constituting part of that tribe's inheritance (Josh 15:58). According to Josephus (*J.W.* 4.516–539), during the first Jewish revolt against Rome (66–73 CE), Simon of Gerasa captured Hebron after disrupting an Idumean force betrayed by Jacob, one of its commanders, at Halhul (Alulus/Alurus).

JASON C. DYKEHOUSE

HALI hay'li [חֲלִי khali]. Second in a list of towns belonging to Asher and constituting part of that tribe's inheritance (Josh 19:25). Hali is almost certainly in the south of Asher.

HALICARNASSUS hal'uh-kahr-nas'uhs [Ἁλικαρνασσός Halikarnassos]. Halicarnassus, modern-day Bodrum in southwest Turkey, was an important city of Caria in Asia Minor during classical times, and home of the historians Herodotus (5th cent. BCE) and Dionysius of Halicarnassus (1st cent. BCE). Founded as a colony of Troezen, it maintained Greek customs under Persian rule, and its importance continued owing to its position on the sea-route from the Aegean to Asia. Its most famous ruler, Mausolus (reigned 377–353 BCE), made the city his capital and constructed his massive family tomb, "the Mausoleum," as the center of his hero-cult. The Mausoleum became one of the Seven Wonders of the World and served as the model for Augustus Caesar's tomb. The city was captured by Alexander the Great in 334 and came under Roman rule in 129 BCE.

The presence of Jews in the city is attested, as elsewhere in Asia Minor, from the 2nd cent. BCE. A letter of the Roman senate to many cities in Asia Minor, including Halicarnassus, requesting protection of the Jews in the cities appears in 1 Macc 15:16-24. Many would have come there following Antiochus III's resettlement (between 212 and 204 BCE) of 2,000 Jews from Babylonia and Mesopotamia (Josephus, *Ant.* 12.148-53).

As an important assize center for the Roman province in Asia Minor, the Romans encouraged stability in the region. A decree by the people of the city (*Ant.* 16.256-58), although clearly under Roman instruction, was issued sometime after 47 BCE permitting the Jews to observe the Sabbath, perform their ancestral rites, and to build places of prayer. These are rights that the Romans encouraged other cities to grant, too. In this decree women are specifically mentioned as being included in these rights, perhaps reflecting a local tradition of high status for women in the Jewish community.

Little is known of the likely early Christian population, but the city became a minor See, and bishops' representatives were sent from it to the early church councils.

JAMES K. AITKEN

HALIF, TEL. The site of Tel Halif (Tell Khuweilifeh) is a 3-acre mound at the southwestern edge of the Judean hills and is strategically located overlooking the Plain of Philistia and the Shephelah to the west and the Negev Desert to the south. Excavations undertaken by the Lahav Research Project identified seventeen Str. of occupation from the Chalcolithic-Early Bronze Age transition to modern times.

During the Early Bronze Age I period, Egyptian-style objects such as bread molds and pottery indicate that Tel Halif participated with sites such as Tel Arad in a regional network of exchange with Egypt. The site was unoccupied during the Early Bronze Age II, but in Early Bronze Age III the town was heavily fortified with the construction of a 3.5 m thick city wall and tower system.

After a gap during the early second millennium BCE, Tel Halif was reoccupied in the Late Bronze Age. The principle building of this time was a large, well-built courtyard house apparently occupied by a wealthy family. In the final Late Bronze Age level dating to the 13th cent. BCE this building and others were covered with a platform of clay and loess up to 2.5 m thick into which were dug several stone-lined storage pits. During this time Tel Halif appears to have become primarily a storage center.

In the Iron Age I, or 12th and 11th cent. BCE, the occupants of Tel Halif continued to use the several storage pits, resembling many other sites of this period. Philistine style potsherds from the late 11th or early 10th cent. indicate that at this time some sort of relationship existed between Tel Halif and Philistia.

The Iron Age II appears to have been an era of prosperity at Tel Halif. The city wall was rebuilt in the 9th cent., this time as a casemate wall whose inner face was integrated with typical Israelite domestic architecture such as four-room houses. The city was destroyed in the late 8th cent., most likely an event associated with Sennacherib's invasion of Judah in 701 BCE, but was reoccupied shortly thereafter. Just south of the tell is a substantial cemetery containing many Iron Age II tombs in the standard Judahite style: a square chamber cut into the rock, with one to three burial benches and hollowed out pits serving as bone repositories.

During the subsequent Persian era, the summit of Tel Halif bore a large building likely related to Persian administration of the region. Some domestic architecture is present from the Hellenistic period. The site then has a gap until the Late Roman–Byzantine period at which point the settlement once again became substantial and prosperous as did the surrounding area.

Although the biblical identification of Tel Halif remains uncertain, two options appear viable. The first is that it constitutes the city of Ziklag given to David by the Philistines. This is based on the site's proximity to nearby Khorvat Rimmon, presumably ancient Rimmon, mentioned in association with Ziklag in the Simeonite inheritance subsequent to the conquest (Josh

15:31-32). The second option is that Tel Halif was itself ancient Rimmon and that the name traveled to the site of Khorvat Rimmon when the area was resettled during the Roman period. Subsequently, evidence from the *Onomasticon* of Eusebius suggests that during the Late Roman–Byzantine era Tel Halif was the Jewish city of Tilla.

JAMES F. OSBORNE

HALL. As an architectural term, *hall* refers to a building or a room within a building, usually one used for special purposes, and usually a large one. In classical architecture two major types of halls found in the ANE are the peristyle hall and the hypostyle hall. The peristyle hall is characterized by columns around the sides of a room or court forming a colonnade. The hypostyle hall has columns throughout the room supporting a roof. Both architectural forms are known from Egypt as early as the New Kingdom and from the Persian Empire. Examples of this type hall are known from the Great Hypostyle Hall in the Temple at Karnak, Egypt, which was begun by Amenophis III, continued by Seti I, and completed by Ramesses II. This huge hall contained 134 large columns, two rows of which were over 20 m high. The hall itself was over 100 m long and over 50 m wide. At nearby Luxor was a temple built by Ramesses II and Amenhotep III. This temple had a pylon leading into a peristyle hall.

In the area of Syria-Palestine, a common monumental building style is the *bit hilani*, a tripartite style with a columned portico or entranceway, a main room, and smaller private rooms toward the rear. In such a plan, the main room could be designated as a hall. At Zincirli, at least four *bit hilani* structures have been excavated on the citadel, two are adjacent, the other two face a common open courtyard.

In the Bible, the NRSV uses *hall* in this manner only a dozen times, five in 1 Kgs 7:6-8, and one each in 1 Sam 9:22; Esth 5:1; 7:8; Dan 5:10; Matt 22:10; Acts 19:9; 25:23. From these limited references one may learn something of the nature of a hall. The three NT occurrences employ three different Greek words: gamos (γάμος, "wedding feast, banquet hall," Matt 22:10); scholē (σχολή, "lecture hall," Acts 19:9); and akroatērion (ἀκροατήριον, "audience hall, auditorium," Acts 25:23). In all three instances the number of people indicated as present suggests a large gathering place. Size does seem to be one factor in determining a hall.

The idea of a BANQUET HALL is seen in two instances in the ·OT. A similar phrase is used in both instances: Hebrew beth mishteh-hayyayin (בֵּית מִשְׁתֵּה־הַיַּיִן), literally, "the house of drinking wine" (Esth 7:8); and Aramaic beth mishteya᾿ (בֵּית מִשְׁתְּיָא), literally, "the house of drinking/feasting" (Dan 5:10). Although the banquet in Esther was just for Haman and the king, the banquet in Daniel was for a

thousand (Dan 5:1) again indicating a large hall. A similar banquet hall is indicated in 1 Sam 9:22, although the size of the gathering is only about thirty. Here the Hebrew term lishkah (לִשְׁכָּה; lit., "room, chamber, hall, cell") is used.

In Esth 5:1 *hall* translates the Hebrew word beth, literally "house." ESTHER enters the inner court of the royal palace opposite the king's hall (beth hammelekh בֵּית הַמֶּלֶךְ, clearly a reference to the throne room). No one entered the royal hall uninvited on pain of death. However, the king held out his royal scepter to Esther, indicating her acceptance. The hall would have been the audience hall of the PALACE where the king received dignitaries. It would correspond to the main room of a *bit hilani.*

The remaining five occurrences of *hall* in the OT use the Hebrew term ᾿ulam (אוּלָם), literally, "porch, vestibule, hall." In other occurrences ᾿ulam refers to the porch or vestibule of the temple, either Solomon's or the temple of Ezekiel's vision (*see* TEMPLE OF SOLOMON). All occur in one context of three verses, 1 Kgs 7:6-8, in the description of Solomon's palace. The palace had a Hall of Pillars (᾿ulam haʿammudhim אוּלָם הָעַמּוּדִים 1 Kgs 7:6), which measured 50 cubits long and 30 cubits wide. This one hall or building had more square footage than the Temple (1,500 sq. cubits, compared to 1,200 sq. cubits [60 × 20] for the Temple, 1 Kgs 6:2). One would assume this Hall of Pillars was roofed, thus a hypostyle hall. It would also be the main room of a *bit hilani.* As such it was probably the primary reception area in the palace complex for guests and dignitaries. It was the second largest space in Solomon's palace, at least in terms of space with measurements given. Only the House of the Forest of the Lebanon at 100 cubits by 50 cubits was larger. Since that space had rows of cedar pillars and was roofed (1 Kgs 7:2-3) it was also a hypostyle hall or a *bit hilani.*

The second hall mentioned in the palace context is the Hall of the Throne (᾿ulam hakkiseh אוּלָם הַכִּסֵּה), also called the Hall of Judgment/Justice (᾿ulam hammishpat אֻלָם הַמִּשְׁפָּט, 1 Kgs 7:7). No dimensions are given for this space. However, one would assume it was a relatively large hall of the throne room. One would also assume that, in addition to royal judgments being rendered here, dignitaries and emissaries from foreign governments would appear before the king here. It is quite possible that this hall in Solomon's palace was the space comparable to the inner court Esther entered in the Persian king's palace (Esth 5:1). This hall would also likely be the main room of a *bit hilani* structure.

The final occurrence of *hall* is to one in the private space of the palace, the royal residence. The private residence was located in another court back of the Hall of the Throne (1 Kgs 7:8). Solomon built a structure like the Hall of the Throne for Pharaoh's daughter, whom he had married (1 Kgs 7:8). One would assume that the queen would use this hall to meet with her guests during royal functions. *See* ARCHITECTURE, NT; ARCHITECTURE, OT; HOUSE; PILLAR.

Bibliography: Dieter Arnold. *Encyclopedia of Ancient Egyptian Architecture* (2003); Sigfried Giedion. *The Eternal Present: The Beginnings of Architecture* (1964); Aharon Kempinski and Ronny Reich, eds. *The Architecture of Ancient Israel* (1992).

JOEL F. DRINKARD, JR.

HALL OF JUSTICE אֻלָם הַמִּשְׁפָּט ʾulam hammishpat]. A building or a chamber in one of the buildings built by Solomon (1 Kgs 7:7). *See* HALL; PRAETORIUM.

HALL OF PILLARS. *See* HALL.

HALL OF THE THRONE. *See* HALL.

HALL OF TYRANNUS. *See* TYRANNUS, HALL OF.

HALLAH חַלָּה khallah]. The ninth tractate of the first order of the Mishnah. The first order of the Mishnah is entitled *Zeraʿim* (seeds), which deals with questions related to agricultural produce. *Hallah* specifically deals with the dough offering mandated in Num 15:18-21.

The biblical text mandates that when the Israelites eat the bread in the land of Israel they are to "set some aside as a gift to the LORD" (Num 15:19). *Hallah* attempts to add specificity to the biblical commandment (e.g., "what of bread made from produce outside the land of Israel?" "what types of dough are subject to this commandment?" "at what point in the production of bread does 'dough' become 'bread' and therefore subject to the commandment?").

PHILLIP MICHAEL SHERMAN

HALLEL hal'el [הַלֵּל hallel]. A term derived from the Hebrew verb "praise" (halal הָלַל) that Jews as early as in the MISHNAH (and so possibly earlier) have used to refer to two collections of psalms, the Egyptian Hallel and the Great Hallel. The Egyptian Hallel includes Pss 113–118 that were recited during the Passover celebration, that is, Pss 113–114 at its beginning and Pss 115–118 at its conclusion, as well as during other major celebrations such as the Festival of Weeks, Festival of Tabernacles, the New Moon festival, and the Feast of the Dedication of the Temple. These psalms commemorate God's deliverance of the Israelites from oppression in Egypt and anticipate God's continued deliverance. One among Pss. 113–118 was possibly the hymn that Jesus and his disciples sang after their eating of the Passover meal (Matt 26:30; Mark 14:26). The Great Hallel refers to Ps 136 and was later extended to include Pss 120–136; it emphasizes thanksgiving to God in a general sense, not just past deliverance from Egyptian oppression.

EMILY R. CHENEY

HALLELUJAH hal'uh-loo'yuh הַלְלוּ־יָהּ halelu-yah; ἀλληλούϊα allēlouia]. This expression is a call to praise Yahweh, found only in the last part of the book of Psalms. It is usually connected with hymns of praise, but the significance of its role (either a liturgical marker or part of the psalm itself) remains a point of discussion.

In Hebrew *Hallelujah* consists of an imperative plural piel form of the verb halal (הָלַל), usually understood as "to praise, shout, sing praise," plus a direct object -yah, an abbreviated form of the personal name of God, Yahweh. This piel form of the verb, appearing some 113 times in the OT, occurs occasionally in noncultic language (e.g., Gen 12:15; Prov 31:31). However, most often it refers to praise of God (or Yahweh), or the name of God (e.g., Joel 2:26; Pss 69:31; 74:21; 113:1; 145:2; 148:5, 13; 149:3; 1 Chr 29:13) is direct object of the verb. The verb occurs approximately twenty times in 1–2 Chronicles, usually in descriptions of the Levites and their worship responsibilities at the Jerusalem Temple; this usage strongly suggests the verb's importance for worship of the Second Temple era.

The verbal form halelu-yah occurs only in the book of Psalms, and more specifically in books 4 and 5, generally considered the last section of the psalter to be edited. This expression usually suggests the action of praise in the hymns of PRAISE. In the Heb. it occurs ten times at the beginning of psalms (Pss 106:1; 111:1; 112:1; 113:1; 135:1; 146:1; 147:1; 148:1; 149:1; 150:1), thirteen times as the conclusion of a psalm (Pss 104:35*c*; 105:45*c*; 106:48*c*; 113:9; 115:18*c*; 116:19;117:2*c*; 135:21*c*; 146:10*c*; 147:20*c*; 148:14*c*; 149:9*c*; 150:6*c*), and once internally (Ps 135:3). *See* HYMNS, OT.

In the LXX the pattern is different. Hallēlouia or Alleluia occurs in a similar collection of psalms, but here always at the beginning of a psalm (LXX 104:1 [Heb., Eng. 105:1]; 105:1 [106:1]; 106:1 [107:1]; 110:1 [111:1]; 111:1 [112:1]; 112:1 [113:1]; 113:1 [114:1]; 114:1 [116:1]; 115:1 [116:10]; 116:1 [117:1]; 118:1 [119:1]; 134:1 [135:1]; 135:1 [136:1]; 145:1 [146:1]; 146:1 [147:1]; 147:1 [147:12]; 148:1 [148:1]; 149:1 [149:1]; 150:1, 6 [150:1, 6]). So in the LXX, "Alleluia" appears to signal the liturgical function at the outset of each psalm.

This subtle difference in usage between the Heb. and LXX has led some scholars to suggest that *Hallelujah* may not constitute an original element of these psalms but rather represents a liturgical formula introduced later into the written text. Others see in the placement of the expression important clues to the editing process of the last two books of the psalter, with theological implications regarding the understanding of praise in the psalter and its relationship to expressions of thanksgiving to God.

In the Apocrypha from the LXX, the Greek equivalent (allēlouia ἀλληλούϊα) of halelu-yah occurs twice: in Tob 13:17 [LXX 13:18] it appears as an exclamation, "all Jerusalem will cry 'Hallelujah! Blessed be the God of Israel!," in a hymn of praise; in 3 Macc 7:13 after the Jews in Alexandria were saved they all "shouted the Hallelujah" using it as a substantive to indicate a type of joyful praise to God.

In the NT the Greek equivalent (allēlouia) of halelu-yah occurs only in Rev 19:1, 3, 4, 6, where it functions in hymns celebrating the victory of God.

The presence of halelu-yah in a psalm usually helps to identify it as a hymn of praise, appropriate for worship in song (both praise and thanksgiving) led by Levites after the exile (suggested by the use of the verb in Chronicles). Earlier scholarship identified this verbal root as the core of the hymns of praise. It is difficult, however, to maintain that the cry halelu-yah itself constituted the earliest indicator of hymns, since this form appears only in later parts of the psalter (books 4 and 5).

Contemporary scholars tend to view the halelu-yah as an indicator of major divisions in the psalter (e.g., the doxology concluding book 4, Ps 106:48c) or discrete collections of psalms within a book. Recent studies of the MT psalter suggest a pattern where halelu-yah concludes one segment, which is followed by a segment beginning with hodhu (הודו, "Give thanks to Yahweh"). For example, Ps 106, which closes book 4, contains halelu-yah in vv. 1, 48 (hodhu as well, in v. 1). Book 5 begins with hodhu in Ps 107:1, opening a segment that by this analysis includes Pss 107–117. Psalm 117:2 concludes with a halelu-yah, completing this segment. Another segment begins in Ps 118:1 ("Give thanks to the LORD") and concludes with the halelu-yah in Ps 135. The next segment begins with Ps 136:1 ("O give thanks to the LORD"). Although it lacks the verbal form halelu-yah, Ps 145 is a hymn of praise, since it contains the substantival form "praise" twice: "Praise. Of David" [v. 1] and "My mouth will speak the praise of the LORD" [v. 21]. Psalms 146–150 do not take up the expected thanksgiving motif but rather form an extended doxology of praise concluding the entire psalter (each of these psalms begins and concludes with halelu-yah).

The Qumran psalms scrolls may demonstrate a similar pattern of halelu-yah and hodhu psalms introducing and concluding psalm segments in the 11QPs^a (11QS). In this text the halelu-yahs generally appear to conclude psalms (even where MT Pss 135, 148, 150 began with halelu-yah, it appears only at the conclusion in the Qumran psalms scroll). This psalter, like the LXX, concludes with a Davidic Ps 151 [(it is a halelu-yah of David in 11QPs^a (11QS), but not in LXX)]. God's deliverance through David is reaffirmed in this collection, and calls for praise.

Throughout this last section of the psalter each segment marked by halelu-yah typically includes psalms of thanksgiving and lament (usually associated with Davidic psalms) and psalms praising God as creator of the cosmos and of Israel (typical of hymns). Thus,

halelu-yah focuses on the interplay among lament, thanksgiving, and praise. Theologically this alternation represents the ongoing movement between thanksgiving for the experience of divine saving presence among God's people and climactic hope buttressed by the power of God as creator (esp. in Pss 148 and 150). *See* PSALMS, BOOK OF.

Bibliography: Peter W. Flint. *The Dead Sea Psalms Scroll and the Book of Psalms* (1997); Gerald H. Wilson. *The Editing of the Hebrew Psalter* (1985); Gerald W. Wilson. "The Qumran Psalms Scroll (11QPs^a) and the Canonical Psalter: Comparison of Canonical Shaping." *CBQ* 59 (1997) 448–64.

JOHN C. ENDRES, S. J.

HALLOHESH huh-loh′hesh [הַלּוֹחֵשׁ *hallokhesh*]. The father of Shallum, who governed half of Jerusalem and who, along with his daughters, helped repair the city wall (Neh 3:12). Hallohesh also appears among leaders of the people whose names were inscribed on the sealed copy of Ezra's covenant (Neh 10:24 [Heb. 10:25]).

HALLOW. *See* CONSECRATE; HOLY, HOLINESS, NT; HOLY, HOLINESS, OT.

HAM, HAMITES ham, ham′it [חָם *kham*, בְּנֵי חָם *bene kham*]. 1. Ham is classically understood as the second son of Noah because of the repeated secondary placement of his name "Shem, Ham, and Japheth" (Gen 5:32; 6:10; 7:13; 9:18; 1 Chr 1:4). Ham "uncovered his father's nakedness" after Noah gets drunk. This is an APHORISM for voyeurism or sexual intercourse. Upon waking up and realizing what transpired, Noah interestingly curses Canaan, Ham's youngest son, instead of Ham (Gen 9:25). The current theory that explains the nature of Ham's sin and the curse of Canaan is that Canaan's birth is the result of Ham's incest with his mother. The curse is the result of Ham's sexual uncovering of his mother (following the connection between the nakedness of a mother and the nakedness of a father in Lev 18:7-8). The repetition of the phrase "Ham the father of Canaan" clarifies this connection (9:18, 22). Some theorists suggested the following ordering of Noah's sons "Shem, Japheth, and Canaan." This is incorrect. Others have argued for Canaan being Noah's fourth son.

2. Ham or Hamites may be related to the Egyptian word kem, a term for Egypt meaning "Black Land." Contemporary African American biblical scholarship has rightfully advocated and challenged the issue of "slavery" and "blackness" being associated with the "Hamite Myth"; a precept that takes its roots in the etymology of Ham, either from Egyptian meaning "black, black land," or from the Hebrew meaning "hot" as the basis and even justification for slavery.

Bibliography: David H. Aaron. "Early Rabbinic Exegesis on Noah's Son Ham and the So-Called 'Hamitic Myth'" *JAAR* 63 (1995) 721–59; John Sietze Bergasma and Scott Walker Hahn. "Noah's Nakedness and the Curse on Canaan (Genesis 9:20-27)." *JBL* 124 (2005) 25–40; Charles B. Copher. "The Black Presence in the Old Testament." *Stony the Road We Trod: African American Biblical Interpretation.* Cain Hope Felder, ed. (1991) 146–64; D. M. Goldenberg. *The Curse of Ham: Race and Slavery in Early Judaism, Christianity, and Islam* (2003); O. Palmer Robertson. "Current Critical Questions Concerning the Curse of Ham (Ge 9:20-27)." *JETS* 41 (1998) 177–88.

JOHN J. AHN

3. A town in the northern Transjordan. According to Gen 14:5, Ham was the dwelling place of the Zuzim. Nothing is known about the Zuzim, who were destroyed during the rebellion against Chedorlaomer. Ham is mentioned as being between Ashteroth-karnaim in Bashan and Shaveh-kiriathaim in the northern Moab. It is commonly associated with the modern village of Ham 4 mi. southwest of Irbid. The town may occur in the topographical list of Thutmose III, although archaeological explorations have revealed no occupation at Ham during the Late Bronze Age. The city of Ham should not be confused with the "land of Ham," which was a poetic way of referring to Egypt (Pss 78:51; 105:23; 106:22).

KEVIN A. WILSON

HAMAM, KHIRBET EL. This site, located near the Dothan Valley in northwestern Samaria, was identified during the Mount Manasseh Regional Survey project conducted in 1978. Subsequent excavations unearthed remains from as early as the site's settlement around the 11th cent. BCE, to as late as the locale's demise in the 1st cent. CE, when it fell victim to Roman besiegement during the First Jewish Revolt. Some have supposed that the city was known as Narbata in this era, an assumption based upon the conclusion that the only known Roman martial conduct in SAMARIA was centered at a place with such a name. The toponym is apparently derivative of ARBATTA, identified in 1 Macc 5:23 as a region inhabited by Jews, and ARUBBOTH, mentioned in 1 Kgs 4:10 as the central city of Solomon's third administrative region. The name presumably persists as ʿArabeh, a village located 3 mi. from the site.

JASON R. TATLOCK

HAMAN hay´muhn [הָמָן haman; Ἀμάν Haman]. King Ahasuerus' highest advisor in the book of Esther. Haman is said to be an Agagite, and thus ancestrally set up against Mordecai and Esther—Benjamites (*see* AGAG, AGAGITE). As foil to Mordecai, Haman's rise to power is tainted by Mordecai's refusal to bow before Haman's royal procession. Haman's hatred for Mordecai spawns a plot to manipulate the king into slaughter-ing all Jews. This proposed genocide was hyperbole at the time; the annihilation of an entire people would be logistically impossible. Haman's characterization of the Jews (3:8) seems a classic in anti-Semitism. As told through the eyes of the Jewish storyteller, Haman cannot come up with anything terrible to say about the people he seeks to annihilate, but only accuses them of being themselves. The accusation is damaging enough to bring their slaughter near.

With irony and poetic justice, Haman and his sons are hanged on the gallows that he had designed for Mordecai, and Mordecai achieves the royal parade that Haman designed for himself. Haman's family line is cut off, but the Jews survive.

NICOLE WILKINSON DURAN

HAMATH, HAMATHITE hay´math, hay´muh-th*i*t [חֲמָת khamath, חֲמָתִי khamathi]. 1. A city-state in central Syria, 214 km north of Damascus, on the Orontes (modern al-ʿAsi) River, mentioned in texts from Ebla, Egypt, Ugarit, and Assyria, as well as Hittite inscriptions from Hamath itself. The name may mean either "fortress" or "warm place."

First settled in the sixth millennium BCE, trade was established with Mesopotamia by the fifth millennium and with Asia Minor by the mid third millennium. Hamath was a major center early in the first millennium and part of a coalition of states, including Israel, that blocked Shalmaneser III's westward expansion from 853–845 BCE. The Assyrians conquered it in 738 BCE. The Seleucids renamed the city Epiphaneia, after Antiochus IV Epiphanes, but the original name was restored after the Muslim conquest in 636 CE. Today it is called Hama.

Its southern border (LEBO-HAMATH, "the entrance to Hamath") is named as part of Israel's northern border (Num 34:8). The region is listed as part of David's and Solomon's kingdoms (1 Kgs 8:65; 1 Chr 13:5), but Hamath remained independent, with King Toi sending congratulatory gifts to David after the latter's defeat of King Hadadezer of Zobah (2 Sam 8:9-10). Although 2 Chr 8:3-4 claims that Solomon conquered Hamath-Zobah, Hamath-Zobah is not mentioned elsewhere in the OT. Israel subsequently lost control of the region, but Jereboam II reestablished Lebo-Hamath as his northern border (2 Kgs 14:25). After the fall of northern Israel, Hamathites were among those forcibly settled in the new Assyrian province of Samaria, bringing their god ASHIMA with them (2 Kgs 17:24, 30). Ezekiel envisioned Lebo-Hamath as the northern boundary of post-exilic Israel (Ezek 47:15-17, 20).

2. Hamathites were citizens of Hamath, descendants of Canaan (Gen 10:18; 1 Chr 1:16).

JOHN L. MCLAUGHLIN

HAMATH-ZOBAH hay´math-zoh´buh [חֲמָת צוֹבָה khamath tsovah]. A location mentioned in 2 Chr 8:3 as having been captured by Solomon. *See* ZOBAH.

HAMID, TELL ABU. Abu Hamid is a Pottery Neolithic and Chalcolithic village located on the eastern side of the Jordan Valley, about halfway between the Dead Sea and the Sea of Galilee at an altitude of ca. 245 ft. below sea level. Three principle phases were noted: Late Neolithic I (Ghrubba phase, ca. 5650 BCE); Late Neolithic II (Wadi Rabah phase, with a C^{14} date of 4932±77 BCE); and Chalcolithic (with two C^{14} dates of 4607±55 and 4486±42 BCE).

The village was small: although the site extended over more than 15 acres, houses were confined to an area of only about 5.75 acres, with the rest devoted to exterior activities and animal enclosures. Houses were oval in the earliest phase, but in the last two phases they were rectangular, made of mudbrick on stone foundations and with beaten earth floors; one Chalcolithic wall bore a fragment of painted plaster (*see* ARCHITECTURE, OT; HOUSE).

Throughout the occupation the subsistence economy was based on domesticated sheep, goats, cattle, and pigs; dogs and donkeys were also present, and hunted gazelle added dietary variety. Plants included olives, wheat, barley, peas, lentils, chickpeas, figs, flax, and vetch (the last for animal feed). *See* AGRICULTURE; ANIMALS OF THE BIBLE; PLANTS OF THE BIBLE.

Bibliography: G. Dollfus and Z. Kafafi. "Recent Researches at Abu Hamid." *ADAJ* 27 (1993) 241–62.

GARY O. ROLLEFSON

HAMILCAR BARCA. Carthaginian general (270–229 BCE) and Hannibal's father. After initial successes against Rome, Hamilcar negotiated for Carthaginian withdrawal from Sicily, ending the First Punic War (264–241 BCE). Before dying in retreat, Hamilcar established a principality in southeastern Spain, facilitating Hannibal's aggressions against Rome during the Second Punic War (218–202 BCE). First Maccabees 8:1-12 might include Hamilcar and his "kingdom" in southeast Spain, which facilitated Hannibal's war with Rome.

JASON C. DYKEHOUSE

HAMMATH ham´ath [חַמַּת khammath]. 1. The ancestor of the Rechabites (1 Chr 2:55).

2. A fortified city of Naphtali (Josh 19:35) that was given to the Levites in Josh 21:32, where it is called HAMMOTH-DOR (1 Chr 6:67 [Heb. 6:61] substitutes HAMMON). Rabbinic references (*b. Meg.* 2.2; *t. ʿErub.* 7:2, 146) indicate it was outside Tiberias on the shore of the Sea of Galilee. Since Hammath means "hot springs," the city is identified with the springs at Hammam Tabariyeh, 3 km south of Tiberias. Excavations to date have revealed three stages of occupation between the 1st cent. BCE and the 8th cent. CE but no evidence of Iron Age settlement. *See* RECHAB, RECHABITES.

JOHN L. MCLAUGHLIN

HAMMEDATHA ham´uh-day´thuh [הַמְּדָתָא hammedhathaʾ; Ἀμαδάθος Amadathos]. Appears only as the father of Haman, an Agagite (Esth 3:1, 10; 8:5; 9:10, 24), and the antagonist in the Esther story. The name also occurs in the Additions to Esther in the LXX (Add Esth 12:6; 16:10, 17).

HAMMER [מַקֶּבֶת maqqeveth, פַּטִּישׁ pattish]. As is the case today, hammers came in various sizes and were employed for various tasks in ancient Israel. However, the claw hammer that could be used to remove nails was not invented until the Roman period when heavier iron nails were employed in construction and for crucifixions. Heavy-duty, mallet-like implements were used for domestic tasks such as driving in tent pegs (Judg 4:21; note the variation MALLET [halmuth הַלְמוּת] in Judg 5:26). Such heavy tools could be and were used as weapons, as Jael demonstrated when she nailed the sleeping Sisera to the floor of her tent. Because of their greater strength, iron implements, including the hammer, were used to chisel and shape stone used in the monumental construction of temples and other public buildings (1 Kgs 6:7). Hammers are used symbolically by the prophets. Jeremiah compared the hammer that breaks a stone to the power of the word of God in the face of the claims of false prophets (23:29). As the skills associated with ironsmiths became more common among the Israelites in the late monarchy period (compare the lack of this technology in 1 Sam 13:19-20), the prophets also used these skills as metaphors for everyday activities. Several of these cases involve the process of casting or shaping the delicate features of idols, a major industry among Israel's neighbors and perhaps among the Israelites. Both Isa 44:12 and Jer 10:4 describe the tiring labor involved in working the metal with hammer and tong (undoubtedly of different weights and sizes). This labor is futile, however, since it is expended in the creation of a metal object of worship with no inherent power of its own. Isaiah 41:7 expands on this theme describing the careful teamwork of goldsmiths and other artisans who use more delicate tools to shape, hammer, and solder an image. Another striking image of a smith working at his anvil is found in Jeremiah's very effective metaphor for Babylon, "the hammer of the whole earth," and the massive destruction imposed on smaller nations by this Mesopotamian superpower (50:23). *See* TOOLS; WAR, METHODS, TACTICS, WEAPONS OF (BRONZE AGE THROUGH PERSIAN PERIOD); WAR, METHODS, TACTICS, WEAPONS OF (HELLENISTIC THROUGH ROMAN PERIODS).

VICTOR H. MATTHEWS

HAMMOLECHETH ha-mol´uh-keth [הַמֹּלֶכֶת hammolekheth]. Gilead's sister, and mother to three sons (Ishhod, Abiezer, and Mahal) in the lineage of Manasseh found in 1 Chr 7. Unlike many of the other mothers in the Chronicler's family lists, no husband is mentioned along with Hammolecheth (1 Chr 7:18).

HAMMON ham'uhn [חַמּוֹן khammon]. 1. A town belonging to Asher and constituting part of that tribe's inheritance (Josh 19:28). Its position in the list suggests a location in northern Asher. Hammon is often identified with Khirbet Umm el-Awamid in Lebanon.

2. A Levitical city within the tribe of Naphtali (1 Chr 6:76).

JASON C. DYKEHOUSE

HAMMOTH-DOR ham'uhth-dor' [חַמֹּת דֹּאר khammoth do'r]. One of the Levitical towns in the land allotted to Naphtali (Josh 21:32). *See* HAMMATH.

HAMMUEL ham'yoo-uhl [חַמּוּאֵל khammu'el]. The son of Mishma and the father of Zaccur, Hammuel appears in a genealogical list of descendants of Simeon (1 Chr 4:26) as a descendant of Shaul, the fifth son of Simeon, although not all biblical lists of Simeon's sons agree with one another.

HAMMURABI ham'uh-rah'bee. The name is probably to be analyzed as Amorite ʿammu–rapi, "The (divine) Kinsman is a healer," though some scholars regard the name as mixed and read the last element as Akkadian rabi, "The (divine) Kinsman is great."

Hammurabi, who ruled Babylon from 1792–1750 BCE (Middle Chronology), was the sixth king in the first dynasty of Babylon and the first to raise Babylon to the level of an imperial power. His father, Sin-muballit, had expanded the territory controlled by Babylon to include the neighboring cities of Borsippa, Kish, and Sippar, but the extent of the kingdom was no more than 60 × 160 km. When Hammurabi came to the throne, Babylon was one of the smaller states in the area. On Babylon's southern border lay the more powerful state of Larsa, which under Rim-Sin (1822–1763 BCE) had unified all of southern and central Babylonia in a single state from the Persian Gulf to the boundary with Babylon. To the east, across the Tigris on the Diyala River was the city-state of Eshnunna, another powerful state. Farther to the east, on the northern shore of the Persian Gulf, sat Elam, at the time richer and more powerful than any of the Mesopotamian states. To the north, Shamshi-Adad (ca. 1808–1776 BCE), another Amorite who had seized the Assyrian throne, ruled over a vast territory of northern Mesopotamia that included the heartland of Assyria along the Tigris, the many small client states in the Habur and Balih River valleys, and Mari and the middle Euphrates region. Shamshi-Adad's westward expansion only stopped near the bend of the Euphrates, impeded by the powerful kingdom of Yamhad centered in Aleppo to the west.

During the first twenty-eight years of his reign, Hammurabi concentrated on the internal develop-

ment of his kingdom, avoiding serious conflict with his more powerful neighbors, yet engaging with them in cautious diplomacy. In 1781 BCE he allied himself as a minor partner with Shamshi-Adad to prevent Eshnunna from gaining control of the Tigris River crossing at Mankisum. When Shamshi-Adad died in 1776 BCE, his northern Mesopotamian kingdom imploded. Zimri-Lim quickly seized Mari, removing Yasmah-Adad, Shamshi-Adad's younger son, and Ishme-Dagan, Shamshi-Adad's older son, had difficulty maintaining himself in Ekallatum in the Assyrian heartland. Eshnunna exploited the situation to expand into northern Mesopotamia, seizing control of much of Shamshi-Adad's former territory. Since both Hammurabi and Zimri-Lim of Mari were threatened by Eshnunna's expansion, they joined forces to keep Eshnunna in check. During this period Elam to the east remained the most powerful nation in the region, though it had seemed uninterested in long-term occupation of Mesopotamian territory. This changed in 1767 BCE, however, when Elam, under the Sukkalmah, Siwe-palar-huppak, and the Sukkal of Susa, Kudu-zulush, decided to conquer and occupy Eshnunna. Elam summoned Mari and Babylon as vassals to assist in this conquest, and in 1766 BCE Elam took Eshnunna. Elam then tried to prohibit diplomatic contact between Mari and Babylon. Elam demanded troops from Hammurabi for a major assault on Larsa, but when Hammurabi discovered that Elam had also demanded troops from Rim-Sin of Larsa for a major attack on Babylon, Hammurabi countered with superior diplomatic moves. Because Elam was also supporting Atamram against Zimri-Lim in northern Mesopotamia, Zimri-Lim joined Hammurabi in an anti-Elamite coalition. In 1765 BCE Elam attacked Upi in the Babylonian territory successfully, though without lasting results, but in 1764 BCE, when Elam tried to take Mankisum, Hammurabi outmanuevered Elam both militarily and diplomatically. With the troops of Mari and Babylon blocking the attack, the troops of Eshnunna, who had been impressed into Elamite service, revolted. In northern Mesopotamia Atamram switched sides and accepted Zimri-Lim as his overlord. Elam in exasperation plundered Eshnunna, but then withdrew to its own territory. Hammurabi and his allies then took Eshnunna, but the puppet king they installed there, Silli-Sin, soon followed his own independent policy.

In the meantime, Hammurabi turned to deal with his southern neighbor, Rim-Sin of Larsa, who had provided no assistance in the war against Elam. In 1763 Hammurabi invaded the south, and after a six-month siege succeeded in capturing Larsa, with assistance from Zimri-Lim, Atamrum, and other allies. Some 40,000 troops fought on the side of Larsa, and, though the exact number is not known, Hammurabi's Babylonian and allied troops probably outnumbered them. By 1762 BCE Hammurabi had restored order in the south, and all of southern Mesopotamia was a part of his realm.

During the same year Hammurabi also attacked Eshnunna again, defeating it, but his control of Eshnunna was not absolute, and he was forced to put down a rebellion there a few years later in 1756.

Nonetheless, with Elam occupied at home, Larsa and its territories annexed, and Eshnunna neutralized, Hammurabi was now ready to deal with Zimri-Lim of Mari, his erstwhile ally. Both Mari and Babylon had an interest in northern Mesopotamia, and by 1762 BCE Hammurabi had a large number of his troops in northern Mesopotamia supporting such vassals as Ishme-Dagan of Ekallatum, a longtime enemy of Zimri-Lim. Even more contentious, however, was the argument over the control of Hit on the Euphrates. Hit was the major source for bitumen needed for boat calking, and Hammurabi wanted to control that source because of the importance of boating for control of his central and southern territories. Zimri-Lim insisted, however, that the legitimacy of his control of the site had been recognized by the Sukkalmah of Elam, and he was unwilling to cede it to Hammurabi. With the elimination of their common enemies there was nothing left to sustain their political friendship, and Hammurabi attacked, capturing Mari and removing Zimri-Lim within four months of his earlier conquest of Eshnunna. His troops systematically looted the palace of Zimri-Lim, and Hammurabi removed any sensitive political correspondence from the Mari archives. Unfortunately, the Mari archives are our most important source for the history of this period, and with the fall of Mari, our sources dry up. Though Babylon has been excavated, the Old Babylonian levels are below the water table, and it is unlikely that Hammurabi's archives in Babylon will ever be recovered. Though we do not know the details, Mari rebelled within a short period, and in 1759 BCE Hammurabi again took the city, this time thoroughly destroying it and burning the palace down.

With the defeat of Mari, Hammurabi's kingdom became the largest and most powerful kingdom in the Middle East. His rule extended from the Persian Gulf, up the Tigris and Euphrates, to incorporate Babylonia and Assyria, the middle Euphrates region, and most of the rest of Mesopotamia, including, in a loose collection of vassal states, the fertile valleys of the Habur and the Balih. The powerful kingdom of Yamhad with its capital at Aleppo west of the Euphrates remained a potential rival, but there is little trace of serious conflict between the two during Hammurabi's last years.

During his final years, Hammurabi devoted himself to administering his empire, to repairing the extensive damages caused to large sections of his empire by the years of war, and to the administration of justice within his kingdom. The prologue to his famous law code enumerates the many cities of his realm that he built

up, restored, repaired, rescued, or otherwise improved: Nippur, Eridu, Babylon, Ur, Sippar, Larsa, Uruk, Kish, Kutha, Borsippa, Dilbat, Kesh, Lagash, Girsu, Hallab, Bet-karkar, Adab, Mashkan-shabrim, Malka, Mari (Mera), Tutul, Akkad, Ashur, and Nineveh. Note that the list includes a number of cities that he captured in battle—Larsa, Mashkan-shabrim, Mari. While he does not specifically mention Eshnunna, he does claim to have brightened the face of Eshnunna's god, Tishpak, and to have saved Tishpak's people from distress, establishing their feet in security in the midst of Babylon. The references in this text about Hammurabi's support for the cults of the various city gods, within his realm, point to the importance of keeping the gods of the realm happy. One of the duties of a Mesopotamian king was to maintain the cults, promoting piety and the goodwill of the divine world. Hammurabi appears to have been successful in this endeavor. Moreover, his attention to maintaining the irrigation canals in central and southern Babylonia brought great prosperity to the region. The fragmentation of the region into quarreling rival states inevitably disrupted the irrigation system for much of the area, so a strong central government was an absolute requirement for the general prosperity of the whole region. Hammurabi was a very good administrator with an admirable attention to detail. He acted quickly when judicial abuses came to his attention, and as a result his people prospered under his rule. It is no fluke or mere propaganda coup that he came to be known as the king of justice.

The year name for his second year indicates that early in his reign Hammurabi acted to establish justice in his land. This is not a reference to his lawcode, which dates to very late in his reign, but to the issuing of a *misharum* edict. This was an edict, usually issued early in an Old Babylonian king's reign and then repeated periodically as the need arose, to prevent the total impoverishment of the poor. The edict typically canceled outstanding debts and released people from debt-slavery, thus relieving economic pressure on the common people that, left unabated, would have seriously impacted the economic well-being of the kingdom.

Hammurabi's more famous lawcode is preserved on a black diorite stela now on display in the Louvre in Paris (*see* HAMMURABI, CODE OF). At the top of the stela Hammurabi is portrayed in a gesture of obeisance before Shamash, the sun god and god of justice. Below the figures are about fifty-one columns of text, containing a prologue, an epilogue, and between them some 275-300 laws. The exact number is unclear, because in the 12th cent. BCE, the Elamite king Shutruk-Nahhunte carted the stela off to Susa and erased a section of the text in preparation for adding his own inscription, though it was never inscribed. This stela originally stood in Sippar, the city of Shamash, and fragments of other stelae, also found in Susa, suggest that Hammurabi had set up similar stelae with his laws in various other cities of his realm. The function of this "lawcode" is still disputed. It is clearly not a code of law in the sense of the Napoleonic Code. It appears to be based on common Near Eastern law; the parallels with the Eshnunna laws and the earlier Sumerian collections are striking. The text itself suggests that the stela served to reassure the wronged that their rightful cases would be heard, and that justice would be done in Hammurabi's realm. Thus Hammurabi's lawcode, whatever its precise legal function, contributed to Hammurabi's self-portrayal and lasting reputation as "the king of justice." *See* ASSYRIA AND BABYLONIA.

Bibliography: Marc Van De Mieroop. *King Hammurabi of Babylon: A Biography* (2005).

J. J. M. ROBERTS

HAMMURABI, CODE OF. A collection of nearly 300 laws promulgated by King Hammurabi, ruler of Babylon, in the 18th cent. BCE. Although these laws are not the earliest ones from Mesopotamia, they are the most comprehensive. Areas covered include some facets of criminal law, business transactions, and property/family matters. Like other ANE laws, however, the Code may have served to express general principles for a just society rather than provide specific legal precedent.

Reunion des Musees Nationaux/Art Resource NY
Figure 1: Stele of the Law Code of Hammurabi

The best-known principle from these laws, "an eye for an eye," requires punishment for an injury that is commensurate with the harm, and it is found in the Bible (see Exod 21:22-25 and Matt 5:38-39). The Code makes distinctions based on social class, and literal compliance only applies to members of the same privileged class. If a member of an upper class injures a member of a lower social class, then a monetary fine is to be paid.

Other similarities between the Code and laws in the Covenant Code (Exod 20:22–23:33) are evident. For example, both codes have laws concerning an ox that gores a human being. Such parallels help to elucidate the ANE background of biblical laws.

CHERYL B. ANDERSON

HAMONAH huh-moh´nuh [הֲמוֹנָה hamonah]. Ezekiel predicts this city, somewhere in the valley of Hamon-Gog, will be the burial site for the armies of GOG (Ezek 39:16). The Hebrew may mean "roar," "murmur," or "abundance." The LXX translation (Poluandrion Πολυάνδριον, "full of men") favors the latter.

HAMON-GOG hay´muhn-gog´ [הֲמוֹן גּוֹג hamon gogh]. A valley where the slain armies of Gog will be buried, a number of dead so extensive that people will not be able to pass through (Ezek 39:11, 15). Perhaps the phrase "valley of Hamon-Gog" was a play on the infamous GEHENNA. *See* HINNOM, VALLEY OF.

PHILLIP MICHAEL SHERMAN

HAMOR hay´mor [חֲמוֹר khamor; Ἐμμώρ Hemmōr]. The father of SHECHEM whom Simeon and Levi killed along with his son in retribution for the rape of DINAH (Gen 34). Jacob bought a plot of land near Shechem from the sons of Hamor and built an altar there (Gen 33:19-20). Stephen (Acts 7:16) apparently confuses this story with Abraham's attempted purchase of MACHPELAH (Gen 23). The name *Hamor* is the Hebrew word for DONKEY.

T. DELAYNE VAUGHN

HAMRAN ham´ran [חַמְרָן khamran]. One of four sons of Seir's grandson Dishon mentioned in a Horite genealogy (1 Chr 1:41). His name appears as HEMDAN in Gen 36:26.

HAMSTRING [עָקַר ʿiqer]. Soldiers would "hamstring" an enemy war horse to disable it, meaning cut the large tendon at the tarsal joint of its hind leg (Josh 11:6, 9; 2 Sam 8:4; 1 Chr 18:4). Oxen could also be hamstrung (Gen 49:6).

HAMUL, HAMULITES hay´muhl, hay´muh-l*i*t [חָמוּל khamul]. 1. The younger son of PEREZ and grandson of Judah and TAMAR (Gen 46:12; 1 Chr 2:5). The name means "spared." However, the Samaritan Pentateuch and LXX forms mean "God protects."

2. Hamul is the ancestral head of the clan of the Hamulites (Num 26:21).

SUSANNA W. SOUTHARD

HAMUTAL huh-my*oo*'tuhl [חֲמוּטַל khamutal]. Married to King Josiah, Hamutal the daughter of Jeremiah of Libnah became the mother of two kings, Jehoahaz and Zedekiah (2 Kgs 23:31; 24:18; Jer 52:1). Sometimes written khamital (חֲמִיטַל), the name could mean "my father-in-law is protection."

HANA hay'nuh ['Aναν Hanan]. A temple servant whose descendants with their families and possessions were escorted to Jerusalem by King Darius' horsemen to ensure their safe return (1 Esd 5:30). Hana is likely a variant of HANAN in parallel lists (e.g., Ezra 2:46). *See* ESDRAS, FIRST BOOK OF.

HANAMEL han'uh-mel [חֲנַמְאֵל khanam'el]. The son of Shallum, Jeremiah's uncle (Jer 32:7-9). Jeremiah bought a field from this cousin at ANATHOTH during the Babylonian siege of Jerusalem. The name may derive from khanan 'el (חָנַן אֵל) meaning "God is gracious."

HANAN hay'nuhn [חָנָן khanan, 'Aναν Hanan]. Means "to be gracious." 1. Shahak's son who descended from Benjamin and lived in Jerusalem (1 Chr 8:23, 28).

2. Azel's son who descended from Saul, a Benjaminite (1 Chr 8:38; 9:44).

3. Maacah's son and one of David's warriors (1 Chr 11:43).

4. Head of a family of Temple servants who returned to Jerusalem after the exile (Ezra 2:46; Neh 7:49; 1 Esd 5:30).

5. A Levite who read and interpreted the Law for the people to understand (Neh 8:7) and whose name was included on the sealed document of the covenant (Neh 10:10 [Heb. 10:11]).

6. A leader whose name was included on the sealed covenant document (Neh 10:22 [Heb. 10:23]).

7. A leader whose name also appeared on the sealed covenant document (Neh 10:26 [Heb. 10:27]).

8. Zacur's son whom Nehemiah appointed as assistant to the Temple treasurers (Neh 13:13).

9. Head of a prophetic guild, who resided in a chamber in the Temple (Jer 35:4).

EMILY R. CHENEY

HANANEL, TOWER OF han'uh-nel [מִגְדַּל חֲנַנְאֵל mighdal khanan'el]. This "tower of the grace/graciousness of God" is mentioned in Jer 31:38; Zech 14:10, and in Neh 3:1 and 12:36 as being at the northwestern border of the newly constructed walls. It has been equated with the "citadel" mentioned in 1 Macc 13:52 and the Antonia Fortress of Herod. Its biblical mention seems to be often in potentially eschatological contexts, perhaps to indicate Israel at peace within safe and secure borders.

PHILLIP MICHAEL SHERMAN

HANANI huh-nay'n*i* [חֲנָנִי khanani; Aνανιας Ananias]. Name of several men: 1. Father of the prophet Jehu

(1 Kgs 16:1, 7; 2 Chr 19:2; 20:34) and probably the seer who told King Asa of Judah the consequences of his lack of trust in God and his reliance on the king of Aram (2 Chr 16:7).

2. Son of HEMAN, the king's seer, who, with his brothers and father, was responsible for music in the Temple and had been trained to sing (1 Chr 25:4-7, 25).

3. Descendant of Immer whom Ezra required to dismiss his foreign wife and children (Ezra 10:20; 1 Esd 9; 21).

4. Nehemiah's brother who told Nehemiah about the need for the walls and the gates in Jerusalem to be rebuilt and whom Ezra placed in charge over Jerusalem (Neh 1:2; 7:2).

5. A musician who participated in the dedication of the Jerusalem wall (Neh 12:36).

EMILY R. CHENEY

HANANIAH han'uh-n*i*'uh [חֲנַנְיָה khananyah, חֲנַנְיָהוּ khananyahu; Aνανιας Ananias]. "Yah/Yahu has been gracious." 1. Zerubbabel's son, father of Pelatiah and Jeshaiah, and a descendant of Solomon (1 Chr 3:19, 21).

2. Shashak's son, a descendant of Benjamin, and a tribal chief living in Jerusalem (1 Chr 8:24).

3. Son of HEMAN, the king's seer, and so served under his direction to provide music for the Lord's house (1 Chr 25:4, 23).

4. A commander of King Uzziah's soldiers (2 Chr 26:11).

5. Descendant of Bebai who sent away his foreign wife and their children according to Ezra's instructions (Ezra 10:28; 1 Esd 9:29).

6. A perfumer who returned to Jerusalem to restore the wall from the Old Gate to the Broad Wall (Neh 3:8).

7. A repairman who worked near Shemaiah and was Shelemiah's son (Neh 3:30). He is possibly the same person as number 6.

8. Governor of the citadel, whom Nehemiah put in charge over Jerusalem (Neh 7:2). This name can also be translated as "my brother HANANI."

9. A Levite who placed his name on the sealed covenant document (Neh 10:23).

10. A priest who played the trumpet during the celebration that dedicated the rebuilding of the Jerusalem wall (Neh 12:12, 41).

11. A false prophet from Gibeon who predicted Nebuchadnezzar's defeat, which he symbolized through breaking the yoke that Jeremiah wore (Jer 28).

12. Father of Zedekiah (Jer 36:12).

13. Grandfather of Irijah who charged and arrested Jeremiah for desertion (Jer 37:13).

14. Daniel's companion who was renamed Shadrach by Ashpenaz, King Nebuchadnezzar's palace master (Dan 1:11, 17, 19).

15. A Levite whose descendants were among Ezra's returnees to Jerusalem (1 Esd 8:48). *See* ANANIAS; SHADRACH, MESHACH, ABEDNEGO; SONG OF THE THREE JEWS.

EMILY R. CHENEY

HANANIEL huh-nan′ee-uhl [Ἀνανιηλ *Hananiēl*]. The paternal grandfather of Tobit of the tribe of Naphtali (Tob 1:1). The Greek text of Tobit also mentions Hananiel as the son of a woman named Deborah, who provided instruction as to proper care of the poor (Tob 1:8). However, the Latin text has Tobiel instead.

JESSICA TINKLENBERG DEVEGA

HAND [יָד *yadh*; χείρ *cheir*]. Predominantly, *hand* refers to the body part in its biblical occurrences, but it also often appears as a metonym for strength and power. Joshua 8:20 reads "they had no hands to flee," although both the NRSV and the KJV translate this in the sense of "they had no power to flee" (see also Ps 78:42; Job 27:11 where God's hand represents God's power). The term *hand* functions to indicate dominion (David went down to "restore his hand at the Euphrates," 2 Sam 8:3; 1 Chr 18:3), to represent a sign or monument (Samuel "set up a hand for himself," 1 Sam 15:12), to identify authority ("for the Lord has delivered them into the hand of Israel," 1 Sam 14:12), to represent an architectural support structure ("two hands for each board," Exod 26:17; see 1 Kgs 7:35, 36), and to euphemize the phallus or penis ("My beloved thrust his hand into the opening", Song 5:4; see also Isa 57:8). The "hand" of a river (Deut 2:37) or a piece of land (Gen 34:21) suggests its side. Washing hands can symbolize ritual cleanliness or blamelessness as stated by the psalmist before the Lord (Ps 26:6) and Pontius Pilate before the mob (Matt 27:24).

The right hand (yamin יָמִין; dexios δεξιός) represents a place of honor or authority (Ps 110:1; Matt 26:64), and it is used to bless (Gen 48:14) and to seal relationships (Isa 62:8; Gal 2:9). Left-handedness (semo′l שְׂמֹאל), because it was less common, provided an advantage in war because the enemy, prepared to attack right-handed opponents, could be caught off guard (Judg 3; 20:16). Kaf (כַּף, "palm of the hand," e.g., 2 Kgs 9:35) is often translated as hand.

DEBORAH A. APPLER

HANDBAG. *See* BAG.

HANDBREADTH [טֹפַח *tofakh*, טֶפַח *tefakh*]. A biblical measure of length, indicating the width of the hand at the base of the fingers (Exod 25:25; 37:12; 1 Kgs 7:26; 2 Chr 4:5; Ps 39:5; Ezek 40:5; 43:13). It was commonly used in the Mishna and often translated as "palm," indicating probably that it contained four fingerbreadths. The exact size is unknown. In Egypt and in Mesopotamia the CUBIT included six (sometimes seven) handbreadths. *See* WEIGHTS AND MEASURES.

RAZ KLETTER

HANDKERCHIEF [σουδάριον *soudarion*]. A small piece of cloth that could be used to wipe the face. The soudaria or "face-cloths" Paul used—soiled napkins or towels, perhaps—were reported to be effective in curing illnesses (Acts 19:12). The dissatisfactory servant in Luke's Parable of the Pounds wrapped his mina (mna μνᾶ, a sum of money equal to 100 denarii [dēnarion δηνάριον]) in a soudarion—a not-terribly-convincing attempt at "hiding" it (Luke 19:20). Dead Lazarus, whose hands and feet were bound with strips of cloth, had a soudarion covering his face when he emerged from the tomb (John 11:44). By contrast, the risen Jesus left his soudarion behind at the tomb (John 20:7).

RICHARD B. VINSON

HANDMAID. *See* MAID, MAIDEN.

HANDPIKE [מַקֵּל יָד *maqqel yadh*]. A rod or staff, named in a list of seven types of weapons used by Israelite soldiers (Ezek 39:9). The name of the implement identifies it as a shock weapon for use in hand-to-hand combat, although it is not clear whether it was a quarterstaff, a thrusting spear or pike, a javelin, or some kind of bludgeon. It is clear that it was at least partially made of wood (Ezek 39:9-10). David's wielding of "sticks" (maqloth מַקְלֹות, 1 Sam 17:43) in combat with Goliath may suggest that the handpike was carried by shepherds.

RALPH K. HAWKINS

HANDS, LAYING ON OF. *See* LAYING ON OF HANDS; ORDINATION, ORDAIN.

HANES hay′neez [חָנֵס *khanes*]. A city in Egypt, probably about 60 mi. south of Cairo, the capital of the twentieth nome of Upper Egypt. The Greeks identified the local deity, Herishef, with Hercules and renamed the city Heracleopolis. In Isa 30, the prophet condemns an apparent alliance with Egypt, saying that the people should not trust in Pharaoh's protection, even though "his envoys reach to Hanes" (Isa 30:4).

T. DELAYNE VAUGHN

HANGING [תָּלָה *talah*; κρεμάννυμι *kremannymi*]. According to the Bible, a criminal who was executed might then be hanged or impaled after death as a means of disgracing the criminal. In Gen 40:19 Joseph predicts that Pharaoh's baker will be beheaded and then impaled. Joshua conquered the city of Ai and hanged its king on a stake for a day but removed the body before sunset (Josh 8:29; 10:26). David had the murderers of ISHBOSHETH killed, mutilated, and hanged (2 Sam 4:12). In these cases, there is mention of the subsequent burial of the corpses. Deuteronomy 21:22-23 specifies that the corpse may not remain on the stake overnight but must be buried lest the land become defiled. This treatment contrasts with that of the Egyptians who allowed the birds to eat the flesh of the baker (Gen 40:19), the Philistines who paraded about with the bodies of Saul and his sons and hanged them on the city wall (1 Sam 31:8-13), and the Gibeonites who left the bodies of their enemies exposed for many days (2 Sam 21:10-14). Josephus states that all criminals were hanged after execution (*Ant.* 4.264–65), but *m. Sanh.* 6:4 testifies to this practice only for blasphemers and idolaters. Tannaitic tradition requires that hanging be minimized to the shortest possible time (*t. Sanh.* 9:6). In the book of Esther, the villain HAMAN and his sons were impaled, but the text does not reveal if they were executed first or if hanging was the means of execution (7:10; 9:14).

CRUCIFIXION was a different form of punishment involving hanging a person while still alive for a prolonged period until death. Pesher Nahum relates how the Pharisees who had invited Demetrius III Eukarus, king of Syria, to invade Judea were crucified by Alexander Janneus for treason (4Q169 3 & 4 I, 6-9; Josephus, *Ant.* 13.380). The Temple Scroll (11Q19 LXIV, 6-9) prescribes crucifixion for a traitor. New Testament authors pictured Jesus' crucifixion at the hands of the Romans as if it were a fulfillment of the biblical command of Deut 21:22-23 (see Matt 27:57-60; Acts 10:39).

LAWRENCE H. SCHIFFMAN

HANGINGS [קְלָעִים qela']. Hangings or curtains refer to portions of the fabric material used in the construction of the Tabernacle. For the portable Tabernacle in the wilderness, solid wall structures to mark the outer court would have been impractical to set up and take down every time the camp moved. The outer court was constructed of pillars at regular intervals and long hangings of fine twisted linen attached to the pillars to mark off the boundaries of the Tabernacle court. The court was 100 cubits north-south and 50 cubits east-west in size, and the hangings were the same (Exod 27:9-12). The hangings were 5 cubits wide (or high, assuming a vertical positioning [Exod 27:18]). The pillars had hooks to attach the hangings (Exod 27:11). Only the east side differed. In the middle of the east side was a gate or opening 20 cubits long. So on either side of the opening, the hangings were 15 cubits long (Exod 27:14-15). The entrance itself had a screen also of fine twisted linen embroidered with brightly colored needlework (Exod 38:18). The linen hangings served as a visible barrier, setting off the holy space inside the court, and also blocking the view to ones outside the court. The linen hangings would have been densely enough woven so that light would not readily pass through. This linen material elsewhere is used for priestly garments (Exod 28:5) and even for a ship's sail (Ezek 27:7). The screen would

similarly block the view inside the court and into the Tabernacle structure proper.

JOEL F. DRINKARD, JR.

HANINAH BEN-DOSA. Legends around this sage, who lived during the era of Shimon ben Gamliel I (ca. 40–80 CE), paint a picture of a man used to having miracles result from his prayers. His wife and his daughter apparently supported his policy of refusing to take advantage of the results of such miracles so as not to forfeit any of their reward in the world to come. *See* RABBI, RABBONI.

JUDITH ABRAMS

HANNAH han'uh [חַנָּה khannah]. Hannah, whose name means "favor," was one of two wives of Elkanah, an Ephraimite (1 Sam 1–2). Hannah had no children, but Elkanah's other wife, Peninnah, did have children. During the annual pilgrimage to SHILOH, Hannah prayed at the shrine, promising that if God gave her a son she would give the son back to God. She then bore a son whom she named SAMUEL. After she weaned him she took him to Eli the priest at Shiloh in fulfillment of her promise. On that occasion she sang the hymn known today as the Song of Hannah (*see* HANNAH, SONG OF).

From a narrative point of view, the Hannah story fits the type scene of the barren wife who bears a special son (*see* BARREN, BARRENNESS). According to the competition model (compare the stories of SARAH and RACHEL), Hannah is her husband's favored wife. The other wife bears children and belittles the childless wife, causing conflict between the two women. Eventually the barren wife bears a son through divine intervention. But unlike Sarah, Hannah does not retaliate against Peninnah's taunts. Unlike Rachel and Leah, Hannah does not compete or bargain with Peninnah for Elkanah's attention.

According to the promise model (compare Sarah, Samson's mother, and the Shunammite woman), Hannah receives a divine promise of a son; the son is born and receives a significant name. In Sarah's case her husband Abraham receives the promise. Samson's mother herself receives the promise of a son through an appearance of the angel of the LORD (Judg 13); the Shunammite woman hears her word of promise from the prophet Elisha (2 Kgs 4). By contrast, the promise to Hannah is uniquely cryptic: the priest Eli accuses her of drunkenness when he sees her lips silently moving, then in response to her protest he gives her a general assurance that her prayer will be answered, without knowing the reason for her prayer.

According to the request model (compare the situations of Rebekah and Rachel), Hannah requests a son, the Lord hears her prayer, and grants her request. In the case of both Rebekah and Rachel, their husbands pray for a son; but Hannah herself prays, and her request is granted.

Hannah's uniqueness in relation to the other barren wives foreshadows her unique role in the history of Israel. She maintained her faithful determination in spite of Peninnah's taunts and Eli's lack of understanding. When she gave Samuel to Eli in fulfillment of her promise, she offered her prayer at the public shrine at Shiloh, where the ark was housed at the time. She prayed the words that we know today as the Song of Hannah (1 Sam 2:1-10), the only sustained prayer of praise offered by a woman in the OT. Her son, Samuel, anointed the first two kings of Israel: Saul and David.

In the aftermath of the Roman destruction of the Temple in 70 CE, Pseudo-Philo expanded the Hannah story, highlighting the divine gift of leaders for the community. In the same period, Luke's Gospel used the narrative framework of the Hannah story in the Infancy Narrative in chaps. 1–2. Mary's song (the Magnificat, Luke 1:47-56) echoes themes from Hannah's song (*see* MAGNIFICAT; MARY).

Bibliography: Joan E. Cook. *Hannah's Desire, God's Design: Early Interpretations of the Story of Hannah* (1999).

JOAN E. COOK

HANNAH, SONG OF. The Song of Hannah is the song of thanks Hannah sang at the shrine at Shiloh (*see* SHILOH, SHILONITE), celebrating the gift of her son SAMUEL (1 Sam 2:1-10). The occasion was her visit to the shrine to leave Samuel with the priest ELI, as she had promised when asking God for a son. In its larger context at the beginning of the books of Samuel, the song rejoices in the nascent monarchy, to which Samuel contributed by anointing Saul and David the first two kings of Israel. Its words offer a theological perspective on the monarchy: the Lord is the ultimate ruler who protects and defends the people, and the divinely appointed king serves as the Lord's regent.

The song's words allude to twofold victory. On a personal level, the Lord overcomes Hannah's barrenness. In the context of the monarchy, the Lord leads Saul and David in their defeat of Israel's enemies. The song rejoices that the divine king upsets the status quo: the strong become weak and the weak strong; the satisfied become hungry while the hungry are satisfied; and the childless woman bears children while the fertile one becomes barren. By these acts the Deity ennobles and honors not only the king but all the faithful.

The song is generally understood as an ancient hymn inserted into the text toward the end of the monarchy. Its themes are similar to those in Ps 113. Early Jewish interpreters expanded the song; e.g., Pseudo-Philo revised it as a testament in *L.A.B.* 51, and the Targum of the Prophets reworked it into an apocalyptic piece. Early Christian interpreters echoed its themes in Mary's song, the Magnificat (Luke 1:47-

56), which Mary sang in the presence of Elizabeth to celebrate the news of her own pregnancy through divine intervention.

JOAN E. COOK

HANNATHON han'uh-thon [חַנָּתֹן khannathon]. Meaning "gracious." Hannathon was a city near the northern border of Zebulun (Josh 19:14) and adjacent to a highway (see EA 8:17, 245:32). According to the annals of Tiglath-pileser III, Hannathon was an important city (no. 18). Since the description of the border of Zebulun is vague and the name was not preserved, the identification of the city is problematic. The preferred identification is Khirbet al-Badawiyye, now Tell Hannaton near Kibbutz Hannaton, 5 km west of Rummane (RIMMON, the previous point in the description of the border). *See* IPHTAH-EL; ZEBULUN, ZEBULUNITE.

Bibliography: Z. Kallai. *Historical Geography of the Bible* (1986) 188.

YOEL ELITZUR

HANNIBAL. The general of the army of Carthage during the Second Punic War (218–202 BCE). When war broke out, he guided the Carthaginians from Spain through the Alps and invaded Italy. Hannibal defeated the Romans in several battles (218–216 BCE) and occupied Roman territory. Unable to defeat Hannibal, Rome resorted to a war of attrition, since Carthage did not send supplies and reinforcements. Finally, SCIPIO AFRICANUS invaded North Africa, forcing Hannibal to return to Carthage, where he was defeated in 202.

Hannibal governed Carthage until Rome forced him into exile. Antiochus III sheltered him in the Seleucid court (190–188 BCE) but after the Romans defeated Antiochus, Hannibal fled to BITHYNIA. Rome demanded Hannibal's return, but the general committed suicide instead.

ADAM L. PORTER

HANNIEL han'ee-uhl [חַנִּיאֵל khanni'el]. The name of two men in the OT, both of whom are given the title nasi' (נָשִׂיא), a PRINCE or CHIEF. The name Hanniel means "God has shown favor." 1. A leader from the tribe of Manasseh. Hanniel son of Ephod was in charge of distributing the tribal inheritance among the clans of Manasseh (Num 34:23).

2. A man from the tribe of Asher (1 Chr 7:39). Hanniel son of Ulla is described as a mighty warrior and one of the leaders of the princes.

KEVIN A. WILSON

HANOCH hay'nok [חֲנֹךְ khanokh]. Four persons in the OT share the Hebrew name khanokh ("Enoch/Hanoch"). Many English translations (e.g., NIV, NRSV) transliterate the name as "Hanoch" only for two of these persons. 1. Third-listed son of Midian (Gen 25:4; 1 Chr 1:33).

2. First-listed son of Jacob's firstborn, Reuben (Gen 46:9; 1 Chr 5:3), and eponymous ancestor of the Hanochite clan (Exod 6:14; Num 26:5).

In other occurrences of khanokh, modern translations render the name ENOCH (e.g., Gen 4:17).

JASON C. DYKEHOUSE

HANUKKAH hah´nuh-kuh [חֲנוּכָּה khanukkah]. The Hebrew title for the Jewish celebration known as the FEAST OF DEDICATION. Commemorated for eight days beginning on the twenty-fifth of the month of CHISLEV (Nov–Dec), Hanukkah celebrates the victory of ancient Judeans over the oppressive and genocidal policies of the Seleucid king, Antiochus IV Epiphanies. Antiochus, for reasons still unclear to modern scholarship, forbade the practice of Judaism and desecrated the Jerusalem Temple. According to 1 Macc 4:36-61 and 2 Macc 10:1-8, a group of Judean rebels under the leadership of Judas Maccabee retook the Temple on the twenty-fifth of Chislev in 165 or 164 BCE and purified the Temple of the desecrations committed by Antiochus.

PHILLIP MICHAEL SHERMAN

HANUN hay´nuhn [חָנוּן khanun]. An adjective meaning "gracious," which is only used to describe an attribute of God. When used this way, it is often paired with the adjective "merciful" (rakhum [רַחוּם]; Exod 34:6; Ps 86:15; 103:8; 2 Chr 30:9; Neh 9:17, 31 and others).

1. Hanun is the name of the son of Nahash, the Ammonite king, who succeeds him on the throne. David sends messengers of goodwill to him, but he humiliates them and sends them back (2 Sam 10:1-4; 2 Chr 19:2-6), rendering "Hanun" a sharply ironic name.

2. An individual who worked in Jerusalem under the leadership of Nehemiah helping to rebuild the Temple and the walls around Jerusalem (Neh 3:13).

3. Another individual who worked under the leadership of Nehemiah (Neh 3:30).

C. MARK MCCORMICK

HAPAX LEGOMENA hah´pahks-luh-gohm´uh-nuh [ἅπαξ λεγόμενα hapax legomena]. A Greek term meaning "once said." This is applied to words in the biblical text, other than proper names, which occur only once. This term emerged when biblical texts were translated from Hebrew in order to denote problematic words that had no other attestation and thus were more liable to mistranslation. The most common solution to these problems comes through comparative philology and the analysis of cognates. The study of comparative Semitic linguistics for this purpose began during the Middle Ages. Typically, Hebrew poetry uses a more eclectic vocabulary and thus contains more instances of hapax legomena. See LINGUISTICS AND BIBLICAL STUDIES.

R. JUSTIN HARKINS

HAPHARAIM haf´uh-ray´im [חֲפָרַיִם khafarayim]. Appearing only once in the Bible, Hapharaim is a town in Issachar's assigned territory (Josh 19:19). Scholars generally locate Hapharaim 9 mi. northwest of Beth-shan at et-Taiyibeh. A less likely traditional location is Khirbet el-Farriyeh, far removed from the rest of Issachar's territory. The suggested connection between Hapharaim and names recorded in the Egyptian conquest lists of Thutmose III and Shishak I at Karnak seems improbable.

SUSANNA W. SOUTHARD

HAPIRU. See HABIRU, HAPIRU.

HAPLOGRAPHY. Phenomenon by which texts are accidentally shortened in the copying process, usually detectable only by comparing versions and manuscripts of biblical texts. This most often occurs when similar words or letters in sequence are copied only once by a scribe. See TEXT CRITICISM, NT; TEXT CRITICISM, OT.

R. JUSTIN HARKINS

HAPPINESS [אֶשֶׁר ʾesher, אָשַׁר ʾashar, שִׂמְחָה simkhah, שָׂשׂוֹן sason; χαίρω chairō, ἀγαλλίασις agalliasis, εὐφροσύνη euphrosynē, ἡδονή hēdonē]. Happiness (gladness, rejoicing) is a relational value: one is made happy "on account of" or by means of something else. In Hebrew, the most basic meaning is related to the verb ʾashar (אָשַׁר), "to go straight, advance," taking on a secondary sense of "blessed." Blessedness is an act of living in balance, taking delight in good things, and moving forward in wholeness, not the result of heaping up possessions or even honor. Such a state can be inspired by festival worship, success, restoration, felicitous relationships, a safe birth, or the end of a time of trial. Even the prophet Jonah feels happy at the protection of a shady bush God provides for him (4:6). A goal of wisdom teaching is to amplify a person's happiness by living in harmony with God's laws and the community's norms, highlighting the social aspect of the concept. The sages often pronounce someone "blessed" (happy) when the person chooses wisdom and knowledge over riches or outward acclaim (Prov 3:13, 18; 8:32, 34; 16:20; 20:7; 28:14; 29:18).

In the NT, such concepts are most especially associated with the good news of Jesus' redemptive work. When the death sentence on humanity is lifted, the result is joy. Jesus' approach in the BEATITUDES takes up where sages left off: now it is the wretched who are first in line for God's abundant blessings, reflecting the overall reversal brought about by God's liberation of the world. See JOY.

CAROLE R. FONTAINE

HAPPIZZEZ hap´uh-zez [הַפִּצֵּץ happitsets]. A priestly clan chief upon whom the eighteenth lot fell when David, Zadok, and Ahimelech divided the descendants of Aaron according to their tasks (1 Chr 24:15). The clan may be connected with BETH-PAZZEZ (Josh 19:21).

HAR HARIF. *See* HARIF, HAR.

HARA hair´uh [הָרָא haraʾ]. This is the name of one of the places listed in 1 Chr 5:26 as the location to which the king of Assyria took the Israelite tribes Reuben, Gad, and the half-tribe of Manasseh into exile. In 1 Chronicles it is listed alongside Hala, Habor, and the river Gozan. The name does not appear in the LXX, or in the Syriac. It also does not appear in the list provided in 2 Kgs 17:6 or 18:11, where instead the text reads "and the cities of the Medes" (weʿare madhay וְעָרֵי מָדָי). The LXX in 2 Kgs 17:6 and 18:11 reads "and the mountains of the Medes," which has led to the conclusion that the Hebrew haraʾ of 1 Chr 5:26 is a corruption of the original har (הַר, "mountain"). If the mountains of the Medes are intended, then the name refers to the mountainous region east of the Tigris River.

C. MARK MCCORMICK

HARADAH huh-ray´duh [חֲרָדָה kharadhah]. One of the places the Israelites camped on their journey from Egypt (Num 33:24-25). The name means "fear" or "trembling."

HARAN hair´uhn [הָרָן haran, חָרָן kharan; Χαρράν Charran]. The word *Haran* in English may refer to two different Hebrew words, one of which is the name of a person and the other of which is most often the name of the town. 1. The personal name Haran (haran) refers to the brother of Abram who died in Ur before Terah and his sons left for the west (Gen 11–12). He was the father of Lot, who traveled with Abram when he left the town Haran for the land of promise (Gen 12).

2. Haran (haran) is also an individual listed in 1 Chr 23:9 as the son of Shimei in the tribe of Levi.

3. Haran (kharan) is listed as the son of Caleb and his concubine, Ephah (1 Chr 2:46).

4. Haran (kharan) refers to a place where the family of Terah settled after leaving Ur. When used referring to the place where Terah and his family made a home, it names an ancient city known through Assyrian and Babylonian records, which contained and ancient sanctuary dedicated to the moon god, Sin.

It is mentioned as far back as the records of HAMMURABI of Babylon (18th cent. BCE), and it played a significant role in the ancestral narratives of the book of Genesis. It is the place from which Abram set forth for Canaan after the death of his father, Terah. This story is cited by Stephen in his sermon, where the name is written **Charran**. Stephen recounts Abraham's departure from Haran as his obedient response to God's call (Acts 7:2, 4). Eliezer, the servant of Abram, went to the Haran area in search of a wife for Isaac and returned with Rebekah (Gen 24). Jacob fled to the area of this town when he had tricked his brother Esau out of his birthright. He settled there for a period of time, working for his uncle Laban for seven years in order to receive the hand of Rachel in marriage. He subsequently married both Rachel and Leah, and decided to depart secretly for his homeland.

The name *Haran* may be a shortening in the Hebrew of the longer Akkadian, harranu, which means "caravan." This could be related to its role as a significant caravanserai, or rest stop on the important trade route from Mesopotamia to the Mediterranean coast.

C. MARK MCCORMICK

HARARITE hair´uh-rit [הֲרָרִי harari, הָאֲרָרִי haʾrari]. A gentilic adjective applied to three individuals in the OT: AGEE (2 Sam 23:11), his son SHAMMAH (2 Sam 23:33; SHAGEE in 1 Chr 11:34), and SHARAR (2 Sam 23:33; SACHAR in 1 Chr 11:35). In every occurrence the designation is somehow associated with one of David's military elite. The appellation could mean something like "mountain dwellers," although the specific location or group to which it refers is uncertain.

NATHAN D. MAXWELL

HARBONA hahr-boh´nuh [חַרְבוֹנָא kharvonaʾ, חַרְבוֹנָה kharvonah]. One of the seven EUNUCHs serving as advisor to King AHASUERUS (Esth 1:10). He recommends the king hang HAMAN on the very gallows that Haman had arranged for Mordecai (Esth 7:9). His name may come from the Persian for "donkey driver."

HARBOR [λιμήν limēn]. A place for ships to take on or remove cargo (1 Macc 14:5; 2 Macc 12:6, 9), traditionally viewed as a safe haven (4 Macc 13:7). Despite Paul's urging to remain in FAIR HAVENS harbor (Acts 27:12), his advice went unheeded, resulting in a shipwreck. *See* SHIPS AND SAILING IN THE NT; SHIPS AND SAILING IN THE OT.

KATHY J. CHAMBERS

HARDEN THE HEART [חִזַּק אֶת־הַלֵּב khizzaq ʾeth-hallev, הִקְשָׁה אֶת־הַלֵּב hiqshah ʾeth-hallev; καρδία πεπωρωμένη kardia pepōrōmenē]. The main locus of the metaphor of the hardened heart is the exodus narratives. God announces that he will harden Pharaoh's heart so that he will not permit the Israelites to leave (Exod 4:21; 7:3; 14:4). The irony here is that God performs dreadful wonders to warn the Egyptians but at the same time refuses them the opportunity to change the course of their actions. Similarly, when Israel enters the land of Canaan, God hardens the heart of the foreign kings, and as a result they engage in battle against Israel and are defeated (Josh 11:20). However, God not only hardens the heart of Israel's enemies but also of the Israelites themselves (Isa 63:17). According to Isa 6:10, God intends to "fatten" the hearts of the Israelites so that they won't give heed to the prophet's words.

In the NT, hardening of the heart is never attributed to God's action. Instead, the pertinent OT passages are cited using a passive voice (compare Ps 95:8, "do not harden your hearts" to 2 Cor 3:14, "their minds were hardened" and Heb 3:13, "so that none of you may be hardened"), and thus the question of agency is left open. In Mark 6:52 and 8:17, the motif of the hardened heart (passive voice of pōroō πωρόω, "to make stubborn, without feeling") is used in the context of Jesus' feeding miracles. Here the disciples see what happens but they are unable to grasp the significance of these events. The metaphor of the hardened heart presupposes a view of the human mind (lev לֵב, "heart") according to which one can observe things with the senses and yet be unable to make use of this data in the exercise of will and judgment. The theological point of the OT seems to be that God uses this gap between perception and judgment to prevent humans from recognizing and responding to his presence in their world.

ANDREAS K. SCHUELE

HARDJEDEF, INSTRUCTION OF PRINCE. A work of didactic literature from the Old Kingdom in EGYPT probably written in the Fifth Dynasty (2450–2300 BCE). Only fragments of the beginning of the manuscript dating to the New Kindgom have been preserved. As with many texts from the instruction genre, it is set up as the teachings of a father, Hardjedef, to his son, Au-ib-re. He urges his son to build himself a house on earth as well as one for the afterlife.

Bibliography: Miriam Lichtheim. *AEL.* Vol. 1. (1973) 58–59.

KEVIN A. WILSON

HARE [אַרְנֶבֶת 'arneveth]. The hare is of the Leporidae family, along with the smaller rabbit, and is native to the Near East. The rabbit is not, arriving via the Romans. Two species of hare are common in Palestine: *Lepus syriacus* in the north and *Lepus aegyptiacus* in the south. The hare is considered unclean because it does not have a cloven hoof (Lev 11:6; Deut 14:7). The ancient Israelites believed erroneously that the hare is a ruminate. Rather, the hare and rabbit eliminate a dropping that may be chewed and swallowed again, allowing the animal to utilize fully plants that are difficult to digest. This activity mocks cud-chewing. The Greco-Roman world associated the hare and rabbit with DIONYSUS, the god of life, death, and fertility. Consequently, the hare and rabbit can often be found on Greco-Roman and Christian funerary monuments, perhaps the origin of the "Easter Bunny." *See* ANIMALS OF THE BIBLE.

F. RACHEL MAGDALENE

HAREPH hair'if [חָרֵף kharef]. Descendant of Caleb identified as the "father" (i.e., founder) of Beth-gader (1 Chr 2:51). Hareph may mean "harvest time" or "autumn," but could also relate to "reproach" or "scorn." Hareph's brothers are identified as founders of the more familiar towns Bethlehem and Kiriath-Jearim (1 Chr 2:50-51).

NATHAN D. MAXWELL

HARHAIAH hahr-hay'yuh [חַרְהֲיָה kharhayah]. After returning from exile, Harhaiah's son UZZIEL participated in the Jerusalem wall repairs under Nehemiah (Neh 3:8). An unlikely textual emendation would replace the personal name Harhaiah with a common noun: "Uzziel, a son (member) of the guild of goldsmiths."

HARHAS hahr'has [חַרְחַס kharkhas]. The grandfather of SHALLUM, who is identified in 2 Kgs 22:14 as the husband of HULDAH the prophetess. In the par. text, 2 Chr 34:22, the grandfather's name is HASRAH. As "Harhas" is somewhat irregular for Hebrew, Hasrah may be the proper form.

HAR-HERES hahr-hihr'iz [הַר־חֶרֶס har-kheres]. Means "Mount of the Sun." The place where the Amorites lived, near Aijalon and possibly an alternate name for BETH-SHEMESH and IR-SHEMESH. The people living there were warring against the Israelites, but Israel prevailed and conscripted the inhabitants into forced labor (Judg 1:35).

HARHUR hahr'huhr [חַרְחוּר kharkhur]. The name of the head of a family of relatively low-ranking temple functionaries known as the NETHINIM who returned from Babylon with Zerubbabel (Ezra 2:51; Neh 7:53). In the par. text in 1 Esd 5:31 the names ASUR and PHARAKIM appear in place of Harhur.

HARIF, HAR. Har Harif is a high (1000 m) Negev plateau on the border with the Sinai Desert. This arid region (c. 150 mm annual rainfall) has no perennial springs, so exploitation of the area depended on rainfall that collected in pools. Surveys and excavations revealed sporadic prehistoric utilization of the plateau over some 20,000 years from Upper Paleolithic (Levantine Aurignacian), Epipaleolithic (late Kebaran), Late Natufian, and Harifian sites. The lone Natufian site (Rosh Horesha) had stone hut foundations that indicated semi-permanent and repeated occupation, and *Dentalium* and other marine shells reflect connections with the Red and Mediterranean Seas. The Harifian sites also had stone hut foundations, and these sites were contemporaneous with the Pre-pottery Neolithic A agricultural sites in the arable lands of the Levant. Climate, however, supported Harifian hunter-gatherers but not farmers.

Bibliography: A. E. Marks, ed. *Prehistory and Paleoenvironments in the Central Negev, Israel.* Vol. 2 (1977).

GARY O. ROLLEFSON

HARIM hair´im [חָרִם kharim; Χαρμή Charmē]. 1. The head of a priestly family that is listed among those that David organized for liturgical service (1 Chr 24:8). Members of this family appear in Ezra 2:39; Neh 7:42; and 1 Esd 5:25 among returnees who left Babylon with Zerubbabel (see also Neh 12:15).

2. The name of a lay family listed in Ezra 2:32 and Neh 7:35. A son of Harim assisted in rebuilding Jerusalem's walls (Neh 3:11). Members of the family divorced their foreign wives according to Ezra's order (Ezra 10:31).

3. A priest who appears as signatory to Ezra's covenant in (Neh 10:5 [Heb. 6]).

4. One of the lay signatories of Ezra's covenant (Neh 10:27 [Heb. 28]).

DEREK E. WITTMAN

HARIPH hair´if [חָרִיף kharif]. A Judahite family patriarch who returned after the Babylonian exile and signed the covenant (Neh 10:19 [Heb. 10:20]). According to the census, the descendants of Hariph numbered 112 "sons" (Neh 7:24). Ezra 2:18 seems to identify JORAH in place of Hariph among the list of returnees.

HARM, TO [רַע ra´, רָעָה ra´ah, רָעַע ra´a´; ἀδικέω adikeō, κακοποιέω kakopoieō, κακόω kakoō]. In the OT, the verb "to harm" is closely associated with the idea of COVENANT (Gen 26:29). God's covenant with Israel often lies behind divine promises of protection (Gen 50:20; Ps 105:15; Isa 27:3; Jer 29:11). Yet protection is not inevitable: God will harm those who reject the covenant (Josh 24:20; Amos 9:4; Mic 3:11). In the NT, Jesus delivers from harm (Acts 18:10), but final deliverance depends on faithfulness until death (Rev 2:11). In both testaments avoiding harm is an ethical imperative (Ps 7:4; 1 Pet 3:13). Jesus insists that to refrain from doing good on the Sabbath is to do harm (Mark 3:4). See VIOLENCE.

DAVID M. MILLER

HARMON hahr´muhn [הַרְמוֹן harmon]. The Hebrew word is a problematic HAPAX LEGOMENA in Amos 4:3. Ancient authorities understood it as a place name, rendering it "the mountain Remman" (LXX) or "mountains of Armenia" (Syr. and Tg.). With emendation, modern interpreters have suggested common nouns including "palaces" (KJV) and "dung heap" (NEB, NAB, NJPS). Of all the suggestions, probably the best is with slight emendation the well-known Mount Hermon (khermon [חֶרְמוֹן], see NJB), a high peak, part of the Bashan range and easily visible from northern Palestine. Reference to this location would form a fitting inclusio with Amos 4:1, "Hear this word, you cows of Bashan who are on Mount Samaria."

MILTON ENG

HARMONIZATION. The process in which scribes involved in the copying and transmission of texts deliberately substitute one reading for another when the copiers believed that the earlier readings were incorrect and needed emendation to "harmonize" the versions of a text and avoid problems of interpretation within the text. See TEXT CRITICISM, NT; TEXT CRITICISM, OT.

R. JUSTIN HARKINS

HARMONY OF THE GOSPELS. See GOSPEL HARMONY; SYNOPTIC PROBLEM.

HARNEPHER hahr´nuh-fuhr [חַרְנֶפֶר kharnefer]. The second of eleven sons of ZOPHAH (1 Chr 7:36) listed in the Asherite genealogy in 1 Chr 7. The name, probably of Egyptian origin and meaning "Horus is merciful," may refer to a clan or village rather than a specific individual.

HARNESS [אָסַר ʾasar, רָתַם ratham]. The act of binding a horse to a chariot (1 Kgs 18:44; Jer 46:4; Mic 1:13).

HAROD hair´uhd [חֲרֹד kharodh, חֲרוֹדִי kharodhi, חֲרוֹרִי kharori]. 1. Site of the camp where Gideon and his army prepare to battle Midian (Judg 7:1). Its actual location is unknown, but it is usually identified with a spring in the vicinity of Mount Gilboa.

2. The hometown of two of the men listed among David's warriors known as the "Thirty" (2 Sam 23:25). Shammah and Elika are both identified as "the Harodite." Some manuscripts read "Harorite," probably due to a scribal error because of the similarity between the Hebrew d (ד) and r (ר).

C. MARK MCCORMICK

HAROEH huh-roh´uh [הָרֹאֶה haro'eh]. A son of Shobal (1 Chr 2:52), possibly identified with REAIAH in 1 Chr 4:2.

HARORITE. See HAROD.

HAROSHETH-HA-GOIIM huh-roh´shith-huh-goi´im [חֲרֹשֶׁת הַגּוֹיִם kharosheth haggoyim]. The home of Sisera, the commander of the army of King Jabin of Hazor (Judg 4:2). The exact location of the site is unknown. The battle between Sisera and Deborah took place in the Wadi Kishon near Mount Tabor, and since Sisera mustered his forces at Harosheth-ha-goiim, it should be nearby, perhaps to the north toward Hazor. It is unclear whether Harosheth-ha-goiim is a town or an area. The name means "forests of the nations," which might suggest that it is a region, similar to Galilee of the Nations in Isa 9:1.

KEVIN A. WILSON

HARP. See MUSICAL INSTRUMENTS.

HARPOON [שֻׂכָּה sukkah]. A term appearing in parallelism with fishing spears (tsiltsal daghim

צֶלְצַל דָּגִים) in Job 41:7 [Heb 40:31], perhaps a barbed iron (KJV). Whatever the exact nature of the instrument, it is cited as an inadequate means by which to snare the sea monster LEVIATHAN. *See* FISHERMEN; FISHING.

HARROW [שָׂדַד sadhadh]. Israelite farmers used oxen to harrow, or smooth, a field after its initial plowing (Job 39:10; Isa 28:24; Hos 10:11). Without evidence of any specialized harrowing tools, scholars have speculated on the process itself. Most likely, harrowing involved leveling and smoothing the soil by dragging forked tree branches over it after sowing the seed. Other possibilities include cross plowing at a right angle to the furrows or making border furrows. *See* AGRICULTURE; PLOW.

SUSANNA W. SOUTHARD

HARSHA hahr'shuh [חַרְשָׁא kharsha'; Χαρεά Charea]. The head of a family of relatively low-ranking temple functionaries known as the NETHINIM who returned to Jerusalem from Babylon along with Zerubbabel (Ezra 2:52; Neh 7:54). A variant of this family name, CHAREA, also appears in a par. text (1 Esd 5:32).

HARSHA, TEL [תֵּל חַרְשָׁא tel kharsha'; Θελερσάς Thelersas]. A town or village in the province of Babylon of unknown location. The site is listed with Tel-Melah, Cherub, Addon, and Immer (Ezra 2:59; Neh 7:61). Jewish exiles deported by the Babylonian king Nebuchadnezzar returned to Jerusalem with Zerubbabel from this location in 520 BCE; however, they could not prove their Israelite lineage and were excluded as being unclean. The site is also mentioned in a list in 1 Esd 5:36.

TERRY W. EDDINGER

HARUM hair'uhm [הָרוּם harum]. The father of AHARHEL, whose families were descendants of their Judahite ancestor KOZ (1 Chr 4:8).

HARUMAPH huh-roo'maf [חֲרוּמַף kharumaf]. JEDAIAH, son of Harumaph, is listed among those who rebuilt the wall under Nehemiah's leadership (Neh 3:10), the only mention of Harumaph. On the basis of the meaning of kharam (חָרַם) in Lev 21:18 or Isa 11:15, the name Harumaph may actually be a moniker meaning broken or split nose.

PHILLIP MICHAEL SHERMAN

HARUPHITE huh-roo'fit [חֲרִיפִי kharifi]. The term is used in 1 Chr 12:6 in connection with the Benjaminite Shephatiah in a list of ambidextrous warriors who joined David while he was at Ziqlag. Following the Masoretic practice known as QERE-KETHIBH (read/written), the term is written one way (kharifi) in the biblical text, but traditionally pronounced another (kharufi חֲרוּפִי). Shephatiah is, perhaps, to be associated with Hareph,

a descendant of Caleb, mentioned in 1 Chr 2:51. It is unclear if the etymology of the term—to taunt or abuse—is significant.

PHILLIP MICHAEL SHERMAN

HARUZ hair'uhz [חָרוּץ kharuts]. Perhaps meaning "golden one," Haruz was the father of MESHULLEMETH, mother of King AMON of Judah (2 Kgs 21:19), and, therefore, Haruz was great-grandfather of King JOSIAH (v. 24). Haruz' residence, JOTBAH, appears to be non-Judahite.

HARVEST [קָצַר qatsar; θερίζω therizō]. A word for harvest occurs frequently in a literal sense in the Bible and other pertinent texts. The GEZER CALENDAR mentions times of gathering or harvest (barley, grains, summer fruit), while scriptural examples include barley (Ruth 1:23; 2 Sam 21:9; Jdt 8:2), wheat (Exod 34:22; Ruth 1:23), olives (Deut 24:20; Isa 17:6), and summer fruits (Isa 16:9 [fruit and grain]; 32:10). *Harvest* could also be used to designate a time in the year (e.g., Gen 8:22; 30:14; Exod 34:21; Josh 3:15), with specific harvests associated with the Festival of Weeks (wheat, Exod 34:22) and the Festival of Booths (the remaining crops, Exod 23:16; Deut 16:13). During harvesttime, reaping to a field's edge and gleaning were forbidden (Lev 19:9; 23:22; Deut 24:19-21), but after the harvest, which ultimately depended upon God (Jer 5:24; Amos 4:7; Jas 5:18), some of the crop was to be left for the poor.

Harvest became a natural metaphor for divine action at the judgment, whether in a negative (e.g., Jer 51:33; Matt 13:39-42; Rev 14:15-16; 4 Ezra 4:28-32, 35) or a positive sense (Matt 9:37-38; Rom 1:13; Jas 3:18).

JAMES C. VANDERKAM

HASADIAH has'uh-di'uh [חֲסַדְיָה khasadhyah; Ἀσαδίος Asadios]. 1. The sixth of the seven sons of Zerubbabel (1 Chr 3:20), listed along with their one sister in 1 Chr 3:19-20.

2. The father of Zedekiah and the son of Hilkiah, Hasadiah appears as an ancestor of Baruch in Bar 1:1.

HASDRUBAL. The name of several different Carthaginian generals. 1. The first and most notable (d. 221 BCE), the son-in-law of Hamilcar Barca, attempted diplomatic relations with Rome.

2. The second (d. 207 BCE), the son of Hamilcar Barca and younger brother of Hannibal. These brothers were involved in the Second Punic War (218–201 BCE) against Rome.

3. Another was in command during the initial years of the HASMONEANS. *See* MACCABEES.

MARY KAY DOBROVOLNY, R.S.M.

HASHABIAH hash'uh-bi'uh [חֲשַׁבְיָה khashavyah, חֲשַׁבְיָהוּ khashavyahu]. 1. A Levite whose descendant served as a musician before the tent of meeting (1 Chr 6:32, 45).

2. A Levite and ancestor of Shemaiah who returned to Jerusalem after the exile (1 Chr 9:14; Neh 11:15).

3. A Levite and one of Jeduthun's sons who played lyres, sang, and prophesied according to David's directions (1 Chr 25:3, 19).

4. Along with his brothers, a Hebronite who managed the area of Israel west of the Jordan River (1 Chr 26:30).

5. Chief officer of the Levites during David's reign (1 Chr 27:17).

6. A chief among the Levites who generously supplied lambs and kids for Passover (2 Chr 35:9; 1 Esd 1:9).

7. A Levitical priest among those whom Iddo sent to join Ezra and who transported temple treasure to Jerusalem (Ezra 8:19, 24-30). This Hashabiah may be the same one who signed the sealed covenant document (Neh 10:11) and who was a Levitical leader (Neh 12:24).

8. A returnee from the exile who rejected his foreign wife (Ezra 10:25).

9. Leader and repairman of part of the district of Keilah (Neh 3:17).

10. Descendant of Asaph and a Levite (Neh 11:22).

11. A priest during the reign of Joiakim (Neh 12:21).

EMILY R. CHENEY

HASHABNAH huh-shab′nuh [חֲשַׁבְנָה khashavnah]. One of the "leaders of the people" (Neh 10:14) who sealed Nehemiah's covenant (Neh 10:25 [Heb 10:26]). Probably a shortened form of the name HASHAB-NEIAH (Neh 3:10; 9:5) or else a corrupted form of HASHABIAH (e.g., 1 Chr 6:45; Ezra 8:19), both meaning "Yahweh has regarded (me)."

T. DELAYNE VAUGHN

HASHABNEIAH hash′uhb-nee′yah [חֲשַׁבְנְיָה khashavneyah]. 1. The father of Hattush, who participated in the reconstruction of Jerusalem's walls under the direction of Nehemiah (Neh 3:10).

2. A Levite who participated in a liturgical blessing of Yahweh that was spoken just prior to the sealing of Ezra's covenant (Neh 9:5). Some suggest that Hashabneiah should be identified with HASHABIAH, whose name appears with some frequency in Ezra and Nehemiah.

DEREK E. WITTMAN

HASHBADDANAH hash-bad′uh-nuh [חַשְׁבַּדָּנָה khashbaddanah]. Nehemiah 8:4 lists this individual as standing to the left of Ezra during the public proclamation of the Torah following the return from exile.

HASHEM hay′shim [הָשֵׁם hashem]. According 1 Chronicles, "sons of Hashem" (11:34; contrast 2 Sam 23:32) are among the heroes known as David's "Thirty." See DAVID'S CHAMPIONS; JASHEN.

HASHMONAH hash-moh′nuh [חַשְׁמֹנָה khashmonah]. A location where the Israelites encamped while traveling between Mithka and Moseroth (Num 33:29-30). Levine suggests (but does not endorse) that Hashmonah may be equivalent to the location Heshmon.

Bibliography: Baruch Levine. *Numbers 21–36: A New Translation with Introduction and Commentary.* AB 4A (2000).

PHILLIP MICHAEL SHERMAN

HASHUBAH huh-shoo′buh [חֲשֻׁבָה khashuvah]. The third son of Zerubabel, the postexilic descendant of the Davidic line (1 Chr 3:20). The BHS suggests that Hashubah may not be a proper name at all, but rather refers to those children born "after his return." Corruption in the Hebrew of the text makes this a possibility, but the reference to the number five at the conclusion of v. 20 makes such emendation difficult.

PHILLIP MICHAEL SHERMAN

HASHUM hay′shuhm [חָשֻׁם khashum; Ἀσόμ Hasom, Ασεμ Asem, Ησαμ Ēsam, Ωσαμ Ōsam]. A postexilic name appearing as the head or eponym of one of the families returning from exile with Zerubbabel (Ezra 2:19; 10:33; Neh 7:22; 8:4; 10:18; 1 Esd 9:33). In a passage parallel to Neh 8:4, 1 Esd 9:44 lists Lothasubus in place of Hashum. NRSV also reads Hashum for the Hebrew khushim (חֻשִׁים) in Gen 46:23 (RSV and KJV, HUSHIM).

T. DELAYNE VAUGHN

HASIDEANS has′uh-dee′uhn. *See* HASIDIM.

HASIDIM has′uh-dim [חֲסִידִים khasidhim; ὅσιοι hosioi, Ἀσιδαῖοι Hasidaioi]. This Hebrew title, which means "pious" or "faithful," appears in transliterated form in the Greek as Hasidaioi, translated "Hasideans" in most English versions (1 Macc 2:42; 7:13; 2 Macc 14:6). It refers to a group of participants who play an important role in the events of the Maccabean revolt. The appearance of the term in Greek transliteration rather than in translated form suggests that a group by that name was present in Second Temple Judaism in the 2nd cent. BCE. The term is not just the translation of the Hebrew adjective to designate some "pious" Jews (*see* MACCABEES, MACCABEAN REVOLT). There is no evidence to support the oft-repeated hypothesis that the Hasidim of 1 Macc 2:42 are the same as those Jews described in 1 Macc 2:29-38 who fled to the desert seeking righteousness and justice during the time of the Antiochian persecution. It is this connection that has frequently been cited to justify the hypothesis that the Hasidim were the predecessors of both the Pharisees and the Essenes. The name essēnoi (Εσσηνοι) has frequently been considered to be derived from the Aram. form, khasidha᾽ (חֲסִידָא), the equivalent of the Hebrew khasidh (חָסִיד). The desert location has been related to the asceticism ascribed to groups associated with the Dead Sea Scrolls. Arguments that these Hasidim were the authors of apocalyptic literature are not convincing.

The Hasidim are rather a synagōgē (συναγωγή "company") who are called ischyroi dynamei (ἰσχυροί δυνάμει), usually translated as "mighty warriors," but which could equally well be translated "mighty men" (see WARRIORS). This group, "all who offered themselves willingly for the law," is described as one more body that allied itself with the Maccabean movement whose origin and growth is described in 1 Macc 2:29-48. This development is described as a reaction to the attack on the Sabbath by the troops of ANTIOCHUS IV on the group of pious Jews who had fled to the desert. This coalition "rescued the law out of the hands of the Gentiles and kings, and they never let the sinner gain the upper hand" (1 Macc 2:48).

The Hasidim are described as a leading group in 1 Macc 7:12-18. They are identified as a company of scribes who are "first among the Israelites" (vv. 12-13). In this Hasmonean dynastic history, however, their significance is discounted (see HASMONEANS). While JUDAS the Maccabee and his brothers refused to listen to Bacchides, the governor and general sent by the king, the Hasidim sought peace with them, because Bacchides was accompanied by ALCIMUS, a priest of the line of Aaron, who had been appointed high priest by the king. Bacchides and Alcimus are able to seize and kill sixty members of the Hasidim, due to the misplaced trust of the Hasidim in Alcimus. In their naïveté the Hasidim have assisted the enemies and their objectives.

In 2 Macc 14:6 the reference to the Hasidim is placed in the mouth of Alcimus, who describes them as a seditious group who will not permit the kingdom to attain tranquility. The epitomist of this history appears to be making positive statements about the Hasidim by placing this charge in the mouth of the impious Alcimus. In this same text Judas is regarded as their leader. In both 1 Macc 2:42 and 2 Macc 14:6 the Hasidim are used as evidence to attest to the historical significance of the Hasmonean subjects of the history, thereby pointing to their significant role in Jewish history of the 2nd cent. BCE. The need to discount directly their importance through the account in 1 Macc 7:12-18 similarly attests to their significance. There is no basis for proposing that the group specified in the sources of the 2nd cent. BCE is attested in biblical materials such as Ps 149:1 ("assembly of the pious") or the other numerous uses of the word khasidh throughout the Psalms. The same can be said for the frequent references to the hosioi (the Gk. translation of khasidhim) in the Psalms of Solomon, especially to the "synagogue of the pious" in 17:16.

The term is attested, however infrequently, in the fragments of the manuscripts from QUMRAN. The appearance of the term in the Messianic Apocalypse (4Q521 2; 4 II, 5, 7) and the Apocryphal Psalms (11QP$_s$^{a} (11QS) XVIII, 12; XIX, 7; XXII, 3, 6) has been used as evidence for this group among the Qumran documents. But it is more likely that this was a common adjective designating piety, since it was a synonym for "the righteous," "the humble," and other such adjectives. The phrase ʾysh khsydym (איש חסידים) is used to describe David in 4Q398 14–17 II, 1. The Hebrew term khasidh is found in early rabbinic literature, in both singular and plural forms. Both HONI the Circle Drawer and HILLEL THE ELDER are described using this adjective (see also HILKIAH THE HASID). HANINAH BEN-DOSA, a miracle-worker in the rabbinic tradition, is sometimes designated a khasidh in the academic literature; however, he is not referred to in that manner in the Tannaitic literature. Some of his activities described in this literature are similar to attributes and events ascribed to the "early Hasidim" in rabbinic literature. The major references to the "first" or "early Hasidim" are m. Ber. 5:1, t. B. Qam. 2:6, b. Nid. 38ab, b. Ned. 10a and b. Menah. 40b–41a. They are used in this literature to illustrate exemplary behavior of exceptional piety rather than as authoritative persons with defined opinions in halakhic disputes or as founders of some religious movement in the 2nd cent. BCE.

Bibliography: Philip R. Davies. "Hasidim in the Maccabean Period." *JJS* 28 (1977) 127–40; John Kampen. *The Hasideans and the Origin of Pharisaism: A Study in 1 and 2 Maccabees* (1988).

JOHN I. KAMPEN

HASMONEAN DYNASTY. *See* HASMONEANS.

HASMONEANS haz′muh-nee′unh [Ἀσαμωναῖος Hasamōnaios]. "Hasmoneans" is the term applied to the family of Maccabees. The family comes from a supposed ancestor, probably something like Hashmon (*m. Mid.* 1:6, which refers to the "Hasmoneans," lit. "sons of Hashmonai": bny khshmwnʾy בני חשמונאי), though we know the name only in Greek (Hasamōnaios) in early sources and not from the books of Maccabees but from Josephus (*Ant.* 12.265). According to Josephus Asamonaios was the great-grandfather of Mattathias. The Hasmoneans led the resistance against the Syrians in the Maccabean Revolt and eventually became high priestly rulers of Judah for the better part of a century until the Romans took over the region. The Hasmoneans formed part of the leadership of Judea even in the period after the fall of Jerusalem in 70 CE.

A. Mattathias and His Sons
B. The Hasmonean Priest-Kings

Hellenistic, Maccabean, and Roman Era Chronology

Because of the fragmentary nature of available literary and archaeological sources, many of the dates are approximate.

332 BCE	Alexander the Great conquers Palestine.
301 BCE	After Alexander's death in 323, Palestine eventually falls under the control of Ptolemy I Soter.
301–198 BCE	Palestine ruled from Egypt by the Ptolemaic dynasty.
198 BCE	The Seleucids, from Damascus, defeat the Ptolemies at the Battle of Panium and take control of Palestine
167 BCE	The Seleucid ruler Antiochus IV Epiphanes uses repression to stop political infighting in Jerusalem. Torah scrolls are burned, circumcision is forbidden, the Sabath is outlawed, participation in Greek religious festivals is forced, Jews are forced to eat pork, the Jerusalem Temple is devoted to Zeus Olympios and other gods.
167 BCE	The priest Mattathias and his sons, known as the Maccabees, revolt against Seleucid repression.
165 BCE	Following the death of Mattathias, his son Judas Maccabeus assumes leadership of the revolt, defeats the Seleucid forces, and reoccupies and cleanses the Temple.
164 BCE	Judas opens negotiations with Roman ambassadors, thus initiating Rome's involvement in the affairs of Judah.
161 BCE	Upon Judas's death, Jonathan Maccabeus continues the resistance against the Seleucids and becomes effective ruler of Judea.
143–135 BCE	The last surviving son of the Maccabees, Simon, becomes high priest and effective ruler of Judea.
143–37 BCE	In the midst of internal political infighting and wars with the Seleucids and other surrounding states, the Hasmoneans (the later name for the Maccabean Dynasty) take control of Palestine, and Judah becomes an independent state.
63 BCE	Political unrest and opposition to Hasmonean rule results in the Roman general Pompey's being invited to intervene. Pompey takes Jerusalem.
37 BCE	The Hasmoneans retain normal rule until the Romans execute Aristobulus (Antigonus Mattathias).
40 BCE	Rome elevates Herod the Great (son of an official in the local Roman government) to kingship.
37 BCE	Herod the Great begins to rule

1. John Hyrcanus (135–104 BCE)
2. Aristobulus I (104–103 BCE)
3. Alexander Janneus (103–76 BCE)
4. Alexandra Salome (76–67 BCE)
5. Hyrcanus II and Aristobulus II (67–63 BCE)
C. The Remaining History of the Hasmoneans
Bibliography

A. Mattathias and His Sons

The first Hasmonean about which we know anything is Mattathias (*see* MATTATHIAS THE MACCABEE, MATTATHIAS MACCABEUS) who began the resistance against the Syrians after Antiochus IV's actions against the Jews, according to 1 Macc 2. Some doubt this scenario, but in any case he did not long survive the initial incidents. At his death the leadership passed to Mattathias's son JUDAS, who was only one of five sons. As it happened all five of the sons (John, Simon, Judas, Eleazar, and Jonathan) died violently in events relating to resistance against Syrian rule and the establishment of Maccabean rule (*see* MACCABEES, MACCABEAN REVOLT).

At the beginning of the Maccabean Revolt (168–165 or 167–164 BCE) the Maccabean resistance seems to have been only annoying rather than a significant thorn in the Seleucid side. The Maccabees and their followers appear to have used guerrilla tactics and to have operated out of Modein, which was not at the center of events in Palestine. At first local commanders were sent against Judas and his fighters, but after they won several spectacular victories (though wholly explicable by normal military tactics) and brought several local Syrian units and their leaders to their deaths, the Seleucid administration began to take them more seriously.

Approximately 165 BCE the vice-regent Lysias came against Judas. The books of Maccabees make this another great Jewish victory, but this seems unlikely. Lysias' army outnumbered the Jewish forces, and when they withdrew, it was in an orderly fashion. More likely than a military defeat is the sudden need for Lysias at Antioch, at which point he made an attempt to resolve the issue by negotiation with the Jews. Once Lysias had left the region Judas now had the opportunity to march to Jerusalem, lay siege to soldiers in the citadel, and retake the temple area and to ritually cleanse it. This action, after the three years of the "abomination of desolation" was a hugely symbolic event for Jews both then and through the ages since, celebrated in the festival of Hanukkah (see FEAST OF DEDICATION).

The Syrians seem to have ignored Judas for a period of time. He got involved with the surrounding peoples in Idumea, Galilee, and Transjordan (1 Macc 2), though the exact cause is debatable. In part Judas was trying to help Jews who were apparently being attacked in these areas by bringing them back to Judah to live. He was also besieging the Jerusalem citadel, which still had a contingent of Seleucid soldiers. This required Lysias to intervene once again. He defeated Judas, though the latter was able to escape capture. However, one of Judas's brothers, named Eleazar, was crushed to death when he attacked and killed a war elephant that then fell on him. Lysias came to terms with the Jews, confirmed their religious freedom, and had the high priest Menelaus executed shortly afterward.

Alcimus was now appointed high priest in place of Menelaus, thus presenting a dilemma to the Maccabees. The original fight had been about religious freedom, which was now restored. There was also a high priest that the vast majority of Jews regarded as legitimate. Many Jews now saw no reason to continue the revolt against the Seleucids and returned to their homes. They had fought for the temple under Maccabean leadership, but that battle was won. For some reason, though, the ambitions of the Hasmoneans had escalated; they wanted nothing less than independence, a state of existence probably not known to them since at least the 8th cent. BCE. It appears that for the next decade or more, the Maccabees carried on their fight with a small number of supporters. Judah himself did not long outlive his restoration of the temple cult. He won a solid victory over the Syrian commander Nicanor, but not long afterward (apparently in the spring

of 161 BCE) an army under the command of Bacchides routed the Jewish army and killed Judas himself.

Judas's brother JONATHAN now assumed leadership, but no longer having the resources of money and manpower coming their way, the Maccabees were not in a position to be able to do much. Furthermore, the Syrian commander Bacchides seems to have regarded Jonathan's group a threat and pursued them relentlessly for a period of time. Jonathan managed to stay ahead of the attackers, but his brother John was killed (by the Nabateans rather than the Syrians, though). The high priest Alcimus died about 160 BCE, evidently of natural causes. For several years there appears to have been no high priest, though speculation has tried to fill the gap. In any case, Jonathan negotiated a truce with Bacchides who left the region. What happened for much of the subsequent decade is not known, but Jonathan no doubt took advantage of the vacuum in leadership to strengthen his position. In 153 BCE an individual named Alexander Balas became a rival for the Syrian throne against Demetrius I (see DEMETRIUS).

It was at this point that Jonathan showed his political skill, and for the rest of his life he used the rivalry over the Seleucid throne to his advantage to advance his position in relation to both the Jews and the Syrians. Demetrius I called on Jonathan for help against Alexander, conceding to him the right to assemble an army. Jonathan set up his headquarters in Jerusalem. Alexander made a counter offer: the office of high priest. This gave Jonathan real power over the Jews, and he took the office at the Festival of Tabernacles that year. Over the next decade Jonathan gained further concessions from the rival dynasties and expanded Jewish rule in the region. He seems to have been moving rapidly toward an independent Jewish state when he was captured in 143 BCE. His brother Simon attempted to ransom him but without success: Jonathan was executed, leaving his brother to take over leadership of the movement.

It was now Simon's turn to lead (see SIMON), as the last of the brothers. Things had changed radically under Jonathan's leadership, though: now the majority of Jews seem to have accepted Maccabean political leadership and also religious leadership, in that the right of the Maccabees to be high priest was apparently not challenged. Simon negotiated with Demetrius II, one of the Seleucid pretenders to the throne, and obtained significant concessions. This included essentially a recognition of Simon's independence and the right to mint his own coins. This formal declaration of liberty is found in 1 Macc 14:4-15 and compares the reign of Simon to that of Solomon. It was a major symbol that the Jews once more constituted their own nation and was indeed a weighty moment in Jewish history, but the reality was that subsequent Seleucid rulers would still assert their lordship over Judah and that Simon himself died a violent death.

An important achievement of Simon's was his finally taking the Jerusalem citadel, expelling its Syrian garrison, and posting his own contingent of Jewish soldiers there. He also sent an army against Antiochus VII (the successor of Demetrius II) who reasserted Seleucid claims to rule Judah and defeated him. It was one of his own men who brought his reign to an end after only eight years. The Jewish general Pompey, Simon's own son-in-law, invited Simon with his family to a banquet. It was a ruse for an ambush in which Simon was killed and his wife and two of his sons were captured. The new Hasmonean dynasty was no different from any other ruling house—there would always be those disputing and challenging their rule. But in this case another son of Simon, John Hyrcanus, had escaped and remained alive to reckon with the challenger.

B. The Hasmonean Priest-Kings

1. John Hyrcanus I (135–104 BCE)

After his father's death, Hyrcanus acceded to the office of high priest and immediately turned the attack on the renegade Jewish commander Ptolemy but besieged him without success; Ptolemy murdered Hyrcanus' mother and brothers before escaping. Soon afterward, Hyrcanus himself was besieged in Jerusalem by Antiochus VII, the reason apparently being the cities that Simon had taken from the Syrians. Antiochus allowed a truce during the Feast of Tabernacles and even sent sacrifices to be offered on his behalf at the Temple. Agreement was finally reached between Antiochus and Hyrcanus that tribute would be paid for Joppa and the other cities on Judea's border. In addition to receiving payment for the cities Antiochus also tore down the defensive walls of Jerusalem. He wanted a Syrian garrison in the city, as well, but Hyrcanus managed to substitute hostages and a further payment of silver instead. In order to obtain the necessary cash, Hyrcanus opened David's tomb and took out a large amount of silver. He used some of this to hire mercenaries, the first Jewish leader to do so.

For most of the rest of his reign Hyrcanus was free to conduct his own affairs with little interference from the Syrians, the reason being the rivalry between the two lines of contenders for the throne. This preoccupation of the Syrian rulers with securing their own throne against rivals allowed Hyrcanus the freedom he needed. He gave no further tribute or help to them after the death of Antiochus VII (129 BCE [*Ant.* 13.273]); instead, he took the opportunity to expand his territory, which he did with considerable success. His most significant acts included the capture of Shechem (ca. 128 BCE), at which time he allegedly destroyed the Samaritan temple, but the archaeology does not support this. He next took some of the major cities of Idumea, extended his rule over the entire country, and is said to have forcibly converted the inhabitants to Judaism. Exactly how this is to be interpreted is difficult. Forced conversion is generally not very successful, yet Josephus states that the Idumeans continued to be Jews (*Ant.* 13.258).

The next area to fall was the city of Samaria itself. After a lengthy siege, the citizens called either on Antiochus VIII (*J.W.* 1.65) or IX (*Ant.* 13.276–78) for help which was readily given; however, Hyrcanus' sons defeated Antiochus' troops and resumed the siege. After a second request by the Samaritans, Antiochus sent a body of soldiers to invade Hyrcanus' territory and conduct guerilla action without directly confronting the Jewish army. This also did not work, and Samaria fell after a year.

The Jews in Palestine were thriving. Nevertheless, opposition developed and Hyrcanus had to spend some time putting down rebels. Exactly what form this rebellion took or when is unclear. In *Jewish War* Josephus refers simply to some of Hyrcanus' "countrymen." In *Jewish Antiquities* he makes the opponents Pharisees, stating that Hyrcanus had himself been a Pharisee but, after falling out with them, became a Sadducee (13.288–99). In any event, he soon reduced the opposition and spent the rest of his reign peacefully, dying a natural death after a rule of thirty-one years. Certain coins have been preserved with the name "Johanan," identified with Hyrcanus I by some; however, others argue that these should be dated to the reign of Hyrcanus II.

2. Aristobulus I (104–103 BCE)

Even though Aristobulus reigned for only one year, most of Josephus's description is taken up with how he was tricked into having his brother Antigonus killed, along with an anecdote about the remarkable prognostications of Judah the Essene. We thus learn little about Aristobulus' reign, yet several points within the brief period are significant: 1) he was the first to actually take the diadem as king, previous Hasmonean high priests having acted as rulers but not having used the actual title; 2) he had the title *Philhellene* (philellēn [φιλέλλην], "lover of the Greeks"), which suggests that he contributed to certain building projects in Greek cities; 3) he took the area of Iturea (in southern Lebanon) and required the inhabitants to adopt circumcision and live according to Jewish law. It has also been suggested that the coins bearing the name "Judah" were minted by Aristobulus, but many argue these should be dated to Aristobulus II.

This all suggests that Aristobulus' reign was significant in various ways despite its brevity. His personal character is pictured as cruel in that he supposedly starved his mother to death. Yet this picture is contradicted by Josephus' own statement that the king was of a "kindly nature" and "wholly given to modesty," a statement then backed up with a quotation from Strabo. There is no confirmation that he was a Philhellene, either from the *Jewish War* or other historians, though one wonders why anyone would have invented the datum if untrue. The statement that he conquered Iturea suggests that he continued with Hyrcanus' policy of expanding the borders of Judah. Again, the forced conversion is a point of interest.

3. Alexander Janneus (103–76 BCE)

Josephus gives more detail about Alexander Janneus than any other Hasmonean ruler. Although the *Jewish Antiquities* gives more information than the *Jewish War*, the overall picture is essentially the same, with one exception: the significance of the Pharisees. Most of what we learn about Alexander's reign is devoted to two issues: further expansion of territory and the internal Jewish opposition to his rule.

At the beginning of his rule, Alexander Janneus besieged the city of Ptolemais. However, the city called on Ptolemy IX Lathyrus (116–96 BCE) from Cyprus who was rival to his mother, Cleopatra III Berenice of Egypt. After an initial attempt by Alexander to trick him into an alliance, Ptolemy invaded Galilee and defeated the Jewish army. At this point Cleopatra intervened and, after a period of maneuvering, forced Ptolemy to return to Cyprus. In concluding a treaty with Cleopatra, Alexander had the help of one of her generals who was himself Jewish (a son of Onias). This left Alexander free to pursue his conquests, which included the cities of Gadara, Amathus, Raphia, and Anthedon. He also took Gaza after a long siege.

At this point in his reign a revolt developed. It began at the Feast of Tabernacles when he was pelted with citrons while sacrificing in his capacity as high priest. The exact reasons for this opposition are not clear. Josephus gives only the trivial charge that his mother had been a captive and, therefore, he was unfit to hold the office (since she would most likely have been raped at the time). This sounds more like a pretext than the true reason. Alexander contained the revolt, killing 6,000 of his opponents, and continued his wars of conquest. This time he moved east, taking Moab and Galaaditis (Gilead). He also attacked the Arab king Obodas I but was decisively beaten and himself almost killed.

The defeat by the Arabs seems to have encouraged his opponents since he now had a civil war on his hands that took up the next six years. (During this time, the territory just taken in Moab and Galaaditis was lost.) The climax came when his opponents called in Demetrius III of Damascus (one of the Seleucid rivals at this time) against him (ca. 88 BCE). Large numbers of Jews fought on both sides in the ensuing engagement. Demetrius seems to have gotten the better of the contest, and Alexander fled. However, when those who had asked for Demetrius' aid now abandoned him and a large number of Jews rallied to Alexander, Demetrius had little choice but to retire from the country. Alexander brought the revolt to a close by driving many of his opponents into the city

Bemeselis and taking it. He then had 800 of the men crucified and their families slaughtered, while he and his concubines feasted and watched the spectacle. The unprecedented action made a great impact on his opponents, and 8000 of them fled the country as long as Alexander was alive. The incident also seems to be referred to in the Qumran commentary on Nah 2:12 (4Q169 3 & 4 I, 4-6).

Soon after the internal revolt was put down, Judah was invaded by the army of Antiochus XII Dionysus (ca. 86 BCE) whose aim seems to have been only to march through to fight against Arabia. Alexander hastily constructed a defensive ditch and wooden wall, which Antiochus had no difficulty pushing though. What he would have done to Judah had his campaign been successful is not clear, but in the event he was defeated and killed. Shortly afterward Aretas III, the Arab king, invaded Judah, but Alexander was able to come to terms with him.

His enemies now out of the way, Alexander Janneus was left to get on with his external military activities for the rest of his reign. He soon developed quartan fever but nevertheless kept to the field until his death. His activities were mainly in the area northeast of the sea of Galilee where he took several cities. According to Josephus (*Ant.* 13.395-97), at the end of Alexander's reign Judah included most of the coastal cities as far north as Caesarea, Idumea, Samaria, Galilee, Moab, and northern Transjordan. If this is correct, Alexander's territory was the largest extent of Israel since that alleged for Solomon. Alexander Janneus died at the age of forty-nine, after reigning twenty-seven years.

At this point in the narrative, there is a significant difference between Josephus' two accounts. The *Jewish Antiquities* claims that before his death, Alexander advised his wife, Alexandra Salome, to make peace with the Pharisees, grant them a certain amount of power, and pretend to have disapproved of her husband's activities. The result was that they gave the king a magnificent funeral with many eulogies. This has led some scholars to infer that most of the opponents of Alexander were Pharisees. Against this are several considerations: 1) the earlier *Jewish War* not only makes no mention of this death-bed incident but makes no mention of the Pharisees at all during Alexander's reign; 2) despite this conclusion to his account in the *Jewish Antiquities*, Josephus himself does not otherwise mention the Pharisees during Alexander's reign; indeed, he at no point suggests that those who opposed, fought, and were killed by Alexander were specifically Pharisees. Therefore, one can only conclude that Pharisaic opponents—which most probably existed—were only a part of the opposition against him. One also suspects that the deathbed scene with regard to the Pharisees was an invention by Josephus to explain the influence of the Pharisees over Alexandra Salome during her rule.

4. Alexandra Salome (76–67 BCE)

Having been the wife of two Hasmonean rulers, Alexandra now became one herself—and one of the few women rulers over Judah in history. The one feature that stands out in both of Josephus' accounts is the extent to which the Pharisees dominated the reign of Alexandra. In much later rabbinic literature there were still preserved traditions of the reign of Alexandra as a golden age (*b. Taʿan.* 23a). Although the *Jewish Antiquities* says that Alexandra "restored" the Pharisaic regulations which John Hyrcanus had abolished (13.408), the *Jewish War* knows nothing of this. As already noted, there is reason to question the extent of Pharisaic influence in Alexander's time, and the ability of the Pharisees to impose their own regulations as law probably originated under Alexandra, as Josephus' earlier account seems to indicate (*J.W.* 1.110). On the other hand, the Pharisees clearly possessed considerable political clout under Alexandra, including the ability to get rid of a number of their enemies. It finally reached the stage that some eminent citizens appealed directly to Alexandra (with the aid of her son Aristobulus) for a guarantee of safety. To appease them she allowed some of the importunates to guard certain of her fortresses.

Alexandra herself was evidently a good administrator, apart from the question of the Pharisees. She doubled the size of the Jewish military forces, in addition to keeping a large mercenary contingent, and as a result was able to maintain peaceful relations with the surrounding rulers. She also concluded terms with Tigranes of Armenia when he was besieging Cleopatra in Ptolemais: evidently, Alexandra supposed that Judea might be his next target. The treaty was never tested, though, since Tigranes had to return quickly to Armenia when Mithradates of Pontus retreated there after being defeated by the Romans.

Although Alexandra could rule, the one thing she could not be was high priest. Her elder son Hyrcanus had been appointed high priest on Alexander Janneus's death and would have been the natural heir to his mother. Yet Aristobulus seems to have been the more dynamic of the two, and there were doubts about Hyrcanus' ability and even desire to rule. When Alexandra became ill, Aristobulus took his chance. He occupied twenty-two fortresses in which a number of his supporters had been made guards, hired a mercenary army, and proclaimed himself king. He apparently used the pretext that if he did not, the Pharisees would seize power on his mother's death. Alexandra quickly responded to this by imprisoning Aristobulus' wife and children, but her illness prevented her from taking further action. As Aristobulus was amassing a large army, she died at the age of seventy-three after a reign of nine years.

5. Hyrcanus II and Aristobulus II (67–63 BCE)

We now enter a period of four years during which the two Hasmonean brothers fought for control of the Jewish throne. Hyrcanus took up the rulership of Judah as soon as his mother died, but only for a short time. Aristobulus quickly attacked and defeated him; Hyrcanus arranged a deal in which he was permitted to live unharmed as a private citizen while the rulership went to his brother. Although such is not made explicit at this point in the narrative, statements elsewhere indicate that Aristobulus also obtained the office of high priest (*Ant.* 14.97; 20.243–44).

At this juncture Josephus introduces a character by the name of Antipater whom he identifies as an Idumean, whose father had been appointed governor of Idumea by Alexander Janneus. Antipater, after a time, persuaded Hyrcanus that he had made a mistake in giving up the kingship and indeed was in danger of being executed by Aristobulus. Receiving a guarantee of safety from Aretas III of Petra, Hyrcanus fled to the Arab ruler. With the aid of an army under Aretas, Hyrcanus attacked Aristobulus, defeated him, and besieged him in Jerusalem to which he had fled. The outcome of the siege was still in the balance when the Romans intervened.

The Roman general Pompey, who was fighting against the Armenians, had sent his lieutenant Scaurus to Syria. As soon as he arrived in Damascus, Scaurus heard of the Jewish civil war and marched south. Delegates from both the sons of Alexandra met him with bribes, but Scaurus sided with Aristobulus and forced Aretas to raise the siege. Shortly afterward Aristobulus defeated Hyrcanus in battle. This was the way things stood until Pompey himself arrived in Syria where he was entreated by both sides. Also appearing was a delegation from "the Jewish nation," asking that Judea be allowed to continue as a theocracy without the high priest also acting as a king. After hearing the different sides, Pompey delayed a decision. This was too much for Aristobulus who set off for Judea. Pompey, taking this as an insult, followed after him. At first the two leaders negotiated, then Pompey ordered Aristobulus to give up his fortresses. Aristobulus reluctantly sent instructions to the various commanders as required by Pompey but then himself withdrew to Jerusalem and prepared for war.

Pompey marched after him before the preparations had advanced very far. Aristobulus realized the folly of resistance and met Pompey on the last leg of his march, promising money as well as entry into Jerusalem. Aristobulus' followers had a different idea, however, and shut the city against the Romans. The people of the city were divided between the supporters of Aristobulus and those of Hyrcanus. The former withdrew into the citadel, cutting the bridge to the upper city, while the latter opened the gates to Pompey. The siege of the citadel lasted three months, apparently until about mid-summer. The Romans took advantage of the Sabbath to advance their siege works since the Jews would not fight if not directly attacked. During this time and even in the final assault when many were being killed, the priests continued their sacrificial duties. When the Romans finally broke through, many of the defenders were slaughtered by their fellow Jews who were adherents of Hyrcanus. Pompey and others of the Romans entered the temple area and even went inside the Holy of Holies, but the Temple itself was respected: neither the vessels nor the temple treasure was touched, and the Temple itself was cleansed and the cult resumed the next day at Pompey's command.

Thus, Judea as an independent kingdom came to an end. Although it was to be a vassal kingdom of Rome for many years under Herod the Great and Agrippa I, it was not again to be a sovereign nation for another two millennia. The territory gained by successive Hasmonean rulers was taken away to leave only the area that roughly made up the province of Judah under the Babylonians and Persians. Although Hyrcanus was restored to the high priesthood, he did not have the title of king, and a heavy tribute was imposed on the country. Aristobulus and his sons were taken captive to Rome (though one son, Alexander, escaped on the way).

C. The Remaining History of the Hasmoneans

The story of the Hasmonean family can be traced for well over a further century, until after the fall of the Temple in 70 CE, but it had lost much of its power. Hasmoneans continued to be part of the upper class of the Jews, though a number of them were also Herodians since the Herodian dynasty married into the Hasmonean line. The story was also played out against the backdrop of the rise of Herod and the Mediterranean-wide events relating to the beginnings of the Roman Empire.

Even though the Romans were now clearly in control of the region, the shortsightedness of Aristobulus II's side of the Hasmonean family was soon demonstrated in several attempts by Aristobulus and his son Alexander (and later Alexander's brother Antigonus) to lead revolts and reestablish their rule. The first attempt was by Alexander at the time Gabinius was appointed governor of Syria in 57 BCE (Josephus, *J.W.* 1.160). Hyrcanus did not have the strength to withstand him. It is clear that there was plenty of sympathy for a native ruler, even if the figures are altogether exaggerated, for Alexander is said to have been able to recruit 10,000 heavy infantry and 1,500 cavalry. He had several fortifications and was even attempting to rebuild the walls of Jerusalem thrown down by Pompey when the Romans intervened. Fighting alongside the Romans were Antipater's own picked troops. After a major defeat in battle, Alexander withdrew to the fortress at Alexandrium where he was besieged by Gabinius. Eventually, he asked for terms and was granted them, though Gabinius demolished his fortresses.

The next year Aristobulus himself, along with his son Antigonus, escaped from Rome and led a new rebellion. As a former priest-king he had no trouble in gaining a large following. Indeed, Peitholaus the "legate" of Jerusalem deserted to him with a thousand men. Aristobulus intended to refortify Alexandrium, but Gabinius came against him too quickly. Aristobulus dismissed all his following who did not have the proper equipment but is still alleged to have had 8,000 armed troops to take a stand against the Romans, indicating the large following collected together in this short time. Unfortunately, the outcome was completely predictable and Aristobulus was returned to Rome as a prisoner.

The two sons, Alexander and Antigonus, were released by the Senate, however, because Gabinius had promised this to their mother when negotiating to have the fortresses surrendered. This soon proved to be a mistake because Alexander revolted a second time. Antipater acted as mediator and managed to persuade many Jews to abandon their following of Alexander; nevertheless, the latter was still left with a large army (said to be 30,000, no doubt grossly exaggerated) with which he met the Romans near Mount Tabor, but again it was to no avail.

It was at this point that the Roman Civil War began in 49 BCE. Caesar released Aristobulus from prison with the intention of putting him at the head of two legions; the plan was thwarted, however, when adherents of Pompey poisoned him before he even left Rome. Likewise, his son Alexander was executed in Antioch at Pompey's orders, but Antigonus and his two sisters were taken under the protection of Ptolemy the Iturean (*Ant.* 14.126; *J.W.* 1.185–86). Josephus says nothing about the activities of Antipater and Hyrcanus at this time; perhaps they wisely bided their time to see which way the war went. After Pompey's death in 48, though, Antipater quite decisively took the side of Caesar and distinguished himself in aiding Mithridates' capture of Egypt. This was done by diplomacy in persuading the Jews in the district of Onias to support Caesar and allow his army through, as well as by military prowess.

Caesar rewarded Antipater and Hyrcanus for their usefulness. Hyrcanus was confirmed in the priesthood and Antipater given Roman citizenship. These honors were increased when Antigonas, Aristobulus' son, foolishly accused Antipater and Hyrcanus before Caesar: Hyrcanus was raised to ethnarch of Judah (but seems to have been called "king" by the Jews themselves [*J.W.* 1.202–3; 1.214; *Ant.* 14.148, 151; 14.157; 14.165; 14.168, 172]) and Antipater made "procurator" of Judea. Permission was also given to rebuild the walls of Jerusalem, which had been in ruins since Pompey's siege.

After Caesar's assassination in 44 BCE, Cassius came to take over the region. Antipater and his sons made themselves useful to him, but other Jewish leaders took the opportunity to plot against them. One was called Malichus, who eventually killed Antipater by poisoning, and another was Helix. Herod succeeded in getting rid of Malichus, but Helix attacked Herod's brother Phasael. Hyrcanus is said to have sided with Helix and to have turned a number of fortresses over to Malichus' brother; these Herod retook as soon as he had recovered. Antigonus, the son of Aristobulus II, had been allowed to return to the area and was aided by Marion the ruler of Tyre. Herod led the campaign against them with considerable success, defeating both.

Herod and Hyrcanus do not seem to have been particularly affected by their support of Cassius in the fight against Antony and Octavian. After Cassius' defeat and death, Antony came to take over rulership of the east (42 BCE). An embassy of leading Jews met him and accused Herod and Phasael of governing the country with Hyrcanus as a mere puppet. Antony ruled in favor of the two brothers, not only because of his personal regard for Herod but also allegedly because of a large bribe. The opposition did not cease, however, and two more delegations came before Antony with accusations. When the second of three made their charges, Antony asked Hyrcanus who were the better rulers of the nation, and the latter indicated Herod and Phasael (presumably, the choice was between the two brothers and the "leading Jews" who made up the delegation). The result was that Antony made Herod and his brother tetrarchs while imprisoning a handful of their opponents.

The Parthian invasion of Syria and Palestine in 40 BCE was the opportunity for the Hasmonean opponents of Herod. Antigonus once more planned to take over Judah, this time with Parthian aid, and many Jews flocked to his banner. After a brief skirmish near Carmel, Antigonus was soon besieging some opponents in the palace in Jerusalem. Evidently, Phasael was not in Jerusalem at the time because he and Herod came to intervene in the siege. It was basically a standoff until Pentecost (Feast of Weeks) when many came to Jerusalem for the festival. Quite a few of these seem to have joined Antigonus at this time, though Herod beat off another concerted attack. This time the Parthians intervened in the person of Pacorus, a Parthian general who claimed to be coming to help settle the fight. Phasael received him cordially and even agreed that he and Hyrcanus should go to discuss matters with the Parthian satrap Barzaphranes near Tyre.

Phasael and Hyrcanus were taken prisoner by the Parthians. The plan was to capture Herod as well, but already wary he received news of what had happened to Phasael and avoided the trap. Instead, he collected his family and followers and fled Jerusalem in the middle of the night to Idumea. He made his way to Petra with the thought of raising ransom money for his brother from King Aretas, but Aretas refused and ordered him out of his territory. Herod then pushed toward Egypt. It was on the way there that he received word of what had happened: the Parthians had given the throne to Antigonus who had mutilated Hyrcanus'

ears so he could no longer be high priest. Phasael had committed suicide.

Herod continued on to Rome, where he was introduced to the Senate by Octavian and Mark Antony, and declared king of Judah in 40 BCE. Antony came to be governor of the east Mediterranean region and to deal with the Parthians. Herod returned with an army to fight Antigonus who seems to have declared himself king of Judah (judging from his coins) with Parthian support. Jerusalem was besieged and fell in 37 BCE. Antony had Antigonus executed, thus bringing formally to an end Hasmonean rule of Judah, a century after the Hasmonean state had been formally declared under Simon Maccabee.

Hyrcanus had been released by the Parthians and was invited to return to Judea by Herod. He could not be high priest now because of his mutilation, and Herod appointed another high priest. This angered Hyrcanus' daughter Alexandra who thought that her own son Aristobulus should have been given the office. She appealed to Cleopatra to use her influence on Antony. Herod decided the best course of action was to accede to this and appointed Aristobulus who was only seventeen. When a year later Aristobulus was drowned while swimming at the palace in Jericho, Alexandra wrote to Cleopatra accusing Herod of his murder. Cleopatra persuaded Antony to summon Herod to answer the charges, but Herod was cleared by Antony.

From now on the Hasmoneans have to be dealt with via the Herodians, for Herod the Great married Mariamme the Hasmonean, and their children were heirs of both the Hasmoneans and the Herodians. Herod executed two of his children by Mariamme over alleged plots to assassinate him, but one of these, Aristobulus, already had several children (grandsons and granddaughters of Herod). One of these was to become Agrippa I. Agrippa's full name was evidently Marcus Julius Agrippa, judging from the name of his son Agrippa II; thus, the common reference to him as "Herod Agrippa" (based on Acts 12:1) is incorrect. Exactly why the author of Acts refers to Agrippa as "Herod" is uncertain; whatever the reason for the confusion, the name "Herod Agrippa" for Agrippa should be deleted from scholarly usage forthwith.

Despite many weaknesses (such as a tendency to being a spendthrift) Agrippa had two traits important for Hasmonean history: he was a friend of the future emperor Caligula in his youth, and he was the heir to the Herodian throne. When Caligula became emperor in 37 BCE, he appointed Agrippa to the tetrarchy of his uncle Philip. He later removed Herod Antipas from his tetrarchy, banished him, and gave the territory to Agrippa. When Caligula decided to erect his statue in the Jerusalem Temple (a much misunderstood episode of Jewish history), Philo and Josephus (though perhaps depending on Philo) say that Agrippa was able to dissuade him. Shortly afterward, after Caligula was assassinated, Agrippa was appointed as an intermediary between Claudius and the Senate to negotiate the arrangements for Claudius to become emperor. Claudius rewarded him not only by leaving his original territories but also by adding the rule of Judah and Samaria to them. It is unfortunate that Agrippa ruled only a short period before dying in 44 CE.

His son Agrippa II was only seventeen at the death of his father, and Claudius unfortunately did not appoint him king over his father's realm. When in 48 CE Herod of Chalcis died, Claudius presented the kingdom to Agrippa (*J.W.* 2.223; *Ant.* 20.104). Included among his privileges were those of appointing the high priests as well as authority over the Temple, even though he did not rule over any Judean territory (*Ant.* 20.15–16). In 53 CE Claudius assigned a new kingdom to the Jewish king, that of his great-uncle Philip (*J.W.* 2.247; *Ant.* 20.137–38); however, rulership of Chalcis was taken away. When Nero came to office, he gave Agrippa the Galilean cities of Tiberias and Tarcheae (*J.W.* 2.252; *Ant.* 20.159).

Agrippa was close to his widowed sister Berenice who lived with him. Both Agrippa and Berenice are mentioned together in Acts 24:24–26:32. When the war with Rome began, Agrippa attempted to dissuade the Jews from carrying through with their folly, but both he and Berenice were forced to withdraw from the city by the people. In the fighting that followed, he led his own troops as an ally of the Romans and helped in crushing the revolt. After the war we hear only sporadic references to him. Josephus corresponded with him about his work and allegedly received his confirmation of their accuracy (*Life* 65.362–67). The date of his death has been disputed, probably about 96/97 CE. *See* ALEXANDRA SALOME; ANTIOCHUS; DEAD SEA SCROLLS; GERIZIM, MOUNT; HESHMON; IDUMEA; JERUSALEM; LYSIAS; MODEIN; SAMARITANS; SON OF MAN

Bibliography: Lester L. Grabbe. *Judaism from Cyrus to Hadrian* (1992).

LESTER L. GRABBE

HASRAH haz′ruh [חַסְרָה khasrah; Ἀσαρά Asara]. 1. The grandfather of the prophet HULDAH's husband. Hasrah appears in 2 Chr 34:22. The name is HARHAS in 2 Kgs 22:14.

2. Head of a postexilic temple servant family, Hasrah is named in 1 Esd 5:31 (but not Ezra 2:49 or Neh 7:51). *See* NETHINIM.

SUSANNA W. SOUTHARD

HASSENAAH. *See* SENAAH.

HASSENUAH has′uh-noo′uh [הַסְּנָאָה, הַסְּנוּאָה hassenu'ah]. A Benjaminite postexilic family name (1 Chr 9:7; Neh 11:9). Judah of the Hassenuah family was second in command (behind Joel son of Zichri)

over Jerusalem (Neh 11:9). SENAAH (Ezra 2:35; Neh 7:38; 1 Esd 5:23) is probably a variant of Hassenuah.

T. DELAYNE VAUGHN

HASSHUB hash′uhb [חַשּׁוּב khashuv]. 1. A Levite, the father of SHEMAIAH, who was among those who settled in Jerusalem after the Babylonian exile (1 Chr 9:14; Neh 11:15).

2. Two men given assignments in the rebuilding of Jerusalem (Neh 3:11, 23). It is possible but uncertain that the same man was given two assignments.

3. A leader of the people who sealed the covenant of Ezra (Neh 10:23).

T. DELAYNE VAUGHN

HASSOPHERETH. *See* SOPHERETH.

HASUPHA huh-soo′fuh [חֲשׁוּפָא, חֲשֻׁפָא khasufa'; Ἀσιφά, Asipha]. Eponymous head of a temple servant family, Hasupha's name appears in the list of exile returnees under Zerubbabel (Ezra 2:43; Neh 7:46; 1 Esd 5:29).

HAT [כַּרְבְּלָא karbela'; πέτασος petasos]. Among the clothing items the three Jews were wearing when they were thrown into the fiery furnace (Dan 3:21) and a sign of Hellenization among the Jews (2 Macc 4:12).

HATCHET [כֵּילַפּוֹת kelappoth]. Hatchet is mentioned only once in the Bible. In Ps 74:6 hatchets, ax-like instruments, are used violently for destruction.

HATE, HATRED [שָׂטַם satam, שָׂנֵא sane'; μισέω miseō]. Hatred is a feeling of intense dislike, loathing, or hostility. One can hate persons, God, or other things. Examples include Esau's hatred (satam, lit. hated, of Jacob, who cheated Esau out of his birthright (Gen 27:41). Leah said that God gave her Simeon because God heard that Leah was hated (sane') (Gen 29:33). Sane' is the general word for hate, while satam is more inclusive, suggesting a deep-seated grudge. Joseph's brothers hated him out of jealousy (Gen 37:4). Absalom hated Ammon for raping Tamar (2 Sam 13:22), which led to Absalom murdering him in revenge. The Israelites claimed that Yahweh hated them and that is why he gave them over to the Amorites to be destroyed (Deut 1:27). Parents who spare the rod hate their children (Prov 13:24). Jesus observes that one cannot serve two masters because he will hate (miseō) one and love the other (Matt 6:24).

Hatred brings negative consequences, such as God taking vengeance on those who hate him (Deut 32:41). Jehu announces to Jehosaphat that there will be violence against the king's house because he loves those who hate Yahweh (2 Chr 19:2). God condemns those who hate the righteous (Ps 34:21). The psalmist prays that the one who hates Zion may be put to shame (Ps 129:5). Those who hate wisdom implicitly love death

(Prov 8:36). God hates robbery and will punish those who do it (Isa 61:8). Whoever hates another believer walks in darkness and has been blinded (1 John 2:11). All those who hate another believer are murderers and murderers do not have eternal life (1 John 3:15).

Hatred is a positive quality in certain situations. Moses is to look for men who fear God and hate dishonest gain (Exod 18:21). Psalm 45 commends the king for hating wickedness (Ps 45:7). The psalmist hates every false way (Ps 119:104). The psalmist hates those who hate God (Ps 139:21). Qoheleth states that there is a time to hate (Eccl 3:8). Amos tells the people to hate evil and love good (Amos 5:15).

God hates as well. God hates abhorrent acts of the nations in Canaan (Deut 12:31). God hates all evildoers (Ps 5:5). According to Proverbs, there are seven things that God hates (Prov 6:16). God hates the festivals of Judah (Isa 1:14). God hates those who devise evil and swear false oaths (Zech 8:17). Malachi states that God hates Esau (Mal 1:3), although God loves Jacob. While interpreters disagree over this verse, it seems best to understand these terms covenantally. God chose Israel and rejected Edom. God also hates divorce (Mal 2:16). Job complains that God hates him (Job 16:9).

The psalmists often pray that God will deliver them from those who hate them (Pss 9:13; 18:17). The psalmists also praise God for giving them victory over those who hate them (Pss 18:40; 44:7). The psalmists often complain that they are hated without cause (Ps 38:19). The psalmists pray often that God would demonstrate care for them visibly in order that their enemies may see it (Ps 86:17) and they expect God to give them victory over those who hate them (Ps 118:6).

Moses commands the Israelites to do good to the animals of those who hate them (Exod 23:5). Jesus commands his followers to love their enemies and do good to those who hate them (Luke 6:27).

Jesus speaks of those who hate him, especially in John's Gospel (John 7:7; 15:18). Several texts predict that Christians will be hated because of Jesus (Matt 10:22; 24:9; Mark 13:13; John 15:19; 17:14). Yet, Jesus' followers are pronounced "blessed" when this occurs (Luke 6:22).

One especially difficult text is Luke 14:26, in which Jesus says that whoever comes after him must hate father, mother, wife, children, siblings, and even life itself. While some scholars suggest that hate here, as in Mal 1:2, is a matter of degree, so that hate means "love less," it is better to take "hate" in full seriousness. Jesus is calling for people to give single-hearted allegiance to him, setting aside family loyalties and identity in order to identify fully with him.

KENNETH D. LITWAK

HATHACH hay′thak [חֲתָךְ hathakh]. One of the EUNUCHs King Ahasuerus appointed to attend to Esther, Hathach served as a messenger between Esther and Mordecai, informing Esther of Haman's plan to destroy the Jews, which he had learned from Mordecai, and then informing Mordecai of her reply (Esth 4:5-6, 9-10).

TRISHA M. WHEELOCK

HATHATH hay′thath [חֲתַת khathath]. Son of OTHNIEL of the tribe of Judah, listed in a genealogy and related to craftsmen of Israel (1 Chr 4:13).

HATIPHA huh-ti′fuh [חֲטִיפָא khatifaʾ; Ἀτιφά Hatipha]. A descendant of the temple servants who returned from Babylon with Zerubbabel (Ezra 2:54; Neh 7:56; 1 Esd 5:32).

HATITA huh-ti′tuh [חֲטִיטָא khatitaʾ]. A descendant of the temple gatekeepers who returned from Babylon with Zerubbabel (Ezra 2:42; Neh 7:45; 1 Esd 5:28).

HATTIL hat′uhl [חַטִּיל khattil]. A descendant of the servants of Solomon who returned from Babylon with Zerubbabel. The "servants of Solomon" were not known before the exile. They were members of the Golah (exile) assembly and were clearly distinguished from slaves (Ezra 2:57; Neh 7:59). See NETHINIM.

HATTUSH hat′uhsh [חַטּוּשׁ hattush; Ἀττούς Hattous]. 1. A descendant of David and Zerubbabel (1 Chr 3:22).

2. A descendant of David among the family heads who returned to Jerusalem with Ezra (Ezra 8:2 and 1 Esd 8:29). He is perhaps the same as number 1 above and perhaps identical with the son of Hashabneiah.

3. A man who worked on Jerusalem's walls (Neh 3:10). He could be the same as number 1.

4. A priest listed among the signatories to Ezra's covenant (Neh 10:4 [Heb. 5]), perhaps identical with a priest who returned to Jerusalem with Zerubbabel and Shealtiel (Neh 12:2).

DEREK E. WITTMAN

HAUGHTINESS [גֵּאָה gaʾah, גָּבַהּ gavah, רוּם rum; ὑπερήφανος hyperēphanos, ὑψηλά hypsēla, φρονεῖν phronein]. There are various Hebrew and Greek expressions translated in the NRSV as "haughty," "haughtiness," and "haughtily." Most of these expressions entail a basic sense of elevation. Further, these various expressions are often used in the context of a spatial, hierarchical metaphor. In this hierarchical metaphor, certain persons are presented as important, and hence they are "lifted up" or "exalted." The God of Israel is frequently portrayed as one located in high places (2 Sam 22:47; Pss 21:13 [Heb. 21:14]; 113:5 [Heb. 113:4]; 138:6; Isa 57:15). Isaiah envisions the deity as enthroned, for instance, describing Yahweh as "high and lofty" (Isa 6:1). Human rulers are also described as exalted (Ps 2:4-6; Job 36:7). Conversely, the poor or oppressed are depicted as low or near the ground (Pss 113:5-8; 138:6).

This hierarchical imagery informs biblical descriptions of the haughty, of haughtiness or of someone acting haughtily. Specifically, these are individuals or actions that show a disregard for proper position and power. A "haughty" person is one who acts "higher" than he or she should in any given situation (*see* PRIDE). Predictably, this haughtiness language is used most frequently to refer to or depict those disobedient to God. Isaiah 2 provides an excellent example of this language and its imagery as the writer predicts the coming of divine judgment, when "the haughty eyes of people will be brought low, and the pride of everyone shall be humbled; and the LORD alone will be exalted" (v. 11). Similar statements occur throughout the prophetic literature in judgment speeches against the nations and against Israel (Isa 3:16; 5:15; 10:12; 37:23; Jer 13:15; 48:29; Ezek 16:50; Mic 2:3; Zeph 3:11).

Whereas the prophets apply this language to nations, the Psalms and Proverbs employ this terminology with reference to individuals or classes of individuals (e.g., the righteous, the humble, the wicked, the fool). The poet in Ps 18 praises the LORD, who "delivers a humble people, but the haughty eyes you bring down" (v. 27 [Heb. v. 28]). Many of these texts maintain the associated spatial metaphor: "For the LORD is high, he regards the lowly; but the haughty he perceives from far away" (Ps 138:6). This is also illustrated in the well-known proverb: "Pride goes before destruction, and a haughty spirit before a fall" (Prov 16:18; compare 18:12). In the Pauline literature of the NT, this imagery is applied in warnings against high-mindedness (Rom 1:30; 12:16; 1 Tim 6:17; compare Rom 12:3). There are also other occurrences where the spatial metaphor is not explicitly present, but the terms signify a related sense of inappropriateness according to one's place or status (3 Macc 1:27; Rev 13:5). As some of the examples mentioned above indicate, this sense is often represented as a "haughty look" or "haughty eyes" (Ps 101:5; Prov 6:17; 21:4, 24; Sir 23:4; 26:9).

The description of someone as "haughty," or of an attitude as "haughtiness," is no doubt appropriate in many circumstances, both in the biblical text and in its contemporary appropriation. Given its hierarchical underpinnings, however, there is also the ironic risk of misapplying such terms. One only has to recall historic instances when women and/or racial and ethnic minorities were considered "haughty" or "high-minded" simply because they dared to assert their rightful "place." Thus, haughtiness can come in many forms and its avoidance requires constant vigilance.

JOSEPH F. SCRIVNER

HAURAN haw'ruhn [חַוְרָן *khawran*]. Hauran is a fertile plateau located in the northeastern part of TRANSJORDAN. It is bounded on the north by Mount Hermon and the river Pharpar, on the east by Jabal ad-Druze, on the south by the Yarmuk River, and on the west by the Sea of Galilee and the Golan Heights. It thus overlaps at least in part with the territory of BASHAN. It is mentioned in the Bible only in Ezek 47:16, 18 where it is described as the northeastern boundary of the restored land of Israel. The name means either "hollow land" (referring to caves) or "black land" (referring to basalt).

The region **huruna** is mentioned in Egyptian texts as early as the Nineteenth Dynasty (13th cent. BCE), and **hauranu** is mentioned in Assyrian texts four cent. later. Shalmaneser III (859–824 BCE) advanced as far as Hauran in 842 BCE, and Tiglath-Pileser III (745–727 BCE) devastated it in 732 BCE and then organized it as a province. Ashurbanipal (669–631 BCE) put down a revolt in the region. During the Persian period, it was part of the large satrapy of Karnaim, but in the Hellenistic period it was formed as the smaller district of Auranitis, a name that it retained through the Roman period of occupation.

The Maccabeans conquered Hauran in the 2nd cent. BCE, but the Nabateans, who settled there as early as 259 BCE, seized control of it from Alexander Jannaeus in 90 BCE. Pompey incorporated it into the DECAPOLIS, and in 23 BCE Augustus assigned it to Herod the Great, who settled Jews from Babylonia there. The region was passed on to Herod Philip, and after his death Tiberius annexed it to the province of Syria. Caligula gave it to Herod Agrippa I in 37 CE. Herod Agrippa II ruled the region until the Jewish revolt. It was ruled by Nabateans again from 85 to 106 CE. When Trajan annexed the Nabatean kingdom, Hauran was included in Provincia Arabia. Today the region still bears the name Hawran.

GREGORY L. LINTON

HAUSTAFELN. *See* HOUSEHOLD CODES.

HAVEN [מָחוֹז *makhoz*, חוֹף *khof*; λιμήν *limēn*]. Havens in the OT and NT are usually associated with harbors, safe places, protected from the wind and rough seas. Genesis 49:13; 1 Esd 5:55; 1 Macc 14:5; 2 Macc 12:6, 9; 14:1; 4 Macc 13:6-7; and Acts 27:8 all refer to harbors as safe havens. Psalm 107:30 uses *haven* in the sense of a small town. *See* FAIR HAVENS; HARBOR.

CHRISTINE D. JONES

HAVILAH hav'uh-luh [חֲוִילָה *khawilah*]. Although it is not certain, this proper name may be related to *sand* (khol חוֹל), and therefore may refer to a land that is characterized by stretches of sand. It is the land surrounded by the river Pishon, noted for gold (Gen 2:11). This name is given for a son of Cush (Gen 10:7 = 1 Chr 1:9), as well as for the son of Joqtan, a descendant of Shem (Gen 10:29 = 1 Chr 1:23).

The location of the land of Havilah is unknown. It is listed as part of the boundary of the territory settled by the Ishmaelites (Gen 25:18), which may indicate a location in the Arabian Peninsula. But it is also given as the boundary of the Amalekite territory (1 Sam 15:7), which may mean it is near Edom or the Sinai region.

C. MARK MCCORMICK

HAVVOTH-JAIR hav′oth-jay′uhr [חַוֺּת יָאִיר khawwoth ya′ir]. "Villages of Jair." A group of villages in the Bashan region of Gilead. They are described as consisting of either thirty villages (Judg 10:4) or a total of sixty villages (Josh 13:30; 1 Chr 2:23), and there are two explanations for their name. Numbers 32:41 and Deut 3:14 indicate Moses assigned the region of Gilead to the descendants of Manasseh and that JAIR captured these villages that were then named for him. Judges 10:4 says that the judge Jair's thirty sons ruled thirty towns, which were identified with their father's name.

C. MARK MCCORMICK

HAWAM, ABU. A complex of sites, principally a major ancient port, at the juncture of the Kishon River and Bay of Haifa, its occupation extending from the Middle Bronze Age (ca. 16th cent. BCE) into the medieval era. The remains of the seaport and several cemeteries, extending over at least 10 acres, are now covered in part by alluvial deposits and the modern city of Haifa. Tell Abu Hawam may be identified with ACHSHAPH or biblical SHIHOR-LIBNATH (Josh 19:26).

The tell has been partially excavated several times as rescue operations. Stratum IIIB–A, with much imported Greek and Cypriot pottery, is the most debated, with estimates of the date ranging from the 10th to the 8th cent. BCE. The site was probably a Phoenician port during the monarchy, perhaps part of the "land of CABUL" ceded by Solomon to HIRAM, king of Tyre (1 Kgs 9:13). Stratum IV belongs to the Philistine horizon. The Late Bronze Age Stratum V is a Canaanite seaport with quantities of luxury imports from Egypt and the eastern Mediterranean world.

Bibliography: J. M. Weinstein. "Was Tell Abu Hawam a Nineteenth Dynasty Naval Base?" *BASOR* 238 (1980) 43–46.

WILLIAM G. DEVER

HAWK [נֵץ nets, קָאַת qa′ath]. Several hawks are found in Palestine, the most common being the sparrow hawk (*Accipiter nisus*), often in olive groves and oases. Among the closely related harriers the most common are the marsh harrier and the hen harrier. "The hawk of any kind" in Lev 11:16 and Deut 14:15 seems to use nets as a generic term, designating all hawks and harriers, perhaps also kestrels. In Job 39:26 the author probably alludes to the migratory habits of some of the smaller hawks, depicting the nets as soar-

ing "towards the south," possibly toward the shores of the Red Sea. *See* BIRDS OF THE BIBLE; NIGHTHAWK; VULTURE.

Bibliography: G. R. Driver. "Birds in the Old Testament: I. Birds in Law." *PEQ* 87 (1955) 5–20.

GÖRAN EIDEVALL

HAY [χόρτος chortos]. Although STRAW, fodder from stalks of grain, was common in the ANE, hay—fodder from GRASS—was evidently not (1 Cor 3:12).

HAZAEL hay′zay-uhl [חֲזָאֵל khaza′el]. King of ARAM (DAMASCUS) from 844 to ca. 800 BCE, Hazael is remembered in the Bible as an implacable enemy of Israel, who fought against kings JORAM, JEHU, and JEHOAHAZ of Israel and JOASH/Jehoash of Judah. Hazael's successes, especially against Jehu and Jehoahaz, gained much formerly Israelite territory for Aram and reduced Israel to a virtual vassal state. The violence of Hazael's conquests was remembered at least a century after his career by the prophet Amos (Amos 1:4).

Hazael's accession to the throne of Damascus was a usurpation instigated by ELISHA (and Yahweh), with Hazael murdering his infirm predecessor, referred to as BEN-HADAD (although Hazael almost certainly followed Hadad-idri, known in Assyrian inscriptions to have been king at this time), as part of Yahweh's plan for the punishment of the apostate Omrides (2 Kgs 8). There is considerable doubt as to the historical accuracy of this episode.

Extra-biblical sources paint a fuller picture of Hazael's career. He withstood three campaigns of SHALMANESER III of Assyria, the mightiest ruler of his era, expanded Damascene influence over much of the Levant, and enjoyed a remarkably long reign.

D. MATTHEW STITH

HAZAIAH huh-zay′yuh [חֲזָיָה khazayah]. Meaning "Yahweh has seen," Hazaiah is listed among the ancestors of Maaseiah, the local leader of a postexilic Jerusalem province (Neh 11:5).

HAZAR-ADDAR. *See* ADDAR; HEZRON.

HAZAR-ENAN hay′zuhr-ee′nuhn [חֲצַר עֵינָן khatsar ′enan, חֲצַר עֵינוֹן khatsar ′enon]. Variant, Hazar-enon. A northern boundary location in Ezekiel's idealized vision of restored Israel (Ezek 47:17), also a marker for the northern boundary of Israel (Num 34:9). Modern identification is uncertain, although Block suggests Quarytein, 70 mi. northeast of Damascus.

Bibliography: Daniel I. Block. *The Book of Ezekiel: Chapters 25–48.* NICOT (1998).

PHILLIP MICHAEL SHERMAN

HAZAR-ENON. *See* HAZAR-ENAN.

HAZAR-GADDAH hay´zuhr-gad´uh [חֲצַר גַּדָּה khatsar gaddah]. A city in southern Judah (Josh 15:27) mentioned between Moladah and Heshmon in the listing of the tribal territories of the clan of Judah. The name may suggest a relation to Gad, the god of fortune familiar from Phoenician and Aramaic sources. *See* GAD, GADITES.

HAZARMAVETH hay´zuhr-may´vith [חֲצַרְמָוֶת khatsarmaweth]. The Semetic son of Joktan and his descendants who settled the area in south Arabia of the Wadi Hadramaut (Gen 10:26; 1 Chr 1:20). The state covered nearly 200 mi. paralleling the Arabian coast along the Indian Ocean. The inhabitants apparently controlled the caravan route of the Arabian incense industry that led to Cana, the major incense port in western Arabia. Excavations in the region revealed two affluent occupation periods (5th cent. BCE; 1st and 2nd cent. CE) with its primary city named Sabteca/Shabwa.

The name of the region is difficult to interpret since little is known of the culture. Literally "enclosure of death," the name carries an ominous tone that may represent the religious culture. A small temple dedicated to the moon god was excavated at Hureidha dating to the 5th through 2nd cent. BCE. In Egyptian religion night represented death while Amun Re, the sun god, brought rebirth. *See* DEITIES, UNDERWORLD.

MICHAEL G. VANZANT

HAZAR-SHUAL hay´zuhr-shoo´uhl [חֲצַר שׁוּעָל khatsar shu`al]. A town in the extreme south of Judah listed among the tribal territories of both Judah (Josh 15:28; Neh 11:27) and Simeon (Josh 19:3; 1 Chr 4:28). Because Simeon was assimilated into Judah at an early date, the Simeonite designation is likely original. The exact location is uncertain, although it is often mentioned in close relationship with BEER-SHEBA (Josh 15:28; 19:3; 1 Chr 4:28). The name means "court of the fox."

T. DELAYNE VAUGHN

HAZAR-SUSAH hay´zuhr-shoo´suh [חֲצַר סוּסָה khatsar susah]. A settlement of the tribe of Simeon in southern Judah (Josh 19:5). Its name and variant Hazar-Susim (1 Chr 4:31), meaning "the court of the horse(s)," may suggest its connection to the cities of the horsemen during the reign of SOLOMON, who is described as one who trafficked in horses (1 Kgs 9:19; 10:28-29). The site is often identified with Sbalat Abu Susein, east of Tell el Farah.

T. DELAYNE VAUGHN

HAZAZON-TAMAR haz´uh-zon-tay´muhr [חַצְצֹן תָּמָר, חַצְצוֹן תָּמָר khatsetson tamar]. An Amorite city conquered by CHEDORLAOMER and his allies (Gen 14:7) and described in conjunction with SODOM and other cities of the plain. Hazazon-tamar is identified with EN-GEDI on the western shore of the Dead Sea in 2 Chr 20:2. It may be the same as the TAMAR that Solomon fortified (1 Kgs 9:18). *See* ZIZ, ASCENT OF.

T. DELAYNE VAUGHN

HAZER-HATTICON hay´zuhr-hat´uh-kon [חֲצֵר הַתִּיכוֹן khatser hattikhon]. A location on the northern border of Ezekiel's idealized vision of restored Israel (Ezek 40–48; see esp. 47:16). The actual location is unknown. Scholars have suggested identification with HAZAR-ENAN (Ezek 47:17).

HAZEROTH huh-zihr´oth [חֲצֵרוֹת khatseroth]. Mentioned several times in the biblical text (Num 11:35; 12:1, 16; 33:17-18; Deut 1:1), Hazeroth is most notable for being the site at which Miriam and Aaron spoke against Moses (Num 12:1-16). In Num 12:16 Hazeroth is situated adjacent to the Wilderness of PARAN, itself consistently located near Edom in the region of the Negeb. Hazeroth is also situated two stations from Mount Sinai. *See* SINAI, MOUNT.

MICHAEL D. OBLATH

HAZIEL hay´zee-uhl [חֲזִיאֵל khazi'el]. One of three sons of SHIMEI in a list of Levites whose families David enrolled for service in the Temple (1 Chr 23:9).

HAZO hay´zoh [חֲזוֹ khazo]. One of the twelve sons of NAHOR, Abraham's brother (Gen 22:22). His mother, MILCAH, had seven other sons with Nahor. Scholars are uncertain whether to understand Hazo as a personal name or as having geographical significance.

HAZOR hay´zor [חָצוֹר khatsor; Ἀσώρ Hasōr]. Tel Hazor (Tel el Qedah, Tel el Waqqas) is the site of an ancient city located in the Hule Valley, 8.5 mi. to the north of the Sea of Galilee on the eastern foot of the upper Galilee ridge. It controls an important branch of the Via Maris, leading from Egypt to Syria and Assyria. The site comprises two distinct parts: an upper tell (100 dunams or 25 acres) and to its north a large enclosure (700 dunams or 175 acres), the lower city of Hazor.

The prominent role of Hazor during the second millennium BCE is reflected in references to the city in the Egyptian Execration texts (19th–18th cent. BCE), the Mesopotamian Mari archive (18th cent. BCE), city lists of the New Kingdom Pharaohs (15th–13th cent. BCE) and the Amarna archive (14th cent. BCE). Hazor is first mentioned in the Bible in the conquest narrative of Joshua, where it is referred to as "once the head of all those kingdoms" (Josh 11:10-13), and again in the prose version of Deborah's wars (Judg 4). Later, Hazor is mentioned among the cities that were built by king Solomon (1 Kgs 9:15), and again as one of the Israelite cities destroyed during the campaign of Tiglath-pileser, king of Assyria in 732 BCE (2 Kgs 15:29). The Lake of Hazor is mentioned in 1 Macc 11:67.

Todd Bolen/BiblePlaces.com
Figure 1: Hazor Solomonic Gate

A. Hazor in the Bronze Age (Strata XXI–XIII)
B. Hazor in the Iron Age (Strata XII–IV)
C. Hazor in Later Periods (Strata III–I)
Bibliography

A. Hazor in the Bronze Age (Strata XXI–XIII)

The first occupation of Hazor, in the third millennium BCE, is attested to by meager architectural features and a rich ceramic assemblage found on the upper tell. In the beginning of the second millennium BCE the lower city is founded and Hazor becomes a prominent Canaanite kingdom. The Middle Bronze Age city (18th–16th cent. BCE) is heavily fortified by huge earthen ramparts, mudbrick walls, and monumental gates. Several temples, whose plans and cultic paraphernalia betray North Syrian influence, were erected in the lower and upper city. The finds attributed to this period include several cuneiform tablets, indication of the high status of Hazor and its far-reaching relations with its northern neighbors. The city was destroyed in a conflagration in the 16th cent. BCE, but its occupation resumed in the Late Bronze Age (16th–13th cent. BCE). Canaanite Hazor reached its peak during the 14th cent. BCE, the time of the Amarna archive. The old temples of the lower city were restored and new ones were constructed. The acropolis was completely rebuilt with the construction of a new ceremonial precinct, consisting of monumental palaces and temples. These royal edifices were lavish and their plan and architectural features show strong north Syrian influences. The finds from this period testify to the wealth and international connections of Hazor's elite, and confirm its prominent status among its peers in the Canaanite city-state system controlled by the Egyptian New Kingdom pharaohs. Hazor's public buildings were destroyed in a violent conflagration in the 13th cent. BCE, following which the lower city was abandoned. This destruction was taken by Yadin to have been done by conquering Israelite tribes, as vividly described in the Bible, but other explanations cannot be ruled out.

B. Hazor in the Iron Age (Strata XII–IV)

The reoccupation of the tell dates to the 11th cent. BCE, when meager architectural remains and many pits were found all over the upper tell. Two small cultic installations, consisting of standing stones and offering altars, were also part of this settlement, which is attributed to the Israelites.

The first Iron Age city is attributed to the united monarchy of Solomonic times, in the 10th cent. BCE (although this dating is currently debated). The city witnesses building activities including the construction of a casemate wall encircling the western part of the upper city, a monumental six-chambered gate and several phases of domestic buildings. This city was destroyed, probably by the Aramean king Ben-Hadad of Damascus (1 Kgs 15:20).

Extensive remains from the next period of Israelite Hazor, in the time of the Omride Dynasty (9th cent. BCE), were uncovered all around the upper tell. Hazor served as an important administrative center of the northern kingdom of Israel, and was fortified by a solid city-wall encircling the entire upper tell. Remains of this period include domestic quarters, administrative storerooms (sometimes interpreted as stables) and public buildings, a fortified citadel on the western tip of the tell, and an impressive water-system cutting almost 30 m down to the water level.

Hazor witnessed several destructions and restorations during the late 9th and early 8th cent. BCE. The public and domestic buildings were reused and sometimes replaced by others, but the overall plan of the city was not considerably changed. Hazor was destroyed in 732 BCE by Tiglath-pileser III, king of Assyria, in his campaign aimed at the northern kingdom of Israel. A squatter settlement, on the ruins of the Israelite city, represents the final phase of Israelite Hazor. The destruction of Samaria and the annihilation of the kingdom of Israel left Israelite Hazor in a state of decline from which it did not recover.

C. Hazor in Later Periods (Strata III–I)

An Assyrian palatial building from the 7th cent. BCE was erected at the foot of the tell, contemporary with an Assyrian military fort that was built on the remains of the Israelite citadel. The fort continued to be used in the Persian period (4th cent. BCE), when numerous graves were also found scattered around the tell. In the Hellenistic period remains of another military fort were found on the western tip of the site. After this limited occupation, Hazor was abandoned.

Bibliography: A. Ben-Tor, ed. *Hazor III-IV: An Account of the Third and Fourth Seasons of Excavation, 1957–1958* (1989); A. Ben-Tor and R. Bonfil, eds. *Hazor V: An Account of the Fifth Season of Excavation, 1968* (1997). Y. Yadin. *Hazor: The Schweich Lectures of the British Academy 1970* (1972); Y. Yadin, et al. *Hazor I: An Account of the First Season of Excavations, 1955, Jerusalem.* (1958); Y. Yadin, et al. *Hazor II: An Account of the Second Season of Excavations, 1956* (1960).

SHARON ZUCKERMAN

HAZOR-HADATTAH hay´zor-huh-dat´uh חֲצוֹר חֲדָתָּה khatsor hadhattah]. A town apportioned to the tribe of Judah, distinguished from another site, "KERIOTH-HEZRON (that is, HAZOR)," mentioned in the same verse and located in the same region (Josh 15:25). The location remains unknown, although a possible association with el-Hudeira has been suggested.

HAZZELELPONI   haz´uh-lel-poh´ni   הַצְלֶלְפּוֹנִי hatselelponi]. The only listed daughter of Etam, who also had four sons, in the lineage of Judah (1 Chr 4:3).

HE hay [ה h]. The fifth letter of the Hebrew ALPHABET, which has an unknown origin and meaning.

HEAD, HEADSHIP [רֹאשׁ ro'sh; κεφαλή kephale]. In the OT, ro'sh most commonly refers to the head as the upper part of the body (Gen 28:11, 18; 40:16-17). People bowed their head in worship or prayer (Gen 24:26, 48; Ps 35:13), and kings (1 Sam 10:1; 2 Kgs 9:3, 6) and priests (Exod 29:7; Lev 21:10) were installed by anointing the head with oil. Mourners put dust or ashes on their head (2 Kgs 10:21; Job 16:4); people covered their heads in shame (Jer 14:3-4); and mockers wagged their head (2 Kgs 19:21; Ps 64:8). Lifting one's head connoted pride (Judg 8:28; Job 10:15), unless it was God who lifted it (Pss 3:3; 27:6). People's evil deeds were said to return upon their head (Josh 2:19; 1 Sam

25:39). The head was also considered to be the seat of a person's intellect (Dan 4:5, 10, 13); and a "head" was one person counted in a census (Num 1:2, 18, 20, 22). Ro'sh also refers to the head of various animals (Gen 3:15; Exod 12:9), other beings (Ezek 10:1, 11; Job 41:7), or statues (1 Sam 5:4); or to the top portion or upper end of an object, whether a bed (Gen 47:31; 1 Sam 19:13), axe (Deut 19:5), or festive table (1 Sam 9:22). Figuratively, ro'sh denotes leaders of families (Exod 6:14, 25), tribes of Israel (Num 1:16; Deut. 1:15), or leaders in general (Num 25:4; Deut 29:10; Josh 23:2), the sense conveyed being that of a position of leadership, authority, or honor.

In the NT, kephale likewise occurs most frequently in a literal sense (e.g., Matt. 5:36; 6:17; 10:30; Mark 12:4; Luke 7:38, 46), including references to Jesus' head (Matt 8:20; 26:7; 27:29; Mark 14:3; Luke 9:58; John 19:2, 30), and Revelation features several references to the heads of various apocalyptic figures (e.g., 4:4; 9:7, 17, 19). In keeping with OT usage, the expression figuratively conveys the notion of leadership or authority in Paul's writings. Hence Paul calls Christ the head of the church (1 Cor 11:3, Eph 1:22; 4:15; 5:23; Col 1:18; 2:10, 19). In 1 Cor 11:3-5, in the context of a passage on head coverings, Christ's headship over the man is cast in terms analogous to the husband-and-wife and God-Christ relationship. What this entails is debated, with some scholars arguing for Paul's affirmation of the "priority" of Christ over men, and of men over women, in some general sense; and others for Christ's authority over men, and of men over women. Continuity with figurative usage in the OT might urge the notion of leadership or authority. As the larger context of 1 Cor 11:2-16 makes clear, either interpretation entails notions of respect and interdependence.

In Ephesians, on the basis of Christ's headship over all things (Eph 1:10), including spiritual rulers and authorities in the heavenly realms, the author, identified in the letter as Paul, construes an analogy between the husband as the head of his wife and Christ as the head of his church (Eph 5:23). Assuming that hypotasso (ὑποτάσσω) refers to "submission (to an authority)," this headship involves both authority (Eph 5:22; compare 1 Pet 2:13, 18; 3:1; 5:5) and loving provision (Eph 5:25-29). Regarding the notion of the husband's headship over his wife, some have maintained on the basis of Eph 5:21 that the NT teaches the husband's and the wife's "mutual submission." Others contend that the submission in view is by the wife to her husband (Eph 5:22; compare Col 3:18; 1 Pet 3:1), while the husband is called to love his wife sacrificially as Christ loves the church (Eph 5:25-27). This latter group also points to the teaching of 1 Cor 11:3, which, similar to the Christ/husband analogy in Eph 5:23, suggests the husband's place of authority, honor, or preeminence in the home, a role expected of the male head of a household in biblical times (passages such as 1 Tim

2:12 and 3:2 are seen as extending this principle to the church; compare 1 Tim 3:4-5). Some of those favoring the idea of "mutual submission" in Eph 5 adduce several classical and patristic passages in which the term kephalē is said to convey the nuance of "source" or "preeminence." Lexical research provides little if any support to a rendering of kephalē as "source." The metaphorical range of usages related to the meaning head—such as "prominent," "uppermost," or "preeminent"—is more plausible. See AUTHORITY; BODY OF CHRIST; CHURCH, LIFE AND ORGANIZATION OF; HOUSEHOLD CODES; HOUSEHOLD, HOUSEHOLDER; JUDGE; MALE AND FEMALE AUTHORITY; PATRIARCHS; TRIBE.

Bibliography: Clinton E. Arnold. "Jesus Christ: 'Head' of the Church (Colossians and Ephesians)." *Jesus of Nazareth: Lord and Christ.* Joel B. Green and Max Turner, eds. (1994) 346–66; Judith M. Gundry-Volf. "Gender and Creation in 1 Cor 11:2–16: A Study in Paul's Theological Method." *Evangelium, Schriftauslegung, Kirche: Festschrift für Peter Stuhlmacher.* J. Ådna, et al., eds. (1997) 151–71; Andreas J. Köstenberger and Thomas R. Schreiner, eds. *Women in the Church* (2005); Max Turner. "Modern Linguistics in the New Testament." *Hearing the New Testament.* Joel B. Green, ed. (1995) 146–74.

ANDREAS J. KÖSTENBERGER

HEAD COVERING [כֶּתֶר kether, מִגְבָּעוֹת mighba'oth, מִצְנֶפֶת mitsnefeth, נֵזֶר nezer, עֲטָרָה 'atarah, פְּאֵר pe'er; διάδημα diadēma, κάλυμμα kalymma, κίδαρις kidaris, στέφανος stephanos]. In the OT several head coverings are mentioned. Aaronic priests, royalty, men, and women sometimes wore a HEADDRESS or HEADBAND (Exod 28:40; 29:9; 39; Lev 8; 13; Isa 3:18, 20). Priests might also wear a linen TURBAN. Turbans were removed in times of mourning (Ezek 24:17, 23). Women could wear a VEIL (Gen 24:65; 38:14). Royalty wore a CROWN or DIADEM (Eccl 11:5).

In 2 Cor 3:13-14, Paul discusses the head covering or veil (kalymma) worn by Moses (Exod 34:33-35), introducing a play on words between what covers the face and what covers understanding. The meaning of 1 Cor 11:4-16 is much debated and controversial. In 1st cent. Roman society (Corinth was a Roman colony), head covering for women indicated a "respectable" status and invited protection from the law against sexual harassment.

Details remain debatable, however. **Kata kephalēs echon** (κατὰ κεφαλῆς ἔχων, 1 Cor 11:4) probably means "with his head covered," but just as possible is "with long hair." **Akatakalyptō tē kephalē** (ἀκατακαλύπτῳ τῇ κεφαλῇ, 1 Cor 11:5) probably means "with head uncovered," but as conceivable is "with long, loose hair." The women's head covering probably denotes a hood but might mean a VEIL. See BODY; CLOTH, CLOTHES.

Bibliography: Dale Martin. *The Corinthian Body* (1995) 229–49; Aline Rousselle. "Body Politics in Ancient Rome." *A History of Women in the West*, vol. 1. G. Duby and M. Perrot, eds. (1992) 296–337; Anthony C. Thiselton. *The First Epistle to the Corinthians* (2000) 800–848.

ANTHONY C. THISELTON

HEADBAND [פְּאֵר pe'er, שְׁבִים shavis]. A headdress of varying material worn in times of joy by men and women of position (Isa 3:18). See HEAD COVERING; SASH.

HEADDRESS [מִצְנֶפֶת mitsnefeth, צַמָּה tsammah, צָנִיף tsanif, צָעִיף tsa'if, רְעָלָה re'alah]. Headdresses were worn by both men and women. Men would wear a TURBAN of cloth wrapped around the head. The priest had a special turban, usually of linen (Exod 28:40; 29:9; 39:28; Lev 8:13). Women would sometimes wear a VEIL or shawl to cover their faces. Veils could hide beauty or enhance beauty (Isa 3:20). A headdress was often a sign of position. See GARLAND; HEAD COVERING.

CHRISTINE D. JONES

HEALING. Healing refers to a restoration to health by any of a number of health care options, including but not limited to the body's capacity to self-heal, prayer and other forms of divine entreaty, and a range of biomedical interventions (e.g., the intercession of a gifted healer, care within the household, use of traditional medicaments, or employment of a professional physician). The Bible explicitly rejects recourse to magic and generally views physicians with disdain. This negative attitude toward physicians serves largely as a commentary on their unenviable status, due especially to their record of success when compared to the efficacy of folk remedies and costs associated with their services. Theologically, healing practices are guided by the recognition that Yahweh alone is the source of life and, therefore, the source of renewed health. Both the OT and NT portray Yahweh as healer, with the NT adding the image of Jesus as God's agent of healing. Healing at the hand of others is consistently attributed to God, to "the name" of the exalted Lord Jesus, or to the Holy Spirit.

A. Perspectives on Healing
B. Ancient Physicians, Ancient Medicine
C. Yahweh as Healer
D. Jesus as Healer
    1. Healing and the historical Jesus
    2. Jesus as healer in the Gospels
E. Other Agents of Healing
Bibliography

A. Perspectives on Healing
"Healing" and "sickness" are notoriously difficult to define, depending on differing cultural and, in some

cases, relatively individual and subjective notions of "health." If "sickness" refers to an unwanted condition or the impairment of normal bodily functions, who decides what is "unwanted" or "normal"? To a degree not often recognized, "sickness" is in the eye of the beholder, so the identification and etiology of sickness, and the therapeutic interventions it warrants, are autobiographically shaped. If "sickness" is any unwanted condition of self or substantial threat of unwanted conditions of self, then notions of health and sickness are tied to how a people measures human well-being.

An immediate implication of this pathological approach is that study of healing in the Bible, particularly but not exclusively in the West, has often been derailed by projecting contemporary biomedical concerns onto accounts of healing from cultures far removed from our own. Too often, focus has fallen on achieving a diagnosis of a presenting problem and its resolution in terms oriented toward the physical body, an approach that turns a blind eye to other definitions of "healing" and "health" assumed in and supported by the biblical materials (see DISEASE).

A useful taxonomy for intercultural study of healing makes distinctions along the following lines. 1) Disease accounts focus on abnormalities located within the body, at or beneath the skin. The problem lies in the structure and functions of bodily organs or systems. In this case, healing requires physical or biomedical intervention. 2) Illness accounts center on the body but also one's networks of relationships and interaction with the larger social environment. The body is not discounted, but placed within a larger web of meaning that includes the embodied lives of persons in community. Healing might require physical intervention, but certainly must address the nesting of persons with others as the target of intervention. 3) Disorder accounts, without neglecting either the body or one's networks of relationships and interactions within a larger social environment, also attend to one's relationship to the world at large, experiences as unbalanced, out of order. The recovery of well-being, in this case, would be tantamount to "putting the world back together," or otherwise redressing a cosmic imbalance. As medical anthropologists are quick to point out, this taxonomy represents ideal categories that, in the lived experience of a people, may overlap; this is almost always the case in the biblical materials.

If contemporary people of the West tend to think of disease preeminently in bodily terms, then they would also imagine that healing requires physical or biomedical intervention. People within biblical accounts, however, tend to think of sickness in more holistic ways. The source of sickness for them lies not only in the bodies of the sick, but also and sometimes especially in their social environments and in the larger cosmos. Accordingly, healing entails alleviating the pressure of one's social relationships, bodily intervention, and/or redress of cosmic imbalances. This means that persons who tend toward a biomedical paradigm for understanding sickness and healing may need to expand what they allow as significant in talk about well-being to include, e.g., concerns with relational integrity and the life of the community. It does not mean that they should jettison concern with the body as though it were unimportant; this would only substitute one form of reductionism for another.

An intercultural perspective is important when reading biblical accounts of healing. For example, in the Bible "leprosy" is rarely if ever true leprosy, or "Hansen's disease," but instead includes any of a number of skin conditions. According to Lev 13–14, LEPROSY is a sign of divine curse on a person, with the result that a person diagnosed by a priest as a leper is relegated to the periphery of human community. In this case, "leprosy" is not life threatening, from a biomedical point of view, nor is this skin disease contagious. Instead, the contagion is ritual impurity. "Leprosy" thus exemplifies how religious, social, and physical considerations coalesce in a single set of symptoms. Jesus' intervention in such cases is classified as "cleansing" rather than healing, since religious impurity is the primary presenting problem, and intervention is followed with instruction like that found in Luke 5:12-14: "Go, show yourself to the priest. . . ." In such an instance, the priest functions as a health care consultant, validating the cure and mediating the former leper's return to community with God's people (see CLEAN AND UNCLEAN).

Cases of exorcism similarly correlate what might appear as discrete spiritual, social, mental, and physical factors, both in the presentation of the disorder and in its resolution. The Gerasene demoniac lived not in a house but among the tombs (apart from human community, as though he were dead, ritually unclean), was naked and uncontrollable (and thus lacking human identity), and his speech moves back and forth between "I" and "we"-statements (so fully is he demonized). Following the exorcism, he sits at the feet of Jesus (self-controlled and submissive), clothed and in his right mind (returned to human identity), and Jesus returns him to his home to declare what God had done for him (restored to his community, with a vocation) (Luke 8:26-39; see DEMON).

The integration of measures of human well-being is also on display in a worldview in which healing and sickness are indicators of Yahweh's favor and displeasure. Although one cannot argue that health is necessarily the direct result of God's favor, nor that sickness is necessarily the direct result of divine punishment, it is nevertheless true that for ancient Israel there could be a causal link from sin to sickness. (See, e.g., Deut 28; 1 Kgs 13:1-25; Prov 3:28-35; 11:19; 13:13-23; 1 Cor 11:29-30. This position is eloquently represented by Job's interlocutors in Job 8:1-22; 11:6; 22:1-30, though in the book of Job their logic is undermined.) In John 9, the disciples assume the causal relation of sin to physical disorder, but Jesus makes no general pronouncement on the subject.

B. Ancient Physicians, Ancient Medicine

Healing practices in Israel centered in the home, where the sick were kept; care might take the form of maintaining vigil and soliciting the help of Yahweh through prayer and fasting (e.g., 2 Sam 12:15-23). Persons with "leprosy," on the other hand, were segregated (Lev 13–14). Women in childbirth received the aid of midwives (e.g., Gen 35:17; 38:28). Only rarely do physicians appear in the OT. When they do, they are typically seen as negative alternatives to Yahweh (e.g., 2 Chr 16:12; Jer 8:22–9:6) or as persons offering worthless advice (Job 13:4). This is consistent with the biblical portrait of Yahweh as the only God. It is also consistent with the state of medical knowledge in antiquity, and thus with the mysteriousness of the human body and its processes, which encouraged hope in magic and/or miracle. Old Testament faith explicitly excluded magic (or sorcery, the manipulation of the spirits) as a remedy, in preference to divine intervention and care (e.g., Lev 19:26-28; Deut 18:10-14; Ezek 13:17-18).

Prejudice against physicians is not unique to the OT world. Due to the association of medicine with the Greeks and an anti-Greek bias characterizing many of the elite of the Roman republic, traditional healing practices among the Romans could be asserted over against Greek medicine. This, together with his disavowal of fee-based medical practices among physicians, explains Cato's advice to his son to stay clear of doctors, preferring instead "a little book of prescriptions for curing those who were sick in his family" (Plutarch, *Cato*, 23.3-6). In rural areas of the empire, snake-charmers and healers with magical powers were the norm. In pandemic times, however, all eyes turned toward the gods for defense and salvation.

Nevertheless, in the world of the NT, physicians were sufficiently common that Jesus can allude to their activity metaphorically (e.g., Mark 2:17 par.). Moreover, reflecting a widespread viewpoint that medical attention should be reserved to one's family and friends, Jesus predicts that some will say, "Doctor, cure yourself"! In effect, he's saying, "Attend to people of your own community and not to outsiders!" (Luke 4:23). Only the wealthy could afford the care of a trained physician, however, and village people were especially vulnerable to the abuse of charlatans who took what little money they had but provided little by way of a cure. Mark 5:26 is illustrative: "She had endured much under many physicians, and had spent all that she had; and she was no better, but rather grew worse."

Village and rural folk depended less on persons who publicly professed the physician's oath (i.e., those of the "profession"), and found the prospect of divine healing especially attractive (e.g., Acts 5:16). Hospitality might take the form of health care (e.g., Luke 10:30-35; Acts 16:33-34), and the author of 1 Timothy, while recognizing the potential of intoxication, nonetheless reflects medical tradition when he advises "a little wine for the sake of your stomach and your frequent ailments" (3:8; 5:3; for an extensive registry of practical medicaments, see Pliny the Elder, *Nat.* 23–32). Relative wealth could not certify medical competence, however. Medical treatises might sneer at root-cutters, drug-sellers, and purveyors of amulets and incantations, but even the best physicians understood little of the ways of the body.

In the Greco-Roman world, the work of healing was claimed by and for "holy men," and for many others, including emperors and philosophers. Again, though, "healing" must be understood broadly. For example, concerning the exploits of Augustus in rescuing "the whole human race exhausted by mutual slaughter," Philo wrote, "This is the Caesar who calmed the torrential storms on every side, who healed pestilences common to Greeks and barbarians . . ." (*Embassy to Gaius* §§144–45). Philosophers were "physicians" since the aim of their teaching was to heal people of their vices and to promote the good health of virtue. Galen (129–ca. 215 CE), the celebrated physician whose writings dominated medicine for almost 1,400 years, entitled one of his books, *That the Best Physician Is also a Philosopher*.

Healing in Greco-Roman antiquity was associated with the ubiquitous gods, especially but not exclusively the cults and shrines honoring the healing deities (see Acts 14:8-13). Exalted to the Greek pantheon, Hercules exercised compassion by healing diseases of all sorts, even raising the dead. The goddess Isis was recognized as dispenser of life, healer, bringer of salvation. Asclepius, the god of healing, was credited with guiding the hands of the physicians. Hygeia (Hygieia Ὑγίεια), health personified, was recognized as Asclepius' daughter. Healing was also claimed to be available by means of magical paraphernalia. Acts records the burning of magical books at Ephesus by former magicians who had become believers (19:18-19), thus disclosing what must have been a characteristic Christian response to such practices.

C. Yahweh as Healer

Throughout the OT, Yahweh's role as healer is paramount: "I am the LORD who heals you" (Exod 15:26; see, e.g., 2 Kgs 5:7; Isa 57:19). This self-attribution comes immediately after the narrator's account of Yahweh's liberation of Israel from Egypt. This demonstrates how broadly the notion of "healing" could be understood—in this instance, to refer to the freedom and formation of a people. Elsewhere in the Pentateuch, Yahweh declares as proof of his singular status, "I kill and I make alive; I wound and I heal" (Deut 32:39).

In the Prophets, we find appeals to God that he might come and heal persons and the nation. Hezekiah prays that God might restore his health (Isa 38:16), and Ezekiel portrays Yahweh as healer of the weak, the sick, and the lost (34:16). The Servant of Yahweh, Isaiah writes, will effect the healing of God's people (53:5). In the Writings, too, God is portrayed as healer. A recurring motif in the Psalms is God's restoring the faithful—sometimes by means of forgiveness, liberation, or renewal (Pss 30:2; 41:4; 103:3; 107:19-20). Yahweh binds up and heals the wounded (Job 5:17-18).

In the NT, the role of God as healer is continued, but with a significant emendation. Healing is a sign of the in-breaking kingdom of God, a reminder that behind the healing ministry of Jesus and others stands Yahweh the healer. Especially in the Gospels and Acts, well-being is a divine gift mediated through Jesus, then through his followers. According to Acts, God worked deeds of power, wonders, and signs through Jesus so as to accredit him as God's authorized agent of salvation (2:22); likewise, the Lord "testified to the word of his grace by granting signs and wonders to be done" through Paul and Barnabas (14:3). Others may participate in God's healing activity, but this does not detract from the essential identification of Yahweh as the source of healing. This is underscored in Acts by means of the theologically significant description of miracles as "signs and wonders," language borrowed from the OT through which the narrator of Acts proclaims the realization of God's saving purpose and bears witness to God's commanding influence in history (e.g., Exod 7:3; Deut 4:34; 7:19; 26:8; Jer 32:20-21; Acts 2:19, 22, 43; 4:30; 5:12; 6:8; 7:36; 8:6, 13; 14:3; 15:12).

D. Jesus as Healer

1. Healing and the historical Jesus

The portrait of Jesus as healer is central to the Gospels and its historicity is strongly advocated by standard criteria of authenticity. With regard to the criterion of dissimilarity, when compared with such Jewish holy men as Honi the Circle-Drawer and HANINA BEN DOSA—as well as the 1st cent. Gentile miracle worker, Apollonius of Tyana—three things distinguish Jesus: 1) the degree to which healing was typical of his ministry, 2) his emphasis on the component of faith (see the phrase, "Your faith has made you well"—e.g., Matt 9:22; Mark 10:52; Luke 17:19), and 3) his unmediated exercise of the saving power of God. Jesus did not ask God to intervene, but pronounced healing directly, in speech-acts that assumed his authority to do so. The character of these speech-acts distinguishes the healing work of Jesus from that of his followers as well; they pronounced healing in the name of Jesus (e.g., Acts 3:6, 16), recoiling from the suggestion that they might be the source of divine power (e.g., Acts 14:14-15).

The portrait of Jesus as healer also satisfies the criterion of multiple attestation. The Gospel of Matthew records nineteen healing and four summary statements naming healing as typical of Jesus' mission. Mark recounts eighteen miracle stories and four summaries, and Luke has twenty stories and three summaries. Taking into account that the Synoptic Gospels occasionally report the same episode, the index is still impressive: six episodes of exorcism and seventeen accounts of healing (including three reports of resuscitation), as well as allusions to unspecified episodes of healing. The Gospel of John refers to miracles as "signs," among which are numbered five episodes of healing (including one resuscitation). We have further testimony from outside the NT. Although Josephus' paragraph concerning Jesus (i.e., the *Testimonium Flavianum*; *Ant.* 18.63–64) has long been under suspicion as a Christian interpolation, recent study supports the theory that an original reference to Jesus in Josephus's work has been embellished. The original reference would have included mention of Jesus' having accomplished "astounding deeds," the charge that he led the people astray, and his crucifixion. To this can be added rabbinic traditions describing Jesus as a magician who deceived and led Israel astray (*b. Sanh.* 107*b*; compare *b. Shabb.* 104*b*), and the pointed statement in *b. Sanh.* 43*a*: "He is going forth to be stoned because he has practiced sorcery and enticed and led Israel astray." According to Origen, Celsus thought that Jesus journeyed to Egypt, learned the secrets of magicians, then returned to Palestine as a deceptive quack (*Cels.* 1.38), and Justin Martyr observed that, though Jesus' healing should have elicited recognition of him as Messiah, some drew the opposite conclusion: "they said it was a display of magic art, for they even dared to say that he was a magician and a deceiver of the people" (*Dia.* 69:7).

While reviewing evidence for multiple sources, we have also garnered evidence in relation to the criterion of Jesus' suffering and death: What about the historical Jesus accounts for his opposition and eventual crucifixion? The material from Josephus and rabbinic texts indicates already that Jesus was charged as a deceiver and false prophet, a parallel to the claims in Luke 23:1-5 that Jesus was delivered to Pilate as one who perverted the people of Israel and led them astray. These charges echo the warning in Deut 13 against false prophets. In other words, the portrait of Jesus as healer helps to explain the hostility he attracted and his execution.

Of perhaps even greater interest is the apparent reality that the locus of debate was not whether these episodes actually occurred, but how to account for them. For some, Jesus engaged in healing as a witch, magician, or quack. According to the Synoptic Gospels, some who recognized Jesus' status as a healer attributed his ministry of exorcism to his association with Satan. In response, Jesus interprets his exorcisms as a sign of the work of the Spirit in his mission, and as a demonstration of God's kingdom (Matt 12:24-33; Mark 2:22-30; Luke 11:14-26). In these exchanges, Jesus' healing ministry signifies the inbreaking kingdom of God. His healing ministry marked the coming of the long-awaited era of salvation (see Luke 4:18-19 [citing Isa 58:6; 61:1-2]; Matt 8:14-17 [citing Isa 53:4]).

2. Jesus as healer in the Gospels

In the Gospels as a whole, the healing ministry of Jesus identifies Jesus as agent of God's beneficence and signifies the enactment of God's saving purpose. Each of the Gospels portrays Jesus as healer with its own emphases.

Healing stories in Matthew congregate especially in Matt 8–9, depicting Jesus as one who makes divine blessing available to those on society's margins—a leper, the slave of a Gentile army officer, an old woman, the demon-possessed, a paralytic, a collector of tolls, a young girl, and the blind. The result is an admixture of references to "healing" as return to physical health, restoration of persons to status within their families and communities, reordering of life around God, and the driving back of demonic forces. Thus, cleansing a leper allowed him new access to God and to the community of God's people (Matt 8:1-4), healing a paralytic was tantamount to forgiving his sins (Matt 9:2-8), extending the grace of God to toll collectors and sinners illustrated the work of a physician (Matt 9:9-13), and recovery of sight signified the insight of faith (Matt 9:27-31). For Matthew, accounts of healing serve also to underscore christological predicates—e.g., Messiah, Lord, Son of David (e.g., 8:2; 9:27-31; 20:29-34)—and to inscribe Jesus' mission into Isaianic anticipation of the new age (e.g., 8:17; 11:4-5; Isa 35:6; 53:4; 61:1).

For the Gospel of Mark, the healing ministry of Jesus is strategically correlated with the message of the cross in the service of Mark's concern with the identity of Jesus. It is precisely as the miracle-worker that Jesus goes to the cross, with Mark portraying him as the powerful, self-giving Son of God. Episodes of healing in Mark sometimes have a parabolic function as well (e.g., a comparison of 8:22-25 with 10:46-52 turns on the metaphorical use of sight and blindness for the presence or absence of the insight of faith).

Healing is pivotal for Jesus' identity and mission in the Gospel of Luke. Jesus' inaugural address tethers healing and teaching together as complementary means of proclaiming the good news (4:16-30). Jesus' role as a healer is a consequence of his anointing by the Spirit (e.g., 4:18-19; 5:17; Acts 10:38), and healing is an important means by which Jesus extends the frontiers of salvation (e.g., 11:17-19). As a whole, the healing ministry of Jesus is portrayed as an assault on the forces of evil (e.g., 13:10-17). The portrait of Jesus as healer in the Gospel of Luke is carefully balanced with parallel accounts of healing in the Acts of the Apostles, authenticating the status of Jesus' witnesses (e.g., compare Luke 5:17-26 with Acts 3:1-10; 14:8-13).

According to John 20:30-31, Jesus' "signs," including incidences of healing, are to cultivate faith in Jesus, Messiah and Son of God. That is, episodes of healing point beyond themselves to the genuine identity and glory of Jesus, verifying his filial relationship with God and demonstrating that the Father sent Jesus (e.g., 5:36-38). Nevertheless, Jesus' healing ministry is received as ambiguous testimony; the Fourth Evangelist typically registers a range of responses (e.g., John 9)—hostility against Jesus, bearing witness to healing apart from a faith-response, and the insight that comes with belief in Jesus.

E. Other Agents of Healing

In the OT, prophets were sometimes portrayed as agents of healing. Elijah was instrumental in restoring a widow's son to life (1 Kgs 17:8-24), and Elisha instructed Naaman, commander of the Syrian army, how to be cured of leprosy (2 Kgs 5:1-15). According to the Synoptic Gospels, Jesus' disciples participated in his ministries of healing and exorcism (Mark 6:7-13 par.), and in Acts the ministries of the apostles, as well as of Stephen, Paul, and Barnabas, are characterized by signs and wonders, including healing. Such healing is performed explicitly in the name of Jesus (e.g., Acts 3:1-10; 9:34; 16:16-18). For Acts, the healing activity of persons like Stephen or Peter functions to convey the blessings of salvation now available through the risen Lord, but also to prove that such persons are the Lord's authorized emissaries.

In 1 Cor 12, Paul lists the gifts of healings and working of miracles as manifestations of the work of the Spirit in the life of the church. In 2 Corinthians, Paul speaks of his having performed "the signs of an apostle" (12:12; compare Rom 15:18-19; 1 Thess 1:5), which presumably would have included healing. Paul, however, is generally reserved in speaking of such matters since weakness is an occasion for identifying with the suffering of Jesus and for communicating the power of the gospel (e.g., Gal 4:13; 2 Cor 12:7).

James directs those who are sick to call for the elders of the church to pray over them, anointing them with oil in the name of the Lord (5:15-16). Correlating confession and healing, James emphasizes healing as integral to the integrity of the Christian community.

Bibliography: Hector Avalos. *Illness and Health Care in the ANE* (1995); Wendy Cotter, ed. *Miracles in Greco-Roman Antiquity* (1999); Robert A. Hahn. *Sickness and Healing: An Anthropological Perspective* (1995); Howard Clark Kee. *Medicine, Miracle and Magic in New Testament Times* (1986); John P. Meier. *A Marginal Jew.* Vol. 2: *Mentor, Message, and Miracles* (1994); Vivian Nutton. *Ancient Medicine* (2004); John J. Pilch. *Healing in the New Testament* (2000); Graham H. Twelftree. *Jesus the Miracle Worker* (1999).

JOEL B. GREEN

HEALTH CARE. One of the most recent developments in the study of illness and disease in the Bible is the shift from the study of biblical "medicine," which historically has emphasized diagnosing biblical illnesses, to the study of "health care" as reflected in biblical and related materials. This shift rests on the premise that healing practices should be treated as part of a healthcare system, which may be defined as a set of interacting resources, institutions, and strategies that are intended to maintain or restore health in a particular community. Such a system includes, but is not limited to, beliefs about the causes of illness, options available to patients, and the role of governments in health care.

Public hygiene, which refers broadly to the organized efforts of a community to promote health and prevent disease, is also part of any health-care system. Closely related is the emerging area of disability studies, which focus on how persons are treated based on presumed or real features of their bodies. Accordingly, this entry will discuss health-care systems in ancient Syria-Palestine in rough chronological order from the prehistoric periods to early Christianity.

    A. Prehistoric Periods
    B. Environment and Health
    C. Identifying Biblical Illnesses
    D. The Israelite Health-care System(s)
    E. The Second Temple Period
    F. Early Christianity
    Bibliography

A. Prehistoric Periods

Health care in the ANE is attested by the end of the Paleolithic, the first period of human material culture ending approximately between 20000–16000 BCE in the Near East. During the Neolithic (ca. 8500–4300 BCE) the domestication of animals probably introduced into human populations new pools of diseases carried by animals (e.g., bovine tuberculosis). Human tuberculosis is reflected in skeletal material from Egypt and Bab edh-Dhra (Jordan) as early as the fourth millennium.

The long existence of healing specialists in Syria-Palestine is reflected in the trephinated skulls at Jericho from at least the Neolithic period. The oldest known surgery for a determinable reason (intercranial infection) is evidenced near Jericho in the Chalcolithic period (ca. 3500 BCE). The activity of healing specialists is also attested by bone spatulas found at Tell Jemmeh (near Gaza) in the early first millennium, and the implantation of a bronze wire in a tooth at Horvat En Ziq, a small Nabatean fortress in the northern Negev in the Hellenistic era. Liver models found at Hazor and Megiddo in the Late Bronze Age may have been used in medical consultations.

The Amarna letters (14th cent. BCE) mention epidemics and the traffic of physicians in Canaanite royal courts. Ugaritic texts (e.g., Kirta epic) indicate that El,

the supreme god at Ugarit, was concerned with healing, especially infertility. In Tyre, Sidon, and other Phoenician city-states of the early first millennium BCE, Eshmun was a healing god whose temples may have provided therapeutic services. Yahweh, Resheph, and other Near Eastern deities brought both disease and healing.

Throughout all prehistoric and historic periods the extended family was probably the main caretaker for the ill. We see this practice in Mesopotamian texts that call upon family members to take care of disabled relatives. The Code of Hammurabi enjoins the family, rather than the state, to care for the ill. A number of biblical episodes also mention the role of the family in taking care of the ill, as in the case of Amnon (2 Sam 13:5-7).

B. Environment and Health

Israel in the pre-exilic period probably shared many of the health problems that were common in many Near Eastern settlements. The inadequate disposal of garbage and human waste was probably a constant threat to public health in Syria-Palestine. Towns (e.g., Gibeon) in areas of poor rainfall had to construct cisterns that were vulnerable to contamination.

Parts of Jericho, Tell Beit Mirsim, and other towns apparently had drains, some of which may have carried sewage, by the Middle or Late Bronze ages. Excavations in Jerusalem have recovered toilet seats, one of which was found in a separate cubicle of a house, dated to about 586 BCE. However, such amenities were probably uncommon in most of Israel.

Although there are many textual references to washing and related hygienic activities (Gen 18:4; Ps 60:8), it is likely that personal hygiene was generally poor in the absence of abundant water supplies. Ruth 3:3 indicates that even bathing was sometimes seen as a special or uncommon event.

C. Identifying Biblical Illnesses

Historically, the study of biblical medicine has focused on providing modern medical diagnoses for ancient conditions. Unfortunately, the precise identification of most diseases in the Bible has been notoriously difficult, especially in cases of epidemics (Num 25; 1 Sam 5:6-12). Nonetheless, many plagues are viewed as the result of Israel's contact with outside groups (e.g., Midianites in Num 25). The stories of the plagues on Egypt in Exod 7–10 also recognize that epidemics can alter the course of history.

Archaeoparasitologists have established the probable existence of certain intestinal diseases (e.g., tapeworm [*Taenia*] and whipworm [*Trichuris trichiura*] infections) in ancient Israel.

The condition usually translated as "leprosy" (tsara‘ath צָרַעַת) receives the most attention in the Bible (Lev 13–14), but it should not be confused with the disease now classified as leprosy, and otherwise known as Hansen's disease. Leprosy, although caused by a microbe (*Mycobacterium leprae*), is not highly contagious. Overall, the Hebrew tsara'ath does not have a simple modern equivalent because it probably encompassed a large variety of diseases that produced a chronic discoloration of the skin.

There are also various references to blindness (2 Sam 5:8) and musculoskeletal disabilities (2 Sam 9:3). Infertility, which is another illness frequently mentioned in the Bible (Gen 16:1-2; 1 Sam 1:5-6), diminished the social status of the afflicted woman (Gen 30:1-20). Some sort of mental disorder seems evidenced by Saul's malady in 1 Sam 16:14-16.

Circumcision, which is depicted as early as 2400 BCE (Fifth Dynasty) in a bas relief from Saqqara, Egypt, often has been explained as medical or hygienic in origin. However, newer research raises serious doubts about this theory. In 1999, the American Academy of Pediatrics declared that it could find no significant medical or hygienic advantages for circumcision. None of the biblical texts used to explain the origin of circumcision (e.g., Gen 17:9-14) provide hygiene as the reason. Accordingly, some scholars view circumcision within the wider practice of slavemarking (Exod 21:6), while others see it as a symbolic expression linked to fertility rituals and kinship solidarity. In any case, the medical problems that may result from ancient circumcision range from infection to being disabled for at least a few days (see Gen 34:25).

D. The Israelite Health-care System(s)

All religious healing systems presumed, of course, that deities could heal, but economics can also explain why certain options were chosen. Most health-care systems in biblical lands had a variety of options that were probably arranged hierarchically, depending, in part, on the needs and means of the patient. Prayer was probably one of the first, and most economical, options chosen by patients in all systems. In general, the management of any illness has two major phases, the first of which is the seeking of information (e.g., cause, diagnosis), and the application of that information in the restoration of health (i.e., therapy).

All health-care systems have an explanatory framework (etiology) for the nature and origin of an illness. The OT has at least two principal explanations for illness. One, represented by Deut 28, affirms that health encompasses a physical state associated with the fulfillment of covenant stipulations that are fully disclosed to the members of the society, and illness stems from the violation of those stipulations. Therapy includes reviewing one's actions in light of the covenant.

The book of Job offers a contrasting yet complementary view that argues that illness may be rooted in divine plans that may not be disclosed to the patient at all, and not in the transgression of published rules. The patient must trust that God's undisclosed reasons are just.

Perhaps the most distinctive feature of the Israelite health-care system depicted in the canonical texts is the division into legitimate and illegitimate consultative options for the patient. This division is partly related to monolatry, insofar as illness and healing rest ultimately upon Yahweh's control (Exod 15:26; Job 5:18), and insofar as non-Yahwistic options are prohibited. The meaning of "magic" is in great dispute in modern scholarship, and there is no agreement on whether distinctions between "legitimate" and "illegitimate" consultants can be classified by the relative use of "magical" or "nonmagical" approaches.

In addition to its presumed efficacy, simple prayer to Yahweh was probably the most common legitimate option for a patient because it required no great economic or physical effort. Petitions and thanksgiving prayers uttered from the viewpoint of the patient are attested in the Bible (e.g., Isa 38:10-20).

Many psalms (e.g., 38, 39, 88, and 102), in particular, may be intended as prayers for use by patients. These psalms also record important Hebrew concepts concerning illness and health care. In Ps 38 the author attributes illness to Yahweh's anger and "hand" (v. 2). This concept is similar to the frequent Mesopotamian use of "the hand" (Akkadian: qatu) of a deity to describe the divine origin of an illness. As in many descriptions of illness in Mesopotamia, the patient in Ps 38:1-4 attributes Yahweh's anger to the patient's own sin. Confession is regarded as part of the therapy (v. 18), and the patient complains about the social consequences of illness (vv. 11-12).

Tangible treatments mentioned in the Bible include "bandages" (Ezek 30:21), "mandrakes" for infertility (Gen 30:14), and "balsam" from Gilead, which may have been an important source of medicinal substances exported to Egypt (Jer 46:11). Incense, oil, and combs found in various sites in various periods (e.g., at Megiddo in the Late Bronze Age, Masada in the Roman period) may have been used to combat lice and other ecto-parasites that may have been significant vectors of disease.

Illegitimate options, which were probably widely used by Israelites, included consultants designated in Hebrew as rof'im (רֹפְאִים, 2 Chr 16:12; NRSV, "physicians"), non-Yahwistic shrines (2 Kgs 1:2-4), and probably a large variety of "sorcerers" (Deut 18:10-12). Female figurines found in most periods in Israel, especially in domestic contexts, may have been involved in fertility rituals. The largest known dog cemetery in the ancient world was uncovered at Ashkelon, and may be associated with a healing cult of the Persian period.

Prophets are probably the foremost legitimate consultants in the canonical texts, and they were often in fierce competition with "illegitimate" consultants. Deuteronomy 18:10-17 seems to advocate the monopoly by the Yahwistic prophet of all the consultation functions, including probable ones for illness, that had been previously distributed in a wide variety of consultants in Canaan. Stories of healing miracles (e.g., 2 Kgs 4; 8) in the Deuteronomistic History may reflect an effort to promote prophets as the sole legitimate consultants. Their function was to provide prognoses (2 Kgs 8:8) and intercede on behalf of the patient (2 Kgs 5:11). Unlike some of the principal healing consultants in other Near Eastern societies, the efficacy of Israelite prophets resided more in their relationship with Yahweh than in technical expertise.

Shrines of Yahweh were probably another significant legitimate option in the pre-exilic period. In 1 Sam 1 Hannah visited the temple at Shiloh to help reverse her infertility. Second Kings 18:4 indicates that prior to Hezekiah the bronze serpent made by Moses as a therapeutic device (Num 21:6-9) was involved in acceptable therapeutic rituals in the Temple of Jerusalem. Metal serpents have been found in temples (e.g., the Asclepieion at Pergamum) known to have been used for therapy during the first millennium BCE. Metal serpents, such as those found in or near shrines at Timna, Tell Mevorakh, and Hazor in the Late Bronze Age, may have been involved in therapeutic rituals, but other functions cannot be excluded.

The centralization of the cult in Jerusalem and the reforms attributed to Hezekiah (715–687 BCE) and Josiah (640–609 BCE) may have wrought significant changes, whether in theory or in practice, to the health-care system. Shrines that may have formerly functioned as therapeutic centers (e.g., Shiloh) may have been destroyed.

The Prayer of Solomon (1 Kgs 8) may be seen, in part, as an attempt to mitigate the loss of the therapeutic roles of the Temple of Jerusalem and outlying shrines. In effect, the Prayer announces that it is not necessary to come to the Temple for therapy, as extending the hands toward the Temple is sufficient to receive healing (1 Kgs 8:38-39). The story of Hezekiah's illness in 2 Kgs 20:1-11 also shows that coming to the Temple was not necessary for healing. Hezekiah, in fact, intends to go to the Temple after he is healed (2 Kgs 20:5).

Newer studies are also emphasizing how authors use disabled characters to promote political and theological agendas in their narratives. Thus, the disability of Saul's descendants may be a sign that they are disqualified from dynastic succession. For example, Saul's daughter, Michal, is infertile in 2 Sam 6:23, and Mephiboshet, Saul's only surviving descendant at one point, is lame (2 Sam 9:3). The auditory perceptiveness of Ahijah, the unsighted prophet (1 Kgs 14), may be part of a larger emphasis on the superiority of hearing over seeing in the Deuteronomistic History.

Of course, throughout the Bible, one finds the use of certain conditions as symbols of unbelief (Isa 43:8), ignorance (Isa 42:16; 56:10), and other moral defects (2 Pet 1:9). In contrast to these negative attitudes, certain persons are said to have done more after they became disabled than before. For example, Samson is said to have killed more people after his eyes were removed than when he was fully sighted (Judg 17:30). There were laws against the mistreatment of the blind (Lev 19:14; Deut 27:18).

E. The Second Temple Period

By the post-exilic period the Priestly Code, which may be viewed as an extensive manual on public health that centralizes in the priesthood the power to define illness and health for an entire state, severely restricted access to the Temple for the chronically ill (e.g., "lepers" in Lev 13–14; compare 2 Sam 5:8 on the blind and the lame) because of fear of "impurity."

Laws concerning pure foods (e.g., in Lev 11) were associated with the maintenance of excellent health in some biblical passages (e.g., Dan 1:15), but the motives for the food laws may not be always restricted to health practices. In particular, many scholars think it unlikely that the fear of infections is responsible for prohibitions against eating pork in ancient Israel (Lev 11:7). Cattle were also susceptible to some infections, but were not prohibited. Other explanations for the prohibition against pork cite economics or the role of pork in maintaining ethnic boundaries.

In any event, the theology of impurity, as a system of social boundaries, could serve to remove socioeconomically burdensome populations, and especially the chronically ill, from society. New demographic groups (those exiled because of chronic illnesses) may have been created by these policies, as the group of "lepers" roaming outside the city in 2 Kgs 7:3 indicates (see also 2 Sam 5:7-8). In effect, the Priestly Code minimizes state responsibility for the chronically ill, leaving the eradication of illness for a future utopia (Ezek 47:12; compare Isa 35:5-6).

Thanksgiving or "well-being" offerings (Lev 7:11-36) after an illness were probably always acceptable and economically advantageous for the Temple, and may have served as public notice of the readmission of previously ostracized patients to the society (Lev 14:1-32).

The demise of the prophetic office in the early Second Temple period probably led to the wide legitimation of the rofʾim (compare Sir 38), but various types of folk healers and midwives (Exod 1:15-21) may actually have been the most common heath-care consultants.

Another important witness to health care in the Second Temple period is found in the Dead Sea Scrolls. Here, one finds at least two distinct attitudes toward the disabled, particularly the blind, deaf, and lame. On the one hand, the Temple Scroll appears to regard the blind and deaf as inherently impure, and expands the restrictions found in Leviticus insofar as the Temple Scroll does not allow the blind access even to the entire city of Jerusalem. Similar restrictions are found in the Rule of the Community (1QSa). On the other hand, the remarkable text called Miqsat Maʿase Ha-Torah ("some precepts of the Torah") appears to object to the presence of the blind and deaf in the Temple because of their inability to execute certain procedures, instead of because they are inherently impure. And while in the OT Yahweh is presumed to be the only sender of disease, in the DSS a complex demonology to explain disease is in evidence. The text identified as 4Q560, e.g., seems to reflect the idea that certain demons were responsible for specific illnesses.

Later, we find such an idea elaborated in *T. Sol.* 18, which may have been originally a Jewish work composed as early as the 1st cent. Here, thirty-six demons are responsible for afflictions of specific body parts (e.g., Artosael affects the eyes). In the apocryphal book of Tobit, we find the demon Asmodeus mentioned as the assassin of bridegrooms.

F. Early Christianity

During the 1st cent. CE there was a variety of health-care systems available in Palestine. These health-care systems included those associated with Isis, the Egyptian goddess, and the Greek god Asclepius. In addition, there were secular Greco-Roman traditions associated with Hippocrates, Celsus, and other physicians. In general, good health in Greco-Roman rational traditions resided in a balance of essential substances in the human body. A good diet was viewed as crucial in maintaining that balance.

Given this plurality of health-care systems, NT authors and stories attempted to address real complaints about health care in the Greco-Roman world. One complaint centered on its cost. Some costly imported medicinal substances (e.g., myrrh) were the subject of sarcastic criticism by Greco-Roman authors (e.g., Pliny). At the same time, medical treatment could entail much pain for little or no gain (see Mark 5:26; Luke 8:43). Accordingly, Christianity may have attracted patients who were too poor to afford the fees charged in many Greco-Roman traditions (see Matt 10:8; compare Acts 8:19-20).

Some Greco-Roman traditions insisted that travel to a shrine was necessary for healing. Yet, the popularity of certain healing centers could result in crowding that effectively denied access for the persons who most needed healing (see John 5:1-9). Other traditions restricted healing to certain days, and physicians could be in short supply in some areas.

While prayer in all Near Eastern religious traditions presupposed belief in a deity who heals, Christianity exhibited some significant differences in the role of prayer in healing. Many Greco-Roman traditions combine prayer with elaborate rituals at healing centers, but Christianity's emphasis on the value of faith alone or on very simple rituals served to eliminate the need for travel to such centers (see Matt 8:8; John 5:1-9). Likewise, Christianity resisted temporal restrictions on when healing could be administered (Mark 3:2-5).

In early Christianity, illness may be caused by numerous demonic entities who are not always acting at Yahweh's command (Matt 15:22; Luke 11:14), and not necessarily by the violation of covenant stipulations (John 9:2). Illnesses mentioned include fevers (Mark 1:30), hemorrhages (Matt 9:20), and what has been identified by some scholars as epilepsy (Mark 9:14-29).

The cure for illness may be found in this world, and not simply in some utopian future. Christian healing procedures could also integrate previous approaches rather than reject them outright. For example, some scholars also see the continuation of Mesopotamian healing traditions in the transfer of demons to swine in Mark 5:12-13, and Asclepius traditions in the use of spittle for healing of the blind man at Bethsaida in Mark 8:22-28.

Early Christianity also may be seen as a critique of the Levitical health-care system. Matthew 10:8; Mark 14:3 and other passages indicate that Jesus and his disciples appear to target the very demographic groups ("lepers," blind, and the lame) who may have been marginalized by the health-care policies reflected in Leviticus.

For example, narratives show how Jesus touches lepers without experiencing any adverse effect (Mark 1:41). Such stories also indicate how Jesus' activities served to reintegrate the sick back into the family.

At the same time, there were other Jewish healers said to be active around the time of Jesus (e.g., Hanina ben Dosa). Indeed, early Christianity preserved many older Hebrew traditions regarding miraculous healings (Acts 5:16; 9:34) and collective health (Jas 5:16). In particular, one may also see Jesus' healing activities as a fulfillment of the arrival of the kingdom of God, which entailed healing the blind, deaf, and lame (compare Isa 35:5-6).

Theological themes could be expressed through healing stories. The progressive healing of the blind man at Bethsaida, for instance, could mirror the progressive revelation of Jesus' messianic mission in Mark. The interplay between blindness/darkness and light has also been linked to the theme of recognizing the divine nature of Jesus and his movement (e.g., John 9:10-11; Acts 9:18).

It is difficult to evaluate one health-care system as better than another because we lack precise data to measure their effectiveness. Some institutions meant to cure may have actually spread diseases by concentrating sick people in small spaces (e.g., Asclepieia). The best medical technology (e.g., scalpels, forceps, dental drills, and splints) may have helped only simple problems (e.g., extraction of lodged weapons). In general, trauma (from accidents, strife), malnutrition, and disease maintained general life expectancy to under forty years during the biblical periods.

In any case, the study of health care is in the midst of a transition from emphasis on determining diagnoses of ancient conditions to more holistic approaches centered on how socioreligious frameworks interact with health care. Disability studies, which focuses on how certain conditions result in the differential valuation of human beings, will probably become increasingly important. Disability studies, in turn, will probably interact more intensely with the study of physiognomy, the ancient art or "science" that judged human character on the basis of physical appearance.

In addition, one is already witnessing the growth of what may be termed "corporeal criticism," which centers on the entire experience of embodiment. Indeed, the integration of medical anthropology, sociology, and biblical studies will probably become more significant in the study of health in ancient Israel and the Near East within the coming decades.

Bibliography: Martin Albl. "'Are Any Among You Sick?' The Health Care System in the Letter of James." *JBL* 121 (2002) 123–43; American Academy of Pediatrics. "Circumcision Policy Statement." *Pediatrics* 103/3 (March 1999) 686–93; Hector Avalos. *Illness and Health Care in the Ancient Near East: The Role of the Temple in Greece, Mesopotamia, and Israel* (1995); Hector Avalos. *Health Care and the Rise of Christianity* (1999); Hector Avalos et al. *This Abled Body: Rethinking Disabilities in Biblical Studies* (forthcoming); Vered Eshed et al. "Tooth Wear and Dental Pathology at the Advent of Agriculture. New Evidence from the Levant." *American Journal of Physical Anthropology* 130 (2006) 130–45; Vivian Nutton. *Ancient Medicine* (2004); Mikeal C. Parsons. "The Character of the Lame Man in Acts 3-4." *JBL* 124 (2005) 295–312; Douglas L. Penney and Michael O. Wise. "By the Power of Beelzebub: An Aramaic Incantation Formula from Qumran (4Q560)." *JBL* 113 (1994) 627–50; John Pilch. *Healing in the New Testament: Insights from Medical and Mediterranean Anthropology* (2000); Maria Barbara Stafford. *Body Criticism: Imaging the Unseen in Enlightenment Art and Medicine* (1997); John Wilkinson. *The Bible and Healing: A Medical and Theological Commentary* (1998); Joseph Zias. "Death and Disease in Ancient Israel." *BA* 54 (1991) 146–59.

HECTOR AVALOS

HEAP OF STONES [אֲבָנִים גַּל gal ʿavanim]. This phrase is used in different ways in the OT. Heaps of stones are markers set up to cause future generations to remember a major event or person. Stones may be set up to mark a covenant agreement, as between Jacob and Laban in Gen 31:46-52. In other instances heaps of stones mark the burial places of three people, Achan, the King of Ai, and Absalom, none of whom are positive figures in the literature (Josh 7:26; 8:29; 2 Sam 18:17).

C. MARK MCCORMICK

HEART [לֵב lev; καρδία kardia]. Most of the inner organs of the human body—throat, nostrils, kidneys,

entrails, and the heart—have specific symbolic meanings in the Bible. The kidneys, e.g., were considered to be the location of conscience, presumably because they are the part of the body that is likely to cause pain for someone with bad conscience. Unlike Western cultures, which primarily associated the heart with feelings and emotions, Near Eastern culture emphasized its role in thinking, reasoning, and planning. The heart characterizes humans first and foremost as "rational beings" that are susceptible to teaching and learning, as Deut 29:3 points out: "Yet to this day, Yahweh has not given you a heart to understand, or eyes to see, or ears to hear." Just as every other part of the human nature has its particular perceptive function so, too, has the heart.

The heart also pertains to human conduct and action. The Shema (Deut 6:4-5) distinguishes three forms in which Israel is supposed to love God: with all its soul (nefesh נֶפֶשׁ), with all its heart (lev), and with all its powers (meʾodh מְאֹד). Assuming that the language here is not merely cumulative, these three capacities point to different ways in which human beings immerse themselves in the world around them. Especially in the psalms the soul expresses human neediness and dependence on natural as well as social environments that support and sustain the life of the individual. By the same token, the soul stands for the human longing and desire to connect with the world of the living—as opposed to the sheʾol (שְׁאוֹל), the Netherworld, to which the soul is headed once it loses this connection. In contrast to this intuitive and existential longing, meʾod emphasizes the physical strength and, occasionally, also the economic power of a human being. Given these two capacities that enable the individual to love God it is safe to assume that the heart, too, expresses a distinct aspect of human vitality.

The heart is also important for theological reflection on the human condition. In the non-priestly parts of the flood narrative humankind is characterized as thoroughly and incurably evil. More specifically it is the "imagination of the thoughts of his heart" that makes a person evil (Gen 6:5). Here the heart stands for the capacity of human beings to act consciously and also strategically—the Hebrew term khashav (חָשַׁב), in a more literal translation, suggests that humans are able to "make plans." However, nothing good springs from what the heart conceives and desires. As Gen 8:21 explains, human wickedness is not merely a product of their socialization, it is with them from the days of their youth on. And this is not as a consequence of human choice, but rather simply seems to be their nature. Note that both Gen 6:5 and 8:21 are observational and not explanatory statements: it is not said that human beings themselves are guilty for their evil hearts, nor that God created them evil. Indeed the question "why" is never asked. One hardly would have understood this as coincidental, but rather as a programmatic omission: no insight or informative power is attributed to this question. Whatever it was that led a person to become evil is irrelevant for the life that that person must lead; it does not change the fact of that person's evil heart.

Other texts that associate human wickedness with the heart are Jer 31:31-34 and Ezek 11:19; 36:26-27. Here, the human inability to act in accordance with Torah is the major defect in human life. However, the prophetic voices express an expectation that contrasts with the flood narrative: God will change the human condition so that the rhythm of the heart and the regulations of the Torah will be in perfect harmony. According to Jeremiah, God will inscribe the Torah on the heart. Ezekiel, on the other hand, suggests that an even more incisive act will be necessary: God will fashion a new heart that will eventually be able to embrace the will of God as expressed in his law. The implication is that, until the formation of the new heart, humanity's creation is both imperfect and incomplete.

In both traditions, the idea of perfection and ongoing divine creation is connected with the image of the new heart. Historically, such a view can be well understood as expressing the hopes and expectations of the early Persian period—a time of restoration and recovery after almost a century of economic and cultural numbness. On the other hand, such a view obviously is in danger of expecting too much, of overstepping the mark, and so of failing to account for the more commonplace realities that would not seem to support the idea of an ultimately perfected and hence unbreakable relationship with God. This is one of the problems with which late biblical prophecy struggled for generations and that eventually could not be resolved.

In wisdom literature it is especially Ecclesiastes' anthropology in which the notion of the heart assumes a central role. In the scenario of a self-experiment the author of Ecclesiastes exposes his heart to the joys and grief of the common person and to the pursuit of wisdom in order to find out where in all of this true happiness could be found (Eccl 1:17; 2:3, 20; 8:9). What connects several of these statements to each other is their use of idioms, according to which one can "transpose" the heart into a particular context where it can learn and perceive things. Thus the wise person has her heart upon the "right side," symbolizing honesty, righteousness, and intelligence, while the fool allows it to sit at her left, her bad side (Eccl 10:2). Qoheleth directs his heart toward an examination of wisdom and foolishness. According to Eccl 2:3, this experiment is even doubled: Qoheleth directs his heart toward the attainment of wisdom, while allowing his "flesh" to share in sensuous delights. Here, heart is that which is able to acquire knowledge and simultaneously weigh and evaluate this knowledge. In a certain sense, it is the cognitive center in distinction

to the "flesh" that bestows upon a person manifest joy or pain. However, the heart also has an emotional component: what the heart sees can lead it to despondency, to "losing heart"—such as in the recognition that goods and property have no permanence under the sun. The heart can also be restless and lack peace when it fails to find fulfillment in that which it does or desires. By occupying itself with wisdom, the heart simultaneously confronts that which moderns call the "burden of existence."

Ecclesiastes presents the most comprehensive account of the heart in the OT. In its view, the heart is that with which a human being perceives the world around herself and responds to it. In that sense Ecclesiastes seems to use "heart" in close analogy to the Greek concept of "mind." However, "heart" implies more than "mind," because, ultimately, it expresses the human striving for the good life. The further a human life progresses, the more it reflects upon its natural striving for happiness. However, Qoheleth is not content with a purely empirical-biographical description, but turns his meditation on the heart in a theological direction: eventually, it is God who places the longing for happiness in the heart. For Qoheleth, it is good fortune when God grants a person the ability to enjoy those things that make life comfortable. Qoheleth even imagines it as the best-case scenario of the good life when a person is completely consumed by such things, when that person has, to a certain degree, no time to think about "the length of his days" (Eccl 5:18-19) and to fall into melancholy thoughts. Indeed, God grants such happiness, though not equally to each person—as Qoheleth notes. On the other hand, God has also placed eternity into the heart (Eccl 3:10-11), and with it the knowledge of one's own finitude and the limitations of knowledge and wisdom. Or in other words: by making human beings aware of the infinite, God throws them back upon their own limitations and thus robs them of the possibility for a carefree life.

As in the OT, the heart (kardia) in NT texts is the seat of rational thought and intentions. Evil intentions come from the heart (Mark 7:21; 15:19), and "what comes out of the mouth proceeds from the heart" (Mark 15:18). Those who are "pure in heart" will be blessed (Matt 5:8), but the evil intentions of the heart are tantamount to sinful deeds (Matt 5:28), and the true inclinations of the heart cannot be hidden from God (1 Cor 4:5; Heb 4:12). The heart is the place from which people understand the true spirit of the law (Mark 10:5; John 12:40), and true forgiveness must come from the heart (Matt 18:35). The heart is also associated with COURAGE in NT passages where listeners are told to "take heart" (Matt 9:2; 14:27) and are praised for not losing heart (2 Cor 4:16; Heb 12:3, 5). To hold something or someone in one's heart is to treasure it (Luke 2:51; Phil 1:7).

Bibliography: Silvia Schroer and Thomas Staubli. *Body Symbolism in the Bible* (2001); Hans-Walter Wolff. *Anthropology of the Old Testament* (1974).

ANDREAS SCHUELE

HEARTH [אֲרִיאֵל ʾariʾel, הַרְאֵל harʾel, יָקוּד yaqudh, מוֹקְדָה moqedhah; ἐσχάρα eschara]. A number of Hebrew and Greek terms in the NRSV are translated "hearth," most often referring to the highest stage or edge of the altar of burnt offering where sacrificial offerings were placed. The term yaqudh (Isa 30:14) probably refers to a domestic hearth, either a hole in the ground or an aboveground oven where a fire was kindled for cooking or warmth.

RALPH K. HAWKINS

HEAT AND COLD [קֹר וָחֹם qor wakhom]. As a word pair, this expression appears in Gen 8:22, but in reverse order "cold and heat." Appearing there in sequence with "seedtime and harvest" and "summer and winter," the phrase has traditionally been understood to denote the cold and hot seasons of the year (as in Pr Azar 1:45). But there is no reason not to interpret the syntagm as referring to the cold and hot portions of a single day in parallel with the fourth word pair, "day and night" (as in Gen 31:40). The Hebrew word for "cold" (qor) is a HAPAX LEGOMENA, and its adjectival derivative never refers to a season, but, e.g., to "cold flowing streams" (Jer 18:14) and "cold water to a thirsty soul" (Prov 25:25). Khom is used in Gen 18:1; 1 Sam 11:11; and 2 Sam 4:5 for "the heat of the day," and for heat that melts snow (Job 24:19) and the warmth of freshly baked bread (1 Sam 21:7). *See* ISRAEL, CLIMATE OF.

MILTON ENG

HEATHEN. *See* NATIONS.

HEAVEN [שָׁמַיִם shamayim, רָקִיעַ raqiʿa; οὐρανός ouranos]. The term *heaven* is used both in an astronomical sense for "sky" or cosmic space and in a theological sense for the divine realm far above the earth.

    A. Heaven in the Ancient Near East
    B. Heaven in the Old Testament
    C. Heaven in the Greco-Roman World
    D. Heaven in the New Testament
    Bibliography

A. Heaven in the Ancient Near East

The people of the ANE believed that the gods resided in the vast cosmic realm, and their quest for knowledge of this realm was one of the driving forces behind their advances in astronomy and theology. Mesopotamian and Egyptian scientists calculated the movements of the celestial bodies (*see* SCIENCE, EGYPT; SCIENCE, MESOPOTAMIA). Because the celestial bodies were regarded as gods, their movements or appearance might foreshadow what would happen on earth.

The people of the Mesopotamian empires did not imagine human beings "going to heaven." Rather, what awaited humans after death was a shadowy existence in the netherworld. Some myths suggest that super mortals might succeed in entering heaven with the permission of the gods, but that was the fate of only a select few. The ancient Egyptians, however, developed elaborate beliefs about heavenly afterlife. The 3rd millennium *Pyramid Texts* reveal that only the Pharaoh—who was regarded as a god during his life—could ascend to heaven to join the celestial circuit after death. In the 2nd millennium *Coffin Texts*, it appears that this heavenly afterlife became available to the royal family and other notables. Finally, in the ultimate democratization of this theme, the 1st millennium *Book of the Dead* relates that even commoners could hope for afterlife in heaven (*see* BOOK OF THE DEAD; EGYPT).

B. Heaven in the Old Testament

The ancient Israelites imagined the cosmos according to the common ANE tripartite model (heaven, earth, netherworld). The Hebrew term shamayim can be translated as either "heaven" (the realm of the gods) or "sky" (the atmosphere or celestial realm). Even though the form is plural, this does not imply that the ancient Hebrews had a notion of multiple heavens. Rather, the plural form stresses the vastness of the heavenly realm from horizon to horizon. The phrase "heaven of heaven(s)" (Neh 9:6) refers not to multiple heavens, but is simply a Hebrew superlative phrase—"vast heaven," or "the highest reaches of the sky." The related term "firmament" (raqiʿa) denotes the region between the divine realm and earth (Gen 1:6-7, 20) where the celestial bodies move (Gen 1:6-8, 14-17). It can also be used as a synonym for shamayim (Gen 1:8).

Biblical tradition asserts that God created the heavens (Gen 1:1; *see* CREATION). That the first ancient Israelites imagined the heavenly realm as a vast cosmic canopy is apparent from the use of the verb natah (נָטָה "stretch out" or "spread") to describe how God "stretched out" this canopy over earth (2 Sam 22:10; Isa 40:22, 42:5, 44:24, 45:12, 51:13, 16; Jer 10:12, 51:15; Zech 12:1; Ps 104:2; Job 9:8). The second image of the material composition of the heavenly realm involves a firm substance. The term raqiʿa "firmament" (from Vulgate's *firmamentum*) is based on the root rqʿ (רקע), which means "stamp out" or "forge." Thus, it may be that some imagined the raqiʿa to be a firm substance on which the celestial bodies rode during their daily journeys across the sky.

It is likely that the ancient Israelites held these and other images together as parts of a large complex of ideas about the heavenly realms. The texts of the OT were composed over hundreds of years and so attest changes in views about humans' relationship to heaven.

The early Israelites believed that heaven was the realm of the divine alone; it had no place for humans (e.g., Ps 115:16-17). These people believed that the dead descended into the netherworld (SHEOL) and did not ascend into heaven. The exclusion from heaven was not based on moral criteria, but it happened to all without discrimination. Even the holy prophet Samuel did not go to heaven; he died and descended into the netherworld (1 Sam 28). The fate of Enoch (Gen 5:21-24) and Elijah (2 Kgs 2:1-18) is ambiguous, and later Jewish and Christian traditions locate them on earth, often at the mystical ends of the earth. It is not until later that the hope for a heavenly afterlife emerged (Ecc 3:21, Dan 12:1-3, and note also Pss 16, 49, 73). This evolution is entirely predictable, however, for these texts were composed when Jews lived under Persian and Greek domination, peoples who had extensive beliefs about heavenly afterlife. Greek beliefs, in particular, had a transformative impact on images of heaven in early Judaism and Christianity. As the early Jewish communities interacted with the Greek cosmologies, they changed the ways they imagined the cosmos and their place in it.

C. Heaven in the Greco-Roman World

Ancient Greek scholars likewise explored heaven (ouranos) in terms of both science and theology/philosophy. As in the ANE, the early Greeks had a tripartite cosmology (heaven, earth, netherworld) and believed that virtually all humans descended into the netherworld at death (e.g., Homer, *Iliad* and *Odyssey*). During the Classical and Hellenistic eras, newer Greek models, based on observations and mathematical calculations, imagined the cosmos as a set of nestled, concentric spheres containing the celestial bodies orbiting the earth, which itself stood at the center of the cosmos. Greek thought placed the gods in heaven, but for the most part the heroes and supermortals resided at the paradisiacal ends of the earth, the Elysian Fields. Due to changes in cosmology that viewed the highest reaches of heaven/sky as the unchanging realm of perfection and purity, after the 5th cent. BCE the Greeks imagined that the soul sought to ascend to heaven after death. The souls were purified as they ascended, and when they arrived at the highest heaven, they were pure and perfect, returning to what the Greeks thought was the soul's original state (*see* GREEK RELIGION AND PHILOSOPHY).

D. Heaven in the New Testament

The early Jewish communities had complex images of heaven that depended both on the images found in the OT and on the images forged from their encounters with Greco-Roman images of the cosmos and of postmortem life in heaven. The statements attributed to Jesus in the canonical gospels seem mostly to imagine heaven after the traditional single heaven model of the OT. In the gospels, people are rewarded in heaven for righteous behavior on earth (Matt 5:12, 6:20), and heaven is a mansion with many rooms (John 14:2). However, in the Gospel of John, Jesus is depicted as a heavenly being that came to earth and returned to heaven after his crucifixion, following a Greco-Roman model. Early Christians likewise believed that after his resurrection, Jesus ascended to heaven, whence they await his return (Acts 1:9-11, compare with the longer ending of Mark, 16:19; and Luke 24:51; *see* ASCENSION). Other early Christian texts evidence similar stress on the heavenly divinity of Jesus and speculation on the punishments and rewards meted out on individuals as they seek to ascend to heaven after death.

Paul's epistles attest Greco-Roman images of cosmology and of heaven as a place for the righteous. In 2 Cor 12:1-4 Paul recounts an ascent to heaven, in which he ascended to the "third heaven," which he also calls "paradise," where he learned secrets he could not recount to mere mortals (2 Cor 12:2, 4). Narratives recounting heavenly ascents became popular during the Greco-Roman era, and Paul is squarely in this tradition. Paul also assuaged the concerns of his followers in Thessalonica about the fate of Christians who die before Jesus' return by telling them that all Christians, the living and the dead, would one day ascend to meet Jesus (1 Thess 4:13-18). These two texts attest that Paul and his churches believed that righteous Christians would enjoy a heavenly afterlife. These texts provide, however, no details about what the righteous do in heaven, whether it is unending contemplation of the divine or joyous reunion with family and friends.

The Book of Revelation, the last book in the Christian Bible, ends with heaven on earth. According to this text God controls all eschatological events from a heavenly throne, with Jesus at God's side (Rev 4:2-3, 9-11; 5:5-7; *see* ESCHATOLOGY OF THE NT). After the complete devastation of the earth and the cosmos, Revelation imagines that righteous Christians will be resurrected and will reign over the earth with Jesus for a millennium (Rev 20:4-6). After this the "new heaven (ouranos) and new earth" replace the old (Rev 21:1). The righteous, however, do not ascend to the new heaven; rather, the new heaven descends to earth in the form of the NEW JERUSALEM (Rev 21:2). The righteous have achieved heavenly existence with God, but it has been achieved by transforming earth and by bringing heaven down to earth.

Christians developed much more elaborate images of heaven that reached their zenith with Dante Alighieri's *The Divine Comedy* in the 13th cent. and that continue to evolve to this day. Jewish, Islamic, and other religious images of heaven are heirs of earlier traditions and yet continue to evolve as they seek to address modern cosmology and modern socio-religious needs. *See* AFTERLIFE; ASTRONOMY, ASTROLOGY; COSMOGNY, COSMOLOGY; DEAD, ABODE OF THE;

DEATH, NT; DEATH, OT; JUDGMENT; PARADISE; RESURRECTION, NT; RESURRECTION, OT; SHEOL.

Bibliography: Alan E. Bernstein. *The Formation of Hell: Death and Retribution in the Ancient and Early Christian Worlds* (1993); Mary Dean-Otting. *Heavenly Journeys: A Study of the Motif in Hellenistic Jewish Literature* (1984); James Evans. *The History & Practice of Astronomy* (1998); Martha Himmelfarb. *Ascent to Heaven in Jewish and Christian Apocalypses* (1993); Wayne Horowitz. *Mesopotamian Cosmic Geography* (1998); Colleen McDannell and Bernhard Lang. *Heaven: A History* (1988); Jeffrey Burton Russell. *A History of Heaven: The Singing Silence* (1997); James D. Tabor. *Things Unutterable: Paul's Ascent to Paradise in its Greco-Roman, Judaic, and Early Christian Contexts* (1986); J. Edward Wright. *The Early History of Heaven* (2000).

J. EDWARD WRIGHT

HEAVEN, ASCENT TO. *See* ASCENT TO HEAVEN.

HEAVEN, HOST OF. *See* HOSTS, HOST OF HEAVEN.

HEAVEN, NEW. *See* NEW HEAVEN, NEW EARTH.

HEAVEN, QUEEN OF. *See* QUEEN OF HEAVEN.

HEAVENLY BODIES [σώματα ἐπουρανία sōmata epourania]. Heavenly or celestial bodies are mentioned and contrasted with "earthly bodies" in 1 Cor 15:40, as part of a Paul's discourse on the nature of the resurrected bodies of believers. Similar discussions about the nature of mortal and immortal bodies are found in Greco-Roman literature. Lucretius, the Epicurean author of the 1ˢᵗ cent. BCE, argues (*De Rerum Natura* 2.991–1022) that human beings originate from an indestructible "celestial seed" ("*caelesti . . . semine*"; see 1 Cor 15:38). Cicero (*De Natura Deorum* 1.18) argues that divine bodies, though similar in form to human bodies, "do not contain blood" (see 1 Cor 15:50). *See* EARTHLY BODIES; RESURRECTION, NT.

HECTOR AVALOS

HEAVENLY FATHER [ὁ πατὴρ ὁ οὐράνοις ho patēr ho ouranois]. Used by Jesus, primarily in Matthew (but Luke 11:13), as a metaphor to portray God as perfect (Matt 5:48) and powerful (Matt 15:13; 18:35), but also as deeply caring for humanity and intimately connected to creation (Matt 6:26-32). *See* FATHER IN HEAVEN; GOD, NAMES OF.

JESSICA TINKLENBERG DEVEGA

HEBER hee'buhr [חֶבֶר khever]. "Companion, association." The name of several individuals in the OT. 1. A son of Beriah, the son of Asher, the son of Jacob by Zilpah, as listed in Gen 46:17-18 and Num 26:45. The genealogy is repeated in 1 Chr 7:31 and 8:17.

2. An individual listed in the extended genealogy of Judah and identified as the father of Soco (1 Chr 4:18).

3. The Kenite husband of JAEL (Judg 4:11, 17; 5:24). In Judg 4, Deborah and Barak battle the Canaanite king Jabin of Hazor, and his general Sisera. The narrative explains that Heber had separated from the other Kenites and was living with his wife in the area of Kadesh, where the battle occurs. Barak engages the Canaanite army and defeats it. Sisera flees the battle and runs to the tent of Jael, the wife of Heber. She invites Sisera into her tent to hide; when he falls asleep, Jael splits his head open with a hammer and tent peg.

C. MARK MCCORMICK

HEBREW BIBLE. Hebrew Bible is a term that has come into widespread use in academic circles and with people engaged in Jewish-Christian dialogue to describe the shared corpus of Jews and Christians and the object of academic study. Increased effort in CHRISTIAN-JEWISH RELATIONS after the Holocaust made Christians, Jews, and biblical scholars more sensitive to ways in which the "Old Testament" implies the incompleteness of the "Old" and the necessity of a "New." Hebrew Bible is an attempt to overcome the problem of the designation "Old Testament," which is an exclusively Christian term, often felt by Jews to be pejorative. The corpus of the Hebrew Bible comprises the books originally written in Hebrew shared by Protestant, Catholic, and Orthodox Christians and Jews, but not the deuterocanonical additions and deuterocanonical books that are canonical in the Orthodox and Catholic traditions (*see* APOCRYPHA, DEUTEROCANONICAL). The term is imperfect because parts of the Hebrew Bible (such as sections of Daniel and Ezra) were written in Aramaic, and because it can misleadingly suggest specialist study of the Hebrew text only, rather than a corpus that can also be studied in translation. However, the term is useful because it avoids the sense of a specifically Jewish text (as in the word TANAKH) or a specifically Christian one (as in the phrase "Old Testament") and emphasizes the commonality of the book. *See* ANTI-JUDAISM.

YVONNE SHERWOOD

HEBREW LANGUAGE. Hebrew is the language in which the OT was originally composed, with the exception of a few sections of the corpus that were written in Aram. (Jer 10:11; Ezra 4:8-6:18; 7:12-26; Dan 2:4*b*-7:28; and one phrase in Gen 31:47; *see* ARAMAIC, ARAMAISM), a relative of Hebrew within the family of Semitic Languages. While the term *Hebrew* (masc. ʿibrî עִבְרִי, fem. ʿibrîyah עִבְרִיָּה) was applied to persons in the Bible (e.g., Gen 14:13, Exod 1:15, and Jer 34:9), the term was not extended to the language of the Israelites until the Second Temple Period, as attested by the use of the Gk. terms Hebraisti (Ἑβραϊστί; "[in] Hebrew"; Sir prologue line 22; John 5:2) and **Hebraidi dialektō**

(Ἑβραΐδι διαλέκτῳ; "Hebrew language"; Acts 21:40) to designate the language, and gegrammenon Hebraisti (γεγραμμενον Ἑβραϊστί; "[in] Hebrew letters"; John 19:20) to indicate the Hebrew script. Sources in later rabbinical literature also use the term ʿibrît (עִבְרִית) to designate the language, in addition to other appellations like lĕšôn haqqodeš (לְשׁוֹן הַקֹּדֶשׁ; "the Holy Tongue"). During the biblical period, the Israelites apparently called the language they spoke the "language (lit., lip) of Canaan" (śĕpaṯ kĕnaʿan [שְׂפַת כְּנַעַן]; Isa 19:18) or "Judahite" (yĕhûdît [יְהוּדִית]; 2 Kgs 18:26, 28//Isa 36:11, 13; Neh 13:24; 2 Chr 32:18), as distinct from a few other languages spoken in the region: "Ashdodite" (ʾašdôdît [אַשְׁדּוֹדִית]; Neh 13:24) and "Aramaic" (ʾărāmît [אֲרָמִית]; 2 Kgs 18:26 //Isa 36:11; Dan 2:4). This article treats primarily the various types of Biblical Hebrew and the contemporaneous vernacular form(s) of Hebrew spoken during the biblical period, although Hebrew has remained a literary, scholarly, and scriptural language within the Jewish community for the past two thousand years (much like the status of Latin within the medieval church). The Modern Hebrew language as spoken in Israel today will not be discussed here.

A. Hebrew Among the Semitic Languages

Hebrew is a member of the Semitic family of languages, itself one of the members of the larger Afro-Asiatic group of languages (which also includes the Chadic, Omotic, Berber, Egyptian, and Cushitic families). Hebrew occupies a privileged position in this family, both because of its long span of attestation and because of the great importance attached to the biblical texts. Because scholars have devoted so much work to the analysis of biblical material, Biblical Hebrew is the most widely studied and well researched of the ancient Semitic languages. The thorough analysis of Hebrew has enabled Semitists to position the language quite accurately within the Semitic family.

The hypothetical linguistic ancestor to which the origins of all Semitic languages can be traced is called Proto-Semitic. This ancestor divided into two branches. Akkadian and Eblaite form the East Semitic branch, while the remainder of languages may be grouped together under the rubric "West Semitic." These West Semitic languages share the innovation whereby the verbal adjective qatala became used as the perfect verb (see §D2c.). The West Semitic group can be further divided between the South Semitic family, in which are found the Ethiopic languages (such as Geʿez, Amharic, Tigrinya, etc.), and the Central Semitic family, distinguished by its use of the yaqtulu form to designate the imperfect. The Central Semitic family is further subdivided into three branches: Arabic, Old (or, Epigraphic) South Arabian, and the Northwest Semitic group, of which Hebrew is a member. Characteristic of Northwest Semitic is the sound change through which initial *w becomes y (see §D1), and the formation of plurals in *qatl, *qitl, and *qutl nouns through the addition of a in the pattern. Both changes can be seen in the Hebrew word /yĕlāḏîm/ילְדִים/"boys." The Northwest Semitic languages include Ugaritic, the various dialects of Aram. (ranging from the oldest epigraphic material, to Imperial Aram., to Syriac, to modern dialects like Turoyo, the dialect of the Deir Alla "Balaam" inscription (see DEIR ALLA, TEXTS), the dialect of ancient Samʾal (modern Zinjirli), and the Canaanite languages. Hebrew is part of the Canaanite group of languages, which includes also Phoenician, Moabite, Ammonite, and Edomite. Common to all these languages is the rounding of original *ā to ō (the so-called "Canaanite Shift"); the change of the 1st c.sg. suffix on the perfect form from *-tŭ to *-tĭ; the leveling of -nŭ as the suffix of the 1st c.pl.; and certain changes in the D (i.e., Hebrew piʿel) and C (hipʿil) stems. Ancient Hebrew is itself by no means a monolithic language, synchronically or diachronically, as a study of its various phases shows.

B. Phases of Hebrew

The term "Biblical Hebrew" covers a period of more than one thousand years, from roughly 1200–150 BCE. During this time, the Hebrew language changed in both its grammar (morphology and syntax) and its lexicon, though these changes were not as drastic as those that have affected, e.g., English in the last thousand years. We can divide Biblical Hebrew language into three major historical phases, called Archaic, Standard, and Late Biblical Hebrew.

Archaic Biblical Hebrew (12th–11th cent. BCE) is represented by a number of poetic biblical passages, including the Song of Deborah (Judg 5), the Song of the Sea (Exod 15), and the Blessings of Jacob (Gen 49), among others. The language of all poetry is naturally different from prose, including the use of rare or archaic words, but these particular texts also preserve archaic grammatical forms that testify to their age. It is presumed that these oldest texts were transmitted orally until they were incorporated into the writing of the biblical books.

The great majority of the preexilic biblical books contain what is usually called Standard Biblical Hebrew (10th–6th cent. BCE). This is the dialect of Judah, which was developed as the literary standard of ancient Israel.

Even before the exile to Babylon in the 6th cent. BCE, the spoken Hebrew language must have been slowly diverging from the written language, as happens naturally with all languages. But the exile itself signified a major turning point in the evolution of Hebrew. The settlement of the Israelite population among a foreign nation logically resulted in changes in the Israelites' language. In particular, Aram. came to have a strong influence on all aspects of Hebrew. Most texts written in the postexilic period (Ezra, Nehemiah, Daniel, Chronicles, Ecclesiastes, and Esther) are of a noticeably different character than preexilic texts, reflecting the evolution of the spoken language. This phase of Hebrew is called Late Biblical Hebrew (6th–2nd cent. BCE). This is not to say that the Hebrew of all postexilic books is identical. In some cases authors attempted to reproduce good Standard Biblical Hebrew (as in Chronicles), while the Hebrew of other late books (especially Song of Songs and Job) reflects what is best called a non-standard dialect of Late Biblical Hebrew.

The diachronic differences of Hebrew discussed above are distinctive, though precise dates cannot be given for the beginning or end of each phase. The language changed gradually over time. But in addition to the diachronic differences of Hebrew, it must also be noted that there were synchronic variations of the language. In each period there were geographic variations of Hebrew that can be called dialects. Usually a distinction is made between Standard Hebrew (also called Southern or Judean) and Northern Hebrew (also called Israelian). Traces of the Northern Hebrew dialect are found in many parts of the Bible, and from all historical periods, ranging from the archaic poem in Judg 5 to late books like Song of Songs. Dialect differences are even referred to in the Bible itself, most famously in the so-called Shibboleth incident (Judg 12:6), where we learn of a difference in pronunciation between the Gileadites and Ephraimites.

Epigraphic Hebrew (*see* INSCRIPTIONS) is probably not to be considered as a separate dialect of Hebrew, but with regards to orthography it is often distinct from the Biblical Hebrew with which it was contemporary. There are even some differences in vocabulary, with words attested in ways that are not found in the Bible. (see §C.)

Hebrew continued to be spoken for several centuries beyond the biblical period, and has remained in use as a written language up to the present day. The Hebrew of the post-biblical period until ca. 5th or 6th cent. CE is known as Rabbinic or Mishnaic Hebrew. This is the language of the Mishnah, Tosefta, and many Midrashim. It is descended from the northern dialect of Hebrew and has been strongly influenced by Aram., which by ca. 3rd cent. CE had completely supplanted Hebrew as a spoken language in Israel.

Even though Hebrew died out as a living spoken language, at no point did it ever cease to be used as a literary language. After the rabbinic period, there is an enormous amount of Hebrew literature attested, in a wide variety of genres, from all over Europe, western Asia, and northern Africa. The many types of texts include liturgical poetry (pîyûṭ פִּיּוּט), secular poetry, philosophy, linguistics, history, scientific treatises, legal texts, and biblical commentaries. Not only was there great variation in genre and place of composition, but also the Hebrew language itself is quite varied in these texts. Some authors imitated the biblical or rabbinic style, while others imitated an Arabic or European style. A large number of words were created from Hebrew roots, while many others were borrowed from local languages (esp. Arabic). This Hebrew, from the rabbinic period until about the 18th cent., can be called Medieval Hebrew, for lack of a better term, though with the caveat that this Hebrew is by no means uniform.

In the late 18th cent., Hebrew entered its modern period, and from this point we begin to see a trend towards secular Hebrew literature. This trend was advanced greatly by the establishment of Hebrew schools and newspapers in Palestine during the 1880s. It was also at this time that there began a revival of Hebrew as a spoken language, a phenomenon which developed very quickly as a result of large-scale Jewish immigration to Palestine in the late 19th and early 20th cent. Hebrew became an official language of British Palestine in 1922, and of the State of Israel upon its establishment in 1948. Today, Israeli Hebrew is a thriving modern language, used for all aspects of life in Israel, while Biblical and Rabbinic Hebrew still play an important role in Jewish religion and learning.

C. Sources and Texts

The largest and most well known source for the study of the Hebrew language from the Iron Age to the Persian and Hellenistic periods is the OT, of which the earliest complete or nearly complete manuscripts of the OT date to ca. 10th and early 11th cent. CE (*see* ALEPPO CODEX; LENINGRAD CODEX). Earlier biblical manuscripts, such as those from the DEAD SEA SCROLLS corpus and some fragments from the Cairo Genizah, provide invaluable witness to the early history of the Bible and its textual traditions. Although these manuscripts reflect some variation in the orthographic practices and the vocalization traditions of the communities in which they were produced, they all preserve Biblical Hebrew in its classical form. Unfortunately, relatively little evidence regarding the Hebrew spoken during the biblical period has survived outside of the biblical text. What little material does remain is found in the form of short epigraphic texts, which provide additional information about Hebrew as it was spoken before the Hellenistic and Roman periods. These texts can be divided schematically into several genres, among which are scribal texts, monumental texts, funerary inscriptions, letters and epistolary texts, economic texts (receipts, etc.), and graffiti. As noted above (see §B), the language of these texts is very similar to that found in the Bible, with occasional minor differences in orthography and vocabulary.

1. Scribal texts

The earliest texts displaying a paleographic style that is demonstrably similar to what later became the specifically Hebrew national script (over against Phoenician or Aram. national scripts) are scribal texts, i.e., texts that seem to have been used as tools for teaching the practice of writing. A late 10th cent. BCE inscription has been found recently at Tel Zayit that lists the alphabet in a non-traditional order (*see* ZAYIT, TEL). However, because there are no lexemes written in this text, the text does not provide any access to the Hebrew language of the preexilic period. Far more important is the so-called GEZER CALENDAR, a text that is usually interpreted as listing the months in the agricultural cycle of the Canaanite highlands. While it cannot be determined with certainty that the language should be called Hebrew, the orthographic conventions are consistent with the plausible historical developments of the Hebrew language (e.g., yrh [ירח] for /yarhu/ or /yarhō/ < *yarhuhŭ "his (one) month," and yrhw [ירחו] for /yarḥêw/ < *yarḥayhŭ "his two months").

2. Monumental texts

As opposed to other Levantine states that have produced several official texts commemorating kings' reigns and accomplishments (building projects completed, battles fought, etc.), ancient Israel and Judah have as yet produced very few authentic cognate exemplars (compare the Aramaean stela from Tell Dan [*see* INSCRIPTION, TELL DAN], the MOABITE STONE, and the Philistine temple inscription from Ekron). Aside from the "Joash stela," which appeared in 2002 and was quickly recognized as a very well crafted forgery (including the chemical "forgery" of the patina; *see* FORGERIES), the only significant monumental inscription written in Hebrew to have been found in Israel and Judah to date is the SILOAM Tunnel inscription,

commemorating the completion of the tunnel during Hezekiah's reign. Because the date of the inscription can be plausibly identified as the late 8th cent. BCE, this relatively long (and reasonably complete) text provides an important witness to the Hebrew language of that time. The language of the inscription is very much like that of Standard Biblical Hebrew, with only a few exceptions, most notably the rendering of the 3rd f.sg. perfect of the verb hyh (היה; "to be") as hyt (הית) rather than the expected hyth (היתה).

3. Funerary inscriptions

In contrast to the many Phoenician funerary texts that have survived nearly intact, few such Hebrew texts marking the burials of important persons have been preserved. Most well known is the tomb inscription from Silwan, which formerly marked the resting place of a royal official (possibly Shebna, Hezekiah's royal steward). Because of its paleographic similarity to the Siloam Tunnel inscription, this inscription provides further evidence as to the linguistic character of Hebrew during the period ca. 700 BCE. Remarkably, the orthography of both inscriptions suggests that in Judahite Hebrew diphthongs had not yet collapsed by this period, so that Biblical Hebrew /bayit/ (בַּיִת) and its construct form /bêt/ (בֵּית) (see §D2a) were at that time both pronounced as /bayt/.

4. Letters and epistolary texts

There are two major corpora of epistolary texts that provide a synchronic view of the Hebrew language during the final years of the Judahite monarchy (ca. 600 BCE). Many of the letters from Tel Arad (*see* ARAD OSTRACA) comprise a group of administrative documents conveying instructions from an unnamed source to officials at the military camp there. These instructions appear both as commands to move troops, and as instructions for the distribution of food supplies. The LACHISH Letters, apparently a series of short communications sent between officials in the western reaches of Judah, provide further insight into the conventions of letter writing in the preexilic period. The MESAD HASHAVYAHU ostracon, also dating to the late 7th cent. BCE, contains an informal plea for justice to a government official.

5. Economic texts

The SAMARIA OSTRACA provide the most thorough epigraphic example of economic texts. While opinion is divided as to their interpretation, the orthographic conventions of these receipts give some indications of linguistic changes that had occurred in northern Israel (as opposed to the southern dialect recorded in the preponderance of biblical texts). For example, the word št (שת; /šat/ < *šant "year") indicates that the northern Israelites used a slightly different lexeme from that of the southern Judahites, who used the word šnh (שנה; /šānâ/ < *šanat). It is interesting to note that the Israelite form šat is the same form used by the Phoenicians. Similarly, the spelling yn (יׁן /yên/ < *yayn "wine") indicates a variant pronunciation from the more conservative Judahite yyn (ייׁן /yayn/). Most economic texts are relatively informal in their presentation and language, thereby providing some data as to written abbreviations.

6. Graffiti

The informality of economic texts is often surpassed only by graffiti, short texts composed not by formally trained scribes, but rather presumably by untrained or under-trained commoners. A graffito was normally written quickly, so that the execution of the inscription itself is less than perfect (often making the text extremely difficult to read), and the linguistic conventions much less standardized than in monumental or funerary inscriptions. Some important Hebrew graffiti have been found at Khirbet Beit Lei and Khirbet el-Qom (see QOM, KHIRBET EL) but the most often cited graffiti in recent study of Hebrew epigraphy have been those from KUNTILLET ʿAJRUD mentioning "YHWH of Teman" or "YHWH of Samaria" and "his Asherah." Opinion is still divided on how best to interpret the phrase "his Asherah," since normally Hebrew does not employ the personal possessive suffix (in this case, 3rd m.sg. -h [ה]) on proper names (nor does it normally admit of proper names being used in the construct state, as is the case with "YHWH of Samaria"). However, this is exactly the value of graffiti: they record the language as it was spoken in everyday life, not just as it was formalized in official texts and inscriptions.

D. Grammar of Biblical Hebrew

1. Phonology

One must talk about the phonology of the Hebrew language both diachronically—i.e., in terms of the various phases of Hebrew—and as a system somewhat distinct from the graphic (alphabetic) and orthographic (spelling) conventions that were used to depict the language. One must keep in mind that the consonantal text of the OT was written and finalized several centuries before the Masoretic scholars of Tiberias "vocalized" the text by adding vowel signs (see MASORETES). While the Tiberian Masoretes were not the first to vocalize the consonantal text, it is their system that remains the standard tradition of vocalization in use among religious and scholarly communities today.

a. Consonants. The Hebrew language of preexilic Israel and Judah likely had at least twenty-five consonantal phonemes (fig. 1a). However, because the Israelites had borrowed the alphabet from the Phoenicians, who had only twenty-two consonants, at least three signs were used to indicate more than one phoneme (see ALPHABET). Ḥêt (ח) indicated both the unvoiced pharyngeal fricative ḥ and the unvoiced uvular fricative ḫ. This distinction in spoken Hebrew persisted perhaps as late as the 2nd cent. CE, and is preserved in the different transcriptions of Hebrew proper names in LXX (e.g., Hezekias [Εζεκιας] for /ḥizqîyāhû/ [חׁזׁקׁיׁהׁוׁ] vs. Achaz [Ἀχάζ] for /ʾāḥāz/ [אׁחׁז]). Similarly, ʿayin (ע) represented both the voiced pharyngeal fricative (ʿ) and the voiced uvular fricative (ġ). The LXX preserves this distinction as well in names such as Aroēr (Ἀροήρ) for /ʿărōʿer/ (עׁרׁעׁר) and Gaza (Γάζα) for /ġazzâ/ (עׁזׁה). Both sets of phonemes eventually merged so that ḥêt and ʿayin each represented only one consonantal phoneme by the time of the Tiberian Masoretes. The letter ש also represents two distinct phonemes in Biblical Hebrew. However, unlike the previous two examples, the contrast was preserved until the time of the Tiberian Masoretes, who marked the distinction with a diacritic: שׁ for /š/ and שׂ for /ś/. A few other signs with more than one phonetic pronunciation may have existed at the time when Hebrew borrowed the

---

Figure 1a: Proto-Hebrew Phonemic Inventory

	bilabial	dental	lateral	palatal	velar	pharyngeal	glottal
voiced stop	ב b	ד d			ג g		
unvoiced stop	פ p	ת t			כ k		א ʾ
emphatic stop		ט ṭ			ק q		
voiced fricative					ע ġ	ע ʿ	
unvoiced fricative			ש ś	ש š (s)	ח ḫ	ח ḥ	ה h
voiced affricate		ז ᵈz					
unvoiced affricate		ס ᵗs					
emphatic affricate		צ ᵗṣ					
approximant	ו w	ר r	ל l	י y			
nasal	מ m	נ n					

Phoenician alphabet (e.g., ז for both /z/ and /ḏ/, as found in Old Aram.), but those phonemes merged before the appearance of the transcriptional evidence that could confirm such a double pronunciation.

Under the influence of the Aram. vernacular spoken by the Jewish community in the postexilic and Hellenistic periods, the Hebrew language developed a conditioned sound change whereby the plosives b, g, d, k, p, and t (ב, ג, ד, כ, פ, and ת; known by the acronym bĕḡaḏkĕp̄at) developed "spirantized" (fricative) allophones when following vowels, except when the consonants were geminate (doubled; see §D2). The plosives (as well as all geminated consonants) are now usually marked with a daghesh (e.g., ב /b/) while the fricatives remain unmarked (e.g., ב /ḇ/) in modern text editions (fig. 1b).

Figure 1b: Tiberian Pronunciation of Hebrew and Transliteration Chart

	bilabial	interdental	dental	lateral	palatal	velar	pharyngeal	glottal
voiced stop	ב b		ד d			ג g		
unvoiced stop	פ p		ת t			כ k		א ʾ (ʾ)
emphatic stop			ט ṭ (t)			ק q (k)		
voiced fricative	ב ḇ (v)	ד ḏ (dh)	ז z			ג ḡ (gh)	ע ʿ (ʿ)	ה h
unvoiced fricative	פ p̄ (f)	ת ṯ (th)	ס s	שׂ ś (s)	שׁ š (sh)	כ ḵ (kh)	ח ḥ (kh)	
emphatic affricate			צ ṣ (ts)					
approximant	ו w		ר r	ל l	י y			
nasal	מ m		נ n					

Most of the Hebrew consonants can be clustered into groups of three, each group a set comprising voiced, unvoiced, and emphatic (usually glottalized) counterparts. For instance, in the series of dental stops (plosives), the group d, t, and ṭ occurs, and g, k, and q appears as the Hebrew series of velar stops. The dental fricative (sibilant) series was probably a comparable series of affricates (ᵈz, ᵗs, ᵗs), of which the voiced and unvoiced members eventually lost their affrication (becoming z/ז and s/ס respectively). The letter šîn (שׁ) was originally pronounced as /s/, but it shifted to the palatal /š/ prior to loss of affrication in sāmek (ס), and perhaps under pressure from this change. That Hebrew maintained a phonological difference between sāmek and šîn is clear because there is rarely, if ever, confusion between the two signs in the consonantal text of the Bible. The same is not true of śîn /ś/ (שׂ, originally a lateral fricative, comparable to the sound signified by *ll* in Welsh), which was articulated as /s/ by the time of the Masoretes. As opposed to šîn, śîn was occasionally confused with sāmek in the consonantal text of the Bible (see, e.g., the alternative spellings of the word for "folly": /śiklût/[שִׂכְלוּת] and /siklût/[סִכְלוּת] in Eccl 1:17 and 2:3, respectively).

Historically, all of these consonants could be geminated (doubled) when required by the morphological pattern (see §D2). However, by the time of the Tiberian Masoretes, Hebrew had lost the possibility of the gemination of the guttural letters ʾ, h, ḥ, ʿ, and r (א ה ח ע and ר). Pattern-conditioned doubling of these consonants was treated in one of two ways: compensatory lengthening (with ʾ, r, and sometimes ʿ), in which the preceding vowel was lengthened; and "virtual" doubling (with h, ḥ, ʿ), in which no changes were made to the adjacent vowels.

b. Vowels. Proto-Hebrew (i.e., the earliest language that had specifically Hebrew characteristics) had three classes of vowel quality (a, i, and u), each of which could be long or short, although all cases of inherited */ā/ had become /ō/ through a distinctive phonetic change called the "Canaanite Shift." Through historical processes, certain environments could cause a-vowels to develop into /e/ and /ā/, i-vowels into /e/ and /ē/, and u-vowels into /o/ and /ō/. The collapse of diphthongs (e.g., */aw/ > /ō/) and triphthongs (*/ayu/ > /ê/) also contributed to changes in the vowel system. Moreover, propretonic vowel reduction in nouns, and pretonic reduction in verbs — both characteristic changes of Hebrew morphology — added an additional semi-vowel to each class (/ă/, /ĕ/, /ŏ/), along with a murmured šĕwâ vowel (ְ —transcribed here as /ĕ/). There may thus be classified fourteen different resulting phonetic vowels (fig. 2).

2. Morphology

As is the case in all Semitic languages, Hebrew conveys meaning through the use of two interconnected systems: 1) triliteral (but sometimes bi- and quadriliteral) roots, which carry the semantic value, and 2) morphological patterns, which carry the grammatical function. That is to say, varying combinations of root consonants (or "radicals") govern the [general semantic field of each word (e.g., the root mlk [מלך] provides the semantic field of "governing" or "ruling"). The specific lexical meaning of each word is then provided

Figure 2: Tiberian Vowel System			
Vowel Class		**Vowel Length**	
	semi-vowel	*short*	*long*
a-vowels	בֲ ă	בַ a	בָ ā = בָה â
i-vowels	בֱ ĕ	בֶ e	בֵ ē = בֵי ê / בְּי ê
		בִ i	בִ ī = בִי î
u-vowels	בֳ ŏ	בָ o	בֹ ō = בוֹ ô
		בֻ u	בֻ ū = בוּ û
reduced	בְ ĕ		

by the insertion (or "intercalation") of vowels between the root radicals, as well as by the addition of affixes. This process results in the provision of a pattern for the root, often described generically with the paradigmatic root QTL (קטל whereby Q symbolizes the first radical of any root $[R_1]$, T the second $[R_2]$, and L the third $[R_3]$; radicals are capitalized here to emphasize the patterning of vowels within each root). Patterns function as templates, and are described according to the inserted vowels and affixes (e.g., QāTaL, QéTeL, maQTāLâ, QaTLūt). These morphological patterns serve to determine the part of speech of the word, and thereby to limit the lexical meaning of the word (e.g., mālak [מָלַךְ] "he ruled"; melek [מֶלֶךְ] "king"; mamlākâ [מַמְלָכָה] "kingdom"; malkût [מַלְכוּת] "reign"). Some patterns exhibit the doubling ("gemination") or repetition ("reduplication") of one of the radicals (e.g., from the root GLL [גלל] are derived the nouns gillûlîm [גִּלּוּלִים], "idols" [gemination of R_2], and galgal [גַּלְגַּל], "wheel" [reduplication of R_1 and R_2]).

a. The noun. Hebrew nouns exhibit several characteristic patterns, among which are the patterns *QvTL (in which *v* denotes any short vowel), *QaTvL, *QaTv̄L (with *v̄* as any long vowel), and so forth. These patterns often include the addition of prefixes (most commonly the consonant m-, but also t-, and ʾ-), or suffixes, such as -ôn. Examples of such nouns include /migdāl/ (מִגְדָּל; "tower," root: gdl [גדל]), /tardēmâ/ (תַּרְדֵּמָה; "deep sleep," root: rdm [רדם]), /ʾezrāḥ/ (אֶזְרָח; "native," root: zrḥ [זרח]), and /rāṣôn/ (רָצוֹן; "pleasure," root: rṣh [רצה]). Furthermore, Hebrew nouns are marked for several grammatical categories: gender, number, and boundness. Adjectives agree with the nouns they modify in gender and number.

i. Gender and number. The m.s. in Hebrew remains unmarked (i.e., no additional affixes are present that specify number or gender other than masculine singular; sometimes this lack of ending is signified -ø). A common paradigmatic noun used in the study of the Hebrew language is /sûs/ (סוס), meaning "horse." Because there is no marker for the fem., the word may

also be translated as the specifically masculine "stallion." The addition of the f. ending /-â/ (ה ָ) to the word /sûsâ/ (סוּסָה) yields the specifically feminine noun /mare." The m.p. is usually marked with the suffix /-îm/ (ים), and the f.p. with the suffix /-ôt/ (ות), e.g., /sûsîm/ (סוּסִים) "horses, stallions" and /sûsôt/ (סוּסוֹת) "mares." In addition to the pl., proto-Hebrew historically had a suffix that denoted the dual, but these had probably become unproductive by the time that Hebrew is attested in written form. The dual as preserved in the OT is limited to cases of paired body parts (e.g., /yādayim/ [יָדַיִם], "two hands"; compare /yād/ [יָד], "hand") and a few other nouns. The dual remains unmarked for gender, nor is there a dual form of the adjective; instead, the plural is used. With the addition of any of these endings, any vowels in "propretonic" position (i.e., the syllable two before the accented syllable) undergo reduction to a šĕwâ (/nābîʾ/[נָבִיא] "prophet," but /nĕbîʾîm/[נְבִיאִים] "prophets").

ii. Definiteness. Unlike English, which has both an indefinite and definite article (compare "a boy" and "the boy"), Hebrew has only a definite article. An unmarked noun like /sûs/ can be translated into English as either "horse" or "a horse," depending on context. The definite article normally takes the shape of /ha-/ plus the doubling of the first consonant of the marked noun (הַ) except in cases where that consonant cannot be doubled; see §D1), e.g., /hassûs/[הַסּוּס] "the horse" and /hassûsîm/[הַסּוּסִים] "the horses." Proper nouns and possessed nouns (e.g., /malkî/[מַלְכִּי] "my king") are considered definite for syntactic purposes.

iii. Boundness ("state"). Like all ancient Semitic languages, Hebrew indicates possession through the juxtaposition of nouns, with the noun designating ownership at the end of the "construct chain" in the absolute state (i.e., the dictionary form). Absolute nouns may be marked as definite with the definite article, or with a personal pronominal suffix. The noun possessed appears in the chain in the bound state, and may not be marked for definiteness, the presence or absence of which is conferred by the final member of the construct phrase. The common endings of the m.sg. (-ø) and f.pl. (-ôt) do not change in the bound state, but the bound state of the f.sg. preserves the original /-at/ (ת ַ) ending (which became /-â/ in the absolute). The m.pl. bound form is marked with the ending /-ê/ (י), in place of the absolute m.pl. suffix /-îm/. Often, there is no formal distinction between the construct and absolute forms of a noun (other than the possible change of suffix), but with the loss of accent on bound forms, propretonic reduction can occur (e.g., *dabár > /dĕbar/[דְּבַר] "word of").

b. The pronoun. Aside from the verbal affixes that indicate person, number, and gender, Hebrew has two types of pronominal forms. The independent pronouns appear as separate words, and always as the subject of a clause. Because the finite verbal forms are inflected specifically for person, number, and gender, the independent pronouns generally are not used in conjunction with verbs, except in cases where emphasis of the pronoun is required (e.g., /mālaktî/[מָלַכְתִּי] "I reigned" but /ʾănî mālaktî/[אֲנִי מָלַכְתִּי] "it is I who reigned"). The independent pronouns are thus used most commonly in verbless clauses (/hammelek ʾănî/ [הַמֶּלֶךְ אָנִי] "I am the king"). The suffixed pronouns occur affixed to prepositions, nouns (in which case they serve as "possessive" pronouns), and verbs (as "object suffixes"). For example, the 2nd m.sg. suffix /-kā/(ךָ-) appears on prepositions (/ʿālêkā/[עָלֶיךָ] "upon/concerning you"), nouns (/malkĕkā/[מַלְכְּךָ] "your king"), and verbs (/šĕmārĕkā/[שְׁמָרְךָ] "he protected you").

c. The verb. As discussed above, the most characteristic morphological feature of Hebrew, and of Semitic in general, is the use of a system of consonantal roots in conjunction with vocalic templates. Nowhere is this more evident than in the verbal system. The overwhelming majority of Hebrew verbal roots have three consonants, though a very few have four. It is the consonantal roots that carry the basic lexical meaning, while the templates—consisting of the vowels and any prefixes or suffixes—carry the grammatical functions. For example, the root ktb (כתב) has a basic meaning associated with writing. From this root we can give the following sample verbal forms: /kātab/ (כָּתַב; "he wrote"), /yiktōb/ (יִכְתֹּב; "he will write"), /kōtēb/ (כֹּתֵב; "is writing"), /kĕtōb/ (כְּתֹב; "write!"), and /kātōb/ (כָּתֹב; "to write").

Within the Hebrew verbal system, there is a basic verbal stem (called paʿal or qal) and a series of derived stems. In all, there are seven major verbal stems: paʿal, nipʿal, piʿel, puʿal, hipʿil, hopʿal, and hitpaʿel. A root can appear in multiple stems, and the meaning of a derived stem verb is often predictable; that is, the derived stems each have a functional value. The nipʿal is most often a passive or middle of the paʿal, e.g., /kātab/ ("he wrote"), /niktab/ (נִכְתַּב; "it was written"). The hipʿil most often expresses a causative, e.g., /gādal/ (גָּדַל; "he was great"), /higdîl/ (הִגְדִּיל; "he made great") and /yārad/ (יָרַד; "he went down"), /hôrîd/ (הוֹרִיד; "he brought down"). The puʿal is always a passive of the piʿel, e.g., /dibber/ (דִּבֶּר; "he spoke"), /dubbar/ (דֻּבַּר; "it was spoken"), and the hopʿal is always a passive of the hipʿil, e.g., /hipqîd/ (הִפְקִיד; "he entrusted"), /hopqad/ (הָפְקַד; "he was entrusted"). The hitpaʿel is often a reciprocal, e.g., /hitrāʾû/ (הִתְרָאוּ; "they looked at each other" (compare paʿal /rāʾâ/ [רָאָה] "he saw"), or a reflexive, e.g., /hitgaddēl/ (הִתְגַּדֵּל; "he magnified himself"). It is hard to pin down a basic meaning for the piʿel; it is sometimes a causative of the paʿal, e.g., /limmēd/ (לִמֵּד; "he taught") from /lāmad/ (לָמַד; "he learned"), and sometimes a denominative, e.g., /šilēš/ (שִׁלֵּשׁ; "divide into three") from /šālôš/ (שָׁלוֹשׁ; "three"), but often it has no deri-

vational function, e.g., /biqqēš/ (בִּקֵּשׁ; "he sought"). In addition to these seven major stems (or *binyanim*, to use the traditional Hebrew term), there are several less common stems (e.g., polel, pilpel, paʿlal), mostly associated with weak verbal roots, as well as a few remnants of archaic stems. For example, the archaic hištapʿel is preserved only for the root ḥwh (חוה).

Within each verbal stem, or *binyan*, there are two basic conjugated forms, traditionally called perfect and imperfect. The perfect form is characterized by a set of suffixes that are attached to a verbal stem. These suffixes, which indicate person, number, and gender (except for 3rd person pl. and 1st person sg. and pl., which are of common gender), are identical for all stems. The imperfect is characterized by a set of prefixes, in some cases combined with an additional suffix, which likewise indicate person, number, and gender. As a general rule, the perfect denotes a past tense, while the imperfect denotes a present or future. But the reality is far more complex. Many scholars see these forms not as tenses at all, but rather as aspectual, denoting a complete vs. incomplete action. There is a vast amount of literature dealing with the nature of the Hebrew tense system, and it is impossible to delve into its various intricacies here. It is safe to say that the Hebrew forms called perfect and imperfect do not fit so neatly into the category that in English we call tense.

There are a variety of other verbal forms in addition to the perfect and imperfect. There exists an imperative form, inflected for person and number, which is limited to the second person only. The form of the imperative is closely connected to that of the imperfect. For the first person there exists a form called the cohortative, which is a lengthened form of the 1st person imperfect. For the 3rd person there is a jussive form, which for most verbs is indistinguishable from the imperfect. The cohortative and jussive can be considered the first and third person counterparts of the imperative. The cohortative is usually best translated as "let me/us . . . ," while the jussive usually has the meaning "may he/she/they . . . " or "let him/her/them. . . ." Together, the imperative, cohortative, and jussive comprise the volitive mood (see §D3).

There are two infinitive forms in Hebrew, known as the infinitive construct and infinitive absolute. The infinitive construct corresponds to what is called the infinitive in English ("to do," "to write," etc.), though it also often corresponds to an English gerund *doing, writing*), especially when it is coupled with a possessive suffix (meaning "my doing," "his writing," etc.). The infinitive absolute is often found in conjunction with a finite verbal form, in which case the infinitive absolute acts as a sort of emphatic, e.g. /bōʾ yabôʾ/ (בֹּא יָבוֹא; "he will surely come"), though it has a variety of other functions.

For each stem there is also an active participle, which in all stems except the paʿal and nipʿal is characterized by a prefixed m- (מ). For the paʿal there is also a passive participle, e.g., /kātûb/ (כָּתוּב; "written"). The active participle has properties of both nouns and verbs. Its form is that of a noun, in that it marks number and gender, but not person; it can take the definite article; and it can be the object of a preposition. But it also functions as a verb, in that it can take a direct or indirect object. Its translation value is often something like an English progressive tense (e.g., "is writing"). In post-biblical Hebrew, including Modern Hebrew, this form has developed into a true present tense.

d. Particles. In addition to nouns, pronouns, adjectives, and verbs, Hebrew has a variety of particles. The most important particles are the prepositions, of which there are two types. The first type comprises the prefixed prepositions. These consist of a single consonant, and are prefixed to the noun that they govern. There are just four of these, but they are extremely common: /bĕ-/ (-בְּ; "in, at, with"), /lĕ-/ (-לְ; "to, for"), /kĕ-/ (-כְּ; "like, as, according to"), and /mi-/ (-מִ; "from"), though this last one is analyzable as a reduced form of the free preposition /min/ (מִן). All other prepositions are free, that is, they are separate words, e.g., /ʿad/ (עַד; "until"), /ʿal/ (עַל; "on, upon"). All prepositions can be combined with pronominal suffixes to indicate a pronominal object, e.g., /lî/ (לִי; "to me") /lĕkā/ (לְךָ; "to you"), /lô/ (לוֹ; "to him"), etc.

The most common conjunction is the prefix /wĕ-/ (וְ–) "and, but, or." Others are /kî/ (כִּי) "that, because, for," /ʾăšer/ (אֲשֶׁר) "that, because, for" (also the relative pronoun), /pen/ (פֶּן) "lest, so that not," /ʾô/ (אוֹ) "or," and /ʾim/ (אִם) "if."

Of the various negative particles, the most common is /lōʾ/ (לֹא), which is used to negate both verbal and verbless clauses (e.g., /lōʾ qārab/ לֹא קָרַב "he did not approach"; /lōʾ mĕraggĕlîm ʾattem/ לֹא מְרַגְּלִים אַתֶּם "you are not spies"), as well as to negate individual words or phrases (/lōʾ ṭāhôr/ לֹא טָהוֹר "not clean"). The particle /ʾal/ (אַל) is most often found in conjunction with a negative imperative (see §D3), but is also used independently on rare occasion. Less common are /(lĕ)biltî/ (לְ)בִלְתִּי) "not," found most commonly before infinitives, and /bal/ (בַּל), confined almost exclusively to poetry (esp. Psalms, Proverbs, and Isaiah).

Hebrew possesses an existential particle /yēš/ (יֵשׁ) "there is/are," which does not decline for gender or number, as well as a negative counterpart, /ʾên/ (אֵין) "there is/are not." To express an explicit past or future tense, a form of the root hyh (היה; "to be") is used in place of the particles /yēš/ and /ʾên/ (e.g., /lōʾ hāyâ šām leḥem/ לֹא הָיָה שָׁם לֶחֶם "there was no bread there").

There are a variety of interjections used in the Bible, including /ʾôy/ (אוֹי) "woe!", /nāʾ/ (נָא) "please!", and /hās/ (הָס) "hush!" Finally, /lōʾ/ (and, less commonly, /ʾal/) can also function independently as interjections (e.g., /lōʾ ʾădōnî/ לֹא אֲדֹנִי "No, my lord").

3. Syntax

The syntax of epigraphic and Biblical Hebrew, like the syntax of any language, is complex and cannot be systematized in any simple manner. However, a few comments here will provide a rough overview of the more important syntactic constructions.

The simplest type of Hebrew clauses are verbless, i.e., the clause itself is a predicative statement in which an equational relationship is made between the subject and the predicate (e.g., /hammelek ʾănî/ הַמֶּלֶךְ אֲנִי/ "I am the king"). While the English translation uses a form of the verb "to be" to relate the elements "I" and "the king," Hebrew juxtaposes the subject ("I") and its predicate ("the king").

In clauses and sentences with an expressed verb, the normal word order is verb-subject (e.g., /hālak hannābîʾ/ הָלַךְ הַנָּבִיא/ "the prophet went"). This is, broadly speaking, the opposite of English, in which the subject precedes the verb. Moreover, in Hebrew (as in English), the direct and indirect objects usually follow this initial unit (e.g., /bārāʾ ʾĕlōhîm ʾet-haššāmayim/ בָּרָא אֱלֹהִים אֶת־הַשָּׁמַיִם "God created the heavens").

In narrative clauses, it is common for Hebrew to use a "waw-consecutive" form of the imperfect to denote past action (/wayyiktōb/ וַיִּכְתֹּב "[and] he wrote"). While this appears to be wa + yiqtōl, with the doubling of the prefix consonant, this is, in fact, an originally distinct, shortened ("apocopated") form of the prefix conjugation. This distinction is preserved only in a few weak roots: compare the imperfect /yibnê/ (יִבְנֶה) "he will build" with the waw-consecutive /wayyíben/ (וַיִּבֶן) "(and) he built." Continuing action in the future is denoted by the waw + perfect (/wĕkātab/ וְכָתַב) "[and] he will write"), but this form is also often used to portray pluperfect circumstantial action in the past ("and he had written"). Again, the two forms appear identical except in certain circumstances, namely, in which the subject is 1st c.sg. or 2nd m.sg. (e.g., /wĕkātabtá/ וְכָתַבְתָּ "you will write" but /wĕkātábtā/ וְכָתַבְתָּ "and you wrote").

Volitive constructions in Hebrew implement many of the same verbal forms already known from the syntactic units of narrative action, as well as a few specifically volitive forms. In the 2nd person, the simple imperative (/lēk/ לֵךְ "go!"), is only used in positive commands. Often, it may be combined with the waw + perfect to form longer imperative sequences (/lēk wĕkātabtá/ לֵךְ וְכָתַבְתָּ "go and write!"). The imperative form is never negated; instead, the sequence ʾal + 2nd person imperfect (and, if it exists, the apocopated form) is used to denote the immediate negative imperative (/ʾal taʿaś/ אַל תַּעַשׂ "do not do [right now]!"), and the sequence lōʾ + 2nd person imperfect conveys the continual prohibition (/lōʾ taʿăśê/ לֹא תַעֲשֶׂה "you shall not do . . . !"). In the 3rd person the "jussive" (which shares its historical development with the apocopated form of the wayyiqtōl preterite; e.g., /yiben/ [יִבֶן] "let him build") serves as the primary volitive form, and the "cohortative" serves the same purpose in the first person (/'ektĕbâ/[אֶכְתְּבָה] "let me write"). A syntactic construction frequently misunderstood by students of Hebrew is the sequence volitive + wĕ + imperfect (most likely originally another volitive), which connotes a purposive sense in the second verb (e.g., /'ērādâ-na' wĕ'er'ê/ [אֵרֲדָה־נָּא וְאֶרְאֶה] "let me go down, so that I may see").

One final common syntactic construction is the temporal construction, which stands at the head of its clause. These clauses are generally composed minimally of a preposition (e.g.,/bĕ-/, /kĕ-/ or /ka'ăšer/ [כַּאֲשֶׁר]), and may be followed by any number of verbal or nominal qualifications.

In short, the syntax of Hebrew is just as complex as the syntax of any other language, and for the complete range of nuances and grammatical possibilities, the reader is referred to the bibliography.

4. Lexicography

The vocabulary of Hebrew is almost totally of Semitic stock, and its core vocabulary is very similar to that of the other Canaanite languages, Phoenician, Moabite, etc. Because the Bible and the contemporary inscriptions form a limited corpus, a large number of words are HAPAX LEGOMENA (i.e., with roots that occur only once), or nearly so, leaving the exact meaning of many Hebrew words unclear. In cases like these, it is comparison with the other Semitic languages that often illuminates our knowledge of Hebrew.

Since the attestation of Biblical Hebrew covers a period of roughly a millennium, it is natural that the lexicon of Hebrew is not uniform. Instead, we find some differences between Archaic, Standard, and Late Biblical Hebrew, as words fall out of use and as new words are introduced. We also find dialectal variations between Standard (Judean) and Northern (Israelian) Hebrew. Differences in vocabulary are even greater when we compare post-biblical dialects of Hebrew.

In all periods of Biblical Hebrew, words were borrowed from neighboring languages, including Egyptian, Akkadian (Babylonian and Assyrian), Persian, and Aram., among others. In the post-biblical period, a great many loanwords entered Hebrew from Gk. and Latin. This is not surprising given Israel's position at the crossroads of the major ancient civilizations, and the fact that Israel was often under the direct or indirect control of one of these nations. Among the earliest loans into Hebrew were those from Egyptian. Examples are /sî/ (צִי) "ship," /'î/ (אִי) "island," /'āḥ/ (אָח) "brazier," /gōme'/ (גֹּמֶא) "reed," /ḥôṭām/ (חוֹתָם) "seal, signet," and several others, including the names of several precious materials and obvious words like /par'ô/ (פַּרְעֹה) "Pharaoh" and /yĕ'ōr/ (יְאֹר) "Nile." Several dozen words have entered Hebrew from Akka-

dian, often via Aram. These include the names of the months (/'ădār/ [אֲדָר], /nîsān/[נִיסָן], /sîwān/[סִיוָן], /tammûz/[תַּמּוּז], etc.), the words /sārîs/(סָרִיס) "eunuch, official," /mekes/(מֶכֶס) "tax," /ṭîṭ/(טִיט) "clay," /miskēn/(מִסְכֵּן) "pauper," and many others. More than a dozen words from Akkadian are ultimately of Sumerian origin, such as /hêkāl/(הֵיכָל) "temple" and /mallāḥ/(מַלָּח) "sailor." Following the Persian conquest of Babylon, that is, during the postexilic period, a number of Persian words found their way into Hebrew. The book of Esther, which is set in the Persian court, contains the greatest number of Persian loans of any biblical book. Examples of Persian words are /pardēs/ (פַּרְדֵּס) "park," /daṭ/ (דָּת) "decree," and a number of governmental terms like /genez/ (גֶּנֶז) "treasury," /partĕmîm/ (פַּרְתְּמִים) "nobles," and /'ăhašdarpan/ (אֲחַשְׁדַּרְפַּן) "satrap."

By the mid-first millennium BCE, Aram. had become a lingua franca in the entire Near East; the Persians even used it as an official language of their empire. Slowly it came to be used more and more in Israel, and eventually Hebrew ceased to function as a living spoken language by the 3rd cent. CE. It is not surprising, therefore, to find that Aram. had a great influence on all aspects of the Hebrew language. Aram. words are found throughout the Bible, but the greatest concentration is found in the later biblical books. A few examples of Aram. loans are /kĕtāb/ (כְּתָב) "writing," /millâ/ (מִלָּה) "word," and / 'āraq/ (עֲרַק) "to flee." As already noted, Aram. was often the direct source of Akkadian loans into Hebrew, e.g., /'iggeret/ (אִגֶּרֶת) "letter," /šûq/ (שׁוּק) "street," and /talmîd/ (תַּלְמִיד) "student." Because Hebrew and Aram. are so closely related, it is often impossible to tell whether a word is Aram. or not. For example, the rare Hebrew verb /'āzal/ (אָזַל) "to go" may be an archaic inherited lexeme, or it may be borrowed from Aram., where it is very common. Aram. is also the source of a large number of loans in all periods of post-biblical Hebrew.

The appearance of loans in Hebrew can actually serve two important purposes for modern scholars. First, loans sometimes help to date the composition of a book. For example, the presence of Persian loans in Esther makes it certain that the book was written after the Persian conquest of Babylon, that is, after 539 BCE. Second, foreign loans in Hebrew can be an excellent aid in uncovering the pronunciation of these words in the source languages. For example, Egyptian loans in Hebrew provide some of the only evidence for the phonetic values of the Egyptian hieroglyphs at the time, not to mention vocalization, which is almost totally unknown for Egyptian until the Coptic period.

Bibliography: Fred W. Dobbs-Allsopp et. al., eds. *Hebrew Inscriptions* (2005); Maximilian Ellenbogen. *Foreign Words in the Old Testament: Their Origin and Etymology* (1962); Sandra Landis Gogel. *A Grammar of*

Epigraphic Hebrew (1998); Frederick E. Greenspahn. *Hapax Legomena in Biblical Hebrew* (1984); Jo Ann Hackett. "Hebrew (Biblical and Epigraphic)." *Beyond Babel: A Handbook for Biblical Hebrew and Related Languages.* John Kaltner and Steven L. McKenzie, eds. (2003) 139–56; John Huehnergard. "Features of Central Semitic." *Biblical and Oriental Essays in Memory of William L. Moran.* Agustinus Gianto, ed. (2005) 155–203; John Huehnergard. "The Early Hebrew Prefix-Conjugations." *Hebrew Studies* 29 (1988) 19–23; Paul Joüon. *A Grammar of Biblical Hebrew.* T. Muraoka, trans. (1996); Geoffrey Khan. "The Tiberian Pronunciation of Biblical Hebrew." *ZAH* 9 (1996) 1–23; E. Kautzsch and A. E. Cowley, eds., *Gesenius' Hebrew Grammar.* 2nd ed. (1910); E. Y. Kutscher. *A History of the Hebrew Language.* Raphael Kutscher, ed. (1982); Thomas O. Lambdin. "Egyptian Loan Words in the Old Testament," *JAOS* 73 (1953) 145–55; Paul V. Mankowski. *Akkadian Loanwords in Biblical Hebrew* (2000); Anson F. Rainey. "The Ancient Hebrew Prefix Conjugation in the Light of Amarnah Canaanite." *Hebrew Studies* 27 (1986) 4–19; Gary Rendsburg. "A Comprehensive Guide to Israelian Hebrew: Grammar and Lexicon." *Orient* 38 (2003) 5-35; Gary A. Rendsburg. "Ancient Hebrew Phonology." *Phonologies of Asia and Africa.* Vol. 1. Alan S. Kaye, ed. (1997) 65–83; Gary Rendsburg. "The Galilean Background of Mishnaic Hebrew." *The Galilee in Late Antiquity.* L. I. Levine, ed. (1992) 225–40; Angel Sáenz-Badillos. *A History of the Hebrew Language.* John Elwolde, trans. (1993); M. H. Segal. *A Grammar of Mishnaic Hebrew* (1927); Bruce K. Waltke and M. O'Connor. *An Introduction to Biblical Hebrew Syntax* (1990); Ronald J. Williams. *Hebrew Syntax: An Outline* (1976).

JEREMY M. HUTTON AND AARON D. RUBIN

HEBREW PEOPLE עִבְרִי ʿivri]. According to Gen 10:24; 11:11-14, EBER is the great grandson of Shem in a genealogy that leads to Abram (Gen 11:26). While Abram/Abraham is generally considered the ancestor of the Hebrew people, the eponymous relationship clearly goes back to Eber (ʿever עֵבֶר).

The Hebrew people is considered another name or designation for Israel, but the use in the OT is generally limited to non-Israelites, or in the context of speaking to non-Israelites (Gen 39:14; 41:12; Jonah 1:9).

The etymology of the word is not clear. It has been explained as connected with the Hebrew verb ʿavar (עָבַר; "to cross over") and derived from references to the ancestors of the Israelites having come from the other side of the Euphrates (Josh 24:2, 3). A once popular theory connected the Hebrew ʿivri with the Akkadian ʿapiru/habiru (*see* HABIRU, HAPIRU) and associated the movements of Abraham and his descendants with references to this group in Mesopotamian and Amarna documents. While there are phonetic similarities between the words, the so-called Habiru

Hypothesis has largely been discredited as careful readings of the appropriate documents has identified **habiru** as a socioeconomic designation and "Hebrew" as an apparent ethnic identifier.

C. MARK MCCORMICK

HEBREW POETRY. *See* POETRY, HEBREW.

HEBREW RELIGION, HISTORY OF. *See* ISRAELITE RELIGION, HISTORY OF.

HEBREW SCRIPTS. *See* ALPHABET.

HEBREW VERSION OF MATTHEW. *See* MATTHEW, HEBREW VERSION OF.

HEBREWS. *See* HEBREW PEOPLE; HEBREWS, LETTER TO THE.

HEBREWS, GOSPEL OF THE. A Jewish-Christian source of widely divergent contents, composed in Greek, probably in ALEXANDRIA, Egypt, in the 2nd cent. CE, available to us today only in fragmentary quotations from early church fathers and medieval scholars. Still unresolved is the exact relationship between this Gospel and other sources (Sayings of Jesus found in the OXYRHYNCHUS PAPYRI; and other Jewish-Christian works, the Gospel of the Ebionites and the Gospel of the Nazarenes), as to whether they are independent or a single work referred to by different titles.

This Gospel is quoted by CLEMENT OF ALEXANDRIA (before 215), ORIGEN (before 254), EUSEBIUS (before 339), Didymus the Blind (4th cent.), CYRIL OF JERUSALEM (4th cent.), EPIPHANIUS (before 403), JEROME (4th–5th cent.), and Nicephorus (Stichometry, before the 9th cent.). These authors offer quotations from Jesus, narratives containing a saying of Jesus, narratives about Jesus, and occasionally a paraphrase of some of its contents. According to Epiphanius, the work was originally about 2,200 lines long. Cyril records that when Christ wanted to come to earth, God the Father summoned a force called Michael, and entrusted Christ to the force, which came into the world as Mary, carried him in her womb for seven months (a perfect period of gestation), and then gave birth to Jesus. He matured, chose and commissioned apostles to preach, incurred the hatred of the Jews who handed him over to the Roman governor, who returned him to the Jews for crucifixion—thus assigning blame to the Jews, in a way similar to the Gospel of John (John 19:16). After the crucifixion, God took him back to heaven.

Jerome offers a story in which Jesus' mother and brothers asked him to go with them to be baptized by John the Baptist for forgiveness of their sins, to which he replied that he had not sinned, and did not need to be baptized unless he did not know what he was talking about when he said that he had no sin. Jerome reports, also, that this Gospel records a prophecy and its fulfillment that as Jesus came up out of the baptismal waters, the full fountain of the Spirit descended upon him, completely embraced him, and claimed that the Lord (Christ) was the Spirit, and that the Spirit addressed him as the firstborn Son whom the prophets anticipated, in whom the Spirit would rest and who would rule forever. This version of the baptism served a Jewish-Christian christology. Rejecting virgin conception (found in Matthew and Luke) as a Greco-Roman myth, early Jewish Christians found in a revised version of the baptism proof that Jesus was God's uniquely appointed agent. This adoptionist view attested that at Jesus' baptism, God certified the unique role of Jesus and his relationship to God by the divine voice (here, intensified by the image of the full union of Jesus and the Spirit). Origen records what he considers a heretical tradition, from this Gospel, that (apparently after Jesus' baptism), the Spirit of God, whom Jesus referred to as his mother, carried him by a single hair of his head up onto Mount Tabor (the traditional mountain of temptation). This is a different version than that of the Synoptic Gospels in which the Spirit (a neuter noun, making it impossible for the Spirit to be Jesus' mother) led Jesus out into the wilderness. The image of being carried by one's hair echoes the prophetic tradition—the Spirit took Ezekiel by his hair to Jerusalem (Ezek 8:3), and carried Habakkuk to Babylon by his hair (Bel 36).

Didymus the Blind says that this Gospel explained the problem of the names Matthew and Levi. In Luke, Jesus called a tax collector named Levi, who followed him (Luke 5:27); however, in the list of disciples there is no Levi, but a Matthew is included (Luke 6:15). Why was Levi not included and where did Matthew come from? This Gospel claimed that the Matthew of Luke was really a different person than the tax collector: he was the Matthias elected to replace Judas (Acts 1:26), and that he went by two names. Jerome reports that this Gospel had a unique testimony about the resurrection. Here, the resurrected Lord handed his grave cloth to a priest's slave (which appears to have intended to offer the Jews proof of Christ's resurrection, and to establish a privileged place for Jewish Christians). Then Christ appeared to James, and administered to him a eucharistic meal, to help fulfill James's vow not to eat until he should see the Lord resurrected. This account made James the first witness to the resurrection, and authenticated the leadership role, which he had in the Jerusalem church and the Jewish-Christian community.

Several of this Gospel's sayings of Jesus, which pertain to the fraternal nature of believers, come to us through Jerome. Jesus said that his followers should only rejoice when they look on a fellow believer with love. Likewise, the worst offense a believer could commit would be to make a fellow believer's spirit sad. Clement of Alexandria quotes a wisdom saying of Jesus that has an esoteric, gnostic quality: "the seeker will

not rest until he finds; and having found, he will be amazed; and having been amazed, he will rule; and having ruled he will come to rest" (virtually identical with Oxyrhynchus Saying 1; also in the Coptic *Gospel of Thomas*). The rhetorical scheme of this saying—using link-terms or catch-words to move by steps from the most elementary stage of wisdom to the climactic stage (seek, find, amaze, rule, rest)—is completely different from the other extant materials from this Gospel, but similar to the rhetorical method of the Letter to the Hebrews and the book of James. It is impossible to draw solid conclusions regarding the scope, plan, and aims of this Gospel, given the fact that it is available to us only in a few fragments that vary greatly in their nature, style, rhetoric, and theological orientation. *See* EBIONITES, GOSPEL OF THE; JESUS, SAYINGS OF; NAZOREANS, GOSPEL OF THE.

Bibliography: Bart D. Ehrman. *Lost Scriptures* (2003); Robert J. Miller, ed. *The Complete Gospels: Annotated Scholars Version* (1994).

RICHARD A. SPENCER

HEBREWS, HISTORY OF. *See* ISRAEL, HISTORY OF.

HEBREWS, LETTER TO THE [Πρὸς Ἑβραίους Pros Hebraious]. The traditional title of this text is misleading on two counts. This text is called a "letter." Elements of a standard letter closing in 13:18-25 (request, benediction, doxology, news and travel plans, conveying greetings, and final farewell) are similar to the closings of other NT letters (see Rom 15:30–16:23; 1 Thess 5:23-28; 2 Tim 4:19-22; 1 Pet 5:10-14). Nevertheless, Hebrews lacks a standard letter opening, starting instead with a sonorous, rhetorically crafted sentence appropriate to an oral speech. The author refers to his text as a "word of exhortation" (13:22), a term associated with the sermon delivered as part of a worship service in Acts 13:15, and assumes that his audience will be "hearing" his text (5:11). It is more helpful, therefore, to consider Hebrews as an example of early (and expert) Christian preaching. The author is unable to present his "word of exhortation" in person (13:19, 23), and so must send the transcript in written form to be read aloud by another party.

Unlike a letter, Hebrews does not name its recipients. "Hebrews" (from Hebraios [Ἑβραῖος]) represents an early guess concerning the intended addressees, perhaps based on the author's extensive use of the Jewish Scriptures and interest in the cultic rites of Israel. An argument centered on the obsolescence of the Old Covenant would seem to be more appropriately directed toward Jewish (Christian) readers than Gentile Christians. On the other hand, Galatians and 1 Peter, both of which are addressed to Gentile Christian audiences, assume that those readers will be able to follow arguments based on the Jewish Scriptures, and will be interested in how those texts can illumine how Gentile believers stand within God's covenant and relate to the particular institutions of the historic people of God, Israel. Moreover, Hebrews refers to a catechism of topics, many of which would be familiar to Jewish converts, but new to Gentile converts (6:1-3). When one adds the likelihood that the congregation addressed had been formed as part of the Pauline mission (the concern over Timothy in 13:23), which had as its explicit goal raising up Gentile believers, it seems prudent not to allow the secondary title to obscure the likelihood that the author addresses a mixed congregation of Jewish and Gentile Christians.

Hebrews begins with a rhetorical affirmation of the ultimacy of God's revelation in the Son who shares in God's divine nature and activity (1:1-4), who has been exalted even above the angels, as the author demonstrates from a chain of recitations from the Psalms and other familiar OT texts (1:5-14), followed by a call to the hearers therefore to take seriously the opportunity for deliverance that the Son has announced (2:1-4). The author thus establishes a pattern that will continue throughout the sermon: discussion of the superior status and achievement of the Son, followed by an exhortation to respond to the Son in a manner befitting that status and achievement.

Jesus is the one in whom the vision of exaltation in Ps 8 has been fulfilled (2:5-9), who leads the many sons and daughters of God on to a share in that glory (2:10-13), and who helps them persevere (2:14-18). Because he enjoys a higher place in God's house than Moses (3:1-6), it is essential for the believers to continue to respond faithfully and single-heartedly to the word that God spoke through him. The author depicts the wilderness generation—those who heard God's word through Moses but failed to follow through in a faithful response—as a negative example to avoid (3:7–4:13).

The middle portion of Hebrews comprises a lengthy exposition of the identity and achievement of Jesus viewed through the lens of priesthood and sacrifice (4:14–10:18). Jesus' appointment and qualification as "priest after the order of Melchizedek" is discussed in 5:1-10, after which the author breaks off in a digression intended to impress upon readers the importance of renewing their commitment to the direction in which God is calling them, lest they bring disgrace upon Jesus and retribution upon themselves by apostasy from the faith (5:11–6:8).

Assuring them that God's promises can indeed be trusted as the basis for their investments (6:9-20), the author returns to his main theme. He compares the obscure figure of Melchizedek with the Levitical priesthood, demonstrating the superiority of the former, and hence the superiority of the successor to Melchizedek, Jesus (7:1-28). This "better" priestly mediator officiates in a "better" sanctuary (the heavenly temple where God's presence dwells in its fullness), and inaugurates a "better covenant" (8:1-13). Jesus' death and his ascen-

sion into heaven are interpreted as the "better sacrifice," a combination of a cosmic DAY OF ATONEMENT and covenant inauguration rite, that makes these benefits effective for those who approach God through Jesus (9:1–10:18). The author accomplishes something of an exegetical coup d'etat as he finds in Ps 40:6-8 the warrant for a unique human sacrifice that was appointed by God to achieve what the animal sacrifices so clearly legislated in the Torah could not (10:1-18).

A climactic exhortation to persevere in a course of action that displays gratitude to God and loyalty to one another in Christian community follows (10:32-39), the models of faith that are held up as praiseworthy in the Jewish Scriptures and Second Temple period traditions (11:1-40), and Jesus himself, the climactic model of faith in action (12:1-3). Their neighbors' attempts to shame them are transformed into an educative, formative process by means of which God shapes them as God's children (12:4-11). Believers are encouraged, therefore, to renew their commitment to staying their course, rather than giving up the joyful and festive access to God that is theirs in Christ for the sake of temporary relief (12:11-24), since the latter would prove ultimately disadvantageous (12:25-29). A series of closing exhortations urges mutual support, accepting the cost of preserving their unique privileges in Christ, and making praise and service offered in Christ's name the central focus of their lives in grateful response to God (13:1-17), followed by an epistolary prescript (13:18-25).

A. Structure
B. Detailed Analysis
  1. Author
  2. Audience and rhetorical situation
  3. Cosmology and eschatology
  4. Jesus, the great high priest
  5. Responding to the divine benefactor
  6. Contours of faith
  7. Obligations of community
C. Theological and Religious Significance
  1. Contributions to early christology
  2. Gift and response
  3. Perfecting the conscience
  4. Faith and freedom
Bibliography

A. Structure
1. 1:1–2:18 First Appeal: Heed the word of God spoken in the Son.
     1:1-14 Thesis and confirmation: God's final and complete word has been spoken through the Son, who has greater honor even than the angels;
     2:1-4 Exhortation to heed the announcement of deliverance made through the Son, drawing "lesser to greater" inference from 1:1-13;

2:5-18 Argument in support of the exhortation: Attachment to Jesus is the path to a share in his honor as well as the path of gratitude for past benefits and Jesus' ongoing mediation.

2. 3:1–4:13 Second Appeal: Honor God's word through trust and perseverance.

3:-6 Argument: Jesus, as Son over God's house, has greater honor than Moses, the servant in God's house;

3:7–4:13 Exhortation against imitating those who failed to trust God's promises and died in the wilderness under the servant, Moses.

3. 4:14–10:18 Central Exposition: The "long and difficult word" about Jesus' priestly work.

4:14-16 Exhortation: Take advantage of the access to God Jesus provides;

5:1-10 Exposition concerning Jesus' appointment to high priesthood;

5:11–6:20 Digression

5:11-14 Interruption and appeal for attentive and responsive hearing;

6:1-3 Exhortation to move forward in Christian journey;

6:4-8 Argument from the contrary in support of exhortation;

6:9-12 Palliation: topics of confidence

6:13-20 Argument confirming cause for confidence;

7:1–10:28 Exposition Resumed: Christians' superior access to God, thanks to Jesus;

7:1-28 Jesus' superior qualifications for priesthood;

8:1-13 Jesus' location in a better sanctuary, mediating a better covenant;

9:1–10:18 Jesus' unique achievement: preparing all the people to enter God's real presence.

4. 10:19–13:25 Exhortation: Persevere in gratitude for the benefactions granted through Jesus.

10:19-25 Exhortation based on this new access;

10:26-31 Rationale for accepting exhortation based on consideration of the contrary;

10:32-39 Exhortation to imitate former endurance and remain constant (show "faith");

11:1–12:3 Encomium on faith, developing the portrait of this virtue in action;

12:4-17 Encouragement to endure opposition

12:18-29 Exhortation to confidence and gratitude;

13:1-21 Specific exhortations for living out this gratitude in everyday life;

13:22-25 Epistolary postscript.

The sermon's alternation between exposition and exhortation has long been recognized as a key to its structure. The outline given above needs to be nuanced somewhat in light of the author's artistry in weaving his work into a unified whole. For example, the close investigation of 4:14-16 and 10:19-22 by Guthrie (1994) reveals that the verses form an *inclusio*, setting off the "long and difficult word" that comprises the centerpiece of the sermon, and that they are both, in fact, transitional sections.

Scholars had formerly questioned the literary unity of the sermon, suggesting that Heb 13, with its relatively brief sentences of practical guidance, was not originally a part of the sermon, which concluded at 12:29. Filson's study (1967) of the thematic and lexical connections between the material in Heb 13 and the remainder of the letter, however, has effectively put an end to this debate in favor of the unity of the text.

B. Detailed Analysis

1. Author

The writer of Hebrews does not give his name. Paul's reputation as a letter-writer and the reference to Timothy (13:22) led early scribes to attribute the letter to Paul. Several factors militate against this ascription, however. Paul came to faith in Christ through direct divine intervention (Gal 1:11-17; 1 Cor 15:3-10), whereas the author of Hebrews did so through other apostles (Heb 2:3-4). Paul never exhibits the attention to rhetorical ornamentation that this author does, and in fact speaks of his own reluctance to engage in such sermon craft (1 Cor 2:1-5). Although the sermon shares topics in common with Paul, they are developed in different ways; the focus on Jesus as high priest and on the Israelite cult, moreover, is quite distinctive.

Clement of Alexandria, Origen, and Tertullian, noting the difference in rhetorical style and content, suggested alternative candidates from among the Pauline team. Barnabas and Apollos often emerge as favorites. Priscilla has become a recent favorite, but the author's use of a self-referential masculine participle argues against this proposal. Origen's conclusion remains the best: "Who wrote the letter? God knows" (quoted in Eusebius, *Hist. eccl.* 6.25.14).

The author comes from the large circle of teachers that constitute the Pauline team (13:23). He appears to have been known to the congregation, to whom he hopes to be restored (13:19). He is expert in the Jewish Scriptures and the art of rhetoric. Only 13:24, the greetings from "those from Italy," provides a clue to his location at the time of writing. It is unclear, however, whether this means that the author is in Italy sending greetings abroad (which seems more likely), or whether he is abroad with others who are away from Italy and sending their greetings back home. Some connection with Roman Christianity is confirmed by the early use of Hebrews by Clement of Rome in 95–96 CE, which also fixes the latest date of composition. The author's question in 10:2 ("would they [the sacrifices] not have ceased being offered?") appears to presuppose that the Levitical sacrifices continue to provide the "annual reminder of sins" (10:3), suggesting a date prior to 70 CE, when the Temple was destroyed by the Roman armies.

2. Audience and rhetorical situation

The addressees came to faith in response to the preaching of early Christian missionaries and the concurrent experience of the Holy Spirit, whose power accompanied the proclamation (2:1-4; compare Gal 3:1-5; 1 Cor 2:1-5). The author speaks of their process of resocialization into the worldview and beliefs of the Christian group (6:1-3), and the author will rely on the addressees' agreement with these foundational beliefs (e.g., the value of faithfulness toward God and the realities of resurrection from the dead and eternal judgment) in the argument.

The addressees had faced attempts to shame them back into conformity with their old, pre-Christian way of life. Non-Christian Jews would be interested in pressuring Jewish Christians whose commitment to the particulars of the Torah was seen to wane to return to a more observant lifestyle. Non-Christian Gentiles would find their Gentile Christian neighbors' withdrawal from worship of the traditional gods and the social contexts where such worship occurred to betoken serious problems for social unity. Neither group would approve of their neighbors' celebration of a crucified revolutionary as the coming king of a new political order.

These opponents used the shaming techniques of their society—verbal abuse, physical assaults, manipulation of the justice system to deprive believers of material wealth—to make a spectacle of the Christians and to make them feel shame at their association with the Christian group (10:32-34). Rather than allow these deviancy-control techniques to pull them away from their new faith, they rallied together instead to support those who had been targeted and boldly continued to associate openly with the followers of Jesus.

Over the long term, loss of status and honor has begun to erode the commitment of at least some members of the congregation(s). Some have ceased to associate openly with the meeting of the Christian assembly (10:25). Others are in danger of "drifting away" (2:1), "neglecting the message" (2:3), "turning away from the living God" (3:12), falling short

of entering God's promised rest and God's gift (4:11; 12:15), "falling away" to the public humiliation of their Redeemer (6:4-6; 10:26-31). There is no indication in the sermon that the addressees face a new wave of persecution, nor a new challenge to "orthodox" belief; rather, they have been made to live too long between the loss of their status, their place, in their host society and their reception of their new status and place in God's eternal realm. As a result, they have begun to question whether God's promises are worth their utter alienation from the way of life and social networks of support they once enjoyed.

In the sections that follow, we will consider prominent elements of the author's rhetorical strategy for addressing these pastoral challenges.

3. Cosmology and eschatology

The author assumes a cosmology in which space is divided into two orders: the visible, material earth and heavens (skies, stars, etc.) and the invisible realm beyond creation ("heaven itself," 9:24). The former is subject to change and to removal (1:10-12), as will in fact happen in the anticipated future in a decisive "shaking" of things "made" (12:26-28). The latter existed prior to creation and will endure into eternity. As is the case in other Jewish texts (e.g., *1 En.* 90:28-29; *T. Levi* 2–5), the cosmos is represented by the desert tabernacle or Temple (6:19-20; 8:1-2; 9:1-11), with the visible creation constituting the outer chamber and courts that must be removed in order for the way into the heavenly Holy of Holies to be revealed (9:8, 24). The author also describes this realm as the "rest" into which God entered after creation (3:7–4:11), the heavenly homeland (11:16), the lasting city (13:14). From the time-bound perspective of human beings, the realm inhabited by God and his angels is "coming" (2:5), but it in fact exists now as a present reality about which the believers can be confident, Jesus having passed through the visible heavens (4:14) to enter the abiding realm as their "forerunner" (6:20).

The author uses elements of Platonic language (e.g., the use of "type" in 8:5 and "shadow" in 10:1) and concepts (visible, material realities have their "true" and "lasting" counterparts in an immaterial realm). However, the author has thoroughly embedded these terms and concepts in a Jewish-Christian apocalyptic framework quite alien to Plato (as is the notion of the penetrability of the two realms, with first Jesus, then the believers, entering the abiding realm).

Based on this cosmology and eschatology, the author can claim that those goods pertaining to God's realm are qualitatively "better" because they are "lasting" (10:34; 11:16; 12:28; 13:14). On this basis, he urges perseverance in faithful response to God. Any losses sustained in that journey are the losses of temporary, fading goods—acceptable losses in view of the abiding goods believers will enjoy in God's realm (10:32-35; 11:24-

26; 13:13-14). Protecting temporary goods at the cost of relinquishing one's hold on eternal goods alienates the divine benefactor by preferring the world's gifts to God's. Such behavior is as foolish as Esau's exchange of his birthright for a single meal (12:16-17).

4. Jesus, the great high priest

The most distinctive contribution of Hebrews to the early church's reflection on Jesus is its author's high priestly christology and, by extension, a much fuller interpretation of Jesus' death and exaltation in terms of priesthood and sacrifice. This theme is announced briefly in 1:3 ("having made purification for sins") and again in 2:17, and is given full attention in 4:14–10:18. Fundamental to the success of his argument is a shared commitment on the part of author and addressees that the oracles of God in the Jewish Scriptures find their ultimate meaning when read in relation to Jesus. Certain texts from the prophets and psalms are spoken *about* Jesus (2 Sam 7:14 in Heb 1:5), spoken *to* Jesus (Ps 2:7; 110:1, 4 in Heb 1:5, 13; 5:5-6), sometimes even spoken *by* Jesus (Ps 22:2; Isa 8:17-18; Ps 40:6-8 in Heb 2:12-13; 10:5-8). At the same time, the author works with a typological model, according to which the institutions and rites of the first covenant, e.g., provide the template for understanding the significance of the mediator of the second covenant and his achievement (*see*, e.g., the use of the rites of the Day of Atonement from Lev 16 and the covenant inauguration ceremony of Exod 24:1-8 to illumine Jesus' accomplishment in Heb 9:1-28). In this way, texts from the Jewish Scriptures (sometimes, as with Ps 40:6-8, clearly relying on the Greek translation) even become witnesses to the invisible stretches of the Son's career (notably, the Son's pre-incarnate activity and his post-resurrection activity). The preamble (1:1-4) reflects this basic hermeneutical presupposition: the Son is the lens through which the piecemeal, diverse moments of illumination from God through the prophets refract into a single, coherent beam of revelation.

Psalms 2:7 and 110:1 play a key role in other NT writings, the first being used to name Jesus as God's "Son" and heir to the Davidic promises, the second establishing Jesus' exaltation to God's right hand and the expectation of the manifestation of his suppression of every opponent (see Acts 2:34-35; 13:33; Matt 22:44; 1 Cor 15:25). This author, however, reads beyond the opening verse of Ps 110:1 to find the same "you" who was named a "son" in Ps 2:7 to be named a "priest forever after the order of Melchizedek" (Ps 110:4; Heb 5:5-6). This leads to a close examination of the obscure figure of Melchizedek (Gen 14:17-20; Heb 7:1-10), and to a reconfiguration of the priestly story of the Jewish Scriptures at the end of which Melchizedek and Levi seem to stand as two principal, equal, alternative paradigms of priesthood—despite the fact that the former is mentioned only twice in the Jewish Scriptures!

Melchizedek emerges here as a Messianic type ("righteousness" and "peace" were typical expectations of the Messiah). It is vitally important that Melchizedek does not hold his priesthood on the basis of fitting into a particular family line, genealogy being the ultimate criterion for priestly service under the Torah. Melchizedek is presented, rather, as one who possesses an unending life, and this becomes the criterion that Jesus (and Jesus alone) can also fulfill. Based on an idiosyncratic reading of Gen 14:17-20, the author also concludes that Melchizedek is a priest of a higher order than that of Levi, which becomes the launching pad for the author's catalogue of the factors that set Jesus above the other priestly mediators sanctioned in God's redemptive history: a priest who never dies, who never sins, whose appointment is confirmed by divine oath, who brokers a better covenant, and who ministers from the better, heavenly sanctuary (7:11–8:13).

The DAY OF ATONEMENT rites of Lev 16 provide a template for understanding Jesus' death and exaltation. Jesus' procession to Calvary "outside the gate" reenacts the scapegoat who bore the people's sins and was driven "outside the camp" (Lev 16:20-22, 27; Heb 13:11-13). Jesus' ascension reenacts the high priest's entrance into the Holy of Holies to apply the sacrificial blood to the ark (Lev 16:15-19; Heb 9:11-14, 23-28). And just as the high priest emerged from the Holy of Holies to bless the people, so Jesus is anticipated to emerge again from "heaven itself," bringing deliverance to those who await him at his coming (9:28).

Jesus' death has opened up an entirely new relationship between God and human beings. Formerly, under the first covenant, access to God was highly limited and the people kept at a distance from the holy God. The author regards the persistence of this limited access to God to be the sign of the failure of the Levitical priesthood (7:11, 18-19a; 9:9; 10:1-2). Jesus' death, however, effects the decisive removal of sin and, the hoped-for new covenant promised by Jeremiah (Jer 31:31-34; see especially Heb 8:12; 10:17). By removing sin from the conscience of the human being ("perfecting" the worshiper, 9:14; 10:10, 14), human beings will come into God's real presence, the heavenly Holy of Holies. All those who, under the Levitical priesthood had no hope even of entering the earthly holy places can now enter "heaven itself."

Jesus' ritual journey is one that the believers are called to embark upon (10:19-25; 13:11-14). The "many sons and daughters" must follow the path pioneered by the Son through suffering to glory (2:10; 6:19-20). The Son's incarnation is interpreted as God's conforming the Son to the experience of human beings, to know their trials and challenges intimately, so as to better offer them assistance from his position as exalted high priest (2:16-18; 4:14-16), Jesus walked the path of suffering because God knew that the "many sons and daughters" would walk such a path as they moved toward their heavenly calling. Throughout his exposition, the author is keenly aware that he is overturning a priesthood, covenant, and sacrificial system established by God's authority. The fact that God announces the appointment of a new "priest after the order of Melchizedek" through "David" (the supposed author of Ps 110) centuries after the giving of the Torah, which established its own priesthood after the order of Levi, shows that God is behind this change of arrangements (7:11, 17-19). Similarly, the oracle of Jer 31 concerning a new covenant is a later divine word that sets aside the previous one (Heb 8:6-13; vv. 7, 13 draw these implications explicitly). Similarly, the oracle of Ps 40:6-8 is a later word that brings an end to the system of sacrifices previously established by another word from God in favor of a new kind of sacrifice (Heb 10:5-8).

5. Responding to the divine benefactor

The heart of the author's rhetorical strategy is to keep the addressees focused on the matchless gifts that have come to them—and will yet come to them—through Jesus' mediation, and thus the value of remaining connected with Jesus as their mediator of God's favor. The social institutions of patronage and benefaction undergird the author's portrayal of Jesus' relationship to the addressees, as well as their proper response of gratitude to this Jesus.

In presenting Jesus as a mediator (8:6; 9:15; 12:24), the author of Hebrews presents him in the social role of "broker," one whose gift is access to another. The details that the author offers about Jesus' proximity to God—in terms of space (at God's right hand), household (a "son" in God's house), and relationship (never sinning against God, alienating God)—all magnify Jesus' value as an effective mediator of God's favor. Angels, Moses, and the Levitical priests were all recognized mediators of God in the Jewish tradition of the author, but Jesus surpasses them all in honor and effectiveness.

On the one hand, connection with this Jesus assures one of continued enjoyment of access to God and finding all the resources one needs to persevere (4:14-16) on the road to enjoying the fullness of what God has for the believers in the abiding realm (2:10; 3:6, 14; etc.). On the other hand, preferring to restore friendship with the unbelieving society at the cost of disloyalty and insult to this Jesus threatens not only the loss of these great benefits but also encountering God as Judge and Avenger of the slighted honor of God's Son (6:4-8; 10:26-31).

The expectation of reciprocity—of returning gratitude (loyalty, thanks, and service or some other appropriate return) for the gifts of great persons—undergirds the warning passages of Hebrews. God's gifts (Heb 6:4-5) are given in the expectation that they will take root in the lives of the recipients and bear pleasant fruit (continued confession of Jesus, along with acts of love and service on behalf of fellow believers; 6:7,

9-10; 13:15-16). Turning away from Jesus amounts to a public testimony concerning the little worth of Jesus and the gifts, secured at the cost of his own life (6:6), a willful insult that could only be expected to result in decisive alienation from God.

The Wilderness Generation illustrates how *not* to respond to God's promises "shrinking back" (10:39) as they did in the face of the obstacles (the story is told in Num 14, and recalled here in the recitation of Ps 95:7-11 [LXX]). Standing on the threshold of Canaan, they considered the opposition too great in alienating themselves from the Divine Patron who merited absolute trust and thus fell short of entering the promised rest (3:7-19).

The author employs these warnings to arouse fear (4:1; 10:27, 31) of the course of action that would lead them to compromise their allegiance to Jesus and to one another for the sake of temporary relief from reproach and deprivation. He positions them, like the wilderness generation, at the threshold of entering God's heavenly holy place, their heavenly homeland, and calls them to make God's promises the foundation and focal point of life since they are, indeed, reliable (6:13-20; 10:36-39).

6. Contours of faith

The sermon is perhaps most celebrated for its portrait of "faith" in action through its rehearsal of how the "heroes of faith" have responded to God's word and promise (Heb 11). This encomium (a laudatory, celebratory speech) on the virtue of faith is thoroughly shaped by the specific challenges facing the addressees. A recurring theme of the examples is that people of faith act in this world with a view to the future intervention of God and reception of God's promises, and with a view to the invisible realities beyond this world (11:1). Thus Noah acts with a view to a disaster yet to come (11:7), Abraham with a view to receiving a homeland in the future (11:8-22), Joseph gives instructions in view of future acts of God (11:22), Moses with regard to God's future acts of liberation on behalf of the Israelites and the reward yet to come (11:23-27). People of faith look to the invisible cause of the visible world (11:3); Moses acted as one who "regarded" the invisible God (11:27). Both of these elements are vitally important in the overall exhortation to the congregation(s), who must conduct themselves in such a way as to negotiate future crises successfully (1:13; 2:3; 10:30-31, 37-39) and to maintain their grasp of goods as yet not seen (3:6, 14; 6:12; 10:34-35; 11:16; 12:28; 13:14).

The examples drive home the lesson that the person of faith accepts temporal loss for the sake of eternal ("abiding," "lasting") gain, and for the sake of the freedom to pursue this greater hope and calling. The author crafts his examples in such a way as to resonate with the addressees' plight. Abraham leaves behind his place at home, accepting the lower status of sojourner and alien in Canaan, mirroring the loss of status within their native cities suffered by the addressees (11:9, 13). Rejection of being "at home" in their native land becomes a source of witness to the "better, heavenly homeland" that Christians seek (11:14-16). Moses also chose not to maintain his status in Pharaoh's household, voluntarily identifying with God's marginalized people and the reproach that befalls them and God's "anointed" in this world (11:24-26; compare 10:32-34; 13:3, 13). Prophets and martyrs (the martyrs whose story is recounted in 2 Macc 6–7 and 4 Macc 5–17) accepted being driven into the margins of society and even the degradation of torture and death out of loyalty to God and in hope of the "better resurrection" that God would bestow upon faithful clients (11:35-38; again compare 10:32-34; 13:3). Jesus crowns the list of examples (12:1-3) by "enduring a cross, despising shame." Responding obediently to God and attaining the reward God set before him involved embracing humiliation (including the "verbal abuse" with which so many of the addressees could relate, 12:3) and suffering, showing that faith looks only to God's approval, and, in so doing, attains eternal honor. The addressees' behavior in the past also fell into this commendable pattern (10:32-34), and the writer urges them to continue that commitment to God and to one another, holding onto God's promises, not temporal goods.

7. Obligations of community

In the midst of a society that discourages continued association with the Christian community and its way of life, the author seeks to mobilize Christians to provide social support for their mutual association. The community has an important role in empowering the perseverance of individuals. The hearers must watch for signs that particular members of the community are succumbing to the pressures of the society (3:12-13; 12:15), and are thus in danger of relinquishing their hold on God and God's gifts. Their failure to become "teachers" by this point (5:11-14) is a failure to take an active role in helping their sisters and brothers to maintain their commitment to the lifestyle of the Christian group.

This mutual support is found when the community gathers together, so that withdrawal of some diminishes the whole (10:24-25). Members of the community show visible and material support for one another, particularly toward those who are most marginalized and therefore in danger of succumbing to society's pressures to return to their former lifestyle (10:32-34; 13:1-3). The sacrifices of the new congregation of the sanctified consist of praise and bold testimony (13:15), as well as acts of kindness and sharing possessions (13:16), especially with fellow Christians. Each community member should allow the plight of others to touch him or her on the basis of their shared humanity, being "embodied" and vulnerable to the same ills and therefore bound to help one another rather than turn a blind eye (or, worse, contribute to another's suffering, 13:3). Taking on the responsibility of family toward one another (13:1), Christians are able to sustain the commitment of individual believers when obedience to the call of God leads them in directions contrary to the ways embraced by their other social networks.

C. Theological and Religious Significance

1. Contributions to early christology

The author has made a lasting contribution to the church's reflection on the person of Jesus and on components of the Christian creed, namely Jesus' death, resurrection, and ascension. The author's high priestly christology and sacrificial interpretation of Jesus' death and exaltation has been explored above, as has the use of texts from the prophetic literature and Psalms to develop a picture of the Son's significance.

Another important body of tradition utilized by the author to express the role and status of the Son is wisdom tradition, particularly the figure of "Wisdom" as she is personified in Prov 8 and Wis 7–9. The author ascribed attributes of Wisdom now to the pre-Incarnate Son. Recalling Wisdom, the Son is now seen as an active agent in Creation (Heb 1:2; see Prov 8:22-31; Wis 7:22; 9:9) and in the ongoing governance of the cosmos ("he sustains all things," Heb 1:3; see Wis 7:27; 8:1). Like Wisdom, who was praised as "the reflection of eternal light" and "the image of God's goodness" (Wis 7:26), the Son manifests the "radiance of God's glory" and is "the exact representation of God's very being" (1:3a). Hebrews 1:1-4 thus adds its voice to the Christ Hymn (Phil 2:6-11), Col 1:15-20, and the prologue to John in pushing Christian reflection toward a christology of Jesus as eternal Son of God.

2. Gift and response

Hebrews highlights the assumption that early Christian teachers shared with their culture, that valuable gifts call forth costly response, indeed that a gift does not have its full effect in its reception but in the response to the gift. The cycle of giving, receiving, and responding constitutes a single, fluid, transformative relationship creating and sustaining movement. Our investment in our response reveals our estimation of the gift (and the Giver), hence the dangerous situation contemplated in 10:26-31, where the response shows the gift and Giver to be held in lesser esteem than enjoying the friendship of the non-Christian society.

Hebrews' articulation of this dynamic assists believers in connecting grace and discipleship, the experience of God's favor and the investment of one's whole self in responding, or in alignment of belief and action. The social dynamic of reciprocity assists disciples in understanding how receiving God's gifts motivates faithfulness, witness, and service. God's gift is not to be treated as something that we receive for our own enjoyment alongside other commodities, but that does not thereby lay a transforming claim on our ambitions and actions.

3. Perfecting the conscience

Hebrews' concept of "perfection" has been the center of much scholarly discussion. Two key uses focus on Jesus' perfection (the process by which he became a sympathetic high priest in God's heavenly holy places) and the perfection of the conscience of the believers (fitting them to enter God's presence along with Jesus). The author touches the heart of Christian religious experience. Jesus has gone further than any other priestly figure into God's space (heaven itself) and further into our space (our conscience, our inner being) to enable us to become completely transparent to God and encounter God more fully. Such spatial and cultic metaphors show that the death and resurrection of Jesus opens up new dimensions of relating to God. Where worship and spiritual direction lead disciples toward religious encounter with God and becoming open before God, the essential vision of the author of Hebrews is realized. Ushering people into the real presence of God, proleptically in access to the "throne of favor" (4:16) and finally at their entrance into the realm beyond time and space is the goal and heart of effective religion (7:19).

This unprecedented possibility of intimate access to God makes "willful sin" so hazardous in the mind of the author (10:26-31). Willful sin becomes a recontamination of the cleansed conscience, bringing back the fear, the distance, the dread of encountering God, displacing the joyful approach to God in the expectation of favor. Hebrews 10:29 names the sin within the willful sin, beneath the particular manifestations of the sin that so often become the focus of attention that disciples miss the root sin—an opportunity to honor God has been lost for the sake of the temporary ease or gratification of the self, or some such lesser good. Once again, the author challenges disciples to connect religious experience with ethical response.

4. Faith and freedom

In a social situation where pressures were being brought to bear to suppress continued participation in the religious and social experiences of Christian congregation(s), exhortations to faithful perseverance are calculated not merely to constrain the hearers but to liberate them. That is, the language of "faith" is the language of freedom from the constraints of one's unbelieving neighbors.

This freedom takes two distinct yet mutually supporting forms. First, faith enables freedom from the tyranny that concern for temporal pleasures and deprivations exercise over the human spirit. Faith weighs anchor in the realm beyond "this creation." Not only does this perspective allow the believer freedom to

consider whether or not life is indeed more than food or clothing but also to move about with freedom from the larger society's systems of rewards and sanctions (its "deviancy-control" techniques).

The second form of freedom is expressed by the author as parrēsia (παρρησία), "boldness," "frank speech." Faith allows the believer not to be cowed into silence (in speech or in living witness) about the value of Jesus, his gifts, and his promises. It is the freedom of Christian witness and solidarity (10:33-35) where the domination systems at work around the believers would silence that witness. Jesus' obedient acceptance of the cross was an act of liberation from the fear of death and all the other sanctions that domination systems use to enforce conformity and cooperation (2:14-15). The author's picture of a response of faith that is willing to live in the margins, to step into places of temporal deprivation and disadvantage for the sake of obediently and single-heartedly pursuing God's promises, and for the sake of solidarity with the people of God, at once speaks of the great freedom that is to be found in Jesus—and of the potential bondage that besets the comfortable Christian that is too well adjusted to his or her social context. *See* CHRISTOLOGY; FAITH; WISDOM IN THE NT.

Bibliography: H. W. Attridge. *The Epistle to the Hebrews* (1989); Herbert W. Bateman IV. *Early Jewish Hermeneutics and Hebrews 1:5-13* (1997); F. F. Bruce. *The Epistle to the Hebrews.* Rev. ed. (1990); F. B. Craddock. "Hebrews." NIB 12 (1998) 1–174; N. C. Croy. *Endurance in Suffering: Hebrews 12:1-13 in Its Rhetorical, Religious, and Philosophical Contexts* (1998); D. A. deSilva. *Despising Shame: Honor Discourse and Community Maintenance in the Epistle to the Hebrews* (1995); D. A. deSilva. *Perseverance in Gratitude: A Socio-Rhetorical Commentary on the Epistle "to the Hebrews"* (2000); P. M. Eisenbaum. *The Jewish Heroes of Christian History: Hebrews 11 in Literary Context* (1997); P. Ellingworth. *The Epistle to the Hebrews* (1993); G. H. Guthrie. *The Structure of Hebrews: A Text-linguistic Analysis* (1994); G. H. Guthrie. *Hebrews.* NIVAC (1998); D. A. Hagner. *Hebrews.* Rev. ed. NIBC (1990); L. D. Hurst. *The Epistle to the Hebrews: Its Background of Thought* (1990); Robert Jewett. *A Letter to Pilgrims: A Commentary on the Epistle to the Hebrews* (1981); Craig Koester. *The Epistle to the Hebrews* (2001); W. L. Lane. *Hebrews 1–8.* WBC 47A (1991); W. L. Lane. *Hebrews 9–13.* WBC 47B (1991); Barnabas Lindars. *The Theology of the Letter to the Hebrews* (1991); Thomas Long. *Hebrews.* Interpretation (1997); V. C. Pfitzner. *Hebrews.* ANTC (1997); J. M. Scholer. *Proleptic Priests: Priesthood in the Epistle to the Hebrews* (1991); J. W. Thompson. *The Beginnings of Christian Philosophy: The Epistle to the Hebrews* (1982).

DAVID A. DESILVA

HEBRON, HEBRONITES hee´bruhn, hee´bruh-n*i*t חֶבְרוֹן khevron, חֶבְרוֹנִי khevroni; Χεβρών Chebrōn, Χεβρωνί Chebrōni]. 1. A geopolitically important city situated at the central high point of the Judean hill country (elevation, 3050 ft.), Hebron is one of the oldest continually occupied cities on earth. Roads ascending from the coastal plain to the west meet near Hebron with the main route connecting Jerusalem, 19 mi. to the north, and Beersheba, 23 mi. to the southwest. The city is associated in biblical tradition with a number of well-known biblical figures. Abraham, Sarah, Isaac, Rebecca, Jacob, Leah and Rachel all sojourned there; Caleb conquered and settled in Hebron; and David chose Hebron as his first royal city. Ancient Hebron, known today variously as Tel Hebron and Tell er-Rumeide, is located on a low spur of Jebel er-Rumeide overlooking the modern city of Hebron spread out before it to the north and east. A spring, which is today called Ein Jedida, served as the ancient city's water source. The site was occupied as early as 3000 BCE and has yielded archaeological evidence of nearly continuous occupation from the beginning of the Middle Bronze Age (ca. 2000 BCE) until the end of the Hellenistic period (ca. 60 BCE), excluding only the Persian period for which evidence of occupation has yet to be unearthed. Hebron probably migrated to the site of the modern city in the valley below Jebel er-Rumeide during the Roman period.

The OT writers usually refer to the city simply as Hebron. Sometimes they explain that it was formerly called KIRIATH-ARBA (Josh 14:15; Judg 1:10), elsewhere they call the city Kiriath-arba adding the note, "that is, Hebron" (Gen 23:2, 35:27; Josh 15:13, 54, 20:7, 21:11). The older name Kiriath-arba persisted into the postexilic period (Neh 11:25), and the choice of designation probably reflects the city's political alignment in different periods. Hebron is also related in some way to MAMRE, a place named only in the book of Genesis.

Above all, Hebron is remembered as the city of Abraham. The modern Arabic name for the city, El-Kahlil, means "the friend [of God]" (see Isa 41:8; 2 Chr 20:7). Indeed, Hebron is the hub around which the earliest stories of Abraham and his descendants revolve. After separating from Lot, Abraham pitched his tents by the oaks of Mamre at Hebron (Gen 13:18). There he dwelt "as an alien" among the Hittites (Gen 35:27), and there he gave hospitality to angels who foretold the wonder of Isaac's birth and revealed the dire fate of Sodom and Gomorrah (Gen 18). Later Abraham moved south to Gerar "in the land of the Philistines" (20:1; 21:34), and then to the area near Beersheba (22:19). Finally, Abraham moved back to Hebron where he and Sarah lived out their days and were buried in the cave of Machpelah that Abraham purchased from the Hittite Ephron (Gen 23; 25:9-10). Isaac settled for a time in Hebron (Gen 35:27). So too Jacob, when he returned from Haran, settled in Hebron (Gen 37:1, 14), and from there he descended into Egypt. Later, when the Israelites fled from Egypt, it was to Hebron that they first sent spies to assess the land and its people.

The spies who visited Hebron brought from the vicinity both evidence of the region's fertility and the report that the Anakites, a tribe of legendary stature and strength said to have descended from the NEPHILIM, inhabited the city (Num 13:33; Deut 9:2). All but one of the spies reported that the inhabitants of the land were too strong and their cities too well fortified to be conquered. Only the spy Caleb encouraged Israel to begin the conquest at once (Num 13:30; Joshua is added as a second faithful spy in Num 14:6, 38). Caleb's faithfulness is rewarded when he is granted Hebron as his possession (Josh 14:6-15; 15:13; Judg 1:20). Responsibility for the conquest of Hebron is attributed variously to the Israelites under Joshua (Josh 10:36-37; 11:21), to the tribe of Judah (Judg 1:10), and to Caleb (Josh 14:6-15; 15:13-14; Judg 1:20). Further conflicts are observable among the traditions detailing the ownership of the city. Some texts assign the city to the Calebites (Josh 14:13-14 and Judg 1:20); some subsume the Calebites under Judah and assign the city to Judah (Josh 15:13, 54); some assign Hebron to the Kohathite clan of Levites, leaving to the Calebites control only of Hebron's surrounding fields and villages (Josh 21:9-11, 13). The Calebite claim on the city probably represents the earliest layer of tradition, and the conflicting perspectives arose as later layers of tradition were added. These later layers probably derive from disputes over the control of this important city at different points in its history. Hebron was also distinguished as a city of refuge (Josh 20:7).

Both Hebron's identity as a Calebite city and its strategic importance in the Judean hill country are apparent in the stories of David's rise to power. After the death of Samuel, David married Abigail, the widow of a wealthy Calebite chieftain (1 Sam 25). Following Saul's death David took over Calebite-controlled Hebron as his residence, apparently by alliance rather than conquest (2 Sam 2:1-4; note that David's Calebite wife Abigail is specifically mentioned). David's alliance with the Calebites coincides with the beginning of his war against the house of Saul (2 Sam 3:1) and with the end of his friendly relations with the Philistines (2 Sam 5:17-21; compare 1 Sam 27). At Hebron the people of Judah acclaimed David king, and David ruled from there for either seven (1 Kgs 2:11) or seven-and-one-half years (2 Sam 2:11). During this time he prospered both in his long war with the house of Saul and in begetting children—six in all. Three, Amnon, Absalom, and Adonijah, were at one time or another contenders for their father's throne (2 Sam 3:2-5). David's reign from Hebron ended when Ishbaal, heir to Saul's throne, was betrayed and assassinated by his own generals. The northern tribes came to David at Hebron and proclaimed him their king (2 Sam 4–5). At this juncture David moved his capital to Jerusalem, a city located adventitiously on the border of the once separate kingdoms.

The length of David's reign at Hebron may have indirectly prompted the editorial note in Num 13:22, "Hebron was built seven years before Zoan in Egypt." Zoan (commonly referred to by its Greek name, "Tanis") is located in upper Egypt and became the royal city of Smendes I in 1070 BCE. The note may be an attempt by an editor, working with only an approximate idea of the actual dates, to coordinate David's establishment of Jerusalem as his capital with Smendes' establishment of his rule at Tanis, thereby suggesting a symbolically important correspondence between Tanis and Jerusalem. Alternatively, the note may simply refer to a phase of refortification of Hebron sometime in the 11th cent. BCE. Archaeological study of Hebron has shown that its first fortification walls were built long before the founding of Tanis.

After David moved his capital to Jerusalem, Hebron continued as an important city within the Israelite-Judean state. In his bid to usurp his father's throne, Absalom chose Hebron as the place to proclaim himself king, a choice no doubt prompted by the city's enduring religious and political importance (2 Sam 15:1-12). Second Chronicles informs us that Hebron was one of fifteen cities fortified and provisioned by Rehoboam (11:5–12). Hebron's importance to the Judean state after 722 is evident in the discovery of some 500 clay jar handles stamped lmlk khbrn, "belonging to the king ... Hebron." Handles bearing this inscription have been found among Iron II debris at several Judean fortress cities, and two have been found at Hebron itself. The handles are usually associated with King Hezekiah's preparation for Sennacherib's attack in 701 BCE, and they suggest that Hebron served Judah as an important administrative or economic center, or perhaps as the site of a royal pottery, long after David's time.

From Rehoboam's time until the exile, Hebron disappears from the biblical narrative, although archaeological evidence shows that it continued to thrive. One final reference to Hebron in the history of Israel and Judah occurs in Neh 11:25, which notes that some returning from Babylon settled in Kiriath-arba, the ancient name reappearing as if to signify a new beginning.

Bibliography: J. R. Chadwick. "Discovering Hebron: The City of the Patriarchs Slowly Yields its Secrets." *BAR* 31.5 (2005) 24–33, 70–71. N. Naʾaman. "'Hebron was Built Seven Years before Zoan in Egypt' (Numbers XIII 22)." *VT* 31 (1981) 488–92.

BRIAN C. JONES

2. The third son of Kohath and grandson of Levi (Exod 6:18; Num 3:19; 1 Chr 6:2, 18 [Heb. 5:28; 6:3]; 23:12). Hebron was the brother of Amram. David

invited 80 descendants of Hebron to take part in the transfer of the ARK OF THE COVENANT to Jerusalem (1 Chr 15:9). In all probability, Hebron the son of Kohath and his children are eponymous ancestors of Levitical families.

3. Hebronites are a Levitical family descended from Hebron the son of Kohath (Num 3:27; 26:58; 1 Chr 26:23). David entrusted 1700 Hebronites with "oversight of Israel west of the Jordan" (1 Chr 26:30). Another group was given similar responsibilities over the Transjordanian tribes (1 Chr 26:32). The two notes possibly reflect and retroactively justify the assumption of secular power by the Levites in the postexilic period. Since a parenthetical note in 1 Chr 26:31 reports that a census conducted in the last year of David's reign found a number of Hebronites (most likely, wealthy landowners) at JAZER in Gilead, 1 Chr 26:30-32 may indicate patterns of Levitical settlement after the exile. The term Hebronites is never used in the Bible as gentilic of the inhabitants of the city of Hebron.

4. The son of MARESHAH, a descendant of Judah (1 Chr 2:42). If the name Mesha in the first part of the same verse is a corruption or variant form of Mareshah (as suggested by the LXX), Hebron was the grandson of Caleb, the son of Hezron, and Judah's descendant five generations removed. Another possibility is that the note introduces Caleb's son Mesha as the father of Ziph and Mareshah as Ziph's son; if so, Hebron was Caleb's great-great-grandson and Judah's descendant seven generations removed. In any case, the verse appears to reflect close ties between the cities of Hebron, Mareshah, and Ziph, or between the clans controlling these cities. First Chronicles 2:43 lists Korah among the descendants of Hebron the son of Mareshah. According to Exod 6:21 (see also 1 Chr 6:22 [Heb 6:7]), Korah was the son of Izhar, the brother of Hebron the Levite.

SERGE FROLOV

HECATAEUS, PSEUDO. *See* HECATAEUS OF ABDERA.

HECATAEUS OF ABDERA. Historian and ethnographer in the time of the Ptolemy I Soter (ca. 300 BCE). His *On the Egyptians*, preserved in part in Diodorus Siculus' *World History*, presents Egypt as the source of all other civilizations. It also includes a treatment of aspects of Jewish history and culture such as the exodus from Egypt and the law of Moses, though scholars attribute some of this material concerning the Jews to other anonymous sources.

SHANE A. BERG

HEDGE [גְּדֵרָה gedherah, מְסוּכָה mesukhah, מְשֻׂכָה mesukkah; φραγμός phragmos]. A hedge is a dense shrub frequently used as a wall or barrier. Hedges are often set around vineyards in the Bible, as e.g., in Isa 5:5 and Matt 21:33. The association between hedges as walls for vineyards might be because planting and maintaining vineyards was a labor-intensive activity and wine was a valuable commodity. Therefore, vineyards were carefully guarded. Not only were they hedged in, but watchtowers were also built in vineyards for protection. Since hedges were used literally as walls, hedges are also employed metaphorically in the Bible to indicate being protected or, alternatively, trapped. For example, Job laments being alive while trapped ("hedged in") by God (Job 3:23). *See* FENCE; VINE; WALLS.

Bibliography: Philip J. King and Lawrence E. Stager. *Life in Biblical Israel* (2001).

JENNIFER L. KOOSED

HEDGEHOG [קִפֹּד qippodh, קִפּוֹד qippodh; ἐχῖνος echinos]. A ft.-long mammal known for rolling its spine-covered body into a ball. The NRSV translates "hedge-hog," following the LXX in several places (Isa 14:23; 34:11), where the meaning may be closer to "bittern," a type of bird (KJV), since it is listed with other birds (Isa 34:11). In Zeph 2:14 the NRSV translates the same term "screech owl." *See* ANIMALS OF THE BIBLE.

ODED BOROWSKI

HEDONISM. The view that pleasure is the highest or only good. Modern philosophy divides hedonism into psychological and ethical types, each capable of taking diverse forms and being combined in various ways. Psychological hedonism tends to emphasize the natural inevitability of pleasure seeking while ethical hedonism tends to rely more on a value theory (e.g., utilitarianism). Utilitarian versions usually aim to maximize pleasure for all sentient beings, while egoistic versions often value one's own pleasure over that of others.

Among ancient thinkers, the hedonistic views of Epicurus (341–270 BCE) are of most relevance to biblical literature. While Aristippus (ca. 435–ca. 360 BCE) taught the ancient equivalent of "if it feels good, do it," without regard to consequences, Epicurus taught that the highest good is the absence of pain and pleasures that lead to painful consequences. This form of hedonism has ascetic aspects, and the highest good is more like happiness than simply pleasure. Despite numerous questionable interpretations, DeWitt demonstrates several striking ethical similarities between Epicurus and Paul. Glad provides an impressive comparison of Epicurean and Pauline practices of psychagogy: "care of souls."

Bibliography: Norman Wentworth DeWitt. *St. Paul and Epicurus* (1954); Clarence E. Glad. *Paul and Philodemus: Adaptability in Epicurean and Early Christian Psychagogy* (1995).

MARK D. GIVEN

HEEL, LIFTED [עָקֵב ʿaqev; πτέρνα pterna]. The phrase appears in Ps 41:9 [Heb. 41:10] where the Hebrew root ʿqb is obscure and has led to different translations. The phrase literally means "to make great the heel." The same root means "heel" in Gen 3:15; 25:26, but in Gen 49:19 and Josh 8:13 it could mean "rear guard." Fisher cites an Egyptian text that offers a useful parallel: "It was he who ate my food that raised troops [against me]" (*ANET,* 418).

Another meaning associated with the root is "fraud, deceit" as in 2 Kgs 10:19. This meaning provides the popular etymology for the name Jacob.

The verse in Ps 41 expresses the ancient code of hospitality where a bond is formed with the one who has shared a meal (bread). Middle Eastern hospitality would require that even your enemy, if he has broken bread with you, should be safe within your home. Whether the phrase is translated as an idiom, "my friend has lifted his heel against me" or "has raised deceit against me" the meaning is the same. A friend has become an enemy.

In the context of the foot washing in John 13:18, Ps 41:10 is cited referring to Judas' betrayal. The Gospel makes significant changes to the LXX, notably changing esthiō (ἐσθίω; "eating") to trōgō (τρώγω), the term used in John 6:51c-58, which is a section of the Bread of Life discourse that many scholars interpret as eucharistic. The Gospel, therefore, links the morsel offered to Judas and the eucharist (see Moloney, 20–22). Menken's analysis of the source for the Johannine version of the Psalm concludes that it is the evangelist's own translation of the Hebrew text based on Jewish exegetical methods of the time.

Bibliography: Loren R. Fisher. "Betrayed by Friends." *Interp* 18 (1964) 20–38; Bruce J. Malina. "The Received View and What It Cannot Do: III John and Hospitality." *Semeia* 35 (1986) 171–89; M. J. J. Menken. "The Translation of Psalm 41:10 in John 13:18." *JSNT* 40 (1990) 61–79; Francis J. Moloney. *Glory not Dishonour: Reading John 13–21* (1998); James B. Pritchard. *ANET.* 2nd ed. (1955) 418.

MARY L. COLOE

HEGAI heg´i [הֵגַי heghe], הֵגָי heghay]. The most prominent of the EUNUCHs who pepper the book of Esther, Hegai is entrusted with the virgins gathered to replace Queen VASHTI. Hegai's position between the two genders makes him a skilled guide from the harem into the court, and Esther relies solely on Hegai's advice to win the king's favor (Esth 2:3-15).

NICOLE WILKINSON DURAN

HEGEMONIDES hej´uh-moh´nuh-deez [Ἡγεμονίδης Hēgemonidēs]. Before leaving to deal with Philip's revolt in Antioch (2 Macc 13:23), Antiochus V is said to have appointed Hegemonides as governor over the Judean territory that stretched from Ptolemais to Gerar (2 Macc 13:24). The geographical location of Gerar is not clear.

HEGESIPPUS [Ἡγήσιππος Hēgēsippos]. A mid-2nd cent. Greek-speaking Christian from Palestine or Syria, perhaps a converted Jew. He traveled by sea to Rome via Corinth collecting authentic apostolic traditions. These he recorded in the five books of his *Hypomnemata*, or *Memoirs*, to safeguard the tradition of apostolic preaching against heresies, especially Gnosticism. This work is now completely lost except for fragments and reports of its contents preserved in EUSEBIUS (*Hist. eccl.* 2.23; 3.11-12, 16, 19-20, 32; and 4.7-8, 11, 21-22). The extant sections deal mostly with the early history of the church at Jerusalem. It is also reported by Eusebius (4.22) that he drew up a succession list of the early bishops of the church of Rome.

MARK DELCOGLIANO

HEGESIPPUS, PSEUDO [Ἡγήσιππος Hēgēsippos]. Anonymous author of a Latin account of the Jewish revolt against Rome in 66–73 CE. Because of the inclusion of apocryphal material the author became associated with Hegesippus, a mid-2nd cent. church historian mentioned by EUSEBIUS, *Hist. eccl.* 4.7-8, etc. Internal evidence indicates a composition date of ca. 370 CE by a Latin-Greek bilingual living in the vicinity of Antioch. The work draws most heavily from Josephus, but also from Greek and Roman historians. The author cites Scripture extensively and is thus a crucial textual witness for the 4th cent. Latin version.

MARK DELCOGLIANO

HEGLAM heg′luhm [הֶגְלָם heghlam]. Only the RSV and NRSV render as a proper name, as an appositive describing Gera (1 Chr 8:7). Other translations understand it as verbal form meaning "caused them to be removed" or "carried them away into exile." The word appears in an obscure genealogy of Benjamin. It follows the listing of three sons of Ehud: Naaman, Ahijah, and Gera, described as the heads of families who lived in Geba, a levitical town of Benjamin (Josh 18:24; 21:17) northwest of the Dead Sea. If rendered as a proper name, Heglam (Gera) is the father of Uzza and Ahihud. If a verb, then perhaps Ehud is their father (JPS Tanakh). There is no scholarly consensus on these textual difficulties.

MARK RONCACE

HEIFER [עֶגְלָה ʿeghlah, עֶגְלַת בָּקָר ʿeghlath baqar]. A young cow that has not borne a calf. Heifers were used for threshing grain (Hos 10:11) and as sacrifices and food. As a sacrifice, it established that Abraham and his descendants would receive the land (Gen 15:8-21). Breaking a heifer's neck is prescribed as the means for atoning for a murder whose perpetrator is unknown (Deut 21:1-9). Its sacrifice also provided the context for the meal after which Samuel anointed David as king (1 Sam 16:1-13). In addition, this animal is used figuratively to describe Samson's wife (Judg 14:18) and Egypt (Jer 46:20), to emphasize

Babylon's wantonness (Jer 50:11), and to represent the stubbornness of the Israelites (Hos 6:16). The phrase rendered in the KJV as "heifer of three years old" (Isa 15:5; Jer 48:34) has been more recently understood as the place EGLATH-SHELISHIYAH. *See* CALF, GOLDEN; RED HEIFER.

EMILY R. CHENEY

HEIR [יוֹרֵשׁ yoresh; κληρονόμος klēronomos]. In the OT, *heir* is generally used literally and having an heir was considered crucial (Judg 21:17), as with Abraham in order for God's promises to be fulfilled (Gen 15:2-4). David is promised that if his heirs follow God, he will never be without a descendant upon the throne of Israel (2 Sam 7:11-13; 1 Kgs 2:4; Luke 1:32-33).

The NT often uses *heir* figuratively. Abraham's heirs are not only those who keep the Law but those who have faith in Jesus (Rom 4:14; Gal 3:29; Eph 3:6). Believers are heirs of God and co-heirs with Christ (Rom 8:17; Titus 3:7; Jas 2:5). Jesus is the heir of all things (Heb 1:2). *See* INHERITANCE IN THE NT; INHERITANCE IN THE OT.

KENNETH D. LITWAK

HELAH hee′luh [חֶלְאָה khel′ah]. One of the two wives of Ashhur, a descendant of Judah and the "father of Tekoa" (1 Chr 4:5).

HELAM hee′luhm [חֵילָם khelam, חֵלְאָם khela′m]. A town east of the Sea of Galilee at which David defeated the Arameans (2 Sam 10:16-17). The conflict arose when David's attempt to comfort Hanun after the death of his father, Nahash, turned sour (2 Sam 10:1-5). Hanun hired Aramean mercenaries to do battle with David's army. The town is identified as ALEMA in 1 Macc 5:26.

STEPHANIE SKELLEY-CHANDLER

HELBAH hel′buh [חֶלְבָּה khelbah]. A town in the territory of the tribe of Asher from which the Israelites were unable to drive out the Canaanite inhabitants (Judg 1:31). It is possible that Helbah, AHLAB (Judg 1:31), and MAHALAB (Josh 19:29) are variants of the same place name.

HELBON hel′bon [חֶלְבּוֹן khelbon]. In his lamentation for Tyre, Ezekiel mentions that Damascus traded the wine produced in Helbon for Tyrian goods (Ezek 27:18). It is generally agreed that Helbon is identified with the modern town of Helbun, several miles north of Dasmascus, where wine production continues to be important.

HELDAI hel′di [חֶלְדַּי khelday]. 1. Commander from Nathophah who was in charge of the army division responsible for serving King David during the twelfth month (1 Chr 27:15). Based on the associated names of commanders, this Heldai may be the same person as the Heled of 1 Chr 11:30, or Heleb in the list of the Thirty (2 Sam 23:29).

2. One of the exiles from whom Zechariah is instructed to collect silver and gold to use to make a crown for the high priest Joshua, the son of Jehozadak (Zech 6:10-14), who will rebuild the Temple. The crown is to be in the care of this Heldai (Hebrew reads Helem in v. 14) and the other exiles, Tobijah, Jedaiah, and Josiah, the son of Zephaniah.

C. MARK MCCORMICK

HELEB. *See* HELDAI.

HELECH hee′lik [חֵילֵךְ khelekh]. Ezekiel 27:11 notes the walls of Tyre manned with foreign soldiers from Helech (NRSV; NIV) and other places. Helech is a transliteration of the Hebrew noun that the KJV and NASB render "your army." Helech as a place is the preferred translation. The annals of the Assyrian king Shalmaneser III first mention Hilakku (858–824 BCE). While the exact location is not certain, Assyrian inscriptions that describe rebellion during the reigns of Sennacherib and Esarhaddon seem to relate Helech to CILICIA in Asia Minor.

The region was known for its lawlessness, thieves, and pirates until the Roman conquest. The possible Hebrew root for Helech carries the sense of wandering or describes a wayfarer. Cilician "warriors" would certainly serve as mercenaries in the defense of Tyre and its important port. Ironically, many of the ships leaving Tyre certainly met Cilician pirates on the waters of the northern Mediterranean.

MICHAEL G. VANZANT

HELED. *See* HELDAI.

HELEK hee′lik [חֵלֶק kheleq]. A descendant of Manasseh and eponymous ancestor of the Helekites, described once as descended from Manasseh through Machir and Gilead (Num 26:29-30), and alternately as among the "sons" of Manasseh receiving a clan allotment (Josh 17:1-2). In comparing these Manassite family relationship accounts with others (e.g., 1 Chr 2:21-24; 7:14-19), the various traditions, exemplified by Helek (meaning "division"), portray Manasseh as a tribe "divided" into a geographic and social puzzle.

JASON C. DYKEHOUSE

HELEM hee′lim [חֵלֶם helem]. The Asherite father of Zophah, Imna, Shelesh, and Amal (1 Chr 7:35).

HELENA [Ἑλένη Helenē]. JUSTIN MARTYR and IRE-NAEUS identified her as the female consort of SIMON Magus, said to be created as "the first conception of his mind." Simonites apparently worshiped the pair as gods. To discredit her, Justin and Irenaeus insisted she was merely a prostitute from Tyre. Irenaeus added that she was trapped in a variety of female bodies, includ-

ing Helen of Troy, in which she suffered numerous defilements.

CARLY DANIEL-HUGHES

HELEPH hee′lif [חֵלֶף khelef]. The first town mentioned in defining the borders of Naphtali (Josh 19:33). It may perhaps be identified with Khirbet ʿIrbadeh, near Mount Tabor, placing the town near the intersection of the borders of Manasseh, Zebulun, and Naphtali.

Bibliography: Y. Aharoni. *The Land of the Bible* (1979) 259.

T. DELAYNE VAUGHN

HELEZ hee′liz [חֶלֶץ khelets]. 1. One of DAVID'S CHAMPIONS ("the Thirty"), called a "Paltite" in the Hebrew of 2 Sam 23:26. In 1 Chr 11:27 and 27:10, he is called a "Pelonite." Additionally, 1 Chr 27 identifies him as an Ephraimite. Some weight may be given to the designation "Pelonite" since some versions of the LXX read "Peleonite" in 2 Sam 23:26.

2. The son of Azariah, a Judahite (1 Chr 2:39).

T. DELAYNE VAUGHN

HELI hee′li [Ἡλί Heli]. In the LXX, Heli is the Gk. form of ELI, the priest to whom Samuel ministered (1 Sam 1–4). In the NT, Heli is listed in Luke's genealogy of Jesus (Luke 3:23-38) as the father of Joseph (3:23).

HELIODORUS hee′lee-uh-dor′uhs [Ἡλιόδωρος Heliodōros]. A chief minister of Seleucus IV Philopator. The name, "gift (dōron δῶρον) of the sun (hēlios ἥλιος)," reflects the popularity of sun worship in Syria. Heliodorus was sent by the king to confiscate the treasury of the Jerusalem Temple, after Simon, the CAPTAIN OF THE TEMPLE, conspired with Apollonius, the governor of Coele-Syria and Phoenicia (2 Macc 3). However, Heliodorus failed to achieve his mission because of divine intervention. Onias III, the high priest in conflict with Simon, offered sacrifice to God on Heliodorus' behalf. This story, marking the beginning of the conflict between Jerusalem and the Seleucids, might be connected with the financial crisis of the Syrian court, which was caused by reparations Rome levied on Antiochus the Great through the treaty of Apamea in 188 BCE. According to 4 Macc 4:1-14, Seleucus IV sent Apollonious, but not Heliodorus, to confiscate the treasury. The attempt of the Seleucid high official to pillage the treasury in Jerusalem is briefly alluded to in Dan 11:20. Appian depicts Heliodorus as an ambitious man, who sought to possess the throne of Syria after assassinating Seleucus IV (*Syrian Wars* 45). Eumenes and Attalus drove out Heliodorus and installed Antiochus IV Epiphanes. *See* SELEUCID EMPIRE.

Bibliography: Jonathan A. Goldstein. *II Maccabees.* AB 41A (1984).

SAMUEL CHEON

HELIOPOLIS hee´lee-op´uh-lis. Heliopolis, located at the southern end of the Nile Delta, just north of modern Cairo, was one of the most important cities in ancient Egypt. Never politically powerful, the city's significance derived from the prominence of its solar cult. Its ancient Egyptian name was *Iunu* (pillar), which came into biblical Hebrew as On (ʾon אוֹן). The city was christened Heliopolis ("city of the sun") by the Greeks. The high priest of Heliopolis was known as "Chief of Seers."

Heliopolis was first occupied in the Predynastic Period, but rose to prominence in the Old Kingdom along with the cult of the sun-god RE. The kings of the Old Kingdom through the New Kingdom demonstrated their devotion to Re by erecting shrines, obelisks, and other monuments or by adding to existing structures. Heliopolis reached its zenith during the Twentieth Dynasty after which it fell into decline. The city suffered significant damage at the hands of the Persians. By the time Strabo visited in the 1st cent. CE, most of its monuments had been plundered or destroyed. The two obelisks erected by Thutmose III are now in London and New York.

The heart of Heliopolis was the temple complex dedicated to Re-Horakhty and Atum with its sacred lake and artificial mound representing the hill of creation. According to the Heliopolitan cosmogony, the creator god (Re or Atum-Re) stood upon the hill of creation in the midst of the primeval waters. The temple complex included a shrine housing the *benben*-stone, symbolizing the hill of creation.

Central to the theology of Heliopolis was the Ennead or Nine. The Nine were the creator and four pairs of gods. They included the earth, sky, and air (moist and dry), as well as four gods associated with the afterlife: Seth, OSIRIS, ISIS, and Nephthys (*see* SETH, EGYPTIAN DEITY).

Heliopolis is less commonly mentioned in the Bible than other Egyptian cities more prominent during the period of the biblical writers, such as Tanis and Memphis, appearing only in the Joseph narrative in Genesis and in oracles against Egypt in Isaiah, Jeremiah, and Ezekiel. With the exception of the oracle in Ezekiel, the references reflect awareness of the city's significance as a cultic site.

Joseph's father-in-law is Potiphera, a priest of On (Gen 41:45, 50; 46:20). The reference does not specify Potiphera's rank or function in the Heliopolitan priesthood, but his name *p3-di-p3-rʿ*, "the one whom Re gives," is most appropriate for a functionary of the temple of Re.

Other than Genesis, Heliopolis is mentioned by name only in Ezek 30:17, where it is pointed ʾawen (אָוֶן), "iniquity, harm, misfortune," instead of ʾon, a pejorative play on words. It is not to be confused with the toponym Aven ʾawen in Hosea and Amos.

In Jer 43, the oracle against Egypt concludes (v. 13) with the shattering of the pillars of the "house

of the sun" (beth shemesh בֵּית שֶׁמֶשׁ), presumably the obelisks of Heliopolis, and the burning of the temples of the Egyptian gods. BETH-SHEMESH refers to one of several locales in Israel elsewhere in the OT. The reference in Isa 19:18 is problematic. The Heb. reads "city of destruction" (ʿir haheres עִיר הַהֶרֶס), which should be emended to read "city of the sun" (ʿir hakheres עִיר הַחֶרֶס).The only difference between the readings is the change of the Hebrew letter h (ה) to the letter kh (ח), two letters that look very similar. Kheres (חֶרֶס) is a rare word for sun, but the reading finds support in some manuscripts and versions. The context is the transition between judgment and salvation in an extended oracle against Egypt. Whereas the politically prominent cities of Tanis and Memphis figure in the judgment, Heliopolis appears in the context of the promised future, when the God of Israel will be worshiped even in Egypt, befitting a city known more for its temples and theology than its military or political might.

CAROLYN HIGGINBOTHAM

HELIOS [Ἥλιος *Helios*]. Greek god of the sun, who is most often artistically portrayed as a charioteer traveling daily from east to west across the sky. A minor deity in the classical period of Greece, Helios became more popular in the Hellenistic era, primarily through associations with other gods (especially APOLLO). Helios' importance peaked in the establishment of the cult of Sol Invictus ("the Invincible Sun") by the Roman emperor Aurelian in 274 CE.

SHANE A. BERG

HELKAI hel´ki [חֶלְקָי *khelqay*]. The head of a clan of priests (MERAIOTH) who served in Jerusalem during the time of JOIAKIM (the son of Zerubbabel's contemporary Jeshua). The name appears in Neh 12:15 in the context of a list of priestly and Levitical clan heads serving at that time.

HELKATH hel´kath [חֶלְקָת *khelqath*]. A town located in the southern part of the tribal possession of Assur (Josh 19:25), probably in the pass that connects the plain of Acco with the Jezreel Valley. It was designated as a Levitical city and given to the Gershonites (Josh 21:31). Helkath does not occur in the list of Gershonite towns in 1 Chr 6:75, but is replaced by HUKOK. The town may be mentioned in Thutmose III's topographical lists at Karnak temple. Two archaeological sites have been proposed for the location Helkath: Tell el-Harbaj and Tell el-Qassis, but a conclusive determination is impossible at this time.

KEVIN A. WILSON

HELKATH-HAZZURIM hel´kath-haz´yoo-rim [חֶלְקָת הַצֻּרִים *khelqath hatsurim*]. Usually translated as "field of sword edges," this more appropriately means "area of cliffs" or possibly "area of adversaries." This is the place near the pool of Gibeon where twelve of Abner's men fought twelve of Joab's men, all piercing the sides of their enemies (2 Sam 2:12-16). Some scholars consequently accept textual corruption and read hatsiddim (הַצִּדִּים) meaning "place of the sides" to better fit the context.

R. JUSTIN HARKINS

HELL. *See* DEAD, ABODE OF THE; GEHENNA.

HELLENISM hel´uh-niz´uhm [Ἑλληνικός Hellēnikos]. Means "Hellenic, Greek." Encompasses the varieties of Greek culture that were diffused and adopted by many groups in antiquity. It can refer distinctly to language, political institutions, and religion. The spread of this culture, hellenization, was a natural process of contact between groups in the ancient world and not exclusively a political or enforced change under ALEXANDER THE GREAT and his successors.

In the Greek of Herodotus (5th cent. BCE), Hellenism denoted the Greek language, although it might have also implied Greek culture. By the early 1st cent. BCE, the author of 2 Maccabees uses the word in opposition to Judaism, referring to foreign influence, especially Greek, in Jerusalem. It was "the height of Hellenism" (2 Macc 4:13) that, the author claims, precipitated the Maccabean revolt, thereby denigrating the Seleucids and attempts to establish Jerusalem as a Greek political state (*see* MACCABEES, MACCABEAN REVOLT). The author's propagandistic language has established in scholarly minds an opposition between Judaism and Hellenism that might well not have existed in antiquity. For some, it is reinforced by the presence in Acts (6:1; 9:29) of two groups, the Hellenists and the Hebraists, although this refers to Greek-speaking versus Hebrew-speaking Jews. The reality in antiquity was complex, and neither Judaism nor Hellenism was a unified entity.

Contact between Jews and Greeks began in the Persian period, and evidence of Greek mercenaries, pottery, and coins is found in Palestine from the early Hellenistic period. But Hellenism refers to more than the presence of Greeks or the Greek language, and includes the fusion of various cultures in the Mediterranean region. The Seleucids themselves merged Greek with Persian traditions, and the Ptolemies Greek with Egyptian, so that it is hard to identify anything that is uniquely Greek in the period. Eventually, Roman influence in these areas was also seen. Nor did Hellenism need to be expressed in Greek, as the early 2nd cent. BCE apocryphal book Sirach demonstrates; its author employed Greek forms, such as his eulogy of the high priest, alluded to Greek sayings (including Homer and Theognis), and gave his name (Ben Sira) in Greek fashion, all while affirming biblical tradition and writing in Hebrew.

Hellenism can be identified, nonetheless, in a number of cultural streams, each transforming Judaism, and subsequently Christianity. Politics is the most obvious external factor affecting Judaism. Since the Babylonian exile in the 6th cent. BCE, Jews lived under foreign rule, leading to aspirations of independence that were partially realized in the Hasmonean dynasty (*see* HASMONEANS). Many of the ideas formed in apocalyptic circles were a response to this foreign rule, and some of the expectations of a messianic figure can be interpreted as a desire for a Jewish ruler. Hellenistic forms of government developed among some Jewish communities, including the establishment of Jewish politeumata (πολιτεύματα) self-governing units, in Egypt. Jerusalem itself might have been established temporarily as a Greek polis (πόλις), city-state, under the Maccabees. Kinship ties that Greeks commonly made between fellow-states were aspirations for some Jews, and the Jews of Jerusalem were said to have made such an alliance with the Spartans (1 Macc 14). Over time the governance of Jews in different locations was modeled on local customs, and regional titles and institutions adopted.

Greek became the main language of diaspora Jews. Its importance can be seen in the translation of the Pentateuch into Greek (the SEPTUAGINT), probably for the Egyptian Jewish community, which displays familiarity with Greek rhetorical techniques. Gradually a large body of Jewish Greek literature was composed. Greek eventually became the dominant language even in Palestine, witnessed by the large number of Greek inscriptions from the early centuries CE in Greek and by the Jewish biblical revisers, notably Aquila and THEODOTION, coming from the region. Greek continued to be used by Jews into the Byzantine Empire, and we might speak properly of the "Hellenistic period" up to this point, or even later. Rabbinic literature is ambiguous on Greek culture, but it is clear that many rabbis were familiar with Greek literature and language. The legal format of the *halakah* (rabbinic law) itself might owe some of its roots to Roman law. The Hellenistic influence on Jewish literature can be seen in the genres that developed, including Jewish novels (JOSEPH AND ASENETH), poetry (Philo the epic poet), tragedy (EZEKIEL THE TRAGEDIAN), philosophy (Wisdom of Solomon, PHILO OF ALEXANDRIA; *see* SOLOMON, WISDOM OF), chronology (Demetrius), religious poetry (Jewish Orphic poems, SIBYLLINE ORACLES), and history (Eupolemus, Justus of Tiberias, Josephus). *See* AQUILA'S VERSION; JOSEPHUS, FLAVIUS.

Architectural forms adopted by Jews for their public buildings and by Christians for churches derive from Hellenistic and Roman building patterns. SYNAGOGUE structures are mostly modeled on Roman civic buildings. In the case of the synagogue in Sardis (modern Turkey), the building probably functioned as a Roman public GYMNASIUM before being converted into a synagogue. Mosaics can be found in a number of early Jewish and Christian meeting places, even a number incorporating the zodiac signs.

It is difficult to gauge the effect on religion from such contacts and literary production. The liturgical language and some of the divine titles found in the LXX and adopted into Jewish and Christian liturgy have their roots in the wider pagan society. In some cases they were used by smaller cults such as those to Isis, Pan, or Demeter rather than within the traditional Greek pantheon. Some Jewish and Christian understandings of death have undoubtedly been influenced by Greek ideas, especially in the philosophical notions of afterlife and the immortality of the soul (first explicated by Jews in the Wisdom of Solomon). These can be seen nevertheless as expressions in a new Greek form of ideas already developing within Judaism that had their roots in the Persian period (*see* GREEK RELIGION AND PHILOSOPHY).

The varying degrees to which Jews were affected by foreign influence, and the difficulty of classing all the ideas as specifically "Greek," render it difficult to identify direct opposition between Judaism and Hellenism. Nonetheless, it became a popular conceptual model of the 19th cent., employed by Mathew Arnold and Heinrich Heine, and has been adopted in more modern times by writers such as Edward Said, and Emmanuel Levinas. It was often used as a way of denigrating Judaism, with the implication that a refined synthesis of biblical religion and Hellenism was the source of triumphant Christianity. Instead, the heritage of Hellenism should be seen in the broad contribution of Greek culture to Judaism and Christianity, balanced by an appreciation of the contributions of eastern elements in the religions. *See* ANTI-SEMITISM; CHRISTIAN-JEWISH RELATIONS; ETHNICITY; GENTILES; GREEK LANGUAGE; JUDAISM; NATIONALITY; NATIONS; RABBINIC LITERATURE.

Bibliography: G. W. Bowersock. *Hellenism in Late Antiquity* (1990); M. Hengel. *Judaism and Hellenism* (1974); L. I. Levine. *Judaism and Hellenism in Antiquity* (1998); A. D. Momigliano. *Alien Wisdom: The Limits of Hellenization* (1971).

JAMES K. AITKEN

HELLENISTIC JEWISH HISTORIANS. Hellenistic Jewish historians are defined here as those Jewish authors of the time between ca. 300 BCE–100 CE who wrote in Greek about the history of the Jews, about specific events in the distant or recent Jewish past, or about individual members of the Jewish people.

Some of the 1st cent. CE Jewish historians are well known. Their writings are preserved more or less intact, especially Josephus in his works: *Jewish War* (*Bellum Judaicum*), about the Jewish revolt; *Jewish Antiquities* (*Antiquitates judaicae*), a history of the Jewish people from the creation to the time before the Jewish revolt; and *The Life* (*Vita*), a description of his own role in the hostilities (*see* JEWISH WARS; JOSEPHUS,

FLAVIUS). Although PHILO OF ALEXANDRIA is better known as a philosopher, some of his writings can also be regarded as Hellenistic Jewish historiography, such as *On the Embassy to Gaius* (*Legatio ad Gaium*) and *Against Flaccus* (*In Flaccum*), both treatises on God's providence containing accounts of the pogrom against the Alexandrian Jews under Nero. Josephus' *Life* and Philo's *Embassy* represent rare autobiographic accounts of events in Jewish history. Philo's biographies of Moses and the patriarchs, *On the Life of Moses* (*De vita Mosis*), *On the Life of Abraham* (*De Abrahamo*), and *On the Life of Joseph* (*De Iosepho*) also represent Hellenistic Jewish historiography, emphasizing Moses' and the patriarchs' preeminence and their cultural importance for the Jews and for all nations.

Most Hellenistic Jewish historians are only known by name and a few quotations or abstracts in other authors; most of their writings having been lost. The fragments of the 3rd cent. BCE chronographer DEMETRIUS (Clement, *Strom.* 1.21; 141.1–2; Eusebius *Praep. ev.* 9.21.1–19; 9.29.1–3, 15–16), and the mid-2nd cent. BCE historian EUPOLEMUS (Clement, *Strom.* 1.21; 141.4–5; Eusebius, *Praep. ev.* 9.26.1; 9.30.1–34.18; 9.34.20; 9.39.215) contain references to biblical events and chronological reckonings into Ptolemaic times. What is left of the Alexandrian ARTAPANUS' (3rd–2nd cent. BCE) strongly syncretistic historical romance *On the Jews* praises the importance of Abraham, Joseph, and Moses as religious leaders and as cultural benefactors of Egypt (Eusebius, *Praep. ev.* 9.18.1; 9.23.1–4; 9.27.1–37). Some of the fragments of ARISTOBULUS, an Alexandrian Jewish philosopher (ca. 170–150 BCE), mention the idea that Plato, Hesiod, Homer, and other Greek authors borrowed from a Greek translation of the Torah (Eusebius, *Praep. ev.* 13.12.1–16). Another Alexandrian is ARISTEAS THE EXEGETE (ca. 100–50 BCE), sometimes called Aristeas the historian, whose only remaining fragment deals with Job (Eusebius, *Praep. ev.* 9.25.1–4).

Although Hellenistic Jewish historians wrote in various styles on a wide range of topics, there are certain common features. Their main sources were the biblical books. These they did not use uncritically but rewrote and interpreted them, eliminating contradictions and adapting them not to the style of Greek historiography. They also used ALLEGORY and references to Greek PHILOSOPHY. Therefore some of the authors could also be called exegetes (Eusebius, *Hist. eccl.* 7.32.16) or philosophers (Eusebius, *Praep. ev.* 9.6.6; *see* EXEGESIS). They used all means available to prove the harmony of the biblical account and the antiquity of the Jewish rites. The authors wished to illustrate the moral, intellectual, and practical preeminence of the Jewish traditions and their beneficial influence on the other Mediterranean cultures. *See* HELLENISM; JEWISH BIBLICAL INTERPRETATION; RIGHTEOUSNESS IN EARLY JEWISH LITERATURE.

Bibliography: James Charlesworth, ed. *OTP.* Vol. 2 (1985) 775–919.

JUTTA LEONHARDT-BALZER

HELLENISTIC JUDAISM. *See* HELLENISM; JUDAISM.

HELLENISTIC PERIOD. The Hellenistic Period (332–63 BCE) is a designation that modern scholars give to a period of time that began with the arrival of ALEXANDER THE GREAT and Greek culture to Palestine (*see* HELLENISM). Though some people actively resisted the cultural changes that were imposed (*see* MACCABEES, MACCABEAN REVOLT), the GREEK LANGUAGE and many concepts from GREEK RELIGION AND PHILOSOPHY eventually made an indelible impression on the culture of the region. Scholars close the Hellenistic period (and begin the ensuing Roman period) with the year 63 BCE, when the Roman general Pompey arrived in Jerusalem. *See* ARCHAEOLOGY.

HELLENISTICUM NOVI TESTAMENTI, CORPUS. C. F. George Heinrici started this project, which uses J. J. Wettstein's compilation of Greek and Latin quotations paralleling NT texts, before World War I. A number of scholars continued the project. When the immensity of Greek and Roman literature to be studied became apparent, the plan for a single volume was replaced with the publication of monographs on the contributions of one Greek or Roman corpus or author to the NT. These parallels demonstrate NT writers were deeply rooted in Hellenistic Roman culture. *See* BIBLICAL INTERPRETATION, HISTORY OF.

Bibliography: W. C. van Unnik. "Corpus Hellenisticum Novi Testamenti." *JBL* 83 (1964) 13–33.

EMILY R. CHENEY

HELLENISTS hel´uh-nist [Ἑλληνιστοί *Hellēnistoi*]. A distinction has to be made between usage in ancient Greek texts and modern usage. *Hellenist* in the NT seems to mean the Greek-speaking Jews in the early church (Acts 6:1). The term has also been applied pejoratively in the context of the Maccabean revolt to those Jews who adopted Greek ways.

The books of Maccabees do not in fact refer to "Hellenists." The noun Hellēn (Ἕλλην) is used to mean a Greek person (1 Macc 1:10; 6:2; 8:18; 2 Macc 4:36; 11:2) and is not applied specifically to Jews. In 2 Macc several terms are used to castigate the adoption of Greek customs, but none of them refers to a person (e.g., "Greek way of life" [4:10], "extreme of Hellenization" [4:13], "Greek forms of prestige" [4:15], "Greek customs" [6:9; 11:24], so primary sources on the Maccabean revolt do not use *Hellenist* in reference to Jews perceived of as compromising their Jewishness.

Hellenist in modern scholarly usage has been applied to two rather diverse groups. The first is Jason and his followers who instituted the "Hellenistic reform" in Jerusalem (2 Macc 4; *see* MACCABEES, MACCABEAN REVOLT). Although adopting many Greek customs, including giving Jerusalem the structure of a Greek city (with a gymnasium and citizenship list), there is no evidence of a clear breach of the law: the Temple and cult continued to function as normal. The author of 2 Maccabees condemned Jason, but can point at most to one event contrary to the law (4:18-20, but even this is doubtful).

The other group is that of Menelaus, who displaced Jason from the high priesthood. The term *Hellenist* may well be a misnomer because there is no evidence that Menelaus followed in Jason's footsteps contining the "Hellenistic reform." However, during Menelaus' term as high priest, Antiochus IV forbade the practice of Judaism, and Jews were forced to take part in Greek forms of worship (2 Macc 6:7-12). Some blamed Menelaus for this, but it is not clear to what extent he was responsible for these measures.

LESTER L. GRABBE

HELMET [כּוֹבַע *kova*ʿ, קוֹבַע *qova*ʿ; περικεφαλαία *perikephalaia*]. A head covering used in warfare that took various shapes according to nationality but also within various armies to denote different units for the leaders to discern in the heat of battle. Materials used to construct the helmet differed according to the stature of the soldier or army. The common Israelite soldier likely wore a leather helmet (2 Chr 26:14; Jer 46:4; Ezek 23:24; 27:10; 38:5), while kings, princes, and heroes wore bronze helmets (Saul and Goliath, 1 Sam 17:5, 38). By the time of Uzziah (2 Chr 26:14) all of the army of Judah wore helmets.

Metaphorically, Ephraim is called God's helmet (Ps 60:7 [Heb. 60:9]; 108:8 [Heb. 108:9]). Isaiah 59:17 describes God as wearing a helmet of salvation with a breastplate of righteousness. These images are transferred to believers in Eph 6:11-17 (see 1 Thess 5:8).

MICHAEL G. VANZANT

HELON hee´lon [חֵלֹן *khelon*, חֵלוֹן *khelon*]. The father of ELIAB, a Zebulunite called at the time of the Mount Sinai census to lead his tribe (Num 1:9; 2:7; 7:24, 29; 10:16).

HELP, NT [ἀντιλαμβάνομαι *antilambanomai*, συναντιλαμβάνομαι *synantilambanomai*]. The verb *help*, related in Greek to the "forms of assistance" of 1 Cor 12:28, appears only three times in the NT. Two of these occurrences are in Luke–Acts, Luke 1:54 and Acts 20:35. The third is found in 1 Tim 6:2. A related compound form of the verb (synantilambanomai) describes the help that Martha wanted Mary to give her (Luke 10:40), and the help that the Spirit gives to one who is weak (Rom 8:26). Immediately after the eschatological reversal proclaimed in Luke 1:51*b*-53, the MAGNIFICAT (Luke 1:46*b*-55) proclaims, "He [the Mighty One] has helped his servant Israel in remembrance of his mercy" (Luke 1:54). Deutero-Isaiah repeatedly identifies Israel as the Lord's servant (Isa 41:8; 42:1; 44:1; 45:4; 52:13). A Deutero-Isaian oracle addresses Israel, "But you Israel, my servant . . . you whom I took" (Isa 41:8-9). Almost immediately afterward the first of the Deutero-Isaian oracles presents Israel, the Lord's servant, as one whom the Lord helps ("whom I uphold," Isa 42:1).

The Song of Mary, replete with biblical motifs, sees the help promised to Israel (see also Ps 118:13) being eschatologically realized in the conception and birth of Jesus. The realization of the promise in this manner stems from God's faithful remembrance of his ongoing mercy to Israel. Recalling the biblical phrase, "He has remembered his steadfast love" (Ps 98:3), the canticle affirms that the birth of the Savior is the realization of the covenant promise. Virtually contemporary with Luke, *Pss. Sol.* 10:4 proclaims that "the Lord will remember his servants in mercy, for the testimony of it is in the Law of the eternal covenant." For Luke, God's affective and active memory results in the birth of the Messiah. Luke refers to Timothy and Erastusas as helpers (diakonountōn [διακονούντων] Acts 19:22).

Paul's farewell discourse to the elders of Ephesus concludes with the apostle saying, "In all this I have given you an example that by such work we must support (= help, antilambanesthai [ἀντιλαμβάνεσθαι]) the weak" (Acts 20:35). Articulated poorly with the immediately preceding sentence, the statement presents Paul as an example of one who helps "the weak," presumably those who cannot provide for themselves. The statement appears to go beyond what Paul says of himself, namely, that he works to support his own ministry (1 Cor 4:12; 9:6; 1 Thess 2:9; see 2 Thess 3:7-9), to present Paul as one who takes care of others in the community. In support of this pattern of behavior, one that is consistent with the mode of action of Luke's ideal community in Jerusalem, the evangelist presents Paul as citing an otherwise unattested saying of Jesus, "It is more blessed to give than to receive."

The portion of a household code appearing in 1 Tim 6:1-2 exhorts believing slaves to be obedient not only to masters who are not believers but also to masters who are believers. Rather than allowing their unity in Christ to deter them from the obedience due to believing masters, Christian slaves are to serve their masters all the more, precisely because these masters are believers and among those whom believing slaves are to love: "they must serve them all the more, since those who benefit (= are helped, antilambanomenoi) by their service are believers and beloved" (1 Tim 6:2*b*). The phraseology of the clause suggests that the equality that exists between master and slave allows both slave

and master to consider that the service that a believing slave renders to a believing master is, in reality, a kind of benefaction. *See* DEACON; DEACONESS; HELP, OT; SERVANT; SERVE, TO.

RAYMOND F. COLLINS

HELP, OT [יָשַׁע yashaʿ, עָזַר ʿazar]. As a verb, *help* means to give assistance or aid. As a noun, it can refer to the act or instance of helping or to the aid itself. *Help* represents a number of Hebrew and Greek words. One of the primary Hebrew words is ʿazar, "to help" or "aid," with its corresponding nouns ʿezer (עֵזֶר) and ʿezrah (עֶזְרָה). Woman is said to be made as a "helper" to man (Gen 2:18), and there are many instances of persons helping one another and of regulations regarding helping (e.g., Exod 23:5; Num 1:24; Deut 22:3-4). While a person can be designated as the one who gives aid, *help* becomes such a characteristic word for God's gracious assistance to his people that it is almost a technical term for such in the OT (e.g., 2 Chr 25:8; Pss 33:20; 40:17; 46:1; 115:9; 121:2; 124:8; Isa 41:13).

Another important word for "help" is yashaʿ, which has the sense of "save" or "deliver," and its derivative forms yehoshiʿa (יְהֹשִׁיעַ) and yeshuʿah (יְשׁוּעָה), "salvation" (e.g., Pss 20:6 [Heb. 20:7]; 21:1, 5 [Heb. 21:2, 6]). The root yshʿ is part of the name Joshua and the Greek form of the name Jesus.

RALPH K. HAWKINS

HELPERS. *See* DEACON; DEACONESS; HELP, NT; HELP, OT.

HEM [שׁוּל shul]. The skirt of a robe. The garment's hem that is described in most detail in the Bible is that of the High Priest (Exod 28:33, 34; 39:24, 25, 26). This hem is ornate, ringed with blue, purple, and red pomegranates, with golden bells interspersed between them. The hem of God's garment is described by Isaiah as "filling the hall of the Temple" (Isa 6:1). Saul rips the hem of Samuel's robes. This symbolizes how Israel will be taken from Saul (1 Sam 15:27-29). *See* CLOTH, CLOTHES.

JUDITH ABRAMS

HEMAN hee′muhn [הֵימָן heman]. Name of several men: 1. Son of Lotan; grandson of Seir, the Horite; and whose name actually should be translated as Hemam (Gen 36:22). In 1 Chr 1:39, the name of this same person is HOMAM.

2. Son of Zerah and grandson of Judah and his wife Tamar (1 Chr 2:6). Probably the same one mentioned as a man of wisdom whom Solomon surpassed, since Ethan, Calcol, and Dara are mentioned in both verses along with Heman (1 Kgs 4:31 [Heb 5:11]). According to 1 Kings he is a son of Mahol, and so belonged to a musical guild.

3. Joel's son and the prophet Samuel's grandson (1 Chr 6:33 [Heb 6:18]) whom the chiefs of the Levites appointed to sing and play the cymbals along with Asaph and Ethan in the celebration of bringing the ARK

OF THE COVENANT to Jerusalem during King David's reign (1 Chr 15:17, 19). As King David's seer, he directed his fourteen sons and three daughters to sing and play harps, lyres, and cymbals for the house of God (1 Chr 25:1, 4-6). He also participated in the celebration of placing the ark of the covenant in the Temple during Solomon's reign (2 Chr 5:12; 35:15).

4. Father of Jehuel and Shimei who cleansed the Temple according to King Hezekiah's instructions (2 Chr 29:14).

EMILY R. CHENEY

HEMDAN hem'dan [חֶמְדָּן khemdan]. A grandson of Seir the Horite and the first-listed son of the clan chief Dishon (Gen 36:26). A parallel passage records the name as HAMRAN (1 Chr 1:41). Hemdan represents part of the indigenous Horite population south of Judah disrupted by immigrating Esauite clans and eventually absorbed into historical Edom.

JASON C. DYKEHOUSE

HEMORRHAGE. *See* FLOW OF BLOOD.

HEMORRHAGING WOMAN. *See* WOMAN WITH FLOW OF BLOOD.

HEN [ὄρνις *ornis*]. The only biblical occurrence of *hen* is in a saying of Jesus that employs the hen's care for her chickens as a powerful metaphor for protection: "as a hen gathers her brood under her wings" (Matt 23:37; Luke 13:34). This Gospel logion is echoed in 2 Esd 1:30, probably a Christian interpolation. Similar metaphors occur in, e.g., Deut 32:11; Ruth 2:12; Pss 17:8; 36:7; 57:1; 61:4; 63:7; 91:4. *See* BIRDS OF THE BIBLE; FOWL; WATER HEN.

GÖRAN EIDEVALL

HENA hen'uh [הֵנַע *hena*ʿ]. A town mentioned during the Assyrian invasion of Judah (2 Kgs 18:34; 19:13) as having been doomed because its god failed to deliver it from the invaders. The Assyrian king, Sennacherib, had dispatched messengers to Hezekiah in order to persuade him not to resist Assyria, citing the example of Hena and nearby towns, including SEPHARVAIM and IVVAH. This incident is related in Isa 37:13. The modern location of Hena is unknown.

R. JUSTIN HARKINS

HENADAD hen'uh-dad [חֵנָדָד khenadhadh]. The eponym of a family whose members were active in the restoration of Jerusalem. It is a theophoric name that references the grace of the storm god Hadad. The descendants of Henadad participated in laying the Temple's foundation under Zerubbabel (Ezra 3:9). Henadad's descendant BINNUI participated in the reconstruction of Jerusalem's walls under Nehemiah (Neh 3:18, 24) and was among the signatories to Ezra's covenant (Neh 10:9 [Heb. 10:10]). *See* HADAD.

DEREK E. WITTMAN

HENNA [כֹּפֶר kofer]. A dwarf shrub 8 to 10 ft. high found in lowland areas of Africa and amid the plants in an oasis like EN-GEDI. Henna (*Lawsonia inermis*) is valued for its fragrant blossoms, which are sometimes collected in a sachet and worn around the neck (Song 1:14; 4:13). Its leaves and flowers are ground into a fine powder containing natural dyeing properties—tannins. The powder is mixed with hot water to produce colorfast orange, red, and brown dyes used for tinting fingernails, toenails, the hair, and skin. The earliest mention of its use is found in the Ugaritic BAAL and ANATH cycle (COS 1.86: 250b) where the goddess decorates herself with "henna (sufficient for) seven girls." *See* CALAMUS; CINNAMON; COSMETICS; FRANKINCENSE; NARD; SAFFRON.

VICTOR H. MATTHEWS

HEPHER hee'fuhr [חֵפֶר khefer]. 1. A Canaanite town probably located on the Sharon plain whose king was defeated by Joshua (Josh 12:17). Later, along with ARUBBOTH and Socoh, it was under the district administration of Ben-hesed during Solomon's reign (1 Kgs 4:10). *See* SOCO, SOCOH.

2. The eponymous head of a clan within the tribe of Manasseh, or Gilead, known as the Hepherites (Num 26:32-33; 27:1; Josh 17:2-3).

3. The son of Ashhur of Tekoa in Judah (1 Chr 4:6).

4. One of DAVID'S CHAMPIONS (1 Chr 11:36) although the parallel text in 2 Sam 23:34 differs (both texts may be corrupt). *See* EPHER.

MICHAEL G. VANZANT

HEPHZIBAH hef'zi-buh [חֶפְצִי־בָהּ kheftsi-vah]. Meaning "in whom I delight," the name for: 1. King Manasseh's mother (2 Kgs 21:1).

2. Metaphorically, the restored city of Jerusalem in a prophetic oracle of Third Isaiah (Isa 62:4). The NRSV translates this name "My delight is in her."

HERACLEON. A leader of GNOSTICISM in Rome (ca. 155 CE) and student of Valentinus, he proposed the division of humanity into three categories: soul/spiritual, psychic, and matter/earth. Heracleon adopted aspects of Christianity in his commentary on the Gospel of John, preserved in 48 fragments that are quoted in ORIGEN's John commentary, including his view of the Logos as the savior of humankind and an allegorical presentation of Jesus meeting the woman at the well.

STEPHANIE BUCKHANON CROWDER

HERACLES. *See* HERCULES.

HERACLIDES. Heraclides was a bishop whose thoughts on the Father, the Son, and the soul were questioned by other bishops. A synod of bishops was summoned in which ORIGEN was asked to provide the orthodox answers to the disputed points. Minutes of the discussion are provided in the *Dialogue with Heraclides*, which does not provide an indication of the place or date of the synod, but was discovered at Tura, south of Cairo, in 1941.

MARY KAY DOBROVOLNY, R.S.M.

HERACLITUS. A Greek philosopher from Ephesus, who, in a fragmentary treatise written ca. 500 BCE, argued that the world consisted of elemental pairs of opposites (e.g., fire and water, hot and cold), ordered and governed according to logos (λόγος) by which he meant a unifying pattern or structure. *See* GREEK RELIGION AND PHILOSOPHY.

SHANE A. BERG

HERAKLES. *See* HERCULES.

HERALD [מְבַשֵּׂר mevasser, מְבַשֶּׂרֶת mevassereth; Aram. כָּרוֹז karoz; κῆρυξ kēryx]. A herald is one who broadcasts a message on behalf of another, or more specifically, a royal official who makes public proclamations. Such proclamation is an apparent necessity in order to effect the legal enactment of a decree. The Aram. karoz of Dan 3:4 clearly reflects this official capacity, and is either a loan word from Greek (kēryx), or perhaps shares a common origin with the latter.

In Hebrew, the participle of the root bsr (בשׂר) (e.g., Isa 40:9), denotes especially the bearer of good news—frequently understood as coming from God. This understanding is carried over into the NT where, in the Pastoral Epistles, *herald* is used in conjunction with the terms *apostle* and *teacher* (1 Tim 2:7; 2 Tim 1:11) to designate one appointed to proclaim the gospel.

PAUL NISKANEN

HERBS [אוֹרָה ʾorah, עֵשֶׂב ʿesev; λάχανον lachanon]. In addition to the cultivated grains (see Gen 41:5-7), ancient Israelites took advantage of the herbs growing wherever they dwelt, grinding their seeds to create condiments. This included both bitter (Exod 12:8; Num 9:11; chicory, eryngo) and spicy herbs (coriander, cumin, mint, dill, rue; Luke 11:42). These items provided flavoring to a bland stew (2 Kgs 4:39). Herb gardens near homes also provided fragrant odors that masked the smells associated with everyday life. *See* BITTER HERBS; PLANTS OF THE BIBLE.

VICTOR H. MATTHEWS

HERCULES. The Latin name of Herakles, the greatest among the Greek heroes, the son of the god Zeus and the mortal Alcmene. Known for his great strength, legends of Hercules include extraordinary events during his birth and childhood, great feats including twelve labors for which he is granted immortality, and legends of his self-immolation and apotheosis. The cult of Hercules dates as early as the 8th cent. BCE; over time he was worshiped both as a hero and a god. Similarities between the legends of Hercules and Samson are striking, as are parallels with some aspects of the Gospels'

accounts of Jesus, something noted by 2nd cent. CE Christian writers.

Bibliography: David E. Aune. "Heracles and Christ: Heracles Imagery in the Christology of Early Christianity." *Greeks, Romans and Christians: Essays in Honor of Abraham J. Malherbe.* David L. Balch, Everett Ferguson, and Wayne A. Meeks, eds. (1990) 3–19.

RUBÉN R. DUPERTUIS

HERD. *See* CATTLE; SHEEP, SHEEPFOLD.

HERDER. *See* SHEPHERD.

HERDSMAN [בּוֹקֵר boqer, רֹעֶה roʿeh; βοσκών boskōn]. From the verb raʿa meaning "to graze," the noun indicates one who watches over a herd of domestic animals such as cattle (Gen 13:7-8; 26:20) or swine (Matt 8:33; Mark 5:14; Luke 8:34). It is alternately translated "herder" or, most often, "SHEPHERD," due to the importance of sheep in OT Israel's pastoral economy. Early OT images of shepherds were of families keeping flocks. Later, animals were raised for commercial purposes resulting in shepherding as a career. Amos 7:14 uses boqer, which is related to oxen. This may be a scribal error since the term noqedh (נֹקֵד) is used in 1:1 to describe Amos as a breeder of sheep (see 2 Kgs 3:4).

Symbolically, roʿeh represented the ones who watched over Israel. Old Testament images include God (Gen 48:15; 49:24; Ps 23:1) and humans by God's choice (2 Sam 5:2; 7:7) as shepherds of Israel. *See* AMOS, BOOK OF; DRESSER OF SYCAMORE TREES; SHEEP, SHEEPFOLD.

MICHAEL G. VANZANT

HEREM. *See* BAN; DESTROY, UTTERLY.

HERES, ASCENT OF hihrʿiz [מַעֲלֵה הֶחָרֶס maʿaleh hekhares]. Means "ascent of the sun." A significant location in one of the Gideon stories (Judg 8:13), but different from HAR-HERES (Judg 1:35). The place is unknown, and there is manuscript evidence that it may well be a confusion of letters from the original "from upon the mountains."

A. HEATH JONES, III

HERESH hihrʿish [חֶרֶשׁ kheresh]. An Asaphite Levite listed among inhabitants of Jerusalem after the exile (1 Chr 9:15). His name is absent from a related list in Neh 11:15-18.

HERESY [αἵρεσις hairesis]. In the Greco-Roman world, **hairesis** indicated a "choice," esp. in terms of the teachings related to a specific philosophical school (Diogenes Laertius, *Vit. phil.* 1.19). This neutral meaning appears in both Philo (*Contempl. Life* 29) and Josephus (*Vita* 12; *Ant.* 18.11; *J.W.* 2.119–21) to designate the different parties within Judaism (e.g., Pharisees, Sadducees, and Essenes). By the late 1st or early 2nd cent. CE, the Hebrew word for hairesis, min (מִין), signified those factions that had deviated from the rabbinic tradition.

Acts refers to the Sadducees and Pharisees as hairesis in the Greco-Roman sense, but the term also bears a pejorative sense in the mouth of Paul's opponents, who disparage the apostle and his group for creating disturbances (5:17; 15:5; 24:5, 14; 26:5; 28:22). Other NT texts lament Christian factionalism because of its corrosive effect on community concord (1 Cor 11:18-19; Gal 5:20; 2 Pet 2:1).

Patristic heresiologists built upon these latter examples, arguing that Christian heresies were deviant, demonic, and unconnected with the "original" and "true" teachings of Jesus and his legitimate successors (apostles, elders, and bishops). Recent studies on early Christian diversity have demonstrated, however, that these polemics reflect theological commitments and are thus historically anachronistic.

DAVID M. REIS

HERETH hihr'ith [חֲרֶת khareth, חֶרֶת khereth]. David takes refuge in the forest of Hereth after the prohet Gad exhorts him to leave Moab (1 Sam 22:5). This place is apparently near KEILAH, although its precise location is unknown. Some scholars identify it with modern Kharas. The LXX and Josephus, *Ant.* 6.249, refer to Hereth (Sarich Σάριχ, Sarin Σάριν) as a city.

R. JUSTIN HARKINS

HERITAGE [נָחַל nakhal, נַחֲלָה nakhalah, יָרַשׁ yarash, יְרֻשָׁה yerushah; κληρονομία klēronomia]. As verbs, nakhal and yarash describe taking possession of property, in particular land (Deut 30:5; Josh 14:1; *see* INHERITANCE). As nouns they describe the people ISRAEL (Ps 74:2; Isa 19:25); the land of Israel (Ps 68:9; Jer 2:7); a portion decreed by the Lord (Ps 37:18; Isa 54:17); what one passes down to children (Ps 2:8); and gifts/rewards (Ps 127:3).

In the NT, as a verb, klēronomeō (κληρονομέω) describes inheriting the earth (Matt 5:5), eternal life (Matt 19:29), or the kingdom of God (Matt 25:34). The noun klēronomia describes material possessions to be handed down (Matt 21:38); the land of Israel (Acts 13:19); a share in eternal life (Gal 3:18).

ARCHIE T. WRIGHT

HERMAS, SHEPHERD OF huhr'muhs [Ποιμήν Poimēn]. An apocryphal apocalypse, The Shepherd of Hermas outlines moral teachings through the visions of an ex-slave, Hermas, in three books: the Visions, Mandates, and Similitudes. It employs allegorical language to express the ethical challenges facing ancient Christians.

In Book 1, Hermas recounts five visions. In the first, Hermas sees his former mistress, Rhoda, who informs him that she is examining him in heaven for a passing thought of lust he once had for her as he attended her; to atone, Hermas must pray for himself and all in his household. He next has a vision of the church in the form of an old woman. In successive visions, the woman becomes progressively younger as Hermas repents for his past transgressions and wins his and his family's redemption. In the fifth vision, she appears, glorious, as the Bride. Throughout, repentance remains a central theme.

In Book 2, twelve mandates pose direct ethical challenges through the "angel of repentance" of Hermas's fourth vision who appears in the guise of a shepherd (hence the work's title). He issues mandates on Christian virtues including faith, charity, prayer, good works, and chastity. No NT work is cited, and the system itself appears based on Jewish traditions. The last book contains ten similitudes (parabolai) or visions explained by the Shepherd. By far the most detailed is the ninth, a vision of a tower explained as an allegory for the church.

Composed in Greek but soon translated into Latin, only the Latin version of the work remains complete today. The Shepherd of Hermas was highly regarded in ancient Christianity, possibly because of its association with Rome. Irenaeus and Tertullian both considered it of canonical authority. The Muratorian fragment includes it as an authorized book. It comprises the final book of the Codex Sinaiticus, while the Codex Claromontanus lists the Shepherd of Hermas between the Acts of the Apostles and the Acts of Paul. Origen considered the book "divinely inspired."

Dating remains uncertain. It was likely composed over a period of time. The text makes reference to the pope Clement I, which could suggest a date of 88–97 CE. Origen sought to connect this Hermas with the Roman Christian of the same name in Rom 16:14. However, an early 2nd cent. CE dating seems more probable, based in part on the author's apparent familiarity with Johannine texts and Revelation. Papyrus fragments of the text derive from the 2nd cent. CE. Three ancient sources attest that Hermas was the brother of Pope Pius I (140–154 CE). The author of the Muratorian fragment claims that Hermas had been written in Rome within his historical memory—a tradition also recorded in the 3rd cent. Liberian Catalogue and a late 3rd cent. CE poem of Pseudo-Tertullian.

The text's warnings that danger faced the Christian community suggest a period of persecution, but the book's emphasis remains on the problem of sin. The Shepherd of Hermas maintains that Christians might obtain forgiveness for sins committed after baptism, but only through repentance.

Bibliography: Carolyn Osiek. *Shepherd of Hermas.* Hermeneia (1999).

NICOLA DENZEY

HERMENEUTICS. *See* CULTURAL HERMENEUTICS; THEOLOGICAL HERMENEUTICS.

HERMES huhr´meez [Ἑρμῆς *Hermēs*]. 1. The Greek divinity with whom Paul is identified by the crowds at Lystra in Acts 14:8-18, while they identified Paul's traveling companion Barnabas as ZEUS. Originally believed to be the spirit residing in boundary markers called herma (ἕρμα), Hermes had become an Olympian deity. He assimilated various roles including the patron of travelers, the conductor of souls to Hades, and the messenger of Zeus. He was also the god of eloquence, which accounts for Paul's identification with him in Acts 14:12: Paul "was the chief speaker." Also supporting this identification was the popular legend of Philemon and Baucis (Ovid, *Metam.* 8.611–724), according to which Hermes and Zeus had at one time visited Lystra and blessed the hospitable couple.

2. A Christian greeted by name by Paul in Rom 16:14. His name would indicate that he was a Gentile and probably a slave or freedman. He was no doubt an influential member of a large HOUSE CHURCH, four other leading members of which are also mentioned by name: ASYNCRITUS, PHLEGON, PATROBAS, and Hermas. This house church contained other unnamed members.

PAUL A. HOLLOWAY

HERMES TRISMEGISTOS. *See* HERMETIC LITERATURE.

HERMETIC LITERATURE. A group of quasi-philosophical and religious texts composed in the 1st–3rd cent. CE, which claim to represent the secret teaching of the Egyptian god Thoth, known in Greek as HERMES. The Egyptian practice of designating the superlative with a triple repetition provided Hermes the epithet, trismegistos (τρισμέγιστος) "thrice-great." Ancient magical papyri contain spells attributed to Hermes.

The religious tracts take the form of a dialogue between the god, sage, or mystagogue and his son or person seeking initiation. The goal of the process is to disentangle the spiritual self from the material world, the body, and the influences of the astrological powers. As the purified soul/mind ascends into the divine realms, it becomes capable of seeing and even becoming the divine. Salvation can be described as a process of regeneration by which the evil powers accumulated through descent into material embodiment are negated. Instead the soul responds to the new powers, which come from loving the divine intellect within. The specific teachings about the origins of the cosmos, the makeup of the human person, and the mechanism(s) for purification and ascent to the divine vary among the different texts. Echoes of a Greek translation of Genesis occur in a few cases, especially, C. H. I (also referred

to as *Poimandres*). Much of the speculative material appears to have its roots in 2nd cent. Platonism. Other passages reflect magical formulas, prayers used in rites of initiation, and speculations of astrological botany. These writings probably originated among the Greek-speaking populace of Roman Egypt and were studied in small groups, which likely engaged in initiation rituals.

By the early 3rd cent., Hermetic treatises had been translated into Latin. Saint Augustine cites passages from the Latin treatise, *Asclepius,* in the 5th cent. A Coptic translation of a previously unknown treatise as well as parts of familiar texts were found at Nag Hammadi. The codex was copied in the mid 4th cent. Citations in Armenian and Syriac indicate that Hermetic writings circulated in those languages by the 6th cent. After Augustine, Hermes does not reappear in the Latin West until the 12th cent., which considered Hermes a contemporary of Moses. The collection or *corpus* of Hermetic texts derives from a Greek Byzantine manuscript translated by Ficino (1471), which contained C. H. I–XIV. Others were added as new manuscripts were discovered. The Platonizing mysticism and the speculations about transforming material substances found in the Hermetic texts made them popular sources of "secret" wisdom throughout the Renaissance with translations into many vernacular languages. *See* PLATO, PLATONISM.

Bibliography: Brian P. Copenhaven. *Hermetica* (1992); Garth Fowden. *The Egyptian Hermes* (1986); A. D. Nock, A. D. Festugière, and J.-M. Festugière. *Corpus Hermeticum. Volumes I–IV.* (1954–60); Douglas M. Parrott. *Nag Hammadi Codices V, 2–5 and VI* (1979).

PHEME PERKINS

HERMOGENES huhr-moj´uh-neez [Ἑρμογένης *Hermogenēs*]. 1. One among "all those in Asia," who with PHYGELUS "turned away" from Paul (2 Tim 1:15). The author of the Pastorals is unclear about the event to which he refers. Scholars debate whether the author cites an episode from Paul's ministry or his own.

2. The name of a Platonizing Christian of the 2nd and 3rd cent. CE. TERTULLIAN challenged his position that matter is eternal and the source of evil.

CARLY DANIEL-HUGHES

HERMON, MOUNT huhr´muhn [הַר חֶרְמוֹן *har khermon*]. The southernmost peak of the Anti-Lebanon Mountains, Hermon was the northernmost reaches of Joshua's conquest (Josh 11:17; 12:1). The name derives from kharam (חָרַם), which can mean "consecrate." Thus the mountain appears to have had sacred connotations from early in Israel's history. It was also called BAAL-HERMON, reflecting its sacred nature to others also (Judg 3:3; 1 Chr 5:23). Deuteronomy 3:9 notes other names for the mountain: SIRION by the Sidonians and SENIR by the Amorites (see Ps 29:6; Ezek

Todd Bolen/BiblePlaces
Figure 1: Mount Hermon and Metulla from the west

27:5). A reference to the "dew of Mount Hermon" may refer to the vegetation-deities of the people around the mount. As early as the 14th cent. BCE, the mountain was known as sacred among the Hittites and Amorites, as seen in a treaty between the two.

Standing 2,813 m, the mountain's three peaks are perpetually covered with snow. The spring and summer runoff on the western slopes provide the main source for one of the headwaters of the Jordan River at modern Banias. Arabs call the mountain Jabel eth-Thalj, "mountain of snow" or Jabel esh-Sheikh, "mountain of the elder/chief."

MICHAEL G. VANZANT

HEROD, FAMILY her′uhd [Ἡρῴδης Hērōdēs]. The Idumean dynasty that played a powerful role in Judean affairs, from 37 BCE to 100 CE, and provided Rome with a number of client rulers (*see* IDUMEA).

A. Sources
B. Family Origins
C. Herod I
  1. Rise to kingship
  2. Consolidation and prosperity
  3. Domestic strife and deterioration
  4. Assessment
D. Archelaus
E. Philip
F. Herod Antipas, Herodias, Salome
G. Agrippa I
H. Agrippa II, Bernice, Drusilla
Bibliography

A. Sources

Our major source for the Herodian family is Flavius Josephus who provides detailed, though often divergent and even opposing, accounts in both his *Jewish War* and *Jewish Antiquities* (*see* JOSEPHUS, FLAVIUS). This Jewish writer is much more positive toward all the Herods in *Jewish War* than in *Jewish Antiquities*. Traditionally, this has been attributed to his use of different sources (in *Jewish War* he was heavily dependent on Nicolas of Damascus, Herod's chief adviser, while in the *Jewish Antiquities* he used a wider range of material, *Ant.* 15.174). This is undoubtedly true, but Josephus was not a slavish copyist and the differences more probably stem from the differing literary aims of each work. The *Jewish War* shows that Jews and their leaders have always understood the need to cooperate with world powers (who rule by God's permission), and that rebellion is alien to Jewish tradition; the material on the Herods illustrates this theme, stressing their loyalty to Rome, and generally tends to view them in a positive light. *Jewish Antiquities*, however, is interested in piety toward the Jewish law, and judges each member of the family accordingly. Although there is doubtless a great deal of solid historical material in Josephus' accounts, we need to treat his record with some caution.

Further information comes from Greco-Roman writers and the NT. The four generations of Herods named below are all mentioned in the Gospels and Acts (albeit briefly); although the dynasty provided the political backdrop to early Christian events, the Christian record is often rather vague and needs, like other sources, careful evaluation.

B. Family Origins

The first reference to a member of the family is to ANTIPAS (the grandfather of Herod I), an Idumean Jew appointed stratēgos (στρατηγός military governor) of IDUMEA by Alexander Jannaeus (103–76 BCE). An earlier generation of the family had presumably been caught up in the forcible subjugation of Idumea by the Hasmonean John Hyrcanus in 127 BCE and converted to Judaism (Josephus, *Ant.* 14.10).

Even in antiquity, however, alternative accounts of the family's origins circulated. Nicolas of Damascus flatteringly claimed that Herod belonged to a leading Jewish family that had returned from Babylon (Josephus, *Ant.* 14.9). Later still, a number of tendentious Christian traditions linked the family with Ascalon, even suggesting that Herod's father was a slave in the temple of Apollo there (Justin, *Dial.* 52.3; Julius Africanus in Eusebius, *Hist. eccl.* 1.7.11-12; Epiphanius, *Pan.* 20.1). Although Kokkinos favors an Ascalon connection, suggesting that the family were Hellenized Phoenicians most treat these alternative traditions with a large degree of skepticism.

Jannaeus was succeeded by his wife, ALEXANDRA SALOME (76–67 BCE). As a woman, she could not combine her rule with the high priesthood as was Hasmonean practice and the office was given to her eldest son, Hyrcanus II (*see* PRIESTS AND LEVITES and HYRCANUS). Shortly before her death in 67, her younger son Aristobulus, after years of plotting, made a successful bid for power and usurped both the throne and the high priesthood (*see* ARISTOBULUS). Hyrcanus II, the rightful heir to the throne, was a docile and unambitious man, and seems to have resigned himself to the new state of affairs. Things changed, however, through the intervention of Antipas' son Antipater, "a man of great energy in the conduct of affairs" (Josephus, *J. W.* 1.226), who had succeeded his father as stratēgos of Idumea. He saw greater opportunities for his own advancement under Hyrcanus than Aristobulus, and did all he could to restore Hyrcanus to power (*see* ANTIPATER).

Antipater was married to Cypros, a woman from a "distinguished Arab (probably Nabatean) family" (Josephus, *Ant.* 14.121) who bore him five children (Phasael, Herod, Joseph, Pheroras, and Salome). Exploiting his family connections, he persuaded Aretas the Nabatean king to send forces to back Hyrcanus, and the country was plunged into a period of unrest that was to last for almost three decades. Both sides appealed to Pompey, now in the midst of his victorious campaign in the east. The Roman general first came to the aid of Aristobulus (who was besieged in the temple), then later backed Hyrcanus (presumably assuming that his weak nature would serve Roman interests better than his warlike brother). Using unrest as a pretext, Pompey took Jerusalem on the Day of Atonement in 63, the land was put under the control of the governor of

Syria, forced to pay tribute, and a drastically reduced Jewish territory was given to Hyrcanus (Josephus, *J.W.* 1.124–54; *Ant.* 14.8–74).

Antipater's fortunes were clearly on the rise. Possessing tremendous foresight, he realized that nothing could be achieved in the political climate of the day without the backing of Rome. He made a point of ostentatious cooperation with Syrian governors, took every opportunity to demonstrate his loyalty to Rome, and was skilled at exploiting situations to his own advantage. Following the death of Pompey in 48 BCE, it now became clear that Julius Caesar would win the civil war in Rome, and Antipater and Hyrcanus realigned their loyalties accordingly; they offered aid to Caesar in his Egyptian campaign and Antipater distinguished himself on the battlefield (Josephus, *J.W.* 1.193). In return, Hyrcanus was confirmed as ethnarch and high priest while Antipater was granted Roman citizenship, exemption from taxes, and appointed procurator (epitropos ἐπίτροπος) of Judea (a post that presumably entailed the safeguarding of Roman financial interests in the region) (Josephus, *J.W.* 1.187–94; *Ant.* 14.127–37, 143). Later that year, Caesar granted certain privileges to diaspora Jews and authorized the rebuilding of the walls of Jerusalem (*Ant.* 14.213–64).

From then on, the power of Antipater and his family rose steadily. He appointed his two oldest sons governors: Phasael over Jerusalem and Herod over Galilee. *Jewish War* stresses Antipater's loyalty and affection toward Hyrcanus, but it is clear that the Idumean was now the real power behind the throne. His loyalty to Rome and ambition were matched only by that of his son, Herod I, who a decade later would oust the Hasmoneans entirely and rule as vassal king.

C. Herod I

1. Rise to kingship

Born in the late 70s BCE, Herod was appointed governor (stratēgos) of Galilee at the age of twenty-five (Josephus, *J.W.* 1.203; *Ant.* 14.158). His natural abilities brought him to the attention of a number of prominent Romans and, like his father, he managed to use civil war in Rome to his own advantage (despite frequently backing the losing side).

His vigorous measures against brigands on the Syrian border came to the notice of the Syrian legate, Sextus Caesar (a relative of Julius Caesar); he protected Herod when Hyrcanus' courtiers persuaded the ethnarch to try him in Jerusalem, and subsequently appointed him stratēgos of Coele-Syria and Samaria (Josephus, *J.W.* 1.204–13; *Ant.* 14.159–80). After the death of Julius Caesar in 44 BCE, Antipater and his sons allied themselves to C. Cassius Longinus (one of Caesar's assassins) who established himself as master of Syria. Cassius needed funds to finance his ever-growing army and Herod gained his favor by being the first to bring his quota from Galilee; in return he was given a military

PALESTINE UNDER THE HERODS

GALILEE Divisions of Israel

HEROD Kingdoms/provinces

Boundary of Herod's kingdom – greatest extent

Division boundaries

0   10   20 Miles
0   10   20 Kilometers

Sidon

DAMASCUS (A CITY OF THE DECAPOLIS)

Sarepta

PHOENECIA

ITURAEA

ABILENE

PROVINCE OF SYRIA

Mt. Hermon

Tyre

Paneas
Danos (Caesarea Philippi)

Kedesh

GAULANITIS

BATANEA

Bathyra?

TRACHANITIS

Gischala
Baca
Merom

Ptolemais

Selame

Chorazim
Capernaum

Bethsaida-Julias

Raphana (a city of the Decapolis)

Shefar'am

Gennesaret
Magdala
(Taricheae)

Gergesa

Hippos

Gamala

Dion?

Mt. Carmel

GALILEE

SEPPHORIS
Nazareth

Jordan R.

Gaba
(Hippeum)

Mt. Tabor

Sennabris
Gadara

Abila

AURANITIS

Dor

Xaloth
Nain

Caesarea
(STRATO'S TOWER)

Scythopolis

Ginaea

Mt. Gilboa

Pella

MARE MAGNUM VEI INTERNUM (MEDITERRANEAN SEA)

HEROD

DECAPOLIS

Plain of Sharon

SEBASTE
(SAMARIA)

Gerasa/Jerash
Amathus

Apollonia
Sozusa

Mt. Ebal
Neopolis
Mt. Gerazim

Jordan River

Jabbok River

Joppa

Antipatris

SAMARIA

Alexandrium

Phasaelis

Gadara

KINGDOM OF

Thamna

Lydda

Gophna

Archelais

PHILADELPHIA
(RABBAH)

Jamnia

Modein
Emmaus
(Nicopolis)

Jericho
Cyprus

Abila
Betharamphtha

Gazara

JERUSALEM

Bethany

Livias

Heshbon

Azotus

JUDEA

Hyrcania

Qumran

Mt. Pisgah

Mt. Nebo

PERAE

Ashkelon
(FREE CITY)

Bethlehem

Herodium

Medeba

Gabalis?

Betogabri

Callirrhae

Marisa
Adora

HEBRON

Machaerus

Gaza

En-gedi

Mare Mortuum

Arnon River

IDUMEA

Masada

KINGDOM

Raphia

Bersabe
(Beer-sheba)

Malatha

Besor Brook

Mampsis

NABATAEAN KINGDOM

Zered Gorge
Zered Brook

NEGEB

The Negeb

N

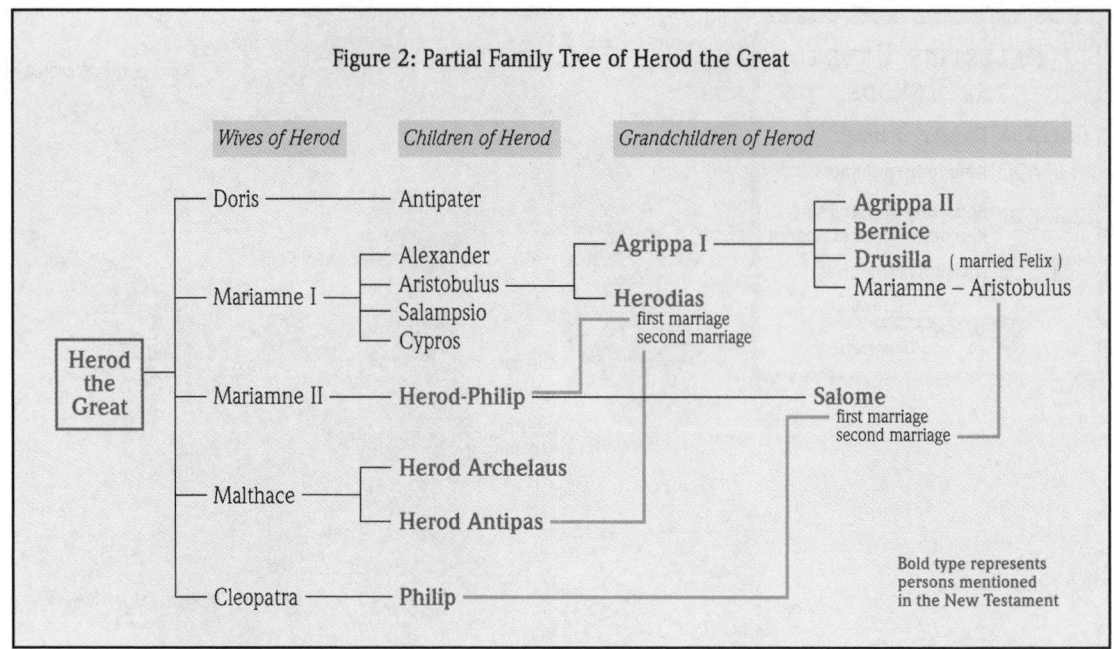

Figure 2: Partial Family Tree of Herod the Great

position and, when Antipater was poisoned, Cassius aided Herod's revenge (Josephus, *J.W.* 1.218–35; *Ant.* 14.277–93). Following Cassius' defeat at Philippi in 42 BCE, the east fell into the hands of Mark Antony. Although the Judeans sent three embassies to complain about Herod and his brother, Antony, who had been on friendly terms with Antipater, appointed the brothers tetrarchs—Phasael over Judea and Herod over Galilee (Josephus, *J.W.* 1.242–44; *Ant.* 14.324–26).

Events further afield were also to aid Herod's ascendancy. In the spring of 40 BCE, the Parthians invaded Asia Minor and Syria. ANTIGONUS saw his opportunity and, with the support of Lysanius (the prince of Chalcis; *see* LYSANIAS), enlisted Parthian support and was installed as king. Antigonus captured HYRCANUS, lacerated his ears to prevent him from acting as high priest (Lev 21:17-23), and took him to Parthia.

Herod, however, had already fled, first to Masada, where he secured his female relatives, then to Rome where he waited on Antony. Once again Antony backed Herod, this time with the support of Octavian (later Augustus), and promised to make him king of the Jews. The two Romans left the Senate house with Herod between them, offered sacrifice, and laid up the decree in the capitol (Josephus, *J.W.* 1.282–85; *Ant.* 14.377–89). Herod returned to Judea in 39 BCE and with the support of C. Sossius, the governor of Syria, took Jerusalem two years later after a five-month siege that was broken only by his marriage to Mariamme, the daughter of Hyrcanus (to whom he had been engaged for five years and through whom he presumably hoped to strengthen his position; Josephus, *J.W.* 1.241, 344; *Ant.* 14.300, 467). Antigonus was put in chains, taken to Antony, and executed. It must now have been clear to everyone that a ruler's authority and legitimacy

depended solely on Roman support. In 37 BCE, three years after his nomination, Herod began his long reign as king of the Jews.

2. Consolidation and prosperity

Herod took his place alongside a number of client kings on Rome's eastern border. The recent conflict, however, along with his lack of kingly pedigree, made his position uneasy. The first few years, therefore, were occupied with securing his realm, both from opposition within (largely from the Hasmoneans and the Jerusalem nobility) and without (from Cleopatra and the changing Roman political stage).

On taking power, Herod executed forty-five of Jerusalem's wealthiest aristocrats who had supported Antigonus; many others fled and their property was confiscated to pay the king's debts (Josephus, *J.W.* 1.358; *Ant.* 15.5). The remaining Hasmoneans also posed a threat. Herod had married Mariamme, but now recalled her grandfather Hyrcanus II from exile in Babylonia, presumably so that he could not be used as the focus for a coup d'etat. Herod needed a high priest: not being of priestly lineage, he could not take on the role himself, nor could Hyrcanus oblige owing to his deformity. Eventually Herod was persuaded by his mother-in-law, Alexandra (with strong support from Cleopatra and Antony), to appoint her sixteen-year-old son ARISTOBULUS to the post. When his popularity became apparent soon afterward, however, Herod had him drowned in a pool at his palace at Jericho (*Ant.* 15.23–26). The episode made it abundantly clear that he could have no security while Hasmoneans still lived, and gradually all remaining members of the family were eliminated: first Hyrcanus in 30 BCE (Josephus, *J.W.* 1.433–34; *Ant.* 15.161–82), then his beloved wife in 29 BCE (see §C3), and her mother, Alexandra, in 28 BCE (*Ant.* 15.247–51). The confiscation of their wealth once again provided the king with badly needed funds.

In place of the Jerusalem nobility and the Hasmoneans, Herod gave prominent leadership roles to his Idumean relatives, cultivated close ties with groups who had been hostile toward his predecessors, and promoted non-Jews to positions in the army and at court. He was intent on bringing all institutions under his control. Paramount in Jewish society was the high priest, who under the Hasmoneans had combined spiritual authority with secular power. Herod abandoned the hereditary principle, appointing and replacing incumbents at will, keeping the sacred high priestly vestments under his own guard, and effectively stripping the position of political power. In the course of his reign, he appointed five men to the post, favoring men of diasporan origins, such as Ananel from Babylonia (*Ant.* 15.22, 39–40) or Simon Boethus from Alexandria (*Ant.* 15.320–22). Their appointment may well have been an attempt by Herod to gain support in some quarters by restoring the high priesthood to its older Zadokite incumbents. At all events, these men and their families formed part of Jerusalem's new aristocracy, an aristocracy dependent solely on Herod, and continued to dominate the high priesthood until the outbreak of revolt a century later.

External threats manifested themselves initially in the person of Cleopatra who, desiring to reconstitute the Ptolemaic Empire of the 3rd cent. BCE, had designs on Herod's land, along with territories in Syria and Arabia. She succeeded in obtaining large parts of the coast of Palestine and Phoenicia in 37/36 BCE and two years later acquired the lucrative plain of Jericho, though Herod was allowed to lease this territory from her (*J.W.* 1.359–63; *Ant.* 15.88–103).

Indirectly, however, Cleopatra's machinations saved Herod from joining Antony at the battle of Actium in 31 BCE. She persuaded Antony to send Herod to war against the Nabateans who had fallen into arrears with their tribute (*J.W.* 1.364–65; *Ant.* 15.108–10). Herod eventually emerged victorious, but was immediately met by a new and serious blow: Octavian had defeated Antony and was now the sole ruler of the Roman world.

In typical fashion, Herod decided to confront the danger and sailed to Rhodes in 30 BCE to present himself before Octavian without his crown, "a commoner in dress and demeanor, but with the proud spirit of a king" (*J.W.* 1.387). He delivered a long speech in which he stressed his loyalty to Antony, and pledged to transfer that loyalty to Octavian. The future emperor AUGUSTUS, who needed a trustworthy man and was in no hurry to depose an effective client king, assured Herod of his safety and confirmed his position. Later, when Augustus passed through Judea on his way to Egypt, Herod entertained him and his troops lavishly and was rewarded by an extended realm (*J.W.* 1.386–

97; *Ant.* 15.187–201, 217). His territory was extended several more times over the next decade until by 20 BCE he ruled over the whole of the former Hasmonean kingdom (*J.W.* 1.398–400).

Herod's rule reached its height in the period 30–12 BCE. It was a time of stability, prosperity, and splendor, with no external wars or threats from within. His friendship with Rome was now at its height: he visited Rome several times between 20–10 BCE, visited M. Vipsanius Agrippa (Augustus' son-in-law and second in command) at Lesbos in 23–21 BCE, and took great pleasure in accompanying him on a tour of his kingdom in 15 BCE. The king delighted in honoring his Roman patrons: he founded cities and named them in honor of Augustus or Agrippa; he erected buildings in celebration of members of the imperial family; and temples were dedicated to the emperor in Panias, Sebaste, and Caesarea. "In short, one can mention no suitable spot within his realm, which he left destitute of some mark of homage to Caesar," commented Josephus (*J.W.* 1.407). Most lavish of all were Sebaste (formerly Samaria) and CAESAREA MARITIMA, both splendid Greco-Roman cities complete with Hellenistic institutions and entertainments; Caesarea boasted a magnificent harbor, a spectacular feat of engineering as large as the Piraeus. The magnificent buildings, however, were not just demonstrations of Herod's loyalty to his Roman patrons; they also showed his subjects that he was a player on the world stage, and warned other nations that he enjoyed the protection of Rome.

Herod presented himself as a Hellenistic monarch (*see* HELLENISIM). He kept a large Hellenistic court in Jerusalem, comprising many non-Jews of Greek education and culture, though he followed ancient oriental counterparts by having a harem (presumably a mark of wealth and honor). Herod wanted to be seen as a great patron and benefactor, an embodiment of magnificence and munificence; it is in this context that we need to view his generosity to cities outside his realm (Rhodes, Antioch, Tyre, Sidon, Damascus, Athens—where his love of Hellenistic culture could find greater scope than at home) and his endowment of the Olympic games. As was common among Hellenistic monarchs, he named a number of cities and monuments after himself and his family: Herodion; Antipatris in memory of his father; a fortress above Jericho named Cypros after his mother; a tower and the city of Phasaelis to his brother; and a tower to his wife Mariamme. In all his projects, Herod used the most lavish and luxurious of Roman methods of construction and design, for which he probably imported builders and artisans from Italy.

Herod needed a capital city that adequately reflected his glory, and during his reign the urban landscape of Jerusalem was completely transformed. He built a luxurious palace in the Upper City; founded Greco-Roman cultural amenities such as a theater, a hippodrome, and an amphitheater; and constructed a council building, monumental tombs, streets, and marketplaces. His most ambitious project, however, and one with which he hoped to win the support of his Jewish subjects, was the rebuilding of the Temple. Begun in 20/19 BCE, he enlarged the Temple Mount to over twice its original size, creating one of the most magnificent temples in the ancient world. "The expenditure devoted to this work was incalculable, its magnificence never surpassed" wrote Josephus (*J.W.* 1.401), and rabbinic writings too expressed awe at the beautiful structure (*b. B. Bat.* 4a). The work provided employment for many and took decades to complete (*see* TEMPLE, HEROD'S).

Yet for all his magnificence, Herod still felt insecure. Early in his reign he rebuilt the fortress-palace of Antonia (named after his then-patron), along with three huge defensive towers in the western part of the city. He continued to rely heavily on a network of spies and informers to keep him apprised of public opinion, and built a series of fortresses (Sebaste, Caesarea, Gaba, Heshbon, and several more throughout the Judean desert) to keep an eye on the people and to quell any uprisings.

3. Domestic strife and deterioration

As Herod's rule was at its height, however, the seeds of destruction were already germinating. The king's problems revolved around succession: he was married ten times, fathered fifteen children, and had at least twenty grandchildren. Augustus had granted him the exceptional right to choose a successor in 23 BCE, but his indecision led to seven changes of his will, dissension among his sons, and the execution of his three eldest boys.

In the earlier part of his reign, Herod's domestic struggles were between the Idumean branch of his family (particularly his mother, Cypros, and his sister, Salome) and his Hasmonean wife and her mother, Alexandra (the daughter of Hyrcanus II). The Hasmoneans were embittered against Herod for the murders of Aristobulus and Hyrcanus, and made no attempt to disguise their hatred of him and their contempt for his family; in revenge, the Idumeans accused Mariamme of adultery. Herod, however, was deeply in love with Mariamme and could not accept the charges until in 29 BCE, faced by what seemed to be incontrovertible evidence, and fueled by the insinuations of his sister (who implicated her own husband/uncle, Joseph), Herod's jealous and suspicious nature overcame him and he ordered her execution. It was not long, however, before Herod bitterly regretted his actions, and became distraught and ill (*Ant.* 15.62–70, 80–87 and 185–86, 202–12 is a doublet of *J.W.* 1.438–44).

The next wave of dissension was caused by the return of Mariamme's eldest sons from their education in Rome in 17 CE. The two boys, Alexander and Aristobulus, were the clear successors and, as Hasmoneans, enjoyed popular support. Herod arranged good

marriages for them: Alexander married the daughter of Archelaus, king of Cappadocia, while Aristobulus married Salome's daughter Bernice. But they inherited their mother's resentment of Herod, and imprudently made it clear that they did not forgive her accusers and wanted revenge. Suspicion and rumor were rife at court, until Herod, fearing the boys were conspiring against him, recalled Antipater, his son by his first wife Doris (a commoner who had been divorced on his marriage to Mariamme) and sent him to Rome to forge connections at court. Realizing that their succession was no longer guaranteed, Mariamme's sons openly vented their wrath, while Antipater—a master insinuator and manipulator—worked on his father until even Augustus became involved in the disputes. Still the situation deteriorated until alleged plots to kill Herod were discovered under torture and the boys were arrested. At Augustus' a suggestion, they were tried at Berytus (ca. 7/6 BCE), condemned (quite possibly unjustly, *J.W.* 1.488), and strangled at Sebaste.

Antipater now had a clear path to the succession, but was unpopular and feared the coming of age of Herod's younger sons. Friction broke out between Herod and his siblings, Salome and Pheroras, all fanned by Antipater. Dissension continued until Pheroras died and it transpired that he had been murdered with a poison intended for Herod by Antipater who, returning from a visit to Rome, was cast in prison and executed only five days before Herod's own death (*J.W.* 1.552–643; *Ant.* 17.1–145).

The last years of Herod's reign witnessed the king's emotional and psychological deterioration. By 4 BCE, aged about seventy, Herod had been seriously ill for some time. One last incident added to the brutality of these final years. Spurred on by rumors of the king's death, two prominent Pharisees persuaded a number of youths to tear down a golden eagle above the Temple gate and smash it to pieces. Despite his failing health, Herod had the perpetrators burned alive (Josephus, *J.W.* 1.648–55; *Ant.* 17.149–64). After an agonizing death, the funeral procession took Herod's body from Jericho to Herodium for burial (Josephus, *J.W.* 1.670–63; *Ant.* 17.196–99). Attempts to diagnose his final illness are hampered by the fact that Josephus' accounts, particularly in the *Jewish Antiquities*, are stereotypical descriptions of the death of an impious ruler.

Matthew's Gospel suggests that Jesus was born approximately two years before the death of Herod, in roughly 6 BCE (Matt 2:1-23); Luke 1:5 refers to "Herod, King of Judea" but it is clear from the reference to Quirinius' census of 6 CE, which occured six months later (2:1-7), that he has Archelaus in mind (*see* CHRONOLOGY OF THE NT; JUDEA, JUDEANS; QUIRINIUS).

Matthew also adds another story from Herod's final years: his massacre of boys under two in and around Bethlehem (Matt 2:16-18; *see* INNOCENTS,

SLAUGHTER OF THE). Herod was certainly capable of such an act, particularly toward the end of his reign, yet it is curious that neither Josephus (whose record of this period, especially in the *Jewish Antiquities*, is particularly detailed) nor Luke (whose whole account is quite different) mention this. Furthermore, Matthew portrays Jesus as a new Moses: just as the family of the Jewish patriarch outwitted an evil ruler (Pharaoh), so too do the family of Jesus (Herod). There are therefore good reasons to be cautious about the historicity of Matthew's account.

4. Assessment

Herod reigned thirty-three years during which time Judea experienced a stability and prosperity it had not known for several decades. Herod's foreign policy was brilliant: his pro-Roman policies and unwavering loyalty were clear from the very beginning, and were at the basis of all his success. Rome needed a powerful ally on its eastern border and found in Herod a capable ruler. Strangely, however, Augustus failed to mention him in his *Res Gestae*, nor was the king given the right to mint either gold or silver coins, facts that suggest that the intimate relationship alleged by Josephus (esp. in Josephus, *J.W.* 1.400 and *Ant.* 15.361) may be rather exaggerated.

The strength of Herod's devotion to Judaism has often been called into question. Clearly some of his actions ran counter to Jewish custom, particularly the Hellenistic entertainment institutions in Jerusalem and the eagle on the Temple (though this may belong to the last, rather deranged part of his life). In general, however, Herod was careful to maintain certain Jewish expectations: no images were used in his realm, nor were any pagan temples erected within Jewish areas; he insisted that anyone marrying into the family be circumcised; and the Jerusalem Temple was built by specially trained priests, so that the building was not defiled. Augustus' quip, preserved in Macrobius, Saturnalia 2.4.11, that he would rather be Herod's pig than his son (based on a pun in Greek), along with Persius' reference to the Sabbath as "Herod's day" (*Saturnalia* 5, 180) suggest that, in pagan eyes at least, Herod was regarded as a Jew.

His kingdom encompassed both Jews and Gentiles, both of whom had reason to fear and suspect him. Gentiles were unhappy to find themselves under Jewish rule, but Herod managed to cultivate them far more than his Hasmonean predecessors, particularly through his Greco-Roman cities and public institutions (gymnasia, halls, porticoes, theaters, fountains, baths, and aqueducts). Decades later, the non-Jews of Caesarea still looked to Herod as the founder of their city (Josephus, *J.W.* 2.266). The Jewish reaction was more mixed. Many Jews had reservations about his Idumean/Arab ancestry, some no doubt disliked his heavy-handed treatment of the high priesthood, and

not everyone shared his enthusiasm for Rome and Hellenistic culture. His rebuilding of the Temple, however, increased pilgrimage to Jerusalem, and DIASPORA Jews (whose rights Herod championed; Josephus, *Ant.* 16.27–65, 160–78) were well disposed toward him (it may have been during his reign that the famous sage Hillel moved to Jerusalem).

Herod was undoubtedly a complex character, a man with an insatiable lust for power, honor, and fame, and a need to be respected by his subjects. He was capable of acts of great generosity (three times he reduced taxes or donated famine relief), and, particularly in his declining years, great brutality. Josephus can speak both of Herod's "noble spirit" and "works of piety" (Josephus, *J.W.* 1.400) and of his "irreligious spirit" and "mind that could not be turned from evil" (Josephus, *Ant.* 16.402–3). That he inspired a wide range of attitudes among his subjects is perhaps only to be expected.

D. Archelaus

On Herod's death, the country plunged into conflict. After decades of iron rule, resentment and frustration broke out against both Herod and the Roman regime of which he was part. Order was finally restored by Varus, the Legate of Syria, though not without high levels of casualties.

Herod's last will divided the country among three of his sons. Roughly half (consisting of Judea, Idumea, and Samaria, but excluding the cities of Gaza, Gadaros, and Hippos) went to Archelaus, the eldest son of Herod's Samaritan wife, Malthace, born in ca. 27 BCE. The remaining half was divided between Antipas (who was to inherit Galilee and Perea) and Philip (who received a number of territories to the north and east of the Sea of Galilee). All three journeyed to Rome to have their succession ratified by the emperor.

ARCHELAUS, after putting down a riot at Passover with excessive force, traveled with his aunt SALOME and her family, though once in Rome they decided to support Antipas, who petitioned Augustus to uphold an earlier will that made him sole heir (*J.W.* 2.20–21; *Ant.* 17.224–27). Fifty prominent Judeans also arrived, requesting direct Roman rule (*J.W.* 2.80–91; *Ant.* 17.299–314). Augustus upheld Herod's wishes, appointing Archelaus ethnarch (with the promise that he would be made king if he proved himself worthy) and Antipas and Philip tetrarchs (*J.W.* 2.93–100; *Ant.* 17.317–23). Salome was proclaimed mistress of the cities of Jamnia, Azotus, and Phasaelis and given the palace of Ascalon (territories overseen by a procurator and bequeathed on her death in ca. 10 CE to the empress Livia).

Once ETHNARCH (or "national ruler"), Archelaus adopted the dynastic title "Herod" (Luke 1:5, though the title "king" is incorrect). Josephus has little to say about Archelaus' short reign (*J.W.* 2.111–16; *Ant.* 17.339–53): he crushed remaining trouble and settled old scores; exercised his power of appointing high priests; and embarked on a rather lackluster building program (restoring the royal winter palace at Jericho, which had been devastated in the recent riots and dedicating a nearby village to himself). He married a woman named MARIAMME (who was probably his niece—endogamous marriages were common within the family), but divorced her to marry Glaphyra, the daughter of King Archelaus of Cappadocia. She, however, had formerly been married to his deceased half-brother Alexander, by whom she had had two sons, making the marriage unlawful.

In the tenth year of his reign, Archelaus was accused in front of the emperor by embassies from both his Jewish and Samaritan subjects and dismissed for excessive brutality, a charge that fits with the reluctance of Mary and Joseph to live under his rule in Matt 2:22. He was banished to Vienne in Gaul in 6 CE and died there (Strabo, *Geogr.* 16.765).

Judea now became a Roman province; governed first by prefects (6–41 CE), then procurators (44–66 CE). However, the Herods seem to have maintained an active role in Judean politics, particularly under the prefects. PHILO OF ALEXANDRIA writes of four Herodian princes who brought certain grievances of the people before first Pontius Pilate (*see* PILATE, PONTIUS) and then the emperor TIBERIUS CAESAR (*Leg.* 299–305; these were probably ANTIPAS, Philip, and two others). Similarly, in the Caligula crisis of 40 CE an embassy supporting Jews of Galilee was led by Herodians, including Agrippa I's younger brother Aristobulus. And if there is any truth to Antipas' involvement in Jesus' trial it should be seen in the same light. The many members of the family remaining in Judea, then, presumably continued to exercise some power as part of the Jerusalem aristocracy.

E. Philip

PHILIP (born ca. 26 BCE) was the younger son of Cleopatra (described by Josephus as a "Jerusalemite") and half-brother to Archelaus and Antipas. He was appointed "TETRARCH" (lit. "ruler of a quarter") over the predominantly Gentile lands of Iturea, Panias, Gaulanitis, Batanea, Trachonitis, and Auranitis by Augustus in 4 BCE (Josephus, *J.W.* 2.95; *Ant.* 17.319; 18.106; Luke 3:1).

Josephus furnishes us with little information regarding Philip, a fact that presumably means that his thirty-seven-year reign was generally successful (Josephus, *Ant.* 18.106–8). He built two cities, naming them after his Roman patrons. In 6/7 CE he renamed Panias, his capital city, Caesarea in honor of AUGUSTUS (it was generally known as CAESAREA PHILIPPI—Mark 8:27; Matt 16:13—to distinguish it from Caesarea Maritima). Soon after he enlarged the village of BETHSAIDA in Gaulanitis into a city, fortifying it and renaming it Julias in honor of Augustus' daughter; when she was ban-

ished in 2 BCE, however, it reverted to Bethsaida (as it is known in the Gospels). Josephus describes the tetrarch as modest, peace-loving, and just (*Ant.* 18.106). He departed from the practice of other Herods by putting images on his coins, but the Gentile character of his territories meant that this caused no offense. Philip is mentioned briefly in the NT, in a statement concerning the beginning of John the Baptist's ministry (Luke 3:1).

Philip's marital life is a subject of much scholarly debate. The NT suggests that he was married to HERODIAS (Mark 6:17 followed by some texts of Matt 14:3), who left him to marry Antipas (see §F.). Josephus, however, more probably gives his wife as Salome, Herodias' daughter (*Ant.* 18.136). When he died in 33/34 CE leaving no heirs, his territory was annexed to Syria (*Ant.* 18.108) before being given to AGRIPPA I (see below).

F. Herod Antipas, Herodias, Salome

Antipas (born ca. 25 BCE) was the son of Herod's wife Malthace the Samaritan, and therefore the full younger brother of Archelaus. Unsuccessful in his bid for sole succession, Antipas was granted the tetrachy of the noncontiguous districts of Galilee and Perea, adopting the dynastic title "Herod" after Archelaus' departure in 6 CE (*J.W.* 2.167; Matt 14:1; Luke 3:19; Mark 6:14 incorrectly refers to him as "king").

Antipas ruled for forty-three years, his long reign exceeded only by that of his great-nephew, Agrippa II. Relations with his subjects were harmonious and no internal disturbances are recorded. At first, he based himself in Perea, perhaps to keep a closer watch on both his brother Archelaus in Judea and the NABATEANS (he entered into a politically expedient marriage with a daughter of the Nabatean king, Aretas IV). After 6 CE, he moved to GALILEE where he refounded and fortified the city of SEPPHORIS, which had been destroyed in the revolt after his father's death. In 19/20 CE he created a new Hellenistic city by the Sea of Galilee, naming it Tiberias in honor of the emperor; he built a lavishly decorated palace and the city became the major seat of power in Galilee. Josephus notes, however, that since the site lay on a former burial ground, Jews refused to move there, and Antipas had difficulty settling it; Jews were moved in by force or bribery and most of the population were of mixed foreign people from surrounding areas (*Ant.* 18.38). The "Herodians" referred to in the gospel are probably supporters of Antipas based in these cities (*see* HEROD ANTIPAS; HERODIANS).

For all his love of Hellenism, however, Antipas, like his father, refrained from putting images on his coins and seems to have regularly attended the feasts in Jerusalem (Luke 23:7). It is true that his palace was decorated with animal sculptures, but no protest seems to have been made until the outbreak of revolt in 66 CE (Josephus, *Life* 65–66).

Jesus' ministry belongs to the reign of Antipas, though he seems to have avoided both the cities and direct confrontation with the tetrarch. Antipas does, however, feature prominently in two NT passages: 1) the death of John the Baptist (Matt 14:1-12; Mark 6:14-29; Luke 3:19-20); 2) Jesus' trial (Luke 23:6-12).

Prior to the execution of JOHN the Baptist, Antipas divorced his Nabatean wife in favor of HERODIAS, the former wife of his half-brother Herod (the son of Mariamme II), though since Herod was still alive the union was unlawful (Josephus, *Ant.* 18.110, 136; Mark 6:17, Matt 14:3). According to the Synoptic Gospels, Antipas imprisoned the Baptist because he criticized his marriage to Herodias. Later, at his birthday party, Herodias' daughter (who Josephus names as Salome, *Ant.* 18.136) bewitched the tetrarch with her dancing and he vowed to give her anything she wanted. After consulting with her mother, the girl asked for the head of the Baptist on a platter; bitterly disappointed, Antipas had no choice but to comply.

Josephus records the same incident, though in his account Antipas, fearing the Baptist's large following would lead to insurrection, had him imprisoned in the fortress of Machaerus, and executed (*Ant.* 18.116–19). The two accounts, however, may be complementary: while elements of the story (particularly in Matthew and Mark) are clearly legendary and evocative of the book of Esther, the central claim that John criticized Antipas' marriage may well be accurate. Antipas would not have wanted a holy man based in Perea drawing attention to his unlawful alliance and politically dangerous divorce from a Nabatean princess, and would have acted quickly to curtail his activities.

Luke has a particular interest in Antipas. In 9:7-9 he hears of Jesus and thinks the Baptist has been raised (so also Matt 14:1-2; Mark 6:14-16); in 9:9 he expresses a wish to see the miracle-worker; and in 13:31-32 a number of Pharisees warn Jesus against Antipas (whom Jesus refers to as a "fox"). Finally, in 23:6-12 Luke records a hearing in front of Antipas as part of Jesus' trial: Pilate, hearing that Jesus belongs to Herod's jurisdiction, tries to relieve himself of the case, but Herod, disappointed that Jesus will not perform a sign, mocks him and sends him back. The historicity of this scene is open to question: there was no legal requirement to send a prisoner to stand trial before a representative of his home territory; and Luke is the only evangelist to record such a meeting. It is possible that the trial has been inserted to parallel the trials of Paul in Acts (who was tried by another Herodian, Agrippa II, see below) and to make Antipas an indirect witness to Jesus' innocence. The reasons for Antipas' enmity with Pilate (Luke 23:12), if historical, are unknown.

In 36 CE, Antipas played host to the Parthian king and the representative of Rome, the Syrian Legate L. Vitellius, on the Euphrates—a sign of the tetrarch's trustworthiness and diplomacy in Roman eyes (Jose-

phus, *Ant.* 18.101–105). Aretas, still angered by Antipas' divorce of his daughter, took advantage of the tetrarch's absence, to invade Perea and defeated Antipas' army, a defeat that Josephus notes was popularly seen as retaliation for Antipas' execution of the Baptist (*Ant.* 18.116, 119). Two years later, after her brother Agrippa had been made king of Philip's territory, Herodias persuaded Antipas to go to Rome and ask for a royal title. Agrippa, however, sent his freedman after them, accusing Antipas of treason. When Antipas was unable to deny that he had been stockpiling arms, the couple lost everything and were exiled to Gaul in 39 CE.

G. Agrippa I

Born in 10/11 BCE, Marcus Julius Agrippa I was the eldest son of Aristobulus (the son of Herod I and Mariamme) and his wife Bernice (Josephus, *Ant.* 18.133–34, though *J.W.* 1.552 suggests his brother Herod of Chalcis was the eldest). He took his name from the recently deceased M. Agrippa, Augustus' heir, and grew up in Rome with his mother who had remained in the city when Archelaus was appointed ethnarch in 4 BCE. He made a number of influential contacts at court, including Tiberius' sister-in-law Antonia, his son Drusus, and the future emperor Claudius. He married Cypros, the granddaughter of Herod's brother Phasael, sometime in the 20s. Josephus credits him with an agreeable disposition and unbounded generosity (*Ant.* 19.330), though his youth was characterized by extravagance and debt.

On his mother's death, Agrippa spent his inheritance, was reduced to poverty, and forced to leave Rome. Cypros wrote to his sister Herodias (now the wife of Antipas), asking for help. She arranged for him to become agoranomos (ἀγορανόμος, overseer of markets) at Tiberias, but the two men soon fell out and Agrippa moved to Antioch, the headquarters of his friend L. Pomponius Flaccus, the legate of Syria. After clashing with him too, Agrippa borrowed money from Alexander the Alabarch (the wealthy brother of Philo) and returned to Italy in 36 CE where Antonia paid off his remaining debts. Arriving in Rome, he began to cultivate the friendship of Gaius (Caligula), but was jailed by Tiberius on suspicion of sedition. Six months later, when Gaius became emperor, he released Agrippa and made him king over the largely Gentile former territories of both his uncle Philip and Lysanias of Abilene (though he arrived in Palestine only in 38 CE), and conferred upon him praetorian rank (Josephus, *J.W.* 2.181; *Ant.* 18.228–37).

In 40 CE, after Antipas' exile (which Agrippa helped to bring about, see §F), Agrippa's domain was substantially enlarged with the addition of the tetrarch's former territories. When Caligula was murdered the following year, Claudius, who had been helped to the throne by Agrippa, added Judea, Idumea, and Samaria to his kingdom. Agrippa was now master of a kingdom larger than his grandfather's and was given consular status

(Dio, *Rom.* 60.8.2). He entered Jerusalem in triumph, offered sacrifices, appointed a new high priest, remitted taxes, and presented the temple with a golden chain given to him by Gaius (Josephus, *Ant.* 19.292–96).

Agrippa's piety is praised by both Josephus (*Ant.* 19.328–31) and rabbinic literature (*m. Sotah* 7, 8; *m. Bik.* 3, 4; *Lev. Rab.* 3, 5). He embarked on a number of building projects in Jerusalem (including finishing a high-level aqueduct started by his grandfather); used his influence with Gaius in 40 CE to block the emperor's attempt to erect a statue of himself in the guise of Jupiter in the Temple (Josephus, *J.W.* 2.185–203; *Ant.* 18.261–309; Philo, *Leg.* 207–333); and cultivated relations with diaspora Jews (Josephus, *Ant.* 19.279, 288, 300–312). His piety earned him popularity amongst his Jewish subjects, as too perhaps did his Hasmonean lineage. Yet his model of rulership was derived not from the Hasmoneans but from his grandfather. Like Herod, he enjoyed presenting himself as a benefactor of Gentile cities, especially Berytus in Syria and, perhaps owing to his upbringing, he was thoroughly at home in Greco-Roman circles. He even put images of himself and the emperor on his coins in Caesarea, and had statues of his daughters erected in the same city (Josephus, *Ant.* 19.357), though he was careful not to infringe the law in Jerusalem.

In 43 CE, Agrippa's all-important relations with his Roman patrons were soured when he held a conference of eastern client kings in TIBERIAS. This was a clear display of independence and power and, coupled with the fact that he was also building a huge "third wall" in Jerusalem, brought C. Vibius Marsus, the Roman legate of Syria, to Tiberias. He broke up the meeting, ordered the client kings to return home, and stopped building work on the wall (Josephpus, *J.W.* 2.218–19; *Ant.* 19.326–27, 338–42). The purpose of this gathering is uncertain: it seems very unlikely that Agrippa was planning a revolt against Rome; perhaps he intended it as a sociable event intended to establish his supremacy among other client kings. Such an action, however, particularly when his uncle had been exiled for treason only a few years earlier, was extremely ill advised.

Agrippa appears in Acts 12:1-4 (which incorrectly calls him "Herod") as a persecutor of early Christian leaders. James Zebedee was killed "by the sword" (that is, for political offenses) and Peter too was imprisoned (though his miraculous escape saved him from execution). The affair is not mentioned by Josephus and Luke clearly uses it to good literary and theological effect (it enables the apostles to leave Jerusalem, facilitating the mission to the diaspora) but there is no reason to question its historicity. Agrippa may have adopted a characteristically Sadducean policy toward the early church, and the fact that CLAUDIUS had persecuted Christians in Rome shortly before may have been a good enough reason for a vassal king anxious to demonstrate his loyalty to do likewise (*see* PERSECUTION).

Acts also mentions Agrippa's demise (12:20-23). In the summer of 44 CE, he moved to Caesarea Maritima and was met by a delegation from Tyre and Sidon with whom he was displeased (we are not told why). On "an appointed day" Agrippa put on his royal robes, took his seat on the throne, and made an oration. When the people acclaimed him as a god, he was immediately smitten by an angel "because he did not give God the glory; and he was eaten by worms and died." Josephus is in substantial agreement with this (*Ant.* 19.343–52), though he situates Agrippa's death at a festival to celebrate Claudius's safe return from Britain, and adds that it was the sun reflecting off his clothing that led the people to acclaim him as a god and that the king died five days later. As with Herod I, there have been a number of attempts to identify the cause of Agrippa's death (peritonitis, an ulcer, even poison?), but as far as our ancient sources are concerned Agrippa died because of an act of impiety.

Agrippa was fifty-four years old at his death, having ruled over the kingdom of his grandfather only three years. His Jewish subjects mourned his passing while the pagan population and his troops celebrated (Josephus, *Ant.* 19.356–59). Agrippa's eldest son, Drusus (born ca. 24 BCE), was already dead, but four children survived: Agrippa II, Bernice, Mariamme, and Drusilla. Since Agrippa II was still a minor, the majority of the kingdom reverted to direct Roman rule (Josephus, *J.W.* 2.220; *Ant.* 19.362). Herod of Chalcis (Agrippa I's brother), however, managed to claim authority over the Jerusalem Temple, its treasury, and the selection of high priest; an arrangement that suited both Rome and the high priestly families, and helped to preserve considerable Herodian interests in Judaea.

H. Agrippa II, Bernice, Drusilla

Marcus Julius Agrippa II, the son of Agrippa I and Cypros, was born in Rome in 27/28 CE, and brought up and educated at Claudius' court. He was judged too young for the Judean throne when his father died in 44 CE, but was given the kingdom of Chalcis along with jurisdiction over Temple affairs following the death of his uncle Herod in 48 CE (Josephus, *J.W.* 2.223; *Ant.* 20.104). In 53 CE, Claudius exchanged Chalcis for larger territories consisting of the former tetrarchies of Philip and Lysanius (Josephus, *J.W.* 2.247; *Ant.* 20.138); and in 55 CE NERO added part of Galilee (including the cities of Tiberias and Tarichea) and a portion of Perea to his land (Josephus, *J.W.* 2.252; *Ant.* 20.159). In gratitude, Agrippa enlarged his capital Panias (Caesarea Philippi) and renamed it Neronias (though the name was dropped following the emperor's death).

Despite his immersion in Greco-Roman culture (Josephus, *Life* 359), Agrippa showed a genuine interest in Jerusalem and Temple affairs from a young age. While still in Rome, he helped a Jewish delegation restore the high priestly robes to Jewish custody (Josephus, *Ant.* 15.407; 20.6–14) and successfully inter-vened before Claudius in a dispute with the Judean procurator Cumanus (Josephus, *J.W.* 2.245–46; *Ant.* 20.134–36). He insisted that husbands of his sisters undergo circumcision, and is said to have discussed Jewish legal matters with R. Eliezer b. Hyrcanus (*Tan. Lekh Lekha* 20; *b. Sukkah* 27a; *b. Pesah.* 107b). From the late 50s CE, Agrippa became increasingly powerful in Judea; he made Jerusalem his home and worked closely with Roman procurators. When the completion of work on the Temple in 63 CE left serious unemploy-ment in Jerusalem, Agrippa had the streets paved with white marble (Josephus, *Ant.* 20.219–22); he also tried to renovate the Temple and save it from subsid-ence, though this was never completed (Josephus, *J.W.* 5.36; *Ant.* 15.391). Not all his initiatives were popular, however. When he enlarged the Hasmonean palace (his Jerusalem residence) with a dining room from which he could observe Temple proceedings, the enraged priests raised the wall of the inner court to block his view. Agrippa enlisted the help of the procurator Festus, who had his own security concerns about the wall; the priests, however, appealed to Nero and the wall was allowed to stay (Josephus, *Ant.* 20.189-95).

Agrippa was particularly close to his sister, BER-NICE. She became a queen through marriage to her uncle, Herod of Chalcis, to whom she bore two sons: Berecianus (b. ca. 46 CE) and Hyrcanus (b. ca. 47 CE). When Herod died, the boys and their mother, now a wealthy widow, went to live with Agrippa. Scurrilous rumors of incest (Juvenal, *Sat.* 6.157-8; Josephus, *Ant.* 20.145) encouraged Bernice to marry Polemo of Cilicia in 63 CE; the marriage, however, did not last and by 65 CE she had returned to her brother's court. Agrippa's sister DRUSILLA was married to Azizus, king of Emesa, but was later seduced by Tiberius Claudius Felix (proc-urator of Judea; *see* FELIX) with whom she contracted an unlawful marriage. The couple had a son, Tiberius Claudius Agrippa (who died along with his wife in the eruption of Vesuvius in 79 CE).

Agrippa and both these sisters appear in Acts in con-nection with Paul. Having been arrested by a Roman tribune (Acts 21:38), Paul was sent to the procurator Felix in Caesarea (23:23-35), and given the opportunity to defend himself (24:10-21). Felix, however, put off the case for two years, during which time he often conversed with Paul, at least once in the presence of Drusilla (24:24-25). Recalled by Nero in 59 or 60 CE, Felix left Paul in prison for his successor, Porcius Festus (*see* FESTUS, PORCIUS). According to Acts 25:13–26:32, Agrippa and Bernice went to Caesarea to pay their respects to the newly appointed procura-tor, on which occasion they too heard Paul's defense. Agrippa is credited with declaring that Paul could have been released had he not appealed to Caesar (26:32).

Following the sudden death of Festus in 62 CE, Agrippa appointed Ananus son of Ananus (ANNAS) to the high priesthood. Ananus executed James, the broth-er of Jesus, and some others; Agrippa was informed and shortly before the arrival of the new procurator, Luc-ceius Albinus, had Ananus replaced, presumably due to his high-handed approach rather than because of any interest in Christianity (*Ant.* 20.200-203). Frequent changes in the high priesthood, however, took its toll, particularly among the upper classes, where competi-tion and division led to internal strife. Matters were made worse still following the disastrous appointment of Gessius Florus as procurator in 64 CE. Agrippa was completely unable to deal with the escalating religious and political tension, and by 66 CE the nation was in revolt against Rome.

Throughout the war, both Agrippa and Bernice remained unswervingly loyal to Rome. Agrippa tried, unsuccessfully, to dissuade the people from rebellion in a long speech preserved by Josephus. Although there is doubtless some exaggeration and artistic license here, the main themes (particularly the might of Rome and the dire consequences of rebellion) presumably go back to Agrippa himself (*J.W.* 2.345–404, 407). Agrippa did what he could to minimize Jewish losses (his media-tion saved Tiberias as well as the lives of some from Tarichea), but he was with Titus throughout the fatal attack on Jerusalem and witnessed the destruction of the Temple in 70 CE. The crushing of Judea and Titus' triumph were celebrated in Agrippa's capital with gladi-atorial spectacles (Josephus, *J.W.* 7.23–24). In return for his loyalty to the Flavians, VESPASIAN increased Agrippa's territory and gave him the rank of praetor (Dio, *Rom.* 66.15.4).

Agrippa and Bernice went to Rome in 75 CE. Ber-nice, who had begun an affair with Titus during the revolt, stayed in Titus' palace as his mistress (Tacitus, *Hist.* 2.2; Quintilian, *Inst.* 4.1). She helped to finance the newly established Flavian dynasty and probably expected to be rewarded by marriage. This would have been the apex of the family's fortunes. As an eastern queen, however, she was deeply unpopular with the people who regarded her as a new Cleopatra, and Titus came under increasing political and social pressure to send her away from Rome (Suetonius, *Tit.* 7). After Titus' death in 81 CE, Bernice left Italy and returned to her brother, after which nothing more is heard of her.

Josephus claims that Agrippa corresponded with him to verify certain aspects of his *Jewish War*, and that the king owned a copy of the work (Josephus, *Life* 362–67; *Ag. Ap.* 51). Agrippa died in 100 CE without an heir, possibly having had his lands reduced by DOMITIAN. After a reign lasting almost half a century, encompass-ing geographical shifts and huge political upheavals (both at home and on the wider world stage), his king-dom was incorporated into the province of Syria. This, along with the incorporation of Nabatea in 106 CE, marked the end of client kingdoms in the east.

Little more is known of the Herod family, though descendants of Alexander, son of Herod I and his Hasmonean wife Mariamme, served in the senate at the end of the 1st and early 2nd cent. CE. *See* HASMONEANS.

Bibliography: David Braund. *Rome and the Friendly King* (1984); Harold Hoehner. *Herod Antipas.* (1972); M. H. Jensen. *Herod Antipas in Galilee* (2006); Nikos Kokkinos. *The Herodian Dynasty* (1998); S. Mason. *Josephus and the New Testament* (2003); E. Schürer. *The History of the Jewish People in the Age of Jesus Christ.* Vol. 1 (1973); D. R. Schwartz. *Agrippa I* (1990); E. M. Smallwood. *The Jews Under Roman Rule* (1976); M. Stern. *CRINT* 1.1:216–307; R. D. Sullivan. *ANRW* 2.8 (1977) 296–354.

HELEN K. BOND

HEROD ANTIPAS her′uhd an′tee-puhs [Ἀντίπας Antipas] (ca. 20 BCE–40 CE). Tetrarch of Galilee and Perea, son of Herod the Great and the Samaritan Malthace. When Herod the Great died in 4 BCE, the emperor Augustus divided his kingdom between his sons Herod Antipas, Archelaus, and Philip. Antipas received the predominantly Jewish tetrarchies of Galilee and Perea, and ruled them for over forty years (ca. 4 BCE–39 CE). Like his father, he was both a shrewd politician (Luke 13:32) and a notable builder, founding the city of Tiberias and rebuilding Sepphoris.

Antipas' late marriage to his niece Herodias had serious repercussions, since it led him to divorce the daughter (Phasaelis) of King Aretas IV of Nabatea, with whom he had formed a dynastic marriage. Aretas avenged this insult by invading Perea in 36 CE. A few years later (ca. 39 CE) Antipas, at Herodias' instigation, appealed to the emperor Caligula to be made king. Caligula deposed and banished him instead, granting his territories to Agrippa I, Antipas's nephew.

Antipas—who is always called Herod in the Gospels and Acts—had dealings with both John the Baptist and Jesus. Antipas imprisoned and beheaded John in MACHAERUS, evidently because he was perceived as a political threat (Josephus, *Ant.* 18.118–19) and because he condemned Antipas's marriage to Herodias (Mark 6:14-29 and par.). Aretas' invasion was popularly regarded as divine retribution for John's death (Josephus, *Ant.* 18.116, 119).

Antipas's response to Jesus was ambiguous. Although he considered Jesus to be John, "raised from the dead" (Matt 14:2), and was eager to see Jesus perform "some sign" (Luke 23:8), he also sought to kill him (Luke 13:31). When Jesus stood trial before him and refused to respond to his questions, Antipas mocked him and sent him back to Pilate (Luke 23:6-12).

Josephus and the Gospels are the principle sources for Antipas's career.

Bibliography: Harold W. Hoehner. *Herod Antipas* (1972).

J. R. C. COUSLAND

HERODIAN ARMY. Herod, an Idumean whose father ANTIPATER had secured influence within the Hasmonean court through his service to Julius Caesar and other Romans, managed to get himself appointed King of the Jews by the Romans after the death of Antipater (43 BCE). To claim the throne, however, Herod first had to defeat the man who would be the last Hasmonean ruler, Antigonus.

In 39 BCE Herod sailed from Italy to Ptolemais, approximately 10 mi. north of Mount Carmel, and mustered an army of both Jews and Gentiles. He first secured the south of the country, then Galilee, and finally, in 37 BCE, with help from the Roman forces of Mark Antony, Jerusalem itself. A Roman legion remained in Jerusalem until 30 BCE but, as the Hasmonean army had not survived, Herod appears to have constructed his army almost from scratch from Judeans, Idumeans, tribes east of the Galilee, recruits from his settlements, and even Babylonian Jews and Europeans. However, most soldiers would have probably been Aramaic speakers and Jewish, and this army lasted through Herod's successors to the First Jewish Revolt.

The most important of Herod's military settlements was Sebaste (Samaria) that consisted initially of 6,000 soldiers, but there were others in Caesarea, Galilee, the northeast, Transjordan, and the Negev. A garrison was stationed at Antonia Fortress built on the northwest corner of the Temple Mount. In addition, Herod maintained a large reserve army by trading land for military service.

LAMONTTE M. LUKER

HERODIAN DYNASTY. *See* HEROD, FAMILY.

HERODIAN FORTRESSES. King Herod, who reigned Judea from 40–4 BCE, built energetically. Many of his construction projects were fortresses or fortified palaces. They are known primarily from Josephus and archaeological excavations.

Herod's fortresses (Antonia, MASADA, Alexandreion, Cypros, Hyrcania, and MACHAERUS) were all originally built by the HASMONEANS. He also built several fortified palaces on new sites, including Herodium, the north palace at Masada and the three towers overlooking his Jerusalem palace, Phaselis, Hippicus, and Mariamme.

One might conclude from the number of fortresses that Herod feared uprisings. However, all the structures that were primarily fortresses were originally built by the Hasmoneans. Josephus makes it clear that the Hasmoneans held power precariously and thus they needed these strategic fortresses.

Herod was unpopular, but there were no rebellions during his reign. Thus, he did not need fortresses to protect himself against his subjects. Nor did the forts protect him from external attacks since they were not located near his borders. According to Richardson, Herod updated the Hasmonean fortresses and improved them by making them more comfortable; they served him as retreats that could be used defensively.

The NT mentions none of these forts by name, but they were used by Herod's successors. Thus, it is likely that Jesus and Paul were tried in the Antonia (*see* ANTONIA, FORTRESS). Herod Antipas executed John the Baptist, perhaps at Machaerus. Later, Jewish rebels used several fortresses during the First Revolt (66–73 CE); their last bastion was Masada.

Bibliography: Peter Richardson. *Herod: King of the Jews and Friend of the Romans* (1996).

ADAM L. PORTER

HERODIANS   hi-roh'dee-uhns   [Ἡρῳδιανοί Hērōdianoi]. Before the 2nd cent. CE, the word *Herodians* occurs only in the Gospels: Mark 3:6; 12:13 (//Matt 22:16). In both incidents, the Herodians are coupled with the Pharisees: in the first, set in Galilee, they plot to kill Jesus after a series of controversies (Mark 2:1–3:5); and the second, set in Jerusalem, introduces the question over payment of tribute (Mark 12:13-17; Matt 22:15-22). Neither John nor Luke mention the Herodians, the latter's silence being surprising given his interest in the Herods.

The Herodians have been explained in a variety of ways: as a religious party claiming one of the Herods as messiah; as a political party seeking the extension of Herodian rule; as scribes, publicans, Essenes, or even SADDUCEES. Mark 8:15's "leaven of Herod" appears in some MSS as "leaven of the Herodians," while Matthew substitutes "Sadducees" (16:6). The reading "Herodians," however, is unlikely to be original; thus there is no connection between the two groups.

By far the likeliest interpretation is that the word is a latinism, *Herodiani*, referring not to an organized party but simply to supporters, servants and officials of Herod. Josephus once uses the proper Gk. form Hērōdeioi (Ἡρῴδειοι) to refer to those around Herod I (*J.W.* 1.319). The term could presumably be understood to refer to whichever member of the dynasty held influence, and during Jesus' ministry denoted supporters of Antipas. *See* HEROD, FAMILY.

Bibliography: J. P. Meier. "The Historical Jesus and the Historical Herodians." *JBL* 119 (2000) 740–46.

HELEN K. BOND

HERODIAS hi-roh'dee-uhs [Ἡρῳδιάς Hērōdias]. Daughter of BERENICE and ARISTOBULUS, Herodias was of combined Hasmonean and Idumean descent, presumably born between 16 and 7 BCE in Judea. She divorced her first husband, with whom she had a daughter, and married HEROD ANTIPAS, her husband's half-brother and TETRARCH over Galilee and Perea.

Herodias is mentioned in the Gospels for two related reasons: John the Baptist apparently criticized her marriage with Herod Antipas (Matt 14:3-4; Mark 6:17-18; Luke 3:19), and in Matthew and Mark she is presented as the one who inspired her daughter to ask Herod for John's head (Matt 14:8; Mark 6:24). Outside of the NT, the most important source of information for her life is Flavius Josephus, who mentions both her marriages, but identifies her first husband as Herod (called Philip according to Matt 14:3 and Mark 6:17) and calls her daughter SALOME (*Ant.* 18.135-36; but Herodias according to some versions of Mark 6:22). Josephus also mentions that Herod had John the Baptist put to death (*Ant.* 18.116-19), but does not mention Herodias in that connection. He further relates that the Roman emperor Gaius CALIGULA sent Herodias, along with her husband, into exile (*Ant.* 18.254). When and where she died is unknown. *See* HEROD, FAMILY.

CAROLINE VANDER STICHELE

HERODION hi-roh'dee-uhn [Ἡρῳδίων Hērōdiōn]. Herodion is one of twenty-six persons Paul names in Romans. Herodion (Rom 16:11), ANDRONICUS, and Junia (16:7) are named Paul's relatives. *See* JUNIA, JUNIAS.

HERODIUM. hi-roh'dee-uhm Rising like a cone-shaped volcano on the horizon, the Herodium (also spelled Herodion) is 15 km south of Jerusalem, about 5 km southeast of Bethlehem, and visible from both. It lies on the border of the Judean hill country and the Judean wilderness so that, conversely, standing on the Herodium one can see the three towers on the Mount of Olives to the north, the churches of Bethlehem to the west, and, looking to the east, the Dead Sea. For any first-time visitor to the Holy Land, it is a marvelous introduction to the geography of Judah in addition to its historical significance.

Todd Bolen/BiblePlaces.com

Figure 1: The Herodium with lower pool in the foreground

When the Herodium was constructed by Herod the Great (37–4 BCE) between 23 and 20, it was the largest palace in the early Roman Empire. It was also a fortress to protect him should he fall out of favor with the Jews

Todd Bolen/BiblePlaces.com
Figure 2: Interior of the Herodium

or with Rome. As such, he leveled the mountain adjacent to the one on which the Herodium is built in order to elevate and reinforce the walls of his fortress-palace, which would serve also as the district capital and eventually his mausoleum. Some have speculated that Jesus had this earth-moving project in mind when he said that anyone with the faith of a mustard seed could move a mountain: if the scoundrel Herod could do it, how much more so God (Matt 17:20; Luke 17:6)? All who had visited the environs of Jerusalem could not have missed the towering Herodium.

The Herodium comprised the upper palace atop the mountain and the lower palace at its base. The upper palace was a circular fortress including one round and three semicircular towers at the east-north-west-south points of the compass, respectively. Excavations have revealed a triclinium, a bathhouse, and cisterns. Much of the official business of the district was probably conducted at the lower palace, which boasted an elaborate pool complex. Josephus reports that upon Herod's death at Jericho, his body was carried by funeral procession to be buried at the Herodium. Archaeologists have discovered a 350-m path, which they think was built for this procession, ending in a monumental building. In 2007 archaeologists discovered the remains of what they believe is Herod's sarcophagus and mausoleum. No inscription has yet been found.

Herod's son, Archelaus (ruled 4 BCE–6 CE), inherited the Herodium, but after his banishment it became the property of the Roman procurators from whom it was seized by Zealots in 66 CE at the outbreak of the First Jewish Revolt. The Zealots fortified themselves in the upper palace where they turned the triclinium into a synagogue and added a mikveh. During the Bar Kokhba Revolt (132–35 CE) it was again occupied by Jewish rebels who constructed a secret system of tunnels. Finally, Byzantine monks transformed it into a monastery and built churches at its base (5th–7th cent. CE). *See* HERODIAN FORTRESSES; HEROD, FAMILY.

LAMONTTE M. LUKER

HERODOTUS [ʽΗρόδοτος Hērodotos]. Herodotus was born in 484 BCE in Halicarnassus (modern Bodrum), located along the Aegean coast of southwest Turkey. He moved to Athens and later relocated to Thurii, an Athenian colony in southern Italy where he died and is buried. He was a Greek historian whom Cicero called the "father of history" (*Leg.* 1.1), though some argue that the Israelites and others produced earlier histories (*see* HISTORY AND HISTORIOGRAPHY, OT). Herodotus' most famous work is *History of the Persian Wars* written in Athens ca. 445 BCE. The title of this work is somewhat misleading because it is more of a compilation of stories, legends, myths, and geography collected during his extensive travels around the Persian Empire after the Peace of Callias in 449 BCE. He is the main source of information about Persian history, although he did greatly exaggerate the size of Xerxes' army. He also provided information about Egypt, Mesopotamia, and the Scythians. He often related a "good" story, even if he thought it was not true, and included contradictory variations of the same account. Herodotus' veracity was challenged in the early 20th cent., but he has been largely vindicated by recent archaeological work.

JOHN D. WINELAND

HERON [אֲנָפָה ʾanafah]. The Hebrew word ʾanafah is often translated *heron* because of its position in the bird lists (Lev 11:19; Deut 14:18), among the water birds, and because of the formulation "of any kind." ʾAnafah may mean *cormorant*, whereas khasidhah (חֲסִידָה) may refer to the heron. *See* BIRDS OF THE BIBLE.

GÖRAN EIDEVALL

Todd Bolen/BiblePlaces.com
Figure 1: Wadi Hesa from the west

HESA, WADI EL. Of the four major east-west wadis in Jordan, Wadi el-Hesa is the southernmost. It is often identified with the Wadi Zered mentioned in the OT (*see* ZERED, WADI). It is a perennial stream that runs 35 mi. in a northwesterly direction and empties into the Ghor at es-Safi near the southern end of the Dead Sea. Its catchment area is 1740 sq. km (672 sq. mi.). The upper portion was occupied by a lake (11 mi. × 2.5 mi.) during the Late Pleistocene era when the Wadi al-Hasa Fault dammed the river. In the Epipaleolithic era, the barrier was breached by tectonic activity or by overtopping caused by silting of the lake. Once the stream crossed the fault, erosion caused by its steep descent incised a deep canyon almost 4,000 ft. from the rim to the bottom. The KING'S HIGHWAY traverses the wadi near its center. The Desert Highway crosses the wadi near its upper extremity through the center of the ancient lake-bed. Since 1979, numerous surveys and excavations have been conducted in its environs. Over a thousand archaeological sites beginning in the Middle Paleolithic era have been discovered.

GREGORY L. LINTON

HESED. hee′sid *See* KHESED; LOVE IN THE OT.

HESHBON hesh′bon [חֶשְׁבּוֹן kheshbon]. Mentioned thirty-seven times in the OT—most notably as an Amorite stronghold conquered by the Israelites under Moses (Num 21:21-31; Deut 2:24; Josh 12:2; Judg 11:19-26). Most scholars agree that the remains of biblical Heshbon can be found at the archaeological site of Tall Hisban (Hesban), a ruin located ca. 10 km (6 mi.) north of the town of Madaba in Transjordan. The site is strategically located on the western edge of the highland plateau with a panoramic view overlooking the Jordan River and the Dead Sea.

RØHR Productions Ltd.
Figure 1: Heshbon aerial view

Due no doubt to its favorable geographic location, abundant water supply, and rich pasture and crop lands (Num 21:22; Song 7:4; Isa 16:8-9) Heshbon and its surrounding hinterland was a valued territory. According to biblical tradition, Sihon, king of the Amorites, took control of Heshbon from the Moabites (Num 21:26) and made it his capital city (e.g. Num 21:34; Deut 1:4; 3:2, 6; 4:46; 29:7; Josh 13:21).

The Israelite tribes subsequently defeated Sihon (Num 21:23), and Heshbon and all its cities were given as an inheritance to the tribe of Reuben (Josh 13:15-23; Num 32:37-38; Judg 11:26). Reubenite claims on Heshbon appear to have been contested by several other neighboring tribes and tribal kinglets, including those of Gad (Josh 21:38-39; 1 Chr 6:80-81), Moab (Isa 15:4; 16:8-9; Jer 48:2, 34, 45) and Ammon (Jer 49:3).

Tall Hisban's archaeological record spans over three millennia, with the earliest excavated stratum dating to the Late Bronze Age/Iron Age I transition. The archaeological data neither support nor refute the biblical tradition, but simply are insufficient, given the present state of our methods and discoveries, to illuminate this part of the biblical record. The vast majority of Tall Hisban's remains reflect the local or "little traditions" by means of which its residents have provided for their livelihoods through the centuries and millennia. The evidence suggests that local inhabitants readily modified

Figure 2: Reservoir

Figure 3: Ammonite Ostracon

their livelihood strategies to cope with changing socio-political and environmental risks and opportunities, alternating between episodes of sedentarization and nomadization.

Tall Hisban's most impressive monumental remains are located on its summit and include a perimeter wall with four towers dating to the Late Hellenistic period; a monumental stairway and acropolis area that included a public building (possibly a temple) from the Roman period; the apse, column bases, and mosaic floors of a Byzantine basilica; and several storage rooms and a bath house likely occupied by the Mamluk governor of Hesban during the 15th cent. CE. Fragments of walls and floors of buildings from other periods—including the Persian, Umayyad, Abbasid, Ayyubid, and Otto-man—have also been found.

The most significant find from the Early Iron Age is a dry-moat from the early 12th cent. CE. This discovery hints at the existence of some sort of stronghold, per-haps a fortified agricultural village during the times of the judges.

The discovery of a 7 m (23 ft.)-deep water reservoir dated to the late 10th/early 9th cent. BCE suggests a pro-cess of growth involving gradual transformation of the earlier fortified village into a larger town, complete with its own large "pools" of water—possibly the "pools of Heshbon" of Song 7:4. For some reason this larger town

ceased to grow, and eventually its buildings became neglected and crumbled. Throughout the latter 9th and 8th cent. BCE these ruins, along with the numerous habitation caves that are located throughout the hill of Hisban, were used by people who lived very simple lives, very likely that of semi-nomadic agriculturalists who camped in the caves and ruins in order to grow wheat and barley in the fertile valleys on both sides of the tell.

In the 7th–5th cent. BCE a large town reemerged on the hill, apparently rebuilt by the Ammonites. Their presence is evidenced by a range of finds, including several ostraca with Ammonite script, pottery typical of their ceramic traditions, and a booming economy based on production and export of vine products. This town came to an end, however, and ruins and caves again became the makeshift dwellings of semi-nomadic agriculturalists.

Archaeological surveys in the region surrounding the site produced numerous examples of vineyards and farms from biblical times (see Isa 5:1-5). This survey data has also enabled project scientists to reconstruct changes over the past several thousand years in the historical landscape, including documentation of the gradual removal of the virgin forests and degradation of the lush pastures that characterized this landscape during biblical times.

ØYSTEIN S. LABIANCA

HESHMON hesh´mon [חֶשְׁמוֹן kheshmon]. Heshmon is among twenty-nine Judahite towns in a list of Negeb towns bordering Edom (Josh 15:27), although the LXX list does not contain Heshmon. Rabbinic tradition (*m. Mid.* 1:6) identifies Heshmon with the HASMONEANS, the name of the Maccabean dynasty.

PHILLIP MICHAEL SHERMAN

HESHVAN [חֶשְׁוָן kheshwan]. The eighth month of the modern Hebrew CALENDAR, corresponding generally with October and November, known in ancient times as MARCHESHVAN.

HESI, TELL EL. A 30-acre archaeological site located roughly halfway between Ashqelon and Beersheba in modern Israel. It is quite famous, for there between 1890 and 1892 W. M. F. Petrie and F. J. Bliss conducted the first scientific archaeological excavation. From 1970 to 1983 the Joint Archaeological Expedition to Tell el-Hesi reexcavated the site.

Although the site was occupied sporadically by the Neolithic period, the first major sedentary occupation was a 25-acre Early Bronze III fortified city. After this city was abandoned in the mid-third millennium BCE the site lay in ruins until about 1550 BCE when a village was established. This village was utterly destroyed about 1150 and the site abandoned. The site was rebuilt as a governmental outpost on Judah's southwestern border in the early or mid-10th cent., and it probably served that function until the early 9th cent. when it was again rebuilt as an imposing fort along the ancient Gaza to Hebron road protecting Judah's border against Philistia. The Assyrians, apparently, destroyed the fort in the late 8th cent. The site again became a village in the 7th and early 6th cent., while in the 5th and 4th cent. it reverted to a governmental purpose for the Persian Empire. Subsequently, the site became a Bedouin cemetery.

The biblical identification of Tell el-Hesi is unknown. Some believe it is one of the villages listed in the Lachish district in Josh 15:37-41, although its former identification as Eglon is now considered doubtful. Edward Robinson and others thought Tell el-Hesi a likely spot for Philip's baptism of the Ethiopian eunuch (Acts 8:26-40), but this, too, is uncertain.

JEFFREY A. BLAKELEY

HESIOD. Greek poet of the Homeric era (ca. 700 BCE). His two most famous works are the *Theogony*, an account of the origins and genealogies of the gods that culminates in Zeus' rise to supremacy; and *Works and Days*, a didactic poem that emphasizes the virtues of hard work and honest living. Both poems contain a wealth of early Greek mythology, and *Works and Days* also yields many rich insights into pre-classical Greek society and culture.

SHANE A. BERG

HETH hayth [חֵת kheth]. A son of Canaan among Noah's descendants (Gen 10:1-15; 1 Chr 1:4-13) and the eponymous ancestor of one of two groups of people called HITTITES. Heth's Hittites inhabited the Hebron area and were the people from whom Abraham negotiated a burial spot for Sarah (Gen 23).

A. HEATH JONES, III

HETHLON heth´lon [חֶתְלֹן khethlon]. A site on the northern boundary of Ezekiel's vision (Ezek 47:15; 48:1) of the idealized and restored borders of Israel. Its connection with "road" or "way" suggests that Hethlon may be a regional term.

HEWERS OF WOOD [חֹטְבֵי עֵצִים khotve ʿetsim]. A group within the servant class of the Israelites, who gathered firewood and are not identical with those servants who chopped down trees for carpentry purposes. Listed as "those who cut your wood" toward the end of the groups assembled to hear the covenant (and thus possessing lowly status), these workers are nonetheless counted as recipients of the covenant (Deut 29:11). The Gibeonites became hewers of wood for the Israelites as punishment for their deception (Josh 9:21, 23, 27). *See* CARPENTER; CRAFTS; DRAWERS OF WATER; SERVANT; SLAVERY.

EMILY R. CHENEY

HEXAPLA [Ἑξαπλα hexapla]. Greek for "sixfold." The Hexapla is a polyglot OT compiled by ORIGEN of Alexandria featuring six versions of the biblical text in parallel columns: the Hebrew, a Greek transliteration of the Hebrew, and four Greek versions (Aquila, Symmachus, SEPTUAGINT, Theodotian). Some books contain one or two additional columns.

CARLY DANIEL-HUGHES

HEXATEUCH. Hexateuch is a term that designates the first six books of the Bible, that is, Genesis, Exodus, Leviticus, Numbers, Deuteronomy, and Joshua, taken as a literary unit. The term has been in common use among scholars beginning in the 19th cent. and continuing throughout much of the 20th cent. The increased use of the term grew out of source critical analysis of the Pentateuch and the adoption of the DOCUMENTARY HYPOTHESIS with its four sources—the Yahwist (J), the Elohist (E), the Deuteronomic source (D), the Priestly author (P)—to explain the origin of the Pentateuch. The success of the Documentary Hypothesis led scholars to search for the sources—J, E, D, and P—beyond the PENTATEUCH into the books that followed. Though there was little agreement regarding the extension of these sources into Joshua, Judges, 1–2 Samuel, and 1–2 Kings, it was generally agreed that one or more of the sources ended with a conquest narrative (J and E) and the distribution of the land (P). The promise of the land is set out early in Genesis (12:7), and the goal of the exodus journey is the land "flowing with milk and honey." Thus it was argued that the events recounted in Joshua are a more likely conclusion to the narrative begun in Genesis than the death of Moses that ends the Pentateuch.

The emergence of Martin Noth's theory of the composition of the DEUTERONOMISTIC HISTORY (the books of Deuteronomy, Joshua, Judges, 1–2 Samuel, 1–2 Kings taken as a literary unit) has undermined scholarly confidence that the Hexateuch ever existed as a literary unit. Martin Noth argued that Deuteronomy is not the conclusion of the Pentateuch, but the introduction to the history that follows in Joshua through 2 Kings and that this complex of books is substantially the work of one author, the Deuteronomistic Historian (DtrH). Noth maintained that the sources JEP do not continue into Joshua, but end in Numbers. Thus originally we had neither a Pentateuch, nor a Hexateuch, but a Tetrateuch (Gen–Num) followed by the Deuteronomistic History (Deuteronomy–2 Kings).

Though Noth's theory has gained widespread acceptance, it continues to be modified and challenged. Many scholars are not convinced that a Tetrateuch existed independent of what follows it. While scholars generally agree that the conquest must be the goal of the narrative begun in the patriarchal stories of Genesis, whether this means that there was a Hexateuch is less certain. Given the weakened position of the Documentary Hypothesis in the field of biblical scholarship, much work needs to be done before there is a consensus about how the books from Genesis to Kings came into existence.

Bibliography: A. Graeme Auld. *Joshua, Moses, and the Land: Tetrateuch-Pentateuch-Hexateuch in a Generation Since 1938* (1980); Martin Noth. *The Deuteronomistic History* (1981); David L. Petersen. "The Formation of the Pentateuch." *Old Testament Interpretation: Past, Present, and Future.* James Luther Mays, David L. Petersen, and Kent Harold Richards, eds. (1995) 31–45.

PAULINE A. VIVIANO

HEZEKIAH hez´uh-ki´uh [חִזְקִיָּהוּ khizeqiyahu, חִזְקִיָּה khizeqiyah, יְחִזְקִיָּהוּ yekhizeqiyahu, יְחִזְקִיָּה yekhizeqiyah]. The name, built on the Hebrew root khazaq (חָזַק), which means "Yahweh is my strength" or more likely "Yahweh has strengthened me." It is the name of three individuals in the OT.

1. An 8th cent. BCE king of Judah. The information from the OT about Hezekiah's reign is extensive and derived primarily from three major portions of texts: 2 Kgs 18–220, Isa 36–39, and 2 Chr 29–32. The material from Isa 36–39 is almost identical with that of Kings. While some of the material in Chronicles parallels that of Kings, there is also much that is different. Additionally, the prophesies of Isaiah of Jerusalem may also reflect events during the reign of Hezekiah.

Hezekiah succeeded his father AHAZ as king of Judah at the age of twenty-five and ruled for twenty-nine years (either ca. 727–699 or 715–687 BCE; 2 Kgs 18:2; 2 Chr 29:1). His mother was Abi (a shortened form of "Abijah" in 2 Chr 29:1), daughter of Zechariah (2 Kgs 18:2). Beyond these introductory materials about his lineage and reign, the biblical writers focus on a number of significant events during Hezekiah's reign: his religious reform, the Assyrian invasion, and his nearly fatal illness. While the account of Hezekiah's reform is brief in Kings, it was obviously an important event for the Deuteronomistic Historian (DtrH) responsible for the material (*see* DEUTERONOMISTIC HISTORY). After noting Hezekiah's parentage and regnal information, DtrH introduces Hezekiah with a standard formula which the historian uses to assess all the kings of Israel and Judah, and in this case a positive assessment: "He did what was right in the sight of the LORD just as his ancestor David had done" (2 Kgs 18:3). The primary reason given for this positive assessment is Hezekiah's religious reform. Hezekiah is credited with removing the high places (*see* HIGH PLACE), shattering the pillars, cutting down the ASHERAH, and destroying the NEHUSHTAN. In addition, Hezekiah is said to have refurbished the Jerusalem temple (2 Kgs 18:16). The reform is also put in the mouth of the Assyrian official, the Rabshakeh, who further notes the centralization of worship in Jerusalem (2 Kgs 18:22).

The Chronicler's account of the reform is noticeably longer and more detailed. While the DtrH does not specify when the reform took place during Hezekiah's reign, the Chronicler sets this as the very first thing that Hezekiah did as soon as he ascended the throne: "In the first year of his reign, in the first month, he opened the doors of the house of the Lord and repaired them" (2 Chr 29:3). To carry out his reform, Hezekiah summons the priests and the Levites and instructs them to purify the temple. In reviewing the history of unfaithfulness of the Israelite people, Hezekiah vows to make a covenant with the Lord to restore proper worship in the temple. When the priests and Levites complete the purification of the temple, a major worship is held, which includes the slaughtering of bulls, rams, and lambs for burnt offering, and the male goats for sin offering on behalf of the royal house, the temple personnel, and the entire nation, and the making of music by the Levites to accompany the sacrifices (*see* PRIESTS AND LEVITES; SACRIFICES AND OFFERINGS). The general public then join in the worship by bringing different kinds of offerings and sacrifices—burnt offerings, consecrated offerings, thank offerings, offerings of well-being, and drink offerings. This major public worship signifies the restoration of regular worship practices in the Jerusalem temple (2 Chr 29:35; *see* TEMPLE, JERUSALEM; WORSHIP, OT).

The Chronicler's depiction of Hezekiah's religious reform continues with Hezekiah observing the Passover in Jerusalem and inviting all Israel, including the northern tribes, from Beer-sheba to Dan to join in the celebration (2 Chr 30). What was originally a festival held in Israelite homes (Exod 12:1-20) is now observed in the central sanctuary of Jerusalem. When the Passover is complete, the people move into places and areas outside of Jerusalem to carry out a wholesale reform by breaking down the pillars, hewing down the Asherim, and pulling down the high places and altars "throughout all Judah and Benjamin, and Ephraim and Manasseh, until they had destroyed them all" (2 Chr 31:1). With the centralization of religious life in Jerusalem, Hezekiah sets about to reorganize the various divisions of priests and Levites and instructs the people to bring their offerings and tithes for the support of the priests and Levites. While the centralization of worship is mentioned only in passing in Kings, it is clearly at the heart of the Chronicler's account. The brief version in Kings does not mention the destruction of local shrines and cultic paraphernalia outside of Jerusalem. For the Chronicler, the religious reform is expansive and widespread.

The theological implication of Hezekiah's reform for both the DtrH and the Chronicler is quite clear. It is the event that defines Hezekiah's successful reign. The theological significance is even more profound when the Chronicler makes this Hezekiah's first royal act immediately following his enthronement. On the basis of this reform, the Chronicler provides a glowing assessment of Hezekiah: "Hezekiah did this throughout Judah, he did what was good and right and faithful before the LORD his God. And every work that he undertook in the service of the house of God, and in accordance with the law and the commandments, to seek his God, he did with all his heart; and he prospered" (2 Chr 31:20-21).

It is often acknowledged that the Chronicler is dependent on DtrH as a source material. Yet, the strikingly different accounts of DtrH and the Chronicler in terms of length and details have raised questions about the historical nature of the Chronicler's account. While earlier scholarship tended to view the Chronicler's account as expansion on theological grounds, a number of recent scholars have argued quite convincingly that the Chronicler was in possession of other independent and accurate sources beyond the DtrH. In fact, scholars have also suggested that the brevity of the reform in the Kings account may have been the result of a later Josianic revision and updating of DtrH, whereby the success of a wholesale reform was credited to JOSIAH.

The second major event during the reign of Hezekiah was the invasion of Judah by SENNACHERIB, king of Assyria. Hezekiah most likely began his reign during a tumultuous period in the history of Syria-Palestine. If the chronology of DtrH is correct, Hezekiah was already king in Judah when the siege of Samaria under Shalmaneser V and its subsequent destruction

took place. Judah's pro-Assyrian policy instituted by Hezekiah's predecessor Ahaz may have saved it from any encroachment by the Assyrians at that time.

According to Assyrian history, Sargon II mounted three campaigns in southern Syria-Palestine during his reign to quell rebellions in the region (720–719, 716–715, 712–711 BCE). Yet, it does not seem that Judah was involved in the rebellions nor was it a target of any of Sargon's campaigns. Hence, it is likely that Hezekiah continued the pro-Assyrian policy of his predecessor during much of this period.

Following the death of Sargon in 705 BCE, rebellions broke out throughout the Assyrian empire, from Babylon to Egypt. Sennacherib's first campaign upon assumption of the throne was directed against Merodach-baladan of Babylon. Either during this period or some years during the twilight of Sargon's reign, Hezekiah's policy in relation to Assyria began to switch. The DtrH summary of Hezekiah's reign notes that "he rebelled against the king of Assyria and would not serve him. He attacked the Philistines as far as Gaza and its territory, from watchtower to fortified city" (2 Kgs 18:7-8). The Philistine territory at that time was under Assyrian jurisdiction and Hezekiah's attack was an act of rebellion against the Assyrians.

In fact, both biblical traditions and archaeological remains attest to Hezekiah's organization of the kingdom in preparation for a revolt. Second Chronicles 32 outlines a number of actions that Hezekiah undertook: "he planned with his officers and his warriors to stop the flow of the springs that were outside the city" (v. 3); he "built up the entire wall that was broken down, and raised towers on it, and outside he built another wall; he also strengthened the Millo in the city of David" (v. 5); he "made weapons and shields in abundance" (v. 5); "he appointed combat commanders over the people" (v. 6); he built "storehouses also for the yield of grain, wine, and oil; and stalls for all kinds of cattle, and sheepfolds" (v. 28). Additionally, 2 Kgs 20:20 notes that "he made the pool and the conduit and brought water into the city." Many of these activities must have been carried out prior to any Assyrian attack.

Archaeological evidence and non-biblical texts lend support to the elaborate planning and fortification that Hezekiah undertook. The Siloam Tunnel in Jerusalem with its famous inscription (ANET 321) describing how the tunnel was constructed can safely be attributed to Hezekiah's preparation for an anticipated siege of Jerusalem. Excavations of Jerusalem have revealed the expansion of the city under Hezekiah, attesting to the significant increase of the population, perhaps including refugees from the north. Another significant piece of archaeological evidence is the discovery in numerous Judean cities of storage jars marked with the inscription lmlk (למלך) "belonging to the king". These jars probably attest to a storage program created by Hezekiah in preparation for revolt. The four storage centers were strategically located: Socoh in the Shephelah, Ziph in the Negeb, Hebron in the southern hill country, and mmsht (מִמְשַׁת an identified place name; see MMŠT) for the Jerusalem vicinity.

As the biblical traditions note, Sennacherib invaded Judah during Hezekiah's reign (2 Kgs 18:13; 2 Chr 32:1). This invasion is dated according to Assyrian texts and chronology to 701 BCE. This invasion is corroborated by one of Sennacherib's texts (*ANET* 287-88). In the Assyrian text, the invasion of Judah was a part of a larger campaign of Sennacherib to crush the revolts throughout Syria-Palestine. The Assyrian text reports that Hezekiah had captured and imprisoned Padi king of Ekron, who was perhaps a loyal vassal of Sennacherib. The Assyrian king notes that he put things back in order when he attacked Ekron, defeating the rebellious faction and reinstalling Padi on the throne. Because of Hezekiah's refusal to surrender, Sennacherib "laid siege to forty-six of his strong fortified cities, and countless small villages in the vicinity, and conquered them by means of well-stamped earth ramps, and battering ramps brought thus near to the walls combined with the attack by foot soldiers, using mines, breaches, as well as sapper work." Of Hezekiah himself, Sennacherib further notes: "Himself I shut up as a prisoner in Jerusalem, his royal residence, like a bird in a cage." Assyrian texts also suggest a heavy tribute imposed on Hezekiah and the Judeans.

History indicates that Jerusalem survived this invasion. Nonetheless, the territory of Judah was significantly reduced. Lachish, one of Judah's largest cities, strategically located in the Shephelah along a major trade route, was lost to Sennacherib, who took pride in depicting the capture of Lachish on a wall relief in his palace in Nineveh (*ANEP* 371–73).

The biblical accounts paint a different picture of this invasion. The Kings account reports that Hezekiah capitulated and paid a hefty penalty imposed by Sennacherib (2 Kgs 18:14-16). The Kings account continues with a long speech of the Assyrian official, the Rabshakeh, to seek the surrender of Hezekiah, whereupon Hezekiah goes into the temple to pray and sends his envoys to seek the prophet Isaiah's advice. Isaiah responds by urging Hezekiah not to be afraid and assuring him that Sennacherib will hear a rumor and return home, where he will be killed. The Rabshakeh sends another message, this time through a letter, to Hezekiah to seek his surrender. Again Hezekiah goes to the temple to pray, and receives a reassurance from Isaiah, who now delivers a message announcing Sennacherib's defeat and Jerusalem's deliverance. Jerusalem is spared when the Assyrian army is slaughtered by an angel of the Lord. Sennacherib returns to Nineveh and is killed by his sons. The Chronicler provides an abbreviated version of the Kings account, without the mention of the Rabshakeh. Also, the Chronicler has both Hezekiah and Isaiah praying together. The theological import of

the biblical narratives is evident. While the Assyrian texts do not tell us why Jerusalem was spared, the biblical traditions attribute it to a direct divine action, brought about by Hezekiah's faith and trust in God.

A third event that the biblical traditions preserved in the narratives of Hezekiah relates to an almost fatal sickness he sustained. When that illness happened during Hezekiah's life is impossible to ascertain, since the traditions introduce the event with an ambiguous temporal formula, "In those days" (2 Kgs 20:1; 2 Chr 32:24; Isa 38:1). According to the longer traditions in Kings and Isaiah, when the prophet Isaiah hears that Hezekiah has taken ill, Isaiah comes with a divine pronouncement that the king will die and not recover from his illness. Thereupon, Hezekiah prays to the Lord and weeps bitterly, reminding the Lord that he has been faithful and done what is right in God's sight. The Lord evidently has a change of heart and instructs Isaiah to return to Hezekiah with a new message that he will be healed and fifteen years will be added to his life, and that Jerusalem will be delivered from the Assyrian invasion. The Isaiah narrative adds at this point a long thanksgiving prayer of Hezekiah (Isa 38:9-20). Then the prophet treats the king's illness with a "lump of figs" (2 Kgs 20:7).

The shorter version in 2 Chronicles does not ascribe any role to Isaiah and does not mention that Hezekiah's life was prolonged by fifteen years. On the other hand, the Chronicler reports that Hezekiah's miraculous healing generates pride in the king leading to God's wrath against the king, Judah, and Jerusalem. When the king humbles himself, he and Jerusalem are spared the divine wrath (2 Chr 32:24-26).

While it is not possible to determine if and when Hezekiah's sickness took place, the theological significance of the narrative is not difficult to discern. The biblical traditions imply that even confronting a certain death and concomitantly the demise of Jerusalem, Hezekiah's faithfulness and humility moves God toward a different course of direction. It is also within a theological framework that the narrative of Hezekiah, the good king, is sandwiched between two evil kings, Ahaz and Manasseh, of whom it is written that he "did not do what was right in the sight of the LORD his God" and "did what was evil in the sight of the LORD," respectively (2 Kgs 16:2; 21:2; 2 Chr 28:1; 33:2).

The chronology relating to the reign of Hezekiah is notoriously challenging. Second Kings 18:9-10 reports that the fall of Samaria to Shalmaneser V occurred in the sixth year of Hezekiah's reign. If Samaria fell in 722/21 BCE according to standard chronology, that would put Hezekiah's accession to 727/26 BCE. However, 2 Kgs 18:13 relates that the invasion of Judah and Jerusalem by Sennacherib occurred in the fourteenth year of Hezekiah's reign. According to Assyrian records, that invasion took place in 701 BCE, putting Hezekiah's accession to 716/15 BCE. The difference between the synchronistic data of the sixth year of Hezekiah and his fourteenth year is eight years, while the dates for the fall of Samaria and the invasion of Sennacherib produce a difference of twenty-one years. These differences are not easily reconcilable.

2. The Hebrew name of ATER, the head of a family of ninety-eight people who returned from the exile in Babylon with Nehemiah (Ezra 2:16; Neh 7:21). He is also one of the signatories of the covenant document of Nehemiah (Neh 10:17 [Heb. 10:18]).

3. The great-great-grandfather of Zephaniah, a 7th cent. BCE prophet (Zeph 1:1). Some scholars have suggested that this Hezekiah is to be identified with the 8th cent. king of Judah (see 2 above).

Bibliography: G. Barkay and A. G. Vaughn. "New Readings of the Hezekian Official Seal Impressions." *BASOR 304* (1996) 29–54; M. Cogan. *Imperialism and Religion: Assyria, Israel, and Judah in the Eighth and Seventh Centuries B.C.E.* (1974); L. L. Grabbe, ed. *"Like a Bird in a Cage": The Invasion of Sennacherib in 701 BCE* (2003); I. Finkelstein and N. A. Silberman. "Temple and Dynasty: Hezekiah, the Remaking of Judah and the Rise of Pan-Israelite Ideology." *JSOT 30* (2006) 259–85; P. K. Hooker. "The Kingdom of Hezekiah: Judah in the Geo-political Context of the Eighth Century B.C.E." Ph.D. diss. Emory University (1993); N. Naʾaman. "Hezekiah and the Kings of Assyria," *TA* 21 (1994) 235–54; N. Naʾaman. "Hezekiah's Fortified Cities and the *LMLK* Stamps." *BASOR* 261 (1986) 5–21; D. Ussishkin. "The Water Systems of Jerusalem during Hezekiah's Reign." *Festgabe für H. Donner zum 16 Februar 1995.* M. Weippert and S. Timm, eds. (1995) 289–303.

JEFFREY KAH-JIN KUAN

HEZION hee′zee-uhn [חֶזְיֹון khezyon]. Ancestor of Syrian king Ben-hadad I (1 Kgs 15:18). Hezion has been identified with names occurring in translations of the Birhadad Stela, and also with Rezon in 1 Kgs 11:23.

HEZIR hee′zuhr [חֵזִיר khezir]. 1. A descendant of Aaron upon whom the seventeenth lot fell when David, Zadok, and Ahimelech organized the priests for performance of liturgical duties (according to 1 Chr 24:15).

2. One of the postexilic heads of the people who signed Ezra's covenant (Neh 10:20 [Heb. 10:21]).

HEZRO hez′roh [חֶצְרֹו khetsro, חֶצְרַי khetsray]. One of David's elite warrior chiefs known as "the Thirty" (2 Sam 23:35; 1 Chr 11:37). Hezro was from Carmel, a town in southern Judah. *See* DAVID'S CHAMPIONS.

HEZRON hez′ruhn [חֶצְרֹון khetsron, חֶצְרֹן khetsron; Ἑσρώμ hesrōm]. 1. Meaning "enclosure," Hezron was a town between Addar and Kadesh-barnea in south Judah (Josh 15:3; "Hazar-addar" in Num 34:4). A

diferent town in southern Judah was named KERIOTH-HEZRON (Josh 15:25).

2. A son of Reuben (Gen 46:9; Exod 6:14) and the eponym for the Hezronites (Num 26:6).

3. The son of Perez (Gen 46:12; Num 26:21; 1 Chr 2:5, 9, 18, 21, 24f.; 4:1). A grandson of Judah, he was an ancestor of David (Ruth 4:18-19) and of Jesus (Matt 1:3; Luke 3:33).

MICHAEL G. VANZANT

HIDDAI hid′i [הִדַּי hidday]. One of David's thirty mighty men (2 Sam 23:30), called Hurai in 1 Chr 11:32, likely due to scribal dittography of the Hebrew dalet (d ד) and resh (r ר). He was from "the wadis of GAASH," below Mount Gaash, located in the hill country of Ephraim (Josh 24:30; Judg 2:9). *See* DAVID'S CHAMPIONS.

RALPH K. HAWKINS

HIDE, HIDDEN. *See* APOCALYPSE; HIDE, TO.

HIDE, TO [חָבָא khavaʾ, טָמַן taman, כָּחַד kakhadh, כָּסָה kasah, סָתַר sathar, עָלַם ʿalam, צָפַן tsafan; ἀποκρύπτω apokryptō, κρύπτω kryptō]. Biblical texts display a broad spectrum of usage of these terms. Moses' mother hides her son (Exod 2:2-3); David hides from Saul (1 Sam 19:2). God's "hiding his face" expresses his withdrawal of support (Deut 31:16-18; Ps 104:29; Isa 8:17; Mic 3:4), whereas people can hide in God's presence for protection (Ps 17:8; 27:5; Isa 49:2; Zeph 2:3). Nothing is hidden from God (Ps 139:15; Isa 40:27; Dan 2:22; Sir 39:19), which is comforting for the penitents (Ps 19:12; 38:9) and devastating for the sinful (Jer 16:17; Amos 9:3; Job 34:22). God by nature is essentially hidden from humans, as are his plans (Deut 29:29; Ps 10:1; Isa 45:15; Job 28:21; Sir 11:4). Therefore, God must reveal God's will. The hiddenness of the divine is presupposed in the NT: God's kingdom is compared with a hidden treasure (Matt 13:44); true knowledge is hidden from the wise (Matt 11:25; Luke 10:21; see also Luke 18:34), yet everything hidden will be disclosed (Mark 4:22 par.). In Jesus, God has revealed his hidden wisdom (1 Cor 2:7); God's hidden mystery must now be proclaimed (Eph 3:9; 1 Col 1:25-26). In a physical sense, Jesus hides from his enemies (John 8:59; see also 12:36), and at the end-times people will be hiding in caves (Rev 6:15). *See* APOCALYPSE; CAVE; REVELATION, BOOK OF.

CECILIA WASSÉN

HIEL hi′uhl [חִיאֵל khiʾel]. Means "El lives." The name may be an abbreviation of yekhiʾel (יְחִיאֵל) "may El live." This man from Bethel is identified as the one who rebuilt the city of Jericho during the reign of King Ahab of Israel and suffered the curse of Joshua for having done so (1 Kgs 16:34; Josh 6:26). The NRSV, with other modern versions, reads that Hiel set the foundation at the cost of his firstborn son, ABIRAM, and the gates of the city at the cost of his youngest son, SEGUB. The way the text relates Hiel's loss of his two sons to the oath made by Joshua is significant. Joshua 6:26 says Joshua swore a curse before Yahweh upon the person who rebuilt the city of Jericho. In 1 Kgs 16:34, this curse is identified as a word of Yahweh, which Yahweh spoke through Joshua, and which Hiel has broken. Within the context of 1 Kgs 16, this text provides another piece of evidence for the negative assessment of Ahab's reign over Israel.

C. MARK MCCORMICK

HIERAPOLIS hi´uh-rap´uhlis [Ἱεραπόλις Hierapolis]. Hierapolis, located in southwest Phrygia, is one of three cities mentioned in Col 4:13, along with COLOSSAE and LAODICEA. If Colossians is accurate, the church at Hierapolis was probably begun by Epaphras, one of Paul's associates (Col 1:7; 4:12; Phil 23). Hierapolis, a center for various Anatolian deities during antiquity, literally means "holy city" or "sacred city" in Greek. Located in the upper Lycus River valley at present-day Pammukkale, Turkey, Hierapolis was 100 mi. east of Ephesus, 12 mi. northwest of Colossae, and 6 mi. north of Laodicea. It is thought that the city had very modest beginnings in the 4th cent. BCE. King Eumenes II of Pergamon (197–159 BCE) granted it city status. When Rome took control of the region in 133 BCE, Hierapolis became a part of the Roman province of Asia. It suffered two earthquakes in 17 CE and 60 CE but flourished in the 2nd and 3rd cent. as a center of Roman jurisprudence. Hierapolis was the birthplace of the Stoic philosopher Epictetus (ca. 55–135 CE).

The city was systematically constructed. A main colonnaded street ran northwest and southwest. A monumental gate stood at both ends of this street. Other streets crossed it at a right angle. A channel that served as a waste disposal ran down the center of each street and other channels conveyed water to different parts of the city.

Hierapolis was visited in antiquity for its medicinal springs. Hot mineral springs overflow and cover the rocks below them with white lime deposits. This natural phenomenon closely resembles a frozen cascade and the city of Pammukkale, which means "cotton castle," might derive its name from this common occurrence. Coins from ancient Hierapolis had images of both Asklepios and Hygieia separately and also together.

Hierapolis was a religious center for several deities in antiquity. For example, Apollo was honored as the city's founder. A 3rd cent. CE temple dedicated to Apollo still remains. The Plutonium was located south of the temple. This cave was believed to be a doorway to the underworld. Carbon dioxide vapors came up from the cave and often proved fatal to visitors. Christians filled in the cave in the 4th cent. CE, but it was rediscovered in the 20th cent. Along with the worship of Apollo, the Roman emperor Caracalla (211–218 CE) declared the city neōkoros (νεωκόρος) an official site of the imperial cult.

Hierapolis was also well known for its textile industry. It was famous for its purple dye from the juice of the madder root (Strabo, *Geogr.* 13.4.14). Epigraphic evidence mentions guilds for carpet weavers and wool washers as well as purple dyers (*Inscriptiones Graecae ad Res Romanas Pertinentes* 4.816; 4.818; 4.821; 4.822), further evidence of a thriving textile industry.

According to Cicero, (*Flac.* 88) and Josephus (*Ant.* 12.147,53), Hierapolis had a significant Jewish population; this is supported by strong epigraphic evidence (*CIJ* 2.775; 2.776; 2.777). Some were craftsmen. Some of the first Christians might have been from this community.

According to Acts 19:10 and Col 4:13, Christianity came to the region in the middle of the 1st cent. CE with Epaphras' ministry in the area. Either Philip the apostle and his daughters or Philip the evangelist and his daughters settled and were buried there in a martyrium (see Acts 21:8-9; Eusebius, *Hist. eccl.* 3.31; 3.39; 5.24). The martyrium, built in the 5th cent., stood immediately outside the city walls to the northeast. The structure was over 180 sq. ft. At its center was an octagonal chamber surrounded by eight chapels. The two Philips may be one and the same person; leading figures in the early church with the same name were often confused.

Papias, bishop of Hierapolis in the early 2nd cent., was a major figure in Christianity, whose study of the sayings of the Lord survives in quotations by Eusebius and Irenaeus. Eusebius reports that Bishop Claudius Apollinaris of Hierapolis addressed an *apologia* to Emperor Marcus Aurelius in 172 CE. This work is lost. The church at Hierapolis sent representatives to the councils of Nicea (325 CE), Ephesus (431 CE), and Chalcedon (451 CE).

Bibliography: J. M. G. Barclay. *Jews in the Mediterranean Diaspora* (1996); C. B. Fant and M. G. Reddish. *A Guide to Biblical Sites in Greece and Turkey* (2003); C. J. Hemer. *The Letters to the Seven Churches of Asia in Their Local Setting* (1986).

THOMAS B. SLATER

HIERARCHY [ἱεραρχία hierarchia]. The word is a transliteration of the Greek hierarchia, the power or rule of a hiearches (hierarchēs ἱεράρχης), a sacred ruler. It designates a divinely constituted, vertically structured social order in which persons at the top are divinely appointed and/or endowed with authority by the deity. In modern usage, the word refers to any social group that is vertically structured with top-down authority. Collectivist societies are usually strongly hierarchical, with a number of ranks and rigid social stratification. In collectivist societies of antiquity this social order was believed to be divinely instituted and included the two focal institutions of politics (including political religion) and kinship (including domestic religion). Persons at the top of the social pyramid, whether in the government, the governmental religion, or the family, were believed to be divinely appointed either by birth or some form of divine election. Monarchical politics, high-priestly political religions, and patriarchal families were replications of this pattern of hierarchical structure. Since appointed by the deity, the persons at the top of the social pyramid spoke in the deity's name and with the deity's authority.

The main symbolic medium of social interaction in hierarchies is power—the ability to have effect on others because of an implied threat of physical force. The dimensions of up and down, high and low, of the vertical, serve as symbols of power and the hierarchy that supports it. In the Bible, the analogy of hierarchy undergirds the designation of God as almighty or all powerful. The same is true of descriptions of God as above, in the sky, as celestial father, as king of heaven and earth. Details of the heavenly hierarchy consisting of God, angelic beings, and subject humans are frequent. *See* COLLECTIVIST PERSONALITY; GENDER; KING, KINGSHIP; PRIESTS AND LEVITES.

Bibliography: Barry Schwartz. *Vertical Classification: A Study in Structuralism and the Sociology of Knowledge* (1981).

BRUCE J. MALINA

HIEROGLYPH. Hieroglyphic writing is a pictographic form of writing used in EGYPT beginning in the 27th cent. BCE.

It was used as late as the Greek period for the decoration of temples and other stone monuments. It was replaced around the 16th cent. BCE by hieratic, a cursive form of hieroglyphs better suited for writing on papyrus with ink.

Signs may be written left to right, right to left, or in columns from top to bottom. One determines the direction for reading by examining the animal and people pictographs and reading from the direction they are

Vanni / Art Resource, NY

Figure 1: Doorway. Hypostyle Hall II. Medinet Habu, Thebes, Egypt

facing. Hieroglyphic writing uses twenty-four signs that represent single letters, although these are rarely used alone. They are combined with signs that represent groupings of two and three letters, along with a determinative that signals the category of the word. As in Hebrew, vowels are only occasionally and partially indicated. *See* WRITING AND WRITING MATERIALS.

KEVIN A. WILSON

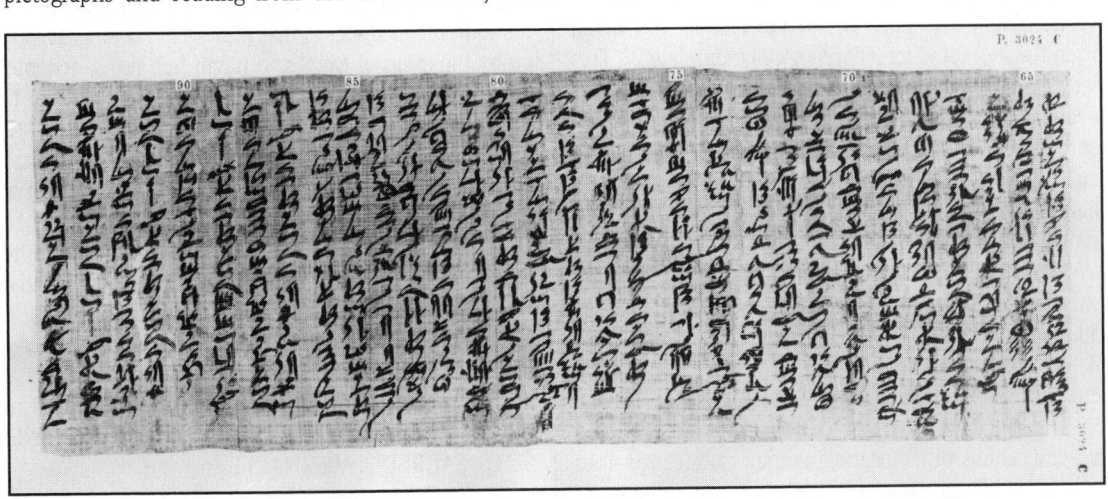

Bildarchiv Preussischer Kulturbesitz / Art Resource, NY

Figure 2: Discourse of a dispirited man with his soul. Papyrus. Hieratic script. Egypt, Twelfth Dynasty, period of Ammenemes III. (Amenemhet III.). Inv. P 3024. Aegyptisches Museum, Staatliche Museen zu Berlin, Berlin, Germany

HIERONYMUS hiʹuh-ronʹuh-muhs [Ἱερώνυμος Hierōnymos]. A Greek military official who served as the governor of a small area during the reign of the Seleucid king ANTIOCHUS V Eupator. He is listed with Timothy, Apollonius, Demophon, and Nicanor as governors who refused to allow the Jews to live quietly and in peace (2 Macc 12:2).

DEREK E. WITTMAN

HIGGAYON. *See* MUSIC.

HIGH PLACE [בָּמָה bamah; ὑψηλόν hypsēlon]. The Hebrew term conventionally translated "high place" is of uncertain derivation and meaning (*see* BAMAH, BAMOTH). In places the meaning "height" makes good sense. In rare instances (e.g., Deut 33:29), it is now understood as a part of the body. Semitic cognates suggest "back," or the like. Most of its hundred or so occurrences refer to a common cultic installation of some kind.

The traditional rendering for cultic bamah, "height, high place," goes back to antiquity (LXX: hypsēlon, Vulgate "excelsus"); however, while "height" (hypsēlon) is the most common translation in the LXX, the term is also on occasion translated "grove," "mound," "idol," "standing stone," and "altar," and in some cases is simply transliterated, indicating possible uncertainty even in antiquity. Until recently most interpreters held either that the bamah was located "high" on a hill, as suggested by several passages in which the term occurs, or that it was itself "high." The first view, prompted by deuteronomistic polemic, assumed that the bamah was a primitive, rustic, open-air precinct that might include an altar, standing stones, and wooden ʾasherim (אֲשֵׁרִים, "asherahs"). This view stated that it was Canaanite in origin and part of a condemnable alien fertility cult (*see* ASHERAH; FERTILITY CULT). In the second view, the bamah was taken to be a constructed raised platform, like the Gk. bēma (βῆμα), "dais, tribunal" (though the words bamah and bēma sound alike, they are etymologically unrelated). This view, perhaps currently the most representative, has been supported by the archaeological discovery in Syria and Palestine of platforms ostensibly associated with cult sites, which are often identified in the plural as bamoth. Whether such identifications are fully warranted remains undecided. A third, less prevalent view to defining the cultic bamah has tried to account for the supposed ambiguity of the word by understanding it as a broad-spectrum term for a "local shrine" of any kind. A fourth view, that the bamah belonged to a funerary cult, has gained little support.

The language used of the bamah in the OT and the indications of its location and appearance together give a different—and not indistinct—impression of the installation. The evidence points to a permanent multi-roomed building in an established settlement.

The bamah was "built" or "made," and could be "torn down" or burned." The bamah could be "entered." In the few cases where it was approached by "going up," the preposition used is not "upon" but "to" or "into," suggesting that in these instances one did not climb a bamah, but rather climbed to it. People performed sacrifices "in" or "at" a bamah, not "on" it. Most bamoth (בָּמוֹת) were located within settlements, not outside them. Jeroboam I had "houses/temples of bamoth" installed in his royal shrines (1 Kgs 12:31) and throughout the cities of his kingdom (1 Kgs 13:32), and he appointed priests to these bamoth and made them serve at the chief shrine of Bethel (1 Kgs 12:32). The kings of Judah followed a similar practice (2 Kgs 23:5, 8-9). The bamoth built east of Jerusalem by Solomon for his wives and those in the Hinnom Valley west of Jerusalem mentioned by Jeremiah had close ties with the Davidic capital. The lishkah (לִשְׁכָּה), "chamber," attached to the bamah in 1 Sam 9:22 is in every other occurrence a part of the permanent structure of a temple, where cultic paraphernalia might be stored. The best-known extra-biblical example of a bamah, found in the MOABITE STONE, is said to have been built by the king "in Qarhoh," usually taken to be an urban precinct or citadel. The frequently adduced connection of bamoth with worship "upon every high hill and under every green tree" is based on sparse attestation. If bamah did indeed mean "height," the Canaanite religious perspective that conceived of shrines as high regardless of their actual location is reason enough to explain the cultic meaning of the term.

Most bamoth mentioned in the Bible are condemned, because most of the references to them occur in the Deuteronomistic History, particularly in 1 and 2 Kings with reference to royal policy, or in Deuteronomistic passages in the Prophets. The Deuteronomistic invective against the bamoth belonged to the drastic policies of radical centralization introduced by Hezekiah and later Josiah. Contrary to this negative view of the bamoth, the evidence is that they were not only accepted by the kings of Israel and Judah but also sanctioned by them as a legitimate feature of local shrines. Prior to the siege of Jerusalem during the reign of HEZEKIAH, Sennacherib's envoys proposed that Hezekiah had betrayed his loyalty to God by ordering the removal of the bamoth; the validity of their charge appears to be underlined when Hezekiah's representatives ask the envoys to speak in Aramaic instead of Hebrew so that nearby Judahites could not understand their argument (2 Kgs 18:17-37). Indeed, given the apparent character of the bamah it is unclear why, apart from this negative deuteronomistic rhetoric, the term is never applied to the Jerusalem Temple itself. *See* SANCTUARY; SHRINE; SITES, SACRED; TABERNACLE.

Bibliography: W. Boyd Barrick. "What Do We Really Know about 'High Places'?" *SEÅ* 45 (1980) 50–57;

Beth Alpert Nakhai. "What's a Bamah? How Sacred Space Functioned in Ancient Israel." *BAR* 20 (1994) 18–29, 77–78; Philip H. Vaughan. *The Meaning of "Bama" in the Old Testament* (1974).

ROBERT B. COOTE

HIGH PRIEST. *See* CHIEF, HIGH PRIEST.

HIGHER CRITICISM. A traditional term for critical analysis of the biblical text using historical and literary methods developed in Germany in the 19th cent. Important examples include Julius Wellhausen's argument for the DOCUMENTARY HYPOTHESIS to explain the literary development of the Pentateuch in light of the history of Israelite religion, and Rudolf Bultmann's critical separation of myth and reality in miracles of Jesus. This approach is often contrasted with "lower" textual criticism that seeks to reconstruct the best original reading of biblical texts by correcting copying mistakes. Higher criticism goes beyond textual criticism by questioning the historical origins and claims of the biblical narrative. *See* HISTORICAL CRITICISM.

BRYAN D. BIBB

HIGHWAY [דֶּרֶךְ derekh, מְסִלָּה mesillah; ὁδός hodos]. Two types of roads are seen in the Hebrew concept of highway. The derekh (Num 20:17, 19; Judg 21:19) was the most common type of road in ancient Israel, formed through continual use compressing the soil and removing vegetation, and sometimes improved. The mesilla (built-up road) was intentionally constructed with a high center and drainage on the edges. This type only became common in the Roman era. The Hebrew tends to relate the two types. Jeremiah 18:15 notes a derekh not "built-up," while Job 19:12 describes a "built-up" derekh.

Highways were also used figuratively (Prov 15:19; 16:17; Jer 18:15; 31:21). Isaiah 35:8 notes a "built-up" derekh called the Highway of Holiness, the route for returning exiles. *See* KING'S HIGHWAY; ROAD; TRAVEL AND COMMUNICATION IN THE NT; TRAVEL AND COMMUNICATION IN THE OT.

MICHAEL G. VANZANT

HILEN hi'luhn [חִילֵן khilez]. A Levitical city of refuge listed in the allotment to Aaron's descendants in 1 Chr 6:58 [Heb. 6:43]. The name appears as HOLON in Josh 15:51.

HILKIAH hil-ki'uh [חִלְקִיָּהוּ khilqiyah, חִלְקִיָּהוּ khilqiyakhu]. The name of several individuals, many of them from the tribe of Levi. 1. The father of Eliakim, a palace administrator during the reign of Hezekiah (2 Kgs 18:18, 26, 37; Isa 22:20; 36:3).

2. Son of Shallum (1 Chr 6:13 [Heb. 5:39]; Ezra 7:1-2), or Meshullam (1 Chr 9:11; Neh 11:11), and father of Azariah. He was the high priest who discovered the Book of the Law during the reign of King Josiah (2 Kgs

22:4-14; 23:4, 8, 24; 2 Chr 34:9-22; 35:8). He was the great-grandfather of Ezra through his son Azariah.

3. The son of Amzi and father of Amaziah, from the clan of Merari, the son of Levi (1 Chr 6:45 [Heb. 6:30]).

4. The second son of Hosah, of the clan of Merari, the son of Levi. He was one of the gatekeepers appointed by David to serve in the house of the Lord (1 Chr 26:11).

5. A Levitical priest from the village of Anathoth who was the father of the prophet Jeremiah (Jer 1:1). It is possible that he was a descendant of Abiathar, the priest banished by Solomon (1 Kgs 2:26-27).

6. The father of Gemariah and companion of Elasah (Jer 29:3).

7. One of the six individuals who stood on the wooden platform on the right hand of Ezra to assist him while he read the words of the Law of Moses to the people (Neh 8:4). The text does not specify whether this Hilkiah belonged to one of the Levitical families.

8. One of the chief priests who returned from Babylon with Zerubbabel and with Jeshua, the high priest (Neh 12:7).

CLAUDE MARIOTTNI

HILKIAH THE HASID. Abba Hilkiah is said to be the grandson of HONI the Circle Drawer. The single story told about him is an elaborate one recounted more fully in the Babylonian Talmud than in the Jerusalem (*b. Taʿan.* 23a-b; *y. Taʿan.* 1:4). He was reputed to have the same miracle-working capacity as Honi. Unlike Honi, Hilkiah seems loath to display his gifts openly. The sages of the time (note that Abba Hilkiah is not described as a sage) send messages to him to pray for rain. Abba Hilkiah tells his wife that he knows the sages have come to ask him to pray for rain and bids her to go onto their roof to pray before they ask him to do so. Rain falls, and Hilkiah asks the sages why they are there since it was already raining. Hilkiah stresses that they should thank God that they had no need of Hilkiah's help. The Babylonian Talmud explains that his wife's prayers are answered first because she stays at home and gives food to the poor, which fulfills their needs at once, but Hilkiah only gives them money. In addition she, like Beruriah, Rabbi Meir's wife (*b. Ber.* 10a), prays for the reformation of criminals rather than their deaths and is therefore more righteous than her husband. *See* MIRACLE; PRAYER; RABBINIC LITERATURE.

JUDITH Z. ABRAMS

HILL, HILL COUNTRY [גִּבְעָה givʿah, הַר har; ὀρεινός oreinos, ὄρος oros, βουνός bounos]. The Hebrew and Greek terms used in the OT and NT to describe natural elevated areas of land that are common in Palestine and the surrounding regions. *Hill* is typically used to denote an individual feature, while "hill country" usually refers to a range of hills. Givʿah is also used as a proper noun for the name of cities built upon hills, the most famous being GIBEAH, the birthplace and residence of King Saul (1 Sam 10:26; 13–15).

The hill country (central highlands) of ancient Israel was part of a distinct geographical region located between the Shephelah (foothills) and the Judean wilderness. The central highlands are a nearly continuous feature that run south from the mountains of Lebanon to the Red Sea. The range is interrupted only by the Plain of Esdraelon south of Nazareth. From their point of origin in Lebanon, their elevation varies from the 3,962 ft. in upper Galilee to less than 2,000 ft. in Southern Judah and the Negev. The hills of the TRANSJORDAN are located along the western edge of its eastern plateau that overlooks the Jordan River valley and Dead Sea and are somewhat higher in elevation than the hill country of Palestine. In the south (biblical Edom) the highest peaks reach 5700 ft.

The higher elevation of a hill country often results in a more moderate climate than in the surrounding areas. The cooler temperatures and greater precipitation of the central highlands of Israel and the hills of the Transjordan produced abundant grain crops for both domestic and animal consumption. Because of their favorable environment and agricultural fertility the hill countries of Israel and the Transjordan were heavily settled throughout antiquity. *See* ISRAEL, GEOGRAPHY OF.

MARK D. GREEN

HILLEL THE ELDER, HOUSE OF HILLEL. Hillel the Elder lived in the early 1st cent. CE and was a forebear of the rabbinic movement. Hillel was not called by the later designation *rabbi* (*see* RABBI, RABBONI), but was titled "elder" (zaqen זָקֵן), as were his contemporaries Shammai and Gamaliel. In later centuries, many rabbinic legends circulated about Hillel as a moral exemplar and a founding father of the rabbinic movement.

Hillel's prestige was such that when the Jewish Patriarchate was founded, the GAMALIEL dynasty traced its lineage back to him. Later, that "lineage" was traced back to King David. The Talmud Yerushalmi (*see* TALMUD, JERUSALEM) imagined Hillel as among the first of the Patriarchs (*y. Pesah* 6:1) and as the originator of certain hermeneutic rules used by later rabbis (*see* RABBINIC LITERATURE). In the Babylonian Talmud (*b. Shabb.* 31a) another cycle of stories is told in the fashion of the Greco-Roman CHREIA, which present Hillel as an originator of the doctrine of two Torahs: one written and one oral (*see* ORAL TORAH; TORAH). These same tales attribute to Hillel a version of the GOLDEN RULE ("what is hateful to you, do not to your colleague") and also relate a story about Hillel and a would-be convert, which parallels a narrative recounted by St. Jerome in the late 4th cent. In several of these narratives, Hillel is presented as the ever-friendly protagonist of the story, while his colleague Shammai is the curmudgeonly antagonist (*see* SHAMMAI THE ELDER).

The abundance of fanciful didactic narratives about Hillel makes suspect the attribution of legal innovations to him. Hillel is claimed to have decreed the *prozbul* (perozbol פְּרוֹזְבּוֹל, a Hellenistic legal device by which rabbinic courts could circumvent the biblically mandated forgiveness of loans in the sabbatical year. *Mishnah ʿEduyyot* (chaps. 1, 4, 5) lists dozens of disagreements between Hillel and Shammai, and between the schools or "houses" of these sages (*see* MISHNAH; RABBINIC INTERPRETATION). In some of these disagreements, the house of Shammai is presented as more lenient, in others, the house of Hillel. In certain of these texts, the house of Hillel is said to revise their original opinions to conform to those of the house of Shammai. It remains remarkably difficult to recover the original traditions behind these later texts.

In the chain of rabbinic tradition found in *Pirqe ʾAvot* (*see* SAYINGS OF THE FATHERS), Hillel and Shammai are recorded as the final of the "pairs" of rabbinic progenitors. The two schools coalesced in Rabbi YONANAN BEN ZAKKAI, "founder" of the first rabbinic disciple-circle at YAVNEH (*see* JAMNIA, COUNCIL OF), in the late 1st cent. CE. *See* ELDER IN THE OT; SAGE.

Bibliography: Henry Fischel. "Studies in Cynicism and the Ancient Near East: The Transformation of a *Chria*." *Numen* 14 (1968) 372–411; Jacob Neusner. *The Rabbinic Traditions about the Pharisees before 70.* 3 vols. (1971); Burton Visotzky. *Fathers of the World: Essays in Rabbinic and Patristic Literatures* (1995).

BURTON L. VISOTZKY

HIN hin [הִין *hin*]. A measure of liquid capacity (Exod 30:24; Lev 19:36; 23:13; Num 28:14; Ezek 4:11; 45:24). Its size is unknown, the biblical hin was perhaps 3 L. *See* WEIGHTS AND MEASURES.

HINGE [צִיר *tsir*]. A metal pole or pivot attached to a DOOR and fitted into a SOCKET, enabling the door to swing open or shut. Proverbs 26:14 compares the lazy person turning in bed to a door turning on its hinges.

HINNOM, VALLEY OF hinʹuhm [גֵּי בֶן הִנֹּם *ge ven hinnom*, גֵּיא בֶן הִנֹּם *geʾ ven hinnom*]. Called "Valley of Hinnom," the literal translation of the Hebrew is "Valley of the Son of Hinnom." This valley, located to the south of Jerusalem outside the Potsherd Gate, marked the boundary between the tribal territory of Benjamin and Judah (Josh 15:8; 18:16; Jer 19:2). It has a long history in the religious life of the kings of Judah and the declarations of the prophet Jeremiah as the place where the TOPHETH was located. In 2 Kgs 23:10, as part of the religious innovations of

Credit: Daniel Frese/BiblePlaces.com
Figure 1: Old City and Hinnom with Sultan's Pool

King Josiah, the king desecrated the Topheth, which is identified as located in the Valley of the Son of Hinnom. The place is notorious for its identification as the place where people "passed their sons and daughters through fire to Molech."

In 2 Chronicles, two kings are denounced for building altars at the Topheth in the Valley of the Son of Hinnom. Ahaz is described as burning incense and passing his sons through the fire in the Valley of the Son of Hinnom (2 Chr 28:3) and Manasseh is said to have passed his son through fire there (2 Chr 33:6).

The abominable nature of the activities associated with the valley and the way that those activities influenced associations with that valley are identified in two oracles from the prophet Jeremiah. In 7:31-32 and 19:6, Jeremiah accuses the people of Judah of sacrificing their sons and daughters at the Topheth in the Valley of the Son of Hinnom to Molech. He announces that the horrors enacted there are so bad that the day will come when that place will no longer be called by Topheth or Valley of the Son of Hinnon, but will be known as the Valley of Slaughter, and it will be used as a cemetery since there will be no other place left.

The characterization of the Valley of the Son of Hinnom in the NT literature seems to bear out the view of Jeremiah. It is called the GEHENNA of fire (geennan tou pyros [γέενναν τοῦ πυρός]; Matt 5:22), characterized as a place of destruction and judgment in Jesus' Sermon on the Mount.

The graves that populate the cliffs that overlook this valley gave rise to the identification of the Valley of Hinnom with the so-called Potter's Field bought with the thirty pieces of silver the remorseful Judas tried to return to the chief priests. They used the field as a burial place for foreigners. Because the money with which the field was bought was considered blood money, the field apparently became known as Blood Field (AKELDAMA) (Matt 27:8; Acts 1:16-20).

C. MARK MCCORMICK

HIPPOCRATES [Ἱπποκράτης Hippokratēs]. Famous 5th cent. Greek physician mentioned in Plato (*Prot.* 311b-c; *Phaedr.* 270c-e) and Aristotle (*Pol.* 1326a). Little is known of his life and writings, though by the 2nd cent. BCE a large body of works (the so-called *Corpus Hippocraticum*) had begun to be collected under his name in Alexandria. It is doubtful that any of these works actually goes back to Hippocrates. Nevertheless, NT scholars are making good use of this corpus today, as among other things it reveals contemporary views of the body, including a number of historically illuminating perspectives on women.

PAUL HOLLOWAY

HIPPOLYTUS. Many scholars today think the evidence favors a division of the once-voluminous, traditional Hippolytan corpus into the works of (at least) two authors: an eastern (probably Asian) author who flourished around the year 200 CE, who may or may not have immigrated to Rome, and a perhaps slightly later author who certainly wrote from Rome or its environs. The former is known for his biblical commentaries on Daniel and the Song of Songs, for such treatises as *The Blessings of Jacob and Moses*, and *On the Antichrist*, and for a polemical work *Against Noetus* (of Smyrna). These compositions are characterized by an exegetical, biblical theology and by several traits that point to Asia Minor (use of typology, knowledge of quartodecimanism, chiliastic eschatology, and the writings of Irenaeus).

Another part of the traditional corpus is assigned by some to a "Hippolytus Romanus," who has been called the last great theologian of Rome to write in

Greek. This writer is credited with a weighty, ten-volume anti-heretical work, *Refutation of All Heresies*, written around 220–25 CE, which also reveals that its author was a Roman church leader who denounced the Roman bishop Callistus. The same author also wrote a philosophical work called *On the Universe*. To one Hippolytus or the other may belong a valuable, early 3rd cent. manual on liturgy and church order, *The Apostolic Tradition*. Whether representing one author or two, the writings associated with Hippolytus remain a highly significant repository of biblical, historical, theological, and ecclesiastical materials from the early 3rd cent.

CHARLES E. HILL

HIPPOPOTAMUS. A four-legged water-dwelling mammal, which is speculated to be the animal mentioned in Job 40:15. This animal, called "behemoth" (behemoth בְּהֵמוֹת), is described as lying in the marsh reeds (Job 40:21), and eating grass like an ox (Job 40:15). Many English translations thus footnote the word *behemoth* by noting the alternate reading "hippopotamus."

JESSICA TINKLENBERG DEVEGA

HIRAH hi'ruh [חִירָה khirah]. A man from Adullam, near Bethlehem. Judah settled near him, became his friend (Gen 38:1, 12), and sent Hirah with payment to TAMAR, who had been disguised as a prostitute (Gen 38:20-23).

HIRAM hi'ruhm [חִירָם khiram]. Two individuals in the OT—both Tyrians—are named Hiram. 1. As king of TYRE in the 10th cent. BCE (ca. 969–936 BCE), and a contemporary of DAVID and SOLOMON, Hiram sent his envoys to David with material and labor for the building of his new royal PALACE (2 Sam 5:11; 1 Chr 14:1). Evidently, Israelite-Tyrian relations continued uninterrupted into the reign of Solomon. While we have only a one-verse description of Hiram's relation with Israel/Judah during the reign of David, the description of the Tyrian-Israelite relationship during the reign of Solomon is more extensive.

According to 1 Kgs, when Hiram received news of Solomon's anointment and accession as king, he sent representatives to pay an official visit to Solomon (1 Kgs 5:1 [Heb. 5:15]). The visit may have been for the purpose of renewing a treaty relationship with a new monarch (1 Kgs 5:12 [Heb. 5:26]). Solomon took advantage of the visit to seek Hiram's assistance in the building of the Temple of Jerusalem, specifically with the request for cedar and cypress from Lebanon. In turn, Solomon would make annual payments of wheat and oil to Hiram. The account provided by Chronicles is a slight variation and expansion of the account in Kings. The contact between Solomon and Hiram did not happen at the time of Solomon's accession but at a later time when he decided to build a temple and a palace. Hence, he contacted Hiram (spelled Huram) to

request materials and skilled labor for the construction projects. As for the payment, in addition to wheat and oil, barley and wine were also included; the payment, however, was not sent to Tyre but given to Hiram's servants (2 Chr 2:1-16 [Heb. 1:18–2:15]). In addition to the building of the Temple, Hiram also supplied Solomon with materials for the construction of his palace. The two building projects took twenty years, at the end of which Solomon gave Hiram twenty cities in the region of Galilee, a gift that apparently offended Hiram (2 Kgs 9:10-14).

Hiram and Solomon also cooperated in maritime trade and commerce. With control of a seaport in Ezion-geber on the Gulf of Aqaba, Solomon sought to use the Red Sea for access to ports in Africa and Arabia. To supplement Solomon's fleet, Hiram provided additional ships and perhaps all the sailors for the seafaring adventures to secure luxury items like gold, silver, ivory, and exotic animals (2 Kgs 9:26-28; 10:11, 22; 2 Chr 8:17-18; 9:10, 21).

It has often been suggested this treaty between Hiram and Solomon, a treaty first established between David and Hiram, was one of parity. However, there is a significant textual variation of 1 Kgs 5:1 [Heb. 5:15] in the LXX, which says that "Hiram the king of Tyre sent his servants to anoint Solomon in place of David his father, for Hiram always loved David." If indeed Hiram initiated this act of anointing, Hiram would have been the suzerain, and the anointing would have been a recognition of the new vassal king's right to rule.

The accounts in both Kings and Chronicles attribute theological significance to Hiram's role. Hiram utters praise to Yahweh (2 Kgs 5:7 [Heb. 5:21]; 2 Chr 2:11-12). Thus, for the writers, the relation between Hiram and Solomon (and David) is more than political; Hiram understands the help he offers Solomon in the building projects as a fulfillment of Yahweh's desire.

2. Hiram is described as a skilled artisan from Tyre who was responsible for the furnishing of Solomon's Temple (1 Kgs 7:13-47; 2 Chr 2:13-16; 4:11-18). First Kings 7:14 describes him as skillful, intelligent, and knowledgeable in metalwork. He is referred to variously as Hiram (1 Kgs 7:13, 45), Hirom (1 Kgs 7:40), Huram (2 Chr 4:11), and Huram-abi (2 Chr 2:13; 4:16). *See* TEMPLE, JERUSALEM; TEMPLE OF SOLOMON.

Bibliography: H. J. Katzenstein. *The History of Tyre: From the Beginning of the Second Millennium B.C.E. until the Fall of the Neo-Babylonian Empire in 538 B.C.E.* (1973); Jeffrey K. Kuan. "Third Kingdoms 5.1 and Israelite-Tyrian Relations during the Reign of Solomon." *JSOT* 46 (1990) 31–46.

KAH-JIN JEFFREY KUAN

HIRI, RUJM EL. This is a unique monumental circular complex in the central Lower Golan, discovered dur-

Mattanyah Zohar

Figure 1: Air view close up. North is on the right.

ing the 1967–68 archaeological survey at the center of the upper Nahal Daliot drainage basin. Whereas the immediate vicinity of the complex appears to be devoid of archaeological remains, the plain is surrounded by basalt flows covered with Chalcolithic villages of the 4th millennium BCE, a large proto-urban settlement dated to the beginning of the Early Bronze Age I A-B/II (ca. 3300–2700 BCE) as well as hundreds of dolmens dated to the Intermediate Bronze Age (ca. 2200–1900 BCE, Fig. 1).

The site consists of four concentric stone circles surrounding a massive central cairn (20 m diameter, 5 m high; Fig. 2 and 3). The outermost circle has a north-south diameter of 156 m by 145 m east-west with a perimeter of ca. 500 m, built with often very large basalt boulders, particularly in the eastern section (Fig. 4), and preserved up to a height of 2 m. This outer wall is interrupted in the northeast and the southeast by gate-like openings, 29 m and 26 m wide, respectively, but blocked by the remains of some tall structure. Standing in the center of the ring, the northeastern gate clearly indicates the summer solstice (Fig. 4), whereas the southeastern gate does not show a recognizable sighting. The stones used in the construction of the inner rings and the perpendicular walls linking them are generally smaller and often later additions.

Excavations at the bases of the various rings reached bedrock after an average soil of only 0.75 m. Very few datable sherds were discovered. The ware of the major-

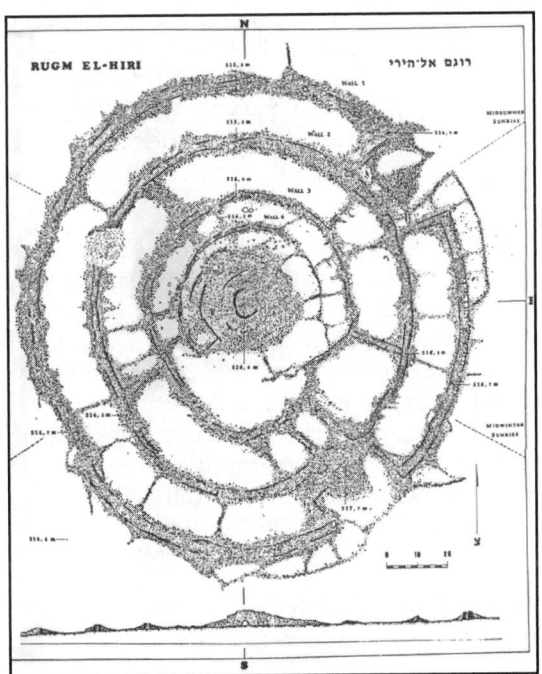

Mattanyah Zohar

Figure 3: Stone-by-stone drawing based on precise measurements

ity of the early pottery appears to date to the last centuries of the fourth and early/middle third millennium BCE. The scarcity of discarded material within the walls suggests that the site seems to have been kept clean for ritual reasons.

The investigation of the central cairn revealed a passage tomb common to the eastern Mediterranean Late Bronze Age, a date confirmed by typical 14th cent. BCE pottery found in the tomb and on a platform surrounding the cairn. The chamber is circular, 2 m in diameter, 1.45 m high (Fig. 6), built of large flat basalt slabs weighing up to 5 tons and forming a semi-corbelled roof, on top of which rested a rough circular cone of equally large stones. The tomb had been robbed in antiquity and only three gold earrings, five bronze arrowheads typical of Late Bronze Age types, and some carnelian beads were found on the floor of the descending passage of 4 m length (Fig. 5). This entire construction was encased by subsequently added rings of support, which might have appeared from the outside as a straight or as a stepped round tower.

Beneath the floor of the tomb and directly on the flat bedrock, an elongated basalt slab (0.85 × 0.30 × 0.1 m) was found in situ, aligned northeast to southwest in the direction of the passage (and the northeastern gate indicating the summer solstice). The symbolic significance of this type of stones (stelae, menhirs, and matseboth representing divinity or venerated ancestors) is well known in the Levant since the Neolithic period and survived into recent times.

Bibliography: C. Epstein and S. Gutman. "The Golan." *Judaea, Samaria, and the Golan—Archaeological Survey 1967–68.* M. Kochavi, ed. (1972) 277–78, site no. 115 (Hebrew); M. Zohar. "Rogem Hiri—A Megalithic Monument in the Golan." *EJ* 30 (1989) 18–31, plates 2–4; Y. Mizrahi, M. Zohar et al. "The 1988–1991 Excavations at Rogem Hiri, Golan Heights." *IEJ* 46 (1996) 167–95.

MATTANYAH ZOHAR

HISS [שָׁרַק sharaq]. The Hebrew verb can be translated "to hiss" or "to whistle" and has two applications: 1) to whistle or to call, as in shepherd summoning sheep (Judg 5:16; NRSV, "piping"), or a metaphorical fly (Isa 7:18), or people (Isa 5:26); 2) more frequently, sharaq is to hiss in shock or derision. In Jer 19:8, e.g., the prophet imagines the severity of the reaction of those who witness the destruction of Jerusalem (see also, e.g., Jer 50:13; Lam 2:15-16; Ezek 27:36; Mic 6:16).

RALPH K. HAWKINS

HISTORIANS, HELLENISTIC JEWISH. *See* HELLENISTIC JEWISH HISTORIANS.

HISTORICAL CRITICISM. An approach to the study of biblical literature that foregrounds questions concerning the "historicity" of the biblical text, and strives to place the biblical literature within the historical context(s) of its production. The method emerged in 19th cent. Germany, primarily in reaction to dogmatic approaches to the interpretation of biblical literature,

and as a result of an increase in relevant comparative materials from the ANE.

PHILLIP MICHAEL SHERMAN

HISTORICAL JESUS. Title for a reconstruction of Jesus that employs the tools of modern historical research. Sources for reconstructing the Jesus of history include: canonical and noncanonical gospels, the letters of Paul, archaeology, and a few non-Christian Jewish and Roman sources. Scholars have proposed various criteria for determining the historical value of information about Jesus in these sources, including attestation in multiple sources and dissimilarity from both 1st cent. Judaism and later Christianity. *See* JESUS CHRIST.

SEAN D. BURKE

HISTORICITY. The question of historicity, when asked of biblical literature, is a question of the AUTHORITY OF SCRIPTURE and the authenticity of its presentation. In some circles, the accuracy of the historical narratives of biblical literature confirm its value for theological constructions. While much of the Bible presents its narrative as a chronology of actual events, the development of the historical-critical method (*see* BIBLICAL INTERPRETATION, HISTORY OF; HISTORICAL CRITICISM), which focused close scholarly attention to the details of the narratives of biblical literature, revealed that the claims of historicity made for the text fall prey to inconsistencies and breaches of coherence and continuity. This realization led to the use of ARCHAEOLOGY and comparative study of texts from contemporary societies in the ANE in attempts to confirm the historicity of the biblical narratives.

While the historicity of biblical narratives has not been entirely set aside, the lack of consistent material evidence and agreement between biblical and non-biblical accounts has yielded new definitions of history and historiography that do not require accuracy of the narrative as a necessary characteristic of history writing (*see* HISTORY AND HISTORIOGRAPHY, NT; HISTORY AND HISTORIOGRAPHY, OT). Consequently, new foundations for textual authority that do not depend upon the historical accuracy of the narrative have found their way into hermeneutical theories and discussions.

C. MARK MCCORMICK

HISTORY AND HISTORIOGRAPHY, NT. There are few more troubled areas of critical biblical studies than the issue of history. The term itself, *history*, is ambiguous, referring to "the past," "study of the past," and "representation of the past." Transitions in the philosophy of history promote different assessments of what qualifies as "good history." For biblical studies generally, questions of genre are discussed with reference to whether a document "intends" history. Since the 18th cent., biblical scholars and theologians alike have largely assumed that theological claims require historical bedrock, pressing scholarship to see the biblical materials as windows into an authoritative past rather than as authoritative witness to the "mighty acts of God." Accordingly, biblical texts were regarded with critical suspicion, and biblical studies became a discipline of "validation" (when the biblical text was judged to represent historical events accurately) or "reconstruction" (when it was not).

The importance of history for NT studies is incontestable. This is not only because the NT includes books, the Gospels and Acts, whose mode of discourse is congruent with ancient traditions of historiography. Additionally, every NT document situates itself in history, whether localized or even oriented toward a particular household church (e.g., Phil 4:2; Rev 2–3) or worldwide (e.g., Luke 2:1-7; 3:1-6; 1 Pet 5:9). The historical dimension of the NT is also realized in its theological declaration: "The Word became flesh and lived among us, and we have seen his glory, the glory as of a father's only son, full of grace and truth" (John 1:14).

In NT studies, historical questions have focused above all on the Gospels and Acts, narratives imagined by many readers to represent what really happened (or not) in the life and mission of Jesus and subsequently of his followers. Paradoxically, it is precisely the concern of the NT writers to situate divine disclosure within their historical context that lies at the root of modern controversy concerning the historical value of these documents. Presupposing the necessary segregation of historical and theological (or religious) interests, modern NT historians have often occupied themselves with carving away from narrated accounts their theological layers so as to expose a historical core.

That the NT includes four Gospels that tell much the same overall story but differ at many points of detail and emphasis raised historical questions from early on. According to Eusebius, Clement of Alexandria (ca. 150–220 CE) observed that Matthew, Mark, and Luke recounted the "physical" facts while John composed a "spiritual Gospel" (*Hist. eccl.* 6.14.7). Similarly, Origen, writing ca. 250 CE of the discrepancies between the Gospel of John and the Synoptic Gospels, concluded, "I conceive it to be impossible for those who admit nothing more than the history in their interpretation to show that these discrepant statements are in harmony with each other" (*Comm. Jo.* 10.15)—a conclusion that cleared the way for the use of additional methods in study of the Gospels.

In modern times, serious challenges to the historical veracity of the Gospels and Acts, as well as the NT as a whole, have been discoveries of additional texts from antiquity, both Jewish and Christian, especially at Nag Hammadi and Qumran. Together, these findings reveal a breadth of diversity within the Judaism of Jesus' day (thus, the increasingly popular reference to early "Judaisms") and within the Christian movement's first centuries. As a result, the relatively monochro-

matic portrait of "the Jews" and the relative priority of Pauline Christianity found generally in the NT have come under increasing scrutiny. Discovery of extant Christian documents or reconsideration of previously known documents has also raised questions about the sources appropriate for historical study of Jesus and the Christian movement. Noncanonical gospels (such as the Gospel of Thomas or the Gospel of Peter) are sometimes championed as containing material with historical priority over or at least comparable to that found in the NT Gospels.

From the mid 20th cent. to the present, scholars have become increasingly polarized in their assessment of the historical veracity of the Acts of the Apostles. The debate has tended to center on a limited number of considerations: the verisimilitude of the narrative of Acts; historical sequence (esp. when events in Acts are mentioned in other contemporary literature), the speeches in Acts, reports of "signs and wonders," and the portrait of Paul in Acts in comparison with the Paul that emerges from the Pauline epistles. This debate has significance primarily because Acts is our sole narrative account of the early church, but also for its bearing on our understanding of such questions as the emergence of the Gentile mission and Pauline chronology. More broadly, how one adjudicates the historicity of Acts, together with parallel decisions about other biblical accounts, gets at the heart of our understanding of the truth claims of the narrative content of the Bible and, then, how to conceive the authority of biblical narrative.

Overlaying such considerations are key scholarly assumptions about history and historical inquiry. First, in an attempt to provide methodological rigor to the study of the historical Jesus at the turn of the 20th cent., Ernst Troeltsch articulated three principles: the historicity of a reported event cannot be assumed (skepticism), the probability of a past event is determined by analogy with the occurrence of a similar event today (analogy), and every historical event is the effect of a historical cause (correlation). Widely adopted, the effect of these principles was to assess the historicity of ancient reports according to modern sensibilities, to rule out of court the possibility of the supernatural or miraculous, and to locate the burden of proof on any claim favoring historical veracity. Subsequent inquiry generated increasingly sophisticated criteria for use in evaluating the historicity of events recorded in the Gospels and Acts.

Second, since these historical methods and practices developed largely from the late 19th through the mid 20th cent., they generally reflect the regnant philosophy of history famously articulated by Leopold von Ranke (1795–1886). Not wanting to pass judgment on the past, he wanted simply to report *wie es eigentlich gewesen*: "how it actually was." Historical inquiry in this tradition has long outlived von Ranke, motivated especially by a desire to emulate the investigative commitments and techniques of the natural sciences. Even if the philosophy of history has moved far beyond this vision of the historical project, this general approach has continued to influence NT studies.

For early Christians, sensibilities regarding the narrative representation of historical events, or historiography, derived from two sources, the tradition of history writing in the Greco-Roman world and historical narrative in the Jewish tradition (both OT and Hellenistic Jewish historiography). From their Jewish precursors, Christians drew especially their interests in the advancement of historical events in the service of God's purpose, the role of historical narrative in instruction, the repetition of patterns in characters and events, and the punctuation of history writing with the awareness of God's continued presence. Interest in preserving the past among the Greeks led to several kinds of historical writing, the most important for our purposes being the "history of great deeds." These "histories," pioneered by Herodotus (ca. 484–425 BCE) but standardized in the work of Thucydides (ca. 460–400 BCE), were concerned not merely with reporting events but with describing and explaining their sequential development. Taking the claims of ancient historians at face value, moderns have tended to characterize Greco-Roman historiographers as dispassionate investigators who rejected the place of myth, the supernatural, and the use of rhetorical tools and aims. To the contrary, their practices reveal their concern to persuade their audiences to a particular reading of the past, and their concomitant employment of a variety of means for sanctioning their accounts—including reference to divine intervention and the supernatural, imitation, and patterns of prediction and recurrence. Discussion of speeches in historiography has centered on a notoriously difficult text on the writing of speeches in Thucydides (1.22.1); some scholars conclude from it that speeches are inventions of the historian, others that historians were constrained by at least general knowledge of what was actually said. Reconsideration of the available evidence suggests, instead, that historians worked to hold in balance artistic and historical appropriateness; speeches documented the speech-event itself but did not provide a transcript of an occasion.

Insofar as biography (focused on a great person) arose out of historiography (focused on great deeds) in the Roman period, it is possible to speak collectively of the historiographical emphases of the Gospels and Acts. Of the several ways the NT writers carried forward their inherited historiographical traditions, three are especially noteworthy: 1) History writing was for them a form of apologetic, demonstrating the antiquity of their faith as well as documenting the continuity of Jesus and the church with the scriptural stories of Abraham, Moses, and/or Isaianic promise in the case of the Synoptic Gospels and Acts, and with the very creation of the cosmos in the case of John (1:1).

2) In their history writing, we find no unbroken chain of natural cause and effect, since, first, the course of history takes its point of beginning from the work and purpose of God in creation and has its telos in the consummation of God's purpose; second, because God makes his purpose known through a variety of media (e.g., prophets, dreams, Scripture); and third, because God continues to work through human agents (e.g., Moses, Deborah), heavenly messengers (e.g., Gabriel), and especially through Christ and the Holy Spirit; 3) In Acts, where they are of particular importance, speeches advance the action of the narrative, provide as hermeneutical asides a commentary on narrative events, and propagate a unified view of God's saving purpose. The author of Acts, following the tradition of Greco-Roman historiographers, composed speeches congruent with the narrative as a whole in terms of content, style, and language, but that would not be anachronistic or out of character with what was known of the person to whom the speech was attributed.

Study of NT historiography can be set on a more sure footing by fresh examinations of the nature of history writing in antiquity and by reflecting critically on its own assumptions and concerns in conversation with contemporary philosophy of history. Among relevant truisms emphasized in contemporary study are the following three: 1) History writing provides us with both more and less than the past—more in that historiography construes events in a web of causal relationships that draw out a significance that is greater than individual episodes might suggest on their own, less in that historians must make ruthless decisions about what to exclude lest the retelling become infinitely detailed. Historiography, then, is inherently partial: providing only a minute segment of the episodes that compose the past, and doing so according to the inescapably subjective aims of the historian; 2) History writing must account for the present to which the past has led. In this sense, all historiography is contemporary, since the historian demonstrates through narrative representation how the present grows organically out of sequences of past events. As a consequence, historiography is a powerful implement of community legitimation, identity formation, and instruction; 3) History writing is a rhetorical exercise in which documentation and interpretation (or signification) are inextricably woven together. Events, which we experience serially as occurrences and situations, acquire a narrative form (arranging what has happened in a web of causation and meaning) that is unavoidably perspectival. As a result, fresh questions should eclipse a narrow focus on "what actually happened," e.g., What choices? What order? What perspective? What organizing principle? What overarching purpose?

Bibliography: E. Breisach. *Historiography: Ancient, Medieval, and Modern.* 2nd ed. (1994); A. Cook. *History/Writing: The Theory and Practice of History in*

Antiquity and in Modern Times (1988); C. W. Fornara. *The Nature of History in Greece and Rome* (1983); J. Marincola. *Authority and Tradition in Ancient Historiography* (1997); C. K. Rothschild. *Luke-Acts and the Rhetoric of History* (2004); C. H. Talbert. "What Is Meant by the Historicity of Acts?" *Reading Luke-Acts in Its Mediterranean Milieu* (2003) 197–217.

JOEL B. GREEN

HISTORY AND HISTORIOGRAPHY, OT.

More than half of the OT is historiography, broadly defined. These portions of the OT display features expected in history writing, such as characterization, cause-and-effect continuum, plot resolution, etc. They also raise challenges for contemporary readers about the origins of such history writing, the rhetorical nature of Hebrew narratology, and the historicity of events described. Many such challenges are resolved when the distinction between ancient and modern historiography is clarified.

  A. Definitions
  B. Israelite Historical Literature
  C. Origins
  D. Methodology
  Bibliography

A. Definitions

Historiography is among the most difficult subjects in biblical studies to define, although many have tried. "History" is itself a word needing clarification, and "historiography" is inherently ambiguous. By the latter, do we mean 1) biblical history, i.e., history according to the Bible or 2) Israelite history, the history of ancient Israel derived from modern research (Tsevat 1980)? The distance between the two is a matter of perspective and debate, but for the purposes of this article, "historiography" will relate to the literary compositions of ancient Israelites rather than to modern reconstructions of Israel's history. Beyond this simple distinction, any treatment of history and historiography as they relate to the OT requires further clarification at the outset.

The word *history* is of Greek origin ("investigations, researches"), and is not itself a biblical term. If we reduce our definitions to simplistic romantic notions prevalent in Western culture, history is made of the events of the past and historiography is the written record of those events. Biblical scholarship has most frequently assumed definitions similar to these, so that Israelite historiography has often been evaluated by criteria assumed of modern historiographers; that is, how accurately and objectively events have been researched and presented. Famously, in the 19th cent., Leopold von Ranke's definition of the discipline of history as an attempt to show "how it really was" took root in the humanities generally. Modern standards of history writing have routinely been applied to ancient authors, assuming the ancients thought about history and wrote history in a way similar to modern historians. Israelite historians were deemed competent or incompetent based upon how exactly they related what happened in the past.

John Van Seters's monograph in 1983 attempted to compare Israelite history writing with that of other peoples of the ancient world (including the Greeks) as a way of studying the nature and origins of history writing in the Bible. The definition he used in his work was that of Johan Huizinga: "History is the intellectual form in which a civilization renders account to itself of its past." From this starting point, Van Seters challenged the assumption that ancient Israelite historians (as well as those of Greece, Mesopotamia, Egypt, and Asia Minor) had the same definition of history and history writing as modern scholars. Although others have objected that Van Seters used Huizinga's definition too narrowly, his work has been influential as a corrective to the assumption that biblical authors understood their task as one of telling what happened in the past. Rather, the purpose of Israelite historiography was theological and aetiological, meaning the authors predominantly set out to "render an account" of their national origins. These authors were not concerned with chronological precision or factual details, which is not to say their records are complete fictions, since the essential historicity of Israel's national epic may be accepted as generally accurate (contra Van Seters). Although Van Seters overstated the case, his work serves as an essential and important corrective, which has placed biblical history writers in their proper perspective as ANE authors, and compels us to read their works on their own terms. In this light, "history" may continue simply to denote events of the past, while "historiography" requires a more nuanced understanding of the purposes and rhetorical techniques of ancient historians writing about those events.

Indeed, rather than historiography as the term is generally used today, we may think of Hebrew narrative as "historiology," or discourse-history. That is, the authors wrote a discursive account, highly rhetorical in nature, that aimed for dramatic, theological, and religious effect more than for historical precision. All Israelite history writing is intensely historiological. Their view of divinity, and hence their theologizing, was embedded in events of the past, including the conviction that the creator God, identified as national Yahweh, had broken into the world of their ancestors and then into the world of their nation, in order to reveal his nature and to save them as a people from slavery. Since the Enlightenment, it has often been assumed that this Israelite ideology would, of necessity, produce history writing that would be concerned to relate the details and realia of those acts of God with precision or with what we might call today historical accuracy. But the assumption that the ancients wrote a literary type similar to our contemporary historiography is precisely where one goes wrong. Israelite authors of history saw the events they described as more than factual events; they narrated acts of the past as the action and will of God in their national history. This theological dimension makes Israelite history writing, from the start, quite another matter altogether than Enlightenment modes of history and historiography.

B. Israelite Historical Literature

Many books of the OT contain portions that are historical narrative, even though the genre of those books is not primarily historiography. For example, there are long stretches of narrative in Jeremiah, and shorter portions in many of the prophets (e.g., Amos 7:10-15), as well as texts cast in narrative form (Job 1–2). In general, however, Israelite history writing is represented by three expansive narrative complexes, which have been interwoven into the present books of the Bible in diverse ways.

First, an early "Israelite epic history," tracing Israel's national origins and early history, has been used in the composition of Genesis, Exodus, and Numbers. The original sources of this epic history have been identified as J (a source referring to God as Yahweh, spelled *Jahwe* in German, hence "J"), E (a source using the divine title ELOHIM, hence "E"), and subsequently as JE, but we may conveniently call the latter the Yahwist's history (*see* DOCUMENTARY HYPOTHESIS; E, ELOHIST; J, YAHWIST). While much debate continues about the nature (even existence) of the original E document, it is clear that the composite work of the Yahwist was an extensive narrative history of elaborate plot and characterization, which played an important role in the development of historiography in ancient Israel. The date of composition of the Yahwist's history was hotly contested in the last quarter of the 20th cent., but the evidence points to a date in the 9th–7th cent. BCE on the basis of analogy to inscriptional evidence, both Northwest Semitic and Assyriological (Emerton). This early historiological epic has been interpolated and combined with priestly materials of diverse sorts into the current books of the Pentateuch.

The second extended history is a unified narrative of preconquest sojourn in the plains of Moab (Deuteronomy), conquest of Canaan (Joshua), and the pre-monarchic settlement period (Judges–Samuel) to monarchic Israel (Samuel–Kings). A long-standing scholarly consensus about this Deuteronomistic History (DtrH) has prevailed since Martin Noth's groundbreaking work of 1943, although many variations of the hypothesis have been offered (*see* DEUTERONOMISTIC HISTORY). Against the so-called Göttingen school's triple redaction or layered-model approach, the simplest and still most persuasive explanation of DtrH is that it was first composed during the reign of Josiah and subsequently revised with additional amounts of more pessimistic material in the early exile, the so-called "double redac-

tion" approach (Nelson). A few variations of this double redaction approach merit particular attention (such as a proposed Hezekian edition; Halpern and Vanderhoft). Based upon the covenantal theological tenets of the book of Deuteronomy, the DtrH recounted Israel's entrance and settlement in the promised land, development as an independent political entity, and eventual collapse and ruin, first at the hands of the Assyrians and then the Babylonians.

The third narrative complex comes from the postexilic period, comprising 1–2 Chronicles and Ezra–Nehemiah (the latter taken as one book). We read them together today largely because of the canonical forms, which are tied together by means of the repetition of 2 Chr 36:22-23 in Ezra 1:1-3a. Indeed, for most of the 19th and 20th cent., scholars believed they originally constituted a single composition, the so-called Chronicler's History. In the last quarter of the 20th cent., however, the consensus changed so the prevailing opinion now is that Chronicles and Ezra–Nehemiah were two separate works (even if by the same author), composed independently and combined at a later time (the previous consensus challenged persuasively by Japhet and Williamson). Shared terms and phrases, as well as common ideology, are best explained at the redactional level. Analogous to the composition of the DtrH, it seems likely that different historical works of separate origins have been combined in a connected narrative. Focused primarily on the restoration of Israel and on the importance of temple worship, this narrative complex covered the distant past (1–2 Chr) and the recent past and present (Ezra–Nehemiah).

Israelite historiographic conventions continued in several works of Second Temple Judaism. In particular, 1 Maccabees, probably written around 100 BCE, relies on carefully researched sources, and gives detail to chronological specifics and characterization. Written several decades later, 2 Maccabees is rhetorically quite different, in some ways a "pathetic" history, in that it emphasizes the emotions of its characters and readers, and is thoroughly didactic (Vanderkam). There were also a few Jewish Greek-writing historians, for which we have only fragmentary remains (e.g., Eupolemus), and these reflect a Hellenistic literary genre emerging among other nations, such as the Babylonian Berossus and the Egyptian Manetho (Walter). But the rhetorical dimensions of Jewish historiography came to full fruition in Flavius Josephus (ca. 37–100 CE). Josephus's extensive writings, especially the *Jewish War* and *Jewish Antiquities* covered all of Jewish history from creation to the revolt against Rome in the historian's own lifetime (66 CE). Although long portions of *Jewish Antiquities* are simple paraphrases of the OT, much of his work was based on extensive research and incorporated painstaking detail. For much of the history of Second Temple Judaism, Josephus is our primary and sometimes only resource. His historiographic conventions included speeches that could encapsulate ideas and perspectives permeating the entire work, as in the DtrH (such as King Agippa's speech [*J.W.* 2.345–401], but he was also influenced by the antiquarian approach of Hellenistic historical traditions, as is more characteristic of *Jewish Antiquities* (Feldman).

C. Origins

Assuming Van Seters's definitions are valid, it is true that historiographical materials have been preserved from Egypt, Mesopotamia, and the Hittites, and yet also true that ancient history writing appears first in Israel, and then (but almost simultaneously) in Greece (Van Seters). The question remains, whence this history-writing impulse in ancient Israel, especially when compared and contrasted to Egypt and Mesopotamia, where ideas of history and historiographical materials are present but where genuine history writing does not make an appearance. Instead, differing views of divinity in Israel and the rest of the ANE apparently resulted in different forms and types of historiography (Arnold).

Van Seters concludes the new genre in Greece and Israel made use of various sorts of lists, royal inscriptions, and chronicles, and yet it did not evolve directly from any one of them or a combination of all of them at once. The first history ever written, therefore, according to Van Seters, was the DtrH, combining a number of historiographical genres into a new genre, "history," in order to "render account" of Israel's past in a sense of identity during the exilic and postexilic periods, needed because of the loss of kingship and the democratization of the notion of election. Subsequently, in Van Seters's reconstruction, the Yahwist was composed in order to supplement DtrH by extending the history back in time to the beginning of the world, and the Chronicler was written last, using the previous two, in an attempt to give account of the "kingdom of God" as preserved in the postexilic community (Damrosch). Van Seters has been severely criticized for his misappropriation or misunderstanding of Huizinga's definition of history. Among these critiques are the fact that the Dutch historian did not intend to limit history writing to a nationalistic exercise, and that Van Seters adopts too facilely a reductionistic historicism inappropriate for ANE materials.

Some have assumed Israelite historiography evolved as a historicizing of older poetic epic, the result of a confluence of such epic literature with chronography, which process was underway in Mesopotamia in the second millennium BCE but came to fruition in genuine history writing only in Israel (Damrosch). This Yahwistic history has often been placed in the 9th cent. BCE, while others tenuously assume a 10th cent. date based on the geographical references in Gen 15:18 (and elsewhere): "from the river of Egypt to the great river, the river Euphrates." Others have argued the Hittites introduced historiography as a literary genre

in the ANE, which was brought to artistic perfection by the Israelite. More likely, the matrix for the origin of history writing in ancient Israel is to be found in the literary and narrative skills embodied in the scribes of the monumental inscriptions in the 9th to 7th cent. BCE (Emerton; Na'aman), a perspective that also supports the idea of a preexilic Yahwistic history (Emerton; contra Van Seters).

D. Methodology

A slow and gradual change began to occur in historical studies generally with the emergence of the Annales School in the late 1920s, and especially in the Braudelian three-tier model's influence on biblical studies (Younger; Kofoed). Named after the journal where it was first expounded, the Annales School is best known for incorporating social scientific methods into the study of the past, rejecting the previous generation's fixation on politics, diplomacy, and warfare. This approach gradually exposed the weaknesses of the established schools of thought related to ancient Israel (both in Germany and in the United States), with their use of biblical texts as the starting point and their inability to use archaeological materials independently of those texts. In the last two decades of the 20th cent., the emphasis of the Annales School on empirical data, positivism, and multidisciplinary studies was combined with an extreme skepticism (or nihilism; some would say a hermeneutic of suspicion) regarding the historical reliability of the OT generally. The result was the so-called "Copenhagen School," with its methodological skepticism of textual evidence and positivistic need to verify data before accepting them in any historical reconstruction.

While the Annales School, and the later Copenhagen School, may be said to be developments within modernism, the turn of the 21st cent. has also given rise to a number of postmodern challenges to traditional historical studies (Barstad; Kofoed). Typically, postmodernist theory asserts that texts have no intrinsic meaning, and at times that "meaning" must be constructed by the reader. Basic principles of modernism, such as "objectivity," the distinction between "primary and secondary sources," and "historical truth" are routinely placed aside in such approaches (Barstad). The conflict with traditional exegetical method has been palpable. Regardless of the varying definitions of postmodernism or its legitimacy as a philosophical movement, the trend has brought into sharp relief the epistemic questions: How do we know what we claim to know about the past and how legitimately can historians today make any claim to objectivity? Although the tenets of postmodernism may be exaggerated (if at times underappreciated), the hermeneutical crisis it has created is pointing toward development of a historical method that is multidisciplinary, incorporating more readily the insights of literary criticism, and that will offer an important corrective to traditional historical studies. Accordingly, an approach that distinguishes between source critical markers of the text and referential markers that help determine the genre of the text may result in more confidence in the reliability of the textual sources of the OT. Another helpful concept that may be useful for future research is the concept of "mnemohistory," which infuses the category of memory into the analysis. To this way of thinking, the biblical traditions of Israel's origins are understood as phenomena of collective cultural memory, creating an identity for the group. The truth of the past encoded in memory "lies in the identity that it shapes."

The current crisis in historical studies has resulted in a great divide between two groups. On the one hand, "revisionists" (minimalists, nihilists) typically reject the biblical account of Israel's history and maintain that the OT contains no reliable historical data and that, in fact, a history of ancient Israel cannot be written and should not be attempted. On the other hand, traditionalists (maximalists, literalists) insist that the referential dimension of the Israelite historical writings is vital and an integral part of interpretation, so that the historical reconstruction of Israel's past is never far removed from the actual events as described in the Bible itself. Despite the polarized rhetoric of these extremes, the challenges of the Copenhagen School and postmodern critiques of the historical enterprise have done a service for mainstream scholars (Bartlett). The methodologies that emerge from this crisis in the future will combine the important observations of genre with a reevaluation of the nature of history writing, the nature of the biblical traditions, and the nature and reliability of the biblical materials.

In the face of historicism's outmoded objectivity, it may be asked whether the historian of Israel's past is well served by an approach that embraces one's subjectivity. In this regard, the proposal of William J. Abraham to modify and redefine the three methodological principles established by Ernst Troeltsch at the turn of the century is still helpful. Troeltsch established "criticism" as a presupposed skepticism toward the sources, "analogy" as a principle in which human experience limits what qualifies as reality in the past, and "correlation" as a limit of historical causation to natural forces or human agency. Instead, Abraham argues that what is needed in the first principle—criticism—is a careful appraisal of data in the context of its source rather than a hermeneutic of suspicion that begins and ends in doubt. The second principle—analogy—must allow plausibility to be determined by reasonable arguments beyond the historian's own personal experience, and must also allow the past to serve as an interpretive key to the present rather than insisting it is only the present that serves as a key to the past. Finally, the third principle—correlation—should be defined formally rather than materially, meaning historical cause-and-

effect and change over time can be effected by personal agency rather than merely natural or human agency, and thus the divine is brought back into the historical project. Although some would object to refining the historical-critical method along theistic lines, there is no inherent truth in the assertion that the atheistic or antitheistic historian has fewer metaphysical assumptions than the theistic historian. Rather, the historian who discounts theological considerations as irrelevant has simply assumed the truth of certain negative theological statements, and is in fact no less theological than the theistic historian. Such a nontheological position at the very least puts the contemporary historian at something of a disadvantage with regard to empathetic evaluation of ancient sources where such beliefs clearly did hold sway. *See* ISRAEL, HISTORY OF; ISRAELITE RELIGION, HISTORY OF; JOSEPHUS, FLAVIUS; PENTATEUCH;.

Bibliography: William J. Abraham. *Divine Revelation and the Limits of Historical Criticism* (1982); Bill T. Arnold. "The Weidner Chronicle and the Idea of History in Israel and Mesopotamia." *Faith, Tradition, and History: Old Testament Historiography in Its Near Eastern Context.* A. R. Millard, James K. Hoffmeier, and David W. Baker, eds. (1994) 129–48; Jan Assmann. *Moses the Egyptian: The Memory of Egypt in Western Monotheism* (1997); James Barr. *History and Ideology in the Old Testament: Biblical Studies at the End of a Millennium* (2000); Hans M. Barstad. "History and the Hebrew Bible." *Can a 'History of Israel' Be Written?* Lester L. Grabbe, ed. (1997) 37–64; John R. Bartlett. "Between Scylla and Charybdis: The Problem of Israelite Historiography." *Biblical and Near Eastern Essays: Studies in Honour of Kevin J. Cathcart.* Carmel McCarthy and John F. Healey, eds. (2004) 180–94; David Damrosch. *The Narrative Covenant: Transformations of Genre in the Growth of Biblical Literature* (1987); John A. Emerton. "The Date of the Yahwist." *In Search of Pre-Exilic Israel: Proceedings of the Oxford Old Testament Seminar.* John Day, ed. (2004) 107–29; John A. Emerton. "The Kingdoms of Judah and Israel and Ancient Hebrew History Writing." *Biblical Hebrew in Its Northwest Semitic Setting: Typological and Historical Perspectives.* Steven E. Fassberg and Avi Hurvitz, eds. (2006) 33–49; Louis H. Feldman. *Studies in Hellenistic Judaism* (1996); Baruch Halpern and David S. Vanderhooft. "The Editions of Kings in the 7th–6th Centuries B.C.E." *HUCA* 62 (1991) 179–244; Johan Huizinga. "A Definition of the Concept of History." *Philosophy and History: Essays Presented to Ernst Cassirer.* Raymond Klibansky and H. J. Paton, eds. (1936) 1–10; Sara Japhet. "The Supposed Common Authorship of Chronicles and Ezra-Nehemiah Investigated Anew." *VT* 18 (1968) 330–71; Jens B. Kofoed. *Text and History: Historiography and the Study of the Biblical Text* (2005); Abraham Malamat. "Doctrines of Causality in

Hittite and Biblical Historiography: A Parallel." *VT* 5 (1955) 1–12; Nadav Na'aman. "Royal Inscriptions and the Histories of Joash and Ahaz, Kings of Judah." *VT* 48 (1998) 333–49; Richard D. Nelson. "The Double Redaction of the Deuteronomistic History: The Case Is Still Compelling." *JSOT* (2005) 319–37. Martin Noth. *The Deuteronomistic History* (1981); Mattiyiahu Tsevat. "Israelite History and the Historical Books of the Old Testament." *The Meaning of the Book of Job and Other Biblical Studies: Essays on the Literature and Religion of the Hebrew Bible* (1980) 177–87; James C. VanderKam. *An Introduction to Early Judaism* (2001); John Van Seters. *In Search of History: Historiography in the Ancient World and the Origins of Biblical History* (1983); Nikolaus Walter. "Jewish-Greek Literature of the Greek Period." *Cambridge History of Judaism. Vol. 2: The Hellenistic Age.* W. D. Davies and Louis Finkelstein, eds. (1990) 385–408. H. G. M. Williamson. *Israel in the Books of Chronicles* (1977); K. L. Younger Jr. "Early Israel in Recent Biblical Scholarship." *The Face of Old Testament Studies: A Survey of Contemporary Approaches.* David W. Baker and Bill T. Arnold, eds. (1999) 176–206.

BILL T. ARNOLD

HISTORY OF ABDIAS, APOSTOLIC. See ABDIAS, APOSTOLIC HISTORY OF.

HISTORY OF JOSEPH THE CARPENTER. *See* JOSEPH THE CARPENTER, HISTORY OF.

HITTITE TEXTS. More than thirty thousand tablet fragments, representing roughly 3000 to 3500 separate tablets, have been recovered from the ruins of the Hittite capital at Boghazköy since excavations began there in 1906, and from recent excavations at the provincial Hittite-period sites of Masat (anc. Tapikka), Kusakli (anc. Sarissa), and Ortaköy (anc. Sapinuwa). The Hittite libraries at Hattusa housed historical documents, treaties, edicts, instructions, laws, myths and legends, medical, ritual and festival prescriptions, oracle texts, lexical lists, and hymns and prayers. In addition, texts in Hattic, Palaic, Luwian, and Hurrian, as well as Sumerian and Akkadian compositions, have been recovered. The scribes also archived a wide variety of more ephemeral documents, including letters, vows, cult inventories, and administrative and economic texts. The common assumption is that the Hittites adopted an Old Babylonian form of the cuneiform script from a north Syrian scribal center sometime at the beginning of the Old Kingdom, however, the script may have arrived in Anatolia considerably earlier than this. A second, hieroglyphic, script was reserved for use on seals and in monumental inscriptions.

The Hittites made especially significant contributions to ANE literature in the genres of historiography, myth, and prayers. The most important of the historiographic texts are the annals, a genre that was a Hittite innovation, and that is best exemplified by the Annals of Mursili II (r. ca. 1321–1295 BCE). Individual historical documents of major importance are Anitta's Chronicle, the Testament of Hattusili I, the Telipinu Proclamation, and the Apology of Hattusili III. This last is perhaps the most famous single composition in the Hittite corpus and has garnered great interest for the folkloristic motifs that it appears to share with biblical (as in the story of David's rise) and other literature as much as for its historical significance.

For the most part, Hittite mythological texts comprise narratives belonging to the Hattian and Hurrian traditions. However, some compositions of Hittite origin are also identifiable, including the Tale of Zalpa, which has been compared with the biblical reports on the minor judges (Judg 10:1-5; 12:7-15), the Appu Myth, which has been compared with the patriarchal stories, and the Tale of the Fisherman. The Kumarbi Cycle of myths has been instrumental in illuminating the path by which Hurro-Mesopotamian literary traditions may have been transmitted to the West.

Although many examples of Hittite hymns are based on Mesopotamian tradition, the Hittites nonetheless developed their own distinctive style. Individual prayers might include protestations of innocence from sin, invocations, petitions, and hymns of praise. The prayers also testify to a Hittite belief in the sins of the father passing to the son.

Other Hittite text genres are of biblical interest. The similarity of the format and terminology of Hittite vassal treaties to the biblical covenants raises the possibility that the latter have their origins in the second millennium. The Hittite Instructions to Priests and Temple Officials offer parallels to the religious regulations in Leviticus. Finally, ideas about redemption and forgiveness of debt found in the Pentateuch are paralleled in the Hittite text of the Hurrian Song of (Debt) Release, which ranks among the finest examples of ANE wisdom literature.

Bibliography: Gary M. Beckman. "Mesopotamians and Mesopotamian Learning at Hattusa." *JCS* 35 (1983) 97–114; Hans G. Güterbock. "A View of Hittite Literature," *JAOS* 84 (1964) 107–15; Hans G. Güterbock. "Hittite Historiography: A Survey." *History, Historiography and Interpretation: Studies in Biblical and Cuneiform Literatures.* H. Tadmor and M. Weinfeld, eds. (1983) 21–35; Harry A. Hoffner Jr. "Hittite-Israelite Cultural Parallels." *COS* 3 (2002) xix–xxxiv; Theo van den Hout. "Another View of Hittite Literature." *Anatolia Antica: Studi in Memoria di Fiorella Imparati* (2002) 857–78; Itamar Singer. "Some Thoughts on Translated and Original Hittite Literature." *Language and Culture in the Near East.* Shlomo Izre'el and Rina Drory, ed. (1995) 123–28.

BILLIE JEAN COLLINS

HITTITES hit´tit [חִתִּי khitti]. "Hittites" comes from the biblical term **khitti**. Neo-Assyrian texts use **khattu** ("Hittite"). The Hittites called their land Hatti, after the population of Hattian-speakers who inhabited it at the beginning of the second millennium BCE, and their capital city Hattusa. They called their language Nesite after the city Kanes in Cappadocia that lay at the heart of early Hittite settlement.

A. History
B. Society
C. Religion
D. Art
E. Hittites in the Bible
Bibliography

A. History

The Hittites ruled a kingdom whose heartland was situated in the bend of the Marassantiya River (classical Halys, modern Kizilirmak) on the Anatolian (Turkish) plateau from the early 17th through the beginning of the 12th cent. BCE. The Hittite capital was located at Hattusa (beneath the modern village of Boghazkale), 180 km east of Ankara. The Indo-European Hittites entered Anatolia sometime in the first half of the third millennium. There they encountered the indigenous Hattian people, whose religion and pantheon merged with their own. As the kingdom grew, what we call Hittite culture came to include not only Hattian and Hittite elements, but Luwian and Hurrian as well, as reflected in the documents from the capital, which reveal much about the political, cultural, and religious life of the kingdom.

Hittites were active in central Anatolia at least as early as the Old Assyrian Colony period, as the letters from Kanes, which contain a few Hittite words, attest. Anitta is the earliest ruler chronicled in the Hittite documents. His connection to the Hittite dynasty that would

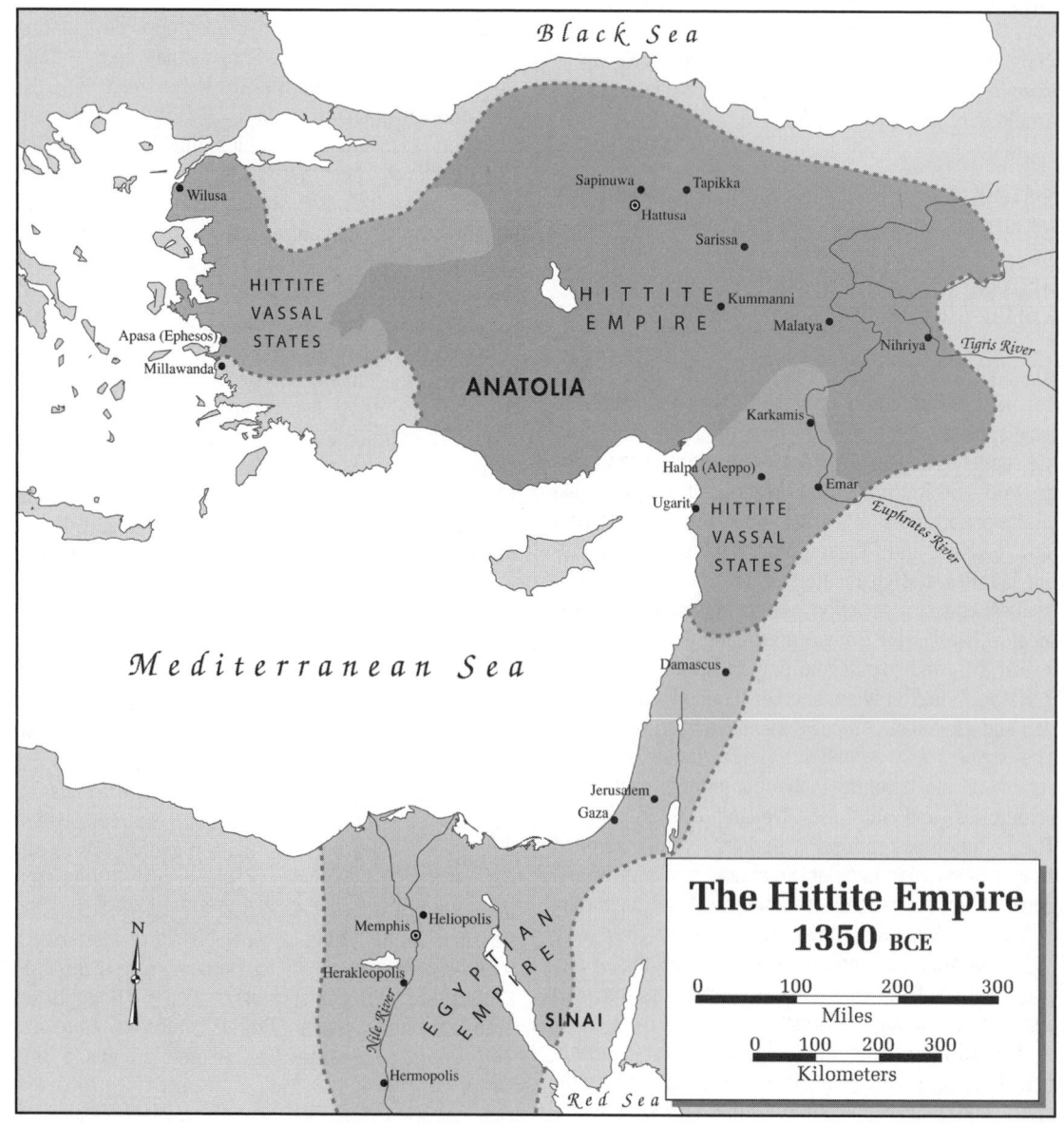

The Hittite Empire
1350 BCE

rule Anatolia for the next 400 years remains unclear. At the beginning of the 17th cent., Hattusili I made Hattusa his capital and continued the task of building a unified kingdom begun by his predecessor, Labarna. His ambition also took him across the Euphrates into North Syria, where he seems to have involved himself in the politics of the region, perhaps in an effort to secure the trade routes. His successor, Mursili I, also crossed the Euphrates. In a raid on Babylon in 1595 BCE (according to the middle chronology), he brought an end to the Old Babylonian dynasty of Hammurabi. This golden era for the Hittites was brought to an abrupt end with Mursili's assassination, which inaugurated a period of internal instability at the Hittite capital. Only the reign of Telipinu offered a respite from the perpetual cycle of assassination and intrigue at court. In this period of limited written sources, Hurrian political influence increased dramatically in the region.

Hittite history is divided between the Old Kingdom (ca. 1670–1400 BCE) and the empire (ca. 1400–1177 BCE), the latter marked by the ascension of Tudhaliya II. Under Suppiluliuma "the Great," the empire attained its greatest extent when Hittite power pushed into Syria, dissolving the empire of Mitanni and establishing a network of Syrian vassal states. Suppiluliuma's son, Mursili II, had a long and troubled reign that included a devastating plague that wiped out much of the population before running its course. Mursili's son, Muwatalli, faced the Egyptians at Qadesh, a confrontation that had been brewing since Suppiluliuma brought the two powers into contact by taking territories adjacent to Egyptian holdings in Syria. A few years later, in 1259 BCE, the usurper Hattusili III concluded a peace treaty with Ramses II inaugurating a period of peace in Syria that would continue until the fall of the Hittite Empire in ca. 1177 BCE. The reign of Tudhaliya IV is one of the best documented artistically as well as historically. The records from this period indicate that the land was suffering from famine and the balance of power within Hatti itself was less and less in the hands of the king as rival claimants pressed their interests. The last known king of the Hittites, Suppiluliuma II, was not able to keep the empire together in the face of internal unrest, prolonged drought and famine, supply and manpower shortages, and the social upheaval that went with them. At some point the capital at Hattusa was abandoned and subsequently burned to the ground, perhaps by Kaska tribesmen from the north.

Although the core of the Hittite kingdom had disintegrated, its second city, CARCHEMISH, whose kings were members of the Hittite royal line, survived the catastrophe with its infrastructure intact. Perhaps under the influence of Carchemish, other Anatolian and north Syrian centers in the Iron Age adopted Luwian hieroglyphs and Hittite architectural and sculptural styles as part of the process of forging a new identity and ideology of kingship that drew on the Hittite past.

Billie Jean Collins
Figure 2: Relief of Tudhaliya IV at Yazilikaya

That these Iron Age rulers considered themselves in some cases the inheritors of Hittite power is evident in their use of royal names from the empire (Qatazili at Gurgum, Uspilulume and Muttallu at Kummuh; Arnuwantis at Malatya; Lubarna and Sapalulme at Unqi) and in the adoption of the title "Great King" by the kings of Carchemish after the collapse of the empire. Although these states were never unified politically, Neo-Assyrian inscriptions nevertheless refer to them individually and together as "Hatti." Owing to the limited subject matter of their monumental inscriptions, a reconstruction of the history of the Neo-Hittite states is dependent almost entirely on Assyrian sources. Each of the states would succumb to Assyrian aggression by the end of the 8th cent., putting an end to Luwian as a written, if not spoken, language. Although the term *Hatti* continued to be used in Babylonian sources, the term by now had become an imprecise geographical designation for territories in the west.

B. Society

The Hittite economy was based on small-scale farming and animal husbandry. Wealth was counted in land and livestock. Villages consisted of a number of households or estates, which included the immediate and extended members of the family as well as the livestock and land holdings of that family. Wealth was funneled both to the central government at Hattusa and redistributed locally via provincial redistributive centers called "palaces" under the oversight of stewards. Other institutions with similar roles were the "stone houses" or mausoleums of deceased kings, and storehouses, literally "seal houses." District governors were responsible for the security and smooth administration of frontier areas. Most of the population lived in small villages either as free, independent farmers, or as dependents of a wealthy landowner or state institution (e.g., a local palace or temple). Villages and estates were levied a sahhan tax, which formed the main source of revenue for the state. In addition, all free persons had to perform corvée labor for the state unless specifically exempted by the king. The work of free or dependent peasants was supplemented by slaves and deportees (civilian prisoners), who became increasingly important to the economy as plague and famine robbed the empire of the human resources it needed to operate effectively.

Beneath the king, a bevy of local administrators—provincial governors, mayors, elders, and civil servants—guaranteed the smooth operation of the kingdom. Texts of instructions ensured that various elements of the administration knew what was expected of them and the administering of oaths offered some security against disloyalty. Vassal kings were bound to the central administration by treaty, but apart from the imposition of a thin layer of imperial bureaucracy, local kings were free to direct their own economic and internal political affairs, so long as they rendered unto the Hittite Great King his due in tribute and services.

The laws of the Hittites focus on a number of legal categories including homicide, assault and battery, abduction of slaves, property damage, burglary, theft, sorcery, sexual offenses, marriage law, wages and fees, and prices. With the exception of a few relatively serious crimes, punishment usually took the form of monetary restitution rather than physical punishment. Under the jurisdiction of local magistrates, courts conducted inquiries and dispensed rulings. The most difficult cases might be appealed to the highest court in the land, that is, the king's court.

C. Religion

The Hittite ruling family was devoutly religious. The state religion involved the active worship, according to their own count, of 1,000 gods. When a state or local cult was neglected, it was the responsibility of the king to make restitution, although this appears to have happened only on a sporadic basis. The king was the representative of the gods on earth and thus his well-being was connected directly to that of his kingdom. About the religion of the lower classes we know much less; however, there is little reason to suppose that they did not actively participate in the worship of their own local gods. In addition, the dozens of magical prescriptions reveal that ritual procedures were in widespread use among all levels of society to deal with the problems of daily life, including illness, impurity, family discord, crop failure, sorcery and other criminal offences (perjury, physical injury), birth, human fertility, and impotence. Many of the magical practices attested in the Hittite texts originated not with the Hittites themselves but with the Hattians, Luwians, and Hurrians, that is, they reflect the composite nature of Hittite society.

Worship took place under the care of priests in official temples, of which thirty (besides the Great Temple) have been identified in excavations at the Hittite capital so far. In addition, open-air sanctuaries were situated in groves, or near springs, or on mountains, that is, in any location imbued with a sense of the sacred. The rock sanctuary of Yazilikaya, just outside the capital, is the best example of one of these.

Humans communicated with the gods through prayer (see HITTITE TEXTS), sacrifice, and divination. The most common form of divination were oracles, although prophecy and dream incubation are also attested. The main techniques for oracular inquiry were augury, extispicy, **KHURRI**-bird oracles, and lot oracles.

Understanding the organization of the Hittite pantheon is complicated by the fact that in addition to the deities who were worshiped locally, the state itself recognized two distinct pantheons. On the one hand are the lists of divine witnesses to the treaties, at the head of which were the main gods of the Hittite pantheon, the storm-god of Hatti and the sun-goddess of Arinna. This divine directory was never fully standardized, but evolved over time to reflect changing political realities. On the other hand, the Hurrian pantheon, adopted by the ruling family to promote the Hurrian element in the empire, is visible in the procession of deities carved on the walls of the rock sanctuary at Yazilikaya. The focal

Billie Jean Collins

Figure 3: Central scene in the inscribed open-air rock sanctuary at Yazilikaya, outside the Hittite Capital

point of this procession is the Hurrian divine triad, Tes-hub (identified with the storm-god), Hebat (identified with the sun-goddess), and Sarruma.

Istanu, the sun-god of heaven, held a high status in the Hittite pantheon as the all-seeing dispenser of justice to humans and animals. Mesopotamian imports of the empire period include Ishtar (Hurrian Sausga), who gained much popularity in Anatolia at the end of the Bronze Age. From Syria comes Ishara, whose epithet "Queen of the Oath" identifies her primary role as divine witness to treaties and vows. The Hittites seem to have picked up the concept of the tutelary, or protective, deity from both the Hattian and Mesopotamian traditions. The underworld was also populated with an abundance of deities, at the head of which was the sun-goddess of the earth (Hurrian Allani).

Festivals were special times when the cult statue of a deity might be transported in procession through the streets and "entertained" with music, dancing, acrobatics, and athletic events, as well as a wide variety of sacrifices and offerings, usually followed by a communal meal uniting deity and worshipers. It might have been one of the few occasions when the average individual had direct access to the gods. The main festivals were the festival of the crocus (AN.TAKH.SHUM), the purulli-festival, the festival of haste (nuntarriyashas), and the festival of the gatehouse (KI.LAM). More than eighty Hittite festivals are known by name. Generally speaking, fall festivals celebrated the harvest in the filling of the storage vessels, while the spring festivals celebrated breaking open these stored goods. Whatever the occasion, festivals must have offered a welcome break from the harshness of life on the Anatolian plateau.

D. Art

Hittite art is both original and recognizable. While some imagery, most notably the Egyptian sphinx and winged sun disk, was imported, and seal engraving and ivory carving were inspired by Syro-Mesopotamian traditions, Hittite art nevertheless has its roots firmly in Anatolia, where artists superimposed their unique style over an existing artistic tradition. Understanding the development of the art has been hampered by an inability to date most of it, which, either because of its architectural setting or because it is unprovenanced has no associated stratigraphy. Early examples of monumental sculpture and relief carving indicate that the Hittite sculptural tradition had a long development. Subjects include mainly divine processions, sacred hunts, and festival celebrations. In the last century of the empire, kings are represented in the protective embrace of their patron deities, or presenting offerings to the gods. In royal portraiture, they are sometimes dressed in the guise of the sun-god. Lions and sphinxes are favorite subjects, and the double-headed eagle, found both at Yazilikaya and Alaca as well as on seals, was probably an emblem of the royal family.

Billie Jean Collins

Figure 4: A Hittite vassal king, Tagasnawa of Mira, is depicted in relief on a rock face at Karabel in western Anatolia.

The Hittites' love of stone is apparent both in the architectural use of monumental blocks of cut stone and in the use of living rock in its natural setting as the canvas for large relief carvings.

In both contexts, the surface of the rock was cut back to expose figures in low relief. In some reliefs, e.g. at Firaktin, the figures are flat with little interior modeling. In others, such as the so-called King's Gate at Hattusa, the reliefs show rounded, plastic forms, and great attention is given to interior details, like musculature and clothing. The city gates at Boghazköy and nearby Alaca Höyük are the best examples of monumental sculpture integrated into an architectural scheme. Lions as gate sculpture continued into the Neo-Hittite period and the idea was even adopted at sites like Hazor in Palestine.

Animal-shaped ceremonial vessels and sculptured vases in metal and clay were a continuation of forms popular in the Assyrian Colony period. A silver vessel in the shape of a stag now in the Metropolitan Museum is a fine example of Hittite expertise in metalwork and relief carving on a small scale. Large ceremonial ceramic vessels from the vicinity of Bitik and Inandik bear tiers of reliefs depicting scenes from religious festivals, probably marriage ceremonies. Representational objects such as these tend to be miniature versions of monumental Hittite sculpture. For example, human figures follow the conventions seen in rock reliefs.

Billie Jean Collins

Figure 5: Hittite rock relief at Firaktin of the King Hattusili and his Queen Puduhepa offering libations to a pair of deities.

Hittite art continues to offer surprises. A vase that has come to light in the vicinity of Hüseyindede bears a relief decoration that points to an Anatolian origin for the "sport" of bull leaping well known from Minoan Crete. In addition, the discovery of frescoes in a temple at Hattusa may indicate the presence of foreign (Mycenaean?) artists in the capital.

A handful of objects of Hittite art have been found in Palestine, but there are also objects of local manufacture in Palestine that show undeniable Hittite influence. A locally manufactured multihandled krater from Raddana features a series of inward-facing bulls' heads projecting from a tubular pipe, a well-known Hittite technique. In addition, a sherd incised with a smiting god whose upturned shoes, pointed hat, and short skirt indicate Hittite inspiration, was found on the surface of the mound at Hazor. Finally, two cult stands with applied decorations from 11th–10th cent. BCE Taanach received their inspiration from Anatolian and Syrian artistic elements.

E. Hittites in the Bible

Of the numerous passages in the OT that mention the Hittites, a handful can be understood as referring to the territories controlled by the Neo-Hittite states of the early first millennium and not to the Late Bronze Age Hittites. These are the references to the kings of the Hittites in 1 Kgs 10:29 (par. 2 Chr 1:17 and 2 Kgs 7:6); Solomon's Hittite wives in 1 Kgs 11:1; and the land of the Hittites in Josh 1:4 and probably Judg 1:26.

Beyond these references, two threads of tradition can be traced. First is the lists of nations, which include the Hittites with the Canaanites, Jebusites (an Amorite tribe?), Hivites (Cilicians), Amorites, Perizzites, and Girgashites (see, e.g., Deut 20:16-17). These peoples arguably reflect the makeup of north Syria and southeastern Anatolia at the end of the Late Bronze Age, when the Hittite Empire was in control of much of the territory to the north of Palestine, including the kingdoms of Amurru and Ugarit. The lists of NATIONS that appear in the Bible, although incorporated into the biblical text only later, retain a historical memory of the earlier period. This memory was preserved in the Canaanite traditions upon which the Israelites were later heavily to depend.

Billie Jean Collins

Figure 6: Monumental gate at Alaça Hoyuk showing sphinx sculptures and carved orthostat blocks.

The rhetorical and ideological use of "Hittites" that we see, e.g., in Ezek 16:3 ("your mother was a Hittite"), on the other hand, appears to relate to the Assyrian rhetoric of Sargon II against the Neo-Hittite cities of northern Syria (he calls them "evil Hittites" repeatedly in his inscriptions). When the Assyrians destroyed Samaria, Israelite refugees moved to Judah. These northerners, who had presumably been exposed both to Canaanite historical memory of Hittites and other groups who had inhabited the territories to their north and also to the more contemporary anti-Hittite Assyrian rhetoric, may have carried both of these traditions with them. The two threads merged and the Hittites became, along with the Jebusites, Hivites, Amorites, and so on, a convenient "Other" imagined as living in the hill country for the "newly arrived" Israelites to conquer. In other words, the Jerusalem-based biblical authors of the late 8th cent. incorporated the Hittites and other groups into their foundational story of Israelite origins. The presence of the Hittites in the narratives of Israelite beginnings is thus rhetorical and ideological rather than historical. At the same time, however, a kernel of historical memory is reflected in the lists of nations, thus establishing some connection between the biblical Hittites and the Hittite Empire of the Late Bronze Age.

The ethnicity of URIAH the Hittite, husband to BATHSHEBA, whom David sent to his death (2 Sam 11), is more difficult to explain. He, with Ahimelech (1 Sam 26:6), could be expatriates from the Neo-Hittite kingdoms. Several etymologies have been proposed for Uriah, including that it comprises the Hittite/Luwian element uri "great" and the Hebrew name of God, Yah ("Great is Yah"), which would fit an ethnic Luwian living in Jerusalem and worshiping the Israelite God. If, however, Uriah is to be identified with Araunah, the Jebusite from whom David purchased the threshing floor, the land on which the Temple would be built, then David's plot to send Uriah to his death so that he can marry Bathsheba is simply a narrative device to legitimate his rule. The motif is paralleled in the story of Abraham's purchase of the cave of Machpelah from Ephron the Hittite. Ephron is willing to turn over the cave without cost, but Abraham insists on paying and thus symbolically legitimizes his residence in the land. Thus, the author may have labeled Uriah a Hittite simply to establish his alterity—that is, as a foreigner, he was expendable. The author may also have had in mind the Neo-Hittite states as a natural point of origin for a character who was so central to his story, perhaps explaining why he was called a Hittite rather than a Jebusite, like Araunah. In either case, Uriah's ethnicity, like that of the Hittites of Genesis, is a narrative device. *See* HORITES.

Bibliography: Trevor Bryce. *Life and Society in the Hittite World* (2004); Trevor Bryce. *The Kingdom of the Hittites* (2005); Billie Jean Collins. *Who Were the Hittites?* (2007); Jack M. Sasson, ed. *Civilizations of the Ancient Near East* (1995).

BILLIE JEAN COLLINS

HIVITES hiv´it [חִוִּי hiwwi]. One of the non-Israelite populations named in the OT, the Hivites make their most frequent appearance in lists of NATIONS inhabiting the LAND before the arrival of the Israelites. The Hivites apparently inhabited the central and northern hill country of Palestine, in locales as far north as Lebo-Hamath (Judg 3:3), down to Shechem (Gen 34:2), Gibeon (Josh 9:3, 7) and environs (2 Sam 24:7). Esau's marriage to a Hivite (Gen 36:2) suggests connections with Edom as well.

The narratives of the Shechem massacre (Gen 34) and the Gibeonites' ruse (Josh 9) offer further information regarding Hivite culture. In both, the Hivites are portrayed as a group with whom the Israelites have a history of making covenants while one of the parties acts deceitfully. At Shechem the story turns on the cultural barrier between Israel and the Shechemites/Hivites, especially that of circumcision. In the Gibeon narrative the Hivites successfully convince Joshua and the Israelites that they come from a distant land and thereby secure a peace treaty. Joshua 9:27 also reveals that the Hivites were involved in the Israelite cult: Joshua appointed them as woodcutters and water-drawers for the sanctuary as a punishment for their deception. Later, they were part of Solomon's conscripted slave labor for his building projects (1 Kgs 9:20).

In the Greek of the LXX information regarding the Hivites appears attenuated when compared with the Hebrew Masoretic Text (MT). In the Greek of Gen 34:2, Hamor is not a Hivite (Euaios Εὐαῖος) but a Horrite (Chorraios Χορραῖος), as are the inhabitants of Gibeon in Josh 9. In Josh 11:19, where the Hebrew MT reports that the Hivites were spared because of the pact of Josh 9, the LXX registers no such report. This discrepancy has prompted a debate over whether the Hivites are a distinct ethnic group or whether the term is merely a corruption of "Horrite." Either way, graphical similarity in the Hebrew forms hwy vs. hry (חוי versus חרי) is likely at the heart of the confusion.

Scholars have had difficulty connecting the Hivites with any extra-biblical group. Some hold that they are connected somehow with the Hurrians because of the LXX evidence (above). Others argue that the term *Hivite* is etymologically connected with the Achaeans known from Homer's *Iliad*. Recently a similar, more plausible connection has been made between the Hivites and Cilicia (southeastern Turkey) on the basis of Egyptian, Akkadian, and Luwian terms for Cilicia—HW, Quwe /Huwe, and Hiyawa, respectively—which may be related to the Hebrew term *Hivite* (hiwwi). If viable, this connection suggests that the Hivite homeland was located in the northeastern Mediterranean, and that some moved down into northern Palestine. *See* GIBEON, GIBEONITES; HORRITES; HURRIANS; ISRAEL, HISTORY OF.

Bibliography: Baruch Halpern. "Gibeon: Israelite Diplomacy in the Conquest Era." *CBQ* 37 (1975) 303–16; Othniel Margalith. "The Hivites." *ZAW* 100 (1988) 60–70; R. North. "The Hivites." *Biblica* 54 (1973) 43–62; Itamar Singer. "The Hittites and the Bible Revisited." *"I Will Speak the Riddles of Ancient Times."* Vol. 2. A. M. Maier and P. de Miroschedji, eds. (2006) 723–56.

CORY DANIEL CRAWFORD

HIZKI hiz′ki [חִזְקִי *khizqi*]. Son of ELPAAL, listed in the genealogy of BENJAMIN (1 Chr 8:17); probably an abbreviated form of HEZEKIAH, meaning "Yah is my strength." The sons of Elpaal are linked with Ono and Lod (1 Chr 8:12), important sites for the post-exilic community.

SAMUEL L. ADAMS

HIZKIAH. *See* HEZEKIAH.

HOBAB hoh′bab [חֹבָב *khovav*]. This name occurs twice in the OT. In Num 10:29, Hobab is defined as the son of Reuel the Midianite, the father-in-law of MOSES, and Hobab is asked by Moses to guide the Israelites through the wilderness. In Judg 4:11 Hobab is identified as the father-in-law of Moses, leading some to see this as a third name for ZIPPORAH's father, adding it to Reuel and Jethro. The identification of Hobab in Judges as Moses' father-in-law in English translations is either the result of misunderstanding the noun khtn (חתן), or of its unfortunate application to Hobab because of misunderstanding its appropriate antecedent in Num 10:29. In Num 10:29, Reuel, not Hobab, is the antecedent for the noun khtn. The misunderstanding surrounding Hobab's relationship to Moses is evidence of the inattention given to the full semantic range of the Hebrew noun khtn, typically translated "father-in-law" (khoten חֹתֵן), or "son-in-law" (khatan חָתָן), respectively. It may be understood as referring to a male related through the wife or daughter (*see* BRIDEGROOM). In this case, there is no reason to limit it to only father-in-law or son-in-law when translating. In the context of Judg 4:11, the noun khtn identifies the relationship between Moses and Hobab. If this Hobab is to be understood as the same Hobab referenced in Num 10:29, then *brother-in-law* is a better translation for khtn. If, on the other hand, this Hobab is a different person from the one referenced in Num 10:29, then the noun could be translated *son-in-law*. The latter suggestion is unworkable, however, since Moses and Zipporah are described as having two sons, Gershom and Eliezer, but no daughters (Exod 18:2-4).

C. MARK MCCORMICK

HOBAH hoh′buh [חוֹבָה *khovah*]. A town north of Damascus (Gen 14:15). In the legendary battle related in Gen 14, the kings of the north under Chedolaomer carry off the kings of Sodom, Gomorrah, Admah, Zeboiim, and Zoar, as well as Abraham's nephew Lot. Abraham raises an army and pursues the kings of the north to Dan, where he engages them in battle. Abraham is victorious and chases the defeated army as far as Hobah.

The location of Hobah is unknown. The only clue in the biblical text is that it lies north of Damascus, and some commentators have seen this as a later gloss with no historical value. Some scholars have compared Hobah to Upe, a region around Damascus known from the Execration Texts (19th cent. BCE) and the Amarna letters (14th cent. BCE) in Egypt. Since Damascus is unknown before the 16th cent., it is argued that another city must have served as the capital of Upe prior to that time. It is argued that such as city could have been called Upe, which the biblical writers may have written Hobah. Tell el-Salihiye (DURA EUROPAS), 10 mi. east of Damascus has been suggested as that city. Extensive excavations at Tell el-Salihiye have revealed no substantial occupation of the site prior to 300 BCE, which precludes it being a candidate for Hobah.

KEVIN A. WILSON

HOBAIAH. *See* HABAIAH.

HOD hod [הוֹד *hodh*]. The seventh of the eleven sons of ZOPHAH in the ASHER genealogy (1 Chr 7:37). The name does not appear in other lists involving this line (Gen 46; Num 26). It means "vigor" or "splendor" and has a military connotation.

HODAVIAH hod′uh-vi′uh [הוֹדַוְיָה *hodhawyah*, הוֹדַוְיָהוּ *hodhawyahu*]. Name of several men: 1. Son of Elioenai and descendant of King David through his son Solomon (1 Chr 3:24).

2. Head of a clan in the half-tribe of Manasseh (1 Chr 5:24).

3. Grandfather of Sallu in the tribe of Benjamin, who lived in Jerusalem (1 Chr 9:7).

4. A Levite and the ancestor of seventy-four Levites who returned with Ezra after the exile (Ezra 2:40; Neh 7:43). Omitted in the parallel list in 1 Esd 5:26. According to Ezra 3:9, with other Levites he was in charge of the workers who rebuilt the Temple.

EMILY R. CHENEY

HODAYOT. *See* THANKSGIVING PSALMS.

HODESH hoh′desh [חֹדֶשׁ *khodhesh*]. Means "new moon." A wife of Shaharaim the Benjaminite, with whom he had seven sons (1 Chr 8:9). Hodesh is called Baara in the previous verse (1 Chr 8:8).

HODEVAH. *See* HODAVIAH.

HODIAH hoh-dĭ'uh [הוֹדִיָּה hodhiyah]. 1. Grandfather of Keilah the Garmite and Eshtemoa the Maacathite married to Naham's sister (1 Chr 4:19).

2. A Levite who interpreted Ezra's public reading of the book of the law of Moses so that the people could understand it (Neh 8:7), led the people in penitential prayer (Neh 9:5), and signed his name on the sealed covenant document (Neh 10:10 [Heb. 10:11]). In 1 Esdr 9:48, the name is Auteas.

3. A Levite who also signed his name on the sealed covenant document (Neh 10:13 [Heb. 10:14]).

4. One of the leaders of the people who signed his name on the sealed covenant document along with the Levites (Neh 10:18 [Heb. 10:19]).

EMILY R. CHENEY

HOE [מַעְדֵּר ma'der]. A hand tool used where topography does not allow the use of a plow, as in mountainous regions (Isa 7:25). In viticulture, the hoe was used to cultivate between rows of vines allowed to spread on the ground (Ezek 17:7) as well as close to the vines and near the vineyard fence. *See* MATTOCK.

RALPH K. HAWKINS

HOGLAH hog'luh [חָגְלָה khoghlah]. One of the five daughters of ZELOPHEHAD (Num 26:33; Josh 3:17). Zelophehad, who had no sons, died in the wilderness, and his daughters appealed to Moses for inheritance rights (Num 27:3-4). Moses brought their case before the LORD, who sided with the daughters' effort to keep their father's property (Num 27:5-12). The sisters marry into their own tribe of Manasseh, preserving the inheritance (Num 36:10). *See* BETH-HOGLAH; INHERITANCE IN THE OT.

JESSICA TINKLENBERG DEVEGA

HOHAM hoh'ham [הוֹהָם hoham]. The Amorite king who joined a coalition with four other rulers to defeat the Gibeonites (Josh 10:3-4). This military action came in response to Joshua's peace agreement with Gibeon. The attack failed, and all five kings were executed (Josh 10:26-27).

HOLIDAY [יוֹם טוֹב yom tov]. Means "a good day." A happy day often celebrated in conjunction with a feast or festival. In the book of Esther, the Jews celebrate PURIM, a holiday commemorating relief from Haman's intended massacre (Esth 8:17; 9:22). On Purim Jews send gifts to one another, give presents to the poor, and are encouraged to drink until they cannot distinguish between "wicked Haman and pious Mordecai" (*b. Meg.* 4*b*). The phrase also occurs in 1 Samuel when David sends his men to Nabal to request provisions during the sheep-shearing festival (25:8). *See* FEASTS AND FESTIVALS.

TRISHA GAMBAIANA WHEELOCK

HOLINESS CODE. *See* H, HOLINESS CODE.

HOLM TREE [תִּרְזָה tirzah]. Compared to the Arabic verb taraza/tariza, "to be hard," the word may indicate a high-grade durable wood, though its origin is unknown. Found only in Isa 44:14 alongside the CEDAR and the OAK, tirzah can be rendered as the holm oak (*Quercus ilex*), a small evergreen mentioned in Sus 58 (prinon πρῖνον). Other translations prefer CYPRESS, oak, and PLANE TREE. The translation "holm tree," however, is doubtful because the holm oak has a limited presence in Palestine. Since the text describes the IDOL maker's preparation of his material, the word seems to connote a stone-like tree, without referring to a specific kind of wood.

WON W. LEE

HOLOCAUST AND BIBLICAL INTERPRETATION. The Holocaust was the systematic, state-sponsored extermination of European Jewry, perpetrated by Nazi Germany and its collaborators between the years 1938–45. Approximately 5.8 million Jewish people were murdered. The Nazis also targeted the Roma and the Sinta, the physically and mentally handicapped, homosexuals, Jehovah's Witnesses, and various political opponents. Post-Holocaust biblical interpretation reads the Scriptures through the lens of this genocide.

The first religious questions to emerge after the Holocaust were theological, concerned particularly with THEODICY. How could an all-powerful and all-good God allow such evil and suffering? Examination of the impact on biblical interpretation emerged later. Whereas Elie Wiesel is a storyteller and a peace activist, his writings were some of the first to grapple with the Bible. In *Messengers of God* and *Five Biblical Portraits*, Wiesel retells biblical stories in light of his Holocaust experience. Wiesel's writings are grounded in traditional Midrashic methods but also break with traditional methods and theologies by challenging God and the world on behalf of the murdered millions.

Emil Fackenheim published a short work entitled *The Jewish Bible after the Holocaust*. Fackenheim argues that the Holocaust was a rupture in the fabric of history, affecting all modes of thought and interpretation. Nothing should remain "seamless" between the pre- and post-Holocaust world. Ultimately, biblical stories must be judged by the extent to which they are beneficial to human welfare.

The central section of David Blumenthal's *Facing the Abusing God* interprets four psalms. Blumenthal enacts the rupture in language that Fackenheim discusses by presenting a series of interpretations of each psalm, some of them contradictory, all on the same page together. Blumenthal's work looks much like a rabbinic Bible or a page of the Talmud. Yet, he employs nontraditional sources in his readings including the testimonies of survivors of the Holocaust and child abuse. This plurivocality is at the core of Blumenthal's exegetical method.

The interpreters above all focus on the Jewish Scriptures (the OT); other scholars have turned their attention to the NT. The work in this vein is concerned primarily with resituating Jesus in his Jewish context and investigating anti-Jewish and anti-Semitic interpretations of the NT. Rosemary Ruether's *Faith and Fratricide* is groundbreaking in this area.

Overall, post-Holocaust biblical interpreters are influenced by the theological challenges of the Holocaust, and are committed to eradicating ANTI-JUDAISM and ANTI-SEMITISM. They also resist interpretations that foreclose on complexity and multiplicity as a way of promoting the value of human life and the ethic of respecting difference. *See* BIBLICAL CRITICISM; BIBLICAL INTERPRETATION, HISTORY OF; JEWISH BIBLICAL INTERPRETATION.

Bibliography: David Blumenthal. *Facing the Abusing God* (1993); Emil Fackenheim. *The Jewish Bible After the Holocaust* (1990); Paula Fredriksen and Adele Reinhartz, eds. *Jesus, Judaism and Christian Anti-Judaism: Reading the New Testament after the Holocaust* (2002); Tod Linafelt, ed. *Strange Fire: Reading the Bible after the Holocaust* (2000); Rosemary R. Ruether. *Faith and Fratricide* (1974); Elie Wiesel. *Messengers of God* (1976); Elie Wiesel. *Five Biblical Portraits* (1981).

JENNIFER L. KOOSED

HOLOCAUSTS. *See* SACRIFICES AND OFFERINGS.

HOLOFERNES hol´uh-fuhr´neez [Ὀφέρνης *Olofernēs*]. "Assyrian" general who theatens the Jews in the fictional book of Judith. The original name in Persian is **Orophernes**, but was altered in transmission to Greek. In the story, he is Nebuchadnezzar's general charged with leading the forces on their western campaign to subdue the populations. Holofernes meets his match in the courageous Israelite widow JUDITH who in many ways is his opposite. He is finally outwitted by her seductive, but ultimately deceptive speech and her determined plan to save her people. The character of Holofernes may be patterned after one or a composite of historical figures. Perhaps the most likely is the general Holofernes of Artaxerxes III who mounted western campaigns in the mid-4th cent. BCE, although others have suggested the Seleucid general NICANOR (1 Macc 7:26-49). *See* JUDITH, BOOK OF.

JUDITH H. NEWMAN

HOLON hoh´lon [חֹלֹן *kholon*]. 1. One of eleven towns in the hill country that was part of the inheritance for the tribe of Judah (Josh 15:51); Holon is named as a Levitical city (Josh 21:15 NRSV). The town HILEN is apparently an alternate form of this name.

2. A Moabite town mentioned in prophetic oracle as a place upon which judgment has come (Jer 48:21).

R. JUSTIN HARKINS

HOLY, HOLINESS, NT [ἅγιος *hagios*, ἁγιωσύνη *hagiōsynē*, ἁγιασμὸς *hagiasmos*, ἁγιότης *hagiotēs*]. The concept of holiness in the NT maintains significant continuity with the OT but reconfigures it in light of God's self-revelation in a crucified, raised, and ascended Messiah who is confessed as LORD (*kurios* κύριος). Holiness primarily, but not exhaustively, refers to the pattern of activity embodied by this Lord who effects the saving, reconciling purposes of the Triune God. The NT people of God are related to this Holy God because they are beneficiaries of this activity and thereby granted a status as *holy*. Enabled by the Holy Spirit, they are called to express this holy status: 1) by corporately modeling God's telos for humanity, exhibiting compassion, reconciliation, joy, and peace; 2) by embodying a pattern of activity analogous to that of their Lord's, becoming channels through which God continues God's reconciling, redeeming purposes.

A. The Second Temple Period
B. The New Testament
   1. Preliminary remarks
   2. The Synoptic Gospels
   3. Acts
   4. The Gospel of John
   5. Paul and the Pauline tradition
   6. The remainder of the NT
Bibliography

A. The Second Temple Period

Although other Greek terms in the Second Temple period (including the NT) express the concept of holiness (*hosios* ὅσιος, *hagnos* ἁγνός, *semnos* σεμνός, *hieros* ἱερός), the primary terminology used is from the *hagios* word group, basically equivalent to the *qadosh* (קָדוֹשׁ) word group in the Hebrew. Hagios and its cognates were rarely used in the Greco-Roman world, and the concept of holiness itself was of little importance. Hosios was most often used to describe things and people associated with cultic activities, but gods and goddesses were seldom described as holy. In contrast, the concept of holiness was so important to Second Temple Judaism and the NT that it provides the implicit background of numerous texts even where explicit holiness language does not appear.

The primary locus of God's presence, and thus of holiness, was widely understood to be the temple from which holiness as a dynamic force radiated outward to the land and people of Israel. As in the OT, there were dangerous consequences for bringing the holy into contact with impurity since impurity too was a dynamic, contagious force and might contaminate God's holy presence. Diminishing the effects of impurity by enlarging the realm of the pure required careful observance of Torah (*see* HOLY, HOLINESS, OT; CLEAN AND UNCLEAN). This led to a purity-based social system whose purpose was to maintain boundaries between pure and impure, to safeguard the conditions under which Israel could experience God's dangerous, yet beneficent, holy presence. With the land politically controlled by impure foreigners (i.e., Syria and then Rome), a heightened concern for holiness could, and did, fuel political resistance. Holiness became increasingly understood in terms of separation, i.e., separating Jew from Gentile, (sources of) life from (sources of) death, pure from impure.

Observant Jews in Israel shared purity concerns about sources of impurity (e.g., unclean foods, corpses, skin diseases, discharges from sexual organs). But some groups intensified purity concerns, dismissing those not observing their HALAKHAH (rabbinic law) as "sinners" excluded from the covenant. This was true of the QUMRAN community and the PHARISEES, both of whom conceived of ideal Israel as a kingdom of priests (see Exod 19:5-6). The Qumran community understood itself to be a holy remnant outside Jewish society, while the Pharisees attempted to maintain holiness within society. The Pharisees sought to extend the holiness of the temple throughout the whole land by extending purity standards appropriate for priests serving in the temple into their daily lives. This was particularly evident in their attempt to maintain their own personal holiness by carefully observing purity practices at meals. Especially in this and in their scrupulous observance of Sabbath regulations, they came into conflict with Jesus.

B. The New Testament
1. Preliminary remarks

Throughout the Bible, divine activity expresses divine essence/character, and holiness is always derived; i.e., people, places or things are holy only insofar as they are in relation to the Holy One whose character defines holiness. The NT as a whole includes Jesus within the unique divine identity of Yahweh (*see* LORD), maintaining that he reveals the character of the God of Israel and thus the nature of holiness. Rarely is holiness explicitly ascribed to God the Father in the NT (1 Peter 1:15-16). However, in Rev 4:8 the character of the Lord God Almighty as exceedingly holy (see Isa 6:3) is concretized in the portrayal of the slaughtered (perfect tense; compare 1 Cor 1:23; Mark 16:6) lamb with whom this God shares the throne (Rev 5:6-10). Hence, the Christ-event reconfigures OT and Second Temple conceptions of holiness along the lines of a cruciform pattern of redemptive activity which reclaims persons for God's reign/lordship and restores their relationship with God, with others, and finally with creation itself.

2. The Synoptic Gospels

Although explicit holiness language is scarce in the Synoptic Gospels, their portrayal of Jesus challenges the whole system of holiness as boundary maintenance. Isa-iah (esp. 40–55) is one lens through which they portray Jesus' activities. Isaiah often calls Yahweh "the Holy One of Israel/the Holy One" (e.g., 1:4; 41:14-20) who is not only transcendent, but also a seeking God whose holiness is expressed in a saving/redeeming pattern of activity (5:16; 43:3, 14-21), a dynamic force whose ultimate goal is a renewed creation (Isa 60:9, 14; 65:17-25). Identified as "the Holy One of God" early in Mark (1:24) and Luke (4:34), some of Jesus' activities are portrayed in the Yahweh-like terms of Deutero-Isaiah. As in Isaiah, the narrated pattern of his salvific activities defines holiness; it is outward looking, saving compassion that finds its culmination on the cross.

As Israel's Messiah anointed with the HOLY SPIRIT, Jesus is both herald and vehicle of God's kingdom. He is not contaminated by impurity but, as bearer of God's Holy Spirit, embodies holiness that is contagious and transforming as it confronts the impure and the sinful. This is particularly exemplified in: 1) Jesus' sharing meals with outsiders/"sinners" (Luke 5:27-39 and //15:1-2; 19:1-10). Whereas the Pharisees require repentance and ritual purity before inclusion within the holy community, Jesus eats with the marginalized so that they might repent and be restored to communion with the Holy God and God's people. 2) Jesus' frequent contact with sources of impurity (e.g., leprosy, blood, corpses) transforms the lives of those affected, enabling their restoration into the community (Mark 1:40-45 and //5:21-43 and //Luke 7:11-17). 3) Jesus' transforming/liberating confrontation with the demonic, sometimes implicitly associated with unrestrained chaotic forces of impurity (Mark 1:23-28 and //esp. 5:1-20 which is immediately preceded by Jesus' encounter with the "chaotic forces" of the sea in 4:35-41).

Jesus' Sabbath activities (mostly healing) also challenge the ideology of holiness as boundary maintenance. They do not undercut Sabbath keeping per se, but privilege its life-giving, salvific purpose over its sociological function of marking out true Israel (Luke 6:6-11, esp. v. 9). This pattern reconfigures what it means to keep Sabbath holy (Luke 6:1-5 par.).

In Luke what makes one "unclean" is the failure to participate in activity that reflects "the justice and love of God" (11:42), practices that flow outward from within one's own character (11:37-44) and that are exemplified in Jesus' compassionate actions and parables (10:25-37; 15:11-31). The Synoptic Gospels do not separate the "internal" from the "external." Rather, holy actions reflect God's character and spring from a pure, undivided internal integrity, a whole-hearted dedication to God's purposes (Matt 5:48; Luke 6:36).

In summary, empowered by the Holy Spirit, Jesus reconfigures holiness by crossing purity boundaries, bringing God's compassion/purifying love to those who have been excluded from God's people. This is a pattern of salvific activity characterized by risk (Luke 7:13; 10:33; 15:20) that culminates with the cross. It seeks to reclaim those on the margins for God's reign/lord-ship and restore their marred relationships with God and with others. Jesus' Spirit empowered activity in the Synoptic Gospels is the means by which the first two parallel petitions in his model prayer are being exemplified; i.e., the Father's name is being "hallowed" as God's reign/kingdom is coming (Matt 6:9-10; Luke 11:2; see LORD'S PRAYER).

3. Acts.

Acts portrays the story of the early community and individuals within it (e.g., Stephen, Paul) as, in some degree, analogous to the story of Jesus in Luke. Luke depicts Pentecost along the lines of Yahweh's restoration of Israel (Ezek 36:16-32; 37:1-14) by the giving of the Holy Spirit onto/into them in order that Yahweh may hallow/sanctify God's name through God's restored people who embody God's holiness before the nations (20:41, 36:23; 37:28). As this restored Israel, the Acts community corporately enacts the eschatological Jubi-lee of God's coming reign (Acts 2:44-45; 4:32-35; com-pare Luke 4:18-19; Deut 15:1-11) and risks acting with compassion toward the marginalized as channels of the Spirit's salvific power (2:33; 3:1-10; 4:1-22). Empow-ered by the same Spirit as their crucified LORD (2:36), they act in his name (3:6) in ways that parallel his own actions. They thereby embody the character of the Holy One of God, and therefore God's own holiness, before the rest of the people and the nations. In Ezekiel-like terms, the Father's name has been hallowed/sanctified by this restored people. As in the OT, God's holiness cannot be abstracted from the character of the people with whom God's name is linked.

The OT and Second Temple Judaism commonly connected sexual immorality with the primary threat to the holiness of God's people, i.e., idolatry. Acts con-tinues this connection portraying holiness also as purity or difference from unbelieving Gentiles, e.g., avoiding sexual immorality and idolatry (15:19, 29).

4. The Gospel of John.

Using logos (λόγος) conceptuality, John's gospel places Jesus within the unique divine identity of Yah-weh (1:1-2). As Son, Jesus reveals the Father's character (1:18) and therefore, as "the Holy One of God" (6:69), the nature of holiness itself. The Father, as the ultimate source of holiness, sanctifies the Son, sending him into the world to exhibit a pattern of saving activity ("the works of my Father") that expresses the essence of the Father's character (10:36-38). Since death and the impurity associated with it is the antonym of holiness, it is fitting that the logos has life in himself (1:4; 11:25). Indeed, it is because Jesus speaks words of eternal life that his disciples know him to be "the Holy One of God" (6:68-69).

Since Yahweh's glory is a manifestation of Yahweh's holiness made visible (e.g., Lev. 10:3), beholding the glory of the logos (1:14a) is to catch a glimpse of the life-giving power and presence of the Holy God (11:4, 40). It is to catch a glimpse of holiness itself displayed in a pattern of redemptive activity. In John's gospel, the primary place where the audience sees Jesus' glory—this holiness made visible—is as he is lifted up on the cross (3:14-16; 12:23-32). This act takes away the sin of the world—the antipathy toward God leading to death (8:24)—transforming it into faith by drawing all to God and thus to life itself (3:16; 6:44). Jesus' laying down his life delivers his flock from death (10:11-15) and is the consummate demonstration of complete/perfect love (see the inclusio formed by 13:1 and 19:28-30; compare 3:14-16). Hence, in John's gospel, divine glory explicates divine holiness in terms of the depths of a divine love that is to be mirrored in community relationships (15:12-17). See GLORY, GLORIFY.

Rather than being contaminated by death's impurity, the Holy One of God, the resurrection and the life, crosses the boundary into death, defeating it from the inside out. Sitting silently in the impurity of the tomb (20:11-13), the essentially mute angels form the shape of the cherubim atop the ark of the covenant. Their silent testimony affirms that death has not contami-nated God's Holy One, but rather, God has swallowed up death and been enthroned in its very presence.

5. Paul and the Pauline tradition

While rejecting some traditional Jewish marks of holiness for his Gentile converts (e.g., circumcision, separate table fellowship), Paul continues to affirm the importance of purity or difference from unbelieving Gentiles, i.e., avoiding sexual immorality (e.g., 1 Thess 4:5) and idolatry (e.g., 1 Cor 10:1-22). However, more fundamental for Paul's understanding of holiness is his conviction that the crucified Messiah is the very revela-tion of the character (2 Cor 5:19; Col 1:15) and thus the holiness of God (1 Cor 1:30). Thus, the nature of human holiness for Paul might best be encapsulated in the word "cruciformity," i.e., becoming like Christ as agents of God's reconciliation (2 Cor 5:18-20) who practice aggressive, self-giving love (Phil 2:6-11).

Paul uses two closely related nouns for holiness, hagiōsynē and hagiasmos (for a fuller treatment of the latter, along with the verb hagiazō [ἁγιάζω], see SANCTIFICATION). The adjective, hagios, is the most common holiness terminology in Paul's letters, and at times he uses it in typical Jewish ways (e.g., Rom 7:12). However, he uses it most often to refer to the Holy Spirit whose actions and essence is holiness. Through this Spirit, God elects, calls, and establishes a people (2 Thess 2:13), conveying on them a status as "holy ones" (hagioi; e.g., 1 Cor 1:2; Rom 1:7; Eph 1:1, 4; see SAINT), an OT term applied to Israel as God's people. By virtue of being "in Christ," all Christians are set apart by God and therefore holy. The body of Christ, the most focused place where the Holy Spirit is at work (e.g., 1 Thess 4:8), is the primary locus of holiness, so much so that Paul can call both the community (1 Cor 3:16-17; 2 Cor 6:16; Eph 1:21) and individuals within it (1 Cor 6:19) the temple of God/Holy Spirit. Human holiness is engendered by the Spirit first and foremost as an ecclesial reality from which individual holiness is then derived (*see* CHURCH, IDEA OF THE).

For Paul, holiness is primarily gift and secondarily task, inextricably linked to SALVATION (Phil 2:12-13). In 1 Cor 1:2, those "in Christ" have already been "made holy" by God (1 Cor 6:11) and, like Israel, are also "called to be holy" (see also Rom 1:7). It is the Holy Spirit who enables those who are "being saved" (1 Cor 1:18) to make expressing corporate and personal holiness their goal. Holiness (hagiōsynē), then, is indeed a state characteristic of those "in Christ," but like salvation, not static. It can be "perfected" (2 Cor 7:1), albeit not simply by human striving. Indeed, Paul implores the Lord to enable the community to increase in self-giving love in order to strengthen the hearts of believers to be blameless in holiness (hagiōsynē) at the Parousia (1 Thess 3:13). As their communal life is constituted by these Spirit empowered (1 Thess 4:8), self-giving actions, the result will be a people of God, "entirely sanctified" and kept blameless both now and at the Parousia (1 Thess 5:23, *see* SANCTIFICATION). While God has already marked them out as holy, they are to become a visible example of the character of the holy God as the Spirit transforms the church as a whole and persons within it into the image of the crucified and risen Son (Rom 8:29-30). Holiness, then, is the beginning, the process, and the culmination (1 Cor 15:42-49; Phil 3:20-21) of salvation itself, a salvation that extends to the whole cosmos (Rom 8:19-22; 2 Cor 5:17; Gal 6:15).

6. The Remainder of the NT

In the remainder of the NT, holiness is particularly emphasized in Hebrews, 1 Peter, and Revelation (although not absent elsewhere, e.g., Jas 4:8; 2 Pet 1:4; 3:11; 1 John 2:20; 3:3). In Hebrews, the ultimate goal of God's redemptive activity in Christ is that the redeemed might "share [God's] holiness" (hagiotēs; Heb 12:10; note the similar conceptuality of becoming "participants of the divine nature" in 2 Pet 1:4). God's salvific activity is described in terms of SANCTIFICATION effected by Jesus' death (e.g., 10:10-14; 13:12). As divine Son, Jesus reflects God's glory (1:3), visibly manifesting God's holiness. And as a truly human high priest, he shares human nature in its fallenness, even to death's defilement (2:14-18). As the visible manifestation of God's holiness, Jesus embraces death's ultimate impurity so that by death's defeat (2:10-18) and sin's removal (10:1-18), life/holiness is conveyed. Ironically this holiness is revealed and conveyed through the defilement of a corpse and what now sanctifies is analogous to the dead corpse outside the camp (13:11-13).

In 1 Peter, the audience is those elected by the Father because of the obedience of the Son, located in the sphere of holiness that the Spirit engenders (1:1-2). Like ancient Israel, they have experienced God's salvation (1:3-12), resulting in the call to be holy in their conduct as God is holy (1:15-16 echoing Lev 19:2). Enabled by the Spirit, they are to embody the calling of ancient Israel as a priestly people, a holy nation who proclaims God's salvific acts (1:9-10), walks in obedience (1:14), and conducts themselves publicly after the pattern of the suffering Christ (e.g., 2:21). As such, they are God's eschatological dwelling place/house (2:4-5), a distinct (not isolated) people who engage their culture with a non-identical repetition of the Son's obedience. Here too, holiness is being reconfigured by the activity of the obedient Son.

In Revelation the creator God is declared absolutely holy (4:8, echoing Isa 6:3), distinct from, and sovereign over, creation. God shares the throne and God's holiness with the exalted Christ, who retains his character as the slaughtered lamb (5:6). As "the Holy One" (3:7) Christ is present among the churches calling them to reject the lure of Rome's system of power and exploitation (18:4) and to follow him by corporately embodying his own holy character as a holy, pure army (14:1-5). Like the high priest with God's name in his headdress, they have the name of the lamb and of the Father written on their foreheads (14:1) marking them off as redeemed priests (e.g., 1:6; 5:10), hagioi/holy ones who wage a public, non-violent battle against Rome's idolatrous culture by acting as prophetic witnesses (13:7; 10) to the sovereignty of God. Paradoxically, like the Holy One they follow, they conquer by being conquered (11:7-12; 12:11). Rather than the values of Babylon/Rome, the vision of God's New Jerusalem (21:1-2) is to provide their orientation. Like the first temple's inner sanctuary (1 Kgs 6:19-20), the New Jerusalem has a perfect cubic shape (21:16) signifying both a people (each one a high priest) and a place (the redeemed, "entirely sanctified" cosmos) permeated with the immediate presence of the Holy God. Anticipating this future, John's churches are to embody its character and values now with their costly testimony that God, not Caesar, reigns. Through corporate and individual witness, they are to embody the character of the Holy One, the slaughtered/cruciform lamb. *See* CHURCH, LIFE AND ORGANIZATION OF; CROSS; MIRACLE; SIGNS AND WONDERS; SPIRITUALITY; WORSHIP, NT CHRISTIAN; WORSHIP IN THE OT; WRATH OF GOD.

Bibliography: Stephen C. Barton. ed. *Holiness Past and Present* (2003); Marcus J. Borg. *Conflict, Holiness and Politics in the Teachings of Jesus* (1998); Kent E. Brower. *Holiness in the Gospels* (2005); Kent E. Brower and Andy Johnson, eds. *Holiness and Ecclesiology in the New Testament* (2007); Hannah K. Harrington.

Holiness: Rabbinic Judaism and the Graeco-Roman World (2001); Gordon Thomas. "A Holy God Among a Holy People in a Holy Place: The Enduring Eschatological Hope." *Eschatology in Bible & Theology: Evangelical Essays at the Dawn of a New Millennium.* Kent E. Brower and Mark W. Elliott, eds. (1997) 53-69; John Webster. *Holiness* (2003); J. B. Wells. *God's Holy People: A Theme in Biblical Theology* (2000).

ANDY JOHNSON

HOLY, HOLINESS, OT [קָדוֹשׁ qadhosh]. An examination of Semitic polytheism (and indeed of any primitive religion) shows that the realm of the gods is never wholly separate from or transcendent to the world of humankind. Natural objects such as specific trees, rivers, stones and the like are invested with supernal force. But this earthbound power is independent of the gods and can be an unpredictable danger to the latter as well as to humankind. *Holy* is thus aptly defined, in any context, as "that which is unapproachable except through divinely imposed restrictions" or "that which is withdrawn from common use."

In opposition to this widespread animism, we notice its absence from the Bible. Holiness there is not innate. The source of holiness is assigned to God alone. Holiness is God's quintessential nature, distinguishing God from all beings (1 Sam 2:2). It acts as the agency of God's will. If certain things are termed holy—such as land (Canaan), person (priest), place (sanctuary), or time (festival day)—they are so by virtue of divine dispensation. Moreover, this designation is always subject to recall. Thus, the Bible exorcises the demonic from nature; it makes all supernatural force coextensive with God. True, as in the polytheistic religions, the holy things of the Bible can cause death to the unwary and the impure who approach them without regard for the regulations that govern their usage (*see* WRATH OF GOD). Indeed, though biblical qadhosh attains new dimensions, it never loses the sense of withdrawal and separation.

The following analysis focuses on the Pentateuchal codes: the Jahwist-Elohist (JE), the Deuteronomic source (D), the Priestly source (P), and the Holiness Code (H). Diachronically, these four codes can be considered as two: JE leading to D, and P leading to H. (*See* D, DEUTERONOMIC, DEUTERONOMISTIC; DOCUMENTARY HYPOTHESIS; E, ELOHIST; H, HOLINESS CODE; J, YAHWIST; P, PRIESTLY WRITERS; SOURCE CRITICISM.)

A. Limited Space, Persons, and Time Can Be Holy: The Priestly Writers
B. All the People of Israel and the Land Can Be Holy: The Holiness Code
C. Covenant and Decalogue Can Make the People Holy: The Yahwist and Elohist Writers
D. Holiness Is Earned by Obeying the Commandments: The Deuteronomic Writers
E. Dynamic Holiness
　1. Holy persons, animals, and space
　2. Holy time
　3. The benefits of divine holiness
F. The Holiness Prescription
Bibliography

A. Limited Space, Persons, and Time Can Be Holy: The Priestly Writers
In the view of "P," the Priestly Writers, only the sanctuary, its holy things, and those authorized to serve them (the priests) are holy by virtue of being sanctified with the sacred anointment oil (Lev 8:10-11, 15, 30; *see* ANOINT). A temporary status of holiness is also bestowed upon the Nazarite as a consequence of his vow of abstinence (Num 6:2-8), especially the prohibition against shaving or trimming his sanctified hair (compare Num 6:5, 7, 9, 18; *see* NAZIR, NAZIRITE). Prior to the selection of Aaron and his descendants, the firstborn served as priests, to judge by the tradition, acknowledged by P, that they were "sanctified" by God (Num 3:13; 8:17; *see* SANCTIFICATION). To be sure, P maintains that they were replaced by Levites, not by priests (*see* PRIESTS AND LEVITES). However, the Levites did not inherit the firstborn's holiness. In fact, P goes out of its way to deny the term qadhosh to the Levites and employs, instead, the neutral verb nathan (נָתַן) "assign" (Num 8:16; 18:6)—an indication of the enduring obsession of the Aaronid priests to deny priestly status to the Levites. The Kohathite Levites, it should be noted, were warned on pain of death not to touch the covered inner holy places but to carry them by their poles and frames (Num 4:15; compare 2 Sam 6:6-7). They were forbidden even to look at them while they were being covered (Num 4:20; compare 1 Sam 6:19). In other words, in regard to the sacred sphere, the Levites were laymen.

The term "holy" (miqra' qodhesh [מִקְרָא קֹדֶשׁ], "a proclamation of holiness") is also bestowed on the fixed festivals (Num 28–29) because they are characterized by the prohibition against work (*see* FEASTS AND FESTIVALS). This term is, therefore, absent from the injunctions concerning the New Moon (Num 28:1-15), which is not a day of rest. It is also missing in P's prescriptions for the Sabbath (Num 28:9-10) despite the fact that it is the day of rest *par excellence*. In this case a different consideration prevails: The Sabbath is not proclaimed—it automatically falls every seventh day—and, hence, the term miqra' (from qara' [קָרָא], "proclaim") does not apply.

In sum, the root qdsh (קדשׁ) in all its forms bears the basic meaning "set apart for God," and applies in P only to certain space, persons, and time.

B. All the People of Israel and the Land Can Be Holy: The Holiness Code
The second part of Leviticus (chaps. 17–26) is sometimes referred to as the Holiness Code or "H" and

is treated as a separate source from the larger Priestly Source (P). H maintains that every Israelite is holy; hence, if he or she contacts impurity, he or she will not survive. To be sure, H postulates a metaphoric, nonritualistic impurity, such as sexual violations (Lev 18, 20), that is cultically irremediable. H does not negate P's cultic impurity but, to the contrary, supports it. H, for example, appends to Lev 16 its own laws, turning P's emergency rite (16:2-3) into an annual one that enjoins abstention from work and fasting upon the entire people (16:29-34a). But it also acknowledges the indispensability of purging the sanctuary of Israel's impurity (v. 33). This means that even the deliberate polluter need not die but can hope that his penitence on that day will effect absolution. Moreover, 15:31 (H) states that polluting the sanctuary incurs death. But if the people are holy, they should be sentenced to death upon contracting impurity. Again, Num 25:22-31 (H) enjoins the purification offering for all inadvertent sins. But if Israel is intrinsically holy, their sacrifice should be of no avail since they are automatically doomed CORBAN. The answer is that the laity is not inherently holy but can become holy by following the commandments. For all Israelites (including priests) holiness is not static, nor endemic, but a goal to be attained (by the laity) or sustained (by the priests).

From a broader perspective, the theme of the entire book of Leviticus is holiness. Chapters 1–10 deal with the sanctuary service; chaps. 11–16, with the purification for access to the sanctuary; chap. 17, with blood on the altar; chaps. 18–22, with how Israel can attain and priests retain holiness and how sexual violations and ancestor worship defile the sanctuary and the land; chap. 23, with the sanctification of time; chap. 24, with Israel's upkeep of the sanctuary and the desecration of Yahweh's holy name; chap. 25, with the laws of the "holy" land; chap. 26, with how breaking the covenant causes God's abandonment of his sanctuaries leading to Israel's exile; and chap. 27, with the laws of consecration (see LEVITICUS, BOOK OF).

H's main distinction from P is that P restricts holiness to sanctified persons (priests) and places (sanctuaries), whereas H extends holiness in both its aspects to persons, the entire people of Israel, and to places, the entire promised (Yahweh's) land. Moreover, Yahweh's holiness is dynamic: Israel must attain it (Lev 19:2; 21:8 LXX; 22:32) and priests must sustain it (21: 15; 22:16).

Israel is enjoined to be holy because Yahweh is holy (19:2). This does not mean that Israel can achieve or even imitate Yahweh's holiness. There is an unbridgeable gap between them. Holiness implies separation, distinction. In the priestly texts, the Masoretes consistently and meticulously distinguish between divine and human (Israelite, priestly, Naziritic) holiness (e.g., Lev. 11:44-45; 19:2; 20:7; 21:8).

But when the prescriptions for holiness in Lev 19 are examined, though most of them are negative (approxi-

mately thirty), many are positive (approximately fourteen). In this latter sense, holiness implies that Israel should emulate God by living a godly life. Observance of the divine commandments leads to God's attribute of holiness, but not to the same degree—not to God but to godliness. Just as the priests, who are innately holy, are qualified to enter into God's presence in the sanctuary, so Israel, by following all Yahweh's commandments (19:37), can attain holiness (19:2) and qualify for admission metaphorically into the providence (i.e., the presence and protection) of God.

Nonetheless, when one examines the holiness contexts outside Lev 19, they are nearly all negative. That is, Israel's separation from God has to be emulated by Israel's separation from other peoples. This is explicitly stated in 20:24-25. As Yahweh has separated Israel from the nations, so Israel must separate itself from them by its dietary system (see also the context of 11:43-45). Conversely, observing the dietary laws will keep Israel from intermingling with others. The necessity to keep apart from the neighboring peoples is spelled out in Lev 18 and 20. Incest and other sexual abominations attributed to Egypt and Canaan are defiling to Israel and to the land (18:24-30).

Mary Douglas defines purity as "adequately segregated." This can also serve as a definition of holiness. Indeed, both purity and holiness have to be carved out of areas of the impure and the profane, respectively, and they must be safeguarded (segregated) against incursions of the ever virulent impurity. The two priestly traditions, P and H, differ in that H ascribes a dynamic quality to holiness, which counters the aggressive, malevolent force of impurity. Thus the notion of segregation (or separation) bridges the two major systems in Leviticus, P's purity (Lev 11–16) and H's holiness (constellated in Lev 19–22). To be sure, since all these qualities in H's monotheistic thought are inert, they possess no intrinsic power. They can be activated only by human deeds. Israel's sins generate impurity, but it can be transmuted into the pure by purificatory rituals. Yahweh has bestowed upon Israel an additional power. It can transmute the pure (and the profane) by observing the divine commandments (see CLEAN AND UNCLEAN).

In H, the root qdsh occurs 66 times in chaps. 19–23. However, God's holiness is implied by God's self-declaration "I am Yahweh your God," especially when it is followed by God's salvific action "who has freed you from the land of Egypt." The addition of these two formulae enlarges the compass of H to Lev 18–26. Furthermore, the root qdsh referring to God and the two formulae are attested within P contexts, inside and outside of Leviticus, in passages also attributable to H (Lev 11:43-44; Exod 6:2-8, 29; 7:5; 12:12; 29:43-46; 31:12-17; Num 3:13, 44-50; 14:26-35; 15:37-41; 35:34). H introduces three radical changes regarding P's notion of holiness. First, it breaks down the barrier between the priesthood and the laity. The attribute of holy is accessible to all Israel. This implies, as aptly noted by Greenberg, that just as the priests qualify for service by learning and obeying the rules of their order, so the folk-priesthood of Israel must learn and follow the divine law commanded to them. Second, holiness is not just a matter of adhering to a regimen of prohibitive commandments, taboos; it embraces positive, performative commandments that are ethical in nature. Third, all of Israel, priests included, enhance or diminish their holiness in proportion to their observance of all of God's commandments. The key to these changes is a new understanding of the holiness of God as expounded in Lev 19.

Leviticus 19 opens with the imperative: "You shall be holy, for I, Yahweh, your God, am holy" (v. 2; *see* GOD, OT VIEW OF; HOLY ONE). This chapter is thereby radically different from the preceding one, which is headed by the divine self-declaration "I am Yahweh your God" (18:2*b*). This formula opens the TEN COMMANDMENTS (Exod 20:2; Deut 5:6). In chap. 19, however, H has altered the formula to emphasize Yahweh's holy nature and that Israel should emulate it. H accepts the prophetic dictum that righteousness is a quintessential component of holiness (Isa 5:16) and fleshes it out in a series of commandments that are a mixture of both rituals and ethics, with ethics taking predominance. Thus, holiness is no longer just a matter of "divinely imposed restrictions" but also embraces positive ethical standards that are illustrative of God's nature: As God relates to divine creation, so should Israel relate to each other. Thus, all the commandments enumerated in Lev 19 fall under the rubric of holiness. It initially comes as a surprise that H never designates God's land as holy. Perhaps if the land were holy, it could be polluted by all forms of impurity—deliberate, accidental, or unconscious. Thus H's metaphoric concept of impurity must break the nexus between impurity and its remedy, ritual purification: the pollution of the land is irreversible by ritual means. A more fundamental reason, however, is H's rejection of the notion that holiness inheres in nature. In this regard it differs sharply with P. Whereas P declares that it was Moses who sanctified the Tabernacle and its priests (with the anointment oil, Lev 8) H states emphatically "I will sanctify the Tent of Meeting and the altar, and I will consecrate Aaron and his sons to serve me as priests" (Exod 29:44).

Thus, H implies that neither is the oil inherently sacred nor is its manipulator, Moses, responsible for the sanctification, but sanctification is generated solely by God's condescending presence (Exod 29:43*b*). In H's view, God does endow Israel with the power to sanctify—not objects but time. The festivals are "proclamations of holiness," whose dates on the CALENDAR are fixed by Israel's decrees (except for the Sabbath, which is independent of the calendar and which was preordained by God to be holy, Gen 2:3). The concession is significant: with time, in contrast to the land, there is no inher-

ent holiness, a notion that can imply a source of power independent of that of God. H also differs sharply from earlier JE and its subsequent evolution into D.

To be sure, some scholars claim that Israel was actually consecrated as priests and a holy people (in fulfillment of Exod 19:6) by the sacrificial blood dashed upon them (Exod 24:8*a*). What consecratory power, however, resides *per se* in blood? The analogy of the priestly consecration (Lev 8:30) actually undermines their case. The sacrificial blood sprinkled upon them and their vestments comes from the altar. That is, the most sacred altar must first transfer its sanctity to the blood (Exod 30:28-29) before it can sanctify the priestly consecrands. Though the Sinaitic covenant rite is still a mystery, it may be related to Gen 15:17, where God passes through severed halves of animals as a sign that God has bound God's self by the covenant struck with Abraham. This, indeed, is what the Sinaitic text explicitly states: "This is the blood of the covenant" (Exod 24:8). The blood, then, has not made Israel priests but confirms that Israel is bound by the covenant. The problem with this solution is that blood plays no part in the Abrahamic covenant (nor in Jer 34:18). The enigma of the blood rite remains unresolved. In any case, it does not sanctify the people. Israel, as the text states explicitly, is an aspirant of holiness (Exod 19:6; compare 22:30) not its possessor.

Israel's "sanctification" is associated with the Exodus (Exod 19:4-6); a similar association is recorded in Lev 11:44-45. The latter, however, confirms not that Israel is holy, but that Israel is enjoined to become holy. The root qdsh appears frequently in the Sinaitic account (Exod 19:10, 14, 22), which ostensibly affirms Israel's sanctity. However, the forms of the verb denote "purify/purify oneself," not "sanctify/sanctify oneself," precisely as Israel proceeds to do by laundering its garments.

The ethical holiness prescribed by Lev 19 contrasts with its ritual counterpart (Exod 19:10-22; Num 11:18; Josh 3:5; 7:13; 2 Chr 30:15-20). Note, however, that these citations are all from epic sources, whereas in P these cultic preparations are called "purification." Thus, in this matter, H is consistent with its P heritage. H polemicizes with the popular notion of a time-bound "consecration." Purification (taher טָהֵר) eliminates impurity, leading to the state of the pure (tohar טֹהַר), a condition required for contact with the holy sphere. H pursues this forward movement further, demanding that the common be transformed into the holy. H's ethical stance on holiness is clearly reflected in the priestly challenge to pilgrims at the entrance to the Temple precincts, as recorded by the psalmist, "who shall stand in his holy place? Those who have clean hands and pure hearts" (Ps 24:3-4; compare Isa 5:16; 33:14-15).

C. Covenant and Decalogue Can Make the People Holy: The Yahwist and Elohist Writers

The Yahwist-Elohist "epic tradition" (JE) proposed that Israel could become a holy people, but only if it would accept the covenantal obligations of the Ten Commandments (Exod 19:6), the two distinctive elements of which are the rejection of idolatry and the observance of the Sabbath (Exod 20:3-11). Implied, therefore, is that nonobservance disqualifies Israel from attaining a holy status, a position that anticipates H, the Holiness Code. In this matter, D, the Deuteronomic source, differs sharply from its demonstrated reliance on E, the Elohist source. The epic tradition also adds abstention from flesh torn because it was prey as a holiness requirement (Exod 22:30). This prohibition is contextually tied to the requirement to dedicate the first of the crops and of the womb of both humans and beasts to Yahweh (vv. 28-29), which by implication are also holy. These three injunctions, abstention from idolatry, Sabbath labor, and torn flesh, are therefore JE's prescription for holiness.

D. Holiness Is Earned by Obeying the Commandments: The Deuteronomic Writers

D, the Deuteronomic source, incorporates the commandments in its holiness prescriptions by its repetition of the Ten Commandments (Deut 5:7-15), its emphasis on the rejection of idolatry (Deut 7:6; 14:2), and its full dietary code (Deut 14:3-21, esp. v. 21). D may not be original. It may have followed the initiative of 8th cent. Isaiah, who referred to the survivors (one-tenth) of God's purge of Israel as zera' qodhesh (זֶרַע קֹדֶשׁ) "a holy seed" (Isa 6:13). Nonetheless, the translation of this idea into law, incumbent on all Israel and not just for a surviving remnant, is the innovation of D. Moreover, D institutes a change of its own: Israel *is* a holy people by virtue of its covenant, and perhaps from the days it was founded by the patriarchs (Deut 7:6-8; 10:15).

In any event, D surely follows the view of its forerunner E that Israel was initiated/"consecrated" into the covenant at Sinai (Exod 24:1-8 E). The priests (Priestly/Holiness Code) harbor no such tradition. Only they were consecrated (Exod 29; Lev 8) but not the people. The people have to "earn" their consecration by obeying Yahweh's commandments. To be sure,

D also acknowledges that Israel's retention of its holy status is dependent on its adherence to Yahweh's commandments (Deut 26:17-19; 28:9). This condition recalls H's view of the priesthood: Though priests are genetically holy, they diminish, and can even forfeit, their holiness by their violation of the commandments. And conversely, by observing the commandments, they augment their holy status. Thus for H, holiness is a dynamic concept, towards which all of Israel, priests and laity alike, must continuously strive: priests to retain it, lay persons to attain it (see below).

Some scholars claim that since Israel's holiness is transmitted from the forefathers genetically; it is unconditional. This view may be implied by the static status of Israel in Deut 7:6; 21:2, 21. However, it is blatantly qualified in the later chapters (by a tradent?) so that if Israel adheres to the commandments, only then will God fulfill God's promise of holiness to the forefathers (26:18-19; 28:9). Hence D moves toward convergence with H on the issue of Israel's holiness.

Nonetheless, this overlap in goal should not mask D's innovation. Whereas H, in agreement with JE (compare Exod 19:6; 21:30), regards holiness only as an ideal towards which Israel should aspire, D establishes Israel's holiness as inherent in its biological nature. Thus, from the diachronic viewpoint, D has extended H's axioms regarding priestly holiness to all of Israel. In D holiness is the reason for the prohibitions; in H, the prohibitions are the means for holiness. Both D and H, however, condition priestly holiness (H) and Israel's holiness (D) on obedience to God's commandments.

E. Dynamic Holiness

1. Holy persons, animals, and space

D's dietary laws are modeled on Lev 11, and the attachment of the holiness ideal to Israel's diet is also the contribution of H. H also bans idolatry and emphasizes the Sabbath as part of its holiness prescriptions (20:1-8; 19:3, 30 and 26:2*a*). H, however, goes much further: It adds many other regulations, ritual

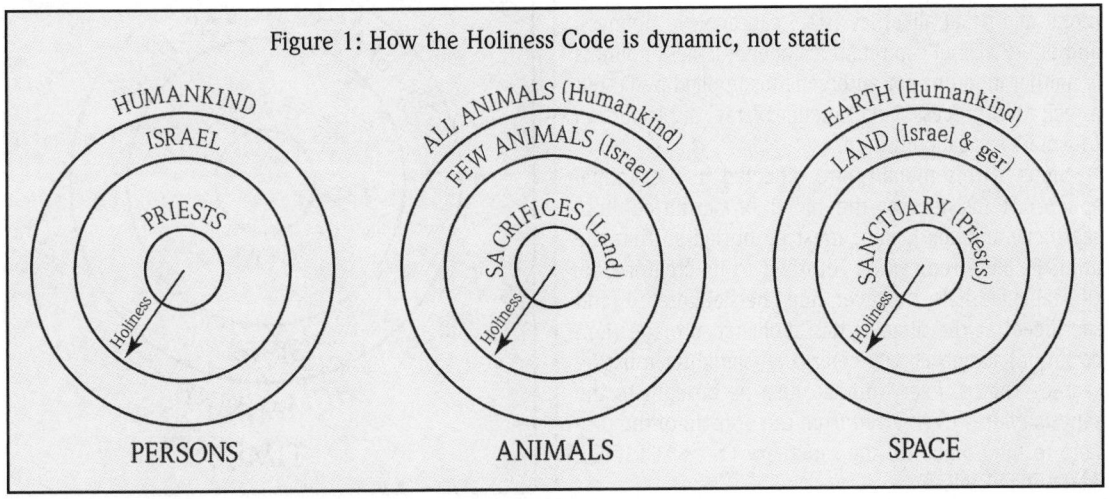

Figure 1: How the Holiness Code is dynamic, not static

PERSONS — HUMANKIND / ISRAEL / PRIESTS / Holiness

ANIMALS — ALL ANIMALS (Humankind) / FEW ANIMALS (Israel) / SACRIFICES (Land) / Holiness

SPACE — EARTH (Humankind) / LAND (Israel & gēr) / SANCTUARY (Priests) / Holiness but mainly ethical, as itemized in Lev 19 (see below), and enjoins the wearing of distinctive tassels as a daily mneumonic that Israel can attain holiness by observing Yahweh's commandments (Num 15:37-41 [H]). Moreover, H polemicizes against P's dogmatic insistence that priestly holiness is unchanging and permanent by implying that the violation of Yahweh's commandments not only bars Israel from attaining holiness but also priests from retaining it. H's dynamic concept of holiness is best explained by resorting to the Figure 1.

In P's world view, the tripartite division of human race corresponds to its three covenants with God: humanity (Gen 9:1-11, including the animals), Israel (via the patriarchs, Gen 17:2; compare Lev 25:42), and the priesthood (Num 25:12-15; compare Jer 33:17-22). The cross-comparison of these three congruent sets of concentric circles reveals, first, that priests, sacrifices and sanctuary (the innermost circles) must be unblemished and unpolluted. They are deliberately set apart from the middle circles, implying that the realms of priests, sacrifices, and sanctuary must never be fused or confused with the realms of Israel, edible animals and holy land, respectively. Humankind is permitted all animals for its diet with the proviso that their blood is drained (Gen 9:3-4). Israel must be in a state of ritual purity to enter the sanctuary or partake of sacred food (Lev 7:20-21; 12:4). Priests are bound to a severe regimen of conduct, especially in regard to mourning and marriage, to warrant their office as sanctuary officiants, and the high priest must live by an even higher standard. These rules are found in H (21:1-15), but it must be presumed to be operative in P.

H breaks apart this static, immutable picture. It declares that the innermost circles are neither fixed nor frozen. All three innermost realms are capable of a centrifugal movement enabling them to incorporate their respective middle circles. According to H, although priests are innately holy, all Israel is enjoined to achieve holiness. Not that Israel is to observe the priestly regimen or attain priestly status in the sanctuary. Rather, by scrupulously observing Yahweh's commandments, moral and ritual alike, lay Israel can achieve holiness, and priestly Israel can retain it. Indeed, Israel's holiness is neither inherent nor automatic (as implied by D) but a reciprocal process. God sanctifies Israel in proportion to Israel's self-sanctification.

Signs of this mobility are reflected in the animal sphere: H insists that the blood of permitted nonsacrificial animals (game) must be buried so that the animal's life force can be returned to its creator. Sacrificeable animals, however, must be slaughtered (and sacrificed) at the altar. H has abolished profane (i.e., common) slaughter. Henceforth all slaughter must be sacred. That is, every animal must be brought to the sanctuary. It is transferred from the domain of the profane to the domain of the sanctuary (see SACRIFICE AND OFFERINGS).

H also harbors an old tradition that the entire camp in the wilderness cannot tolerate severe impurity (Num 5:1-4; compare 31:19). This tradition is echoed in D, which explicitly stipulates that the camp must be holy (Deut 23:10-15). It is H, however, that extends this view, logically and consistently, to the future residence of Israel—the Promised Land. Hence, impurities produced by Israel by violating Yahweh's prohibitions pollute not only the sanctuary but the entire land. Because God dwells in the land as well as in the sanctuary (e.g., 25:23; 26:11; compare Josh 22:19; Hos 9:3-4), the land cannot abide pollution (e.g., 18:25-30; compare Num 35:33-34). It is therefore no accident that H enjoins upon both the Israelite and the resident alien, that is to say, all who live on the land, to keep the land holy by guarding against impurity and following the prescribed purificatory procedures (e.g., Num 15:27-29; 19:10*b*-13;) so that Yahweh will continue to reside in it and bless the land and its inhabitants with fertility and security (26:3-11; see SOJOURNER; STRANGER).

The dynamic catalyst that turns H's view of Yahweh's covenant from a static picture into one of flux is its concept of holiness. For H, the ideal of holiness is not only embodied in a limited group (priests), animals (sacrifices), and space (sanctuary) but affects all who live on God's land: persons and animals, Israel and the resident alien.

There is one other obligatory dimension for Israel: time. Figure 2 contains only two concentric circles. The holiest day is the SABBATH; it is Yahweh's (Exod 16:23; 20:10; 35:2; 23:3). It was sanctified at creation (Gen 2:3), and its observance is theoretically available to all persons, but is obligatory for every Israelite household and every living thing in his charge (Exod 20:8-11). The Sabbath's holiness is defined by stoppage of all labor.

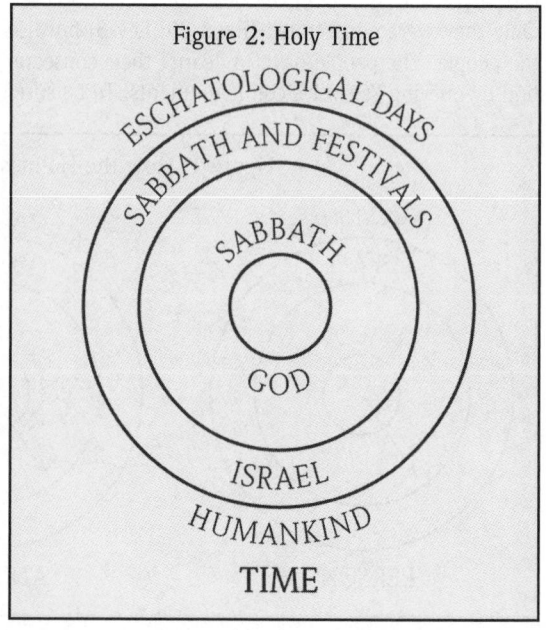

Figure 2: Holy Time

ESCHATOLOGICAL DAYS
SABBATH AND FESTIVALS
SABBATH
GOD
ISRAEL
HUMANKIND
TIME

2. Holy time

The festivals are not Yahweh's. They are miqra'e qodesh, "proclamations of holiness"' because they too require the stoppage of labor (but, with the exception of the Day of Purgation, not to the same degree as the Sabbath). Set by the lunar calendar, they do not occur with the regularity of the Sabbath. Therefore, it is the responsibility of Israel to fix these days. In P's calendar the Sabbath is not a miqra'e qodhesh; it falls automatically on every seventh day and need not be proclaimed. NEW MOON is not a "sacred occasion" for a different reason: it is a work day (Num 28:11-15).

H declares the Sabbath a miqra'e qodhesh (Lev 23:3). Israel was in exile. Being subject to the Babylonian calendar, whose days were ordered by the month—not the week—the exiles might have overlooked the advent of the Sabbath; it had to be proclaimed.

In the priestly system, the nations were not required to observe time. Only the prophets, in their eschatological visions, project a period when all peoples will pilgrimage to Jerusalem to worship Yahweh on Sabbaths and New Moons (Isa 66:23) and on the Festival of Booths (Zech 14:16; see BOOTHS, FEAST OR FESTIVAL OF).

Figure 2 contains no arrow, hence, no movement. In the time dimension H is not dynamic in relation to P in contrast with the dimensions of person, animals, and space (above). H accepts P's concept of the holy Sabbath and festivals and the obligation of Israel to sanctify them by the same differentiated work stoppage. H only differs with P by proclaiming the Sabbath.

Just as Yahweh's presence in the sanctuary does not continue to sanctify the priests who serve within or the layperson when he enters, neither does Yahweh's presence in the land sanctify its inhabitants. Indeed, as the blessings of Lev 26:11-13 indicate, Yahweh's walking about (v.12) the land is for purpose of fertility, vv. 1-5*a*, 9-10, and protection (vv. 4*b*-8). Israelites and priests alike are sanctified by virtue of their own effort, namely, by their adherence to the divine commandments.

3. The benefits of divine holiness

As noted above, the commandments, the observance of which generates holiness, are performative as well as prohibitive, ethical as well as ritual. In contrast with P, which touches on the dangerous, even fatal aspect of the sancta (e.g., 10:1-4; Num 4:15, 17-20), H focuses exclusively on the beneficial aspects of divine holiness. It generates blessing and life; it is the antonym and ultimate conqueror of impurity, the symbol of death. This dynamic power of holiness can also be represented diagrammatically:

Persons and objects are subject to four possible states: holy, common, pure, and impure. Two of them can exist simultaneously: pure things may be either holy or common and common things may be pure or impure. (These relationships are represented in adjoining boxes in the diagram.) However, the holy may not come into contact with the impure. (Their respective boxes do not touch.) These latter two categories are mutually antagonistic. Moreover, they are dynamic: They seek to extend this influence and control over the other two categories, the common and the pure. In contrast to the holy and impure, the common and pure are static. They cannot transfer their state; they are not contagious. Indeed, in effect they are secondary categories. They take their identity from their antonyms. Purity is the absence of impurity; commonness is the absence of holiness. Hence, the boundaries between the holy and the common and between the pure and impure are permeable, represented by a broken line. There is no fixed boundary. Israel by its behavior can move the boundaries either way. But it is enjoined by H to move in one direction only: to advance the holy into the realm of the common and to diminish the impure, thereby enlarging the realm of the pure. This accounts for the formulaic expression "between holy and common and between impure and pure" (Ezek 44:23; Lev 10:10). Besides the fact that it exemplifies the priestly affection for chiasm, (compare 11:47; 20:25), it emphasizes that the first member in each clause (AB') is dynamic and the second static (BA').

The same rationale or, more precisely, its complement obtains here. The bodily impurities focus on four phenomena: death, blood, semen, and scale disease. Their common denominator is death. Vaginal blood and semen represent the forces of life; their loss represents

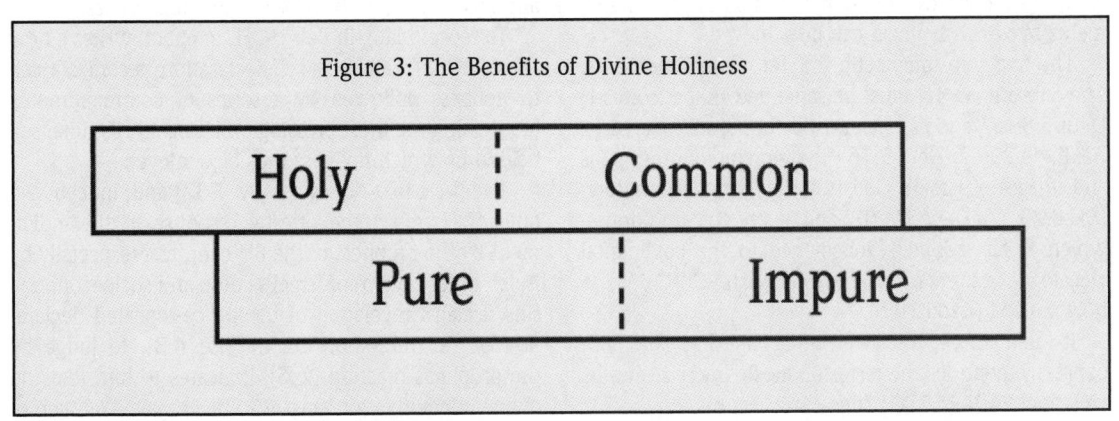

Figure 3: The Benefits of Divine Holiness

Holy	Common

Pure	Impure

death. In the case of scale disease, this symbolism is made explicit: Aaron prays for his stricken sister, "Let her not be like a corpse" (Num 19:14). The wasting of the body, the common characteristic of all biblically impure skin diseases, symbolizes the death process as much as the loss of blood and semen. The antonymy of life and death (muth מוּת) is graphically underscored by the rationale for not engaging in certain mourning rites for the dead (Deut 14:1-2): "for you are a holy people." The previous word is lameth לָמֵת "for the dead," making the juxtaposition—rather, the opposition—of "holy" and "death" striking.

Thus tumʿah (טֻמְאָה) and qedhushah (קְדֻשָׁה), biblical impurity and holiness, are semantic opposites. And as the quintessence and source of qedhusha resides with God, it is imperative for Israel to control the occurrence of impurity lest it impinge upon the realm of the holy God. The forces pitted against each other in the cosmic struggle are no longer the benevolent and demonic deities who populate the mythologies of Israel's neighbors but the forces of life and death set loose by people themselves through their obedience to or defiance of God's commandments. Among all of the diachronic changes that occur in the development of Israel's impurity laws, this clearly is the most significant: the total severance of impurity from the demonic and its reinterpretation as a symbolic system reminding Israel of its imperative to cleave to life and reject death.

Another duality in the concept of holiness is "defective" and "whole." This undoubtedly holds within the sanctuary where priests and sacrifices must be unblemished. But outside the sanctuary this antinomy does not prevail. In fact, Israel's access to the sanctuary or to sacred food is independent of any physical defect (mum מוּם). Note that in the detailed program for achieving holiness (Lev 19) there is no mention of any physical imperfection. One may, however, say that by not following this program Israel sustains moral imperfection.

F. The Holiness Prescription

Leviticus 19 provides the prescription to effect a transformation to holiness. Under the call to holiness (v. 2), it enumerates sixteen units containing commandments by which holiness can be achieved.

The first two units echo the Ten Commandments. The Sabbath (v. 3*b*) must be sanctified (Exod 20:8-11; Deut 5:8-15), and parents must be honored, revered (v. 3*a*; Exod 20:12; Deut 5:16); the worship of other gods and images of Israel's God (v. 4) are strictly forbidden (Exod 20:3-6; Deut 5:7-10); and by the epic tradition—which H has adopted—obedience to the covenantal Decalogue renders Israel a goy qadhosh (גּוֹי קָדוֹשׁ) "a holy nation" (Exod 19:6).

In unit three, the well-being offering (vv. 5-8) expressly mentions the terms qodhesh "sacred" and its violation, khillel (חִלֵּל) "desecrate" (v. 8).

Unit four, dealing with horticultural holiness (vv. 9-10), lacks these terms, but its inclusion under the call to holiness is significant. The emulation of God's holiness must include materializing God's concern for the indigent. Also, setting aside part of the harvest might be equivalent to firstfruits and tithes; thereby, symbolically, Yahweh has assigned some of his due to the poor.

Unit five concerns ethical deeds (vv. 11-13) and includes oath desecration (v. 12), implying the concomitant diminution in holiness.

The remainder of this ethical series (vv. 14-18) includes unit six: exploitation of the helpless (v. 14); unit seven: injustice and indifference (vv. 15-16), and unit eight: reproof and love (vv. 17-18), all of which emphasize the divine attribute of compassion, essential to God's holy nature. As neatly encapsulated by the rabbis: "As he (the Lord) is gracious and compassionate (compare Exod 34:6) so you should be gracious and compassionate" (*b. Sabb.* 133*b*). "As he clothes the naked (Gen 3:21), you should clothe the naked; as he nurses the sick (Gen 18:1), you should nurse the sick; as he comforts the mourners (Gen 25:11), you should comfort the mourners; as he buries the dead (Deut 34:5), so you should bury the dead" (*b. Sotah* 14a).

Unit nine, concerning mixtures (v. 19), proscribes the breeding of different animals, sowing mixed seed, or weaving fabrics made from mixed seed because these mixtures are reserved for the sacred sphere, the sanctuary and the priests. Unit ten concerns the betrothed slave-woman (vv. 20-22) and involves reparation offering prescribed in cases of desecration (5:14-16). In unit eleven, horticultural holiness (vv. 23-25) focuses on the fruit of the fourth year, which is declared "sacred" and belongs to Yahweh (v. 24). Unit twelve eschews the chief form of impurity, death and the dead (vv. 26-28), essential in adhering to the God of holiness—life.

Unit thirteen states that prostitution (v. 29) is a form of desecration (compare 22:7, 9). Units fourteen to sixteen discuss sabbath and sanctuary (also 26:2), consulting the dead (also 20:1-7), and respecting elders (vv. 30-32) parallel the opening verses (vv. 3-4) and, hence, echo the Decalogue, the basic prescription for holiness. Units seventeen to eighteen, the resident alien and business ethics (vv. 33-37), are appendices.

To recapitulate, in Lev 19, H, in effect, writes a new "Decalogue." Yahweh's self-declaration becomes a call to holiness, followed by a series of commandments (addressing the most pressing problems in H's time; see below) by which holiness may be achieved.

The basic text of Lev 19 (vv. 1-32) and, indeed, the bulk of H reflect the priestly response to the indictment by the prophets of the 8th cent. BCE (especially by Isaiah of Jerusalem) of Israel's cultic and socioeconomic sins. Isaiah's revelation of the thrice-repeated declaration of Yahweh's holy nature (Isa 6:3), to judge by the prophet's reaction (v. 5), indicates to him that the divine imperative for Israel is to be ethical: "Yahweh of hosts shall be exalted by his judgment and the holy God shall be shown holy by his righteousness" (Isa 5:16), a statement which is both a prediction of doom upon unrighteous Israel (vv. 24-30) and an indictment of the moral failings of Israel's corrupt judicial leaders, who blur the distinction between right and wrong (5:20) and pervert justice for the sake of bribes (5:22). Isaiah's indictment of the leadership includes the prophet and the priest (28:2), but it is especially directed against the civil leaders (3:14) and the rich (5:8) who rob the poor and seize their land. That is to say, Isaiah's "Holy, holy, holy" implies that Yahweh, who governs the world by justice, expects Israel to do the same. In Isaiah's gloomy forecast, only those who do not participate in these social evils will survive the forthcoming purge, and these few—provided they truly repent—will be called "holy" and be admitted into the New Zion (4:3).

The text of H testifies that its priestly authors have been stung by their fellow Jerusalemite's rebuke. Their response is twofold: First, they adopt Isaiah's revelation that Yahweh's holiness implies that Israel must be ethical, and then they go beyond Isaiah by prescribing specific commandments (Lev 19) by which holiness can be attained and by prescribing a revolutionary program that will reverse the extant socioeconomic wrongs (Lev 25). Moreover, H takes issue with Isaiah's pessimism concerning Israel's inability to repent. Note that after pronouncing Israel's irrevocable doom in chap. 6, Isaiah never again calls upon his people to repent. In Lev 19, H brims with hope that all Israel will heed the divine call to holiness, and hence there is no reason to anticipate a purge of the nation (the dour forecast of Lev 26 has not yet dawned).

The rabbis follow up on H's insight and extend it into new dimensions. To be sure, they accept the Torah's basic notion that holiness implies separation and withdrawal, and hence, they interpret the injunction to be holy to mean that Israel mst separate itself from the nations of the world and its abominations (compare *Mek.* 63*a*; *Sifra Qedoshim* 93*b*), but they add, in agreement with H: "Be holy, for as long as you fulfill my commandments you are sanctified, but if you neglect them you become profaned" (*Num. Rab.* 17:6); "when the Omnipresent enjoins a new precept upon Israel, he adds holiness to them" (*Mek. Kaspa* 20); and the rabbis exemplify these statements by specifying that holiness is added to Israel by observing the Sabbath (19:3b, 30a; *Mek. Shabbata* 1) and by wearing tassels (Num 15:37-41; *Sifre Num.* 115).

The rabbis also enjoin a superior kind of holiness: "Sanctify yourselves even in what is permitted" (*b. Yebam.* 20*a*).

For example, note this expansion of the Decalogue's prohibition against adultery: "The eye of the adulterer waits for nightfall" (Job 24:15) teaches us that an unchaste look is also to be considered as adultery; and the verse "so that you do not follow your heart and your eyes in your lustful urge" (Num 15:39) teaches that an unchaste look or even an unchaste thought is also to be regarded as adultery (*Lev. Rab.* 23:12; compare Matt 5:27).

Archaeological evidence—the profusion of stone vessels from the 2nd cent. BCE through the 2nd cent. CE, especially in Jerusalem and its environs but also throughout the land—indicates that ordinary people were observing a form of nonsacred purity, that is, not just in handling sacred food (prescribed by Scripture, Lev 7:19-21) but in ordinary, daily food. Stone is impervious to impurity, and thus the abundance of jars, mugs, pitchers, bowls, and measuring cups for containing the food and drink for daily meals indicates the extent to which the people-at-large, and not just the Pharisees, went in order to conduct their lives according to a more stringent form of purity.

Furthermore, the sectaries of QUMRAN prescribe a nonbiblical, one-day ablation for the corpse-contaminated (11Q20 XIV, 15), also adumbrated in Tob 2:9; Jud 12:6-10, so that he/she would not be contaminated by food or drink. Archaeology confirms this practice by its unearthing of ritual baths (miqwaʾoth מִקְוָאֹת) built alongside of burial caves and graveyards, which must have served the same purpose (*see* MIQVAH, MIQVAʾOTH).

What drove the common people to adopt such stringent measures? Their motivation likely came from the biblical commandment for all Israel to become holy (Lev 19:2; compare Exod 19:6; Deut 14:2, 21).

Bibliography: G. Alon. *Jews, Judaism, and the Classical World* (1977); Mary Douglas. *Leviticus as Literature* (1999); E. S. Gerstenberger. *Leviticus* OTL (1996); M. Greenberg. "Three Conceptions of Torah in Hebrew Scriptures." *Die hebräische Bibel und ihre zweifache Nachgeschicht.* E. Blum, ed. (1990) 365–78; M. Greenberg. "The Value of Controversy," *Judaism and Humanism.* N. Guber, ed. (1996) 4–9; J. E. Hartley. *Leviticus* WBC 4 (1992); G. F. Hasel. "The Meaning of the Animal Rite in Genesis 15." *JSOT* 19 (1981) 61–78; I. Knohl. *The Sanctuary of Silence: The Priestly Torah and the Holiness School* (1995); R. A. Kugler. "Holiness, Purity, the Body and Society: The Evidence for Theological Conflict in Leviticus." *JSOT* 76 (1997) 3–27; J. Milgrom. "Did Isaiah Prophesy During the Reign of Uzziah?" *VT* 14 (1964):164–82; J. Milgrom. "Profane Slaughter and a Formulaic Key to the Composition of Deuteronomy." *HUCA* 47 (1976) 1–17; J. Milgrom. "Studies in the Temple Scroll." *JBL* 97 (1978) 501–23; J. Milgrom. *Numbers.* JPS Torah Commentary (1990); J. Milgrom. *Leviticus 1-16.* AB 3 (1991); J. Milgrom. *Leviticus 17-22.* AB 3a (2000); E. W. Nicholson. "The Covenant Ritual in Exodus XXIV 3–8." *VT* 32 (1982) 74–86; E. Regev. "Non-priestly Purity and its Religious Perspectives according to the Historical Sources and Archaeological Findings." *Purity and Holiness; the Heritage of Leviticus.* M. J. H. M. Poorthuis and J. Schwartz, eds. (2000) 223–44; B. J. Schwartz. *The Holiness Legislation* (1999).

JACOB MILGROM

HOLY ARRAY. *See* ARRAY, HOLY.

HOLY COMMUNION. *See* COVENANT (OT AND NT); EUCHARIST; LAST SUPPER, THE; LORD'S SUPPER.

HOLY GHOST. *See* HOLY SPIRIT.

HOLY OF HOLIES ["Αγια 'Αγίων Hagia Hagiōn]. The inner sanctum of the Temple containing the golden altar of incense and the ARK OF THE COVENANT, also called the MOST HOLY PLACE. The high priest alone was allowed to enter the adytum once a year, on the DAY OF ATONEMENT (compare Lev 16). *See* HOLY PLACE; TEMPLE, JERUSALEM.

RALPH K. HAWKINS

HOLY ONE [קָדוֹשׁ qadosh; ἅγιος hagios]. The epithet "Holy One," without additional qualification, is used of God several times in the OT (1 Sam 2:2; Prov 9:10; Job 6:10; Isa 40:25; Hab 3:3; Hos 11:12 [Heb. 12:1]), along with the more common variant, "Holy One of Israel" (thirty-three times, twenty-five in Isaiah), but also "the Holy One of Jacob" (Isa 29:23), and the possessive forms "my Holy One" (Hab 1:12), "your Holy One" (Isa 43:15), and "his Holy One (Isa 10:17; 49:7). The overwhelming majority of the occurences is in the Isaiah tradition, which is not surprising, given the proclamation "Holy, Holy, Holy" in the prophet's inaugural vision of transcendent divine kingship (Isa 6). "Holy" denotes something or someone that is set apart, extraordinary (*see* HOLY, HOLINESS, OT).

The association of the epithet with God's kingship is suggestive, since in Ugaritic literature, El, the celestial king and ruler of the divine council, is also called "the Holy One" (CTU 1.2.I.20-21; 1.16.I.11, 22; 1.17.I.3, 8, 12, 22). Thus, too, the designation "Holy One" in the Bible is sometimes juxtaposed with the term ʾel (Pss 78:41; 89:7; Hos 11:9; 12:1). Given the connotation of divine transcendence and kingship, the assertion that God is "the Holy One in your midst" (Hos 11:9) is a daring theological claim, as is the designation of God as Israel's own "Holy One"—the transcendent God being nevertheless among a people and relating to a people.

The Gospels refer to Jesus as "the Holy One of God" (Mark 1:24; Luke 4:34; John 6:69), though Luke, citing OT texts, also refers to Jesus, the incarnate presence of God, simply as "the Holy One" (Acts 2:27; 13:35). *See* GOD, NAMES OF.

C. L. SEOW

HOLY PLACE [קֹדֶשׁ qodhesh, מָקוֹם קָדֹשׁ maqom qadhosh]. The larger of the two divisions of both the tabernacle and the Temple, containing the lampstand(s) and the tables of showbread (compare Exod 25–40; 1 Kgs 6–7). "Holy place" is also used as a general term for the Temple (e.g., Ezra 9:8; Ps 24:3), the inside of the Temple (2 Chr 29:5), and even the Temple grounds (Ezek 45:4). *See* MOST HOLY PLACE; TEMPLE, JERUSALEM.

RALPH K. HAWKINS

HOLY SEPULCHRE. The church in the middle of the Old City of Jerusalem that is built over the place of Christ's crucifixion and the tomb from which he rose. Although questioned by partisans of the Garden Tomb, the authenticity of the location is now accepted by many experts. In the 1st cent. the site was an abandoned quarry outside the north wall of Jerusalem. Golgotha protruded from the east wall of the quarry, while a catacomb, whose innermost part still survives, had been cut into the west wall. Traces of fruits were found in the earth covering the quarry bed. This is precisely the situation described in John 19:41-42; in the place where Jesus was crucified there was a garden, and in it an empty tomb; there they laid him because it was close.

The 1st cent. *Lives of the Prophets* attests that pious Jews prayed at the graves of holy persons. It is probable, therefore, that Jesus' disciples visited his tomb. "See the place where they laid him" (Mark 16:6) may reflect a liturgy in the tomb. The memory of the location was intensified by bitterness when in 135 CE Hadrian made it inaccessible by filling in the quarry to create a podium for the Capitoline Temple of Aelia Capitolina.

The temple was demolished and excavated to bedrock on the orders of Constantine in 325. The discovery of a tomb is documented by Eusebius of Caesarea and Cyril of Jerusalem who were present. In all probability it was identified as the tomb of Christ by graffiti, as was the tomb of St. Peter in the Vatican. Byzantine texts and modern excavations permit a detailed reconstruction of the great church that was dedicated on September 17, 335 CE. Golgotha stood under a baldachino in the southwest corner of an open courtyard on the east side of a circular building housing the tomb of Christ, which had been freed from the overburden and the surrounding rock. East of the courtyard was a five-aisled basilica.

Attacks on the complex culminated in the systematic destruction by the Fatimid Caliph in Egypt, al-Hakim, in 1009. The tomb was severely damaged, and the stones of the buildings were levered from their courses. Restoration of the rotunda and courtyard began in 1012, but the basilia had to be abandoned. What remained of the rock-cut tomb was enshrined in an edicule. The Crusaders gave the building its present shape by erecting a Romanesque church over the court-

Todd Bohlen/BiblePlaces.com
Figure 1: The Church of the Holy Sepulchre from Lutheran Tower.

yard between 1163 and 1169. Extensive renovation carried out between 1955 and 1997 was necessitated by the great fire of 1808 and the earthquake of 1927. The existing edicule dates only from 1810 and is in danger of imminent collapse. *See* GOLGOTHA.

Bibliography: M. Biddle. *The Tomb of Christ* (1999); J. Murphy-O'Connor. "Restoration and Discovery: Bringing to Light the Constantinian Holy Sepulchre Church." *Patterns of the Past, Prospects for the Future: The Christian Heritage in the Holy Land.* Thomas Hummel, Kevork Hintlian, and Ulf Carmesund, eds. (1999) 69–84.

JEROME MURPHY-O'CONNOR.

HOLY SPIRIT. In the Bible's opening words, the Spirit of God hovers over the face of the deep, brooding perhaps like a mother eagle (Gen 1:2). In the scripture's closing lines, the Spirit and the bride—the church—offer an invitation to taste the water of life (Rev 22:17). Between the opening and closing of the Bible's curtain lies a rich and jagged spiritual terrain to which the Spirit of God lends a measure of focus.

Three challenges beset any effort to transfer ancient concepts of spirit into contemporary language and thought. The first is raised as early as Gen 1:2, in which the meaning of **ruakh** (רוּחַ) is elusive; the word can just as easily be translated with "spirit" as "wind." The challenge for modern interpreters is that the Hebrew and Greek words, **ruakh** and **pneuma** (πνεῦμα), encompass a wide range of realities: divine energy and presence (e.g., Ps 139:7); the human core (e.g., Ps 77:6); breath (e.g., Isa 40:7); the waxing and waning of life itself (Judg 15:19; Ezek 10:17; Job 34:14); a disposition, as in "spirit of lust" (Hos 4:12); an angelic being (e.g., Ps 104:4); a demonic being (e.g., 1 Sam 16:16); and wind (e.g., Num 11:31). Although Hebrew literature, for example, may play upon the overlap between spirit and wind (Num 11:17, 31; Ps 104:4) or breath and spirit (Isa 40:7), contemporary translators are compelled to choose one English word and, at best, to relegate the other to a footnote.

Second, there existed no single technical term for the divine spirit in Israelite, Jewish, and Christian antiquity. The expression, "Holy Spirit," occurs only twice—and with very different connotations—in the OT. In Heb. Ps 51:13, the Holy Spirit (**ruakh qodhshekha** [רוּחַ קָדְשְׁךָ]; "your holy spirit") resides within the individual psalmist; in Isa 63:10-11, God places the Holy Spirit (**ruakh qodhsho** [רוּחַ קָדְשׁוֹ]; "his holy spirit") within the community of Israel. These two occurrences show how disparate conceptions of the Spirit can be, notwithstanding a shared epithet. The Spirit could, further, be identified in many ways: "Spirit" without qualifiers (e.g., Isa 34:16; Ezek 11:1; 1 Chr 12:18);

"Spirit of God" (e.g., Gen 1:2; Exod 31:3; 2 Chr 15:1); "Spirit of wisdom" (e.g., Exod 28:3; Deut 34:9); "Spirit of the LORD" (e.g., Judg 3:10; Mic 3:8); good Spirit (Ps 143:10; Neh 9:20); my [God's] Spirit (e.g., Isa 42:1; Ezek 39:29); "Spirit of the holy gods" or "Spirit of the holy God" (e.g., Dan 4:8); extraordinary (e.g., Dan 5:12).

In early Jewish literature, the term "Holy Spirit" occurs with enormous fluidity. The Dead Sea Scrolls caution "not to defile your holy spirit," by which they mean not to forfeit one's integrity (e.g., 4Q416 2 II, 6). They speak of the "spirit of holiness" that cleanses new members of the community (1QS III, 7-8). They refer to "spirits of holiness" (1QH[a] XVI, 12). Josephus and Philo tend to prefer the moniker "divine Spirit" for the Spirit in Israelite literature (e.g., Philo, *Her.* 265; Josephus, *Ant.* 6.166).

In the NT, the expressions, "Holy Spirit" (to pneuma to hagion τὸ πνεῦμα τὸ ἅγιον, to hagion pneuma τὸ ἅγιον πνεῦμα, etc.) and "Spirit of Holiness" (pneuma hagiōsunēs πνεῦμα ἁγιωσύνης in Rom 1:4) occur alongside the more frequent use of the word *spirit* (pneuma), without qualifiers.

The third challenge is of a different nature. There exists an unfortunate tendency to drive a wedge between the divine Spirit and the human spirit, although ancient authors were less prone to do so. This unfortunate bifurcation has an historical point of origin. During the mid-19th cent., German idealists understood *Geist* (spirit) as absolute self-consciousness. Hermann Gunkel, in the mid 1880's corrected this perception. Gunkel focused upon the effects—mysterious and overpowering symptoms—that led ancient observers to identify the work of the holy spirit. By doing so, he recaptured claims to the inexplicable and independent activities of the holy spirit that occur in the NT. Unfortunately, this has led to an overshadowing of those experiences that were not ecstatic or remarkable. Further, subsequent studies have tended to expand Gunkel's beneficial findings, which were limited to the NT, to the OT. Consequently, the allegedly charismatic judges and ecstatic prophets would become the gold standard from which the Spirit's presence would be judged. This perspective lays too much emphasis upon the extraordinary and occasional onslaught of God's spirit and too little upon God's spirit as the divine energy that resides in all living and breathing human beings.

A. Old Testament

1. Torah

At its most fundamental level, the spirit marks the borderland between life and death. The treachery of this boundary is poignantly portrayed in the flood narrative, in which God plots the demise of "all flesh in which is the spirit of life" (Gen 6:17; 7:15; compare 7:22).

This belief in the spirit as the source of physical life shades into the conviction that the spirit within is the source of skill and wisdom. The Egyptian Pharaoh recognizes that Joseph, who can interpret dreams, is one "in whom is the spirit" (Gen 41:38). Of Bezalel (and Oholiab), lead architects of the tabernacle, God says: "See, I have called by name Bezalel . . . and I have filled him with (the) spirit-of-God, with ability, intelligence, and knowledge in every kind of craft, to devise artistic designs, to work in gold, silver, and bronze, in cutting stones for setting, and in carving wood, in every kind of craft" (Exod 31:1-3). Later in the Torah, Moses is told to lay his hands upon Joshua because Joshua is "a man in whom is the spirit" (Num 27:18); according to a later version, "Joshua son of Nun was full of spirit of wisdom, because Moses laid his hands on him; and the Israelites obeyed him, doing as the LORD had commanded Moses" (Deut 34:9).

These statements are liable to one of two interpretations. They may suggest, on the one hand, that God gave the spirit as a subsequent, temporary endowment to equip these heroic Israelites in particular tasks: Joseph to interpret dreams, Bezalel to lead in construction of the tabernacle, and Joshua to take over from Moses. On the other hand, they may point to the belief that certain people had cultivated the spirit that was theirs from birth. This interpretation is supported by the contrast between Pharaoh's troubled spirit and Joseph's divine one (Gen 41:8; 38), both of which, presumably, are theirs from birth. Bezalel is selected because he already possesses the spirit of God and skills that he has cultivated; further, spirit and heart—an endowment from birth—are set repeatedly in parallel positions in this narrative, e.g., "I filled him with spirit of God . . . for every craft" (Exod 35:31), and "I filled them with wisdom of heart . . . to do every craft" (35:35). Heart and spirit are tandem permanent endowments that have been cultivated by select Israelites. The scenario is little different with respect to Joshua in Num 27:18: Joshua is chosen because he already possesses the vigor that qualifies him to become Moses' successor without the need for a further endowment.

Deuteronomy 34:9, in which Joshua is filled with a spirit of wisdom when Moses lays his hands upon him, may be an exception to this pattern that can be explained by the influence of the Deuteronomic perspective, which dominates the so-called Deuteronomistic History (Former Prophets without Ruth). In these stories, the Spirit comes as a subsequent and spectacular endowment that effects liberation and skill. Deuteronomy 34:9 is aligned with the mystifying story of Balaam, upon whom the Spirit comes as a temporary, subsequent endowment. Balaam blesses Israel—though Balak of Moab intends to pay him handsomely for cursing Israel—when the Spirit comes upon him (Num 24:2; also LXX Num 23:7).

Another perplexing story occurs in Num 11. God tells an exhausted Moses, "I will take from the spirit that is on you and put it on them; and they shall bear the burden of the people along with you . . ." (11:17). Subsequently, Moses gathers the elders; the LORD "took [some] of the spirit that was on him and put it on the seventy elders; and when the spirit rested upon them, they prophesied. But they did not do so again" (11:25). Scholars have typically understood prophesying here as an ecstatic, even crazed, phenomenon, but the parallel between bearing the burden of the people and prophesying suggests that the gift is administrative. Further, the distribution of the spirit is an indication that Moses' gift

of leadership is being passed on to them. Finally, the verb "rest" expresses a different form of presence from "rush upon," as in the story of Saul's prophesying. The story continues when two elders who did not gather with the seventy, Eldad and Medad, prophesy; Moses, rather than being alarmed at this excess of leadership, tells Joshua he wishes all Israelites were prophets "and that the LORD would put his spirit upon them" (11:29).

The Torah, then, contains several significant depictions of the spirit: 1) the source of physical LIFE from birth; 2) the source of wisdom and insight for those who cultivated this spirit (*see* WISDOM IN THE OT); 3) a subsequent, temporary endowment; and 4) a distribution of the capacity for prophetic leadership (*see* PROPHET, PROPHECY).

2. Prophets
a. Former Prophets. In the so-called Former Prophets (Joshua–2 Kings, except Ruth), the spirit—typically the "Spirit of the LORD," occasionally the "Spirit of God"—develops explosive dimensions when it comes upon Israel's leaders, particularly the judges, to empower them to liberate the tribes of Israel, usually through warfare. The spirit "was upon" Othniel (Judg 3:10) and Jephthah (11:29), "clothed" Gideon (6:34), "began to trouble" (13:25) and "rushed upon" Samson (14:6, 19; 15:14). These moments of inspiration lead to a military victory or eventual liberation. In other words, the spirit inspires leaders of oppressed Israel to defeat the enemy. In a provocative, if not altogether convincing study, M. Welker contends instead that the spirit in Judges does not initiate violence but restores Israelite solidarity by raising the oppressed.

With Israel's first king, a scenario that is reminiscent of the judges re-emerges when the "Spirit of the LORD" rushes upon Saul, and he cuts an ox yoke into twelve, sending it to the twelve tribes in a declaration of war (1 Sam 11:5-11). There are, however, new developments in the pattern of Judges.

First, the verb, "rushed upon" (tsalakh צָלַח), which refers in Judges to a transitory experience that leads to liberation, is no longer only temporary and liberative but transformative and permanent. Samuel predicts that the spirit of the LORD will come upon Saul and he will prophesy and be transformed into another person. This inaugural onrush of the spirit draws Saul into the circle of prophets who "prophesy." What this experience entails is difficult to pinpoint. In a similar experience, after he has forfeited this Spirit to David, Saul lies naked and crazed (1 Sam 19:23-24). The difficulty in drawing a parallel between Saul's initial and final experiences is that the spirit in the latter may be an evil spirit; this experience of possession may not be true prophesying at all but a caricature of prophetic possession.

A less ambiguous association of the verb, "rush," with permanence, attends the anointing of David. The transition from Saul's to David's leadership occurred when "the spirit of the LORD rushed upon David from that day forward" (1 Sam 16:13).

The second development is the conceptualization of the Spirit as an angelic being, a counterpart to evil spirits. Strong correspondences link evil and good spirits. 1) Both are referred to as "spirit of God" in 10:10; 11:6; 16:15, 16, 23a; 18:10; 19:20, 23, or "spirit of the LORD" in 10:6, 16:13, 16:14a (compare 16:14b); 19:9. 2) Both "rush upon" Saul in 10:6, 10; 11:6; 16:13; 18:10. 3) Both can have the same effect, depicted by the same verb, prophesy, in the hithpael (hithnabbeʾ הִתְנַבֵּא). 4) Both "depart" from Saul in 16:14, 23b.

The third development that distinguishes the stories of kings from those of judges is the ability of the Spirit to leave one person to inhabit another—as in the story of Saul and David. This reality emerges also in the puzzling story of Micaiah ben Imlah, which encapsulates the Deuteronomic concern with true and false prophecy (1 Kgs 18:15-22): God inspires Micaiah, the true prophet, and also places a lying spirit in the mouths of the false prophets. In this narrative, Zedekiah, chief of the false royal prophets asks, "Which way [where] did the spirit of the LORD pass from me to you?" (1 Kgs 22:24). This passing of the spirit from Saul to David, or Zedekiah to Micaiah, is different from succession narratives, such as when Elisha receives a double portion of Elijah's spirit—his vitality and extraordinary abilities—in 2 Kgs 2:9, 15.

b. Latter Prophets. In comparison with the Former Prophets, the so-called writing prophets offer precious little about experiences of the spirit. During the 8th cent., Micah laid claim to being filled "with power, with the spirit of the LORD, and with justice and might" (3:7-8). This claim is difficult to interpret. Micah may claim here a subsequent filling with the spirit, but the parallel drawn between the spirit and power, justice, and might suggests otherwise. Knowledge of justice, for example, is hardly due to a special endowment; it is cultivated, learned, studied (compare 6:8). So, presumably, is the spirit that fills him cultivated through learning. Micah may be saying, therefore, that the spirit which fills him—the spirit that he has strengthened and cultivated—trumps the claims to inspiration of false prophets (3:5-8).

A later 8th cent. prophet, Hosea, criticizes Israel for the vague saying, "The prophet is a fool; the man of the spirit is mad!" (9:7). Exilic prophets offer slightly more. Deutero-Isaiah commands a hearing because "the LORD God has sent me and his spirit" (48:16), while Ezekiel claims that "the spirit lifted me up" (3:12, 14) and that "the spirit of the LORD fell upon me" (11:5).

i. Resting. More plentiful than their autobiographical accounts are the prophets' vivid statements about the spirit, which appear principally in Isaiah, Ezekiel, Joel, Haggai, and Zechariah. In the Isaiah corpus, the sense of a permanent endowment comes to fullest flower. During a politically unstable era, Isaiah imagined that a root, a future king, would emerge from Jesse's stump, from all that Assyria left. "The spirit of the LORD shall rest on him, the spirit of wisdom and understanding, the spirit of counsel and might, the spirit of knowledge and the fear of the LORD" (Isa 11:2). The image is one of anointing for superb leadership. The spirit of the LORD that rests upon him will grant: 1) intellectual and practical skills needed for peacetime leadership (understanding and wisdom); 2) the skills of developing military strategies and leading in battle (counsel and courage or might; though in Prov 8:14 this pair is used of peacetime leadership); and 3) devotion to God, presumably through the appropriate participation in worship (knowledge and fear of God). (See also 9:6-9).

Centuries later, Jerusalem would fall to Babylon in 587 BCE, and exiles would cry, "My way is hidden from the LORD, and my justice is disregarded by my God" (Isa 40:27). An heir to Isaiah's prophecies answered this by presenting Israel with God's servant: "Here is my [God's] servant, whom I uphold, my chosen, in whom my soul delights; I have put my spirit upon him; he will bring forth justice to the nations" (42:1). This servant would restore the balance of justice, not only to Israel, but to the entire world. In what manner? With a quiet voice. "He will not cry or lift up his voice, or make it heard in the street." By what means? By persistent teaching. "He will not grow faint or be crushed until he has established justice in the earth; and the coastlands wait for his teaching" (42:2-4). It is difficult to identify this servant, who could represent the nation Israel (41:8-10), a remnant of Israel, a prophetic individual, or Cyrus, a Persian ruler designated the LORD's anointed (45:1), who would restore the exiles to the land. Regardless of who this servant was, a new association emerges during the exile between the Spirit and the sort of quiet and persistent teaching that will restore the universal balance of justice (see JUSTICE; PEACE IN THE OT).

Perhaps later still, another prophet would claim, "The spirit of the Lord God is upon me, because the LORD has anointed me . . ." (Isa 61:1) This mission is rooted in the understanding and wisdom of the inspired messiah (Isa 11:1-4) and the justice that lies at the core of the exilic servant's teaching (Isa 42:1-4). Now, however, it is not the place of Judah among the nations that is pre-eminent but the visceral quality of liberating the poor within Judah: he preaches good news to the oppressed, release to prisoners, comfort for those who weep in Jerusalem, even perhaps the liberating year of Jubilee (Lev 25:8-17; Isa 48:16; see MESSIAH, JEWISH; SERVANT OF THE LORD).

ii. Recreation. Another prophet lived during a period that spanned the destruction of Jerusalem in 587 BCE. Prior to 587, in response to the proverb, "The parents have eaten sour grapes, and the children's teeth are set on edge" (Ezek 18:2), Ezekiel tells the Israelites that each individual is responsible for his or her own destiny. He commands them to repent and to "make yourselves a new heart and a new spirit!" (18:31). The impetus for recreation, the catalyst for transformation, lies entirely with individuals.

At another point prior to the fall of Jerusalem, as the glory departs from the temple (8:1-11:25), there occurs a vision of the ingathering of those who will inevitably be exiled: "Thus says the Lord God: I will gather you from the peoples. . . . When they come there, they will remove from it all its detestable things and all its abominations. I will give them one heart, and put a new spirit within them; I will remove the heart of stone from their flesh and give them a heart of flesh, so that they may follow my statutes and keep my ordinances and obey them" (11:17-21). At this point in time, the initiative for recreation lies both with Israelites, who can repent, and God, who will give heart and a new spirit.

Following the destruction of Jerusalem in 587 BCE, responsibility for recreation shifts wholly to God. The promise is reiterated, though with complete emphasis upon divine initiative: "A new heart I will give you, and a new spirit I will put within you; and I will remove from your body the heart of stone and give you a heart of flesh. I will put my spirit within you, and make you follow my statutes and be careful to observe my ordinances" (36:26-27). This emphasis is due to the moribund state of Israel, which is vividly depicted in the following vision of the valley of dry bones. Israel is dead, impure, bleached bones. In this horrific valley, Ezekiel discovers hope that resides in the power of the spirit to revivify: "Then he said to me, "Prophesy to these bones, and say to them: O dry bones, hear the word of the LORD. Thus says the Lord God to these bones: I will cause spirit to enter you, and you shall live. I will lay sinews on you, and will cause flesh to come upon you, and cover you with skin, and put spirit in you, and you shall live; and you shall know that I am the LORD" (37:4-6). With these words, Ezekiel peers beyond the cusp of death to a world with bones clattering, into sinews, flesh, and skin. Still, the Israelites have "no spirit in them" (37:8), so God commands, "'Prophesy to the breath, prophesy, mortal, and say to the spirit: Thus says the Lord God: Come from the four winds, O spirit, and breathe into these slain, that they may live.' I prophesied as he commanded me, and the spirit came into them, and they lived, and stood on their feet, a vast multitude" (37:9-10). This is Gen 2:7 in a new key. This is the command to make for oneself a new heart and spirit. In an unrivalled play upon the word, ruakh, Ezekiel dramatizes the grand collective, even cosmic, action that is taking place to vivify, not just individuals, but a nation that lies in ruins: the spirit is not renewed but replaced entirely, as the winds scurry to reinvigorate Israel with new BREATH.

ii. Outpouring. Israel's prophets also envisaged the future outpouring of the spirit upon Israel. According to Isaiah, the outpouring marks the shift between the desolation of Jerusalem and the restoration of justice: ". . . until a spirit from on high is poured out on us, and the wilderness becomes a fruitful field . . . then justice will dwell in the wilderness . . . My people will abide in peaceful habitation . . ." (32:15-20). His prophetic heir comforts the "servant" with the promise, "For I will pour water on the thirsty land . . . I will pour my spirit upon your descendants, and my blessing on your offspring. They shall spring up like a green tamarisk . . ." (44:3-4; compare 59:20-21). Ezekiel transforms this outpouring into a surprising climax of his belief that Israel will be returned to a purified homeland: "and I will never again hide my face from them, when I pour out my spirit upon the house of Israel, says the Lord God" (39:25-29). The latest (perhaps postexilic) and most dramatic development of this theme is Joel (2:28-29; [Heb. 3:1-2]). Though the book as a whole is preoccupied with Judah, the breadth of this promise appears to be wider: "Then afterward I will pour out my spirit on all flesh; your sons and your daughters shall prophesy, your old men shall dream dreams, and your young men shall see visions. Even on the male and female slaves, in those days, I will pour out my spirit." Taking his cue from Moses' hope that all Israel would prophesy (Num 11:29), Joel envisages an outpouring that will enable all people to receive revelations of God through prophecies, dreams, and visions. Israel's conceptions of the outpouring of the spirit, then, encompassed a renewal of the natural world (Isa 32:15-30), a renewal of Israel akin to natural renewal (Isa 44:3-4), a purification and resurrection of Israel (Ezekiel 36–39), and revelation to all people (Joel 3:1-2). In a related text, Zechariah promises that God "will pour out a spirit of compassion and supplication;" this will be necessary because the people will mourn for the one whom they pierced (12:10).

iv. Exodus. Since reflection upon the exodus inevitably catalyzed Israelite traditions, conceptions of the spirit fell under the sway of this tradition during the postexilic period. Nehemiah inserts the spirit directly into this tradition: "You gave your good spirit to instruct them, and did not withhold your manna from their mouths, and gave them water for their thirst" (Neh 9:20). Isaiah 63:7-14 sets the spirit into a context replete with allusions to the exodus, wilderness wanderings, and conquest. An initial reference to "God's presence" (63:9) which delivered Israel is followed by three references to the spirit. "But they rebelled and grieved his holy spirit" (63:10) is rooted in the command not to "rebel" against the angel whom God appoints to go "in front of you, to guard you on the way . . . " (Exod 23:20; compare. Num 20:16). "Where is the one who put within them his holy spirit?" (63:11) is rooted in traditions that refer to an angel and God's own presence which "will go with you" (Exod 33:15; compare. Deut 4:37-38). "Like cattle that go down into the valley, the spirit of the LORD gave them rest" (63:14) is rooted in God's promise to Moses, "My presence will go with you, and I will give you rest" (Exod 33:14).

The placement of the spirit within Israel (Isa 63:11) corresponds to another postexilic text, Hag 2:4-5, which consoles the leaders of those recently returned to the promised land, "for I am with you, says the LORD of hosts, according to the promise I made you when you came out of Egypt: my spirit stands in your midst. Do not fear." There is no promise in the exodus tradition of the spirit understood as something to be poured (e.g., Isa 32:14-15; 44:1-3; Ezek 39:28-29; Joel 3:1-2) or used to anoint a leader (e.g., Isa 11:1-2; 42:1; 59:21; 61:1-2) or placed within to renew a people (e.g., Ezek 36:26-27). There is the promise of God's angel and presence to lead Israel (Exod 23:20-23; 32:34; 33:2, 14-15). Haggai's exhortation is a reaffirmation of God's presence in the postexilic community, though the fresh language he adopts is rooted in the exodus tradition, less in God's angel or presence, as in Isa 63, than in the pillar and cloud that stood at the entrance of the tent of presence (Exod 33:9-10). If Isa 63 addresses an uncertain future by amalgamating the traditions of the spirit and the angelic presence during the uncertain times of wilderness wanderings, Hag 2 addresses such uncertainty by amalgamating the spirit with the presence of the pillar and cloud—though these traditions were not inseparable.

Zechariah, which is probably a composite book, contains several references to the spirit. This book presents Zerubbabel as the sole figure responsible for the rebuilding of the temple, which was accomplished "not by might, not by power, but by my spirit" (4:6). This is reminiscent of Micah, though Micah's understanding of the spirit has been transformed. Micah drew a relationship between the spirit, his knowledge, and power, which suggests that he understood the spirit as a permanent endowment from birth. Zechariah draws a contrast between the spirit and power, which suggests that he understands the spirit as a fresh temporary endowment. In Zech 7:12, a typical postexilic review (e.g., Neh 9:30) recounts how the people hardened their hearts against the words that God "had sent by his spirit through the former prophets."

The latest prophetic text, where references to the spirit occur in the third person, is an anomaly. Successive episodes are modeled upon the Joseph novella, for Daniel, like Joseph, has a "spirit of god(s)" in him (Gen 41:38; Dan 5:14). As in Gen 41, so in the book of Daniel, the spirit is his own from birth, for this "spirit of God" is depicted as well as "an excellent spirit, knowledge, and understanding." "Excellent" barely captures the connotations of yattirah יַתִּירָה (quantity and quality, vitality and character combined). Daniel

is full to the brim with an exceptional spirit (5:12), with extraordinary wisdom (5:14). Through his faithful discipline, he has cultivated this reservoir full of an extraordinary spirit and stunning wisdom.

3. Writings

This association of the spirit and wisdom comes to fullest flower in the book of Job, which embodies the belief that the spirit is the source of wisdom and virtue. Though embittered, Job claims, "as long as my breath is in me and the spirit of God is in my nostrils, my lips will not speak falsehood, and my tongue will not utter deceit. . . . until I die I will not put away my integrity from me" (27:2-5; compare on the spirit and physical life, Pss 104:29-30; 146:3-4; Job 33:4, 6; 34:14-15; Ecc 12:10). The subtle implication of Job's claim, that the spirit of God has something to do with truth, comes to full flower in Elihu's claim to possess wisdom although he is young, "I am young in years, and you are aged. . . . But truly it is the spirit in a mortal, the breath of the Almighty that makes for understanding. It is not the old that are wise, nor the aged that understand what is right" (Job 32:6-9). Slightly later, he claims, "For I am full of words; the spirit within me constrains [lays siegeworks against] me. My heart is indeed like wine that has no vent; like new wineskins, it is ready to burst" (32:18-19). This parallel between the spirit and the human heart is kin to the story of Bezalel and Ps 51, both of which place heart and spirit in tandem positions and associate them with virtue. Further, the sense of bursting with spirit, having to hold back wise words, resembles the stories featuring Daniel, who is full of an extraordinarily wise spirit—though Elihu's claim to wisdom, in contrast to the description of Daniel, is pretension.

Psalm 51 sets the familiar parallel between a holy spirit and the human heart into a context of recreation: "Create in me a clean heart, O God, and put a new and right spirit within me. Do not cast me away from your presence, and do not take your holy spirit from me. Restore to me the joy of your salvation, and sustain in me a generous spirit" (Ps 51:10-12; Heb. 51:12-14). This prayer for purification is atypical; the psalmist begins, not with public temple worship or private devotion, but with creation, even the word, create, as in Gen 1:1. In this context, the words, "your holy spirit"—the earliest reference to "holy spirit" in Israelite literature, since Isa 63:11 is probably later—represent the spirit which the psalmist has from birth. This spirit parallels the heart, representing the essence of the psalmist that must be cleansed, instructed, and redirected. The relationship between these two core realities, heart and spirit, is apparent in the taut parallels between a "clean heart" and "right spirit" (51:10 [Heb. 51:12]), and particularly between a "broken spirit" and "broken . . . heart" (51:17 [Heb. 51:19]), where the same word, broken, describes in close succession both spirit and heart. Tainted now by sin, the psalmist prays that this spirit will be recreated, corrected, and made generous, even broken so that it can be made acceptable to God.

Several other postexilic texts associate the spirit with prophets (Neh 9:30; see Zech 7:12) and select individuals (1 Chr 12:18; 2 Chr 20:14; 24:20).

B. Early Jewish Literature

1. The Vitality of Early Judaism

A misperception that Judaism was the spiritually infertile soil in which Christianity took root has characterized much of NT scholarship. As recently as 1992, F. W. Horn cited alleged evidence of the universal consciousness of the loss of prophecy or loss of the spirit. This consensus arose from the piecing together of a diverse collection of literary texts, including: Ps 74:9; 1 Macc 4:46, 9:27, and 14:41; Josephus's *Ag. Ap.* 1.37-41; *2 Bar.* 85:3; *Prayer of Azariah* 15; and *t. Sotah* 13.2-4.

The focus of this interpretation is *t. Sotah* 13.2-4: "When Haggai, Zechariah, and Malachi, the last of the prophets, died, the Holy Spirit ceased in [from] Israel. Nevertheless, a Bath Qol was heard by them: It once happened that the sages entered a house in Jericho and they heard a Bath Qol saying, 'There is a man here who is worthy of the Holy Spirit, but there is no one in his generation righteous.' Thereupon, they set their eyes upon Hillel. . . ." The first difficulty that attends the use of this text to demonstrate the spiritual aridity of early Judaism is its late date; this belongs to the Tosefta, which was compiled as late as the 4th cent. CE.

More serious is the misinterpretation of this text, which is incorrectly interpreted to mean that, with the end of the succession of the canonical prophets, the Holy Spirit was replaced by a voice, the **bath qol** (בַּת קוֹל). The *bath qol* (lit. "daughter of the voice") informs the sages who are gathered together that Hillel is worthy of the Spirit but cannot receive it because of the evil generation to which he belongs. This interpretation violates the literary context of *t. Sotah* 13.2-4, which illustrates a straightforward principle: "When a righteous person comes into the world, good comes into the world . . . and retribution departs from the world (10:1)." *Tosefta Sotah* 13:2-4, understood according to this principle, indicates that the Holy Spirit is present because one person, Hillel, is worthy of it. This affirms the spirit's presence—not its absence (*see* HILLEL THE ELDER, HOUSE OF HILLEL).

This misrepresentation of Judaism, furthermore, disregards an abundance of texts that evince spiritual vitality. Only some of these are discussed below.

2. Dead Sea Scrolls and related pseudepigrapha

The Dead Sea Scrolls offer a range of contexts in which the holy spirit plays a significant role. The term, "holy spirit," first of all, is the human spirit that can be defiled. In CD VII, 4 and 5, 11-13, the term, "holy spirit," replaces the biblical term, **nefesh** (נֶפֶשׁ Lev 11:43;

20:25), to describe that which can be defiled. One wisdom author instructs, ". . . do not for any money exchange your holy spirit, for no price is adequate" (4Q416 2 II, 6-7). This belief that the spirit within can be "holy spirit" has affinities with the apocryphal book of Susannah, in which God raises the "holy spirit" of Daniel (see below).

The association of the spirit and prophecy reemerges in the Scrolls. Following from Neh 9:30 and Zech 7:12, 1QS VIII, 15-16 glances retrospectively at the prophets of Israel: "This is the study of the law which he commanded . . . in order to act in compliance with all that has been revealed from age to age, and according to what the prophets have revealed through his holy spirit." In Jubilees, Jacob blessed Levi and Judah when "a spirit of prophecy came down upon his mouth" (Jub 31:12; see 25:14). A section of the Enoch cycle of literature begins when Enoch commands, "Now, my son Methuselah . . . gather together to me all the sons of your mother; for a voice calls me, and the spirit is poured over me so that I may show you everything that shall happen to you forever" (*1 En.* 91:1).

The spirit is associated with initiation into the community. The hymn writer praises God for choosing "to purify me with your holy spirit" (1QH[a] VIII, 20). He thanks God that ". . . in your kindness toward humankind/you have enlarged his share with the spirit of your holiness./Thus, you make me approach your intelligence,/and to the degree that I approach/my fervour against all those who act wickedly . . ." (1QH[a] VI, 13-14). The eighth hymn is particularly rich with such language: ". . . to be strengthened by the spirit of holiness/to adhere to the truth of your covenant/to serve you in truth, with a perfect heart . . . to purify me with your holy spirit/to approach your will according to the extent of your kindnesses" (1QH[a] VIII, 15-20).

In the foundational *Community Rule*, the spirit is associated with purity, individual conversion, and initiation into the community. Although in 1QS IV, 21, purification occurs in the context of final judgment, purification occurs typically in the present: "by the spirit of holiness which links him with the truth he is cleansed of all his sins. And by the spirit of uprightness and of humility his sin is atoned" (1QS III, 7-8; see 1QS IX, 3-4). The spirit in this context of initiation (1QS I, 21–III, 12) also has a communal dimension: "And it is by the holy spirit of the community, in its truth, that he is cleansed of all his iniquities" (1 QS III, 6). The community even believed itself to be a spirit-filled temple: "When these exist in Israel in accordance with these rules in order to establish the spirit of holiness in truth eternal, in order to atone for the guilt of iniquity and for the unfaithfulness of sin, and for approval for the earth, without the flesh of burnt offerings and without the fats of sacrifice . . . in order to form a most holy community, and a house of the Community for Israel, those who walk in perfection" (1QS IX, 3-6).

The spirit effects communal purity in *Jub.* 1:20-21, where Moses, recalling Ps 51, intercedes for Israel, "O Lord, let your mercy be lifted up upon your people, and create for them an upright spirit. . . . Create a pure heart and a holy spirit for them. And do not let them be ensnared by their sin henceforth and forever." God responds (1:22-25) in turn by recalling Ps 51 and Ezek11:19-20: "And I shall create for them a holy spirit, and I shall purify them so that they will not turn away from following me from that day and forever. And their souls will cleave to me and to all my commandments."

Conceptions from the Isaiah corpus reemerge in 11Q13 II, 16-18), in which the herald of Isa 52:7 is identified with the anointed one in Dan 9:25. From this combination emerges a warrior figure who will destroy Belial and his entourage of evil spirits. Consequently, an emphasis upon power supplants the Isaianic emphasis upon justice.

A distinctive portion of the Community Rule is the so-called Teaching on the Two Spirits, which is spun from Gen 2:7: "God created humanity to rule the world and placed within him two spirits so that he would walk with them until the moment of his visitation: they are the spirits of truth and of deceit. From the spring of light stem the generations of truth, and from the source of darkness the generations of deceit. And in the hand of the Prince of Lights is dominion over all the sons of justice; they walk in paths of light. And in the hand of the Angel of Darkness is total dominion over the sons of deceit; they walk in paths of darkness" (3:17-21). Three levels of struggle coexist in this teaching: anthropological (two spirits struggling within); collective (two opposing generations); and cosmic (the Prince of Lights and the angel of Darkness). This teaching differs substantially from the Qumran Hymns, so there is a debate about its significance. Some scholars deem this central to Qumran theology; others think this was early on supplanted by teachings such as those of the Qumran Hymns.

Finally, the QUMRAN community believed that their interpretation of scripture was inspired. A hymn writer, perhaps the Teacher of Righteousness, traced this inspired interpretations to the spirit: "And I, the Instructor, have known you, my God, through the spirit which you gave (in)to me, and I have listened loyally to your wonderful secret through your holy spirit. You have opened within me knowledge of the mystery of your wisdom, the source of your power . . ." (1QH^a XX, 11-13). This hymn evokes powerful images of inspired knowledge and wisdom. By designating himself an "instructor," the hymn writer evokes images of the renowned scribe Ezra, who instructed Israel (Ezra 8:8, 13; 9:20). The words, "your holy spirit," are sandwiched between references to "your wonderful secret" and "knowledge of the mystery of your wisdom." The content of such inspired interpretation may be evident in such texts as the Habakkuk Commentary, in which ancient scripture applies directly to the recent past and immediate future of the community (*see* DEAD SEA SCROLLS).

3. Apocrypha

a. Sirach. Decades before the emergence of the Qumran community Ben Sira associated a spirit of wisdom with interpretation when he described the scribal calling: " . . . he will be filled by a spirit of understanding/he will pour out his own words of wisdom . . . He will make known the instruction of what he has learned . . ." (Sir 39:6-8). What is the source of this interpretation? It may be that a scribe succumbs to the extraordinary influence of an external spirit of wisdom; it is also possible that he cultivates the spirit within so that he is eventually filled with a spirit that is rich with wisdom. The latter is more likely, for Ben Sira repudiates visions and claims to revelation (Sir 34:1-2, 5a); disciplined study and life-experience alone are the legitimate sources of insight into scripture. This portrait of the scribe, therefore, shares affinities with the story of Daniel (see below), whose spirit increases in knowledge, or Bezalel, who is filled with spirit of God, with skill and intelligence, or the perspective of Elihu, who believes that the spirit or breath within brings wisdom, or perhaps even Micah, who is filled with spirit of the LORD, power, and intelligence.

b. Wisdom of Solomon. A wisdom author of a different sort reflected the context, not of Palestine, but of Egyptian Judaism, which was permeated by Stoicism. The author retains the traditional perspective on the spirit as a gift: "I prayed . . . and the spirit of wisdom came to me" (7:7); and "Who has learned your counsel, unless you . . . sent your holy spirit from on high" (9:17). Yet this spirit is Stoic in character: ". . . the spirit of the Lord has filled the world, and that which holds all things together knows what is said . . . " (1:7-8). In Stoicism, **pneuma** is the cohesive force of the universe. (See B.4 below.)

c. Judith. In 16:14, Gen 2:7, combined with Ps 104:29-30, influences the depiction of the spirit as that which creates humankind: "You sent forth your spirit, and it formed (built) them/there is none that can resist your voice." Intriguing in this metamorphosis is that the verb in Gen 2:7, "form," is supplanted by the verb, "build," from Gen 2:22. Consequently, the formation of woman, not man, becomes the paradigm of creation in the victory song of a Jewish heroine.

d. Susannah. In this novella, God raises up "the holy spirit" of a youthful Daniel (Sus 44-45). As in CD VII, 4; V, 11-13, and 4Q416 2 II, 6, the spirit which humans possess from birth is a holy spirit. Daniel's is pure; Qumran teachers caution that one's holy spirit must remain pure.

e. Fourth Ezra. This post-70 CE apocalypse contains a vivid depiction of inspiration. In response to Ezra's prayer for the holy spirit (*4 Ezra* 14:22), Ezra is given the promise that the lamp of understanding will remain lit throughout his experience, during which he dictates ninety-four books. The process itself begins as he drinks the cup given to him, and his heart pours forth understanding, and wisdom increases within him. Following his experience, it is said that these ninety-four books contain "the spring of understanding, the fountain of wisdom, and the river of knowledge" (14:47). This is an experience of inspiration in which the mind is made more alert, not less. This impression is confirmed by the significant detail that Ezra's understanding and wisdom overflowed because his own spirit retained its memory. From start to finish, then, Ezra composed ninety-four books through an experience of the Holy Spirit that heightened his intellectual acuity.

4. Philo

PHILO OF ALEXANDRIA, a Jewish philosopher, makes much of the inbreathing of Gen 2:7 by interpreting it as the impartation of the rational mind and the capacity for virtue. This represents the influence of Stoicism; Seneca believed that a holy spirit resides within, providing the capacity for virtue if it is well-tended (Philo, *Leg.* 1.31-42; Seneca, *Ep.* 41). The Stoic character of the spirit comes to fullest flower in Philo's interpretation of the spirit that inspired Bezalel (Exod 31:3) as "susceptible of neither severance nor division, diffused in its fullness everywhere and through all things" (*Gig.* 27). Alexander of Aphrodisias, summarizing the view of the renowned Stoic thinker, Chrysippus, writes that **pneuma** is that "which wholly pervades it [the cosmos] and by which the universe is made coherent and kept together . . ." (*Mixt.* 216.14-17). See STOICS, STOICISM.

The association of the spirit and prophecy also comes to full flower in Philo's commentaries, though again with a decidedly Greco-Roman flair. In his interpretation of the word ekstasis (ἐκστάσις) in LXX Gen 15:12, he writes, "This is what regularly befalls the fellowship of the prophets. The mind is evicted at the arrival of the divine Spirit, but when that departs the mind returns to its tenancy" (*Her.* 265; see *Spec.* 1.65; 4.49; *QG* 3.9). Though Moses would differ from the prophetic race by his ability to speak without losing control of his mind, he too experienced "that divine possession in virtue of which he is chiefly and in the strict sense considered a prophet" (*Mos.* 2.191).

An intensification of prophetic inspiration is evident in an interpretation of Balaam that Philo shares with Josephus, though probably independently. Both emphasize the total passivity of Balaam. In Philo's interpretation, the angel predicts: ". . . I shall prompt the needful words without your mind's consent, and direct your organs of speech as justice and convenience require. I shall guide the reins of speech, and, though you understand it not, employ your tongue for each prophetic

utterance" (*Mos.* 1.274; see Num 22:35). This prediction is fulfilled when Balaam "advanced outside, and straightway became possessed, and there fell upon him the truly prophetic spirit which banished utterly from his soul his art of wizardry" (*Mos.* 1.277). Balaam, in Josephus' version, explains to Balak: ". . . that spirit gives utterance to such language and words as it will, whereof we are all unconscious" (*Ant.* 4.120). This radical form of prophetic passivity is a novelty of the Greco-Roman era; it approximates a view held by of Ammonius, in Plutarch's *On the Defection of Oracles*, in which "the god himself after the manner of ventriloquists . . . enters into the bodies of his prophets and prompts their utterances, employing their mouths and voices as instruments" (414E).

On other occasions, prophetic inspiration takes on the characteristics of a magnificent rhetor. Abraham, though not of noble lineage, "whenever he was possessed, everything in him changed to something better, eyes, complexion, stature, carriage, movements, voice. For the divine spirit which was breathed upon him from on high made its lodging in his soul, and invested his body with singular beauty, his voice with persuasiveness, and his hearers with understanding." In such a state, he was "ranked among the prophets" (*Virt.* 217-19).

Philo even attributes his own interpretation of scripture to prophetic inspiration. In *Spec.* 3:1-6, he is wafted on the winds of knowledge through the ascent of his mind; during these episodes, he peers into the deepest meaning of Moses' writings. In *Somn.* 2.252, Philo claims to be taught by his customary friend, the spirit. In this autobiographical reflection, the immediate task is to solve an exegetical dilemma, such as why the biblical text refers to two, rather than to one, cherubim. The conundrum is solved when the spirit teaches him with instruction that is directed toward his alert mind. (See also *Cher.* 27-29; *Somn.* 1.164-65; and *Fug.* 53-58). The word, "customary," with which Philo describes the divine spirit, is evocative of Socrates' daemon, which Plato refers to as "the customary prophetic inspiration of the daemon" (*Apol.* 40A), "the daemonic and customary sign" (*Phaedr.* 242B), and "my customary daemonic sign" (*Euthyd.* 272e; see further *Gen. Socr.* 589d). The affinities between the renowned Socrates and Philo, in Philo's estimation at least, include an untroubled mind which is taught by the presence of a customary friend.

This description of the divine spirit along the lines of Socrates' daemon, taken together with the easy identification of the angel with the divine spirit in Philo and Josephus' interpretation of Balaam, points toward an understanding of the spirit as an angelic presence. Isaiah 63:7-14 and Hag 2:4-5, furthermore, anticipated this by amalgamating the spirit with the exodus traditions of the angel of God's presence and the pillars of cloud and fire.

These writings evince a remarkable flexibility in the interpretation of pneuma by a Jewish author during the Greco-Roman era. The spirit can be the quintessential expression of Stoic pneuma, a force that possesses akin to Greco-Roman prophets, an angelic presence not unlike Socrates' customary daemon, and the source of inspiration that prompts the philosophical ascent of the mind (*Spec.* 3.1-6).

5. Flavius Josephus

The taut association of the spirit with prophecy is evident in Josephus' revision of Israelite literature, his *Jewish Antiquities*, in which he adds references to prophecy in scriptural contexts that refer only to the spirit (*see* JOSEPHUS, FLAVIUS). For example, while 1 Sam 16:13 recounts that "the spirit of the LORD came mightily upon David from that day forward," Josephus adds that David, "when the divine spirit had removed to him, began to prophesy" (*Ant.* 6.166). Zedekiah, the false prophet, asks Micaiah in LXX 1 Kgs 22:24, "What sort of spirit of the Lord speaks in you?" Josephus relates the spirit to prophecy: "But you shall know whether he is really a true prophet and has the power of the divine spirit" (*Ant.* 8.408). Although there are less references to the spirit in his version of the book of Daniel, Josephus still refers to Daniel as "one of the greatest prophets" (*Ant.* 10.266).

Though with less intensity than Philo, Josephus claims to be an inspired interpreter of scripture. In a fascinating instance of self-exoneration, he explains why he surrendered to Rome: "and Josephus . . . was an interpreter of dreams and skilled in divining the meaning of ambiguous utterances of the Deity . . . not ignorant of the prophecies in the sacred books. At that hour he was inspired to read their meaning . . ." (*J.W.* 3.351–53).

6. Pseudepigrapha

The association of the spirit with prophecy characterizes many Jewish pseudepigrapha. These are essential documents, even though the dates of origin of some of them and the question of whether they were originally Jewish documents remain a matter of debate.

One statement of a sibyl, in what was undoubtedly a Jewish literary text, the Greco-Roman counterpart of the Jewish prophet, sounds like the Stoic affirmation of Wis. Sol. 1:6-7: "Nor is anything left unaccomplished that God so much as puts in mind/for the spirit of God which knows no falsehood is throughout the world" (*Sib. Or.* 3.696-701).

Replete with spirit-references is an imaginative retelling of Israelite scripture, *Liber Antiquitatum Biblicarum*. The spirit, not surprisingly, inspires prophecy: Miriam is the recipient of a dream in which the birth of Moses is predicted (*L.A.B.* 9:10); Deborah is said to have predicted Sisera's demise by the inspiration of the spirit (31:9); to the military accomplishments of the first judge, Othniel (Judg 3:9-10), are added a prophetic experience (*L.A.B.* 28:6): "when they had sat down, a holy spirit came upon Kenaz . . . and he began to prophesy." Even an abbreviated account of Saul's pursuit of David contains an extra-biblical reference to prophecy: "And (a) spirit abided in Saul, and he prophesied" (*L.A.B.* 62:2).

As in the writings of Philo and Josephus, inspired prophecy in *L.A.B.* begins to look less like Israelite prophecy and more like the inspiration associated with Delphi and a variety of Greco-Roman prophetic figures. The inspiration of Joshua in *L.A.B.* 20:3, for example, melds biblical and Greco-Roman ingredients. To Deut 34:9*a*, "Joshua son of Nun was full of the spirit of wisdom," *L.A.B.* adds, "his mind was afire and his spirit was moved, and he said . . ." (20:3). These added elements reflect the hallmarks of enthusiasm in a classic text, Cicero's *Div.* 1.114, where the winged soul is "inflamed and aroused," or Plutarch's *Def. orac.* 432e-f, in which the "soul becomes hot and fiery, and throws aside the caution that human intelligence lays upon it."

The novella, *Joseph and Aseneth*, spins from Gen 41:45 a tale of love that culminates in Aseneth's conversion to Israelite faith. Prior to their marriage, "they kissed each other for a long time . . . And Joseph kissed Aseneth and gave her spirit of life, and he kissed her the second time and gave her spirit of wisdom, and he kissed her the third time and gave her spirit of truth" (19:10-11).

Depictions of the anticipated messianic deliverer that are rooted in the Isaianic vision emerge in other pseudepigrapha. *Psalms of Solomon* 17:37 preserves the association of the spirit and wisdom: "And he will not weaken in his days, (relying) upon his God/for God made him powerful in the holy spirit/and wise in the counsel of understanding/with strength and righteousness." So too does the author of the *Testament of Levi:* "And the glory of the Most High shall burst forth upon him./And the spirit of understanding and sanctification/shall rest upon him . . . /And he shall open the gates of paradise/he shall remove the sword that has threatened since Adam/and he will grant to the saints to eat of the tree of life./The spirit of holiness shall be upon them./And Beliar shall be bound by him./And he shall grant to his children the authority to trample on wicked spirits" (*T. Levi* 18:7, 10-12). *First Enoch* 37–71, the only portion of the Ethiopic Enoch cycle of literature not discovered among the Dead Sea Scrolls, contains a depiction of the Elect One that is reminiscent of Isa 11. In contrast to 11Q13, emphasis lies not upon power but upon wisdom: "The Elect One stands before the Lord of the Spirits; his glory is forever and ever and his power is unto all generations. In him dwells the spirit of wisdom, the spirit which gives thoughtfulness, the spirit of knowledge and strength, and the spirit of those who have fallen asleep in righteousness" (*1 En.* 49:2-3).

A Jewish apocalypse composed after 70 CE, the *Syriac Apocalypse of Baruch*, recalls Gen 1:2, though with greater attention to the process of creation. Baruch prays, ". . . you who created the earth, the one who fixed the firmament by the word and fastened the height of heaven by the spirit . . ." (21:4). God responds, "For my spirit creates the living" (23:5). In both statements, the spirit is an active participant in creation, as in Jud 16:14.

7. Mishnah

The purifying power of the spirit is central to *Sotah* 9:15: "Heedfulness leads to cleanliness, and cleanliness leads to purity, and purity to abstinence, and abstinence leads to holiness, and holiness leads to humility, and humility leads to the shunning of sin, and the shunning of sin leads to saintliness, and saintliness leads to [the gift of] the Holy Spirit, and the Holy Spirit leads to the resurrection of the dead." The gift of the spirit does not, however, effect purification; it is instead a gift given in response to purification, holiness, and humility.

8. Summary

In light of this sampling of texts, it would be injudicious to conclude that early Christianity emerged from the arid soil of Judaism. Among the many directions in which belief in the spirit of God was taken by Judaism during the Greco-Roman era, several rise to the surface: 1) the divine inbreathing of Gen 2:7 is interpreted in creative ways; 2) the human spirit continues to be understood as a "holy spirit;" 3) the spirit is associated with the phenomenon of prophecy to a degree that far outstrips Israelite prophecy; 4) such prophecy takes on Greco-Roman hues; 5) a new conception gains momentum—the inspired interpretation of scripture.

C. New Testament

Early Christian authors shared much in common with respect to their beliefs in the holy spirit, while many left their distinctive marks as well. This portion of the entry examines both.

1. Common features

a. The Spirit received. The simple expression, "receive the spirit," had wide currency among early Christian communities. Three times the Fourth Gospel refers in shorthand to "receiving the spirit" (7:39; 14:17; 20:22). In the final occurrence, Jesus, raised from the dead, commissions the disciples and, as in Gen 2:7, "breathed into them" and said, "Receive (the) holy spirit." The disciples are created anew, as in Gal 6:15, in which the phrase, "new creation," pithily gathers together the theological pieces of Galatians, particularly those claims to the spirit that link the paragraphs of the letter, from 3:1 to 6:15.

The tenor of Acts is even more palpably shaped by this phrase. At pivotal junctures—PENTECOST (2:33, 38), the extension of the gospel to Samaria (8:15, 17, 19), the outpouring of the spirit to Gentiles in the wake of Cornelius' vision (10:47), and the reception of the spirit by John the Baptist's disciples, who have not yet heard of the holy spirit (19:2)—this phrase tersely conveys the experience of filling with the Holy Spirit. These are profound transitions that were promised at the story's beginning: "But you will receive power when the Holy Spirit has come upon you; and you will be my witnesses in Jerusalem, in all Judea and Samaria, and to the ends of the earth" (Acts 1:8).

Paul himself employed this expression in Rom 8:15; 1 Cor 2:12; Gal 3:2 (see 2 Cor 11:4).

b. The Spirit given. Early Christian authors made frequent use of some form of the formula, "God gave the spirit in us" (e.g., Acts 5:32; 15:8; Rom 11:8; 2 Cor 1:22; 5:5; 2 Tim 1:7; 1 John 3:24; 4:13). The language stems probably from Ezek 36:26-27, although the odd occurrence of the preposition "into" rather than "in" in 1 Thess 4:8 almost certainly stems from Ezek 37:5, 14. The phrase, "God gave the Spirit," was not an unfamiliar expression; it is adopted as well in hymns in the Dead Sea Scrolls (1QH^a IV, 17; V, 25; VIII, 19-20; XX, 11-12). Since the gift of the spirit is to individuals, it is questionable whether Ezekiel's vision of national recreation still remains in view; perhaps the language is merely a remnant.

c. The Spirit as teacher and guide. Some Israelite and Jewish authors, we observed, tended to attribute somewhat more personality to the spirit. Isaiah 63:7-14 remembers that "the spirit of the LORD gave them rest" (63:14), and Haggai encourages, "my spirit stands in your midst. Do not fear" (Hag 2:5). Further, the psalmist prays, "Let your good spirit lead me on a level path" (Ps 143:10), while Nehemiah recalls, "You gave your good spirit to instruct them" (Neh 9:20). Josephus and Philo, in independent ways, identify the angel that stood before Balaam (Num 22:25) with the divine spirit that would come upon him (24:2); this is an angelic spirit (Philo, *Mos.* 1.274–77; Josephus, *Ant.* 4.108). Philo's customary friend resembles Socrates' customary sign, the daemon (*Somn.* 2.252).

Similar perceptions of the spirit as an individual figure characterize many early Christian references to the spirit. The spirit teaches (Luke 12:12 John 14:25-26, 16:13; 1 Cor 2:13), speaks (John 16:13; Acts 8:29; 10:19; 11:12; 13:2; Heb 3:7 [=Ps 95:7-11]), testifies (Acts 20:23 [through prophets]; Jn 15:26 [along with the disciples]; Heb 10:15 [through scripture]), leads (Gal 5:18; Rom 8:14), reveals (Luke 2:27; 1 Cor 2:6-16; Eph 3:5; Heb 9:8), forbids (Acts 16:6-7), predicts (1 Tim 4:1), searches God's depths (1 Cor 2:11), and participates in prayer by crying Abba (Gal 4:6) and interceding with wrenching sighs for those in a state of weakness (Rom 8:26-27). The spirit also functions as a leader by sending out apostles (Acts 13:2-4), appointing overseers (Acts 20:28), and distributing spiritual gifts (1 Cor 12:11).

There are no certain grounds for attributing these actions to a trinitarian view of the holy spirit. Although nascent trinitarianism may be briefly evident in the formulae in Matt 28:18-20; 1 Cor 12:4-6; and 2 Cor 13:13, these activities emerge from Israelite scripture, in which the spirit guides, leads, and teaches, and from the world of Judaism, in which the angelic spirit inspires prophecy or the interpretation of scripture.

d. Opposition to the Holy Spirit. The indictment, "But they rebelled and grieved his holy spirit" (Isa 63:10) roots opposition to the Holy Spirit in the exodus tradition, in which Israel is ordered not to "rebel" against the angel who leads and guards Israel following the exodus (Exod 23:20; compare Num 20:16). The unfortunate reality of opposition to the Holy Spirit emerges as well in several early Christian texts. Ephesians 4:30 commands, "and do not grieve the Holy Spirit of God." The context, which urges the need for gracious words rather than bitterness, wrangling, and slander, provides a poignant counterpoint to the Israelites, who complained bitterly of their plight.

In the Synoptic Gospels, Jesus exorcises a demon in a mute (and blind, in Matt 12:22) man. Some are amazed; others accuse him of alignment with Beelzebul, the ruler of demons. Jesus responds that a house divided cannot stand, that Satan cannot disarm himself, and that he exorcises by the spirit (Matt 12:28) or finger of God (Luke 12:10; see Exod 8:15 [Heb.]). In Mark and Matthew's Gospels, the puzzling statement that blasphemy against the Holy Spirit comprises the unpardonable sin occurs directly after this confrontation (Mark 3:28-30; Matt 12:31-32). The implication is that the Jewish leaders who accuse Jesus of being aligned with Satan are blaspheming the Holy Spirit. Luke, in contrast, places the word about blasphemy in another context altogether that has to do with testimony under constraint rather than Jesus' ministry (12:8-12). It is not the Jewish leaders who blaspheme, as in the gospels of Mark and Matthew; it is believers brought before the authorities who will be pressed to blaspheme the Holy Spirit (12:8-10). For those who do not, there is no need to worry: ". . . for the Holy Spirit will teach you at that very hour what you ought to say" (12:11-12).

Opposition to the spirit occurs twice in Acts. Peter accuses Ananias of being filled with Satan and lying to the Holy Spirit because he and Sapphira held back some of the money they received from selling their property (Acts 5:1-3). The verb, "hold back" (nosphizein νοσφίζειν), occurs in the Septuagintal translation of Hebrew scripture only in the story of Achan, whose holding back of booty had a dreadful impact upon Israel's fortunes at war (Josh 7:1). This parallel points to the communal dimension of the Spirit; to deceive the community is to lie against its driving force, the Holy Spirit.

Stephen, following the lead of Neh 9:29-30 and Zech 7:12, indicts his "stiff-necked" hearers for "forever opposing the Holy Spirit, just as your ancestors used to do" (Acts 7:51). Stephen, who is "filled with the Holy Spirit" (7:55), becomes another instance of Israel's recalcitrance. Because "they could not withstand the wisdom and the Spirit with which he spoke" (6:10), they stoned him.

The possibility of grieving the Holy Spirit extends to the community addressed in Heb 10:28-29. Slightly earlier, the author expressed his view that those who had been enlightened, tasty the heavenly gift, "shared in the Holy Spirit," and tasted the word of God would have enormous difficulty repenting (6:4-6). In a similar vein, he reproaches those who persist in sin "after having received the knowledge of the truth." Such believers have nothing but judgment ahead, no sacrifice for sin, because they "have spurned the Son of God, profaned the blood of the covenant by which they were sanctified, and outraged [enybrisas ἐνυβρίσας] the Spirit of grace." The inclusion of the Spirit in both texts alongside enlightenment, Jesus, and his blood, is an indication of how integral the Spirit is to the process of initiation and the prospect of future salvation.

Although the Holy Spirit, therefore, can be received and fill believers, it can also be the object of resistance. For Matthew, Luke, and Stephen, the Jewish leaders oppose the Spirit. Yet the gospel of Luke, Acts, Ephesians, and Hebrews together indicate that followers of Jesus also have the potential to oppose the Spirit—to blaspheme, to lie to it, to grieve it, and to outrage it.

e. Prayer. Luke associates the Holy Spirit with prayer and praise. Elizabeth and Zechariah praise God when they are filled with the Holy Spirit (1:41-42, 67). Jesus receives the Spirit at his baptism while he is praying (3:21-22). When the seventy return from their mission, he rejoices in the Holy Spirit and addresses God in prayer (10:21). In instructions about prayer, Jesus asks, ". . . how much more will the heavenly Father give the Holy Spirit to those who ask him?" (11:13).

This Lukan promise of the Spirit is fulfilled, not during Jesus' own lifetime, but after his resurrection—and then in good measure—when believers are filled with the Holy Spirit and begin to recite God's powerful acts (Acts 2:1-13; see 10:44-48). Following prayer, the newly founded community prays for boldness and is immediately filled with the Spirit (4:31). Later, Peter receives the programmatic vision of Cornelius while he prays at lunchtime (10:9-16).

Prayer in the Holy Spirit is also a topic in NT letters. Paul explains that the Holy Spirit intercedes with groans beyond words in the process of agonizing prayer, in which a believer does not know how he or she ought to pray (Rom 8:26-27). The author of Ephesians urges readers to alertness and persistence as they pray on behalf of all the saints. The author of Jude recalls the predictions of the apostles, that those "devoid of the Spirit" would be lustful and divisive, and he encourages his readers, in contrast, to build themselves up "on your most holy faith" and to "pray in the Holy Spirit" (20). It is not possible to determine conclusively whether prayer in the Spirit refers to the sort of mindless prayer in tongues, as in 1 Cor 14:13-15, or to comprehensible prayer; prayer in Ephesians 6 seems comprehensible, for it concerns intercession for the saints.

f. Prophecy. The association of prophecy and the Holy Spirit occurs in many early Christian texts, though prophecy has a variety of meanings. At times, inspired prophecy refers to Israelite literature. Paul says, in Acts 28:25, that the Holy Spirit spoke through the prophet Isaiah. The author of 1 Peter offers a telling description of the phenomenon of prophecy; prophets searched salvation beforehand, "inquiring about the person or time that the Spirit of Christ within them indicated when it testified in advance to the sufferings destined for Christ and the subsequent glory" (1:11). How the spirit of Christ, before his appearance on earth, could speak through the prophets, is unclear, though the author moves quickly to more traditional language in the following clauses (1 Pet 1:12), when he attributes such predictions to the Holy Spirit, as does 2 Pet 1:21.

Luke portrays John the Baptist as a figure who, filled with the Spirit from before birth, comes in the spirit and power of Elijah (Luke 1:15, 17). Zechariah, his father, prophesies once he is filled with the Spirit (Luke 1:67). Jesus himself, according to Luke, claims the endowment of Isa 61, and Matthew interprets Jesus' power to heal as a fulfillment of Isa 42:1-4.

Prophecy is paradigmatic in Acts. In his explanation of the events of Pentecost, Peter amends the quotation of Joel that describes the outpouring of the Spirit by adding, "and they shall prophesy" (Acts 2:17-18). Various prophets show up in the ensuing narratives: an Agabus who predicts a famine (11:28), and another Agabus who predicts Paul's imprisonment (21:11; see 20:23). It may be that prophets, in the context of prayer and fasting, are those through whom the spirit instructs Paul and Barnabas to begin their journeys (13:1-2).

Paul himself offers advice on SPIRITUAL GIFTS and urges the Corinthians to pursue the gift of prophecy because it is comprehensible, edifying for the church, rather than speaking in tongues, which is not (1 Cor 14). He recognizes that prophecies may be false and, consequently, instructs the Thessalonians not to quench the Spirit, by which he means that the community should neither despise prophecy nor accept it without discernment (1 Thess 5:19-21).

Other letters, some possibly post-Pauline, also value prophecy. Ephesians 3:5 regards latter-day apostles and prophets as recipients of a revelation that eluded past generations. A swirl of prophetic activity surrounds Timothy's call. The author charges him to wage the good fight "in accordance with the prophecies made earlier about you" (1 Tim 1:18). He is instructed not to neglect the gift "which was given you through

prophecy with the laying on of hands by the council of elders" (1 Tim 4:14).

Such discernment remains the critical issue in other letters. Although the problem of false prophets emerges in Matthew's Gospel (7:21-23), in the community of 1 John it becomes pivotal in the battle for the truth because a real-life crisis is still fresh. To navigate this crisis, the author commends a principle of discernment: "Beloved, do not believe every spirit, but test the spirits to see whether they are from God; for many false prophets have gone out into the world. By this you know the Spirit of God: every spirit that confesses that Jesus Christ has come in the flesh is from God, and every spirit that does not confess Jesus is not from God. And this is the spirit of the antichrist, of which you have heard that it is coming; and now it is already in the world" (4:1-3). Though minimal, this is an irrefutable, verifiable principle of discernment that is related to the confession that Jesus Christ came in the flesh. Its function is similar to the confession, "Jesus is Lord" and Paul's contention that "no one can say, 'Jesus is Lord' except by the Holy Spirit" (1 Cor 12:3). Amidst a variety of itinerant prophets and prophetic messages, and the spirits that inspire them, it is difficult to discern the truth, and so this is the dividing line, the test of truth: Jesus is from God and in the flesh.

The author of 2 Peter faces a similar situation and responds by condemning the false prophets "who arose among the people" (2:1), though he offers no principle of discernment. Instead he argues that false prophets misinterpret prophecy (Israelite and perhaps early Christian). This is anathema "because no prophecy ever came by human will, but men and women moved by the Holy Spirit spoke from God" (2 Pet 1:19-2:3). If prophets were inspired, the interpreters must be as well—though the content of that interpretation is left inchoate.

The problem of distinguishing between true and false prophets came to dominate the skyline or the early church, so much so that the *Didache* offers practical markers for identifying false prophets, e.g., staying more than three days, asking for money, not living as they taught, ordering a meal and actually eating it.

The problem is raw as well in the book of Revelation, which is designated a prophecy (22:7, 19; 1:3, based, perhaps by way of oral tradition, upon the blessing Luke 11:28), and in which John is, like Ezekiel, commanded to eat a scroll, that is, to prophesy to the nations (10:8-10). Even the introduction of the four visions by the same phrase "in the spirit" recollects the book of Ezekiel (e.g., 3:12).

True prophets populate the pages of this self-proclaimed prophecy. Some are OT prophets (10:7; 11:18). Others are joined with saints and apostles (18:20; see 22:6-9). The essence of true prophecy is defined in Rev 19:10: "For the testimony of Jesus is the spirit of prophecy." Prophecy may entail visions—revelations—and prophetic insight, but at its core, the spirit of prophecy inspires testimony on behalf of Jesus, witness in the face of persecution by all believers rather than by a specific group of prophets. This testimony concerns the resurrection of Jesus, if other NT texts provide a clue: 1 Cor 12:3; 1 John 4:2-3; John 15:26-27. The book of Revelation alleges to comprise, then, an inspired prophetic testimony to the risen Christ.

2. Canonical Gospels

The presence of the holy spirit in the life of Jesus is attested by all four canonical gospels and appears in every alleged source (Q, Mark, so-called L and M material, and in both the narrative and farewell discourses of the Fourth Gospel). This material deals both with the Holy Spirit in the experience of Jesus and the relationship of the Holy Spirit to Jesus' followers.

a. The experience of Jesus. A later summation from the book of Acts offers a salient précis of Jesus' experience of the holy spirit: " . . . how God anointed Jesus of Nazareth with the Holy Spirit and with power; how he went about doing good and healing all who were oppressed by the devil, for God was with him" (Acts 10:38). The canonical gospels align neatly with this summary, which identifies three principal points of reference for the Holy Spirit in Jesus' public ministry: 1) anointing (his baptism, testing, and early preaching); 2) doing good; and 3) exorcisms.

Despite some differences, the gospels are unified in identifying the presence of the Holy Spirit with the initiatory experiences of Jesus. a) John the Baptist predicts or recognizes that Jesus will baptize with the Holy Spirit (Mark 1:8 John 1:32-33); this prediction in Luke and Matthew has an added note of judgment through the addition of "and fire"—Jesus will baptize "with the Holy Spirit and fire" (Matt 3:11/Luke 3:16; see Isa 4:4); b) The Holy Spirit descends upon Jesus like a dove (in bodily form, according to Luke) during or after his water BAPTISM by John the Baptist (Mark 1:10-11/Matt 3:16-17/Luke 3:21-22/John 1:29-34); c) The Holy Spirit accompanies Jesus in the wilderness during a time of testing (Mark 1:12-13/Matt 4:1-11/Luke 4:1-13). In Mark, the Spirit drives Jesus out violently to live peaceably among the animals, perhaps in contrast to the primeval pair, who were driven out of Eden into a world of enmity with beasts. Matthew and Luke's reference to forty days of testing recalls Israel's emergence from Egypt and their forty years of wilderness wandering. This may account for Luke's description of Jesus as "led by the Spirit in the wilderness," rather than being driven by the Spirit into the wilderness (Luke 4:1-2; see Isa 63:7-14). Further, in Luke's gospel, Jesus enters this period of testing full of the Spirit (4:1); he returns filled with the Spirit, and he teaches in the synagogues of Galilee (4:14), where he claims the Spirit in his work of preaching good news to the poor (4:18-19).

The words at Jesus' baptism, "my beloved," offer a subtle reminiscence of the Isaianic servant (Isa 42:1). Luke continues this appeal to the later oracles of Isaiah with Jesus' first public sermon, in which he claims such an anointing with a quotation of Isa 61:1-2: "The Spirit of the Lord is upon me, because he has anointed me to bring good news to the poor . . ." The text continues with release to prisoners, sight for the blind, freedom for the oppressed (see Isa 58:6), and proclamation of God's favorable year.

Matthew also connects the baptism of Jesus with the public doing of good, though in a typically Matthean manner. After a summary statement about Jesus' curing all of the sick, Matthew concludes with the characteristic formula, "This was to fulfill what had been spoken through the prophet Isaiah," and a quotation from Isa 42:1-4, 9, which begins, "Here is my servant, whom I have chosen, my beloved, with whom my soul is well pleased. I will put my Spirit upon him . . ." (See also Jesus' response to John the Baptist's messengers in Matt 11:2-6; Luke 7:18-23.) Both Matthew and Luke, then, in part through allusions to the so-called servant passages of Isaiah, draw a taut association between the anointing of Jesus by the Holy Spirit at his baptism and his ongoing vocation of doing good.

Controversy following an exorcism in Matt 12:22 leads to Jesus' statement, "But if it is by the Spirit of God that I cast out demons, then the kingdom of God has come to you" (Matt 12:28). Luke's version, surprisingly in light of his interest in the Spirit, lacks a reference to the spirit: "But if it is by the finger of God that I cast out the demons ..." (Luke 11:20). The occurrence of the word, finger, rather than Spirit of God, draws the reader directly to the confrontation brought about by the plagues in Exod 8:19; Heb. 8:15: "And the magicians said to Pharaoh, 'This is the finger of God!'" This reminiscence suits Luke's New Exodus theme perfectly.

b. The experience of believers. In contrast to the pivotal role the holy spirit plays in Jesus' initiation, his doing good, and his authority to exorcise, far less in the Gospels serves to explain the function of the Holy Spirit in the life of believers. Jesus' followers, in fact, do not receive the Holy Spirit during his lifetime. Although the period prior to his birth exhibits, according to the birth narratives, a flurry of Spirit-induced activity (Luke 1:15, 17, 41-42, 67; 2:25, 27, 28-35, 36-38 [Anna a prophet]; Matt 1:18, 20), only after his resurrection are Jesus' followers said to receive the Holy Spirit, and this in a variety of ways. Mark's longer ending does not mention the Holy Spirit, but Jesus predicts signs that suggest the spirit's presence, including new tongues, picking up snakes and drinking poison unharmed, and healing the sick (Mark 16:17-18). In Matthew's final lines, Jesus commands his disciples to baptize in the name of the father, son, and holy spirit (Matt 28:16-20).

In Luke's Gospel, even when the disciples return from a remarkable mission during which the seventy exercised authority over snakes, scorpions, Satan, and spirits, the holy spirit is associated not with their feats but with Jesus' response of rejoicing: "At that same hour Jesus rejoiced in the Holy Spirit and said, 'I thank you, Father . . .'" (Luke 10:17-21; similarly 1:41-42; 1:67; 2:28-35). Jesus' followers must wait for power from on high (24:49), and this does not occur until Acts (1:4-8; 2:1-13).

In the Fourth Gospel, Jesus talks to Nicodemus about the spirit and new birth (3:5-8), to the Samaritan woman about living water that wells up (4:10-14; see 7:37-39), and to the disciples about his own words as spirit and life (6:63). In a narrative aside, the author notes, "Now he said this about the Spirit, which believers in him were to receive; for as yet there was no Spirit, because Jesus was not yet glorified" (7:39). Only after the resurrection, however, does Jesus enter a locked room and "breathe into" (see Gen 2:7; 1 Kgs 17:17-24; Ezek 37:1-10) his disciples, with the words, "Receive the Holy Spirit" (20:19-23).

The principal promise of the Holy Spirit in the Gospels concerns public testimony, though each Gospel gives the promise its own emphasis. Mark's single promise occurs in a context in which Jesus predicts that families will be splintered by betrayal, in which only the one who endures will be saved (13:12-13). In this highly-charged context, Jesus says, "When they bring you to trial and hand you over, do not worry beforehand about what you are to say; for it is not you who speak, but the Holy Spirit" (13:11). This is not a vague promise of joy; it is a promise to a desperate, persecuted and betrayed people who stand before governors and kings in the service of the gospel (13:9-10). They may not survive, but they can endure faithfully to the end.

Matthew preserves a similar saying: "for it is not you who speak, but the Spirit of your Father speaking through you" (10:20). This is the true father, in contrast to the father who betrays his own child to the authorities (10:21).

Luke gives this promise gravity by placing it directly after the saying about blasphemy against the Holy Spirit. Those who do not blaspheme but remain faithful need not worry about what they will say in defense, ". . . for the Holy Spirit will teach you at that very hour what you ought to say" (12:11-12). This emphasis upon teaching corresponds to a key theme of Luke's christology: the importance of Jesus as teacher.

3. Paul

a. Issues of method. Several issues of method attend the interpretation of Paul's letters: 1) His pneumatology was in flux and subject to development; for example, although 1 Thessalonians, an early letter, prizes the spirit, many characteristic features, such as the contrast between flesh and spirit, are missing; 2) External sources of Paul's pneumatology are not easily identifiable. Hypotheses include Greco-Roman mystery religions, popular Greco-Roman philosophical traditions, rabbinic Judaism, nascent Gnosticism, and Ezek 36-37, with its post-biblical interpreters; 3) The importance of Paul's experience is debated. The role of the third-person narrative, Acts 9, and possible autobiographical reflection in 2 Cor 4:4-6, are especially debatable; 4) The relationship between Pauline pneumatology and the book of Acts is difficult to ascertain. Some scholars drive a wedge between Paul's pneumatology, which is believed to focus upon an initial soteriological act, and Luke's pneumatology, which is said to catalyze a subsequent experience related to mission. This alleged borderline is faulty, however, for the boundary between new creation and continuing life in the spirit is porous in Paul's letters. Notwithstanding these thorny issues, it is possible to identify dominant Pauline emphases.

b. Characteristic contrasts. Although Paul adopts the early church's language of "receiving" the spirit, he typically employs his own "not-but" pattern. In this way, Paul invests traditional language of receiving the Spirit with a concrete and clear statement of specific consequences.

Reception of the Spirit is not identified by euphoria, ecstasy, or a spectacular gift, but by a divine humility, a wisdom that flows from a gospel of Christ crucified (1 Cor 2:12). This is a new creation in which the truly spiritual (hoi pneumatikoi οἱ πνευματικοί), as opposed to the merely human (hoi psychikoi οἱ ψυχικοί), are not the world's privileged rulers, with their own coterie of sycophants, but the weak of the world who sacrifice status for unity, who forego prestige for the power of the cross (1 Cor 1:18-3:23). The concrete context of the spiritual life, then, is framed by the ignominious death and reprehensible weakness of Jesus rather than the apparent victory and strength of alleged rulers.

Reception of the Spirit drives a wedge as well between works of Torah and faith. In trying to wrest the Galatians from an apparently superfluous adherence to Torah and the practice of circumcision without a thorough transformation of the heart, Paul raises a series of rhetorical questions, including, "Did you receive the spirit by doing the works of the law or by believing what you heard? . . . Having started with the spirit, are you now ending with the flesh? Did you experience so much for nothing?" (Gal 3:2-5). For Paul, the bedrock of faith is the Spirit—"having started with the Spirit . . ." The ongoing life of faith is due equally to the generosity of the Spirit—"did you experience so much ..." Even the experiences of faith and miracles find their headwaters in the Spirit—"does God supply you with the Spirit and work miracles among you?" How can the Galatians have forgotten that they now dwell in a sphere in which "neither circumcision nor uncircumcision is anything; but a new creation is everything" (6:15)? How can they forget that they have received the Spirit (3:3, 14: 4:6), been made alive by the Spirit (3:14, 21-22), received the promise of the Spirit through faith (4:14-15) been given birth by the Spirit (4:29), lived by the Spirit (5:25), begun to walk by the spirit (5:16, 18, 25), and received a divine inheritance through the Spirit in their hearts (4:6-7)? This is indeed a good deal to forget.

This Galatian shift is inconceivable to Paul because the Spirit simultaneously inaugurates a new creation and covenant (6:15; 2 Cor 5:16-17). This is the arena not of Hagar the slave but Sarah the daughter (Gal 3), not of the earthy first Adam but the life-giving resurrected second Adam (1 Cor 15:35-49), not of Torah written on tablets of stone but of Christ whose spirit inscribes Torah on human hearts (2 Cor 3:7-18; see Jer 31:31-34; Ezek 34). Yet this new covenant and creation does not permit a denigration of Hagar or Moses or Sinai, but reconciliation with them, an ambassadorial service in the territory of the recalcitrant, in which believers cannot characterize others as merely human or judge them to be inferior. The Spirit that writes Torah on human hearts is no cause for arrogance; the Spirit is a gracious gift (charisma χάρισμα) that does what human effort could not accomplish: to fulfil the altogether just demands of Torah (Rom 7:1-6; 8:1-2).

The concreteness of this contrast lies in Paul's conception of two spheres, the arena of virtuous fruits of the Spirit in contrast to a life dominated by the despicable works of the flesh (Gal 5:18-26; Rom 8:1-17). Once again, this contrast ought not lead to judgment and arrogance. The spirit ought to engender cooperation rather than conceit, gentle patience with the fallen rather than judgment toward them (Gal 6:1). The spirit accomplishes what human beings—the flesh—could not, to inspire believers to embody the love of God (Rom 5:5), to bear each other's burdens "and thus fulfill the law of Christ" (Gal 6:2). *See* FLESH IN THE NT.

This contrast of spirit and flesh is accompanied in Rom 8 by another contrast between the spirit of adoption and the spirit of slavery; one leads to assurance, the other to fear. This contrast, too, is concrete, for it is learned through hard-fought prayer: when believers "cry, 'Abba, Father,'" they understand that the Spirit leads to adoption rather than to slavery (Rom 8:15). The spirit intercedes "in our weakness; for we do not know how to pray as we ought, but that very Spirit intercedes with sighs too deep for words" (Rom 8:26). A rich life in the spirit is framed by ongoing, wrenching prayer.

Life in the Spirit could hardly be more concrete than this. Reception of the Spirit issues in concrete ways of living: humility rather than arrogance (1 Cor 1-3); miracles (Gal 3); reconciliation of resisters (2 Cor 5); restoration, in a spirit of gentleness, of those who stumble (Gal 6); and agonizing, speechless prayer (Rom 8), in which the Spirit groans within.

Although he sets out these contrasts, Paul still recognizes that the struggle is not over, that the new creation still lies in the future. Creation continues to groan. The inbreathing of Gen 2:7 will yield a new breath; the first Adam was earthy, while Christ, the second Adam, is "life-giving" Spirit (pneuma zōopoioun [πνεῦμα ζῳοποιοῦν]; 1 Cor 15:45). People, sown now in weakness, will be raised in power; "it is sown a physical body, it is raised a spiritual body (sōma pneumatikon σῶμα πνευματικόν)" (1 Cor 15:44).

These contrasts suggest that the work of the Spirit resides principally within individuals. Yet Paul understands that the Spirit transcends the concrete activities of individuals, for which reason he adopts the metaphors of temple and body to describe the communal presence of the spirit.

c. Spirit and temple. When he argues that the church can exist only as an organic whole and that, consequently, the Corinthians must reject all schisms, Paul reminds them, "Do you not know that you are God's temple and that God's Spirit dwells in you? If anyone destroys God's temple, God will destroy that person. For God's temple is holy, and you are that temple" (1 Cor 3:16-17). Those who believe that discrete portions—schismatic pockets—of the church are Spirit-filled, while others are not, are temple-destroyers. With this metaphor, Paul launches a frontal critique upon the splintering tendencies of those who shatter the church by their failure to appreciate and to appropriate the unifying presence of Christ in their midst.

Paul adopts this metaphor later in the letter when his attentions have shifted from schisms to sexual matters. Addressing dalliances with prostitutes, he writes, "Or do you not know that your body is a temple of the Holy Spirit within you, which you have from God, and that you are not your own? For you were bought with a price; therefore glorify God in your body" (6:19). Many interpreters (e.g., Fee, 135-36) assume that Paul here applies the communal metaphor of the church as a spiritual temple, from 1 Cor 3, to the individual believer. Sex with prostitutes is a violation of the individual body, understood as a Spirit-filled temple. Yet there remains an unavoidable communal residue in Paul's discussion, for the words, BODY (sōma σῶμα) and members (melē μέλη), are dominant Pauline metaphors for the church community and its constituent parts in 1 Cor 12-14. Along these lines, illicit sexual activity may provide another example of the Corinthians' inability to grasp the communal dimension of the spirit. Sex with a prostitute is not an individual matter; it pollutes the entire temple.

In 2 Cor 6:14-7:1, Paul adopts the metaphor a third time, though without an explicit reference to the spirit. The wedge he drives between righteousness and lawlessness, light and darkness, Christ and Beliar, believer and unbeliever, is uncharacteristic. At the forefront of this assault, which has more in common with the language of the Dead Sea Scrolls than 2 Corinthians, is holiness. The Corinthians may not have grasped, in

Paul's opinion, the meaning of the metaphor in his earlier letter ("For God's temple is holy, and you are that temple" in 1 Cor 3:17*b*) or the thrust of his instructions about prostitutes (1 Cor 6).

d. Spirit and body. In response to a Corinthians question on the topic of spiritual gifts, Paul depicts the church as a spiritual body composed of many diverse members. Before he begins, however, he lays down a fundamental assertion that attributes perhaps the earliest Christian creed to the spirit: "no one speaking by the Spirit of God every says, 'Let Jesus be cursed!' and no one can say 'Jesus is Lord' except by the Holy Spirit" (1 Cor 12:3). Slightly later he returns again to early tradition when he roots the diverse community in water baptism, which he understands as a work of the spirit: "For in the one Spirit we were all baptized into one body—Jews or Greeks, slaves or free—and we were all made to drink of one Spirit" (1 Cor 12:13).

The Spirit that inspires a singularly unifying confession and provides the basis for diversity in the church through participation in baptism becomes in this context also the spirit that distributes gifts to the church. Once again, the spirit inspires unity, this time in the recognition that the range of SPIRITUAL GIFTS are distributed by one spirit: "Now there are varieties of gifts, but the same spirit" (12:4). With these assertions Paul undermines the Corinthian penchant for one gift in particular, glossolalia, at the expense of other gifts (e.g., prophecy, which he personally commends). The Spirit fills the church, in much the same way that pneuma was believed to permeate a physical body, and inspires a variety of gifts, a diverse array of members, who function much like body parts, all of which are necessary to a healthy body.

e. Seal and pledge. In 2 Corinthians, Paul adopts two metaphors which underline this certainty of resurrection in the future: "to seal" (sphragizein σφραγίζειν) and "guarantee" (ho arrabōn ὁ ἀρραβῶν) (2 Cor 1:22). A "seal" may have been a religious metaphor that explains circumcision, baptism, or wearing a mark or seal of the god. More likely, it was a commercial metaphor: an imprint set in wax that denoted ownership and, by extension, protection; in legal documents, such as a will, a safeguard against premature violation; or validation of a document. The metaphor of a guarantee or down-payment may belong to commercial life, where it functioned as a deposit or first installment paid for services or rent or wages or goods. Both the giver and the recipient were under a legal obligation to complete the contract. The Spirit, understood in commercial terms, is God's guarantee of the whole of salvation.

Another possible commercial foreground is the story of Judah and Tamar in Gen 38. Judah asks, "What pledge ('eravon עֵרָבוֹן) shall I give you?" The first item Judah leaves in pledge is his seal (pathil פְּתִיל). Genesis 38:18 is the single instance in the OT where the words, "seal" (more literally, the cord that holds the seal) and "pledge," occur together. This association, however, is obscured by the Septuagint, which translates "seal" anomalously as "ring" (ton daktylion sou τόν δακτύλιόν σου), although typically it is translated in the Septuagint by the Greek word, "seal" (sphragis σφράγις). Had Paul been familiar with the Hebrew of Gen 38:18 or a more typical translation than LXX Gen 38:18, he would have recognized the association of "pledge" and "seal" and discerned a story that encapsulates the certainty of God's promise. If the promise of God is forwarded in this remarkable story of a bereft widow who becomes the ancestor of David, the messiah, by playing the part of prostitute, it can also be forwarded through the flawed but determined mission of Paul. (See Eph 1:13-14.)

4. Acts

The holy spirit in Acts marks the fulfillment of Jesus' promise at the conclusion of Luke's gospel: the disciples must wait in Jerusalem until they "have been clothed with power from on high" (24:49). In a programmatic promise at the beginning of Acts, Jesus associates this power with the Holy Spirit, verbal witness, and the ever-expanding mission of the church: "you will receive power when the Holy Spirit has me upon you; and you will be my witnesses in Jerusalem, in all Judea and Samaria, and to the ends of the earth" (1:8). This is the onset of mission, and the spirit functions principally in Acts as the inspiration for mission.

This mission takes place primarily through the inspired interpretation of Israel's scripture, which commences at Pentecost. While gathered together in Jerusalem, events that are reminiscent of the gift of Torah (Exod 19–24) at Sinai transpire: violent wind; fire; and loud sounds. The loud wind fills the entire house. Tongues as of fire are distributed among the believers. The Holy Spirit fills them and gives them the ability to recite God's powerful acts in other languages, so that Jews gathered from far flung regions of the Dispersion are able to understand their message in their own dialects. This experience leads to a division among the crowds between those who think they are drunk and those who wonder about the meaning of this event (2:1-13).

Peter answers this question at first by explaining that this experience is what the prophet Joel (LXX 3:1-5) described—though Peter adapts this quotation in telling ways. Whereas Joel places the outpouring "at some time," Peter sees it as a signal of "the last days" (2:17). He also tightens the association of the Spirit with prophecy by adding, "and they shall prophesy."

The sort of prophecy that the holy spirit inspires consists of the inspired interpretation of scripture. Peter's speech at Pentecost features a catena of scripture references, each of which is interpreted to demonstrate that the experience of Pentecost fulfills Israelite scripture (e.g., Joel 3:1-5; LXX, Ps 15:8-11; and Ps 109:1).

This model of inspiration sets the pattern for Acts. In Acts 4:8-13, for example, Peter, once he is "filled with the Holy Spirit," delivers a speech that turns on the inspired interpretation of Ps 118:22: "This Jesus is 'the stone that was rejected by you, the builders; it has become the cornerstone.'"

The next scene offers an extension of Pentecost. Following the release of Peter and John from prison, the community quotes Ps 2:1-2 in a prayer for boldness, after which "the place in which they were gathered together was shaken; and they were all filled with the Holy Spirit and spoke the word of God with boldness" (Acts 4:31). Everything to this point in the story, including the content of their prayer, leads to the presumption that their speech will consist of an inspired interpretation of Scripture that applies scripture to the events of their own day.

Saul, too, according to Ananias, will regain his sight and "be filled with the Holy Spirit" (9:17). The effect of this infilling is Paul's ability to muster scriptures persuasively: "Saul became increasingly more powerful and confounded the Jews who lived in Damascus by proving that Jesus was the Messiah" (9:22). The participle, "proving" (symbibazōn συμβιβάζων) connotes bringing together or marshalling arguments from scripture that demonstrate Jesus' messiahship.

Even Paul's (Saul's) subsequent condemnation of the false prophet, Bar-Jesus, which occurs when he is "filled with the holy spirit," consists of a catena of scriptural quotations and allusions (Gen 32:11; 1 Chr 21:1; Job 1:6; Sir 1:30; and 1 Sam 7:13 in Acts 13:10-11). Even the climax of the spirit-inspired speech is an amalgamation of LXX Prov 10:9 and LXX Hos 14:10: "will you not stop making crooked the straight paths of the Lord?"

The Holy Spirit in Acts, then, does inspire invasive prophetic speech. Yet these experiences of inspiration consist, more specifically, of the inspired interpretation of scripture intended to explain recent events, from the life of Jesus to the experiences of the early church. This is the characteristic impact of the Holy Spirit in the book of Acts.

The Holy Spirit, consequently, has less in Acts to do with salvation than with mission, less to do with notions of new creation and new covenant, such as can be found in Paul's letters, than with the centripetal movement of the church. Even the offer of the Holy Spirit to the Jews gathered at Pentecost is neither the offer of conversion—moving from one religion to another—nor the promise of salvation understood as a shift in eternal destiny. Peter's offer (Acts 2:37-39) contains allusions to Isa 57:19, Joel 3:5, and Deut 32:5; it is an offer of healing to those near and far, of repentance and baptism, of realignment with those in Israel who rightly understand God by following the crucified, risen, and ascended Jesus, who pours out the Spirit (Acts 2:33) upon old and young, female and male slaves, Israel's sons and daughters (2:17-21).

5. Other NT Letters

Among those letters of debated authorship, Ephesians preserves the predominance of traditional NT emphases. The spirit is associated with the church understood as body and temple, although these are not metaphors of the local church, as in 1 Corinthians, but of the church as a universal reality composed of Jew and Gentile (2:18, 22; 4:3-4). As in 2 Cor 1:22, believers have the seal and pledge of the Spirit (1:13-14; see 4:30). They must not "grieve the Holy Spirit" (4:30), as in the gospels and Acts, nor, in recollection of Pentecost (Acts 2:13), be drunk with wine but filled with the Spirit (5:18), perhaps through prayer (6:18). The Spirit is also tied to wisdom and revelation, both in the church's past, which was populated by apostles and prophets (3:5), and the present, through the reception of divine mystery (1:17; see Col 1:9; 1 Cor 2:10) and proclamation, for the sword of the Spirit is the word of God (Eph 6:17).

The pastoral letters also preserve much of traditional early Christian belief. One creedal affirmation reads: "He was revealed in flesh, vindicated in Spirit (en pneumati ἐν πνεύματι) . . ." (1 Tim 3:16). This association of the Spirit with Jesus' resurrection is reminiscent of the traditional formulation incorporated by Paul in Rom 1:3-4: "descended from David according to the flesh . . . declared to be Son of God with power according to the Spirit of holiness by resurrection from the dead."

Titus underscores the traditional association of the Spirit with baptism: "through the water of rebirth and renewal by the Holy Spirit" (3:5; see 1 Cor 12:13). Rebirth or regeneration principally refers to initial transformation, while renewal, which is a characteristically Pauline term, evokes an ongoing process of transformation, as in Rom 12:2 and 2 Cor 4:16.

The pastorals also reflect the widespread early Christian adoption of the LXX, though 2 Tim 3:16-17 alone describes its inspiration: "all Scripture is inspired [theopneustos θεόπνευστος] by God . . ." This is not a philosophical statement of the nature of Scripture but an expression of the usefulness of the Septuagint for equipping believers to live competently and with character: "All Scripture is inspired by God and is useful for teaching, for reproof, for correction, and for training in righteousness, so that everyone who belong to God may be proficient, equipped for every good work."

A principal element of 1–2 Timothy is Timothy's call, which was accompanied by prophecies (1 Tim 1:18) that perhaps occurred alongside the laying on of the elders' hands (4:14)—though Timothy's gift is also attributed to the laying on of Paul's hands, presumably without prophetic mediation (2 Tim 1:6-7). The Spirit is said to predict stormy days ahead that will require courage (1 Tim 4:1). Timothy must, therefore, guard the deposit of faith "with the help of the Holy Spirit living in us" (2 Tim 1:14). From start to finish, then,

Timothy's is an inspired calling that demands persistence and courage.

James 4:5 cites a non-existent scriptural text to support the separation of believers from the world: "God yearns jealously for the Spirit that he has made to dwell in us." This is probably the clearest NT reference to the Spirit that God gives human beings at birth.

In Hebrews the principal means by which the Spirit instructs the community is through the pronouncement of OT scripture (3:7; 9:8; 10:15). The Spirit is here both the source of OT citations and the direct way in which they address the author's community. The author also adopts traditional early Christian beliefs: the widespread conviction that believers could oppose the Holy Spirit (Heb 10:38-39); and the Pauline belief that the Spirit distributes gifts to the church (Heb 2:4; 1 Cor 12:4-11). The purpose of these gifts is to authenticate early Christian belief. This reference to God's signs, wonders, and miracles, therefore, resembles Acts, or even Gal 3:1-5, more than 1 Cor 12, in which the purpose of gifts is to edify the local church. Hebrews also contains an unusual reference to the "eternal Spirit" by which Jesus offered himself up; this may be a simple moniker for the Holy Spirit or it may be an attempt to describe Jesus' indomitable and unquenchable spirit. Perhaps the author believed that Jesus did not need a subsequent gift of the Spirit, as normal believers do, because he remained without blemish (9:14).

1 Peter also adopts traditional conceptions. The spirit features in the sanctification of believers, as in Rom 15:16 and 1 Cor 6:11; it is set alongside God's choice and the sprinkling of Jesus' blood (1 Pet 1:2). The traditional association of spirit and resurrection (Rom 1:3-4; 1 Tim 3:16) occurs in 1 Pet 3:18: "He was put to death in the flesh, but made alive in the Spirit . . ." The result of this is association is unique; after being made alive in the spirit, Jesus was believed to preach to the spirits in prison (3:19).

Each of these letters, with the exception of James, absorbs and passes on traditional conceptions of the Holy Spirit that were widespread in the early church, often with slight shifts in emphases. These letters do not indicate the emergence of an allegedly spiritually deficient early Catholicism. They preserve many traditional expressions of faith while offering as well fresh applications of traditional beliefs that inform their new interests in the church universal (Ephesians), the inspiration of scripture (Hebrews; 2 Timothy), and the precarious future that lay ahead (1–2 Timothy). *See* CHURCH, IDEA OF THE.

6. The Fourth Gospel

Although the most familiar saying about the spirit deals with rebirth or birth from above—words directed to Nicodemus in John 3:6-8—the most distinctive conception of the Holy Spirit in the Fourth Gospel surfaces later in four related portions of the Farewell Discourse: 14:15-17; 14:25-26; 15:25-26; and 16:7-15. The first saying, may be, from a tradition-historical perspective, the source of the other sayings: "If you love me, you will keep my commandments. And I will ask the Father, and he will give you another Advocate [ho paraklētos ὁ παράκλητος], to be with you forever (*see* PARACLETE). This is the Spirit of truth [to pneuma tēs alētheias τὸ πνεῦμα τῆς ἀληθείας], whom the world cannot receive, because it neither sees him nor knows him. You know him, because he abides with you, and he will be in you" (14:16-17). This initial promise telegraphs key themes: the Spirit is identified as another paraclete; the spirit indwells and accompanies the disciples but is unavailable to unbelievers; and the Spirit is described by the term, Spirit of truth, in a context rife with rejection of the world.

The promise of another paraclete is significant in two ways. First, the word, paraklētos, explains the unique formulation that the spirit of truth will not only be in the disciples but remain with them, for the compound word, para + klētos, suggests a "calling alongside." There is meager consensus about precisely how this spirit accompanies. Alternatives include intercessor and mediator, helper or comforter or consoler, exhorter, teacher, representative, and advocate (see 1 John 2:1). Whatever its precise meaning, the occurrence of paraclete in tandem with "another" is an indication that the paraclete will function in Jesus' stead; Jesus was the first to exist in solidarity with the disciples, this other paraclete will also accompany them.

Second, this correspondence to Jesus anticipates the role of the paraclete as a teacher who guides the disciples into all truth. This is no orgy of new revelation but a clear vocation of reminding the disciples what Jesus said and then helping them to interpret his life in Jesus' absence. This is the essence of John 14:26, according to which the Holy Spirit "will teach you everything, and remind you of all that I have said to you." The Spirit will both recall Jesus' words and interpret them.

Twice this process appears in the gospel. Jesus' saying, "Destroy this temple, and in three days I will raise it up," is misunderstood, since the Herodian Temple took forty-six years to build. Yet John ventures, "But he was speaking of the temple of his body. After he was raised from the dead, his disciples remembered that he had said this; and they believed the scripture and the word that Jesus had spoken" (2:19-22). This narrative aside illuminates the process of recollection that leads to understanding. Later, Jesus enters Jerusalem triumphantly. As in the Synoptic Gospels, John sees this triumphal entrance as the fulfillment of Zechariah's words. However, unlike them, he explains how the disciples came to see this event in relation to Zechariah: "His disciples did not understand these things at first; but when Jesus was glorified, then they remembered that these things had been written of him and had been done to him" (12:16). Again, the fingerprints of the paraclete are evident in this aside, in which there is recollection and increased understanding. In this way, perhaps, the typically briefer sayings of Jesus in the Synoptic Gospels that accompanied events such as the feeding of the multitude became a the lengthy discourses that characterize the Fourth Gospel, discourses that offer, not merely—to adopt John's language—the basic meaning of "the flesh" but the richer meaning of "the Spirit" (6:60-63).

Another element of the first saying, the expression, "Spirit of Truth," introduces the presence of an alien world: "the Spirit of Truth, whom the world cannot receive, because it neither sees him nor knows him" (14:17). The disciples are not led to expect a cease-fire between them and the world around them. If the Spirit of Truth will indwell and accompany them, it will function differently with respect to the unbelieving world by convicting the world of its sin, of what righteousness means in Jesus absence, and the inevitability of judgment, since the ruler of this age has already been judged (16:7-11). The Holy Spirit, therefore, has an irenic inner function among the disciples and a corrective, even combative, relationship with the world.

A similar antipathy underlies the letter of 1 John, although now the divide is between two sets of Christian believers, between those who remained and those "who went out from us" (1 John 2:19). These are liars, deceivers, even the antichrist (2:22; 4:1-6; 2 John 7). In the drawing of these battle-lines, there are two spirits, the Spirit of Truth, as in John 14:17, and the spirit of error: "We are from God. Whoever knows God listens to us, and whoever is not from God does not listen to us. From this we know the Spirit of Truth and the spirit of error" (1 John 4:6). This divided world resembles the Teaching on the Two Spirits in the *Community Rule* (1 QS III–IV), which contrasts the sons of light with the sons of darkness.

In this epistolary confrontation, the author of 1 John offers subtle clues to buttress his claim to the high ground. First, he writes, "And by this we know that he abides in us, by the Spirit that he has given us" (1 John 3:24); the use of a traditional expression, "has given to us," situates his coterie, and not his opponents, squarely in the early church. Second, the unique prepositional phrase in 1 John 4:13, "from the Spirit," roots his claim in an experience that enabled Moses' elders to prophesy. In that story, God took "from the Spirit" that was upon Moses and distributed it. The author and his community are identified, in this way, as the legitimate heirs of Moses and his prophetic elders. Third, he offers a principle of discernment between true and false prophets: the confession that Jesus Christ has come in the flesh from God (4:1-3).

The author presumably depicts this experience of the Spirit as an anointing that renders teaching through recollection—hallmarks of the Fourth Gospel—superfluous: "As for you, the anointing that you received

from him abides in you, and so you do not need anyone to teach you. But as his anointing teaches you about all things . . ." (1 John 2:27; see 2:18-20). The claim is that the vision of Jeremiah—Torah fully written on the human heart—is fulfilled presumably by this small and battered corner of the early church (Jer 31:34).

7. Revelation

Although conceptions of the spirit are dominated by the problem of true and false prophecy (see above), additional dimensions do emerge. Predominant among these is the fluidity of the language of pneuma; the plural, pneumata (πνεύματα), can, for example, denote demons (16:13-14; 18:2) or "the seven spirits of God" (1:4; 3:1; 4:5; 5:6). This fluidity is apparent moreover in the letters to the seven churches, where the refrain, "Let anyone who has an ear listen to what the Spirit is saying to the churches," may mean that the reader should listen to each angel that is given charge over each church (e.g., 2:1) or to the angel that explains matters to John (e.g., 22:1) or to the spirit understood in more traditional terms as the Holy Spirit.

The present literary shape of Revelation is framed by four occurrences of the formula, "in [the] spirit" (en pneumati ἐν πνεύματι). This prepositional phrase may signal a vision "in the Spirit," or simply a vision "in spirit" (i.e., visionary) rather than "in body." If the former is correct, then four times John is transported when he is "in [the] Spirit" (1:10; 4:2; 17:3; 21:10): while worshiping on Patmos; to the heavenly throne; to a wilderness, where he views the prostitute Babylon; and to a high mountain, where he sees the new Jerusalem. Each leads to a fresh vision of Jesus: the ancient of days (e.g., Dan 7); the lion and slain lamb; the conqueror; the lamb on the heavenly throne.

George Montague contends that the river of life in the new Jerusalem (Rev 22:1) is the outpouring predicted in John 7:37-39. More certain are two instances in which the Spirit speaks, both in formulaic language: after a beatitude for the dead, the Spirit responds that they will indeed rest (14:13); the Spirit and the Bride (i.e., the church), in the book's epilogue, offer an invitation to the thirsty that is reminiscent of the grand invitation to the battered exiles in Isa 55:1: "Ho, everyone who thirsts, come to the waters; and you that have no money, come, buy and eat!" *See* CONSUMING FIRE; JESUS CHRIST; KINGDOM OF GOD, KINGDOM OF HEAVEN; PROPHET, PROPHECY; TONGUES, GIFT OF.

Bibliography: David E. Aune. *Prophecy in Early Christianity and the Ancient Mediterranean World* (1983); C. K. Barrett. *The Holy Spirit and the Gospel Tradition.* 2nd ed (1966); Cornelis Bennema. *The Power of Saving Wisdom: An Investigation of Spirit and Wisdom in Relation to the Soteriology of the Fourth Gospel* (2002); James D. G. Dunn. *Baptism in the Holy Spirit:*

A Re-examination of the New Testament Teaching on the Gift of the Spirit in Relation to Pentecostalism Today (1970); James D. G. Dunn. *Jesus and the Spirit: A Study of the Religious and Charismatic Experience of Jesus and the First Christians as Reflected in the New Testament* (1975); Gordon Fee. *God's Empowering Presence: The Holy Spirit in the Letters of Paul* (1994); Hermann Gunkel. *The Influence of the Holy Spirit: The Popular View of the Apostolic Age and the Teaching of the Apostle Paul* (1979); Moyer V. Hubbard. *New Creation in Paul's Letters and Thought* (2002); John R. Levison. "Did the Spirit Withdraw From Judaism? An Evaluation of the Earliest Jewish Data." *NTS* 43 (1997) 35–57; John R. Levison. *The Spirit in First Century Judaism* (1997); David Lull. *The Spirit in Galatia: Paul's Interpretation of Pneuma as Divine Power* (1980); Dale B. Martin. *The Corinthian Body* (1995); Robert P. Menzies. *The Development of Early Christian Pneumatology: With Special Reference to Luke-Acts* (1991); George T. Montague. *Holy Spirit: Growth of a Biblical Tradition* (1976); Finny Philip. *The Origins of Pauline Pneumatology: The Eschatological Bestowal of the Spirit upon Gentiles in Judaism and in the Early Development of Paul's Theology* (2005); G. Stanton, B. W. Longenecker, and S. C. Barton. *The Holy Spirit and Christian Origins: Essays in Honor of James D. G. Dunn* (2004); M. M. B. Turner. *Power from on High: The Spirit in Israel's Restoration and Witness in Luke-Acts* (1996); M.M. B. Turner. *The Holy Spirit and Spiritual Gifts in the New Testament Church and Today* (1996); Keith Warrington. *Discovering the Holy Spirit in the New Testament* (2005); Michael Welker. *God the Spirit* (1994).

JOHN R. LEVISON

HOLY WAR. Scholars use two related expressions to conceptualize the relationship between God and warfare in the OT. *Divine Warrior* refers to descriptions of the LORD as a warrior god who fights for (or even against) Israel. *Holy war* designates the actual or hypothetical practice of warfare as a religious activity.

A. Holy War as Theological Concept
B. Holy War as God's Action
C. Holy War as Human Action
D. Holy War in Biblical Literature
   1. Theophany poems
   2. Exodus
   3. Deuteronomy
   4. Joshua
   5. Judges
   6. 1 and 2 Samuel
   7. Psalms
   8. Prophets
   9. Later literature
Bibliography

A. Holy War as Theological Concept

Unlike *crusade* or *jihad*, which signify human struggles to achieve what is thought to be divine will, *holy war* describes the military activity of God in which humans could sometimes assist in a secondary fashion (*see* TERRORISM). To avoid misunderstanding, some prefer the expressions *Yahweh war* or *sacral war*. The OT has no general expression for holy war, but does speak of "the wars" or "battles of the LORD" (Num 21:14; 1 Sam 18:17; 25:28; compare Exod 17:16) and of the LORD as warrior (Exod 15:3; compare Ps 78:65; Isa 42:13; Zeph 3:17). Adversaries are expressly the LORD's enemies (Judg 5:31; 1 Sam 30:26). Evidence indicates that holy war was never a uniform or normative sequence of practices but a constellation of religiously oriented military procedures and customs that varied according to time and circumstance. Nor was holy war something distinctive or unique to Israel's culture and religion. Holy war was not only, or even primarily, a set of actual military practices, but more foundationally a theological construct intended to relate belief in the LORD as cosmic warrior to Israel's narrative traditions, national identity, and insecure position in the world.

B. Holy War as God's Action

Old Testament texts describe the LORD marching forth from southern mountain regions (Judg 5:4) leading a supernatural army into battle (Judg 5:20; 2 Sam 5:22-25; 2 Kgs 6:15-17; Zech 14:5) and thus bearing the title "LORD of hosts" (*See* HOSTS, HOST OF HEAVEN). The LORD's presence in battle is centered in the ARK OF THE COVENANT (1 Sam 4:3-7), from which the LORD sets off and to which the LORD returns (Num 10:35-36). When battle is joined on the human level, the LORD may provide oracular guidance on the conduct of battle (Judg 1:1-2; 20:18; 1 Sam 14:36-37; 23:2, 4, 9-11; 2 Sam 5:23-24; 1 Kgs 20:13-14) and its positive outcome (Judg 7:9-14; 1 Sam 23:12; 30:7-8; 2 Sam 5:19; 1 Kgs 22:5-6, 11-12; 2 Kgs 3:15-19; often using the phrase "give into your hand"). The LORD accompanies Israel's army at its head (Deut 20:4; Judg 4:14; 2 Sam 5:24). The LORD may use natural forces as weapons: east wind (Exod 14:21; Ps 48:7), hail stones (Josh 10:11), storm (Judg 5:21), lightning (2 Sam 22:15; Ps 18:15; 77:18-19; Hab 3:11). The LORD's attack may take place at dawn (Exod 14:21; Ps 46:5). The LORD's most characteristic weapon is panic let loose to demoralize the enemy, the classic example being Gideon's victory in Judg 7:19-23 (also Exod 23:27-28; Deut 2:25; 7:23; Josh 5:1; 10:10; Judg 4:15; 1 Sam 7:10). The LORD achieves decisive victory and gives the enemy into Israel's "hand" (Judg 3:10, 28; 7:15). Because God was conceived of as the primary actor in holy war (Exod 14:14; Deut 1:30; Judg 20:35; 1 Sam 14:23), human roles were deemphasized by the notion that the size of Israel's army was immaterial (Judg 7:2-8; 1 Sam 14:6).

C. Holy War as Human Action

For its part, Israel is described as carrying the ark into battle (Num 10:35-36; Josh 6; 1 Sam 4), blowing war trumpets (Num 10:9; 31:6; Judg 3:27; 6:34; 1 Sam 13:3), and practicing special taboos (Deut 20:5-8; 23:10-14) including abstinence from sex (1 Sam 21:5-6; 2 Sam 11:11). Israel's task is to finish off the disorganized remnants of the panicked foe (Josh 10:10; Judg 4:15-16; 1 Sam 7:10). Holy war also entails special treatment of booty and captured persons (Num 21:1-3; Josh 6; 1 Sam 13; see BAN; DESTROY, UTTERLY). The appropriate human reaction is to admire God's triumphs in silent, submissive faith (Exod 14:13-14; 2 Chr 20:17; Ps 46:10; Isa 7:4, 9; 30:15). Israel is not to fear but believe (Deut 20:3; Judg 7:3). To this catalogue of characteristic motifs some would add charismatic leadership (Judg 11:29; 1 Sam 11:6), mustering the people by a trumpet blast (Judg 6:34) or distributing pieces of butchered flesh (Judg 19:29; 1 Sam 11:7), consecration of the army (Josh 3:5) and its weapons (2 Sam 1:21; perhaps 1 Sam 21:5), and offering sacrifice (1 Sam 7:9; 13:9, 12).

Presumably, the custom of holy war was a historical reality, and Israel in the premonarchical and early monarchic periods sought oracular guidance in warfare, practiced special taboos, and used the ark as a war palladium (the latter two practices are revealed incidentally in 2 Sam 11:11). Israel was certainly not alone in conceiving of its national god as its leader in war, for this is a common motif in Ugaritic and Mesopotamian texts. The 9th cent. BCE MOABITE STONE (*ANET* 320–21; *COS* 2.23) shares concepts and vocabulary with OT holy war texts, especially with the book of Joshua (divine command to fight, divinely assisted victory, attack at dawn, devotion of the enemy population to destruction, acquisition of territory). It is noteworthy that Mesha refers to recent events rather than a tradition about the distant past. Yet the Mesha Inscription, like Joshua, is primarily a theological text, intended to substantiate ownership of the national territory and to honor the national god. Scholars presume that the practices of holy war (as distinct from its theological aspects) tended to disappear when warfare became a royal responsibility and standing professional armies became more important than Israel's citizen militia called together on an impromptu basis. The controversies reported in 1 Sam 15 and 1 Kgs 20:31-43 suggests a struggle between older tradition and the newer imperatives of the monarchy. Some infer that the predominance of holy war motifs in Deuteronomy and Deuteronomic literature reflects a restoration of the citizen militia and older warfare patterns under the resurgent nationalism of Josiah.

D. Holy War in Biblical Literature

1. Theophany poems

Holy war motifs cluster in particular literary types and in certain books. Theophany poems (Deut 33:2-3; Judg 5:4-5; Ps 68:8-9, 18; Hab 3:3-7) are a form of doxology, extolling the LORD as a warrior in order to celebrate the LORD's power and willingness to defend Israel. The LORD advances to battle from Sinai and the southern mountain regions (Deut 33:2; Judg 5:4; Ps 68:8, 18; Hab 3:3). The LORD is portrayed as a storm-god (Judg 5:4; Ps 68:5, 9-10, 34) attended by awe-inspiring natural phenomena (Judg 5:5; Ps 68:9; Hab 3:4-6, 10) and leading a supernatural army into battle (Deut 33:2-3; Judg 5:20; Ps 68:18; Hab 3:5). Creation motifs are reflected in the LORD's victorious struggle with chaotic waters and sea (Hab 3:8, 15). Cosmic powers freeze in awe (Hab 3:10-11; compare Josh 10:12-13).

2. Exodus

The Red Sea event is conceptualized in holy war terms. The prose description of chap. 14 utilizes the motifs of calm and silent faith (vv. 13-14), east wind (v. 21), engagement in the morning (v. 24), and divinely induced panic (v. 24). The poetic chap. 15 declares "the LORD is a warrior" (v. 3) who acts as storm-god (vv. 8, 10) and brings terror to the foe (vv. 14-16). Holy war narratives appear in Exod 17:8-13 (divine aid) and Num 21:1-3 (devotion of the enemy to destruction).

3. Deuteronomy

Peculiarities in Deuteronomy's presentation of holy war are immediately apparent. The ark does not represent the presence of the LORD as warrior, but serves simply as a law depository (contrast Num 10:35-36 with Deut 10:1-5; 31:9). Priests have no sacral or oracular duties in warfare, but merely deliver a reassuring oration before battle (contrast Num 10:1-9 or 1 Sam 23:9-12 with Deut 20:2-4). Yet holy war motifs permeate Deuteronomy and function in a variety of ways. Chapters 1–3 use narratives of successful and unsuccessful holy wars to teach a lesson in faith and obedience. Deuteronomy 2:26-37 retells the story of victory over Sihon from Num 21:21-26, in the process emphasizing and adding elements of holy war ideology (oracle in Deut 2:31; divine action, vv. 33, 36; devotion to destruction, vv. 34-35) to an earlier, sparse account that lacked these features. This act of redaction is a clear indication that the motifs of holy war were at least as much a function of theology and literary activity as they were reflections of actual tradition and practice. In the admonitions and laws of Deut 7, 13, and 20, the traditions of holy war and the practice of devoting the foe to destruction are directed internally in order to combat unorthodox altars and religious objects (7:1-5, 16-26) and participants in disloyal worship (13:12-18; 20:16-18). Deuteronomy's laws of holy war promote an appreciation of God's gifts (20:5-8), humane behavior (20:19-20; 21:10-14), and appropriate propriety in the war camp (23:9-14).

4. Joshua

Joshua recounts tales of holy war conquest to praise the LORD's power and graciousness and to solidify Israel's national identity and its claim to the land. Battle narratives reflect a repeated pattern. A statement of assurance from the LORD (6:2; 8:1-2, 18; 10:8, 19; 11:6) is followed by a victory won by varying proportions of divine and human effort, sometimes involving the motif of dawn attack (6:15; 8:10; 10:9) and the marvelous exploits of God as warrior (6:20; 10:11-14). Commands about the annihilation of booty and the enemy population are carefully obeyed (6:24; 8:26-27; 11:14). The book stresses the inevitability and totality of the LORD's victory. In this sense, Joshua is a theological confession, summarized in the creedal statement: "Yahweh fought for Israel" (10:14, 42; 23:3, 10).

5. Judges

The book of Judges utilizes holy war motifs to narrate the victories of Deborah and Barak (oracle, 4:6-7; panic, v. 15; supernatural participants and natural forces, 5:20-21) and Gideon (oracle, 6:36-40; 7:9-14; panic, vv. 21-22). In chap. 20 Israel engages in an internal holy war directed against Benjamin (oracle, vv. 18, 23, 27-28; sacrifice, v. 26; devotion to destruction, v. 48).

6. 1 and 2 Samuel

Samuel's victory over the Philistines is preceded by a sacrifice and won by divinely induced panic (1 Sam 7:9, 10). Holy war motifs also appear in the battles of Jonathan and Saul against the Philistines (oracle and divine guidance, 1 Sam 14:8-10, 18-19; panic and earthquake, v. 15). Saul is rejected because of his failure to carry out the requirement that booty and enemy captives be devoted to destruction (1 Sam 15). Saul, who must face defeat because he can obtain no oracle from God (1 Sam 28:6) contrasts starkly with David, who receives a favorable oracle (30:7-8). Holy war elements also appear in the narrative of David's defeat of the Philistines in 2 Sam 5:17-25 (oracle, vv. 19, 23; supernatural host, v. 24).

7. Psalms

Holy war motifs function in a striking way in three Zion psalms that celebrate the LORD's defense of Jerusalem (Pss 46, 48, 76). The city is beset by human kings (48:5) and the mythic powers of chaos (46:3-4). God is present in Jerusalem (46:5-6; 48:2-4; 76:3) to defend it at dawn (46:6) through cosmic power (46:6; 76:4) and divinely induced panic (48:5-6; 76:6-7). Mortals are instructed "be still and know that I am God" (46:11).

7. Prophets

Isaiah of Jerusalem reflects the themes of these Zion psalms with his call to stillness and faith in the face of the Assyrian onslaught (Isa 7:4, 9; 30:15). Yet in a striking reversal of standard holy war ideology, Isaiah also speaks of the LORD using enemy armies against Judah to punish it (5:26-30; 10:5-11), something also typical of other prophets (e.g., Jer 6:1-5; Ezek 5:5-17; Mic 1:10-16; Hab 1:5-17). Ezekiel's description of the attack of Gog of Magog employs the holy war motifs of panic, earthquake, and hail (Ezek 38:19-22). Micah 1:3-7 reverses the theophany description of God's approach as a warrior so that the LORD comes not to defend the nation but to attack it. The characteristic prophetic theme of the DAY OF THE LORD seems to have emerged, at least in part, from the ideology of holy war. Thus Isaiah compares the day of the LORD's victory to the "day of Midian" (Isa 9:4; Judg 7). Traditionally the occasion of the LORD's decisive defeat of Israel's enemies (Isa 13:6-9; Ezek 30:1-4; Obad 15), the Day of the LORD became for Amos (5:18-20) and Zephaniah (1:7-18) the catastrophic time when the LORD would turn in judgment against Israel and Judah.

9. Later literature

The books of Maccabees use characteristic features of holy war to describe Jewish victories over the Greeks (1 Macc 3:18-19, 22; 4:30-32; 7:41-42; 2 Macc 10:27-31; 11:6-12). The notion of a final struggle between good and evil cosmic powers became a characteristic theme of Jewish and Christian apocalyptic literature (2 Esd 13:5-50; Rev 16:14-16; 17:14; 20:8-9). At QUMRAN, the War Scroll (1QM) continued the heritage of holy war in its instructions for the conduct of the final battle of the sons of light against the sons of darkness. Heavenly hosts join humans in this struggle to achieve climactic victory.

Modern readers often experience discomfort with the notion of divinely directed warfare. However, we should remember that Israel was always threatened by the loss of its land and spent much of its history under the domination of militarily superior foreign rulers. Menaced by outside forces that were politically and technically its superior, Israel's faith that its God had the power to give victory in battle must have been essential for national survival.

Bibliography: Peter C. Craigie. *The Problem of War in the Old Testament* (1978); T. R. Hobbs. *A Time for War: A Study of Warfare in the Old Testament* (1989); Philip P. Jenson. *The Problem of War in the Old Testament* (2002); Sa-Moon Kang. *Divine War in the Old Testament and the Ancient Near East* (1989); Millard Lind. *Yahweh Is a Warrior: The Theology of Warfare in Ancient Israel* (1980); Patrick D. Miller. *The Divine Warrior in Early Israel* (1973); Richard D. Nelson. "Divine Warrior Theology in Deuteronomy."

A God So Near (2003) 241–59; Susan Niditch. *War in the Hebrew Bible: A Study in the Ethics of Violence* (1993); Gerhard von Rad. *Holy War in Ancient Israel* (1991); Charles Sherlock. *The God Who Fights: The War Tradition in Holy Scripture* (1993).

RICHARD D. NELSON

HOMAM hoh´mam [הוֹמָם homam]. A son of the clan chief Lotan according to 1 Chr 1:39.

HOMER hoh´muhr [חֹמֶר khomer]. 1. The largest dry measure of capacity in the Bible (Exod 8:10; Num 11:32; Lev 27:16; Isa 5:10; Hos 3:2). The name derives from the Akkadian imeru ("ass-load"). The homer contained 10 BATH (= 10 EPHAH; Ezek 45:10, 11, 14); if so, the homer and the COR were equal (roughly 190 L). *See* WEIGHTS AND MEASURES.

RAZ KLETTER

2. Poet to whom the ancient world attributed the *Iliad* and the *Odyssey*, the earliest epics of Greek literature. The *Iliad* focuses on a few weeks in the tenth year of the Trojan War, exploring the consequences of Achilles' rage, hubris, fate, and what it means to act heroically. The *Odyssey* follows the wanderings and sufferings of another hero, Odysseus, as he struggles to return to his home in Ithaca after the war. Written in dactylic hexameter, both works stand out among other early Greek epics for their striking unity, literary sophistication, and artistry; indeed, part of the puzzle of Homer is how the earliest works of Western literature can also be among the greatest.

The ancients imagined Homer as a blind bard, much like his character Demodocus in book eight of the *Odyssey*, but there is virtually no reliable historical information about him. Almost everything about the composition of the poems has been and continues to be the subject of intense debate. One view is that the poems were composed in the 8th cent. BCE, but some scholars date them later. Whereas much of 18th and 19th cent. scholarship saw multiple sources behind the epics, since the work of Milman Parry in the 1920s on oral storytelling techniques, scholars now see the Homeric epics as growing out of a centuries-long storytelling tradition. Whether the epics as we have them were composed in performance by an oral singer/poet or whether Homer was the first to write them down is still debated, but not the oral poetic techniques for composition. Some question whether the two poems are the work of the same person.

Whatever their origin, the significance and influence of Homer's *Iliad* and *Odyssey* in subsequent Western culture has been enormous. The two epics became the preeminent literary texts of the Greek and later Roman world, pervading all aspects of culture and all levels of society. Homer's place in Greek literary education was unrivaled. Usually the first author students would

encounter in the elementary stages of education, Homer remained a staple of education, rhetorical training, and literary practice, his epics serving as literary models that Hellenistic and Roman authors imitated and sought to surpass. Not surprisingly, there are more than twice the number of extant manuscripts of the *Iliad* and the *Odyssey* dating from the Greco-Roman world than any other Greek author. Given Homer's ubiquity, indirect influence on Jewish and Christian literature of the Hellenistic and Roman periods is to be expected. In keeping with the compositional practices of the period, it also follows that Homer served as a literary model for some of the earliest Christian writings.

Bibliography: Albert B. Lord. *Singer of Tales.* Stephen Mitchell and Gregory Nagy, eds. 2nd ed. (2000); Dennis R. MacDonald. *The Homeric Epic and the Gospel of Mark* (2000); Milman Parry. *The Making of Homeric Verse: The Collected Papers of Milman Parry.* Adam Parry, ed. (1987).

RUBÉN R. DUPERTUIS

HOMICIDE. *See* CRIMES AND PUNISHMENT (OT AND NT).

HOMILY. *See* FORM CRITICISM, NT; KERYGMA; PREACHING.

HOMOIOTELEUTON hoh-moi´oh-tel´yoo-ton. A Greek term that means "like ending," indicating an error in which a scribe copying texts has overlooked a portion of a text because of similar words or letters at the end of a block of that text. As a result, the copied text is shorter than the original. *See* TEXT CRITICISM, NT; TEXT CRITICISM, OT.

R. JUSTIN HARKINS

HOMOSEXUALITY. The topic of homosexuality occasions very little attention from the biblical writers. Indeed, whereas the status of same-sex relations is one of the most divisive ethical issues in the modern church, it is barely of passing interest to the ancient biblical authors. There are basically six passages in the Bible that refer directly to homoerotic relations, three in the OT: Gen 19:1-11; Lev 18:22; 20:13; and three in the NT: Rom 1:26-27; 1 Cor 6:9; and 1Tim 1:10.

The famous story of the destruction of Sodom and Gomorrah in Gen 19 includes a passage stating that the men of the city wanted "to know" (yadha‘ יָדַע) Lot's guests. Lot calls their desire "wicked" and offers his daughters for them "to know," indicating that the term "to know" here connotes sexual relations (similar to Adam "knowing" his wife Eve in Gen 4:1). The men apparently want to rape Lot's foreign male guests by way of demeaning them. Little do the men of the city realize, of course, that their evil desire only confirms God's judgment against the city, a judgment the visiting angelic guests soon carry out (*see* SODOM).

Some scholars point to the violation of hospitality as the primary issue in the passage, but Lot's offer of his daughters suggests overtones of sexual violence as well (a similar passage is found in Judg 19:14-29).

The two passages from Lev 18:22 and 20:13 occur within the context of the Holiness Code (Lev 17–26), where the Israelites receive instructions on how they shall conduct themselves upon entering the promised land (*see* H, HOLINESS CODE). Both passages give clear prohibitions against same-sex relations between men, though no reason for the proscription is given. The second prohibition in 20:13 adds the punishment of death to men engaged in same-sex relations. There are many other prohibitions in the Holiness Code (e.g., crossbreeding of animals, sowing two kinds of seed in one field, wearing garments made of two different fabrics, rounding off the hair of one's temples, receiving a tattoo; Lev 19:19, 27-28; 21:5). It appears that these various practices were perhaps markers for the previous idolatrous inhabitants of the land. In modern discussions the rationales for these various prohibitions, including same-sex relations, form a significant issue of debate.

All of the NT passages come from Pauline letters. The Rom 1:26-27 passage is the most important, as here Paul clearly views homoerotic behavior (male or female) as a consequence of idolatry, unnatural, and an expression of excessive lust. Most scholars acknowledge that Paul knew of homoeroticism indirectly and in stereotypic terms—that is, with reference to Gentile practices of pederasty and male prostitution—a view that receives support from 1 Cor 6:9, where homoeroticism is included in a typical vice-list of prohibited behaviors. Issues of translation are particularly important here, as there was no word in ancient Greek corresponding to our modern term *homosexuality* (which was coined at the end of the 19th cent.). Literally translated, the terms in question, malakoi (μαλακοὶ) and arsenokoitai (ἀρσενοκοῖται), mean "soft people" and something like "men who go to bed," respectively. These terms may be euphemisms for the passive and active partners in same-sex activity, whether in relation to pederasty or male prostitution, but the exact meanings of the terms are disputed. Modern translations, however, often mislead the reader by rendering these terms as "sodomites" (reading the Sodom and Gomorrah story into the text; e.g., NRSV, NKJV, NAB) or as "homosexuals" (anachronistically reading modern understandings of sexual orientation into the text; e.g, NIV, NKJV). It may well be that Paul derives the term arsenokoitai from the LXX version of Lev 20:13 (meta arsenos koitēn μετὰ ἄρσενος κοίτην). The passage in 1 Tim 1:10 also refers to arsenokoitai in the context of a vice list, with the same overtones as in 1 Cor 6.

The relative lack of attention to homosexuality in the biblical writings means that the few passages where it does arise have been subjected to extensive scrutiny and interpretive debate in recent decades. Debates about how to use the Bible to address homosexuality in the modern era are further complicated by: 1) issues of translation, 2) differing contextual understandings of same-sex relations in antiquity, and 3) placing homosexuality within the larger frameworks of biblical approaches to human sexuality. As seen above, how best to translate both the terms and the understanding of homoerotic sexuality in the biblical texts into modern English (or any other language) is a significant issue, especially in relation to 1 Cor 6:9. This difficulty is directly related to changing understandings of same-sex relations over time. Whereas in antiquity same-sex relations were typically understood as exploitive and a perversion of the natural order, many modern understandings of homosexuality differ significantly—particularly in terms of mutuality rather than exploitation and in terms of people having different naturally occurring sexual orientations. Here it is important to note that, even though homoerotic behavior is clearly prohibited in biblical texts, the concepts of heterosexuality and homosexuality as sexual orientations are modern constructs not found in antiquity.

Another issue is how the biblical materials should be understood in light of the modern psycho-social and biological sciences regarding human sexuality. The larger frameworks of human sexuality from biblical perspectives also come into view. The Bible includes various sanctioned sexual relationships that in the modern world are generally understood as unethical (e.g., polygamy, levirate marriage). Thus Christian communities across the ages have had to discern the leading of God's Spirit regarding appropriate and inappropriate expressions of human sexuality. At present many churches are deeply divided regarding the full inclusion of gay, lesbian, bisexual, and transgender Christians within church leadership and within church-sanctioned committed relationships. *See* ETHICS IN THE NT; ETHICS IN THE OT; GAY INTERPRETATION; GENDER; GENDER STUDIES; LESBIAN INTERPRETATION; PROSTITUTION; SEX, SEXUALITY.

Bibliography: Robert Brawley. *Biblical Ethics and Homosexuality: Listening to Scripture* (1996); Bernadette Brooten. *Love Between Women: Early Christian Responses to Female Homoeroticism* (1996); Kenneth Dover. *Greek Homosexuality* (1978); Victor P. Furnish. *The Moral Teaching of Paul.* 2nd ed. (1985); Robert Gagnon. *The Bible and Homosexual Practice: Texts and Hermeneutics* (2001); M. Nissinen. *Homoeroticism in the Biblical World: A Historical Perspective* (1998); Jack Rogers. *Jesus, The Bible, and Homosexuality* (2006); Choon Leong Seow. *Homosexuality and Christian Community* (1996); Jeffrey S. Siker, ed. *Homosexuality in the Church: Both Sides of the Debate* (1994); Jeffrey S. Siker, ed. *The Encyclopedia* of *Religion and Homosexuality* (2006); Dan Via and Robert Gagnon. *Homosexuality and the Bible: Two Views* (2003).

JEFFREY S. SIKER

HONESTY. The quality or condition of being honest; exhibiting integrity, trustworthiness, and truthfulness. The word itself is rare in English Bible translations. Biblical literature has much more to say about the opposite of honesty: DECEIVE and its cognates occur over 150 times.

The topic of honesty is more prevalent than occurrences of the word would suggest. Strikingly, its first appearance in the temptation narrative (Gen 3) is profoundly theological. The serpent insinuates that God has not been honest about his motives for forbidding Adam and Eve the fruit of the tree of knowledge. Affirming God's trustworthiness and JUSTICE will be a major theme in biblical literature. Even the practical command to have honest (i.e., *just*, tsedheq [צֶדֶק], dikaios [δίκαιος]) weights and measures (Lev 19:36; Deut 25:15; Ezek 45:10) is grounded in the righteousness (tsedhaqah צְדָקָה, dikaiosynē δικαιοσύνη) of a God who abhors all dishonesty (Deut 26:16).

Among other examples, many passages affirm the basic virtue of speaking and behaving honestly (e.g., Prov 12:17; 24:26; Isa 59:4; Eph 4:28), and the pretended honesty of spies plays a role in a couple of contexts (Gen 42:11-34; Luke 20:20). *See* LYING; SINCERITY; TRUST; TRUTH.

MARK D. GIVEN

HONEY [דְּבַשׁ devash; μέλι meli]. Honey in the ANE and the Bible referred to either a sweet substance made from such fruits as dates, grapes, or figs, or to honey from bees, either wild or domesticated. Honey appears in the Bible literally and figuratively. While the Egyptians and Hittites cultivated bees for honey, it appears Israel took several centuries to begin beekeeping.

Manna tasted like wafers made with honey (Exod 16:31). Samson found honey in a lion's carcass (Judg 14:8). John the Baptist ate locusts and honey (Matt 3:4; Mark 1:6).

Honey is often used metaphorically to describe the land of Canaan as a wonderful place flowing with "milk and honey" (Exod 3:8; 13:5; Lev 20:24; Num 13:27; 14:8; 16:14; Deut 6:3; Josh 5:6; Ezek 20:6). Honey figures as a symbol of abundance and fertility. God's words are compared with honey (Ps 19:10; 119:103).

KENNETH D. LITWAK

HONI [חוני המעגל khwny hm'gl]. The name of a famous Jewish wonder-worker (akin to HANINAH BEN DOSA) of the 1st cent. BCE known from both Josephus (*Ant.* 14.22) and from various references in rabbinic literature (*m. Taan* 3:8; *y. Taan* 3:9; *b. Taan* 23a). He is known as the "circle-drawer" because of his refusal to vacate a circle he had drawn around himself until

it rained. He was stoned to death during the civil war between Hyracanus II and Aristobulus II. A number of later legends grew up around this figure: his prayers were especially powerful, he claimed to have a unique relationship as "son" of God, and the assertion that the land of Israel was punished because of his death. One legend, found in Josephus, pictures Honi (Onias) as falling asleep for some seventy years.

PHILLIP MICHAEL SHERMAN

HONOR [כָּבֵד khavedh; τιμή timē]. Honor has been emphasized in modern biblical scholarship as a pivotal value in the ancient (and even modern) Mediterranean world (*see* ANTHROPOLOGY, CULTURAL, NT; ANTHROPOLOGY, CULTURAL, OT). For example, Luke 20:46 indicates that there were places reserved for distinguished guests, and the advice on table manners at Luke 14:8-10 assumes that honor (not food, drink, talk) were the diners' and the hearers' overriding concern. (Plutarch, *Mor.* 149AB, says much the same.) Among other examples of concern for honor are 1 Sam 15:30; 1 Chr 19:3; Job 29–30; Ps 91:15; or references to God's acting purely for reputation's sake (e.g., Ezek 36:22; Isa 48:11).

According to a widely utilized honor/shame theory, only men could possess honor. Men had worth only in terms of the respect others accorded them. Honor must be earned, and it could be lost. Moreover, one gained honor at the expense of others' honor. Men vied for respect, which could only be won at the expense of downgrading others. It was a "zero-sum" game. Women were simply vulnerable, liable to forfeit their men's honor by their own shameful actions. This concentration on "face" (rather than "guilt") is an unfamiliar concept to many in the Western world.

As important as these insights may be, they demand qualification. For example, a gracious woman could receive honor (Prov 11:16), and Plutarch wrote a whole treatise on honored women, who were extolled for excellences men aspire to. Both father and mother were to be honored (Exod 20:12; Deut 5:16; Matt 15:4; 19:19; Mark 7:10; Luke 18:20).

The worst dishonor is said to be SLAVERY, a fate for many who were heavily indebted or had been captured as prisoners of war, yet people would pay the taxes that betokened slavery, and would accept full-scale slavery rather than death. A livelihood could matter more than respect; and, while a livelihood might gain one respect, it could be sought at the cost of respect. Moreover, the "shameful" state of POVERTY could be adopted deliberately, as the way to true well-being, as it was by CYNICS, and, it would seem, by Jesus (e.g., Luke 12:22-34).

Mattathias refused the offer of high honor in exchange for loyalty to the law (1 Macc 22:18-22). Jesus upheld the example of the poor widow above that of the honored scribes (Luke 20:46). Jesus is constantly "dishonored" by disciples at odds with him (e.g., Mark 8:32), and he even loses an argument with a woman (Mark 7:28-29). In Luke's version of the parable of the Wedding Feast, clearly the host loses face if he has no guests; yet what he does is to counter the honor system by bringing in lowly replacements (Luke 14:15-24).

A related concept is "honor-virtue," that is, one's own sense of self-worth. Such self-worth includes knowing that one has kept faith, that one is not envious, and that one trusts God, whether others are aware of it or not (Ps 18:23-24; Job 31:5-23).

There was readily available in the ancient Mediterranean a notion of empty respect, "vainglory," the only achievement of those deliberately seeking honor. It was a point made by Cynics in particular, but by others, as well. In the Jesus tradition (in Q and Mark, in Matthew and Luke separately, and in Paul), the leading critical term for vainglory is "HYPOCRISY" (lit., "play-acting"). Lucian used this term in the same way (*Nigr.* 24). In Luke 6:41-42 Jesus' audience is told to avoid "play-acting," not to secure honor, but to enable usefulness. When Paul reprimands Cephas and the rest (Gal 2:14-15), it is precisely for aiming to make a formal good impression. That is, seeking honor is not itself universally honored. And, of course, though Jesus does come to glory and honor, it is only by despising honor (Heb 2:9; 12:2; Phil 2:5-11; 2 Pet 1:17). *See* SHAME.

Bibliography: P. Bourdieu. *The Disenchantment of the World* (1979); F. Gerald Downing. "'Honor' among Exegetes." *CBQ* 61 (1999), 53–73; F. Gerald Downing. *Making Sense in (and of) the First Christian Century* (2000) 19–42; L. J. Lawrence. "'For Truly I Tell You, They Have Their Reward.' Investigating Honor Precedence and Honor Virtue." *CBQ* 64 (2002) 687–702; B. J. Malina. *The New Testament World: Insights from Cultural Anthropology* (2001).

F. GERALD DOWNING

HOOK [וָו waw, חָח khakh, חַכָּה khakkah, צִנּוֹת tsinoth; ἄγκιστρον ankistron]. The Tabernacle (Exod 26:32, 37; 27:10; 36:36, 38; 38:10-12, 17, 19, 28) contained portable walls made of poles and curtains (also screens and veils) held by gold or silver hooks (waw). The Hebrew letter WAW (w ו) is hooked-shaped, thus one name for the hooks.

A hook (khakkah) and line were used by the Israelites for fishing (Isa 19:8; Hab 1:15; *see* FISHHOOK). Job 41:1 notes that Leviathan cannot be caught with a hook. Peter probably fished with the same type of hook (Matt 17:27). Fishhooks and hooks (tsinoth) were used to lead the Samaritans into exile (Amos 4:2). Hooks (khakh) were used for capturing and retaining captives, land, and water creatures (2 Chr 33:11; Ezek 19:4, 9; 29:4; 38:4; Job 41:2) by inserting the hooks through the nose (2 Kgs 19:28) or jaw.

The PRUNING HOOK was shaped like a curve-bladed sword attached to a wooden handle, with the inner edge sharpened (Joel 3:10; Isa 2:4; Mic 4:3) for reaping (Isa 18:5).

MICHAEL G. VANZANT

HOOPOE hoo'poo [דּוּכִיפַת dukhifath]. Several of the birds mentioned in the lists in Lev 11 and Deut 14 are notoriously difficult to identify, but the hoopoe seems to be an exception. Scholars agree unanimously that the Hebrew word dukifath refers to this migratory bird. With its characteristic sound (represented in Lat. *upupa* and Eng. hoopoe, as well as in its Hebrew name) and its conspicuous head crest set with plumes, the hoopoe was reportedly common in all parts of Palestine. Since the hoopoe has a reputation of being filthy, frequently "feeding on dunghills," it is not surprising that the ancient Israelites counted it among the unclean birds (Lev 11:19; Deut 14:18). *See* BIRDS OF THE BIBLE.

GÖRAN EIDEVALL

HOPE [בָּטַח betakh, חָסָה khasah, יָחַל yakhal, קָוָה qawah, πείθω peithō, ἐλπίζω elpizō]. Hope is looking forward with confidence to a future good. Hope can be an act of hoping, an object desired, or a subject in which one has trust. In the Bible, hope is founded upon Israel's religious memories in which Yahweh, the "hope of Israel" (Jer 14:8), makes covenants with Israel. Christian hope for inclusion in the kingdom of God is based on the belief that Christ is the Messiah, the fulfillment of these OT covenants (*see* MESSIAH, JEWISH).

A. Hope in the Old Testament
  1. Vocabulary
  2. Pentateuch and historical books
  3. Psalter and Job
  4. Prophets
  5. Eschatological hope
B. Hope in the New Testament
  1. Vocabulary
  2. Gospels and Acts of the Apostles
  3. Epistles and Revelation

A. Hope in the Old Testament
1. Vocabulary

In the OT, the concept of hope is most often expressed by the words betakh, khasah, yakhal, and qawah. Batakh has connotations that are both positive (to rely on someone), and negative (to have false security). This is reflected particularly in the LXX translation of Ps 115 (LXX Ps 113) by the uses of both peithō and elpizō. Khasah connotes shelter, and the LXX generally renders it with words related to "confidence." It is often found in laments (Ps 57:2 [Heb. 57:3]) and in eschatological texts (Isa 4:6). A derivative of yakhal, tohkheleth (תּוֹחֶלֶת), is the waiting for an expected good object, often Yahweh (Mic 7:7); those who receive evil after waiting have cause for complaint (Job 30:26). Its most frequent LXX renderings are elpizō and hypomenō (ὑπομένω). Nearly half of the occurrences of tiqwah (תִּקְוָה), a derivative of qawah, are found in Job. The word generally emphasizes waiting, often with the temporal limits of life in view. Only twice does the LXX use elpizō for tiqwa, preferring various forms of menō (μένω), emphasizing the aspect of waiting. The themes of hope, however, are not restricted to passages that use these words.

2. Pentateuch and historical books

In the OT, hope is founded on the religious narratives of Israelite history. These narratives are punctuated by the promises of Yahweh expressed as covenants with all God's creation and with Israel. Yahweh is the creator, preserver, liberator, and benefactor of Israel, desiring their prosperity and shalom (שָׁלוֹם; "welfare, completeness, peace"). God is faithful and just in response to unfaithfulness. The creation narratives (Gen 1–2) express Yahweh's fundamental relationship to humanity, offering prosperity and shalom (Gen 1:28-31). The FLOOD narrative (Gen 6:5–9:17) demonstrates Yahweh's willingness and ability to intervene within history to bring an end to an intolerable situation (Gen 6:11). After Noah is preserved, God makes an unconditional covenant with creation (Gen 8:22), assuring Noah that "day and night shall not cease" (Gen 8:22). After Abraham left his family and came to Canaan in response to divine call, Yahweh enters into a covenant with him; he is promised numerous descendants and the land of Canaan (Gen 15, 17). In the accounts of Israel's ancestors, barrenness threatened this promise of land and lineage (see ABRAHAM, OT). However, Yahweh is faithful, and Israel's barren matriarchs, Sarah, Rebekah, and Rachel, are given sons (Gen 21:2; 25:21; 30:22). The exodus event (Exod 12–15), memorialized in the festival of Passover, shows that Yahweh can overcome oppressive structures. The formula often used in divine address represents the emphasis placed on remembrance that leads to trust in Yahweh: "I am the Lord your God which brought you out of the land of Egypt" (Lev 19:36; 25:38; 26:13; Exod 20:2; Num 15:41; compare Lev 23:33). On the basis of Yahweh's act of liberation, Israel enters into a conditional covenant with Yahweh at Sinai. This Mosaic Covenant is a divine promise that Israel will be Yahweh's treasured possession if they will keep the law (Exod 19:5). The gift of the fertile land, a fulfillment of the Abrahamic covenant, is also a reversal of the curse of infertile land as a response to Adam's sin (Gen 3:17). In the exodus from Egypt and conquest of Canaan, Yahweh is presented as a warrior for Israel. In light of the horrific nature of modern warfare, the image of Yahweh as the divine warrior should not be accepted uncriti-

cally, but neither should it be entirely dismissed, as it is an image that provided hope for Israel (see GOD, OT VIEWS OF).

Throughout its history, Israel struggled with the covenantal requirement of monotheism. Yet hope can be derived from the deuteronomistic, cyclical pattern that is intensely presented in Judges: apostasy, oppression by a foreign nation, arrival of a judge, and deliverance from oppression (Judg 2:11-19). The pattern demonstrates the conditional/unconditional nature of Yahweh's covenants with Israel; the actualization of shalom requires covenantal fidelity of Israel, and Yahweh is faithful to preserve Israel even in spite of their apostasy. After the time of the judges, David becomes a prototype for a righteous king, and Yahweh makes an unconditional covenant with him (2 Sam 7). The promise that a Davidic king will always occupy the throne of Judah will become significant after the Babylonian exile, for it provides a nationalistic hope for dispossessed Israel. Further, it was essential in the post-exilic development of messianic hope, eventually becoming a component of the Christian message.

3. Psalter and Job

The belief that Yahweh will intervene to end the suffering of the present crisis is strongly present in the lament psalms. One-third of the psalms are in the language of a grievance designed to summon Yahweh to action, which is an expression of the incongruity of the memory of Yahweh's faithfulness in light of current crises. These expressions are hopeful because they are a rejection of the current crisis, and an expectation that Yahweh can, should, and will rectify the situation. The psalms of LAMENT can be a demand for salvation from enemies (e.g., Ps 7:6 [Heb. 7:7]), a complaint against the perceived neglect by Yahweh (e.g., Ps 44:9-16), a desire for a resting place (e.g., Ps 27:4-5), or the preemptive praise for what one expects to be accomplished (e.g., Ps 35:9). In many psalms, the image of Yahweh as warrior and monarchical supporter provided hopeful language (e.g., Ps 24:8).

The author of Job presents a complex hope for a "redeemer" (19:21-29), which is ambiguous and open to several interpretations. Christians have generally seen a nascent hope of resurrection in the book of Job and even a prophetic messianic hope in the statement, "For I know that my Redeemer lives" (Job 19:25), as conveyed by the capital "R" in modern translations. For many Jewish exegetes, it is Yahweh himself who set to be the redeemer, as is demonstrated in the epilogue (see REDEEM, REDEEMER). Yahweh lives, waiting to bless the childless Job with prosperity (42:10), children (42:13), and longevity (42:16-17). Job seems to reject the possibility of resurrection, noting that a tree has more hope than a person of life after being cut down (14:7).

4. Prophets

The monarchical prophets also illustrate a pattern of judgment and preservation that mirrors the nature of conditional/unconditional covenants. Because of the covenantal relationship, Yahweh is concerned with Israel more than all other nations (Amos 3:2) and will bring an inescapable judgment (Amos 9:1; Mic 3:9-12) in response to their neglect of justice, righteousness, and Yahweh worship. The imagery of spousal infidelity (Hos 1–3), which describes Israel's neglect of Yahweh, is one of the most familiar metaphors in the OT. However, the pronouncements of inevitable judgment are followed by the promise of restoration. Yahweh is a faithful husband, wooing an unfaithful wife, hoping for reconciliation (Hos 2:19), or a loving parent who still seeks to help the ever disobeying child (Hos 11:1-9). The land will be blessed with overwhelming fertility and filled with rebuilt and repopulated cities (Amos 9:11-14). Other nations will gather in Jerusalem (Mic 4:1-2), the home of both the Davidic king (Amos 9:11) and Yahweh. International war will cease (Mic 4:3), and the restored nation of Israel will be superior to its neighbors (Mic 5:8). The religious and nationalistic expectations are inextricable. The hope given to Israel through the pre-exilic prophets is a corporate, nationalistic hope centered on a this-worldly restoration of the kingdom (see PROPHETS, PROPHECY).

The exile deprived Judah of the monarchy, Temple, and land that were their visible connections to Yahweh. This catastrophe is presented in the OT as the most theologically jarring of all crises. Surprisingly, the theological response was literature of hope, rather than despair. The language and imagery suggest a fundamental change in the nature of the hope for restoration. Jeremiah presents a hope of return even before the deportation. While refusing to marry (Jer 16:1), a prophetic enactment of the coming judgment, Jeremiah purchases land, expressing the certitude of return (32:9-15). Upon Israel's return, Yahweh will make a new covenant with them and restore the land (32:37-44). The sovereignty of Yahweh, evidenced by his creative acts (Isa 42:5), shows that he is capable of bringing about this newness. A "new exodus" is prepared by Cyrus the Persian king, who is called God's messiah in Deutero-Isaiah (Isa 45:1). The newness may be accomplished by an intermediary being, as Isaiah introduces the enigmatic figure of Yahweh's servant (Isa 53). To some, these pronouncements were incredible. Ezekiel answers this doubt with a famous metaphor: the valley of dry bones (Ezek 37:1-14; see VALLEY OF DRY BONES). The metaphor emphasizes the hope of return and new life for Israel, but only by the intervention of Yahweh. The prophets of the exile share the hopes of previous prophets, which are nationalistic, but use imagery and themes that express newness or change: a new covenant, a messianic foreign king, and servant of Yahweh who

absorbs violence directed toward others in order to bring about the end of suffering (Isa 53:5).

The message of the prophets who returned to Israel presented a restoration that was increasingly distant from their present reality. The restored kingdom will be wealthier and the Temple more splendid than during Solomon's reign (Hag 2:9). In contrast to the years of vassal status, the wealth of the nations will be directed into Judah (Hag 2:7). They hoped that "on that day" (Zech 14:6, 8, 20) a future divine intervention will bring the beginning of a new existence on the earth. Third Isaiah tells of "a new heaven and a new earth" (Isa 65:17) where "the cry of distress" shall not be heard (Isa 65:19).

In the span of prophetic literature, this-worldly hope that tends to be corporate and nationalistic develops into hope for inclusion of righteous individuals in a new world.

5. Eschatological hope

The unfulfilled expectations of the post-exilic prophets provided the basis for the various forms of eschatology that are found in the apocalyptic literature surrounding the Maccabean period. These disappointments fueled a growing doubt that Yahweh's promises could be realized within history; therefore, hope began to be expressed as the expectation of the end of history. These writings provided hope in dire circumstances such as the cultural conflict with Hellenism or persecution. Using heavenly visions and angelic mediators these writings sought to assure the reader of the coming eschaton of a postmortem judgment and the reward of a transcendent world. These writings are the apex of the growing eschatological character of OT hope, and provide the immediate context for the 1st cent. Judaism, out of which the NT was produced (see ESCHATOLOGY IN EARLY JUDAISM; ESCHATOLOGY OF THE NT; ESCHATOLOGY OF THE OT).

In contrast to earlier corporate nationalistic hope, apocalyptic writings are more individualistic and emphasize piety. The author of Daniel encourages personal piety in times of trouble through the example of the young exiles in Babylon who are successful (1:20) because they refuse to defile themselves for the sake of assimilation (1:8). Further, the righteous will be resurrected. Righteous individuals will endure the persecution to see victory, and even those who lose their lives can have hope of eternal life, while their oppressors will be raised for eternal shame (Dan 12:1-2; 2 Macc 7).

Apocalyptic literature generally presents deliverance via intervention of heavenly being. The "son of man" of Dan 7 is the most well-known example. This figure is ambiguous, being inferior to the Ancient of Days (7:13) but having divine authority (7:14). Intertestamental literature presents savior figures who are less ambiguous, like the "king, god and man" who will save the world (*T. Sim.* 7:2). The Messiah is linked to the tribes of Levi and Judah (*T. Naph.* 5; *T. Jud.* 24), presented as two separate messiahs or as a conflation.

B. Hope in the New Testament

New Testament hope is integrally related to the covenantal hope of the OT, and is particularly influenced by the eschatological nature of 1st cent. Judaism. Jesus is the fulfillment of OT covenants and apocalyptic messianic expectations. Since God has been faithful to the OT covenants, Christians can have hope in the fulfillment of the new covenant made with all humanity. By faith in Christ's resurrection, Christians can have hope for an eternal life in the kingdom of God. New Testament hope is framed within the eschatological tension created by the "already but not yet" nature of the kingdom of God.

1. Vocabulary

The words elpis (ἐλπίς) and elpizō are the primary Greek words for hope. Surprisingly, these words are virtually absent from the Gospels. Elpis is only found eight times in Acts and not at all in the Gospels. **Elpizo** is used a total of seven times from Matthew through Acts. This, of course, does not mean that hope is absent from the NT narratives. The words are much more frequently used outside of the Gospels and Acts, with the exception of 2 Timothy, James, 2 Peter, Jude, and Revelation, which do not use the words at all.

2. Gospels and Acts of the Apostles

The Gospels and Acts inspire hope in the reader by demonstrating that the eschatological kingdom promised in prophetic literature has been made manifest by the presence, words, and deeds of Jesus the Messiah. His death and resurrection is a salvific event that assures eternal life for believers.

The kingdom of God that Jesus proclaimed, preached, and actualized is one of HEALING and liberation. It is the good news, the gospel, which provides hope to those oppressed by demonic power. The good news is that in the kingdom of God, which has already begun with Jesus' presence, their sins are forgiven, illness is healed, hunger is satisfied, and bonds are released (Luke 4:16-30).

The MIRACLES reported in the Gospels and Acts are a rejection of the status quo, and provide hope for those who are oppressed. The miracles performed by Jesus and his disciples are both a prefigurement and proof of the kingdom. For example, Jesus rejects that there is not enough bread and fish to feed all the needy, for in the kingdom there is enough for all (Mark 6:35-44). Similarly, Jesus objects to the presence of illness (e.g., Matt 8:1-4), deformity (e.g., Matt 12:9-14), and demonic oppression (e.g., Matt 9:32-34) in the newly inaugurated kingdom. The revivification of the dead (e.g., Matt 9:23-26), particularly the Lazarus narrative

(John 11), demonstrates the radical newness of the kingdom of God. Healing and liberation have communal and spiritual aspects as well as physical; Jesus brings the socially marginalized back into community (e.g., Matt 8:4) and displays the divine prerogative to forgive sins (e.g., Matt 9:2).

The resurrection of Christ provides the greatest hope because it is the glorification of Jesus and vindication of his ministry and preaching (Acts 2:32-36). It is the hopeful testimony for the forgiveness of sins (Acts 10:42-43) and opportunity of eternal life (John 14:19). Resurrection is assured, because it is related to belief in Jesus (John 11:25), and those who believe can live by participating in his life (John 14:19). The righteous and the socially oppressed will be rewarded both here and in heaven, while the unrighteous will be condemned (Matt 5:3-12; 8:11; 25:31-46; Luke 6:35; 16:19-31; 23:43; John 14:2-3).

The Gospels present Jesus' ministry as only the beginning, not the consummation of the kingdom. The church participates in the consummation of the kingdom through evangelization (Matt 28:19-20) and its ministry of healing until Jesus' return, or parousia (παρουσία; *see* PAROUSIA). Jesus promises (John 14:18; 16:16; compare Acts 1:11) that he will return in the future, when he is sent by God at the time of the universal restoration (Acts 3:21). Although the world will become a perilous place, those he has chosen will be gathered up and saved (Matt 24:30-31; Mark 13:27). Jesus promises to remain with his followers through all of this (Matt 28:20) and will send the HOLY SPIRIT to empower and comfort them (John 14:16-17; Luke 24:49; Acts 1:8).

The early church was a community of hope. The Holy Spirit received at Pentecost (Acts 2:1-4) enabled them to continue the healing and liberating ministry begun by Jesus. The church grew (Acts 6:1; 12:24; 15:41; 19:20) as healings (e.g., Acts 3:6), exorcisms (e.g., Acts 8:7), and revivifications of the dead (e.g., Acts 20:10) exemplified the reality of the eschatological kingdom (*see* CHURCH, IDEA OF THE).

3. Epistles and Revelation

Though more eschatologically focused, the hope of the Epistles and Revelation is consistent with the hope presented in the Gospels and Acts. Jesus' life is an eschatological event, the fulfillment of the OT covenants, and so "the ends of the ages has come" (1 Cor 10:11). Still, Christians need to wait until the time they can gain the "inheritance of the saints," their share of the kingdom into which they have already been transferred (Col 1:12-13). When the kingdom is fully established by Jesus' **parousia** at the end of the world, believers will share in his glory and resurrection.

As people who live between eschatological events, hope is necessary for daily living. One could not have this hope without faith (Heb 11:1; Rom 8:24). It is faith in Christ and in his resurrection that allows Christians to have hope, unlike unbelievers (Eph 2:11-12; 1 Thess 4:13). Christians can expect to experience persecution, but this is a proof of righteousness (2 Tim 3:12). This suffering is a privilege (Phil 1:29) and a blessing (1 Pet 3:14), and the hope that enables endurance should be a witness to others (1 Pet 3:15). Suffering leads to hope (Rom 5:3-5) and is to be rejoiced in because "we suffer with him so that we may also be glorified with him" (Rom 8:17). Further, although suffering is present in this life, the Christian can have hope that God will console (2 Cor 1:5) and save from earthly perils (2 Cor 1:10). The hope of resurrection even transforms grief, as loved ones will live again (1 Thess 4:13-15). For Christ, suffering was only the penultimate reality; he was glorified by his resurrection. Therefore, the Christian may expect glorification of resurrection by participating in his suffering (Phil 3:10).

The power of hope is not limited to the realm of suffering; the promises of forgiveness (Eph 1:7; Col 1:14) and empowerment by the Spirit (1 Cor 12:4-31; Eph 4:11-13) are key to the continued growth of the Christian community. In fact, Paul asserts that it is the Spirit that allows him to hope. Because the Spirit has been given as a guarantee, the Christian is assured of future immortality (2 Cor 5:4-5). The famous triad of faith, hope, and love (1 Cor 13:13) are interconnected by their relationship to the Spirit.

Though Christians have hope to endure until the parousia, the greatest hope is in resurrection and participation in the fullness of the kingdom. The evil in this world is as diametrically opposed to the kingdom as Babylon is to Zion (Rev 14). Because of the incompatibility of the kingdom with evil, a new heaven and earth will make room for a new Jerusalem (Rev 21:1-2). At the advent of this new heavenly existence, there will be a reversal of fortunes; those who afflict suffering will be consigned to judgment while those who suffered will be comforted (2 Thess 1:6-7). Believers will be "caught up in the clouds" (1 Thess 4:17) and taken to their eternal homeland (2 Cor 5:1-2; Phil 3:20). *See* COMFORT; CONSOLATION; COVENANT, NT AND OT; PARACLETE; SUFFERING AND EVIL.

Bibliography: Johan Christiaan Beker. *Suffering and Hope: The Biblical Vision and the Human Predicament* (1994); David M. Bossman. "Paul's Mediterranean Gospel: Faith, Hope, Love." *BTB* 25 (1995) 71–78; Walter Brueggemann. *Hope within History* (1987); Walter Brueggemann. "The Hope of Heaven . . . on Earth." *BTB* 29 (1999) 99–111; Ronald E. Clements. "The Messianic Hope in the Old Testament." *JSOT* 43 (1989) 3–19; Donald E. Gowan. *Eschatology in the Old Testament* (2000); Louis C. Jonker. "Hope beyond the Pre-exilic Period: The Interrelationship of the Creation and Temple/Zion Traditions during the Monarchical and Exilic Periods." *Scriptura* 66 (1998) 199–213; Bernd Kollmann. "Images of Hope." *Wonders Never Cease*. Michael Labahn and Bert Jan Lietaert Peerbolte, eds. (2006) 244–64; Hans Schwarz. *Eschatology* (2000); David Starling. "The Messianic Hope in the Psalms." *RTR* 58 (1999) 121–34; Peter Stuhlmacher and Douglas C. Mohrmann. "Eschatology and Hope in Paul." *EvQ* 72 (2000) 315–33; Lindsay Wilson. "Realistic Hope or Imaginative Exploration? The Identity of Job's 'Arbiter.'" *Pacifica* 9 (1996) 243–52.

SEUNG AI YANG

HOPHNI AND PHINEHAS hof'ni, fin'ee-huhs [חָפְנִי khofni, פִּנְחָס] pinekhas, פִּינְחָס pinekhas]. Hophni (Egyptian "tadpole") and Phinehas (Egyptian "the Southerner"), the two sons of ELI, are noted for their despicable and worthless behavior (bene veliya'al [בְּנֵי בְלִיָּעַל], "sons of BELIAL"). They treat the sacrificial laws with disrespect, and they have sex with the young women who work at the sanctuary door (1 Sam 2:12-17).

The house of Eli stands in contrast to the preferred priests in the DEUTERONOMISTIC HISTORY. The sons of Eli are presented as a contrast with the boy Samuel, who is as loyal as they are incorrigible. After the man of God denounces the Elide house (1 Sam 2:27-36) and the judgment is completed during the battle of Aphek (1 Sam 4:11-18), SAMUEL becomes the judge and priest for Israel.

The wife of Phinehas, however, produces a son, ICHABOD, whose brother AHITUB is the father of the priests at Nob during the reign of Saul (1 Sam 14:3). When they are punished for helping David (1 Sam 22:20), Abiathar, a grandson of Ahitub, escapes and joins David. This Abiathar is banished from Jerusalem by Solomon for supporting Adonijah's attempt to become king (1 Kgs 2:26). The text explains this banishment and the preference for Zadok as priest fulfilled "the word of Yahweh which he spoke concerning the house of Eli at Shiloh."

C. MARK MCCORMICK

HOPHRA hof'ruh [חָפְרַע hofra']. Apries, biblical "Hophra" (Jer 44:30), fourth king of the Egyptian Twenty-sixth Dynasty, was an ally of King ZEDEKIAH of Judah against Babylon. Apries continued his predecessors' policy of active engagement in Syria-Palestine to counter Babylonian expansion.

An initial campaign by Apries into Lebanon met with little resistance and encouraged King Zedekiah of Judah to rebel against Babylon. The results were disastrous, especially for Judah, as the Egyptian army was unable to lift the siege of Jerusalem and returned home in defeat (Jer 37:5-8). Babylonian reprisals may have included a foray into Egypt proper in 582 BCE. Later campaigns along the Phoenician coast (574–571 BCE) were more successful but short lived. Failure of a campaign against the Libyan coastal town of Cyrene in 570 BCE led to mutiny by native Egyptian troops and the ouster of Apries in favor of Amasis. *See* EGYPT; PHARAOH.

CAROLYN HIGGINBOTHAM

HOPPING LOCUST. *See* LOCUSTS.

HOR hor [הֹר hor]. From the same root as "mountain" (har הַר). Hor is always written in combination with hahar (הָהָר), "the mountain," thus Mount Hor is understood. Two mountains are named in the biblical text. 1. The most important Mount Hor is noted in the exodus tradition as the burial place of Aaron (Num 20:22; 21:4; 33:37; Deut 32:50), yet Deut 10:6 states that Aaron died and was buried at Moserah. The apparent conflict is eased when moserah (מוֹסֵרָה) is interpreted through its root meaning of "discipline/chastisement." The notation about Aaron's burial (Deut 10:6) is recorded in the midst of Moses' speech regarding the broken tablets of the Law at Sinai. Also, Num 20:24 and Deut 32:51 state that Aaron died on Mount Hor in Edom due to the rebellion at Meribah. Therefore, Moserah may describe the events of Aaron's death and burial rather than the location of the mountain.

Mount Hor is described as on the Edomite border in Transjordan (Num 20:23). The Edomites, with a show of force, emphatically refused to allow the Israelites to cross their territory when the Israelites journey toward Moab (Num 20:17-21). Moses agreed to circumvent Edom to the east by way of the desert.

Josephus (*Ant.* 4.82–84) moved the location of Aaron's tomb to the central highlands of Edom near Petra. It is now called Jebel Nebi Haroun, "the Mount of the prophet Aaron." This rugged sandstone mountain has two peaks that reach nearly 1,460 m. A Christian church from the time of Justinian (527–565 CE) marks the traditional site, now converted into a tomb and a Muslim mosque. This traditional location is in tension with the biblical text's presentation of the story. Josephus' account requires the Israelites to have crossed through Edom. Jebel Haroun is too high and isolated for the account of transference of priestly authority "in the sight of the whole people" (Num 20:23-28).

Another suggestion for Aaron's Mount Hor is Jebel Madurah about 15 mi. northeast of Kadesh, at the northwestern boundary of ancient Edom. Its topography would allow all Israel to observe the priestly transfer from Aaron to Eleazar.

2. The northern limit of Israel's territory (Num 34:7-8). Most likely the peak was part of the Lebanon Mountains, with Mount Hermon and Jebel Akkar as possible locations.

MICHAEL G. VANZANT

HORAM hor´am [הֹרָם horam]. The king of Gezer who was killed by Joshua when Horam sought to assist Lachish during the conquest period (Josh 10:33). *See* GEZER, GEZERITES.

HOREB, MOUNT. *See* SINAI, MOUNT.

HOREM hor´em [חֳרֵם khorem]. Means "consecrated," this was one of the "fortified towns" allotted to the Naphtali tribe in the book of Joshua (19:38). It was probably situated in upper Galilee.

HORESH hor´esh [חֹרְשָׁה khorshah]. An uncertain area southwest of Hebron within the rugged terrain of the wilderness of Ziph. Eluding Saul, David covenanted with Jonathan and remained within "the strongholds of Horesh" (thicketed, rocky encampments) until Ziphites informed Saul of David's specific location on the hill of Hachilah (1 Sam 23:15-19).

JASON C. DYKEHOUSE

HOR-HAGGIDGAD hor-huh-gid´gad [חֹר־הַגִּדְגָּד khor-haggidhgadh]. It may be that Gudgodah (Deut 10:7) is a variant spelling of this site along the Israelites' journey from Egypt (Num 33:32-33). If the itinerary site detail is even close to accurate it would appear that the source for both lists is filling the space between Sinai, located near Edom (*see* SINAI, MOUNT), and the Gulf of Elath with a rather large number of stations. This might best be explained as a later anachronistic expansion of a tradition believed to have originated in Egypt, thus requiring a great number of stops to reach EZION-GEBER. *See* EXODUS, ROUTE OF.

MICHAEL OBLATH

HORI hor´i [חֹרִי khori, חוֹרִי khori]. 1. Son of Lotan (Gen 36:22; 1 Chr 1:39) and grandson of "Seir the Horite" (Gen 36:20).

2. Father of Shaphat of the tribe of Simeon, Hori was one of twelve spies sent by Moses into Canaanite territory (Num 13:5). *See* HORITES.

HORITES hor´it [חֹרִי khori, חוֹרִי khori]. This is a Gentilic name of the ancient inhabitants of Edom (Gen 14:6; 36:20; Deut 2:12, 20). It often occurs with the definite article as in "Seir the Horite" (hakhori הַחֹרִי) (Gen 36:21). The name has been identified as possibly derived from the root khor (חוֹר) meaning "hole," and therefore referring to cave dwellers in the southern region of Edom. This etymology is increasingly identified as incorrect. The name is more correctly associated with the HURRIANS, known in the ANE from the third millennium. Hurrians were clearly in the central region around Jerusalem during the Amarna period, as Egyptians referred to the territory as Hur, and the o-u shift is linguistically insignificant as a distinction. The Horites of the OT are to be identified as well with the HIVITES, based on the interchanging of the terms in Gen 36:2.

C. MARK MCCORMICK

HORMAH hor´muh [חׇרְמָה khormah]. A town in the Negev of Judah, probably close to Arad. After the abortive attempt to invade Canaan from the south, the Amalekites and Canaanites pursued the Israelites as far as Hormah (Num 14:45). The name of the town means "destruction," and the OT provides two etiologies for this name. Numbers 21:3 explains the meaning by saying that the Israelites destroyed the Canaanite towns in the area. According to Judg 1:17, however, the city was originally called ZEPHAT, but its name was changed after Judah helped Simeon destroy it. In the conquest, the city was assigned to the territory of both Judah (Josh 15:30) and Simeon (Josh 19:4; 1 Chr 14:30). Hormah was one of the cities with which David shared the spoils of war when he was raiding Philistine settlements (1 Sam 30:30).

KEVIN A. WILSON

HORN. *See* ALTAR; MUSICAL INSTRUMENTS.

HORN OF MOSES. *See* MOSES, HORN OF.

HORNET [צִרְעָה *tsir'ah*]. In Israel one hornet (Hymenoptera, Vespidae, *Vespa orientalis*) and seven WASP species (*Dolychovespula germanica* and six *Polistes* species) are found. The oriental hornet is well adapted to the dry climate widely spread from the east Mediterranean to central Asia. In Israel this species is found all over the country; their subterraneous nests can be up to 1 m in diameter with tens of thousands of individuals. It is slightly larger and more aggressive than the European hornet (*Vespa crabro*), which is also found as an invasive species in the United States. Stings are painful, but even multiple stings are rarely fatal.

Hornets were used in battles, by imbedding them into clay vessels, "canonballs," which were catapulted into the rows of enemies at an early stage of the fight. It was an efficient instrument of psychological warfare causing great confusion, panic, and terror, though there was probably little actual physical damage. This kind of strategy explains Josh 24:12. This has also a metaphorical meaning where the NRSV translates tsir'ah as PESTILENCE (Exod 23:28; Deut 7:20). *See* BEE; INSECTS OF THE BIBLE.

AXEL HAUSMANN AND GÜNTER C. MÜLLER

HORONAIM hor'uh-nay'im [חוֹרֹנַיִם *khoronayim*, חֹרֹנַיִם *khoronayim*, חֹרֹנָיִם *khoronayim*]. Literally means "two hollows," Horonaim (2 Sam 13:34) was a town in southern Moab (Jer 48:3, 34; Isa 15:5), located at the foot of an ascent (Jer 48:5). Moab was on the Transjordanian plateau east of the Jordan River. Mesha's (2 Kgs 3) Moabite Inscription states that Chemosh, god of Moab, commanded Mesha to "go down" and fight against the town. With these references to descent and ascent, the town may have stood at the base of one of the dry riverbeds that led from the plateau to the Arabah/Rift Valley below. Alexander Janneus (103–76 BCE) conquered "Oroniam" (Ōrōnaim Ωρωναιμ), but

Hyrcannus gave it back to the Arab, Aretus. *See* BETH-HORON; HORONITE; MOABITE STONE.

MICHAEL G. VANZANT

HORONITE hor'uh-nit [חֹרֹנִי *khoroni*]. A resident of Horonaim (or perhaps Beth-horon). The term is used in Neh 2:10, 19; and 13:28 to denote the place of origin of SANBALLAT, a prominent opponent of Nehemiah in his efforts to restore Jerusalem. Sanballat enjoyed considerable political clout under Persian rule in his position as Samaria's governor.

DEREK E. WITTMAN

HORSE [סוּס *sus*; ἵππος *hippos*]. The horse appears in the Bible as a domesticated animal used for riding and pulling chariots. Unlike other equids such as the donkey and the mule, the horse was considered a prestigious animal used only for military purposes.

    A. Domestication
    B. Uses and Care of the Horse
      1. Use
      2. Care
    C. Stabling Horses
    D. Chariotry and Horseback Riding
    E. Horses in Canaan and in the Bible
    F. Horses and Chariots in the ANE
    Bibliography

A. Domestication

Cave paintings in France and Spain indicate that the horse (*Equus caballus*) has been part of human culture since the Magdalenian phase of the Upper Paleolithic (35000–18000 BCE). Some scholars date the horse's domestication to 2500 BCE, while others to 4200–4000 BCE, possibly in the Ukrainian steppes, north of the Black Sea. Horse bones from the Chalcolithic (3500–3200 BCE) Negev sites of Shiqmim and Gerar suggest that the horse was already domesticated by that time and that vehicles with spoked wheels were in use.

B. Uses and Care of the Horse
  1. Use

By the Middle Bronze Age I (2000–1750 BCE) the domestic horse was present in southern Iran. The horse was harnessed to draw chariots as well as to serve in the cavalry. The appearance of the chariot in the Near East in the second millennium BCE is associated with the arrival of the Kassites, Hittites and Hurrians, who dominated western Asia. The chariot, which during the New Kingdom became a well-known symbol of pharaonic might, was introduced into Egypt probably during the Hyksos period (ca. 1650–1550 BCE).

  2. Care

Harnessing the horse in the service of human culture was not without certain difficulties. Horses are very delicate animals and need much care to be in top shape. In antiquity horses were highly pampered, and this is seen by the grooming and decorations with which they were lavished as reflected in artistic representations, written documents, and in archaeological finds. Horses' hooves (ʿiqqeve sus [עִקְּבֵי־סוּס], Judg 5:22; parsoth abbirayw [פַּרְסוֹת אַבִּירָיו], Jer 47:3) need protection; however, it is not clear when horseshoes originated.

C. Stabling Horses

Biblical and extra-biblical sources mention horses used for military purposes in Canaan (later Israel). However, neither the Bible, nor any other source gives a detailed description of horses. This is especially important when trying to define the function of the structures labeled "The Megiddo Stables" and the other tripartite buildings. One of the main arguments advanced by those opposing the identification of the structures as stables is that the side rooms, where the horses were supposed to be stabled, are too narrow and could not accommodate horses of the size with which we are familiar. This problem might be resolved if, in fact, small horses (such as Przewalski's horse, *Equus ferus przewalskii* or *Equus przewaskii* and the Caspian Miniature Horse, both of which are native to the region) were stabled in these buildings. Their discovery and identification add support to the possibility that horses smaller than present-day horses were used in antiquity for a variety of functions, including riding and pulling chariots. Illustrations of small horses used for such functions appear in the reliefs at Persepolis (5th cent. BCE) and on a royal seal of Darius.

D. Chariotry and Horseback Riding

It has been suggested that early domestic horses were small in stature and were more commonly used for pulling chariots than for riding. This does not seem reasonable, because horseback riding probably started in the Ukrainian steppes ca. 3800–3500 BCE, well before the introduction of carts at about 3500 BCE. During that time, the horse was utilized by herding societies for moving and transporting materials from one locale to another.

Biblical references suggest that horseback riding was practiced at the end of the Late Bronze Age. The "Song of the Sea" in Exod 15:1, which is considered to be an early composition, describes the Israelites' victory over the Egyptians at the Sea of Reeds saying "horse and rider (sus werokhevo סוּס וְרֹכְבוֹ) he has hurled into the sea" (see also Exod 15:21). This reference suggests that horseback riding was known in the Near East, at least, as early as the 13th cent. BCE. Some argue that Egyptian military rode horses for scouting purposes. Egyptian art from the time of Seti I and Rameses II depicts mounted Asiatics, Syrians, and Hittites, probably also serving as mounted scouts. Several examples show horses with reins and harness and riders on a cloth-saddle, a few on a sidesaddle, and most of them are in military context, representing perhaps the earliest known examples of cavalry.

E. Horses in Canaan and in the Bible

The employment of cavalry and chariotry became prevalent in Canaan even before 1000 BCE. That the Egyptians used both is well known and the biblical record alludes to it (Josh 24:6). The Bible suggests that the Canaanites used chariotry to their disadvantage against the Israelites (Judg 4; 5:28). Also the Philistines are said to have used them in large numbers (1 Sam 13:5; 2 Sam 1:6). Even before its formation it was expected of the Israelite monarchy to make use of these military forces (1 Sam 8:11). According to the biblical account, King David did not know what to do with the chariot horses he captured from Hadadezer the Rehobite, king of Zobah, and by hamstringing most of them he took them out of commission (2 Sam 8:4). But Solomon seems to have used horses for CHARIOTs and CAVALRY (1 Kgs 5:6; 9:19). He built chariot cities (1 Kgs 10:26), and was involved in horse and chariot trading, serving as a middleman between Egypt, Que, the Hittites, and the Arameans (1 Kgs 10:28-29; 2 Chr 1:17). Chariotry became a means of displaying the highest level of military investment because it required large teams of trained soldiers, auxiliary forces engaged in the building and maintenance of the chariotry, weaponry, and horses. When Adonijah wanted to become king, he employed chariots and cavalry (1 Kgs 1:5) because this was a sign of royalty. Solomon was no exception, because in addition to other functions, his regional governors "provided also barley and straw, each according to his duty, for the horses and chariot-horses where it was required" (1 Kgs 4:28).

Using horses for chariotry (1 Kgs 5:8; Mic 1:13) and cavalry (2 Kgs 7:14) in the military became very popular in the 10th–7th cent. BCE. The biblical record devotes much space to descriptions of such activities. The Arameans were well known for their mounted forces. David destroyed a large number of these forces (2 Sam 10:18); the Ammonites hired Aramean mounted forces (1 Chr 19:6-7, 18). Shalmaneser III's (858–824 BCE) annalistic reports testify to the power of the Aramean and Israelite chariotry and cavalry. One such report states in part: "1,200 chariots, 1,200 cavalrymen, 20,000 foot soldiers of Adad-ʾidri (i.e., Hadadezer) of Damascus, . . . 700 chariots, 700 cavalrymen, 10,000 foot soldiers of Irhuleni from Hamath, 2,000 chariots, 10,000 foot soldiers of Ahab, the Israelite." The biblical records show also that the kings of Judah and Israel employed cavalry and chariotry in many of their wars (1 Kgs 16:9; 2 Chr 21:9). The prophets describe the mounted forces of the Judahite kings (Jer 17:25; 22:4) as well as those of the enemies (Isa 22:6-7; 31:1; Jer 46:9; Ezek 26:7). That the kings of Judah possessed chariots is also illustrated on Sennacherib's palace reliefs, where a chariot is seen taken away from Lachish by the Assyrians as booty.

While the Egyptians used chariotry on the battlefield to their advantage, as recorded by Thutmoses III after the Battle of Megiddo (1485 BCE) and by Ramesses II after the Battle of Qadesh (ca. 1280 BCE), the Assyrians developed the use of cavalry as well as nonmilitary mounted messengers. In their army, the Assyrians incorporated prisoners of war who were skilled in the arts of chariotry and cavalry. Thus, after conquering Samaria in 722 BCE, Sargon II incorporated from the prisoners a contingent of fifty chariots in his royal corps.

The extensive use of horses for chariotry and cavalry demanded large numbers of animals. Solomon, who had a large force of cavalry and chariotry, acquired them by trade with Egypt (1 Kgs 10:28-29; 2 Chr 1:17) and Isaiah was also aware of the fact that Egypt was a source of horses (Isa 31:1, 3). In the Bible, the horse functioned only as a military machine and not as a power source for agricultural or other daily tasks. The description of the horse's strength in Job 39:19-25 and even the depictions of horses in apocalyptic literature (Zech 6:2-6; Rev 9:7-17; 19:14, 18) are characteristic of the horse's use as a military instrument.

In the realm of Israelite cultic practices, archaeological evidence such as clay figurines of horses with or without riders, and the biblical account in 2 Kgs 23:11 suggest that the horse was somehow connected with sun worship.

F. Horses and Chariots in the Ancient Near East

The earliest mention of chariot and horses used in Egypt is in a text "The Expulsion of the Hyksos," where Pharaoh is described as having a chariot. The Hyksos introduced into Egypt horses and chariots and the Egyptians adopted them. In his reports on the Asiatic campaigns, Thutmoses III describes the major role played by horses. His enemies' horses and chariots were captured and the list of booty he carried off from Megiddo includes "2,041 horses, 191 foals, 6 stallions, . . . colts" and chariots totaling 924. The Barkal Stele summarizing Thutmoses" achievements states, "tribute: gold and silver, all their horses which were with them, their great chariots of gold and silver." At every one of Thutmoses' campaigns he took booty that included horses and chariots. When Amen-hotep II (1447–1421 BCE) reports on his Asiatic campaigns, he claims that near the Orontes river he captured two princes and six maryanu with "their chariots, their teams, and their weapons of warfare," and on his return to Memphis, the list of booty includes "horses: 820; chariots: 730." More horses and chariots were taken as booty at the battles of Aphek and at Iteren and Migdol-yen (unknown sites).

The Assyrians were also using military campaigns to replenish their chariotry and cavalry needs. Tiglath-Pileser I (1114–1076 BCE) and Ashurbanipal II (883–859 BCE) brought back horses from their campaigns. Shalmaneser III (858–824 BCE), in his so-called "Monolith Inscription" describes the large numbers of mounted forces involved in these conflicts: nearly 15,000 chariots and 2,000 cavalrymen.

Other Assyrian kings including Tiglath-Pileser III (744–727 BCE), Sennacherib (704–681 BCE), and Ashurbanipal (668–633 BCE) brought back from their campaigns in the Levant, among other livestock, countless horses as booty and tribute. *See* ANIMALS OF THE BIBLE.

Bibliography: O. Borowski. *Every Living Thing: Daily Use of Animals in Ancient Israel* (1998); J. B. Pritchard. *Ancient Near Eastern Texts Relating to the Old Testament* (1969).

ODED BOROWSKI

HORSE GATE [שַׁעַר הַסּוּסִים shaʿar hassusim]. A gate of Jerusalem mentioned in Jeremiah's description of a rebuilt, expanded city (31:40) that appears in association with the repairs being carried out by priests in Neh 3:28. It was located on the eastern side of the city near the Temple/palace complex and opened toward the KIDRON VALLEY. *See* JERUSALEM.

DEREK E. WITTMAN

HORSEMAN [פָּרָשׁ parash, רַכָּב rakkav, רֹכֵב סוּס rokhev sus; ἱππεύς hippeus]. Usually refers to a soldier mounted on a horse prepared for war (e.g., Josh 24:6; Acts 23:23). *See* CAVALRY; CHARIOT; HORSE; WAR, METHODS, TACTICS, WEAPONS OF (BRONZE AGE THROUGH PERSIAN PERIOD); WAR, METHODS, TACTICS, WEAPONS OF (HELLENISTIC THROUGH ROMAN PERIODS).

HORVAT RIMMON. *See* RIMMON, HORVAT.

HORVAT ʿUZA. *See* ʿUZA, HORVAT.

HOSAH hoh´suh [חֹסָה khosah]. 1. Part of the tribe of Asher's allotment (Josh 19:29); it is most likely the biblical name for the Tyrian suburb Usu (Tell Rashidiyeh), which, according to the *Annals of Sennacherib*, was conquered in 701 BCE.

2. A man, who along with male family members, was appointed by David to serve as gatekeeper at Yahweh's sanctuary in Jerusalem. By the casting of lots, these descendants of Levi were assigned to the western side of the holy site (1 Chr 16:38; 26:10, 11, 16).

Bibliography: Yohanan Aharoni. *The Land of the Bible.* A. F. Rainey, transl. and ed. (1979); A. Leo Oppenheim. "Babylonian and Assyrian Historical Texts." *ANET* (1969) 287.

JASON R. TATLOCK

HOSANNA hoh-zan´uh [נָא הוֹשִׁיעָה hoshi'ah na']; Aram. נָא הוֹשַׁע hosha' na'; ὡσαννά hōsanna]. The word *hosanna* is a transliteration of the Aram. words hosha' na'. Hosha' na' is the equivalent of the Hebrew hoshi'ah na in Ps 118:25-26, which reads, "Save now (hoshi'ah na), we beseech thee, O LORD! O LORD, we beseech thee, give us success! Blessed be he who enters in the name of the LORD! We bless you from the house of the LORD."

The Aram. term, with the Hebrew behind it, is well known to Christians as part of the shout of the crowd when Jesus entered the city of Jerusalem. Mark's paraphrase "Hosanna! Blessed is he who comes in the name of the Lord!" (Mark 11:9) thus represents the first part of each verse of Ps 118:25-26. The LXX does not transliterate, but translates sōson dē (σῶσον δή; "Save now!" Ps 117:25). Accordingly, the Markan evangelist's use of the Aram. hosha' na' argues for authenticity of the tradition, rather than as a later Christian gleaning of the LXX. Literally and originally, *hosanna* is a request for help. Because the hosha' of hosha' na' and the Hebrew/Aramaic meaning of Jesus' name are derived from the verb "save," some commentators think that the cry *hosanna* was specifically directed to Jesus, rather than to God. This could be correct, for shouts of "hosanna" to Israel's kings are found in Scripture. For example, the woman of Tekoa cries out hoshi'ah hammelekh (הוֹשִׁיעָה הַמֶּלֶךְ; "Save, O king!"), which in the LXX is rendered sōson basileu sōson (Σῶσον βασιλεῦ σῶσον; "Save, O king, save"; e.g., 2 Sam 14:4); or the cry of a famished woman hoshi'ah 'adhoni hammelekh (הוֹשִׁיעָה אֲדֹנִי הַמֶּלֶךְ; "Save, O lord king!"), which in the LXX is rendered sōson kyrie basileu (Σῶσον κύριε βασιλεῦ; 2 Kgs 6:26). Nevertheless, the addressee of the hoshi'ah na' of Ps 118:25 is God, so it is more likely that the people accompanying Jesus are crying out to God to fulfill the promised deliverance (through Jesus, God's agent of deliverance) and the kingdom of David.

The expression "hosanna" evoked kingly associations, and Ps 118, the passage that lies behind the cry in Jesus' entry into Jerusalem, was itself later interpreted with reference to the recognition of David as Israel's rightful king. According to the Aramaic version: "Blessed is the one who comes in the name of the Word of the Lord, said David" (*Tg. Ps.-J.* 118:26). The Davidic orientation of Ps 118 thus coheres with the crowd's paraphrase: "Blessed is the kingdom of our father David that is coming" (Mark 11:10).

Bibliography: J. A. Fitzmyer. "Aramaic Evidence Affecting the Interpretation of *Hosanna* in the New Testament." *Tradition and Interpretation in the New Testament.* G. F. Hawthorne and O. Betz, eds. (1987) 110–18.

CRAIG A. EVANS

HOSEA. *See* HOSEA, BOOK OF.

HOSEA, BOOK OF hoh-zay´uh [הוֹשֵׁעַ hoshae']. Hosea was the only prophet with a book by his name who was a native of the northern kingdom of Israel and who proclaimed his message there. He began his ministry sometime around 750 BCE and ended it just prior to the Assyrian conquest of the Northern Kingdom in 722 BCE. The book by his name is the first in the Book of the Twelve, a collection of shorter prophetic books that make up the final portion of the Hebrew canon called *nevi'im* or "the Prophets." The beginning of Hosea's ministry is contemporary with that of Amos although it extends through a much longer period of time. His message is about God's judgment on Israel, particularly for its sin of idolatry, viewed as an adulterous relationship with Canaanite religion, particularly the worship of Baal. However, his message of judgment is tempered by a strong concept of God's love for Israel and a divine willingness to redeem the relationship.

A. Text and Translation
B. Structure, Form, and Contents
C. Hosea's Marriage and Children
D. Historical Context
E. Message of Hosea
  1. God's covenant and the knowledge of God
  2. Opposition to idolatry
  3. Corruption of political and social institutions
  4. God's judgment
  5. God's love and redemption
F. Enduring Significance and Challenge
Bibliography

A. Text and Translation

The book of Hosea is regarded as second only to Job in the difficulty of its text and the problems it poses to translators. It is often suggested that the obscure vocabulary and unusual grammatical constructions are due to textual corruption in the transmission of the text. The LXX version seems equally difficult and obscure, as do the other ancient versions, suggesting that these ancient translators were struggling with the difficulty of the text as well. Small fragments from the first two chapters of Hosea are found in the Qumran texts (4Q78, 4Q79; 4Q82; 4Q167), but they are very close to the MT and seem to indicate that Hosea's textual peculiarities are ancient in origin and not due to corruption as the text was handed on through the generations.

An increasing number of scholars believe that the peculiar difficulties of the text of Hosea stem from our lack of familiarity with the Hebrew dialect of northern Israel. It is probable that the oracles of Hosea are the only genuinely northern Hebrew material of any extent in the Hebrew canon. Even Amos, who preached in the north, was from Tekoa in the tribal territory of Judah.

What translators encounter as difficulties may not stem from corruptions of errors in transmission, but from a genuinely different dialect of ancient Hebrew. A number of recent studies and commentaries have begun to draw on linguistic understandings from the comparative study of northwest Semitic languages and texts, particularly Ugaritic. This approach seems to promise helpful explanations of obscure texts in Hosea without the assumption that the text is corrupt.

B. Structure, Form, and Contents

Anyone reading through the books of the Prophets in the Hebrew canon will quickly recognize that Hosea does not employ the same stylized patterns of prophetic speech that are reflected in most of the other prophetic books. There are two chapters of prose narrative (Hos 1 and 3), and the rest of the book is in the form of collections of short oracles sometimes grouped thematically within larger sections. The full prophetic messenger formula ("Thus says the Lord") does not appear in Hosea, although a shortened oracle formula ("says the Lord") appears four times (2:13, 16, 21; 11:1). There are two instances of a divine lawsuit pattern (4:1; 12:2). Many of Hosea's oracles are in the first person, as if the Lord is directly addressing Israel (e.g., 4:1-14).

Hosea's oracles were probably edited into final form in Judah after the collapse of the northern kingdom of Israel, which also marks the end of Hosea's preaching. Several references to Judah seem added to give meaning to Hosea's oracles for a Judean audience (e.g., 1:7; 3:5).

There are three major sections of the book. Chapters 1–3 tell the story of Hosea's marriage to Gomer and the birth of their children. The prophet uses his personal experience to reflect on God's experience with Israel using imagery of husband and wife. Chapters 4–11 are Hosea's oracles of judgment on Israel's covenant transgressions in cult and politics, and introduce, esp. in chap. 11, imagery of God as parent and Israel as rebellious child. Chapters 12–14 reflect the final days of the Northern Kingdom when its collapse seems inevitable, and the prophet sees this as the result of God's judgment. Each of these sections, although speaking of God's judgment, ends with chapters that speak of God's enduring love for Israel and the redemption and forgiveness that God intends beyond judgment (chaps. 3, 11, 14). There are also scattered references to hope and redemption within these sections (e.g., 2:14-23; 9:10-16).

Hosea 1:1–3:5 Hosea and Gomer; God and Israel
  1:1-11 Go, Take for Yourself a Wife
    1:1-9 Hosea, Gomer, and Their Children
    1:10-11 God's New Future
  2:1-23 Not My Wife, Not Her Husband
    2:1-13 Judgment on Israel's Adultery
    2:14-23 Restoration and Renewal of Relationship
  3:1-5 Go, Love a Woman Again

Hosea 4:1–11:11 God's Judgment on Israel's Idolatry
                    and Political Corruption
  4:1-11a There Is No Knowledge of God
    4:1-3 God's Lawsuit
    4:4-11a Charges against the Priests
  4:11b-19 Though You Play the Whore, O Israel
    4:11b-14 The Lord Condemns Idolatry
    4:15-19 The Prophet's Warning
  5:1-7 God Judges Israel's Leaders
    5:1-2 Hear, O Priests and Kings
    5:3-7 They Do Not Know the Lord
  5:8–6:6 Steadfast Love, Not Sacrifice
    5:8-15 War for Israel and Judah
    6:1-3 Let Us Return to the Lord
    6:4-6 God's Desired Response
  6:7–7:16 They Call Upon Egypt; They Go to
                    Assyria
    6:7–7:7 The Corruption of Ephraim
    7:8-12 Israel's Pride and Folly
    7:13-16 God's Outcry
  8:1-14 Israel Has Spurned the Good
    8:1-3 Warning Is Sounded
    8:4-14 Israel's Sins of Kings and Idolatry
  9:1-17 The Prophet Is a Sentinel
    9:1-6 The Prophet Condemns Israel
    9:7-9 The Prophet Condemned and Upheld
    9:10-16 God Remembers Israel
    9:17 Announcement of God's Judgment
  10:1-8 Israel Is a Luxuriant Vine
    10:1-2 Israel's Apostasy
    10:3-4 Loss of a King
    10:5-8 Worship of a Calf
  10:9-15 The Sin of Gibeah
    10:9-10 The Violence of Gibeah
    10:11-12 Ephraim as a Heifer
    10:13-15 War Shall Rise against Your People
  11:1-11 When Israel Was a Child
    11:1-4 Israel as God's Child
    11:5-7 Israel as Rebelious Child
    11:8-11 God Loves and Restores Israel

Hosea 11:12–14:9 Israel Judged but Restored
  11:12–12:14 The Punishment of Jacob
    11:12–12:1 Ephraim Herds the Wind
    12:2-6 Israel as Jacob I
    12:7-11 Deceptive Behavior
    12:12-14 Israel as Jacob II
  13:1-16 God Will Destroy
    13:1-3 Idolatrous Ephraim Doomed
    13:4-8 Indictment and Punishment
    13:9-11 God's Disputation with Israel
    13:12-16 Ephraim Refuses Life
  14:1-9 Israel Restored By God
    14:1-3 Confession and Repentance
    14:4-8 God's Salvation as Luxuriant Garden
    14:9 Final Advice for the Wise Reader

C. Hosea's Marriage and Children

Hosea was the son of Beeri, and his ministry was in the northern kingdom of Israel, although no precise locations are known. He was probably already a prophet when God called him to marry a promiscuous woman ('esheth zenunim [אֵשֶׁת זְנוּנִים], 1:2). In response, he marries Gomer, the daughter of Diblaim (1:3). The nature of Gomer's promiscuity has been the subject of speculation and debate throughout the history of the interpretation of the book. Many translations and interpreters have treated Gomer as a prostitute. The Hebrew word for a prostitute is zonah (זֹנָה) derived from the verb zanah (זָנָה). This verb covers a range of sexual transgressions by women outside of marriage: ADULTERY by a married woman, fornication by unmarried daughters or sisters, and PROSTITUTION by women giving sex for economic payment. The noun, however, is primarily used for prostitutes, and Gomer is never simply labeled a zonah. To be an 'esheth zenunim seems to be less a designation as a professional prostitute than as a woman who acts in promiscuous or adulterous ways. It is occasionally suggested that Gomer was engaged in the prostitution that is sometimes claimed as a part of Canaanite religious practice. There is little evidence for this in the text of Hosea. Worship practices associated with Baal or other Canaanite deities are only mentioned in the God/Israel analogy and not in reference to Hosea's own relationship to Gomer. It is most likely that Hosea has married a woman with a reputation for promiscuity, who is probably continuing such behavior after the marriage. It is clear that God's command to marry such a woman is intended as an analogy to God's relationship with Israel, who has also been adulterous and forsaken loyalty to God (1:2).

Gomer bears three children to Hosea: a son, a daughter, and another son. If the marriage to Gomer symbolizes Israel's sin, the names of the children represent the consequences of that sin. The first son is named Jezreel. It is the name of a fertile valley located between the hills of Galilee and the hills of Samaria, and also the name of an important Israelite city in that valley, but it has a bloody history. It is associated with the violent overthrow of the house of Omri by Jehu (2 Kgs 9–10). The idolatrous reign of Ahab was ended with the deaths of kings in Judah and Samaria, the throwing of Jezebel to the dogs, and the gruesome display of the heads of Ahab's seven sons. There was also a massacre of Baal worshipers launched by Jehu with prophetic support. The dynasty of Jehu is still on the throne at the time of Hosea, in the person of Jeroboam II. Yet, in the naming of Hosea's son it is stated that Jehu's dynasty will also come to an end, and its power will be broken. The Israel of Jehu's dynasty has become as deserving of judgment as the dynasty he overthrew. Since we later learn that, like the reign of Ahab and Jezebel, the chief sin for which Israel is judged in Hosea's time is idolatry, the implication is that the boy Jezreel will be a reminder of God's judgment on any idolatrous generation.

The second child is a daughter, and her name is to be LO-RUHAMAH (1:6). In Hebrew this means "No compassion" or "Not pitied." The verb related to this noun (rukhamah רֻחָמָה) means "compassion" and is related to the Hebrew word for a woman's womb (rekhem רֶחֶם). It is a word used to suggest that God's compassion encompasses the covenant partner like a mother's womb, but the naming of Hosea's daughter indicates that God's compassion is exhausted, the time for forgiveness is passed.

The third child, a son, is named LO-AMMI, which means "Not My People." This is a reversal of the covenantal formula "I will be your God and you will be my people" (compare Exod 6:7; Lev 26:12; Deut 26:17). Israel's sin has nullified the covenant with God and ended the special relationship as God's people.

In Hos 2 we see more fully the manner in which Hosea's marriage and family have become metaphors in his message for the idolatrous relationship of Israel to the Lord. The poetic imagery of Hosea's preaching makes clear that it is Israel's attraction to the worship of Baal and the implied promise in Canaanite religion of the fertility and productivity of the land that God regards as the unfaithful taking of lovers and the forsaking of covenant commitment to the Lord (2:5-9, 13). Israel does not know that the gifts of the land come from the Lord (2:8).

The images of God's judgment are harsh and reflect the accepted behavior of a wounded and angry husband toward an adulterous wife in Israel's time. The chapter moves from accusation (2:2-5) to consequences, which include public stripping and humiliation, followed by isolation and restricting of the wife's freedom in an effort to control her sexuality. Such actions today would be considered abusive and unacceptable. They reflect a view of women and marriage in which husbands exercised control of the freedom and sexuality of women, and this justified harsh penalties to women judged guilty of ADULTERY. We can acknowledge the pain and vulnerability that surfaces in broken relationships when promises and loyalties are set aside, and all parties— husband, wife, children—suffer consequences. But we must firmly reject the appropriateness of physically or emotionally abusive responses to such brokenness in the effort to regain control, even when such responses have been attributed to God.

Beneath the adultery metaphor lays the issue of IDOLATRY. Hosea's metaphor of husband and wife points to God's covenant relationship with Israel and the demand for loyalty to the Lord alone. Hosea seems to be familiar with the Decalogue (compare 4:1-3), and there is no room for shared loyalty to BAAL and the Lord. Further, such split loyalty is motivated out of a desire for material gain (2:5). For Hosea and God, in whose voice he speaks, to pursue the Baals is to forget the Lord (2:13).

If the language of consequence in Hosea's use of the husband-wife metaphor is problematic, we must also acknowledge that the language of continued love and divine resolve for renewal is moving and passionate. In 2:14-23 the imagery shifts from indictment to forgiveness and redemption. If we say a firm no to abusive responses to broken relationship, then the images of these verses become a testimony to loving and constructive alternatives for response to woundedness and pain in broken promises. Hosea speaks of wooing and tenderness while remembering the beginnings of relationship (2:14-15). The Baals are not needed to acknowledge the gifts of creation (vv. 16-18). Recommitment and renewal become possible through a litany of qualities on which genuine relationship is built: righteousness, justice, steadfast love, compassion, and faithfulness (vv. 19-20), and in these qualities Israel may know the Lord (v. 20). In this vision of restoration, the names of the children are reversed from images of judgment to images of renewal and hope (vv. 21-23). Jezreel fulfills the true meaning of his name, "God sows." "Not-pitied" becomes "You shall have pity," and "Not my people" becomes "You are my people."

There is a final cryptic note to the story of Hosea's marriage in 3:1-5. Speaking in the first person, Hosea says that God commanded him to "Go, love again a woman who has a lover and is an adulteress." The word again applies to the verb and not, as in the NRSV, to God's command. The likelihood is that the unnamed woman here is Gomer, whose behavior has led her into difficult circumstances that require Hosea to redeem her for a price. A few scholars believe this is a reference to a second woman. The verses of this chapter are unclear. The payment to redeem her is also obscure. Is Hosea simply supplying silver for clothes and food because he stripped her of these things, as reflected in the judgment of God in chap. 2? Or has she gone to her lovers and ended in difficulty, perhaps servitude, from which she must be redeemed? In the end this brief chapter leaves these questions unresolved, but what is clear is that Hosea has been moved to act redemptively in restoring relationship. He does not force his attentions upon her but insists she no longer have lovers, and the suggestion is that he waits for her own return to him (3:4-5). The chapter shows marks of later editing as well.

D. Historical Context

Hosea began preaching during the relatively peaceful and prosperous reign of Jeroboam II (786–746 BCE) in the northern kingdom of Israel (1:1). Most scholars would date the beginning of his ministry somewhere around 750 BCE. Hosea shared with his contemporary Amos the conviction that beneath the seemingly calm surface of Jeroboam II's reign all was not well. In spite of scattered references to Judah (many of which are later editorial additions), Hosea preached only in the northern kingdom of Israel. Chapters 1–4 are probably from the early years of his ministry and reflect his concern that idolatry, particularly in relation to the Canaanite god Baal, was eroding loyalty to the Lord, Israel's covenant God. The result of moral erosion as well as knowledge of God diminished in Israel's people and leaders (see esp. Hos 4).

Even the external well-being of Jeroboam's reign was ended with his death. Israel fell into a brutal period of struggle and intrigue focused on the throne. Between 746 BCE and the end of the kingdom in 722 BCE, six different kings sat on the throne. None held it for more than a few years and some only for months. Hosea's message during this period added political intrigue and corruption to the list of Israel's transgressions. Hosea came to see the kingship itself as sinful and ill considered (7:7; 8:4).

Unfortunately Israel's internal political woes coincided and were exacerbated by a growing period of international intrigue. Assyria was in an expansive period of empire building begun by the accession of Tiglath-pileser III to the Assyrian throne in 745 BCE. Menachem (745–738 BCE) felt the pressure of Assyrian campaigns in the region in 743 BCE and paid a large tribute in submission to Assyria. This angered wealthy landowners who supported the murder of Menachem's son and the seizing of the throne by Pekah in 737 BCE. Pekah, in alliance with the Syrian king in Damascus, formed an Egyptian-backed coalition against Assyria and tried to force Judah and its king, Ahaz, to join them. Ahaz (with the encouragement of the prophet Isaiah) refused and appealed to Assyria for help. This gave Tiglath-pileser III opportunity to subdue Syrian and Israelite territory. Much of Israel's land was occupied in 733, and many people were deported, but Samaria and its surrounding territory was spared when Pekah was overthrown by Hoshea ben Elah (732–724), who paid immediate tribute to Assyria and averted total disaster. Much of Hosea's preaching in chaps. 5–8 seems to reflect the turbulent political dealings of this period. Some also believe the more hopeful oracles of chaps. 9–11 come from the brief time of calm under the reign of Hoshea.

Hoshea, however, was drawn into intrigue with Egypt at the time Assyria went through some of its own inner turmoil over succession to the throne in 727 BCE. He withheld tribute, but in 724 a new Assyrian king, Shalmaneser V, gained control and invaded rebellious Israel. He captured Hoshea and laid siege to Samaria. The final chapters of Hosea come against the backdrop of these final days of the northern kingdom of Israel (Hos 12–14). Nothing in the book of Hosea seems to know of Samaria's fall in 722 or the deportation of the kingdom's population, so it is usually thought his preaching ended just prior to these final events.

E. Message of Hosea

1. God's covenant and the knowledge of God

Hosea's message constantly operates out of the understanding that God has willingly entered into a covenant partnership with Israel. In this respect he is similar to most of the other prophets, esp. those of the 8th cent. For Hosea this covenant understanding seems rooted in the Sinai tradition of Moses and the law since 4:1-2 seems to clearly draw upon the Decalogue. The reason for Israel's judgment is clearly related to this tradition in 8:1, "because they have broken my covenant and transgressed my law" (compare also 6:1). This covenant partnership was understood to lay obligations on both parties, God and Israel, and much of Hosea's preaching grows out of the conviction that Israel has failed in its obligations while God has remained faithful to the divine commitment (*see* COVENANT, NT AND OT).

Although Hosea shares the assumption of covenant partnership with contemporary and later prophets, his vocabulary for covenant commitment is somewhat different. The prominent concepts of justice and righteousness as the demand of covenant obedience are present in Hosea but not extensively used (as by his contemporary, Amos, who was preaching in the north). He refers to the pair in his restored marriage metaphor in 2:19, to justice paired with love in 12:6, and to righteousness paired with love in 10:12.

Hosea's primary term for the quality demanded by covenant loyalty is "the knowledge of God." It is what God desires more than sacrifice (6:6). Covenant disobedience and God's judgment are the result of its lack: "My people are destroyed for lack of knowledge (4:6*a*). Nurturing and cultivating the knowledge of God is the special responsibility of the priests, and they are judged for not carrying out this task (4:6). To know God is to enter into the understanding and experiencing of God's relationship to Israel, including the traditions of the past from Egypt through the wilderness (11:1-4; 13:4-5). It is a relational term and implies intimacy between related partners, including the marital relationship that is such an important metaphor in Hosea's message. It is most often paired in Hosea's preaching with the terms for "steadfast love" and "faithfulness," words also associated elsewhere in the Prophets with covenant loyalty, but that are especially prominent in Hosea (4:1; 6:6; 12:6). God shows these qualities of knowledge, love, and faithfulness toward Israel and expects Israel to return them in relationship to God, just as a husband and wife would expect in their relationship (*see* LOVE IN THE OT; MARRIAGE, OT).

2. Opposition to idolatry

In the statement of covenant obligations represented by the Decalogue, the foremost responsibility of Israel as covenant partner is loyalty to the Lord alone (Exod 20:3), and the second commandment strictly forbids the making and worshiping of idols of any kind (Exod 20:4-6). For Hosea, the central charge against Israel for the breaking of covenant is that they engage in worshiping human-made objects of wood and metal that are no gods at all (4:12, 17). Specifically, the people of Israel have been drawn to the worship of Baal (11:2) and engage in Canaanite practices at their sacred sites (4:13) with hopes of receiving the material blessings of fertility in the land that Canaanite religion promises (2:5). For Hosea, it was the Lord who provided the gifts of the land and worship of Baal was not choosing life, but death (2:8-9; 13:1-2).

Perhaps because of his own marriage experience, Hosea saw Israel's idolatry through the metaphor of a wife taking lovers in disloyalty to her husband. Israel, in worshiping Baal, has become an adulteress and engaged in whore-like behavior (2:4-5, 13; 4:12-13; 5:3; 9:1). Some scholars conjecture that worship of Baal and the fertility of the land associated with him included sexual rites considered immoral by Israel's prophets (*see* FERTILITY CULT). Israel's unfaithfulness has broken the relationship to the Lord. God is in the role of a wounded marital partner.

The sin of idolatry is particularly laid at the feet of the priests in Hosea's preaching. They were to guard the integrity of Israel's worship and promote the knowledge of God. Since they had not done so, they were particularly worthy of judgment (4:4-6; 5:1-2). Some may have thought that proper sacrificial ritual would ensure the Lord's favor in spite of idolatrous practice, but Hosea makes clear that God desires steadfast love and knowledge of God more than sacrifice or offerings (6:6).

3. Corruption of political and social institutions

After the death of Jeroboam II (746 BCE), the kingdom of Israel entered a period of political intrigue and corruption that increasingly led Hosea to see Israel's sins as great in the political as well as the cultic realm. Like his contemporary, Amos, he saw a general moral breakdown in social behavior that did not accord with the responsibilities toward the neighbor demanded of God's covenant partners. Wholesale disregard for the fundamental commandments of the Decalogue are reflected in 4:2 (see 6:7-8).

It is, however, against the kings of Israel and the leaders associated with them that Hosea speaks with particular venom. They have not trusted in the Lord but in their own military might and political maneuvering (7:7; 10:13-14). He particularly believes that the kings' attempts to gain advantage by manipulating alliances with Assyria and Egypt were ill advised and dangerous (7:11; 8:9; 12:1). Such actions betray a lack of trust in the Lord. The motive for such actions is not covenant obedience but the personal gain of wealth or power that can be gained through corruption and duplicity (7:3). The chaos of these final years for the

Northern Kingdom seems to have led Hosea to a negative evaluation of kingship as such. He indicates that the beginning of Israel's corrupt and sinful state began at Gibeah, the capital city of Israel's first king, Saul (9:9; 10:9). Kingship, in Hosea's view, was not from God but from the lack of trust of the people (8:4). The false security promoted by the kings would bring Israel to destruction, a view that unfortunately seems vindicated in Hosea's own time (13:10-11).

4. God's judgment

Although his listing of Israel's sins was somewhat different than his contemporary, Amos, Hosea agrees with the other 8th cent. prophets that the breaking of covenant has become so widespread and grievous that God has determined to bring the kingdom to an end. God's judgment was not a passing reprimand but an announcement of the end of the nation. In the oracles that probably come from the earlier part of Hosea's preaching, the images of God's judgment often fit the offense. If the people falsely believed that idolatrous worship of Baal would bring them the bounteous gifts of the land, then judgment would take the form of a refusal of the land to yield its gifts and to languish rather than flourish (2:9; 4:3). If kings sought to secure their own future through military might, political manipulation, or false alliances then they would suffer the fate of conquest (7:11-16; 8:7-16).

Toward the end of Hosea's ministry, as the political events become more desperate and chaotic, his message moves from one poetic image of disaster to another. He opines that Israel's future among the nations will be as ephemeral as morning mist, early dew, swirling chaff, or smoke drifting from a window (13:3). He comes to believe that the nation cannot be saved. "I will destroy you, O Israel; who can help you? Where now is your king that he may save you?" (13:9-10a). Chapter 13 piles up image after image for the end of Israel, and may reflect Hosea's experience of the kingdom's final days. Hosea's preaching and the end of Israel by Assyrian conquest came very close together. Nothing in the book of Hosea indicates a perspective after the end of the kingdom, but the prophet's clear view of Israel's impending fate is surely one of the things that commended his preaching for preservation as a word to future generations.

5. God's love and redemption

One of the striking differences between Hosea and Amos is the passionate message that God's love transcended God's judgment. Again, the metaphor drawn out of Hosea's own marriage experience seems influential here. Beyond anger and woundedness, beyond the ruptures of broken relationship, Hosea saw the husband desiring restored and renewed relationship. Whatever the full nature of the events reflected in Hos 3, it is clear that Hosea acted with a personal intent to redeem and restore. The same is true when God acts to restore and renew the relationship with Israel (2:14-23). The images of hope and love as God's final word literally spill out of this passage: tenderness, peace, safety, righteousness, justice, steadfast love, mercy, and knowledge of God.

Each major section of the book of Hosea ends with a chapter devoted to hope, restoration, and affirmation of God's love (3; 11; 14). This placement suggests that Hosea saw the testimony to God's love and grace as the final word, not the witness to judgment and brokenness. God has remained faithful to covenant promises through and in spite of Israel's sin that made judgment inevitable.

Hosea's gift for striking imagery is as evident in his message of God's love and redemption as in that of judgment. In chap. 11 he shifts from his major metaphor of husband/wife to the language of parent/child and movingly speaks of the enduring power of parental love in spite of the actions of a rebellious child. Chapter 14 ends with a magnificent description of the day when Israel returns to the Lord and meets with forgiveness. They return from death to the flourishing life described as a garden grown from God's love. "I will love them freely, for my anger has turned from them" (14:4). Israel's future is to flourish like the garden of God's love, which stands, in spite of Israel's idolatry, like a faithful evergreen cypress (14:8).

F. Enduring Significance and Challenge

Throughout the history of its interpretation Hosea has suffered neglect because the frankness of its metaphors drawn from human sexual relationships has been considered embarrassing, or at least difficult to use in the life of religious communities. This embarrassment has been compounded by the offense of the language of abuse treated as the right of an aggrieved husband toward an unfaithful wife. Further, issues of idolatry, associated with Baal, have been considered archaic and not directly applicable to modern experience. These issues make Hosea a challenging book in terms of its significance for modern readers of religious communities.

More recent commentary on Hosea has suggested that, although challenging, Hosea's message might well reward a closer reading. Idolatry, in Hosea's time and our own, is closely associated with cultural accommodation and materialistic lifestyles. These in turn are often supported and encouraged by self-serving political manipulation and even violence to maintain power and attempt to secure our own well-being. Hosea's message of judgment on such patterns is still needed. God's love can redeem self-serving patterns of idolatry and greed and lead to a flourishing life. Beyond the challenges of reading Hosea and the differences in his time and ours, the basic issues are timeless, and the basic truths of his message still needed.

Bibliography: F. I. Anderson and D. N. Freedman. *Hosea.* AB 24 (1980); W. Brueggemann. *Tradition for Crisis: A Study in Hosea* (1968); M. J. Buss. *The Prophetic Word of Hosea: A Morphological Study* (1969); J. Cathey. *Hosea 2: Metaphor and Rhetoric in Historical Perspective* (2005); G. I. Davies. *Hosea* (1993); G. I. Emmerson. *Hosea: An Israelite Prophet in Judean Perspective* (1984); J. Limburg. *Hosea-Micah.* Interpretation (1988); J. L. Mays. Hosea: A Commentary. OTL (1969); J. L. McKenzie. "Divine Passion in Hosea? Osee." *CBQ* 17 (1955) 167–79; J. L. McKenzie. "Knowledge of God in Hosea." *JBL* 74 (1955) 22–27; B. Oestreich. *Metaphors and Similes for Yahweh in Hosea 14:2-9 (1-8): A Study of Hoseanic Pictorial Language* (1998); Y. Sherwood. *The Prostitute and the Prophet: Hosea's Marriage in Literary-Theoretical Perspective* (1996); D. Simundson. *Hosea, Joel, Amos, Obadiah, Jonah, Micah* (2005); C. P. Staton, ed. *Interpreting Hosea for Teaching and Preaching* (1993); D. Stuart. *Hosea-Jonah.* WBC 31 (1987); M. Sweeney. *The Twelve Prophets* (2000); J. M. Ward. *Hosea: A Theological Commentary* (1966); J. M. Ward. "The Message of Hosea." *Int.* 23 (1969) 387–407; H. W. Wolff. *Hosea.* Hermeneia. (1974); G. A. Yee. *Composition and Tradition in the Book of Hosea* (1987); G. A. Yee. "Hosea: Introduction, Commentary and Reflection." NIB 7 (1996); E. Ben Zvi. *Hosea.* FOTL (2005).

BRUCE C. BIRCH

HOSHAIAH. *See* HOSEA, BOOK OF.

HOSHAMA hosh′uh-muh [הוֹשָׁמָע *hoshama*ʿ]. Sixth son of King JECONIAH (JEHOIACHIN) of Judah, as recorded in the Chronicler's genealogy of Davidic descendants (1 Chr 3:18).

HOSHEA hoh-shee′uh [הוֹשֵׁעַ *hoshe*ʿa]. The name of five individuals in the OT. 1. Hoshea was the original name of Joshua, son of Nun, which Moses changed (Num 13:8, 16). In Deut 32:44, the Hebrew reads Hoshea, while many of the translations read Joshua.

2. The last king of the northern kingdom of Israel (732–722 BCE). Hoshea, the son of Elah, came to power during the course of Tiglath-pileser III's (733–732 BCE) campaign against Rezin, the king of Damascus, and Pekah, the king of Israel. This expedition culminated in the annexation of Damascus into the Assyrian Empire. As for Israel, it lost all of the Transjordan, Galilee, and the coastal plain, everything except the area around Samaria. In the midst of this Assyrian invasion, according to 2 Kgs 15:30, Hoshea took advantage to plot the assassination of Pekah, the son of Remaliah (750–732 BCE), which he successfully carried out. According to one of his inscriptions (Summary Inscription 4, lines 17Nb–18Na; *COS* 2:287-288), Tiglath-pileser III states: "[I/they killed] Pekah, their king, and I installed Hoshea [as king] over them." The restoration of the verb describing Pekah's fate is uncertain. The possible restorations include "they killed" or "I killed." But the first person singular verb "I installed" (*ashkun*) clearly indicates Tiglath-pileser's claim of involvement in the events that brought Hoshea to power in Israel. Thus it was with clear Assyrian backing that Hoshea gained the throne.

After his installation, Hoshea (or more likely his representative) seems to have made obeisance to Tiglath-pileser in the town of Sarrabanu, the capital of the Chaldean tribe of Bit-Shilani, in southern Babylonia, which was besieged and captured by Tiglath-pileser in 731.

When Shalmaneser V (727–722) succeeded his father, Tiglath-pileser III, Hoshea continued his tribute payments as he had done (2 Kgs 17:4). But Hoshea sent messengers to So, king of Egypt (identity debated), and rebelled against Shalmaneser V. Hoshea was arrested and taken prisoner to Assyria at the very beginning of the siege of Samaria. The Israelite king may have come forth to plead for forgiveness from Shalmaneser hoping to be reinstated (which occasionally the kings of Assyria did; Tiglath-pileser III had done this with Hanunu of Gaza earlier, see *COS* 2:288). But in this case, he was sadly mistaken. After a three-year siege, Shalmaneser V conquered Samaria (722 BCE). A few years later (720 BCE), Sargon II recaptured the city after its brief rebellion.

The internal biblical chronology is very difficult, with contradictory statements given in connection to Hezekiah's reign, resulting in great confusion. Scholars are divided in how to understand these statements: some give priority to 2 Kgs 18:1, 9-10; others give priority to 2 Kgs 18:13 and Isa 36:1. In favor of 2 Kgs 18:13 is the fact that it unquestionably synchronizes with well-established Assyrian chronology, namely with the "third campaign" of Sennacherib in 701 BCE. There is also disagreement about how best to understand the "ninth year" of Hoshea: some understand it as 724, i.e., the year that Hoshea was arrested and the siege of Samaria began; others understand it as 722, i.e., the year that Shalmaneser V captured the city.

3. Hoshea, son of Azaziah, was the chief officer of Ephraim during the time of David (1 Chr 27:20).

4. A signatory on behalf of the entire community, committing the people to obedience to the covenant of God in the context of Ezra's work (Neh 10:23 [Heb. 10:24]).

5. The 8th cent. northern kingdom prophet whose name is commonly transliterated Hosea. His ministry dated from the time of Uzziah and Jeroboam II until the reign of Hezekiah (Hos 1:1). Since there is dispute over the dates of Hezekiah, there is some uncertainty about the end of his prophetic career. He was certainly active throughout the prosperity of Jeroboam's reign, the tensions of the Syro-Ephraimite War, and the turmoil of the 720s, possibly until the fall of Samaria in 722. *See* HOSEA, BOOK OF.

Bibliography: B. Becking. *The Fall of Samaria: An Historical and Archaeological Study* (1992); M. Cogan and H. Tadmor. *II Kings.* AB 11 (1988); H. Tadmor. *The Inscriptions of Tiglath-pileser III King of Assyria* (1994).

K. LAWSON YOUNGER, JR.

HOSPITALITY [ξενία xenia, φιλοξενία philoxenia]. The ancient custom of hospitality revolved around the welcoming and assisting of strangers or travelers. By extending hospitality to a traveler, the host generally committed himself or herself to provide the guest with provisions and protection while the guest remained in the region. Moreover, within a context of hospitality, hosts and guests often forged long-term, reciprocal relationships, which are commonly referred to as guest-friendships.

Among the Greeks, Homer's *Odyssey* helped to shape this custom, which was believed to have been monitored closely by Zeus (*Od.* 6.207-210). Typically, meritorious Greek hosts would feed, house, bathe, and clothe their guests (*Od.* 3.4-485). Furthermore, when it was time to depart, the host would equip the guest with provisions and escort the guest out of the region (*Od.* 13.47-125). Not surprisingly, the Greek term for hospitality, xenia, is closely linked to the Greek term for STRANGER, xenos (ξένος).

Hospitality was also a valued custom among the ancient Israelites. While the terminology varied, expressions of this custom were fairly consistent. For example, Abraham's hospitality served as the paradigm for subsequent hosts. Even though Abraham's guests stayed for only a brief time, he served them an extravagant feast (Gen 18:1-16). Conversely, the men of Sodom attempted to abuse Lot's guests (Gen 19:1-11).

The NT also contains numerous references to hospitality (e.g., Luke 7:36-50; Acts 28:1-10; Heb 13:2). Early Christian missionaries routinely depended upon hospitable hosts as they spread their message (e.g., Luke 10:1-16; 3 John 5-8; *Did.* 11-12). Early Christian hospitality also helped to bridge the cultural gap between Jews and Gentiles. This dynamic can be seen most clearly when Cornelius, a Roman centurion, converts to Christianity in Acts 10:1-48. *See* HOUSE-HOLD, HOUSEHOLDER.

Bibliography: Andrew Arterbury. *Entertaining Angels: Early Christian Hospitality in its Mediterranean Setting* (2005).

ANDREW E. ARTERBURY

HOSTAGE [בְּנֵי הַתַּעֲרֻבוֹת bene hatta‘aruvoth; ὅμηρος homēros, υἱοὺς τῶν συμμίξεων huious tōn summixeōn]. A person held against his or her will for political leverage. As a Hebrew phrase, it literally means "sons of pledging" (2 Kgs 14:14; 2 Chr 25:24). The phrase was mistranslated in the LXX as "sons

of commingling." Specifically, the passages refer to those persons in Jerusalem whom King Jehoash took as captives after he had defeated King Amaziah at Beer-Shemesh. **Homeros** refers to the captives whom the Romans took from those among the people they conquered (1 Macc 8:7), and to the sons of the leading men whom Baccides took and placed under guards in Jerusalem (1 Macc 9:53). As a settlement to the people of Gaza, Jonathan took their rulers' sons and held them in Jerusalem (1 Macc 11:62). Trypho demanded Jonathan's two sons as part of the strategy to ensure that Jonathan, when released, would not lead a revolt against him (1 Macc 13:16). This type of captivity differs from the practice of SURETY since the goal is to quell fighting, whereas surety aims to settle a debt.

EMILY R. CHENEY

HOSTS, HOST OF HEAVEN [צְבָאוֹת tseva’oth; Σαβαώθ Sabaōth]. "Hosts" is a plural noun from tsava’ (צָבָא), which commonly designates military service or troops. The plural form occurs as an epithet of Yahweh some 285 times as "Yahweh/Lord of Hosts" (*see* LORD OF HOSTS). The majority of the occurrences of the epithet are in the prophetic books. For example, "Hosts" is never used apart from the divine name and makes its way into the NT as "Lord of Hosts" (kyrios Sabaōth κύριος Σαβαώθ; Rom 9:29; Jas 5:4). The origins of the phrase remain debated, but it seems to express the sovereignty and power of Yahweh and is closely associated with his name (Amos 4:13; 5:27; Isa 47:4; Jer 10:16; 31:5; etc.). One occurrence explicitly designates Yahweh as the leader of the armies of Israel (1 Sam 17:45). Many scholars trace the origins of this epithet to the cultus at Shiloh, where it was associated with the ark (*see* ARK OF THE COVENANT; 1 Sam 1:3, 11; 4:4).

The term *host* occurs in the singular approximately 200 times, most commonly referring to either a military unit or army, both earthly and heavenly. The "host of heaven" (tsava’ hashamayim צְבָא הַשָּׁמַיִם) commonly refers to the heavenly bodies, the sun, moon, and stars, which Israel was forbidden to worship (Deut 4:19; 17:4), though there is ample reference to syncretistic practices (2 Kgs 17:16; 21:3; 23:5; Jer 19:13; Zeph 1:5; etc.). Indeed, there are a number of passages that suggest that astral deities might have been associated with the Yahwistic cult (Job 38:6-7; Isa 14:13; Dan 8:9-11; Zeph 1:5). Both sun and moon could be invoked as members of Yahweh's heavenly armies (Josh 10:12). In Josh 5:13-15, Joshua has an encounter with a being who identifies himself as "the commander of the host of Yahweh."

Not all uses of the term necessarily imply a military function. In a number of passages the "Host of Heaven" constitute the members of Yahweh's heavenly court. In the vision of Micaiah, the prophet sees Yahweh enthroned and surrounded by "all the host of heaven" (1 Kgs 22:19-22). A similar scene occurs in Isa 6:1-8, where the "host" is replaced by CHERUBIM. Psalms 103:19-22 and 148:1-2 present the angels as among the host praising Yahweh (compare Luke 2:13; *see* ANGEL). It is not uncommon that prophetic traditions relate prophetic authority to participation in this council (Amos 3:7; Jer 23:18, 22). In Ps 82:1, God stands in the "assembly of El" and passes judgment on the heavenly entourage, identified as "gods" and "sons of Elyon/the most high" (*see* ELYON). The hosts of heaven are also understood as part of Yahweh's creation (Gen 2:1; Neh 9:6). *See* HOLY WAR..

E. THEODORE MULLEN, JR.

HOSTS, LORD OF. *See* LORD OF HOSTS.

HOTHAM hoh'thuhm [חוֹתָם khotham]. 1. Son of HEBER, one of the descendants of Asher (1 Chr 7:32), who seems to be the same person as HELEM (1 Chr 7:35).

2. An Aroerite (Transjordan region) and father of two of David's warriors (1 Chr 11:44).

HOTHIR hoh'thuhr [הוֹתִיר hothir]. One of the fourteen sons of HEMAN appointed to prophesy with instruments (1 Chr 25:4), chosen by lot (1 Chr 25:28). In the context of temple worship, these sons were "under the direction of their father for the music in the house of the Lord with cymbals, harps, and lyres" (1 Chr 25:6). This sequence of names (1 Chr 25:9-31) can be read in Hebrew as a liturgical prayer. *See* MUSIC.

SAMUEL L. ADAMS

HOUR [ὥρα hora]. A modern hour is 1/24 of the astronomical day, but ancients commonly divided daylight into twelve equal hours and night into twelve equal hours. Thus, a civic hour varied in length depending on latitude and season: in summer, an hour was about 5/4 of a modern hour, but in winter, an hour was about 3/4 of a modern hour. Dividing the day into hours is attested in Egypt as early as 2100 BCE.

Hour appears in the NT and the Apocrypha as a synonym for "time" and does not specify an exact period (e.g., "the hour has come"). Occasionally it specifies a metaphorically short period of time ("add a single hour to your life"). It is often used in eschatological contexts (Matt 24:36, 44, 50; Rev 3:3; 14:17; 18:10). *See* DAY, NT; DAY, OT; ESCHATOLOGY IN THE NT.

ADAM L. PORTER

HOUSE [בַּיִת bayith; οἰκία oikia, οἶκος oikos]. A house is both a physical structure in which individuals live (Mark 7:24) as well as a communal term that applies to a kinship group made up of current members and their ancestors (*see* FAMILY). Throughout its existence a household's identity and its kinship ties

are associated with its house (equaling its members, its inheritable property, and its social standing; see Exod 20:17; Num 1:20). It is referred to as the (beth 'av בֵּית אָב; Gen 38:11), the "father's house," reflecting the leadership and social responsibilities of the father of the house. Thus David's *house* expresses his immediate and extended family, the line of all those descended from David's line (Zech 13:1; Luke 1:27), as well as the "everlasting covenant" in which God made a house of David and granted divine right to rule Israel (2 Sam 7:11).

Household associations also have negative connotations, as exemplified in Sheba's cry in 2 Sam 20:1— "We have no portion in David, no share in the son of Jesse! Everyone to your tents, O Israel!"

When speaking of God's temple, *house* may refer to any place dedicated to God's worship. Its sacred character is based on its serving as the *house* of the deity (1 Kgs 6:14; Ezra 1:5; Matt 12:4; John 2:16), and the priests who serve in this place are often described as members of the "house of Aaron" or the "house of Levi" (Ps 135:19). In the same way, a tribe or the entire nation can be referred to as the "house of Judah" (Isa 22:21) or the "house of Jacob" (Isa 10:20). This is a common practice in the prophetic literature, since it allows the prophet to speak collectively about the wickedness of the people (see Jer 5:11; Hos 7:1; Mic 3:1) and to condemn other nations as well (see "house of Esau," where Esau stands for Edom in Obad 1:18).

During much of the biblical period (13th–6th cent. BCE), the most common dwelling in unwalled villages and small towns was the pillared, two-story, four-room house, which allowed extended families to live together. The three broad rooms created by a row of pillars were further divided into chambers radiating out from the central courtyard, allowing for some privacy while designating specific space for housing animals separate from human quarters and the cooking area. The lower walls, often 2 m thick, were built of field stones with the exterior plastered with lime to prevent erosion. The upper story consisted of mud bricks. The roof served as additional living space (2 Kgs 4:10) and a work area (Josh 2:5). A series of such dwellings, standing next to one another provided opportunities for social discourse and some protection against raiders. In walled cities, both four-room houses and the city's casemate walls provided housing,m as well as storage space, accommodating the needs of the populace and commercial interests (e.g., Rahab's house in Josh 2:15).

Legal texts demonstrate that the various architectural features of a house were given additional social meaning. For instance, when Isaiah counsels king Hezekiah to "put his house in order" the reference is to tying up one's legal affairs as they relate to his household (Isa 38:1). In another case, the covenantal obligation placed on every Israelite "house" is symbolized by placing a scroll on the doorpost (Deut 11:20).

The doorpost is also the setting for economic transactions, such as the ritual transformation of a free person into a perpetual servant of a house (Deut 15:16-17). Even judicial procedures occur on the doorstep, as is the case when a woman who has been proven to be unfaithful is stoned on her father's doorstep, to demonstrate the shaming of that house (Deut 22:13-21). *See* ARCHITECTURE, NT; ARCHITECTURE, OT; GATE; HOUSE CHURCH; HOUSEHOLD, HOUSEHOLDER; KINSHIP.

Bibliography: David Balch and Cynthia Osiek. *Families in the New Testament World: Households and House Churches* (1997); Leo Perdue, et al. *Families in Ancient Israel* (1997).

VICTOR H. MATTHEWS

HOUSE CHURCH. Scholars now use the term *house church* in reference to the practice among many Christian groups of meeting in homes of wealthier members in the 1st cent. The earliest evidence for this practice comes from the Pauline epistles, where we find variations on the phrase "the church in their house" (he kat' oikon autōn ekklēsia [ἡ κατ' οἶκον αὐτῶν ἐκκλησία]; 1 Cor 16:19; Phlm 2; Col 4:15; compare Rom 16:5, 10-16, 23). Attention to the household-based meetings of the early Christians may shed further light on issues concerning divisions among various house churches at one particular locale, such as those at Corinth (e.g., 1 Cor 1–4). The book of Acts confirms the importance of household meetings (1:13-14; 2:46; 20:7-12, 20), as well as the "conversion" or baptism of entire households along with the head of the family (10:2; 11:14; 16:15, 31-34; 18:8; compare 1 Cor 1:16; 16:15). As certain Christians began to define internal structures more clearly around the turn of the 2nd cent., structures of the Greco-Roman household played a significant role in defining hierarchy and leadership in Christian gatherings, as evidenced by the HOUSEHOLD CODES (e.g., 1 Tim 3:4-5; Col 3:18–4:1; Eph 5:2–6:9; 1 Pet 2:18–3:7). *See* CHURCH, LIFE AND ORGANIZATION OF; CONGREGATION.

Bibliography: Wayne Meeks. *The First Urban Christians: The Social World of the Apostle Paul* (1983) 75–84; David Balch and Carolyn Osiek. *Families in the New Testament World: Households and House Churches* (1997).

PHILLIP A. HARLAND

HOUSE OF DAVID INSCRIPTION. *See* INSCRIPTION, TEL DAN.

HOUSE OF THE FOREST OF LEBANON [בֵּית יַעַר הַלְּבָנוֹן beth ya'ar hallebanon]. The House of the Forest of Lebanon is one of the buildings constructed by Solomon in Jerusalem after the completion of the Temple (1 Kgs 7:2). It is described as 150 ft. long, 75 ft. wide, 45 ft. high.

The name of the building provides an interesting double meaning. The materials for its construction had been transported from the forests of Lebanon (1 Kgs 5:20, 22-24). It was, therefore, a structure made from the forest of Lebanon. The name could also refer to the visual impression created by the arrangement of three (Heb. reads "four") 150 ft.-long rows of cedar pillars to support the cedar beams and planks of the roof. This would have created the visual effect of the dense cedar forest of Lebanon. While there is no archaeological evidence for the structure, and the use of rare Hebrew words makes reconstruction difficult, the verbal description contributes to the dramatic nature of Solomon's construction projects in Jerusalem and emphasizes the glory of his reign.

The function of the building is not entirely clear. On the one hand it seems to be some sort of treasury, decorated with shields, where gold vessels were housed (1 Kgs 10:17, 21; compare 2 Chr 9:16, 20). On the other hand, if Isaiah's reference to "the House of the Forest" (beth hayya'ar בֵּית הַיָּעַר) is to be read as an abbreviated name for this structure, then it appears that it may have functioned as an armory (Isa 22:8).

C. MARK MCCORMICK

HOUSEHOLD, HOUSEHOLDER. Across the biblical period, households as family units differ significantly from contemporary forms of family. Israel's households were the smallest social unit composing larger clans (often village-centered) and tribes (Josh 7:16-18; 1 Sam 10:20-21). Social circumstances and location (rural, urban; elite or non-elite status) meant diverse patterns, but general features can be noted.

Households in ancient Israel were formally patriarchal (under the authority of the head male), patrilineal (descent through the male line), and patrilocal (a wife joined her husband's household). The primary designation for the household was "house of the father" (Num 25:15; 1 Chr 24:31), with the head male (father or grandfather) exercising power over household members (e.g., Jephthah's daughter, Judg 11:29-40). Stories, though, indicate women influencing males, often through informal or subversive ways (e.g., Rebekah, Gen 24–27). Several references denote a "mother's household" (Gen 24:28; Ruth 1:8; Song 3:4; 8:2). Households were multigenerational involving grandparents, adult male children, wives, their children, the unmarried, divorced, and widowed. Also included were persons to whom care was extended: debt servants (Exod 21:1-11), resident aliens (Deut 24:17-20), day laborers (Lev 25:6), orphans (Isa 1:17), the sick (1 Kgs 17:17-24), Levites (Deut 26:12-13), and their relatives (Deut 5:12-15; 16:11-14). Connections with dead ancestors were also important to some people (Judg 2:10), though opposed as necromancy (Isa 8:19-20; Lev 19:31; Deut 18:11).

The economic role of households was vital for survival in an agrarian society. Land, transferred from generation to generation, sustained the household with crops and animals that provided food and materials for textiles. Any surplus was bartered with other households for needed supplies, stored against crop failure, and sown for next year's crop (*see* AGRICULTURE). Hard work, interdependence, and commitment to the collective good composed the household ethos. In this context, procreation, education of children in household skills and customs, religious observances, and judicial settlements (arranging marriages, assigning tasks, settling disputes, etc.), took place. Males generally performed agricultural labor while females performed household tasks (preparing food, producing textiles, etc.), though the survival of the household required flexibility in roles.

The household was central to theological reflection in the OT. God was portrayed in household roles (father and creator of life, Ps 139:13-16; mother, Deut 32:18; husband, Ezek 16; Hos 2; provider for the marginalized, Ps 146; redeemer from slavery, Exod 15:13; lawgiver and judge, Exod 20:2-17; owner of land, Lev 25:23-24). Israel's identity and covenant relationship with God was also understood in household terms (son, Exod 4:22; daughter Jerusalem, Lam 2:13; wife, Hos 2; slave, Deut 6:12-13). The covenant relationship was primarily lived out in households: the possession and use of LAND (Lev 25:18-34; Josh 13–19), labor and SABBATH rest (Gen 2:15; 3:17-19; Exod 20:8-11), religious practices (festivals such as Weeks and first-fruits offerings, Deut 26), and morality as household practices (care for the outsider, Deut 10:17-19). In and through the household, God was encountered and life was shaped accordingly (*see* FEASTS AND FASTS; HOSPITALITY).

In the NT period, similar household structures and values exist. They are evident in Jesus' parables (male sower, Matt 13:3-4; household slaves, Matt 13:27; 24:45-51; woman baking bread, Matt 13:33; vineyard owner, Matt 21:28-32; tenants, Matt 21:33-41; marriage, Matt 25:1-10; inheritance, Luke 15:11-32). Other parables reflect the harsh realities of urban households (day laborers hired in the marketplace, Matt 20:1-16; care for marginal persons, Luke 14:13, 21-24; 16:19-31; 18:18-30). Households comprise blood relatives as well as dependents such as slaves and clients ("free" persons who were reliant on a patron or wealthy householder). As economic and social units, households defined identity and allegiance. Texts likewise use household language for theological insights about God (father, Rom 8:15; Matt 6:9; over 100 times in John), about Jesus (son, Mark 1:1, 11), and about the identity (children of God, Rom 8:14-17; adoption, John 1:12-13) and tasks of disciples (love, John 13:34-35; practical care of the brother and sister in need, 1 John 3:17).

One commonly used image for both God and discipleship is that of the (male) householder or head of the household. A householder who does not secure his house against a thief highlights the need for disciples to be ready (vigilant and faithful) for the return of the Son of Man (Matt 24:43/Luke 12:39). Frequently the image presents God and/or Jesus in conventional household roles: sowing seed/gathering disciples in the world (Matt 13:27, 37-38); preventing entrance to the household/kingdom (Luke 13:25); inviting the poor and marginalized (Luke 14:21-24); producing the new and the old (Matt 13:52); demanding appropriate return/way of life from tenants (Matt 21:33-41). Yet the image also embraces the unconventional. A householder conventionally hires workers for his vineyard (Matt 20:1) but surprisingly pays them all equally (Matt 20:11-12), exemplifying the disruptive and socially transformative impact of God's reign.

While there are reflections of conventional household structures in NT texts, the texts attest considerable ambivalence about conventional structures. Instructions about household management, called household codes, imitate common views in mandating patriarchal households in which the husband/father/master represents the household in society and rules over domesticated wife, children, and slaves (Eph 5:21–6:9; Col 3:18–4:1; 1 Pet 3:1-7). Jesus sometimes supports conventional structures by, e.g., instructing disciples to care for aged parents (Matt 15:4-6; 19:19). Yet much more often, Jesus subordinates household obligations to commitment to himself (Mark 3:31-35 and par.). He calls disciples to leave parents and household economies (Mark 1:16-20 and par., though Peter has a house and wife, Matt 8:14). He recognizes that his call causes antagonism among households (Luke 12:51-53) and requires a radical rearranging of priorities in which disciples "hate" household members to follow Jesus (Luke 14:25-27). Following Jesus means constituting an alternative household centered on Jesus (Matt 12:46-50). Matthew 19–20 speaks of conventional household topics (marriage, children, wealth, slaves) but subverts the patriarchal, cultural norms by advocating marriage with limited male power, discipleship modeled on powerless children, wealth redistributed to the poor, and being slaves. Paul recognizes advantages in being unmarried for serving God (1 Cor 7:32-40). The harsh realities of surviving everyday life undermined any idealization of household life for non-elites who composed most of the population. While occupying small quarters in multistoried apartment blocks, or rooms above or behind small workshops attached to large villas, all household members worked to ensure survival. It was in such physical settings that early Christians met to worship. *See* FAMILY; HOUSEHOLD CODES; HOUSEHOLD OF GOD.

Bibliography: David Balch and Carolyn Osiek. *Families in the New Testament World: Households and House*

Churches (1997); Warren Carter. *Matthew and the Margins* (2000) 376–410; Leo Perdue, Joseph Blenkinsopp, John Collins, Carol Meyers. *Families in Ancient Israel* (1997).

WARREN CARTER

HOUSEHOLD CODES.

    A. Definition and Extent
    B. Form
    C. Origin
    D. Historical Meaning
    E. Contemporary Meaning
    Bibliography

A. Definition and Extent

The NT contains a number of lists of duties of members of the household (husbands and wives, slaves and masters, parents and children). Luther's section heading *Haustafel* (plural, *Haustafeln*, lit. *household table*, i.e., *table of household duties*) in his translation of Eph 5:21–6:9 and Col 3:18–4:1 has been adopted as a technical term for such *household codes* also in English-language scholarship. The list of texts designated by these terms has sometimes been expanded to include those texts that deal with the believers' duties within the Christian community and society at large, with congregation and political community conceived in terms of the larger family (compare, e.g., 1 Tim 3:15). Texts usually listed in this broadened category include Col 3:18–4:1; Eph 5:21–6:9; 1 Tim 2:1-15; 3:1-15; 5:1-21; 6:1-2; Titus 2:1-10; 1 Pet 2:13–3:7). The pattern continued to be reflected in Patristic writings, though there are no exact formal parallels to NT household codes (e.g., *Did.* 4:9-11; *Barn.* 19:5-7; *1 Clem.* 1:3; 21:6-9; Ign. *Pol.* 4:1–6:1; Pol. *Phil.* 4:2–6:3).

B. Form

The texts listed above are bound together more by common content than by strictly formal considerations. However, Col 3:18–4:1, reflected in the later Pauline tradition (esp. Eph 5:21–6:9), does have a distinctive form: the threefold schema of wife/ husband, children/ father, slave/master, with each pair addressed directly in second-person imperatives, subordinate member addressed first, but with reciprocal obligations.

C. Origin

The NT household codes are not derived from the OT, the teaching of Jesus, or the letters of Paul. The undisputed letters of Paul contain no household codes, though the household codes are in continuity with Paul's own teaching. A tension between accommodation to social conventions and resisting them in the name of the new life given in Christ is present in Paul's letters from the very beginning. While it was fundamental to Paul's understanding of the Christian life that it not be conformed to this world (Rom 12:2),

Paul was also concerned that the churches adapt to the structures God has established in creation. The virtue and vice catalogues show that Paul adopted and adapted ethical models from the prevailing culture to help the church adapt to the ethical codes of the time (Rom 1:29-31; 13:13; 1 Cor 5:10-11; 6:9-10; 13:4-7; 2 Cor 6:6-7; 12:20-21; Gal 5:19-21, 22-23; Phil 4:8). Romans 13:1-7 documents Paul's challenge to the churches to adapt to the social and political structures God had established in creation. The letter to Philemon shows that for Paul, Christian freedom does not abolish the prevailing social structures, but that disciples of Jesus must live within them in ways that manifest their new life in Christ. Paul repeatedly urged Christians to live responsible, ethical lives within the social structures in which they have been called (1 Cor 7:17, 20, 24).

While reflecting Pauline concerns, the NT household codes do not represent direct literary dependence on Paul or one another, except in the case of Ephesians, which is directly dependent on Colossians. The later Christian household codes do manifest some influence from the earlier ones, with Col 3:18–4:1 representing the beginning of the Christian *Haustafel* tradition. This tradition as a whole, however, represents a number of Christian authors' adoption and adaptation of materials and traditions from the philosophical and ethical currents of the Hellenistic world. It is generally agreed that these codes originated in the philosophy of the Greco-Roman world and had already been accepted and modified in Hellenistic Judaism prior to their use by NT authors. It has been debated whether the household codes adopted and adapted by second- and third-generation Christianity are more directly derived from the Stoic, Palestinian Jewish, Hellenistic Jewish, or Aristotelian traditions. It now seems most likely that the NT codes were influenced by the Hellenistic discussion peri oikonomias (περὶ οἰκονομίας, "concerning household management"), esp. as outlined by Aristotle (*Pol.* 1.1253b 1-14). Aristotle delineates how three pairs of social groups are to relate to each other, arguing that in each case one group is to be subordinate to the other. Hellenistic Jews had already adapted some of these materials; when some of these Jews became Christians, they brought these materials and perspectives with them into the church. There are, however, no close formal parallels to the *Haustafeln* that first made an appearance in Christian circles in Col 3:18–4:1. It thus appears that the material and general pattern for the household codes came from the Hellenistic milieu, including its precursors in Hellenistic Judaism, but that Christian teachers first gave them the stylized forms found in the NT.

D. Historical Meaning

While some points remain disputed, the following observations are generally accepted by scholars as representing the reasons early Christianity adopted and adapted household codes: The material represents a traditional schema, and thus cannot be directly used to portray the particular situations in the churches to which the letters containing them are addressed.

The household codes represent a decline from the first generation's eschatological fervor, which saw the present structures of this world passing away (1 Cor 7:31). Later generations needed direction for coming to terms with a world that was going to endure for some time. Though an important factor, this itself was not the decisive impulse. Hellenistic Jews had already adopted such codes.

The kind of religious enthusiasm that threatened to break down all social conventions in the name of the new life of the Spirit was sometimes regarded as a danger. Early Christian communities needed patterns and models for ethical conduct that manifested both the newness of the Christian life to which they had been called and exhibited to the world that their manner of life conformed to general social expectations (ta kathēkonta, [τὰ καθήκοντα] Rom 1:28). The formulation and adoption of such models had both the internal purpose of providing needed ethical norms and the missionary purpose, both evangelistic and apologetic, of showing to the world that the Christian faith did not undermine family and society but affirmed its highest values. The household codes taught insiders and reassured outsiders that Christians did not flee from the world but assumed a responsible place within it.

E. Contemporary Meaning

The household codes calling for the subordination of wives, children, and slaves to their husbands, fathers, and masters—often the same person, the *pater familias*—has proven to be a problem for interpreters in later generations where differing social mores prevail. On the one hand, these texts have been cited as biblical instruction for divine approval of patriarchy and slavery, while other readers have found them to be an embarrassment, scandal, or evidence of the repressive nature of biblical faith. The following suggestions, originally framed from the perspective of interpreting 1 Pet 2:13–3:7 in the modern world, may have some general validity. The household codes are a reminder that faith does not lift one out of the givenness of one's historical situation, and that the life of faith must always come to terms with the realities of society and history rather than fleeing into internal individualism or eschatological extremism. The historical structures themselves are neither justified nor condemned, but accepted as the given historical reality of their time and place.

Commands to be subordinate affirm that God the Creator has established order in the world, which is always better than chaos. The commands do not establish any particular social order as given by God.

The NT codes are always presented in the context of letters addressed to a particular situation, do not purport to give valid rules for every time and place, and must be reinterpreted anew in every situation.

In the NT codes, especially in Colossians, Ephesians, and 1 Peter, instruction is given in terms of mutuality and not merely hierarchy.

All members of the Christian community, whether master or slave, male or female, old or young, are called to live their lives with the mission of the community to the world as a higher priority than individualistic rights. Mission, not submission, is the focus of NT household codes. *See* FAMILY; FATHER; HOUSEHOLD, HOUSEHOLDER.

Bibliography: David L. Balch. "Household Codes." *Greco-Roman Literature and the New Testament: Selected Forms and Genres.* David E. Aune, ed. (1988) 25–50; M. Eugene Boring. "Christian Existence and Conduct in the Given Structures of Society." *1 Peter.* ANTC (1999) 102–28; James E. Crouch. *The Origin and Intention of the Colossian Haustafel* (1972).

M. EUGENE BORING

HOUSEHOLD DUTIES, LIST OF. *See* HOUSEHOLD CODES; LISTS, ETHICAL.

HOUSEHOLD GOD [תְּרָפִים terafim]. Statues or other material representations of familial or local deities called TERAPHIM were enshrined and consulted in an effort to make decisions (Zech 10:2), by both foreigners (Ezra 21:21) and Israelites (Judg 18:14-31). Hosea condemns the practice of having household gods (3:4). The significance of teraphim in religious life is evident in the story of RACHEL, who takes them from the tent of her father LABAN, hides them under her camel's saddle, and then tricks him into not searching her with a ruse about menstruating (Gen 31:19-35). Her willingness to deceive Laban suggests that the household gods were of some great importance to her; it may be that they were her own gods, or that the objects themselves had the power to transmit her legitimacy to Jacob's household. MICHAL also uses her teraphim for deception; she places her household god in David's bed as a substitute to deceive Saul's army when they come to kill him (1 Sam 19:13-16). *See* GODS, GODDESSES; IDOL; IDOLATRY.

Bibliography: Moshe Greenberg. "Another Look at Rachel's Theft of the Teraphim." *JBL* 81 (1962) 239–48; Ktziah Sanier. "Rachel's Theft of the Teraphim: Her Struggle for Family Primacy." *VT* 42 (1992) 404–12.

JESSICA TINKLENBERG DEVEGA

HOUSEHOLD OF GOD. *See* GOD, HOUSEHOLD OF.

HOWLING CREATURE [אֹחִים ʼokhim]. The NRSV's translation of an obscure word in Isa 13:21, found only in the plural. The animal to which it refers (singular:

'oakh [חֹאֵ]), can also be translated as OWL or JACKAL, perhaps named for the sound it makes.

HOZAI hoh'zi [חֹוזָי khozay]. The author of a chronicle on the deeds of King Manasseh (2 Chr 33:19), apparently cataloging the king's transgressions "before he humbled himself." The Greek translator, followed by the NRSV, RSV, and KJV, did not read khozay as the name of an individual, but a group of "seers" (khozim). The description of the king's prayer is the inspirational source for the apocryphal *Prayer of Manasseh. See* BOOKS REFERRED TO IN THE BIBLE; MANASSEH, PRAYER OF.

SAMUEL L. ADAMS

HUBBAH huh'buh [*Kethiv* יַחְבָּה yakhbah; *Qere* וְחֻבָּה wekhubbah]. Some translations go with the *Kethibh* (the way a word is written), Jehubbah, but the NRSV uses the *Qere* (the way a word is to be pronounced when read aloud), "and Hubbah," one of the sons of Shemer and a descendant of Asher (1 Chr 7:34). Neither of the names appears in the parallel Asherite genealogical lists in Gen 46 or Num 26. The name may mean "hidden one."

TRISHA GAMBAIANA WHEELOCK

HUKKOK huh'kok [חֻקֹק khuqoq]. A border town in the territory of Naphtali near the territories of Zebulun and Asher (Josh 19:34).

HUKOK. *See* CHINNERETH, CHINNEROTH.

HUL huhl [חוּל khul]. The second son of Aram and a grandson of Shem (Gen 10:23); but listed as Aram's brother in 1 Chr 1:17.

HULDAH huhl'duh [חֻלְדָּה khuldhah]. A prophet of Jerusalem, and wife of Shallum (2 Kgs 22:14; 2 Chr 34:22). Huldah was consulted by the High Priest HILKI-AH and the officials of Josiah's court after the "book of the law" was recovered from the Temple (2 Kgs 22:8-11; 2 Chr 34:14-21). Her prophecy announced tragedy for the people of the kingdom, who had made offerings to idols, but offered a peaceful death to Josiah (2 Kgs 22:20; 2 Chr 34:28). The words of her prophecy encouraged the king to make a covenant to be obedient to the law (2 Kgs 23:1-4; 2 Chr 34:29-33), and to initiate other religious reforms. Huldah's designation as a "prophetess" in (nevi'ah נְבִיאָה) is shared by both MIRIAM (Exod 15:20) and DEBORAH (Judg 4:4).

JESSICA TINKLENBERG DEVEGA

HUMAN SACRIFICE. *See* SACRIFICE, HUMAN.

HUMANITY, NT. In the NT, humans are wholly dependent upon and yet estranged from God, the creator; they are created in God's image, but do not live according to that nature. As creatures, humans are seen in relation to God, whether in their transitory nature in comparison to God, in their disobedience to God's will, or in their election by God. As dependent creatures, humans are not immortal by nature, even though God may grant them eternal life. Humans are social creatures and so fullness of life comes only when one is in community with others. Thus, the NT envisions salvation occurring within the church as the community of God's people rather than as an isolated, individual experience. While the NT does not use the expression "image of God" for humanity, it speaks of believers being conformed to the "image of Christ" as the fulfillment of their humanity. What it means to possess the *imago Dei* is defined by Christ. Jesus is human, even while being the unique revelation of God to humanity.

A. Sin and Human Nature
B. The Value of Human Beings
C. Pauline Anthropology
D. Terms Used for Aspects of Humanity
Bibliography

A. Sin and Human Nature

Within the NT's apocalyptic framework humans are a central site of the battle between God and the forces of evil. They are caught between opposing powers. Sin pervades the world so that it is inescapably a part of all human existence. All have been seduced and entrapped by evil and are unable to free themselves to live in their rightful relationship with God. While they are trapped, they are also complicit with sin because they sin willingly. Sin is both a power outside people and the evil acts people commit. One of the most basic realities of human existence is that people both sin and are captives of the power of sin; all are sinners and are incapable of rectifying this debilitating circumstance.

In distinction from much Western thought, the biblical ideal of human existence is not the autonomous person. The NT sees humans as too dependent for such a vision to be realistic. All are dominated by either sin or God. To serve God is to live according to one's created nature as exemplified in the life of Jesus. Only this way of being brings true life in the present and eternal life beyond death.

B. The Value of Human Beings

The NT has a very positive view of humanity. While no NT writer takes up the subject of the nature of humanity for its own sake, but always in the service of explicating other teachings, the value it places on humanity remains clear. Humans are creatures who are intimately related to God and responsible for their behavior. The NT sets a high moral standard for humans and expects them to fulfill it. Only a high view of the value and nature of humans allows such demands to be reasonable. Since humans do not live up to this God-given nature, they are all culpable before God. In the Gospels, Jesus always refers to humans as so valuable he comes to deliver God's message and to give himself for them. At the same time, humanity is oppressed by evil powers that entrap and harm, whether through causing people to sin or by illness or demon possession. Jesus comes to free the people of this oppression. Still, Jesus sees humans as intelligent, morally responsible, and in possession of free will. Yet, all are also sinners who fail to live up to their vocation of being children of God.

C. Pauline Anthropology

Paul provides more reflection on humanity than any other NT writer, even as his discussions of the topic always serve his explications of soteriology. Paul recognizes the struggles and contradictions, even hopelessness, of the human situation without surrendering humanity's dignity. He retains that dignity by consistently maintaining that humans are valuable enough, intelligent enough, and in possession of their own will to such an extent that they are responsible to God for their behavior and commitments. Romans 7 reveals the depth of the struggle humans experience when trying to live up to their nature (and the salvation granted them in Christ) in a world that is dominated by sin, a power that has infused every aspect of the world. Paul sometimes assumes and sometimes presents evidence for the universal sinfulness of humanity. The failure of every person is more the result of living in the environment ruled by sin than it is the result of an ontological fault in human nature. While this distinction receives no explicit articulation, Paul maintains the moral responsibility of humans, even as he recognizes that they are trapped in circumstances that lead every person to sin and so to enslavement under sin's power and estrangement from God. Part of Paul's understanding of Christ's work is that he defeats the powers of evil so that humans can begin to live for God.

D. Terms Used for Aspects of Humanity

The NT uses several terms to speak of various aspects of human nature. Among these are heart, mind, flesh, body, life/soul, and spirit. These terms have overlapping and varying meanings that simple English translations cannot adequately capture. These terms do not refer to "parts" that make up a person, but to different ways to think about humans and their actions.

The Gospels and Acts use heart (kardia καρδία) to refer to the inner self of a person or a people (Matt 15:8; Acts 4:32). It is the seat of feelings and commitment, but also of thought and forgiveness (Mark 2:6; Matt 18:35). It determines one's attitude toward God; it can be hardened (Mark 6:52; John 12:40) or be in accord with God's will (Mark 12:30). The heart combines emotions and thought as people have "thoughts in their hearts" (Mark 2:6; Luke 24:38). In the Pauline corpus, the term can refer to the whole person into

whom God sends the Spirit (2 Cor 1:22; Gal 4:6; Eph 3:17). It is also a place faith (Rom 10:10) or disbelief can be located. It can reveal one's orientation of life and so be fleshly (2 Cor 3:3) or blinded (2 Cor 3:15), or it can generate praise (Col 3:16; Eph 5:19).

In comparison with heart, terms for the mind (nous νοῦς, dianoia διάνοια) occur much less often. Nous appears outside the Pauline corpus once in the Gospels and twice in Revelation. The mind can be the center of thinking, but also of attitude and orientation. Similarly, dianoia is used seldom in the NT, mostly in the Catholic epistles. It also represents the home of both thought and orientation of life.

New Testament writers often use psyche (ψυχή) to refer to the inner self or the whole of one's existence. While it is often translated "soul," it does not designate a part of a person that is distinct from the body or the flesh. It can simply point to the whole person (2 Cor 12:15; 1 Pet 3:20; 2 Pet 2:8). The Synoptics, Paul, Acts, and Hebrews use it to translate the Hebrew term nefesh (נֶפֶשׁ, Matt 22:37; Mark 14:3; Luke 10:27; Acts 2:27; Rom 11:3; Heb 10:38). So it designates the life force that one is or possesses. Jesus gives his psyche as a ransom for others (Mark 10:45; Matt 20:28; 1 John 3:16; compare John 10:11), its loss means death (Luke 12:20), one may lose or gain (Matt 10:39) or risk it for the gospel (Phil 1:27). Hebrews 10:39 describes attaining salvation as obtaining psyche, life (also compare 1 Pet 1:22). The psyche can be the object of salvation (Jas 5:20), but animals also possess it (Rev 8:9; 16:3; Rom 2:9). So when Hebrews distinguishes psyche from pneuma (πνεῦμα, SPIRIT), it is speaking metaphorically, not designating the component parts of human nature. Still, psyche focuses on the inner self that may be pierced by sorrow (Luke 2:35), may praise God (Luke 1:46), and may trust God (1 Pet 4:19; Heb 6:19; compare Matt 11:29). Revelation also uses the term in multiple ways. In Rev 6:9 it refers to the life the martyrs possess under the altar until the parousia, but it also denotes earthly existence (12:11). Clearly this is not a technical term that bears a precise definition in the NT. It has meanings that overlap with pneuma and sarx (σάρξ, "flesh").

Sarx can also refer to the whole person (1 Cor 7:28), but it sometimes has theological and cosmic meanings. "Flesh and blood" designates humans as distinct from God (Matt 16:17; Luke 3:16; John 1:13; 17:2; Acts 2:17; 1 Pet 1:24). Flesh also refers to the aspect of life that is joined in marriage (Matt 19:5-6; Mark 13:20; 1 Cor 6:16). Sarx may designate human weakness (Matt 26:41; Mark 14:38, where the spirit is willing but the flesh is weak), but is not necessarily evil because the Word becomes flesh in John 1:14 (compare 2 John 7). Having flesh also distinguishes the resurrected Christ from a ghost in Luke (24:39; see references to the flesh of the dead in Acts 2:26, 31). See FLESH IN THE NT.

Paul uses sarx (flesh) for the physical aspect of a person (Rom 1:3; 2:28; Phil 3:3), but also as an aspect that cannot participate in the eschatological reality (1 Cor 15:50). Paul often makes sarx a moral and eschatological category so that it refers to the orientation of humans who oppose God. To live or think "according to the flesh" (kata sarka κατὰ σάρκα) is to reject the standards of conduct and evaluation that God intends. Living in this manner is incompatible with Christian existence. Even beyond designating a way of life in rebellion against God, Paul can use sarx to speak of a power to which humans can fall victim (Rom 8:12; Gal 5:13, 17-24). Such uses of sarx are distinctive to Paul in the NT, but constitute the more common ways Paul uses the term. When sarx and sōma (σῶμα, body) seem synonymous in Paul (1 Cor 6:16; 2 Cor 4:10-11), their meanings do not involve rejection of God. Both terms can simply signify human creatureliness.

New Testament writers usually use sōma in its literal sense to speak of a BODY (alive or dead), though at times it refers to the whole self (Matt 5:29-30; 6:25; Luke 12:22-23). To emphasize how the Christian's entire being participates in sanctification and the resurrection, Paul speaks of God sanctifying their "spirit and life (psychē) and body" (1 Thess 5:23). James, in the most dualistic use of the term, speaks of the body being dead without the spirit (2:26; similarly see 2 Cor 5:6-8). But Matthew can speak of the bodies of the dead saints appearing in Jerusalem following the death of Jesus (Matt 27:52). The body itself is neither good nor evil in Paul. It can be a temple for God's Spirit (1 Cor 6:19) and it will be redeemed (Rom 8:23). The true purpose of the body is to honor God (1 Cor 6:13). But it can be captured or given to the powers of evil such that its practices are sinful (Rom 8:13). Such behavior dishonors the body and consequently one's whole self (Rom 1:24). Paul uses "body" in ways that are metaphoric. Just as various ancient writers used sōma to designate the corporate identity of a group (e.g., a city's population), so Paul uses body as a metaphor for the church. Beyond this, Paul uses "body" to refer to the human situation viewed as captured by evil. He speaks of what must be crucified in baptism as the "body of sin" (Rom 6:6) and calls out to be rescued from this "body of death" (Rom 7:24) as he contemplates human subjection to the powers of evil. Despite his use of such metaphors, he does not see the physical body itself as evil.

The great majority of times, NT writers use pneuma to designate the divine Spirit (Holy Spirit, Spirit of God/Christ) or other beings in the spirit world (demons, etc.). Just as in the case of sarx, pneuma can refer to something personal or something cosmic (see Gal 5:17). When NT writers do use pneuma to refer to humans, the spirit is a place of feeling emotion, whether distress or comfort (John 11:33; 13:21; 1 Cor 16:18; 2 Cor 2:13), and of self-knowledge (1 Cor 2:11). The spirit can be dominated by either evil or good (1 Cor 7:34). Pneuma is another way to refer to one's inner self where self-consciousness and knowledge reside.

Pneuma sometimes designates the self that is open to God. In Luke's writings, the pneuma gives a person life. When Jesus raises the young girl, Luke says her spirit returned to her (8:58), and when Jesus and Stephen die, each gives up his spirit (Luke 23:46; Acts 7:59; compare Acts 23:8; similarly, Jas 2:26; Rev 13:15). In Paul, the spirit can be that inner self, but may also be equated with the flesh (compare 2 Cor 2:13 and 7:5). More metaphorically, Paul can be present in spirit while absent in body (1 Cor 5:3, 4; also Col 2:5).

The coherence in the NT's understanding of humanity is not found in common language but in the ways humanity is seen in its value to God, its intended relationship with God, its sinfulness, and God's love for us. While NT writers envision the salvation of humanity as a reclamation of their true nature and as given in the present (a particular emphasis in John), they also recognize that humans do not attain the fullness of their humanity until the eschaton. Only then will they no longer be fettered by the power of sin in the world. Only then will they receive the fullness of likeness to Christ who is the paradigm for truly and fully human existence. See ANTHROPOLOGY, NT THEOLOGICAL; HEART; MIND; SALVATION; SIN, SINNER; SOUL; SPIRIT.

Bibliography: Klaus Berger. *Identity and Experience in the New Testament* (2003); Rudolf Bultmann. *Theology of the New Testament*, vol. 1 (1954); Robert Gundry. *Sōma in Biblical Theology: With Emphasis on Pauline Anthropology* (1976); Robert Jewett. *Paul's Anthropological Terms: A Study of Their Use in Conflict Settings* (1971); Udo Schnelle. *The Human Condition: Anthropology in the Teachings of Jesus, Paul, and John* (1996).

JERRY L. SUMNEY

HUMANITY, OT. The Bible hosts a wide variety of discourses about the nature of humankind and about their place and purpose in the world. What connects most of these discourses is an understanding that a human being belongs at the same time to different natural, social, and cosmic realms that characterize the human person as a being with a body, heart/mind, soul, and spirit. Biblical traditions differ especially on the meaning of the Hebrew terms as well as on which of these individual characteristics in particular capture the essence of human existence.

A. Body, Soul, and Spirit
B. Human Nature and Human Righteousness
C. Human Wisdom and Human Civilization

A. Body, Soul, and Spirit

More than any other book of the Bible, the psalter offers a number of different views of humanity and of the respective worldviews from which they emerge.

Cultic psalms, e.g., place special emphasis on humans as composed of BODY and SOUL (Pss 16; 73; 84). The body defines the place of human beings in the natural world and also puts them in a relationship with their fellow human beings. The soul, on the other hand, is that part of a human person that is oriented toward God (Ps 130:6) and that constantly seeks God's presence as the source of life (Ps 42:1-3). The worldview to which this understanding of humankind is tied sees the temple and the temple mountain as the axis of the four world corners that centers all of life and toward which all ensouled life gravitates. The language of body and soul that describes a human person implies a complex notion of what it means to live at the same time in the natural and social world (*coram mundo*) and before God (*coram deo*). This view of humanity also includes a particular understanding of death and dying: as a bodily creature, a human being lives for a limited period of time at the end of which the body decays and its connection with the soul dissolves. Note that nowhere in the OT is the soul considered to be immortal. On the contrary, it too dies, and in the imagery of the ancient world this is pictured as a fading away into SHEOL, the underworld. Although the soul does not die in the same way as the body (through disintegration and decay), nonetheless it no longer shares in life. Dying also has a social connotation. It is not only disease and death that make the soul lose the connection with the living God, but also enemies and hostile social environments are able to "ensnare" the soul and drag it down "to the pit."

In the NT as well the human being is regarded as consisting in a body and a soul. Here, however, it is not a cultic background but rather the influence of Greek philosophy that stands behind the view in some parts of the NT that the human soul is something able to exist apart from the body and thus to exist beyond death; compare Matt 10:28: "Do not fear those who kill the body but cannot kill the soul; rather fear him who can destroy both soul and body in hell" (compare also Matt 16:26//Mark 8:36-37; Heb 10:39; Jas 5:20). Second Peter 1:13-14 describes the human body as a "tent" that we inhabit for a time but which, in death, we eventually put off and leave behind.

Yet another OT understanding of human life occurs in traditions that see God's presence in the cosmos not as confined to one particular place, but as indwelling all of created life. In particular, major creation texts such as Ps 104 and Deutero-Isaiah take positions that scholars have called "cosmotheistic": that is to say, it is through the SPIRIT that God enlivens matter and brings forth living beings such as humans and animals: "When you hide your face, they are dismayed; when you take away their breath, they die and return to their dust. When you send forth your spirit, they are created; and you renew the face of the ground" (Ps 104:29-30; compare also Isa 40:7; 42:5). Living, dying, and the emergence of new life are determined by the movement of the divine spirit. This concept has significant implications for understanding humankind in relation to their fellow creatures. Humans, by their nature, are no different from animals since animals, too, possess the life-giving spirit. Ecclesiastes phrases this insight in the form of a rhetorical question: "Who knows whether the human spirit goes upward and the spirit of animals goes downward to the earth?" (Eccl 3:21). The implicit answer according to Ecclesiastes is not only does nobody know if there is any difference between the spirit of humans and that of animals but also any form of life is characterized by the temporary union of matter and spirit. According to this line of tradition, any living being is composed around two elliptical poles: one that is material and connects them according to their emergence from the dust of the earth, and one that characterizes them specifically as God's creatures. In this view, spirit is what forms matter into a particular living entity. Once this connection dissolves, however, nothing remains. Neither matter nor the spirit carry an individual signature of what once was a living being.

Both the cultic and the cosmotheistic concepts of humankind with their respective emphases on soul and spirit may be termed "uneschatological" and even "antieschatological," since their views of humankind do not extend beyond the horizon of the present world. The ideas of an afterlife and of an immortal soul develop late in the inter-testamental period, e.g., in the Wisdom of Solomon (Wis 8:19; 9:15) and in parts of the Qumran literature (4Q418).

B. Human Nature and Human Righteousness

More than being a mere depiction of the origins of the world, the "primeval history" (Gen 1–11) provides a thick mythic description of humanity. What is said here about humankind "at the beginning" provides a multi-layered reflection on the essential nature of human beings, their relationship with other living creatures, and their relationship with God. The priestly report on Creation (Gen 1:1–2:4a) introduces a categorical distinction between humankind, which God creates "in his own image and likeness," and plants and animals, which are made and then procreate "according to their own kinds." Implied in such a distinction is the fact that each human being is considered as an individual rather than as a mere specimen of its kind. Hence, the priestly writers (P) focus on particular forms that characterize human life and distinguish it from other creatures: gender (Gen 1:27-28), the bonds between parents and their children (Gen 5:1-3), and, on a more general level, the relationship between neighbors (Gen 9:4-6). By using the concepts of the "image of God" and humanity's "dominion over the earth," P develops a framework that lays out the specificities of human life and so sets the table for what follows in the Pentateuch: the ancestral traditions, the exodus narrative, and the Sinai pericope. At the same time, P emphasizes what connects humans with their fellow creatures. Like other creatures humans are "flesh"—a term that assumes theological significance especially in the flood narrative. There, P states that all flesh was corrupted and as a result the world was filled with violence (Gen 6:12). It is because of their fleshly constitution—their being a part of the physical world—that humans are susceptible to the spreading of violence, and in this way they are no different from the rest of creation (see FLESH IN THE OT). It is noteworthy that P does not try to ease the tension between its view of humankind as made in the image of God and entrusted with dominion over the earth on the one hand, and humanity's fallible, physical nature on the other. On the contrary, P seems intentionally to highlight this tension as a characteristic of the human condition. P also recognizes that there are exceptional human beings who are able to live up to their created purpose. In the primeval history, it is Noah who exemplifies the true image of God in that he is "righteous," "without flaw," and "walking with God." Like the rest of creation, human existence emerges from chaos and is therefore imperfect. Yet humans also have the ability to sustain and promote the order that God established in creating order from chaos. "Righteousness" is the term that characterizes a way of life that is in accordance with the created world order.

The non-priestly texts in the flood narrative, on the other hand, give a different account of the human condition. The reason for the existence of evil in the world is not because of the nature of created life in general, but rather because of a defect peculiar to humankind. Humans, from their youth on, have "evil hearts" (Gen 6:5; 8:21)—even Noah who on this account is no different from the rest of humanity. No expectation is expressed that this defect would eventually subside or that God would intervene to correct. (Such an expectation, however, is expressed in the prophetic voices that envision God to either manipulate the human heart or replace the old "heart of stone" with a "heart of flesh"; compare Jer 31:33; Ezek 11:19; 36:26). Consequently, the ability of humans to be righteous has a different nuance than in P. Since humans cannot escape this original defect, their thoughts and actions will always be tainted by their evil hearts. Nonetheless, the hope is articulated that, despite their wickedness, humans will find favor in God's eyes (Gen 6:8).

The debate about human righteousness that shapes important parts of the primeval history can also be found in other parts of the OT, especially in the book of Job. In the prologue, Job is characterized with exactly the same words that P uses for its depiction of Noah: Job is an exemplary blameless and righteous human being (Job 1:1, 8). But, unlike P, the prologue of Job does not express any hope that through the agency of such exceptional human beings righteousness and

peace will flourish in the world. The thematic focus shifts to a different concern: even the righteous person faces the reality of evil and bad fate; even for such a person the world does not function in a way that ensures that the good acts and a pure heart will be reciprocated accordingly. On the other hand, the viewpoint of the prologue of Job that there may be such righteous persons is questioned especially by the speeches of Eliphaz: "What are mortals, that they can be clean? Or those born of woman, that they can be righteous? God puts no trust even in his holy ones, and the heavens are not clean in his sight; how much less one who is abominable and corrupt, one who drinks iniquity like water!" (Job 15:14-16). Placing humans at the low end of the cosmic order, this position stands in direct opposition to the traditions in the OT that view humans as only "little lower than divine" and as endowed with "glory and honor" (Ps 8:5-6).

C. Human Wisdom and Human Civilization

A leitmotif that characterizes humankind throughout major parts of the biblical Scriptures is their striving for wisdom. The Garden of Eden story (Gen 2–3) introduces this motif in terms of a conflict between the humans and God: the tree of the knowledge of good and evil was "to be desired to make one wise" (Gen 3:6). Although major parts of the Christian tradition have associated such desire with sin, nowhere in the OT do the Hebrew terms used in Gen 3 suggest that wisdom is an inappropriate or even sinful thing for human beings to strive for. Quite the contrary, it is such wisdom that allows them to inhabit the world that is given to them. Wisdom, as introduced in the primeval history, includes a variety of characteristics: it enables—and requires—humans to cultivate the soil and it also turns them into moral agents, with all the risks that the knowledge of good and evil and, hence, the ability to do the good and the evil entail. Wisdom is best understood as that which allows humans to build civilization as their own distinct way of inhabiting the world. This raises the question, however, how civilization correlates with the ways in which God ordered the world. In Gen 2–3 this question is fashioned in form of a dilemma: humans cannot obey God's law and have wisdom at the same time. Although both law and wisdom are viewed as powers that give human life orientation and direction, they stand, to some extent, in tension with each other. Humans exist before God, but they also have to live a life of their own and, in that sense, without God. Other OT traditions display a more homogenous view of the world as God's creation and as human civilization. Proverbs 8:1-36 depicts wisdom as that which God had created as "the beginning of his work, the first of his acts of long ago" (Prov 8:22). Wisdom was there when God made the world, beholding his work and rejoicing in all that came to inhabit the cosmos. The point of this text is to say that the same wisdom that comprises knowledge of God's creation is also the kind of wisdom that humans should strive for in creating their own world. Civilization, then, is a microcosm fashioned in accordance with the larger world in which it is embedded. *See* ANTHROPOLOGY, OT THEOLOGICAL; HUMANITY, NT; WISDOM IN THE OT.

ANDREAS SCHUELE

HUMANITY OF JESUS. The church's consensus that Jesus was both fully human and fully divine emerged centuries after the NT was written. The NT contains a variety of understandings of Jesus' humanity and divinity. In the Gospels this diversity comes to the fore, particularly in the PASSION NARRATIVES. While all four Gospels, to varying degrees, depict Jesus as having both human and divine qualities, the crucifixion is a test case for the degree of humanity and divinity that each Gospel accords to Jesus as the Christ. Mark's Gospel portrays Jesus' physical and emotional anguish on the cross when he doubts God's continued care in a very human way. In the Gospel of John, Jesus' divine foreknowledge of what his death accomplishes takes the edge off of his immediate suffering, referred to as "glorification" (12:23; 17:4). Luke also shows a Jesus much more in control, apparently acting as God in forgiving his crucifiers and admitting his fellow convict into paradise (23:34, 43). Among other NT writers, the apostle Paul seems to have cared little for the traditions emerging from Jesus' earthly ministry, but found the human moment of Jesus' crucifixion key to Christian faith (2 Cor 2:22; 5:16).

Elsewhere, Jesus' humanity, even in his suffering is eclipsed by his place in the history of salvation. In Hebrews, Jesus' earthly life disappears, and even his death occurs in a heavenly realm. In Revelation, Jesus is often indistinguishable from God, as eternal king and judge.

Seeing the human Jesus on the cross draws the reader into questions of the politics of his death, whereas seeing Christ redeeming humanity on the cross tends to push the political questions aside (*see* DIVINITY OF CHRIST). If Jesus' death was accomplished or allowed by God in order to atone for sin, then the political realities of Roman occupation and 1st cent. Jewish factionalism are trivial by comparison. If Jesus' death is to be read in human terms, however, then the story of his betrayal by his own followers, his having made enemies of the occupied elite, and in particular the politics of his execution by imperial forces, is of ultimate relevance. *See* CHRISTOLOGY; JESUS CHRIST; INCARNATION; SON OF MAN.

NICOLE WILKINSON DURAN

HUMILITY [עֲנָוָה 'anawah; ταπεινός tapeinos]. In antiquity these terms primarily denote the low social status of those who have been humiliated or suffer oppression and who cry out to God for relief from this condition.

A. Definition
B. Old Testament and Apocrypha
  1. Social and cultural adversity
  2. Humiliation before God
C. New Testament
  1. Gospels
  2. Pauline and Post-Pauline letters
  3. 1 Peter and James
Bibliography

A. Definition

Humility as a "self-effacement" or "humbleness" that is admirable or a virtue to be cultivated rarely appears in the biblical tradition. While one may humble oneself before others or before God in repentance or trust, more often the word denotes an action or socio-economic and political situation marked by insignificant status, suffering, and deprivation. The situation can be caused by God, political-imperial powers, or the wealthy and powerful. Lowly status can be positive as reversal by God's saving work, or it can be negative as experience of God's judgment.

"Humility/humiliation" is to be distinguished from "meekness," the condition of those who suffer poverty and oppression but look for God's deliverance (see Ps 37, quoted in Matt 5:5). It is also distinguished from "patience" which denotes primarily faithful endurance in adversity. While recognizing the interrelatedness of these and other terms, this entry will focus on the primary Greek word group for "humility/humiliation," tapeinos and its cognates. This term renders various Hebrew words, the most common being 'anah (עָנָה, "to afflict" or "oppress"), and shafal (שָׁפֵל, "to be abased" or "brought low"). Translating this word group into English is difficult. No single English word adequately expresses the range and nuance of usage.

B. Old Testament and Apocrypha

The verb 'anawah occurs most frequently in the Psalms and Isaiah. Few biblical references require a person to humble themselves or be subservient to another human being. In two occurrences, humans are to be subservient to a person of greater power. In Gen 16:9, the angel commands Hagar to submit to her mistress Sarai; in Sir 4:7, Sirach maintains elite hierarchical society by requiring submission to a great man.

More often, one humbles or "denies" oneself before God in worship, as on the DAY OF ATONEMENT (Lev 16:29, 31; 23:29, 32) and in fasting and repentance (Ezra 8:21; Ps 35:13-14; Isa 58:3, 5; Jdt 4:9; Sir 18:21). Eliphaz urges Job to repent (Job 22:23). The repentant David declares God's pleasure in a "contrite/humbled" heart (Ps 51:17), an example of the great man who must humble himself before God to find God's favor (Sir 3:18; also 2:17). Isaiah instructs that fasting is false without acts of mercy and justice such as feeding the hungry, housing the homeless, and freeing the oppressed (Isa 58:3-10). Self-humbling or humility denotes dependence on God marked by obedience. Thus Hezekiah humbles his proud heart before God (2 Chr 32:26), as does Manasseh (2 Chr 33:12) and Josiah (2 Chr 34:27), but the disobedient, image-worshiping Amnon refuses (2 Chr 33:23).

1. Social and cultural adversity

The verb does not indicate religious activity primarily. Its uses denote a wide range of personal, societal, and political experiences. These situations comprise temporary calamities, or permanent low social status in hierarchical societies controlled by wealthy imperial powers. Suffering often marks the experience of the "lowly" or "humble." In Ps 38:8 the psalmist is "crushed/humbled/humiliated" by disease (38:3-7); in 39:2 "distressed/humbled" by the wicked as God's punishment (39:9-11), and in 51:8 "crushed" by sin (see SUFFERING AND EVIL). Frequently the verb denotes humiliating women sexually (Gen 31:50; Ezek 22:10-11) including Shechem's rape of Dinah (Gen 34:2), the rape of betrothed and unbetrothed virgins (Deut 22:24, 29), and of a virgin daughter and a concubine (Judg 19:24; 20:5), Amnon's rape of Tamar (2 Sam 13:12, 14, 22, 32), and the rape of women taken in battle (Deut 21:14; Lam 5:11).

The verb also denotes military oppression. Philistines attempt to "subdue" Samson (Judg 16:5-6, 19), Israelites "subdue" Philistines (1 Sam 7:13; 1 Chr 20:4), Judah "subdues" Israel (2 Chr 13:18). David orders that Saul is not to be "destroyed"/humiliated (killed, 1 Sam 26:9). The people are "humbled/oppressed" in SLAVERY to Egypt (Gen 15:13; Exod 1:12; Deut 26:6; 1 Sam 12:8; Jdt 5:11). In Isa 51:21 the verb denotes exiles "wounded/humiliated" by Babylon, and in Isa 58:10 those of low status "afflicted" by injustice and deprived of basic needs. They are "crushed/humiliated" by the unjust actions of the proud and wicked (Ps 94:5), and "oppressed/humbled" and "crushed" by enemies (Ps 106:42; 143:3) including the lofty Assyrians (Isa 10:33), insolent tyrants like Babylon (Isa 13:11), proud Moabites (Isa 25:11-12), and the ungodly (Sir 7:17).

The adjective *humble*, used more than sixty times, most commonly in Psalms, Isaiah, and Sirach, denotes the same realities. It refers to the socially lowly, poor, powerless, vulnerable, and insignificant. For example, the psalmist prays, "Give justice to the weak and orphan; maintain the right of the 'lowly/humbled' and the destitute. Rescue the weak and needy; deliver them from the hand of the wicked" (Ps 82:3-4). The lowly are opposed by the wicked and are associated with the weak, orphaned, destitute, and needy who look to God to intervene on their behalf (see POVERTY).

Antonyms oppose the humble/lowly to the proud or haughty (Pss 18:27; 138:6; Prov 30:14) and to the scorners, the wicked, and stubborn fools (Prov 3:34). The "poor/humble" and needy are endangered by the lofty (Prov 30:13-14) and by wicked villains (Isa 32:7). The unjust wealthy maltreat the POOR and "push the 'afflicted/humiliated' out of the way" (Amos 2:7). Twice in Sir 13:21-22 the rich man is contrasted with the humble, suggesting that the latter comprise the poor and socially lowly. This meaning is supported by Sirach's command to pay alms to the one in "humble/ lowly circumstances" (Sir 29:8).

2. Humiliation before God

Humiliation can be attributed to God. Naomi attributes the "calamity" of the deaths of her husband and sons to God (Ruth 1:21). Jabez instructs people to pray against God bringing "harm/humiliation" (1 Chr 4:10). The psalmist protests God's unjust "breaking/humiliating" of those faithful to the covenant (Ps 44:19). And God promises a time when there will be no more "affliction" for Israel (1 Chr 17:9-10).

More often, humiliation is regarded as God's punishment. God "brings Judah low" as punishment for King Ahaz's actions (2 Chr 28:19), God's "putting down" is judgment (Ps 75:7), God "afflicts" the people (Ps 90:15) with disease (Isa 3:17). In anger God has enemies "oppress/humble" them (Ps 106:42), God "humbles" them because of idolatry (Isa 2:9), "punishes" them with foreign occupation, devastated cities, and a destroyed temple (Isa 60:14) as well as with exile (Jer 13:18; Lam 1:5, "made her suffer," 8, "despised," 12, "inflicted;" 3:32-34, "causes grief," "crushed"). *See* WRATH OF GOD.

These humiliations can lead to new encounter with God's SALVATION. In "severe affliction/humiliation," people seek God's help (Pss 119:107; 142:6) and experience it (Ps 116:6). God works to "bring low"/humble (1 Sam 2:7) imperial powers and beneficiaries of unjust social structures. So God "crushes" the mighty (Job 34:25), "brings low/humbles the high tree" (Ezek 17:24), and the rich into poverty (Sir 6:12). Frequently God's action of "bringing low" is directed against the haughty and proud (Prov 29:23), including Saul (2 Sam 22:28], proud Israel (Isa 2:11, 17; 5:15), and proud Moabites (25:11-12). God "subdues"/humiliates King Jabin of Canaan (Judg 4:23) and Israel's enemies and oppressors (1 Chr 17:10; Ps 81:14), "brings low" Assyria (Isa 10:33), "lays low" Babylon (Isa 13:11; 51:21, 23) and Moab (Isa 25:11-12), bends low "those who oppressed/humiliated you" (Isa 60:14), "humbles" enemies (1 Macc 12:15) and those who do not fear God (Ps 55:19), "crushes" oppressors (Ps 72:4, through the king), "casts down" the wicked (Ps 147:6), and "punishes/humbles" the ungodly (Sir 7:17). Instead, God exalts the lowly (Ezek 17:24; 21:26; Sir 7:11). This is God's salvific action.

God's "humbling/saving" work can lead to repentance and obedience (*see* REPENTANCE IN THE OT). Solomon recognizes drought and famine as God's punishment/humiliation for sin that requires repentance and confessional prayer (1 Kgs 8:35; 2 Chr 6:26). The imprisonment and hard labor that "bowed down/ humiliated their hearts" in exile brings a cry for God's mercy (Ps 107:12, 17). The psalmist rejoices in being "humbled" by God because he now lives a life marked by studying and obeying God's word (Ps 119:67, 71, 75).

In beseeching God's saving intervention against the Assyrians, Judith addresses God as "God of the lowly/ humbled/humiliated." The following four phrases not only define God but also elaborate the vulnerable circumstances of the objects of God's favor: "helper of the oppressed, upholder of the weak, protector of the forsaken, savior of those without hope" (Jdt 9:11). Other synonyms present the "crushed in spirit/humiliated" as the "brokenhearted" and righteous afflicted by the wicked (Ps 34:18), "the needy" (Isa 32:7), and "storm-tossed and not comforted" in Babylonian exile (Isa 54:11).

In these contrasts God's favor lies with the humble/ lowly (Prov 3:34; Isa 11:4 [2x] through God's agent). Saul offers David his daughter in marriage, but the response of David, God's chosen, is classic, "I am a poor/humble man and of no repute" (1 Sam 18:23). God exalts the humble/lowly (Job 5:11) and "brings low"/humbles the haughty (Isa 2:11) and lofty (Isa 26:5-6; see also Ezek 17:24; 21:26). The humble seek God's help through obedience and doing justice (Zeph 2:3; 3:12) and glorify God (Sir 3:20). They are the "oppressed" who rely on God's justice (Ps 10:18), the "needy" who find refuge from the nations in Zion (Isa 14:32), the "poor" who find a refuge in God (Isa 25:4), the "suffering ones" in exile to whom is directed God's compassion or saving power (Isa 49:13; 54:11). God heeds their prayer (Ps 102:17) and honors the "lowly in spirit" (Prov 29:23, using a related adjective).

The most distinctive usage of the noun occurs in clauses that denote God's gracious interventions. God "has [graciously] given heed to" or God "has looked [with favor] on" or God "has [mercifully] seen" the affliction, misery, suffering or humiliation of an individual or people. The situations in which God intervenes involve a considerable range of "afflictions." God heeds Hagar's struggle with Sarai and Hagar conceives (Gen 16:11). Leah's "affliction" is Jacob's greater love for Rachel, yet God enables Leah to bear a son (Gen 29:32). Jacob's affliction is fourteen years of labor for Laban (Gen 31:42). Joseph's "misfortunes" involve his time in Egypt, yet God grants two sons (Gen 41:52). Hannah promises that if God heeds her "misery" of childlessness, she will dedicate the child to God's service (1 Sam 1:11). God sees the "humiliation" of slavery in Egypt and delivers the people (Deut 26:7;

Neh 9:9). God sees the "suffering" inflicted by the Philistines and sends Saul (1 Sam 9:16). David wishes God to look on his "distress" comprising Absalom's revolt and Shimei's cursing (2 Sam 16:12). God sees Israel's "distress" under Jeroboam (2 Kgs 14:26). Jerusalem's "humiliation/term" in Babylonian exile has ended with God freeing the people (Isa 40:2). The people experienced "affliction" before exile and "suffering" and "affliction" in exile (Lam 1:3, 7, 9).

The psalms refer to further situations, often of conflict, and ask God to "be gracious" and "heed," "consider," or "see" the "suffering" (Ps 9:13), "affliction" (Ps 90:3, "turned to dust/affliction"), or "misery" (Ps 119:92). The scenarios are generalized but some details emerge. In Ps 25:18 the "affliction" results from the violent hatred of others, in 31:7 from enemies and persecutors, and in Ps 119:153 the "misery" also results from persecutors. In these circumstances, the psalmist experiences God's comfort or salvation. In 119:50 he receives comfort from God's promise in his "affliction" and in 119:92 God's word keeps him alive in his "misery."

C. New Testament

Only thirty-four instances of this word group occur in the NT, the Gospels, and Acts (thirteen times), the Pauline (nine times) and post-Pauline letters (four), James (four) and 1 Peter (four). The verb appears fourteen times (Matthew three; Luke five; 2 Corinthians two; Philippians two; James one; 1 Peter one), the adjective eight times (Matthew one; Luke one; Romans one; 2 Corinthians two; James two; 1 Peter one), and the noun four times (Luke, Acts, Philippians, James). A related noun, tapeinophrosynē (ταπεινοφροσύνη), appears seven times (Acts 1; Ephesians 1; Phillippians 1; Colossians 3; 1 Peter 1) and an adjective, tapeinophron (ταπεινόφρων), once (1 Pet 3:8).

1. Gospels

The word group appears twice in Mary's Magnificat. Luke 1:48 employs the noun tapeinōsis (ταπείνωσις) with a verb of seeing that recalls the pervasive OT sense of God's gracious intervention. God has seen Mary's "lowliness" or low social position as one of the nonelites, the powerless and insignificant in the Roman imperial world. Her hymn of praise celebrates it as God's general salvific work of choosing "the lowly" and bringing down the powerful (1:52). In Luke 3:5 (citing Isa 40:4), God "brings low" hills and mountains as part of the commencement of John the Baptist's activity and manifestation of God's salvation for all people. The four subsequent uses emphasize the eschatological reversal of current societal structures. God's favor does not legitimize the status quo but reverses it. The (self-)exalting will be humbled (by God) and the (self-)humbling will be exalted. This vision of God's distinct activity in God's kingdom contrary to cultural norms is consistent with OT patterns. The point is illustrated by a wedding feast parable and subverted meal conventions (Luke 14:11) and in another parable contrasting the self-exalting Pharisee with the tax collector who humbles himself and seeks God's mercy (Luke 18:14, twice). The parables advocate identification with the powerless and lowly in the present as preparation for judgment (14:10; 18:13).

Matthew's use of the same saying in Matt 23:12 and Matt 18:4 also emphasizes its eschatological and ethical-communal dimensions. Mathew 23:12 follows the exhortation to be slaves of one another in seeking the other's well-being (23:11). In Matt 18:4, the eschatological dimension is being greatest in the kingdom. The image of dependent children points to dependence on God. The communal dimension is also evident in the comparison to a child. Up to fifty percent of the children, the most vulnerable in the population, died by age ten.

Matthew's remaining use is christological. In 11:29, Jesus describes himself as "meek/suffering and lowly/ humble in heart." The first word, used in Matt 5:5 quoting Ps 37:11, 22, 29, denotes the powerless righteous who suffer because of the wicked powerful. God will vindicate the former. As we have seen, this term closely approximates one significant meaning of the "humble/humiliated" word group. "Lowly in heart" synonymously emphasizes Jesus' low social position, conflict with the powerful, and anticipates God's vindication. But the phrase "in heart" adds a further dimension noted above, namely openness to and dependence on God. In adversity, Jesus expresses his commitment to God's purposes that exalt the lowly and bring down the powerful.

The word group appears twice in Acts. In 8:33, the quotation from Isa 53:8 evokes the scenarios of suffering noted above. God's servant is opposed by the powerful, is denied justice, is humiliated, killed, but vindicated by God. Philip interprets the Isaiah passage as a reference to Jesus. In Acts 20:19 Paul describes his service to the Lord. A translation "with every humiliation" that emphasizes his circumstances, rather than "with all humility" that emphasizes his character, seems more consistent with his references to tears and trials (20:19) and to "not shrinking" from preaching (20:20). That is, as is typical of the biblical usage, the term expresses difficult circumstances in serving God.

2. Pauline and Post-Pauline letters

The four uses in 2 Corinthians denote Paul's difficult relations with the Corinthian church. In 7:6 he finds God's comfort in being "downcast" over his "afflictions," described in 7:5 as "disputes without" (conflict with Corinth) and "fears within," perhaps at their reception to his "painful" letter of rebuke carried by Titus (2:2-3, 13; 7:8). The reference in 10:1 to being "humble/lowly" may reflect their criticism of him that he seemed powerless when with them. In 11:7-9 his "humbling/humiliating himself" to exalt them imitates God's way of working. It refers to his not following the cultural pattern of taking money from their patronage, resulting probably in the wealthy believers despising him for his low-status reliance on manual labor (1 Cor 4:12), and money from other churches. In 12:21, his fear of God "humiliating me" is difficult. Recalling the range of meanings described above, perhaps it refers to punishment for not accomplishing his task or his suffering at seeing their nonresponsiveness.

Such apostolic sufferings supply the content for Phil 4:12. Paul knows what it is to "be abased," to "have little," or be scorned as lowly. This lowly status is to mark relationships of mutual deference and to seek the well-being of others in the believing community (Phil 2:3; see also Rom 12:16). Two factors shape this way of being. It is appropriate to the current human condition, which is "lowly" compared to the resurrection glory to come (Phil 3:21). And it is the behavior that Christ evidenced in humbling himself in obedience to God, taking the form of a servant, suffering in death, and being vindicated by God (Phil 2:8).

Ephesians (4:2) and Colossians (3:12) similarly call believers to participate with the suffering lowly who look to God's justice (Eph 4:2). Colossians includes two other references—"self-abasement" (2:18) and "humility" (2:23).

3. 1 Peter and James

First Peter's four usages emphasize deference to others as part of one's love within the community of believers (3:8; 5:5a). The justification for this way of living is God's opposition to the proud (5:5b); its basis is submission to and dependence on God (5:5b). James evokes the OT emphasis on God's just favor for the lowly (poor, suffering, deprived) and humiliation of the rich whose exploitative way of life is ending (Jas 1:9-10). As with 1 Peter, James recalls God opposition to the proud and favor for the lowly (4:6) who must depend on and submit to God to be exalted (4:10). *See* MEEKNESS; PATIENCE.

Bibliography: K. Wengst. *Humility-Solidarity of the Humiliated: The Transformation of an Attitude and Its Social Relevance in Graeco-Roman, Old Testament-Jewish and Early Christian Tradition* (1988).

WARREN CARTER

HUMOR. The term *humor* refers to both the expression and the perception of the comic dimension of life. Until recently, pious attitudes toward Holy Scripture, its subject matter, its character portrayals, and its purposes have precluded readers from perceiving any humor that may be expressed in the Bible. Indeed, the common association of humor with silliness, entertainment, and the baser elements of human experience contravenes expectation that the Bible contains expressions of humor. However, not only does the Bible itself offer ample evidence to the contrary, but reflection on the nature of the comic dimension of life also draws attention to the suitability of humor as an authentic expression of aspects of the human character and condition and of the story of God's involvement in the story of humanity.

A. Features of Humor
B. Functions of Humor
C. Comic Mechanisms
   1. Paranomaisia
   2. Hyperbole
   3. Irony
   4. Sarcasm
   5. Parody and Satire
   6. Turnabouts
Bibliography

A. Features of Humor

Comedy involves a number of characteristic features. It represents a perception of incongruity coupled with an awareness of what would constitute congruity. The recognition of a delightfully imbalanced situation implies the ability to understand circumstances that would constitute balance. In essence, comic awareness fulfills a truth-telling function that can work subversively, pointing to an alternative reality. The catharsis that comedy often produces testifies to this truth-telling, even prophetic, function.

Closely related to this subversive component is the experience of comedy (via one's "sense of humor") ecstatically and intrusively. A response to humor is often irrational and beyond the subject's control. The typical response to humor is laughter, an autonomous, involuntary reaction to comic stimulus. Humor, as the perception of incongruity, often depends on the contextual, cultural definition of propriety; e.g., the transgression of boundaries defining gender and class roles is a typical comic theme. As such, the sense of humor, the capacity to comprehend incongruity, is subjective. If one is unfamiliar, e.g., with the norm subverted in a humorous expression, either because the norm belongs to a foreign time, place, or culture, or because of some other limitation (ignorance of vocabulary, custom, etc.), one will likely fail to perceive the incongruity. Such ignorance of language, culture, and role expectations confronts readers of the Bible at every turn.

B. Functions of Humor

As the recognition of incongruity and the imagination of alternative realities, humor lends itself to several clear psychological and social functions—all evident in Scripture. In an aggressive function, humor highlights the contrast between "is" and "ought." This prophetic and subversive role of humor appears,

e.g., in Isaiah's comparison of the people's efforts to achieve deliverance to a woman giving birth to flatus (Isa 26:18), or when Balaam finds himself listening to his donkey telling him what to do (Num 22:22-35), or Jesus' disputations with the Pharisees in which he lures them into logical and exegetical conundrums, thereby subjecting them to the ridicule of the people (Mark 12:12-40 and par.). Humor can function to include, as when the reluctant and buffoonish prophet Jonah leaves a string of converts in his path, despite his best efforts to the contrary (Jonah 1–4), or when Matthew subverts expectations by inserting into Jesus' genealogy five women noteworthy for their unwillingness to be consigned to the margins (Matt 1:1-16).

Alternatively, humor can demarcate boundaries. For example, the wordplay on ʾadham (אָדָם, humankind) and ʾadhamah (אֲדָמָה, earth, dirt, red clay) reminds readers of the boundary between human beings, animated clay figures, and the Creator (Gen 2:7). Defensively, humor can also serve as a coping mechanism allowing for the sublimation of fears. Humorous treatments of the enemy render them harmless, or a least manageable (e.g., the Esther story).

The Bible exhibits the full range of comic character types: tricksters (Tamar and Jael), simpletons (the young David, eager to please Saul and ready to trust him despite contrary evidence), buffoons (drunken Noah), and clowns (Jesus' disciples arguing over preeminence as Jesus travels toward his fate).

C. Comic Mechanisms

The Bible utilizes a wide range of humorous techniques and mechanisms to express the comic dimension. The more prominent include:

1. Paranomasia

Wordplay, often impossible to convey in translation, characterizes Semitic storytelling. For example, note the wordplay in Hebrew when Abimelech observes Isaac (yitskhaq יִצְחָק) "sporting" (metsakheq מְצַחֵק) with his "sister" Rebekah (Gen 26:8). With a similar wordplay in Greek, Jesus announces that Simon is called Peter (Petros Πέτρος), and his confession the rock (petra πέτρα) upon which Jesus will establish the church (Matt 16:18).

2. Hyperbole

In an outlandish exaggeration, the Agagite Haman proposes to hang the Jew Mordecai on a gallows 50 cubits (75 ft.) tall (Esth 5:14; compare 6:4; 7:9-10; 8:7; 9:13, 25). Proverbs compares a beautiful woman who is without discretion to "a gold ring in a pig's snout" (Prov 11:22). Jesus advises those who would reprove another first to remove the beams of wood from their own eyes (Matt 23:27).

3. Irony

The Philistines discover the discrepancy between expectation and reality when their capture of the ark of Yahweh does not, in fact, grant them control over either the box or the God of Israel (1 Sam 6). John's Gospel raises the question as to who is truly blind, the man born who comes to see, or the Pharisees, born with sight but unable to discern the significance of Jesus' healing ministry (John 9). In a dream at the tanner's house (ironically a ceremonially unclean setting), Peter, who had argued with God concerning the propriety of consuming unclean foods, is surprised that his Gentile audience believes and receives the Holy Spirit (Acts 10).

4. Sarcasm

Amos encourages citizens of the Northern Kingdom to "come to Bethel [to worship] and transgress" (Amos 4:4). Twice (Gal 5:11-12; Phil 3:2-3), Paul taunts the Judaizers who would require Gentile converts to Christianity to submit to circumcision (peritomēn περιτομὴν, lit. "cutting around"), suggesting, instead, that if they are so eager to cut, they should mutilate themselves (apokoptein [ἀποκόπτειν], lit. to "cut off," Gal 5:12; katatomen [κατατομήν], lit. "to cut into").

5. Parody and satire

In addition to the story of Jonah, the anti-prophet, and Esther's ridiculous account of the excesses of the Persian court, the Bible includes parodies on the imperfect judge, anti-Nazirite Samson (Judg 14–16), and a number of wisdom sayings that satirize the arrogant (Prov 23:1-8) and the drunken (23:29-35). Elijah ridicules Baal and his prophets in the contest on Mount Carmel (1 Kgs 18), just as the prophet Isaiah derides the arrogant king of Babylon (Isa 14).

6. Turnabouts

Joseph, once despised and sold into slavery but now vizier of all Egypt, toys with his unsuspecting brothers (Gen 42–44). The naive shepherd-boy, David, innocently bests wily and powerful Saul (1 Sam 16–30). The Syro-Phoenician woman, through wit and tenacity, gains the boon she seeks (Mark 7:24-30; Matt 15:21-28). Indeed, salvation history, itself, can be regarded as a grand comic plot of reversed fortune.

Bibliography: Douglas Adams. *The Prostitute in the Family Tree: Discovering Humor and Irony in the Bible* (1997); Peter Berger. *Redeeming Laughter* (1997); H. Comier. *The Humor of Jesus* (1977); C. R. Gruner. *Understanding Laughter* (1978); M. C. Hyers. *And God Created Laughter: The Bible as Divine Comedy* (1987); J. Johnsson. *Humour and Irony in the New Testament* (1985); Karl-Josef Kuschel. *Laughter: A Theological Essay* (1994); J. Morreall. *Comedy, Tragedy, and Religion* (1999); Yehuda T. Radday and Athalya Brenner, eds. *On Humour and the Comic in the Hebrew Bible* (1990); J. Whedbee. *The Bible and the Comic Vision* (1998).

MARK E. BIDDLE

HUMTAH huhm′tuh [חֻמְטָה khumtah]. A town in Judah's central hill country (Josh 15:54), located somewhere between Hebron and Aphekah.

HUNCHBACK [גִּבֵּן gibben]. A physical deformity included among a list of others (lameness, blindness, etc.) that disqualify a Levite from offering sacrifices to Yahweh (Lev 21:16-23). However, such deformities do not prohibit the individual from eating from the offerings themselves.

HUNDRED. *See* NUMBERS, NUMBERING.

HUNDRED, TOWER OF THE. *See* TOWER OF THE HUNDRED.

HUNGER, HUNGRY [רָעָב ra‛av; λιμός limos]. References to hunger in the Bible alternate between the literal meaning of physical need for food and the metaphorical meaning of spiritual or emotional desire. Hunger and starvation were among the greatest threats to ancient people because their diet depended on unpredictable rainfall and harvest conditions and could be threatened by natural disasters and war. Biblical authors assume that God is the source of all agricultural blessings and is therefore ultimately responsible for the presence or absence of adequate food.

The OT describes hunger as a condition from which God saves people and as God's punishment for disobeying the law. In Deuteronomy, Moses recalls the episode of manna in the wilderness by saying that God "humbled you by letting you hunger, then by feeding you with manna" (Deut 8:3). Later, Moses warns that God will send hunger along with disease and pestilence against rebellious people (Deut 28:48). The prophets also reflect these convictions, alternately picturing divine punishment as FAMINE (Isa 5:13; Mic 6:14) and predicting that God will rescue people from hunger (Isa 49:10; Ezek 34:29). Proverbs 10:3 assures the reader that God "does not let the righteous go hungry." The OT also argues that people should feed those who are hungry, especially when they are weak or vulnerable (Isa 58:7-10), and even if they are enemies (Prov 25:21). In most of these passages, physical hunger is a marker for a deeper spiritual need for the knowledge and presence of God.

The Gospels emphasize the physical hunger of Jesus in order to demonstrate his truly human nature (Mark 11:12; Matt 21:18). His concern for the needs of his followers leads to the miraculous feeding of the crowd (Mark 8:3). Jesus also echoes the Jewish ethic of feeding those who are hungry and of tending to the needy in general (Matt 25:34-40). Jesus uses hunger in a metaphorical sense in the Sermon on the Mount: "Blessed are those who hunger and thirst for righteousness" (Matt 5:6). Revelation extends this metaphorical use of hunger to the time of final redemption for those who persevere during the tribulation, promising that "they will hunger no more" because the risen Christ will lead them to nourishment (Rev 7:16-17). In life, followers of God hunger for God's righteousness to be revealed in the world, and in God's final victory their desires are fully satisfied. *See* FOOD; POOR.

BRYAN D. BIBB

HUNTING [צַיִד tsayidh, צוּד tsudh]. Among the earliest depictions of hunting from ancient Mesopotamia is the "Hunt Stele" from Uruk (ca. 3000 BCE), which shows a king spearing one lion and shooting arrows into another. Inscriptions on Egyptian seals and commemorative scarabs and in tomb paintings reinforce the idea that big game hunting was generally a sport reserved for the wealthy and the nobility. For example, the New Kingdom pharaoh Amenophis III (1387–1350 BCE) boasts that during his first ten years as ruler of Egypt, he personally slew 102 wild lions. Typical official artistic renderings found on the funerary temple of Ramesses III at Medinet Habu depict the pharaoh in heroic mode, with wounded lions, bristling with arrows, lying at the feet of his chariot, and the king warding off others with his spear. In these land-based struggles, kings and their favorites ride in their chariots to the hunt with bows and spears while beaters drive the animals, including lions and gazelles, from cover. In some cases, hunting preserves were created for royal sport with fencing installed to keep the animals within prescribed limits. Swamp hunting took place on flat-bottomed boats, allowing the participants to seek out hippopotami, crocodiles, wild bulls, and a variety of water bird species. In some cases, the birds were stunned with throwing sticks. More often, however, these detailed tomb illustrations portray hunters using fowling nets or snares to capture their prey. These traps consisted of a net spread over a wooden frame that was supported by a stick in such a way that it fell with the slightest touch (Ps 91:3; Amos 3:5). There were also draw nets that required a team of hunters to coordinate the pulling of drawstrings that would close the device around a flock of wading birds (see the net in Job 18:8 that enmeshes the legs of the unwary). In addition to the thrill associated with the sport, hunting also had symbolic and political connotations, since the successful royal hunter demonstrated his dexterity and strength, and he also participated in a ritual performance, which reinforced and clearly defined his role as the protector of his people and their resources. By slaying a wild bull in the marshes, the pharaoh could claim that he had saved the farmers from being mauled and their fields from being destroyed. Thus the title given to the ancient king Nimrod, "a mighty hunter before the Lord" (Gen 10:9), evokes this image of a larger-than-life personage.

The fact that the biblical narrative chooses virtually to ignore hunting practices may be the result of the storytellers' attempt to draw distinctions between the Israelites and their neighbors. This could also help explain why the major characters that are identified as having prowess in hunting are characterized in such negative tones. Thus, Nimrod the "mighty hunter" (Gen 10:9) is listed in the genealogy of Ham and is the founder of Mesopotamian cities that will eventually bring disaster on Israel and Judah. Ishmael, Abraham's son by the slave woman Hagar, hones his skills as an archer in order to survive in the wilderness, but he is an outcast from the covenant community (Gen 21:20). In the same narrative vein, the other great hunter of game animals, Esau, Jacob's twin, is able to please his father, Isaac, with his hunting activities and the game meat that he supplies, but he is supplanted in his role as heir by his younger brother (Gen 25:27–27:33). Despite the shaping of the narrative in this way, hunting must have existed in ancient Israel, given the injunction in the Holiness Code that enjoins hunters, even resident aliens, to drain the blood from their game before consuming the meat (Lev 17:13).

Wisdom literature also reminds hunters that the incautious or lazy stalker will have nothing to roast at the end of the day (Prov 12:27). Surveys of animal bones found in the excavation of Israelite towns and villages indicate that wild animals were hunted, including roebuck, deer, and gazelle. It may be assumed that Israelite families preferred to supplement their diet with game meat rather than draw an animal from the herd. The familiarity with hunting techniques also gives rise to its use by the prophets, as they draw analogies between laying a trap for birds or animals and attempting to snare an unwary or innocent man (Jer 18:22-23) or catching one's "brother" with a net (Mic 7:2). Ezekiel draws on this hunting language in describing how God will cast a net over the people of Judah, ensnaring them and carrying them off to Babylonian captivity (12:13). Similarly, Isaiah compares the mindless flight of a "hunted gazelle" to the wicked that are pursued by God's wrath (13:14). *See* GAME; TRAPS AND SNARES.

Bibliography: W. Decker. *Sports and Games of Ancient Egypt* (1987).

VICTOR H. MATTHEWS

HUPHAM, HUPHAMITES hyoo´fuhm, hyoo´fuhmits [חוּפָם khufam, חוּפָמִי khufami]. A descendant of Benjamin and the head of a clan whose members were called Huphamites (Num 26:39). The name is HUPPIM in a parallel list (Gen 46:21).

HUPPAH hup´uh [חֻפָּה khuppah]. A priestly clan chief upon whom the thirteenth lot fell when David, Zadok, and Ahimelech divided the descendants of Aaron according to their tasks (1 Chr 24:13).

HUPPIM hup´im [חֻפִּים khuppim]. Ancestor of the Huphamites (Num 26:39). Huppim is listed as a son of Benjamin (Gen 46:21), but elsewhere he appears as a grandson or later descendant (Num 26:39; 1 Chr 7:15). The apparent contradiction may be explained by the use of the Hebrew word for SON (ben בֵּן), which can refer to a male descendant beyond the first generation (e.g., Gen 31:28). The name Hupham refers to the same individual (Num 26:39); the difference is due either to scribal error or to variant forms of the name (*see* HUPHAM, HUPHAMITES).

RALPH K. HAWKINS

HUR huhr [חוּר khur]. The name of five men in the OT. The meaning of the name is unclear, but a number of Ugaritic, Phoenician, and Aramaic names contain the element khr probably derived from the Egyptian god Horus, which may be true for the Hebrew names as well. 1. An assistant of Moses who, with Aaron, held up Moses' arms when they became tired during the battle against the Amalekites (Exod 17:8-13). Moses left Aaron and Hur behind to adjudicate disputes while he went up on Mount Sinai (Exod 24:14).

2. The grandfather of Bezalel, a Judahite in charge of making the tabernacle and the associated cultic apparatus (Exod 31:1-5; 38:22). Hur's father was Caleb and his mother Ephrath (1 Chr 2:18-20). First Chronicles 4:1-4 provides an alternative genealogy for this Hur, a son of Judah instead of Caleb, and whose mother was Ephrathah.

3. One of the kings of Midian killed by the Israelites (Num 31:8; Josh 13:21).

4. One of Solomon's officials in charge of Ephraim was called Ben-Hur, "son of Hur" (1 Kgs 4:8). Whether the man's name was Ben-Hur is unclear, although why the text would provide only the patronymic is unknown.

5. The father of Rephaiah, an official in charge of half of Jerusalem in the postexilic period (Neh 3:9).

KEVIN A. WILSON

HURAI. *See* HIDDAI.

HURAM, HURAM-ABI hyoor´uhm, hyoor´uhm-ay´bi [חוּרָם khuram, חוּרָם־אָבִי khuram ʾavi]. 1. Huram is the name of the craftsman who made the bronze implements for the Temple according to 2 Chr 4:11 (Huram-abi 4:16). In 1 Kgs 7 he is identified as HIRAM (khirom חִירוֹם).

2. The name of the king of Tyre, who is a contemporary of David and Solomon. He is first described as sending the materials and craftsmen to build the palace of David at the beginning of his reign in Jerusalem (1 Chr 14:1; *Khetibh* = khyrm חירם; *see* QERE-KHETIBH). Later, during the reign of Solomon, he is Solomon's benefactor of materials and craftsmanship for the Temple and palaces built in Jerusalem (2 Chr 2:10, 11). In the parallel passages in Samuel and Kings, the name of the King is HIRAM (khiram חִירָם; see 2 Sam 5; 1 Kgs 5; 9; 10). The shift between the names may be attributable to the similarity between the Hebrew letters WAW (w ו)and YOD (y י).

3. A Benjaminite identified as the son of Bela, who is the firstborn of Benjamin (1 Chr 8:1, 5).

C. MARK MCCORMICK

HURI hyoor´i [חוּרִי khuri]. A Gadite and father of Abihail (1 Chr 5:14). Explanations for the name vary, with some linking it to the Egyptian cult of Horus, others to the Akkadian huru, "child," and still others to the Hebrew root khwr (חור), "to be/become white."

HURRIANS hoor´ee-uhn. The Hurrians were a group of people who lived in northern Mesopotamia during the late third and second millennia BCE. Originally from the region to the west and south of Lake Van in Armenia, they spoke a language unrelated either to the Semitic languages or to HITTITES. The only Near Eastern language related to Hurrian is Urartian, used in the kingdom of Urartu (biblical ARARAT), in the Lake Van vicinity, in the first half of the first millennium BCE.

Our knowledge of both the language and the history of the Hurrians is incomplete. The most important Hurrian texts, which are usually written in Babylonian cuneiform, come from the Hittite capital Hattusha in central Anatolia and El-Amarna in Egypt (*see* AMARNA, TELL EL), and smaller numbers of texts in Hurrian have been found at MARI and EMAR in northern Mesopotamia and at Ugarit on the Mediterranean coast. Personal names with Hurrian linguistic elements and Hurrian deities are attested elsewhere throughout the ANE in the second millennium BCE, at such important sites as NUZI and ALALAKH. This range shows the extent of Hurrian influence. The zenith of Hurrian political power was in the mid-second millennium BCE, when for a century or so the Hurrian kingdom of MITANNI became a major power whose domain extended across the northern part of the Fertile Crescent from the Mediterranean Sea to the Euphrates River. From their capital, Washshukanni, which has still not been identified, they ruled over a large region of southeastern Anatolia and northern Syria, at times controlling even Assyrian territory to the east and Hittite territory to the west.

The longest Hurrian text known is from Tell El-Amarna in Egypt, one of a dozen letters between kings of Mitanni and pharaohs of the Eighteenth Dynasty (*see* AMARNA LETTERS). This letter (EA 24) is from Tushratta, the king of Mitanni, to the pharaoh Amenophis III (1390–1352 BCE). In the 15th cent. BCE, the kingdom of Mitanni was Egypt's only serious rival in the Levant. Its subjects included the city-states of Nuzi, Alalakh, Emar, and Aleppo. The kings of Mitanni and Egypt were equals ("brothers"), and their relationship had been enhanced by marriages of several Mitanni princesses to various pharaohs. Nevertheless, as the other letters show, the relationship had its problems, despite extravagant exchanges between the two courts.

The Mitanni kings were especially interested in gold ore from Egypt, for which they traded luxury goods. In several Amarna letters, Tushratta wrote to the pharaoh that "gold is as plentiful as dirt" in Egypt, and there are long lists of what he promised to send in return, such as a gold goblet with lapis-lazuli inlays in its handle; elaborate necklaces, one of which consisted of twenty pieces of lapis lazuli and nineteen pieces of gold around a centerpiece of lapis lazuli set in gold; ten teams of horses; ten fully equipped chariots; and thirty slaves.

At the same time, the Mitanni kingdom under Tushratta was experiencing problems. The major threat came from the Hittites to the west, whose king Suppiluliumas led several campaigns deep into Mitanni territory and captured Washshukanni. Tushratta was murdered by one of his sons, and Mitanni soon became a vassal state of the Hittites. But Hittite power itself was waning, and the Assyrians took over Mitanni in the early 13th cent. BCE.

Despite the loss of power by Mitanni, however, Hurrian influence continued to make itself felt, especially in Hatti, the land of the Hittites, where Hurrian deities were prominent in the Hittite pantheon. An important collection of Hurrian texts, many of which are unfortunately broken, comes from the archives of the Hittite capital of Hattusha (modern Bogazkoy). These Hurrian texts are mostly ritual and mythological in content.

Some of the texts appear to have been sung, perhaps during rituals. One, addressed to the "primeval gods," tells of an ongoing struggle in the pantheon between Kurmarbi, the son of the sky god, and Teshub, the storm god. One of the songs recounts how Kumarbi assumed supreme power among the gods by defeating the Mesopotamian sky-god Anu, biting off and swallowing his testicles. Kumarbi then became pregnant with Teshub and other future enemies. The motif is later found in Greek mythology, where Kronos, the father of the storm-god Zeus, castrates his own father, Ouranos (Sky). In the Greek version, the struggle is intergenerational, but in the Hurrian myth it seems to be between rival families of deities, similar to that found in Ugaritic mythology. In a sequel, Teshub defeats Kumarbi. Again, there are Greek reflexes (for Zeus supplanted his father, Kronos), and Near Eastern ones as well, as in the replacement of the deity El as king of the gods by the storm-god BAAL in Ugaritic myth, and the assumption of power by the storm-god MARDUK in Mesopotamia. Other fragments tell how Kumarbi attempted repeatedly to regain his power.

Like the Canaanite storm-god Baal, Teshub is often depicted with weapons in his hands, frequently including lightning bolts, and is sometimes standing on a bull. Teshub's consort was Hepat, the queen of heaven, whose name occurs in an element in the name of the ruler of Jerusalem in the Amarna letters, Abdi-Hepa.

Hurrian influence is also evident at such sites as Alalakh and Nuzi, where many individuals also have

Bridgeman-Giaudon / Art Respirce, NY

Figure 1: God Teshub. Relief on the Gate of the King. 13th c. BCE. Location: Hattusa (Boghazkov), Turkey.

Hurrian names, although the texts themselves are in Babylonian. Although Mitanni may not have exercised total control of these city-states, they were clearly within its sphere of influence, and, as in the Hittite region, Hurrian influence continued after the decline of Mitanni. In fact, at Emar, the texts in Hurrian date after Mitanni had lost power. A few Hurrian texts have also been found at ancient Ugarit, including what appears to be the earliest writing of musical notation.

An identification of the Hurrians with the biblical Horites (in some passages also translated "Horim"), based largely in part on the similarity of the names, was proposed by several scholars in the 20th cent. but is now questioned by many. One reason against the identification is the location of the Horites in the Bible. In the few times they are mentioned (Gen 14:6; 36:20-30; Deut 2:12, 22), they are always associated with the region of Seir in southern Transjordan, a region where the Hurrians had no direct influence. *See* HIVITES; HORITES; JEBUS, JEBUSITES; NURI.

Bibliography: Giorgio Buccellati and Marilyn Kelly-Buccellati. "Urkesh: The First Hurrian Capital." *BA* 60 (1997) 77–96; Harry A. Hoffner, Jr. "Hurrian Myths." *Hittite Myths* (1998) 40–80; Amelie Kuhrt. "Mitanni and the Hurrians." *The Ancient Near East, 3000–330 BC* (1995) 283–300; Gernod Wilhelm. *The Hurrians* (1989).

MICHAEL D. COOGAN

HURRICANE [סוּפָה sufah; τυφωνικός typhōnikos]. Psalm 83:15 calls on God's hurricane to terrify enemies. Paul's ship faced violent winds at sea (Acts 27:14). *See* STORM; WHIRLWIND.

HUSBAND AND WIFE. *See* FAMILY; MARRIAGE, NT; MARRIAGE, OT.

HUSHAH hoosh´uh [חוּשָׁה khushah]. 1. A town in Judah, west of Bethlehem; two of David's commanders,

Mebunnai (2 Sam 23:27) and Sibeccai (2 Sam 21:18), were associated with Hushah as Hushathites.

2. The Son of Ezer in the genealogy of Judah (1 Chr 4:4).

HUSHAI hoosh´*i* [חוּשַׁי khushay]. 1. Hushai is a friend of King DAVID who remains loyal during the rebellion of Absalom (2 Sam 15–17). As David flees Jerusalem, he meets Hushai, who intends to join the king's entourage. David sends Hushai back into Jerusalem with instructions that he is to return to the palace and swear his loyalty to ABSALOM in order to confuse and undermine the counsel that Absalom receives from Ahithophel (2 Sam 15:32-37).

After Hushai assures Absalom that he will be loyal to him and will serve him just as he had served David (2 Sam 16:17-19), Ahithophel encourages Absalom to put together a force of 12,000 troops and to pursue David immediately, before he can organize his resistance. When Absalom checks this advice with Hushai, he encourages just the opposite. He suggests that Absalom not go after David immediately, but rather that he wait until all of Israel has gathered to follow Absalom, and then to fall upon David and destroy him. Hushai's advice seems better to Absalom, and this gives David time to organize his resistance to Absalom's army. After undermining Ahithophel's counsel, Hushai sends word to David through the sons of Zadok and Abiathar, so that David knows what is being planned in the camp of Absalom.

2. The name of the father of Baana, one of Solomon's officials (1 Kgs 4:16).

C. MARK MCCORMICK

HUSHAM hoosh´uhm [חֻשָׁם khusham, חוּשָׁם khusham]. The third ruler mentioned in the list of non-dynastic Edomite "kings" (Gen 36:31-39; 1 Chr 1:43-51) and the first with a specified region of origin.

HUSHATHITE. *See* HUSHAH.

HUSHIM hoosh´im [חֻשִׁים khushim, חוּשִׁים khushim]. 1. Son of Aher, a descendant of Benjamin (1 Chr 7:12), possibly a plural reference.

2. Wife of Shaharaim, mother of Abitub and Elpaal (1 Chr 8:8, 11).

HUSN, TELL EL. A site in Jordan approximately 20 mi. south of the Sea of Galilee near PELLA (Tabaqat Fahl). Excavation of preclassical levels has shown that occupation of the main mound of Pella expanded southward to Tell el-Husn. A massive defensive wall, stone platforms, and a gateway with stone buttresses indicate that the Early Bronze Age fortification system included Tell el-Husn. Child burials (ca. Middle Bronze IIC) were found in a settlement destroyed by an earthquake (Late Bronze II); thereafter, there is a gap in occupation until the classical period.

Bibliography: Stephen J. Bourke. "Pre-classical Pella in Jordan: A Conspectus of Ten Years' Work (1985–1995)." *PEQ* 129 (1997) 94–115.

SUZANNE RICHARD

HYDASPES h*i*-das´peez [Ὑδάσπης Hydaspēs]. Judith 1:6 names the Hydaspes river along with the Euphrates, the Tigris, and the plain of Elymais. While a river named Hydaspes exists, it is in the Punjab and not in the area described in Judith. The author may have intended the Choaspes River (modern Karkheh).

MARY KAY DOBROVOLNY, RSM

HYENA [צָבוּעַ tsavu‘a, ὕαινα huaina]. The NRSV uses "hyena" for various other Hebrew animal terms, often following the LXX (e.g., Isa 13:22; 34:14; Jer 50:39). *See* ANIMALS OF THE BIBLE.

HYKSOS hik´sohs. *Hyksos* is the conventional designation for the Fifteenth Egyptian Dynasty that ruled Middle and Lower EGYPT from the mid-17th to the mid-16th cent. BCE.

A. The Hyksos in Tradition
B. The History of the Fifteenth Dynasty
C. The Expulsion of the Hyksos
D. The Hyksos and the Bible
Bibliography

A. The Hyksos in Tradition

Egyptian tradition remembered the Hyksos as barbaric invaders and the Fifteenth Dynasty as a time of chaos and oppression. These sources depict the Hyksos from the perspective of their Theban adversaries who drove them from power. The fullest surviving account comes from the 3rd cent. BCE priest-historian Manetho who wrote a history of Egypt in Greek. Manetho described the Hyksos as "shepherd-kings" who invaded from the east, razing cities and temples and massacring and enslaving the populace. Greco-Roman folk etymologies derived the Greek term Hyksos (Hyksōs Ὑκσώς) from the Egyptian for "king-shepherd" or "captive shepherd." The term actually derives from the Egyptian title ḥk3-ḫ3swt, "ruler of foreign lands." Previously, it was a term that designated foreigners ruling in their native lands, but in the Second Intermediate Period (1650–1550 BCE), the title was adopted by chieftains of foreign descent in the Egyptian Delta. One such chieftain extended his dominion south and west, eventually capturing Memphis and founding the Fifteenth Dynasty.

New Kingdom and Greco-Roman sources betray a tendency to xenophobic hyperbole in their condemnations of the Hyksos, ascribing to the period all the features of the conventional "time of troubles"—chaos, immorality, injustice, oppression, destruction, and neglect of the gods. Manetho termed the Hyksos anthrōpoi to genos asēmoi (ἄνθρωποι τὸ γένος ἄσημοι, "doomed men," not "men of obscure race" as traditionally translated), which represents the Egyptian convention of execration. When naming an enemy, whether individual or collective, the enemy should be characterized as ḫsi, doomed to destruction.

B. The History of the Fifteenth Dynasty

The Hyksos dynasty had its origins in a trading emporium in the northeastern Delta. Late in the Twelfth Dynasty Tell ed-Dabʿa was settled by Asiatic immigrants who exercised a monopoly over trade between Egypt and Syria-Palestine. The site's material culture—architecture, burials, pottery, etc.—was Middle Bronze Age II, indicating that the population was predominantly Syro-Palestinian rather than Egyptian. Later levels demonstrate a gradual Egyptianization of the culture. Linguistic analysis of their names places them within the West Semitic (Amorite) language group.

The end of the twelfth Dynasty inaugurated an era of political disintegration during which the rulers of various cities and nomes vied for power. The rulers of Tell ed-Dabʿa, backed by the economic engine of their vast trade networks, rose to prominence, conquering Lower and Middle Egypt. Although they assumed the title "King of Upper and Lower Egypt," the Hyksos' control over Upper Egypt was nominal at best.

Throughout the Fifteenth Dynasty, the Delta was a key trading hub, linking Egypt and Nubia to Syria-Palestine, Crete and Cyprus. The location of Tell ed-Dabʿa on the Pelusiac branch of the Nile provided access to Mediterranean sea routes while the desert oases allowed Hyksos trading caravans to bypass Upper Egypt as they traveled back and forth to Nubia.

Tell ed-Dabʿa is particularly known for its donkey burials and palaces with Minoan frescoes. The practice of donkey burials is known from contemporary sites in southern Canaan and represents a key cultural link between the two regions. The decoration of the Hyksos palaces with Minoan frescoes suggests close political and economic ties with Knossos on the island of Crete. Excavations at Tell el-Yahudiyya, also located in the eastern Delta, revealed a distinctive type of black pottery with incised white dots. Called Tell el-Yahudiyya ware by archaeologists, this pottery was produced in both Egypt and southern Canaan and was found throughout the Hyksos sphere of influence.

C. The Expulsion of the Hyksos

The Fifteenth Dynasty ended when the princes of Thebes, the dominant city in Upper Egypt, rebelled. The first phase of the rebellion, which resulted in the death of Seqenenre Taʿo by means of a Syro-Palestinian battle-ax, is memorialized in the Tale of Apophis and Seqenenre. His successor, Kamose, campaigned as far north as Avaris, but was unable to capture the city. Kamose died soon after and was succeeded by his younger brother Ahmose. Ahmose proceeded by steps to capture Memphis, Heliop-

olis, the border fortress of Sile, and finally Avaris itself. Ahmose continued his campaign into southern Canaan where he captured the city of Sharuhen.

The ultimate fate of the Hyksos is unclear. Tell ed-Dabʿa was rebuilt as a purely Egyptian settlement. Its Middle Bronze population disappears from the archaeological record. Manetho claims that the Hyksos, recognizing the inevitability of defeat, concluded a treaty with the Thebans and fled to Syria. Yet there is little evidence of the Hyksos retreat at sites in Syria-Palestine. Many sites were destroyed at the end of the Middle Bronze Age, but those destructions appear to have been spread over an extended period of time. Only the destruction of Tell el-ʿAjjul (ancient Sharuhen) can be definitively linked to the campaign of King Ahmose.

D. The Hyksos and the Bible

Could the Hyksos be the source for the biblical narrative of Joseph and the sojourn of the Hebrew people in Egypt (Gen 37–50)? In both cases, Semitic peoples settle in the Delta for economic reasons (trade or famine) where they rise to positions of power (king or vizier). The rise of a new king leads to their expulsion or flight.

The problems with this theory are insurmountable. The biblical account does not mention the Hyksos or offer any historical details linking the story to this or any other particular time period. There is too great a gap between the expulsion of the Hyksos and the appearance of Israel in Palestine. Furthermore, the differences far exceed the similarities. The Hyksos were merchant-kings who came to power through military conquest and fell by the same means. Joseph was a lone Semitic official in a thoroughly Egyptian court who rose to power through faithful service. His descendants were enslaved for generations before escaping.

Bibliography: Manfred Bietak. "Avaris and Pi-ramesse." *Proceedings of the British Academy* 65 (1979) 225–90; Eliezer Oren, ed. *The Hyksos: New Historical and Archaeological Perspectives* (1997).

CAROLYN HIGGENBOTHAM

HYMENAEUS hīˈmuh-neeˈuhs [Ὑμέναιος Hymenaios]. First Timothy identifies Hymenaeus and Alexander as Ephesian Christians who had strayed from the "sound teachings" of the gospel: "by rejecting conscience" they "suffered shipwreck in the faith" that the author seeks to correct (1:19-20; 1:10-11; see 1 Cor 5:5). Second Timothy refers to Hymanaeus in conjunction with Philetus, contending that both had "swerved from the truth" by claiming the resurrection had already occurred (2:17-18). This Gnostic-like teaching apparently had some success in Ephesus (2 Tim 2:18), and Timothy receives instruction to avoid this "profane chatter" that leads people into "more and more impiety" (2 Tim 2:16).

DAVID M. REIS

HYMN OF THE PEARL. Preserved in the *Acts of Thomas*, the *Hymn* was composed as a separate poem. Usually interpreted as gnostic, it recounts the travels of a king's son in search of the pearl. He journeys to Egypt where he nearly forgets his lineage but attains the pearl and becomes heir to his father's kingdom. *See* GNOSTICISM; NAG HAMMADI; THOMAS, ACTS OF.

CARLY DANIEL-HUGHES

HYMN OF THE THREE YOUNG MEN. *See* SONG OF THE THREE JEWS.

HYMNS, NT [ὕμνος hymnos]. St. Augustine declared, "A hymn is a song containing praise of God" (*Enarrat. Ps.* 148). Early Christians were instructed to bring hymns to worship (1 Cor 14:26; Eph 5:19; Col 3:16). Judging by the praise embedded in the prose of the NT, there was a considerable repertoire to choose from. The NT contains both complete hymns and fragmentary outbursts of praise such as those found at Luke 2:14 and 19:38. There are also doxologies and acclamations scattered liberally throughout Revelation (e.g., Rev 4:11), and the writings of Paul (e.g., Rom 11:36).

Hymns, more narrowly defined, can be discerned by their apparent metric form, by the parallelism so characteristic of Hebrew poetry, or by vocabulary or concepts different from the surrounding prose. These hymns may be examples of early Christian praise or may have been composed by the authors of the books in which they are found. Even where the latter is true, these hymns might have been modeled on praise that was current in the church.

Some NT hymns stand in continuity with the praise of Israel; chief among them are the hymns of Luke's infancy narratives (Luke 1:46-55, 68-79; 2:29-32). These hymns adhere so exactly to OT hymnic patterns of declaration of praise and substantiation that they can be assigned to OT form-critical categories (*see* HYMNS, OT). Moreover the phrases that make up these hymns are a catena of OT references, and they may have been composed in Hebrew or Aramaic. The chief difficulty here is not proving that they are Jewish, but that they are Christian. The prevailing view in recent scholarship is that these are hymns of the very early Jewish Christian church. Some of the praise in Revelation also follows OT patterns of declaration and substantiation (Rev 11:17-18; 12:10-12; 15:3-4).

Hymns in the NT also declare the new and the specifically Christian. Hymns both reflect and form the core identity of a worshiping community. The identity of the early churches was expressed in the confession that Jesus is Lord. The concepts of praise and confession overlap; the verbs homologeō (ὁμολογέω) and exomologeō (ἐξομολογέω) can mean both "praise" and "confess" (*see* CONFESSION; PRAISE). Most notable among hymnic confessions is the Christ hymn of Phil 2:5-11. This hymn describes in elevated lan-

guage the cosmic ministry of Jesus and culminates in the characteristic confession of Jesus as Lord. Similarly, the *Logos* hymn of John 1:1-18 lays out the central christological convictions of an early Christian community (*see* CHRISTOLOGY).

The hymns of the NT have often been studied form-critically to investigate the churches behind the text (*see* FORM CRITICISM, NT). They also should be read in their canonical context as part of the theology of the author of the works in which they are found. *See* BENEDICTUS; MAGNIFICAT; MUSIC; NUNC DIMITTIS; WORSHIP, EARLY JEWISH; WORSHIP, NT CHRISTIAN.

Bibliography: S. Farris. *The Hymns of Luke's Infancy Narratives: Their Origin, Meaning and Significance* (1985); Hermann Gunkel. *An Introduction to the Psalms* (1998 [1933]); Ralph P. Martin. *A Hymn of Christ: Philippians 2:5-11 in Recent Interpretation and in the Setting of Early Christian Worship* (1997).

STEPHEN FARRIS

HYMNS, OT [שִׁיר shir, תְּהִלָּה tehillah; ὕμνος hymnos]. The translators of the LXX used the Gk. term hymnos "hymn, ode, in praise of gods and heroes," (as well as psalmos [ψαλμός], ōdē [ᾠδή], and ainesis [αἴνεσις], and related verbs) to gloss the various Hebrew designations for praise songs in the Bible (e.g., tehillah and shir; compare Ps 64:2 [LXX]; Isa 42:10). *Hymn* has since been used as a broad ranging genre term for similar kinds of poetry in many literary traditions.

Hymns were especially common in the ANE, where gods, kings and heroes, and even temples could be the focus of a hymn's exaltation. R. Lowth's 18th cent. characterization of the biblical Hebrew hymn still provides an insightful orientation to this important kind of verse. For Lowth, the hymn is the quintessential specimen of lyric verse that expresses passions of the mind, love, joy, and admiration. A hymn enacts "an effusion of praise" expressed with energy and exultation. And even when it deals with somber subjects, it has about it a sweetness and tenderness expressed in colorful imagery. The essential formal criterion identified by Lowth—that a hymn is written as verse (although apparently in late antiquity the Gk. hymnos could be written in prose)—typifies the hymnic literature from the ANE and the Bible, and practically distinguishes the hymn from other textual means of praise or celebration (e.g., royal inscriptions).

The enactment of "an effusion of praise" is perhaps the definitive thematic marker of the genre. The intent to PRAISE is often made explicit, either in a first person declaration of praise (e.g. Ps 45:1, 17; Exod 15:1-3), or, more frequently, as throughout the Psalms (e.g., Ps 117:1), in a call upon others to give praise. The remainder of the hymn is given over to substantiating the exaltation, providing the reason for praise which itself becomes part of the expression of praise. The combination of the two (declaration or call plus the substantiation) marks the most explicit and fullest expression of the shape of praise in biblical hymns.

The great frequency of this bifold way of shaping praise in the psalmic hymns in particular has sometimes misled scholars into reifying these criteria as definitive of the genre, a temptation which nowadays is more often resisted. Variation is the watchword of hymnic literature. Not only are the biblical hymns that contain these elements otherwise often very diverse (formally, stylistically, thematically), there are many hymns without one or the other, or even both, of these elements. Indeed, there are hymns where the intent to praise is only implied, as in Ps 93. Such hymns are nonetheless expressive of their origin and abiding nature.

Lowth also calls attention to the hymn's typical "sweetness" and musicality. That is, the hymn is often distinguished by its celebratory and radiant tones and mood, its sense (variously signaled) of untroubled contentment, delight, and buoyancy—a general sensibility that contrasts most vividly, for example, with the more somber laments and dirges, or the didacticism of so much wisdom poetry. And it is in the hymnic literature of the Bible that we find our most explicit references to song, singing, and musical instruments (e.g., Ps 98:4-6), from which the sung quality of this kind of verse may be inferred (see MUSIC).

Yahweh, the God of Israel and Judah, is the most prominent subject of praise and exaltation in the liturgical hymns of the OT. Yahweh is hymned for any number of reasons: in celebration of a military victory (Exod 15), on account of the glory and wonders of creation (Ps 104), in thanksgiving for the perception of divine deliverance (Ps 18:4; 56:13-14; compare also 1 Sam 2:1-10). The traditional form-critical distinction between hymns of praise and songs of thanksgiving should not be pressed too hard. Praise and thanksgiving are closely interrelated in Israel's hymnic idiom, as shown by the parallelism involving these notions (e.g., Ps 35:18; 69:31; 92:2; 100:4; 106:1). The so-called royal hymns (Pss 47; 93; 96-99; 146) specifically celebrate Yahweh's divine kingship. Zion, the temple mount, comes in for special attention in the "songs of Zion" (Psalm 137:3; see esp. Psalms 46, 48)—analogous in some respects to the temple hymns from Mesopotamia, though even here adoration of Yahweh remains the psalmist's ultimate preoccupation. Hymns focused on the praise of human beings are rare in the Bible. Examples include celebration of the king in Ps 45 and of the capable woman in Prov 31:10-31, and the lovers in the Song of Songs exult in and praise one another (Song 6:9; compare also Song 1:9-16; 2:1-3; 4:1-7; 5:10-16). See DEAD SEA SCROLLS; HYMNS, NT; POETRY, HEBREW; PSALMS, BOOK OF; SOLOMON, PSALMS OF; SONG OF SONGS; WORSHIP, OT.

Bibliography: H. Gunkel. *An Introduction to the Psalms* (1998 [1933]); R. Lowth. *Lectures on the Sacred Poetry of the Hebrews* (1829 [1753]); P. D. Miller. *They Cried to the Lord* (1994); K. Seybold. *Introducing the Psalms* (1990); C. Westermann. *Praise and Lament in the Psalms* (1967).

FRED W. DOBBS-ALLSOP

HYPOCORISTIC NAMES. Hypocorism (from hypokorismos ὑποκόρισμος) is the use of a pet name or diminutive (e.g., in English, *Liz* for *Elizabeth* or *Will* for *William*). It is frequently applied in a more general sense to indicate any shortened name.

Hypocoristic names are well attested in the Hebrew of the OT. The phenomenon of hypocorism in Hebrew is paralleled in related Northwest Semitic languages as well as in other Semitic languages. One finds similar, sometimes even identical, hypocoristic names in Amorite, Ugaritic, Phoenician, and Aramaic. The similarity in the use of noun classes, suffixes, and deletion of elements demonstrates the common Northwest Semitic cultural background from which these names developed. The formation of hypocoristic names may be divided into three general classes.

The first class contains contracted names formed by the deletion of a word or part of a word. This is the case in many theophoric names, where the theophoric element may be dropped entirely, i.e., word-initial yeho-/ yo- (יְהוֹ/יוֹ) and word-final –yah(u) (יָהוּ/יָה), -ʾel (אֵל). This phenomenon is confirmed by pairs of names referring to the same person, one with the theophoric element and one without, e.g., yozavadh (יוֹזָבָד) "Yahweh has given" (2 Kgs 12:22) vs. zavadh (זָבָד, 2 Chr 24:26); mikhayah (מִיכָיָה) "Who is like Yahweh" (Neh 12:35) vs. mikhah (מִיכָה, Neh 11:17); paltiʾel (פַּלְטִיאֵל) "El has delivered" (2 Sam 3:15) vs. palti (פַּלְטִי, 1 Sam 25:44). In some cases it is not certain what the original theophoric element was, e.g., is ʾuri (אוּרִי) from ʾuriyah(u) (אוּרִיָהוּ) "Yahweh is my light/flame" or is it from ʾuriʾel (אוּרִיאֵל) "El is my light/flame?" Sometimes one cannot be certain whether the theophoric element was ever explicitly present, as in the case of the following two verbal forms: yaʿaqov (יַעֲקֹב) "He (Yahweh) supplants/protects," yivkhar (יִבְחָר) "He (Yahweh, El?) chooses." Evidence from the later books of the OT and the Dead Sea Scrolls demonstrates that the theophoric form –yahu tended to be shortened to –yah (יָה) in the Second Temple Period, e.g., yirmeyahu (יִרְמְיָהוּ) "Yahweh founded" (Jer 1:1) vs. yirmeyah (יִרְמְיָה, 1 Chr 12:11); yeshaʿyahu (יְשַׁעְיָהוּ) "Yahweh has saved" (2 Kgs 19:2) vs. yeshaʿyah (יְשַׁעְיָה, 1 Chr 3:21). One can also find possible examples of the shortening of the nontheophoric element, e.g., yekhizeqiyahu(u) (יְחִזְקִיָּהוּ) "Yahweh has strengthened me" vs. khizeqiyah(u) (חִזְקִיָּהוּ); yekhoneyahu (יְכָנְיָהוּ) "May Yahweh be enduring" vs. konanyah(u)

(בְּנִיָהוּ), though both of these shorter forms may be explained differently.

The second class contains names in a noun pattern different from that of the full name, e.g., qattul (more common in the Second Temple Period than in the First Temple Period): shallum (שַׁלּוּם) vs. shelemyahu (שֶׁלֶמְיָהוּ) "Yahweh gives a replacement" (2 Kgs 15:10-15); shammuʿa (שַׁמּוּעַ) vs. shemaʿyah(u) (שְׁמַעְיָהוּ) "Yahweh has listened" (Num 13:4); zakkur (זַכּוּר) vs. zekharyah (זְכַרְיָה) "Yahweh has remembered"; qetel: zekher (זֶכֶר) vs. zekharyah(u) (זְכַרְיָהוּ); khesedh (חֶסֶד) vs. khasadhyah (חֲסַדְיָה) "Yahweh has been gracious"; qatul: barukh (בָּרוּךְ) vs. berekhyah(u) (בֶּרֶכְיָהוּ) "Yahweh has blessed" (Jer 36:4-32); rakhum (רָחוּם) vs. yerakhmeʾel (יְרַחְמְאֵל) "El has had compassion."

The third class contains names with a diminutive suffix. Common endings are –ay (יָ): ʾamittay (אֲמִתַּי, Jonah 1:1), zakkay (זַכַּי, Ezra 2:9), khaggay (חַגַּי); -a (א , ה —with final alef or he), ʿavdhaʾ (עַבְדָּא), ʿuzzaʾ (עֻזָּא, 2 Kgs 21:18), ʿuzzah (עֻזָּה in some Hebrew manuscripts, 2 Sam 6:3-8), shevnaʾ (שֶׁבְנָא), shevnah (שֶׁבְנָה); -i (יָ): ʾimri (אִמְרִי), zikhri (זִכְרִי), zimri (זִמְרִי, 1 Kgs 16:9-20); -on (וֹן): ʾamnon (אַמְנוֹן, 2 Sam 13:7-8), shimʿon (שִׁמְעוֹן), shimshon (שִׁמְשׁוֹן). Less common are -o (וֹ): ʿiddo (עִדּוֹ), yiddo (יִדּוֹ), shelomoh (שְׁלֹמֹה); -an (ָן): ʾarnan (אַרְנָן), ʿazzan (עַזָּן), shiftan (שִׁפְטָן); -am (ָם): ʾakhuzzam (אֲחֻזָּם), zetham (זֵיתָם), -om (וֹם): gereshom (גֵּרְשֹׁם, Exod 2:22; also gereshon (גֵּרְשׁוֹן), Exod 6:16). It has been suggested that the hypocoristic names ending with a vowel are of vocative origin. The following suffixes on feminine names have also been viewed as hypocoristic: –ath (ָת , ַת): bekhorath (בְּכוֹרַת), shimʿath (שִׁמְעָת), shimrath (שִׁמְרָת); –al / -ayil (ָיִל / ָל): ʾavighal (אֲבִיגַל), ʾavighayil (אֲבִיגַיִל), ʾavihayil (אֲבִיחַיִל), ʾavital (אֲבִיטָל), khamutal (חֲמוּטַל).

It is not always possible to identify from which full name a hypocoristic has been formed. For example, there are several hypocoristic names based on the root shmʿ (שמע, "hear") (shemaʿ שֶׁמַע, shamaʿ שָׁמָע, shimeʿi שִׁמְעִי, shimeʿaʾ שִׁמְעָא) that might have been derived from one or more of the following attested fuller forms: yishmaʿyah(u) (יִשְׁמַעְיָהוּ), shemaʿyah(u) (שְׁמַעְיָהוּ), ʾelishamaʿ (אֱלִישָׁמָע), or yishmaʿeʾl (יִשְׁמָעֵאל). See NAME, NAMING.

Bibliography: Frank L. Benz. Personal Names in the Phoenician and Punic Inscriptions (1972); Jeaneane D. Fowler. Theophoric Personal Names in Ancient Hebrew: A Comparative Study (1988); G. Buchanan Gray. Studies in Hebrew Proper Names (1896); Richard S. Hess. Amarna Personal Names (1993); Scott C. Layton. Archaic Features of Canaanite Personal Names in the Hebrew Bible (1990); Michael H. Silverman. Religious Values in the Jewish Proper Names at Elephantine (1985); Ran Zadok. On West Semites in Babylonia during the Chaldean and Achaemenian Periods: An Onomastic Study (1977).

STEVEN E. FASSBERG

HYPOCRISY, HYPOCRITE. The literal meaning of hypocrisy/hypocrite is a "judgment, sentence, or power of distinguishing" (krisis κρίσις) or "a decider, judge or umpire" (kritēs κριτής) from "below, beneath, or behind" (hypo- ὑπό-).

The most common usage of this term in antiquity was to designate an "actor" (hypokritēs ὑποκριτής). A person who made "judgments" about the characters they played from "behind" a mask was considered "acting," "playing a role," or "performing on a stage" (hypokrisē ὑποκρισή). Thus, in popular understanding, the term came to denote metaphorically persons who pretended to be like someone they were not.

There is no equivalent word in the OT; however, in two passages in the LXX of Job, the LXX translators used hypokritēs for khanef (חָנֵף), a Hebrew term which generally means "profane" or "irreligious" (Job 34:30; 36:13). The term is not uncommon in later books of the LXX. The author of 2 Maccabees utilized various forms of the word to describe Apollonius as one who "pretended" (hypokrinomai ὑποκρίνομαι) to be a person of peace after entering Jerusalem. Then, when the Sabbath day arrived, he ordered his troops to attack the Jews (2 Macc 5:25). On another occasion, the agents of Antiochus attempted to convince Eleazar, a well-respected scribe, to "pretend" as if he were eating the flesh of sacrificial meat ordered by the king (2 Macc 6:21; 4 Macc 6:15). But Eleazar refused: "Such pretense is not worthy of our time of life" (2 Macc 6:24).

In the NT, the term is used only negatively. Hypocrite occurs only in the Gospel narratives; hypocrisy occurs in the Gospels (Matt 23:38; Mark 12:15; Luke 12:1) and in three other places in the NT (Gal 2:13; 1 Tim 4:2; 1 Pet 2:1).

In the Synoptic Gospels, the use of hypocrite occurs most frequently in Matthew (Mark uses the term only once; Luke 3 times; Matthew 14 times), a gospel that reflects a much more tense relationship between the synagogue and the church. Among synoptic characters, only Jesus uses the term. The clearest usage to the idea of the play-actor occurs in Jesus' references in the Sermon on the Mount: When you give alms (6:2), pray (6:5), or fast (6:16), do not follow the actions of the "hypocrites" who "sound trumpets" when they give (6:2), "stand and pray" in synagogues and street corners (6:5), and "disfigure their faces" so that their fasting may be noticeable. These activities suggest the pretension of these persons; they offer expressions of religiosity but, in reality, are insincere. The Didache takes Jesus' teaching one step farther: the disciples' fasting should not occur on the same days as the "hypocrites'" (Did. 8.1-2).

Elsewhere within the Gospels, Jesus uses the term as a direct charge (and slander) against the Pharisees and scribes, his leading "opponents" (compare Matt 15:7//Mark 7:6; Matt 22:18; 23:13, 14, 15, 23, 25, 27, 29). In one exception, Jesus charges a "synagogue ruler" (and others) with hypocrisy for criticizing his healing of a crippled woman on the Sabbath (Luke 13:15). The charge would be severe, given evidence that many Jews held actors in contempt. The Greek verb hypokrinomai ("to reply" or "to reply on stage")—"to pretend" or "to make believe"—occurs only one time in the NT. According to Luke, the scribes and chief priests sent spies who "pretended" to be righteous so that they might entrap Jesus (Luke 20:20; compare the use of synypokrinomai [συνυποκρίνομαι] in Gal 2:13).

Elsewhere within the NT, the term *hypocrisy* is rare. First, Paul charges Barnabas, and other Jewish Christians, with hypocrisy for joining Peter in the cessation of their table-fellowship practices, of eating with the Gentiles, after certain representatives of James arrived in Antioch (Gal 2:13): "If you, though a Jew, live like a Gentile and not like a Jew, how can you compel the Gentiles to live like Jews?" Peter questioned their desire to live consistently with the truth of the gospel. Second, in a later Pauline document, the "Pastor" charges opponents with hypocrisy for forbidding marriage and requiring abstinence (1 Tim 4:2). Finally, the term is included in a list of vices that obedient Christians should remove (1 Pet 2:1).

The Greek negation of the term, anypokritos (ἀνυπόκριτος, "without hypocrisy"), occurs as an adjective of love (Rom 12:9; 2 Cor 6:6; 1 Tim 1:5; 1 Pet 1:22), of faith (2 Tim 1:5), and of wisdom (Jas 3:17), a word the NRSV translators render as "genuine" or "sincere." *See* DECEIT; HONOR; LYING.

Bibliography: R. Batey. "Jesus and the Theatre." *NTS* 30 (1984) 563–74.

EMERSON B. POWERY

HYPOSTASIS OF THE ARCHONS. This anonymous Nag Hammadi text is preserved in a single Coptic papyrus manuscript in the Sahidic dialect. Dating from the 4th cent. CE, the Coptic text translates a Greek original, whose composition is tentatively dated to the 3rd cent. CE. Features from the Jewish/Christian story of the creation, the fall of humanity, and the flood (Gen 1–6) are adapted to describe the role of the Rulers and Authorities in the foundation of the world. These mythological figures play a prominent role in gnostic texts and are mentioned in the NT as the evil powers that compete with the forces of righteousness for the control of humanity. Brief citations to these figures from the "great apostle" (Paul) introduce the document: Col 1:13; Eph 6:12, and are the only overt Christian allusions in the text. The

text seems best described as a Jewish/gnostic writing superficially Christianized. The text is in two parts: a gnostic midrash on Gen 1–6 to which is appended a dialogue between a mystagogue and an initiate.

The narrative elaborates Genesis from a gnostic perspective. The creator is actually a lesser divine figure called Samael (Yaldabaoth, Sakla); he is the blind chief of the Rulers, an arrogant figure who thinks that he alone rules over the Entirety. The rulers fashion an Adam powerless to move because he is only endowed with soul. The (true) Father, however, endows him with spirit and Adam becomes a living spirit. He is placed in the garden to cultivate it and is forbidden under the penalty of death to eat of the tree that gives the ability to recognize good and evil.

Upon the creation of Eve, the spirit principle of Adam departs and comes to reside in Eve and then into the snake. The snake teaches Adam and Eve that eating the fruit of the forbidden tree will not bring death but rather enlightenment by which they will become like the gods. They were forbidden to eat because of the chief ruler's jealousy. Adam and Eve are put out of the garden, and Eve begets Norea, a figure from the realm of imperishable light. The Rulers try to defile her, but she calls up to the God of the Entirety for help. The great Angel Eleleth (also called Sagacity and Understanding) comes to aid her. He informs her that she and her offspring will exist in the world until the true all-powerful man shall come and free them from the bondage of the rulers' error, and they will then ascend into the limitless light. *See* GNOSTICISM; NAG HAMMADI TEXTS.

Bibliography: Roger A. Bullard. *The Hypostasis of the Archons* (1970).

CHARLES W. HEDRICK

HYPSIPHRONE. *Hypsiphrone* is a fragmentary treatise in the Nag Hammadi library recounting Hypsiphrone's ("the high-minded one") revelations during her descent from a virginal state into the material world. *See* NAG HAMMADI.

HYRCANUS hihr-kay'nuhs [Ὑρκανος Hyrkanos].
1. A prominent, wealthy person identified as the son of Tobias (2 Macc 3:11). When Seleucus IV Philopator sent Heliodorus to extract wealth from the Temple in Jerusalem, the high priest informed HELIODORUS that Hyrcanus had deposited a sum of money there.

2. John Hyrcanus I, a nephew of Judas the Maccabee, was a high priest of the Hasmonean dynasty who reigned in Jerusalem from 134–104 BCE.

3. Hyrcanus II was the son of the Hasmonean high priest Alexander Jannaeus and the grandson of John Hyrcanus I. *See* HASMONEANS.

DEREK E. WITTMAN

HYSSOP his′uhp [אֵזוֹב ’ezov; ὕσσωπος hyssopōs]. A small plant of unknown identity used to apply blood to door frames in preparation for Passover (Exod 12:22) and often associated with cleansing (e.g., Lev 14:4; Num 19:6; Ps 51:7). John reports that a sponge of wine vinegar was offered to Jesus on a hyssop branch (John 19:29). *See* LEPROSY; PASSOVER AND FEAST OF UNLEAVENED BREAD; RED HEIFER.

RALPH K. HAWKINS

ABBREVIATIONS

GENERAL ABBREVIATIONS

*	reconstructed prototype of hypothetical letter or word form
Akkad.	Akkadian
AM	Anno Mundi (creation of the world)
ANE	Ancient Near East
Aram.	Aramaic
b.	born
BCE	Before the Common Era (replaces B.C.)
C	centigrade
c.	common
ca.	circa
CE	Common Era (replaces A.D.)
cent.	century
chap(s).	chapter(s)
Chr	Chronicler
cm	centimeter(s)
d.	died
D	Deuteronomist source (of the Pentateuch)
Dtr	Deuteronomistic
DtrH	Deuteronomistic Historian
E	Elohist source (of the Pentateuch)
ed(s).	editor(s), edited by
e.g.	*exempli gratia,* for example
esp.	especially
et al.	*et alii,* and others
etc.	*et cetera,* and the rest
f. or fem.	feminine
fig.	figure
frag.	fragment
ft.	feet (measurement)
FS	Festschrift
g	grams
Gk.	Greek, referring to lexical forms
ha.	Hectare(s)
HB	Hebrew Bible
Heb.	Hebrew
i.e.	*id est,* that is
in.	inch(es)
J	Jahwist or Yahwist source (of the Pentateuch)
km	kilometers
L	liters
LB	Late Bronze

lb(s)	pound(s)
lit.	literally
LXX	Septuagint (the Greek Old Testament)
m	meters
m. or masc.	masculine
MB	Middle Bronze
mi.	miles
mm	millimeters
MS(S)	manuscript(s)
MT	Masoretic Text (of the Hebrew Bible)
n(n).	note(s)
n.d.	no date
n.p.	no place; no publisher; no page
NHC	Nag Hammadi Codex
NS	new series
NT	New Testament
OT	Old Testament
P	Priestly source (of the Pentateuch)
P. Oxy.	Oxyrhyncus Papyri
p(p).	page(s)
par. or //	parallel
Q	Qumran (or Quelle)
repr.	reprinted
rev.	revised (by)
ser.	series
sq. mi.	square mile(s)
suppl.	supplement
Tg(s).	Targum(s); Targumic
trans.	translator, translated by;
v(v).	verse(s)
vol(s).	volume(s)
yd(s).	yard(s)

BIBLE TRANSLATIONS

ASV	American Standard Version
CEV	Contemporary English Version
CSB	Catholic Study Bible
GNB	Good News Bible
JB	Jerusalem Bible
KJV	King James Version
LB	The Living Bible
NAB	New American Bible
NCB	New Century Bible
NEB	New English Bible
NIV	New International Version
NJB	New Jerusalem Bible
NJPS	New Jewish Publication Society Tanakh
NKJV	New King James Version
NLB	New Living Bible
NOAB	New Oxford Annotated Bible
NRSV	New Revised Standard Version
REB	Revised English Bible
RSV	Revised Standard Version

TEV	Today's English Version
TNK	Tanakh

OLD TESTAMENT

Gen	Genesis
Exod	Exodus
Lev	Leviticus
Num	Numbers
Deut	Deuteronomy
Josh	Joshua
Judg	Judges
Ruth	Ruth
1–2 Sam	1–2 Samuel
1–2 Kgs	1–2 Kings
1–2–3–4 Kgdms	1–2–3–4 Kingdoms (LXX)
1–2 Chr	1–2 Chronicles
Ezra	Ezra
Neh	Nehemiah
Esth	Esther
Job	Job
Ps(s)	Psalm(s)
Prov	Proverbs
Eccl	Ecclesiastes
Song	Song of Songs (Song of Solomon, or Canticles)
Isa	Isaiah
Jer	Jeremiah
Lam	Lamentations
Ezek	Ezekiel
Dan	Daniel
Hos	Hosea
Joel	Joel
Amos	Amos
Obad	Obadiah
Jonah	Jonah
Mic	Micah
Nah	Nahum
Hab	Habakkuk
Zeph	Zephaniah
Hag	Haggai
Zech	Zechariah
Mal	Malachi

NEW TESTAMENT

Matt	Matthew
Mark	Mark
Luke	Luke
John	John
Acts	Acts
Rom	Romans
1–2 Cor	1–2 Corinthians
Gal	Galatians

Eph	Ephesians
Phil	Philippians
Col	Colossians
1–2 Thess	1–2 Thessalonians
1–2 Tim	1–2 Timothy
Titus	Titus
Phlm	Philemon
Heb	Hebrews
Jas	James
1–2 Pet	1–2 Peter
1–2–3 John	1–2–3 John
Jude	Jude
Rev	Revelation

APOCRYPHA AND SEPTUAGINT

Bar	Baruch
Add Dan	Additions to Daniel
Pr Azar	Prayer of Azariah
Bel	Bel and the Dragon
Sg Three	Song of the Three Jews
Sus	Susanna
1–2 Esdras	1–2 Esdras
Add Esth	Additions to Esther
Ep Jer	Epistle of Jeremiah
Jdt	Judith
1–2–3–4 Macc	1–2–3–4 Maccabees
Pr Man	Prayer of Manasseh
Ps 151	Psalm 151
Sir	Sirach (Ecclesiasticus)
Tob	Tobit
Wis	Wisdom of Solomon

PSEUDEPIGRAPHICAL AND EARLY PATRISTIC BOOKS

Ahiqar	*Ahiqar*
Apoc. Ab.	*Apocalypse of Abraham*
Apoc. Adam	*Apocalypse of Adam*
Apoc. Dan.	*Apocalypse of Daniel*
Apoc. El. (C)	Coptic *Apocalypse of Elijah*
Apoc. El. (H)	Hebrew *Apocalypse of Elijah*
Apoc. Mos.	*Apocalypse of Moses*
Apoc. Sedr.	*Apocalypse of Sedrach*
Apoc. Zeph.	*Apocalypse of Zephaniah*
Apocr. Ezek.	*Apocrypon of Ezekiel*
Aris. Ex.	Aristeas the Exegete
Aristob.	Aristobulus
Artap.	Artapanus
Ascen. Isa.	*Mart. Ascen. Isa. 6–11*
As. Mos.	*Assumption of Moses*
2 Bar.	*2 Baruch (Syriac Apocalypse)*
3 Bar.	*3 Baruch (Greek Apocalypse)*
4 Bar.	*4 Baruch (Paraleipomena Jeremiou)*

Bk. Noah	*Book of Noah*
Cav. Tr.	*Cave of Treasures*
Cl. Mal.	Cleodemus Malchus
Dem.	Demetrius (the Chronographer)
El. Mod.	*Eldad and Modad*
1 En.	*1 Enoch (Ethiopic Apocalypse)*
2 En.	*2 Enoch (Slavonic Apocalypse)*
3 En.	*3 Enoch (Hebrew Apocalypse)*
Eup.	Eupolemus
Ezek. Trag.	Ezekiel the Tragedian
4 Ezra	*4 Ezra*
5 Apoc. Syr. Pss.	*Five Apocryphal Syriac Psalms*
Gk. Apoc. Ezra	*Greek Apocalypse of Ezra*
Hec. Ab.	Hecataeus of Abdera
Hel. Syn. Pr.	*Hellenistic Synagogal Prayers*
Hist. Jos.	*History of Joseph*
Hist. Rech.	*History of the Rechabites*
Jan. Jam.	*Jannes and Jambres*
Jos. Asen.	*Joseph and Aseneth*
Jub.	*Jubilees*
L.A.B.	*Liber antiquitatum biblicarum* (Pseudo-Philo)
L.A.E.	*Life of Adam and Eve*
Lad. Jac.	*Ladder of Jacob*
Let. Aris.	*Letter of Aristeas*
Liv. Pro.	*Lives of the Prophets*
Lost Tr.	*The Lost Tribes*
3 Macc.	*3 Maccabees*
4 Macc.	*4 Maccabees*
5 Macc.	*5 Maccabees* (Arabic)
Mart. Ascen. Isa.	*Martyrdom and Ascension of Isaiah*
Mart. Isa.	*Mart. Ascen. Isa.* 1–5
Odes Sol.	*Odes of Solomon*
Ph. E. Poet	Philo the Epic Poet
Pr. Jac.	*Prayer of Jacob*
Pr. Jos.	*Prayer of Joseph*
Pr. Man.	*Prayer of Manasseh*
Pr. Mos.	*Prayer of Moses*
Ps.-Eup.	Pseudo-Eupolemus
Ps.-Hec.	Pseudo-Hecataeus
Ps.-Orph.	Pseudo-Orpheus
Ps.-Phoc.	Pseudo-Phocylides
Pss. Sol.	*Psalms of Solomon*
Ques. Ezra	*Questions of Ezra*
Rev. Ezra	*Revelation of Ezra*
Sib. Or.	*Sibylline Oracles*
Syr. Men.	*Sentences of the SyriacMenander*
T. 12 Patr.	*Testaments of the Twelve Patriarchs*
T. Ash.	*Testament of Asher*
T. Benj.	*Testament of Benjamin*
T. Dan	*Testament of Dan*
T. Gad	*Testament of Gad*
T. Iss.	*Testament of Issachar*
T. Jos.	*Testament of Joseph*
T. Jud.	*Testament of Judah*

T. Levi	*Testament of Levi*
T. Naph.	*Testament of Naphtali*
T. Reu.	*Testament of Reuben*
T. Sim.	*Testament of Simeon*
T. Zeb.	*Testament of Zebulun*
T. 3 Patr.	*Testaments of the Three Patriarchs*
T. Ab.	*Testament of Abraham*
T. Isaac	*Testament of Isaac*
T. Jac.	*Testament of Jacob*
T. Adam	*Testament of Adam*
T. Hez.	*Testament of Hezekiah (Mart. Ascen. Isa.* 3:13–4:22*)*
T. Job	*Testament of Job*
T. Mos.	*Testament of Moses*
T. Sol.	*Testament of Solomon*
Theod.	Theodotus, *On the Jews*
Treat. Shem	*Treatise of Shem*
Vis. Ezra	*Vision of Ezra*

PHILO OF ALEXANDRIA

Latin title		English title	
Abr.	*De Abrahamo*	*Abraham*	*On the Life of Abraham*
Aet.	*De aeternitate mundi*	*Eternity*	*On the Eternity of the World*
Agr.	*De agricultura*	*Agriculture*	*On Agriculture*
Anim.	*De animalibus*	*Animals*	*Whether Animals Have Reason (= Alexander)*
Cher.	*De cherubim*	*Cherubim*	*On the Cherubim*
Conf.	*De confusione linguarum*	*Confusion*	*On the Confusion of Tongues*
Congr.	*De congressueru ditionis gratia*	*Prelim. Studies*	*On the Preliminary Studies*
Contempl.	*De vita contemplativa*	*Contempl. Life*	*On the Contemplative Life*
Decal.	*De decalogo*	*Decalogue*	*On the Decalogue*
Deo	*De Deo*	*God*	*On God*
Det.	*Quod deterius potiori insidari soleat*	*Worse*	*That the Worse Attacks the Better*
Deus	*Quod Deus sit immutabilis*	*Unchangeable*	*That God Is Unchangeable*
Ebr.	*De ebrietate*	*Drunkenness*	*On Drunkenness*
Exsecr.	*De exsecrationibus*	*Curses*	*On Curses (= Rewards 127–72)*
Flacc.	*In Flaccum*	*Flaccus*	*Against Flaccus*
Fug.	*De fuga et inventione*	*Flight*	*On Flight and Finding*
Gig.	*De gigantibus*	*Giants*	*On Giants*
Her.	*Quis rerum divinarum heres sit*	*Heir*	*Who Is the Heir?*
Hypoth.	*Hypothetica*	*Hypothetica*	*Hypothetica*
Ios.	*De Iosepho*	*Joseph*	*On the Life of Joseph*
Leg. 1, 2, 3	*Legum allegoriae* I, II, III	*Alleg. Interp.* 1, 2, 3	*Allegorical Interpretation* 1, 2, 3
Legat.	*Legatio ad Gaium*	*Embassy*	*On the Embassy to Gaius*
Migr.	*De migratione Abrahami*	*Migration*	*On the Migration of Abraham*
Mos. 1, 2	*De vita Mosis* I, II	*Moses* 1, 2	*On the Life of Moses* 1, 2
Mut.	*De mutatione nominum*	*Names*	*On the Change of Names*
Opif.	*De opificio mundi*	*Creation*	*On the Creation of the World*
Plant.	*De plantatione*	*Planting*	*On Planting*
Post.	*De posteritate Caini*	*Posterity*	*On the Posterity of Cain*
Praem.	*De praemiis et poenis*	*Rewards*	*On Rewards and Punishments*
Prob.	*Quod omnis probus liber sit*	*Good Person*	*That Every Good Person Is Free*
Prov. 1, 2	*De providentia* I, II	*Providence* 1, 2	*On Providence* 1, 2
QE 1, 2	*Quaestiones et solutiones in Exodum* I, II	*QE* 1, 2	*Questions and Answers on Exodus* 1, 2

QG 1, 2, 3, 4	*Quaestiones et solutiones in Genesin* I, II, III, IV	*QG* 1, 2, 3, 4	*Questions and Answers on Genesis* 1, 2, 3, 4
Sacr.	*De sacrificiis Abelis et Caini*	*Sacrifices*	*On the Sacrifices of Cain and Abel*
Sobr.	*De sobrietate*	*Sobriety*	*On Sobriety*
Somn. 1, 2,	*De somniis* I, II	*Dreams* 1, 2	*On Dreams* 1, 2
Spec. 1, 2, 3, 4	*De specialibus legibus* I, II, III, IV	*Spec. Laws*	*On the Special Laws* 1, 2, 3, 4
Virt.	*De virtutibus*	*irtues*	*On the Virtues*

JOSEPHUS

Latin title		**English title**	
A.J.	*Antiquitates judaicae*	*Ant.*	*Jewish Antiquities*
B.J.	*Bellum judaicum*	*J.W.*	*Jewish War*
C. Ap.	*Contra Apionem*	*Ag. Ap.*	*Against Apion*
Vita	*Vita*	*Life*	*The Life*

DEAD SEA SCROLLS AND RELATED TEXTS

Number	**Abbreviation**	**Name**
	CD	Cairo Genizah copy of the *Damascus Document*
	1Qap Gen^{ar}	*Genesis Apocryphon*
	1QH^a	*Hodayot*^{a} or *Thanksgiving Hymns*^{a}
	1QpHab	*Pesher Habakkuk*
	1QM	*Milhamah, War Scroll, War Rule*
	1QS	*Serek Hayahad* or *Rule of the Community*
	1QIsa^a	Isaiah^a
	1QIsa^b	Isaiah^b
1Q21	1QTLevi ar	*Aramaic Levi Document*
1Q22	1QDM(apocrMoses^a)	*Dibrê Moshe, Words of Moses*
1Q26		*Instruction*
1Q28a	1QSa	*Rule of the Congregation*
1Q28b	1QSb	*Rule of Benedictions*
1Q32	1QJN ar	*New Jerusalem*
1Q34	1QLiturgical Prayers	*Prières pour les fêtes, Festival Prayers*
2Q22	2QapDavid?	*Apocryphon of David?*
2Q24	2QJN ar	*New Jerusalem*
3Q7	3QTJuda?	*Testament of Judah?*
3Q15		*Copper Scroll*
4Q17	4QExod-Lev^f	
4Q22	4QpaleoExod^m	*paleoExod^m*
4Q30	4QDeut^c	Deuteronomy^c
4Q37	4QDeut^j	Deuteronomy^j
4Q51	4QSam^a	Samuel^a
4Q71	4QJer^b	Jeremiah^b
4Q72a	4QJer^d	Jeremiah^d
4Q78	4QXII^c	*Minor Prophets^c*
4Q79	4QXII^d	*Minor Prophets^d*
4Q82	4QXII^g	*Minor Prophets^g*
4Q127	4QpapParaExod gr	*pap4QParaExodus gr*
4Q156	4QtgLev	*Targum of Leviticus*
4Q157	4QtgJob	*Targum of Job*
4Q159	4QOrd^a	*Ordinances*
4Q160	4QVisSam	*Vision of Samuel*

4Q161	4QpIsa*a*	*Pesher to Isaiah*
4Q164	4QpIsa*d*	*Pesher Isaiah*[d]
4Q166	4QpHos*a*	*Hosea Pehser*[a]
4Q167	4QpHos*b*	*Hosea Pesher*[b]
4Q169	4QpNah	*Pesher Nahum*
4Q171	4QpPs*a*	*Pesher Psalms*[a]
4Q174	4QFlor	*Florilegium*
4Q175	4QTest	*Testimonia*
4Q177	4QCatena*a*	*Catena (A)*
4Q180	4QAgesCreat	*Ages of Creation*
4Q181	4QAgesCreat	*Ages of Creation*
4Q182	4QCatena*b* (MidrEschatc)	*Catena*[b], also *Midrash on Eschatology*[c]
4Q185		Sapential Work
4Q196–199	4QTob*a-d* ar	*Tobit* [a-d]
4Q200	4QTob*e* hebr	*Tobit* [e]
4Q201–207	4QEn*a-f* ar	Enoch[a-f]
4Q212	4QEn*g* ar	Enoch[g]
4Q213–14	4QLevi*a* ar	*Aramaic Levi Document*[a-f]
4Q225–27	4QpsJub*a-c*	*pseudoJubilees*[a-c]
4Q238		*Words of Judgement*
4Q242	4QPrNab ar	*Prayer of Nabonidus ar*
4Q243–45	4QpsDan*a-c* ar	*Pseudo-Daniel*[a-c]
4Q246		*Aramaic Apocalypse*
4Q252	4QcommGen A	*Commentary on Genesis A*
4Q256	4QS*b*	*Rule of the Community*[b]
4Q258	4QS*d*	*Rule of the Community*[d]
4Q264a		*Halakhah* B
4Q265	4QSD	*Miscellaneous*
4Q266–73	4QD*a-h*	*Damascus Document*[a-h]
4Q274	4QTorohot A	*Purification Rules A*
4Q275		*Communal Ceremony*
4Q276	4QTorohot B*a*	*Purification Rules B* [a]
4Q277	4QTorohot B*b*	*Purification Rules B* [b]
4Q278	4QTorohot C?	*Purification Rules C*
4Q280		*Curses*
4Q284		*Purification Liturgy*
4Q284a		*Harvesting*
4Q285	4QSM	*Sepher ha-Milhamah*
4Q286–90	4QBer*a-e*	*Berakhot*[a-e]
4Q299	4QMysta	*Mysteries*[a]
4Q302	4QpapAdmonitory Parable	*Admonitory Parable*
4Q303		*Mediation on Creation A*
4Q304		*Meditation on Creation B*
4Q305		*Meditation on Creation C*
4Q319		*Otot*
4Q320		*Calendrical Doc. A*
4Q321		*Calendrical Doc. B*[a]
4Q322		*Calendrical Doc. C*[a]
4Q322a		*Historical Text H?*
4Q323		*Calendrical Doc. C*[b]
4Q324		*Calendrical Doc. C*[c]
4Q325		*Calendrical Doc. D*
4Q326		*Calendrical Doc. E*[a]
4Q327		*Calendrical Doc. E*[b]

4Q328		*Calendrical Doc. F^a*
4Q329		*Calendrical Doc. F^b*
4Q329a		*Calendrical Doc. G*
4Q330		Calendrical Doc. H
4Q331	4QpapHistoricalC	*Historical Text C*
4Q332		*Historical* Text D
4Q333		*Historical* Text E
4Q339	4QList of False Prophets ar	*List of False Prophets*
4Q365	4QRP^c	*Reworked Pentateuch^c*
4Q369	4QPEnosh?	*Prayer of Enosh*
4Q371–373	4QapocrJoseph^{a-c}	*Narrative and Poetic Composition^{a-c}*
4Q375	4QapocrMoses^a	*Apocryphon of Moses^a*
4Q376	4QapocrMoses^b?	*Apocryphon of Moses^b?*
4Q378–79	4QapocrJoshua^{a-b}	*Apocryphon of Joshua^{a-b}*
4Q380–81		Non-Canonical Psalms A–B
4Q382		*Paraphrase of Kings*
4Q383–84	4QapocJer A–B	*Apocryphon of Jeremiah A–B*
4Q385	4QpsEzek^a	*Pseudo-Ezekiel^a*
4Q385a	4QapocJer C^a	*Apocryphon of Jeremiah C^a*
4Q385b	4QpsEzek^c	*Pseudo-Ezekiel^c*
4Q385c	4QpsEzek	*Pseudo-Ezekiel:Unid. Frags.*
4Q386	4QpsEzek^b	*Pseudo-Ezekiel^b*
4Q387	4QapocJer C^b	*Apocryphon of Jeremiah C^b*
4Q387a	4QapocJer C^f	*Apocryphon of Jeremiah C^f*
4Q388	4QpsEzek^d	*Pseudo-Ezekiel^d*
4Q388a	4QapocJer C^c	*Apocryphon of Jeremiah^c*
4Q389	4QapocJer C^d	*Apocryphon of Jeremiah^d*
4Q390	4QapocJer C^e	*Apocryphon of Jeremiah^e*
4Q391	4Qpap psEzek^e	*Pseudo-Ezekiel^e*
4Q394–399	4QMMT	*Miqsat Maase ha-Torah*
4Q400–407	4QShirSabb^{a-h}	*Songs of the Sabbath Sacrifice^a*
4Q408	4QapocrMoses^c?	*Apocryphon of Moses^c?*
4Q411		*Sapiential Hymn*
4Q414	4QRitPur A	*Ritual Purity A*, formerly *Baptismal Liturgy*
4Q415–17		*Instruction^{a-c}*
4Q418	4QInstruction^a	*Instruction^a*, formerly *Sapiental Work A^a*
4Q418a		*Instruction^e*
4Q418c		*Instruction^f?*
4Q422	4QParaphrase of Gen and Exod	*Paraphrase of Genesis and Exodus*
4Q423		*Instruction^g*
4Q424		*Instruction-like composition B*
4Q434	4QBarki Nafshi^a	*BarkhiNafshi^a*
4Q440		*Hodayot-Like Text C*
4Q444		*Incantation*
4Q445		*Lament A*
4Q448	4QApocry. Psalm and Prayer	*Apocryphal Psalm and Prayer*
4Q457b		*Eschatological Hymn*
4Q460		*Narrative Work and Prayer*
4Q462		*Narrative C^a*
4Q464		*Exposition on the Patriarchs*
4Q468e		*Historical Text F*
4Q475		*Renewed Earth*
4Q484	4QpapTJud?	*Testament of Judah?*
4Q502	4QpapRitMar	*Ritual of Marriage*

4Q503	4QpapPrQuot	*Daily Prayers*
4Q504	4QDibHam[a]	*Dibre Ha-Me'orot[a], Words of the Luminaries[a]*
4Q505	4QpapDibHam[b]	*Dibre Ha-Me'orot[b], Words of the Luminaries[b]?*
4Q506	4QpapDibHam[c]	*Dibre Ha-Me'orot[c], Words of the Luminaries[c]*
4Q507	4QPrFêtes[a]?	*Prieres pour les fete, Festival Prayers[a] (?)*
4Q508	4QPrFêtes[b]	*Prieres pour les fete, Festival Prayers[b]*
4Q510	4QShir[a]	*Songs of the Sage[a]*
4Q511	4QShir[b]	*Songs of the Sage[b]*
4Q521		*Messianic Apocalypse*
4Q522	4QapocrJosué[c]?	*Prophétie de Josué*
4Q524	4QT[b]	*Temple Scroll[b]*
4Q525	4QBéat	*Beatitudes*
4Q541	4QapocrLevi[b]? ar	*Apocrypon of Levi[b]*
4Q543–48		*Visions of Amram[a-f]*
4Q549		*Visions of Amram[g]?*
4Q550	4QPrEsther[a] ar	*Proto-Esther[a]*
4Q550a-e	4QprEsther[b-f] ar	*Proto-Esther[b-f]*
4Q551	4QDanSuz? ar	*Daniel-Suzanna (?) ar*
4Q552–53	4QFour Kingdoms[a-b] ar	*4QFour Kingdoms[a-b] ar*
4Q554	4QNJ[a] ar	*New Jerusalem[a]*
4Q554a	4QNJ[b] ar	*New Jerusalem[b]*
4Q555	4QNJ[c] ar	*New Jerusalem[c]*
4Q559	4QpapBibChronology ar	*Biblical Chronology*
4Q560		*Exorcism*
4Q577		*Text Mentioning the Flood*
5Q12	5QD	*Damascus Document*
5Q15	5QNJ ar	*New Jerusalem*
6Q15	6QD	*Damascus Document*
8Q5		*Hymn*
11Q1	11QpaleoLev[a]	*Paleo-Leviticus*
11Q5	11QPs[a]	*Psalms Scroll*
11Q10	11QtgJob	*Targum Job*
11Q11	11QapocrPs	*apocryphal Psalms*
11Q13	11QMelch	*Melchizedek*
11Q17	11QShirShabb	*Songs of the Sabbath Sacrifice*
11Q18	11QNJ ar	*New Jerusalem*
11Q19–20	11QT[a-b]	*Temple Scroll[a-b]*
11Q21	11QT[c]?	*Temple Scroll[c]?*
Mas11	apocJosh	Masada copy of the *Apocryphon of Joshua*

MISHNAH, TALMUD, AND RELATED LITERATURE

Abbreviations distinguish the versions of the Talmudic tractates: *y.* for Jerusalem and *b.* for Babylonian. A pre-fixed *t.* denotes the tractates of the Tosefta and an *m.* those of the Mishnah. A prefixed *bar.* denotes a baraita (an authoritative Tannaitic rule external to the Mishnah).

Abod. Zar.	*Avodah Zarah*
Abot	*Avot*
Arak.	*Arakhin*
B. Bat.	*Bava Batra*
B. Metz.	*Bava Metzia*
B. Qam.	*Bava Qamma*
Bek.	*Bekhorot*

Ber.	Berakhot
Betzah	Betzah (= Yom Tov)
Bik.	Bikkurim
Demai	Demai
Eruv.	Eruvin
Ed.	Eduyyot
Git.	Gittin
Hag.	Hagigah
Hal.	Hallah
Hor.	Horayot
Hul.	Hullin
Kelim	Kelim
Ker.	Keritot
Ketub.	Ketubbot
Kil.	Kilayim
Maas. S.	Maaser Sheni
Maas.	Maaserot
Mak.	Makkot
Makh.	Makhshirin
Meg.	Megillah
Meil.	Meilah
Menah.	Menahot
Mid.	Middot
Mikw.	Mikwaot
Moed	Moed
Moed Qat.	Moed Qatan
Nash.	Nashim
Naz.	Nazir
Ned.	Nedarim
Neg.	Negaim
Nez.	Neziqin
Nid.	Niddah
Ohal.	Ohalot
Or.	Orlah
Parah	Parah
Peah	Peah
Pesah.	Pesahim
Qinnim	Qinnim
Qidd.	Qiddushin
Qod.	Qodashim
Rosh. Hash.	Rosh HaShanah
Sanh.	Sanhedrin
Shabb.	Shabbat
Shev.	Sheviit
Shevu.	Shevuot
Seder	Seder
Sheq.	Sheqalim
Sotah	Sotah
Sukkah	Sukkah
Taan.	Taanit
Tamid	Tamid
Tehar.	Teharot
Tem.	Temurah
Ter.	Terumot

T. Yom	*Tevul Yom*
Uq.	*Uqtzin*
Yad.	*Yadayin*
Yev.	*Yevamot*
Yoma	*Yoma (= Kippurim)*
Zabim	*Zabim*
Zevah.	*Zevahim*
Zera.	*Zeraim*

TARGUMIC TEXTS

Tg. Onq.	*Targum Onqelos*
Tg. Neb.	*Targum of the Prophets*
Tg. Ket.	*Targum of the Writings*
Frg. Tg.	*Fragmentary Targum*
Sam. Tg.	*Samaritan Targum*
Tg. Isa.	*Targum Isaiah*
Tg. Neof.	*Targum Neofiti*
Tg. Ps.-J.	*Targum Pseudo-Jonathan*
Tg. Yer. I, II	*Targum Yerushalmi I, II*
Yem. Tg.	*Yemenite Targum*
Tg. Esth. I, II	*First or Second Targum of Esther*

OTHER RABBINIC WORKS

Avad.	*Avadim*
Avot. R. Nat.	*Avot of Rabbi Nathan*
Ag. Ber.	*Aggadat Bereshit*
Bab.	*Babylonian*
Der. Er. Rab.	*Derekh Eretz Rabbah*
Der. Er. Zut.	*Derekh Eretz Zuta*
Gem.	*Gemara*
Gerim	*Gerim*
Kallah	*Kallah*
Kallah Rab.	*Kallah Rabbati*
Kutim	*Kutim*
Mas. Qet.	*Massekhtot Qetannot*
Mek.	*Mekilta*
Mez.	*Mezuzah*
Midr.	*Midrash*
Midr. Tann.	*Midrash Tannaim*
Pal.	*Palestinian*
Pesiq. Rab.	*Pesiqta Rabbati*
Pesiq. Rab Kah.	*Pesiqta of Rab Kahana*
Pirqe R. El.	*Pirqe Rabbi Eliezer*
Rab.	*Rabbah*
S. Eli. Rab.	*Seder Eliyahu Rabbah*
S. Eli. Zut.	*Seder Eliyahu Zuta*
Sem.	*Semahot*
Sef. Torah	*Sefer Torah*
Sifra	*Sifra*
Sifre	*Sifre*
Tzitz.	*Tzitzit*

Sof.	*Soferim*
S. Olam. Rab	*Seder Olam Rabbah*
Tanh.	*Tanhuma*
Tef.	*Tefillin*
Yal.	*Yalqut*

Apostolic Fathers

Barn.	*Barnabas*
1–2 Clem.	*1–2 Clement*
Did.	*Didache*
Diogn.	*Diognetus*
Herm. *Mand.*	Shepherd of Hermas, *Mandate*
Herm. *Sim.*	Shepherd of Hermas, *Similitude*
Herm. *Vis.*	Shepherd Hermas, *Vision*
Ign. *Eph.*	Ignatius, *To the Ephesians*
Ign. *Magn.*	Ignatius, *To the Magnesians*
Ign. *Phld.*	Ignatius, *To the Philadelphians*
Ign. *Pol.*	Ignatius, *To Polycarp*
Ign. *Rom.*	Ignatius, *To the Romans*
Ign. *Smyrn.*	Ignatius, *To the Smyrnaeans*
Ign. *Trall.*	Ignatius, *To the Trallians*
Mart. Pol.	*Martyrdom of Polycarp*
Pol. *Phil*	Polycarp, *To the Philippians*

Nag Hammadi Codices

Nag Hammadi Codices are identified by the codex number (I) followed by the treatise number (1).

Act Pet.	*Act of Peter* (BG, 4)
Acts Pet. 12 Apos.	*Acts of Peter and the Twelve Apostles* (VI, 1)
Allogenes	*Allogenes* (XI, 3)
Ap. Jas.	*Apocryphon of James* (I, 2)
Ap. John	*Apocryphon of John* (II, 1), (III, 1), (IV, 1), (BG, 2)
Apoc. Adam	*Apocalypse of Adam* (V, 5)
1 Apoc. Jas.	*(First) Apocalypse of James* (V, 3)
2 Apoc. Jas.	*(Second) Apocalypse of James* (V, 4)
Apoc. Paul	*Apocalypse of Paul* (V, 2)
Apoc. Pet.	*Apocalypse of Peter* (VII, 3)
Asclepius	*Asclepius 21–29* (VI, 8)
Auth. Teach.	*Authoritative Teaching* (VI, 3)
Dial. Sav.	*Dialogue of the Savior* (III, 5)
Disc. 8–9	*Discourse on the Eighth and Ninth* (VI, 6)
Ep. Pet. Phil.	*Letter of Peter to Philip* (VIII, 2)
Eugnostos	*Eugnostos the Blessed* (III, 3), (V, 1)
Exeg. Soul	*Exegesis of the Soul* (II, 6)
Frm.	*Fragments* (XII, 3)
Gos. Eg.	*Gospel of the Egyptians* (III, 2), (IV, 2)
Gos. Mary	*Gospel of Mary* (BG, 1)
Gos. Phil.	*Gospel of Philip* (II, 3)
Gos. Thom.	*Gospel of Thomas* (II, 2)
Gos. Truth	*Gospel of Truth* (I, 3), (XII, 2)
Great Pow.	*Concept of our Great Power* (VI, 4)

Hyp. Arch.	*Hypostasis of the Archons* (II, 4)
Hypsiph.	*Hypsiphrone* (XI, 4)
Interp. Know.	*Interpretation of Knowledge* (XI, 1)
Marsanes	*Marsanes* (X)
Melch.	*Melchizedek* (IX, 1)
Norea	*Thought of Norea* (IX, 2)
On Anointing	*On the Anointing* (XI, 2*a*)
On Bap. A	*On Baptism A* (XI, 2*b*)
On Bap. B	*On Baptism B* (XI, 2*c*)
On Euch. A	*On the Eucharist A* (XI, 2*d*)
On Euch. B	*On the Eucharist B* (XI, 2*e*)
Orig. World	*On the Origin of the World* (II, 5), (XIII, 2)
Paraph. Shem	*Paraphrase of Shem* (VII, 1)
Plato Rep.	Plato, *Republic 588b-589b* (VI, 5)
Pr. Paul	*Prayer of the Apostle Paul* (I, 1)
Pr. Thanks.	*Prayer of Thanksgiving* (VI, 7)
Sent. Sextus	*Sentences of Sextus* (XII, 1)
Soph. Jes. Chr.	*Sophia of Jesus Christ* (III, 4), (BG, 3)
Steles Seth	*Three Steles of Seth* (VII, 5)
Teach. Silv.	*Teachings of Silvanus* (VII, 4)
Testim. Truth	*Testimony of Truth* (IX, 3)
Thom. Cont.	*Book of Thomas the Contender* (II, 7)
Thund.	*Thunder: Perfect Mind* (VI, 2)
Treat. Res.	*Treatise on the Resurrection* (I, 4)
Treat. Seth	*Second Treatise of the Great Seth* (VII, 2)
Tri. Trac.	*Tripartite Tractate* (I, 5)
Trim. Prot.	*Trimorphic Protennoia* (XIII, 1)
Val. Exp.	*Valentinian Exposition* (XI, 2)
Zost.	*Zostrianos* (VIII, 1)

NEW TESTAMENT APOCRYPHA AND PSEUDEPIGRAPHA

Acts Andr.	*Acts of Andrew*
Acts Andr. Mth.	*Acts of Andrew and Matthias*
Acts Andr. Paul	*Acts of Andrew and Paul*
Acts Barn.	*Acts of Barnabas*
Acts Jas.	*Acts of James the Great*
Acts John	*Acts of John*
Acts John Pro.	*Acts of John (by Prochorus)*
Acts Paul	*Acts of Paul (or Acts of Paul and Thecla)*
Acts Pet.	*Acts of Peter*
Acts Pet. (Slav.)	*Acts of Peter (Slavonic)*
Acts Pet. Andr.	*Acts of Peter and Andrew*
Acts Pet. Paul	*Acts of Peter and Paul*
Acts Phil.	*Acts of Philip*
Acts Phil. (Syr.)	*Acts of Philip (Syriac)*
Acts Pil.	*Acts of Pilate*
Acts Thad.	*Acts of Thaddaeus*
Acts Thom.	*Acts of Thomas*
Apoc. Pet.	*Apocalypse of Peter*
Ap. John	*Apocryphon of John*
Apoc. Dosith.	*Apocalypse of Dositheus*
Apoc. Messos	*Apocalypse of Messos*
Apoc. Thom.	*Apocalypse of Thomas*

Apoc. Vir.	Apocalypse of the Virgin
(Apocr.) Ep. Tit.	Apocryphal Epistle of Titus
(Apocr.) Gos. John	Apocryphal Gospel of John
Apos. Con.	Apostolic Constitutions and Canons
Ps.-Abd.	Apostolic History of Pseudo-Abdias
(Arab.) Gos. Inf.	Arabic Gospel of the Infancy
(Arm.) Gos. Inf.	Armenian Gospel of the Infancy
Asc. Jas.	Ascents of James
Assum. Vir.	Assumption of the Virgin
Bk. Barn.	Book of the Resurrection of Christ by Barnabas the Apostle
Bk. Elch.	Book Elchasai
Cerinthus	Cerinthus
3 Cor.	3 Corinthians
Ep. Alex.	Epistle to the Alexandrians
Ep. Apos.	Epistle to the Apostles
Ep. Chr. Abg.	Epistle of Christ and Abgar
Ep. Chr. Heav.	Epistle of Christ from Heaven
Ep. Lao.	Epistle to the Laodiceans
Ep. Lent.	Epistle of Lentulus
Ep. Paul Sen.	Epistles of Paul and Seneca
Gos. Barn.	Gospel of Barnabas
Gos. Bart.	Gospel of Bartholomew
Gos. Bas.	Gospel of Basilides
Gos. Bir. Mary	Gospel of the Birth of Mary
Gos. Eb.	Gospel of the Ebionites
Gos. Eg.	Gospel of the Egyptians
Gos. Eve	Gospel of Eve
Gos. Gam.	Gospel of Gamaliel
Gos. Heb.	Gospel of the Hebrews
Gos. Marcion	Gospel of Marcion
Gos. Mary	Gospel of Mary
Gos. Naass.	Gospel of the Naassenes
Gos. Naz.	Gospel of the Nazarenes (Nazoreans)
Gos. Nic.	Gospel of Nicodemus
Gos. Pet.	Gospel of Peter
Ps.-Mt.	Gospel of Pseudo-Matthew
Gos. Thom.	Gospel of Thomas
Gos. Trad. Mth.	Gospel and Traditions of Matthias
Hist. Jos. Carp.	History of Joseph the Carpenter
Hymn Dance	Hymn of the Dance
Hymn Pearl	Hymn of the Pearl
Inf. Gos. Thom.	Infancy Gospel of Thomas
Inf. Gos.	Infancy Gospels
Mart. Bart.	Martyrdom of Bartholomew
Mart. Mt.	Martyrdom of Matthew
Mart. Paul	Martyrdom of Paul
Mart. Pet.	Martyrdom of Peter
Mart. Pet. Paul	Paul Martyrdom of Peter and Paul
Mart. Phil.	Martyrdom of Philip
Melkon	Melkon
Mem. Apos.	Memoria of Apostles
Pre. Pet.	Preaching of Peter
Prot. Jas.	Protevangelium of James
Ps.-Clem.	Pseudo-Clementines

Rev. Steph.	*Revelation of Stephen*	
Sec. Gos. Mk.	*Secret Gospel of Mark*	
Vis. Paul	*Vision of Paul*	

WORKS IN GREEK AND LATIN, SOME WITH ENGLISH TRANSLATIONS

ACHILLES TATIUS

Leuc. Clit.	*Leucippe et Clitophon*	*The Adventures of Leucippe and Clitophon*

AELIAN

Nat. an.	*De natura animalium*	*Nature of Animals*
Var. hist.	*Varia historia*	

AESCHINES

Ctes.	*In Ctesiphonem*	*Against Ctesiphon*
Fals. leg.	*De falsa legatione*	*False Embassy*
Tim.	*In Timarchum*	*Against Timarchus*

AESCHYLUS

Ag.	*Agamemnon*	*Agamemnon*
Cho.	*Choephori*	*Libation-Bearers*
Eum.	*Eumenides*	*Eumenides*
Pers.	*Persae*	*Persians*
Prom.	*Prometheus vinctus*	*Prometheus Bound*
Sept.	*Septem contra Thebas*	*Seven against Thebes*
Suppl.	*Supplices*	*Suppliant Women*

AESOP

Fab.	*Fabulae*	*Fables*

ALBINUS

Epit.	*Epitome doctrinae platonicae*	*Handbook of Platonism*
Intr.	*Introductio in Platonem*	*Introduction to Plato*

ALEXANDER OF APHRODISIAS

De an.	*De anima*
Comm. An. post.	*In Analytica posteriora commentariorum fragmenta*
Comm. An. pr.	*In Aristotelis Analyticorum priorum librum i commentarium*
Comm. Metaph.	*In Aristotelis Metaphysica commentaria*
Comm. Mete.	*In Aristotelis Meteorologicorum libros commentaria*
Comm. Sens.	*In librum De sensu commentarium*
Comm. Top.	*In Aristotelis Topicorum libros octo commentaria*
Fat.	*De fato*

Mixt.	*De mixtione*	
Probl.	*Problemata*	

AMBROSE

Abr.	*De Abraham*	
Apol. Dav.	*Apologia prophetae David*	
Aux.	*Sermo contra Auxentium de basilicis*	
	tradendis	
Bon. mort.	*De bono mortis*	Death as a Good
Cain	*De Cain et Abel*	
Enarrat. Ps.	*Enarrationes in XII Psalmos davidicos*	
Exc.	*De excessufratris sui Satyri*	
Exh. virginit.	*Exhortatio virginitatis*	
Fid.	*De fide*	
Exp. Isa.	*Expositio Isaiae prophetae*	
Exp. Luc.	*Expositio Evangelii secundum Lucam*	
Exp. Ps. 118	*Expositio Psalmi CXVIII*	
Expl. symb.	*Explanatio symboli ad initiandos*	
Fid. Grat.	*De fide ad Gratianum*	
Fug.	*De fuga saeculi*	Flight from the World
Hel.	*De Helia et Jejunio*	
Hex.	*Hexaemeron libri sex*	Six Days of Creation
Hymn.	*Hymni*	
Incarn.	*De incarnationis dominicae sacramento*	Sacrament of the Incarnation of the Lord
Instit.	*De institutione virginis*	
Isaac	*De Isaac vel anima*	Isaac, or the Soul
Jac.	*De Jacob et vita beata*	Jacob and the Happy Life
Job	*De interpellatione Job et David*	Prayer of Job and David
Jos.	*De Joseph patriarcha*	
Myst.	*De mysteriis*	The Mysteries
Nab.	*De Nabuthae historia*	
Noe	*De Noe et arca*	
Ob. Theo.	*De obitu Theodosii*	
Ob. Val.	*De obitu Valentianiani consolatio*	
Off.	*De officiis ministrorum*	
Paen.	*De paenitentia*	
Parad.	*De paradiso*	Paradise
Patr.	*De benedictionibus patriarcharum*	The Patriarchs
Sacr.	*De sacramentis*	The Sacraments
Sacr. regen.	*De sacramento regenerationis sive de philosophia*	
Spir.	*De Spiritu Sancto*	The Holy Spirit
Symb.	*Explanatio symboli*	
Tob.	*De Tobia*	
Vid.	*De viduis*	
Virg.	*De virginibus*	
Virginit.	*De virginitate*	

ANAXIMENES OF LAMPSACUS

Rhet. Alex.	*Rhetorica ad Alexandrum (Ars rhetorica)*

ANDRONICUS

    [Pass.]   *De passionibus*   *The Passions*

ANTH. PAL.

                         Anthologia palatina   *Palatine Anthology*

ANTH. PLAN.

                         Anthologia planudea   *Planudean Anthology*

ANTONINUS LIBERALIS

    Metam.   *Metamorphôseôn synagôgê*

APOLLONIUS OF RHODES

    Argon.   *Argonautica*   *Argonautica*

APOLLONIUS SOPHISTA

    Lex. hom.   *Lexicon homericum*   *Homeric Lexicon*

APPIAN

    Bell. civ.   *Bella civilia*   *Civil Wars*
    Hist. rom.   *Historia romana*   *Roman History*

APULEIUS

    Apol.   *Apologia (Pro se de magia)*   *Apology*
    De deo Socr.   *De deo Socratico*
    Dogm. Plat.   *De dogma Platonis*
    Flor.   *Florida*
    Metam.   *Metamorphoses*   *The Golden Ass*

ARATUS

    Phaen.   *Phaenomena*

ARCHIMEDES

    Aequil.   *De planorum aequilibriis*   *Equilibriums of Planes*
    Aren.   *Arenarius*   *The Sand-reckoner*
    Assumpt.   *Liber assumptorum*
    Bov.   *Problema bovinum*
    Circ.   *Dimensio circuli*   *Measurement of a Circle*
    Con. sph.   *De conoidibus et sphaeroidibus*   *On Conoids and Spheroids*
    Eratosth.   *Ad Eratosthenem methodus*   *To Eratosthenes on the Mechanical*
                                                     Method Theorems

Fluit.	*De corporibus fluitantibus*	*On Floating Bodies*
Quadr.	*Quadratura parabolae*	*Quadrature of the Parabola*
Sph. cyl.	*De sphaera et cylindro*	*On the Sphere and Cylinder*
Spir.	*De lineis spiralibus*	*On Spirals*
Stom.	*Stomachion*	

ARETAEUS

Cur. acut.	*De curatione acutorum morborum*
Cur. diut.	*De curatione diuturnorum morborum*
Sign. acut.	*De causis et signis acutorum morborum*
Sign. diut.	*De causis et signis diuturnorum morborum*

ARISTOPHANES

Ach.	*Acharnenses*	*Acharnians*
Av.	*Aves*	*Birds*
Eccl.	*Ecclesiazusae*	*Women of the Assembly*
Eq.	*Equites*	*Knights*
Lys.	*Lysistrata*	*Lysistrata*
Nub.	*Nubes*	*Clouds*
Pax	*Pax*	*Peace*
Plut.	*Plutus*	*The Rich Man*
Ran.	*Ranae*	*Frogs*
Thesm.	*Thesmophoriazusae*	
Vesp.	*Vespae*	*Wasps*

ARISTOTLE

De an.	*De anima*	*Soul*
An. post.	*Analytica posteriora*	*Posterior Analytics*
An. pr.	*Analytica priora*	*Prior Analytics*
Ath. pol.	*Athēnain politeia*	*Constitution of Athens*
[Aud.]	*De audibilibus*	*Sounds*
Cael.	*De caelo*	*Heavens*
Cat.	*Categoriae*	*Categories*
Col.	*De coloribus*	*Colors*
Div. somn.	*De divinatio per somnum*	*Prophesying by Dreams*
Ep.	*Epistulae*	*Letters*
Eth. eud.	*Ethica eudemia*	*Eudemian Ethics*
Eth. nic.	*Ethica nichomachea*	*Nichomachean Ethics*
Gen. an.	*De generatione anamalium*	*Generation of Animals*
Gen. corr.	*De generatione et corruptione*	*Generaion of Corruption*
Hist. an.	*Historia animalium*	*History of Animals*
Inc. an.	*De incessu animalium*	*Gait of Animals*
Insomn.	*De insomniis*	
Int.	*De interpretatione*	*Interpretation*
Juv. sen.	*De juventute et senectute*	*Youth and Old Age*
[Lin. ins.]	*De lineis insecabilibus*	*Indivisible Lines*
Long. brev.	*De longitudine et brevitate vitae*	*Longevity and Shortness of Life*
[Mag. mor.]	*Magna moralia*	
[Mech.]	*Mechanica*	*Mechanics*
Mem. rem.	*De memoria et reminiscentia*	*Memory and Reminiscence*

Metaph.	Metaphysica	Metaphysics
Mete.	Meteorologica	Meteorology
[Mir. ausc.]	De mirabilibus auscultationibus	On Marvelous Things Heard
Mot. an.	De motu animalium	Movement of Animals
[Mund.]	De mundo	World
[Oec.]	Oeconomica	Economics
Part. an.	De partibus animalium	Parts of Animals
Phys.	Physica	Physics
[Physiogn.]	Physiognomonica	Physiognomonics
[Plant.]	De plantis	Plants
Poet.	Poetica	Poetics
Pol.	Politica	Politics
[Probl.]	Problemata	Problems
Protr.	Protrepticus	
Resp.	De respiratione	Respiration
Rhet.	Rhetorica	Rhetoric
[Rhet. Alex.]	Rhetorica ad Alexandrum	Rhetoric to Alexander
Sens.	De sensuet sensibilibus	Sense and Sensibilia
Somn.	De somniis	Dreams
Somn. vig.	De somno et vigilia	Sleep and Waking
Soph. elench.	Sophistici elenchi	Sophistical Refutations
[Spir.]	De spiritu	Spirit
Top.	Topica	Topics
[Vent.]	De ventorum situ et nominibus	Situations and Names of Winds
[Virt. vit.]	De virtutibus et vitiis	Virtues and Vices
Vit. mort.	De vita et morte	Life and Death
[Gorg.]	De Gorgia	
[Xen.]	De Xenophane	
[Zen.]	De Zenone	

ARRIAN

Anab.	Anabasis
Epict. diss.	Epicteti dissertationes
Peripl. M. Eux.	Periplus Maris Euxini
Tact.	Tactica

ARTEMIDORUS DALDIANUS

Onir.	Onirocritica

ATHANASIUS

Apol. Const.	Apologia ad Constantium	Defense before Constantius
Apol. sec.	Apologia secunda (= Apologia contra Arianos)	Defense against the Arians
[Apoll.]	De incarnatione contra Apollinarium	On the Incarnation against Apollinarius
C. Ar.	Orationes contra Arianos	Orations against the Arians
C. Gent.	Contra gentes	Against Pagans
Decr.	De decretis	Defense of the Nicene Definition
Dion.	De sententia Dionysii	On the Opinion of Dionysius
Ep. Adelph.	Epistula ad Adelphium	Letter to Adelphius
Ep. Aeg. Lib.	Epistula ad episcopos Aegypti et Libyae	Letter to the Bishops of Egypt and Libya

Ep. Afr.	*Epistula ad Afros episcopos*	*Letter to the Bishops of Africa*
Ep. Amun	*Epistula ad Amun*	*Letter to Ammoun*
Ep. cler. Alex.	*Epistula ad clerum Alexandriae*	*Letter to the Clergy of Alexandria*
Ep. cler. Mareot.	*Epistula ad clerum Mareotae*	*Letter to the Clergy of Mareotis*
Ep. Drac.	*Epistula ad Dracontium*	*Letter to Dracontius*
Ep. encycl.	*Epistula encyclica*	*Circular Letter*
Ep. Epict.	*Epistula ad Epictetum*	*Letter to Epictetus*
Ep. fest.	*Epistulae festales*	*Festal Letters*
Ep. Jo. Ant.	*Epistula ad Joannem et Antiochum presbyteros*	*Letter to John and Antiochus*
Ep. Jov.	*Epistula ad Jovianum*	*Letter to Jovian*
Ep. Marcell.	*Epistula ad Marcellinum de interpretatione Psalmorum*	*Letter to Marcellinus on the Interpretation of the Psalms*
Ep. Max.	*Epistula ad Maximum*	*Letter to Maximus*
Ep. mon. 1	*Epistula ad monachos i*	*First Letter to Monks*
Ep. mon. 2	*Epistula ad monachos ii*	*Second Letter to Monks*
Ep. mort. Ar.	*Epistula ad Serapionem de more Arii*	*Letter to Seapion Concerning Death of Arius*
Ep. Ors. 1	*Epistula ad Orsisium i*	*First Letter to Orsisius*
Ep. Ors. 2	*Epistula ad Orsisium ii*	*Second Letter to Orsisius*
Ep. Pall.	*Epistula ad Palladium*	*Letter to Palladius*
Ep. Rufin.	*Epistula ad Rufinianum*	*Letter to Rufinianus*
Ep. Serap.	*Epistulae ad Serapionem*	*Letters to serapion concerning the Holy Spirit*
Ep. virg. (Copt.)	*Epistula ad virgines (Coptice)*	*First (Coptic) Letter to Virgins*
Ep. virg. (Syr.)	*Epistula ad virgines (Syriace)*	*Second (Syriac) Letter to Virgins*
Ep. virg. (Syr./Arm.)	*Epistula ad virgines (Syriace et Armeniace)*	*Letter to Virgins*
Ep. virg. (Theod.)	*Epistula exhortatora ad virgines apud Theodoretum*	*Letter to Virgins*
Fug.	*Apologia de fuga sua*	*Defense of His Flight*
H. Ar.	*Historia Arianorum*	*History of the Arians*
Hen. sōm.	*Henos sōmatos*	*Encyclical Letter of Alexander concerning the Deposition of Arius*
Hom. Jo. 12:27	*In illud Nunc anima mea turbata est*	*Homily on John 12:27*
Hom. Luc. 12:10	*In illud Qui dixerit verbum in filium*	*Homily on Luke 12:10*
Hom. Matt. 11:27	*In illud Omnia mihi tradita sunt*	*Homily on Matt 11:27*
Inc.	*De incarnatione*	*On the Incarnation*
Mor. et val.	*De morbo et valitudine*	*On Sickness and Health*
Narr. fug.	*Narratio ad Ammonium episcopum de fuga sua*	*Report of Athanasius concerning Theodorus*
Syn.	*De synodis*	*On the Councils of Arimimum and Seleucia*
Tom.	*Tomus ad Antiochenos*	*Tome to the People of Antioch*
Vit. Ant.	*Vita Antonii*	*Life of Antony*

ATHENAEUS

Deipn.	*Deipnosophistae*

ATHENAGORAS

Leg.	*Legatio pro Christianis*
Res.	*De resurrectione*

AUGUSTINE

Acad.	Contra Academicos	Against the Academics
Adim.	Contra Adimantum	Agaiinst Adimantus
Adnot. Job	Adnotationum in Job liber I	Annotations on Job
Adv. Jud.	Tractatus adversus Judaeos	In Answer to the Jews
Agon.	De agone christiano	Christian Combat
An. orig.	De anima et eius origine	The Soul and Its Origin
Arian.	Contra sermonem Arianorum	
Bapt.	De baptismo contra Donatistas	
Beat.	De vita beata	Baptism
Bon. conj.	De bono conjugali	The Good Marriage
Brev. coll.	Breviculus collationis cum Donatistas	
C. du. ep. Pelag.	Contra duas epistulas Pelagianorum ad Bonifatium	Against the Two Letters of the Pelagians
C. Jul.	Contra Julianum	Against Julian
C. Jul. op. imp.	Contra secundam Juliani responsionem imperfectum opus	Against Julian: Opus Imperfectum
C. litt. Petil.	Contra litteras Petiliani	
C. mend.	Contra mendacium	Against Lying (to Consentius)
Catech.	De catechizandis rudibus	Catechizing the Uninstructed
Civ.	De civitate Dei	The City of God
Coll. Max.	Collatio cum Maximino Arianorum episcopo	
Conf.	Confessionum libri XIII	Confessions
Cons.	De consensu evangelistarum	Harmony of the Gospels
Contin.	De continentia	Continence
Corrept.	De correptione et gratia	Admonition and Grace
Cresc.	Contra Cresconium Donatistam	
Cur.	De cura pro mortuis gerenda	The Care to Be Taken for the Dead
Dial.	Principia dialecticae	
Disc.	De disciplina christiana	
Div.	De divinitate daemonum	The Divination of Demons
Div. quaest. LXXXIII	De diversis quaestionibus LXXXIII	Eighty-three Different Questions
Div. quaest. Simpl.	De diversis quaestionibus ad Simplicianum	
Doctr. chr.	De doctrina christiana	Christian Instruction
Don.	Post collationem adversus Donatistas	
Duab.	De duabus animabus	Two Souls
Dulc.	De octo Dulcitii quaestionibus	The Eight Questions of Dulcitius
Emer.	De gestis cum Emerino	
Enarrat. Ps.	Enarrationes in Psalmos	Enarrations on the Psalms
Enchir.	Enchiridion de fide, spe, et caritate	Enchiridion on Faith, Hope, and Love
Exp. Gal.	Expositio in epistulam ad Galatas	
Exp. quaest. Rom.	Expositio quarumdam quaestionum in epistula ad Romanos	
Faust.	Contra Faustum Manichaeum	Against Faustus the Manichaean
Fel.	Contra Felicem	Against Felix
Fid.	De fide rerum quae non videntur	Faith in Thiings Unseen
Fid. op.	De fide et operibus	Faith and Works
Fid. symb.	De fide et symbolo	Faith and the Creed
Fort.	Contra Fortunatum	Against Fortunatus
Fund.	Contra epistulam Manichaei quam vocant Fundamenti	Against the Letter of the Manichaeans That They Call "The Basics"

Gaud.	*Contra Gaudentium Donatistarum episcopum*	*Against Gaudentius the Donatist Bishop*
Gen. imp.	*De Genesi ad litteram imperfectus liber*	*On the Literal Interpretation of Genesis: An Unfinished Book*
Gen. litt.	*De Genesi ad litteram*	*On Genesis Litarally Interpreted*
Gen. Man.	*De Genesi contra Manichaeos*	*On Genesis Against the Manicheans*
Gest. Pelag.	*De gestis Pelagii*	*Proceedings of Pelagius*
Gramm.	*De grammatica*	
Grat.	*De gratia et libero arbitrio*	*Grace and Free Will*
Grat. Chr.	*De gratia Christi, et de peccato originali*	*The Grace of Christ and Original Sin*
Haer.	*De haeresibus*	*Heresies*
Immort. an.	*De immortalitate animae*	*The Immortality of the Soul*
Incomp. nupt.	*De incompetentibus nuptiis*	*Adulterous Marriages*
Leg.	*Contra adversarium legis et prophetarum*	
Lib.	*De libero arbitrio*	*Free Will*
Locut. Hept.	*Locutionum in Heptateuchum libri septem*	
Mag.	*De magistro*	
Man.	*De moribus Manichaeorum*	*The Morals of the Manichaeans*
Maxim.	*Contra Maximinum Arianum*	*Against Maximimus the Arian*
De mend.	*De mendacio*	*On Lying*
Mor. eccl.	*De moribus ecclesiae catholicae*	*The Way of Life of the Catholic Church*
Mor. Manich.	*De moribus Manichaeorum*	*The Way of the Life of the Manichaeans*
Mus.	*De musica*	*Music*
Nat. bon.	*De natura boni contra Manichaeos*	*The Nature of the Good*
Nat. grat.	*De natura et gratia*	*Nature and Grace*
Nat. orig.	*De natura et origine animae*	*The Nature and Origin of the Soul*
Nupt.	*De nuptiis et concupiscentia ad Valerium comitem*	*Marriage and Concupiscence*
Oct. quaest. Vet. Test.	*De octo quaestionibus ex Veteri Testamento*	*Eight Questions from the Old Testament*
Op. mon.	*De opere monachorum*	*The Work of Monks*
Ord.	*De ordine*	
Parm.	*Contra epistulam Parmeniani*	
Pat.	*De patientia*	*Patience*
Pecc. merit.	*De peccatorum meritis et remissione*	*Guilt and Remission of Sins*
Pecc. orig.	*De peccato originali*	*Original sin*
Perf.	*De perfectione justitiae hominis*	*Perfection in Human Righteousness*
Persev.	*De dono perseverantiae*	*The Gift of Perseverance*
Praed.	*De praedestinatione sanctorum*	*The Predestination of the Saints*
Priscill.	*Ad Orosium contra Priscillianistas et Origenistas*	*To Orosius against the Priscillianists and the Origenists*
Psal. Don.	*Psalmus contra partem Donati*	
Quaest. ev.	*Quaestionum evangelicarum libri II*	
Quaest. Hept.	*Quaestiones in Heptateuchum*	
Quaest. Matt.	*Quaestiones in evangelium Matthaei*	
Quant. an.	*De quantitate animae*	*The Magnitude of the Soul*
Reg.	*Regula ad servos Dei*	
Retract.	*Retractationum libri II*	*Retractions*
Rhet.	*De rhetorica, Rhetores Latini*	
Secund.	*Contra Secundinum Manichaeum*	
Serm.	*Sermones*	
Serm. Dom.	*De sermone Domini in monte*	*Sermon on the Mount*

Solil.	Soliloquiorum libri II	Soliloquies
Spec.	De scriptura sancta speculum	
Spir. et litt.	De spiritu et littera	The Spirit and the Letter
Symb.	De symbolo ad catechumenos	The Creed: For Catechumens
Tract. ep. Jo.	In epistulam Johannis ad Parthos tractatus	Tractates on the First Epistle of John
Tract. Ev. Jo.	In Evangelium Johannis tractatus	Tractates on the Gospel of John
Trin.	De Trinitate	The Trinity
Unic. bapt.	De unico baptismo	
Unit. eccl.	De unitate ecclesiae	The Unity of the Church
Util. cred.	De utilitate credendi	The Usefulness of Believing
Util. jej.	De utilitate jejunii	The Usefulness of Fasting
Ver. rel.	De vera religione	True Religion
Vid.	De bono viduitatis	The Excellence of Widowhood
Virginit.	De sancta virginitate	Holy virginity
Vit. Christ.	De vita christiana	The Christian Life

AULUS GELLIUS

Bell. afr.	Bellum africum	African War
Bell. alex.	Bellum alexandrinum	Alexandrian War
Noct. att.	Noctes atticae	Attic Nights

BION

Epitaph. Adon.	Epitaphius Adonis	Lament for Adonis
[Epith. Achil.]	Epithalamium Achillis et Deidameiae	To Achilles and Deidamea

CAESAR

Bell. civ.	Bellum civile	Civil War
Bell. gall.	Bellum gallicum	Gallic War

CALLIMACHUS

Aet.	Aetia (in P.Oxy. 2079)	Causes
Epigr.	Epigrammata	Epigrams
Hec.	Hecala	Hecale
Hymn.	Hymni	Hymns
Hymn. Apoll.	Hymnus in Apollinem	Hymn to Apollo
Hymn. Cer.	Hymnus in Cererem	Hymn to Ceres or Demeter
Hymn. Del.	Hymnus in Delum	Hymn to Delos
Hymn. Dian.	Hymnus in Dianam	Hymn to Diana or Artemis
Hymn. Jov.	Hymnus in Jovem	Hymn to Jove or Zeus
Hymn. lav. Pall.	Hymnus in lavacrum Palladis	Hymn to the Baths of Pallas

CAN. AP.

	Canones apostolicae	Apostolic Canons

CATO

Agr.	De agricultura (De re rustica)	Agriculture
Orig.	Origines	Origins

CEB. TAB.

Cebetis Tabula

CHARITON

Chaer.   De Chaerea et Callirhoe   Chaereas and Callirhoe

CHRYSOSTOM (See John Chrysostom)

CICERO

Acad.   Academicae quaestiones
Acad. post.   Academica posteriora (Lucullus)
Acad. pr.   Academica priora
Agr.   De Lege agraria
Amic.   De amicitia
Arch.   Pro Archia
Att.   Epistulae ad Atticum
Aug.   De auguriis
Balb.   Pro Balbo
Brut.   Brutus or De claris oratoribus
Caecin.   Pro Caecina
Cael.   Pro Caelio
Cat.   In Catalinam
Clu.   Pro Cluentio
Corn.   Pro Cornelio de maiestate
Deiot.   Pro rege Deiotaro
Div.   De divinatione
Div. Caec.   Divinatio in Caecilium
Dom.   De domo suo
Ep. Brut.   Epistulae ad Brutum
Epigr.   Epigrammata
Fam.   Epistulae ad familiares
Fat.   De fato
Fin.   De finibus
Flac.   Pro Flacco
Font.   Pro Fonteio
Har. resp.   De haruspicum responso
Inv.   De inventione rhetorica
Leg.   De legibus
Leg. man.   Pro Lege manilia (De imperio Cn. Pompeii)
Lig.   Pro Ligario
Lim.   Limon
Mar.   Marius
Marcell.   Pro Marcello
Mil.   Pro Milone
Mur.   Pro Murena
Nat. d.   De natura deorum
Off.   De officiis
Opt. gen.   De optimo genere oratorum
De or.   De oratore
Or. Brut.   Orator ad M. Brutum
Parad.   Paradoxa Stoicorum

Part. or.	Partitiones oratoriae	
Phil.	Orationes philippicae	
Pis.	In Pisonem	
Planc.	Pro Plancio	
Prov. cons.	De provinciis consularibus	
Quinct.	Pro Quinctio	
Quint. fratr.	Epistulae ad Quintum fratrem	
Rab. Perd.	Pro Rabirio Perduellionis Reo	
Rab. Post.	Pro Rabirio Postumo	
Red. pop.	Post reditum ad populum	
Red. sen.	Post reditum in senatu	
Rep.	De republica	
Rosc. Amer.	Pro Sexto Roscio Amerino	
Rosc. com.	Pro Roscio comoedo	
Scaur.	Pro Scauro	
Sen.	De senectute	
Sest.	Pro Sestio	
Sull.	Pro Sulla	
Tim.	Timaeus	
Tog. cand.	Oratio in senatu in toga candida	
Top.	Topica	
Tull.	Pro Tullio	
Tusc.	Tusculanae disputationes	
Vat.	In Vatinium	
Verr.	In Verrem	

CLEMENT OF ALEXANDRIA

Ecl.	Eclogae propheticae	Extracts from the Prophets
Exc.	Excerpta ex Theodoto	Excerpts from Theodotus
Paed.	Paedagogus	Christ the Educator
Protr.	Protrepticus	Exhortation to the Greeks
Quis div.	Quis dives salvetur	Salvation of the Rich
Strom.	Stromata	Miscellanies

COD. JUSTIN.

Codex justinianus

COD. THEOD.

Codex theodosianus

COLUMELLA

Arb.	De arboribus
Rust.	De re rustica

CONST. AP.

Constitutiones apostolicae   Apostolic Constitutions

CORNUTUS

Nat. d.	*De natura deorum (Epidrôme ton kata tēn Hellēniken theologian paradedomenôn)*	*Summary of the Traditions concerning Greek Mythology*

CORP. HERM.

	Corpus hermeticum	

COSMAS INDICOPLEUSTES

Top.	*Topographia christiana*	*Christian Topography*

CYPRIAN

Demetr.	*Ad Demetrianum*	*To Demetrian*
Dom. or.	*De dominica oratione*	*The Lord's Supper*
Don.	*Ad Donatum*	*To Donatus*
Eleem.	*De opere et eleemosynis*	*Works and Almsgiving*
Fort.	*Ad Fortunatum*	*To Fortunatus: Exhortation to Martyrdom*
Hab. virg.	*De habitu virginum*	*The Dress of Virgins*
[Idol.]	*Quod idola dii non sint*	*That Idols Are Not Gods*
Laps.	*De lapsis*	*The Lapsed*
Mort.	*De mortalitate*	*Mortality*
Pat.	*De bono patientiae*	*The Advantage of Patience*
Sent.	*Sententiae episcoporum de haereticis baptizandis*	
Test.	*Ad Quirinum testimonia adversus Judaeos*	*To Quirinius: Testimonies against the Jews*
Unit. eccl.	*De catholicae ecclesiae unitate*	*The Unity of the Catholic Church*
Zel. liv.	*De zelo et livore*	*Jealousy and Envy*

DEMETRIUS

Eloc.	*De elocutione (Peri hermeneias)*	*Style*

DEMOSTHENES

Andr.	*Adversus Androtionem*	*Against Androtion*
[Apat.]	*Contra Apatourium*	*Against Apaturius*
1–3 Aphob.	*In Aphobum*	*1–3 Against Aphobus*
Aristocr.	*In Aristocratem*	*Against Aristocrates*
1–2 Aristog.	*In Aristogitonem*	*1–2 Against Aristogeiton*
1 [2] Boeot.	*Contra Boeotum i–ii*	*1–2 Against Boeotos*
C. Phorm.	*Contra Phormionem*	*Against Phormio*
Call.	*Contra Calliclem*	*Against Callicles*
[Callip.]	*Contra Callipum*	*Against Callipus*
Chers.	*De Chersoneso*	*On the Chersonese*
Con.	*In Cononem*	*Against Canon*
Cor.	*De corona*	*On the Crown*
Cor. trier.	*De corona trierarchiae*	*On the Trierarchic Crown*

[Dionys.]	Contra Dionysodorum	Against Dionysodorus
Epitaph.	Epitaphius	Funeral Oration
[Erot.]	Eroticus	Eroticus
Eub.	Contra Eubulidem	Against Eubulides
[Everg.]	In Evergum et Mnesibulum	Against Evergus and Mnesibulus
Exord.	Exordia (Prooemia)	
Fals. leg.	De falsa legatione	False Embassy
Halon.	De Halonneso	On the Halonnesus
[Lacr.]	Contra Lacritum	Against Lacritus
[Leoch.]	Contra Leocharem	Against Leochares
Lept.	Adversus Leptinem	Against Leptines
[Macart.]	Contra Macartatum	Against Macartatus
Meg.	Pro Megalopolitanis	For the Megalopolitans
Mid.	In Midiam	Against Meidias
Naus.	Contra Nausimachum et Xenopeithea	Against Nausimachus
[Neaer.]	In Neaeram	Against Neaera
Nicostr.	Contra Nicostratum	Against Nicostratus
[Olymp.]	In Olympiodorum	Agaiinst Olympiodorus
1–3 Olynth.	Olynthiaca i–iii	1–3 Olynthiac
1–2 Onet.	Contra Onetorem	1–2 Against Onetor
De pace	De pace	On the Peace
Pant.	Contra Pantaenetum	Against Pantaenetus
1–3 [4] Philip.	Philippica i–iv	1–4 Philippic
Pro Phorm.	Pro Phormione	For Phormio
[Poly.]	Contra Polyclem	Against Polycles
Rhod. lib.	De Rhodiorum libertate	On the Liberty of the Rhodians
Spud.	Contra Spudiam	Against Spudia
1 [2] Steph.	In Stephanum i–ii	1–2 Against Stephanus
Symm.	De symmoriis	On the Symmories
[Syntax.]	Peri syntaxeōs	On Organization
[Theocr.]	In Theocrinem	Against Theocrines
[Tim.]	Contra Timotheum	Against Timotheus
Timocr.	In Timocratem	Against Timocrates
Zenoth.	Contra Zenothemin	Against Zenothemis

DIDYMUS

Comm. Eccl.	Commentarii in Ecclesiasten
Comm. Job	Commentarii in Job
Comm. Oct. Reg.	Commentarii in Octateuchum et Reges
Comm. Ps.	Commentarii in Psalmos
Comm. Zach.	Commentarii in Zachariam
Dial. haer.	Dialogus Didymi Caeci cum haeretico
Enarrat. Ep. Cath.	In Epistulas Catholicas brevis enarratio
Fr. Cant.	Fragmentum in Canticum canticorum
Fr. 1 Cor.	Fragmenta in Epistulam i ad Corinthios
Fr. 2 Cor.	Fragmenta in Epistulam ii ad Corinthios
Fr. Heb.	Fragmentum in Epistulam ad Hebraeos
Fr. Jer.	Fragmenta in Jeremiam
Fr. Jo.	Fragmenta in Joannem
Fr. Prov.	Fragmenta in Proverbia
Fr. Ps.	Fragmenta in Psalmos
Fr. Rom.	Fragmenta in Epistulam ad Romanos
In Gen.	In Genesim

Incorp.	*De incorporeo*	
Man.	*Contra Manichaeos*	
Philos.	*Ad philosophum*	
Trin.	*De Trinitate*	

DIG.

	Digesta	

DINARCHUS

Aristog.	*In Aristogitonem*	*Against Aristogiton*
Demosth.	*In Demosthenem*	*Against Demosthenes*
Phil.	*In Philoclem*	*Against Philocles*

DIO (CASSIUS DIO)

Rom.	*Romaika*	

DIO CHRYSOSTOM

Achill.	*Achilles (Or. 58)*	*Achilles and Cheiron*
Admin.	*De administratione (Or. 50)*	*His Past Record*
Aegr.	*De aegritudine (Or. 16)*	*Pain and Distress of Spirit*
Alex.	*Ad Alexandrinos (Or. 32)*	*To the People of Alexandria*
Apam.	*Ad Apamenses (Or. 41)*	*To the Apameians*
Aud. aff.	*De audiendi affectione (Or. 19)*	*Fondness for Listening*
Avar.	*De avaritia (Or. 17)*	*Covetousness*
Borysth.	*Borysthenitica (Or. 36)*	*Borysthenic Discourse*
Cel. Phryg.	*Celaenis Phrygiae (Or. 35)*	*At Celaenae in Phrygia*
Charid.	*Charidemus (Or. 30)*	
Chrys.	*Chryseis (Or. 61)*	
Compot.	*De compotatione (Or. 27)*	*Symposia*
Conc. Apam.	*De concordia cum Apamensibus (Or. 40)*	*On Concord with Apamea*
Consuet.	*De consuetudine (Or. 76)*	*Custom*
Consult.	*De consultatione (Or. 26)*	*Deliberation*
Cont.	*Contio (Or. 47)*	*In the Public Assembly at Prusa*
In cont.	*In contione (Or. 48)*	*Political Address in the Assembly*
[Cor.]	*Corinthiaca (Or. 37)*	*Corinthian Discourse*
Def.	*Defensio (Or. 45)*	*Defense*
Dei cogn.	*De dei cognitione (Or. 12)*	*Olympic Discourse*
Dial.	*Dialexis (Or. 42)*	*In His Native City*
Dic. exercit.	*De dicendi exercitatione (Or. 18)*	*Training for Public Speaking*
Diffid.	*De diffidentia (Or. 74)*	*Distrust*
Diod.	*Ad Diodorum (Or. 51)*	*To Diodorus*
Divit.	*De divitiis (Or. 79)*	*Wealth*
Exil.	*De exilio (Or. 13)*	*Banishment*
Fel.	*De felicitate (Or. 24)*	*Happiness*
Fel. sap.	*De quod felix sit sapiens (Or. 23)*	*The Wise Man is Happy*
Fid.	*De fide (Or. 73)*	*Trust*
1 Fort.	*De fortuna i (Or. 63)*	*Fortune 1*

2 Fort.	De fortuna ii (Or. 64)	Fortune 2
3 Fort.	De fortuna iii (Or. 65)	Fortune 3
Gen.	De genio (Or. 25)	The Guiding Spirit
1 Glor.	De gloria i (Or. 66)	Reputation
2 Glor.	De gloria ii (Or. 67)	Popular Opinion
3 Glor.	De gloria iii (Or. 68)	Opinion
Grat.	Gratitudo (Or. 44)	Friendship for Native Land
Hab.	De habitu (Or. 72)	Personal Appearance
Hom.	De Homero (Or. 53)	Homer
Hom. Socr.	De Homero et Socrate (Or. 55)	Homer and Socrates
Invid.	De invidia (Or. 77/78)	Envy
Isthm.	Isthmiaca (Or. 9)	Isthmian Discourse
De lege	De lege (Or. 75)	Law
Lib.	De libertate (Or. 80)	Freedom
Lib. myth.	Libycus mythos (Or. 5)	A Libyan Myth
1 Melanc.	Melancomas i (Or. 29)	Melancomas 1
2 Melanc.	Melancomas ii (Or. 28)	Melancomas 2
Ness.	Nessus (Or. 60)	Nessus, or Deianeira
Nest.	Nestor (Or. 57)	Homer's Portrayal of Nestor
Nicaeen.	Ad Nicaeenses (Or. 39)	To the Nicaeans
Nicom.	Ad Nicomedienses (Or. 38)	To the Nicomedians
De pace	De pace et bello (Or. 22)	Peace and War
Philoct. arc.	De Philoctetae arcu (Or. 52)	Appraisal of the Tragic Triad
Philoct.	Philoctetes (Or. 59)	
De philosophia	De philosophia (Or. 70)	Philosophy
De philosopho	De philosopho (Or. 71)	The Philosopher
Pol.	Politica (Or. 43)	Political Address
Pulchr.	De pulchritudine (Or. 21)	Beauty
Rec. mag.	Recusatio magistratus (Or. 49)	Refusal of the Office of Archon
Regn.	De regno (Or. 56)	Kingship
1 Regn.	De regno i (Or. 1)	Kingship 1
2 Regn.	De regno ii (Or. 2)	Kingship 2
3 Regn.	De regno iii (Or. 3)	Kingship 3
4 Regn.	De regno iv (Or. 4)	Kingship 4
Regn. tyr.	De regno et tyrannide (Or. 62)	Kingship and Tyranny
Rhod.	Rhodiaca (Or. 31)	To the People of Rhodes
Sec.	De secessu (Or. 20)	Retirement
Serv.	De servis (Or. 10)	Servants
1 Serv. lib.	De servitute et libertate i (Or. 14)	Slavery and Freedom 1
2 Serv. lib.	De servitute et libertate ii (Or. 15)	Slavery and Freedom 2
Socr.	De Socrate (Or. 54)	Socrates
1 Tars.	Tarsica prior (Or. 33)	First Tarsic Discourse
2 Tars.	Tarsica altera (Or. 34)	Second Tarsic Discourse
Troj.	Trojana (Or. 11)	Trojan Discourse
Tumult.	De tumultu (Or. 46)	Protest against Mistreatment
Tyr.	De tyrannide (Or. 6)	On Tyranny, or Diogenes
Ven.	Venator (Or. 7)	The Hunter
Virt. (Or. 8)	De virtute (Or. 8)	Virtue
Virt. (Or. 69)	De virtute (Or. 69)	Virtue

DIODORUS SICULUS

Bib. Hist.	Biblioteca Historica	

DIOGENES LAERTIUS

Vit. Phil.	*Vitae philosophorum*	*Lives of the Philosophers*

DIONYSIUS OF HALICARNASSUS

1–2 Amm.	*Epistula ad Ammaeum i–ii*
Ant. or.	*De antiquis oratoribus*
Ant. rom.	*Antiquitates romanae*
Comp.	*De compositione verborum*
Dem.	*De Demosthene*
Din.	*De Dinarcho*
Is.	*De Isaeo*
Isocr.	*De Isocrate*
Lys.	*De Lysia*
Pomp.	*Epistula ad Pompeium Geminum*
[Rhet.]	*Ars rhetorica*
Thuc.	*De Thucydide*
Thuc. id.	*De Thucydidis idiomatibus*

DIOSCORIDES PEDANIUS

[Alex.]	*Alexipharmaca*
Mat. med.	*De materia medica*

EPICTETUS

Diatr.	*Diatribai (Dissertationes)*
Ench.	*Enchiridion*
Gnom.	*Gnomologium*

EPIPHANIUS

Pan.	*Panarion (Adversus haereses)*	*Refutation of All Heresies*

EURIPIDES

Alc.	*Alcestis*	
Andr.	*Andromache*	
Bacch.	*Bacchae*	*Bacchanals*
Cycl.	*Cyclops*	
Dict.	*Dictys*	
El.	*Electra*	
Hec.	*Hecuba*	
Hel.	*Helena*	*Helen*
Heracl.	*Heraclidae*	*Children of Hercules*
Herc. fur.	*Hercules furens*	*Madness of Hercules*
Hipp.	*Hippolytus*	
Hyps.	*Hypsipyle*	
Iph. aul.	*Iphigenia aulidensis*	*Iphigenia at Aulis*
Iph. taur.	*Iphigenia taurica*	*Iphigenia at Tauris*
Med.	*Medea*	*Medea*

Orest.	Orestes	Phoenician Maidens
Phoen.	Phoenissae	
Rhes.	Rhesus	
Suppl.	Supplices	
Tro.	Troades	Daughters of Troy

EUSEBIUS

Chron.	Chronicon	Chronicle
Coet. sanct.	Ad coetum sanctorum	To the Assembly of Saints
Comm. Isa.	Commentarius in Isaiam	Commentary on Isaiah
Comm. Ps.	Commentarius in Psalmos	Commentary on Psalms
Dem. ev.	Demonstratio evangelica	Demonstration of the Gospel
Eccl. theol.	De ecclesiastica theologia	Ecclesiastical Theology
Ecl. proph.	Eclogae propheticae	Extracts from the Prophets
Hier.	Contra Hieroclem	Against Hierocles
Hist. eccl.	Historia ecclesiastica	Church History
Laud. Const.	De laudibus Constantini	Praise of Constantine
Marc.	Contra Marcellum	Against Marcellus
Mart. Pal.	De martyribus Palaestinae	The Martyrs of Palestine
Onom.	Onomasticon	List of Names
Praep. ev.	Praeparatio evangelica	Preparations for the Gospel
Theoph.	Theophania	Divine Manifestation
Vit. Const.	Vita Constantini	Life of Constantine

FIRMICUS MATERNUS

| Err. prof. rel. | De errore profanarum religionum |
| Math. | Mathesis |

GAIUS

| Inst. | Institutiones |

GORGIAS

| Hel. | Helena |
| Pal. | Palamedes |

GREGORY OF NAZIANZUS

| Ep. | Epistulae |
| Or. Bas. | Oratio in laudem Basilii |

GREGORY OF NYSSA

| Deit. | De deitate Filii et Spiritus Sancti |

GREGORY THE GREAT

| Moral. | Expositio in Librum Job, sive Moralium libri xxv | Moralia |

HELIODORUS

Aeth.	*Aethiopica*

HERACLITUS

All.	*Allegoriae (Quaestiones homericae)*

HERODOTUS

Hist.	*Historiae*	*Histories*

HESIOD

Op.	*Opera et dies*	*Works and Days*
[Scut.]	*Scutum*	*Shield*
Theog.	*Theogonia*	*Theogony*

HIERONYMUS (See Jerome)

HIPPOCRATES

Acut.	*De ratione victus in morbis acutis*	*Regimen in Acute Diseases*
Aff.	*De affectionibus*	*Affections*
Alim.	*De alimento*	*Nutriment*
Aph.	*Aphorismata*	*Aphorisms*
Arte	*De arte*	*The Art*
Artic.	*De articulis reponendis*	*Joints*
Carn.	*De carne*	*Fleshes*
Coac.	*Praenotiones coacae*	
Decent.	*De habitu decenti*	*Decorum*
Dent.	*De dentitione*	*Dentition*
Epid.	*Epidemiae*	*Epidemics*
Fist.	*Fistulae*	*Fistulas*
Fract.	*De fracturis*	*Fractures*
Genit.	*Genitalia*	*Genitals*
Int.	*De affectionibus internis*	*Internal Affections*
Jusj.	*Jus jurandum*	*The Oath*
Lex	*Lex*	*Law*
Liq.	*De liquidorum usu*	*Use of Liquids*
Loc. hom.	*De locis in homine*	*Places in Man*
Med.	*De medico*	*The Physician*
Mochl.	*Mochlichon*	*Instruments of Reduction*
Morb.	*De morbis*	*Diseases*
Morb. sacr.	*De morbo sacro*	*The Sacred Disease*
Mul.	*De morbis mulierum*	*Female Diseases*
Nat. hom.	*De natura hominis*	*Nature of Man*
Nat. mul.	*De natura muliebri*	*Nature of Woman*
Nat. puer.	*De natura pueri*	*Nature of the Chile*
Oct.	*De octimestri partu*	
Off.	*De officina medici*	*In the Surgery*
Praec.	*Praeceptiones*	*Precepts*
Progn.	*Prognostica*	*Prognostic*

Prorrh.	Prorrhetica	Prorrhetic
Septim.	De septimestri partu	
Steril.	De sterilitate	Sterility
Vet. med.	De vetere medicina	Ancient Medicine
Vict.	De victu	Regimen
Vict. salubr.	De ratione victus salubris	Regimen in Health

HIPPOLYTUS

Antichr.	De antichristo	
Ben. Is. Jac.	De benedictionibus Isaaci et Jacobi	
Can. pasch.	Canon paschalis	
In Cant.	In Canticum canticorum	
Cant. Mos.	In canticum Mosis	
Chron.	Chronicon	
Comm. Dan.	Commentarium in Danielem	
Fr. Prov.	Fragmenta in Proverbia	
Fr. Ps.	Fragmenta in Psalmos	
Haer.	Refutatio omnium haeresium (Philosophoumena)	Refutation of All Heresies
Helc. Ann.	In Helcanam et Annam	
Noet.	Contra haeresin Noeti	
Trad. ap.	Traditio apostolica	The Apostolic Tradition
Univ.	De universo	

HOMER

Il.	Ilias	Iliad
Od.	Odyssea	Odyssey

HORACE

Ars	Ars poetica	
Carm.	Carmina	Odes
Ep.	Epistulae	Epistles
Epod.	Epodi	Epodes
Saec.	Carmen saeculare	
Sat.	Satirae	Satires

IRENAEUS

Epid.	Epideixis tou apostolikou kerygmatos	Demonstration of the Apostolic Preaching
Haer.	Adversus haereses	Against Heresies

ISOCRATES

Aeginet.	Aegineticus (Or. 19)	
Antid.	Antidosis (Or. 15)	
Archid.	Archidamus (Or. 6)	
Areop.	Areopagiticus (Or. 7)	
Big.	De bigis (Or. 16)	On the Team of Horses
Bus.	Busiris (Or. 11)	

Callim.	In Callimachum (Or. 18)	Agaiinst Callimachus
De pace	De pace (Or. 8)	
Demon.	Ad Demonicum (Or. 1)	
Ep.	Epistulae	
Euth.	In Euthynum (Or. 21)	
Evag.	Evagoras (Or. 9)	
Hel. enc.	Helenae encomium (Or. 10)	
Loch.	In Lochitum (Or. 20)	
Nic.	Nicocles (Or. 3)	
Ad Nic.	Ad Nicoclem (Or. 2)	
Panath.	Panathenaicus (Or. 12)	
Paneg.	Panegyricus (Or. 4)	
Phil.	Philippus (Or. 5)	
Plat.	Plataicus (Or. 14)	
Soph.	In sophistas (Or. 13)	
Trapez.	Trapeziticus (Or. 17)	On the Banker

JEROME

Chron.	Chronicon Eusebii a Graeco Latine redditum et continuatum
Comm. Abd.	Commentariorum in Abdiam liber
Comm. Agg.	Commentariorum in Aggaeum liber
Comm. Am.	Commentariorum in Amos libri III
Comm. Eccl.	Commentarii in Ecclesiasten
Comm. Eph.	Commentariorum in Epistulam ad Ephesios libri III
Comm. Ezech.	Commentariorum in Ezechielem libri XVI
Comm. Gal.	Commentariorum in Epistulam ad Galatas libri III
Comm. Habac.	Commentariorum in Habacuc libri II
Comm. Isa.	Commentariorum in Isaiam libri XVIII
Comm. Jer.	Commentariorum in Jeremiam libri VI
Comm. Joel.	Commentariorum in Joelem liber
Comm. Jon.	Commentariorum in Jonam liber
Comm. Mal.	Commentariorum in Malachiam liber
Comm. Matt.	Commentariorum in Matthaeum libri IV
Comm. Mich.	Commentariorum in Michaeum libri II
Comm. Nah.	Commentariorum in Nahum liber
Comm. Os.	Commentariorum in Osee libri III
Comm. Phlm.	Commentariorum in Epistulam ad Philemonem liber
Comm. Ps.	Commentarioli in Psalmos
Comm. Soph.	Commentariorum in Sophoniam libri III
Comm. Tit.	Commentariorum in Epistulam ad Titum liber
Comm. Zach.	Commentariorum in Zachariam libri III
Did. Spir.	Liber Didymi de Spiritu Sancto
Epist.	Epistulae
Expl. Dan.	Explanatio in Danielem
Helv.	Adversus Helvidium de Mariae virginitate perpetua
Hom. Matth.	Homilia in Evangelium secundum Matthaeum
Interp. Job	Libri Job versio, textus hexaplorum
Jo. Hier.	Adversus Joannem Hierosolymitanum liber
Jov.	Adversus Jovinianum libri II
Lucif.	Altercatio Luciferiani et orthodoxi seu dialogus contra Luciferianos
Mon. Pachom.	Monitorum Pachomii versio latina
Monogr.	Tractatus de monogrammate
Nom. hebr.	De nominibus hebraicis (Liber nominum)

Orig. Hom. Cant.	*Homiliae II Origenis in Canticum canticorum Latine redditae*
Orig. Hom. Luc.	*In Lucam homiliae XXXIX ex Graeco Origenis Latine conversae*
Orig. Jer. Ezech.	*Homiliae XXVIII in Jeremiam et Ezechielem Graeco Origenis Latine redditae*
Orig. Princ.	*De principiis*
Pelag.	*Adversus Pelagianos dialogi III*
Psalt. Hebr.	*Psalterium secundum Hebraeos*
Qu. hebr. Gen.	*Quaestionum hebraicarum liber in Genesim*
Reg. Pachom.	*Regula S. Pachomii, e Graeco*
Ruf.	*Adversus Rufinum libri III*
Sit.	*De situ et nominibus locorum Hebraicorum (Liber locorum)*
Tract. Isa.	*Tractatus in Isaiam*
Tract. Marc.	*Tractatus in Evangelium Marci*
Tract. Ps.	*Tractatus in Psalmos*
Tract. var.	*Tractatus varii*
Vigil.	*Adversus Vigilantium*
Vir. ill.	*De viris illustribus*
Vit. Hil.	*Vita S. Hilarionis eremitae*
Vit. Malch.	*Vita Malchi monachi*
Vit. Paul.	*Vita S. Pauli, primi eremitae*

JOHN CHRYSOSTOM

Adfu.	*Adversus eos qui non adfuerant*	
Aeg.	*In martyres Aegyptios*	
Anna	*De Anna*	
Anom.	*Contra Anomoeos*	
Ant. exsil.	*Sermo antequam iret in exsilium*	
Ascens.	*In ascensionem domini nostri JesuChristi*	
Bab.	*De sancto hieromartyre Babyla*	*Babylas the Martyr*
Bab. Jul.	*De Babyla contra Julianum et gentiles*	
Bapt.	*De baptismo Christi*	
Barl.	*In sanctum Barlaam martyrem*	
Bern.	*De sanctis Bernice et Prosdoce*	
Catech. illum.	*Catecheses ad illuminandos*	
Catech. jur.	*Catechesis de juramento*	
Catech. ult.	*Catechesis ultima ad baptizandos*	
Cath.	*Adversus Catharos*	
Coemet.	*De coemeterio et de cruce*	
Comm. Isa.	*Commentarius in Isaiam*	
Comm. Job	*Commentarius in Job*	
Comp. reg. mon.	*Comparatio regis et monachi*	
Compunct. Dem.	*Ad Demetrium de compunctione*	
Compunct. Stel.	*Ad Stelechium de compunctione*	
Cruc.	*De cruce et latrone homiliae II*	
Cum exsil.	*Sermo cum iret in exsilium*	
Dav.	*De Davide et Saule*	
Delic.	*De futurae vitae deliciis*	
Diab.	*De diabolo tentatore*	
Diod.	*Laus Diodori episcopi*	
Dros.	*De sancta Droside martyre*	
Educ. lib.	*De educandis liberis*	
El. vid.	*In Eliam et viduam*	
Eleaz. puer.	*De Eleazaro et septem pueris*	

Eleem.	*De eleemosyna*
Ep. carc.	*Epistula ad episcopos, presbyteros et diaconos in carcere*
Ep. Cyr.	*Epistula ad Cyriacum*
1 Ep. Innoc.	*Ad Innocentium papam epistula I*
2 Ep. Innoc.	*Ad Innocentium papam epistula II*
Ep. Olymp.	*Epistulae ad Olympiadem*
Ep. Theod.	*Letter to Theodore*
Eust.	*In sanctum Eustathium Antiochenum*
Eutrop.	*In Eutropium*
Exp. Ps.	*Expositiones in Psalmos*
Fat. prov.	*De fato et providentia*
Fem. reg.	*Quod regulares feminae viris cohabitare non debeant*
Fr. Ep. Cath.	*Fragmenta in Epistulas Catholicas*
Freq. conv.	*Quod frequenter conveniendum sit*
Goth. concin.	*Homilia habita postquam presbyter Gothus concionatus fuerat*
Grat.	*Non esse ad gratiam concionandum*
Hom. Act.	*Homiliae in Acta apostolorum*
Hom. Act. 9:1	*De mutatione nominum*
Hom. Col.	*Homiliae in epistulam ad Colossenses*
Hom. 1 Cor.	*Homiliae in epistulam i ad Corinthios*
Hom. 1 Cor. 7:2	*In illud: Propter fornicationes autem unusquisque suam uxorem habeat*
Hom. 1 Cor. 10:1	*In dictum Pauli: Nolo vos ignorare*
Hom. 1 Cor. 11:19	*In dictum Pauli: Oportet haereses esse*
Hom. 2 Cor.	*Homiliae in epistulam ii ad Corinthios*
Hom. 2 Cor. 4:13	*In illud: Habentes eundem spiritum*
Hom. 2 Cor. 11:1	*In illud: Utinam sustineretis modicum*
Hom. Eph.	*Homiliae in epistulam ad Ephesios*
Hom. Gal.	*Homiliae in epistulam ad Galatas commentarius*
Hom. Gal. 2:11	*In illud: In faciem ei restiti*
Hom. Gen.	*Homiliae in Genesim*
Hom. Heb.	*Homiliae in epistulam ad Hebraeos*
Hom. Isa. 6:1	*In illud: Vidi Dominum*
Hom. Isa. 45:7	*In illud Isaiae: Ego Dominus Deus feci lumen*
Hom. Jer. 10:23	*In illud: Domine, non est in homine*
Hom. Jo.	*Homiliae in Joannem*
Hom. Jo. 5:17	*In illud: Pater meus usque modo operatur*
Hom. Jo. 5:19	*In illud: Filius ex se nihil facit*
Hom. Matt.	*Homiliae in Matthaeum*
Hom. Matt. 9:37	*In illud: Messis quidem multa*
Hom. Matt. 18:23	*De decem millium talentorum debitore*
Hom. Matt. 26:39	*In illud: Pater, si possibile est, transeat*
Hom. Phil.	*Homiliae in epistulam ad Philippenses*
Hom. Phlm.	*Homiliae in epistulam ad Philemonem*
Hom. princ. Act.	*In principium Actorum*
Hom. Ps. 48:17	*In illud: Ne timueris cum dives factus fuerit homo*
Hom. Rom.	*Homiliae in epistulam ad Romanos*
Hom. Rom. 5:3	*De gloria in tribulationibus*
Hom. Rom. 8:28	*In illud: Diligentibus deum omnia cooperantur in bonum*
Hom. Rom. 12:20	*In illud: Si esurierit inimicus*
Hom. Rom. 16:3	*In illud: Salutate Priscillam et Aquilam*
Hom 1 Thess.	*Homiliae in epistulam i ad Thessalonicenses*
Hom. 2 Thess.	*Homiliae in epistulam ii ad Thessalonicenses*
Hom. 1 Tim.	*Homiliae in epistulam i ad Timotheum*
Hom. 1 Tim. 5:9	*In illud: Vidua eligatur*

Hom. 2 Tim.	*Homiliae in epistulam ii ad Timotheum*	
Hom. 2 Tim. 3:1	*In illud: Hoc scitote quod in novissimis diebus*	
Hom. Tit.	*Homiliae in epistulam ad Titum*	
Hom. Tit. 2:11	*In illud: Apparuit gratia dei omnibus hominibus*	
Ign.	*In sanctum Ignatium martyrem*	
Inan. glor.	*De inani gloria*	
Iter. conj.	*De non iterando conjugio*	
Adv. Jud.	*Adversus Judaeos*	*Discourses against Judaizing Christians*
Jud. gent.	*Contra Judaeos et gentiles quod Christus sit deus*	
Jul.	*In sanctum Julianum martyrem*	
Juv.	*In Juventinum et Maximum martyres*	
Kal.	*In Kalendas*	
Laed.	*Quod nemo laeditur nisi a se ipso*	*No One Can Harm the Man Who Does Not Injure Himself*
Laud. Max.	*Quales ducendae sint uxores (=De laude Maximi)*	
Laud. Paul.	*De laudibus sancti Pauli apostoli*	
Laz.	*De Lazaro*	
Lib. repud.	*De libello repudii*	
Liturg.	*Liturgia*	
Lucian.	*In sanctum Lucianum martyrem*	
Macc.	*De Maccabeis*	
Mart.	*De sanctis martyribus; Homilia in martyres*	
Melet.	*De sancto Meletio Antiocheno*	
Natal.	*In diem natalem Christi*	
Non desp.	*Non esse desperandum*	
Oppugn.	*Adversus oppugnatores vitae monasticae*	
Ordin.	*Sermo cum presbyter fuit ordinatus*	
Paenit.	*De paenitentia*	
Paralyt.	*In paralyticum demissum per tectum*	
Pasch.	*In sanctum pascha*	
Pecc.	*Peccata fratrum non evulganda*	*Against Publicly Exposing the Sins of the Brethren*
Pelag.	*De sancta Pelagia virgine et martyre*	
Pent.	*De sancta pentecoste*	
Phoc.	*De sancto hieromartyre Phoca*	
Praes. imp.	*Homilia dicta praesente imperatore*	
Prod. Jud.	*De proditione Judae*	
Prof. evang.	*De profectu evangelii*	*Lowliness of Mind*
Proph. obscurit.	*De prophetarum obscuritate*	
Quatr. Laz.	*In quatriduanum Lazarum*	
1 Redit.	*Post reditum a priore exsilio sermo I*	
2 Redit.	*Post reditum a priore exsilio sermo II*	
Regr.	*De regressu*	
Reliq. mart.	*Homilia dicta postquam reliquiae martyrum*	
Res. Chr.	*Adversus ebriosos et de resurrectione domini nostri JesuChristi*	
Res. mort.	*De resurrectione mortuorum*	
Rom. mart.	*In sanctum Romanum martyrem*	
Sac.	*De sacerdotio*	*Priesthood*
Sanct. Anast.	*Homilia dicta in templo sanctae Anastasiae*	

Saturn.	*Cum Saturninus et Aurelianus acti essent in exsilium*	
Scand.	*Ad eos qui scandalizati sunt*	
Serm. Gen.	*Sermones in Genesim*	
Stag.	*Ad Stagirium a daemone vexatum*	
Stat.	*Ad populum Antiochenum de statuis*	
Stud. praes.	*De studio praesentium*	
Subintr.	*Contra eos qui subintroductas habent virgines*	
Terr. mot.	*De terrae motu*	
Theatr.	*Contra ludos et theatra*	
Theod. laps.	*Ad Theodorum lapsum*	*Exhortation to Theodore after His Fall*
Vid.	*Ad viduam juniorem*	*To the Young Widow*
Virginit.	*De virginitate*	

John Malalas

Chron.	*Chronographia*

John Philoponus

Comm. De an.	*In Aristotelis De anima libros commentaria*

Josephus (See p. 935)

Justin

1 Apol.	*Apologia i*	*First Apology*
2 Apol.	*Apologia ii*	*Second Apology*
Dial.	*Dialogus cum Tryphone*	*Dialogue with Trypho*

Justinian

Edict.	*Edicta*
Nov.	*Novellae*

Juvenal

Sat.	*Satirae*	*Satires*

Lactantius

Epit.	*Epitome divinarum institutionum*	*Epitome of the Divine Institutes*
Inst.	*Divinarum institutionum libri VII*	*The Divine Institutes*
Ir.	*De ira Dei*	*The Wrath of God*
Mort.	*De morte persecutorum*	*The Deaths of the Persecutors*
Opif.	*De opificio Dei*	*The Workmanship of God*

Longinus

[Subl.]	*De sublimitate*	*On the Sublime*

LONGUS

Daphn.	*Daphnis et Chloe*	*Daphnis and Chloe*

LUCIAN

Abdic.	*Abdicatus Disowned*	*Disowned*
Alex.	*Alexander (Pseudomantis)*	*Alexander the False Prophet*
[Am.]	*Amores*	*Affairs of the Heart*
Anach.	*Anacharsis*	
[Asin.]	*Asinus (Lucius)*	*Lucius, or The Ass*
Astr.	*Astrologia*	*Astrology*
Bis acc.	*Bis accusatus*	*The Double Indictment*
Cal.	*Calumniae non temere credendum*	*Slander*
Cat.	*Cataplus*	*The Downward Journey, or The Tyrant*
Char.	*Charon*	
Demon.	*Demonax*	
Deor. conc.	*Deorm concilium*	*Parliament of the Gods*
Dial. d.	*Dialogi deorum*	*Dialogues of the Gods*
Dial. meretr.	*Dialogi meretricii*	*Dialogues of the Courtesans*
Dial. mort.	*Diologi mortuorum*	*Dialogues of the Dead*
Dom.	*De domo*	*The Hall*
Electr.	*De electro*	*Amber, or The Swans*
[Encom. Demosth.]	*Demosthenous encomium*	*Praise of Demosthenes*
Eunuch.	*Eunuchus*	*The Eunuch*
Fug.	*Fugitivi*	*The Runaways*
Gall.	*Gallus*	*The Dream, or The Cock*
Hermot.	*Hermotimus (De sectis)*	*Hermotimus, or Sects*
Icar.	*Icaromenippus*	
Imag.	*Imagines*	*Essays in Portraiture*
Pro imag.	*Pro imaginibus*	*Essays in Portraiture Defended*
Ind.	*Adversus indoctum*	*The Ignorant Book-Collector*
Jud. voc.	*Judicium vocalium*	*The Consonants at Law*
Jupp. conf.	*Juppiter confutatus*	*Zeus Catechized*
Jupp. trag.	*Juppiter tragoedus*	*Zeus Rants*
Laps.	*Pro lapsu inter salutandum*	*A Slip of the Tongue in Greeting*
Lex.	*Lexiphanes*	
Luct.	*De luctu*	*Funerals*
Men.	*Menippus (Necyomantia)*	*Menippus, or Descent into Hades*
Merc. cond.	*De mercede conductis*	*Salaried Posts in Great Houses*
Musc. laud.	*Muscae laudatio*	*The Fly*
Nav.	*Navigium*	*The Ship, or The Wishes*
Nigr.	*Nigrinus*	
Par.	*De parasito*	*The Parasite*
Peregr.	*De morte Peregrini*	*The Passing of Peregrinus*
Phal.	*Phalaris*	
[Philopatr.]	*Philopatris*	*The Patriot*
Philops.	*Philopseudes*	*The Lover of Lies*
Pisc.	*Piscator*	*The Dead Come to Life, or The Fisherman*
Pseudol.	*Pseudologista*	*The Mistaken Critic*
Rhet. praec.	*Rhetorum praeceptor*	*A Professor of Public Speaking*
Sacr.	*De sacrificiis*	*Sacrifices*
Salt.	*De saltatione*	*The Dance*
Sat.	*Saturnalia*	*Conversation with Cronius*

Scyth.	Scytha	The Scythian, or The Consul
Somn.	Somnium (Vita Luciani)	The Dream
Lucians Career		
Symp.	Symposium	The Carousal
Lapiths		
Syr. d.	De syria dea	The Goddess of Syria
Tim.	Timon	
Tox.	Toxaris	
Tyr.	Tyrannicida	The Tyrannicide
Ver. hist.	Vera historia	A True Story
Vit. auct.	Vitarum auctio	Philosophies for Sale

MARTIAL

Epi.	Epigramma

MENANDER

Dysk.	Dyskolos
Epitr.	Epitrepontes
Georg.	Georgos
Mis.	Misoumenos
Mon.	Monostichoi
Perik.	Perikeiromenē
Phasm.	Phasma
Sam.	Samia
Sik.	Sikyonios
Thras.	Thrasonidis

METHODIUS OF OLYMPUS

Lib. arb.	De libero arbitrio
Res.	De resurrectione
Symp.	Symposium (Convivium decem virginum)

MINUCIUS FELIX

Oct.	Octavius

NEPOS

Ag.	Agesilaus
Alc.	Alciabiades
Arist.	Aristides
Att.	Atticus
Cat.	Cato
Chabr.	Chabrias
Cim.	Cimon
Con.	Conon
Dat.	Datames
Di.	Dion
Epam.	Epaminondas

Eum.	*Eumenes*
Ham.	*Hamilcar*
Han.	*Hannibal*
Iph.	*Iphicrates*
Lys.	*Lysander*
Milt.	*Miltiades*
Paus.	*Pausanias*
Pel.	*Pelopidas*
Phoc.	*Phocion*
Reg.	*De regibus*
Them.	*Themistocles*
Thras.	*Thrasybulus*
Timol.	*Timoleon*
Timoth.	*Timotheus*

NICANDER

Alex.	*Alexipharmaca*
Ther.	*Theriaca*

NICOLAUS OF DAMASCUS

Hist. univ.	*Historia universalis*	*Universal History (in Athanaeus)*
Vit. Caes.	*Vita Caesaris*	

NONNUS

Dion.	*Dionysiaca*
Paraphr. Jo.	*Paraphrasis sancti evangelii Joannei*

ORAC. CHALD.

	De oraculis chaldaicis	*Chaldean Oracles*

ORIGEN

Adnot. Deut.	*Adnotationes in Deuteronomium*	
Adnot. Exod.	*Adnotationes in Exodum*	
Adnot. Gen.	*Adnotationes in Genesim*	
Adnot. Jes. Nav.	*Adnotationes in Jesum filium Nave*	
Adnot. Judic.	*Adnotationes in Judices*	
Adnot. Lev.	*Adnotationes in Leviticum*	
Adnot. Num.	*Adnotationes in Numeros*	
Cant. (Adulesc.)	*In Canticum canticorum (libri duo quos scripsit in adulescentia)*	
Cels.	*Contra Celsum*	*Against Celsus*
Comm. Cant.	*Commentarius in Canticum*	
Comm. Gen.	*Commentarii in Genesim*	
Comm. Jo.	*Commentarii in evangelium Joannis*	
Comm. Matt.	*Commentarium in evangelium Matthaei*	
Comm. Rom.	*Commentarii in Romanos*	
Comm. ser. Matt.	*Commentarium series in evangelium*	

	Matthaei	
Dial.	*Diologus cum Heraclide*	Dialogue with Heraclides
Enarrat. Job	*Enarrationes in Job*	
Engastr.	*De engastrimytho*	Witch of Endor
Ep. Afr.	*Epistula ad Africanum*	
Ep. Greg.	*Epistula ad Gregorium Thaumaturgum*	
Ep. ign.	*Epistula ad ignotum (Fabianum Romanum)*	
Exc. Ps.	*Excerpta in Psalmos*	
Exp. Prov.	*Expositio in Proverbia*	
Fr. Act.	*Fragmentum ex homiliis in Acta apostolorum*	
Fr. Cant.	*Libri x in Canticum canticorum*	
Fr. 1 Cor.	*Fragmenta ex commentariis in epistulam i ad Corinthios*	
Fr. Eph.	*Fragmenta ex commentariis in epistulam ad Ephesios*	
Fr. Exod.	*Fragmenta ex commentariis in Exodum*	
Fr. Ezech.	*Fragmenta ex commentariis in Ezechielem*	
Fr. Heb.	*Fragmenta ex homiliis in epistulam ad Hebraeos*	
Fr. Jer.	*Fragmenta in Jeremiam*	
Fr. Jo.	*Fragmenta in evangelium Joannis*	
Fr. Lam.	*Fragmenta in Lamentationes*	
Fr. Luc.	*Fragmenta in Lucam*	
Fr. Matt.	*Fragmenta ex commentariis in evangelium Matthaei*	
Fr. Os.	*Fragmentum ex commentariis in Osee*	
Fr. Prin.	*Fragmenta de principiis*	
Fr. Prov.	*Fragmenta ex commentariis in Proverbia*	
Fr. Ps.	*Fragmenta in Psalmos 1–150*	
Fr. 1 Reg.	*Fragmenta in librum primum Regnorum*	
Fr. Ruth	*Fragmentum in Ruth*	
Hex.	*Hexapla*	
Hom. Cant.	*Homiliae in Canticum*	
Hom. Exod.	*Homiliae in Exodum*	
Hom. Ezech.	*Homiliae in Ezechielem*	
Hom. Gen.	*Homiliae in Genesim*	
Hom. Isa.	*Homiliae in Isaiam*	
Hom. Jer.	*Homiliae in Jeremiam*	
Hom. Jes. Nav.	*In Jesu Nave homiliae xxvi*	
Hom. Job	*Homiliae in Job*	
Hom. Judic.	*Homiliae in Judices*	
Hom. Lev.	*Homiliae in Leviticum*	
Hom. Luc.	*Homiliae in Lucam*	
Hom. Num.	*Homiliae in Numeros*	
Hom. Ps.	*Homiliae in Psalmos*	
Hom. 1 Reg.	*Homiliae in I Reges*	
Mart.	*Exhortatio ad martyrium*	Exhortation to Martyrdom
Or.	*De oratione (Peri proseuchēs)*	Prayer
Pasch.	*De pascha*	The Pascha
Philoc.	*Philocalia*	
Princ.	*De principiis (Peri archōn)*	First Principles
Res.	*De resurrectione libri ii*	
Schol. Apoc.	*Scholia in Apocalypsem*	
Schol. Cant.	*Scholia in Canticum canticorum*	
Schol. Luc.	*Scholia in Lucam*	
Schol. Matt.	*Scholia in Matthaeum*	
Sel. Deut.	*Selecta in Deuteronomium*	
Sel. Exod.	*Selecta in Exodum*	

Sel. Ezech.	*Selecta in Ezechielem*
Sel. Gen.	*Selecta in Genesim*
Sel. Jes. Nav.	*Selecta in Jesum Nave*
Sel. Job	*Selecta in Job*
Sel. Judic.	*Selecta in Judices*
Sel. Lev.	*Selecta in Leviticum*
Sel. Num.	*Selecta in Numeros*
Sel. Ps.	*Selecta in Psalmos*

OVID

Am.	*Amores*
Ars	*Ars amatoria*
Fast.	*Fasti*
Hal.	*Halieutica*
Her.	*Heroides*
Ib.	*Ibis*
Med.	*Medicamina faciei femineae*
Metam.	*Metamorphoses*

PAUSANIAS

Descr.	*Graeciae description*	*Description of Greece*

PERIPL. M. RUBR.

	Periplus Maris Rubri	*The Periplus of the Erythraean Sea*

PERSIUS

Sat.	*Satirae*

PHILO OF ALEXANDRIA (See pp. 934-35)

PHILODEMUS OF GADARA

Adv. Soph.	*Adversus sophistas*
D.	*De Diis*
Hom.	*De bono rege secundum Homerum*
Ir.	*De ira*
Lib.	*De libertate dicendi*
Mort.	*De morte*
Mus.	*De musica*
Piet.	*De pietate*
Rhet.	*Volumina rhetorica*
Sign.	*De signis*
Vit.	*De vitiis X*

PHILOSTRATUS

Ep.	*Epistulae*
Gymn.	*De gymnastica*
Imag.	*Imagines*

Vit. Apoll.	*Vita Apollonii*	
Vit. soph.	*Vitae sophistarum*	

PHOTIUS

Lex.	*Lexicon*	

PINDAR

Isthm.	*Isthmionikai*	*Isthmian Odes*
Nem.	*Nemeonikai*	*Nemean Odes*
Ol.	*Olympionikai*	*Olympian Odes*
Paean.	*Paeanes*	*Hymns*
Pyth.	*Pythionikai*	*Pythian Odes*
Thren.	*Threnoi*	*Dirges*

PLATO

[Alc. maj.]	*Alcibiades major*	*Greater Alcibiades*
Apol.	*Apologia*	*Apology of Socrates*
[Ax.]	*Axiochus*	
Charm.	*Charmides*	
Crat.	*Cratylus*	
[Def.]	*Definitiones*	*Definitions*
Ep.	*Epistulae*	*Letters*
[Epin.]	*Epinomis*	
Euthyd.	*Euthydemus*	
Euthyphr.	*Euthyphro*	
Gorg.	*Gorgias*	
Hipparch.	*Hipparchus*	
Hipp. maj.	*Hippias major*	*Greater Hippias*
Hipp. min.	*Hippias minor*	*Lesser Hippias*
Lach.	*Laches*	
Leg.	*Leges*	*Laws*
Menex.	*Menexenus*	
[Min.]	*Minos*	
Parm.	*Parmenides*	
Phaed.	*Phaedo*	
Phaedr.	*Phaedrus*	
Phileb.	*Philebus*	
Pol.	*Politicus*	*Statesman*
Prot.	*Protagoras*	
Resp.	*Respublica*	*Republic*
Soph.	*Sophista*	*Sophist*
Symp.	*Symposium*	
Theaet.	*Theaetetus*	
Tim.	*Timaeus*	

PLAUTUS

Amph.	*Amphitruo*	
Asin.	*Asinaria*	
Aul.	*Aulularia*	
Bacch.	*Bacchides*	

Capt.	Captivi
Cas.	Casina
Cist.	Cistellaria
Curc.	Curculio
Epid.	Epidicus
Men.	Menaechmi
Mil. glor.	Miles gloriosus
Most.	Mostellaria
Pers.	Persae
Poen.	Poenulus
Pseud.	Pseudolus
Rud.	Rudens
Stic.	Sticus
Trin.	Trinummus
Truc.	Truculentus
Vid.	Vidularia

PLINY THE ELDER

Nat.	Naturalis historia	Natural History

PLINY THE YOUNGER

Ep.	Epistulae
Ep. Tra.	Epistulae ad Trajanum
Pan.	Panegyricus

PLOTINUS

Enn.	Enneades

PLUTARCH

Adol. poet. aud.	Quomodo adolescens poetas audire debeat
Adul. am.	De adulatore et amico
Adul. amic.	Quomodo adulator ab amico internoscatur
Aem.	Aemilius Paullus
Ag. Cleom.	Agis et Cleomenes
Ages.	Agesilaus
Alc.	Alcibiades
Alex.	Alexander
Alex. fort.	De Alexandri magni fortuna aut virtute
Am. prol.	De amore prolis
Amat.	Amatorius
[Amat. narr.]	Amatoriae narrationes
Amic. mult.	De amicorum multitudine
An. corp.	Animine an corporis affectiones sint peiores
[An ignis]	Aquane an ignis utilior
An. procr.	De animae procreatione in Timaeo
An. procr. epit.	Epitome libri de procreatione in Timaeo
An seni	An seni respublica gerenda sit
An virt. doc.	An virtus doceri possit

An vit.	*An vitiositas ad infelicitatem sufficiat*	
Ant.	*Antonius*	
[Apoph. lac.]	*Apophthegmata laconica*	
Arat.	*Aratus*	
Arist.	*Aristides*	
Art.	*Artaxerxes*	
Brut.	*Brutus*	
Brut. an.	*Bruta animalia ratione uti*	
Caes.	*Caesar*	
Cam.	*Camillus*	
Cat. Maj.	*Cato Major*	*Cato the Elder*
Cat. Min.	*Cato Minor*	*Cato the Younger*
Cic.	*Cicero*	
Cim.	*Cimon*	
Cleom.	*Cleomenes*	
Cohib. ira	*De cohibenda ira*	
Adv. Col.	*Adversus Colotem*	
Comm. not.	*De communibus notitiis contra stoicos*	
Comp. Aem. Tim.	*Comparatio Aemilii Paulli et Timoleontis*	
Comp. Ag. Cleom. cum Ti. Gracch.	*Comparatio Agidis et Cleomenis cum Tiberio et Gaio Graccho*	
Comp. Ages. Pomp.	*Comparatio Agesilai et Pompeii*	
Comp. Alc. Cor.	*Comparatio Alcibiadis et Marcii Coriolani*	
Comp. Arist. Cat.	*Comparatio Aristidis et Catonis*	
Comp. Arist. Men. compend.	*Comparationis Aristophanis et Menandri compendium*	
Comp. Cim. Luc.	*Comparatio Cimonis et Luculli*	
Comp. Dem. Cic.	*Comparatio Demosthenis et Ciceronis*	
Comp. Demetr. Ant.	*Comparatio Demetrii et Antonii*	
Comp. Dion. Brut.	*Comparatio Dionis et Bruti*	
Comp. Eum. Sert.	*Comparatio Eumenis et Sertorii*	
Comp. Lyc. Num.	*Comparatio Lycurgi et Numae*	
Comp. Lys. Sull.	*Comparatio Lysandri et Sullae*	
Comp. Nic. Crass.	*Comparatio Nicae et Crassi*	
Comp. Pel. Marc.	*Comparatio Pelopidae et Marcelli*	
Comp. Per. Fab.	*Comparatio Periclis et Fabii Maximi*	
Comp. Phil. Flam.	*Comparatio Philopoemenis et Titi Flaminini*	
Comp. Sol. Publ.	*Comparatio Solonis et Publicolae*	
Comp. Thes. Rom.	*Comparatio Thesei et Romuli*	
Conj. praec.	*Conjugalia Praecepta*	
[Cons. Apoll.]	*Consolatio ad Apollonium*	
Cons. ux.	*Consolatio ad uxorem*	
Cor.	*Marcius Coriolanus*	
Crass.	*Crassus*	
Cupid. divit.	*De cupiditate divitiarum*	
Curios.	*De curiositate*	
De esu	*De esu carnium*	
De laude	*De laude ipsius*	
Def. orac.	*De defectu oraculorum*	
Dem.	*Demosthenes*	
Demetr.	*Demetrius*	
Dion	*Dion*	
E Delph.	*De E apud Delphos*	
Eum.	*Eumenes*	

Exil.	*De exilio*
Fab.	*Fabius Maximus*
Fac.	*De facie in orbe lunae*
Flam.	*Titus Flamininus*
Fort.	*De fortuna*
Fort. Rom.	*De fortuna Romanorum*
Frat. amor.	*De fraterno amore*
Galb.	*Galba*
Garr.	*De garrulitate*
Gen. Socr.	*De genio Socratis*
Glor. Ath.	*De gloria Atheniensium*
Her. mal.	*De Herodoti malignitate*
Inim. util.	*De capienda ex inimicis utilitate*
Inv. od.	*De invidia et odio*
Is. Os.	*De Iside et Osiride*
Lat. viv.	*De latenter vivendo*
Lib. aegr.	*De libidine et aegritudine*
[Lib. ed.]	*De liberis educandis*
Luc.	*Lucullus*
Lyc.	*Lycurgus*
Lys.	*Lysander*
Mar.	*Marius*
Marc.	*Marcellus*
Max. princ.	*Maxime cum principibus philosophiam esse disserendum*
Mor.	*Moralia*
Mulier. virt.	*Mulierum virtutes*
[Mus.]	*De musica*
Nic.	*Nicias*
Num.	*Numa*
Oth.	*Otho*
Parsne an fac.	*Parsne an facultas animi sit vita passiva*
Pel.	*Pelopidas*
Per.	*Pericles*
Phil.	*Philopoemen*
Phoc.	*Phocion*
[Plac. philos.]	*De placita philosophorum*
Pomp.	*Pompeius*
Praec. ger. rei publ.	*Praecepta gerendae rei publicae*
Prim. frig.	*De primo frigido*
Princ. iner.	*Ad principem ineruditum*
Publ.	*Publicola*
Pyrrh.	*Pyrrhus*
Pyth. orac.	*De Pythiae oraculis*
Quaest. conv.	*Quaestionum convivialum libri IX*
Quaest. nat.	*Quaestiones naturales (Aetia physica)*
Quaest. plat.	*Quaestiones platonicae*
Quaest. rom.	*Quaestiones romanae et graecae (Aetia romana et graeca)*
Rect. rat. aud.	*De recta ratione audiendi*
[Reg. imp. apophth.]	*Regum et imperatorum apophthegmata*
Rom.	*Romulus*
Sept. sap. conv.	*Septem sapientium convivium*
Sera	*De sera numinis vindicta*
Sert.	*Sertorius*
Sol.	*Solon*

Soll. an.	*De sollertia animalium*
Stoic. abs.	*Stoicos absurdiora poetis dicere*
Stoic. rep.	*De Stoicorum repugnantiis*
Suav. viv.	*Non posse suaviter vivi secundum Epicurum*
Sull.	*Sulla*
Superst.	*De superstitione*
Them.	*Themistocles*
Thes.	*Theseus*
Ti. C. Gracch.	*Tiberius et Caius Gracchus*
Tim.	*Timoleon*
Tranq. an.	*De tranquillitate animi*
Trib. r. p. gen.	*De tribus rei publicae generibus*
Tu. san.	*De tuenda sanitate praecepta*
Un. rep. dom.	*De unius in republica dominatione*
Virt. mor.	*De virtute morali*
Virt. prof.	*Quomodo quis suos in virtute sentiat profectus*
Virt. vit.	*De virtute et vitio*
Vit. aere al.	*De vitando aere alieno*
[Vit. poes. Hom.]	*De vita et poesi Homeri*
Vit. pud.	*De vitioso pudore*
[Vit. X orat.]	*Vitae decem oratorum*

POLLUX

Onom.	*Onomasticon*

PORPHYRY

Abst.	*De abstinentia*
Agalm.	*Peri agalmatôn*
Aneb.	*Epistula ad Anebonem*
Antr. nymph.	*De antro nympharum*
Christ.	*Contra Christianos*
Chron.	*Chronica*
Comm. harm.	*Eis ta harmonika Ptolemaiouhypomnēma*
Comm. Tim.	*In Platonis Timaeum commentaria*
Exp. Cat.	*In Aristotelis Categorias expositio per interrogationem et responsionem*
Isag.	*Isagoge sive quinque voces*
Marc.	*Ad Marcellam*
Philos. orac.	*De philosophia ex oraculis*
Quaest. hom.	*Quaestiones homericae*
Quaest. hom. Odd.	*Quaestionum homericarum ad Odysseam pertinentium reliquiae*
Sent.	*Sententiae ad intelligibilia ducentes*
Vit. Plot.	*Vita Plotini*
Vit. Pyth.	*Vita Pythagorae*

PTOLEMY (THE GNOSTIC)

Flor.	*Epistula ad Floram*	Letter to Flora

Quintilian

Decl.	*Declamationes*
Inst.	*Institutio oratoria*

Res gest. divi Aug.

	Res gestae divi Augusti

Rhet. Her.

	Rhetorica ad Herennium

Rufinus

Adam. Haer.	*Adamantii libri Contra haereticos*
Anast.	*Apologia ad Anastasium papam*
Apol. Hier.	*Apologia adversus Hieronymum*
Apol. Orig.	*Eusebii et Pamphyli Apologia Origenis*
Basil. hom.	*Homiliae S. Basilii*
Ben. patr.	*De benedictionibus patriarcharum*
Clem. Recogn.	*Clementis quae feruntur Recognitiones*
Greg. Orat.	*Gregorii Orationes*
Hist.	*Eusebii Historia ecclesiastica a Rufino translata et continuata*
Hist. mon.	*Historia monachorum in Aegypto*
Orig. Comm. Cant.	*Origenis Commentarius in Canticum*
Orig. Comm. Rom.	*Origenis Commentarius in epistulam ad Romanos*
Orig. Hom. Exod.	*Origenis in Exodum homiliae*
Orig. Hom. Gen.	*Origenis in Genesism homiliae*
Orig. Hom. Jos.	*Origenis Homiliae in librum Josua*
Orig. Hom. Judic.	*Origenis in librum Judicum homiliae*
Orig. Hom. Lev.	*Origenis Homiliae in Leviticum*
Orig. Hom. Num.	*Origenis in Numeros homiliae*
Orig. Hom. Ps.	*Origenis Homiliae in Psalmos*
Orig. Princ.	*Origenis Libri Peri archōn seu De principiis libri IV*
Sent. Sext.	*Sexti philosophi Sententiae a Rufino translatae*
Symb.	*Commentarius in symbolum apostolorum*

Sallust

Bell. Cat.	*Bellum catalinae*
Bell. Jug.	*Bellum jugurthinum*
Hist.	*Historiae*
Rep.	*Epistulae ad Caesarem senem de re publica*

Seneca

Ag.	*Agamemnon*
Apol.	*Apolocyntosis*
Ben.	*De beneficiis*

Clem.	*De clementia*
Dial.	*Dialogi*
Ep.	*Epistulae morales*
Helv.	*Ad Helviam*
Herc. fur.	*Hercules furens*
Herc. Ot.	*Hercules Otaeus*
Ira	*De ira*
Lucil.	*Ad Lucilium*
Marc.	*Ad Marciam de consolatione*
Med.	*Medea*
Nat.	*Naturales quaestiones*
Phaed.	*Phaedra*
Phoen.	*Phoenissae*
Polyb.	*Ad Polybium de consolatione*
Thy.	*Thyestes*
Tranq.	*De tranquillitate animi*
Tro.	*Troades*
Vit. beat.	*De vita beata*

Sextus Empiricus

Math.	*Adversus mathematicos*	*Against the Mathematicians*
Pyr.	*Pyrrhoniae hypotyposes*	*Outlines of Pyrrhonism*

Sophocles

Aj.	*Ajax*
Ant.	*Antigone*
El.	*Elektra*
Ichn.	*Ichneutae*
Oed. col.	*Oedipus coloneus*
Oed. tyr.	*Oedipus tyrannus*
Phil.	*Philoctetes*
Trach.	*Trachiniae*

Stobaeus

Ecl.	*Eclogae*
Flor.	*Florilegium*

Strabo

Geogr.	*Geographica*

Suetonius

Aug.	*Divus Augustus*
Cal.	*Gaius Caligula*
Claud.	*Divus Claudius*
Dom.	*Domitianus*
Galb.	*Galba*
Gramm.	*De grammaticis*
Jul.	*Divus Julius*
Nero	*Nero*

Otho	*Otho*	
Poet.	*De poetis*	
Rhet.	*De rhetoribus*	
Tib.	*Tiberius*	
Tit.	*Divus Titus*	
Vesp.	*Vespasianus*	
Vit.	*Vitellius*	

TACITUS

Agr.	*Agricola*	
Ann.	*Annales*	
Dial.	*Dialogus de oratoribus*	
Germ.	*Germania*	
Hist.	*Historiae*	

TERENCE

Ad.	*Adelphi*	
Andr.	*Andria*	
Eun.	*Eunuchus*	
Haut.	*Hauton timorumenos*	
Hec.	*Hecyra*	
Phorm.	*Phormio*	

TERTULLIAN

An.	*De anima*	*The Soul*
Apol.	*Apologeticus*	*Apology*
Bapt.	*De baptismo*	*Baptism*
Carn. Chr.	*De carne Christi*	*The Flesh of Christ*
Cor.	*De corona militis*	*The Crown*
Cult. fem.	*De cultu feminarum*	*The Apparel of Women*
Exh. cast.	*De exhortatione castitatis*	*Exhortation to Chastity*
Fug.	*De fuga in persecutione*	*Flight in Persecution*
Herm.	*Adversus Hermogenem*	*Against Hermogenes*
Idol.	*De idololatria*	*Idolatry*
Jejun.	*De jejunio adversus psychicos*	*On Fasting, against the Psychics*
Adv. Jud.	*Adversus Judaeos*	*Against the Jews*
Marc.	*Adversus Marcionem*	*Against Marcion*
Mart.	*Ad martyras*	*To the Martyrs*
Mon.	*De monogamia*	*Monogamy*
Nat.	*Ad nationes*	*To the Heathen*
Or.	*De oratione*	*Prayer*
Paen.	*De paenitentia*	*Repentance*
Pall.	*De pallio*	*The Pallium*
Pat.	*De patientia*	*Patience*
Praescr.	*De praescriptione haereticorum*	*Prescription against Heretics*
Prax.	*Adversus Praxean*	*Against Praxeas*
Pud.	*De pudicitia*	*Modesty*
Res.	*De resurrectione carnis*	*The Resurrection of the Flesh*
Scap.	*Ad Scapulam*	*To Scapula*
Scorp.	*Scorpiace*	*Antidote for Scorpian's Sting*

Spect.	*De spectaculis*	*The Shows*
Test.	*De testimonio animae*	*The Soul's Testimony*
Ux.	*Ad uxorem*	*To His Wife*
Val.	*Adversus Valentinianos*	*Against the Valentinians*
Virg.	*De virginibus velandis*	*The Veiling of Virgins*

THEOCRITUS

Id.	*Idylls*

THEODORET

Car.	*De caritate*	
Hist. eccl.	*Historia ecclesiastica*	*Ecclesiastical History*
Phil. hist.	*Philotheos historia*	*History of Monks of Syria*

THEON OF ALEXANDRIA

Comm. Alm.	*Commentarium in Almagestum*	*Commentary on the Almagest*

THEOPHILUS

Autol.	*Ad Autolycum*	*To Autolycus*

THEOPHRASTUS

Caus. plant.	*De causis plantarum*
Char.	*Characteres*
Hist. plant.	*Historia plantarum*
Sens.	*De sensu*

TYCONIUS

Reg.	*Liber regularum*

VARRO

Rust.	*De re rustica*

VIRGIL

Aen.	*Aeneid*
Ecl.	*Eclogae*
Georg.	*Georgica*

XENOPHON

Ages.	*Agesilaus*
Anab.	*Anabasis*
Apol.	*Apologia Socratis*
[Ath.]	*Respublica atheniensium*
Cyn.	*Cynegeticus*
Cyr.	*Cyropaedia*
Eq.	*De equitande ratione*

Eq. mag.	*De equitum magistro*
Hell.	*Hellenica*
Hier.	*Hiero*
Lac.	*Respublica Lacedaemoniorum*
Mem.	*Memorabilia*
Oec.	*Oeconomicus*
Symp.	*Symposium*

PERIODICALS, REFERENCE WORKS, AND SERIALS

AA	*Archäologischer Anzeiger*
AAA	Annals of Archaeology and Anthropology
AAeg	*Analecta aegyptiaca*
AAHG	*Anzeiger für die Altertumswissenschaft*
AARDS	American Academy of Religion Dissertation Series
AAS	*Acta apostolicae sedis*
AASF	Annales Academiae scientiarum fennicae
AASOR	Annual of the American Schools of Oriental Research
AASS	*Acta sanctorum quotquot toto orbe coluntur.* Antwerp, 1643–
AB	Anchor Bible
AB	*Assyriologische Bibliothek*
ABAT2	*Altorientalische Bilder zum Alten Testament.* Edited by H. Gressmann. 2d ed. Berlin, 1927
ABAW	Abhandlungen der Bayrischen Akademie der Wissenschaften
AbB	*Altbabylonische Briefe in Umschrift und Übersetzung.* Edited by F. R. Kraus. Leiden, 1964–
ABC	*Assyrian and Babylonian Chronicles.* A. K. Grayson. TCS 5. Locust Valley, New York, 1975
ABD	*Anchor Bible Dictionary.* Edited by D. N. Freedman. 6 vols. New York, 1992
ABL	*Assyrian and Babylonian Letters Belonging to the Kouyunjik Collections of the British Museum.* Edited by R. F. Harper. 14 vols. Chicago, 1892–1914
ABQ	*American Baptist Quarterly*
ABR	*Australian Biblical Review*
ABRL	Anchor Bible Reference Library
AbrN	*Abr-Nahrain*
AbrNSup	Abr-Nahrain: Supplement Series
ABW	*Archaeology in the Biblical World*
ABZ	*Assyrisch-babylonische Zeichenliste.* Rykle Borger. 3d ed. AOAT 33/33A. Neukirchen-Vluyn, 1986
ACCS	Ancient Christian Commentary on Scripture
ACEBT	*Amsterdamse Cahiers voor Exegese en bijbelse Theologie*
ACNT	Augsburg Commentaries on the New Testament
ACO	*Acta conciliorum oecumenicorum.* Edited by E. Schwartz. Berlin, 1914–
AcOr	*Acta orientalia*
ACR	*Australasian Catholic Record*
AcT	*Acta theologica*
ACW	Ancient Christian Writers. 1946–
ADAJ	*Annual of the Department of Antiquities of Jordan*
ADD	*Assyrian Deeds and Documents.* C. H. W. Johns. 4 vols. Cambridge, 1898–1923
ADOG	Abhandlungen der deutschen Orientgesellschaft
AE	*Année épigraphique*
AEB	*Annual Egyptological Bibliography*
Aeg	*Aegyptus*
AEL	*Ancient Egyptian Literature.* M. Lichtheim. 3 vols. Berkeley, 1971–1980
AEO	*Ancient Egyptian Onomastica.* A. H. Gardiner. 3 vols. London, 1947
AER	*American Ecclesiastical Review*
Aev	*Aevum: Rassegna de scienze, storiche, linguistiche, e filologiche*

ÄF	Ägyptologische Forschungen
AfK	*Archiv für Keilschriftforschung*
AfO	*Archiv für Orientforschung*
AfOB	Archiv für Orientforschung: Beiheft
ÄgAbh	Ägyptologische Abhandlungen
AGBL	*Aus der Geschichte der lateinischen Bibel (= Vetus Latina: Die Reste der altlateinischen Bibel: Aus der Geschichte der lateinischen Bibel).* Freiburg: Herder, 1957–
AGJU	Arbeiten zur Geschichte des antiken Judentums und des Urchristentums
AGSU	Arbeiten zur Geschichte des Spätjudentums und Urchristentums
AHAW	Abhandlungen der Heidelberger Akademie der Wissenschaften
AHR	*American Historical Review*
AHw	*Akkadisches Handwörterbuch.* W. von Soden. 3 vols. Wiesbaden, 1965–1981
AION	*Annali dell'Istituto Orientale di Napoli*
AIPHOS	*Annuaire de l'Institut de philologie et d'histoire orientales et slaves*
AJA	*American Journal of Archaeology*
AJAS	*American Journal of Arabic Studies*
AJBA	*Australian Journal of Biblical Archaeology*
AJBI	*Annual of the Japanese Biblical Institute*
AJBS	*African Journal of Biblical Studies*
AJP	*American Journal of Philology*
AJSL	*American Journal of Semitic Languages and Literature*
AJSR	*Association for Jewish Studies Review*
AJSUFS	Arbeiten aus dem Juristischen Seminar der Universität Freiburg, Schweiz
AJT	*American Journal of Theology*
AJT	*Asia Journal of Theology*
ALASP	Abhandlungen zur Literatur Alt-Syren-Palästinas und Mesopotamiens
ALBO	Analecta lovaniensia biblica et orientalia
ALGHJ	Arbeiten zur Literatur und Geschichte des hellenistischen Judentums
Altaner	Altaner, B. *Patrologie.* 8th ed. Freiburg, 1978
ALUOS	*Annual of Leeds University Oriental Society*
AMS	*Acta martyrum et sanctorum Syriace.* Edited by P. Bedjan. 7 vols. Paris, 1890–1897
AMWNE	*Apocalypticism in the Mediterranean World and the Near East. Proceedings of the International Colloquium on Apocalypticism.* Edited by D.Hellholm. Uppsala, 1979
Anám	*Anámnesis*
AnBib	Analecta biblica
AnBoll	Analecta Bollandiana
ANEP	*The Ancient Near East in Pictures Relating to the Old Testament.* Edited by J. B. Pritchard. Princeton, 1954
ANESTP	*The Ancient Near East: Supplementary Texts and Pictures Relating to the Old Testament.* Edited by J. B. Pritchard. Princeton, 1969.
ANET	*Ancient Near Eastern Texts Relating to the Old Testament.* Edited by J. B. Pritchard. 3d ed. Princeton, 1969
ANF	*Ante-Nicene Fathers*
Ang	*Angelicum*
AnL	*Anthropological Linguistics*
AnOr	Analecta orientalia
AnPhil	*L'année philologique*
ANQ	*Andover Newton Quarterly*
ANRW	*Aufstieg und Niedergang der römischen Welt: Geschichte und Kultur Roms im Spiegel der neueren Forschung.* Edited by H. Temporini and W. Haase. Berlin, 1972–
AnSt	*Anatolian Studies*
ANTC	Abingdon New Testament Commentaries
ANTF	Arbeiten zur neutestamentlichen Textforschung
AnthLyrGraec	*Anthologia lyrica graeca.* Edited by E. Diehl. Leipzig, 1954–

ANTJ	Arbeiten zum Neuen Testament und Judentum
Anton	*Antonianum*
Anuari	*Anuari de filología*
ANZSTR	Australian and New Zealand Studies in Theology and Religion
AO	*Der Alte Orient*
AOAT	Alter Orient und Altes Testament
AÖAW	Anzeiger der Österreichischen Akademie der Wissenschaften
AOBib	Altorientalische Bibliothek
AoF	Altorientalische Forschungen
AOS	American Oriental Series
AOSTS	American Oriental Society Translation Series
AOT	*The Apocryphal Old Testament.* Edited by H. F. D. Sparks. Oxford, 1984
AOTAT	*Altorientalische Texte zum Alten Testament.* Edited by H. Gressmann. 2d ed. Berlin, 1926
APAT	*Die Apokryphen und Pseudepigraphen des Alten Testaments.* Translated and edited by E. Kautzsch. 2 vols. Tübingen, 1900
APF	*Archiv für Papyrusforschung*
APHM	Grohmann, A. *Arabic Papyri from Hirbet el-Mird.* Bibliothèque du Muséon 52. Louvain: Publications Universitaires, 1963.
APOT	*The Apocrypha and Pseudepigrapha of the Old Testament.* Edited by R. H. Charles. 2 vols. Oxford, 1913
APSP	*American Philosophical Society Proceedings*
AR	*Archiv für Religionswissenschaft*
ARAB	*Ancient Records of Assyria and Babylonia.* Daniel David Luckenbill. 2 vols. Chicago, 1926–1927
ArBib	The Aramaic Bible
Arch	*Archaeology*
ARE	*Ancient Records of Egypt.* Edited by J. H. Breasted. 5 vols. Chicago, 1905–1907. Reprint, New York, 1962
ARG	*Archiv für Reformationsgeschichte*
ARI	*Assyrian Royal Inscriptions.* A. K. Grayson. 2 vols. RANE. Wiesbaden, 1972–1976
ARM	Archives royales de Mari
ARMT	Archives royales de Mari, transcrite et traduite
ArOr	*Archiv Orientální*
ArSt	Arabian Studies
AS	Assyriological Studies
ASAE	*Annales duservice des antiquités de l'Egypte*
ASAW	Abhandlungen der Sächsischen Akademie der Wissenschaften
ASNU	Acta seminarii neotestamentici upsaliensis
ASOR	American Schools of Oriental Research
ASP	*American Studies in Papyrology*
Asp	*Asprenas: Rivista di scienze teologiche*
ASS	*Acta sanctae sedis*
AsSeign	*Assemblées du Seigneur*
ASSR	*Archives de sciences sociales des religions*
ASTI	*Annual of the Swedish Theological Institute*
AsTJ	*Asbury Theological Journal*
AT	*Annales theologici*
ATA	Alttestamentliche Abhandlungen
ATANT	Abhandlungen zur Theologie des Alten und Neuen Testaments
ATD	Das Alte Testament Deutsch
ATDan	Acta theologica danica
ATG	*Archivo teológico granadino*
AThR	*Anglican Theological Review*
Atiqot	ʿ*Atiqot*

ATJ	*Ashland Theological Journal*
ATLA	American Theological Library Association
ATR	*Australasian Theological Review*
Aug	*Augustinianum*
AugStud	*Augustinian Studies*
AuOr	*Aula orientalis*
AUSS	*Andrews University Seminary Studies*
AVTRW	Aufsätze und Vorträge zur Theologie und Religionswissenschaft
AzTh	Arbeiten zur Theologie
B&R	*Books and Religion*
BA	*Biblical Archaeologist*
Bab	*Babyloniaca*
BAC	Biblioteca de autores cristianos
BAG	Bauer, W., W. F. Arndt, and F. W. Gingrich. *Greek-English Lexicon of the New Testament and Other Early Christian Literature.* Chicago, 1957
BAGB	*Bulletin de l'Association G. Budé*
BAGD	Bauer, W., W. F. Arndt, F. W. Gingrich, and F. W. Danker. *Greek-English Lexicon of the New Testament and Other Early Christian Literature.* 2d ed. Chicago, 1979
BaghM	*Baghdader Mitteilungen*
BAIAS	*Bulletin of the Anglo-Israel Archeological Society*
BAP	*Beiträge zum altbabylonischen Privatrecht.* Bruno Meissner. Leipzig, 1893
BAR	*Biblical Archaeology Review*
BARead	*Biblical Archaeologist Reader*
Bar-Ilan	*Annual of Bar-Ilan University*
BASOR	*Bulletin of the American Schools of Oriental Research*
BASORSup	Bulletin of the American Schools of Oriental Research: Supplement Series
BASP	*Bulletin of the American Society of Papyrologists*
BASPSup	Bulletin of the American Society of Papyrologists: Supplement
BAT	Die Botschaft des Alten Testaments
BBB	Bonner biblische Beiträge
BBB	*Bulletin de bibliographie biblique*
BBET	Beiträge zur biblischen Exegese und Theologie
BBMS	Baker Biblical Monograph Series
BBR	*Bulletin for Biblical Research*
BBS	*Bulletin of Biblical Studies*
BCH	*Bulletin de correspondance hellénique*
BCPE	*Bulletin du Centre protestant d'études*
BCR	Biblioteca di cultura religiosa
BCSR	*Bulletin of the Council on the Study of Religion*
BDAG	Bauer, W., F. W. Danker, W. F. Arndt, and F. W. Gingrich. *Greek-English Lexicon of the New Testament and Other Early Christian Literature.* 3d ed. Chicago, 1999
BDB	Brown, F., S. R. Driver, and C. A. Briggs. *A Hebrew and English Lexicon of the Old Testament.* Oxford, 1907
BDF	Blass, F., A. Debrunner, and R. W. Funk. *A Greek Grammar of the New Testament and Other Early Christian Literature.* Chicago, 1961
BE	Milik, J. T. *The Books of Enoch.* Oxford: Clarendon, 1976.
BEATAJ	Beiträge zur Erforschung des Alten Testaments und des antiken Judentum
BEB	*Baker Encyclopedia of the Bible.* Edited by W. A. Elwell. 2 vols. Grand Rapids, 1988
BeO	*Bibbia e oriente*
Ber	*Berytus*
BerMatÖAI	Berichte und Materialien des Österreichischen archäologischen Instituts
BETL	Bibliotheca ephemeridum theologicarum lovaniensium
BEvT	Beiträge zur evangelischen Theologie
BFCT	Beiträge zur Förderung christlicher Theologie

BFT	Biblical Foundations in Theology
BGBE	Beiträge zur Geschichte der biblischen Exegese
BGU	*Aegyptische Urkunden aus den Königlichen Staatlichen Museen zu Berlin, Griechische Urkunden.* 15 vols. Berlin, 1895–1983.
BHEAT	*ulletin d'histoire et d'exégèse de l'Ancien Testament*
BHG	*Bibliotheca hagiographica Graece.* Brussels, 1977
BHH	*Biblisch-historisches Handwörterbuch: Landeskunde, Geschichte, Religion, Kultur.* Edited by B. Reicke and L. Rost. 4 vols. Göttingen, 1962–1966
BHK	*Biblia Hebraica.* Edited by R. Kittel. Stuttgart, 1905–1906, 1925^2, 1937^3, 1951^4, 1973^{16}
BHL	*Bibliotheca hagiographica latina antiquae et mediae aetatis.* 2 vols. Brussels, 1898–1901
BHLen	*Biblia Hebraica Leninradensia.* Edited by A. Dotan. Peabody, Mass., 2001.
BHO	*Bibliotheca hagiographica orientalis.* Brussels, 1910
BHS	*Biblia Hebraica Stuttgartensia.* Edited by K. Elliger and W. Rudolph. Stuttgart, 1983
BHT	Beiträge zur historischen Theologie
BI	*Biblical Illustrator*
Bib	*Biblica*
BibB	Biblische Beiträge
BiBh	*Bible Bhashyam*
BibInt	*Biblical Interpretation*
BibLeb	*Bibel und Leben*
BibOr	Biblica et orientalia
BibS(F)	Biblische Studien (Freiburg, 1895–)
BibS(N)	Biblische Studien (Neukirchen, 1951–)
BIES	*Bulletin of the Israel Exploration Society* (= *Yediot*)
BIFAO	*Bulletin de l'Institut français d'archéologie orientale*
Bijdr	*Bijdragen: Tijdschrift voor filosofie en theologie*
BIN	*Babylonian Inscriptions in the Collection of James B. Nies*
BIOSCS	*Bulletin of the International Organization for Septuagint and Cognate Studies*
BiPa	Biblia Patristica: Index des citations et allusions bibliques dans la littérature. Paris, 1975–
BJ	*Bonner Jahrbücher*
BJPES	*Bulletin of the Jewish Palestine Exploration Society*
BJRL	*Bulletin of the John Rylands University Library of Manchester*
BJS	Brown Judaic Studies
BJVF	*Berliner Jahrbuch für Vor- und Frühgeschichte*
BK	*Bibel und Kirche*
BKAT	Biblischer Kommentar, Altes Testament. Edited by M. Noth and H. W. Wolff
BL	*Bibel und Liturgie*
BLE	*Bulletin de littérature ecclésiastique*
BLit	*Bibliothèque liturgique*
BMes	Bibliotheca mesopotamica
BN	*Biblische Notizen*
BNTC	Black's New Testament Commentaries
BO	*Bibliotheca orientalis*
Böhl	Böhl, F. M. Th. de Liagre. *Opera minora: Studies en bijdragen op Assyriologisch en Oudtestamentisch terrein.* Groningen, 1953
BOR	*Babylonian and Oriental Record*
Bousset-Gressmann	Bousset, W., and H. Gressmann, *Die Religion des Judentums im späthellenistischen Zeitalter.* 3d ed. Tübingen, 1926
BR	*Biblical Research*
BRev	*Bible Review*
BRL2	*Biblisches Reallexikon.* 2d ed. Edited by K. Galling. HAT 1/1. Tübingen, 1977
BSAA	*Bulletin de la Société archéologique d'Alexandrie*
BSac	*Bibliotheca sacra*
BSAC	*Bulletin de la Société d'archéologie copte*

BSC	Bible Student's Commentary
BSGW	Berichte der Sächsischen Gesellschaft der Wissenschaften
BSOAS	*Bulletin of the School of Oriental and African Studies*
BT	*The Bible Translator*
BTB	*Biblical Theology Bulletin*
BThAM	*Bulletin de théologie ancienne et médiévale*
BTS	*Bible et terre sainte*
BTZ	*Berliner Theologische Zeitschrift*
Budé	Collection des universités de France, publiée sous le patronage de l'Association Guillaume Budé
Burg	*Burgense*
BurH	*Buried History*
BV	*Biblical Viewpoint*
BVC	*Bible et vie chrétienne*
BW	*The Biblical World: A Dictionary of Biblical Archaeology.* Edited by C. F. Pfeiffer. Grand Rapids, 1966
BWA(N)T	Beiträge zur Wissenschaft vom Alten (und Neuen) Testament
BWL	*Babylonian Wisdom Literature.* W. G. Lambert. Oxford, 1960
ByF	*Biblia y fe*
Byzantion	*Byzantion*
ByzF	*Byzantinische Forschungen*
ByzZ	*Byzantinische Zeitschrift*
BZ	*Biblische Zeitschrift*
BzA	Beiträge zur Assyriologie
BZAW	Beihefte zur Zeitschrift für die alttestamentliche Wissenschaft
BZNW	Beihefte zur Zeitschrift für die neutestamentliche Wissenschaft
BZRGG	Beihefte zur Zeitschrift für Religions- und Geistesgeschichte
CA	*Convivium assisiense*
CAD	*The Assyrian Dictionary of the Oriental Institute of the University of Chicago.* Chicago, 1956–
CaE	*Cahiers évangile*
CAGN	*Collected Ancient Greek Novels.* Edited by B. P. Reardon. Berkeley, 1989
CAH	Cambridge Ancient History
CahRB	Cahiers de la Revue biblique
CahT	Cahiers Théologiques
CANE	*Civilizations of the Ancient Near East.* Edited by J. Sasson. 4 vols. New York, 1995
CAP	Cowley, A. E. *Aramaic Papyri of the Fifth Century B.C.* Oxford, 1923
Car	*Carthagiensia*
CAT	Commentaire de l'Ancien Testament
CB	*Cultura bíblica*
CBC	Cambridge Bible Commentary
CBET	Contributions to Biblical Exegesis and Theology
CBM	Chester Beatty Monographs
CBQ	*Catholic Biblical Quarterly*
CBQMS	Catholic Biblical Quarterly Monograph Series
CBTJ	*Calvary Baptist Theological Journal*
CC	Continental Commentaries
CCath	Corpus Catholicorum
CCCM	Corpus Christianorum: Continuatio mediaevalis. Turnhout, 1969–
CClCr	*Civiltà classica e cristiana*
CCSG	Corpus Christianorum: Series graeca. Turnhout, 1977–
CCSL	Corpus Christianorum: Series latina. Turnhout, 1953–
CCT	*Cuneiform Texts from Cappadocian Tablets in the British Museum*
CDME	*A Concise Dictionary of Middle Egyptian.* Edited by R. O. Faulkner. Oxford, 1962
CF	*Classical Folia*
CGTC	Cambridge Greek Testament Commentary

CGTSC	Cambridge Greek Testament for Schools and Colleges
CH	*Church History*
CHJ	*Cambridge History of Judaism.* Ed. W. D. Davies and Louis Finkelstein. Cambridge, 1984–
Chm	*Churchman*
CHR	*Catholic Historical Review*
ChrCent	*Christian Century*
ChrEg	*Chronique d'Egypte*
ChrLit	*Christianity and Literature*
CIC	*Corpus inscriptionum chaldicarum*
CIG	*Corpus inscriptionum graecarum.* Edited by A. Boeckh. 4 vols. Berlin, 1828–1877
CII	*Corpus inscriptionum iudaicarum.* Edited by J. B. Frey. 2 vols. Rome, 1936–1952
CIJ	*Corpus inscriptionum judaicarum*
CIL	*Corpus inscriptionum latinarum*
CIS	*Corpus inscriptionum semiticarum*
CJ	*Classical Journal*
CJT	*Canadian Journal of Theology*
Cmio	*Communio: Commentarii internationales de ecclesia et theologia*
CML	*Canaanite Myths and Legends.* Edited by G. R. Driver. Edinburgh, 1956. Edited by J. C. L. Gibson, 1978[2]
CNS	*Cristianesimo nella storia*
CNT	Commentaire du Nouveau Testament
Coll	*Collationes*
Colloq	*Colloquium*
ColT	*Collectanea theologica*
Comm	*Communio*
Comp	*Compostellanum*
ConBNT	Coniectanea neotestamentica or Coniectanea biblica: New Testament Series
ConBOT	Coniectanea biblica: Old Testament Series
Cont	*Continuum*
COS	William W. Hallo, ed., *The Context of Scripture.* (3 vols.; Leiden: E. J. Brill, 1997–)
COut	Commentaar op het Oude Testament
CP	*Classical Philology*
CPG	*Clavis patrum graecorum.* Edited by M. Geerard. 5 vols. Turnhout, 1974–1987
CPJ	*Corpus papyrorum judaicorum.* Edited by V. Tcherikover. 3 vols. Cambridge, 1957–1964.
CPL	*Clavis patrum latinorum.* Edited by E. Dekkers. 2d ed. Steenbrugis, 1961
CQ	*Church Quarterly*
CQ	*Classical Quarterly*
CQR	*Church Quarterly Review*
CRAI	Comptes rendus de l'Académie des inscriptions et belleslettres
CRBR	*Critical Review of Books in Religion*
CRINT	Compendia rerum iudaicarum ad Novum Testamentum
CRTL	Cahiers de la Revue théologique de Louvain
Crux	*Crux*
CSCO	Corpus scriptorum christianorum orientalium. Edited by I. B. Chabot et al. Paris, 1903–
CSEL	Corpus scriptorum ecclesiasticorum latinorum
CSHB	Corpus scriptorum historiae byzantinae
CSJH	Chicago Studies in the History of Judaism
CSR	*Christian Scholar's Review*
CSRB	*Council on the Study of Religion: Bulletin*
CT	*Cuneiform Texts from Babylonian Tablets in the British Museum*
CTA	*Corpus des tablettes en cunéiformes alphabétiques découvertes à Ras Shamra-Ugarit de 1929 à 1939.* Edited by A. Herdner. Mission de Ras Shamra 10. Paris, 1963
CTAED	*Canaanite Toponyms in Ancient Egyptian Documents.* S. Ahituv. Jerusalem, 1984
CTJ	*Calvin Theological Journal*

CTM	*Concordia Theological Monthly*
CTQ	*Concordia Theological Quarterly*
CTR	*Criswell Theological Review*
CTU	*The Cuneiform Alphabetic Texts from Ugarit, Ras Ibn Hani, and Other Places.* Edited by M. Dietrich, O. Loretz, and J. Sanmartín. Münster, 1995.
CUL	*A Concordance of the Ugaritic Literature.* R. E. Whitaker. Cambridge, Mass., 1972
CurBS	*Currents in Research: Biblical Studies*
CurTM	*Currents in Theology and Mission*
CV	*Communio viatorum*
CW	*Classical World*
CWS	Classics of Western Spirituality. New York, 1978–
DACL	*Dictionnaire d'archéologie chrétienne et de liturgie.* Edited by F. Cabrol. 15 vols. Paris, 1907–1953
DB	*Dictionnaire de la Bible.* Edited by F. Vigouroux. 5 vols. 1895–1912
DBAT	*Dielheimer Blätter zum Alten Testament und seiner Rezeption in der Alten Kirche*
DBSup	*Dictionnaire de la Bible: Supplément.* Edited by L. Pirot and A. Robert. Paris, 1928–
DBT	*Dictionary of Biblical Theology.* Edited by X. Léon-Dufour. 2d ed. 1972
DCB	*Dictionary of Christian Biography.* Edited by W. Smith and H. Wace. 4 vols. London, 1877–1887
DCG	*Dictionary of Christ and the Gospels.* Edited by J. Hastings. 2 vols. Edinburgh, 1908
DCH	*Dictionary of Classical Hebrew.* Edited by D. J. A. Clines. Sheffield, 1993–
DDD	*Dictionary of Deities and Demons in the Bible.* Edited by K. van der Toorn, B. Becking, and P. W. van der Horst. Leiden, 1995
DHA	*Dialogues d'histoire ancienne*
Di	*Dialog*
Did	*Didaskalia*
DISO	*Dictionnaire des inscriptions sémitiques de l'ouest.* Edited by Ch. F. Jean and J. Hoftijzer. Leiden, 1965
DissAb	Dissertation Abstracts
DivThom	*Divus Thomas*
DJD	Discoveries in the Judaean Desert (of Jordan)
DJG	*Dictionary of Jesus and the Gospels.* Edited by J. B. Green and S. McKnight. Downers Grove, 1992
DLE	*Dictionary of Late Egyptian.* Edited by L. H. Lesko and B. S. Lesko. 4 vols. Berkeley, 1982–1989
DLNT	*Dictionary of the Later New Testament and Its Developments.* Edited by R. P. Martin and P. H. Davids. Downers Grove, 1997
DNP	*Der neue Pauly: Enzyklopädie der Antike.* Edited by H. Cancik and H. Schneider. Stuttgart, 1996–
DNWSI	*Dictionary of the North-West Semitic Inscriptions.* J. Hoftijzer and K. Jongeling. 2 vols. Leiden, 1995
DOP	*Dumbarton Oaks Papers*
DOTT	*Documents from Old Testament Times.* Edited by D. W. Thomas, London, 1958
DPAC	*Dizionario patristico e di antichità cristiane.* Edited by A. di Berardino. 3 vols. Casale Monferrato, 1983–1988
DPL	*Dictionary of Paul and His Letters.* Edited by G. F. Hawthorne and R. P. Martin. Downers Grove, 1993
DRev	*Downside Review*
DrewG	*Drew Gateway*
DSD	*Dead Sea Discoveries*
DSSSE	*Dead Sea Scrolls: Study Edition.* Edited by F. H. Martínez and E. J. C. Tigchelaar. New York, 1997–1998.
DTC	*Dictionnaire de théologie catholique.* Edited by A. Vacant et al. 15 vols. Paris, 1903–1950
DTT	*Dansk teologisk tidsskrift*

Duchesne	Duchesne, L., ed. *Le Liber pontificalis*. 2 vols. Paris, 1886, 1892. Reprinted with 3d vol. by C. Vogel. Paris, 1955–1957
DunRev	*Dunwoodie Review*
EA	El-Amarna tablets. According to the edition of J. A. Knudtzon. *Die el-Amarna-Tafeln*. Leipzig, 1908–1915. Reprint, Aalen, 1964. Continued in A. F. Rainey, *El-Amarna Tablets, 359–379*. 2d revised ed. Kevelaer, 1978
EAEHL	*Encyclopedia of Archaeological Excavations in the Holy Land*. Edited by M. Avi-Yonah. 4 vols. Jerusalem, 1975
EB	Echter Bibel
EBib	*Etudes bibliques*
ECR	*Eastern Churches Review*
ECT	*Egyptian Coffin Texts*. Edited by A. de Buck and A. H. Gardiner. Chicago, 1935–1947
EdF	Erträge der Forschung
EDNT	*Exegetical Dictionary of the New Testament*. Edited by H. Balz, G. Schneider. ET. Grand Rapids, 1990–1993
EEA	*L'epigrafia ebraica antica*. S. Moscati. Rome, 1951
EEC	*Encyclopedia of Early Christianity*. Edited by E. Ferguson. 2d ed. New York, 1990
EECh	*Encyclopedia of the Early Church*. Edited by A. di Berardino. Translated by A. Walford. New York, 1992
EfMex	*Efemerides mexicana*
EFN	Estudios de filología neotestamentaria. Cordova, Spain, 1988–
EgT	*Eglise et théologie*
EHAT	Exegetisches Handbuch zum Alten Testament
EKKNT	Evangelisch-katholischer Kommentar zum Neuen Testament
EKL	*Evangelisches Kirchenlexikon*. Edited by Erwin Fahlbusch et al. 4 vols. 3d ed. Göttingen, 1985–1996
Elenchus	*Elenchus bibliographicus biblicus* of *Biblica,* Rome, 1985–
ELKZ	*Evangelisch-Lutherische Kirchenzeitung*
EMC	*Echos dumonde classique/Classical Views*
Enc	*Encounter*
EnchBib	*Enchiridion biblicum*
EncJud	*Encyclopaedia Judaica*. 16 vols. Jerusalem, 1972
EPap	*Etudes de papyrologie*
Epiph	*Epiphany*
EPRO	Etudes préliminaires auxreligions orientales dans l'empire romain
ER	*The Encyclopedia of Religion*. Edited by M. Eliade. 16 vols. New York, 1987
ERAS	*Epithètes royales akkadiennes et sumériennes*. M.-J. Seux. Paris, 1967
ERE	*Encyclopedia of Religion and Ethics*. Edited by J. Hastings. 13 vols. New York, 1908–1927. Reprint, 7 vols., 1951
ErIsr	*Eretz-Israel*
ErJb	*Eranos-Jahrbuch*
EstAg	*Estudio Agustiniano*
EstBib	*Estudios bíblicos*
EstEcl	*Estudios eclesiásticos*
EstMin	*Estudios mindonienses*
EstTeo	*Estudios teológicos*
ETL	*Ephemerides theologicae lovanienses*
ETR	*Etudes théologiques et religieuses*
ETS	Erfurter theologische Studien
EuroJTh	*European Journal of Theology*
Even-Shoshan	Even-Shoshan, A., ed. *A New Concordance of the Bible.* Jerusalem, 1977, 1983
EvJ	*Evangelical Journal*
EvK	Evangelische Kommentare
EvQ	*Evangelical Quarterly*

EvT	*Evangelische Theologie*
ExAud	*Ex auditu*
Exeg	*Exegetica* [Japanese]
ExpTim	*Expository Times*
FAT	Forschungen zum Alten Testament
FB	Forschung zur Bibel
FBBS	Facet Books, Biblical Series
FBE	Forum for Bibelsk Eksegese
FC	Fathers of the Church. Washington, D.C., 1947–
FCB	Feminist Companion to the Bible
FF	*Forschungen und Fortschritte*
FF	Foundations and Facets
FGH	*Die Fragmente der griechischen Historiker.* Edited by F. Jacoby. Leiden, 1954–1964
FHG	Fragmenta historicorum graecorum. Paris, 1841–1870
FiE	*Forschungen in Ephesos*
FMSt	Frühmittelalterliche Studien
FO	*Folia orientalia*
FoiVie	*Foi et vie*
ForFasc	*Forum Fascicles*
Foster, *Muses*	Foster, Benjamin R. *Before the Muses: An Anthology of Akkadian Literature.* 2 vols. Bethesda, 1993
FOTL	Forms of the Old Testament Literature
Fran	*Franciscanum*
FRLANT	Forschungen zur Religion und Literatur des Alten und Neuen Testaments
FT	*Folia theologica*
Fund	*Fundamentum*
FZPhTh	*Freiburger Zeitschrift für Philosophie und Theologie*
GAG	*Grundriss der akkadischen Grammatik.* W. von Soden. 2d ed. Rome, 1969
GAT	Grundrisse zum Alten Testament
GBS	Guides to Biblical Scholarship
GCDS	*Graphic Concordance to the Dead Sea Scrolls.* Edited by J. H. Charlesworth et al. Tübingen, 1991
GCS	Die griechische christliche Schriftsteller der ersten [drei] Jahrhunderte Gesenius
Gesenius, Thesaurus	Gesenius, W. *Thesaurus philologicus criticus linquae hebraeae et chaldaeae Veteris Testamentia* Vols. 1-3. Leipzig, 1829–1842.
GKC	*Gesenius' Hebrew Grammar.* Edited by E. Kautzsch. Translated by A. E. Cowley. 2d. ed. Oxford, 1910
Gn	*Gnomon*
GNS	*Good News Studies*
GNT	Grundrisse zum Neuen Testament
GOTR	*Greek Orthodox Theological Review*
GP	*Géographie de la Palestine.* F. M. Abel. 2 vols. Paris, 1933
GR	*Greece and Rome*
GRBS	*Greek, Roman, and Byzantine Studies*
Greg	*Gregorianum*
GS	*Gesammelte Studien*
GTA	Göttinger theologischer Arbeiten
GTT	*Gereformeerd theologisch tijdschrift*
GTTOT	*The Geographical and Topographical Texts of the Old Testament.* Edited by J. J. Simons. Studia Francisci Scholten memoriae dicata 2. Leiden, 1959
GVG	*Grundriss der vergleichenden Grammatik der semitischen Sprachen.* C. Brockelmann, 2 vols. Berlin, 1908–1913. Reprint, Hildesheim, 1961
HAL	Koehler, L., W. Baumgartner, and J. J. Stamm. *Hebräisches und aramäisches Lexikon zum Alten Testament.* Fascicles 1–5, 1967–1995 (KBL3). ET: *HALOT*

HALOT	Koehler, L., W. Baumgartner, and J. J. Stamm, *The Hebrew and Aramaic Lexicon of the Old Testament.* Translated and edited under the supervision of M. E. J. Richardson. 4 vols. Leiden, 1994–1999
HAR	*Hebrew Annual Review*
Harris	Harris, Z. S. *A Grammar of the Phoenician Language.* AOS 8. New Haven, 1936. Reprint, 1990
HAT	Handbuch zum Alten Testament
HBC	*Harper's Bible Commentary.* Edited by J. L. Mays et al. San Francisco, 1988.
HBD	*HarperCollins Bible Dictionary.* Edited by P. J. Achtemeier et al. 2d ed. San Francisco, 1996
HBT	*Horizons in Biblical Theology*
HDR	Harvard Dissertations in Religion
Hell	*Hellenica: Recueil d'épigraphie, de numismatique et d'antiquités grecques*
Hen	*Henoch*
Herm	*Hermanthena*
Hesperia	*Hesperia: Journal of the American School of Classical Studies at Athens*
HeyJ	*Heythrop Journal*
HibJ	*Hibbert Journal*
HKAT	Handkommentar zum Alten Testament
HKL	*Handbuch der Keilschriftliteratur.* R. Borger. 3 vols. Berlin, 1967–1975
HKNT	Handkommentar zum Neuen Testament
HNT	Handbuch zum Neuen Testament
HNTC	Harper's New Testament Commentaries
HO	Handbuch der Orientalistik
Hok	*Hokhma*
HolBD	*Holman Bible Dictionary.* Edited by T. C. Butler. Nashville, 1991
Hor	*Horizons*
HR	*History of Religions*
HRCS	Hatch, E. and H. A. Redpath. *Concordance to the Septuagint and Other Greek Versions of the Old Testament.* 2 vols. Oxford, 1897. Suppl., 1906. Reprint, 3 vols. in 2, Grand Rapids, 1983
HS	*Hebrew Studies*
HSAT	*Die Heilige Schrift des Alten Testaments.* Edited by E. Kautzsch and A. Bertholet. 4th ed. Tübingen, 1922–1923
HSCP	*Harvard Studies in Classical Philology*
HSem	Horae semiticae. 9 vols. London, 1908–1912
HSM	Harvard Semitic Monographs
HSS	Harvard Semitic Studies
HT	*History Today*
HTB	Histoire du texte biblique. Lausanne, 1996–
HTh	*Ho Theológos*
HTKNT	Herders theologischer Kommentar zum Neuen Testament
HTR	*Harvard Theological Review*
HTS	Harvard Theological Studies
HUCA	*Hebrew Union College Annual*
HUCM	Monographs of the Hebrew Union College
HumTeo	Biblioteca humanística e teológica
HUT	Hermeneutische Untersuchungen zur Theologie
HvTSt	*Hervormde teologiese studies*
IAR	Iraq Archaeological Reports
IATG[2]	Schwertner, Siegfried M. *Internationales Abkürzungsverzeichnis für Theologie und Grenzgebeite.* 2d ed. Berlin, 1992
IB	*Interpreter's Bible.* Edited by G. A. Buttrick et al. 12 vols. New York, 1951–1957
IBC	Interpretation: A Bible Commentary for Teaching and Preaching.

IBHS	*An Introduction to Biblical Hebrew Syntax.* B. K. Waltke and M. O'Connor. Winona Lake, Indiana, 1990
IBS	*Irish Biblical Studies*
ICC	International Critical Commentary
ICUR	*Inscriptiones christianae urbis Romae.* Edited by J. B. de Rossi. Rome, 1857–1888
IDB	*The Interpreter's Dictionary of the Bible.* Edited by G. A. Buttrick. 4 vols. Nashville, 1962
IDBSup	*Interpreter's Dictionary of the Bible: Supplementary Volume.* Edited by K. Crim. Nashville, 1976
IDS	*In die Skriflig*
IEJ	*Israel Exploration Journal*
IESS	*International Encyclopedia of the Social Sciences.* Edited by D. L. Sills. New York, 1968–
IG	*Inscriptiones graecae.* Editio minor. Berlin, 1924–
IJT	*Indian Journal of Theology*
IKaZ	*Internationale katholische Zeitschrift*
IKZ	*Internationale kirchliche Zeitschrift*
ILCV	*Inscriptiones latinae christianae veteres.* Edited by E. Diehl. 2d ed. Berlin, 1961
Imm	*Immanuel*
Int	*Interpretation*
IOS	*Israel Oriental Society*
IPN	*Die israelitischen Personennamen.* M. Noth. BWANT 3/10. Stuttgart, 1928. Reprint, Hildesheim, 1980
Iran	*Iran*
Iraq	*Iraq*
Irén	*Irénikon*
IRT	Issues in Religion and Theology
ISBE	*International Standard Bible Encyclopedia.* Edited by G. W. Bromiley. 4 vols. Grand Rapids, 1979–1988
Isd	*Isidorianum*
Istina	*Istina*
IstMitt	*Istanbuler Mitteilungen*
Itala	*Itala: Das Neue Testament in altlateinischer Überlieferung.* 4 vols. Berlin, 1938–1963
ITC	International Theological Commentary
Iter	*Iter*
Itin (Italy)	*Itinerarium* (Italy)
Itin (Portugal)	*Itinerarium* (Portugal)
ITP	Hayim Tadmor, *The Inscriptions of Tiglath-Pileser III, King of Assyria.* Jerusalem, 1994
ITQ	*Irish Theological Quarterly*
IZBG	*Internationale Zeitschriftenschaufür Bibelwissenschaft und Grenzgebiete*
JA	*Journal asiatique*
JAAL	*Journal of Afroasiatic Languages*
JAAR	*Journal of the American Academy of Religion*
JAARSup	Journal of the American Academy of Religious Supplement Series
JAC	Jahrbuch für Antike und Christentum
JACiv	*Journal of Ancient Civilizations*
Jahnow	Jahnow, J. *Das hebräische Leichenlied im Rahmen der Völkerdichtung.* Giessen, 1923
JAL	Jewish Apocryphal Literature Series
JANESCU	*Journal of the Ancient Near Eastern Society of Columbia University*
JAOS	*Journal of the American Oriental Society*
JAS	*Journal of Asian Studies*
Jastrow	Jastrow, M. *A Dictionary of the Targumim, the Talmud Babli and Yerushalmi, and the Midrashic Literature.* 2d ed. New York, 1903
JB	Jerusalem Bible
JBC	*Jerome Biblical Commentary.* Edited by R. E. Brown et al. Englewood Cliffs, 1968
JBL	*Journal of Biblical Literature*

JBQ	*Jewish Bible Quarterly*
JBR	*Journal of Bible and Religion*
JCS	*Journal of Cuneiform Studies*
JdI	*Jahrbuch des deutschen archäologischen Instituts*
JDS	Jewish Desert Studies
JDS	Judean Desert Studies
JDT	*Jahrbuch für deutsche Theologie*
JE	*The Jewish Encyclopedia.* Edited by I. Singer. 12 vols. New York, 1925
JEA	*Journal of Egyptian Archaeology*
JECS	*Journal of Early Christian Studies*
Jeev	*Jeevadhara*
JEH	*Journal of Ecclesiastical History*
JEOL	*Jaarbericht van het Vooraziatisch-Egyptisch Gezelschap (Genootschap) Ex oriente lux*
JES	*Journal of Ecumenical Studies*
JESHO	*Journal of the Economic and Social History of the Orient*
JET	*Jahrbuch für Evangelische Theologie*
JETS	*Journal of the Evangelical Theological Society*
JFSR	*Journal of Feminist Studies in Religion*
JHI	*Journal of the History of Ideas*
JHNES	Johns Hopkins Near Eastern Studies
JHS	*Journal of Hellenic Studies*
Jian Dao	*Jian Dao*
JJA	*Journal of Jewish Art*
JJP	*Journal of Juristic Papyrology*
JJS	*Journal of Jewish Studies*
JJT	*Josephinum Journal of Theology*
JLA	*Jewish Law Annual*
JLCRS	Jordan Lectures in Comparative Religion Series
JMedHist	*Journal of Medieval History*
JMES	*Journal of Middle Eastern Studies*
JMS	*Journal of Mithraic Studies*
JNES	*Journal of Near Eastern Studies*
JNSL	*Journal of Northwest Semitic Languages*
JÖAI	*Jahreshefte des Österreichischen archäologischen Instituts*
JOTT	*Journal of Translation and Textlinguistics*
Joüon	Joüon, P. *A Grammar of Biblical Hebrew.* Translated and revised by T. Muraoka. 2 vols. Subsidia biblica 14/1–2. Rome, 1991
JPJ	*Journal of Progressive Judaism*
JPOS	*Journal of the Palestine Oriental Society*
JPS	Jewish Publication Society
JQR	*Jewish Quarterly Review*
JQRMS	Jewish Quarterly Review Monograph Series
JR	*Journal of Religion*
JRAS	*Journal of the Royal Asiatic Society*
JRE	*Journal of Religious Ethics*
JRelS	*Journal of Religious Studies*
JRH	*Journal of Religious History*
JRitSt	*Journal of Ritual Studies*
JRS	*Journal of Roman Studies*
JRT	*Journal of Religious Thought*
JSem	*Journal of Semitics*
JSHRZ	*Jüdische Schriften aus hellenistisch-römischer Zeit*
JSJ	*Journal for the Study of Judaism in the Persian, Hellenistic, and Roman Periods*
JSNT	*Journal for the Study of the New Testament*
JSNTSup	Journal for the Study of the New Testament: Supplement Series

JSOR	*Journal of the Society of Oriental Research*
JSOT	*Journal for the Study of the Old Testament*
JSOTSup	Journal for the Study of the Old Testament: Supplement Series
JSP	*Journal for the Study of the Pseudepigrapha*
JSPSup	Journal for the Study of the Pseudepigrapha: Supplement Series
JSQ	*Jewish Studies Quarterly*
JSS	*Journal of Semitic Studies*
JSSEA	*Journal of the Society for the Study of Egyptian Antiquities*
JSSR	*Journal for the Scientific Study of Religion*
JTC	*Journal for Theology and the Church*
JTS	*Journal of Theological Studies*
JTSA	*Journal of Theology for Southern Africa*
Jud	Judaica
Judaica	*Judaica: Beiträge zum Verständnis des jüdischen Schicksals in Vergangenheit und Gegenwart*
Judaism	*Judaism*
JWSTP	*Jewish Writings of the Second Temple Period: Apocrypha, Pseudepigrapha, Qumran Sectarian Writings, Philo, Josephus.* Edited by M. E. Stone. CRINT 2.2. Assen/Philadelphia, 1984
K&D	Keil, C. F., and F. Delitzsch, *Biblical Commentary on the Old Testament.* Translated by J. Martin et al. 25 vols. Edinburgh, 1857–1878. Reprint, 10 vols., Peabody, Mass., 1996
KAH 1	*Keilschrifttexte aus Assur historischen Inhalts.* L. Messerschmidt. Vol. 1. WVDOG 16. Leipzig, 1911
KAH 2	*Keilschrifttexte aus Assur historischen Inhalts.* O. Schroeder. Vol. 2. WVDOG 37. Leipzig, 1922
KAI	*Kanaanäische und aramäische Inschriften.* H. Donner and W. Röllig. 2d ed. Wiesbaden, 1966–1969
Kairós	*Kairós*
KAR	*Keilschrifttexte aus Assur religiösen Inhalts.* Edited by E. Ebeling. Leipzig, 1919–1923
KAT	Kommentar zum Alten Testament
KB	*Keilinschriftliche Bibliothek.* Edited by E. Schrader. 6 vols. Berlin, 1889–1915
KBANT	Kommentare und Beiträge zum Alten und Neuen Testament
KBL	Koehler, L., and W. Baumgartner, *Lexicon in Veteris Testamenti libros.* 2d ed. Leiden, 1958
KBo	*Keilschrifttexte aus Boghazköi.* WVDOG 30, 36, 68–70, 72–73, 77–80, 82–86, 89–90. Leipzig, 1916–
KD	*Kerygma und Dogma*
KEK	Kritisch-exegetischer Kommentar über das Neue Testament (Meyer-Kommentar)
Kerux	*Kerux*
KHC	Kurzer Hand-Commentar zum Alten Testament
KI	*Kanaanäische Inschriften (Moabitisch, Althebraisch, Phonizisch, Punisch).* Edited by M. Lidzbarski. Giessen, 1907
KK	*Katorikku Kenkyu*
KlPauly	*Der kleine Pauly*
KlT	Kleine Texte
KS	*Kirjath-Sepher*
KTU	*Die keilalphabetischen Texte aus Ugarit.* Edited by M. Dietrich, O. Loretz, and J. Sanmartín. AOAT 24/1. Neukirchen-Vluyn, 1976. 2d enlarged ed. of *KTU: The Cuneiform Alphabetic Texts from Ugarit, Ras Ibn Hani, and Other Places.* Edited by M. Dietrich, O. Loretz, and J. Sanmartín. Münster, 1995 (= *CTU*)
KUB	*Keilschrifturkunden aus Boghazköi*
Kuhn	Kuhn, K. G. *Konkordanz zuden Qumrantexten.* Göttingen, 1960
KVRG	Kölner Veroffentlichungen zur Religionsgeschichte
L&N	Louw and Nida. *Greek-English Lexicon of the New Testament: Based on Semantic Domains.* Edited by J. P. Louw and E. A. Nida. 2d ed. New York, 1989

LAE	*Literature of Ancient Egypt.* W. K. Simpson. New Haven, 1972
LAE[3]	*Literature of Ancient Egypt.* W. K. Simpson. 3d rev. ed. New Haven, 2003
Lane	Lane, E. W. *An Arabic-English Lexicon.* 8 vols. London. Reprint, 1968
LAPO	Littératures anciennes du Proche-Orient
LASBF	*Liber annuus Studii biblici franciscani*
Laur	*Laurentianum*
LÄ	*Lexikon der Ägyptologie.* Edited by W. Helck, E. Otto, and W. Westendorf. Wiesbaden, 1972
LB	*Linguistica Biblica*
LCC	Library of Christian Classics. Philadelphia, 1953–
LCL	Loeb Classical Library
LD	Lectio divina
LEC	Library of Early Christianity
Leš	*Lešonénu*
Levant	*Levant*
LexSyr	*Lexicon syriacum.* C. Brockelmann. 2d ed. Halle, 1928
LIMC	*Lexicon iconographicum mythologiae classicae.* Edited by H. C. Ackerman and J.-R. Gisler. 8 vols. Zurich, 1981–1997
List	*Listening: Journal of Religion and Culture*
LJPSTT	Literature of the Jewish People in the Period of the Second Temple and the Talmud
LQ	*Lutheran Quarterly*
LR	*Lutherische Rundschau*
LS	*Louvain Studies*
LSJ	Liddell, H. G., R. Scott, H. S. Jones, *A Greek-English Lexicon.* 9th ed. with revised supplement. Oxford, 1996
LSS	*Leipziger semitische Studien*
LTK	*Lexicon für Theologie und Kirche*
LTP	*Laval théologique et philosophique*
LTQ	*Lexington Theological Quarterly*
LUÅ	Lunds universitets årsskrift
Lum	*Lumen*
LumVie	*Lumière et vie*
LW	*Living Word*
MAAR	Memoirs of the American Academy in Rome
Maarav	*Maarav*
MAMA	*Monumenta Asiae Minoris Antiqua.* Manchester and London, 1928–1993
Mandl	Mandelkern, S. *Veteris Testamenti concordantiae hebraicae atque chaldaicae, etc.* Reprint, 1925. 2d ed. Jerusalem, 1967
MAOG	Mitteilungen der Altorientalischen Gesellschaft
MARI	*Mari: Annales de recherches interdisciplinaires*
MBPF	Münchener Beiträge zur Papyrusforschung und antiken Rechtsgeschichte
MBS	Message of Biblical Spirituality
McCQ	*McCormick Quarterly*
MCom	*Miscelánea Comillas*
MCuS	*Manchester Cuneiform Studies*
MDAI	*Mitteilungen des Deutschen archäologischen Instituts*
MDB	*Mercer Dictionary of the Bible.* Edited by W. E. Mills. Macon, 1990
MdB	*Le Monde de la Bible*
MDOG	Mitteilungen der Deutschen Orient-Gesellschaft
MEAH	*Miscelánea de estudios arabes y hebraicos*
Med	*Medellin*
MEFR	*Mélanges d'archéologie et d'histoire de l'école français de Rome*
MelT	*Melita theologica*
MGWJ	*Monatschrift für Geschichte und Wissenschaft des Judentums*
MH	*Museum helveticum*

Mid-Stream	*Mid-Stream*
Mils	*Milltown Studies*
MIO	*Mitteilungen des Instituts für Orientforschung*
MM	Moulton, J. H., and G. Milligan. *The Vocabulary of the Greek Testament.* London, 1930. Reprint, Peabody, Mass., 1997
MNTC	Moffatt New Testament Commentary
MPAIBL	Mémoires présentés à l'Academie des inscriptions et belleslettres
MS	*Mediaeval Studies*
MScRel	*Mélanges de science religieuse*
MSJ	*The Master's Seminary Journal*
MSL	*Materialien zum sumerischen Lexikon.* Benno Landsberger, ed.
MSU	Mitteilungen des Septuaginta-Unternehmens
MTSR	*Method and Theory in the Study of Religion*
MTZ	*Münchener theologische Zeitschrift*
Mursurillo	Mursurillo, H., ed. and trans. *The Acts of the Christian Martyrs.* Oxford, 1972
Mus	*Muséon: Revue d'études orientales*
MUSJ	*Mélanges de l'Université Saint-Joseph*
MVAG	Mitteilungen der Vorderasiatisch-ägyptischen Gesellschaft. Vols. 1–44. 1896–1939
NABU	*Nouvelles assyriologiques breves et utilitaires*
NAC	New American Commentary
NAWG	*Nachrichten (von) der Akademie der Wissenschaften in Göttingen*
NBD[2]	*New Bible Dictionary.* Edited by J. D. Douglas and N. Hillyer. 2d ed. Downers Grove, 1982
NBf	*New Blackfrairs*
NCB	New Century Bible
NCE	*New Catholic Encyclopedia.* Edited by W. J. McDonald et al. 15 vols. New York, 1967
NE	*Handbuch der nordsemitischen Epigraphik.* Edited by M. Lidzbarski. Weimar, 1898. Reprint, Hildesheim, 1962
NEAEHL	*The New Encyclopedia of Archaeological Excavations in the Holy Land.* Edited by E. Stern. 4 vols. Jerusalem, 1993
NEchtB	Neue Echter Bibel
NedTT	*Nederlands theologisch tijdschrift*
Nem	*Nemalah*
Neot	*Neotestamentica*
NETR	*Near East School of Theology Theological Review*
NewDocs	*New Documents Illustrating Early Christianity.* Edited by G. H. R. Horsley and S. Llewelyn. North Ryde, N.S.W., 1981–
NFT	New Frontiers in Theology
NGTT	*Nederduitse gereformeerde teologiese tydskrif*
NHC	Nag Hammadi Codices
NHL	*Nag Hammadi Library in English.* Edited by J. M. Robinson. 4th rev. ed. Leiden, 1996
NHS	Nag Hammadi Studies
NIB	*The New Interpreter's Bible*
NIBCNT	New International Biblical Commentary on the New Testament
NIBCOT	New International Biblical Commentary on the Old Testament
NICNT	New International Commentary on the New Testament
NICOT	New International Commentary on the Old Testament
NIDB	*New International Dictionary of the Bible.* Edited by J. D. Douglas and M. C. Tenney. Grand Rapids, 1987
NIDBA	*New International Dictionary of Biblical Archaeology.* Edited by E. M. Blaiklock and R. K. Harrison. Grand Rapids, 1983
NIDNTT	*New International Dictionary of New Testament Theology.* Edited by C. Brown. 4 vols. Grand Rapids, 1975–1985
NIDOTTE	*New International Dictionary of Old Testament Theology and Exegesis.* Edited by W. A. VanGemeren. 5 vols. Grand Rapids, 1997

NIGTC	New International Greek Testament Commentary
NJahrb	*Neue Jahrbücher für das klassische Altertum (1898–1925); Neue Jahrbücher für Wissenschaft und Jugendbildung (1925–1936)*
NJBC	*The New Jerome Biblical Commentary.* Edited by R. E. Brown et al. Englewood Cliffs, 1990
NKZ	*Neue kirchliche Zeitschrift*
Notes	*Notes on Translation*
NovT	*Novum Testamentum*
NovTSup	Novum Testamentum Supplements
NovTSup	Supplements to Novum Testamentum
NPNF[1]	*Nicene and Post-Nicene Fathers,* Series 1
NPNF[2]	*Nicene and Post-Nicene Fathers,* Series 2
NRTh	*La nouvelle revue théologique*
NTA	*New Testament Abstracts*
NTAbh	Neutestamentliche Abhandlungen
NTD	Das Neue Testament Deutsch
NTF	Neutestamentliche Forschungen
NTG	New Testament Guides
NTGF	New Testament in the Greek Fathers
NTL	New Testament Library
NTOA	Novum Testamentum et Orbis Antiquus
NTS	*New Testament Studies*
NTT	*Norsk Teologisk Tidsskrift*
NTTS	New Testament Tools and Studies
NumC	*Numismatic Chronicle*
Numen	*Numen: International Review for the History of Religions*
NuMu	*Nuevo mundo*
NV	*Nova et vetera*
OBO	Orbis biblicus et orientalis
ÖBS	Österreichische biblische Studien
OBT	Overtures to Biblical Theology
OCD	*Oxford Classical Dictionary.* Edited by S. Hornblower and A. Spawforth. 3d ed. Oxford, 1996
OCP	*Orientalia christiana periodica*
OCT	Oxford Classical Texts/Scriptorum classicorum bibliotheca oxoniensis
OCuT	Oxford Editions of Cuneiform Texts
ODCC	*The Oxford Dictionary of the Christian Church.* Edited by F. L. Cross and E. A. Livingstone. 2d ed. Oxford, 1983
OEANE	*The Oxford Encyclopedia of Archaeology in the Near East.* Edited by E. M. Meyers. New York, 1997
OECT	Oxford Early Christian Texts. Edited by H. Chadwick. Oxford, 1970–
OGIS	*Orientis graeci inscriptiones selectae.* Edited by W. Dittenberger. 2 vols. Leipzig, 1903–1905
OiC	*One in Christ*
OIC	*Oriental Institute Communications*
OIP	Oriental Institute Publications
OLA	Orientalia lovaniensia analecta
OLP	Orientalia lovaniensia periodica
OLZ	*Orientalistische Literaturzeitung*
Or	*Orientalia* (NS)
OrAnt	*Oriens antiquus*
OrChr	*Oriens christianus*
OrChrAn	Orientalia christiana analecta
Orita	*Orita*
OrSyr	*L'orient syrien*
OTA	*Old Testament Abstracts*

OTE	*Old Testament Essays*
OTG	Old Testament Guides
ÖTK	Ökumenischer Taschenbuch-Kommentar
OTL	Old Testament Library
OTM	Old Testament Message
OTP	*Old Testament Pseudepigrapha.* Edited by J. H. Charlesworth. 2 vols. New York, 1983
OTS	Old Testament Studies
OtSt	*Oudtestamentische Studiën*
PAAJR	*Proceedings of the American Academy of Jewish Research*
Pacifica	*Pacifica*
PapyCast	Papyrologica Castroctaviana, Studia et textus. Barcelona, 1967–
Parab	*Parabola*
ParOr	*Parole de l'orient*
PaVi	*Parole di vita*
Payne Smith	*Thesaurus syriacus.* Edited by R. Payne Smith. Oxford, 1879–1901
PDM	*Papyri demoticae magicae.* Demotic texts in *PGM* corpus as collated in H. D. Betz, ed. *The Greek Magical Papyri in Translation, including the Demotic Spells.* Chicago, 1996
PEFQS	Palestine Exploration Fund Quarterly Statement
PEQ	*Palestine Exploration Quarterly*
Per	*Perspectives*
PerTeol	*Perspectiva teológica*
PG	Patrologia graeca [= Patrologiae cursus completus: Series graeca]. Edited by J.-P. Migne. 162 vols. Paris, 1857–1886
PGL	*Patristic Greek Lexicon.* Edited by G. W. H. Lampe. Oxford, 1968
PGM	*Papyri graecae magicae: Die griechischen Zauberpapyri.* Edited by K. Preisendanz. Berlin, 1928
Phil	*Philologus*
Phon	*Phonetica*
PIASH	Proceedings of the Israel Academy of Sciences and Humanities
PIBA	Proceedings of the Irish Biblical Association
PJ	*Palästina-Jahrbuch*
PL	Patrologia latina [= Patrologiae cursus completus: Series latina]. Edited by J.-P. Migne. 217 vols. Paris, 1844–1864
Pneuma	*Pneuma: Journal for the Society of Pentecostal Studies*
PNTC	Pelican New Testament Commentaries
PO	Patrologia orientalis
POut	De Prediking van het Oude Testament
Presb	*Presbyterion*
ProEccl	*Pro ecclesia*
Proof	*Prooftexts: A Journal of Jewish Literary History*
Protest	*Protestantesimo*
Proy	*Proyección*
PRSt	*Perspectives in Religious Studies*
PRU	*Le palais royal d'Ugarit*
PS	Patrologia syriaca. Rev. ed. I. Ortiz de Urbina. Rome, 1965
PSB	*Princeton Seminary Bulletin*
PSTJ	*Perkins (School of Theology) Journal*
PTMS	Pittsburgh Theological Monograph Series
PTS	Patristische Texte und Studien
PVTG	Pseudepigrapha Veteris Testamenti Graece
PW	Pauly, A. F. *Paulys Realencyclopädie der classischen Altertumswissenschaft.* New edition G. Wissowa. 49 vols. Munich, 1980
PWSup	Supplement to PW
PzB	*Protokolle zur Bibel*

Qad	*Qadmoniot*
QC	*Qumran Chronicle*
QD	Quaestiones disputatae
QDAP	*Quarterly of the Department of Antiquities in Palestine*
QR	*Quarterly Review*
Quasten	Quasten, J. *Patrology.* 4 vols. Westminster, 1953–1986
R&T	*Religion and Theology*
RA	*Revue d'assyriologie et d'archéologie orientale*
RAC	*Reallexikon für Antike und Christentum.* Edited by T. Kluser et al. Stuttgart, 1950–
RANE	Records of the Ancient Near East
RAr	*Revue archéologique*
RÄR	*Reallexikon der ägyptischen Religionsgeschichte.* H. Bonnet. Berlin, 1952
RawlCu	*The Cuneiform Inscriptions of Western Asia.* Edited by H. C. Rawlinson. London, 1891
RB	*Revue biblique*
RBB	*Revista biblica brasileira*
RBén	*Revue bénédictine*
RBL	*Ruch biblijny i liturgiczny*
RBPH	*Revue belge de philologie et d'histoire*
RCB	*Revista de cultura bíblica*
RCT	*Revista catalana de teología*
RdT	*Rassegna di teologia*
RE	*Realencyklopädie für protestantische Theologie und Kirche*
REA	*Revue des études anciennes*
REAug	*Revue des études augustiniennes*
REB	*Revista eclesiástica brasileira*
RechBib	Recherches bibliques
RechPap	*Recherches de papyrologie*
RefLitM	*Reformed Liturgy and Music*
RefR	*Reformed Review*
REg	*Revue d'égyptologie*
REG	*Revue des études grecques*
REJ	*Revue des études juives*
RelArts	Religion and the Arts
RelEd	*Religious Education*
RelS	*Religious Studies*
RelSoc	*Religion and Society*
RelSRev	*Religious Studies Review*
RelStTh	*Religious Studies and Theology*
RES	*Répertoire d'épigraphie sémitique*
RES	*Revue des études sémitiques*
ResQ	*Restoration Quarterly*
RET	*Revista española de teología*
RevExp	*Review and Expositor*
RevistB	*Revista bíblica*
RevPhil	*Revue de philologie*
RevQ	*Revue de Qumran*
RevScRel	*Revue des sciences religieuses*
RGG	*Religion in Geschichte und Gegenwart.* Edited by K. Galling. 7 vols. 3d ed. Tübingen, 1957–1965
RHA	*Revue hittite et asianique*
RHE	*Revue d'histoire ecclésiastique*
RHPR	*Revue d'histoire et de philosophie religieuses*
RHR	*Revue de l'histoire des religions*
RIBLA	*Revista de interpretación bíblica latino-americana*

RIDA	*Revue internationale des droits de l'antiquité*
RIM	The Royal Inscriptions of Mesopotamia Project. Toronto
RIMA	The Royal Inscriptions of Mesopotamia, Assyrian Periods
RIMB	The Royal Inscriptions of Mesopotamia, Babylonian Periods
RIME	The Royal Inscriptions of Mesopotamia, Early Periods
RIMS	The Royal Inscriptions of Mesopotamia, Supplements
RISA	*Royal Inscriptions of Sumer and Akkad.* Edited by G. A. Barton. New Haven, 1929
RivB	*Rivista biblica italiana*
RivSR	*Rivista di scienze religiose*
RlA	*Reallexikon der Assyriologie.* Edited by Erich Ebeling et al. Berlin, 1928–
RLV	*Reallexikon der Vorgeschichte.* Edited by M. Ebert. Berlin, 1924–1932
RNT	Regensburger Neues Testament
RocT	*Roczniki teologiczne*
RomBarb	*Romanobarbarica*
RoMo	Rowohlts Monographien
RQ	*Römische Quartalschrift für christliche Altertumskunde und Kirchengeschichte*
RR	*Review of Religion*
RRef	*La revue réformée*
RRelRes	*Review of Religious Research*
RS	Ras Shamra
RSC	*Rivista di studi classici*
RSém	*Revue de sémitique*
RSF	*Rivista di studi fenici*
RSO	*Rivista degli studi orientali*
RSP	*Ras Shamra Parallels*
RSPT	*Revue des sciences philosophiques et théologiques*
RSR	*Recherches de science religieuse*
RST	Regensburger Studien zur Theologie
RStB	*Ricerche storico bibliche*
RTAM	*Recherches de théologie ancienne et médiévale*
RThom	*Revue thomiste*
RTL	*Revue théologique de Louvain*
RTP	*Revue de théologie et de philosophie*
RTR	*Reformed Theological Review*
RuBL	*Ruch biblijnu i liturgiczny*
RUO	*Revue de l'université d'Ottawa*
SA	Studia anselmiana
SAA	State Archives of Assyria
SAAB	*State Archives of Assyria Bulletin*
SAAS	State Archives of Assyria Studies
SAC	Studies in Antiquity and Christianity
SacEr	*Sacris erudiri: Jaarboek voor Godsdienstwetenschappen*
Salm	*Salmanticensis*
SANT	Studien zum Alten und Neuen Testaments
SAOC	Studies in Ancient Oriental Civilizations
Sap	*Sapienza*
SAQ	Sammlung ausgewählter Kirchen- und dogmengeschichtlicher Quellenschriften
SB	*Sammelbuch griechischer Urkunden aus Aegypten.* Edited by F. Preisigke et al. Vols. 1– , 1915–
SB	Sources bibliques
SBA	Studies in Biblical Archaeology
SBAB	Stuttgarter biblische Aufsatzbände
SBAW	Sitzungsberichte der bayerischen Akademie der Wissenschaften
SBB	Stuttgarter biblische Beiträge

SBFLA	*Studii biblici Franciscani liber annus*
SBL	Society of Biblical Literature
SBLABib	Society of Biblical Literature Academia Biblica
SBLABS	Society of Biblical Literature Archaeology and Biblical Studies
SBLBAC	Society of Biblical Literature The Bible and American Culture
SBLBMI	Society of Biblical Literature The Bible and Its Modern Interpreters
SBLBSNA	Society of Biblical Literature Biblical Scholarship in North America
SBLCP	Society of Biblical Literature Centennial Publications
SBLDS	Society of Biblical Literature Dissertation Series
SBLEJL	Society of Biblical Literature Early Judaism and Its Literature
SBLGPBS	Society of Biblical Literature Global Perspectives on Biblical Scholarship
SBLHS	*The SBL Handbook of Style,* Edited by P. Alexander et al. Peabody, Mass., 1999
SBLMasS	Society of Biblical Literature Masoretic Studies
SBLMS	Society of Biblical Literature Monograph Series
SBLNTGF	Society of Biblical Literature The New Testament in the Greek Fathers
SBLRBS	Society of Biblical Literature Resources for Biblical Study
SBLSBS	Society of Biblical Literature Sources for Biblical Study
SBLSC	Society of Biblical Literature Septuagint and Cognate Studies
SBLSP	*Society of Biblical Literature Seminar Papers*
SBLStBL	Society of Biblical Literature Studies in Biblical Literature
SBLSymS	Society of Biblical Literature Symposium Series
SBLTCS	Society of Biblical Literature Text-Critical Studies
SBLTT	Society of Biblical Literature Texts and Translations
SBLWAW	Society of Biblical Literature Writings from the Ancient World
SBLWGRW	Society of Biblical Literature Writings from the Greco-Roman World
SBM	Stuttgarter biblische Monographien
SBS	Stuttgarter Bibelstudien
SBT	Studies in Biblical Theology
SC	Sources chrétiennes. Paris: Cerf, 1943–
ScC	*La scuola cattolica*
ScEccl	*Sciences ecclésiastiques*
ScEs	*Science et esprit*
SCH	Studies in Church History
SCHNT	Studia ad corpus hellenisticum Novi Testamenti
Schol	*Scholastik*
Scr	*Scripture*
SCR	*Studies in Comparative Religion*
ScrB	*Scripture Bulletin*
ScrC	*Scripture in Church*
ScrHier	Scripta hierosolymitana
ScrTh	*Scripta theologica*
ScrVict	*Scriptorium victoriense*
SD	Studies and Documents
SDAW	Sitzungen der deutschen Akademie der Wissenschaften zu Berlin
SE	*Studia evangelica I, II, III* (= TU 73 [1959], 87 [1964], 88 [1964]. etc.)
SEÅ	*Svensk exegetisk årsbok*
SEAug	Studia ephemeridis Augustinianum
SecCent	*Second Century*
Sef	*Sefarad*
SEG	Supplementum epigraphicum graecum
SEL	*Studi epigrafici e linguistici*
Sem	*Semitica*
Semeia	*Semeia*
SemeiaSt	Semeia Studies

SFulg	*Scripta fulgentina*
SHANE	Studies in the History of the Ancient Near East
SHAW	Sitzungen der heidelberger Akademie der Wissenschaften
Shofar	*Shofar*
SHR	Studies in the History of Religions (supplement to *Numen*)
SHT	Studies in Historical Theology
SIDIC	*SIDIC* (Journal of the Service internationale de documentation judeo-chrétienne)
SIG	*Sylloge inscriptionum graecarum.* Edited by W. Dittenberger. 4 vols. 3d ed. Leipzig, 1915–1924
SJ	Studia judaica
SJLA	Studies in Judaism in Late Antiquity
SJOT	*Scandinavian Journal of the Old Testament*
SJT	*Scottish Journal of Theology*
SK	*Skrif en kerk*
SKKNT	Stuttgarter kleiner Kommentar, Neues Testament
SL	*Sumerisches Lexikon.* Edited by A. Deimel. 8 vols. Rome, 1928–1950
SLJT	*St. Luke's Journal of Theology*
SMBen	Série monographique de Benedictina: Section paulinienne *SMSR Studi e materiali di storia delle religioni*
SMSR	*Studi e materiali di storia delle religioni*
SMT	*Studii Montis Regii*
SNT	Studien zum Neuen Testament
SNTA	Studiorum Novi Testamenti Auxilia
SNTSMS	Society for New Testament Studies Monograph Series
SNTSU	Studien zum Neuen Testament und seiner Umwelt
SO	Symbolae osloenses
SÖAW	Sitzungen der österreichischen Akademie der Wissenschaften in Wien
Sobornost	*Sobornost*
SOTSMS	Society for Old Testament Studies Monograph Series
Sound	*Soundings*
SP	Sacra pagina
SPap	*Studia papyrologica*
SPAW	Sitzungsberichte der preussischen Akademie der Wissenschaften
Spec	*Speculum*
SPhilo	*Studia philonica*
SQAW	Schriften und Quellen der alten Welt
SR	*Studies in Religion*
SSEJC	*Studies in Early Judaism and Christianity*
SSN	Studia semitica neerlandica
SSS	Semitic Study Series
ST	*Studia theologica*
St	*Studium*
StABH	Studies in American Biblical Hermeneutics
StC	Studia catholica
STDJ	*Studies on the Texts of the Desert of Judah*
SThU	*Schweizerische theologische Umschau*
SThZ	*Schweizerische theologische Zeitschrift*
STJ	*Stulos Theological Journal*
STK	*Svensk teologisk kvartalskrift*
StOR	Studies in Oriental Religions
StPat	*Studia patavina*
StPatr	Studia patristica
StPB	Studia post-biblica
Str	*Stromata*

Str-B	Strack, H. L., and P. Billerbeck. *Kommentar zum Neuen Testament aus Talmud und Midrasch.* 6 vols. Munich, 1922–1961
STRev	*Sewanee Theological Review*
StSin	Studia Sinaitica
StudBib	Studia Biblica
StudMon	Studia monastica
StudNeot	Studia neotestamentica
StudOr	Studia orientalia
StZ	Stimmen der Zeit
Su	*Studia theological varsaviensia*
SubBi	*Subsidia biblica*
Sumer	*Sumer: A Journal of Archaeology and History in Iraq*
SUNT	Studien zur Umwelt des Neuen Testaments
SVF	*Stoicorum veterum fragmenta.* H. von Arnim. 4 vols. Leipzig, 1903–1924
SVTP	Studia in Veteris Testamenti pseudepigraphica
SVTQ	*St. Vladimir's Theological Quarterly*
SWBA	Social World of Biblical Antiquity
SwJT	*Southwestern Journal of Theology*
SymBU	Symbolae biblicae upsalienses
T&K	*Texte & Kontexte*
TA	*Tel Aviv*
TAD	*Textbook of Aramaic Documents from Ancient Egypt. Newly Copied, Edited and Translated into Hebrew and English.* Edited by Bazalel Porten and Ada Yardeni. Winona Lake, IN *(1986–1993)*
TAPA	*Transactions of the American Philological Association*
Tarbiz	*Tarbiz*
TB	Theologische Bücherei: Neudrucke und Berichte aus dem 20. Jahrhundert
TBC	Torch Bible Commentaries
TBei	*Theologische Beiträge*
TBl	*Theologische Blätter*
TBT	*The Bible Today*
TCL	Textes cunéiformes. Musée du Louvre
TCS	Texts from Cuneiform Sources
TCW	*Tydskrif vir Christelike Wetenskap*
TD	*Theology Digest*
TDNT	*Theological Dictionary of the New Testament.* Edited by G. Kittel and G. Friedrich. Translated by G. W. Bromiley. 10 vols. Grand Rapids, 1964–1976
TDOT	*Theological Dictionary of the Old Testament.* Edited by G. J. Botterweck and H. Ringgren. Translated by J. T. Willis, G. W. Bromiley, and D. E. Green. 8 vols. Grand Rapids, 1974–
TdT	Themen der Theologie
Teol	*Teología*
Teubner	Bibliotheca scriptorum graecorum et romanorum teubneriana
Text	*Textus*
TF	*Theologische Forschung*
TGI	*Textbuch zur Geschichte Israels.* Edited by K. Galling. 2d ed. Tübingen, 1968
TGl	*Theologie und Glaube*
TGUOS	Transactions of the Glasgow University Oriental Society
THAT	*Theologisches Handwörterbuch zum Alten Testament.* Edited by E. Jenni, with assistance from C. Westermann. 2 vols., Stuttgart, 1971–1976
Them	*Themelios*
Theo	*Theologika*
Theof	*Theoforum*
Theol	*Theologica*

ThH	Théologie historique
THKNT	Theologischer Handkommentar zum Neuen Testament
ThPQ	*Theologisch-praktische Quartalschrift*
ThSt	Theologische Studiën
ThT	*Theologisch tijdschrift*
ThTo	*Theology Today*
ThViat	*Theologia viatorum*
ThWAT	*Theologisches Wörterbuch zum Alten Testament.* Edited by G. J. Botterweck and H. Ringgren. Stuttgart, 1970–
TI	*Teologia iusi*
TimesLitSupp	*Times Literary Supplement*
TJ	*Trinity Journal*
TJT	*Toronto Journal of Theology*
TLG	*Thesaurus linguae graecae: Canon of Greek Authors and Works.* Edited by L. Berkowitz and K. A. Squitier. 3d ed. Oxford, 1990
TLL	*Thesaurus linguae latinae*
TLNT	*Theological Lexicon of the New Testament.* C. Spicq. Translated and edited by J. D. Ernest. 3 vols. Peabody, Mass., 1994
TLOT	*Theological Lexicon of the Old Testament.* Edited by E. Jenni, with assistance from C. Westermann. Translated by M. E. Biddle. 3 vols. Peabody, Mass., 1997
TLZ	*Theologische Literaturzeitung*
TNTC	Tyndale New Testament Commentaries
TOTC	Tyndale Old Testament Commentaries
TP	*Theologie und Philosophie*
TPINTC	TPI New Testament Commentaries
TPQ	*Theologisch-praktische Quartalschrift*
TQ	*Theologische Quartalschrift*
Transeu	*Transeu phratène*
TRE	*Theologische Realenzyklopädie.* Edited by G. Krause and G. Müller. Berlin, 1977–
TRev	*Theologische Revue*
TRSR	Testi e ricerche di scienze religiose
TRu	*Theologische Rundschau*
Trumah	*Trumah*
TS	Texts and Studies
TS	*Theological Studies*
TSAJ	Texte und Studien zum antiken Judentum
TSK	*Theologische Studien und Kritiken*
TTE	*The Theological Educator*
TThSt	Trierer theologische Studien
TTJ	*Trinity Theological Journal*
TTKi	*Tidsskrift for Teologi og Kirke*
TTZ	*Trierer theologische Zeitschrift*
TU	Texte und Untersuchungen
TUAT	*Texte aus der Umwelt des Alten Testaments.* Edited by Otto Kaiser. Gütersloh, 1984–
TUGAL	Texte und Untersuchungen zur Geschichte der altchristlichen Literatur
TUMSR	Trinity University Monograph Series in Religion
TV	*Teología y vida*
TVM	Theologische Verlagsgemeinschaft: Monographien
TvT	*Tijdschrift voor theologie*
TWNT	*Theologische Wörterbuch zum Neuen Testament.* Edited by G. Kittel and G. Friedrich. Stuttgart, 1932–1979
TWOT	*Theological Wordbook of the Old Testament.* Edited by R. L. Harris, G. L. Archer Jr. 2 vols. Chicago, 1980
TynBul	*Tyndale Bulletin*

TZ	*Theologische Zeitschrift*
UBL	Ugaritisch-biblische Literatur
UF	*Ugarit-Forschungen*
UHP	*Ugaritic-Hebrew Philology.* M. Dahood. 2d ed. Rome, 1989
UJEnc	*The Universal Jewish Encyclopedia.* Edited by I. Landman. 10 vols. New York, 1939–1943
UNP	*Ugaritic Narrative Poetry.* Edited by Simon B. Parker. SBLWAW 9. Atlanta, 1997
UNT	Untersuchungen zum Neuen Testament
UrE	Ur Excavations
UrET	Ur Excavations: Texts
USQR	*Union Seminary Quarterly Review*
UT	*Ugaritic Textbook.* C. H. Gordon. AnOr 38. Rome, 1965
UUA	Uppsala Universitets arskrift
VAB	Vorderasiatische Bibliothek
VAT	Vorderasiatische Abteilung Tontafel. Vorderasiatisches Museum, Berlin
VC	*Vigiliae christianae*
VCaro	*Verbum caro*
VD	*Verbum domini*
VE	*Vox evangelica*
VF	*Verkündigung und Forschung*
VH	*Vivens homo*
Vid	*Vidyajyoti*
VL	*Vetus Latina: Die Reste der altlateinischen Bibel.* Edited by E. Beuron, 1949–
VR	*Vox reformata*
VS	*Verbum Salutie*
VS	*Vox scripturae*
VSpir	*Vie spirituelle*
VT	*Vetus Testamentum*
VTSup	Supplements to Vetus Testamentum
WÄS	*Wörterbuch der ägyptischen Sprache.* A. Erman and H. Grapow. 5 vols. Berlin, 1926–1931. Reprint, 1963
WBC	Word Biblical Commentary
WC	Westminster Commentaries
WD	*Wort und Dienst*
WDB	*Westminster Dictionary of the Bible*
Wehr	Wehr, H. *A Dictionary of Modern Written Arabic.* Edited by J. M. Cowan. Ithaca, 1961, 1976[3]
WHAB	*Westminster Historical Atlas of the Bible*
WHJP	World History of the Jewish People
WKAS	*Das Wörterbuch der klassischen arabischen Sprache.* Edited by M. Ullmann. 1957– .
WMANT	Wissenschaftliche Monographien zum Alten und Neuen Testament
WO	*Die Welt des Orients*
WTJ	*Westminster Theological Journal*
WTM	*Das Wörterbuch über die Talmudim und Midraschim.* J. Levy. 2d ed. 1924
WUANT	Wissenschaftliche Untersuchungen zum Alten und Neuen Testament
WUNT	Wissenschaftliche Untersuchungen zum Neuen Testament
WUS	*Das Wörterbuch der ugaritischen Sprache.* J. Aistleitner. Edited by O. Eissfeldt. 3d ed. Berlin, 1967
WVDOG	Wissenschaftliche Veröffentlichungen der deutschen Orientgesellschaft
WW	*Word and World*
WZ	*Wissenschaftliche Zeitschrift*
WZKM	*Wiener Zeitschrift für die Kunde des Morgenlandes*
WZKSO	*Wiener Zeitschrift für die Kunde Süd- und Ostasiens*
YCS	Yale Classical Studies
YOS	Yale Oriental Series, Texts

YOSR	Yale Oriental Series, Researches
ZA	*Zeitschrift für Assyriologie*
ZABeih	Zeitschrift für Assyriologie: Beihefte
ZABR	*Zeitschrift für altorientalische und biblische Rechtgeschichte*
ZAC	*Zeitschrift für Antikes Christentum/Journal of Ancient Christianity*
ZAH	*Zeitschrift für Althebräistik*
ZÄS	*Zeitschrift für ägyptische Sprache und Altertumskunde*
ZAW	*Zeitschrift für die alttestamentliche Wissenschaft*
ZB	Zürcher Bibel
ZBK	Zürcher Bibelkommentare
ZDMG	*Zeitschrift der deutschen morgenländischen Gesellschaft*
ZDMGSup	Zeitschrift der deutschen morgenländischen Gesellschaft: Supplementbände
ZDPV	*Zeitschrift des deutschen Palästina-Vereins*
ZEE	*Zeitschrift für evangelische Ethik*
ZHT	*Zeitschrift für historische Theologie*
Zion	*Zion*
ZKG	*Zeitschrift für Kirchengeschichte*
ZKT	*Zeitschrift für katholische Theologie*
ZKunstG	*Zeitschrift für Kunstgeschichte*
ZNW	*Zeitschrift für die neutestamentliche Wissenschaft und die Kunde der älteren Kirche*
Zorell	Zorell, F. *Lexicon hebraicum et aramaicum Veteris Testamenti.* Rome, 1968
ZPE	*Zeitschrift für Papyrologie und Epigraphik*
ZPEB	*Zondervan Pictorial Encyclopedia of the Bible.* Edited by M. C. Tenney. 5 vols. Grand Rapids, 1975
ZRGG	*Zeitschrift für Religions- und Geistesgeschichte*
ZS	*Zeitschrift für Semitistik und verwandte Gebiete*
ZST	*Zeitschrift für systematische Theologie*
ZTK	*Zeitschrift für Theologie und Kirche*
ZWKL	*Zeitschrift für Wissenschaft und kirchliches Leben*
ZWT	*Zeitschrift für wissenschaftliche Theologie*

Charts, Illustrations, and Maps